When They Read

Manuscripts:

1. **How the manuscript's form and contents depict the idea**

2. **A writing style that informs, entertains, and touches the reader**

3. **Verifiable research (in nonfiction)**

4. **Anecdotes and quotes from your interviews with people**

5. **How the manuscript will serve their readers and the market**

6. **Perfect copy; SASE enclosed**

1988 Writer's Market

Acknowledgement
The editor wishes to thank Becky Williams,
1987 Writer's Market *editor, and Sheila
Freeman,* 1987 Writer's Market *assistant
editor, for their efforts in planning and
preparing much of this edition.*

*Distributed in Canada by Prentice-Hall of
Canada Ltd., 1870 Birchmount Road,
Scarborough, Ontario M1P 2J7.*

*Managing Editor, Market Books Department:
Constance J. Achabal*

*Library of Congress Catalog Number
31-20772
International Standard Serial Number
0084-2729
International Standard Book Number
0-89879-274-6*

1988

Writer's Market

Where to Sell What You Write

Editor: **Glenda Tennant Neff**

Assistant Editor: **Robin Gee**
Editorial Coordinator: **Kathleen Vonderhaar**

Cincinnati, Ohio

The Writing Profession

1   **From the Editors**
3   **Using *Writer's Market***
5   **Getting Published: A Conflict of Views,**
     by Glenda Tennant Neff
9   **The Writer/Editor Relationship: Taking Charge,**
     by William Brohaugh

The Markets

13   **Book Publishers**

55   **Close-up:**
     Tama Janowitz, Author
     How can writers take an active part in marketing their books? The author of Slaves of New York tells her way.

127   **Close-up:**
     Chuck Perry, Peachtree Publishers
     This executive editor tells why finding a good unsolicited manuscript and publishing a variety of books are important.

186   **Book Packagers and Producers**

189   **Close-up:**
     Paul Fargis, American Book Producers Association
     The president of American Book Producers offers advice for writers who want to work with book producers.

191   **Subsidy Publishers**

192   **Consumer Publications**

193   *Animal*

202   *Art*

206   *Association, Club and Fraternal*

214   *Astrology and Metaphysical*

216   *Automotive and Motorcycle*

Contents

223 Aviation

226 Business and Finance

238 Career, College and Alumni

247 Child Care and Parental Guidance

253 Comic Books

255 Close-up:
Diana Schutz, Comico
An editor looks for comic book writers who can put together dramatic stories that will also be visually interesting.

257 Consumer Service and Business Opportunity

260 Detective and Crime

262 Disabilities

265 Entertainment

272 Ethnic/Minority

277 Close-up:
Stephanie Stokes Oliver, Essence
This editor explains why she looks for substantive articles on a wide range of topics of interest to black women.

283 Food and Drink

286 Games and Puzzles

289 General Interest

300 Health and Fitness

310 History

316 Hobby and Craft

335 Home and Garden

343 Humor

344 Close-up:
Robert Orben, Orben's Current Comedy
A 40-year veteran tells humor writers why it's important to hear material performed live.

346 In-Flight

350 Juvenile

365 Literary and "Little"

388 Men's

393 Military

401 Music

410 Mystery

410 Nature, Conservation and Ecology

417 Personal Computers

425 Photography

427 Politics and World Affairs

432 Psychology and Self-Improvement

435 Regional

449 Close-up:
Stephen Petranek, The Washington Post Magazine
Articles that touch emotional and human values are top priorities for this managing editor.

493 Relationships

500 *Religious*

534 *Retirement*

538 *Romance and Confession*

539 **Close-up:**
Nathasha Brooks, Black Romance
An editor of romance magazines tells writers exactly what kinds of stories she is looking for.

542 *Rural*

544 *Science*

548 *Science Fiction, Fantasy and Horror*

551 **Close-up:**
James Gunn, Author
An award-winning author advises writers to draw upon their imaginations as well as their experiences.

555 *Sports*
Archery and Bowhunting, Bicycle, Boating, Bowling, Gambling, General Interest, Golf, Guns, Horseracing, Hunting and Fishing, Martial Arts, Miscellaneous, Skiing and Snow Sports, Soccer, Tennis, Water Sports

607 *Teen and Young Adult*

616 *Travel, Camping and Trailer*

631 *Women's*

641 **Close-up:**
Karen Larson, Redbook
One piece of advice from this senior editor is to know a magazine's audience as well as its content when submitting manuscripts.

645 **Trade, Technical and Professional Journals**

646 *Advertising, Marketing and PR*

651 *Art, Design and Collectibles*

653 *Auto and Truck*

659 *Aviation and Space*

661 *Beverages and Bottling*

662 *Book and Bookstore Trade*

664 *Brick, Glass and Ceramics*

665 *Building Interiors*

667 *Business Management*

672 *Church Administration and Ministry*

675 *Clothing*

676 *Coin-Operated Machines*

678 *Confectionery and Snack Foods*

678 *Construction and Contracting*

683 *Dental*

684 *Drugs, Health Care and Medical Products*

685 *Education and Counseling*

689 Close-up:
Leanna Landsmann, Instructor Magazine
What are the practical ideas for teachers—and articles on educational trends—that interest this editor and publisher?

693 Electronics and Communication

700 Energy and Utilities

702 Engineering and Technology

704 Entertainment and the Arts

708 Farm
Agricultural Equipment, Crops and Soil Management, Dairy Farming, Livestock, Management, Miscellaneous, Regional

719 Finance

723 Fishing

724 Florists, Nurseries and Landscaping

726 Government and Public Service

731 Groceries and Food Products

736 Hardware

737 Home Furnishings and Household Goods

741 Hospitals, Nursing and Nursing Homes

743 Hotels, Motels, Clubs, Resorts, Restaurants

747 Industrial Operations

751 Information Systems

758 Insurance

760 International Affairs

761 Jewelry

762 Journalism and Writing

775 Laundry and Dry Cleaning

775 Law

780 Leather Goods

781 Library Science

783 Lumber

784 Machinery and Metal

786 Maintenance and Safety

787 Management and Supervision

792 Marine and Maritime Industries

794 Medical

804 Mining and Minerals

805 Music

808 Office Environment and Equipment

809 Paint

809 Paper

810 Pets

811 Photography Trade

814 Plumbing, Heating, Air Conditioning, Refrigeration

817 Printing

820 Real Estate

823 *Resources and Waste Reduction*

823 *Selling and Merchandising*

827 *Sport Trade*

832 *Stone and Quarry Products*

833 *Toy, Novelty and Hobby*

834 *Transportation*

835 *Travel*

839 *Veterinary*

841 **Scriptwriting**

841 *Business and Educational Writing*

856 *Playwriting*

887 *Screenwriting*

893 **Gag Writing**

901 **Greeting Card Publishers**

906 Close-up:
Perri Ardman, Maine Line
An editor looks for humorous cards that express emotions but allow readers to laugh at themselves and their relationships.

910 **Syndicates**

Services & Opportunities

920 **Author's Agents**

961 **Contests and Awards**

Appendix

979 **The Business of Freelancing**

979 *Developing a plan*

980 *Tools of the trade*

982 *Approaching markets*

983 *Sample magazine query*

984 *Sample book query*

986 *Manuscript mechanics*

987 *Mailing submissions*

988 *U.S. postage by the page*

989 *Canadian postage by the page*

990 *Recording submissions*

991 *Bookkeeping*

991 *Tax information*

992 *Rights and the writer*

997 *How much should I charge?*

1004 **Glossary**

1007 **Book Publishers Subject Index**

1007 *Nonfiction*

1020 *Fiction*

1023 **Index**

The Writing Profession

From the Editors

Welcome to the 59th edition of _Writer's Market_. We are here to help you in your search for markets to publish your work. We also can supply important information about the publishing industry and provide you with insights and tips from editors and fulltime writers.

Our work

We began preparing this edition by asking writers, editors and publishers about the industry and the changes in publishing during the past year. We also contacted more than 4,000 new and established markets for information on their submission policies and manuscript needs.

In addition, the 1988 _Writer's Market_ features:
● Upfront articles on taking charge of the writer/editor relationship and dealing with the dilemmas of submitting unsolicited manuscripts.
● A new section on book packagers, producers and developers, and the opportunities they offer writers.
● Close-up interviews with 12 writers and editors who share their experience, advice and insights on the writing profession.
● Sample queries for a magazine article and a book manuscript in the revised and expanded Business of Freelancing Appendix.
● A new version of Using _Writer's Market_ featuring a sample listing and a step-by-step approach to reading listings and using all the information available in this book.

Your use of _Writer's Market_

You may be a student, a part-time writer or a fulltime freelancer relying on writing for your income. Experienced freelancers use _Writer's Market_ as the source for complete information on current freelance opportunities. Those who rely on writing for a little extra income and a lot of self-satisfaction find it an important tool in identifying markets that buy their type of writing. And beginners trying to break in to print find it indispensable for its details on how to approach editors and submit manuscripts and for the wide variety of market listings.

You'll find markets for consumer and trade publications, as well as scriptwriting, gag writing, greeting cards and syndicates. Be sure to read the introductions to each market section and category. You'll find helpful information on trends, industry practices, related sections and special methods for submitting your material.

Services and Opportunities contains information about author's agents and contests for writers. The Appendix at the back of the book answers questions about the business side of writing, ranging from manuscript preparation to current rates for freelance work.

We hope you understand that between the time this book goes to press and the time you read it, some details in the market listings may change. We make additions, corrections and changes in the listings until the book is sent to the printer, but often publishers go out of business, editors find other jobs, and publications change their focuses, payment or submission policies. Listings for new markets and changes in others can be found throughout the year in *Writer's Digest*, the monthly magazine for freelance writers.

As editors we appreciate readers who send us information they discover about new market opportunities. And we want to know if you have complaints about nonpayment or lack of response from any market we've listed. Always enclose a self-addressed, stamped envelope if you expect a reply.

Best wishes for success in your writing.

Glenda Tennant Neff

Robin L. Gee

Kathleen Vonderhaar

Important

● Listings are based on editorial questionnaires and interviews. They are *not* advertisements; publishers do not pay for their listings. The markets are *not* endorsed by *Writer's Market* editors.

● All listings have been verified before publication of this book. If a listing has not changed from last year, then the editor told us the market's needs have not changed and the previous listing continues to accurately reflect its policies. We require documentation in our files for each listing and never run a listing without its editorial office's approval.

● *Writer's Market* reserves the right to exclude any listing.

● When looking for a specific market, check the index. A market may not be listed for one of these reasons:

1. It doesn't solicit freelance material.
2. It doesn't pay for material.
3. It has gone out of business.
4. It has failed to verify or update its listing for the 1988 edition.
5. It was in the middle of being sold at press time, and rather than disclose premature details, we chose not to list it.
6. It hasn't answered *Writer's Market* inquiries satisfactorily. (To the best of our ability, and with our readers' help, we try to screen out dishonest listings.)
7. It buys few manuscripts, thereby constituting a very small market for freelancers.

_____ Using Writer's Market

If you've browsed through the Table of Contents, you've already found several sections that interest you. Before you plunge into the listings which follow, however, take time to read this section. It will allow you to make full use of the individual market listings and will explain the symbols and abbreviations used throughout the book.

Symbols and abbreviations are explained in the box at the end of this section. The most important abbreviation is SASE—self-addressed, stamped envelope. *Always* enclose one when you write to an editor or publisher. This requirement is not included in the individual market listings because it's a "given" that you *must* follow if you expect to receive a reply.

Review the following sample listing and the explanation section that accompanies it. This listing is from the 1987 edition and should not be used to submit articles to the market.

	(1) ‡**SPLASH, Art and Contemporary Culture**, Crandall Enterprises, Inc.
contact names	458A N. Tamiami Trail, Osprey FL 33559. **(2)** (813)966-5137. **(3)** Editor:
size of market	Jordan Crandall. Managing Editor: Lisa D. Black. **(4)** 75% freelance written.
publication's	**(5)** A bimonthly magazine covering the arts, "but we are eclectic. *Splash* is
emphasis and	devoted to art and contemporary culture. Our audience is generally
readership	well-educated and interested in the arts. There is no special slant, per se, but we
	dare to be controversial and are decidedly progressive in our thinking." Circ.
rights purchased	5,000. **(6)** Pays 30 days after publication. Publishes ms an average of 4 months
submission	after acceptance. Byline sometimes given. Buys first rights. **(7)** Submit
requirements	seasonal/holiday material 4 months in advance. Simultaneous and photocopied
reporting time	submissions OK. **(8)** Reports in 2 weeks on queries; 1 month on mss. **(9)** Sample
	copy $3; free writer's guidelines.
types of nonfiction	**(10)** Nonfiction: **(11)** Essays; expose; general interest; historical/nostalgic;
needed	humor; interview/profile; opinion; personal experience; photo feature;
	religious; travel; and reviews (art, music, film, books, dance). Does not want
	anything in a strictly journalistic mode—no newspaper-type mss will be
	considered. **(12)** Buys 50-60 mss/year. **(13)** Query with or without published
word length	clips, or send complete ms. **(14)** Length: 250-2,000 words. **(15)** Pays $50-350.
payment rates	**(16)** Sometimes pays expenses of writers on assignment, but generally does not
	assign freelance writers.
photo requirements,	**Photos:** **(17)** State availability or send photos with submission. Reviews b&w
rates and policies	glossy prints, any size. Offers $5-25/photo. Captions, model releases and
	identification of subjects required. Buys one-time rights; photo essays, first
	time rights only.
column/department	**Columns/Departments:** **(18)** Expo (reviews on *all* the arts—local as well as
needs, rates and	national), 500-750 words; Opine (educated opinions on politics, art, religion,
policies	current issues), 750-1,250 words; Arena (short sophisticated humor), 250-500
	words; Studio (introduction to new and/or emerging talents in all the arts),
	500-1,000 words. Buys 25 mss/year. Query with published clips. Length:
	250-1,250 words. Pays $50-250.
fiction needs, rates	**Fiction: (19)** "We use very *little* fiction at present." Confession, experimental,
and policies	fantasy, novel excerpts and slice-of-life vignettes. "No lengthy stories (no
	book-size texts)—the shorter the fiction, and the more avant garde, the better the
	chances are that we will use it." Buys 5 mss/year. Query with published clips.
	Length: 250-1,000 words. Pays $50-350.
poetry needs, rates	**Poetry: (20)** "We use very little poetry at present." No traditional,
and policies	Victorian-type verse; "the shorter and more avant garde, the better." Buys 5
	poems/year. Submit maximum 10 poems. Length: 5-75 lines. Pays $15-75.
filler needs and rates	**Fillers: (21)** Anecdotes, facts and short humor. Buys 10/year. Length: 150-500
	words. Pays $15-75.
inside information	**Tips: (22)** "Our style is progressive, avant garde. In a word, our magazine is
from the editor	*style-oriented* and decidedly *not* journalistic. If a manuscript is approached
	aesthetically as opposed to journalistically it has a much better chance of being
	published. Sample writings ought to be sent and perhaps a cover letter stating
	interests, etc. All areas are open to freelancers. Reviews must be topical,
	interesting, insightful and succinct. The interviews we do are generally with
	accomplished, well-known people in all fields—art, literature, politics,
	entertainment. As above, we require progressive writers and not journalists."

(1) One or more symbols (*, ‡,□) may precede the name and address of the publication or market; check the key at the end of this section for their meanings. (This double dagger signifies a new listing.)

(2) A phone number in a listing does not mean the market accepts phone queries. Make a phone query only when your story's timeliness would be lost by following the usual procedures. As a rule, don't call unless you have been invited to do so.

(3) In most listings, names of contact persons are given in the first paragraph or under the bold subheadings. Address your query or submission to a specific name when possible. If the name is not easily recognizable by gender, use the full name (e.g., Dear Dale Smith:). If no contact name is given, consult a sample copy. As a last resort, you can address your query to "Articles editor" or what is appropriate. For more information, read Approaching Markets in the Appendix.

(4) A market's general openness to writers is indicated by the percentage of freelance material used or by the percentage of published manuscripts from new, unagented writers. Since most publications are copyrighted, the information is only given in this spot when the publication is not copyrighted. For information on copyrighting your own work, see Rights and the Writer in the Appendix.

(5) A description of the market provides the focus and audience. The date a market was established can help you evaluate its stability. New markets may be open to freelancers, but they can also be riskier. Circulation figures listed are the total of subscriptions plus off-the-shelf sales.

(6) General business policies give information about rights purchased and time of payment. For more information on types of rights for sale, see Rights and the Writer in the Appendix.

(7) Submission requirements include how far in advance to submit seasonal material and whether or not previously published and photocopied material will be considered. Send manuscripts or queries to one market at a time unless it indicates simultaneous submissions are OK. If you send your manuscript to more than one market at a time, always mention in your cover letter that it is a simultaneous submission. Computer printouts and electronic submissions are mentioned only if the market accepts them. See Tools of the Trade in the Appendix for more information.

(8) Reporting times indicate how soon a market will respond to your query or manuscript, but times listed are approximate. Quarterly publications, book publishers, literary magazines and all new listings may be slow to respond. Wait four weeks beyond the stated reporting time before you send a polite inquiry.

(9) If you're interested in writing for a particular market, request the writer's guidelines and/or a sample copy if the market indicates availability. "Writer's guidelines for SASE" means that a business-size envelope with one First Class stamp will be adequate. You should request a sample copy if you are unable to find the publication at a newsstand or library. A sample copy or book catalog is often available for a 9x12 self-addressed envelope with a specified number of stamps or International Reply Coupons. Most publishers will send, at no extra charge, writer's guidelines with sample copies if you request them.

(10) Subheads in bold (Nonfiction, Photos, etc.) guide you to requirements for those types of materials.

(11) The specific material desired (and often material *not* desired) is listed. Follow the guidelines. Do not send fiction to a publication that only uses nonfiction; do not send a children's book manuscript to a publisher of men's adventure novels.

(12) The number of manuscripts purchased per issue or per year will give you an idea of how easy or difficult it may be to sell your work to a particular market. With new listings, these figures may change dramatically depending on the submissions they receive or changes in policy.

(13) If the market wants to see queries, that's what you should send. The same goes for outlines and sample chapters, etc. Don't send a complete manuscript unless the listing indicates it's acceptable.

(14) Editors know the length of most material they buy; follow their range of words or pages. If your manuscript is longer or shorter (by a wide margin) than the stated requirements, find another market.

(15) Payment ranges tell you what the market usually paid at the time *Writer's Market* was published.

(16) Whether a market sometimes or usually pays expenses of writers on assignment is listed. No mention is made when a market does not pay expenses.

(17-21) Needs, rates and policies for specified material.

(22) Helpful suggestions are listed under the subhead Tips in many listings. They describe the best way to submit manuscripts or give special insight into needs and preferences of the market.

Key to Symbols and Abbreviations

‡ New listing in all sections

* Subsidy publisher in Book Publishers section

□ Cable TV market in Scriptwriting section

ms-manuscript; mss-manuscripts

b&w-black and white (photo)

SASE-self-addressed, stamped envelope

SAE-self-addressed envelope

IRC-International Reply Coupon, for use on reply mail in Canada and foreign markets.

Getting Published: A Conflict of Views

by Glenda Tennant Neff

We've always considered *Writer's Market* a meeting ground where writers and the publishing industry come together. That's why this year we read with concern a number of letters from our readers voicing complaints against the industry.

When *Publishers Weekly* ran a series of heated guest editorials from writers, publishers and agents, we decided it was time to investigate.

The last months have been spent talking and corresponding with writers, editors and agents. What follows is an attempt to show both sides of the controversy over unsolicited and unagented submissions. The *Writer's Market* editorial staff can't solve these complicated problems or harmonize all the viewpoints. But we know writers and the publishing industry can't survive without each other and feel this discussion can promote more understanding of each side's perspective. On the plus side for writers—our research has turned up some tried and true advice for marketing work and we're pleased to be able to pass it on to you.

Publishing's Catch-22s

To many writers, the world of book publishing seems like a series of Catch-22s. First, you're told it will be difficult to get your book published unless you've already had something else published. But you can't get published until someone considers your submissions, and many publishers won't (or can't) read unsolicited or unagented submissions. So you try to get an agent, but none will consider you as a client until you've had something published.

Initially, you should recognize that you're not alone in your frustration. "I would like to know why it's so hard for a good writer to get anything published," one writer tells us. "It seems people who commit crimes or do some silly thing which makes headlines get publishers running to publish their books, but a legitimate person who wants to write more than anything can't get a toe in the door. I've sent in dozens of short stories, articles and have written three novels, none of which has been given the time of day by an agent or publisher or magazine editor. Do they even read anything from someone totally unknown?"

Unsolicited submissions

Even some published writers consider the odds overwhelming for an unagented or unsolicited manuscript or query. Author Gila Berkowitz[1] says she sent query letters for her cookbook to 25 major publishers. "A dozen of these responded with requests for more material. Three publishers made serious offers. But what still makes me mad is the attitude of the 13 publishers who never even gave me a fighting chance. Seven of these didn't bother to answer my query at all. Of the six who responded, not one publisher rejected my query on the grounds that the book seemed uninteresting, poorly written and organized or inappropriate for their list. The sole reason offered for rejection was that they *refused to consider unsolicited material*."

When refusing to consider unsolicited or unagented submissions, publishers and editors point to the economics of publishing. Ann Finlayson[2] says: "The publishing business operates on an extremely slender profit margin. To survive, it pays its employees on a wage scale that compares favorably *only* to the earnings of after-school grocery baggers at the supermarket. No one who has not sat down, day after day, and shuffled through the stuff that comes in unsolicited can imagine how unspeakably godawful most of it is. Occasionally out of that vast sea of heaving slop a bit of usable material can be fished up—but not often enough to make it worth the cost of trolling." Finlayson, a freelance copy editor and proofreader for more than 30 years, adds that it's not publishers or agents, but writers who submit unpublishable manuscripts who are the "enemies" of publishable writers.

Book producer Paul Fargis echoes her thoughts. "It's so hard for me, on the other side, to read the letters from writers in *Publishers Weekly* about the slush pile and 'How can they do this to me?' "says Fargis. "I've been on the receiving end, and for years I used to go through the slush, searching for the gem. You can't believe what's in there—the awful material. You can tell the writer has no conception of what can be published and what will sell. Writers don't want to hear that, but they really need to."

An agent can help

In order to move their manuscripts out of the slush pile of unsolicited material, writers should seek representation by an agent, say several writers and agents. "It is possible to get published without an agent," says Lori Perkins[3]. "But why should a writer teach him- or herself about the publishing industry, when he or she could work with someone who knows the field inside out?"

Author Richard Cummings points to other benefits of having an agent. "My agent has stimulated me to think of new subjects and new markets. She has made contacts for me that I could not have made myself, particularly in the field of television. I sell my own work because of its quality, but my agent gets that work to the editors. Without her, what I have written might never be read."

But many writers say finding a good agent is difficult unless the writer is already published. "A good author/agent fit takes more luck than a Hollywood marriage, and most writers are several volumes into their careers before they find a suitable representative," Berkowitz says.

Perkins, a literary agent with Barbara Lowenstein Associates, contends that writers' problems in finding the right agent often stem from a lack of serious effort or recognition of competition. "Writers often complain that getting an agent is as difficult as getting published, but most writers don't take the process of obtaining an agent as seriously as they take getting published. The literary agency I work in receives at least 100 query letters and unsolicited manuscripts a month. Most of them are awful, but we read through them anyway, hoping to find that gem in the middle of the slush pile. If a literary agency receives 100 queries a month, you can imagine how many letters and manuscripts a publishing house receives."

Another agent, Barbara W. Yedlin, says she worked for "friends, friends of friends, and local writers" until she opened her agency and listed it in the 1987 *Writer's Market*. "Little did I dream what the results of a listing would produce quantitatively, how many writers and would-be writers were existing in the U.S. landscape, and how many of them wanted help and representation." Of the "hundreds of queries and manuscripts" she's received, Yedlin says: "I have found five writers worth working for. Only one of these is talented, prolific, and published—the other four have at least one of these qualities and merit assistance."

Author John E. Stith says he succeeded in getting an agent to sell his science fiction book *Scapescope* by carefully planning his search. "First, I wrote and sold about a dozen short stories and articles. Second, I completed my novel. Third, I formed two lists of agents: those who were mentioned in *Writer's Market* as being open to new clients, and those who represented writers in Science Fiction Writers of America. Agents I found on both lists went onto my final list. Fourth, I sent a one-page query to the first agent on the list. The letter mentioned my credits and described the novel. That agent said he wasn't taking on new clients unless personally recommended by one of his existing clients. The second (agent) said he would be willing to look at the novel. After that, he proceeded to sell it. I've been pleased and impressed with his efforts ever since."

Other writers have not had good experiences with agents, however, and prefer to market their manuscripts over the transom. "I went through three (agents) when I was starting out and all they did was let me think I was being represented so I didn't hustle for myself," says author Tony Fennelly. "After the last agent dropped me, I finally sold my first book, *The Glory Hole Murders*, on my own via an over the transom query. It was nominated for an Edgar and after that, selling came easy." J. Birney Dibble contends that writers can get published without agents. "Don't believe anyone who tells you differently. The key is persistence. My first novel went to a dozen publishers over a three-year period before being accepted."

Other ways to market

Some writers and editors suggest marketing work to small publishing houses since they often are willing to consider unsolicited or unagented submissions. "Small press publishers are the answer to your question," says Audrey Parente, 1986-87 president of Small Press Writers' and Artists' Organization. "If writers as a block are to survive, apart from the handful of superstars and conglomerates, there is a need for reliable, approachable small press publishers. These are the publishers who will take an unsolicited query or manuscript from the as-yet-unknown writer. The industry is small scale, not big bucks. If the writer moves into the big bucks after his small press book has achieved a reputation, an agent can be acquired."

Small publishing house editors, however, caution writers against assuming they are an easy mark for less than first-rate submissions. Although many small houses consider unsolicited manuscripts, "We are probably more selective, not less, about what we publish than the big houses, simply because we have fewer slots per year to fill," says Charles Fortier, senior editor at North Country Press.

Author K.T. Anders also reminds authors that some of the larger publishing houses are still open to unsolicited submissions. "I sent my first novel, a spy thriller entitled *Legacy of Fear*, to an agent who took three months to reject it. The next agent took five months before sending it back. I wasn't getting any younger, and worried that I'd be old and gray before finding a middleman to handle my book, I submitted it over the transom, to Avon. Four months and only two gray hairs later, I had sold my first book. I didn't know it couldn't be done."

Published writers also tell *Writer's Market* they stress the importance of sending a good query letter. "I'm convinced that editors do read queries carefully," says Deborah Gorman. "Writers should take as much care in writing and polishing a query letter as a final manuscript." Tony Fennelly agrees. "Editors do read queries," he says. "And if yours is arresting enough, it will rise to the top of the slush pile."

Author William Brittain urges writers to be flexible and willing to revise their manuscripts. "If any publisher expresses interest but asks if you'd consider revisions—or even a complete rewrite—say yes! Few publishers will consider a new author who believes his work is so marvelous as to be 'untouchable.' "

Whether you're submitting a query, complete manuscript or an outline with sample chapters, it's important to follow the publisher's guidelines, tailor your submission to the needs and requirements of the house, and show the kind of courtesy you want to receive. "Unsolicited manuscripts are our lowest priority and those without a SASE are a burden to us," says Gilbert Campbell, editor/publisher of Filter Press. "We have received 10-pound manuscripts with a 22 cent stamp for reply."

On the other side, we continue to hear that writers long for more feedback from publishers. "Large, reputable houses say they want to see the entire manuscript. You send it, and it's as if they disappeared off the face of the earth," says author Nathan Aaseng[4]. "I resent the attitude that publishers are doing 'a work of charity' by reading my proposals. Do they consider it charity when a bookstore agrees to stock their books?"

Writer Harold Emanuel concurs. "My problem is not finding publishers to read my manuscript. My problem is determining the reason my manuscript was rejected. The editor says my manuscript isn't strong enough. I would be happy to strengthen my manuscript if I knew exactly what they would require to make my manuscript publishable. An unpublished author is working in the dark. We need someone to provide us with a flashlight and give us some guidance on how to reach sunlight.''

Even though a rejection can be only an unilluminating form letter, William Brittain urges writers to continue perfecting their work and marketing their manuscripts. "Don't be discouraged by rejection slips. They don't represent a rejection of your way of life, your religion and your political philosophy. They mean merely that *this* particular publisher is not interested in *this* particular work at *this* particular time. Keep trying. My first book for kids, *All the Money in the World*, was rejected by five publishers before Harper & Row took a flyer on my unsolicited manuscript. It ended up winning the Charlie May Simon Award in the state of Arkansas and being adapted for ABC-TV.''

The end-all solution

You've read many perspectives now and probably agree there is no easy solution to the frustrations of all sides. But there is one positive action writers can take that never fails: Make sure the submission, whether agented or over the transom, is your best writing. "There's one surefire way to get into print," says Tony Fennelly. "Just write better than 90 percent of the professionals working in the same genre. Master your craft and you'll succeed.''

Editor's note: The author wishes to recognize the help of *Publishers Weekly* Executive Editor Daisy Maryles, Science Fiction Writers of America, Small Press Writers' and Artists' Organization, National Writers Club, Romance Writers of America, Mystery Writers of America, Western Writers of America and all the writers who shared their experiences and helped in compiling this article.

[1]All quotes by Gila Berkowitz are excerpted from "Open Up That Transom!" *Publishers Weekly*, April 4, 1986.

[2] Excerpted from "Why We Call It Slush," *Publishers Weekly*, May 16, 1986.

[3] All quotes by Lori Perkins are excerpted from "The Truth About Agents," *Publishers Weekly*, March 6, 1987.

[4] Excerpted from "The Standard Line," *Publishers Weekly*, Aug. 8, 1986.

The Writer-Editor Relationship: Taking Charge

by William Brohaugh

I can roughly translate many of the questions I field from writers into a single question: *How can I light fires under editors?*

The need for such editorial ignition stems from a variety of problems: the editors (or agents) in question are slow to respond, to take notice and even to pay. The writers who encounter procrastinating or inefficient or (and it sometimes happens) uncaring editors want responses to their queries and especially payment within a reasonable time. They also want to be given the courtesy they deserve as working professionals, and they want to be able to have control over their situations.

There are a variety of ways to solve these problems, to gain control, to light fires. Some of them involve specific negotiation tactics, which I'll describe in a moment. Most, however, involve a general attitude you must employ in dealing with editors. It's a businesslike, professional and *distanced* attitude that will first give you perspective on the problems you're encountering, and will next allow you to handle the problems without placing a self-destructive fire under *yourself*.

The writer-editor debt

The first step in approaching problems with editors is to identify which situations warrant fire-starting and which don't. Sometimes you're far better off ignoring a "problem" (because it isn't one, or isn't one worth correcting), or shrugging it off, or dealing with it in a more constructive way. To make that identification, remember that there are two types of responses an editor gives you:

- those the editor owes you, and
- those the editor does not owe you.

For example, an editor does not, in any sense of binding obligation, owe you a response to an unsolicited query. And here I'm not talking matters of courtesy. Professional courtesy does indeed dictate that the editor respond to you, as quickly as possible. But the editor does not *owe* you a response. You have approached him, without being asked, with a business proposition. If the editor isn't interested, that's the end of it. Nor does the editor *owe* you immediate response to unsolicited material. With all the proofreading and business meetings and budget work and correspondence with writers on assignment and personnel work and everything else an editor does to get a magazine to press or a book in the stores, unsolicited material often must be given low priority.

Therefore, if an editor is slow to respond or doesn't respond at all, take professional umbrage at lack of courtesy, then calmly and systematically move on to the next editor. Don't berate the editor for his apparent lackadaisicalness. Don't try to light fires. In this case, you're only heating up tempers.

If the material was *solicited*, on the other hand, the editor does indeed owe you an answer.

William Brohaugh is editor of Writer's Digest *magazine and author of* Professional Etiquette for Writers *(Writer's Digest Books).*

By asking you to send it, the editor has made an implicit commitment to consider the work and to let you know what he thinks of it—within a reasonable amount of time. Here's where you can and should bring out the matches if you feel you're not being treated well.

Therefore, when you have a problem with an editor, first determine whether it's a problem that you can do anything about in the first place. To do that, translate the situation into something closer to home—at your doorstep, to be more precise: the traveling salesperson.

Assume that you're not a writer, but someone selling magazine subscriptions door to door. Assume that the editor is a customer behind one of those doors. Then ask what the editor should be required to do when the magazine salesperson comes aknockin'. Ask yourself what *you* would do in that particular situation.

• If the salesperson leaves a flyer at your door detailing the magazines available, would you be obligated to specifically inform the salesperson if you're not interested?

• If you turn down the magazine offer, are you obligated to tell the salesperson exactly *why* you're saying no?

• If you buy the magazine and pay for it, would you be offended if the salesperson tried to dictate how soon you read it?

• If you buy the magazine but don't pay for it right away, does the salesperson have the right to demand payment?

The answers vary. But phrasing the questions in this way gives you some perspective on the writer-editor relationship, and helps you determine a reasonable course of action.

Problem-solving

I must stress that we aren't speaking matters of courtesy here; we're speaking *obligations*. You can't ignite courtesy. It just won't happen. "Be courteous to me," you shout, shaking your fist. You can guess the response to that. You *can* ignite fulfillment of obligations, however.

To do that, take these steps:

1. Inquire politely about the problem. Don't place blame—in fact, you might want to deflect potential confrontation by shifting blame elsewhere. The post office, for instance, is a common scapegoat. "I haven't heard from you, and I wondered if you even received my query."

2. Inquire more firmly. "It's been some weeks since I mailed the manuscript, and I haven't received a response. What's its status?"

3. Call. Sometimes problems can be solved quickly and easily on the phone; sometimes not. Sometimes it prompts immediate action (it's harder to dodge things in conversation than through correspondence); sometimes it only aggravates the problem, especially when the editor fields several nagging phone calls he doesn't think are justified. It's this very chanciness of using the phone that makes it inappropriate as a first step.

4. Determine if you want to pursue the matter further. If not, withdraw the manuscript or query, or back away from the situation as appropriate (obviously you don't want to do that if money is involved). If so, make your third mail inquiry the firmest. "I still haven't received a response, and though I'd like to work with you, I need to know if you'll be buying my manuscript or if I should market it elsewhere."

5. Look to others for help:

• Might a letter to the editor's boss prompt some action? Go over someone's head only as a last resort, however. Such a fire under an editor can burn a tender place, and he will blame you for it. It could mean the end of a relationship.

• Would someone with less authority (and perhaps a less demanding schedule) be able to check into things for you? For example, a managing editor—who monitors production schedules—might be able to answer your questions.

• Would an invoice to the accounting department spur payment? This is often an effective way of securing overdue payment.

- Would a letter from your lawyer open some eyes? The lawyer might not be able to do anything specifically, but no one, including an editor, wants to get into legal squabbles.
- Would a trip to small claims court be appropriate? Not if you're seeking the contributor copies the editor promised, but perhaps if that payment check has been slow in coming.

Pre-ignition

Perhaps one of the best ways of lighting fires is to have them burning from the very start of your working relationship with an editor. Give the editor every reason to *want* to work with you efficiently and responsibly, to respond and pay quickly, to treat you with courtesy. To do that, *be a professional*. Professionals want to work with—and are generally far more responsive to—other professionals. Here's how to get editors to want to work with you, and to keep *you* happy:

- Remember that courtesy, though it can't be ignited, can be bred—with courtesy. Certainly don't genuflect before editors, but do treat them with the respect you'd accord to anyone else you have business dealings with.
- Try to eliminate possible problems early on. If the editor hasn't said when or how much you will be paid, ask, and get the answer on paper. If you want to see prepublication galleys, negotiate for that right before you finalize the assignment. If the article you're submitting is timely, request an answer within a specified time so that the manuscript won't go stale.
- Learn as much as you can about the business so that you'll know what to expect: what ways of handling things are standard operating procedures, what ways vary from situation to situation, what ways are unusual? Much of this education simply comes with time and experience; more comes from doing a little reading. I recommend these books: *The Awful Truth About Publishing*, by John Boswell; *Books: From Writer to Reader*, by Howard Greenfeld; *How to Understand & Negotiate a Book Contract or Magazine Agreement* and *A Writer's Guide to Book Publishing*, by Richard Balkin; and *Magazine Editing and Production*, by J.W. Click and Russell N. Baird.
- Enclose a self-addressed, stamped envelope in all correspondence. The SASE not only invites response, but also instills in your correspondent a feeling of obligation to respond.
- Don't whine, gnash teeth, moan or scream during negotiations or even when complaining. State your case clearly and vigorously, but unemotionally. Remember that you're two businesspeople at this point, not two temperamental geniuses locking creative horns.
- Don't go in with the attitude that the editor is trying to rip you off. Sure, some disreputable editors are out there. Some disreputable writers are out there, too. But not many, and not enough to worry about. Paranoia about having your work stolen only gives off the wrong signals to the people you're working with, and wastes *your* time.
- Don't insult the editor by trying to trick or manipulate him. I recently heard of a writer who submitted manuscripts single-spaced, typed to every margin, not because the writer didn't understand the conventions of basic manuscript preparation, but because the writer wanted to preclude editing by not giving the editor space in which to make editing marks. Trickery and manipulation always backfire. As clever or as compelling as you think you're being—from inserting a page upside down to see if the editor has read the manuscript to threatening to cancel your subscription if the editor doesn't buy the piece—the editor has likely seen it all before.

Taking control

There are also ways to gain control that don't depend on the editor. For example:
- Some writers complain of editors who lose or damage manuscripts. The solution: don't depend on the editor to send your manuscript back. Just don't send an important copy in the first place—that is, keep the original, and send a photocopy, one that, if lost or damaged, you can replace.

• Some writers worry about editors changing the titles of their manuscripts without consulting them. The solution: give the editor a choice of titles. Better yet, write a title that is very much in the style of the magazine you're selling to. (You might also negotiate for the right to approve the title before you finalize the magazine assignment or before you sign the book contract.)

• Some writers want to conduct business with great speed. The solution: set a deadline for a response from an editor. But don't force the deadline on the editor unless nothing else has worked and you're ready to go into your "or-else" mode ("I need a response by the 15th or else I'll be forced to withdraw the manuscript"). In your own mind, set a deadline. If you don't hear from the editor by that date, assume the editor isn't interested and move on to the next. If the editor eventually says no, you haven't wasted any time waiting for the answer. If the editor says yes, you have the choice of working with that editor or with an editor you moved on to who said yes.

• Some writers get peeved by lack of editorial courtesy. The solution: simplistic, maybe, but just don't get peeved. Decide on a list of things you Won't Worry About. Sure, it's aggravating when you send first-class postage for the return of your manuscript and it comes back fourth class. But why worry about it? You're out a few cents, maybe a couple of bucks. Consider it a part of the business, and worry about something more important. That and supposedly filched paper clips and the like are inconsequential. This is related to the concept of knowing what editors do and don't owe you. Yes, on an absolute bottom-line basis, they owe you that postage and those paper clips. But is worrying about it, fretting over it, complaining about it going to gain you anything?

In other words, sometimes putting a fire under the editor doesn't solve anything. In the long run, the most important thing is for you to take charge, in a professional way, of your own writing career.

The Markets

Book Publishers

Book publishers tell us they receive too many manuscripts that are clones of current bestsellers, manuscripts that have no audience or are not yet publishable. Writers in turn let us know they blame editors and publishers for not giving adequate attention to their manuscripts.

How can you overcome the obstacles to being published? First, understand some facts about the industry as a whole. Book publishing is a blend of business and intuition that varies from one publishing house to the next. In deciding which books to publish, most rely on a combination of an editor's enthusiasm for a manuscript and statistics from those who analyze each book's sales potential. Some publishers consider only books that look like bestsellers. Others are proud to produce a few literary novels that will have only moderate sales compared to the other books on their list.

Like most businesses, publishing companies have been at the mercy of economic changes in the last few years. Don't suppose that as a writer you are not affected when two publishers merge or when a conglomerate or foreign investor buys a publishing firm. Those changes are made for economic reasons and the usual effect is belt tightening while firms try to produce a profitable operation.

As a result, many publishers now have smaller editorial staffs that are unable to review every query, proposal and manuscript. It's no longer possible for them to consider hundreds, or thousands, of manuscripts each year. That's why many editors rely on agents to sift through the stacks of proposals before they pass on the best ones. This situation affects all writers, but especially beginners who have no publishing track record.

As you continue writing and trying to sell your books, take time to learn more about the publishing industry. Once you understand the role of editors and the complexities of the business, you'll see how you can improve your queries and manuscripts. Your study of specific publishers also will be a good investment in your writing future.

Trends and transitions

Although publishers plan titles years in advance, predicting popular topics and types of books is always risky. Current events and population trends will certainly influence the types of books published in 1988. As a writer, you'll need to keep up with the most recent information and events.

Here are some trends that may affect what editors buy:

● Self-help, how-to and home and garden books continue to attract reader interest. Books that teach readers or show them how to improve their lives and surroundings are popular. If you know your subject well and can express yourself clearly, editors will be interested.

● Biographies, including sports and celebrity life stories, are pushing their way onto the bestseller lists with increasing frequency.

● Business books are popular, ranging from up-to-date office technology books, to those on business scandals, mistakes and the inside politics of international corporations.

- Books for and about children should find a ready market for the next few years. First-time parents want to know more about child care, development and parenting topics. They also want to provide good books for their children.
- Books about and by celebrities and experts help readers satisfy their curiosity about people and events in the news. They also must provide a glimpse behind the scenes to sustain reader interest.
- Books about reincarnation, astrology and the occult have become extremely popular. One publisher said "phenomenal interest" in the areas began with publication of Shirley Mac-laine's biography, *Out on a Limb*.

Study the market

Don't spend years writing a book and only a few days looking for a publisher. Give your book the best publisher possible. For some writers, the best is a publisher whose books regularly appear on the bestseller lists. For others, the best is a small press where each author gets personal attention from the editor.

No matter what type of book you've written, the Book Publisher section can help you. You'll find more than 800 publishers listed. Not all of them buy the kind of work you write, but studying the subject indexes at the back of the book will tell you which ones do.

When you read the detailed listings of publishers, choose two or three that buy what you're writing. Send for their catalogs and writer's guidelines. You'll learn the most current information about the books they've published, as well as their preferences for receiving manuscripts. Try to read a couple of the publishers' books; a visit to the library is all that's necessary.

You may be frustrated by the manuscript preparation or writer's guidelines you receive; it seems that each publisher prefers a different type of submission. Some will read only a query letter; some want a query with an outline or synopsis; others want a one-page proposal. If editors accept submissions only through agents, don't waste their time and yours by submitting material directly.

Most editors like specific information in query letters. Show that you understand their concerns by mentioning the audience for your book, the competition, and why your book is different. The editor also will want to know if you have previous publishing experience or special training relevant to the book. Do not claim to have written the next blockbuster bestseller—even if you think you have.

Remember that only a fraction of today's writers sell a book to the first place it's submitted. Prepare a list of at least a dozen publishers that might be interested in your book. Learn more about them; send for catalogs and guidelines a few at a time. If your submission comes back with a rejection, send it to the next publisher on your list.

You may be able to speed up this process with simultaneous submissions of your query letter or manuscript. It's usually acceptable to send queries to several editors at the same time—as long as each letter is individually addressed. Never send a form letter as a query. If more than one editor responds favorably, you may be able to submit your manuscript simultaneously. Some publishers, however, refuse to consider simultaneous submissions; their *Writer's Market* listings and their guidelines will tell you their policies. Otherwise, you can send your manuscript to two or more publishers at the same time—but you must notify the editors that it's a simultaneous submission.

Subsidy publishing

At the *Writer's Market* office, we receive many calls and letters asking about subsidy publishing and self-publishing. As you read more about the publishing industry, you'll undoubtedly find advertisements and articles describing the benefits of these alternatives. Be cautious. Know what you want from your writing.

Most writers want to make money from the books they write; not many succeed at first. Those who aspire to be professional writers know that it may take years to perfect a book, find the right publisher and receive royalty payments. They are willing to invest their time and efforts to meet that goal.

Some writers are more impatient. They've tried to sell a book and have met only rejection—encouraging rejection, maybe, but still rejection. They know they haven't written best-sellers, but they don't believe their books can be improved by further revision. They believe a specific market exists, and they want their books published.

Other writers simply write for their own satisfaction or for the pleasure of family and friends. Their writing may be just a hobby, but with some encouragement they begin to wonder if they could be published. They haven't tried to market a manuscript before and are confused about the differences between royalty publishers, subsidy publishers and self-publishing.

As a rule, we suggest you work with publishers that pay writers. Most publishers do this through a royalty arrangement, paying the author 3-25% of the wholesale or retail price. These publishers actively market their books; you'll find them in bookstores and libraries, read about them in the newspaper and sometimes see the author on TV. Whenever a copy of one of these books is sold, both the writer and the publisher make money.

Subsidy publishers, on the other hand, expect writers to pay part or all of the cost of producing a book. They may ask for $1,000 or sometimes as much as $18,000, explaining that current economic conditions in the industry necessitate it. Subsidy publishers rarely market books as effectively as major publishing companies. They make money by selling their services to writers, not by selling their products to bookstores and libraries. Some subsidy publishers offer royalties but expect the writer to pay for promotion expenses.

Problems can arise when writers don't understand the policies and terms of a subsidy publisher's proposal or contract. Don't sign anything unless you understand and are comfortable with the terms. If you are willing to pay to have your book published, you should be willing to hire an attorney to advise you on a contract.

Subsidy publishers are sometimes called "vanity" presses because the company appeals to a writer's ego in wanting to have his book published. Most subsidy publishers are offended when they are called vanity presses, but we don't distinguish between the two. Any publishing effort that asks the writer to pay all or part of the cost is identified as a subsidy publisher. Companies that ask authors to pay subsidies on more than 50% of the books they publish each year are listed in *Writer's Market* at the end of the Book Publishers section.

This doesn't mean that subsidy publishing is always a bad choice. In Canada, for example, books are often subsidized by government grants. In the U.S., a special interest book may be subsidized by the writer's friends, a foundation or church. Sometimes a royalty publisher or university press will offer a subsidy arrangement to a writer whose talent outweighs the marketing potential of the book. Companies that do this 50% of the time or less are identified with an asterisk before the listings.

Self-publishing

Self-publishing is another option for writers. Are you willing to pay for a few hundred to several thousand copies of your book? Can you supervise all stages of its production? Do you have the time and energy to promote and distribute the book yourself?

Your consideration of self-publishing should include answering these questions. The successful self-published book has a potential audience and fills a need not filled by current books on the topic. If you have submitted the manuscript to a publisher and had it rejected, you should also analyze the reasons for rejection. If your manuscript needs polishing, do that before you self-publish it. If a large publisher determined that it would not generate enough sales, however, remember that books do not have to sell in the same quantities for a self-published book to make money as for a large publisher to profit.

Writers interested in self-publishing also may approach a small press publisher and agree to split the cost of a press run. Some companies also call themselves self-publishers. More often, writers contract with a local printer to produce a specific number of books for a specific price.

As with subsidy publishing, be sure you know what's involved. "Done properly, self-publishing is an exciting and viable way to get your book into print," say Marilyn and Tom Ross, authors of *The Complete Guide to Self-Publishing* (Writer's Digest Books).

Marketing your manuscript

If you receive a number of rejections, don't give up. Many successful writers submit a manuscript to dozens of publishers before finding one to publish their book.

First, be sure you've done everything to improve your book's chances. Study writing and revision techniques and continue to study the markets. Many writers also find classes and writer's groups helpful in putting them in touch with other people who share their interest in writing.

No matter which method you choose—royalty, subsidy or self-publishing—remember that the writing of the book comes first. Think of your book as a manuscript in transition and help it evolve into the best book it can be while you search for the best possible publisher.

AASLH PRESS, American Association for State and Local History, 172 2nd Ave. N., Nashville TN 37201. (615)255-2971. Director of Programs: Candace Floyd. Publishes hardcover and softcover originals and reprints. Averages 6 titles/year; receives 20-30 submissions annually. 50% of books from first-time authors; 100% of books from unagented writers. Pays 5-10% royalty on retail price. Publishes book an average of 1 year after acceptance. Photocopied submissions OK. Computer printout submissions acceptable; prefers letter-quality to dot-matrix. Reports in 3 months on submissions. Free book catalog.
Nonfiction: How-to, reference, self-help and textbook. "We publish books, mostly technical, that help people do effective work in historical societies, sites and museums, or do research in, or teach, history. No manuscripts on history itself—that is, on the history of specific places, events, people." Submit outline/synopsis and sample chapters. Reviews artwork/photos.
Recent Nonfiction Title: *Museum Visitor Evaluation*, by Ross J. Loomis (how-to hardcover).
Tips: "Explain why our market will buy your book, use it, need it."

‡ABBEY PRESS, Publishing Division, St. Meinrad IN 47577. (812)357-8011. Publisher: Keith McClellan O.S.B. Publishes mass market paperback originals. Averages 10 titles/year. Receives 200 submissions/year. 40% of books from first-time authors; 100% of books from unagented writers. Pays 10% royalty on retail price. Publishes book an average of 1 year after acceptance. Photocopied submissions OK. Computer printout submissions OK; prefers letter-quality. Reports in 1 month on queries; 6 weeks on mss. Free book catalog. Ms guidelines for SASE.
Nonfiction: How-to, humor, illustrated book, juvenile and self-help. Subjects include psychology and religion. Especially looking for "manuscripts on marriage and family life, with specific attention to ways to enrich, support, and strengthen them through communication, counseling, activities, etc. No manuscripts with an anti-religious or anti-Christian bias." Query with outline/synopsis and sample chapters.
Recent Nonfiction Title: *Alzheimer's Disease: A Call to Courage for Caregivers*, by Martha O. Adams.
Fiction: All fiction must have religious values underlying the story. Will consider adventure, ethnic, fantasy, historical, mystery, religious and science fiction. "We're looking for religious fiction that gives evidence of human and spiritual values within life; generally, values should be implied instead of being badly stated. We do not want to see fiction that is filled with preaching and scripture quotes that do not flow naturally from the storyline. We seek religious fiction that helps the reader to discover or be awakened to religious experience in the midst of ordinary life." Query or submit complete ms.
Recent Fiction Title: *To Love and To Honor*, by B.J. Hoff (historical romance).
Tips: "Our audience includes Christian women and married couples who believe in the traditional family and are working to enrich their own marital and family relationships. These Christians, however, are not necessarily 'activists.' Religious titles as well as self-help continue to do well for us."

ABBOTT, LANGER & ASSOCIATES, 548 1st St., Crete IL 60417. (312)672-4200. President: Dr. Steven Langer. Small press. Publishes trade paperback originals and loose-leaf books. Averages 14 titles/year; receives 25 submissions annually. 75% of books from first-time authors; 100% of books from unagented writers.

Pays 10-15% royalty; no advance. Publishes book an average of 1 year after acceptance. Photocopied submissions OK. Query for electronic submissions. Computer printout submissions acceptable. Book catalog for 6x9 SAE with 39¢ postage. Reports in 2 weeks on queries; 1 month on mss.

Nonfiction: How-to, reference, technical on some phase of personnel administration, industrial relations, sales management, etc. Especially needs "a very limited number (3-5) of books dealing with very specialized topics in the field of personnel management, wage and salary administration, sales compensation, training, recruitment, selection, labor relations, etc." Publishes for personnel directors, wage and salary administrators, training directors, sales/marketing managers, security directors, etc. Query with outline. Reviews artwork/photos.

Recent Nonfiction Title: *Available Pay Survey Reports*, by S. Langer (annotated bibliography).

Tips: "A how-to book in personnel management, sales/marketing management or security management has the best chance of selling to our firm."

ABINGDON PRESS, 201 8th Ave. S., Box 801, Nashville TN 37202. (615)749-6403. Director of Publishing: Ronald P. Patterson. Senior Editor Trade Books: Michael E. Lawrence. Senior Editor Reference/Academic Books: Carey J. Gifford. Senior Editor Church Resources: Jean Crawford-Lee. Editor/Professional Books Editor: Robert Conn. Children's Books Editor: Etta Wilson. Publishes paperback originals and reprints; church supplies. Receives approximately 2,500 submissions annually. Published 100 titles last year. 10% of books from first-time authors; 90-95% of books from unagented writers. Average print order for a writer's first book is 4,000-5,000. Pays royalty. Publishes book an average of 18 months after acceptance. Query for electronic submissions. Computer printout submissions acceptable; prefers letter-quality to dot-matrix. Ms guidelines for SASE. Reports in 6 weeks.

Nonfiction: Religious-lay and professional, children's religious books and academic texts. Length: 32-300 pages. Query with outline and samples only. Reviews artwork/photos.

Recent Nonfiction Title: *Raising PG Kids in an X-Rated Society*, by Tipper Gore.

Fiction: Juveniles only. Reviews artwork/photos.

Recent Fiction Title: *Night Pleas*, by Martin Bell.

ACADEMY CHICAGO, 425 N. Michigan Ave., Chicago IL 60611. (312)644-1723. Editorial Director/Senior Editor: Anita Miller. Publishes hardcover and paperback originals and reprints. Averages 60 titles/year; receives approximately 2000 submissions annually. 10% of books from first-time authors; 25% of books from unagented writers. Average print order for a writer's first book 1,500-3,500. Pays 7-10% royalty; no advance. Publishes book an average of 18 months after acceptance. Photocopied submissions OK; no simultaneous submissions. No computer printout submissions. Book catalog for 8½x11 SAE with 59¢ postage; guidelines for #10 SAE with 1 first class stamp. Submit cover letter with first four chapters. Reports in 2 months.

Nonfiction: Adult, travel, and historical. No how-to, cookbooks, self help, etc. Query and submit first four consecutive chapters. Reviews artwork/photos.

Recent Nonfiction Title: *Ramage in South Italy*, edited by Edith Clay (travel).

Fiction: "Mysteries, mainstream novels." No "romantic," children's, young adult, religious or sexist fiction; nothing avant-garde.

Recent Fiction Title: *Judges' Chambers*, by Lowell Komie (short stories).

Tips: "The writer has the best chance of selling our firm a good mystery, because the response to these is predictable, relatively."

ACCELERATED DEVELOPMENT INC., 3400 Kilgore Ave., Muncie IN 47304. (317)284-7511. President: Dr. Joseph W. Hollis. Executive Vice President: Marcella Hollis. Publishes textbooks/paperback originals and software. Averages 10-15 titles/year; receives 120 submissions annually. 50% of books from first-time authors; 100% of books from unagented writers. Query for electronic submissions. Computer printout submissions acceptable; prefers letter-quality to dot-matrix. Pays 6-15% royalty on net price. Publishes book an average of 1 year after acceptance. Reports in 3 months. Book catalog for 9x12 SAE with 39¢ postage.

Nonfiction: Reference books and textbooks on psychology, counseling, guidance and counseling, teacher education and death education. Especially needs "psychologically-based textbook or reference materials, death education material, theories of counseling psychology, techniques of counseling, and gerontological counseling." Publishes for professors, counselors, teachers, college and secondary students, psychologists,

ALWAYS submit manuscripts or queries with a self-addressed, stamped envelope (SASE) within your country or International Reply Coupons purchased from the post office for other countries.

death educators, psychological therapists, and other health-service providers. "Write for the graduate level student." Submit outline/synopsis, 2 sample chapters, prospectus, and author's resume. Reviews artwork/ photos.

Recent Nonfiction Title: *Dictionary of Abbreviations and Acronyms in the Helping Professions*, by Joseph W. Hollis (mental health/dictionary).

Tips: "Freelance writers should be aware of American Psychological Association style of preparing manuscripts."

ACCENT BOOKS, A division of Accent Publications, 12100 W. 6th Ave., Box 15337, Denver CO 80215. (303)988-5300. Managing Editor: Mary B. Nelson. Publishes evangelical Christian paperbacks, the majority of which are nonfiction. Averages 18-24 titles/year. 30% of books from first-time authors; 100% of books from unagented writers. Pays royalty on cover price. Publishes book an average of 9 months after acceptance. Computer printout submissions acceptable; no dot-matrix. Query or submit 3 sample chapters with a brief synopsis and chapter outline. Do not submit full ms unless requested. Reports in 3 months. Book catalog for 9x6 SAE with 37¢ postage.

Recent Nonfiction Title: *Grown-Up Kids*, by Shirley Cook (adult friendships with adult children).

Fiction: "Fiction titles have strong evangelical message woven throughout plot and characters, and are either contemporary mystery/romance or frontier romance."

Recent Fiction Title: *Storm at Daybreak*, by B.J. Hoff.

Tips: "How-to books designed for personal application of Biblical truth and/or dealing with problems/solutions of philosophical, societal, and personal issues from a Biblical perspective have the best chance of selling to our firm. We also consider books for the professional and volunteer in church ministries."

ACE SCIENCE FICTION, The Berkley Publishing Group, 200 Madison Ave., New York NY 10016. (212)686-9820. Publishes paperback originals and reprints. Publishes 120 titles/year.

Fiction: Science fiction and fantasy. Query with outline and 3 sample chapters. Reports in 3 months.

ACROPOLIS BOOKS, LTD., Subsidiary of Colortone Press, 2400 17th St. NW, Washington DC 20009. (202)387-6805. Publisher: Alphons J. Hackl. Publishes hardcover and trade paperback originals. Averages 25 titles/year. Pays individually negotiated royalty. Publishes book an average of 7 months after acceptance. Query for electronic submissions. Computer printout submissions acceptable; prefers letter-quality to dot-matrix. Reports in 2 months. Free book catalog.

Nonfiction: How-to, reference and self-help. Subjects include health, beauty/fashion and money management. "We will be looking for manuscripts dealing with fashion and beauty, and self development. We also will be continuing our teacher books for early childhood education. Our audience includes general adult consumers, professional elementary school teachers and children." Submit outline/synopsis and sample chapters. Reviews artwork/photos as part of ms package.

Recent Nonfiction Title: *Earn College Credit for What you Know*, by Susan Simosko.

ACS PUBLICATIONS, INC., Box 16430, San Diego CA 92116-0430. (619)297-9203. Editorial Director: Maritha Pottenger. Small press. Publishes trade paperback originals and reprints. Averages 8 titles/year; receives 400 submissions annually. 50% of books from first-time authors; 95% of books from unagented writers. Average print order for a writer's first book is 3,000. Pays 15% royalty "on monies received through wholesale and retail sales." No advance. Publishes book an average of 2 years after acceptance. Photocopied submissions OK "if neat." Query for electronic submissions. Computer printout submissions acceptable; prefers letter-quality to dot-matrix. Reports in 1 month on queries; 2 months on mss. Book catalog and guidelines for 9x12 SAE with 56¢ postage.

Nonfiction: Astrology, self-help and New Age. Subjects include astrology, holistic health alternatives, psychology, numerology, and psychic understanding. "Our most important market is astrology. We are seeking pragmatic, useful, immediately applicable contributions to field; prefer psychological approach. Specific ideas and topics should enhance people's lives. Research also valued. No determinism ('Saturn made me do it.') No autobiographies. No airy-fairy 'space cadet' philosophizing. Keep it grounded, useful, opening options (not closing doors) for readers." Query or submit outline and 3 sample chapters.

Recent Nonfiction Title: *Complete Horoscope Interpretation*, by Maritha Pottenger (astrological reference).

Tips: "The most common mistake writers make when trying to get their work published is to send works to inappropriate publishers. We get too many submissions outside our field or contrary to our world view."

‡*ADAMS, HOUMES AND WARD BOOK PUBLISHERS, 660 West Fairbanks Ave., Winter Park FL 32789. (305)740-7359. Editor: Terry Houmes-Ward. Publishes hardcover and trade paperback originals. Averages 10 titles/year. Receives 50+ submissions/year. 95% of books from first-time authors. 90% of books from unagented writers. Subsidy publishes 40% of books. "If an author would like his book published in order to promote his business, practice or himself, we recommend self-publishing. And we offer assistance in helping authors go through this process. Other self (or subsidy) projects we work with are short runs of family histories, poetry, memoirs, reminiscences, etc." Pays 10-15% royalty; offers $1,000 average advance. Publishes book an average of 6 months after acceptance. Simultaneous and photocopied submissions OK. Reports in 3 weeks on queries; 2 months on mss. Free book catalog.

Nonfiction: Biography, how-to, self-help. Subjects include career, family histories, business histories, memoirs, autobiographies, reminiscences, poetry, and business and economics. "For our own publication (non-subsidy), we are interested in business and career books of the how-to and self-help variety." No computer books. Submit complete ms with descriptive cover letter. Reviews artwork/photos as part of ms package.

Recent Nonfiction Title: *By the Sun and Stars*, by Wladek Wagner (cruise sailing book).

Tips: Writers should be aware of "the growing popularity of 'recipe' type career and business self-help books that resemble workbooks or kits. We plan to publish more of these. Also books with a long shelf life. Another area we plan to explore in the near future is subjects for older Americans market. We will consider submissions in that area. I would not try to market a book on a subject area that I was not already active in as a professional or at least an enthusiast. A manuscript that is accomplished by a detailed plan on how the author can help market his book gets our attention."

‡BOB ADAMS, INC., 840 Summer St., Boston MA 02127. (617)268-9570. Managing Editor: Brandon Toropov. Publishes hardcover and trade paperback originals. Averages 7 titles/year. Receives 25 submissions/year. 25% of books from first-time authors. 25% of books from unagented writers. Variable royalty "determined on case-by-case basis." Publishes book an average of 12-18 months after acceptance. Computer printout submissions OK; prefers letter-quality. Reports in 6 months "if interested. We accept no responsibility for unsolicited manuscripts." Book catalog for 9x12 SAE with $2.40 postage.

Nonfiction: Reference books on careers and business. Query.

Recent Nonfiction Title: *Knock 'Em Dead*, by Martin Yate (interview techniques).

ADDISON-WESLEY PUBLISHING CO., INC., General Books Division, Jacob Way, Reading MA 01867. Publisher: Ann Dilworth. Publishes hardcover and paperback originals. Publishes 45-50 titles/year. Pays royalty. Simultaneous and photocopied submissions OK. Reports in 1 month. Free book catalog.

Nonfiction: Biography, history, business/economics, health, how-to, politics, psychology and science. Query, then submit outline/synopsis and 1 sample chapter.

Recent Nonfiction Title: *Lessons, An Autobiography*, by Dr. An Wang, founder of Wang Laboratories, with Eugene Linden.

Tips: Queries/mss may be routed to other editors in the publishing group.

AFFIRMATION BOOKS, 109 Woodland St., Natick MA 01760. (617)651-3893. Executive Editor: Marie Kraus. Publishes trade paperback originals. Publishes 4 titles/year; receives 75 submissions annually. 50% of books from first-time authors; 100% of books from unagented writers. Pays 5-10% royalty on retail or wholesale price. Publishes book an average of 1 year after acceptance. Simultaneous and photocopied submissions OK. Computer printout submissions acceptable; no dot-matrix. Reports in 3 months on queries; 6 months on mss. Book catalog for #10 SAE and 1 first class stamp.

Nonfiction: Self-help. Subjects include psychology (combined with religion) and religion (combined with psychology; Christian, no dogma). "Affirmation Books is part of the ministry of the House of Affirmation, international therapeutic residential centers for clergy and religious suffering from emotional unrest (not alcohol or drug problems). We need books for an audience that is primarily clergy and religious or lay people working in or for the church. Topics on healthy emotional living that will help people improve the quality of their lives. Not pop psychology; some research or mention of previous literature in the field." No personal journeys, alcohol or drug problems, or books aimed at parents only. Query or submit outline/synopsis and sample chapters. Reviews artwork/photos.

Recent Nonfiction Title: *Holy Mirth*, by Richard Cote.

Tips: "We are primarily a mail-order business although we are looking to expand our bookstore outlets. Because we have a specific audience, clergy, men and women religious, lay people in ministry, none of our backlist has gone out of print. We are interested in expanding our audience. The writer has the best chance of selling our firm a book that combines psychology and Christianity in a way that helps our audience improve the quality of their lives. No autobiographical material or personal journeys."

AGLOW PUBLICATIONS, A ministry of Women's Aglow Fellowship International, Box I, Lynnwood WA 98046-1557. (206)775-7282. Editor: Gwen Weising. Publishes mass market paperback originals. Averages 10

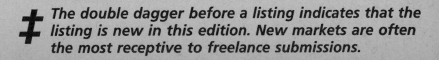

The double dagger before a listing indicates that the listing is new in this edition. New markets are often the most receptive to freelance submissions.

titles/year; receives 1,000 submissions annually. 50% of books from first-time authors; 95% of books from un-agented writers. Average print order of a writer's first book is 10,000. Pays up to 7½% maximum royalty on retail price "depending on amount of editorial work needed"; buys some mss outright. No advance. Publishes book 1 year after acceptance. Photocopied submissions OK. Computer printout submissions acceptable; prefers letter-quality to dot-matrix. Reports in 1 month on queries; 2 months on mss. Book catalog and guidelines for 9x12 SAE with 47¢ postage.

Nonfiction: Bible studies, self-help and inspirational. Subjects include religion (Christian only). "Familiarize yourself with our materials before submitting. Our needs and formats are very specific." Query or submit outline/synopsis and first 3 sample chapters.

Recent Nonfiction Title: *How to Pray for Your Children*, by Quin Sherrer.

Tips: "The writer has the best chance of selling our firm a book that shows some aspect of the Christian life."

AHSAHTA PRESS, Boise State University, Dept. of English, 1910 University Dr., Boise ID 83725. (208)385-1246. Co-Editor: Tom Trusky. Small press. Publishes trade paperback originals. Averages 3 titles/year; receives 500 submissions annually. 75% of books from first-time authors; 75% of books from unagented writers. Pays 25% royalty on retail price. "Royalty commences with third printing." Publishes books an average of 8 months after acceptance. Simultaneous and photocopied submissions OK. Computer printout submissions acceptable; prefers letter-quality to dot-matrix. Reports in 2 weeks on queries; 3 months on mss. Book catalog and ms guidelines for 9x12 SASE.

Poetry: Contemporary Western American (cultural ecological or historical) poetry collections only. No "rhymed verse, songs of the sage, buckaroo ballads, purple mountain's majesty, coyote wisdom; Jesus-in-the-prairie, or 'nice' verse." Accepts poetry translations from native American languages, Spanish and Basque. Submit 15 samples between February and April. "Write incredible, original poetry."

Recent Poetry Title: *Westering*, by Thomas Hornsby Ferril (poetry).

*ALASKA NATURE PRESS, Box 632, Eagle River AK 99577. Editor/Publisher: Ben Guild. Publishes hardcover and paperback originals. Plans to offer subsidy publishing "as needed—estimated 10%." Averages 2-6 titles/year. 75-80% of books from first-time authors; 100% of books from unagented writers. Pays 10% royalty on retail price; no advance. Publishes book 24-30 months after acceptance. Simultaneous and photocopied submissions OK. Computer printout submissions acceptable; prefers letter-quality to dot-matrix. Reports in 4 months. Guidelines for SASE.

Nonfiction: Alaska material only: animals, biography, history, how-to, juveniles, nature, photography, poetry, recreation, wildlife and self-help. No hunting or fishing tales. Query or submit outline/synopsis and 2-3 sample chapters or complete ms. Reviews artwork/photos as part of ms package. "As a specialty publishing house (we take *only* Alaskans' material) the work *must* have an impact on Alaska or people interested in Alaska—for Alaska."

Recent Nonfiction Title: *The Fool-Proof-Four-Edible Wild Mushrooms* (nature/field guide).

Fiction: Alaska material only—adventure, historical, romance and suspense. Query editor/publisher. Reports in 4 months.

ALASKA NORTHWEST PUBLISHING, 130 Second Ave. S., Edmonds WA 98020. Editor/Publisher: Robert A. Henning. Publishes primarily paperback originals. Averages 12 titles/year; receives 250 submissions annually. 80% of books from first-time authors; 95% of books from unagented writers. Most contracts call for 10% royalty. "Rejections are made promptly, unless we have three or four possibilities in the same general field, and it's a matter of which one gets the decision. That could take three months." Publishes book an average of 2 years after acceptance. Computer printout submissions acceptable; prefers letter-quality to dot-matrix. Free book catalog.

Nonfiction: "Alaska, northern British Columbia, the Yukon, Northwest Territories and northwest U.S. are our subject areas. Emphasis is on life in the last frontier, history, biography, cookbooks, travel, field guides and outdoor subjects. Writers must be familiar with the area first-hand. We listen to any ideas." Query with outline, sample chapters, and any relevant photographs. Reviews artwork/photos as part of ms package.

Tips: "First-person nonfiction, preferably resource- but not development-oriented, and informal prose (well organized, syntax reasonably good) have the best chance of selling to our firm."

An asterisk preceding a listing indicates that subsidy publishing or co-publishing (where author pays part or all of publishing costs) is available. Firms whose subsidy programs comprise more than 50% of their total publishing activities are listed at the end of the Book Publishers section.

ALBA HOUSE, 2187 Victory Blvd., Staten Island, New York NY 10314. (212)761-0047. Editor-in-Chief: Anthony L. Chenevey. Publishes hardcover and paperback originals and reprints. Specializes in religious books. "We publish shorter editions than many publishers in our field." Averages 15 titles/year; receives 1,000 submissions annually. 50% of books from first-time authors; 80% of books from unagented writers. Pays 10% royalty on retail price. Publishes book an average of 9 months after acceptance. Computer printout submissions acceptable; prefers letter-quality to dot-matrix. Query. State availability of photos/illustrations. Simultaneous and photocopied submissions OK. Reports in 1 month. Book catalog and ms guidelines for SASE. Reviews artwork/photos.
Nonfiction: Publishes philosophy, psychology, religion, sociology, textbooks and Biblical books. Accepts nonfiction translations from French, German or Spanish. Submit outline/synopsis and 1-2 sample chapters.
Tips: "We look to new authors." Queries/mss may be routed to other editors in the publishing group.

THE ALBAN INSTITUTE, INC., 4125 Nebraska Ave. NW, Washington DC 20016. (202)244-7320. Director of Publications: Celia A. Hahn. Small press. Publishes trade paperback originals. Averages 7 titles/year; receives 100 submissions annually. 100% of books from unagented writers. Pays 7% royalty on books; $50 on publication for 2- to 8-page articles relevant to congregational life—practical—ecumenical. Publishes book an average of 1 year after acceptance. Computer printout submissions acceptable; prefers letter-quality to dot-matrix. Reports in 2 months. Prefers queries. Book catalog and ms guidelines for SAE with 39¢ postage.
Nonfiction: Religious—focus on local congregation—ecumenical. Must be accessible to general reader. Research preferred. Needs mss on the task of the ordained leader in the congregation, the career path of the ordained leader in the congregation, problems and opportunities in congregational life, and ministry of the laity in the world and in the church. No sermons, devotional, children's titles, inspirational type or prayers. Query or submit outline/synopsis and sample chapters.
Recent Nonfiction Title: *The Life Cycle of a Congregation*, by Martin Saarinen.
Tips: "Our audience is intelligent, probably liberal mainline Protestant and Catholic clergy and lay leaders, executives and seminary administration/faculty—people who are concerned with the local church at a practical level and new approaches to its ministry."

ALLEN PUBLISHING CO., 7324 Reseda Blvd., Reseda CA 91335. Publisher: Michael Wiener. Small press. Publishes paperback originals. Averages 3 titles/year; receives 50 submissions annually. 50% of books from first-time authors; 100% of books from unagented writers. Pays 10% royalty on net price; no advance. Publishes book an average of 6 months after acceptance. Simultaneous and photocopied submissions OK. Computer printout submissions acceptable; prefers letter-quality to dot-matrix. "Author queries welcome from new or established writers. Do not send manuscript or sample chapter." Reports in 2 weeks. SASE "essential." Ms guidelines for #10 SASE.
Nonfiction: Self-help material, 20,000-30,000 words, aimed at wealth-builders. "We want to reach the vast audience of opportunity seekers who, for instance, purchased *Lazy Man's Way to Riches*, by Joe Karbo. Material must be original and authoritative, not rehashed from other sources. Most of what we market is sold via mail order in softcover book form. No home fix-it, hobby hints, health or 'cure' books, or 'faith' stories, poetry or fiction. We are a specialty publisher and will not consider any book not fitting the above description." Reviews artwork/photos as part of ms package.
Recent Nonfiction Title: *How to Turn $15 into a Money-Making Business*, by Jack Erbe.
Tips: "We are looking for books that appeal to down-and-out people who want to start a business of their own or otherwise turn around their financial status. We do not aim at the sophisticated, highly-educated person looking for such things as tax shelters and complicated investments. Our audience is looking for uncomplicated answers to their financial problems. Although we are a specialty publisher producing self-help books, we continuously receive queries and samples of poetry, fiction, autobiography, etc. What a waste of time and effort."

ALMAR PRESS, 4105 Marietta Dr., Binghamton NY 13903. (607)722-0265. Editor-in-Chief: A.N. Weiner. Managing Editor: M.F. Weiner. Publishes hardcover and paperback originals and reprints. Averages 8 titles/year; receives 200 submissions annually. 75% of books from first-time authors; 100% of books from unagented writers. Average print order for a writer's first book is 2,000. Pays 10% royalty; no advance. Publishes book an average of 3 months after acceptance. Prefers exclusive submissions; however, simultaneous (if so indicated) and photocopied submissions OK. Query for electronic submissions. Computer printout submissions acceptable; prefers letter-quality to dot-matrix. Reports in 1 month. Book catalog for 8½x11 SAE with 56¢ postage. "*Submissions must include SASE for reply and return of manuscript.*"
Nonfiction: Publishes business, technical, and consumer books and reports. "These main subjects include general business, financial, travel, career, technology, personal help, hobbies, general medical, general legal, and how-to. *Almar Reports* are business and technology subjects published for management use and prepared in 8½x11 and book format. Publications are printed and bound in soft covers as required. Reprint publications represent a new aspect of our business." Submit outline/synopsis and sample chapters. Reviews artwork/pho-

tos as part of ms package. Looks for information in the proposed book that makes it different or unusual enough to attract book buyers. Reviews artwork/photos.

Recent Nonfiction Title: *How to Buy, Install and Maintain Your Own Telephone Equipment*, by La Carrubba and Zimmer.

Tips: "We look for timely subjects. The type of book the writer has the best chance of selling to our firm is something different or unusual—*no* poetry or fiction, also *no* first-person travel or family history. The book must be complete and of good quality."

‡***ALPHA PUBLISHING COMPANY**, Division of Special Edition, Inc., 3497 E. Livingston Ave., Columbus OH 43227. (614)231-4088. Publisher: Dr. Y. Hayon. Small press. Publishes hardcover and trade paper originals. Averages 6 titles/year. Subsidy publishes 30% of books. Decision to subsidy publish "depending on anticipated sales." Pays 10-25% royalty on wholesale price. Simultaneous and photocopied submissions OK. Reports on queries in 2 weeks. Book catalog for SASE.

Nonfiction: Biography, how-to, reference, technical and textbook. Subjects include history, philosophy, religion, sociology and Judaica. Seeking Hebraica, Judaica, Christianity books. Query.

Recent Nonfiction Title: *Weddings: A Complete Guide to All Religious and Interfaith Marriage Services*, by Abraham Klausner (reference on weddings).

‡***ALPINE PUBLICATIONS, INC.**, 214 19th St. SE, Loveland CO 80537. (303)667-2017. Publisher: B.J. McKinney. Publishes hardcover and trade paperback originals. Averages 12 titles/year. Subsidy publishes 2% of books when "book fits into our line but has a market so limited (e.g. rare dog breed) that we would not accept it on royalty terms." No advance. Pays 7-15% royalty. Publishes book an average of 2 years after acceptance. Computer printout submissions OK; prefers letter-quality. Reports in 2 weeks on queries; 2 months on mss.

Nonfiction: How-to books about animals. "We need comprehensive breed books on the more popular AKC breeds, books for breeders on showing, breeding, genetics, gait, new training methods, and cat and horse books. No fiction or fictionalized stories of real animals; no books on reptiles; no personal experience stories except in case of well-known professional in field." Submit outline/synopsis and sample chapters or complete ms. Reviews artwork/photos as part of manuscript package.

Recent Nonfiction Title: *The Arab: An Owner's Guide*, by Byford.

Tips: "Writers should have experience in their field; and be able to provide a neat, easy to read ms with samples of high quality photos and illustrations to be included in text."

***ALYSON PUBLICATIONS, INC.**, 40 Plympton St., Boston MA 02118. (617)542-5679. Publisher: Sasha Alyson. Small press. Publishes trade paperback originals and reprints. Averages 20 titles/year; receives 500 submissions annually. 50% of books from first-time authors; 80% of books from unagented writers. Average print order for a writer's first book is 6,000. Subsidy publishes 5% of books. Pays 8-15% royalty on net price; buys some mss outright for $200-1,000; offers average $600 advance. Publishes book an average of 15 months after acceptance. Computer printout submissions acceptable; no dot-matrix. Reports in 2 weeks on queries; 5 weeks on mss. Looks for "writing ability and content suitable for our house." Book catalog and ms guidelines for business-size SAE and 3 first class stamps.

Nonfiction: Gay/lesbian subjects. "We are especially interested in nonfiction providing a positive approach to gay/lesbian issues." Accepts nonfiction translations. Submit one-page synopsis. Reviews artwork/photos as part of ms package.

Recent Nonfiction Title: *The Men With the Pink Triangle*, by Heinz Heger (history).

Fiction: Gay novels. Accepts fiction translations. Submit one-page synopsis.

Recent Fiction Title: *Between Friends*, by Gillian E. Hanscombe (lesbian fiction).

Tips: "We publish many books by new authors. The writer has the best chance of selling to our firm well-researched, popularly-written nonfiction on a subject (e.g., some aspect of gay history) that has not yet been written about much. With fiction, create a strong storyline that makes the reader want to find out what happens. With nonfiction, write in a popular style for a non-academic audience."

AMERICAN ASTRONAUTICAL SOCIETY, (Univelt, Inc., Publisher), Box 28130, San Diego CA 92128. (619)746-4005. Editorial Director: H. Jacobs. Publishes hardcover originals. Averages 8 titles/year; receives 12-15 submissions annually. 5% of books from first-time authors; 5% of books from unagented writers. Average print order for a writer's first book is 600-2,000. Pays 10% royalty on actual sales; no advance. Publishes book an average of 4 months after acceptance. Simultaneous and photocopied submissions OK. Computer printout submissions acceptable; prefers letter-quality to dot-matrix. Reports in 1 month. Free book catalog; ms guidelines for SAE and 39¢ postage.

Nonfiction: Proceedings or monographs in the field of astronautics, including applications of aerospace technology to Earth's problems. "Our books must be space-oriented or space-related. They are meant for technical libraries, research establishments and the aerospace industry worldwide." Submit outline/synopsis and 1-2 sample chapters. Reviews artwork/photos as part of ms package.

Recent Nonfiction Title: *Soviet Space Programs 1980-1985*, by N.L. Johnson.

*AMERICAN ATHEIST PRESS, American Atheists, Box 2117, Austin TX 78768-2117. (512)458-1244. Editor: R. Murray-O'Hair. Small press. Imprints include Gusttav Broukal Press. Publishes trade paperback originals and trade paperback reprints. Averages 12 titles/year; receives 200 submissions annually. 40-50% of books from first-time authors; 100% of books from unagented writers. Pays 5-10% royalty on retail price. Publishes book an average of 8 months after acceptance. Simultaneous and photocopied submissions OK. Computer printout submissions acceptable; prefers letter-quality to dot-matrix. Reports in 3 weeks on queries; 6 weeks on submissions. Book catalog for 6½x9½ SAE.
Nonfiction: Biography, humor, reference and general. Subjects include history (of religion and Atheism, of the effects of religion historically); philosophy and religion (from an Atheist perspective, particularly criticism of religion); politics (separation of state and church, religion and politics); Atheism (particularly the lifestyle of Atheism; the history of Atheism; applications of Atheism). "We are interested in hard-hitting and original books expounding the lifestyle of Atheism and criticizing religion. We would like to see more submissions dealing with the histories of specific religious sects, such as the L.D.S., the Worldwide Church of God, etc. We are generally not interested in biblical criticism." Submit outline/synopsis and sample chapters or complete ms. Reviews artwork/photos.
Recent Nonfiction Title: *Essays on American Atheism*, by Jon G. Murray (activist Atheism).
Fiction: Humor (satire of religion or of current religious leaders); anything of particular interest to Atheists. "We rarely publish any fiction. But we have occasionally released a humorous book." No mainstream. "For our press to consider fiction, it would have to tie in with the general focus of our press, which is the promotion of Atheism and free thought." Submit outline/synopsis and sample chapters.
Tips: "At our press, the single most common mistake made by authors is 'toning down' their opinions and conclusions to complete blandness. Somehow some writers think that their work will only sell if it can offend no one."

AMERICAN CATHOLIC PRESS, 1223 Rossell Ave., Oak Park IL 60302. (312)386-1366. Editorial Director: Father Michael Gilligan. Publishes hardcover originals and hardcover and paperback reprints. "Most of our sales are by direct mail, although we do work through retail outlets." Averages 4 titles/year. Pays by outright purchase of $25-100; no advance. Publishes book an average of 8 months after acceptance. Simultaneous and photocopied submissions OK. Computer printout submissions acceptable. Reports in 2 months.
Nonfiction: "We publish books on the Roman Catholic liturgy—for the most part, books on religious music and educational books and pamphlets. We also publish religious songs for church use, including Psalms, as well as choral and instrumental arrangements. We are interested in new music, meant for use in church services. Books, or even pamphlets, on the Roman Catholic Mass are especially welcome. We have no interest in secular topics and are not interested in religious poetry of any kind." Query.
Recent Nonfiction Title: *The Role of Music in the New Roman Liturgy*, by W. Herring (educational).

AMERICAN FEDERATION OF INFORMATION PROCESSING SOCIETIES, INC. (AFIPS), 1899 Preston White Dr., Reston VA 22091. (703)620-8918. Director: Chris Hoelzel. Publishes hardcover and trade paperback originals. Averages 6 titles/year; receives 15 submissions annually. Simultaneous and photocopied submissions OK. Query for electronic submissions. Computer printout submissions acceptable; prefers letter-quality to dot-matrix. Free book catalog.
Nonfiction: Reference, technical and textbook on computing. Query. Reviews artwork/photos.
Recent Nonfiction Title: *Information Processing in the U.S.* (reference).
Tips: "The writer has the best chance of selling to our firm books on current computer technology (cutting edge), for use by computing professionals."

THE AMERICAN PSYCHIATRIC PRESS, INC. (associated with the American Psychiatric Association), 1400 K St. NW, Washington DC 20005. (202)682-6268. Editor-in-Chief: Carol C. Nadelson, M.D. Publishes hardcover and trade paperback originals. Averages 40 titles/year, 2-4 trade books/year; receives about 300 submissions annually. About 10% of books from first-time authors; 95% of books from unagented writers. Pays 10% minimum royalty based on all money actually received, maximum varies; offers average $3,000-5,000 advance. Publishes book an average of 9 months after acceptance. Simultaneous and photocopied submissions OK (if made clear in cover letter). Query for electronic submissions. Computer printout submissions acceptable; no dot-matrix. Reports in 6 weeks "in regard to an *initial* decision regarding our interest. A *final* decision requires more time." Ms guidelines for SASE.
Nonfiction: Reference, self-help, technical, textbook and general nonfiction. Subjects include psychology/psychiatry and sociology (as it relates to psychiatry). Authors must be well qualified in their subject area. Especially looking for books that discuss major psychiatric topics for the general public. No first-person accounts of mental illness or anything not clearly related to psychiatry. Query with outline/synopsis and sample chapters.
Recent Nonfiction Title: *Cocaine*, by Roger D. Weiss, M.D., and Steven M. Mirin, M.D.
Tips: "Because we are a specialty publishing company, books written by or in collaboration with a psychiatrist have the best chance of acceptance. Make it authoritative and professional."

‡AMERICAN REFERENCES INC., 919 N. Michigan, Chicago IL 60611. (312)951-6200. President: Les Krantz. Publishes hardcover and trade paperback originals. Averages 4-10 titles/year. Payment negotiable. Simultaneous and photocopied submissions OK. Reports in 6 weeks on queries.
Nonfiction: Illustrations and reference. Subjects include art and photography.
Nonfiction Title: *The New York Art Review*, 1982, 2nd ed.

‡AMERICAN STUDIES PRESS, INC., 13511 Palmwood Lane, Tampa FL 33624. (813)961-7200 or 974-2857. Imprints include ASP Books, Harvest Books and Marilu Books (Marilu imprint includes Herland—Poems by women about women—and Woman). Editor-in-Chief: Donald R. Harkness. Small press. Publishes trade paperback originals. Receives 40-50 submissions/year. 80% of books from first-time authors. 100% of books from unagented writers. Averages 6 titles/year. Pays 10 copies plus 10% royalty on retail price after printing cost is met. Publishes book an average of 6 months after acceptance. Computer printout submissions OK; prefers letter-quality. Reports in 2 weeks on queries; 2 months on mss. Book catalog for #10 SASE.
Nonfiction: Biography, humor and illustrated book. Subjects include Americana, business and economics, history, politics, psychology, sports and travel. "I might consider a book or two of generalized family history, of interest to an audience wider than the immediate circle of relatives." Query or submit outline/synopsis and sample chapters or complete ms. Reviews artwork/photos as part of ms package.
Recent Nonfiction Title: *Everyperson's Guide to Strange People in Public Places*, by Max Krill (satire).
Poetry: Submit 6 poems or submit complete ms.
Recent Poetry Title: *The Ambivalent Journey*, by Hans Juergensen.
Tips: "Our audience is intelligent and appreciative college graduates, not taken in by the slick and fancy package but more concerned with content. Good poetry, or satire—that's what I like best."

ANCESTRY INCORPORATED, Box 476, Salt Lake City UT 84110. (801)531-1790. Managing Editor: Robert J. Welsh. Publishes hardcover and mass market paperback originals. Averages 10 titles/year; receives 10-20 submissions annually. 70% of books from first-time authors; 100% of books from unagented writers. Pays 8-12% royalty; purchases mss outright for varying amount or pays royalty on gross sales. Offers variable advance. Publishes book an average of 1 year after acceptance. Simultaneous and photocopied submissions OK. Query for electronic submissions. Computer printout submissions acceptable. Reports in 1 month on queries; 2 months on mss. Free book catalog and ms guidelines.
Nonfiction: Biography, how-to, reference, and genealogy. Subjects include Americana; history (family and local); and hobbies (genealogy). "Our publications are almost exclusively genealogical in nature. We consider everything from short monographs to book length works on immigration, migration, record collections, etc. Good local histories and heraldic topics are considered." No mss that are not genealogical or historical. Query, or submit outline/synopsis and sample chapters, or complete ms. Reviews artwork/photos.
Recent Nonfiction Title: *Plymouth Colony: Its History & People, 1620-1691*, by Eugene Aubrey Stratton (reference).
Tips: "Genealogical reference, how-to, and descriptions of source collections have the best chance of selling to our firm. Be precise in your description."

‡AND BOOKS, 702 S. Michigan, South Bend IN 46618. (219)219-3134. Editor: Janos Szebedinszky. Small press. Publishes trade paperback originals. Averages 10 titles/year. Receives 1,000 submissions/year. 50% of books from first-time authors. 90% of books from unagented writers. Pays 6-10% royalty on retail price. Simultaneous and photocopied submissions OK. Publishes book an average of 1 year after acceptance. Query for electronic submissions. Reports in 1½ months. Book catalog for #10 SASE.
Nonfiction: Cookbook, how-to, illustrated book and self-help. Subjects include health, music, nature, politics (current issues), recreation, travel and general adult nonfiction. Especially needs books on computers and the law and electronic publishing. No biography, financial planning, religious experience/inspirational works or diet books.
Recent Nonfiction Title: *Murder Next Door*, by John O'Brien and Edward Bauman (crime stories).
Tips: "Attempt to get an intro or foreword by a well-known individual in the field about which you are writing, or some good review comments. A little preliminary legwork and market investigation can go a long way to influence a potential publisher."

‡*ANDERSON PUBLISHING CO., Suite 501, 602 Main St., Cincinnati OH 45201. (513)421-4393. Editorial Director: Jean Martin. Publishes hardcover, paperback originals, journals and software and reprints. Publishes 13-15 titles/year. Subsidy publishes 10% of books. Pays 15-18% royalty; "advance in selected cases." Publishes book an average of 7 months after acceptance. Simultaneous and photocopied submissions OK. Computer printout submissions acceptable; prefers letter-quality to dot-matrix. Reports in 2 months. Book catalog for 8½x11 SASE; guidelines for SASE.
Nonfiction: Law and law-related books, and criminal justice criminology texts (justice administration legal series). Query or submit outline/chapters with vitae.
Recent Nonfiction Title: *Economic Damages*, by Michael L. Brookshire, Ph.D. (law/economics).

ANDREWS, McMEEL & PARKER, 4900 Main St., Kansas City MO 64112. Editorial Director: Donna Martin. Publishes hardcover and paperback originals. Averages 30 titles/year. Pays royalty on retail price. "Query only. No unsolicited manuscripts. Areas of specialization include humor, how-to, and consumer reference books, such as *The Writer's Art* by James J. Kilpatrick, and *Roger Ebert's Movie Home Companion*."

APPALACHIAN MOUNTAIN CLUB, 5 Joy St., Boston MA 02108. (617)523-0636. Senior Editor: Diane Welebit. Small press. Imprints include AMC Books. Publishes hardcover and trade paperback originals. Averages 3-6 titles/year; receives 30 submissions annually. 80% of books from first-time authors; 99% of books from unagented writers. Pays 10% royalty on retail price; offers $500-1,000 advance. Publishes book 1 year after acceptance. Simultaneous and photocopied submissions OK. Query for electronic submissions. Computer printout submissions acceptable; prefers letter-quality to dot-matrix. Reports in 6 weeks on queries; 3 months on mss. Book catalog for 9x12 SAE.
Nonfiction: How-to, illustrated book, reference and guidebook. Subjects include history (Northeast, mountains), nature, photography, recreation, "self-propelled" outdoors activities, and travel. "We want manuscripts about the outdoors, ecology, the environment, mountains and their history and culture, non-motorized recreation, and guidebooks and field guides. We would also like to see semi-philosophical works on the outdoors. Relevant fiction will be considered, too." No physical fitness manuals. Query or submit outline/synopsis and sample chapters only. Reviews artwork/photos.
Recent Nonfiction Title: *Southern Snow*, by Randy Johnson (guide to skiing and mountaineering in the south).
Tips: "We are expanding into the Southeast (North Carolina, South Carolina, Washington DC, Maryland, Virginia, West Virginia), with basically the same interests as here in New England. Be patient. The AMC makes decisions slowly, mainly because it cannot afford to take financial risks."

APPLEZABA PRESS, Box 4134, Long Beach CA 90804. (213)591-0015. Publisher: D.H. Lloyd. Small press. Publishes trade paperback originals. Averages 3 titles/year; receives 800-1,000 submissions annually. 10% of books from first-time authors; 100% of books from unagented writers. Pays 8-12% royalty on retail price plus several author copies. Seldom offers advance. Publishes book an average of 3 years after acceptance. Simultaneous and photocopied submissions OK. Computer printout submissions acceptable; prefers letter-quality to dot-matrix. Reports in 1 month on queries; 2 months on mss. Free book catalog (when available).
Nonfiction: "Our needs are not great here." Cookbook and humor. Subjects include cooking and foods. Query. Reviews artwork/photos.
Recent Nonfiction Title: *Hungry Poets' Cookbook*, edited by Glenda McManus (cookbook).
Fiction: Experimental, humor, mainstream, novella and short story collections. "We prefer to see short, novella length, or short story collections. No confession, gothic, horror or western manuscripts. Submit outline/synopsis and sample chapters.
Recent Fiction Title: *Flight to Freedom*, by F.N. Wright (novel of the 1960s).
Poetry: "The poetry that attracts us is *usually* short, conversational prose poems. We don't let this limit us, however." No traditional forms. Submit complete ms.
Recent Poetry Title: *Save Save Save Save*, by Nichola Manning (experimental poetry).
Tips: The freelancer has the best chance of publishing collections of poetry or short fiction. "They are economical enough for us to produce, and we have developed a market for them."

ARBOR HOUSE, Division of the Hearst Corporation. 235 E. 45th St., New York NY 10017. President and Publisher: Eden Collinsworth. Publishes hardcover and trade paperback originals and selected reprints. Averages 50-60 titles/year. Pays standard royalty; offers negotiable advance. Publishes book an average of 9 months after acceptance. Computer printout submissions acceptable; prefers letter-quality to dot-matrix. Free book catalog.
Nonfiction: Autobiography, cookbook, how-to and self-help. Subjects include Americana (possibly), art (possibly), business and economics, cooking and foods, health, history, politics, psychology, recreation, inspiration and sports. Query first to "The Editors." Reviews artwork/photos as part of ms package.
Recent Nonfiction Title: *The Equilibrium Plan: Balancing Diet and Exercise*, by Sally Edwards.

❝ *A writer can never be truly certain of the quality of his/her writing. But from the beginning you should be certain that no one else is as perfectly suited to write your book as you are.* **❞**

—Felice Picano
author of House of Cards

Fiction: "Quality fiction—everything from romance to science fiction, fantasy, adventure and suspense." Query or submit outline/synopsis and sample chapters to "The Editors."
Recent Fiction Title: *Poison*, by Ed McBain.
Tips: "Freelance writers should be aware of a greater emphasis on agented properties and market resistance to untried fiction."

‡**ARCHITECTURAL BOOK PUBLISHING CO., INC.**, 268 Dogwood Lane, Stamford CT 06903. (203)322-1460. Editor: Walter Frese. Averages 10 titles/year; receives 400 submissions annually. 80% of books from first-time authors; 95% of books from unagented writers. Average print order for a writer's first book is 5,000. Royalty is percentage of retail price. Publishes book an average of 10 months after acceptance. Computer printout submissions acceptable; no dot-matrix. Prefers queries, outlines and 2 sample chapters with number of illustrations. Reports in 2 weeks.
Nonfiction: Publishes architecture, decoration, and reference books on city planning and industrial arts. Accepts nonfiction translations. Also interested in history, biography, and science of architecture and decoration. Reviews artwork/photos.

ARCsoft PUBLISHERS, Box 132, Woodsboro MD 21798. (301)845-8856. Publisher: Anthony R. Curtis. Publishes trade paperback originals. Averages 20 titles/year. "We now offer only 'buyout' contracts in which all rights are purchased. Typically, an advance of 20 percent is paid at contract signing and 80 percent at acceptable completion of work. Royalties are no longer offered since writers suffer under royalty contracts for small-volume technical books." Offers variable advance. Publishes book an average of 6 months after acceptance. Computer printout submissions acceptable; no dot-matrix. Reports in 1 month on queries; 10 weeks on mss. Free book catalog.
Nonfiction: Technical. "We publish technical books including space science, personal computers and hobby electronics, especially for beginners." Accepts nonfiction translations. Query or submit outline/synopsis and 1 sample chapter. Reviews artwork/photos as part of ms package.
Recent Nonfiction Title: *1987 Space Satellite Handbook*, by A.R. Curtis.
Tips: "We look for the writer's ability to cover our desired subject thoroughly, writing quality and interest."

*****M. ARMAN PUBLISHING, INC.**, 28 N. Ridgewood Ave., Rio Vista, Ormond Beach FL 32074. (904)673-5576. Mailing address: Box 785, Ormond Beach FL 32074. Contact: Mike Arman. Publishes trade paperback originals, reprints and software. Averages 6-8 titles/year; receives 20 submissions annually. 20% of books from first-time authors; 100% of books from unagented writers. Average print order for a writer's first book is 1,500. Subsidy publishes 20% of books. Pays 10% royalty on wholesale price. No advance. Publishes book (on royalty basis) an average of 8 months after acceptance; 6 weeks on subsidy basis. Photocopied submissions OK. "We now set type directly from author's disks. Our equipment can read many CPM 5¼ formats, and can read IBM disks if the file is ASC II. We can do this for our own books, and we can save subsidy publishers 40-50% on their typesetting bills." Computer printout submissions acceptable. Reports in 1 week on queries; 3 weeks on mss. Book catalog for business size SAE with 1 first class stamp.
Nonfiction: How-to, reference, technical, and textbook. "Motorcycle and aircraft technical books only." Accepts nonfiction translations. Publishes for enthusiasts. Submit complete ms. Reviews artwork/photos as part of ms package.
Recent Nonfiction Title: *V-Twin Thunder*, by Carl McClanahan (motorcycle performance manual).
Fiction: "Motorcycle or aircraft-related only." Accepts fiction translations. Immediate needs are "slim," but not non-existent. Submit cover letter and complete ms.
Tips: "The type of book a writer has the best chance of selling to our firm is how-to fix motorcycles—specifically Harley-Davidsons. We have a strong, established market for these books."

ART DIRECTION BOOK COMPANY, 10 E. 39th St., 6th Floor, New York NY 10016. (212)889-6500. Editorial Director: Don Barron. Senior Editor: Loren Bliss. Publishes hardcover and paperback originals. Publishes 10 titles/year. Pays 10% royalty on retail price; offers average $1,000 advance. Publishes book an average of 1 year after acceptance. Photocopied submissions OK. Computer printout submissions acceptable; no dot-matrix. Reports in 3 months. Book catalog for 6x9 SAE.
Nonfiction: Commercial art, ad art how-to and textbooks. "We are interested in books for the professional advertising art field—that is, books for art directors, designers, etc.; also entry level books for commercial and advertising art students in such fields as typography, photography, paste-up, illustration, clip-art, design, layout and graphic arts." Query with outline/synopsis and 1 sample chapter. Reviews artwork/photos as part of ms package.
Recent Nonfiction Title: *American Corporate Identity #2*, by D.E. Carter.

ASHER-GALLANT PRESS, (formerly Caddylak Publishing), Division of Caddylak Systems, Inc., 60 Shames Dr., Westbury NY 11590. (516)333-7440. Publisher: Edward Werz. Publishes softcover and loose-leaf-format originals (sold mostly through direct marketing). Averages 20 titles/year; receives 150 submissions annually.

75% of books from first-time authors. 95% of books from unagented writers. "Many of our authors are first-time authors when they begin working with us, but write several subsequent books for us. Payment for each project is treated individually, but generally, the rights to smaller works (up to about 25,000 words) are purchased on a flat fee basis, and rights to larger works are purchased on a royalty basis." Advance varies by project. Publishes books an average of 6 months after acceptance. Simultaneous and photocopied submissions OK. Computer printout submissions acceptable; prefers letter-quality to dot-matrix. Ms returned only if requested. "We prefer to keep a writer's sample on file for possible future assignments." Reports negative results in 2 weeks on queries; 1 month on mss. Free book catalog.

Nonfiction: How-to, reference, audio cassette programs and business directories. Subjects include business (general) and management topics. "We plan to do 35 to 40 new titles during the next two years. The list will consist of individual business titles, more technical management reports, and longer, more comprehensive books that will be published in binder format. All subject matter must be appropriate to our broad audience of middle-level corporate managers. No sensational, jazzy nonfiction without solid research behind it." Submit outline/synopsis and sample chapters.

Recent Nonfiction Title: *Complete Portfolio of Tests for Hiring Office Personnel*, by Mary Healey (business how-to).

Tips: "The deciding factors in whether or not we publish a certain book are: (1) we believe there will be a very sizeable demand for the book, (2) the outline we review is logically structured and very comprehensive, and (3) the sample chapters are concisely and clearly written and well-researched."

‡***ASHLEY BOOKS, INC.**, 30 Main St., Port Washington NY 11050. (516)883-2221. Associate Editor: Gwen Costa. Other imprints include South Group USA. Publishes hardcover and trade paperback originals. Averages 25-35 titles/year. Receives 200-300 submissions/year. 75% of books from first-time authors. 70% of books from unagented writers. Subsidy publishes 1% of books. Pays 10-15% royalty on retail price. "Advances are negotiated with the agent or the author individually." Publishes book an average of 20 months after acceptance. Simultaneous and photocopied submissions OK. Reports in 2 months on mss. Book catalog for business size SASE.

Nonfiction: Biography, cookbook, how-to, humor, reference, self-help and technical. Subjects include Americana, animals, business and economics, cooking and foods, health (avant garde and/or controversial), vitamins and diets for health, history, hobbies, music, nature, philosophy, politics, psychology, recreation, religion, sociology, sports and travel. "We're especially interested in controversy and really love material on medicine, health, vitamins, diet and natural foods. Books on how to make money, biographies and molding one's life to get the most out of it, are always exciting to us, too. We're not particularly interested in art books, photography or cartoon books." Submit complete ms. Reviews artwork/photos as part of ms package.

Recent Nonfiction Title: *Taxi—The Harry Chapin Story*, by Peter Coan (biography).

Fiction: Adventure, confession, ethnic, gothic, historical, horror, humor, mainstream, mystery, religious, romance, science fiction, suspense, western and gay books. "We need emotional fiction, books that make the reader feel emotion—fear, anger, or happiness—page turners that tempt the reader, educate, entertain, books that make one feel. We want nothing flat that does not satisfy or that leaves the reader hanging. We're also not interested in porn or erotica." Submit complete ms.

Recent Fiction Title: *Ashlawn*, by R.A. Osbourne (saga of Irish immigrant family).

Poetry: "We buy poetry very selectively." Submit complete ms.

Recent Poetry Title: *Footprints in the Sand*, by Ann Frost (nature).

Tips: "We publish for laymen, professionals and people who are addicted to reading. Health and self-doctoring will be of major importance to our list. If I were a writer trying to market a book today, I would find a way to pique an editor's interest by trying it in, whether fiction or nonfiction, to a current event or something trendy happening in society, be it real life, a parody of real life or something similar in the news. I would try to find a handle or a hook that would make an editor want to take a second look. Don't send manuscripts that weigh 10 lbs. without a query."

***ASSOCIATED FACULTY PRESS, INC.**, Rt. 100, Millwood NY 10546. (914)762-2200. President: Dr. Richard Koffler. Publishes hardcover originals and reprints. Averages 20-30 titles/year; receives 150 submissions annually. 30% of books from first-time authors; 95% of books from unagented writers. May subsidy publish, "but only after careful editorial review." Publishes book an average of 18 months after acceptance. Simultaneous submissions of proposal OK. Computer printout submissions acceptable; no dot-matrix. Reports in 1 month on queries; 3 months on mss. Book catalog for 9x12 SAE with 2 first class stamps.

Imprints: Kennikat (nonfiction reprints), Richard Koffler, president. National Universities Publications (nonfiction), Richard Koffler, president.

Nonfiction: Biography; reference; monographs; supplementary legal texts; business and economics; health-related (not medicine); history; modern literary criticism; politics (public administration); sociology; and law and criminal justice. "We are rather backed up for at least one full year. Do not submit manuscript without first sending proposal." No trade books or academic books in fields not indicated above. Query or submit academic vita, table of contents and proposal.

Recent Nonfiction Title: *Regaining the Lead*, by Herbert Stinner (economic policy).
Tips: "Our audience is college and university libraries, law libraries, scholars in fields listed above, and discriminating general readers. We are not trade publishers. In general, purely scholarly books are having a harder time of it."

ATHENEUM CHILDREN'S BOOKS, Subsidiary of Macmillan, Inc., 866 3rd Ave., New York NY 10022. (212)702-7894. Editorial Director: Jonathan J. Lanman or Editors: Marcia Marshall and Gail Paris. Publishes hardcover originals. Averages 60 titles/year; receives 7,000-8,000 submissions annually. 8-12% of books from first-time authors; 50% of books from unagented writers. Pays 10-12½% royalty on retail price; offers average $2,000-3,000 advance. Publishes book an average of 18 months after acceptance. Photocopied submissions (outline and first 3 chapters only, please) OK. Computer printout submissions acceptable; prefers letter-quality to dot-matrix. Reports in 2 weeks on queries; 4-6 weeks on outline and sample chapters. Book catalog and ms guidelines for 7x10 SAE and 2 first class stamps.
Nonfiction: Biography, how-to, humor, illustrated book, juvenile (pre-school through young adult) and self-help, all for juveniles. Subjects include: Americana, animals, art, business and economics, cooking and foods, health, history, hobbies, music, nature, philosophy, photography, politics, psychology, recreation, religion, sociology, sports, and travel, all for young readers. "Do remember, most publishers plan their lists as much as two years in advance. So if a topic is 'hot' right now, it may be 'old hat' by the time we could bring it out. It's better to steer clear of fads. Some writers assume juvenile books are for 'practice' until you get good enough to write adult books. Not so. Books for young readers demand just as much 'professionalism' in writing as adult books. So save those 'practice' manuscripts for class, or polish them before sending them." Query, submit outline/synopsis and sample chapters. Reviews artwork/photos as part of ms package; prefers photocopies of artwork.
Recent Nonfiction Title: *Dead Serious*, by Jane Mersky Leder (teenage suicide).
Fiction: Adventure, ethnic, experimental, fantasy, gothic, historical, horror, humor, mainstream, mystery, romance, science fiction, suspense, and western, all in juvenile versions. "We have few specific needs except for books that are fresh, interesting and well-written. Again, fad topics are dangerous, as are works you haven't polished to the best of your ability. (The competition is fierce.) We've been inundated with dragon stories (misunderstood dragon befriends understanding child), unicorn stories (misunderstood child befriends understanding unicorn), and variations of 'Ignatz the Egg' (Everyone laughs at Ignatz the egg [giraffe/airplane/accountant] because he's square [short/purple/stupid] until he saves them from the eggbeater [lion/storm/I.R.S. man] and becomes a hero). Other things we don't need at this time are safety pamphlets, ABC books, and rhymed narratives. We have little need for children's poetry. In writing picture book texts, avoid the coy and 'cutesy.' " Query, submit outline/synopsis and sample chapters, or complete ms.
Recent Fiction Title: *The Return*, by Sonia Levitin (young adult novel).
Poetry: "At this time there is *very* little market for children's poetry. We don't anticipate needing any for the next year or two, especially rhymed narratives."
Tips: "Our books are aimed at children from pre-school age, up through high school. Our young adult novels and much of our science fiction and fantasy also cross over into adult markets. Government cut-backs to schools and city libraries have impacted heavily on publishers of quality books for children. We're having to cut down on the number of books we take on and, unfortunately, this usually hits new authors hardest."

ATHENEUM PUBLISHERS, 866 3rd Ave., New York NY 10022. Editor-in-Chief: Susan Ginsburg. Receives 10,000 submissions annually. 5% of books from first-time authors; 1% of books from unagented writers. Average print order for a writer's first book is 5,000. Publishes book an average of 1 year after acceptance. Simultaneous and photocopied submissions OK. Electronic submissions OK, but requires hard copy also. Computer printout submissions acceptable; prefers letter-quality to dot-matrix. Reports in 6 weeks.
Nonfiction: General trade material dealing with politics, psychology, history, cookbooks, sports, biographies and general interest. Length: 40,000 words minimum. Query or submit outline/synopsis and a sample chapter.
Tips: "We would prefer not to have artwork or photographs accompany unsolicited manuscripts."

ATHLETIC PRESS, Box 80250, Pasadena CA 91108. (213)283-3446. Editor-in-Chief: Donald Duke. Publishes paperback originals. Averages 3 titles/year. Pays 10% royalty; no advance. Publishes book an average of 1 year after acceptance. Query or submit complete ms. "Illustrations will be requested when we believe manuscript is publishable." Simultaneous and photocopied submissions OK. Computer printout submissions acceptable. Reports in 1 month. Free book catalog.
Nonfiction: Specializes in sports conditioning books.

ATLANTIC MONTHLY PRESS, 420 Lexington Ave., New York NY 10170. (212)557-6030. Publisher: Carl Navarre. Editorial Director: Gary Fisketjon. Executive Editor: Upton Birnie Brady. Senior Editors: Ann Godott and Edward Weeks (Boston). Assistant Editors: Marjorie Brauman and Anne Rumsey. Averages 50 titles/year; receives 3,000 submissions annually. 20% of books from first-time authors; 10% of books from unagented writers. "Advance and royalties depend on the nature of the book, the stature of the author, and the subject matter." Publishes book an average of 9 months after acceptance. Computer printout submissions acceptable; no dot-matrix.

Nonfiction: Publishes general nonfiction, biography, autobiography, science, philosophy, the arts, belles lettres, history and world affairs. Looks for "intelligence, coherence, organization, good writing (which comes first), neatness of presentation—and a covering letter." Length: 70,000-200,000 words. Query with sample chapter. Reviews artwork/photos as part of manuscript package.

Recent Nonfiction Title: *Light Years*, by Gary Kinder.

Fiction: Publishes general fiction and poetry. Prefers complete fiction and poetry mss.

Recent Fiction Title: *Not Fade Away*, by Jim Dodge.

AUGSBURG PUBLISHING HOUSE, 426 S. 5th St., Box 1209, Minneapolis MN 55440. (612)330-3432. Director, Book Department: Roland Seboldt. Publishes hardcover and paperback originals and paperback reprints. Publishes 45 titles/year; receives 5,000 submissions annually. 20% of books from first-time authors; 95% of books from unagented writers. Average print order for a writer's first book is 5,000. Pays 10-15% royalty on retail price; offers variable advance. Publishes book an average of 1 year after acceptance. Simultaneous and photocopied submissions OK. Computer printout submissions acceptable; no dot-matrix. Book catalog and ms guidelines for SASE. Reports in 6 weeks.

Nonfiction: Health, psychology, religion, self-help and textbooks. "We are looking for manuscripts that apply scientific knowledge and Christian faith to the needs of people as individuals, in groups and in society;" also good contemporary stories with a Christian theme for the young readers in age categories 8-11, 12-14, and 15 and up. We prefer writers submit a prospectus: statement of objective, author vita, outline and sample chapter." Reviews artwork/photos.

Recent Nonfiction Title: *Confidence: How to Succeed at Being Yourself*, by Alan Loy McGinnis.

Recent Fiction Title: *Wild, Blue Berries*, by Edna Hong (mystery novel).

AUTO BOOK PRESS, P.O. Bin 711, San Marcos CA 92069. (619)744-3582. Editorial Director: William Carroll. Publishes hardcover and paperback originals. Averages 3-5 titles/year; receives 24 submissions annually. 75% of books from first-time authors; 100% of books from unagented writers. Pays 15% royalty; offers variable advance. Publishes book an average of 1 year after acceptance. Simultaneous and photocopied submissions OK. Computer printout submissions OK; prefers letter-quality to dot-matrix. Reports in 2 weeks.

Nonfiction: Automotive material only: technical or definitive how-to. Query with outline/synopsis and 3 sample chapters.

Tips: "The most common mistake writers make is not taking time to research the potential market."

AVALON BOOKS, Imprint of Thomas Bouregy & Co., Inc., 401 Lafayette St., New York NY 10003. Editor: Rita Brenig. Publishes 60 titles/year. Pays $500 advance which is applied against sales of the first 3,500 copies of the book. Computer printout submissions acceptable; no dot-matrix. Reports in 5 months. Book catalog and guidelines for SASE.

Fiction: "We want well-plotted, fast-moving light romances, romance-mysteries, gothics, westerns, and nurse-romance books of about 50,000 words." Submit one-page synopsis with SASE, or submit complete ms with manuscript-size SASE. No sample chapters or long outlines.

Recent Fiction Title: *Love's Sweet Echo*, by Louise Bergstrom.

Tips: "We print romances mostly, and there must be suspense about the outcome of the romance until the end. Writers often let us know much too early that the guy really only likes the heroine—and vice versa. We like writers to focus on the plot, drama, and characters, not the background."

AVI PUBLISHING CO., 250 Post Rd. E., Box 831, Westport CT 06881. (203)226-0738. Senior Editor: James R. Ice, Ph.D. Imprint of Van Nostrand Reinhold. Publishes hardcover and paperback originals. Publishes 30 titles/year; receives 100+ submissions annually. 50+% of books from first-time authors; 90+% of books from unagented writers. Pays 10% royalty based on list price on the first 3,000 copies sold; offers average $5,000 advance (paid only on typing and art bills). Publishes book an average of 15 months after acceptance. Query for electronic submissions. Computer printout submissions acceptable; no dot-matrix. Reports in 1 month. Free book catalog and ms guidelines.

Nonfiction: Specializes in books on foods, agriculture, nutrition and health, scientific, technical, textbooks and reference works. Accepts nonfiction translations. Query or "submit a 500-word summary, a preface, a table of contents, estimated number of pages in manuscript, 1-2 sample chapters, when to be completed and a biographical sketch." Reviews artwork/photos as part of ms package.

Tips: "The writer has the best chance of selling our firm books on technology or science—areas in which our company specializes."

AVIATION BOOK CO., 1640 Victory Blvd., Glendale CA 91201. (818)240-1771. Editor: Walter P. Winner. Publishes hardcover and paperback originals and reprints. Averages 5 titles/year; receives 25 submissions annually. 90% of books from first-time authors; 10% of books from unagented writers. Pays royalty on retail price. No advance. Query with outline. Publishes book an average of 9 months after acceptance. Computer printout submissions acceptable; prefers letter-quality to dot-matrix. Reports in 2 months. Book catalog for 9x12 SAE with $1 postage.

Nonfiction: Aviation books, primarily of a technical nature and pertaining to pilot training. Young adult level and up. Also aeronautical history. Asks of ms, "Does it fill a void in available books on subject?" or, "Is it better than available material?" Reviews artwork/photos as part of ms package.

Recent Nonfiction Title: *Airman's Information Manual*, by W. Winner (aeronautics).

AVON BOOKS, 105 Madison, New York NY 10016. Editorial Director: Linda Cunningham. Publishes paperback originals and paperback reprints. Averages 300 titles/year. Pay and advance are negotiable. Publishes ms an average of 2 years after acceptance. Simultaneous and photocopied submissions OK. Computer printout submissions acceptable; prefers letter-quality to dot-matrix. Reports in 2 months. Book catalog for SASE.

Nonfiction: Biography, business/economics, health, history, how-to, politics, popular psychology, reference, self-help, sports, and war. No textbooks.

Recent Nonfiction Title: *No Laughing Matter*, by Joseph Heller and Speed Vogel.

Fiction: Men's adventure, fantasy, historical romance, mainstream, mystery, science fiction, suspense and western. Submit query letter only.

Recent Fiction Title: *A Heart So Wild*, by Johanna Lindsey.

AVON FLARE BOOKS, Young Adult Imprint of Avon Books, a division of the Hearst Corp., 105 Madison Ave., New York NY 10016. (212)399-1384. Editorial Director: Ellen Krieger. Publishes mass market paperback originals and reprints. Imprint publishes 24 new titles annually. 10-15% of books from first-time authors; 25% of books from unagented writers. Pays 6-8% royalty; offers average $2,000 advance. Publishes book an average of 15 months after acceptance. Simultaneous and photocopied submissions OK. Computer printout submissions acceptable; prefers letter-quality to dot-matrix. Reports in 10 weeks. Book catalog and manuscript guidelines for 8x10 SASE and 98¢ postage.

Nonfiction: General. Query or submit outline/synopsis and 6 sample chapters. "*Very* selective with young adult nonfiction."

Fiction: Adventure, ethnic, experimental, fantasy, humor, mainstream, mystery, romance, suspense and contemporary. "Very selective with science fiction, fantasy and mystery." Mss appropriate to ages 12-18. Query with sample chapters or synopsis.

Recent Fiction Title: *Breaking Up Is Hard to Do*, by Bruce and Carole Hart.

‡AZTEX CORP., 1126 N. 6th Ave., Box 50046, Tucson AZ 85703. (608)882-4656. Publishes hardcover and paperback originals. Averages 15 titles/year; receives 250 submissions annually. 100% of books from unagented writers. Average print order for a writer's first book is 3,500. Pays 10% royalty. Publishes book an average of 18 months after acceptance. Electronic and disk submissions OK but inquire about compatibility; requires hard copy also. Computer printout submissions acceptable; prefers letter-quality to dot-matrix. Reports in 3 months. Free catalog. *Author-Publisher Handbook* for $3.95.

Nonfiction: "We specialize in transportation subjects (how-to and history) and early childhood education (nonfiction)." Accepts nonfiction translations. Submit outline/synopsis and 2 sample chapters or complete ms. Reviews artwork/photos as part of ms package.

Recent Nonfiction Title: *The Amateur Astronomer's Catalog of 500 Deep-Sky Objects*, by Ronald J. Morales.

Tips: "We look for accuracy, thoroughness and interesting presentation."

BAEN PUBLISHING ENTERPRISES, Distributed by Simon & Schuster, 260 Fifth Ave., New York NY 10001. (212)532-4111. Senior Editor: Elizabeth Mitchell. Publishes hardcover trade paperback and mass market paperback originals and mass market paperback reprints. Averages 80-100 titles/year; receives 1,000 submissions annually. 5% of books from first-time authors; 2% of books from unagented writers. Pays 6-12% royalty on cover price. Simultaneous and photocopied submissions OK, although they will not receive as serious consideration as originals. Computer printout submissions acceptable if letter-quality. Reports in 2 weeks on queries; 2 months on mss. Ms guidelines for SASE.

Nonfiction: No high tech science or futuristic topics such as space technology, artificial intelligence, etc. Submit outline/synopsis and sample chapters.

Recent Nonfiction Title: *Artificial Intelligence*, by F. David Peat.

Fiction: Fantasy and science fiction, high tech adventure. Submit outline/synopsis and sample chapters or complete ms.

Recent Fiction Title: *Roma Mater*, by Poul and Karen Anderson.

Tips: "Our audience includes those who are interested in *hard* science fiction and quality fantasy pieces that instruct as well as entertain."

BAKER STREET PRODUCTIONS LTD., 216 Belgrade Ave., Box 3610, Mankato MN 56001. (507)625-2482. Contact: Karyne Jacobsen. Small Press. Publishes hardcover and trade paperback originals and software. Averages 8 titles/year; receives 500 submissions annually. 10% of books from first-time authors; 80% of books from unagented writers. Publishes book an average of 9 months after acceptance. Photocopied submissions OK. Computer printout submissions acceptable; prefers letter-quality to dot-matrix. Book catalog and ms guidelines for SASE. Reports in 2 months on queries; 2 months on mss.
Fiction: Adventure, fantasy, humor and mystery. Needs juvenile materials, grades 1-3. No science fiction. Submit synopsis and sample chapters. "No manuscripts longer than 2,000 words." Reviews artwork/photos as part of ms package.
Recent Fiction Title: *My Friend George*, by Keefe.

BALE BOOKS, Division of Bale Publications, Box 2727, New Orleans LA 70176. Editor-in-Chief: Don Bale Jr. Publishes hardcover and paperback originals and reprints. Averages 10 titles/year; receives 25 submissions annually. 50% of books from first-time authors; 90% of books from unagented writers. Average print order for a writer's first book is 1,000. Offers standard 10-12½-15% royalty contract on wholesale or retail price; sometimes purchases mss outright for $500. Offers no advance. Publishes book an average of 3 years after acceptance. Will consider photocopied submissions. Computer printout submissions acceptable; no dot-matrix. "Send manuscript by registered or certified mail. Be sure copy of manuscript is retained." Book catalog for SAE and 39¢ postage.
Nonfiction: Numismatics. "Our specialty is coin and stock market investment books; especially coin investment books and coin price guides. Most of our books are sold through publicity and ads in the coin newspapers. We are open to any new ideas in the area of numismatics. The writer should write for a teenage through adult level. Lead the reader by the hand like a teacher, building chapter by chapter. Our books sometimes have a light, humorous treatment, but not necessarily." Looks for "good English, construction and content, and sales potential." Submit outline and 3 sample chapters.
Recent Nonfiction Title: *A Gold Mine in Gold*, by Bale (discusses gold coins as an investment).

‡BALLANTINE/EPIPHANY BOOKS, Imprint of Ballantine Books, 201 E. 50th St., New York NY 10022. (212)572-2266. Editor: Toni Simmons. Publishes hardcover and trade paperback originals, mass market paperback originals and reprints. Averages 20 titles/year. Receives 520 submissions/year. 30% of books from first-time authors. Subsidy publishes 10% of books. Pays 8-10% royalty on retail price. Publishes book an average of 1 year after acceptance. Simultaneous and photocopied submissions OK. Reports in 6 weeks. Book catalog for 9x12 SASE with 2 first class stamps.
Nonfiction: Biography, cookbook, how-to, humor and self-help. Subjects include health, psychology, religion, sociology and sports. "Nonfiction proposals should enrich the Christian's life in some way and be written in a style that will also appeal to and be accessible to nonChristians." No poetry, sermons, eschatology, devotionals, books for children or books on controversial issues. Query or submit outline/synopsis and sample chapters. Reviews artwork/photos as part of ms package.
Recent Nonfiction Title: *Inspiring Parenthood*, by Janice Presser (self-help).
Fiction: Adventure, mainstream, mystery, religious and suspense. "We publish very little fiction; while it need not be overly religious, our fiction must contain some inspirational qualities." No "fiction for children, fiction about the end of time, prairie romances, inspirational romances or biblical/historical fiction." Query or submit outline/synopsis and sample chapters.
Recent Fiction Title: *An Educated Death*, by Gaylord Larsen (mystery).
Tips: "Examine possible similar books already on the market, then compare your own manuscript to others. Be sure to write for a general audience; Epiphany does not publish books of limited interest to a small segmented audience. A common mistake writers make is that they state how much of an advance they want in their query letters."

BALLINGER PUBLISHING CO., Subsidiary of Harper & Row, 54 Church St., Harvard Square, Cambridge MA 02138. (617)492-0670. President: Carol Franco. Publishes hardcover and paperback originals. Averages 50 titles/year. Pays royalty by arrangement. Simultaneous and photocopied submissions OK. Computer printout submissions acceptable; prefers letter-quality to dot-matrix. Reports in 1 month. Free book catalog.
Nonfiction: Professional and reference books in economics, business, finance, high technology, and international relations. Submit synopsis and sample chapters or submit complete ms.
Recent Nonfiction Title: *Megamergers*, by Kenneth Davidson.

BANKERS PUBLISHING CO., 210 South St., Boston MA 02111. (617)426-4495. Executive Editor: Jack A. Bruggeman. Publishes hardcover originals. Averages 7 titles/year; receives 20-30 submissions annually. 50% of books from first-time authors; 100% of books from unagented writers. Average print order for a writer's first book is 2,000. Pays 10-15% royalty on both wholesale and retail price; buys some mss outright for negotiable fee. Publishes book an average of 8 months after acceptance. Computer printout submissions acceptable; prefers letter-quality to dot-matrix. Reports in 2 months. Book catalog and ms guidelines for 5½x8½ SAE and 2 first class stamps.

Nonfiction: How-to reference texts on banking only, for banking professionals. "Because of their nature, our books remain useful for many years (it is not unusual for a title to remain in print for 5-10 years). However, some of our technical titles are revised and updated frequently." Looks for "the ability of the author to communicate practical, how-to technical knowledge to the reader in an understanding way." Submit outline/synopsis and 2 sample chapters.

Recent Nonfiction Title: *Bank Marketing Handbook*, by Robert J. McMahon.

Tips: "As long as a book contains technical, necessary information about doing a particular banking job, it does well. We try to provide bankers with information and guidance not available anywhere else. A common mistake writers make is failing to evaluate strengths and weaknesses of competing books. Most of our writers are experienced bankers, but we are willing to consider a professional researcher/writer for some projects. We seek to work with new authors."

BANKS-BALDWIN LAW PUBLISHING CO., 1904 Ansel Rd., Cleveland OH 44106. (216)721-7373. Editor-in-Chief: P.J. Lucier. Publishes law books and services in a variety of formats. Averages approximately 5 titles/year; receives 5-10 submissions annually. 5% of books from first-time authors; 90% of books from unagented writers. "Most titles include material submitted by outside authors." Pays 10-15% royalty or fee. Offers advance not to exceed 25% of anticipated royalty or fee. Publishes book an average of 18 months after acceptance. Photocopied submissions OK. Query for electronic submissions. Computer printout submissions acceptable; prefers letter-quality to dot-matrix. Reports in 3 weeks on queries; 6 weeks on submissions. Free book catalog; ms guidelines for SASE.

Nonfiction: Reference, law/legal. Query.

Recent Nonfiction Title: *Kentucky Mineral Law*, by David Short and Rick Thomas (law).

Tips: "We publish books for attorneys, government officials and professionals in allied fields. Trends in our field include more interest in handbooks, less in costly multi-volume sets; electronic publishing. Writer has the best chance of selling us a book on a hot new topic of law. Check citations and quotations carefully."

BANTAM BOOKS, INC., 666 5th Ave., New York NY 10103. Imprints include Skylark, For Young Readers, Sweet Dreams, Peacock Press, Loveswept, New Age Books, Spectra Windstone, and Bantam Classics. (212)765-6500. President of Bantam-Doubleday, Dell Publishing Group CEO: Alberto Vitale. President of Bantam Publishing Division (Publisher/Editor-in-Chief): Linda Grey. Vice President and Editorial Director/Adult Fiction and Nonfiction Books: Steve Rubin; Associate Editor: Amy Stout (horror, science fiction); Senior Editors: Barbara Alpert (women's fiction); Harriet Fier (business, politics, general nonfiction); Beverly Lewis (women's fiction); Greg Tobin (westerns, general fiction).

Nonfiction: Michelle Rapkin (religion); Toni Burbank, Executive Editor (women's studies, school and college); Fred Klein, Vice President and Executive Editor/Media; Senior Editors: Coleen O'Shea (cookbooks, health); Deborah Futter (school and college, Bantam New Fiction, classics); Nessa Rapoport (Bantam Jewish Bookshelf).

Fiction: Elizabeth Perle, Trade and HC Association Publisher; Peter Guzzardi (sports and general fiction); Carolyn Nichols (Loveswept); Lou Aronica, Editor, Spectra Science Fiction and Fantasy; Kate Miciak, Senior Editor (general fiction, mysteries); Betsy Gould, Associate Publisher for young readers; Judy Gitenstein, books for young readers; Nina Hoffman, Vice President Director of Subsidiary Rights); Linda Biagi, Associate Director of Subsidiary Rights); Kenzi Sugihara, Director Bantam Electronic Publishing.

BARNES & NOBLE, Division of Harper & Row, 10 E. 53rd St., New York NY 10022. (212)207-7000. Editor: Jeanne Flagg. Publishes paperback originals and paperback reprints. Pays standard paperback royalties for reprints; offers variable advance. Simultaneous and photocopied submissions OK. Computer printout submissions acceptable. Reports in 1 month.

Nonfiction: Education paperbacks. Query or submit outline/synopsis and sample chapters. Looks for "an indication that the author knows the subject he is writing about and that he can present it clearly and logically."

‡BASIL BLACKWELL, INC., Subsidiary of Basil Blackwell, Ltd., Suite 1503, 432 Park Ave. S., New York NY 10016. (212)684-2890. Editorial Director: Peter J. Dougherty. Publishes hardcover and trade paperback originals. Averages 250 titles/year. Pays royalty on net receipts in the U.S. and United Kingdom. Publishes book an average of 9 months after acceptance. Simultaneous and photocopied submissions OK. Computer printout submissions OK; prefers letter-quality. Reports in 1 week on queries; 3 weeks on mss. Free book catalog and ms guidelines for SASE.

Nonfiction: Biography, reference, textbook, scholarly and professional books. Subjects include business and economics, history, philosophy, politics, psychology, religion and sociology.

BEACON HILL PRESS OF KANSAS CITY, Box 419527, Kansas City MO 64141. Book division of Nazarene Publishing House. Coordinator: Betty Fuhrman. Publishes hardcover and paperback originals. Averages 65-70 titles/year. Offers "standard contract (sometimes flat rate purchase). Advance on royalty is paid on first 1,000 copies at publication date. On standard contract, pays 10% on first 10,000 copies and 12% on subsequent cop-

ies at the end of each calendar year.'' Publishes book an average of 2 years after acceptance. Computer printout submissions acceptable; prefers letter-quality to dot-matrix. Reports in 4-8 months unless immediately returned. "Book Committee meets quarterly to select from the manuscripts which will be published."
Nonfiction: Inspirational, Bible-based. Doctrinally must conform to the evangelical, Wesleyan tradition. Conservative view of Bible. No autobiography, poetry, devotional collections, or children's picture books. Accent on holy living; encouragement in daily Christian life. Popular style books usually under 128 pages. Query. Textbooks "almost exclusively done on assignment." Full ms or outline/sample chapters. Length: 20,000-40,000 words.
Recent Nonfiction Title: *Keeping Love in the Family*, by Leslie Parrott.
Recent Fiction Title: *God and the Timber Wolf*, by G. Franklin Allee.

BEACON PRESS, 25 Beacon St., Boston MA 02108. (617)742-2110. Director: Wendy J. Strothman. Publishes hardcover originals and paperback reprints. Averages 50 titles/year; receives 4000 submissions annually. 10% of books from first-time authors; 70% of books from unagented writers. Average print order for a writer's first book is 3,000. Offers royalty on net retail price; advance varies. Publishes book an average of 1 year after acceptance. Simultaneous and photocopied submissions OK. Computer printout submissions acceptable; prefers letter-quality to dot-matrix. Return of materials not guaranteed without SASE. Reports in 2 months. Query or submit outline/synopsis and sample chapters to Editorial Department.
Nonfiction: General nonfiction including works of original scholarship, religion, women's studies, philosophy, current affairs, literature communications, sociology, psychology, history, political science, art.
Recent Nonfiction Title: *Shared Destiny: Fifty Years of Soviet-American Relations*.
Tips: "We probably accept only one or two manuscripts from an unpublished pool of 4,000 submissions per year. No fiction or poetry submissions invited. No children's books. Authors should have academic affiliation."

‡BEAR AND CO., INC., Drawer 2860, Santa Fe NM 87504-2860. (505)983-9868. Editorial Director: Barbara Clow. Small press. Publishes trade paperback originals and reprints. Averages 12 titles/year. Receives 250 submissions/year. 20% of books from first-time authors; 80% of books from unagented writers. Pays 8-10% royalty. Publishes book an average of 18 months after acceptance. Simultaneous and photocopied submissions OK. Query for electronic submissions. Computer printout submissions OK; prefers letter-quality. Reports in 1 week on queries; 6 weeks on mss. Book catalog free.
Nonfiction: Illustrated books, science, theology, mysticism, religion and ecology. "We publish books to 'heal and celebrate the earth.' Our interest is in creation theology, western mystics, new science, ecology. Many of our books have a Christian bias, but this is not required. We are not interested in how-to, self-help, etc. Our readers are people who are open to new ways of looking at the world. They are spiritually oriented but not necessarily religious; interested in healing of the earth, peace issues, and receptive to New Age ideas." Query or submit outline/synopsis and sample chapters. Reviews artwork/photos as part of ms package.
Recent Nonfiction Title: *A Painter's Quest*, by Peter Rogers (art, spirituality).

BEAUFORT BOOKS PUBLISHERS, 9 E. 40th St., New York NY 10016. (212)685-8588. Publisher: Susan Suffes. Publishes hardcover and trade paperback originals. Averages 30-40 titles/year; receives 1,000 submissions annually. 5% of books from unagented writers. Pays 7½-15% royalty on retail price; offers variable advance. Publishes book an average of 1 year after acceptance. Simultaneous and photocopied submissions OK. Reports in 1 month on queries; 2 months on mss. Book catalog for 10x12 SAE with 70¢ postage.
Nonfiction: Subjects include biography, health, business, sports, travel, history, music, and recreation. Query, or submit outline synopsis and 3 sample chapters or complete ms.
Recent Nonfiction Title: *Cousteau*, by Axel Madsen (biography).
Fiction: Mystery, thrillers, contemporary and literary novels. "No first novels, no science fiction." Query only.
Recent Fiction Title: *The Complete Short Stories of L.P. Hartley*.

*THE BENJAMIN COMPANY, INC., One Westchester Plaza, Elmsford NY 10523. (914)592-8088. President: Ted Benjamin. Publishes hardcover and paperback originals. Averages 20-25 titles/year. 90-100% of books from unagented writers. "Usually commissions author to write specific book; seldom accepts proffered manuscripts." Subsidy publishes (nonauthor) 100% of books. Publishes book an average of 6 months after acceptance. Buys mss by outright purchase. Offers advance. Simultaneous and photocopied submissions OK. Query for electronic submissions. Computer printout submissions acceptable; prefers letter-quality to dot-matrix. Reports in 2 months.
Nonfiction: Business/economics, cookbooks, cooking and foods, health, hobbies, how-to, self-help, sports and consumerism. "Ours is a very specialized kind of publishing—for clients (industrial and association) to use in promotional, PR, or educational programs. If an author has an idea for a book and close connections with a company that might be interested in using that book, we will be very interested in working together with the author to 'sell' the program and the idea of a special book for that company. Once published, our books do get

trade distribution through a distributing publisher, so the author generally sees the book in regular book outlets as well as in the special programs undertaken by the sponsoring company. We do not encourage submission of manuscripts. We usually commission an author to write for us. The most helpful thing an author can do is to let us know what he or she has written, or what subjects he or she feels competent to write about. We will contact the author when our needs indicate that the author might be the right person to produce a needed manuscript." Query. Submit outline/synopsis and 1 sample chapter. Looks for "possibility of tie-in with sponsoring company or association."
Recent Nonfiction Title: *Commitment to Excellence*, for Amway.

BENNETT & MCKNIGHT PUBLISHING CO., Division of Glencoe Publishing Co., 809 W. Detweiller Dr., Peoria IL 61615. (309)691-4454. Vice President/Publisher: David W. Whiting. Publishes hardcover and paperback originals. Specializes in textbooks and related materials. Averages 50 titles/year. Receives 25 submissions annually. 10% of books from first-time authors; 100% of books from unagented writers. Pays up to 10% royalty for textbooks "based on cash received, less for supplements." Publishes book an average of 2 years after acceptance. Photocopied submissions OK. Computer printout submissions acceptable. Reports in 1 month. Free book catalog and ms guidelines.
Nonfiction: Publishes textbooks and related items for home economics, industrial and technology, education, career education, and art education, allied health occupations and vocational training in schools, junior high through post-secondary. Wants "content with good coverage of subject matter in a course in one of our fields; intelligent organization; and clear expression." Query "with 1-2 sample chapters that represent much of the book; not a general introduction if the ms is mostly specific 'how-to' instructions."
Recent Nonfiction Title: *Wood: Technology and Processes*.

THE BERKLEY PUBLISHING GROUP, (publishers of Berkley/Berkley Trade Paperbacks/Jove/Charter/Second Chance at Love/Pacer; Ace Science Fiction), 200 Madison Ave., New York NY 10016. (212)686-9820. Senior Vice President/Publisher: Roger Cooper. Editor-in-Chief: Ed Breslin. Publishes paperback originals and reprints. Publishes approximately 900 titles/year. Pays 6-10% royalty on retail price; offers advance. Publishes book an average of 18 months after acceptance. "We don't accept unsolicited material."
Nonfiction: How-to, inspirational, family life, philosophy and nutrition.
Recent Nonfiction Title: *The One Minute Manager*.
Fiction: Adventure, historical, mainstream men's adventure, young adult, suspense, western, occult, romance and science fiction. Submit outline/synopsis and first 3 chapters (for Ace Science Fiction only).
Recent Fiction Title: *The Accidental Tourist*, by Anne Tyler.
Young Adult Fiction Title: *The Lone Wolf*, by Joe Dever and Gary Chalk.

BETHANY HOUSE PUBLISHERS, Subsidiary of Bethany Fellowship, Inc. 6820 Auto Club Rd., Minneapolis MN 55438. (612)944-2121. Editorial Director: Carol Johnson. Publishes hardcover and paperback originals and reprints. "Contracts negotiable." Averages 60 titles/year; receives 1,200 submissions annually. 15% of books from first-time authors; 95% of books from unagented writers. Publishes book an average of 9-18 months after acceptance. Simultaneous and photocopied submissions OK. Electronic submissions OK; "no limitation regarding compatibility—we hire a transfer from other companies if necessary." Computer printout submissions acceptable. Reports in 1-2 months. Book catalog and ms guidelines for 9x12 SAE with 98¢ postage.
Nonfiction: Publishes reference (lay-oriented); devotional (evangelical, charismatic); and personal growth books. Submit outline and 2-3 sample chapters. Looks for "provocative subject, quality writing style, authoritative presentation, unique approach, sound Christian truth." Reviews artwork/photos as part of ms package.
Recent Nonfiction Title: *Finding the Freedom of Self-Control*, by William Backus (personal growth).
Fiction: Well-written stories with a Christian message. No poetry. Submit synopsis and 2-3 sample chapters to Nathan Unseth, Acquisitions Editor. Guidelines available.
Recent Fiction Title: *The Gates of Zion*, by Bodie Thoene.
Tips: "The writer has the best chance of selling our firm a book that will market well in the Christian bookstore. In your query, list other books in this category (price, length, main thrust), and tell how yours is better or unique."

BETTER HOMES AND GARDENS BOOKS, Division of the Meredith Corporation. Imprints include Sedgewood Press, 1716 Locust St., Des Moines IA 50336. Managing Editor: David A. Kirchner. Publishes hardcover and trade paperback originals. Averages 40 titles/year. "Ordinarily we pay an outright fee for work (amount depending on the scope of the assignment). If the book is the work of one author, we sometimes offer royalties in addition to the fee." Will consider photocopied submissions. Reports in 6 weeks.
Nonfiction: "We publish nonfiction in many family and home service categories, including gardening, decorating and remodeling, crafts, money management, handyman's topics, cooking and nutrition, Christmas activities, and other subjects of home service value. Emphasis is on how-to and on stimulating people to action. We require concise, factual writing. Audience is primarily husbands and wives with home and family as their

main center of interest. Style should be informative and lively with a straightforward approach. Stress the positive. Emphasis is entirely on reader service. We approach the general audience with a confident air, instilling in them a desire and the motivation to accomplish things. Food book areas that we have already dealt with in detail are currently overworked by writers submitting to us. We rely heavily on a staff of home economist editors for food books. We are interested primarily in nonfood books that can serve mail order and book club requirements (to sell at least for $9.95 and up) as well as trade. Publisher recommends careful study of specific Better Homes and Gardens Books titles before submitting material." Prefers outline and sample chapters.
Tips: "Writers often fail to familiarize themselves with the catalog/backlist of the publishers to whom they are submitting." Queries/mss may be routed to other editors in the publishing group.

BETTERWAY PUBLICATIONS, INC., White Hall VA 22987. (804)823-5661. Senior Editor: Robert F. Hostage. Publishes hardcover and trade paperback originals. Averages 14-15 titles/year; receives 1,200 submissions annually. 50-60% of books from first-time authors; 90% of books from unagented writers. Pays 10-16% royalty on wholesale price; offers $500-1,000 advance. Publishes book an average of 8 months after acceptance. Simultaneous and (quality copies please) photocopied submissions OK. Query for electronic submissions. Computer printout submissions acceptable; no dot-matrix. Reports in 6 weeks on queries; 2 months on mss. Book catalog and ms guidelines for 9x12 SAE with 56¢ postage.
Nonfiction: How-to, illustrated book, juvenile, reference, and self-help on business and economics, cooking and foods, health, hobbies, psychology, sociology, genealogy, small businesses, all aspects of homebuilding and ownership ("e.g., contracting your own home, securing the right mortgage loan, avoiding foreclosure of home, farm, or business."). "We are seeking to expand our list in small and home-based business guides or handbooks, parenting books, genealogy books (advanced how to), books that present career, lifestyle, family choices to women." No cookbooks. Submit outline/synopsis and sample chapters. Reviews artwork/photos.
Recent Nonfiction Title: *The Complete Guide to Remodeling Your Home*.
Tips: "The audience we envision for our books is typically adults of both sexes who are looking for useful and practical books that will enhance their homes and their business and personal lives. If I were a writer trying to market a book today, I would determine that there was a market for the book I intended to write and that the market was not already saturated."

*BINFORD & MORT PUBLISHING, 1202 N.W. 17th Ave., Portland OR 97209. (503)221-0866. Publisher: James Gardenier. Publishes hardcover and paperback originals and reprints. Receives 500 submissions annually. 60% of books from first-time authors; 90% of books from unagented writers. Average print order for a writer's first book is 5,000. Pays 10% royalty on retail price; offers variable advance (to established authors). Publishes about 10-12 titles annually. Occasionally does some subsidy publishing (10%), at author's request. Publishes book an average of 1 year after acceptance. Reports in 4 months. Computer printout submissions acceptable; prefers letter-quality to dot-matrix.
Nonfiction: Books about the Pacific Coast and the Northwest. Western Americana, biography, history, nature, recreation, reference, and travel. Query with sample chapters and SASE. Reviews artwork/photos as part of ms package.
Recent Nonfiction Title: *Stepping Stones: The Pilgrims' Own Story*, edited by Adelia White Notson and Robert Carver Notson.

‡*BIRKHÄUSER BOSTON, Subsidiary of Birkhauser-Basel/Spinger-Verlag, New York, Inc., 380 Green St., Cambridge MA 02139. (617)876-2333. Editorial Director: George Adelman. Publishes hardcover originals. Averages 50 titles/year. 10% of titles subsdized by organizations. Pays 10% royalty on retail price. Reports in 2 weeks on queries; 1 month on mss. Free book catalog.
Nonfiction: Technical and textbooks. Professional books on mathematics, physics, computer science and neuroscience. Especially needs "scholarly monographs or collections in mathematics, physics and neuroscience for professionals and special libraries. No trade books." Submit outline/synopsis and sample chapters.
Recent Nonfiction Title: *Renormalization Groups*, edited by A. Jaffe (physics).

JOHN F. BLAIR, PUBLISHER, 1406 Plaza Dr., Winston-Salem NC 27103. (919)768-1374. President: Margaret Couch. Publishes hardcover originals, trade paperbacks and occasionally reprints; receives 1,000 submissions annually. 20-30% of books from first-time authors; 90% of books from unagented writers. Average print order for a writer's first book is 3,500. Royalty to be negotiated. Publishes book an average of 2 years after acceptance. Query for electronic submissions. Computer printout submissions acceptable; no dot-matrix. Reports in 2 months. Book catalog and ms guidelines for large manila SAE and 56¢ postage.
Nonfiction: Especially interested in well-researched adult biography and history. Preference given to books dealing with Southeastern United States. Also interested in environment and Americana; query on other nonfiction topics. Looks for utility and significance. Submit synopsis/outline and first 3 chapters or complete ms. Reviews artwork/photos as part of ms package.
Recent Nonfiction Title: *The Lee Girls*, by Mary P. Coulling (biography).
Fiction: "We are most interested in serious novels of substance and imagination. Preference given to material

related to Southeastern United States." No category fiction, juvenile fiction, picture books or poetry.
Recent Fiction Title: *The Hatterask Incident*, by John D. Randall.

‡**BNA BOOKS**, Division of The Bureau of National Affairs, Inc., 1231 25th St., NW, Washington DC 20037. (202)452-4276. Assistant to the Publisher: Francis Hill Slowinski. Publishes hardcover and softcover originals. Averages 30 titles/year. Receives 200 submissions/year. 20% of books from first-time authors. 95% of books from unagented writers. Pays 5-15% royalty on retail price; offers $1,000 average advance. Simultaneous submissions OK. Publishes book an average of 1 year after acceptance. Reports in 2 months on queries; 3 months on mss. Book catalog and ms guidelines free on request.
Nonfiction: Reference and professional/scholarly. Subjects include business law and regulation, environment and safety, legal practice, labor relations and human resource management. No biographies, bibliographies, cookbooks, religion books, humor or trade books. Submit detailed table of contents or outline.
Recent Nonfiction Title: *Supreme Court Practice*, sixth edition, by Stern, Gressman and Shapiro (law).
Tips: "Our audience is practicing lawyers and business executives; managers, federal, state, and local government administrators; unions; and libraries. We look for authoritative and comprehensive works on subjects of interest to executives, professionals, and managers, that relate to the interaction of government and business."

BOOKCRAFT, INC., 1848 W. 2300 S., Salt Lake City UT 84119. (801)972-6180. Editorial Manager: Cory H. Maxwell. Publishes (mainly hardcover) originals and reprints. Pays standard 7½-12½-15% royalty on retail price; "we rarely give a royalty advance." Averages 35-40 titles/year; receives 500-600 submissions annually. 25% of books from first-time authors; 100% of books from unagented writers. Publishes book an average of 6 months after acceptance. Will consider photocopied submissions. Computer printout submissions acceptable; prefers letter-quality to dot-matrix. Reports in about 3 months. Will send general information to prospective authors on request; ms guidelines for SASE.
Nonfiction: "We publish for members of The Church of Jesus Christ of Latter-Day Saints (Mormons) and do not distribute to the national market. All our books are closely oriented to the faith and practices of the LDS church, and we will be glad to review such mss. Mss which have merely a general religious appeal are not acceptable. Ideal book lengths range from about 64 to 224 pages or so, depending on subject, presentation, and age level. We look for a fresh approach—rehashes of well-known concepts or doctrines not acceptable. Mss should be anecdotal unless truly scholarly or on a specialized subject. Outlook must be positive. We do not publish anti-Mormon works. We also publish short and moderate length books for Mormon youth, about ages 14 to 19, mostly nonfiction. These reflect LDS principles without being 'preachy'; must be motivational. 30,000-45,000 words is about the right length, though good longer mss are not entirely ruled out. This is a tough area to write in, and the mortality rate for such mss is high. We publish only 2 or 3 new juvenile titles annually." No "poetry, plays, personal philosophizings, family histories, or personal histories." Query. "Include contents page with manuscript."
Recent Nonfiction Title: *The Life Beyond*, by Robert L. Millet and Joseph Fielding McConkie.
Fiction: Must be closely oriented to LDS faith and practices.
Recent Fiction Title: *The Morning Comes Singing*, by Kristen D. Randle.

BOOKMAKERS GUILD, INC., Suite 202, 1430 Florida Ave., Longmont CO 80501. (303)442-5774. Executive Editor: Normandi Ellis. Publishes hardcover and trade paperback originals, and hardcover and trade paperback reprints. Averages 8-10 titles/year; receives 500 submissions annually. 30% of books from first-time authors; 90% of books from unagented writers. Pays 10% royalty on net. Publishes books an average of 12-18 months after acceptance. Photocopied submissions OK. Letter-quality computer printout submissions acceptable. Mss will not be returned without SASE. Reports in 2 weeks on queries; 2 months on mss after query, 4 months on ms without query. Free book catalog and guidelines.
Nonfiction: Adult reference; self-help; contemporary and social issues; health; nature (general interest and professional); and psychology (focus on children and family). "We see a continuing focus on families, children and youth, especially books on child advocacy, behavior and education. Potential growth areas are the natural sciences. No how to, cookbooks, local history, novels, poetry, sci-fi, computers, fashion, sports or works ill-written and ill-conceived." Query or submit outline/synopsis and sample chapters. Sometimes reviews artwork/photos.
Recent Nonfiction Title: *39 Forever*, by Levitt and Guralnick.
Fiction: Juvenile, age 8 and up. "We seek fantasy folklore, and saga along classical themes with educational merit." 100 page minimum required. No picture books, but will look at collections of stories that could make a good volume. Query first.
Recent Fiction Title: *The Silver Trumpet*, by Owen Barfield.
Tips: "We are specifically seeking educational nonfiction in the natural sciences for young adults, as well as nonfiction for adults that addresses the issues for the well-being of the adolescent, the aged, and the family. Books that are sensitively written, well-researched, and on topics that are not already flooding the market have the best chance of selling to our firm."

*BOREALIS PRESS, LTD., 9 Ashburn Dr., Nepean, Ontario K2E 6N4 Canada. Editorial Director: Frank Tierney. Senior Editor: Glenn Clever. Publishes hardcover and paperback originals. Averages 4 titles/year; receives 400-500 submissions annually. 80% of books from first-time authors; 100% of books from unagented writers. Subsidy publishes (nonauthor) 5% of books. Pays 10% royalty on retail price; no advance. Publishes book an average of 18 months after acceptance. "No multiple submissions or electronic printouts on paper more than 8½ inches wide." Computer printout submissions acceptable; prefers letter-quality to dot-matrix. Reports in 4 months. SAE and IRCs. Book catalog $1.
Nonfiction: "Only material Canadian in content." Query. Reviews artwork/photos as part of ms package. Looks for "style in tone and language, reader interest, and maturity of outlook."
Recent Nonfiction Title: *How Parliament Works*, by Bejermi (politics).
Fiction: "Only material Canadian in content and dealing with significant aspects of the human situation." Query.
Recent Fiction Title: *Rose of the North* by Friesen (novel).
Tips: "Ensure that creative writing deals with consequential human affairs, not just action, sensation, or cutesy stuff."

THE BORGO PRESS, Box 2845, San Bernardino CA 92406. (714)884-5813. Publisher: Robert Reginald. Editor: Mary A. Burgess. Publishes hardcover and paperback originals. Averages 30 titles/year; receives 200+ submissions annually. 5% of books from first-time authors; 50% of books from unagented writers. Pays royalty on retail price: "10% of gross, with a 12% escalator." No advance. Publishes book an average of 1-2 years after acceptance. "Virtually all of our sales are to the library market." Accept diskettes compatible with IBM PC using MS—Dos 2.1 with WordStar; requires hard copy also. Computer printout submissions acceptable. Reports in 3 months. Book catalog and writer's guidelines for SAE and 39¢ postage.
Nonfiction: Publishes literary critiques, bibliographies, historical research, film critiques, theatrical research, interview volumes, biographies, social studies, political science, and reference works for library and academic markets. Query with letter or outline/synopsis and 1 sample chapter. "All of our books, without exception, are published in open-ended, numbered, monographic series. Do not submit proposals until you have looked at our catalogs and publications. We are not a market for fiction, poetry, popular nonfiction, artwork, or anything else except scholarly monographs in the humanities and social sciences. We discard unsolicited manuscripts from outside of our subject fields which are not accompanied by SASEs."
Recent Nonfiction Title: *Existentially Speaking*, by Colin Wilson.

*DON BOSCO PUBLICATIONS, 475 N. Ave., Box T, New Rochelle NY 10802. (914)576-0122. Subsidiaries include Salesiana Publishers. Editorial Director: John Malloy. Publishes hardcover and trade paperback originals. Averages 6-10 titles/year; receives 50 submissions annually. 15% of books from first-time authors; 100% of books from unagented writers. Average print order for a writer's first book is 3,000. Subsidy publishes 10% of books. Subsidy publishes (nonauthor) 30% of books. "We judge the content of the manuscript and quality to be sure it fits the description of our house. We subsidy publish for nonprofit and religious societies." Pays 5-10% royalty on retail price; offers average $100 advance. Publishes book an average of 10 months after acceptance. Computer printout submissions acceptable; no dot-matrix. Reports in 2 weeks on queries; 2 months on mss. Free book catalog.
Nonfiction: Biography, juvenile and textbook on Roman Catholic religion. "Biographies of outstanding Christian men and women of today. We are a new publisher with wide experience in school marketing, especially in religious education field." Accepts nonfiction translations from Italian and Spanish. Query or submit outline/synopsis and 2 sample chapters. Occasionally reviews artwork/photos as part of ms package.
Recent Nonfiction Title: *Dreams, Visions and Prophecies of Don Bosco*, edited by Rev. Gene Brown.
Tips: Queries/mss may be routed to other editors in the publishing group.

THE BOSTON MILLS PRESS, 132 Main St., Erin Ontario N0B 1T0 Canada. (519)833-2407. President: John Denison. Publishes hardcover and trade paperback originals. Averages 16 titles/year; receives 100 submissions annually. 75% of books from first-time authors; 90% of books from unagented writers. Pays 6-10% royalty on retail price; no advance. Publishes book an average of 8 months after acceptance. Simultaneous and photocopied submissions OK. Query for electronic submissions. Computer printout submissions acceptable. Reports in 2 weeks on queries; 1 month on mss. Free book catalog.
Nonfiction: Illustrated book. Subjects include history. "We're interested in anything to do with Canadian or American history—especially transportation. We like books with a small, strong market." No autobiographies. Query. Reviews artwork/photos as part of ms package.
Recent Nonfiction Title: *Next Stop Grand Central*, by Stan Fischler (railway history).
Tips: "We can't compete with the big boys so we stay with short-run specific market books that bigger firms

can't handle. We've done well this way so we'll continue in the same vein. We tend to accept books from completed manuscripts."

THOMAS BOUREGY AND CO., INC., 401 Lafayette St., New York NY 10003. Editor: Rita Brenig. Imprint includes Avalon Books (fiction). Offers advance on publication date. Averages 60 titles/year. Reports in 5 months. Computer printout submissions acceptable; no dot-matrix. Book catalog and guidelines for SASE.
Fiction: Romances, nurse/romances, westerns and gothic novels. Avoid sensationalist elements. Send one-page synopsis with SASE. No sample chapters. Length: about 50,000 words.
Recent Fiction Title: *Caprice in Love*, by Jean Woodward.
Tips: "Maintain suspense about the romance outcome of the plot. Writers let us know too soon—too definitely—that the man, the heroine wants, really wants her. Knowing this too soon kills the story. There is supposed to be an obstacle between the guy and the girl until the very end."

BRADBURY PRESS affiliate of Macmillan, Inc., 866 3rd Ave., New York NY 10022. (212)702-9809. Editor-in-Chief: Barbara Lalicki. Publishes hardcover originals for children and young adults. Averages 30 titles/year. Pays royalty and offers advance. No simultaneous submissions. Reports in 3 months. Book catalog and ms guidelines for 9x12 SAE with 88¢ postage.
Fiction: Picture books, concept books, photo essays and novels. Also "stories about real kids; special interest in realistic dialogue." No adult ms. No fantasy or religious material. Submit complete ms.
Recent Fiction Title: *The Moonlight Man*, by Paula Fox (novel).

‡ALLEN D. BRAGDON PUBLISHERS, INC., 153 W. 82nd St., New York NY 10024. (212)787-6886. Subsidiaries include Brownstone Library and Munchie Books. Publisher: Allen Bragdon. Publishes hardcover originals and reprints and trade paperback originals. Averages 8-20 titles/year. Receives 15-20 submissions/year. 25% of books from first-time authors. 75% of books from unagented writers. Buys some mss outright for $500-7,500 and share of profit. Publishes book an average of 1 year after acceptance. Computer printout submissions OK; prefers letter-quality. Reports in 1 week on queries; 2 months on mss. Book catalog free on request.
Nonfiction: Cookbook, how-to and illustrated book. Subjects include Americana, cooking and foods and hobbies. "We welcome contacts from illustrated cooking authors and Americana crafts for future publications. We are looking for good how-to illustrators and skilled professionals or amateurs in non-academic how-to." Query with table of contents, outline and sample illustrations. Requires artwork/photos as part of ms package.
Recent Nonfiction Title: *Joy Through the World*, by UNICEF.
Tips: "We are looking for old-time Americana and European home skills with color photos or illustrations."

BRANDEN PRESS, INC., 17 Station St., Box 843, Brookline Village MA 02147. (617)734-2045. President: Adolph Caso. Small press. Subsidiaries include International Pocket Library and Popular Technology, Four Seas and Brashear. Publishes hardcover and trade paperback originals, hardcover and trade paperback reprints and software. Averages 10 titles/year; receives 400 submissions annually. 80% of books from first-time authors; 90% of books from unagented writers. Average print order for a writer's first book is 3,000. Pays 5-10% royalty on wholesale price; offers $1,000 maximum advance. Publishes book an average of 10 months after acceptance. Electronic submissions OK if compatible with IBM PC, but requires hard copy also. Computer printout submissions acceptable; prefers letter-quality to dot-matrix. Reports in 1 week on queries; 2 months on mss. Book catalog for SASE.
Nonfiction: Biography, illustrated book, juvenile, reference, technical and textbook. Subjects include Americana, art, health, history, music, photography, politics, sociology and classics. Especially looking for "about 10 manuscripts on national and international subjects, including biographies of well-known individuals." No religion or philosophy. Prefers paragraph query with author's vita; no unsolicited mss. Reviews artwork/photos as part of ms package.
Recent Nonfiction Title: *"Bitch!" Autobiography of Lady Lawford*.
Fiction: Adventure (well-written, realistic); ethnic (histories, integration); historical (especially biographies); mainstream (emphasis on youth and immigrants); religious (historical-reconstructive); romance (novels with well-drawn characters); and books about computers and software. No science, mystery or pornography. Paragraph query with author's vita; no unsolicited mss.
Recent Fiction Title: *Sarah M. Peale*, by King (fictionalized biography).
Poetry: No religious, humorous or autobiographical poetry books. Submit 5 poems.
Recent Poetry Title: *Tid-Bits*, by Brook (epigrams).
Tips: "Branden publishes only manuscripts determined to have a significant impact on modern society. Our audience is a well-read general public, professionals, college students, and some high school students. If I were a writer trying to market a book today, I would thoroughly investigate the number of potential readers interested in the content of my book."

GEORGE BRAZILLER, INC., 60 Madison Ave., New York NY 10010. 25% of books from first-time authors; 10% of books from unagented writers. Average print order for a writer's first book is 3,000; receives 500 submissions annually. Averages 30 titles/year. Offers standard 10-12½-15% royalty contract; offers variable advance depending on author's reputation and nature of book. Publishes book an average of 1 year after acceptance. Computer printout submissions acceptable; prefers letter-quality to dot-matrix. No unsolicited mss. Reports in 6 weeks. Book catalog and guidelines for SASE.

Fiction and Nonfiction: Publishes general fiction and nonfiction; subjects include literature, art, philosophy and history. Accepts nonfiction and fiction.   Query.

Recent Nonfiction Title: *Winnie Mandela*, by Nancy Harrison (biography).

Recent Fiction Title: *Telcaihua/The Windeater*, by Ken Hulme (stories).

*BRETHREN PRESS, 1451 Dundee Ave., Elgin IL 60120. (312)742-5100. Owned and managed by The Church of the Brethren General Board. Book Editor: David Eller. Publishes hardcover and trade paperback originals, and trade paperback reprints. Averages 10-12 titles/year; receives 150 queries/submissions annually. 30% of books from first-time authors; 90% of books from unagented writers. Subsidy publishes (nonauthor) 30% of books. Payment depends on target market, "some manuscripts are purchased outright." Typical contract: up to $1,000 advance against 10% net royalties for first 5,000 copies; 12% net on 5,001 copies and up. Publishes book an average of 1 year after acceptance. Simultaneous and photocopied submissions OK. Query for electronic submissions. Computer printout submissions acceptable; prefers letter-quality to dot-matrix. Reports in 2 months on queries; 6 months ("hopefully") on mss. Book catalog and mss guidelines for 9x12 SAE with 37¢ postage.

Nonfiction: Subjects include business and economics, health, history, philosophy, politics, psychology, religion and sociology. All titles should be from a faith perspective. Needs theology, Bible study, devotional, peace-related, practical discipleship, social issues, simple living, family life, "Plain People" heritage, and current and international events. Query or submit outline/synopsis and sample chapters. Reviews artwork/photos as part of ms package.

Recent Nonfiction Title: *The Family Farm*, by Shantilal Bughat.

Fiction: Religious. "The only fiction published in recent years were inspirational, with historical settings in 'Pennsylvania Dutch'/Plain People context." No romances. Query.

Tips: "We prefer timely issues with solid theological content, well-written for the average reader. Adhere to *Chicago Manual* style and *Church of the Brethren Handbook of Style*."

BREVET PRESS, INC., Box 1404, Sioux Falls SD 57101. Publisher: Donald P. Mackintosh. Managing Editor: Peter E. Reid. Publishes hardcover and paperback originals and reprints. Receives 40 submissions annually. 50% of books from first-time authors; 100% of books from unagented writers. Average print order for a writer's first book is 5,000. Pays 5% royalty; advance averages $1,000. Publishes book an average of 1 year after acceptance. Simultaneous and photocopied submissions OK. Computer printout submissions acceptable. Reports in 2 months. Free book catalog.

Nonfiction: Specializes in business management, history, place names, and historical marker series. Americana (A. Melton, editor); business (D.P. Mackintosh, editor); history (B. Mackintosh, editor); and technical books (Peter Reid, editor). Query; "after query, detailed instructions will follow if we are interested." Reviews artwork/photos; send copies if photos/illustrations are to accompany ms.

Recent Nonfiction Title: *Challenge*, by R. Karolevitz (history).

Tips: "Write with market potential and literary excellence. Keep sexism out of the manuscripts by male authors."

*BRIARCLIFF PRESS PUBLISHERS, 11 Wimbledon Ct., Jericho NY 11753. Editorial Director: Trudy Settel. Senior Editor: J. Frieman. Publishes hardcover and paperback originals. Averages 5-7 titles/year; receives 250 submissions annually. 10% of books from first-time authors; 60% of books from unagented writers. Average print order for a writer's first book is 5,000. Subsidy publishes 20% of books. Pays $4,000-5,000 for outright purchase; offers average of $1,000 advance. Publishes book an average of 6 months after acceptance. Computer printout submissions acceptable; no dot-matrix. "We do not use unsolicited manuscripts. Ours are custom books prepared for businesses, and assignments are initiated by us."

Nonfiction: How-to, cookbooks, sports, travel, fitness/health, business and finance, diet, gardening and crafts. "We want our books to be designed to meet the needs of specific businesses." Accepts nonfiction translations from French, German and Italian. Query. Submit outline and 2 sample chapters. Reviews artwork/photos as part of ms package.

BRICK HOUSE PUBLISHING CO., Subsidiary of Mont Chat, Inc., 3 Main St., Andover MA 01810. (617)475-9568. Publisher: Robert Runck. Small press. Publishes hardcover and trade paperback originals. Averages 12 titles/year; receives 100 submissions annually. 20% of books from first-time authors; 100% of books from unagented writers. Pays 10-15% royalty on wholesale price. Offers average $1,000 advance. Publishes book an average of 6 months after acceptance. Simultaneous and photocopied submissions OK. Electronic submissions OK, but requires hard copy also. Computer printout submissions acceptable; prefers letter-quality to dot-matrix. Reports in 2 weeks on queries; 3 months on mss. Book catalog and ms guidelines for 9x12 SAE with 39¢ postage.

Nonfiction: How-to, reference, technical and textbook. Subjects include business and consumer advice. "We are looking for writers to do books in the following areas: practical guidance and information for people running small businesses, consumer trade books on money and job topics, and college business textbooks." Query with synopses.

Recent Nonfiction Title: *Personal Financial Planning*, by Byron Woodman, et al. (consumer advice).

Tips: "A common mistake writers make is not addressing the following questions in their query/proposals: What are my qualifications for writing this book? Why would anyone want the book enough to pay for it in a bookstore? What can I do to help promote the book?"

BRIDGE PUBLISHING, INC., 2500 Hamilton Blvd., South Plainfield NJ 07080. (201)754-0745. Editor: Stephen R. Clark. Publishes trade and mass-market paperback originals and reprints, and cloth originals. Averages 12-20 titles/year; receives 1,000 submissions annually. 10% of books from first-time authors; 90% of books from unagented writers. Average print order for a writer's first book is 5,000. Pays negotiable royalty. Assigns projects to writers. Publishes book an average of 1 year after acceptance. Photocopied submissions OK. Computer printout submissions acceptable; prefers letter-quality to dot-matrix. Reports in 1 month. Book catalog $2; ms guidelines for SASE.

Nonfiction: How-to, self-help and religious/Christian (nondenominational). Subjects include current events, health, religion and social issues. Especially looking for books with spiritual emphasis. Query with outline/synopsis and at least 2 sample chapters or submit complete ms, and always include SASE.

Recent Nonfiction Title: *Help For the Battered Woman*, by Lydia Savina, Ph.D.

Tips: "We are especially (though not exclusively) interested in self-help books dealing with sensitive issues, such as divorce, rape, abortion, suicide, alcoholism, homosexuality, abuse, addiction, sexuality, pornography, mental and emotional illness, terminal illness, incest, aging and unemployment. We are looking for mss authoritatively written, dealing with the subjects head-on, and offering real answers and serious help for both teen and adult readers. In addition to issues-oriented books, we are looking for mss on Bible study, doctrine, spiritual growth, evangelism that exhibit careful scholarship solidly grounded in God's word. While we are not generally accepting any fiction or poetry, we will consider mss of *exceptional merit*. Authors must already have material published in significant periodicals and/or other books published by reputable publishers. The work should be written from a Biblical Christian world view but does not necessarily need to be explicitly religious in nature. Only completed fiction and poetry mss will be considered."

BROADMAN PRESS, 127 9th Ave. N, Nashville TN 37234. Editorial Director: Harold S. Smith. Publishes hardcover and paperback originals (85%) and reprints (15%). Averages 80 titles/year. Pays 10% royalty on retail price; no advance. Photocopied submissions OK "only if they're sharp and clear." Computer printouts acceptable; prefers letter-quality to dot-matrix. Reports in 2 months.

Nonfiction: Religion. "We are open to freelance submissions in the children's and inspirational areas. Materials in both areas must be suited for a conservative Protestant readership. No poetry, biography, sermons, or anything outside the area of the Protestant tradition." Query, submit outline/synopsis and sample chapters, or submit complete ms. Reviews artwork/photos as part of ms package.

Fiction: Religious. "We publish almost no fiction—less than five titles per year. For our occasional publication we want not only a very good story, but also one that sets forth Christian values. Nothing that lacks a positive Christian emphasis; nothing that fails to sustain reader interest." Submit complete ms with synopsis.

Tips: "Bible study is very good for us, but our publishing is largely restricted in this area to works that we enlist on the basis of specific author qualifications. Preparation for the future and living with life's stresses and complexities are trends in the subject area."

BROADWAY PRESS, Suite 407, 120 Duane St., New York NY 10007. (212)693-0570. Publisher: David Rodger. Small press. Publishes trade paperback originals. Averages 5-10 titles/year; receives 20-30 submissions annually. 50% of books from first-time authors; 75% of books from unagented writers. Pays negotiable royalty. Publishes book an average of 18 months after acceptance. Simultaneous and photocopied submissions OK. Computer printout submissions acceptable. Reports in 1 month on queries. Book catalog and ms guidelines for 9x12 SAE with 39¢ postage.

Nonfiction: Reference and technical. Subjects include theatre and the performing arts. "We're looking for professionally oriented and authored books for technical theatre and the performing arts. Most of our books are in-house publications, but we will accept author's queries for titles fitting the above criteria." Submit outline/synopsis and sample chapters.

Recent Nonfiction Title: *The New York Theatrical Sourcebook*, by The Association of Theatrical Artists & Craftspeople (reference book for services and supplies).

Tips: "A common mistake writers make is not following up on submissions and queries."

‡BROOK HOUSE PRESS, Box 709, Holbrook NY 11741. (516)542-4344. Senior Editor: Amanda McIntyre. Publishes hardcover originals. Publishes 3-5 titles per year. 99% of books from unagented writers. Pays 10% royalty. Publishes ms an average of 18 months after acceptance. Simultaneous and photocopied submissions

OK. Query for electronic submissions. Responds in 4-6 weeks on queries, 4-6 months on submissions. Book catalog for #10 SAE with one first class stamp; writer's guidelines for SASE.

Nonfiction: "We are seeking books which deal broadly with important aspects of the human condition, be it cultural, social, political or philosophical. They do not have to be scholarly, but may be so provided they are well written and devoid of jargon. We do not want the usual conservative or radical discourses on the current political scene, nor do we want books catering to special interest groups. Do not write about the CIA in South America, write about the idea of power among nations, etc." Submit complete ms according to guidelines.

Recent Nonfiction Title: *The Goroon's Head*, by Donald Navin (Social commentary).

Fiction: "We believe that fiction should not only put forth broad cultural, social and philosophical ideas, but should also be conceived and executed as art. Thus we are open to all ideas about the human condition . . . and to all genres and style provided these are interestingly and imaginatively executed. We do not want to see the current novels about a writer writing about a writer writing about a writer, nor do we want to see special interest or regional fiction." Submit complete ms according to guidelines.

Recent Fiction Title: *In Tynan's House*, by Jon Burkhardt (experimental).

Poetry: "As with fiction and nonfiction, we want to see poetry that puts forth significant ideas about the human condition. We are partial to poetry which makes use of symbolism, allegory, myth, and is stylistically imaginative. This includes narrative poems and prose poems." Submit complete ms.

Recent poetry title: *The City of Light*, by S.J. Speranza (prose poem).

Tips: "We cater to first time and little known authors."

BRUNNER/MAZEL, PUBLISHERS, Box 419, 1889 Palmer Ave., Larchmont NY 10538. (914)834-3920. Senior Editor: Ms. Ann Alhadeff. Publishes hardcover originals. Averages 30-35 titles/year; receives 400 submissions annually. Offers average $1,000 advance. Publishes book an average of 1 year after acceptance. Simultaneous submissions OK. Computer printout submissions acceptable; prefers letter-quality to dot-matrix. Reports in 1 week on queries; 2 weeks on mss. Free ms guidelines.

Nonfiction: Clinical psychology and psychiatry on health, psychology, social work, child development, psychiatry, hypnosis and family therapy. No submissions for a general audience. Submit outline/synopsis and sample chapters.

Recent Nonfiction Title: *The Evolution of Psychotherapy*, edited by Jeffrey K. Zeig, Ph.D. (psychotherapy).

*BYLS PRESS, Department of Bet Yoatz Library Services, 6247 N. Francisco Ave., Chicago IL 60659. (312)262-8959. President: Daniel D. Stuhlman. Publishes trade paperback originals and computer programs. Averages 3 titles/year; receives 10-20 submissions annually. Subsidy publishes variable percentage of books. Pays 7½-15% on wholesale price; no advance. Photocopied submissions OK. Query for electronic submissions. Writers may submit via computer bulletin board. Computer printout submissions acceptable; prefers letter-quality. Reports in 1 week on queries; reporting time on mss "depends on material." Free book catalog for #10 SASE.

Nonfiction: How-to (for teachers), and juvenile. Subjects include baking and religion ("stories aimed at children for Jewish holidays"). "We're looking for children's books for Jewish holidays that can be made into computer personalized books. In particular we need books for Sukkot, Shabbat and Purim. We need titles for our teacher education series." Query with synposes; "no agents, authors only. Do not submit ideas without examining our books. Ask yourself if a book idea fits what we are looking for."

Recent Nonfiction Title: *Subject*, by Daniel Stuhlman (computer program for library subject headings).

Fiction: Religious (stories for Jewish children). No expository fiction. "All unsolicited manuscripts are returned only if return postage is included."

C Q PRESS, Imprint of Congressional Quarterly, Inc., 1414 22nd St. NW, Washington DC 20037. (202)887-8642. Director: Joanne Daniels. Publishes hardcover and paperback originals. Receives 20-30 submissions annually. 90% of books from unagented writers. Pays standard college royalty on wholesale price; offers college text advance. Publishes book an average of 5 months after acceptance of final ms. Simultaneous and photocopied submissions OK. Computer printout submissions acceptable; no dot-matrix. Reports in 3 months. Free book catalog.

Nonfiction: College text. All levels of political science texts. "We are one of the most distinguished publishers in the area of political science textbooks." Submit outline and sample chapter.

*CAMBRIDGE UNIVERSITY PRESS, 32 E. 57th St., New York NY 10022. Editorial Director: Colin Day. Publishes hardcover and paperback originals. Publishes 1,000 titles/year; receives 1,000 submissions annually. 50% of books from first-time authors; 99% of books from unagented writers. Subsidy publishes (nonauthor) 8% of books. Pays 10% royalty on receipts; 8% on paperbacks; no advance. Publishes book an average of 1 year after acceptance. Electronic submissions OK via most IBM/IBM compatible/Apple microcomputer 5¼" disks; most dedicated W.P. systems; some tapes to prearranged specifications, but requires hard copy also. Computer printout submissions acceptable. Reports in 4 months.

Nonfiction: Anthropology, archeology, economics, life sciences, mathematics, psychology, physics, art history, upper-level textbooks, academic trade, scholarly monographs, biography, history, and music. Looking for academic excellence in all work submitted. Department Editors: Elizabeth Maguire (humanities); Susan Milmoe (psychology); Rufus Neal (physical sciences); Frank Smith (history, political science); Ellen Shaw (English as second language); Colin Day (economics); Terence Moore (philosophy); and Peter-John Leone (earth sciences). Query. Reviews artwork/photos.
Recent Nonfiction Title: *Colonial American Portraiture*, by Wayne Craven.

CAMELOT BOOKS, Children's Book Imprint of Avon Books, a division of the Hearst Corp., 105 Madison Ave., New York NY 10016. (212)399-1384. Editorial Director: Ellen Krieger. Publishes paperback originals and reprints. Averages 36 titles/year; receives 1,500-2,000 submissions annually. 10-15% of books from first-time authors; 25% of books from unagented writers. Pays 6-8% royalty on retail price; offers minimum advance $1,500. Publishes book an average of 15 months after acceptance. Simultaneous and photocopied submissions OK. Computer printout submissions acceptable; prefers letter-quality to dot-matrix. Reports in 10 weeks. Free book catalog and ms guidelines for 8x10 SAE and 98¢ postage.
Fiction: Subjects include adventure, fantasy, humor, mainstream, mystery, science fiction ("very selective with mystery and science fiction") and suspense. Submit entire ms or 3 sample chapters and a brief "general summary of the story, chapter by chapter."
Recent Fiction Title: *Search for Grissi*, by Mary Francis Shur.

‡*CANADIAN PLAINS RESEARCH CENTER, University of Regina, Regina, Saskatchewan S4S 0A2 Canada. (306)584-4795. Manager: Gillian Wadsworth Minifie. Publishes scholarly and trade paperback originals. Averages 6-8 titles/year; receives 45-50 submissions annually. 35% of books from first-time authors; 90% of books from unagented writers. Subsidy publishes 80% (nonauthor) of books. Determines whether an author should be subsidy published through a scholarly peer review. Pays 5-10% royalty on retail price. "Occasionally academics will waive royalties in order to maintain lower prices." Publishes book an average of 18 months after acceptance. Query for electronic submissions. Reports in 2 weeks. Free book catalog and ms guidelines.
Nonfiction: Biography, "coffee table" book, illustrated book, technical, textbook and scholarly. Subjects include animals, business and economics, history, nature, politics and sociology. "The Canadian Plains Research Center publishes the results of research on topics relating to the Canadian Plains region, although manuscripts relating to the Great Plains will be considered. Material *must* be scholarly. Do not submit health, self-help, hobbies, music, sports, psychology, recreation or cookbooks unless they have a scholarly approach. For example, we would be interested in acquiring a pioneer manuscript cookbook, with modern ingredient equivalents, if the material relates to the Canadian Plains/Great Plains region. Submit complete ms. Reviews artwork/photos as part of ms package.
Recent Nonfiction Title: *1885 and After: Native Society in Transition*, edited by Barron and Waldram (native studies).
Tips: "Pay great attention to manuscript preparation and accurate footnoting."

*CANTERBURY PRESS, Box 2151C, Berkeley CA 94702. (415)843-1860. Editors: Ian Faircloth and Norine Brogan. Small press. Publishes hardcover and trade paperback originals. Averages 3-4 titles/year; receives approximately 100 submissions annually. 75% of books from first-time authors; 90% of books from unagented writers. Subsidy publishes 50% of books; 25% non-author subsidized. Pays 5-8% royalty on wholesale price. Offers average $500 advance. Publishes book an average of 4 months after acceptance. Simultaneous and photocopied submissions OK. Electronic submissions via disk or modem acceptable—"we are compatible with all systems"; but hard copy must accompany an electronic submission. Computer printout submissions acceptable; prefers letter-quality to dot-matrix. Reports in 1 month on queries; 2 months on manuscripts. Book catalog and ms guidelines for #10 SASE.
Nonfiction: Subjects include philosophy, politics and sociology. "We need work which highlights social injustice, and political strategies to alleviate this. Studies on 'third world' peoples, people with disabilities, native Americans and other minority groups—works which evidence the plight of the underprivileged." Query with outline; all unsolicited mss are returned unopened.
Recent Nonfiction Title: *Living Outside Inside*, by Susan Hannaford (a social study on the plight of disabled people).
Fiction: Adventure, experimental, fantasy and humor. "We need fiction works of a high literary standard which offer a social, political and/or cultural insight. No predictable material which really has nothing to offer the type of reader we would like to attract." Query; all unsolicited mss are returned unopened.
Recent Fiction Title: *Peregrina*, by Laura Mars (children's bilingual Spanish/English book).
Tips: "The audience we envision for our books is a mature adult audience that appreciates good literature, but realizes that we are in a developing society which can be influenced by that literature—an audience that appreciates innovative writing which may bring new ideas and important insights. If I were a writer trying to market a book today, I would remain confident in my work and persevere—there's always an opening somewhere."

‡*ARISTIDE D. CARATZAS, PUBLISHER, Box 210/30 Church St., New Rochelle NY 10801. (914)632-8487. Managing Editor: John Emerich. Publishes hardcover originals and reprints. Averages 12 titles/year; receives over 100 submissions annually. 35% of books from first-time authors; 80% of books from unagented writers. Subsidy publishes 25% of books. "We seek grants/subsidies for limited run scholarly books; granting organizations are generally institutions or foundations." Pays royalty; offers $1,500 average advance. Publishes book an average of 18 months after acceptance. Simultaneous and photocopied submissions OK. Query for electronic submissions. Computer printout submissions OK. Reports in 1 month on queries; 3 months on mss. Free book catalog.
Nonfiction: Reference, technical and textbook. Subjects include art, history, politics, religion, travel, classical languages (Greek and Latin), archaeology and mythology. Nonfiction book ms needs for the next year include "scholarly books in archaeology; mythology; ancient and medieval history; and art history." Query or submit outline/synopsis and sample chapters. Reviews artwork/photos as part of ms package.
Recent Nonfiction Title: *Spartan Twilight*, by L. Piper (history).

‡CAREER PUBLISHING, INC., Box 5486, Orange CA 92613-5486. (714)771-5155. Contact: Senior Editor. Publishes paperback originals and software. Averages 6-20 titles/year; receives 300 submissions annually. 80% of books from first-time authors; 90% of books from unagented writers. Average print order for a writer's first book is 1,500. Pays 10% royalty on wholesale price; no advance. Publishes book an average of 6 months after acceptance. Simultaneous (if so informed with names of others to whom submissions have been sent) and photocopied submissions OK. Query for electronic submissions. Computer printout submissions acceptable; prefers letter-quality to dot-matrix. Reports in 2 months. Book catalog for 6x9 SAE with 39¢ postage; ms guidelines for SAE and 1 first class stamp.
Nonfiction: Microcomputer material, educational software, word processing, guidance material, allied health, dictionaries, etc. "Textbooks should provide core upon which class curriculum can be based: textbook, workbook or kit with 'hands-on' activities and exercises, and teacher's guide. Should incorporate modern and effective teaching techniques. Should lead to a job objective. We also publish support materials for existing courses and are open to unique, marketable ideas with schools in mind. Reading level should be controlled appropriately—usually 8th-9th grade equivalent for vocational school and community college level courses. Any sign of sexism or racism will disqualify the work. No career awareness masquerading as career training." Submit outline/synopsis, 2 sample chapters/and table of contents or complete ms. Reviews artwork/photos as part of ms package. If material is to be returned, enclose SAE and return postage.
Recent Nonfiction Title: *The Voting Machine*, by Barry Kerns.
Tips: "Authors should be aware of vocational/career areas with inadequate or no training textbooks, submit ideas and samples to fill the gap. Trends in book publishing that freelance writers should be aware of include education—especially for microcomputers."

CAROLINA BIOLOGICAL SUPPLY CO., 2700 York Rd., Burlington NC 27215. (919)584-0381. Head, Scientific Publications: Dr. Phillip L. Owens. Publishes paperback originals. Averages 15 titles/year; receives 30 submissions annually. 25% of books from first-time authors; 100% of books from unagented writers. Pays 10% royalty on sales. Publishes book an average of 1½ years after acceptance. Simultaneous and photocopied submissions OK. Query for electronic submissions. Computer printout submissions acceptable; no dot-matrix. Reports in 2 weeks on queries.
Nonfiction: Self-help, technical, field and study guides on animals, health, nature, biology and science. "We will consider short (10,000 words) manuscripts of general interest to high school and college students on health, computers, biology, physics, astronomy, microscopes, etc. Longer manuscripts less favored but will be considered." Query. Reviews photos/artwork as part of ms package.
Recent Nonfiction Title: *AIDS*, by Donald Armstrong.

‡CAROLRHODA BOOKS, INC., 241 1st Ave. N., Minneapolis MN 55401. (612)332-3344. Submissions Editor: Rebecca Poole. Publishes hardcover originals. Averages 25-30 titles/year. Receives 1,300-1,500 submissions/year. 25% of books from first-time authors. 90% of books from unagented writers. Pays royalty on wholesale price, makes outright purchase, or negotiates cents per printed copy. Publishes book an average of 18 months after acceptance. Simultaneous and photocopied submissions OK. Computer printout submissions OK; no dot-matrix. Reports in 1 month. Book catalog free on request; ms guidelines for SASE.
Nonfiction: Biography, illustrated books and juvenile. Publishes only children's books. Subjects include animals, art, history, music and nature. Needs "biographies in story form on truly creative individuals—20 manuscript pages in length." Query. Reviews artwork/photos as part of ms package.
Recent Nonfiction Title: *Life of the Butterfly*, by H.&A. Fischer-Nagel (butterflies/science).
Fiction: Children's historical. No anthropomorphized animal stories. Submit complete ms.
Recent Fiction Title: *The Boy and the Devil*, by Erica Magnus (folklore/picture book).
Poetry: For children.
Recent Poetry Title: *To Bathe a Boa*, by C. Ionbior Kudrna (humorous/picture book).
Tips: "Our audience is children; grades kindergarten through twelve. Nonfiction science topics, particularly

nature, do well for us as do photo-essays, picture books on farm machinery and other large equipment, nature, geology and easy-reader. It's faster for us to slot a manuscript into an existing series. Spend time developing your idea in a unique way or from a unique angle and describe it briefly.''

CARROLL & GRAF PUBLISHERS, INC., 260 5th Ave., New York NY 10001. (212)889-8772. Contact: Kent Carroll. Small press. Publishes hardcover, trade and mass market paperback originals, and trade paperback, and mass market paperback reprints. Averages 100 titles/year; receives 1,000 submissions annually. 10% of books from first-time authors; 10% of books from unagented writers. Pays 6-10% royalty on retail price. Publishes book an average of 1 year after acceptance. Photocopied submissions OK. Computer printout submissions acceptable; prefers letter-quality to dot-matrix. Reports in 2 weeks on queries; 1 month on mss. Book catalog for 9x6 SASE.
Nonfiction: Biography. Query. Reviews artwork/photos as part of ms package.
Fiction: Adventure, erotica, fantasy, humor, mainstream, mystery, and suspense. Query.

CARSTENS PUBLICATIONS, INC., Hobby Book Division, Box 700, Newton NJ 07860. (201)383-3355. Publisher: Harold H. Carstens. Publishes paperback originals. Averages 5 titles/year. 100% of books from unagented writers. Pays 10% royalty on retail price; offers average advance. Publishes book an average of 2 years after acceptance. Query for electronic submissions. Computer printout submissions acceptable; prefers letter-quality to dot-matrix. Book catalog for SASE.
Nonfiction: Model railroading, toy trains, model aviation, railroads and model hobbies. "We have scheduled or planned titles on several railroads as well as model railroad and model airplane books. Authors must know their field intimately since our readers are active modelers. Our railroad books presently are primarily photographic essays on specific railroads. Writers cannot write about somebody else's hobby with authority. If they do, we can't use them." Query. Reviews artwork/photos as part of ms package.
Tips: "No fiction. We need lots of good b&w photos. Material must be in model, hobby, railroad field only."

‡THE CATHOLIC HEALTH ASSOCIATION, 4455 Woodson Rd., St. Louis MO 63134. (314)427-2500. Books Editor: Robert J. Stephens. Publishes hardcover originals and reprints, trade paperback originals and reprints. Averages 20 titles/year. Receives 50 submissions/year. 5% of books from first-time authors. 100% of books from unagented writers. Pays 10-15% royalty on net proceeds. Offers variable advance. Publishes book an average of 9 months after acceptance. Query for electronic submissions. Reports in 1 month on queries; 3 months on mss. Book catalog for 9x12 SASE.
Nonfiction: Textbook, ethics and management. Subjects include health and religion. Needs manuscripts for pamphlets on ethical health care topics for lay people and religious practices in health care, health care management and financing. No books for nonprofessionals. Submit outline/synopsis and sample chapters. Reviews artwork/photos as part of ms package.
Recent Nonfiction Title: *Marketing Religious Health Care*, by Mac Strovie (marketing).

CATHOLIC UNIVERSITY OF AMERICA PRESS, 620 Michigan Ave. NE, Washington DC 20064. (202)635-5052. Director: Dr. David J. McGonagle. Marketing Manager: Cynthia Miller. Averages 15-20 titles/year; receives 100 submissions annually. 50% of books from first-time authors; 100% of books from unagented writers. Average print order for a writer's first book is 1,000. Pays variable royalty on net receipts. Publishes book an average of 1 year after acceptance. Query for electronic submissions. Computer printout submissions acceptable; no dot-matrix. Reports in 2 months. Book catalog for #10 SASE.
Nonfiction: Publishes history, biography, languages and literature, philosophy, religion, church-state relations, political theory and social sciences. No unrevised doctoral dissertations. Length: 200,000-500,000 words. Query with sample chapter plus outline of entire work, along with curriculum vitae and list of previous publications. Reviews artwork/photos.
Recent Nonfiction Title: *Peace in a Nuclear Age*, edited by Charles Reid (public policy).
Tips: Freelancer has best chance of selling "scholarly monographs and works suitable for adoption as supplementary reading material in courses."

THE CAXTON PRINTERS, LTD., 312 Main St., Box 700, Caldwell ID 83605. (208)459-7421. Vice President: Gordon Gipson. Small press. Publishes hardcover and trade paperback originals. Averages 6-10 titles/year; receives 250 submissions annually. 50% of books from first-time authors; 60% of books from unagented writers. Audience includes Westerners, students, historians and researchers. Pays royalty; advance $500-2,000. Publishes book an average of 18 months after acceptance. Simultaneous and photocopied submissions OK. Computer printout submissions acceptable; no dot-matrix. Reports in 2 weeks on queries; 2 months on mss. Book catalog for 9x12 SASE.
Nonfiction: Coffee table, Americana and Western Americana. "We need good Western Americana, especially the Northwest, preferably copiously illustrated with unpublished photos." Query. Reviews artwork/photos as part of ms package.
Recent Nonfiction Title: *Encyclopedia of Western Railroad History*, by Donald B. Robertson.

*CAY-BEL PUBLISHING COMPANY, Thompson-Lyford Bldg., 2nd Fl., 45 Center St., Brewer ME 04412. (207)989-3820. Editor-in-Chief: John E. Cayford. Imprints include C&H Publishing Co. Publishes hardcover and trade paperback originals, and hardcover and trade paperback reprints. Averages 8 titles/year; receives 350 submissions annually. 50% of books from first-time authors; 100% of books from unagented writers. Average print order for a writer's first book is 2,000-5,000. Subsidy publishes 2% of books when authors "want us to put their manuscript in a book form, to typeset it and print it, but want to handle their own sales." Pays 10-15% royalty on retail price. Publishes book an average of 6-8 months after acceptance. Simultaneous and photocopied submissions OK. Computer printout submissions acceptable; prefers letter-quality to dot-matrix. Reports in 1 month on queries; 2 months on mss. Book catalog for #10 SASE; ms guidelines for #10 SASE and $1.
Nonfiction: Biography, cookbook, reference and maritime. Subjects include Americana, cooking and foods, history, vital records and genealogy. "Our book schedule is well filled for the next year, but we will give very careful consideration to any book about a Maine personage or to a Maine history." No poetry or pornography. Query. Reviews artwork/photos.
Recent Nonfiction Title: *Village Memories*, by W. Lawrence Stone.

*CBP PRESS, Subsidiary of Christian Board of Publication, Box 179, St. Louis MO 63166. (314)231-8500. Editor: Herbert H. Lambert. Publishes trade paperback originals and trade paperback reprints. Averages 12 titles/year; receives 400 submissions annually. 50% of books from first-time authors; 100% of books from unagented writers. "We subsidy publish about one or two books in ten, and the subsidy usually comes from friends, foundations, or church agencies." An author should be subsidy published "when projected sales are under 3,000, and the book is needed." Pays 17% royalty on wholesale price; offers no advance. Publishes book an average of 1 year after acceptance. Simultaneous and photocopied submissions OK. Computer printout submissions acceptable; prefers letter-quality to dot-matrix. Reports in 6 weeks. Free book catalog.
Nonfiction: Biography, how-to, humor, and self-help on religion. "We are looking for books of Bible theology spirituality, worship, and practical Christianity. These books may be primarily for clergy or laity of mainline Protestant and Roman Catholic groups." Submit outline/synopsis and sample chapters.
Recent Nonfiction Title: *Only By Grace*, by Tom S. Sampson.
Tips: "Deal with some current theme that has not been adequately discussed in other books. We look for books on personal devotions or lay Christianity that have a unique approach."

‡CCC PUBLICATIONS,20306 Tau Place, Chatsworth CA 91311. (818)407-1661. Editor: Cliff Carle. Publishes trade paperback originals and mass market paperback originals. Averages 5-10 titles/year; receives 50-100 mss/year. 50% of books from first time authors; 50% of books from unagented writers. Pays 5-10% royalty on wholesale price. Publishes book an average of 1 year after acceptance. Simultaneous and photocopied submissions OK. Computer printout submissions OK; prefers letter quality to dot matrix. Reports in 1 month on queries; reports in 3 months on mss. Book catalog for 8½x11 SAE with 2 first class stamps.
Nonfiction: How-to, humor, self-help. "We are looking for anything *original*, *clever* and *current* that is not too limited in audience appeal or that will have a limited shelf life. All of our titles are as marketable 5 years from now as they are today. No 'rip-offs' of previously published books, or too special interest mss." Query or submit complete ms. Reviews artwork/photos as part of ms package.
Recent Nonfiction Title: *No Hang-Ups*, by John Carfi and Cliff Carle (humor).
Tips: "Humor—we specialize in the subject and have a good reputation with retailers and wholesalers for publishing super-impulse titles."

CELESTIAL ARTS, Division of Ten Speed Press, Box 7327, Berkeley CA 94707. (415)524-1801. Editorial Director: David Hinds. Editor: Paul Reed. Publishes paperback originals. Publishes 30 titles/year; receives 12,000 submissions annually. 50% of books from first-time authors; 90% of books from unagented writers. Average print order for a writer's first book is 5,000. Publishes book an average of 1 year after acceptance. Simultaneous and photocopied submissions OK. Computer printout submissions acceptable; prefers letter-quality to dot-matrix. Reports in 3 months. Book catalog for 9x12 SAE with $1.92 postage.
Nonfiction: Publishes biography, cookbooks/cooking, health, psychology, social sciences, new age, philosophy, gay, and self-help. No poetry. "Submit 2-3 sample chapters and outline; no original copy. If return requested, include postage. We do not want to see the same manuscripts submitted to both Ten Speed Press and Celestial Arts." Reviews artwork/photos.
Recent Nonfiction Title: *The Black Butterfly*, by Richard Moss, M.D. (philosophy/new age).
Tips: "Common mistakes that writers make are that they're impatient with reporting time and they send out material that's incomplete and not well thought out."

‡CENTER FOR MIGRATION STUDIES OF NEW YORK, INC., 209 Flagg Pl., Staten Island NY 10304. (718)351-8800. Director of Publications: Maggie Sullivan. Publishes hardcover and trade paperback originals. Averages 12 titles/year. Receives 250 submissions/year. 1% of books from first-time authors. 100% of books from unagented writers. Pays 7-12% royalty on retail price. Publishes book an average of 20 months after acceptance. Computer printout submissions OK; prefers letter-quality. Reports in 3 weeks on queries; 4 months on mss. Free book catalog and guidelines.

Nonfiction: Technical and textbook. Subjects include business and economics, history, politics, psychology, sociology, migration and refugees. Especially needs mss "on migration theory and policy on newest immigrant groups. Our audience includes college and university students, policy makers, voluntary agencies and anyone interested in population movements." Submit complete ms. Reviews artwork/photos as part of ms package.

Recent Nonfiction Title: *Global Trends in Migration*, by Mary Kritz, et al.

‡CHARIOT BOOKS, Imprint of David C. Cook Publishing Co., 850 N. Grove Ave., Elgin IL 60120. (312)741-2400. Editorial Assistant: Jeannie Harmon. Publishes hardcover, trade paperback and mass market paperback originals. Averages 60 titles/year; receives 1,500 submissions annually. 20% of books from first-time authors; 90% of books from unagented writers. Pays royalty on retail price and outright purchase. Publishes book an average of 18 months after acceptance. Simultaneous submissions OK. Computer printout submissions OK; no dot-matrix. Reports in 3 weeks on queries; 3 months on mss. Book catalog for 10x13 SAE with 44¢ postage.

Nonfiction: Juvenile. Subjects include animals, art, hobbies, nature, recreation, religion and sports. "For young readers, we are looking for books that illuminate the Bible, including parts not previously made understandable to this age group. For all readers, books may incorporate fun facts and activities." Query or submit outline/synopsis and sample chapters. All unsolicited mss are returned unopened. Reviews artwork/photos as part of ms package.

Recent Nonfiction Title: *God, You Fill Us Up With Joy*, by Elspeth Murphy.

Fiction: Adventure, fantasy, historical, humor, mainstream, mystery, religious, science fiction, suspense and western. "For preschool, we prefer stories for picture books that talk about familiar things, avoid complicated plot and abstract concepts, and help the young child understand basic spiritual truths. For primary age children, we're interested in storybooks that illuminate biblical truths, and parts of the Bible not previously made understandable for such a young age group. Use of humor is sometimes appropriate. These books may be either for independent reading or to be read to children." Query or submit outline/synopsis and sample chapters.

Recent Fiction Title: *Potter*, by Walter Wangerin.

Tips: "We pay special attention to a writer who has researched our market and knows how the manuscript compares to what is out there."

*CHATHAM PRESS, Box A, Old Greenwich CT 06870. Publishes hardcover and paperback originals, reprints and anthologies relating to New England and the Atlantic coastline. Averages 15 titles/year; receives 50 submissions annually. 30% of books from first-time authors; 75% of books from unagented writers. Subsidy publishes (non-author) 15% of books. "Standard book contract does not always apply if the book is heavily illustrated. Average advance is low." Publishes book an average of 6 months after acceptance. Query for electronic submissions. Computer printout submissions acceptable; prefers letter-quality to dot-matrix. Reports in 2 weeks. Book catalog and ms guidelines for 6x9 SAE with 50¢ postage.

Nonfiction: Publishes mostly "regional history and natural history, involving mainly Northeast seaboard to the Carolinas, mostly illustrated, with emphasis on conservation and outdoor recreation." Accepts nonfiction translations from French and German. Query with outline and 3 sample chapters. Reviews artwork/photos as part of ms package.

Recent Nonfiction Title: *Exploring Old Martha's Vineyard*, by H. Whitman and R. Fox (illustrated guidebook).

Recent Poetry Title: *Weapons Against Chaos*, by M. Ewald.

Tips: "Illustrated New England-relevant titles have the best chance of selling to our firm."

CHELSEA GREEN, Box 283, Chelsea VT 05038. (802)685-3108. Editor: Ian Baldwin Jr. Publishes hardcover and trade paperback originals and reprints. Averages 6 titles/year. Publishes book an average of 9 months after acceptance. Simultaneous and photocopied submissions OK. Query for electronic submissions. Computer printout submissions acceptable. Free book catalog.

Nonfiction: Biography, art history, nature, politics and travel. Query or submit outline/synopsis and sample chapter.

Recent Nonfiction Title: *Permanent Parisians* by Judi Culbertson and Tom Randall.

Fiction: Query or submit outline/synopsis and sample chapter.

Recent Fiction Title: *The Automotive History of Lucky Kellerman*, by Stephen Heller.

‡CHELSEA HOUSE PUBLISHERS-EDGEMONT, Subsidiary of Chelsea House Publishers, Box 419, Edgemont PA 19028. (215)353-6625. Editorial Director: Susan Williams. Publishes Hardcover originals. Entire firm averages 300 titles/year; this division averages 96 titles/year. 50% of books from first-time authors; 100% of books from unagented writers. Makes outright purchase of $1,500-1,750; offers advance of $500. Publishes ms an average of 6 months after acceptance. Query for electronic submissions. Computer printout submissions OK; prefers letter-quality. Does not return unsolicited material "We use work for hire (by assignment) only." Free book catalog; ms guidelines for SASE.

Nonfiction: Biography, "coffee table" book, illustrated book and reference. Subjects include art, history, government, geography and ethnic groups.

Recent Nonfiction Title: *Magnolia*, by Rebecca Stefoff (geography series).

Tips: "The Chelsea House books are sold to school libraries and public libraries and are targeted to junior high school readers."

CHICAGO REVIEW PRESS, 814 N. Franklin, Chicago IL 60610. (312)337-0747. Editor: Linda Matthews. Publishes hardcover and trade paperback originals. Averages 30 titles/year; receives 200+ submissions annually. 60% of books from first-time authors; 80% of books from unagented writers. Pays 10-15% royalty. Offers average $1,500 advance. Publishes book an average of 6 months after acceptance. Simultaneous and photocopied submissions OK. Electronic submissions OK if CPM compatible. Computer printout submissions acceptable; no dot-matrix. Reports in 1 month on queries; 3 months on mss. Book catalog free on request.

Nonfiction: Cookbook, how-to, humor, reference, self-help and guidebooks on cooking and foods, recreation, travel and popular science, study guides, and regional. Needs regional Chicago material and how-to, travel, popular science, family, cookbooks for the national audience. Query or submit outline/synopsis and sample chapters. Reviews artwork/photos.

Recent Nonfiction Title: *The Straight Dope*, by Cecil Adams (humor).

Tips: "The audience we envision for our books is adults and young people 15 and older, educated readers with special interests, do-it-yourselfers, travellers, students, and young professionals. A trend we have noticed is the comeback of the successful short-run title, study guides and practical information, and the popularization of technical subjects, and information."

CHILTON BOOK CO., Chilton Way, Radnor PA 19089. Editorial Director: Alan F. Turner. Publishes hardcover and trade paperback originals. Publishes 90 titles/year. Pays royalty; average advance. Simultaneous and photocopied submissions OK. Electronic submissions OK, decided "case by case." Computer printout submissions acceptable. Reports in 3 weeks.

Nonfiction: Business/economics, crafts, how-to and technical. "We only want to see any manuscripts with informational value." Query or submit outline/synopsis and 2-3 sample chapters.

Recent Nonfiction Title: *Banking Strategies for Businesses*, by Bryan E. Milling.

*CHINA BOOKS AND PERIODICALS, INC., 2929 24th St., San Francisco CA 94110. (415)282-2994. Editorial Director: Foster Stockwell. Publishes hardcover and trade paperback originals. Averages 6 titles/year; receives 40 submissions annually. 50% of books from first-time authors; 80% of books from unagented writers. Subsidy publishes 2% of books. Pays 2-10% royalty on retail price. Offers average $1,000 advance. Publishes book an average of 6 months after acceptance. Simultaneous and photocopied submissions OK. Query for electronic submissions. Computer printout submissions acceptable; prefers letter-quality to dot-matrix. Reports in 2 weeks. Free book catalog.

Nonfiction: Biography, coffee table book, cookbook, how-to, juvenile and reference, all related to China. Query or submit outline/synopsis and sample chapters. Reviews artwork/photos as part of ms package.

Recent Nonfiction Title: *Shopping in China*, by Roberta Stalberg (travel).

Fiction: Publishes only fiction subjects related to China. Query or submit outline/synopsis and sample chapters.

Recent Fiction Title: *Love Must Not Be Forgotten*, by Zhang Jie (short stories).

Tips: "Our audience includes tourists, art collectors and China scholars."

CHOSEN BOOKS PUBLISHING CO., LTD., Imprint of Fleming H. Revell Co., 184 Central Ave., Old Tappan NJ 07675. (201)768-8060. Editor: Jane Campbell. Publishes hardcover and trade paperback originals. Averages 16 titles/year; receives 500 submissions annually. 15% of books from first-time authors; 99% of books from unagented writers. Pays royalty on retail price—7½% average on quality paper; 10% on hardcover. Publishes book an average of 9 months after acceptance. Simultaneous and photocopied submissions OK. Computer printout submissions acceptable; prefers letter-quality to dot-matrix. Reports in 2 months on queries; 3 months on mss. Occasionally makes work-for-hire assignments. Book catalog not available; ms guidelines for SASE.

Nonfiction: How-to, self-help, and "teaching" or first-person narrative on religion. "We publish books reflecting the current acts of the Holy Spirit in the world and books with a charismatic Christian orientation, whether teaching or first-person narrative." No poetry, fiction, or children's books. Submit synopsis, chapter outline and 2 sample chapters.

Recent Nonfiction Title: *A Closer Walk*, by Catherine Marshall (spiritual growth).

Tips: "Narratives don't do as well as 'teaching' books, which are what the Christian audience is looking for. Check out other Chosen titles to see the style of writing and subject matter we print. State the theme clearly in your proposal, and structure the manuscript, chapter by chapter, around this theme."

CHRISTIAN ED. PUBLISHERS, Subsidiary of Success With Youth Publications, Box 261129, San Diego CA 92126. (619)578-4700. Subsidiaries include Rainbow Publishers. Editorial Director: Dr. Lon F. Ackelson. Publishes trade paperback originals. Averages 20-30 titles/year; receives 100 submissions annually. 10% of books from first-time authors; 100% of books from unagented writers. Makes outright purchase. No advances. Publishes book an average of 1 year after acceptance. Photocopied submissions OK. Computer printout submissions acceptable; no dot-matrix. Reports in 3 weeks on queries; 2-3 months on mss. Book catalog for 9x12 SAE and 3 first class stamps; ms guidelines for SASE.
Nonfiction: How-to, illustrated book, juvenile and reference on evangelical, non-denominational religion. Looks for nonfiction ms on parties, games, activities and devotionals for children and youth; program book articles for children's and youth's expressional training sessions. Just starting program for two's to three's, and a junior take-home feature. No topics that do not dovetail with our Christian education product line. No articles that are not directly tied to scriptural principles for life.   Query or submit outline/synopsis and sample chapters. Reviews artwork/photos as part of ms package.

*THE CHRISTOPHER PUBLISHING HOUSE, 106 Longwater Dr., Norwell MA 02061. (617)878-9336. Managing Editor: Susan Lukas. Small press. Publishes hardcover and trade paperback originals. Averages 20-30 titles/year; receives over 300-400 submissions annually. 30% of books from first-time authors; 100% of books from unagented writers. Subsidy publishes 50% of books. Pays 5-30% of royalty on wholesale price; offers no advance. Publishes book an average of 2 years after acceptance. Simultaneous and photocopied submissions OK. Query for electronic submissions. Computer printout submissions acceptable; prefers letter-quality to dot-matrix. Reports in 1 month. Book catalog for #10 SAE with 39¢ postage; ms guidelines for SASE.
Nonfiction: Biography, how-to, reference, self-help, textbook and religious. Subjects include Americana, animals, art, business and economics, cooking and foods (nutrition), health, history, philosophy, politics, psychology, religion, sociology and travel. "We will be glad to review all nonfiction manuscripts, particularly college textbook and religious-oriented. Submit complete ms. Reviews artwork/photos.
Recent Nonfiction Title: *Krinkelt-Rocherath, the Battle for the Twin Villages*, by William C.C. Cavanagh (military).
Poetry: "We will review all forms of poetry." Submit complete ms.
Recent Poetry Title: *Drumbeats and Whispers*, by Thomas V. Simpkins.
Tips: "Our books are for a general audience, slanted toward college-educated readers. There are specific books targeted toward specific audiences when appropriate."

CHRONICLE BOOKS, Chronicle Publishing Co., 1 Hallidie Plaza, San Francisco CA 94102. (415)777-7240. Senior Editor: William LeBlond. Publishes hardcover and trade paperback originals. Averages 55 titles/year; receives 300 submissions annually. 40% of books from first-time authors; 70% of books from unagented writers. Pays 6-10% royalty on retail price. Offers average $3,000 advance. Publishes book an average of 1½ years after acceptance. Simultaneous and photocopied submissions OK. Computer printout submissions acceptable; prefers letter-quality to dot-matrix. Reports in 1 month on queries; 2 months on mss. Book catalog for 9x12 SAE with 3 first class stamps.
Nonfiction: Coffee table book, cookbook, and regional California on art, cooking and foods, nature, photography, recreation, and travel. Query or submit outline/synopsis and sample chapters. Reviews artwork/photos.
Recent Nonfiction Title: *Pasta Classica*, by Julia Delan Croce (cookbook).

CITADEL PRESS, Subsidiary of Lyle Stuart Inc., 120 Enterprise Ave., Secaucus NJ 07094. (212)736-0007. Editorial Director: Allan J. Wilson. Publishes hardcover originals and paperback reprints. Averages 60-80 titles/year. Receives 800-1,000 submissions annually. 7% of books from first-time authors; 50% of books from unagented writers. Average print order for a writer's first book is 5,000. Pays 10% royalty on hardcover, 5-7% on paperback; offers average $3,000 advance. Publishes book an average of 6 months after acceptance. Simultaneous and photocopied submissions OK. Computer printout submissions acceptable; no dot-matrix. Reports in 2 months. Book catalog for $1 and 8½x11 SAE with 50¢ postage.
Nonfiction: Biography, film, psychology, humor and history. Also seeks "off-beat material," but no "poetry, religion, politics." Accepts nonfiction and fiction translations. Query. Accepts outline/synopsis and 3 sample chapters. Reviews artwork/photos.
Recent Nonfiction Title: *Barbra: The 2nd Decade*, by Karen Swenson (filmography).
Tips: "We concentrate on biography, popular interest, and film, with limited fiction (no romance, religion, poetry, music)."

CLARION BOOKS, Ticknor & Fields: a Houghton Mifflin Company. 52 Vanderbilt Ave., New York NY 10017. Editor and Publisher: James C. Giblin. Senior Editor for Nonfiction: Ann Troy. Publishes hardcover originals. Averages 18-20 titles/year. Pays 5-10% royalty on retail price; $1,000-3,000 advance, depending on whether project is a picture book or a longer work for older children. Photocopied submissions OK. No multiple submissions. Computer printout submissions acceptable; no dot-matrix. Reports in 2 months. Publishes book an average of 18 months after acceptance. Book catalog and guidelines for 9x12 SASE.

Nonfiction: Americana, biography, holiday, humor, nature, photo essays and word play. Prefers books for younger children. Reviews artwork/photos as part of ms package. Query.
Recent Nonfiction Title: *Cowboys of the Wild West*, by Russell Freedman.
Fiction: Adventure, fantasy, humor, mystery, strong character studies, and suspense. "We would like to see more humorous contemporary stories that young people of 8-12 or 10-14 can identify with readily." Accepts fiction translations. Query on ms of more than 50 pages. Looks for "freshness, enthusiasm—in short, life" (fiction and nonfiction).
Recent Fiction Title: *On My Honor*, by Marion Dane Bauer (ages 9-12).

*ARTHUR H. CLARK CO., Box 230, Glendale CA 92109. (213)245-9119. Editorial Director: Robert A. Clark. Publishes hardcover originals. Averages 8 titles/year; receives 40 submissions annually. 40% of books from first-time authors; 100% of books from unagented writers. Subsidy publishes 15% of books based on whether they are "high-risk sales." Subsidy publishes (nonauthor) 5% of books. Pays 10% minimum royalty on wholesale price. Publishes book an average of 9 months after acceptance. Photocopied submissions OK. Computer printout submissions acceptable; prefers letter-quality to dot-matrix. Reports in 1 week on queries; 2 months on mss. Book catalog for 6x9 SAE.
Nonfiction: Biography, reference and historical nonfiction. Subjects include Americana and history. "We're looking for documentary source material in Western American history." Query or submit outline/synopsis and 3 sample chapters. Looks for "content, form, style." Reviews artwork/photos as part of ms package.
Recent Nonfiction Title: *The Notorious*, (Western historical biography).
Tips: "Western Americana (nonfiction) has the best chance of selling to our firm."

*CLEANING CONSULTANT SERVICES, INC., 1512 Western Ave., Seattle WA 98101. (206)682-9748. President: William R. Griffin. Small press. Publishes trade paperback originals and reprints. Averages 4-6 titles/year; receives 15 submissions annually. 75% of books from first-time authors; 100% of books from unagented writers. Subsidy publishes 5% of books. "If they (authors) won't sell it and won't accept royalty contract, we offer our publishing services and often sell the book along with our books." Pays 5-15% royalty on retail price or outright purchase, $100-2,500, depending on negotiated agreement. Publishes book an average of 6-12 months after acceptance. Photocopied submissions OK. Computer printout submissions acceptable; prefers letter-quality to dot-matrix. Reports in 6 weeks on queries; 3 months on mss. Free book catalog; ms guidelines for SASE.
Nonfiction: How-to, illustrated book, reference, self-help, technical, textbook and directories. Subjects include business, health, and cleaning and maintenance. Needs books on anything related to cleaning, maintenance, self-employment or entrepreneurship. Query or submit outline/synopsis and sample chapters or complete ms. Reviews artwork/photos.
Recent Nonfiction Title: *Food Service, Health Sanitation and Safety*, by Bruce Jackson (how-to).
Tips: "Our audience includes those involved in cleaning and maintenance service trades, opportunity seekers, schools, property managers, libraries—anyone who needs information on cleaning and maintenance. How-to and self-employment guides are doing well for us in today's market."

*CLEVELAND STATE UNIVERSITY POETRY CENTER, R.T. 1815, Cleveland State University, Cleveland OH 44115. (216)687-3986. Co-Editor: Leonard M. Trawick. Small press. Publishes trade paperback originals. Averages 5 titles/year; receives 400 queries, 300 mss annually. 60% of books from first-time authors; 100% of books from unagented writers. 30% of titles subsidized by CSU, 30% by government subsidy. CSU poetry series pays 10% royalty plus 50 copies on wholesale price if sold by bookseller, on retail price if sold by CSU Poetry Center; Cleveland Poetry Series (Ohio poets only) pays 100 copies. $1,000 prize for best manuscript each year. No advance. Publishes book an average of 1 year after acceptance. Simultaneous and photocopied submissions OK. Computer printout submissions acceptable; prefers letter-quality to dot-matrix. Reports in 2 weeks on queries; 6 months on mss. Book catalog for 6x9 SAE; ms guidelines for SASE.
Poetry: No light verse, "inspirational," or greeting card verse. ("This does not mean that we do not consider poetry with humor or philosophical/religious import.") Query—ask for guidelines. Submit only December-February. Reviews artwork/photos if applicable (i.e., concrete poetry).
Recent Poetry Title: *The Appassionata Doctrines*, by David Citino (humorous surface dealing with profound, serious human matters—sex, society, religion).
Tips: "Our books are for serious readers of poetry, i.e. poets, critics, academics, students, people who read *Poetry*, *Field*, *American Poetry Review*, *Antaeus*, etc." Trends include "movement from 'confessional' poetry; greater attention to form and craftsmanship. Try to project an interesting, coherent personality; link poems so as to make coherent unity, not just a miscellaneous collection." Especially needs "poems with *mystery*, i.e., poems that reflect profound thought, but do not tell all—suggestive, tantalizing, enticing."

‡CLIFFHANGER PRESS, Box 29527, Oakland CA 94604-9527. (415)763-3510. Book publisher and independent book producer/packager. Subsidiaries include ed-it productions. Editor: Nancy Chirich. Small press. Publishes trade paperback originals. Averages 5 titles/year. Pays 8% royalty on retail price. Publishes book an average of 6 months after acceptance. Simultaneous and photocopied submissions OK. Reports in 1 month. Book catalog for #10 SASE. Query for electronic submissions. Computer printout submissions OK; prefers letter-quality.

Fiction: Mystery and suspense. "Manuscripts should be about 75,000 words, heavy on American regional or foreign atmosphere. No cynical, hardboiled detectives or spies." Submit outline and sample chapters.

Recent Fiction Title: *The Mystic Policeman*, by James P. O'Neill.

Tips: "Mystery/suspense is our only specialty. Have believable characters, a strong, uncomplicated story and heavy regional or foreign atmosphere. No justified right margins on manuscripts submitted. They're very hard to read at length."

CLIFFS NOTES, INC., Box 80728, Lincoln NE 68501. (402)477-6971. General Editor: Michele Spence. Notes Editor: Gary Carey. Publishes trade paperback originals. Averages 20 titles/year. 100% of books from unagented writers. Pays royalty on wholesale price. Buys some mss outright; "full payment on acceptance of ms." Publishes book an average of 1 year after acceptance. Computer printout submissions acceptable. Reports in 1 month. Free book catalog. "We provide specific guidelines when a project is assigned."

Nonfiction: Self-help, and textbook. "We publish self-help study aids directed to junior high through graduate school audience. Publications include *Cliffs Notes*, *Cliffs Test Preparation Guides*, *Cliffs Teaching Portfolios*, and other study guides. Most authors are experienced teachers, usually with advanced degrees. *Teaching Portfolio* authors are experienced high school English teachers who can provide practical, proven classroom material designed for junior high and high school English teachers. Some books also appeal to a general lay audience." Query.

Recent Nonfiction Title: Cliffs Teaching Portfolio for *The Grapes of Wrath*.

COACH HOUSE PRESS, INC., Box 458, Morton Grove IL 60053. (312)967-1777. Publisher/President: David Jewell. Small press. Publishes production script originals. Averages 3-8 titles/year; receives 150-200 submissions annually. 50% of books from first-time authors; 95% of books from unagented writers. Pays 10% royalty on receipts from book sales; 50% royalty on performance. Publishes book an average of 3-15 months after acceptance. Simultaneous and photocopied submissions OK. Query for electronic submissions. Computer printout submissions acceptable; prefers letter-quality to dot-matrix. Reports in 1 month on queries; 3 months on mss. Script catalog and guidelines for 9x12 SAE with 73¢ postage.

Nonfiction: Drama production guides and aids. Query with synopsis.

Recent Nonfiction Title: *Acting Up! An Innovative Guide to Creative Drama for Older Adults*, by Telander, Verson and Quinlan.

Fiction: Plays for children's theatre, one-act plays for high school contest and plays for senior adults. Query with synopsis and production history.

Recent Fiction Title: *Alien Equation*, by Annie Macoby/Jeff Church (junior high school play).

Tips: "Plays which sell best to today's producers respect children as intelligent, alert and informed, and *avoid* stereotyping any group as evil, stupid or immature. Playwrights need to get their plays production-tested. They help themselves by including production history and personal biography with cover letter. Don't send adult scripts to a child-drama publisher."

COLES PUBLISHING CO., LTD., 90 Ronson Dr., Rexdale, Ontario M9W 1C1 Canada. (416)243-3132. Publishing Assistant: Janina Lucci. Publishes hardcover and paperback originals and reprints. Averages 10 titles/year; receives 350 submissions annually. 20% of books from first-time authors; 100% of books from unagented writers. Average print order for a writer's first books is 5,000. "We are a subsidiary company of 'Coles, the Book People,' a chain of 235 bookstores throughout Canada and America." Pays by outright purchase of $500-$2,500; advance averages $1,000. Publishes book an average of 8 months after acceptance. Simultaneous and photocopied submissions OK. Reports in 1 month. SAE and International Reply Coupons.

Nonfiction: "We publish in the following areas: education, language, science, math, pet care, gardening, occult, business, reference, technical and do-it-yourself, crafts and hobbies, games, and sports. We also publish a complete line of literary study aids sold worldwide." No philosophy, religion, history or biography. Submit outline/synopsis and sample chapters.

Recent Nonfiction Title: *Canadian Job Hunting Guide*.

Tips: "The writer has the best chance of selling us wide appeal, practical self-help books."

COLLECTOR BOOKS, Division of Schroeder Publishing Co., Inc., Box 3009, Paducah KY 42001. Editor: Steve Quertermous. Publishes hardcover and paperback originals. Publishes 35-40 titles/year. 50% of books from first-time authors; 100% of books from unagented writers. Average print order for a writer's first book is 5,000. Pays 5% royalty on retail; no advance. Publishes book an average of 8 months after acceptance. Computer printout submissions acceptable; no dot-matrix. Reports in 1 month. Free book catalog.

Nonfiction: "We only publish books on antiques and collectibles. We require our authors to be very knowledgeable in their respective fields and have access to a large representative sampling of the particular subject concerned." Query. Accepts outline and 2-3 sample chapters. Reviews artwork/photos as part of ms package.

Recent Nonfiction Title: *Collector's Guide to Baseball Memorabilia*, by Don Raycraft and Stew Salowitz.
Tips: Common mistakes writers make include "making phone contact instead of written contact and assuming an accurate market evaluation."

COMMUNICATION SKILL BUILDERS, INC., Box 42050, Tucson AZ 85733. (602)323-7500. Acquisitions Manager: Patti Hartmann. Publishes paperback originals, kits, games, software and audio cassettes. Averages 40 titles/year; receives 150 submissions annually. 50% of books from first-time authors; 100% of books from unagented writers. Pays negotiable royalty on cash received. Publishes book an average of 9 months after acceptance. No simultaneous submissions; photocopied submissions OK. Query for electronic submissions. Computer printout submissions acceptable. Reports in 2 months. Free book catalog—Speech-Language/Special Education/Early Childhood Education.
Nonfiction: Speech-Language/Special Education/Early Childhood Education material: Articulation therapy, language remediation and development; hearing impaired; adult communicative disorders; physically handicapped/developmentally delayed; professional resources; assessment materials. Reviews artwork/photos as part of ms package. "If a material is illustrated, costs for the photographs or drawings are the responsibility of the author."
Recent Nonfiction Title: *Practicing Individual Concepts of Language*.

‡**COMPACT BOOKS**, 2131 Hollywood Blvd., Hollywood FL 33020. (305)925-5242. Publisher: Donald L. Lessne. Publishes hardcover and trade paperback originals. Averages 15 titles/year; receives 1,000 submissions annually. 25% of books from first-time authors; 25% of books from unagented writers. Pays royalty. Publishes book an average of 2 years after acceptance. Simultaneous and photocopied submissions OK. Query for electronic submissions. Computer printout submissions OK. Reports in 6 months on mss. Free book catalog.
Nonfiction: Cookbook, how-to, humor, reference and self-help. Subjects include business and economics, cooking and foods, health, hobbies, psychology, recreation, religion and sociology. "We're looking for easy-to-read, general interest books on current issues and health." Submit outline/synopsis and sample chapters. Reviews artwork/photos as part of ms package.
Recent Nonfiction Title: *Teenage Alcoholism and Substance Abuse*, by Bartimole (family/child care).

COMPUTE! BOOKS, A Division of COMPUTE! Publications, Inc., A subsidiary of ABC Consumer Magazine, Inc. one of the ABC Publishing Companies, Box 5406, Greensboro NC 27403. (919)275-9809. Book editor: Stephen Levy. Publishes trade paperback originals and software. Averages 36-48 titles/year. Pays 15% of gross wholesale receipts as royalty on one-author books; pro rata share of 7½% of gross receipts on collections. Photocopied submissions OK. Publishes ms an average of 6 months after acceptance. Query for electronic submissions. Computer printout submissions acceptable (dot-matrix OK if clear). Reports in 3 months.
Nonfiction: Books on computers. "We publish books for the home computer user and are always looking for reference books, teaching books, and books of useful programs for small computers. Books must be aimed at the users of a *specific* computer with a specific and limited purpose in mind. For instance, our *Mapping the 64* covers Commodore 64 memory locations clearly and completely with general tips for using them but does not attempt to provide any full-fledged programs. If you have unusual expertise or inside knowledge of a particular subject, then we might well be interested in a highly technical reference book on the order of *Atari BASIC Sourcebook*, but usually we try to aim our books at nontechnical users who are learning to use their computers in their own way and at their own pace. Writers should think of their audience as intelligent people who want their computers to improve their lives and the lives of their loved ones. We are also interested in entertainment programs and programming; home applications; educational programs; and books that teach programming at different levels—if a family or individual would find them useful and interesting." Submit outline and synopsis with sample chapters. "Writers who are known to us through articles in *COMPUTE! Magazine* and *COMPUTE!'s Gazette* already have our trust—we know they can come through with the right material—but we have often bought from writers we did not know, and from writers who had never published anything before."
Recent Nonfiction Title: *Mastering Microsoft Works*, by Sharon Aker.
Tips: "If I were trying to create a marketable computer book today, I would become intimately familiar with one computer, then define a specific area to explain to less-familiar computer users, and write a clear, concise outline of the book I meant to write, along with a sample chapter from the working section of the book (not the introduction). Then send that proposal to a publisher whose books you believe are excellent and who targets the same audience you are aiming at. Once the proposal was in the mail, I'd forget about it. Keep learning more about the computer and develop another book proposal. *Don't write a book without a go-ahead from a publisher*. The chances are too great that you will spend 6 months writing a book, only to discover that there are nine on the market with the same concept by the time your manuscript is ready to send out."

COMPUTER SCIENCE PRESS, INC., 1803 Research Blvd., Rockville MD 20850. (301)251-9050. President: Barbara B. Friedman. Editor-in-Chief: Dr. Arthur D. Friedman. Publishes hardcover and paperback originals and software. Averages 20 titles/year. 25% of books from first-time authors; 98% of books from unagented writers. Pays royalty on net price; no advance. Publishes book an average of 6 months after acceptance. Computer printout submissions acceptable. Reports ASAP. Free book catalog.

Nonfiction: "Technical books in all aspects of computer science, computer engineering, computer chess, electrical engineering, computers and math, and telecommunications. Both text and reference books. Will also consider public appeal 'trade' books in computer science, manuscripts and diskettes for computer education at all levels: elementary, secondary and college and professional." Also publishes bibliographies in computer science areas and the irregular periodicals *Journal of VLSI Systems & Computations* and *Journal of Telecommunication Networks*. Query or submit complete ms. "We prefer 3 copies of manuscripts." Looks for "technical accuracy of the material and the reason this approach is being taken. We would also like a covering letter stating what the author sees as the competition for this work and why this work is superior."

Recent Nonfiction Title: *Elements of Artificial Intelligence*, by Tanimoto.

CONSUMER REPORTS BOOKS, Subsidiary of Consumers Union. #1301, 110 E. 42nd St., New York NY 10017. (212)682-9280. Contact: Director, Consumer Reports Books. Publishes trade paperback originals, and trade paperback reprints. Averages 30-35 titles/year; receives 1,000 submissions annually. Most of books from unagented writers. Pays variable royalty on retail price; buys some mss outright. Publishes book an average of 9 months after acceptance. Simultaneous and photocopied submissions OK. Computer printout submissions acceptable; prefers letter-quality to dot-matrix. Reports in 1 month on queries; 2 months on mss. Free book listing.

Nonfiction: Cookbook, how-to, reference, self-help and technical, and how-to books for children. Subjects include business and economics, cooking and foods, health, music and consumer guidance. Submit outline/synopsis and 1-2 sample chapters.

‡CONTEMPORARY BOOKS, INC., 180 N. Michigan Ave., Chicago IL 60601. (312)782-9182. Subsidiaries include Congdon & Weed. Editorial Director: Nancy J. Crossman. Publishes hardcover originals and trade paperback originals and reprints. Averages 100 titles/year; receives 1,000+ submissions annually. 25% of books from first-time authors; 25% of books from unagented writers. Pays 6-15% royalty on retail price. Publishes book an average of 10 months after acceptance. Query for electronic submissions. Computer printout submissions OK. Simultaneous and photocopied submissions OK. Reports in 3 weeks. Free book catalog; ms guidelines for SASE.

Nonfiction: Biography, cookbook, how-to, humor, reference and self-help. Subjects include business and economics, cooking and foods, health, music, photography, psychology, sports, travel, fitness, nutrition, popular culture and women's studies. Submit outline/synopsis and sample chapters. Reviews artwork/photos as part of ms package.

Fiction: Adult science fiction and sports only. Submit outline/synopsis and sample chapters.

Recent Fiction Title: *She's On First*, by Barbara Gregorich (sports).

COPLEY BOOKS, A division of The Copley Press, Inc., (Copley Newspapers), Box 957, La Jolla CA 92038. (619)454-1842, 454-0411. Manager/Editor: Jean I. Bradford. Publishes hardcover originals. Averages 1-2 titles/year; receives 60 submissions annually. 25% of books from first-time authors; 100% of books from unagented writers. Pays royalty; "individual agreement with author for each publication." Publishes book a minimum of 1 year after acceptance. Simultaneous and photocopied submissions OK. Computer printout submissions acceptable; prefers letter-quality to dot-matrix. Reports in "a few weeks." Free book catalog.

Nonfiction: Well-researched, historical narratives of California (including Baja) and the Southwest. Will consider manuscripts which provide newly-discovered or little-known facts about this region's history and which present the material in a clear, interesting manner for the general reader. Subject matter must have broad enough appeal for reasonably large volume sales potential. Illustrations are important, so a list of available artwork should be submitted with query, outline/synopsis, and perhaps one or two sample chapters.

CORNELL MARITIME PRESS, INC., Box 456, Centreville MD 21617. Editor: Willard A. Lockwood. Imprint includes Tidewater Publishers. Publishes original hardcover and quality paperbacks. Averages 15-18 titles/year; receives 150 submissions annually. 41% of books from first-time authors; 99% of books from unagented writers. Payment is negotiable but royalties do not exceed 10% for first 5,000 copies, 12½% for second 5,000 copies, 15% on all additional. Royalties for original paperbacks and regional titles are invariably lower. Revised editions revert to original royalty schedule. Publishes book an average of 10 months after acceptance. Electronic submissions OK via disk, but requires hard copy also. Computer printout submissions acceptable; prefers letter-quality to dot-matrix. Send queries first, accompanied by writing samples and outlines of book ideas. Reports in 1 month. Free book catalog and ms guidelines.

Nonfiction: Marine subjects (highly technical); manuals; and how-to books on maritime subjects. Tidewater Publishers imprint publishes books on regional history, folklore and wildlife of the Chesapeake Bay and the Delmarva Peninsula.

Recent Nonfiction Titles: *Shiphandling With Tugs*, by Capt. G.H. Reid (professional text/reference) published by Cornell Maritime Press; and *Steamboat on the Chesapeake: Emma Giles & the Tolchester Line*, by D.C. Holly (regional history for general reader) published by Tidewater Publishers.

COUNCIL OAK BOOKS, 8424 S. St. Louis, Tulsa OK 74120. (918)587-6454. President: Sally Dennison. Small press. Publishes hardcover and softcover originals and reprints. Averages 5 titles/year; receives approximately 700 submissions annually. 50% of books from first-time authors; 95% of books from unagented writers. Pays royalty on retail price. Simultaneous and photocopied submissions OK. Computer printout submissions acceptable; prefers letter-quality to dot-matrix. Reports in 1 month on queries; 3 months on mss. Book catalog and ms guidelines for 9½x5 SAE with 56¢ postage.
Nonfiction: Biography, memoir, cookbook, how-to, humor, illustrated book and self-help. Subjects include Americana, animals, art, business and economics, cooking and foods, health, history, hobbies, music, nature, philosophy, photography, politics, psychology, recreation, sociology, sports and travel. Query. "We cannot consider nonfiction of fewer than 20,000 words. No unsolicited nonfiction." Reviews artwork/photos.
Recent Nonfiction Title: *Libby*, by Elizabeth Beaman John (journal/art).
Fiction: Historical, humor and mainstream; novels. "Any *upscale* fiction. It must be intelligent, and have an honest heart." No standard genre fiction—"the romance, the sci-fi, the western, the mystery, etc."—religious or devotional. Submit first 10 pages. "We do not publish poetry, children's books, novellas or short fiction collections. No fiction under 50,000 words."
Recent Fiction Title: *Kiss the Son*, by Mary Thralls.
Tips: "Non-genre fiction and upscale market nonfiction have the best chance of selling to us. A well-written 'sales' letter is no substitute for a well-written book."

CRAFTSMAN BOOK COMPANY, 6058 Corte Del Cedro, Box 6500, Carlsbad CA 92009. (619)438-7828. Editor-in-Chief: Laurence D. Jacobs. Publishes paperback originals. Averages 8-12 titles/year; receives 20 submissions/year. 50% of books from first-time authors; 98% of books from unagented writers. Pays 12.5% royalty on wholesale price; pays 12.5% royalty on retail price "when we retail by mail." Offers $300-800 average advance. Publishes book an average of 18 months after acceptance. Simultaneous and photocopied submissions OK. Query for electronic submissions. Computer printout submissions OK; prefers letter-quality. Reports in 1 month on queries; 10 weeks on mss. Free book catalog and guidelines.
Nonfiction: How-to and technical. All titles are related to construction for professional builders. Submit outline/synopsis and sample chapters. Reviews artwork/photos as part of ms package.
Recent Nonfiction Title: *Carpentry Estimating*, by W.P. Jackson.
Tips: "The book should be loaded with step-by-step instructions, illustrations, charts, reference data, forms, samples, cost estimates, rules of thumb, and examples that solve actual problems in the builder's office and in the field. The book must cover the subject completely, become the owner's primary reference on the subject, have a high utility-to-cost ratio, and help the owner make a better living in his chosen field."

‡CRCS PUBLICATIONS, Box 20850, Reno NV 89515. (702)358-2850. Contact: Editorial Dept. Small press. Publishes trade paperback originals and reprints. Averages 4 titles/year. Receives 50 submissions/year. 40% of books from first-time authors. 98% of books from unagented writers. Pays 6-9% royalty on retail price. Offers various advance. Publishes book an average of 18 months after acceptance. Computer printout submissions OK; prefers letter-quality. Reports in 6 weeks on queries; 3 months on mss. Book catalog free on request.
Nonfiction: Cookbook and self-help. Subjects include cooking and food, health, psychology. Query or submit outline/synopsis and sample chapters. Reviews artwork/photos as part of ms.
Recent Nonfiction Title: *The Ancient Art of Geomancy*, by N. Pennick (earth science).
Tips: "Research what is already available and who is publishing in your areas of interest."

‡CREDO PUBLISHING CORPORATION, Suite 103, 19623-56th Ave., Langley, British Columbia V3A 3X7 Canada. (604)533-3770. Book Editor: Jocelyn E. Cameron. Imprint includes CEDAR Books. Publishes trade paperback originals and reprints. Publishes 3-4 titles/year. Receives 25-50 submissions/year. 60% of books from first-time authors. 90% of books from unagented writers. Pays 10% royalty on wholesale price. Publishes book an average of 1 year after acceptance. Photocopied submissions OK. Computer printout submissions OK; prefers letter-quality. Reports in 2 weeks on queries; 1 month on mss. Book catalog and ms guidelines for SASE.
Nonfiction: Biography, how-to, reference and self-help. Subjects include psychology, self-help, religion and sociology. Query or submit outline and sample chapters.
Recent Nonfiction Title: *Manuel, the Continuing Story*, by Hugh Steven.
Fiction: Mainstream.
Tips: "Learn how to write, have something to say and say it with clarity and purpose. It's been my experience that writers don't think through to their target audience—what they have to say is for 'everyone' instead of 'someone.'"

CRITIC'S CHOICE PAPERBACKS, Subsidiary of Lorevan Publishing, Inc., 31 E. 28th St., New York NY 10016. (212)685-1550. Editor-in-Chief: Norman Goldfind. Publishes mass market paperback originals and reprints. Averages 96 titles/year; receives 100 submissions annually. 1% of books from first-time authors; 5% of books from unagented writers. Pays 6-8% royalty on retail price. Offers average $1,000 advance. Publishes book an average of 18 months after acceptance. Computer printout submissions acceptable; no dot-matrix. Reports in 2 weeks on queries; 2 months on mss. Book catalog for #10 SAE with 37¢ postage.

Nonfiction: Humor.

Fiction: Adventure, historical, horror, mainstream, mystery, science fiction, suspense, western, spy/espionage, thriller, and action. Query or submit outline/synopsis and sample chapters; all unsolicited mss are returned unopened.

THE CROSSING PRESS, 22-D Roache Rd., Box 207, Freedom CA 95019. (408)722-0711. Co-Publishers: Elaine Goldman Gill, John Gill. Publishes hardcover and trade paperback originals. Averages 20 titles/year; receives 500 submissions annually. 20% of books from first-time authors; 90% of books from unagented writers. Pays royalty. Publishes book an average of 18 months after acceptance. Simultaneous and photocopied submissions OK. Query for electronic submissions. Computer printout submissions acceptable. Reports in 2 months on queries; 3 months on mss. Free book catalog.

Nonfiction: Cookbook, how-to, literary and feminist. Subjects include cooking, health, gays and feminism. Submissions to be considered for the feminist series must be written by women. Submit outline and sample chapter. Reviews artwork/photos as part of ms package.

Recent Nonfiction Title: *Salad Dressings*, by Jane M. Dieckmann (cookbook).

Fiction: Feminism (good literary material). Submit outline and sample chapter.

Recent Fiction Title: *Class Porn*, by Molly Hite (novel).

Tips: "Simple intelligent query letters do best. No come-ons, no cutes. It helps if there are credentials. Authors should research the press first to see what sort of books it publishes."

CROSSWAY BOOKS, Subsidiary of Good News Publishers, 9825 W. Roosevelt Rd., Westchester IL 60153. Managing Editor: Ted Griffin. Publishes hardcover and trade paperback originals. Averages 25 titles/year; receives 3,500 submissions annually. 10% of books from first-time authors; 50% of books from unagented writers. Average print order for a writer's first book is 3,000. Pays negotiable royalty; offers negotiable advance. Publishes book an average of 1 year after acceptance. Send query and synopsis, not whole manuscript. Reports in 2 months. Book catalog and ms guidelines for 6x9 SAE and $1 postage.

Nonfiction: Subjects include issues on Christianity in contemporary culture, Christian doctrine, and church history. Accepts translations from European languages. "All books must be written out of Christian perspective or world view." No unsolicited mss. Query with synopsis.

Recent Nonfiction Title: *Poverty and Wealth*, by Ronald Nash.

Fiction: Mainstream; science fiction; fantasy (genuinely creative in the tradition of C.S. Lewis, J.R.R. Tolkien and Madeleine L'Engle); and juvenile age 6 and up to young adult. No formula romance. Query with synopsis. "All fiction must be written from a genuine Christian perspective."

Recent Fiction Title: *Taliesin* (first of three in Pendragon Cycle), by Stephen R. Lawhead.

Tips: "The writer has the best chance of selling our firm a book which, through fiction or nonfiction, shows the practical relevance of biblical doctrine to contemporary issues and life."

CROWN PUBLISHERS, INC., 225 Park Ave. S., New York NY 10003. (212)254-1600. Imprints include Clarkson N. Potter, Arlington House, Harmony and Julian Press. Publishes hardcover and paperback originals. Publishes 250 titles/year. Simultaneous submissions OK. Reports in 2 months.

Nonfiction: Americana, animals, art, biography, cookbooks/cooking, health, history, hobbies, how-to, humor, juveniles, music, nature, philosophy, photography, politics, psychology, recreation, reference, science, self-help and sports. Query with letter only.

*HARRY CUFF PUBLICATIONS LIMITED, 1 Dorset St., St. John's, Newfoundland A1B 1W8 Canada. (709)726-6590. Editor: Harry Cuff. Hardcover and trade paperback originals. Averages 12 titles/year; receives 50 submissions annually. 50% of books from first-time authors; 100% of books from unagented writers. Subsidy publishes (nonauthor) 30% of books. Pays 10% royalty on retail price. No advance. Publishes book an average of 8 months after acceptance. Photocopied submissions OK. Computer printout submissions acceptable; no dot-matrix. Reports in 6 months on mss. Book catalog for 5x9 SAE.

Nonfiction: Biography, humor, illustrated book, juvenile, reference, technical, and textbook, all dealing with Newfoundland. Subjects include history, photography, politics and sociology. Query.

Recent Nonfiction Title: *Sea Stories from Newfoundland*, by Michael Harrington.

Fiction: Ethnic, historical, humor and mainstream. Needs fiction about Newfoundlanders or Newfoundland. "No erotica under any circumstances." Submit complete ms.

Recent Fiction Title: *Ned 'n' Me*, by Mike Murphy.

Tips: "We are currently dedicated to publishing Newfoundlanders. The writer has the best chance of selling our firm well-written memoirs. There are many books of this genre, but few are well-written."

Close-up

Tama Janowitz
Writer

"I've run into trouble with people saying it's not right for a serious writer to get any attention, that you should sit at your desk with glasses and have a nice little braid and keep your mouth shut and be very, very timid," says Tama Janowitz. Janowitz's collection of interrelated stories, *Slaves of New York*, was published in 1986 by Crown and has won her enormous acclaim and publicity.

It was after *Slaves of New York* was published that she realized the importance of taking an active part in the book's marketing. "When you have a chance, finally, to have people actually read your book, then I think you'd better be glad, when you're sitting in some photo shoot and three hours have gone by, that someone is interested enough in you to take your picture," she says. "I felt this was not only a chance to get my book out there and let people read it, but to see and do so much. I've always been broke and sitting at my typewriter, but now people send me around the country and call me up, and it's pretty neat—it's all material in any event."

Janowitz's success was definitely not immediate. Her first novel, *American Dad*, was published in 1981 but was remaindered, like many first novels, within a few months. "When I published *American Dad*, I thought it would be easy—you just publish a book and use the money to live for a year," Janowitz says. "But then I wrote four books that I couldn't publish. I didn't have enough energy to get up and write from 6 to 8 and then work a 9-to-5 job, so I just figured I would take being broke and probably not making it, in return for doing what I wanted to do. I was extremely lucky—I would always get a grant or prize or publish something at the last minute that kept me going."

It was the appearance of several of her stories in *The New Yorker* that interested her editor at Crown in publishing the collection. "I was publishing stories in places like East Village underground magazines and literary magazines," she says. "Then *The New Yorker* started taking them, and people would come up to me at parties and say, 'Oh, you wrote that story that was in *The New Yorker*.' It was the first time I really felt that I was in the presence of people who had read my work, as opposed to these literary magazines with a 3,000 circulation. You're writing alone and people are reading alone, and you don't get that feeling that they're reading what you've done. But I certainly did with *The New Yorker*."

One of Janowitz's unpublished novels, *A Cannibal in Manhattan*, which she revised during her year at Princeton as the Alfred Hodder Fellow, was published by Crown in the fall of '87, and *American Dad* reappeared in paperback earlier in June.

Janowitz emphasizes the importance of persistence in both writing and marketing and says talent may not be the most important factor in determining which writers' books are published. "I get letters saying, 'Dear Tama, I am interested in becoming a short story writer. Do you think I should get the contract first, or write the stories?' Well, you better just be doing it because you like to write and forget the rest of it. If you can't place your first novel, sit down and write your second one. Even if you weren't meant to be a writer, after your tenth book you can produce *something* publishable."

—*Laurie Henry*

‡CYNTHIA PUBLISHING COMPANY, Suite 1106, 4455 Los Feliz Blvd., Los Angeles CA 90027. (213)664-3165. President: Dick Mitchell. Small press. Publishes mass market paperback originals. Averages 10-20 titles/year. Receives 50-100 submissions/year. 50% of books from first-time authors. 80% of books from unagented writers. Pays royalty on retail price. Offers $2,000 average advance. Simultaneous and photocopied submissions OK. Query for electronic submissions. Computer printout submissions OK; prefers letter-quality. Reports in 1 week on queries; 2 months on mss. Book catalog for #10 SAE.
Nonfiction: Technical. Subjects include sports and investments. "We need one title per month on subject of strategic investing (stock market, commodities, options, horse racing, sports betting). No narratives—must include specific strategy." Query.
Recent Nonfiction Title: *Thoroughbred Handicapping, as an Investment*, by Dick Mitchell (investing at the racetrack).

*DANCE HORIZONS, Imprint of Princeton Book Co., Publishers, Box 109, Princeton NJ 08542. (609)737-8177. Editorial Director: Richard Carlin. Publishes hardcover and paperback originals and paperback reprints. Averages 20 titles/year; receives 50-75 submissions annually. 50% of books from first-time authors; 100% of books from unagented writers. Subsidy publishes 20% of books. Pays 10% royalty on net receipts; offers no advance. Publishes book an average of 18 months after acceptance. Simultaneous and photocopied submissions OK. Computer printout submissions acceptable; no dot-matrix. Reports in 3 months. Free book catalog.
Nonfiction: "Anything dealing with dance." Query first. Reviews artwork/photos.
Recent Nonfiction Title: *The Hidden You*, by Mabel Todd.

*JOHN DANIEL, PUBLISHER, Box 21922, Santa Barbara CA 93121. (805)962-1780. Imprints include Fithian Press. Independent book producer/packager. Publisher: John Daniel. Publishes trade paperback originals. Averages 12 titles/year; receives 300 submissions annually. 50% of books from first-time authors; 100% of books from unagented writers. Subsidy publishes 50% of titles. "If we like a book but don't feel its commercial possibilities justify a financial risk, we offer the Fithian Press contract: author pays major production costs in exchange for a 50%-of-net royalty." Pays 10-50% royalty on wholesale price. Publishes book an average of 6 months after acceptance. Simultaneous and photocopied submissions OK. Query for electronic submissions. Computer printout submissions acceptable. Reports in 6 weeks on queries; 2 months on mss. Book catalog and ms guidelines for SASE.
Nonfiction: Autobiography, biography, cookbook, humor, self-help, travel, nature, philosophy and essays. "We'll look at anything, but are particularly interested in books in which literary merit is foremost—as opposed to books that simply supply information. No libelous, obscene, poorly written, or unintelligent manuscripts." Query or submit outline and sample chapters. Reviews artwork/photos.
Recent Nonfiction Title: *Mister Raja's Neighborhood*, by Jeff Greenwald (travel).
Fiction: Adventure, ethnic, experimental, fantasy, historical, humor, mainstream and mystery. "We do best with books by authors who have demonstrated a clear, honest, elegant style. No libelous, obscene, poorly written, or boring submissions." Query or submit synopsis and sample chapters.
Recent Fiction Title: *City of Roses*, by Mary Jane Moffat (short stories).
Poetry: "We're open to anything, but we're very cautious. Poetry's hard to sell." Submit complete ms.
Recent Poetry Title: *Milking the Earth*, by Perie Longo.
Tips: "If I were a writer trying to market a book today, I would envision my specific audience and approach publishers who demonstrate that they can reach that audience. Writing is not always a lucrative profession; almost nobody makes a living off of royalties from small-press publishing houses. That's why the authors we deal with are dedicated to their art and proud of their books—but don't expect to appear on the Carson show. Small-press publishers have a hard time breaking into the bookstore market. We try, but we wouldn't be able to survive without a healthy direct-mail sale."

DANTE UNIVERSITY OF AMERICA PRESS, INC., Box 843, Brookline MA 02147. Contact: Manuscripts Editor. Publishes hardcover originals and reprints, and trade paperback originals and reprints. Averages 5 titles/year; receives 50 submissions annually. 50% of books from first-time authors; 50% of books from unagented writers. Average print order for a writer's first book is 3,000. Pays royalty; offers negotiable advance. Publishes book an average of 10 months after acceptance. Simultaneous and photocopied submissions OK. Query for electronic submissions. Computer printout submissions acceptable. Reports in 2 weeks on queries only; 2 months on mss.
Nonfiction: Biography, reference, reprints, and nonfiction and fiction translations from Italian and Latin. Subjects include general scholarly nonfiction, Renaissance thought and letter, Italian language and linguistics, Italian-American history and culture, and bilingual education. Query first. Reviews artwork/photos as part of ms package.
Poetry: "There is a chance that we would use Renaissance poetry translations."
Recent Poetry Title: *The Inferno*, by Dante (epic poetry).

DARTNELL CORP., 4660 N. Ravenswood Ave., Chicago IL 60640. (312)561-4000. Editorial Director: Scott Pemberton. Averages 4 titles/year; receives 150-200 submissions annually. 50% of books from first-time au-

thors; 99% of books from unagented writers. Average print order for a writer's first book is 2,000. Pays in royalties on sliding scale based usually on retail price. Publishes book an average of 1 year after acceptance. Query for electronic submission. Computer printout submissions acceptable; no dot-matrix. Reports in 1 month. Ms guidelines for SASE.
Nonfiction: Publishes business manuals, reports and handbooks. Interested in new material on business skills and techniques in management, sales management, marketing, supervision, administration, advertising, etc. Submit outline and sample chapter.
Recent Nonfiction Title: *Building a Winning Sales Force*, by George Lumsden.

*MAY DAVENPORT, PUBLISHERS, 26313 Purissima Rd., Los Altos Hills CA 94022. (415)948-6499. Editor/Publisher: May Davenport. Imprint includes md Books (nonfiction and fiction). Hardcover and trade paperback originals. Averages 3-4 titles/year; receives 1,000-2,000 submissions annually. 95% of books from first-time authors; 95% of books from unagented writers. Subsidy publishes (non-author) 20% of books. Pays 15% royalty on retail price; no advance. Publishes book an average of 1-3 years after acceptance. Reports in 3 weeks. Book catalog and ms guidelines for 6x9 SAE with 63¢ postage.
Nonfiction: Juvenile and textbook. Subjects include Americana, animals, art, music and nature. Our readers are students in elementary and secondary public school districts, as well as correctional institutes of learning, etc." No "hack writing." Query.
Recent Nonfiction Title: *The Rabbit Under the Wisteria Bush*, by Joyce Deedy (lifecycle of rabbit).
Fiction: Adventure, ethnic, fantasy. "We're overstocked with picture books and first readers; prefer closetplays for the TV-oriented teenagers (one act). "Be entertaining while informing." No sex or violence. Query.
Recent Fiction Title: *Kate's Scarf*, by Virginia Deans (growing up).
Tips: "Make people laugh. Humor has a place, too."

‡DAVIS PUBLICATIONS, INC., 50 Portland St., Worcester MA 01608. (617)754-7201. Acquisitions Editor: Wyatt Wade. Averages 5-10 titles/year. Pays 10-15% royalty. Publishes book an average of 1 year after acceptance. Computer printout submissions acceptable; prefers letter-quality to dot-matrix. Write for copy of guidelines for authors.
Nonfiction: Publishes art, design and craft books. Accepts nonfiction translations. "Keep in mind the intended audience. Our readers are visually oriented. All illustrations should be collated separately from the text, but keyed to the text. Photos should be good quality original prints. Well selected illustrations should explain, amplify, and enhance the text. We average 2-4 photos/page. We like to see technique photos as well as illustrations of finished artwork. Recent books have been on papermaking, airbrush painting, jewelry, design, puppets, quilting, and watercolor painting." Submit outline, sample chapters and illustrations. Reviews artwork/photos as part of ms package.

STEVE DAVIS PUBLISHING, Box 190831, Dallas TX 75219. (214)823-8660. Publisher: Steve Davis. Publishes hardcover and trade paperback originals. Averages 4 titles/year. Query for electronic submissions. Computer printout submissions acceptable. "Manuscripts should be professionally proofed for style, grammar and spelling before submission." Reports in 3 weeks on queries *if interested*. Not responsible for unsolicited material. Book catalog and ms guidelines for #10 SASE.
Nonfiction: Books on modern technology, communications, current social issues and some reference books. "We are very selective about our list. We look for material that is professionally prepared, takes a fresh approach to a timely topic, and offers the reader helpful information." No religious or occult topics, no sports, and no mass market material such as diet books, joke books, exercise books, etc. Query with outline/summary, sample chapter and SASE. "We can only respond to projects that interest us."
Recent Nonfiction Title: *The Facts on Fax*, by Lawrence Robinson (business communications).

DAW BOOKS, INC., 1633 Broadway, New York NY 10019. Editor: Betsy Wollheim. Publishes science fiction paperback originals and reprints. Publishes 62 titles/year. Pays 6% royalty; offers $2,500 advance—more on arrangement. Simultaneous submissions "returned at once, unread." Computer printout submissions acceptable; prefers letter-quality to dot-matrix. Reports in 6 weeks. Free book catalog.
Fiction: "We are interested in science fiction and fantasy novels only. We do not publish any other category of fiction. We are not seeking collections of short stories or ideas for anthologies. We do not want any nonfiction manuscripts." Submit complete ms.

‡*DAWN PUBLICATIONS, (formerly Ananda Publications), 14618 Tyler Foote Rd., Nevada City CA 95959. (916)292-3482. Imprints include Joyful Arts and Crystal Hermitage. Manager: Richard McCord. Publishes trade paperback originals. Averages 3 titles/year. Receives 50-100 submissions/year. 10-20% of books from first-time authors. 100% of books from unagented writers. Subsidy publishes 50% of books—25% subsidized by authors, 25% subsidized by other organizations. "Books that we do not view as part of our main line, or books for which we merely provide publishing consulting services, are subsidy-published on a case-by-case basis." Pays 8-15% royalty on wholesale or retail price. Publishes book an average of 5 months after acceptance. Simultaneous and photocopied submissions OK. Computer printout submissions OK; no dot-matrix. Reports in 1 month. Book catalog for 6x9 SAE with 2 first class stamps.

Nonfiction: Cookbook and self-help. Subjects include cooking and foods, health, nature, religion and spirituality. Most likely to consider "uplifting spiritual books and how-tos on spiritual, health and nature topics. No UFO's or extraterrestrials, spirit guides, channeling or recovery from 'fatal' diseases." Query.

Recent Nonfiction Title: *Education for Life*, by J. Donald Watters (alternative education).

Fiction: Children's spirituality. "We don't consciously seek fiction, but would consider a query if it fit our directions." Query.

Tips: "We do serious books on spirituality, health, and nature awareness. At this time, that's all we're considering, but we're open to other 'up' topics. The writer should tune in to one or more of our books before querying to make sure his/her book is compatible. With the query, give us lots of straight shooting and no hype. Answer the question, 'What is unique about your book?' "

DEL REY BOOKS, Imprint of Ballantine Books, 201 E. 50th St., New York NY 10022. (212)572-2677. Editor-in-Chief: Owen Lock. Fantasy Editor: Lester del Rey. Publishes hardcover, trade paperback and mass market originals and mass market paperback reprints. Averages 80 titles/year; receives 1,000 submissions annually. 10% of books from first-time authors; 40% of books from unagented writers. Pays royalty on retail price. Offers competitive advance. Publishes book an average of 1 year after acceptance. Photocopied submissions OK. Computer printout submissions acceptable; prefers letter-quality to dot-matrix. Reports in 1 month on queries; 1 year on mss.

Fiction: Fantasy ("should have the practice of magic as an essential element of the plot") and science fiction ("well-plotted novels with good characterization, exotic locales, and detailed alien cultures. Novels should have a 'sense of wonder' and be designed to please readers"). Will need "144 original fiction manuscripts of science-fiction and fantasy suitable for publishing over the next two years. No flying-saucers, Atlantis, or occult novels." Submit complete ms.

Recent Fiction Title: *The Smoke Ring*, by Larry Niven (original science-fiction hardcover).

Tips: "Del Rey is a reader's house. Our audience is anyone who wants to be pleased by a good entertaining novel. We do very well with original fantasy novels, in which magic is a central element, and with hard-science science-fiction novels. Pay particular attention to plotting and a satisfactory conclusion. It must be/feel believable. They're what the readers like."

DELACORTE PRESS, Imprint of Dell Publishing and division of Bantam/Doubleday/Dell, 245 E. 47th St., New York NY 10017. (212)605-3000. Editor-in-Chief: Jackie Farber. Publishes hardcover originals. Publishes 25 titles/year. Pays 10-12½-15% royalty; average advance. Publishes book an average of 2 years after acceptance. Simultaneous and photocopied submissions OK. Computer printout submissions acceptable; prefers letter-quality to dot-matrix. Reports in 2 months. Book catalog and guidelines for SASE.

Fiction and Nonfiction: *Query, outline or brief proposal, or complete ms accepted only through an agent;* otherwise returned unopened. No mss for children's or young adult books accepted in this division.

Recent Nonfiction Title: *Enter Talking*, by Joan Rivers.

Recent Fiction Title: *Fine Things*, by Danielle Steel.

DELL PUBLISHING CO., INC., Subsidiary of Bertelsman. 1 Dag Hammarskjold Plaza, New York NY 10017. Imprints include Dell, Delacorte Press, Delta Books, Dell Trade Paperbacks, Laurel, Delacorte Press Books for Young Readers, Yearling and Laurel Leaf. Publishes hardcover and paperback originals and reprints. Publishes 500 titles/year. Pays royalty on retail price. "General guidelines for unagented submissions. Please adhere strictly to the following procedure: 1) Do not send manuscript, sample chapters or art work; 2) Do not register, certify or insure your letter; 3) Send only a 4-page synopsis or outline with a cover letter stating previous work published or relevant experience." Simultaneous and photocopied submissions OK. Reports in 3 months. Book catalog and guidelines for SASE.

Nonfiction: "Because Dell is comprised of several imprints, each with its own editorial department, we ask you to carefully review the following information and direct your submission to the appropriate department. Your envelope must be marked, Attention: (blank) Editorial Department—Proposal. Fill in the blank with one of the following: Delacorte: Publishes in hardcover. Looks for popular nonfiction (*SON*). Delta and Dell Trade: Publishes in trade paperback; rarely publishes original fiction; looks for useful, substantial guides (*Getting Work Experience*); entertaining, amusing nonfiction (*Nice Guys Sleep Alone*); serious work in the area of modern society. Yearling and Laurel Leaf: Publishes in paperback and hardcover for children and young adults, grades 7-12.

Fiction: Refer to the above guidelines. Delacorte: Publishes top-notch commercial fiction in hardcover (e.g., *Fine Things*). Dell: Publishes mass-market paperbacks; rarely publishes original nonfiction; looks for family sagas, historical romances, sexy modern romance, adventure and suspense, thrillers, occult/horror and war novels.

DELMAR PUBLISHERS, INC., Subsidiary of International Thomson Publishing Inc., 2 Computer Dr. W., Box 15015, Albany NY 12212-5015. (518)459-1150. Vice President of Publishing: G.C. Spatz. Publishes hardcover and paperback textbooks and educational software. Averages 50 titles/year; receives 150 submissions annually. 35% of books from first-time authors; 100% of books from unagented writers. Average print order for a writer's first book is 5,000. Pays royalty on wholesale price. Publishes book an average of 3 years after acceptance. Electronic submissions acceptable on IBM PC or WordStar, but requires hard copy also. Computer printout submissions acceptable; no dot-matrix. Reports in 2 weeks on queries; 2 months on submissions. Book catalog for 8½x11 SASE; guidelines for SASE.

Nonfiction: Subjects include business and data processing, allied health/nursing, childcare, mathematics, agriculture/horticulture texts, and textbooks for most vocational and technical subjects. Books are used in secondary and postsecondary schools. Query and submit outline/synopsis and 2-3 sample chapters. Reviews artwork/photos as part of ms package.

Recent Nonfiction Title: *Technology In Your World*, by Michael Hacker and Robert Barden (technology education).

Tips: Vocational textbooks have the best chance of selling for Delmar Publishers. Queries/mss may be routed to other editors in the publishing group.

DELTA BOOKS, Division of Dell Publishing Co., 1 Dag Hammarskjold Plaza, New York NY 10017. (212)605-3000. Editor-in-Chief: Jackie Farber. Publishes trade paperback reprints and originals. Averages 10 titles/year. Pays 6-7½% royalty; offers advance. Simultaneous and photocopied submissions OK. Computer printout submissions acceptable; prefers letter-quality to dot-matrix. Reports in 2 months. Book catalog for 8½x11 SASE.

Nonfiction: Consciousness, health, how-to, humor, music, New Age, photography, politics, recreation, reference, science, self-help and sports. "We would like to see books on the arts, social history, social criticism and analysis, and child care. We do not want to see biography, philosophy, academic books, textbooks, juveniles, or poetry books." Query or submit outline/synopsis and sample chapters. *Prefers submissions through agents.*

Fiction: "We are looking for original, innovative and contemporary novels." Submit through an agent.

DEMBNER BOOKS, Division of Red Dembner Enterprises, Corp., 80 8th Ave., New York NY 10011. (212)924-2525. Associate Editor: Therese Eiben. Publishes hardcover and trade paperback originals, and hardcover and trade paperback reprints. Averages 10-15 titles/year; receives 500-750 submissions annually. 20% of books from first-time authors; 75% of books from unagented writers. Pays 10-15% royalty on hardcover; 6-7½% royalty on paperback, both on retail price. Offers average $1,000-5,000 advance. Publishes book an average of 1 year after acceptance. Simultaneous and photocopied submissions OK. Computer printout submissions acceptable; no dot-matrix. Reports in 2 weeks on queries; 10 weeks on mss. Book catalog available from W.W. Norton, 500 5th Ave., New York NY 10110.

Nonfiction: How-to, reference, self-help. Subjects include animals, health, film, history (popular), music, psychology, sports and social causes. "We want books written by knowledgeable authors that focus on a problem area (health/home/handicapped) and offer an insightful guidance toward solutions." No surveys or collections—books that do not focus on one specific, promotable topic. Also, no books on heavily published topics, such as weight loss and exercise programs. Query. Reviews artwork/photos.

Recent Nonfiction Title: *A Consumer's Guide to Vintage Clothing*, by Terry McCormick.

Fiction: Adventure, mystery, suspense and literary. "We look for genre fiction (mystery, suspense, etc.), that keeps pace with the times, deals with contemporary issues, and has three-dimensional characters. Occasionally we publish literary novels, but the writing must be of excellent quality." No indulgent, self-conscious fiction. Query or submit outline/synopsis and sample chapters.

Recent Fiction Title: *In Siberia It Is Very Cold*, by Lester Goldberg.

Tips: "We take a great deal of pride in the books we publish. We are interested in serving a need as well as entertaining. We publish books worth reading and even worth keeping. Small hardcover houses such as ourselves are being very careful about the books they choose for publication primarily because secondary rights sales have dropped, and the money is less. Quality is of utmost importance."

T.S. DENISON & CO., INC., 9601 Newton Ave., S. Minneapolis MN 55431. Editor-in-Chief: Sherrill B. Flora. Publishes teacher aid materials; receives 500 submissions annually. 90% of books from first-time authors; 100% of books from unagented writers. Average print order for a writer's first book is 2,000. Royalty varies; no advance. Publishes book an average of 1-2 years after acceptance. Photocopied submissions OK. Computer printout submissions acceptable; no dot-matrix. Reports in 1 month. Book catalog and ms guidelines for SASE.

Nonfiction: Specializes in early childhood teaching aids. Send prints if photos are to accompany ms. Submit complete ms. Reviews artwork/photos as part of ms package.

DENLINGER'S PUBLISHERS, LTD., Box 76, Fairfax VA 22030. (703)830-4646. Publisher: William W. Denlinger. Publishes hardcover and trade paperback originals, hardcover and trade paperback reprints. Averages 12 titles/year; receives 250 submissions annually. 5% of books from first-time authors; 95% of books from unagented writers. Average print order for a writer's first book is 3,000. Pays variable royalty. No advance. Publishes book an average of 18 months after acceptance. Simultaneous and photocopied submissions OK. Query for electronic submissions. Computer printout submissions acceptable; prefers letter-quality to dot-matrix. Reports in 1 week on queries; 6 weeks on mss. Book catalog for SASE.

Nonfiction: How-to and technical books. Subjects include dogs and Americana. Query. Reviews artwork/photos.

Recent Nonfiction Title: *Bird Dogs and Upland Game Birds*, by Jack Stuart.

Fiction: Southern historical.

Recent Fiction Title: *Mandingo*.

‡*DEVIN-ADAIR PUBLISHERS, INC., 6 N. Water St., Greenwich CT 06830. (203)531-7755. Editor: Jane Andrassi. Publishes hardcover and paperback originals, reprints and software. Averages 20 titles/year; receives up to 500 submissions annually. 30% of books from first-time authors; 70% of books from unagented writers. Average print order for a writer's first book is 7,500. Subsidy publishes 5% of books. Royalty on sliding scale, 5-25%; "average advance is low." Publishes book an average of 9 months after acceptance. No simultaneous submissions. Query for electronic submissions. Computer printout submissions acceptable; prefers letter-quality to dot-matrix. Book catalog and guidelines for 6x9 SAE with $1 postage.

Nonfiction: Publishes Americana, business, how-to, conservative politics, history, medicine, nature, economics, sports and travel books. New lines: personal computer books and homeopathic books. Accepts translations. Query or submit outline/synopsis and sample chapters. Looks for "early interest, uniqueness, economy of expression, good style, and new information." Reviews artwork/photos as part of ms package.

Recent Nonfiction Title: *Haiti: The Black Republic*, by S. Rodman (guidebook and art history).

Tips: "We seek to publish books of high quality manufacture. We spend 8% more on production and design than necessary to ensure a better quality book. Trends include increased specialization and a more narrow view of a subject. General overviews in computer publishing are now a thing of the past. Better a narrow subject in depth than a wide superficial one."

*DEVONSHIRE PUBLISHING CO., Box 7066, Chicago IL 60680. (312)242-3846. Vice President: Don Reynolds. Publishes hardcover and trade paperback originals. Averages 3-5 titles/year; receives 300 submissions annually. 75% of books from first-time authors; 75% of books from unagented writers. Subsidy publishes 15% of books. "Although we do not generally subsidy publish we will enter into 'cooperative publishing agreements' with an author if the subject matter is of such limited appeal that we doubt its profitability, or the author desires a more extravagant finished product than we planned to produce." Pays 10-15% royalty on retail price. "Royalty would be higher if author engaged in cooperative venture." Offers negotiable advance. Publishes book an average of 1 year after acceptance. Simultaneous and photocopied submissions OK. Computer printout submissions acceptable; prefers letter-quality to dot-matrix. Reports in 1 month on queries; 2 months on submissions. Book catalog for 9x12 SAE with 39¢ postage; guidelines for #10 SASE.

Nonfiction: Illustrated book, reference, technical and textbook. Subjects include business and economics, history, hobbies, nature, psychology, religion and sociology. "We will be looking for books that have an impact on the reader. A history or religious book will have to be more than just a recitation of past events. Our books must have some relation to today's problems or situations." No works of personal philosophy or unverifiable speculation. Query and/or submit outline/synopsis and sample chapters.

Recent Nonfiction Title: *Soul Quest*, by M. Giffiotti (biography).

Fiction: Erotica, experimental, historical, horror, religious and science fiction. "All works must have some relevance to today's reader and be well written. We hope to produce one or two titles, but our main thrust will be in the nonfiction area. However, if a work is thought-provoking and/or controversial, we may give it priority. Query and/or submit outline/synopsis and sample chapters.

Recent Fiction Title: *Transcripts of the Trial of Jesus of Nazareth*, by N. Kristensen (religious).

Tips: "Since we are a small publishing company (and new), we can aim for the smaller, more specialized market. We envision that the audience for our books will be well educated with a specific area of interest. Because we are new, we can afford to look at work that other publishers have passed over. Although we are not looking for works that are controversial just for the sake of controversy, we are looking for topics that go beyond the norm. If it is documented and has a strong basis or foundation, we will endeavor to publish it."

DIAL BOOKS FOR YOUNG READERS, Division of NAL Penguin Inc., 2 Park Ave., New York NY 10016. (212)725-1818. Editor: Paula Wiseman. Imprints include Dial Easy-to-Read Books and Dial Very First Books. Publishes hardcover originals. Averages 60 titles/year; receives 20,000 submissions annually. 15% of books from first-time authors. Pays variable royalty and advance. Simultaneous and photocopied submissions OK, but not preferred. Computer printout submissions acceptable. Reports in 2 weeks on queries; 3 months on mss. Book catalog and ms guidelines for 9x12 SASE.

Nonfiction: Juvenile picture books and young adult books. Especially looking for "quality picture books and well-researched young adult and middle-reader mss." Not interested in alphabet books, riddle and game

books, and early concept books." Query with outline/synopsis and sample chapters. Reviews artwork/photos.
Recent Nonfiction Title: *Mountains*, by Clive Catchpole (picture book).
Fiction: Adventure, fantasy, historical, humor, mystery, romance (appropriate for young adults), and suspense. Especially looking for "lively and well written novels for middle grade and young adult children involving a convincing plot and believable characters. The subject matter or theme should not already be overworked in previously published books. The approach must not be demeaning to any minority group, nor should the roles of female characters (or others) be stereotyped, though we don't think books should be didactic, or in any way message-y." No "topics inappropriate for the juvenile, young adult, and middle grade audiences. No plays or poetry." Submit complete ms.
Recent Fiction Title: *Through the Hidden Door*, by Rosemary Wells.
Tips: "Our readers are anywhere from preschool age to teenage. Picture books must have strong plots, lots of action, unusual premises, or universal themes treated with freshness and originality. Humor works well in these books. A very well thought out and intelligently presented book has the best chance of being taken on. Genre isn't as much of a factor as presentation."

DILLON PRESS, INC., 500 S. 3rd St., Minneapolis MN 55415. (612)333-2691. Editorial Director: Uva Dillon. Senior Editor: Tom Schneider. Juvenile Fiction Editor: Alice Herber. Nonfiction Editor: Kathryn Shupe. Publishes hardcover originals. Averages 30-40 titles/year; receives 3,000 submissions annually. 50% of books from first-time authors; 90% of books from unagented writers. Average print order for a writer's first book is 3,000-5,000. Pays royalty and by outright purchase. Publishes book an average of 1 year after acceptance. Computer printout submissions acceptable; no dot-matrix. Reports in 6 weeks. Book catalog for 10x12 SAE with 73¢ postage.
Nonfiction: "We are actively seeking mss for the juvenile educational market." Subjects include foreign countries, U.S. states and cities, contemporary and historical biographies for elementary and middle grade levels, unusual approaches to science topics for primary grade readers, wildlife, sports biographies, and contemporary issues of interest and value to young people. Submit complete ms or outline and 1 sample chapter; no query letters. Reviews artwork/photos as part of ms package.
Recent Nonfiction Title: *One Woman's Power: A Biography of Gloria Steinem*, by Emily Taitz and Sondra Henry.
Fiction: "We are looking for fiction mss that appeal to fourth through ninth grade readers." Subjects include mysteries, adventure, fantasy, science fiction. Also interested in historical fiction based on actual events. No picture books.
Recent Fiction Title: *How I Saved the World*, by Dennis Fradin.
Tips: "Before writing, authors should check out the existing competition for their book idea to determine if it is really needed and stands a reasonable chance for success, especially for a nonfiction proposal."

DIMENSION BOOKS, INC., Box 811, Denville NJ 07834-0811. (201)627-4334. Contact: Thomas P. Coffey. Publishes 25 titles/year; receives 450-500 submissions annually. 10% of books from first-time authors; 60% of books from unagented writers. Pays "regular royalty schedule" based on retail price; advance is negotiable. Publishes book an average of 3-5 months after acceptance. Computer printout submissions acceptable. Book catalog and guidelines for SAE and 2 first class stamps. Reports in 2 weeks.
Nonfiction: Publishes general nonfiction including religion, principally Roman Catholic. Also psychology. Accepts nonfiction translations. Query. Accepts outline/synopsis and 3 sample chapters. Length: 40,000 words minimum. Reviews artwork/photos.
Recent Nonfiction Title: *The Enneagram: A Journey of Self-Discovery*, by Beesing, Nogosek, and O'Leary.

DODD, MEAD & CO., 71 5th Ave., New York NY 10003. (212)627-8444. President: John Harden. Publisher: Lynn Lumsden. Senior Editors: Mary Kennan, Allen T. Klots, Margaret Norton and Cynthia Vartan. Editors: Chris Fortunato, Barbara Beckman, Cynthia Merman and Betsey Perry. Averages 200 titles/year. Pays 10-15% royalty; advances vary, depending on the sales potential of the book. A contract for nonfiction books is offered on the basis of a query, a suggested outline and a sample chapter. Write for permission before sending mss. Adult fiction, history, philosophy, the arts, current events, management and religion should be addressed to Editorial Department. Publishes book an average of 9 months after acceptance. Electronic submissions OK "only on exceptional occasions when submission can be used on equipment of our suppliers." Reports in 6 weeks.
Fiction and Nonfiction: Publishes book-length mss. Length: 70,000-100,000 words average. Looks for high quality; mysteries and romantic novels of suspense, business, nature and science, travel, yachting and other sports, music and other arts. Very rarely buys photographs or poetry. Publishes books for juveniles. Children's Books Editors: Jo Ann Daly, Rosanne Laury and Betty Ann Schwartz. Length: 1,500-75,000 words.
Tips: "Freelance writers should be aware of trends toward nonfiction and the difficulty of publishing marginal or midlist fiction."

DOLL READER, Subsidiary of Hobby House Press, Inc., 900 Frederick St., Cumberland MD 21502. (301)759-3770. Subsidiaries include *Doll Reader* and *The Teddy Bear and Friends Magazine*. Publisher: Gary R. Ruddell. Publishes hardcover originals. Averages 24 titles/year. 20% of books from first-time authors; 90% of books from unagented writers. Pays royalty. Publishes book an average of 24 months after acceptance. Simultaneous and photocopied submissions OK. Computer printout submissions acceptable; prefers letter-quality to dot-matrix. Reports in 1 month. Ms guidelines for 9x12 SAE.
Nonfiction: Doll-related books. "We publish books pertaining to dolls, teddy bears and crafts as a collector's hobby; we also publish pattern books. The *Doll Reader* is published 8 times a year dealing with the hobby of doll collecting. We appeal to those people who are doll collectors, miniature collectors, as well as people who sew for dolls. Our magazine has a worldwide circulation of close to 65,000." Query or submit outline/synopsis. Reviews artwork/photos as part of ms package. *The Teddy Bear and Friends Magazine* is published bimonthly.
Recent Nonfiction Title: *7th Blue Book of Dolls and Values*, by Jan Foulke (price guide for dolls).

‡THE DONNING COMPANY/PUBLISHERS, INC., 5659 Virginia Beach Blvd., Norfolk VA 23502. (804)461-8909. Publisher: Robert S. Friedman. Publishes hardcover and trade paperback originals. Averages 35-40 titles/year; receives 350 submissions/year. 50% of books from first-time authors; 50% of books from unagented writers. Pays 7-15% royalty on retail price. Offers $2,000 average advance. Publishes book an average of 1 year after acceptance. Simultaneous and photocopied submissions OK. Computer printout submissions OK; prefers letter-quality. Reports in 2 weeks on queries; 2 months on mss. Ms guidelines for SASE.
Nonfiction: "Coffee table" book, cookbook, how-to, humor, illustrated book, reference and self-help. Subjects include Americana, cooking and foods, health, history, philosophy, photography and travel. "Americana, regional cookbooks, pictorial histories of cities and counties and metaphysical self-help are what we seek. No textbooks, music, art appreciation, sports, sociology or religion." Submit outline/synopsis and sample chapters or complete ms.
Recent Nonfiction Title: *Robotech Art I*, by Kay Reynolds (illustrated fantasy).
Fiction: Adventure, fantasy, mainstream, mystery, romance, science fiction. "No western, religious, historical, horror, erotica, gothic or experimental manuscripts." Submit outline/synopsis and sample chapters and complete ms.
Recent Fiction Title: *Fortune's Friends*, by Kay Reynolds (mystery).
Tips: "Regional pictorials, cookbooks, and self-help books have the best chance of selling because there is less competition in manuscript production. Writing about a fairly unique subject will always get attention, and including information on the marketing potential will help in making decision."

DOUBLEDAY & CO., INC., 245 Park Ave., New York NY 10167. Publishes hardcover and paperback originals. Offers royalty on retail price; offers variable advance. Reports in 2½ months. "At present, Doubleday and Co. is *only* able to consider fiction for mystery/suspense, science fiction, and romance imprints." Send *copy* of complete manuscript (60,000-80,000 words) to Crime Club Editor, Science Fiction Editor, or Starlight Romance Editor as appropriate. Sufficient postage for return via fourth class mail must accompany manuscript.

DOUGLAS & MCINTYRE PUBLISHERS, 1615 Venables St., Vancouver, British Columbia V5L 2H1 Canada. (604)254-7191. Manuscript Editor: Shaun Oakey. Imprints include Groundwood Books. Publishes hardcover originals and trade paperback originals; and trade paperback reprints. Averages 50 titles/year; receives 600 submissions annually. 50% of books from first-time authors; 90% of books from unagented writers. Pays 8-15% royalty on retail price; offers average $500 advance. Simultaneous and photocopied submissions OK. Reports in 1 month on queries; 2 months on mss. Book catalog for SASE.
Nonfiction: Biography, cookbook, illustrated book, juvenile and Canadian history. Subjects include Canadiana, art, business and economics, cooking and foods, history, and Canadian politics and medical/health. No how-to or outdoor guides. Query with outline/synopsis and sample chapters or complete ms.
Recent Nonfiction Title: *Beyond Forget*, by Mark Abley.
Fiction: Ethnic, experimental and literary/women's. No mass market-type material—romance, gothic, etc. Submit outline/synopsis and sample chapters or complete ms.
Tips: "For our fiction and general trade lists we prefer Canadian authors."

DOWN EAST BOOKS, Division of Down East Enterprise, Inc., Box 679, Camden ME 04843. (207)594-9544. Editor: Karin Womer. Publishes hardcover and trade paperback originals and trade paperback reprints. Averages 10-14 titles/year; receives 400 submissions annually. 50% of books from first-time authors; 90% of books from unagented writers. Average print order for a writer's first book is 2,500. Pays 10-15% on receipts. Offers average $200 advance. Publishes book an average of 12 months after acceptance. Simultaneous and photocopied submissions OK. Computer printout submissions acceptable; prefers letter-quality to dot-matrix. Reports in 2 weeks on queries; 2 months on mss. Book catalog and ms guidelines for 9x12 SAE with 39¢ postage.

Nonfiction: Regional biography, cookbooks, illustrated books, juvenile, reference and guidebooks. Subjects include Americana, art, cooking and foods, history, nature, traditional crafts and recreation. "All of our books must have a Maine or New England emphasis." Query. Reviews artwork/photos as part of ms package.

Recent Nonfiction Title: *Glaciers and Granite: A Guide to Maine's Landscape and Geology*, by D. Kendall.

Fiction: "We publish no fiction except for an occasional juvenile title (average 1/year)."

Recent Fiction Title: *Crystal: The Story of a Real Baby Whale*, by Karen Smyth.

*DRAGON'S TEETH PRESS, El Dorado National Forest, Georgetown CA 95634. (916)333-4224. Editor: Cornel Lengyel. Publishes trade paperback originals and software. Averages 6 titles/year; receives 100+ submissions annually. 50% of books from first-time authors; 75% of books from unagented writers. Subsidy publishes 25% of books; applies "if book has high literary merit, but very limited market." Pays 10% royalty on retail price, or in copies. Publishes book an average of 1 year after acceptance. Simultaneous and photocopied submissions OK. Computer printout submissions acceptable. Reports in 2 weeks on queries; 1 month on mss. Book catalog for SAE with 63¢ postage.

Nonfiction: Music and philosophy. Publishes for 500 poets, or potential poets. Query or submit outline/synopsis and sample chapters. Reviews artwork/photos as part of ms package.

Poetry: "Highly original works of potential literary genius. No trite, trivial or trendy ego exhibitions." Submit 10 samples or the complete ms.

DRAMA BOOK PUBLISHERS, Box 816, Gracie Station, New York NY 10028. (212)517-4455. Contact: Ralph Pine or Judith Holmes. Publishes hardcover and paperback originals and reprints. Averages 4-15 titles/year; receives 500 submissions annually. 70% of books from first-time authors; 90% of books from unagented writers. Royalty varies; advance varies; negotiable. Publishes book an average of 18 months after acceptance. Computer printout submissions acceptable; prefers letter-quality to dot-matrix. Reports in 1 to 2 months. Book catalog for 6x9 SAE.

Nonfiction: Books—texts, guides, manuals, directories, reference—for and about performing arts theory and practice: acting, directing; voice, speech, movement, music, dance, mime; makeup, masks, wigs; costumes, sets, lighting, sound; design and execution; technical theatre, stagecraft, equipment; stage management; producing; arts management, all varieties; business and legal aspects; film, radio, television, cable, video; theory, criticism, reference; playwriting; theatre and performance history. Accepts nonfiction, drama and technical works in translations also. Query; accepts 1-3 sample chapters; no complete mss. Reviews artwork/photos as part of ms package.

Fiction: Professionally produced plays and musicals.

DUNDURN PRESS LTD., 1558 Queen St. E., Toronto, Ontario, M4L 1E8 Canada. (416)461-1881. Publisher: Kirk Howard. Publishes hardcover, trade paperback and hardcover reprints. Averages 15 titles/year; receives 500 submissions annually. 45% of books from first-time authors; 100% of books from unagented writers. Average print order for a writer's first book is 3,000. Pays 10% royalty on retail price; 8% royalty on some paperback children's books. Publishes book an average of 1 year after acceptance. "Easy-to-read" photocopied submissions OK. Computer printout submissions acceptable; prefers letter-quality to dot-matrix.

Nonfiction: Biography, "coffee table" books, juvenile, literary and reference. Subjects include Canadiana, art, history, hobbies, Canadian history and literary criticism. Especially looking for Canadian biographies. No religious or soft science topics. Query with outline/synopsis and sample chapters. Reviews artwork/photos as part of ms package.

Tips: "Publishers want more books written in better prose styles. If I were a writer trying to market a book today, I would visit book stores and watch what readers buy and what company publishes that type of book 'close' to my manuscript."

*DUQUESNE UNIVERSITY PRESS, 600 Forbes Ave., Pittsburgh PA 15282. (412)434-6610. Averages 9 titles/year; receives 400 submissions annually. 25% of books from first-time authors; 90% of books from unagented writers. Average print order for a writer's first book is 1,500. Subsidy publishes 20% of books. Pays 10% royalty on net sales; no advance. Publishes book an average of 1 year after acceptance. Electronic submissions OK but check with publisher; but requires hard copy also. Computer printout submissions acceptable; no dot-matrix. Query. Reports in 3 months.

Nonfiction: Scholarly books in the humanities, social sciences for academics, libraries, college bookstores and educated laypersons. Length: open. Looks for scholarship.

Recent Nonfiction Title: *Imaginative Thinking*, by Edward L. Murray.

DUSTBOOKS, Box 100, Paradise CA 95969. (916)877-6110. Publisher: Len Fulton. Publishes hardcover and paperback originals. Averages 7 titles/year. Offers 15% royalty. Offers average $500 advance. Simultaneous and photocopied submissions OK if so informed. Computer printout submissions acceptable. Reports in 2 months. Free book catalog.

Nonfiction: Technical. "DustBooks would like to see manuscripts dealing with microcomputers (software, hardware) and water (any aspect). Must be technically sound and well-written. We have at present no titles in these areas. These represent an expansion of our interests." Submit outline/synopsis and sample chapters.

E.P. DUTTON, Division of NAL-Penguin, Inc., 2 Park Ave., New York NY 10016. (212)725-1818. Publisher, Children's Books: Christopher Franceschelli. Averages 45 titles/year. 15% of books from first-time authors; 85% of books from unagented writers. Pays royalty on list price; offers variable advance. Considers unsolicited mss. Computer printout submissions acceptable; prefers letter-quality to dot-matrix. "Please send query letter first on all except picture book manuscripts."
Nonfiction: Nonfiction for ages 6-14.
Fiction: Picture books; beginning readers; novels for ages 8-12; young adult novels for ages 12 and up. Reviews artwork/photos as part of ms package. Emphasis on good writing and quality for all ages.
Tips: Queries/mss may be routed to other editors in the division.

EAKIN PUBLICATIONS, INC., Box 23066, Austin TX 78735. (512)288-1771. Imprints include Nortex. Editorial Director: Edwin M. Eakin. Publishes hardcover and paperback originals and reprints. Averages 40 titles/year; receives 500 submissions annually. 80% of books from first-time authors; 90% of books from unagented writers. Average print order for a writer's first book is 2,000. Pays 10-12-15% in royalty. Publishes book an average of 1 year after acceptance. Simultaneous and photocopied submissions OK. Query for electronic submissions. Computer printout submissions acceptable; prefers letter-quality to dot-matrix. Reports in 3 months. Book catalog and ms guidelines for SASE.
Nonfiction: History, juvenile history, contemporary, and regional. Specifically needs biographies of well-known Texas people, current Texas politics and history for grades 3-9. Query, or submit outline/synopsis and sample chapters. Reviews artwork/photos.
Recent Nonfiction Title: *Willie Nelson, An Authorized Biography*, by Susie Nelson.
Fiction: Historical fiction for school market. Specifically needs juveniles that relate to Texas. Query, or submit outline/synopsis and sample chapters.
Recent Fiction Title: *Trader Wooly*, by Tom Townsend.

‡*EDICIONES UNIVERSAL, 3090 S. W. 8th St., Miami FL 33135. (305)642-3355. Director: Juan M. Salvat. Publishes trade paperback originals in Spanish. Publishes 50 titles/year; receives 150 submissions/year. 40% of books from first-time authors. 90% of books from unagented writers. Subsidy publishes 10% of books. Pays 5-10% royalty on retail price. Publishes book an average of 9 months after acceptance. Simultaneous and photocopied submissions OK. Computer printout submissions OK; prefers letter-quality. Reports in 1 month on queries; 2 months on mss. Book catalog free.
Nonfiction: Biography, cookbook, humor and reference. Subjects include cooking and foods, philosophy, politics, psychology and sociology. "We specialize in Cuban topics." All manuscripts must be in Spanish. Submit outline/synopsis and sample chapters. Reviews artwork/photos as part of ms package.
Recent Nonfiction Title: *Cuba: Destiny as Choice*, by Wilfredo del Prado.
Fiction: "We will consider everything as long as it is written in Spanish." Submit outline/synopsis and sample chapters.
Recent Fiction Title: *El Rumbo*, by Joaquin Delgado-Sanchez.
Poetry: "We will consider any Spanish-language poetry." Submit 3 or more poems.
Recent Poetry Title: *Antologia De Poesia Infantil*, by Ana Rosa Nunez.
Tips: "Our audience is composed entirely of Spanish-language readers. This is a very limited market. Books on Cuban or Latin American topics have the best chance of selling to our firm."

*EDUCATION ASSOCIATES, Division of The Daye Press, Inc., Box 8021, Athens GA 30603. (404)542-4244. Editor, Text Division: D. Keith Osborn. Publishes hardcover and trade paperback originals. Averages 2-6 titles/year; receives 200 submissions annually. 1% of books from first-time authors; 100% of books from unagented writers. Subsidy publishes 5% of books. "We may publish a textbook which has a very limited audience and is of unusual merit . . . but we still believe that the book will make a contribution to the educational field." Buys mss "on individual basis." Publishes book an average of 9 months after acceptance. Photocopied submissions OK. Computer printout submissions acceptable; no dot-matrix. Reports in 1 month on queries.
Nonfiction: How-to and textbook. Subjects include psychology and education. "Books in the fields of early childhood and middle school education. Do not wish basic textbooks. Rather, are interested in more specific areas of interest in above fields. We are more interested in small runs on topics of more limited nature than general texts." Query only with one-page letter; do not send manuscript. If interested will request synopsis and sample chapters. Absolutely no reply unless SASE is enclosed. Do not telephone with query.
Recent Nonfiction Title: *Computer MAT*, by A.B. Wilson.
Tips: College textbooks—usually dealing with early childhood, middle school, or child development—have the best chance of selling to *Education Associates*.

*WILLIAM B. EERDMANS PUBLISHING CO., Christian University Press, 255 Jefferson Ave. SE, Grand Rapids MI 49503. (616)459-4591. Editor-in-Chief: Jon Pott. Managing Editor: Charles Van Hof. Publishes hardcover and paperback originals and reprints. Averages 65-70 titles/year; receives 3,000-4,000 submissions annually. 25% of books from first-time authors; 95% of books from unagented writers. Average print order for a writer's first book is 4,000. Subsidy publishes 1% of books. Pays 7½-10% royalty on retail price; usually no advance. Publishes book an average of 1 year after acceptance. Simultaneous and photocopied submissions OK if noted. Computer printout submissions acceptable; no dot-matrix. Reports in 3 weeks for queries; 4 months for mss. Looks for "quality and relevance." Free book catalog.
Nonfiction: Reference, textbooks and tourists guidebooks. Subjects include history, philosophy, psychology, religion, sociology, regional history and geography. "Approximately 80% of our publications are religious—specifically Protestant—and largely of the more academic or theological variety (as opposed to the devotional, inspirational or celebrity-conversion type of book). Our history and social studies titles aim, similarly, at an academic audience; some of them are documentary histories. We prefer that writers take the time to notice if we have published anything at all in the same category as their manuscript before sending it to us." Accepts nonfiction translations. Query. Accepts outline/synopsis and 2-3 sample chapters. Reviews artwork/photos.
Recent Nonfiction Title: *On Moral Medicine*, by Stephen Lammers and Allen Verhey (textbook).

‡ELYSIUM GROWTH PRESS, 5436 Fernwood Ave., Los Angeles CA 90027. (213)455-1000. Publishes hardcover and paperback originals, and hardcover and trade paperback reprints. Averages 4 titles/year; receives 20 submissions/year. 20% of books from first-time authors. 100% of books from unagented writers. Pays $5,000 average advance. Publishes book an average of 18 months after acceptance. Photocopied submissions OK. Query for electronic submissions. Computer printout submissions OK; no dot-matrix. Reports in 2 weeks on queries; 6 weeks on submissions. Book catalog free on request; ms guidelines for SASE.
Nonfiction: Illustrated book, self-help and textbook. Subjects include health, nature, philosophy, photography, psychology, recreation, sociology and travel. Needs books on "body self-image, body self-appreciation, world travel and the nudist way." Query. All unsolicited mss are returned unopened. Reviews artwork/photos as part of ms package.
Recent Nonfiction Title: *Family Naturism in Europe*, by Lange (nudist/naturist).

ENSLOW PUBLISHERS, Bloy St. and Ramsey Ave., Box 777, Hillside NJ 07205. (201)964-4116. Editor: Ridley Enslow. Publishes hardcover and paperback originals. Averages 30 titles/year. Pays 10-15% royalty on retail price or net price; offers $500-5,000 advance. Publishes book an average of 8 months after acceptance. Photocopied submissions OK. Computer printout submissions acceptable. Reports in 2 weeks. Free book catalog.
Nonfiction: Interested in manuscripts for young adults and children on science topics and social issues. Also, biography, business/economics, health, hobbies, how-to, juveniles, philosophy, psychology, recreation, reference, science, self-help, sociology, sports and technical. Accepts nonfiction translations. Submit outline/synopsis and 2 sample chapters. Reviews artwork/photos as part of ms package.
Recent Nonfiction Title: *Birth of The Constitution*, by E. Lindop.

ENTELEK, Ward-Whidden House/The Hill, Box 1303, Portsmouth NH 03801. Editor-in-Chief: Albert E. Hickey. Small press. Publishes paperback originals. Offers royalty on retail price of 5% trade; 10% textbook. No advance. Averages 5 titles/year. Photocopied and simultaneous submissions OK. Submit outline and sample chapters or submit complete ms. Reports in 1 week. Book catalog for SASE.
Nonfiction: Publishes computer books and software of special interest to educators. Length: 3,000 words minimum.
Recent Nonfiction Title: *Sea Experience*, edited by A. Hickey (education).

ENTERPRISE PUBLISHING CO., INC., 725 Market St., Wilmington DE 19801. (302)654-0110. Publisher: T.N. Peterson. Editor: Ann Faccenda. Publishes hardcover and paperback originals, "with an increasing interest in newsletters and periodicals." Averages 8 titles/year; receives 150 submissions annually. 50% of books from first-time authors; 90% of books from unagented writers. Pays royalty on wholesale or retail price. Offers $1,000 average advance. Publishes book an average of 6 months after acceptance. Simultaneous and photocopied submissions OK, but "let us know." Query for electronic submissions. Computer printout submissions acceptable; prefers letter-quality to dot-matrix. Catalog and ms guidelines for SASE.
Nonfiction: "Subjects of interest to small business executives/entrepreneurs. They are highly independent and self-sufficient, and of an apolitical to conservative political leaning. They need practical information, as opposed to theoretical: self-help topics on business, including starting and managing a small enterprise, advertising, marketing, raising capital, public relations, tax avoidance and personal finance. Business/economics, legal self-help and business how-to." Queries only. All unsolicited mss are returned unopened. Reviews artwork/photos.
Recent Nonfiction Title: *Complete Book of Employee Forms*, by Arnold S. Goldstein, Esq.

*PAUL S. ERIKSSON, PUBLISHER, 208 Battell Bldg., Middlebury VT 05753. (802)388-7303; Summer: Forest Dale VT 05745. (802)247-8415. Publisher/Editor: Paul S. Eriksson. Associate Publisher/Co-Editor: Peggy Eriksson. Publishes hardcover and paperback trade originals and paperback trade reprints. Averages 5-10 titles/year; receives 1,500 submissions annually. 25% of books from first-time authors; 95% of books from unagented writers. Average print order for a writer's first book is 3,000-5,000. Subsidy publishes 1% of books. Pays 10-15% royalty on retail price; advance offered if necessary. Publishes book an average of 6 months after acceptance. Photocopied submissions OK. Computer printout submissions acceptable; prefers letter-quality to dot-matrix. Reports in 3 weeks. Free book catalog.

Nonfiction: Americana, birds (ornithology), art, biography, business/economics, cookbooks/cooking/ foods, health, history, hobbies, how-to, humor, music, nature, philosophy, photography, politics, psychology, recreation, self-help, sociology, sports and travel. Submit outline/synopsis and sample chapters.

Recent Nonfiction Title: *How to Save Your Child From Drugs*, by Harold M. Voth, M.D. and Gabriel G. Nahas, M.D.,Ph.D.

Fiction: Mainstream. Submit outline/synopsis and sample chapters.

Recent Fiction Title: *The Headmaster's Papers*, by Richard A. Hawley.

Tips: "We look for intelligence, excitement and salability. We prefer manuscripts written out of deep, personal knowledge or experience."

*ETC PUBLICATIONS, Drawer ETC, Palm Springs CA 92263. (619)325-5352. Editorial Director: LeeOna S. Hostrop. Senior Editor: Dr. Richard W. Hostrop. Publishes hardcover and paperback originals. Averages 6-12 titles/year; receives 100 submissions annually. 75% of books from first-time authors; 90% of books from unagented writers. Average print order for a writer's first book is 2,500. Subsidy publishes 5-10% of books. Offers 5-15% royalty, based on wholesale and retail price. No advance. Publishes book an average of 1 year after acceptance. Simultaneous and photocopied submissions OK. Computer printout submissions acceptable; prefers letter-quality to dot-matrix. Reports in 3 weeks.

Nonfiction: Business management, educational management, gifted education, books for writers and text-books. Accepts nonfiction translations in above areas. Submit complete ms. Reviews artwork/photos as part of ms package.

Recent Nonfiction Title: *Memo To the Boss: From Mack—A Contemporary Rendering of The Prince by Niccolo Machiavelli*, by W.T. Brahmstedt (business management).

Tips: "ETC will seriously consider textbook manuscripts in any knowledge area in which the author can guarantee a first-year adoption of not less than 500 copies. Special consideration is given to those authors who are capable and willing to submit their completed work in camera-ready, typeset form."

‡M. EVANS AND CO., INC., 216 E. 49 St., New York NY 10017. Editor-in-Chief: George C. deKay. Publishes hardcover originals. Royalty schedule to be negotiated. Averages 30-40 titles/year. 5% of books from unagented writers. Publishes book an average of 8 months after acceptance. Will consider photocopied submissions. Computer printout submissions OK; no dot-matrix. "No mss should be sent unsolicited. A letter of inquiry is essential." Reports in 8 weeks. SASE essential.

Nonfiction and Fiction: "We publish a general trade list of adult fiction and nonfiction, cookbooks and semireference works. The emphasis is on selectivity since we publish only 30 titles a year. Our fiction list represents an attempt to combine quality with commercial potential. Our most successful nonfiction titles have been related to health and the behavioral sciences. No limitation on subject. A writer should clearly indicate what his book is all about, frequently the task the writer performs least well. His credentials, although important, mean less than his ability to convince this company that he understands his subject and that he has the ability to communicate a message worth hearing." Reviews artwork/photos.

Tips: "Writers should review our catalog (available for 9x12 envelope with 3 first class stamps) or the *Publishers Trade List Annual* before making submissions."

FABER & FABER, INC., Division of Faber & Faber, Ltd., London, England; 50 Cross St., Winchester MA 01890. (617)721-1427. Editor-in-Chief: Douglas W. Hardy. Publishes hardcover and trade paperback originals, and hardcover and trade paperback reprints. Averages 20 titles/year; receives 600 submissions annually. 10% of books from first-time authors; 25% of books from unagented writers. Pays 7½-10% royalty on wholesale or retail price; advance varies. Publishes book an average of 1 year after acceptance. Simultaneous and photocopied submissions OK. Computer printout submissions acceptable; prefers letter-quality to dot-matrix. Reports in 3 weeks on queries; 6 weeks on mss. Book catalog for 9x12 SAE and 5 first class stamps.

Nonfiction: Biography, "coffee table" book, how-to, humor, illustrated book, juvenile, contemporary culture, self-help and business. Subjects include Americana, animals, art, health, history, hobbies, music, photography, politics, sociology and travel. Query with synopsis and outline. Reviews artwork/photos as part of ms package.

Recent Nonfiction Title: *Driving Passion*, by Peter Marsh and Peter Callett (psychology/culture).

Fiction: Ethnic, experimental, historical, mainstream, mystery and regional. No historical/family sagas. Query with synopsis and outline.

Recent Fiction Title: *Shelter*, by Marty Asher.
Tips: "We are a growing publisher, and we acquire manuscripts and publish books with great care. Writers with books on very obscure topics should look elsewhere. We take journalists seriously as possible book authors; many of our titles are house-generated with a writer brought on later."

FACTS ON FILE, INC., 460 Park Ave. S., New York NY 10016. (212)683-2244. Executive Editor: Gerard Helferich. Publishes hardcover originals and hardcover reprints. Averages 110 titles/year; receives approximately 1,000 submissions annually. 25% of books from unagented writers. Pays 10-15% royalty on retail price. Offers average $10,000 advance. Simultaneous and photocopied submissions OK. Query for electronic submissions. Computer printout submissions acceptable; prefers letter-quality to dot-matrix. Reports in 2 weeks on queries; 1 month on mss. Book catalog free on request.
Nonfiction: Reference and other informational books on animals, business and economics, cooking and foods (no cookbooks), health, history, hobbies (but no how-to), music, nature, philosophy, psychology, recreation, religion language and sports. "We need serious, informational books for a targeted audience. All our books must have strong library interest, but we also distribute books effectively to the book trade." No cookbooks, biographies, pop psychology, humor, do-it-yourself crafts or poetry. Query or submit outline/synopsis and sample chapters. Reviews artwork/photos.
Recent Nonfiction Title: *The Visual Dictionary*.
Tips: "Our audience is school and public libraries for our more reference-oriented books and libraries, schools and bookstores for our less reference-oriented informational titles."

*FAIRCHILD BOOKS & VISUALS, Book Division, Subsidiary of Capital Cities, Inc., 7 E. 12th St., New York NY 10003. Manager: E.B. Gold. Publishes hardcover and paperback originals. Offers standard minimum book contract; no advance. Pays 10% of net sales distributed twice annually. Averages 12 titles/year; receives 100 submissions annually. 50% of books from first-time authors; 99% of books from unagented writers. Subsidy publishes 2% of books—1% subsidized by authors, 1% by organizations. Publishes book an average of 1 year after acceptance. Photocopied submissions OK. Computer printout submissions acceptable; prefers letter-quality to dot-matrix. Book catalog and ms guidelines for 9x12 SASE.
Nonfiction: Publishes business books and textbooks relating to fashion, electronics, marketing, retailing, career education, advertising, home economics and management. Length: Open. Query, giving subject matter, brief outline and at least 1 sample chapter. Reviews artwork/photos as part of ms package.
Recent Nonfiction Title: *Basic Pattern Skills for Fashion Design*, by Zamkoff and Price.
Tips: "The writer has the best chance of selling our firm fashion, retailing or textile related books that can be used by both the trade and schools. If possible, the writer should let us know what courses would use the book."

*FAIRLEIGH DICKINSON UNIVERSITY PRESS, 285 Madison Ave., Madison NJ 07940. (201)593-8564. Chairperson, Editorial Committee: Harry Keyishian. Publishes hardcover originals. Averages 30 titles/year; receives 300 submissions annually. 33% of books from first-time authors; 100% of books from unagented writers. Average print order for a writer's first book is 1,000. "Contract is arranged through Associated University Presses of Cranbury, New Jersey. We are a *selection* committee only." Subsidy publishes (nonauthor) 2% of books. Publishes book an average of 18 months after acceptance. Computer printout submissions acceptable; prefers letter-quality to dot-matrix. Reports in 2 weeks on queries; 4 months on mss. Free book catalog.
Nonfiction: Reference and scholarly books. Subjects include art, business and economics, history, literary criticism, music, philosophy, politics, psychology, sociology and women's studies. Looking for scholarly books in all fields. No nonscholarly books. Query with outline/synopsis and sample chapters. Reviews artwork/photos as part of ms package.
Recent Nonfiction Title: *Gilbert and Sullivan: The Creative Conflict*, by David Eden.
Tips: "Research must be up to date. Poor reviews result when authors' bibliographies and notes don't reflect current research."

*FALCON PRESS, Subsidiary of J.W. Brown, Suite 295, 2210 Wilshire Blvd., Santa Monica CA 90403. (213)821-3540. Vice President: J. Reinhold. Publishes hardcover and trade paperback originals, and hardcover and trade paperback reprints. Averages 15 titles/year; receives 120 submissions annually. 20-25% of books from first-time authors; 70% of books from unagented writers. Subsidy publishes 20% of books. Subsidy publishes if author is unknown or had poor performance on previous titles. Pays 4-10% royalty on retail price. Offers average $500 advance. Publishes book an average of 13 months after acceptance. Simultaneous and photocopied submissions OK. Computer printout submissions acceptable; prefers letter-quality to dot-matrix. Reports in 1 month. Book catalog for 9x12 SAE with 2 first class stamps.
Nonfiction: Biography, how-to, illustrated book, reference, self-help, technical and textbook on business and economics, health, history, nature, philosophy, politics, psychology, religion, sociology, and metaphysics. Needs mss on psychology, sociology, new age, and the occult. Submit synopsis and sample chapters.
Recent Nonfiction Title: *Hinduism and Jungian Psychology*, by J. Marvin Spiegelman (psychology).

Fiction: Adventure, confession, erotica, ethnic, experimental, fantasy, historical, horror, mainstream, mystery, religious, science fiction and suspense. Needs science-fiction, fantasy, and experimental mss. Submit synopsis and sample chapters.
Recent Fiction Title: *The Downside of Up*, by Marian Greenberg (fantasy).

*FALCON PRESS PUBLISHING CO., INC., 27 Neill Ave., Box 731, Helena MT 59624. (406)442-6597. Publisher: Bill Schneider. Publishes hardcover and trade paperback originals. Averages 10-15 titles/year. Subsidy publishes 30% of books. Pays 8-15% royalty on net price or flat fee. Publishes book an average of 6 months after ms is in final form. Reports in 3 weeks on queries. Free book catalog.
Nonfiction: "We're primarily interested in ideas for recreational guidebooks and books on regional outdoor or geographic subjects—especially on Colorado and California—to go in a series of books on those states." No fiction or poetry. Query only; do not send ms.
Recent Nonfiction Title: *California State Parks*, by Kim Heacox.

*THE FAMILY ALBUM, Rt. 1, Box 42, Glen Rock PA 17327. (717)235-2134. Contact: Ron Lieberman. Publishes hardcover originals and reprints and software. Averages 4 titles/year; receives 150 submissions annually. 30% of books from first-time authors; 100% of books from unagented writers. Average print order for a writer's first book is 1,000. Subsidy publishes 20% of books. Pays royalty on wholesale price. Publishes book an average of 10 months after acceptance. Simultaneous and photocopied submissions OK. Query for electronic submissions. Computer printout submissions acceptable; prefers letter-quality to dot-matrix. Reports in 2 months.
Nonfiction: "Significant works in the field of (nonfiction) bibliography. Worthy submissions in the field of Pennsylvania-history, biography, folk art and lore. We are also seeking materials relating to books, literacy, and national development. Special emphasis on Third World countries, and the role of printing in international development." No religious material. Submit outline/synopsis and sample chapters.

FARRAR, STRAUS AND GIROUX, INC., 19 Union Sq. W., New York NY 10003. Publisher, Books for Young Adults: Stephen Roxburgh. Publishes hardcover originals. Receives 3,000 submissions annually. Pays royalty; advance. Publishes book an average of 18 months after acceptance. Photocopied submissions OK. Computer printout submissions acceptable; prefers letter-quality to dot-matrix. Reports in 3 months. Catalog for SAE and 56¢ postage.
Nonfiction and Fiction: "We are primarily interested in fiction picture books and novels for children and young adults." Submit outline/synopsis and sample chapters. Reviews artwork/photos as part of ms package.
Recent Nonfiction Title: *Grace in the Wilderness*, by Aranka Siegal.
Recent Fiction Title: *Many Waters*, by Madeleine L'Engle.
Recent Picture Book Title: *Froggie Went A-Courting*, by Chris Conover.
Tips: Fiction of all types has the best chance of selling to this firm. Farrar, Straus and Giroux publishes a limited number of nonfiction titles.

FEARON EDUCATION, Subsidiary of David S. Lake Publishers, 19 Davis Dr., Belmont CA 94002. (415)592-7810. Editorial Director: Carol Hegarty. Editorial and Marketing Director, Fearon Teacher Aids: Ina Tabibian. Averages 100-120 titles/year. Pays royalty or fee outright. Photocopied submissions OK. Computer printout submissions acceptable; prefers letter-quality to dot-matrix. Reports in 1 month. Book catalog and ms guidelines for 9x12 SASE.
Nonfiction: Educational. Query or submit synopsis.
Recent Nonfiction Title: *Getting Smarter*, by Greene/Jones-Bamman, (study skills).
Fiction: "Fearon Education is looking for easy-to-read fiction suitable for middle school and up. We prefer the major characters to be young adults or adults. Solid plotting is essential." Length: varies with series; write for specific guidelines.
Recent Fiction Title: *Ship of Doom*, by Dan J. Marlowe (hi-lo historical fiction).

‡FREDERICK FELL PUBLISHERS, INC., 2131 Hollywood Blvd., Hollywood FL 33020. (305)925-5242. Publisher: Donald L. Lessne. Publishes hardcover and trade paperback originals and reprints. Averages 15 titles/year; receives 1,000 submissions annually. 20% of books from first-time authors; 20% of books from unagented writers. Pays royalty. Publishes book an average of 1 year after acceptance. Simultaneous and photo-copied submissions OK. Query for electronic submissions. Computer printout submissions OK. Reports in 6 months on mss. Free book catalog.

Nonfiction: Biography, "coffee table" book, cookbook, how-to, humor, self-help, technical and textbook. Subjects include business and economics, cooking and foods, health, hobbies, philosophy, psychology, recreation, religion and sociology. Especially looking for manuscripts on current issues of interest; how-to, health and business. Submit outline/synopsis and sample chapters. Reviews artwork/photos as part of ms package.

Recent Nonfiction Title: *The Complete Guide to Eye Care, Eyeglasses and Contact Lenses*, by Zinn and Solomon.

‡*FICTION COLLECTIVE, Manuscript Central, English Department, University of Colorado, Boulder CO 80302. Contact: Managing Editor. Publishes hardcover and trade paperback originals. Averages 6 titles/year; receives 100-150 submissions/year. 30% of books from first-time authors. 50% of books from unagented writers. Subsidy publishes (nonauthor) 50% of books. Pays 10% royalty on wholesale price after production costs are covered. Publishes book an average of 15 months after acceptance. Simultaneous and photocopied submissions OK. Computer printout submissions OK; no dot-matrix. Reports in 2 months on queries; 6 months on submissions. Free book catalog.

Fiction: Ethnic and experimental. "We publish high-quality, innovative fiction (novels and story collections) completely on the basis of literary merit. We are always looking for quality fiction, but can publish only a very small percentage of what we receive. No genre fiction." Query or submit complete ms.

Recent Fiction Title: *My Amputations*, by Clarence Major (novel).

FIDDLEHEAD POETRY BOOKS & GOOSE LANE EDITIONS, 132 Saunders St., Fredericton, New Brunswick E3B 1N3 Canada. (506)454-8319. General Editor: Peter Thomas. Small press. Publishes hardcover and trade paperback originals. Averages 12 titles/year; receives 250 submissions annually. 33⅓% of books from first-time authors; 75-100% of books from unagented writers. Pays royalty on retail price. Small advances. Computer printout submissions acceptable. Reports in 3 weeks on queries; 2 months on mss. Book catalog free on request.

Imprints: Goose Lane Editions (nonfiction and fiction), Peter Thomas, general editor.

Nonfiction: Coffee table book and reference on Canadian and maritime provinces, history, photography, regional literature and linguistics. Submit sample chapters.

Recent Nonfiction Title: *Silver Harvest*, by F. Wentworth and R. Wilbur (social history).

Fiction: Experimental, mainstream, and "first" novel authors. "Erotica, confession, or dull or immature fiction is not required. SASE absolutely necessary for return of manuscript." Submit sample chapters or complete ms.

Recent Fiction Title: *Leaping Up, Sliding Away*, by Kent Thompson (short stories).

Poetry: Open to collections of poetry; modern/experimental preferable. Submit complete ms with SASE.

Recent Poetry Title: *Tiger in the Skull*, by Douglas Lockhead.

Tips: "No one will ever grow rich by publishing poetry. We have a much easier time marketing fiction and nonfiction but feel a cultural obligation as a small literary press."

‡*THE FILTER PRESS, Box 5, Palmer Lake CO 80133. (303)481-2523. President: G.L. Campbell. Imprints include Filter Press and Wild and Woolly West Books. Publishes hardcover and trade paperback originals and reprints. Averages 8 titles/year; receives 100 submissions/year. 90% of books from first-time authors. 100% of books from unagented writers. Subsidy pubishes 10% of books based on "the subject, readability and marketability of the work. We will not embarrass a writer (or ourselves) by doing a poorly written book." Pays 10% royalty on wholesale price. Publishes book an average of 10 months after acceptance. Simultaneous and photocopied submissions OK. Computer printout submissions OK; no dot-matrix. Reports in 1 month on queries. Book catalog and writer's guidelines for SASE.

Nonfiction: Cookbook, how-to, humor, illustrated book and reference. Subjects include Western Americana, art, cooking and foods, history, hobbies, photography, recreation and travel. "Our mix of reprints and new material on Western Americana is pretty well covered by material on hand. We probably will accept one or two books this year, but don't need them. There are far too many diaries of recent ancestors submitted to us. Usually these are only of local or family interest so we must reject. Most are not satisfactory for either subsidy or royalty printing." Query. Reviews artwork/photos as part of ms package.

Recent Nonfiction Title: *Mexican Recipe Shortcuts*, by Helen C. Duran.

FIREBRAND BOOKS, 141 The Commons, Ithaca NY 14850. (607)272-0000. Publisher: Nancy K. Bereano. Publishes hardcover and trade paperback originals and hardcover and trade paperback reprints. Averages 6-8 titles/year; receives 200-300 submissions annually. 50% of books from first-time authors; 75% of books from unagented writers. Pays 7-9% royalty on retail price, or makes outright purchase. Publishes book an average of 18 months after acceptance. Simultaneous and photocopied submissions OK "with notification." Computer printout submissions acceptable; prefers letter-quality to dot-matrix. Reports in 2 weeks on queries; 2 months on mss. Book catalog free on request.

Nonfiction: Criticism and essays. Subjects include feminism and lesbianism. Submit complete ms.
Recent Nonfiction Title: *Getting Home Alive*, by Aurora Levins Morales and Rosario Morales.
Fiction: Will consider all types of feminist and lesbian fiction.
Recent Fiction Title: *Tender Warriors*, by Rachel Guido deVries.
Recent Poetry Title: *Living as a Lesbian*, by Cheryl Clarke.
Tips: "Our audience includes feminists, lesbians, ethnic audiences, and other progressive people."

*FITZHENRY & WHITESIDE, LTD.,195 Allstate Parkway, Markham, Ontario L3R 4T8 Canada. (416)477-0030. Vice-President: Robert Read. Trade Editor: Helen Heller. Publishes hardcover and paperback originals and reprints. Royalty contract varies; advance negotiable. Publishes 50 titles/year, text and trade. Subsidy publishes (non-author) 5% of books. Photocopied submissions OK. Reports in 1-3 months. Enclose return postage.
Nonfiction: "Especially interested in topics of interest to Canadians, and by Canadians." Textbooks for elementary and secondary schools, also biography, business, history, health, fine arts. Submit outline and sample chapters. Length: open.
Recent Title: *Northrop Frye on Shakespeare*.

‡*FJORD PRESS, Box 16501, Seattle WA 98116. (206)625-9363. Publisher: Steve Murray. Small press. Publishes trade paperback originals. Averages 3-6 titles/year; receives 150 submissions/year. 80% of books from unagented writers. Subsidy publishes (non-author) 50% of books. Pays 2-12½% royalty on retail price. Small advance possible. Publishes book an average of 2 years after acceptance. Simultaneous submissions OK if so advised. Computer printout submissions OK; no dot-matrix. Reports in 3 weeks on queries; 3 months on submissions. Book catalog for #10 SASE.
Nonfiction: Biography. Subjects include European history, music (rock, R&B, blues), film & video, popular science. "We are looking for popular science books dealing with the cutting edge of new technologies." Query with synopsis and sample chapter.
Recent Nonfiction Title: *Evening Light*, by Stephan Hermlin (autobiography).
Fiction: Ethnic, mainstream, mystery (hardboiled; no British-style); science fiction (set on Earth only—in the Dick tradition); suspense (with international setting); and by women and Northwest writers. Needs "more women's novels." Will also consider poetry. Query with synopsis and sample chapter.
Recent Fiction Title: *Stolen Spring*, by Hans Scherfig (satire).
Recent Poetry Title: *The Dear Dance of Eros*, by Mary Mackey (erotic poetry).
Tips: "Our audience has been described as 'upscale'—people who want to read books of quality in any genre and are interested in what is happening in the rest of the world. We are moving into doing original American books, not only translations, though we will continue to consider queries from translators as well."

FLEET PRESS CORP., 160 5th Ave., New York NY 10010. (212)243-6100. Editor: Phoebe Scott. Publishes hardcover and paperback originals and reprints; receives 200 submissions annually. 10% of books from first-time authors; 25% of books from unagented writers. Royalty schedule and advance "varies." Publishes book an average of 15 months after acceptance. Computer printout submissions acceptable; no dot-matrix. Reports in 2 weeks. Free book catalog.
Nonfiction: History, biography, arts, religion, general nonfiction and sports. Length: 45,000 words. Publishes juveniles. Stresses social studies and minority subjects; for ages 8-15. Length: 25,000 words. Query with outline; no unsolicited mss. Reviews artwork/photos.

FLORA AND FAUNA PUBLICATIONS, Division of E.J. Brill Publishing Co., Suite 100, 4300 NW 23rd Ave., Gainesville FL 32606. (904)371-9858. Publisher: Ross H. Arnett, Jr. Book publisher/packager. Publishes hardcover and trade paperback originals. Entire firm publishes 350 annually; imprint averages 10-12 titles/year; receives 70 submissions annually. 50% of books from first-time authors; 100% of books from unagented writers. Average print order for a writer's first book is 500. Pays 10% royalty on list price; negotiable advance. Publishes book an average of 1 year after acceptance. Photocopied submissions OK. Query for electronic submissions. Computer printout submissions acceptable; prefers letter-quality to dot-matrix. Reports in 2 weeks on queries; 3 months on mss. Book catalog for #10 SASE.
Nonfiction: Reference, technical, textbook and directories. Subjects include plants and animals (for amateur and professional biologists), and natural history. Looking for "books dealing with kinds of plants and animals, new nature guide series underway. No nature stories or 'Oh My' nature books." Query with outline and 2 sample chapters. Reviews artwork/photos as part of ms package.

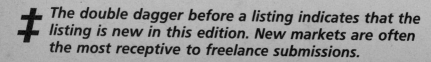

The double dagger before a listing indicates that the listing is new in this edition. New markets are often the most receptive to freelance submissions.

Recent Nonfiction Title: *Reptiles and Amphibians*, by R.L. Bartlett.
Tips: "Well-documented books, especially those that fit into one of our series, have the best chance of selling to our firm—biology, natural history, no garden books."

J. FLORES PUBLICATIONS, Box 14, Rosemead CA 91770. (818)287-2195. Editor: Eliezer Flores. Publishes trade paperback originals and reprints. Averages 10 titles/year. 99% of books from unagented writers. Pays 10-15% royalty on net sales; no advance. Publishes book an average of 8 months after acceptance. Simultaneous and photocopied submissions OK. Computer printout submissions acceptable; prefers letter-quality to dot-matrix. Reports in 1 month on queries; 6 weeks on mss. Book catalog and ms guidelines for 6x9 SAE with 39¢ postage.
Nonfiction: How-to, illustrated book and self-help. "We need original nonfiction manuscripts on military science, weaponry, current events, self-defense, survival, police science, the martial arts, guerrilla warfare and military history. How-to manuscripts are given priority." No pre-World War II material. Query with outline and 2-3 sample chapters. Reviews artwork/photos. "Photos are accepted as part of the manuscript package and are strongly encouraged."
Recent Nonfiction Title: *How to Train a Guard Dog*, by John Larson.
Tips: "Trends include illustrated how-to books on a specific subject. Be thoroughly informed on your subject and technically accurate."

FLORICANTO PRESS, INC., Box 4273, Berkeley CA 94704. (818)990-1886. Editor: Claire Splan. Publishes hardcover and trade paperback originals. Averages 5-10 titles/year; receives 50-100 submissions annually. 90% of books from first-time authors; 90% of books from unagented writers. Pays 5% royalty on net receipts. Publishes book an average of 9 months after acceptance. Simultaneous and photocopied submissions OK. Query for electronic submissions. Computer printout submissions acceptable; prefers letter-quality to dot-matrix. Reports in 2 months on queries; 3 months on mss. Book catalog and ms guidelines for 4½x6 SAE with 37¢ postage.
Nonfiction: Reference. "Our nonfiction book manuscript needs include reference works related to Hispanics in the United States—directories, bibliographies, studies." No submissions unrelated to Hispanics. Submit complete ms.
Recent Nonfiction Title: *El Libro de Calo: Dictionary of Chicano Slang*.
Fiction: Ethnic and Hispanic-related adult. Children's fiction. No submissions unrelated to Hispanics. Submit complete ms.
Recent Fiction Title: *Bring Me a Story*, by Sally Benforado (short story collection).
Tips: "Our audience includes professionals serving Hispanics, and the Hispanic community."

‡FOCAL PRESS, Subsidiary of Butterworth Publishers, 80 Montvale Ave., Stoneham MA 02180. (617)438-8464. Editor: Arlyn S. Powell, Jr. Imprint/publishes hardcover and trade paperback originals and reprints. Averages 20-25 titles/year; entire firm averages 40-50 titles/year; receives 150 submissions annually. 25% of books from first-time authors; 90+% of books from unagented writers. Pays 10-17% royalty on net receipts; offers $1,500 average advance. Publishes book an average of 1 year after acceptance. Simultaneous and photocopied submissions OK. Computer printout submissions OK; dot-matrix OK "if of decent quality." Reports in 3 months. Free book catalog; ms guidelines for SASE.
Nonfiction: How-to, reference, technical and textbooks on photography, communications, audiovisual, film and cinematography, and broadcasting. "We are looking, first, for undergraduate textbooks in filmmaking, broadcasting, photography and audio/visual (in order of importance). We are also looking for professional handbooks and reference books on the same subjects. High-level scientific/technical monographs are third priority. We generally do not publish collections of photographs or books composed primarily of photographs. Our books are text-oriented, with artwork serving to illustrate and expand on points in the text." Query preferred, or submit outline/synopsis and sample chapters or complete ms. Reviews artwork/photos as part of ms package.
Recent Nonfiction Title: *Live TV: An Inside Look at Directing and Producing*, by Tony Verna.

FODOR'S TRAVEL PUBLICATIONS, INC., Subsidiary of Random House, 201 E. 50th St., New York NY 10022. Publisher: Richard T. Scott. Publishes paperback travel guides. Averages 130+ titles/year.
Nonfiction: "We are the publishers of periodic travel guides—regions, countries, cities, and special tourist attractions. We do not solicit manuscripts on a royalty basis, but we are interested in travel writers and/or experts who will and can cover an area of the globe for Fodor's for a fee." Submit credentials and samples of work.
Recent Nonfiction Title: *Fodor's Florence & Venice*.

*FORDHAM UNIVERSITY PRESS, University Box L, Bronx NY 10458. (212)579-2320. Director: H.G. Fletcher. Averages 8 titles/year. Subsidy publishes 0-5% of books. Pays royalty on sales income. Publishes book an average of 2 years after acceptance. Computer printout submissions acceptable; no dot-matrix. Reports in 1 week. Free book catalog.

Nonfiction: Humanities. "We would like the writer to use the *MLA Style Sheet*, latest edition. We do not want dissertations or fiction material." Send written queries only; do not send unsolicited manuscripts. "We prefer abstract, description and examples."

Recent Nonfiction Title: *Irish Green & Union Blue: The Civil War Letters of Peter Welsh.*

FORMAN PUBLISHING, Suite 206, Brentwood Sq., 11661 San Vicente Blvd., Los Angeles CA 90049. President: Len Forman. Publishes hardcover and trade paperback. Averages 6 titles/year; receives 1,000 submissions/year. 100% of books from first-time authors. 90% of books from unagented writers. Pays 6-15% royalty. Simultaneous and photocopied submissions OK. Publishes book an average of 18 months after acceptance. Reports in 2 weeks on queries; 3 months on mss. Book catalog free for business size SASE.

Nonfiction: "Coffee table" book, cookbook, how-to and self-help. Subjects include art, business and economics, cooking and foods, health, nature and psychology. No diet (especially low cholesterol) or how-to books. Submit outline/synopsis and sample chapters. Reviews artwork/photos as part of ms package.

Recent Nonfiction Title: *Dr. Susan Larks PMS Book.*

‡FORTRESS PRESS, Subsidiary of Board of Publication, Lutheran Church in America. 2900 Queen Lane, Philadelphia PA 19129. (215)848-6800. Editorial Director: Harold W. Rast. Publishes hardcover and paperback originals. Averages 70-80 titles/year. Receives 1,000 submissions annually. 10% of books from first-time authors; 95% of books from unagented writers. Average print order for a writer's first book is 3,500. Pays 7½% royalty on paperbacks; 10% on hardcover; modest advance. Publishes book an average of 1 year after acceptance. Photocopied submissions OK. Computer printout submissions acceptable; prefers letter-quality to dot-matrix. Reports in 90 days. Free book catalog; ms guidelines for SAE and 50¢ postage.

Nonfiction: Publishes theology, religious and counseling books. Specializes in general religion for laity and clergy; academic texts and monographs in theology (all areas). Accepts nonfiction translations. Mss must follow Chicago *Manual of Style* (13th edition). Query. Accepts outline/synopsis and 2 sample chapters. No religious poetry or fiction.

Recent Nonfiction Title: *Jesus and Judaism*, by E.P. Sanders (early Christian origins, critical study of Jesus).

THE FRASER INSTITUTE, 626 Bute St., Vancouver, British Columbia V6E 3M1 Canada. (604)688-0221. Assistant Director: Sally Pipes. Publishes trade paperback originals. Averages 4-6 titles/year; receives 30 submissions annually. Pays honorarium. Publishes book an average of 6 months after acceptance. Simultaneous and photocopied submissions OK. Query for electronic submissions. Computer printout submissions acceptable; prefers letter-quality to dot-matrix. SAE and IRC. Reports in 6 weeks. Free book catalog; ms guidelines for SASE.

Nonfiction: Analysis, opinion, on economics, social issues and public policy. Subjects include business and economics, politics, religion and sociology. "We will consider submissions of high-quality work on economics, social issues, economics and religion, public policy, and government intervention in the economy." Submit complete ms.

Recent Nonfiction Title: *Tax Facts*, by Sally C. Pipes and Michael A. Walker (economics).

Tips: "Our books are read by well-educated consumers, concerned about their society and the way in which it is run and are adopted as required or recommended reading at colleges and universities in Canada, the U.S. and abroad. Our readers feel they have some power to improve society and view our books as a source of the information needed to take steps to change unproductive and inefficient ways of behavior into behavior which will benefit society. Recent trends to note in book publishing include affirmative action, banking, broadcasting, insurance, healthcare and religion. A writer has the best chance of selling us books on government, economics, finance, or social issues."

SAMUEL FRENCH, INC., 45 W. 25th St., New York NY 10010. (212)206-8990. Subsidiaries include Samuel French Ltd. (London); Samuel French (Canada) Ltd. (Toronto); Samuel French, Inc. (Hollywood); and Baker's Plays (Boston). Editor: Lawrence Harbison. Publishes paperback acting editions of plays. Averages 80-90 titles/year; receives 1,200 submissions annually, mostly from unagented playwrights. About 10% of publica-

 An asterisk preceding a listing indicates that subsidy publishing or co-publishing (where author pays part or all of publishing costs) is available. Firms whose subsidy programs comprise more than 50% of their total publishing activities are listed at the end of the Book Publishers section.

tions are from first-time authors; 20% from unagented writers. Pays 10% book royalty on retail price. Pays 90% stock production royalty; 80% amateur production royalty. Offers variable advance. Publishes book an average of 6 months after acceptance. Simultaneous and photocopied submissions OK. Computer printouts acceptable; no dot-matrix. Reports immediately on queries; from 6 weeks to 8 months on mss. Book catalog $1.25; ms guidelines $3.

Nonfiction: Acting editions of plays.

Tips: "Broadway and Off-Broadway hit plays, light comedies and mysteries have the best chance of selling to our firm. Our market is theater producers—both professional and amateur and actors. Read as many plays as possible of recent vintage to keep apprised of today's market; write small-cast plays with good female roles; and be one hundred percent professional in approaching publishers and producers (see guidelines)."

FRONT ROW EXPERIENCE, 540 Discovery Bay Blvd., Byron CA 94514. (415)634-5710. Editor: Frank Alexander. Publishes trade paperback originals. Averages 2-3 titles/year; receives 20 submissions annually. 90% of books from first-time authors; 100% of books from unagented writers. Average print order for a writer's first book is 500. Pays 5-10% royalty on net sales. Publishes book an average of 1 year after acceptance. Simultaneous and photocopied submissions OK. Computer printout submissions acceptable; no dot-matrix. "We return submissions but not without a SASE." Reports in 1 week on queries; 1 month on mss. Book catalog for 9½x4¼ SAE with 44¢ postage.

Nonfiction: Curriculum guides for movement education, special education, educational games, and perceptual-motor development. Especially needs innovative curriculum guides. Publishes for elementary physical education directors, elementary, junior high, and preschool teachers, YMCA activity directors, occupational therapists, physical therapists, curriculum directors, and childhood development professionals in general. Accepts nonfiction translations from any language in subject areas we specialize in. No mss outside of movement education, special education, educational games, and perceptual-motor development. Reviews artwork/photos as part of ms package. Query. Submit outline/synopsis and 3 sample chapters.

Recent Nonfiction Title: *Holiday Movement Activities*, by Jean Stangl (curriculum guide in movement education).

Tips: "We accept *only* movement education, special education, perceptual-motor development and educational games manuscripts. There is a greater chance of manuscript acceptance, if the author gives or participates in workshops, conventions, symposiums, seminars, etc., and would be willing to spread the word about her book and even sell copies herself."

‡FULCRUM, INC., #510, 350 Indiana St., Golden CO 80401. (303)277-1623. Contact: Hunter Holloway or Jay Staten. Publishes hardcover originals and reprints. Averages 12-16 titles/year; receives 100 submissions/year. 75% of books from first-time authors. 75% of books from unagented writers. Pays 8-12% royalty on wholesale or retail price based on discount; offers $3,000 average advance. Publishes book an average of 6 months after acceptance. Query for electronic submissions. Computer printout submissions OK; no dot-matrix. Reports in 1 month on queries; 6 weeks on mss. Book catalog for 8x10 SASE with 3 first class stamps; ms guidelines for SASE.

Nonfiction: Biography and self-help. Subjects include animals, business and economics, history, nature, philosophy, photography, politics, recreation, travel, natural resources and other issues. "We welcome submissions on nature/outdoor/environmental issues. We're interested in more self-help. No sports, cookbooks or religion." Query or submit outline/synopsis and sample chapters. Reviews artwork/photos as part of ms package.

Recent Nonfiction Title: *Hatteras Journal*, by Jan DeBlieu (nature narrative).

Fiction: Adventure, historical, western and nature. "We presently do not publish fiction, but would consider mss complimentary for our product line." Query or submit outline/synopsis and sample chapters.

Tips: "Our audience includes those interested in land, nature and the outdoors, as the foundation of America; also college students and graduates aware of what is vital and happening in our world. Issue focused books on natural resources have the best chance of selling to our firm."

GAMBLING TIMES, 1018 N. Cole, Hollywood CA 90038. (213)466-5261. Marketing Director: Lee Muir. Publishes hardcover and softcover. Averages 12 titles/year; receives 200-250 submissions annually. 5-10% of books from first-time authors; 99% of books from unagented writers. Pays 9-11% royalty on retail price for hardcover; 4-6% on softcover. Publishes book an average of 9 months after acceptance. Simultaneous and photocopied submissions OK. Computer printout submissions acceptable; no dot-matrix. Reports in 3 months. Ms guidelines for SASE.

Nonfiction: How-to. "Straight gambling material related to gambling systems, betting methods, etc. Also interested in political, economic and legal issues surrounding gambling inside and outside the US." Submit sample chapters. Reviews artwork/photos. Gambling-related books only.

Tips: "Technical books on gambling strategy, odds, etc., have the best chance of selling to our firm. (We have basic books on all areas of gambling.) You should play the game you write about. Don't invent strategies that are mathematically unsound."

GARBER COMMUNICATIONS, INC., (affiliates: Steinerbooks, Spiritual Fiction Publications, Spiritual Science Library, Rudolf Steiner Publications, Freedeeds Library, Biograf Publications), 5 Garber Hill Rd., Blauvelt NY 10913. (914)359-9292. Editor: Bernard J. Garber. Publishes hardcover and paperback originals and reprints. Does not accept unsolicited submissions. "We will refuse and return unsolicited submissions at the author's expense." Averages 15 titles/year; receives 250 submissions annually. 10% of books from first-time authors; 10% of books from unagented writers. Average print order for a writer's first book is 500-1,000 copies. Pays 5-7% royalty on retail price; offers average $500 advance. Publishes book an average of 1 year after acceptance. Will consider photocopied submissions.

Nonfiction: Spiritual sciences, occult, philosophical, metaphysical and ESP. These are for our Steiner Books division only. Serious nonfiction. Philosophy and Spiritual Sciences: Bernard J. Garber. Query only (with SASE or no response).

Fiction: Patricia Abrams, editor, the new genre called Spiritual Fiction Publications. "We are now looking for original manuscripts or rewrites of classics in modern terms." Query only with SASE.

GARDEN WAY PUBLISHING, Storey Communications, Inc., Schoolhouse Rd., Pownal VT 05261. (802)823-5811. Editor: Deborah Burns. Publishes hardcover and paperback originals. "We are looking at audio and video cassettes." Publishes 18 titles/year; receives 2,000 submissions annually. 50% of books from first-time authors; 90% of books from unagented writers. Average print order for a writer's first book is 7,500. Offers a flat fee arrangement varying with book's scope, or royalty, which usually pays author 8% of book's net price. Advances are negotiable, but usually range from $1,500 to $3,000. "We stress continued promotion of titles and sales over many years." Emphasizes direct mail sales and sales to specialty stores, plus sales to bookstores through Harper and Row. Publishes book 1 year after acceptance. Photocopied submissions OK. Computer printout submissions acceptable; no dot-matrix. Book catalog and ms guidelines for 9x12 SAE with 2 first class stamps.

Nonfiction: Books on gardening (both vegetable and ornamental), cooking, nutrition, house building and remodeling, animals, country living, and country business. Emphasis should be on how-to. Length requirements are flexible. "The writer should remember the reader will buy his book to learn to do something, so that all information to accomplish this must be given. We are publishing specifically for the person who is concerned about natural resources and a deteriorating life style and wants to do something about it." Query with outline and 2-3 sample chapters. Reviews artwork/photos as part of ms package.

Recent Nonfiction Title: *The Pleasure of Herbs*, by Phyllis V. Shaudys (month-by-month guide to growing, using and cooking with herbs).

Tips: "We look for comprehensive, authoritative manuscripts. Authors should look at our other books to see how theirs would suit our line, and tell us who they feel the audience for their book would be."

‡GAY SUNSHINE PRESS, Box 40397, San Francisco CA 94140. (415)824-3184. Editor: Winston Leyland. Publishes hardcover and trade paperback originals and trade paperback reprints. Averages 10 titles/year. Pays royalty or makes outright purchase. Photocopied submissions OK. Reports in 3 weeks on queries; 1 month on mss. Book catalog $1.

Nonfiction: How-to and gay lifestyle topics. "We're interested in innovative literary nonfiction which deals with gay lifestyles." No long personal accounts (e.g., "how I came out"), academic or overly formal titles. No books that are too specialized (e.g., homosexuality in the ancient world). Query. "After query is returned by us, submit outline/synopsis and sample chapters. All unsolicited mss are returned unopened."

Recent Nonfiction Title: *Calamus Lovers: Walt Whitman's Working Class Camerados*.

Fiction: Erotica, ethnic, experimental, historical, mystery, science fiction and gay fiction in translation. "Interested in well-written novels on gay themes; also short story collections. We have a high literary standard for fiction." Query. "After query is returned by us, submit outline/synopsis and sample chapters. All unsolicited mss are returned unopened."

‡*GENEALOGICAL PUBLISHING CO., INC., 1001 N. Calvert St., Baltimore MD 21202. (301)837-8271. Editor-in-Chief: Michael H. Tepper, Ph.D. Publishes hardcover originals and reprints. Subsidy publishes 10% of books. Averages 80 titles/year; receives 400 submissions annually. 50% of books from first-time authors; 100% of books from unagented writers. Average print order for a writer's first book is 2,000-3,000. Offers straight 10% royalty on retail price. Publishes book an average of 6 months after acceptance. Photocopied submissions OK. Computer printout submissions acceptable; no dot-matrix. Reports "immediately." Enclose SAE and return postage.

Nonfiction: Reference, genealogy, and immigration records: "Our requirements are unusual, so we usually treat each author and his subject in a way particularly appropriate to his special skills and subject matter. Guidelines are flexible, but it is expected that an author will consult with us in depth. Most, though not all, of our original publications are offset from camera-ready typescript. Since most genealogical reference works are compilations of vital records and similar data, tabular formats are common. We hope to receive more ms material covering vital records and ships' passenger lists. We want family history compendia, basic methodology in genealogy, heraldry, and immigration records." Prefers query first, but will look at outline and sample chapter or complete ms. Reviews artwork/photos as part of ms package.

GENERAL HALL, INC., 5 Talon Way, Dix Hills NY 11746. (516)243-0155. Publisher: Ravi Mehra. Small press. Publishes hardcover and trade paperback originals for the college market. Averages 5-6 titles/year; receives 100-300 submissions annually. 10% of books from first-time authors; 100% of books from unagented writers. Pays 10-15% royalty. Publishes book an average of 10 months after acceptance. Simultaneous and photocopied submissions OK. Computer printout submissions acceptable; no dot-matrix. Reports in 6 weeks. Book catalog for 5½x8½ SASE.
Nonfiction: Reference and textbook. Subjects include Americana, blacks, business and economics, politics, psychology and sociology. Submit complete ms. Reviews artwork/photos.
Recent Nonfiction Title: *Sociological Theory from Enlightenment to Present*, by Calvin J. Larson.

THE C.R. GIBSON COMPANY, 32 Knight St., Norwalk CT 06856. (203)847-4543. Senior Editor: Jayne Bowman. Publishes hardcover originals. Averages 25 titles/year; receives 230 submissions annually. Pays royalty or outright purchase. Publishes book an average of 18 months after acceptance. Simultaneous and photocopied submissions OK. Reports in 3 weeks on queries; 2 months on mss. Free book catalog.
Nonfiction: Juvenile and gift books. Subject includes religion/inspiration. Query or submit outline/synopsis and sample chapter. Reviews artwork/photos.
Tips: "Religious inspirational books or books suitable for special occasion gift-giving have the best chance of selling to our firm."

GIFTED EDUCATION PRESS, The Reading Tutorium, 10201 Yuma Ct., Box 1586, Manassas VA 22110. (703)369-5017. Publisher: Maurice D. Fisher. Small press. Publishes mass market paperback originals. Averages 5 titles/year; receives 50 submissions annually. 100% of books from first-time authors; 100% of books from unagented writers. Pays royalty of $1 per book. Publishes book an average of 4 months after acceptance. Simultaneous and photocopied submissions OK. Computer printout submissions acceptable; prefers letter-quality to dot-matrix. Reports in 1-2 months on queries; 3 months on mss. Book catalog and ms guidelines for #10 SAE with 2 first class stamps.
Nonfiction: How-to. Subjects include philosophy, psychology, education of the gifted; and how to teach children to read. "Need books on how to educate gifted children—both theory and practice. Also, we are searching for books on using computers with the gifted, and how to teach children with learning problems to read. Need rigorous books on procedures, methods, and specific curriculum for the gifted." Query with outline.
Recent Nonfiction Title: *Creative Ways to Improve Reading and Language Skills in Gifted Students*, by Win Wenger.
Tips: "If I were a writer trying to market a book today, I would develop a detailed outline based upon intensive study of my field of interest. Present creative ideas in a rigorous fashion. Be knowledgeable about and comfortable with ideas."

‡GLENBRIDGE PUBLISHING LTD., 1303 West Adams, Macomb IL 61455. (309)833-5704. Editor: James A. Keene. Publishes hardcover originals and reprints, and trade paperback originals. Publishes 6 titles/year. Pays 10% royalty. Publishes book an average of 1 year after acceptance. Simultaneous and photocopied submissions OK. Computer printout submissions OK; prefers letter-quality. Reports in 1 week on queries; 1 month on mss. Ms guidelines for SASE.
Nonfiction: Reference and textbook. Subjects include Americana, business and economics, history, music, philosophy, politics, psychology and sociology. "Academic and scholarly" looks desired. Query or submit outline/synopsis and sample chapters.
Recent Nonfiction Title: *Reminiscences of Mendelssohn*, by Eloise Poko (reprint).

‡GLENMARK PUBLISHING, 5041 Byrne Rd., Oregon WI 53575. (608)255-1812. Editor-in-Chief: Glenn Schaeffer. Publishes mass market paperback originals. Averages 8-12 titles/year; receives 100 submissions annually. 100% of books from first-time authors; 100% of books from unagented writers; buys mss outright for $1,000-5,000. Publishes book an average of 6 months after acceptance. Simultaneous and photocopied submissions OK. Computer printout submissions acceptable; no dot-matrix. Reports in 1 week.
Nonfiction: How-to and self-help. Subjects include business and economics, cooking and foods, health, hobbies, psychology, recreation, religion, travel, adventure, making money, sexuality, mysticism and many others. "We specialize in selling books and reports by mail. We are looking for exciting manuscripts of 500-50,000 words. The subject can be of any nature, just so it strikes a chord in some segment of the population." Query.
Recent Nonfiction Title: *The Best Things in Life Are Free*, by Mike Pearlman (how to get things free).
Fiction: "Although we haven't dealt with fiction, we do not preclude it."

‡*GLOBE PRESS BOOKS, Box 2045, Madison Sq. Station, New York NY 10159. (212)362-3720. Publisher: Joel Friedlander. Imprint includes Fourth Way Books. Publishes hardcover and trade paperback originals. Averages 4 titles/year; receives 12 submissions/year. 25% of books from first-time authors. 50% of books from unagented writers. Subsidy publishes (nonauthor) 20% of books. Pays royalty on retail price. Publishes book an average of 1 year after acceptance. Simultaneous submissions OK. Query for electronic submissions. Computer printout submissions OK; prefers letter-quality. Reports in 6 weeks. Book catalog for #10 SAE with 1 first class stamp.

Nonfiction: Self-help and esoteric psychology. Subjects include history, philosophy and psychology. "We want manuscripts on east/west psychology and esoteric thought. No economics, politics or how-to books." Query or submit outline/synopsis and sample chapters. Reviews artwork/photos as part of ms package.

Recent Nonfiction Title: *Body Types*, by Friedlander (esoteric psychology).

Tips: "Well written, well thought-out mss on esoteric approaches to psychology, art, literature and history are needed."

GOLD EAGLE BOOKS, Imprint of Worldwide Library, a division of Harlequin Books, 225 Duncan Mill Rd., Don Mills, Ontario M3B 3K9 Canada. (416)445-5860. Editorial Director: Randall Toye. Publishes mass market paperback originals and reprints. Averages 72 titles/year; receives 1,100 submissions annually. 20% of books from first-time authors; 25% of books from unagented writers. Offers negotiable royalty on retail price; offers average $5,000-10,000 advance. Publishes book an average of 1 year after acceptance. Photocopied submissions OK. Reports in 1 month on queries; 2 months on mss. Book catalog for 8½x11 SASE.

Fiction: Espionage, crime/suspense thriller, adventure and mystery. "The Gold Eagle list is expanding, and in 1988 we expect to publish a minimum of 24 espionage novels in addition to our program of action adventure series. We will also be adding mystery fiction to the list." Preferred length: a minimum of 120,000 words. Prefers complete ms; will accept synopsis and first 3 chapters.

Recent Fiction Title: *Foxcatcher*, by William H. Hallahan (espionage).

Tips: "We are an excellent market for well-written espionage and spy fiction."

GOLDEN BOOKS, Western Publishing Co., Inc., 850 3rd Ave., New York NY 10022. Publisher, Children's Books: Doris Duenewald. Averages 200 titles/year; receives 1,000 submissions annually. 10-15% of books from first-time authors; 50% of books from unagented writers. Pays royalty; buys some mss outright. Publishes book an average of 3 months after acceptance. Computer printout submissions acceptable; prefers letter-quality to dot-matrix.

Nonfiction: Adult nonfiction, limited to cookbooks and nature guides. Children's books, including picturebooks, concept books, novelty books, and information books. Query before submitting ms. Looks for "completeness, an indication that the author knows his subject and audience." Reviews artwork/photos.

Fiction: Children's picturebooks and young fiction. Query before submitting ms.

GOLDEN WEST BOOKS, Box 80250, San Marino CA 91108. (213)283-3446. Editor-in-Chief: Donald Duke. Managing Editor: Vernice Dagosta. Publishes hardcover and paperback originals. Receives 50 submissions annually. 50% of books from first-time authors; 100% of books from unagented writers. Pays 10% royalty contract; no advance. Publishes book an average of 3 months after acceptance. Simultaneous and photocopied submissions OK. Computer printout submissions acceptable; prefers letter-quality to dot-matrix. Reports in 1 month. Free book catalog.

Nonfiction: Publishes selected Western Americana and transportation Americana. Query or submit complete ms. "Illustrations and photographs will be examined if we like manuscript."

GOLDEN WEST PUBLISHERS, 4113 N. Longview, Phoenix AZ 85014. (602)265-4392. Editor: Hal Mitchell. Small press. Publishes trade paperback originals. Averages 4-5 titles/year; receives 400-500 submissions annually. 50% of books from first-time authors; 100% of books from unagented writers. Average print order for a writer's first book is 5,000. Pays 6-10% royalty on retail price or makes outright purchase of $500-2,500. No advance. Publishes book an average of 6 months after acceptance. Simultaneous and photocopied submissions OK. Query for electronic submissions. Computer printout submissions acceptable; no dot-matrix. Reports in 2 weeks on queries; 1 month on mss. Book catalog for business size SAE and 1 first class stamp.

Nonfiction: Cookbooks, books on the Southwest and West. Subjects include cooking and foods. Query or submit outline/synopsis and sample chapters. Prefers query letter first. Reviews artwork/photos as part of ms package.

Recent Title: *On the Arizona Road with Bill Leverton*, (people and places).

GOVERNMENT INSTITUTES, INC., Suite 24, 966 Hungerford Dr., Rockville MD 20850. (301)251-9250. Director, Publications Department: G. David Williams. Publishes hardcover and softcover originals. Averages 24 titles/year; receives 20 submissions annually. 50% of books from first-time authors; 100% of books from unagented writers. Pays variable royalty or fee. No advance. Publishes book an average of 4 months after acceptance. Simultaneous and photocopied submissions OK. Computer printout submissions acceptable; prefers letter-quality to dot-matrix. Reports in 1 month on queries; 2 months on mss. Book catalog and ms guidelines for #10 SAE.

Nonfiction: Reference and technical. Subjects include environmental law and energy. Needs professional-

level titles in environmental law and energy. Submit synopsis in narrative style and sample chapters. Reviews artwork/photos.
Recent Nonfiction Title: *Environmental Law Handbook, 9th Edition*, by J. Gordon Arbuckle, et al. (professional).

‡**GRAPEVINE PUBLICATIONS, INC.**, Box 118, Corvallis OR 97339. (503)754-0583. Editor: Chris Coffin. Publishes trade paperback originals. Averages 3-5 titles/year; receives 5-10 submissions/year. 50% of books from first-time authors. 100% of books from unagented writers. Pays 9-10% royalty on retail price. Offers variable advance. Publishes book an average of 6 months after acceptance. Simultaneous and photocopied submissions OK. Query for electronic submissions. Computer printout submissions OK; prefers letter-quality. Reports in 6 weeks on queries; 10 weeks on mss. Book catalog for 8½x11 SAE with 2 first class stamps.
Nonfiction: How-to, self-help, technical and textbook. Subjects include math, science, computers and calculators. "We are looking for books on calculators and computers that fit our style (i.e., friendly, understandable writing in no-jargon terms). We are also looking for textbooks written in similar style, but no dry, highly technical, jargon-riddled or dense books on technical topics." Submit outline and sample chapters. Reviews artwork/photos as part of ms package.
Recent Nonfiction Title: *The HP Business Consultant Training Guide*, by Chris Coffin and Ted Wadman.
Tips: "The writer should make sure no similar books exist. If other books on the topic do exist, the writer must make his/her book 100% more unique, easy to read, and full of wit. Common mistakes writers make are assuming their work is done once the manuscript is accepted, and omitting table of contents, index, illustrations and diagrams from their submissions."

GRAPHIC ARTS CENTER PUBLISHING CO., 3019 NW Yeon Ave., Box 10306, Portland OR 97210. (503)226-2402. General Manager and Editor: Douglas Pfeiffer. Publishes hardcover originals. Averages 3-6 titles/year. Makes outright purchase, averaging $3,000.
Nonfiction: "All titles are pictorials with text. Text usually runs separately from the pictorial treatment. Authors must be previously published and are selected to complement the pictorial essay." Query.

‡**GREAT NORTHWEST PUBLISHING AND DISTRIBUTING COMPANY, INC.**, Box 10-3902, Anchorage AK 99510-3902. (907)373-0121. President: Marvin H. Clark Jr. Publishes hardcover and trade paperback originals. Averages 3 titles/year; receives 22-25 submissions annually. 30% of books from first-time authors; 100% of books from unagented writers. Pays 10% royalty on retail price. Publishes book an average of 1 year after acceptance. Simultaneous and photocopied submissions OK. Query for electronic submissions. Computer printout submissions OK; no dot-matrix. Reports in 2 weeks on queries; 2 months on mss. Free book catalog.
Nonfiction: Biography and how to. Subjects include sports, Alaska and hunting. "Alaskana and hunting books by very knowledgeable hunters and residents of the Far North interest our firm." Query.
Recent Nonfiction Title: *Head Winds*, by Willy L. Warbelow.
Tips: "Pick a target audience first, subject second. Provide crisp, clear journalistic prose on desired subject matter."

GREAT OCEAN PUBLISHERS, 1823 N. Lincoln St., Arlington VA 22207. (703)525-0909. President: Mark Esterman. Publishes hardcover and trade paperback originals and hardcover reprints. Averages 3 titles/year; receives 350 submissions annually. 10% of books from first-time authors; 50% of books from unagented writers. Average print order for a writer's first book is 3,000-5,000. Pays 8-10% hardcover royalty; 6-8% paperback on retail price; occasionally offers advance. Publishes book an average of 1 year after acceptance. Simultaneous (if so indicated) and photocopied submissions OK. Computer printout submissions acceptable; prefers letter-quality to dot-matrix. Reports in 3 weeks.
Nonfiction: Biography, how-to, illustrated book, reference, self-help and technical. Subjects include art, business and economics, child care/development, health, history, music, philosophy, politics and religion. "Any subject is fine as long as it meets our standards of quality." Submit outline/synopsis and sample chapters. "SASE *must* be included with all material to be returned." Looks for "1) good writing, 2) clear evidence that manuscript is intended as a *book*, not a long collection of weakly organized small pieces, and 3) good organization—not to mention a worthwhile, interesting subject." Accepts nonfiction translations—query first. Reviews artwork/photos.
Recent Nonfiction Title: *Beethoven Remembered*.
Tips: "Nonfiction with a real theme and a mature knowledgeable point of view has the best chance of selling to Great Ocean. If you have to ask . . ."

GREEN HILL PUBLISHERS, INC., 722 Columbus St., Ottawa IL 61350. (815)434-7905. (Distributed by Kampmann & Co.). Publisher: Jameson G. Campaigne. Publishes hardcover, trade paper and mass market paperback originals. Publishes 10 titles/year. Pays 6-15% royalty. Advance averages $2,500. Simultaneous and "clean" photocopied submissions OK. Query for electronic submissions. Computer printout submissions acceptable; prefers letter-quality to dot-matrix. Reports in 2 months on queries; 4 months on mss. Book catalog for 6x9 SAE with 2 first class stamps.

Nonfiction: Biography (of major subjects), business and economics, history, politics, Chicago themes.

Recent Nonfiction Title: *Constitutional Journal*, by Jeffrey St. John (current events).

Fiction: The Frontier Library—American, "mountain man, early fur trade, and frontiersmen stories." Query or submit complete ms.

Recent Fiction Title: *Buckskin Brigades*, by L. Ron Hubbard (Frontier Library).

Tips: "Concentrate on literacy, historical accuracy, vocabulary, grammar, basic story telling and narrative skills. Don't submit poor pitch letters stressing word counts and other irrelevancies."

GREEN TIGER PRESS, 1061 India St., San Diego CA 92101. (619)238-1001. Editor: Harold Darling. Imprints include Star and Elephant (nonfiction and fiction). Publishes hardcover and trade paperback originals and reprints. Averages 12 titles/year; receives 2,500+ submissions annually. 5% of books from first-time authors; 80% of books from unagented writers. Pays 10% maximum royalty on retail price. Publishes book an average of 1 year after acceptance. Simultaneous and photocopied submissions OK. Computer printout submissions acceptable; prefers letter-quality to dot-matrix. Reports in 4 weeks on queries; 4 months on mss. Guidelines for SASE.

Tips: "We are publishers of children's picture books. We look for manuscripts containing a romantic, visionary or imaginative quality, often with a mythic feeling where fantasy and reality co-exist. Since we are a visually-oriented house, we look for manuscripts whose texts readily conjure up visual imagery."

*WARREN H. GREEN, INC., 8356 Olive Blvd., St. Louis MO 63132. Editor: Warren H. Green. Imprint includes Fireside Books. Publishes hardcover originals. Offers "10-20% sliding scale of royalties based on quantity distributed. All books are short run, highly specialized, with no advance." Subsidy publishes about 1% of books, e.g., "books in philosophy and those with many color plates." Averages 30 titles/year; receives 200+ submissions annually. 15% of books from first-time authors; 100% of books from unagented writers. "37% of total marketing is overseas." Will send a catalog to a writer on request. Publishes book an average of 10 months after acceptance. Will consider simultaneous and photocopied submissions. Computer printout submissions acceptable; no dot-matrix. Query or submit outline and sample chapters. "Publisher requires 300- to 500-word statement of scope, plan, and purpose of book, together with curriculum vitae of author." Reports in 60-90 days.

Nonfiction: Medical and scientific. "Specialty monographs for practicing physicians and medical researchers. Books of 160 pages upward. Illustrated as required by subject. Medical books are non-textbook type, usually specialties within specialties, and no general books for a given specialty. For example, separate books on each facet of radiology, and not one complete book on radiology. Authors must be authorities in their chosen fields and accepted as such by their peers. Books should be designed for all doctors in English speaking world engaged in full or part time activity discussed in book. We would like to increase publications in the fields of radiology, anesthesiology, pathology, psychiatry, surgery and orthopedic surgery, obstetrics and gynecology, and speech and hearing." Also interested in books on health, philosophy, psychology and sociology. Reviews artwork/photos as part of ms package.

‡THE STEPHEN GREENE PRESS/LEWIS PUBLISHING, 15 Muzzey St., Lexington MA 02173. (802)257-7757. Editorial Director: Thomas Begner. Publishes hardcover and paperback originals, and hardcover and paperback reprints. Averages 30 titles/year. Royalty "variable; advances are small." Send contact sheet or prints to illustrate ms. Photocopied submissions OK. Reports in 3 months.

Nonfiction: How-to (self-reliance); nature and environment; recreation; self-help; sports (outdoor and horse); popular technology; popular psychology and social science; and regional (New England). "We see our audience as mainly college-educated men and women, 30 and over. They are regular book buyers and readers. They probably have pronounced interests, hobby or professional, in subjects that our books treat. Authors can assess their needs by looking critically at what we have published."

‡GREENHAVEN PRESS, INC., 577 Shoreview Park Rd., St. Paul MN 55126. (612)482-1582. Subsidiaries include New Day. Senior Editor: Terry O'Neill. Publishes hard and softcover educational supplementary materials and (nontrade) juvenile nonfiction. Averages 20-30 titles/year; receives 36 submissions/year. 50% of juvenile books from first-time authors; 100% of juvenile books from unagented writers. Makes outright purchase for $1,000-2,000. Publishes book an average of 1 year after acceptance. Simultaneous "if specified" and clear photocopied submissions OK. Computer printout submissions OK; prefers letter-quality. Book catalog for 9x12 SAE with 39¢ postage.

Nonfiction: Biography, illustrated book, juvenile, reference and textbook. Subjects include animals, business and economics, history, nature, philosophy, politics, psychology, religion and sociology. "We produce book series for young people grades 3-5 and 6-8. Each series has specific requirements. Potential writers should familiarize themselves with our catalog and senior high material. No unsolicited manuscripts." Query or submit outline/synopsis and sample chapters. Reviews artwork/photos as part of manuscript package.

Recent Nonfiction Title: *Terrorism: Opposing Viewpoints*, edited by Bonnie Szumski (anthology).

GREENLEAF CLASSICS, INC., Box 20194, San Diego CA 92120. Editor: Meredith Gorman. Publishes paperback originals. Publishes 450 titles/year; receives 1,000-2,000 submissions annually. 15% of books from first-time authors; 90% of books from unagented writers. Pays by outright purchase about 4 months after acceptance. Computer printout submissions acceptable; no dot-matrix. Reports in 1-2 months. "No manuscripts will be returned unless accompanied by return postage." Ms guidelines for SASE.
Fiction: Specializes in adult erotic novels. "All stories must have a sexual theme. They must be contemporary novels dealing with the serious problems of everyday people. All plots are structured so that characters must get involved in erotic situations. Write from the female viewpoint (third person). Request our guidelines before beginning any project for us." Preferred length: 35,000 words. Send complete ms (preferred); or at least 3 sample chapters.

‡GRYPHON HOUSE, INC., 3706 Otis St., Box 275, Mt. Rainier MD 20712. (301)779-6200. President Editor: Larry Rood. Publishes trade paperback originals. Averages 3 titles/year; receives 250-400 submissions annually. 80% of books from first-time authors; 100% of books from unagented writers. Average print order for a writer's first book is 3,000-4,000. Pays 10-12½% royalty on retail price; offers average $300 advance. Photocopied submissions OK. Computer printout submissions OK; prefers letter-quality to dot-matrix. Reports in 2 weeks. Book catalog for 9x12 SAE and 3 first class stamps. Writer's guidelines for SASE.
Nonfiction: How-to and creative educational activities for teachers to do with preschool children, ages 1-5. "We are specialty publishers and do not consider anything at present out of the above category. Our audience includes teachers in preschools, nursery schools, day care centers and kindergartens." Query or submit outline/synopsis and 1 sample chapter. Looks for "brevity, clarity and an explanation of how this book is unique."

*GUERNICA EDITIONS, Box 633, Station N.D.G., Montreal, Quebec H4A 3R1 Canada. (514)481-5569. President/Editor: Antonio D'Alfonso. Publishes hardcover and trade paperback originals, hardcover and trade paperback reprints and software. Averages 10 titles/year; receives 1,000 submissions annually. 5% of books from first-time authors. Average print order for a writer's first book is 750-1,000. Subsidy publishes (non-author) 50% of titles. "Subsidy in Canada is received only when the author is established, Canadian-born and active in the country's cultural world. The others we subsidize ourselves." Pays 3-10% royalty on retail price. Makes outright purchase of $200-5,000. Offers 10¢/word advance for translators. Photocopied submissions OK. IRCs required. "American stamps are of no use to us in Canada." Reports in 1 month on queries; 6 weeks on mss. Free book catalog.
Nonfiction: Biography, humor, juvenile, reference and textbook. Subjects include art, history, music, philosophy, politics, psychology, recreation, religion and Canadiana.
Fiction: Ethnic, historical, mystery. "We wish to open up into the fiction world. No country is a country without its fiction writers. Canada is growing some fine fiction writers. We'd like to read you. No first novels." Query.
Poetry: "We wish to have writers in translation. Any writer who has translated Italian poetry is welcomed. Full books only. Not single poems by different authors, unless modern, and used as an anthology. First books will have no place in the next couple of years." Submit samples.
Recent Poetry Title: *French Poets of Today* (anthology).

GUIDANCE CENTRE, University of Toronto, 10 Alcorn Ave., Toronto, Ontario M4V 2Z8 Canada. (416)978-3210. Editorial Director: L. Miller. Coordinating Editor: Gethin James. Publishes hardcover and paperback originals. Averages 25 titles/year; receives 50 submissions annually. 5% of books from first-time authors; 5% of books from unagented writers. Pays in royalties. Publishes book an average of 6 months after acceptance. Query for electronic submissions. Computer printout submissions acceptable; prefers letter-quality to dot-matrix. Reports in 1 month. Submissions returned "only if Canadian postage is sent." Free book catalog.
Nonfiction: "The Guidance Centre is interested in publications related to career planning and guidance and in measurement and evaluation. Also general education. No manuscripts which have confined their references and illustrations to United States material." Submit complete ms. Consult Chicago *Manual of Style*.
Recent Nonfiction Title: *Managing Common Classroom Problems*, by Julienne Barber and John Allan.

*GULF PUBLISHING CO., Book Division, Box 2608, Houston TX 77001. (713)529-4301. Vice President: C.A. Umbach Jr. Editor-in-Chief: William J. Lowe. Imprints include Gulf (sci-tech and business/management) and Lone Star Books (regional Texas books). Publishes hardcover and large format paperback originals and software. Averages 40-50 titles/year; receives 300 submissions annually. 60% of books from first-time authors; 95% of books from unagented writers. Subsidy publishes 5% of books. Pays 10% royalty on net income; offers $300-2,000 advance. Publishes book an average of 10 months after acceptance. Simultaneous and photocopied submissions OK. Computer printout submissions OK; no dot-matrix. Reports in 2 months. Free book catalog; ms guidelines for SASE.
Nonfiction: Popular science, business, management, reference, regional trade, scientific and technical. Sub-

mit outline/synopsis and 1-2 sample chapters. Reviews artwork/photos as part of ms package.

Recent Nonfiction Title: *Managing Cultural Differences*, by Harris and Moran (management and intercultural awareness).

Tips: "Common mistakes writers make include calling first, not having a marketing plan of their own, and not matching publishers with their subject. Tell us the market, and how it can be reached at *reasonable* cost."

H.P. BOOKS, Subsidiary of Knight-Ridder Newspapers, Box 5367, Tucson AZ 85703. Publisher: Rick Bailey. Publishes hardcover and paperback originals. Imprints include The Body Press and Knight-Ridder Press. Entire firm averages 75-80 titles/year; H.P. Books averages 55 titles/year. Pays royalty on wholesale price; advance negotiable. Publishes ms an average of 9 months after acceptance. Simultaneous and photocopied submissions OK. "We delight in disk submissions but must be 8" diskette compatible with Wang VS 100 system or transfer directly to computer via telephone modem." Reports in 1 month. Book catalog for 8½x11 SAE.

Nonfiction: Specializes in how-to and leisure-time books in several fields, most photo-illustrated. Cookbooks, cooking and foods, gardening, hobbies, how-to, leisure activities, photography, automotive, health, sports, family medicine, recreation, self-help, computer and technical books. Most books are 160 pages minimum; "word count varies with the format." Query only and state number and type of illustrations available. Submit comprehensive outline and 1 sample chapter. "We *require* author to supply photos and illustrations to our specifications."

Recent Nonfiction Title: *Healthy High-Fiber Cooking*, by Jeanette P. Egan.

ALEXANDER HAMILTON INSTITUTE, 1633 Broadway, New York NY 10019. (212)397-3580. Senior Editor: Brian L.P. Zevnik. Publishes 3-ring binder and paperback originals. Averages 18 titles/year; receives 200+ submissions annually. 40% of books from first-time authors; 90% of books from unagented writers. "We pay advance against negotiated royalty or straight fee (no royalty)." Offers average $2,000 advance. Publishes book an average of 10 months after acceptance. Simultaneous submissions OK. Computer printout submissions acceptable; no dot-matrix. Reports in 1 month on queries; 2 months on mss.

Nonfiction: How-to, reference and skills building. Subjects include business and management. "Since we publish only a specific type of book, we have very select needs. We want only 'how-to' books in the management area aimed at an overseas executive audience. We do *not* want traditional textbooks." Query or submit outline/synopsis and sample chapters. "We prefer outlines, chapter titles and three paragraphs on contents of each chapter, including lists, graphics, charts and sample cases."

Recent Nonfiction Title: *Profitable Purchasing Strategies*.

Tips: "We sell exclusively by direct mail to managers and executives around the world. A writer must know his/her field and be able to communicate practical systems and programs."

HANLEY & BELFUS, INC., 210 S. 13th St., Philadelphia PA 19107. (215)546-4995. President: John J. Hanley. Executive Vice President: Linda C. Belfus. Publishes hardcover and trade paperback originals. Averages 10 titles/year; receives 200 submissions annually. 50% of books from first-time authors; 100% of books from unagented writers. Pays 10% royalty on retail price. Publishes book an average of 9 months after acceptance. Simultaneous and photocopied submissions OK. Query for electronic submissions. Computer printout submissions acceptable; prefers letter-quality to dot-matrix. Reports in 1 week on queries; 2 weeks on mss. Free ms guidelines.

Nonfiction: Reference, textbook, medical manuals and atlases. Subjects include health. Especially looking for textbooks for medical students, nursing students and allied health students, and selected reference books for practicing doctors. Query or submit outline/synopsis and sample chapters. Reviews artwork/photos.

HARBOR HOUSE PUBLISHERS, 221 Water St., Boyne City MI 49712. (616)582-2814. Chairman: Jacques LesStrang. Publishes hardcover and trade paperback originals and hardcover and trade paperback reprints. Averages 20 titles/year. Pays 10-15% royalty on wholesale price. Advance varies. Photocopied submissions OK. Reports in 1 month. Book catalog free on request.

Nonfiction: "Coffee table" book, illustrated book, and maritime. Subjects include business and economics, cooking and foods, and Great Lakes subjects. "Our manuscript needs include pictorials of all kinds, books conceived within the Great Lakes region and maritime subjects." Submit outline/synopsis and sample chapters or complete ms.

‡**HARCOURT BRACE JOVANOVICH**, Trade Division, 1250 6th Ave., San Diego CA 92101. (619)231-6616. Editor-in-Chief: Rubin Pfeffer. Imprints include Harvest/HBJ Paperbacks (adult), Gulliver Books (children) and Voyager/HBJ Paperbacks (children). Publishes hardcover and trade paperback originals and trade paperback reprints. Averages 200 titles/year; receives 2,000 submissions/year. 5% of books from first-time authors. 5% of books from unagented writers. Pays 6-15% royalty on retail price; offers $5,000 average advance. Publishes book an average of 1 year after acceptance. Simultaneous and photocopied submissions OK. Computer printout submissions OK; prefers letter-quality. Reports in 3 weeks on queries; 6 weeks on submissions.

Book catalog and guidelines for 8x10 SASE.

Nonfiction: Biography, cookbook, illustrated book, juvenile, reference, self-help and technical. Subjects include Americana, business and economics, health, history, nature, philosophy, politics, psychology, religion, sociology, sports and travel. "We're looking for extraordinary historical accounts, biographies and autobiographies, books on current affairs and reference books." Submit outline/synopsis and sample chapters. Reviews artwork/photos as part of ms package.

Recent Nonfiction Title: *How I Grew*, by Mary McCarthy (autobiography).

Fiction: Ethnic, fantasy, historical, mystery, science fiction and suspense. "Quality fiction; no formula or romance." Submit outline/synopsis and sample chapters.

Recent Fiction Title: *Show Me a Hero*, by Alfred Coppel (novel).

‡**MAX HARDY—PUBLISHER**, Box 28219, Las Vegas NV 89126-2219. (702)368-0379. Owner: Max Hardy. Publishes trade paperback originals. Averages 5 titles/year; receives few submissions/year. Small percentage of books from first-time authors. 100% of books from unagented writers. Pays 10% royalty on retail price. Publishes book an average of 8 months after acceptance. Query for electronic submissions. Computer printout submissions OK; prefers letter-quality. Reports in 2 weeks. Book catalog free on request.

Nonfiction: Textbooks on bridge. Especially needs "quality educational material preferably from known bridge authorities. No other topics." Query.

Recent Nonfiction Title: *Better Bidding With Bergen*, by Marty Bergen.

Fiction: Bridge fiction only. Query.

Recent Fiction Title: *The Jake of Diamonds*, by Don Von Elsner (bridge novel).

HARLEQUIN BOOKS, Subsidiary of Torstar, 225 Duncan Mill Rd., Don Mills, Ontario M3B 3K9 Canada. (416)445-5860. Subsidiaries include Worldwide Library and Silhouette Books, editorial offices, 300 E. 42nd St., New York NY 10017. Vice President and Editorial Director: Star Helmer. Publishes mass market paperback originals. Averages 675 titles/year; receives 10,000 submissions annually. 10% of books from first-time authors; 20% of books from unagented writers. Pays 6-10% "escalating" royalty on retail price. Offers advance. Publishes book an average of 1 year after acceptance. Photocopied submissions OK. Computer printout submissions acceptable; prefers letter-quality to dot-matrix. Reports in 2 weeks on queries; 2 months on mss. Free ms guidelines.

Imprints: Harlequin Books of North America, 6 fiction series. Harlequin Romance. Presents. American Romance. Superromance. Intrigue and Temptation. Silhouette Books, 5 fiction series. Romance. Desire. Special Edition. Intimate Moments.

Fiction: Gothic, Regency, intrigue, traditional, short contemporary sensuals, long contemporary romances. "We're always looking for new authors." Query.

Tips: "Harlequin readership comprises a wide variety of ages, backgrounds, income and education levels. The audience is predominantly female. Because of the high competition in women's fiction, readers are becoming very discriminating. They look for a quality read. If I were a writer trying to market a book today, I would read as many recent romance books as possible in all series to get a feel for the scope, new trends, acceptable levels of sensuality, etc."

HARPER & ROW JUNIOR BOOKS GROUP, 10 E. 53rd St., New York NY 10022. (212)207-7044. Imprints include: Harper & Row Junior Books, including Charlotte Zolotow Books; T.Y. Crowell; Lippincott and Harper Carousel Books; and Trophy Junior Books. Publisher: Elizabeth Gordon. Editors: Charlotte Zolotow, Nina Ignatowizz, Marilyn Kriney, Barbara Fenton, Laura Geringer, Robert O. Warren, Antonia Q. Markiet and Pamela D. Hastings. Publishes hardcover originals and paperback reprints—board books, picture books, easy-to-read, middle-grade, teenage, and young adult novels. Published 72 titles in 1987 (Harper, cloth); 89 titles (Harper-Trophy, paperback); 24 titles (Crowell); 10 titles (Lippincott). Query; submit complete ms; submit outline/synopsis and sample chapters; or submit through agent. Photocopied submissions OK. Computer printout submissions acceptable. "Please identify simultaneous submissions." Reports in 2-3 months. Pays average royalty of 10%. Royalties on picture books shared with illustrators. Offers advance. Book catalog for self-addressed label. Writer's guidelines for SASE.

Nonfiction: Science, history, social studies, and sports. Reviews artwork/photos as part of ms package.

Fiction: Fantasy, animal, spy/adventure, science fiction, problem novels, contemporary. Needs picture books, easy-to-read, middle-grade, teenage and young adult novels.

Recent Titles: *After the Dancing Days*, by Margaret I. Rostkowski (Harper); *Street Family*, by Adrienne Jones (Charlotte Zolotow Book); *Wake Up, Vladimir*, by Felicia Bond (Crowell); *Someone to Love Me*, by Jeannette Everly (Lippincott).

Tips: "Write from your own experience and the child you once were. Read widely in the field of adult and children's literature. Realize that writing for children is a difficult challenge."

HARPER & ROW PUBLISHERS, INC., 10 E. 53rd St., New York NY 10022. (212)207-7000. Imprints include Barnes & Noble; Harper & Row-San Francisco (religious books only); Perennial Library; and Torchbooks. Managing Editor: Coral Tysliava. Publishes hardcover and paperback originals, and paperback reprints. Publishes 300 titles/year. Pays standard royalties; advances negotiable. No unsolicited queries or mss. Reports on solicited queries in 6 weeks.

Nonfiction: Americana, animals, art, biography, business/economics, cookbooks, health, history, how-to, humor, music, nature, philosophy, politics, psychology, reference, religion, science, self-help, sociology, sports and travel.

Fiction: Adventure, fantasy, gothic, historical, mystery, science fiction, suspense, western and literary. "We look for a strong story line and exceptional literary talent."

Tips: "Strongly suggest that you go through a literary agent before submitting any ms. Any unsolicited query or ms will be returned unread."

‡**HARPER JUNIOR BOOKS GROUP, WEST COAST**, Division of Harper & Row Publishers, Box 6549, San Pedro CA 90734. (213)547-4292. Executive Editor, West Coast: Linda Zuckerman. Publishes hardcover originals. Averages 15 titles/year; receives 800 submissions annually. 10% of books from first-time authors. 40% of books from unagented writers. Pays royalty on invoice price. Advance negotiable. Publishes book an average of 18 months after acceptance. Simultaneous and photocopied submissions OK. Computer printout submissions OK; no dot-matrix. Reports in 3 months. Book catalog and guidelines for 10x13 SAE with 69¢ postage.

Nonfiction: Juvenile. Query or submit complete ms. Reviews artwork/photos as part of ms package.

Recent Nonfiction Title: *Deadline/From News to Newspapers*, by Gail Gibbons (picture book).

Fiction: Juvenile. Submit complete ms only. No queries.

Recent Fiction Title: *After the Dancing Days*, by Margaret Rostkowski.

Poetry: No Dr. Seuss-type verse. Submit complete ms.

Recent Poetry Title: *Pass the Poetry, Please!*, by Lee Bennett Hopkins (poetry collections).

Tips: "Our audience is categorized into children, ages 3-6; 4-8; 8-12; 10-14; 12-16. Read contemporary children's books at all age levels; try to take some writing or children's literature courses; talk to children's librarians and booksellers in independent bookstores; read *Horn Book*, *Booklist*, *School Library Journal* and *Publishers Weekly*; take courses in book illustration and design.

HARROW AND HESTON, Stuyvesant Plaza, Box 3934, Albany NY 12203. (518)442-5223. Editor-in-Chief: Graeme Newman. Small press. Publishes hardcover and trade paperback originals and paperback reprints. Averages 4 titles/year; receives 10-20 submissions annually. 80% of books from first-time authors; 100% of books from unagented writers. Pays 10% royalty on wholesale price. Publishes book an average of 3 months after acceptance. Simultaneous and photocopied submissions OK. Query for electronic submissions. Computer printout submissions acceptable. Reports in 2 months on queries; 6 months on mss. Ms guidelines for SASE.

Nonfiction: Textbooks on sociology and criminal justices. Query.

Recent Nonfiction Title: *Delinquency and Identity*, by Jim Sheu (delinquency in Chinatown).

Tips: "Submissions must be clearly written with no jargon, and directed to upper undergraduate or graduate criminal justice students, on central criminal justice topics."

THE HARVARD COMMON PRESS, 535 Albany St., Boston MA 02118. (617)423-5803. President: Bruce P. Shaw. Publishes hardcover and trade paperback originals and reprints. Averages 6 titles/year; receives "thousands" of submissions annually. 75% of books from first-time authors; 75% of books from unagented writers. Average print order for a writer's first book is 7,500. Pays royalty; offers average $1,000 advance. Publishes book an average of 9 months after acceptance. Simultaneous and photocopied submissions OK. Computer printout submissions acceptable; no dot-matrix. Reports in 1 month. Book catalog for 9x11½ SAE and 56¢ postage; ms guidelines for SASE.

Nonfiction: Travel, cookbook, how-to, reference and self-help. Subjects include Americana, business, cooking and foods, and travel. "We want strong, practical books that help people gain control over a particular area of their lives, whether it's family matters, business or financial matters, health, careers, food or travel. An increasing percentage of our list is made up of books about travel and travel guides; in this area we are looking for authors who are well traveled, and who can offer a different approach to the series guidebooks. We are open to good nonfiction proposals that show evidence of strong organization and writing, and clearly demonstrate a need in the marketplace. First-time authors are welcome." Accepts nonfiction translations. Submit outline/synopsis and 1-3 sample chapters. Reviews artwork/photos.

Recent Nonfiction Title: *Paradores of Spain/Ponsadas of Portgual*, by Sam and Jane Ballard (travel).

*****HARVARD UNIVERSITY PRESS**, 79 Garden St., Cambridge MA 02138. (617)495-2600. Director: Arthur J. Rosenthal. Editor-in-Chief: Maud Wilcox. Publishes hardcover and paperback originals and reprints. Publishes 120 titles/year. Subsidy publishes 3% of books; 1% by government subsidy, 2% from other organizations. Publishes ms an average of 1 year after acceptance. Query for electronic submissions. Computer printout submissions acceptable; no dot-matrix. Book catalog and ms guidelines for 9x12 SAE with $1.75 postage.

Nonfiction: "We publish only scholarly nonfiction." No fiction. Query.

HARVEST HOUSE PUBLISHERS, 1075 Arrowsmith, Eugene OR 97402. (503)343-0123. Managing Editor: Eileen L. Mason. Manuscript Coordinator: Nancy Alson. Publishes hardcover, trade paperback and mass market originals and reprints. Averages 55-60 titles/year; receives 1,200+ submissions annually. 10% of books from first-time authors; 90% of books from unagented writers. Pays 14-18% royalty on wholesale price. Publishes book an average of 1 year after acceptance. Simultaneous and photocopied submissions OK. Computer printout submissions acceptable; prefers letter-quality to dot-matrix. Reports in 10 weeks. Book catalog for 8½x11 SAE with 2 first class stamps; manuscript guidelines for SASE.
Nonfiction: Biography, how-to, illustrated book, juvenile, reference, self-help, textbook and gift books on Evangelical Christian religion. No cookbooks, theses, dissertations or music.
Fiction: Historical, mystery and religious. No romances or short stories. Query or submit outline/synopsis and sample chapters.
Tips: Audience is women ages 25-40 and high school youth—evangelical Christians of all denominations.

‡*HAWKES PUBLISHING, INC.**, 3775 S. 5th W., Salt Lake City UT 84115. (801)262-5555. President: John Hawkes. Publishes hardcover and trade paperback originals. Averages 24 titles/year; receives 200 submissions annually. 70% of books from first-time authors; 90% of books from unagented writers. Average print order for a writer's first book is 2,000. Subsidy publishes 25-50% of books/year based on "how promising they are." Pays varying royalty of 10% on retail price to 10% on wholesale; no advance. Publishes book an average of 6 months after acceptance. Photocopied submissions OK. Computer printout submissions acceptable; prefers letter-quality to dot-matrix. Reports in 1 month on queries; 3 months on mss. Free book catalog.
Nonfiction: Cookbook, how-to and self-help. Subjects include cooking and foods, health, history, hobbies and psychology. Query or submit outline/synopsis and sample chapters. Reviews artwork/photos.

HAZELDEN FOUNDATION, Dept. of Educational Materials, Imprint of Harper & Row, Box 176, Center City MN 55012. (612)257-4010. Managing Editor: Linda Peterson. Publishes trade paperback originals and pamphlets. Averages 100 titles/year. Pays 7-9% royalty on retail price; buys some mss outright; offers $150-300+ advance. Publishes ms an average of 10 months after acceptance. Simultaneous and photocopied submissions OK. Computer printout submissions acceptable. "We immediately acknowledge receipt of ms. A decision is usually made within 2 months." Ms guidelines for SAE.
Nonfiction: Reference, self-help, psychology, sociology and addictions. "We are seeking manuscripts of pamphlet or booklet length. The subject matter, ideally, will center around alcoholism, drug abuse or other addictions. The focus would be on the prevention, recovery from, or understanding of an addiction or chronic illness." Publishes for people recovering from an addiction and those close to them; people seeking information about addiction or chronic illness; and professionals who help such people. No personal stories or poetry. Submit detailed outline, introduction and 2 sample chapters.
Recent Nonfiction Title: *Codependent No More*, by Melodie Beattie.
Tips: "Common mistakes writers make include not doing their homework; i.e., they do not thoroughly investigate existing works on their topic and are unaware that they have reinvented the wheel. They do not investigate the publisher's niche and submit totally inappropriate proposals."

HEALTH PROFESSION DIVISION, McGraw-Hill Book Co., 1221 Avenue of the Americas, New York NY 10020. General Manager: Thomas Kothman. Publishes 40 titles/year. Pays on royalty basis. Free book catalog and ms guidelines.
Nonfiction: Textbooks, major reference books and continuing education materials in the field of medicine. Submit outline and synopsis.
Recent Nonfiction Title: *Harrison's Principles of Internal Medicine*, by Braunwald, et al.

*HEART OF THE LAKES PUBLISHING**, 2989 Lodi Rd., Interlaken NY 14847-0299. (607)532-4997. Imprints include Empire State Books. Contact: Walter Steesy. Publishes hardcover and trade paperback originals and hardcover and trade paperback reprints. Averages 20-25 titles/year; receives 15-20 submissions annually. 100% of books from unagented writers. Average print order for a writer's first book is 500-1,000. Subsidy publishes 50% of books, "depending on type of material and potential sales." 15% author subsidized; 35% non-author subsidized. Payment is "worked out individually." Publishes book an average of 1-2 years after acceptance. Simultaneous and photocopied submissions OK. Query for electronic submissions. Computer printouts acceptable. Reports in 1 week on queries; 2 weeks on mss. Current books flyer for business size SAE and 1 first class stamp; full catalog $3.
Nonfiction: New York state and New England history and genealogy. Query. Reviews artwork/photos.
Recent Nonfiction Title: *Madison County (NY) Revolutionary War Veterans*, by Isabel Bracy.
Fiction: Will review only fiction that deals with New York state historical subjects.
Recent Fiction Title: *Yankee Boy*, by Ethel Comins.

D.C. HEATH & CO., Raytheon Co., 125 Spring St., Lexington MA 02173. (617)862-6650. President: Loren A. Korte. General Manager College Division: Bruce Zimmerli. General Manager Lexington Books: Robert D.

Bovenschulte. General Manager School Division: Albert Bursma, Jr. College Division. Editor-in-Chief: Barbara Piercecchi. Director of Development School Division: Roger Rogalin. Publishes hardcover and paperback textbooks (grades kindergarten through college), professional scholarly, and software. Averages 300 titles/year. Offers standard royalty rates. Query. Publishes book an average of 1 year after acceptance. Query for electronic submissions. Computer printout submissions acceptable; prefers letter-quality to dot-matrix.

Nonfiction: Texts at the college level in history, political science, chemistry, math, biology, physics, economics, modern languages, English, business, and computer science. Also publishes professional books and research-based studies in the social sciences, business and economics, political science and international relations (Lexington Books). Length varies.

Tips: "We generally look for writers who freelance parts of already approved educational projects." Queries/mss may be routed to other editors in the publishing group.

HEINLE & HEINLE PUBLISHERS, INC., Subsidiary of Linguistics International, Inc., 20 Park Plaza, Boston MA 02216. (617)451-1940. President: Charles H. Heinle. Editor-in-Chief: Stanley Galek. Publishes books, video and software. Averages 15-20 titles/year; receives 50-60 submissions annually. 50% of books from first-time authors; 100% of books from unagented writers. Pays 6-15% royalty on net price; no advance. Publishes book an average of 18 months after acceptance. Query for electronic submissions. Computer printout submissions acceptable; prefers letter-quality to dot-matrix. Reports immediately on queries; 2 weeks on mss. Free book catalog; ms guidelines for SASE.

Nonfiction: Textbook. "Foreign language and English as a second or foreign language text materials. Before writing the book, submit complete prospectus along with sample chapters, and specify market and competitive position of proposed text."

Recent Nonfiction Title: *Interaction/Intersection*, by Susan S. St. Onge, David W. King and Ronald R. St. Onge.

Tips: "Introductory and intermediate college foreign language textbooks have the best chance of selling to our firm. A common mistake writers make is planning the project and/or writing the book without first reviewing the market and product concept with the publisher."

‡HERALD PRESS, Subsidiary of Mennonite Publishing House, 616 Walnut Ave., Scottdale PA 15683. (412)887-8500. General Book Editor: Paul M. Schrock. Publishes hardcover, trade and mass market paperback originals, trade paperback and mass market paperback reprints. Averages 30 titles/year; receives 700 submissions annually. 15% of books from first-time authors. 95% of books from unagented writers. Pays minimum royalty of 10% wholesale, maximum of 12% retail. Advance seldom given. Publishes book an average of 14 months after acceptance. Photocopied submissions OK. Query for electronic submissions. Computer printout submissions OK; no dot-matrix. Reports in 3 weeks on queries; 2 months on submissions. Book catalog 50¢.

Nonfiction: Cookbook, how-to, juvenile, reference, self-help and textbook. Subjects include cooking and foods, church history, Christian philosophy, social concerns, religion and Christian sociology. "We need books of Christian inspiration, Bible study, current issues, missions and evangelism, peace, self-help, and juveniles (mostly ages 9-14)." No drama or poetry. Query or submit outline/synopsis and sample chapters. Reviews artwork/photos as part of ms package.

Recent Nonfiction Title: *Journey Towards Holiness*, by Alan Kreider (peace/piety).

Fiction: Religious. Needs some fiction for youth and adults reflecting themes similar to those listed in nonfiction, also "compelling stories that treat social and Christian issues in a believable manner." No fantasy. Query or submit outline/synopsis and sample chapters.

Recent Fiction Title: *Rachel's Hope*, by Carole Gift Page (adult fiction).

HERALD PUBLISHING HOUSE, Division of Regorganized Church of Jesus Christ of Latter-Day Saints. 3225 South Noland Rd., Box HH, Independence MO 64055. (816)252-5010. Imprints include Independence Press. Editorial Director: Roger Yarrington. Publishes hardcover and trade paperback originals and hardcover and trade paperback reprints. Averages 30 titles/year; receives 700 submissions annually. 20% of books from first-time authors; 100% of books from unagented writers. Pays 5% maximum royalty on retail price. Offers average $400 advance. Publishes book an average of 14 months after acceptance. Computer printout submissions

66 *Gimmicks are one of the quickest ways to rejection. The fact of the matter is that there is no substitute for good writing. A good manuscript needs no gimmick and no gimmick can save a bad manuscript.* **99**

—*Jonathan J. Lanman*
editorial director, Atheneum Children's Books

acceptable; no dot-matrix. Reports in 3 weeks on queries; 2 months on mss. Book catalog for 9x12 SASE.
Nonfiction: Self-help and religious (RLDS Church). Subjects include Americana, history and religion. Herald House focus: history and doctrine of RLDS Church. Independence Press focus: regional studies (Midwest, Missouri). No submissions unrelated to RLDS Church (Herald House) or to Midwest regional studies (Independence Press). Query. Use *Chicago Manual of Style*. Reviews artwork/photos as part of ms package.
Recent Nonfiction Title: *The Conferring Church* by Richard and Marjorie Troeh (church procedures).
Tips: The audience for Herald Publishing House is members of the Reorganized Church of Jesus Christ of Latter Day Saints; for Independence Press, persons living in the Midwest or interested in the Midwest.

HERE'S LIFE PUBLISHERS, INC., Subsidiary of Campus Crusade for Christ, Box 1576, San Bernardino CA 92404. (714)886-7981. President: Les Stobbe. Editorial Director: Dan Benson. Publishes hardcover and trade paperback originals and mass market paperback originals. Averages 30 titles/year; receives 400 submissions annually. 40% of books from first-time authors; 100% of books from unagented writers. Average print order for a writer's first book is 5,000. Pays 15% royalty on wholesale price. Publishes book an average of 1 year after acceptance. Simultaneous and photocopied submissions OK. Query for electronic submissions. Computer printout submissions acceptable; no dot-matrix. Reports in 1 month on queries; 3 months on mss. Ms guidelines for 8½x11 SAE with 44¢ postage.
Nonfiction: Biography, how-to, illustrated book, reference and self-help. Needs "books in the areas of evangelism, Christian growth and family life; must reflect basic understanding of ministry and mission of Campus Crusade for Christ. No metaphysical or missionary biography." Query or submit outline/synopsis and sample chapters. Reviews artwork/photos.
Recent Nonfiction Title: *Megatruth*, by David L. McKenna (trends).
Tips: "The writer has the best chance of selling our firm a sharply focused how-to book, that provides a Biblical approach to a felt need."

*HERITAGE BOOKS, INC., 3602 Maureen, Bowie MD 20715. (301)464-1159. Editorial Director: Laird C. Towle. Publishes hardcover and paperback originals and reprints. Averages 60 titles/year; receives 100 submissions annually. 25% of books from first-time authors; 100% of books from unagented writers. Subsidy publishes 5% or less of books. Pays 10% royalty on retail price; no advance. Publishes book an average of 9 months after acceptance. Simultaneous and photocopied submissions OK. Computer printout submissions acceptable; prefers letter-quality to dot-matrix. Reports in 1 month. Book catalog for SAE.
Nonfiction: "We particularly desire nonfiction titles dealing with history and genealogy including how-to and reference works, as well as conventional histories and genealogies. The titles should be either of general interest or restricted to Eastern US. Material dealing with the present century is usually not of interest. We prefer writers to query, submit an outline/synopsis, or submit a complete ms, in that order, depending on the stage the writer has reached in the preparation of his work." Reviews artwork/photos.
Recent Nonfiction Title: *Tempestuous Voyage*, by Annah Maud Gould, edited by Laura Penny.
Tips: "The quality of the book is prime importance; next is its relevance to our fields of interest."

‡HERMES HOUSE PRESS, 39 Adare Place, Northampton MA 01060. (413)584-8402. Editor: Richard Mandell. Small press. Publishes trade paperback originals. Averages 8 titles/year; receives 45 submissions annually. 50% of books from first-time authors. "Pays in copies; after cost of publication is covered by income, pays small royalty." Publishes book an average of 8 months after acceptance. Photocopied submissions OK. Query for electronic submissions. Computer printout submissions OK; prefers letter-quality. Reports in 2 weeks on queries; 2 months on mss. Book catalog for #10 SAE.
Fiction: Ethnic, experimental, feminist, historical, mainstream and science fiction. "Although we are presently backed up with submissions, we are always willing to read high quality work. Literary fiction, with some attention made to language, has the best chance of selling to our firm." Query or submit complete ms.
Recent Fiction Title: *The Deadly Swarm & Other Stories*, by LaVerne Harrell Clark (short fiction).
Poetry: "We plan on publishing one or two books per year. No purely confessional poems." Submit 5-10 poems.
Recent Poetry Title: *Going West*, by Stanley Diamond (narrative).

‡HEROICA BOOKS, 4286 Redwood Hwy., San Rafael CA 94903. (415)897-6067. Editor: Judith Bonair. Division includes Modern Studies Group. Publishes hardcover and trade paperback originals. Averages 5 titles/year. 50% of books from first-time authors. 100% of books from unagented authors. Pays 7-15% royalty on retail price. Publishes book an average of 7 months after acceptance. Computer printout submissions OK; prefers letter-quality. Reports in 2 weeks on queries; 1 month on mss. Book catalog for #10 SAE with 2 first class stamps.
Nonfiction: Reference and textbook. Subjects include politics, psychology and sociology. "We seek well-researched, clearly written nonfiction that addresses significant psychological, sociological, or political issues. We do *not* want to see how-to fads." Query. Reviews artwork/photos as part of ms package.
Recent Nonfiction Title: *Hunger for Power*, by André Bacard (sociology/psychology).

Fiction: Historical, mainstream, mystery and literary. "We welcome literary and historical novels that combine major sociopolitical themes (e.g., human rights) with insightful character development. We do *not* want to see fiction that lacks a social message." Query.
Recent Fiction Title: *League of Liars*, by Maritza Pick (historical/mystery).
Tips: "Our audience prefers lasting books that make a difference, rather than fads. Heroica Books believes that literacy has a future in America. And our books appeal to readers who agree."

HEYDAY BOOKS, Box 9145, Berkeley CA 94709. (415)549-3564. Publisher: Malcolm Margolin. Small press. Publishes hardcover and trade paperback originals, trade paperback reprints. Averages 4-9 titles/year; receives 200 submissions annually. 50% of books from first-time authors; 75% of books from unagented writers. Pays 8-15% royalty on retail price; offers average $1,000 advance. Publishes book an average of 8 months after acceptance. Computer printout submissions acceptable; no dot-matrix. Reports in 1 week on queries; up to 5 weeks on mss. Book catalog for 7x9 SASE and 2 first class stamps.
Nonfiction: How-to and reference. Subjects include Americana, history, nature and travel. "We publish books about native Americans, natural history, history, and recreation, with a strong California focus." Query with outline and synopsis. Reviews artwork/photos.
Recent Nonfiction Title: *Strawberries in November*, by Judith Goldsmith.
Tips: "Give good value, and avoid gimmicks. A useful, factual book about some aspect of California has the best chance of selling to our firm."

‡*HIPPOCRENE BOOKS INC.,171 Madison Ave., New York NY 10016. (212)685-4371. President: George Blagowidow. Publishes hardcover originals and trade paperback originals and reprints. Averages 100 titles/year. Receives 150 submissions annually. 25% of books from first-time authors; 50% of books from unagented writers. Subsidy publishes 2% of books. Will consider subsidy publishing "an important title without sufficient commercial potential." Pays 6-15% royalty on retail price. Offers "few thousand" dollar advance. Publishes book an average of 11 months after acceptance. Simultaneous submissions OK. Free book catalog; ms guidelines for SASE.
Nonfiction: Biography, how-to, reference, self-help, travel guides. Subjects include history, recreation and travel. Submit outline/synopsis and 2 sample chapters. Reviews artwork/photos as part of ms package.
Recent Nonfiction Titles: *Travel Trivia Test.*

HOLIDAY HOUSE, INC., 18 E. 53rd St., New York NY 10022. (212)688-0085. Editorial Director: Margery Cuyler. Publishes hardcover originals. Averages 35-40 titles/year. Pays in royalties based on retail price; offers variable advance. Photocopied submissions OK. Computer printout submissions acceptable. Reports in 2 months.
Nonfiction and Fiction: General fiction and nonfiction for young readers—pre-school through high school. "It's better to submit the ms without art." Submit outline/synopsis and 3 sample chapters or complete ms. "No certified, insured or registered mail accepted."
Recent Nonfiction Title: *Ellis Island*, by Leonard Everett Fisher.
Recent Fiction Title: *The Hounds of the Morrigan*, by Pat O'Shea.

‡HOMESTEAD PUBLISHING, Box 193, Moose WY 83102. Editor: Carl Schreier. Publishes hardcover and trade paperback originals and trade paperback reprints. Averages 5 titles/year; receives 100 submissions annually. 60% of books from first-time authors. 90% of books from unagented writers. Pays 12% royalty on retail price; offers $1,000 average advance. Publishes book an average of 1 year after acceptance. Simultaneous and photocopied submissions OK. Query for electronic submissions. Computer printout submissions OK. Reports in 2 weeks on queries; 2 months on submissions. Book catalog for #10 SAE with 39¢ postage.
Nonfiction: Biography, "coffee table" book, illustrated book, juvenile and reference. Subjects include animals, art, history, nature, photography and travel. Especially needs natural history and nature books for children. No textbooks. Query; or submit outline, synopsis and sample chapters or complete ms. Reviews artwork/photos as part of ms package.
Recent Nonfiction Title: *Yellowstone's Geysers, Hot Springs and Fumaroles.*
Fiction: "Westerns based upon historical incidents." Query.
Tips: "Illustrated books on natural history are our specialty. Our audiences includes professional, educated people with an interest in natural history, conservation, national parks, and western art. Underneath the visual aspects, a book should be well written, with a good grasp of the English language."

HOUGHTON MIFFLIN CO., Divisions include Ticknor & Fields; School Division; College Division; Educational Software Division; and Riverside Publishing Co./Reference Division, 2 Park St., Boston MA 02108. (617)725-5000. Editor-in-Chief: Nan A. Talese. Submissions Editor: Janice Harvey. Hardcover and paperback originals and paperback reprints. Royalty of 6-7½% on retail price for paperbacks; 10-15% on sliding scale for standard fiction and nonfiction; advance varies widely. Publishes book an average of 18 months after acceptance. Publishes 100 titles/year. Simultaneous submissions OK. Computer printout submissions acceptable; no dot-matrix. SASE required with all submissions. Reports in 2 months. Book catalog for 8½x11 SAE.

Nonfiction: Natural history, biography, health, history, current affairs, psychology and science. Query.
Recent Nonfiction Title: *The Cycles of American History*, by Arthur M. Schlesinger, Jr.
Fiction: Historical, mainstream and literary. Query.
Recent Fiction Title: *The Prince of Tides*, by Pat Conroy.
Tips: "No unsolicited manuscripts will be read. Submit query letter and outline or synopsis to Submissions Editor. (Include one sample chapter for fiction.) The query letter should be short and to the point—that is, it should *not* incorporate the book's synopsis. The letter should say who the writer is (including information on previous publications in magazines or wherever) and the subject of the book."

*HOUNSLOW PRESS, A Division of Anthony R. Hawke Limited, 124 Parkview Ave., Willowdale, Ontario M2N 3Y5 Canada. (416)225-9176. President: Anthony Hawke. Publishes hardcover and trade paperback originals and reprints. Averages 6 titles/year; receives 500 submissions annually. 5% of books from first-time authors; 80% of books from unagented writers. Subsidy publishes (nonauthor) 10% of titles. Average print order for a writer's first book is 1,000. Pays 5-10% royalty on retail price; rarely offers advance. Publishes book an average of 18 months after acceptance. Simultaneous and photocopied submissions OK. Reports in 2 weeks on queries; 1 month on mss. Free book catalog.
Nonfiction: Biography, "coffee table" book, cookbook, how-to, humor, illustrated book, juvenile, reference and self-help. Subjects include animals, art, business and economics, cooking and foods, health, history, hobbies, nature, philosophy, photography, politics, psychology, recreation, religion and travel. Publishes for a general audience. "We do well with cookbooks and photography books about Canadian themes." Query. Submit outline/synopsis and 4 sample chapters. Reviews artwork/photos.
Recent Nonfiction Title: *Island Kitchens*.
Fiction: Adventure, humor and mainstream. Query.
Poetry: Query.
Recent Poetry Title: *The Proper Lover*, by William Gough.
Tips: "Selp-help, humor, and controversial nonfiction sell the best in the retail market. We really want exceptional material from outstanding, talented writers—our standards are high."

HUDSON HILLS PRESS, INC., Suite 1308, 230 5th Ave., New York NY 10001. (212)889-3090. President/Editorial Director: Paul Anbinder. Publishes hardcover and paperback originals. Averages 10 titles/year; receives 50-100 submissions annually. 15% of books from first-time authors; 90% of books from unagented writers. Average print order for a writer's first book is 3,000. Offers royalties of 5-8% on retail price. Average advance: $5,000. Publishes book an average of 1 year after acceptance. Simultaneous and photocopied submissions OK. Computer printout submissions acceptable; prefers letter-quality to dot-matrix. Reports in 1 month. Book catalog for SAE with 39¢ postage.
Nonfiction: Art and photography. "We are only interested in publishing books about art, and photography and monographs." Query first, then submit outline/synopsis and sample chapters. Reviews artwork/photos.
Recent Nonfiction Title: *Young America: A Folk Art History*.

HUMAN KINETICS PUBLISHERS, INC., Box 5076, Champaign IL 61820. (217)351-5076. Publisher: Rainer Martens. Imprints include Leisure Press and Life Enhancement Publications. Publishes hardcover and trade paperback originals. Averages 80 titles/year; receives 300 submissions annually. 50% of books from first-time authors; 97% of books from unagented writers. Pays 10-15% royalty on wholesale price; offers average $500 advance. Publishes book an average of 1 year after acceptance. Simultaneous and photocopied submissions OK. Query for electronic submissions. Computer printout submissions acceptable; prefers letter-quality to dot-matrix. Reports in 2 months. Free book catalog and ms guidelines.
Nonfiction: How-to, reference, self-help, technical and textbook. Subjects include health; recreation; sports, sport sciences and sports medicine; and physical education. Especially interested in books on wellness, including stress management, weight management, leisure management, and fitness; books on all aspects of sports technique or how-to books and coaching books; books which interpret the sport sciences and sports medicine, including sport physiology, sport psychology, sport pedagogy and sport biomechanics. No sport biographies, sport record or statistics books or regional books. Submit outline/synopsis and sample chapters. Reviews artwork/photos as part of ms package.
Recent Nonfiction Title: *Eating on the Run*, by Evelyn Tribole (how-to).
Tips: "Books which accurately interpret the sport sciences and health research to coaches, athletes and fitness enthusiasts have the best chance of selling to us."

HUMANICS LIMITED, Suite 201, 1389 Peachtree St. NE, Atlanta GA 30309. (404)874-2176. President: Gary B. Wilson. Contact: Sarah L. Gregory, Executive Editor. Publishes softcover, educational and trade paperback originals. Averages 12 titles/year; receives 500 submissions annually. 20% of books from first-time authors; 100% of books from unagented writers. Average print order for a writer's first book is 5,000. Pays average 10% royalty on net sales; buys some mss outright. Publishes book an average of 1 year after acceptance. Computer printout submissions acceptable; prefers letter-quality to dot-matrix. Reports in 4 months. Book catalog and ms guidelines for SASE.

Nonfiction: Self-help and teacher resource books. Subjects include health, psychology, sociology, education, business and New Age. Submit outline/synopsis and at least 3 sample chapters. Reviews artwork/photos as part of ms package.

Recent Nonfiction Title: *Inner Bridges*, by Fritz Frederick Smith (New Age).

Tips: "We are actively seeking authors with New Age material."

‡**CARL HUNGNESS PUBLISHING**, Box 24308, Speedway IN 46224. (317)244-4792. Editorial Director: Carl Hungness. Publishes hardcover and paperback originals. Pays "negotiable" outright purchase. Reports in 3 weeks. Free book catalog.

Nonfiction: Stories relating to professional automobile racing. No sports car racing or drag racing material. Query.

****HUNTER HOUSE, INC., PUBLISHERS**, Box 1302, Claremont CA 91711. General Manager: K.S. Rana. Publishes hardcover and trade paperback originals. Averages 8 titles/year; receives 200 submissions annually. 50% of books from first-time authors; 50% of books from unagented writers. Subsidy publishes 10% of books. "We determine whether an author should be subsidy published based upon subject matter, quality of the work, and if a subsidy is available." Pays $7\frac{1}{2}$-$12\frac{1}{2}$% royalty on retail price. Offers $50 advance. Publishes book an average of 12-18 months after acceptance. Simultaneous and photocopied submissions OK. Query for electronic submissions. Computer printout submissions acceptable. Reports in 2 months on queries; 6 months on mss. Book catalog and ms guidelines for 9x12 SAE with 56¢ postage.

Nonfiction: How-to, juvenile, and self-help. Subjects include health, psychology and "new science." Needs mss on "family and health, especially emerging areas in women's health, men's opening up and single parenting, older people, young adult, especially on health and intergenerational concerns." No evangelical, political, Americana or esoteric. Query or submit outline/synopsis and sample chapters. Reviews artwork/photos.

Recent Nonfiction Title: *Not Another Diet Book*, by Bobbe Sommer, Ph.D.

Fiction: Erotica, and ethnic fiction and fantasy. Needs one or two historical/mythical/fantasy books by and for women. Query or submit outline/synopsis and sample chapters.

Recent Fiction Title: *Rastus on Capitol Hill*, by Samuel Edison.

Tips: "Manuscripts on family and health, or psychology for an aware public do well for us. Write simply, with established credentials and imagination. We respect writers and do not mistreat them. We ask for the same consideration."

‡**HUNTER PUBLISHING, INC.**, 155 Riverside Dr., New York NY 10024. (212)595-8933. President: Michael Hunter. Averages 100 titles/year; receives 300 submissions annually. 10% of books from first-time authors. 75% of books from unagented writers. Pays 10-15% royalty on wholesale price; offers $2,000-5,000 average advance. Publishes book an average of 9 months after acceptance. Simultaneous submissions OK. Query for electronic submissions. Computer printout submissions OK. Reports in 3 weeks on queries; 1 month on submissions. Book catalog for #10 SAE with 69¢ postage.

Nonfiction: Reference. Subjects include history, travel, foreign language and dictionaries. "We need travel guides to areas covered by few competitors: Caribbean Islands, Pacific Islands, Canada, Mexico, regional U.S. from an active 'adventure' perspective. Walking & climbing guides to all areas—from Australia to India." No personal travel stories or books not directed to travellers. Query or submit outline/synopsis and sample chapters. Reviews artwork/photos as part of ms package.

Recent Nonfiction Title: *France on Backroads*, (guidebook).

Tips: "Study what's out there, pick some successful models, and identify ways they can be made more appealing. We need active adventure-oriented guides and more specialized guides for travellers in search of the unusual."

HUNTINGTON HOUSE, INC., Box 78312, Shreveport LA 71137. (318)221-2767. President: Bill Keith. Publishes hardcover, trade paperback, and mass market paperback originals, trade paperback reprints and software. Averages 10-20 titles/year; receives 200 submissions annually. 50% of books from first-time authors; 20% of books from unagented writers. Average print order for a writer's first book is 10,000. Pays 10-15% royalty on wholesale and retail price, or $50; offers $100-2,500 advance. Publishes book an average of 6 months after acceptance. Simultaneous and photocopied submissions OK. Electronic submissions OK. Computer printout submissions acceptable. Reports in 2 months on queries; 3 months on mss. Free book catalog and ms guidelines.

Nonfiction: Biography, self-help and religious. "We publish self-help books and Christian growth books oriented to the Christian community." No New Age, occult, humanism or liberal theology. Query. Reviews artwork/photos.

Tips: "Write clear, crisp, exciting self-help or teaching manuscripts. Current Christian concerns books have the best chance of selling to our firm."

****HURTIG PUBLISHERS LTD.**, 10560 105th St., Edmonton, Alberta T5H 2W7 Canada. (403)426-2359. Editor-in-Chief: Elizabeth Munroe. Hardcover and paperback originals and reprints. Averages 12 titles/year; re-

ceives 1,000 submissions annually. 15% of books from first-time authors; 90% of books from unagented writers. Subsidy publishes (non-author) 10% of books. Typically pays 10% royalty on first 7,500 copies; 12% on next 7,500; 15% thereafter. Offers $500-1,000 advance on first book. Letter of inquiry first. Reports in 2-3 months. Free book catalog.

Nonfiction: Publishes biographies of well-known Canadians, Canadian history, humor, nature, topical Canadian politics and economics, reference (Canadian), and material about native Canadians "aimed at the nationalistic Canadian interested in politics, the North and energy policy." No poetry or original fiction. Query first. Very few unsolicited mss published. Looks for "suitability of topic to general publishing program; market interest in topic; qualifications of writer to treat that topic well; quality of writing." State availability of photos and/or illustrations to accompany ms.

Recent Nonfiction Title: *Pitseolak: A Canadian Tragedy*, by David F. Raine.

Tips: "Submissions must appeal to a very wide general audience, since the Canadian market is small."

‡ILR PRESS, Division of The New York State School of Industrial and Labor Relations, Cornell University, Ithaca NY 14851-0952. (607)255-3061. Managing Editor: E. Fox. Publishes hardcover originals and reprints, and trade paperback originals and reprints. Averages 5-10 titles/year. Pays royalty. Photocopied submissions OK. Computer printout submissions acceptable; no dot-matrix. Reports in 2-3 weeks on queries; 8-12 weeks on mss. Free book catalog.

Nonfiction: All titles must relate to labor history and industrial relations. Biography, reference, technical, academic books in industrial and labor relations. Subjects include history, sociology of work and the workplace and business and economics. Book manuscript needs for the next year include "manuscripts on workplace problems, employment policy, women and work, personnel issues, and dispute resolution that will interest academics and practitioners." Query or submit outlines/synopsis and sample chapters or complete ms.

Recent Nonfiction Title: *Hard Times Cotton Mill Girls: Personal Histories of Womanhood and Poverty in the South*, by Victoria Byerly (oral history).

Tips: "We are interested in manuscripts that address topical issues in industrial and labor relations that concern both academics and the general public. These must be well documented to pass our editorial evaluation, which includes review by academics in the industrial and labor relations field."

IMAGINE, INC., Box 9674, Pittsburgh PA 15226. (412)571-1430. President: R.V. Michelucci. Publishes trade paperback originals. Averages 3-5 titles/year; receives 50 submissions annually. 50% of books from first-time authors; 75% of books from unagented writers. Pays 6-10% royalty on retail price. Offers average $500 advance. Publishes book an average of 8-12 months after acceptance. Photocopied submissions OK. Computer printout submissions acceptable; no dot-matrix. Reports in 2 weeks on queries; 2 months on mss. Book catalog for #10 SAE with 1 first class stamp.

Nonfiction: "Coffee table" book, how-to, illustrated book and reference. Subjects include films, science fiction, fantasy and horror films. Submit outline/synopsis and sample chapters or complete ms with illustrations and/or photos.

Recent Nonfiction Title: *Forrest J. Ackerman, Famous Monster of Filmland*.

Tips: "If I were a writer trying to market a book today, I would research my subject matter completely before sending a manuscript. Our audience is between ages 18-45 and interested in film, science fiction, fantasy and the horror genre."

INCENTIVE PUBLICATIONS, INC., 3835 Cleghorn Ave., Nashville TN 37215. (615)385-2934. Editor: Sally Sharpe. Publishes paperback originals. Averages 15-25 titles/year; receives 350 submissions annually. 25% of books from first-time authors; 95% of books from unagented writers. Pays royalty or makes outright purchase. Publishes book an average of 1 year after acceptance. Photocopied submissions OK. Computer printout submissions acceptable; prefers letter-quality to dot-matrix. Reports in 2 weeks on queries; 3 weeks on mss. Book catalog and ms guidelines for 9x12 SAE.

Nonfiction: Teacher resources and books on educational areas relating to children. Submit outline/synopsis and sample chapters. Query with synopsis and detailed outline. Reviews artwork/photos as part of ms package.

Recent Nonfiction Title: *The I'm Ready to Learn Series*, by Imogene Forte, (early childhood skills-based activity books).

Tips: "A common mistake writers make is demanding too much, such as the inclusion of their own artwork. Often they overwhelm the editor with too much copy—a short synopsis often receives much more attention."

*INDIANA UNIVERSITY PRESS, 10th & Morton Sts., Bloomington IN 47405. (812)337-4203. Director: John Gallman. Publishes hardcover and paperback originals and paperback reprints. Averages 110 titles/year. 30% of books from first-time authors. 98% from unagented writers. Average print order for a writer's first book is 1,500. Subsidy publishes (nonauthor) 9% of books. Pays maximum 10% royalty on retail price; offers occasional advance. Publishes book an average of 18 months after acceptance. Photocopied submissions OK. Electronic submissions OK if IBM compatible, but requires hard copy also. Computer printout submissions acceptable; no dot-matrix. Reports in 2 months. Free book catalog and ms guidelines.

Nonfiction: Scholarly books on humanities, history, philosophy, religion, Jewish studies, Black studies, translations, semiotics, public policy, film, music, linguistics, social sciences, regional materials, African studies, women's studies, and serious nonfiction for the general reader. Query or submit outline/synopsis and sample chapters. "Queries should include as much descriptive material as is necessary to convey scope and market appeal to us." Reviews artwork/photos.

Recent Nonfiction Title: *Semiotics and the Philosophy of Language*, by Umberto Eco.

Fiction: Query or submit outline/synopsis.

INDUSTRIAL PRESS INC., 200 Madison Ave., New York NY 10016. (212)889-6330. Director of Marketing: Woodrow Chapman. Small press. Publishes hardcover originals. Averages 3 titles/year; receives 15 submissions annually. 2% of books from first-time authors; 100% of books from unagented writers. Publishes book an average of 1 year after acceptance of finished ms. Query for electronic submissions. Computer printout submissions acceptable; no dot-matrix. Reports in 1 month. Free book catalog.

Nonfiction: Reference and technical. Subjects include business and economics, science and engineering. "We envision professional engineers, plant managers, on-line industrial professionals responsible for equipment operation, professors teaching manufacturing, engineering, technology related courses as our audience." Especially looking for material on manufacturing technologies and titles on specific areas in manufacturing and industry. Computers in manufacturing are a priority. No energy-related books or how-to books. Query.

Recent Nonfiction Title: *Engineered Work Measurement*, by Delmar W. Karger and Franklin H. Bayha.

INFORMATION RESOURCES PRESS, A Division of Herner and Company, Suite 700, 1700 N. Moore St., Arlington VA 22209. (703)558-8270. Vice President/Publisher: Ms. Gene P. Allen. Publishes hardcover originals. Averages 6 titles/year; receives 25 submissions annually. 80% of books from first-time authors; 100% of books from unagented writers. Pays 10-15% royalty on net cash receipts after returns and discounts. Publishes book an average of 1 year after acceptance. Simultaneous and photocopied submissions OK. Query for electronic submissions. Reports in 2 weeks on queries; 2 months on mss. Free book catalog and ms guidelines.

Nonfiction: Reference, technical and textbook. Subjects include health and library and information science. Needs basic or introductory books on information science, library science, and health planning that lend themselves for use as textbooks. Preferably, the mss will have been developed from course notes. No works on narrow research topics (nonbasic or introductory works). Submit outline/synopsis and sample chapters or complete ms.

Recent Nonfiction Title: *Federal Health Information Resources*, edited by Melvin S. Day. Reviews artwork/photos.

Tips: "Our audience includes libraries (public, special, college and university); librarians, information scientists; college-level faculty; schools of library and information science; health planners, graduate-level students of health planning, and administrators; economists. Our marketing program is slanted toward library and information science and health planning, and we can do a better job of marketing in these areas."

*INSTITUTE FOR THE STUDY OF HUMAN ISSUES, (ISHI Publications), 210 S. 13th St., Philadelphia PA 19107. (215)732-9729. Director of Publications: Betty Crapivinsky-Jutkowitz. Associate Director: Edward A. Jutkowitz. Managing Editor: Brad Fisher. Publishes hardcover and paperback originals and paperback reprints. Averages 18 titles/year; receives 150 submissions annually. 5-10% of books from first-time authors; 75% of books from unagented writers. Publishes 10% of books by partial subsidy. Pays 10-12½% royalty on wholesale price; no advance. Publishes book an average of 15 months after acceptance. Photocopied submissions OK. Query for electronic submissions. Computer printout submissions acceptable; no dot-matrix. Reports in 3 months. Book catalog and ms guidelines for SASE.

Nonfiction: Books on political science, history, anthropology, folklore, sociology, economics and drug studies, suitable for students and scholars in these fields. Accepts nonfiction translations. Submit outline/synopsis for initial consideration. Reviews artwork/photos as part of ms package.

Recent Nonfiction Title: *The President and Economic Policy*, edited by James Pfiffner.

Tips: "Latin American politics and current events, or Regional Americana are our strongest markets. Use up-to-date sources, documented controversies, good maps or photos, and a foreword by a well-known figure."

INTERCULTURAL PRESS, INC., Box 768, Yarmouth ME 04096. (207)846-5168. Contact: David S. Hoopes, Editor-in-Chief, 130 North Rd., Vershire VT 05079. (802)685-4448. Publishes hardcover and trade paperback originals. Averages 5-7 titles/year; receives 50-80 submissions annually. 50% of books from first-time authors; 95% of books from unagented writers. Pays royalty; occasionally offers small advance. Publishes book an average of 2 years after acceptance. Simultaneous and photocopied submissions OK. Electronic submissions OK, but requires hard copy also. Computer printout submissions acceptable; prefers letter-quality to dot-matrix. Reports in "several weeks" on queries; 2 months on mss. Free book catalog and ms guidelines.

Nonfiction: How-to, reference, self-help, textbook and theory. Subjects include business and economics, philosophy, politics, psychology, sociology, travel, or "any book with an international or domestic intercultural, multicultural or cross-cultural focus, i.e., a focus on the cultural factors in personal, social, political or eco-

nomic relations. We want books with an international or domestic intercultural or multicultural focus, especially those on business operations (how to be effective in intercultural business activities) and education (textbooks for teaching intercultural subjects, for instance). Our books are published for educators in the intercultural field, business people who are engaged in international business, and anyone else who works in an international occupation or has had intercultural experience. No manuscripts that don't have an intercultural focus." Accepts nonfiction translations. Query "if there is any question of suitability (we can tell quickly from a good query)," or submit outline/synopsis. Do not submit mss unless invited.
Recent Nonfiction Title: *Understanding Arabs*, by Margaret Nydell.

‡**INTERNATIONAL FOUNDATION OF EMPLOYEE BENEFIT PLANS**, Box 69, Brookfield WI 53008. (414)786-6700. Director of Publications: Dee Birschel. Publishes hardcover and trade paperback originals. Averages 30 titles/year; receives 10 submissions annually. 10% of books from first-time authors. 75% of books from unagented writers. Pays 5-15% royalty on wholesale and retail price. Publishes book an average of 1 year after acceptance. Photocopied submissions OK. Computer printout submissions OK; no dot-matrix. Reports in 3 months on queries. Book catalog free on request; ms guidelines for SASE.
Nonfiction: Reference, technical and textbook. Subjects include business and economics and employee benefits. "We publish general and technical monographs on all aspects of Employee benefits—pension plans, health insurance, etc." Query with outline.
Recent Nonfiction Title: *Flexible Benefits—A How-To Guide*, by Richard E. Johnson.
Tips: "Interview people in the field to determine subjects of interest."

INTERNATIONAL MARINE PUBLISHING CO., Division of Highmark Publishing, Ltd., 21 Elm St., Camden ME 04843. Imprints include Seven Seas Press. Editor-in-Chief: Jonathan Eaton. Publishes hardcover and paperback originals. Averages 22 titles/year; receives 500-700 submissions annually. 50% of books from first-time authors; 80% of books from unagented writers. Pays standard royalties, based on net price, with advances. Publishes book an average of 8 months after acceptance. Computer printout submissions acceptable; prefers letter-quality to dot-matrix. Reports in 6 weeks. Book catalog and ms guidelines for SASE.
Nonfiction: "Mostly marine nonfiction but a wide range of subjects within that category: boatbuilding, boat design, yachting, seamanship, boat maintenance, maritime history, etc." All books are illustrated. "Material in all stages welcome. We prefer queries first with outline and 2-3 sample chapters." Reviews artwork/photos as part of ms package.
Recent Nonfiction Title: *Stroke! A Guide to Recreational Rowing*, by Bruce Brown.
Fiction: "Marine fiction of excellence will be considered."
Tips: "Freelance writers should be aware of the need for clarity, accuracy and interest. Many progress too far in the actual writing, with an unsalable topic."

INTERNATIONAL PUBLISHERS CO., INC., #1301, 381 Park Ave. S., New York NY 10016. (212)685-2864. President: Betty Smith. Publishes hardcover and trade paperback originals and trade paperback reprints. Averages 15-20 titles/year; receives 200 submissions annually. 15% of books from first-time authors. Pays 5% royalty on paperbacks; 10% royalty on cloth. No advance. Publishes book an average of 6 months after acceptance. Simultaneous and photocopied submissions OK. Computer printout submissions acceptable; prefers letter-quality to dot-matrix. Reports in 1 month on queries; 6 months on mss. Free book catalog; ms guidelines for SASE and $1.
Nonfiction: Biography, reference and textbook. Subjects include Americana, economics, history, philosophy, politics, social sciences, and Marxist-Leninist classics. "Books on labor, black studies and women's studies based on Marxist science have high priority." Query or submit outline and sample chapters. Reviews artwork/photos as part of ms package.
Recent Nonfiction Title: *Warwords*, by David Eisenhower and John Murray.
Fiction: "We publish very little fiction." Query or submit outline and sample chapters.
Recent Fiction Title: *Home For Supper*, by Phillip Bonosky (short stories).
Poetry: "We rarely publish individual poets, usually anthologies."
Recent Poetry Title: *New and Old Voices of Wah'Kon-Tah*, editors Dodge and McCullough (contemporary native American Indian poetry).

INTERNATIONAL SELF-COUNSEL PRESS, LTD., 1481 Charlotte Rd., North Vancouver, British Columbia V7J 1H1 Canada. (604)986-3366. President: Diana R. Douglas. Senior Editor: Ruth Wilson. Publishes trade paperback originals. Averages 10-15 titles/year; receives 100 submissions annually. 50% of books from first-time authors; 100% of books from unagented writers. Average print order for a writer's first book is 4,000. Pays 10% royalty on wholesale price; no advance. Publishes book an average of 9 months after submission of contracted ms. Simultaneous and photocopied submissions OK. Computer printout submissions acceptable; prefers letter-quality to dot-matrix. Reports in 6 weeks. SAE with IRCs. Book catalog for 9x6 SASE.
Nonfiction: Specializes in self-help and how-to books in law, business, reference, and psychology for lay person. Submit outline and sample chapters. Follow *Chicago Manual of Style*.

Recent Nonfiction Title: *Marketing Your Service*, by Withers and Vipperman (business—how-to).

INTERNATIONAL WEALTH SUCCESS, Box 186, Merrick NY 11566. (516)766-5850. Editor: Tyler G. Hicks. Averages 10 titles/year; receives 100+ submissions annually. 100% of books from first-time authors; 100% of books from unagented writers. Average print order for a writer's first book "varies from 500 and up, depending on the book." Pays 10% royalty on wholesale or retail price. Buys all rights. Usual advance is $1,000, but this varies, depending on author's reputation and nature of book. Publishes book 4 months after acceptance. Photocopied and dot-matrix submissions OK. Query for electronic submissions. Computer printout submissions acceptable. Reports in 1 month. Book catalog and ms guidelines for 9x12 SAE with 56¢ postage.
Nonfiction: Self-help and how-to. "Techniques, methods, sources for building wealth. Highly personal, how-to-do-it with plenty of case histories. Books are aimed at the wealth builder and are highly sympathetic to his and her problems." Financing, business success, venture capital, etc. Length: 60,000-70,000 words. Query. Reviews artwork/photos as part of ms package.
Recent Nonfiction Title: *Money Agency Planning Guide*, by Brisky (how-to).
Tips: "The writer has the best chance of selling our firm self-help moneymaking titles directed at small business ventures. Writing too stuffily is a common mistake— that is writing for bankers when the market is the man or woman in the street. Books that sell are hands-on. They tell people how to do something quickly and easily, without trying to impress with big words that most readers don't understand."

*THE INTERSTATE PRINTERS & PUBLISHERS, INC., 19 N. Jackson St., Box 50, Danville IL 61834-0050. (217)446-0500. Acquisitions/Vice President-Editorial: Ronald L. McDaniel. Hardcover and paperback originals and software. Publishes about 50 titles/year. 50% of books from first-time authors; 100% of books from unagented writers. Subsidy publishes 5% of books; 3% non-author subsidy. Usual royalty is 10%; no advance. Markets books by mail and exhibits. Publishes book an average of 9 months after acceptance. Computer printout submissions acceptable; prefers letter-quality to dot-matrix. Reports in 3-4 months. Book catalog for 9x12 SAE.
Nonfiction: Publishes high school and undergraduate college-level texts in vocational education (agriculture and agribusiness, trade and industrial education, home economics and business education). Also publishes professional references, texts, and supplementary materials in special education (including speech-language pathology, audiology, learning disabilities, neurological impairment) and in corrections education. "We favor, but do not limit ourselves to, works that are designed for class—quantity rather than single-copy sale." Query or submit synopsis and 2-3 sample chapters. Reviews artwork/photos as part of ms package.
Recent Nonfiction Title: *Arts & Humanity: An Introduction to Applied Aesthetics.*
Tips: "Freelance writers should be aware of strict adherence to the use of nonsexist language; fair and balanced representation of the sexes and of minorities in both text and illustrations; and discussion of computer applications wherever applicable. Writers commonly fail to identify publishers who specialize in the subject areas in which they are writing. For example, a publisher of textbooks isn't interested in novels, or one that specializes in elementary education materials isn't going to want a book on auto mechanics."

INTERURBAN PRESS/TRANS ANGLO BOOKS, Box 6444, Glendale CA 91205. (213)240-9130. Subsidiaries include PRN/PTJ Magazines and Interurban Films. President: Mac Sebree. Publishes hardcover and trade paperback originals. Averages 10-12 titles/year; receives 50-75 submissions yearly. 35% of books from first-time authors; 99% of books from unagented writers. Average print order for a writer's first book is 2,000. Pays 5-10% royalty on retail price; offers no advance. Computer printout submissions acceptable. Reports in 2 weeks on queries; 2 months on mss. Free book catalog.
Nonfiction: Western Americana and transportation. Subjects include Americana, business and economics, history, hobbies and travel. "We are interested only in manuscripts about railroads, local transit, local history, and Western Americana (gold mining, logging, early transportation, etc.). Also anything pertaining to preservation movement, nostalgia." Query. Reviews artwork/photos.
Recent Nonfiction Title: *By Rail to the Boardwalk*, by Gladulich (history).
Tips: "Our audience is comprised of hobbyists in the rail transportation field ('railfans'); those interested in Western Americana (logging, mining, etc.); and students of transportation history, especially railroads and local rail transit (streetcars)."

*INTERVARSITY PRESS, Division of Intervarsity Christian Fellowship, Box 1400, Downers Grove IL 60515. (312)964-5700. Managing Editor: Andrew T. LePeau. Small press. Publishes hardcover and paperback originals and reprints. Averages 50 titles/year; receives 800 submissions annually. 25% of books from first-time authors; 95% of books from unagented writers. Subsidy publishes (non-author) 6% of books. Pays average 10% royalty on retail price; offers average $1,000 advance. Sometimes makes outright purchase for $600-2,500. Publishes book an average of 15 months after acceptance of final draft. "Indicate simultaneous submissions." Computer printout submissions acceptable; no dot-matrix. Reports in 3 months. Book catalog and ms guidelines for SASE.
Nonfiction: "InterVarsity Press publishes books geared to the presentation of Biblical Christianity in its vari-

ous relations to personal life, art, literature, sociology, psychology, philosophy, history and so forth. Though we are primarily publishers of trade books, we are cognizant of the textbook market at the college, university and seminary level within the general religious field. The audience for which the books are published is composed primarily of adult Christians. Stylistic treatment varies from topic to topic and from fairly simple popularizations to scholarly works primarily designed to be read by scholars." Accepts nonfiction translations. Query or submit outline/synopsis and 2 sample chapters.

Recent Nonfiction Title: *Beating the Churchgoing Blahs*, by Robert Thornton Henderson (Christian living).

Fiction: Fantasy, humor, mainstream, religious, science fiction. "While fiction need not be explicit Christian or religious, it should rise out of a Christian perspective." Submit outline/synopsis and sample chapters.

Recent Fiction Title: *The Magic Bicycle*, by John Bibee (juvenile fantasy).

Tips: "Religious publishing has become overpublished. Books that fill niches or give a look at a specific aspect of a broad topic (such as marriage or finances or Christian growth) are doing well for us. Also, even thoughtful books need lower reading levels, more stories and illustrative materials. If I were a writer trying to market a book today, I would read William Zinsser's *On Writing Well* and do as he says. Writers commonly send us types of mss that we don't publish, and act as if we should publish their work—being too confident of their ideas and ability."

IRON CROWN ENTERPRISES, Box 1605, Charlottesville VA 22902. (804)295-3918. Managing Editor: Terry K. Amthor. Imprint includes Questbooks (fiction)—John Ruemmler, editor. Publishes 8½x11" paperback and mass market paperback originals. Averages 20 titles/year; receives 20 submissions annually. 50% of books from first-time authors; 100% of books from unagented writers. Pays 2-4% royalty on wholesale price, or makes outright purchase for $1,000-2,000. Offers average $500 advance. Publishes book an average of 2-12 months after acceptance. Photocopied submissions OK. Computer printout submissions acceptable; prefers letter-quality to dot-matrix. Reports in 1 month on queries; 3 months on mss. Book catalog and ms guidelines for 4x9½ SASE.

Fiction: Fantasy and science fiction fantasy role-playing supplements. Query. "We do not accept unsolicited manuscripts."

Recent Fiction Title: *Lords of Middle-Earth*, by Pete Fenlon (resource game book).

Tips: "Our basic audience is role-players, who are mostly aged 12-25. Iron Crown Enterprises publishes only a very specific sub-genre of fiction, namely fantasy role-playing supplements. We own the exclusive worldwide rights for such material based on J.R.R. Tolkien's *Hobbit* and *Lord of the Rings*. We also have a line of science-fiction supplements and are planning a line of fantasy books of our own. With our Questbooks we have a growing crossover into a general Fantasy readership. Questbooks, more similar to standard fiction, allow the reader to choose courses for the main character as he proceeds through alternative plotlines in the book. We are currently concentrating on a very specific market, and potential submissions must fall within stringent guidelines. Due to the complexity of our needs, please query. Extensive research is necessary."

*ISHIYAKU EUROAMERICA, INC., Subsidiary of Ishiyaku Publishers, Inc., Tokyo, Japan: 11559 Rock Island Court, St. Louis MO 63043. (314)432-1933. President: Manuel L. Ponte. Publishes hardcover originals. Averages 15 titles/year; receives 50 submissions annually. Subsidy publishes (nonauthor) 100% of books. 75% of books from first-time authors; 100% of books from unagented writers. Average print order for a writer's first book is 3,000. Pays 10% minimum royalty on retail price or pays 35% of all foreign translation rights sales. Offers average $1,000 advance. Simultaneous submissions OK. Query for electronic submissions. Computer printout submissions acceptable; no dot-matrix. Reports in 2 weeks on queries; 1 week on mss. Free book catalog; ms guidelines for SASE.

Nonfiction: Reference and medical/nursing textbooks. Subjects include health (medical and dental); psychology (nursing); and psychiatry. Especially looking for "all phases of nursing education, administration and clinical procedures." Query, or submit outline/synopsis and sample chapters or complete ms. Reviews artwork/photos.

Recent Nonfiction Title: *Handbook of Pediatric Infectious Diseases*, by A.D. Friedman (medicine).

Tips: "Medical authors often feel that their incomplete works deserve to be published; dental authors have a tendency to overstress facts, thereby requiring considerable editing. We prefer the latter to the former."

*JALMAR PRESS, INC., A subsidiary of B.L. Winch & Associates, 45 Hitching Post Dr., Bldg. 2, Rolling Hill Estates CA 90274-4297. (213)547-1240. Editorial Director: B.L. Winch. Senior Editor: Suzanne Mikesell. Publishes trade paperback originals. Averages 4-8 titles/year. Pays 5-15% on net sales. Subsidy publishes 10% of books; subsidy publishes (nonauthor) 20% of books. Publishes book an average of 18 months after acceptance. Simultaneous and photocopied submissions OK. Query for electronic submissions. Computer printout submissions acceptable. Reports in 3 months. Book catalog for 8½x11 SAE with 69¢ postage.

Nonfiction: Positive self-esteem materials for parenting and teaching; right-brain/whole-brain learning materials; peacemaking skills activities for parenting and teaching; and inspirational titles or self-concept and values. Reviews artwork/photos as part of ms package. "Prefer completed ms."

Recent Nonfiction Title: *Openmind/Wholemind: Parenting and Teaching Tomorrow's Children Today*, by Bob Samples.

JAMESTOWN PUBLISHERS, INC., Box 9168, Providence RI 02940. (401)351-1915 or 1-800-USA-READ. Senior Editor: Ted Knight. Publishes paperback and hardcover supplementary reading text/workbooks. Averages 20 titles/year; receives 100 + submissions annually. 10% of books from first-time authors; 100% of books from unagented writers. Average print order for a writer's first book is 10,000. Pays 10% royalty on retail price; buys some mss outright; offers variable advance. Publishes book an average of 1 year after acceptance. Computer printout submissions acceptable; prefers letter-quality to dot-matrix. Reports in 1 month. Free book catalog.

Nonfiction: Textbook. "Materials for improving reading and study skills for kindergarten through twelfth grade, college, and adult education." Submit synopsis and sample chapters. Reviews artwork/photos as part of ms package.

Recent Nonfiction Title: *Heroes*, by Henry and Melissa Billings (middle school reading text).

Fiction: "We occasionally use original fiction as the basis for comprehension exercises and drills." Submit synopsis and sample chapters.

Tips: "We operate in a very clearly, narrowly defined subject area. The writer should know this field well and the more familiar he or she is with our products, the better. Reading/study skills material paralleling our current skills breakdown, and exceptional and innovative/groundbreaking material in the same areas have the best chance of selling to our firm."

JH PRESS, Box 294, Village Station, New York NY 10014. Publisher: Terry Helbing. Publishes trade paperback originals. Averages 3 titles/year. Pays 6-10% royalty on retail price; offers average $100 advance. Publishes book an average of 1 year after acceptance. Simultaneous and photocopied submissions OK. Reports in 2 weeks.

Nonfiction: Subjects include drama and theater. Studies of gay theater or gay plays. Query. Reviews artwork/photos as part of ms package.

Recent Nonfiction Title: *Gay Theatre Alliance Directory of Gay Plays*, by Terry Helbing.

Fiction: Drama and theater. Gay plays that have been produced but not previously published. Query.

Recent Fiction Title: *Last Summer at Bluefish Cove*, by Jane Chambers (play).

JOHNSON BOOKS, Johnson Publishing Co., 1880 S. 57th Ct., Boulder CO 80301. (303)443-1576. Imprint, Spring Creek Press. Editorial Director: Michael McNierney. Spring Creek Press, Scott Roederer. Publishes hardcover and paperback originals and reprints. Publishes 8-10 titles/year; receives 500 submissions annually. 30% of books from first-time authors; 90% of books from unagented writers. Average print order for a writer's first book is 5,000. Royalties vary. Publishes book an average of 1 year after acceptance. Good computer printout submissions acceptable; prefers letter-quality to dot-matrix. Reports in 1-2 months. Book catalog and ms guidelines for 9x12 SASE.

Nonfiction: General nonfiction, books on the West, environmental subjects, natural history, paleontology, geology, archaeology, travel, guidebooks, and outdoor recreation. "We are publishing a new series of books on fly-fishing under a separate imprint, Spring Creek Press." Accepts nonfiction translations. "We are primarily interested in books for the informed popular market, though we will consider vividly written scholarly works. As a small publisher, we are able to give every submission close personal attention." Query first or call. Accepts outline/synopsis and 3 sample chapters. Looks for "good writing, thorough research, professional presentation and appropriate style. Marketing suggestions from writers are helpful." Reviews artwork/photos.

Recent Nonfiction Title: *Field Guide to Mammal Tracking in North America*, by James Halfpenny.

Tips: "We are looking for nature titles with broad national, not just regional, appeal."

JONATHAN DAVID PUBLISHERS, 68-22 Eliot Ave., Middle Village NY 11379. (718)456-8611. Editor-in-Chief: Alfred J. Kolatch. Publishes hardcover and paperback originals. Averages 25-30 titles/year; receives 600 submissions annually. 50% of books from first-time authors; 75% of books from unagented writers. Pays standard royalty. Publishes book an average of 1 year after acceptance. Computer printout submissions acceptable; no dot-matrix. Reports in 3 weeks. Book catalog for 8½x5½ SASE.

Nonfiction: Adult nonfiction books for a general audience. Cookbooks, cooking and foods, how-to, baseball and football, reference, self-help, Judaica. Query.

Recent Nonfiction Title: *Great Jews in Music*, by Darryl Lyman (biographical reference).

‡KALEIDOSCOPIX INC. CHILDREN'S BOOK DIVISION, Box 389, Franklin MA 02038. (617)528-6211. President: J.A. Kruza. Averages 6-10 titles/year. Buys some ms outright for $300-500, or royalty basis. Photocopied submissions OK. Query for electronic submissions. Computer printout submissions OK. Reports in 2 weeks on queries; 2 months on mss. Free writer's guidelines for #10 SAE with 1 first class stamp.

Nonfiction: Humor, juvenile and self-help. Subjects include history, travel and nautical. "We're looking for

children's books, tourism and nautical books." Query or submit complete ms.
Fiction: Adventure, historical, humor and mainstream. Needs children's books for ages 3-7.

KALMBACH PUBLISHING CO., 1027 N. 7th St., Milwaukee WI 53233. (414)272-2060. Books Editor: Bob Hayden. Publishes hardcover and paperback originals and paperback reprints. Averages 6 titles/year; receives 25 submissions annually. 85% of books from first-time authors; 100% of books from unagented writers. Offers 5-8% royalty on retail price. Average advance: $1,000. Publishes book an average of 18 months after acceptance. Computer printout submissions acceptable; prefers letter-quality to dot-matrix. Reports in 2 months. Book catalog for 9x12 SAE with 39¢ postage.
Nonfiction: Hobbies, how-to, and recreation. "Our book publishing effort is in railroading and hobby how-to-do-it titles *only*." Query first. "I welcome telephone inquiries. They save me a lot of time, and they can save an author a lot of misconceptions and wasted work." In written query, wants to see "a detailed outline of two or three pages and a complete sample chapter with photos, drawings, and how-to text." Reviews artwork/photos.
Recent Nonfiction Title: *Guide to Tourist Railroads and Railroad Museums*, by George H. Drury (railroads).
Tips: "Our books are about half text and half illustrations. Any author who wants to publish with us must be able to furnish good photographs and rough drawings before we'll consider contracting for his book."

KAR-BEN COPIES INC., 6800 Tildenwood Ln., Rockville MD 20852. (301)984-8733. President: Judy Groner. Publishes hardcover and trade paperback originals. Averages 8-10 titles/year; receives 150 submissions annually. 25% of books from first-time authors; 100% from unagented writers. Average print order for a writer's first book is 5,000. Pays 6-8% royalty on gross sales; makes negotiable outright purchase; offers average $1,000 advance. Publishes book an average of 1 year after acceptance. Computer printout submissions acceptable. Reports in 1 week on queries; 1 month on mss. Free book catalog; ms guidelines for SASE.
Nonfiction: Jewish juvenile. Especially looking for books on Jewish life-cycle, holidays, and customs for children—"early childhood and elementary." Send only mss with Jewish content. Query with outline/synopsis and sample chapters or submit complete ms. Reviews artwork/photos as part of ms package.
Recent Nonfiction Title: *Ima on the Bimah— My Mommy is a Rabbi*, by Mindy Avra Portnoy (juvenile Judaica).
Fiction: Adventure, fantasy, historical and religious (all Jewish juvenile). Especially looking for Jewish holiday and history-related fiction for young children. Submit outline/synopsis and sample chapters or complete ms.
Recent Fiction Title: *Nathan's Hanukkah Bargain*.
Tips: "We envision Jewish children and their families, and juveniles interested in learning about Jewish subjects, as our audience."

WILLIAM KAUFMANN, INC., 95 1st St., Los Altos CA 94022. Editor-in-Chief: William Kaufmann. Hardcover and paperback originals. "Generally offers standard minimum book contract of 10-12½-15% but special requirements of book may call for lower royalties"; no advance. Reports in 1-2 months. Free book catalog.
Nonfiction: "We look primarily for originality and quality." Publishes Americana, art, business, computer science, economics, history, how-to, humor, medicine and psychiatry, scientific, and textbooks. Does not want to see cookbooks, novels, poetry, inspirational/religious or erotica. Query. Discourages submission of unsolicited manuscripts.
Recent Nonfiction Title: *What's So Funny About Business?*, by Sidney Harris (cartoons).

*KENT STATE UNIVERSITY PRESS, Kent State University, Kent OH 44242. (216)672-7913. Director: John T. Hubbell. Editor: Jeanne West. Publishes hardcover and paperback originals and some reprints. Averages 12-15 titles/year. Subsidy publishes (non-author) 20% of books. Standard minimum book contract on net sales; rarely offers advance. "Always write a letter of inquiry before submitting manuscripts. We can publish only a limited number of titles each year and can frequently tell in advance whether or not we would be interested in a particular manuscript. This practice saves both our time and that of the author, not to mention postage costs. If interested we will ask for complete manuscript. Decisions based on in-house readings and two by outside scholars in the field of study." Computer printout submissions acceptable; prefers letter-quality. Reports in 6-10 weeks. Enclose return postage. Free book catalog.
Nonfiction: Especially interested in "scholarly works in history of high quality, particularly any titles of regional interest for Ohio. Also will consider scholarly biographies, literary studies, archeological research, the arts, and general nonfiction."
Recent Nonfiction Title: *The Cautious Diplomat: Charles E. Bohlen and the Soviet Union, 1929-1969*, by T. Michael Ruddy (history/biography).

‡KERN INTERNATIONAL INC., Suite G-1, 100 Weymouth St., Rockland MA 02370. (617)871-4982. Senior Editor: Pam Korites. Publishes trade paperback originals and microcomputer software. Averages 12 titles/year; receives 75 submissions annually. 50% of books from first-time authors. Average print order for a writer's first book is 500. Pays 15% royalty on revenues received. Publishes book an average of 3 months after acceptance. Simultaneous and photocopied submissions OK. Query for electronic submissions. Computer printout submissions acceptable. Reports in 2 weeks. Book catalog and ms guidelines for 8½x11 SASE.

Nonfiction: How-to, technical, textbook and computer software in book form. Subjects include recreation, business, finance, science and engineering. We are interested in books that include computer program listings. Of special interest are how-to books in this area. We are also interested in nontechnical books and programs, such as business applications, as long as they relate to microcomputers. Of special interest are computer-aided design and manufacturing, robotics, computer graphics, and computer-aided instruction. Also, our publications must be of immediate interest to the computer and educational communities and must be highly professional in technical content. No mss of merely academic interest." Query or submit outline/synopsis and sample chapters. Reviews artwork/photos.

Recent Nonfiction Title: *Stock Market Charting*, by A. Hogue (investment).

MICHAEL KESEND PUBLISHING, LTD., 1025 5th Ave., New York NY 10028. (212)249-5150. Director: Michael Kesend. Publishes hardcover and trade paperback originals, and hardcover and trade paperback reprints. Averages 4-6 titles/year; receives 150 submissions annually. 50% of books from first-time authors; 50% of books from unagented writers. Pays 3-12½% royalty on wholesale price or retail price, or makes outright purchase for $500 minimum. Advance varies. Publishes book an average of 18 months after acceptance. Computer printout submissions acceptable; prefers letter-quality to dot-matrix. Reports in 2 months on queries; 3 months on mss. Book catalog and guidelines for #10 SASE.

Nonfiction: Biography, how-to, illustrated book, self-help and sports. Subjects include animals, health, history, hobbies, nature, sports, travel, the environment, and guides to several subjects. Needs sports, health self-help and environmental awareness guides. No photography mss. Submit outline/synopsis and sample chapters. Reviews artwork/photos.

Recent Nonfiction Title: *Emergency Care for Cats and Dogs*, by Craton Burkholder, D.V.M. (pet care).

Fiction: Literary fiction only. No science fiction or romance. No simultaneous submissions. Submit outline/synopsis and 2-3 sample chapters.

Recent Fiction Title: *Asylum Piece*, by Anna Kavan (literary fiction).

*B. KLEIN PUBLICATIONS, Box 8503, Coral Springs FL 33065. (305)752-1708. Editor-in-Chief: Bernard Klein. Hardcover and paperback originals. Specializes in directories, annuals, who's who type of books, bibliography, business opportunity, reference books. Averages 5 titles/year. Subsidy publishes 25% of books. Pays 10% royalty on wholesale price, "but we're negotiable." Advance "depends on many factors." Markets books by direct mail and mail order. Simultaneous and photocopied submissions OK. Reports in 1-2 weeks. Book catalog for #10 SASE.

Nonfiction: Business, hobbies, how-to, reference, self-help, directories and bibliographies. Query or submit outline/synopsis and sample chapters or complete ms.

Recent Nonfiction Title: *Mail Order Business Directory* 14th edition.

KNIGHTS PRESS, Box 454, Pound Ridge NY 10576. Publisher: Elizabeth G. Gershman. Publishes trade paperback originals. Averages 10 titles/year; receives 500 submissions annually. 50% of books from first-time authors; 75% of books from unagented writers. Pays 10 plus escalating royalty on retail price; offers average $500 advance. Publishes book an average of 1 year after acceptance. Photocopied submissions OK. Computer printout submissions acceptable; prefers letter-quality to dot-matrix. Reports in 1 month on queries; 3 months on mss. Book catalog and ms guidelines for business size SASE.

Fiction: Adventure, erotica (very soft-core considered), ethnic, experimental, fantasy, gothic, historical, humor, mystery, romance, science fiction, suspense and western. "We publish *only* gay men's fiction; must show a positive gay lifestyle or positive gay relationship." No young adult or children's; no pornography; no formula plots, especially no formula romances; or no hardcore S&M. No lesbian fiction. Query a must. Submit outline/synopsis and sample chapters. Do not submit complete manuscript unless requested.

Recent Fiction Title: *The Vanilla Kid*, by Daniel McVay (gay humor).

Tips: "We are interested in well-written, well-plotted gay fiction. We are looking only for the highest quality gay literature."

ALFRED A. KNOPF, INC., 201 E. 50th St., New York NY 10022. (212)751-2600. Senior Editor: Ashbel Green. Children's Book Editor: Ms. Frances Foster. Publishes hardcover and paperback originals. Averages 196 titles annually. 15% of books from first-time authors; 40% of books from unagented writers. Royalties and advance "vary." Publishes book an average of 10 months after acceptance. Simultaneous (if so informed) and photocopied submissions OK. Reports in 1 month. Book catalog for SASE.

Nonfiction: Book-length nonfiction, including books of scholarly merit. Preferred length: 40,000-150,000 words. "A good nonfiction writer should be able to follow the latest scholarship in any field of human knowledge, and fill in the abstractions of scholarship for the benefit of the general reader by means of good, concrete, sensory reporting." Query. Reviews artwork/photos.

Recent Nonfiction Title: *The Fatal Shore*, by R. Hughes (history).
Fiction: Publishes book-length fiction of literary merit by known or unknown writers. Length: 30,000-150,000 words. Submit complete ms.
Recent Fiction Title: *Sphere*, by M. Crichton.

KNOWLEDGE INDUSTRY PUBLICATIONS, INC., 701 Westchester Ave., White Plains, NY 10604. (914)328-9157. Assistant Vice President: Margaret Csenge. Publishes hardcover and paperback originals. Averages 10 titles/year; receives 30 submissions annually. 50% of books from first-time authors; 100% of books from unagented writers. Average print order for a writer's first book is 2,500. Offers 5-10% royalty on net price; also buys mss by outright purchase for minimum $500. Offers negotiable advance. Publishes book an average of 6 months after acceptance. Photocopied submissions OK. Electronic submissions OK via IBM, but requires hard copy also. Computer printout submissions acceptable; no dot-matrix. Reports in 2 weeks. Free book catalog; ms guidelines for SASE.
Nonfiction: Business and economics. Especially needs TV and video. Query first, then submit outline/synopsis and sample chapters. Reviews artwork/photos as part of ms package.
Recent Nonfiction Title: *Lighting Techniques for Video Production*, by Tom LeTourneau (theory and applications).

JOHN KNOX PRESS, 341 Ponce de Leon Ave. NE, Atlanta GA 30365. (404)873-1549. Editorial Director: Walter C. Sutton. Acquisitions Editor: John G. Gibbs. Averages 18 nonfiction titles/year. Pays royalty on income received; no advances. 20% of books from first-time authors; 100% of books from unagented writers. Publishes book an average of 9-12 months after acceptance. Query for electronic submissions. Computer printout submissions acceptable. Book catalog and "Guidelines for a Book Proposal" for 9x12 SASE.
Nonfiction: "We publish textbooks, resource books for ministry, and books to encourage Christian faith, in subject areas including biblical studies, theology, ethics, psychology, counseling, worship, and the relationship of science and technology to faith." Query or submit outline/synopsis and sample chapters.
Recent Nonfiction Title: *Hope Within History*, by W. Brueggemann (biblical theology).

ROBERT E. KRIEGER PUBLISHING CO. INC., Box 9542, Melbourne FL 32902-9542. (305)724-9542. Subsidiary, Orbit Book Company (space technology). Executive Assistant: Marie Bowles. Publishes hardcover and paperback originals and reprints. Averages 120 titles/year; receives 50-60 submissions annually. 30% of books from first-time authors; 100% of books from unagented writers. Pays royalty on net realized price. Publishes book an average of 8 months after acceptance. Computer printout submissions acceptable; prefers letter-quality to dot-matrix. Reports in 1 month. Free book catalog.
Nonfiction: College reference, technical, and textbook. Subjects include business, history, music, philosophy, psychology, recreation, religion, sociology, sports, chemistry, physics, engineering and medical. Reviews artwork/photos.
Recent Nonfiction Title: *Public History: An Introduction*, edited by Barbara J. Howe and Emory Kemp.

* PETER LANG PUBLISHING, 62 W. 45th St., New York NY 10036. (212)302-6740. Subsidiary of Verlag Peter Lang AG, Bern, Switzerland. Executive Director: Brigitte D. McDonald. Editor-in-Chief: Jay Wilson. Publishes hardcover and trade paperack originals, and hardcover and trade paperback reprints. Averages 120 titles/year; receives 600 submissions annually. 75% of books from first-time authors; 98% of books from unagented writers. Subsidy publishes 50% of books. All subsidies are guaranteed repayment plus profit (if edition sells out) in contract. Subsidy published if ms is highly specialized and author relatively unknown. Pays 10-30% royalty on net price. Translators get flat fee plus percentage of royalties. No advance. Publishes book an average of 1 year after acceptance. Photocopied submissions OK. Computer printout submissions acceptable; prefers letter-quality to dot-matrix. Reports in 2 months on queries; 4 months on mss. Free book catalog and ms guidelines.
Nonfiction: Biography, reference, textbook and scholarly monograph. Subjects include Americana, art, business and economics, health, history, music, philosophy, politics, psychology, religion, sociology and biography. All books are scholarly monographs, textbooks, reference books, reprints of historic texts, critical editions or translations. "We are expanding and are receptive to any scholarly project in the humanities and social sciences." No mss shorter than 200 pages; college textbooks. Submit complete ms.
Fiction: Critical editions and English translations of classics in any language. "We publish primarily nonfiction." Submit outline/synopsis and complete ms.
Poetry: Scholarly critical editions only. Submit complete ms.
Tips: "Besides our commitment to specialist academic monographs, we are one of the few U.S. publishers who publish books in most of the modern languages."

LEARNING PUBLICATIONS, INC., 5351 Gulf Dr., Holmes Beach FL 33510. (813)778-5524. Publisher: Edsel Erickson. Publishes hardcover and trade paperback originals. Averages 24 titles/year; receives 500+ submissions/year. 75% of books from first-time authors; 90% of books from unagented writers. Average print order for a writer's first book is 3,000. Pays 5% royalty on income received from sales. No advance. Publishes book an average of 18 months after acceptance. Photocopied submissions OK. Query for electronic submissions. Computer printout submissions acceptable; prefers letter-quality to dot-matrix. Reports in 3 weeks on queries; 3 months on mss. Book catalog and ms guidelines for 9x12 SASE.

Nonfiction: How-to (for professionals); self-help (for general public); technical; textbooks on art, psychology, sociology; and reference books for counselors, teachers, and school administrators. Books to help parents of children with reading problems and special needs (impaired, gifted, etc.), or art activity books for teachers. Query with outline/synopsis and sample chapters.

Recent Nonfiction Title: *101 Reading Games*, by Eleanor Miller.

Fiction: Query with outline/synopsis and sample chapters.

Recent Fiction Title: *First Story Book of Opera*, by C. Biscardi.

LEE'S BOOKS FOR YOUNG READERS,813 West Ave., Box 111, O'Neil Professional Bldg., Wellington TX 79095. (806)447-5445. Independent book producer/packager. Publisher: Lee Templeton. Small press. Publishes hardcover originals. Averages 8 titles/year; receives 60 submissions annually. 20% of books from first-time authors; 100% of books from unagented writers. Average print order for a writer's first book is 1,000. Pays 10% minimum royalty on wholesale price. No advance. Publishes book an average of 1 year after acceptance. Computer printout submissions acceptable; no dot-matrix. Free book catalog.

Nonfiction: Biography. "Our books are nonfiction history of young heroes. All our books are written for 'reluctant' readers in junior high school market (10-14 age group), to be sold to junior (middle) school libraries. We will consider queries about young American heroes, male or female, that historians overlooked." Query; all unsolicited mss are returned unopened. Reviews artwork/photos.

Recent Nonfiction Title: *Pilot Boy*, by Lee Templeton (autobiography).

Fiction: Query; all unsolicited mss are returned unopened.

Recent Fiction Title: *Albert Geronimo*, by Lee Templeton (humorous animal story).

Tips: "Tell a beautiful story about a young person (under age 19) who performed a heroic deed that affected history. The only books we publish are nonfiction —about 'Young Heroes of America' preferably under 200 pages, with good illustrations and pictures."

LEISURE BOOKS, Division of Dorchester Publishing Co., Inc., Suite 900, 6 E. 39th St., New York NY 10016. (212)725-8811. Editor: Katherine Carlon. Publishes mass market paperback originals and reprints. Averages 144 titles/year; receives thousands of submissions annually. 50% of books from first-time authors; 60% of books from unagented writers. Pays royalty on retail price or makes outright purchase. Offers average $1,000 advance. Publishes book an average of 18 months after acceptance. Computer printout submissions acceptable; no dot-matrix. Reports in 2 weeks on queries; up to 2 months on mss. Book catalog and ms guidelines for SASE.

Nonfiction: "Our needs are minimal as we publish perhaps four nonfiction titles a year." Query.

Fiction: Historical (120,000+ words); horror (90,000-100,000+ words); mainstream (up to 100,000+ words); and historical romantic suspense (75,000-90,000 words). "We are strongly backing the horror, historical romance and contemporary women's fiction." No sweet romance, science fiction, western, erotica or male adventure. Query or submit outline/synopsis and sample chapters.

Recent Fiction Title: *Summer Storm*, by Catherine Hart (historical romance).

Tips: "Horror and historical romance are our best sellers."

LEISURE PRESS, Box 5076, Champaign IL 61820. (217)351-5076. Director: Vic Mackenzie. Publishes hardcover, trade paperback and mass market paperback originals. Averages 30 titles/year; receives 100-150 submissions annually. 80% of books from first-time authors; 90% from unagented writers. Pays 10-15% royalty on wholesale price. Offers average $1,000 advance. Publishes ms an average of 9 months after acceptance. Simultaneous submissions OK. Query for electronic submissions. Computer printout submissions OK; prefers letter-quality to dot-matrix. Reports in 2 weeks on queries; 6 weeks on ms. Free book catalog; writer's guidelines for SASE.

Nonfiction: How-to, reference, technical. Subjects include sports, fitness and wellness. "We want coaching-related books, technique books on sports and fitness. No fitness or coaching books that are not based on sound physical education principles and research." Reviews artwork/photos as part of ms package. Query or submit outline/synopsis and sample chapters.

Recent Nonfiction Title: *Baby Swim Book*, by Kochen/McCabe (fitness/technique).

Tips: "Our audience is coaches, athletes and physical education students. Target my audience and cater to their needs."

HAL LEONARD PUBLISHING CORP.,8112 W. Bluemound Rd., Box 13819, Milwaukee WI 53213. (414)774-3630. Imprints include Hal Leonard Books and Robus Books. Managing Editor: Glenda Herro. Publishes hardcover and trade paperback originals. Averages 20 titles/year; receives 25 submissions annually. 95% of books from unagented writers. Pays 5-10% royalty on wholesale or retail price. Publishes book an average of 1 year after acceptance. Simultaneous and photocopied submissions OK. Reports in 2 months on queries; 3 months on mss. Free book catalog.

Nonfiction: Biography, "coffee table" book, how-to, illustrated book, reference and technical. "The majority of our titles are music or entertainment-industry related." Especially interested in "subject matter related to pop and rock music, Broadway theatre, film and television personalities, and general interest material in the music and entertainment industry." Query. Reviews artwork/photos.

Recent Nonfiction Title: *Billboard Top 1000 Singles 1955-1986*, by Joel Whitburn (popular music).

Tips: "Our books are for all age groups interested in music and entertainment. Robus Books (rock photo-biographies) are geared to the juvenile and young adult markets."

LEXIKOS,4079 19th Ave., San Francisco CA 94132. (415)584-1085. Imprints include Don't Call It Frisco Press. Editor: Mike Witter. Publishes hardcover and trade paperback originals and trade paperback reprints. Averages 3 (growing each season) titles/year; receives 200 submissions annually. 50% of books from first-time authors; 90% of books from unagented writers. Average print order for a writer's first book is 5,000. Royalties vary from 8-12½% according to book sold. "Authors asked to accept lower royalty on high discount (50% plus) sales." Offers average $1,000 advance. Publishes book an average of 10 months after acceptance. Simultaneous and photocopied submissions OK. Computer printout submissions acceptable. Reports in 1 month. Book catalog and ms guidelines for 6x9 SAE and 2 first class stamps.

Nonfiction: "Coffee table" book, illustrated book. Subjects include regional, outdoors, oral histories, Americana, history and nature. Especially looking for 50,000-word "city and regional histories, anecdotal in style for a general audience; books of regional interest about *places*; adventure and wilderness books; annotated reprints of books of Americana; Americana in general." No health, sex, European travel, diet, broad humor, fiction, quickie books (we stress backlist vitality), religion, children's or nutrition. Submit outline/synopsis and sample chapters. Reviews artwork/photos.

Recent Nonfiction Title: *From Satori to Silicon Valley*, by Theodore Roszak (history of Silicon Valley).

Tips: "A regional interest or history book has the best chance of selling to Lexikos. Submit a short, cogent proposal; follow up with letter queries. Give the publisher reason to believe you will help him *sell* the book (identify the market, point out the availability of mailing lists, distinguish your book from the competition). Avoid grandiose claims."

LIBERTY PUBLISHING COMPANY, INC., 50 Scott Adam Rd., Cockeysville MD 21030. (301)667-6680. Publisher: Jeffrey B. Little. Publishes hardcover and mostly trade paperback originals and software. Averages 10-15 titles/year; receives 500 submissions annually. 10% of books from first-time authors; 95% of books from unagented writers. Average print order for a writer's first book is 4,000-6,000. Pays 6-12% royalty of wholesale or retail price; buys some mss outright for $500-2,000; offers average $400 advance. Publishes book an average of 6-12 months after acceptance. Computer printout submissions acceptable; prefers letter-quality to dot-matrix. Reports in 3 weeks on queries; 1-2 months on mss. "Exclusive distribution arrangements with self-publishers possible. We are also seeking tie-ins with software and videos."

Nonfiction: Biography, cookbook, how-to, illustrated book and self-help. Subjects include Americana, business, cooking and foods, history, hobbies, photography (b&w only), recreation, sports, travel, educational, videos and computer software. Accepts nonfiction translations. "How-to or self-help books dealing with concrete advice written by people qualified to address the subject. Extensive graphic possibilities preferred. No self-improvement books dealing with psychology and mind improvement. No poetry, please." Query with author biography or submit outline/synopsis and 3 sample chapters. Reviews artwork/photos as part of ms package.

Recent Nonfiction Title: *Winning at the Track*, by David L. Christopher (horse race handicapping).

Tips: Author has best chance with how-to. "Know your competition and tell us why your book is better."

*LIBRA PUBLISHERS, INC., Suite 383, 3089C Clairemont Dr., San Diego CA 92117. (619)581-9449. Contact: William Kroll. Publishes hardcover and paperback originals. Specializes in the behavioral sciences. Averages 15 titles/year; receives 300 submissions annually. 60% of books from first-time authors; 85% of books from unagented writers. 10-15% royalty on retail price; no advance. "We will also offer our services to authors who wish to publish their own works. The services include editing, proofreading, production, artwork, copyrighting, and assistance in promotion and distribution." Publishes book an average of 8 months after acceptance. Computer printout submissions acceptable; prefers letter-quality to dot-matrix. Reports in 2 weeks. Free book catalog.

Nonfiction: Mss in all subject areas will be given consideration, but main interest is in the behavioral sciences. Prefers complete manuscript but will consider outline/synopsis and 3 sample chapters. Reviews artwork/photos as part of ms package.

Recent Nonfiction Title: *Hidden Bedroom Partners: Needs & Motives that Destroy Sexual Pleasure*, by Frank Hajcak, Ph.D. and Patricia Garwood, M.D.

LIBRARIES UNLIMITED, Box 263, Littleton CO 80160. (303)770-1220. Imprints include Ukranian Academic Press. Editor-in-Chief: Bohdan S. Wynar. Small press. Publishes hardcover and paperback originals. Averages 40 titles/year; receives 100-200 submissions annually. 10-20% of books from first-time authors. Average print order for a writer's first book is 2,000. 10% royalty on net sales; advance averages $500. Publishes book an average of 1 year after acceptance. Reports in 2 months. Free book catalog and ms guidelines.

Nonfiction: Publishes reference and library science text books. Looks for professional experience. Query or submit outline and sample chapters; state availability of photos/illustrations with submission. All prospective authors are required to fill out an author questionnaire.

Recent Nonfiction Title: *Women's Studies*, by Loeb, Searing and Stineman.

‡**LIFE CYCLE BOOKS**, Subsidiary of Life Cycle Books, Ltd., Toronto, Canada. Box 792, Lewiston NY 14092-0792. (416)690-5860. President: Paul Broughton. Publishes trade paperback originals and reprints, brochures and pamphlets. Receives 150 submissions annually. 30% of books from first time authors. 100% of books from unagented authors. Averages 5-10 titles/year. Pays 8% royalty on net price for books; makes outright purchase of $200-1,000 for pamphlets and books. Offers average $150 advance. Publishes book an average of 18 months after acceptance. Photocopied submissions OK if good quality reproduction. Computer printout submissions acceptable; no dot-matrix. Reports in 2 weeks on queries; 2 months on mss. Free book catalog.

Nonfiction: Health, history, politics, religion, sociology. Specifically "We publish materials on human life issues (i.e. abortion, infanticide, euthanasia, child abuse, sex education, etc.) written from a pro-life perspective." Query for books; submit complete ms for pamphlets or brochures. Reviews artwork/photos as part of ms package.

Recent Nonfiction Titles: *Abortion, the Bible and the Church*, by T. J. Bosgra.

LIGUORI PUBLICATIONS, Book and Pamphlet Dept., 1 Liguori Dr., Liguori MO 63057. (314)464-2500. Editor-in-Chief: Rev. Christopher Farrell, C.SS.R. Managing Editor: Thomas Artz, C.SS.R. Publishes paperback originals. Specializes in Catholic-Christian religious materials. Averages 35 titles/year; receives about 200 submissions annually. About 40% of books from first-time authors; 95% of books from unagented writers. Average print order for a writer's first book is 10,000-16,000. Pays royalty on books; flat fee on pamphlets and teacher's guides. Publishes book an average of 8 months after acceptance. Query for electronic submissions. Computer printout submissions acceptable; no dot-matrix. Reports in 5 weeks. Book catalog and ms guidelines for 9x12 SAE with 73¢ postage.

Nonfiction: Publishes doctrinal, inspirational, biblical, self-help and educational materials. Looks for "thought and language that speak to basic practical religious concerns of contemporary Catholic Christians." Query or submit synopsis and 1 sample chapter; "never submit total book."

Recent Nonfiction Title: *The Single Life: A Christian Challenge.*

Tips: "Simply written and short self-help/educational material that is easily understood and can relate to the 'ordinary' Catholic has the best chance of selling to our firm. Writers often do not understand the focus of a publisher, and send a good manuscript to the wrong publisher."

LINCH PUBLISHING, INC., Box 75, Orlando FL 32802. (305)647-3025. Vice President: Dolores W. Neville. Editor: Val Lynch. Publishes hardcover and trade paperback originals. Averages 10 titles/year; receives 100 submissions annually. 25% of books from first-time authors; 25% of books from unagented writers. Pays 6-10% royalty on retail price. Rarely pays advances. Publishes book an average of 9 months after acceptance. Simultaneous and photocopied submissions OK. Computer printout submissions acceptable; prefers letter-quality to dot-matrix. Reports in 6 weeks. Book catalog for $1 and #10 SAE with 39¢ postage.

Nonfiction: Specializes in books on estate planning and legal how-to books which must be applicable in all 50 states. "We are interested in a book on getting through probate, settling an estate, and minimizing federal estate and/or state inheritance taxes." Query editor by phone before submitting mss—"we could have already accepted a manuscript and be in the process of publishing one of the above."

Recent Nonfiction Title: *Family Affairs: A Record Keeping Book.*

Tips: Currently interest is mainly estate planning.

LITTLE, BROWN AND CO., INC., 34 Beacon St., Boston MA 02108. Contact: Editorial Department, Trade Division. Publishes hardcover and paperback originals and paperback reprints. Averages 100+ titles/year. "Royalty and advance agreements vary from book to book and are discussed with the author at the time an offer is made. Submissions only from authors who have had a book published or have been published in professional or literary journals, newspapers or magazines." Computer printout submissions acceptable; prefers letter-quality to dot-matrix. Reports in 3 months for queries/proposals.

Nonfiction: "Some how-to books, distinctive cookbooks, biographies, history, science and sports." Query or submit outline/synopsis and sample chapters. Reviews artwork/photos as part of ms package.

Recent Nonfiction Title: *Ford, the Men and the Machine*, by Robert Lacey.

Fiction: Contemporary popular fiction as well as fiction of literary distinction. "Our poetry list is extremely limited; those collections of poems that we do publish are usually the work of poets who have gained recognition through publication in literary reviews and various periodicals." Query or submit outline/synopsis and sample chapters.

Recent Fiction Title: *In the Land of Dreamy Dreams*, by Ellen Gilchrist.

*LLEWELLYN PUBLICATIONS, Division of Chester-Kent, Inc., Box 64383-WM88, St. Paul MN 55164-0383. (612)291-1970. President: Carl L. Weschcke. Publishes hardcover and trade paperback originals and reprints, audio and video cassettes and software. Averages 15-18 titles/year; receives 300 submissions annually. 50% of books from first-time authors; 95% of books from unagented writers. Subsidy publishes 10% or less of books; "generally the subsidized book is well-written and makes a valuable contribution to the subject area, but we feel the market potential to be too small for our investment in publication, or the book is too expensive or too slow in turnover." Pays 10-15% royalty. Publishes book an average of 1 year after acceptance. Simultaneous and photocopied submissions OK. Computer printout submissions acceptable; no dot-matrix. Reports in 3 months. Book catalog $2; ms guidelines for $1 and SASE.
Nonfiction: "Coffee table" book, how-to, reference, self-help and textbook. Subjects include astrology and occultism. Especially looking for self-help through astrology and occultism, with the emphasis on practicality, readability, and wide market. No pseudo or "pop" approaches to the subjects; no "satanism." Submit outline/synopsis and sample chapters. Reviews artwork/photos.
Recent Nonfiction Title: *Psionics 101*, by Charles Cosimano (parapsychology).
Tips: " 'Real' self-help or how-to books (tapes and software also) dealing with aspects of astrology, magic, psychic development, spiritual development, lunar gardening, past life regression, hypnosis and self-hypnosis, etc. have the best chance of selling to our firm. The writer should show that he or she understands the market as well as the subject area—so that the book is written to fulfill a marketable need."

LODESTAR BOOKS, Division of E. P. Dutton, 2 Park Ave., New York NY 10016. (212)725-1818. Editorial Director: Virginia Buckley. Editor: Rosemary Brosnan. Hardcover originals. Publishes juveniles, young adults, fiction and nonfiction; nonfiction picture books. Averages 20 titles/year; receives 800 submissions annually. 10-20% of books from first-time authors; 25-30% of books from unagented writers. Average print order for a writer's first book is 4,000-5,000. Pays royalty on invoice list price; advance offered. Publishes book an average of 18 months after acceptance. Photocopied submissions OK. Electronic submissions OK, but requires hard copy also. Computer printout submissions acceptable; prefers letter-quality to dot-matrix. Reports in 2-4 months. Ms guidelines for SASE.
Nonfiction: Query or submit outline/synopsis and 2-3 sample chapters including "theme, chapter-by-chapter outline, and 1 or 2 completed chapters." State availability of photos and/or illustrations. Queries/mss may be routed to other editors in the publishing group. Reviews artwork/photos as part of ms package.
Fiction: Publishes only for young adults and juveniles: adventure, fantasy, historical, humorous, contemporary, mystery, science fiction, suspense and western books. Submit complete ms.
Tips: "A young adult novel that is literary, fast-paced, well-constructed (as opposed to a commercial novel) and well-written nonfiction on contemporary issues have the best chance of selling to our firm."

LOMOND PUBLICATIONS, INC., Box 88, Mt. Airy MD 21771. (301)829-1496. Publisher: Lowell H. Hattery. Publishes hardcover originals. Averages 3-10 titles/year; receives 30 submissions annually. 50% of books from first-time authors; 100% of books from unagented writers. Pays 10% royalty on net price or makes outright purchase. No advance. Publishes book an average of 6-18 months after acceptance. Simultaneous submissions OK. Computer printout submissions acceptable. Reports in 1 month. Free book catalog.
Nonfiction: Technical, professional and scholarly. Subjects include business and economics, politics, sociology, public policy, technological change and management. Query or submit complete ms.
Recent Nonfiction Title: *Management's Hidden Enemy*, by Prof. David S. Brown (cause and cure for dysfunctionalism).
Tips: "We publish for the scholarly, professional, and well-informed lay readers of all countries. We publish only English titles, but many are subsequently reprinted and translated in other languages. A writer's best bet with us is an interdisciplinary approach to management, technology or public policy."

‡LONE EAGLE PUBLISHING CO., 9903 Santa Monica Blvd., Beverly Hills CA 90212. (213)471-8066. President: Joan V. Singleton. Small press. Publishes hardcover and trade paperback originals. Averages 3-4 titles/year; receives 8-10 submissions annually. 100% of books from unagented writers. Pays 10% royalty minimum on net price, wholesale and retail. Offers $250 average advance. Publishes a book an average of 1 year after acceptance. Simultaneous and photocopied submissions OK. Query for electronic submissions. Computer printout submissions OK; prefers letter-quality. Book catalog for #10 SAE and 1 first class postage stamp.
Nonfiction: Self-help, technical, how-to, and reference. Subjects include movies. "We are looking for technical books in the motion picture and video field by professionals. No unrelated topics or biographies." Submit outline/synopsis and sample chapters. Reviews artwork/photos as part of ms package.
Recent Nonfiction Title: *Film Directors: A Complete Guide*, by M. Singer (reference).
Tips: "A well-written, well-thought-out book on some technical aspect of the motion picture (or video) industry has the best chance: for example, script supervising, editing, special effects, costume design, production design. Pick a subject that has not been done to death, make sure you know what you're talking about, get someone well-known in that area to endorse the book and prepare to spend a lot of time publicizing the book."

LONGMAN FINANCIAL SERVICES PUBLISHING, 520 N. Dearborn, Chicago IL 60610. (312)836-0466. Senior Editor, Real Estate Textbooks: Richard Hagle. Executive Editor, Trade and Professional Books: Kathy Welton. Acquisitions Editor, Financial Services Textbooks: Paul Revenko-Jones. Associate Publisher Subscription Services: Sheila Frank. Imprints include Real Estate Education Co., Farnsworth Publishing, R&R Newkirk, Educational Methods, Inc., Longman Trade and Longman Financial Services Publishing. Publishes hardcover and paperback originals and subscription products for consumers, investors and professionals in real estate, insurance, financial planning, securities and all other financial services industries (includes standard and client newsletters and loose leaf services). Averages 100 titles/year; receives 200 submissions annually. 60% of books from first-time authors; 99% of books from unagented writers. Average print order for a writer's first book is 500-3,000. Pays 5-15% royalty; no advance. Publishes book an average of 1 year after acceptance. Simultaneous and photocopied submissions OK. Computer printout submissions acceptable; prefers letter-quality to dot-matrix. Reports in 2 months. Free book catalog and ms guidelines.
Nonfiction: "Publishes books for real estate professionals and other financial services professionals (banking, financial planning, insurance, securities). Also publishes on financial and investment topics for consumers and investors. Any topics appropriate for this market are of interest." Submit outline and 1-3 sample chapters (but not the first chapter) or complete ms. Reviews artwork/photos as part of ms package.
Recent Nonfiction Title: *Financial Planning Under the New Rules: An Investor's Guide to the Tax Reform Act of 1986.*
Tips: "We seek well-targeted books and proposals for course books, professional how-to, investor how-to, and reference books in all segments of the financial services industry. The writer must know the market, and, more importantly, the competitive books. Once a proposal is signed, authors often lose their market focus. We recommend close, careful attention be paid to a detailed chapter-by-chapter outline."

LONGMAN, INC., 95 Church St., White Plains NY 10601. (914)993-5000. President: Bruce S. Butterfield. Publishes hardcover and paperback originals. Publishes 200 titles/year. Pays variable royalty; offers variable advance. Photocopied submissions OK. Reports in 6 weeks.
Nonfiction: Textbooks only (elementary/high school, college and professional): world history, political science, economics, communications, social sciences, education, English, Latin, foreign languages, English as a second language. No trade, art or juvenile.

LOTHROP, LEE & SHEPARD BOOKS, Division of William Morrow & Company, 105 Madison Ave., New York NY 10016. (212)889-3050. Editor-in-Chief: Dorothy Briley. Hardcover original children's books only. Royalty and advance vary according to type of book. Averages 60 titles/year; receives 4,000 submissions annually. Less than 2% of books from first-time authors; 25% of books from unagented writers. Average print order for a writer's first book is 6,000. State availability of photos to accompany ms. Publishes book an average of 2 years after acceptance. Photocopied submissions OK, but originals preferred. No simultaneous submissions. Computer printout submissions acceptable; no dot-matrix. Responds in 6 weeks. Book catalog and guidelines for 9x12 SAE with 88¢ postage.
Fiction and Nonfiction: Publishes picture books, general nonfiction, and novels. Submit outline/synopsis and sample chapters for nonfiction. Juvenile fiction emphasis is on novels for the 8-12 age group. Submit complete ms for fiction. Looks for "organization, clarity, creativity, literary style."
Recent Nonfiction Title: *Reaching for Dreams*, by Susan Kuklin (photo essay about a ballet).
Recent Fiction Title: *Mufaro's Beautiful Daughters*, by John Steptie (illustrated picture book).
Tips: "Trends in book publishing that freelance writers should be aware of include the demand for books for children under age three and the shrinking market for young adult books, especially novels."

*LOYOLA UNIVERSITY PRESS, 3441 N. Ashland Ave., Chicago IL 60657. (312)281-1818. Editorial Director: George A. Lane. Imprints include Campion Books. Publishes hardcover and trade paperback originals, and hardcover and trade paperback reprints. Averages 15 titles/year; receives 100 submissions annually. 40% of books from first-time authors; 95% of books from unagented writers. Subsidy publishes 5% of books. Pays 5-10% royalty on wholesale price; offers no advance. Publishes book an average of 1 year after acceptance. Simultaneous and photocopied submissions acceptable. Query for electronic submissions. Computer printout submissions acceptable; prefers letter-quality to dot-matrix. Reports in 1 month on queries; 1 month on mss. Book catalog for 6x9 SASE.
Nonfiction: Biography and textbook. Subjects include art (religious); history (church); and religion. The four subject areas of Campion Books include Jesuitica (Jesuit history, biography and spirituality); Literature-Theology interface (books dealing with theological or religious aspects of literary works or authors); contemporary Catholic concerns (books on morality, spirituality, family life, pastoral ministry, prayer, worship, etc.); and Chicago/art (books dealing with the city of Chicago from historical, artistic, architectural, or ethnic perspectives, but with religious emphases). Query before submitting ms. Reviews artwork/photos.
Recent Nonfiction Titles: *Spiritual Development*, by Daniel Helminiak (theology/psychology).
Tips: "Our audience is principally the college-educated reader with religious, theological interest."

‡**LURAMEDIA**, Box 261668, 10227 Autumnview Lane, San Diego CA 92126. (619)578-1948. Editorial Director: Lura Jane Geiger. Publishes trade paperback originals and reprints. Averages 3-4 titles/year; receives 100 submissions annually. 75% of books from first-time authors. 100% of books from unagented writers. Pays 10-15% royalty on wholesale price. Publishes book an average of 6 months after acceptance. Photocopied submissions OK. Query for electronic submissions. Computer printout submissions OK; prefers letter-quality. Reports in 1 week on queries; 3 weeks on mss. Book catalog and guidelines for SASE.
Nonfiction: Self-help. Subjects include health, philosophy, psychology, and creativity. "Books on renewal . . . body, mind spirit . . . using the right brain and relational material. Books on creativity, journaling, women's issues, relationships. I want well digested, thoughtful books. No 'Jesus Saves' literature; books that give all the answers; poetry; or strident politics." Submit outline/synopsis and sample chapters. Reviews artwork/photos as part of ms package.
Recent Nonfiction Title: *Guerrillas of Grace: Prayers for the Battle*, by Ted Loder (prayer/meditation).
Tips: "Our audience is people who want to grow and change; who want to get in touch with their spiritual side; who want to relax; who are creative and want creative ways to live."

MARGARET K. McELDERRY BOOKS, Macmillan Publishing Co., Inc., 866 3rd Ave., New York NY 10022. Editor: Margaret K. McElderry. Publishes hardcover originals. Publishes 20-25 titles/year; receives 1,200-1,300 submissions annually. 8% of books from first-time authors; 45% of books from unagented writers. The average print order is 6,000-7,500 for a writer's first teen book; 7,500-10,000 for a writer's first picture book. Pays royalty on retail price. Publishes book an average of 1½ years after acceptance. Reports in 6 weeks. Computer printout submissions acceptable; no dot-matrix. Ms guidelines for SASE.
Nonfiction and Fiction: Quality material for preschoolers to 16-year-olds. Looks for "originality of ideas, clarity and felicity of expression, well-organized plot (fiction) or exposition (nonfiction) quality." Reviews artwork/photos as part of ms package.
Recent Title: *I Have a Friend*, by Keiko Narahashi.
Tips: "There is not a particular 'type' of book that we are interested in above others; rather, we look for superior quality in both writing and illustration." Freelance writers should be aware of the swing away from teen-age problem novels to books for young readers.

McFARLAND & COMPANY, INC., PUBLISHERS, Box 611, Jefferson NC 28640. (919)246-4460. President and Editor-in-Chief: Robert Franklin. Business Manager: Rhonda Herman. Editor: Virginia Hege. Publishes hardcover and "quality" paperback originals; a non-"trade" publisher. Averages 65 titles/year; receives 700 submissions annually. 70% of books from first-time authors; 95% of books from unagented writers. Average print order for a writer's first book is 1,000. Pays 10-12½% royalty on gross receipts; no advance. Publishes book an average of 15 months after acceptance. Computer printout submissions acceptable; prefers letter-quality to dot-matrix. Reports in 2 weeks.
Nonfiction: Reference books and scholarly, technical and professional monographs. Subjects include Americana, art, business, chess, drama/theatre, health, cinema/radio/TV (very strong here), history, literature, librarianship (very strong here), music, parapsychology, religion, sociology, sports/recreation, women's studies, and world affairs (very strong here). "We will consider *any* scholarly book—with authorial maturity and competent grasp of subject." Reference books are particularly wanted—fresh material (i.e., not in head-to-head competition with an established title). "We don't like manuscripts of fewer than 200 double-spaced typed pages. Our market consists mainly of libraries." No memoirs, poetry, children's books, devotional/inspirational works or personal essays. Query or submit outline/synopsis and sample chapters. Reviews artwork/photos as part of ms package.
Recent Nonfiction Title: *Commonsense Copyright: A Guide to the New Technologies*, by R.S. Talab (comprehensive handbook for teachers and librarians).
Tips: "We do *not* accept novels or fiction of any kind. Don't worry about writing skills—we have editors. What we want is well-organized *knowledge* of an area in which there is not good information coverage at present, plus reliability so we don't feel we have to check absolutely everything."

McGRAW-HILL BOOK CO., College Division, 1221 Avenue of the Americas, New York NY 10020. (212)512-2000. Editors-in-Chief: Philip Butcher (social sciences and humanities); Kay Pace (business and economics); Eric Munson (engineering and computer science); David Boleio (science, math, nursing). Publishes hardcover and softcover technical material and software for the college market.
Nonfiction: The College Division publishes textbooks. The writer must know the college curriculum and course structure. Also publishes scientific texts and reference books in business and economics, computers, engineering, social sciences, physical sciences, nursing, and mathematics. Material should be scientifically and factually accurate. Most, but not all, books should be designed for existing courses offered in various disciplines of study. Books should have superior presentations and be more up-to-date than existing textbooks.

MACMILLAN PUBLISHING COMPANY, Children's Book Department, 866 3rd Ave., New York NY 10022. Publishes hardcover originals. Averages 65 titles/year. Will consider juvenile submissions only. Fiction and nonfiction. Enclose return postage.

MADRONA PUBLISHERS, INC., Box 22667, Seattle WA 98122. (206)325-3973. President: Daniel J. Levant. Editorial Director: Sara Levant. Publishes hardcover and paperback originals and paperback reprints. Averages 6-8 titles/year; receives 1,000 submissions annually. 80% of books from first-time authors; 95% of books from unagented writers. Average print order for a writer's first book is 5,000. Pays 15-17½% royalty on net sales; offers $1,000 average advance. Publishes book an average of 1 year after acceptance. Computer printout submissions acceptable; prefers letter-quality to dot-matrix. Reports in 2 months. Book catalog and guidelines for SASE.

Nonfiction: Americana, biography, cooking and foods, health, history, hobbies, how-to, humor, photography, politics, psychology, recreation, self-help and travel. Query, submit outline/synopsis and at least 2 sample chapters or complete ms. Accepts nonfiction and fiction translations. Reviews artwork/photos (if appropriate) as part of ms package.

Recent Nonfiction Title: *The Marriage Bed*, by William Womack, M.D. (marriage self-help).

Tips: "*Good* popular psychology on subjects of current interest—family, alcoholism, parenting, social problems, etc.—has the best chance of selling to our firm."

THE MAIN STREET PRESS, William Case House, Pittstown NJ 08867. (201)735-9424. Editorial Director: Martin Greif. Publishes hardcover and trade paperback originals. Averages 30 titles/year; receives 750 submissions annually. 50% of books from first-time authors; 50% of books from unagented writers. Pays 5-7½% royalty on paperbacks, 10-15% on a sliding scale for hardcover books; advance varies widely. Sometimes makes outright purchase. Publishes book an average of 1 year after acceptance. Simultaneous and photocopied submissions OK. Computer printout submissions OK. Reports in 2 months on queries; 3 months on mss. Reviews artwork/photos (photocopies OK) as part of ms package. Book catalog $1.25.

Nonfiction: Subjects include Americana, art, hobbies, gardening, film, architecture, popular culture, humor and design. "We publish *heavily illustrated* books on almost all subjects; we publish *only* illustrated books." Especially needs how-to quilting books. "We do not want to consider any nonfiction book with fewer than 75 illustrations." Query or submit outline/synopsis and sample chapters. "We will *not* return queries without SASE, and we will *not* return unsolicited manuscripts without return postage."

Recent Nonfiction Title: *How to Be a Happy Cat*, by Charles Platt.

Tips: "Our books are for the 'carriage trade'."

MARATHON INTERNATIONAL PUBLISHING COMPANY, INC., Dept. WM, Box 33008, Louisville KY 40232. President: Jim Wortham. Publishes hardcover originals, and trade paperback originals, trade paperback reprints. Averages 10 titles/year. Pays 10% royalty on wholesale. Publishes book an average of 10 months after acceptance. Simultaneous and photocopied submissions OK. Computer printout submissions acceptable. Reports in 2 weeks. Book catalog for 6x9 SAE and 4 first class stamps.

Nonfiction: Cookbooks, how-to, self-help. Especially needs how-to make extra money-type mss; self-improvement; how a person can be happier and more prosperous. No biography, textbooks or poetry. Query. Reviews artwork/photos as part of ms package.

‡MARLOR PRESS, 4304 Brigadoon Dr., St. Paul MN 55126. (612)483-1588. Editors: L. Theovin and M. Bree. Publishes trade paperback originals. Averages 4-5 titles/year; receives 100+ submissions annually. 10% of books from first-time authors. 100% of books from unagented writers. Pays 5-10% royalty on net sales. Publishes book an average of 1 year after acceptance. Simultaneous and photocopied submissions OK. Computer printout submissions OK. Reports in 1 month on queries. Book catalog for #10 SAE and 1 first class stamp.

Nonfiction: Travel books. Query or submit outline/synopsis and sample chapters or complete ms. Reviews artwork/photos as part of ms package.

Recent Nonfiction Title: *London for the Independent Traveler*, by Ruth Humleker (self-guided tours).

Tips: "Our books are targeted toward the independent traveler who likes to plan ahead and learn about options. We are interested in books dealing with all aspects of travel, particularly affordable travel. We might also be interested in travel-related gift books."

‡MAYNARD-THOMAS PUBLISHING, INC., Box 14753, Orlando FL 32857-4753. (305)658-1539. President: Beth Brennan. Publishes trade paperback originals. Averages 3 titles/year; receives 15 submissions annually. 50% of books from first-time authors; 50% of books from unagented writers. Pays 5-10% royalty on wholesale or retail price. No advance. Publishes book and average of 1 year after acceptance. Simultaneous and photocopied submissions OK. Computer printout submissions OK; prefers letter-quality to dot-matrix. Reports in 2 months on queries; 3 months on mss. Book catalog for #10 SAE and 1 first class stamp.

Nonficton: Self-help, juvenile and textbook. Subjects include animals and elementary drama. "We want compilations of unique and interesting stories involving animals and how-to books involving animals. No stories about one individual pet." Submit complete ms. Reviews artwork/photos as part of ms package.

Recent Nonfiction Title: *Pet Heroes*, by Elizabeth Seafoss (trade paperback).

MAZDA PUBLISHERS, Box 2603, 2991 Grace Ln., Costa Mesa CA 92626. (714)751-5252. Editor-in-Chief/ Publisher: Ahmad Jabbari. Publishes hardcover and trade paperback originals and trade paperback reprints. Averages 6 titles/year; receives approximately 25 submissions annually. 90% of books from first-time authors; 100% of books from unagented writers. Pays royalty on wholesale price; no advance. Publishes book an average of 4 months after acceptance. Photocopied submissions OK. Query for electronic submissions. Computer printout submissions acceptable; prefers letter-quality to dot-matrix. Reports in 2 weeks on queries; 6 weeks on mss. Free book catalog; ms guidelines for SASE.
Nonfiction: Cookbook, juvenile, reference, textbook, scholarly books. Subjects include art, business and economics, cooking and foods, history, politics, sociology, and social sciences in general. "Our primary objective is to publish scholarly books and other informational books about the Middle East and North Africa. All subject areas will be considered with priority given to the scholarly books." Query with outline/synopsis and sample chapters. Reviews artwork/photos as part of ms package.
Recent Nonfiction Title: *Timurid Architecture in Khurasan*, by Bernard O'Kane (art and architecture).
Poetry: Translations and scholarly presentation of poetry from the poets of the Middle Eastern countries only. Submit 5 poems.
Recent Poetry Title: *The Homely Touch: Folk Poetry of Old India* (translated from Sanscrit).
Tips: "We publish books for an academic audience and laymen."

‡MEADOWBROOK PRESS, 18318 Minnetonka Blvd., Deephaven MN 55391. (612)473-5400. Contact submissions editor. Publishes trade paperback originals and reprints. Averages 10-15 titles/year. Receives 250 queries annually. 25% of books from first-time authors. 75% of books from unagented writers. Pays 5-7.5% royalty; offers $2,000 average advance. Publishes book an average of 1 year after acceptance. Simultaneous and photocopied submissions OK. Computer printout submissions OK. Reports in 2 weeks on queries; 1 month on mss. Book catalog and ms guidelines for business size SASE.
Nonfiction: How-to, humor, juvenile, illustrated book and reference. Subjects include health; hobbies; travel; recreation; parenting (baby and child care); consumer information; and relationships. No academic, autobiography, semi-autobiography or fiction. Query with outline and sample chapters. "We prefer a query first; then we will request an outline and/or sample material."
Recent Nonfiction Title: *Practical Single Parenting*, by Anne Wayman (advice).
Tips: "We like how-to books in a simple, accessible format and any new advice on parenting. We look for a fresh approach to overcoming traditional problems (e.g. potty training."

‡MEDIA PRODUCTIONS AND MARKETING, INC., Subsidaries include Pine Mountain Press and Midgard Press, 2440 O Street, Suite 202, Lincoln NE 68510. (402)474-2676. President: Jerry Kromberg. Publishes hardcover originals and trade paperback originals and reprints. Averages 6-10 titles annually. Receives 200 submissions/year. 60% of books from first-time writers; 95% from unagented writers. Pays 2-15% royalty based on net sales. Makes some work-for-hire assignments. "Midgard Press is contract publishing; PMP has done cooperative publishing." Publishes book an average of 6 months after acceptance. Simultaneous submissions Ok; photocopied submissions OK. Computer printout submissions acceptable. Reports in 1 month. Free book catalog.
Nonfiction: Biography, "coffee table," cookbook, how-to, reference, self-help, textbook. Subjects include Americana, history, politics, sociology and general interest. "We will consider manuscripts of general interest with good commercial appeal to regional or special interest markets." Query or submit outline/synopsis and sample chapters or complete ms. Reviews artwork/photos as part of ms package.
Recent Nonfiction Title: *I Couldn't Put It Down*, Catherine Kidwell (how to write quality fiction).

MEDICAL ECONOMICS BOOKS, Division of Medical Economics Co., 680 Kinderkamack Rd., Oradell NJ 07649. Acquisitions Editors: Thomas Bentz and Esther Gumpert. Publishes hardcover, paperback, and spiral bound originals. Company also publishes magazines and references for doctors, nurses, pharmacists and laboratorians. Averages 25 titles/year; receives 100 submissions annually. 95% of books from unagented writers. Pays by individual arrangement. Publishes book an average of 11 months after acceptance. Simultaneous and photocopied submissions OK. Query for electronic submissions. Computer printout submissions acceptable; prefers letter-quality to dot-matrix. Reports in 6 weeks. Free book catalog; ms guidelines for SASE. Tests freelancers for rewriting, editing, and proofreading assignments.
Nonfiction: Clinical and practice—financial management references, handbooks, and manuals. Medical— primary care—all fields; obstetrics and gynecology, laboratory medicine and management. Critical care nursing. Submit table of contents and prospectus. Reviews artwork/photos as part of ms package.
Recent Nonfiction Title: *Interpreting Cardiac Dysrhythmias*, by J. Marcus Wharton, M.D., and Nora Goldschlager, M.D.
Tips: "Books addressed to and written by MDs and health-care managers and financial professionals have the best chance of selling to our firm." Queries/mss may be routed to other editors in the publishing group.

MELIUS AND PETERSON PUBLISHING, INC.,(formerly Tensleep Publications), Subsidiary of Video Resources, Inc., Rm. 524, Citizens Building, Box 925, Aberdeen SD 57401. (605)226-0488. Publisher: Ken Melius (nonfiction). Juvenile Editor: Victoria Peterson. Publishes hardcover and trade paperback originals. Averages 5 titles/year; receives 1,000 submissions annually. 95% of books from first-time authors; 100% of books from unagented writers. Pays 6-12% royalty on retail price. Offers negotiable advance. Publishes book an average of 1 year after acceptance. Simultaneous and photocopied submissions OK. Computer printout submissions acceptable. Reports in 3 weeks on queries; 2 months on mss. Book catalog and guidelines for SASE.
Nonfiction: How-to, reference and self-help. Subjects include business and economics, cooking and foods, hobbies, nature, recreation, travel and juvenile (preschool to age 9). "We are seeking works especially on time management and the concept of time. We need a unique approach to the concept of time as a commodity, how time can be used effectively, how it can be wasted—and the effects. Also seeking specific reference books for specific types of businesses." No music, art and religion. Query or submit outline/synopsis and sample chapters. Reviews artwork/photos as part of ms package.
Recent Nonfiction Title: *America's Favorites, Naturally*, by V. Cavalier.
Fiction: Juvenile, preschool to age 9. "We need well written, creative manuscripts with engaging characters that lend themselves to serial possibilities. No 'cutsie', poorly conceived manuscripts that talk down to children." Query or submit complete ms.
Tips: "Writers should pay more attention to a book's market and realize that a publisher has to efficiently sell that book to a specific audience. We envision an audience in need of specific information about certain business activities or practices, information about travel and recreation. Cookbooks should appeal to a broad cross-section of the public. We seek books with a two to three year shelf life. Books aimed at specific, easily identifiable audiences seem to be a trend. Travel books continue to do well in today's market. In the future, we need unique, informative books written for a certain market whether it be business, travel or recreation markets. Juvenile books should not only be unique but should reflect current interests of children."

MENASHA RIDGE PRESS, INC., Box 59257, Birmingham AL 35259. (205)991-0373. Publisher: R.W. Sehlinger. Small press. Publishes hardcover and trade paperback originals. Averages 10-15 titles/year; receives 600-800 submissions annually. 50% of books from first-time authors; 90% of books from unagented writers. Average print order for a writer's first book is 4,000. Pays 10% royalty on wholesale price or purchases outright; offers average $1,000 advance. Publishes book an average of 8 months after acceptance. Simultaneous and photocopied submissions OK. Query for electronic submissions. Computer printout submissions acceptable; prefers letter-quality to dot-matrix. Reports in 1 month. Book catalog for 9x12 SAE and 4 first class stamps; ms guidelines for SASE.
Nonfiction: How-to, reference, self-help, consumer, outdoor recreation, travel guides and small business. Subjects include business and economics, health, hobbies, recreation, sports, travel and consumer advice. No biography or religious copies. Submit outline/synopsis. Reviews artwork/photos.
Recent Nonfiction Title: *Kayak*, by William Nealy (outdoor how-to).
Tips: Audience: age 25-60, 14-18 years' education, white collar and professional, $30,000 median income, 75% male, 75% east of Mississippi River.

‡*MERCER UNIVERSITY PRESS, Macon GA 31207. (912)744-2880. Director: Edd Rowell. Publishes hardcover originals. Averages 40 titles/year. Receives 250 submissions annually. 10% of books from first-time authors. 100% of books from unagented writers. Subsidy publishes 50% of books. "We usually ask for a subsidy from the author's insitution (university). We do not accept personal subsidies from the authors themselves." Pays 10% royalty. Publishes book an average of 1 year after acceptance. Simultaneous and photocopied submissions OK. Computer printout submissions acceptable; no dot-matrix. Reports in 1 month on queries; 3 months on mss. Free book catalog; writer's guidelines for SASE.
Nonfiction: Biography, reference, textbook and scholarly monographs. Subjects include history (of the American South); philosophy; religion and sociology. "We are very interested in Southern history, biblical studies and theology. We also favor books that may be adapted as textbooks in college courses. Our audience includes professors, students, researchers and libraries." Query or submit outline/synopsis and sample chapters or complete ms. Reviews artwork/photos as part of ms package.
Recent Nonfiction Title: *To See the Promised Land: The Faith Pilgrimage of Martin Luther King, Jr.*, by Frederick L. Downing.
Tips: "In scholarly publising, there has been a substantial increase in the cost of books and decrease in print runs. We see more university presses publishing 'coffee table books' that appeal to a general audience rather than to a scholarly one. Writers have the best chance of selling us scholarly monographs or original research in theology, religion, or history. Extensive footnotes, bibliography, and a manuscript addressed to a specific (usually academic) market usually impress us."

MERIWETHER PUBLISHING LTD., 885 Elkton Dr., Colorado Springs CO 80907. (303)594-4422. Editor/President: Arthur L. Zapel. Small press. Publishes trade paperback originals and reprints. Averages 25-30 titles/year; receives 1,100 submissions annually. 80% of books from first-time authors; 95% of books from unagented writers. Pays 10% royalty on wholesale or retail prices or makes outright purchase. "We occasionally make work-for-hire assignments; usually only with writers we have published before." Publishes books an average of 7 months after acceptance. Simultaneous and photocopied submissions OK. Reports in 3 weeks on queries; 1 month on mss. Book catalog and ms guidelines for 8½x11 SAE and $1 postage.

Nonfiction: How-to, self-help, textbook and one-act plays. Subjects include religion, speech, drama and English. "We specialize in books dealing with the communication arts: drama, speech, theatre, English, etc. We also publish how-to books for youth activities. Books of short plays are our specialty." We are looking for humorous, self-help or instructional books. Query. Reviews artwork/photos.

Recent Nonfiction Title: *Theatre Games for Young Performers*, by Maria Novelly.

Fiction: Religious plays or comedy one-act plays or comedy musicals.

Recent Fiction Title: *Dave*, by Hank Beebe (two book set—story and musical score.)

Tips: "We are primarily play publishers but we also publish how-to books relating to speech, drama and youth activities, and nonfiction religious books. A writer should be sure that he/she has a fresh idea—a unique theme or concept. We look for writers who are ahead of the trends."

MERRILL PUBLISHING CO., a Bell & Howell Co., 1300 Alum Creek Dr., Columbus OH 43216. (614)890-1111. Education Division, Editor-in-chief: Ann Turpie. College Division, Editor-in-chief: Timothy McEwen. Publishes hardcover and paperback originals and software. Averages 400 titles/year; receives 200 submissions annually. 50% of books from first-time authors; the majority of books from unagented writers. Publishes book an average of 2 years after acceptance. "Royalties and contract terms vary with the nature of the material. They are very competitive within each market area. Some projects are handled on an outright purchase basis." Will accept simultaneous submissions if notified. Query for electronic submissions. Computer printout submissions acceptable; prefers letter-quality to dot-matrix. Reports in 1-3 months.

Nonfiction: Education Division publishes textbooks, workbooks, software, and other supplementary materials for elementary, junior high and high schools in the subject areas of language arts and reading, mathematics, science, health, and social studies (no juvenile stories or novels). Bilingual materials (Spanish) are also published for mathematics and science. College Division publishes college texts and related materials in the areas of education, special education and humanities, business, mathematics, science and technology. Submit outline/synopsis and 3 sample chapters. Reviews artwork/photos.

METAMORPHOUS PRESS, Subsidiary of Metamorphosis, Inc., 3249 NW 29th Ave., Box 10616, Portland OR 92710. (503)228-4972. Editor: David Balding. Publishes hardcover, trade paperback originals and hardcover and trade paperback reprints. Averages 8-12 titles/year; receives 600 submissions annually. 90% of books from first-time authors; 100% of books from unagented writers. Average print order for a writer's first book is 2,000-5,000. Pays minimum 10% profit split on wholesale prices. No advance. Publishes book an average of 8 months after acceptance. Simultaneous and photocopied submissions OK. Electronic submissions OK, but requires hard copy also. Computer printout submissions acceptable; prefers letter-quality to dot-matrix. Free book catalog; ms guidelines for SASE.

Nonfiction: Biography, how-to, illustrated book, reference, self-help, technical and textbook—all related to behavioral science and personal growth. Subjects include business and sales, health, psychology, sociology, education, children's books, science and new ideas in behavioral science. "We are interested in any well-proven new idea or philosophy in the behavioral science areas. Our primary editorial screen is 'will this book further define, explain or support the concept that we create our reality literally or assist people in gaining control of their lives.'" Submit idea, outline, and table of contents only. Reviews artwork/photos as part of ms package.

Recent Nonfiction Title: *Performance Management*, by Michael D. McMaster (business).

METHUEN, INC., Imprint of Methuen, Inc., 29 W. 35th St., New York NY 10001. (212)244-3336. Eight subject editors in the U.K. Editorial Director: William P. Germano. Philosophy and Social Science Editor: Maureen MacGrogan. Imprints include Ark, Arkana, Pandora Press, Rutledge and Kegan Paul, Methuen, Chapman and Hall, Tavistock, Croom Helm and Theatre Arts Books. Pandora Press publishes both fiction and nonfiction and deals with topics of interest to women. Arkana publishes primarily books on popular religious topics, especially Eastern religions and occult. Methuen and Rutledge and Kegan Paul publishes scholarly books on humanities. Chapman and Hall publishes science and technology books. Tavistock publishes books on social sciences. Publishes hardcover and trade paperback originals and reprints. Averages 400 titles/year; receives 5,000+ submissions annually. 10% of books from first-time authors; 50-70% of books from unagented writers. Pays 7½-10% royalty on retail price; offers average $1,000 advance. Publishes book an average of 1 year after acceptance. Inquire about electronic submissions. Simultaneous and photocopied submissions OK. Computer printout submissions acceptable; prefers letter-quality to dot-matrix. Reports in 3 weeks on queries; 6 weeks on mss. Book catalog 73¢; ms guidelines for SASE.

Nonfiction: Academic monograph and textbook. Subjects include biography, illustrated book, reference, self-help, social sciences, philosophy, history, travel, psychology, women's studies, mind/body/spirit, education, geography, economics and literary criticism. No Biblical prophecies. Monograph length: 100,000 words maximum. Query and/or submit outline/synopsis and sample chapters.

Recent Nonfiction Title: *Rough Guide to Greece*, by Mark Ellingham (travel).
Fiction: Routledge & Kegan Paul no longer publishes fiction. Fiction appears only under its imprint, Pandora Press.

*MEYERBOOKS, PUBLISHER, Box 427, Glenwood IL 60425. (312)757-4950. Publisher: David Meyer. Publishes hardcover and trade paperback originals and hardcover and trade paperback reprints. Averages 3 titles/year; receives 25 submissions annually. 50% of books from first-time authors; 100% of books from unagented writers. Is willing to subsidy publish. Pays 5-10% royalty on wholesale price or retail price or makes outright purchase for minimum $500. Offers average $250 advance. Publishes book an average of 15 months after acceptance. Simultaneous and photocopied submissions OK. Computer printout submissions acceptable; prefers letter-quality to dot-matrix. Reports in 3 months on queries; 6 months on mss. Book catalog for #10 SASE.
Nonfiction: History, reference and self-help. Subjects include Americana, cooking and foods, health (natural healing), history (theatre), hobbies (magic) and nature. "We publish books for limited, specialized markets. No technical books, esoteric subjects, or books which might be better published by large New York publishers." Query or submit outline/synopsis and sample chapters. Reviews artwork/photos.
Recent Nonfiction Title: *Sachet, Potpourri and Incense Recipes*, by C. Meyer (how-to).

THE MGI MANAGEMENT INSTITUTE, INC., 378 Halstead Ave., Harrison NY 10528. (914)835-5790. President: Dr. Henry Oppenheimer. Averages 10-15 titles/year; receives 3-4 submissions annually. 50% of books from first-time authors; 100% of those books from unagented writers. Pays 3-5% royalty on retail price of correspondence course (price is usually in $100 range) or 10-15% for conventional book. Publishes book an average of 6 months after acceptance. Electronic submissions OK on IBM PC, Wordstar, but requires hard copy also. Computer printout submissions acceptable. Reports in 2 weeks. Free book catalog.
Nonfiction: How-to, technical and correspondence courses. Subjects include business and economics, electrical engineering, computer, and manufacturing-related topics. Needs correspondence courses in audit management, purchasing, manufacturing management, computers, artificial intelligence and marketing professional services. Reviews artwork/photos.
Recent Nonfiction Title: *Basics of Inventory Management*, by G. Sanderson (correspondence course).
Tips: "We are interested in textbooks also if specific market can be identified. Our audience includes audit managers, purchasing managers, graduate engineers and architects, manufacturing supervisors and managers, and real estate investors."

‡*MICHIGAN STATE UNIVERSITY PRESS, Room 25, 1405 S. Harrison Rd., East Lansing MI 48824. (517)355-9543. Director: Richard Chapin. Publishes hardcover and softcover originals. Averages 12 titles annually. Receives 100 submissions/year. 95% of books from first-time writers; 100% from unagented writers. Pays 10% royalty on net sales. Publishes ms an average of 9 months after acceptance. Photocopied submissions OK. Query for electronic submissions. Computer printout submissions OK; prefers letter-quality to dot-matrix. Book catalog and manuscript guidelines for SASE.
Nonfiction: Reference, software, technical, textbook and scholarly. Subjects include agriculture, business and economics, history, literature, philosophy, politics and religion. Looking for "scholarly publishing representing strengths of the university." Query with outline/synopsis and sample chapters. Reviews artwork/photos.
Recent Nonfiction Title: *Diego Rivera*, by D. McMeekin (science in art).

‡MILADY PUBLISHING CORPORATION, Subsidiary MPC Educational Publishers, 3839 White Plains Rd., Bronx NY 10467. (212)881-3000. President: Thomas R. Severance. Publishes technical books, particularly for occupational education. Averages 10 titles/year; receives 12 submissions annually. 25% of books from first-time authors; 100% of books from unagented writers. Pays 8-12% royalty on wholesale price. Offers average $750 advance. Publishes book an average of 1 year after acceptance. Photocopied submissions OK. Computer printout submissions acceptable; prefers letter-quality to dot-matrix. Reports in 6 weeks. Book catalog for $1.
Nonfiction: How-to, reference, textbook, workbooks and exam reviews on occupational education. No academic. Query or submit outline/synopsis and sample chapters. Reviews artwork/photos.
Tips: "Our audience is vocational students."

‡MILLS & SANDERSON, PUBLISHERS, Subsidiary of The Huenefeld Co., Inc., Suite 5, 442 Marrett Rd., Lexington MA 02173. (617)861-0992. Publisher: Georgia Mills. Publishes trade paperback originals. Publishes 8 titles/year; receives 150 submissions annually. 50% of books from first-time authors; 75% of books from unagented writers. Pays 12½-13% royalty on wholesale price; offers average $1,000 advance. Publishes book an average of 6 months after acceptance. Simultaneous and photocopied submissions OK. Query for electronic submissions. Computer printout submissions OK; prefers letter-quality to dot-matrix. Reports in 1 month on queries; 2 months on mss. Free ms guidelines.

Nonfiction: Cookbook, how-to and self-help. Subjects include cooking and foods, health, sociology, travel and contemporary issues. "All our books are aimed at improving individual's life in some way. No religion, music, art or photography." Query.

Recent Nonfiction Title: *The Cruise Answer Book*, by Charlanne Herring.

Tips: "We only publish nonfiction with broad general consumer appeal because it normally is less chancy than fiction. It must be an interesting subject with broad appeal by an author whose credentials indicate he/she knows a lot about the subject, be well researched and most importantly, must have a certain uniqueness about it."

‡MISTY HILL PRESS, 5024 Turner Rd., Sebastopol CA 95472. (415)892-0789. Managing editor: Sally C. Karste. Publishes trade paperback originals. Averages 1 title/year. 90% of books from first-time authors. 90% of books from unagented writers. Pays 10% royalty on retail price. Publishes book an average of 1 year after acceptance. Simultaneous submissions OK. Computer printout submissions OK; prefers letter-quality to dot-matrix. Reports in 6 weeks on mss. Book catalog for 6x9 SAE and 39¢ postage; writer's guidelines for $2.

Nonfiction: Biography, humor and juvenile. Subjects include Americana, religion, animals, history and nature. "We want social studies, juvenile grades 5-7, complementary support books for American history." Submit outline/synopsis and sample chapters. Reviews artwork/photos as part of ms package.

Recent Nonfiction Title: *Tales Fledgling Homestead*, by Joe E. Armstrong (contemporary California homesteading).

Fiction: Adventure, fantasy, historical and humor. "Historical fiction for young readers in grades 5-7 to colorfully supplement the American social studies program. No picture books requiring elaborate color reproduction." Submit outline/synopsis and sample chapters.

Recent Fiction Title: *Trails to Poosey*, by Olive R. Cook (historical fiction-juvenile).

Poetry: Holiday poems for children of all ages. Submit 3-10 samples.

Tips: "We are interested in nature-juvenile, history and biography because our market reaches these areas of readers. We require careful attention to accurate information presented in positive, interesting format."

*MIT PRESS, Imprint of Massachusetts Institute of Technology, 28 Carleton St., Cambridge MA 02142. (617)253-5646. Acquisitions Coordinator: Cristina Sanmartin. Averages 115 titles/year. Subsidy publishes (nonauthor) 8% of books. "Subsidies are sometimes provided by cultural agencies but not by author." Pays 8-10% royalty on wholesale or retail price; $500-1,000 advance. Advances are rare. Publishes book an average of 18 months after acceptance. Computer printout submissions acceptable; prefers letter-quality to dot-matrix. Reports in 6 weeks. Book catalog and guidelines for SASE.

Nonfiction: Computer science/artificial intelligence/robotics, cognitive science, linguistics, continental philosophy, architecture, design arts, economics, history, and philosophy of science. "We are a scholarly publisher active in areas above. We do not publish fiction, poetry, literary criticism, education, pure philosophy, history, personal philosophies, or children's books." Submit abstract (synopsis), resume and table of contents (outline) only.

Recent Nonfiction Title: *Scientific Discovery: An Account of the Creative Process*, by Langley.

MODERN LANGUAGE ASSOCIATION OF AMERICA, 10 Astor Pl., New York NY 10003. (212)475-9500. Director of Book Publications: Walter S. Achtert. Publishes hardcover and trade paperback originals. Averages 20 titles/year; receives 100 submissions annually. 100% of books from unagented writers. Pays 5-15% royalty on net proceeds. Offers average $100 advance. Publishes book an average of 11 months after acceptance. Photocopied submissions OK. Electronic submissions OK via MS-DOS, CPM, or Apple 5¼ disks, but requires hard copy also. Computer printout submissions acceptable; prefers letter-quality to dot-matrix. Reports in 3 weeks on queries; 3 months on mss. Book catalog free on request.

Nonfiction: Reference and professional. Subjects include language and literature. Needs mss on current issues in research and teaching of language and literature. No critical monographs. Query or submit outline/synopsis and sample chapters.

Recent Nonfiction Title: *Helping Students Write Well*, by Barbara E. Fassler Walvoord.

MONITOR BOOK CO., INC., 9441 Wilshire Blvd., Beverly Hills CA 90212. (213)271-5558. Editor-in-Chief: Alan F. Pater. Hardcover originals. Pays 10% minimum royalty or by outright purchase, depending on circumstances; no advance. Reports in 4 months. Book catalog for SASE.

Nonfiction: Americana, biographies (only of well-known personalities), law and reference books. Send prints if photos and/or illustrations are to accompany ms.

---

*An asterisk preceding a listing indicates that subsidy publishing or co-publishing (where author pays part or all of publishing costs) is available. Firms whose subsidy programs comprise more than 50% of their total publishing activities are listed at the end of the Book Publishers section.

*MOREHOUSE-BARLOW CO., INC., Divison of B&C Co., 78 Danbury Rd., Wilton CT 06897. Publisher: E. Allen Kelley. Publishes hardcover and paperback originals. Averages 20 titles/year; receives 500 submissions annually. 40% of books from first-time authors; 75% of books from unagented writers. Pays 10% royalty on retail price. Publishes book an average of 8 months after acceptance. Computer printout submissions acceptable; no dot-matrix. Book catalog for 9x12 SAE with 2 first class stamps.
Nonfiction: Specializes in Christian publishing (with an Anglican emphasis). Theology, ethics, church history, pastoral counseling, liturgy, religious education and children's books; beginning tapes and videos. No poetry or drama. Accepts outline/synopsis and 2-4 sample chapters. Reviews artwork/photos as part of ms package.
Recent Nonfiction Title: *Banners for Beginners*, by Cory Atwood, (craft book—religious subjects).

WILLIAM MORROW AND CO., 105 Madison Ave., New York NY 10016. Publisher: Sherry W. Arden. Imprints include Greenwillow Books (juveniles), Susan Hirschman, editor. Lothrop, Lee and Shepard (juveniles), Dorothy Briley, editor. Morrow Junior Books (juveniles), David Reuther, editor. Quill (trade paperback), Douglas Stumpf and Andrew Ambraziejus, editors. Affiliates include Hearst Books (trade). Editorial Director: Ann Bramson. Hearst Marine Books (nautical). Connie Roosevelt, editor, Beech Tree Books, James D. Landis, Publisher. Receives 10,000 submissions annually. 30% of books from first-time authors; 5% of books from unagented writers. Payment is on standard royalty basis. Publishes book an average of 1-2 years after acceptance. Computer printout submissions acceptable; prefers letter-quality to dot-matrix. Query letter on all books. *No* unsolicited mss or proposals. Mss and proposals should be submitted through a literary agent.
Nonfiction and Fiction: Publishes adult fiction, nonfiction, history, biography, arts, religion, poetry, how-to books and cookbooks. Length: 50,000-100,000 words. Query only; mss and proposals should be submitted only through an agent.
Recent Fiction Title: *Windmills of the Gods*, by Sidney Sheldon.

MORROW JUNIOR BOOKS, Division of William Morrow & Company, Inc., 105 Madison Ave., New York NY 10016. (212)889-3050. Editor-in-Chief: David L. Reuther. Executive Editor: Meredith Charpentier. Senior Editor: Andrea Curley. Publishes hardcover originals. Publishes 50 titles/year. All contracts negotiated separately; offers variable advance. Book catalog and guidelines for 8½x11 SAE with 2 first class stamps.
Nonfiction: Juveniles (trade books). No textbooks. Query. Reviews artwork/photos as part of ms package.
Recent Nonfiction Title: *Story of Rock 'n' Roll*, by Pete Forntale (history of rock music).
Fiction: Juveniles (trade books).
Recent Fiction Title: *After the Rain*, by Norma Fox Mazer (young adult novel).
Tips: "We are not accepting unsolicited manuscripts until after Jan. 1, 1988."

MOSAIC PRESS MINIATURE BOOKS, 358 Oliver Rd., Cincinnati OH 45215. (513)761-5977. Publisher: Miriam Irwin. Publishes hardcover originals. Averages 4 titles/year; receives 150-200 submissions annually. 49% of books from first-time authors. Average print order for a writer's first book is 2,000. Buys mss outright for $50. Publishes book an average of 30 months after acceptance. Computer printout submissions acceptable; no dot-matrix. Reports in 2 weeks; "but our production, if manuscript is accepted, often takes 2 or 3 years." Book catalog $3.
Nonfiction: Biography, cookbook, humor, illustrated book and satire. Subjects include Americana, animals, art, business and economics, cooking and foods, health, history, hobbies, music, nature, sports and travel. Interested in "beautifully written, delightful text. If factual, it must be extremely correct and authoritative. Our books are intended to delight, both in their miniature size, beautiful bindings and excellent writing." No occult, pornography, science fiction, fantasy, haiku, or how-to. Query or submit outline/synopsis and sample chapters or complete ms. Reviews artwork/photos as part of ms package.
Recent Nonfiction Title: *Scrimshaw*, by Carolyn G. Orr.
Tips: "I want a book to tell me something I don't know."

‡MOTHER COURAGE PRESS, 1533 Illinois St., Racine WI 53405. (414)634-1047. Managing editor: Barbara Lindquist. Small press. Publishes trade paperback originals. Averages 2-4 titles/year; receives 10-20 submissions annually. 100% of books from first-time authors. 100% of books from unagented writers. Pays 10-15% royalty on wholesale and retail price; offers $250 average advance. Publishes book an average of 9-12 months after acceptance. Simultaneous and photocopied submissions OK. Query for electronic submissions. Computer printout submissions OK. Reports in 2 weeks on queries; 6 weeks on mss. Free book catalog.

> **❝ I receive more rejection letters now as an established writer than when I started out. Why? Because I send out more queries. ❞**
>
> *—Florence Temko, author*

Nonfiction: Biography, how-to and self-help. Subjects include health, psychology and sociology. "We are looking for books on difficult subjects—explaining death to children (no talking animals); teen pregnancy; sexual abuse (no personal stories); and rape." Submit outline/synopsis and sample chapters or complete ms. Reviews artwork/photos as part of ms package.
Recent Nonfiction Title: *Fear or Freedom, A Woman's Options in Social Survival and Physical Defense*, by Susan E. Smith.
Fiction: Adventure, fantasy, historical, humor, mystery, romance, science fiction and lesbian. "We are looking for lesbian/feminist or strictly feminist, themes. Don't send male-oriented fiction of any kind." Submit outline/synopsis and sample chapters or complete ms.
Recent Fiction Title: *News*, by Heather Conrad (suspense fiction).

MOTORBOOKS INTERNATIONAL PUBLISHERS & WHOLESALERS, INC., Box 2, Osceola WI 54020. Director of Publications: Tim Parker. Senior Editor: Barbara K. Harold. Hardcover and paperback originals. Averages 20 titles/year. 100% of books from unagented writers. Offers 7-15% royalty on net receipts. Offers average $2,500 advance. Publishes book an average of 7-10 months after acceptance. Simultaneous and photocopied submissions OK. Query for electronic submissions. Computer printout submissions acceptable; prefers letter-quality to dot-matrix. Reports in 3 months. Free book catalog; ms guidelines for SASE.
Nonfiction: Biography, history, how-to, photography, and motor sports (as they relate to cars, trucks, motorcycles, motor sports and aviation—domestic and foreign). Accepts nonfiction translations from German/Italian. Submit outline/synopsis, 1-2 sample chapters and sample of illustrations. "State qualifications for doing book." Reviews artwork/photos as part of ms package.
Recent Nonfiction Title: *The Harley-Davidson Motor Company*, by David Wright.

‡MOTT MEDIA, INC., PUBLISHERS, 1000 E. Huron, Milford MI 48042. (313)685-8773. Senior Editor: George Mott. Hardcover and paperback originals and reprints. Averages 15 titles/year; receives 900 submissions annually. 20% of books from first-time authors; 100% of books from unagented writers. Average print order for a writer's first book is 3,500-5,000. Pays variable 7-10% royalty on retail, depending on type of book, and makes outright purchases. Publishes book an average of 20 months after acceptance. Simultaneous and photocopied submissions OK. Computer printout submissions acceptable; no dot-matrix. Reports in 2 months. Book catalog for 8½x11 SAE with 39¢ postage; ms guidelines for SASE.
Nonfiction: Specializes in religious books, including trade and Christian school textbooks. Publishes Americana (religious slant); biography (for juveniles on famous Christians, adventure-filled; for adults on Christian people, scholarly, new slant for marketing); how-to (for pastors, Christian laymen); juvenile (biographies, 30,000-40,000 words); politics (conservative, Christian approach); religious (conservative Christian); self-help (religious); and textbooks (all levels from a Christian perspective, all subject fields). No preschool materials. Main emphasis of all mss must be religious. Wants to know "vocation, present position and education of author; brief description of the contents of the book; basic readership for which the manuscript was written; brief explanation of why the manuscript differs from other books on the same subject; the author's interpretation of the significance of this manuscript." Submit outline/synopsis and sample chapters or complete ms.
Recent Nonfiction Title: *Process Theology*, by Ron Nash.

THE MOUNTAINEERS BOOKS, The Mountaineers, 306-2nd Ave W., Seattle WA 98119. (206)285-2665. Manager: Donna DeShazo. Publishes hardcover and trade paperback originals (85%) and reprints (15%). Averages 10-15 titles/year; receives 150-250 submissions annually. 25% of books from first-time authors; 98% of books from unagented writers. Average print order for a writer's first book is 2,000-5,000. Offers 17½% royalty based on net sales. Offers advance on occasion. Publishes book an average of 1 year after acceptance. Dot-matrix submissions are acceptable with new ribbon and double spaced. Reports in 2 months. Book catalog and ms guidelines for 9x12 SAE with 39¢ postage.
Nonfiction: Recreation, non-competitive sports, and outdoor how-to books. "We specialize only in books dealing with mountaineering, hiking, backpacking, skiing, snowshoeing, canoeing, bicycling, etc. These can be either how-to-do-it, where-to-do-it (guidebooks), or accounts of mountain-related experiences." Does *not* want to see "anything dealing with hunting, fishing or motorized travel." Submit outline/synopsis and minimum of 2 sample chapters. Accepts nonfiction translations. Looks for "expert knowledge, good organization."
Recent Nonfiction Title: *Moments of Doubt*, by David Roberts (essays).
Fiction: "We might consider an exceptionally well-done book-length manuscript on mountaineering." Does *not* want poetry or mystery. Query first.
Tips: "The type of book the writer has the best chance of selling our firm is an authoritative guidebook (*in our field*) to a specific area not otherwise covered; or a first-person narrative of outdoor adventure otherwise unduplicated in print."

MULTNOMAH PRESS, A division of Multnomah School of The Bible, 10209 SE Division St., Portland OR 97266. (503)257-0526. Editorial Manager: Rodney L. Morris. Publishes hardcover and trade paperback originals, and trade paperback reprints. Averages 30 titles/year; receives 500 submissions annually. 30% of books from first-time authors; 100% of books from unagented writers. Pays royalty on wholesale price. Publishes books an average of 9 months after acceptance. Photocopied submissions OK. Query for electronic submissions. Computer printout submissions acceptable; no dot-matrix. Reports in 6 weeks on queries; 10 weeks on mss. Book catalog and ms guidelines for SASE.

Nonfiction: "Coffee table" book and self-help. Subjects include religion. "We publish issue-related books linking social/ethical concerns and Christianity; books addressing the needs of women from a Christian point of view; books addressing the needs of the traditional family in today's society; and books explaining Christian theology in a very popular way to a lay audience." No daily devotional, personal experience, Scripture/photo combinations or poetry. Submit outline/synopsis and sample chapters. Reviews artwork/photos.

Recent Nonfiction Title: *Desiring God: Meditations of a Christian Hedonist*, by John Piper (Christian social-ethical).

Tips: "We have a reputation for tackling tough issues from a Biblical view; we need to continue to deserve that reputation. Avoid being too scholarly or detached. Although we like well-researched books, we do direct our books to a popular market, not just to professors of theology."

MUSEUM OF NEW MEXICO PRESS, Box 2087, Santa Fe NM 87503. (505)827-6454. Director: James Mafchir. Editor-in-Chief: Mary Wachs. Hardcover and paperback originals (90%) and reprints (10%). Averages 4-6 titles/year; receives 100 submissions annually. 50% of books from first-time authors; 75% of books from unagented writers. Average print order for a writer's first book is 2,000-5,000. Royalty of 10% of list after first 1,000 copies; no advance. Publishes book an average of 1 year after acceptance. Computer printout submissions acceptable; no dot-matrix. Reports in 1-2 months. Free book catalog.

Nonfiction: "We publish both popular and scholarly books on regional anthropology, history, fine and folk arts; geography, natural history, the Americas and the Southwest; regional cookbooks; art, biography (regional and Southwest); music; nature; reference, scientific and technical." Accepts nonfiction translations. Prints preferred for illustrations; transparencies best for color. Sources of photos or illustrations should be indicated for each. Query or submit outline/synopsis and sample chapters to Sarah Nestor, Editor-in-Chief. Mss should be typed double-spaced, follow Chicago *Manual of Style*, and be accompanied by information about the author's credentials and professional background. Reviews artwork/photos as part of ms package.

*MUSEUM OF NORTHERN ARIZONA PRESS, Subsidiary of Museum of Northern Arizona, Box 720, Rt. 4, Flagstaff AZ 86001. (602)774-5211. Publisher: Diana Clark Lubick. Publishes hardcover and trade paperback originals, and also quarterly magazine. Averages 10-12 titles/year; receives 35 submissions annually. 10% of books from first-time authors; 100% of books from unagented writers. Subsidy publishes (nonauthor) 15% of books. Pays one-time fee on acceptance of ms. No advance. Publishes book an average of 1 year after acceptance. Queries only. Electronic submissions OK via IBM PC or Macintosh. Computer printout submissions acceptable; prefers letter-quality to dot-matrix. Reports in 1 month. Book catalog and ms guidelines for 8½x11 SAE.

Nonfiction: Coffee table book, reference and technical. Subjects include Southwest, art, nature, science. "Especially needs manuscripts on the Colorado Plateau that are written for a well-educated general audience." Query or submit outline/synopsis and 3-4 sample chapters. Reviews artwork/photos.

Recent Nonfiction Title: *Wildlife of the Colorado Plateau*, by Steven Brothers (natural history).

MUSTANG PUBLISHING CO., Box 9327, New Haven CT 06533. (203)624-5485. President: Rollin Riggs. Publishes hardcover and trade paperback originals. Averages 6 titles/year; receives 1,000 submissions annually. 50% of books from first-time authors; 100% of books from unagented writers. Pays 7-10% royalty on retail price. Publishes book an average of 1 year after acceptance. Simultaneous and photocopied submissions OK. No electronic submissions. Computer printout submissions acceptable; prefers letter-quality to dot-matrix. Reports in 1 month. Book catalog available from our distributor: Kampmann & Company, 9 E. 40th St., New York NY 10016.

Nonfiction: How-to, humor and self-help. Subjects include Americana, hobbies, recreation, sports and travel. "Our needs are very general—humor, travel, how-to, nonfiction, etc.—for the 18-to 35-year-old market." Query or submit synopsis and sample chapters.

Recent Nonfiction Title: *Prove It All Night: The Bruce Springsteen Trivia Book*, by Deborah Mayer.

Tips: "Some writers don't go to bookstores, and they don't ask themselves, 'How many times have I and my friends actually bought this type of book?' "

‡THE MYSTERIOUS PRESS, 129 W. 56th St., New York NY 10019. (212)765-0901. Managing editor: William Malloy. Subsidiaries include Penzler Books (non-mystery fiction by mystery authors) and *The Armchair Detective* (magazine). Publishes hardcover originals, trade paperback reprints and mass market paperback reprints. Averages 40-50 titles/year; receives 750 submissions annually. 10% of books from first-time authors. 5% of books from unagented writers. Pays standard, but negotiable, royalty on retail price; amount of advance varies widely. Publishes a book an average of 1 year after acceptance. Photocopied submissions OK. Computer printout submissions OK; prefers letter-quality. Reports in 2 months. Book catalog and guidelines for 8½x11 SAE with $1 postage.

Nonfiction: Reference books on criticism and history of crime fiction. "Especially needs reprints of worthy hardcover books dealing with literary criticism and history of mystery/detective fiction." Submit complete ms. Reviews artwork/photos as part of ms package.

Recent Nonfiction Title: *A Talent to Deceive: An Appreciation of Agatha Christie*, by Robert Barnard (mystery/reference).

Fiction: Mystery, suspense and espionage. "We will consider publishing any outstanding crime/espionage/suspense/detective novel that comes our way. No short stories." Submit complete mss.

Recent Fiction Title: *Out on the Rim*, by Ross Thomas (suspense).

THE NAIAD PRESS, INC., Box 10543, Tallahassee FL 32302. (904)539-9322. Editorial Director: Barbara Grier. Publishes paperback originals. Averages 12 titles/year; receives 255 submissions annually. 20% of books from first-time authors; 99% of books from unagented writers. Average print order for a writer's first book is 12,000. Pays 15% royalty on wholesale or retail price; no advance. Publishes book an average of 1 year after acceptance. Reports in 2 months. Book catalog and ms guidelines for #10 SAE and 39¢ postage.

Fiction: "We publish lesbian fiction, preferably lesbian/feminist fiction. We are not impressed with the 'oh woe' school and prefer realistic (i.e., happy) novels. We emphasize fiction and are now heavily reading manuscripts in that area. We are working in a lot of genre fiction—mysteries, science fiction, short stories, fantasy—all with lesbian themes, of course." Query.

Recent Fiction Title: *Memory Board*, by Jane Rule.

‡NATIONAL ASSOCIATION OF SOCIAL WORKERS, 7981 Eastern Ave., Silver Springs MD 20910. Contact: Director of Publications. Averages 8 titles/year; receives 100 submissions annually. 20% of books from first-time authors. 100% of books from unagented writers. Pays 10-15% royalty on net prices. Publishes book an average of 1 year after acceptance. Computer printout submissions OK; prefers letter-quality. Reports in 3 months on submissions. Free book catalog and ms guidelines.

Nonfiction: Textbooks of interest to professional social workers. "We're looking for books on social work in health care, mental health and occupational social work. Books must be directed to the professional social worker and build on the current literature." Submit outline/synopsis and sample chapters. Rarely reviews artwork/photos as part of ms package.

Recent Nonfiction Title: *The Vulnerable Social Worker*, by Douglas Besharov (textbook on liability).

Tips: "Our audience includes social work practitioners, educators, students and policy makers. They are looking for practice-related books that are well grounded in theory. The books that do well are those that have direct application to the work our audience does. New technology will be of increasing interest to our readers."

‡NATIONAL BOOK COMPANY, Division of Educational Research Associates, 333 SW Park Ave., Portland OR 97205-3784. (503)228-6345. Imprints include Halcyon House. Editorial Director: Carl W. Salser. Senior Editor: John R. Kimmel. Manager of Copyrights: Lucille Fry. Publishes hardcover and paperback originals, paperback reprints, and software. Averages 23 titles/year. Pays 5-15% royalty on wholesale or retail price; no advance. Publishes book an average of 1 year after acceptance. Computer printout submissions acceptable. Reports in 2 months. Free catalog for 9x12 SAE with 2 first class stamps.

Nonfiction: Only materials suitable for educational uses in all categories. Art, business/economics, health, history, music, politics, psychology, reference, science, technical and textbooks. "The vast majority of titles are multimedia Individualized Instruction/Mastery Learning programs for educational consumers. Prospective authors should be aware of this and be prepared for this type of format, although content, style and appropriateness of subject matter are the major criteria by which submissions are judged. We are most interested in materials in the areas of the language arts, social studies and the sciences." Query, submit outline/synopsis and 2-5 sample chapters or complete ms. Reviews artwork/photos as part of ms package.

Recent Nonfiction Title: *The Vocabulary of Physics*, by William S. Rothwell.

*NATIONAL GALLERY OF CANADA, Publications Division, 75 Albert St., R-330, Ottawa, Ontario K1A 0M8 Canada. (613)990-0540. Acting Head: Gyde Shepherd. Editorial Coordinator: Irene Lillico. Publishes hardcover and paperback originals. Averages 15 titles/year. Subsidy publishes (non-author) 100% of books. Pays in outright purchase of $1,500-2,500; offers average $700 advance. Photocopied submissions OK. Reports in 3 months. Free sales catalog.

Nonfiction: "In general, we publish only *solicited* manuscripts on art, particularly Canadian art, and must publish them in English and French. Exhibition catalogs are commissioned, but we are open (upon approval by Curatorial general editors) to manuscripts for the various series, monographic and otherwise, that we publish. All manuscripts should be directed to our Editorial Coordinator, who doubles as manuscript editor. Since we publish translations into French, authors have access to French Canada and the rest of Francophonia. Because our titles are distributed by the University of Chicago Press, authors have the attention of European as well as American markets."

Recent Nonfiction Title: *European and American Painting, Sculture and Decorative Arts in The National Gallery Of Canada, Volume 1, 1300-1800*, general editors: Myron Laskin, Jr. and Michael Pantazzi.

NATIONAL PRESS, INC., 7508 Wisconsin Ave., Bethesda MD 20814. (301)657-1616. Publisher: Joel D. Joseph. Publishes hardcover and trade paperback originals, and hardcover and trade paperback reprints. Averages 10-12 titles/year. 50% of books from first-time authors; 50% of books from unagented writers. Pays 5-10% royalty on retail price. Offers variable advance. Publishes book an average of 9 months after acceptance. Computer printout submissions acceptable; prefers letter-quality to dot-matrix. Simultaneous and photocopied submissions OK. Reports in 2 months. Free book catalog.
Nonfiction: Biography, law, consumer guides, cookbooks, how-to, illustrated books, juvenile, picture books, reference and self-help. Subjects include business and economics, cooking and foods, health, recreation and sports. Query and/or submit outline/synopsis and sample chapters. Do not send more than 20 pages.
Recent Nonfiction Title: *Katherine The Great*, by Deborah Davis.

NATIONAL PUBLISHERS OF THE BLACK HILLS, INC., 47 Nepperhan Ave., Elmsford NY 10523. Editorial Director: Ellen Schneid Coleman. Publishes trade and text paperback originals and software. Averages 15 titles/year. Pays negotiable royalty; offers negotiable advance. Publishes book an average of 9 months after acceptance. Computer printout submissions acceptable. Reports in 3 weeks on queries; 5 weeks on mss.
Nonfiction: Technical, business and economics texts, medical administrative assisting, computer science texts, travel and hospitality, and general texts aimed at the post-secondary school market. Immediate needs include basic electronics texts, algebra, hospitality and remedial math. Query or submit outline/synopsis and a sample chapter, or complete ms. Reviews artwork/photos as part of ms package.
Recent Nonfiction Title: *Prose and Cons: The Do's and Don'ts of Technical and Business Writing*, by Carol Barnam.

NATIONAL TEXTBOOK CO., 4255 W. Touhy Ave., Lincolnwood IL 60646. (312)679-5500. Editorial Director: Leonard I. Fiddle. Publishes originals for education and trade market, and software. Averages 100-150 titles/year; receives 200+ submissions annually. 10% of books from first-time authors; 80% of books from unagented writers. Mss purchased on either royalty or buy-out basis. Publishes book an average of 6-12 months after acceptance. Computer printout submissions acceptable; no dot-matrix. Reports in 4 months. Book catalog and ms guidelines for SAE and 2 first class stamps.
Nonfiction: Textbook. Major emphasis being given to foreign language and language arts areas, especially secondary level material, and business and career subjects (marketing, advertising, sales, etc.). Judith Clayton, Language Arts Editor. Michael Ross, Foreign language and ESL. Michael Urban, Career Guidance. Harry Briggs, Business Books. Send sample chapter and outline or table of contents.
Recent Nonfiction Title: *Building Real Life English Skills*, by Penn and Starkey (survival reading and writing).

NATUREGRAPH PUBLISHERS, INC., Box 1075, Happy Camp CA 96039. (916)493-5353. Imprint, Prism Editions. Editor: Barbara Brown. Trade books. Averages 5 titles/year; receives 200 submissions annually. 75% of books from first-time authors; 100% of books from unagented writers. Average print order for a writer's first book is 2,500. "We offer 10% of wholesale; 12½% after 10,000 copies are sold. Publishes book an average of 18 months after acceptance. Photocopied submissions OK. Computer printout submissions acceptable; prefers letter-quality to dot-matrix. Reports in 2 months. Free book catalog; ms guidelines for SASE.
Nonfiction: Primarily publishes nonfiction for the layman in 7 general areas: natural history (biology, geology, ecology, astronomy); American Indian (historical and contemporary); outdoor living (backpacking, wild edibles, etc.); land and gardening (modern homesteading); crafts and how-to; holistic health (natural foods and healing arts); and PRISM Editions (Baha'i and other New Age approaches to harmonious living). All material must be well-grounded; author must be professional, and in command of effective style. Our natural history and American Indian lines can be geared for educational markets. To speed things up, queries should include summary, detailed outline, comparison to related books, 2 sample chapters, availability and samples of any photos or illustrations, and author background. Send manuscript only on request." Reviews artwork/photos.
Recent Nonfiction Title: *The Mushroom Manual—Tops!*, by Lorentz C. Pearson.

NAVAL INSTITUTE PRESS, Annapolis MD 21402. Manager, Acquisitions and Subsidiary Rights: Deborah Guberti Estes. Press Director: Thomas F. Epley. Averages 35 titles/year; receives 400-500 submissions annually. 80% of books from first-time authors; 70% of books from unagented writers. Average print order for a writer's first book is 4,000. Pays 14-18-21% royalty based on net sales; advance. Publishes book an average of 10 months after acceptance. Computer printout submissions acceptable; no dot-matrix. Reports in 2 weeks on queries; 6-8 weeks on other submissions. Free book catalog; ms guidelines for SASE.
Nonfiction: "We are interested only in naval and maritime subjects: tactics, strategy, navigation, naval history, biographies of naval leaders and naval aviation." Reviews artwork/photos as part of ms package.
Recent Nonfiction Title: *Icebound: The Jeanette Expedition's Quest for the North Pole*, by Leonard Gattridge (adventure/history).

Fiction: Limited, very high quality fiction on naval and maritime themes.
Recent Fiction Title: *Flight of the Intruder*, by Stephen Coonts.

NC PRESS, Suite 401, 260 Richmond St. W., Toronto, Ontario M5V 1W5 Canada. (416)593-6284. Editorial Director: Caroline Walker. Publishes hardcover and paperback originals and reprints and a limited line of children's books. Averages 10-15 titles/year; receives 500 submissions annually. 50% of books from first-time authors; 80% of books from unagented writers. Average print order for a writer's first book is 2,500. Pays royalty on list under 50% discount. Computer printout submissions acceptable. Include IRCs with submissions. Ms guidelines for SASE.
Nonfiction: "We generally publish books of social/political relevance either on contemporary topics of concern (current events, ecology, etc.), or historical studies and popular health books. We publish primarily Canadians. We cannot publish a U.S. author without U.S. co-publisher." Submit outline/synopsis and 1-2 sample chapters.
Recent Nonfiction Title: *Choices: For People Who Have A Terminal Illness, Their Families and Their Caregivers*.

THOMAS NELSON PUBLISHERS, Nelson Place at Elm Hill Pike, Nashville TN 37214. (615)889-9000. Editorial Vice President: Bruce A. Nygren. Publishes hardcover and paperback originals and reprints. Averages 55 titles/year. Pays royalty or makes outright purchase. Publishes book an average of 1 year after acceptance. Computer printout submissions acceptable. Reports in 2 months. SASE must accompany submissions or unable to respond.
Nonfiction: Adult trade and reference books on religion. Accepts outline/synopsis and 3 sample chapters.
Recent Nonfiction Title: *Meadowlark*, by Meadowlark Lemon, with Jerry Jenkins.

NELSON-HALL PUBLISHERS, 111 N. Canal St., Chicago IL 60606. (312)930-9446. Editorial Director: Harold Wise, Ph.D. Publishes hardcover and paperback originals. Averages 105 titles/year. Pays 15% maximum royalty on retail price; offers average advance. Photocopied submissions OK. Reports in 1 month. Free book catalog.
Nonfiction: Textbooks and general scholarly books in the social sciences. Query.
Recent Nonfiction Title: *Sociology: the Science of Human Organization*, by Jonathan H. Turner.

NEW AMERICAN LIBRARY, 1633 Broadway, New York NY 10019. (212)397-8000. Imprints include Signet, Mentor, Signet Classics, Plume, Meridian, D.A.W Books, Onyx and NAL Books. Publisher: Elaine Koster. Editor-in-Chief: Maureen Baron. Editor-in-Chief/Trade Books: Arnold Dolin. Editor-in-Chief/Hardcover: Michaela Hamilton. Publishes hardcover and paperback originals and hardcover reprints. Publishes 350 titles/year. Royalty is "variable"; offers "substantial" advance. Query letters *only*. Replies in 1 month. Free book catalog.
Tips: Queries may be routed to other editors in the publishing group.

THE NEW ENGLAND PRESS, INC., Box 575, Shelburne VT 05482. (802)863-2520/985-2569. President: Alfred Rosa. Small press. Publishes hardcover and trade paperback orignals and trade paperback reprints. Averages 6-12 titles/year; receives 200+ submissions annually. 25% of books from first-time authors; 75% of books from unagented writers. Pays 10-15% royalty on wholesale price. Publishes ms an average of 1 year after acceptance. Photocopied submissions OK. Computer printout submissions acceptable; no dot-matrix. Reports in 2 weeks on queries; 1 month on mss. Free book catalog.
Nonfiction: Biography, cookbook, how-to, nature and illustrated book. Subjects include Americana (Vermontiana and New England); cooking and foods, history (New England orientation); and essays (New England orientation). No juvenile or psychology. Query or submit outline/synopsis and sample chapters. Reviews artwork/photos.
Recent Nonfiction Title: *The Vermont Quiz Book*, by Frank and Melissa Bryan (history in anecdote quiz form).
Fiction: Historical (New England orientation). No novels. Query.

‡NEW HARBINGER PUBLICATIONS, INC., 5674 Shattuck Ave., Oakland CA 94609. (415)465-1435. Acquisitions Editor: Carol Talpers. Publishes hardcover and trade paperback originals and trade paperback reprints. Averages 4 titles/year; receives 50 submissions annually. 40% of books from first-time authors. 100% of books from unagented writers. Pays 15% royalty on wholesale price; offers $1,000 average advance. Publishes book an average of 1 year after acceptance. Simultaneous and photocopied submissions OK. Computer printout submissions OK; prefers letter-quality. Reports in 2 months. Free book catalog. Reviews artwork/photos as part of ms package.
Nonfiction: Self-help on psychology and health. "We're primarily interested in the cognitive behavior approach to specific emotional problems. Ms should be of interest to both therapists and lay public. Make it clear, step-by-step, with good examples." Submit outline/synopsis and sample chapters or artwork/photos as part of

ms package. "We prefer a detailed chapter by chapter outline."
Recent Nonfiction Title: *Beyond Grief*, by Staudacher.

NEW LEAF PRESS, INC., Box 311, Green Forest AR 72638. Editor-in-Chief: Harriett Dudley. Hardcover and paperback originals. Specializes in charismatic books. Publishes 15 titles/year; receives 236 submissions annually. 15% of books from first-time authors; 90% of books from unagented writers. Average print order for a writer's first book is 10,000. Pays 10% royalty on first 10,000 copies, paid once a year; no advance. Send photos and illustrations to accompany ms. Publishes book an average of 10 months after acceptance. Simultaneous and photocopied submissions OK. Electronic submissions OK via 128 Commodore, but requires hard copy also. Computer printout submissions acceptable. Reports in 3 months. Reviews artwork/photos. Book catalog and guidelines for 8½x11 SAE with $1 postage.
Nonfiction: Biography and self-help. Charismatic books; life stories, and how to live the Christian life. Length: 100-400 pages. Submit complete ms.
Recent Nonfiction Title: *Smashing Gates of Hell*, by David Lewis (non-fiction/prophecy).
Tips: "Biographies, relevant nonfiction, and Bible-based fiction have the best chance of selling to our firm. Honest and real-life experience help make a book or query one we can't put down."

NEW READERS PRESS, Publishing division of Laubach Literacy International, Box 131, Syracuse NY 13210. Acquisitions Editor: Kay Koschnick. Publishes paperback originals. Averages 30 titles/year; receives 200 submissions annually. 40% of books by first-time authors; 100% of books by unagented writers. Average print order for a writer's first book is 5,000. "Most of our sales are to high school classes for slower learners, special education, and adult basic education programs, with some sales to volunteer literacy programs, private human-services agencies, prisons, and libraries with outreach programs for poor readers." Pays royalty on retail price, or by outright purchase. "Rate varies according to type of publication and length of manuscript." Advance is "different in each case, but does not exceed projected royalty for first year." Publishes book an average of 1 year after acceptance. Photocopied submissions OK. Query for electronic submissions. Computer printout submissions acceptable; prefers letter-quality to dot-matrix. Reports in 2 months. Free book catalog and authors' brochure.
Nonfiction: "Our audience is adults and older teenagers with limited reading skills (6th grade level and below). We publish basic education materials in reading and writing, math, social studies, health, science, and English-as-a-second-language for double illiterates. We are particularly interested in materials that fulfill curriculum requirements in these areas. Manuscripts must be not only easy to read (3rd-6th grade level) but mature in tone and concepts. We are not interested in poetry or anything at all written for children." Submit outline and 1-3 sample chapters. Reviews artwork/photos as part of ms package.
Recent Nonfiction Title: *In the Know: The Informational Reading Series*, by Michael P. O'Donnell and Margo Wood (supplementary reading practice).
Fiction: Short novels (12,000-15,000 words) at third grade reading level on themes of interest to adults and older teenagers. Submit synopsis.

*NEW SOCIETY PUBLISHERS, 4722 Baltimore Ave., Philadelphia PA 19143. (215)726-6543. Collectively managed. Publishes hardcover and trade paperback originals and reprints. Averages 18 titles/year; receives 200 submissions annually. 80% of books from first-time authors; 95% of books from unagented writers. Subsidy publishes (nonauthor) 10% of books. Pays 10% royalty on net receipts. Offers average $500 advance. Publishes book an average of 18 months after acceptance. Photocopied submissions OK. Computer printout submissions acceptable; prefers letter-quality to dot-matrix. Reports in 1 month on queries; 3 months on mss. Book catalog and ms guidelines for #10 SASE.
Nonfiction: Biography, humor, illustrated book, social self-help and books on nonviolent action (case studies). Subjects include history, philosophy, politics, psychology, religion, sociology, feminism, ecology, worker self-management, group dynamics and peace issues. No books about the damage which will be done by nuclear war. Query *only*; "all unsolicited mss are thrown in trash." Reviews artwork/photos as part of ms package.
Recent Nonfiction Title: *The Power of the People*, by Robert Coouey (pictorial history).

‡NEW VICTORIA PUBLISHERS, Box 27, Norwich VT 05055. (802)649-5297. Editor: Claudia Lamperti. Publishes trade paperback originals. Averages 3-4 titles/year; receives 25 submissions/year. 100% of books from first-time authors; 100% of books from unagented writers. Pays 10% royalty on wholesale price. Publishes book an average of 6 months after acceptance. Photocopied submissions OK. Query for electronic submissions. Computer printout submissions OK. Reports on queries in 2 weeks; on mss in 1 month. Free book catalog.
Nonfiction: History. "We are interested in feminist history or biography and interviews with or topics relating to lesbians. No poetry." Submit outline/synopis and sample chapters.
Recent Nonfiction Title: *Radical Feminists of Htereodoxy*, by Judith Schwarz (feminist history).
Fiction: Adventure, erotica, fantasy, historical, humor, mystery, romance, science fiction and western. "We

will consider most anything if it is well written and appeals to lesbian/feminist audience. Submit outline/synopsis and sample chapters.
Recent Fiction Title: *Something Shady*, by Sarah Dreher (mystery adventure).
Tips: "Try to appeal to a specific audience and not write for the general market."

*NEW YORK ZOETROPE, INC., 838 Broadway, New York NY 10003. (212)420-0590. Contact: James Monaco. Publishes hardcover and trade paperback originals, hardcover and trade paperback reprints and software. Averages 25-35 titles/year; receives 25-50 submissions annually. 25% of books from first-time authors; 75% of books from unagented writers. Subsidy publishes (nonauthor) 3% of books. Pays 10-20% royalty on wholesale prices or makes outright purchase of $500-1,000. Offers average $1,000 advance. Publishes book an average of 9 months after acceptance. Simultaneous and photocopied submissions OK. Query for electronic submissions. Computer printout submissions acceptable; prefers letter-quality to dot-matrix. Reports in 2 weeks on queries; 2 months on mss. Book catalog and guidelines for 6x9 SAE.
Nonfiction: Coffee table book, reference, technical and textbook. Subjects include computers, travel and media. Interested especially in film and computer subjects. No fiction. Query with a synopsis and outline.
Recent Nonfiction Title: *Louise Brooks: Portrait of an Anti-Star*, by Roland Jaccard, editor; English translation by Gideon Y. Schein.
Tips: "Film- or media-oriented (academic and popular) tie-ins have the best chance of selling to our firm. Media books are our strongest line."

NEWCASTLE PUBLISHING CO., INC., 13419 Saticoy, North Hollywood CA 91605. (213)873-3191. Editor-in-Chief: Alfred Saunders. Publishes trade paperback originals and reprints. Averages 10 titles/year; receives 300 submissions annually. 70% of books from first-time authors; 95% of books from unagented writers. Average print order for a writer's first book is 3,000-5,000. Pays 5-10% royalty on retail price; no advance. Publishes book an average of 8 months after acceptance. Simultaneous and photocopied submissions OK. Computer printout submissions acceptable; prefers letter-quality to dot-matrix. Reports in 3 weeks on queries; 6 weeks on mss. Free book catalog; ms guidelines for SASE.
Nonfiction: How-to, self-help, metaphysical and New Age. Subjects include health (physical fitness, diet and nutrition), psychology and religion. "Our audience is made up of college students and college-age nonstudents; also, adults ages 25 and up. They are of above average intelligence and are fully aware of what is available in the bookstores." No biography, travel, children's books, poetry, cookbooks or fiction. Query or submit outline/synopsis and sample chapters. Looks for "something to grab the reader so that he/she will readily remember that passage."
Recent Nonfiction Title: *Authentic I Ching*, by Henry Wei, Ph.D (translation of I Ching by a Chinese national).
Tips: "Check the shelves in the larger bookstores on the subject of the manuscript being submitted. A book on life extension, holistic health, or stress management has the best chance of selling to our firm."

NIMBUS PUBLISHING LIMITED, Subsidiary of H.H. Marshall Ltd., Box 9301, Station A, Halifax, Nova Scotia B3K 5N5 Canada. (902)454-8381. Contact: Dorothy Cooper. Imprints include: Petheric Press (nonfiction and fiction). Publishes hardcover and trade paperback originals and trade paperback reprints. Averages 10 titles/year; receives 60 submissions annually. 50% of books from first-time authors; 100% of books from unagented writers. Average print order for a writer's first book is 3,000. Pays 4-10% royalty on retail price. Publishes book an average of 2 years after acceptance. Photocopied submissions OK. Electronic submissions OK, but requires hard copy also. Computer printout submissions acceptable. IRCs. Reports in 2 months on queries; 4 months on mss. Free book catalog.
Nonfiction: Biography, "coffee table" books, cookbooks, how-to, humor, illustrated books, juvenile and books of regional interest. Subjects include art, cooking and foods, history, nature, travel and regional. "We do some specialized publishing, otherwise, our audience is the tourist and trade market in Nova Scotia." Query or submit outline/synopsis and a minimum of 1 sample chapter. Reviews artwork/photos as part of ms package.
Tips: "Titles of regional interest, with potential for national or international sales, have the best chance of selling to our firm."

NITTY GRITTY COOKBOOKS, 447 E. Channel Rd., Box 2008, Benicia CA 94510. (707)746-0800. President: Earl Goldman. Publishes trade and mass market paperback originals. Averages 4 titles/year; receives 100 submissions annually. 50% of books from first-time authors; 100% of books from unagented writers. Pays standard royalty. Offers average $500 advance. Publishes book an average of 6 months after acceptance. Simultaneous and photocopied submissions OK. Computer printout submissions acceptable. Reports in 2 weeks. Free book catalog and ms guidelines.
Nonfiction: Books on cooking and foods. "We publish cookbooks only." Query or submit outline/synopsis and sample chapters.
Recent Nonfiction Title: *The Barbecue Book*, by Callahan.

NORTH COUNTRY PRESS, Imprint of Thorndike Press, One Mile Rd., Box 159, Thorndike ME 04986. (207)948-2962. Senior Editor: Charles Fortier. Publishes hardcover and paperback originals and reprints. Averages 10 titles/year; receives 500 submissions annually. 10% of books from first-time authors; 90% of books from unagented writers. Average print order for writer's first book is 2,000. Offers 6-10% of list; or makes outright purchase for $500-2,000. Offers average $1,000 advance. Publishes book an average of 18 months after acceptance. Electronic submissions OK on IBM PC compatible disks. Computer printout submissions acceptable; prefers letter-quality to dot-matrix. Unsolicited submissions not accompanied by SASE with proper postage will not be returned. Reports in 2 months. Book catalog for 9x12 SAE and 56¢ postage.

Nonfiction: Biography, animals, outdoors how- and where-to, nature, and all subjects of New England regional interest. Especially needs "manuscripts relating to the wilderness and oudoor recreation (hunting, fishing, etc.) in the Northeast U.S." *No* poetry, young adult, adventure suspense, cookbooks, science fiction, erotica, history, romance, crafts, drama, computer, engineering, religion, Gothic, mass market titles or children's books. Submit outline/synopsis and 2-3 sample chapters. Reviews artwork/photos as part of ms package.

Recent Nonfiction Title: *Hawks at My Wing Tip*, by Bill Welch (bird watching).

Fiction: Humor (New England), and serious regional fiction (Maine and New England). "We will always consider exceptional manuscripts in our areas of interest, but 90% of the submissions we receive are not appropriate to our line. We prefer short works." No young adult or children's books; no poetry. Submit outline/synopsis and 2-3 sample chapters.

Recent Fiction Title: *Sea Stories*, by Colcord (anthology).

Tips: "I wish authors who have been turned down repeatedly would not send such oft-rejected material here in hope that 'well, maybe . . .' As a small publisher, we are probably *more* selective, not less, than the big houses, simply because we have fewer slots per year to fill. What we *are* looking for, and seek queries on, is New England nature and outdoors guidebooks that take a how-to and/or where-to-go approach to a specific activity, as well as New England regional biography, humor, and serious (or 'literary') general fiction."

NORTH LIGHT, Imprint of F&W Publications, 1507 Dana Ave., Cincinnati OH 45207. Editorial Director: David Lewis. Publishes hardcover and trade paperback originals. Averages 20-25 titles/year. Pays 10% royalty on net receipts. Offers $3,000 advance. Simultaneous submissions OK. Reports in 3 weeks on queries; 2 months on mss. Free book catalog.

Nonfiction: Art and graphic arts instruction books. Interested in books on watercolor painting, oil painting, basic drawing, pen and ink, airbrush, markers, basic design, color, illustration techniques, layout and typography. Do not submit coffee table art books with no how-to art instruction. Query or submit outline/synopsis and examples of artwork (photographs of artwork are OK).

Recent Nonfiction Title: *Dynamic Airbrush*.

NORTH POINT PRESS, 850 Talbot Ave., Berkeley CA 94706. (415)527-6260. Contact: Kathleen Moses. Publishes hardcover and trade paperback originals, and trade paperback reprints. Averages 30 titles/year; receives 4,000 submissions annually. 5% of books from first-time authors; 40% of books from unagented writers. Photocopied submissions OK. Publishes book an average of 10 months after acceptance. Computer printout submissions acceptable; no dot-matrix. Reports in 3 months. Material not accompanied by postage will not be returned. Free book catalog; ms guidelines for SASE.

Nonfiction: Biography, cooking and foods, history, nature, philosophy, sociology (cultural anthropology), and travel (literary travel). No heavily illustrated books, children's books, how-tos, technical, academic, cookbooks, or "western"-genre biographies. Query.

Recent Nonfiction Title: *Home Economics*, by Wendell Berry.

Fiction: Serious literature and fiction in translation. No genre or children's fiction. Query.

Recent Fiction Title: *Adventures with Julia*, by Candace Denning.

Poetry: No unsolicited poetry manuscripts.

Recent Poetry Title: *Left Out in the Rain*, by Gary Snyder.

NORTHWORD, Imprint of Paperback Press Inc., Box 128, Ashland WI 53705. (608)231-2355. Editor: Pat Klein. Publishes trade paperback originals and trade paperback reprints. Averages 10 titles/year; receives approximately 100 submissions annually. 10-15% of books from first time authors; 40-50% unagented submissions. Pays 15% royalty on wholesale price. Offers negotiable advance. Publishes book an average of 1 year after acceptance. Computer printout submissions acceptable; prefers letter-quality to dot-matrix. Simultaneous submissions OK *only* if we are so informed. "It takes me forever to reply to most submissions. I do not object to polite periodic reminders, however." Average report time 12-18 months. Free book catalog.

Nonfiction: Natural history, natural heritage. "We publish titles with a national nature focus, and Midwest oriented nature and history titles. We are always looking for guidebooks of various types to our region—travel, recreation, sporting activities, historical sights, natural landmarks, etc." No religion. Submit outline and sample chapters. Reviews artwork/photos as part of ms package.

Recent Nonfiction Title: *Birds of Prey*, by John P.S. MacKenzie.

Tips: "In general, our audience is a literate, curious, well-educated group interested in enjoying life in our region to the fullest."

W.W. NORTON CO., INC., 500 5th Ave., New York NY 10110. (212)354-5500. Managing Editor: Sterling Lawrence. Imprint includes Shoreline Books. Publishes 213 titles/year; receives 5,000 submissions annually. Often publishes new and unagented authors. Royalty varies on retail price; advance varies. Publishes book an average of 1 year after acceptance. Photocopied and simultaneous submissions OK. Computer printout submissions acceptable. Submit outline and/or 2-3 sample chapters for fiction and nonfiction. Return of material not guaranteed without SASE. Reports in 1 month. Book catalog and guidelines for 8½x11 SAE with 39¢ postage.
Nonfiction and Fiction: "General, adult fiction and nonfiction of all kinds on nearly all subjects and of the highest quality possible within the limits of each particular book." Last year there were 93 book club rights sales; 36 mass paperback reprint sales; and "innumerable serializations, second serial, syndication, translations, etc." Looks for "clear, intelligent, creative writing on original subjects or with original characters."
Recent Nonfiction Title: *The Rotation Diet*, by Martin Kathahn, Ph.D. (diet).
Recent Fiction Title: *God's Snake*, by Irini Spanidou.
Tips: "Long novels are too expensive—keep them under 350 (manuscript) pages."

NOYES DATA CORP., Imprints include Noyes Press and Noyes Publications, Noyes Bldg., Park Ridge NJ 07656. Publishes hardcover originals. Averages 60 titles/year. Pays 10%-12% royalty on retail price; advance varies, depending on author's reputation and nature of book. Reports in 2 weeks. Free book catalog.
Nonfiction: Noyes Press publishes art, classical studies, archeology, and history. "Material directed to the intelligent adult and the academic market." Noyes Publications publishes technical books on practical industrial processing, science, economic books pertaining to chemistry, chemical engineering, food, textiles, energy, electronics, pollution control—primarily of interest to the business executive. Length: 50,000-250,000 words. Query Editorial Department.

OAK TREE PUBLICATIONS, Vizcom, Inc., Suite 202, 9601 Aero Dr., San Diego CA 92123. (619)560-5163. Subsidiaries include: Value Tale Comunications. Editor: Beth Ingram. Publishes hardcover originals. Averages 10 titles/year; receives hundreds of submissions annually. 5% of books from first-time authors; 50% of books from unagented writers. Pays variable royalty on wholesale price; offers $500 average advance. Publishes book an average of 8 months after acceptance. Simultaneous submissions OK. Computer printout submissions OK; prefers letter-quality. Reports in 1 month on queries; 6 weeks on mss. Book catalog for 8½x11 SAE with 66¢ postage; ms guidelines for SASE.
Fiction: "Juvenile picture books with mass market appeal and licensed toy tie-in." Submit outline/synopsis and sample chapters. Reviews artwork/photos as part of ms package.
Recent Fiction Title: *I Wish I Had A Computer That Makes Waffles*, by Dobson.

‡OASIS PRESS, Subsidiary of PSI Research, 720 S. Hillview Dr., Milpitas CA 95035. (408)263-9671. Publisher: Emmett Ramey. Publishes hardcover originals. Averages 25-30 titles/year; receives 25-30 submissions annually. 10% of books from first-time authors. 95% of books from unagented writers. Pays 8-15% royalty on wholesale price. Offers no advance. Publishes book an average of 10 months after acceptance. Simultaneous submissions OK. Query for electronic submissions. Computer printout submissions OK. Reports in 1 week. Book catalog free on request.
Nonfiction: How-to and self-help. Subjects include business and economics.
Recent Nonfiction Title: *Career Builder*, by McLeod (self-help).

OCTAMERON ASSOCIATES, 820 Fontaine St., Alexandria VA 22302. (703)823-1882. Editorial Director: Karen Stokstad. Publishes trade paperback originals. Averages 15 titles/year; receives 100 submissions annually. 10% of books from first-time authors; 100% of books from unagented writers. Average print order for a writer's first book is 8,000-10,000. Pays 7½% royalty on retail price. Publishes book an average of 6 months after acceptance. Simultaneous submissions OK. Electronic submissions OK via IBM PC, Microsoft and Word Software, but requires hard copy also. Computer printout submissions acceptable; prefers letter-quality to dot-matrix. Reports in 2 weeks. Book catalog and guidelines for #10 SAE with 39¢ postage.
Nonfiction: Reference, career and post-secondary education subjects. Travel guides. Especially interested in "paying-for-college and college admission guides." Query. Submit outline/synopsis and 2 sample chapters. Reviews artwork/photos as part of ms package.
Recent Nonfiction Title: *Top Dollars For Technical Scholars*, by Clark Robinson.

ODDO PUBLISHING, INC., Box 68, Redwine Rd., Fayetteville GA 30214. (404)461-7627. Managing Editor: Genevieve Oddo. Publishes hardcover and paperback originals. Averages 2-6 titles/year; receives 300 + submissions annually. 25% of books from first-time authors; 100% of books from unagented writers. Average print order for a writer's first book is 3,500. Makes outright purchase. "We judge all scripts independently."

Royalty considered for special scripts only. Publishes book an average of 2-3 years after acceptance. Computer printout submissions acceptable; no dot-matrix. Reports in 4 months. Book catalog for 9x12 SAE with $1.07 postage.

Nonfiction and Fiction: Publishes juvenile books in language arts, workbooks in math, writing (English), photophonics, science (space and oceanography), and social studies for schools, libraries, and trade. Interested in children's supplementary readers in the areas of language arts, math, science, social studies, etc. "Texts run from 1,500 to 3,500 words. Ecology, space, patriotism, oceanography and pollution are subjects of interest. Manuscripts must be easy to read, general, and not set to outdated themes. They must lend themselves to full color illustration. No stories of grandmother long ago. No love angle, permissive language, or immoral words or statements." Submit complete ms. Reviews artwork/photos as part of ms package.

Recent Fiction Title: *Bobby Bear and The Friendly Ghost*, by Marilue (children's U.S. geography book).

Tips: "We feel it is important to produce books that will make children feel good."

‡**OHARA PUBLICATIONS, INC.**, 1813 Victory Place, Box 7728, Burbank CA 91510-7728. Contact: Editor. Publishes trade paperback originals. Averages 12 titles/year. Pays royalty. Photocopied submissions OK. Write for guidelines. Reports in 3 weeks on queries; 8 weeks on mss.

Nonfiction: Martial arts. "We decide to do a book on a specific martial art, then seek out the most qualified martial artist to author that book. 'How to' books are our mainstay, and we will accept no manuscript that does not pertain to martial arts systems (their history, techniques, philosophy, etc.)." Query first, then submit outline/synopsis and sample chapter. Include author biography and copies of credentials.

Recent Nonfiction Title: *Chinese Gung Fu*, by Bruce Lee (how-to).

‡**OHIO PSYCHOLOGY PUBLISHING CO.**, 131 N. High St., Columbus OH 43215. (614)224-3288. Vice President: Henry Saeman. Publishes hardcover and trade paperback originals. Averages 3 titles/year; receives 10 submissions annually. 90% of books from first-time authors. Pays 10-14% royalty on retail price; offers $200 average advance. Publishes book an average of 6 months after acceptance. Photocopied submissions OK. Computer printout submissions OK. Reports in 2 months on submissions. Book catalog and guidelines for SASE.

Nonfiction: Self-help and textbook. Subjects include health, psychology, parenting and gifted children. Especially looking for "practical, how-to, self-help books concerning gifted/creative children, or concerning parenting in general. Our audience includes parents, teachers of gifted children, psychologists, guidance counselors and social workers." Submit outline/synopsis and sample chapters.

Recent Nonfiction Title: *Guiding the Gifted Child*, by Webb, Mecksroth and Tolan.

OHIO STATE UNIVERSITY PRESS, 1050 Carmack Rd., Columbus OH 43210. (614)292-6930. Director: Peter J. Givler. Pays royalty on wholesale or retail price. Averages 30 titles/year. Reports in 3 months; ms held longer with author's permission.

Nonfiction: Publishes history, biography, science, philosophy, the arts, political science, law, literature, economics, education, sociology, anthropology, geography, and general scholarly nonfiction. Query with outline and sample chapters.

Recent Nonfiction Title: *Paintings from Books: Art and Literature in Britain, 1760-1900*, by Richard D. Altick.

Tips: Publishes some poetry and fiction.

OHIO UNIVERSITY PRESS, Scott Quad, Ohio University, Athens OH 45701. (614)593-1153. Imprints include Ohio University Press and Swallow Press. Director: Duane Schneider. Publishes hardcover and paperback originals and reprints. Averages 25-30 titles/year. No advance. Photocopied submissions OK. Reports in 5 months. Free book catalog.

Nonfiction: "General scholarly nonfiction with particular emphasis on 19th century literature and culture. Also history, social sciences, philosophy, western regional works and miscellaneous categories." Query.

Recent Nonfiction Title: *The Manyfaced Glass: Tennyson's Dramatic Monologues*, by Linda K. Hughes.

‡*OISE PRESS**, Subsidiary of Ontario Institute for Studies in Education, 252 Floor, W., Toronto, Ontario M5S 1V6 Canada. (416)923-6641, ext. 2531. Editor-in-Chief: Hugh Oliver. Publishes trade paperback originals. Averages 25 titles/year; receives 100 submissions annually. 20% of books from first-time authors. 90% of books from unagented writers. Subsidy publishes (non-author) 5% of books. Pays 10-15% royalty; rarely offers an advance. Simultaneous and photocopied submissions OK. Query for electronic submissions. Computer printout submissions OK; prefers letter-quality. Reports in 1 week on queries; 2 months on submissions. Book catalog and guidelines free on request.

Nonfiction: Textbooks and educational books. "Our audience includes educational scholars; educational administrators, principals and teachers and students. In the future, we will be publishing fewer scholarly books and more books for teachers and students." Submit complete ms. Reviews artwork/photos as part of ms package.

Recent Nonfiction Title: *Reaching the Gifted Child*, by Barbara Dixon, John R. Meyer and Allan Hardy.

‡**THE OLD ARMY PRESS**, Box 2243, Ft. Collins CO 80522. (303)484-5535. General Manager: Dee Koury. Publishes hardcover and trade paperback originals; hardcover and trade paperback reprints. Averages 6 titles/year; receives 20 submissions annually. 50% of books from first-time authors. 100% of books from unagented writers. Pays 5-10% royalty on wholesale price. Publishes book an average of 18 months after acceptance. Photocopied submissions OK. Query for electronic submissions. Computer printout submissions OK; prefers letter-quality. Reports in 3 weeks on queries; 3 months on submissions.
Nonfiction: Biography and reference—all related to western military history. Especially needs mss on Indian wars and Texas history. Query. Reviews artwork/photos as part of ms package.
Recent Nonfiction Title: *Indian Campaigns*, by Harry H. Anderson, ed.

101 PRODUCTIONS, 834 Mission St., San Francisco CA 94103. (415)495-6040. Editor-in-Chief: Jacqueline Killeen. Publishes paperback originals. Offers standard minimum book contract on retail prices. Averages 12 titles/year; receives 200 submissions annually. 10% of books from first-time authors; 90% of books from unagented writers. Publishes book an average of 1 year after acceptance. Photocopied submissions OK. "We are equipped to edit and typeset from electronic disks, providing the software is compatible with Wordstar"; requires hard copy also. Computer printout submissions acceptable; prefers letter-quality to dot-matrix. No unsolicited mss will be read. Free book catalog.
Nonfiction: Mostly how-to: cookbooks, home, gardening, outdoors, and travel. Heavy emphasis on graphics and illustrations. Query. Reviews artwork/photos as part of ms package. Most books are 192 pages.
Recent Nonfiction Title: *The New Harvest*, by Pappas (cookbook).

*****OPEN COURT PUBLISHING CO.**, Box 599, Peru IL 61354. Publisher: M. Blouke Carus. General Manager: Dr. André Carus. Averages 20 titles/year; receives 300 submissions annually. 20% of books from first-time authors; 80% of books from unagented writers. Subsidy publishes 15% of books; 10% non-author subsidy. Royalty contracts negotiable for each book. Publishes book an average of 18 months after acceptance. Query for electronic submissions. Computer printout submissions acceptable; prefers letter-quality to dot-matrix. Guidelines for 9x12 SAE.
Nonfiction: Philosophy, psychology, Jungian analysis, science and history of science, mathematics, public policy, comparative religions,education, Orientalia, and related scholarly topics. Accepts nonfiction translations. "This is a publishing house run as an intellectual enterprise, to reflect the concerns of its staff and as a service to the world of learning." Query or submit outline/synopsis and 2-3 sample chapters. Reviews artwork/photos as part of ms package.
Recent Nonfiction Title: *On Being Mindless: Buddhist Meditation and the Mind-Body Problem*, by Paul J. Griffiths.
Tips: "Many writers do not follow up with phone calls or letters once they have submitted their ms."

*****ORBIS BOOKS**, Maryknoll NY 10545. (914)941-7590. Executive Director: Robert J. Gormley. Publishes cloth and paperback originals and translations. Publishes 40 titles/year. Subsidy publishes (nonauthor) 20% of books. Pays 7-8½-10% royalty on retail prices; offers average $1,000 advance. Query with outline, 2 sample chapters, and prospectus. Query for electronic submissions. Reports in 6 weeks. Enclose return postage.
Nonfiction: "Religious developments in Asia, Africa and Latin America. Christian missions. Justice and peace. Christianity and world religions."
Recent Nonfiction Title: *Sanctuary: The New Underground Railroad*.

*****OREGON STATE UNIVERSITY PRESS**, 101 Waldo Hall, Corvallis OR 97331. (503)754-3166. Hardcover and paperback originals. Averages 6 titles/year; receives 100 submissions annually. 75% of books from first-time authors; 100% of books from unagented writers. Average print order for a writer's first book is 1,500. Subsidy publishes (nonauthor) 40% of books. Pays royalty on wholesale price. No advance. Publishes book an average of 1 year after acceptance. Electronic submissions OK; query first. Computer submissions acceptable; no dot-matrix. Reports in 1 month. Book catalog for 6x9 SAE with 30¢ postage.
Nonfiction: Publishes scholarly books in history, biography, geography, literature, social science, marine and freshwater sciences, life sciences, geology, education, and bibliography, with strong emphasis on Pacific or Northwestern topics. Submit outline/synopsis and sample chapters.
Recent Nonfiction Title: *William L. Finley: Pioneer Wildlife Photographer*, by Worth Mathewson (biography/photos).

ORTHO INFORMATION SERVICES, Subsidiary of Chevron Chemical Co., 575 Market St., San Francisco CA 94105. (415)894-0277. Editorial Director: Robert J. Dolezal. Imprints include California Culinary Academy (nonfiction), Sally Smith, project editor. Publishes hardcover and trade paperback originals and reprints and quarterly Chevron Automobile Travel Magazine. Averages 20-30 titles/year; receives 100+ submissions annually. 10% of books from first-time authors; 20% of books from unagented writers. Makes outright purchase. Publishes book an average of 2 years after acceptance. Simultaneous submissions OK. Electronic submissions OK via IBM-PC format/XyWrite, but requires hard copy also. Computer printout submissions acceptable; prefers letter-quality to dot-matrix. Reports in 3 weeks on queries; 1 month on mss. Book catalog and guidelines for 9x12 SAE with 39¢ postage.

Nonfiction: Cookbook, how-to, illustrated book and reference. Subjects include cooking and foods, hobbies, nature, gardening and home repair. "All our projects are internally generated from project proposals—assignment of author, photographers, some illustration from project outline, including outside submissions." No anecdotal/biographical gardening, how-to, cooking or previously covered topics. Query. "We prefer outline following query with synopsis." All unsolicited mss are returned unopened.

Recent Nonfiction Title: *Upholstery*, by Karin Shakery (how-to).

OUR SUNDAY VISITOR, INC., 200 Noll Plaza, Huntington IN 46750. (219)356-8400. Director: Robert Lockwood. Publishes paperback originals and reprints. Averages 20-30 titles a year; receives 75 submissions annually. 10% of books from first-time authors; 90% of books from unagented writers. Pays variable royalty on net receipts; offers average $500 advance. Publishes book an average of 1 year after acceptance. Query for electronic submissions. Computer printout submissions acceptable; prefers letter-quality to dot-matrix. Reports in 1 month on most queries and submissions. Author's guide and catalog for SASE.

Nonfiction: Catholic viewpoints on current issues, reefence and guidance, Bibles and devotional books, and Catholic heritage books. Prefers to see well-developed proposals as first submission with "annotated outline, three sample chapters, and definition of intended market." Reviews artwork/photos as part of ms package.

Recent Nonfiction Title: *Strange Gods: Contemporary Religious Cults in America*, by William Whalen.

Tips: "Solid devotional books that are not first person, well-researched church histories or lives of the saints and self-help for those over 55 have the best chance of selling to our firm. Make it solidly Catholic, unique, without pious platitudes."

OUTBOOKS INC., 217 Kimball Ave., Golden CO 80401. Contact: William R. Jones. Small press. Publishes trade paperback originals and reprints. Averages 10 titles/year. Pays 5% royalty on retail price. Computer printout submissions acceptable. Reports in 1 month on queries. Book catalog for $1.

Nonfiction: Regional books on Americana, history, nature, recreation and travel. Publishes for "lay enthusiasts in American history, outdoors, and natural history, ecology, and conservation." Query only; send no ms until requested.

Recent Nonfiction Title: *Oh, Ranger*, by Albright (national park interest).

OWL CREEK PRESS, 1620 N. 45th St., Seattle WA 98103. Editor: Rich Ives. Small press. Publishes hardcover, trade paperback and mass market paperback originals, and mass market paperback reprints. Averages 5-10 titles/year; receives 2,000 submissions annually. 50% of books from first-time authors; 95% of books from unagented writers. Pays 10-20% royalty on wholesale price (cash or equivalent in copies). If paid in copies, royalty is advanced. Photocopied submissions OK. Computer printout submissions acceptable; prefers letter-quality to dot-matrix. Reports in 2 months. Book catalog for #10 SASE.

Nonfiction: Photography. "Our selections are made solely on the basis of lasting artistic quality." No cookbooks, how-to, juvenile, self-help, technical or references. Submit outline/synopsis and sample chapters.

Recent Nonfiction Title: *The Truth About the Territory*, edited by Rick Ives (anthology-Northwest).

Fiction: "We seek writing of lasting artistic merit in all areas. Writing genre is irrelevant, although we avoid easy approaches and formula work. We are not interested in writing that attempts to fulfill genre requirements or comply with preconceived notions of mass market appeal. If it's work of lasting quality we will try to find and build a market for it." Submit outline/synopsis and sample chapters.

Recent Fiction Title: *Glove of Passion, Voice of Blood*, by Jean Muno (stories).

Poetry: "We publish both full-length and chapbook titles. Selections are based solely on the lasting quality of the manuscripts. No manuscripts where genre category or preconceived ideas of mass market appeal dominate the work." Submit complete ms, unsolicited through contests only.

Recent Poetry Title: *The Green Duck*, by Mildred Weston (poetry).

Tips: "We attempt to reach the reader with a somewhat discerning taste first. Future plans include further expansion into fiction and translated titles (both poetry and fiction) as well as maintaining a continued series of both full-length and chapbook poetry originals. We are nonprofit, dedicated to the promotion of literary art."

‡P.A.R. INCORPORATED, Subsidiary of Abbott Park Associates, 290 Westminister St., Providence RI 02903. (401)331-0130. Senior Editor: Carol A. Long. Publishes educational hardcover and paperback text/workbooks. Averages 6-10 titles/year. 65% of books from first-time authors. 100% of books from unagented writers. Pays 5-10% royalty on wholesale price. Sometimes makes outright purchase. Publishes book an aver-

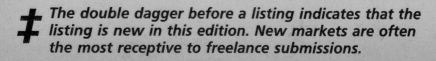

The double dagger before a listing indicates that the listing is new in this edition. New markets are often the most receptive to freelance submissions.

age of 1 year after acceptance. Simultaneous and photocopied submissions OK. Computer printout submissions OK; prefers letter-quality. Reports in 1 month. Book catalog free on request.
Nonfiction: Textbooks for the post-secondary business and technical school market. Subjects include business, education and developmental studies—reading, writing and business math. Especially needs manuscripts on "developmental studies for post-secondary career students: Communication skills, travel, career development, getting a job, basic math and basic skills." Submit outline/synopsis and sample chapters.
Recent Nonfiction Title: *Developing Writing Skills*, by Farrell (developmental writing text/workbook).
Tips: "We look for innovative manuscripts which are easily presented in a workshop format. Manuscripts with text content plus a workshop outline preferrable. Readability of manuscripts must be appropriate for community college, electronic school, secretarial, etc. populations."

P.P.I. PUBLISHING, 835 E. Congress Park, Box 335, Dayton OH 45459. (513)433-2709. Vice President: Kim Brooks. Publishes mass market paperback originals (booklets). Averages 30-40 titles/year; receives 250 submissions annually. 45% of books from first-time authors; 100% of books from unagented writers. Average print order for a writer's first book is 1,000. Pays 10% royalty on retail selling price to customer (some customer discounts). Publishes book an average of 3 months after acceptance. Simultaneous and photocopied submissions OK. Computer printout submissions acceptable but not preferable; no dot-matrix. Reports in 3 weeks on queries; 10 weeks on mss. Book catalog with guidelines for SAE and 3 first class stamps; ms guidelines only for SASE.
Nonfiction: Juvenile and teens, and self-help. Subjects include health and sociology. "We publish nonfiction booklets of 20,000 words or larger for junior and senior high schools, libraries, colleges, universities and other specialized markets such as social service organizations. Our main subjects include controversial issues and items in the news. Topics that students are preparing for research papers or debates are of particular interest. We keep our markets informed on what's happening today in the world, in the home, in schools, and for the future. Some recent topics that were published include how to deal with freshman stress for the college student, euthanasia, prescription drug abuse, teens, drinking and driving, food irradiation, teenage suicide, the Klan, television, etc. We are especially looking for 20,000-word manuscripts or larger on current events. We're not interested in how-to, technical material, travel or cookbooks." Submit outline/synopsis, sample chapters or complete ms. "For new authors we prefer outlines or queries to save them time and trouble." Reviews artwork/photos as part of ms package on a limited basis.
Recent Nonfiction Titles: *Teenage Drinking and Driving: A Deadly Duo*, by Elaine Fantle Shimberg.
Tips: "Find out how today's events and news affect students and people in general, and what the future outlook is for social issues, world issues and family. One of our largest markets is high schools."

PACIFIC BOOKS, PUBLISHERS, Box 558, Palo Alto CA 94302. (415)856-0550. Editor: Henry Ponleithner. Averages 6-12 titles/year. Royalty schedule varies with book. No advance. Send complete ms. Computer printout submissions OK "if clean, typewriter-quality." Reports "promptly." Book catalog and guidelines for 9x12 SAE.
Nonfiction: General interest, professional, technical and scholarly nonfiction trade books. Specialties include western Americana and Hawaiiana. Looks for "well-written, documented material of interest to a significant audience." Also considers text and reference books; high school and college. Accepts artwork/photos and translations.
Recent Nonfiction Title: *Economic and Political Change In The Middle East*, by Elias H. Tuma (economics).

PACIFIC PRESS PUBLISHING ASSOCIATION, Book Division, Seventh-day Adventist Church, Box 7000, Boise ID 83707. (208)465-2595. Vice President of Editorial Development: Ken McFarland. Publishes hardcover and trade paperback originals and hardcover and trade paperback reprints. Averages 50 titles/year; receives 800 submissions annually. Up to 50% of books from first-time authors; 100% of books from unagented writers. Pays 5-7% royalty on retail price. Offers average $300 advance. Publishes books an average of 6 months after acceptance. Photocopied submissions OK. Electronic submissions OK ("We have an Altertext disk reader and can read all major systems"); requires hard copy also. Computer printout submissions acceptable; prefers letter-quality to dot-matrix. Reports in 1 month on queries; 2 months on mss. Ms quidelines for SASE.
Nonfiction: Biography, cookbook (vegetarian), how-to, juvenile, self-help and textbook. Subjects include cooking and foods (vegetarian only), health, nature, religion, and family living. "We are an exclusively religious publisher. We are looking for practical, how-to-oriented manuscripts on religion, health, and family life that speak to human needs, interests and problems from a Biblical perspective. We can't use anything totally secular or written from other than a Christian perspective." Query or submit outline/synopsis and sample chapters. Reviews artwork/photos as part of ms package.
Recent Nonfiction Title: *How Jesus Treated People*, by Morris L. Vendem.
Tips: "Our primary audiences are members of our own denomination (Seventh-day Adventist), the general Christian reading market, and the secular or nonreligious reader. Books that are doing well for us are those that

relate the Biblical message to practical human concerns and those that focus more on the experiential rather than theoretical aspects of Christianity."

THE PAGURIAN CORPORATION LIMITED, 13 Hazelton Ave., Toronto, Ontario M5R 2E1 Canada. (416)968-0255. Editor-in-Chief: Christopher Ondaatje. Publishes paperback and hardcover originals and reprints. Averages 2 titles/year. Offers negotiable royalty contract. Advance negotiable. Publishes book an average of 6 months after acceptance. Photocopied submissions OK. Computer printout submissions acceptable; prefers letter-quality to dot-matrix. Submit 2-page outline, synopsis or chapter headings and contents. Reports "immediately." SAE with IRC.
Nonfiction: Publishes general interest trade and art books. Will consider fine arts, outdoor and cookbook. Length: 40,000-70,000 words. Reviews artwork/photos as part of ms package.
Tips: "We are publishing *fewer* books, and all are Canadian art or art history themes."

PALADIN PRESS, Box 1307, Boulder CO 80306. (303)443-7250. President/Publisher: Peder C. Lund. General Manager: Kim R. Hood. Editorial Director: Rose-Marie Strassberg. Publishes hardcover and paperback originals and paperback reprints. Averages 36 titles/year. 50% of books from first-time authors; 100% of books from unagented writers. Pays 10-12-15% royalty on net sales. Publishes book an average of 1 year after acceptance. Simultaneous and photocopied submissions OK. Computer printout submissions acceptable. Reports in 2 months. Free book catalog.
Nonfiction: "Paladin Press primarily publishes original manuscripts on martial arts, military science, weaponry, self-defense, police science, action careers, guerrilla warfare, fieldcraft and 'creative revenge' humor. How-to manuscripts are given priority. Manuals on building weapons, when technically accurate and clearly presented, are encouraged. If applicable, send sample photographs and line drawings with complete outline and sample chapters." Query or submit outline/synopsis and sample chapters.
Recent Nonfiction Title: *Secrets of Hakkoryu Jujutsu.*
Tips: "We need lucid, instructive material aimed at our market and accompanied by sharp, relevant illustrations and photos. As we are primarily a publisher of 'how-to' books, a manuscript which has step-by-step instructions, written in a clear and concise manner (but not strictly outline form) is desirable. No fiction, first-person accounts, children's, religious or joke books."

PANDORA PRESS, Imprint of Routledge and Kegan Paul, 29 W. 35th St., New York NY 10001. (212)244-3336. Editor: Philippa Brewster. Publishes hardcover and trade paperback originals and trade paperback reprints. Averages 50 titles/year. 40% of books from first-time authors; 30% of books from unagented writers. Pays 7½-10% royalty on retail price; offers average $3,500 advance. Publishes book an average of 1 year after acceptance. Simultaneous and photocopied submissions OK. Computer printout submissions acceptable. Reports in 2 months on queries; 3 months on mss. Book catalog free on request; ms guidelines for SASE.
Nonfiction: Biography, reference, self-help, general interest and popular women's studies. Subjects include art, health, history, current issues, literary criticism, photography, cinema and politics. "Pandora is a feminist press which addresses a range of interests in the U.S., in the U.K. and internationally. Manuscripts of subjects listed above will be considered." No mss that do not fit these categories. Query or submit outline/synopsis and sample chapters. Reviews artwork/photos as part of ms package.
Recent Nonfiction Title: *Half The Earth: A Woman's Guide to Travel Worldwide*, by Miranda Davies (travel).
Fiction: Contemporary, adventure, ethnic, crime and humor. Query or submit outline/synopsis and 2 sample chapters.
Recent Fiction Title: *This Place*, by Andrea Freud Loewenstein (first novel).
Tips: "The writer has the best chance of selling our firm challenging accessible feminist works in a range of areas. That is the audience Pandora tries to reach and the contribution the Press makes in the best traditions of women's creativity. The books which are most successful address an important contemporary social issue and/or uncover a new area of interest to women. And the fiction is to entertain, above all."

PANJANDRUM BOOKS, Suite 1, 11321 Iowa Ave., Los Angeles CA 90025. (213)477-8771. Subsidiaries include Panjandrum Books Inc. Editor/Publisher: Dennis Koran. Publishes hardcover and trade paperback originals. Averages 4-5 titles/year. Pays 7-10% royalty on retail price. Computer printout submissions acceptable. Reports in 2 weeks on queries; 2 months on mss. Book catalog for 7x10 SAE and 2 first class stamps.
Nonfiction: Biography, cookbook, how-to, juvenile and reference. Subjects include cooking, health, hobbies, music, philosophy, theater and drama, herbs, vegetarianism, and childhood sexuality. "We're looking for manuscripts of cookbooks, health books, music (how-to) and drama, and are open to queries on other subjects." No religious or humorous. Query or submit outline/synopsis and sample chapters.
Recent Nonfiction Title: *Alfred Jarry: The Man with the Axe*, by Lennon (literary biography).
Fiction: Avant-garde, experimental, surreal and translations of European literature (not previously translated into English). Query with sample chapter.
Recent Fiction Title: *Fighting Men*, by Manus (post-Vietnam novel).

Poetry: Submit maximum 5 poems.
Recent Poetry Title: *Visions of the Fathers of Lascaux*, by Eshleman.

PANTHEON BOOKS, Division of Random House, Inc., 201 E. 50th St., New York NY 10022. Averages 90 titles/year. Pays royalty on invoice price (retail price minus freight pass-through, usually 50¢). Publishes book an average of 1 year after acceptance (longer if ms not written/completed when contract is signed). Address queries to Adult Editorial Department (28th Floor). "We prefer to work with experienced writers who have already published at least one book or several articles. In addition to a description of the book, queries must include a brief market study detailing how the book proposed will be different from other books available on the subject." Computer printout submissions acceptable; prefers letter-quality to dot-matrix.
Nonfiction: Emphasis on Asia, international politics, radical social theory, history, medicine, women's studies, and law. Recreational guides and practical how-to books as well. Query letters only. No mss accepted. Publishes some juveniles.
Recent Nonfiction Title: *War Without Mercy*, by John W. Dower.
Fiction: Publishes fewer than 5 novels each year, primarily mysteries and foreign fiction in translation. Queries on fiction not accepted.

*PARAGON HOUSE PUBLISHERS, 2 Hammarskjold Plaza, New York NY 10017. (212)223-6433. Editor-in-Chief: Ken Stuart. Publishes hardcover and trade paperback originals and reprints. Averages 80 titles/year; receives 1,000 submissions annually. 10-20% of nonfiction from first-time authors; 50% of books from unagented writers. Subsidy publishes 2% of books/year (mostly translations). Whether an author is subsidy published is determined by "how much subsidy there is, as well as how much market." Royalty and advance negotiable. Simultaneous and photocopied submissions OK. Query for electronic submissions. Computer printout submissions acceptable; no dot-matrix. Reports in 2 weeks on queries; 6 weeks on mss. Book catalog free on request.
Nonfiction: Biography, illustrated book, reference and textbook. Subjects include Americana, history, music, philosophy, politics, religion, and literature. Especially needs history, biography and serious nonfiction. No self help, diet, gardening, crafts, occult or humor. Query or submit outline/synopsis and sample chapters. Reviews artwork/photos as part of ms package.
Recent Nonfiction Title: *American Journals: Albert Camus*.
Poetry: Journals and letters only. No new or unestablished writers.
Recent Poetry Title: *The Poet's Craft*, by Bill Packard (interviews with Auden, Ginsberg, Ashbery, etc.)
Tips: "We are looking for books that fall between the cracks, such as books which are too mid-list for trade houses and not scholarly enough for university presses."

PARENTING PRESS, INC., 7744 31st Ave, NE, Seattle WA 98115. (206)527-2900. Editor: Shari Steelsmith. Publishes hardcover and trade paperback originals. Averages 10 titles/year; receives 50 submissions annually. 80% of books from first-time authors; 100% of books from unagented writers. Pays 8-10% royalty on retail price. Offers average $150 advance. Publishes book an average of 9 months after acceptance. Simultaneous and photocopied submissions OK. Computer printout submissions acceptable; no dot-matrix. Reports in 3 weeks on queries; 6 weeks on mss. Book catalog and ms guidelines for #10 SASE.
Nonfiction: Illustrated book, juvenile, self-help and parenting. "We need books that build competence in parents and children and improve the quality of family life. No fiction or 'should' books—we instead like to see manuscripts that provide a variety of ways to do things—not just one 'right' way." Submit outline/synopsis and sample chapters or complete ms. Reviews artwork/photos as part of ms package.
Recent Nonfiction Title: *Why Does That Man Have Such A Big Nose?*, by Mary Beth Quinsey (parenting).
Tips: "Our audience is thinking adults who are looking for ways to improve the quality of family life. The writer has the best chance of selling our firm a book that provides alternatives in child guidance and child-rearing issues. We are 'alternative' oriented. Books on child guidance are doing well for us. Make certain there is a wide enough need for the book before writing, and field test it yourself. I would say field testing the manuscript with parents and children improves it immensely."

‡PARKER & SON PUBLICATIONS, INC., Box 60001, Los Angeles CA 90060. (213)727-1088. President: James A. Hughes. Publishes hardcover and trade paperback originals. Averages 35 titles/year; receives 50 submissions annually. 20% of books from first-time writers; 90% of books from unagented writers. Pays 7½-20% royalty on retail price. Publishes book an average of 6 months after acceptance. Query for electronic submissions. Computer printout submissions OK; prefers letter-quality. Reports in 1 month on queries; 6 weeks on mss. Free book catalog and "Special Note to Authors."
Nonfiction: Technical law books and practice guidebooks for attorneys in active practice and their office personnel. Submit outline/synopsis and sample chapters. Reviews artwork/photos as part of ms package.
Recent Nonfiction Title: *Federal Courtroom Procedure*, by E. Niles.

‡PARNASSUS IMPRINTS, INC., 21 Canal Rd., Box 335, Orleans MA 02653. (617)255-2932. General Manager: Trumbull Huntington. Publishes hardcover and trade paperback originals and mass market paperback reprints. Averages 5 titles/year; receives 25 submissions annually. 75% of books from unagented writers. Pays royalty on retail price; offers $1,000 average advance. Publishes book an average of 9 months after acceptance. Computer printout submissions OK. Reports in 2 weeks on queries; 1 month on submissions. Book catalog free on request.

Nonfiction: Subjects include art, cooking and food, nature and New England topics. Especially looking for mss on environmental themes, New England and cooking. Query or submit outline/synopsis and sample chpaters.

Recent Nonfiction Title: *Gardening by the Sea*, by Dan Foley.

‡**PASSPORT PRESS**, Box 1346, Champlain NY 12919. (514)937-8155. Publisher: B. Houghton. Publishes trade paperback originals. Averages 3 titles/year; receives 12 submissions annually. 25% of books from first-time authors; 100% of books from unagented writers. Pays 8-12% royalty on retail price. Publishes book an average of 9 months after acceptance. Simultaneous and photocopied submissions OK. Query for electronic submissions. Computer printout submissions OK. Reports in 3 weeks. Free book catalog.

Nonfiction: Travel books only. Especially looking for manuscripts on practical travel subjects and travel guides on specific countries. Query. Reviews artwork/photos as part of ms package.

Recent Nonfiction Title: *Costa Rica*, by Paul Glassman (travel guide).

*****PAULIST PRESS**, 997 Macarthur Blvd., Mahwah NJ 07430. (201)825-7300. Publisher: Rev. Kevin A. Lynch. Managing Editor: Donald Brophy. Publishes hardcover and paperback originals and paperback reprints. Averages 90-100 titles/year; receives 500 submissions annually. 5-8% of books from first-time authors; 95% of books from unagented writers. Subsidy publishes (nonauthor) 1-2% of books. Pays royalty on retail price. Occasionally offers advance. Publishes book an average of 8 months after acceptance. Photocopied submissions OK. Query for electronic submissions. Computer printout submissions acceptable; prefers letter-quality to dot-matrix. Reports in 1 month.

Nonfiction: Philosophy, religion, self-help and textbooks (religious). Accepts nonfiction translations from German, French and Spanish. "We would like to see theology (Catholic and ecumenical Christian), popular spirituality, liturgy, and religious education texts." Submit outline/synopsis and 2 sample chapters. Reviews artwork/photos as part of ms package.

Recent Nonfiction Title: *The Mothers Songs*, by Meinrad Craighead (feminist spirituality).

‡**PETER PAUPER PRESS, INC.**, 202 Mamaroneck Ave., White Plains NY 10601. (914)681-0144. Co-Publisher: Nick Beilenson. Publishes hardcover originals. Averages 8 titles/year; receives 20 submissions annually. Buys some mss outright for $1,000. Offers no advance. Publishes ms an average of 9 months after acceptance. Simultaneous and photocopied submissions OK. Computer printout submissions OK. Reports in 2 weeks. Book catalog for #10 SAE.

Nonfiction: Cookbook and humor. Subjects include Americana, cooking and foods, inspirational, and religion. Submit complete ms. Reviews artwork/photos as part of ms package.

Recent Nonfiction Title: *Wit & Wisdom of Famous American Women* (collection).

Tips: Books on women's subjects have done well for Peter Pauper Press.

PBC INTERNATIONAL INC., Subsidiaries include Pisces Books and The Photographic Book Company, 1 School St., Glen Cove NY 11542. (516)676-2727. Editorial Director: H. Taylor. Imprints include Library of Applied Design (nonfiction) and Pisces Books (nonfiction). Publishes hardcover and trade paperback originals. Averages 15 titles/year; receives 100-200 submissions annually. Most of books from first-time authors and unagented writers, done on assignment. Pays royalty and/or flat fees. Simultaneous and photocopied submissions OK. Computer printout submissions acceptable; prefers letter-quality to dot-matrix. Book catalog for 8½x11 SASE.

Nonfiction: Subjects include design and commercial art, nature (marine only), treasure hunting, underwater photography, and skin diving. Library of Applied Design needs books that show the best in current design trends in all fields. Pisces Books needs books for snorklers and skin divers, on marine life, travel, diver safety, etc. No submissions not covered in the above listed topics. Query with outline/synopsis and sample chapters. Reviews artwork/photos as part of ms package.

Recent Nonfiction Title: *Treasure of the Atocha*, by R. Duncan Mathewson.

PEACHTREE PUBLISHERS, LTD., 494 Armour Circle NE, Atlanta GA 30324. (404)876-8761. Executive Editor: Chuck Perry. Publishes hardcover and trade paperback originals. Averages 20-25 titles/year; receives up to 1,000 submissions annually. 75% of books from first-time authors; 95% of books from unagented writers. Average print order for a writer's first book is 5,000-10,000. Publishes book an average of 1 year after acceptance. Computer printout submissions acceptable; prefers letter-quality to dot-matrix. Reports in 1 week on queries; 5 months on mss. Book catalog for SAE with 56¢ postage; ms guidelines for SASE.

Nonfiction: General and humor. Subjects include cooking and foods, history, recreation and travel. No business, technical, reference, art and photography, juvenile or animals. Submit outline/synopsis and sample chap-

Close-up

Chuck Perry
Executive Editor
Peachtree Publishers

"I am very proud of the mix of books we have published—from quality fiction to biography, cookbooks, self-help, and coffee-table books," says Chuck Perry. As executive editor of Peachtree Publishers, Perry says he wants to keep the Atlanta house "strong enough to avoid being forced into a niche, as many small publishers are. By remaining broad-based, both in our list and our sales, I want Peachtree to be known as *the* Southern publisher. I also want to continue to provide the close editorial attention which many writers say is missing today in larger publishing operations."

Perry spent 16 years as a writer, editor and manager in newspapers before moving to book publishing. "My experience in the newsroom, where one is forced to make decisions about relative values in a short time, has proven to be invaluable in my role as executive editor of Peachtree," he says. "You have a little more time to make decisions, but the pace is just as fast here as in newspapers." In addition to his newspaper experience, Perry has a master's degree in English literature and "the advantage of being married to novelist Emily Ellison, which makes me more empathetic with writers' situations."

Perry's time in the office is spent checking the status of various book projects, talking with current and prospective authors about books and "attending the details of the business of publishing." He says at least 95 percent of his reading is done outside the office, "preferably away from the phone."

As executive editor, his favorite part of the job is "finding a great manuscript or proposal in the unsolicited pile." Although Perry encourages queries first, Peachtree accepts unsolicited submissions—and receives 1,500 of them each year. Response on unsolicited submissions can take up to 15 weeks, Perry says, but the submission will be considered. Of 25 titles published annually by Peachtree, about five are from the stack of unsolicited submissions. Perry finds it equally rewarding to "approach a published author whose work you admire and have them respond 'Yes, I've heard of you and I'm impressed by the works you've published.' Mutual respect is a nice starting place for a professional relationship." Perry says his greatest frustration is finding a good manuscript "but not being able to find an adequate market for it. Close behind is the frustration of explaining to writers that their work is good, but not good enough to make a publishing list; the competition is so keen, and often marketing considerations make the difference in books of equal quality."

When evaluating proposals, Perry says he looks for "quality work, a biographical sketch which tells me if I'm dealing with an unknown or a celebrity, and some consideration of the market for the proposed book. I think it's an author's responsibility in nonfiction to know if there are three other books on the same subject already in bookstores." Perry, like other editors, doesn't want to see "a cover letter which tells me that the enclosed book is going to make me rich and famous." And authors "should *not* include complimentary rejections from other publishers as an endorsement for their work," he says. "I've written some of those letters myself."

—Glenda Tennant Neff

ters. Reviews artwork/photos as part of ms package.

Recent Nonfiction Title: *The Blue Chip Graduate/How You Become One*, by Bill Osher and Sioux Henley Campbell.

Fiction: Literary, humor and mainstream. "We are particularly interested in fiction with a Southern feel." No fantasy, juvenile, science fiction or romance. Submit complete manuscript.

Recent Fiction Title: *Any Cold Jordan*, by David Bottoms.

Tips: "We're looking for mainstream fiction and nonfiction of general interest; although our books are sold throughout the United States, our principal market is the Southeastern region—Virginia to Texas."

PELICAN PUBLISHING COMPANY, 1101 Monroe St., Box 189, Gretna LA 70053. (504)368-1175. Assistant Editor: Dean Shapiro. Publishes hardcover, trade paperback and mass market paperback originals and reprints. Averages 30-40 titles/year; receives 1,800 submissions annually. 30% of books from first-time authors; 97% of books from unagented writers. Pays royalty on wholesale price. Publishes book an average of 18 months after acceptance. Photocopied submissions OK. Computer printout submissions acceptable; no dot-matrix. Reports in 3 weeks on queries; 4 months on mss. Guidelines for SASE.

Nonfiction: Biography, "coffee table" book (limited), cookbook, how-to, humor, illustrated book, juvenile, self-help, motivational, inspirational, and Scottish. Subjects include Americana (especially Southern regional, Ozarks, Texas and Florida); business and economics (popular how-to and motivational); cooking and food; health; history; music (American artforms: jazz, blues, Cajun, R&B); politics (special interest in conservative viewpoint); recreation; religion (for popular audience mostly, but will consider others); and travel. *Travel*: Regional and international (especially areas in Pacific). *Motivational*: with business slant. *Inspirational*: author must be someone with potential for large audience. *Cookbooks*: "We look for authors with strong connection to restaurant industry or cooking circles, i.e. someone who can promote successfully." *How-to*: will consider broad range. Query. "Although our company does accept and review unsolicited manuscripts, we prefer that a query be made first. This greatly expedites the review process and can save the writer additional postage expenses." Reviews artwork/photos as part of ms package.

Recent Nonfiction Title: *Guide to Sacramento and the Gold Country*, by Faren Maree Bachelis (travel).

Fiction: Historical, humor, mainstream, Southern, juvenile and young adult. "Fiction needs are *very* limited. One novel is probably the maximum we would publish in the next year or two. We are most interested in Southern novels. We are also looking for good mainstream juvenile/young adult works." No romance, science fiction, fantasy, gothic, mystery, erotica, confession, horror; no sex or violence. Submit outline/synopsis and sample chapters.

Recent Fiction Title: *Henry Hamilton, Graduate Ghost*, by Marilyn Redmond (juvenile novel).

Tips: "We do extremely well with travel, motivational, cookbooks, and children's titles. We will continue to build in these areas. The writer must have a clear sense of the market and this includes knowledge of the competition."

THE PENKEVILL PUBLISHING COMPANY, Box 212, Greenwood FL 32443. (904)569-2811. Director: Stephen H. Goode. Publishes hardcover originals. Averages 10-12 titles/year; receives approximately 20 submissions annually. 40% of books from first-time authors; 100% of books from unagented writers. Pays 10-15% royalty on wholesale price. Publishes book an average of 15 months after acceptance. Simultaneous and photocopied submissions OK. Computer printout submissions acceptable; prefers letter-quality to dot-matrix. Reports in 2 weeks on queries; 6 weeks on submissions. Free book catalog.

Nonfiction: Reference, textbook and scholarly/critical. Subjects include history (19th, 20th Century American and European; Civil War and current interest); psychology; sociology (of current interest, divorce, terrorism); and literature and the arts and humanities. "Substantively, there are three areas of current interest: 1. Scholarly and critical works in the arts and humanities from the Renaissance forward; 2. 19th and 20th century American and Continental history, such as the American Civil War (e.g. Wheeler's Last Raid or a collection of essays on the literature, film, and art arising from the Vietnam war); 3. modern social currents, such as divorce, terrorism, the [Jewish] Holocaust, etc. (e.g., an annual bibliography and survey of divorce in America; an annual bibliography of terrorism, etc.). On another level, we are interested in the following genres: diaries, correspondence, histories of movements, biographies, critical and scholarly editions, sources (e.g. Faulkner's library); and in the following kinds of reference works; bibliographies, preferably annotated, checklists; dictionaries (of authors' works, such as a Proust dictionary), etc." Query.

Recent Nonfiction Title: *Jewish Holocaust Studies—A Directory*, by Martin Savel (Judaica).

Tips: "The type of book a writer has the best chance of selling to us is something unique in modern letters; that is, that hasn't been done before—such as the *Art and Artists of Protest: The Vietnam War*, (a forthcoming title); the sources of Melville [either externally (his personal library) or internally (an examination of references in his works) arrived at]; or an index to the magazines that are members of the CCLM (a forthcoming annual title that indexes 350+ literary magazines that are members of the Council of Literary Magazines, etc."

‡*PENNSYLVANIA HISTORICAL AND MUSEUM COMMISSION, The official history agency for the Commonwealth of Pennsylvania, Box 1026, Harrisburg PA 17108-1026. (717)787-8312. Chief,

Marketing, Sales and Publications Division: Douglas H. West. Publishes hardcover originals and reprints, trade paperback originals and reprints, mass market paperback originals and reprints. Averages 6 titles/year; receives 50 submissions annually. 50% of books from first-time authors; 95% of books from unagented writers. Pays 5-10% royalty on wholesale or retail price. May make outright purchase of $500-10,000; sometimes makes special assignments; offers $350 average advance. Publishes book an average of 15 months after acceptance. Simultaneous and photocopied submissions OK. Query for electronic submissions. Computer printout submissions OK. Reports in 6 weeks on queries; 3 months on mss. Manuscripts prepared according to the Chicago *Manual of Style*.

Nonfiction: All books must be related to Pennsylvania, its history and its culture. Biography, "coffee table" book, cookbook, how-to, illustrated book, reference, technical, visitor attractions and historic travel guidebooks. "The Commission is seeking manuscripts on Pennsylvania in general, but most specifically on archaeology, history, art (decorative and fine), politics, religion, travel, photography, nature, sports, history, and cooking and food." Query or submit outline/synopsis and sample chapters.

Recent Nonfiction Title: *William Penn: Architect of a Nation*, by John B.B. Trussel (biography of Penn).

Tips: "Our audience is diverse—professional and avocational historians, students and scholars, specialists and generalists—all of whom are interested in one or more aspects of Pennsylvania's history and culture. Manuscripts must be well researched and documented (footnotes not necessarily required depending on the nature of the manuscript) and interestingly written. Because of the expertise of our reviewers, manuscripts must be factually accurate, but in being so, writers must not sacrifice style. We have always had a tradition of publishing scholarly and reference works, and although we intend to continue doing so, we want to branch out with more popularly styled books which will reach an even broader audience."

‡THE PERFECTION FORM CO., Suite 15, 8350 Hickman Rd., Des Moines IA 50322. (515)278-0133. Publishes 60 titles/year. Buys mss outright or negotiates royalty with small advance. Average print run for first release is 2,500. Computer printout submissions acceptable; prefers letter-quality to dot-matrix. Reports in 6 months. Book catalog for 8½x11 SAE with $2.40 postage.

Nonfiction: Publishes supplementary educational materials, grades kindergarten-12 social studies and language arts, cross curriculum K-6. Submit complete ms for K-6 material to Virginia Murphy; K-12 social studies to Douglas M. Rife; and 7-12 language arts to M. Kathleen Myers.

Recent Nonfiction Title: *Reading Beyond the Basal*, by Doris Roettger (teacher guide).

‡PERSPECTIVES PRESS, 905 W. Wildwood Ave., Ft. Wayne IN 46807. (219)456-8411. Publisher: Pat Johnston. Small press. Publishes hardcover and trade paperback originals. Averages 2-5 titles/year; receives 50 queries annually. 95% of books from first-time authors. 95% of books from unagented writers. Pays 5-15% royalty on net sales. Publishes book an average 6 months after acceptance. Simultaneous and photocopied submissions OK. Computer printout submission OK; no dot-matrix. Reports in 2 weeks on queries; 2 months on mss. Book catalog and writer's guidelines for #10 SAE and 2 first class stamps.

Nonfiction: How-to, juvenile and self-help books on health, psychology and sociology—all related to adoption or infertility. Query.

Recent Nonfiction Title: *Our Baby: A Birth and Adoption Story* by Janice Koch (children's).

Fiction: Adoption/infertility for adults or children. Query.

Recent Fiction Title: *The Miracle Seekers: An Anthology of Infertility*, by Mary Martin Mason.

Tips: "For adults we are seeking decision-making materials, books dealing with parenting issues, books to use with children, books to share with others to help explain infertility or adoption or foster care, special programming or training manuals, etc. For children we will consider manuscripts that are appropriate for preschoolers, for early elementary, for later elementary or middle school children, for high schoolers. While we would consider a manuscript from a writer who was not personally or professionally involved in these issues, we would be more inclined to accept a manuscript submitted by an infertile person, an adoptee, a birthparent, an adoptive parent, a professional working with any of these."

PETROCELLI BOOKS, INC., Research Park, 251 Wall St., Princeton NJ 08540. (609)924-5851. Editorial Director: O.R. Petrocelli. Senior Editor: Rick Batlan. Publishes hardcover and paperback originals. Publishes 20 titles/year. Offers 12½-18% royalties. No advance. Simultaneous and photocopied submissions OK. Computer printout submissions acceptable; prefers letter-quality to dot-matrix. Reports in 1 month. Free book catalog.

Nonfiction: Business/economics, reference, technical, and textbooks. Submit outline/synopsis and 1-2 sample chapters.

Recent Nonfiction Title: *A Layman's Guide to Robotics*, by Derek Kelly.

PHAROS BOOKS, Publisher of *The World Almanac*, 200 Park Ave., New York NY 10166. (212)692-3824. Editor-in-Chief: Hana Umlauf Lane. Senior Acquisitions Editor: Beverly Jane Loo. Publishes hardcover and trade paperback originals. Averages 30 titles/year. Pays 5-15% on retail price. Publishes book an average of 1 year after acceptance. Computer printout submissions acceptable; prefers letter-quality to dot-matrix. Reports in 3 weeks. Free book catalog.

Nonfiction: "We look for books under three imprints: Pharos Books for nonfiction with strong consumer interest; World Almanac for innovative reference books; Topper for humor books. We expect at least a synopsis/outline and sample chapters, and would like to see the completed manuscript." Reviews artwork/photos as part of ms package.

PHILOMEL BOOKS, Division of The Putnam Publishing Group, 51 Madison Ave., New York NY 10010. (212)689-9200. Editor-in-Chief: Patricia Lee Gauch. Editor: Victoria Rock. Associate Editor: Wendy Steinhacker. Publishes hardcover originals. Publishes 25-30 titles/year; receives 2,600 submissions annually. 15% of books from first-time authors; 30% of books from unagented writers. Pays standard royalty. Advance negotiable. Publishes book an average of 1-2 years after acceptance. Computer printout submissions acceptable; no dot-matrix. Reports in 1 month on queries. Book catalog for 8½x11 SAE with 90¢ postage. Request book catalog from marketing department of Putnam Publishing Group.
Nonfiction: Young adult and children's picture books. No alphabet books or workbooks. Query first. Looks for quality writing, unique ideas, suitability to our market.
Recent Nonfiction Title: *Anno's Sundial*, by Mitsumassa Anno.
Fiction: Young adult and children's books on any topic. Particularly interested in fine regional fiction and quality picture books. Query to department.
Recent Fiction Title: *Miracle of Clements Pond*, by Patricia Pendergraff.
Tips: "We prefer a very brief synopsis that states the basic premise of the story. This will help us determine whether or not the manuscript is suited to our list. If applicable, we'd be interested in knowing the author's writing experience or background knowledge. We are interested in the beauty of language—books written with a child's vision that celebrate human spirit."

*PICKWICK PUBLICATIONS, 4137 Timberlane Dr., Allison Park PA 15101. Editorial Director: Dikran Y. Hadidian. Small press. Publishes paperback originals and reprints. Averages 6-8 titles/year; receives 10 submissions annually. 50% of books from first-time authors; 90% of books from unagented writers. Subsidy publishes 10% of books. Publishes book an average of 18-24 months after acceptance. Photocopied submissions OK. Computer printout submissions acceptable. Reports in 4 months. Free book catalog.
Nonfiction: Religious and scholarly mss in Biblical archeology, Biblical studies, church history and theology. Also reprints of outstanding out-of-print titles and original texts and translations. Accepts nonfiction translations from French or German. No popular religious material. Query or submit outline/synopsis and 2 sample chapters. Consult *MLA Style Sheet* or Turabian's, *A Manual for Writers*.
Recent Nonfiction Title: *Theology Beyond Christendom*, edited by John Thompson.

‡*THE PILGRIM PRESS, Subsidiary of United Church Press, 132 W. 31st St., New York NY 10001. (212)239-8700. Publisher: Larry E. Kalp. Publishes trade paperback originals and reprints. Averages 25 titles/year; receives 150 submissions annually. 65% of books from first-time authors. 90% of books from unagented writers. Subsidy publishes 15% of books. Authors may be subsidy if there is "no clearly identifiable, reachable market." Pays 5-12% royalty on retail price or negotiable; offers negotiable advance. Simultaneous and photocopied submissions OK. Computer printout submissions OK. Reports on queries and mss "as work allows." Book catalog and ms guidelines for #10 SASE.
Nonfiction: Religious and social issues. Subjects include business and economics; philosophy; religion and sociology. Needs 10-15 religious or social issues manuscripts per year. Query.
Recent Nonfiction Title: *For Crying Out Loud*, by Lefkowitz (women and poverty).

PILOT BOOKS, 103 Cooper St., Babylon NY 11702. (516)422-2225. Publishes paperback originals. Averages 20-30 titles/year; receives 300-400 submissions annually. 20% of books from first-time authors; 90% of books from unagented writers. Average print order for a writer's first book is 3,000. Offers standard royalty contract based on wholesale or retail price. Usual advance is $250, but this varies, depending on author's reputation and nature of book. Publishes book an average of 8 months after acceptance. Computer printout submissions acceptable; prefers letter-quality to dot-matrix. Reports in 1 month. Book catalog and guidelines for SASE.
Nonfiction: Financial, business, travel, career, personal guides and training manuals. "Our training manuals are utilized by America's major corporations as well as the government." Directories and books on travel and moneymaking opportunities. Wants "clear, concise treatment of subject matter." Length: 8,000-30,000 words. Send outline. Reviews artwork/photos as part of ms package.
Recent Nonfiction Title: *The Travel and Vacation Discount Guide*, by Paige Palmer.

PINEAPPLE PRESS, INC., Box 314, Englewood FL 33533. (813)475-2238. Editor: June Cussen. Publishes hardcover and trade paperback originals. Averages 10-12 titles/year; receives 600 submissions annually. 20% of books from first-time authors; 80% of books from unagented writers. Pays 6½-15% royalty on retail price. Seldom offers advance. Publishes book an average of 1 year after acceptance. Simultaneous and photocopied submissions OK. Query for electronic submissions. Computer printout submissions acceptable; no dot-matrix

unless high quality. Reports in 1 month on queries; 6 weeks on mss. Book catalog for SAE and 39¢ postage.
Nonfiction: Biography, how-to, reference, nature and young adult. Subjects include animals, cooking and foods, history and nature. "We will consider all nonfiction topics, but not those heavily illustrated. We are seeking quality nonfiction on diverse topics for the library and book trade markets." No heavily illustrated submissions, pop psychology, or autobiographies. Query or submit outline/synopsis and sample chapters.
Recent Nonfiction Title: *Voice of the River*, by Marjory Stoneman Douglas (autobiography).
Fiction: Experimental, historical and mainstream. No romance, science fiction, or children's (below the young adult level). Query or submit outline/synopsis and sample chapters.
Recent Fiction Title: *Cunuman*, by Omar Castaneda (novel).
Tips: "If I were a writer trying to market a book today, I would learn everything I could about book publishing and book publicity and agree to actively participate in promoting my book. A query on a novel without a brief synopsis seems useless."

PLATT & MUNK PUBLISHERS, Division of Grosset & Dunlap, 51 Madison Ave., New York NY 10010. Editor-in-Chief: Bernette G. Ford. Publishes hardcover and paperback originals. Averages 10-20 titles/year; receives more than 10,000 submissions annually. Pays $1,000-2,000 in outright purchase; advance negotiable. Publishes book an average of 18 months after acceptance. Simultaneous and photocopied submissions OK. Reports in 10 weeks.
Nonfiction: Juveniles. Submit proposal or query first. "Nature, science, and light technology are of interest." Looks for "new ways of looking at the world of children."
Fiction: Juveniles, picture books for 3-7 age group and some higher. Also interested in anthologies and collections with a fresh approach.
Tips: "Nonfiction that is particularly topical or of wide interest in the mass market; a new concept for novelty format for preschoolers; and very well-written fiction on topics that appeal to parents of preschoolers have the best chance of selling to our firm. We want something new—a proposal for a new series for the ordinary picture book. You have a better chance if you have new ideas."

*PLAYERS PRESS, INC., Box 1132, Studio City CA 91604. (818)789-4980. Vice President, Editorial: Robert W. Gordon. Publishes hardcover and trade paperback originals, and trade paperback reprints. Averages 15-25 titles/year; receives 75-300 submissions annually. 10% of books from first-time authors; 90% of books from unagented writers. Subsidy publishes 1% of books; subsidy publishes (non-author) 2% of books. Pays royalty on retail price. Publishes book an average of 20 months after acceptance. Simultaneous and photocopied submissions OK. Reports in 4 months. Book catalog and guidelines for 6x9 SAE and 56¢ postage.
Nonfiction: Juvenile and theatrical drama/entertainment industry. Subjects include the performing arts. Needs quality plays and musicals, adult or juvenile. Submit complete ms. Reviews artwork/photos as part of ms package.
Fiction: Adventure, confession, ethnic, experimental, fantasy, historical, horror, humor, mainstream, mystery, religious, romance, science fiction, suspense and western. Submit complete ms for theatrical plays only. "No novels are accepted. We publish plays only."
Recent Fiction Title: *Mother Love Me*, by Martha Monigle (drama).
Tips: "Plays, entertainment industry texts and children's story books have the best chance of selling to our firm."

‡PLENUM PUBLISHING, 233 Spring St., New York NY 10013. (212)620-8018. Senior Editor, Trade Books: Linda Greenspan Regan. Imprint includes Da Capo. Publishes hardcover originals. Averages 350 titles/year; trade division publishes 10. Receives 250 submissions annually. 50% of books from first-time authors. 90% of books from unagented writers. Publishes book an average of 8 months after acceptance. Simultaneous and photocopied submissions OK. Query for electronic submissions. No computer printout submissions. Reports in several months on queries; several months on mss.
Nonfiction: Subjects include business and economics, politics, psychology, current events, sociology and science. "We need popular books in the social sciences, sciences and the humanities." Da Capo division publishes art, music, photography, dance and film. Query only.
Recent Nonfiction Title: *100 Predictions for the Baby Boom: The Next 50 Years*, by Cheryl Russell.
Tips: "Our audience is intelligent laymen and professionals. Authors should be experts on subject matter of book. They must compare their books with competitive works, explain how theirs differs, and define the market for their books."

PLEXUS PUBLISHING, INC., (formerly World Natural History Publications), 143 Old Marlton Pike, Medford NJ 08055. (609)654-6500. Editorial Director: Thomas Hogan. Publishes hardcover and paperback originals. Averages 4-5 titles/year; receives 10-20 submissions annually. 70% of books from first-time authors; 90% of books from unagented writers. Pays 10-20% royalty on wholesale price; buys some booklets outright for $250-1,000. Offers $500-1,000 advance. Simultaneous and photocopied submissions OK. Computer printout submissions acceptable; prefers letter-quality to dot-matrix. Reports in 2 months. Book catalog and guidelines for SASE.

Nonfiction: Biography (of naturalists) and reference. Subjects include plants, animals, nature and life sciences. "We will consider any book on a nature/biology subject, particularly those of a reference (permanent) nature that would be of lasting value to high school and college audiences, and/or the general reading public. Authors should have authentic qualifications in their subject area, but qualifications may be by experience as well as academic training." No gardening; no philosophy or psychology; generally not interested in travel but will consider travel that gives sound ecological information. Also interested in mss of about 20-40 pages in length for feature articles in *Biology Digest* (guidelines available with SASE). Always query. Reviews artwork/photos as part of ms package.
Recent Nonfiction Title: *The Natural History of Living Mammals,* by W. Voelker (reference).
Tips: "We will give serious consideration to well-written manuscripts that deal even indirectly with biology/ nature subjects. For example, *Exploring Underwater Photography* (a how-to for divers) and *The Literature of Nature* (an anthology of nature writings for college curriculum) were accepted for publication."

POCKET BOOKS, 1230 Avenue of the Americas, New York NY 10020. Imprints include Washington Square Press (high-quality mass market), and Poseidon Press (hardcover fiction and nonfiction). Publishes paperback originals and reprints, mass market and trade paperbacks. Averages 300 titles/year; receives 750 submissions annually. 15% of books from first-time authors. Pays royalty on retail price. Publishes book an average of 1 year after acceptance. No unsolicited mss or queries. "All submissions must go through a literary agent."
Nonfiction: History, biography, reference and general nonfiction.
Fiction: Adult (mysteries, science fiction, romance, westerns).

PORTER SARGENT PUBLISHERS, INC., 11 Beacon St., Boston MA 02108. (617)523-1670. Publishes hardcover and paperback originals, reprints, translations and anthologies. Averages 4 titles/year. Pays royalty on retail price. "Each contract is dealt with on an individual basis with the author." Computer printout submissions acceptable. Book catalog for SASE.
Nonfiction: Reference, special education and academic nonfiction. "Handbook Series and Special Education Series offer standard, definitive reference works in private education and writings and texts in special education. The Extending Horizons Series is an outspoken, unconventional series which presents topics of importance in contemporary affairs and the social sciences." This series is particularly directed to the college adoption market. Accepts nonfiction translations from French and Spanish. Contact: Peter M. Casey. Send query with brief description, table of contents, sample chapter and information regarding author's background.
Recent Nonfiction Title: *11th Directory for Exceptional Children (1987/88)*, (reference).

POSEIDON PRESS, Division of Simon and Schuster, 1230 Avenue of the Americas, New York NY 10020. (212)698-7290. Vice President/Publisher: Ann E. Patty. Publishes hardcover and trade paperback originals. Averages 15-20 titles/year; receives 1,000 submissions annually. 20% of books from first-time authors; none from unagented writers. Pays 10-15% royalty on hardcover retail price. Publishes book an average of 1 year after acceptance. Computer printout submissions acceptable; no dot-matrix. Does not accept unsolicited material.
Nonfiction: Biography, cookbook and self-help. Subjects include business and economics, culture, history, psychology and sociology. No religious/inspirational or humor.
Fiction: Literary, historical, contemporary and mainstream.

POTENTIALS DEVELOPMENT FOR HEALTH & AGING SERVICES, 775 Main St., Buffalo NY 14203. (716)842-2658. Publishes paperback originals. Averages 6 titles/year; receives 30-40 submissions annually. 90% of books from first-time authors; 100% of books from unagented writers. Average print order for a writer's first book is 1,500. Pays 5% royalty on sales. Publishes book an average of 1 year after acceptance. Computer printout submissions acceptable; no dot-matrix. Reports in 6 weeks. Free book catalog and ms guidelines for SASE.
Nonfiction: "We seek material of interest to those working with elderly people in the community and in institutional settings. We need tested, innovative and practical ideas." Query or submit outline/synopsis and 3 sample chapters to J.A. Elkins. Looks for "suitable subject matter, writing style and organization." Reviews artwork/photos as part of ms package.
Recent Nonfiction Title: *Music and Memories*, by Karen Bauman (activity book).
Tips: "The writer has the best chance of selling us materials of interest to those working with elderly people in nursing homes, senior and retirement centers. Our major market is activity directors. Give us good reasons why activity directors would want or need the material submitted."

CLARKSON N. POTTER, INC., 225 Park Ave., New York NY 10003. (212)254-1600. Vice President/Editorial Director: Carol Southern. Publishes hardcover and trade paperback originals. Averages 55 titles/year; receives 1,500 submissions annually. 18% of books from first-time authors, but many of these first-time authors are well-known and have had media coverage. Buys no unagented submissions. Pays 10% royalty on hardcover; 5-7½% on paperback; 5-7% on illustrated hardcover, varying escalations; advance depends on type of

book and reputation or experience of author. No unagented mss can be considered. Photocopied submissions OK. Computer printout submissions acceptable. Reports in 1 month. Book catalog for 7x10 SASE.
Nonfiction: Publishes art, autobiography, biography, cooking and foods, how-to, humor, juvenile, nature, photography, self-help, style and annotated literature. Accepts nonfiction translations. "Manuscripts must be cleanly typed on 8½x11 nonerasable bond; double-spaced. Chicago *Manual of Style* is preferred." Query or submit outline/synopsis and sample chapters. Reviews artwork/photos as part of ms package.
Recent Nonfiction Title: *Weddings*, by Martha Stewart.
Fiction: Will consider "quality fiction."
Recent Fiction Title: *Doctors and Women*, by Susan Cheever.

THE PRAIRIE PUBLISHING COMPANY, Box 264, Postal Station C, Winnipeg, Manitoba R3M 3S7 Canada. (204)885-6496. Publisher: Ralph Watkins. Publishes trade paperback originals. Averages 4 titles/year; receives 25 submissions annually. 4% of books from first-time authors; 85% of books from unagented writers. Average print order for a writer's first book is 2,000. Pays 10% royalty on retail price. Photocopied submissions OK. Computer printout submissions acceptable; no dot-matrix. Reports in several weeks. Book catalog and guidelines for 8x10½ SASE.
Nonfiction: Biography and cookbook. Subjects include cooking and foods. "We would look at any submissions." Reviews artwork/photos as part of ms package.
Recent Nonfiction Title: *My Name Is Marie Anne Gabaury*, by Mary Jordan.

PRAKKEN PUBLICATIONS, INC., Box 8623, Ann Arbor MI 48107. (313)769-1211. Publisher/executive editor: Alan H. Jones. Publishes hardcover and trade paperback originals. Averages 5 titles/year; receives 50 submissions annually. 50% of books from first-time authors; 100% of books from unagented writers. Pays 10% royalty on net price. Publishes book an average of 6 months after acceptance. Simultaneous and photocopied submissions OK. Computer printout submissions acceptable; prefers letter-quality to dot-matrix. Reports in 2 weeks on queries; 1 month on mss. Book catalog for #10 SASE.
Nonfiction: General education, vocational and technical education. "We are interested in manuscripts with broad appeal in any of the specific subject areas of the industrial arts, vocational-technical education, and in the general education field." Submit outline/synopsis and sample chapters. Reviews artwork/photos as part of ms package.
Recent Nonfiction Title: *Global Images of Peace and Education*, by T.M. Thomas, David R. Contrad, and Gertrude F. Langsam.

PRENTICE-HALL, Books for Young Readers, A Division of Simon & Schuster, 1230 Avenue of the Americas, New York NY 10020. Editorial Director: Grace Clarke. Manuscripts Editor: Rose Lopez. Publishes hardcover and paperback originals. Publishes 30 hardcovers/year, 15 paperbacks/year. Pays royalty. Offers advance. Reports in 2 months. Book catalog and guidelines for 9x12 SASE.
Nonfiction: All subjects, all age groups to age 12, but special interest in unusual approach and accessible style. Query. Accepts outline/synopsis and 5-6 sample chapters from published writers; entire ms from unpublished writers. Art or illustration submissions should be copies,not originals.
Recent Nonfiction Title: *Amazing Mouths and Menus*, by Mary Blocksma, illustrated by Lee Ames.
Fiction: Humor, mainstream and mystery. Special interest in young fiction. Submit outline/synopsis and sample chapters.
Recent Fiction Title: *Dogsled To Dread*, by Robert Quackenbush (detective mystery, ages 6-9).
Picture Books: Accent on humor.
Recent Picture Book: *Timothy and the Night Noises*.

PRENTICE-HALL CANADA, INC., College Division, Subsidiary of Simon & Schuster, 1870 Birchmount Road, Scarborough, Ontario M1P 2J7 Canada. (416)293-3621. Executive Editor: Cliff Newman. Publishes hardcover and paperback originals and software. Averages 30 titles/year. Receives 200-300 submissions annually. 30-40% of books from first-time authors; 100% of books from unagented writers. Pays 10-15% royalty on net price. Publishes book an average of 14 months after acceptance. Electronic submissions OK via IBM PC disk, but requires hard copy also. Computer printout submissions acceptable; prefers letter-quality to dot-matrix.
Nonfiction: The College Division publishes textbooks suitable for the community college and large university market. Most submissions should be designed for existing courses in all disciplines of study. Will consider software in most disciplines, especially business and sciences. Canadian content is important. The division also publishes books in computer science, technology and mathematics.
Recent Nonfiction Title: *Accounting: A Decision Approach*, by L.S. Rosen.

PRENTICE-HALL CANADA, INC., Secondary School Division, A subsidary of Simon & Schuster, 1870 Birchmount Road, Scarborough, Ontario M1P 2J7 Canada. (416)293-3621. General Manager: Rob Greenaway. Averages 30 titles annually.

Nonfiction: Publishes texts, workbooks, and instructional media including computer courseware for junior and senior high schools. Subjects include business, computer studies, geography, history, language arts, mathematics, science, social studies, technology, and French as a second language. Query.
Recent Nonfiction Title: *Science 9: An Introductory Study*, by W.A. Andrews (science textbook).

PRENTICE-HALL CANADA, INC., Trade Division, 1870 Birchmount Road, Scarborough, Ontario M1P 2J7 Canada. (416)293-3621. Acquisitions Editor: Iris Skeoch. Publishes hardcover and trade paperback originals. Averages 15 titles/year; receives 750-900 submissions annually. 40% of books from first-time authors; 40% of books from unagented writers. Negotiates royalty and advance. Publishes book an average of 9 months after acceptance. Query for electronic submissions. Computer printout submissions acceptable; prefers letter-quality to dot-matrix. SAE and IRCs. Reports in 10 weeks. Ms guidelines for SASE.
Nonfiction: Subjects of Canadian and international interest; art, politics and current affairs, business, travel, health and food. Send outline and sample chapters. Reviews artwork/photos as part of ms package.
Recent Nonfiction Title: *Lions in Winter*, by Chrys Goyens and Allan Turowetz (hockey).
Tips: Needs general interest non-fiction books on topical subjects. "Present a clear, concise thesis, well-argued with a thorough knowledge of existing works."

PRENTICE-HALL, INC., Business & Professional Books Division, Gulf & Western, Inc., A division of Simon & Schuster, Sylvan Ave., Englewood Cliffs NJ 07632. (201)592-2000. Vice President: Ted Nardin. Publishes hardcover and trade paperback originals. Averages 150 titles/year; receives 1,000+ submissions annually. 50% of books from first-time authors; 95% of books from unagented writers. Pays royalty: 5% on cash received on *mail order*, or 10-15% on all *trade* sales. Offers $3,000-5,000 advance, sometimes more. Publishes book an average of 8 months after acceptance. Simultaneous and photocopied submissions OK. Query for electronic submissions. Computer printout submissions acceptable; prefers letter-quality to dot-matrix. Reports in 3 weeks. Book catalog and ms guidelines for 8½x11 SASE.
Nonfiction: How-to, reference, self-help and technical. Subjects include all aspects of management, business, real estate, accounting, computers, education, electronics and engineering. Needs business, professional, technical and educational references, for sale primarily via direct mail. Query or submit outline and sample chapters. Reviews artwork/photos as part of ms package.
Recent Nonfiction Title: *Managing by Influence*, by Schatz and Schatz.
Tips: "We seek high-level, practical references that command high prices and that can be sold to targeted markets via direct mail."

PRENTICE HALL/REGENTS PUBLISHING CO., INC., (formerly Regents Publishing Co.), Englewood Cliffs NJ 07632. Acquisitions: Tina Carver. 5% of books from first-time authors; 100% of books from unagented writers. Average print order for a writer's first book is 5,000. Publishes English as a second language textbooks, computer-assisted instruction programs for the same market, and software. Averages 50 titles/year; receives 250 submissions annually. Publishes book an average of 1 year after acceptance. Query for electronic submissions. Computer printout submissions acceptable; no dot-matrix.
Nonfiction: Textbooks. Publishes ESL/EFL for all ages. Produces ESP materials for business, science, language arts, etc. Prefers complete proposals, including description of target market, comparison with similar materials already on the market, description of age/grade/difficulty level, as well as table of contents and at least 3 sample units.
Recent Nonfiction Title: *ExpressWays* (an adult contemporary/functional grammar ESL series).
Tips: Freelance writers should be aware of English as second language trends and market needs in education.

THE PRESERVATION PRESS, National Trust for Historic Preservation, 1785 Massachusetts Ave. NW, Washington DC 20036. Director: Diane Maddex. Publishes nonfiction books on historic preservation (saving and reusing the "built environment"). Averages 6 titles/year; receives 30+ submissions annually. 40% of books from first-time authors; 50% of books from unagented writers. Books are often commissioned by the publisher. Publishes book an average of 2 years after acceptance. Query for electronic submissions. Computer printout submissions acceptable; no dot-matrix. Book catalog for 9x12 SASE.
Nonfiction: Subject matter encompasses architecture and architectural history, building restoration and historic preservation. No local history. Looks for "relevance to national preservation-oriented audience; educational or instructional value; depth; uniqueness; need in field." Query. Reviews artwork/photos as part of ms package.
Recent Nonfiction Title: *America's Architectural Roots*, edited by Dale Upton (architectural history).
Tips: "The writer has the best chance of selling our firm a book clearly related to our mission—historic preservation— that covers new ideas and is unique and practical. If it fills a clear need, we will know immediately."

PRESIDIO PRESS, 31 Pamaron Way, Novato CA 94947. (415)883-1373. Editor-in-Chief: Adele Horwitz. Senior Editor: Joan Griffin. Publishes hardcover and paperback. Averages 17 titles/year. Receives 150 submissions annually. 90% of books from first-time authors; 95% of books from unagented writers. Pays 15% royalty

on net price. Offers nominal advance. Publishes book an average of 10 months after acceptance. Photocopied submissions OK. Electronic submissions OK, but requires hard copy also. Reports in 3 months. Free book catalog.
Nonfiction: Military history. No scholarly. Fiction with military background considered. Accepts nonfiction translations. Query or submit outline/synopsis and 3 sample chapters. Reviews artwork/photos as part of ms package.
Tips: "Have the proper experience or qualifications for the subject."

‡*PRESS PORCÉPIC, #235-560 Johnson St., Victoria British Columbia V8W 3C6 Canada. (604)381-5502. Acquisitions Editor: Terri Jack. Imprints include Softwords and Porcepic Books. Imprint publishes hardcover and trade paperback originals. Averages 1-6 titles/year; receives 300 submissions annually. 20% of books from first-time authors. 90% of books from unagented writers. Subsidy publishes (nonauthor) 100% of books. Pays 10% royalty on retail price; offers $300-500 advance. Publishes a book an average of 10 months after acceptance. Simultaneous (if so advised) and photocopied submissions OK. Computer printout submissions OK; prefers letter-quality. Reports in 1 week on queries; 3 months on mss.
Nonfiction: "Not actively soliciting nonfiction books."
Fiction: Experimental, science fiction and children's literature. "We are interested in hearing from new Canadian writers of mainstream or experimental fiction. Children's books have the best chance of selling to our firm."
Recent Fiction Title: *Tesseracts*, edited by Judith Merril (Canadian science fiction stories).
Poetry: "We're interested in new Canadian poets for *New Poet Series*, as well as established Canadian poets. No work poetry or poetry which is weak in use of language and/or structure." Submit complete ms.
Recent Poetry Title: *The Self Completing Tree*, by Dorothy Livesay (collection of selected poetry, from an author's total career).
Tips: "Make sure the manuscript is well written. We see so many mss that only the unique and excellent can't be put down."

PRICE/STERN/SLOAN INC., PUBLISHERS, 360 N. La Cienega Blvd., Los Angeles CA 90048. Imprints include Serendipity Books, Bugg Books, Wee Sing Books, Troubador Press and Laughter Library. Associate Editor: L. Spencer Humphrey. Publishes trade paperback originals. Averages 200 titles/year; receives 6,000+ submissions annually. 20% of books from first-time authors; 60% of books from unagented writers. Pays royalty on wholesale price, or by outright purchase. Offers small or no advance. Publishes book an average of 1 year after acceptance. Computer printout submissions acceptable; no dot-matrix. Reports in 3 months. Ms guidelines for SASE.
Nonfiction: Subjects include humor, self-help (limited), and satire (limited). Juveniles. Query *only*. "Most titles are unique in concept as well as execution and are geared for the so-called gift market." Reviews artwork/photos as part of ms package.
Tips: "Humor and satire were the basis of the company's early product and are still the mainstream of the company."

‡PRIMA PUBLISHING AND COMMUNICATIONS, Cal Co Am., Inc., Box 1260, Rocklin CA 95677. (916)624-5718. Publisher: Ben Dominitz. Publishes hardcover and trade paperback originals and trade paperback reprints. Publishes 30+ titles/year. Receives 100 queries/year. Buys 15% of books from first-time authors; 65% from unagented writers. Pays 15-20% royalty on wholesale price. Advance varies. Publishes books an average of 6-9 months after acceptance. Simultaneous and photocopied submissions OK. Query for electronic submissions. Computer printout submissions OK; no dot-matrix. Reports in 1 month.
Nonfiction: Biography, coffee table book, cookbook, how-to, humor, illustrated book, self-help. Subjects include business and economics, cooking and foods, health, music, politics, psychology and travel. "We want books with originality, written by highly qualified individuals. No fiction at this time." Query.
Recent Nonfiction Title: *Winning Them Over*, by Jim Robinson (business how-to).
Tips: "Prima strives to reach the primary and secondary markets for each of its books. We are known for promoting our books aggressively. Books that genuinely solve problems for people will always do well if properly promoted. Try to picture the intended audience while writing the book. Too many books are written to an audience that doesn't exist."

PRINCETON ARCHITECTURAL PRESS, 2 Research Way, Forrestal Center, Princeton NJ 08540. (609)924-7911. Editor: Robert Wechsler. Publishes hardcover and trade paperback originals and hardcover reprints. Averages 10 titles/year; receives 20 submissions annually. 50% of books from first-time authors; 100% of books from unagented writers. Subsidy publishes 10% of books; subsidy publishes (nonauthor) 20% of books. Pays 6-10% royalty on wholesale price. Simultaneous and photocopied submissions OK. Electronic submissions OK on IBM and Altos compatibles, but requires hard copy also. Computer printout submissions acceptable; no dot-matrix. Reports in 1 month. Book catalog and guidelines for 8½x11 SAE with 59¢ postage.
Nonfiction: "Coffee table" book, illustrated book and textbook. Subjects include art, history and architec-

ture. Needs texts on architecture, landscape architecture, architectural monographs, and texts to accompany a possible reprint, architectural history and urban design. Submit outline/synopsis and sample chapters or complete ms. Reviews artwork/photos as part of ms package.
Recent Nonfiction Title: *The Writing on the Walls*, by Anthon Vidler (architectural history).
Tips: "Our audience is architects, designers, urban planners, architectural theorists, and architectural-urban design historians, and many academicians and practitioners."

PRINTEMPS BOOKS, INC., Box 746, Wilmette IL 60091. (312)251-5418. Secretary/Treasurer: Beatrice Penovich. Publishes trade paperback originals. Averages 3 titles/year. Pays royalty or makes outright purchase, "to be agreed upon." Offers no advance. Reports in 1 month on mss.
Fiction: Children's short stories, adventure, ethnic, fantasy, humor, mystery and suspense. "Our aim is to both entertain and educate students who have less than average reading skills. We envision publication of a collection of short stories and plays suitable for high school students who have a limited vocabulary." Publishes for school systems and over-the-counter purchases. No novel-length works accepted. Submit complete ms.

‡PROBUS PUBLISHING CO., 118 N. Clinton, Chicago IL 60606. (312)346-7985. Vice President: J. Michael Jeffers. Publishes hardcover originals and trade paperback reprints. Averages 40 titles/year; receives 75 submissions annually. 50% of books from first-time authors; 100% of books from unagented writers. Pays 10-15% royalty on wholesale price; offers average $1,500 advance. Publishes book an average of 5 months after acceptance. Simultaneous and photocopied submissions OK. Query for electronic submissions. Computer printout submissions acceptable; prefers letter-quality. Reports in 1 weeks on queries; 1 month on mss. Free book catalog; ms guidelines for SASE.
Nonfiction: How-to and technical. Subjects include business, economics and investments. Query or submit outline/synopsis and sample chapters.
Recent Nonfiction Title: *The Intelligent Investor's Guide to Profiting from Stock Market Inefficiencies*, by D. Robert Coulson.

‡PROFESSIONAL PUBLICATIONS, INC. 1250 Fifth Ave., Belmont CA 94002. (415)593-9119. Acquisitions Editor: Michael Lindeburg. Publishes hardcover and paperback originals. Averages 6 titles/year; receives 10-20 submissions annually. Pays 8-12% royalty on wholesale price; offers $2,000 average advance. Sometimes makes outright purchase for $1,000-$2,000. Publishes book an average of 6-18 months after acceptance. Simultaneous and photocopied submissions OK. Query for electronic submissions. Computer printout submissions OK; prefers letter-quality. Reports in 2 weeks on queries; 1 month on mss. Free book catalog.
Nonfiction: Reference, technical and textbook. Subjects include business and economics, engineering, accounting, architecture, contracting and building. Especially needs "licensing examination review books for architects, general contractors and lawyers." Query or submit outline/synopsis and sample chapters or complete ms. Reviews artwork/photos as part of ms package.
Recent Nonfiction Title: *Getting Started as a Consulting Engineer*, by D.G. Sunar (how-to).
Tips: "We specialize in books for working professionals: engineers, architects, contractors, accountants, etc. The more complex technically the manuscript is the happier we are. We love equations, tables of data, complex illustrations, mathematics, etc. In technical/professional book publishing, it isn't always obvious to us if a market exists. We can judge the quality of a ms, but the author should make some effort to convince us that a market exists. Facts, figures, and estimates about the market—and marketing ideas from the author—will help sell us on the work."

‡PROLINGUA ASSOCIATES, 15 Elm St., Brattleboro VT 05301. (802)207-7779. Publisher: Arthur A. Burrows. Publishes text paperback originals. Averages 6 titles/year; receives 10 submissions annually. 25% of books from first-time authors. 100% of books from unagented writers. Pays 5-10% royalty on wholesale price; offers $200 average advance. Publishes book an average of 12 months after acceptance. Simultaneous and photocopied submissions OK. Computer printout submissions OK; prefers letter-quality. Reports in 2 weeks on queries; 3 months on mss. Free book catalog.
Nonfiction: Reference and textbook. Subjects include English as a second language, French and Spanish. "We are always willing to consider innovative language texts and language teacher resources which fit with our approach to language teaching. Also interested in intercultural training." Query or submit outline/synopsis and sample chapters.
Recent Nonfiction Title: *Language Teaching Techniques*, by R.C. Clark (reference).
Tips: "Get a catalog of our books, take a couple of books by ProLingua out of the library or from a nearby language department, ask about ProLingua, and in general try to determine whether your book would fit into ProLingua's list."

PRUETT PUBLISHING CO., 2928 Pearl, Boulder CO 80301. Managing Editor: Gerald Keenan. Averages 20 titles/year; receives 200 submissions annually. 50% of books from first-time authors; 100% of books from unagented writers. Average print order for a writer's first book is 2,000-3,000. Pays royalty on wholesale price.

"Most books that we publish are aimed at special interest groups. As a small publisher, we feel most comfortable in dealing with a segment of the market that is very clearly identifiable, and one we know we can reach with our resources." Publishes book an average of 10 months after acceptance. Legible photocopies acceptable. Query for electronic submissions. Computer printout submissions acceptable; no dot-matrix. Reports in 1 month. Free catalog on request; ms guidelines for #10 SASE.

Nonfiction: Publishes general adult nonfiction and textbooks. Subjects include travel in the Western US, outdoor activities related to the Intermountain West, western Americana and pictorial railroad histories. Textbooks with a regional (intermountain) aspect for preschool through college level. "Like most small publishers, we try to emphasize quality from start to finish, because, for the most part, our titles are going to a specialized market that is very quality conscious. We also feel that one of our strong points is the personal involvement ('touch') so often absent in a much larger organization." Accepts outline/synopsis and 3 sample chapters. Mss must conform to the Chicago *Manual of Style*. Reviews artwork/photos as part of ms package.

Recent Nonfiction Title: *Letters from Honeyhill*, by Wahl.

*PSG PUBLISHING CO., INC.,545 Great Rd., Littleton MA 01460. (617)486-8971. President/Publisher: Frank Paparello. Publishes hardcover and paperback originals. Averages 25 titles/year. Receives 100 submissions annually. 50% of books from first-time authors; 100% of books from unagented writers. Subsidy publishes (nonauthor) 10% of books. Pays royalty on net revenues. Specializes in publishing medical and dental books, newsletters and journals for the professional and student markets. Pays 10-15% royalty. Publishes book an average of 8 months after acceptance. Simultaneous submissions OK. Electonic submissions OK via IBM PC, but requires hard copy also. Computer printout submissions acceptable; prefers letter-quality to dot-matrix. Reports in 1 month. Book catalog and ms guidelines for 8½x11 SAE.

Nonfiction: Medical and dental books, newsletter and journals. Request proposal form. Query or submit complete ms. Reviews artwork photos as part of ms package.

Recent Nonfiction Title: *Occupational Stress*, by Stewart G. Wolfe (clinical monography for physicians).

Tips: "Books on clinical medicine for practicing professionals have the best chance of selling to our firm." Queries/mss may be routed to other editors in the publishing group.

‡PUBLISHERS ASSOCIATES, Box 160361, Las Colinas TX 75016. (817)572-7400. Subsidiaries include Liberal Arts Press; The Liberal Press; Scholars Books; Tangelwild Press; Nicole Graphics; Monument Press and The Galaxy Group. Senior Editor: Art Frederic. Publishes trade paperback originals. Entire firm averages 10 or more titles/year; receives 100 submissions annually. 80% of books from first-time authors; 100% of books from unagented writers. Pays 4-8% royalty on wholesale price at end of each year. Publishes book an average of 6 months after acceptance. No simultaneous submissions; photocopied submissions OK. Computer printout submissions OK; prefers letter-quality. Reports in 1 month on queries; 3 months on mss. Free book catalog.

Nonfiction: Subjects include Americana, art, business and economics, health, history, music, philosophy, politics, psychology, religion and sociology. "We are especially interested in any aspect of woman's history (chronology, nation—no biographies); any aspect of gay history (chronology, period, theme, etc.); any aspect of prison life (history, sociology, psychology); and liberal theology. No diaries, biographies, or anything related to conservative politics or (fundamentalist) religion/theology. Query. Reviews artwork/photos as part of ms package.

Recent Nonfiction Title: *Unfolding Misconceptions: A Study of the Arkansas Prison System*, by Clyde Crosley.

Tips: "We publish only liberal academic books. A well-prepared abstract with outline will catch our attention. Always query first. We advertise and sell internationally. Each press in the consortium is independent but we work together. The consortium (Publishers Associates) recommends manuscripts to the individual presses."

‡PUCKERBRUSH PRESS, 76 Main St., Orono ME 04473. (207)581-3832/866-4808. Publisher/Editor: Constance Hunting. Publishes trade paperback originals. Averages 2-3 titles/year; receives 500-1,000 submissions annually. 60% of books from first-time authors; 50% of books from unagented writers. Average print order for a writer's first book is 500-1,000. Pays 10-15% royalty on retail price. Publishes book an average of 1 year after acceptance. Simultaneous submissions OK. Computer printout submissions acceptable; prefers letter-quality to dot-matrix. Reports in 1 month. Free book list.

Nonfiction: Literary. Subjects include religion ("lively, interesting; no Bible verse listing"). Submit outline/synopsis and sample chapters or complete ms.

Recent Nonfiction Title: *The Rocking Horse*, by Douglas Young (sermons for children).

Fiction: Literary—"anything fresh, written (as opposed to confused or automated)." No California fantasy or Midwest realism. Submit outline/synopsis and sample chapters or complete ms.

Recent Fiction Title: *The Police Know Everything*, by Sanford Phippen (downeast, bizarre stories).

Poetry: "Anything nontemporary." No "confessional, feminist, or 20th century imitation." Submit complete ms.

Recent Poetry Title: *Palace of Earth*, by Sonya Dorman (Pushcart Foundation Small Press Promotion selection).

Tips: "We have a small, literate, widely-read audience."

PURDUE UNIVERSITY PRESS, South Campus Courts, Bldg. D, West Lafayette IN 47907. (317)494-2035. Managing Editor: Verna Emery. Publishes hardcover and trade paperback originals and trade paperback reprints. Averages 6 titles/year; receives 100 submissions annually. Pays 10% royalty on retail price. No advance. Publishes book an average of 15 months after acceptance. Photocopied submissions OK. Computer printout submissions acceptable; no dot-matrix. Reports in 8 weeks on mss. Book catalog and ms guidelines for SASE.

Nonfiction: Biography, textbook, scholarly and regional. Subjects include Americana (especially Indiana), business and economics, history, philosophy, politics, religion, sociology, theories of biology and literary criticism. "The writer must present good credentials, demonstrate good writing skills, and above all explain how his/her work will make a significant contribution to scholarship/regional studies. Our purpose is to publish scholarly and regional books. We are looking for manuscripts on these subjects: theory of biography, Balkan and Danubian history, interdisciplinary, regional interest, horticulture, history, literature, criticism, and effects of science and technology on society. No cookbooks, nonbooks, textbooks, theses/dissertations, manuals/pamphlets, or books on how-to, fitness/exercise or fads." Submit complete ms. Reviews artwork/photos as part of ms package.

Recent Nonfiction Title: *The Broken Window*, by Jane Alison Hale (critical analysis of Samuel Beckett's dramatic perspective).

Poetry: "We publish one poetry book per year. No 'McKuenesque' poetry." Submit complete ms.

Recent Poetry Title: *A Season of Loss*, by Jim Barnes.

Tips: "Scholarly publishers are gearing books in the humanities especially toward the educated layperson so as to widen their audiences, make academic knowledge more accessible, and increase sales. In the future I hope to see academic jargon abolished so that books are in plain English. If I were a writer trying to market a book today, I would show a press why publishing my book would help them meet their own long-term goals."

Q.E.D. INFORMATION SCIENCES, INC., 170 Linden St., Box 181, Wellesley MA 02181. (617)237-5656. Manager of Publishing/Software: Jerry Murphy. Publishes computer books and software for MIS professionals. Averages 20 titles/year. Pays 10-15% royalty on net receipts. Publishes book an average of 4-6 months after acceptance. Query for electronic submissions. Preliminary reports in 1 week on queries; 3 weeks on mss. Free book catalog.

Nonfiction: Technical. Subjects include computers, personal computing, and database technology. "Our books are read by data processing managers and technicians." Submit outline/synopsis and 2 sample chapters. Reviews artwork/photos as part of ms package.

Recent Nonfiction Title: *How to Use CICS to Create On-Line Applications*, by B. Musteata.

‡QUALITY PUBLICATIONS, Box 2633, Lakewood OH 44107-0633. Editor: Gary S. Skeens. Publishes mass market paperbak originals and reprints. Averages 4 titles/year; receives 96 submissions annually. 75% of books from first-time authors; 100% from unagented writers. Pays 15-25% royalty on retail price. Publishes book average of 1 year after acceptance. Simultaneous and photocopied submissions OK. Computer printout submissions acceptable. Reports on queries in 1 week; 2-4 months on submissions. Book catalog for #10 SAE with first class stamp; ms guidelines for SASE.

Fiction: Adventure, erotica, historical, mainstream and western. "I'm looking for westerns, and more Vietnam—related stories. Never any pornography." Query or submit outline/synopsis and sample chapters. Reviews artwork/photos.

Recent Fiction Title: *As Any Mountain Of Its Snows*, by Joseph Davey (story collection).

Tips: "Our books reach a wide spectrum of the public from blue-collar working people to academics; a pretty fair split of men and women; and through all age ranges from early 20's on up. A writer should simply treat his/her writing as a business, and a tough one at that—that I say from personal experience as a writer."

QUE CORPORATION, 7999 Knue Rd., Indianapolis IN 46250. (317)842-7162. Executive Editor/Acquisitions: Pegg Kennedy. Publishes tutorials and application books on popular business software, and trade paperback originals, programming languages and systems and technical books. Receives 700 submissions/year. 80% of books from first-time authors; 100% of books from unagented writers. Pays 8-15% escalating royalty on net price. Publishes book an average of 4 months after acceptance. Simultaneous (if so advised) and photocopied submissions OK. Computer printout submissions acceptable; prefers letter-quality to dot-matrix. Reports in 1 month. Free book catalog.

Nonfiction: How-to, technical, and reference books relating to microcomputers; textbooks on business use of microcomputers; software user's guides and tutorials; operating systems user's guides; computer programming language reference works; books on microcomputer systems, spreadsheet software business applications, word processing, data base management, time management, popular computer programs for the home, computer graphics and game programs, networking, communications, languages, educational uses of microcomputers, computer-assisted instruction in education and business and course-authoring applications. "We will consider books on most subjects relating to microcomputers." Query or submit outline/synopsis and sample chapters. Reviews artwork/photos as part of ms package.

Recent Nonfiction Title: *Word Perfect Tips, Tricks and Traps*, by Charles Stewart and Daniel Rosenbaum.

QUILL, Imprint of William Morrow and Co., Inc., subsidiary of The Hearst Corporation, 105 Madison Ave., New York NY 10016. (212)889-3050. Managing Editor: Andrew Ambraziejus. Publishes trade paperback originals and reprints. Averages 40 titles/year; receives over 2,000 submissions annually. 40% of books from first-time authors; 5% of books from unagented writers. Pays royalty on retail price. Offers variable advance. Publishes ms an average of 1 year after acceptance. Simultaneous and photocopied submissions OK. Computer printout submissions acceptable; prefers letter-quality to dot-matrix. No unsolicited mss or proposals; mss and proposals should be submitted through a literary agent. Reports in 1 month.
Nonfiction: Biography and trade books. Subjects include cooking and foods, history, music, psychology, science, and puzzles and games. Needs nonfiction trade paperbacks with enduring importance; books that have backlist potential and appeal to educated people with broad intellectual curiosities. No fiction, poetry, fitness, diet, how-to, self-help or humor. Query.

‡RACZ PUBLISHING COMPANY, Box 287, Oxnard CA 93041. (702)795-8922. Business Manager: Jeanette Racz. Publishes hardcover originals and reprints and trade paperback originals. Averages 1-10 titles/year. 100% of books from unagented writers. Pays 5-15% royalty on wholesale or retail price. Publishes ms an average of 18 months after acceptance. Simultaneous submissions and photocopied submissions OK. Computer printout submissions OK; prefers letter quality to dot-matrix. Reports on queries in 2 weeks; reports on submissions in 1 month. Free book catalog.
Nonfiction: Biography, coffee table book, how-to book, illustrated book, juvenile, reference, self-help, technical and textbooks. Subjects include Americana, business and economics, history, hobbies, recreation and sports. Query or submit outlines/synopsis and sample characters.
Recent Nonfiction Title: *You Can Learn Metric Easily*, by Joan Follendore.
Fiction: Adventure, ethnic, experimental, historical, mainstream, mystery, science fiction, suspense and western. Query or submit outline/synopsis and sample chapters.
Recent Fiction Title: *The Bronc Rider*, by William Crawford.

RAINBOW BOOKS, Box 1069, Moore Haven FL 33471. (813)946-0293. Associate: B. Lampe. Publishes hardcover and trade paperback originals. Averages 8-10 titles/year; receives 600 submissions annually. 70% of books from first-time authors; 68% of books from unagented writers. Publishes book an average of 8 months after acceptance. Reports in 1 week. Book catalog and ms guidelines for 9x6 SAE with 56¢ postage.
Nonfiction: Reference and resource books plus some well-targeted how-to. Query.
Recent Nonfiction Title: *Parental Kidnapping: An International Resource Directory*, by Margaret Strickland.

RAINTREE PUBLISHERS INC., 310 W. Wisconsin Ave., Milwaukee WI 53203. (414)273-0873. Editor-in-Chief: Russell Bennett. Publishes hardcover originals. Usually makes outright purchase. Simultaneous and photocopied submissions OK. Computer printout submissions acceptable; prefers letter-quality to dot-matrix. Reports in approximately 2 months.
Nonfiction: Juvenile and reference. Subjects include animals, health, history, nature, photography and science. "We publish school and library books in series." Query with outline/synopsis and sample chapters.
Fiction: Adventure, historical and science fiction. Query with outline/synopsis and sample chapters.

‡RANDOM HOUSE, INC., Subsidary of Advance Publications, 201 E. 50th St., New York NY 10022. Random House Trade Division publishes 120 titles/year; receives 3,000 submissions annually. Pays royalty on retail price. Simultaneous and photocopied submissions OK. Reports on 3 weeks on queries; 6 weeks on mss. Free book catalog.
Nonfiction: Biography, cookbook, humor, illustrated book, self-help. Subjects include Americana, art, business and economics, cooking and foods, health, history, music, nature, politics, psychology, religion, sociology and sports. No juveniles or textbooks (separate division). Query with outline/synopsis and sample chapters.
Fiction: Adventure, confession, experimental, fantasy, historical, horror, humor, mainstream, mystery, and suspense. Submit outline/synopsis and sample chapters.
Tips: "If I were a writer trying to market a book today, I would get an agent."

‡THE REAL COMET PRESS, Subsidiary of Such a Deal Corporation, #410, 3131 Western Ave, Seattle WA 98121. (206)283-7827. Publisher: Catherine Hillenbrand. Publishes hardcover and trade paperback originals and trade paperback reprints. Averages 5 titles/year; receives 100 submissions annually. 30% of books from first-time authors; 50% from unagented writers. Pays royalty on list or wholesale price. Publishes book average of 15-24 months after acceptance. Simultaneous and photcopied submissions OK. Computer printout submissions OK. Free book catalog; writer's guidelines for SASE.
Nonfiction: Visual books, humor, exhibition catalog and political commentary. Subjects include art, contemporary culture, music, photography, politics and sociology. "Art books, comics, critique, political commentary, and books on popular culture have the best chance of selling to our firm." Submit outline/synopsis and sample chapters. Reviews artwork/photos.
Recent Nonfiction Title: *The 100th Boyfriend*, by Daly and Skeels (humor/belles lettres).

REFERENCE SERVICE PRESS, Suite 310, 3540 Wilshire Blvd., Los Angeles CA 90010. (213)251-3743. President: Dr. Gail Schlachter. Publishes hardcover and paperback originals. Averages 10 titles/year; receives 30-50 submissions annually. 90% of books from unagented writers. Average print order for a writer's first book is 1,000. Pays 10-20% royalty on net price, depending upon form of submission. Publishes book an average of 9 months after acceptance. Photocopied submissions OK. Electronic submissions OK via IBM, but requires hard copy also. Computer printout submissions acceptable; prefers letter-quality to dot-matrix. Reports in 45 days. Book catalog and ms guidelines for SASE.

Nonfiction: Reference works (directories, dictionaries, handbooks, guides, bibliographies, encyclopedias, almanacs, serials, etc.), particularly in the area of financial aid. Query or submit outline/prospectus and 2-3 sample chapters. Reviews artwork/photos as part of ms package.

Recent Nonfiction Title: *Directory of Financial Aids for Women, 1987-88*, by Gail Schlachter (reference book).

‡REGAL BOOKS, Division of Gospel Light Publications, 2300 Knoll Dr., Ventura CA 93003. Managing Director Acquisitions: Keith Wintermute. Publishes hardcover and paperback originals. Averages 15 titles/year. Receives 5,000 submissions annually. 20% of books from first-time authors, 90% of books from unagented writers. Average print order for writer's first book is 5,000. Pays 10% royalty on paperback titles, 10% net for curriculum books. Publishes book an average of 11 months after acceptance. Buys all rights. Computer printout submissions acceptable; prefers letter-quality to dot-matrix. Reports in 3 months. Book catalog and ms guidelines for 8½x11 SAE and $2 postage.

Nonfiction: Bible studies (Old and New Testament), Christian living, counseling (self-help), contemporary concerns, evangelism (church growth), marriage and family, youth, inspirational/devotional, communication resources, teaching enrichment resources, Bible commentary for Laymen Series, and missions. Query or submit detailed outline/synopsis and 2-3 sample chapters; no complete mss.

Recent Nonfiction Title: *Extra Innings: The Don Sutton Story*, by Sutton, Timmons (biography).

REGNERY/GATEWAY, INC., Imprints/divisions include Cahill and Co., Gateway Distribution and Fullfillment Services and Gateway Editions, 950 N. Shore Drive, Lake Bluff IL 60044. President: Alfred S. Regnery. Vice President: Thomas A. Palmer. Publishes hardcover and paperback originals and paperback reprints. Averages 6-12 titles/year. Pays royalty. Simultaneous and photocopied submissions OK. Computer printout submissions acceptable. "Responds only to submissions in which there is interest." Book catalog for 8½x11 SAE.

Nonfiction: Biography, economics, history, philosophy, politics, psychology, religion, science, sociology and education (teaching). Accepts nonfiction translations. "We are looking for books on current affairs—of either political, legal, social, environmental, educational or historical interest—or children's literature. Books heavy on sex and obscene brutality should not be submitted." Queries preferred. Additional information if requested. No unsolicited mss accepted. Looks for "a novel approach to the subject, expertise of the author, clean, respectable writing, salability of the proposed work."

Recent Nonfiction Title: *Swift Walker*, by Lloyd Wendt.

RELIGIOUS EDUCATION PRESS, 1531 Wellington Rd., Birmingham AL 35209. (205)879-4040. Editor: James Michael Lee. Publishes trade paperback originals. Averages 5 titles/year; receives 120 submissions annually. 40% of books from first-time authors; 100% of books from unagented writers. Pays 10% royalty on actual selling price. "Many of our books are work for hire. We do not have a subsidy option." Offers no advance. Photocopied submissions OK. Information on request for electronic submissions. Computer printout submissions OK; no dot-matrix. Reports in 1 month on queries; 2 months on mss. Free book catalog.

Nonfiction: Technical and textbook. Scholarly subjects on religion and religious education. "We publish serious, significant and scholarly books on religious education and pastoral ministry." No mss under 200 pages, books on Biblical interpretation, or "popular" books. Query. Reviews artwork/photos as part of ms package.

Recent Nonfiction Title: *Faith Development and Fowler*, by Craig Dykstra and Sharon Parks.

Tips: "Write clearly, reason exactly and connectively, and meet deadlines."

RENAISSANCE HOUSE PUBLISHERS, Subsidiary of Jende-Hagan, Inc., Box 177, 541 Oak St., Frederick CO 80530. (303)833-2030. Editor: Eleanor Ayer. Publishes hardcover and trade paperback originals and trade paperback reprints. Averages 12 titles/year; receives 125 submissions annually. 60% of books from first-time authors; 75% of books from unagented writers. Pays 10-15% royalty on wholesale price. Offers average advance of 10% of anticipated first printing royalties. May consider work for hire for experts in specific fields of interest. Publishes book an average of 18 months after acceptance. Simultaneous and photocopied submissions OK. Query for electronic submissions. Computer printout submissions acceptable. Reports in 1 month on queries; 2 months on mss. Book catalog free on request.

Nonfiction: Biography and general interest nonfiction. Subjects include Americana, history, and naturalist philosophy. No personal reminiscences, general traditional philosophy, children's books, general cookbooks, books on topics totally unrelated to subject areas specified above. Submit outline/synopsis and sample chapters. Reviews artwork/photos as part of ms package.

Recent Nonfiction Title: *A Child of Hitler: Germany in the Days When God Wore a Swastika*, by Alfan Stleck (history).

*RESOURCE PUBLICATIONS, INC., Suite 290, 160 E. Virginia St., San Jose CA 95112. Editorial Director: Kenneth E. Guentert. Publishes paperback originals. Publishes 14 titles/year; receives 100-200 submissions annually. 30% of books from first-time authors; 99% of books from unagented writers. Average print order of a writer's first book is 2,000. Subsidy publishes 10% of books. "If the author can present and defend a personal publicity effort or otherwise demonstrate demand and the work is in our field, we will consider it." Pays 8% royalty; offers no advance. Publishes book an average of 18 months after acceptance. Photocopied submissions (with written assurance that work is not being submitted simultaneously) OK. Query for electronic submissions. Computer printout submissions acceptable; prefers letter-quality to dot-matrix. Reports in 2 months.

Nonfiction: "We look for creative source books for the religious education, worship, religious art, and architecture fields. How-to books, especially for contemporary religious art forms, are of particular interest (dance, mime, drama, choral reading, singing, music, musicianship, bannermaking, statuary, or any visual art form). No heavy theoretical, philosophical, or theological tomes. Nothing utterly unrelated or unrelatable to the religious markets as described above." Query or submit outline/synopsis and sample chapters. "Prepare a clear outline of the work and an ambitious schedule of public appearances to help make it known and present both as a proposal to the publisher. With our company a work that can be serialized or systemically excerpted in our periodicals is always given special attention." Accepts translations. Reviews artwork/photos as part of ms package.

Fiction: "Light works providing examples of good expression through the religious art forms. Any collected short works in the areas of drama, dance, song, stories, anecdotes or good visual art." Query or submit outline/synopsis and sample chapters.

Tips: "Books that provide readers with practical, usable suggestions and ideas pertaining to worship, education, and the religious arts have the best chance of selling to our firm."

FLEMING H. REVELL CO., Subsidiary of Guideposts, Inc., Central Ave., Old Tappan NJ 07675. Imprints include Power Books and Spire. Vice President/Editor-in-Chief: Gary A. Sledge. Managing Editor: Norma F. Chimento. Publishes hardcover and paperback originals and reprints. Averages 90 titles/year. 10% of books from first-time authors; 95% of books from unagented writers. Pays royalty on retail price; sometimes offers advance. Publishes book an average of 1 year after acceptance. Computer printout submissions acceptable if letter-quality. No unsolicited mss. Must query.

Nonfiction: Religion and inspirational. "All books must appeal to Protestant-evangelical readers." Query. Reviews artwork/photos as part of ms package.

Recent Nonfiction Title: *Back on Course*, by Gavin MacLeod.

Fiction: Protestant-evangelical religion and inspiration. Query.

Recent Fiction Title: *Lambs of the Lie*, by Lissa Halls Johnson.

Tips: "The writer has the best chance of selling our firm Christian books if she or he has credentials, degree and area of professional expertise."

REVIEW AND HERALD PUBLISHING ASSOCIATION, 55 West Oak Ridge Dr., Hagerstown MD 21740. Acquisition Editor: Penny Wheeler. Publishes hardcover and paperback originals and software. Specializes in religious-oriented books. Averages 30-40 titles/year; receives 300 submissions annually. 15% of books from first-time authors; 100% of books from unagented writers. Average print order for a writer's first book is 5,000-7,500. Pays 5-10% royalty on retail price; offers average $500 advance. Publishes book an average of 1 year after acceptance. Computer printout submissions acceptable; prefers letter-quality to dot-matrix. Reports in 3 months. Free brochure; ms guidelines for SASE.

Nonfiction: Juveniles (religious-oriented only), nature, and religious, all 20,000-60,000 words; 128 pages average. Query or submit outline/synopsis and 2-3 sample chapters. Prefers to do own illustrating. Looks for "literary style, constructive tone, factual accuracy, compatibility with Adventist theology and lifestyle, and length of manuscript." Reviews artwork/photos as part of ms package.

Tips: "Familiarize yourself with Adventist theology because Review and Herald Publishing Association is owned and operated by the Seventh-day Adventist Church. We are accepting fewer but better-written manuscripts."

REYMONT ASSOCIATES, Box 2013, Boca Raton FL 33427. Editor-in-Chief: D.J. Scherer. Managing Editor: Felicia Scherer. Publishes soft cover originals. Averages 4 titles annually. Receives 30 submissions annually. 20% from first-time authors; 100% from unagented writers. Average print order for a writer's first book is 1,000. Pays 10-12-15% royalty on wholesale price; no advance. Publishes book an average of 3 months after acceptance. Computer printout submissions acceptable. Reports in 2 weeks. Book catalog for #10 SASE.

Nonfiction: Publishes business reports, how-to, unique directories, and bibliographies. " 'Net' writing; no rhetoric. Aim for 7,500-10,000 words." Submit outline/synopsis and sample chapter.

Recent Nonfiction Title: *Radon in the Home*, (guide to dealing with risks from radon).

Tips: Trends in book publishing that freelance writers should be aware of include "the need for sharply focused single-subject reports of 7,000-8,000 words in length."

‡RICHBORO PRESS, Box 1, Richboro PA 18954. (215)364-2212. Editor: George Moore. Publishes hardcover, trade paperback originals and software. Averages 6 titles/year; receives 500 submissions annually. 90% of books from unagented writers. Average print order for a writer's first book is 500. Pays 10% royalty on retail price. Publishes book an average of 1 year after acceptance. Query for electronic submissions. Computer printout submissions acceptable. Reports in 6 weeks on queries; 3 months on mss. Free book catalog; ms guidelines $1 with SASE.

Nonfiction: Cookbook, how-to and gardening. Subjects include cooking and foods. Query.

Recent Nonfiction Title: *Classified Advertising*, 4th Edition, by Blair.

THE RIVERDALE COMPANY, INC., PUBLISHERS, Suite 102, 5506 Kenilworth Ave., Riverdale MD 20737. (301)864-2029. President: John Adams. Vice President: Adele Manuel. Editor: Mary Power. Publishes hardcover originals. Averages 16-18 titles/year; receives 50 submissions annually. 20% of books from first-time authors; 100% of books from unagented writers. Pays 0-15% royalty on wholesale price. Publishes book an average of 8 months after acceptance. Computer printout submissions acceptable; prefers letter-quality to dot-matrix. Reports in 1 week on queries; 2 months on mss. Book catalog and ms guidelines for SASE.

Nonfiction: "We publish technical and social science books for scholars, students, policymakers; and tour, restaurant and recreational guides for the mass market." Subjects include economics, history, humanities, politics, psychology, sociology and travel. Especially needs social science and travel mss on South Asia or Africa. Will consider college text proposals in economics and Third World studies; travel guides of any sort. Query. Accepts outline/synopsis and 2-3 sample chapters.

Recent Nonfiction Title: *The Travelers Almanac: Planning Your Vacation Around the Weather—North America*, by H. Bernard.

ROCKY TOP PUBLICATIONS, Subsidiary of Rocky Top Industries, Box 33, Stamford NY 12167. President/Publisher: Joseph D. Jennings. Publishes hardcover and paperback originals. Averages 4-6 titles/year. 70% of books from first-time authors; 95% of books from unagented writers. Pays 4-10% royalty (may vary) on wholesale price. Publishes book an average of 6 months after acceptance. Photocopied submissions OK. Computer printout submissions acceptable; prefers letter-quality to dot-matrix. Reports in 2 weeks on queries; 4 months on mss. Book catalog and ms guidelines for SASE.

Nonfiction: How-to, reference, self-help and technical. Subjects include animal health; health; hobbies (crafts); medical; nature; philosophy (Thoreau or environmental only); and science. "We are actively looking for exposé-type material on science, medicine and health—well written and researched only." No autobiographies, biographies, business "get rich quick" or fad books. Submit outline/synopsis (sample chapters or complete ms after approval). Reviews artwork/photos as part of ms package.

Recent Nonfiction Title: *The Hydroponic Workbook*, by J. Gooze (technical).

Tips: "Our readers range from self-sufficiency people, to medical and health professionals, environmentalists, and gardeners. Scientific, medical, health, pharmaceutical, and environmental (conservation, naturalist) books have the best chance of selling to us."

RODALE PRESS, Prevention Health Books Div., 33 E. Minor St., Emmaus PA 18049. (215)968-5171. Senior Editors: Carol Keough and Debora Tkac. Publishes hardcover and trade paperback originals and reprints. Averages 20 titles/year; receives 100 submissions annually. 10% of books from first-time authors; 1% of books from unagented writers. Pays royalty on retail price: 10-15% trade hardcover; 7½% trade paperback; or 2% major mail order. Offers average $7,500 advance. Publishes book an average of 1 year after acceptance. Simultaneous and photocopied submissions OK. Will discuss electronic submissions with author, but requires hard copy also. Computer printout submissions acceptable; prefers letter-quality to dot-matrix. Reports in 1 month. Free book catalog.

Nonfiction: Cookbook, how-to, reference, self-help—all health books. Subjects include health, psychology and fitness. Especially interested in "how-to books on health care with practical, self-help information by doctors and other health professionals, or a careful author using primary medical studies." No technical, textbook, non-health related books. Query with outline/synopsis and sample chapters. Reviews artwork/photos.

Recent Nonfiction Title: *Future Youth: How to Reverse The Aging Process*, editors of Prevention Health books (diet and fitness).

Tips: "Our audience is over 50 years of age, health conscious, mostly women. Writers have the best chance of selling us health books in their field of expertise. They must have the ability to turn technical information into friendly, easy-to-understand copy."

THE ROSEN PUBLISHING GROUP, 29 E. 21st St., New York NY 10010. (212)777-3017. President: Roger Rosen. Imprints include Pelion Press (music titles). Publishes hardcover originals. Entire firm averages 46 titles/year; young adult division averages 4-35 titles/year. 45% of books from first-time authors; 80% of books from unagented writers. Pays royalty or makes outright purchase. Publishes book an average of 9 months after acceptance. Simultaneous and photocopied submissions OK. Computer printout submissions acceptable; prefers letter-quality to dot-matrix. Reports in 1 month. Book catalog and guidelines for 8½x11 SAE with 56¢ postage.

Nonfiction: Young adult, reference, self-help and textbook. Subjects include art, health (coping), and music. "Our books are geared to the young adult audience whom we reach via school and public libraries. Most of the books we publish are related to career guidance and personal adjustment. We also publish material on the theatre, music and art, as well as journalism for schools. Interested in supplementary material for enrichment of school curriculum." Mss in the young adult nonfiction areas include vocational guidance, personal and social adjustment, journalism and theatre. For Pelion Press, mss on classical music, emphasis on opera and singing." Query or submit outline/synopsis and sample chapters. Reviews artwork/photos as part of ms package.
Recent Nonfiction Title: *Coping with Suicide*, by Smith (young adult/self help).
Tips: "The writer has the best chance of selling our firm a book on vocational guidance or personal social adjustment."

ROSS BOOKS, Box 4340, Berkeley CA 94704. President: Franz Ross. Small press. Publishes hardcover and paperback originals, paperback reprints, and software. Averages 7-10 titles/year; receives 200 submissions annually. 90% of books from first-time authors; 99% of books from unagented writers. Average print order for a writer's first book is 5,000-10,000. Offers 8-12% royalty on net price. Offers average advance of 2% of the first print run. Publishes book an average of 1 year after acceptance. Simultaneous and photocopied submissions OK. Query for electronic submissions. Computer printout submissions acceptable; prefers letter-quality to dot-matrix. Reports in 1 month. Book catalog for 6x9 SAE with 37¢ postage.
Nonfiction: Popular how-to on science, business, general how-to. No political, religious or children's books. Accepts nonfiction translations. Submit outline or synopsis of no more than 3 pages and 1 sample chapter with SASE. Reviews artwork/photos as part of ms package.
Recent Nonfiction Title: *How to Plan and Book Meetings and Seminars*, by Williams (business).

*ROWMAN & LITTLEFIELD, PUBLISHERS, Division of Littlefield Adams & Co., 81 Adams Dr., Totowa NJ 07512. Managing Director: Arthur Hamparian. Publishes hardcover and paperback originals and reprints. Receives 500 submissions annually. 50% of books from first-time authors; 100% of books from unagented writers. Subsidy publishes 5% of books; subsidy publishes (nonauthor) 5% of books. Pays 8-10% royalty on net sales; offers no advance. Publishes book an average of 9 months after acceptance. Query for electronic submissions. Computer printout submissions acceptable; prefers letter-quality to dot-matrix. Reports in 2 months. Free book catalog; ms quidelines for SASE.
Nonfiction: Scholarly and academic books. Subjects include philosophy, social sciences, women's studies, economics and finance, health care, criminology and legal studies, public affairs, geography, computer science and statistics. "Our authors are typically academics writing for other professionals, for government bodies and other organizations which utilize primary research." Submit outline/synopsis and sample chapters.
Recent Nonfiction Title: *The Social Reconstruction of the Feminine Character*, by Sondra Farganis.

ROXBURY PUBLISHING CO., Box 491044, Los Angeles CA 90049. (213)458-3493. Executive Editor: Claude Teweles. Publishes hardcover and paperback originals and reprints. Averages 20 titles/year. Pays royalty; offers negotiable advance. Simultaneous, photocopied and computer printout submissions OK. Reports in 1 month.
Nonfiction: College-level textbooks only. Subjects include business and economics, humanities, philosophy, psychology, social sciences and sociology. Query, submit outline/synopsis and sample chapters, or submit complete ms.
Recent Nonfiction Title: *The Writing Cycle*, by Celia Allphin-Hoggatt.

RPM PRESS, INC., Box 157, Verndale MN 56481. Publisher: David A. Hietala. Publishes trade paperback originals, and audio-cassette training programs (with workbook) and selected software. Averages 18-24 titles/year; receives 75-150 submissions annually. 75% of books from first-time authors; 100% of books from unagented writers. Average print order for a writer's first book is 1,000-5,000. Pays 5-15% royalty on retail price or makes outright purchases of $200-1,500. Offers average advance to established authors of $500. Publishes book/training program an average of 6-9 months after acceptance. Simultaneous and photocopied submissions OK. Electronic submissions OK; prefers IBM-PC-readable diskettes in ASC II files—and hard copy also. Computer printout submissions OK; no dot-matrix. Reports in 5 weeks on queries; 2 months on mss (usually sooner for both). Book catalog for 9x12 SAE with 56¢ postage.
Nonfiction: How-to, reference, technical, and audio-cassette training programs on business, applied management, finance, program development, client programming, and engineering geared toward managing the nonprofit workcenter (for the handicapped). "We are looking for how-to books and audio-tape training programs that tell how to set up new business ventures; improve present management practice in this specialized setting; how-to training programs on setting up quality assurance programs, marketing rehabilitation services, or developing innovative types of service delivery mechanisms. People who buy our books and training programs are managers and concerned professionals looking to improve the management practice of their nonprofit business enterprises or programs, so we obviously like to hear from writers who have spent some time in the management of these business and service organizations (or who can speak assertively as if they had). We real-

ize that few writers have the hard-won experience that we are looking for—that's why we offer *extensive* editorial assistance to the few authors we end up working with. If you want to work with us, please note the sort of marketplace we're serving and the type of material we seek. We receive hundreds of query letters each year that are outside our area of specific interest. We have no upper limit on the number of books we publish annually—our limit is based on the number of on-target manuscripts we have available. We are entirely receptive to hearing all ideas and are interested in working with new or established authors who, once they establish themselves with us, are willing to work with us on a long-term basis. We would also like to identify software developers that would like to freelance with us on projects in this market—IBM and Apple II only.'' Query.
Recent Nonfiction Title: *Job Accommodation Handbook*, by P. McCray, Board of Directors.

*RUSSICA PUBLISHERS, INC., 799 Broadway, New York NY 10003. (212)473-7480. Contact: David A. Daskal. Publishes trade paperback originals and reprints. Averages 15 titles/year. Subsidy publishes 10% of books; subsidy publishes (nonauthor) 10% of books. Pays 10-15% royalty on retail price. Photocopied submissions OK. Reports in 2 weeks. Free book catalog.
Nonfiction: Biography and humor. Subjects include history. "We're looking for biographies of prominent Russians or Slavs written in English. All other mss must be in Russian only."
Fiction: Adventure, erotica, ethnic, horror, humor, mystery and suspense. "Russian language manuscripts only." Submit complete ms.
Poetry: Modern Russian poetry. Submit complete ms.

‡RUTGERS UNIVERSITY PRESS, 109 Church St., New Brunswick NJ 08901. Averages 50 titles/year; receives 600 submissions annually. 30% of books from first-time authors; 90% of books from unagented writers. Average print order for a writer's first book is 2,000. Pays royalty on retail price. Publishes book an average of 1 year after acceptance. Query for electronic submissions. Computer printout submissions acceptable; no dot-matrix. Final decision depends on time required to secure competent professional reading reports. Book catalog and ms guidelines for 9x12 SAE with 76¢ postage.
Nonfiction: Scholarly books in history, literary criticism, film studies, art history, anthropology, sociology, science, technology, women's studies and criminal justice. Regional nonfiction must deal with mid-Atlantic region with emphasis on New Jersey. Length: 60,000 words minimum. Query. Reviews artwork/photos as part of ms package.
Recent Nonfiction Title: *The Tenant Movement in New York City, 1904-1984*, by Ronald Lawson, editor (American history).

‡*RUTLEDGE HILL PRESS, 513 Third Ave. S, Nashville TN 37210. (615)244-2700. President: Lawrence Stowe. Vice President: Ron Pitkin. Publishes hardcover and trade paperback originals and hardcover and trade paperback reprints. Averages 20 titles/year; receives 250 submissions annually. 40% of books from first-time authors; 90% of books from unagented writers. Subsidy publishes (nonauthor) 5% of books. Pays 10-20% royalty on wholesale price. Publishes book an average of 10 months after acceptance. Photocopied submissions OK. Computer printout submissions OK; prefers letter-quality. Reports in 5 weeks on queries; 3 months on mss. Book catalog for 9x12 SAE and 56¢ postage.
Nonfiction: Biography, "coffee table", cookbook, humor, reference and self-help. "The book must have a market that is primarily in the Southeast." Submit outline/synopsis and sample chapters. Reviews artwork/photos as part of ms package.
Recent Nonfiction Title: *The Quilts of Tennessee*, by Betsy Ramsey, and Merikay Waldroge.

RYND COMMUNICATIONS, National Health Publishing, National Law Publishing, 99 Painters Mill Rd., Owings Mills MD 21117. (301)363-6400. Acquisitions Editor: Sara Mansure. Publishes hard and soft cover originals. Averages 15-20 titles/year and quarterly subscription services. Receives 75 submissions annually. 30% of books from first-time authors; 100% of books from unagented writers. Pays 8-12% royalty on retail price. Offers average $300 advance. Publishes book an average of 1 year after acceptance. Query for electronic submissions. Computer printout submissions acceptable; prefers letter-quality to dot-matrix. Reports in 2 weeks on queries; 10 weeks on mss. Book catalog for 5½x8½ SAE with 39¢ postage.
Nonfiction: Reference, technical and textbook. Subjects include health and nursing administration; health finance; and health law. Needs publications on long term care management; nurse management and administration; home health care; finance; and adult day care. Management oriented rather than clinical; prefers works that can be used as professional references and textbooks. Query or submit table of contents, resume and sample chapters.
Recent Nonfiction Title: *Cost Containment and DRGs*, by Allen D. Spiegel, Ph.D. and Florence Kavaler, M.D. (professional textbook).
Tips: "We are a growing house devoted to health care. We welcome new authors, whether or not they have already published; we look for academic and experience background and a clear writing style. We also welcome topics which reflect new trends in health care."

S. C. E.-EDITIONS L'ETINCELLE, Suite 206, 4920 Blvd. de Maisonneuve W. Westmount, Montreal, Quebec H3Z 1N1 Canada. (514)488-9531. President: Robert Davies. Publishes trade paperback originals in French translation. Averages 12 titles/year; receives 200 submissions annually. 10% of books from first-time authors; 80% of books from unagented writers. Average print order for a writer's first book is 4,000. Pays 8-12% royalty on retail price; offers average $1,000 advance. Publishes book an average of 1 year after acceptance. Simultaneous and photocopied submissions OK. Query for electronic submissions. Computer printout submissions acceptable. Reports in 2 months on queries; 4 months on mss. Book catalog and ms guidelines for 9x12 SAE with 2 IRCs.
Imprints: L'Etincelle (nonfiction and fiction). Memoire Vive (microcomputer books).
Nonfiction: Biography, cookbook, how-to, humor, reference and self-help. Subjects include animals, business and economics, cooking and foods, health, history, hobbies, microcomputers, nature, philosophy, politics, psychology, recreation, sociology, sports and travel. Accepts nonfiction translations. "We are looking for about five translatable works of nonfiction, in any popular field. Our audience includes French-speaking readers in all major markets in the world." No topics of interest only to Americans. Query or submit outline/synopsis and 3 sample chapters. Reviews artwork/photos as part of ms package.
Recent Nonfiction Title: *Astrography: The New Personalized Astrology*, by Alan Rosenthal.

ST. ANTHONY MESSENGER PRESS, 1615 Republic St., Cincinnati OH 45210. Editor-in-Chief: The Rev. Norman Perry, O.F.M. Publishes paperback originals. Averages 12 titles/year; receives 250 submissions annually. 10% of books from first-time authors; 100% of books from unagented writers. Pays 6-8% royalty on retail price; offers average $600 advance. Publishes book an average of 8 months after acceptance. Books are sold in bulk to groups (study clubs, high school or college classes, and parishes) and in bookstores. Photocopied submissions OK if they are not simultaneous submissions to other publishers. Query for electronic submissions. Computer printout submissions acceptable; no dot-matrix. Book catalog and ms guidelines for 9x12 SAE with 39¢ postage.
Nonfiction: Religion. "We try to reach the Catholic market with topics near the heart of the ordinary Catholic's belief. We want to offer insight and inspiration and thus give people support in living a Christian life in a pluralistic society. We are not interested in an academic or abstract approach. Our emphasis is on popular writing with examples, specifics, color and anecdotes." Length: 25,000-40,000 words. Query or submit outline and 2 sample chapters. Reviews artwork/photos as part of ms package.
Recent Nonfiction Title: *Living With Sickness: A Struggle Toward Meaning*, by Susan Saint Sing (inspirational).
Tips: "The book cannot be the place for the author to think through a subject. The author has to think through the subject first and then tell the reader what is important to know. Style uses anecdotes, examples, illustrations, human interest, 'colorful' quotes, fiction techniques of suspense, dialogue, characterization, etc. Address practical problems, deal in concrete situations, free of technical terms and professional jargon."

*ST. BEDE'S PUBLICATIONS, Subsidiary of St. Scholastice Priory, Box 545, Petersham MA 01366. (617)724-3407. Editorial Director: Sr. Mary Joseph, OSB. Publishes hardcover originals, trade paperback originals and reprints. Averages 8-12 titles/year; receives 100 submissions annually. 30-40% of books from first-time authors; 90% of books from unagented writers. Subsidy publishes (nonauthor) 10% of books. Pays 5-10% royalty on wholesale price or retail price. No advance. Publishes book an average of 2 years after acceptance. Simultaneous and photocopied submissions OK. Query for electronic submissions. Computer printout submissions acceptable; no dot-matrix. Reports in 2 weeks on queries; 3 months on mss. Book catalog and ms guidelines for #10 SAE and 39¢ postage.
Nonfiction: Textbook (theology), religion, prayer, spirituality, hagiography, theology, philosophy, church history and related lives of saints fields. "We are always looking for excellent books on prayer, spirituality, liturgy, church or monastic history. Theology and philosophy are important also. We publish English translations of foreign works in these fields if we think they are excellent and worth translating." No submissions unrelated to religion, theology, spirituality, etc. Query or submit outline/synopsis and sample chapters.
Recent Nonfiction Title: *Old Testament Priests and the New Priest*, by Albert Vanhoye, S J.
Fiction: Historical (only if religious) and religious. "Generally we don't do fiction—but we are willing to look over a manuscript if it fits into our categories." No fiction submissions unrelated to religion. Query or submit outline/synopsis and sample chapters.
Tips: For our theology/philosophy titles our audience is scholars, colleges and universities, seminaries, etc. For our other titles (i.e. prayer, spirituality, lives of saints, etc.) the audience is above-average readers interested in furthering their knowledge in these areas. Theology seems to be swinging back to studying more conservative lines. We're finding a lot of excellent books being published in France and are getting the rights to translate these. Also, there's a great, general interest in prayer and spirituality so we try to publish really excellent titles in these areas, too. New material, or newly translated material, gets priority."

*ST. LUKE'S PRESS, Subsidiary of Tickle Inc., Mid-Memphis Tower, 1407 Union, Memphis TN 38104. (901)357-5441. Subsidiaries include Shelby House. Managing Editor: Roger Easson, Ph.D. Averages 8-10 titles/year; receives 3,000 submissions annually. 50% of books from unagented writers. Average print order for a writer's first book is 5,000. Subsidy publishes (nonauthor) 10% of books. Pays 10% minimum royalty on monies received; offers average $100-500 advance. Publishes book an average of 2 years after acceptance. Query for electronic submissions. Computer printout submissions acceptable. Reports in 3 months. Book catalog $1.

Nonfiction: Biography. Accepts translations. Submit story line and 3 sample chapters. Reviews artwork/photos as part of ms package.

Recent Nonfiction Title: *A.J.'s Tax Court: Who Won, Who Lost and Why*, by A.J. Cook.

Fiction: Submit story line and 3 sample chapters.

Recent Fiction Title: *The Himmler Plaque*, by Jackson Collins.

ST. MARTIN'S PRESS, 175 5th Ave., New York NY 10010. Averages 900 titles/year; receives 3,000 submissions annually. 15-20% of books from first-time authors; 30% of books from unagented writers. Electronic submissions OK, but requires hard copy also. Computer printout submission acceptable; prefers letter-quality to dot-matrix. Reports "promptly."

Nonfiction and Fiction: General and textbook. Publishes general fiction and nonfiction; major interest in adult fiction and nonfiction, history, self-help, political science, popular science, biography, scholarly, popular reference, etc. Query. Reviews artwork/photos as part of ms package. "It takes very persuasive credentials to prompt us to commission a book or outline."

Recent Title: *Isak Dinesen*, by Judith Thurmon.

Tips: "We do almost every kind of book there is—trade, textbooks, reference and children's books. Crime fiction has the best chance of selling to our firm—over fifteen percent of all the trade books we published are this category."

*ST. VLADIMIR'S SEMINARY PRESS, 575 Scarsdale Rd., Crestwood NY 10707. (914)961-8313. Managing Editor: Theodore Bazil. Publishes hardcover and trade paperback originals and reprints. Averages 15 titles/year. Subsidy publishes 20% of books. Market considerations determine whether an author should be subsidy published. Pays 7% royalty on retail price. Simultaneous and photocopied submissions OK. Computer printout submissions acceptable; prefers letter-quality to dot-matrix. Reports in 3 months on queries; 6 months on mss. Free book catalog and ms guidelines.

Nonfiction: Religion dealing with Eastern Orthodox theology. Query. Reviews artwork/photos as part of ms package.

Tips: "We have an interest in books that stand on firm theological ground; careful writing and scholarship are basic."

SANDLAPPER PUBLISHING, INC., Box 1932, Orangeburg SC 29116. (803)531-1658. Acquisitions: Frank N. Handal. Publishes hardcover and trade paperback originals and reprints. Averages 6 titles/year; receives 200 submissions annually. 80% of books from first-time authors; 90% of books from unagented writers. Pays 15% maximum royalty on wholesale price. Publishes book an average of 18 months after acceptance. Photocopied submissions OK; simultaneous submissions OK if informed ("please inform us of other offers"). Computer printout submissions acceptable; no dot-matrix. Reports in 1 month on queries; 6 months on mss. Book catalog and ms guidelines for 9x12 SASE with 73¢ postage.

Nonfiction: Biography, "coffee table" book, cookbook, humor, illustrated book, juvenile, reference and textbook. Subjects are limited to South Carolina history, culture and cuisine. "We are looking for manuscripts that show a new facet of our state, by both South Carolinians and residents of other states. If it is not related to South Carolina, we don't want to see it. I refuse to read self-help books, children's books about divorce, kidnapping, etc., and we are not looking at any 'growing up poor and Southern' manuscripts at this time. Absolutely no religious manuscripts." Query or submit outline/synopsis and sample chapters "if you're not sure it's what we're looking for, otherwise complete ms." Reviews artwork/photos as part of ms package.

Recent Nonfiction Title: *Charleston Ironwork*, by Charles N. Bayless (photo survey).

Fiction: Does not need fiction submissions at this time, "but I will look at good strong fiction by South Carolinians and/or about South Carolina. Also, good, strong juvenile fiction about South Carolina history, and fiction showing new facets of our state and its heritage. No romance, no horror, no science fiction, no religious fiction, etc." Query or submit outline/synopis and sample chapters.

Recent Fiction Title: *The Treasure of Pawley's Island*, by Celia Childress Halford (adventure).

Tips: "Our readers are South Carolinians, visitors to the state's tourist spots, and friends and family that live out-of-state. We are rapidly becoming the regional publisher for South Carolina. Authors frequently try to convince us of the merits of their works in the course of a telephone call, before sending the manuscript. Such promotion is pointless. We must read a manuscript and make a judgment ourselves."

‡SANDPIPER PRESS, Box 286, Brookings OR 97415. (503)469-5588. Editor: Marilyn Riddle. Publishes trade paperback originals. Averages 1-3 titles/year. 100% from unagented writers. Buys some mss outright for $10 per article/story in anthologies plus two free copies of books. Simultaneous and photocopied submissions

OK. Computer printout submissions OK. Reports in 2 weeks on queries; 2 months on mss. Book catalog and ms guidelines for #10 SAE and 1 first-class stamp.

Fiction: Fantasy and mainstream. "We are seeking Rod Serling-type short-short stories and first person handicapped accounts of going from what 'I can't do' to what 'I can do'." Submit complete ms.

Recent Fiction Title: *Unicorns For Everyone*, by Marilyn Reed Riddle.

Tips: "All our books are in 18-point large type for vision impaired. The Rod Serling-type stories are not to be scary or technical science fiction but in the original Serling vein, surprise ending, irony, modern morality plays. The anthology of personal experiences of physically challenged people starts with being faced with what they cannot do anymore and finding what they *can* do which will stir the hopes and imaginations of readers who are faced with similar challenges. For the Rod Serling short-short story anthology the editorial slant is anti-nuclear, anti-war, and pro-brotherhood, as was Serling."

SANTA BARBARA PRESS, Suite C, 815 Dela Vina St., Santa Barbara CA 93101. (805)966-2060. Editor-in-Chief: George Erikson. Publishes hardcover and trade paperback originals, and trade paperback reprints. Averages 12 titles/year; receives 75 submissions annually. 50% of books from first-time authors; 50% of books from unagented writers. Pays 5-10% royalty. Offers maximum $1,000 advance. Publishes book an average of 1 year after acceptance. Simultaneous submissions OK. Query for electronic submissions. Computer printout submissions acceptable; no dot-matrix. Reports in 3 weeks on queries; 3 months on mss. Book catalog for 4x9 SAE with 2 first class stamps.

Nonfiction: Biography, how-to and self-help. Subjects include philosophy, religion, sociology, sports and travel. "Our nonfiction book manuscript needs include biography and autobiographies." No humor, juvenile or cookbooks. Query.

Recent Nonfiction Title: *Women's Winning Doubles*, by Blaskower/Williams (sports).

SAYBROOK PUBLISHING CO., 4223 Cole Ave., Dallas TX 75205. (214)521-2375. Managing Editor: Nathan Mitchell. Publishes hardcover and trade paperback originals and reprints. Averages 8 titles/year; receives 700 submissions annually. 25% of books from first-time authors; 50% of books from unagented writers. Average print order for a writer's first book is 5,000. Pays 6-12% royalty on retail price. Publishes book an average of 10 months after acceptance. Photocopied submissions OK. Query for electronic submissions. Computer printout submissions acceptable; prefers letter-quality to dot-matrix. Reports in 3 months.

Nonfiction: Biography and literary human science. Subjects include business and economics, health, nature, philosophy, politics, psychology, sociology, women's studies and environmental studies. "Especially interested in scholarly studies in the human sciences which are also exciting, marketable dramatic literature written for substantial sales in the trade." Submit outline/synopsis and query letter. No sample chapters or mss unless requested.

Recent Nonfiction Title: *The Human Adventure*, by Norman Cousins.

Fiction: "We limit our fiction publishing to 2-3 titles per year. Send query letter *only*; we will ask for ms if interested."

Recent Fiction Title: *No Marble Angels*, by Joanne Leedom-Ackerman.

Tips: "Our books are for the intelligent, curious, general reader. Seek to tell the truth about human beings by any means. The times in which we live demand it. If your submission is important and you can convince us that you are determined to do the very best work you are capable of, we will work with you all the way for as long as it takes."

SCARECROW PRESS, INC., 52 Liberty St., Metuchen NJ 08840. Vice President, Editorial: Norman Horrocks. Senior Editor: Barbara Lee. Publishes hardcover originals. Averages 110 titles/year; receives 600-700 submissions annually. 70% of books from first-time authors; 100% of books from unagented writers. Average print order for a writer's first book is 1,000. Pays 10% royalty on net of first 1,000 copies; 15% of net price thereafter. Offers no advance. Publishes book 10-12 months after receipt of ms. Photocopied submissions OK. Query for electronic submissions. Computer printout submissions acceptable. Reports in 2 weeks. Free book catalog.

Nonfiction: Books about music. Needs reference books and meticulously prepared annotated bibliographies, indexes, women's studies and movies. Query. Occasionally reviews artwork/photos as part of ms package.

‡*SCHENKMAN BOOKS INC., Box 1570, Harvard Square, Cambridge MA 02238. (617)492-4952. Editor-in-Chief: Joseph Schenkman. Publishes hardcover and paperback originals. Specializes in textbooks and professional and technical books. Averages 20 titles/year. Subsidy publishes 3% of books. Royalty varies on net sales, but averages 10%. "In some cases, no royalties are paid on first 2,000 copies sold." No advance. State availability of photos and/or illustrations. Publishes book an average of 1 year after acceptance. Computer printout submissions acceptable. Reports in 1-2 months. Free book catalog.

Nonfiction: Publishes economics, history, psychology, sociology, Third World, women's studies, political science, textbooks and professional and technical books. Reviews artwork/photos as part of ms package. Query.

Recent Nonfiction Title: *One Korea Via Permanent Neutrality*, by In K. Hwang.

SCHIRMER BOOKS, Macmillan Publishing Co., Inc., 866 3rd Ave., New York NY 10022. Senior Editor: Maribeth Anderson Payne. Publishes hardcover and paperback originals, paperback reprints and some software. Averages 20 books/year; receives 250 submissions annually. 40% of books from first-time authors; 95% of books from unagented writers. Average print order for a writer's first book is 3,000-5,000. Pays royalty on wholesale or retail price; offers small advance. Submit photos and/or illustrations "if central to the book, not if decorative or tangential." Publishes book an average of 1 year after acceptance. Electronic submissions OK, requirements "determined on a per project basis"; but requires hard copy also. Computer printout submissions acceptable; prefers letter-quality to dot-matrix. Reports in 2 months. Book catalog and ms guidelines for SASE.
Nonfiction: Publishes college texts, biographies, scholarly, reference and how-to on the performing arts specializing in music, also dance and theatre. Needs texts or scholarly mss for college or scholarly audience. Submit outline/synopsis and sample chapters and current vita. Reviews artwork/photos as part of ms package.
Recent Nonfiction Title: *Soundings: Music in the Twentieth Century*, by Glenn Watkins (scholarly trade).
Tips: "The writer has the best chance of selling our firm a music book with a clearly defined, reachable audience, either scholarly or trade. Must be an exceptionally well-written work of original scholarship prepared by an expert in that particular field who has a thorough understanding of correct manuscript style and attention to detail (see the Chicago *Manual of Style*)."

‡*SCHOCKEN BOOKS, INC., 62 Cooper Square, New York NY 10003. (212)475-4900. President: David L. Rome. Publishes hardcover and trade paperback originals and hardcover and trade paperback reprints. Averages 40 titles/year; receives 300 submissions annually. 5% of books from first-time authors; 5% of books from unagented writers. Subsidy publishes 1% of books; subsidy publishes (nonauthor) 15% of books. Publishes book an average of 18 months after acceptance. Simultaneous and photocopied submissions OK. Computer printout submissions OK; prefers letter-quality. Reports in 6 weeks. Book catalog for 6x9 SAE with 60¢ postage.
Nonfiction: Biography and reference. Subjects include Judaica, Americana, women's studies, health, history, philosophy, politics, psychology, religion and sociology. "We are especially looking for critical analyses on forefront of philosophy, politics, sociology and religion, but not too specialized for the general reader. No fiction, children's books, human interest or personal odysseys." Query or submit outline/synopsis and sample chapters. Reviews artwork/photos as part of ms package.
Recent Nonfiction Title: *Radical Citizenship*, by David Bouchier (political science/current affairs).
Tips: "Our audience is scholars, historians, students, libraries and families interested in current issues and historical themes. Make it relevant, well-written, intelligent and issue-oriented."

*ABNER SCHRAM LTD., 36 Park St., Montclair NJ 07042. (201)744-7755. President: Frances Schram. Executive Editor: Arthur Hamparian. Publishes hardcover and paperback originals. Averages 33 titles/year. Subsidy publishes 3-4% books. Offers 7½-10% royalty; very limited advance. Simultaneous and photocopied submissions OK. Reports in 2 months. Book catalog for 8x10½ SASE.
Nonfiction: "Our main thrust is art and art history." Also interested in the slight outer periphery of art history and wants some idea of photos that could illustrate the book. Query first.
Recent Nonfiction Title: *Bibloclasm*, by Marc Drogin (the mythical origins, magic powers, and perishability of the written word).

CHARLES SCRIBNER'S SONS, Children's Books Department, 866 Third Ave., New York NY 10022. (212)702-7885. Editorial Director, Children's Books: Clare Costello. Publishes hardcover originals, and paperback reprints of own titles. Averages 40 titles/year. Pays royalty on retail price; offers advance. Publishes book an average of 1 year after acceptance. Computer printout submissions acceptable. Free book catalog.
Nonfiction: Subjects include animals, art, biography, health, hobbies, humor, nature, photography, recreation, science and sports. Query. Reviews artwork/photos as part of ms package.
Recent Nonfiction Title: *Digging To The Past*, by John W. Hackwell.
Fiction: Adventure, fantasy, historical, humor, mainstream, mystery, science fiction and suspense. Submit outline/synopsis and sample chapters.
Recent Fiction Title: *The Solitary*, by Lynn Hall.

SECOND CHANCE AT LOVE, 200 Madison Ave., New York NY 10016. (212)686-9820. Subsidiary of Berkley Publishing Group. Editor: Joan Marlow. Publishes mass market paperback original category romances. Averages 24 titles/year; receives 1,200 submissions annually. 10% of books from first-time authors; 15% of books from unagented writers. Pays 2-6% royalty. Photocopied submissions OK. Computer printout submissions acceptable; prefers letter-quality to dot-matrix. Reports in 6 weeks. Ms guidelines for SASE.
Fiction: Contemporary romance. Accepts 3 sample chapters and detailed chapter-by-chapter outline, but prefers complete ms from unpublished writers. Query and request ms guidelines.
Recent Fiction Title: *One From the Heart*, by Cinda Richards.

SECOND CHANCE PRESS/PERMANENT PRESS, Rd. A2, Noyac Rd., Sag Harbor NY 11963. (516)725-1101. Editor: Judith Shepard. Publishes hardcover and trade paperback originals, hardcover trade paperback, and mass market paperback reprints. "Second Chance Press devotes itself exclusively to re-publishing fine books that are out of print and deserve continued recognition." Averages 12 titles/year; receives 700 submissions annually. 25% of books from first-time authors; 75% of books from unagented writers. Average print order for a writer's first book is 2,000. Pays 10% maximum royalty on wholesale price; offers average $200 advance. Publishes book an average of 18 months after acceptance. Simultaneous and photocopied submissions OK. Computer printout submissions acceptable; prefers letter-quality to dot-matrix. Reports in 2 weeks on queries; 3 months on mss. Book catalog for $2 postage.
Nonfiction: Biography and current events. Subjects include Americana, history, philosophy and politics. No scientific and technical material or academic studies. Query.
Recent Nonfiction Title: *Kal Flight 007: The Hidden Story*, by Oliver Clubb.
Fiction: Adventure, confession, ethnic, experimental, fantasy, historical, humor, mainstream, mystery, and suspense. Especially looking for fiction with a unique point of view—"original and arresting." suitable for college literature classes. No mass market romance. Query.
Recent Fiction Title: *The Great Equalizer*, by Rick Borsten.

SELF-COUNSEL PRESS, INC., Subsidiary of International Self-Counsel Press Ltd., 1303 N. Northgate Way, Seattle WA 98133. Senior Editor: Ruth Wilson. Publishes trade paperback originals. Averages 15 new titles/year; receives 100 submissions annually. 50% of books from first-time authors; 99% of books from unagented writers. Pays 10% royalty on wholesale price. Publishes book an average of 10 months after acceptance. Query for electronic submissions. Computer printout submissions acceptable; prefers letter-quality. Reports in 1 month on queries; 2 months on mss. Free book catalog.
Nonfiction: How-to, reference and self-help. Subjects include business and economics and business-oriented psychology. Especially looking for mss on "business trends that can sell in both Canada and US. Avoid psychology lines." Query or submit outline/synopsis and sample chapters. Reviews artwork/photos as part of ms package.
Recent Nonfiction Title: *Arrested! Now What?*, by Stephen Blake.

SERVANT PUBLICATIONS, 840 Airport Blvd., Box 8617, Ann Arbor MI 48107. (313)761-8505. Editor: Ann Spangler. Publishes hardcover, trade and mass market paperback originals and trade paperback reprints. Averages 30 titles/year. 5% of books from first-time authors; 95% of books from unagented writers. Pays 8-10% royalty on retail price. Publishes book an average of 1 year after acceptance. Computer printout submissions acceptable. Reports in 2 months. Free book catalog.
Nonfiction: Subjects include religion. "We're looking for practical Christian teaching, scripture, current problems facing the Christian church, and inspiration." No heterodox or non-Christian approaches. Query or submit brief outline/synopsis and 1 sample chapter. All unsolicited mss are returned unopened. Reviews artwork/photos as part of ms package.
Recent Nonfiction Title: *God In Our Midst*, by J.I. Packer.

*SEVEN LOCKS PRESS, INC., Box 27, Cabin John MD 20818. (301)320-2130. Publisher: Calvin Kytle. Small press. Publishes hardcover and trade paperback originals, and hardcover and trade paperback reprints. Averages 6-9 titles/year; receives 100 submissions annually. 50% of books from first-time authors; 50% of books from unagented writers. Subsidy publishes 30% of books; 20% nonauthor subsidy. Whether an author will be subsidy published depends on the "type of manuscript and cost of production." Pays 10% royalty of gross sales. Simultaneous and photocopied submissions OK. Computer printout submissions acceptable; no dot-matrix. Reports in 1 month on queries; 3 months on mss. Free book catalog.
Nonfiction: Biography, reference and textbook. Subjects include Americana, business and economics, history, international relations, nature, politics, religion and sociology. Especially needs "books that promise to enlighten public policy; also, books of regional interest that are entertaining." Query or submit outline/synopsis and sample chapters. Reviews artwork/photos as part of ms package.
Recent Nonfiction Title: *Main Street America and The Third World*, by Jack M. Hamilton (international affairs).
Tips: "Literate, intelligent, socially conscious men and women are our readers."

SEVEN SEAS PRESS, Subsidiary of Highmark Publishing, Ltd. 2 Dean Ave., Newport RI 02840. (401)847-1683. Editor: James Gilbert. Other divisions include International Marine. Publishes hardcover and paperback originals. Averages 5-12 titles/year; receives 350 submissions annually. 50% of books from first-time authors; 90% of books from unagented writers. Average print order for a writer's first book is 3,000. Pays 8-12½% on gross receipts. Offers average $1,500 advance. Publishes book an average of 14 months after acceptance. Computer printout submissions acceptable; prefers letter-quality to dot-matrix. Reports in 1 month. Book catalog for SASE.

Nonfiction: "Coffee table" book, cookbook, how-to, humor, illustrated book, reference and technical. "All our titles are in the nautical/marine field. We specialize in informative books that help cruising sailors, in particular, enjoy their sport." Also publishes a line of nonfiction nautical high adventure books. Query or submit outline/synopsis and sample chapters. Reviews artwork/photos as part of ms package.

SHAMELESS HUSSY PRESS, Box 3092, Berkeley CA 94703. (415)547-1062. Editor: L. Bosserman. Publishes trade paperback originals and reprints. Averages 1-3 titles/year; receives 1,600 submissions annually. 85% of books from first-time authors; 100% of books from unagented writers. Pays 10% royalty on net profits and 100 copies. Publishes book an average of 3 years after acceptance. Simultaneous and photocopied submissions OK. Computer printout submissions acceptable; prefers letter-quality to dot-matrix. Reports in 6 months. Free book catalog; guidelines for SASE.

Nonfiction: Biography, illustrated book and juvenile. Subjects include Americana, history, psychology and sociology. Needs feminist interviews and biographies. No pornography or anything oppressive to anyone. Submit outline/synopsis and 2 sample chapters. Reviews artwork/photos as part of ms package.

Recent Nonfiction Title: *Home Front: Women and Vietnam*, by B. Byrd (interviews).

Fiction: Adventure, confession, ethnic, experimental, historical, humor and religious. Submit outline/synopsis and 2 sample chapters.

Recent Fiction Title: *Lavinia*, by George Sand (novel).

Poetry: Feminist, mystical, and other. No pornography or oppressive poetry. Submit 5-10 samples.

Recent Poetry Title: *Neither of Us*, by J.O. Simon (poems).

‡SHAPOLSKY BOOKS,(formerly Steimatzky Publications of North America, Inc.), 56 East 11th St., New York NY 10003. (212)505-2505. Editorial Director: Isaac Mozeson. Publishes hardcover and paperback originals, mass market paperback originals, hardcover and trade paperback reprints. 60% originals and 40% reprints. Averages 12 titles/year; receives 300 submissions annually. 60% of books from first-time authors; 40% of books from unagented writers. Subsidy publishes 2% of books. Pays 5-10% royalty on retail price. Offers average $1,000 advance. Publishes ms an average of 15 months after acceptance. Simultaneous and photocopied submissions OK. Query for electronic submissions. Computer printout submissions OK; prefers letter-quality to dot-matrix. Reports on queries in 3 weeks; 5 weeks on ms. Free book catalog.

Nonfiction: Subjects include art, cooking and foods, history, philosophy, photography, politics, religion, sports and travel. "The major thrust of our list is light and lively Judaica. No memoirs." Query or submit outline/synopsis and sample chapters. Reviews artwork/photos as part of ms package.

Recent Nonfiction Title: *The Jewish Celebrity Hall of Fame*, by Tim Boxer (biographies).

Fiction: "Must be by a well established author." Query.

Recent Fiction Title: *Hinkl and Other Shlemiel Stories*, by Miriam Chaikin.

Tips: "Religious and ethnic books enjoy a growing demand. 95% of our titles are for the general Jewish readership. We are presently expanding into general publishing for the mass market."

HAROLD SHAW PUBLISHERS, 388 Gundersen Dr., Box 567, Wheaton IL 60189. (312)665-6700. Director of Editorial Services: Ramona Cramer Tucker. Publishes hardcover and trade paperback originals and reprints. Averages 22 titles/year; receives 2,000 submissions annually. 10% of books from first-time authors; 90% of books from unagented writers. Offers 5-10% royalty on retail price; offers average $250 advance. Sometimes makes outright purchase for $1,000-2,500; "negotiable if big-time author." Publishes book an average of 15 months after acceptance. Photocopied submissions OK. Query for electronic submissions. Computer printout submissions OK; no dot-matrix. Reports in 1 month on queries; 6 weeks on mss. Book catalog and ms guidelines for 9x12 SAE with $1 postage.

Nonfiction: Biography, "coffee table," juvenile (Bible studies only), reference and self-help. Subjects include history (of religious movements/evangelical/charismatic), psychology (self-help) and religion (Bible study guides and general religion). "We are looking for general, nonfiction, with different twists—self help manuscripts on issues and topics with fresh insight and colorful, vibrant writing style. We already have how to forgive yourself, or defend yourself, and how to deal with cancer, death and handicaps. No autobiographies or self help books on authors, fixing mechanical stuff, cookbooks, or aerobics books. Must have an evangelical Christian perspective for us even to review the ms." Query. Reviews artwork/photos as part of ms package.

Recent Nonfiction Title: *Child Sexual Abuse: A Hope for Healing*, by Karen Mains and Maxine Hancock (self-help for adult victims).

Tips: "Get an editor who is not a friend or a spouse who will tell you honestly whether your book is marketable. It will save a lot of your time and money and effort. Then do an honest evaluation of yourself and the book. Most writers who send in mss say this is for everyone. Most books that are written are for no one but the writer. Evaluate who would actually read the book other than yourself—will it do others enough good to sell 5,000 copies?"

SHINING STAR PUBLICATIONS, Subsidiary of Good Apple Inc., Box 1329, Jacksonville OR 97530. (503)899-7121. Editor: Becky Daniel. Averages 18 titles/year; receives 100 submissions annually. 50% of books from first-time authors; 100% of books from unagented writers. Makes outright purchase. No advance. Publishes book an average of 1 year after acceptance. Photocopied submissions OK. Computer printout submissions acceptable. Reports in 1 month. Book catalog for 9x12 SAE and 2 first class stamps to Donna Borst, Shining Star, Box 299, Carthage IL 62321. Ms guidelines for SASE.
Nonfiction: Workbooks on Christian education, grades preschool through 8th. Submit complete ms.
Recent Nonfiction Title: *Celebrate Easter*, by Kelly Riley (Christian education).
Fiction: Religious (Bible-based stories). Submit complete ms.
Tips: "Submissions should be single spaced with art suggestions."

THE SHOE STRING PRESS, 925 Sherman Ave., Box 4327, Hamden CT 06514. (203)248-6307. President: James Thorpe III. Imprints include Archon and Library Professional Publications. Publishes hardcover and trade paperback originals. Publishes 40 titles/year; receives 700 submissions annually. 15% of books from first-time authors; 95% of books from unagented writers. Pays 15% royalty on wholesale price. Publishes book an average of 10 months after acceptance. Photocopied submissions OK. Query for electronic submissions. Computer printout submissions OK. Reports in 2 weeks on queries; 3 months on mss. Book catalog and ms guidelines for SASE.
Nonfiction: Biography, reference, technical, textbook and general. Subjects include Americana, art, business and economics, history, music, nature, philosophy, politics, psychology, religion, travel, literature and military. Will consider "any good scholarly or general nonfiction, reference or professional library literature." No "flying saucers, reincarnation, or inspiration." Submit outline/synopsis and sample chapters. Reviews artwork/photos as part of ms package.
Recent Nonfiction Title: *Kurt Vonnegut, Jr.*, by Pieratt (reference).

‡SHOE TREE PRESS, 405 Front St., Box 356, Belvidere NJ 07823. (201)475-4751. Publisher/Editor: Joyce McDonald. Hardcover and trade paperback originals and reprints. Averages 3-4 titles/year. 25% of books from first-time authors; 25% of books from unagented writers. Pays 10-15% royalty; "sometimes on wholesale price, usually on retail price. Maximum royalty on hardcover only." Advance negotiable. Publishes book an average of 18 months after acceptance. Simultaneous and photocopied submissions OK. Computer printout submissions OK; prefers letter-quality. Reports in 1 month on queries; 3 months on mss. Book catalog and guidelines for #10 SAE and 1 first class stamp.
Nonfiction: Juvenile books on Americana, animals, art, cooking and foods, health, history, hobbies, music, nature, recreation, sports and travel. "Books focusing on the problems of growing up have the best chance of being considered. We are also looking for nature and environmental books. No textbook manuscripts." Query. Reviews artwork/photos as part of ms package. "We currently have two nonfiction titles under contract, but they will not be out until Fall 1989."
Fiction: Juvenile adventure, fantasy, historical, humor, mainstream, mystery and science fiction. "Humorous novels and adventure stories are preferred. Occasionally we publish a picture book or YA. No 'formula' books." Query or submit outline/synopsis and sample chapters.
Recent Fiction Title: *Summer Captive*, by Penny Pollock (young adult).
Tips: "Authors have the best chance of selling us timely nonfiction or humorous novels for 8-11 year-olds."

SIERRA CLUB BOOKS, 730 Polk St., San Francisco CA 94109. (415)776-2211. Editor-in-Chief: Daniel Moses. Publishes hardcover and paperback originals and reprints. Averages 20 titles/year; receives 500 + submissions annually. 50% of books from unagented writers. Pays 7-12½% royalty on retail price. Offers average $3,000-5,000 advance. Publishes book an average of 12-18 months after acceptance. Computer printout submissions acceptable. Reports in 2 months. Free book catalog.
Nonfiction: Animals; health; history (natural); how-to (outdoors); juveniles; nature; philosophy; photography; recreation (outdoors, nonmechanical); science; sports (outdoors); and travel (by foot or bicycle). "The Sierra Club was founded to help people to explore, enjoy and preserve the nation's forests, waters, wildlife and wilderness. The books program looks to publish quality trade books about the outdoors and the protection of natural resources. Specifically, we are interested in nature, environmental issues such as nuclear power, self-sufficiency, natural history, politics and the environment, and juvenile books with an ecological theme." Does *not* want "personal, lyrical, philosophical books on the great outdoors; proposals for large color photographic books without substantial text; how-to books on building things outdoors; books on motorized travel; or any but the most professional studies of animals." Query first, submit outline/synopsis and sample chapters. Reviews artwork/photos ("duplicates, not originals") as part of ms package.
Fiction: Adventure, historical, mainstream and ecological science fiction. "We do very little fiction, but will consider a fiction manuscript if its theme fits our philosophical aims: the enjoyment and protection of the environment." Does *not* want "any manuscript with animals or plants that talk; apocalyptic plots." Query first, submit outline/synopsis and sample chapters, or submit complete ms.

‡**SIGO PRESS**, 77 N. Washington St., Boston MA 02114. (617)523-2321. Publisher: Sisa Sternback. Publishes hardcover and trade paperback originals. Averages 4 titles/year; receives 100 submissions annually. 10% of books from first time authors. 90% of books from unagented writers. Pays variable royalty on retail price; offers variable advance. Publishes book an average of 14 months after acceptance. Simultaneous and photocopied submissions OK. Computer printout submissions OK; prefers letter-quality. Reports in 4 months on queries; 1 month on mss. Free book catalog.
Nonfiction: Self-help and psychology. "We only want to see mss on psychology, specifically Jungian psychology." Query.
Recent Nonfiction Title: *The Grail Legend*, by Emma Jung and M.L. Von Franz.

SILHOUETTE BOOKS, Division of Harlequin Enterprises. 300 E. 42nd St., New York NY 10017. (212)682-6080. Vice President and Editor-in-Chief: Karen Solem. Publishes mass market paperback originals. Averages 312 titles/year; receives 4,000 submissions annually. 10% of books from first-time authors; 25% of books from unagented writers. Pays royalty. Publishes book an average of 1 year after acceptance. Computer printout submissions acceptable; no dot-matrix. No unsolicited mss. Send query letter; 2 page synopsis and SASE to head of imprint. Ms guidelines for SASE.
Imprints: Silhouette Romances (contemporary adult romances), Tara Hughes, Senior Editor; 53,000-58,000 words. Silhouette Special Editions (contemporary adult romances), Leslie Kazanjian, Senior Editor; 75,000-80,000 words. Silhouette Desires (contemporary adult romances), Isabel Swift, Senior Editor and Editorial Coordinator; 55,000-65,000 words. Silhouette Intimate Moments (contemporary adult romances), Leslie Wainger, Senior Editor; 80,000-85,000 words. Crosswinds (contemporary young adult novels), Nancy Jackson, Senior Editor and Editorial Coordinator; 40,000-50,000 words.
Fiction: Romance (contemporary romance for adults and young adults). "We are interested in seeing submissions for all our lines. No manuscripts other than contemporary romances of the type outlined above." Ms should "follow our general format, yet have an individuality and life of its own that will make it stand out in the readers' minds."
Recent Fiction Title: *Carved In Stone*, by Kathleen Engle.
Tips: "The contemporary romance market is constantly changing, so when you read for research, read the latest books and those that have been recommended to you by those knowledgeable in the genre."

‡**SILVER BURDETT PRESS**, Imprint of Simon & Schuster Supplementary Education Unit. 250 James St., Morristown NJ 07960. (201)285-8100. Executive Vice President and Publisher: Dan Wasp. Product Development Editor: Walter Kossmann. Publishes hardcover and trade paperback originals. Averages 65-80 titles/year; receives 500 submissions annually. 5% of books from first-time authors; 80% of books from unagented writers. Pays variable royalty on wholesale price; occasionally makes outright purchase. Publishes book an average of 1 year after acceptance. Offers variable advance. Simultaneous submissions OK. Computer printout submissions OK. Reports in 4 months. Book catalog free on request; ms guidelines for SASE.
Nonfiction: Biography and juvenile. Subjects include Americana, animals, health, history, nature, religion, sports and geography. "We're primarily interested in nonfiction for elementary school students on subjects compatible with classroom curricula—biography, social studies, science, mathematics." Query or submit outline/synopsis and sample chapters. Reviews artwork/photos as part of ms package.
Recent Nonfiction Title: *Hiroshima*, by Martin McPhillips (children's nonfiction).
Fiction: Adventure, ethnic and historical. Needs minimal fiction. Will only consider those titles that may be related to classroom curricula.
Tips: "Our audience is children and juveniles utilizing books as the basis of research or for learning. Our principal markets are libraries and classrooms, with some retail bookstore sales."

SIMON & SCHUSTER, Trade Books Division, 1230 Avenue of the Americas, New York NY 10020. "If we accept a book for publication, business arrangements are worked out with the author or his agent and a contract is drawn up. The specific terms vary according to the type of book and other considerations. Royalty rates are more or less standard among publishers. All unsolicited manuscripts will be returned unread. Only manuscripts submitted by agents or recommended to us by friends or actively solicited by us will be considered. In such cases, our requirements are as follows: All manuscripts submitted for consideration should be marked to the attention of a specific editor. It usually takes at least three weeks for the author to be notified of a decision—often longer. Sufficient postage for return by first-class registered mail, or instructions for return by express collect, in case of rejection, should be included. Manuscripts must be typewritten, double-spaced, on one side of the sheet only. We suggest margins of about one and one half inches all around the standard 8x11 typewriter paper." Computer printout submissions acceptable; prefers letter-quality to dot-matrix.
Nonfiction and Fiction: "Simon and Schuster publishes books of general adult fiction, history, biography, science, philosophy, the arts and popular culture, running 50,000 words or more. Our program does not, however, include school textbooks, extremely technical or highly specialized works, or, as a general rule, poetry or plays. Exceptions have been made for extraordinary manuscripts of great distinction or significance."
Tips: Queries/mss may be routed to other editors in the publishing group.

*GIBBS M SMITH INC., Peregrine Smith Books, Box 667, Layton UT 84041. (801)544-9800. Editorial Director: Madge Baird. Publishes hardcover and paperback originals and reprints. Averages 20-25 titles/year; receives 1,000 + submissions annually. 41% of books from first-time authors; 50% of books from unagented writers. Subsidy publishes 5% (nonauthor) of books. Average print order for a writer's first book is 3,000-5,000. Starts at 10% royalty on wholesale price. Offers average $2,000 advance. Publishes book an average of 1 year after acceptance. Photocopied submissions OK. Reports in 2 months. Book catalog for 6x9 SAE with 56¢ postage.

Nonfiction: "Subjects include western American history, natural history, American architecture, photography, art history and fine arts. "We consider biographical, historical, descriptive and analytical studies in all of the above. Much emphasis is also placed on pictorial content." Query. Consult Chicago *Manual of Style*. Reviews artwork/photos as part of ms package.

Recent Nonfiction Title: *Blessed By Light: Visions of the Colorado Plateau*, edited by Stephen Trimble.

Fiction: "We publish contemporary literary fiction." Looks for "style, readable, intelligent, careful writing, contribution to the social consciousness of our time. Must be geared to a competitive commercial market." Query.

Recent Fiction Title: *Grandmother Club*, by Alan Cheuse (novel).

Tips: "Write seriously. If fiction, no potboilers, and no science fiction. If nonfiction, well-organized, clear ideas; we're open to a wide range of nonfiction subjects. Some authors send in an early draft that they admit isn't in top shape. They should work it over several times before submitting so they don't have to send along an apology for the roughness."

SOS PUBLICATIONS, Division of Bradley Products, Inc., U.S.A. 4223-25 W. Jefferson Blvd., Los Angeles CA 90016. (213)730-1815. Publisher: Paul Bradley. Imprints include Private Library Collection (fiction). Publishes mini-bound originals only. Averages 48 titles/year; receives 800-1,000 submissions annually. 40% of books from first-time authors; 40% of books from unagented writers. Average print order for a writer's first book is 30,000. Pays 6-15% royalty on net selling price. Publishes book an average of 9 months after acceptance. Photocopied submissions OK. Computer printout submissions acceptable; no dot-matrix. SASE which will *enclose* the manuscript *must* accompany submission. Any queries *must* also include SASE. "Due to both the large number of manuscripts we receive and our limited reading staff, we report as soon as possible—but allow approximately 4-5 months." Book catalog for 8½x11 SAE with 39¢ postage.

Fiction: Kathy Clear, fiction editor. Mystery, adventure, romance and suspense. "Our Private Library Collection consists of the Mini-Bound, a hardcover book the size of a mass-market paperback. It showcases original titles, illustrations and new authors. There are four categories: the novel, mystery, romance, and adventure. Don't send any science fiction or westerns *before* the winter of 1989. It is suggested to query first when that time of year arrives." Especially needs mainstream mss. No horror or occult. Send complete ms. Must have minimum 85,000 words.

Recent Fiction Title: *The Secret Past*, by Arnold Harmor (mystery).

Tips: "Well-written romance and mystery does well for us, but we need mainstream. There is no particular style that we *must* have, but our reviewer's list includes *The New York Times*. Study the *New York Times* trends to review. If I were a writer trying to market a book today I would follow guidelines *exactly*. I would *not* call an editor. I would not take a rejection personally."

‡SOUND VIEW PRESS, Subsidiary of P. Hastings Falk, Inc., 36 Webster Point, Madison CT 06443. (203)245-2246. President: Peter Falk. Small press. Publishes hardcover and trade paperback originals. Averages 2-3 titles/year; receives 4-5 submissions annually. Pays royalty or outright purchase. Advance varies. Publishes book an average of 1 year after acceptance. Simultaneous and photocopied submissions OK. Computer printout submissions OK; prefers letter-quality. Reports in 1 week on queries; 2 weeks on mss.

Nonfiction: Reference. Exclusively American art. "We are seeking manuscripts on forgotten American artists from 1860-1940." No mss on contemporary artists. Query or submit complete ms. Reviews artwork/photos as part of ms package.

Recent Nonfiction Title: *Who Was Who in American Art*, by Peter Falk (reference).

*SOUTH END PRESS, 116 St. Botolph, Boston MA 02115. (617)266-0629. Small press. Publishes trade paperback and hardcover originals and trade paperback reprints. Averages 15 nonfiction titles/year; receives 900 submissions annually. 50% of books from first-time authors; 90% of books from unagented writers. Subsidy publishes (nonauthor) 7% of books. Pays 10% royalty on net price. Publishes book an average of 6 months after acceptance. Simultaneous submissions OK. Computer printout submissions acceptable. Reports in 2 months. Free book catalog.

Nonfiction: Subjects include politics, economics, feminism, social change, radical cultural criticism, explorations of race, class, and sex oppression and liberation. No conservative political themes. Submit outline/synopsis and 1-2 sample chapter(s).

SOUTHERN ILLINOIS UNIVERSITY PRESS, Box 3697, Carbondale IL 62901. (618)453-2281. Director: Kenney Withers. Averages 50 titles/year; receives 500 submissions annually. 50% of books from first-time authors; 99% of books from unagented writers. Publishes book an average of 1 year after acceptance. Computer printout submissions acceptable; no dot-matrix. Reports in 6 weeks. Free book catalog.

Nonfiction: "We are interested in scholarly nonfiction on the humanities, social sciences and contemporary affairs. No dissertations or collections of previously published articles." Accepts nonfiction translations from French, German, Scandinavian and Hebrew. Query.

Recent Nonfiction Title: *The Spontaneous Poetics of Jack Kerouac*, by Regina Weinreich (literary criticism).

SPARROW PRESS, Subsidiaries include Sparrow Poverty Pamphlets and Vagrom Chap Books, 103 Waldron St., West Lafayette IN 47906. (317)743-1991. Editor/Publisher: Felix Stefanile. Publishes trade paperback originals. Averages 3 pamphlets and 1-3 chapbooks/year; receives 1,200 submissions annually. 25% of books from first-time authors; 100% of books from unagented writers. Pays $25 advance on royalties, 20% of profits after cost is recovered. No simultaneous submissions. Publishes book an average of 10 months after acceptance. Reports in 1 month on queries; 6 weeks on mss. Book catalog and ms guidelines for SASE. Sample pamphlet $2.

Imprints: Sparrow Poverty Pamphlets (poetry), Felix Stefanile, editor/publisher. Vagrom Chap Books (poetry, by invitation), Felix Stefanile, editor/publisher.

Poetry: "We need the best poetry we can find. We plan at least three volumes a year. We are not interested in seeing any humor, or religious verse. We don't want prose poems. We do not want cut-up prose confessional poems." 28 page typescript only, one poem/page. "If we want to see more, we'll ask." *No* queries answered without SASE. Send complete ms.

Recent Poetry Title: *Boys Who Go Aloft*, by Daniel Bourne (traditional free verse).

Tips: "Our readers are contemporary-minded fellow poets, creative writing students, serious readers and teachers. Poetry is becoming more formal again, more literate. The better poets write out of their hearts, and find their own genuine, if not too large, following. One of our poets has gone through three printings, another two. Recent Sparrow poets have won the Guggenheim, the Carl Sandburg Memorial Award, etc."

‡THE SPEECH BIN, INC., 231 Clarksville Road, Box 218, Princeton Junction NJ 08550-0218. (609)799-3935. Senior Editor: Jan Binney. Publishes trade paperback originals. Publishes 5-10 titles/year. Receives 50-75 manuscripts per year. 50% of books from first-time authors; 90% from unagented writers. Pays negotiable royalty on wholesale price. Publishes ms average of 6 months after acceptance. Photocopied submissions OK. Query for electronic submissions. Computer printout submissions acceptable. Reports in one month on queries, six weeks on manuscripts. Free book catalog.

Nonfiction: How-to, illustrated book, juvenile, reference, textbook, educational material and games. Subjects include health, communication disorders and education for handicapped persons. Query or submit outline synopsis and sample chapters. Reviews artwork/photos as part of ms package.

Recent Nonfiction Title: *Getting Through: Communicating When Someone You Care for Has Alzheimer's Disease*, by Elizabeth Ostuni and Dr. Mary Jo Santo Pietro.

Fiction: Booklets or books "for children and adults about handicapped persons, especially with communication disorders." Query or submit outline/synopsis and sample chapters. "This is a potentially new market for The Speech Bin."

Tips: "Our audience is special educators, speech-language pathologists and audiologists, parents, caregivers, and teachers of children and adults with developmental and post-trauma disabilities. Books and materials must be research-based, clearly presented, well written, competently illustrated, and unique."

SPINSTERS/AUNT LUTE BOOKS, Box 410687, San Francisco CA 94141. (415)558-9655. Editors: Sherry Thomas and Joan Pinkvoss. Publishes trade paperback originals and reprints. Averages 6-8 titles/year; receives 200 submissions annually. 50% of books from first-time authors; 95% of books from unagented writers. Pays 7-12% royalty on retail price. Publishes book an average of 1 year after acceptance. Photocopied submissions OK. Computer printout submissions acceptable; prefers letter-quality to dot-matrix. Reports in 3 weeks on queries; 6 months on mss. Free book catalog; ms guidelines for SASE.

Nonfiction: Self-help and feminist analysis for positive change. Subjects include women's issues. "We are interested in books that not only name the crucial issues in women's lives, but show and encourage change and growth. We do not want to see work by men, or anything that is not specific to women's lives (ie. humor, childrens' books, etc.). We do not want genre fiction (romances, etc.)". Query. Reviews artwork/photos as part of ms package.

Recent Nonfiction Title: *Letters from Nicaragua*, by Rebecca Gordon.

Fiction: Query.

Recent Fiction Title: *Leave A Light On For Me*, by Jean Swallow.

Tips: "Writers have the best chance with feminist fiction and innovative nonfiction that encourages change and growth."

‡SQUARE ONE PUBLISHERS, Box 4385, Madison WI 53711. (608)255-8425. Editorial Director: Lyn Miller-Lachman. Imprints include Stamp Out Sheep Press. Publishes trade paperback and originals. Averages 2 titles/year. Receives 300 submissions annually. 50% of books from first time authors. 100% of books from un-agented authors. Pays 5-6% royalties on retail price. Offers $200 advance. Publishes book an average of 1 year after acceptance. Simultaneous and photocopied submissions OK. Computer printout submissions acceptable; prefers letter-quality to dot-matrix. Book catalog and ms guidelines for SASE.

Fiction: Young adult fiction. "We're looking for contemporary novels with an international focus and novels that deal realistically with teenage lives and problems. No traditional young adult romance or novels that glorify war or reinforce ethnic, race or sex stereotypes; no novels that belittle teens who don't conform or that give pat answers to problems without encouraging teen to think and question. The book has to be unique, with characters who are compelling and memorable because of the challenges they face and the choices they make. Teenagers have to do neat things that are in some way out of the ordinary." Query (phone queries OK), or submit outline/synopsis and sample chapters, or complete ms.

Recent Fiction Title: *Cassandra Robbins, Esq.*, by Pat Costa Viglucci.

Tips: "The writer must think for him/herself rather than follow formulas. Teenagers are by nature rebellious, so there's no law that they will read books that try to shove them into narrow roles and way of behaving. Write for a teenager whose mind you respect. Manuscripts considered for publication are read by teenagers before they are accepted. Manuscripts submitted by teenagers receive special attention and additional comments."

ST PUBLICATIONS, Book Division, 407 Gilbert Ave., Cincinnati OH 45202. (513)421-4050. Book Division Coordinator: Carole Singleton. Publishes hardcover and trade paperback originals and hardcover reprints. Averages 3-5 titles/year; receives 15-20 submissions annually. 50% of books from first-time authors; 100% of books from unagented writers. Pays royalty on wholesale price: 10% until recovery of production costs; 12½% thereafter; and 15% on straight reprints. Publishes book an average of 9 months after acceptance. Photocopied submissions OK. Computer printout submissions acceptable. Reports in 6 weeks on queries; 2 months on mss. Free book catalog and ms guidelines.

Nonfiction: How-to, reference, technical and textbook. Subjects include art (collections of copyright-free artwork suitable for sign, display or screen printing industries). "We need technical how-to books for professionals in three specific industries: the sign industry, including outdoor advertising, electric and commercial signs; the screen printing industry, including the printing of paper products, fabrics, ceramics, glass and electronic circuits; and the visual merchandising and store design industry. We are not interested in submissions that do not relate specifically to those three fields." Submit outline/synopsis and sample chapters. Reviews artwork/photos as part of ms package.

Recent Nonfiction Title: *Control Without Confusion: Troubleshooting Screen Printed Process Color*, by Joe Clarke (4-color screen printing).

Tips: "The writer has the best chance of selling our firm how-to books related to our industries: signs, screen printing, and visual merchandising. These are the fields our marketing and distribution channels are geared to. Request copies of, and thoroughly absorb the information presented in, our trade magazines (*Signs of the Times*, *Visual Merchandising*, and *Screen Printing*). Our books are permanent packages of this type of information."

STACKPOLE BOOKS, Company of Commonwealth Communications Services, Box 1831, Harrisburg PA 17105. Executive Vice President and Editorial Director: Chet Fish. Publishes hardcover and paperback originals. Publishes approximately 30 titles/year. "Proposals should begin as a one-page letter, leading to chapter outline only on request. If author is unknown to Stackpole, supply credentials." Publishes book an average of 9 months after acceptance. Computer printout submissions acceptable; prefers letter-quality to dot-matrix. Ms guidelines for SASE.

Nonfiction: Outdoor-related subject areas—fishing, hunting, firearms, wildlife, adventure, outdoor skills, military guides, decoy carving/woodcarving, and space exploration. Reviews artwork/photos as part of ms package.

Recent Nonfiction Title: *Reflections on the Wall: The Vietnam Veteran Memorial*, by Smithsonian Institution (short essays and commentary).

STANDARD PUBLISHING, A division of Standex International Corp., 8121 Hamilton Ave., Cincinnati OH 45231. (513)931-4050. Publisher/Vice President: Eugene H. Wigginton. Publishes hardcover and paperback originals and reprints. Specializes in religious books. Averages 125 titles/year; receives 1,500 submissions annually. 25% of books from first-time authors; 90% of books from unagented writers. Average print order for a writer's first book is 7,500. Pays 10% royalty on wholesale price "for substantial books. Lump sum for smaller books." Offers $200-1,500 advance. Publishes book an average of 1 year after acceptance. Query for electronic submissions. Computer printout submissions acceptable; no dot-matrix. Reports in 2-3 months. Ms guidelines for SASE.

Nonfiction: Publishes how-to; crafts (to be used in Christian education); juveniles; reference; Christian education; quiz; puzzle and religious books; and college textbooks (religious). All mss must pertain to religion. Query or submit outline/synopsis and 2-3 sample chapters. Reviews artwork/photos as part of ms package.

Recent Nonfiction Title: *Strengthening the Family*, by Wayne Rickerson.

Fiction: Religious, devotional books.

Recent Fiction Title: *Another Jennifer*, by Jane Sorenson.

Tips: "Children's books, Christian education, activity books, and helps for Christian parents and church leaders are the types of books writers have the best chance of selling to our firm."

*STANFORD UNIVERSITY PRESS, Imprint of Stanford University, Stanford CA 94305. (415)723-9434. Editor: William W. Carver. Averages 65 titles/year; receives 900 submissions annually. 40% of books from first-time authors, 95% of books from unagented writers. Subsidy publishes (nonauthor) 65% of books. Pays up to 15% royalty ("typically 10%, often none"); sometimes offers advance. Publishes book an average of 13 ("typically a year") months after acceptance. Photocopied submissions OK. Electronic submissions by agreement only; requires hard copy also. Computer printout submissions acceptable; no dot-matrix. Reports in 3 weeks on queries; 5 weeks on mss. Free book catalog.

Nonfiction: Scholarly books in the humanities, social sciences, and natural sciences: European history; history and culture of China, Japan, and Latin America; biology, natural history and taxonomy; anthropology, linguistics, and psychology; literature, criticism, and literary theory; political science and sociology; archaeology and geology; and classical studies. Also high-level textbooks and books for a more general audience. Query. "We like to see a prospectus and an outline." Reviews artwork/photos as part of ms package.

Recent Nonfiction Title: *The Butterflies of North America*, by James A. Scott.

Tips: "We are interested in seeing syntheses, upper division texts, handbooks, and general interest. The writer's best chance is a work of original scholarship with an argument of some importance and an appeal to a broad audience."

‡STARBLAZE, Imprint of The Donning Company/Publishers, 5659 Virginia Beach Blvd., Norfolk VA 23502. (804)461-8090. Editor: Mary Gray. Publishes trade paperback originals. Averages 20-25 titles/year; receives 100-150 submissions annually. 5% of books from first-time authors. 80% of books from unagented writers. Pays 8-15% royalty on retail price; offers $2,500-7,500 average advance. Photocopied submissions OK. Computer printout submissions OK; no dot-matrix. Reports in 2 months on queries; 6 months on mss. Free book catalog; writer's guidelines for SASE.

Fiction: Fantasy, horror and science fiction. "We are seeking good, strong novels in SF & F field with interesting characters and high entertainment value—original work, not rehashes." No post-apocalypse novels, near future thrillers, WW III novels, historical or romance fiction with fantasy "dressing," cut and slash horror or "generic quest" fantasies. Query. Reviews artwork/photos as part of graphic novel mss.

Recent Fiction Title: *M.Y.T.H. Inc. Link* by Robert L. Asprin.

Tips: "Our audience is young to middle-age adults, well-educated, knowledgable about SF and fantasy and avid readers. Graphic and illustrated novels are really taking off. Comics are in a period of growth, artistically, and graphic novels appeal to the more mature reader as well as readers who have 'grown away' from comics. Know the market and try to submit something appropriate but original—not just more of the same."

STEIN AND DAY PUBLISHERS, Scarborough House, Briarcliff Manor NY 10510. Averages 60 titles/year. Offers standard royalty contract.

Nonfiction & Fiction: Publishes general adult fiction and nonfiction books; no juvenile or college. All types of nonfiction except technical. Quality fiction. No unsolicited mss without querying first. Nonfiction, send outline or summary and sample chapter. *Must* furnish SASE with all fiction and nonfiction queries. Minimum length: 65,000 words.

Recent Nonfiction Title: *Reducing the Risk of Alzheimer's*, by Dr. Michael A. Weiner.

Recent Fiction Title: *Black Money*, by George H. Rosen.

STERLING PUBLISHING, 2 Park Ave., New York NY 10016. (212)532-7160. Acquisitions Manager: Sheila Anne Barry. Publishes hardcover and paperback originals and reprints. Averages 80 titles/year. Pays royalty; offers advance. Publishes book an average of 8 months after acceptance. Computer printout submissions acceptable; prefers letter-quality to dot-matrix. Reports in 6 weeks. Guidelines for SASE.

Nonfiction: Alternative lifestyle, fiber arts, games and puzzles, health how-to, business, foods, hobbies, how-to, children's humor, occult, pets, photography, recreation, reference, self-help, sports, theatre (how-to), technical, collecting, wine and woodworking. Query or submit complete chapter list, detailed outline/synopsis and 2 sample chapters with photos if necessary. Reviews artwork/photos as part of ms package.

Recent Nonfiction Title: *Windows on the World Complete Wine Course*, by Kevin Zraly.

‡STEWART, TABORI AND CHANG, 740 Broadway, New York NY 10003. (212)460-5000. Editor-in-chief: Leslie Stoker. Publishes hardcover and trade paperback originals. Averages 15 titles/year. Receives 100 submissions annually. 30-40% of books from first-time authors. 30% from unagented authors. Royalty paid on wholesale price. Average advance is 6-10% of receipts. Publishes book average of 1 year after acceptance. Simultaneous and photocopied submissions OK. Makes some work-for-hire assignments. Computer printout submissions OK; prefers letter-quality to dot-matrix. Reports on queries in 2 weeks; on submissions in 2 months. Free book catalog.

Nonfiction: "Coffee-table" book, cookbook, illustrated book. Subjects include Americana, art, cooking and foods, nature, photography, travel, popular science, design and decorating. Do not submit non-illustrated mss. Submit outline/synopsis and sample chapters or complete ms. Reviews artwork/photos as part of package.
Recent Nonfiction Title: *Visions of Paradise*, by Marina Schinz (photo essay on gardens).

‡**STILL POINT PRESS**, Imprint of Whaley Enterprises, Inc., 4222 Willow Grove Rd., Dallas TX 75220. (214)352-8282. Editor/Publisher: Charlotte T. Whaley. Publishes hardcover originals. Averages 3-4 titles/year; receives 25 submissions annually. 1% of books from first-time authors. 100% of books from unagented writers. Pays 10-15% royalty on retail price. Advance negotiable. Publishes book an average of 9 months after acceptance. Simultaneous and photocopied submissions OK. Computer printout submissions OK; prefers letter-quality. Reports in 1 month. Free book catalog.
Nonfiction: Biography and fine limited editions. Subjects include Americana, cooking and foods, and history. "We are interested in manuscripts in virtually all areas of the humanities, particularly history and biography. No textbooks, how-to books, business or economics." Query or submit outline/synopsis and sample chapters. Reviews artwork/photos as part of ms package.
Recent Nonfiction Title: *Remembering Carl Hertzog*, by Al Lowman (limited edition).
Fiction: Ethnic, historical, mainstream and short story collections. "We are interested in good collections of short stories and other well-written fiction manuscripts. No horror, erotica or confession." Query.
Recent Fiction Title: *Prize Stories: Texas Institute of Letters*, by Marshal Terry, ed.
Tips: "The author should be open to suggestions from the editors/publishers regarding editorial changes or additions, reorganization of content, and title of the work."

STILLPOINT PUBLISHING, INC., Subsidiary of Dutton/New American Library, Box 640 Meetinghouse Rd., Walpole NH 03608. (603)756-3508. Imprints include Angelfood (juvenile fiction). Editorial Assistant: Jean Etter. Small press. Publishes hardcover originals and trade paperback originals and reprints. Averages 10-15 titles/year; receives 750 submissions annually. 60% of books from first-time authors; 15% of books from unagented writers. Pays 7.5-15% royalty on retail price. No advances. Publishes book an average of 1 year after acceptance. Photocopied submissions OK. Query for electronic submissions. Reports in 2 weeks on queries; 2 months on mss. Call (800)847-4014 for free book catalog.
Nonfiction: Self-help, health and healing, personal/spiritual development. Subjects include health, philosophy, psychology, religion, and channeled material. "We are looking for quality mss dealing with spirituality, life transformation, and personal development, whether the transformation is through sports, meditation, or a near-death experience or being in contact with higher dimensions of being." No submissions that do not deal with spirituality or personal development. Also interested in acquisitions and out of print titles. Submit complete ms.
Recent Nonfiction Title: *Seth Dreams and Projection of Consciousness*, by Jane Roberts (spirituality).
Fiction: Non-secular religion, dealing with what mankind might become. "We are looking for quality mss that show mankind's evolving spirituality, or aspects of personal or planetary growth." Submit complete ms.
Tips: "If I were a writer trying to market a book today, I would try to match my book to the proper publisher. We have a very specific market and appreciate hearing from authors who write books concerning how mankind is changing spiritually and what we might be heading toward. We've noticed a trend to trade paperbacks. We do well with channeled material—information that comes through from the non-physical realm. Books of the caliber of Jane Roberts and *Agartha* by Meredith Young are coming to us to be published. Our audience is interested in the spiritual quality of their lives, and the integration of mind, body and spirit."

STIPES PUBLISHING CO., 10-12 Chester St., Champaign IL 61820. (217)356-8391. Contact: Robert Watts. Publishes hardcover and paperback originals. Averages 15-30 titles/year; receives 150 submissions annually. 50% of books from first-time authors; 100% of books from unagented writers. Pays 15% maximum royalty on retail price. Publishes book an average of 4 months after acceptance. Computer printout submissions acceptable; prefers letter-quality to dot-matrix. Reports in 2 weeks on queries; 2 months on mss.
Nonfiction: Technical (some areas), textbooks on business and economics, music, chemistry, agriculture/horticulture, and recreation and physical education. "All of our books in the trade area are books that also have a college text market." No "books unrelated to educational fields taught at the college level." Submit outline/synopsis and 1 sample chapter.
Recent Nonfiction Title: *Creative Piano Teaching*, by James Lyke and Evonne Enoch (piano pedagogy).

STOEGER PUBLISHING COMPANY, 55 Ruta Court, S. Hackensack NJ 07606. (201)440-2700. Subsidiary includes Stoeger Industries. Publisher: Robert E. Weise. Publishes trade paperback originals. Averages 12-15 titles/year. Royalty varies, depending on ms. Simultaneous and photocopied submissions OK. Reports in 1 month on queries; 3 months on mss. Book catalog for SASE.
Nonfiction: Cookbook, how-to and self-help. Subjects include sports, outdoor sports, cooking and foods, and hobbies. Especially looking for how-to books relating to hunting, fishing, or other outdoor sports. Submit outline/synopsis and sample chapters.
Recent Nonfiction Title: *Shooters Bible*, William S. Jarrett, editor.

STONE WALL PRESS, INC., 1241 30th St., NW, Washington DC 20007. President/Publisher: Henry Wheelwright. Small press. Publishes hardcover and trade paperback originals. Averages 2-3 titles/year; receives 50 submissions annually. 75% of books from first-time authors; 95% of books from unagented writers. Average print order for a writer's first book is 3,000-4,000. Pays standard royalty; offers minimal advance. Publishes book an average of 6 months after acceptance. Computer printout submissions acceptable; no dot-matrix. Reports in 2 weeks. Book catalog for business size SAE and 1 first class stamp.

Nonfiction: How-to and environmental/outdoor. "Unique, practical, illustrated how-to outdoor books (nature, camping, fishing, hiking, hunting, etc.) and environmental books for the general public." Query. Looks for "concise, sharp writing style with humorous touches; a rough table of contents for an idea of the direction of the book, a new approach or topic which hasn't been done recently." Accepts outline/synopsis and several sample chapters. Reviews artwork/photos as part of ms package.

Recent Nonfiction Title: *Stalking Trout*, by Hill and Marshall.

STONEYDALE PRESS PUBLISHING CO., 205 Main St., Stevensville MT 59870. (406)777-2729. Publisher: Dale A. Burk. Publishes hardcover and trade paperback originals. Averages 4-6 titles/year; receives 75-100 submissions annually. 20% of books from first-time authors; 100% of books from unagented writers. Pays 10-12% royalty on actual price or makes outright purchase. Publishes book an average of 14 months after acceptance. Query for electronic submissions. Computer printout submissions acceptable. Reports in 1 month. Book catalog for SAE and $1 postage.

Nonfiction: Outdoor recreation, nature, and wildlife with emphasis on hunting and fishing. Good photo illustrations required. "We're looking for good outdoor recreation book ideas for our area, which encompasses the Rocky Mountains and the Pacific Northwest. We are open to ideas if we can be convinced that a market exists for the specific book." Query. Artwork/photos reviewed as part of ms package.

Recent Nonfiction Title: *Bowhunting for Mule Deer*, by Dwight Schuh.

*LYLE STUART, INC., 120 Enterprise Ave., Secaucus NJ 07094. (201)866-0490. (212)736-1141. Subsidiaries include Citadel Press and University Books. President: Lyle Stuart. Publisher: Carole Stuart. Editor-in-Chief: Mario Satori. Publishes hardcover and trade paperback originals, and trade paperback reprints. Averages 80 titles/year; receives 700-1,000 submissions annually. 60% of books from first-time authors; 60% of books from unagented writers. Subsidy publishes 5% of books. Pays 10-12% royalty on retail price; offers "low advance." Publishes book an average of 10 months after acceptance.

Nonfiction: Biography, "coffee table" book, how-to, humor, illustrated book and self-help. Subjects include Americana, art, business and economics, health, history, music and politics. "The percentage of acceptable over-the-transom manuscripts has been so low during the years that we rarely read unsolicited material." Reviews artwork/photos as part of ms package.

Recent Nonfiction Title: *On the Run*, by Philip Agee.

Recent Fiction Title: *The Rain Maiden*.

Tips: "The writer has the best chance of selling a book that is controversial—and professionally written."

STUDIO PRESS, Box 1268, Twain Harte CA 95383. (209)533-4222. Publisher: Paul Castle. Publishes hardcover and paperback originals. Averages 3-5 titles/year; receives 10-15 submissions annually. 100% of books from first-time authors; 100% of books from unagented writers. Average print order for a writer's first book is 2,000-3,000. Pays 15% royalty on wholesale or retail price; no advance. Publishes book an average of 3-6 months after acceptance. Simultaneous and photocopied submissions OK. Computer printout submissions acceptable; prefers letter-quality to dot-matrix. Reports in 1 month. Ms guidelines for #10 SASE.

Nonfiction: Photography. "We are always interested in good manuscripts on technique and the business of photography. We especially want manuscripts on *marketing* one's photography. We don't want manuscripts on art criticism of photography, collections of art photos, basic photo teaching books, or anything other than books on the technique and/or business of photography. Query; if the idea is good, we'll ask for outline and sample chapters." Reviews artwork/photos as part of ms package. "Artwork/photos are essential to acceptance."

Recent Nonfiction Title: *Successful Business Practices for Studio Photographers*, by Charles "Bud" Haynes.

Tips: "We need more anecdotes and word illustrations to amplify the writer's points. We particularly look for skilled photographers who are doing something very well and can communicate their expertise to others. We are willing to work with such individuals on extensive re-write and editing, if what they have to say is valuable."

SUCCESS PUBLISHING, 2812 Bayonne Dr., Palm Beach Gardens FL 33410. (305)626-4643. President: Allan H. Smith. Publishes trade paperback originals. Averages 6 titles/year; receives 50 submissions annually. 50% of books from first-time authors; 65% of books from unagented writers. Pays variable royalty on wholesale price (10% minimum) or makes minimum outright purchase of $1,000. Publishes book an average of 4 months after acceptance. Simultaneous submissions OK. Computer printout submissions acceptable; prefers letter-quality to dot-matrix. Reports in 1 month on queries; 6 weeks on mss. Book catalog and writer's guidelines for SAE and 1 first class stamp.

Nonfiction: How-to, juvenile, self-help and craft. Subjects include business and economics and hobbies. Especially looking for mss interesting to home-based business people; middle school and high school children, and those interested in sewing and crafts. No poetry, cult, religious or technical books. Query and/or submit outline/synopsis and sample chapters.

Recent Nonfiction Title: *Business for Profits*, by Allan Smith (business).

SHERWOOD SUGDEN & COMPANY, PUBLISHERS, 315 Fifth St., Peru IL 61354. (815)223-1231. Publisher: Sherwood Sugden. Publishes hardcover and trade paperback originals and reprints. Averages 6 titles/year. Pays 4-12% royalty. Simultaneous and photocopied submissions OK. Computer printout submissions acceptable. Reports in 3 weeks on queries; 3 months on mss. Book catalog for business size SAE.

Nonfiction: Subjects include history, philosophy, politics, religion (Christian, especially Roman Catholic), and literary criticism. "We're looking for lucid presentations and defenses of orthodox Roman Catholic doctrine, Church history and lives of the Saints aimed at the average intelligent reader. (Possibly one or two scholarly works of the same sort as well.) Works of criticism of British or American authors; perhaps a biography or two; also a work in elementary syllogistic logic. The audience for our books ranges from the bright high school student with a curiosity about ideas through the mature general reader. Certain of our titles (perhaps 30% of our annual output) will appeal chiefly to the advanced student or scholar in the relevant disciplines." Submit outline/synopsis and 1 sample chapter. "We prefer a four or more paragraph synopsis to a skeletal listing of chapter titles, which some authors take to be the meaning of outline."

Recent Nonfiction Title: *Cosmos & Transcendence: Breaking Through the Barriers of Scientistic Belief*, by Wolfgang Smith.

‡*SUNFLOWER UNIVERSITY PRESS, formerly MA/AH Publishing, Subsidiary of Journal of the West, Inc., 1531 Yuma, Box 1009, Manhattan KS 66502-4228. (913)532-6733. Associate Publisher: Carol A. Williams. Imprints include MA/AH Publishing and Wheatland Books. Publishes trade paperback originals and trade paperback reprints. Averages 3-6 titles/year; receives 25+ submissions annually. 90% of books from first-time authors; 100% of books from unagented writers. Subsidy publishes 20% of books. Pays 10% royalty on retail price. Publishes book an average of 9 months after acceptance. Computer printout submissions acceptable on approval; prefers letter-quality. Reports in 1 week on queries; 1 month on ms. Book catalog and guidelines for 6x9 SASE.

Nonfiction: Biography, reference and textbook. Subjects include Americana (Western American history); and history (military, naval, American aviation). Prefers manuscripts on military subjects: memoirs, studies of battle action, and technological advances. No undocumented studies. Query or submit outline/synopsis and sample chapters or complete ms.

Recent Nonfiction Title: *The Rise of the Wheat State: A History of Kansas Agriculture 1861-1986*, George Ham and Robin Higham, editors.

Tips: "Our audience includes scholars and history buffs."

THE SUNSTONE PRESS, Box 2321, Santa Fe NM 87504-2321. (505)988-4418. Editor-in-Chief: James C. Smith Jr. Publishes paperback originals; few hardcover originals. Averages 16 titles/year; receives 400 submissions annually. 70% of books from first-time authors; 100% of books from unagented writers. Average print order for writer's first book is 2,000-5,000. Pays royalty on wholesale price. Publishes book an average of 1 year after acceptance. Computer printout submissions acceptable; prefers letter-quality to dot-matrix. Reports in 2 months.

Nonfiction: How-to series craft books. Books on the history and architecture of the Southwest. Looks for "strong regional appeal (Southwestern)." Reviews artwork/photos as part of ms package.

Recent Nonfiction Title: *The Dilemma of Wilderness*, by Carry McDonald.

Fiction: Publishes "material with Southwestern theme."

Recent Nonfiction Title: *The Land*, by Robert K. Swisher, Jr.

Poetry: Traditional or free verse. Poetry book not exceeding 64 pages. Prefers Southwestern theme.

Recent Poetry Title: *Thin Ice*, by Marcia Muth.

SYBEX, INC., 2021 Challenger Dr., Alameda CA 94501. (415)848-8233. Editor-in-Chief: Dr. Rudolph S. Langer. Acquisitions Editor: Chuck Ackerman. Publishes paperback originals. Offers averages 60 titles/year. Royalty rates vary. Offers average $2,500 advance. Publishes book an average of 3 months after acceptance. Simultaneous and photocopied submissions OK. "We prefer hard copy for proposal evaluations and encourage our authors to submit WordStar diskettes upon completion of their manuscripts. WordStar word processor diskettes preferred." Computer printout submissions acceptable. Reports in 2 months. Free book catalog.

Nonfiction: Computer and electronics. "Manuscripts most publishable in the field of personal computers, personal computer applications, microprocessors, hardware, programming, languages, applications, and telecommunications." Submit outline/synopsis and 2-3 sample chapters. Accepts nonfiction translations from

French or German. Looks for "clear writing; technical accuracy; logical presentation of material; and good selection of material, such that the most important aspects of the subject matter are thoroughly covered; well-focused subject matter; and well-thought-out organization that helps the reader understand the material. And marketability." Reviews artwork/photos as part of ms package.

Recent Nonfiction Title: *Mastering Symphony.*

Tips: Queries/mss may be routed to other editors in the publishing group.

*SYMMES SYSTEMS, Box 8101, Atlanta GA 30306. Editor-in-Chief: E. C. Symmes. Publishes hardcover and paperback originals. 50% of books from first-time authors; 100% of books from unagented writers. Pays 10% royalty on wholesale price. "Contracts are usually written for the individual title and may have different terms." No advance. Subsidy publishes 40% of books. Publishes book an average of 14 months after acceptance. Will consider photocopied and simultaneous submissions. Computer printout submissions acceptable; no dot-matrix. Acknowledges receipt of submission in 10 days; evaluates within 1 month.

Nonfiction: Nature. "Our books have mostly been in the art of bonsai (miniature trees). We are publishing quality information for laypersons (hobbyists). Most of the titles introduce information that is totally new for the hobbyist." Text must be topical, showing state-of-the-art. All books so far have been illustrated with photos and/or drawings. Would like to see more material on self-help business subjects; also photography and collecting photographica. Length: open. Query. Reviews artwork/photos as part of ms package.

Recent Nonfiction Title: *The Physician's Guide to Nutritional Therapy*, by Anderson.

*SYRACUSE UNIVERSITY PRESS, 1600 Jamesville Ave., Syracuse NY 13244-5160. (315)423-2596. Director: Luther Wilson. Averages 25-30 titles/year; receives 350 submissions annually. 40% of books from first-time authors; 95% of books from unagented writers. Subsidy publishes (nonauthor) 20% of books. Pays royalty on net sales. Publishes book an average of 10 months after acceptance. Simultaneous and photocopied submissions OK "if we are informed." Computer printout submissions acceptable. Reports in 2 weeks on queries; "longer on submissions." Book catalog and ms guidelines for SASE.

Nonfiction: "The best opportunities in our nonfiction program for freelance writers are books on New York state. We have published regional books by people with limited formal education, but authors were thoroughly acquainted with their subjects, and they wrote simply and directly about them. Provide precise descriptions about subjects, along with background description of project. The author must make a case for the importance of his or her subject." Query. Accepts outline/synopsis and at least 2 sample chapters. Reviews artwork/photos as part of ms package.

Recent Nonfiction Title: *The Man Who Tried to Burn New York*, by Nat Brandt (history/Civil War).

TAB BOOKS, INC., Blue Ridge Summit PA 17214. (717)794-2191. Vice President: Ray Collins. Publishes hardcover and paperback originals and reprints. Publishes 200 titles/year; receives 400 submissions annually. 50% of books from first-time authors; 85% of books from unagented writers. Average print order for writer's first book is 10,000. Pays variable royalty; buys some mss outright for a negotiable fee. Offers advance. Photocopied submissions OK (except for art). Query for electronic submissions. Computer printout submissions acceptable; prefers letter-quality to dot-matrix. Reports in 6 weeks. Free book catalog and ms guidelines.

Nonfiction: TAB publishes titles in such fields as computer hardware, computer software, business, solar and alternate energy, marine line, aviation, automotive, music technology, consumer medicine, electronics, electrical and electronics repair, amateur radio, shortwave listening, model railroading, toys, hobbies, drawing, animals and animal power, woodworking, practical skills with projects, building furniture, basic how-to for the house, building large structures, calculators, robotics, telephones, model radio control, TV servicing, audio, recording, hi-fi and stereo, electronic music, electric motors, electrical wiring, electronic test equipment, video programming, CATV, MATV and CCTV, broadcasting, photography and film, appliance servicing and repair, advertising, antiques and restoration, bicycles, crafts, farmsteading, hobby electronics, home construction, license study guides, mathematics, metalworking, reference books, schematics and manuals, small gasoline engines, two-way radio and CB, military fiction, and woodworking. Accepts nonfiction translations. Query with outline/synopsis. Reviews artwork/photos as part of ms package.

Tips: "Many writers believe that a cover letter alone will describe their proposed book sufficiently; it rarely does. The more details we receive, the better the chances are that the writer will get published by us. We expect a writer to tell us what the book is about, but many writers actually fail to do just that."

TAPLINGER PUBLISHING CO., INC., 132 W. 22nd, New York NY 10011. (212)741-0801. Editors: Ms. Bobs Pinkerton and Roy E. Thomas. Publishes hardcover originals. Publishes 75 titles/year. 2% of books from first-time authors; 1% of books from unagented writers. Average print order for a writer's first book is 3,000-5,000. Pays standard royalty; offers variable advance. Publishes book an average of 1 year after acceptance. Simultaneous and photocopied submissions OK. Computer printout submissions acceptable; no dot-matrix. Reports in 10 weeks.

Imprints: Crescendo (music).

Nonfiction: Art, biography, calligraphy, history, theatre and belles-lettres. No juveniles. Query.

Fiction: Serious contemporary quality fiction. Accepts fiction translations. No juveniles.

‡**JEREMY P. TARCHER, INC.**, Suite 250, 9110 Sunset Blvd., Los Angeles CA 90069. (213)273-3274. Editor-in-chief: Jeremy P. Tarcher. Assistant Editor: Laurie S. Held. Publishes hardcover and trade paperback originals and hardcover and trade paperback reprints. Averages 30 titles/year; receives 2,000 submissions annually. 50% of books from first-time authors; 15% of books from unagented writers. Pays royalty with variable advance. Publishes book an average of 1 year after acceptance. Simultaneous and photocopied submissions OK. Computer printout submissions OK; no dot-matrix. Reports in 3 weeks on queries; 6 weeks on mss. Book catalog and guidelines for SASE.
Nonfiction: Cookbook, how-to and self-help. Subjects include business and economics, cooking and foods, health, nature, politics, psychology, recreation, sociology and sports. "We're looking for practical, self-help titles on a variety of health and psychology-related subjects. We continue to be interested in books on consciousness and creativity, science for the layperson, adult relationships, parenting, etc. No humor books, art books, children's books, Hollywood exposes, astrology books, textbooks, puzzle or game books." Submit outline/synopsis and sample chapters.
Recent Nonfiction Title: *Drawing on the Right Side of the Brain*, by Betty Edwards, Ph.D.
Tips: "It's important to us that the author has authority in his or her field and that this is conveyed in the proposal. Authors should pay particular attention to what makes their book different and exciting, and to why they're the ideal author for the book. One of the most important ingredients in a proposal, as far as we're concerned, is the market survey which lists competing books (refer to *Books in Print*) and describes the potential audience. This survey lets us know that the author has a clear picture of his or her audience and can deliver a saleable book. We're opening up new areas such as lyrical science and nature writing, and more commercial books."

TAYLOR PUBLISHING COMPANY, Subsidiary of Insilco, 1550 W. Mockingbird Ln., Dallas TX 75235. (214)637-2800. Editorial Assistant—Trade Books Division. Publishes hardcover and softcover originals. Averages 24 titles/year; receives 1,000 submissions annually. 25% of books from first-time authors; 10% of books from unagented writers. Buys some mss outright. Publishes book 1 year after acceptance. Simultaneous and photocopied submissions OK. Computer printout submissions acceptable. Reports in 6 weeks on queries and unsolicited mss. Book catalog and ms guidelines for 7x9 SASE.
Nonfiction: Biography, true crime, true adventure, "coffee table" book, cookbook, sports, natural history, politics, gardening, and Americana. Submit outline/synopsis and sample chapters. Reviews artwork/photos as part of ms package.
Recent Nonfiction Title: *Careless Whispers*, by Carlton Stowers.

****TEACHERS COLLEGE PRESS**, 1234 Amsterdam Ave., New York NY 10027. (212)678-3929. Director: Carole P. Saltz. Publishes hardcover and paperback originals and reprints. Averages 50 titles/year. Subsidy publishes (nonauthor) 26% of books. Pays royalty. Publishes book an average of 1 year after acceptance. Reports in 1 year. Free book catalog.
Nonfiction: "This university press concentrates on books in the field of education in the broadest sense, from early childhood to higher education: good classroom practices, teacher training, special education, innovative trends and issues, administration and supervision, film, continuing and adult education, all areas of the curriculum, comparative education, computers, guidance and counseling and the politics, economics, nursing, philosophy, sociology and history of education. The press also issues classroom materials for students at all levels, with a strong emphasis on reading and writing." Submit outline/synopsis and sample chapters.
Recent Nonfiction Title: *Children's Mathematical Thinking*, by Arthur J. Baroody.

TEN SPEED PRESS, Box 7123, Berkeley CA 94707. Imprints include Celestial Arts. Publisher: P. Wood. Editors: G. Young and J. Wan. Publishes trade paperback originals and reprints. Averages 40 titles/year; receives 12,000 submissions annually. 50% of books from first-time authors; 90% of books from unagented writers. Average print order for a writer's first book is 5,000-10,000. Offers standard royalties. Offers advance. Publishes book an average of 10 months after acceptance. Computer printout submissions acceptable; prefers letter-quality to dot-matrix. Reports in 1 month. Book catalog and ms guidelines for 9x12 SAE with $1.92 postage.
Nonfiction: Americana, gardening, careers, cookbooks, business, cooking and foods, life guidance, history, humor, nature, self-help, how-to, hobbies, recreation and travel. Subjects range from bicycle books to business. "We will consider any first-rate nonfiction material that we feel will have a long shelf life and be a credit to our list." No set requirements. Submit outline and sample chapters. Reviews artwork/photos as part of ms package.
Recent Nonfiction Title: *Kill as Few Patients as Possible*, by Oscar London, M.D. (essays).
Tips: "Do not send duplicate submissions to our subsidiary, Celestial Arts."

‡***TEXAS A&M UNIVERSITY PRESS**, Drawer C, College Station TX 77843. (409)845-1436. Director: Lloyd G. Lyman. Publishes 30 titles/year. Subsidy publishes 3% of books; subsidy publishes (nonauthor) 15% of books. Pays in royalties. Publishes book an average of 1 year after acceptance. Query for electronic submis-

sions. Computer printout submissions acceptable; prefers letter-quality to dot-matrix. Reports in 1 week on queries; 1 month on submissions. Free book catalog.

Nonfiction: History, natural history, environmental history, economics, agriculture and regional studies (including fiction). Receives artwork/photos as part of ms package. "We do not want poetry." Query. Accepts outline/synopsis and 2-3 sample chapters. "We prefer an introductory statement, table of contents, and sample chapter, which may be a combination of a synopsis and an outline." Reviews artwork/photos as part of ms package.

Recent Nonfiction Title: *East of Chosin*, by R.E. Appleman (history).

Recent Fiction Title: *Thank You, Queen Isabella*, by John Works (novel).

*TEXAS CHRISTIAN UNIVERSITY PRESS, Box 30783, TCU, Fort Worth TX 76129. (817)921-7822. Editor: Judy Alter. Publishes hardcover originals, some reprints. Averages 8 titles/year; receives 100 submissions annually. 10% of books from first-time authors; 75% of books from unagented writers. Subsidy publishes (nonauthor) 10% of books. Pays royalty. Publishes book an average of 16 months after acceptance. Computer printout submissions acceptable; no dot-matrix. Reports "as soon as possible."

Nonfiction: American studies, Texana, literature and criticism. "We are looking for good scholarly monographs, other serious scholarly work and regional titles of significance." Query. Reviews artwork/photos as part of ms package.

Recent Nonfiction Title: *Dream of Empire: A Human History of the Republic of Texas*, by J.E. Weems (scholarly and popular history).

Fiction: Adult and young adult regional fiction. Query.

Recent Fiction Title: *Wanderer Springs*, by Robert Flynn (regional novel).

Tips: "Regional and/or Texana-nonfiction or fiction have best chance of breaking into our firm."

TEXAS MONTHLY PRESS, INC., Subsidiary of Mediatex Communications Corp., Box 1569, Austin TX 78767. (512)476-7085. Director/Vice President: Scott Lubeck. Publishes hardcover and trade paperback originals, and trade paperback reprints. Averages 30 titles/year; receives 400 submissions annually. 60% of books from first-time authors; 85% of books from unagented writers. Pays royalty; offers advance. Publishes book an average of 1 year after acceptance. Simultaneous and photocopied submissions OK. Query for electronic submissions. Computer printout submissions acceptable. Reports in 2 weeks on queries; 2 months on mss. Free book catalog.

Nonfiction: Politics and history with comtemporary subject matter, biography, "coffee table" book, cookbook, humor, guidebook, illustrated book and reference. Subjects include Southwest, art, business and economics, cooking and foods, nature, photography, recreation, sports and travel. Query or submit outline/synopsis and 3 sample chapters. Reviews artwork/photos as part of ms package.

Recent Nonfiction Title: *Thunder in America: The Improbable Presidential Campaign of Jesse Jackson*, by Bob Faw and Nancy Skelton (politics).

Fiction: Ethnic, mainstream. "All stories must be set in the South or Southwest." No experimental, erotica, confession, gothic, romance or poetry. Query or submit outline/synopsis and 3 sample chapters. No unsolicited mss.

Recent Fiction Title: *A Flatland Fable: A Novel*, by Joe Coomer.

TEXAS WESTERN PRESS, Imprint of The University of Texas at El Paso, El Paso TX 79968-0633. (915)747-5688. Director: Dale L. Walker. Editor: Nancy Hamilton. Publishes hardcover and paperback originals. Publishes 7-8 titles/year. "This is a university press, 33 years old; we do offer a standard 10% royalty contract on our hardcover books and on some of our paperbacks as well. We try to treat our authors professionally, produce handsome, long-lived books and aim for quality, rather than quantity of titles carrying our imprint." Photocopied submissions OK. Free book catalog and ms guidelines. Reports in 1-3 months.

Nonfiction: Scholarly books. Historic and cultural accounts of the Southwest (West Texas, New Mexico, northern Mexico and Arizona). Occasional scientific titles. "Our *Southwestern Studies* use manuscripts of up to 30,000 words. Our hardback books range from 30,000 words up. The writer should use good exposition in his work. Most of our work requires documentation. We favor a scholarly, but not overly pedantic, style. We specialize in superior book design." Query with outlines. Follow Chicago *Manual of Style*.

Recent Nonfiction Title: *The Spanish Mustang*, by Don Worcester.

Fiction: Occasional literary titles.

Recent Fiction Title: *Will Henry's West*, by Will Henry (collection of stories, essays).

THEATRE ARTS BOOKS, An imprint of Methuen, Inc., 29 West 35th St., New York NY 10001. (212)244-3336. Editorial Director: William P. German. Publishes trade paperback originals. Averages 1-2 titles/year; receives 100 submissions annually. 100% of books from unagented writers. Pays royalty. No advance. Publishes ms an average of 1 year after acceptance. Photocopied submissions OK. Computer printout submissions acceptable; no dot-matrix. "Report time varies—2-3 weeks in slow seasons, 3 months in busy seasons." Use *Chicago Manual of Style* for ms guidelines.

Nonfiction: Drama and theatre. Subjects include acting, directing, lighting, costume, dance, staging, etc. "We publish only books of broad general interest to actors, directors and theatre technicians, especially books that could be useful in college classrooms. Most of our authors have had long experience in professional theatre. Topics that are very narrowly focused (a costume book on women's shoes in the eighteenth century, for example) would not be acceptable. We no longer publish original plays." Query with outline, synopsis and author's qualifications.

*THE THEOSOPHICAL PUBLISHING HOUSE, Subsidiary of The Theosophical Society in America, 306 W. Geneva Rd., Wheaton IL 60189. (312)665-0123. Imprint, Quest (nonfiction). Senior Editor: Shirley Nicholson. Publishes trade paperback originals. Averages 12 titles/year; receives 750-1,000 submissions annually. 50-60% of books from first-time authors; 95% of books from unagented writers. Average print order for a writer's first book is 5,000. Pays 10-12% royalty on retail price; offers average $1,500 advance. Publishes book an average of 8 months after acceptance. Simultaneous and photocopied submissions OK. Computer printout submissions acceptable; prefers letter-quality to dot-matrix. Reports in 2 weeks on queries, 2 months on mss. Free book catalog; ms guidelines for SASE.
Nonfiction: Subjects include self-development, self-help, philosophy (holistic), psychology (transpersonal), Eastern and Western religions, comparative religion, holistic implications in science, health and healing, yoga, meditation and astrology. "TPH seeks works which are compatible with the theosophical philosophy. Our audience includes the 'new age' consciousness community seekers in all religions, general public, professors, and health professionals. No submissions which do not fit the needs outlined above." Accepts nonfiction translations. Query or submit outline/synopsis and sample chapters. Reviews artwork/photos as part of ms package.
Recent Nonfiction Title: *Self-Transformation through Music*, by Joanne Crandall.
Tips: "The writer has the best chance of selling our firm a book which illustrates a connection between spiritually-oriented philosophy or viewpoint and some field of current interest."

*THISTLEDOWN PRESS, 668 E. Place, Saskatoon, Saskatchewan S7J 2Z5 Canada. (306)477-0556. Editor-in-Chief: Paddy O' Rourke. Publishes hardcover and trade paperback originals by resident Canadian authors *only*. Averages 8 titles/year; receives 150 submissions annually. 50% of books from first-time authors; 100% of books from unagented writers. Average print order for a writer's first (poetry) book is 750 or (fiction) 1,000. Subsidy publishes (nonauthor) 100% of books. Pays standard royalty on retail price. Publishes book an average of 18-24 months after acceptance. Computer printout submissions acceptable; no dot-matrix. Reports in 2 weeks on queries; 2 months on poetry mss; 3 months on fiction mss. Book catalog and guidelines for #10 SAE with IRC.
Fiction: Literary. Interested in fiction mss from resident Canadian authors only. Minimum of 30,000 words.
Recent Fiction Title: *Small Regrets*, by Dave Margoshes (short stories).
Poetry: "The author should make him/herself familiar with our publishing program before deciding whether or not his/her work is appropriate." No poetry by people *not* citizens and residents of Canada. Submit complete ms. Minimum of 60 pages. Prefers poetry mss that have had some previous exposure in literary magazines.
Recent Poetry Title: *The Beekeeper's Daughter*, by Bruce Hunter (contemporary Canadian).
Tips: "We prefer a book that has literary integrity and a distinct voice."

THOMAS PUBLICATIONS, Subsidiary of Thomas Graphics, Inc., Box 33244, Austin TX 78764. (512)832-0355. Contact: Ralph D. Thomas. Publishes trade paperback originals and trade paperback reprints. Averages 8-10 titles/year; receives 20-30 submissions annually. 90% of books from first-time authors; 90% of books from unagented writers. Pays 10-15% royalty on wholesale or retail price, or makes outright purchase of $500-2,000. Publishes book an average of 1 year after acceptance. Simultaneous and photocopied submissions OK. Computer printout submissions acceptable; no dot-matrix. Reports in 2 weeks on queries; 1 month on mss. Book catalog $1.
Nonfiction: How-to, reference and textbook. Subjects include sociology and investigation and investigative techniques. "We are looking for hardcore investigative methods books, manuals on how to make more dollars in private investigation, private investigative marketing techniques, and specialties in the investigative professions." Query or submit outline/synopsis and sample chapters. Reviews artwork/photos as part of ms package.
Recent Nonfiction Title: *How to Find Anyone Anywhere*, by Ralph Thomas (investigation).
Tips: "Our audience includes private investigators, those wanting to break into investigation, related trades such as auto repossessors, private process servers, news reporters, and related security trades."

*THREE CONTINENTS PRESS, 1636 Connecticut Ave. NW, Washington DC 20009. Publisher/Editor-in-Chief: Donald E. Herdeck. General Editor: Norman Ware. Publishes hardcover and paperback originals and reprints. Averages 12-14 titles/year. Receives 200 submissions annually. 15% of books from first-time authors; 100% of books from unagented writers. Average print order for a writer's first book is 1,000. Subsidy publishes (nonauthor) 10% of books. Pays 10% royalty; advance "only on delivery of complete manuscript which is found acceptable; usually $300." Photocopied (preferred) and simultaneous submissions OK. State availability of photos/illustrations. Computer printout submissions acceptable; prefers letter-quality to dot-matrix. Reports in 2 months. Book catalog and guidelines for 8x11 SAE.

Nonfiction and Fiction: Specializes in African, Caribbean and Middle Eastern (Arabic and Persian) literature and criticism and translation, Third World literature and history. Scholarly, well-prepared mss; creative writing. Fiction, poetry, criticism, history and translations of creative writing. "We search for books which will make clear the complexity and value of non-western literature and culture, including bilingual texts (Arabic language/English translations). We are always interested in genuine contributions to understanding non-western culture." Length: 50,000-125,000 words. Query. "Please do not submit manuscript unless we ask for it. We prefer an outline, and an annotated table of contents, for works of nonfiction; and a synopsis, a plot summary (one to three pages), for fiction. For poetry, send two or three sample poems." Reviews artwork/photos as part of ms package.

Recent Nonfiction Title: *The Ensphering Mind,* by J. Wieland (criticism).

Recent Fiction Title: *Worl' Do For Fraid,* a play by Nabie Swaray.

Tips: "We need a *polished* translation, or original prose or poetry by non-Western authors *only.*"

THUNDER'S MOUTH PRESS, 93-99 Greene St., New York NY 10012. (212)226-0277. Publisher: Neil Ortenberg. Publishes hardcover and trade paperback originals and reprints. Averages 6 titles/year; receives 1,000 submissions annually. 50% of books from unagented writers. Average print order for a writer's first book is 2,000. Pays 5-10% royalty on retail price; offers average $200 advance. Publishes book an average of 8 months after acceptance. Reports in 3 weeks on queries. Book catalog for SAE and 22¢ postage.

Nonfiction: Biography. Publishes for "college students, academics, politically left of center, ethnic, social activists, women, etc. We basically do poetry and fiction now but intend to start doing nonfiction over the next few years." Query only.

Fiction: Erotica, ethnic, experimental, historical, humor, science fiction and political. "We are interested in doing anywhere from 3-5 novels per year, particularly highly literary or socially relevant novels." No romance. Query only.

Poetry: "We intend to publish 3-5 books of poetry per year. No elitist, rhymes or religious poetry." Submit complete ms.

TIMBER PRESS, 9999 S.W. Wilshire, Portland OR 97225. (503)292-0745. Imprints include Dioscorides Press (botany) and Amadeus Press (music). Editor: Richard Abel. Small press. Publishes hardcover and paperback originals. Publishes 20 titles/year; receives 300-400 submissions annually. 90% of books from first-time authors; 100% of books from unagented writers. Pays 10-20% royalty; sometimes offers advance to cover costs of artwork and final ms completion. Publishes book an average of 1 year after acceptance. Query for electronic submissions. Computer printout submissions acceptable; prefers letter-quality to dot-matrix. Reports in 2 months. Book catalog and ms guidelines for 9x12 SAE with 56¢ postage.

Nonfiction: Arts and crafts, natural history, Northwest regional material, forestry and horticulture. Accepts nonfiction translations from German. Query or submit outline/synopsis and 3-4 sample chapters. Reviews artwork/photos as part of ms package.

Recent Nonfiction Title: *Gardening with Dwarf Trees and Shrubs,* by Bartels (horticulture).

Tips: "The writer has the best chance of selling our firm good books on botany, horticulture, forestry, agriculture and serious music."

TIMES BOOKS, Division of Random House, Inc., 201 East 50 St., New York NY 10022. (212)872-8110. Vice President and Editorial Director: Jonathan B. Segal. Senior Editors: Elisabeth Scharlatt and Hugh O'Neill. Publishes hardcover and paperback originals and reprints. Publishes 45 titles/year. Pays royalty; average advance. Publishes book an average of 1 year after acceptance. Computer printout submissions acceptable.

Nonfiction: Business/economics, science and medicine, history, biography, women's issues, the family, cookbooks, current affairs, cooking, self-help and sports. Accepts only solicited manuscripts. Reviews artwork/photos as part of ms package.

Recent Nonfiction Title: *Tales of a New America,* by Robert B. Reich.

TOR BOOKS, Subsidiary of St. Martin's Press, 9th Floor, 49 W. 24th St., New York NY 10010. (212)564-0150. Editor-in-Chief: Beth Meacham. Publishes mass market hardcover and trade paperback originals and reprints. Averages 100 books/year. Pays 6-8% royalty; offers negotiable advance. Book catalog for 9x12 SASE.

Fiction: Horror, science fiction, occult, chillers, suspense, espionage, historical and fantasy. "We prefer a extensive chapter-by-chapter synopsis." Prefers agented mss or proposals.

Recent Fiction Title: *Speaker for the Dead,* by Orson Scott Card (science fiction novel).

Tips: "We're pretty broad in the occult, horror and fantasy but more straightforward in science fiction and thrillers, tending to stay with certain authors and certain types of work."

‡*TRANSACTION BOOKS, Rutgers University, New Brunswick NJ 08903. (201)932-2280. President: I.L. Horowitz. Publisher: Scott Bramson. Book Division Director: Mary E. Curtis. Publishes hardcover and paperback originals and reprints. Specializes in scholarly social science books. Averages 135 titles/year; receives

700-800 submissions annually. 15% of books from first-time authors; 85% of books from unagented writers. Average print order for a writer's first book is 1,000. Subsidy publishes 10% of books. Royalty "depends almost entirely on individual contract; we've gone anywhere from 2-15%." No advance. Publishes book an average of 8 months after acceptance. Electronic submissions OK, but requires hard copy also. Computer printout submissions acceptable; prefers letter-quality to dot-matrix. Reports in 4 months. Book catalog and ms guidelines for SASE.
Nonfiction: Americana, biography, economics, history, law, medicine and psychiatry, music, philosophy, politics, psychology, reference, scientific, sociology, technical and textbooks. "All must be scholarly social science or related." Query or submit outline/synopsis. "Do not submit sample chapters. We evaluate complete manuscripts only." Accepts nonfiction translations. Use Chicago *Manual of Style*. Looks for "scholarly content, presentation, methodology, and target audience." State availability of photos/illustrations and send one photocopied example. Reviews artwork/photos as part of ms package.
Recent Nonfiction Title: *The Gun in Politics*, by J. Bowyer Bell (military history).

TRANSNATIONAL PUBLISHERS, INC., Box 7282, Ardsley-on-Hudson NY 10503. (914)693-0089. Publisher: Ms. Heike Fenton. Publishes hardcover originals. Averages 10-15 titles/year; receives 50 submissions annually. 10% of books from first-time authors; 100% of books from unagented writers. Pays 5-10% royalty. Publishes book an average of 6 months after acceptance. Simultaneous and photocopied submissions OK. Computer printout submissions acceptable. Reports in 2 weeks on queries; 1 month on mss. Book and ms guidelines free on request.
Nonfiction: Reference, textbook and books for professionals. Subjects include politics, international law, criminal law, human rights, women's studies and political theory. Needs scholarly works in the area of international law and politics. No submissions on topics other than those listed above. Submit outline/synopsis and sample chapters.
Recent Nonfiction Title: *International Law: Process and Prospect*, by A. D'Amato.
Tips: "The audience for our books includes law libraries, public libraries, universities, government personnel, military personnel, college students and women's rights groups."

TRAVEL KEYS, Box 160691, Sacramento CA 95816. (916)452-5200. Publisher: Peter B. Manston. Publishes hardcover and trade paperback originals. Averages 4 titles/year; receives 8 submissions annually. 20% of books from first-time authors; 90% of books from unagented writers. Pays 6-15% royalty ("rarely, we mostly use work for hire"); or makes outright purchase for $500 minimum. Offers minimum $500 advance. Publishes book an average of 6 months after acceptance. Simultaneous and photocopied submissions OK. Query for electronic submissions. Reports in 1 month. Book catalog for #10 SAE with 1 first class stamp.
Nonfiction: How-to on travel, antiques and flea market guides. "We need carefully researched, practical travel manuscripts. No science or technical submissions." Submit outline/synopsis and sample chapters. Reviews artwork/photos as part of ms package.
Recent Nonfiction Titles: *Manston's Travel Key Europe*, by Manston.
Tips: "Most of our titles, so far, are staff written. Our audience is travelers looking for easily accessible, down-to-earth, practical information. If I were a writer, I would research well, double-check facts and write clearly."

‡TRILLIUM PRESS, Subsidiaries include Cloud 10, Box 209, Monroe NY 10950. (914)783-2999. Editor: William Neuman. Publishes hardcover and trade paperback originals. Averages 100 titles/year; receives 200 submissions annually. 33% of books from first-time authors; 95% of books from unagented writers. Pays 10% royalty on wholesale price; no advance. Publishes book an average of 1 year after acceptance. Photocopied submissions OK. Computer printout submissions OK; prefers letter-quality. Reports in 1 month on queries. Book catalog and guidelines for 8½x11 SAE and 56¢ postage.
Nonfiction: Self-help and textbook. Subjects include inspirational and education. Submit complete ms. Review artwork/photos as part of ms.
Recent Nonfiction Title: *Feel the Laughter*, by Sharon Komlos.
Fiction: Children's. Submit complete ms.
Recent Fiction Title: *Mother, I'm Mad*, by Daniel.

TROUBADOR PRESS, Subsidiary of Price/Stern/Sloan, Publishers, Inc., 410 N. La Cienega Blvd., Los Angeles CA 90048. (213)657-6100. Publishes paperback originals. Averages 4 titles/year; receives 300 submissions annually. 95% of books from unagented writers. Average print order for a writer's first book is 10,000. Pays royalty. Offers average $500 advance. Publishes book an average of 6 months after acceptance. Computer printout submissions acceptable; prefers letter-quality to dot-matrix. Reports in 1 month. Book catalog and ms guidelines for SASE.
Nonfiction: "Troubador Press publishes mainly, but is not limited to, children's activity books: coloring, cut-out, mazes, games, paper dolls, etc. All titles feature original art and exceptional graphics. We like books which have the potential to develop into series." Query or submit outline/synopsis and 2-3 sample chapters

with conciseness and clarity of a good idea. Reviews artwork as part of ms package.

Recent Nonfiction Title: *The Second Dinosaur Action Set*, by M. Whyte and artist Dan Smith (dinasours punch-out and play book with dinosour dictionary text incorporated).

Tips: "We continue to publish new authors along with established writers/artists. We feel the mix is good and healthy." Queries/mss may be routed to other editors in the publishing group.

TWAYNE PUBLISHERS, Subsidiary of Macmillan, Inc., a division of G.K. Hall & Co., 70 Lincoln St., Boston MA 02111. (617)423-3990. Publishes hardcover and paperback originals. Publishes 100+ titles/year; receives 1,000 submissions annually. 5% of books from first-time authors; 10% of books from unagented writers. Average print order for a writer's first book is 1,000. Pays royalty. Reports in 5 weeks.

Nonfiction: Publishes scholarly books and volumes in and out of series for the general reader. Literary criticism, biography, history; women's studies, art history, current affairs and science. Query only with outline and 2 sample chapters.

Recent Nonfiction Title: *Big Daddy from the Pedernales: Lyndon B. Johnson*, by Paul K. Conkin.

Tips: Queries may be routed to other editors in the publishing group. Unsolicited mss will not be read.

*TYNDALE HOUSE PUBLISHERS, INC., 336 Gundersen Dr., Wheaton IL 60187. (312)668-8300. Editor-in-Chief/Acquisitions: Wendell Hawley. Publishes hardcover and trade paperback originals and hardcover and mass paperback reprints. Averages 100 titles/year; receives 3,000 submissions annually. 15% of books from first-time authors; 99% of books from unagented writers. Average print order for a writer's first book is 7,000-10,000. Subsidy publishes 2% of books. Pays 10% royalty; offers negotiable advance. Publishes book an average of 18 months after acceptance. Computer printout submissions acceptable; no dot-matrix. Reports in 6 weeks. Free book catalog; ms guidelines for SASE.

Nonfiction: Religious books only: personal experience, family living, marriage, Bible reference works and commentaries, Christian living, devotional, inspirational, church and social issues, Bible prophecy, theology and doctrine, counseling and Christian psychology, Christian apologetics and church history. Submit table of contents, chapter summary, preface, first 2 chapters and 1 later chapter.

Fiction: Biblical novels. Submit outline/synopsis and sample chapters.

‡ULI, THE URBAN LAND INSTITUTE, 1090 Vermont Ave. N.W., Washington DC 20005. (202)289-8500. Director of Publications: Frank H. Spink, Jr. Publishes hardcover and trade paperback originals. Averages 15-20 titles/year. Receives 20 submissions annually. No books from first-time authors; 100% of books from unagented authors. Pays 10% royalty on gross sales. Offers advance of $1,500-2,000. Publishes book an average of 6 months after acceptance. Query for electronic submissions. Computer printout submissions acceptable; prefers letter-quality to dot matrix.

Nonfiction: Technical books on real estate development and land planning. "The majority of mss are created in-house by research staff. We acquire two or three outside authors to fill schedule and subject areas where our list has gaps. We are not interested in real estate sales, brokerages, appraisal, making money in real estate, opinion, personal point of view, or mss negative toward growth and development." Query. Reviews artwork/photos as part of ms package.

Recent Nonfiction Title: *Hotel/Motel Development*, by Leventhal and Horwath.

ULTRALIGHT PUBLICATIONS, INC., Box 234, Hammelstown PA 17036. (717)566-0468. Editor: Michael A. Markowski. Imprints includes Aviation Publishers and Medical Information Systems Division. Publishes hardcover and trade paperback originals. Averages 6 titles/year; receives 30 submissions annually. 50% of books from first-time authors; 100% of books from unagented writers. Average print order for a writer's first book is 5,000. Pays 10-15% royalty on wholesale price; buys some mss outright. Offers average $1,000-1,500 advance. Publishes book an average of 6 months after acceptance. Simultaneous and photocopied submissions OK. Computer printout submissions acceptable; no dot-matrix. Reports in 3 weeks on queries; 2 months on mss. Book catalog and ms guidelines for #10 SAE with 39¢ postage.

Nonfiction: How-to, technical on hobbies (model airplanes, model cars, and model boats) and aviation. Publishes for "aviation buffs, dreamers and enthusiasts. We are looking for titles in the homebuilt, ultralight, sport and general aviation fields. We are interested in how-to, technical and reference books of short to medium length that will serve recognized and emerging aviation needs." Also interested in automotive historical, reference and how-to; popular health, medical, and fitness for the general public. Self-help, motivation and success are also areas of interest. Query or submit outline/synopsis and 3 sample chapters. Reviews artwork/photos as part of ms package.

Recent Nonfiction Title: *Canard: A Revolution in Flight*, by Lennon (aviation history).

UMI RESEARCH PRESS, University Microfilms, Inc., Bell & Howell, 300 N. Zeeb Road, Ann Arbor MI 48106. Acquisitions Editor: Christine B. Hammes. Small press. Publishes hardcover originals and revised dissertations. Averages 75 titles/year; receives 300 submissions annually. 70% of books from first-time authors. Average print order for a writer's first book is 500. Pays 5% royalty on net sales. Offers average $100 advance.

Publishes book an average of 9 months after acceptance. Photocopied submissions OK. Query for electronic submissions. Computer printout submissions acceptable "if good quality." Ms guidelines available.

Nonfiction: Scholarly and professional research and critical studies in arts and humanities. Subjects include architecture; cinema (theory and aesthetics); art (theory, criticism, and history); theatre (history and theory); musicology; photography (theory); American material culture; religion; literary criticism and women's studies. Especially looking for "scholarly works, original conclusions resulting from careful academic research. Primarily aimed at graduate, post-graduate and professional level. Academics, research librarians, art, music, and literary communities, are our audience." No mass market books. Query.

Recent Nonfiction Title: *Only a Paper Moon: The Theatre of Billy Rose*, by Stephen Nelson.

Tips: "Send letters of inquiry to appropriate publishers *before* devoting hours to a manuscript. Get feedback at the outline/prospectus stage."

‡**THE UNICORN PUBLISHING HOUSE, INC.**, 1148 Parsippany Blvd., Parsippany NJ 07054. (201)334-0353. Associate Juvenile Editor: Heidi K. L. Corso. Publishes hardcover originals. Averages 10 titles/year; receives 75 submissions annually. 25% of books from first-time authors; 90% of books from unagented writers. Negotiates payment. Publishes book an average of 18 months after acceptance. Simultaneous and photocopied submissions OK. Computer printout submissions OK. Reports in 2 weeks on queries; 1 month on mss. Guidelines for SASE.

Nonfiction: Biography, "coffee table," illustrated, juvenile, and self-help. Subjects include animals, art, health, music and photography. "We are seeking juvenile, arts and entertainment and current issues books." Query or submit outline/synopsis and sample chapters or complete ms. Reviews artwork/photos as part of ms.

Recent Nonfiction Title: *A Question of Innocence*, by L. Spiegel (contemporary issues).

Fiction: Adventure and fantasy. "We want books for juveniles ages 4-15." Query or submit outline/synopsis and sample chapters or complete ms.

Recent Fiction Title: *Come Play With Peter Cottontail*, by Ed J. Scrocco (touch and feel).

Poetry: No adult books. Submit complete ms.

Tips: "Juvenile fiction constitutes the bulk of what we publish."

‡***UNION OF AMERICAN HEBREW CONGREGATIONS**, 838 5th Ave., New York NY 10021. (212)249-0100. Managing Director: Stuart L. Benick. Publishes hardcover and trade paperback originals. Averages 15 titles/year. 50% of books from first-time authors; 90% of books from unagented writers. Subsidy publishes 40% of books. Pays 5-15% royalty on wholesale price. Publishes book an average of 9 months after acceptance. Simultaneous and photocopied submissions OK. Computer printout submissions OK. Book catalog and ms guidelines for SASE.

Nonfiction: Illustrated, juvenile and Jewish textbooks. Subjects include Jewish religion. "We need Jewish textbooks which fit into our curriculum." Reviews artwork/photos as part of ms package.

Fiction: Jewish religion. "We publish books that teach values."

***UNIVELT, INC.**, Box 28130, San Diego CA 92128. (619)746-4005. Publisher: H. Jacobs. Publishes hardcover originals. Averages 8 titles/year; receives 20 submissions annually. 5% of books from first-time authors; 5% of books from unagented writers. Subsidy publishes (nonauthor) 10% of books. Average print order for a writer's first book is 1,000-2,000. Pays 10% royalty on actual sales; no advance. Publishes book an average of 4 months after acceptance. Computer printout submissions acceptable; prefers letter-quality to dot-matrix. Reports in 1 month. Book catalog and ms guidelines for SASE.

Nonfiction: Publishes in the field of aerospace, especially astronautics and technical communications, but including application of aerospace technology to Earth's problems, also astronomy. Submit outline/synopsis and 1-2 sample chapters. Reviews artwork/photos as part of ms package.

Recent Nonfiction Title: *Soviet Space Programs 1980-1985.*

Tips: "Writers have the best chance of selling manuscripts on the history of astronautics (we have a history series) and astronautics/space/light subjects. We publish for the American Astronautical Society." Queries/mss may be routed to other editors in the publishing group.

***UNIVERSE BOOKS**, 381 Park Ave. S., New York NY 10016. (212)685-7400. Editorial Director: Louis Barron. Publishes hardcover and paperback originals and reprints. Averages 40-50 titles/year; receives 1,000 submissions annually. 15% of books from first-time authors; 75% of books from unagented writers. Average print order for a writer's first book is 3,000-4,000. Offers 10-15% royalty on retail price (hardbound books). "On a few extra-illustrated art books and on special studies with a limited market we may pay a smaller royalty." Offers $1,000-4,000 advance. "If a book makes a genuine contribution to knowledge but is a commercial risk, we might perhaps accept a subsidy from a foundation or other organization, but not directly from the author." Publishes book an average of 9 months after acceptance. Simultaneous and photocopied submissions OK. Computer printout submissions acceptable; no dot-matrix. "Will not return material without postage-paid SAE." Reports in 2 weeks. Book catalog for 8½x11 SAE with 5 first-class stamps.

Nonfiction: Animals, art, economics, history, linguistics, nature, performing arts, politics and reference.

Universe also pays secondary attention to biography, health and how-to. Also uses "monographs on specific animal, bird or plant species; social histories of specific types of artifacts or social institutions; art histories of specific types of artifacts or symbols. We publish books in the following categories: antiques, crafts and collectibles, art, architecture and design, history, horticulture, ballet, music, contemporary problems, and social sciences (especially books on survival, appropriate technology, and the limits to growth). We do not publish fiction, poetry, cookbooks, criticism or belles lettres." Accepts nonfiction French and German translations. Submit outline/synopsis and 2-3 sample chapters. Reviews artwork/photos as part of ms package.
Recent Nonfiction Title: *The Bald Eagle*, by Stalmaster (natural history).

‡UNIVERSITY ASSOCIATES, INC., 8517 Production Ave., San Diego CA 92121. (619)578-5900. President: J. William Pfeiffer. Publishes paperback originals and reprints. Averages 12-15 titles/year. Specializes in practical materials for human resource development, consultants, etc. Pays average 10% royalty; no advance. Publishes book an average of 6 months after acceptance. Markets books by direct mail. Simultaneous submissions OK. Computer printout submissions acceptable; no dot-matrix. Reports in 4 months. Book catalog and guidelines for SASE.
Nonfiction: Richard Roe, Vice President, Publications. Publishes (in order of preference) human resource development and group-oriented material, management education and community relations and personal growth, and business. No materials for grammar school or high school classroom teachers. Use *American Psychological Association Style Manual*. Query. Send prints or completed art or rough sketches to accompany ms.
Recent Nonfiction Title: *The 1987 Annual: Developing Human Resources*, J.W. Pfeiffer, editor.

*UNIVERSITY OF ALABAMA PRESS, Box 2877, University AL 35486. Director: Malcolm MacDonald. Publishes hardcover originals. Averages 40 titles/year; receives 200 submissions annually. 80% of books from first-time authors; 100% of books from unagented writers. "Pays maximum 10% royalty on wholesale price; no advance." Publishes book an average of 16 months after acceptance. Computer printout submissions acceptable. Free book catalog; ms guidelines for SASE.
Nonfiction: Biography, history, philosophy, politics, religion, sociology and anthropology. Considers upon merit almost any subject of scholarly interest, but specializes in linguistics and philology, political science and public administration, literary criticism and biography, philosophy and history. Accepts nonfiction translations. Reviews artwork/photos as part of ms package.
Recent Nonfiction Title: *Black Eagle: General Daniel "Chappie", James* (biography).

THE UNIVERSITY OF ALBERTA PRESS, 141 Athabasca Hall, Edmonton, Alberta T6G 2E8 Canada. (403)432-3662. Imprint, Pica Pica Press. Director: Norma Gutteridge. Publishes hardcover and trade paperback originals, and trade paperback reprints. Averages 10 titles/year; receives 200-300 submissions annually. 60% of books from first-time authors; majority of books from unagented writers. Average print order for a writer's first book is 1,000. Pays 10% royalty on retail price. Publishes book an average of 1 year after acceptance. Query for electronic submissions. Computer printout submissions acceptable; no dot-matrix. Reports in 1 week on queries; 3 months on mss. Free book catalog and ms guidelines.
Nonfiction: Biography, how-to, reference, technical, textbook, and scholarly. Subjects include art, history, nature, philosophy, politics, and sociology. Especially looking for "biographies of Canadians in public life, and works analyzing Canada's political history and public policy, particularly in international affairs. No pioneer reminiscences, literary criticism (unless in Canadian literature), reports of narrowly focused studies, unrevised theses." Submit complete ms. Reviews artwork/photos as part of ms package.
Recent Nonfiction Title: *Founders: Innovators in Education 1830-1980*, by Ernest Stabler (education).
Tips: "We are interested in original research making a significant contribution to knowledge in the subject."

UNIVERSITY OF ARIZONA PRESS, 1615 E. Speedway, Tucson AZ 85719. (602)621-1441. Director: Stephen Cox. Publishes hardcover and paperback originals and reprints. Averages 40 titles/year; receives 300-400 submissions annually. 30% of books from first-time authors; 90% of books from unagented writers. Average print order is 1,500. Royalty terms vary; usual starting point for scholarly monograph is after sale of first 1,000 copies. Publishes book an average of 1 year after acceptance. Photocopied submissions OK. Query for electronic submissions. Computer printout submissions acceptable; no dot-matrix. Reports in three months. Book catalog for 9x12 SAE; ms guidelines for #10 SAE.
Nonfiction: Scholarly books about the American West, Mexico and natural history, and about subjects strongly identified with the universities in Arizona—anthropology, philosophy, arid lands studies, space sciences, Asian studies, Southwest Indians, Mexico and creative nonfiction. Query and submit outline, list of illustrations and sample chapters. Reviews artwork/photos as part of ms package.
Recent Nonfiction Title: *Blue Desert*, by Charles Bowden.
Tips: "Perhaps the most common mistake a writers might make is to offer a book manuscript or proposal to a house whose list he or she has not studied carefully. Editors rejoice in receiving material that is clearly targeted to the house's list, 'I have approached your firm because my books complements your past publications in. . .', presented in a straightforward, businesslike manner."

THE UNIVERSITY OF ARKANSAS PRESS, 201 Ozark St., Fayetteville AR 72701. (501)575-3246. Director: Miller Williams. Publishes hardcover and trade paperback originals and hardcover reprints. Averages 16 titles/year; receives 4,000 submissions annually. 30% of books from first-time authors; 100% of books from un-agented writers. Pays 10% royalty on net receipts. Publishes book an average of 18 months after acceptance. Simultaneous (if so informed) and photocopied submissions OK. Electronic submissions OK on CPT disk *only*; requires hard copy also. Computer printout submissions OK; no dot-matrix. Reports in 3 weeks on queries; 6 weeks on mss.

Nonfiction: Biography and literature. Subjects include Americana, animals, history, humanities, nature, general politics and history of politics, and sociology. "Our current needs include literary criticism—especially on contemporary authors, history and biography. We won't consider manuscripts for texts, juvenile or religious studies, or anything requiring a specialized or exotic vocabulary." Query or submit outline/synopsis and sample chapters.

Recent Nonfiction Title: *John Ciardi: Measure of the Man*, by Vince Clemente, Ed. (contemporary views of the poet and his work).

Fiction: "Works of high literary merit; short stories; rarely novels. No genre fiction." Query.

Recent Fiction Title: *All My Trials*, by John Corrington (two novellas, southern setting).

Poetry: "Because of small list, query first."

Recent Poetry Title: *The Made Thing*, by Leon Stokesbury, Ed. (anthology of contemporary southern poetry).

‡*THE UNIVERSITY OF CALGARY PRESS, Library Tower, 2500 University Drive NW, Calgary, Alberta T2N 1N4 Canada. (403)220-7578. Assistant Director: Linda D. Cameron. Publishes scholarly paperback originals. Averages 12-16 titles/year; receives 70 submissions annually. 50% of books from first-time authors; 100% of books from unagented authors. Subsidy publishes (nonauthor) 100% of books. "As with all Canadian University presses, UGP does not have publication funds of its own. Money must be found to subsidize each project. We do not consider publications for which there is no possibility of subvention." Publishes book an average of 1 year after acceptance. Pays negotiable royalties. "Ms must pass a two tier review system before acceptance." Photocopied submissions OK. Query for electronic submissions. Computer printout submissions OK; prefers letter-quality to dot-matrix. Reports in 2 weeks on queries; 2 months on mss. Free book catalog and guidelines.

Nonfiction: Reference, technical, textbook and scholarly. Subjects include Canadiana, business and economics, health, history, nature, philosophy, politics, psychology, religion, communications, energy research and engineering. "Especially looking for scholarly works in the humanities, social sciences, communication, natural history, library sciences, energy research and engineering." Query or submit complete ms.

Recent Nonfiction Title: *Greek Tragedy and Its Legacy*, edited by M. Cropp, E. Fantham and S. Scully.

Tips: "If I were trying to market a book today, I would prepare my manuscript on a word processor and submit a completed prospectus, including projected market, to the publisher."

UNIVERSITY OF CALIFORNIA PRESS, 2120 Berkeley Way, Berkeley CA 94720. Director: James H. Clark. Assistant Director: Lynne E. Withey. Los Angeles office: Suite 613, 10995 Le Conte Ave., UCLA, Los Angeles CA 94995. New York office: Room 513, 50 E. 42 St., New York NY 10017. London office: University Presses of California, Chicago, Harvard and MIT, 126 Buckingham Palace Rd., London SW1W 9SD England. Publishes hardcover and paperback originals and reprints. "On books likely to do more than return their costs, a standard royalty contract beginning at 10% is paid; on paperbacks it is less." Published 230 titles last year. Queries are always advisable, accompanied by outlines or sample material. Accepts nonfiction translations. Send to Berkeley address. Reports vary, depending on the subject. Enclose return postage.

Nonfiction: "Most of our publications are hardcover nonfiction written by scholars." Publishes scholarly books including art, literary studies, social sciences, natural sciences and some high-level popularizations. No length preferences.

Fiction and Poetry: Publishes fiction and poetry only in translation, usually in bilingual editions.

*UNIVERSITY OF ILLINOIS PRESS, 54 E. Gregory, Champaign IL 61820. (217)333-0950. Director/Editor: Richard L. Wentworth. Publishes hardcover and trade paperback originals, and hardcover and trade paperback reprints. Averages 85-90 titles/year. 50% of books from first-time authors; 95% of books from unagented writers. Subsidy publishes (nonauthor) 30% of books. Pays 0-15% royalty on net sales; offers average $1,000-1,500 advance (rarely). Publishes book an average of 1 year after acceptance. Simultaneous and photocopied submissions OK. Electronic submissions OK via IBM-PC, but requires hard copy also. Computer printout submissions acceptable; no dot-matrix. Reports in 1 week on queries; 3 months on mss. Free book catalog; ms guidelines for SASE.

Nonfiction: Biography, reference and scholarly books. Subjects include Americana, business and economics, history (especially American history), music (especially American music), politics, sociology, sports and literature. Always looking for "solid scholarly books in American history, especially social history; books on American popular music, and books in the broad area of American studies." Query with outline/synopsis.

Recent Nonfiction Title: *Music At The White House: A History Of The American Spirit*, by Elise Kirk (music).

Fiction: Ethnic, experimental and mainstream. "We publish four collections of stories by individual writers each year. We do not publish novels." Query.

Recent Fiction Title: *Pastorale*, by Susan Engberg (stories).

Tips: "Serious scholarly books that are broad enough and well-written enough to appeal to non-specialists are doing well for us in today's market. Writers of nonfiction whose primary goal is to earn money (rather than get promoted in an academic position) are advised to try at least a dozen commercial publishers before thinking about offering the work to a university press."

UNIVERSITY OF IOWA PRESS, Westlawn, Iowa City IA 52242. (319)353-3181. Director: Paul Zimmer. Publishes hardcover and paperback originals. Averages 20-28 titles/year; receives 300-400 submissions annually. 30% of books from first-time authors; 95% of books from unagented writers. Average print order for a writer's first book is 1,200-1,500. Pays 7-10% royalty on net price. "We market mostly by direct mailing of flyers to groups with special interests in our titles and by advertising in trade and scholarly publications." Publishes book an average of 1 year after acceptance. Electronic submissions OK for tape, but requires hard copy also. Readable computer printout submissions acceptable. Reports in 4 months. Free book catalog and ms guidelines.

Nonfiction: Publishes anthology, archaeology, British and American literary studies, history (Victorian, U.S., German, medieval, Latin American), and natural history. Currently publishes the Iowa School of Letters Award for Short Fiction. Looks for "evidence of original research; reliable sources; clarity of organization, complete development of theme with documentation and supportive footnotes and/or bibliography; and a substantive contribution to knowledge in the field treated." Query or submit outline/synopsis. Use Chicago *Manual of Style*. Reviews artwork/photos as part of ms package.

UNIVERSITY OF MASSACHUSETTS PRESS, Box 429, Amherst MA 01004. (413)545-2217. Director: Bruce Wilcox. Acquisitions Editor: Richard Martin. Publishes hardcover and paperback originals, reprints and imports. Averages 30 titles/year; receives 600 submissions annually. 20% of books from first-time authors; 90% of books from unagented writers. Average print order for a writer's first book is 1,500. Royalties generally 10% of net income. Advance rarely offered. No author subsidies accepted. Publishes book an average of 1 year after acceptance. Electronic submissions OK, but requires hard copy also. Computer printout submissions acceptable; prefers letter-quality to dot-matrix. Preliminary report in 1 month. Free book catalog.

Nonfiction: Publishes Afro-American studies, art and architecture, biography, criticism, history, natural history, philosophy, poetry, psychology, public policy, sociology and women's studies in original and reprint editions. Accepts nonfiction translations. Submit outline/synopsis and 1-2 sample chapters. Reviews artwork/photos as part of ms package.

Recent Nonfiction Title: *Archibald MacLeish: Reflections*, edited by Bernard A. Orabeck and Helen E. Ellis; foreward by Richard Wilbur.

Tips: "As members of AAUP, we sometimes route (queries/mss) to other university presses."

‡UNIVERSITY OF MICHIGAN PRESS, 839 Greene St., Ann Arbor MI 48106. (313)764-4394. Editorial Director: Walter E. Sears. Senior Editor: Mary C. Erwin. Publishes hardcover and paperback originals and reprints. Averages 35-40 titles/year. Pays 10% royalty on retail price but primarily on net; offers advance. Electronic submissions OK, but requires hard copy also. Computer printout submissions acceptable; no dot-matrix. Reports in 2 weeks. Free book catalog.

Nonfiction: Americana, art, business/economics, health, history, music, philosophy, photography, psychology, recreation, reference, science, sociology, technical, textbooks and travel. No dissertations. Query first.

‡UNIVERSITY OF NEBRASKA PRESS, 901 N. 17th St., Lincoln NE 68588-0520. Editor-in-Chief: Willis G. Regier. Publishes hardcover and paperback originals and hardcover and paperback reprints. Specializes in scholarly nonfiction, some regional books; reprints of Western Americana; and natural history. Averages 50 new titles, 30 paperback reprints (*Bison Books*)/year; receives 700 submissions annually. 25% of books from first-time authors; 95% of books from unagented writers. Average print order for a writer's first book is 1,000. Royalty is usually graduated from 10% on wholesale price for original books; no advance. Computer printout submissions acceptable; prefers letter-quality to dot-matrix. Reports in 4 months. Book catalog and guidelines for 8½x11 SAE with $1.08 postage.

Nonfiction: Publishes Americana, biography, history, nature, photography, psychology, sports, literature, agriculture and American Indian themes. Accepts nonfiction and fiction translations. Query. Accepts outline/synopsis, 2 sample chapters and introduction. Looks for "an indication that the author knows his subject thoroughly and interprets it intelligently." Reviews artwork/photos as part of ms package.

Recent Nonfiction Title: *Soldiers West*, by Andrew Hutton (history).

Recent Fiction Translation: *Winter's Child*, by Dea Trier Morch (maternity).

UNIVERSITY OF NEVADA PRESS, Reno NV 89557. (702)784-6573. Director: John F. Stetter. Editor: Nicholas M. Cady. Publishes hardcover and paperback originals and reprints. Averages 12 titles/year; receives 100 submissions annually. 20% of books from first-time authors; 100% of books from unagented writers. Average print order for a writer's first book is 2,000. Pays 5-10% royalty on net price. Publishes book an average of 2 years after acceptance. Computer printout submissions acceptable; high quality dot-matrix is OK. Preliminary report in 2 months. Free book catalog and ms guidelines.
Nonfiction: Specifically needs regional history and natural history, anthropology, biographies and Basque studies. "We are the first university press to sustain a sound series on Basque studies—New World and Old World." No juvenile books. Submit complete ms. Reviews photocopies of artwork/photos as part of ms package.
Recent Nonfiction Title: *Bacon, Beans, and Galantines*, by Joseph Conlin (western history).

THE UNIVERSITY OF NORTH CAROLINA PRESS, Box 2288, Chapel Hill NC 27514. (919)966-3561. Editor-in-Chief: Iris Tillman Hill. Publishes hardcover and paperback originals. Specializes in scholarly books and regional trade books. Averages 50 titles/year. 70% of books from first-time scholarly authors; 90% of books from unagented writers. Royalty schedule "varies." Occasional advances. Photocopied submissions OK. Query for electronic submissions. Computer printout submissions acceptable; letter-quality or good dot-matrix preferred. Publishes book an average of 1 year after acceptance. Reports in 5 months. Free book catalog; ms guidelines for SASE.
Nonfiction: "Our major fields are American history and Southern studies." Also, scholarly books in legal history, literary studies, classics, oral history, political science, urban studies, religious studies, historical sociology and Latin American studies. Special focus on general interest books on the lore, crafts, cooking, gardening and natural history of the Southeast. Submit outline/synopsis and sample chapters; must follow Chicago *Manual of Style*. Looks for "intellectual excellence and clear writing. We do *not* publish poetry or original fiction." Reviews artwork/photos as part of ms package.
Recent Nonfiction Title: *Bill Neal's Southern Cooking*, by Bill Neal.

‡*UNIVERSITY OF NOTRE DAME PRESS**, Notre Dame IN 46556. (219)239-6346. Editor: Ann Rice. Publishes hardcover originals; trade paperback originals and reprints. Averages 35-40 titles/year; receives 700 submissions annually. 10% of books from first-time authors; 95% of books from unagented writers. Subsidy publishes (nonauthor) 12-17% of books. Subsidy determined by origin of publication; market potential. Pays 10-15% royalty on wholesale price. Publishes book an average of 11 months after acceptance. Photocopied submissions OK. Query for electronic submissions. Computer printout submissions OK; prefers letter-quality to dot-matrix. Book catalog free on request; ms guidelines for SASE.
Nonfiction: Reference and textbook. Subjects include business and economics, history, philosophy, religion and sociology. No science or technology manuscripts.
Tips: "Our audience is educated general readers and college students. Philosophy books sell well; some theology also."

*UNIVERSITY OF PENNSYLVANIA PRESS**, University of Pennsylvania, Blockley Hall, 418 Service Dr., Philadelphia PA 19104. (215)898-6261. Director: Thomas M. Rotell. Publishes hardcover and paperback originals and reprints. Averages 60 titles/year; receives 600 submissions annually. 10-20% of books from first-time authors; 99% of books from unagented writers. Subsidy publishes (nonauthor) 4% of books. Subsidy publishing is determined by evaluation obtained by the press from outside specialists; work approved by Faculty Editorial Committee; subsidy approved by funding organization. Royalty determined on book-by-book basis. Publishes book an average of 9 months after acceptance. Photocopied submissions OK. Query for electronic submissions. Computer printout submissions acceptable; prefers letter-quality to dot-matrix. Reports in 3 months. Free book catalog; ms guidelines for SASE.
Nonfiction: Publishes Americana, biography, business, economics, history, medicine, biological sciences, computer science, physical sciences, law, anthropology, folklore and literary criticism. "Serious books that serve the scholar and the professional." Follow the Chicago *Manual of Style*. Query with outline and letter describing project, state availability of photos and/or illustrations to accompany ms, with copies of illustrations.
Recent Nonfiction Title: *Law, Ethics and the Visual Arts*, by John Merryman and Albert E. Elsen.
Tips: Queries/mss may be routed to other editors in the publishing group.

*THE UNIVERSITY OF TENNESSEE PRESS**, 293 Communications Bldg., Knoxville TN 37996. Contact: Acquisitions Editor. Averages 30 titles/year; receives 750 submissions annually. 50% of books from first-time authors; 99% of books from unagented writers. Average print order for a writer's first book is 1,250. Subsidy publishes (nonauthor) 2% of books. Pays negotiable royalty on retail price. Publishes book an average of 10 months after acceptance. Photocopied submissions OK. Computer printout submissions acceptable; no dot-matrix. Reports in 2 weeks on queries; "in 1 month on submissions we have encouraged." Book catalog for 75¢ and 12x16 SAE; ms guidelines for SASE.

Nonfiction: American history, political science, religious studies, sports studies, literary criticism, Black studies, women's studies, Caribbean, anthropology, folklore and regional studies. Prefers "scholarly treatment and a readable style. Authors usually have Ph.D.s." Submit outline/synopsis, author vita, and 2 sample chapters. No fiction, poetry or plays. Reviews artwork/photos as part of ms package.

Recent Nonfiction Title: *Guerrilla Minstrels: John Lennon, Joe Hill, Woody Guthrie and Bob Dylan*, by Wayne Hampton.

Tips: "Our market is in several groups: scholars; educated readers with special interests in given scholarly subjects; and the general educated public interested in Tennessee, Appalachia and the South. Not all our books appeal to all these groups, of course, but any given book must appeal to at least one of them."

UNIVERSITY OF TEXAS PRESS, Box 7819, Austin TX 78713. Managing Editor: Barbara Spielman. Averages 60 titles/year; receives 1,000 submissions annually. 50% of books from first-time authors; 99% of books from unagented writers. Average print order for a writer's first book is 1,000. Pays royalty usually based on net income; occasionally offers advance. Publishes book an average of 18 months after acceptance. Electronic submissions OK, but requires hard copy also. Computer printout submissions acceptable; no dot-matrix. Reports in 2 months. Free book catalog and writer's guidelines.

Nonfiction: General scholarly subjects: astronomy, natural history, economics, Latin American and Middle Eastern studies, native Americans, classics, films, medical, biology, contemporary architecture, archeology, Chicano studies, physics, health, sciences, international relations, linguistics, photography, twentieth-century and women's literature. Also uses specialty titles related to Texas and the Southwest, national trade titles, and regional trade titles. Accepts nonfiction and fiction translations (generally Latin American fiction). Query or submit outline/synopsis and 2 sample chapters. Reviews artwork/photos as part of ms package.

Recent Nonfiction Title: *Austin City Limits*, by C. Endres.

Recent Poetry Translation: *100 Love Sonnets*, by Neruda (translation from Spanish).

Tips: "It's difficult to make a manuscript over 400 double-spaced pages into a feasible book. Authors should take special care to edit out extraneous material." Looks for sharply focused, in-depth treatments of important topics.

UNIVERSITY OF UTAH PRESS, University of Utah, 101 University Services Bldg., Salt Lake City UT 84112. (801)581-6771. Director: David Catron. Publishes hardcover and paperback originals and reprints. Averages 18 titles/year; receives 500 submissions annually. 30% of books from first-time authors. Average print order for writer's first book is 1,000. Subsidy publishes (nonauthor) 10% of books. Pays 10% royalty on net sales on first 2,000 copies sold; 12% on 2,001 to 4,000 copies sold; 15% thereafter. Publishes book an average of 18 months after acceptance. Computer printout submissions acceptable. Reports in 10 weeks. Free book catalog; ms guidelines for SASE.

Nonfiction: Scholarly books on Western history, philosophy, anthropology, Mesoamerican studies, folklore, and Middle Eastern studies. Accepts nonfiction translations. Popular, well-written, carefully researched regional studies for Bonneville Books Series. Query with synopsis and 3 sample chapters. Author should specify ms length in query. Reviews artwork/photos as part of ms package.

Recent Nonfiction Title: *Indians of Yellowstone*, by Joel Janetski.

UNIVERSITY OF WISCONSIN PRESS, 114 N. Murray St., Madison WI 53715. (608)262-4928 (telex: 265452). Director: Allen N. Fitchen. Acquisitions Editors: Barbara J. Hanrahan and Gordon Lester-Massman. Publishes hardcover and paperback originals, reprints and translations. Averages 50 titles/year. Pays standard royalties on retail price. Reports in 3 months.

Nonfiction: Publishes general nonfiction based on scholarly research. Looks for "originality, significance, quality of the research represented, literary quality, and breadth of interest to the educated community at large." Accepts nonfiction translations. Follow Chicago *Manual of Style*. Send complete ms.

Recent Nonfiction Title: *Joyce's Book Of The Dark: Finnegans Wake*, by John Bishop.

UNIVERSITY PRESS OF AMERICA, INC., 4720 Boston Way, Lanham MD 20706. (301)459-3366. Publisher: James E. Lyons. Publishes hardcover and paperback originals and reprints. Averages 450 titles/year. Pays 5-15% royalty on retail price; occasional advance. No computer printout submissions. Reports in 6 weeks. Book catalog and guidelines for SASE.

Nonfiction: Scholarly monographs, college, and graduate level textbooks in history, economics, business, psychology, political science, African studies, Black studies, philosophy, religion, sociology, music, art, literature, drama and education. No juvenile, elementary or high school material. Submit outline.

Recent Nonfiction Title: *Thomas Jefferson: A Strange Case of Mistaken Identity*, by Alf J. Mapp Jr. (biography).

*UNIVERSITY PRESS OF MISSISSIPPI, 3825 Ridgewood Rd., Jackson MS 39211. (601)982-6205. Director: Richard Abel. Acquisitions Editor: Seetha Srinivasan. Publishes hardcover and paperback originals and reprints. Averages 25 titles/year; receives 150 submissions annually. 50% of books from first-time authors;

100% of books from unagented writers. Subsidy publishes (nonauthor) 25% of books. Customarily pays 10% net royalty. No advance. Publishes book an average of 9 months after acceptance. Computer printout submissions acceptable. Reports in 2 months. Free book catalog.

Nonfiction: Americana, biography, history, politics, sociology, literary criticism, ethnic studies and popular culture. Interested in regional studies and literary studies. Submit outline/synopsis and sample chapters and curriculum vita to Acquisitions Editor. "We prefer a proposal that describes the significance of the work and a chapter outline." Reviews artwork/photos as part of ms package.

Recent Nonfiction Title: *Walker Percy: A Southern Wayfarer*, by William Rodney Allen.

‡*UNIVERSITY PRESS OF NEW ENGLAND, 3 Lebanon St., Hanover NH 03755. (603)646-3349. "University Press of New England is a consortium of university presses. Some books—those published for one of the consortium members—carry the joint imprint of New England and the member: Dartmouth, Brandeis, Brown, Tufts, Clark, Universities of Connecticut, New Hampshire, Vermont and Rhode Island." Director: Thomas L. McFarland. Editor: Charles Backus. Publishes hardcover and trade paperback originals and trade paperback reprints. Averages 35 titles/year. Subsidy publishes (nonauthor) 80% of books. Pays standard royalty; occasionally offers advance. Query for electronic submissions. Computer printout submissions acceptable. Reports in 1 month. Book catalog and guidelines for SASE.

Nonfiction: Americana (regional—New England), art, biography, history, music, nature, politics, psychology, reference, science, sociology, and regional (New England). No festschriften, memoirs, unrevised doctoral dissertations, or symposium collections. Submit outline/synopsis and 1-2 sample chapters.

Recent Nonfiction Title: *Shaker Communities, Shaker Lives*, by Priscilla Brewer (social history).

*UNIVERSITY PRESS OF VIRGINIA, Box 3608, University Station, Charlottesville VA 22903. (804)924-3468. Publishes hardcover and paperback originals and reprints. Averages 50 titles/year; receives 250 submissions annually. 70% of books from first-time authors; 100% of books from unagented writers. Average print order for a writer's first book is 1,000. "We subsidy publish 35% of our books, based on cost versus probable market." Royalty on retail depends on the market for the book; sometimes none is made. Publishes book an average of 1 year after acceptance. Computer printout submissions acceptable; no dot-matrix. Returns rejected material within a week; reports on acceptances in 2 months. Free catalog; ms guidelines for SASE.

Nonfiction: Publishes Americana, business, history, law, medicine and psychiatry, politics, reference, bibliography, and decorative arts books. "Write a letter to the director, describing content of the manuscript, plus length. Also specify if maps, tables, illustrations, etc., are included." No educational, sociological or psychological mss. Reviews artwork/photos as part of ms package.

Recent Nonfiction Title: *Keeper of the Rules: Congressman Howard W. Smith of Virginia*, By Bruce J. Dierenfield.

‡*UNLIMITED PUBLISHING CO., Rt. 17K, Box 240, Bullville NY 10915. (914)361-1299. Publisher: John J. Prizzia Jr. Imprints includes UPC Publications, Inc. Publishes trade paperback originals. Averages 12 titles/year; receives 25 submissions annually. 90% of books from first-time; 95% of books from unagented writers. Subsidy publishes 20% of books. Pays 10-40% royalty on retail price or makes outright purchase for $500-4,000; offers $1,000 average advance. Publishes book an average of 6 months after acceptance. Photocopied submissions OK. Computer printout submissions OK; prefers letter-quality. Reports in 1 month on queries; 6 months on submissions. Book catalog for SASE.

Nonfiction: Biography, cookbook, how-to, humor, illustrated book, reference, self-help and technical. Subjects include business and economics, cooking and foods, hobbies, nature and sociology. "Prefers self-help and how-to books pertaining to cooking, traveling, hobbies, small business, advertising for small business, start your own business, etc." Submit outline/synopsis and sample chapters or complete ms.

Recent Nonfiction Title: *Twins*, by Donald Helms (life drama).

Fiction: Adventure, experimental, historical, humor and mystery. "War stories, adventures of successful business people, the beginnings of millionaires, etc." Submit outline/synopsis and sample chapters or complete ms.

Recent Fiction Title: *Nicaragua Incident*, by Joseph Musso.

‡*UTAH STATE UNIVERSITY PRESS, Utah State University, Logan UT 84322. (801)750-1362. Director: Linda Speth. Publishes hardcover and trade paperback originals and hardcover and trade paperback reprints. Averages 6 titles/year; receives 170 submissions annually. 8% of books from first-time authors. Average print

Market conditions are constantly changing! If this is 1989 or later, buy the newest edition of **Writer's Market** *at your favorite bookstore or order directly from* **Writer's Digest Books.**

order for a writer's first book is 1,500. Subsidy publishes 10% of books; subsidy publishes (nonauthor) 45% of books. Pays 10-15% royalty on retail price; no advance. Publishes book an average of 18 months after acceptance. Electronic submissions OK on Televideo 803, but requires hard copy also. Computer printout submissions acceptable; prefers letter-quality to dot-matrix. Reports in 2 weeks on queries; 2 months on mss. Free book catalog; ms guidelines for SASE.

Nonfiction: Biography, reference and textbook on Americana, history, politics and science. "Particularly interested in book-length scholarly manuscripts dealing with Western history, Western literature (Western Americana). All manuscript submissions must have a scholarly focus." Submit complete ms. Reviews artwork/photos as part of ms package.

Recent Nonfiction Title: *Folk Groups*, by Elliot Oring (folklore).

Poetry: "At the present time, we have accepted several poetry manuscripts and will not be reading poetry submissions for one year."

Recent Poetry Title: *Stone Roses: Poems from Transylvania*, by Keith Wilson.

VALLEY OF THE SUN PUBLISHING COMPANY, Subsidiary of The Sutphen Corporation, Box 38, Malibu CA 90265. Contact: Sharon Boyd. Publishes trade paperback originals. Averages 6-12 titles/year; receives 100 submissions annually. 50% of books from first-time authors; 100% of books from unagented writers. Pays variable royalty, "usually 8% of what we receive—80% of our books are sold directly to the consumer via mail order program"; averages $1,000 advance. Publishes book an average of 6 months after acceptance. Simultaneous and photocopied submissions OK. Computer printout submissions acceptable; prefers letter-quality to dot-matrix. Reports in 6 weeks on submissions. Book catalog for 9x12 SAE with 85¢ postage.

Nonfiction: Metaphysical, primarily reincarnation. "We are interested primarily in books about reincarnation from *very* knowledgeable writers. Must be documented material and offer something new on the subject. We will consider other metaphysical subjects, but this material usually comes from those who actually work in the field. No 'channeled' material—we won't even consider it. No general reincarnation information explaining how it all works." Submit complete ms. Reviews artwork/photos as part of ms package.

ALFRED VAN DER MARCK EDITIONS, Suite 1301, 1133 Broadway, New York NY 10010. (212)645-5150. Editorial Director: Robert Walter. Publishes hardcover and paperback originals and reprints. Averages 10-20 titles/year; receives 500+ submissions annually. 30% of books from first-time authors; 20% of books from unagented writers. Pays 3-12% royalty on wholesale or retail price. Offers average $5,000 advance. Publishes book an average of 1 year after acceptance. Simultaneous and photocopied submissions OK. Query for electronic submissions. Computer printout submissions acceptable; prefers letter-quality to dot-matrix. Reports in 1 month on queries; 2 months on mss. Free book catalog.

Nonfiction: Contemporary art, coffee table book, photography, and cultural history only. Subjects include art (contemporary); cultural history; photography; religion (comparative religion and mythology). Needs mss on "interesting conceptual projects on the cutting edge of contemporary cultural activities, as well as timeless reference works. No conventional illustrated books, 'how-I-spent-a-year-of-my-life' photography." Query or submit outline/synopsis and sample chapters. Submit complete ms through agents only. Reviews artwork/photos as part of ms package.

Recent Nonfiction Title: *Beyond Boundaries: New York's New Art*, by J. Saltz (contemporary art).

Poetry: Seminal collections and anthologies *only*. Submit query.

Recent Poetry Title: *The Poet Exposed*, by Chris Felver.

Tips: "The audience for our books is a general audience with interest in contemporary and timeless culture."

VANCE BIBLIOGRAPHIES, 112 N. Charter, Box 229, Monticello IL 61856. (217)762-3831. Imprints include Architecture Series (bibliography) and Public Administration Series (bibliography). Publisher: Judith Vance. Small press. Publishes trade paperback originals. Averages 450 titles/year; receives 500 submissions annually. 10% of bibliographies from first-time authors; 100% of bibliographies from unagented writers. Average print order for a writer's first bibliography is 200. Pays $100 honorarium and 10-20 author's copies. Publishes bibliography an average of 4 months after acceptance. Photocopied submissions OK. Computer printout submissions acceptable; prefers letter-quality to dot-matrix. Reports in 1 week on queries; 2 weeks on mss. Free book catalog; ms guidelines for SASE.

Nonfiction: Bibliographies on public administration and/or architecture and related subject areas. Publishes for "graduate students and professionals in the field; primary customers are libraries." Query or submit complete ms.

Recent Nonfiction Title: *Housing from Redundant Buildings: A Select Bibliography*, by V.J. Nurcombe.

VEHICULE PRESS, Box 125, Place du Parc Station, Montreal, Quebec H2W 2M9 Canada. (514)844-6073. Imprints include Signal Editions (poetry) and Dossier Quebec (history, memoirs). President/Publisher: Simon Dardick. Publishes trade paperback originals by Canadian authors *only*. Averages 8 titles/year; receives 250 submissions annually. 20% of books from first-time authors; 95% of books from unagented writers. Pays 10-15% royalty on retail price; offers $200-500 advance. Publishes book an average of 1 year after acceptance.

Photocopied submissions OK. Query for electronic submissions. Computer printout submissions acceptable; prefers letter-quality to dot-matrix. "We would appreciate receiving an IRC with SAE rather than U.S. postage stamps which we cannot use." Reports in 1 month on queries; 2 months on mss. Free book catalog.

Nonfiction: Biography and memoir. Subjects include Canadiana, history, politics, social history and literature. Especially looking for Canadian social history. Query. Reviews artwork/photos as part of ms package.

Recent Nonfiction Title: *The Life of a Document: A Global Approach to Archives and Records Management*, by Carol Couture and J-Y Rousseau.

Fiction: Short stories only. Query.

Recent Fiction Title: *Voyage to the Other Extreme*, by Marilu Mallet (short stories).

Poetry: Contact Michael Harris, editor. Looking for Canadian authors only. Submit complete ms.

Recent Poetry Title: *Power to Move*, by Susan Glickman.

Tips: "We are only interested in Canadian authors."

‡*VEND-O-BOOKS/VEND-O-PRESS, Box 3736, Ventura CA 93006-3736. (805)642-2355. Editor: Dr. Bill Busche. Publishes trade paperback and mass market paperback originals and hardcover reprints. Averages 10 titles/year; receives 80-90 submissions annually. 20% of books from first-time authors; 50% of books from unagented writers. Subsidy publishes (nonauthor) 5% of books. Pays 7½-15½% royalty on retail price. Publishes book an average of 2 years after acceptance. Photocopied submissions OK. Computer printout submissions acceptable; prefers letter-quality to dot-matrix. Book catalog for size 11 SAE and 2 first class stamps.

Nonfiction: Cookbook, how-to and humor. No educational, religious or historical. Query.

Fiction: Fantasy, humor, mystery, science fiction, suspense and western. Query.

Tips: How-to and humor are most open to freelancers.

‡THE VESTAL PRESS, LTD., 320 N. Jensen Rd., Box 97, Vestal NY 13850. (607)797-4872. Editors: Harvey N. Roehl and Gil Williams. Publishes hardcover and trade paperback originals and reprints. Averages 6 titles/year; receives 30 submissions annually. 40% of books from first-time writers; 95% of books from unagented authors. Pays 5-10% royalty "based on net dollars received (adding retail and wholesale receipts)." Publishes books average of 1 year after acceptance. Photocopied submissions OK. Query for electronic submissions. Computer printout submissions OK; prefers letter-quality to dot-matrix. Reports back on queries in 1 week; on submissions in 3 weeks. Book catalog for $2; free ms guidelines.

Nonfiction: Biography, how-to, humor, illustrated books, juvenile, reference and technical. Subjects include history, hobbies and music. "We will always look for quality manuscripts relating to automatic music (music boxes, player pianos, etc.), to the piano and organ. We are also interested in film history, postcard history, Americana and antiques, and nautical history. A writer has the best chance of selling us a book related to a collecting hobby, or Americana, 1870-1950. We have a firm handle on certain aspects of American life, and wish to remain in that area." Query with outline/synopsis and sample chapters. Reviews artwork/photos as part of ms package.

Recent Nonfiction Title: *Nickelodeon Theatres and Their Music*, by Q. David Bowers.

Tips: "We hope the author will write clearly and cover his subject completely. It's good to see quality photos supplied, or diagrams, and attention to bibliography, a list of suppliers, etc."

VGM CAREER HORIZONS, (Division of National Textbook Co.), 4255 W. Touhy Ave., Lincolnwood IL 60646-1975. (312)679-4210. Editorial Director: Leonard Fiddle. Senior Editor: Michael Urban. Publishes hardcover and paperback originals and software. Averages 20-30 titles/year; receives 150-200 submissions annually. 10% of books from first-time authors; 95% of books from unagented writers. Pays royalty or makes outright purchase. Advance varies. Publishes book an average of 1 year after acceptance. Simultaneous and photocopied submissions OK. Query for electronic submissions. Computer printout submissions OK, prefers letter-quality to dot-matrix. Reports in 6 weeks. Book catalog and ms guidelines for SASE.

Nonfiction: Textbook and general trade on careers and jobs. Nonfiction book manuscript needs are for careers in agriculture, biotechnology, sales and marketing, liberal arts, information technology, etc. Query or submit outline/synopsis and sample chapters. Reviews artwork/photos as part of ms package.

Recent Nonfiction Title: *Careers in Business*, by Stair and Domkowski.

Tips: "Our audience is job seekers, career planners, job changers, and students and adults in education and trade markets."

‡WADSWORTH PUBLISHING COMPANY, Division of Wadsworth, Inc., 10 Davis Dr., Belmont CA 94002. (415)595-2350. Other divisions include Brooks/Cole Pub. Co., Kent Pub. Co., Prindle, Weber and Schmidt Pub. Co. Editor-in-Chief for Wadsworth Publishing Company: Stephen D. Rutter. Publishes hardcover and paperback originals and software. Publishes 600 titles/year. 50% of books from first-time authors; 100% of books from unagented writers. Pays 5-15% royalty on net price. Advances not automatic policy. Publishes ms an average of 1 year after acceptance. Simultaneous and photocopied submissions OK. Query for electronic submissions. Computer printout submissions acceptable; prefers letter-quality to dot-matrix. Reports in 2 weeks. Ms guidelines available.

Nonfiction: Textbook: higher education only. Subjects include mathematics, music, social sciences, economics, philosophy, religious studies, speech and mass communications, English, and other subjects in higher education. "We need books that use fresh teaching approaches to all courses taught at schools of higher education throughout the U.S. and Canada. We specifically do not publish textbooks in art and history." Query or submit outline/synopsis and sample chapters.

J. WESTON WALCH, PUBLISHER, Box 658, Portland ME 04104. (207)772-2846. Managing Editor: Richard S. Kimball. Editor: Jane Carter. Computer Editor: Robert Crepeau. Publishes paperback originals and software. Averages 120 titles/year; receives 300 submissions annually. 10% of books from first-time authors; 95% of books from unagented writers. Average print order for a writer's first book is 700. Offers 10-15% royalty on gross receipts; buys some titles by outright purchase for $100-2,500. No advance. Publishes book an average of 18 months after acceptance. Query for electronic submissions. Computer printout submissions acceptable; prefers letter-quality to dot-matrix. Reports in 3 weeks. Book catalog for 9x12 SAE with $1.05 postage; ms guidelines for SASE.
Nonfiction: Subjects include art, business, computer education, economics, English, foreign language, government, health, history, mathematics, music, psychology, recreation, science, social science, sociology, special education and sports. "We publish only supplementary educational material for sale to secondary schools throughout the U.S. and Canada. Formats include books, posters, ditto master sets, visual master sets (masters for making transparencies), cassettes, filmstrips, microcomputer courseware and mixed packages. Most titles are assigned by us, though we occasionally accept an author's unsolicited submission. We have a great need for author/artist teams and for authors who can write at third- to tenth-grade levels. We do *not* want basic texts, anthologies or industrial arts titles. Most of our authors—but not all—have secondary teaching experience. I cannot stress too much the advantages that an author/artist team would have in approaching us and probably other publishers." Query first. Looks for "sense of organization, writing ability, knowledge of subject, skill of communicating with intended audience." Reviews artwork/photos as part of ms package.
Recent Nonfiction Title: *150 Great Books: Synopses, Quizzes and Tests for Independent Reading*, by Bonnie A. Helms.

WALKER AND CO., Division of Walker Publishing Co., 720 5th Ave., New York NY 10019. Contact: Submissions Editor. Hardcover and trade paperback originals and reprints of British books. Averages 100 titles/year; receives 3,500 submissions annually. 50% of books from first-time authors; 50% of books from unagented writers. Pays 10-12-15% royalty on retail price or makes outright purchase. Advance averages $1,000-3,000 "but could be higher or lower." Photocopied submissions OK. Do not telephone submissions editors. Material without SASE will not be returned. Book catalog and guidelines for 8½x11 SAE with 56¢ postage.
Nonfiction: Publishes Americana, art, biography, business, histories, juveniles, science and natural history, medicine and psychiatry, music, nature, sports, parenting, psychology, recreation, reference, popular science, and self-help books. Query or submit outline/synopsis and sample chapter. Reviews artwork/photos as part of ms package (photographs). Do not send originals.
Recent Nonfiction Title: *Counterclockwise*, by Michael Drury.
Fiction: Mystery, romantic suspense, regency romance, historical romance, western, action adventure/suspense, espionage, science fiction and fantasy.
Recent Fiction Title: *A Deceptive Clarity*, by Aaron J. Elkins.
Tips: "We also need preschool to young adult nonfiction, science fiction, historical novels, biographies and middle-grade novels. Query."

WALLACE—HOMESTEAD BOOK CO., American Broadcasting Company, Inc., 580 WatersEdge, Lombard IL 60148. (312)953-1100. General Manager: William N. Topaz. Publishes hardcover and trade paperback originals. Averages 30 titles/year; receives 300 submissions annually. 50% of books from first-time authors; 95% of books from unagented writers. Pays royalty on net price. Publishes book an average of 8 months after receipt of acceptable manuscript and materials. "Consult with production manager about electronic submissions." Computer printout submissions acceptable; prefers letter-quality to dot-matrix. Simultaneous and photocopied submissions OK. Reports in 1 month. Free book catalog and ms guidelines.
Nonfiction: Cookbook, how-to and reference. Subjects include Americana, art, business and economics, cooking and food, hobbies and crafts, photography, needlecraft, antiques and collectibles. Especially looking for mss on antiques, collectibles, memorabilia, quilting, cookbooks, and other specialty areas. No school or textbook material. Submit outline/synopsis and sample chapters. Reviews artwork/photos as part of ms package.
Recent Nonfiction Title: *Wallace-Homestead Price Guide to American Country Antiques*, 6th edition, (antiques and collectibles).
Tips: "Our books are intended for an adult nontechnical audience."

‡*WASHINGTON STATE UNIVERSITY PRESS*,Washington State University, Pullam WA 99164-5910. (509)335-3518. Editor-in-chief: Fred C. Bohm. Publishes hardcover originals, trade paperback originals and

reprints. Averages 10-15 titles/year; receives 50-75 submissions annually. 50% of books from first-time writers; 100% of books from unagented authors. Subsidy publishes 20% of books. "The nature of the manuscript and the potential market for the manuscript determine whether it should be subsidy published." Pays 10% royalty. Publishes book average of 1 year after acceptance. Simultaneous and photocopied submissions OK. Query for electronic submissions. Computer printout submissions are acceptable. Reports on queries in 1 month; on submissions in 1-4 months.

Nonfiction: Biography, academic and scholarly. Subjects include Americana, art, business and economics, history (especially of the American West and the Pacific Northwest), nature, philosophy, politics, psychology, and sociology. Needs for the next year are "quality manuscripts that focus on the development of the Pacific Northwest as a region, and on the social and economic changes that have taken place and continue to take place as the region enters the 21st century. No romance novels, historical fiction, how-to books, gardening books, or books specifically written as classroom texts." Submit outline/synopsis and sample chapters. Reviews artwork/photos as part of ms package.

Recent Nonfiction title: *Formulary 1987*, by Christine Schultz (veterinary medicine formulary).

Tips: "Our audience is scholars, specialists and informed general readers who are interested in well-documented research presented in an attractive format." Writers have the best chance of selling to our firm "completed manuscripts on regional history. We have developed our marketing in the direction of regional and local history and have attempted to use this as the base around which we hope to expand our publishing program. In regional history, the secret is to write a good narrative—a good story—that is substantiated factually. It should be told in an imaginative, clever way. Have visuals (photos, maps, etc) available to help the reader envision what has happened. Tell the local or regional history story in a way that ties it to larger, national, and even international events. Weave it into the large pattern of history."

‡FRANKLIN WATTS, INC., Subsidiary of Trade and Professional Books Division of Grolier, Inc., 387 Park Ave. S, New York NY 10016. (212)686-7070. Editor-in-Chief: Ed Breslin. Publishes hardcover originals. Entire firm publishes 200 titles/year; trade and professional division publishes 40. 10% of books from first-time authors; 2% of books from unagented writers. Pays royalty on wholesale or retail price. Simultaneous and photocopied submissions OK. Reports in 3 weeks on queries; 6 weeks on submissions. Free book catalog.

Nonfiction: Biography and business. Subjects include Americana, business and economics, history, politics and sports. No humor, coffee-table books, cookbooks or gardening books. Query.

Fiction: Mainstream, mystery and science fiction. Query.

Tips: "If I were a writer trying to market a book, I would research the market first, the agent second, the publisher third and the editor fourth (and between the first and second step I would make sure the book receives a truly critical and objective read). Watts is more likely to be interested in nonfiction from first-time authors. Corners should not be cut on the research; neither first nor second drafts should be sent."

‡SAMUEL WEISER INC., Box 612, York Beach ME 03910. (207)363-4393. Editor: Susan Smithe. Publishes hardcover originals and trade paperback originals and reprints. Publshes 18-20 titles/year; receives 100-200 submissions annually. 50% of books from first-time authors; 98% of books from unagented writers. Pays 10% royalty on wholesale or retail price; offers average $500 advance. Publishes book an average of 1-1½ years after acceptance. Query for electronic submissions. Computer printout submissions OK; prefers letter-quality to dot-matrix. Reports in 3 months. Free book catalog.

Nonfiction: How-to and self-help. Subjects include health, music, philosophy, psychology and religion. "We look for strong books in our specialty field—written by teachers and people who know the subject. Don't want a writer's rehash of all the astrology books in the library, only texts written by people with strong background in field. No poetry or novels." Submit complete ms. Reviews artwork/photos as part of ms package.

Recent Nonfiction Title: *Development of the Personality*, by Liz Greene/Howard Sasportas.

Tips: "Most new authors do not check permissions, nor do they provide proper footnotes. If they did, it would help."

WESTERN MARINE ENTERPRISES INC., Division of ProStar Publications, Suite 14, 4051 Glencoe Ave., Marina Del Ray CA 90292. (213)306-2094. Editor: William Berssen. Publishes hardcover and trade paperback originals. Averages 4 titles/year. Pays 15% royalty on net price. Offers no advance. Computer printout submissions acceptable; prefers letter-quality to dot-matrix. Reports in 3 weeks.

Nonfiction: Boating. "We specialize in boating books—mainly how-to and when-to." No "simple narrative accounts of how someone sailed a boat from here to there." First-time book authors should submit complete ms.

Recent Nonfiction title: *Landfalls of Paradise*, by Earl Hinz (cruising guide to Pacific Islands).

*WESTERN PRODUCER PRAIRIE BOOKS, Division of Western Producer Publications, Box 2500, Saskatoon, Saskatchewan S7K 2C4 Canada. Publishing Director: Rob Sanders. Publishes hardcover and paperback originals and reprints. Averages 17-20 titles/year; receives 400-500 submissions annually. 20% of books from first-time authors; 80% of books from unagented writrs. Average print order for a writer's first book is 4,000.

Subsidy publishes (nonauthor) 15% of books. Pays negotiable royalty on list price. Publishes book an average of 1 year after acceptance. Query for electronic submissions. Computer printout submissions acceptable; no dot-matrix. Reports in 4 months. Free book catalog; ms guidelines for SAE with IRCs.

Nonfiction: Publishes history, nature, photography, biography, reference, agriculture, economics, politics and cookbooks. Accepts nonfiction and fiction translations. Submit outline, synopsis and 2-3 sample chapters with contact sheets or prints if illustrations are to accompany ms. Reviews artwork/photos as part of ms package.

Recent Nonfiction Title: *The Long and the Short and the Tall*, by R. Collins (autobiography).

Fiction: Young adult and juvenile novels. Accepts fiction translations.

Recent Fiction Title: *Last Chance Summer.* by D. Wieler (young adult fiction).

WESTERN TANAGER PRESS, 1111 Pacific Ave., Santa Cruz CA 95060. (408)425-1111. Publisher: Hal Morris. Publishes hardcover and trade paperback originals and reprints. Averages 3 titles/year; receives 50-100 submissions annually. 25% of books from first-time authors; 100% of books from unagented writers. Average print order for a writer's first book is 3,000. Publishes book an average of 6 months after acceptance. Computer printout submissions acceptable; prefers letter-quality to dot-matrix.

Nonfiction: Biography and history. "We are looking for works of local and regional history dealing with California. This includes biography, natural history, art and politics. Also interested in travel, hiking, biking guides and touring books." Query. Looks for "a well-written, well-thought-out project with a specific audience in mind." Reviews artwork/photos as part of ms package.

WESTERNLORE PRESS, Box 35305, Tucson AZ 85740. Editor: Lynn R. Bailey. Publishes 6-12 titles/year. Pays standard royalties on retail price "except in special cases." Query. Reports in 2 months. Enclose return postage with query.

Nonfiction: Publishes Western Americana of a scholarly and semischolarly nature: anthropology, history, biography, historic sites, restoration, and ethnohistory pertaining to the greater American West. Re-publication of rare and out-of-print books. Length: 25,000-100,000 words.

‡*WESTVIEW PRESS, 5500 Central Ave., Boulder CO 80301. (303)444-3541. Publisher/President: F.A. Praeger. Hardcover and paperback originals, lecture notes, reference books, and paperback texts. Specializes in scholarly monographs or conference reports with strong emphasis on applied science, both social and natural. 0-10% royalty on net price, depending on market. Accepts subsidies for a small number of books, "but only in the case of first class scholarly material for a limited market when books need to be priced low, or when the manuscripts have unusual difficulties such as Chinese or Sanskrit characters; the usual quality standards of a top-flight university press apply, and subsidies must be furnished by institutions, not by individuals." Averages 300 titles/year. Markets books mainly by direct mail. State availability of photos and/or illustrations to accompany manuscript. Reports in 1-4 months. Free book catalog.

Nonfiction: Agriculture/food, agricultural economics, public policy, energy, natural resources, international economics and business, international law, international relations, area studies, development, science and technology policy, sociology, anthropology, reference, military affairs, national security, health, Asia and the Pacific, comparative politics, social impact assessment, women's studies, Latin America and Caribbean, Soviet Union and Eastern Europe, Middle East, Africa, and Western Europe. Looks for "scholarly excellence and scientific relevance." Query and submit 2 sample chapters and tentative table of contents and curriculum vitae. Use Chicago *Manual of Style*. "Unsolicited manuscripts receive low priority; inquire before submitting projects."

Recent Nonfiction Title: *The Business of Book Publishing*, by Geiser.

*WHITAKER HOUSE, Pittsburgh and Colfax Sts., Springdale PA 15144. (412)274-4440. Publishes mass paperback originals and reprints. Averages 12-20 titles/year. Subsidy publishes (author and nonauthor) 25% of books. "We publish only Christian books for the adult reader." Unsolicited mss returned. Book catalog for 9x12 SAE with 39¢ postage. Ms guidelines for SASE.

Nonfiction: How-to and personal growth books centered on biblical teaching and related to everyday life. Looking for teaching books supported by author's research and personal experience. Wants typewritten copy or computer printout, double-spaced, 50,000-90,000 words. Prefers synopsis of chapters with query letter. Interested in receiving queries from Christian leaders with a recognized ministry. No booklets, poetry, or children's books considered.

Recent Nonfiction Title: *How to Find Your Purpose in Life*, by Bill Greenman.

THE WHITSTON PUBLISHING CO., Box 958, Troy NY 12181. (518)283-4363. Editorial Director: Jean Goode. Publishes hardcover originals. Averages 20 titles/year; receives 100 submissions annually. 50% of books from first-time authors; 100% of books from unagented writers. Pays 10-12-15% royalty on wholesale price; no advance. Publishes book an average of 30 months after acceptance. Computer printout submissions acceptable; no dot-matrix. Reports in 1 year. Book catalog for 7x10 SAE.

Nonfiction: "We publish scholarly and critical books in the arts, humanities and some of the social sciences. We also publish reference books, bibliographies, indexes, checklists and monographs. We do not want author bibliographies in general unless they are unusual and unusually scholarly. We are, however, much interested in catalogs and inventories of library collections of individuals, such as the catalog of the Evelyn Waugh Collection at the Humanities Research Center, the University of Texas at Austin; and collections of interest to the specific scholarly community, such as surveys of early Black newspapers in libraries in the U.S., etc." Query or submit complete ms. Reviews artwork/photos as part of ms package.
Recent Nonfiction Title: *The Newspaper Verse of Philip Freneau*, compiled by Judith Hiltner.

WILDERNESS PRESS, 2440 Bancroft Way, Berkeley CA 94704. (415)843-8080. Editorial Director: Thomas Winnett. Publishes paperback originals. Averages 5 titles/year; receives 150 submissions annually. 20% of books from first-time authors; 95% of books from unagented writers. Average print order for a writer's first book is 5,000. Pays 8-10% royalty on retail price; offers average $1,000 advance. Publishes book an average of 6 months after acceptance. Computer printout submissions acceptable; prefers letter-quality to dot-matrix. Reports in 2 weeks. Book catalog for 9x12 SAE.
Nonfiction: "We publish books about the outdoors. Most of our books are trail guides for hikers and backpackers, but we also publish how-to books about the outdoors and perhaps will publish personal adventures. The manuscript must be accurate. The author must thoroughly research an area in person. If he is writing a trail guide, he must walk all the trails in the area his book is about. The outlook must be strongly conservationist. The style must be appropriate for a highly literate audience." Query, submit outline/synopsis and sample chapters, or submit complete ms demonstrating "accuracy, literacy, and popularity of subject area." Reviews artwork/photos as part of ms package.
Recent Nonfiction Title: *Afoot and Afield in San Diego County*, by Jerry Schad (outdoor guide).

‡JOHN WILEY & SONS, INC., 605 3rd Ave., New York NY 10158. (212)850-6000. Editor: Katherine S. Bolster. Publishes hardcover and trade paperback originals. Receives 150 submissions annually. 40% of books from first-time authors; 65% of books from unagented writers. Pays 7.5-15% royalty on wholesale price; offers $3,000 advance. Publishes book an average of 18 months after acceptance. Photocopied submissions OK. Query for electronic submissions. Computer printout submissions OK; prefers letter-quality to dot-matrix. Reports in 2 weeks on queries; 6 weeks on mss. Manuscript guidelines for SASE.
Nonfiction: How-to, reference and self-help. Subjects include business and economics, travel and careers. Needs travel, small business, finance, business management, and careers. "In all areas information needs to be new and it is important to do a thorough competitive search to determine how your manuscript is different from other books on the subject. No sales skills, low-level business books or crafts." Submit outline/synopsis and sample chapters.
Recent Nonfiction Title: *Be Your Own Financial Planner*, by Shane (financial planning). Reviews artwork/photos as part of ms package.
Tips: "It is important to have as complete a proposal as possible—information on the audience, competition, how the book will be used, and how the reader will benefit from reading the book."

WILLIAMSON PUBLISHING CO., Box 185, Church Hill Rd., Charlotte VT 05445. (802)425-2102. Editorial Director: Susan Williamson. Publishes trade paperback originals. Averages 12 titles/year; receives 250 submissions annually. 50% of books from first-time authors; 80% of books from unagented writers. Average print order for a writer's first book is 5,000-10,000. Pays 10-12% royalty on sales dollars received or makes outright purchase if favored by author. Advance negotiable. Publishes book an average of 1 year after acceptance. Simultaneous and photocopied submissions OK. Computer printout submissions acceptable; prefers letter-quality to dot-matrix. Reports in 1 month on queries; 3 months on mss. Book catalog for 6x9 SAE and 2 first class stamps.
Nonfiction: How-to, cookbook, illustrated book and self-help. Subjects include gardening, building, animals, business, education, cooking and foods, health, travel, hobbies, nature landscaping, and children. "Our areas of concentration are people-oriented business and psychology books, cookbooks, travel books, gardening, small-scale livestock raising, family housing (all aspects), health and education." No children's books, photography, politics, religion, history, art or biography. Query with outline/synopsis and sample chapters. Reviews photos as part of ms package.
Recent Nonfiction Title: *Building Fences of Wood, Stone, Metal and Plants*, by John Vivian (how-to).
Tips: "Some writers assume they are in charge of not only the manuscript, but also layout, cover design, and graphics and photography. We have a highly skilled staff to develop the look of our books."

‡WILLOW CREEK PRESS, Box 300, Wautoma WI 54982. (414)787-3005. Editor-in-chief: Chuck Petrie. Publishes hardcover original and reprints. Averages 5-7 titles/year. 10% of books from first time authors; 80% of books from unagented writers. Pays 10-15% royalties on wholesale or retail price depending on individual contract. Offers average advance of $2,000-5,000. Publishes book an average of 1 year after acceptance. Simultaneous and photocopied submissions OK. Computer printout submissions OK. Reports in 5 weeks on queries; 6 weeks on mss. Book catalog for 8½x11 SAE with 56¢ postage.

Nonfiction: "Coffee table" book, cookbook, how-to, humor, illustrated and technical books. Subjects include wildlife, cooking wild game, nature, hunting and fishing. "We do not want to see submissions on dog training, taxidermy or fly tying, any compilations of stories previously published in outdoor magazines or any submissions not suitable for publishing in trade hardcover format." Submit outline/synopsis and sample chapters. Reviews artwork/photos as part of ms package.

Recent Nonfiction Title: *Grouse of the North Shore*, by Gordon Gullion.

Fiction: Historical and humorous fiction, all related to hunting and fishing. "No mss concerning hunting and/or fishing in 'exotic' countries." Submit outline/synopsis and sample chapters.

Recent Fiction Title: *Last Stories of the Old Duck Hunters*, by Gordon MacQuarrie.

Tips: "Our editorial needs for the next three years are already filled with scheduled titles, but we will consider over-the-transom submissions in the fields where we specialize. Writers wishing to be published by Willow Creek Press should familiarize themselves with the types of books we have published and not submit proposals or mss outside those catagories."

‡WILSHIRE BOOK CO., 12015 Sherman Rd., North Hollywood CA 91605. (213)875-1711. Editorial Director: Melvin Powers. Publishes paperback originals and reprints. Publishes 50 titles/year; receives 6,000 submissions annually. 25% of books from first-time authors; 75% of books from unagented writers. Average print order for a writer's first book is 5,000. Pays standard royalty; offers variable advance. Computer printout submissions acceptable; no dot-matrix. Reports in 2 weeks. Book catalog for SASE.

Nonfiction: Health, hobbies, how-to, psychology, recreation, self-help, entrepreneurship, how to make money, and mail order. "We are always looking for self-help and psychological books such as *Psycho-Cybernetics* and *Guide to Rational Living*. We need manuscripts teaching mail order, entrepreneur techniques, how to make money and advertising. We publish 70 horse books. "All that I need is the concept of the book to determine if the project is viable. I welcome phone calls to discuss manuscripts with authors." Reviews artwork/photos as part of ms package.

Recent Nonfiction Title: *The Magic of Thinking Success*, by David J. Schwartz, Ph.D. (inspirational).

Tips: "We are looking for such books as *Jonathan Livingston Seagull*, *The Little Prince*, and *The Greatest Salesman in the World*."

WINDSOR BOOKS, Subsidary of Windsor Marketing Corp., Box 280, Brightwaters NY 11718. (516)666-4631. Managing Editor: Stephen Schmidt. Publishes hardcover and trade paperback originals, reprints, and very specific software. Averages 8 titles/year; receives approximately 40 submissions annually. 60% of books from first-time authors; 90% of books from unagented writers. Pays 10% royalty on retail price; 5% on wholesale price (50% of total cost); offers variable advance. Publishes book an average of 9 months after acceptance. Simultaneous and photocopied submissions OK. Computer printout submissions acceptable; prefers letter-quality to dot-matrix. Reports in 2 weeks on queries; 3 weeks on mss. Free book catalog and ms guidelines.

Nonfiction: How-to and technical. Subjects include business and economics (investing in stocks and commodities). Interested in books on strategies, methods for investing in the stock market, options market, and commodity markets. Query or submit outline/synopsis and sample chapters. Reviews artwork/photos as part of ms package.

Recent Nonfiction Title: *Profitable No-Load Mutual Fund Trading Techniques*, by Norman Mallory (investing).

Tips: "Our books are for serious investors; we sell through direct mail to our mailing list and other financial lists. Writers must keep their work original; this market tends to have a great deal of information overlap among publications."

WINDSOR PUBLICATIONS, 8910 Quartz Ave., Box 9071, Northridge CA 91328. Senior Publications Editor: Lin Schonberger. Receives 50 submissions annually. 25% of books from first-time authors; 100% of books from unagented writers. "We publish pictorial civic publications, business directories, and relocation guides for chambers of commerce, boards of realtors, etc. Our audience is anyone considering relocating or visiting another part of the country, and our publications document in pictures and words every aspect of a city or area. Writers and photographers work on assignment only, after having demonstrated ability through samples. Publications are annual or biennial, vary in size and are titled with the name of a city. Circulation is controlled. Writers and writer/photographers with strong interview, reporting and travel writing experience are especially sought." Publishes book an average of 10 months after acceptance.

Nonfiction: "All mss assigned. Unsolicited manuscripts and/or photos not wanted." Queries, stating writing and/or photography experience and including tearsheets, are welcome. Length: 3,000-10,000 words. Pays $500-2,400 on acceptance for all rights. Photography for each publication usually assigned to photographer on per-day rate plus expenses. Also purchases stock, speculative and existing photos on one-time use basis if they pertain to future publications. 35mm and larger color transparencies, b&w contact sheets and negatives or b&w prints (5x7 to 8x10) are acceptable; no color prints. Fully descriptive captions required.

WINE APPRECIATION GUILD LTD., Vintage Image, Wine Advisory Board, 155 Connecticut St., San Francisco CA 94107. (514)864-1202. Director: Maurice Sullivan. Imprints include Vintage Image and Wine Advisory Board (nonfiction). Publishes hardcover and trade paperback originals, trade paperback reprints, and software. Averages 26 titles/year; receives 30-40 submissions annually. 30% of books from first-time authors; 100% of books from unagented writers. Pays 5-15% royalty on wholesale price or makes outright purchase; offers average $1,000 advance. Publishes book an average of 18 months after acceptance. Simultaneous and photocopied submissions OK. Electronic submissions OK via IBM PC etc., but requires hard copy also. Reports in 2 months. Book catalog for $2.

Nonfiction: Cookbook and how-to—wine related. Subjects include wine, cooking and foods and travel. Must be wine-related. Submit outline/synopsis and sample chapters. Reviews artwork/photos as part of ms package.

Tips: "Our books are read by wine enthusiasts—from neophytes to professionals, and wine industry and food industry people. We are interested in anything of a topical and timely nature connected with wine, by a knowledgeable author. We do not deal with agents of any type. We prefer to get to know the author as a person and to work closely with him/her."

WINGBOW PRESS, Subsidiary of Bookpeople, 2929 Fifth St., Berkeley CA 94710. (415)549-3030. Editor: Randy Fingland. Small press. Publishes trade paperback originals. Averages 2-4 titles/year; receives 450 submissions annually, "mostly fiction and poetry, which we aren't even considering." 50% of books from first-time authors; 100% of books from unagented writers. Pays 7-10% royalty on retail price; offers average $250 advance. Publishes book an average of 15 months after acceptance. Photocopied submissions OK. Query for electronic submissions. Computer printout submissions OK; prefers letter-quality. Reports in 2 weeks on queries; 2 months on mss. Book catalog for #10 SAE and 1 first-class stamp.

Nonfiction: Reference and self-help. Subjects include philosophy/metaphysics, psychology and women's issues. "We are currently looking most seriously at women's studies; religion/metaphysics/philosophy; psychology and personal development. Our readers are receptive to alternative/New Age ideas. No business/finance how-to." Query or submit outline/synopsis and sample chapters.

Recent Nonfiction Title: *The Motherpeace Tarot Playbook*, by Vicki Noble and Jonathan Tenney.

*WINSTON-DEREK PUBLISHERS, Pennywell Dr., Box 90883, Nashville TN 37209. (615)329-1319/321-0535. Publisher: James W. Peebles. Pubishes hardcover, trade, and mass market paperback originals. Averages 40-45 titles/year; receives 2,500+ submissions annually. 60% of books from first-time authors; 80% of books from unagented authors. Average print order for writer's first book is 3,000-5,000. "We will co-publish exceptional works of quality and style only when we reach our quota in our trade book division." Subsidy publishes 15% of books. Pays 10-15% of the net amount received on sales. Advance varies. Simultaneous and photocopied submissions OK. Computer printout submissions acceptable; prefers letter-quality to dot-matrix. Queries and mss without SASE will be discarded. Reports in 1 month on queries; 2 months on mss. Book catalog and guidelines for 9x12 SASE.

Nonfiction: Biography (current or historically famous) and behavioral science and health (especially interested in mss of this category for teenagers and young adults). Subjects include Americana; theology; philosophy (nontechnical with contemporary format); religion (noncultist); and inspirational. Length: 50,000-60,000 words or less. Submit outline and first 2 or 4 chapters. Reviews artwork/photos as part of manuscript package. No political or technical material.

Recent Nonfiction Title: *The Christian Church and The Equal Rights Amendment*, by Edward R. Robbins.

Fiction: Ethnic (non-defamatory); religious (theologically sound); suspense (highly plotted); and Americana (minorities and whites in positive relationships). Length: 50,000 words or less. "We can use fiction with a semi-historical plot; it must be based or centered around actual facts and events—Americana, religion, gothic and science fiction. We are looking for juvenile books on relevant aspects of growing up and understanding life's situations. No funny animals talking." Children's/juvenile books must be of high quality. Submit complete ms for children and juvenile books with illustrations, which are optional.

Recent Fiction Title: *With Wings of an Eagle*, by James H. Goodman.

Poetry: Should be inspirational and with meaning. Poetry dealing with secular life should be of excellent quality. "We will accept unusual poetry books of exceptional quality and taste. We do not publish avant-garde type poetry." Submit complete ms. No single poems.

Recent Poetry Title: *Touching Fingers with God*, by Fr. Benedict Auer.

Tips: "We do not publish material that advocates violence or is derogative of other cultures or beliefs. Outstanding biographies are quite successful, as are books dealing with the simplicity of man and his relationship with his environs. Our imprint Scythe Books for children needs material for adolescents within the 9-13 age group. These manuscripts should help young people with motivation for learning and succeeding at an early age, goal setting and character building. Biographies of famous women and men as role models are always welcomed. Stories must have a new twist and be provocative."

ALAN WOFSY FINE ARTS, Box 2210, San Francisco CA 94126. Publishes hardcover and paperback originals and hardcover reprints. Subsidy publishes 15% of books. Specializes in art reference books, specifically catalogs of graphic artists; bibliographies related to fine presses and the art of the book. Pays negotiable fee on

retail price; offers advance. Publishes 5 titles annually. Reports in 1 month. Free book catalog.
Nonfiction: Publishes reference books on art. Seeking catalogs of (i.e., reference books on) collectibles. Query. Reviews artwork/photos as part of ms package.

‡**WOODBINE HOUSE**, 10400 Connecticut Ave., 512, Kensington MD 20895. (301)949-3590. Editor: Terry Rosenberg. Publishes hardcover and trade paperback originals. Averages 8-10 titles/year; receives 200-300 submissions annually. 60% of books from first-time authors; 60% of books from unagented writers. Pays royalty; buys some mss outright. Publishes book an average of 18 months after acceptance. Simultaneous and photocopied submissions OK. Query for electronic submissions. Computer printout submissions OK; prefers letter-quality. Reports in 1 month on queries; 3 months on mss. Free book catalog.
Nonfiction: Biography, humor, reference and self-help. Subjects include Americana, health, history, hobbies, sociology, parents' guides for special needs children. Especially needs parents' guides for special needs children, history and Americana. No exercise or diet books. Submit outline/synopsis and sample chapters. Review artwork/photos as part of ms.
Recent Nonfiction Title: *Babies with Down's Syndrome*, by Karen Stray Gunderson.
Fiction: Historical, mainstream and mystery. "Our fiction needs are very limited. I'd have to fall in love with a manuscript." No horror or science fiction. Submit outline/synopsis and sample chapters.
Recent Fiction Title: *Yordim*, by Micha Lev (mainstream).
Tips: "Writers must know their subjects and audience. We don't have time to do their market research."

WOODLAND BOOKS, 500 N. 1030 W. Lindon UT 84603. (801)785-8100. President: Al Lisonbee. Publishes hardcover and paperback originals. Averages 12-20 titles/year; receives 200 submissions annually. 10% of books from first-time authors; 100% of books from unagented writers. Pays 8-12% royalty on net price; no advance. Publishes book an average of 1 year after acceptance. Reports in 2 weeks on queries; 1 month on mss. Free book catalog.
Nonfiction: Cookbook, how-to, reference, self-help and textbook. Subjects include cooking and foods, health and nature. "We're looking for reputable, professionally-done, well-researched manuscripts dealing in health, natural medicine, etc." Submit outline/synopsis and sample chapters or complete ms. Reviews artwork/photos as part of ms package.
Recent Nonfiction Title: *Today's Healthy Eating*, by Louise Tenney.
Tips: "The health field is just now dawning. Health-related books of quality research are in demand."

*****WOODSONG GRAPHICS, INC.**, Box 238, New Hope PA 18938. (215)794-8321. Editor: Ellen P. Bordner. Publishes hardcover and trade paperback originals. Averages 6-8 titles/year; receives 2,500-3,000 submissions annually. 40-60% of books from first-time authors; 100% of books from unagented writers. Average print order for writer's first book is 2,500-5,000. Will occasionally consider subsidy publishing based on "quality of material, motivation of author in distributing his work, and cost factors (which depend on the type of material involved), plus our own feelings on its marketability." Subsidy publishes 20% of books. Pays royalty on net price; offers average $100 advance. Publishes book an average of 1 year after acceptance. Simultaneous submissions OK. Computer printout submissions acceptable; prefers letter-quality to dot-matrix. Reports in 1 month on queries; reports on full mss *can* take several months, depending on the amount of material already in house. "We do everything possible to facilitate replies, but we have a small staff and want to give every manuscript a thoughtful reading." Book catalog for #10 SAE and 1 first class stamp.
Nonfiction: Biography, cookbook, how-to, humor, illustrated book, juvenile, reference, and self-help. Subjects include cooking and foods, hobbies, philosophy and psychology. "We're happy to look at anything of good quality, but we're not equipped to handle lavish color spreads at this time. Our needs are very open, and we're interested in seeing any subject, provided it's handled with competence and style. Good writing from unknowns is also welcome." No pornography; only minimal interest in technical manuals of any kind. Query or submit outline/synopsis and at least 2 sample chapters. Reviews artwork/photos as part of ms package.
Recent Nonfiction Title: *The Herb Gardener's Mail Order Source Book*, by Elayne Moos.
Fiction: Adventure, experimental, fantasy, gothic, historical, humor, mainstream, mystery, romance, science fiction, suspense and western. "In fiction, we are simply looking for books that provide enjoyment. We want well-developed characters, creative plots, and good writing style." No pornography or "sick" material. Submit outline/synopsis and sample chapters.
Poetry: "We are unable to take on any new poetry manuscripts for the time being."
Tips: "Good nonfiction with an identified target audience and a definite slant has the best chance of selling to our firm. We rarely contract in advance of seeing the completed manuscript. We prefer a synopsis, explaining what the thrust of the book is without a chapter-by-chapter profile. If the query is interesting enough, we'll look at the full manuscript for further details."

*****WORD BEAT PRESS**, Box 22310, Flagstaff AZ 86002. Editor: Allen Woodman. Publishes trade paperback originals and reprints. Averages 4 titles/year; receives 500 submissions annually. 50% of books from first-time authors; 80% of books from unagented writers. Average print order for a writer's first book is 500-1,000. Subsidy publishes (nonauthor) 20% of books. Pays 10% royalty on wholesale price. Offers average $100 advance. Publishes book an average of 1 year after acceptance. Computer printout submissions acceptable; prefers letter-quality to dot-matrix. Reports in 5 weeks on queries; 3 months on mss. Book catalog and guidelines for legal size SAE and 1 first class stamp.

Fiction: Short story collections and novellas; "open to fine writing in any category." Query first.

Recent Fiction Title: *Four-Minute Fictions: Best Short-Short Stories from The North American Review*, edited by Robley Wilson, Jr.

Tips: "We hold annual fiction book competitions judged by nationally recognized writers. Past judges have included George Plimpton, Eve Shelnutt, Janet Burroway, Joy Williams and Robley Wilson, Jr. Send SASE for details. Writers have the best chance of selling short story collections."

WORD BOOKS PUBLISHER, Division of Word Inc., subsidiary of ABC, 4800 W. Waco Dr., Waco TX 76703. (817)772-7650. Managing Editor: Al Bryant. Publishes hardcover and trade paperback originals, and hardcover, trade paperback, and mass market paperback reprints. Averages 75 titles/year; receives 2,000 submissions annually. 15% of books from first-time authors; 98% of books from unagented writers. Pays 7½-15% royalty on retail price; offers average $2,000 advance. Publishes book an average of 1 year after acceptance. Photocopied submissions OK. Query for electronic submissions. Computer printout submissions acceptable; no dot-matrix. Reports in 1 month on queries; 2 months on mss. Free book catalog and ms guidelines for 9x12 SAE with 54¢ postage.

Nonfiction: Biography, "coffee table" book, cookbook, how-to, reference, self-help and textbook. Subjects include health, history (church and Bible), philosophy, politics, psychology, religion, sociology, and sports. Especially looking for "religious books that help modern-day Christians cope with the stress of life in the 20th century. We welcome queries on all types of books." Query with outline/synopsis and sample chapters. Reviews artwork/photos as part of ms package.

Recent Nonfiction Title: *Welcome Home, Davey*, by Dave Roever (overcoming serious injury).

Fiction: Religious, romance and science fiction. No non-religious fiction. Submit outline/synopsis and sample chapters.

Recent Fiction Title: *Penross Manor*, by Joan Winmill Brown (gothic novel).

‡*WORDWARE PUBLISHING, INC., Suite 101, 1506 Capital Ave., Plano TX 75074. (214)423-0090. Book packager producing 5 titles/year. Editor: Cydney C. Martin. Publishes hardcover and trade paperback originals. Averages 40 titles/year; receives 400+ submissions annually. 40% of books from first-time authors; 95% of books from unagented writers. Subsidy publishes 5% of books. "We review manuscripts on a case-by-case basis. We are primarily a trade publisher dealing with authors on a royalty basis." Pays royalty on wholesale price; advance varies. Publishes book an average of 1 year after acceptance. Simultaneous and photocopied submissions OK. "We require electronic submissions." Reports in 2 weeks. Free book catalog.

Nonfiction: Technical. Subjects include business and economics and computer. "I am always interested in books that improve upon specific software documentation. Additionally, I am willing to consider manuscripts on any new software products or 'hot' topics in the field of computers. I do not want to see anything that is not computer or business related." Query or submit outline/synopsis and sample chapters. Reviews artwork/photos as part of ms package.

Recent Nonfiction Title: *The Illustrated Turbo Pascal Book*, by Paul Schlieve (reference).

Tips: "Our audience covers the spectrum from computer novice to the professional who needs advanced reference manuals. We have very stringent deadlines that our authors must meet to access the window of opportunity for our products. So many computer books are time-sensitive and any author interested in signing with me should expect to give an all-out effort to his manuscript."

*WRIGHT PUBLISHING COMPANY, INC., Suite 303, 1422 W. Peachtree St., Atlanta GA 30309. (404)876-1900. Editor-in-Chief: Yvonne Bowman Wright. Small Press. Publishes hardcover, trade paperback, and mass market paperback originals and reprints. Averages 5 titles/year; receives 500 submissions annually. 75% of books from first-time authors; 95% of books from unagented writers. Subsidy publishes 50% of books. "We determine whether an author should be subsidy published based on the book's potential marketability and the author's financial resources." Pays 12-17% royalty on wholesale price, makes outright purchase of $2,000 maximum, or author pays for production. Offers average 20% advance. Publishes book an average of 10 months after acceptance. Computer printout submissions acceptable; no dot-matrix. Reports in 2 months on queries; 2 months on mss. Ms guidelines for #10 SASE.

Nonfiction: Biography, cookbook, how-to, humor, illustrated book, juvenile, self-help, technical, and textbook. Subjects include business and economics, cooking and foods, health, and sports. "We are especially interested in biographies and/or autobiographies, technical, business, economics, juvenile, sports, health and beauty, and cookbooks." Submit outline/synopsis and sample chapters or complete ms. Reviews artwork/photos as part of ms package.

Recent Nonfiction Title: *Confessions of a Car Salesman*, by Frank Hardy.

Fiction: Adventure, confession, erotica, ethnic, fantasy, horror, humor, mainstream, mystery, romance, science fiction, and suspense. Submit outline/synopsis and sample chapters or complete ms.

WRITER'S DIGEST BOOKS, Imprint of F & W Publications, 1507 Dana Ave., Cincinnati OH 45207. Editorial Director: David Lewis. Publishes hardcover and paperback originals (nonfiction only). Averages 45 titles/year. Pays advance and 10% royalty on net receipts. Simultaneous (if so advised) and photocopied submissions OK. Computer printout submissions OK; prefers letter-quality to dot-matrix. Publishes book an average of 1 year after acceptance. Enclose return postage. Book catalog for SASE.

Nonfiction: Writing, photography, music, and other creative pursuits, as well as general-interest subjects. "We're seeking up-to-date, how-to treatments by authors who can write from successful experience. Should be well-researched, yet lively and readable. Query or submit outline/synopsis and sample chapters. Be prepared to explain how the proposed book differs from existing books on the subject. We are also very interested in republishing self-published nonfiction books and good instructional or reference books that have gone out of print before their time. No fiction or poetry. Send sample copy, sales record, and reviews if available. If you have a good idea for a book that needs updating often, try us. We're willing to consider freelance compilers of such works." Reviews artwork/photos as part of ms package.

Recent Nonfiction Title: *Successful Lyric Writing: A Step-By-Step Course and Workbook.*

YANKEE BOOKS, Subsidiary of Yankee Publishing Inc., Main St., Dublin NH 03444. (603)563-8111. Subsidiaries include *Yankee Magazine* and *The Old Farmers' Almanac*. Editor: Clarissa M. Silitch. Publishes trade paperback and hardcover originals. Averages 10-15 titles/year. 50% of books from first-time authors; 30% of books from unagented writers. Average print order for a writer's first book is 5,000-10,000. Pays royalty with $1,000-5,000 advance. Publishes book an average of 18 months after acceptance. Query for electronic submissions. Computer printout submissions acceptable; no dot-matrix. Reports in 1 month on queries; 6 weeks on mss. Book catalog for 9x12 SASE with 90¢ postage.

Nonfiction: Cookbooks, how-to, country matters, nature, animals, subjects related in one way or another to New England: nostalgia, and nostalgic humor, Americana, antiques, cooking, crafts, gardening, the outdoors, essays, folklore and popular history, photographs, today and old-time, travel in the Northeast U.S., the sea, boats, sailors, et al. No scholarly history, even slightly off-color humor, highly technical works, or biographies of persons not strikingly interesting. Query or submit outline/synopsis and sample chapters or complete ms. Reviews artwork/photos as part of ms package.

Recent Nonfiction Title: *Whales and Man*, by Tim Dietz.

Fiction: Mystery, horror, adventure and selected fiction.

Recent Fiction Title: *Dear Lily*, by Malcolm Greenough (historical fiction).

‡YEE WEN PUBLISHING COMPANY, Subsidiary of Yee Wen Publishing Company, Ltd., Republic of China, 21 Vista Court, San Francisco CA 94080. (415)873-7167. Acquisitions Editor: Jammy Yen. Publishes hardcover originals and reprints. Averages 2-5 titles/year; receives 2 submissions annually. 10% of books from first-time authors; 100% of books from unagented writers. Pays 15% royalty on wholesale price and 10 free copies of the book. Publishes book an average of 1 year after acceptance. Simultaneous and photocopied submissions OK. Query for electronic submissions. Computer printout submissions OK; prefers letter-quality. Reports in 1 month on queries; 6 weeks on mss. Book catalog and ms guidelines for SASE.

Nonfiction: Technical and textbook. Subjects include art, history, philosophy, religion, sociology and archaeology, all of China. "We are seeking a small number of manuscripts by specialists in the studies of China either in English or in Chinese. We do not have enough submissions. We do not want manuscripts unrelated to Chinese culture." Submit outline/synopsis and sample chapters. Reviews artwork/photos as part of ms package.

Recent Nonfiction Title: *The Society of Ancient China*, by James Hsu.

Tips: "We like to get general interest books with fresh ideas and a creative approach about Chinese culture."

YORK PRESS LTD., Box 1172, Fredericton, New Brunswick E3B 5C8 Canada. (506)458-8748. General Manager/Editor: Dr. S. Elkhadem. Publishes trade paperback originals. Averages 10 titles/year; receives 25 submissions annually. 10% of books from first-time authors; 100% of books from unagented writers. Pays 5-10% royalty on wholesale price. Publishes book an average of 6 months after acceptance. Photocopied submissions OK. Computer printout submissions acceptable; prefers letter-quality to dot-matrix. Reports in 1 week on queries; 1 month on ms. Free book catalog; ms guidelines for $1.50.

Nonfiction: Reference, textbook and scholarly. Especially needs literary criticism, comparative literature and linguistics. Query.

Recent Nonfiction Title: *Eugene O'Neill*, by F. Hirsch (literary criticism).

Tips: "If I were a writer trying to market a book today, I would spend a considerable amount of time examining the needs of a publisher *before* sending my manuscript to him. Scholarly books are the only kind we publish. The writer must adhere to our style manual and follow our guidelines exactly."

ZEBRA BOOKS, Subsidiary of Kensington Publishing Corp., 475 Park Ave. S., New York NY 10016. (212)889-2299. Editorial Director: Leslie Gelbman. Publishes mass market paperback originals and reprints. Averages 600 titles/year; receives thousands of submissions annually. 50% of books from first-time authors.

Pays royalty on retail price or makes outright purchase. Publishes book an average of 12-18 months after acceptance. Simultaneous and photocopied submissions OK. Computer printout submissions acceptable; no dot-matrix. Reports in 3 months on queries; 4 months on mss. Book catalog for business size SAE and 39¢ postage.
Nonfiction: Biography, how-to, humor and self-help. Subjects include health, history and psychology. "We are open to many areas, especially self-help, stress, money management, child-rearing, health, war (WWII, Vietnam), and celebrity biographies." No nature, art, music, photography, religion or philosophy. Query or submit outline/synopsis and sample chapters.
Fiction: Adventure, men's action, confession, erotica, gothic, historical, horror, humor, mainstream, medical novels, romance and suspense. Tip sheet on historical romances, gothics, family sagas, adult romances and women's contemporary fiction is available. No poetry or short story collections. Query with synopsis and several sample chapters. SASE is a must.

THE ZONDERVAN CORP., 1415 Lake Drive, SE, Grand Rapids MI 49506. (616)698-6900. Publishes hardcover and trade and mass market paperback originals, and trade and mass market paperback reprints. Averages 100 titles/year; receives 3,500 submissions annually. 30% of books from first-time authors; 98% of books from unagented writers. Average print order for a writer's first book is 5,000. Pays royalty of 14% of the net amount received on sales of cloth and softcover trade editions and 12% of net amount received on sales of mass market paperbacks. Offers variable advance. Computer printout submissions are acceptable; prefers letter-quality to dot-matrix. The author should separate the perforated pages. Reports in 6 weeks on queries; 3 months on proposals. Book catalog for 9x12 SASE and $1.22 postage. Ms guidelines for SASE. Send proposals to Lori Walburg, manuscript review editor.
Nonfiction: Biography, "coffee table" book, how-to, humor, illustrated book, reference, devotional and gift, self-help, youth books, Bible study, inspirational romance, history books for charismatics, textbooks on philosophy, psychology, religion and sociology. All from religious perspective (evangelical). Immediate needs include "books that take a fresh approach to issues and problems in the evangelical community; that offer new insights into solving personal and interpersonal problems; and that encourage readers to mature spiritually." No mss written from an occult point of view. Query or submit outline/synopsis and 2 sample chapters.
Recent Nonfiction Title: *Choice Changes*, by Joni Eaveckson Tada (autobiography).
Fiction: Books that deal realistically and creatively with relevant social and religious issues. No mss for new children's books or poetry. Query or submit outline/synopsis and 2 sample chapters.
Recent Fiction Title: *Captain, My Captain*, by Deborah Meroff.

❝ *Rejections can be terribly depressing. I find that the best thing to do first is to get out and about. Go to a movie, have lunch with a friend. Then start in again. If you have a sense of purpose, you will overcome the rejections.* **❞**

—*Richard Cummings*
author of The Pied Piper: Allard K. Lowenstein
and the Liberal Dream

Book Packagers
and Producers

As a writer, you may have heard of book packagers, book producers or book developers, but you may not be sure what they do or what the difference is between the three. And, more importantly, you may not know what opportunities they provide for writers.

It's generally acknowledged in the industry that book packaging originated in England and moved to the U.S. in the 1940s. Until the 1970s, however, book packagers were small in number and in their impact on book publishing. When the industry experienced a tremendous increase in the amount of packagers and producers in the 1980s, *Writer's Market* identified them within the Book Publishers section. With the 1988 edition, we are classifying book packagers and producers in a separate section.

While they originally were known as book packagers, today many firms prefer to be called book producers or book developers. The terms most often refer to a company that provides a book publisher with services ranging from hiring writers, photographers or artists, to editing and delivering the finished book. In most instances, a book packager or producer develops a book proposal, assembles the people to prepare it and submits it to a publisher. When a proposal is accepted by a publisher, the producer serves several functions. When the manuscript is in preparation, the producer is an editor. As the manuscript and illustration or photo package are put together, the function changes to managing editor. Then the producer takes over coordination of production and may also serve as a sales consultant for the project. In other cases, a book publisher will contract with a book packager or producer to perform one or more of these functions instead of doing it inhouse.

The term book developer may be used to refer to a book packager or producer, or it may apply to a literary agent who joins with writers to provide writing and editorial services. An agent who functions as a book packager or developer often provides additional writing support for the author as they work together to produce a proposal. Then the agent uses his contacts within the industry to sell the work. Agents who work in book packaging have that information included in their listings in the Author's Agents section.

What makes book packagers' and producers' services so attractive to publishers? Primarily, it's speed and specialties. Many publishers with small editorial staffs use packagers and producers as extensions of their companies. An inhouse staff member can provide 20% of the work on the book and rely on the packager to produce the remaining 80%. This frees the staff member to move on to other projects. In some cases, publishers work with packagers to provide resources or knowledge they don't need fulltime but do need for a specific book. Many book packagers and producers also are experts at producing high quality illustrated books, an area where small publishers often lack inhouse expertise.

Writers who want to work in the field should be aware of differences between book publishers and book packagers. Publishers accept book proposals and ideas for books submitted to them by writers. Book packagers and agents who act as book packagers most often assign topics to writers. If you are an expert in an area, let the packager or agent know. Writers who are trying to establish themselves in the industry may consider this an attractive option but should be aware that it doesn't always provide you with credit for your writing since many books require several writers. Book producers and packagers often make outright purchases of writing or offer a large advance and low royalty percentage. Don't expect to receive a book catalog from a book producer or book packager; they produce books for other publishers' catalogs. You may ask for a sample of titles they've produced, and you may be surprised to find some bestsellers on the list. *The Joy of Sex*, by Alex Comfort, probably is still the most widely known of the titles by book packagers.

Today, it's estimated that more than 150 book packagers, producers and agents work in this field. Most, however, prefer to make their own contacts with writers and do not accept unsolicited queries. In this section, we've only included those who say they are interested in being contacted by writers. For a list of other book packagers and producers, see the latest edition of *Literary Market Place* in your local library.

‡**BYRON PREISS VISUAL PUBLICATIONS, INC.**, Subsidiaries include General Licensing Co., 12th Floor, 24 West 25th St., New York NY 10010. (212)645-9870. Senior Editor: David M. Harris. Publishes hardcover, trade paperback and mass market paperback originals. Averages 30 titles/year; receives 30-50 submissions annually. 2% of books from first-time authors; 30% of books from unagented writers. Pays 2-6% royalty on retail price; offers $3,000 average advance. Publishes book an average of 1 year after acceptance. Photocopied submissions OK. Computer printout submissions OK; prefers letter-quality to dot-matrix. Reports in 1 month on queries; 6 weeks on mss.
Nonfiction: Biography and juvenile. Subjects include history and science. "All of our books are commissioned. We need authors who are familiar with a specialized field and capable of writing for younger readers. Series under development at present include dinosaurs and biographies of prominent figures from the sciences and sports. Since all our books are commissioned, no completed manuscripts should be submitted." Query. Reviews artwork/photos as part of ms package.
Recent Nonfiction Title: *The Planets*, by Byron Preiss, ed. (astromony).
Fiction: Adventure, fantasy, historical, horror, mystery and science fiction. "We need people who can work to our specifications and who are familiar with the conventions of genre fiction." Query.
Recent Fiction Title: *Legacy of Lehr*, by Katherine Kurtz (science fiction).
Tips: "Science fiction is doing particularly well for us lately, as part of the resurgence of category fiction in the market. Interactive fiction seems to be consolidating as a part of the publishing scene, and may be moving from young adult into the mainstream."

‡**CARPENTER PUBLISHING HOUSE**, Suite 4602, 175 E. Delaware Place, Chicago IL 60611. (312)787-3569. President: Allan Carpenter. Develops hardcover originals. Averages 25 titles/year. "We develop on contract for major publishers. We assign work to a stable of authors and artists." Makes outright purchase "depending on nature of work." Negotiates advance/fee. "We are looking for authors to write but we might consider nonfiction proposals." Query for electronic submissions. Reports in 1 week on queries.
Nonfiction: Biography, juvenile, reference and supplementary texts. Subjects include Americana, history, directory/resource annuals, and travel. "We do not solicit mss. We specialize in books in large series. We would consider proposals for American biographies for school use." Query or submit concepts. All unsolicited mss are returned unopened. Reviews artwork/photos as part of ms package.
Recent Nonfiction Title: *All About the U.S.A.*, by Allan Carpenter, ed. (supplementary text).

***GRUNWALD AND RADCLIFF PUBLISHERS**, Division of Global Communications Associates, Inc., Suite 344, 5049 Admiral Wright Rd., Virginia Beach VA 23462. (804)490-1132. President and Publisher: Stefan Von Rath-Grunwald, Ph.D. Publishes hardcover and trade paperback originals, and hardcover and trade paperback reprints. Averages 10-12 titles/year; receives 120 submissions annually. 80% of books from first-time authors; "many" from unagented writers. Subsidy publishes (nonauthor) 90% of books. Pays 6-25% royalty on net receipts. Offers average $500 advance. Publishes book an average of 1 year after acceptance. Simultaneous and photocopied submissions OK. Query for electronic submissions. Computer printout submissions a must; prefers letter-quality to dot-matrix. Reports in 1 month. Book catalog for 8½x4 SAE with 1 first class stamp, plus $1.75 postage; guidelines for 10x4 SASE.
Imprints: Ben-Gurion Books and Media Productions (nonfiction and fiction), Reba A. Karp, editor. Pennsylvania Publishers (nonfiction), Michael Manfred, editor.
Nonfiction: "Coffee table" book, cookbook, reference and scholarly books. Subjects include New Age, art, cooking and foods, health, history (Civil War), philosophy and religion. "We are looking for manuscripts in the areas indicated, which can also be converted into media productions (video, audio)." No highly technical texts or topics not listed above. Query with one page synopsis only. Reviews artwork/photos as part of ms package.
Recent Nonfiction Title: *Handbook of Ayuruedic Medicine*, by Tillerson (medicine/reference).
Fiction: Query.
Recent Fiction Title: *Atlantis*, by Cuffee (New Age/novel).

‡**LUCAS-EVANS BOOKS**, 1123 Broadway, New York NY 10010. (212)929-2583. Contact: Barbara Lucas. Publishes hardcover, trade paperback originals and mass market paperback originals. Averages 10-15 titles/year. 10% of books from first-time authors. Pays 1-8% royalty, "depends on contract agreement with publisher." Makes work-for-hire assignments. Offers $3,000 average advance. Reports in 1 month on queries; 2 months on mss.
Nonfiction: Reference. "We are looking for juvenile books: preschool through high school, prefer picture book and middle grade novels." Submit complete ms.
Recent Nonfiction Title: *So Can I*, by Margery Facklam (preschool).
Fiction: Preschool through high school. No rhyming verse.

‡**LUNA VENTURES**, Box 1064, Suisun CA 94585. Editor: Paul Doerr. Publishes hardcover originals and reprints. Averages 10 titles/year; receives 100 submissions annually. "Most" of books from unagented writers. Pays percentage of 50% of profit on sales. Simultaneous and photocopied submissions OK. Query for electronic submissions. Computer printout submissions OK; prefers letter-quality to dot-matrix. Reports in 1 month. Book catalog for #10 SAE with 1 first class stamp; guidelines for #10 SASE.
Nonfiction: Biography, cookbook, how-to, reference, self-help, technical and textbook. "We will consider any subject, new or reprint. No anti-gun, anti-American or anti-space manuscripts." Query or submit outline/synopsis and sample chapters. Reviews artwork/photos as part of ms package.
Recent Nonfiction Title: *En Ballistac.*
Tips: "Write on space colonization, mining, entrepreneurs, science, technical (fiction or nonfiction). We will operate as agent also. We will offer subsidy, co-op options and a 'prestige press' service. We pay on sales. All payments are on retail (or on wholesale if we sell wholesale—we haven't yet.) We buy one print right but keep publication 'in print.' "

*****MAVERICK PUBLICATIONS**, Drawer 5007, Bend OR 97708. (503)382-6978. Publisher: Ken Asher. Publishes hardcover and trade paperback originals. Averages 15 titles/year; receives 200 submissions annually. "Like every other publisher, the number of books we can publish is limited. We would like to suggest to any writer who has a timely manuscript and is having trouble getting it published to consider publishing it themselves. We will be glad to discuss this alternative with anyone who might be interested." 40% of books from first-time authors; 95% of books from unagented writers. Pays 15% royalty on net selling price. Publishes book an average of 6 months after acceptance. Simultaneous and photocopied submissions OK. Computer printout submissions acceptable; prefers letter-quality to dot-matrix. Reports in 2 weeks on queries; 3 weeks on mss. Book catalog on request.
Nonfiction: Biography, cookbook, illustrated book, self-help and technical. Subjects include Americana, cooking and foods, health, history, hobbies, music and travel. Query. Reviews artwork/photos.
Recent Nonfiction Title: *The All Natural Baby Cookbook*, by Judy Stoffer (cookbook).
Fiction: Adventure, historical, mystery and science fantasy. "We have no specific needs, but prefer stories based on facts." Submit outline/synopsis and sample chapters.
Recent Fiction Title: *Skyhawk*, by Ted Tate and Tom Tweddale (novel).
Tips: "Book publishing trends include direct marketing by independent publishers of quality material to an intelligent public. A timely, well-researched exposé of national or at least regional importance has the best chance of selling to our firm."

OTTENHEIMER PUBLISHERS, INC., 300 Reisterstown Rd., Baltimore MD 21208. (301)484-2100. President: Allan T. Hirsh Jr. Vice-President: Allan T. Hirsh III. Managing Editor: Emeline Kroiz. Publishes hardcover and paperback originals and reprints. Publishes 250 titles/year; receives 500 submissions annually. 20% of books from first-time authors; 100% of books from unagented writers. Average print order for a writer's first book is 15,000. Negotiates royalty and advance, sometimes makes outright purchase for $25-3,000. Publishes book an average of 6 months after acceptance. Photocopied submissions OK. Computer printout submissions acceptable; prefers letter-quality to dot-matrix. Reports in 3 months.
Nonfiction: Cookbooks, reference, gardening, home repair and decorating, children's nonfiction activities, automotive and medical for the layperson. Submit outline/synopsis and sample chapters or complete ms. Reviews artwork/photos as part of ms package.
Tips: "We're looking for nonfiction adult books in the how-to information area, for mass market—we're a packager."

‡**JAMES PETER ASSOCIATES, INC.**, Box 772, Tenafly NJ 07670. (201)568-0760. President: Bert Holtje. Packages hardcover and trade paperback originals. Averages 8-12 titles/year; receives 35-50 submissions annually. 10% of books from first-time authors; 90% of books from unagented writers. Pays 30-50% royalty "on income to J.P.A. Inc." Offers $8,000-15,000 average advance. Publishes ms an average of 1 year after acceptance. Photocopied submissions OK. Query for electronic submissions. Computer printout submissions OK. Reports in 2 weeks on queries; 2 months on mss.
Nonfiction: How-to, reference, self-help and technical. Subjects include business and economics, health,

Close-up

Paul Fargis
President
American Book Producers Association

"It's a paradox," says Paul Fargis, president of the 55-member American Book Producers Association. "In a way, our members aren't really a market for writers. We're always *looking* for writers . . . but we don't want them coming to us with ideas or material."

Book producers (also called packagers or developers) usually begin a book project with their own ideas; they research the market and develop the concept for a new book before a writer is ever involved. Several bestsellers have been created by book producers. So how do you get a chance to work with a book producer?

Fargis, who is also head of The Stonesong Press, suggests that you look at what a producer has done and make sure your areas of capability fit what it publishes. Then prepare a one-page letter telling what you've done. "No query, no outline, no sample chapter, no full manuscript, no SASE," Fargis advises. "You're probably not going to get a response. Most book producers are very small and can't keep up with their mail."

The one-page letter should focus on your writing specialty, research skills, publications, work experience and area of expertise. "Tell me about your capabilities," says Fargis, speaking as a typical book producer. "Tell me what you have had published, the kind of books you want to write, the subjects that interest you, what really turns you on. Maybe even what you *don't* want to do. Tell me what your terms are; or if you're doing work for hire, or if you want to do a book on royalty, tell me what you want to get paid."

Book producers also like to know if you have a word processor or if you can use a personal computer to research information and provide it in different forms. If you know how to code a manuscript for computerized typesetting, be sure to mention that skill, too.

Don't be discouraged if you don't receive a reply. Months—or even years—may pass before the book producer happens to develop a concept that fits your interests and qualifications. Fargis says he and other ABPA members usually keep information on file about compatible writers "unless their letters are written on a 1942 Smith-Corona with a faded ribbon and Xs through the typos." Fargis shakes his head. "I get some like that. It's obvious I'm going to throw them out, because the writer didn't care enough."

Like many other book producers, Fargis prefers to work with experienced writers. "Ninety-nine percent of the time I'm not going to work with a writer who hasn't been published in some form somewhere." He suggests that unpublished writers get some credentials in trade magazines and newspapers before they approach a book producer.

When Fargis says that book producers aren't a typical market, he means they won't pay for something the writer's already written, no matter how creative or topical. Instead, book producers are more interested in the writer's ability to understand the requirements of a specific book proposal and deliver the finished manuscript in a professional manner. For writers who follow the rules, working with a book producer can be as satisfying and rewarding as any other market in the publishing industry.

—Becky Hall Williams

psychology and sociology. "We're looking for psychological subjects for general readers. Must be done by, or with professional psychologist, psychiatrist. No rehashes of pop-psych subjects." Query or submit outline/synopsis and sample chapters. All unsolicited mss are returned. Reviews artwork/photos as part of ms package.

Recent Nonfiction Title: *Personnel Administrator's Desk Book*, by Marc Dorio.

Tips: "Show us that the idea is fresh. New slants are critical! Why? The business and psychology fields are glutted with clones!"

‡POLICE BOOKSHELF,Box 122, Concord NH 03301. (603)224-6814. Director: Massad Ayoob. Publishes hardcover originals and reprints; trade paperback originals. Averages 3-6 titles/year; receives 20-30 submissions annually. "We feel a special author will earn more (and write better) if he has a financial stake from the beginning. To date, however, we have not subsidy published." Pays 10-15% royalty on retail price. Publishes book an average of 18 months after acceptance. Query for electronic submissions. Computer printout submissions OK; prefers letter-quality. Reports in 3-4 weeks on queries; 1-2 months on ms. Book catalog for 8½x11 SAE and 2 first-class stamps.

Nonfiction: Biography, how-to, reference, self-help and technical. Subjects include law enforcement and personal protection. "We want top-flight work on armed and unarmed combat, arrest procedures, court and trial techniques, officer survival and personal protection—preferably by authorities in the given field." No philosophy on crime in America or future of the criminal justice system. Submit outline/synopsis and sample chapters. Reviews artwork/photos as part of ms package.

Recent Nonfiction Title: *Street Smart Gun Book*, by John Farnam.

Tips: "Our readers want professional, nonfiction guides to police work and self-protection. We demand documentation, citations, clear illustrations and readability."

QUINLAN PRESS, 131 Beverly St., Boston MA 02114. (617)227-4870/1-800-551-2500. Executive Editor: Sandra E. Bielawa. Publishes hardcover and trade paperback originals. Averages 25-40 titles/year; receives 1,500 submissions annually. 75% of books from first-time authors; 90% of books from unagented writers. Pays 7-12% royalty on retail price; buys one ms outright for $1,000-5,000. Offers average $500 advance. Publishes book 1 year after acceptance. Simultaneous submissions OK. Query for electronic submissions. Computer printout submissions acceptable. Reports in 5 weeks on queries; 2 months on mss. Guidelines for SASE.

Nonfiction: Biography, humor, illustrated book and self-help. Subjects include Americana, animals, history, hobbies, music, photography, politics, recreation, religion, sociology and sports. "We are interested in publishing any nonfiction book we feel is consumable by the population in general. Nothing too esoteric." Submit outline/synopsis and sample chapters. Reviews artwork/photos as part of ms package.

Recent Nonfiction Title: *Rebound: The Autobiography of K.C. Jones and an Inside Look at the Champion Boston Celtics*, by K.C. Jones, with Jack Warner.

Tips: "Trends in book publishing over the last few years have included novelty items, for example our trivia series, which have been well-received as the reading public looks for a light-hearted approach to learning. For the future what we're looking toward is more nonfiction, and alternative portrayals of both stories and instructive material. Our audience is those with an interest in reading works depicting true-life experiences which are not necessarily sensational, but rather realistic and entertaining in their own right. As a publisher of many first-time authors, books stand a very good chance if their content is true-to-life and, in some way, the first of their kind."

‡ISIDORE STEPHANUS SONS, PUBLISHING, Box 6772, Ithaca NY 14851. (607)272-0056. Co-Publisher: James McGrath Morris. Publishes hardcover and trade paperback originals. Averages 3-5 titles/year; receives 5-10 submissions annually. 50% of books from first-time authors; 50% of books from unagented writers. Pays 5-15% royalty on retail price; offers $600 average advance. Publishes book an average of 6 months after acceptance. Photocopied submissions OK. Query for electronic submissions. Computer printout submissions OK; prefers letter-quality to dot-matrix. Reports in 2 weeks on queries; 1 month on mss.

Nonfiction: Biography, cookbook and illustrated book. Subjects include cooking and foods, history, politics and travel. "We are interested in regional travel books such as literary walking tours." Query. Reviews artwork/photos as part of ms package.

Recent Nonfiction Title: *Thomas Jefferson's European Travel Diaries*, by T. Jefferson (history/travel).

T.F.H. PUBLICATIONS, INC., 211 W. Sylvania Ave., Neptune City NJ 07753. (201)988-8400. Managing Editor: Neal Pronek. Publishes hardcover originals. Averages 40 titles/year; receives 200 submissions annually. 80% of books from first-time authors; 95% of books from unagented writers. Royalty varies, depending on type of book, etc. Also makes outright purchase of up to $20 per page. Offers advance of ½ of total based upon estimation of total pages in final printed work. Publishes book an average of 1 year after acceptance. Simultaneous and photocopied submissions OK. Electronic submissions OK if compatible with three major DOS's, Editwriters and Multimate. Computer printout submissions acceptable; prefers letter-quality to dot-matrix. Reports in 3 weeks. Book catalog for 8½x11 SAE with 56¢ postage; guidelines for #10 SAE with 1 first class stamp.

Nonfiction: "Coffee table" book, how-to, illustrated book, reference, technical and textbook. Subjects include animals. "Our nonfiction book manuscript needs are for books that deal with specific guidelines for people who own or are interested in purchasing a particular breed of animal. No books exclusively devoted to personal experiences with a particular pet, for example, *My Pet Sam*." Submit outline/synopsis and sample chapters. Reviews artwork/photos as part of ms package.

Recent Nonfiction Titles: *The World of Doberman Pinschers*, by Anna Katherine Nicholas.

Tips: "Our audience is any and everyone who owns a pet. We do well with books that have a lot of photographs, and those that offer good sound advice for caring for a particular breed."

WINGRA WOODS PRESS, Box 9601, Madison WI 53715. Acquisitions Editor: M.G. Mahoney. Publishes trade paperback originals. Averages 6-10 titles/year; receives 200+ submissions annually. 70% of books from first-time authors; 100% of books from unagented writers. Pays 10-12% royalty on retail price, sometimes makes outright purchase of $500-10,000. Publishes book an average of 18 months after acceptance. Simultaneous and photocopied submissions OK. Computer printout submissions acceptable. Reports in 6 weeks. Book catalog for 9x12 SAE with $1 postage.

Nonfiction: "Coffee table," cookbook, how-to, juvenile, self-help. Subjects include Americana, popular history and science, animals, art, and nature. Especially looking for popularized book-length treatments of specialized knowledge; interested in proposals from academics and professionals. Query with outline/synopsis. Do not send complete ms. Reviews artwork/photos as part of ms package.

Recent Nonfiction Title: *The Christmas Cat*.

Tips: "Put your 'good stuff' in the very first paragraph . . . tell us why we should care. Consider page 1 of the query as distilled flap copy. Then follow up with facts and credentials."

Subsidy Publishers

The following publishers produce more than 50% of their books on a subsidy basis. What they charge and what they offer to each writer varies, so you'll want to judge each publisher on its own merit. Because subsidy publishing can cost you several thousand dollars, make sure the number of books, the deadlines and services offered by a publisher are detailed in your contract. If you are willing to pay to have your book published, you should be willing to hire an attorney to review the contract. This step prevents misunderstandings between you and your prospective publisher. *Don't ever agree to terms you don't understand*. For more information on subsidy publishing, consult the Book Publishers introduction in this book.

Aegina Press and University Editions
4937 Humphrey Rd., Huntington WV 25704
Amereon Ltd.
Box 1200, Mattituck NY 11952.
Authors' Unlimited
#204, 3330 Barham Blvd., Los Angeles CA 90068
Brunswick Publishing Company
Box 555, Lawrenceville VA 23868
Carlton Press, Inc.
11 W. 32nd St., New York NY 10001
De Young Press
Box 7252, Spencer IA 57301-7252
Dow Jones-Irwin
1818 Ridge Rd., Homewood IL 60430
The Golden Quill Press
Avery Rd., Francestown NH 03043
Helix Press
4410 Hickey, Corpus Christi TX 78413
Moon Publications
722 Wall St., Chico CA 95928

R & E Publishers, Inc.
936 Industrial Ave., Palo Alto CA 94303
Peter Randall Publisher
500 Market St., Box 4726, Portsmouth NH 03801
Ronin Publishing Inc.
Box 1035, Berkeley CA 94701.
Howard W. Sams and Co., Inc.
4300 W 62nd St., Indianapolis IN 46268
Summa Publications
Box 20725, Birmingham AL 35216
University of Alaska Press
Signers' Hall, Fairbanks AK 99775-1580
Vantage Press
516 W. 34th St., New York NY 10001.
Wimmer Brothers
Box 18408, 4210 B.F. Goodrich Blvd., Memphis TN 38118
Writers Publishing Service Co.
1512 Western Ave., Seattle WA 98101

Consumer Publications

Consumer publications covered in this section are the magazines bought at the newsstand or by subscription. People read them for both information and entertainment. Consumer magazines often are slanted toward a special interest, like sports or gardening, or a particular age group, like children, women or senior citizens. Look at the Table of Contents to see how these publications are categorized. Be sure to read the brief introductions at the beginning of each section for suggestions on related markets.

Consumer magazines are a changing market. Editorial departments, focuses and formats are often restructured. New magazines are started every day, but magazines depend on income from advertisers and subscribers to keep them going. Industry statistics indicate that 9 of 10 magazine startups fail.

To keep pace with changes and startups, make regular trips to your local bookstore, newsstand or library. Read magazines like *Writer's Digest*, *Folio* and other publications that report on magazines to learn the changes that have occurred since this edition of *Writer's Market* went to press. Read the publications you find interesting and be sure to write for a sample copy if you can't locate a recent issue locally.

You'll also want to keep in mind some industry trends that affect the type of material purchased.

● A number of general interest and specialized regional magazines have started publication. Regional home and garden, sports, women's and business magazines are a few of the areas that enjoy popularity. About 50 regional women's magazines have started up in the past few years, but industry experts are uncertain how many of them will be sustained by subscribers and advertisers. Regional business magazines focus on the local impact of national policies as well as detailing mergers, acquisitions and other developments that affect the local business economy.

● Women's magazines continue to evolve, with publishers hoping to attract a broader base for both traditional women's magazines and those that target career-oriented women. In addition, the number of parenting, grandparenting and retirement magazines is increasing.

● Cooking magazines are adapting to readers' fast-paced lifestyles, new interest in gourmet food and consciousness about nutritious meals.

● Health and fitness magazines reflect a changing emphasis on individual sports and recreation, including bicycling, skiing, walking and backpacking.

● Avant-garde and alternative city magazines are enjoying a renewal. While they tend to show an irreverence for institutions, many are placing a premium on fashion and design pieces.

● In fiction, most magazines are buying shorter stories and some are discontinuing fiction. Scan the categories in the Fiction subhead—science fiction, mystery, romance, men's, women's, juvenile, teen and literary—for a listing of fiction requirements. You'll find complete information on the fiction field in *Fiction Writer's Market* (Writer's Digest Books).

● An increasing emphasis on graphics remains strong in the magazine industry. Short articles and attention to the visual impact of articles and photographs are stressed. Writers who can provide quality photographs with their manuscripts have an advantage.

As you think about magazine trends, try to develop as many options as possible for your work. You can diversify the topics you write about by expanding your knowledge on a variety of subjects. The result will be more marketing opportunities and a greater depth in your writing.

You can also increase the value of your ideas by expanding the number of publications for which you write. An easy way to accomplish this is by revising or changing the slant of one article to make it suitable for a second or third magazine. See the Trade section of this book for suggestions on writing and/or adapting consumer articles for those publications.

Remember to follow the requirements of the magazines listed in *Writer's Market*. If an editor specifically requests queries—and most of them do—don't send a complete manuscript. As you read the listings, look for those that accept simultaneous submissions and previously published material. Using these marketing techniques, you may be able to sell your writing to more magazines—and have it read by more people.

Animal

The publications in this section deal with pets, racing and show horses, other pleasure animals and wildlife. Magazines about animals bred and raised for the market are classified in the Farm category. Publications about horse racing can be found in the Sports section.

AMERICAN FARRIERS JOURNAL, The Laux Company Publishers, Inc., 63 Great Rd., Maynard MA 01754. (617)897-5552. Contact: Editor. Published 7 times/year. Magazine covering horseshoeing, horse health related to legs and feet of horses and metalworking for a professional audience of full-time horseshoers, veterinarians and horse trainers. Circ. 4,000. Pays on publication. Byline given. Buys all rights. Submit material 3 months in advance. Computer printout submissions acceptable; dot-matrix submissions accepted only when double-spaced. Reports in 4 weeks on queries; 2 weeks on mss. Writer's guidelines for SAE and 1 first class stamp.
Nonfiction: Book excerpts, general interest, historical/nostalgic, how-to, interview/profile, new product, personal experience, photo feature and technical. Buys 50 mss/year. Send complete ms. Length: 800-3,000 words. Pays 30¢ per published line.
Photos: Send photos with ms. Reviews b&w contact sheets, b&w negatives, 35mm color transparencies, and 8x10 b&w or color prints. Pays $10 per published photo. Captions and identification of subjects required. Buys one-time rights.

ANIMAL KINGDOM, New York Zoological Society,185 St. and Southern Blvd., Bronx NY 10460. (212)220-5121. Editor: Eugene J. Walter, Jr. Executive Editor: Penelope J. O'Prey. 89% freelance written. A bimonthly magazine on zoology, animal behavior and conservation. Circ. 155,000. Pays on acceptance. Byline given. Offers $100 kill fee. Buys all rights. Submit seasonal/holiday material 9 months in advance. Simultaneous submissions OK. Computer printout submissions OK; prefers letter-quality to dot-matrix. Reports in 1 month. Sample copy $2 with 9x12 SAE and 4 first class stamps. Free writer's guidelines.
Nonfiction: Nancy Simmons Christie, articles editor. Book excerpts, essays, historical, how-to, humor, personal experience, photo feature and travel. No pet stories. Buys 24 mss/year. Query with published clips. Length: 1,500-2,500 words. Pays $550-800 for assigned and unsolicited articles. Pays in copies "at request of author."
Photos: State availability of photos with submission. Reviews transparencies. Offers $35-200 per photo. Identification of subjects required. Buys one-time rights.
Columns/Departments: Bookshelf (reviews of wildlife books for adults/children); Images (reviews of art shows, TV, films related to wildlife); both 300-600 words. Buys 18 mss/year. Query with published clips. Pays $75-150.

‡ANIMALS, Massachusetts Society for the Prevention of Cruelty to Animals, 350 S. Huntington Ave., Boston MA 02130. (617)522-7400. Editor: Joni Praded. Managing Editor: Paula Abend. 90% freelance written. Bimonthly magazine covering animals. "*Animals* publishes articles on wildlife (American and international), domestic animals, controversies involving animals, conservation, animal welfare issues, pet health and pet care." Circ. 50,000. Pays on publication. Publishes ms an average of 5 months after acceptance. Byline given.

Offers negotiable kill fee. Buys one-time rights or makes work-for-hire assignments. Submit seasonal/holiday material 6 months in advance. Photocopied submissions OK. Computer printout submissions OK; prefers letter-quality. Reports in 1 month. Sample copy $2.50 with 9x12 SAE and $1.20 postage. Writer's guidelines for #10 SAE and 1 first class stamp.

Nonfiction: Essays, expose, general interest, how-to, opinion and photo feature. "*Animals* does not want to see sentimental, personal stories such as those describing an individual's relationship with a pet or stories of nursing baby wild animals back to health. *Animals* also does not publish poetry or fiction." Buys 36 mss/year. Query with published clips. Length: 3,000 words maximum. Pays $300 maximum for assigned and unsolicited articles. Sometimes pays the expenses of writers on assignment.

Photos: State availability of photos with submission. Reviews contact sheets, 35mm transparencies and 5x7 or 8x10 prints. Offers $60 per photo. Captions, model releases and identification of subjects required. Buys one-time rights.

Columns/Departments: Books (book reviews of books on animals and animal-related subjects), 300 words; Guest Appearance (personal opinion on animal or conservation issues), 600 words. Buys 18 mss/year. Query with published clips. Length: 300 words maximum. Pays $75 maximum.

Tips: "Present a well-researched proposal. Be sure to include clips that demonstrate the quality of your writing. Stick to categories mentioned in *Animals'* editorial description. Combine well-researched facts with a lively, original writing style. Feature stories are written almost exclusively by freelancers."

APPALOOSA WORLD, Appaloosa World Magazine, Inc., Box 1035, Daytona Beach FL 32029. (904)767-6284. Editor: Gerald A. Matacale. 75% freelance written. A monthly magazine highlighting Appaloosa breed show news, results and events. Features training and breeding articles as well as the breed's leading personalities and horses. Circ. 40,112. Pays on acceptance. Byline given. Offers 100% kill fee. Buys first rights and second serial (reprint) rights, and makes work-for-hire assignments. Photocopied and previously published submissions OK. Computer printout submissions acceptable; prefers letter-quality to dot-matrix. Reports in 1 week. Sample copy $5; free writer's guidelines.

Nonfiction: How-to (horse or rider training) and interview/profile (on assignment only). No articles written for children, or horse lovers as opposed to horse owners. Buys 200-300 mss/year. Query with published clips. Length: 1,000-5,000 words. Pays $8/double-spaced pica typewritten page. Pays expenses of writers on assignment.

Photos: Send photos with submission. Reviews 4x5 or larger prints. Offers $5/photo. Captions required. Buys one-time rights.

Tips: "The best approach is a telephone call to the editor."

ARABIAN HORSE TIMES, Adams Corp., Rt. 3, Waseca MN 56093. (507)835-3204. Editor: Marian Studer-Johnson. Managing Editor: Ronda Morehead. 20% freelance written. Works with a small number of new/unpublished writers each year. Monthly magazine about Arabian horses. Editorial format includes hard news (veterinary, new products, book reports, etc.), lifestyle and personality pieces, and bloodline studies. Circ. 19,000. Pays on publication. Publishes ms an average of 6 months after acceptance. Byline given. Offers 33% kill fee. Buys first serial rights. Submit seasonal/holiday material 3 months in advance. Simultaneous queries OK. Computer printout submissions acceptable; prefers letter-quality to dot-matrix. Reports in 3 weeks on queries; 6 weeks on mss. Free sample copy and writer's guidelines.

Nonfiction: General interest, how-to, interview/profile, new product and photo feature. Buys at least 12 mss/year. Query with published clips. Length: 1,000-5,000 words. Pays $75-350. Sometimes pays expenses of writers on assignment.

Photos: Prefers 5x7 color prints. Payment depends on circumstances. Captions and identification of subjects required. Buys one-time rights.

Fiction: Will look at anything about horses except erotica. Buys 1-2 mss/year. Send complete ms. Length: 1,500-5,000 words. Pays $75-250.

Poetry: Horse-related poetry only. Buys 1-2 poems/year. Submit maximum of 1 poem. Pays $25.

Fillers: Buys 12/year. Length: 100-500 words. Pays $10-75.

Tips: "As our periodical is specific to Arabian horses, we are interested in anyone who can write well and tightly about them. Send us something timely. Also, narrow your topic to a specific horse, incident, person or problem. 'Why I Love Arabians' will not work."

BIRD TALK, Dedicated to Better Care for Pet Birds, Fancy Publications, Box 6050, Mission Viejo CA 92690. (714)240-6001. Editor: Karyn New. 85% freelance written. Works with a small number of new/unpublished writers each year. Monthly magazine covering the care and training of cage birds for men and women who own any number of pet or exotic birds. Circ. 100,000. Pays latter part of month in which article appears. Publishes ms an average of 4 months after acceptance. Byline given. Buys first North American serial rights. Submit seasonal/holiday material 5 months in advance. Photocopied and previously published submissions OK. Computer printout submissions acceptable; prefers letter-quality to dot-matrix. Reports in 3 weeks on queries; 8 weeks on mss. Sample copy $3; writer's guidelines for 9x12 SAE and 1 first class stamp.

Nonfiction: General interest (anything to do with pet birds); historical/nostalgic (of bird breeds, owners, cages); how-to (build cages, aviaries, playpens and groom, feed, breed, tame); humor; interview/profile (of bird and bird owners); new product; how-to (live with birds—compatible pets, lifestyle, apartment adaptability, etc.); personal experience (with your own bird); photo feature (humorous or informative); travel (with pet birds or to see exotic birds); and articles giving medical information, legal information, and description of breeds. No juvenile or material on wild birds not pertinent to pet care; everything should relate to *pet* birds. Buys 150 mss/year. Query or send complete ms. Length: 500-3,000 words. Pays 3-5¢/word.

Photos: State availability of photos. Reviews b&w contact sheets. Pays $75-150 for color transparencies; $15 minimum for 8x10 b&w prints. Model release and identification of subjects required. Buys one-time rights.

Columns/Departments: Editorial (opinion on a phase of owning pet birds) and Small Talk (short news item of general interest to bird owners). Buys 20 mss/year. Send complete ms. Length: 300-1,200 words. Pays 3¢/word and up.

Fiction: "Only fiction with pet birds as primary focus of interest." Adventure, fantasy, historical, humorous, mystery, suspense. No juvenile, and no birds talking unless it's their trained vocabulary. Buys 6 mss/year. Send complete ms. Length: 2,000-3,000 words. Pays 3¢/word and up.

Tips: "Send grammatical, clean copy on a human-interest story about a pet bird or about a medical or health-related topic. We also need how-tos on feather crafts; cage cover making; aviary, perch and cage building; and planting plants in aviaries safe and good for birds. Keep health, nutrition, lack of stress in mind regarding pet birds. Study back issues to learn our style."

CAT FANCY, Fancy Publications, Inc., Box 6050, Mission Viejo CA 92690. (714)240-6001. Editor: Linda W. Lewis. 80-90% freelance written. Monthly magazine for men and women of all ages interested in all phases of cat ownership. 80 pages. Circ. 200,000. Pays after publication. Publishes ms an average of 6 months after acceptance. Buys first American serial rights. Byline given. Submit seasonal/holiday material 4 months in advance. Computer printout submissions acceptable. Reports in 6 weeks. Sample copy $3; writer's guidelines for SASE.

Nonfiction: Historical, medical, how-to, humor, informational, personal experience, photo feature and technical. Buys 5 mss/issue. Query or send complete ms. Length: 500-3,000 words. Pays 3-5¢/word.

Photos: Photos purchased with or without accompanying ms. Pays $15 minimum for 8x10 b&w glossy prints; $50-150 for 35mm or 2¼x2¼ color transparencies. Send prints and transparencies. Model release required.

Fiction: Adventure, fantasy, historical and humorous. Nothing written with cats speaking. Buys 1 ms/issue. Send complete ms. Length: 500-3,000 words. Pays 5¢/word.

Fillers: Newsworthy or unusual; items with photo and cartoons. Buys 10 fillers/year. Length: 100-500 words. Pays $20-35.

Tips: "We receive more filler-type articles than we can use. It's the well-researched, hard information article we need."

CATS MAGAZINE, Cats Magazine Inc., Box 290037, Port Orange FL 32029. (904)788-2770. Editor: Linda J. Walton. 50% freelance written. A monthly magazine for cat lovers, veterinarians, breeders and show enthusiasts. Circ. 120,000. Pays on publication. Byline given. Buys one-time rights. Submit seasonal/holiday material 7 months in advance. Reports in 1 month on queries; 3 months on manuscripts (sometimes longer depending on the backlog.) Free sample copy and writer's guidelines.

Nonfiction: Book excerpts; general interest (concerning cats); how-to (care for cats); humor; interview/profile (on cat owning personalities); new product; personal experience; photo feature; and technical (veterinarian writers). No talking cats. Buys 36 mss/year. Send complete ms. Length 800-2,500 words. Pays $25-300.

Photos: Send photos with submission. Reviews transparencies. Offers $5-25/photo. Identification of subjects required. Buys one-time rights.

Fiction: Fantasy, historical, mystery, science fiction, slice-of-life vignettes and suspense. "We rarely use fiction, but are not averse to using it if the cat theme is handled in smooth, believable manner. All fiction must involve a cat or relationship of cat and humans, etc." No talking cats. Buys 4-6 mss/year. Send complete ms. Length: 800-2,500 words. Pays $25-300.

Poetry: Avant-garde, free verse, haiku, light verse and traditional. Length: 4-64 lines. Pays 50¢/line.

Tips: "Fiction and articles are the freelancer's best bet. Writers must at least like cats. Writers who obviously don't, miss the mark."

THE CHRONICLE OF THE HORSE, The Chronicle of the Horse, Inc., Box 46, Middleburg VA 22117. (703)687-6341. Editor: John Strassburger. Managing Editor: Nancy Comer. 80% freelance written. Weekly magazine about horses. "We cover English riding sports, including horse showing, grand prix jumping competitions, steeplechase racing, foxhunting, dressage, endurance riding, handicapped riding and combined training. We are the official publication for the national governing bodies of many of the above sports. We feature news of the above sports, and we also publish how-to articles on equitation and horse care, and interviews with leaders in the various fields." Circ. 22,000. Pays for features on acceptance; news and other items on publication. Publishes ms an average of 3 months after acceptance. Byline given. Buys first North American rights and makes work-for-hire assignments. Submit seasonal/holiday material 3 months in advance. Computer printout submissions acceptable only if double-spaced, 8½x11 format; prefers letter-quality. Simultaneous queries and photocopied submissions OK. Reports in 2 weeks. Sample copy $2; free writer's guidelines.

Nonfiction: General interest; historical/nostalgic (history of breeds, use of horses in other countries and times, art, etc.); how-to (trailer, train, design a course, save money, etc.); humor (centered on living with horses or horse people); interview/profile (of nationally known horsemen or the very unusual); technical (horse care, articles on feeding, injuries, care of foals, shoeing, etc.); and news (of major competitions, clear assignment with us first). Special issues include Steeplechasing; Grand Prix Jumping; Combined Training; Dressage; Hunt Roster; Junior and Pony; and Christmas. No Q&A interviews, clinic reports, Western riding articles, personal experience, or wild horses. Buys 300 mss/year. Query or send complete ms. Length: 300-1,225 words. Pays $25-200.

Photos: State availability of photos. Reviews 5x7 b&w prints. Pays $10-25. Identification of subjects required. Buys one-time rights.

Columns/Departments: Dressage, Combined Training, Horse Show, Horse Care, Polo, Racing, Racing over Fences, Young Entry (about young riders, geared for youth), Horses and Humanities, and Hunting. Query or send complete ms. Length: 300-1,225 words. Pays $25-200.

Poetry: Light verse and traditional. No free verse. Buys 100 mss/year. Length: 5-30 lines. Pays $15.

Fillers: Anecdotes, short humor, newsbreaks and cartoons. Buys 250 mss/year. Length: 50-175 lines. Pays $10-25.

Tips: "Get our guidelines. Our readers are sophisticated, competitive horsemen. Articles need to go beyond common knowledge. Freelancers often attempt too broad or too basic a subject. We welcome well-written news stories on major events, but clear the assignment with us."

DOG FANCY, Fancy Publications, Inc., Box 6050, Mission Viejo CA 92690. (714)240-6001. Editor: Linda Lewis. 75% freelance written. Eager to work with unpublished writers. "We'd like to see a balance of both new and established writers." Monthly magazine for men and women of all ages interested in all phases of dog ownership. Circ. 120,000. Pays after publication. Publishes ms an average of 9 months after acceptance. Buys first American serial rights. Byline given. Submit seasonal/holiday material 4 months in advance. Computer printout submissions acceptable; prefers letter-quality to dot-matrix. Sample copy $3; writer's guidelines for SASE.

Nonfiction: Historical, medical, how-to, humor, informational, interview, personal experience, photo feature, profile and technical. "We're planning one or two *major* features covering significant events in the dog world. We'll be looking for (and paying more for) high quality writing/photo packages on topics outside of our normal range of features. Interested writers should query with topics." Buys 5 mss/issue. Query or send complete ms. Length: 500-3,000 words. Pays 5¢/word. Sometimes pays the expenses of writers on assignment.

Photos: Photos purchased with or without accompanying ms. Pays $15 minimum for 8x10 b&w glossy prints; $50-150 for 35mm or 2¼x2¼ color transparencies. Send prints and transparencies. Model release required.

Fiction: Adventure, fantasy, historical and humorous. Buys 5 mss/year. Send complete ms. Length: 500-3,000 words. Pays 5¢/word.

Fillers: "Need short, punchy photo fillers and cartoons." Buys 10 fillers/year. Pays $20-35.

Tips: "We're looking for the unique experience that communicates something about the dog/owner relationship—with the dog as the focus of the story, not the owner. Articles that provide hard information (medical, etc.) through a personal experience are appreciated. Note that we write for a lay audience (non-technical), but we do assume a certain level of intelligence: no talking down to people. If you've never seen the type of article you're writing in *Dog Fancy*, don't expect to."

‡**EASTERN HORSE WORLD**, Garri Publications, Inc., 114 West Hills Rd., Box 249, Huntington Station NY 11746. (516)549-3557. Editor: Diana DeRosa. 25% freelance written. A magazine, published 18 times per year, on horses. Circ. 16,500. Pays on publication. Byline given. Buys first North American serial rights. Submit seasonal/holiday material 6 months in advance. Query for electronic submissions. Computer printout submissions OK; no dot-matrix. Reports in 3 months on queries. Sample copy $3.50; writer's guidelines for #10 SAE with 1 first class stamp.

Nonfiction: Interview/profile and new product. Buys 25 mss/year. Query with published clips. Length: 100-2,000 words. Pays $5-125 or offers complimentary ad in directory as payment.

Photos: State availability of photos with submission or send photos with submission. Reviews 5x7 prints. Offers $5-10 per photo. Captions, model releases and identification of subjects required. Buys one-time rights.

Columns/Departments: Horse Tidbits. Query with published clips. Length: 500-1,000 words. Pays $75 maximum.

Fillers: Anecdotes, facts, gags to be illustrated by cartoonist, and short humor. Buys 18/year. Length: 25 words minimum. Pays $5 maximum.

Tips: "We are an information center for horse people. Write for guidelines. We like to work with writers and artists who are new and are not necessarily looking for money but rather a chance to be published."

‡**THE GREYHOUND REVIEW**, Box 543, Abilene KS 67410. (913)263-4660. Editor: Gary Guccione. Managing Editor: Tim Horan. 20% freelance written. A monthly magazine covering greyhound breeding, training and racing. Circ. 6,300. Pays on acceptance. Byline given. Buys first rights. Submit seasonal/holiday material 2 months in advance. Query for electronic submissions. Computer printout submissions acceptable. Reports in 1 week on queries; 3 weeks on mss. Sample copy $2.50. Free writer's guidelines.

Nonfiction: How-to, interview/profile and personal experience. "Articles must be targeted at the greyhound industry: from hard news, special events at racetracks to the latest medical discoveries." Do not submit gambling systems. Buys 24 mss/year. Query. Length: 1,000-10,000 words. Pays $50-150. Sometimes pays the expenses of writers on assignment.

Photos: State availability of photos with submission. Reviews 35mm transparencies and 8x10 prints. Offers $10-50 per photo. Identification of subjects required. Buys one-time rights.

‡**THE HORSE DIGEST, The News and Business Journal of the Horse Industry**, Sport Horse Publishing, Inc., 3 Royal St. SE, Leesburg VA 22075. (703)777-6508. Editorial Director: Bob Naylor. Managing Editor: Cathy Laws. 80% freelance written, "including reprints from other horse publications, for which we usually pay writer $35." Works with a small number of new/unpublished writers each year. Monthly magazine covering all aspects of all breeds and disciplines of the horse industry, with primary focus on North America. "We reach subscribers nationwide and in Canada; average age 39.5; average household income $49,764; 61.3% female; 96.3% own horses." Circ. 21,000. Pays on acceptance. Publishes ms an average of 3 months after acceptance. Byline given. Kill fees paid only under special prior arrangement. Buys one-time rights. Submit seasonal/holiday material 3 months in advance. Simultaneous queries, and simultaneous, photocopied, and previously published submissions OK. Computer printout submissions acceptable; prefers letter-quality to dot-matrix. Reports in 6 weeks. Sample copy for 8x10 SAE with $1.25 postage.

Nonfiction: Book excerpts; expose; general interest; how-to (horse management, equine health, conditioning, equipment, and farm or horse business management); humor (rarely, except for short items); interview (questions and answers with trendsetters in the horse industry); new product (query us first); and technical. Special issues include breeding (January); horse sales and auctions (March); and others to be scheduled. "No first-person pieces on writer's love affair or experiences with Old Dobbin; no articles too specific to one breed, region or discipline or addressed to unsophisticated audience." Buys 40 mss/year. Query with published clips. Length: 800-2,500 words. Pays $75-200. "We also pay for news tips." Pays expenses of writers on assignment.

Photos: State availability of photos with query or ms. Reviews contact sheets, 8x10 b&w glossy prints and 2¼x2¼ color transparencies. Pays $150-200 color (cover); $15-50 b&w prints. Identification of subjects required. Buys one-time rights.

Columns/Departments: Interview (questions and answers with equine industry pacesetters, trendsetters); Experts Speak (3 experts' approaches to common problem); and The Topic Is (5-7 different perspectives on trends or events in or affecting the industry). Buys 40-50 mss/year. Query with published clips. Length: 750-1,000 words. Pays $75-125; "often pays some documented phone expenses, too."

Fillers: Clips, anecdotes and newsbreaks. Buys approximately 50/year, "but mostly from regular correspondents." Length: 100-250 words. "We usually rewrite them." Pays $10-50.

Tips: "We are actively recruiting business and medical writers with horse industry knowledge. Writers have a better chance of breaking in with short, lesser-paying articles and fillers because we use more of them and we are always hungry for news items—trends spotted in the bud, scams and scandals, mergers, high-dollar syndications or sales, etc. Also, send us a résumé and best clips (no more than six). We may need you as a regional correspondent. Correspondents feed us clippings, items picked up through contacts and press releases; help research regional aspects of national stories upon request; and handle one to three feature assignments per year."

HORSE ILLUSTRATED, The Magazine for Responsible Horse Owners, Fancy Publications, Inc., Box 6050, Mission Viejo CA 92680. (714)240-6001. Editor: Jill-Marie Jones. 90% freelance written. Prefers to work with published/established writers but are eager to work with new/unpublished writers. Monthly magazine covering all aspects of horse ownership. "Our readers are adult women between the ages of 18 and 40; stories should be geared to that age group and reflect responsible horse care." Circ. 65,000. Pays on publication. Publishes ms an average of 8 months after acceptance. Byline given. Buys one-time rights. Submit seasonal/holiday material 6 months in advance. Computer printout submissions acceptable; prefers letter-quality to dot-matrix. Reports in 6 weeks on queries; 2 months on mss. Sample copy $3. Writer's guidelines for SAE with 1 first class stamp.

Nonfiction: How-to (horse care, training, veterinary care), humor, personal experience and photo feature. No "little girl" horse stories; "cowboy and Indian" stories; anything not *directly* relating to horses. "We are beginning to look for longer, more in-depth features on trends and issues in the horse industry. (See our three-part series on equestrian colleges, May to July, 1987.) Such articles must be queried first with a detailed outline of the article and clips." Buys 100 mss/year. Query or send complete ms. Length: 1,000-2,500 words. Pays $100-250 for assigned articles. Pays $50-200 for unsolicited articles. Sometimes pays telephone bills for writers on assignment.

Photos: Send photos with submission. Reviews contact sheet, 35mm transparencies and 5x7 prints. Offers no additional payment for photos accepted with ms.

Tips: "Freelancers can break in at this publication with feature articles on Western and English training methods and trainer profiles (including training tips); veterinary and general care how-to articles; and horse sports articles. While we use personal experience articles (six to eight times a year), they must be extremely well-written and have wide appeal; humor in such stories is a bonus. Submit photos with training and how-to articles whenever possible. We have a very good record of developing new freelancers into regular contributors/columnists. We are always looking for fresh talent, but certainly enjoy working with established writers who 'know the ropes' as well."

HORSEPLAY, Box 130, Gaithersburg MD 20877. (301)840-1866. Editor: Cordelia Doucet. 50% freelance written. Works with published/established writers and a small number of new/unpublished writers each year. Monthly magazine covering horses and English horse sports for a readership interested in horses, show jumping, dressage, combined training, hunting, and driving. 60-80 pages. Circ. 48,000. Pays end of publication month. Buys all rights, first North American serial rights, and second serial (reprint) rights. Offers kill fee. Byline given. Query before sending finished work. Deadline is 2 months prior to issue date. Nothing returned without SASE. Computer printout submissions acceptable; no dot-matrix. Reports within 3 weeks. Sample copy $2.95; free writer's and photographer's guidelines.

Nonfiction: Instruction (various aspects of horsemanship, course designing, stable management, putting on horse shows, etc.); competitions; interview; photo feature; profile and technical. Length: 1,000-3,000 words. Pays 9¢/word, all rights; 8¢/word, first North American serial rights; 7¢/word, second rights. Sometimes pays extra to writers on assignment.

Photos: Cathy Heard, art director. Purchased on assignment. Write captions on separate paper attached to photo. Query or send contact sheet, prints or transparencies. Pays $20 for 8x10 b&w glossy prints; $175 for color transparencies for cover; $45 for inside color.

Tips: Don't send fiction, Western riding, or racing articles.

HORSES ALL, Box 550, Nanton Alberta T0L 1R0 Canada. (403)646-2271. Editor: Jacki French. 30% freelance written. Eager to work with new/unpublished writers. Monthly tabloid for horse owners, 75% rural, 25% urban. Circ. 11,200. Pays on publication. Publishes ms an average of 6 months after acceptance. Buys one-time rights. Phone queries OK. Submit seasonal material 3 months in advance. Simultaneous, photocopied (if clear), and previously published submissions OK. Computer printout submissions acceptable; no dot-matrix. Reports on queries in 5 weeks; on mss in 6 weeks. Sample copy $2.

Nonfiction: Interview, humor and personal experience. Query. Pays $20-100. Sometimes pays the expenses of writers on assignment.

Photos: State availability of photos. Captions required.

Columns/Departments: Open to suggestions for new columns/departments. Send query to Doug French. Length: 1-2 columns.

Fiction: Historical and western. Query. Pays $20-100.

Tips: "We use more short articles. The most frequent mistakes made by writers in completing an article assignment for us are poor research, wrong terminology, and poor (terrible) writing style."

LONE STAR HORSE REPORT, Box 14767, Fort Worth TX 76117. (817)834-3951. Editor: Henry L. King. 15-20% freelance written. Monthly magazine on horses and horse people in and around Dallas/Ft. Worth metroplex. Circ. 6,364. Pays on publication. Publishes ms an average of 2 months after acceptance. Byline given. Buys first rights and second serial (reprint) rights to material originally published elsewhere. Submit seasonal/holiday material 2 months in advance. Photocopied and previously published submissions OK. Computer printout submissions OK; prefers letter quality. Reports in 2 weeks on queries; 4 weeks on mss. Sample copy $1; free writer's guidelines.

Nonfiction: How-to (how a specific horseman trains horses for specific events); interview/profile (horsemen living in trade area); photo feature (horses, farms, arenas, facilities, people in trade area). Buys 30-40 mss/year. Query with published clips or send complete ms. Length: 200-2,000 words. Pays $15-60. Sometimes pays the expenses of writers on assignment.

Photos: State availability of photos. Pays $5 for 5x7 b&w prints. Buys one-time rights.

Tips: "We need reports of specific horse-related events in north Texas area such as trail rides, rodeos, play days, shows, etc., and also feature articles on horse farms, outstanding horses and/or horsemen. Emphasis on local events as opposed to events which would attract national coverage is a trend that writers should be aware of. If Texas voters pass a referendum on pari-mutuel racing, we will place more emphasis on racing and race-horse breeding."

THE MORGAN HORSE, American Morgan Horse Association, Box 1, Westmoreland NY 13490. (315)735-7522. Editor: James Bloomquist. 55% freelance written. Prefers to work with published/established writers. Monthly breed journal covering the training, showing, and vet care of Morgan horses. Circ. 10,000. Pays on publication. Publishes ms an average of 2½ months after acceptance. Byline given. Rights vary with submission. Submit seasonal/holiday material 3 months in advance. Simultaneous queries and simultaneous, photocopied, and previously published submissions OK (subject to editor's discretion). Computer printout submissions acceptable; prefers letter-quality to dot-matrix. Reports in 3 months. Sample copy $4; writer's guidelines for business size SAE and 1 first class stamp.

Nonfiction: How-to (trailering, driving, training, etc.); human interest (if highly unusual); interview/profile (of respected Morgan personalities); veterinary articles. Special issues include Morgan Grand National, Stallion, Mare, Gelding, Foal, International. No articles dealing with half-bred Morgans. "We have few fillers we can print but always seem to receive more than our share of them." Buys 15-20 mss/year. Query with clips of published work. Length: 500-3,000 words. Pays 5¢/word and up. "Infrequently" pays the expenses of writers on assignment.

Photos: Send photos with ms. Pays $5 minimum for 8x10 b&w prints, $25 for color. Captions, model releases and identification of subjects required.

Tips: "We like to see complete manuscripts from new writers and welcome articles on veterinary breakthroughs and training."

NATIONAL SHOW HORSE, (formerly *National Show Horse News*), National Show Horse Registry, Suite 237, 10401 Linn Station Rd., Louisville KY 40223. (502)423-1902. Editor: Mary Kirkman. News Editor: Les Sellnow. 10-20% freelance written. Prefers to work with published/established writers, but works with a small number of new/unpublished writers each year. A magazine covering "all aspects of the horse industry as it applies to National Show Horse." Circ. 5,000. Pays on acceptance. Byline given. Buys one-time rights. Computer printout submissions acceptable; prefers letter-quality to dot-matrix. Reports within 2 weeks. Free sample copy and writer's guidelines.

Nonfiction: How-to (training the English style show horse); interview/profile (of successful breeders/exhibitors or persons involved in the field—artist, photographers, etc.); and photo feature (must tie directly to some aspect of National Show Horse World). "We also need in-depth features of well-known National Show Horses and NSH-nominated Arabian and Saddlebred stallions or mares being used in NSH breeding programs, including analysis of pedigrees and show records, and historical retrospectives of great horses in Arabian and Saddlebred breeds, including their influence on the National Show Horse breed." Query. Length: 3,000-5,000 words. Pays $100-250. Sometimes pays the expenses of writers on assignment.

Photos: State availability of photos with query letter or ms. Reviews transparencies and prints. Pays $10. Captions and identification of subjects required. Buys one-time rights.

PACIFIC COAST JOURNAL, Pacific Coast Quarter Horse Association, Gate 12, Cal-Expo, Box 25482, Sacramento CA 95825. (916)924-7265. Editor: Jill L. Scopinich. 20% freelance written. A monthly magazine covering Cutting and Quarter Horses on the Pacific Coast published by and for members of two equine groups which concentrate on Cutting and Quarter Horses. "It is more technical than most equine publications and our readers are extremely knowledgeable on the subject." Circ. 8,000. Pays on acceptance. Byline given. Offers 50% kill fee. Buys first rights and second serial (reprint) rights. Simultaneous, photocopied and previously published submissions OK. Computer printout submissions acceptable; no dot-matrix. Reports in 3 months. Sample copy for 9x12 SAE with $1.50 postage. Writer's guidelines for #10 SAE with 1 first class stamp.

Nonfiction: How to train Quarter or Cutting Horses, make or care for tack, trailers, etc. No articles that are aimed at newcomers to the horse industry, or that are about other breeds. Buys 36 mss/year. Send complete ms. Length: 750-3,000 words. Pays $100-300 for assigned articles; $50-175 for unsolicited articles; will trade advertising if writer requests. Sometimes pays expenses of writers on assignment.

Photos: Send photos with submission. Reviews contact sheets, transparencies, and 5x7 prints. Offers no additional payment for photos accepted with ms unless negotiated in advance. Captions, model releases, and identification of subjects required. Buys one-time rights.

Columns/Departments: Bookshelf (reviews of books written by professionals concerning the Quarter or Cutting Horse industries). Buys 12 mss/year. Send complete ms. Length: 300-500 words. Pays $35-50.

Fillers: Anecdotes, facts and short humor. Buys 24/year. Length: 50-100 words. Pays $20-40.

Tips: "Send examples of your work that have been published in other equine magazines, or send a cover letter explaining your expertise in the field you are writing about. It is important to our readers that our writers are knowledgeable in the fields of Cutting and Quarter horses. At all times remember that our readers are well-educated in the industry and the majority is professionals, so never speak down to them."

PAINT HORSE JOURNAL, American Paint Horse Association, Box 18519, Fort Worth TX 76118. (817)439-3400. Editor: Bill Shepard. 10% freelance written. Works with a small number of new/unpublished writers each year. For people who raise, breed and show Paint horses. Monthly magazine. Circ. 12,000. Pays on acceptance. Publishes ms an average of 3 months after acceptance. Buys first North American serial rights plus reprint rights occasionally. Pays negotiable kill fee. Byline given. Phone queries OK, but prefers written query. Submit seasonal/holiday material 3 months in advance. Photocopied and previously published submissions OK. Computer printout submissions acceptable; prefers letter-quality to dot-matrix. Reports in 1 month. Sample copy for $1 in postage; writer's guidelines for SAE and 1 first class stamp.

Nonfiction: General interest (personality pieces on well-known owners of Paints); historical (Paint horses in the past—particular horses and the breed in general); how-to (train and show horses); photo feature (Paint horses); and articles on horse health. Buys 4-5 mss/issue. Send complete ms. Pays $50-250.

Photos: Send photos with ms. Offers no additional payment for photos accepted with accompanying ms. Uses 3x5 or larger b&w glossy prints; 35mm or larger color transparencies. Captions required.

Tips: "*PHJ* needs breeder-trainer articles, Paint horse marketing and timely articles from areas throughout the U.S. and Canada. Photos with copy are almost always essential. Well-written first person articles are welcomed. Submit well-written items that show a definite understanding of the horse business. Use proper equine terminology and proper grounding in ability to communicate thoughts."

‡PRACTICAL HORSEMAN, PERFORMANCE HORSEMAN, Gum Tree Store Press, Gum Tree Corner, Unionville PA 19375. (215)857-1101. Editor: Pamela Goold. Articles Editor: Miranda Lorraine. 30% freelance written. Monthly magazine covering English riding (*Practical Horseman*); and Western riding (*Performance Horseman*). Circ. 60,000 (*Practical*); 30,000 (*Performance*). Pays on acceptance. Publishes ms an average of 3 months after acceptance. Byline given. Offers $50 kill fee. Buys first or simultaneous rights. Query for electronic submissions. Computer printout submissions OK; prefers letter-quality to dot-matrix. Reports in 2 weeks on queries; 2 months on mss. Free sample copy and writer's guidelines.

Nonfiction: How-to and interview/profile. Query with published clips, or send complete ms. Length: approximately 3,000 words. Pays $200-500 for assigned articles. Sometimes pays the expenses of writers on assignment.

Photos: State availability of photos with submission. Reviews contact sheets, transparencies and 5x7 prints. Offers $10-25 for b&w; $35-75 for color, "depending on quality." Identification of subjects required. Buys one-time rights.

PURRRRR! THE NEWSLETTER FOR CAT LOVERS, The Meow Company, HCR 227 Rd., Islesboro ME 04848. (207)734-6745. Publisher/Editor Agatha Cabaniss. 85% freelance written. Works with a small number of new/unpublished writers each year. A bimonthly newsletter for the average cat owner, *not* breeders. "The publication is designed to amuse while providing cat lovers with information about the care, feeding and enjoyment of house cats." Circ. 2,000 +. Pays on acceptance. Publishes ms an average of 4-5 months after acceptance. Byline given. Buys first serial rights and second serial (reprint) rights. Submit seasonal/holiday material 6 months in advance. Photocopied and previously published submissions OK unless it's been published in a competing publication, such as *Cats* and *Cat Fancy*. Query for electronic submissions. Computer printout submissions acceptable; prefers letter-quality to dot-matrix. Reports in 2 weeks. Sample copy $2; writer's guidelines for business size SAE and 1 first class stamp.

Nonfiction: General interest; historical; how-to; literary cat lovers (have featured Colette, Mark Twain and May Sarton); humor; interview/profile; new product; travel, off-beat unusual. "We want a humorous slant wherever possible; writing should be tight and professional. Avoid the first person." Special Christmas issue. No shaggy cat stories, sentimental stories, "I taught Fluffy to roll over" cutsie material, or no "reformed cat hater" stories. "We would like to receive articles on humane societies and animal rescue leagues." Absolutely no fiction. Buys 50/mss year. Query with published clips, or send complete ms. *Do not call*. Length: 250-1,500 words. Pays: $15-100.

Photos: Avoid "cute" photos. State availability of photos. Pays $5-10 for 5x8 b&w prints. Buys one-time rights.

Poetry: Accepts some poetry.

Fillers: Clippings, anecdotes, short humor and newsbreaks. Buys 20/year. Length: 25-75 words. Pays $5.

Tips: "You should know pet cats, their foibles and personalities. We are interested in good writing but also in a good story about a cat. We will work with a writer who has an interesting cat story. We are not interested in show cats or breeding. Query or send article and a SASE for reply."

THE QUARTER HORSE JOURNAL, Box 32470, Amarillo TX 79120. (806)376-4811. Editor-in-Chief: Audie Rackley. 5% freelance written. Prefers to work with published/established writers. Official publication of the American Quarter Horse Association. Monthly magazine. Circ. 70,000. Pays on acceptance. Publishes ms an average of 3 months after acceptance. Buys first North American serial rights. Submit seasonal/holiday material 2 months in advance. Computer printout submissions acceptable; no dot-matrix. Reports in 2 weeks. Free sample copy and writer's guidelines.

Nonfiction: Historical ("those that retain our western heritage"); how-to (fitting, grooming, showing, or anything that relates to owning, showing, or breeding); informational (educational clinics, current news); interview (feature-type stories—must be about established horses or people who have made a contribution to the business); personal opinion; and technical (equine updates, new surgery procedures, etc.). Buys 20 mss/year. Length: 800-2,500 words. Pays $50-250.

Photos: Purchased with accompanying ms. Captions required. Send prints or transparencies. Uses 5x7 or 8x10 b&w glossy prints; 2¼x2¼ or 4x5 color transparencies. Offers no additional payment for photos accepted with accompanying ms.

Tips: "Writers must have a knowledge of the horse business. We will be purchasing more material on quarter horse racing."

RURAL HERITAGE (formerly *The Evener*), Freiberg, Frederick Press, 29 and College, Box 7, Cedar Falls IA 50613. (319)277-3475. Editor: Bill Freiberg. Managing Editor: Suzanne Seedorff. 98% freelance written. Works with a small number of new/unpublished writers each year. Quarterly magazine covering individuals dedicated to preserving traditional American life. Circ. 10,000. Pays on publication. Publishes ms an average of 6-12 months after acceptance. Byline given. Offers $15 kill fee. Buys first North American or second serial (reprint) rights. Submit seasonal/holiday material 12 months in advance. Photocopied and previously published submissions OK. Computer printout submissions acceptable. Reports in 2 months. Sample copy $3; writer's guidelines for business size SAE and 1 first class stamp.

Nonfiction: Essays; historical/nostalgic; how-to (all types of crafting and farming); interview/profile (especially people using draft animals); photo feature; and travel (emphasizing our theme "rural heritage"). No articles on *modern* farming. Buys 100 mss/year. Send complete ms. Length: 500-1,500 words. Pays $15-400. Sometimes pays expenses of writers on assignment.

Photos: Send photos with ms. Reviews contact sheets, transparencies and 5x7 prints. No negatives. Pays $5-40. Captions, model releases and identification of subjects (if applicable or pertinent) required. Buys one-time rights.

Columns/Departments: Self-Sufficiency (modern people preserving traditional American lifestyle), 500-1,500 words; Drafter's Features (draft horses and mules used for farming, horse shows and pulls—their care), 500-2,000 words; and Crafting (new designs and patterns), 500-1,500 words. Buys 75 mss/year. Send complete ms. Pays $15-125.

Fiction: Historical and slice-of-life vignettes. "Nothing on modern farming." Buys 50 mss/year. Send complete ms. Length: 500-1,500 words. Pays $15-225.

Poetry: Traditional. Pays $5-25.

Fillers: Anecdotes and short humor. Pays $15-25.

Tips: "Profiles/articles on draft horses and draft horse shows and pulling events are *very* popular with our readers."

‡TROPICAL FISH HOBBYIST, "The World's Most Widely Read Aquarium Monthly," TFH Publications, Inc., 211 W. Sylvania Ave., Neptune City NJ 07753. (201)988-8400. Editor: Ray Hunziker. Managing Editor: Neal Pronek. 75% freelance written. Monthly magazine covering the tropical fish hobby. "We favor articles well illustrated with good color slides and aimed at both the neophyte and veteran tropical fish hobbyist." Circ. 50,000. Pays on acceptance. Publishes ms an average of 4 months after acceptance. Byline given. Buys all rights. Submit seasonal/holiday material 4 months in advance. Photocopied submissions OK. Computer printout submissions acceptable; no dot-matrix. Reports in 2 weeks. Sample copy $2.50; free writer's guidelines.

Nonfiction: General interest, how-to, photo feature, technical, and articles dealing with beginning and advanced aspects of the aquarium hobby. No "how I got started in the hobby" articles that impart little solid information. Buys 20-30 mss/year. Length: 500-2,500 words. Pays $25-100.

Photos: State availability of photos or send photos with ms. Pays $10 for 35mm color transparencies. Identification of subjects required. "Originals of photos returned to owner, who may market them elsewhere."

Fiction: "On occasion, we will review a fiction piece relevant to the aquarium hobby."

Tips: "We cater to a specialized readership—people knowledgeable in fish culture. Prospective authors should be familiar with subject; photography skills are a plus. It's a help if an author we've never dealt with queries first or submits a short item."

THE WESTERN HORSEMAN, Box 7980, Colorado Springs CO 80933. Editor: Randy Witte. 40% freelance written. Works with a small number of new/unpublished writers each year. Monthly magazine covering western horsemanship. Circ. 156,092. Pays on acceptance. Publishes ms an average of 5 months after acceptance. Buys first serial rights. Byline given. Computer printout submissions acceptable; prefers letter-quality to dot-matrix. Submit seasonal/holiday material 3 months in advance. Reports in 3 weeks. Sample copy $1.95.

Nonfiction: How-to (horse training, care of horses, tips, etc.); and informational (on rodeos, ranch life, historical articles of the West emphasizing horses). Length: 1,500 words. Payment begins at $125; "sometimes higher by special arrangement."

Photos: Send photos with ms. Offers no additional payment for photos. Uses 5x7 or 8x10 b&w glossy prints and 35mm transparencies. Captions required.

Tips: "Submit clean copy with professional quality photos. Stay away from generalities. Writing style should show a deep interest in horses coupled with a wide knowledge of the subject."

Art

Listed here are publications about art, art history, specific art forms and contemporary culture written for art patrons and artists. Publications addressing the business and management side of the art industry are listed in the Art, Design and Collectibles category of the Trade section.

‡AMERICAN INDIAN ART MAGAZINE, American Indian Art, Inc., 7314 E. Osborn Dr., Scottsdale AZ 85251. (602)994-5445. Managing Editor: Roanne P. Goldfein. 97% freelance written. Works with a small number of new/unpublished writers each year. Quarterly magazine covering Native American art, historic and contemporary, including new research on any aspect of Native American art. Circ. 15,000. Pays on publication. Publishes ms an average of 3 months after acceptance. Byline given. Buys one-time and first rights. Submit seasonal/holiday material 6 months in advance. Simultaneous queries OK. Computer printout submissions OK; prefers letter-quality to dot-matrix. Reports in 2 weeks on queries; 2 months on mss. Writer's guidelines available.
Nonfiction: New research on any aspect of Native American art. No previously published work or personal interviews with artists. Buys 12-18 mss/year. Query. Length: 1,000-2,500 words. Pays $75-300.
Tips: "The magazine is devoted to all aspects of Native American art. Some of our readers are knowledgeable about the field and some know very little. We seek articles that offer something to both groups. Articles reflecting original research are preferred to those summarizing previously published information."

ART TIMES, Cultural and Creative News, Box 730, Mount Marion NY 12456. (914)246-5170. Editor: Raymond J. Steiner. 10% (just fiction and poetry) freelance written. Prefers to work with published/established writers; works with a small number of new/unpublished writers each year; and eager to work with new/unpublished writers. Monthly tabloid covering the arts (visual, theatre, dance, etc.). "*Art Times* covers the art fields and is distributed in locations most frequented by those enjoying the arts. Our 15,000 copies are distributed throughout three upstate New York counties rich in the arts as well as in most of the galleries in Soho, 57th Street and Madison Avenue in the metropolitan area; locations include theatres, galleries, museums, cultural centers and the like. Our readers are mostly over 40, affluent, art-conscious and sophisticated." Circ. 15,000. Pays on publication. Publishes ms an average of 8 months after acceptance. Byline given. Buys first serial rights. Submit seasonal/holiday material 6 months in advance. Simultaneous queries, and simultaneous and photocopied submissions OK. Computer printout submissions OK; prefers letter-quality to dot-matrix. Reports in 1 month on queries; 3 months on mss. Sample copy for 9x12 SAE and 3 first class stamps; writer's guidelines for business size envelope and 1 first class stamp.
Fiction: "We're looking for short fiction that aspires to be *literary*. No excessive violence, sexist, off-beat, erotic, sports, or juvenile fiction." Buys 8-10 mss/year. Send complete ms. Length: 1,500 words maximum. Pays $15 maximum (honorarium).
Poetry: Poet's Niche. Avant-garde, free verse, haiku, light verse and traditional. "We prefer well-crafted 'literary' poems. No excessively sentimental poetry." Buys 30-35 poems/year. Submit maximum 6 poems. Length: 20 lines maximum. Offers contributor copies.
Tips: "We are now receiving 200 to 250 poems and 30-40 short stories per month. We only publish 2 to 3 poems and one story each issue. Competition is getting very great. We only pick the best. Be familiar with *Art Times* and its special audience. *Art Times* has literary leanings with articles written by a staff of scholars knowledgeable in their respective fields. Our readers expect quality. Although an 'arts' publication, we observe no restrictions (other than noted) in accepting fiction/poetry other than a concern for quality writing—subjects can cover anything and not specifically arts."

THE ARTIST'S MAGAZINE, F&W Publishing Co., 1507 Dana Ave., Cincinnati OH 45207. Editor: Michael Ward. 80% freelance written. Works with a small number of new/unpublished writers each year. Monthly magazine covering primarily two-dimensional art instruction for working artists. "Ours is a highly visual approach to teaching the serious amateur artist techniques that will help him improve his skills and market his work. The style should be crisp and immediately engaging." Circ. 180,000. Pays on acceptance. Publishes ms an average of 4 months after acceptance. Byline given; bionote given for feature material. Offers 20% kill fee. Buys first North American serial rights and second serial (reprint) rights. Simultaneous queries, and photocopied and previously published submissions OK "as long as noted as such." Computer printout submissions acceptable; prefers letter-quality to dot-matrix. Reports in 2 months. Sample copy $2.50 with 9x12 SAE with 50¢ postage; free writer's guidelines.

Nonfiction: Instructional only—how an artist uses a particular technique, how he handles a particular subject or medium, or how he markets his work. "The emphasis must be on how the reader can learn some new method of improving his artwork, or the marketing of it." No unillustrated articles; no seasonal/holiday material; no travel articles; no profiles of artists. Buys 60 mss/year. Query first; all queries must be accompanied by slides, transparencies, prints or tearsheets of the artist's work as well as the artist's bio, and the writer's bio and clips. Length: 1,000-2,500 words. Pays $100-350 and up. Sometimes pays the expenses of writers on assignment.
Photos: "Color transparencies or slides are required with every accepted article since these are essential for our instructional format. Full captions must accompany these." Buys one-time rights.
Departments: Three departments are open to freelance writers: The Artist's Life, Books and P.S. The Artist's Life (profiles and brief items about artists and their work, also art-related games and puzzles and art-related poetry). Query first for profiles; send complete ms for other items. Length: 600 words maximum. Pays $50-100 for profiles; up to $25 for brief items and poetry. Books (200-word maximum reviews of newly-published books on art and artists). Query first with title of book. Pays $30 per review. P.S. (a humorous look at art from the artist's point of view, or at least sympathetic to the artist). Send complete ms. Pays $50-100 and up.
Tips: "Look at several current issues and read the author's guidelines carefully. Remember that our readers are working fine and graphic artists."

ARTVIEWS, Visual Arts Ontario, 439 Wellington St. W, Toronto, Ontario M5V 1E7 Canada. (416)591-8883. Editor: Fred Gaysek. 25% freelance written. "We are backlogged with submissions and prefer not to receive unsolicited submissions at this time, but we are open to proposals for articles." Quarterly magazine "exploring the current visual arts scene—issues, events, major exhibitions—particularly as they pertain to Ontario's art community." Circ. 8,000. Pays on acceptance. Publishes ms an average of 2 months after acceptance. Byline given. Offers 25% kill fee. Buys one-time rights. Computer printout submissions OK; prefers letter-quality to dot-matrix. Reports in 1 month on queries. Free sample copy and writer's guidelines if SASE is provided (postage in Canadian funds $1.50).
Nonfiction: Interview/profile, opinion, photo feature, art issues. No exhibition reviews. Buys 8 mss/year. Query with published clips if available. Length: 500-1,500 words. Pays $50-150.
Photos: State availability of photos. Pays $10-25 for 8x10 b&w prints. Captions and identification of subjects required.
Fillers: Newsbreaks, art, cartoons. Buys variable number/year. Length: 200-500 words. Pays $5-25.

‡**LAST ISSUE**, Last Issue Publishing Society, #604, 815 1st St. SW, Calgary, Alberta T2P 1N3 Canada. (403)263-3232. Editor: Heather Elton. 75% freelance written. A semiannual magazine of visual art, fiction, commentary, satire, poetry, interviews and essays. Circ. 4,000. Pays on publication. Byline given. Offers 50% kill fee. Buys first rights or second serial (reprint) rights. Submit seasonal/holiday material 3 months in advance. Simultaneous, photocopied and previously published submissions OK. Computer printout submissions OK. Sample copy for 9x12 SAE with IRCs.
Nonfiction: Book excerpts, essays, expose, general interest, historical/nostalgic, humor, opinion and photo feature. Buys 8 mss/year. Query with or without published clips, or send complete ms. Length: 800-2,500 words. Pays $5-150.
Photos: Send photos with submission. Offers no additional payment for photos accepted with ms. Buys one-time rights.
Fiction: Erotica, ethnic, experimental, fantasy, humorous, novel excerpts, science fiction, slice-of-life vignettes. Buys 25 mss/year. Query with published clips. Length: 800-2,500 words. Pays $50 honorarium.
Fillers: Anecdotes, short humor. Buys 10 mss/year. Length: 50-400 words. Pays $50 honorarium.
Tips: "Be thought-provoking and stylish. Read the magazine and query within our field of interest—arts and culture."

METROPOLIS, The Architecture and Design Magazine of New York, Bellerophon Publications, 177 E. 87th St., New York NY 10128. (212)722-5050. Editor: Susan S. Szenasy. Managing Editor: Claude Lubroth. 60% freelance written. A monthly (except bimonthly January/February and July/August) magazine for consumers interested in architecture and design. Circ. 15,110. Pays on acceptance. Publishes ms an average of 3-6 months after acceptance. Byline given. Buys first rights or makes work-for-hire assignments. Submit calendar material 6 weeks in advance. Photocopied submissions OK. Computer printout submissions acceptable; prefers letter-quality to dot-matrix. Reports in 2 weeks on queries; 1 month on mss. Sample copy $3.50 including postage.
Nonfiction: Book excerpts; essays (design, residential interiors); historical (New York); opinion (design architecture); and profile (only well-known international figures in USA). No profiles on individuals or individual architectural practices, technical information, information from public relations firms, fine arts, or things outside of the New York area. Buys approximately 30 mss/year. Query with published clips. Length: 1,500-3,000 words. Pays $350-500.

Photos: State availability, or send photos with submission. Reviews contact sheets, 35mm or 4x5 transparencies, or 8x10 b&w prints. Payment offered for certain photos. Captions required. Buys one-time rights.

Columns/Departments: Insites (Manhattan miscellany: information on design and architecture around New York), 100-600 words; In Print (book review essays), 600-750 words. Buys approximately 10 mss/year. Query with published clips. Pays $50-100.

Tips: "Keep in mind that we are *only* interested in the consumer end of architecture and design. Send query with examples of photos explaining how you see illustrations working with article. Also, be patient and don't expect an immediate answer after submission of query."

THE ORIGINAL ART REPORT, Box 1641, Chicago IL 60690. Editor and Publisher: Frank Salantrie. 1% freelance written. Eager to work with new/unpublished writers. Emphasizes "visual art conditions from the visual artists' and general public's perspectives." Newsletter; 6-8 pages. Pays on publication. Reports in 4 weeks. Sample copy $1.25 and 1 first class stamp.

Nonfiction: Expose (art galleries, government agencies ripping off artists, or ignoring them); historical (perspective pieces relating to now); humor (whenever possible); informational (material that is unavailable in other art publications); inspirational (acts and ideas of courage); interview (with artists, other experts; serious material); personal opinion; technical (brief items to recall traditional methods of producing art); travel (places in the world where artists are welcomed and honored); philosophical, economic, aesthetic, and artistic. "We would like to receive investigative articles on government and private arts agencies, and nonprofits, too, perhaps hiding behind status to carry on for business. No vanity profiles of artists, arts organizations, and arts promoters' operations." Buys 4-5 mss/year. Query or submit complete ms. Length: 1,000 words maximum. Pays 1¢/word.

Columns/Departments: In Back of the Individual Artist. "Artists express their views about non-art topics. After all, artists are in this world, too." WOW (Worth One Wow), Worth Repeating, and Worth Repeating Again. "Basically, these are reprint items with introduction to give context and source, including complete name and address of publication. Looking for insightful, succinct commentary." Submit complete ms. Length: 500 words maximum. Pays ½¢/word.

Tips: "We get excited when ideas address substantive problems of individual artists in the art condition and as they affect the general population. Send original material that is direct and to the point, opinionated and knowledgeable. Write in a factual style with clarity. No straight educational or historical stuff. All material must be original or unique."

PROFESSIONAL STAINED GLASS, Edge Publishing Group, Room 701, 270 Lafayette St., New York NY 10012. (212)966-6694. Editor: Albert Lewis. Monthly magazine covering stained glass. "Our readers are stained glass professionals, retailers and hobbyists. We are interested in articles that are useful to them, rather than merely interesting." Circ. 12,700. Pays on publication. Byline given. Offers $25 kill fee. Buys first North American serial rights. Simultaneous queries, and simultaneous, photocopied and previously published submissions OK. Computer printout submissions acceptable. Reports in 2 weeks on queries; 1 month on mss. Sample copy for 9x12 SAE and $1 postage; writer's guidelines for 4x9½ SAE and 1 first class stamp.

Nonfiction: How-to (anything related to stained glass); interview/profile (of stained glass craftsmen); new product; and technical. "We like articles on techniques, features on individuals who are doing interesting work in glass (with emphasis on the technical aspects of their work), and marketing tips. We also want articles on subjects other than glass, which would be of use to hobbyists, e.g., cabinetmaking, lighting techniques and glass photography. We are not interested in nonpractical articles, such as stories about church windows or Louis Tiffany." Buys 30 mss/year. Query. Length: 750-2,000 words. Pays $50-200.

Photos: State availability of photos. Pays $5-25 for color contact sheets, transparencies and 8x10 prints. Identification of subjects required. Buys one-time rights.

Tips: "Freelancers should have a reasonable understanding of the crafts field, particularly stained glass. We get too many articles from people who are not familiar with their subject."

SOUTHWEST ART, Box 13037, Houston TX 77219. (713)850-0990. Editor: Susan Hallsten McGarry. 80% freelance written. Prefers to work with published/established writers. Emphasizes art—paintings, sculpture and fine art photography. Monthly. Pays on acceptance. Publishes an average of 8 months after acceptance. Buys all rights to ms (not artwork). Photocopied submissions OK. Query for electronic submissions. Computer printout submissions acceptable; no dot-matrix. Reports in 4 months. Sample copy $6; writer's guidelines for #10 SASE.

Nonfiction: Informational, interview, personal opinion and profile. "We publish articles about artists and art trends, concentrating on a geographical area west of the Mississippi River. Articles should explore the artist's personality, philosophy, media and techniques, and means by which they convey ideas." Buys 100 mss/year. Must submit 20 color prints/transparencies along with a full outline biography of the artist. If artist is accepted, article length is 1,600-2,000 words minimum. Pays on sliding scale to $400. Sometimes pays the expenses of writers on assignment.

Tips: The writer has a better chance of breaking in at *Southwest Art* with short, lesser-paying articles and fillers (rather than with major features) because "short pieces, skillfully handled, are an excellent gauge of feature writing potential. Submit both published and unpublished samples of your writing. An indication of how quickly you work and your availability on short notice are helpful."

SPLASH, International Magazine, Art and Contemporary Culture, #4B, 561 Broadway, New York NY 10012. (212)966-3218. Editor-in-Chief: Jordan Crandall. Editor: Lisa D. Black. 75% freelance written. A bimonthly magazine covering the arts, "but we are eclectic. *Splash* is devoted to art and contemporary culture. Our audience is generally well-educated and interested in the arts. There is no special slant, per se, but we dare to be controversial and are decidedly progressive in our thinking." Circ. 25,000. Pays on acceptance. Publishes ms an average of 4 months after acceptance. Byline sometimes given. Buys first rights. Submit seasonal/holiday material 4 months in advance. Simultaneous and photocopied submissions OK. Computer printout submissions OK; prefers letter-quality to dot-matrix. Reports in 1 month on queries; 6 weeks on mss. Sample copy $3; writer's guidelines for SASE.
Nonfiction: Essays; expose; general interest; humor; interview/profile; opinion; personal experience; photo feature; and reviews (art, music, film, books, dance). "We would also like to receive social satire (subtle, dry, educated wit); absurdist and/or surreal literature or humor; and political pieces written without an *obvious* bias, but one in which the point of view is *intimated* by the reader—in other words, no polemics." Does not want anything in a strictly journalistic mode—no newspaper-type mss will be considered. Buys 50-60 mss/year. Query with published clips, or send complete ms. Length: 250-2,000 words. Pays $50-350.
Photos: State availability or send photos with submission. Reviews b&w glossy prints, any size. Offers $5-50/photo. Captions, model releases and identification of subjects required. Buys one-time rights; photo essays, first time rights only.
Columns/Departments: Expo (reviews on *all* the arts—national as well as international), 500-850 words; Opine (educated opinions on politics, art, religion, current issues), 750-1,250 words; Arena (short, sophisticated humor), 150-500 words; Studio (introduction to new and/or emerging talents in all the arts), 250-500 words. Buys 25 mss/year. Query with published clips. Length: 250-1,250 words. Pays $50-250.
Fiction: "We use *very little* fiction at present." Confession, experimental, fantasy, novel excerpts and slice-of-life vignettes. "No lengthy stories (no book-size texts)—the shorter the fiction, and the more avant garde, the better the chances are that we will use it." Buys 5 mss/year. Query with published clips. Length: 250-1,000 words. Pays $50-350.
Poetry: "We use very little poetry at present." No traditional, Victorian-type verse; "the shorter and more avant garde, the better." Buys 2 poems/year. Submit maximum 5 poems. Length: 5-75 lines. Pays $15-75.
Fillers: Anecdotes, facts, and short humor. Buys 10/year. Length: 150-500 words. Pays $15-75.
Tips: "As we are distributed world-wide, we will be looking for more international material on all subjects. Our style is progressive, avant garde. In a word, our magazine is *style-oriented* and decidedly *not* journalistic. If a manuscript is approached aesthetically as opposed to journalistically it has a much better chance of being published. Sample writings ought to be sent and perhaps a cover letter stating interests, etc. All areas are open to freelancers. Reviews must be topical, interesting, insightful and succinct. The interviews we do are generally with accomplished, well-known people in all fields—art, literature, politics, entertainment. We require progressive writers and not journalists."

‡THE STATE OF ART, The State of Texas Art Inc., Suite 107, 13910 Champion Forest Dr., Houston TX 77069. (713)440-8025. Editor: Mildred Cheek. Managing Editor: Susan Embry. Monthly tabloid covering the visual arts, art shows, artists, art-related events. "Our publication is directed toward the art collector, the artist and dealer." Circ. 15,000. Pays on acceptance. Publishes ms an average of 3 months after acceptance. Byline sometimes given. Not copyrighted. Buys all rights. Simultaneous submissions OK. Computer printout submissions OK; no dot-matrix. Reports in 1 week on mss. Free sample copy and writer's guidelines.
Nonfiction: Interview/profile. Buys 10-12 mss/year. Query with published clips. Length: 700-1,000 words. Pays $35-100 for assigned articles or offers "trade for advertising."
Photos: State availability of photos with submission. Reviews 4x5 prints. Offers no additional payment for photos accepted with ms. Captions required. Buys all rights.
Columns/Departments: Query with published clips.

WESTART, Box 6868, Auburn CA 95604. (916)885-0969. Editor-in-Chief: Martha Garcia. Emphasizes art for practicing artists and artists/craftsmen; students of art and art patrons. Semimonthly tabloid; 20 pages. Circ. 7,500. Pays on publication. Buys all rights. Byline given. Phone queries OK. Photocopied submissions OK. Sample copy $1; free writer's guidelines.
Nonfiction: Informational, photo feature and profile. No hobbies. Buys 6-8 mss/year. Query or submit complete ms. Length: 700-800 words. Pays 50¢/column inch.
Photos: Purchased with or without accompanying ms. Send b&w prints. Pays 50¢/column inch.
Tips: "We publish information which is current—that is, we will use a review of an exhibition only if exhibition is still open on the date of publication. Therefore, reviewer must be familiar with our printing deadlines and news deadlines."

WOMEN ARTISTS NEWS, Midmarch Associates, Box 3304 Grand Central Station, New York NY 10163. Editor: Judy Seigel. 70-90% freelance written. Works with small number of new/unpublished writers each year; eager to work with new/unpublished writers. Bimonthly magazine for "artists and art historians, museum and gallery personnel, students, teachers, crafts personnel, art critics and writers." Circ. 5,000. Buys first serial rights only when funds are available. "Token payment as funding permits." Publishes ms an average of 2 months after acceptance. Byline given. Submit seasonal material 2 months in advance. Computer printout submissions acceptable; no dot-matrix. Reports in 1 month. Sample copy $3.
Nonfiction: Features, informational, historical, interview, opinion, personal experience, photo feature and technical. Query or submit complete ms. Length: 500-2,500 words.
Photos: Used with or without accompanying ms. Query or submit contact sheet or prints. Pays $5 for 5x7 b&w prints when money is available. Captions required.

Association, Club and Fraternal

Association publications allow writers to write for national audiences while covering local stories. If your town has a Kiwanis, Lions or Rotary Club chapter, one of its projects might merit a story in the club's magazine. Some association magazines circulate worldwide. These publications link members who live continents away from one another or just across town. They keep members and friends informed about the ideas, objectives, projects and activities of the club. Club-financed magazines that carry material not directly related to the group's activities are classified by their subject matter in the Consumer and Trade sections.

CALIFORNIA HIGHWAY PATROLMAN, California Association of Highway Patrolmen, 2030 V St., Sacramento CA 95818. (916)452-6751. Editor: Carol Perri. 80% freelance written. Will work with established or new/unpublished writers. Monthly magazine. Circ. 20,000. Pays on publication. Publishes ms an average of 1 year after acceptance. Buys one-time rights. Submit seasonal/holiday material 6 months in advance. Computer printout submissions acceptable. Reports in 3 months. Sample copy and writer's guidelines for 9x12 SAE and 98¢ postage.
Nonfiction: Publishes articles on transportation safety, driver education, consumer interest, California history, humor and general interest. "Topics can include autos, boats, bicycles, motorcycles, snowmobiles, recreational vehicles and pedestrian safety. We are also in the market for California travel pieces and articles on early California. We are *not* a technical journal for teachers and traffic safety experts, but rather a general interest publication geared toward the layman." Pays 2½¢/word.
Photos: "Illustrated articles always receive preference." Pays $2.50/b&w photo. Captions required.
Tips: "If a writer feels the article idea, length and style are consistent with our magazine, submit the manuscript for me to determine if I agree. We are especially looking for articles for specific holidays."

CATHOLIC FORESTER, Catholic Order of Foresters, 425 W. Shuman Blvd., Naperville IL 60566. (312)983-4920. Editor: Barbara Cunningham. 35% freelance written. Prefers to work with published/established writers; works with a small number of new/unpublished writers each year. A bimonthly magazine of short, general interest articles and fiction for members of the Order, which is a fraternal insurance company. Family type audience, middle class. Circ. 150,000. Pays on acceptance. Publishes ms an average of 6 months after acceptance. Byline given. Buys one-time rights, second serial (reprint) rights, and simultaneous rights. Submit seasonal/holiday material 6 months in advance. Simultaneous, photocopied, and previously published submissions OK. Computer printout submissions acceptable; prefers letter-quality to dot-matrix. Reports in 6 weeks on ms. Sample copy for 8½x11 SAE and 73¢ postage; free writer's guidelines.
Nonfiction: General interest; historical/nostalgic; humor; inspirational; interview/profile; new product; opinion; personal experience; photo feature; technical (depends on subject); and travel. "Short feature articles of interest to the all-American type are most open to freelancers." No blatant sex nor anything too violent. Send complete ms. Length: 1,000-3,000 words. Pays 5¢/word; more for excellent ms.

Photos: Prefers something of unusual interest or story-telling. State availability of photos, or send photos with ms. Reviews any size b&w and color prints. Payment to be determined. Captions, model releases, and identification of subjects required. Buys one-time rights.

Columns/Departments: Needs unusual items on what is going on in the world; new, interesting products, discoveries or happenings. Send complete ms. Length: 1,000 words. Payment to be determined.

Fiction: Adventure, historical, humorous, mainstream, mystery, religious (Catholic), suspense and western. No sex or extreme violence. Length: up to 3,000 words (prefers shorter fiction). Pays 5¢/word; more for excellent ms.

Poetry: Free verse, haiku, light verse and traditional. Submit maximum 5 poems. Payment to be determined.

Fillers: Cartoons, jokes, anecdotes and short humor. Length: 300-500 words. Payment to be determined.

CBIA NEWS, Journal of the Connecticut Business and Industry Association, CBIA Service Corp., 370 Asylum St., Hartford CT 06103. (203)547-1661. Editor: Kimberly Dillon. 30% freelance written. A monthly tabloid (except combined July/August and December/January issue) covering business in Connecticut for approximately 6,500 member companies. Half of the *News* is about the association and written in-house. Other half is about how to run your business better; interesting businesspeople in Connecticut, and business trends here. These are sometimes written by freelancers. Circ. 7,200. Pays on acceptance. Publishes ms an average of 5 months after acceptance. Byline given. Offers 20% kill fee. Buys variable rights; can be negotiable. Photocopied and previously published submissions OK if not published in competing publication. Computer printout submissions acceptable; prefers letter-quality to dot-matrix. Reports in 2 weeks. Free sample copy.

Nonfiction: Book excerpts, how-to (run your business better in some specific way); interview/profile (must be a Connecticut person). Buys approximately 20 mss/year. Query with published clips. Length and payment vary with the subject.

Photos: State availability of photos with query or ms. Reviews b&w contact sheets. Pays negotiable rate. Model release and identification of subjects required.

Tips: "Write to me including resume and clips. They do *not* have to be from business publications. If I'm interested, I'll contact you and describe fees, rules, etc."

CHARIOT, Ben Hur Life Association, Box 312, Crawfordsville IN 47933. (317)362-4500. Editor: Loren Harrington. 15-20% freelance written. "We are backlogged with submissions and prefer not to receive unsolicited submissions at this time." A quarterly magazine covering fraternal activities of membership plus general interest items. Circ. 11,000. Usually pays on acceptance, sometimes on publication. Publishes ms an average of 1 year after acceptance. Byline and brief biography given. Not copyrighted. Buys variable rights. Submit seasonal/holiday material 10 months in advance. Simultaneous queries, and simultaneous and photocopied submissions OK. Computer printout submissions acceptable; prefers letter-quality to dot-matrix. Reports in 2 weeks on queries; 1 month on mss. Sample copy for 9x12 SAE and 4 first class stamps—for *serious* inquiries only; writer's guidelines for business size SAE and 2 first class stamps.

Nonfiction: General interest, historical and how-to. "Absolutely *nothing* of a smutty, sexually-oriented, gay, etc. nature. Only items of benefit to our readers and/or family would be considered." Query with or without published clips. Length: 300-3,500 words. Pays 3-20¢/word. Sometimes pays the expenses of writers on assignment.

Photos: State availability of photos with query letter or ms. "We would like to have quality photo with query. We will return if rejected." Reviews b&w and color contact sheets and prints. Payment for photos included in payment for mss. Captions, model releases and identification of subjects required. Buys one-time rights.

Columns/Departments: Columns are editorial or insurance-related. "We would consider a query piece, but it would have to be extremely applicable."

Fiction: Especially interested in "really good, *short* fiction. It must have theme of helping another person or benefitting a worthy cause. Absolutely *nothing* of a smutty, sexually-oriented, gay, etc. nature. Only stories of benefit to our readers and/or family would be considered." Query with or without published clips or send complete ms. Length: 300-2,500 words. Pays 3-20¢/word.

Fillers: No fillers considered at present—will take a look at cartoons.

Tips: "Our requirements are very tightly edited and professionally written with a wide appeal to our particular audience, self-help volunteer and charity. Those items that we can give our local units to encourage their fraternal participation and projects would be considered more than any other single submitted features."

CLUB COSTA MAGAZINE, Club Costa Corp., Suite 535, 9200 Ward Parkway, Kansas City MO 64114. (816)361-8404. Editor: Norman F. Rowland. 50-65% freelance written. Prefers to work with published/established writers; works with a small number of new/unpublished writers each year. A quarterly magazine available only to club members covering discounted accommodations, travel and other savings available through Club Costa. "We offer airline employee 'discount' prices to our members on a variety of accommodations, flights, car rentals and activities. Our format features money-saving tips for vacation and destination features for the areas in which we have properties available. Readers are reasonably sophisticated travelers with above average incomes." Circ. 2,000 + . Pays on publication. Publishes ms an average of 3 months after acceptance.

Byline given. Buys one-time rights, simultaneous rights and second serial (reprint) rights. Submit seasonal/holiday material 6 months in advance. Simultaneous, photocopied, and previously published submissions OK. Computer printout submissions acceptable. Reports in 6 weeks. Sample copy $3; writer's guidelines for SASE.

Nonfiction: Travel-related historical/nostalgic, how-to, personal experience and humor. "Articles may relate to saving money while on vacation. We need features about destinations, activities, background/history of area(s), bargain purchases, how to plan a vacation, and tips for the business or leisure traveler." No camping, hunting, fishing, or "my favorite vacation" articles. Buys 15-20 mss/year. Query with SASE. Length: 1,200 words, features; up to 500 words, shorts. Pays $25-125.

Photos: Photos are required with most articles. State availability.

Tips: "We need short travel-related humor and shorts that give an insight to an area or its people."

‡D.A.C. NEWS, Detroit Athletic Club, 241 Madison Ave., Detroit MI 48226. Editor: John H. Worthington. 5% freelance written. Prefers to work with published/established writers. For business and professional men. Much of the magazine is devoted to member activities, including social events and athletic activities at the club. Magazine published 9 times/year. Pays after publication. Publishes ms an average of 2 months after acceptance. Buys first rights. Byline given. Computer printout submissions OK; no dot-matrix. Reports in 1 month. Sample copy for 9x12 SAE with $1.07 postage.

Nonfiction: General interest articles, usually male-oriented, about sports (pro football, baseball, squash, golf, skiing and tennis); travel (to exclusive resorts and offbeat places); drama; personalities; health (jogging and coronary caution); some nostalgia (football greats, big band era are best examples). "We publish three special issues per year—on Florida, on Northern Michigan, and on Detroit's annual Grand Prix race." Buys 5-6 unsolicited mss/year. Send complete ms. Length: 750-2,500 words. Pays $50-300.

Photos: Send photos with ms. Offers no additional payment for photos accepted with ms.

Tips: "Bear in mind this is a highly affluent, sophisticated, well-traveled readership. Tell us your story idea and where you have been published previously. Give us a brief synopsis of one idea. Quality, not length, is the factor. Express a cheerful willingness to rewrite along our lines."

THE ELKS MAGAZINE, 425 W. Diversey, Chicago IL 60614. Executive Editor: Fred D. Oakes. 50% freelance written. Prefers to work with published/established writers. Emphasizes general interest with family appeal. Magazine published 10 times/year. 48 pages. Circ. 1,600,000. Pays on acceptance. Publishes ms an average of 4 months after acceptance. Buys first North American serial rights. Computer printout submissions acceptable; no dot-matrix. Reports in 6 weeks. Sample copy and writer's guidelines for 9x12 SASE.

Nonfiction: Articles of information, business, contemporary life problems and situations, nostalgia, or just interesting topics, ranging from medicine, science, and history, to sports. "The articles should not just be a rehash of existing material. They must be fresh, thought-provoking, well-researched and documented." No fiction, political articles, fillers or verse. Buys 2-3 mss/issue. Query; no phone queries. Length: 1,500-3,000 words. Pays from $100.

Tips: "Requirements are clearly stated in our guidelines. Loose, wordy pieces are not accepted. A submission, following a query letter go-ahead, should include several b&w prints if the piece lends itself to illustration. We offer no additional payment for photos accepted with manuscripts. We expect to continue targeting our content to an older (50+) demographic."

FEDCO REPORTER, A Publication Exclusively for FEDCO Members, 9300 Santa Fe Springs Rd., Santa Fe Springs CA 90670. (213)946-2511. Editor: Michele A. Brunmier. 90% freelance written. Works with a small number of new/unpublished writers each year. A monthly catalog/magazine for FEDCO department store members. Circ. 1,900,000. Pays on acceptance. Publishes ms an average of 3 months after acceptance. Byline given. Offers $50 kill fee. Buys first rights. Query for electronic submissions. Computer printout submissions acceptable; prefers letter-quality to dot-matrix. Reports in 6 weeks. Sample copy for 9x12 SASE; writer's guidelines for SASE.

Nonfiction: General interest, historical, interview/profile. The magazine publishes material on "historical events (especially relating to California); historical personality profiles; general interest (we do numerous stories on common, everyday items with an unusual background or interesting use); seasonal stories; and articles about areas of California." No first person narrative. Buys 75 mss/year. Query with published clips. Length: 450-650 words. "The length of the majority of our stories is 450 words." Pays $100-250.

Photos: State availability of photos. Reviews b&w and color slides. No payment, byline only.

Fillers: Historical anecdotes or everyday information.

Tips: "We will publish excellent writing that is well-researched regardless of prior writings. Articles should be of topical interest to consumers."

4-H LEADER—the National Magazine for 4-H, 7100 Connecticut Ave., Chevy Chase MD 20815. (301)961-2800. Editor: Suzanne M. Carney. 20% freelance written. Monthly magazine for "volunteers of a wide range of ages who lead 4-H clubs; most with college education whose primary reason for reading us is their interest in working with kids in informal youth education projects, ranging from aerospace to sewing, and almost anything in between." Circ. 70,000. Pays on acceptance. Publishes ms an average of 3 months after acceptance. Buys first serial rights or one-time rights. Submit seasonal material 1 year in advance. Reports in 1 month. Free sample copy and writer's guidelines.

Nonfiction: Education and child psychology from authorities, written in light, easy-to-read fashion with specific suggestions on how the layman can apply principles in volunteer work with youth; how-to pieces about genuinely new and interesting crafts of any kind. "Craft articles must be fresh in style and ideas, and tell how to make something worthwhile—almost anything that tells about kids having fun and learning outside the classroom, including how they became interested, most effective programs, etc., always with enough detail and examples, so reader can repeat project or program with his or her group, merely by reading the article. Speak directly to our readers without preaching. Tell them in a conversational manner how they might work better with kids to help them have fun and learn at the same time. Use lots of genuine examples (although names and dates are not important) to illustrate points. Use contractions when applicable. Write in a concise, interesting way. Our readers have other jobs and not a lot of time to spend with us. Will not print personal reminiscences, stories on 'how this 4-H club made good' or about state or county fair winners." Length: 3-8 pages, typewritten, double-spaced. Payment up to $200, depending on quality and accompanying photos or illustrations.

Photos: State availability of photos. "Photos must be genuinely candid, of excellent technical quality and preferably shot in 'available light' or in that style; must show young people or adults and young people having fun learning something. How-to photos or drawings must supplement instructional texts. Photos do not necessarily have to include people. Photos are usually purchased with accompanying ms, with no additional payment. Captions required. If we use an excellent single photo, we generally pay $25 and up."

Tips: "We are very specialized, and unless a writer has been published in our magazine before, he more than likely doesn't have a clue to what we can use. When a query comes about a specific topic, we often can suggest angles that make it usable. There will be more emphasis on interpersonal skills, techniques for working with kids, more focus on the family. Write for a sample copy. We judge a writer's technical skills by the grammar and syntax of his query letter. We seldom ask for a manuscript we think will require extensive reorganization or heavy editing."

KIWANIS, 3636 Woodview Trace, Indianapolis IN 46268. Executive Editor: Chuck Jonak. 90% of feature articles freelance written. Magazine published 10 times/year for business and professional men and their families. Circ. 300,000. Pays on acceptance. Buys first North American serial rights. Pays 20-40% kill fee. Publishes ms an average of 6 months after acceptance. Byline given. Computer printout submissions acceptable. Reports within 2 months. Sample copy and writer's guidelines for 9x12 SAE and 75¢ postage.

Nonfiction: Articles about social and civic betterment, business, science, education, religion, family, sports, health, recreation, etc. Emphasis on objectivity, intelligent analysis and thorough research of contemporary problems. Positive tone preferred. Concise, lively writing, absence of cliches, and impartial presentation of controversy required. When applicable, information and quotation from international sources are required. Avoid writing strictly to a U.S. audience. Especially needs articles on business and professional topics that will directly assist the readers in their own businesses (generally independent retailers and companies of less than 25 employees) or careers. "We have an increasing need for articles of international interest and those that will enlighten our readers about the health needs and safety of children." Length: 2,500-3,000 words. Pays $400-1,000. "No fiction, personal essays, fillers, or verse of any kind. A light or humorous approach is welcomed where the subject is appropriate and all other requirements are observed." Usually pays the expenses of writers on assignment.

Photos: "We accept photos submitted with manuscripts. Our rate for a manuscript with good photos is higher than for one without." Model release and identification of subjects required. Buys one-time rights.

Tips: "We will work with any writer who presents a strong feature article idea applicable to our magazine's audience and who will prove he or she knows the craft of writing. First, obtain writer's guidelines and a sample copy. Study for general style and content. Present well-researched, smoothly written manuscript that contains a 'human quality' with the use of anecdotes, practical examples, quotation, etc. When querying, present detailed outline of proposed manuscript's focus, direction, and editorial intent. Indicate expert sources to be used for attribution, as well as article's tone and length."

THE LION, 300 22nd St., Oak Brook IL 60570. (312)986-1700. Editor-in-Chief: Roy Schaetzel. Senior Editor: Robert Kleinfelder. 35% freelance written. Works with a small number of new/unpublished writers each year. Covers service club organization for Lions Club members and their families. Monthly magazine; 48 pages. Circ. 670,000. Pays on acceptance. Publishes ms an average of 5 months after acceptance. Buys all rights. Byline given. Phone queries OK. Photocopied submissions OK. Computer printout submissions acceptable; no dot-matrix. Reports in 2 weeks. Free sample copy and writer's guidelines.

Nonfiction: Informational (stories of interest to civic-minded individuals) and photo feature (must be of a Lions Club service project). No travel, biography, or personal experiences. No sensationalism. Prefers anecdotes in articles. Buys 4 mss/issue. Query. Length: 500-2,200. Pays $50-400. Sometimes pays the expenses of writers on assignment.

Photos: Purchased with or without accompanying ms or on assignment. Captions required. Query for photos. B&w and color glossies at least 5x7 or 35mm color slides. Total purchase price for ms includes payment for photos, accepted with ms. "Be sure photos are clear and as candid as possible."

Tips: "Incomplete details on how the Lions involved actually carried out a project and poor quality photos are the most frequent mistakes made by writers in completing an article assignment for us."

THE MODERN WOODMEN, Public Relations Department, Mississippi River at 17th St., Rock Island IL 61201. (309)786-6481. Editor: Gloria Bergh. Address manuscripts to Sandy Howell, staff writer. 5-10% freelance written. Works with both published and new writers. "Our publication is for families who are members of Modern Woodmen of America. Modern Woodmen is a fraternal life insurance society, and most of our members live in smaller communities or rural areas throughout the United States. Various age groups read the magazine." Quarterly magazine, 24 pages. Circ. 350,000. Not copyrighted. Pays on acceptance. Publishes ms an average of 6 months after acceptance. Buys one-time rights or second serial (reprint) rights to material. Photocopied and simultaneous submissions OK. Reports in 1 month if SASE included. Sample copy and guidelines for 8½x11 SAE and 2 first class stamps.

Nonfiction: For children and adults. "We seek lucid style and rich content. We need manuscripts that center on family-oriented subjects, human development, and educational topics."

Fiction: "Most of the fiction we publish is for children and teens. We stress plot and characterization. A moral is a pleasant addition, but not required." Length: about 1,200 words. Pays $50 minimum.

Tips: "We want articles that appeal to young families, emphasize family interaction, community involvement, and family life. We also consider educational, historical and patriotic articles. We don't want religious articles, teen romances, or seasonal material. Focus on people, whether the article is about families or is educational, historical or patriotic."

‡MOOSE MAGAZINE, Loyal Order of Moose, Supreme Lodge Building, Mooseheart IL 60539. (312)859-2000. Managing Editor: Raymond Dickow. A monthly (10 issues/year) fraternal magazine "distributed to men, ages 21 and older, who are members of 2,300 Moose lodges located throughout the U.S. and Canada." Circ. 1,300,000. Pays on acceptance. Byline given. Not copyrighted. Buys first North American serial rights. Submit seasonal/holiday material 4 months in advance. Photocopied submissions OK. No computer printout submissions. Reports in 5 weeks on mss.

Nonfiction: General interest, historical/nostalgic and sports. No politics or religion. Send complete ms. Length: 1,000-2,000 words. Pays $300-1,000 for unsolicited articles.

Photos: Send photos with submission. Offers no additional payment for photos accepted with ms.

Tips: Freelancers can best break in at this publication with "feature articles involving outdoor sports (fishing, hunting, camping) as well as golf, bowling, baseball, football, etc., and with articles of general interest reflective of community and family living in addition to those of nostalgic interest. Features should include anecdotes and provide the kind of information that is interesting, educational, and entertaining to our readers. Style of writing should show rather than tell. Submit appropriate photo(s) with manuscript whenever possible."

THE OPTIMIST MAGAZINE, Optimist International, 4494 Lindell Blvd., St. Louis MO 63108. (314)371-6000. Editor: James E. Braibish. Assistant Editor: Patricia A. Gamma. 10% freelance written. Eager to work with new/unpublished writers. Monthly magazine about the work of Optimist clubs and members for the 155,000 members of the Optimist clubs in the United States and Canada. Circ. 155,000. Pays on acceptance. Publishes ms an average of 4 months after acceptance. Buys first North American serial rights. Submit seasonal material 3 months in advance. Photocopied and previously published submissions OK. Computer printout submissions acceptable; prefers letter-quality to dot-matrix. Reports in 1 week. Sample copy and writer's guidelines for SAE and 4 first class stamps.

Nonfiction: "We want articles about the activities of local Optimist clubs. These volunteer community-service clubs are constantly involved in projects, aimed primarily at helping young people. With over 4,000 Optimist clubs in the U.S. and Canada, writers should have ample resources. Some large metropolitan areas boast several dozen clubs. We are also interested in feature articles on individual club members who have in some way distinguished themselves, either in their club work or their personal lives. Good photos for all articles are a plus and can mean a bigger check. We are no longer a market for general-interest articles." Buys 2-3 mss/issue. Query. "Submit a letter that conveys your ability to turn out a well-written article and tells exactly what the scope of the article will be and whether photos are available." Length: 1,000-1,500 words. Pays $150 and up.

Photos: State availability of photos. Payment negotiated. Captions preferred. Buys all rights. "No mug shots or people lined up against the wall shaking hands. We're always looking for good color photos relating to Optimist activities that could be used on our front cover. Colors must be sharp and the composition must be suitable to fit an 8½x11 cover."

Tips: "Find out what the Optimist clubs in your area are doing, then find out if we'd be interested in an article on a specific club project. All of our clubs are eager to talk about what they're doing. Just ask them and you'll probably have an article idea."

PERSPECTIVE, Pioneer Clubs, Division of Pioneer Ministries, Inc., Box 788, Wheaton IL 60189-0788. (312)293-1600. Editor: Susan Zitzman. 15% freelance written. Works with a small number of new/unpublished writers each year. "All subscribers are volunteer leaders of clubs for girls and boys in grades K-12. Clubs are sponsored by evangelical churches throughout North America." Quarterly magazine; 32 pages. Circ. 24,000. Pays on acceptance. Publishes ms an average of 8 months after acceptance. Buys first North American serial rights and second serial (reprint) rights to material originally published elsewhere. Submit seasonal/holiday material 9 months in advance. Simultaneous submissions OK. Computer printout submissions acceptable if double-spaced; prefers letter-quality to dot-matrix. Reports in 6 weeks. Writer's packet for 9x12 SAE and $1.50; includes writer's guidelines and sample magazine.
Nonfiction: How-to (projects for clubs, crafts, cooking, service); informational (relationships, human development, mission education, outdoor activities); inspirational (Bible studies, adult leading youths); interview (Christian education leaders); personal experience (of club leaders). Buys 4-10 mss/year; 3 unsolicited/year. Byline given. Query. Length: 200-1,500 words. Pays $10-60. Sometimes pays expenses of writers on assignment.
Columns/Departments: Storehouse (craft, game, activity, outdoor activity suggestions—all related to club projects for any age between grades 1-12). Buys 4-6 mss/year. Submit complete ms. Length: 150-250 words. Pays $8-20.
Tips: "We only assign major features to writers who have proven previously that they know us and our constituency. Submit articles directly related to club work, practical in nature, i.e., ideas for leader training in communication, Bible knowledge, teaching skills. They must have practical application. We want substance—not ephemeral ideas. In addition to a summary of the article idea and evidence that the writer has knowledge of the subject, we want evidence that the author understands our purpose and philosophy. We're doing more and more inhouse writing—less purchasing of any freelance."

PORTS O' CALL, Box 530, Santa Rosa CA 95402. (707)542-0898. Editor: William A. Breniman. Newsbook of the Society of Wireless Pioneers. Society members are mostly early-day wireless "brass-pounders" who sent code signals from ships or manned shore stations handling wireless or radio traffic. Biannually. Not copyrighted. Pays on acceptance. No computer printout or disk submissions. Reports on submissions "within 30 days (depending on workload)."
Nonfiction: Articles about early-day wireless as used in ship-shore and high power operation; radar, electronic aids, SOS calls, etc. Early-day ships, records, etc. "Writers should remember that our members have gone to sea for years and would be critical of material that is not authentic. We are not interested in any aspect of amateur radio. We are interested in authentic articles dealing with ships (since about 1910)." Oddities about the sea and weather as it affects shipping. Buys 45 unsolicited mss/year. Query. Length: 500-2,000 words. Pays 1-5¢/word.
Photos: Paul Dane, department editor. Purchased with mss. Unusual shots of sea or ships. Wireless pioneers. Prefers b&w, "4x5 would be the most preferable size but it really doesn't make too much difference as long as the photos are sharp and the subject interests us." Fine if veloxed, but not necessary. Pays $2.50-10; "according to our appraisal of our interest." Ship photos of various nations, including postcard size, if clear, 25¢-$1 each.
Poetry: Ships, marine slant (not military), shipping, weather, wireless. No restrictions. Pays $1-$2.50 each.
Tips: "Material will also be considered for our *Ports O' Call* biannual and *Sparks Journal*, a quarterly tabloid newsletter. *Sparks* (published yearly) takes most of the contents used in *Ports O' Call*, published now every 2 years in encyclopedic format and content. *The Sparks Journal*, published quarterly in tabloid form, carries much of the early days, first hand history of wireless (episodes and experiences). Also, *Wireless Almanac* contains much nautical data relating to radio and wireless used at sea."

RECREATION NEWS, Official Publication of the League of Federal Recreation Associations, Inc., Icarus Publishers, Inc., Box 32335, Washington DC 20007. (202)965-6960. Editor: Annette Licitra. 50% freelance written. Prefers to work with published/established writers. A monthly guide to leisure activities for federal workers covering outdoor recreation, federal issues, money, travel, fitness and health, and indoor pastimes. Circ. 106,000. Pays on publication. Publishes ms an average of 3 months after acceptance. Byline given. Offers 20% kill fee on 4th assignment (first 3 on speculation). Buys one-time rights, all rights, first rights and second serial (reprint) rights. Submit seasonal/holiday material 5 months in advance. Simultaneous queries, simultaneous, photocopied, and previously published submissions OK. Computer printout submissions acceptable, prefers letter-quality. Reports in 3 weeks on queries; 1 month on mss. Sample copy for 9x12 SAE with 56¢ postage; writer's guidelines for SASE.
Nonfiction: Richard Koman, articles editor. Book excerpts (on recreation, travel, federal government); exposé (relating to federal workers); general interest (on recreation, outdoors); historical/nostalgic (Washington-related); humor (on working, home life); interview/profile (sports or government angle); opinion (on federal worker issues); and personal experience (with recreation, life in Washington). Special issues feature skiing (December); Annapolis, Maryland (summer); education (August) and federal worker health care (November). No inhouse propaganda from government agencies. Buys 45 mss/year. Query with clips of published work.

Length: 500-3,000 words. Pays $50-300. Sometimes pays the expenses of writers on assignment.
Photos: Kathy Velis, photo editor. State availability of photos with query letter or ms. Reviews contact sheets, transparencies, and 5x7 b&w prints. Pays $25-40/b&w photo ordered from contact sheet, $50-100 for color. Captions and identification of subjects required.
Columns/Departments: Richard Koman, columns, departments editor. Books (recreation, outdoors, hobbies, travel); Good sport (first person sports/recreation column); Money (personal finance); Reflections (column on home life, work); Health. Buys 15-20 mss/year. Query with clips of published work or send complete ms (on speculation only). Length: 500-1,200 words. Pays $25-75.
Tips: "Our writers generally have a few years of professional writing experience and their work runs to the lively and conversational. We're growing. We'll need more manuscripts in a wider range of recreational topics, including the off-beat. The areas of our publication most open to freelancers are general articles, and the Reflections column. *Reflections* is introspective, while main pieces are action-oriented."

REVIEW, A Publication of North American Benefit Association, North American Benefit Association, 1338 Military St., Box 5020, Port Huron MI 48061-5020. (313)985-5191, ext. 77. Editor: Virginia E. Farmer. Associate Editor: Patricia Pfeifer. 10-15% freelance written. Prefers to work with published/established writers, and works with a small number of new/unpublished writers each year. Quarterly trade journal on insurance/fraternal deeds. Family magazine. Circ. 35,000. Pays on acceptance. Publishes ms an average of 2 years after acceptance. Byline given. Not copyrighted. Buys one-time rights, simultaneous rights, and second serial (reprint) rights. Submit seasonal/holiday material 6 months in advance. Simultaneous, photocopied and previously published submissions OK. Computer printout submissions acceptable; no dot-matrix. Reports in 6 weeks. Sample copy for SAE.
Nonfiction: General interest, historical/nostalgic, how-to (improve; self-help); humor; inspirational; personal experience; and photo feature. No political/controversial. Buys 4-10 mss/year. Send complete ms. Length: 600-1,500 words. Pays 3-5¢/word.
Photos: Prefers ms with photos if available. Send photos with ms. Reviews 5x7 or 8x10 b&w prints and color slides or prints. Pays $10-15. Model release and identification of subjects required. Buys one-time rights.
Fiction: Adventure, humorous and mainstream. Buys 2-4 mss/year. Send complete ms. Length: 600-1,500 words. Pays 3-5¢/word.
Tips: "We like articles with accompanying photos; articles that warm the heart; stories with gentle, happy humor. Give background of writer as to education and credits. Manuscripts and art material will be carefully considered, but received only with the understanding that North American Benefit Association shall not be responsible for loss or injury."

THE ROTARIAN, Official Magazine of Rotary International, 1600 Ridge Ave., Evanston IL 60201. (312)328-0100. Editor: Willmon L. White. 50% freelance written. Works with published and unpublished writers. For Rotarian business and professional men and their families; for schools, libraries, hospitals, etc. Monthly. Circ. 508,000. Usually buys all rights. Pays on acceptance. Query preferred. Computer printout submissions acceptable; prefers letter-quality to dot-matrix. Reports in 1 month. Sample copy for SAE and 7 first class stamps; writer's guidelines for SAE and first class stamp.
Nonfiction: "The field for freelance articles is in the general interest category. These run the gamut from guidelines for daily living to such concerns as world hunger, the nuclear arms race, and preservation of environment. Recent articles have dealt with the office of the future, eradication of polio, and hidden illiteracy. Articles should appeal to an international audience and should in some way help Rotarians help other people. An article may increase a reader's understanding of world affairs, thereby making him a better world citizen. It may educate him in civic matters, thus helping him improve his town. It may help him to become a better employer, or a better human being. We are interested in articles on unusual Rotary club projects or really unusual Rotarians. We carry debates and symposiums, but are careful to show more than one point of view. We present arguments for effective politics and business ethics, but avoid expose and muckraking. Controversy is welcomed if it gets our readers to think but does not offend minority, ethnic or religious groups. In short, the rationale of the organization is one of hope and encouragement and belief in the power of individuals talking and working together." Query preferred. Length: 1,000-2,000 words. Payment varies. Seldom pays the expenses of writers on assignment.
Photos: Purchased with mss or with captions only. Prefers 2¼x2¼ or larger color transparencies, but also uses 35mm. B&w prints and photo essays. Vertical shots preferred for covers. Scenes of international interest. Color cover.

‡**SCOUTING**, Boy Scouts of America, 1325 Walnut Hill Ln., Irving TX 75038-3096. (214)580-2355. Editor: Walter Babson. Managing Editor: Ernest Doclar. 90% freelance written. A bimonthly magazine on scouting activities for adult leaders of the Boy Scouts. Circ. 1 million. Pays on acceptance. Publishes ms an average of 4 months after acceptance. Byline given. Buys first North American serial rights. Submit seasonal/holiday material 4 months in advance. Computer printout submissions OK; no dot-matrix. Reports in 2 weeks. Sample copy for #10 SAE with 60¢ postage; writer's guidelines for #10 SAE with 1 first class stamp.

Nonfiction: Buys 60 mss/year. Query with published clips. Length: 1,500-2,000 words. Pays $300-600 for assigned articles; pays $200-500 for unsolicited articles. Pays expenses of writers on assignment.
Photos: State availability of photos with submission. Reviews contact sheets and transparencies. Identification of subjects required. Buys one-time rights.
Columns/Departments: Family Quiz (quiz on topics of family interest), 1,000 words; and Way it Was (scouting history), 1,200 words. Buys 6 mss/year. Query. Pays $200-300.

THE SERTOMAN, Sertoma International, 1912 E. Meyer Blvd., Kansas City MO 64132. (816)333-8300. Editor: M. Megan Linhares. 1% freelance written. Quarterly magazine with "service to mankind" as its motto edited for business and professionals. Circ 30,000. Pays on acceptance. Publishes ms an average of 3 months after acceptance. Byline given. Buys one-time rights. Submit seasonal material 6 months in advance. Simultaneous, photocopied and previously published submissions OK. Computer printout submissions acceptable. Reports in 1 month. Free sample copy.
Nonfiction: "We're especially interested in articles on speech and hearing, Sertoma's international sponsorship and local Sertoma Clubs across the U.S., Canada and Mexico." Query with clips of previously published work. Length: 500-2,000 words. Pays $25-100.
Photos: Pays $5 minimum/5x7 b&w glossy prints. Captions and model release required. Buys one-time rights.

THE SONS OF NORWAY VIKING, Sons of Norway, 1455 W. Lake St., Minneapolis MN 55408. (612)827-3611. Editor: Gaelyn Beal. 10% freelance written. "We are backlogged with submissions and prefer not to receive unsolicited manuscripts at this time." Prefers to work with published/established writers. A monthly magazine for the Sons of Norway, a fraternal and cultural organization, covering Norwegian culture, heritage, history, Norwegian-American topics, modern Norwegian society, genealogy and travel. "Our audience is Norwegian-Americans (middle-aged or older) with strong interest in their heritage and anything Norwegian. Many have traveled to Norway." Circ. 77,000. Pays on publication. Publishes ms an average of 8 months after acceptance. Byline given. Offers $25 kill fee. Buys first North American serial rights and second serial (reprint) rights. Submit seasonal/holiday material 4 months in advance. Photocopied and previously published submissions OK. Computer printout submissions acceptable; prefers letter-quality to dot-matrix. Reports in 6 weeks on queries; 8 weeks on mss. Free sample copy on request.
Nonfiction: General interest, historical/nostalgic, humor, interview/profile, and travel—all having a Norwegian angle. "Articles should not be personal impressions nor a colorless spewing of facts, but well-researched and conveyed in a warm and audience-involving manner. Does it entertain *and* inform?" Buys 10 mss/year. Query. Length: 1,500-3,000 words. Pays $75-250.
Photos: Reviews transparencies and prints. Pays $10-20/photo; pays $100 for cover color photo. Identification of subjects required. Buys one-time rights.
Tips: "Show familiarity with Norwegian culture and subject matter. Our readers are somewhat knowledgeable about Norway and quick to note misstatements. Articles about modern Norway are most open to freelancers— the society, industries—but historical periods also okay. Call before a scheduled trip to Norway to discuss subjects to research or interview while there. The *Viking* will purchase more articles because more editorial pages have been added."

WOODMEN OF THE WORLD MAGAZINE, 1700 Farnam St., Omaha NE 68102. (402)342-1890, ext. 302. Editor: Leland A. Larson. 20% freelance written. Works with a small number of new/unpublished writers each year. Published by Woodmen of the World Life Insurance Society for "people of all ages in all walks of life. We have both adult and child readers from all types of American families." Monthly. Circ. 467,000. Not copyrighted. Buys 20 mss/year. Pays on acceptance. Byline given. Buys one-time rights. Publishes ms an average of 2 months after acceptance. Will consider photocopied and simultaneous submissions. Computer printout submissions acceptable; prefers letter-quality to dot-matrix. Submit seasonal material 3 months in advance. Reports in 5 weeks. Free sample copy.
Nonfiction: "General interest articles which appeal to the American family—travel, history, art, new products, how-to, sports, hobbies, food, home decorating, family expenses, etc. Because we are a fraternal benefit society operating under a lodge system, we often carry stories on how a number of people can enjoy social or recreational activities as a group. No special approach required. We want more 'consumer type' articles, humor, historical articles, think pieces, nostalgia, photo articles." Buys 15-24 unsolicited mss/year. Submit complete ms. Length: 2,000 words or less. Pays $10 minimum, 5¢/word depending on count.
Photos: Purchased with or without mss; captions optional "but suggested." Uses 8x10 glossy prints, 4x5 transparencies ("and possibly down to 35mm"). Payment "depends on use." For b&w photos, pays $25 for cover, $10 for inside. Color prices vary according to use and quality. Minimum of $25 for inside use; up to $150 for covers.
Fiction: Humorous and historical short stories. Length: 1,500 words or less. Pays "$10 minimum or 5¢/word, depending on count."

— *Astrology and Metaphysical*

The following publications regard astrology, psychic phenomena, metaphysical experiences and related subjects as sciences or as objects of serious study. Each has an individual personality and approach to these phenomena. If you want to write for these publications, be sure to read them first.

‡**ASTRO SIGNS**, T-Square Publications, 566 Westchester Ave., Rye Brook NY 10573. (914)939-2111. Editor: Nancy Frederick Sussan. 20% freelance written. Monthly miniature magazine (2½x3") covering astrology. Estab. 1986. Circ. 1,000,000. Pays on publication. Byline given (listing on masthead). Buys all rights. Submit seasonal/holiday material 6 months in advance. Computer printout submissions OK. Reports in 2 weeks. Sample copy and writer's guidelines for 25¢.
Nonfiction: General interest, humor, technical, travel and sun sign articles. "We use upbeat, positive articles focusing on sun signs as a way to make the reader's life better." Buys 60 mss/year. Query or send complete ms to the editor at 8377 Clinton Ave., West Hollywood CA 90048. Pays $100 minimum.
Tips: "A writer must have some astrological sophistication as well as a positive, helpful approach. Usually a query letter is best and then a phone call. We need at least two small features a month on love, travel, health, etc."

‡**COMMON GROUND**, Box 34090, Station D, Vancouver, British Columbia V6J 4M1 Canada. (604)733-2215. Editor: Joseph Roberts. 20% freelance written. Quarterly tabloid covering "personal growth, health and healing, peace, environment, relationships, holistic, humor. Average age of reader: 38 years; 53% female, 47% male; well educated, socially conscious; favorite TV station: PBS; favorite pastime: reading." Circ. 65,000. Pays on publication. Publishes ms an average of 1-3 months after acceptance. Byline given. Buys one-time rights or second serial (reprint) rights. Submit seasonal/holiday material 3 months in advance. Simultaneous, photocopied and previously published submissions OK. Computer printout submissions OK; prefers letter-quality to dot-matrix. Reports in 1 month. Sample copy $1.
Nonfiction: Book excerpts, expose, humor, inspirational (non-sectarian, please), interview/profile, personal experience and photo feature (b&w). No poetry or self-promotional material. Buys 10 mss/year. Query with published clips. Length: 800-1,600 words. Pays $50-100 (in Canadian funds).
Photos: Send photos with submission. Reviews transparencies, b&w contact sheets and prints. Offers $25-50 per photo. Captions, model releases and identification of subjects required. Buys one-time rights.
Columns/Departments: Health Matters (alternative medicine, high touch rather than high tech), 500-900 words; Book Reviews (positive, life enhancing, personal, professional and global), 300-400 words. Buys 8 mss/year. Query or send complete ms. Length: 600-1,000 words. Pays $25-75.
Fiction: Experimental and humorous. Buys 4 mss/year. Length: 600-1,200 words. Pays $50-90.
Fillers: Gags to be illustrated by cartoonist. Buys 4/year. Length: 200-600 words. Pays $20-40.
Tips: "First find out if we want the subject material and if we want your particular style of writing."

FATE, Clark Publishing Co., 500 Hyacinth Place, Highland Park IL 60035. Editor: Mary Margaret Fuller. 70% freelance written. Monthly. Buys all rights; occasionally North American serial rights only. Byline given. Pays on publication. Query. Reports in 2 months.
Nonfiction and Fillers: Personal psychic experiences, 300-500 words. Pays $10. New frontiers of science, and ancient civilizations, 2,000-3,000 words; also parapsychology, occultism, witchcraft, magic, spiritual healing miracles, flying saucers, etc. Must include complete authenticating details. Prefers interesting accounts of single events rather than roundups. "We very frequently accept manuscripts from new writers; the majority are individuals' first-person accounts of their own psychic experience. We do need to have all details, where, when, why, who and what, included for complete documentation." Pays minimum of 5¢/word. Fillers should be fully authenticated. Length: 100-300 words.
Photos: Buys good glossy prints with mss. Pays $5-10.

‡**HIGH TIMES**, Trans High Corp., Floor 20, 211 E. 43rd St., New York NY 10017. (212)972-8484. Editor: John Howell. 75% freelance written. Monthly magazine covering marijuana. Circ. 200,000. Pays on publication. Byline given. Offers 20% kill fee. Buys one-time rights, all rights, or makes work-for-hire assignments. Submit seasonal/holiday material 6 months in advance. Simultaneous and photocopied submissions OK. Computer printout submissions OK; prefers letter-quality to dot-matrix. Reports in 1 month on queries; 2 months on

mss. Sample for $4 and SASE; writer's guidelines for SASE.
Nonfiction: Book excerpts, expose, humor, interview/profile, new product, personal experience, photo feature and travel. Special issues include indoor Growers issue in September. No poetry or stories on "my drug bust." Buys 30 mss/year. Send complete ms. Length: 1,000-10,000 words. Pays $150-400. Sometimes pays in trade for advertisements. Sometimes pays expenses of writers on assignment.
Photos: Send photos with submission. Pays $50-300. Captions, model releases and identification of subjects required. Buys all rights.
Fiction: Adventure, fantasy, humorous and stories on smuggling. Buys 5 mss/year. Send complete ms. Length: 2,000-5,000 words. Pays $250-400.
Fillers: John Holmstrom, news editor. Gags to be illustrated by cartoonist, newsbreaks and short humor. Buys 10/year. Length: 100-500 words. Pays $10-50.
Tips: "All sections are open to good, professional writers."

HOROSCOPE GUIDE, Box 70, West Springfield MA 01090. Editor: Susan Gaetz. 50% freelance written. Prefers to work with published/established writers; works with a small number of new/unpublished writers each year. For persons interested in astrology as it touches their daily lives; all ages. Monthly. Circ. 50,000. Publishes ms an average of 6 months after acceptance. Pays on publication. Buys all rights. Byline given. Submit seasonal material 6 months in advance. Sample copy $2.50.
Nonfiction and Fillers: Wants anything of good interest to the average astrology buff, preferably not so technical as to require more than basic knowledge of birth sign by reader. Mss should be light, readable, entertaining and sometimes humorous. Not as detailed and technical as other astrology magazines, "with the astro-writer doing the interpreting without long-winded reference to his methods at every juncture. We are less reverent of astrological red tape." Wants mss about man-woman relationships, preferably in entertaining and occasionally humorous fashion. No textbook-type material. Does not want to see a teacher's type of approach to the subject. Buys 40 mss/year. Submit complete ms. Length: 900-4,000 words. Pays 2-3¢/word.
Tips: "Best way to break in with us is with some lively Sun-sign type piece involving some area of man-woman relationships—love, sex, marriage, divorce, differing views on money, religion, child-rearing, in-laws, vacations, politics, lifestyles, etc."

INNER LIGHT, Enlightment in the New Age, Global Communications, GPO Box 1994, New York NY 10001. (212)685-4080. Editor: Timothy Beckley. Managing Editor: Diane Tessman. 50% freelance written. A quarterly magazine with an "upbeat approach showing how metaphysical/New Age studies can assist readers in leading better, more prosperous lives and educating them to the fact that there are other dimensions they can tap into to make this reality better." Circ. 50,000. Pays on publication. Publishes ms an average of 3 months after acceptance. Byline given. Buys first North American serial rights and second serial (reprint) rights. Simultaneous queries, photocopied and previously published submissions OK. Reports in 1 month. Sample copy $1.25.
Nonfiction: How-to, inspirational, interview/profile and personal experience. "We are also looking for full-length manuscripts related to revelations." Pays small advance and royalties. Sells primarily to its own mailing list. No rehashing of material that has been in print. Buys 25 mss/year. Send complete ms. Length: 1,800-2,500 words. Pays $50 maximum.
Photos: Send photos with accompanying query or ms. Reviews b&w prints. Pays $5-10. Identification of subjects required. Buys one-time rights.
Fillers: Revelations (letters about personal experiences). Pays $5.

METAPSYCHOLOGY, The Journal of Discarnate Intelligence, Box 3295, Charlottesville VA 22903. Editor: Tam Mossman. 90% freelance written. Eager to work with new/unpublished writers. Quarterly journal/review on channeling—transmission of spirit writings and messages through Ouija board, automatic writing, trance, etc. For those interested in Jane Roberts' Seth books, Ramtha, Lazaris, and other wisdom from spirit entities. Circ. 3,700. Pays on publication. Publishes ms an average of 5 months after acceptance. Byline given. Buys first serial rights only. Submit seasonal/holiday material 6 months in advance. Simultaneous queries, and simultaneous and photocopied submissions OK. Computer printout submissions acceptable. Reports in 2 weeks on queries; 1 month on mss. Sample copy $5; writer's guidelines (included in sample issue).
Nonfiction: Book excerpts (first serial); channeled essays; how-to (only by trance psychics); encounters with spirits; interview/profile (of trance psychics); personal experience; and use of mind for personal evolution. "We would also like to receive interviews with 'name' channelers and articles by professionals in the medical and psychological fields, including ones who take a skeptical or critical view of the channeling phenomenon. No fiction, poetry, self-aggrandizement, religious treatises, articles with a religious axe to grind (pro or con), personal opinion pieces, or pointless voyages into autobiographical thickets." Buys 35 mss/year, most are channeled material. Query with samples of channeled material. "We serialize book-length pieces, but query first. Don't send book-length mss we have not asked to see." Pays 3¢/word. No length limit.
Photos: Photos used only on cover. No unsolicited photos.
Columns/Departments: Questions and Answers—trance psychics should write for guidelines.

Tips: "First, read a sample copy of *Metapsychology*. If your material, or writing, or insight, is up to our standards, then you have an excellent chance of getting published—especially if you channel spirit messages yourself. Few other publications accept trance material. Interviews with 'professional' channelers would be welcomed, but interviews with spirit guides would be preferred. We also want interviews with psychiatrists and psychologists who are supportive of channeling."

PSYCHIC GUIDE MAGAZINE, Island Publishing Co. Inc., Box 701, Providence RI 02901. (401)351-4320. Editor: Paul Zuromski. Managing Editor: John Kramer. 75% freelance written. Prefers to work with published/ established writers; works with many new/unpublished writers each year. Bimonthly magazine covering New Age, natural living, and metaphysical topics. "Our editorial is slanted toward assisting people in their self-transformation process to improve body, mind and spirit. We take a holistic approach to the subjects we present. They include spirituality, health, healing, nutrition, new ideas, interviews with new age people, travel, books, music, even a psychic weather report. We avoid sensationalizing and present material with the idea that an individual should decide what he should or shouldn't accept or believe." Circ. 150,000. Pays on publication. Publishes ms an average of 3-6 months after acceptance. Byline given. Offers negotiable kill fee. Buys first North American serial rights. Submit seasonal/holiday material 8 months in advance. Simultaneous queries OK. Computer printout submissions acceptable. Reports in 2 months on queries; 4 months on mss. Sample copy $3.95 with 9x12 SAE and $1 postage; writer's guidelines for SAE and 1 first class stamp.
Nonfiction: Book excerpts, historical/nostalgic (research on the roots of the New Age movement and related topics); how-to (develop psychic abilities, health, healing, proper nutrition, etc., based on holistic approach); inspirational; interview/profile (of New Age people); new product (or services offered in this field—must be unique and interesting); opinion (on any New Age, natural living or metaphysical topic); and travel (example: to Egypt based on past life research). Don't send "My life as a psychic" or "How I became psychic" articles. Buys 10-15 mss/year. Query with published clips. Length: 4,000-5,000 words. Pays $100-300. Sometimes pays the expenses of writers on assignment.
Photos: State availability of photos with query. Pays $10-20 for b&w contact sheets. Captions, model releases and identification of subjects required. Buys one-time rights.
Fillers: Clippings, anecdotes or newsbreaks on any interesting or unusual New Age, natural living, or metaphysical topic. Buys 20-30 fillers/year. Length: 500 words maximum. Pays $10-40.
Tips: "Examine our unique approach to the subject matter. We avoid sensationalism and overly strange or unbelievable stories. Reading an issue should give you a good idea of our approach to the subject. We are increasing the number of health-related features."

THE UNEXPLAINED, The Unknown Visited and Explained, National Publishing, Box 8042, Van Nuys CA 91409. (818)366-1090. Editor: Hank Krastman. 90% freelance written. Eager to work with new/unpublished writers. Quarterly magazine of unusual places (Egypt, India, Tibet, South America) and the occult, astrology, mystic. Circ. 30,000. Pays on publication. Publishes ms an average of 3 months after acceptance. Byline given. Buys all rights. Submit seasonal/holiday material 3 months in advance. Simultaneous queries, and simultaneous and photocopied submissions OK. Computer printout submissions acceptable; no dot-matrix. Reports in 2 weeks. Sample copy for 8½x11 SASE.
Nonfiction: General interest, how-to, photo feature, and travel. Buys 40 mss/year. Send complete ms. Length: open. Pays 3-5¢/word. Sometimes pays the expenses of writers on assignment.
Photos: Cherry Krastman, photo editor. Send photos with query or ms. Reviews 8½x11 b&w prints. Pays $5-10. Captions, model releases and identification of subjects required. Buys all rights.
Tips: "We need good researched articles with photos, drawings or witnesses. No ghost stories, please!"

— Automotive and Motorcycle

Publications in this section detail the maintenance, operation, performance, racing and judging of automobiles and recreational vehicles. Publications that treat vehicles as means of transportation or shelter instead of as a hobby or sport are classified in the Travel, Camping and Trailer category. Journals for service station operators and auto and motorcycle dealers are located in the Trade Auto and Truck section.

AMERICAN MOTORCYCLIST, American Motorcyclist Association, Box 6114, Westerville OH 43081-6114. (614)891-2425. Executive Editor: Greg Harrison. For "enthusiastic motorcyclists, investing considerable time and money in the sport. We emphasize the motorcyclist, not the vehicle." Monthly magazine. Circ. 134,000. Pays on publication. Rights purchased vary with author and material. Pays 25-50% kill fee. Byline given. Query with SASE. Submit seasonal/holiday material 4 months in advance. Reports in 1 month. Sample copy $1.25.

Nonfiction: How-to (different and/or unusual ways to use a motorcycle or have fun on one); historical (the heritage of motorcycling, particularly as it relates to the AMA); interviews (with interesting personalities in the world of motorcycling); photo feature (quality work on any aspect of motorcycling); and technical or how-to articles. No product evaluations or stories on motorcycling events not sanctioned by the AMA. Buys 20-25 mss/year. Query. Length: 500 words minimum. Pays minimum $4/published column inch.

Photos: Purchased with or without accompanying ms, or on assignment. Captions required. Query. Pays $20 minimum per published photo.

Tips: "Accuracy and reliability are prime factors in our work with freelancers. We emphasize the rider, not the motorcycle itself. It's always best to query us first and the further in advance the better to allow for scheduling."

ATV SPORTS MAGAZINE, The Original All Terrain Vehicle Magazine, (formerly *3 Wheeling Magazine*), Wright Publishing Co., 2949 Century Pl., Box 2260, Costa Mesa CA 92626. (714)979-2560. Editor: Bruce Simurda. Managing Editor: Rick Busenkell. 5% freelance written. Works with a small number of new/unpublished writers each year. Monthly magazine covering all terrain vehicles. Circ. 75,000. Pays on publication. Publishes ms an average of 3 months after acceptance. Byline given. Buys all rights. Submit seasonal/holiday material 3 months in advance. Simultaneous queries and simultaneous submissions OK. Computer printout submissions acceptable; no dot-matrix. Reports in 1 month. Sample copy for 9x12 SAE and 5 first class stamps.

Nonfiction: General interest, how-to, new product, personal experience, technical and travel. Especially interested in articles on specific off-road riding areas. Buys 10 mss/year. Query. Length: 600-900 words. Pays $60-90. Sometimes pays the expenses of writers on assignment.

Photos: State availability of photos. Reviews b&w contact sheets and 35mm color transparencies. Captions, model releases and identification of subjects required.

Columns/Departments: All freelance columns on contract basis only. Buys 36 mss/year. Query. Length: 600-650 words. Pays $60-90.

BMX PLUS MAGAZINE, Daisy/Hi-Torque Publishing Co., Inc., 10600 Sepulveda Blvd., Mission Hills CA 91345. (714)545-6012. Editor: John Ker. Monthly magazine covering the sport of bicycle motocross for a youthful readership (95% male, aged 8-25). 3% freelance written. Prefers to work with published/established writers. Circ. 102,000. Pays on publication. Byline given. Buys one-time rights. Submit seasonal/holiday material 4 months in advance. Simultaneous queries and manuscripts OK. Computer printout submissions acceptable; prefers letter-quality. Reports in 2 months. Publishes ms an average of 3 months after acceptance. Sample copy $2; writer's guidelines for business size SAE and 1 first class stamp.

Nonfiction: Historical/nostalgic, how-to, humor, interview/profile, new product, photo feature, technical, travel. "No articles for a general audience; our readers are BMX fanatics." Buys 20 mss/year. Send complete ms. Length: 500-1,500 words. Pays $30-250.

Photos: "Photography is the key to our magazine. Send us some exciting and/or unusual photos of hot riders in action." Send photos with ms. Pays $40-50 for color photo published; $25 for b&w photos. Reviews 35mm color transparencies and b&w negatives and 8x10 prints. Captions and identification of subjects required.

Tips: "We would like to receive more material on hot freestylers from areas other than California. Photo/story submissions would be welcomed. We also need more material about racing and freestyle from foreign countries. The sport of BMX is very young. The opportunities for talented writers and photographers in this field are open. Send us a good interview or race story with photos. Race coverage is the area that's easiest to break in to. It must be a *big* race, preferably national or international in scope. Submit story within one week of completion of race."

CAR AND DRIVER, 2002 Hogback Rd., Ann Arbor MI 48104. (313)971-3600. Editor: Don Sherman. For auto enthusiasts; college-educated, professional, median 24-35 years of age. Monthly magazine; 160 pages. Circ. 900,000. Pays on acceptance. Rights purchased vary with author and material. Buys all rights or first North American serial rights. Buys 10-12 unsolicited mss/year. Submit seasonal material 4 months in advance. Reports in 2 months.

Nonfiction: Non-anecdotal articles about the more sophisticated treatment of autos and motor racing. Exciting, interesting cars. Automotive road tests, informational articles on cars and equipment; some satire and humor. Personalities, past and present, in the automotive industry and automotive sports. "Treat readers as intellectual equals. Emphasis on people as well as hardware." Informational, how-to, humor, historical, think articles, and nostalgia. Query with clips of previously published work. Length: 750-2,000 words. Pays

$200-1,500. Also buys mini-features for FYI department. Length: about 500 words. Pays $100-500.
Photos: B&w photos purchased with accompanying mss with no additional payment.
Tips: "It is best to start off with an interesting query and to stay away from nuts-and-bolts stuff since that will be handled in-house or by an acknowledged expert. Our goal is to be absolutely without flaw in our presentation of automotive facts, but we strive to be every bit as entertaining as we are informative."

CAR COLLECTOR/CAR CLASSICS, Classic Publishing, Inc., Suite 144, 8601 Dunwoody Pl., Atlanta GA 30338. Editor: Donald R. Peterson. 90% freelance written. Works with a small number of new/unpublished writers each year. For people interested in all facets of collecting classic, milestone, antique, special interest and sports cars; also mascots, models, restoration, garaging, license plates and memorabilia. Monthly magazine; 68 pages. Circ. 35,000. Pays on publication. Publishes ms an average of 4 months after acceptance. Buys first serial rights. Submit seasonal/holiday material 4 months in advance. Photocopied submissions OK. Computer printout submissions acceptable; no dot-matrix. Reports in 2 months. Sample copy for $2; writer's guidelines for SAE and 1 first class stamp.
Nonfiction: General interest, historical, how-to, humor, inspirational, interview, nostalgia, personal opinion, profile, photo feature, technical and travel. Buys 75-100 mss/year; buys 24-36 unsolicited mss/year. Query with clips of published work. Length: 300-2,500 words. Pays 5¢/word minimum. Sometimes pays the expenses of writers on assignment.
Photos: "We have a continuing need for high-quality color positives (e.g., 2¼ or 35mm) *with* copy." State availability of photos with ms. Offers additional payment for photos with accompanying mss. Uses b&w glossy prints; color transparencies. Pays a minimum of $75 for cover and centerfold color; $10 for inside color; $5 for inside b&w. Captions and model releases required.
Columns/Departments: "Rarely add a new columnist but we are open to suggestions." Buys 36 mss/year. Query with clips of published work. Length: 2,000 maximum; prefers 1,000-2,000 words. Pays 5¢/word minimum.
Tips: "The most frequent mistakes are made by writers who are writing to a 'Sunday supplement' audience rather than to a sophisticated audience of car collectors and who are submitting stories that are often too basic and assume no car knowledge at all on the part of the reader."

CORVETTE FEVER, Prospect Publishing Co., Inc., Box 44620, Ft. Washington MD 20744. (301)839-2221. Publisher: Patricia E. Stivers. 30-40% freelance written. Works with a small number of new/unpublished writers each year. Bimonthly magazine; 64-84 pages. Circ. 35,000. Pays on publication. Publishes ms an average of 4-6 months after acceptance. Buys first and second serial (reprint) rights. Byline given. Phone queries OK. Submit seasonal/holiday material 4 months in advance. Photocopied submissions OK. Computer printout submissions OK; prefers letter-quality to dot-matrix. Reports in 1 month. Sample copy and writer's guidelines $2.
Nonfiction: General interest (event coverage, personal experience); historical (special or unusual Corvette historical topics); how-to (technical and mechanical articles, photos are a must); humor (Corvette-related humor); interview (with important Corvette persons, race drivers, technical persons, club officials, etc.); nostalgia (relating to early Corvette car and development); personal experiences (related to Corvette car use and experiences); profile (prominent and well-known Corvette personalities wanted for interviews and articles); photo feature (centerspread in color of Corvette and female Vette owner); photo essays on renovation, customizing and show cars); technical (any aspect of Corvette improvement or custom articles); and travel (relating to Corvette use and adventure). Buys 4-6 mss/issue. Query or send complete ms. Length: 500-2,500 words. Pays $40-300. Sometimes pays the expenses of writers on assignment.
Photos: Send photos with ms. Pays $5 for 5x7 b&w glossy prints; $10 for color contact sheets and transparencies. Captions preferred; model release required.
Columns/Departments: Innovative Ideas, In Print, Model Shop, Pit Stop, and Tech Vette. Buys 3 mss/issue. Send complete ms. Length: 300-800 words. Pays $24-200.
Fiction: "Any type of story as long as it is related to the Corvette." Buys 1-2 mss/issue. Send complete ms. Length: 500-2,500 words. Pays $40-200.
Fillers: Clippings, anecdotes, short humor and newsbreaks. Buys 2-3/issue. Length: 25-150 words. Pays $2-15.

CORVETTE NEWS, % GM Photographic, 30005 Van Dyke Ave., Warren MI 48090. Managing Editor: Kari Plyer. 50% freelance written. Prefers to work with published/established writers. For Corvette owners worldwide. Quarterly magazine. Circ. 150,000. Buys all rights. Pays on publication. Publishes ms an average of 4 months after acceptance. Query for electronic submissions. Computer printout submissions acceptable; prefers letter-quality to dot-matrix. Sample copy and editorial guidelines for 10x12 SAE with 80¢ postage.
Nonfiction: "Articles must be of interest to audience. Subjects considered include technical articles dealing with restorations, engines, paint, body work, suspension, parts searches, etc.; competition, 'Vettes vs. 'Vettes, or 'Vettes vs. others; profiles of Corvette owners/drivers; general interest articles, such as the unusual history of a particular early model Corvette, and perhaps its restoration; one owner's do-it-yourself engine repair procedures, maintenance procedures; Corvettes in unusual service, hobbies involving Corvettes, sports involving

Corvettes; celebrity owner profiles; Corvettes in motor sports such as races, drags, rallies, concours, gymkhanas, slaloms; travel, in USA or abroad, via Corvette. No articles negative to cars in general and Corvette in particular or articles not connected, in some way, to Corvette. Send an approximately 100-word query on the proposed article and add a statement about how you are prepared to supplement it with drawings or color transparencies." Length: 1,200-3,600 words. Query. Pays $100/published page. Sometimes pays the expenses of writers on assignment.

Photos: Color transparencies are preferred when submitted with ms; 35mm smallest format accepted.

Tips: "We are always looking for new ideas and stimulating writing approaches. But the writer must have a solid knowledge about Corvettes—either owns one, has driven one, or comes in contact with people who do own the car. We need writers who have an ability to translate very technical subjects into readable prose."

‡CYCLE WORLD, CBS Magazines, 1499 Monrovia Ave., Newport Beach CA 92663. (714)720-5300. Editor: Paul Dean. 20% freelance written. For active motorcyclists, "young, affluent, educated, very perceptive." Subject matter includes "road tests (staff-written), features on special bikes, customs, racers, racing events; technical and how-to features involving mechanical modifications." Monthly. Circ. 300,000. Pays on acceptance. Publishes ms an average of 3 months after acceptance. Buys all rights. Query for electronic submissions. Computer printout submissions acceptable. Reports in 1 week on queries; 1 month on mss. Sample copy $2; free writer's guidelines.

Nonfiction: Buys informative, well-researched, technical, theory and how-to articles; interviews; profiles; humor; and historical pieces. Buys 20 mss/year. Query. Length: 1,000-2,000 words. Pays variable rates. Sometimes pays the expenses of writers on assignment.

Photos: Purchased with or without ms, or on assignment. "We need funny photos with a motorcycle theme." Reviews contact sheets and transparencies. Pays $75 minimum. Buys one-time rights and reprint rights.

Tips: "Area most open to freelancers is short nonfiction features. they must contain positive and fun experience regarding motorcycle travel, sport and lifestyle."

‡4-WHEEL & OFF-ROAD, Petersen Publishing Co., 8490 Sunset Blvd., Los Angeles CA 90069. (213)854-2360. Editor: Steve Campbell. Managing Editor: Cecily Chittick. A monthly magazine covering four-wheel-drive vehicles, "devoted to new-truck tests, buildups of custom 4x4s, coverage of 4WD racing, trail rides and other competitions." Circ. 275,000. Pays on acceptance. Publishes ms an average of 4 months after acceptance. Byline given. Pays 20% kill fee. Buys first North American serial rights or all rights. Submit seasonal/holiday material 4 months in advance. Computer printout submissions OK. Reports in 3 weeks. Free writer's guidelines.

Nonfiction: How-to (on four-wheel-drive vehicles—engines, suspension, drive systems, etc.), new product, photo feature, technical and travel. Buys 12-16 mss/year. Send complete ms. Length: 1,000-2,500 words. Pays $200-500 for assigned and unsolicited articles. Sometimes pays the expenses of writers on assignment.

Photos: Send photos with submission. Reviews transparencies and 7x9 prints. Offers no additional payment for photos accepted with ms. Captions, model releases and identification of subjects required. Buys all rights.

Fillers: Anecdotes, facts, gags, newsbreaks and short humor. Buys 12-16/year. Length: 50-150 words. Pays $15-50.

Tips: "Attend 4x4 events, get to know the audience. Present material only after full research. Manuscripts should contain *all* of the facts pertinent to the story. Technical/how-to articles are most open to freelancers."

FOUR WHEELER MAGAZINE, 6728 Eton Ave., Canoga Park CA 91303. (818)992-4777. Publisher: Dave Cohen. Editor: John Stewart. 20% freelance written. Works with a small number of new/unpublished writers each year. Emphasizes four-wheel-drive vehicles, competition and travel/adventure. Monthly magazine; 164 pages. Circ. 222,835. Pays on publication. Publishes ms an average of 4 months after acceptance. Buys all rights. Submit seasonal/holiday material at least 4 months in advance. Query for electronic submissions. Computer printout submissions acceptable; prefers letter-quality to dot-matrix. Sample copy for SASE.

Nonfiction: 4WD competition and travel/adventure articles, technical, how-tos, and vehicle features about unique four-wheel drives. "We like the adventure stories that bring four wheeling to life in word and photo: mud-running deserted logging roads, exploring remote, isolated trails, or hunting/fishing where the 4x4 is a necessity for success." See features by Bruce Smith, Gary Wescott, Don Biggs and Dick Stansfield for examples. Query with photos before sending complete ms. Length: 1,200-2,000 words; average 4-5 pages when published. Pays $100/page minimum for complete package. Sometimes pays the expenses of writers on assignment.

Photos: Requires professional quality color slides and b&w prints for every article. Captions required. Prefers Kodachrome 64 or Fujichrome 50 in 35mm or 2¼ formats. "Action shots a must for all vehicle features and travel articles."

Tips: "Show us you know how to use a camera as well as the written word. The easiest way for a new writer/photographer to break in to our magazine is to read several issues of the magazine, then query with a short vehicle feature that will show his or her potential as a creative writer/photographer."

FRIENDS MAGAZINE, Ceco Communications, Inc., 30400 Van Dyke Blvd., Warren MI 48093. (313)575-9400. Editor: Michael Brudene. "*Friends* is a magazine for Chevrolet owners." 75-85% freelance written. Prefers to work with published/established writers. Monthly magazine; 52 pages. Circ. 1,000,000. Pays on acceptance. Publishes ms an average of 6 months after acceptance. Buys first rights in most cases. Computer printout submissions acceptable; no dot-matrix. Submit seasonal/holiday material 6 months in advance. Simultaneous and photocopied submissions OK. Reports in 1 month. Free sample copy and writer's guidelines.
Nonfiction: Travel (by automobile; U.S. only); celebrity profiles; unusual use of Chevrolet products; humor (travel-related); entertainment; and photo features (strong travel-tied photo essays). "We're looking for freelancers who can focus and produce lively copy and write a story that will interest or excite the general reader. Query by mail only. Sometimes pays expenses of writers on assignment.
Photos: State availability of photos. Pays $200/page. Transparencies only. "About the only time we'll consider black and white is when the article is an early historical piece." Captions and model release required.
Tips: "Writing style must be 'people' oriented with plenty of quotes and conversational tone. Avoid 'dry' narrative. We're particularly interested in seeing queries about auto trips or tours that can be done in 72 hours or less. Most auto travelers prefer 'long weekend' vacations."

HOT BIKE, McMullen Publishing Co., 2145 W. Le Palme, Anaheim CA 92632. (714)635-9040. Editor: Tod Knuth. 20-50% freelance written. Prefers to work with published/established writers; eager to work with a small number of new/unpublished writers. Monthly magazine that is a serious, tech-oriented, high performance motorcycle publication with emphasis on Harley-Davidson motorcycles, plus coverage of race events, and classics. Circ. 80,000. Pays on publication. Publishes ms an average of 3 months after acceptance. Byline given. Buys one-time rights. Submit seasonal/holiday material 3 months in advance. Photocopied submissions OK. Computer printout submissions acceptable. Reports in 2 weeks. Sample copy $1.25; writer's guidelines for SAE with 1 first class stamp.
Nonfiction: Historical/nostalgic (classic bikes and events); how-to (tech article, high performance engine, suspension, etc.); interview/profile (top racers and builders); new products (for new product section); and photo feature (high-performance street and track machine). Exclusives on hot new performance bikes, particularly Harley-Davidson. Also, European Harley coverage. Buys 40 mss/year. Send complete ms. Length: 500-3,000 words. Pays $50-300. Sometimes pays the expenses of writers on assignment.
Photos: "For cover consideration, a female model helps—no nudes—keep it sexy but tasteful. Photos should be dramatic if they are race oriented." Pays $20-50 for b&w contact sheets, negatives and prints (5x7 or 8x10); $30-100 for color transparencies (35mm or 2¼). Captions, model releases and identification of subjects required.
Tips: "Have a hot subject, hot photos, clear and concise writing. Bad photos ruin most freelance submissions. Read the magazine and study format style and subject matter. We are always willing to give new writers a chance."

NISSAN DISCOVERY, The Magazine for Nissan Owners, Donnelley Marketing, Box 4617, N. Hollywood CA 91607. (213)877-4406. Editor: Wayne Thoms. 50% freelance written. Prefers to work with published/established writers and photographers. Bimonthly magazine for Nissan owners and their families. Circ. 500,000. Pays on acceptance. Publishes ms an average of 3-6 months after acceptance. Byline given. Buys first North American serial rights. Submit seasonal/holiday material 5 months in advance. Photocopied and previously published submissions OK. Computer printout submissions acceptable; no dot-matrix. Reports in 1 month. Sample copy $1.50 in cash or stamps, 9x12 SAE, and 80¢ postage; writer's guidelines for business size SAE and 22¢ postage.
Nonfiction: Historical/nostalgic, humor, photo feature, travel. "We need general family interest material with heavy emphasis on outstanding color photos: travel, humor, food, lifestyle, sports, entertainment." Buys 25 mss/year. Query. Length: 1,300-1,800 words. Pays $300-1,000. Sometimes pays the expenses of writers on assignment.
Photos: State availability of photos. Reviews 2¼" and 35mm color transparencies. No b&w photos. "Payment usually is part of story package—all negotiated." Captions and identification of subjects required. Buys one-time rights.
Tips: "A freelancer can best break in to our publication by submitting a brief idea query with specific information on color slides available. Offer a package of copy and art."

‡**OFF-ROAD'S THUNDER TRUCKS AND TRUCK PULLS**, Argus Publishing, Suite 316, 12301 Wilshire Blvd., Los Angeles CA 90025. (213)820-3601. Editor: Stephanie Wolfe. 35% freelance written. Quarterly magazine covering truck pulls, monster events and mud bogging. Pays on publication. Publishes ms an average of 3-8 months after acceptance. Byline given. Kill fee varies. Buys second serial (reprint) rights. Submit seasonal/holiday material 4 months in advance. Simultaneous submissions OK. Query for electronic submissions. Computer printout submissions OK; prefers letter-quality to dot-matrix. Reports in 2 weeks on mss. Free writer's guidelines.
Nonfiction: Book excerpts, historical/nostalgic, how-to, humor, interview/profile, new product, personal

experience, photo feature, technical and travel. Query. Pays $50-400 for assigned articles.

Photos: Send photos with submission. Reviews contact sheets, negatives, transparencies and prints. Captions, model releases and identification of subjects required. Buys all rights.

Columns/Departments: Video and Book Reviews. Query. Payment varies.

‡OPEN WHEEL MAGAZINE, Lopez Publications, Box 715, Ipswich MA 01938. (617)356-7030. Editor: Dick Berggren. 80% freelance written. Bimonthly magazine. "*OW* covers sprint cars, midgets, supermodifieds and Indy cars. *OW* is an enthusiast's publication which speaks to those deeply involved in oval track automobile racing in the United States and Canada. *OW*'s primary audience is a group of men and women actively engaged in competition at the present time, those who have recently been in competition and those who plan competition soon. That audience includes drivers, car owners, sponsors and crew members who represent perhaps 50-70 percent of our readership. The rest who read the magazine are those in the racing trade (part manufacturers, track operators and officials) and serious fans who see 30 or more races per year." Circ. 150,000. Pays on publication. Publishes ms an average of 3-6 months after acceptance. Byline given. Buys first rights. Submit seasonal/holiday material 2 months in advance. Computer printout submissions OK; prefers letter-quality. Reports in 3 weeks on queries. Free sample copy and writer's guidelines.

Nonfiction: General interest, historical/nostalgic, how-to, humor, interview/profile, new product, photo feature and technical. "We don't care for features that are a blow-by-blow chronology of events. The key word is interest. We want features which allow the reader to get to know the main figure very well. Our view of racing is positive. We don't think all is lost, that the sport is about to shut down and don't want stories that claim such to be the case, but we shoot straight and avoid whitewash." Buys 125+ mss/year. Query with or without published clips, or send complete ms.

Photos: State availability of photos with submission. Reviews contact sheets, negatives, transparencies and prints. Buys one-time rights.

Fillers: Anecdotes, facts and short humor. Buys 100+/year. Length: 1-3 pages, double-spaced. Pays $35.

Tips: "Virtually all our features are submitted without assignment. An author knows much better what's going on in his backyard than we do. We ask that you write to us before beginning a story theme. If nobody is working on the theme you wish to pursue, we'd be glad to assign it to you if it fits our needs and you are the best person for the job. Judging of material is always a combination of a review of the story and its support illustrations. Therefore, we ask for photography to accompany the manuscript on first submission."

POPULAR CARS, The Complete Street Machine Magazine, McMullen Publishing, Inc., 2145 W. La Palma, Anaheim CA 92801-1785. (714)635-9040. Editor: Jim Kelso. 25% freelance written. Prefers to work with published/established automotive writers. Monthly magazine on contemporary, high performance, domestic automobiles. "Our main emphasis is on 'street machines' (owner-modified cars) and 60s and 70s 'muscle' cars and related subjects." Circ. 85,000. Pays on publication. Publishes ms an average of 3 months after acceptance. Byline given. Kill fee negotiated in advance. Buys first serial rights. Submit material 3 months in advance. Computer printout submissions acceptable; prefers letter-quality to dot-matrix. Reports in 3 weeks on queries; 1 month on mss. Sample copy $2.50; free photographer's guidelines.

Nonfiction: Historical/nostalgic (60s, 70s muscle cars); how-to (street performance and drag racing); interview/profile (of people associated with automotive performance subjects); new product (new cars—2 page maximum, performance cars *only*); photo feature (on peoples' street machines); technical (street performance); and drag race and street machine event coverage. Special issues on Ford '64-'70 Mustangs, Corvettes, '55-'57, Chevys, Pro Streeters. No new car tests. Buys 36-40 mss/year. Query with published clips. Length: 435-1,175 words. Pays $75-300.

Photos: Reviews 35mm color transparencies and 5x7 b&w prints. Pays $20-75 for transparencies; $0-20 for prints. Captions, model releases, and identification of subjects required. Buys all rights.

Tips: "A freelancer can best break in to our publication with a query, submission of past work, good quality manuscripts, reputation, and good 'car features'."

RIDER, 29901 Agoura Rd., Agoura CA 91301. Editor: Tash Matsuoka. 60% freelance written. Works with a small number of new/unpublished writers each year. For owners and prospective buyers of motorcycles to be used for touring, sport riding, and commuting. Monthly magazine; 100-160 pages. Buys first-time rights only. Pays on publication. Publishes ms average of 6 months after acceptance. Query first. Submit seasonal material 3 months in advance. Photocopied submissions OK. Computer printout submissions acceptable; no dot-matrix. Reports in 1 month. Sample copy $2; writer's guidelines for SAE with 1 first class stamp.

Nonfiction: Articles directly related to motorcycle touring, camping, commuting and sport riding including travel, human interest, safety, novelty, do-it-yourself and technical. "Articles which portray the unique thrill of motorcycling." Should be written in clean, contemporary style aimed at a sharp, knowledgeable reader. Buys informational how-to, personal experience, profile, historical, nostalgia and personal opinion. Length is flexible. Pays $100 for Favorite Ride feature and $150-450 for major articles. Sometimes pays expenses of writers on assignment.

Photos: Offers no additional payment for photos purchased with ms. Captions required. "Quality photographs are critical. Graphics are emphasized in *Rider*, and we must have photos with good visual impact."

‡ROAD & TRACK, 1499 Monrovia Ave., Newport Beach CA 92663. Editor: John Dinkel. 10% freelance written. For knowledgeable car enthusiasts. Monthly magazine. Publishes ms up to 2 years after acceptance. Buys first rights. Computer printout submissions acceptable. Reports in 6 weeks.
Nonfiction: "The editor welcomes freelance material, but if the writer is not thoroughly familiar with the kind of material used in the magazine, he is wasting both his time and the magazine's. *Road & Track* material is highly specialized and that old car story in the files has no chance of being accepted. We publish more serious, comprehensive and in-depth treatment of particular areas of automotive interest." Query. Pays 25-50¢/word minimum depending upon subject covered and qualifications and experience of author.
Tips: "Freelancer must have intimate knowledge of the magazine. Unless he can quote chapter and verse for the last 20 years of publication, he's probably wasting his time and mine."

ROAD KING MAGAZINE, Box 250, Park Forest IL 60466. Editor-in-Chief: George Friend. 10% freelance written. Eager to work with new/unpublished writers each year. Truck driver leisure reading publication. Quarterly magazine; 72 pages. Circ. 224,000. Pays on acceptance. Publishes ms an average of 2 months after acceptance. Usually buys all rights; sometimes buys first serial rights. Byline given "always on fiction—if requested on nonfiction—copyright mentioned only if requested." Submit seasonal/holiday material 3 months in advance. Simultaneous and photocopied submissions OK. Sample copy for 7x10 SAE with 73¢ postage or get free sample copy at any Unocal 76 truck stop.
Nonfiction: Trucker slant or general interest, humor, and photo feature. No articles on violence or sex. Name and quote release required. No queries. Submit complete ms. Length: 500-1,200 words. Pays $50-400.
Photos: Submit photos with accompanying ms. No additional payment for b&w contact sheets or 2¼x2¼' color transparencies. Captions preferred. Buys first rights. Model release required.
Fiction: Adventure, historical, humorous, mystery, rescue-type suspense and western. Especially about truckers. No stories on sex and violence. "We're looking for quality writing." Buys 4 mss/year. Submit complete ms. Length: approximately 1,200 words. Pays up to $400. Writer should quote selling price with submission.
Fillers: Jokes, gags, anecdotes and short humor about truckers. Buys 20-25/year. Length: 50-500 words. Pays $5-100.
Tips: "No collect phone calls or postcard requests. Never phone for free copy as we will not handle such phone calls. We don't appreciate letters we have to answer. Do not submit manuscripts, art or photos using registered mail, certified mail or insured mail. Publisher will not accept such materials from the post office. Publisher will not discuss refusal with writer. Nothing personal, just legal. Do not write and ask if we would like such and such article or outline. We buy only from original and complete manuscripts submitted on speculation. Do not ask for writer's guidelines. See above and/or get a copy of the magazine and be familiar with our format before submitting anything. We are a trucker publication whose readers are often family members and sometimes Bible Belt. We refrain from violence, sex, nudity, etc. "

STOCK CAR RACING MAGAZINE, Box 715, Ipswich MA 01938. Editor: Dick Berggren. 80% freelance written. Eager to work with new/unpublished writers. For stock car racing fans and competitors. Monthly magazine; 116 pages. Circ. 400,000. Pays on publication. Publishes ms an average of 3 months after acceptance. Buys all rights. Byline given. Query for electronic submissions. Computer printout submissions acceptable; prefers letter-quality to dot-matrix. Reports in 6 weeks. Free sample copy and writer's guidelines.
Nonfiction: General interest, historical/nostalgic, how-to, humor, interviews, new product, photo features and technical. "Uses nonfiction on stock car drivers, cars, and races. We are interested in the story behind the story in stock car racing. We want interesting profiles and colorful, nationally interesting features. We are looking for more technical articles, particularly in the area of street stocks and limited sportsman." Query with or without published clips, or submit complete ms. Buys 50-200 mss/year. Length: 100-6,000 words. Pays up to $450.
Photos: State availability of photos. Pays $20 for 8x10 b&w photos; up to $250 for 35mm or larger color transparencies. Captions required.
Fillers: Anecdotes and short humor. Buys 100+ each year. Pays $35.
Tips: "We get more queries than stories. We just don't get as much material as we want to buy. We have more room for stories than ever before. We are an excellent market with 12 issues per year. Virtually all our features are submitted without assignment. An author knows much better what's going on in his backyard than we do. We ask that you write to us before beginning a story theme. If nobody is working on the theme you wish to pursue, we'd be glad to assign it to you if it fits our needs and you are the best person for the job. Judging of material is always a combination of a review of the story and its support illustration. Therefore, we ask for photography to accompany the manuscript on first submission."

VOLKSWAGEN'S WORLD, Volkswagen of America, 888 W. Big Beaver Rd., Box 3951, Troy MI 48007. Editor: Marlene Goldsmith. 75% freelance written. Magazine published 5 times/year for Volkswagen owners in the United States. Circ. 340,000. Pays on acceptance. Buys first North American serial rights. Byline given. Query on electronic submissions. Computer printout submissions acceptable; no dot-matrix. Reports in 6 weeks. Free writer's guidelines.

Nonfiction: "Interesting stories on people using Volkswagens; travel pieces with the emphasis on people, not places; Volkswagenmania stories; personality pieces, including celebrity interviews; and inspirational and true adventure articles. The style should be light. Our approach is subtle, however, and we try to avoid obvious product puffery, since *Volkswagen's World* is not an advertising medium. We prefer a first-person, people-oriented handling. No basic travelogues; stay away from Beetle stories. With all story ideas, query first. All unsolicited manuscripts will be returned unopened. Although queries should be no longer than 2 pages, they ought to include a working title, a short, general summary of the article, and an outline of the specific points to be covered. We strongly advise writers to read at least 2 past issues before working on a story." Buys 10-12 mss/year. Length: 1,000 words maximum; "shorter pieces, some as short as 450 words, often receive closer attention." Pays $150 per printed page for photographs and text; otherwise, a portion of that amount, depending on the space allotted. Most stories are 2 pages; some run 3 or 4 pages.

Photos: Submit photo samples with query. Photos purchased with ms; captions required. "We prefer color transparencies, 35mm or larger. All photos should carry the photographer's name and address. If the photographer is not the author, both names should appear on the first page of the text. Where possible, we would like a selection of at least 40 transparencies. It is recommended that at least one show the principal character or author. Quality photography can often sell a story that might be otherwise rejected. Every picture should be identified or explained." Model releases required. Pays $350 maximum for front cover photo.

Fillers: "Short, humorous anecdotes about current model Volkswagens." Pays $15.

Tips: "Style of the publication and its content are being structured toward more upscale, affluent buyers. VW drivers are not the same as those who used to drive the Beetle."

Aviation

Professional and private pilots and aviation enthusiasts read the publications in this section. Editors at aviation magazines want material for audiences who know commercial aviation. Magazines for passengers of commercial airlines are grouped in the In-Flight category. Technical aviation and space journals and publications for airport operators, aircraft dealers and others in aviation businesses are listed under Aviation and Space in the trade section.

AERO, Fancy Publications, Box 6050, Mission Viejo CA 92690. (714)240-6001. Editor: Dennis Shattuck. Executive Editor: Steve Kimball. 85% freelance written. Works with a small number of new/unpublished writers each year. For owners of private aircraft. "We take a unique, but limited view within our field." Circ. 75,000. Buys first North American serial rights. Buys about 30-50 mss/year. Pays after publication. Publishes manuscript an average of 3 months after acceptance. Will consider photocopied submissions if guaranteed original. Query for electronic submissions. Computer printout submissions OK. Reports in 2 months. Sample copy $3; writer's guidelines for SASE.

Nonfiction: Material on aircraft products, developments in aviation, specific airplane test reports, travel by aircraft, development and use of airports. All must be related to general aviation field. Query. Length: 1,000-4,000 words. Pays $75-250. Sometimes pays expenses of writers on assignment.

Photos: Pays $15 for 8x10 b&w glossy prints purchased with mss or on assignment. Pays $150 for color transparencies used on cover.

Columns/Departments: Weather flying, instrument flight refresher, new products.

Tips: "Freelancer must know the subject about which he is writing; use good grammar; know the publication for which he's writing; remember that we try to relate to the middle segment of the business/pleasure flying public. We see too many 'first flight' type of articles. Our market is more sophisticated than that. Most writers do not do enough research on their subject. We would like to see more material on business-related flying, more on people involved in flying."

AIR & SPACE MAGAZINE, Joe Bonsignore-Smithsonian, 900 Jefferson Dr., Washington DC 20560. (202)357-4414. Editor: George C. Larson. Managing Editor: Philip Hayward. 80% freelance written. Prefers to work with published/established writers. A bimonthly magazine covering aviation and aerospace for a nontechnical audience. "Features are slanted to a technically curious, but not necessarily technically knowledgeable audience. We are looking for unique angles to aviation/aerospace stories, history, events, personalities, current and future technologies, that emphasize the human-interest aspect." Circ. 300,000. Pays on acceptance. Byline given. Offers kill fee. Buys first North American serial rights. Photocopied submissions OK. Reports in 5 weeks. Sample copy for $3.50 plus 9½x13 SASE; writer's guidelines for #10 SASE.
Nonfiction: Book excerpts, essays, general interest (on aviation/aerospace), historical/nostalgic, how-to, humor, interview/profile, photo feature and technical. Buys 50 mss/year. Query with published clips. Length: 1,500-3,000 words. Pays $2,000 maximum. Pays the expenses of writers on assignment.
Photos: State availability of photos with submission. Reviews 35mm transparencies. Photos are assigned separately.
Columns/Departments: Above and Beyond (first person), 2,000-2,500 words; Flights and Fancy (whimsy, insight), approximately 1,200 words; Groundling's Notebook (looking upward), length varies. Buys 25 mss/year. Query with published clips. Pays $1,000 maximum. Soundings (brief items, timely but not breaking news), 500-800 words. Pays $300.
Tips: Soundings is the section most open to freelancers.

‡**ALASKA FLYING MAGAZINE**, Pacific Quest Publishing, Inc., Pouch 112010, Anchorage AK 99511. (907)344-3331. Editor: Beth Burgos. Managing Editor: Wayne Adair. 60% freelance written. Eager to work with new/unpublished writers. A monthly magazine on Alaskan aviation and lifestyles. "For both pilots and nonpilots, *Alaska Flying* covers a wide variety of topics related to Alaska aviation, including hunting and fishing, adventures, historical articles, character sketches, how aircraft are used in Alaska, etc." Circ. 65,000. Pays 60 days after publication. Publishes manuscript an average of 5 months after acceptance. Byline given. Pays $40 kill fee. Buys first North American rights and makes work-for-hire assignments. Submit seasonal/holiday material 4 months in advance. Simultaneous, photocopied and previously published submissions OK. Computer printout submissions OK. Reports in 4 weeks on queries. Sample copy for 8½x11 SAE with 3 first class stamps.
Nonfiction: General interest, historical/nostalgic, how-to, humor, new product, personal experience, photo feature, technical, travel and flying techniques. Buys 60 mss/year. Send complete ms. Length: 1,000-3,000 words. Pays $100-200 for assigned articles. Pays $75-125 for unsolicited articles. Sometimes pays the expenses of writers on assignment.
Photos: Send photos with submission. Reviews contact sheets, negatives, transparencies and prints. Offers no additional payment for photos accepted with ms. Captions and identification of subjects required. Buys one-time rights.
Tips: "Make sure your story has a strong *Alaska lifestyle* connection—not too technical—with strong photo support."

AOPA PILOT, 421 Aviation Way, Frederick MD 21701. (301)695-2350. Editor: Thomas A. Horne. 15% freelance written. Prefers to work with published/established writers; works with a small number of new/unpublished writers each year. For aircraft owners, pilots, and the complete spectrum of the general aviation industry. Official magazine of the Aircraft Owners and Pilots Association. Monthly. Circ. 260,000. Pays on acceptance. Publishes ms an average of 3 months after acceptance. Buys first North American serial rights. Computer printout submissions acceptable; prefers letter-quality to dot-matrix. Sample copy $2.
Nonfiction: Factual articles up to 2,500 words that will inform, educate and entertain pilots and aircraft owners ranging from the student to the seasoned professional. These pieces should be generously illustrated with good quality photos, diagrams or sketches. Quality and accuracy are essential. Topics covered include maintenance, operating technique, reports on new and used aircraft, avionics and other aviation equipment, governmental policies (local, state and federal) relating to general aviation. Additional features on weather in relation to flying, legal aspects of aviation, flight education, pilot fitness, and aviation history are used occasionally. No commonplace first-solo or fly-in/local-event stories. Query. Pays up to $400.
Photos: Pays $25 minimum for each photo or sketch used. Original b&w negatives or color slides should be made available.

AVIATION/USA, Randall Publishing Company, Box 2029, Tuscaloosa AL 35403. (205)349-2990. Editor: Claude Duncan. 25-50% freelance written. Eager to work with new/unpublished writers. Biweekly magazine on general aviation (small planes, not jets). "Most of our readers are private pilots who like to read about other pilots, their planes, equipment and adventures." Circ. 10,000. Pays on acceptance. Publishes ms an average of 1 month or less after acceptance. Byline given. Offers 100% kill fee. Not copyrighted. Buys first serial rights, one-time rights, second serial (reprint) rights and simultaneous rights. Simultaneous and previously published (updated) submissions OK. Computer printout submissions acceptable; prefers letter-quality to dot-matrix. Reports in 2 weeks. Free sample copy and writer's guidelines.

Nonfiction: General interest (with general aviation angle); historical/nostalgic (except combat stories); how-to (overcome flight problems); humor (with pilot angle); interview/profile (with general aviation angle); personal experience (with pilots); technical (planes); travel (related to small planes); and small local airports. Buys 100 mss/year. Send complete ms. Length: 250-1,000 words. Pays $10-50. Sometimes pays expenses of writers on assignment.

Photos: Send photos with query or ms. Prefers b&w or color prints; commercially processed OK if sharp. Pays $5.

Tips: "We encourage pilots to write. Submitting art with copy gives a definite edge. Nothing is too local if it's interesting. Our major focus is on single-engine planes, and increasingly I prefer articles by licensed pilots or mechanics."

FLIGHT REPORTS, Peter Katz Productions, Inc., 1280 Saw Mill River Rd., Yonkers NY 10710. (914)423-6000. Editor: David Sampugnaro. Managing Editor: Peter J. Katz. 50% freelance written. Works with a small number of new/unpublished writers each year. Monthly travel magazine for pilots and aircraft owners. Pays on publication. Publishes ms an average of 1 month after acceptance. Byline given. Buys all rights. Submit seasonal/holiday material 2 months in advance. Computer printout submissions OK; prefers letter-quality. Reports in 2 weeks. Sample copy $1.

Nonfiction: Destination reports include what to do, where to stay, and airport facilities for domestic travel and Canada only. No foreign travel. Buys variable number of mss/year. Query. Length: 750-1,500 words. Pays $25-50.

Photos: State availability of photos. Pays $5 for 3½x5½ b&w and color prints. Captions required.

Tips: "Pilot's license and cross country flying experience are helpful. Some aviation background is required."

KITPLANES, "Featuring Fast-Build Aircraft for the Home Craftsman," Fancy Publications, Box 6050, Mission Viejo CA 92690. (714)240-6001. Editor: Dennis Shattuck. Managing Editor: Dave Martin. 70% freelance written. Eager to work with new/unpublished writers. Monthly magazine covering self-construction of private aircraft for pilots and builders. Circ. 45,000. Pays on publication. Publishes ms an average of 3 months after acceptance. Byline given. Offers negotiable kill fee. Buys first North American serial rights. Submit seasonal/holiday material 6 months in advance. Query for electronic submissions. Computer printout submissions acceptable; dot-matrix must be caps and lower case printing. Reports in 2 weeks on queries; 6 weeks on mss. Sample copy $3; writer's guidelines for business size SAE.

Nonfiction: How-to, interview/profile, new product, personal experience, photo feature, technical and general interest. "We are looking for articles on specific construction techniques, the use of tools, both hand and power, in aircraft building, the relative merits of various materials, conversions of engines from automobiles for aviation use, installation of instruments and electronics." No general-interest aviation articles, or "My First Solo" type of articles. Buys 80 mss/year. Query. Length: 500-5,000 words. Pays $100-400.

Photos: Send photos with query or ms, or state availability of photos. Pays $10-75 for b&w prints; $20-150 for color transparencies and color prints. Captions and identification of subjects required. Buys one-time rights.

Tips: "*Kitplanes* contains very specific information—a writer must be extremely knowledgeable in the field. Major features are entrusted only to known writers. I cannot emphasize enough that articles must be directed at the individual aircraft constructor. We will not accept or even consider articles about personal experiences in flight."

PRIVATE PILOT, Fancy Publications Corp., Box 6050, Mission Viejo CA 92690. (714)240-6001. Editor: Dennis Shattuck. Managing Editor: April E. Hay. 60% freelance written. Works with a small number of new/unpublished writers each year. For owner/pilots of private aircraft, for student pilots and others aspiring to attain additional ratings and experience. "We take a unique, but limited view within our field." Circ. 85,000. Buys first North American serial rights. Pays on publication. Publishes manuscript average of 6 months after acceptance. Will consider photocopied submissions if guaranteed original. No simultaneous submissions. Query for electronic submissions. Computer printout submissions acceptable "if double-spaced and have upper and lower case letters." Reports in 2 months. Sample copy $3; writer's guidelines for SASE.

Nonfiction: Material on techniques of flying, developments in aviation, product and specific airplane test reports, travel by aircraft, development and use of airports. All must be related to general aviation field. No personal experience articles. Buys about 60-90 mss/year. Query. Length: 1,000-4,000 words. Pays $75-300.

Photos: Pays $15 for 8x10 b&w glossy prints purchased with mss or on assignment. Pays $150 for color transparencies used on cover.

Columns/Departments: Business flying, homebuilt/experimental aircraft, pilot's logbook. Length: 1,000 words. Pays $50-125.

Tips: "Freelancer must know the subject about which he is writing; use good grammar; know the publication for which he's writing; remember that we try to relate to the middle segment of the business/pleasure flying public. We see too many 'first flight' type of articles. Our market is more sophisticated than that. Most writers do not do enough research on their subject. We would like to see more material on business-related flying, more on people involved in flying."

Business and Finance

Business publications give executives and consumers a range of information from local reports to national overviews. These publications cover business trends, computers in business, and the general theory and practice of business and financial management. National and regional publications are listed below in separate categories. Magazines that have a technical slant are in the Trade section under Business Management, Finance, Industrial Operations or Management and Supervision categories.

National

‡**BARRON'S Business and Financial Weekly**, Dow Jones and Co. Inc., 200 Liberty St., New York NY 10028. (212)416-2759. Editor: Alan Abelson. Managing Editor: Kathryn M. Welling. 10% freelance written. Weekly tabloid covering the investment scene. *"Barron's* is written for active participants in and avid spectators of the investment scene. We require top-notch reporting *and* graceful, intelligent and irreverent writing." Circ. 296,000. Pays on publication. Byline given. Offers 25% kill fee. Buys all rights. Computer printout submissions OK; no dot-matrix. Reports in 1 month. Writer's guidelines for SASE.
Nonfiction: Kathryn M. Welling, managing editor. Book excerpts, general interest and interview/profile. Publishes quarterly mutual fund sections. Buys 100 mss/year. Query with published clips. Length: 1,500-2,000 words. Pays $500-2,000 for assigned articles. Pays expenses of writers on assignment.
Photos: State availability of photos with submission. Reviews contact sheets, negatives and 8x10 prints. Offers $150-300/photo (day rate). Model releases and identification of subjects required. Buys one-time rights.
Columns/Departments: Richard Donnelly, column/department editor. Barron's on Books (business/investment books). Buys 100 mss/year. Query with published clips. Length: 250-500 words. Pays $150.

BETTER BUSINESS, National Minority Business Council, Inc., 235 E. 42nd St., New York NY 10017. (214)573-2385. Editor: John F. Robinson. 50% freelance written. Semiannual magazine covering small/minority business issues. Circ. 10,000. Pays on publication. Publishes ms an average of 2 months after acceptance. Byline given. Buys first North American serial rights and all rights. Submit seasonal material 1 month in advance. Computer printout submissions acceptable; prefers letter-quality to dot-matrix. Sample copy $5 and 9x12 SAE with $1.50 postage; free writer's guidelines.
Nonfiction: Interview/profile and technical. Buys 5 mss/year. Query with clips. Length: 3,000-5,000 words. Pays $200-250.
Photos: State availability of photos. Reviews b&w prints. Captions required. Buys all rights.

BUSINESS AGE, The Magazine for Small Business, Business Trends Communications Corp., Box 11597, Milwaukee WI 53211. (414)332-7507. Editor: Margaret A. Brickner. Associate Editors: Katherine L. Steinbach and Julie M. Sobieski. 10% freelance written. Monthly magazine for owners/managers of businesses with 1-100 employees. Articles should emphasize useful information for effective business operation. Circ. 100,000+. Pays on publication. Publishes ms an average of 2 months after acceptance. Byline given. Buys first North American serial rights or second serial (reprint) rights. Computer printout submissions acceptable; prefers letter-quality to dot-matrix. Reports in 1 month. Sample copy for $3, 8x11 SAE and 5 first class stamps. Writer's guidelines for business size SAE with 1 first class stamp.
Nonfiction: How-to (finance, accounting, marketing, management, business law, personnel management, customer relations, planning, taxes, international businesses); interview/profile (successful businesses and small business advocates). All articles should have clear application to small business. Query or send complete ms. State availability of photos. Length: 1,500-2,000 words. Pays $100-450. Sometimes pays expenses of writers on assignment.
Tips: "Keep in mind that small business owners want to increase profits and productivity. Emphasize the how-to and tailor your piece to benefit the reader."

‡**BUSINESS MONTH**, (formerly *Dun's Business Month*), 875 3rd Ave., New York NY 10022. (212)605-9400. Editor: Arlene Hershman. 20% freelance written. Prefers to work with published/established writers. Emphasizes business, management and financial trends for a readership "concentrated among senior

executives of those companies that have a net worth of $1 million or more." Monthly magazine. Circ. 301,000. Pays on acceptance. Buys all rights. Submit seasonal/holiday material 3 months in advance. Photocopied submissions OK. Computer printout submissions OK; prefers letter-quality to dot-matrix. Reports in 1 month. Sample copy $3.50.

Nonfiction: Business and government, historical (business; i.e., law or case history), management (new trends, composition), finance and accounting, informational, interview, personal opinion and company profile. Buys 12 mss/year. Query first. Length: 1,200-2,500 words. Pays $200 minimum. Pays expenses of writers on assignment.

Photos: Contact art director. Photos purchased with accompanying ms. Query first. Pays $75 for b&w photos; $150 for color.

Tips: "Make your query short and clearly to the point. Also important—what distinguishes proposed story from others of its type?"

D&B REPORTS, The Dun & Bradstreet Magazine for Small Business Management, Dun & Bradstreet, 299 Park Ave., 24th Floor, New York NY 10171. (212)593-6723. Editor: Patricia W. Hamilton. 10% freelance written. Works with a small number of new/unpublished writers each year. A bimonthly magazine for small business. "Articles should contain useful information that managers of small businesses can apply to their own companies. *D&B Reports* focuses on companies with $10 million in annual sales and under." Circ. 76,000. Pays on acceptance. Publishes ms an average of 2 months after acceptance. Byline given. Buys all rights. Query for electronic submissions. Computer printout submissions acceptable. Reports in 3 weeks on manuscripts. Free sample copy and writer's guidelines.

Nonfiction: How-to (on management); and interview/profile (of successful entrepreneurs). Buys 5 mss/year. Query. Length: 1,500-2,500 words. Pays $500 minimum. Sometimes pays expenses of writers on assignment.

Photos: State availability of photos with submission. Identification of subjects required. Buys one-time rights.

Tips: "The area of our publication most open to freelancers is profiles of innovative companies and managers."

EXECUTIVE FEMALE, NAFE, 1041 Third Ave., New York NY 10021. (212)371-0740. Editor: Mary E. Terzella. Emphasizes "upbeat and useful career and financial information for the upwardly mobile female." 30% freelance written. Prefers to work with published/established writers; works with a small number of new/unpublished writers each year. Bimonthly magazine; 64 pages. Circ. 180,000. Byline given. Pays on publication. Publishes ms an average of 4 months after acceptance. Submit seasonal/holiday material 6 months in advance. Buys first rights, first North American serial rights, one-time rights, all rights, simultaneous rights and second serial (reprint) rights to material originally published elsewhere. Simultaneous and photocopied submissions OK. Computer printout submissions acceptable; no dot-matrix. Reports in 3 months. Sample copy $2.50; free writer's guidelines.

Nonfiction: "Articles on any aspect of career advancement and financial planning are welcomed." Needs how-tos for managers and articles about coping on the job, trends in the workplace, financial planning, trouble shooting, business communication, time and stress management, career goal-setting, and get-ahead strategies. "We would also like to receive humorous essays dealing with aspects of the job/workplace." Written queries only. Length: 1,000-2,500 words. Pays $50-200 minimum. Sometimes pays the expenses of writers on assignment.

Columns/Departments: Profiles (interviews with successful women in a wide range of fields, preferably nontraditional areas for women); Entrepreneur's Corner (successful female business owners with unique ideas); Horizons (career planning, personal and professional perspectives and goal-setting); More Money (specific financial issues, social security, tax planning); and Your Executive Style (tips on health and lifestyle). Department length: 800-1,200 words. Pays $25-50 minimum.

FACT, The Money Management Magazine, 305 E. 46th St., New York NY 10017. Contact: Editor. 25% freelance written. Monthly personal money management and investment magazine for sophisticated readers. Circ. 50,000. Pays on acceptance. Publishes ms an average of 2 months after acceptance. Byline given. Offers 25% kill fee. Buys first rights, nonexclusive (reprint) rights and second serial (reprint) rights. Simultaneous queries OK. Computer printout submissions acceptable; prefers letter-quality to dot-matrix. Reports in 6 weeks. Free sample copy.

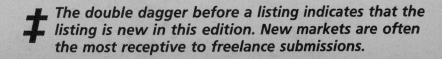

The double dagger before a listing indicates that the listing is new in this edition. New markets are often the most receptive to freelance submissions.

Nonfiction: General interest (specific money management topics); how-to (invest in specific areas); and new product. No business articles; no "how to balance your checkbook" articles. Writers must be knowledgeable and use lots of sidebars and tables. Buys 25-35 mss/year. Query with published clips. Length: 1,000-2,500 words. Pays $50-250.

Columns/Departments: Stocks, mutual funds, precious metals, bonds, real estate, collectibles, taxes, insurance, cash management and banking. Buys 10-20 mss/year. Query with published clips. Length: 1,500-1,800 words. Pays $50-250.

Tips: "Show writing credentials and expertise on a specific subject. Try something fresh. Read the magazine. Our readers are sophisticated about investments and money management."

FORBES, 60 5th Ave., New York NY 10011. (212)620-2200. Managing Editor: Sheldon Zalaznick. "We occasionally buy freelance material. When a writer of some standing (or whose work is at least known to us) is going abroad or into an area where we don't have regular staff or bureau coverage, we have given assignments or sometimes helped on travel expenses." Pays negotiable kill fee. Byline usually given.

HOME BUSINESS NEWS, The Magazine for Home-based Entrepreneurs, 12221 Beaver Pike, Jackson OH 45640. (614)988-2331. Editor: Ed Simpson. 60% freelance written. Works with a small number of new/unpublished writers each year. A bimonthly magazine covering home-based businesses and marketing. Pays on publication. Publishes ms an average of 2 months after acceptance. Byline sometimes given. Buys first North American serial rights and second serial (reprint) rights. Submit seasonal/holiday material 4 months in advance. Simultaneous, photocopied and previously published submissions OK. Query for electronic submissions. Computer printout submissions acceptable; prefers letter-quality to dot-matrix. Reports in 1 week on queries; 5 weeks on mss. Sample copy $2; writer's guidelines for SAE with 1 first class stamp.

Nonfiction: Book excerpts, inspirational, interview/profile (of home business owners), new products, personal experience, computer-based home businesses and mail order success stories. Buys 15-20 mss/year. Query with published clips. Length: 800-3,000 words. Pays $20-100; will pay with ad space if agreed upon.

Photos: State availability of photos with submission. Offers no additional payment for photos accepted with ms. Captions and identification of subjects required. Buys one-time rights.

Columns/Departments: Home Business Profiles (profiles of home business owners), 2,000 words. Buys 15-20 mss/year. Query with published clips. Pays $20-100.

Fillers: Facts and newsbreaks. Buys 10/year. Length: 50-300 words. Pays $5-10.

INC MAGAZINE, The Magazine for Growing Companies, INC Publishing Corp., 38 Commercial Wharf, Boston MA 02110. (617)227-4700. Editor: George Gendron. Executive Editor: Bo Burlingham. Managing Editor: Sara P. Noble. 10% freelance written. Prefers to work with published/established writers. A monthly business magazine for chief executive officers and managers of growing companies up to $100 million in sales. Circ. 625,000. Pays on acceptance. Publishes ms an average of 2 months after acceptance. Byline given. Offers 33% kill fee. Buys first North American serial rights. Submit seasonal/holiday material 3 months in advance. Electronic submissions OK via ASCII, 300 or 1200 BPS Hayes Smart modem, but requires hard copy also. Computer printout submissions acceptable; prefers letter-quality to dot-matrix. Reports in 6 weeks on queries; 1 month on mss.

Nonfiction: Interview/profile and opinion. Buys 8 mss/year. Query with published clips. Length: 1,000-4,000 words. Pays $150-2,500. Pays expenses of writers on assignment.

Columns/Departments: Insider, Hands On, Management Columns. Buys 10 mss/year. Query with published clips. Length: 350-1,200 words. Pays $150-800.

Tips: "We are cutting back on freelance submissions in general, tending to work with those freelancers with whom we presently have a working relationship."

THE INTERNATIONAL ADVISOR, WMP Publishing Company, Suite 103, 2211 Lee Road, Winter Park FL 32789. (305)628-5300. Editor: Dennis Hardaker. Executive Editor: Gerald Schomp. 15% freelance written. Prefers to work with published/established writers. A monthly newsletter on global diversification in investments. This investment advisory publication selects, analyzes, and recommends the most promising world stocks and monitors the world's stock markets, offering its readers the chance to participate in these gains. Pays on publication. Publishes ms an average of 2 months after acceptance. Byline given. Buys all rights. Photocopied submissions OK. Computer printout submissions acceptable; prefers letter-quality to dot-matrix. Reports in 3 weeks. Free sample copy and writer's guidelines.

Nonfiction: Opinion and technical on market analyses, exchanges and stock recommendations, investment trends, foreign markets, etc. No politically liberal submissions. Buys 40 mss/year. Send complete ms. Length: 1,200 words. Pays 20¢/word. Very seldom pays expenses of writers on assignment.

Tips: "All articles should be as timely as deadlines permit and must draw obvious conclusions."

INVESTigate, The Journal of Investment Protection, Investment Publishing Group, Suite 103, 2211 Lee Rd., Winter Park FL 32789. (305)628-5300. Associate Editor: Mike Ketcher. Managing Editor: Jerry

Schomp. 50% freelance written. Prefers to work with published/established writers; works with a small number of new/unpublished writers each year. A monthly newsletter on investment fraud and protection of assets. Circ. 25,000. Pays on publication. Publishes ms an average of 2 months after acceptance. Byline given. Buys all rights. Photocopied submissions OK. Computer printout submissions acceptable; prefers letter-quality to dot-matrix. Reports in 2 weeks. Free sample copy and writer's guidelines.

Nonfiction: Exposé (investment industry, related areas) and how-to (protect assets; rights of investors, etc.). Buys 40 mss/year. Query with published clips. Length: 800-2,500 words. Pays 20¢/word. Sometimes pays expenses of writers on assignment.

Tips: "We will be looking for more positive articles on what to do to invest wisely (rather than what not to do). *INVESTigate* focuses on alerting subscribers to dishonesty, misrepresentation, bad deals, and even criminal fraud in the investment arena, and then educating and directing them toward worthwhile opportunities."

‡MBA, The Magazine for Business Professionals, 18 N. Main St., Box 8001, Chagrin Falls OH 44022-8001. (216)622-4444. Editor: Paul H. Oppmann, Jr. Managing Editor: Mary E. Mihaly. 90% freelance written. Monthly magazine covering all interests of MBA degree holders. Estab. 1986. Circ. 120,000. Pays on publication. Publishes ms an average of 2 months after acceptance. Byline given. Offers up to a 40% kill fee. Buys one-time rights or second serial (reprint) rights. Submit seasonal/holiday material 5 months in advance. Simultaneous and previously published submissions OK. Computer printout submissions OK; prefers letter-quality, but dot-matrix OK "if highest quality." Reports in 1 month. Writer's guidelines for SAE with 1 first class stamp.

Nonfiction: Essays, exposé, general interest, humor (business-related), interview/profile, photo feature, technical, travel, cartoons, surveys, reportage. No poetry, religion, or how-to. Buys 250 mss/year. Query with published clips, or send complete ms. Length: 200-2,500 words. Pays $100-2,000. Pays expenses of writers on assignment.

Photos: State availability of photos with query, or send photos with submission. Reviews contact sheets, transparencies, prints and slides. Offers $50-800 per photo. Model releases and identification of subjects required. Buys one-time rights.

Columns/Departments: Book Reviews (business-related), 200-500 words; Humor or Essay (business-related), 500-700 words; Education (interesting continuing education alternatives for MBAs), up to 1,500 words. Will consider ideas and samples submitted by freelancers. Query with published clips, or send complete ms. Pays $100-1,500.

Fillers: Anecdotes, facts, newsbreaks and short humor. Length: 50-250 words. Pays $50-200.

Tips: "Query with clips that show a good understanding of business issues and professional writing skills. First submissions to us will be on speculation; once we know a writer can fill our needs, work is on an assignment basis. We look for a sophisticated but lively, intelligent tone."

THE NCFE MOTIVATOR, National Center for Financial Education, Inc. (NCFE), Suite 3100 West, 50 Fremont St., San Francisco CA 94105. (415)777-0460. Editor: Paul Richard. 25% freelance written. Works with published/established writers and new/unpublished writers; eager to work with new/unpublished writers. A monthly newsletter covering personal finance information. "This is *not* a publication for the sophisticated investor, rather it is for novices, beginners, those who hope to become investors, as well as high school students." Circ. 3,500 (estimated total after client reprint is 85,000). Pays on publication. Publishes ms an average of 3 months after acceptance. Byline given. Submit seasonal/holiday material 4 months in advance. Simultaneous, photocopied and previously published submissions OK. Computer printout submissions acceptable; prefers letter-quality to dot-matrix. Reports in 3 weeks on queries; 6 weeks on mss. Sample copy for #10 SAE with 1 first class stamp; writer's guidelines for #10 SAE with 1 first class stamp.

Nonfiction: How-to (finance, credit, debt, savings, insurance, banking, wills) and interview/profile. Buys 10-20 mss/year. Query first with published clips and SASE. Length: 250-1,000 words. Pays $25-75 for assigned articles; pays $10-30 for unsolicited articles.

Photos: State availability of photos with submission. Reviews contact sheets. Offers no additional payment for photos accepted with ms. Captions and identification of subjects required.

Fillers: Facts and newsbreaks. Buys 15-25/year. Length: 50-100 words. Pays $5-40.

SYLVIA PORTER'S PERSONAL FINANCE MAGAZINE, 380 Lexington Ave., New York NY 10017. (212)557-9100. Editor: Patricia Schiff Estess. Executive Editor: Greg Daugherty. 50% freelance written. Prefers to work with published/established writers. Monthly (10 issues/year). Pays on acceptance. Publishes ms an average of 3 months after acceptance. Byline given. Offers 20% kill fee. Buys all rights. Submit seasonal/holiday material at least 4 months in advance. No simultaneous, photocopied or previously published submissions. Computer printout submissions acceptable; prefers letter-quality. Reports in 1 month. Writer's guidelines for SAE and 1 first class stamp. Sample copy for 9x12 envelope with $1.98 postage.

Nonfiction: General interest (financial). Only articles dealing with personal finance; no financially technical articles. "Send a cover letter with original ideas or slants about personal finance articles you'd like to do for us, accompanied by clippings of your previously published work. The features section is most open to freelancers."

We will be covering topics such as financial planning, investing, real estate, taxes, and entrepreneurship in each issue." Buys 100 mss/year. Query with published clips. Length: 500-2,000 words. Pays negotiable rates ($500-2,000). Sometimes pays the expenses of writers on assignment.

Columns/Departments: Hot Tips (timely items), 100-300 words; Travel (money-saving strategies), Investing, and Real Estate, all 1,000 words. Buys 80 mss/year. Query with published clips. Length: 100-1,500 words. Pays $100-750.

Tips: "Explain why your topic is important to our reader and why now. Demonstrate a grasp of our subject matter—through your query or through previously published work or both. Because our material is fairly technical, we're not an easy market for beginners."

TECHNICAL ANALYSIS OF STOCKS AND COMMODITIES, The Trader's Magazine, 9131 California Ave. SW, Box 46518, Seattle WA 98146-0518. (206)938-0570. Editor: John Sweeney. 75% freelance written. Eager to work with new/unpublished writers. Magazine covers methods of investing and trading stocks, bonds and commodities (futures), options, mutual funds, and precious metals. Circ. 15,000. Pays on publication. Publishes ms an average of 3 months after acceptance. Byline given. Offers 50% kill fee. Buys all rights; however, second serial (reprint) rights revert to the author, provided copyright credit is given. Photocopied and previously published submissions OK. Electronic submissions via phone 300/1200 baud or Apple II, Macintosh, IBM PC computer disk, but requires hard copy also. Computer printout submissions acceptable; prefers letter-quality to dot-matrix. Reports in 3 weeks on queries; 1 month on mss. Sample copy $5; detailed writer's guidelines for business size SAE and 1 first class stamp.

Nonfiction: Reviews (new software or hardware that can make a trader's life easier; comparative reviews of software books, services, etc.); how-to (trade); technical (trading and software aids to trading); utilities (charting or computer programs, surveys, statistics, or information to help the trader study or interpret market movements); humor (unusual incidents of market occurrences, cartoons). No newsletter-type, buy-sell recommendations. The article subject must relate to trading psychology, technical analysis, charting or a numerical technique used to trade securities or futures. Virtually requires graphics with every article. Buys 80 mss/year. Query with published clips if available, or send complete ms. Length: 1,000-4,000 words. Pays $100-500. (Applies per inch base rate and premium rate—write for information). Sometimes pays expenses of writers on assignment.

Photos: Christine M. Napier, photo editor. State availability of photos. Pays $10-100 for 5x7 b&w glossy prints or color slides. Captions, model releases and identification of subjects required. Buys one-time rights.

Columns/Departments: Buys 10 mss/year. Query. Length: 800-1,600 words. Pays $50-200.

Fillers: Melissa J. Hughes, fillers editor. Jokes and cartoons, on investment humor. Must relate to trading stocks, bonds, options, mutual funds, or commodities. Buys 50/year. Length: 100-500 words. Pays $10-50.

Tips: "Describe how to use technical analysis, charting, or computer work in day-to-day trading of stocks, bonds, mutual funds, options or commodities. A blow-by-blow account of how a trade was made, including the trader's thought processes, is, to our subscribers, the very best received story. One of our prime considerations is to instruct in a manner that the layperson can comprehend. We are not hyper-critical of writing style. The completeness and accuracy of submitted material are of the utmost consideration. Write for detailed writer's guidelines."

TRAVEL SMART FOR BUSINESS, Communications House, 40 Beechdale Rd., Dobbs Ferry NY 10522. (914)693-8300. Editor/Publisher: H.J. Teison. Managing Editor: L.M. Lane. 20% freelance written. Monthly newsletter covering travel and information on keeping travel costs down for business travelers and business travel managers. Circ. 2,000. Pays on publication. Publishes ms an average of 6 weeks after acceptance. No byline given. "Writers are listed as contributors." Buys first North American serial rights. Computer printout submissions acceptable; prefers letter-quality to dot-matrix. Reports in 6 weeks. Sample copy for business size SAE and 2 first class stamps; writer's guidelines for business size SAE and 1 first class stamp.

Nonfiction: "Inside" travel facts for companies that travel; how-to (pick a meeting site, save money on travel); reviews of facilities and restaurants; analysis of specific trends in travel affecting business travelers. No general travel information, backgrounders, or non-business-oriented articles. "We're looking for value-oriented, concise, factual articles." Buys 20 mss/year. Query with clips of published work. Length: 250-1,500 words. Pays $20-150.

Tips: "We are primarily staff written, with a few regular writers. Know the travel business or have business travel experience. People with a specific area of experience or expertise have the inside track."

‡THE WORKSTEADER NEWS, LA Features, 2396 Coolidge Way, Rancho Cordova CA 95670. (916)635-8764. Editor: Lynie Arden. 20% freelance written. Works with a small number of new/unpublished writers each year. Monthly newsletter serving as "an advocate of working at home whether in a business or job." Circ. 5,000. Pays on publication. Publishes ms an average of 1 month after acceptance. Byline given. Buys first rights or second serial (reprint) rights. Simultaneous, photocopied and previously published submissions OK. Query for electronic submission requirements. Computer printout submissions OK; prefers letter-quality to dot-matrix. Reports in 2 weeks on queries; 1 month on mss. Sample copy $1.

Nonfiction: Book excerpts, exposé, humor, inspirational, interview/profile, new product, personal experience and how-to (marketing ideas, starting a home-based business). Our readers are either working at home now and want to enhance the experience or are looking for the opportunity to do so. Length: 250-1,000 words. Pays $10-50 for assigned articles. Sometimes pays with "one-year subscription to amateurs with good information, but no writing ability (piece has to be rewritten)." Sometimes pays expenses of writers on assignment.

Columns/Departments: Electronic Cottage (home work opportunities using computers), 250-750 words; Nothing for Something (consumer alert to work-at-home ripoffs), 500 words; and Reviewing (books on working at home, low-cost marketing), 250-750 words. Buys 20 mss/year. Query. Pays $10-50.

WORLD MARKET PERSPECTIVE, WMP Publishing Company, Suite 103, 2211 Lee Rd., Winter Park FL 32789. (305)628-5300. Editor: Jerry Schomp. Associate Editor: Jack Holsomback. 60% freelance written. Prefers to work with published/established writers. A monthly newsletter covering research in economic science and world markets. Circ. 25,000. Pays on publication. Publishes manuscript on average of 1-2 months after acceptance. Byline given. Buys all rights. Photocopied submissions OK. Computer printout submissions acceptable; prefers letter-quality. Reports in 2 weeks. Free sample copy and writer's guidelines.
Nonfiction: Opinion and technical on market analysis, stock recommendations, investment trends, etc. No politically liberal submissions. Buys 40 mss/year. Query first. Length: 1,200-6,000 words. Pays $120-1,200.
Tips: *"World Market Perspective* studies the global markets for specific and general economic trends and analyzes them so that our subscribers can use the information to make better investment decisions. We follow the Austria school of economics, and prefer that articles reflect this viewpoint. However, we occasionally print material of a different viewpoint if we feel it is of interest to our readership."

Regional

‡**BC BUSINESS**, Canasus Communications, 200-550 Burrard St., Vancouver, British Columbia, V6C 2J6 Canada. (604)669-1721. Editor: Richard A. Murray. Managing Editor: Bonnie Irving. 95% freelance written. Monthly magazine publishing business profiles and information focusing on British Columbia. Circ. 25,000. Pays on publication. Publishes manuscript an average of 2 months after acceptance. Byline given. Offers 50% kill fee. Buys first North American serial rights. Submit seasonal/holiday material 3 months in advance. Photocopied and previously published submissions OK. Computer printout submissions OK. Reports in 3 weeks. Sample copy for 8½x11 SASE. Free writer's guidelines.
Nonfiction: Book excerpts (BC oriented or how-to business); how-to (business only), interview/profile (BC people/companies only). Buys 96 mss/year. Query with published clips. Length: 1,500-3,000 words. Pays $300-800. Sometimes pays the expenses of writers on assignment.
Photos: State availability of photos with submission. Offers no additional payment for photos accepted with ms. Identification of subjects required.
Tips: "Come up with a good or novel idea and send samples of published magazine articles that demonstrate an ability to write well. We are open to any article ideas dealing with business in British Columbia."

‡**BOSTON BUSINESS JOURNAL**, P&L Publications, 393 D. St., Boston MA 02210-1907. (617)268-9880. Executive Editor: Peter Kadzis. Managing Editor: John P. Mello, Jr. 20% freelance written. Weekly newspaper covering business in Greater Boston. "Our audience is top managers at small, medium and Fortune 500 companies." Circ. 42,000. Pays on publication. Publishes ms an average of 2 weeks after acceptance. Byline given. Offers 50% kill fee. Buys all rights. Submit seasonal/holiday material 1 month in advance. Photocopied and previously published submissions OK. Query for electronic submissions. Computer printout submissions OK; prefers letter-quality to dot-matrix. Reports in 1 week on queries; in 2 weeks on mss.
Nonfiction: Expose, humor, interview/profile, opinion, and photo features. Real estate supplement (3rd week of each month); special focus on hotels, skiing and the office. Buys 100 mss/year. Query with published clips. Length: 600-1,500 words. Pays $125-250 for assigned articles; $125-150 for unsolicited articles. Pays expenses of writers on assignment.
Photos: State availability of photos with submission. Reviews 8x10 prints. Pays $30-75 per photo. Identification of subjects required. Buys one-time rights and reprint rights.
Columns/Departments: Small Business (how to deal with problems faced by small businesses); Investments (where and how to invest your money); Technology (computer and computer-related topics). Buys 100 mss/year. Query. Length: 1,000 words. Pays $125-175.
Tips: "Read *Wall Street Journal.* Look for hard news angle versus feature angle. Use 'numbers' liberally in the story."

BOULDER COUNTY BUSINESS REPORT, (formerly *Boulder Business Report*), Box 8005-265, Boulder CO 80306. (303)440-4950. Editor: Vicki Cooper. 60% freelance written. Prefers to work with published/established writers; works with a small number of new/unpublished writers each year. Monthly newspaper covering Boulder County business issues. Offers "news tailored to a monthly theme and read primarily by Colorado businesspeople and by some investors nationwide. Philosophy: Descriptive, well-written prose of educational value." Circ. 10,000. Pays on publication. Publishes ms an average of 1 month after acceptance. Byline given. Offers 10% kill fee. Buys one-time rights and second serial (reprint) rights. Simultaneous queries and photocopied submissions OK. Query for electronic submissions. Computer printout submissions acceptable; prefers letter-quality to dot-matrix. Reports in 1 month on queries; 2 weeks on mss. Sample copy $1.75.

Nonfiction: Book excerpts, interview/profile, new product, photo feature of company, examination of competition in a particular line of business. "All our issues are written around a monthly theme. No articles are accepted in which the subject has not been pursued in depth and both sides of an issue presented in a writing style with flair." Buys 60 mss/year. Query with published clips. Length: 250-2,000 words. Pays $25-200.

Photos: State availability of photos with query letter. Reviews b&w contact sheets; prefers "people portraits." Pays $10 maximum for b&w contact sheet. Identification of subjects required. Buys one-time rights and reprint rights.

Tips: "It would be difficult to write for this publication if a freelancer was unable to localize a subject. In-depth articles are written by assignment. The freelancer located in the Colorado area has an excellent chance here."

BUSINESS ATLANTA, Communication Channels Inc., 6255 Barfield Rd., Atlanta GA 30328. (404)256-9800. Editor: Barrie Rissman. 80% freelance written. A monthly magazine covering Atlanta and Georgia. Circ. 27,000. Pays on publication. Publishes ms an average of 3 months after acceptance. Byline given. Offers 10% kill fee. Buys first North American serial rights and second serial (reprint) rights. Submit seasonal/holiday material 4 months in advance. Reports in 6 months on queries; 3 months on manuscripts. Sample copy $2.

Nonfiction: Humor and interview/profile. No product-related material or case studies. Buys 150 mss/year. Query with published clips. Length: 1,000-4,000 words. Pays $250-800. Sometimes pays the expenses of writers on assignment. Buys one-time rights and reprint rights.

Columns/Departments: Southern Stocks (review of publicly traded Atlanta-based company); Profile (interview with local business person); Enterprise (analysis of a local business); and Marketing (analysis of a local business's marketing approach), all 1,500-1,800 words. Buys 85 mss/year. Query with published clips. Pays $300-350.

Tips: "We do not use writers from outside the state of Georgia except in very rare cases. The back-of-the-book departments are most open to new writers. Our initial assignments are made on speculation only."

THE BUSINESS TIMES, For Connecticut Executives, The Business Times, Inc., 544 Tolland St., East Hartford CT 06108. (203)289-9341. Editor: Mark Isaacs. 20% freelance written. A monthly tabloid covering general business news, information and feature articles for upper-level executives in Connecticut. Circ. 25,000. Pays on publication. Publishes ms an average of 3 months after acceptance. Byline given. Buys all rights in Connecticut. Simultaneous, photocopied and previously published submissions OK. Reports in 1 month. Sample copy $2.

Nonfiction: Interview/profile and opinion. No humor, product information, or highly technical articles; no articles on selling, or anything aimed at "middle management." Buys 3-5 mss/year. Query with published clips. Length: 500-1,400 words; prefers 600-1,000 words. Pays $50-300 for assigned articles; pays $30-200 for unsolicited articles.

Photos: State availability of photos with submission. Reviews contact sheets. Offers $10-30/photo. Identification of subjects required. Buys one-time rights.

Columns/Departments: Viewpoint (any area of controversy in business, finance and sometimes economic issues) and Management (articles useful to upper-level management to improve productivity, etc.). Buys 3-5 mss/year. Query with published clips and/or send complete ms. Length: 500-800 words. Pays $30-75.

Tips: "We are geographically-oriented to Connecticut-based businesses, so the most important thing is that the story appeal to our audience. Writers outside of the area might consider concentrating on an area of interest (national legislation or issue, for example) that has a Connecticut tie-in or might impact in a unique way on Connecticut business. Also, we prefer articles with very specific examples to support arguments. Most open to freelancers is our op-ed or Viewpoint section, for which we almost always look for new, fresh articles on controversial subjects related to business from a free market perspective. This does not require a Connecticut tie-in."

BUSINESS TO BUSINESS, North Florida's Business Magazine, Business to Business, Inc., Box 6085, Tallahassee FL 32314. (904)222-7072. Editor: Robert Mellon Singer. 75% freelance written. Eager to work with new/unpublished writers and works with a number of new/unpublished writers each year. Monthly tabloid covering business in the North Florida-South Georgia Big Bend region. Circ. 16,000. Pays on acceptance. Byline given "generally. We purchase rights depending on the article, author and costs." Submit seasonal/holiday material 4 months in advance. Reprints welcomed. Computer printout submissions acceptable. Reports in

2 weeks on queries; 3 weeks on mss. Sample copies and writer's guidelines for 9x12 SAE and 6 first class stamps.

Nonfiction: Book excerpts (reviews of business related books—*Megatrends*, *Positioning*); In Search of Excellence (topics of interest to business-minded people); historical/nostalgic (only pertaining to the Big Bend); how-to (select the right typewriter, adding machine, secretary, phone system, insurance plan); new products; technical (articles on finance marketing, investment, advertising and real estate as it applies to small business). "We also solicit articles on controversial topics relating to business and government." Special "inserts" planned: advertising, office of the future, consulting, taxes. "No really basic material. Writers must assume that readers have some idea of business vocabulary. No new business profiles, or material without a local handle." After Work section contains a wide array of "lifestyle" pieces—health, food, hobbies, travel, recreation, etc. Buys 100-200 mss/year. Query with published clips if available. Length: 500-2,000 words. Pays $25-300. "Articles with photos and/or artwork pay more."

Photos: State availability of photos. Pays $5-20 for b&w contact sheets and b&w prints. Identification of subjects required.

Columns/Departments: "Shorts accepted on all aspects of doing business. Each story should tackle one topic and guide reader from question to conclusion. General appeal for all trades and industries." Buys 75-100 mss/year. Query with published clips if available. Length: 500-1,000 words. Pays $25-100.

Tips: "Send a query with past writing sample. If it seems that a writer is capable of putting together an interesting 500- to 800-word piece dealing with small business operation, we're willing to give him/her a try. Meeting deadlines determines writer's future with us. We're open to short department pieces on management, finance, marketing, investments, real estate. Articles must be tightly written—direct and to the point; keep it casual, but put in the facts."

BUSINESS VIEW, (formerly *Business View of SW Florida*), Florida Business Publications Inc., Box 9859, Naples FL 33941. (813)263-7525. Editor: Meg Andrew. 100% freelance written. Prefers to work with published/established writers; works with a small number of new/unpublished writers each year. A monthly magazine covering business trends and issues in southwest Florida. Circ. 14,200. Pays on publication. Publishes ms an average of 3-6 months after acceptance. Byline given. Buys all rights or makes work-for-hire assignments. Simultaneous, photocopied and previously published submissions OK. Computer printout submissions acceptable; prefers letter-quality to dot-matrix. Reports in 2 months. Sample copy $2 with 8½x11 SAE and 8 first class stamps; free writer's guidelines.

Nonfiction: Book excerpts (business); how-to (management); humor (business); interview/profile (regional); and technical. "No jokes, puzzles, or whimsy, unless it pertains directly to business." Buys 24-36 mss/year. Query with published clips. Length: 100-3,000 words. Pays $15-350 for assigned articles; pays $15-200 for unsolicited articles. Sometimes pays the expenses of writers on assignment.

Photos: State availability of photos with submission. Reviews contact sheets and 5x7 prints. Offers $25-35/photo. Buys one-time rights.

Columns/Departments: Personal Finance (general investment opportunities); Management; and Computers (software information that helps business people—"high level material—stay away from ABC computer level"). Buys 12-20 mss/year. Send complete ms. Length: 750-1,200 words. Pays $25-100.

Fillers: Facts and newsbreaks. Buys 36/year. Length: 75-200 words. Pays $15-25.

Tips: "Our readers like specific answers to specific problems. Do not send generalized how-to articles that do not offer concrete solutions to management problems. Our readers are busy, so be concise and upbeat in style. Profiles of southwest Florida business leaders are most open to freelance writers. These are short (500 words) articles that present local, interesting personalities. How-to articles in the areas of management, personal finance, retailing, accounting, investing, computers, personnel, and stress management are also open. We have recently entered the Sarasota market and are actively looking for articles about businesses in that area."

CRAIN'S CLEVELAND BUSINESS, 140 Public Square, Cleveland OH 44114. (216)522-1383. Editor: Brian Tucker. Prefers to work with published/established writers; works with a small number of new/unpublished writers each year. Weekly tabloid about business in the 7-county area surrounding Cleveland and Akron for upper-income executives, professionals and entrepreneurs. Circ. 26,000. Average issue includes 2-3 freelance news or feature articles. Pays on publication. Publishes ms an average of 1 month after acceptance. Byline given. Buys first North American serial rights. Phone queries OK. Query for electronic submissions. Computer printout submissions OK; prefers letter-quality to dot-matrix. Reports in 3 weeks. Sample copy for 9x12 SAE; writer's guidelines for #10 SAE and 2 first class stamps.

Nonfiction: "We are interested in business and political events and their impact on the Cleveland area business community." Query. Length: 500-1,200 words. Pays $5/column inch for news stories; $3/column inch for special section features.

Photos: State availability of photos. Reviews 5x7 b&w glossy prints. Pays $10/photo used. Captions required. Buys one-time rights.

Tips: "We want stories that have a strong local twist, either a national trend filled with local quotes and anecdotes, or perhaps a statewide piece with the same focus."

‡CRAIN'S DETROIT BUSINESS,Crain Communications, Inc., 1400 Woodbridge, Detroit MI 48207. (313)446-0419. Editor: Peter Brown. Managing Editor: Matt Gryczan. 20% freelance written. Weekly tabloid covering Detroit area businesses. *"Crain's Detroit Business* reports the activities of local businesses. Our readers are mostly executives; many of them own their own companies. They read us to keep track of companies not often reported about in the daily press—privately held companies and small public companies. Our slant is hard news and news features. We do not report on the auto companies, but other businesses in Wayne, Oakland, Macomb, and Washtenaw counties are part of our turf." Circ. 33,500. Pays on publication. Byline given. Offers negotiable kill fee. Buys first rights and "the right to make the story available to the other 25 Crain publications, and the right to circulate the story through the Crain News Service, which to date has 22 subscribers." Photocopied submissions OK. Query for electronic submissions. Computer printout submissions OK; prefers letter-quality to dot-matrix. Sample copy 50¢; free writer's guidelines.

Nonfiction: Cindy Goodaker, articles editor. Book excerpts and interview/profile. No "how-tos, new product articles, or fiction." Buys 200 mss/year. Query. Length: 800 words average. Pays $6/inch and expenses for assigned articles. Pays $6/inch without expenses for unsolicited articles. Pays expenses of writers on assignment.

Photos: State availability of photos with submission. Offers no additional payment for photos accepted with ms. Identification of subjects required. "Buys the right to re-use photo at will."

Tips: "What we are most interested in are specific news stories about local businesses. The fact that Widget Inc. is a great company is of no interest to us. However, if Widget Inc. introduced a new product six months ago and sales have gone up from $20 million to $30 million, then that's a story. The same is true if sales went down from $20 million to $10 million. I would strongly encourage interested writers to contact me directly. Although we don't have a blanket rule against unsolicited manuscripts, they are rarely usable. We are a general circulation publication, but we are narrowly focused. A writer not familiar with us would have trouble focusing the story properly. In addition, writers may not have a business relationship with the company they are writing about."

‡DALLAS MAGAZINE, The Dallas Chamber, 1507 Pacific Ave., Dallas TX 75201. (214)954-1390. Editor: D. Ann Shiffler. Managing Editor: Jeff Hampton. 50% freelance written. A monthly consumer business journal. Circ. 30,000. Pays on publication. Publishes ms an average of 2 months after acceptance. Byline given. Buys first North American serial rights and first rights. Submit seasonal/holiday material 3 months in advance. Simultaneous submissions OK. Query for electronic submissions. Computer printout submissions OK; prefers letter-quality to dot-matrix. Reports in 2 months. Free sample copy and writer's guidelines.

Nonfiction: General interest, how-to, interview/profile, new product. Buys 24 mss/year. Query with published clips. Length: 1,000-2,500 words. Pays $100-600. Sometimes pays expenses of writers on assignment.

Photos: State availability of photos with submission. Identification of subjects required. Buys one-time rights.

Columns/Departments: Issues (business trends); Portrait (interesting business personality); Enterprise (upstart company). Length: 1,000-1,500 words. Query with published clips. Pays $100.

Fillers: Anecdotes, facts, newsbreaks and short humor. Buys 2/year. Length: 50 words maximum. Pays $20-50.

Tips: "Send queries. Do not send articles for the magazine. First, contact the magazine for editorial calendar."

INDIANA BUSINESS, 1000 Waterway Blvd., Indianapolis IN 46202. (317)633-2026. Managing Editor: Brian Burton. 50% freelance written. Statewide publication focusing on business in Indiana. "We are a general business publication that reaches 30,000 top executives in Indiana, covering all business categories." Circ. 30,000. Pays 30-60 days after acceptance. Publishes ms an average of 2 months after acceptance. Rights negotiable. Submit seasonal/holiday material 4 months in advance. Photocopied submissions OK. Computer printout double-spaced submissions acceptable. Byline given. Reports in 1 month. Sample copy $1.75.

Nonfiction: Expose; interview/profile; and opinion (does not mean letters to the editor). No first person experience stories. "All articles must relate to Indiana business and must be of interest to a broad range of business and professional people." Especially interested in articles on agribusiness, international affairs as they affect Indiana business, executive health issues, new science and technology projects happening in Indiana. "We would like to hear about business success stories but only as they pertain to current issues, trends (i.e., a real estate company that has made it big because they got in on the Economic Development Bonds and invested in renovation property)." Buys 40-50 mss/year. Query. Length: 500-2,500 words. Pay negotiable. Pays expenses of writers on assignment.

Photos: State availability of photos. Reviews contact sheets, negatives, transparencies and 5x7 prints. Pay negotiable for b&w or color photos. Captions, model releases and subject identification required.

Columns/Departments: "Writers need to check with us. We may publish a column once a year or six times a year, and we will consider any business-related subject." Buys 30 mss/year. Query. Length: 1,000-1,500 words. Pays $50-200.

Fillers: Anecdotes and newsbreaks. Length: 125-250 words. Pays $50 maximum.

Tips: "Give us a concise query telling us not only why we should run the article but why you should write it. Be sure to indicate available photography or subjects for photography or art. We look first for good ideas. Our readers are sophisticated businessmen who are interested in their peers as well as how they can run their businesses better. We will look at non-business issues if they can be related to business in some way."

‡**LA CROSSE CITYBUSINESS, The Independent Business Newspaper for the La Crosse/Winona Area**, MCP Inc., Suite 217, 505 King St,. LaCrosse WI 54601. (608)782-2130. Editor: Vickie Lojek. *CityBusiness* is a tabloid-sized publication about and for business and community leaders in the tri-state area of Wisconsin-Minnesota-Iowa. "We write for small business owners as well as those in middle and upper management." Circ. 8,000. Pays 30 days after publication. Publishes ms an average of 2-3 months after acceptance. Byline given. Buys first North American serial rights. Simultaneous and photocopied submissions OK. Legible computer printouts acceptable. Sample copy available upon request.
Nonfiction: Financial, governmental, other items of general business interest. Buys approximately 75 mss/year. Query. Length: 750-1,500 words. Pays $35-50. Occasionally pays expenses of writers on assignment.

MEMPHIS BUSINESS JOURNAL, Mid-South Communications, Inc., Suite 102, 88 Union, Memphis TN 38103. (901)523-0437. Editor: Barney DuBois. 10% freelance written. Works with a small number of new/unpublished writers each year. Weekly tabloid covering industry, trade, agribusiness and finance in west Tennessee, north Mississippi, east Arkansas, and the Missouri Bootheel. "Articles should be timely and relevant to business in our region." Pays on acceptance. Publishes ms an average of 2 weeks after acceptance. Byline given. Pays $50 kill fee. Buys one-time rights, and makes work-for-hire assignments. Submit seasonal/holiday material 2 months in advance. Simultaneous queries and submissions OK. Computer printout submissions acceptable; prefers letter-quality to dot-matrix. Reports in 2 weeks. Free sample copy.
Nonfiction: Exposé, historical/nostalgic, interview/profile, business features and trends. "All must relate to business in our area." Buys 130 mss/year. Query with or without clips of published work, or send complete ms. Length: 750-2,000 words. Pays $80-200. Sometimes pays the expenses of writers on assignment.
Photos: State availability of photos or send photos with ms. Pays $25-50 for 5x7 b&w prints. Identification of subjects required. Buys one-time rights.
Tips: "We are interested in news—and this means we can accept short, hard-hitting work more quickly. We also welcome freelancers who can do features and articles on business in the smaller cities of our region. We are a weekly, so our stories need to be timely."

NEVADA BUSINESS JOURNAL, Nevada's Only State-wide Business Magazine, H&M Publications, Suite 270, 2375 E. Tropicana, Las Vegas NV 89109. (702)454-1669. Editor: Henry C. Holcomb. Managing Editor: Jeffrey Hunter. 90% freelance written. A monthly magazine covering business in Nevada. Estab. 1986. Circ. 15,000. Pays on acceptance. Publishes ms an average of 2 months after acceptance. Byline given. Offers $75 kill fee. Buys all rights. Submit seasonal/holiday material 3 months in advance. Photocopied submissions OK. Computer printout submissions acceptable; prefers letter-quality to dot-matrix. Reports in 1 week. Free sample copy and writer's guidelines.
Nonfiction: Essays; general interest (business); how-to (execute specific business activities); interview/profile; photo feature; and technical. No exposé, humor, religious or travel. Buys 108 mss/year. Query with or without published clips. Length: 2,000-3,000 words. Pays $150-300. Sometimes pays expenses of writers on assignment; always pays telephone expenses.
Photos: Send photos with submission. Reviews 35mm or 2¼x2¼ transparencies and 5x7 or 8x10 prints. Offers no additional payment for photos accepted with ms. Captions and identification of subjects required. Rights purchased depend on assignment.
Tips: Company, executive and industry profiles are most open to freelancers.

NEW BUSINESS MAGAZINE, Clubhouse Publishing, Box 3312, Sarasota FL 33581. (813)366-8225. Editor: Dan Denton. Managing Editor: Pam Daniel. A bimonthly business publication for business people in Sarasota and Manatee counties. "*New Business* provides a review and digest of local business events; profiles, commentary, perspective, and reporting on people, trends, and issues in area business. Reporting of local business from an intelligent, questioning perspective is the key to our stories; we're not interested in puff pieces or in very general how-to." Circ. 10,000. Pays on publication. Byline given. Offers variable kill fee. Buys first North American serial rights or second serial (reprint) rights. Previously published submissions sometimes OK. Computer printout submissions acceptable; prefers letter-quality to dot-matrix. Reports in 1 month on queries; 6 weeks on manuscripts. Sample copy $3.
Nonfiction: Humor (short essays with a business slant); interview/profile; new product (if local); and opinion. "No general business articles about national trends—we're very local." Buys 25 mss/year. Query with or without published clips. Length 350-3,000 words. Pays $50-400 for assigned articles; pays $50-150 for unsolicited articles. Sometimes pays the expenses of writers on assignment.
Photos: State availability of photos with submission. Offers $25 minimum/photo. Buys one-time rights.

Columns/Departments: Backtalk (humor about business trends and attitudes), 500-800 words; and Comment (essays with a strong point of view about local business events or trends), 800-1,300 words. Buys 6 mss/year. Query with or without published clips, or send complete ms. Pays $50-100.

NEW JERSEY BUSINESS, 310 Passaic Ave., Fairfield NJ 07006. (201)882-5004. Executive Editor: James Prior. Emphasizes business in the state of New Jersey. Monthly magazine. Pays on acceptance. Buys all rights. Simultaneous and previously published work OK. Reports in 3 weeks. Sample copy $1.
Nonfiction: "All freelance articles are upon assignment, and they deal with business and industry either directly or more infrequently, indirectly pertaining to New Jersey." Buys "a few" mss/year. Query or send clips of published work. Pays $150-200.
Photos: Send photos with ms. Captions preferred.

OHIO BUSINESS, Business Journal Publishing Co., 3rd floor, 1720 Euclid Ave., Cleveland OH 44115. (216)621-1644. Editor: Robert W. Gardner. Managing Editor: Michael E. Moore. 10% freelance written. Prefers to work with published/established writers. A monthly magazine covering general business topics. "*Ohio Business* serves the state of Ohio. Readers are business executives in the state engaged in manufacturing, agriculture, mining, construction, transportation, communications, utilities, retail and wholesale trade, services, and government." Circ. 35,000. Pays for features on acceptance; news on publication. Publishes ms an average of 4 months after acceptance. Byline sometimes given. Kill fee can be negotiated. Buys first serial rights; depends on projects. Submit seasonal/holiday material 3-4 months in advance. Simultaneous queries, and simultaneous, photocopied, and previously published submissions OK. Computer printout submissions acceptable; prefers letter-quality to dot-matrix. Reports in 2 weeks on queries; 1 month on mss. Sample copy $2; writer's guidelines for SAE and 1 first class stamp.
Nonfiction: Book excerpts, general interest, how-to, interview/profile, opinion and personal experience. "In all cases, write with an Ohio executive in mind. Stories should give readers useful information on business within the state, trends in management, ways to manage better, or other developments which would affect them in their professional careers." Buys 14-20 mss/year. Query with published clips. Length: 100-2,500 words. Pays $25 minimum. Sometimes pays expenses of writers on assignment.
Photos: State availability of photos. Reviews b&w and color transparencies and prints. Captions and identification of subjects required. Buys variable rights.
Columns/Departments: News; People (features Ohio business execs); High-Tech (leading edge Ohio products and companies); Made in Ohio (unusual Ohio product/services). Query with published clips. Length: 100-600 words. Pays $50 minimum.
Tips: "Features are most open to freelancers. Come up with new ideas or information for our readers: Ohio executives in manufacturing and service industries. Writers should be aware of the trend toward specialization in magazine publishing with strong emphasis on people in coverage."

ORANGE COUNTY BUSINESS JOURNAL, Scott Publishing, 1112 E. Chestnut, Santa Ana CA 92701. (714)835-9692. Editor: Vickora Clepper. 10% freelance written. Works with a small number of new/unpublished writers each year. A biweekly tabloid covering Orange County, California business. "We address top-level business executives." Circ. 20,000. Pays on publication. Publishes ms an average of 2 months after acceptance. Byline given. Buys first rights. Computer printout submissions acceptable; prefers letter-quality to dot-matrix. Reports in 3 weeks on queries. Free sample copy.
Nonfiction: How-to (business), interview/profile, and opinion. All submissions must be business-oriented. Buys 24 mss/year. Query. Length: 750-1,500 words. Pays $50-150. Sometimes pays the expenses of writers on assignment.
Photos: State availability of photos with submission. Reviews contact sheets. Offers $5/photo. Captions and identification of subjects required. Buys one-time rights.
Columns/Departments: Commentary (general interest business events), 750-1,000 words. Buys 8 mss/year. Query. Pays $50.

OREGON BUSINESS, MIF Publications, Suite 500, 208 SW Stark, Portland OR 97204. (503)223-0304. Editor: Robert Hill. 60% freelance written. Works with a small number of new/unpublished writers each year. Monthly magazine covering business in Oregon. Circ. 20,000. Pays on publication. Publishes ms an average of 4 months after acceptance. Byline given. Buys first rights. Submit seasonal/holiday material 3 months in advance. Photocopied and previously published submissions OK. Electronic submissions OK; query for details. Computer printout submissions acceptable; prefers letter-quality to dot-matrix. Reports in 1 month. Sample copy for 9x12 SAE and $1.05 postage.
Nonfiction: General interest (real estate, business, investing, small business); interview/profile (business leaders); and new products. Special issues include tourism, world trade, finance. "We need articles on real estate or small business in Oregon, outside the Portland area." Buys 24 mss/year. Query with published clips. Length: 900-2,000 words. Pays 10¢/word minimum; $200 maximum. Sometimes pays expenses of writers on assignment.

‡**ORLANDO MAGAZINE,**Box 2207, Orlando FL 32802. (305)644-3355. 2% freelance written. Monthly magazine covering city growth, development, trends, entertainment. "We use first-person experiential pieces on subjects of interest to people in central Florida. Our business, personality and trends stories are staff written." Circ. 28,000. Pays on acceptance. Publishes ms an average of 6-9 months after acceptance. Byline given. Offers 100% kill fee. Makes work-for-hire assignments. Submit seasonal/holiday material 6 months in advance. Simultaneous and photocopied submissions OK. Computer printout submissions OK. Reports in 3 weeks. Sample copy $3; free writer's guidelines.
Nonfiction: General interest, historical/nostalgic, photo feature, travel, and trends in central Florida. Buys 25 mss/year. Send complete ms. Length: 750-2,000 words. Pays $75-150 for assigned articles; $75-100 for unsolicited articles.
Photos: Send photos with submission. Reviews prints. Offers $5 per photo. Captions and identification of subjects required. Buys one-time rights.

PROFIT, Making it in Broward, Ft. Lauderdale/Broward County Chamber of Commerce, 208 SE 3rd Ave., Ft. Lauderdale FL 33301. (305)463-4500. Editor: Mary C. Brooks. 60% freelance written. A bimonthly magazine covering business subjects for Broward County, Florida. Circ. 15,000. Pays on publication. Publishes ms an average of 4 months after acceptance. Byline given. Buys first rights. Free sample copy.
Nonfiction: On local business. Buys 25 mss/year. Query with published clips. Length: 800-1,500 words. Pays $75-500 for assigned articles.
Photos: Send photos with submission. Reviews 35mm transparencies and 8x10 prints. Offers no additional payment for photos accepted with ms. Captions, model releases, and identification of subjects required.

REGARDIES: THE MAGAZINE OF WASHINGTON BUSINESS, 1010 Wisconsin Ave., NW, Washington DC 20007. (202)342-0410. Editor: Brian Kelly. 80% freelance written. Works with a small number of new/unpublished writers each year. Monthly magazine covering business and general features in the Washington DC metropolitan area for Washington business executives. Circ. 60,000. Pays within 30 days after publication. Publishes ms an average of 2 months after acceptance. Byline given. Offers variable kill fee. Buys first serial rights and second serial (reprint) rights. Computer printout submissions acceptable; prefers letter-quality to dot-matrix. Submit seasonal/holiday material 3 months in advance. Reports in 3 weeks.
Nonfiction: Profiles (of business leaders), investigative reporting, real estate, advertising, politics, lifestyle, media, retailing, communications, labor issues, and financial issues—all on the Washington business scene. "If it isn't the kind of story that could just as easily run in a city magazine or a national magazine like *Harper's*, *Atlantic*, *Esquire*, etc., I don't want to see it." Also buys book mss for excerpt. No how-to. Narrative nonfiction only. Buys 90 mss/year. Length: 4,000 words average. Buys 5-6/issue. Pays negotiable rate. Pays the expenses of writers on assignment.
Columns/Departments: Length: 1,500 words average. Buys 8-12/issue. Pays negotiable rates.
Tips: "The most frequent mistake writers make is not including enough information and data about business which, with public companies, is easy enough to find. This results in flawed analysis and a willingness to accept the 'official line'."

TIDEWATER VIRGINIAN, 711 W. 21st St., Norfolk VA 23517. Editor: Sally Kirby Hartman. 80% freelance written. Prefers to work with published/established writers. Published by two Hampton area chambers of commerce. Monthly magazine for business management people. Circ. 15,000. Buys first serial rights and second serial (reprint) rights to material originally published elsewhere. Byline given. Buys 60 mss/year. Pays on publication. Publishes ms an average of 4 months after acceptance. Photocopied and simultaneous submissions OK. Computer printout submissions acceptable; prefers letter-quality to dot-matrix. Reports in 4 weeks. Sample copy $1.95.
Nonfiction: Articles dealing with business and industry in Virginia, primarily the surrounding area of southeastern Virginia (Hampton Roads area). Profiles, how-to articles, successful business operations, new products, merchandising techniques and business articles. Query or submit complete ms. Length: 500-2,500 words. Pays $25-150.
Tips: "Send writing samples and resume; call for an interview. We continue to stress a local angle on most articles, with the possible exception of how-to articles."

WESTERN INVESTOR, Western States Investment Information, Willamette Publishing, Inc., Suite 1115, 400 SW 6th Ave., Portland OR 97204. (503)222-0577. Editor/Publisher: S.P. Pratt. Managing Editor: Donna Walker. 5% freelance written. Quarterly magazine for the investment community of the 13 western states. For stock brokers, corporate officers, financial analysts, trust officers, CPAs, investors, etc. Circ. 13,000. Pays on publication. Publishes ms an average of 6 months after acceptance. Byline given. Buys one-time and second serial (reprint) rights and makes work-for-hire assignments. Simultaneous queries and simultaneous, photocopied and previously published submissions OK. Computer submissions acceptable; prefers letter-quality to dot-matrix. Sample copy $1.50 with SAE and $1.24 postage.
Nonfiction: General business interest ("trends, people, public, listed in our instrument data section"). "Each

issue carries a particular industry theme." Query. Length: 200-2,000 words. Pays $50 minimum.
Photos: State availability of photos. Pays $10 minimum for 5x7 (or larger) b&w prints. Buys one-time rights.
Tips: "All editorial copy must pertain or directly relate to companies and/or industry groups included in our listed companies. Send us a one-page introduction including your financial writing background, story ideas, availability for assignment work, credits, etc. What we want at this point is a good working file of authors to draw from; let us know your special areas of interest and expertise. Newspaper business-page writers would be good candidates. If you live and work in the West, so much the better."

WESTERN NEW YORK MAGAZINE, Greater Buffalo Chamber of Commerce, 107 Delaware Ave., Buffalo NY 14202. (716)852-7100. Editor: J. Patrick Donlon. 10% freelance written. Monthly magazine of the Buffalo-Niagara Falls area. "Tells the story of Buffalo and Western New York, with special emphasis on business and industry and secondary emphasis on quality of life subjects." Circ. 8,000. Pays on acceptance. Publishes ms an average of 3 months after acceptance. Byline given. Offers $150 kill fee. Not copyrighted. Buys all rights. Submit seasonal/holiday material 3 months in advance. Simultaneous queries OK. Computer printout submissions acceptable; no dot-matrix. Reports in 1 month. Sample copy for $2, 9x12 SAE and 3 first class stamps; writer's guidelines for business size SAE and 1 first class stamp.
Nonfiction: General interest (business, finance, commerce); historical/nostalgic (Buffalo, Niagara Falls); how-to (business management); interview/profile (community leader); and Western New York industry, quality of life. "Broad-based items preferred over single firm or organization. Submit articles that provide insight into business operations, marketing, finance, promotion, and nuts-and-bolts approach to small business management. No nationwide or even New York statewide articles or pieces on specific companies, products, services." Buys 30 mss/year. Query with published clips. Length: 1,000-2,500 words. Pays $150-300. Sometimes pays the expenses of writers on assignment.
Photos: Pamela Mills, art director. State availability of photos. Reviews contact sheet. Pays $10-25 for 5x7 b&w prints.

— Career, College and Alumni

Three types of magazines are listed in this section: university publications written for students, alumni and friends of a specific institution; publications about college life; and publications on career and job opportunities.

ALABAMA ALUMNI MAGAZINE, University of Alabama, Box 1928, Colonial Dr., University AL 35486. (205)348-1548. Editor: James M. Kenny. Managing Editor: Julie L. Griffin. 20% freelance written. Eager to work with new/unpublished writers. A quarterly alumni magazine. "We present a positive but factual look at the University of Alabama and its faculty, staff, students and alumni. Our audience consists of alumni and supporters of the University of Alabama" Circ. 20,000. Pays on acceptance. Publishes ms an average of 3 months after acceptance. Byline given. Not copyrighted. Buys first rights. Submit seasonal/holiday material 4 months in advance. Photocopied submissions OK. Electronic submissions OK via IBM XT; prefers hard copy accompanying electronic submissions. Computer printout submissions OK; prefers letter-quality. Reports in 1 week on queries; 2 weeks on mss. Free writer's guidelines.
Nonfiction: Alumni (general interest), historical/nostalgic about university, and interview/profile. "We want only articles about the university, its alumni and students." Buys 8 mss/year. Query by mail or phone. Length: 400-4,000 words. Pays $20-300. Sometimes pays the expenses of writers on assignment.
Photos: State availability of photos with submission. Reviews prints. Payment offered on photos (depends on situation). Captions, model releases, and identification of subjects required. Buys one-time rights.
Columns/Departments: Who's Who (profiles of Alabama alumni), 600-1,200 words; Games (sports, especially shorties), 100-1,200 words; and Quest (university research), 600-1,200 words. Buys up to 8 mss/year. Query. Pays $5-50.
Tips: "Let us know when you come across a story idea connected with the University of Alabama, which is in Tuscaloosa—*not* Birmingham. We want freelancers to be our extension into the world at large, so we're interested in any workable ideas. Just make sure it has some connection with the right school. A freelancer could break in most easily by writing a suitable department article. We are especially looking for interesting profiles of alumni. It would be very easy to make a quick five or ten bucks by sending in a short notice on some athlete connected with this school (seen Joe Namath out jogging lately?). Similarly, do you know a professor/scientist with a 'Bama connection?"

ALCALDE, Box 7278, Austin TX 78713. (512)471-3799. Editor: Ernestine Wheelock. 20% freelance written. Works with a small number of new/unpublished writers each year. Bimonthly magazine. Circ. 48,000. Pays on publication. Publishes ms an average of 6 months after acceptance. Buys all rights. Submit seasonal/holiday material 5 months in advance. Electronic submissions OK via Xerox 860 disk or Macintosh disk, but requires hard copy also. Computer printout submissions acceptable; prefers letter-quality to dot-matrix. Reports in 1 month.

Nonfiction: General interest; historical (University of Texas, research, and faculty profile); humor (humorous University of Texas incidents or profiles that include background data); interviews (University of Texas subjects); nostalgia (University of Texas traditions); profile (students, faculty or alumni); and technical (University of Texas research on a subject or product). No subjects lacking taste or quality, or not connected with the University of Texas. Buys 12 mss/year. Query. Length: 1,000-2,400 words. Pays according to importance of article.

‡THE ATO PALM, Alpha Tau Omega Fraternity, 4001 W. Kirby Ave., Champaign IL 61821. (217)351-1865. Editor: Robert Vogele. Associate Editor: Steve A. Glaser. 20% freelance written. Works with small number of new/unpublished writers each year. A quarterly tabloid focusing on leadership and fraternity news. Circ. 100,000. Pays on acceptance. Publishes ms an average of 6 months after acceptance. Byline given. Buys first North American serial rights and/or second serial (reprint) rights. Simultaneous, photocopied and previously published submissions OK. Query for electronic submissions. Computer printout submissions OK; prefers letter-quality to dot-matrix. "This is our first venture into soliciting freelance material. All queries will be responded to as soon as possible but actual response time will depend upon number received. Right now *The Palm* is in a state of experimentation and may change."

Nonfiction: Historical, humor, interview/profile and articles dealing with some aspect of leadership. Can be profiles of leaders (preferably ATO members) showing their leadership, research on leadership, etc. Leadership is *not* the same as management. "Leadership deals with a person's ability to inspire, motivate and communicate goals and ideals." Plans to buy 8-12 mss/year. Query. Length: 750-1,200 words. Pays $25-50 for assigned articles. Sometimes pays the expenses of writers on assignment.

Photos: State availability of photos with query. Send photos with submission. Reviews contact sheets. Offers $5-15 per photo. Model releases and identification of subjects required. Buys one-time or all rights.

Tips: "We are looking for articles which give insight into some aspect of leadership. We love pieces that are novel or unusual."

THE BLACK COLLEGIAN, The National Magazine of Black College Students, Black Collegiate Services, Inc., 1240 S. Broad St., New Orleans LA 70125. (504)821-5694. Editor: K. Kazi-Ferrouillet. 40% freelance written. Magazine for black college students and recent graduates with an interest in black cultural awareness, sports, news, personalities, history, trends, current events and job opportunities. Published bimonthly during school year; (4 times/year). 160 pages. Circ. 121,000. Buys one-time rights. Byline given. Pays on publication. Photocopied submissions OK. Computer printout submissions acceptable. Submit seasonal and special material 2 months in advance of issue date (Careers, September; Computers/Grad School and Travel/Summer Programs, November; Engineering and Black History Programs, January; Finance and Jobs, March). Reports in 3 weeks on queries; 1 month on mss. Writer's guidelines for #10 SAE and 1 first class stamp.

Nonfiction: Material on careers, sports, black history, news analysis. Articles on problems and opportunities confronting black college students and recent graduates. Book excerpts, exposé, general interest, historical/nostalgic, how-to (develop employability), opinion, personal experience, profile, inspirational, humor. Buys 40 mss/year (6 unsolicited). Query with published clips or send complete ms. Length: 500-2,500 words. Pays $25-350.

Photos: State availability of photos with query or ms, or send photos with query or ms. B&w photos or color transparencies purchased with or without mss. 8x10 b&w prints preferred. Captions, model releases and identification of subjects required. Pays $35/b&w; $50/color.

Tips: "Career features area is most open to freelancers."

CAMPUS VOICE, The National College Magazine, 13-30 Corporation, 505 Market St., Knoxville TN 37902. (615)521-0646. Senior Editor: Elise Nakhnikian. Managing Editor: Barbara Penland. 80% freelance written. Works with small number of new/unpublished student writers each year. Quarterly magazine. "The purpose of *Campus Voice* is to define and reflect the college experience of the '80s, and to take a lively, irreverent and informed look at the issues that interest students." Circ. 1.2 million. Pays on acceptance. Publishes ms an average of 3 months after acceptance. Byline given. Offers 25% kill fee. Buys first North American serial rights. Submit seasonal/holiday material 6 months in advance. Computer printout submissions acceptable; no dot-matrix. Reports in 6 weeks. Sample copy $2, 10x12 SAE and 6 first class stamps. Writer's guidelines for business size SAE, and 1 first class stamp.

Nonfiction: Book excerpts, exposé, general interest, how-to (careers/academics with news angles), humor, interview/profile, personal experience, photo feature, cartoons, short reviews, sports and finance. No inspirational, obvious college-oriented ideas. Buys 100 mss/year. Query with published clips. Length: 750-4,000 words. Pays $500-3,000. Pays expenses of writers on assignment.

Fiction: Fiction by college students.

Tips: "Don't think of our readers as students—they're 18- to 24-year-olds with sophisticated tastes. If you pitch a college-based idea, make it original. Area most open to freelancers is Campus Beat. Be relevant, offbeat, original. Look for news/entertainment ideas with a twist."

CARNEGIE-MELLON MAGAZINE, Carnegie Mellon University, Pittsburgh PA 15213. (412)578-2900. Editor: Ann Curran. Alumni publication issued fall, winter, spring, summer covering university activities, alumni profiles, etc. Circ. 46,000. Pays on acceptance. Byline given. Not copyrighted. Reports in 1 month.

Nonfiction: Book reviews (faculty alumni); general interest; humor; interview/profile; photo feature. "We use general interest stories linked to CMU activities and research." No unsolicited mss. Buys 5 features and 5-10 alumni profiles/year. Query with published clips. Length: 2,500-6,000 words. Pays $250 or negotiable rate.

Poetry: Avant-garde or traditional. No previously published poetry. No payment.

Tips: "Consideration is given to professional writers among alumni."

CIRCLE K MAGAZINE, 3636 Woodview Trace, Indianapolis IN 46268. Executive Editor: Karen J. Pyle. 60% freelance written. "Our leadership consists almost entirely of above-average college students interested in voluntary community service and leadership development. They are politically and socially aware and have a wide range of interests." Published 5 times/year. Magazine; 16 pages. Circ. 10,000. Pays on acceptance. Normally buys first North American serial rights. Byline given. Submit seasonal/holiday material 6 months in advance. Computer printout submissions acceptable; no dot-matrix. Reports in 1 month. Sample copy and writer's guidelines for large SASE.

Nonfiction: Articles published in *Circle K* are of two types—serious and light nonfiction. "We are interested in general-interest articles on topics concerning college students and their lifestyles, as well as articles dealing with community concerns and leadership development." No "first-person confessions, family histories, or travel pieces." Recent article example: "Combating Campus Crime" (January/February 1987). Queries are preferred. Length: 2,000-2,500 words. Pays $175-250.

Photos: Purchased with accompanying ms. Captions required. Query. Total purchase price for ms includes payment for photos.

Tips: "Query should indicate author's familiarity with the field and sources. Subject treatment must be objective and in-depth, and articles should include illustrative examples and quotes from persons involved in the subject or qualified to speak on it. Queries also should reflect a familiarity with our magazine and its style."

‡COLLEGE ENTERTAINMENT GUIDE, Alan Weston Communications, Suite 600, 303 N. Glenoaks Blvd., Burbank CA 91502. (818)848-4666. Editor: Charlotte Wolter. 100% freelance written. Prefers to work with published/established writers; works with small number of new/unpublished writers each year. A quarterly magazine covering entertainment for the college audience "primarily ages 18-26. They want lively reports on current trends and personalities in popular entertainment." Circ. 1.2 million. Pays ½ on acceptance and ½ on publication. Publishes ms an average of 3 months after acceptance. Byline given. Offers 50% kill fee. Buys first North American serial rights. Submit seasonal/holiday material 3 months in advance. Simultaneous, photocopied and previously published submissions OK. Query for electronic submission requirements. Computer printout submissions OK. Reports in 2 months on queries. Sample copy for 9x12 SAE with 50¢ postage. Free writer's guidelines.

Nonfiction: General interest, humor and interview/profile. No fiction or how-tos. Buys 15 mss/year. Query. Length: 600-2,500 words. Pays $100-500 for assigned articles. Sometimes pays expenses of writers on assignment.

Photos: State availability of photos with submission. Offers $25-100 per photo. Identification of subjects required. Buys one-time rights.

Columns/Departments: Books (new books of interest to college students); Short Subjects (news and issues in entertainment on campus—not local productions but rather film contests, campus radio and TV, etc. Buys 10 mss/year. Query. Length: 50-250 words. Pays $25-100.

Tips: "The writer needs to have experience writing about entertainment, access to entertainment figures, interesting writing style and point of view on the entertainment subjects they cover. Living in New York or Los Angeles helps, but is not necessary. We're looking for very individual, lively writing styles. The best areas for freelancers are special topics in music, film or humor—such as a unique personality that the writer has access to, or a topic or issue relevant to college, such as the growth of college radio, an article we recently published."

‡COLLEGE OUTLOOK AND CAREER OPPORTUNITIES, Special editions include Business, Education, Academic Honors, Computer/High Tech, Christian, Minority, and Junior College Transfer, Townsend Outlook Publishing Co., Box 239, Liberty MO 64068. (816)781-4941. Editor: Linn Brown. 20% freelance written. Student information publications on subjects of interest to college or college-bound students. "*College*

Outlook attempts to inform students on college admissions, financial aid, career opportunities, academic subjects, study techniques and other topics of interest to college-bound students." Circ. 2.5 million regular, plus special editions. Publishes ms an average of 3 months after acceptance. Byline given. Buys all rights and second (reprint) rights. Computer printout submissions acceptable; prefers letter-quality to dot-matrix. Reports as soon as possible. Sample copy for SAE and 90¢ postage; writer's guidelines for business size SAE and 1 first class stamp.

Photos: State availability of photos. "We prefer to see photos with focus on students." Model release required. Buys all rights.

Fillers: Newsbriefs. Buys up to 4 mss/year. Length: 100-500 words. Pay is negotiable.

‡COLLEGE WOMAN, Alan Weston Communications, Suite 600, 303 N. Glenoaks Blvd., Burbank CA 91502. (818)848-4666. Editor: Charlotte Wolter. 95% freelance written. Prefers to work with published/established writers; works with small number of new/unpublished writers each year. "A quarterly service magazine for college women ages 18-26 featuring lively, pointed articles on current issues, personalities, careers, academics, health, humor, beauty and fashion." Circ. 500,000. Pays ½ on acceptance and ½ on publication. Publishes ms an average of 3 months after acceptance. Byline given. Offers 50% kill fee. Buys first North American serial rights. Submit seasonal/holiday material 3 months in advance. Simultaneous, photocopied and previously published submissions OK. Query for electronic submissions. Computer printout submissions OK. Reports in 2 months on queries. Sample copy and writer's guidelines for 9x12 SAE and $1 postage.

Nonfiction: General interest, humor, interview/profile, opinion and personal experience. Buys 40 mss/year. Query with published clips. Length: 600-2,500 words. Pays $100-500 for assigned articles. Sometimes pays expenses of writers on assignment.

Photos: State availability of photos with submission. Offers $25-100. Identification of subjects required. Buys one-time rights.

Columns/Departments: Health (fitness, new medical info, sex) 600-800 words; Humor (on-campus humor) 600-800 words; Careers (info or opinion for those new to job market) 150-1,200 words; Up Front (news and issues, on and off campus) 50-150 words. Buys 20 mss/year. Query. Pays $100-250.

Tips: "My audience is bright and sophisticated, but inexperienced. They want articles which will help them make it on campus and in the world. The use of humor is important with this audience. I like a one-page, brief article idea, with a quick outline of topics to be covered. Articles on current issues, serious personalities, campus issues, and careers are very open to freelancers, if they can tailor their material very specifically to the college market and if they have some experience with their chosen topic area."

COLLEGIATE CAREER WOMAN, For Career-Minded Women, Equal Opportunity Publications, Inc., 44 Broadway, Greenlawn NY 11740. (516)261-8917. Editor: Anne Kelly. 80% freelance written. Works with small number of new/unpublished writers each year. Magazine published 3 times/year (fall, winter, spring) covering career-guidance for college women. Strives "to aid women in developing career abilities to the fullest potential; improve job hunting skills; present career opportunities; provide personal resources; help cope with discrimination." Audience is 92% college juniors and seniors; 8% working graduates. Circ. 10,500. Controlled circulation, distributed through college guidance and placement offices. Pays on publication. Publishes ms an average of 3-12 months after acceptance. Byline given. Buys first North American serial rights. Simultaneous queries and submissions OK. Computer printout submissions acceptable; prefers letter-quality. Free sample copy and writer's guidelines.

Nonfiction: "We want career-related articles describing for a college-educated woman the how-tos of obtaining a professional position and advancing her career." Looks for practical features detailing self-evaluation techniques, the job-search process, and advice for succeeding on the job. Emphasizes role-model profiles of successful career women. Needs manuscripts presenting information on professions offering opportunities to young women—especially the growth professions of the future. Special issues emphasize career opportunities for women in fields such as health care, communications, sales, marketing, banking, insurance, finance, science, engineering, and computers, as well as opportunities in government, military and defense. Query first.

Photos: Send with mss. Prefers 35mm color slides, but will accept b&w prints. Captions and identification of subjects required. Buys all rights.

Tips: Articles should focus on career-guidance, role model, and industry prospects for women and should have a "snappy, down-to-earth writing style."

THE COMPUTER & ELECTRONICS GRADUATE, The Entry-Level Career & Information Technology Magazine for CS, Systems, and EE Graduates, Equal Opportunity Publications, Inc., 44 Broadway, Greenlawn NY 11740. (516)261-8917. Editor: James Schneider. A career-guidance magazine published three times a year for computer science/systems and electrical/electronics engineering students and professionals. "We strive to aid our readers in developing career abilities to the fullest potential; improve job-hunting skills; present career opportunities; provide personal resources." Circ. 18,000 (controlled circulation, distributed through college guidance and placement offices). Pays on publication. Byline given. Buys first North

American serial rights. Deadline: fall, June 1; winter, Aug. 1; spring, Oct. 15. Simultaneous queries and simultaneous, photocopied, and previously published submissions OK. Computer printout submissions acceptable; no dot-matrix. Reports in 1 month. Sample copy and writer's guidelines for 8½x11 SAE and 60¢ postage.

Nonfiction: Book excerpts (on job search techniques, role models, success stories, employment helps); general interest (on special concerns to computer science/systems, and electrical/electronics engineering students and professionals); how-to (on self-evaluation, job-finding skills, adjustment, coping with the real world); humor (student or career related); interview/profile (of successful computer science/systems and electrical/electronics engineering students and professionals); new product (new career opportunities); personal experience (student and career experiences); technical (on career fields offering opportunities); travel on overseas job opportunities; and coverage of other reader interests. Special issues include careers in industry and government in computer science, computer systems, electrical engineering, software systems, robotics, artificial intelligence, as well as opportunities in the military and in defense. No sensitive or highly technical material. Buys 20-25 mss/year. Query. Length: 1,250-3,000 words. Pays 10¢/word.

Photos: Anne Kelly, photo editor. State availability of photos or send photos with query or ms. Prefers 35mm color slides, but will accept b&w. Captions and identification of subjects required.

Tips: "Articles should focus on career-guidance, role model, and industry prospects for computer science, computer systems and electrical and electronics engineering students and professionals."

EQUAL OPPORTUNITY, The Nation's Only Multi-Ethnic Recruitment Magazine for Black, Hispanic, Native American & Asian American College Grads, Equal Opportunity Publications, Inc., 44 Broadway, Greenlawn NY 11740. (516)261-8917. Editor: James Schneider. 50% freelance written. Prefers to work with published/established writers. Magazine published 3 times/year (fall, winter, spring) covering career-guidance for minorities. "Our audience is 90% college juniors and seniors, 10% working graduates. An understanding of educational and career problems of minorities is essential." Circ. 15,000. Controlled circulation, distributed through college guidance and placement offices. Pays on publication. Publishes ms an average of 1 month after acceptance. Byline given. Buys first North American serial rights. Deadline dates: fall, June 15; winter, Aug. 15; spring, Nov. 1. Simultaneous queries, and simultaneous, photocopied and previously published submissions OK. Computer printout submissions acceptable; no dot-matrix. Free sample copy and writer's guidelines for SAE and 4 first class stamps.

Nonfiction: Book excerpts and articles (on job search techniques, role models); general interest (on specific minority concerns); how-to (on job-hunting skills, personal finance, better living, coping with discrimination); humor (student or career related); interview/profile (minority role models); new product (new career opportunities); opinion (problems of minorities); personal experience (professional and student study and career experiences); technical (on career fields offering opportunities for minorities); travel (on overseas job opportunities); and coverage of Black, Hispanic, Native American and Asian American interests. Special issues include career opportunities for minorities in industry and government in fields such as banking, insurance, finance, communications, sales, marketing, engineering and computers, as well as careers in the government, military and defense. Query or send complete ms. Length: 1,250-3,000 words. Sometimes pays the expenses of writers on assignment.

Photos: Prefers 35mm color slides and b&w. Captions and identification of subjects required. Buys first North American serial rights.

Tips: "Articles must be geared toward questions and answers faced by minority and women students."

‡FLORIDA LEADER MAGAZINE, Box 14081, Gainesville FL 32604. (804)373-6907. Editor: W.H. Oxendine, Jr. Managing Editor: Vincent Alex Brown. 100% freelance written. "We are the nation's largest college magazine produced and owned by students—we're feature-oriented and specialize in story interviews with leaders from all walks of life." Published every 2 months; 6 times a year. Circ. 25,000. Publishes ms an average of 5 months after acceptance. Byline given. Buys first rights. Submit seasonal/holiday material 6 months in advance. Simultaneous, photocopied and previously published submissions OK. Query for electronic submissions. Reports in 1 month on queries. Sample copy for SAE with $1.08 postage. Free writer's guidelines.

Nonfiction: How-to, humor, interview/profile and photo feature. Special issues include Homecoming edition (October); Back-to-School (August). No submissions "written by non-students." Buys 40 mss/year. Query. Length: 2,000 words. Payment varies; may pay writers with contributor copies or other premiums rather than cash. Sometimes pays the expenses of writers on assignment.

Photos: State availability of photos with submission. Reviews negatives and transparencies. Offers $2 per photo. Captions, model releases and identification of subjects required. Buys one-time rights.

MISSISSIPPI STATE UNIVERSITY ALUMNUS, Mississippi State University, Alumni Association, Editorial Office, Box 5328, Mississippi State MS 39762. (601)325-3442. Editor: Linsey H. Wright. 10% freelance written ("but welcome more"). Works with small number of new/unpublished writers each year. Emphasizes articles about Mississippi State graduates and former students. For well-educated and affluent audience.

Quarterly magazine; 36 pages. Circ. 15,650. Pays on publication. Publishes ms 3-6 months after acceptance. Buys one-time rights. Pays 25% kill fee. Byline given. Phone queries OK. Submit seasonal/holiday material 3 months in advance. Simultaneous, photocopied and previously published submissions OK. Computer printout submissions acceptable; prefers letter-quality to dot-matrix. Reports in 1 month. Free sample copy.

Nonfiction: Historical, humor (with strong MSU flavor; nothing risque), informational, inspirational, interview (with MSU grads), nostalgia (early days at MSU), personal experience, profile and travel (by MSU grads, but must be of wide interest to other grads). Buys 5-6 mss/year ("but welcome more submissions.") Send complete ms. Length: 500-2,000 words. Pays $50-150 (including photos, if used).

Photos: Offers no additional payment for photos purchased with accompanying ms. Captions required. Uses 5x7 and 8x10 b&w photos and color transparencies of any size.

Columns/Departments: Statements, "a section of the *Alumnus* that features briefs about alumni achievements and professional or business advancement. We do not use engagements, marriages or births. There is no payment for Statements briefs."

Tips: "All stories *must* be about Mississippi State University or its alumni. We welcome articles about MSU grads in interesting occupations and have used stories on off-shore drillers, miners, horse trainers, etc. We also want profiles on prominent MSU alumni and have carried pieces on Senator John C. Stennis, comedian Jerry Clower, professional football players and coaches, and Eugene Butler, former editor-in-chief of *Progressive Farmer* magazine. We feature 2-4 alumni in each issue, alumni who have risen to prominence in their fields or who are engaged in unusual occupations or who are involved in unusual hobbies. We're using more short features (500-700 words) to vary the length of our articles in each issue. We pay $50-75 for these, including 1 b&w photo."

‡MOVING UP, Alan Weston Communications, Suite 600, 303 N. Glenoaks Blvd., Burbank CA 91502. (818)848-4666. Editor: Charlotte Wolter. 100% freelance written. Prefers to work with published/established writers; works with small number of new/unpublished writers each year. A quarterly magazine for college men, ages 21-28. "A magazine to help them make the transition from college to the 'real world.' Topics include careers, relationships, academics, stereo, fitness, fashion, opinion." Estab. 1986. Circ. 500,000. Pays ½ on acceptance; ½ on publication. Publishes ms an average of 3 months after acceptance. Byline given. Offers 50% kill fee. Buys first North American serial rights. Submit seasonal/holiday material 3 months in advance. Simultaneous, photocopied and previously published submissions OK. Query for electronic submissions. Computer printout submissions OK. Reports in 2 months. Sample copy and writer's guidelines for 9x12 SAE and $1 postage.

Nonfiction: General interest, humor, interview/profile, opinion and personal experience. Buys 40 mss/year. Query with published clips. Length: 600-2,500 words. Pays $100-350 for assigned articles. Sometimes pays expenses of writers on assignment.

Photos: State availability of photos with submission. Offers $25-100 per photo. Identification of subjects required. Buys one-time rights.

Columns/Departments: Health (fitness, new medical info, sex); Electronics (latest in stereo, video, etc.); Arts (commentary on issues in music, film, etc.); Money (info on how to manage personal finances); Issues (commentary on politics, personal ethics, other). Buys 20 mss/year. Query with published clips. Length: 600-1,200 words. Pays $100-250.

Tips: "Features are most open to freelancers, especially those with access to a personality or a special topic of interest to college upperclassmen. Humor is also open to freelancers, although it had better be sophisticated for this audience. I like authors who show they know what's going on on campus today and articles which give my readers real information they can use in their daily lives and careers."

NATIONAL FORUM: THE PHI KAPPA PHI JOURNAL, The Honor Society of Phi Kappa Phi, 216 Petrie Hall, Auburn University AL 36849. Editor: Stephen W. White. Managing Editor: Betty Barrett. 20% freelance written. Prefers to work with published/established writers. Quarterly interdisciplinary, scholarly journal. "We are an interdisciplinary journal that publishes crisp, nontechnical analyses of issues of social and scientific concern as well as scholarly treatments of different aspects of culture." Circ. 112,000. Pays on publication. Publishes ms an average of 6 months after acceptance. Byline given. Buys exclusive rights with exceptions. Submit seasonal/holiday material 6 months in advance. Electronic submissions acceptable; can accept 5¼" diskettes compatible with Lanier No-Problem Shared System. Telecommunications capabilities if author has compatible equipment/software. Computer printout submissions acceptable; no dot-matrix. Reports in 6 weeks on queries; 2 months on mss. Sample copy $1.65; free writer's guidelines.

Nonfiction: General interest, interview/profile and opinion. No how-to or biographical articles. Each issue is devoted to the exploration of a particular theme. Upcoming theme issues: "The Human Brain," "Curricular Reform," "News and the Media." Query with clips of published work. Buys 5 unsolicited mss/year. Length: 1,500-2,000 words. Pays $50-200.

Photos: State availability of photos. Identification of subjects required. Buys one-time rights.

Columns/Departments: Educational Dilemmas of the 80s and Book Review Section. Buys 8 mss/year for Educational Dilemmas, 40 book reviews. Length: Book reviews—400-800 words. Educational

Dilemmas—1,500-1,800 words. Pays $15-25 for book reviews; $50/printed page, Educational Dilemmas.
Fiction: Humorous and short stories. No obscenity or excessive profanity. Buys 2-4 mss/year. Length: 1,500-1,800 words. Pays $50/printed page.
Poetry: Free verse, haiku, light verse, traditional. No love poetry. Buys 20 mss/year. Submit 5 poems maximum. Prefers shorter poems.

‡**THE NEW HAMPSHIRE ALUMNUS**, University of New Hampshire Alumni Association, Elliott Alumni Center, Durham NH 03824. (603)862-2040. Editor: Patricia M. Kelly. Assistant Editor: Virginia Walter. 25% freelance written. *"The Alumnus* provides the alumni audience (65,000) of the University of New Hampshire with features, news, and notes on alumni achievements nationwide and on university people and programs three times/year." Circ. 59,000. Pays on acceptance. Publishes ms an average of 6 months after acceptance. Byline given. Kill fee to be negotiated. Not copyrighted. Makes work-for-hire assignments. Submit seasonal/holiday material 4 months in advance. Simultaneous and previously published submissions OK. Query for electronic submissions. Computer printout submissions OK; prefers letter-quality. Free sample copy and writer's guidelines.
Nonfiction: General interest, how-to, humor, interview/profile, photo feature. Buys variable mss/year. Query with published clips. Length: 350-1,500 words. Pays $75-200 for assigned articles; pays $50-150 for unsolicited articles. Sometimes pays the expenses of writers on assignment.
Photos: State availability of photos with submission. Reviews negatives and 5x8 prints. Identification of subjects required. Buys one-time rights.
Columns/Departments: Alumni Profile (UNH alumni achievements). Query with published clips. Length: 350-750 words. Pays $200 maximum.
Fillers: Gags. Payment varies.
Tips: "We give preference to University of New Hampshire (alumni and campus) features, articles, and news briefs. We have just recently started working with freelancers, so payments and guidelines are negotiable. We like writers to submit samples of work first with story ideas and fee requirements."

NOTRE DAME MAGAZINE, University of Notre Dame, Room 415, Administration Bldg., Notre Dame IN 46556. (219)239-5335. Editor: Walton R. Collins. Managing Editor: Kerry Temple. 75% freelance written. Quarterly magazine covering news of Notre Dame and education and issues affecting the Roman Catholic Church. "We are interested in the moral, ethical and spiritual issues of the day and how Christians live in today's world. We are universal in scope and Catholic in viewpoint and serve Notre Dame alumni, friends and other constituencies." Circ. 102,000. Pays on acceptance. Publishes ms an average of 6-12 months after acceptance. Byline given. Kill fee negotiable. Buys first rights. Simultaneous queries OK. Electronic submissions OK with IBM, Phillips on Apple Micro compatibility, but requires hard copy also. Computer printout submissions acceptable; prefers letter-quality to dot-matrix. Reports in 1 month. Free sample copy.
Nonfiction: Opinion, personal experience, religion. "All articles must be of interest to Christian/Catholic readers who are well educated and active in their communities." Buys 35 mss/year. Query with clips of published work. Length: 600-2,000 words. Pays $500-1,500. Sometimes pays the expenses of writers on assignment.
Photos: State availability of photos. Reviews b&w contact sheets, color transparencies, and 8x10 prints. Model releases and identification of subjects required. Buys one-time rights.

‡**PANACHE, The College Magazine That Sizzles**, Win Records and Video, 45-50 38th St., Long Island City NY 11101. (718)937-8813. Editor: Michael Weiss. Managing Editors: Catie Lott and Robin Clark. A quarterly magazine focusing on college students and events. Circ. 556,000. Pays on publication. Byline given. Buys first rights. Submit seasonal/holiday material 3 months in advance. Simultaneous and photocopied submissions OK. Computer printout submissions OK; no dot-matrix. Sample copy $1.95. Free writer's guidelines.
Nonfiction: Essays, humor, interview/profile, personal experience and personality profiles of outstanding college students. Buys 3 mss/year. Query. Length: 500-2,500 words. Pays $60-150 for assigned articles; pays $30-100 for unsolicited articles. Sometimes pays the expenses of writers on assignment.
Photos: State availability of photos with submission. Reviews contact sheets, negatives, 1x1³⁄₈ transparencies and 3x5 prints. Captions, model releases and identification of subjects required. Buys one-time rights.
Columns/Departments: Living in the Real World (articles about people who have just graduated from college); On Location (exciting events—parties, concerts, athletic events that take place on college campus). Buys 5 mss/year. Query with published clips. Length: 500-1,500 words. Pays $30-100.
Fiction: Robin Clark, fiction editor. Confession, erotica, humorous, romance and slice-of-life vignettes. Buys 5 mss/year. Query with published clips. Length: 1,000-2,000 words. Pays $50-100.

PRINCETON ALUMNI WEEKLY, Princeton University Press, 41 William St., Princeton NJ 08540. (609)452-4885. Editor: Charles L. Creesy. Managing Editor: Margaret M. Keenan. 50% freelance written.

Eager to work with new/unpublished writers. Biweekly (during the academic year) magazine covering Princeton University and higher education for Princeton alumni, students, faculty, staff and friends. "We assume familiarity with and interest in the university." Circ. 51,000. Pays on publication. Publishes ms an average of 3 months after acceptance. Byline given. Offers $100 kill fee. Buys first serial rights and one-time rights. Submit seasonal/holiday material 2 months in advance. Simultaneous queries or photocopied submissions OK. Electronic submissions OK but requirements must be clarified with publisher—"too complex to summarize here." Computer printout submissions acceptable; prefers letter-quality to dot-matrix. Sample copy for 9x12 SAE and 71¢ postage.

Nonfiction: Book excerpts, general interest, historical/nostalgic, interview/profile, opinion, personal experience, photo feature. "Connection to Princeton essential. Remember, it's for an upscale educated audience." Special issue on education and economics (February). Buys 20 mss/year. Query with clips of published work. Length: 1,000-6,000 words. Pays $100-600. Pays expenses of writers on assignment.

Photos: State availability of photos. Pays $25-50 for 8x10 b&w prints; $50-100 for color transparencies. Reviews (for ordering purposes) b&w contact sheet. Captions and identification of subjects required.

Columns/Departments: "Columnists must have a Princeton connection (alumnus, student, etc.)." Buys 50 mss/year. Query with clips of published work. Length: 750-1,500 words. Pays $75-150.

‡PRINCETON PARENTS, Princeton University, Nassau St., Stanhope Hall, Princeton NJ 08544. (609)452-5734. 12% freelance written. Works with small number of new/unpublished writers each year. A quarterly newsletter covering topics of concern to parents of Princeton undergraduates and recent graduates with positive information about educational opportunities and developments at Princeton University. Circ. 14,000. Pays on acceptance. Publishes ms an average of 2 months after acceptance. Byline given. Buys one-time rights and makes work-for-hire assignments. Simultaneous, photocopied and previously published submissions OK. Query for electronic submission requirements. Computer printout submissions OK. Reports in 1 week. Sample copy for #10 SAE with 1 first class stamp.

Nonfiction: Essays, interview/profile, opinion and personal experience. Buys 4 mss/year. Query with published clips. Pays $100 maximum for assigned articles. Sometimes pays the expenses of writers on assignment.

Photos: Send photos with submission. Reviews contact sheets. Offers $25 maximum per photo. Captions, model releases and identification of subjects required. Buys one-time rights.

Tips: "Be a Princeton graduate and/or parent, or write about something that will interest Princeton students and their parents. Quote real people about specific current issues."

THE PURDUE ALUMNUS, Purdue Alumni Association, Purdue Memorial Union 160, West Lafayette IN 47907. (317)494-5184. Editor: Gay L. Totten. 30% freelance written. Prefers to work with published/established writers; works with small number of new/unpublished writers each year. Magazine published 9 times/year (except February, June, August) covering subjects of interest to Purdue University alumni. Circ. 72,000. Pays on publication. Publishes ms an average of 2 months after acceptance. Byline given. Buys first rights and makes work-for-hire assignments. Submit seasonal/holiday material 3 months in advance. Simultaneous queries, and simultaneous, photocopied, and previously published submissions OK. Computer printout submissions acceptable; prefers letter-quality to dot-matrix. Reports in 1 week on queries; 2 weeks on mss. Free sample copy.

Nonfiction: Book excerpts, general interest, historical/nostalgic, humor, interview/profile, personal experience. Focus is on campus news, issues, opinions of interest to 72,000 members of the Alumni Association. Feature style, primarily university-oriented. Issues relevant to education. Buys 12-20 mss/year. Length: 1,500-2,500 words. Pays $25-250. Sometimes pays expenses of writers on assignment.

Photos: State availability of photos. Reviews b&w contact sheet or 5x7 prints.

Tips: "We are moving away from the exclusively campus-focused coverage of the past, toward a broader, societal focus. Our stories will be issue-based, endeavoring to fit university values into the problems and issues facing educated individuals. For instance, while we will do a story on the university's research on aging, we would also like a human interest piece on the joys, or travails, of dealing with an aging parent. We will be doing more pairing of stories in this vein, as well as seeking more thoughtful, creative material of relevance to educated readers."

‡RIPON COLLEGE MAGAZINE, Box 248, Ripon WI 54971. (414)748-8115. Editor: Andrew G. Miller. 10% freelance written. "*Ripon College Magazine* is a bimonthly publication that contains information relating to Ripon College. It is mailed to alumni and friends of the college." Circ. 12,500. Pays on publication. Publishes ms an average of 3 months after acceptance. Byline given. Not copyrighted. Makes work-for-hire assignments. Query for electronic submission requirements. Computer printout submissions OK; no dot-matrix. Reports in 2 weeks.

Nonfiction: Historical/nostalgic and interview/profile. Buys 4 mss/year. Query with or without published clips, or send complete ms. Length: 250-1,000 words. Pays $25-500.

Photos: State availability of photos with submission. Reviews contact sheets. Offers no additional payment

for photos accepted with ms. Captions and model releases are required. Buys one-time rights.
Tips: "Story ideas must have a direct connection to Ripon College."

SCORECARD, Falsoft, Inc., 9509 US Highway 42, Box 385, Prospect KY 40059. (502)228-4492. Editor: John Crawley. Assistant Editor: Garry Jones. 50% freelance written. Prefers to work with published/established writers. A weekly sports fan tabloid covering University of Louisville sports only. Circ. 3,000. Pays on publication. Publishes ms an average of 1 month after acceptance. Byline given. Buys first rights. Submit seasonal/holiday material 1 month in advance. Previously published submissions OK "rarely." Computer printout submissions acceptable; prefers letter-quality to dot-matrix. Reports in 2 weeks. Sample copy for $1 and SAE.
Nonfiction: Assigned to contributing editors. Buys 100 mss/year. Query with published clips. Length: 750-1,500 words. Pays $20-50. Sometimes pays expenses of writers on assignment.
Photos: State availability of photos.
Columns/Departments: Notes Page (tidbits relevant to University of Louisville sports program or former players or teams). Buys 25 mss/year. Length: Approximately 100 words. Pay undetermined.
Tips: "Be very familiar with history and tradition of University of Louisville sports program. Contact us with story ideas. Know the subject."

‡SHIPMATE, U.S. Naval Academy Alumni Association Magazine, Alumni House, Annapolis MD 21402. (301)263-4469. Editor: Col. J.W. Hammond, Jr., USMC (retired). 100% freelance written. A magazine published ten times a year by and for alumni of the U.S. Naval Academy. Circ. 31,000. Pays on publication. Byline given. Buys first North American serial rights. Submit seasonal/holiday material 10 months in advance. Computer printout submissions OK; prefers letter-quality. Reports in 1 week. Sample copy for 8½x11 SAE with $1.41 postage.
Nonfiction: Buys 50 mss/year. Send complete ms. Length: 2,000-7,500 words. Pays $100 for unsolicited articles.
Photos: Send photos with submission. Offers no additional payment for photos accepted with ms. Identification of subjects required. Buys one-time rights.
Tips: "The writer should be a Naval Academy alumnus (not necessarily a graduate) with first-hand experience of events in the Naval Service."

THE STUDENT, 127 9th Ave. N., Nashville TN 37234. Editor: Milt Hughes. 20% freelance written. Works with a small number of new/unpublished writers each year. Publication of National Student Ministries of the Southern Baptist Convention. For college students; focusing on freshman and sophomore levels. Published 12 times during the school year. Circ. 25,000. Buys all rights. Payment on acceptance. Publishes ms an average of 10 months after acceptance. Mss should be double-spaced on white paper with 50-space line, 25 lines/page. Reports usually in 6 weeks. Computer printout submissions acceptable; no dot-matrix. Sample copy and guidelines for SASE.
Nonfiction: Contemporary questions, problems, and issues facing college students viewed from a Christian perspective to develop high moral and ethical values. Cultivating interpersonal relationships, developing self-esteem, dealing with the academic struggle, coping with rejection, learning how to love, developing a personal relationship with Jesus Christ. Prefers complete ms rather than query. Length: 800 words maximum. Pays 5¢/word after editing with reserved right to edit accepted material.
Fiction: Satire and parody on college life, humorous episodes; emphasize clean fun and the ability to grow and be uplifted through humor. Contemporary fiction involving student life, on campus as well as off. Length: 900 words. Pays 5¢/word.

‡TEXAS COLLEGE STUDENT, Box 162464, Austin TX 78716-2464. (512)472-3893. Managing Editor: Tracy Duncan. Associate Managing Editor: David Elliot. 50% freelance written. Monthly magazine covering regional (Texas) 18- to 24-year-old college students. Estab. 1987. Circ. 210,000. Pays on publication. Byline given sometimes. Buys first rights. Submit seasonal/holiday material 3 months in advance. Photocopied submissions OK. Query for electronic submission requirements. Computer printout submissions OK; prefers letter-quality. Sample copy $1.
Nonfiction: How-to, (i.e. buy a used car, get a credit card, etc.); interview/profile (with interesting or famous Texans). Special issues include February—Guide to Spring Break; March—Guide to South Padre Island; April—Summer Activities. No general interest stories. Send complete ms. Length: 250-2,500 words. Pays $0-50. Sometimes pays expenses of writers on assignment.
Photos: State availability of photos with submission. Reviews negatives, 4x5 transparencies and 8x10 prints. Offers no additional payment for photos accepted with ms. Captions, model releases, and identification of subjects required. Buys one-time rights.
Columns/Departments: Spotlight, (unique aspects of life at a particular Texas college or university—i.e. weird, strange, or unusual things the students do), 750 words. Send complete ms. Length: 500-1,500 words. Pays $0-50.

Fillers: Gags to be illustrated by cartoonist. Buys 8/year. Pays $0-30.
Tips: "Stories about fascinating students are encouraged. All areas are open to freelancers."

U MAGAZINE, (formerly *HIS Magazine*), Box 1450, Downers Grove IL 60515. (312)964-5700. Editor: Verne Becker. 60% freelance written. Works with a small number of new/unpublished writers each year. Issued monthly from October-April for college students, with "a Christian approach to the needs and issues they face." Pays on acceptance. Publishes ms an average of 1 year after acceptance. Buys first rights and second (reprint) rights to material originally published elsewhere. Reports in 3 months. Computer printout submissions acceptable; prefers letter-quality to dot-matrix.
Nonfiction and Fiction: "Articles dealing with practical aspects of Christian living on campus, relating contemporary issues to Biblical principles. Student-related articles on the relationship between Christianity and various fields of study and career options, Christian doctrine and missions. Every article must relate to the needs of a typical college student. We like material that shows students struggling with real problems and, as a result, learning and growing. No theological dissertations." Query. Buys 35 unsolicited mss/year. Length: 2,000 words maximum. Pays $50-200. Sometimes pays expenses of writers on assignment.
Poetry: Pays $20-50.
Tips: "Direct your principles and illustrations at college students. Avoid preachiness and attacks on various Christian ministries or groups; share your insights on a peer basis."

WPI JOURNAL, Worcester Polytechnic Institute, 100 Institute Rd., Worcester MA 01609. Editor: Kenneth McDonnell. 75% freelance written. A quarterly alumni magazine covering science and engineering/education/business personalities for 16,000 alumni, primarily engineers, scientists, managers; parents of students, national media. Circ. 22,500. Pays on publication. Publishes ms an average of 3 months after acceptance. Byline given. Buys one-time rights. Submit seasonal/holiday material 3 months in advance. Simultaneous queries, and simultaneous, photocopied and previously published submissions OK. Electronic submissions OK via disk compatible with DEC or NBI, but requires hard copy also. Computer printout submissions acceptable; prefers letter-quality to dot-matrix. Reports in 2 weeks on queries; 1 month on mss.
Nonfiction: Book excerpts; exposé (education, engineering, science); general interest; historical/nostalgic; how-to (financial, business-oriented); humor; interview/profile (people in engineering, science); personal experience; photo feature; and technical (with personal orientation). Query with published clips. Length: 1,000-4,000 words. Pays negotiable rate. Sometimes pays the expenses of writers on assignment.
Photos: State availability of photos with query or ms. Reviews b&w contact sheets. Pays negotiable rate. Captions required.
Fillers: Cartoons. Buys 4/year. Pays $75-100.
Tips: "Submit outline of story and/or ms of story idea or published work. Features are most open to freelancers."

————— Child Care and Parental Guidance

People used to learn how to care for their children from their own parents, but research and new options are changing practices. Today many career-oriented couples are starting families later and having fewer children. Parents are hearing terms their parents didn't: single-parent households, gifted children, bonding, etc. Readers want information on new research about pregnancy, infancy, child development and family issues written for parents and people who care for children. Child care magazines address these and other issues. Other markets that buy articles about child care and the family are included in the Education, Religious and Women's sections.

‡**BABY TALK MAGAZINE**, Parenting/Excellence, 185 Madison Ave., New York NY 10016. (212)679-4400. Editor: Patricia D. Irons. 50% freelance written. Monthly magazine covering "topics of interest to expectant and new parents—baby care—child development." Circ. 975,000. Pays on acceptance. Publishes ms an average of 3-6 months after acceptance. Byline given. Buys one-time rights. Submit

seasonal/holiday material 3-6 months in advance. Previously published submissions sometimes OK. Computer printout submissions OK; no dot-matrix. Reports in 4 weeks. Sample copy for SAE with 37¢ postage; writer's guidelines for SAE.

Nonfiction: Essays (on parental topics); how-to (on baby care); opinions; personal experience; photo feature; and travel. No articles under 1,000 words, hand-written articles, humor or fiction. Buys 40 mss/year. Query or send complete ms. Length: 1,500-3,000 words. Pays $50-200.

Photos: Send photos with submission. Reviews transparencies or b&w prints. Offers $25-75 per photo. Captions and model releases required. Buys one-time rights.

Columns/Departments: Budgets and Children's Health (young parents' concerns, written by M.D. or R.N.) Length: 1,500-3,000 words. Buys 6-8 mss/year. Query or send complete ms. Pays $50-200.

Tips: "Writing for *Baby Talk* is highly competitive. Due to a lack of available editorial space, less than one in 100 submitted manuscripts can be accepted."

‡**CHILD**,The New York Times Magazine Group, 110 6th Ave., New York NY 10011. (212)463-1000. Editor-in-Chief: Jacqueline Leo. Executive Editor: Nancy Clark. 75% freelance written. Bimonthly magazine covering parents and children. "*Child* is written for sophisticated parents who want the best for their children—the best information, health care, products, etc." Estab. 1986. Circ. 200,000. Pays on acceptance. Publishes ms an average of 3 months after acceptance. Byline given. Offers 25% kill fee. Buys first North American serial rights, one-time rights or second serial (reprint) rights. Submit seasonal/holiday material 6 months in advance. Simultaneous and photocopied submissions OK. Computer printout submissions OK; prefers letter-quality to dot-matrix. Reports in 6-8 weeks. Sample copy $1.50; writer's guidelines for SASE.

Nonfiction: Book excerpts, humor, interview/profile, personal experience, and travel. No poetry, children's stories, fiction. Buys 75 mss/year. Query with published clips. Length: 1,000-2,500 words. Pays $500-1,000 for assigned articles. Pays $300-750 for unsolicited mss. Sometimes pays expenses of writers on assignment.

Photos: State availability of photos with submission. Offers $25-100 per photo. Identification of subjects required. Buys one-time rights.

Columns/Departments: Family Fortunes (money management from parent's point of view); Manners and Morals (ethics and values); Child's Play (toys, child-related businesses, activities); Behavior (psychological issues); and Health (medical concerns for parents). Buys 30 mss/year. Query with published clips. Length: 1,500-2,000 words. Pays $500-1,000.

THE EXCEPTIONAL PARENT, Children with Disabilities/Practical Information, Psy/Ed Corp., 605 Commonwealth Ave., Boston MA 02215. (617)536-8961. Editor: Maxwell Schleifer. Managing Editor: Christine Sandulli. 30% freelance written. Magazine published 8 times/year covering issues of concern to parents of disabled children. "Our editorial goal is to provide practical guidance and help to those interested in the growth and development of people with disabilities. We bring together people with different perspectives to present the most comprehensive view of the individual, to generate new solutions to old problems, to create visions." Circ. 35,000. Pays on publication. Byline given. Buys all rights. Submit seasonal/holiday material 3 months in advance. Simultaneous, photocopied and previously published submissions OK. Computer printout submissions acceptable; prefers letter-quality to dot-matrix. Reports in 6 months maximum. Sample copy for $3; free writer's guidelines.

Nonfiction: Book excerpts; essays; how-to (adapt toys, fix wheelchairs, etc.); inspirational (family stories); new product; personal experience; and travel. Buys 40 mss/year. Send complete ms. Length: 500-5,000 words. Pays $25-75.

Photos: Send photos with submission. Reviews 3x5 or larger prints. Offers no additional payment for photos accepted with ms. Model releases required. Buys one-time rights.

Tips: "We welcome articles by parents, disabled individuals, professionals, and anyone else—including children."

EXPECTING, 685 3rd Ave., New York NY 10017. Editor: Evelyn A. Podsiadlo. Assistant Editor: Grace Lang. Issued quarterly for expectant mothers. Circ. 1,200,000. Buys all rights. Byline given. Pays on acceptance. Reports in 1 month. Free writer's guidelines.

Nonfiction: Prenatal development, layette and nursery planning, budgeting, health, fashion, husband-wife relationships, naming the baby, minor discomforts, childbirth, expectant fathers, working while pregnant, etc. Length: 800-1,600 words. Pays $200-400 for feature articles.

Fillers: Short humor and interesting or unusual happenings during pregnancy or at the hospital; maximum 100 words, $15 on publication; submissions to "Happenings" are not returned.

Poetry: Occasionally buys subject-related poetry; all forms. Length: 12-64 lines. Pays $10-30.

GIFTED CHILDREN MONTHLY, For the Parents of Children with Great Promise, Box 115, Sewell NJ 08080. (609)582-0277. Editor: Dr. James Alvino. Managing Editor: Robert Baum. 50% freelance written. Prefers to work with published/established writers. Monthly newsletter covering parenting and education of gifted children for parents. Circ. 50,000. Pays on acceptance. Publishes ms an average of 3-6 months after acceptance. Buys all rights and first rights. Submit seasonal/holiday material 4 months in advance. Simultaneous queries, and simultaneous, photocopied, and previously published submissions OK. Computer printout submissions acceptable; prefers letter-quality to dot-matrix. Reports in 1 month on queries; 2 months on mss. Sample copy and writer's guidelines for 9x12 SAE and 51¢ postage.

Nonfiction: Book excerpts; personal accounts; how-to (on parenting of gifted kids); research into practice; outstanding programs; interview/profile; and opinion. Also puzzles, brainteasers and ideas for children's Spin-Off section. "Our Special Reports and Idea Place sections are most accessible to freelancers." Query with clips of published work or send complete ms. Buys 36 unsolicited mss/year. Length: Idea Place 500-750 words; Special Reports 1,000-2,500 words. Pays $10-200. Sometimes pays expenses of writers on assignment.

Tips: "We look forward to working with both new and veteran writers who have something new to say to the parents of gifted and talented children. It is helpful if freelancers provide copies of research papers to back up the article."

GROWING PARENT, Dunn & Hargitt, Inc., 22 N. 2nd St., Box 1100, Lafayette IN 47902. (317)423-2624. Editor: Nancy Kleckner. 40-50% freelance written. Works with a small number of new/unpublished writers each year. "We do receive a lot of unsolicited submissions but have had excellent results in working with some unpublished writers. So, we're always happy to look at material and hope to find one or two jewels each year." A monthly newsletter which focuses on parents—the issues, problems, and choices they face as their children grow. "We want to look at the parent as an adult and help encourage his or her growth not only as a parent but as an individual." Pays on acceptance. Publishes ms an average of 6 months after acceptance. Byline given. Buys first North American serial rights; maintains exclusive rights for three months. Submit seasonal/holiday material 6 months in advance. Photocopied submissions and previously published submissions OK. Computer printout submissions acceptable; prefers letter-quality to dot-matrix. Reports in 2 weeks. Sample copy and writer's guidelines for 9x6 SAE with 37¢ postage.

Nonfiction: "We are looking for informational articles written in an easy-to-read, concise style. We would like to see articles that help parents deal with the stresses they face in everyday life—positive, upbeat, how-to-cope suggestions. We rarely use humorous pieces, fiction or personal experience articles. Writers should keep in mind that most of our readers have children under three years of age." Buys 15-20 mss/year. Query. Length: 1,500-2,000 words; will look at shorter pieces. Pays 8-10¢/word (depends on article).

Tips: "Submit a very specific query letter with samples."

HOME EDUCATION MAGAZINE, Box 1083, Tonasket WA 98855. Editors: Mark J. Hegener and Helen E. Hegener. 80% freelance written. Eager to work with new/unpublished writers each year. A monthly magazine covering home-based education. "We feature articles which address the concerns of parents who want to take a direct involvement in the education of their children—concerns such as socialization, how to find curriculums and materials, testing and evaluation, how to tell when your child is ready to begin reading, what to do when home schooling is illegal in your state, teaching advanced subjects, etc." Circ. 3,500. Pays on publication. Publishes ms an average of 2-3 months after acceptance. Byline given. Buys first North American serial rights, first rights, one-time rights, second serial (reprint) rights, simultaneous rights, all rights, and makes work-for-hire assignments. Submit seasonal/holiday material 3 months in advance. Simultaneous, photocopied and previously published submissions OK. Query for electronic submission requirements. Computer printout submissions acceptable; prefers letter-quality. Reports in 6-8 weeks. Sample copy $2.50; writer's guidelines for SASE.

Nonfiction: Book excerpts, essays, how-to (related to home schooling), humor, inspirational, interview/profile, personal experience, photo feature, religious and technical. "No off-color submissions. We are a family publication." Buys 40-50 mss/year. Query with or without published clips, or send complete ms. Length: 250-2,500 words. Pays $5/500 words; up to 6 copies of the issue author's work appears in at discount. Sometimes pays expenses of writers on assignment.

Photos: Send photos with submission. Reviews 5x7, 35mm prints and b&w snapshots. Write for photo rates. Identification of subjects required. Buys one-time rights.

Tips: "We would especially welcome interviews with or articles about home schooling leaders. Articles are most open to freelancers, but know what you're talking about. We would like to see how-to articles (that don't preach, just present options); articles on testing, accountability, working with the public schools, socialization, learning disabilities, resources, support groups, legislation; and humor. We need answers to the questions that home schoolers ask."

HOME LIFE, Sunday School Board, 127 9th Ave. N., Nashville TN 37234. (615)251-2271. Editor-in-Chief: Reuben Herring. 40-50% freelance written. Prefers to work with published/established writers; eager to work with new/unpublished writers. Emphasizes Christian marriage and Christian family life. For married adults of all ages, but especially newlyweds and middle-aged marrieds. Monthly magazine; 64 pages. Circ. 800,000. Pays on acceptance. Publishes ms an average of 15 months after acceptance. Buys first serial rights, first North American serial rights and all rights. Byline given. Phone queries OK, but written queries preferred. Submit seasonal/holiday material 1 year in advance. Computer printout submissions acceptable; prefers letter-quality to dot-matrix. Reports in 6 weeks. Sample copy $1; free writer's guidelines.

Nonfiction: How-to (good articles on marriage and family life); informational (about some current family-related issue of national significance such as "Television and the Christian Family" or "Whatever Happened to Family Worship?"); personal experience (informed articles by people who have solved marriage and family problems in healthy, constructive ways); marriage and family life with a masculine slant. "No column material. We are not interested in material that will not in some way enrich Christian marriage or family life." Buys 150-200 mss/year. Query or submit complete ms. Length: 600-2,400 words. Pays up to 5¢/word.

Fiction: "Fiction should be family-related and should show a strong moral about how families face and solve problems constructively." Buys 12-20 mss/year. Submit complete ms. Length: 1,000-2,400 words. Pays up to 5¢/word.

Tips: "Study the magazine to see our unique slant on Christian family life. We prefer a life-centered case study approach, rather than theoretical essays on family life. Our top priority is marriage enrichment material."

L.A. PARENT, The Magazine for Parents in Southern California, Box 3204, Burbank CA 91504. (818)846-0400. Editor: Jack Bierman. 80% freelance written. Prefers to work with published/established writers, and works with a small number of new/unpublished writers each year. Monthly tabloid covering parenting. Circ. 100,000. Pays on publication. Publishes ms an average of 4 months after acceptance. Byline given. Buys all rights. Submit seasonal/holiday material 3 months in advance. Simultaneous queries and previously published submissions OK. Query for electronic submission requirements. Computer printout submissions acceptable. Reports in 1 month. Sample copy $2; free writer's guidelines.

Nonfiction: David Jameison, articles editor. General interest, how-to. "We focus on southern California activities for families, and do round-up pieces, i.e., a guide to private schools, fishing spots." Buys 60-75 mss/year. Query with clips of published work. Length: 700-1,200 words. Pays $100 plus expenses.

Tips: "We will be using more contemporary articles on parenting's challenges. If you can write for a 'city magazine' in tone and accuracy, you may write for us. The 'Baby Boom' has created a need for more generic parenting material."

LIVING WITH CHILDREN, Baptist Sunday School Board, 127 9th Ave. N., Nashville TN 37234. (615)251-2229. Editor: SuAnne Bottoms. 50% freelance written. Works with a small number of new/unpublished writers each year. Quarterly magazine covering parenting issues for parents of elementary-age children (ages 6 through 11). "Written and designed from a Christian perspective." Circ. 50,000. Pays on acceptance. Publishes ms an average of 2 years after acceptance. Byline given. "We generally buy all rights to mss; first serial rights on a limited basis. First and reprint rights may be negotiated at a lower rate of pay." Submit seasonal/holiday material 1 year in advance. Previously published submissions (on limited basis) OK. Computer printout submissions acceptable; no dot-matrix. Reports in 1 month on queries; 2 months on mss. Sample copy for 9x12 manila SASE; free writer's guidelines.

Nonfiction: How-to (parent), humor, inspirational, personal experience, and articles on child development. No highly technical material or articles containing more than 15-20 lines quoted material. Buys 60 mss/year. Query or send complete ms (queries preferred). Length: 800-1,800 words (1,450 words preferred). Pays 5¢/word.

Photos: "Submission of photos with mss is strongly discouraged."

Fiction: Humorous (parent/child relationships); and religious. "We have very limited need for fiction." Buys maximum of 4 mss/year. Length: 800-1,450 words. Pays 5¢/word.

Poetry: Light verse and inspirational. "We have limited need for poetry and buy only all rights." Buys 15 poems/year. Submit maximum 3 poems. Length: 4-30 lines. Pays $1.75 (for 1-7 lines) plus $1 for each additional line; pays $4.50 for 8 lines and more plus 65¢ each additional line.

Fillers: Jokes, anecdotes and short humor. Buys 15/year. Length: 100-400 words. Pays $5 minimum, 5¢/word.

Tips: "Articles must deal with an issue of interest to parents. A mistake some writers make in articles for us is failing to write from a uniquely Christian perspective; that is very necessary for our periodicals. Material should be 850, 1,450 or 1,800 words in length. All sections, particularly articles, are open to freelance writers. Only regular features are assigned."

LIVING WITH PRESCHOOLERS, Baptist Sunday School Board, 127 9th Ave. N., Nashville TN 37234. (615)251-2229. Editor: SuAnne Bottoms. 50% freelance written. Works with a small number of new/unpublished writers each year. Quarterly magazine covering parenting issues for parents of preschoolers (infants through 5-year-olds). The magazine is "written and designed from a Christian perspective." Circ. 152,000. Pays on acceptance. Publishes manuscript an average of 2 years after acceptance. Byline given. "We generally buy all rights to manuscripts. First and reprint rights may be negotiated at a lower rate of pay." Submit seasonal/holiday material 2 years in advance. Previously published submissions (on limited basis) OK. Computer printout submissions acceptable; no dot-matrix. Reports in 1 month on queries; 2 months on mss. Sample copy for 9x12 manila SASE; free writer's guidelines.

Nonfiction: How-to (parent), humor, inspirational, personal experience, and articles on child development. No highly technical material or articles containing more than 15-20 lines quoted material. Buys 60 mss/year. Query or send complete ms (queries preferred). Length: 800-1,800 words (1,450 words preferred). Pays 5¢/word for manuscripts offered on all-rights basis.

Photos: "Submission of photos with mss is strongly discouraged."

Fiction: Humorous (parent/child relationships); and religious. "We have very limited need for fiction." Buys maximum of 4 mss/year. Length: 800-1,450 words. Pays 5¢/word.

Poetry: Light verse and inspirational. "We have limited need for poetry and buy only all rights." Buys 15 poems/year. Submit maximum 3 poems. Length: 4-30 lines. Pays $1.75 (for 1-7 lines) plus $1 for each additional line; pays $4.50 for 8 lines and more plus 65¢ each additional line.

Fillers: Jokes, anecdotes and short humor. Buys 15/year. Length: 100-400 words. Pays $5 minimum, 5¢/word maximum.

Tips: "Articles must deal with an issue of interest to parents. A mistake some writers make in writing an article for us is failing to write from a uniquely Christian perspective; that is very necessary for our periodicals. Material should be 850, 1,450, or 1,800 words in length. All sections, particularly articles, are open to freelance writers. Only regular features are assigned."

NETWORK, For Public Schools, National Committee for Citizens in Education, Suite 301, 10840 Little Patuyent Pkwy., Columbia MD 21044. (301)997-9300. Editor: Chrissie Bamber. 10% freelance written. Works with a small number of new/unpublished writers each year. Published 6 times during the school year covering parent/citizen involvement in public schools. Circ. 6,000. Pays on publication. Publishes ms an average of 6 months after acceptance. Byline given. Buys first serial rights, first North American serial rights, one-time rights, second serial (reprint) rights, simultaneous rights, all rights and makes work-for-hire assignments. Submit seasonal/holiday material 3 months in advance. Simultaneous queries and photocopied submissions OK. Computer printout submissions OK; prefers letter-quality. Reports in 6 weeks. Free sample copy; writer's guidelines for #10 SAE and 39¢ postage.

Nonfiction: Book excerpts (elementary and secondary public education); exposé (of school systems which attempt to reduce public access); how-to (improve schools through parent/citizen participation); humor (related to public school issues); opinion (school-related issues); personal experience (school-related issues). "It is our intention to provide balanced coverage of current developments and continuing issues and to place the facts about schools in a perspective useful to parents. No highly technical or scholarly articles about education; no child rearing articles or personal opinion not backed by research or concrete examples." Buys 4-6 mss/year. Query with clips of published work or send complete ms. Length: 1,000-1,500 words. Pays $25-100. Sometimes pays the expenses of writers on assignment.

Tips: "We are seeking more local examples of parent/community and school partnerships that have succeeded in raising student achievement. Readers want articles of substance with information they can use and act on, not headlines which promise much but deliver only the most shallow analysis of the subject. Information is first, style second. A high personal commitment to public schools and preferably first-hand experience are the greatest assets. A clear and simple writing style, easily understood by a wide range of lay readers, is a must."

PEDIATRICS FOR PARENTS, The Newsletter for Caring Parents, Pediatrics for Parents, Inc., 176 Mt. Hope Ave., Bangor ME 04401. (207)942-6212. Editor: Richard J. Sagall, M.D. 20% freelance written. Eager to work with new/unpublished writers. Monthly newsletter covering medical aspects of rearing children and educating parents about children's health. Circ. 2,800. Pays on publication. Publishes ms an average of 3-4 months after acceptance. Byline given. Buys first North American serial rights, first and second rights to the same material, and second (reprint) rights to material originally published elsewhere. Rights always include right to publish article in our books on "Best of . . ." series. Submit seasonal/holiday material 6 months in advance. Simultaneous queries, and simultaneous, photocopied and previously published submissions OK. Electronic submissions OK compatible with Apple-PFS. Computer printout submissions acceptable. Reports in 1 month on queries; 6 weeks on mss. Sample copy for $2; writer's guidelines for business size SAE and 39¢ postage.

Nonfiction: Book reviews; how-to (feed healthy kids, exercise, practice wellness, etc.); new product; technical (explaining medical concepts in shirtsleeve language). No general parenting articles. Query with published clips or submit complete ms. Length: 25-1,000 words. Pays 2-5¢/edited word.

Columns/Departments: Book reviews; Please Send Me (material available to parents for free or at nominal cost); Pedia-Tricks (medically-oriented parenting tips that work). Send complete ms. Pays $15-250. Pays 2¢/edited word.

Tips: "We are dedicated to taking the mystery out of medicine for young parents. Therefore, we write in clear and understandable language (but not simplistic language) to help people understand and deal intelligently with complex disease processes, treatments, prevention, wellness, etc. Our articles must be well researched and documented. Detailed references must always be attached to any article for documentation, but not for publication. We strongly urge freelancers to read one or two issues before writing."

SEATTLE'S CHILD, Box 22578, Seattle WA 98122. (206)322-2594. Editor: Ann Bergman. 85% freelance written. Works with a small number of new/unpublished writers each year. Monthly tabloid of articles related to being a parent of children age 12 and under. Directed to parents and professionals involved with children 12 and under. Circ. 10,000. Pays on publication. Publishes ms an average of 3 months after acceptance. Byline given. Offers 50% kill fee. Buys first North American serial rights or all rights. Submit seasonal/holiday material 6 months in advance. Simultaneous queries, and simultaneous and photocopied submissions OK. Electronic submissions OK via IBM PC, 1200 baud, but requires hard copy also. Computer printout submissions acceptable. Reports in 6 weeks on queries; 4 weeks on mss. Sample copy $1.50 with 10x13 envelope; writer's guidelines for business size SAE and 1 first class stamp.

Nonfiction: Needs reports on political issues affecting families. Exposé, general interest, historical/nostalgic, how-to, humor, interview/profile, new product, opinion, personal experience, travel, record, tape and book reviews, and educational and political reviews. Articles must relate to parents and parenting. Buys 120 mss/year. Send complete ms (preferred) or query with published clips. Length: 400-2,500 words. Pays $25-500. Sometimes pays the expenses of writers on assignment.

Photos: Robert Cole, photo editor. Send photos with query or ms. Reviews 5x7 b&w prints. Pays $25-125. Model release required. Buys one-time rights or all rights.

Tips: "We prefer concise, critical writing and discourage overly sentimental pieces. Don't talk down to the audience. Consider that the audience is sophisticated and well-read. We also consider articles for a network of 'parent' publications, total circulation 250,000, call *Parenting News Network*."

‡THE SINGLE PARENT, Parents Without Partners, Inc., 8807 Colesville Rd., Silver Spring MD 20910. (301)588-9354. Assistant Editor: Jackie Conciatore. 20% freelance written. Works with small number of new/unpublished writers each year. Magazine, published 6 times/year; 48 pages. Emphasizes single parenting, family, divorce, widowhood and children. Distributed to members of Parents Without Partners, plus libraries, universities, psychologists, psychiatrists, subscribers, etc. Circ. 200,000. Pays on publication. Publishes ms an average of 6-9 months after acceptance. Buys one-time rights. Simultaneous, photocopied, and previously published submissions OK. Query for electronic submissions. Computer printout submissions acceptable; no dot-matrix. Reports in 2 months. Sample copy and writer's guidelines for 10x12 SAE with 50¢ postage.

Nonfiction: Informational (parenting, legal issues, single parents in society, programs that work for single parents, children's problems); how-to (raise children alone, travel, take up a new career, cope with life as a new or veteran single parent; short lists of how-to tips). No first-hand accounts of bitter legal battles with former spouses. Buys 20 unsolicited mss/year. Query. Length: 1,000-2,000 words. Payment negotiable.

Columns/Departments: "We are starting a new section, F.Y.I., for short news items, reports on research, and tips on how to do things better."

Photos: Purchased with accompanying ms. Query. Pays negotiable rates. Model release required.

Tips: "We get far too many articles that are too general. We are the only magazine for single parents, and we have to be much more specific for our readers. We already know about 'Children and Divorce'; we need to know about 'Divorce and Bad Parent Guilt—What to Do'. We need specific, fresh ideas."

TWINS, The Magazine for Parents of Multiples, Twins Magazine, Inc., Box 12045, Overland Park KS 66212. (913)722-1090. Editor: Barbara C. Unell. 100% freelance written. Eager to work with new/unpublished writers. A bimonthly magazine covering parenting of multiples. Circ. 30,000. Pays on publication. Publishes ms an average of 6 months after acceptance. Byline given. Buys all rights. Submit seasonal/holiday material 10 months in advance. Simultaneous, photocopied and previously published submissions OK. Computer printout submissions acceptable; prefers letter-quality to dot-matrix. Reports in 6 weeks on queries; 2 months on mss. Sample copy $3.50 plus $1.50 postage and handling; writer's guidelines for #10 SAE with 1 first class stamp.

Nonfiction: Book excerpts, general interest, how-to, humor, interview/profile, personal experience and photo feature. "No articles which substitute the word 'twin' for 'child'—those that simply apply the same research to twins that applies to singletons without any facts backing up the reason to do so." Buys 150 mss/year. Query with or without published clips, or send complete ms. Length: 1,250-3,000 words. Payment varies; sometimes pays in contributor copies or premiums instead of cash. Sometimes pays the expenses of writers on assignment.

Photos: Send photos with submission. Reviews contact sheets, 4x5 transparencies, and all size prints. Captions, model releases, and identification of subjects required. Buys all rights.

Columns/Departments: Resources, Supertwins, Prematurity, Family Health, Twice as Funny, Double Focus (series from pregnancy through adolescence), Personal Perspective (first-person accounts of beliefs about a certain aspect of parenting multiples), Caring for You (ways parents can feel as good as can be as people, not just parents), Feelings on Fatherhood, Research, On Being Twins (first-person accounts of growing up as a twin), On Being Parents of Twins (first-person accounts of the experience of parenting twins), Double Takes (fun photographs of twins), and Education Matters. Buys 70 mss/year. Query with published clips. Length: 1,250-2,000 words. Payment varies.

Fillers: Anecdotes and short humor. Length: 75-750 words. Payment varies.

Tips: "Features and columns are both open to freelancers. Columnists write for *Twins* on a continuous basis, so the column becomes their column. We are looking for a wide variety of the latest, well-researched practical information. There is no other magazine of this type directed to this market." We are interested in "personal interviews with celebrity twins or celebrity parents of twins, and tips on rearing twins from experienced parents and/or twins themselves."

Comic Books

Comic markets differ from other magazine markets—they present stories visually. This doesn't mean you have to be an artist to write for comic books. Most of these publishers want to see a synopsis of one to two double-spaced pages. Highlight the story's beginning, middle and end, and tell how events will affect your main character emotionally. Be concise. Comics use few words.

Once your synopsis is accepted, either an artist will draw the story from your plot, returning these pages to you for dialogue and captions, or you will be expected to write a script. Scripts run approximately 23 typewritten pages and include suggestions for artwork as well as dialogue. Try to imagine your story on actual comic book pages and divide your script accordingly. The average comic has six panels per page, with a maximum of 35 words per panel.

If you're submitting a proposal to Marvel or DC, your story should center on an already established character. If you're dealing with an independent publisher, characters are often the property of their creators. Your proposal should be for a new series. Include a background sheet for main characters who will appear regularly, listing origins, weaknesses, powers or other information that will make your character unique. Indicate an overall theme or direction for your series. Submit story ideas for the first three issues. If you're really ambitious, you may also include a script for your first issue. As with all markets, read a sample copy before making a submission.

‡AMAZING HEROES, Fantagraphics Books, 4359 Cornell Rd., Agoura CA 91301. (818)706-7606. Editor: Kim Thompson. 80% freelance written. Eager to work with new/unpublished writers. A biweekly magazine for comic book fans of all ages and backgrounds. "*Amazing Heroes* focuses on both historical aspects of comics and current doings in the industry." Circ. 15,000. Pays on publication. Publishes ms an average of 2 months after acceptance. Byline given. Offers $25 kill fee. Buys first North American serial rights and second serial (reprint) rights. Submit seasonal/holiday material 3 months in advance. Photocopied and previously published submissions OK. Computer printout submissions OK; prefers letter-quality to dot-matrix. Reports in 2 weeks on queries; 1 month on mss. Sample copy $2.50.
Nonfiction: Essays, historical/nostalgic, interview/profile, new product. Query with published clips. Length: 300-7,500 words. Pays $5-125 for assigned articles; pays $5-75 for unsolicited articles. Pays writers with double payment in Fantagraphics book merchandise if requested. Sometimes pays the expenses of writers on assignment.
Photos: State availability of photos on profile pieces and interviews.

CARTOON WORLD, Box 30367, Dept. WM, Lincoln NE 68503. Editor: George Hartman. 100% freelance written. Works with published/established writers and a small number of new/unpublished writers each year. "Monthly newsletter for professional and amateur cartoonists who are serious and want to utilize new cartoon markets in each issue." Buys only from paid subscribers. Circ. 150-300. Pays on acceptance. Publishes ms an average of 2 months after acceptance. Byline given. Buys second (reprint) rights to material originally published elsewhere. Not copyrighted. Submit seasonal/holiday material 3 months in advance. Simultaneous submissions OK. Computer printout submissions acceptable; no dot-matrix. Reports in 1 month. Sample copy $5.
Nonfiction: "We want only positive articles about the business of cartooning and gag writing." Buys 10 mss/year. Query. Length: 1,000 words. Pays $5/page.

‡COMICO THE COMIC COMPANY, 1547 DeKalb St., Norristown PA 19401. (215)277-4305. Editor-in-Chief: Diana Schutz. 100% freelance written. "We work only with writers, published or unpublished, who can tell a strong, solid, and visual story." One-shot, limited and continuing series comic books. Circ. approximately 70,000 per title. Pays 5 days after acceptance. Publishes ms an average of 9-12 months after acceptance. Byline given. Buys first rights, makes work-for-hire assignments or offers creator ownership contracts. Simultaneous, photocopied and previously published submissions OK. Computer printout submissions OK; no dot-matrix. Reports in 1 month on queries; 2 months on mss. Sample copy for $1.50 and 7½x10½ SAE and 56¢ postage. Free writer's guidelines.
Fiction: Various genres. "We are always interested in seeing submissions of new and innovative material. Due to the words-and-pictures format of comic books, it is usually preferable, though not essential, that the writer submit material in conjunction with an artist of his or her choice." No pornography or dogma. Buys 100 mss/year. Query. Length: 26 story pages. Payment varies.
Tips: "Our industry in general and our company in particular are beginning to look more and more at the limited series and graphic novel formats as means of properly conveying solid stories, beautifully illustrated for the adult marketplace, as opposed to the standard continuing serials. Be familiar with comics medium and industry. Show that writer can write in script format and express intentions to artist who will create images based on writer's descriptions. The area of licensed properties is most open to freelancers. Writer must be faithful to licensed characters, to licensor's wishes, and be willing to make any requested changes."

‡EAGLE, Box 447, Sicklerville NJ 08081. (609)629-6091. Managing Editor: Neil D. Vokes. 100% freelance written. Monthly magazine. Estab. 1986. Circ. 25,000. Pays on acceptance. Publishes ms an average of 1-2 months after acceptance. Byline given. Simultaneous, photocopied and previously published submissions OK. Computer printout submissions OK; no dot-matrix. Free sample copy.
Fiction: Adventure, fantasy, horror, humorous, mainstream, mystery, science fiction, suspense and western. No parodies. "*Eagle* is a blend of these categories." Query. Writers who are also artists should submit "at least three pages showing story continuity with realistic people and backgrounds." Submit story ideas for already established characters and original characters.
Tips: "Make sure all submissions contain correct spelling and punctuation; otherwise we don't take you seriously."

ECLIPSE COMICS, Box 1099, Forestville CA 95436. (707)887-1521. Publisher: Dean Mullaney. Editor-in-Chief: Catherine Yronwode. 100% freelance written. Works with a small number of new/unpublished writers each year. Publishers of various four-color comic books. *Eclipse* publishes comic books with high-quality paper and color reproduction, geared toward the discriminating comic book fan; and sold through the "direct sales" specialty store market. Circ. varies (35,000-85,000). Pays on acceptance (net 30 days). Publishes ms an average of 3 months after acceptance. Byline given. Buys first North American serial rights, second serial (reprint) rights with additional payment, and first option on collection and non-exclusive rights to sell material to South American and European markets (with additional payments). Simultaneous queries, and simultaneous and photocopied submissions OK. Computer printout submissions acceptable; no dot-matrix. Reports in 2 months. Sample copy $1.75; writer's guidelines for business-size SAE and 1 first class stamp.
Fiction: "All of our comics are fictional." Adventure, fantasy, mystery, romance, science fiction, horror, western. "No sexually explicit material, please." Buys approximately 250 mss/year (mostly from established comics writers). Send sample science fiction or horror script or plot synopsis. Length: 8-11 pages. Pays $30 minimum/page.
Tips: "At the present time we are publishing as many adventure and super-heroic series as our schedule permits. Because all of our comics are creator-owned, we do not buy fill-in plots or scripts for these books. We do have two comics open to new writers, however. These are *Alien Encounters*, a bimonthly science fiction anthology, and *Tales of Terrors*, a bimonthly horror anthology. The stories in these titles vary from 1-page fillers to short stories of 8 or more pages each, with a maximum length of 11 pages. Plot synopsis of less than a page can be submitted; we will select promising concepts for development into full script submissions. All full script submissions should be written in comic book or 'screenplay' form for artists to illustrate. Science fiction themes we need include outer-space, UFOs, alien invasions, time travel, inter-dimensional travel, nuclear holocaust aftermath, future-science exploration, robots, cyborgs, end-of-world, etc. Horror themes we need include vampires, werewolves, zombies, walking dead, monsters in the sewers, revenge from beyond the grave, 'murder will out' stories, and assorted slimy, creepy, gooey, demonic and horrific stuff. 85% of the stories in these anthologies have downbeat twist endings of the kind popularized by O. Henry and the EC comic books of the 1950s. The other 15% start off in that mold but lead to an unexpected upbeat resolution. Our special needs at the moment are for moody, romantic, character-oriented pieces with overtones of humanism, morality, political opinion, philosophical speculation, and/or social commentary. Comic book adaptations (by the original authors) of previously published science fiction and horror short stories are definitely encouraged."

Close-up

Diana Schutz
Editor-in-chief
Comico

"The purpose of a comic book is to tell a story through
the use of words *and* pictures," says Diana Schutz, editor-
in-chief of Comico. "A writer for comic books must have
a strong *visual* sense. Furthermore, since comics tend to be
produced via an 'assembly-line' process—one person
writes, another draws the story in pencil, another lays
down the ink line, another puts in speech balloons and let-
tering, and yet another colors the story—a comic book writer must not only be able to function as a member of a team, but should ideally tailor the work to the various strengths and
weaknesses of his fellow creative personnel. Since most comics are published on a monthly
schedule, a comic book writer must be able to meet deadlines.

"A writer interested in comic books can become acquainted with the field by visiting any
of the 5,000 comic book specialty stores in the U.S. and Canada. They provide a wide sampling of what is currently available. Comic book retailers are avid comic buffs, usually, and
can give novitiates resource material, or often the exact information they are seeking."

What is the most common mistake writers make when submitting their work to Schutz?
"Submitting *too* much. A series proposal should consist of no more than five pages. If the
writer cannot 'hook' the editor within those five pages, then they've failed at one important
aspect of the job. A submission should be brief and describe the intended format—continuing
or limited series, graphic novel, or one-shot; total number of story pages per issue; premise
and/or theme of the series; central characters; and plot synopsis." Although Schutz says it's
easier to work with a writer who is also an artist, artistic ability isn't absolutely necessary.
"It's always advisable to team up with an artist before making a submission. If a story is too
outstanding to pass up, Comico will make every effort to match up the writer with an artist.
When submitting, photocopies of artwork are always a plus, in light of the demands of our
particular medium. No submissions should be attempted over the phone, and we prefer *no*
telephone follow-ups to submission presentations. It may take us time to respond, but we *will*
respond.

"I prefer to see writers tell stories with compelling human drama. The comic book field has
grown and grown *up* throughout its forty years of existence, and more and more titles are directed toward the adult reader. The primary market, with its emphasis on clear-cut definitions
of good versus evil, still tends to cater to male adolescents. However, my personal interests
lie with stories built around serious themes, complex inter-personal relationships and emotional depth. Writers should avoid storylines that have no visually stimulating counterpart.
The comics medium functions on high visual impact, and writers must constantly weave their
stories around what is, or can be made, visually interesting. A story that consists of two 'talking heads' expounding back and forth rarely works in comics. The comics industry suffers
from a dearth of good writers, while enjoying a multitude of talented artists. At Comico, we
recognize and stress the importance of solid stories and we pride ourselves on the fact that all
our writers are exceptional."

—Sheila Freeman

FIRST COMICS, INC., includes *American Flagg!*, *Jon Sable*, *Grimjack*, *Nexus*, *Dreadstar*, *The Enchanted Apples of Oz*, *Elric*, 435 N. LaSalle St., Chicago IL 60610. (312)670-6770. Managing Editor: Richard Oliver. 100% freelance written. Works with small number of new/unpublished writers each year. Comic book magazines published monthly, bimonthly, one-shot and trade paperbacks. Circ. 4,000,000. Pays between acceptance and publication. Publishes ms an average of 6 months after acceptance. Byline given. Buys negotiable rights. Submit seasonal/holiday material 9 months in advance. Simultaneous queries OK. Computer printout submissions acceptable; prefers letter-quality to dot-matrix. "We only respond to new writer queries—brief, with SASE." Reports in 6 months.
Fiction: In comic art format, subjects include adventure, experimental, fantasy, historical, mystery, science fiction and suspense. Query. Payment negotiable. Sometimes pays the expenses of writers on assignment.
Tips: "The writer has a better chance of getting our attention by including a short synopsis (no more than one paragraph) summarizing the concept and highlighting interesting aspects. Ever buy a paperback because you liked the blurb on the back cover? That's what we want to see."

MARVEL COMICS, 387 Park Ave. S., New York NY 10016. (212)576-9200. Editor-in-Chief: James Shooter. 99% freelance written. Publishes 60 comics and magazines per month, 6-12 graphic novels per year, and specials, storybooks, industrials, and paperbacks for all ages. Over 9 million copies sold/month. Pays a flat fee for most projects, plus a royalty type incentive based upon sales. Also works on advance/royalty basis on many projects. "Top regular writers make up to $300,000 per year." Pays on acceptance. Publishes manuscript an average of 6 months after acceptance. Byline given. Offers variable kill fee. Rights purchased depend upon format and material. Submit seasonal/holiday material 1 year in advance. Simultaneous and photocopied submissions OK. Computer printout submissions OK; no dot-matrix. Reports in 6 months. Sample copy and writer's guidelines for SASE. Additional guidelines on request.
Fiction: Super hero, action-adventure, science fiction, fantasy, and other material. No noncomics. Buys 600-800 mss/year. Query with brief plot synopses only. Do not send scripts, short stories or long outlines. A plot synopsis should be less than two typed pages; send two synopses at most. Pays expenses of writers on assignment.

‡NOW COMICS, Caputo Publishing/Now Comics, Suite 401, 525 S. Dearborn, Chicago IL 60605. (312)786-9013. Editor: Brian Augustyn. Managing Editor: Michael Dimpsey. 100% freelance written. Publishes monthly, bimonthly and semiannual comic books and graphic novels. Estab. 1986. Circ. 200,000. Pays on publication. Publishes ms an average of 2 months after acceptance. Byline given. Offers 10% kill fee. Buys all rights and makes work-for-hire assignments. Submit seasonal/holiday material 6 months in advance. Photocopied submissions OK. Computer printout submissions OK; prefers letter-quality to dot-matrix. Reports in 6 weeks. Sample copy for 8x10 SAE with 2 first class stamps. Writer's guidelines for #10 SAE with 1 first class stamp.
Photos: State availability of photos with submission. Reviews 3x5 prints. Offers no additional payment for photos accepted with ms. Identification of subjects required.
Columns/Departments: Nanette Injeski, column/department editor. Now News (news on Now Comics, conventions, and interviews with creators). Length: 100-500 words. Buys 10 mss/year. Query with published clips. Pays $20-50.
Fiction: Adventure, fantasy, horror, humorous, mystery, science fiction, serialized novels, suspense, social parodies and Japanimation. Themes include outer space, future science and teenage exploits. Comic books published by our company include Ralph Snart Adventures, Vector, Speed Racer, Syphons and Dai-Kamikaze. No erotica, religious or romance. Submit story ideas for already established characters. Buys 1,000 mss/year. Send complete ms. Length: 100-600 words. Pays $100-600.
Fillers: Contact Nanette Injeski. Facts, gags to be illustrated by cartoonist, newsbreaks and short humor. Buys 20/year. Length: 20-200 words. Pays $10-50.
Tips: "Writers should think of a script for a motion picture when writing for comics. The words and pictures have to work together to create a quality product. For our bimonthly *Now News* newspaper, we are looking for new and different articles on comics and animation. For comics: think creative. Characterization is important as well as the relation between picture and words. For *Now News*: think original—new ways of saying the same old thing."

‡RENEGADE PRESS,3908 E. 4th St., Long Beach CA 90814. (213)433-4874. Editor: Wendi Lee. 100% freelance written. Publishes 16 titles including *Ms. Tree*, *The Silent Invasion*, *Cases of Sherlock Holmes* and *Flaming Carrot*. "We cater to an eclectic audience; most of our readers are between the ages of 20 and 40, college-educated, professionals. We have a larger female audience than most comic book companies." Pays 30 days from shipment. Publishes ms an average of 3 months to one year after acceptance. Byline given. Simultaneous and photocopied submissions OK. Computer printout submissions OK; prefers letter-quality to dot-matrix. Reports in 2 months. Sample copy $2; free writer's guidelines.
Fiction: Adventure, animal parodies, fantasy, horror, humor, mystery, romance, science fiction, slice-of-life vignettes, social parodies, suspense and western. "All must be written with comic book art in mind. Please

send comic book scripts; no novels or short story form. We prefer it if you have an artist in mind to work with—or are an artist." Prefers story ideas for original characters. Writer supplies full script that the artist follows when drawing the story. Buys 5-10 mss/year. Query. Pays royalty.

Tips: "Comic books are unlike any other medium—story married to art. Pick up the titles of a company you are interested in submitting to and read them. This will help you understand the trend that comic books are taking today. Comic books are a lot different today as opposed to 20 years ago. Originality is what *Renegade* applauds. Too many submissions are based on out-moded notions of comic books. We look for a fresh approach to an old idea. After all there are only about 8 original plots—it's what you do with a plot to make it your own."

‡**VORTEX**, 367 Queen St. W., Toronto, Ontario M5V 2A4 Canada. (416)977-4151. Editor: Lou Stathis. Managing Editor: Deborah Marks. 100% freelance written. Works with a small number of new/unpublished writers each year. Publishes bimonthly comic books. Circ. 16,000. Pays 30 days after publication. Publishes ms an average of 4 months after acceptance. Byline given. Buys first rights and makes work-for-hire assignments. Simultaneous, photocopied and previously published submissions OK. Computer printout submissions OK; prefers letter-quality to dot-matrix. Reports in 2 weeks on queries; 1 month on mss. Sample copy $2.

Nonfiction: General interest, historical/nostalgic and humor. Pays $40. Sometimes pays the expenses of writers on assignment.

Fiction: Adventure, experimental, horror, humorous, slice-of-life vignettes and suspense. No science fiction or fantasy. Buys 25 mss/year. Query.

Consumer Service and Business Opportunity

Some of these magazines are geared to investing earnings or starting a new business; others show how to make economical purchases. Publications for business executives and consumers interested in business topics are listed under Business and Finance. Those on how to run specific businesses are classified by category in the Trade section.

BUSINESS TODAY, Meridian Publishing Inc., Box 10010, Ogden UT 84409. (801)394-9446. Editor: Robyn Walker. 65% freelance written. Monthly magazine covering all aspects of business. Particularly interested in profiles of business personalities. Pays on acceptance. Publishes ms an average of 8 months after acceptance. Byline given. Buys first rights, second serial (reprint) rights and nonexclusive reprint rights. Computer printout submissions acceptable; prefers letter-quality to dot-matrix. Reports in 6 weeks. Sample copy for $1 and 9x12 SAE; writer's guidelines for legal-size SAE and 1 first class stamp. All requests for samples and guidelines should be addressed Attn: Editorial Assistant.

Nonfiction: General interest articles about employee relations, management principles, advertising methods and financial planning. Articles covering up-to-date practical business information are welcome. Cover stories are often profiles of people who have expertise and success in a specific aspect of business. Buys 40 mss/year. Query. Length: 1,000-1,400 words. Pays 15¢/word for first rights plus non-exclusive reprint rights. Payment for second rights is negotiable.

Photos: State availability of photos or send photos with query. Reviews 35mm or longer transparencies. Pays $35 for inside photo; pays $50 for cover photo. Captions, model releases and identification of subjects required.

Tips: "The key is a well-written query letter that: 1) demonstrates that the subject of the article is tried-and-true and has national appeal 2) shows that the article will have a clear, focused theme 3) outlines the availability (from writer or a photographer or a PR source) of top-quality color photos 4) gives evidence that the writer/photographer is a professional, even if a beginner."

CHANGING TIMES, The Kiplinger Magazine, 1729 H St. NW, Washington DC 20006. Editor: Ted Miller. Less than 10% freelance written. Prefers to work with published/established writers. For general, adult audience interested in personal finance and consumer information. Monthly. Circ. 1,350,000. Pays on acceptance. Publishes ms an average of 2 months after acceptance. Buys all rights. Reports in 1 month. Query for electronic submissions. Computer printout submissions acceptable; prefers letter-quality to dot-matrix. Thorough documentation required for fact-checking.

Nonfiction: "Most material is staff-written, but we accept some freelance." Query with clips of published work. Pays expenses of writers on assignment.

Tips: "We are looking for a heavy emphasis on personal finance topics."

CONSUMER ACTION NEWS, Suite 208, 1106 E. High St., Springfield OH 45505. (513)325-2001. Editor: Victor Pence. 10% freelance written. Eager to work with new/unpublished writers. A monthly newsletter circulated in the state of Ohio for readers who are interested in knowing how to handle any type of consumer complaint. "We handle consumer complaints and publish results in newsletter." Circ. 5,000. Pays on acceptance. Publishes ms an average of 4 months after acceptance. Byline given. Copyrighted. Buys one-time rights. Simultaneous queries, and simultaneous, photocopied, and previously published submissions OK. Computer printout submissions acceptable; prefers letter-quality to dot-matrix. Reports in 6 weeks.

Nonfiction: Send complete ms. No maximum length. Pays $10-100.

Tips: "Every area is open to freelancers. We want only experiences with complaints that name the company and people involved and the outcome. If the problem has not been solved, we will offer possible solutions to the problem anywhere in the U.S. and Canada at no charge."

CONSUMERS DIGEST MAGAZINE, Consumers Digest, Inc., 5705 N. Lincoln Ave., Chicago IL 60659. (312)275-3590. Executive Editor: Elliott H. McCleary. 75% freelance written. Prefers to work with published/established writers. Emphasizes anything of consumer interest. Monthly magazine. Circ. 1,000,000. Pays on acceptance. Publishes ms an average of 3 months after acceptance. Buys all rights. Computer printout submissions acceptable; prefers letter-quality to dot-matrix. Reports in 1 month. Free guidelines for SAE and 1 first class stamp to published writers only.

Nonfiction: Product-testing, evaluating; general interest (on advice to consumers, service, health, home, business, investments, insurance and money management); new products and travel. Query. Length: 1,200-3,000 words. Also buys shorter, more topical pieces (300-800 words) for Consumer Scope. Fees negotiable. First-time contributors usually are paid 25¢/word. Pays expenses of writers on assignment.

Tips: "Send short query with samples of published work. Assignments are made upon acceptance of comprehensive outline."

ECONOMIC FACTS, The National Research Bureau, Inc., 424 N. 3rd St., Burlington IA 52601. Editor: Rhonda Wilson. Editorial Supervisor: Doris J. Ruschill. 25% freelance written. Eager to work with new/unpublished writers; works with a small number of new/unpublished writers each year. Magazine for industrial workers of all ages. Published 4 times/year. Pays on publication. Publishes ms an average of 1 year after acceptance. Buys all rights. Byline given. Submit seasonal/holiday material 7 months in advance of issue date. Previously published submissions OK. Computer printout submissions acceptable; prefers letter-quality to dot-matrix. Reports in 1 week. Writer's guidelines for SASE.

Nonfiction: General interest (private enterprise, government data, graphs, taxes and health care). Buys 3-5 mss/year. Query with outline of article. Length: 400-600 words. Pays 4¢/word.

ENTREPRENEUR MAGAZINE, 2311 Pontius Ave., Los Angeles CA 90064. (213)478-0437. Publisher: Wellington Ewen. Editor: Rieva Lesonsky. 40% freelance written. "We are eager to work with any writer (new or established) who takes the time to see *Entrepreneur*'s special 'angle' and who turns in copy on time." For a readership looking for profitable opportunities in small businesses, as owners, franchisees. Monthly magazine with "tips and tactics on running a small business." Circ. 200,000. Pays on acceptance. Publishes ms an average of 3-5 months after acceptance. Buys all rights. Byline given. Submit seasonal/holiday material 6 months in advance of issue date. Photocopied submissions OK. Accepts electronic submissions; query for details. Computer printout submissions acceptable; prefers letter-quality to dot-matrix. Reports in 2 months. Sample copy $3; free writer's guidelines.

Nonfiction: How-to (in-depth start-up details on "hot" business opportunities like tanning parlors or computer stores). Buys 60-70 mss/year. Query with clips of published work. Length: 750-2,000 words. Payment varies.

Photos: "We need good b&w glossy prints or color transparencies to illustrate articles." Offers additional payment for photos accepted with ms. Uses 8x10 b&w glossy prints or standard color transparencies. Captions preferred. Buys all rights. Model release required.

Columns/Departments: Business Primer, News and Views. Query. Length: 200-500 words. Payment varies.

Tips: "We are upgrading our editorial slant and including more articles for people already established in their own businesses. It's rewarding to find a freelancer who reads the magazine *before* he/she submits a query. We get so many queries with the wrong angle. I can't stress enough the importance of reading and understanding our magazine and our audience before you write. We're looking for writers who can perceive the difference between *Entrepreneur* and 'other' business magazines."

FDA CONSUMER, 5600 Fishers Lane, Rockville MD 20857. (301)443-3220. Editor: William M. Rados. 20% freelance written. Prefers to work with experienced health and medical writers. Monthly magazine. December/January and July/August issues combined. For "all consumers of products regulated by the Food and Drug Administration." A federal government publication. Circ. 16,000. Pays after acceptance. Publishes ms an average of 3 months after acceptance. Byline given. Not copyrighted. Pays 50% kill fee. "All purchases automatically become part of public domain." Buys 10-20 freelance mss a year. "We cannot be responsible for any work by writer not agreed upon by prior contract." Electronic submissions OK via Wang or Macintosh. Computer printout submissions acceptable; prefers letter-quality to dot-matrix. Free sample copy.

Nonfiction: "Articles of an educational nature concerning purchase and use of *FDA regulated* products and specific FDA programs and actions to protect the consumer's health and pocketbook. Authoritative and official agency viewpoints emanating from agency policy and actions in administrating the Food, Drug and Cosmetic Act and a number of other statutes. All articles subject to clearance by the appropriate FDA experts as well as acceptance by the editor. Articles based on health topics with the proviso that the subjects be connected to food, drugs, medicine, medical devices, and other products regulated by FDA. All articles based on prior arrangement by contract." Query. Length: 2,000-2,500 words. Pays $1,000 average. Sometimes pays the expenses of writers on assignment.

Photos: B&w photos are purchased on assignment only.

Tips: "Besides reading the feature articles in *FDA Consumer*, a writer can best determine whether his/her style and expertise suit our needs by submitting a query letter, resume and sample clips for our review."

INCOME OPPORTUNITIES, 380 Lexington Ave., New York NY 10017. Editor: Stephen Wagner. Managing Editor: Paula Nichols. 90% freelance written. Works with a small number of new/unpublished writers each year. Monthly magazine. For all who are seeking business opportunities, full- or part-time. Publishes ms an average of 5 months after acceptance. Buys all rights. Two special directory issues contain articles on selling techniques, mail order, import/export, franchising and business ideas. Query for details on electronic submissions. Computer printout submissions acceptable. Reports in 2 weeks.

Nonfiction and Photos: Regularly covered are such subjects as mail order, home business, direct selling, franchising, party plans, selling techniques and the marketing of handcrafted or homecrafted products. Wanted are ideas for the aspiring entrepreneur; examples of successful business methods that might be duplicated. No material that is purely inspirational. Buys 50-60 mss/year. Query with outline of article development. Length: 800 words for a short; 2,000-3,000 words for a major article. "Payment rates vary according to length and quality of the submission." Sometimes pays expenses of writers on assignment.

Tips: "Study recent issues of the magazine. Best bets for newcomers: Interview-based report on a successful small business venture."

PUBLIC CITIZEN, Public Citizen, Inc., Box 19404, Washington DC 20036. Editor: Catherine Baker. 20% freelance written. Prefers to work with published/established writers. Bimonthly magazine covering consumer issues for "contributors to Public Citizen, a consortium of five consumer groups established by Ralph Nader in the public interest: Congress Watch, the Health Research Group, the Critical Mass Energy Project, the Litigation Group, and the Tax Reform Group. Our readers have joined Public Citizen because they believe the consumer should have a voice in the products he or she buys, the quality of our environment, good government, and citizen rights in our democracy." Circ. 42,000. Pays on publication. Publishes ms an average of 3 months after acceptance. Byline given. Buys first North American serial rights, second serial (reprint) rights and simultaneous rights. Submit seasonal/holiday material 3 months in advance. Query for electronic submission requirements. Computer printout submissions acceptable; prefers letter-quality to dot-matrix. Reports in 1 month on queries; 2 months on mss. Sample copy available.

Nonfiction: Exposé (of government waste and inaction and corporate wrongdoing); general interest (features on how consumer groups are helping themselves); how-to (start consumer groups such as co-ops, etc.); interview/profile (of business or consumer leaders, or of government officials in positions that affect consumers); and photo feature (dealing with consumer power). "We are looking for stories that go to the heart of an issue and explain how it affects individuals. Articles must be in-depth investigations that expose poor business practices or bad government or that call attention to positive accomplishments. Send us stories that consumers will feel they learned something important from or that they can gain inspiration from to continue the fight for consumer rights. All facts are double checked by our fact-checkers." No "fillers, jokes or puzzles." Query or send complete ms. Length: 500-10,000 words. Pays $750 maximum/article. Sometimes pays the expenses of writers on assignment.

Photos: State availability of photos. Reviews 5x7 b&w prints. "Photos are paid for with payment for ms." Captions required. Buys one-time rights.

Columns/Departments: Reliable Sources ("book reviews"). Query or send complete ms—"no clips." Length: 500-1,000 words. Pays $125 maximum/article.

Tips: No first-person articles, political rhetoric, or "mood" pieces; *Public Citizen* is a highly factual advocacy magazine. Knowledge of the public interest movement, consumer issues, and Washington politics is a plus.

TOWERS CLUB, USA NEWSLETTER, The Original Information-By-Mail, Direct-Marketing Newsletter, TOWERS Club Press, Box 2038, Vancouver WA 98668. (206)574-3084. Editor: Jerry Buchanan. 5-

10% freelance written. Works with a small number of new/unpublished writers each year. Newsletter published 10 times/year (not published in August or December) covering entrepreneurism (especially selling useful information by mail). Circ. 5,000. Pays on publication. Publishes ms an average of 2 months after acceptance. Byline given. Buys one-time rights. Submit seasonal/holiday material 10 weeks in advance. Simultaneous, photocopied, and previously published submissions OK. Computer printout submissions or 7'' diskettes with TRS-80 Scriptsit software OK. Reports in 2 weeks. Sample copy for $3 and 6x9 SAE with 56¢ postage.

Nonfiction: Exposé (of mail order fraud); how-to (personal experience in self-publishing and marketing); book reviews of new self-published nonfiction how-to-do-it books (must include name and address of author). "Welcomes well-written articles of successful self-publishing/marketing ventures. Must be current, and preferably written by the person who actually did the work and reaped the rewards. There's very little we will not consider, *if* it pertains to unique money-making enterprises that can be operated from the home." Buys 10 mss/year. Send complete ms. Length: 500-1,000 words. Pays $10-35. Pays extra for b&w photo and bonus for excellence in longer manuscript.

Tips: "The most frequent mistake made by writers in completing an article for us is that they think they can simply rewrite a newspaper article and be accepted. That is only the start. We want them to find the article about a successful self-publishing enterprise, and then go out and interview the principal for a more detailed how-to article, including names and addresses. We prefer that writer actually interview a successful self-publisher. Articles should include how idea first came to subject; how they implemented and financed and promoted the project; how long it took to show a profit and some of the stumbling blocks they overcame; how many persons participated in the production and promotion; and how much money was invested (approximately) and other pertinent how-to elements of the story. Glossy photos (b&w) of principals at work in their offices will help sell article."

VENTURE, For Entrepreneurial Business Owners and Investors, Venture Magazine, Inc., 521 5th Ave., New York NY 10175. (212)682-7373. Editor: Jeannie Mandelker. 80% freelance written. Prefers to work with published/established writers. Monthly magazine about entrepreneurs for people owning their own businesses, starting new businesses or investing in entrepreneurial businesses. Publishes ms an average of 3 months after acceptance. Query for electronic submission. Computer printout submissions OK; prefers letter-quality to dot-matrix.

Nonfiction: "We use current news on new business areas, venture capital and entrepreneurs by assignment only." No unsolicited material. Query. Pays expenses of writers on assignment.

—————— Detective and Crime

Fans of detective stories want to read accounts of actual criminal cases and espionage. The following magazines specialize in nonfiction, but a few buy some fiction. Markets specializing in crime fiction are listed under Mystery publications.

DETECTIVE CASES, Detective Files Group, 1350 Sherbrooke St. W., Montreal, Quebec H3G 1J1 Canada. Editor-in-Chief: Dominick A. Merle. Bimonthly magazine. See *Detective Files*.

DETECTIVE DRAGNET, Detective Files Group, 1350 Sherbrooke St. W., Montreal, Quebec H3G 1J1 Canada. Editor-in-Chief: Dominick A. Merle. Bimonthly magazine; 72 pages. See *Detective Files*.

DETECTIVE FILES, Detective Files Group, 1350 Sherbrooke St. W., Montreal, Quebec H3G 1J1 Canada. Editor-in-Chief: Dominick A. Merle. 100% freelance written. Bimonthly magazine; 72 pages. Pays on acceptance. Publishes ms an average of 3 months after acceptance. Buys all rights. Photocopied submissions OK. Include international reply coupons. Reports in 1 month. Free sample copy and writer's guidelines.

Nonfiction: True crime stories. "Do a thorough job; don't double-sell (sell the same article to more than one market); and deliver, and you can have a steady market. Neatness, clarity and pace will help you make the sale." Query. Length: 3,500-6,000 words. Pays $250-350.

Photos: Purchased with accompanying ms; no additional payment.

ESPIONAGE MAGAZINE, Leo II Publications, Ltd., Box 1184, Teaneck NJ 07666. (201)836-9177. Editor: Jackie Lewis. 90% freelance written. A bimonthly magazine "totally devoted to spy stories of international intrigue, suspense, blackmail, confused loyalties, deception, and other things immoral. Fiction and nonfiction stories by top writers in the world of espionage." Pays on publication. Publishes ms usually many months after acceptance. Byline given. Buys all rights, first North American serial rights and second serial (reprint) rights. Photocopied and previously published submissions OK. Computer printout submissions acceptable; no dot-matrix. Reports in about 1 month. Sample copy $3, 6x9 SAE, and 90¢ postage; writer's guidelines for business size SAE and 1 first class stamp.

Nonfiction: Spy oriented only: book excerpts, exposé, historical/nostalgic, interview/profile and personal experience. Anything relating to spy stories. Buys approximately 10 mss/year. Send complete ms. Length: 1,000-10,000 words. Pays 5-6¢/word depending on amount of editing needed. Sometimes pays the expenses of writers on assignment.

Fiction: Spy oriented only: adventure, condensed novels, confession, fantasy, historical, humorous, mystery, excerpts from published novels, romance, science fiction, suspense and western. Anything relating to intrigue, international suspense about spies. Buys 40 mss/year. Send complete ms. Length: 1,000-10,000 words. Pays 5-6¢/word depending on the amount of editing needed.

Fillers: Spy oriented only: anecdotes. Length: 20-100 words. Pays $5.

Tips: "We are interested in any writer of fiction or nonfiction who writes spy stories. We will not accept explicit sex or gratuitous gore." First-person stories are preferred, but stories from any perspective will be considered. Heroes can be any age, gender, nationality, or walk of life. "Send *no* subject, however, unless it is spy oriented."

FRONT PAGE DETECTIVE, Official Detective Group, R.G.H. Publishing Corp., 20th Floor, 460 W. 34th St., New York NY 10001. (212)947-6500. Editor: Rose Mandelsberg. Managing Editor: Halima Nooradeen. Monthly magazine covering true crime stories. "We publish complete murder stories with an emphasis on all phases of police work that went into solving the case from embryonic stage of murder to completion (trial and conviction)." Pays on acceptance. Publishes ms an average of 2 months after acceptance. Byline given. Buys first North American serial rights. Query for electronic submissions. Computer printout submissions OK; prefers letter-quality. Reports in 2 weeks on queries; 3 weeks on manuscripts. Free writer's guidelines.

Nonfiction: "True crime stories with a lot of detective work and mystery." The focus of these two publications is similar to the others in the Official Detective Group. "We now use post-trial stories; rarely are pre-trial ones published." Buys 350 mss/year. Query. Length: 5,000-11,000 words. Pays $250-500. Pays expenses of writers on assignment.

Photos: Send photos with submission of mss. Reviews contact sheets. Captions and identification of subjects required. Offers $12.50 per photo used. Buys all rights.

Tips: "We are always looking to develop new writers from the United States and abroad. Read the five detective magazines: *True Detective, Official Detective, Master Detective, Inside Detective* and *Front Page Detective*; know police procedures; and familiarize yourself with district attorneys, captains, detectives, etc."

HEADQUARTERS DETECTIVE, Detective Files Group, 1350 Sherbrooke St. W., Montreal, Quebec H3G 1J1 Canada. Editor-in-Chief: Dominick A. Merle. Bimonthly magazine; 72 pages. See *Detective Files*.

‡**INSIDE DETECTIVE**, Official Detective Group, R.G.H. Publishing Corp., 460 W. 34th St., New York NY 10001. (212)947-6500. Editor: Rose Mandelsberg. Managing Editor: Robyn Burland. Monthly magazine. Circ. 90,000. Pays on acceptance. Publishes ms an average of 3 months after acceptance. Byline given. Buys first rights and one-time world rights. Query for electronic submissions. Computer printout submissions OK. Reports in 2 weeks. Free writer's guidelines.

Nonfiction: Buys 120 mss/year. Query. Pays $250. Length: 5,000-6,000 words (approx. 20 typed pages).

MASTER DETECTIVE, Official Detective Group, R.G.H. Publishing Corp., 460 W. 34th St., New York NY 10001. Editor-in-Chief: Art Crockett. Managing Editor: Christos K. Ziros. 100% freelance written. Bimonthly. Circ. 350,000. Buys 9 mss/issue. See *Official Detective*.

OFFICIAL DETECTIVE, Official Detective Group, R.G.H. Publishing Corp., 460 W. 34th St., New York NY 10001. (212)947-6500. Editor-in-Chief: Art Crockett. Managing Editor: Christos Mirtsopoulos. 100% freelance written. Monthly magazine "for detective story or police buffs whose tastes run to *true*, rather than fictional crime/mysteries." Circ. 500,000. Pays on acceptance. Buys all rights. Byline given. Reports in 2 weeks.

Nonfiction: "Only *fact* detective stories. We are actively trying to develop new writers, and we'll work closely with those who show promise and can take the discipline required by our material. It's not difficult to write, but it demands meticulous attention to facts, truth, clarity, detail. Queries are essential with us, but I'd say the quickest rejection goes to the writer who sends in a story on a case that should never have been written for us because it lacks the most important ingredient, namely solid, superlative detective work. We also dislike pieces with multiple defendants, unless all have been convicted." Buys 150 mss/year. Query. Length: 5,000-6,000 words. Pays $250 ($500 for double-length mss).

Photos: Purchased with accompanying mss. Captions required. Send prints for inside use; transparencies for covers. Pays $12.50 minimum for 4 x 5 b&w glossy prints. Pays $200 minimum for 2¼x2¼ or 35mm transparencies. Model release required for color photos used on cover.

Tips: Send a detailed query on the case to be submitted. Include: locale; victim's name; type of crime; suspect's name; status of the case (indictment, trial concluded, disposition, etc.); amount and quality of detective work; dates; and availability and number of pictures. "We're always impressed by details of the writer's credentials."

STARTLING DETECTIVE, Detective Files Group, 1350 Sherbrooke St. W., Montreal, Quebec H3G 1J1 Canada. Editor-in-Chief: Dominick A. Merle. Bimonthly magazine; 72 pages. See *Detective Files*.

TRUE DETECTIVE, Official Detective Group, R.G.H. Publishing Corp., 460 W. 34th St., New York NY 10001. (212)947-6500. Editor-in-Chief: Art Crockett. Managing Editor: Christos Mirtsopoulos. Monthly. Circ. 500,000. Buys 10 mss/issue. Byline given.

TRUE POLICE CASES, Detective Files Group, 1350 Sherbrooke St. W., Montreal, Quebec H3G 1J1 Canada. Editor-in-Chief: Dominick A. Merle. Bimonthly magazine; 72 pages. Buys all rights. See *Detective Files*.

Disabilities

Some of these magazines are written for disabled individuals; others are designed for parents and professionals who work with the disabled. Many feature music, literature and fine arts produced by persons with physical disabilities. On some, writing is restricted to disabled authors. All avoid sentimental treatises in favor of helpful how-to articles on solving problems and overcoming barriers.

DIALOGUE, The Magazine for the Visually Impaired, Dialogue Publications, Inc., 3100 Oak Park Ave., Berwyn IL 60402. (312)749-1908. Editor: Bonnie Miller. 50% freelance written. Works with published/established writers and a small number of new/unpublished writers each year. Quarterly magazine of issues, topics and opportunities related to the visually impaired. Pays on acceptance. Publishes ms an average of 6 months after acceptance. Byline given. Buys all rights "with generous reprint rights." Submit seasonal/holiday material 6 months in advance. Photocopied submissions OK. Computer printout submissions acceptable; no dot-matrix. Reports in 2 weeks on queries; 1 month on mss. Free sample copy to visually impaired writers. Writer's guidelines in print for business size SAE and 1 first class stamp; send a 60-minute cassette for guidelines on tape.

Nonfiction: "Writers should indicate nature and severity of visual handicap." How-to (cope with various aspects of blindness); humor; interview/profile; new product (of interest to visually impaired); opinion; personal experience; technical (adaptations for use without sight); travel (personal experiences of visually impaired travelers); and first person articles about careers in which individual blind persons have succeeded. No "aren't blind people wonderful" articles; articles that are slanted towards sighted general audience. Buys 60 mss/year. Query with published clips or submit complete ms. Length: 3,000 words maximum. Prefers shorter lengths but will use longer articles if subject warrants. Pays $10-50. Sometimes pays the expenses of writers on assignment.

Columns/Departments: ABAPITA ("Ain't Blindness a Pain in the Anatomy")—short anecdotes relating to blindness; Recipe Round-Up; Around the House (household hints); Vox Pop (see magazine); Puzzle Box (see magazine and guidelines); book reviews of books written by visually impaired authors; Beyond the Armchair (travel personal experience); and Backscratcher (a column of questions, answers, hints). Buys 80 mss/year. Send complete ms. Payment varies.

Fiction: "Writers should state nature and severity of visual handicap." Adventure, fantasy, historical, humorous, mainstream, mystery, science fiction, and suspense. No plotless fiction or stories with unbelievable characters; no horror; no explicit sex and no vulgar language. Buys 12 mss/year. Send complete ms. Length: 3,000 words maximum; shorter lengths preferred. Pays $10-50.

Poetry: "Writers should indicate nature and severity of visual impairment." Free verse, haiku, and traditional. No religious poetry or any poetry with more than 20 lines. Buys 30 poems/year. Submit maximum 3 poems. Length: 20 lines maximum. Pays in contributor's copies.

Fillers: Jokes, anecdotes, and short humor. Buys few mss/year. Length: 100 words maximum. Payment varies.

Tips: "*Dialogue* cannot consider manuscripts from authors with 20/20 vision or those who can read regular print with ordinary glasses. Any person unable to read ordinary print who has helpful information to share with others in this category will find a ready market. We believe that blind people are capable, competent, responsible citizens, and the material we publish reflects this view. This is not to say we never sound a negative note, but criticism should be constructive. The writer sometimes has a better chance of breaking in at our publication with short articles and fillers. We are interested in material that is written for a general-interest magazine with visually impaired readers. As we move into a cassette version, we must tighten our format, this means fewer articles used, therefore they must be of the highest quality. We are *not* interested in scholarly journal-type articles; 'amazing blind people I have known,' articles written by sighted writers; articles and fiction that exceed our 3,000-word maximum length; and material that is too regional to appeal to an international audience. No manuscript can be considered without a statement of visual impairment, nor can it be returned without a SASE."

HANDICAP NEWS, Burns Enterprises, #342, 3060 E. Bridge St., Brighton CO 80601. (303)659-4463. Editor/Publisher: Phyllis Burns. 30% freelance written. Eager to work with new/unpublished writers and any handicapped writer. Monthly newsletter on handicaps. "*Handicap News* is written for people with handicaps and those people working with them. Material should be written in an 'upbeat' mode." Circ. 500. Pays on publication. Publishes ms an average of 7 months after acceptance. Credit is given for pieces written by handicapped people. In the news section, no credit is given. Not copyrighted. Buys one-time rights. Simultaneous, photocopied, and previously published submissions OK. Reports in 1 month. Sample copy $2 with #10 SAE and 1 first class stamp. Writer's guidelines with sample copy only.

Nonfiction: How-to, humor, inspiration, medical breakthroughs, new product, opinion, personal experience, physical/occupation therapy developments, research findings, technical and travel. "We request a copy of the study, report or news article which was the source of information. We are sometimes asked for more information by the readers so we must have a file copy." No pessimistic articles. Buys 10-20 mss/year. Send complete ms. Length: 75-300 words. Pays in 2 copies of the newsletter in which the article appeared.

Fiction: Fantasy, historical, humorous, mainstream, religious, science fiction and western. "All fiction must deal directly with the subject (handicapped people and how they respond to certain conditions.) This section must be written by handicapped people or their families." Query. Length: 500-800 words. Pays in 2 copies of publication in which the article appeared.

Poetry: Will consider any type, length or style as long as it is written by handicapped people or their families. Nothing pessimistic or downbeat. Buys 20-30/year. Submit maximum 4 poems. Pays in 2 copies.

Tips: "In the medical, product, travel, and therapy section, anyone may study the format and submit the material with their documentation. In the poems, experiences, inspirational, and fiction, the material must come from the handicapped person and family. (A letter must be enclosed stating who is handicapped, etc.) In the latter, we will accept almost any material as long as it falls within the guidelines and is optimistic. We look forward to receiving material from handicapped writers but wish more of them would learn the basic format to sending articles to publications. We do not appreciate paying postage on material we receive from you. If possible, type it. If not, write in a 'readable' manner."

KALEIDOSCOPE, International Magazine of Literature, Fine Arts, and Disability, Kaleidoscope Press, 326 Locust St., Akron OH 44302. (216)762-9755, ext. 27. Editor: Darshan C. Perusek, Ph.D. 75% freelance written. Works with a small number of new/unpublished writers each year; eager to work with new/unpublished writers. Semiannual magazine with international collection of literature and art by disabled/nondisabled people for writers, artists, and anyone interested in fine art and literature and disability. Circ. 1,500. Pays on publication. Publishes ms an average of 6 months after acceptance. Byline given. Buys first North American serial rights. Simultaneous queries, and photocopied and previously published submissions OK. Computer printout submissions acceptable; no dot-matrix. Reports in 3-6 months. Free sample copy; writer's guidelines for SAE and 1 first class stamp.

Nonfiction: Book excerpts, reviews, historical/nostalgic, humor, articles spotlighting arts/disability, interview/profile (on prominent disabled people in the arts), opinion, the craft of fiction, personal experience, photo feature and travel. Publishes 14 mss/year. Query with clips if available or send complete ms. Length: 5,000 words maximum. Payment of up to $25. All contributors receive 3 complimentary copies.

Photos: Pays up to $25/photo. Reviews 3x5, 5x7, 8x10 b&w and color prints. Captions and identification of subjects required.

Fiction: Experimental, fantasy, historical, horror, humorous, mainstream, mystery, romance, science fiction, suspense. Short stories, plays, novel excerpts. Publishes 16 mss/year; purchases 4/year. Query with clips if available or send complete ms. Length: 5,000 words maximum.

Poetry: Avant-garde, free verse, haiku, light verse and traditional. Publishes 30 poems/year. Submit maximum 6 poems. Pays up to $50 for a body of work.

Fillers: Anecdotes and short humor. Length: open.

Tips: "Avoid the maudlin and sentimental. Treatment of subject should be fresh, original and thoughtful; humor welcome. Fiction and poetry are open to freelancers. For fiction, have strong, believable characterizations. Poetry should be vivid and free of cliches. Non-disabled writers who write disability-related literature are considered."

‡**MAINSTREAM, Magazine of the Able-Disabled**, Exploding Myths, Inc., 2973 Beech St., San Diego CA 92102. (619)234-3138. Editor: Cyndi Jones. 100% freelance written. Eager to develop writers who have a positive outlook on disability. A magazine published 10 times/year (monthly except January and June) covering disability-related topics, geared to disabled consumers. Circ. 15,500. Pays on publication. Publishes ms an average of 3 months after acceptance. Byline given. Buys all rights. Submit seasonal/holiday material 4 months in advance. Computer printout submissions OK; prefers letter-quality to dot-matrix. Reports in 2 months. Sample copy $2.75. Writer's guidelines for #10 SAE with 1 first class stamp.

Nonfiction: Book excerpts, exposé, how-to (daily independent living tips), humor, interview/profile, personal experience (dealing with problems/solutions), photo feature, technical, travel and legislation. "All must be disability-related, directed to disabled consumers." No articles on " 'my favorite disabled character', my most inspirational disabled person, poster child stories." Buys 50 mss/year. Query with or without published clips, or send complete ms. Length: 6-12 pages. Pays $50-100. May pay subscription if writer requests. Sometimes pays the expenses of writers on assignment by prior arrangement.

Photos: State availability of photos with submission. Reviews contact sheets, 1½x¾ transparencies and 5x7 or larger prints. Offers $5-25 per b&w photo. Captions and identification of subjects required. Buys all rights.

Columns/Departments: Creative Solutions (unusual solutions to common aggravating problems); Personal Page (deals with personal relations: dating, meeting people). Buys 10 mss/year. Send complete ms. Length: 500-800 words. Pays $25-50.

Fiction: Humorous. Must be disability-related. Buys 4 mss/year. Send complete ms. Length: 800-1,200 words. Pays $50-100.

Tips: "It seems that politics and disability are becoming more important."

A POSITIVE APPROACH, A National Magazine for the Physically Challenged, 1600 Malone St., Municipal Airport, Millville NJ 08332. (609)327-4040. Editor: Patricia M. Johnson. 80% freelance written. A bimonthly magazine for the physically disabled/handicapped. "We're a positive profile on living and for the creation of a barrier-free lifestyle. Each profile is aimed at encouraging others with that same handicap to better their situations and environments. Covers all disabilities." Estab. 1986. Circ. 150,000. Pays on publication. Publishes ms an average of 2 months after acceptance. Byline given. Buys one-time rights and second serial (reprint) rights. Submit seasonal/holiday material 2-3 months in advance. Simultaneous, photocopied and previously published submissions OK. Computer printout submissions acceptable; no dot-matrix. Reports in 2 weeks on queries; 3 weeks on mss. Sample copy $2; free writer's guidelines.

Nonfiction: Ann Miller, articles editor. Book excerpts, general interest, how-to (make life more accessible), humor, inspirational, interview/profile, personal experience, photo feature and travel (for the disabled). No depressing, poorly researched, death and dying articles. Buys 60-70 mss/year. Query with or without published clips, or send complete ms. Length: 500-800 words. Pays 20¢/word for assigned articles; pays 10¢/word for unsolicited articles. Sometimes pays the expenses of writers on assignment.

Photos: State availability of photos with submission. Reviews 3x5 or larger prints. Offers $5/photo. Identification of subjects required. Buys one-time rights.

Columns/Departments: Ann Miller, column/department editor. Hair Styling (easy hairdo for the disabled), 500 words; Wardrobe (fashionable clothing/easy dressing), 500 words; Travel (accessible travel throughout U.S. and Europe), 500-700 words; Workshops (employment, self-improvement), 500 words; and Profiles (positive approach on life with goals), 500 words. Buys 30 mss/year. Query with published clips or send complete ms. Pays 10¢/word.

Tips: "Research newspapers. Learn what problems exist for the physically challenged. Know that they want to better their lifestyles and get on with their lives to the best of their abilities. Learn their assets and write on what they can do and not on what can't be done! The area of our publication most open to freelancers is profiles."

‡**WAYS**, First Publications, Inc., Box 5072, Evanston IL 60204. (312)869-7210. Editor: Mark Russell. Managing Editor: Tom Terez. A bimonthly magazine written for parents/professionals who care for people who are mentally retarded, developmentally disabled, or mentally ill. Pays on publication. Byline given. Offers 25% kill fee. Buys all rights. Submit seasonal/holiday material 4-5 months in advance. Photocopied submissions OK. Computer printout submissions OK; prefers letter-quality. Reports in 1 month on queries. Sample copy for 9x12 SAE with $1.24 postage.

Nonfiction: General interest, how-to, interview/profile, personal experience. Buys 50 mss/year. Query with published clips, or send complete ms. Length: 800-3,000 words. Pays $100-600. Pays with contributor copies "if writer prefers." Sometimes pays the expenses of writers on assignment.

Photos: Send photos with submission. Reviews contact sheets, negatives, transparencies and prints. Offers no additional payment for photos accepted with ms. Model releases and identification of subjects required. Buys one-time rights.

Columns/Departments: Close-up (personal profile of unusual person); Health (leading edge in medicine); Money, all 1,000 words. Buys 15 mss/year. Query with published clips, or send complete ms. Length: 800-1,500 words. Pays $75-300.

Entertainment

This category's publications cover live, filmed or videotaped entertainment, including home video, TV, dance, theater and adult entertainment. Besides celebrity interviews, most publications want solid reporting on trends and upcoming productions. For those publications with an emphasis on music and musicians, see the Music section. For markets covering video games, see Games and Puzzles.

AMERICAN FILM, American Film Institute, MD Publications, 3 E. 54th St., New York NY 10022. Editor: Peter Biskind. 80% freelance written. Prefers to work with published/established writers; works with small number of new/unpublished writers each year. For film professionals, students, teachers, film enthusiasts, culturally oriented readers. Monthly magazine. Circ. 140,000. Buys first North American serial rights, and first and second rights to the same material. Pays kill fee. Byline given. Pays 3 months after acceptance. Publishes ms an average of 4 months after acceptance. Will consider photocopied submissions. Computer printout submissions acceptable; prefers letter-quality to dot-matrix. Submit material 3 months in advance. Reports in 1 month. Sample copy $2.50.

Nonfiction: In-depth articles on film and television-related subjects. "Our articles require expertise and first-rate writing ability." Buys informational, profile, historical and "think" pieces. No film reviews. Buys 10 unsolicited mss/year. Query. Length: 500-4,000 words. Pays $100-1,500. Pays expenses of writers on assignment.

Tips: "No 'my favorite moments in films' or other 'fanzine' type pieces."

AMERICAN SQUAREDANCE, Burdick Enterprises, Box 488, Huron OH 44839. (419)433-2188. Editors: Stan and Cathie Burdick. 10% freelance written. Works with a small number of new/unpublished writers each year; eager to work with new/unpublished writers. Monthly magazine of interviews, reviews, topics of interest to the modern square dancer. Circ. 23,000. Pays on publication. Publishes ms an average of 3-6 months after acceptance. Byline given. Buys all rights. Submit seasonal/holiday material 3 months in advance. Computer printout submissions acceptable; prefers letter-quality to dot-matrix. Reports in 2 weeks on queries. Sample copy for 6x9 SAE; free writer's guidelines.

Nonfiction: General interest, historical/nostalgic, humor, inspirational, interview/profile, new product, opinion, personal experience, photo feature, travel. Must deal with square dance. Buys 6 mss/year. Send complete ms. Length: 1,000-1,500 words. Pays $10-35.

Photos: Send photos with ms. Reviews b&w prints. Captions and identification of subjects required.

Fiction: Subject related to square dancing only. Buys 1-2 mss/year. Send complete ms. Length: 2,000-2,500 words. Pays $25-35.

Poetry: Avant-garde, free verse, haiku, light verse, traditional. Square dancing subjects only. Buys 6 poems/year. Submit maximum 3 poems. Pays $1 for 1st 4 lines; $1/verse thereafter.

ARTSLINE, G/F Publications, Inc., 2518 Western Ave., Seattle WA 98121. (206)441-0786. Executive Editor: Sonia Grunberg. Editor: Alice Copp Smith. 80% freelance written. Monthly arts magazine serving as program magazine for seven Seattle-Tacoma theatres, concert and dance presenters. "We feature performing and visual arts nationwide but with an emphasis on the Pacific Northwest." Circ. 73,000. Pays on acceptance. Publishes ms an average of 4 months after acceptance. Byline given. Offers 50% kill fee. Buys first North American serial rights. Submit seasonal/holiday material 6 months in advance. Simultaneous queries and photocopied submissions OK. Computer printout submissions acceptable; prefers letter-quality to dot-matrix. Reports in 3 weeks. Sample copy for 9x12 SAE and 3 first class stamps; writer's guidelines for SASE.

Nonfiction: Book excerpts; humor; interview/profile (arts-related only); opinion (arts-related only); photo feature (arts-related only); and performing or visual arts features. No crafts; no arts pieces of regional interest only, when region is not Pacific Northwest. Buys 18 features/year. Query with or without published clips or send complete ms. Length: 1,500-2,000 words. Pays $150-200.

Photos: Send photos with query or ms. Reviews b&w contact sheets. Pays $25-50 for 35mm or 4x5 color transparencies; $25-50 for 8x10 b&w prints. Captions and identification of subjects required. Buys one-time rights. Photo credit given.

Fillers: Jokes, anecdotes, short humor (arts-related only). Length: 150 words maximum.

Tips: "A freelancer can best break in to our publication by sending well-written material that fits our format. Feature articles are most open to freelancers. First submission from a writer new to us has to be on speculation; thereafter, we're willing to assign. Know your subject and the Northwest arts scene. Be aware of the increasing sophistication of Pacific Northwest readers and their strong support of the arts."

‡CINEFANTASTIQUE MAGAZINE, The review of horror, fantasy and science fiction films, Box 270, Oak Park IL 60303. (312)366-5566. Editor: Frederick S. Clarke. 100% freelance written. Eager to work with new/unpublished writers. A bimonthly magazine covering horror, fantasy and science fiction films. Circ. 25,000. Pays on publication. Publishes ms an average of 6 months after acceptance. Byline given. Buys all magazine rights. Simultaneous queries and photocopied submissions OK. Computer printout submissions acceptable. Sample copy for $2 and 9x12 SAE. Reports in 2 months or longer.

Nonfiction: Historical/nostalgic (retrospects of film classics); interview/profile (film personalities); new product (new film projects); opinion (film reviews, critical essays); technical (how films are made). Buys 100-125 mss/year. Query with published clips. Length: 1,000-10,000 words. Sometimes pays the expenses of writers on assignment.

Photos: State availability of photos with query letter or ms.

Tips: "Develop original story suggestions; develop access to film industry personnel; submit reviews that show a perceptive point-of-view."

DALLAS OBSERVER, Observer Publications, Box 190289, Dallas TX 75219. (214)521-9450. Editor: Bob Walton. 50% freelance written. Weekly tabloid covering local news, arts, lifestyle issues and entertainment. Circ. 70,000. Pays on publication. Publishes ms an average of 2 months after acceptance. Byline given. Offers 50% kill fee. Buys first serial rights. Submit seasonal/holiday material 2 months in advance. Simultaneous queries and photocopied submissions OK. Computer printout submissions acceptable; prefers letter-quality to dot-matrix. Reports in 1 month. Sample copy for $1.50, 8x10 SAE and 5 first class stamps.

Nonfiction: Interview/profile (Dallas only) and arts features. "Write intelligently about local Dallas arts and entertainment subjects." Buys 400 mss/year. Query with published clips. Length: 500-5,000 words. Pays $20-400.

Columns/Departments: Local Dallas arts and entertainment news. Buys 100 mss/year. Query with published clips. Length: 500-1,000 words. Pays $20-100.

Tips: "Freelancers can best break in at our publication with thought-provoking essays or short articles."

‡DANCE MAGAZINE, 33 W. 60th St., New York NY 10023. (212)245-9050. Editor-in-Chief: William Como. Managing Editor: Richard Philip. 25% freelance written. Monthly magazine covering dance. Circ. 51,000. Pays on publication. Byline given. Offers up to $150 kill fee (varies). Makes work-for-hire assignments. Submit seasonal/holiday material 3 months in advance. Computer printout submission OK; no dot-matrix. Reports in "weeks." Sample copy and writer's guidelines for 8x10 SAE.

Nonfiction: Interview/profile. Publishes annual video issue. Buys 24 mss/year. Query with or without published clips, or send complete ms. Length: 300-1,500 words. Pays $15-350. Sometimes pays expenses of writers on assignment.

Photos: State availability of photos with submission. Reviews transparencies and prints. Offers $15-285/photo. Captions and identification of subjects required. Buys one-time rights.

Columns/Departments: News Editor: Gary Parks. Presstime News (topical, short articles on current dance world events) 150-400 words. Buys 24 mss/year. Query with published clips. Pays $20-75.

Tips: Writers must have "thorough knowledge of dance and take a sophisticated approach."

DANCE TEACHER NOW, SMW Communications, Inc., University Mall, Suite 2, 803 Russell Blvd., Davis CA 95616. (916)756-6222. Publisher: Susan M. Wershing. Editor: Martin A. David. 75% freelance written. Works with small number of new/unpublished writers each year. Magazine published 9 times/year for professional teachers of ballet, modern, jazz, tap, ballroom, and fitness dance in private studios, college departments, fitness centers, etc. Circ. 6,000. Average issue includes 6-8 feature articles, departments, and calendar sections. Pays on publication but hopes to return to "on acceptance" soon. Byline given. Buys all rights, "but we are reasonable as long as a writer is not reselling to our competitors." Submit seasonal material 6 months in advance. Query for electronic submissions. Computer printout submissions acceptable, "as long as the cover letter assures us the author is not shotgunning the article to a dozen publications at once"; no dot matrix. Reports in 2 months. Sample copy $2.25; writer's guidelines for SASE.

Nonfiction: Dance techniques, legal issues, health and dance injuries, business, advertising, taxes and insurance, curricula, student/teacher relations, government grants, studio equipment, concerts and recitals, competitions, departmental budgets, etc. "The writer must choose subject matter suitable to the knowledgeable, professional people our readers are." Buys 4-6 mss/issue. Query with published clips. Length: 1,000-3,000 words. Pays $100-300.

Photos: Photos to accompany articles only. Pays $20 maximum for 5x7 b&w glossy prints. Model releases required.

Columns/Departments: Practical Tips (3-4 paragraphs, short items of immediate practical use to the teacher) and Ballroom Technique.

Tips: "We like complete reportage of the material with all the specifics, but personalized with direct quotes and anecdotes. The writer should speak one-to-one to the reader but keep the national character of the magazine in mind. To achieve the practical quality in each article, the most important question in any interview is 'How?' We do not want consumer magazine personality profiles. Articles must include material of practical value to the reader. We do not want philosophical or 'artsy' articles; straightforward reporting only."

DIAL, The Magazine for Public Television, East/West Network, 34 E. 51st St., New York NY 10022. (212)888-5900. Editor: Lisa Schwarzbaum. 25% freelance written. Prefers to work with published/established writers. Monthly magazine covering public television. "*Dial* goes to 1.2 million subscribers to public television in 12 cities: New York, Boston, Washington D.C., Los Angeles, Dallas, Seattle, Tampa, Portland, Miami, Salt Lake City, Indianapolis and New Orleans." Pays on acceptance. Publishes ms an average of 2 months after acceptance. Byline given. Offers 25% kill fee. Buys first North American serial rights and promotional rights. Computer printout submissions acceptable; no dot-matrix. Reports in 1 month.

Nonfiction: "All material must have some connection with public television programming." Interview/profile; background pieces on shows. "A freelancer can best break in to our publication by being aware of upcoming public television programming." Query with published clips. Direct queries to editor-in-chief. Length: 500-800 words. Pays $500-750.

Tips: "Watch public television, read *Dial*, and get an informed sense of both. We're running shorter pieces—400-700 words."

DRAMATICS MAGAZINE, International Thespian Society, 3368 Central Pkwy., Cincinnati OH 45225. (513)559-1996. Editor-in-Chief: Donald Corathers. 70% freelance written. Works with small number of new/unpublished writers. For theatre arts students, teachers and others interested in theatre arts education. Magazine published monthly, September through May; 44-52 pages. Circ. 32,000. Pays on acceptance. Publishes ms an average of 3 months after acceptance. Buys first North American serial rights. Byline given. Submit seasonal/holiday material 3 months in advance. Simultaneous, photocopied and previously published submissions OK. Query for electronic submission. Computer printout submissions acceptable; prefers letter-quality to dot-matrix. Reports in 1 month. Sample copy for $2 and a 9x12 SAE with 90¢ postage; free writer's guidelines.

Nonfiction: How-to (technical theatre), informational, interview, photo feature, humorous, profile and technical. Buys 30 mss/year. Submit complete ms. Length: 750-3,000 words. Pays $30-150. Rarely pays expenses of writers on assignment.

Photos: Purchased with accompanying ms. Uses b&w photos and color transparencies. Query. Total purchase price for ms includes payment for photos.

Fiction: Drama (one-act plays). No "plays for children, Christmas plays, or plays written with no attention paid to the playwriting form." Buys 5-9 mss/year. Send complete ms. Pays $50-200.

Tips: "The best way to break in is to know our audience—drama students, teachers and others interested in theatre—and to write for them. Writers who have some practical experience in theatre, especially in technical areas, have a leg-up here, but we'll work with anybody who has a good idea. Some freelancers have become regular contributors. Others ignore style suggestions included in our writer's guidelines."

‡DRAMATIKA, 429 Hope St., Tarpon Springs FL 33589. Editor: John Pyros. Magazine; 40 pages. For persons interested in the theater arts. Published 2 times/year. Circ. 500-1,000. Buys all rights. Pays on publication. Query. Reports in 1 month. Sample copy $2.

Fiction: Wants "performable pieces—plays, songs, scripts, etc." Will consider plays on various and open themes. Query first. Length: 20 pages maximum. Pays about $25/piece; $5-10 for smaller pieces.

Photos: Submit 8x11 b&w photos with ms. Captions required. Pays $5.

EMMY MAGAZINE, Suite 800, Academy of Television Arts & Sciences, Suite 700, 3500 W. Olive, Burbank CA 91505-4628. (213)506-7885. Editor and Publisher: Hank Rieger. Managing Editor: Deborah Clark Yeseta. 100% freelance written. Works with a small number of new/unpublished writers each year. Bimonthly magazine on television—a "provocative, critical—though not necessarily fault-finding—treatment of television and its effects on society." Circ. 10,000. Pays on publication. Publishes ms an average of 3 months after acceptance. Byline given. Offers 20% kill fee. Buys first North American serial rights. Computer printout submissions acceptable; no dot-matrix. Reports in 3 weeks on queries; 1 month on mss. Free sample copy.

Nonfiction: Provocative and topical articles, nostalgic, humor, interview/profile, opinion—all dealing with television. Buys 40 mss/year. Query with published clips. Length: 2,000-3,000 words. Pays $500-1,000. Sometimes pays expenses of writers on assignment.

Columns/Departments: Opinion or point-of-view columns dealing with TV. Buys 18-20 mss/year. Query with published clips. Length: 800-1,500 words. Pays $200-400.

Tips: "Query with a thoughtful description of what you wish to write about. Or call. In either case, we can soon establish whether or not we can do business. The most frequent mistake made by writers in completing an article for us is that they misread the magazine and send fan-magazine items."

FANGORIA: Horror in Entertainment, Starlog Group, 475 Park Ave. South, 8th Floor, New York NY 10016. (212)689-2830. Editor: Anthony Timpone. 80% freelance written. Works with a small number of new/unpublished writers each year. Published 10 times/year. Magazine covering horror films, TV projects and literature and those who create them. Pays on publication. Publishes ms an average of 3 months after acceptance. Byline given. Buys first North American serial rights with option for second serial (reprint) rights to same material. Submit seasonal/holiday material 6 months in advance. Simultaneous queries OK. Query for electronic submissions. Computer printout submissions acceptable; no dot-matrix. Reports in 6 weeks. "We provide an assignment sheet (deadlines, info) to writers, thus authorizing queried stories that we're buying." Sample copy $3; writers' guidelines for SASE.

Nonfiction: Book excerpts, interview/profile of movie directors, makeup FX artists, screenwriters, producers, actors, noted horror novelists and others—with genre credits. No "think" pieces, opinion pieces, reviews, or sub-theme overviews (i.e., vampire in the cinema). Buys 100 mss/year. Query with published clips. Length: 1,000-3,000 words. Pays $100-225. Rarely pays the expenses of writers on assignment. Avoids articles on science fiction films—see listing for sister magazine *Starlog* in *Writer's Market* science fiction magazine section.

Photos: State availability of photos. Reviews b&w and color transparencies and prints. "No separate payment for photos provided by film studios." Captions or identification of subjects required. Photo credit given. Buys all rights.

Columns/Departments: Monster Invasion (news about new film productions; must be exclusive, early information; also mini-interviews with filmmakers and novelists). Query with published clips. Length: 300-500 words. Pays $25-35.

Fiction: "We do *not* publish any fiction. *Don't* send any."

Tips: "Other than recommending that you study one or several copies of *Fangoria*, we can only describe it as a horror film magazine consisting primarily of interviews with technicians and filmmakers in the field. Be sure to stress the interview subjects' words—not your own opinions. We're very interested in small, independent filmmakers working outside of Hollywood. These people are usually more accessible to writers, and more cooperative. *Fangoria* is also sort of a *de facto* bible for youngsters interested in movie makeup careers and for young filmmakers. We are devoted only to *reel* horrors—the fakery of films, the imagery of the horror fiction of a Stephen King or a Peter Straub—we *do not* want nor would we *ever* publish articles on real-life horrors, murders, etc. A writer must *like* and *enjoy* horror films and horror fiction to work for us. If the photos in *Fangoria* disgust you, if the sight of (*stage*) blood repels you, if you feel 'superior' to horror (and its fans), you aren't a writer for us and we certainly aren't the market for you. *Fangoria*'s frequency has increased over the last years and, with an editorial change reducing staff written articles, this has essentially doubled the number of stories we're buying. In 1988, we expect such opportunities only to increase for freelancers. *Fangoria* will try for a lighter, more "Gonzo" tone in the year ahead."

FILM QUARTERLY, University of California Press, Berkeley CA 94720. (415)642-6333. Editor: Ernest Callenbach. 100% freelance written. Eager to work with new/unpublished writers. Quarterly. Buys all rights. Byline given. Pays on publication. Publishes ms an average of 3 months after acceptance. Query; "sample pages are very helpful from unknown writers. We must have hard-copy printout and don't care how it is produced, but we cannot use dot-matrix printouts unless done on one of the new printers that gives type-quality letters."

Nonfiction: Articles on style and structure in films, articles analyzing the work of important directors, historical articles on development of the film as art, reviews of current films and detailed analyses of classics, book reviews of film books. Must be familiar with the past and present of the art; must be competently, although not necessarily breezily, written; must deal with important problems of the art. "We write for people who like to think and talk seriously about films, as well as simply view them and enjoy them. We use no personality pieces or reportage pieces. Interviews usually work for us only when conducted by someone familiar with most of a filmmaker's work. (We don't use performer interviews.)" Length: 6,000 words maximum. Pay is about 2¢/word.

Tips: "*Film Quarterly* is a specialized academic journal of film criticism, though it is also a magazine (with pictures) sold in bookstores. It is read by film teachers, students, and die-hard movie buffs, so unless you fall into one of those categories, it is very hard to write for us. Currently, we are especially looking for material on independent, documentary, etc. films not written about in the national film reviewing columns."

‡**MAGICK THEATRE, Magazine of Diverse Film Esoterica**, Box 0446, Baldwin NY 11510-0129. Editor: Raymond Young. Managing Editor: Christine Young. 25% freelance written. A semiannual magazine covering film history, criticism and obscure and neglected films/filmmakers. "Our audience is fans, filmmakers and writers—not casual moviegoers. Our magazine is slanted against the grain of the contemporary, commercial mainstream to allow forgotten artists to speak up and gain their due recognition." Circ. 3,000. Pays on publication. Publishes ms an average of 8 months after acceptance. Byline given. Buys first, one-time and second serial (reprint) rights. Photocopied and previously published submissions OK. Reports in 1 month. Free sample copy and writer's guidelines.

Nonfiction: Book excerpts, expose, general interest, historical/nostalgic, interview/profile, opinion, personal experience and photo feature. "No articles dealing with contemporary, commercial, mainstream films." Buys 5-20 mss/year. Send complete ms. Length: 1,500-8,000 words. Pays $25-200 for assigned articles. May pay writers with contributor copies if writer requests.

Photos: Send photos with submission. Reviews negatives and 8x10 prints. Offers no additional payment for photos accepted with ms. Identification of subjects required. Buys one-time rights.

Columns/Departments: R. Zimmerman, editor. Books (film books reviewed), 400-900 words; Film-A (film reviews—dates of release unimportant), 400-900 words; Film-B (capsule film reviews—date of release unimportant), 50-300 words; and Magazines (film magazines reviewed—capsule and lengthy), 50-500 words. Buys 10 mss/year. Send complete ms. Pays $5-25.

Fillers: R. Zimmerman, editor. Facts, gags and newsbreaks. Buys 15/year. Length: 50-300 words. Pays $5-20.

Tips: "Writers must be dedicated and studious towards the subject, as we will not accept articles on subjects frequently covered elsewhere. A lot of research is involved, but it is rewarding, since we usually run material unavailable in other publications. We are 'Open House' and do encourage any first-timers to simply write us."

MOVIE COLLECTOR'S WORLD, The Marketplace For Film & Video Collectors, 151 E. Birch St., Annandale MN 55302. (612)274-5230. Editor: Jon E. Johnson. 90% freelance written. Eager to work with new/ unpublished writers. Biweekly tabloid covering film-collecting movie and video reviews, profiles, features and technical subjects. "We strive to serve the varied interests of our readers, ranging from film and video enthusiasts to still and poster collectors." Circ. 10,000. Pays on publication. Publishes ms an averge of 3 months after acceptance. Byline given. Buys first serial rights and second serial (reprint) rights. Submit seasonal/dated material 3 months in advance. Photocopied submissions OK. Computer printout submissions OK "if close to double-spaced;" prefers letter quality to dot matrix. Reports in 6 weeks. Sample copy and writer's guidelines for 9x12 SAE and 4 first class stamps.

Nonfiction: Book excerpts; expose (investigative or extensive profile-type submissions); how-to; new product (uses and technical review); opinion (in the form of reviews or commentary); technical subjects ("one very popular feature we ran was on Cinemascope"). "We'd like to see more historical retrospective-type pieces on films. For instance our stories on *The Thin Man* series and *Ma and Pa Kettle* were two recent favorites." No personal experience/first person articles other than interview, profile or general interest. "We do not need very elementary pieces on 'buying your first VCR' or humorous commentary." Send complete ms or query. Pays 3¢/word or $100 maximum.

Photos: State availability of photos with query or ms. Pays $3-5 for 8x10 b&w prints. Model release required. Buys one-time rights.

Columns/Departments: Book (film/video-related topics) and tape/disc reviews. Send ms or query. Pays $5 minimum for short reviews, word rates for longer pieces.

Tips: "We're looking for more historical-type retrospectives and interviews, rather than currently available video reviews that can be found anywhere. *MCW* uses freelance material for nearly its entire content, and as a result it is very easy for a freelancer to break in to the publication, provided his/her material suits our needs and they know what they're writing about. Once writers get a feel for what *MCW* is, and we get an idea of their work, they tend to become one of our 'family' of regular contributors. Writers who know and care about their subject should have no problem when it comes to writing for *MCW* (providing it suits our needs). We actually encourage unsolicited submissions. A look at your wares just might land you a quicker sale than if there has to be a lot of counseling, advising or hand-holding involved. With a biweekly schedule we work quick."

‡**MOVIELINE MAGAZINE**,1141 S. Beverly Dr., Los Angeles CA 90035. (213)282-0711. Editor: Laurie Halpern Smith. Managing Editor: Julie Richard. 75% freelance written. Biweekly magazine covering motion pictures. Circ. 100,000. Pays on publication. Publishes ms an average of 1 month after acceptance. Byline given. Offers variable kill fee. Buys first North American serial rights or simultaneous rights ("if not in our market"). Submit seasonal/holiday material 1½ months in advance. Simultaneous submissions OK. Computer printout submissions OK. Reports in 1 month. Free sample copy and writer's guidelines.

Nonfiction: Book excerpts, essays, humor and interview/profile. Buys 75-100 mss/year. Query with published clips. Length: 150-2,500 words. Pays $35-500. Sometimes pays expenses of writers on assignment.

Photos: State availability of photos with submission. Reviews contact sheets, 2¼ transparencies and 5x7 photos. Offers $10-100/photo. Identification of subjects required. Buys one-tiome rights.

Columns/Departments: Buzz (short, funny pieces on movie-related personalities or anecdotes) 150-300 words; Festival Phile (reports from world film festivals) 500-1,000 words; La Dolce Video (articles about video releases) 1,000 words. Buys 75 mss/year. Pays $35-350.

Tips: "*Movieline* is a consumer-oriented publication devoted to film. We publish interviews with actors and actresses, directors, cinematographers, producers, writers, costume designers, and others with a creative involvement in motion pictures; we also seek behind-the-scenes stories relating to the movie business; fresh, insightful overviews of trends and genres; on-location pieces; and short, anecdotal items relating to any of the above. We consider our audience to be seasoned moviegoers, and consequently look for a knowledgeable, sophisticated approach to the subject; avoid a breathless, "fan"-like attitude, especially in star interviews. Pieces should be exciting, stylish and, because of our space limitations, tightly written."

THE OPERA COMPANION, 40 Museum Way, San Francisco CA 94114. (415)626-2741. Editor: James Keolker, Ph.D. 25% freelance written. Eager to work with new/unpublished writers. A magazine published 14 times yearly covering "opera in particular, music in general. We provide readers with an in depth analysis of 14 operas per year—the personal, philosophical, and political content of each composer and his works." Circ. 8,000. Pays on acceptance. Publishes ms an average of 2 months after acceptance. Byline given. Buys first rights. Photocopied submissions OK. Computer printout submissions acceptable; prefers letter-quality to dot-matrix. Reports in 1 week on queries; 1 month on mss. Free sample copy and writer's guidelines.

Nonfiction: Essay, historical/nostalgic, humor and interview/profile (opera composers, singers, producers and designers). No Master's or Doctoral theses. Buys 10 mss/year. Query with published clips. Length: 500-5,000 words. Pays $50-250.

Fillers: Anecdotes and short humor. Buys 25/year. Length: 150-500 words. Pays $50-250.

Tips: "Be pointed, pithy in statement, accurate in research. Avoid florid, excessive language. Writers must be musically sensitive, interested in opera as a continuing vocal art. Enthusiasm for the subject is important. Contact us for which operas/composers we will be featuring each year. It is those areas of research, anecdote, analysis and humor, we will be filling first."

‡PLAYBILL, Playbill Inc., Suite 320, 71 Vanderbilt Ave., New York NY 10169. (212)557-5757. Editor: Joan Alleman. 50% freelance written. Monthly magazine covering NYC, Broadway and Off-Broadway theatre. Circ. 1,040,000. Pays on acceptance. Publishes ms an average of 2 months after acceptance. Byline given. Offers $150 kill fee. Buys all rights. Computer printout submissions OK; no dot-matrix. Reports in 2 months.

Nonfiction: Book excerpts, humor, interview/profile, personal experience—must all be theatre related. Buys 10 mss/year. Query with published clips. Length: 1,500-1,800 words. Pays $250-500.

Photos: State availability of photos with submission. Offers no additional payment for photos accepted with ms. Identification of subjects required.

Fillers: Anecdotes, facts and short humor. Buys 10 mss/year. Length: 350-700 words. Pays $50-100. Must all be theatre related.

‡RAVE, The Comedy Performance Magazine, Rave Communications, 40 Prince Street, New York NY 10012. (212)925-7560. Editor: Ronald L. Smith. 50% freelance written. Monthly magazine covering comedy. "We're the *Playbill* of the comedy clubs. When patrons visit top national comedy clubs (Caroline's in New York, Second City in Chicago, The Improv in Los Angeles) they receive our magazine free. We're totally adsupported." Pays on publication. Publishes ms an average of 1-2 months after acceptance. Byline given. Offers 25% kill fee. Buys one-time rights. Submit seasonal/holiday material 3 months in advance. Simultaneous, photocopied and previously published (in local newspaper) submissions OK. Computer printout submissions OK; prefers letter-quality to dot-matrix. Reports in 2 weeks. Sample copy for 5x7 SAE.

Nonfiction: Cy Kottick, articles editor. Interview/profile and photo feature. "No essays on why the world needs to laugh or first person stories on my favorite jokes or the day I performed stand-up etc. Only interviews with comics." Buys 24 mss/year. Query with or without published clips, or send complete ms. Length: 300-1,200 words. Pays $50-300. Sometimes pays expenses of writers on assignment.

Photos: State availability of photos with submission. Reviews transparencies (2x2). Offers no additional payment for photos accepted with ms. Identification of subjects required. Buys one-time rights.

Tips: "We buy two types of nonfiction: interviews with comedians who tour nationally or are outstanding local prospects and general pieces about comedy and stand-up. These include odd history (the Arrapajo Indian Crazy Society), occasional mainstream (recipes from comedians) and compilation ('football kicks,' about the various football routines of a dozen comics)."

Satellite ORBIT, CommTek Publishing, 9440 Fairview Ave., Box 53, Boise ID 83707. (208)322-2800. Editor: Ray Bennett. 60% freelance written. A monthly guide for the Satellite TV viewer, featuring articles an profiles dealing with all aspects of home-screen entertainment. Circ. 500,000. Pays on acceptance. Publishes ms an average of 2 months after acceptance. Byline given. Offers 30% kill fee. Buys first North American serial rights. Submit seasonal/holiday material 3 months in advance. Photocopied submissions OK. Query for electronic submissions. Computer printout submissions acceptable; no dot-matrix. Reports in 2 weeks on queries;

3 weeks on manuscripts. Sample copy $5.

Nonfiction: Television-related themes, issues and personalities. Buys 75 mss/year. Query with published clips. Length: 1,500-2,000 words. Pays $750-1,750 for assigned articles. Sometimes pays the expenses of writers on assignment.

Photos: State availability of photos with submission. Reviews contact sheets and transparencies. Identification of subjects required.

Columns/Departments: Tuning In (short items—offbeat, funny or newsworthy items relating to satellite TV and dish owners). Pays $50 on acceptance. Taking Off (preview of upcoming programs on satellite TV). Pays $350-700. Length: 1,000 words. Query with published clips.

Tips: "Most writing is assigned. We use accomplished authoritative writers who know the field. A detailed query with published clips is essential."

SOAP OPERA DIGEST, 254 W. 31st St., New York NY 10001. Executive Editor: Meredith Brown. 25% freelance written. Works with published/established writers. Biweekly magazine; 144 pages. Circ. 850,000. Pays on acceptance. Publishes ms an average of 2 months after acceptance. Buys all rights. Submit seasonal/holiday material 4 months in advance of issue date. Computer printout submissions acceptable; prefers letter-quality to dot-matrix. Reports in 1 month.

Nonfiction: Lynn Davey, managing editor, freelance material. "Articles only directly related to daytime and nighttime personalities or soap operas." Interview (no telephone interviews); nostalgia; profiles; special interest features: health and beauty with soap opera personalities and industry news with a strong interest in nighttime soaps. "We are a 'newsy' magazine—not gossipy—and are highly interested in timely news stories. No poorly written material that talks down to the audience." Buys 2-3 mss/issue. Query with clips of previously published work. Length: 1,000-2,000 words. Pays $225 and up. Sometimes pays the expenses of writers on assignment.

Photos: State availability of photos with query. Captions preferred. Buys all rights.

Tips: "Writers must be good at in-depth personality profiles. Pack as much info as possible into a compact length. Also want humor pieces."

TV GUIDE, Radnor PA 19088. Editor (National Section): David Sendler. Editor (Local Sections): Roger Youman. Managing Editor: R.C. Smith. 70% freelance written. Prefers to work with published/established writers; works with a small number of new/unpublished writers each year; eager to work with new/unpublished writers. Weekly. Circ. 16.9 million. Publishes ms an average of 2 months after acceptance. Computer printout submissions acceptable; prefers letter-quality to dot-matrix.

Nonfiction: Wants offbeat articles about TV people and shows. This magazine is not interested in fan material. Also wants stories on the newest trends of television, but they must be written in clear, lively English. Study publication. Query to Andrew Mills, assistant managing editor. Length: 1,000-2,000 words.

Photos: Uses professional high-quality photos, normally shot on assignment by photographers chosen by *TV Guide*. Prefers color. Pays $350 day rate against page rates—$450 for 2 pages or less.

VIDEOMANIA, "The Newspaper For Video Nuts", Legs Of Stone Publishing Co., Box 359, Princeton WI 54968. Editor: Robert Katerzynske. 40% freelance written. Eager to work with new/unpublished writers. A monthly tabloid for the home video hobbyist. "Our readers are very much 'into' home video: they like reading about it—including both video hardware and software. A large number also collect video (movies, vintage TV, etc.)." Circ. 5,000. Pays on publication. Publishes ms an average of 3 months after acceptance. Byline given. Buys all rights; may reassign. Submit seasonal/holiday material 4 months in advance. Computer printout submissions acceptable; prefers letter-quality to dot-matrix. Reports in 3 weeks on mss. Sample copy for $2 and 9x12 SASE.

Nonfiction: Book excerpts, videotape and book reviews, expose, general interest, historical/nostalgic, how-to, humor, interview/profile, new product, opinion, personal experience, photo feature, technical and travel. "All articles should deal with video and/or film. We always have special holiday issues in November and December." No "*complicated* technical pieces." Buys 24 mss/year. Send complete ms. Length: 500-2,500 words. Pays $2.50 maximum. "Contributor copies given for mss deemed interesting but not as 'newsworthy' as others."

Photos: Send photos with submissions. Reviews contact sheets and 3x5 prints. Offers no additional payment for photos accepted with ms. Model releases and identification of subjects required. Buys all rights; may reassign.

Fiction: Adventure, horror and humorous. "We want short, video-related fiction only on an occasional basis. Since we aim for a general readership, we do not want any pornographic material." Buys 5 mss/year. Send complete ms. Length: 500-2,500 words. Pays $2.50 maximum plus copies.

Tips: "We want to offer more reviews and articles on offbeat, obscure and rare movies, videos and stars. Write in a plain, easy-to-understand style. We're not looking for a highhanded, knock-'em-dead writing style . . . just something good! We want more short video, film and book reviews by freelancers."

X-IT, A general arts and entertainment magazine, Image Design, Box 102, St. John's, Newfoundland A1C 5H5 Canada. (709)753-8802. Editor: Ken J. Harvey. Managing Editor: Sol Christian. 100% freelance written. Eager to work with new/unpublished writers. A triannual entertainment magazine concentrating on new ideas and thoughts in arts and literature (written and visual) for the general public. Circ. 3,000. Pays on publication. Publishes ms an average of 3 months after acceptance. Byline given. Buys one-time rights. Submit seasonal/holiday material 2 months in advance. Simultaneous, photocopied and previously published submissions OK. Computer printout submissions acceptable; no dot matrix. Reports in 3 weeks on queries; 1 month on mss. Sample copy $3 and 2 IRCs.
Nonfiction: All nonfiction is assigned by the editor. Query. Sometimes pays the expenses of writers on assignment.
Fiction: Adventure, erotica, experimental, fantasy, horror, humorous, mystery, science fiction and suspense. "We are open to practically all areas of literature. Our only demand is quality." Buys 12 mss/year. Send complete ms. Length: 1,500-4,800 words. Pays $10-150.
Poetry: Allela English, poetry editor. Avant-garde, free verse, light verse and traditional. Buys 30 poems/ year. Submit maximum 10 poems. Length: open. Pays $10-50. "*X-IT* also produces a yearly anthology of poetry. Submit up to five poems. Sixteen lines maximum per poem. Notification in two weeks. Send short bio and SASE or IRC. Cash prizes are awarded. $200 first place; $100 second place; $50 for third and fourth place. Submissions are continually accepted for this year's and next year's anthologies. Quality a *must.*"
Fillers: Jokes and short humor. Buys 12/year. Length: "preferably short." Pays $5-25.
Tips: "Send along a short bio with submissions and a cover letter describing how work would fit in with the publication. Fiction and poetry are most open to freelancers. We need fillers."

Ethnic/Minority

Traditions are kept alive, new ones become established and people are united by ethnic publications. Some ethnic magazines seek material that unites people of all races. Ideas, interests and concerns of nationalities and religions are covered by publications in this category. General interest lifestyle magazines for these groups are also included. Additional markets for writing with an ethnic orientation are located in the following sections: Career, College and Alumni; Juvenile; Men's; Women's and Religious.

AIM MAGAZINE, AIM Publishing Company, 7308 S. Eberhart Ave., Chicago IL 60619. (312)874-6184. Editor: Ruth Apilado. Managing Editor: Dr. Myron Apilado. 75% freelance written. Works with a small number of new/unpublished writers each year. Quarterly magazine on social betterment that promotes racial harmony and peace for high school, college and general audience. Circ. 10,000. Pays on publication. Publishes ms an average of 3 months after acceptance. Offers 60% of contract as kill fee. Not copyrighted. Buys one-time rights. Submit seasonal/holiday material 6 months in advance. Simultaneous queries, and simultaneous and photocopied submissions OK. Computer printout submissions acceptable; prefers letter-quality to dot-matrix. Reports in 6 weeks on queries. Writer's guidelines for $3, 8½x11 SAE and 85¢ postage.
Nonfiction: Exposé (education); general interest (social significance); historical/nostalgic (Black or Indian); how-to (help create a more equitable society); and profile (one who is making social contributions to community); and book reviews and reviews of plays "that reflect our ethnic/minority orientation." No religious material. Buys 16 mss/year. Send complete ms. Length: 500-800 words. Pays $25-35.
Photos: Reviews b&w prints. Captions and identification of subjects required.
Fiction: Ethnic, historical, mainstream, and suspense. Fiction that teaches the brotherhood of man. Buys 20 mss/year. Send complete ms. Length: 1,000-1,500 words. Pays $25-35.
Poetry: Avant-garde, free verse, light verse. No "preachy" poetry. Buys 20 poems/year. Submit maximum 5 poems. Length: 15-30 lines. Pays $3-5.
Fillers: Jokes, anecdotes and newsbreaks. Buys 30/year. Length: 50-100 words. Pays $5.
Tips: "Interview anyone of any age who unselfishly is making an unusual contribution to the lives of less fortunate individuals. Include photo and background of person. We look at the nation of the world as part of one family. Short stories and historical pieces about blacks and Indians are the areas most open to freelancers. Subject matter of submission is of paramount concern for us rather than writing style. Articles and stories showing the similarity in the lives of people with different racial backgrounds are desired."

THE AMERICAN CITIZEN ITALIAN PRESS, 13681 V St., Omaha NE 68137. (402)896-0403. Publisher/Editor: Diana C. Failla. 40% freelance written. Eager to work with new/unpublished writers. Quarterly newspaper of Italian-American news/stories. Circ. 5,600. Pays on publication. Publishes ms an average of 3 months after acceptance. Byline given. Not copyrighted. Buys first North American serial rights. Submit seasonal/holiday material 2 months in advance. Previously published submissions OK. Computer printout submissions acceptable; prefers letter-quality to dot-matrix. Reports in 1 month. Free sample copy.
Nonfiction: Book excerpts, general interest, historical/nostalgic, opinion, photo feature, celebrity pieces, travel, fashions, profiles and sports (Italian players). Query with published clips. Length: 400-600 words. Pays $15-20. Sometimes pays the expenses of writers on assignment.
Photos: State availability of photos. Reviews b&w prints. Pays $5. Captions and identification of subjects required. Buys all rights.
Columns/Departments: Query.
Fiction: Query. Pays $15-20.
Poetry: Traditional. Submit maximum 5 poems. Pays $5-10.
Tips: Human interest stories are the most open to freelancers.

AMERICAN DANE, The Danish Brotherhood in America, 3717 Harney St., Box 31748, Omaha NE 68131. (402)341-5049. Editor: Jerome L. Christensen. Managing Editor: Pamela K. Dorau. 50% freelance written. Prefers to work with published/ established writers; works with a small number of new/unpublished writers each year. The monthly magazine of the Danish Brotherhood in America. All articles must have Danish ethnic flavor. Circ. 10,000. Pays on publication. Publishes ms an average of 1 year after acceptance. Byline given. Not copyrighted. Buys first rights. Submit seasonal/holiday material 1 year in advance. Photocopied submissions OK. Computer printout submissions acceptable; prefers letter-quality to dot-matrix. Reports in 2 weeks on queries. Sample copy $1 with 9½x4 SAE and 55¢ postage; writer's guidelines for 9½x4 SAE with 1 first class stamp.
Nonfiction: Historical, humor, inspirational, personal experience, photo feature and travel, all with a Danish flavor. Buys 12 mss/year. Query. Length: 1,500 words maximum. Pays $50 maximum for unsolicited articles.
Photos: Send photos with submission. Reviews prints. Offers no additional payment for photos accepted with ms. Captions and identification of subjects required. Buys one-time rights. .
Fiction: Adventure, historical, humorous, mystery, romance and suspense, all with a Danish flavor. Buys 6-12 mss/year. Query with published clips. Length: 1,500 words maximum. Pays $50 maximum.
Poetry: Traditional. Buys 1-6 poems/year. Submit maximum 6 poems. Pays $35 maximum.
Fillers: Anecdotes and short humor. Buys 0-12/year. Length: 300 words maximum. Pays $15 maximum.
Tips: "Feature articles are most open to freelancers."

‡ARARAT, The Armenian General Benevolent Union, 585 Saddle River Rd., Saddle Brook NJ 07662. Editor-in-Chief: Leo Hamalian. 80% freelance written. Emphasizes Armenian life and culture for Americans of Armenian descent and Armenian immigrants. "Most are well-educated; some are Old World." Quarterly magazine. Circ. 2,400. Pays on publication. Publishes ms an average of 1 year after acceptance. Buys first North American serial rights and second (reprint) rights to material originally published elsewhere. Submit seasonal/holiday material at least 3 months in advance. Photocopied and previously published submissions OK. Computer printout submissions acceptable. Reports in 6 weeks. Sample copy $3 plus $1 postage.
Nonfiction: Historical (history of Armenian people, of leaders, etc.); interviews (with prominent or interesting Armenians in any field, but articles are preferred); profile (on subjects relating to Armenian life and culture); personal experience (revealing aspects of typical Armenian life); and travel (in Armenia and Armenian communities throughout the world and the US). Buys 3 mss/issue. Query. Length: 1,000-6,000 words. Pays $25-100.
Columns/Departments: Reviews of books by Armenians or relating to Armenians. Buys 6/issue. Query. Pays $25. Open to suggestions for new columns/departments.
Fiction: Any stories dealing with Armenian life in America or in the old country. Buys 4 mss/year. Query. Length: 2,000-5,000 words. Pays $35-75.
Poetry: Any verse that is Armenian in theme. Buys 6/issue. Pays $10.
Tips: "Read the magazine, and write about the kind of subjects we are obviously interested in, e.g., Kirlian photography, Aram Avakian's films, etc. Remember that we have become almost totally ethnic in subject matter, but we want articles that present (to the rest of the world) the Armenian in an interesting way. The most frequent mistake made by writers in completing an article for us is that they are not sufficiently versed in Armenian history/culture. The articles are too superficial for our audience."

ATTENZIONE, The Italian Lifestyle Magazine, Adam Publications, Inc., 152 Madison Ave., New York NY 10016. (212)683-9000. Senior Editor: Denise Gorga. 75% freelance written. Prefers to work with published/established writers; eager to work with new/unpublished writers. A bimonthly magazine which "celebrates the Italian lifestyle in design, fashion, travel, food, and addresses an audience of Italian Americans *and* Italophiles." Circ. 93,400. Pays 60 days after publication. Publishes ms an average of 3 months after acceptance. Byline given. Offers 25% kill fee. Buys first North American serial rights. Submit seasonal/holiday material 4 months in advance. Computer printout submissions acceptable; prefers letter-quality to dot-matrix. Reports in 2 months. Sample copy $3.50 with SASE; free writer's guidelines.

Nonfiction: Book excerpts, essays, general interest, historical/nostalgic, humor, interview/profile, photo feature and travel. Special issues include Food (December); Travel (April, October); Fashion (March, September). No family recollections. Query with or without published clips. Length: 1,500-3,000 words. Pays $200-500 for assigned articles; pays $150-350 for unsolicited articles. Sometimes pays the expenses of writers on assignment.

Photos: State availability of photos with submission. Offers no additional payment for photos accepted with ms. Identification of subjects required. Buys one-time rights.

Columns/Departments: Media, Insight, and Report From Italy (all should have Italian-American link, e.g., how ethnic stereotyping can be fought; new scientific advances in Italy, etc.). Buys 5 mss/year. Query. Length: 1,500-2,000 words. Pays $150-300.

Tips: "*Attenzione* prefers a well-written query and published clips to unsolicited manuscripts. All queries are answered if accompanied by a SASE. Travel articles and interviews are most open to freelancers. We are always looking for an unusual slant even if it is an often covered subject, e.g., where the literati gather in Milan."

BALTIMORE JEWISH TIMES, 2104 N. Charles St., Baltimore MD 21218. (301)752-3504. Editor: Gary Rosenblatt. 25% freelance written. Weekly magazine covering subjects of interest to Jewish readers. "*Baltimore Jewish Times* reaches 20,000 Baltimore-area Jewish homes, as well as several thousand elsewhere in the U.S. and Canada; almost anything of interest to that audience is of interest to us. This includes reportage, general interest articles, personal opinion, and personal experience pieces about every kind of Jewish subject from narrowly religious issues to popular sociology; from the Mideast to the streets of Brooklyn, to the suburbs of Baltimore. We run articles of special interest to purely secular Jews as well as to highly observant ones. We are Orthodox, Conservative, and Reform all at once. We are spiritual and mundane. We are establishment and we are alternative culture." Circ. 20,000. Pays on publication. Publishes ms an average of 2 months after acceptance. Byline given. Buys one-time rights. Submit seasonal/holiday material 2 months in advance. Simultaneous queries, and photocopied and previously published submissions OK. Computer printout submissions acceptable; prefers letter-quality to dot-matrix. "We will not return submissions without SASE." Reports in 6 weeks. Sample copy $2.

Nonfiction: Barbara Pash, editorial assistant. Book excerpts, exposé, general interest, historical/nostalgic, humor, interview/profile, opinion, personal experience and photo feature. "We are inundated with Israel personal experience and Holocaust-related articles, so submissions on these subjects must be of particularly high quality." Buys 100 mss/year. "Established writers query; others send complete manuscript." Length: 1,200-6,000 words. Pays $25-150.

Photos: Kim Muller-Thym, graphics editor. Send photos with ms. Pays $10-35 for 8x10 b&w prints.

Fiction: Barbara Pash, editorial assistant. "We'll occasionally run a high-quality short story with a Jewish theme." Buys 6 mss/year. Send complete ms. Length: 1,200-6,000 words. Pays $25-150.

‡BLACK ENTERPRISE MAGAZINE, Black America's Guidebook for Success, Earl G. Graves Publishing Co., 130 5th Ave., New York NY 10011. (212)242-8000. Editor: Earl G. Graves. Managing Editor: Sheryl Hilliard. Monthly magazine covering career and money management advice and Black economic development and entrepreneurship for a highly-educated, affluent, Black, middle-class audience interested in business, politics, careers and international issues. Circ. 234,000. Pays on acceptance. Byline given. Offers negotiable kill fee. Buys all rights. Submit seasonal/holiday material 4 months in advance. Simultaneous queries OK. No unsolicited mss. Reports in 6 weeks on queries. Free sample copy and writer's guidelines.

Nonfiction: Expose, general business, career and personal finance interest, how-to, interview/profile, technical, travel, and short, hard-news items about Black business, career and personal finance interest. "We emphasize the how-to aspect." Special issues include: Careers, February; Top 100 Black Businesses, June; Money Management, October; and Auto Guide, November. "No fiction or poetry; no 'rags-to-riches,' ordinary-guy stories, please." Buys 30-40 feature length mss/year. Query with clips of published work. Send "a short, succinct letter that lets us know the point of the piece, the elements involved, and *why* our readers would want to read it." Length: 600-3,000 words. Buys 40 mss/year. Pays $100-800/article.

Columns/Departments: Alfred Edmond, associate editor. In the News (short, hard-news pieces on issues of Black interest); and Verve (lifestyle and leisure articles. Ed Smith, Verve editor). Query with clips of published work. Length: 300-1,000 words. Pays $75-300/article.

Tips: "We have stayed away from trivia and first-person pieces on the belief that our readers want hard-nosed reporting and innovative analysis of issues that concern them. *Black Enterprise* has a mission of informing, educating and entertaining an upscale, affluent audience that wants issues addressed from its unique perspective. We are most open to 'In the News,' an expression of a sensitivity to issues/events/trends that have an impact on Black people."

BLACK FAMILY, Black Family Publications, Inc., Box 1046, Herndon VA 22070-1046. (703)860-3411. Editor: Frank C. Kent. Managing Editor: Evelyn Ivery. 90% freelance written. Eager to work with new/unpublished writers. A bimonthly magazine for and about black families. "This is a total family magazine. Submissions must be positive, promoting traditional family values. Stories about people who succeed against the odds are especially desirable." Circ. 250,000. Pays on publication. Publishes ms an average of 4 months after acceptance. Byline given. Offers 50% kill fee. Buys first rights, second serial (reprint) rights, all rights, and makes work-for-hire assignments. Submit seasonal/holiday material 4 months in advance. Simultaneous submissions OK. Mss on disk (IBM compatible DOS) accepted. Disk returned. Computer printout submissions acceptable; no dot-matrix. Reports in 1 month. Sample copy for 9x12 SAE with $1.50 postage; writer's guidelines for #10 SAE with 1 first class stamp.
Nonfiction: Address to attention: nonfiction. General interest, historical/nostalgic, how-to, humor, inspirational, interview/profile, opinion (from scholars or well known blacks), personal experience, photo feature, religious and travel. Special issues include Holiday issue (Nov.), Christmas (Dec.), Black History (Feb.), Martin Luther King's Birthday (Jan.) and Travel (June). No material which does not promote stable family life (i.e. swinging singles, etc.). Buys 25 mss/year. Send complete ms. Length: 750-3,500 words. Pays $150-300 for assigned articles; pays $300 maximum for unsolicited articles. Pays expenses of writers on assignment.
Photos: State availability of photos with submission. "On assignments, we will supply the photographer or make arrangements with writers." Offers no additional payment for photos accepted with ms. Captions, model releases and identification of subjects required.
Columns/Departments: Outstanding People (Black Americans who are doing exciting things in their communities. Especially senior citizens). Also Kids Games and About Black History. 500 words plus photo(s). Buys 12 mss/year. Query with published clips. Pays $25-50.
Fiction: Humorous and slice-of-life vignettes. "No erotica, horror, etc. We look for stories which would be published in *Woman's Day* or *Ladies' Home Journal*." Buys 12 mss/year. Send complete ms only. Length: 2,500-5,000 words. Pays $250 flat fee if accepted.
Poetry: Avant-garde, free verse, light verse and traditional. "We are open. Just remember we are a family magazine." Buys varying number of poems/year. "No set number of poems per submission. Use common sense or it won't be read." Length: 8 lines minimum.
Tips: "Use *Reader's Digest*, *Woman's Day*, *LHJ*, etc., as guides—only slant stories for interest to black families."

B'NAI B'RITH JEWISH MONTHLY, B'nai B'rith International, 1640 Rhode Island Ave., N.W., Washington DC 20036. (202)857-6645. Editor: Marc Silver. 75% freelance written. Works with a small number of new/unpublished writers each year. A monthly magazine covering Jewish issues. "We have a Jewish family audience. Our magazine covers the Jewish world: politics, lifestyles, culture, religion and history." Circ. 200,000. Pays on publication. Publishes ms an average of 3 months after acceptance. Byline given. Offers 25% kill fee. Buys first North American serial rights. Submit seasonal/holiday material 6 months in advance. Computer printout submissions acceptable; prefers letter-quality to dot-matrix. Reports in 2 weeks on queries; 1 month on manuscripts. Free writer's guidelines.
Nonfiction: Book excerpts, essays, exposé, general interest, historical/nostalgic, how-to, humor, inspirational, interview/profile, new product, opinion, personal experience, photo feature, religious and travel. No immigrant reminiscences. Buys 35 mss/year. Query with published clips. Length: 300-5,000 words. Pays 10-25¢/word. Sometimes pays the expenses of writers on assignment.
Photos: State availability of photos with submission. Reviews contact sheets and transparencies. Offers $25-75/photo. Captions, model releases, and identification of subjects required. Buys one-time rights.
Columns/Departments: Arts (reviews, interviews with writers, artists, filmmakers, etc.), 300-1,000 words; Kol-Bo (humorous and offbeat material), 300-800 words; and Up Front (brief political items), 300-500 words. Buys 25 mss/year. Query with published clips. Length: 300-500 words. Pays $30-100.

CONGRESS MONTHLY, American Jewish Congress, 15 E. 84th St., New York NY 10028. (212)879-4500. Editor: Maier Deshell. 90% freelance written. Magazine published 7 times/year covering topics of concern to the American Jewish community representing a wide range of views. Distributed mainly to the members of the American Jewish Congress; readers are intellectual, Jewish, involved. Circ. 35,000. Pays on publication. Publishes ms an average of 3 months after acceptance. Byline given. Buys one-time rights. Submit seasonal/holiday material 2 months in advance. No photocopied or previously published submissions. Computer printout submissions acceptable; prefers letter-quality to dot-matrix. Reports in 2 months.
Nonfiction: General interest ("current topical issues geared toward our audience"). No technical material. Send complete ms. Length: 2,000 words maximum. Pays $100-150/article.
Photos: State availability of photos. Reviews b&w prints. "Photos are paid for with payment for ms."
Columns/Departments: Book, film, art and music reviews. Send complete ms. Length: 1,000 words maximum. Pays $100-150/article.

‡**CRISIS**, Crisis Publishing Co., #206, 6515 Sunset Blvd., Los Angeles CA 90028. (213)465-4512. Editor: Fred Beauford. 50% freelance written. "The *Crisis* is a monthly magazine published by the NAACP. We con-

sider it the magazine of ideas, issues and the arts from a black point of view." Circ. 300,000. Pays on publication. Publishes ms an average of 2 months after acceptance. Byline given. Buys first North American serial rights. Reports in 1 month on queries; 2 weeks on mss. Sample copy for 9x11 SAE with $1.70 postage.

Nonfiction: Essays, exposé, historical/nostalgic, opinion, travel. Buys 15 mss/year. Query with published clips. Length: 500-10,000 words. Pays $300-500 for assigned articles. Pays $75-500 for unsolicited articles. Sometimes pays the expenses of writers on assignment.

Photos: State availability of photos with submission. Reviews contact sheets and 8x11 prints. Pays $35 per photo. Captions, model releases and identification of subjects required. Buys all rights.

Tips: "Write for a list of topics. We plan our editorial material a year in advance."

‡**DÄN SHA NEWS**, (formerly *The Yukon Indian News*), Ye Sa To Communications Society ("Voice of the People"), #22 Nisutlin Dr., Whitehorse, Yukon Territory Y1A 3S5 Canada. (403)667-7631 or (403)667-2775. Editor: Jessica Carr. 20% freelance written. Monthly newspaper tabloid covering all Yukon Indian issues. Circ. approximately 2,500. Pays on publication. Byline given. Buys one-time rights or makes work-for-hire assignments. Submit seasonal/holiday material 2 months in advance. Simultaneous and photocopied submissions OK. Query for electronic submissions. Reports in "weeks" on queries; "months" on mss. Free sample copy.

Nonfiction: Essays, expose, general interest, historical/nostalgic, interview/profile and photo feature. No anti-native articles or vitriolic opinion pieces. Buys 80-100 mss/year. Query with published clips. Length: 500-2,000 words. Pays $5-50. Sometimes pays the expenses of writers on assignment.

Photos: State availability of photos with submission or send photos with submission. Reviews contact sheets, negatives and 3x5 prints. Offers $5 per photo. Captions and identification of subjects required. Buys one-time rights.

Columns/Departments: Yukon Notes (short clips of Yukon Native events), Outside Notes (24 short clips per issue of native events outside the territory); Native Language Lessons (language lessons of 7 Yukon languages); Community News (information from Yukon native community about events, etc.). Buys 30 mss/year. Query. Length: 250-500 words. Pays $10-50.

Fiction: Native ethnic. No violence or erotica. Buys 15 mss/year. Query with published clips. Length: 250-1,000 words. Pays $10-50.

Poetry: Avant-garde, free verse, light verse and traditional. Buys 30 poems/year. Submit maximum 20 poems. Length: 10-50 lines. Pays $0-10.

Fillers: Facts and newsbreaks. Buys 15/year. Length: 10-30 words.

Tips: Areas of our publication most open to freelancers are factual features (with lots of interviews and quotes), poetry and news.

ESSENCE, 1500 Broadway, New York NY 10036. (212)730-4260. Editor-in-Chief: Susan L. Taylor. Editor: Stephanie Stokes Oliver. Executive Editor: Cheryll V. Greene. Senior Editor: Elsie B. Washington. Edited for Black women. Monthly magazine; 150 pages. Circ. 850,000. Pays on acceptance. Makes assignments on work-for-hire basis. 3 month lead time. Pays 25% kill fee. Byline given. Submit seasonal/holiday material 6 months in advance. Computer printout submissions acceptable. Reports in 2 months. Sample copy $1.50; free writer's guidelines.

Features: "We're looking for articles that inspire and inform Black women. Our readers are interested and aware; the topics we include in each issue are provocative. Every article should move the *Essence*·woman emotionally and intellectually. We welcome queries from good writers on a wide range of topics: general interest, health and fitness, historical, how-to, humor, self-help, relationships, work, personality interview, personal experience, political issues, business and finances and personal opinion." Buys 200 mss/year. Query. Length: 1,000-3,000 words. Pays $500 minimum.

Photos: Gregory Gray, art director. State availability of photos with query. Pays $100 for b&w page; $300 for color page. Captions and model release required. "We particularly would like to see photographs for our travel section that feature Black travelers."

Columns/Departments: Query department editors: Contemporary Living (home, food, lifestyle, consumer information): Harriette Cole, Contemporary Living, editor; Arts & Entertainment: Pamela Johnson; Health & Fitness: Marjorie Whigham; Business and Finance: Nancy Anita Williams; Travel: Dari Giles Salter. Query. Length: About 1,000 words. Pays $100 minimum. "We are interested in buying short poetry to be used as filler material."

Tips: "We're looking for quality fiction; more self-improvement pieces, 'relationship' articles, career information and issues important to Black women."

‡**FINNISH CONNECTION**, Box 1531, Vancouver WA 98668. (206)695-7807. Editor: Eugene Messer. 90% freelance written. Bimonthly newspaper covering "literature, arts, travel, history, business and cultural news and information—Finland and American/Canadian/Finnish. Our publication has as its main purpose the dissemination of information regarding Finland (both Finnish and Swedish/Finnish Finland) and the activities and

Close-up

Stephanie Stokes Oliver
Editor
Essence

"There is nothing touching the lives of black women—AIDS, South Africa, parenting—that we are not willing to go in to," says Stephanie Stokes Oliver, editor of *Essence* magazine.

Although some publications designed for specific audiences are limited in scope, Oliver says *Essence* is bound only by a commitment to its readers.

"At first we were a fashion magazine, but our readers wouldn't have it. They wanted more substantive articles," she says. "We are looking for articles that move the reader forward."

Writers should not only be creative in the way they handle a topic, but also in the choice of topics to explore, she says.

Since the magazine covers everything from relationships to politics, Oliver advises writers to stay current. "Often a query will expand on an idea an editor already has in mind." A recent query on the effects of love on men did just that and it resulted in an assignment.

The magazine's broad range of subject matter forces Oliver to rely on her journalism training from Howard University. She finds the mechanics of hard news and feature writing similar.

"Journalism makes writing very specific," she says. "The first paragraph should say in a nutshell what the story is about . . . I look for the same thing in the first paragraph of a query. It should begin with 'I want to do a story on.'

"The query should also include at least three key points and supporting facts, statistics and quotes from experts. The writer should include a paragraph outlining writing experience."

Oliver's interest in the query process is two-fold. As an editor she says she does not have the time to weed through lengthy background material to get to the point of a proposal. As a writer she relies on queries to help make her own sales.

Oliver has freelanced throughout her career. In fact, she was an editor at *Glamour* magazine when she sold an article to *Essence*. The editors liked her work so much they offered her a position. After working as *Essence*'s West Coast editor and Mothering editor, she became Editor in 1986.

Oliver, the only person who reads the entire publication, is aware not only of the content needs but also of its overall tone. She advises writers to develop a feel for the relationship between the publication and its readers.

"Writers should *read* the magazine to see how we speak to the reader. We are very concerned with how we talk to her—never down to her, more like a sister, yet not too familiar."

Fiction writers should also be aware of the tone and philosophy of the magazine. "I have not been able to find much quality fiction. I receive many submissions with negative, destructive endings or a lack of self achievement.

"I would like to see stories that reflect the contemporary black woman—with a sense of winning, getting ahead. I'm interested in mysteries, science fiction, anything showing black women doing wonderful things. The stories should take readers in a direction they want to go."

—Robin Gee

lives of Americans and Canadians of Finnish descent." Circ. 5,000 + . Pays on publication. Publishes ms an average of 2-3 months after acceptance. Byline given. Buys one-time or second serial (reprint) rights. Submit seasonal/holiday material 4 months in advance. Photocopied and previously published submissions OK. Computer printout submissions OK; no dot-matrix. Reports in 1 month. Sample copy for 9½x12½ SAE with 1 first class stamp; writer's guidelines for SAE and 1 first class stamp.

Nonfiction: Book excerpts, essays, general interest, historical/nostalgic, humor, interview/profile, new product, personal experience, photo feature, travel, art, design and crafts, business, history and culture. Buys 10+ mss/year. Query with or without published clips, or send complete ms. Pays $20 minimum for assigned and unsolicited articles.

Photos: Send photos with submissions. Reviews prints. Offers no additional payment for photos accepted with ms. Offers $10 per photo. Captions, model release and identification of subjects required. Buys one-time rights.

Columns/Departments: A Touch of the Poet (poetry on any subject); Chefs of the Baltic (food and preparation of regional dishes); My Story (immigration to all parts of the world from Finland); From the Bookshop and the Cinema (reviews of materials with regional interest). Send complete ms. Pays $20 minimum.

Fiction: Ethnic, historical, humorous and slice-of-life vignettes. "All with a theme relating to Finnish or Finnish/Swedish heritage." Buys 6 mss/year. Send complete ms. Pays $20 minimum.

Poetry: Avant-garde, free verse, light verse and traditional. No scatological poetry. Buys 6-12 poems/year. Submit maximum 3 poems. Pays in copies.

Fillers: Anecdotes, facts, newsbreaks and short humor. Pays in copies.

Tips: "Submit articles with a new approach or with fresh information. Everyone knows about saunas, the War debt and Sibelius. Tell us something new about Finland and Finnish ways. We are very interested in stories of out-of-the-way travel in Finland or immigration adventures. All areas are open and we accept stories in Finnish and Swedish as well as English. However we want the articles in any of the three languages to be clear and grammatical and told in a fresh style."

FRIDAY (OF THE JEWISH EXPONENT), 226 S. 16th St., Philadelphia PA 19102. (215)893-5745. Editor: Jane Biberman. 100% freelance written. Eager to work with new/unpublished writers. Monthly literary supplement for the Jewish community of Greater Philadelphia. Circ. 100,000. Pays after publication. Publishes ms an average of 6 months after acceptance. Byline given. Offers 25% kill fee. Buys first serial rights. Submit seasonal/holiday material 3 months in advance. Photocopied submissions OK. Computer printout submissions acceptable; no dot-matrix. Reports in 3 weeks. Sample copy and writer's guidelines for SASE.

Nonfiction: "We are interested only in articles on Jewish themes, whether they be historical, thought pieces, Jewish travel or photographic essays. Topical themes are appreciated." Buys 25 unsolicited mss/year. Length: 6-20 double-spaced pages. Pays $75 minimum.

Fiction: Short stories on Jewish themes. Length: 6-20 double-spaced pages. Pays $75 minimum.

Poetry: Traditional forms, blank verse, free verse, avant-garde and light verse; must relate to Jewish theme. Length varies. Pays $15 minimum.

GREATER PHOENIX JEWISH NEWS, Phoenix Jewish News, Inc., Box 26590, Phoenix AZ 85068. (602)870-9470. Executive Editor: Flo Eckstein. Managing Editor: Leni Reiss. 10% freelance written. Prefers to work with published/established writers. Weekly tabloid covering subjects of interest to Jewish readers. Circ. 7,000. Pays on publication. Publishes ms an average of 3 months after acceptance. Byline given. Submit seasonal/holiday material 3 months in advance. Simultaneous queries, and simultaneous, photocopied, and previously published submissions OK. Computer printout submissions acceptable; prefers letter-quality to dot-matrix. (Must be easy to read, with upper and lower case.) Reports in 1 month. Sample copy $1.

Nonfiction: General interest, issue analysis, interview/profile, opinion, personal experience, photo feature and travel. Special sections include Fashion and Health; House and Home; Back to School; Summer Camps; Party Planning; Bridal; Travel; Business and Finance; and Jewish Holidays. Buys 25 mss/year. Query with published clips or send complete ms. Length: 1,000-2,500 words. Pays $15-75 for simultaneous rights; $1.50/column inch for first serial rights. Sometimes pays the expenses of writers on assignment.

Photos: Send photos with query or ms. Pays $10 for 8x10 b&w prints. Captions required.

Tips: "We are looking for lifestyle and issue-oriented pieces of particular interest to Jewish readers between ages 25-40. Our newspaper reaches across the religious, political, social and economic spectrum of Jewish residents in this burgeoning southwestern metropolitan area. We look for fairly short (maximum 1,500 words) pieces of a serious nature, written with clarity and balance. We stay away from cute stories as well as ponderous submissions."

HADASSAH MAGAZINE, 50 W. 58th St., New York NY 10019. Executive Editor: Alan M. Tigay. 60% freelance written. Works with small number of new/unpublished writers each year. Monthly, except combined issues (June-July and August-September). Circ. 370,000. Publishes ms 1-18 months after acceptance. Buys first rights (with travel articles, we buy all rights). Computer printout submissions acceptable. Reports in 6 weeks. Sample copy $3 with 9x12 SAE; writer's guidelines for SASE.

Nonfiction: Primarily concerned with Israel, Jewish communities around the world, and American civic affairs. Buys 10 unsolicited mss/year. Length: 1,500-2,000 words. Pays $200-400, less for reviews. Sometimes pays the expenses of writers on assignment.

Photos: "We buy photos only to illustrate articles, with the exception of outstanding color from Israel which we use on our covers. We pay $175 and up for a suitable cover photo." Offers $50 for first photo; $35 for each additional. "Always interested in striking cover (color) photos, especially of Israel and Jerusalem."

Columns/Departments: "We have a Parenting column and a Travel column, but a query for topic or destination should be submitted first to make sure the area is of interest and the story follows our format."

Fiction: Contact Zelda Shluker. Short stories with strong plots and positive Jewish values. No personal memoirs, "schmaltzy" fiction, or women's magazine fiction. "We continue to buy very little fiction because of a backlog. We are also open to art stories that explore trends in Jewish art, literature, theatre, etc." Length: 3,000 words maximum. Pays $300 minimum.

Tips: "While we work with established writers for most of our regular columns, we are open to reading unsolicited mss and are always seeking writers with fresh ways of looking at the Jewish community and its interests."

THE HIGHLANDER, Angus J. Ray Associates, Inc., Box 397, Barrington IL 60011. (312)382-1035. Editor: Angus J. Ray. Managing Editor: Ethyl Kennedy Ray. 20% freelance written. Works with a small number of new/unpublished writers each year. Bimonthly magazine covering Scottish history, clans, genealogy, travel/history, and Scottish/American activities. Circ. 35,000. Pays on acceptance. Publishes ms an average of 6 months after acceptance. Byline given. Buys first North American serial rights and second serial (reprint) rights to material originally published elsewhere. Submit seasonal/holiday material 6 months in advance. Photocopied and previously published submissions OK. Computer printout submissions acceptable; no dot-matrix. Reports in 1 month. Sample copy $1. Free writer's guidelines.

Nonfiction: Historical/nostalgic. "No fiction; no articles unrelated to Scotland." Buys 20 mss/year. Query. Length: 750-2,000 words. Pays $75-150. Sometimes pays the expenses of writers on assignment.

Photos: State availability of photos. Pays $5-10 for 8x10 b&w prints. Reviews b&w contact sheets. Identification of subjects required. Buys one-time rights.

Tips: "Submit something that has appeared elsewhere."

INSIDE, The Jewish Exponent Magazine, Federation of Jewish Agencies of Greater Philadelphia, 226 S. 16th St., Philadelphia PA 19102. (215)893-5700. Editor: Jane Biberman. Managing Editor: Jodie Green. 95% freelance written (by assignment). Works with published/established writers and a small number of new/unpublished writers each year. Quarterly Jewish community magazine—for a 25 years and older general interest Jewish readership. Circ. 100,000. Pays on acceptance. Publishes ms an average of 2 months after acceptance. Byline given. Offers 20% kill fee. Buys one-time rights. Submit seasonal/holiday material 3 months in advance. Simultaneous queries OK. Computer printout submissions acceptable; no dot-matrix. Reports in 2 weeks on queries; 3 weeks on mss. Sample copy $3.50; free writer's guidelines.

Nonfiction: Book excerpts, general interest, historical/nostalgic, humor, interview/profile. Philadelphia angle desirable. No personal religious experiences or trips to Israel. Buys 100 mss/year. Query. Length: 600-3,000 words. Pays $200-700. Pays the expenses of writers on assignment.

Fiction: Short stories. Query.

Photos: State availability of photos. Reviews color and b&w transparencies. Identification of subjects required.

Tips: "Personalities—very well known—and serious issues of concern to Jewish community needed. We can use 600-word 'back page' pieces—humorous, first person articles."

THE ITALIAN TIMES, Italian-American Publications, Inc., Box 20241, Baltimore MD 21284-2024. (301)254-1300. Publisher: Stephen J. Ferrandi. Managing Editor: Jodi Barke. 55% freelance written. Eager to work with new/unpublished writers. Monthly magazine covering anything of interest to Italian-Americans. Circ. 32,500. Pays on publication. Publishes ms an average of 3 months after acceptance. Byline given. Buys first rights, one-time rights, or second serial (reprint) rights. Submit seasonal/holiday material 5 months in advance. Simultaneous and previously published submissions OK. Computer printout submissions acceptable; no dot-matrix. Reports in 6 weeks on queries; 1 month on mss. Sample copy $1.

Nonfiction: Essays, exposé, general interest, historical/nostalgic, humor, interview/profile, opinion, personal experience, travel and young Italian-American success stories. Special issues include Italian Easter; all

ALWAYS submit manuscripts or queries with a self-addressed, stamped envelope (SASE) within your country or International Reply Coupons purchased from the post office for other countries.

Italy issue with personal experiences, travel hints, food and wine featured (August); and Italian Christmas. Buys 30 mss/year. Send complete ms. Length: 100-10,000 words. Pays $2-100; mainly pays in copies "if new author with only average writing skills but good idea." Sometimes pays the expenses of writers on assignment.
Photos: Send photos or slides with submission. Reviews 8x10 prints. Captions and identification of subjects required.
Fiction: Ethnic, humorous and slice-of-life vignettes. All fiction submissions must have an Italian or Italian-American theme. Buys 8 mss/year. Send complete ms. Length: 3,750 words maximum. Pays $2-50.
Poetry: F. Joseph Sebastian, poetry editor. Free verse, haiku, light verse and traditional. Buys 6 poems/year. Length: 50 lines maximum. Pays $2-25.
Fillers: Anecdotes, facts, newsbreaks and short humor. Buys 100/year. Length: 750 words maximum. Pays $2-25.
Tips: "We encourage good writers who haven't been published to send a manuscript for consideration. Stories and articles should be fast paced, easily digested and worth reading a second time. We welcome phone calls to answer any questions (9-5). We publish mostly freelance general interest and cover stories."

‡**THE JEWISH MONTHLY**, B'nai B'rith International, 1640 Rhode Island Ave. NW, Washington DC 20036. (202)857-6645. Editor: Marc Silver. 75% freelance written. Prefers to work with published/established writers. A monthly magazine covering Jewish politics, lifestyles, religion and culture for a family audience. Circ. 180,000. Pays on publication. Publishes ms an average of 4 months after acceptance. Byline given. Offers 25% kill fee. Buys first North American serial rights. Submit seasonal/holiday material 6 months in advance. Photocopied submissions OK. Query for electronic submissions. Computer printout submissions acceptable; prefers letter-quality to dot-matrix. Reports in 2 weeks on queries; 1 month on mss. Sample copy $1; free writer's guidelines.
Nonfiction: Book excerpts, general interest, historical/nostalgic, humor, interview/profile, opinion, personal experience, photo feature, religious and travel. "I am looking for articles that offer fresh perspectives on familiar issues in the Jewish community (such as assimilation, Middle East conflict, religious tensions) and articles that focus on new trends and problems." No immigrant reminiscences. Buys 25 mss/year. Query with published clips. Length: 500-5,000 words. Pays 10-25¢/word. Sometimes pays the expenses of writers on assignment.
Photos: State availability of photos with submission. Reviews contact sheets, transparencies and prints. Offers $25-75/photo. Captions, model releases, and identification of subjects required. Buys one-time rights.

JEWISH NEWS, Suite 240, 20300 Civic Center Dr., Southfield MI 48076. (313)354-6060. Editor: Gary Rosenblatt. News Editor: Alan Hitsky. 10% freelance written. Works with a small number of new/unpublished writers each year. A weekly tabloid covering news and features of Jewish interest. Circ. 17,000. Pays on publication. Publishes ms an average of 3 months after acceptance. Byline given. No kill fee "unless stipulated beforehand." Buys first North American serial rights. Simultaneous queries and photocopied submissions OK. Computer printout submissions acceptable; prefers letter-quality to dot-matrix. Reports in 2 weeks on queries; 1 month on mss. Sample copy $1.
Nonfiction: Book excerpts, humor, and interview/profile. Buys 10-20 mss/year. Query with or without published clips, or send complete ms. Length: 500-2,500 words. Pays $40-125.
Fiction: Ethnic. Buys 1-2 mss/year. Send complete ms. Length: 500-2,500 words. Pays $40-125.

KOREAN CULTURE, Korean Cultural Service, 5505 Wilshire Blvd., Los Angeles CA 90036. (213)936-7141. Editor: Kyounghee Yoon Lee. 100% freelance written. Prefers to work with published/established writers. A quarterly magazine covering historical and modern culture of Korea. "An illustrated academic journal, it is distributed free of charge world-wide to both institutions and individuals. Readers include scholars and educated lay persons." Circ. 12,000. Pays on publication. Publishes ms an average of 6 months after acceptance. Byline given. Makes work-for-hire assignments. Submit seasonal/holiday material 6 months in advance. Computer printout submissions acceptable; prefers letter-quality to dot-matrix. Reports in 2 weeks on queries; 2 months on mss. Free sample copy and writer's guidelines.
Nonfiction: Essays, historical/nostalgic, interview/profile, photo feature, religious and travel. No personal experience travelogues; technically complex submissions in linguistics, sociology, or political science; unresearched materials of any type. Buys 4 mss/year. Query with or without published clips, or send complete ms. Length: 3,000 minimum. Pays $100-250.
Photos: Send photos with submission. Reviews transparencies and prints. Offers no additional payment for photos accepted with ms. Captions and identification of subjects required. Buys all rights.
Columns/Departments: Review (publications, cultural events, films, exhibitions may be considered). Reviews should be well researched, and should place the item reviewed into the larger context of Korean culture. Buys 2 mss/year. Query with published clips. Length: approximately 3,000 words. Pays $100-250.
Tips: "*Korean Culture* is designed to educate the Western audience to the unique qualities of Korea. Specialists in Korean studies, or those with a sophisticated grounding in Korean affairs, will therefore have the best chance of submitting acceptable typescripts. Specialists in other fields (e.g., film, sports, travel, international

trade) should be prepared to research their topic thoroughly prior to submission. Reviews of a variety of cultural events are needed most frequently; these are sometimes scattered across the United States and abroad, wherever a sizable Korean community exists. Some of these may be of interest to *Korean Culture*, but authors should inquire in advance, and obtain specific advice about the best method of approach for the topic."

LECTOR, The Hispanic Review Journal, Hispanic Information Exchange, Box 4273, Berkeley CA 94704. (818)990-1886. Editor: Roberto Cabello-Argandona. Managing Editor: Claire Splan. 95% freelance written. Works with a small number of new/unpublished writers each year and is eager to work with new/unpublished writers. A semiannual journal of Hispanic cultural articles and English reviews of books in Spanish. "We desire cultural articles, particularly of Hispanic arts and literature, written for a popular level (as opposed to an academic level). Articles are to be nonsexist, nonracist." Circ. 3,000. Pays on publication. Publishes ms an average of 6-12 months after acceptance. Byline given. Buys first rights or makes work-for-hire assignments. Photocopied submissions OK; previously published submissions sometimes accepted. Computer printout submissions acceptable; prefers letter-quality to dot-matrix. Reports in 3 months. Sample copy $3; writer's guidelines for SASE.
Nonfiction: Interview/profile, photo feature and articles on art, literature and Latino small presses. No personal experience, religious or how-to. Buys 25 mss/year. "No unsolicited manuscripts; query us first." Length: 2,000-3,500 words. Pays $50-150. "Writers, along with payment, always get five copies of magazine."
Photos: Send photos with submission. Reviews contact sheets. Captions required. Buys one-time rights.
Columns/Departments: Publisher's Corner (covers publishing houses in Latin America or U.S. [Latin]), 2,000-2,500 words; Perspective (cultural articles dealing with aspect of Hispanic art/lit), 2,500-3,500 words; Events in Profile (occasional column covering particular event in Chicano Studies), 1,500-2,000 words; Feature Review (in-depth review of particularly important published work), 2,500-3,000 words, Author's Corner (interview with recently published author), 1,500-2,000 words, and Inquiry (literary criticism) 2,000-2,500 words. Buys 15 mss/year. Query with published clips. Pays $50-150.

MIDSTREAM, A Monthly Jewish Review, 515 Park Ave., New York NY 10022. Editor: Joel Carmichael. 90% freelance written. Works with a small number of new/unpublished writers each year. Monthly. Circ. 10,000. Buys first North American serial rights. Byline given. Pays after publication. Publishes ms an average of 6 months after acceptance. Computer printout submissions acceptable; no dot-matrix. Reports in 2 months. Fiction guidelines for SAE with 1 first class stamp.
Nonfiction: "Articles offering a critical interpretation of the past, searching examination of the present, and affording a medium for independent opinion and creative cultural expression. Articles on the political and social scene in Israel, on Jews in Russia, the U.S. and elsewhere; generally it helps to have a Zionist orientation." Buys historical and think pieces, primarily of Jewish and related content. Pays 5¢/word.
Fiction: Primarily of Jewish and related content. Pays 5¢/word.
Tips: "A book review is a good way to start. Send us a sample review or a clip, let us know your area of interest, suggest books you would like to review. For longer articles, give a brief account of your background or credentials in this field. Send query describing article or ms with cover letter. Since we are a monthly, we look for critical analysis rather than a 'journalistic' approach."

‡NIGHTMOVES, Chicago's Free Biweekly, Nightmoves Publishing Co., Suite 1100, 105 W. Madison, Chicago IL 60602. (312)346-7765. Editor: Howard Wilson. Managing Editor: Gayle Soucek. 75% freelance written. Eager to work with new/unpublished writers. Biweekly tabloid of politics, entertainment, and social issues. "We reach a Black, primarily urban audience ages 18-40." Circ. 50,000. Pays on publication. Publishes ms an average of 3 months after acceptance. Byline given. Not copyrighted. "We rarely kill an article without giving the writer ample opportunity to re-write it." Buys first rights and second serial (reprint) rights. Submit seasonal/holiday material 2 months in advance. Photocopied and previously published submissions OK. Computer printout submissions acceptable; no dot-matrix. Reports in 3 weeks on queries; 1 month on mss. Sample copy for 9x12 SAE and 3 first class stamps. Writer's guidelines for #10 SAE and 1 first class stamp.
Nonfiction: Expose (almost any subject, but must be carefully documented); general interest; humor (mostly sophisticated, such as political satire); and interview/profile. No personal opinion or travel. "While we enjoy articles of national interest, our distribution is in the Chicago area only, so we cannot use articles on local issues from other areas, *unless* they relate closely to a broader theme." Buys 120+ mss/year. Query or send complete ms (prefers queries). Length: 750-2,500 words. Pays 3-5¢/word. Sometimes pays expenses of writers on assignment.
Photos: State availability of photos with query letter or ms. "We are a very visually-oriented publication, so photos are welcomed, but they must be good quality. Good photos will help sell us on a story idea." Prefers 5x7 or 8x10 b&w prints. Pays $10-20. Captions and model releases required. Buys one-time rights.
Columns/Departments: Movie and Theatre Reviews, Chicago-area restaurant reviews, etc. "This is a lim-

ited area for freelancers, and we prefer queries only." Buys 10-15 mss/year. Query. Length: 750-1,250 words. Pays 3-5¢/word.

Tips: "We receive too much 'light' material and not enough well-researched, hard-hitting cover story material. Articles are usually too vague and all-encompassing, lacking a definite focus and adequate research and documentation."

PRESENT TENSE: The Magazine of World Jewish Affairs, 165 E. 56th St., New York NY 10022. (212)751-4000. Editor: Murray Polner. 95% freelance written. Prefers to work with published/established writers. For college-educated, Jewish-oriented audience interested in Jewish life throughout the world. Bimonthly magazine. Circ. 45,000. Buys all rights. Byline given. Buys 60 mss/year. Pays on publication. Publishes ms an average of 6 months after acceptance. Computer printout submissions acceptable. Reports in 2 months. Sample copy $4.50.

Nonfiction: Quality reportage of contemporary events (a la *Harper's, New Yorker,* etc.). Personal journalism, reportage, profiles and photo essays. Query. Length: 3,000 words maximum. Pays $150-250. Sometimes pays the expenses of writers on assignment.

Tips: "Read our magazine."

RECONSTRUCTIONIST, 270 W. 89th St., New York NY 10024. (212)496-2960. Editor: Dr. Jacob Staub. 50% freelance written. Works with a small number of new/unpublished writers each year. A general Jewish religious and cultural magazine. Monthly. Circ. 8,500. Buys first serial rights. Pays on publication. Publishes ms of 12-18 months after acceptance. Computer printout submissions acceptable. Free sample copy.

Nonfiction: Publishes literary criticism, reports from Israel and other lands where Jews live, and material of educational or communal interest. Query. Buys 35 mss/year. Preferred length is 2,000-3,000 words. Pays $36.

Fiction: Uses a small amount of fiction as fillers.

Poetry: Used as fillers.

THE UKRAINIAN WEEKLY, Ukrainian National Association, 30 Montgomery St., Jersey City NJ 07302. (201)434-0237. Editor: Roma Hadzewycz. 30% freelance written. "We are backlogged with submissions and prefer not to receive unsolicited submissions at this time." A weekly tabloid covering news and issues of concern to Ukrainian community. Circ. 7,000. Pays on publication. Publishes ms an average of 1-2 months after acceptance. Byline given. Buys first North American serial rights, second serial (reprint) rights or makes work-for-hire assignments. Submit seasonal/holiday material 1 month in advance. Reports in 1 month. Free sample copy.

Nonfiction: Book excerpts, essays, exposé, general interest, historical/nostalgic, interview/profile, opinion, personal experience, photo feature and news events. Special issues include Easter, Christmas, anniversary of Helsinki Accords, anniversary of Ukrainian Helsinki monitoring group. Buys 80 mss/year. Query with published clips. Length: 500-2,000 words. Pays $45-100 for assigned articles. Pays $25-100 for unsolicited articles. Sometimes pays the expenses of writers on assignment.

Photos: Send photos with submission. Reviews contact sheets, negatives and 3x5, 5x7 or 8x10 prints. Offers no additional payment for photos accepted with ms.

Columns/Departments: News & Views (commentary on news events), 500-1,000 words. Buys 10 mss/ year. Query. Pays $25-50.

Tips: "Become acquainted with the Ukrainian community in the U.S. and Canada. The area of our publication most open to freelancers is community news—coverage of local events."

‡VISTA, Focus on Hispanic Americans, Suite 301, 2355 Salzedo St., Coral Gables FL 33314. (305)442-2462. Editor: Harry Caicedo. Managing Editor: Renato Pérez. 95% freelance written. Prefers to work with published/established writers. An English-language monthly directed at Hispanic Americans. It appears as a supplement to 27 newspapers across the country with a combined circulation of 1,118,300 in cities with large Latin populations. Pays on publication. Publishes ms an average of 2 months after acceptance. Byline given. Offers 25% of original price kill fee. Buys first rights. Submit seasonal/holiday material 4 months in advance. Photocopied submissions OK. Computer printout submissions OK; prefers letter-quality to dot-matrix. Reports in 1 week on queries; 2 weeks on mss. Sample copy and writer's guidelines for 11½x12½ SAE with 56¢ postage.

Nonfiction: General interest, historical/nostalgic, inspirational, interview/profile, opinion and travel. No articles without a Hispanic American angle. Buys 90 mss/year. Query with published clips. Length: 100-2,000 words. Pays $50-400. Sometimes pays the expenses of writers on assignment.

Photos: State availability of photos with submission. Reviews contact sheets, negatives, transparencies and prints. Offers negotiable payment per photo. Identification of subjects required. Buys one-time rights.

Columns/Departments: Vistascopes (Hispanic people in the news), 100 words; Spotlight (profile of a Hispanic notable for his/her accomplishments), 500-750 words; Voices (personal views on matters affecting Hispanic Americans), 500 words. Buys 48 mss/year. Query with published clips. Length: 100-750 words. Pays $50-200.

Fiction: Slice-of-life vignettes. Buys 2 mss/year. Send complete ms. Length: 1,000 words maximum. Pays 20¢ per word.

Tips: "Be aware of topics and personalities of interest to Hispanic readers. We need profiles of Hispanic Americans in unusual or untypical roles and jobs. Anticipate events; profiles should tell the reader what the subject will be doing at the time of publication. Keep topics upbeat and positive: no stories on drugs, crime. A light, breezy touch is needed for the profiles. Express your opinion in the Voices pages but be scrupulously impartial and accurate when writing articles of general interest. Don't be militant; *Vista* is *not* a soapbox. Keep standards high; *Vista* editors are a critical bunch."

Food and Drink

Magazines appealing to gourmets are classified here. Journals aimed at food processing, manufacturing and retailing are in the Trade section. Many magazines in General Interest and Women's categories also buy articles on these topics.

‡AMERICAN BREWER, The Micro-Brewer/Brew Pub Magazine, Box 713, Hayward CA 94541. (415)886-9823. Editor: Scott Schoepp. 100% freelance written. Quarterly magazine covering micro beer brewing. Circ. 2,000. Pays on acceptance. Byline given. Buys first North American serial rights. Submit seasonal/holiday material 3 months in advance. Accepts electronic submissions; query for details. Computer printout submissions OK; prefers letter-quality. Reports in 2 weeks. Sample copy $3.
Nonfiction: Book excerpts, general interest, how-to, personal experience. Plans special issue on regional breweries and beers. Buys 10 mss/year. Query. Length: 1,000-2,000 words. Pays $50-100. Pays expenses of writers on assignment.
Photos: State availability of photos with submission. Reviews contact sheets. Offers no additional payment for photos accepted with ms. Captions are required. Buys one-time rights.

BON APPETIT, America's Food and Entertaining Magazine, Knapp Communications Corporation, 5900 Wilshire Blvd., Los Angeles CA 90036. (213)937-1025. Editor: William J. Garry. 70% freelance written. Works with small number of new/unpublished writers each year. Monthly magazine. "Our articles are written in the first person voice and are directed toward the active cook. Emphasis on recipes intended for use by the dedicated amateur cook." Circ. 1,300,000. Pays on acceptance. Publishes ms an average of 6 months after acceptance. Byline given. Buys first North American serial rights and all rights. Submit seasonal/holiday material 6 months in advance. Computer printout submissions acceptable; no dot-matrix. Reports in 1 month. Writer's guidelines for 4x8 SAE with 22¢ postage.
Nonfiction: Barbara Fairchild, senior editor. How-to (cooking) and travel. No articles which are not food related. Buys 120 mss/year. Query with published clips. Length: 1,000-3,000 words. Pays $600-2,000. Sometimes pays the expenses of writers on assignment.
Photos: State availability of photos with submission. Reviews 35mm transparencies. Offers $175-550/photo. Captions, model releases and identification of subjects required. Buys one-time rights.
Columns/Departments: Laurie Glenn Buckle, column/department editor. Bon Voyage (travel articles featuring a specific city which cover, in a lively manner, interesting sights and landmarks and, especially, local restaurants and foods of note). Will need recipes from these restaurants. Buys 12 mss/year. Query. Length: 1,000-2,000 words. Pays $600-1,200.

‡CHOCOLATIER, The Haymarket Group/Ion International, #407, 45 W. 34th St., New York NY 10001. (212)239-0855. Editor-in-Chief: Barbara Albright. Managing Editor: Susan Spedalle. 33% freelance written. A bimonthly magazine "devoted to people who exemplify their passion for the good life by their love of fine chocolate. While *Chocolatier* focuses on a national indulgence, feature articles cover food, travel, spirits, and all aspects of entertaining." Circ. 350,000. Pays on acceptance. Publishes ms an average of 6 months after acceptance. Byline given. Offers 25% kill fee. Buys first worldwide serial rights (publication elsewhere not earlier than 4 months after publication in *Chocolatier*). Submit seasonal/holiday material 8 months in advance. Simultaneous and photocopied submissions OK. Computer printout submissions acceptable; prefers letter-quality to dot-matrix. Reports in 2 months. Free writer's guidelines.
Nonfiction: Interview/profile, new products, food/recipe, technical and travel. Buys 35-50 mss/year. Query with published clips. Length: 500-2,500 words. Pays $100-1,000.

Photos: State availability of photos with submission. Identification of subjects required. Buys one-time rights.

Columns/Departments: Submit ideas for departments. Query with published clips. Length: 500-1,000 words. Pays variable rates.

COOK'S, The Magazine of Cooking in America, Pennington Publishing, 2710 North Ave., Bridgeport CT 06604. (203)366-4155. Editor: Judith Hill. Managing Editor: Sheila O'Meara Lowenstein. 50% freelance written. Prefers to work with published/established writers. A bimonthly magazine covering food and cooking in America. *"Cook's* publishes lively informative articles that describe food and restaurant trends in the U.S. or that describe hands-on cooking techniques. Almost all of our articles include recipes." Circ. 165,000. Pays on publication. Publishes ms an average of 8 months after acceptance. Byline given. Offers 50% kill fee. Buys all rights. Submit seasonal/holiday material 10 months in advance. Photocopied submissions OK. Computer printout submissions acceptable; prefers letter-quality to dot-matrix. Reports in 2 months. Sample copy for 10x13 SAE with $1.18 postage; writer's guidelines for #10 SAE with 1 first class stamp.

Nonfiction: Mary Caldwell, articles editor. Food and cooking. No travel, personal experience or nostalgia pieces, history of food and cuisine, or recipes using prepared ingredients (e.g., canned soups, "instant" foods, mixes, etc.). Buys 25-30 mss/year. Query with clips and sample original recipes. Length: 500-3,000 words plus recipes. Pays $75-375. Rarely pays expenses of writers on assignment.

Columns/Departments: Mary Caldwell, articles editor. Peak Produce (article plus 8-10 recipes focusing on a specific seasonal ingredient or type of ingredient), 500-1,000 words plus recipes. Buys about 9 mss/year. Query with published clips or unpublished writing sample. Length: 500-2,500 words. Pays $250-300.

‡KASHRUS MAGAZINE, The Bimonthly for the Kosher Consumer, Yeshiva Birkas Reuven, Box 96, Parkville Station, Brooklyn NY 11204. (718)998-3201. Editor: Rabbi Yosef Wikler. 25% freelance written. Prefers to work with published/established writers, and is eager to work with new/unpublished writers. Bimonthly magazine covering kosher food industry. Circ. 10,000. Pays on acceptance. Publishes ms an average of 2 months after acceptance. Byline given. Offers 50% kill fee. Buys first or second serial (reprint) rights. Submit seasonal/holiday material 2 months in advance. Simultaneous, photocopied and previously published submissions OK. Query for electronic submissions. Computer printout submissions OK; prefers letter-quality. Reports in 1 week on queries; 2 weeks on mss. Free sample copy and writer's guidelines.

Nonfiction: General interest, interview/profile, new product, personal experience, photo feature, religious, technical and travel. Special issues feature International Kosher Travel (October, 1987) and Passover (March, 1988). Buys 3 mss/year. Query with published clips. Length: 1,000-2,000 words. Pays $100-250 for assigned articles; pays $0-100 for unsolicited articles. Sometimes pays the expenses of writers on assignment.

Photos: State availability of photos with submission. Offers no additional payment for photos accepted with ms. Buys one-time rights.

Columns/Departments: Book Review (cooking books, food technology, kosher food), 250-500 words; People in the News (interviews with kosher personalities), 1,000-2,000 words; Regional Kosher Supervision (report on kosher supervision in a city or community), 1,000-3,000 words; Food Technology (new technology or current technology with accompanying pictures), 1,000-2,000 words. Buys 5 mss/year. Query with published clips. Pays $50-250.

Tips: *"Kashrus Magazine* will do more writing on general food technology, production, and merchandising as well as human interest and regional writing in 1988 than we have done in the past. Areas most open to freelancers are interviews, food technology, regional reporting."

VINTAGE, The Magazine of Food, Wine and Gracious Living, Wine News, Inc., Suite 370, E. 76th St., New York NY 10021. Editor: Philip Seldon. 80% freelance written. A monthly magazine covering food, wine, travel, etc. Circ. 100,000. Pays on publication. Byline given. Buys all rights. Submit seasonal/holiday material 6 months in advance. Simultaneous, photocopied and previously published submissions OK. Computer printout submissions acceptable; prefers letter-quality to dot-matrix. Reports in 1 month. Sample copy $2 with 9x12 SAE; writer's guidelines for #10 SAE with 1 first class stamp.

Nonfiction: Book excerpts, exposé, how-to, interview/profile, new product, personal experience, photo feature and travel, all food and wine related. Buys 10-12 mss/year. Query with published clips, or send complete ms. Length: 750-4,000 words. Pays $100-500 for assigned articles; $50-250 for unsolicited articles. May pay in wine.

Photos: State availability of photos with submission or send photos with submission. Reviews contact sheets or transparencies. Offers no additional payment for photos accepted with ms. Captions, model releases and identification of subjects required. Buys one-time rights.

Fiction: Historical, humorous, mystery, slice-of-life vignettes and suspense, all food and wine-related. Buys 10-12 mss/year. Query with published clips or send complete ms. Length: 500-4,000 words.

WINE & SPIRITS BUYING GUIDE, Winestate Publications, Inc., Box 1548, Princeton NJ 08542. (609)921-2196. Editor: Joshua Greene. 60% freelance written. A bimonthly magazine covering wine and spirits tasting. Circ. 52,000. Pays on publication. Publishes ms an average of 3 months after acceptance. Byline given. Buys first North American serial rights. Computer printout submissions acceptable; prefers letter-quality to dot-matrix. Sample copy for 9x12 SAE with $1.07 postage; writer's guidelines for letter-size SAE with 1 first class stamp.

Nonfiction: Interview/profile (of a winemaker, importer, or wine personality) and travel (to wine related areas, vineyards, wineries, distilleries, etc.). Only wine or spirits related submissions. Buys 25 mss/year. Query with published clips. Length: 1,000-2,000 words. Pays $200-250 for assigned articles; pays $100-150 for unsolicited articles. Sometimes pays the expenses of writers on assignment.

Photos: Send photos with submission. Offers $25/photo. Model releases and identification of subjects required. Buys one-time rights.

THE WINE SPECTATOR, M. Shanken Communications, Inc., Opera Plaza Suite 2040, 601 Van Ness Ave., San Francisco CA 94102. (415)673-2040. Executive Editor: Harvey Steiman. Managing Editor: Jim Gordon. 35-40% freelance written. Prefers to work with published/established writers. Twice monthly consumer newspaper covering wine. Circ. 70,000. Pays on publication. Publishes ms an average of 2 months after acceptance. Byline given. Buys first rights and makes work-for-hire assignments. Submit seasonal/holiday material 3 months in advance. Query for electronic submissions. Computer printout submissions acceptable "as long as they are legible." Reports in 3 weeks. Sample copy $1.75; free writer's guidelines.

Nonfiction: General interest (news about wine or wine events); humor; interview/profile (of wine, vintners, wineries); opinion; and photo feature. No "winery promotional pieces or articles by writers who lack sufficient knowledge to write below just surface data." Query. Length: 100-2,000 words average. Pays $50-300.

Photos: Send photos with ms. Pays $25 minimum for b&w contact sheets, negatives, transparencies, and 5x7 prints. Captions, model releases and identification of subjects required. Buys all rights.

Tips: "A solid knowledge of wine is a must. Query letters help, detailing the story idea; many freelance writers do not understand what a query letter is and how important it is to selling an article. New, refreshing ideas which have not been covered before stand a good chance of acceptance. *The Wine Spectator* is a consumer-oriented *newspaper* but we are interested in some trade stories; brevity is essential."

WINE TIDINGS, Kylix Media Inc., 5165 Sherbrooke St. W., 414, Montreal, Quebec H4A 1T6 Canada. (514)481-5892. Publisher: Judy Rochester. Editor: Barbara Leslie. 90% freelance written. Works with small number of new/unpublished writers each year. Magazine published 8 times/year primarily for men with incomes of more than $50,000. "Covers anything happening on the wine scene in Canada." Circ. 28,000. Pays on publication. Publishes ms an average of 3-4 months after acceptance. Byline given. Buys all rights. Submit seasonal/holiday material 3 months in advance. Computer printout submissions acceptable; prefers letter-quality to dot-matrix. Reports in 1 month.

Nonfiction: General interest; historical; humor; interview/profile; new product (and developments in the Canadian and U.S. wine industries); opinion; personal experience; photo feature; and travel (to wine-producing countries). "All must pertain to wine or wine-related topics and should reflect author's basic knowledge of and interest in wine." Buys 20-30 mss/year. Send complete ms. Length: 500-2,000 words. Pays $35-300.

Photos: State availability of photos. Pays $20-100 for color prints; $10-25 for b&w prints. Identification of subjects required. Buys one-time rights.

WINE WORLD MAGAZINE, Suite 412, 6433 Topanga Blvd., Canoga Park CA 91303. Editor-Publisher: Dee Sindt. For the wine-loving public (adults of all ages) who wish to learn more about wine. Quarterly magazine; 48 pages. Buys first North American serial rights. Buys about 50 mss/year. Pays on publication. No photocopied submissions. Simultaneous submissions OK "if spelled out." Send $2 for sample copy and writer's guidelines.

Nonfiction: "Wine-oriented material written with an in-depth knowledge of the subject, designed to meet the needs of the novice and connoisseur alike—wine technology advancements, wine history, profiles of vintners the world over. Educational articles only. No first-person accounts. Must be objective, informative reporting on economic trends, new technological developments in vinification, vine hybridizing, and vineyard care. New wineries and new marketing trends. We restrict our editorial content to wine, and wine-oriented material. Will accept restaurant articles—good wine lists. No more basic wine information. No articles from instant wine experts. Authors must be qualified in this highly technical field." Query. Length: 750-2,000 words. Pays $50-100.

WOMEN'S CIRCLE HOME COOKING, Box 198, Henniker NH 03242. Editor: Susan Hankins Andrews. 95% freelance written. Eager to work with new/unpublished writers. For women (and some men) of all ages who really enjoy cooking. "Our readers collect and exchange recipes. They are neither food faddists nor gourmets, but practical women and men trying to serve attractive and nutritious meals. Many work fulltime, and most are on limited budgets." Monthly magazine; 72 pages. Circ. 225,000. Pays on publication. Publishes ms an average of 6-12 months after acceptance. Buys all rights. Submit seasonal/holiday material 6 months in advance. Computer printout submissions acceptable; prefers letter-quality to dot-matrix. Reports in 2 months. Sample copy for 8x5 SAE with 59¢ postage.

Nonfiction: Exposé, historical, how-to, informational, inspirational, nostalgia, photo feature and travel. "We like a little humor with our food, for the sake of digestion. Keep articles light. Stress economy and efficiency. Remember that at least half our readers must cook after working a fulltime job. Draw on personal experience to write an informative article on some aspect of cooking. We're a reader participation magazine. We don't go in for fad diets, or strange combinations of food which claim to cure anything. Good articles discuss some aspect of cooking and provide several recipes." No medical advice or sick or gross humor. Buys 12-15 mss/year. Query. Length: 50-1,000 words. Pays 2-5¢/word.

Photos: State availability of photos. Pays $5 for 4x5 b&w or color sharp glossy prints; $35 minimum for 35 mm, 2¼x2¼ and 4x5 transparencies used on cover. Pays $75 for cover photos.

Fiction: Humorous fiction related to cooking and foods. Length: 1,000 words maximum. Pays 2-5¢/word.

Poetry: Light verse related to cooking and foods. Length: 20 lines. Pays $5-10/verse.

Fillers: Short humorous fillers. Length: 100 words. Pays 2-5¢/word. Cartoons related to cooking and dining. Pays $20/cartoon.

Tips: "We promise readers 80-100 recipes per issue and are doing less and less freelance material per issue—stressing reader-submitted recipes (non-compensated). Recipes, if chosen for publication, are eligible for consideration as the 'Recipe of the Month' which pays $25."

Games and Puzzles

These publications are written by and for game enthusiasts interested in both traditional games and word puzzles and newer role-playing adventure, computer and video games. Crossword fans also will find markets here. Additional home video game publications are listed in the Entertainment section. Other puzzle markets may be found in the Juvenile section.

‡ABYSS, 921 E. 49½ St., Austin TX 78751. (512)467-2806. Editor: David F. Nalle. Managing Editor: Jon Schuller. 40% freelance written. Eager to work with new and unpublished writers. Bimonthly magazine covering games (fantasy, science fiction, historical). "*Abyss* provides game background and theory articles for adult game players interested in expanding their sources and ideas, particularly in the area of interactive role-playing games. Our orientation is toward college-age gamers who take the hobby seriously as an educational and enlightening pursuit. We ask only for an open mind and an active imagination." Circ. 1,200-1,500. Pays on publication. Publishes ms an average of 5 months after acceptance. Byline given. Buys one-time rights and first rights. Submit seasonal/holiday material 8 months in advance. Query for electronic submissions. Computer printout submissions acceptable; prefers letter-quality to dot-matrix. Reports in 2 weeks on queries; 6 weeks on mss. Sample copy $2; writer's guidelines for SASE.

Nonfiction: Expose (concentrate on major game companies like TSR, FGU, SJG, etc.); historical (preferably pre-20th century game-oriented); humor (preferably game or fantasy related); new product reviews (games and small press items only); opinion (any gaming topic); technical (game design, game publishing, game variants); and articles on any gaming-related topic from a range of approaches. "Also bibliographical fantasy." No "why my campaign is wonderful" or "articles too closely wedded to only one game system." Buys 30 mss/year. Send complete ms. Length: 1,000-5,000 words. Pays $5-100. Sometimes pays the expenses of writers on assignment.

Columns/Departments: John R. Davies, column/department editor. Berserkergang (opinion/expose); Worlds of . . . (fantasy or science fiction bibliographical relevant to gaming); In the Pentacle (demonscopy, send for sample); and In the Speculum (reviews of games, magazines and books). Buys 18 mss/year. Query. Length: 400-3,000 words. Pays $5-40.

Fiction: P. Fitch, fiction editor. Adventure, fantasy and mythology. "We really are not looking for any science fiction this year. No derivative, pastiche or game-based fiction." Buys 8 mss/year. Send complete ms. Length: 1,000-5,000 words. Pays $5-100.

Tips: "The best way to break in to *Abyss* is by writing good, short commentary or opinion articles with new information or perspectives. The areas most open to freelancers are In the Speculum (reviews must include copy of product or be assigned) and Worlds of. . . . Most major features are left to staff writers." The most frequent mistakes made by writers are "not querying just to find out current needs or taking a prosaic or too conventional approach."

CHESS LIFE, United States Chess Federation, 186 Route 9W, New Windsor NY 12550. (914)562-8350. Editor: Larry Parr. 15% freelance written. Works with a small number of new/unpublished writers each year. Monthly magazine covering the chess world. Circ. 60,000. Pays variable fee. Publishes ms an average of 5 months after acceptance. Byline given. Offers kill fee. Buys first or negotiable rights. Submit seasonal/holiday material 8 months in advance. Simultaneous queries, and simultaneous, photocopied and previously published submissions OK. Computer printout submissions acceptable. Reports in 1 month. Free sample copy and writer's guidelines.

Nonfiction: General interest, historical, interview/profile, and technical—all must have some relation to chess. No "stories about personal experiences with chess." Buys 30-40 mss/year. Query with samples "if new to publication." Length: 3,000 words maximum. Sometimes pays the expenses of writers on assignment.

Photos: Reviews b&w contact sheets and prints, and color prints and slides. Captions, model releases and identification of subjects required. Buys all or negotiable rights.

Fiction: "Chess-related, high quality." Buys 1-2 mss/year. Pays variable fee.

Tips: "Articles must be written from an informed point of view—not from view of the curious amateur. Most of our writers are specialized in that they have sound credentials as chessplayers. Freelancers in major population areas (except New York and Los Angeles, which we already have covered) who are interested in short personality profiles and perhaps news reporting have the best opportunities. We're looking for more personality pieces on chessplayers around the country; not just the stars, but local masters, talented youths, and dedicated volunteers. Freelancers interested in such pieces might let us know of their interest and their range. Could be we know of an interesting story in their territory that needs covering."

‡COMPUTER GAMING WORLD, The Journal of Computer Gaming, Golden Empire Publications, Inc., Suite C, 515 S. Harbor Blvd., Anaheim CA 92805. (714)535-4435. Editor: Russell Sipe. 75% freelance written. Works with a small number of new/unpublished writers each year. Monthly (except February, July, September) magazine covering computer games. "CGW is read by an adult audience looking for detailed reviews and information on strategy, adventure and action games." Circ. 20,000. Pays on publication. Publishes ms an average of 3 months after acceptance. Byline given. Buys first rights. Submit seasonal/holiday material 4 months in advance. Query for electronic submissions; electronic submissions preferred, but not required. Computer printout submissions OK. Reports in 1 month. Sample copy $3.50. Free writer's guidelines.

Nonfiction: Reviews, strategy tips, industry insights. Buys 60 mss/year. Query. Length: 500-3,500 words. Pays $10-150. Sometimes pays the expenses of writers on assignment.

Photos: State availability of photos with submission. Reviews contact sheets. Offers $5-25 per photo. Buys one-time rights.

DRAGON® Magazine, Monthly Adventure Role-Playing Aid, TSR, Inc., Box 110, 201 Sheridan Springs Rd., Lake Geneva WI 53147. (414)248-8044. Editor: Roger E. Moore. 90% freelance written. Prefers to work with published/established writers, but eager to work with new/unpublished writers. Monthly magazine of fantasy and science-fiction role-playing games. "Most of our readers are intelligent, imaginative and under the age of 18." Circ. about 100,000. Pays on publication; pays on acceptance for fiction only. Publishes ms an average of 6 months after acceptance. Byline given. Offers kill fee. Buys first rights for fiction; all rights for most articles. Submit seasonal/holiday material 8 months in advance. Photocopied submissions OK. Computer printout submissions acceptable if clearly legible; prefers letter-quality to dot-matrix. Reports in 1 month on queries; 2 months on submissions. Sample copy $4.50; writer's guidelines for #10 SAE and 1 first class stamp.

Nonfiction: Articles on the hobby of gaming and fantasy role-playing. No general articles on gaming hobby; "our article needs are *very* specialized. Writers should be experienced in gaming hobby and role-playing. No strong sexual overtones or graphic depictions of violence." Buys 120 mss/year. Query. Length: 1,000-8,000 words. Pays $75-600 for assigned articles; pays $50-400 for unsolicited articles. Sometimes pays the expenses of writers on assignment.

Fiction: Patrick Price, fiction editor. Adventure, fantasy and suspense. "No strong sexual overtones or graphic depictions of violence." Buys 8-12 mss/year. Send complete ms. Length: 2,000-8,000 words. Pays $150-650.

Tips: "*Dragon Magazine* and the related publications of Dragon Publishing are *not* periodicals that the 'average reader' appreciates or understands. A writer must *be* a reader and must share the serious interest in gaming our readers possess."

GAMES, PSC Games Limited Partnership, 1350 Ave. of the Americas, New York NY 10019. Editor: Wayne Schmittberger. 50% freelance written. Bimonthly magazine featuring games, puzzles, mazes and brainteasers for people 18-49 interested in verbal and visual puzzles, trivia quizzes and original games. Circ. 550,000.

Average issue includes 5-7 feature puzzles, paper and pencil games and fillers, bylined columns and 1-2 contests. Pays on publication. Publishes ms an average of 6 months after acceptance. Byline given. Offers 25% kill fee. Buys all rights, first rights, first and second rights to the same material, and second (reprint) rights to material originally published elsewhere. Submit seasonal material 6 months in advance. Book reprints considered. Computer printout submissions acceptable. Reports in 6 weeks. Writer's guidelines for SASE.
Nonfiction: "We are looking for visual puzzles, rebuses, brainteasers and logic puzzles. We also want newsbreaks, new games, inventions, and news items of interest to game players." Buys 4-6 mss/issue. Query. Length: 500-2,000 words. Usually pays $125/published page.
Columns/Departments: Wild Cards (25-200 words, short brainteasers; 25-100 wordplay, number games, anecdotes and quotes on games). Buys 6-10 mss/issue. Send complete ms. Length: 25-200 words. Pays $10-100.
Fillers: Will Shortz, editor. Crosswords, cryptograms and word games. Pays $25-100.

GIANT CROSSWORDS, Scrambl-Gram, Inc., Puzzle Buffs International, 1772 State Road, Cuyahoga Falls OH 44223. (216)923-2397. Editors: C.J. Elum and C.R. Elum. Managing Editor: Carol L. Elum. 40% freelance written. Eager to work with new/unpublished writers. Crossword puzzle and word game magazines issued quarterly. Pays on acceptance. Publishes ms an average of 10 days after acceptance. No byline given. Buys all rights. Simultaneous queries OK. Reports in several weeks. "We furnish constructors' kits, master grids and clue sheets and offer a 'how-to-make-crosswords' book for $17.50 postpaid."
Nonfiction: Crosswords only. Query. Pays according to size of puzzle and/or clues.
Tips: "We are expanding our syndication of original crosswords and our publishing schedule to include new titles and extra issues of current puzzle books."

OFFICIAL CROSSWORD PUZZLES, DELL CROSSWORD PUZZLES, POCKET CROSSWORD PUZZLES, DELL WORD SEARCH PUZZLES, OFFICIAL WORD SEARCH PUZZLES, DELL PENCIL PUZZLES & WORD GAMES, OFFICIAL PENCIL PUZZLES & WORD GAMES, DELL CROSSWORD SPECIAL, DELL CROSSWORDS AND VARIETY PUZZLES, DELL CROSSWORD YEARBOOK, OFFICIAL CROSSWORD YEARBOOK, DELL CROSSWORD ANNUAL, FAST 'N' FUN CROSSWORDS AND VARIETY PUZZLES, DELL CROSSWORD SUPER SPECIAL, DELL CROSSWORD EXTRAVAGANZA, DELL PENCIL PUZZLES & WORD GAMES YEARBOOK, BEST OF DELL, Dell Puzzle Publications, 245 E. 47th St., New York NY 10017. Editor-in-Chief: Rosalind Moore. For "all ages from 8 to 80—people whose interests are puzzles, both crosswords and variety features." 95+% freelance written. Buys all rights. Computer printout submissions acceptable; no dot-matrix.
Puzzles: "We publish puzzles of all kinds, but the market here is limited to those who are able to construct quality pieces that can compete with the real professionals. Study our magazines; they are the best guide to our needs. We publish quality puzzles which are well-conceived and well-edited, with appeal to solvers of all ages and in almost every walk of life. We are the world's leading name in puzzle publications and are distributed in many countries around the world in addition to the continental U.S. However, no foreign language puzzles. Our market for regular crosswords and Anacrostics is very small, since long-time contributors supply most of the needs in those areas. However, we are always willing to see material of unusual quality, or with a new or original approach. We are in the market for expert-level 21x21 crosswords and very easy 13x13 crosswords. Since most of our publications feature variety puzzles in addition to the usual features, we are especially interested in seeing picture features, and new and unusual puzzle features of all kinds. Do *not* send us remakes of features we are now using. Send only one sample, please, and make sure your name and address are on each page submitted. Nothing without an answer will be considered. Do not expect an immediate reply. Prices vary with the feature, but ours are comparable with the highest in the puzzle business. We are seeking creative people who have a love of puzzles. Submissions, however, must show the constructor's familiarity with our magazines and our particular style."

POKER CHIPS, Official Publication of the International Home & Private Poker Player's Association, Scotty Barclay Poker Products, Rt. 2, Box 2845, Manistique MI 49854. (906)341-5468. Editor: Tony Wuehle. Works with a small number of new/unpublished writers each year. A quarterly tabloid covering recreational poker. "We are a publication for the serious home and private club poker player. Our readers are not professionals, but they do know and understand poker." Circ. 2,000. Pays on publication. Publishes ms an average of 6 months after acceptance. Byline given. Buys first rights. Photocopied submissions OK. Computer printout submissions acceptable; prefers letter-quality to dot-matrix. Reports in 2 weeks on queries; 1 month on mss. Sample copy $1.
Nonfiction: Essays; how-to (play various poker games well); new product (related to poker); and news of home and private poker groups. "No bad beat poker stories." Buys 4 mss/year. Query with or without published clips, or send complete ms. Length: 400-1,000 words. Pays $10-40 for articles; pays in copies for news of clubs.
Photos: Send photos with submission. Reviews 5x7 b&w prints. Offers no additional payment for photos accepted with ms. Captions, model releases, and identification of subjects required. Buys one-time rights.

"We will probably use photos of club members only."

Fillers: Anecdotes, facts and short humor. Length: 25-100 words. Pays in copies at this time.

Tips: "Articles on experience in tournament play, whether it be in a private or public game, are probably most open to freelancers. We will probably be interested in court decisions regarding poker games and possibly the poker games which are spread at the Native American casinos."

General Interest

General interest magazines need writers who can appeal to a varied audience—teens and senior citizens, wealthy readers and the unemployed. Some general interest publications do appeal to a specific audience, such as *Connoisseur* or *Grit*. Each magazine has a personality that suits its audience—one that a writer should study before sending material to an editor. Some markets for general interest material are in these Consumer categories: Ethnic/Minority, In-Flight, Men's, Regional and Women's.

AMERICAN ATHEIST, American Atheist Press, Box 2117, Austin TX 78768. (512)458-1244. Editor: R. Murray-O'Hair. Managing Editor: Jon Garth Murray. 20-40% freelance written. Monthly magazine covering atheism and topics related to it and separation of Church and State. Circ. 50,000. Publishes ms an average of 3-6 months after acceptance. Byline given. Buys one-time and all rights. Submit seasonal/holiday material 3 months in advance. Simultaneous queries and simultaneous, photocopied and previously published submissions OK. Query for electronic submissions. Computer printout submissions acceptable; prefers letter-quality to dot-matrix. Reports in 3 weeks on queries; 6 weeks on mss. Publishes ms an average of 4 months after acceptance. Sample copy and writer's guidelines for 9x12 SAE.

Nonfiction: Book excerpts, expose, general interest, historical, how-to, humor, interview/profile, opinion, personal experience and photo feature, but only as related to State/Church or atheism. "We receive a great many Bible criticism articles—and publish very few. We would advise writers not to send in such works. We are also interested in fiction with an atheistic slant." Buys 40 mss/year. Send complete ms. Length: 400-10,000 words. Pays in free subscription or 15 copies for first-time authors. Repeat authors paid $15 per 1,000 words. Sometimes pays the expenses of writers on assignment.

Columns/Departments: Atheism, Church/State separation and humor. Send complete ms. Length: 400-10,000 words.

Poetry: Avant-garde, free verse, haiku, light verse and traditional. Submit unlimited poems. Length: open. Pays $10 per thousand words maximum.

Fillers: Jokes, short humor and newsbreaks. Length: 800 words maximum, only as related to State/Church separation or atheism.

Tips: "We are primarily interested in subjects which bear directly on atheism or issues of interest and importance to atheists. This includes articles on the atheist lifestyle, on problems that confront atheists, the history of atheism, person experiences of atheists, separation of state and church, theopolitics and critiques of atheism in general and of particular religions. We are starting to have issues which focus on lifestyle topics relevant to atheism. For instance, our February 1987 issue featured black atheists. We would like to receive more articles on current events and lifestyle issues. Critiques of *particular* religions would also be likely candidates for acceptance."

THE AMERICAN LEGION MAGAZINE, Box 1055, Indianapolis IN 46206. (317)635-8411. Editor: Michael D. La Bonne. Monthly. 95% freelance written. Prefers to work with published/established writers, eager to work with new/unpublished writers, and works with a small number of new/unpublished writers each year. Circ. 2,600,000. Buys first North American serial rights. Computer printout submissions acceptable; prefers letter-quality to dot-matrix. Reports on submissions "promptly." Pays on acceptance. Publishes ms an average of 6 months after acceptance. Byline given.

Nonfiction: Query first, but will consider unsolicited mss. "Prefer an outline query. Relate your article's thesis or purpose, tell why you are qualified to write it, the approach you will take and any authorities you intend to interview. War remembrance pieces of a personal nature (vs. historic in perspective) should be in ms form." Uses current world affairs, topics of contemporary interest, little-known happenings in American history, 20th century war-remembrance pieces, and 750-word commentaries on contemporary problems and points of view. No personality profiles, or regional topics. Buys 60 mss/year. Length: 1,800 words maximum. Pays $100-

1,500. Pays expenses of writers on assignment.

Photos: On assignment.

Fillers: Short, tasteful jokes and humorous anecdotes. Pays $15.

Tips: Query should include author's qualifications for writing a technical or complex article. Also include thesis, length, outline and conclusion. "Send a thorough query. Submit material that is suitable for us, showing that you have read several issues. Attach a few clips of previously published material. *The American Legion Magazine* considers itself '*the* magazine for a strong America.' Any query reflective of this theme (which includes strong economy, educational system, moral fiber, infrastructure and armed forces) will be given priority. Humor is welcomed—must touch on universal themes applicable to most people."

A BETTER LIFE FOR YOU, The National Research Bureau, Inc., 424 N. 3rd St., Burlington IA 52601. (319)752-5415. Editor: Rhonda Wilson. Editorial Supervisor: Doris J. Ruschill. 75% freelance written. Works with a small number of new/unpublished writers each year, and is eager to work with new/unpublished writers. For industrial workers of all ages. Quarterly magazine. Pays on publication. Publishes ms an average of 1 year after acceptance. Buys all rights. Submit seasonal/holiday material 7 months in advance of issue date. Previously published submissions OK. Computer printout submissions acceptable; no dot-matrix. Reports in 3 weeks. Writer's guidelines for SASE.

Nonfiction: General interest (steps to better health, on-the-job attitudes); and how-to (perform better on the job, do home repair jobs, and keep up maintenance on a car). Buys 10-12 mss/year. Query or send outline. Length: 400-600 words. Pays 4¢/word.

Tips: "Writers have a better chance of breaking in at our publication with short articles and fillers because all of our articles are short."

BRENNAN PARTNERS, INC., Suite 1042, 485 5th Ave., New York NY 10017. (212)867-9291. Editor: Peter J. Brennan. Managing Editor: Richard J. Anobile. 100% freelance written. Prefers to work with published/established writers. "Special supplements run in all types of publications. The frequency depends upon the sponsor. Topics range from industrial developments to support of culture." Pays an advance, plus part on acceptance, and final on publication. Publishes ms an average of 3 months after acceptance. Byline given. Offers 100% kill fee. Buys all rights. Electronic submissions OK on TRS 80 Model I, IBM PC compatible, and CPM, but requires hard copy also. Computer printout submissions acceptable; prefers letter-quality to dot-matrix. Writer's guidelines for 10x13 SAE with 4 first class stamps.

Nonfiction: General interest, how-to, new product, technical and travel. "Our business is one-shot nonfiction specials for many publications." Buys 6 mss/year. Query. "We do not want *any* unsolicited manuscripts. We assign all work." Length: 1,500 words minimum. Pays $2,400 minimum for solicited mss. Pays the expenses of writers on assignment.

Photos: State availability of photos with submission. Reviews contact sheets, transparencies and prints. Offers no additional payment for photos accepted with ms. Captions, model releases, and identification of subjects required. Buys one-time rights.

Tips: "Read the special supplements we have produced. In particular, read our guidelines and comply with the requirements. We will not acknowledge or return unsolicited material without SASE. Show evidence that you can handle complex topics in depth."

CAPPER'S, Stauffer Communications, Inc., 616 Jefferson St., Topeka KS 66607. (913)295-1108. Editor: Nancy Peavler. 25% freelance written. Works with a small number of new/unpublished writers each year. Emphasizes home and family for readers who live in small towns and on farms. Biweekly tabloid. Circ. 385,000. Pays for poetry on acceptance; articles on publication. Publishes ms an average of 3 months after acceptance. Buys first serial rights only. Submit seasonal/holiday material 2 months in advance. Computer printout submissions OK; prefers letter-quality to dot-matrix. Reports in 1 month; 8 months for serialized novels. Sample copy 75¢.

Nonfiction: Historical (local museums, etc.), inspirational, nostalgia, travel (local slants) and people stories (accomplishments, collections, etc.). Buys 35 mss/year. Submit complete ms. Length: 700 words maximum. Pays $1/inch.

Photos: Purchased with accompanying ms. Submit prints. Pays $5-10 for 8x10 or 5x7 b&w glossy prints. Total purchase price for ms includes payment for photos. Limited market for color photos (35mm color slides); pays $25 each.

Columns/Departments: Heart of the Home (homemakers' letters, recipes, hints), and Hometown Heartbeat (descriptive). Submit complete ms. Length: 300 words maximum. Pays $2-10.

Fiction: "We have begun to buy some fiction pieces—longer than short stories, shorter than novels." Mystery, adventure and romance mss. No explicit sex, violence or profanity. Buys 4-5 mss/year. Query. Pays $150-200.

Poetry: Free verse, haiku, light verse, traditional, nature and inspiration. "The poems that appear in *Capper's* are not too difficult to read. They're easy to grasp. We're looking for everyday events, and down-to-earth themes." Buys 4-5/issue. Limit submissions to batches of 5-6. Length: 4-16 lines. Pays $3-5.

Tips: "Study a few issues of our publication. Most rejections are for material that is too long, unsuitable or out of character for our paper (too sexy, too much profanity, etc.). On occasion, we must cut material to fit column space."

THE CHRISTIAN SCIENCE MONITOR, 1 Norway St., Boston MA 02115. (617)450-2303. Contact: Submissions. International newspaper issued daily except Saturdays, Sundays and holidays in North America; weekly international edition. Special issues: travel, winter vacation and international travel, summer vacation, autumn vacation, and others. March and September: fashion. Circ. 200,000. Buys all newspaper rights for 3 months following publication. Buys limited number of mss, "top quality only." Publishes original (exclusive) material only. Pays on acceptance or publication, "depending on department." Submit seasonal material 2 months in advance. Reports in 1 month. Submit complete original ms or letter of inquiry. Writer's guidelines available.
Nonfiction: Roderick Nordell, feature editor. In-depth features and essays. Please query by mail before sending mss. "Style should be bright but not cute, concise but thoroughly researched. Try to humanize news or feature writing so reader identifies with it. Avoid sensationalism, crime and disaster. Accent constructive, solution-oriented treatment of subjects. Home Forum page buys essays of 400-900 words. Pays $70-140. Education, arts, real estate, travel, living, garden, books, sports, food, furnishings, and science pages will consider articles not usually more than 800 words appropriate to respective subjects." Pays $75-100.
Poetry: Traditional, blank and free verse. Seeks poetry of high quality and of all lengths up to 75 lines. Pays $25 average.
Tips: "We prefer neatly typed originals. No handwritten copy. Enclosing an SAE and postage with ms would be helpful."

THE CONNOISSEUR, The Hearst Corp., 224 W. 57th St., New York NY 10019. (212)262-5595. Editor-in-Chief: Thomas Hoving. Executive Editor: Philip Herrera. Managing Editor: Ellen Rosenbush. 90% freelance written. Prefers to work with published/established writers. Monthly magazine of the arts—fine, decorative and performing. "*Connoisseur* is written and designed for people who value excellence. It is informed by lively scholarship, a keen critical eye, and a civilized sense of fun. It covers a wide range of subjects and provides our audience with first-hand access to our topics and pertinent service data." Circ. 320,000. Pays on acceptance. Publishes ms an average of 3 months after acceptance. Offers 15% kill fee. Buys first English language rights. Submit seasonal/holiday material 3 months in advance. Query for electronic submissions. Computer printout submissions acceptable; no dot-matrix. Reports in 1 month. For back issues phone (212)262-8485 or write 250 W. 55th St., New York NY 10019.
Nonfiction: Travel; the arts—fine, decorative, performing; food; wine; architecture; fashion and jewelry. Buys 120 mss/year. Query with published clips. Length: 350-2,500 words. Pays $100-2,000. Pays expenses of writers on assignment.
Photos: Phyllis Levine, photo editor. Captions, model releases and identification of subjects required. Buys one-time rights.
Columns/Departments: Connoisseur's World, Lively Arts and Up & Coming. Buys 50 mss/year. Query with published clips. Length: 1,500-2,000 words. Pays $500-750.
Tips: "A freelancer can best break in to our publication with a strong, original proposal backed by good clips. Be aware of what we *have been doing*—read the magazine. Connoisseur's World and Up & Coming—short, timely proposals that are miniature magazine features—are the areas most open to freelancers."

EQUILIBRIUM, Everyone's Entertainment, Eagle Publishing Productions, Box 162, Golden CO 80402. Editor: Gary A. Eagle. "Featuring version of opposites. Themes range practically from anything to everything—from nonfiction to fiction comed to drama, short stories to features serious to light, conservative to liberal, idealogy to scientific and from sports to intellectual." 30% freelance written. Pays on acceptance. Publishes ms an average of 1 year after acceptance. "We prefer to hold ms on file until we publish it." Byline given. Offers 50% kill fee; varies for ghosts. Buys first rights. Computer printout submissions acceptable; no dot-matrix. Simultaneous queries, and simultaneous, photocopied, and previously published submissions OK. Reports in 3 months on queries; 6 months on mss. Sample copy for $3 with 9x12 SAE and 4 first class stamps; writer's guidelines for business size SAE and 1 first class stamp.
Nonfiction: How-to (physics, psychology, political science, medical, evolution, economics, philosophical, religion, actual UFO occurrences with photo); photo feature (any photo to show balance of something, with article or without); and technical. Think of opposites and equal values. Inquire about special issues. Modern events are accepted. Buys 20 mss/year. Query. Length: 50-1,000 words; more than 1,000 words if article series. Pays $50-500.
Photos: State availability or send photos with query or ms. Pays $20-40 for 1" b&w and color slides, and b&w and color prints.
Columns/Departments: Especially wants editorials, children's material, love stories. Length: 250 words. Pays $50-100.
Poetry: Light verse and traditional. "None will be accepted if not dealing with the balance of the universe." Submit maximum 10 poems. Length: 5-20 lines. Pays $10-50.

Fillers: Clippings, jokes, gags, short humor, cartoons. Buys 20/year. Length: 5-20 words. Pays $10-50.
Tips: "We encourage new writers. We read everything that comes in. Although our program has been geared toward the philosophical, we are receptive to a variety of subjects and our needs are flexible. Controversial material is acceptable. The most frequent mistakes made by writers in completing an article for us are that they fail to illustrate *or* demonstrate the opposites and equals. There are many types of opposites, such as reverses, equals, balances, etc. They do not have to be scientific. Explain in your query why readers will enjoy your article. Ideas for future articles are also welcome. The shorter the article the better. Play-science welcome. Send in your own thought of today or philosophical quote; it must be original."

EQUINOX: THE MAGAZINE OF CANADIAN DISCOVERY, Equinox Publishing, 7 Queen Victoria Dr., Camden East, Ontario K0K 1J0 Canada. (613)378-6651. Editor: Barry Estabrook. Managing Editor: Bart Robinson. Bimonthly magazine. "We publish in-depth profiles of people, places and wildlife to show readers the real stories behind subjects of general interest in the fields of science and geography." Circ. 150,000. Pays on acceptance. Byline given. Offers 50% kill fee. Buys first North American serial rights only. Submit seasonal queries 1 year in advance. SAE, IRCs. Computer printout submissions acceptable; prefers letter-quality to dot-matrix. Reports in 6 weeks. Sample copy $5; free writer's guidelines.
Nonfiction: Book excerpts (occasionally), geography, science and art. No travel articles. Buys 40 mss/year. Query. "Our biggest need is for science stories. We do not touch unsolicited feature manuscripts." Length: 5,000-10,000 words. Pays $1,500-negotiated.
Photos: Send photos with ms. Reviews color transparencies—must be of professional quality; no prints or negatives. Captions and identification of subjects required.
Columns/Departments: Nexus (current science that isn't covered by daily media) and Habitat (Canadian environmental stories not covered by daily media). Buys 80 mss/year. Query with clips of published work. Length: 200-300 words. Pays $200.
Tips: "Submit Habitat and Nexus ideas to us—the 'only' route to a feature is through these departments if writers are untried."

FORD TIMES, 1 Illinois Center, Suite 1700, 111 E. Wacker Dr., Chicago IL 60601. Editor: Thomas A. Kindre. 85% freelance written. Works with a small number of new/unpublished writers each year. "General-interest magazine designed to attract all ages." Monthly. Circ. 1,200,000. Pays on acceptance. Publishes ms an average of 8-9 months after acceptance. Buys first rights only. Offers kill fee. Byline given. Submit seasonal material 6 months in advance. Computer printout submissions acceptable; prefers letter-quality to dot-matrix. Reports in 1 month. Sample copy and writer's guidelines for 9x12 SASE.
Nonfiction: "Almost anything relating to contemporary American life that is upbeat and positive. Topics include lifestyle trends, outdoor activities and sports, profiles, food, narrow-scope destination stories, and the arts.   We are especially interested in subjects that appeal to readers in the 18-35 age group. We strive to be colorful, lively and, above all, interesting. We try to avoid subjects that have appeared in other publications or in our own." Buys 100 mss/year. Length: 1,700 words maximum. Query required unless previous contributor. Pays $550 minimum for full-length articles. Usually pays the expenses of writers on assignment.
Photos: "Speculative submission of high-quality color transparencies and b&w photos with mss is welcomed. We need bright, graphically strong photos showing people. We need releases for people whose identity is readily apparent in photos."

FRIENDLY EXCHANGE, Meredith Publishing Services, Locust at 17th, Des Moines IA 50336. Publication Office: (515)284-2008. Editor (702)786-7419. Editor: Adele Malott. 80% freelance written. Works with a small number of new/unpublished writers each year. Quarterly magazine exploring travel and leisure topics of interest to active western families. For policyholders of Farmers Insurance Group of Companies. "These are traditional families (median adult age 39) who live in the area bounded by Ohio on the east and the Pacific Ocean on the west." Circ. 4.5 million. Pays on acceptance. Publishes ms an average of 5 months after acceptance. Offers 25% kill fee. Buys all rights. Submit seasonal/holiday material 1 year in advance. Simultaneous queries and photocopied queries OK. Query for electronic submissions. Computer printout submissions acceptable; prefers letter-quality to dot-matrix. Reports in 2 months. Sample copy for 9x12 SAE and 5 first class stamps; writer's guidelines for business size SAE and 1 first class stamp.
Nonfiction: Travel and leisure activities such as gardening, crafts, pets, photography, etc.—topics of interest to the western family. "Travel and leisure topics can be addressed from many different perspectives, including health and safety, consumerism, heritage and education. Articles offer a service to readers and encourage them to take some positive action such as taking a trip. Style is colorful, warm, and inviting, making liberal use of anecdotes and quotes. The only first-person articles used are those assigned; all others in third person. Domestic locations in the western half of the continent are emphasized." Buys 8 mss/issue. Query. Length: 600-1,800 words. Pays $300-800/article, plus agreed-upon expenses.
Photos: Peggy Fisher, art director. Pays $150-250 for 35mm color transparencies; and $50 for b&w prints. Cover photo payment negotiable. Pays on publication.
Columns/Departments: All columns and departments rely on reader-generated materials; none used from

professional writers.
Tips: "We are now concentrating exclusively on the travel and leisure hours of our readers. Study articles: 'Watery Vacations,' 'The RV Lifestyle,' and 'Burglar-Proof Your Home' (February 1987) and 'Disneyland's Dreamkeepers' and 'Great American Markets' (August 1986). Do not use destination approach in travel pieces—instead, for example, tell us about the people, activities, or events that make the location special. Concentrate on what families can do together."

FUTURIFIC MAGAZINE, 280 Madison Ave., New York NY 10016. (212)684-4913. Editor-in-Chief: Balint Szent-Miklosy. 50-75% freelance written. Monthly. "Futurific, Inc. is an independent, nonprofit organization set up in 1976 to study the future, and *Futurific Magazine* is its monthly report on findings. We report on what is coming in all areas of life from international affairs to the arts and sciences. Readership cuts across all income levels and includes government, corporate and religious people." Circ. 10,000. Pays on publication. Publishes ms an average of 1 month after acceptance. Byline given in most cases. Buys one-time rights and will negotiate reprints. Computer printout submissions OK; prefers letter-quality to dot-matrix. Reports within 1 month. Sample copy for $2 and 9x12 SAE.
Nonfiction: All subjects must deal with the future: book, movie and theatre reviews, general interest, how to forecast the future—seriously, humor, interview/profile, new product, photo feature and technical. No historical, opinion or gloom and doom. Send complete ms. Length: 5,000 words maximum. Payment negotiable. Sometimes pays the expenses of writers on assignment.
Photos: Send photos with ms. Reviews b&w prints. Pay negotiable. Identification of subjects required.
Columns/Departments: Medical breakthroughs, new products, inventions, book, movie and theatre reviews, etc. "Anything that is new or about to be new." Send complete ms. Length: 5,000 words maximum.
Poetry: Avant-garde, free verse, haiku, light verse and traditional. "Must deal with the future. No gloom and doom or sad poetry." Buys 6/year. Submit unlimited number of poems. Length: open. Pays in copies.
Fillers: Clippings, jokes, gags, anecdotes, short humor, and newsbreaks. "Must deal with the future." Length: open. Pays in copies.
Tips: "It's not who you are; it's what you have to say that counts with us. We seek to maintain a light-hearted, professional look at forecasting. Be upbeat and show a loving expectation for the marvels of human achievement. Take any subject or concern you find in regular news magazines and extrapolate as to what the future will be. Use imagination. Get involved in the excitement of the international developments, social interaction. Write the solution—not the problem."

‡**GLOBE**, 5401 N.W. Broken Sound Blvd., Boca Raton FL 33431. Stories Editor: Donald McLachlan. "For everyone in the family. *Globe* readers are the same people you meet on the street and in supermarket lines, average hard-working Americans who prefer easily digested tabloid news." Weekly national tabloid newspaper. Circ. 2,000,000. Byline given.
Nonfiction and Fillers: "We want features on well-known personalities, offbeat people, places, events and activities. No personal essays. Current issue is best guide. Stories are best that don't grow stale quickly. No padding. Remember—we are serving a family audience. All material must be in good taste. If it's been written up in a major newspaper or magazine, we already know about it." Buys informational, how-to, interview, profile, inspirational, humor, historical, exposé, photo, and spot news. Length: 1,000 words maximum; average 500-800 words. Pays $250 maximum (special rates for "blockbuster" material).
Photos: Ron Haines, photo editor. Photos are purchased with or without ms, and on assignment. Captions are required. Pays $50 minimum for 8x10 b&w glossy prints. "Competitive payment on exclusives."
Tips: "*Globe* is constantly looking for human interest subject material from throughout the United States, and much of the best comes from America's smaller cities and villages, not necessarily from the larger urban areas. Therefore, we are likely to be more responsive to an article from a new writer than many other publications. This, of course, is equally true of photographs. A major mistake of new writers is that they have failed to determine the type and style of our content, and in the ever-changing tabloid field this is a most important consideration. It is also wise to keep in mind that what is of interest to you or to the people in your area may not be of equal interest to a national readership. Determine the limits of interest first. And, importantly, the material you send us must be such that it won't be 'stale' by the time it reaches the readers."

GOOD READING, for Everyone, Henrichs Publications, Inc., Box 40, Sunshine Park, Litchfield IL 62056. (217)324-3425. Editor: Peggy Kuethe. Managing Editor: Garth Henrichs. 80% freelance written. Works with a small number of new/unpublished writers, and is eager to work with new/unpublished writers each year. A monthly general interest magazine with articles and stories based on a wide range of current or factual subjects. Circ. 7,500. Pays on acceptance. Publishes ms an average of 6 months after acceptance. Byline given. Buys first North American serial rights. Submit seasonal/holiday material 5 months in advance. Photocopied submissions OK. Computer printout submissions acceptable; prefers letter-quality to dot-matrix. Reports in 2 months. Sample copy 50¢; writer's guidelines for #10 SAE with 1 first class stamp.
Nonfiction: General interest, historical/nostalgic, humor, photo feature and travel. Also stories about annual festivals, new products, people who make a difference. "No material that deals with the sordid side of life,

nothing about alcohol, smoking, drugs, gambling. Nothing that deals with the cost of travel, or that is too technical." Send complete ms. Length: 100-1,000 words. Pays $20-100 for unsolicited articles.
Photos: Send photos with submission. Reviews contact sheets and 3x5, 5x7, or 8x10 prints. Offers no additional payment for photos accepted with ms. Identification of subjects required. Buys one-time rights.
Columns/Departments: Youth Today (directed at young readers), 100 words maximum. Buys 6-9 mss/year. Send complete ms. Pays $10-50.
Poetry: Light verse. No limit to number of poems submitted at one time. Length: 4-16 lines. Pays in copies.
Fillers: Anecdotes, facts and short humor. Length: 50-150 words. Pays $10-30.
Tips: "The tone of *Good Reading* is wholesome; the articles are short. Keep writing informal but grammatically correct. *Good Reading* is general interest and directed at the entire family—so we accept only material that would be of interest to nearly every age group."

GRIT, Stauffer Communications, Inc., 208 W. 3rd St., Williamsport PA 17701. (717)326-1771. Editor: Naomi L. Woolever. 33% freelance written. Eager to work with new/unpublished writers. For a general readership of all ages in small town and rural America. Tabloid newspaper. Weekly. Circ. 600,000. Buys first and second rights to the same material. Byline given. Buys 1,000-1,500 mss/year. Pays on acceptance for freelance material; on publication for reader-participation feature material. Publishes ms an average of 1 month after acceptance. Query for electronic submissions. Computer printout submissions acceptable; no dot-matrix. Reports in 1 month. Sample copy $1; free writer's guidelines.
Nonfiction: Alvin Elmer, news editor. "We want mss about six basic areas of interest: people, religion, jobs (how individuals feel about their work), recreation, spirit of community (tradition or nostalgia that binds residents of a town together), and necessities (stories about people and how they cope—food, shelter, etc.). Also want sociological pieces about rural transportation and health problems or how a town deals effectively with vandalism or crime. Also first-person articles of 300 words or less about a person's narrowest escape, funniest moment, a turning point in life, or recollections of something from the past, i.e., a flood, a fire, or some other dramatic happening that the person experienced." Want good Easter, Christmas and holiday material. Mss should show some person or group involved in an unusual and/or upbeat way. "We lean heavily toward human interest, whatever the subject. Writing should be simple and down-to-earth." No "articles promoting alcoholic beverages, immoral behavior, narcotics, or unpatriotic acts." Query or submit complete ms. Length: 500 words maximum. Pays 12¢/word for first or exclusive rights; 6¢/word for second or reprint rights.
Photos: Photos purchased with or without ms. Looks for photos "outstanding in composition and technical quality." Captions required. No "deep shadows on (photo) subjects." Prefers 8x10 prints (*no* negatives or contact prints) for b&w, but will consider 5x7. Transparencies only for color. Pays $25 for b&w photos accompanying ms; $100 for front cover color transparencies.
Poetry: Joanne Decker, poetry editor. Buys traditional forms of poetry and light verse. "We want poems on seasonal, human interest and humorous topics. We'd also like to see poems about the holidays." Length: preferably 20 lines maximum. Pays $6 for 4 lines and under, plus 50¢/line for each additional line.
Tips: "The freelancer would do well to write for a copy of our Guidelines for Freelancers. We are planning an editorial calendar geared to gardening, travel, home improvement, arts and crafts, canning, health, and money management. Everything is spelled out there about how-tos, submission methods, etc. All manuscripts should include in upper right-hand corner of first page the number of words and whether it's first or second rights."

HARPER'S MAGAZINE, 666 Broadway, 11th Floor, New York NY 10012. (212)614-6500. Editor: Lewis H. Lapham. 40% freelance written. For well-educated, socially concerned, widely read men and women who value ideas and good writing. Monthly. Circ. 176,000. Rights purchased vary with author and material. Pays negotiable kill fee. Pays on acceptance. Computer printout submissions acceptable if double-spaced. Reports in 2 weeks. Publishes ms an average of 3 months after acceptance. Sample copy $2.50.
Nonfiction: "For writers working with agents or who will query first only, our requirements are: public affairs, literary, international and local reporting, and humor." No interviews; no profiles. Complete mss and queries must include SASEs. No unsolicited poems will be accepted. Publishes one major report per issue. Length: 4,000-6,000 words. Publishes one major essay per issue. Length: 4,000-6,000 words. "These should be construed as topical essays on all manner of subjects (politics, the arts, crime, business, etc.) to which the author can bring the force of passionately informed statement." Generally pays 50¢-$1/word.
Photos: Deborah Rust, art director. Occasionally purchased with mss; others by assignment. Pays $50-500.

IDEALS MAGAZINE, Box 141000, Ideals Publishing, Nelson Place at Elm Hill Pike, Nashville TN 37214. (615)889-9000. Editor: Ramona Richards. 95% freelance written. A magazine published eight times a year. "Our readers are generally women over 50. The magazine is mainly light poetry and short articles with a nostalgic theme. The eight issues are seasonally oriented, as well as being thematic." Pays on publication. Publishes ms an average of 1 year after acceptance. Byline given. Buys one-time North American serial and subsidiary rights. Submit seasonal/holiday material 8 months in advance. Simultaneous, photocopied, and previously published submissions OK. Computer printout submissions acceptable; prefers letter-quality to dot-matrix. Reports in 3 months. Writer's guidelines for #12 SAE with 1 first class stamp.

Nonfiction: Essays, historical/nostalgic, how-to (crafts), humor, inspirational and personal experience. "No down beat articles or social concerns." Buys 40 mss/year. Query with or without published clips, or send complete ms. Length: 400-800 words. Pays $40-80.

Photos: Send photos with submission. Reviews transparencies and b&w prints. Offers no additional payment for photos accepted with ms. Captions, model release, and identification of subjects required. Buys one-time rights.

Fiction: Slice-of-life vignettes. Buys 2 mss/year. Query. Length: 400-800 words. Pays $40-80.

Poetry: Light verse and traditional. "No erotica or depressing poetry." Buys 250 poems/year. Submit maximum 15 poems. Pays $10.

Tips: "Poetry is the area of our publication most open to freelancers. It must be oriented around a season or theme. The basic subject of *Ideals* is nostalgia, and poetry must be optimistic (how hard work builds character—not how bad the Depression was)."

LIFE, Time & Life Bldg., Rockefeller Center, New York NY 10020. (212)522-1212. Managing Editor: Judith Daniels. Articles Editor: Jeff Wheelwright. 10% freelance written. Prefers to work with published/established writers, and works with a small number of new/unpublished writers each year. Monthly general interest picture magazine for people of all ages, backgrounds and interests. Circ. 1.5 million. Average issue includes one short and one long text piece. Pays on acceptance. Publishes ms an average of 3 months after acceptance. Byline given. Buys first North American serial rights. Submit seasonal material 4 months in advance. Simultaneous and photocopied submissions OK. Computer printout submissions acceptable; prefers letter-quality to dot-matrix. Reports in 6 weeks.

Nonfiction: "We've done articles on anything in the world of interest to the general reader and on people of importance. It's extremely difficult to break in since we buy so few articles. Most of the magazine is pictures. We're looking for very high quality writing. We select writers whom we think match the subject they are writing about." Query with clips of previously published work. Length: 2,000-6,000 words.

MACLEAN'S, Maclean Hunter Bldg., 777 Bay St., 7th, Toronto, Ontario M5W 1A7 Canada. (416)596-5386. Contact: Section Editors (listed in masthead). 15% freelance written. Works with a small number of new/unpublished writers each year. For news-oriented audience. Weekly newsmagazine; 90 pages. Circ. 650,000. Frequently buys first North American serial rights. Pays on acceptance. Publishes ms "immediately" after acceptance. "Query with 200- or 300-word outline before sending material." Reports in 2 weeks. Query for electronic submissions. Computer printout submissions acceptable. SAE and IRCs. Sample copy for 9x12 SAE.

Nonfiction: "We have the conventional newsmagazine departments (Canada, world, business, people, plus science, medicine, law, art, music, etc.) with roughly the same treatment as other newsmagazines. We specialize in subjects that are primarily of Canadian interest, and there is now more emphasis on international—particularly US—news. Most material is now written by staffers or retainer freelancers, but we are open to suggestions from abroad, especially in world, business and departments (like medicine, lifestyles, etc.). Freelancers should write for a free copy of the magazine and study the approach." Length: 400-3,500 words. Pays $300-1,500. Pays expenses of writers on assignment.

NATIONAL EXAMINER, Globe Communications, Inc., 5401 N.W. Broken Sound Blvd., Boca Raton FL 33431. (305)997-7733. Editor: Bill Burt. Associate Editor: Cliff Linedecker. 15% freelance written. Works with a small number of new/unpublished writers each year. "We are a weekly supermarket tabloid that covers celebrity news, human interest features, medical breakthroughs, astrology, UFOs and the supernatural. Nonfiction stories should be well researched and documented, concise and fun to read." Circ. 1,000,000 + . Pays on acceptance. Publishes ms an average of 1 month after acceptance. Byline given. Buys first North American serial rights. Submit seasonal/holiday material 2 months in advance. Photocopied submissions OK. Computer printout submissions acceptable; prefers letter-quality to dot-matrix.

Nonfiction: Historical/nostalgic; interview/profile (of celebrities); photo feature (color preferred); and the supernatural. No fillers or political material. Buys 200 mss/year. Query with published clips. Length: 250-750 words. Pays $25-300.

Photos: Send photos with submission. Reviews contact sheets, 35mm transparencies, and 8x10 prints. Offers $35-100/photo. Captions and identification of subjects required. Buys one-time rights.

Tips: "Send us a well crafted, carefully documented story. The areas of our publication most open to freelancers are celebrity interviews and color photo spreads featuring celebrities or general subjects."

NATIONAL GEOGRAPHIC MAGAZINE, 17th and M Sts. NW, Washington DC 20036. Editor: Wilbur E. Garrett. Approximately 50% freelance written. Prefers to work with published/established writers, and works with a small number of new/unpublished writers each year. For members of the National Geographic Society. Monthly. Circ. more than 10,000,000. Query for electronic submissions. Computer printout submissions OK; prefers letter-quality to dot-matrix.

Nonfiction: *National Geographic* publishes first-person, general interest, heavy illustrated articles on science, natural history, exploration and geographical regions. Almost half of the articles are staff-written. Of the freelance writers assigned, most are experts in their fields; the remainder are established professionals. Fewer than one percent of unsolicited queries result in assignments. Query (500 words) by letter, not by phone, to Senior Assistant Editor (Contract Writers). Do not send manuscripts. Before querying, study recent issues and check a *Geographic Index* at a library since the magazine seldom returns to regions or subjects covered within the past ten years. Pays expenses of writers on assignment.

Photos: Photographers should query in care of the Illustration Division.

NEW AGE JOURNAL, Rising Star Associates, 342 Western Ave., Brighton MA 02135. (617)787-2005 Associate Publisher: Florence Graves. Editorial Manager: Gail Whitney. 95% freelance written. Works with a small number of new/unpublished writers each year. A bimonthly magazine emphasizing "personal fulfillment and social change. The audience we reach is college-educated, social-service/hi-tech oriented, 25-45 years of age, concerned about social values, humanitarianism, spirituality and balance in personal life." Payment negotiated. Publishes ms an average of 5 months after acceptance. Byline given. Offers 25% kill fee. Buys first North American serial rights and reprint rights. Submit seasonal/holiday material 6 months in advance. Simultaneous and photocopied submissions OK. Computer printout submissions are acceptable provided they are double-spaced "and dark enough." No dot-matrix. Reports in 2 months on queries. Sample copy $3; writer's guidelnes for letter-size SAE with 1 first class stamp.

Nonfiction: Book excerpts, expose, general interest, how-to (travel on business, select a computer, reclaim land, plant a garden, behavior, trend pieces), humor, inspirational, interview/profile, new product, food, sci-tech, nutrition, holistic health, education and personal experience. Buys 60-80 mss/year. Query with published clips. "Written queries only—no phone calls. The process of decision making takes time and involves more than one editor. An answer cannot be given over the phone." Length: 500-4,000 words. Pays $50-2,500. Pays the expenses of writers on assignment.

Photos: State availability of photos with submission. Model releases and identification of subjects required. Buys one-time rights.

Columns/Departments: Body/Mind; Reflections; First Person. Buys 60-80 mss/year. Query with published clips. Length: 750-1,500 words. Pays $100-800.

Tips: "Submit short, specific news items to the Upfront department. Query first with clips. A query is one to two paragraphs—if you need more space than that to *present* the idea, then you don't have a clear grip on it. The next open area is columns: First Person and Reflections often take first-time contributors. Read the magazine and get a sense of type of writing run in these two columns. In particular we are interested in seeing inspirational, first-person pieces that highlight an engaging idea, experience or issue. We are also looking for new cutting edge thinking."

THE NEW YORKER, 25 W. 43rd St., New York NY 10036. Editor: Robert Gottlieb. Weekly. Circ. over 500,000. Reports in 2 months. Pays on acceptance. Computer printout submissions acceptable; prefers letter-quality to dot-matrix.

Nonfiction, Fiction, Poetry, and Fillers: Long fact pieces are usually staff-written. So is "Talk of the Town," although ideas for this department are bought. Pays good rates. Uses fiction, both serious and light. About 90% of the fillers come from contributors with or without taglines (extra pay if the tagline is used).

OPENERS, America's Library Newspaper, American Library Association, 50 E. Huron St., Chicago IL 60611. (312)944-6780. Editor: Deborah G. Robertson. 80% freelance written. Quarterly tabloid covering "what's great to read," about books, sports, art, music, TV and radio, movies, health, etc., as they relate/tie into the library. No first-person articles or tomes on the importance of reading and libraries. Distributed free. Circ. 250,000. Pays on publication. Publishes ms an average of 6 months after acceptance. Byline given. Buys all rights. Submit seasonal/holiday material 3 months in advance. Simultaneous queries, and simultaneous and photocopied submissions OK. Computer printout submissions acceptable; prefers letter-quality to dot-matrix. Reports in 2 months. Sample copy for 9x12 SAE.

Nonfiction: General interest, how-to and humor relating to reading or books. "Send us an outline first." Buys 25+ mss/year. Query with published clips. Length: 200-800 words. Pays $25-100.

PARADE, Parade Publications, Inc., 750 3rd Ave., New York NY 10017. (212)573-7000. Editor: Walter Anderson. Weekly magazine for a general interest audience. 90% freelance written. Circ. 30 million. Pays on acceptance. Publishes ms an average of 3 months after acceptance. Kill fee varies in amount. Buys first North American serial rights. Computer printout submissions acceptable. Reports in 5 weeks on queries. Writer's guidelines for 4x9 SAE and 1 first class stamp.

Nonfiction: General interest (on health, trends, social issues, business or anything of interest to a broad general audience); interview/profile (of news figures, celebrities and people of national significance); and "provocative topical pieces of news value." Spot news events are not accepted, as *Parade* has a 6-week lead time. No fiction, fashion, travel, poetry, quizzes, or fillers. Address three-paragraph queries to Articles Editor. Length: 800-1,500 words. Pays $1,000 minimum. Pays expenses of writers on assignment.

Tips: "Send a well-researched, well-written query targeted to our market. Please, no phone queries. We're interested in well-written exclusive manuscripts on topics of news interest. The most frequent mistake made by writers in completing an article for us is not adhering to the suggestions made by the editor when the article was assigned."

PEOPLE IN ACTION, Meridian Publishing Company, Inc., Box 10010, Ogden UT 84409. (801)394-9446. Editor: Marjorie Rice. 65% freelance written. A monthly inhouse magazine featuring personality profiles. Circ. 70,000. Pays on acceptance. Publishes ms an average of 8 months after acceptance. Byline given. Buys first rights, second serial (reprint) rights and non-exclusive reprint rights. Simultaneous, photocopied and previously published submissions OK. Computer printout submissions acceptable. Reports in 6 weeks. Publishes ms an average of 6 months after acceptance. Sample copy for $1 and 9x12 SAE; writer's guidelines for SAE and 1 first class stamp. All requests for sample copies and guidelines should be addressed Attn: Editorial Assistant.

Nonfiction: General interest personality profiles. Cover stories focus on nationally noted individuals in the fine arts, literature, entertainment, communications, business, sports, education, health, science and technology. The lives of those featured exemplify positive values; overcoming obstacles, helping others, advancing culture, creating solutions. Buys 40 mss/year. Query. Length: 1,000-1,400 words. Pays 15¢/word for first rights plus non-exclusive reprint rights. Payment for second rights is negotiable.

Photos: State availability of photos or send photos with query. Pays $35/inside photo, $50/cover photo; uses glossy professional-quality color prints and transparencies (slides to 8x10). Captions, model releases and identification of subjects required.

Columns/Departments: Regular column features: a 700-word profile of a gourmet chef, first-class restaurant manager, food or nutrition expert, or a celebrity who is also a top-notch cook; a recipe and 1-2 good color transparencies are essential. Buys 10 mss/year. Query. Pays 15¢/word.

Tips: "The key is a well-written query letter that: 1) demonstrates that the subject of the article has national appeal; 2) shows that a profile of the person interviewed will have a clear, focused theme; 3) outlines the availability (from the writer, photographer or PR source) of top-quality color photos; and 4) gives evidence that the writer/photographer is a professional, even if a beginner."

READER'S DIGEST, Pleasantville NY 10570. Monthly. Circ. 16.5 million. Publishes general interest articles "as varied as all human experience." The *Digest* does not read or return unsolicited mss. Address proposals and tearsheets of published articles to the editors. Considers only previously published articles; pays $900/*Digest* page for World Digest rights. (Usually split 50/50 between original publisher and writer.) Tearsheets of submitted article must include name of original publisher and date of publication.

Columns/Departments: "Original contributions become the property of *Reader's Digest* upon acceptance and payment. Life-in-these-United States contributions must be true, unpublished stories from one's own experience, revealing adult human nature, and providing appealing or humorous sidelights on the American scene." Length: 300 words maximum. Pays $300 on publication. True and unpublished stories are also solicited for Humor in Uniform, Campus Comedy and All in a Day's Work. Length: 300 words maximum. Pays $300 on publication. Towards More Picturesque Speech—the first contributor of each item used in this department is paid $40 for original material, $35 for reprints. Contributions should be dated, and the source must be given. For items used in Laughter, the Best Medicine, Personal Glimpses, Quotable Quotes, and elsewhere in the magazine payment is as follows; to the *first* contributor of each from a published source, $35. For original material, $20 per *Digest* two-column line, with a minimum payment of $50. Send complete anecdotes to excerpt editor."

READERS REVIEW, The National Research Bureau, Inc., 424 N. 3rd St., Burlington IA 52601. Editor: Rhonda Wilson. Editorial Supervisor: Doris J. Ruschill. 75% freelance written. Works with a small number of new/unpublished writers each year, and is eager to work with new/unpublished writers. "For industrial workers of all ages." Quarterly magazine. Pays on publication. Publishes ms an average of 1 year after acceptance. Buys all rights. Previously published submissions OK. Computer printout submissions acceptable; prefers letter-quality to dot-matrix. Submit seasonal/holiday material 7 months in advance of issue date. Reports in 3 weeks. Writer's guidelines for SASE.

Nonfiction: General interest (steps to better health, attitudes on the job); how-to (perform better on the job, do home repairs, car maintenance); and travel. No articles on car repair, stress and tension. Buys 10-12 mss/year. Query with outline or submit complete ms. Length: 400-600 words. Pays 4¢/word.

Tips: "Writers have a better chance of breaking in at our publication with short articles and fillers because all of our articles are short."

THE SATURDAY EVENING POST, The Saturday Evening Post Society, 1100 Waterway Blvd., Indianapolis, IN 46202. (317)636-8881. Editor: Cory SerVaas, M.D. Executive Editor: Ted Kreiter. 40% freelance written. A family-oriented magazine published 9 times/year covering preventive medicine and health care. Circ. 700,000. Pays on publication. Byline given. Buys all rights. Submit seasonal/holiday material at least 3 months in advance. Simultaneous, photocopied and previously published submissions OK. Computer printout submissions acceptable. Reports in 1 month on queries; 6 weeks on mss. Writer's guidelines for business size SAE and 1 first class stamp.

Nonfiction: Barbara Potter, articles editor. General interest, health, interview/profile, religious. "No political articles, or articles containing sexual innuendo or hypersophistication." Buys 40-60 mss/year. Query with published clips. Length: 750-2,500 words. Pays $100 minimum. Sometimes pays the expenses of writers on assignment.

Photos: State availability of photos with submission. Reviews negatives and transparencies. Model releases and identification of subjects required. Buys one-time rights or all rights. Payment and rights negotiable.

Columns/Departments: Money Talk and Gardening/Home Improvement, Travel (tourism-oriented). "See recent issues for topics and slant." Query with published clips. Length: 750-1,000 words. Pays $150 minimum.

Fiction: Rebecca Whitney, fiction editor. Adventure, historical, humorous, and mainstream. "Anything except humor has only a *remote* chance." Buys approximately 2 mss/year. Send complete ms. Length: 2,500 words. Pays $150 minimum.

Fillers: Jack Gramling, Post Scripts editor. Anecdotes, short humor and light verse. Buys 200 + /year. Length: 300 words maximum. Pays $15.

Tips: The areas most open to freelancers are "Post Scripts—no cute kiddy sayings; keep submissions up-to-date—no put downs of hippies, etc. when submitting, let the editor make up his own mind whether your material is humorous—and Travel—no first person—it's egocentric, thus boring; select mainstream locales; and have lots of pictures or know where to find them."

SELECTED READING, The National Research Bureau, Inc., 424 N. 3rd St., Burlington IA 52601. Editor: Rhonda Wilson. Editorial Supervisor: Doris J. Ruschill. 75% freelance written. Eager to work with new/unpublished writers, works with a small number of new/unpublished writers each year. For industrial workers of all ages. Quarterly magazine. Pays on publication. Publishes ms an average of 1 year after acceptance. Buys all rights. Previously published submissions OK. Computer printout submissions acceptable; prefers letter-quality to dot-matrix. Submit seasonal/holiday material 6-7 months in advance of issue date. Reports in 3 weeks. Writer's guidelines for SASE.

Nonfiction: General interest (economics, health, safety, working relationships); how-to; and travel (out-of-the way places). No material on car repair. Buys 10-12 mss/year. Query. A short outline or synopsis is best. Lists of titles are no help. Length: 400-600 words. Pays 4¢/word.

Tips: "Writers have a better chance of breaking in at our publication with short articles and fillers because all of our articles are short."

SEVEN, The Lifestyle Magazine of Caesars, Caesars World, Inc., Suite 2600, 1801 Century Park E., Los Angeles CA 90067. (213)552-2711. Editor: Stewart Weiner. Managing Editor: Nancy Gottesman. 99% freelance written. Works with a small number of new/unpublished writers each year. A bimonthly magazine covering attractions and events at Caesars World properties. Circ. 130,000. Pays on acceptance. Publishes ms an average of 1 month after acceptance. Byline given. Offers 25% kill fee. Buys first North American serial rights. Submit seasonal/holiday material 6 months in advance. Simultaneous submissions OK. Computer printout submissions acceptable; prefers letter-quality to dot-matrix. Reports in 6 weeks on queries. Sample copy for 6 first class stamps.

Nonfiction: Book excerpts, essays, historical/nostalgic, how-to, humor, interview/profile, new product and photo feature. "All features have to relate to either gaming or Caesars." Buys 20 mss/year. Query with published clips. No unsolicited ms. Length: 150-2,000 words. Sometimes pays $500-1,000. Sometimes pays the expenses of writers on assignment.

Photos: State availability of photos with submission. Offers $100-500/photo. Captions, model releases, and identification of subjects required. Buys one-time rights.

Columns/Departments: Gaming (how-to, historical, fiction), and Caesars People (celebrities interviewed or profiled), both 500-2,000 words. Query with or without published clips. Length: 500-2,000 words. Pays $500-1,000.

Fiction: Slice-of-life vignettes. No fiction without a reference to gaming or Caesars. Buys 3 mss/year. Query with published clips. Length: 500-2,000 words. Pays $500-1,000.

Fillers: Buys 10/year. Length: 25-150 words. Pays $75-100.

Tips: "Writers should have an interest in gaming and in the attractions and events associated with Caesars properties."

SMITHSONIAN MAGAZINE, 900 Jefferson Drive, Washington DC 20560. Articles Editor: Marlane A. Liddell. 90% freelance written. Prefers to work with published/established writers. For "associate members of the Smithsonian Institution; 85% with college education." Monthly. Circ. 2 million. Buys first North American serial rights. Payment for each article to be negotiated depending on our needs and the article's length and excellence. Pays on acceptance. Publishes ms an average of 6 months after acceptance. Submit seasonal material

3 months in advance. Computer printout submissions acceptable; no dot-matrix. Reports in 6 weeks.
Nonfiction: "Our mandate from the Smithsonian Institution says we are to be interested in the same things which now interest or should interest the Institution: cultural and fine arts, history, natural sciences, hard sciences, etc." Query. Length: 750-4,500 words. Payment negotiable. Pays expenses of writers on assignment.
Photos: Purchased with or without ms and on assignment. Captions required. Pays $400/full color page.

THE STAR, 660 White Plains Rd., Tarrytown NY 10591. (914)332-5000. Editor: Leslie Hinton. Executive Editor: Richard Kaplan. 40% freelance written. Prefers to work with published/established writers. "For every family; all the family—kids, teenagers, young parents and grandparents." Weekly magazine; 56 pages. Circ. 3.5 million. Publishes ms an average of 1 month after acceptance. Buys first North American serial rights, occasional second serial book rights. Query for electronic submissions. Computer printout submissions acceptable; prefers letter-quality to dot-matrix. Pays expenses of writers on assignment.
Nonfiction: William Ridley, managing editor. Exposé (government waste, consumer, education, anything affecting family); general interest (human interest, consumerism, informational, family and women's interest); how-to (psychological, practical on all subjects affecting readers); interview (celebrity or human interest); new product; photo feature; profile (celebrity or national figure); health; medical; and diet. No first-person articles. Query or submit complete ms. Length: 500-1,000 words. Pays $50-1,500.
Photos: Alistair Duncan, photo editor. State availability of photos with query or ms. Pays $25-100 for 8x10 b&w glossy prints, contact sheets or negatives; $150-1,000 for 35mm color transparencies. Captions required. Buys one-time or all rights.

SUNSHINE MAGAZINE, Henry F. Henrichs Publications, Box 40, Sunshine Park, Litchfield IL 62056. (217)324-3425. Editor: Peggy Kuethe. Managing Editor: Garth Henrichs. 95% freelance written. Eager to work with new/unpublished writers. A monthly magazine. "Primarily human interest and inspirational in its appeal, *Sunshine Magazine* provides worthwhile reading for all the family." Circ. 70,000. Pays on acceptance. Publishes ms an average of 6 months after acceptance. Byline given. Buys first North American serial rights or one-time rights. Submit seasonal/holiday material 6 months in advance. Photocopied submissions OK. Computer printout submissions acceptable; prefers letter-quality to dot-matrix. Reports in 2 months. Sample copy 50¢; writer's guidelines for #10 SAE with 1 first class stamp.
Nonfiction: Essays, historical/nostalgic, inspirational and personal experience. "No material dealing with specifically religious matters or that is depressing in nature (divorce, drug abuse, alcohol abuse, death, violence, child abuse)." Send complete ms. Length: 200-1,250. Pays $10-100.
Columns/Departments: Extraordinary Experience (personal experience), 500 words; Let's Reminisce (reminiscent, nostalgia), 500 words; Guidelines (inspirational), 200 words; and Favorite Meditation (inspirational essay), 200 words. Buys 85-90 mss/year. Send complete ms. Pays $15-50.
Fiction: Inspirational and human interest. Buys 75-80 mss/year. Send complete ms.
Poetry: Light verse and traditional. No avant-garde, free verse or haiku. Buys 12-15 poems/year. No limit to the number of poems submitted at one time. Length: 4-16 lines. Pays $15-80, or may pay in copies.
Fillers: Anecdotes and short humor. Buys 1-5/year. Length: 50-150 words. Pays $10-20.
Tips: "Make a note that *Sunshine* is not religious—but it is inspirational. After reading a sample copy, you should know that we do not accept material that is very different from what we've been doing for over 60 years. Don't send a manuscript that is longer than specified or that is 'different' from anything else we've published—that's not what we're looking for. The whole magazine is written primarily by freelancers. We are just as eager to publish new writers as they are to get published."

TOWN AND COUNTRY, 1700 Broadway, New York NY 10019. (212)903-5000. Managing Editor: Jean Barkhorn. For upper-income Americans. Monthly. Pays on acceptance. Not a large market for freelancers. Always query first.
Nonfiction: Frank Zachary, department editor. "We're always trying to find ideas that can be developed into good articles that will make appealing cover lines." Wants provocative and controversial pieces. Length: 1,500-2,000 words. Pay varies. Also buys shorter pieces for which pay varies.

WEBB TRAVELER MAGAZINE, The Webb Co., 1999 Shepard Rd., St. Paul MN 55116. (612)690-7228. Editor: George Ashfield. 90% freelance written. Quarterly magazine emphasizing money management, consumer and American and foreign travel and food articles for a high-income audience 30-60 years of age. Pays on acceptance. Publishes ms an average of 4 months after acceptance. Buys one-time rights and nonexclusive reprint rights. Submit seasonal/holiday material 1 year in advance. Photocopied submissions OK. Computer printout submissions acceptable. Reports on queries and mss in 6 weeks. Free sample copy and writer's guidelines.
Nonfiction: Nonfiction only. No first person or personal experience. Query. Length: 1,000-2,000 words. Pays $200-600.
Photos: Contact Julie Hally at (612)690-7396 for current rates.

WHAT MAKES PEOPLE SUCCESSFUL, The National Research Bureau, Inc., 424 N. 3rd St., Burlington IA 52601. Editor: Rhonda Wilson. Editorial Supervisor: Doris J. Ruschill. 75% freelance written. Eager to work with new/unpublished writers, and works with a small number of new/unpublished writers each year. For industrial workers of all ages. Published quarterly. Pays on publication. Publishes ms an average of 1 year after acceptance. Buys all rights. Previously published submissions OK. Computer printout submissions acceptable; prefers letter-quality to dot-matrix. Submit seasonal/holiday material 8 months in advance of issue date. Reports in 3 weeks. Writer's guidelines for SASE.

Nonfiction: How-to (be successful); general interest (personality, employee morale, guides to successful living, biographies of successful persons, etc.); experience; and opinion. No material on health. Buys 3-4 mss/issue. Query with outline. Length: 400-600 words. Pays 4¢/word.

Tips: Short articles and fillers (rather than major features) have a better chance of acceptance because all articles are short.

Health and Fitness

The magazines listed here specialize in covering health and fitness topics for a general audience. Magazines covering health topics from a medical perspective are listed in the Medical category of Trade. Also see the Sports/Miscellaneous section where publications dealing with health and particular sports may be listed. Many general interest publications are potential markets for health or fitness articles.

ACCENT ON LIVING, Box 700, Bloomington IL 61702. (309)378-2961. Editor: Betty Garee. 75% freelance written. Eager to work with new/unpublished writers. For physically disabled persons and rehabilitation professionals. Quarterly magazine; 128 pages. Circ. 18,000. Buys first rights and second (reprint) rights to material originally published elsewhere. Byline usually given. Buys 50-60 unsolicited mss/year. Pays on publication. Publishes ms an average of 6 months after acceptance. Photocopied submissions OK. Computer printout submissions acceptable; prefers letter-quality to dot-matrix. Reports in 2 weeks. Sample copy $2; writer's guidelines for SAE and 1 first class stamp.

Nonfiction: Betty Garee, editor. Articles about new devices that would make a disabled person with limited physical mobility more independent; should include description, availability, and photos. Medical breakthroughs for disabled people. Intelligent discussion articles on acceptance of physically disabled persons in normal living situations; topics may be architectural barriers, housing, transportation, educational or job opportunities, organizations, or other areas. How-to articles concerning everyday living, giving specific, helpful information so the reader can carry out the idea himself/herself. News articles about active disabled persons or groups. Good strong interviews. Vacations, accessible places to go, sports, organizations, humorous incidents, self improvement, and sexual or personal adjustment—all related to physically handicapped persons. No religious-type articles. "We are looking for upbeat material." Query. Length: 250-1,000 words. Pays 10¢/word for article as it appears in magazine (after editing and/or condensing by staff).

Photos: Pays $5 minimum for b&w photos purchased with accompanying captions. Amount will depend on quality of photos and subject matter. "We need good-quality transparencies or slides with submissions—or b&w photos."

Tips: "Ask a friend who is disabled to read your article before sending it to *Accent*. Make sure that he/she understands your major points and the sequence or procedure."

‡AIMplus, Arthritis Information Magazine, The Haymarket Group, Inc., Suite 407, 45 West 34th St., New York NY 10001. (212)239-0855. Editor: Tim Moriarty. Associate Editor: Gayle Turim. 75% freelance written. Prefers to work with published/established writers, and works with a small number of new/unpublished writers each year. Magazine published 10 times/year covering arthritis and general interest topics for the 50+ population. Writers should keep in mind that many of our readers have a sedentary lifestyle. Estab. 1986. Circ. 200,000. Pays on acceptance. Byline given. Offers 25% kill fee. Buys first North American serial rights. Submit seasonal/holiday material 5 months in advance. Computer printout submissions OK; no dot-matrix. Reports in 6 weeks on queries. Sample copy $2.50 with 9x12 SAE and 3 first class stamps.

Nonfiction: Health (especially relating to arthritis), book excerpts, general interest, historical/nostalgic, how-to, humor, interview/profile, new product and personal experience. No travel (our travel editor covers this), no clippings, no articles slanted to those 50 and under. Query with published clips. Length: 800-1,500 words. Pays $400-750 for assigned articles; pays $300-500 for unsolicited articles. Usually pays expenses of writers on assignment.

Photos: State availability of photos with submission. Identification of subjects required. Buys one-time rights.

Fillers: Anecdotes, facts and short humor. Length: 50-300 words. Pays $25-60.

Tips: "Send a detailed, well-written query. Easiest way to break in is through the general interest category. Avoid the obvious. Queries that convey a sense of humor stand out; we need upbeat material."

AMERICAN HEALTH MAGAZINE, Fitness of Body and Mind, American Health Partners, 80 Fifth Ave., New York NY 10011. (212)242-2460. Editor-in-Chief: T. George Harris. Editor: Joel Gurin. 70% freelance written. Prefers to work with published/established writers. 10 issues/year. General interest magazine that covers both scientific and "lifestyle" aspects of health, including laboratory research, clinical advances, fitness, holistic healing and nutrition. Circ. 1,000,000. Pays on acceptance. Publishes ms an average of 4-6 months after acceptance. Byline given. Offers 25% kill fee. Buys first North American serial rights, "and certain other rights that are negotiable, in some cases." Computer printout submissions acceptable. Reports in 2 months. Sample copy for $3; writer's guidelines for 4x9 SAE and 1 first class stamp.

Nonfiction: Mail to Editorial/Features. Book excerpts; how-to; humor (if anyone can be funny, yes); interview/profile (health or fitness related); photo feature (any solid feature or news item relating to health); and technical. No first-person narratives, mechanical research reports, weight loss plans or recipes. "Stories should be written clearly, without jargon. Information should be new, authoritative and helpful to the readers." Buys 60-70 mss/year. Query with 2 clips of published work. "Absolutely *no* complete mss." Length: 1,000-3,000 words. Pays $600-2,000 upon acceptance. Pays the expenses of writers on assignment.

Photos: Mail to Editorial/Photo. Send photos with query. Pays $100-600 for 35mm transparencies and 8x10 prints "depending on use." Captions and identification of subjects required. Buys one-time rights.

Columns/Departments: Mail to Editorial/News. Consumer Alert, Medical News (technological update), Fitness Report, Nutrition Report, Mind/Body News, Family Report, Family Pet, Tooth Report, and Skin, Scent and Hair. Other news sections included from time to time. Buys about 300 mss/year. Query with clips of published work. Prefers 2 pages-500 words. Pays $125-375 upon acceptance.

Fillers: Mail to Editorial/Fillers. Anecdotes and newsbreaks. Buys 30/year. Length: 20-50 words. Pays $10-25.

Tips: "*American Health* has no full-time staff writers; we have chosen to rely on outside contributors for almost all our articles. The magazine needs good ideas, and good articles, from professional journalists, health educators, researchers and clinicians. Queries should be short (no longer than a page), snappy and to the point. Think short; think news. Give us a good angle and a paragraph of background. Queries only. We do not take responsibility for materials not accompanied by SASE."

BESTWAYS MAGAZINE, Box 2028, Carson City NV 89702. Editor/Publisher: Barbara Bassett. 20% freelance written. Prefers to work with published/established writers, and works with a small number of new/unpublished writers each year. Emphasizes health, diet and nutrition. Monthly magazine; 64 pages. Circ. 300,000. Pays on publication. Publishes ms an average of 8 months after acceptance. Byline given. Buys first North American serial rights. Submit seasonal/holiday material 6 months in advance. Computer printout submissions acceptable; prefers letter-quality to dot-matrix. Reports in 6 weeks. Writer's guidelines for SASE.

Nonfiction: General interest (nutrition, physical fitness, preventive medicine, supplements, natural foods); how-to (diet and exercise); and technical (vitamins, minerals, weight control and nutrition). "No direct or implied endorsements of refined flours, grains or sugar, tobacco, alcohol, caffeine, drugs or patent medicines." Buys 4 mss/issue. Query. Length: 1,500 words. Pays 10¢/word. Sometimes pays the expenses of writers on assignment.

Photos: State availability of photos with query. Pays $7.50 for 4x5 b&w glossy prints; $15 for 2¼x2¼ color transparencies. Captions preferred. Buys all rights. Model releases required.

‡BETTER HEALTH, Better Health Press, 1485 Chapel St., New Haven CT 06511. (203)789-3974. Editor: Deborah Turton. Managing Editor: Kelly Anthony. 50% freelance written. Prefers to work with published/established writers; works with small number of new/unpublished writers each year. A bimonthly magazine covering health related topics. Circ. 120,000+. Pays on acceptance. Byline sometimes given. Offers $50 kill fee. Buys first and second serial rights. Submit seasonal/holiday material 2 months in advance. Simultaneous, photocopied and previously published submissions OK. Query for electronic submissions. Computer printout submissions OK; no dot-matrix. Sample copy $1.25.

Nonfiction: Medical general interest, humor, inspirational and personal experience. Buys 20 mss/year. Query with published clips. Length: 800-3,000 words. Pays $100-400.

Photos: State availability of photos with submission. Reviews contact sheets. Offers no additional payment for photos accepted with ms.

BETTER HEALTH & LIVING, Decathlon Corp., 800 2nd Ave., New York NY 10017. (212)986-9026. Editor: Julie Davis. Managing Editor: Sharon Schwartzman. 80% freelance written. Prefers to work with published/established writers. Bimonthly magazine on fitness, health and lifestyle. The magazine focuses on "how to make the most of your lifestyle in a healthy way and still enjoy yourself. Moderation is the key." Circ. 100,000. Publishes ms an average of 4 months after acceptance. Byline given. Buys first North American serial rights. Submit seasonal/holiday material 4 months in advance. Exclusive queries and submissions preferred. Computer printout submissions OK; prefers letter-quality to dot-matrix. Reports in 1-2 months. Sample copy $2.50 with SAE and $1.75 postage.

Nonfiction: Book excerpts, general interest, interview/profile, new product, opinion, personal experience, photo feature and travel. No technical writing. Buys 50 mss/year. Query with published clips. Length: 500-3,000 words. Pays $250-1,000. Sometimes pays the expenses of writers on assignment.

Photos: Cornelia Walworth, art director. State availability of photos. Reviews 35mm b&w and color transparencies. Fees depend upon usage. Model releases and identification of subjects required. Buys one-time rights.

Columns/Departments: Better Living—items on beauty/grooming, stress management, fitness, lifestyle, illustrated health news; Healthwire—hard news items on health, fitness, medicine; Fitworks—new tools, gadgets, videos, books (highly photographed); Fitness to Go—away from home fitness. Buys 200 mss/year. Query with published clips. Length: 100-500 words. Pays $25-200.

Tips: "Send query with clips after familiarizing yourself with format. Submissions should be both male/female oriented. Healthwire and Better Living columns are most open to freelancers."

DAZZLE, The Webb Company, 1999 Shepard Rd., St. Paul MN 55116. (612)690-7200. Editor: Gayle Bonneville. 95% freelance written. Works with a small number of new/unpublished writers each year. A quarterly magazine for the general public covering dentistry and dental and general health for the layperson. Circ. 50,000. Pays on acceptance. Publishes ms an average of 3 months after acceptance. Byline given. Offers 25% kill fee. Buys limited rights in work-for-hire. Submit seasonal/holiday material at least 6 months in advance. Simultaneous, photocopied, and previously published submissions OK, "but original, first-time articles have a much better chance of acceptance." Electronic submissions OK via ASCII file, MS DOS. Computer printout submissions acceptable; prefers letter-quality to dot-matrix. Reports in 1 month. Sample copy for 6x9 SAE with 56¢ postage; free writer's guidelines with SAE.

Nonfiction: General health, nutrition and dental health. Also, book excerpts, essays, historical/nostalgic, humor, interview/profile and new product—if dental related. No opinion, technical dental or medical stories, stories negative to dentistry, or religious articles. Buys approximately 20 mss/year. Query with published clips. Resume is helpful. Length: 500-1,400 words. Pays $250-500. Pays certain expenses of writers on assignment.

Photos: State availability of photos with submission. Reviews 35mm or 2¼ transparencies. Pays variable rate for photos. Buys one-time rights.

Columns/Departments: Tongue in Cheek (lighthearted, witty look at dentistry, dental history, dental trivia, dental essay), 500-800 words; and Marketplace Update (new products page, usually staff-written).

Tips: Most needed are good Tongue in Cheek essays. Don't send stories that are negative toward dentistry. Since *Dazzle* is no longer affiliated with Delta Dental Plans, we can now cover a broader range of dental topics—and the manuscript approval/payment processes can now be accelerated."

EAST WEST, The Journal of Natural Health & Living, Kushi Foundation, Inc., 17 Station St., Box 1200, Brookline Village MA 02147. (617)232-1000. Editor: Mark Mayell. 40% freelance written. Works with a small number of new/unpublished writers each year. Monthly magazine emphasizing natural health for "people of all ages seeking balance in a world of change." Circ. 70,000. Pays on publication. Publishes ms an average of 6 months after acceptance. Buys first serial rights or second (reprint) rights. Byline given. Submit seasonal/holiday material 6 months in advance. Simultaneous and photocopied submissions OK. Computer printout submissions acceptable; prefers letter-quality to dot-matrix. Reports in 1 month. Sample copy $1; writer's guidelines for SAE and 1 first class stamp.

Nonfiction: Major focus is on issues of natural health and diet; interviews and features (on the natural foods industry, sustainable farming and gardening, natural healing, human-potential movement, diet and fitness). No negative, politically-oriented, or New Age material. "We're looking for original, first-person articles without jargon or opinions of any particular teachings; articles should reflect an intuitive approach." Buys 15-20 mss/year. Query. Length: 2,000-3,000 words. Pays 8-12¢/word. Sometimes pays expenses of writers on assignment.

Photos: Send photos with ms. Pays $15-40 for b&w prints; $15-175 for 35mm color transparencies (cover only). Captions preferred; model releases required.

Columns/Departments: Body, Whole Foods, Natural Healing, Gardening, and Cooking. Buys 15 mss/year. Submit complete ms. Length: 1,500-2,000 words. Pays 8-12¢/word.

Tips: "Read another issue. Too many freelancers don't take the time to truly understand their market and thus waste their time and ours with inappropriate submissions."

HEALTHPLEX MAGAZINE, The Magazine for Healthier Living, Methodist Hospital/Childrens Hospital, 8303 Dodge St., Omaha NE 68114. (402)390-4528. Managing Editor: Gini Goldsmith. 80% freelance written. Prefers to work with published/established writers. Most articles are written on assignment. Quarterly magazine on health information and medical subjects. Focuses on current health care topics, wellness-related articles, etc. Circ. 60,000. Pays on acceptance. Publishes ms an average of 3 months after acceptance. Byline given. Buys all rights and first serial rights; makes work-for-hire assignments. Submit seasonal/holiday material 3 months in advance. Photocopied submissions OK. Computer printout submissions acceptable; prefers letter-quality to dot-matrix. Reports in 1 month. Free sample copy.

Nonfiction: Only health/wellness articles. Buys 24 mss/year. Query with published clips or send complete ms. Length: 1,000-3,000 words. Pays $50-200. Sometimes pays the expenses of writers on assignment.

Photos: State availability of photos. Reviews b&w contact sheets and color transparencies. Pays $100-250. Model release required. Buys all rights.

Columns/Departments: Feelin' Good (wellness articles) and Health Updates (short topics on current health topics, new technology, etc.).

Tips: "This is a corporate publication so all articles must have a broad consumer appeal and not be on an obscure medical topic. Since most articles are written on assignment, it is preferable to send a topic query or a submission of published articles for writing style selection."

IMC JOURNAL, The Health Publication of International Medical Center, International Medical Center, Suite 333, 1515 N.W. 167th St., Miami FL 33169. (305)623-1091. Editor: Marcia J. Maze. 30% freelance written. A magazine covering health maintenance, preventive medicine and fulfilled living. "We publish easy to read, human interest articles covering positive attitudes on aging and health; and articles slanted to inspire the reader to change their habits or lifestyles for the better." Circ. 170,000. Pays on publication. Publishes ms an average of 4 months after acceptance. Byline given. Buys first rights and second serial (reprint) rights. Submit seasonal/holiday material 4 months in advance. Photocopied submissions OK. Query for electronic submissions. Computer printout submissions acceptable; prefers letter-quality to dot-matrix. Reports in 1 month. Free sample copy.

Nonfiction: Historical/nostalgic (on medicine); interview/profile; personal experience; and health and medicine. Buys 15 mss/year. Query with published clips. Length: 500-2,500 words. Pays $75-450 for assigned articles.

Photos: State availability of photos with submission. Reviews contact sheets and transparencies. Offers $25-55/photo. Captions required. Buys one-time rights.

Columns/Departments: Travel (health-related cruises, adventures), Diet and Nutrition (recipes, tips for dieting and personal experience), Fitness and Exercise (tips for keeping active, personal experience). Buys 10 mss/year. Query with published clips. Length: 500-1,500 words. Pays $75-200.

Tips: "A writer must exhibit a sensitivity and understanding toward aging and living a full life. Send a cover letter first, preferably with five article ideas, and you will be contacted within one month."

LET'S LIVE MAGAZINE, Oxford Industries, Inc., 444 N. Larchmont Blvd., Box 74908, Los Angeles CA 90004. (213)469-3901. Editor: Keith Stepro. Emphasizes nutrition. 40% freelance written. Works with a small number of new/unpublished writers each year. Monthly magazine; 96 pages. Circ. 135,000. Pays on publication. Publishes ms an average of 4 months after acceptance. Buys first North American serial rights. Byline given. Submit seasonal/holiday material 4 months in advance. Computer printout submissions acceptable; prefers letter-quality to dot-matrix. Reports in 3 weeks on queries; 6 weeks on mss. Sample copy for $2.50 and 10x13 SAE with $1 postage; writer's guidelines for SAE and 1 first class stamp.

Nonfiction: General interest (effects of vitamins, minerals and nutrients in improvement of health or afflictions); historical (documentation of experiments or treatment establishing value of nutrients as boon to health); how-to (acquire strength and vitality, improve health of adults and/or children and prepare tasty health-food meals); inspirational (first-person accounts of triumph over disease through substitution of natural foods and nutritional supplements for drugs and surgery); interview (benefits of research in establishing prevention as key to good health); advertised new product (120-180 words plus 5x7 or glossy of product); personal opinion (views of orthomolecular doctors or their patients on value of health foods toward maintaining good health); and profile (background and/or medical history of preventive medicine, M.D.s or Ph.D.s, in advancement of nutrition). "We do not want kookie first-person accounts of experiences with drugs or junk foods, faddist healers or unorthodox treatments. Manuscripts must be well-researched, reliably documented, and written in a clear, readable style." Buys 8-10 mss/issue. Query with published clips. Length: 750-1,200 words. Pays $50-150. Sometimes pays expenses of writers on assignment.

Photos: State availability of photos with ms. Pays $17.50 for 8x10 b&w glossy prints; $35 for 8x10 color prints and 35mm color transparencies; and $150 for good cover shot. Captions and model releases required.

Tips: "We want writers with experience in researching nonsurgical medical subjects and interviewing experts with the ability to simplify technical and clinical information for the layman. A captivating lead and structural flow are essential. The most frequent mistakes made by writers are in writing articles that are too technical; in poor style; written for the wrong audience (publication not thoroughly studied) or have unreliable documentation or overzealous faith in the topic reflected by flimsy research and inappropriate tone."

LISTEN MAGAZINE, 6830 Laurel St. NW, Washington DC 20012. (202)722-6726. Editor: Gary B. Swanson. 75% freelance written. Works with a small number of new/unpublished writers each year. Specializes in drug prevention, presenting positive alternatives to various drug dependencies. "*Listen* is used in many high school classes, in addition to use by professionals: medical personnel, counselors, law enforcement officers, educators, youth workers, etc." Monthly magazine, 32 pages. Circ. 100,000. Buys first rights. Byline given. Pays on acceptance. Publishes ms an average of 5 months after acceptance. Computer printout submissions acceptable; prefers letter-quality to dot-matrix. Reports in 4 weeks. Sample copy $1; send large manila SASE; free writer's guidelines.

Nonfiction: Seeks articles that deal with causes of drug use such as poor self-concept, family relations, social skills or peer pressure. Especially interested in youth-slanted articles or personality interviews encouraging nonalcoholic and nondrug ways of life. Teenage point of view is essential. Popularized medical, legal and educational articles. Also seeks narratives which portray teens dealing with youth conflicts, especially those related to the use of or temptation to use harmful substances. Growth of the main character should be shown. "We don't want typical alcoholic story/skid-row bum, AA stories. We are also being inundated with drunk-driving accident stories. Unless yours is unique, consider another topic." Buys 75-100 unsolicited mss/year. Query. Length: 500-1,500 words. Pays 5-7¢/word. Sometimes pays the expenses of writers on assignment.

Photos: Purchased with accompanying ms. Captions required. Color photos preferred, but b&w acceptable.

Fillers: Word square/general puzzles are also considered. Pays $15.

Tips: "True stories are good, especially if they have a unique angle. Other authoritative articles need a fresh approach. In query, briefly summarize article idea and logic of why you feel it's good."

‡**MASSAGE MAGAZINE**, Box 1969, Kealakekua HI 96750. (808)329-2433. Editor: Robert Calvert. 60% freelance written. Prefers to work with published/established writers, and works with a small number of new/unpublished writers each year. A bimonthly magazine on massage-bodywork and related healing arts. Circ. 15,000. Pays (for some articles) on publication. Publishes ms an average of 6 months after acceptance. Byline given. Buys first North American or second serial (reprint) rights or makes work-for-hire assignments. Simultaneous and previously published submissions OK. Query for electronic submissions. Computer printout submissions OK; no dot-matrix. Reports in 1 month on queries; 2 months on mss. Sample copy $4. Free writer's guidelines.

Nonfiction: Book excerpts, essays, general interest, historical/nostalgic, how-to, humor, inspirational, interview/profile, new product, photo feature, technical and travel. "No 'cure stories,' how so and so was healed by . . ." Query. Length: 200-1,000 words. Pays $25-150. Sometimes pays the expenses of writers on assignment.

Photos: State availability of photos with submission. Reviews contact sheets. Offers no additional payment for photos accepted with ms. Captions and identification of subjects required. Buys one-time rights.

Columns/Departments: Mental Massage (what happens in a session), 800 words; Business (all aspects of starting, doing, expanding, massage), 600 words; Practices World Wide (massage practices in other countries), 800 words; Academics (technical pieces directly related to soft tissue work), 1,000 words. Query. Length: 400-800 words. Pays $25-200.

Fillers: Anecdotes, facts, newsbreaks and short humor. Buys 5/year. Length: 100 words. Pays $25 maximum.

Tips: "For first articles accepted, we don't pay much, but as a writer establishes with us, we pay more. Wholesome stories with facts, interviews and industry insight are welcomed. We're leaning away from a strong emphasis on the touch professions to more consumer (general) touch-related materials."

‡**MEMBERS, Health and Racquet Club Members**, The Mercator Corp., Suite 400, 15 Bank St., Stamford CT 06901. (203)964-0084. Publisher: T. Richard Gascoigne. 35% freelance written. Quarterly lifestyle magazine distributed to members of privately-owned and operated health, fitness and racquet clubs. Estab. 1986. Circ. 750,000. Pays on publication. Publishes ms an average of 3 months after acceptance. Byline given. Buys all rights. Submit seasonal/holiday material 4 months in advance. Previously published submissions OK. Computer printout submissions OK; no dot-matrix. Reports in 6 months on queries; 3 months on mss. Free sample copy and writer's guidelines.

Nonfiction: Peggy Vick, articles editor. General interest; how-to (sports, exercise, business, finance); humor; interview/profile; travel; health and self-improvement. "*Members* is not a body and sweat magazine, but an upscale, lifestyle magazine of general subject interest to 'yuppie' health and racquet club members." No religious articles. Buys 12 mss/year. Query. Length: 250-1,250 words. Pays $250 maximum. Sometimes pays the expenses of writers on assignment.

Photos: State availability of photos with submission. Reviews contact sheets. Captions and model releases required.

Fillers: Peggy Vick, fillers editor. Gags to be illustrated by cartoonist. Buys 10/year.

Tips: Travel and leisure, self-improvement (general psychology), general health and fitness are topics most open to freelancers.

MEN'S FITNESS, (formerly *Sports Fitness*), Men's Fitness, Inc., 21100 Erwin St., Woodland Hills CA 91367. (818)884-6800. Editor-in-Chief: David Rivas. Managing Editor: Chris Weygandt. 75% freelance writ-

ten. Works with small number of new/unpublished writers each year. A monthly magazine for health-conscious men between the ages of 18 and 45. Provides reliable, entertaining guidance for the active male in all areas of lifestyle. Writers often share bylines with professional experts. Pays 30 days after acceptance. Publishes ms an average of 4 months after acceptance. Offers 20% kill fee. Buys all rights. Submit seasonal material 4 months in advance. Reports in 1 month. Computer printout submissions OK; no dot-matrix. Sample copy and writer's guidelines for 8½x11 SAE with $1.46 postage.
Nonfiction: Service, informative, inspirational, scientific studies written for men. Few interviews, regional news unless extraordinary. Query with published clips. Buys 50 mss/year. Length: 2,000-3,000 words. Pays $300-500. Occasionally buys mss devoted to specific fitness programs, including exercises, e.g. 6-week chest workout, aerobic weight-training routine. Buys 10-15 mss/year. Pays $250-300.
Columns/Departments: Nutrition, Sporting Life, Sports Science, Grooming, Sex, Prevention, Adventure. Length: 1,250-2,000 words. Buys 40-50 mss/year. Pays $250-300.
Tips: "Articles are welcomed in all facets of men's health; they must be well-researched, entertaining and intelligent."

NEW BODY, The Magazine of Health & Fitness, GCR Publishing Group, Inc., 888 7th Ave., New York NY 10106. (212)541-7100. Editor: Constance Boze. Managing Editor: Sandra Kosherick. 75% freelance written. Works with a small number of new/unpublished writers each year. A bimonthly magazine covering fitness and health for young, middle-class women. Circ. 125,000. Pays on publication. Publishes ms an average of 6 months after acceptance. Byline given. Offers negotiable kill fee. Buys first North American serial rights. Submit seasonal/holiday material 6 months in advance. Simultaneous and photocopied submissions OK. Computer printout submissions acceptable; prefers letter-quality to dot-matrix. Reports in 2 months.
Nonfiction: Book excerpts, exposé (investigational health issues); general interest; how-to (exercise, health); photo feature (exercise, food, fashion); and travel (spas, health clubs, exercise vacations). "We are interested in specific methods or programs of exercises designed by professionals to accomplish specific purposes. We do not cover bodybuilding—please no queries." No articles on "How I do exercises." Buys 75 mss/year. Query with published clips. Length: 1,000-2,500 words. Pays $100-300 for assigned articles; $50-150 for unsolicited articles.
Photos: Reviews contact sheets, transparencies and prints. Model releases and identification of subjects required. Buys one-time rights.
Tips: "We are moving toward more general interest women's material on relationships, emotional health, travel, etc. We look for a fresh angle—a new way to present the material. Relationships, celebrity profiles, tips, and health news are good topics to consider. Make a clean statement of what your article is about, what it would cover—not why the article is important. We're interested in new ideas, new trends or new ways of looking at old topics."

OSTOMY QUARTERLY, United Ostomy Association, Inc., Suite 120, 36 Executive Park, Irvine CA 92714. Editor: TennieBee M. Hall. 20% freelance written. Works with a small number of new/unpublished writers each year and is eager to work with new/unpublished writers. Quarterly magazine on ostomy surgery and living with ostomies. "The *OQ* is the official publication of UOA and should cover topics of interest to patients who underwent abdominal ostomy surgery (ileostomy, colostomy, urostomy). Most articles should be 'upbeat' in feeling; also, we cover new surgical techniques in ostomy surgery." Circ. 50,000. Pays on publication. Publishes ms an average of 6 months after acceptance. Byline given. Buys first North American serial rights; makes work-for-hire assignments. Submit seasonal/holiday material 3 months in advance. Simultaneous queries and photocopied submissions OK. Computer printout submissions acceptable; prefers letter-quality to dot-matrix. Print must be dark and readable. Reports in 3 months. Sample copy for $2.50 and 8½x11 SAE with $1.41 postage; writer's guidelines and editorial calendar for SASE.
Nonfiction: General interest (parenting, psychology); humor (coping humorously with problems with ostomies); interview/profile (important MDs in gastroenterology, urology); personal experience (living with abdominal ostomies); technical (new surgical techniques in ostomy); and travel (with ostomies). No testimonials from members, "How I overcame . . . with ostomy and life is great now." Buys 6 mss/year. Query. Length: 800-2,400 words. Usually asks for pages of copy. Pays $50-150 maximum. Sometimes pays the expenses of writers on assignment but no more than $150 total (expenses plus fee) per article will be paid. No kill fee offered.
Photos: Reviews b&w and color transparencies. "We like to use photographs with articles, but price for article includes use of photos. We return photos on request." Captions and model releases required.
Columns/Departments: Book reviews (on ostomy care, living with ostomies); Ostomy World (any news items relating to ostomy, enterostomal therapy, medical); Q&A (answers medical questions from members); nutrition; financial; psychology. Primarily staff-written.
Tips: "We will be looking mainly for articles from freelancers about ostomy management, ostomy advances, people important to ostomates. Send different topics and ideas than we have published for 24 years. Be willing to attend free meeting of UOA chapter to get a 'flavor' of the group. UOA is a nonprofit association which ac-

counts for the fees offered. The *OQ* might be re-evaluated in terms of focus. The association might want to expand its focus to include the medical professionals who relate to people with ostomies (discharge planners, visiting nurses, ET nurses, pharmacists, etc.)."

RX BEING WELL, Biomedical Information Corp., 800 Second Ave., New York NY 10017. (212)599-3400. Editor: Mark Deitch. 50-75% freelance written. Prefers to work with published/established writers. A bimonthly magazine "covering health and medicine and reaching readers primarily in physicians' waiting rooms. Articles usually have a physician coauthor." Circ. 350,000. Pays on acceptance. Publishes ms an average of 3-6 months after acceptance. Byline given. Offers ⅓ kill fee. Buys all rights. Computer printout submissions OK; prefers letter-quality to dot-matrix. Reports in 1 month. Sample copy and writer's guidelines for 9x12 SAE with 90¢ postage.
Nonfiction: Health and medical. No personal experience ("My Gall Bladder Operation") or speculative therapies ("Ginseng Cures Heart Disease"). Buys 40-50 mss/year. Query with or without published clips, or send complete ms. SASE a must. Length: 1,000-2,000 words. Pays $500 minimum for assigned articles. Pays the expenses of writers on assignment within reasonable limits.
Tips: "Our editorial aim is health/medical education: providing authoritative (not trendy or speculative) information on disease treatment and prevention, nutrition, sports medicine, pre- and post-natal care, psychological health, and related topics. Your best bet is to include (with your query) the name or names of established medical experts who might serve as coauthor or interview subject."

SHAPE, Merging Mind and Body Fitness, Weider Enterprises, 21100 Erwin St., Woodland Hills CA 91367. (818)715-0600. Editor: Christine MacIntyre. 10% freelance written. Prefers to work with published/ established writers, works with a small number of new/unpublished writers each year, and is eager to work with new/unpublished writers. Monthly magazine covering women's health and fitness. Circ. 560,000. Pays on publication. Publishes ms an average of 6 months after acceptance. Offers 1/3 kill fee. Buys all rights and reprint rights. Submit seasonal/holiday material 8 months in advance. Computer printout submissions acceptable; prefers letter-quality to dot-matrix. Reports in 2 months.
Nonfiction: Book excerpts; exposé (health, fitness related); how-to (get fit); interview/profile (of fit women); travel (spas). "We use health and fitness articles written by professionals in their specific fields. No articles which haven't been queried first." Query with clips of published work. Length: 500-2,000 words. Pays negotiable fee. Pays expenses of writers on assignment.

SLIMMER, R/G Communications, 801 Second Ave., New York NY 10017. (212)986-5100. Editor-in-Chief: Nancie S. Martin. Executive Editor: Rhonda J. Wilson. 75% freelance written. A bimonthly magazine. "We are a fitness lifestyle publication presenting articles and features on health, beauty, fashion, nutrition, diet and exercise in the hopes of presenting a head-to-toe approach to fitness. We attempt to excite the complacent woman about fitness and the idea of improving herself." Circ. 250,000. Pays on publication. Byline given. Offers 15% kill fee. Not copyrighted. Buys first rights, one-time rights and second serial (reprint) rights. Submit seasonal holiday material 6 months in advance. Photocopied submissions OK. Sample copy for 8½x11 SAE with 3 first class stamps; free writer's guidelines.
Nonfiction: Book excerpts (health, fitness, nutrition, celebrity workout books); exposé (such as the real Herbalife story); general interest; how-to (exercise, beauty, nutrition, etc.); inspirational ("How I lost 200 pounds"; "How I overcame chocolate craving"); interview/profile (celebrities relating beauty, fashion, fitness); personal experience (on makeovers, etc.); photo feature (on fashion, beauty, celebrities) and travel (spas, resorts, health retreats, bicycling paths, etc.). "No basic or general stories on aerobics, jogging, swimming—sports or ideas that we have obviously covered from a general nature many times over." Query with or without published clips or send complete ms. Length: 2,000-4,000 words. Pays $150-300 for assigned articles. Sometimes pays the expenses of writers on assignment.
Photos: State availability of photos with submission. Captions required.
Columns/Departments: The Sporting Life (rising female sports stars); Trim Tales (before and after success stories); Quiz (health and nutrition); BodyWorks (how the body works); Fitness Forum (compendium of fitness, health, beauty, nutrition features); and Overtime (humorous first person perspective on fitness). Query. Length: 850-1,500 words. Pays $150-250.
Fillers: Facts and newsbreaks. Buys few fillers. Length: 50-200 words. Pays $25-100.
Tips: "Find a new angle on an obvious story. Be creative. Look for authorities to quote in the article. Be persistent. Stories must be full of information and presented in a thought-provoking manner."

TOTAL HEALTH, Body, Mind and Spirit, Trio Publications, Suite 300, 6001 Topanga Cyn Blvd., Woodland Hills CA 91367. (818)887-6484. Editor: Robert L. Smith. Managing Editor: Rosemary Hofer. Prefers to work with published/established writers. 80% freelance written. A bimonthly magazine covering fitness, diet (weight loss), nutrition and mental health—"a family magazine about wholeness." Circ. 70,000. Pays on publication. Publishes ms an average of 2 months after acceptance. Byline given. Buys first rights. Submit seasonal/holiday material 4 months in advance. Photocopied submissions OK. Reports in 1 month. Sample copy $1 with SAE; writer's guidelines for SAE.

Nonfiction: Exposé; how-to (pertaining to health and fitness); and religious (Judeo-Christian). Especially needs articles on skin and body care and power of positive thinking articles. No personal experience articles. Buys 48 mss/year. Send complete ms. Length: 2,000-3,000 words. Pays $50. Sometimes pays the expenses of writers on assignment.

Photos: State availability of photos with submission. Offers no additional payment for photos accepted with ms. Captions, model releases and identification of subjects required.

Columns/Departments: Query with or without published clips. Length: 1,000 words maximum. Pays $50 maximum.

Tips: "Feature-length articles are most open to freelancers."

‡VEGETARIAN JOURNAL, Box 1463, Baltimore MD 21203. (301)752-VEGV. Editors: Charles Stahler/Debra Wasserman. A monthly newsletter on vegetarianism and animal rights. "*Vegetarian* issues include health, nutrition, animal rights and world hunger. Articles related to nutrition should be documented by established (mainstream) nutrition studies." Circ. 2,000. Pays on publication. Publishes ms an average of 3-5 months after acceptance. Byline given. Makes work-for-hire assignments. Submit seasonal/holiday material 6 months in advance. Computer printout submissions OK; prefers letter-quality to dot-matrix. Reports in 1 month. Sample copy for #10 SAE with 2 first class stamps.

Nonfiction: Book excerpts, expose, how-to, interview/profile, new products, travel. "At present we are only looking for in-depth articles on selected nutrition subjects from registered dieticians or M.D.'s Please query with your background. Possibly some in-depth practical and researched articles from others. No miracle cures or use of supplements." Buys 1-5 mss/year. Query with or without published clips or send complete ms. Length: 2,500-8,250 words. Pays $10-25. Sometimes pays writers with contributor copies or other premiums "if not a specific agreed upon in-depth article." Sometimes pays the expenses of writers on assignment.

Photos: State availability of photos with submission. Reviews prints. Offers no additional payment for photos accepted with ms. Identification of subjects required. Buys one-time rights.

Poetry: Avant-garde, free verse, haiku, light verse, traditional "Poetry should be related to vegetarianism, world hunger, or animal rights. No graphic animal abuse. We do not want to see the word, blood, in any form." Pays in copies.

Tips: "We are most open to vegan-oriented medical professionals or vegetarian/animal rights activists who are new to freelancing."

VEGETARIAN TIMES, Box 570, Oak Park IL 60303. (312)848-8100. Executive Editor: Sally Hayhow. Managing Editor: Lucy Moll. 30% freelance written. Prefers to work with published/established writers; works with small number of new/unpublished writers each year. Monthly magazine. Circ. 150,000. Rights purchased vary with author and material. Buys first serial rights or all rights ("always includes right to use article in our books or 'Best of' series"). Byline given unless extensive revisions are required or material is incorporated into a larger article. Pays on publication. Publishes ms an average of 8 months after acceptance. Photocopied and simultaneous submissions OK. Query for electronic submissions. Computer printout submissions acceptable; prefers letter-quality to dot-matrix. Submit seasonal material 6 months in advance. Reports in 1 month. Query. Sample copy $2.

Nonfiction: Features concise articles related to vegetarian cooking, health foods and articles about vegetarians. "All material should be well documented and researched. It would probably be best to see a sample copy." Informational, how-to, personal experience, interview, profile, historical, successful health food business operations and restaurant reviews. Length: average 1,500 words. Pays 5-20¢/word. Will also use 500- to 1,000-word items for regular columns. Sometimes pays expenses of writers on assignment.

Photos: Prefers b&w ferrotype. Pays $25 for b&w; $25 for color photos used.

Tips: "The worst thing about freelance writers is that everybody who can type thinks they are writers. And the less experience a writer has the more he/she hates to be edited. Some writers scream bloody murder when you delete their paragraphs or add words to make the copy flow better. Nevertheless, many writers have broken in to print in our magazine. Write query with brevity and clarity."

WALKWAYS, Update on Walkers and Walking, The WalkWays Center, #427, 733 15th St., NW, Washington DC 20005. (202)737-9555. Editor: Marsha L. Wallen. 50% freelance written. Works with a small number of new/unpublished writers each year, and is eager to work with new/unpublished writers. A bimonthly newsletter on walking. Circ. 4,000. Pays on publication. Publishes ms an average of 1 month after acceptance. Byline given. Offers 50% kill fee. Buys first North American serial rights. Submit seasonal/holiday material 6 months in advance. Simultaneous and photocopied submissions OK. Computer printout submissions OK. Reports in 2 weeks. Sample copy $1.50 with #10 SASE.

Nonfiction: Essays, how-to, humor, interview/profile, opinion, personal experience and travel. "No general travelogues, how walking is a religious experience, or narrow-scope articles about a type of walking with no examples of where it can be done in other places." Buys 8 mss/year. Send complete ms. Length: 200-750 words. Pays $20-75.

Photos: State availability of photos with submissions. Photos should include people walking or some other activity; should not be just scenery. Reviews contact sheets, 35mm transparencies, and 5x7 and 8x10 prints. Offers $10/photo. Captions required. Buys one-time rights.

Columns/Departments: Health notes, 350 words maximum, with art or photo; Networking (an information sharing department on specific subjects to familiarize readers, such as Volksmarching, race walking, how to form walking club), 350 words maximum, with art or photo; and Footloose (a walk or series of walks in special places with how-to and sidebar information on how to get there, best time, best places to see, who was leader, etc.), 750 words maximum, with art or photo. Buys 32 mss/year. Send complete ms. Offers $10/photo.

Fiction: Humorous. Send complete ms. Length: 200 words maximum. Pays $10-20.

Fillers: Medical facts and short humor. Length: 30-50 words. Pays $5.

Tips: "We need writers who can concentrate more on the walk and less about the scenery and extraneous details, although they are appreciated. If writing about a walking trip or experience, give details on how to get there, costs, etc., plus *other* places you can do similar walks. We like to approach themes versus single event or experiences, if possible and applicable."

WEIGHT WATCHERS MAGAZINE, 360 Lexington Ave., New York NY 10017. (212)370-0644. Editor-in-Chief: Lee Haiken. Articles Editor: Nelly Edmondson. 50% freelance written. Works with a small number of new/unpublished writers each year. Monthly publication for those interested in weight loss and weight maintenance through sensible eating and health/nutrition guidance. Circ. 902,525. Buys first North American serial rights only. Pays on acceptance. Publishes ms an average of 6 months after acceptance. Computer printout submissions acceptable; prefers letter-quality to dot-matrix. Reports in 1-2 months. Sample copy and writer's guidelines $1.75.

Nonfiction: Subject matter should be related to food, fitness, health or weight loss, but not specific diets or recipes. Would like to see researched articles related to the psychological aspects of weight loss and control and suggestions for making the battle easier. Inspirational success stories of weight loss following the Weight Watchers Program or other *sensible* weight-loss regimens also accepted. "We want to do more in-depth nutrition, psychology, and health pieces. Writers should interview top experts." Send detailed queries with published clips and SASE. No full-length mss; send feature ideas, as well as before-and-after weight loss story ideas dealing either with celebrities or "real people." Length: 1,500 words maximum. Pays $200-600. Sometimes pays the expenses of writers on assignment.

Tips: "It's rewarding giving freelancers the rough shape of how an article should look and seeing where they go with it. It's frustrating working with writers who don't pay enough attention to revisions that have been requested and who send back second drafts with a few changes. We rarely use fillers. Writers can break in if their writing is lively, tightly constructed, and shows an understanding of our audience."

WHOLE LIFE, A Journal for Personal Health and Natural Living, Whole Life Enterprises, Inc., Suite 600, 89 5th Ave., New York NY 10003. (212)741-7274. Editor and Publisher: Marc Medoff. 25% freelance written. Prefers to work with published/established writers and works with a small number of new/unpublished writers each year. Tabloid covering holistic health, environment, and including some material on world peace. Circ. 60,000. Pays 60 days after publication. Publishes ms 3-12 months after acceptance. Byline given. Buys first North American serial rights, all rights, and second serial (reprint) rights, and makes work-for-hire assignments; depends on topic and author. Submit seasonal/holiday material 6 months in advance. Simultaneous queries, and simultaneous, photocopied, and previously published submissions OK. Reports in 2 months. Sample copy $4; writer's guidelines for 4x9 SASE.

Nonfiction: Book excerpts (health, environment, community activism); general interest (health sciences, holistic health, environment, alternative economics and politics); how-to (exercise, relaxation, fitness, appropriate technology, outdoors); interview/profile (on assignment); and new product (health, music, spiritual, psychological, natural diet). No undocumented opinion or narrative. Buys 40-80 mss/year. Query with published clips and resume. Length: 1,150-3,000 words. Pays $25-150. Sometimes pays expenses of writers on assignment.

Photos: Reviews b&w contact sheets, any size b&w and color transparencies and any size prints. Model releases and identification of subjects required. Buys all rights.

Columns/Departments: Films, Recipes, Herbs & Health, Resources, Whole Health Network, Living Lightly (appropriate technology), Peacefronts, News Views, Whole Life Person, Music, In the Market, Animal Rights—Human Wrongs, Whole Life Experience, Healthy Travel, Restaurant Review, Alternative Fitness, Whole Foods in the News, Whole Frauds in the News, People and Food. Buys 40-80 mss/year. Query with published clips and resume. Length: 150-1,000 words. Pays $25-80.

WHOLISTIC LIVING NEWS, Association for Wholistic Living, Box 16346, San Diego CA 92116. (619)280-0317. Editor: Judith Horton. 75% freelance written. Works with a small number of new/unpublished writers each year. Bimonthly newspaper covering the wholistic field from a wholistic perspective. Circ. 80,000. Pays on publication. Publishes ms an average of 2-4 months after acceptance. Byline given. Not copyrighted. Buys first serial rights and second serial (reprint) rights to material originally published elsewhere. Submit seasonal/

holiday material 6 months in advance. Simultaneous queries, and simultaneous, photocopied, and previously published submissions OK. Computer printout submissions acceptable; prefers letter-quality to dot-matrix. Reports in 1 month on queries; 2 months on mss. Sample copy $1.50; free writer's guidelines.

Nonfiction: General interest (wholistic or new age overviews of a general topic); and how-to (taking responsibility for yourself—healthwise). No profiles, individual companies, personal experience or first person articles. Buys 100 mss/year. Query with published clips. Length: 200-1,500 words. Pays $10-45. Sometimes pays the expenses of writers on assignment.

Photos: Send photos with query. Pays $7.50 for 5x7 b&w prints. Model releases and identification of subjects required.

Tips: "Study the newspaper—the style is different from a daily. The articles generally provide helpful information on how to feel your best (mentally, spiritually, physically) and how to live in harmony with the planet. Any of the sections are open to freelancers: Creative Living, Health & Fitness, Arts, Nutrition and Network (recent events and upcoming ones). One of the main aspects of the paper is to promote the concept of a wholistic lifestyle and help people integrate it into their lives by taking simple steps on a daily basis. We are becoming somewhat more political in our outlook—exploring the political aspects of the topics we discuss. Animal rights, Central America and food irradiation are examples."

THE YOGA JOURNAL, California Yoga Teachers Association, 2054 University Ave., Berkeley CA 94704. (415)841-9200. Editor: Stephan Bodian. 75% freelance written. Bimonthly magazine covering yoga, holistic health, conscious living, spiritual practices, and nutrition. "We reach a middle-class, educated audience interested in self-improvement and higher consciousness." Circ. 30,000. Pays on publication. Publishes ms an average of 6 months after acceptance. Byline given. Offers $35 kill fee. Buys first North American serial rights only. Submit seasonal/holiday material 4 months in advance. Simultaneous queries and photocopied submissions OK. Reports in 6 weeks on queries; 2 months on mss. Sample copy $3; free writer's guidelines.

Nonfiction: Book excerpts; how-to (exercise, yoga, massage, etc.); inspirational (yoga or related); interview/profile; opinion; personal experience; photo feature; and travel (if about yoga). "Yoga is our main concern, but our principal features in each issue highlight other new age personalities and endeavors. Nothing too far-out and mystical. Prefer stories about Americans incorporating yoga, meditation, etc., into their normal lives." Buys 40 mss/year. Query. Length: 750-3,500 words. Pays $35-150.

Photos: Diane McCarney, art director. Send photos with ms. Pays $100-150 for color cover transparencies; $15-25 for 8x10 b&w prints. Model release (for cover only) and identification of subjects required. Buys one-time rights.

Columns/Departments: Forum; Food (vegetarian, text and recipes); Health; Music (reviews of new age music); and Book Reviews. Buys 12-15 mss/year. Pays $25-50.

Tips: "We always read submissions. We are very open to freelance material and want to encourage writers to submit to our magazine. We're looking for out-of-state contributors, particularly in the Midwest and east coast."

YOUR HEALTH, Meridian Publishing Inc., Box 10010, Ogden UT 84409. (801)394-9446. Editor: Ms. Caroll McKanna Halley. 65% freelance written. A monthly in-house magazine covering personal health, customized with special imprint titles for various businesses, organizations and associations. "Articles should be timeless, noncontroversial, upscale and positive, and the subject matter should have national appeal." Circ. 40,000. Pays on acceptance. Publishes ms an average of 8 months after acceptance. Byline given. Buys first rights and non-exclusive reprint rights. Simultaneous, photocopied, and previously published submissions OK. Computer printout submissions acceptable; prefers letter-quality to dot-matrix. Reports in 6 weeks. Sample copy $1 with 9x12 SAE; writer's guidelines for business size SAE with 1 first class stamp. (All requests for sample copies and guidelines should be addressed to—Attention: Editorial Assistant.)

Nonfiction: General interest stories about individual's health care needs, including preventative approaches to good health. Topics include advances in medical technology, common maladies and treatments, fitness and nutrition, hospital and home medical care, and personality profiles of both health care professionals and exceptional people coping with disability or illness. "We almost never use a first person narrative. No articles about chiropractic, podiatry or lay midwifery articles." Medical pieces must be accompanied by a list of checkable resources. Buys 40 mss/year. Query. Length: 1,000-1,200 words. Pay 15¢/word for first rights plus non-exclusive reprint rights. Payment for second rights is negotiable. Authors retain the right to resell material after it is printed by *Your Health*.

Photos: Send photos or state availability with submission. Reviews 35mm and 2¼x2¼ transparencies and 5x7 or 8x10 prints. Offers $35/inside photo and $50/cover photo. Captions, model releases and identification of subjects required.

Tips: "The key for the freelancer is a well-written query letter that demonstrates that the subject of the article has national appeal; establishes that any medical claims are based on interviews with experts and/or reliable documented sources; shows that the article will have a clear, focused theme; outlines the availability (from the writer, photographer, or a PR source) of top-quality color photos; and gives evidence that the writer/photographer is a professional, even if a beginner. The best way to get started as a contributor to *Your Health* is to prove that you can submit a well-focused article, based on facts, written cleanly per AP style, along with a variety of beautiful color transparencies to illustrate the story."

‡**YOUR HEALTH & FITNESS**, General Learning Corp., 3500 Western Ave., Highland Park IL 60035. (312)432-2700. Editor: Laura Ruckberg. Managing Editor: Carol Lezak. 90-95% freelance written. Prefers to work with published/established writers. A bimonthly magazine covering health and fitness. Needs "general, educational material on health, fitness and safety that can be read and understood easily by the layman." Circ. 1,000,000. Pays within 30 days after acceptance. Publishes ms an average of 6 months after acceptance. No byline given. Offers 50% kill fee. Buys all rights. Submit seasonal/holiday material 6 months in advance. Computer printout submissions OK; no dot-matrix. Sample copy for 9x12 SAE with 2 first class stamps. Free writer's guidelines.
Nonfiction: General interest. "All article topics assigned; send resumes and writing samples. All topics are determined a year in advance of publication by editors; no unsolicited manuscripts." Buys approximately 65 mss/year. Length: 350-1,400 words. Pays $100-700 for assigned articles. Sometimes pays the expenses of writers on assignment.
Photos: Offers no additional payment for photos accepted with ms.
Tips: "Write to a general audience which has only a surface knowledge of health and fitness topics. Possible subjects include exercise and fitness, psychology, nutrition, safety, disease, drug data and health concerns."

History

Listed here are magazines and other periodicals written for historical collectors, genealogy enthusiasts, historic preservationists and researchers. Editors of history magazines look for fresh accounts of past events in a readable style. Some publications cover an era or a region; others deal with historic perservation.

AMERICAN HERITAGE, 60 Fifth Ave., New York NY 10011. Editor: Byron Dobell. 70% freelance written. Bimonthly. Circ. 200,000. Usually buys first North American rights or all rights. Byline given. Pays on acceptance. Publishes ms an average of 6-12 months after acceptance. Before submitting material, "check our index to see whether we have already treated the subject." Submit seasonal material 1 year in advance. Electronic submissions acceptable ("any disk—to be converted by us in house"). Computer printout submissions acceptable; prefers letter-quality to dot-matrix. Reports in 1 month. Writer's guidelines for SAE and 1 first class stamp.
Nonfiction: Wants "historical articles by scholars or journalists intended for intelligent lay readers rather than for professional historians." Emphasis is on authenticity, accuracy and verve. "Interesting documents, photographs and drawings are always welcome. Query." Style should stress "readability and accuracy." Buys 30 uncommissioned mss/year. Length: 1,500-5,000 words. Sometimes pays the expenses of writers on assignment.
Tips: "We have over the years published quite a few 'firsts' from young writers whose historical knowledge, research methods and writing skills met our standards. The scope and ambition of a new writer tell us a lot about his or her future usefulness to us. A major article gives us a better idea of the writer's value. Everything depends on the quality of the material. We don't really care whether the author is 20 and unknown, or 80 and famous, or vice versa."

AMERICAN HISTORY ILLUSTRATED, Box 8200, Harrisburg PA 17105. (717)657-9555. Editor: Ed Holm. 75% freelance written. Willing to work with new/unpublished writers. "We are backlogged with submissions and prefer not to receive unsolicited submissions at this time." A magazine of cultural, social, military and political history published for a general audience. Monthly except July/August. Circ. 125,000 + . Pays on acceptance. Publishes ms 5 months after acceptance. Byline given. Buys all rights. Query for electronic submissions. Computer printout submissions acceptable; no dot-matrix. Reports in 10 weeks on queries; 16 weeks on mss. Writer's guidelines for business size SAE and 1 first class stamp; sample copy and guidelines $3 (amount includes 3rd class postage) or $2.50 and 9x12 SAE with 4 first class stamps.
Nonfiction: Regular features include American Profiles (biographies of noteworthy historical figures); Artifacts (stories behind historical objects); Portfolio (pictorial features on artists, photographers and graphic subjects); Digging Up History (coverage of recent major archaeological and historical discoveries); and Testaments to the Past (living history articles on major restored historical sites). "Material is presented on a popular

rather than a scholarly level." Writers are required to query before submitting ms. "Query letters should be limited to a concise 1-2 page proposal defining your article with an emphasis on its unique qualities." Buys 60 mss/year. Length: 1,000-3,000 words depending on type of article. Pays $100-500. Sometimes pays the expenses of writers on assignment.

Photos: Occasionally buys 8x10 glossy prints with mss; welcomes suggestions for illustrations. Pays for the reproduced color illustrations that the author provides.

Tips: "Key prerequisites for publication are thorough research and accurate presentation, precise English usage and sound organization, a lively style, and a high level of human interest. We are especially interested in publishing 'Testaments to the Past' articles (on significant ongoing living history sites), as well as top-quality articles on significant American women, on the Vietnam era, and on social/cultural history. Submissions received without return postage will not be considered or returned. Inappropriate materials include: fiction, book reviews, travelogues, personal/family narratives not of national significance, articles about collectibles/antiques, living artists, local/individual historic buildings/landmarks and articles of a current editorial nature."

ANCESTRY NEWSLETTER, Ancestry, Inc., Box 476, Salt Lake City UT 84110. (801)531-1790. Editor-in-Chief: Scott R. Woodruff. 95% freelance written. Eager to work with new/unpublished writers. A bimonthly newsletter covering genealogy and family history. "We publish practical, instructional, and informative pieces specifically applicable to the field of genealogy. Our audience is the active genealogist, both hobbyist and professional." Circ. 7,000. Pays on publication. Publishes ms an average of 5 months after acceptance. Byline given. Buys first North American serial rights or all rights. Submit seasonal/holiday material 4 months in advance. Simultaneous and photocopied submissions OK. Computer printout submissions acceptable; prefers letter-quality to dot-matrix. Reports in 2 weeks on queries; 2 months on mss. Free sample copy and writer's guidelines.

Nonfiction: General interest (genealogical); historical; how-to (genealogical research techniques); instructional; and photo feature (genealogically related). No unpublished or published family histories, genealogies; the "story of my great-grandmother," etc. or personal experiences. Buys 25-30 mss/year. Send complete ms. Length: 1,000-2,500 words. Pays $50-100.

Photos: Send photos with submission. Reviews contact sheets and 5x7 prints. Offers no additional payment for photos accepted with ms. Identification of subjects required. Buys one-time rights.

Tips: "You don't have to be famous, but you must know something about genealogy. Our readers crave any information which might assist them in their ancestral quest."

THE ARTILLERYMAN, Cutter & Locke, Inc., Publishers, 4 Water St., Box C, Arlington MA 02174. (617)646-2010. 60% freelance written. Editor: C. Peter Jorgensen. Quarterly magazine covering antique artillery, fortifications, and crew-served weapons 1750 to 1900 for competition shooters, collectors and living history reenactors using muzzleloading artillery; "emphasis on Revolutionary War and Civil War but includes everyone interested in pre-1900 artillery and fortifications, preservation, construction of replicas, etc." Circ. 3,100. Pays on publication. Publishes ms an average of 3-6 months after acceptance. Byline given. Not copyrighted. Buys one-time rights. Simultaneous queries, and simultaneous, photocopied and previously published submissions OK. Computer printout submissions acceptable; prefers letter-quality to dot-matrix. Reports in 3 weeks. Sample copy and writer's guidelines for 8½x11 SAE and 4 first class stamps.

Nonfiction: Historical/nostalgic; how-to (reproduce ordnance equipment/sights/implements/tools/accessories, etc.); interview/profile; new product; opinion (must be accompanied by detailed background of writer and include references); personal experience; photo feature; technical (must have footnotes); and travel (where to find interesting antique cannon). Interested in "artillery *only*, for sophisticated readers. Not interested in other weapons, battles in general." Buys 24-30 mss/year. Send complete ms. Length: 300 words minimum. Pays $20-60. Sometimes pays the expenses of writers on assignment.

Photos: Send photos with ms. Pays $5 for 5x7 and larger b&w prints. Captions and identification of subjects required.

Tips: "We regularly use freelance contributions for Places-to-Visit, Cannon Safety, The Workshop and Unit Profiles departments. Also need pieces on unusual cannon or cannon with a known and unique history. To judge whether writing style and/or expertise will suit our needs, writers should ask themselves if they could knowledgeably talk *artillery* with an expert. Subject matter is of more concern than writer's background."

BACKWOODSMAN MAGAZINE, The Publication for 20th Century Frontiersmen, Route 8, Box 579, Livingston TX 77351. Editor: Charlie Richie. 50% freelance written. Bimonthly magazine covering buckskinning, 19th century crafts, muzzleloading, homesteading and trapping. Circ. 5,000. Pays after publication. Publishes ms an average of 4 months after acceptance. Byline given. Buys all rights. Computer printout submissions acceptable; prefers letter-quality to dot-matrix. Reports in 2 weeks on queries. Sample copy $2.

Nonfiction: Historical/nostalgic (1780 to 1900); how-to (19th century crafts, muzzle-loading); inspirational (wilderness survival); interview/profile (real-life backwoodsmen); new product (buckskinning field); and travel (American historical). "We want 19th century craft how-tos—mostly the simple kinds of everyday woodslore-type crafts." Buys 30-40 mss/year. Send complete ms. Length: 3-4 double-spaced pages. Pays $20 maximum.

Photos: ''We prefer that at least one b&w photo or illustration be submitted with ms.''

Tips: ''We want established buckskinning and backwoodsing writers—no fanciful first-time material will be accepted. We publish articles by real backwoodsmen and prefer that the writer just be himself and not Hemingway.''

BLUE & GRAY MAGAZINE, "For Those Who Still Hear the Guns," Blue & Gray Enterprises, Inc., 130 Galloway Rd. Galloway OH 43119. (614)870-1861. Editor: David E. Roth. 25% freelance written. Works with a small number of new/unpublished writers each year. Bimonthly magazine on the Civil War era and current Civil War-related activities. ''Our philosophy is color, quality and broad-based reporting. Included in this 'broad-based' reporting is the full range of Civil War-related topics, such as pure history articles, relic hunting, collectibles, wargaming, book reviews, new discoveries, and tour guides of historical sites. Our distribution is international in scope and appeals to both a popular and scholarly market.'' Circ. 20,000 (with a 5% growth per issue). Pays on acceptance. Publishes ms an average of 6 months after acceptance. Byline given. Usually buys all rights. Submit seasonal/holiday material 6 months in advance. Computer printout submissions acceptable; no dot-matrix. Reporting time varies with query/manuscripts. Writer's guidelines for SAE with 1 first class stamp.

Nonfiction: Expose (history); historical/nostalgic; interview/profile (Civil War descendant); opinion (history); photo feature (history); technical (history, relic hunting, etc.); travel (Civil War sites); or article on Civil War history. Query with or without published clips or send complete ms. Length: 1,000-6,000 words. Pays $25-350.

Photos: State availability of photos, or send photos with query or mss. Captions and identification of subjects required. Buys non-exclusive rights for continued use.

Columns/Departments: Book Reviews, Relic Hunting, Controversy, Profile, etc. Query with or without published clips, or send complete ms. Length: 1,000-4,000 words. Pays $25-250.

Tips: ''Submit an appropriate Civil War-related ms with sources listed (footnotes from original sources preferred), and photos or photo suggestions. All areas of our publication are open to freelancers except Tour Guides which is somewhat restricted because of already firm commitments.''

CANADIAN WEST, Box 3399, Langley, British Columbia V3A 4R7 Canada. (604)576-6561. Editor-in-Chief: Damian Inwood. 80-100% freelance written. Works with a small number of new/unpublished writers each year. Emphasizes pioneer history, primarily of British Columbia, Alberta and the Yukon. Quarterly magazine; 48 pages. Circ. 8,000. Pays on publication. Publishes ms an average of 3 months after acceptance. Buys first North American serial rights. Phone queries OK. Electronic submissions acceptable via IBM compatible disks, but requires hard copy also. Computer printout submissions acceptable; prefers letter-quality to dot-matrix. Previously published submissions OK. Reports in 2 months. Sample copy and writer's guidelines for $1.50.

Nonfiction: How-to (related to gold panning and dredging); historical (pioneers, shipwrecks, massacres, battles, exploration, logging, Indians, ghost towns, mining camps, gold rushes and railroads). No American locale articles. Buys 28 mss/year. Submit complete ms. Length: 2,000-3,500 words. Pays $100-300.

Photos: All mss must include photos or other artwork. Submit photos with ms. Pays $10 per b&w photo and $20 per color photo. Captions preferred. ''Photographs are kept for future reference with the right to re-use. However, we do not forbid other uses, generally, as these are historical prints from archives.''

Columns/Departments: Open to suggestions for new columns/departments.

CHICAGO HISTORY, The Magazine of the Chicago Historical Society, Chicago Historical Society, Clark St. at North Ave., Chicago IL 60614. (312)642-4600. Editor: Russell Lewis. Associate Editor: Meg Walter. Editorial Assistant: Aleta Zak. 100% freelance written. Works with a small number of new/unpublished writers each year. A quarterly magazine covering Chicago history: cultural, political, economic, social, architectural. Circ. 5,500. Pays on publication. Publishes ms an average of 6-12 months after acceptance. Byline given. Buys all rights. Submit seasonal/holiday material 9 months in advance. Photocopied submissions OK. Electronic submissions OK if IBM compatible, but requires hard copy also. Computer printout submissions acceptable; no dot-matrix. Reports in 6 weeks. Sample copy $3.25; free writer's guidelines.

Nonfiction: Book excerpts, essays, historical/nostalgic, interview/profile and photo feature. Articles to be ''analytical, informative, and directed at a popular audience with a special interest in history.'' No ''cute'' articles. Buys 16-20 mss/year. Query; send complete ms. Length: approximately 4,500 words. Pays $250.

Photos: State availability of photos with submission and submit photocopies. Would prefer no originals. Offers no additional payment for photos accepted with ms. Identification of subjects required.

Columns/Departments: Book Reviews (Chicago and/or urban history), 500-750 words; and Review Essays (author reviews, comparatively, a compilation of several books on same topic—Chicago and/or urban history), 2,500 words. Buys 20 mss/year. Query; send complete ms. Pays $75-100 ''but book review authors receive only one copy of book, no cash.''

Tips: ''A freelancer can best break in by 1) calling to discuss an article idea with editor; and 2) submitting a detailed outline of proposed article. All sections of *Chicago History* are open to freelancers, but we suggest that authors do not undertake to write articles for the magazine unless they have considerable knowledge of the subject and are willing to research it in some detail. We require a footnoted manuscript, although we do not publish the notes.''

CIVIL WAR TIMES ILLUSTRATED, 2245 Kohn Rd., Box 8200, Harrisburg PA 17105. (717)657-9555. Editor: John E. Stanchak. 90% freelance written. Works with a small number of new/unpublished writers each year. Magazine published monthly except July and August. Circ. 120,000. Pays on acceptance. Publishes ms an average of 12-18 months after acceptance. Buys all rights, first rights or one-time rights, or makes work-for-hire assignments. Submit seasonal/holiday material 1 year in advance. Query for electronic submissions. Computer printout submissions acceptable; prefers letter-quality to dot-matrix. Reports in 2 weeks on queries; 3 months on mss. Sample copy $3; free writer's guidelines.
Nonfiction: Profile, photo feature, and Civil War historical material. "Positively no fiction or poetry." Buys 20 mss/year. Length: 2,500-5,000 words. Query. Pays $75-450. Sometimes pays the expenses of writers on assignment.
Photos: Jeanne Collins, art director. State availability of photos. Pays $5-50 for 8x10 b&w glossy prints and copies of Civil War photos; $400-500 for 4-color cover photos; and $100-250 for color photos for interior use.
Tips: "We're very open to new submissions. Querying us after reading several back issues, then submitting illustration and art possibilities along with the query letter is the best 'in.' Never base the narrative solely on family stories or accounts. Submissions must be written in a popular style but based on solid academic research. Manuscripts are required to have marginal source annotations.''

EL PALACIO, THE MAGAZINE OF THE MUSEUM OF NEW MEXICO, Museum of New Mexico Press, Box 2087, Santa Fe NM 87504. (505)827-6794. Editor-in-Chief: Sarah Nestor. 15% freelance written. Prefers to work with published/established writers. Emphasizes the collections of the Museum of New Mexico and anthropology, ethnology, history, folk and fine arts, Southwestern culture, and natural history as these topics pertain to the Museum of New Mexico and the Southwest. Triannual magazine; 48 pages. Circ. 2,500. Pays on publication. We hope "to attract professional writers who can translate scholarly and complex information into material that will fascinate and inform a general educated readership." Acquires first North American serial rights. Byline given. Phone queries OK. Submit seasonal/holiday queries 1 year in advance. Photocopied submissions OK. Query for electronic submissions. Computer printout submissions acceptable; no dot-matrix. Reports in 6 weeks. Sample copy $4; free writer's guidelines.
Nonfiction: Historical (on Southwest; substantive but readable—not too technical); folk art; archeology (Southwest); photo essay; anthropology; material culture of the Southwest. Buys 3-4 unsolicited mss/year. Recent articles documented the history of Las Vegas, New Mexico; women in New Mexico; collections of the Museum of New Mexico; and contemporary photography. "Other articles that have been very successful are a photo-essay on Chaco Canyon and other archeological spots of interest in the state and an article on Indian baskets and their function in Indian life." Query with credentials. Length: 1,750-4,000 words. Pays $50 honorarium minimum. Sometimes pays the expenses of writers on assignment.
Photos: Photos often purchased with accompanying ms, some on assignment. Prefers b&w prints. Informative captions required. Pays "on contract" for 5x7 (or larger) b&w photos and 5x7 or 8½x11 prints or 35mm color transparencies. Send prints and transparencies. Total purchase price for ms includes payment for photos.
Columns/Departments: New Acquisitions; Curator's Choice; Photo Essay; and Books (reviews of interest to *El Palacio* readers).
Tips: "*El Palacio* magazine offers a unique opportunity for writers with technical ability to have their work published and seen by influential professionals as well as avidly interested lay readers. The magazine is highly regarded in its field. The writer should have strong writing skills, an understanding of the Southwest and of the field written about. Be able to communicate technical concepts to the educated reader. We like to have a bibliography, list of sources, or suggested reading list with nearly every submission.''

‡MEDIA HISTORY DIGEST, Media History Digest Corp., % Editor and Publisher, 11 W. 19th St., New York NY 10011. Editor: Hiley H. Ward. 100% freelance written. Semiannual (will probably return to being quarterly) magazine. Circ. 2,000. Pays on publication. Publishes ms an average of 4 months after acceptance. Byline given. Buys first or second serial (reprint) rights. Submit seasonal/holiday material 8 months in advance. Previously published submissions OK. Reports in 2 months. Sample copy $2.
Nonfiction: Historical/nostalgic (media); humor (media history); and puzzles (media history). Buys 15 mss/year. Query. Length: 1,500-3,000 words. Pays $125 for assigned articles; pays $100 for unsolicited articles. Pays in contributor copies for articles prepared by university graduate students. Sometimes pays the expenses of writers on assignment.
Photos: Send photos with submission. Buys first or reprint rights.
Columns/Departments: Quiz Page (media history) and "Media Hysteria" (media history humor). Query. Pays $50-125 for humor; $25 for puzzles.
Fillers: Anecdotes and short humor on topics of media history.
Tips: "Present in-depth enterprising material targeted for our specialty—media history, pre-1970."

‡MILITARY IMAGES, RD2, Box 2542, East Stroudsburg PA 18301. (717)476-1388. Editor: Harry Roach. 100% freelance written. A bimonthly journal reaching a broad spectrum of military historians, antiquarians, collectors and dealers. *MI* covers American military history from 1839 to 1900, with heavy concentration on the Civil War. Circ. 3,000. Pays on publication. Byline given. Buys first North American serial rights. Submit seasonal/holiday material 2 months in advance. Photocopied submissions OK. Query for electronic submissions. Computer printout submissions OK; prefers letter-quality. Reports in 2 weeks on queries; 1 month on mss. Free sample copy and writer's guidelines.
Nonfiction: Book excerpts, historical, humor, interview/profile, photo feature and technical. No articles not tied to, or illustrated by, period photos. Buys 36 mss/year. Query. Length: 1,000-12,000 words. Pays $40-200.
Photos: State availability of photos with submission, or send photocopy with query. Reviews 5x7 or larger b&w prints. Offers no additional payment for photos accepted with ms. Captions required.
Columns/Departments: The Darkroom (technical, 19th-century photo processes, preservation), 1,000 words. Buys 6 mss/year. Query. Length: 1,000-3,000 words. Pays $20-75.
Tips: "Concentrate on details of the common soldier, his uniform, his equipment, his organizations. We do not publish broad-brush histories of generals and campaigns. Articles must be supported by period photos."

‡OLD MILL NEWS, Society for the Preservation of Old Mills, 604 Ensley Dr., Rt. 29, Knoxville TN 37920. (615)577-7757. Editor: Michael LaForest. 70% freelance written. Quarterly magazine covering "water, wind, animal, steam power mills (usually grist mills)." Circ. 2,500. Pays on acceptance. Byline given. Buys first North American serial rights or first rights. Simultaneous and photocopied submissions OK. Computer printout submissions OK; prefers letter-quality. Reports in 2 weeks. Sample copy $2.
Nonfiction: Historical and technical. "No poetry, recipes, mills converted to houses, commercial, or alternative uses, nostalgia." Buys 8 mss/year. Query with or without published clips, or send complete ms. Length: 400-1,000 words. Pays $15-50.
Photos: Send photos with submission. "At least one recent photograph of subject is highly recommended." Reviews prints. Offers $5-10 per photo. Identification of subjects required. Buys one-time rights.
Fillers: Short humor. Buys 3-4/year. Length: 50-200 words. Pays $10 maximum.
Tips: "An interview with the mill owner/operator is usually necessary. Accurate presentation of the facts and good English are required."

OLD WEST, Western Periodicals, Inc., Box 2107, Stillwater OK 74076. (405)743-3370. Quarterly magazine. Byline given. See *True West*.

PERSIMMON HILL, 1700 NE 63rd St., Oklahoma City OK 73111. Editor: Marcia Preston. 70% freelance written. Prefers to work with published/established writers and works with a small number of new/unpublished writers each year. For an audience interested in Western art, Western history, ranching and rodeo, historians, artists, ranchers, art galleries, schools, and libraries. Publication of the National Cowboy Hall of Fame and Western Heritage Center. Quarterly. Circ. 15,000. Buys first rights. Byline given. Buys 12-14 mss/year. Pays on scheduling of article. Publishes ms an average of 6 months after acceptance. Reporting time on mss varies. Computer printout submissions acceptable; no dot-matrix. Sample copy $5 plus $1 postage.
Nonfiction: Historical and contemporary articles on famous Western figures connected with pioneering the American West, Western art, rodeo, cowboys, etc. (or biographies of such people), stories of Western flora and animal life, and environmental subjects. "We want thoroughly researched and historically authentic material written in a popular style. May have a humorous approach to subject. No "broad, sweeping, superficial pieces; i.e., the California Gold Rush or rehashed pieces on Billy the Kid, etc." Length: 2,000-3,000 words. Query. Pays $100-250; special work negotiated.
Photos: B&w glossy prints or color transparencies purchased with or without ms, or on assignment. Pays according to quality and importance for b&w and color photos. Suggested captions appreciated.

PRESERVATION NEWS, National Trust for Historic Preservation, 1785 Massachusetts Ave. NW, Washington DC 20016. (202)673-4075. Editor: Arnold M. Berke. 30% freelance written. Prefers to work with published/established writers. A monthly tabloid covering preservation of historic buildings in the U.S. "We cover efforts and controversies involving historic buildings and districts. Most entries are news stories, features or essays." Circ. 175,000. Pays on publication. Publishes ms an average of 1 month after acceptance. Byline given. Offers variable kill fee. Buys one-time rights. Simultaneous queries, and photocopied and previously published submissions OK. Computer printout submissions acceptable. Reports in 1 month on queries. Sample copy for $1 and 10x14 SAE with 56¢ postage; writer's guidelines for SAE and 1 first class stamp.
Nonfiction: Historical/nostalgic, humor, interview/profile, opinion, personal experience, photo feature and travel. Buys 12 mss/year. Query with published clips. Length: 500-1,000 words. Pays $75-150. Sometimes pays the expenses of writers on assignment.
Photos: State availability of photos with query or ms. Reviews b&w contact sheet. Pays $25-100. Identification of subjects required.
Columns/Departments: "We seek an urban affairs reporter who can give a new slant on development con-

flict throughout the United States." Buys 6 mss/year. Query with published clips. Length: 600-1,000 words. Pays $75-150.

Tips: "The writer has a better chance of breaking in at our publication with short articles and fillers because we like to try them out first. Don't submit dull articles that lack compelling details."

TIMELINE, Ohio Historical Society, 1985 Velma Ave., Columbus OH 43211. (614)297-2360. Editor: Christopher S. Duckworth. 90% freelance written. Works with a small number of new/unpublished writers each year. A bimonthly magazine covering history, natural history, archaeology, and fine and decorative arts. Circ. 11,000. Pays on acceptance. Publishes ms an average of 1 year after acceptance. Byline given. Offers $75 minimum kill fee. Buys first North American serial rights or all rights. Submit seasonal/holiday material 6 months in advance. Photocopied submissions OK. Electronic submissions OK on PC/DOS, but requires hard copy also. Computer printout submissions acceptable; no dot-matrix. Reports in 3 weeks on queries; 6 weeks on manuscripts. Sample copy $4; free writer's guidelines.

Nonfiction: Book excerpts, essays, historical, profile (of individuals) and photo feature. Buys 22 mss/year. Query. Length: 500-6,000 words. Pays $100-900.

Photos: State availability of photos with submission. Will not consider submissions without ideas for illustration. Reviews contact sheets, transparencies, and 8x10 prints. Captions, model releases, and identification of subjects required. Buys one-time rights.

Tips: "We want crisply written, authoritative narratives for the intelligent lay reader. An Ohio slant may strengthen a submission, but it is not indispensable. Contributors must know enough about their subject to explain it clearly and in an interesting fashion. We use high-quality illustration with all features. If appropriate illustration is unavailable, we can't use the feature. The writer who sends illustration ideas with a manuscript has an advantage, but an often-published illustration won't attract us."

TRUE WEST, Western Periodicals, Inc., Box 2107, Stillwater OK 74076. (405)743-3370. Editor: John Joerschke. 100% freelance written. Works with a small number of new/unpublished writers each year. Magazine on Western American history before 1920. "We want reliable research on significant historical topics written in lively prose for an informed general audience." Circ. 100,000. Pays after acceptance. Publishes ms an average of 4 months after acceptance. Byline given. Buys first North American serial rights. Submit seasonal/holiday material 6 months in advance. Simultaneous queries OK. Computer printout submissions acceptable; prefers letter-quality to dot-matrix. Reports in 1 month on queries; 6 weeks on mss. Sample copy $1; writer's guidelines for #10 SAE and 1 first class stamp.

Nonfiction: Historical/nostalgic, how-to, photo feature, travel, and western movies. "We do not want rehashes of worn-out stories, historical fiction, or history written in a fictional style." Buys 150 mss/year. Query. Length: 500-4,500 words. Pays 3-5¢/word.

Photos: Send photos with accompanying query or manuscript. Pays $10 for b&w prints. Identification of subjects required. Buys one-time rights.

Columns/Departments: Kelli Rhoads, assistant editor. Western Roundup—200-300 word short articles on historically oriented places to go and things to do in the West with one b&w print. Buys 12-16 mss/year. Send complete ms. Pays $35.

Tips: "Do original research on fresh topics. Stay away from controversial subjects unless you are truly knowledgeable in the field. Read our magazines and follow our writer's guidelines. A freelancer is most likely to break in with us by submitting thoroughly researched, lively prose on relatively obscure topics. First person accounts rarely fill our needs."

VIRGINIA CAVALCADE, Virginia State Library, Richmond VA 23219. (804)786-2312. Primarily for readers with an interest in Virginia history. 90% freelance written. "Both established and new writers are invited to submit articles." Quarterly magazine; 48 pages. Circ. 12,000. Buys all rights. Byline given. Pays on acceptance. Publishes ms an average of 6-12 months after acceptance. Rarely considers simultaneous submissions. Submit material 15-18 months in advance. Reports in 1-3 months. Computer printout submissions acceptable; prefers letter-quality to dot-matrix. Sample copy $2; free writer's guidelines.

Nonfiction: "We welcome readable and factually accurate articles that are relevant to some phase of Virginia history. Art, architecture, literature, education, business, technology and transportation are all acceptable subjects, as well as political and military affairs. Articles must be based on thorough, scholarly research. We require footnotes but do not publish them. Any period from the age of exploration to the mid-20th century, and any geographical section or area of the state may be represented. Must deal with subjects that will appeal to a broad readership, rather than to a very restricted group or locality. Articles must be suitable for illustration, although it is not necessary that the author provide the pictures. If the author does have pertinent illustrations or knows their location, the editor appreciates information concerning them." Buys 12-15 mss/year. Query. Length: 3,500-4,500 words. Pays $100.

Photos: Uses 8x10 b&w glossy prints; color transparencies should be at least 4x5.

Tips: "*Cavalcade* employs a narrative, anecdotal style. Too many submissions are written for an academic audience or are simply not sufficiently gripping."

Hobby and Craft

Craftspeople and hobbyists always need new ideas while collectors need to know what is most valuable and why. Collectors, do-it-yourselfers and craftspeople look to these magazines for inspiration, research and information. Publications covering antiques and miniatures are also listed here. Publications for electronics and radio hobbyists are included in the science classification.

AMERICAN BOOK COLLECTOR, Box 1080, Ossining NY 10562. (914)941-0409. Editor: Bernard McTigue. 50-75% freelance written. Eager to work with new/unpublished writers. Monthly magazine on book collecting from the 15th century to the present for individuals, rare book dealers, librarians, and others interested in books and bibliomania. Circ. 3,500. Pays on publication. Publishes ms an average of 6 months after acceptance. Submit seasonal material 3 months in advance. Photocopied and previously published submissions OK. Electronic submissions OK if IBM PC, but requires hard copy also. Computer printout submissions acceptable; prefers letter-quality to dot-matrix. Reports in 6 weeks. Sample copy and writer's guidelines for $5.
Nonfiction: General interest (some facet of book collecting: category of books; taste and technique; artist; printer; binder); interview (prominent book collectors; producers of contemporary fine and limited editions; scholars; librarians); and reviews of exhibitions. Buys 20-30 unsolicited mss/year. "We absolutely require queries with clips of previously published work." Query should include precise description of proposed article accompanied by description of author's background plus indication of extent of illustrations. Length: 1,500-4,500 words. Pays 5¢/word. Sometimes pays the expenses of writers on assignment.
Photos: State availability of photos. Prefers b&w glossy prints of any size. Offers no additional payment for photos accompanying ms. Captions and model release required. Buys one-time rights.
Columns/Departments: Contact editor. Reviews of books on book collecting, and gallery exhibitions.
Tips: "We look for knowledgeable writing. A purely journalistic (i.e., learned while writing) approach is unlikely to be of value."

AMERICAN CLAY EXCHANGE, Page One Publications, Box 2674, La Mesa CA 92041. (619)697-5922. Editor: Susan N. Cox. 95% freelance written. Eager to work with new/unpublished writers. Biweekly newsletter on subjects relating to American made pottery—old or new—with an emphasis on antiques and collectibles for collectors, buyers and sellers of American made pottery, earthenware, china, dinnerware, etc. Pays on acceptance. Publishes ms an average of 2 months after acceptance. Byline given. Buys all rights; will consider first serial rights. Submit seasonal/holiday material 4 months in advance. Computer printout submissions acceptable; no dot-matrix. Reports in 1 month on queries; 2 months on mss. Sample copy $1.50; free writer's guidelines.
Nonfiction: Book reviews (on books pertaining to American made pottery, china, earthenware); historical/nostalgic (on museums and historical societies in the U.S. if they handle pottery, etc.); how-to (identify pieces, clean, find them); and interview/profile (if artist is up-and-coming). No "I found a piece of pottery for 10¢ at a flea market" types. Buys 40-50 mss/year. Query or send complete ms. Length: 1,000 words maximum. Pays $125 maximum.
Photos: Send photos with ms. Pays $5 for b&w prints. Captions required. Does not accept color slides. Buys all rights; will consider one-time rights.
Tips: "Know the subject being written about, including marks and values of pieces found. Telling a reader what 'marks' are on pieces is most essential. The best bet is to write a short (200-300 word) article with a few photos and marks. We are a small company willing to work with writers who have good, salable ideas and know our product. Any article that deals effectively with a little-known company or artist during the 1900-1950 era is most sought after. We have added a section devoted to dinnerware, mostly from the 1900-1950 era—same guidelines."

‡THE AMERICAN COLLECTORS JOURNAL, Box 407, Kewanee IL 61443. (308)853-8441. Editor: Carol Saridge. 55% freelance written. Eager to work with new/unpublished writers. A bimonthly tabloid covering antiques and collectibles. Circ. 46,302. Pays on acceptance. Publishes ms an average of 4 months after acceptance. Byline given. Not copyrighted. Buys first North American serial rights. Submit seasonal/holiday material 6 months in advance. Photocopied submissions OK. Computer printout submissions OK. Reports in 3 weeks. Sample copy for 4x9 SAE with 74¢ postage.
Nonfiction: Carol Harper, articles editor. General interest, interview/profile, new product, photo feature and

technical. Buys 12-20 mss/year. Query or send complete ms. Pays $10-35 for unsolicited articles.
Photos: Send photos with submission. Reviews 5x7 prints. Offers no additional payment for photos accepted with ms. Captions required. Buys one-time rights.
Tips: "We are looking for submissions with photos in all areas of collecting and antiquing, unusual collections, details on a particular kind of collecting or information on antiques."

THE ANTIQUARIAN, Box 798, Huntington NY 11743. (516)271-8990. Editor-in-Chief: Marguerite Cantine. Publisher: Elizabeth Kilpatrick. Emphasizes antiques and 19th-century or earlier art. Monthly. 15% freelance written. Circ. 15,000. Pays on publication. Publishes ms an average of 3 months after acceptance. Buys all rights. Pays 10% kill fee. Byline given. Submit seasonal/holiday material 3 months in advance. Computer printout submissions acceptable; no dot-matrix. Reports in 6 weeks. Sample copy for 9x12 SAE with $1 postage attached. No checks.
Nonfiction: How-to (repair glass, restore old houses, restore paintings, rebind books, etc.); general interest (relations of buyers and dealers at antique shows/sales, auction reports); historical (data, personal and otherwise, on famous people in the arts and antiques field); interview; photo feature (auctions, must have caption on item including selling price); profile (wants articles around movie stars and actors who collect antiques; query); and travel (historical sites of interest in New York, New Jersey, Michigan, Indiana, Virginia, Massachusetts, Connecticut, Pennsylvania and Delaware). Wants concise articles, accurate research; no material on art deco, collectibles, anything made after 1900, cutesy things to 'remake' from antiques, or flea markets and crafts shows. Buys 6 mss/year. Submit complete ms. Length: 200-1,000 words. Pays 3¢/word.
Photos: Pays 50¢-$1 for 3½x5 glossy b&w prints. Captions required. Buys all rights. Model releases required.
Tips: "Don't write an article unless you *love* this field. Write as though you were carrying on a nice conversation with your mother. No pretentions. No superiority. It's frustrating when freelancers don't read, follow instructions, or send an SASE, call the office and *demand* answers to questions, or act unprofessionally. We won't deal with anyone who calls us via telephone."

ANTIQUE MONTHLY, Boone, Inc., Drawer 2, Tuscaloosa AL 35402. (205)345-0272. Editor/Publisher: Gray D. Boone. Senior Editor: Joe Forsthoffer. 20% freelance written. Eager to work with new/unpublished writers. Monthly tabloid covering art, antiques, and major museum shows. "More than half of our audience are college graduates, over 27% have post-graduate degrees; 59 percent are in $35,000 and over income bracket. Average number of years readers have been collecting art/antiques is 20.5." Circ. 65,100. Pays on publication. Publishes ms an average of 4 months after acceptance. Buys all rights. Submit seasonal/holiday material 2 months in advance. Photocopied submissions OK. Computer printout submissions acceptable; prefers letter-quality to dot-matrix. Reports in 1 month on queries and mss. Sample copy 90¢.
Nonfiction: Discussions of current trends in antiques marketplace; coverage of antiques shows and auctions; profiles of important collectors and dealers; descriptions of decorative arts exhibitions; and book reviews. No personal material. Buys 6-10 unsolicited mss/year. Length: 1,000 words. Pays $125 minimum/article. Sometimes pays expenses of writers on assignment.
Photos: State availability of photos. Prefers color transparencies or slides and 5x7 b&w prints. "We rarely pay for photos; usually we pay only for costs incurred by the writer, and this must be on prior agreement." Captions required.
Tips: "Freelancers are important because they offer the ability to cover stories that regular staff and correspondents cannot cover. A story is more likely to interest the editors if there is a timely news peg—if the story is related to a recent or current event or trend in the antiques world. Write in a crisp, newsy style and have a working knowledge of the antiques and decorative arts field."

ANTIQUE REVIEW, Box 538, Worthington OH 43085. Editor: Charles Muller. (614)885-9757. 60% freelance written. Eager to work with new/unpublished writers. For an antique-oriented readership, "generally well-educated, interested in folk art and other early American items." Monthly tabloid. Circ. 8,000 in all 50 states. Pays on publication date assigned at time of purchase. Publishes ms an average of 3 months after acceptance. Buys first North American serial rights, and second (reprint) rights to material originally published elsewhere. Byline given. Phone queries OK. Computer printout submissions acceptable; prefers letter-quality to dot-matrix. Reports in 1 month. Free sample copy and writer's guidelines.
Nonfiction: "The articles we desire concern history and production of furniture, pottery, china, and other quality Americana. In some cases, contemporary folk art items are acceptable. We are also interested in reporting on antique shows and auctions with statements on conditions and prices. We do not want articles on contemporary collectibles." Buys 5-8 mss/issue. Query with clips of published work. Query should show "author's familiarity with antiques and an interest in the historical development of artifacts relating to early America." Length: 200-2,000 words. Pays $80-125. Sometimes pays the expenses of writers on assignment.
Photos: State availability of photos with query. Payment included in ms price. Uses 5x7 or larger glossy b&w prints. Captions required. Articles with photographs receive preference.
Tips: "Give us a call and let us know of specific interests. We are more concerned with the background in an-

tiques than in writing abilities. The writing can be edited, but the knowledge imparted is of primary interest. A frequent mistake is being too general, not becoming deeply involved in the topic and its research.''

THE ANTIQUE TRADER WEEKLY, Box 1050, Dubuque IA 52001. (319)588-2073. Editor: Kyle D. Husfloen. 50% freelance written. Works with a small number of new/unpublished writers each year. For collectors and dealers in antiques and collectibles. Weekly newspaper; 90-120 pages. Circ. 90,000. Publishes ms an average of 6 months after acceptance. Buys all rights. Payment at beginning of month following publication. Photocopied and simultaneous submissions OK. Computer printout submissions acceptable; no dot-matrix. Submit seasonal/holiday material 4 months in advance. Sample copy 50¢; free writer's guidelines.
Nonfiction: "We invite authoritative and well-researched articles on all types of antiques and collectors' items and in-depth stories on specific types of antiques and collectibles. No human interest stories. We do not pay for brief information on new shops opening or other material printed as a service to the antiques hobby." Buys about 60 mss/year. Query or submit complete ms. Pays $5-75 for feature articles; $75-150 for feature cover stories.
Photos: Submit a liberal number of good b&w photos to accompany article. Uses 35mm or larger color transparencies for cover. Offers no additional payment for photos accompanying mss.
Tips: "Send concise, polite letter stating the topic to be covered in the story and the writer's qualifications. No 'cute' letters rambling on about some 'imaginative' story idea. Writers who have a concise yet readable style and know their topic are always appreciated. I am most interested in those who have personal collecting experience or can put together a knowledgeable and informative feature after interviewing a serious collector/authority.''

ANTIQUES & AUCTION NEWS, (formerly *Joel Sater's Antiques and Auction News*), Route 230 West, Box 500, Mount Joy PA 17552. (717)653-9797. Editor: Doris Ann Johnson. Prefers to work with published/established writers, and works with a small number of new/unpublished writers each year. A weekly tabloid for dealers and buyers of antiques, nostalgics and collectibles, and those who follow antique shows, shops and auctions. Buys 200 mss annually. Averages 32 pages/issue. Circ. 40,000. Pays on publication. Publishes ms an average of 1 month after acceptance. Buys all rights. Phone queries OK. Submit seasonal/holiday material 3 months in advance. Computer printout submissions OK; no dot-matrix. Reports in 6 weeks. Free sample copy available if you mention *Writer's Market*. Writer's guidelines for business size SASE.
Nonfiction: "Our readers are interested in collectibles and antiques dating approximately from the Civil War to the present, originating in the U.S. or western Europe. We normally will consider any story on a collectible or antique if it is well-written, slanted toward helping collectors, buyers and dealers learn more about the field, and is focused on the aspect of collecting. This could be an historical perspective, a specific area of collecting, an especially interesting antique or unusual collection. Issues have included material on old Christmas ornaments, antique love tokens, collections of fans, pencils and pottery, and 'The Man from U.N.C.L.E.' books and magazines. Articles may be how-to, informational research, news and reporting and even an occasional photo feature." Length: 1,000 words or less preferred, but will consider up to 2,000 words. Pays $12.50 for articles without photos; $15 for articles with usable photos. "We also accept an occasional short article—about one typed page, with a good photo—for which we will pay $7.50."
Photos: Purchased as part of ms package. "We prefer b&w photos, usually of a single item against a simple background. Color photos can be used if there is good contrast between darks and lights." Captions required.

THE ARCTOPHILE, Bear-in-Mind, Inc., 20 Beharrell St., Concord MA 01742. (617)369-1167. Editor: Fran Lewis. Managing Editor: Judy Knoll. 25% freelance written. Works with a small number of new/unpublished writers each year. Quarterly newsletter on Teddy Bears and Teddy collecting. For adult Teddy Bear collectors who are interested in heartwarming or poignant tales about what Teddys mean to them or how they have helped to share feelings or comfort them in times of need. Circ. 10,000. Pays on publication. Publishes ms an average of 3 months after acceptance. Byline given. Buys first North American serial rights. Submit seasonal/holiday material 6 months in advance. Simultaneous, photocopied and previously published submissions OK. Computer printout submissions acceptable; no dot-matrix. Reports in 2 months. Sample copy for SAE and 1 first class stamp.
Nonfiction: Book excerpts, historical/nostalgic, humor, inspirational, interview/profile, personal experience and photo feature. Buys 12-24 mss/year. Send complete ms. Length: 300-500 words. Pays 4-6¢/word.
Fiction: Fantasy and humorous. Buys 12-24 mss/year. Send complete ms. Length: 300-500 words. Pays 4-6¢/word.
Poetry: Avant-garde, free verse, haiku, light verse and traditional. Buys 4 poems/year. Submit maximum 2 poems. Length: 6-10 lines. Pays $10-15.
Fillers: Jokes, gags, anecdotes, short humor and newsbreaks—all Teddy related. Buys 8-10/year. Length: 15-30 words. Pays $5-10.
Tips: Articles, and fiction and poetry submissions must be Teddy Bear related. Writing should be direct and crisp.

BANK NOTE REPORTER, Krause Publications, 700 E. State St., Iola WI 54990. (715)445-2214. Editor: Robert F. Lemke. 30% freelance written. Works with a small number of new/unpublished writers each year, and is eager to work with new/unpublished writers. Monthly tabloid for advanced collectors of U.S. and world paper money. Circ. 4,250. Pays on publication. Publishes ms an average of 2 months after acceptance. Byline given. Buys first North American serial rights and reprint rights. Photocopied submissions acceptable. Electronic submissions OK with special arrangements. Computer printout submissions acceptable; prefers letter-quality to dot-matrix. Reports in 2 weeks. Sample copy for 8½x11 SAE and 3 first class stamps.
Nonfiction: "We review articles covering any phase of paper money collecting including investing, display, storage, history, art, story behind a particular piece of paper money and the business of paper money." News items not solicited. "Our staff covers the hard news." Buys 6 mss/issue. Send complete ms. Length: 500-3,000 words. Pays 3¢/word to first-time contributors; negotiates fee for later articles. Pays the expenses of writers on assignment.
Photos: Pays $5 for 5x7 b&w glossy prints. Captions and model releases required.
Tips: "The writer has a better chance of breaking in at our publication with short articles due to the technical nature of the subject matter and sophistication of our readers. Material about bank notes used in a writer's locale would be interesting, useful, encouraged. We like new names."

BASEBALL CARDS, Krause Publications, 700 E. State St., Iola WI 54990. (715)445-2214. Editor: Bob Lemke. 50% freelance written. Eager to work with new/unpublished writers. A monthly magazine covering sports memorabilia collecting. "Geared for the novice collector or general public who might become interested in the hobby." Circ. 120,000. Pays on publication. Publishes ms an average of 2-3 months after acceptance. Byline given. Buys first North American serial rights and second serial (reprint) rights. Submit seasonal/holiday material 6 months in advance. Photocopied submissions OK. Computer printout submissions acceptable; no dot-matrix. Reports in 2 weeks. Sample copy for 8½x11 SAE with 3 first class stamps.
Nonfiction: General interest, historical/nostalgic, how-to (enjoy or enhance your collection) and photo feature. No personal reminiscences of collecting baseball cards as a kid or articles that relate to baseball, rather than cards. Buys 24-36 mss/year. Query. Length: 2,000-4,000 words. Pays up to $250.
Photos: Send photos with submission. Reviews contact sheets and transparencies. Offers no additional payment for photos accepted with ms. Identification of subjects required.
Tips: "We would like to receive knowledgeable features on specific collectibles: card sets, team items, etc. A heavier emphasis on 1980s collectibles will affect the types of freelance material we buy in 1988."

THE BLADE MAGAZINE, Box 22007, Chattanooga TN 37422. Editor: J. Bruce Voyles. 90% freelance written. For knife enthusiasts who want to know as much as possible about quality knives and edged weapons. Bimonthly magazine. Pays on publication. Publishes ms an average of 3-6 months after acceptance. Buys all rights. Submit seasonal/holiday material 6 months in advance. Previously published submissions OK. Computer printout submissions acceptable; no dot-matrix. Reports in 2 months. Sample copy $2.75.
Nonfiction: How-to; historical (on knives and weapons); adventure on a knife theme; interview (knifemakers); celebrities who own knives; knives featured in movies with shots from the movie, etc.; new product; nostalgia; personal experience; photo feature; profile and technical. "We would also like to receive articles on knives in adventuresome life-saving situations." No poetry. Buys 75 unsolicited mss/year. "We evaluate complete manuscripts and make our decision on that basis." Length: 1,000-2,000 words. Pays 5¢/word minimum, more for better writers. "We will pay top dollar in the knife market." Sometimes pays the expenses of writers on assignment.
Photos: Send photos with ms. Pays $5 for 8x10 b&w glossy prints, $25-75 for 35mm color transparencies. Captions required.
Tips: "We are always willing to read submissions from anyone who has read a few copies and studied the market. The ideal article for us is a piece bringing out the romance, legend, and love of man's oldest tool—the knife. We like articles that place knives in peoples' hands—in life saving situations, adventure modes, etc. (Nothing gory or with the knife as the villain). People and knives are good copy. We are getting more and better written articles from writers who are reading the publication beforehand. That makes for a harder sell for the quickie writer not willing to do his homework."

THE COIN ENTHUSIAST'S JOURNAL, Masongate Publishing, Box 1383, Torrance CA 90505. Editor: William J. Cook. 40% freelance written. Prefers to work with published/established writers, and works with a small number of new/unpublished writers each year. Monthly newsletter covering numismatics (coin collecting) and bullion trading. "Our purpose is to give readers information to help them make sound investment decisions in the areas we cover and to help them get more enjoyment out of their hobby." Circ. 2,000 + . Pays on publication. Publishes ms an average of 2 months after acceptance. Byline given. Offers $25 kill fee. Buys all rights. Submit seasonal/holiday material 3 months in advance. Simultaneous queries and simultaneous and photocopied submissions OK. Computer printout submissions acceptable; prefers letter-quality to dot-matrix. Reports in 2-3 weeks on queries; 3 weeks on mss. Sample copy for SAE and 2 first class stamps; writer's guidelines for SAE and 1 first class stamp.

Nonfiction: How-to (make money from your hobby and be a better trader); opinion (what is the coin market going to do?); personal experience (insiders' "tricks of the trade"); and technical (why are coin prices going up [or down]?). No "crystal ball" predictions, i.e., "I see silver going up to $200 per ounce by mid-1988." Query with published clips. Length: 500-2,500 words. Buys 20 mss/year. Pays $50-200; fees negotiable. Also looking for "staff writers" who will submit material each month or bimonthly.
Photos: State availability of photos with query. Pays $5-25 for b&w prints. Buys one-time rights.
Tips: "We run few short articles. Be able to show an in-depth knowledge and experience in numismatics and also show the ability to be creative in developing new ideas for the coin industry."

COINS, Krause Publications, 700 E. State St., Iola WI 54990. (715)445-2214. Editor: Arlyn G. Sieber. 75% freelance written. Eager to work with new/unpublished writers. Monthly magazine about U.S. and foreign coins for all levels of collectors, investors and dealers. Circ. 65,000. Computer printout submissions acceptable; prefers letter-quality to dot-matrix.
Nonfiction: "We'd like to see articles on any phase of the coin hobby; collection, investing, displaying, history, art, the story behind the coin, unusual collections, profiles on dealers and the business of coins." No news items. "Our staff covers the hard news." Buys 8 mss/issue. Send complete ms. Length: 500-5,000 words. Pays 3¢/word to first-time contributors; fee negotiated for later articles. Sometimes pays the expenses of writers on assignment.
Photos: Pays $5 minimum for b&w prints. Pays $25 minimum for 35mm color transparencies used. Captions and model releases required. Buys first rights.

COLLECTOR EDITIONS QUARTERLY, Collector Communications Corp., 170 5th Ave., New York NY 10010. Editor: R. C. Rowe. 25% freelance written. Works with a small number of new/unpublished writers each year. Quarterly magazine for collectors, mostly aged 30-65 in any rural or suburban, affluent area; reasonably well-educated. Quarterly. Circ. 80,000. Rights purchased vary with author and material. Buys first North American serial rights, and sometimes second serial (reprint) rights. "First assignments are always done on a speculative basis." Pays within 30 days of acceptance. Publishes ms an average of 6 months after acceptance. Photocopied submissions OK. Computer printout submissions acceptable; no dot-matrix. Reports in 2 months. Sample copy $2; writer's guidelines for SAE and 1 first class stamp.
Nonfiction: "Short features about collecting, written in tight, newsy style. We specialize in contemporary (postwar) collectibles. Values for pieces being written about should be included." Informational, how-to, interview, profile, exposé, and nostalgia. Buys 8-10 mss/year. Query with sample photos. Length: 500-2,500 words. Pays $100-300. Sometimes pays expenses of writers on assignments.
Columns/Departments: Columns cover stamps and coins, porcelain, glass, auction reports and artist profiles. Query. Length: 750 words. Pays $75.
Photos: B&w and color photos purchased with accompanying ms with no additional payment. Captions are required. "We want clear, distinct, full-frame images that say something."
Tips: "Unfamiliarity with the field is the most frequent mistake made by writers in completing an article for us."

COLLECTORS NEWS & THE ANTIQUE REPORTER, 506 2nd St., Box 156, Grundy Center IA 50638. (319)824-5456. Editor: Linda Kruger. 20% freelance written. Works with a small number of new/unpublished writers each year. A monthly tabloid covering antiques, collectibles and nostalgic memorabilia. Circ. 15,000. Byline given. Pays on publication. Publishes ms an average of 1 year after acceptance. Buys first rights and makes work-for-hire assignments. Submit seasonal material (holidays) 3 months in advance. Computer printout submissions acceptable. Reports in 2 weeks on queries; 6 weeks on mss. Sample copy for $2 and 9x12 SAE; free writer's guidelines.
Nonfiction: General interest (any subject re: collectibles, antique to modern); historical/nostalgic (relating to collections or collectors); how-to (display your collection, care for, restore, appraise, locate, add to, etc.); interview/profile (covering individual collectors and their hobbies, unique or extensive; celebrity collectors, and limited edition artists); technical (in-depth analysis of a particular antique, collectible or collecting field); and travel (coverage of special interest or regional shows, seminars, conventions—or major antique shows, flea markets; places collectors can visit, tours they can take, museums, etc.). Special issues include January and June show/flea market issues; and usual seasonal emphasis. Buys 100 mss/year. Query with sample of writing. Length: 1,200-1,600 words. Pays 75¢/ column inch; $1/column inch for color features.
Photos: Reviews b&w prints and 35mm color slides. Payment for photos included in payment for ms. Captions required. Buys first rights.
Tips: Articles most open to freelancers are on celebrity collectors; collectors with unique and/or extensive collections; music collectibles; transportation collectibles; advertising collectibles; bottles; glass, china and silver; primitives; furniture; toys; political collectibles; and movie memorabilia.

‡**CRAFTS 'N THINGS**, 14 Main St., Park Ridge IL 60068. (312)825-2161. Editor: Nancy Tosh. Associate Editor: Jackie Thielen. Bimonthly magazine covering quality crafts for today's creative woman. Circ. 250,000.

Pays on publication. Byline, photo and brief bio given. Buys first North American serial rights. Submit season-al/holiday material 6 months in advance. Reports in 1 month. Free sample copy.

Nonfiction: How-to (do a craft project). Buys 7-14 mss/issue. "Send in a photo of the item and complete directions. We will consider it and return if not accepted." Length: 1-4 magazine pages. Pays $50-200, "depending on how much staff work is required."

Photos: "Generally, we will ask that you send the item so we can photograph it ourselves."

Tips: "We're looking more for people who can craft than people who can write."

‡**CROCHET WORLD OMNIBOOK**, House of White Birches Inc., 306 E. Parr Rd., Berne IN 46711. (603)474-2404. Editor: Susan Hankins Andrews. 90% freelance written. A quarterly magazine on crocheting. "Readers are low to middle income, young and old, but all love to crochet and spend most of their free time doing so. Keep articles easy to understand, patterns complete and using standard crochet abbreviations." Circ. 50,000. Pays on publication. Publishes ms an average of 6-12 months after acceptance. Byline given. Buys all rights. Submit seasonal/holiday material 6 months in advance. Computer printout submissions OK; prefers letter-quality to dot-matrix. Reports in 1 month on queries; 6 weeks on mss. Sample copy for 8½x11 with 59¢ postage. Free writer's guidelines.

Nonfiction: General interest, historical, how-to, humor, personal experience and technical. No previously copyrighted patterns. Buys 6-10 mss/year. Send complete ms. Length: 500-2,000 words. Pays $20-75 for unsolicited articles.

Photos: Buys no photos. Writer must send crocheted item for staff photography.

Columns/Departments: Pineapple Potpourri (pineapple crochet); Antique Attic (crocheted patterns more than 50 years old); Editor's Award (1st and 2nd prize chosen for each issue, $75 and $60 respectively. Recent winners include: sugar and spice baby set, filet beach cover, fan pillow.) Length: up to 2,000 words. Send complete ms. Pays competitive designer rates.

Poetry: Light verse and traditional. Buys 6 poems/year. Submit maximum 2 poems. Length: 5-20 lines. Pays $5-20.

Fillers: Anecdotes, crochet cartoons, facts and short humor. Buys 24/year. Length: 35-70 words. Pays $5-20.

Tips: "Our readers are crochet lovers who spend most of their free time crocheting. We're looking for articles on how to improve on our craft, tips on marketing finished work, new trends in crochet, designing how-to, and personal stories on how crochet 'changed, enhanced, etc., my life.' Remember, we're mainly a pattern magazine, so articles should relate to this fact. Send completed crochet item with mss. We will return the item, if return postage is included. An awareness of current trends in fashion, home decor, toys, dolls and doll clothes will give the crochet designer ideas on what to create."

‡**DECORATIVE ARTIST'S WORKBOOK**, F&W Publishing, 1507 Dana Ave., Cincinnati OH 45207. Editor: Phil Myer. 75% freelance written. Bimonthly magazine covering tole and decorative painting and related art forms. Offers "straightforward, personal instruction in the techniques of tole and decorative painting." Estab. 1987. Circ. 25,000. Pays on acceptance. Byline given. Offers 20% kill fee. Buys first North American serial rights. Submit seasonal/holiday material 6 months in advance. Photocopied submissions OK. Computer printout submissions OK; no dot-matrix. Reports in 4 weeks. Sample copy for $2.95 with 9x12 SAE and 7 first class stamps.

Nonfiction: How-to (related to tole and decorative painting), new product and technical. No profiles and/or general interest topics. Buys 30 mss/year. Query with slides and/or transparencies. Length: 1,200-1,800 words. Pays 10-15¢/word. Sometimes pays the expenses of writers on assignment.

Photos: State availability of photos with submission or send photos with submission. Reviews 35mm or 4x5 transparencies. Offers no additional payment for photos accepted with ms. Captions required. Buys one-time rights.

Poetry: Light verse. Buys 6 poems/year. Submit maximum 4 poems. Length: 5-25 lines. Pays $5-25.

Fillers: Anecdotes, facts and short humor. Buys 10/year. Length: 50-200 words. Pays $10-20.

Tips: "The more you know—and can prove you know—about decorative painting the better your chances. I'm looking for experts in the field who, through their own experience, can artfully describe the techniques involved. How-to articles are most open to freelancers. Be sure to query with slides or transparencies, and show that you understand the extensive graphic requirements for these pieces, and are able to provide progressives—slides that show works in progress."

DOLLS, The Collector's Magazine, Collector Communications Corp., 170 5th Ave., New York NY 10010. (212)989-8700. Editorial Director: Krystyna Poray Goddu. 75% freelance written. Works with a small number of new/unpublished writers each year. Bimonthly magazine covering doll collecting "for collectors of antique, contemporary and reproduction dolls. We publish well-researched, professionally written articles that are illustrated with photographs of high quality, color or black-and-white." Circ. 55,000. Pays within 30 days of acceptance. Publishes ms an average of 6 months after acceptance. Byline given. "Almost all first manuscripts are on speculation. We rarely kill assigned stories, but fee would be about 33% of article fee." Buys first serial rights, first North American serial rights ("almost always"), second serial rights if piece has appeared in a noncompeting publication. Submit seasonal/holiday material 6 months in advance. Photocopied submissions considered (not preferred); previously published submissions OK. Computer printout submissions acceptable; no dot-matrix. Reports in 2 months. Sample copy $2; writer's guidelines for SAE and 1 first class stamp.

Nonfiction: Book excerpts; historical (with collecting angle); interview/profile (on collectors with outstanding collections); new product (just photos and captions; "we do not pay for these, but regard them as publicity"); opinion ("A Personal Definition of Dolls"); technical (doll restoration advice by experts only); and travel (museums and collections around the world). "No sentimental, uninformed 'my doll collection' or 'my grandma's doll collection' stories or trade magazine-type stories on shops, etc. Our readers are knowledgeable collectors." Query with clips. Length: 500-2,500 words. Pays $100-350. Sometimes pays expenses of writers on assignment.

Photos: Send photos with accompanying query or ms. Reviews 4x5 color transparencies; 4x5 or 8x10 b&w prints. "We do not buy photographs submitted without manuscripts unless we have assigned them; we pay for the manuscript/photos package in one fee." Captions required. Buys one-time rights.

Columns/Departments: Doll Views—a miscellany of news and views of the doll world includes reports on upcoming or recently held events. "*Not* the place for new dolls, auction prices or dates; we have regular contributors or staff assigned to those columns." Query with clips if available or send complete ms. Length: 200-500 words. Pays $25-75. Doll Views items are rarely bylined.

Fillers: "We don't really use fillers but would consider them if we got something very good. Hints on restoring, for example, or a nice illustration." Length: 500 words maximum. Pays $25-75.

Tips: "We need experts in the field who are also good writers. The most frequent mistake made by writers in completing an article assignment for us is being unfamiliar with the field; our readers are very knowledgeable. Freelancers who are not experts should know their particular story thoroughly and do background research to get the facts correct. Well-written queries from writers outside the NYC area are especially welcomed. Non-experts should stay away from technical or specific subjects (restoration, price trends). Short profiles of unusual collectors or a story of a local museum collection, with good photos, might catch our interest. Editors want to know they are getting something from a writer they cannot get from anyone else. Good writing should be a given, a starting point. After that, it's what you know."

EARLY AMERICAN LIFE, Historical Times, Inc., Box 8200, Harrisburg PA 17105. Editor: Frances Carnahan. 60-70% freelance written. Bimonthly magazine for "people who are interested in capturing the warmth and beauty of the 1600 to 1900 period and using it in their homes and lives today. They are interested in arts, crafts, travel, restoration and collecting." Circ. 350,000. Buys all rights. Buys 50 mss/year. Pays on acceptance. Publishes ms an average of 1 year after acceptance. Photocopied submissions OK. Computer printout submissions OK; no dot-matrix. Free sample copy and writer's guidelines. Reports in 1 month. Query or submit complete ms. SASE.

Nonfiction: "Social history (the story of the people, not epic heroes and battles), traditional crafts such as woodworking and needlepoint, travel to historic sites, country inns, antiques and reproductions, refinishing and restoration, architecture and decorating. We try to entertain as we inform and always attempt to give the reader something he can do. While we're always on the lookout for good pieces on any of our subjects, the 'travel to historic sites' theme is most frequently submitted. Would like to see more how-to-do-it (well-illustrated) on how real people did something great to their homes." Buys 50 mss/year. Query or submit complete ms. Length: 750-3,000 words. Pays $50-400. Pays expenses of writers on assignment.

Photos: Pays $10 for 5x7 (and up) b&w photos used with mss, minimum of $25 for color. Prefers 2¼x2¼ and up, but can work from 35mm.

Tips: "Our readers are eager for ideas on how to bring early America into their lives. Conceive a new approach to satisfy their related interests in arts, crafts, travel to historic sites, and especially in houses decorated in the early American style. Write to entertain and inform at the same time, and be prepared to help us with illustrations, or sources for them."

‡EDGES, The Official Publication of the American Blade Collectors, American Blade, Inc., 2835 Hickory Valley Rd., Chattanooga TN 37421. Editor: J. Bruce Voyles. Bimonthly tabloid covering the knife business. Circ. 20,000. Pays on publication. Byline given. Buys all rights. Submit seasonal/holiday material 6 months in advance. Simultaneous queries, and photocopied and previously published submissions OK "as long as they are exclusive to our market." Reports in 5 months. Acknowledges receipt of queries and ms in 2 months. Sample copy $1.

Nonfiction: "Emphasis on pocket knives and folders." Book excerpts, expose, general interest, historical (well-researched), how-to, humor, new product, opinion, personal experience, photo feature, and technical. "We look for articles on all aspects of the knife business, including technological advances, profiles, knife shows, and well-researched history. Ours is not a hard market to break into if the writer is willing to do a little research. To have a copy is almost a requirement." Buys 150 mss/year. Send complete ms. Length: 50-3,000 words "or more if material warrants additional length." Pays 5¢/word.

Photos: Pays $5 for 5x7 b&w prints. Captions and model release required (if persons are identifiable).

Fillers: Clippings, anecdotes and newsbreaks.

Tips: "If writers haven't studied the publication they shouldn't bother to submit an article. If they have studied it, we're an easy market to sell to." Buys 80% of the articles geared to "the knife business."

FIBERARTS, The Magazine of Textiles, 50 College St., Asheville NC 28801. (704)253-0467. Editor: Kate Mathews. 85% freelance written. Eager to work with new/unpublished writers; works with a small number of new/unpublished writers each year. Bimonthly magazine covering textiles as art and craft (weaving, quilting, surface design, stitchery, knitting, fashion, crochet, etc.) for textile artists, craftspeople, hobbyists, teachers, museum and gallery staffs, collectors and enthusiasts. Circ. 26,000. Pays on publication. Publishes ms an average of 4 months after acceptance. Byline given. Rights purchased are negotiable. Submit seasonal/holiday material 8 months in advance. Editorial guidelines and style sheet available. Computer printout submissions acceptable; prefers letter-quality to dot-matrix. Reports within 2 weeks. Sample copy $3 and 10x12 SAE with 39¢ postage; writer's guidelines for SAE with 39¢ postage.
Nonfiction: Book excerpts; historical/nostalgic; how-to; humor; interview/profile; opinion; personal experience; photo feature; technical; travel (for the textile enthusiast, e.g., collecting rugs in Turkey); and education, trends, exhibition reviews and textile news. Buys 25-50 mss/year. Query. "Please be very specific about your proposal. Also an important consideration in accepting an article is the kind of photos—35mm slides and/or b&w glossies—that you can provide as illustration. We like to see photos in advance." Length: 250-1,200 words. Pays $40-300, depending on article. Sometimes (rarely) pays the expenses of writers on assignment.
Tips: "Our writers are very familiar with the textile field, and this is what we look for in a new writer. Familiarity with textile techniques, history or events determines clarity of an article more than a particular style of writing. The writer should also be familiar with *Fiberarts*, the magazine. We outline our upcoming issues in regular Editorial Agendas far enough in advance for a prospective writer to be aware of our future needs."

FINESCALE MODELER, Kalmbach Publishing Co., 1027 N. 7th St., Milwaukee WI 53233. (414)272-2060. Editor: Bob Hayden. 80% freelance written. Eager to work with new/unpublished writers. Bimonthly magazine "devoted to how-to-do-it modeling information for scale modelbuilders who build non-operating aircraft, tanks, boats, automobiles, figures, dioramas, and science fiction and fantasy models." Circ. 58,000. Pays on acceptance. Publishes ms an average of 14 months after acceptance. Byline given. Buys all rights. Computer printout submissions acceptable; prefers letter-quality to dot-matrix. Reports in 1 month on queries; 2 months on mss. Sample copy for 9x12 SAE and 3 first class stamps; free writer's guidelines.
Nonfiction: How-to (build scale models); and technical (research information for building models). Query or send complete ms. Length: 750-3,000 words. Pays $30/published page minimum.
Photos: Send photos with ms. Pays $7.50 minimum for color transparencies and $5 minimum for 5x7 b&w prints. Captions and identification of subjects required. Buys one-time rights.
Columns/Departments: *FSM* Showcase (photos plus description of model); and *FSM* Tips and Techniques (modelbuilding hints and tips). Buys 25-50 Tips and Techniques/year. Query or send complete ms. Length: 100-1,000 words. Pays $5-75.
Tips: "A freelancer can best break in first through hints and tips, then through feature articles. Most people who write for *FSM* are modelers first, writers second. This is a specialty magazine for a special, quite expert audience. Essentially, 99% of our writers will come from that audience."

‡THE FRANKLIN MINT ALMANAC, Franklin Center PA 19091. (215)459-7016. Editor-in-Chief: Barbara Caddy. Editor: Samuel H. Young. 90% freelance written. Bimonthly magazine covering collecting, fashion, and fine and decorative arts for members of Franklin Mint Collectors Society who are regular customers and others who request. Circ. 1,200,000. Pays on acceptance. Publishes ms an average of 5 months after acceptance. Byline given. Pays negotiable kill fee. Buys one-time rights. Submit seasonal/holiday material 9 months in advance. Simultaneous queries, and simultaneous, photocopied, and previously published submissions OK. Computer printout submissions acceptable; prefers letter-quality to dot-matrix. Reports in 1 week on queries.
Nonfiction: General interest (topics related to products offered by the Franklin Mint); interview/profile (with eminent collectors); and types of collections. Buys 30 mss/year. Query. Length: 1,500-2,000 words. Pays $750 average/article. Pays expenses of writers on assignment.
Photos: State availability of photos.
Tips: "Solid writing credentials and a knowledge of collecting are a plus. A frequent mistake made by writers is poor organization—they haven't thought through the structure and flow of the piece or else they become bogged down in biographical/historical details."

‡FRESHWATER AND MARINE AQUARIUM MAGAZINE, R/C Modeler Corp., Box 487, 144 W. Sierra Madre Blvd., Sierra Madre CA 91024. (818)355-1476. Editor: Don Dewey. Managing Editor: Patricia Crews. 70% freelance written. Eager to work with new/unpublished writers. A monthly magazine covering freshwater or marine aquarium keeping. Circ. 32,000. Pays on publication. Publishes ms an average of 4 months after acceptance. Byline given. Offers $100 kill fee. Buys first North American serial rights. Submit seasonal/holiday material 4 months in advance. Computer printout submissions OK; prefers letter-quality to dot-matrix. Reports in 2 weeks. Sample copy and writer's guidelines for 9x12 SAE with $1 postage.

Nonfiction: General interest, historical/nostalgic, how-to, interview/profile, opinion, personal experience, photo feature and technical. Buys 75 mss/year. Send complete ms. Length: 750-7,500 words. Pays $50-400 for assigned articles; pays $25-300 for unsolicited articles. Pays with free subscription only for ideas published in "For What It's Worth." Sometimes pays the expenses of writers on assignment.

Photos: Send photos with submission. Offers $10-15 per photo. Captions and identification of subjects required. Buys one-time rights.

Tips: "Freelance writers should be knowledgeable aquairists with a working background in the hobby. 'How-to' type articles geared toward the beginning-intermediate hobbyist; construction ideas, time and money saving ideas, etc. are needed."

‡HANDS-ON ELECTRONICS, Gernsback Publications, Inc., 500B Bi-County Blvd., Farmingdale NY 11735. (516)293-3000. Editor: Julian Martin. 95% freelance written. Monthly magazine covering hobby electronics—"features, projects, ideas related to audio, CB, radio, experimenting, test equipment, antique radio, communications, state-of-the-art, etc." Circ. 60,000. Pays on acceptance. Byline given. Buys all rights. Submit seasonal/holiday material 5 months in advance. Simultaneous, photocopied and previously published submissions OK. Query for electronic submissions. Computer printout submissions OK; prefers letter-quality to dot-matrix. Reports in 2 weeks. Free sample copy, "include label." Writer's guidelines for SASE.

Nonfiction: General interest, how-to, photo feature and technical. Buys 200 + mss/year. Query or send complete ms. Length: 1,000-3,500 words. Pays $100-350.

Photos: Send photos with submission. Reviews contact sheets or 5x7 prints. Offers no additional payment for photos accepted with ms. Captions required. Buys all rights.

Fiction: "Very little purchased." Experimental, historical, humorous and science fiction. Buys 5 mss/year. Query or send complete ms. Length: 1,000-2,000 words. Pays $100-200.

Tips: "It's all in the selling. Give us a new idea and prove to us you can deliver, and the job is yours!"

HANDWOVEN, from Interweave Press, 306 N. Washington, Loveland CO 80537. (303)669-7672. Editor: Jane Patrick. 75% freelance written. Bimonthly magazine (except July) covering handweaving, spinning and dyeing. Audience includes "practicing textile craftsmen. Article should show considerable depth of knowledge of subject, although tone should be informal and accessible." Circ. 32,000. Pays on publication. Publishes ms an average of 8 months after acceptance. Byline given. Pays 50% kill fee. Buys first North American serial rights. Simultaneous queries and photocopied submissions OK. Computer printout submissions acceptable; prefers letter-quality to dot-matrix. Sample copy $4.50; writer's guidelines for SASE.

Nonfiction: Historical and how-to (on weaving and other craft techniques; specific items with instructions); and technical (on handweaving, spinning and dyeing technology). "All articles must contain a high level of in-depth information. Our readers are very knowledgeable about these subjects." Query. Length: 500-2,000 words. Pays $35-150. Sometimes pays the expenses of writers on assignment.

Photos: State availability of photos. Identification of subjects required.

Tips: "We prefer work written by writers with an in-depth knowledge of weaving. We're particularly interested in articles about new weaving and spinning techniques as well as applying these techniques to finished products."

HOME MECHANIX, 1515 Broadway, New York NY 10036. (212)719-6630. Editor: Joseph R. Provey. Executive Editor: Harry Wicks. Managing Editor: Jim Wigdahl. 50% freelance written. Prefers to work with published/established writers. "If it's good, we're interested, whether writer is new or experienced." Monthly magazine for the home and car manager. "Articles on maintenance, repair, and renovation of the home and family car. Information on how to buy, how to select products useful to homeowners/car owners. Emphasis in home-oriented articles is on good design, inventive solutions to styling and space problems, useful home-workshop projects." Circ. 1.6 million. Pays on acceptance. Publishes ms an average of 3 months after acceptance. Byline given. Buys first North American serial rights. Computer printout submissions acceptable; prefers letter-quality to dot-matrix.

Nonfiction: Feature articles relating to homeowner/car owner, 1,500-2,500 words. "This may include personal home-renovation projects, professional advice on interior design, reports on different or unusual construction methods, energy-related subjects, outdoor/backyard projects, etc. We are no longer interested in high-tech subjects such as aerospace, electronics, photography or military hardware. Most of our automotive features are written by experts in the field, but fillers, tips, how-to repair, or modification articles on the family car are welcome. Workshop articles on furniture, construction, tool use, refinishing techniques, etc., are also sought. Pays $300 minimum for features; fees based on number of printed pages, photos accompanying mss., etc." Pays expenses of writers on assignment.

Photos: Photos should accompany mss. Pays $600 and up for transparencies for cover. Inside color: $300/1 page, $500/2, $700/3, etc. Home and Shop hints illustrated with 1 photo, $40. Captions and model releases required.

Fillers: Tips and fillers useful to tool users or for general home maintenance. Pays $25 and up for illustrated and captioned fillers.

Tips: "The most frequent mistake made by writers in completing an article assignment for *Home Mechanix* is not taking the time to understand its editorial focus and special needs."

‡**JUGGLER'S WORLD**, International Jugglers Association, Box 443, Davidson NC 28036. (704)892-1296. Editor: Bill Giduz. 50% freelance written. A quarterly magazine on juggling. "*Juggler's World* publishes news, feature articles, fiction, and poetry that relates to juggling. We also encourage 'how to' articles describing how to learn various juggling tricks." Circ. 2,700. Pays on acceptance. Publishes ms an average of 6 months after acceptance. Byline given. Buys all rights. Submit seasonal material 6 months in advance. Simultaneous, photocopied and previously published submissions OK. Query for electronic submissions. Computer printout submissions OK. Reports in 1 week. Sample copy for 8½x11 SAE with 90¢ postage.
Nonfiction: Essays, general interest, historical/nostalgic, how-to, humor, interview/profile, opinion, personal experience, photo feature and travel. Buys 10 mss/year. Query. Length: 500-2,000 words. Pays $50-100 for assigned articles. Pays expenses of writers on assignment.
Photos: State availability of photos with submission. Reviews contact sheets, negatives and prints. Offers no additional payment for photos accepted with ms. Captions required. Buys one-time rights.
Fiction: Ken Letko, fiction editor. Adventure, fantasy, historical, humorous, science fiction and slice-of-life vignettes. Buys 2 mss/year. Query. Length: 250-1,000 words. Pays $25-50.
Tips: "The best approach is a feature article on or an interview with a leading juggler. Article should include both human interest material to describe the perfomer as a individual and technical juggling information to make it clear to a knowledgeable audience the exact tricks and skits performed."

THE LEATHER CRAFTSMAN, Target Marketing and Publishing, Box 1386, Fort Worth TX 76101. (817)560-2396. Editor: Stanley Cole. Managing Editor: Nancy Sawyer. 95% freelance written. Eager to work with new/unpublished writers. A bimonthly magazine covering leathercrafting or leather art. "We are dedicated to the preservation of leather craft and leather art. Each issue contains articles on leather crafters, helpful hints and projects that our readers try at home or in their businesses." Circ. 10,000. Pays on publication. Publishes ms an average of 6-12 months after acceptance. Byline given. Buys first rights. Submit seasonal/holiday material 6 months in advance. Computer printout submissions acceptable; prefers letter-quality to dot-matrix. Reports in 2 weeks on queries; 1 month on mss. Sample copy $2.25; free writer's guidelines.
Nonfiction: How-to on leathercrafting projects. No articles not related to leather in some way. Send complete ms. Pays $25-200.
Photos: Send photos or completed project with submission. Reviews transparencies and prints. Offers no additional payment for photos accepted with ms. Captions required.
Tips: "*The Leather Craftsman* is dedicated to the preservation of leather craft and leather art. All aspects of the craft including carving, stamping, dyeing, sewing, decorating, etc., are presented to our readers through the use of step by step instructions. We are interested in more articles concerning leather apparel."

LOOSE CHANGE, Mead Publishing Co., 1515 S. Commerce St., Las Vegas NV 89102-2703. (702)387-8750. Publisher: Daniel R. Mead. 10-20% freelance written. Eager to work with new/unpublished writers. Monthly magazine covering gaming and coin-op machines. Slot machines; trade stimulators; jukeboxes; gumball and peanut vendors; pinballs; scales, etc. "Our audience is predominantly male. Readers are all collectors or enthusiasts of coin-operated machines, particularly slot machines and jukeboxes. Subscribers are, in general, not heavy readers." Circ. 3,000. Pays on acceptance. Publishes ms an average of 2-3 months after acceptance. Byline given. Prefers to buy all rights, but also buys first and reprint rights. "We may allow author to reprint upon request in noncompetitive publications." Photocopied submissions OK. Previously published submissions must be accompanied by complete list of previous sales, including sale dates. Query for electronic submissions. Computer printout acceptable; prefers letter-quality to dot-matrix. Reports in 1 month on queries; 6 weeks on mss. Sample copy $1; writer's guidelines for SASE.
Nonfiction: Historical/nostalgic, how-to, interview/profile, opinion, personal experience, photo feature and technical. "Articles illustrated with clear, black and white photos are always considered much more favorably than articles without photos (we have a picture-oriented audience). The writer must be knowledgeable about subject matter because our readers are knowledgeable and will spot inaccuracies." Buys up to 50 mss/year. Length: 900-6,000 words; 3,500-12,000 for cover stories. Pays $100 maximum, inside stories; $200 maximum, cover stories.
Photos: "Captions should tell a complete story without reference to the body text." Send photos with ms. Reviews 8x10 b&w glossy prints. Captions required. "Purchase price for articles includes payment for photos."
Fiction: "All fiction must have a gambling/coin-operated-machine angle. Very low emphasis is placed on fiction. Fiction must be exceptional to be acceptable to our readers." Buys maximum 4 mss/year. Send complete ms. Length: 800-2,500 words. Pays $60 maximum.

‡**MANUSCRIPTS**, The Manuscript Society, Department of History, University of South Carolina, Columbia SC 29208. (803)777-6525. Editor: David R. Chesnutt. 10% freelance written. A quarterly magazine for collectors of autographs and manuscripts. Circ. 1,400. Pays on acceptance. Publishes ms an average of 6-18

months after acceptance. Byline given. Buys all rights. Query for electronic submissions. Computer printout submissions OK; prefers letter-quality to dot-matrix. Reports in 2 weeks on queries; 1 month on mss.

Nonfiction: Historical, personal experience and photo feature. Buys 4-6 mss/year. Query. Length: 1,500-3,000 words. Pays $50-250 for unsolicited articles.

Photos: State availability of photos with submission. Reviews contact sheets and prints. Offers $15-30/photo. Captions and identification of subjects required. Buys one-time rights.

Tips: "The Society is a mix of autograph collectors, dealers and scholars who are interested in manuscripts. Good illustrations of manuscript material are essential. Unusual documents are most often the basis of articles. Scholarly apparatus may be used but is not required. Articles about significant collections of documents (or unusual collections) would be welcomed. Please query first."

MINIATURE COLLECTOR, Collector Communications Corp., 170 5th Ave., New York NY 10010. (212)989-8700. Editor: Louise Fecher. 25% freelance written. Works with a small number of new/unpublished writers each year. Quarterly magazine; 56 pages. Circ. 25,000. Byline given. Buys first North American serial rights and occasionally second (reprint) rights to material originally published elsewhere. Pays within 30 days of acceptance. Publishes ms an average of 4 months after acceptance. Submit seasonal/holiday material 4 months in advance. Photocopied submissions OK. Computer printout submissions acceptable; no dot-matrix. Reports in 2 months. Sample copy $2; writer's guidelines for business-size SASE.

Nonfiction: How-to (detailed furniture and accessories projects in l/12th scale with accurate patterns and illustrations); interview (with miniaturists, well-established collectors, museum curators; include pictures); new product (very short-caption type pieces—no payment); photo feature (show reports, heavily photographic, with captions stressing pieces and availability of new and unusual pieces); and profile (of collectors, with photos). Buys 1-2 mss/issue. Query. Length: 800-1,000 words. Pays $100-175. "Most short pieces, such as news stories, are staff written. We welcome both short and long (1,000 words) stories from freelancers." First manuscripts usually on speculation. Sometimes pays the expenses of writers on assignment.

Photos: Send photos with ms; usually buys photo/manuscript package. Buys one-time rights. Captions required.

Tips: "The most frequent mistake made by writers submitting an article to us is that they write with too general a focus; our magazine is for a highly specialized audience, so familiarity with miniatures is a very big plus. Many writers are also unaware of the high quality of the pieces featured in our magazine."

MODEL RAILROADER, 1027 N. 7th St., Milwaukee WI 53233. Editor: Russell G. Larson. For hobbyists interested in scale model railroading. Monthly. Buys exclusive rights. Study publication before submitting material. Reports on submissions within 1 month.

Nonfiction: Wants construction articles on specific model railroad projects (structures, cars, locomotives, scenery, benchwork, etc.). Also photo stories showing model railroads. Query. First-hand knowledge of subject almost always necessary for acceptable slant. Pays base rate of $66/page.

Photos: Buys photos with detailed descriptive captions only. Pays $7.50 and up, depending on size and use. Pays: double b&w rate for color; full color cover earns: $210.

MOUNTAIN STATES COLLECTOR, Spree Publishing, Box 2525, Evergreen CO 80439. Editor: Carol Fertig. Managing Editor: Peg DeStefano. 85% freelance written. A monthly tabloid covering antiques and collectibles. Circ. 8,000. Pays on publication. Publishes ms an average of 3 months after acceptance. Byline given. Not copyrighted. Buys first rights, one-time rights or second serial (reprint) rights to material published elsewhere. Submit seasonal/holiday material at least 3 months in advance. Simultaneous and previously published submissions OK. Computer printout submissions acceptable; prefers letter-quality to dot-matrix. Reports in 3-6 weeks. Sample copy for 9x12 SAE with 4 first class stamps; writer's guidelines for SASE.

Nonfiction: Book excerpts, historical/nostalgic, how-to (collect), interview/profile (of collectors) and photo feature. Buys 75 mss/year. Query with or without published clips, or send complete ms. Length: 500-1,500 words. Pays $15. Sometimes pays the expenses of writers on assignment.

Photos: Send photos with submission. Reviews contact sheets, and 5x7 b&w prints. Offers $5/photo used. Captions required. Buys one-time rights.

Tips: "Writers should know their topics well or be prepared to do in-depth interviews with collectors. We prefer a down home approach. We need articles on antiques and on collectors and collections; how-to articles on collecting; how a collector can get started; or clubs for collectors. We would like to see more articles in 1988 with high-quality b&w photos."

NEEDLEPOINT NEWS, EGW International Corp., Box 5967, Concord CA 94524. (415)671-9852. Editor: Gerri Eggers. 95% freelance written. A bimonthly magazine covering needlepoint. Circ. 15,000. Pays on publication. Publishes ms an average of 6 months after acceptance. Byline given. Buys first serial rights. Submit seasonal/holiday material 3 months in advance. Simultaneous queries and submissions, and photocopied submissions OK. Computer printout submissions acceptable; no dot-matrix. Reports in 6 weeks. Sample copy $2 with 9x12 SAE and 90¢ postage; writer's guidelines for #10 SASE.

Nonfiction: How-to (original designs and projects), interview/profile, new product, personal experience, photo feature, and technical. Buys 50 mss/year. Query with or without published clips. Length: 500-1,500 words. Pays $35/published page; pays $70/published page for two-time rights.

Photos: Send photos with accompanying query or ms. Reviews color negatives, 4x5 transparencies, and 5x7 b&w prints. Pays $25 maximum. Captions and identification of subjects required. Buys one-time rights.

Tips: "*Needlepoint News* is devoted exclusively to the art of needlepoint and is especially interested in original designs and projects. We look for articles on any subject related to needlepoint that aids the stitcher, from original projects to technical articles. In the past, we have published a wealth of topics, both brief and extensive, and some in a series. We also provide information for the serious stitcher on how to sell one's work or open a business."

‡THE NEW YORK ANTIQUE ALMANAC, The New York Eye Publishing Co., Inc., Box 335, Lawrence NY 11559. (516)371-3300. Editor-in-Chief: Carol Nadel. Tabloid published 10 times/year. Emphasizes antiques, art, investments and nostalgia. 30% freelance written. Circ. 52,000. Pays on publication. Buys all rights. Byline given. Phone queries OK. Submit seasonal/holiday material "whenever available." Previously published submissions OK but must advise. Computer printout submissions acceptable; no dot-matrix. Reports in 6 weeks. Publishes ms an average of 6 months after acceptance. Free sample copy.

Nonfiction: Expose (fraudulent practices); historical (museums, exhibitions, folklore, background of events); how-to (clean, restore, travel, shop, invest); humor (jokes, cartoons, satire); informational; inspirational (essays); interviews (authors, shopkeepers, show managers, appraisers); nostalgia ("The Good Old Days" remembered various ways); personal experience (anything dealing with antiques, art, investments, nostalgia); opinion; photo feature (antique shows, art shows, fairs, crafts markets, restoration); profile; technical (repairing, purchasing, restoring); travel (shopping guides and tips); and investment (economics, and financial reviews). Buys 9 mss/issue. Query or submit complete ms. Length: 3,000 words maximum. Pays $15-75. "Expenses for accompanying photos will be reimbursed."

Photos: "Occasionally, we have photo essays (auctions, shows, street fairs, human interest) and pay $5/photo with caption."

Fillers: Personal experiences, commentaries, anectdotes. "Limited only by author's imagination." Buys 45 mss/year. Pays $5-15.

Tips: "Articles on shows or antique coverage accompanied by photos are definitely preferred."

NOSTALGIAWORLD, for Collectors and Fans, Box 231, North Haven CT 06473. (203)269-8502. Editor: Bonnie Roth. Managing Editor: Stanley N. Lozowski. 50-75% freelance written. Works with a small number of new/unpublished writers each year; eager to work with new/unpublished writers. Bimonthly tabloid covering entertainment collectibles. "Our readership is interested in articles on all eras—everything from early Hollywood, the big bands, country/western, rock 'n' roll to jazz, pop, and rhythm and blues. Many of our readers belong to fan clubs." Circ. 5,000. Pays on publication. Publishes ms an average of 8 months after acceptance. Byline given. Buys all rights, one-time rights, second serial (reprint) rights, and simultaneous rights. Submit seasonal/holiday material 6 months in advance. Simultaneous queries, and simultaneous, photocopied, and previously published submissions OK. Computer printout submissions acceptable; prefers letter-quality to dot-matrix. Reports in 1 month on queries; 6 weeks on mss. Sample copy $2; writer's guidelines for business size SASE.

Nonfiction: Historical/nostalgic; how-to (get started in collecting); and interview/profile (of movie, recording, or sport stars). "Articles must be aimed toward the collector and provide insight into a specific area of collecting. *Nostalgiaworld* readers collect records, gum cards, toys, sheet music, movie magazines, posters and memorabilia, personality items, comics, baseball, and sports memorabilia. We do *not* cater to antiques, glass, or other nonentertainment collectors." Buys 20-30 unsolicited mss/year.

Photos: Send photos with ms. Pays $5-15 for 5x7 b&w prints; reviews b&w contact sheets. Captions and identification of subjects required. Buys all rights.

Columns/Departments: Video Memories (early TV); and 78 RPM-For Collectors Only (advice and tips for the collector of 78 RPM recordings; prices, values, outstanding rarities). Buys varying number of mss/year. Query or send complete ms. Length: 500-1,500 words. Pays $10-25.

Tips: "We have purchased numerous articles from beginning writers who have contacted us through *Writer's Market*. Most of the articles we reject are from writers who *do not read our requirements* and 'think' they know what we want. One sample issue will illustrate what we are looking for. We look forward to working with new writers, and find they supply us with some of our best material."

‡THE NUMISMATIST, American Numismatic Association, 818 N. Cascade Ave., Colorado Springs CO 80903. (303)632-2646. Editor: N. Neil Harris. Managing Editor: Barbara Gregory. Monthly magazine "for collectors of coins, medals, tokens and paper money." Circ. 35,000. Pays on publication. Publishes ms an average of 1 year after acceptance. Byline given. Buys first North American serial rights or second serial (reprint) rights. Submit seasonal/holiday material 1 year in advance. Simultaneous and previously published submissions OK. Computer printout submissions OK. Reports in 1 month on queries; 6 weeks on mss. Free sample

copy and writer's guidelines.
Nonfiction: Essays, expose, general interest, historical/nostalgic, humor, interview/profile, new product, opinion, personal experience, photo feature and technical. No articles that are lengthy non-numismatic. Buys 48-60 mss/year. Send complete ms. Length: 4,800-32,000 words. Pays "on rate-per-published-page basis." Sometimes pays the expenses of writers on assignment.
Photos: Send photos with submission. Reviews contact sheets and 4x5 or 5x7 prints. Offers $2.50-5/photo. Captions and identification of subjects required. Buys one-time rights.
Columns/Departments: Buys 6 mss/year. Length: 3,240-9,720 words. "Pays negotiable flat fee per column."

NUTSHELL NEWS, for the complete miniatures hobbyist, Boynton & Associates, Inc., Clifton House, Clifton VA 22024. (703)830-1000. Editor: Bonnie Schroeder. Managing Editor: Mel Frantz. 90% freelance written. A monthly magazine covering 1" scale dollhouse miniatures. "All articles must be related to the miniatures field. We do not use first-person submissions, and prefer a personal slant of the subject, with quotes. Our readers want to feel they know the subject after reading the article." Circ. 30,000. Pays on publication. Publishes ms an average of 1 year after acceptance. Byline given. Offers $25 kill fee. Buys all rights. Submit seasonal/holiday material 6 months in advance. Computer printout submissions acceptable; prefers letter-quality to dot-matrix. Reports in 2 months on queries; 3 months on mss. Sample copy $3; free writer's guidelines.
Nonfiction: How-to (on making miniatures) and interview/profile. "No articles that do not deal with quality hand-crafted miniatures." Buys 175 mss/year. Query with published clips. Length: 600-2,000 words. Pays 10¢/word.
Photos: Send photos with submission. Reviews 35mm transparencies and b&w prints. Offers $10/color photo and $7.50/b&w.
Columns/Departments: Book Reviews (books dealing directly with the miniatures field or reference books that can be used by miniaturists when reproducing full-size items), 100-300 words. Buys 30 mss/year. Send complete ms. Pays 10¢/word.
Tips: "Our readership is dedicated to this magazine and their hobby, and want to see articles on fine craftsmanship and outstanding miniatures collections. Even though this is an expensive hobby, our readers already know this, so don't stress 'dollars.' Artisan profiles, articles on collections and miniatures related how-to articles are areas most open to freelancers. How-tos should have step-by-step instructions with photos and diagrams. Articles on miniatures museums and miniatures show coverage are also accepted, as well as articles on decorating styles and periods."

‡THE OLD BOTTLE MAGAZINE/POPULAR ARCHAEOLOGY, Box 243, Bend OR 97709. (503)382-6978. Editor: Shirley Asher. For collectors of old bottles, insulators and relics. Monthly. Circ. 3,500. Buys all rights. Byline given. Buys 35 mss/year. Pays on acceptance. Sample copy $2. Reports in 1 month.
Nonfiction, Photos and Fillers: "We are soliciting factual accounts on specific old bottles, canning jars, insulators and relics." Stories of a general nature on these subjects not wanted. "Interviews of collectors are usually not suitable when written by noncollectors. A knowledge of the subject is imperative. Would highly recommend potential contributors study an issue before making submissions. Articles that tie certain old bottles to a historical background are desired." Submit complete ms. Length: 250-2,500 words. Pays $10/published page. B&w glossy prints and clippings purchased separately. Pays $5.
Tips: "We are accepting stories about all relics of the Industrial Age and industrial or urban archaeology."

OLD CARS PRICE GUIDE, Krause Publications, 700 E. State St., Iola WI 54990. (715)445-2214. Editor: Dennis Schrimpf. 5% freelance written. Eager to work with new/unpublished writers. Bimonthly magazine of old car prices for old car hobbyists and investors. Circ. 90,000. Pays on acceptance. Publishes ms an average of 2 months after acceptance. Byline given. Buys first North American serial rights. Submit seasonal/holiday material 3 months in advance. Computer printout submissions acceptable; prefers letter-quality to dot-matrix. Reports in 1 week. Sample copy $2.25 and 8x10 SASE.
Nonfiction: How-to (buy and sell collector cars); opinion (on car values market); technical (how to fix a car to increase value); and investment angles. "All articles should be car-value related and include information or actual price lists on recent sales (of more than one car). Articles about brands or types of cars *not* covered in regular price lists are preferred. Plenty of research and knowledge of the old car marketplace is usually essential. Photos required with all articles. No historic or nostalgic pieces." Buys 15-20 mss/year. Send complete ms. Length: 600-1,000 words. Pays $75-150.
Photos: Send photos with ms. Pays $50 minimum for 4x4 color transparencies used on cover; $5 for b&w prints; "undetermined for color." Captions and identification of subjects required. Buys one-time rights.

OLD CARS WEEKLY, Krause Publications, 700 E. State St., Iola WI 54990. (715)445-2214. Editor: John Gunnell. 50% freelance written. Weekly tabloid; 44-48 pages. Circ. 80,000. Pays on publication. Publishes ms an average of 2 months after acceptance. Buys all rights. Phone queries OK. Byline given. Computer printout submissions OK; prefers letter-quality to dot-matrix. Reports in 2 weeks. Sample copy $1.

Nonfiction: Short (2-3 pages) timely news reports on old car hobby with 1 photo. Buys 20 mss/issue. Query. Pays 3¢/word. Sometimes pays the expenses of writers on assignment.
Photos: Pays $5 for 5x7 b&w glossy prints. Captions required. Buys all rights.
Fillers: Newsbreaks. Buys 50/year. Pays 3¢/word. Pays $10 bonus for usable news tips.
Tips: "We have converted basically to a news package and buy only news. This would include post-event coverage of antique auto shows, summary reports on auctions with list of prices realized, and 'hard' news concerning old cars or people in the hobby. Buying and selling trends within the old car marketplace will affect the types of freelance material we buy in 1988. "

PIPE SMOKER, Journal of Kapnismology, Pipe Collectors International Inc., 6172 Airways Blvd., Box 22085, Chattanooga TN 37422. (615)892-7277. Editor: C. Bruce Spencer. 20% freelance written. Works with a small number of new/unpublished writers each year who are already involved with collectibles. A quarterly magazine about collecting smoking pipes and tobacciana. Features articles relative to the past, present and future of smoking pipes, tobacciana and the people and companies involved. Circ. 6,500. Pays on publication. Publishes ms an average of 6 months after acceptance. Byline given. Buys all rights; other use with permit. Submit seasonal/holiday material 3 months in advance. Sample copy $2.
Nonfiction: Historical/nostalgic, how-to, interview/profile and new product. No anti-smoking articles. Buys 8-10 mss/year. Send complete ms. Length: 1,500 words maximum. Pays 5¢/word. Sometimes pays the expenses of writers on assignment.
Photos: Send photos with submission. Reviews contact sheets; contract on color. Offers $5 maximum/b&w photo. Captions, model releases and identification of subjects required. Buys one-time rights.
Tips: "Features on related subjects are most open to freelancers, especially if writer is a pipe smoker."

POPULAR WOODWORKING, EGW Publishing Co., 1300 Galaxy Way, Concord CA 94520. (415)671-9852. Editor: David M. Camp. 99% freelance written. Eager to work with new/unpublished writers. A bimonthly magazine covering woodworking. "Our readers are the woodworking hobbyist and small woodshop owner. Writers should have a knowledge of woodworking, or be able to communicate information gained from woodworkers." Circ. 20,000. Pays on publication. Publishes ms an average of 10-12 months after acceptance. Byline given. Buys first North American serial rights and second-time rights ("at our discretion"). Submit seasonal/holiday material 6 months in advance. Photocopied submissions OK. Computer printout submissions acceptable; prefers letter-quality to dot-matrix. Reports in 6 weeks. Sample copy $2.95; writer's guidelines for SASE.
Nonfiction: How-to (on woodworking projects, with plans); humor (woodworking anecdotes); and technical (woodworking techniques). "No home-maintenance articles or stories about bloody accidents." Buys 120 mss/year. Query with or without published clips, or send complete ms. Pays $45-75/published page.
Photos: Send photos with submission. Reviews contact sheets, 4x5 transparencies, 5x7 glossy prints and 35mm color slides. Offers no additional payment for photos accepted for ms; $50 extra for cover photos only. Captions and identification of subjects required. Buys one-time rights.
Columns/Departments: Jig Journal (how to make special fixtures to help a tool do a task), 500-1,500 words. Buys 6 mss/year. Query. Pays $75 maximum/published page.
Fillers: Anecdotes, facts, short humor and shop tips. Buys 15/year. Length: 50-500 words. Pays $45 maximum/published page.
Tips: "Show a technical knowledge of woodworking. Sharp close-up black and white photos of a woodworker demonstrating a technique impress me. We really need project with plans articles. Describe the steps in making a piece of furniture (or other project). Provide a cutting list and a rough diagram (we can redraw). If the writer is not a woodworker, he should have help from a woodworker to make sure the technical information is correct."

‡POSTCARD COLLECTOR, Krause Publications, 700 E. State St., Iola WI 54990. (715)445-2214. Editor: Diane Allmen. 70% freelance written. Monthly magazine. "Publication is for postcard collectors; all editorial content relates to postcards in some way." Pays on publication. Publishes ms an average of 8 months after acceptance. Byline given. Offers $15 kill fee. Buys perpetual, but nonexclusive rights. Submit seasonal/holiday material 5 months in advance. Computer printout submissions OK; prefers letter-quality to dot-matrix. Reports in 2 weeks on queries; 1 month on mss. Free sample copy and writer's guidelines.
Nonfiction: Historical/nostalgic, how-to (e.g. preservatives) and technical. Buys 100 mss/year. Query. Length: 200-1,800 words. Pays $25-150 for assigned articles; pays $2-150 for unsolicited articles.

ALWAYS submit manuscripts or queries with a self-addressed, stamped envelope (SASE) within your country or International Reply Coupons purchased from the post office for other countries.

Photos: State availability of postcards with submission. Offers $1-3/photo. Captions and identification of subjects required. Buys perpetual, but nonexclusive rights.
Columns/Departments: Where Is It (interesting subject on unidentified real photo postcard), 50-150 words. Buys 35-45 mss/year. Query. Pays $2.
Tips: "We publish information about postcards written by expert topical specialists. The writer must be knowledgeable about postcards and have acquired 'expert' information." Areas most open to freelancers are feature-length articles on specialized areas (600-1,800 words) with 1-10 illustrations.

THE PROFESSIONAL QUILTER, Oliver Press, Box 4096, St. Paul MN 55104. (612)488-0974. Editor: Jeannie M. Spears. 80% freelance written. Works with a small number of new/unpublished writers each year. Quarterly magazine on the quilting business. Emphasis on small business, preferably quilt related. Circ. 2,000. Payment negotiated. Publishes ms an average of 6 months after acceptance. Byline given. Buys first North American serial rights, first serial rights, and second serial (reprint) rights. Simultaneous queries, and photocopied and previously published submissions OK. Computer printout submissions acceptable; prefers letter-quality to dot-matrix. Reports in 2 weeks on queries; 1 month on mss. Sample copy $4; writer's guidelines for #10 SASE.
Nonfiction: How-to (quilting business); humor; interview/profile; new product; opinion; and personal experience (of problems and problem-solving ideas in a quilting business). No quilting or sewing *techniques* or quilt photo spreads. Buys 20 mss/year. Query or send complete ms. Length: 500-1,500 words. Pays $25-75.
Tips: "Each issue will focus in depth on an issue of concern to the professional quilting community, such as ethics, art vs. craft, professionalism, etc. We would also like to receive articles on time and space (studio) organization, stress and family relationships. Remember that our readers already know that quilting is a time-honored tradition passed down from generation to generation, that quilts reflect the life of the maker, that quilt patterns have revealing names, etc., etc. Ask yourself: If my grandmother had been running a quilting business for the last five years, would she have found this article interesting? Send a letter describing your quilt, craft or business experience with a query or manuscript."

QUILTWORLD, House of White Birches, 306 E. Parr Rd., Berne IN 46711. Editor: Sandra L. Hatch. 90% freelance written. Works with a small number of new/unpublished writers each year. Bimonthly magazine covering quilting. Also publishes the quarterly *Quilt World Omnibook*. "We use patterns of both contemporary and traditional quilts and related articles." Circ. 90,000. Pays on publication. Publishes ms an average of 6 months after acceptance. Byline given. Buys all rights. Submit seasonal/holiday material 6 months in advance. Computer printout submissions are acceptable. Reports in 1 month. Sample copy $1.75; writer's guidelines for SASE.
Nonfiction: How-to, interview/profile (quilters), new product (quilt products) and photo feature. Buys 18-24 mss/year. Query with or without published clips, or send complete ms. Length: open. Pays $25-150.
Photo: Send photos with submission. Reviews 35mm, 2¼x2¼ or larger transparencies and 3x5 prints. Offers $10/photo (except covers). Identification of subjects required. Buys all rights.
Poetry: Free verse and traditional. Buys 10-12 poems/year. Submit maximum of 2 poems. Length: 6-30 lines. Pays $10-25.
Fillers: Gags to be illustrated by cartoonist and short humor. Buys 10-12/year. Length: 50-100 words. Pays $25-40.
Tips: "Send list of previous articles published with resume and a SASE. List ideas which you plan to base your articles around."

QUILTER'S NEWSLETTER MAGAZINE, Box 394, Wheatridge CO 80033. Editor: Bonnie Leman. Monthly. Circ. 150,000. Buys first North American serial rights or second rights. Buys 15 mss/year. Pays on publication, sometimes on acceptance. Reports in 5 weeks. Free sample copy.
Nonfiction: "We are interested in articles on the subject of quilts and quiltmakers *only*. We are not interested in anything relating to 'Grandma's Scrap Quilts' but could use fresh material." Submit complete ms. Pays 3¢/word minimum, usually more.
Photos: Additional payment for photos depends on quality.
Fillers: Related to quilts and quiltmakers only.
Tips: "Be specific, brief, and professional in tone. Study our magazine to learn the kind of thing we like. Send us material which fits into our format but which is different enough to be interesting. Realize that we think we're the best quilt magazine on the market and that we're aspiring to be even better, then send us the cream off the top of your quilt material."

RAILROAD MODEL CRAFTSMAN, Box 700, Newton NJ 07860. (201)383-3355. Editor: William C. Schaumburg. 75% freelance written. Works with a small number of new/unpublished writers each year. For model railroad hobbyists, in all scales and gauges. Monthly. Circ. 97,000. Buys all rights. Buys 50-100 mss/year. Pays on publication. Publishes ms an average of 9 months after acceptance. Submit seasonal material 6 months in advance. Computer printout submissions acceptable; prefers letter-quality to dot-matrix. Sample copy $2; writer's and photographer's guidelines for SASE.

Nonfiction: "How-to and descriptive model railroad features written by persons who did the work are preferred. Almost all our features and articles are written by active model railroaders. It is difficult for non-modelers to know how to approach writing for this field." Pays minimum of $1.75/column inch of copy ($50/page).

Photos: Purchased with or without mss. Buys sharp 8x10 glossy prints and 35mm or larger color transparencies. Pays minimum of $10 for photos or $2/diagonal inch of published b&w photos, $3 for color transparencies and $100 for covers which must tie in with article in that issue. Caption information required.

Tips: "We would like to emphasize freight car modeling based on actual prototypes, as well as major prototype studies of them."

‡R/C MODELER MAGAZINE, R/C Modeler Corp., Box 487, 144 W. Sierra Madre Blvd., Sierra Madre CA 91024. (818)355-1476. Publisher: Don Dewey. Editor: Patricia Crews. 70% freelance written. A monthly magazine covering radio control model aircraft, helicopters, boats and cars. Circ. 132,000. Pays on publication. Byline given. Offers $100 kill fee. Buys first North American serial rights. Submit seasonal/holiday material 4 months in advance. Computer printout submissions OK; prefers letter-quality. Reports in 2 weeks. Free sample copy and writer's guidelines.

Nonfiction: General interest, historical/nostalgic, how-to (on any aspect of radio control), personal experience, photo feature, technical and full construction articles. Buys 75-100 mss/year. Send complete ms. Length: 500-7,500 words. Pays $75-400. Sometimes pays the expenses of writers on assignment.

Photos: Send photos with submission. Offers no additional payment for photo accepted with ms. Captions, model releases and identification of subjects required. Buys one-time rights.

Tips: "The writer should be experienced in radio controlled model building and operating. Our primary purchases are full construction articles from modelers/readers."

‡SAGEBRUSH JOURNAL, The Best Danged Western Newspaper Going!, Allied Publishing, 430 Haywood Rd., Asheville NC 28806. Editor: Ralph Roberts. Publisher: Bill Hagan. 90% freelance written. A monthly tabloid covering Western genre films and print (books and magazines). "We are oriented toward people who love the thrill of the Western genre—from the glorious B westerns of yesteryear, pulp stories and novels, to the Western revival of today." Estab. 1986. Circ. 5,000. Pays on publication. Byline given. Buys first North American serial, one-time and second serial (reprint) rights. Submit seasonal/holiday material 6 months in advance. Photocopied and previously published submissions OK. Query for electronic submissions. Computer printout submissions OK; prefers letter-quality to dot-matrix. Reports in 2 weeks on queries; 2 months on mss. Sample copy $2.50. Writer's guidelines for business-size SAE with 1 first class stamp.

Nonfiction: General interest, historical/nostalgic, humor, interview/profile, personal experience, photo feature, Western convention reports, reviews of Western films and books. Buys 40-50 mss/year. Query with or without published clips, or send complete ms. Length: 200-5,000 words. Pays 25¢/column inch.

Photos: Send photos with submission. Reviews prints. Offers 25¢/column inch for photo (included with article payment); "no separate photos." Captions and identification of subjects required. Buys one-time rights.

Fillers: Judy Hagan, fillers editor. Western-related anecdotes, facts, newsbreaks and short humor. Buys 15-20/year. Length: 50-200 words. Pays 25¢/column inch.

SCOTT STAMP MONTHLY, Box 828, Sidney OH 45365. (513)498-2111. Editor: Richard L. Sine. 30% freelance written. Works with a small number of new/unpublished writers each year. For stamp collectors, from the beginner to the sophisticated philatelist. Monthly magazine; 84 pages. Circ. 24,000. Rights purchased vary with author and material; usually buys first North American serial rights. Byline given. Buys 50 unsolicited mss/year. Pays on publication. Publishes ms an average of 7 months after acceptance. Submit seasonal or holiday material 6 months in advance. Computer printout submissions acceptable; prefers letter-quality to dot-matrix. Electronic submissions OK via IBM PC format—300/1200 baud ASCII, but requires hard copy also. Reports in 1 month.

Nonfiction: "We are in the market for articles, written in an engaging fashion, concerning the remote byways and often-overlooked aspects of stamp collecting. Writing should be clear and concise, and subjects must be well-researched and documented. Illustrative material should also accompany articles whenever possible." Query. Pays about $100.

Photos: State availability of photos. Offers no additional payment for b&w photos used with mss.

Tips: "It's rewarding to find a good new writer with good new material. Because our emphasis is on lively, interesting articles about stamps, including historical perspectives and human interest slants, we are open to writers who can produce the same. Of course, if you are an experienced philatelist, so much the better. We do not want stories about the picture on a stamp taken from a history book or an encyclopedia and dressed up to look like research. If an idea is good and not a basic rehash, we are interested."

SEW NEWS, The fashion magazine for people who sew, PJS Publications, Inc., News Plaza, Box 1790, Peoria IL 61656. (309)682-6626. Editor: Linda Turner Jones. 90% freelance written. Works with a small number of new/unpublished writers each year. Monthly newspaper covering fashion-sewing. "Our magazine is for the beginning home sewer to the professional dressmaker. It expresses the fun, creativity and excitement of sewing." Circ. 150,000. Pays on acceptance. Publishes ms an average of 6 months after acceptance. Byline given. Buys all rights. Submit seasonal/holiday material 6 months in advance. Photocopied submissions OK. Computer printout submissions acceptable; no dot-matrix. Reports in 2 months. Sample copy $3; writer's guidelines free.

Nonfiction: Historical/nostalgic (fashion, textiles history); how-to (sewing techniques); and interview/profile (interesting personalities in home-sewing field). Buys 200-240 ms/year. Query with published clips. Length: 500-2,000 words. Pays $25-400. Rarely pays expenses of writers on assignment.

Photos: State availability of photos. Prefers b&w contact sheets and negatives. Payment included in ms price. Identification of subjects required. Buys all rights.

Fillers: Anecdotes and sewing-related cartoons. Buys 12/year. Length: 50-100 words. Pays $10-25.

Tips: "Query first with writing sample. Areas most open to freelancers are how-to and sewing techniques; give explicit, step-by-step instructions plus rough art."

SPIN-OFF, Interweave Press, 306 N. Washington, Loveland CO 80537. (303)669-7672. Send submissions to Lee Raven, 1227 Monterey Ave., Berkeley CA 94707. (415)525-3574. Editors: Lee Raven and Anne Bliss. 10-20% freelance written. Quarterly magazine covering handspinning, dyeing, techniques and projects for using handspun fibers. Audience includes "practicing textile/fiber craftsmen. Article should show considerable depth of knowledge of subject, although the tone should be informal and accessible." Circ. 10,000. Pays on publication. Publishes ms an average of 6 months after acceptance. Byline given. Pays 50% kill fee. Buys first North American serial rights. Simultaneous queries and photocopied submissions OK. Computer printout submissions acceptable; prefers letter-quality to dot-matrix. Sample copy $3.50 and 8½x11 SAE; free writer's guidelines.

Nonfiction: Historical and how-to (on spinning; knitted, crocheted, woven projects from handspun fibers with instructions); interview/profile (of successful and/or interesting fiber craftsmen); and technical (on spinning, dyeing or fiber technology, use, properties). "All articles must contain a high level of in-depth information. Our readers are very knowledgeable about these subjects." Query. Length: 2,000 words. Pays $15-100.

Photos: State availability of photos. Identification of subjects required.

Tips: "You should display an in-depth knowledge of your subject, but you can tailor your article to reach beginning, intermediate, or advanced spinners. Try for thoughful organization, a personal informal style, and an article or series segment that is self-contained. New approaches to familiar topics are welcomed."

SPORTS COLLECTORS DIGEST, Krause Publications, 700 E. State St., Iola WI 54990. (715)445-2214. Editor: Steve Ellingboe. 70% freelance written. Eager to work with new/unpublished writers; works with a small number of new/unpublished writers each year. Sports memorabilia magazine published weekly. "We serve collectors of sports memorabilia—baseball cards, yearbooks, programs, autographs, jerseys, bats, balls, books, magazines, ticket stubs, etc." Circ. 35,000. Pays after publication. Publishes ms an average of 3 months after acceptance. Byline given. Buys first North American serial rights only. Submit seasonal/holiday material 3 months in advance. Simultaneous queries and photocopied submissions OK. Computer printout submissions acceptable; prefers letter-quality to dot-matrix. Reports in 5 weeks on queries; 2 months on mss. Free sample copy; writer's guidelines for business-size SASE.

Nonfiction: General interest (new card issues, research on older sets); historical/nostalgic (old stadiums, old collectibles, etc.); how-to (buy cards, sell cards and other collectibles, display collectibles, ways to get autographs, jerseys, and other memorabilia); interview/profile (well-known collectors, ball players—but must focus on collectibles); new product (new card sets) and personal experience ("what I collect and why"-type stories). No sports stories. "We are not competing with *The Sporting News, Sports Illustrated* or your daily paper. Sports collectibles only." Buys 200-300 mss/year. Query. Length: 300-3,000 words; prefers 1,000 words. Pays $20-75.

Photos: Unusual collectibles. State availability of photos. Pays $5-15 for b&w prints. Identification of subjects required. Buys all rights.

Columns/Departments: "We have all the columnists we need but welcome ideas for new columns." Buys 100-150 mss/year. Query. Length: 600-3,000 words. Pays $15-60.

Tips: "If you are a collector, you know what collectors are interested in. Write about it. No shallow, puff pieces; our readers are too smart for that. Only well-researched articles about sports memorabilia and collecting. Some sports nostalgia pieces are OK. Write only about the areas you know about."

SUNSHINE ARTISTS USA, The Voice Of The Nation's Artists and Craftsman, Sun Country Enterpises, 1700 Sunset Dr., Longwood FL 32750. (305)323-5937. Editor: Joan L. Wahl. Managing Editor: 'Crusty' Sy. A monthly magazine covering art and craft shows in the United States. "We are a top marketing magazine for professional artists, craftspeople and photographers working street and mall shows. We list 10,000+ shows a year, critique many of them and publish articles on marketing, selling, and improving arts and crafts. Circ. 16,000+. Pays on publication. Publishes ms an average of 6 months after acceptance. Byline given. Buys first North American serial rights. Reports in 2 weeks on queries; 6 weeks on manuscripts. Sample copy $2.50.

Nonfiction: "We are interested in articles that relate to artists and craftsmen traveling the circuit. Although we have a permanent staff of 40 writers, we will consider well-written, thoroughly researched articles on successful artists making a living with their work, new ways to market arts and crafts, and rags to riches profiles. Attend some art shows. Talk to the exhibitors. Get ideas from them." No how-tos. Buys 12+ mss/year. Query. Length: 550-2,000 words. Pays $10-50 for assigned articles.

Photos: State availability of photos with submission. Offers no additional payment for photos accepted with ms. Captions, model releases, and identification of subjects required.

‡**TEDDY BEAR REVIEW**, Collector Communications Corp., 170 5th Ave., New York NY 10010. Editorial Director: Krystyna Poray Goddu. 50% freelance written. Works with a small number of new/unpublished writers each year. A quarterly magazine on teddy bears. Estab. 1986. Pays 30 days after acceptance. Byline given. Buys first North American serial rights. Submit seasonal/holiday material 6 months in advance. Photocopied and previously published submissions OK if not published in a competing publication. Computer printout submissions OK; no dot-matrix. Reports in 2 months. Writer's guidelines for #10 SASE.

Nonfiction: Book excerpts, historical, how-to and interview/profile. No nostalgia on childhood teddy bears. Buys 20 mss/year. Query with published clips. Length: 500-1,500 words. Pays $75-250. Sometimes pays the expenses of writers on assignment "if approved ahead of time."

Photos: Send photos with submission. Reviews transparencies and b&w prints. Offers no additional payment for photos accepted with ms. Captions required. Buys one-time rights.

Tips: "We are interested in good, professional writers around the country with a strong knowledge of teddy bears. Historical profile of bear companies, profiles of contemporary artists and knowledgeable reports on museum collections are of interest."

‡**THE TRUMPETER**, Croatian Philatelic Society, 1512 Lancelot, Borger TX 79007. (806)273-7225. Editor: Eck Spahich. 50% freelance written. Eager to work with new/unpublished writers. A quarterly magazine covering stamps, coins, currency, military decorations and collectibles of the Balkans, and of central Europe. Circ. 800. Pays on publication. Publishes ms an average of 9 months after acceptance. Byline given. Buys first and one-time rights. Submit seasonal/holiday material 6 months in advance. Simultaneous and photocopied submissions OK. Computer printout submissions acceptable; no dot-matrix. Reports in 2 months on queries; 1 month on mss. Sample copy $2.50; free writer's guidelines.

Nonfiction: Book excerpts, general interest, historical/nostalgic, how-to (on detecting forged stamps, currency etc.) interview/profile, photo features and travel. Special issues include spring issue (1988): Spotlight will be on Albania, its philatelic, numismatic history, especially pre-1950 period. Buys 15-20 mss/year. Send complete ms. Length: 500-1,500 words. Pays for $10-30 for assigned articles; pays $5-25 for unsolicited articles. Sometimes pays the expenses of writers on assignment.

Photos: State availability of photos with submission. Reviews 3x5 prints. Offers $5-10/photo. Captions and identification of subjects required. Buys one-time rights.

Columns/Departments: Book Reviews (stamps, coins, currency of Balkans), 200-400 words; Forgeries (emphasis on pre-1945 period), 500-1,000 words. Buys 10 mss/year. Send complete ms. Length: 100-300 words. Pays $5-25.

Fillers: Facts. Buys 15-20/year. Length: 20-50 words. Pays $1-5.

Tips: "We desperately need features on Zara, Montenegro, Serbia, Bulgaria, Bosnia, Croatia, Romania and Laibach."

WESTERN & EASTERN TREASURES, People's Publishing Co., Inc., Box 1095, Arcata CA 95521. Editor: Rosemary Anderson. Emphasizes treasure hunting and metal detecting for all ages, entire range in education, coast-to-coast readership. 90% freelance written. Monthly magazine. Circ. 70,000. Pays on publication. Publishes ms an average of 1 year after acceptance. Buys all rights. Computer printout submissions acceptable; no dot-matrix. Sample copy and writer's guidelines for $2.

Nonfiction: How-to "hands on" use of metal detecting equipment, how to locate coins, jewelry and relics, prospect for gold, where to look for treasures, rocks and gems, etc., "first-person" experiences. "No purely historical manuscripts or manuscripts that require two-part segments or more." Buys 200 unsolicited mss/year. Submit complete ms. Length: maximum 1,500 words. Pays 2¢/word—negotiable.

Photos: Purchased with accompanying ms. Captions required. Submit b&w prints or 35mm Kodachrome color transparencies. Pays $5 maximum for 3x5 and up b&w glossy prints; $35 and up for 35mm Kodachrome cover slides. Model releases required.

Tips: "The writer has a better chance of breaking in at our publication with short articles and fillers as these give the readers a chance to respond to the writer. The publisher relies heavily on reader reaction. Not adhering to word limit is the main mistake made by writers in completing an article for us. Also, not following what the editor has emphasized as needed material to be clearly covered."

WOMEN'S CIRCLE, COUNTED CROSS STITCH, House of White Birches, Inc., 306 E. Parr Rd., Berne IN 46711. Editor: Sandra L. Hatch. 100% freelance written. Eager to work with new/unpublished writers. Quarterly magazine covering cross-stitch. Circ. 50,000. Pays on publication. Publishes ms an average of 6 months after acceptance. Byline given. Buys all rights. Submit seasonal/holiday material 6 months in advance. Computer printout submissions OK; prefers letter-quality to dot-matrix. Reports in 1 month. Sample copy $1.75; writer's guidelines for SASE.
Nonfiction: How-to, interview/profile, new product and charted designs. Buys 12-15 mss/year. Query with published clips. Length: open. Pays $25-100.
Photos: Send photos with submission. Reviews 35mm, 2¼x2¼ or larger transparencies or 3x5 or larger prints. Offers $10/photo "except covers." Identification of subjects required. Buys all rights.
Fiction: Fantasy, humorous and slice-of-life vignettes (all related to cross-stitch). Buys 4-8 mss/year. Send complete ms. Length: 100-600 words. Pays $25-75.
Poetry: Light verse and traditional (related to cross-stitch). Buys 8-12 poems/year. Submit maximum 2 poems. Length: 6-30 lines. Pays $15-30.
Fillers: Facts and short humor. Buys 4-8/year. Length: 50-150 words. Pays $20-40.
Tips: "We'd like more complicated designs using the latest techniques and products."

‡**WOMEN'S HOUSEHOLD CROCHET**, House of White Birches, Inc., 306 E. Parr Rd., Berne IN 46711. Editor: Susan Hankins Andrews. 90% freelance written. A quarterly magazine. "We appeal to crochet lovers—young and old, city and country, thread and yarn lovers alike. Our readers crochet for necessity as well as pleasure. Articles are 90% pattern-oriented. We need patterns for all expertise levels—beginner to expert. No knit patterns please." Circ. 75,000. Pays on publication. Publishes ms an average of 1 year after acceptance. Byline given. Buys all rights. Submit seasonal/holiday material 6 months in advance. Computer printout submissions OK. Reports in 1 month on queries; 6 weeks on mss. Sample copy for 8x11 SAE with 59¢ postage; free writer's guidelines.
Nonfiction: General interest, historical/nostalgic, how-to, humor, personal experience and technical. Needs seasonal patterns by March 1. Christmas Annual (December). Must be Christmas oriented. "Nothing of explicit sexual nature—our readers are true Bible-belt types. Even articles of a suggestive nature are apt to offend. Stay away from themes having to do with alcohol." Buys 10 mss/year. Send complete ms. Length: 500-2,000 words. Pays $20-75 for unsolicited articles.
Photos: Buys no photos. Must send crocheted item for staff photography.
Columns/Departments: Designer's Debut Contest (1st and 2nd prizes chosen each issue for crochet design). Buys 8 mss/year. Send complete ms. Length: 500-2,000 words. Pays competitive designer rates.
Poetry: Light verse and traditional. "No long poems over 20 lines. None of a sexual nature." Buys 6 poems/year. Submit maximum 2 poems. Length: 5-20 lines. Pays $5-20.
Fillers: Anecdotes, crochet cartoons, facts and short humor. Buys 24/year. Length: 35-70 words. Pays $5-20.
Tips: "Freelancers have the best chance of selling articles incorporating new trends in crochet. Look around you at the latest fashions, home decor, etc., for ideas—how to make money at crocheting (success stories from those who have marketed their needlework successfully) and patterns (keep materials inexpensive or moderately priced). Make sure crochet directions are complete and exact (no errors). Use standard crochet abbreviations. Send crocheted items with manuscripts; we will return them if return postage is included."

THE WORKBASKET, 4251 Pennsylvania Ave., Kansas City MO 64111. Editor: Roma Jean Rice. Issued monthly except bimonthly June-July and November-December. Buys first rights. Pays on acceptance. Reports in 6 weeks.
Nonfiction: Step-by-step directions for craft projects (400-500 words) and gardening articles (200-500 words). Query. Pays 7¢/word.
Photos: Pays $7-10 for 8x10 glossies with ms.
Columns/Departments: Readers' Recipes (original recipes from readers); and Making Cents (short how-to section featuring ideas for pin money from readers).

WORKBENCH, 4251 Pennsylvania Ave., Kansas City MO 64111. (816)531-5730. Editor: Robert Hoffman. 75% freelance written. Prefers to work with published/established writers; works with a small number of new/unpublished writers each year. For woodworkers. Circ. 830,000. Pays on acceptance. Publishes ms an average of 1 year after acceptance. Byline given if requested. Buys all rights then returns all but first rights upon request, after publication. Computer printout submissions acceptable; prefers letter-quality to dot-matrix. Reports in 2 months. Sample copy for 8x10 SAE wtih $1.25 postage; free writer's guidelines.
Nonfiction: "We have continued emphasis on home improvement, home maintenance and alternate energy projects. Our readers are do-it-yourselfers. So we provide in-progress photos technical drawings and how-to text for all projects. Because most of our readers own their own homes, we stress 'retrofitting' of energy-saving devices, rather than saying they should rush out and buy or build a solar home. Energy conservation is another subject we cover thoroughly; insulation, weatherstripping, making your own storm windows. We still are very strong in woodworking, cabinetmaking and furniture construction. Projects range from simple toys to compli-

cated reproductions of furniture now in museums. We would like to receive more contemporary furniture items (like those sold in the unfinished furniture stores) that can be easily duplicated by beginning do-it-yourself woodworkers." Query. Pays $175/published page, up or down depending on quality of submission. Additional payment for good color photos. "If you can consistently provide good material, including photos, your rates will go up and you will get assignments. If we pay less than the rate, it's because we have to supply photos, information, drawings or details the contributor has overlooked."

Columns/Departments: Shop Tips bring $30 maximum with a line drawing and/or B&W photo. Workbench Solver pays $50 to experts providng answers to readers problems related to do-it-yourself projects and home repair.

Tips: "Our magazine will focus on wood working, covering all levels of ability. We will continue to present home improvement projects from the do-it-yourselfer's viewpoint, emphasizing the most up-to-date materials and procedures. We would like to receive articles on indoor home improvements and remodeling, home improvement on manufactured and mobile homes, and/or simple contemporary furniture. Our editors are skilled woodworkers, do-it-yourselfers and photographers. We have a complete woodworking shop at the office, and we use it often to check out construction details of projects submitted to us."

WORLD COIN NEWS, Krause Publications, 700 E. State, Iola WI 54990. (715)445-2214. Editor: Colin Bruce. 30% freelance written. Works with a small number of new/unpublished writers each year. Weekly newsmagazine about non-U.S. coin collecting for novices and advanced collectors of foreign coins, medals, and other numismatic items. Circ. 15,000. Pays on publication. Publishes ms an average of 1 month after acceptance. Byline given. Buys first North American serial rights and reprint rights. Submit seasonal material 1 month in advance. Simultaneous and photocopied submissions OK. Computer printout submissions acceptable; no dot-matrix. Reports in 2 weeks. Free sample copy.

Nonfiction: "Send us timely news stories related to collecting foreign coins and current information on coin values and markets." Send complete ms. Buys 30 mss/year. Length: 500-2,000 words. Pays 3¢/word to first-time contributors; fees negotiated for later articles. Sometimes pays the expenses of writers on assignment.

Photos: Send photos with ms. Pays $5 minimum for b&w prints. Captions and model release required. Buys first rights and first reprint rights.

YESTERYEAR, Yesteryear Publications, Box 2, Princeton WI 54968. (414)787-4808. Editor: Michael Jacobi. 25% freelance written. Prefers to work with published/established writers. For antique dealers and collectors, people interested in collecting just about anything, and nostalgia buffs. Monthly tabloid. Circ. 7,000. Pays on publication. Publishes ms an average of 2-3 months after acceptance. Buys all rights. Byline given. Submit seasonal/holiday material 3 months in advance. Simultaneous, photocopied and previously published submissions OK. Computer printout submissions acceptable; prefers letter-quality to dot-matrix. Reports in 1 month for queries; 1 month for mss. Sample copy $1.

Nonfiction: General interest (basically, anything pertaining to antiques, collectible items or nostalgia in general); historical (again, pertaining to the above categories); and how-to (refinishing antiques, how to collect). The more specific and detailed, the better. "We do not want personal experience or opinion articles." Buys 24 mss/year. Send complete ms. Pays $5-25. Pays expenses of writers on assignment.

Photos: Send photos with ms. Pays $5 for 5x7 b&w glossy or matte prints; $5 for 5x7 color prints. Captions preferred.

Columns/Departments: "We will consider new column concepts as long as they fit into the general areas of antiques and collectibles." Buys 2 mss/issue. Send complete ms. Pays $5-25.

Home and Garden

Some magazines here concentrate on gardens; others on the how-to of interior design. Still others focus on homes and gardens in specific regions.

AUSTIN HOMES & GARDENS, Duena Development Corp., 900 West Ave., Austin TX 78701. (512)479-8936. Publisher: Hazel W. Gulley. Senior Editor: Marsia Hart Reese. 30-50% freelance written. Prefers to work with published/established writers; works with a small number of new/unpublished writers each year. Monthly magazine emphasizing Austin, Texas homes, people, gardens, and events for current, former, and prospective residents. Circ. 25,000. Average issue includes 16 articles. Pays on publication. Publishes ms an average of 6 months after acceptance. Buys all rights. Byline given. "The material that we buy becomes the sole property of AH&G and cannot be reproduced in any form without written permission." Photocopied submissions OK. Electronic submissions OK via IBM PC (or compatible), PC Write software, but requires hard copy also. Computer printout submissions acceptable; prefers letter-quality to dot-matrix. Reports in 1 month. Sample copy $3.

Nonfiction: General interest (interior design and architecture; trends in home furnishings and landscaping; arts and crafts); historical (local); how-to (on home or garden); and fashion feature. "We are looking for brief, lively, Austin-lifestyle-oriented articles that are aimed at a younger, informed, educated market; we wish to expand our readership as Austin expands and grows." Query with samples of published articles. Length: 700-1,500 words. Pays $100 minimum.

Columns/Departments: Departments include Portfolio (unusual local businesses or services); Travel; and People (interesting Austin people). Query. Length: 500-1,000 words. Pays $100 minimum.

Tips: "Always looking for good freelancers, but prefer Austin area writers familiar with city and area."

BETTER HOMES AND GARDENS, 1716 Locust St., Des Moines IA 50336. (515)284-3000. Editor (Building): Joan McCloskey. Editor (Furnishings): Shirley Van Anate. Editor (Foods): Nancy Byal. Editor (Travel): Mark Ingelbrentson. Editor (Garden Outdoor Living): Doug Jimerson. Editor (Health & Education): Paul Krantz. Editor (Money Management, Automotive, Features): Margaret Daly. 10-15% freelance written. Pays on acceptance. Buys all rights. "We read all freelance articles, but much prefer to see a letter of query rather than a finished manuscript."

Nonfiction: Travel, education, health, cars, money management, and home entertainment. "We do not deal with political subjects or with areas not connected with the home, community, and family." Pays rates "based on estimate of length, quality and importance."

Tips: Direct queries to the department that best suits your story line.

CANADIAN WORKSHOP, The How-to Magazine, Camar Publications (1984) Inc., 130 Spy Ct., Markham, Ontario L3R 5H6 Canada. (416)475-8440. Editor: Bob Pennycook. 90% freelance written. Monthly magazine covering the "do-it-yourself market including projects, renovation and restoration, gardening, maintenance and decoration. Canadian writers only." Circ. 85,000. Pays on publication. Publishes ms an average of 5 months after acceptance. Byline given. Offers 75% kill fee. Buys first serial rights only. Submit seasonal/holiday material 6 months in advance. Simultaneous queries OK. Computer printout submissions acceptable; no dot-matrix. Reports in 3 weeks. Sample copy $2; free writer's guidelines.

Nonfiction: How-to (home and home machinery maintenance, renovation projects, and woodworking projects). Buys 20-40 mss/year. Query with clips of published work. Length: 1,500-4,000 words. Pays $225-600. Pays expenses of writers on assignment.

Photos: Send photos with ms. Pays $20-150 for 2¼x2¼ color transparencies; covers higher; $10-50 for b&w contact sheets. Captions, model releases, and identification of subjects required.

Tips: "Freelancers must be aware of our magazine format. Product-types used in how-to articles must be readily available across Canada. Deadlines for articles are 5 months in advance of cover date. How-tos should be detailed enough for the amateur but appealing to the experienced. We work with the writer to develop a major feature. That could mean several rewrites, but we've found most writers to be eager. A frequent mistake made by writers is not directing the copy towards our reader. Stories sometimes have a tendency to be too basic."

‡COLORADO HOMES & LIFESTYLES, Suite 154, 2550 31st St., Denver CO 80216. (303)433-6533. Editor: Ania Savage. 60% freelance written. Bimonthly magazine covering Colorado homes and lifestyles for upper-middle-class and high income households as well as designers, decorators, and architects. Circ. 30,000. Pays on acceptance. Publishes ms an average of 4 months after acceptance. Byline given. Buys all rights. Submit seasonal/holiday material 6 months in advance. Simultaneous queries and photocopied submissions OK. Query for electronic submissions. Computer printout submissions acceptable; prefers letter-quality to dot matrix. Reports in 1 month. Free writer's guidelines.

Nonfiction: Fine home furnishings, interesting personalities and lifestyles, gardening and plants, decorating and design, fine food and entertaining—all with a Colorado slant. Buys 40 mss/year. Send complete ms. Length: 1,000-2,000 words. "For celebrity features (Colorado celebrity and home) pay is $300-800. For unique, well-researched pieces on Colorado people, places, etc., pay is 15-25¢/word. For regular articles, 10¢/word. The more specialized and Colorado-oriented your article is, the more generous we are." Sometimes pays the expenses of writers on assignment.

Photos: Send photos with ms. Reviews 35mm, 4x5 and 2¼ color transparencies and b&w glossy prints. Identification of subjects required.

Tips: "The more interesting and unique the subject the better. A frequent mistake made by writers is failure to provide material with a style and slant appropriate for the magazine, due to poor understanding of the focus of the magazine."

FARMSTEAD MAGAZINE, Box 111, Freedom ME 04941. Business offices: (207)382-6200. Editorial offices: (207)382-6200. Publisher: George Frangoulis. Managing Editor: Heidi Brugger. 50% freelance written.

Prefers to work with published/established writers. Magazine published 6 times/year covering home gardening, shelter/construction, woodworking and DIY crafts, alternative energy, recipes, small-scale livestock (breeds and care), tools, homesteading and country lifestyles. Circ. 150,000. Pays on publication. Publishes ms an average of 6 months after acceptance. Buys first serial rights and second serial (reprint) rights; second serial right may be used in an anthology and/or for another issue published by The Farmstead Press. Submit seasonal material 1 year in advance. Computer printout submissions acceptable; no dot-matrix. Reports in 3 months. Free sample copy and writer's guidelines with appropriate size SASE.

Nonfiction: General interest (related to rural living and gardening); how-to (gardening, farming, shelter, energy—especially wood heat—construction, conservation, wildlife, livestock, crafts, and rural living); interview (with interesting and/or inspirational people involved with horticulture, or commitment to country living). "We would like to see short subjects related to traditional country skills and knowledge or to new trends and ideas that improve country living today." No sentimentality or nostalgia. Buys 60 mss/year. Submit complete ms. Phone queries OK. Length: 700-5,000 words. Pays 5¢/word. Sometimes pays the expenses of writers on assignment.

Photos: State availability of photos with ms. Pay starts at $10 for each 5x7 b&w print used; starts at $25 for color; $100 for each color transparency used on cover.

Tips: "Contribute a thorough well-researched or first-hand experience article. B&w photos of good quality, 35mm color transparencies or careful diagrams or sketches are a boon. We look for an unusual but practical how-to article. Send short factual pieces with good photos. Our market is a highly competitive one. As a result we are constantly fine-tuning our focus. For a writer, this will mean a potential shift in acceptable subject matter due to changes in the percentages of topics in the editorial mix. All unsolicited manuscripts must have SASE or we cannot guarantee their return."

FLOWER AND GARDEN MAGAZINE, 4251 Pennsylvania, Kansas City MO 64111. Editor-in-Chief: Rachel Snyder. 50% freelance written. Works with a small number of new/unpublished writers each year. For home gardeners. Bimonthly. Picture magazine. Circ. 600,000. Buys first rights only. Byline given. Pays on acceptance. Publishes ms an average of 6-12 months after acceptance. Computer printout submissions acceptable; no dot-matrix. Free writer's guidelines. Reports in 6 weeks. Sample copy $2; writer's guidelines for SASE.

Nonfiction: Interested in illustrated articles on how to do certain types of gardening and descriptive articles about individual plants. Flower arranging, landscape design, house plants, patio gardening are other aspects covered. "The approach we stress is practical (how-to-do-it, what-to-do-it-with). We try to stress plain talk, clarity, and economy of words. An article should be tailored for a national audience." Buys 20-30 mss/year. Query. Length: 500-1,500 words. Pays 7¢/word or more, depending on quality and kind of material.

Photos: Pays up to $12.50/5x7 or 8x10 b&w prints, depending on quality, suitability. Also buys color transparencies, 35mm and larger. "We are using more four-color illustrations." Pays $30-125 for these, depending on size and use.

Tips: "The prospective author needs good grounding in gardening practice and literature. Offer well-researched and well-written material appropriate to the experience level of our audience. Use botanical names as well as common. Illustrations help sell the story. Describe special qualifications for writing the particular proposed subject."

GARDEN DESIGN, The Fine Art of Residential Landscape Architecture, American Society of Landscape Architects, 1733 Connecticut Ave. NW, Washington DC 20009. (202)466-7730. Editor: Susan Rademachee Frey. Managing Editor: Duke Johns. 80% freelance written. Works with a small number of new/unpublished writers each year. A quarterly magazine focusing on the design of public and private gardens. "Our attitude is that garden design is a fine art and craft, and that gardening is a way of life." Circ. 33,000. May pay part on acceptance if long interval between acceptance and publication. Publishes ms an average of 4 months after acceptance. Byline given. Offers $100 kill fee. Buys first North American and second serial (reprint) rights. Submit seasonal/holiday material 6 months in advance. Computer printout submissions OK; no dot-matrix. Reports in 3 weeks on queries; 6 weeks on mss. Sample copy $2.50; free writer's guidelines.

Nonfiction: "We look for literate, imaginative writing that conveys how a specific garden's design works, both how it was achieved and the experience it provides." No how-to, such as gardening techniques. Buys 35 mss/year. Query with published clips. Length: 1,000-2,500 words. Pays $300 maximum. Sometimes pays the expenses of writers on assignment.

Photos: Send photos with submission. Reviews transparencies and prints. Offers $50-250/photo. Captions and identification of subjects required. Buys one-time rights.

Columns/Departments: Particulars (things in the garden, i.e., how to use ornaments, materials), 1,000 words; Plant Page (design application of specific plant or type), 1,000 words; Ex Libris (book review), 1,500; Focal Point (guest opinion/editorial/personal point of view), 1,000 words; Eclectic (compendium of interesting bits and pieces of news), 250 words. Buys 16-20 mss/year. Query with published clips or send complete ms. Pays $50-200.

Tips: "Our greatest need is for small to mid-size private gardens, designed by professionals in collaboration with owners. Scouting locations is a valuable service freelancers can perform, by contacting designers and garden clubs in the area, visiting gardens and taking snapshots for our review. It helps to submit a plan drawing of the garden's layout (the designer usually can supply this). All feature articles are open to freelancers, as well as Focal Point, Ex Libris, Plant Page and Particulars. Writing should be intelligent and well-informed, a pleasure to read. Avoid pretension and flowery devices. Check proper plant names in Hortus III.''

GARDEN MAGAZINE, The Garden Society, A Division of the New York Botanical Garden, Bronx Park, Bronx NY 10458. Editor: Ann Botshon. 50% freelance written. Works with a small number of new/unpublished writers each year. Bimonthly magazine, emphasizing horticulture, environment and botany for a diverse readership, largely college graduates and professionals united by a common interest in plants and the environment. Most are members of botanical gardens and arboreta. Circ. 30,000. Publishes ms an average of 1 year after acceptance. Buys first North American serial rights. Submit seasonal/holiday material 6 months in advance. Photocopied submissions OK. Query for electronic submissions. Computer printout submissions acceptable; prefers letter-quality to dot-matrix. Reports in 2 months. Sample copy $3; guidelines for SASE.
Nonfiction: Ann Botshon, editor. "All articles must be of high quality, meticulously researched and botanically accurate." Exposé (environmental subjects); how-to (horticultural techniques, must be unusual and verifiable); general interest (plants in art and history, botanical news, ecology); humor (pertaining to botany and horticulture); and travel (great gardens of the world). Buys 15-20 unsolicited mss/year. Query with clips of published work. Length: 1,000-2,500 words. Pays $100-300. Sometimes pays the expenses of writers on assignment.
Photos: Jessica Snyder, associate editor. Pays $35-50/5x7 b&w glossy print; $40-150/4x5 or 35mm color transparency. Captions preferred. Buys one-time rights.
Tips: "We appreciate some evidence that the freelancer has studied our magazine and understands our special requirements. A writer should write from a position of authority that comes from either personal experience (horticulture); extensive research (environment, ecology, history, art); adequate scientific background; or all three. Style should be appropriate to this approach."

GURNEY'S GARDENING NEWS, A Family Newsmagazine for Gurney Gardeners, Gurney Seed and Nursery Co., 2nd and Capitol, Yankton SD 57079. (605)665-4451. Editor: Pattie Vargas. 85% freelance written. Prefers to work with published/established writers; works with a small number of new/unpublished writers each year. Bimonthly newsmagazine covering gardening, horticulture and related subjects for home gardeners. Circ. 65,000. Pays on acceptance. Publishes ms an average of 9-12 months after acceptance. Byline given. "We buy first North American serial rights and reprint rights for materials we might reprint or excerpt in our own publications, i.e., customer service bulletins or catalogs. Second rights are assigned to the writer and he is free to resell the material to any publication once we have printed the article." Will also consider second serial (reprint) rights to material originally published elsewhere. Submit seasonal/holiday material 6 months in advance. Computer printout submissions acceptable; no dot-matrix. Reports in 1 month on queries; 2 months on mss. Sample copy for 9x12 SAE and 4 first class stamps; writer's guidelines and themes for each issue for business size SAE.
Nonfiction: "We are interested in well-researched, well-written and illustrated articles on all aspects of home gardening. We prefer articles that stress the practical approach to gardening and are easy to understand. We don't want articles which sound like a rehash of material from a horticultural encyclopedia or how-to-garden guide. We rarely buy articles without accompanying photos or illustrations. We look for a unique slant, a fresh approach, new gardening techniques that work and interesting anecdotes. Especially need short (300-500 words) articles on practical gardening tips, hints, and methods. We are interested in: how-to (raise vegetables, flowers, bulbs, trees); interview/profile (of gardeners); profiles of celebrity gardeners; photo feature (of garden activities); and technical (horticultural-related)." Buys 70 unsolicited mss/year. Query. Length: 700-1,250 words. Pays $50-125. Also buys articles on gardening projects and activities for children. Length: 500-1,000 words. Pays $30-100.
Photos: Purchases photos with ms. Also buys photo features, essays. Pays $10-25 for 5x7 or 8x10 b&w prints or contact sheets. Captions, model releases, and identification of subjects required. Buys one-time rights.
Tips: "Time articles to coincide with the proper season. Read Gurney's Seed and Nursery catalogs and be familiar with Gurney's varieties before you submit an article on vegetables, fruits, flowers, trees, etc. We prefer that it be Gurney's. Our readers know gardening. If you don't, don't write for us. *Gurney's Gardening News* also sponsors an annual garden writers of the year contest."

THE HOMEOWNER, America's How-to Magazine, Family Media Inc., 3 Park Ave., New York NY 10016. Editor-in-chief: Joe Carter. Managing Editor: Michael Chotiner. 75% freelance written. Monthly (combined Jan/Feb; July/Aug) magazine on home improvement, maintenance. Aimed at men and women who want to successfully complete home improvement (even ambitious remodeling) and repair projects. Circ. 700,000. Pays on acceptance. Publishes ms an average of 5 months after acceptance. Byline given. Offers variable kill fee. Buys first North American serial rights. Computer printout submissions acceptable. Reports in 1 month. Sample copy $1.95 and 8x10 SAE; writer's guidelines for #10 SASE.
Nonfiction: How-to (remodeling, home repair and maintenance); personal experience (hands-on experience

with building a home, remodeling or carpentry project); and some technical information on products, materials, how things work. Length: 1,500 maximum. Pays $35 plus some expenses of writers on assignment.

HORTICULTURE, The Magazine of American Gardening, 755 Boylston St., Boston MA 02116. Published by the Horticulture Associates. Editor: Thomas C. Cooper. 90% freelance written. Works with a small number of new/unpublished writers each year. Monthly. Buys first North American serial rights. Byline given. Pays on acceptance. Publishes ms an average of 7 months after acceptance. Computer printout submissions OK; prefers letter-quality to dot-matrix. Reports in 6 weeks.
Nonfiction: All aspects of gardening. "We cover indoors and outdoors, edibles and ornamentals, garden design, noteworthy gardens and gardeners." Length: 1,500-3,500 words. Query. Study publication. Pays expenses of writers on assignment.
Photos: Color transparencies and top quality b&w prints, 8x10 only; "accurately identified." Buys one-time rights.
Tips: "We'd like to see some writing by accomplished vegetable gardeners. We continue to seek good pieces on garden design."

HOUSE BEAUTIFUL, The Hearst Corp., 1700 Broadway, New York NY 10019. (212)903-5000. Editor: JoAnn Barwick. Executive Editor: Margaret Kennedy. Editorial Director: Mervyn Kaufman. Director of Copy/Features: Carol Cooper Garey. (212)903-5236. 15% freelance written. Prefers to work with published/established writers. Emphasizes design, architecture and building. Monthly magazine; 200 pages. Circ. 840,000. Pays on acceptance. Publishes ms an average of 4 months after acceptance. Byline given. Submit seasonal/holiday material 4 months in advance of issue date. Computer printout submissions acceptable; prefers letter-quality to dot-matrix. Reports in 5 weeks.
Nonfiction: Historical (landmark buildings and restorations); how-to (kitchen, bath remodeling service); interview; new product; and profile. Submit query with detailed outline or complete ms. Length: 300-1,000 words. Pays varying rates.
Photos: State availability of photos or submit with ms.

‡LOG HOMES, Annual Buyer's Guide, Home Buyer Publications, Inc., Suite 500, 610 Herndon Parkway, Box 370, Herndon VA 22070. Editor: Richard V. Nunn. Publisher: John Kepferer. Annual magazine covering log homes and the log home industry. "We publish articles on how to build, buy, and maintain a log home: practical, nuts-and-bolts approaches for log home buyers and owners." Circ. 125,000. Pays an acceptance. Publishes ms an average of 6 months after acceptance. Byline sometimes given. Buys all rights. Computer printout submissions OK; prefers letter-quality to dot-matrix. Reports in 2 weeks. Sample copy $6 with 10x12 SAE and $2 postage.
Nonfiction: How-to, new product and technical. Buys 10 mss/year. Query. Length: 1,000-2,500 words. Pays $200-1,000 for assigned articles; pays $50-500 for unsolicited articles. Sometimes pays the expenses of writers on assignment.
Photos: Send photos with submission. Reviews 4x5 prints. Offers $10-50/photo. Captions, model releases and identification of subjects required. Buys all rights.
Tips: "Articles on construction, buying, selling and maintaining log homes are open."

NATIONAL GARDENING, Magazine of the National Gardening Association, 180 Flynn Ave., Burlington VT 05401. (802)863-1308. Editor: Katharine Anderson. 65% freelance written. Willing to work with new/unpublished writers. Monthly tabloid covering food gardening and food trees. "We publish not only how-to-garden techniques, but also news that affects gardeners, like science advances. Specific, experienced-based articles with carefully worked-out techniques for planting, growing, harvesting, using garden fruits and vegetables sought. Most of our material is for gardeners with several years' experience." Circ. 200,000. Pays on acceptance. Publishes ms an average of 9 months after acceptance. Byline given. Buys first serial rights and occasionally second (reprint) rights to material originally published elsewhere. Submit seasonal/holiday material 4 months in advance. Photocopied and previously published submissions OK. Computer printout submissions acceptable; prefers letter-quality to dot-matrix. Reports in 2 weeks on queries; 1 month on mss. Sample copy $1; writer's guidelines for SASE.
Nonfiction: How-to, humor, inspirational, interview/profile, new product, personal experience, photo feature and technical. "All articles must be connected with food/gardening." Buys 80-100 mss/year. Query. Length: 300-3,500 words. Pays $30-450/article. Sometimes pays the expenses of writers on assignment.
Photos: Vicki Congdon, photo manager. Send photos with ms. Pays $20-40 for b&w photos; $40 for color photos. Captions, model releases and identification of subjects required.
Tips: "Wordiness is a frequent mistake made by writers. Few writers understand how to write 'tight'. The most irritating easily correctable problem is careless grammar and poor spelling, often even in otherwise well-written pieces."

N.Y. HABITAT MAGAZINE, For Co-op, Condominium and Loft Living, The Carol Group, Ltd., 928 Broadway, New York NY 10010. (212)505-2030. Editor: Carol J. Ott. Managing Editor: Tom Soter. 75%

freelance written. Prefers to work with published/established writers. Published 8 times/year, covering co-op, condo and loft living in metropolitan New York. "Our primary readership is boards of directors of co-ops and condos, and we are looking for material that will help them fulfill their responsibilities." Circ. 10,000. Pays on publication. Publishes ms an average of 3 months after acceptance. Byline given. Offers negotiable kill fee. Buys first North American serial rights. Submit seasonal/holiday material 3 months in advance. Computer printout submissions acceptable. Reports in 3 weeks. Sample copy for $4, 9x12 SAE and 5 first class stamps; writer's guidelines for business size SASE.

Nonfiction: Only material relating to co-op and condominium living in New York metropolitan area. Buys 20 mss/year. Query with published clips. Length: 750-1,500 words. Pays $25-1,000. Sometimes pays the expenses of writers on assignment.

Tips: "We would like to receive manuscripts dealing with co-op or condo management."

1,001 HOME IDEAS, Family Media, Inc., 3 Park Ave., New York NY 10016. (212)340-9250. Editor: Ellen Frankel. Executive Editor: Kathryn Larson. 40% freelance written. Prefers to work with published/established writers. A monthly magazine covering home furnishings, building, remodeling and home equipment. "We are a family shelter magazine edited for young, mainstream homeowners, providing ideas for decorating, remodeling, outdoor living, and at-home entertaining. Emphasis on ideas that are do-able and affordable." Circ. 1,500,000. Pays on acceptance. Publishes ms an average of 6 months after acceptance. Byline given. Offers 25% kill fee. Buys first North American serial rights, second serial (reprint) rights, or makes work-for-hire assignments. Submit seasonal/holiday material 12 months in advance. Computer printout submissions acceptable. Reports in 1 month. Sample copy $2.50; writer's guidelines for business size SASE.

Nonfiction: Book excerpts (on interior design and crafts only); how-to (on decorating, remodeling and home maintenance); interview/profile (of designers only); new product; photo feature (on homes only); crafts; home equipment; and home furnishings and decor. No travel, religious, technical or exposés. Buys 15 mss/year. Query with or without published clips, or send complete ms. Length: 300-2,000 words. Pays $100-750 for assigned articles; pays $100-500 for unsolicited articles. Sometimes pays the expenses of writers on assignment.

Photos: State availability of photos with submission. Reviews transparencies and prints. Offers $10-100/photo. Captions, model releases, and identification of subjects required. Buys one-time rights.

Columns/Departments: Kathie Robitz, column/department editor. 1,001 Ways to Save $$$ (consumer buymanship, housing, finance, home furnishings, products, etc.) 1,500 words. Buys 12 mss/year. Query. Pays $300-400.

Tips: "The idea is what sells an article to us . . . good ideas for decorating, remodeling and improving the home, and well-researched information on how-to, with any necessary directions and patterns, to help the reader carry out the idea. The department, 1,001 Ways to Save, is the area most open to freelance writers. We also look for features which we can turn into photo features on decorating, remodeling and improving the home."

PHOENIX HOME & GARDEN, Arizona Home Garden, Inc., 3136 N. 3rd Ave., Phoenix AZ 85013. (602)234-0840. Editor: Manya Winsted. Managing Editor: Nora Burba. 50% freelance written. Works with a small number of new/unpublished writers each year. Monthly magazine covering homes, furnishings, entertainment, lifestyle and gardening for Phoenix area residents interested in better living. Circ. 35,000. Pays on publication. Publishes ms an average of 2 months after acceptance. Byline given. Buys all rights. Submit seasonal/holiday material 6 months in advance. Query for electronic submissions. Computer printout submissions acceptable; no dot-matrix. Reports in 6 weeks on queries. Sample copy $2, plus $2.10 postage.

Nonfiction: General interest (on interior decorating, architecture, gardening, entertainment, food); historical (on furnishings related to homes); some how-to (on home improvement or decorating); health, beauty, fashion; and travel (of interest to Phoenix residents). Buys 100 or more mss/year. Query with published clips. Length: 1,200 words maximum. Pays $75-300/article. Pays expenses of writers on assignment.

Tips: "It's not a closed shop. I want the brightest, freshest, most accurate material available. Study the magazine to see our format and style. Major features are assigned to staff and tried-and-true freelancers."

PRACTICAL HOMEOWNER, Rodale Press, 33 E. Minor St., Emmaus PA 18049. Articles Editor: John Viehman. 75% freelance written. Eager to work with new/unpublished writers; works with a small number of new/unpublished writers each year. Magazine published 9 times/year about practical homes. Circ. 700,000. Pays on acceptance. Publishes ms an average of 3 months after acceptance. Buys all rights. Submit seasonal material at least 6 months in advance. Electronic submissions OK via IBM "XYWrite III", but requires hard copy also. Computer printout submissions acceptable; no dot-matrix. Reports in 6 weeks. Writer's guidelines for SASE.

Nonfiction: "We are the magazine of innovative, yet practical, home designs and projects of use to our audience of advanced do-it-yourselfers. We are looking for the work of innovators who are at the cutting edge of affordable housing, alternate energy, water and resource conservation, etc. Our subtitle is, "Practical Ideas for the Homeowner," and that really says it all. We don't want run-of-the-mill, wooden how-to prose. We want lively writing about what real people have done with their homes, telling how and why our readers should do the same." No hobby/craft or overly general, simplistic articles. Query with clips of previously published work. Length: 1,000-2,000 words. Rate of payment depends on quality of ms. Sometimes pays the expenses of writers.

Photos: Mitch Mandel, photo editor. State availability of photos. Pays $75-200 depending on the size for color or transparencies. Captions and model releases required.

SAN ANTONIO HOMES & GARDENS, Duena Development Corp., 900 West Ave., Austin TX 78701. (512)479-8936. Publisher: Hazel W. Gully. Monthly magazine emphasizing San Antonio homes, people, events and gardens for current, former and prospective residents. Anticipated circulation 22,000. See *Austin Homes & Gardens* for format, departments, rates and requirements.

Tips: Looking for steady freelancers in the San Antonio, Texas, area.

SAN DIEGO HOME/GARDEN, Westward Press, Box 1471, San Diego CA 92101. (714)233-4567. Editor: Peter Jensen. Managing Editor: Dirk Sutro. 50% freelance written. Works with a small number of new/unpublished writers each year. Monthly magazine covering homes, gardens, food, and travel for residents of San Diego city and county. Circ. 36,000. Pays on publication. Publishes ms an average of 3 months after acceptance. Byline given. Buys first North American serial rights only. Submit seasonal material 3 months in advance. Photocopied submissions OK. Computer printout submissions acceptable; prefers letter-quality to dot-matrix. Reports in 1 month. Free writer's guidelines for SASE.

Nonfiction: Residential architecture and interior design (San Diego-area homes only); remodeling (must be well-designed—little do-it-yourself), residential landscape design; furniture; other features oriented towards upscale readers interested in living the cultured good life in San Diego. Articles must have local angle. Buys 5-10 unsolicited mss/year. Query with published clips. Length: 700-2,000 words. Pays $50-200. Sometimes pays expenses of writers on assignment.

Tips: "No out-of-town, out-of-state subject material. Most freelance work is accepted from local writers. Gear stories to the unique quality of San Diego. We try to offer only information unique to San Diego—people, places, shops, resources, etc."

SELECT HOMES MAGAZINE, 1450 Don Mills Dr., Don Mills, Ontario M3B 2X7 Canada. (416)445-6641. Editor: Jim Adair (East). 40% freelance written. Prefers to work with published/established writers; works with a small number of new/unpublished writers each year for news items and short features (700 words). Magazine published 8 times/year covering decorating, energy, and how-to as applied to homes for mostly upper-income single-family homeowners. Circ. 160,000. Pays on acceptance. Publishes ms an average of 5 months after acceptance. Buys 80 or more text/photo packages/year. Byline and photo credits given. Usually buys first Canadian serial rights; simultaneous rights, first rights, or second serial (reprint) rights, if explained. Submit seasonal/holiday material 3-12 months in advance. Simultaneous queries, and simultaneous, photocopied and previously published submissions OK if explained. Computer printout submissions acceptable; no dot-matrix. SASE or SAE, IRCs. Reports in 1 month. Sample copy for $1 and magazine size SAE; writer's guidelines for SAE.

Nonfiction: How-to, humor, and personal experience on decorating, interior design, energy, financial matters and architecture. Special sections include kitchen, spring; bathroom, fall. "We would like to receive humor columns for Back Porch (650 words maximum), relating specifically to home ownership. No lifestyle essays. No business profiles or home gardening articles. Buys 80 or more mss/year. Query with published clips. Length: 650-1,500 words. Pays $50 (news and some reprints)-600 (occasionally higher). Pays expenses of writers on assignment.

Photos: State availability of photos. Reviews contact sheets and 2¹/₄x2¹/₄ transparencies. Pays $50-250, color. "We pay mostly on a negotiable per-day rate, but we like to work from stock lists, too." Captions and model release requested. Buys one-time rights.

Fillers: Newsbreaks. Buys 10/year. Length: 100-500 words. Pays $15-150.

Tips: "We're looking for more renovation how-to articles—query first with clips. Submit clips and outline and tell us what special interests you have (decorating, energy, how-to). The editors generate 75% of the magazine's article ideas and assign them to writers whose style or background matches. We actively solicit book excerpts and reprints; please mention if your material is one of these. We retain stringers throughout Canada."

‡THE SPROUTLETTER, Sprouting Publications, Box 62, Ashland OR 97520. (503)488-2326. Editor: Michael Linden. 50% freelance written. Quarterly newsletter covering sprouting, live foods and indoor food gardening. "We emphasize growing foods (especially sprouts) indoors for health, economy, nutrition and food self-sufficiency. We also cover topics related to sprouting, live foods and holistic health." Circ. 2,500. Pays on publication. Publishes ms an average of 3 months after acceptance. Byline given. Offers 50% kill fee. Buys North American serial rights and second (reprint) rights to material originally published elsewhere. Submit seasonal/holiday material 3 months in advance. Previously published submissions OK. Computer printout submissions acceptable; prefers letter-quality to dot-matrix. Reports in 2 weeks on queries; 3 weeks on mss. Sample copy $4.50; writer's guidelines for business size SAE and 2 first class stamps.

Nonfiction: General interest (raw foods, sprouting, holistic health); how-to (grow sprouts, all kinds of foods indoors; build devices for sprouting or indoor gardening); personal experience (in sprouting or related areas); and technical (experiments with growing sprouts). No common health food/vitamin articles or growing ornamental plants indoors (as opposed to food producing plants). Buys 4-6 mss/year. Query. Length: 500-2,400 words. Pays $15-50. Trades for merchandise are also considered.

Columns/Departments: Book Reviews (books oriented toward sprouts, nutrition or holistic health). Reviews are short and informative. News Items (interesting news items relating to sprouts or live foods); Recipes (mostly raw foods). Buys 5-10 mss/year. Query. Length: 100-450 words. Pays $3-10.

Fillers: Short humor and newsbreaks. Buys 3-6/year. Length: 50-150 words. Pays $2-6.

Tips: "Writers should have a sincere interest in holistic health and in natural whole foods. We like writing which is optimistic, interesting and very informative. Consumers are demanding more thorough and accurate information. Articles should cover any given subject in depth in an enjoyable and inspiring manner. A frequent mistake is that the subject matter is not appropriate. Also buys cartoon strips and singles. Will consider series."

TEXAS GARDENER, The Magazine for Texas Gardeners, by Texas Gardeners, Suntex Communications, Inc., Box 9005, Waco TX 76714. (817)772-1270. Editor: Chris S. Corby. 80% freelance written. Works with a small number of new/unpublished writers each year. Bimonthly magazine covering vegetable and fruit production, ornamentals and home landscape information for home gardeners in Texas. Circ. 37,000. Pays on publication. Publishes ms an average of 4 months after acceptance. Byline given. Buys first North American serial rights and all rights. Submit seasonal/holiday material 6 months in advance. Query for electronic submissions. Computer printout submissions acceptable; prefers letter-quality to dot-matrix. Reports in 6 weeks. Sample copy $2.75; writer's guidelines for business size SASE.

Nonfiction: How-to, humor, interview/profile and photo feature. "We use feature articles that relate to Texas gardeners. We also like personality profiles on hobby gardeners and professional horticulturists who are doing something unique." Buys 50-100 mss/year. Query with clips of published work. Length: 800-2,400 words. Pays $50-200.

Photos: "We prefer superb color and b&w photos; 90% of photos used are color." State availability of photos. Pays negotiable rates for 2¼ color transparencies and 8x10 b&w prints and contact sheets. Model release and identification of subjects required.

Tips: "First, be a Texan. Then come up with a good idea of interest to home gardeners in this state. Be specific. Stick to feature topics like 'How Alley Gardening Became a Texas Tradition.' Leave topics like 'How to Control Fire Blight' to the experts. High quality photos could make the difference. We would like to add several writers to our group of regular contributors and would make assignments on a regular basis. Fillers are easy to come up with in-house. We want good writers who can produce accurate and interesting copy. Frequent mistakes made by writers in completing an article assignment for us are that articles are not slanted toward Texas gardening, show inaccurate or too little gardening information or lack good writing style. We will be doing more 'people' features and articles on ornamentals."

‡YANKEE HOMES, Yankee Publishing Incorporated, Main St., Dublin NH 03444. (603)563-8111. Editor: Jim Collins. 75% freelance written. Prefers to work with published/established writers. "*Yankee Homes* is a monthly publication geared toward people interested in buying, owning, and restoring New England homes. Feature articles tend to be factual and service-oriented, with an emphasis on information." Circ. 35,000. Pays on acceptance. Publishes ms an average of 2 months after acceptance. Byline given. Kill fee varies. Buys first and second serial (reprint) rights. Query for electronic submissions. Computer printout submissions OK. Reports in 1 weeks on queries; 2 weeks on mss. Free sample copy.

Nonfiction: Essays, historical/nostalgic, how-to, interview/profile and new product. "No meditations on "How I built my dream house," or anything we've already seen in *Better Homes and Gardens* and *Country Living*. Buys 35 mss/year. Query with or without published clips, or send complete ms. Length: 400-2,000 words. Pays $200-600 for assigned articles; pays $150-400 for unsolicited articles. Sometimes pays the expenses of writers on assignment.

Photos: State availability of photos with submission. Reviews 5x7 prints. Offers no additional payment for photos accepted with ms. Identification of subjects required. Buys one-time rights.

Columns/Departments: Mary-Jo Haronian, mail order products. A View From Our House (first-person thoughts and reminiscences on some concept of "home" in New England. Generally assigned), 400-800 words; The Advisor (concise, informational articles on trends, new products), 200-600 words. Buys 15 mss/year. Send complete ms. Pays $100-250.

Tips: "Feature articles that focus on unusual or new or atypical topics relating to homes in New England are most open to freelancers. Articles should be both entertaining and informative. In some cases, timeliness can be very important. *Yankee Homes* only publishes black and white photographs."

YOUR HOME, Meridian Publishing, Inc., Box 10010, Ogden UT 84409. (801)394-9446. Editor: Marjorie H. Rice. 65% freelance written. A monthly in-house magazine covering home/garden subjects. Circ. 112,000.

Pays on acceptance. Publishes ms an average of 8 months after acceptance. Byline given. Buys first rights and second serial (reprint) rights. Eight-month lead time. Submit seasonal material 10 months in advance. Simultaneous, photocopied and previously published submissions OK. Computer printout submissions acceptable; prefers letter-quality to dot-matrix. Reports in 6 weeks. Sample copy for $1 and 9x12 SAE; writer's guidelines for business size SASE. All requests for samples and guidelines should be addressed Attn: Editorial Assistant.

Nonfiction: General interest articles about fresh ideas in home decor, ranging from floor and wall coverings to home furnishings. Subject matter includes the latest in home construction (exteriors, interiors, building materials, design), the outdoors at home (landscaping, pools, patios, gardening), remodeling projects, home management and home buying and selling. Buys 40 mss/year. Length: 1,000-1,400 words. Pays 15¢/word for first rights plus nonexclusive reprint rights. Payment for second serial rights is negotiable.

Photos: State availability of photos with query. Reviews 35mm or larger transparencies and 5x7 or 8x10 "sharp, professional-looking" color prints. Pays $35 for inside photo; pays $50 for cover photo. Captions, model releases and identification of subjects required.

Tips: "The key is a well-written query letter that: (1) demonstrates that the subject of the article is practical and useful and has national appeal; (2) shows that the article will have a clear, focused theme and will be based on interviews with experts; (3) outlines the availability (from the writer, a photographer or a PR source) of top-quality color photos; (4) gives evidence that the writer/photographer is a professional."

Humor

Publications listed here specialize in gaglines or prose humor. Other publications that use humor can be found in nearly every category in this book. Some have special needs for major humor pieces; some use humor as fillers; many others are interested in material that meets their ordinary fiction or nonfiction requirements but has a humorous slant. Other markets for humorous material can be found in the Comic Books and Gag Writing sections. For a closer look at writing humor, consult *How to Write and Sell (Your Sense of) Humor*, by Gene Perret and *The Craft of Comedy Writing*, by Sol Saks (Writer's Digest Books).

LONE STAR HUMOR, Lone Star Publications of Humor, Suite 103, Box 29000, San Antonio TX 78229. (512)271-2632. Editor: Lauren I. Barnett. Less than 25% freelance written. Eager to work with new/unpublished writers. A humor book-by-subscription for "the general public and 'comedy connoisseur' as well as the professional humorist." Pays on publication, "but we try to pay before that." Publishes ms an average of 8 months after acceptance. Buys variable rights. Submit seasonal/holiday material 6 months in advance. Photocopied submissions and sometimes previously published work OK. Query for electronic submissions. Computer printout submission acceptable; no dot-matrix. Reports in 2 months on queries; 3 months on mss. Inquire for prices and availability of sample copy. Writer's guidelines for business size SASE.

Nonfiction: Humor (on anything topical/timeless); interview/profile (of anyone professionally involved in humor); and opinion (reviews of stand-up comedians, comedy plays, cartoonists, humorous books, *anything* concerned with comedy). "Inquire about possible theme issues." Buys 15 mss/year. Query with clips of published work if available. Length: 500-1,000 words; average is 700-800 words. Pays $5-20 and contributor's copy.

Fiction: Humorous. Buys variable mss/year. Send complete ms. Length: 500-1,000 words. Pays $5-20 and contributor's copy.

Poetry: Free verse, light verse, traditional, clerihews and limericks. "Nothing too 'artsy' to be funny." Buys 10-20/year. Submit maximum 5 poems. Length: 4-16 lines. Inquire for current rates.

Fillers: Clippings, jokes, gags, anecdotes, short humor and newsbreaks—"must be humorous or humor-related." Buys 20-30 mss/year. Length: 450 words maximum. Inquire for current rates.

Tips: "Our needs for freelance material will be somewhat diminished; writers should inquire (with SASE) before submitting material. We will be generating more and more of our humor inhouse, but will most likely require freelance material for books and other special projects. If the words 'wacky, zany, or crazy' describe the writer's finished product, it is *not* likely that his/her piece will suit our needs. The best humor is just slightly removed from reality."

MAD MAGAZINE, E.C. Publications, 485 Madison Ave., New York NY 10022. (212)752-7685. Editors: John Ficarra and Nick Meglin. 100% freelance written. Magazine published 8 times/year on humor, all forms.

Close-up

Robert Orben
Editor
Orben's Current Comedy

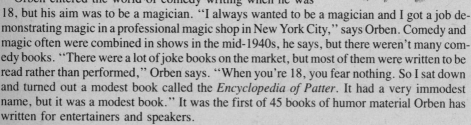

You may not know Robert Orben, but he's probably made you laugh.

His 40-year comedy writing career has spanned show business, politics and business. Orben continues to provide public speakers with material through his bimonthly humor newsletter, *Orben's Current Comedy*.

Orben entered the world of comedy writing when he was 18, but his aim was to be a magician. "I always wanted to be a magician and I got a job demonstrating magic in a professional magic shop in New York City," says Orben. Comedy and magic often were combined in shows in the mid-1940s, he says, but there weren't many comedy books. "There were a lot of joke books on the market, but most of them were written to be read rather than performed," Orben says. "When you're 18, you fear nothing. So I sat down and turned out a modest book called the *Encyclopedia of Patter*. It had a very immodest name, but it was a modest book." It was the first of 45 books of humor material Orben has written for entertainers and speakers.

In the 1960s, Orben wrote for Jack Paar in New York, then moved to Hollywood to write for the Red Skelton Hour. He became a consultant to Congressman Gerald Ford and when Ford became President, Orben was named a speechwriter and eventually director of the White House speechwriting department. Whether it's for entertainment, business or politics, Orben says humor "is a tool people use to reach out to an audience, make the audience like them, and make the audience listen." In each area, "there are certain similarities, but each provides its own unique challenges. A lot of jokes Red Skelton could do wouldn't work for a businessman or the President."

Now settled in Arlington, Virginia, Orben continues to speak to business and communications groups nationwide while editing *Orben's Current Comedy*. "You can't write humor in a vacuum," Orben says. "You have to know what a live audience will respond to. A lot of people watch situation comedies on television and that's where they get their ideas of what's funny and what's not. The only problem with that is many of them are not shot before a live audience. And even when they are, a laugh track is added."

Writers for *Current Comedy* must keep the live audience in mind, Orben says. "*Current Comedy* requires a special approach. This service is meant to be used by speakers, performers, ministers and politicians—anyone who has to stand up and say a few words or give regular speeches. It has to be performable and get an out-and-out laugh from listeners. This is the hardest part about writing performable comedy. Smiles don't make it."

Orben doesn't consider sexist, off-color material, ethnic jokes, puns or poems, and all material must be original. "Make sure you send what the market needs and not just what you're working on at the time," he urges. A good comedy writer also will do material in front of a live audience or sit in an audience to listen to the reaction, Orben says. Finally, Orben urges writers to work on the construction of their comedy writing. "It is the hardest aspect to learn and takes years of trial and error and practical experience to acquire," he says. "I've been in the business 40 years and I'm still learning."

—*Glenda Tennant Neff*

Circ. 1½ million. Pays on acceptance. Publishes ms an average of 6 months after acceptance. Byline given. Buys all rights. Submit seasonal/holiday material 6 months in advance. Photocopied submissions OK. Computer printout submissions acceptable; prefers letter-quality to dot-matrix. Reports in 1 month. Writer's guidelines for business size SASE.

Nonfiction: Humor. "We're always on the lookout for new ways to look at hot trends—music, computers, etc." No text pieces. "No formats we're already doing or have done to death like . . . 'You know you're _____ when . . .'." Buys 400 mss/year. Query or send complete ms. Pays $300/*MAD* page. Sometimes pays the expenses of writers on assignment.

Columns/Departments: Don Martin and department ideas. Buys 30 mss/year. Send complete ms. Pays $300/MAD page.

Fiction: Humorous. No text pieces. "We're a visually-oriented magazine." Buys 100 mss/year. Query or send complete ms. Pays $300/MAD page.

Poetry: Free verse, light verse, traditional and parody. Buys 20/year. Pays $300/*MAD* page.

Fillers: Short humor. Buys 100/year. Pays $300/*MAD* page.

Tips: "Freelancers can best break into our magazine with nontopical material (no movie or TV spoofs). If we see even a germ of talent, we will work with that person. We like outrageous but *clean* humor."

NATIONAL LAMPOON, National Lampoon Inc., 635 Madison Ave., New York NY 10022. (212)688-4070. Executive Editor: Larry Sloman. 50% freelance written. Works with small number of new unpublished writers each year. But "We are backlogged with submissions and prefer not to receive unsolicited submissions at this time." A bimonthly magazine of "offbeat, irreverent satire." Circ. 400,000. Pays on acceptance. Publishes ms an average of 4 months after acceptance. Byline given. Offers 20% kill fee. Buys first North American serial rights. Simultaneous submissions OK. Computer printout submissions acceptable; prefers letter-quality to dot-matrix. Reports in 2-3 months. Sample copy $3.95 with SAE.

Nonfiction: Humor. Buys 60 mss/year. Query with published clips. Length: approximately 2,000 words. Pays 20-40¢/word. Pays the expenses of writers on assignment.

Columns/Departments: John Bendel, column/department editor. True Facts (weird true-life stories). Special True Facts issue during first quarter of each year. Buys 240/year. Send complete ms. Length: 200 words maximum. Pays $10/item; $20/photo. Offers t-shirt for ideas, $10 and t-shirt for photos.

Tips: "We use very few new freelancers for major articles." True Facts section is most open to freelancers.

ORBEN'S CURRENT COMEDY, 1200 N. Nash St., #1122, Arlington VA 22209. (703)522-3666. Editor: Robert Orben. Biweekly. For "speakers, toastmasters, businessmen, public relations people, communications professionals." Pays at the end of the month for material used in issues published that month. Buys all rights. Computer printout submissions acceptable. "Unused material will be returned to the writer within a few days if SASE is enclosed. We do not send rejection slips. If SASE is not enclosed, all material will be destroyed after being considered except for items purchased."

Fillers: "We are looking for funny, performable one-liners, short jokes and stories that are related to happenings in the news, fads, trends and topical subjects. The accent is on laugh-out-loud comedy. Ask yourself, 'Will this line get a laugh if performed in public?' Material should be written in a conversational style, and if the joke permits it, the inclusion of dialogue is a plus. We are particularly interested in material that can be used by speakers and toastmasters: lines for beginning a speech, ending a speech, acknowledging an introduction, specific occasions, anything that would be of use to a person making a speech. We can use lines to be used at roasts, sales meetings, presentations, conventions, seminars and conferences. Short, sharp comment on business trends, fads and events is also desirable. Please do not send us material that's primarily written to be read rather than spoken. We have little use for definitions, epigrams, puns, etc. The submissions must be original. If material is sent to us that we find to be copied or rewritten from some other source, we will no longer consider material from the contributor. Material should be typed and submitted on standard size paper. Leave three spaces between each item." Pays $8.

Tips: "Follow the instructions in our guidelines. Although they are quite specific, we have received everything from epic poems to serious novels."

‡THE P.U.N., Play on Words, The Silly Club, Box 536-583, Orlando FL 32853. (305)898-0463. Editor: Danno Sullivan. 15% freelance written. Eager to work with new/unpublished writers. A bimonthly newsletter for a nonexistant organization, The Silly Club. "The P.U.N. readers enjoy humor bordering on intellectual, all the way down or up to just plain silliness. Politeness, though, above all." Circ. 250. Pays on acceptance. Publishes ms an average of 2 months after acceptance. Byline given "listed in credits." Buys one-time rights. Submit seasonal/holiday material 1-2 months in advance. Simultaneous, photocopied and previously published material OK. Computer printout submissions OK; prefers letter-quality. Reports in 3 weeks on mss. Sample copy for business size SAE.

Nonfiction: Humor. "Nothing rude, no foul language and no naughty things." Buys 10-25 mss/year. Send complete ms. Length: 10-2,000 words. Pays $1-25 for unsolicited articles.

Columns/Departments: Letters to the Emperor (usually concerning past P.U.N. articles, but frequently not), 100 words; Write That Story (an occasional feature, which invites readers to write the next short chapter of an ongoing story), 1,000 words. Buys 10-15 mss/year. Send complete ms. Length: 10-100 words. Pays $1-25.

Fiction: Humorous. Buys 3-5 mss/year. Send complete ms. Length: 10-2,000 words. Pays $1-25. Also single panel cartoons.

Poetry: Humorous poetry. Buys 5 poems/year. Submit maximum 10 poems. Pays $1-10.

Fillers: Gags and short humor. Buys 15/year. Pays $1-25.

TRIFLE MAGAZINE, Imaginary News Reported by Real People, Box 182, Dover NH 03820. (603)749-5114. Editor: Mary Pat Kingsbury. 100% freelance written. "We work with published and unpublished writers." A semiannual magazine of humorous fictional news. "*Trifle Magazine* presents a satirical version of our nation's most venerable news magazines using standard news magazine format." Circ. 50,000. Pays on publication. Publishes ms an average of 4 months after acceptance. Byline given. Buys one-time rights. Previously published submissions OK. Computer printout submissions acceptable. Reports in 4 months on mss. Sample copy $3; writer's guidelines for letter size SASE.

Photos: Black and white prints, and illustrations should accompany ms.

Columns/Departments: Spouting Off (writers vent frustrations, disillusionment, etc. on social issues, daily life, the human condition—nonfiction with a humorous tone) 150-750 words; and Newsnotes (brief, fictional news items) 100-200 words. Buys 15 mss/year. Send complete ms. Pays $15-75.

Fiction: Adventure, ethnic, fantasy, historical, humorous, mainstream, mystery, religious, science fiction, slice-of-life vignettes, fictional book, movie, music, concert, theatre, reviews, and fictional articles on politics and world events. All categories should be written in news article format. "No sex, violence or discussion of abortion. Material should be in good taste. We aim to make people laugh out loud." Buys 50 mss/year. Send complete ms. Length: 200-2,000 words. Pays $25-150.

Poetry: Avant-garde, free verse, light verse and traditional. Nothing serious, erotic, violent or melancholy. Poetry is used as filler. Buys 5 poems/year. Length: 20 lines maximum. Pays $10-25.

Fillers: Illustrated gags (illustration must accompany ms) and short humor. Buys 10/year. Length: 25-50 words. Pays $10-25.

Tips: "Because of the unusual nature of *Trifle* we suggest writers see a copy before submitting material. The mistake most often made is submission of newpaper style rather than magazine style reporting. We are very approachable, but we do appreciate good organization, neatness, and correct grammar and spelling."

In-flight

Most major in-flight magazines cater to business travelers and vacationers who will be reading, during the flight, about the airline's destinations and other items of general interest. Airline mergers and acquisitions have affected these magazines. The writer should watch for airline announcements in the news and in ads and read newest sample copies and writer's guidelines for current information.

AIR WISCONSIN, MIDSTATE, JET AMERICA, MIDWAY AIRLINES, FLIGHT CRAFT, GOLDEN PACIFIC, GREAT AMERICAN AIRWAYS, HORIZON AIR, SAN JUAN AIRWAYS, SCENIC AIRWAYS, WINGS WEST and WEST AIR ,Skies America Publishing Co., 9600 SW Oak St., Portland OR 97223. (503)244-2299. Editor: Robert E. Patterson. Managing Editor: Anne Siegel. 80% freelance written. Works with a small number of new/unpublished writers each year. Monthly and bimonthly inflight magazines for regional airlines in the United States and the Virgin Islands. "Our readers are affluent (median income is $40,159; 72% own property in excess of $100,000), well-educated (49% engaged in postgraduate study), businessmen/executives (78% are in professional/technical and managerial/administration fields), with a wide variety of interests and activities." Circ. 1.5 million. Pays on publication. Publishes ms an average of 3 months after acceptance. Byline given. Offers $50 kill fee. Buys first serial rights. Submit seasonal/holiday material 3 months in advance. Simultaneous queries OK. Computer printout submissions acceptable. Reports in 2 weeks. Sample copy for 8½x11 SAE and $3; writer's guidelines for business size SASE.

Nonfiction: Attractions in the West, Midwest, Florida, the Virgin Islands, and most major air hub cities: business, city features, general interest, health/medicine, historical, investing, humor, corporate profile, interview/profile, new product, photo feature, sports, technical and travel. Buys 60 mss/year. Query. Length:

1,000-1,500 words. Pays $200-400. Sometimes pays the expenses of writers on assignment.

Photos: Prefers that photography accompany articles. State availability of photos. Reviews 35mm transparencies. Pays $25-50 for b&w and color photos. Captions and identification of subjects required. Buys one-time rights.

Tips: We would like to see colorful profiles of entrepreneurs, local celebrities and unusual businesses in Miami, Minneapolis, Cleveland, Boston, New York, Indianapolis, Washington, D.C., Detroit, Kansas City, the U.S. Virgin Islands, New Orleans, Dallas, Chicago, Denver, Las Vegas and Atlanta.

AMERICA WEST AIRLINES MAGAZINE, Skyword Marketing, Inc., Suite 236, 7500 N. Dreamy Draw Dr., Phoenix AZ 85020. (602)997-7200. Editor: Michael Derr. Assistant Editor: Donald Slutes. 80% freelance written. Works with small number of new/unpublished writers each year. A monthly "general interest magazine emphasizing the western and southwestern U.S. Some midwestern, northwestern and eastern subjects also appropriate. We look for ideas and people that celebrate opportunity, and those who put it to positive use." Estab. 1986. Pays on publication. Publishes ms an average of 4 months after acceptance. Byline given. Offers 33% kill fee. Buys first North American rights. Submit seasonal/holiday material 6-8 months in advance. Simultaneous submissions OK, "if indicated as such." Query for electronic submissions. Computer printout submissions OK; prefers letter quality to dot-matrix. Reports in 1 month on queries; 5 weeks on mss. Sample copy for $2; writer's guidelines for 9x12 SAE with 56¢ postage.

Nonfiction: General interest, creative leisure, events, profile, photo feature, science, sports, travel and trends. Also considers essays, how-to and humor. No puzzles, reviews or highly controversial features. Buys 72-80 mss/year. Query with published clips. Length: 500-2,200. Pays $200-750. Pays some expenses.

Photos: State availability of photos. Offers $25-250/photo. Captions, model releases and identification of subjects required. Buys one-time rights.

Columns/Departments: All need strong regional connections. Achievers (mini-profiles of entrepreneurs); Dateline (one aspect of travel); Wild West (natural resources). Buys 30-40 mss/year. Query with published clips. Length: 500-1,500 words. Pays $200-350.

Fiction: Will consider exceptional pieces with a regional slant. No horror, inspirational or political. Send complete ms. Length: 800-1,800. Pays $200-500.

AMERICAN WAY, Mail Drop 2G23, Box 619616, Dallas/Fort Worth Airport TX 75261-9616. (817)355-1583. Editor: Charles Marsh. 98% freelance written. Prefers to work with published/established writers. Fortnightly inflight magazine for passengers flying with American Airlines. Pays on acceptance. Publishes ms an average of 6 months after acceptance. Buys exclusive world rights; splits reprint fee 50/50 with the author. Simultaneous queries and photocopied submissions OK. Computer printout submissions acceptable; prefers letter-quality to dot-matrix. Free sample copy; writer's guidelines for SASE.

Nonfiction: Business and CEO profiles, the arts and entertainment, sports, personalities, technology, food, science and medicine, and travel. "We are amenable to almost any subject that would be interesting, entertaining or useful to a passenger of American Airlines." Also humor, trivia, trends, and will consider a variety of ideas. Buys 300-350 mss/year. Query with published clips. Length: 2,500 words. Pays $500 and up; shorter items earn $100 or more. Sometimes pays the expenses of writers on assignment.

Photos: Pays $50 for each published photograph made by a writer while researching an article.

DELTA SKY, Inflight Magazine of Delta Air Lines, Halsey Publishing Co., 12955 Biscayne Blvd., N. Miami FL 33181. (305)893-1520. Editor: Lidia de Leon. 90% freelance written. "*Delta Sky* is a monthly general-interest magazine with a business/finance orientation thats main purpose is to entertain and inform business travelers aboard Delta Air Lines." Circ. 410,000. Pays on acceptance. Publishes ms an average of 2 months after acceptance. Byline given. Offers 100% kill fee when cancellation through no fault of writer. Buys first North American serial rights. Submit seasonal/holiday material 9 months in advance. Simultaneous and photocopied submissions OK. Computer printout submissions acceptable; prefers letter-quality to dot-matrix. Reports in 1 month. Sample copy for 9x12 SAE; free writer's guidelines.

Nonfiction: General interest. No reprints, religious or first-person/experiential. Buys 160 mss/year. Query with published clips. Length: 1,500-2,500 words. Pays $350-600 for assigned articles; pays $300-500 for unsolicited articles. Pays expenses of writers on assignment.

Photos: State availability of photos with submission. Reviews 5x7 prints. Offers $25-100/photo. Captions, model releases and identification of subjects required. Buys one-time rights.

Columns/Departments: On Management (managerial techniques/methods with current appeal), 1,700 words. Query with published clips. Pays $300-400.

Tips: "Send a comprehensive, well-detailed query tied in to one of the feature categories of the magazine, along with clips of previously published work. Since our lead times call for planning of editorial content 6-9 months in advance, that should also be kept in mind when proposing story ideas. We are always open to good feature-story ideas that have to do with business and technology. Next in order of priority would be leisure, sports, entertainment and consumer topics."

‡**EASTERN REVIEW**, In-flight Magazine for Eastern Airlines, 34 E. 51st Street, New York NY 10022. (212)888-5900. Editor: John Atwood. 10% freelance written. Monthly magazine. *"Eastern Review* features reprinted articles from national consumer magazines." Circ. 360,000. Pays on acceptance. Publishes ms an average of 3 months after acceptance. Byline given. Buys second serial (reprint) rights. Submit seasonal/holiday material 3 months in advance. Simultaneous, photocopied and previously published submissions OK. Reports in 2 months. Sample copy $3.

Nonfiction: Book excerpts, general interest (on New York, Boston, Washington D.C.), historical/nostalgic (on New York, Boston, Washington D.C.), travel to South America. Buys 15 mss/year. Query with published clips. Length: 1,500-2,500 words. Pays $300-600 for assigned articles; pays $200-800 for unsolicited articles. Pays expenses of writers on assignment.

Photos: State availability of photos with submission. Identification of subjects required. Buys one-time rights.

‡**ECHELON, The Magazine For Corporate Executives**, Halsey Publishing Co., 12955 Biscayne Blvd., North Miami FL 33181. (305)893-1520. Editor: Debra Silver. 95% freelance written. Monthly general interest magazine for upscale audience; distributed by Butler Aviation to corporate executives. Estab. 1986. Circ. 40,000. Pays 1 month prior to publication. Publishes ms an average of 2 months after acceptance. Byline given. Negotiable kill fee. Buys first North American serial rights. Simultaneous submissions OK. Computer printout submissions OK; prefers letter-quality to dot-matrix. Reports in 1-2 months. Sample copy $3.

Nonfiction: Essays, expose, general interest, historical/nostalgic, humor, interview/profile, personal experience, photo feature, technical and travel. "Since the audience is intelligent and refined, so is the editorial content. Business orientation is fine but our focus includes artistic, historical, educational and current events." Buys 90 mss/year. Query with published clips, or send complete ms. Length: 2,000-2,500 words. Pays $500 for assigned articles.

Photos: State availability of photos with submission. Reviews transparencies. Identification of subjects required.

Fiction: Adventure, ethnic, experimental, fantasy, historical, horror, humorous, mainstream, mystery, science fiction, slice-of-life vignettes, suspense and western. Query. Length: 2,000-2,500 words. Pays $500.

Tips: The editor offers encouragement and will consider submissions that are in accord with the editorial focus of *Echelon*. All feature sections are open to freelancers. Remember that *Echelon's* audience is comprised of upscale business executives whose range of interest is diverse.

MIDWAY MAGAZINE, Skies America Publishing Co., Suite 310, 9600 S.W. Oak St., Portland OR 97223. (503)244-2299. Editor: Robert Patterson. Managing Editor: Ann Siegel. 75% freelance written. Monthly magazine. Estab. 1986. Circ. approximately 40,000. Pays on publication. Publishes ms an average of 2 months after acceptance. Byline given. Offers $50 kill fee. Buys one-time rights. Submit seasonal/holiday material 6 months in advance. Simultaneous submissions OK. Computer printout submissions acceptable; prefers letter-quality to dot-matrix. Reports in 1 month. Sample copy $3 with SASE; writer's guidelines for SASE.

Nonfiction: Interview/profile, photo feature and travel. "Business features should be timely, well-researched and well-focused. Corporate profiles and personality profiles are encouraged. Travel destination pieces should be original, detailed and lively. No stale pieces that sound like canned promotions." Buys 24 mss/year. Query with published clips. Length: 1,000-2,500 words. Pays $150-400 for assigned articles; pays $150-250 for unsolicited articles. Sometimes pays the expenses of writers on assignment.

Photos: Send photos with submission. Reviews color transparencies and 8x10 b&w prints. Offers no additional payment for photos accepted with ms. Identification of subjects required. Buys one-time rights.

Columns/Departments: Epicure (food department focusing on regional cuisines or individual restaurants that are unusual or outstanding). Buys 10 mss/year. Query with published clips. Length: 1,000-1,500 words. Pays $150-300.

Tips: "The cities we focus on are: New York; Boston; Chicago; Indianapolis; Miami; Minneapolis; Dallas; Cleveland; Detroit; New Orleans; Washington, D.C.; Orlando; Virgin Isands; Cincinnati; Kansas City; Philadelphia; Las Vegas; Denver and Atlanta. Write to us with specific ideas relating to these cities. A fresh, original idea with excellent photo possibilities will receive our close attention. Areas most open to freelancers are corporate profiles; destination travel pieces with an unusual slant; personality profiles on businessmen and women, entrepreneurs."

PACE MAGAZINE, Piedmont Airlines Inflight Magazine, Fisher-Harrison Publications Inc., 338 N. Elm St., Greensboro NC 27401. (919)378-6065. Editor: Davis A. March. Freelance written. Monthly magazine covering travel, trends in business for the present and the future and other business-related articles. Circ. 2.5 mlllon. Pays on acceptance. Publishes ms an average of 8 months after acceptance. Byline given. Buys first serial rights. Submit holiday/seasonal material 6 months in advance. Computer printout submissions acceptable; no dot-matrix. Reports in 2 months. Sample copy for $4 and SAE; writer's guidelines for SASE.

Nonfiction: Travel (within the Piedmont flight route), trends in business, business management, employee relations, business psychology and self-improvement as related to business and other business-related articles.

No personal, religious, historical, nostalgic, humor, or interview/profile pieces. No cartoons. Buys 40 mss/ year. Send query or complete ms. No telephone queries. Length: 1,500-4,000 words. Pays $100-750.
Photos: Send photos with accompanying ms. Captions required.
Tips: "Major features are assigned; I would rarely accept an unsolicited major feature. Writers frequently do not perceive the audience correctly—they must not be unfamiliar with our magazine."

‡PSA MAGAZINE, East/West Network, Inc., Suite 800, 5900 Wilshire Blvd., Los Angeles CA 90036. (213)937-5810. Editor: Al Austin. 90% freelance written. Monthly magazine; 140 pages. Pays within 60 days after acceptance. Buys first rights only. Pays 25% kill fee. Byline given. Submit seasonal/holiday material 4 months in advance of issue date. Simultaneous and photocopied submissions OK. Computer printout submissions acceptable; prefers letter-quality to dot-matrix. Publishes ms an average of 3 months after acceptance. Sample copy $2.
Nonfiction: Prefers California/West Coast slant. General interest; interview (top-level government, entertainment, sports figures); new product (trends, survey field); profile and business (with California and West Coast orientation). Buys 6 mss/issue. Query. Length: 500-2,000 words. Pays $150-800.
Photos: State availability of photos with query. Pays ASMP (American Society of Magazine Photographers) rates for b&w contact sheets or negatives and 35mm or 2¼x2¼ color transparencies. Captions required. Buys one-time rights. Model release required.
Columns/Departments: Business Trends. Buys 1 ms/issue. Query. Length: 700-1,500 words. Pays $250-500.

REVIEW MAGAZINE, Eastern Airline's Inflight Magazine, East/West Network, 34 E. 51st St., New York NY 10022. Editor: John Atwood. Associate Editor: Madeline Johnson. 30% freelance written. Prefers to work with published/established writers. Monthly magazine featuring reprints of articles previously published in leading consumer magazines, plus book excerpts and original articles. Circ. 1 million. Pays on acceptance. Publishes ms an average of 6 months after acceptance. Byline given. Buys one-time rights. Photocopied and previously published submissions should be submitted by original publication, not by individuals. Computer printout submissions acceptable; no dot-matrix. Reports in 2 weeks on queries; 3 weeks on mss. Sample copy $3.
Nonfiction: General interest, historical/nostalgic, humor, and photo feature. No how-to or violence-related material. Buys 40 mss/year. Query. Length: 2,000-3,000 words. Pays $500-750 for original articles. Sometimes pays the expenses of writers on assignment.
Photos: Nancy Campbell, art director. State availability of photos. Pays $75-600 for color transparencies; $75-500 for b&w prints. Identification of subjects required.
Tips: "We are always on the lookout for 2,000-word service and essay pieces on New York, Boston, and Washington, especially subjects of interest to passengers on Eastern Air-Shuttle."

‡SKIES AMERICA, Publisher for the Nation's Business Airlines, Suite 310, 9600 S.W. Oak St., Portland OR 97223. (503)244-2299. Editor: Robert E. Patterson. Managing Editor: Anne M. Siegel. 75% freelance written. Some editions published monthly; some published bimonthly. "Published primarily for educated business travelers." Circ. 1,500,000. Pays on publications. Publishes ms an averaged of 3 months after acceptance. Byline given. Offers kill fee of up to $100. Buys first North American serial rights and second serial (reprint) rights. Submit seasonal/holiday material 3 months in advance. Simultaneous, photocopied and previously published submissions OK. Reports in 3 weeks. Sample copy $3. Writer's guidelines for SASE.
Nonfiction: General interest, humor, interview/profile, new product, technical, and travel. No fiction. Buys 75 mss/year. Query with or without published clips. Length: 500-2,000 words. Pays $100-400. Sometimes pays expenses of writers on assignment.
Photos: State availability of photos with submission. Reviews transparencies (35mm and over) and prints. Offers $25-50/photo. Identification of subjects required. Buys "one time rights for all 12 magazines we publish."
Fillers: Facts, short humor. Buys 12/year. Length: 100-500 words. Pays $50-100.
Tips: "Most of our readers are businessmen under 45 years of age. Any business or vocational type article would be welcome."

‡SKY, Inflight Magazine of Delta Air Lines, Halsey Publishing Co., 12955 Biscayne Blvd., N. Miami FL 33181. (305)893-1520. Editor: Lidia De Leon. 90% freelance written. Monthly magazine. "Delta *SKY* is a general interest, nationally oriented magazine with a primary editorial focus on business and management, with the main purpose to entertain and inform business travelers aboard Delta Air Lines." Circ. 410,000. Pays on acceptance. Publishes ms an average of 2 months after acceptance. Byline given. Offers 100% kill fee when cancellation is through no fault of the writer. Buys first North American serial rights. Submit seasonal/holiday material 9 months in advance. Simultaneous and photocopied submissions OK. Computer printout submissions OK; prefers letter-quality to dot-matrix. Reports in 1 month. Sample copy for 9x12 SAE; free writer's guidelines.

Nonfiction: General interest and photo feature. "No excerpts, essays, personal experience, opinion, religious, reviews, poetry, fiction or fillers." Buys 200 mss/year. Query with published clips. Length: 1700-2500 words. Pays $300-500 for assigned articles; pays $300-450 for unsolicited articles. Pays expenses of writers on assignment.

Photos: State availability of photos with submission. Reviews transparencies (4x5) and prints (5x7). Offers $25-50/photo. Captions, model releases and identification of subject required. Buys one-time rights.

Columns/Departments: On Management (managerial techniques, methods of topical nature). Buys 40 mss/year. Query with published clips. Length: 1500-1800 words. Pays $300-400.

Tips: "Send a comprehensive, well detailed query tied in one of the feature categories of the magazine along with clips of previously published work. Since our lead times call for planning of editorial content 6-9 months in advance, that should also be kept in mind when proposing story ideas. We are always open to good feature story ideas that have to do with business and technology. Next in order of priority would be leisure, sports, entertainment and consumer topics. All feature story categories (Business, Lifestyle, Sports, Arts/Entertainment, Consumer, Technology, and Collectibles) are open to freelancers, with the exceptions of Travel (areas are predetermined by the airline) and the executive Profile Series (which is also predetermined)."

SOUTHWEST SPIRIT, East/West Network, Suite 800, 5900 Wilshire Blvd., Los Angeles CA 90036. (213)937-5810. Editor: Gabrielle Cosgriff. Assistant Editor: David Stolberg. 90% freelance written. Prefers to work with published/established writers. The monthly magazine of Southwest Airlines covering the Southwest, primarily Texas. Pays on acceptance. Publishes ms an average of 2 months after acceptance. Byline given. Offers 25% kill fee. Buys first North American serial rights. Simultaneous and photocopied submissions OK. Computer printout submissions acceptable; prefers letter-quality to dot-matrix. Reports in 1 month. Sample copy $3; writer's guidelines for SASE.

Nonfiction: Essays (issue-oriented); general interest; profile (business); new product (technology, medicine); photo feature (occasionally); travel (very limited); and sports. No historical/nostalgic, personal experience, or unsolicited travel pieces. Buys approximately 120 mss/year. Query with published clips. Length: 250-3,500 words. Pays $150-900. Pays the expenses of writers on assignment.

Photos: State availability of photos with submission. Reviews color transparencies and b&w prints. Identification of subjects required. Buys one-time rights.

Columns/Departments: Cutting Edge (new products, the arts, innovative businesses and ideas—"newsy and energetic"), 250-600 words; Wining & Dining (briefs on Southwest foods, wines, restaurants, chefs, etc.), 500-1,000 words; and Only In . . . (colorful essays on one-of-a-kind places and people in the Southwest), 1,000 words. Buys 60 mss/year. Query with published clips. Pays $150-350.

USAIR MAGAZINE, Halsey Publishing Co., 600 3rd Ave. New York NY 10016. Editor: Richard Busch. Senior Editor: Mark Orwoll. 95% freelance written. Prefers to work with published/established writers. A monthly general interest magazine published for airline passengers, many of whom are business travelers, male, with high incomes and college educations. Circ. 200,000. Pays on acceptance. Publishes ms an average of 4 months after acceptance. Buys first rights only. Submit seasonal material 6 months in advance. Photocopied submissions OK. Computer printout submissions acceptable; prefers letter-quality to dot-matrix. Reports in 2 weeks. Sample copy $3; free writer's guidelines with SASE.

Nonfiction: Travel, business, sports, health, food, personal finance, nature, the arts, science/technology and photography. "No downbeat stories or controversial articles." Buys 100 mss/year. Query with clips of previously published work. Length: 1,500-2,800 words. Pays $400-750. Pays expenses of writers on assignment.

Photos: Send photos with ms. Pays $75-150/b&w print, depending on size; color from $100-250/print or slide. Captions preferred; model release required. Buys one-time rights.

Columns/Departments: Sports, food, money, health, business, living and science. Buys 3-4 mss/issue. Query. Length: 1,200-1,800 words. Pays $300-450.

Tips: "Send irresistible ideas and proof that you can write. It's great to get a clean manuscript from a good writer who has given me exactly what I asked for. Frequent mistakes are not following instructions, not delivering on time, etc."

Juvenile

Just as children change and grow, so do juvenile magazines. Children's magazine editors stress that writers must read recent issues. This section lists publications for children ages 2-12. Magazines for young people 13-19 appear in the Teen and Young Adult category. Many of the following publications are produced by religious groups and, where possible, the specific denomination is given. For the writer with a story or article slanted to a specific age group, the following children's index is a quick reference to markets for each age group.

Juvenile publications classified by age

Two- to Five-Year Olds: *Chickadee, Children's Playmate, The Friend, Highlights for Children, Humpty Dumpty, Our Little Friend, Owl, Turtle Magazine for Preschool Kids, Wee Wisdom.*
Six- to Eight-Year Olds: *Boys' Life, Chickadee, Child Life, The Children's Album, Children's Digest, Children's Playmate, Cobblestone, Cricket, Discoveries, The Dolphin Log, The Electric Company, Faces, The Friend, Highlights for Children, Humpty Dumpty, Jack and Jill, National Geographic World, Noah's Ark, Odyssey, Our Little Friend, Owl, Pennywhistle Press, Pockets, Primary Treasure (see Our Little Friend), RADAR, Ranger Rick, 3-2-1 Contact, Touch, Wee Wisdom, Young American, Young Author.*
Nine- to Twelve-Year Olds: *Action, Boys' Life, Chickadee, Child Life, The Children's Album, Children's Digest, Clubhouse, Cobblestone, Cricket, Current Health I, Discoveries, The Dolphin Log, The Electric Company, Enfantaisie, Faces, The Friend, High Adventure, Highlights for Children, Junior Trails, National Geographic World, Noah's Ark, Odyssey, On the Line, Owl, Pennywhistle Press, Pockets, Primary Treasure (see Our Little Friend), RADAR, Ranger Rick, 3-2-1 Contact, Touch, Venture, Wee Wisdom, Young American, Young Author.*

ACTION, Dept. of Christian Education, Free Methodist Headquarters, 901 College Ave., Winona Lake IN 46590. (219)267-7656. Editor: Vera Bethel. 100% freelance written. Weekly magazine for "57% girls, 43% boys, ages 9-11; 48% city, 23% small towns." Circ. 25,000. Pays on publication. Rights purchased vary; may buy simultaneous rights, second (reprint) rights or first North American serial rights. Submit seasonal/holiday material 3 months in advance. Simultaneous and previously published submissions OK. Computer printout submissions acceptable; no dot-matrix. SASE must be enclosed. Reports in 1 month. Free sample copy and writer's guidelines for 6x9 SASE.
Nonfiction: How-to (make gifts and craft articles); informational (nature articles with pictures); and personal experience (my favorite vacation, my pet, my hobby, etc.). Buys 50 mss/year. Submit complete ms with photos. Length: 200-500 words. Pays $15.
Fiction: Adventure, humorous, mystery and religious. Buys 50 mss/year. Submit complete ms. Length: 1,000 words. Pays $25. SASE must be enclosed; no return without it.
Poetry: Free verse, haiku, light verse, traditional, devotional and nature. Buys 20/year. Submit maximum 5-6 poems. Length: 4-16 lines. Pays $5.
Tips: "Send interview articles with children about their pets, their hobbies, a recent or special vacation—all with pictures if possible. Kids like to read about other kids. A frequent mistake made by writers is using words too long for a 10-year-old and *too many* long words."

BOYS' LIFE, Boy Scouts of America, 1325 Walnut Hill Lane, Irving TX 75038-3096. Editor-in-chief: William B. McMorris. 75% freelance written. Prefers to work with published/established writers; works with small number of new/unpublished writers each year. Monthly magazine covering activities of interest to all boys ages 8-18. Most readers are Scouts or Cub Scouts. Circ 1.4 million. Pays on acceptance. Publishes ms an average of 6-12 months after acceptance. Buys one-time rights. Computer printout submissions OK; prefers letter-quality to dot-matrix. Reports in 2 weeks. Sample copy for 9x12 SAE and $1 postage.
Nonfiction: Major articles run 1,200-2,000 words; preferred length is about 1,500 words. Pays minimum $500 for text. Uses strong photo features with about 750 words of text; pays minimum $350 for text. Separate payment or assignment for photos. "Much better rates if your really know how to write for our market." Buys 60 major articles/year. Also needs how-to features and hobby and crafts ideas. "We pay top rates for ideas accompanied by sharp photos, clean diagrams, and short, clear instructions." Query first in writing. Buys 30-40 how-tos/year. Query all nonfiction ideas in writing. Pays expenses of writers on assignment. Also buys freelance comics pages and scripts. Query first.
Columns: "Food, Health, Pets, Bicycling and Magic Tricks are some of the columns for which we use 500-750 words of text. This is a good place to show us what you can do. Query first in writing." Pays $150 minimum. Buys 75-80 columns/year.
Fiction: Short stories 1,500 words; occasionally longer. Send complete ms. Pays $500 minimum. Buys 15 short stories/year.
Tips: "We strongly recommend reading at least 12 issues of the magazine and learning something about the

programs of the Boy Scouts of America before you submit queries. We are a good market for any writer willing to do the necessary homework."

CHICKADEE MAGAZINE, For Young Children from *OWL*, The Young Naturalist Foundation, 56 The Esplanade, Suite 306, Toronto, Ontario M5E 1A7 Canada. (416)868-6001. Editor: Janis Nostbakken. 25% freelance written. Magazine published 10 times/year (except July and August) for 4-9 year-olds. "We aim to interest young children in the world around them in an entertaining and lively way." Circ. 100,00 Canada; 50,000 U.S. Pays on publication. Byline given. Buys all rights. Submit seasonal/holiday material up to 1 year in advance. Computer printout submissions acceptable. Reports in 2½ months. Sample copy for $1.95 and IRCs; writer's guidelines for IRC.
Nonfiction: How-to (arts and crafts for children); personal experience (real children in real situations); and photo feature (wildlife features). No articles for older children; no religious or moralistic features. Sometimes pays the expenses of writers on assignment.
Photos: Send photos with ms. Reviews 35mm transparencies. Identification of subjects required.
Fiction: Adventure (relating to the 4-9 year old). No science fiction, fantasy, talking animal stories or religious articles. Send complete ms. Pays $100-300.
Tips: "A frequent mistake made by writers is trying to teach too much—not enough entertainment and fun."

‡CHILD LIFE, Children's Better Health Institute, 1100 Waterway Blvd Box 567, Indianapolis IN 46206. (317)636-8881. Editor: Steve Charles. 80% freelance written. Monthly (except bimonthly Feb/Mar, Apr/May, June/July, August/September) magazine covering "children—some health oriented." Pays on publication. Publishes ms an average of 8 months after acceptance. Byline given. Buys all rights. Submit seasonal/holiday material 8 months in advance. Photocopied submissions OK. Computer printout submissions OK; prefers letter-quality to dot-matrix. Reports in 3 months. Sample copy 75¢; writer's guidelines for SASE.
Nonfiction: How-to (simple crafts), anything children might like—health topics preferred. Buys 20 mss/year. Send complete ms. Length: 400-1,500. Pays 6¢/word (approx). "Readers chosen for Young Author Story receive copies."
Photos: Send photos with submission. Reviews transparencies and prints. Offers $10 for inside b&w; $20 for inside color photo, $50 for front cover. Captions, model releases and identification of subjects required. Buys one time rights.
Fiction: Adventure, ethnic, fantasy, historical, humorous, mystery, science fiction and suspense. All must be geared to children. Health-related fiction stories preferred (explain how character handles disease, how character's health is reinforced by good habits, etc.). Buys 20-25 mss/year. Send complete ms. Length: 500-1,800 words. Pays 6¢/word (approx).
Poetry: Free verse, haiku, light verse and traditional. No long "deep" poetry not suited for children. Buys 4-5 poems/year. Submit maximum 5 poems. "We have used some verse 'stories'—500+ words." Pays approx. 50¢/line.
Fillers: We do accept puzzles, games, mazes, etc." Variable pay.
Tips: "Present health related items in an interesting, non-textbook manner. The approach to health fiction can be subtle—tell a good story first. We also consider non-health items—makes them fresh and enjoyable for children."

‡THE CHILDREN'S ALBUM, Incorporating *Butterflies* (poetry), and *Children's Crafts*, EGW Publishing Co., Box 6086, Concord CA 94524. (415)671-9852. Literary Editor: Debra Wittenberg. Literary Crafts Editor: Kathy Madsen. Managing Editor: Wayne Lin. 95% freelance written. A quarterly magazine of stories and plays written for children ages 8-14. "Adult input includes discussion of writing techniques, terms and examples, book reviews and fillers (anagrams, cartoons, etc.) on literature, writing or other topics of general education." Pays on publication. Publishes ms an average of 1 year after acceptance. Byline given. Buys all rights. Submit seasonal/holiday material 6 months in advance. Simultaneous and photocopied submissions OK. Reports in 2 months on mss. Sample copy $3; writer's guidelines for letter-size SASE.
Nonfiction: *Open to all adults.* How-to (on improving your writing, overcoming writer's block); technical (writing tips); book reviews and literary terms defined and exemplified. "We cannot accept any articles on creative writing that are too erudite. Our readers are children ages 8-14." Buys 15 mss/year. Send complete ms. Length: 100-800 words. Pays $35/published page.
Columns/Departments: Write On! (tips for writing better fiction and poetry; thinking like a writer/poet; unblocking writer's block; stimulating creativity); Coming to Terms (literary terms defined, with examples). Buys 8 mss/year. Send complete ms. Length: 100-800 words. Pays $35/published page.
Fiction: *Open only to children 8-14.* Adventure, ethnic, experimental, fantasy, horror, humorous, mainstream, mystery, religious, romance, science fiction, slice-of-life vignettes, suspense and western. Length: 50-1,000 words.
Fillers: Anecdotes, facts, short humor, crossword puzzles, mazes, quizzes, sayings, anagrams and cartoons. Buys 30/year. Length: 100-100 words. Pays $5-20.
Tips: "We are writer-friendly. We review each submission carefully and encourage new writers. Children—use your imagination. Adults—remember we are geared to children 8-14."

CHILDREN'S DIGEST, Children's Better Health Institute, Box 567, Indianapolis IN 46206. (317)636-8881. Editor: Elizabeth Rinck. 85% freelance written. Works with a small number of new/unpublished writers each year. Magazine published 8 times/year covering children's health for children ages 8-10. Pays on publication. Publishes ms an average of 1 year after acceptance. Byline given. Buys all rights. Submit seasonal/holiday material 8 months in advance. Submit *only* complete manuscripts. "No queries, please." Photocopied submissions acceptable (if clear). Computer printout submissions acceptable; prefers letter-quality to dot-matrix. Reports in 2 months. Sample copy 75¢; writer's guidelines for business size SASE.

Nonfiction: Historical, interview/profile (biographical), craft ideas, health, nutrition, hygiene, exercise and safety. "We're especially interested in factual features that teach readers about the human body or encourage them to develop better health habits. We are *not* interested in material that is simply rewritten from encyclopedias. We try to present our health material in a way that instructs *and* entertains the reader." Buys 15-20 mss/year. Send complete ms. Length: 500-1,200 words. Pays 6¢/word. Sometimes pays the expenses of writers on assignment.

Photos: State availability of full color or b&w photos. Payment varies. Model releases and identification of subjects required. Buys one-time rights.

Fiction: Adventure, humorous, mainstream and mystery. Stories should appeal to both boys and girls. "We need some stories that incorporate a health theme. However, we don't want stories that preach, preferring instead stories with implied morals. We like a light or humorous approach." Buys 15-20 mss/year. Length: 500-1,800 words. Pays 6¢/word.

Poetry: Pays $7 minimum.

Tips: "Many of our readers have working mothers and/or come from single-parent homes. We need more stories that reflect these changing times while communicating good values."

CHILDREN'S PLAYMATE, 1100 Waterway Blvd., Box 567, Indianapolis IN 46206. (317)636-8881. Editor: Elizabeth Rinck. 75% freelance written. Eager to work with new/unpublished writers. "We are looking for articles, stories, and activities with a health, safety, exercise, or nutritionally oriented theme. Primarily we are concerned with preventative medicine. We try to present our material in a positive—not a negative—light, and we try to incorporate humor and a light approach wherever possible without minimizing the seriousness of what we are saying." For children ages 5-7. Magazine published 8 times/year. Buys all rights. Byline given. Pays on publication. Publishes ms an average of 1 year after acceptance. Submit seasonal material 8 months in advance. Computer printout submissions acceptable; prefers letter-quality to dot-matrix. Reports in 2 months. Sometimes may hold mss for up to 1 year, with author's permission. Write for guidelines. "Material will not be returned unless accompanied by a self-addressed envelope and sufficient postage." Sample copy 75¢; free writer's guidelines with SASE.

Nonfiction: Beginning science, 600 words maximum. A feature may be an interesting presentation on animals, people, events, objects or places, especially about good health, exercise, proper nutrition and safety. Include number of words in articles. Buys 30 mss/year. "We do not consider outlines. Reading the whole manuscript is the only way to give fair consideration. The editors cannot criticize, offer suggestions, or review unsolicited material that is not accepted." No queries. Pays about 6¢/word.

Fiction: Short stories for beginning readers, not over 700 words. Seasonal stories with holiday themes. Humorous stories, unusual plots. "We are interested in stories about children in different cultures and stories about lesser-known holidays (not just Christmas, Thanksgiving, Halloween, Hanukkah)." Vocabulary suitable for ages 5-7. Submit complete ms. Include number of words in stories. Pays about 6¢/word.

Fillers: Puzzles, dot-to-dots, color-ins, hidden pictures and mazes. Buys 30 fillers/year. Payment varies.

Tips: Especially interested in stories, poems and articles about special holidays, customs and events.

CLUBHOUSE, Your Story Hour, Box 15, Berrien Springs MI 49103. (616)471-3701. Editor: Elaine Meseraull. 75% freelance written. Works with a small number of new/unpublished writers each year. Magazine published 10 times/year covering many subjects with Christian approach, though not associated with a church. "Stories and features for fun for 9-14 year-olds. Main objective: To provide a psychologically 'up' magazine that lets kids know that they are acceptable, 'neat' people." Circ. 15,000. Pays on acceptance. Publishes ms an average of 1 year after acceptance. Byline given. Buys first serial rights or first North American serial rights, one-time rights, simultaneous rights, and second serial (reprint) rights. Simultaneous queries, and simultaneous, photocopied, and previously published submissions OK. Computer printout submissions acceptable; prefers letter-quality to dot-matrix. Reports in 3 weeks. Sample copy for 6x9 SAE and 3 first class stamps; writer's guidelines for business size SASE.

Nonfiction: How-to (crafts), personal experience and recipes (without sugar or artificial flavors and colors). "No stories in which kids start out 'bad' and by peer or adult pressure or circumstances are changed into 'good' people." Send complete ms. Length: 750-800 words ($25); 1,000-1,200 words ($30); feature story 1,200 words ($35).

Photos: Send photos with ms. Pays on publication according to published size. Buys one-time rights.

Columns/Departments: Body Shop (short stories or "ad" type material that is anti-smoking, drugs and alcohol and pro-good nutrition, etc.); and Jr. Detective (secret codes, word search, deduction problems, hidden pictures, etc.). Buys 20/year. Send complete ms. Length: 400 words maximum for Jr. Detective; 1,000 maximum for Body Shop. Pays $10-30.

Fiction: Adventure, historical, humorous and mainstream. "Stories should depict bravery, kindness, etc., without overt or preachy attitude." No science fiction, romance, confession or mystery. Buys 60 mss/year. Send query or complete ms (prefers ms). Length: 750-800 words ($20); 1,000-1,200 words ($30); lead story ($35).

Poetry: Free verse, light verse and traditional. Buys 8-10/year. Submit maximum 5 poems. Length: 4-24 lines. Pays $5-20.

Fillers: Cartoons. Buys 20/year. Pay $12 maximum.

Tips: "All material for any given year is accepted during April-May in the previous year. Think from a kid's point of view and ask, 'Would this story make me glad to be a kid?' Keep the stories moving, exciting, bright and tense. Stay within length guidelines."

COBBLESTONE, Cobblestone Publishing, Inc., 20 Grove St., Peterborough NH 03458. (603)924-7209. Editor-in-Chief: Carolyn P. Yoder. 100% freelance written (approximately 2 issues/year are by assignment only). Prefers to work with published/established writers; works with small number of new/unpublished writers each year. Monthly magazine covering American history for children ages 8-14. "Each issue presents a particular theme, approaching it from different angles, making it exciting as well as informative. Half of all subscriptions are for schools." Circ. 45,000. Pays on publication. Publishes ms an average of 4 months after acceptance. Byline given. Buys all rights; makes work-for-hire assignments. All material must relate to monthly theme. Simultaneous and previously published submissions OK. Computer printout submissions acceptable; prefers letter-quality to dot-matrix. Sample copy $3.95; writer's guidelines for SASE.

Nonfiction: Historical/nostalgic, how-to, interview, plays, biography, activities and personal experience. "Request a copy of the writer's guidelines to find out specific issue themes in upcoming months." No material that editorializes rather than reports. Buys 5-8 mss/issue. Length: 800-1,200 words. Supplemental nonfiction 200-800 words. Query with published clips, outline and bibliography. Pays up to 15¢/word. Rarely pays expenses of writers on assignment.

Fiction: Adventure, historical, humorous and biographical fiction. "Has to be very strong and accurate." Buys 1-2 mss/issue. Length: 800-1,200 words. Request free editorial guidelines that explain upcoming issue themes and give query deadlines. "Message" must be smoothly integrated with the story. Query with written samples. Pays up to 15¢/word.

Poetry: Free verse, light verse and traditional. Buys 6 mss/year. Submit maximum 2 poems. Length: 5-100 lines. Pays on an individual basis.

Tips: "All material is considered on the basis of merit and appropriateness to theme. Query should state idea for material simply, with rationale for why material is applicable to theme. Request writer's guidelines (includes themes and query deadlines) before submitting a query. Include SASE."

CRICKET, The Magazine for Children, Open Court Publishing Co., 315 5th St., Peru IL 61354. (815)224-6643. Editor: Marianne Carus. Monthly magazine. Circ. 120,000. Pays on publication. Byline given. Buys first North American serial rights. Submit seasonal/holiday material 8 months in advance. Photocopied and previously published submissions OK. Computer printout submissions acceptable; prefers letter-quality to dot-matrix. Reports in 2 months. Sample copy $2; writer's guidelines for SASE.

Nonfiction: Historical/nostalgic, lively science, personal experience travel and well-researched. Send complete ms. Length: 200-1,200 words. Pays $50-300.

Fiction: Adventure, ethnic, fantasy, historical, humorous, mystery, novel excerpts, science fiction, suspense and western. No didactic, sex, religious, or horror stories. Buys 24-36 mss/year. Send complete ms. Length: 200-1,500 words. Pays $50-375.

Poetry: Buys 8-10 poems/year. Length: 100 lines maximum. Pays $3/line on publication.

‡CURRENT HEALTH I, The Beginning Guide to Health Education, General Learning Corporation, 3500 Western Avenue, Highland Park IL 60035. (312)432-2700. Executive Editor: Laura Ruekberg. Associate Editor: Ellen Blum Barish. 95% freelance written. An educational health periodical. Published monthly 9 times per year, September-May. "Our audience is fourth through seventh grade health education students. Articles should be written at a fifth grade reading level. As a curriculum supplementary publication, info should be accurate, timely, accessible and highly readable." Circ. 100,000. Pays on publication. Publishes ms an average of 9 months after acceptance. Offers 50% kill fee. Buys all rights.

Nonfiction: General interest, interview/profile, new product, and educational. Buys 100 mss/year. "We accept no queries or unsolicited mss. *Articles are on assignment only.* Send introductory letter, resume and clips. Length: 800-2,000 words. Pays $100-700 for assigned articles. Sometimes pays expenses of writers on assignment.

Tips: "We are looking for good writers with an education and health background preferably, who can write for the age group in a firm, accessible and medically/scientifically accurate way. Ideally, the writer should be an expert in the area in which he or she is writing. Topics open to freelancers are disease, drugs, fitness and exercise, psychology, safety, nutrition and personal health. We are in need of drug writers in particuler."

‡**DISCOVERIES**, 6401 The Paseo, Kansas City MO 64131. Editor: Cheryl Turner. 75% freelance written. For boys and girls ages 9-12 in the Church of the Nazarene. Weekly. Publishes ms an average of 1 year after acceptance. Buys first serial rights and second (reprint) rights. "We process only letter-quality manuscripts; word processing with letter-quality printers acceptable. Minimal comments on pre-printed form are made on rejected material." Reports in 4 weeks. Guidelines for SAE with two first class stamps.
Fiction: Stories with Christian emphasis on high ideals, wholesome social relationships and activities, right choices, Sabbath observance, church loyalty, and missions. Informal style. Submit complete ms. Length: 500-700 words. Pays 3½¢/word for first serial rights and 2¢/word for second (reprint) rights.
Photos: Color photos only.
Tips: "The freelancer needs an understanding of the doctrine of the Church of the Nazarene and the Sunday school material for third to sixth graders."

THE DOLPHIN LOG, The Cousteau Society, 8440 Santa Monica Blvd., Los Angeles CA 90069. (213)656-4422. Editor: Pamela Stacey. 60% freelance written. Prefers to work with published/established writers; works with a small number of new/unpublished writers each year. Bimonthly magazine covering marine biology, ecology, environment, natural history, and water-related stories. "The *Dolphin Log* is an educational publication for children ages 7-15 offered by The Cousteau Society. Subject matter encompasses all areas of science, history and the arts which can be related to our global water system. The philosophy of the magazine is to delight, instruct and instill an environmental ethic and understanding of the interconnectedness of living organisms, including people." Circ. 60,000. Pays on publication. Publishes ms an average of 1 year after acceptance. Byline given. "We do not make assignments and therefore have no kill fee." Buys one-time and translation rights. Submit seasonal/holiday material 4 months in advance. Query for electronic submissions. Computer printout submissions acceptable; prefers letter-quality to dot-matrix. Reports in 2 months. Sample copy for $2 with 9x12 SAE and 56¢ postage; writer's guidelines for SASE.
Nonfiction: General interest (per guidelines); how-to (water-related crafts or science); personal experience (ocean related); and photo feature (marine subject). "Of special interest are articles on specific marine creatures, and games involving an ocean/water-related theme which develop math, reading and comprehension skills. Humorous articles and short jokes based on scientific fact are also welcome. Experiments that can be conducted at home and demonstrate a phenomenon or principle of science are wanted as are clever crafts or art projects which also can be tied to an ocean theme. Try to incorporate such activities into any articles submitted." No fiction or "talking" animals. Buys 8-12 mss/year. Query or send complete ms. Length: 500-1,000 words. Pays $10-150.
Photos: Send photos with query or ms (duplicates only). Prefers underwater animals, water photos with children, photos that explain text. Pays $25-100/photo. Identification of subjects required. Buys one-time and translation rights.
Columns/Departments: Discovery (science experiments or crafts a young person can easily do at home), 50-500 words; Creature Feature (lively article on one specific marine animal) 500-700 words. Buys 1 mss/year. Send complete ms. Pays $10-150.
Poetry: No "talking" animals. Buys 1-2 poems/year. Pays $10-100.
Tips: "Find a lively way to relate scientific facts to children witout anthropomorphizing. We need to know material is accurate and current. Articles should feature an interesting marine creature and yet contain factual material that's fun to read."

THE ELECTRIC COMPANY MAGAZINE, Children's Television Workshop, 1 Lincoln Plaza, New York NY 10023. (212)595-3456. Editor: Randi Hacker. Associate Editor: Christina Meyer. 10% freelance written. Works with small number of new/unpublished writers each year. Magazine published 10 times/year. "We are a humor/reading/activity magazine for children 6-10 years old." Circ. 250,000+. Pays on acceptance. Publishes ms an average of 8 months after acceptance. Byline given. Offers 50% kill fee. Buys all rights. Submit seasonal/holiday material at least 6 months in advance. Simultaneous and photocopied submissions OK. Computer printout submissions acceptable. Reports in 2 weeks. Sample copy for 9x12 SAE with $1.25 postage.
Nonfiction: General interest, humor and photo feature. Buys 5-6 mss/year. Query with or without published clips, or send complete ms. Length: 500 words maximum. Pays $50-200.
Photos: State availability of photos with submission. Reviews transparencies. Offers $75 maximum/photo. Model releases and identification of subjects required.
Fiction: Adventure, fantasy, historical, humorous, mystery and western. "No stories with heavy moral messages; or those about child abuse, saying 'no,' divorce, single parent households, handicapped children, etc." Buys 3 mss/year. Query or send complete ms. Length: 750-1,000 words. Pays $200 maximum.
Tips: "Just think about what you liked to read about when you were a kid and write it down. No stories about doggies, bunnies or kitties. No stories with heavy moral message."

ENFANTAISIE, La Revue Des Jeunes, 2603 SE 32nd Ave., Portland OR 97202. (503)235-5304. Editor: Viviane Gould. 20%freelance written. Eager to work with new/unpublished writers. Managing Editor: Michael Gould. Bimonthly educational/classroom children's magazine for learning French. Circ. 2,000. Pays on publication. Publishes ms an average of 6 months after acceptance. Byline given. Buys first rights. Submit seasonal/holiday material 5 months in advance. "We do not publish material relating to religious holidays." Simultaneous, photocopied and previously published submissions OK. Electronic submissions OK via Macintosh disk. Computer printout submissions acceptable. Reports in 2 weeks on queries; 4 weeks on mss. Sample copy $3 with 9x12 SAE and 4 first class stamps; free writer's guidelines with SASE.
Nonfiction: Personal experience, photo feature and French culture pedagogical. No religious, how-to, technical, inspirational, exposé or book excerpts. Buys 5 mss/year. Query. Length: 1,000 words. Pays $15-25.
Photos: State availability of photos with submission. Offers no additional payment for photos accepted with ms. Buys one-time rights.
Columns/Departments: Teachers' Forum (practical essay on an aspect of teaching French—for example, teaching reading, making visual aids, using games, etc.). Buys 5 mss/year. Send complete ms. Length: 500-600 words. Pays 3 complimentary copies.
Fiction: Adventure, humorous, family situations, and sibling relations. Buys 10 mss/year. Send complete ms. Length: 1,000 words. Pays $15-25.
Tips: "As we are widely used in the classroom, features submitted in English will be translated into simplified French. All features are adapted to suit our linguistic/pedagogical criteria. Write for children 12-16 years old."

FACES, The Magazine about People, Cobblestone Publishing, Inc., 20 Grove St., Peterborough NH 03458. (603)924-7209. Editor: Carolyn P. Yoder. 95% freelance written. Prefers to work with published/established writers. A magazine published 10 times/year covering world cultures for 8 to 14-year-olds. Articles must relate to the issue's theme. Circ. approximately 10,000. Pays on publication. Byline given. Buys all rights. Simultaneous and photocopied submissions OK. Previously published submissions rarely accepted. Computer printout submissions acceptable; prefers letter-quality to dot-matrix. Sample copy $3.50; writer's guidelines for SASE.
Nonfiction: Book excerpts, essays, expose, general interest, historical/nostalgic, how-to (activities), humor, interview/profile, personal experience, photo feature, technical and travel. Articles must relate to the theme. No religious, pornographic, biased or sophisticated submissions. Buys approximately 50 mss/year. Query with published clips. Length: 250-1,000 words. Pays up to 15¢/word. Rarely pays expenses of writers on assignment.
Photos: State availability of photos with submission. Reviews contact sheets and 8x10 prints. Offers $5-10/photo. Buys one-time and all rights.
Fiction: All fiction must be theme-related. Buys 10 mss/year. Query with published clips. Length: 500-1,000 words. Pays 10-15¢/word.
Poetry: Light verse and traditional. No religious or pornographic poetry or poetry not related to the theme. Buys 10 poems/year. Submit maximum 1 poem. Pays on individual basis.
Tips: "Writers must have an appreciation and understanding of people. All manuscripts for *Faces* are reviewed by the American Museum of Natural History. Writers must not condescend to our readers."

THE FRIEND, 50 East North Temple, Salt Lake City UT 84150. Managing Editor: Vivian Paulsen. 60% freelance written. Eager to work with new/unpublished writers as well as established writers. Appeals to children ages 4-12. Monthly publication of The Church of Jesus Christ of Latter-Day Saints. Circ. 200,000. Pays on acceptance. Buys all rights. Submit seasonal material 8 months in advance. Computer printout submissions acceptable. Publishes ms an average of 1 year after acceptance. Free sample copy and writer's guidelines.
Nonfiction: Subjects of current interest, science, nature, pets, sports, foreign countries, and things to make and do. Special issues for Christmas and Easter. "Submit only complete ms—no queries, please." Length: 1,000 words maximum. Pays 8¢/word minimum.
Fiction: Seasonal and holiday stories and stories about other countries and their children. Wholesome and optimistic; high motive, plot, and action. Also, simple but suspense-filled mysteries. Character-building stories preferred. Length: 1,200 words maximum. Stories for younger children should not exceed 700 words. Pays 8¢/word minimum.
Poetry: Serious, humorous and holiday. Any form with child appeal. Pays $15.
Tips: "Do you remember how it feels to be a child? Can you write stories that appeal to children ages 4-12 in today's world? We're interested in stories with an international flavor and those that focus on present-day problems. Send material of high literary quality slanted to our editorial requirements. Let the child solve the problem—not some helpful, all-wise adult. No overt moralizing. Nonfiction should be creatively presented—not an array of facts strung together. Beware of being cutesy."

HIGH ADVENTURE, Assemblies of God, 1445 Boonville, Springfield MO 65802. (417)862-2781, ext. 1497. Editor: Johnnie Barnes. Eager to work with new/unpublished writers. Quarterly magazine "designed to provide boys with worthwhile, enjoyable, leisure reading; to challenge them in narrative form to higher ideals and greater spiritual dedication; and to perpetuate the spirit of the Royal Rangers program through stories, ideas, and illustrations." Circ. 78,000. Pays on acceptance. Byline given. Buys one-time rights. Submit seasonal/holiday material 6-9 months in advance. Simultaneous queries, and simultaneous, photocopied, and previously published submissions OK. Computer printout submission OK; prefers letter-quality to dot-matrix. Reports in 1 month. Sample copy for 9x12 SAE with 56¢ postage; free writer's guidelines.

Nonfiction: Historical/nostalgic, how-to, humor and inspirational. Buys 25-50 mss/year. Query or send complete ms. Length: 1,200 words. Pays 2¢/word.

Photos: Reviews b&w negatives, transparencies and prints. Identification of subjects required. Buys one-time rights.

Fiction: Adventure, historical, humorous, religious and western. Buys 25-50 mss/year. Query or send complete ms. Length: 1,200 words maximum. Pays 2¢/word.

Fillers: Jokes, gags and short humor. Pays $2 for jokes; others vary.

HIGHLIGHTS FOR CHILDREN, 803 Church St., Honesdale PA 18431. Editor: Kent L. Brown Jr. 80% freelance written. Magazine published 11 times/year for children ages 2-12. Circ. 2,000,000. Pays on acceptance. Publishes ms an average of 18 months after acceptance. Buys all rights. Computer printout submissions acceptable; prefers letter-quality to dot-matrix. Reports in about 2 months. Sample copy $2.25; writer's guidelines for SASE.

Nonfiction: "We prefer factual features, including history and natural, technical and social science, written by persons with rich background and mastery in their respective fields. Contributions always welcomed from new writers, especially engineers, scientists, historians, teachers, etc., who can make useful, interesting and authentic facts accessible to children. Also writers who have lived abroad and can interpret the ways of life, especially of children, in other countries. Sports material, biographies and general articles of interest to children. Direct, original approach, simple style, interesting content, without word embellishment; not rewritten from encyclopedias. State background and qualifications for writing factual articles submitted. Include references or sources of information. Length: 900 words maximum. Pays $65 minimum. Also buys original party plans for children ages 7-12, clearly described in 400-700 words, including drawings or sample of items to be illustrated. Also, novel but tested ideas in crafts, with clear directions and made-up models. Projects must require only free or inexpensive, easy-to-obtain materials. Especially desirable if easy enough for early primary grades. Also, fingerplays with lots of action, easy for very young children to grasp and parents to dramatize. Avoid wordiness. Pays minimum $30 for party plans; $15 for crafts ideas; $25 for fingerplays.

Fiction: Unusual, meaningful stories appealing to both girls and boys, ages 2-12. Vivid, full of action. "Engaging plot, strong characterization, lively language." Seeks stories that the child ages 8-12 will eagerly read, and the child ages 2-7 will begin to read and/or will like to hear when read aloud. "We publish stories in the suspense/adventure/mystery and humor category, and short (200 words and under) stories for the beginning reader, with an interesting plot and a number of picturable situations. Also need rebuses, stories with urban settings, stories for beginning readers (500 words), humorous and horse stories. We also would like to see more material of 1-page length (300-500 words), both fiction and factual. We need creative-thinking puzzles that can be illustrated, optical illusions, body teasers, and other 'fun' activities. War, crime and violence are taboo. Some fantasy stories published." Length: 400-900 words. Pays $65 minimum.

Tips: "We are pleased that many authors of children's literature report that their first published work was in the pages of *Highlights*. It is not our policy to consider fiction on the strength of the reputation of the author. We judge each submission on its own merits. With factual material, however, we do prefer either authorities in their field or people with first-hand experience. In this manner we can avoid the encyclopedic article that merely restates information readily available elsewhere. We don't make assignments. Query with simple letter to establish whether the nonfiction *subject* is likely to be of interest. A beginning writer should first become familiar with the type of material which *Highlights* publishes. We are most eager for easy stories for very young readers, but realize that this is probably the most difficult kind of writing. Include special qualifications, if any, of author. Write for the child, not the editor."

HUMPTY DUMPTY'S MAGAZINE, Children's Health Publications, 1100 Waterway Blvd., Box 567, Indianapolis IN 46206. Editor: Christine French Clark. 90% freelance written. "We try not to be overly influenced by an author's credits, preferring instead to judge each submission on its own merit." Magazine published 8 times/year stressing health, nutrition, hygiene, exercise and safety for children ages 4-6. Combined issues: February/March, April/May, June/July, and August/September. Pays on publication. Publishes ms at least 8 months after acceptance. Buys all rights. Submit seasonal material 8 months in advance. Computer printout submissions OK; prefers letter-quality to dot-matrix. Reports in 10 weeks. Sample copy 75¢; writer's guidelines for SASE.

Nonfiction: "We are open to nonfiction on almost any age-appropriate subject, but we especially need material with a health theme—nutrition, safety, exercise, hygiene. We're looking for articles that encourage readers to develop better health habits without preaching. Very simple factual articles that creatively teach readers about their bodies. We use simple crafts, some with holiday themes. We also use several puzzles and activities in each issue—dot-to-dot, hidden pictures, *simple* crosswords, and easy-to-play 'board' games. Keep in mind that most our readers are just *beginning* to learn to read and write, so word puzzles must be very basic." Submit complete ms. "Include number of words in manuscript and Social Security number." Length: 600 words maximum. Pays 6¢/word.

Fiction: "We're primarily interested in stories in rhyme and easy-to-read stories for the beginning reader. Currently we need seasonal stories with holiday themes. We use contemporary stories and fantasy, some employing a health theme. We try to present our health material in a positive light, incorporating humor and a light approach wherever possible. Avoid sexual stereotyping. Characters in contemporary stories should be realistic and up-to-date. Remember, many of our readers have working mothers and/or come from single-parent homes. We need more stories that reflect these changing times but at the same time communicate good, wholesome values." Submit complete ms. "Include number of words in manuscript and Social Security number." Length: 600 words maximum. Pays 6¢/word.

Poetry: Short, simple poems. Pays $7 minimum.

JACK AND JILL, 1100 Waterway Blvd., Box 567, Indianapolis IN 46206. (317)636-8881. Editor: Christine French Clark. 85% freelance written. Magazine published 8 times/year for children ages 6-8. Pays on publication. Publishes ms an average of 8 months after acceptance. Buys all rights. Byline given. Submit seasonal material 8 months in advance. Computer printout submissions acceptable. Reports in 10 weeks. May hold material seriously being considered for up to 1 year. "Material will not be returned unless accompanied by self-addressed envelope with sufficient postage." Sample copy 75¢; writer's guidelines for SASE.

Nonfiction: "Because we want to encourage youngsters to read for pleasure and for information, we are interested in material that will challenge a young child's intelligence *and* be enjoyable reading. Our emphasis is on good health, and we are in particular need of articles, stories, and activities with health, safety, exercise and nutrition themes. We are looking for well-written articles that take unusual approaches to teaching better health habits and scientific facts about how the body works. We try to present our health material in a positive light—incorporating humor and a light approach wherever possible without minimizing the seriousness of what we are saying." Straight factual articles are OK if they are short and interestingly written. "We would rather see, however, more creative alternatives to the straight factual article. For instance, we'd be interested in seeing a health message or facts presented in articles featuring positive role models for readers. Many of the personalities children admire—athletes, musicians, and film or TV stars—are fitness or nutrition buffs. Many have kicked drugs, alcohol or smoking habits and are outspoken about the dangers of these vices. Color slides, transparencies, or black and white photos accompanying this type of article would greatly enhance salability." Buys 25-30 nonfiction mss/year. Length: 500-1,200 words. Pays approximately 6¢ a word.

Photos: When appropriate, photos should accompany ms. Reviews sharp, contrasting b&w glossy prints. Sometimes uses color slides, transparencies, or good color prints. Pays $10 for b&w. Buys one-time rights.

Fiction: May include, but is not limited to, realistic stories, fantasy adventure—set in past, present or future. All stories need a well-developed plot, action and incident. Humor is highly desirable. "Currently we need stories with holiday themes. Stories that deal with a health theme need not have health as the primary subject. We would like to see more biographical fiction." Length: 500-1,500 words, short stories; 1,500 words/installment, serials of two parts. Pays approximately 6¢ a word. Buys 20-25 mss/year.

Fillers: Puzzles (including various kinds of word and crossword puzzles), poems, games, science projects, and creative craft projects. Instructions for activities should be clearly and simply written and accompanied by models or diagram sketches. "We also have a need for recipes. Ingredients should be healthful; avoid sugar, salt, chocolate, red meat, and fats as much as possible. In all material, avoid references to eating sugary foods, such as candy, cakes, cookies and soft drinks."

Tips: "We are constantly looking for new writers who can tell good stories with interesting slants—stories that are not full of out-dated and time-worn expressions. Our best authors are writers who know what today's children are like. Keep in mind that our readers are becoming 'computer literate', living in an age of rapidly developing technology. They are exploring career possibilities that may be new and unfamiliar to our generation. They are faced with tough decisions about drug and alcohol use. Many of them are latch-key children because both parents work or they come from single-parent homes. We need more stories and articles that reflect these changing times but that also communicate good, wholesome values. Obtain *current* issues of the magazines and *study* them to determine our present needs and editorial style."

JUNIOR TRAILS, Gospel Publishing House, 1445 Boonville Ave., Springfield MO 65802. (417)862-2781. Editor: Kathy Ketcher. 100% freelance written. Eager to work with new/unpublished writers. Weekly tabloid covering religious fiction; and biographical, historical, and scientific articles with a spiritual emphasis for boys and girls ages 10-11. Circ. 75,000. Pays on acceptance. Publishes ms an average of 9-12 months after acceptance. Byline given. Not copyrighted. Buys simultaneous rights, first rights, or second (reprint) rights to material originally published elsewhere. Submit seasonal/holiday material 1 year in advance. List Social Security number and number of words in ms. Simultaneous and previously published submissions OK. Computer printout submissions acceptable; prefers letter-quality to dot-matrix. Reports in 6 weeks on queries; 2 months on mss. Sample copy and writer's guidelines for 9x12 SAE and 2 first class stamps.

Nonfiction: Biographical, historical and scientific (with spiritual lesson or emphasis). "Junior-age children need to be alerted to the dangers of drugs, alcohol, smoking, etc. They need positive guidelines and believable examples relating to living a Christian life in an ever-changing world. Buys 30-40 mss/year. Send complete ms. Length: 500-1,000 words. Pays 2-3¢/word.

Fiction: Adventure (with spiritual lesson or application); and religious. "We're looking for fiction that presents believable characters working out their problems according to Biblical principles. No fictionalized accounts of Bible stories or events." Buys 60-80 mss/year. Send complete ms. Length: 1,000-1,800 words. Pays 2-3¢/word.

Poetry: Free verse and light verse. Buys 6-8 mss/year. Pays 20¢/line.

Fillers: Anecdotes (with spiritual emphasis). Buys 15-20/year. Length: 200 words maximum. Pays 2-3¢/word.

Tips: "We like to receive stories showing contemporary children positively facing today's world. These stories show children who are aware of their world and who find a moral solution to their problems through the guidance of God's Word. They are not 'super children' in themselves. They are average children learning how to face life through God's help. We tend to get settings in stories that are out of step with today's society. We will tend to turn more and more to purely contemporary settings unless we are using a historical or biographical story. We will have the setting, characters and plot agree with each other in order to make it more believable to our audience."

NATIONAL GEOGRAPHIC WORLD, National Geographic Society, 17th & M Sts. NW, Washington DC 20036. (202)857-7000. Editor: Pat Robbins. Associate Editor: Margaret McKelway. 80% freelance written. Monthly magazine of factual stories of interest to children ages 8-13 years. "*World* is a strongly visual magazine; all stories must have a visual story line; no unillustrated stories are used." Circ. 1.2 million. Pays on publication. No byline given. Offers variable kill fee. Buys all rights. Submit seasonal/holiday material 1 year in advance. Free sample copy.

Nonfiction: Subject matter is factual. Subjects include animals, conservation, science and technology, geography, history, sports, outdoor adventure and children's activities. No fiction, poetry, book reviews, TV or current events. Humor, shorts, and game ideas are welcome. Query first. Inquire in writing to Pat Robbins regarding freelance assignments. Include resume and published work. "Writing is always done after pictures are in hand. Freelance assignments are made on a contract basis."

Photos: "Freelance photography is handled in a variety of ways. Photo story submissions are reviewed by the illustrations editor. Photographers who want assignments should send a query letter first. Include a brief description of the proposed story and list the picture possibilities. If the magazine is interested, the illustrations editor will review the photographer's portfolio."

‡NOAH'S ARK, A Newspaper for Jewish Children, 7726 Portal, Houston TX 77071. (713)771-7143. Editors: Debbie Israel Dubin and Linda Freedman Block. A monthly tabloid that "captures readers' interest and reinforces learning about Jewish history, holidays, laws and culture through articles, stories, recipes, games, crafts, projects, Hebrew column and more." For Jewish children, ages 6-12. Circ. 450,000. Pays on acceptance. Byline given. Buys first North American serial rights. Submit seasonal/holiday material 4 months in advance. Simultaneous and photocopied submissions OK. Computer printout submissions OK; prefers letter-quality to dot-matrix. Reports in 6 weeks on queries; 2 months on mss. Sample copy and writer's guidelines for #10 SASE.

Nonfiction: Historical/nostalgic, how to (craft projects, recipes), humor and interview/profile, all related to the needs of Jewish children. Send complete ms. Length: 350 words maximum. Pays usually 5¢/word.

Photos: State availability of photos with submission or send photos with submission. Offers no additional payment for photos accepted with ms. Identification of subjects required. Buys one-time rights.

Fiction: Historical, humorous, religious (Jewish), slice-of-life vignettes. Any and all suitable for Jewish children. Buys 2-3 mss/year. Send complete ms. Length: 700 words maximum. Pays 5¢/word.

Poetry: Light verse and traditional. Buys 1 poem/year. Submit maximum 1 poem. Payment varies.

Fillers: Anecdotes, facts, gags, short humor and games. Buys 3-5/year. Payment varies.

Tips: "We're just looking for high quality material suitable for entertainment as well as supplemental religious school use." Encourages freelancers to take an "unusual approach to writing about holidays."

ODYSSEY, Kalmbach Publishing Co., 1027 N. 7th St., Milwaukee WI 53233. (414)276-2689. Editor: Nancy Mack. 50% freelance written. Works with a small number of new/unpublished writers each year. Monthly magazine emphasizing astronomy and outer space for children ages 8-12. Circ. 100,000. Pays on publication. Publishes ms an average of 8 months after acceptance. Buys first serial or one-time rights. Submit seasonal/holiday material 4 months in advance. Photocopied and previously published submissions OK. Computer printout submissions acceptable; prefers letter-quality to dot-matrix. Reports in 8 weeks. "Material with little news connection may be held up to one year." Sample copy and writer's guidelines for 8½x12½ SAE and $1.24 postage.

Nonfiction: General interest (astronomy, outer space, spacecraft, planets, stars, etc.); how-to (astronomy projects, experiments, etc.); and photo feature (spacecraft, planets, stars, etc.). "We like short, off-beat articles with some astronomy or space-science tie-in. A recent example: an article about a baseball game that ended with the explosion of a meteorite over the field. Study the styles of the monthly columnists. No general overview articles; for example, a general article on the Space Shuttle, or a general article on stars. We do not want science fiction articles.'' Buys 12 mss/year. Query with published clips. Length: 750-2,000 words. Pays $100-350 depending on length and type of article. Sometimes pays expenses of writers on assignment.

Photos: State availability of photos. Buys one-time rights. Captions preferred; model releases required. Payment depends upon size and placement.

Tips: ''Since I am overstocked and have a stable of regular writers, a query is very important. I often get several manuscripts on the same subject and must reject them. Write a very specific proposal and indicate why it will interest kids. If the subject is very technical, indicate your qualifications to write about it. I will be buying short articles almost exclusively in 1988 because most major features are being handled by staff or contributing editors. Frequent mistakes writers make are trying to fudge on material they don't understand, using outdated references, and telling me their articles are assignments for the Institute of Children's Literature.''

ON THE LINE, Mennonite Publishing House, 616 Walnut Ave., Scottdale PA 15683-1999. (412)887-8500. Editor: Virginia A. Hostetler. 100% freelance written. Works with a small number of new/unpublished writers each year. Weekly magazine for children ages 10-14. Circ. 10,000. Pays on acceptance. Publishes ms an average of 1 year after acceptance. Byline given. Buys one-time rights. Submit seasonal/holiday material 6 months in advance. Simultaneous, photocopied and previously published submissions OK. Computer printout submissions acceptable; prefers letter-quality to dot-matrix. Reports in 1 month.

Nonfiction: How-to (things to make with easy-to-get materials); and informational (500-word articles on wonders of nature, people who have made outstanding contributions). Buys 95 unsolicited mss/year. Send complete ms. Length: 500-1,200 words. Pays $10-24.

Photos: Photos purchased with or without ms. Pays $10-25 for 8x10 b&w photos. Total purchase price for ms includes payment for photos.

Columns/Departments: Fiction, adventure, humorous and religious. Buys 52 mss/year. Send complete ms. Length: 800-1,200 words. Pays $15-30.

Poetry: Light verse and religious. Length: 3-12 lines. Pays $5-15.

Tips: ''Study the publication first. We need short well-written how-to and craft articles. Don't send query; we prefer to see the complete manuscript.''

OUR LITTLE FRIEND, PRIMARY TREASURE, Pacific Publishing Association, Box 7000, Boise ID 83707. (208)465-2581. Editor: Aileen Andres Sox. 99% freelance written. Works with small number of new/unpublished writers each year. Weekly for youngsters of the Seventh-day Adventist church. *Our Little Friend* is for children ages 2-6; *Primary Treasure*, ages 7-9. Buys first serial rights (international), first North American serial rights; one-time rights, second serial (reprint) rights; and simultaneous rights. Byline given. Publishes ms an average of 6 months or more after acceptance. ''The payment we make is for one magazine right. In most cases, it is for the first one. But we make payment for second and third rights also.'' Simultaneous submissions OK. Computer printout submissions acceptable; no dot-matrix.

Nonfiction: All stories must be based on fact, written in story form. True, character-building stories written from viewpoint of child and giving emphasis to lessons of life needed for Christian living. Nature or science articles, but no fantasy; science must be very simple. All material should be educational or informative and stress moral attitude and religious principle. Buys 300 unsolicited mss/year. Length: 700-1,000 words for *Our Little Friend*; 600-1,200 for *Primary Treasure*. Pays $15-25.

Photos: 8x10 glossy prints for cover. Photo payment: sliding scale according to quality.

Poetry: Juvenile poetry. Up to 12 lines. Pays $1/line.

Tips: ''Authors must understand a Christian perspective and portray it in an upbeat fashion to be published. We want true stories presented in narrative form. By truth we mean that the characters actually live or have lived, that they had the problem you say they had, and that they solved it the way you say they solved it.''

OWL MAGAZINE, The Discovery Magazine for Children, The Young Naturalist Foundation, 56 The Esplanade, Suite 306, Toronto, Ontario M5E 1A7 Canada. (416)868-6001. Editor: Sylvia Funston. 25% freelance written. Works with small number of new/unpublished writers each year. Magazine published 10 times/year (no July or August issues) covering science and nature. Aims to interest children in their environment through accurate, factual information about the world around them presented in an easy, lively style. Circ. 150,000. Pays on publication. Publishes ms an average of 3 months after acceptance. Byline given. Buys all rights; makes work-for-hire assignments. Submit seasonal/holiday material 1 year in advance. Computer printout submissions acceptable; no dot-matrix. Reports in 10 weeks. Sample copy $1.95; free writer's guidelines. Send SAE (large envelope if requesting sample copy) and IRC (no stamps please).

Nonfiction: How-to (activities, crafts); personal experience (real life children in real situations); photo feature (natural science, international wildlife, and outdoor features); and science and environmental features. No folk tales, problem stories with drugs, sex or moralistic views, fantasy or talking animal stories. ''We accept short, well-written articles about up-to-the-minute science discoveries or developments for our Hoot Club

News section." Query with clips of published work.

Photos: State availability of photos. Reviews 35mm transparencies. Identification of subjects required.

Tips: "Write for editorial guidelines first; know your topic. Our magazine never talks down to children."

PENNYWHISTLE PRESS, Gannett Co., Inc., Box 500-P, Washington DC 20044. (703)276-3796. Editor: Anita Sama. 15% freelance written. Works with a very small number of new/unpublished writers each year. A weekly tabloid newspaper supplement with stories and features for children ages 6-12. Circ. 2,900,000. Pays on acceptance. Publishes ms an average of 1 year after acceptance. Byline given. Buys all rights. Submit seasonal/holiday material 3-6 months in advance. Reports in 3 months. Sample copy for 75¢, SAE and 2 first class stamps; writer's guidelines for SASE.

Nonfiction: How-to (sports, crafts). Buys 15 mss/year. Length: 500 words maximum. Pays variable rate.

Fiction: For children. Buys 25 mss/year. Send complete ms. Length: 250-850 words. Pays variable rate.

Poetry: Traditional poetry for children. Buys 5-10 poems/year. Submit maximum 1 poem. Pays variable rate.

Tips: Fiction is most open to freelancers.

POCKETS, The Upper Room, 1908 Grand Ave., Box 189, Nashville TN 37202. (615)327-2700. Editor: Willie S. Teague. 40% freelance written. Eager to work with new/unpublished writers. A monthly themed magazine (except combined January and February issues) covering children's and families spiritual formation. "We are a Christian, non-denominational publication for children 6 to 12 years of age." Circ. 70,000. Pays on acceptance. Byline given. Offers 4¢/word kill fee. Buys first North American serial rights. Submit seasonal/holiday material 1 year in advance. Photocopied and previously published submissions OK. Computer printout submissons acceptable; prefers letter-quality to dot-matrix. Reports in 10 weeks on manuscripts. Sample copy for 10½x7½ SAE with 4 first class stamps; writer's guidelines and themes for business size SASE.

Nonfiction: Shirley Paris, articles editor. Interview/profile, religious (retold scripture stories); and personal experience. List of themes for special issues available with SASE. No violence or romance. Buys 3 mss/year. Send complete ms. Length: 600-1,500 words. Pays 7¢-10¢/word.

Photos: Send photos with submission. Reviews contact sheets, transparencies and prints. Offers $25-50/photo. Buys one-time rights.

Columns Departments: Refrigerator Door (poetry and prayer related to themes), 25 lines; Pocketsful of Love (family communications activities), and Loaves and Fishes (simplified lifestyle and nutrition) both 300 words. Buys 20 mss/year. Send complete ms. Pays 7¢-10¢/word; recipes $25.

Fiction: Adventure; ethnic; and slice-of-life. "Stories should reflect the child's everyday experiences through a Christian approach. This is often more acceptable when stories are not preachy or overtly Christian." Buys 15 mss/year. Send complete ms. Length: 750-1,600 words. Pays 7-10¢/word.

Poetry: Buys 3 poems/year. Length: 4-25 lines. Pays $25-50.

Tips: "Theme stories, role models and retold scripture stories are most open to freelancers. Poetry is also open, but we rarely receive an acceptable poem. It's very helpful if writers send for our themes. These are *not* the same as writer's guidelines."

R-A-D-A-R, 8121 Hamilton Ave., Cincinnati OH 45231. (513)931-4050. Editor: Margaret Williams. 75% freelance written. Prefers to work with published/established writers; works with a small number of new/unpublished writers each year. Weekly for children in grades 3-6 in Christian Sunday schools. Rights purchased vary with author and material; prefers buying first serial rights, but will buy second (reprint) rights. Occasionally overstocked. Pays on acceptance. Publishes ms an average of 1 year after acceptance. Submit seasonal material 1 year in advance. Computer printout submissions acceptable; prefers letter-quality to dot-matrix. Reports in 1-2 months. Free sample copy; writer's guidelines for business size SASE.

Nonfiction: Articles on hobbies and handicrafts, nature, famous people, seasonal subjects, etc., written from a Christian viewpoint. No articles about historical figures with an absence of religious implication. Length: 500-1,000 words. Pays 3¢/word maximum.

Fiction: Short stories of heroism, adventure, travel, mystery, animals and biography. True or possible plots stressing clean, wholesome, Christian character-building ideas, but not preachy. Make prayer, church attendance and Christian living a natural part of the story. "We correlate our fiction and other features with a definite Bible lesson. Writers who want to meet our needs should send for a theme list." No talking animal stories, science fiction, Halloween stories or first-person stories from an adult's viewpoint. Length: up to 1,000 words. Pays 3¢/word maximum.

RANGER RICK, National Wildlife Federation, 1412 16th St. NW, Washington DC 20036. (703)790-4274. Editorial Director: Trudy D. Farrand. 50% freelance written. Works with a small number new/unpublished writers each year. Monthly magazine for children from ages 6-12, with the greatest concentration in the 7-10 age bracket. Buys all world rights. Byline given "but occasionally, for very brief pieces, we will identify author by name at the end. Contributions to regular departments usually are not bylined." Pays on acceptance. Publishes ms an average of 18 months after acceptance. Computer printout submissions acceptable; no dot-matrix. Reports in 2 weeks. "Anything written with a specific month in mind should be in our hands at least 10 months before that issue date."

Nonfiction: "Articles may be written on anything related to nature, conservation, the outdoors, environmental problems or natural science." Buys 20-25 unsolicited mss/year. Query. Pays from $10-350, depending on length and content (maximum length, 900 words). Rarely pays expenses of writers on assignment.

Fiction: "Same categories as nonfiction plus fantasy and science fiction. The attributing of human qualities to animals is limited to our regular feature, 'The Adventures of Ranger Rick,' so please do not humanize wildlife. The publisher, The National Wildlife Federation, discourages keeping wildlife as pets."

Photos: "Photographs, when used, are paid for separately. It is not necessary that illustrations accompany material."

Tips: "Include in query details of what manuscript will cover; sample lead; evidence that you can write playfully and with great enthusiasm, conviction and excitement (formal, serious, dull queries indicate otherwise). Think of an exciting subject we haven't done recently, sell it effectively with query, and produce a manuscript of highest quality. Read past issues to learn successful styles and unique approaches to subjects. If your submission is commonplace in any way we won't want it."

3-2-1 CONTACT, Children's Television Workshop, One Lincoln Plaza, New York NY 10023. (212)595-3456. Senior Editor: Jonathan Rosenbloom. Associate Editor: Richard Chevat. 40% freelance written. Magazine published 10 times/year covering science and technology for children ages 8-14. Circ. 375,000. Pays on acceptance. Publishes ms 6 months after acceptance. Buys all rights "with some exceptions." Submit seasonal material 8 months in advance. Simultaneous, photocopied, and previously published submissions OK if so indicated. Computer printout submissions acceptable; prefers letter-quality to dot-matrix. Reports in 1 month. Sample copy $1.25; free writer's guidelines.

Nonfiction: General interest (space exploration, the human body, animals, computers and the new technology, current science issues); profile (of interesting scientists or children involved in science or with computers); photo feature (centered around a science theme); and role models of women and minority scientists. No articles on travel not related to science. Buys 5 unsolicited mss/year. Query with published clips. Length: 700-1,000 words. Pays $150-400. Sometimes pays expenses of writers on assignment.

Photos: Reviews 8x10 b&w prints and 35mm color transparencies. Model releases required.

Tips: "I prefer a short query, without manuscript, that makes it clear that an article is interesting. When sending an article, include your telephone number. Don't call us, we'll call you. Many submissions we receive are more like college research papers than feature stories. We like articles in which writers have interviewed kids or scientists, or discovered exciting events with a scientific angle. Library research is necessary; but if that's all you're doing, you aren't giving us anything we can't get ourselves. If your story needs a bibliography, chances are, it's not right for us."

TOUCH, Box 7259, Grand Rapids MI 49510. Editor: Joanne Ilbrink. 80% freelance written. Prefers to work with published/established writers. Monthly magazine. Purpose of publication is to show girls ages 7-14 how God is at work in their lives and in the world around them. "The May/June issue annually features the material written by our readers." Circ. 14,000. Pays on acceptance. Publishes ms an average of 1 year after acceptance. Byline given. Buys second serial (reprint) rights and first North American serial rights. Submit seasonal/holiday material 9 months in advance. Simultaneous, photocopied and previously published submissions OK. Computer printout submissions acceptable; no dot-matrix. Reports in 6 weeks. Free sample copy and writer's guidelines for 9x12 SASE and 3 first class stamps.

Nonfiction: How-to (crafts girls can make easily and inexpensively); informational (write for issue themes); humor (need much more); inspirational (seasonal and holiday); interview; multicultural materials; travel; personal experience (avoid the testimony approach); and photo feature (query first). "Because our magazine is published around a monthly theme, requesting the letter we send out twice a year to our established freelancers would be most helpful. We do not want easy solutions or quick character changes from bad to good. No pietistic characters. Constant mention of God is not necessary if the moral tone of the story is positive. We do not always want stories that have a good ending." Buys 36-45 unsolicited mss/year. Submit complete ms. Length: 100-1,000 words. Pays 2¢/word, depending on the amount of editing.

Photos: Purchased with or without ms. Reviews 5x7 clear b&w (only) glossy prints. Appreciate multicultural subjects. Pays $5-25 on publication.

Fiction: Adventure (that girls could experience in their hometowns or places they might realistically visit); humorous; mystery (believable only); romance (stories that deal with awakening awareness of boys are appreciated); suspense (can be serialized); and religious (nothing preachy). Buys 20 mss/year. Submit complete ms. Length: 300-1,500 words. Pays 2¢/word.

Poetry: Free verse, haiku, light verse and traditional. Buys 10/year. Length: 50 lines maximum. Pays $5 minimum.

Fillers: Puzzles, short humor and cartoons. Buys 3/issue. Pays $2.50-7.

Tips: "Prefers not to see anything on the adult level, secular material or violence. Writers frequently over-simplify the articles and often write with a Pollyanna attitude. An author should be able to see his/her writing style as exciting and appealing to girls ages 7-14. The style can be fun, but also teach a truth. The subject should be current and important to *Touch* readers. We would like to receive material that features a multi-cultural slant."

TURTLE MAGAZINE FOR PRESCHOOL KIDS, Children's Better Health Institute, Benjamin Franklin Literary & Medical Society, Inc., 1100 Waterway Blvd., Box 567, Indianapolis IN 46206. (317)636-8881. Editor: Beth Wood Thomas. 95% freelance written. Monthly magazine (bimonthly February/March, April/May, June/July, August/September) for preschoolers emphasizing health, safety, exercise and good nutrition. Pays on publication. Publishes ms an average of 1 year after acceptance. Byline given. Buys all rights. Submit seasonal/holiday material 8 months in advance. Reports in 10 weeks. Sample copy 75¢; writer's guidelines for business size SASE.

Fiction: Fantasy, humorous and health-related stories. "Stories that deal with a health theme need not have health as the primary subject but should include it in some way in the course of events." No controversial material. Buys 40 mss/year. Submit complete ms. Length: 700 words maximum. Pays approximately 6¢/word.

Poetry: "We use many stories in rhyme—vocabulary should be geared to a 3- to 5-year-old. Anthropomorphic animal stories and rhymes are especially effective for this age group to emphasize a moral or lesson without 'lecturing'." Pays variable rates.

Tips: "We are primarily concerned with preventive medicine. We try to present our material in a positive—not a negative—light and to incorporate humor and a light approach wherever possible without minimizing the seriousness of what we are saying. We would like to see more stories, articles, craft ideas and activities with the following holiday themes: New Year's Day, Valentine's Day, President's Day, St. Patrick's Day, Easter, Independence Day, Thanksgiving, Christmas and Hannukah. We like new ideas that will entertain as well as teach preschoolers. Publishing a writer's first work is very gratifying to us. It is a great pleasure to receive new, fresh material."

‡**VENTURE**, Christian Service Brigade, Box 150, Wheaton IL 60189. (312)665-0630. Managing Editor: Steven P. Neideck. 15% freelance written. Works with a small number of new/unpublished writers each year. "Venture is a bimonthly company publication published to support and compliment *CSB's* Stockade and Battalion programs. We aim to provide wholesome, entertaining reading for boys ages 10-15." Circ. 25,000. Pays on publication. Publishes ms an average of 4-6 months after acceptance. Byline given. Offers $35 kill fee. Buys first North American serial, one-time and second serial (reprint) rights. Submit seasonal/holiday material 6 months in advance. Photocopied submissions and previously published submissions OK. Computer printout submissions OK; prefers letter-quality. Reports in 2 weeks. Sample copy $1.50 with 9x12 SAE and 73¢ postage, writer's guidelines for #10 SASE.

Nonfiction: Expose, general interest, historical/nostalgic, humor, inspirational, interview/profile, personal experience, photo feature and religious. Buys 10-12 mss/year. Query. Length: 1,000-1,500 words. Pays $75-125 for assigned articles; pays $40-100 for unsolicited articles. Sometimes pays expenses of writers on assignment.

Photos: Send photos with submission. Reviews contact sheets and 5x7 prints. Offers $35-125/photo. Buys one-time rights.

Fiction: Adventure, humorous, mystery and religious. Buys 10-12 mss/year. Query. Length: 1,000-1,500 words. Pays $40-125.

Tips: "Talk to young boys. Find out the things that interest them and write about those things. We are looking for material relating to our 1987-88 theme: Building Men to Serve Christ."

WEE WISDOM, Unity Village MO 64065. Editor: Ms. Verle Bell. 90% freelance written. "We are happy to work with any freelance writers whose submissions and policies match our needs." Magazine published 10 times/year "for children aged 13 and under, dedicated to the truth that each person has an inner source of wisdom, power, love and health that can be applied in a practical manner to everyday life." Circ. 175,000. Publishes ms an average of 8 months after acceptance. Submit seasonal/holiday material 8 months in advance. Pays on acceptance. Byline given. Buys first serial rights only. Computer printout submissions acceptable; no dot-matrix. Sample copy and editorial policy for 5¾x8¾ SAE and 3 first class stamps.

Nonfiction: Entertaining nature articles or projects/activities to encourage appreciation of all life. Wants only completed mss. Pays 4¢/word minimum.

Fiction: Character-building stories that encourage a positive self-image. Although entertaining enough to hold the interest of the older child, they should be readable by the third grader. "Characters should be appealing; plots should be imaginative but plausible, and all stories should be told without preaching. Life combines fun and humor with its more serious lessons, and our most interesting and helpful stories do the same thing. Language should be universal, avoiding the Sunday school image." Length: 500-800 words. Pay 4¢/word minimum.

Poetry: Very limited. Prefers short, seasonal or humorous poems. Pays $15 minimum, 50¢ per line after 15 lines. Rhymed prose (read aloud) stories are paid at about the same rate as prose stories, depending on excellence.

Fillers: Pays $5-15 for puzzles and games.

WONDER TIME, 6401 The Paseo, Kansas City MO 64131. (816)333-7000. Editor: Evelyn Beals. 75% freelance written. "Willing to read and consider appropriate freelance submissions." Published weekly by

Church of the Nazarene for children ages 6-8. Pays on acceptance. Publishes ms an average of 1 year after acceptance. Byline given. Buys first serial rights, second serial (reprint) rights; simultaneous rights and all rights for curriculum assignments. Computer printout submissions acceptable; prefers letter-quality to dot-matrix. Sample copy and writer's guidelines for 9x12 SAE with 3 first class stamps.

Fiction: Buys stories portraying Christian attitudes without being preachy. Uses stories for special days—stories teaching honesty, truthfulness, kindness, helpfulness or other important spiritual truths, and avoiding symbolism. Also, stories about real life problems children face today. "God should be spoken of as our Father who loves and cares for us; Jesus, as our Lord and Savior." Buys 100/mss year. Length: 350-550 words. Pays 3½¢/word on acceptance.

Poetry: Uses verse which has seasonal or Christian emphasis. Length: 4-8 lines. Pays 25¢/line, minimum $2.50.

Tips: "Any stories that allude to church doctrine must be in keeping with Nazarene beliefs. Any type of fantasy must be in good taste and easily recognizable. We are overstocked now with poetry and stories with general themes. We plan to reprint more than before to save art costs, therefore we will be more selective and purchase fewer manuscripts."

YOUNG AMERICAN, America's Newspaper for Kids, Young American Publishing Co., Inc., Box 12409, Portland OR 97212. (503)230-1895. Editor: Kristina T. Linden. 20% freelance written. Eager to work with new/unpublished writers. A tabloid-size newspaper supplement to suburban newspapers for children and their families. Circ. 130,000. Pays on publication. Publishes ms an average of 6 months after acceptance. Byline given. Buys first North American serial rights and makes work-for-hire assignments. Submit seasonal/holiday material 3 months in advance. Photocopied submissions OK. Computer printout submissions acceptable; prefers letter-quality to dot-matrix. Reports in 4 months on mss. Sample copy $1.50 with 9x12 SAE; writer's guidelines for SASE.

Nonfiction: General interest; historical/nostalgic; how-to (crafts, fitness); humor; interview/profile (of kids, or people particularly of interest to them); and newsworthy kids. No condescending articles or articles relating to religion, sex, violence, drugs or substance abuse. Buys 100 mss/year. No queries; send complete ms. Length: 350 words maximum. Pays $5-75. Sometimes pays the expenses of writers on assignment.

Photos: Send photos with submission. Offers $5 maximum/photo. Identification of subjects required. Buys one-time rights.

Columns/Departments: You and the News (stories about newsworthy kids), science (new developments, things not covered in textbooks), and book reviews (for kids and young teens). Length 350 words maximum. Buys 40 mss/year. Send complete ms. Pays $5-75.

Fiction: Adventure, ethnic, fantasy, humorous, mystery, science fiction, suspense, western and lore. No condescending stories or stories relating to religion, sex, drugs or substance abuse. Buys 24 mss/year. Send complete ms. Length: 500-1,000 words. Pays $35-75.

Poetry: Light verse and traditional. No "heavy" or depressing poetry. Buys 30 poems/year. Length: 4 lines, 500 words maximum. Pays $5-35.

Fillers: Facts and short humor. Buys 20/year. Length: 30-300 words. Pays $2.10-21.

Tips: "The *Young American* is particularly interested in publishing articles about newsworthy kids and in publishing children's work. These articles should be under 350 words and accompanied by photos—we prefer color or transparencies to black and white. The *Young American* focus is on children—and they are taken seriously. Articles are intended to inform, entertain, stimulate and enlighten. They give children a sense of being a part of today's important events and a recognition which is often denied them because of age. If applicable, photos, diagrams, or information for illustration helps tremendously as our publication is highly visual. The fiction we have been receiving is excellent. However, it is more abundant than we can publish. Personal notes are written to those who we sincerely hope will consider us again. As we are now publishing twice monthly we are accepting approximately twice as much material."

YOUNG AUTHOR'S MAGAZINE, Theraplan, Incorporated, 3015 Woodsdale Blvd., Lincoln NE 68502. (402)421-3172. Managing Editor: Traci Austin. A bimonthly literary magazine focusing on creative writing by gifted children. Circ. 18,000. Pays on publication. Publishes ms an average of 4 months after acceptance. Pays on publication. Byline given. Not copyrighted. Buys all rights. Submit seasonal/holiday material 6 months in advance. Photocopied submissions OK. Computer printout submissions acceptable. Reports in 3-4 months. Sample copy $3; writer's guidelines for SASE.

Nonfiction: General interest, how-to, interview/profile, personal experience and photo feature. "The November issue of each year is our 'international' issue which features the creative writing of young authors in other countries, as well as the U.S." Nothing with excessive violence. Buys 60 mss/year. Send complete ms. Length: 1,000-2,500 words. Pays $15 minimum.

Photos: Reviews 8x10 prints. Pays $20 for b&w; $20-50 for color. Identification of subjects and model releases required. Buys one-time rights.

Columns/Departments: Send complete ms. Length of columns and payment varies.

Fiction: Adventure, fantasy, humorous, mystery, science fiction and suspense. Send complete ms. Length and payment varies.

Poetry: Avant-garde, free verse, haiku, light verse and traditional. Buys 200 poems/year. No maximum limit on number of poems submitted. Pays $5.

Tips: "The entire publication is open to young writers. We try not to go over 16 years of age—mostly upper elementary to junior high."

_____ *Literary and "Little"*

Literary and "little" magazines contain fiction, poetry, book reviews, essays and literary criticism. Many are published by colleges and universities and have a regional or scholarly focus.

Literary magazines launch many writers into print. Serious literary writers will find great opportunities here; some agents read the magazines to find promising potential clients, and many magazines also sponsor annual contests. Writers who want to get a story printed may have to be patient. Literary magazines, especially semiannuals, will buy good material and save it for future editions. Submitting work to a literary, the writer may encounter frequent address changes or long response times. On the other hand, many editors read submissions several times and send personal notes to writers.

Many literary magazines do not pay writers or pay in contributor's copies. Only literary magazines which pay are included in *Writer's Market* listings. However, *Fiction Writer's Market*, published by Writer's Digest Books, includes nonpaying fiction markets and has in-depth information about fiction techniques and markets. Literary and "little" magazine writers will notice that again this year *Writer's Market* does not contain a Poetry section. Writer's Digest Books also publishes *Poet's Market*, edited by Judson Jerome, with detailed information for poets.

ALASKA QUARTERLY REVIEW, College of Arts & Sciences, University of Alaska Anchorage, Dept. of English, 3221 Providence Dr., Anchorage AK 99508. (907)786-1731. Editor: Ronald Spatz. 100% freelance written. Prefers to work with published/established writers; eager to work with new/unpublished writers. A semiannual magazine publishing fiction and poetry, both traditional and experimental styles, and literary criticism and reviews, with an emphasis on contemporary literature. Circ. 1,000. Pays honorariums on publication when funding permits. Publishes ms an average of 6 months after acceptance. Byline given. Buys first North American serial rights. Upon request, rights will be transferred back to author after publication. Photocopied submissions OK. Computer printout submissions acceptable; prefers letter-quality to dot-matrix. Reports in 4 months. Sample copy $2.50; writer's guidelines for legal-size SAE.

Nonfiction: James Jakob Liszka, articles editor. Literary criticism, reviews and philosophy of literature. No essays. Buys 1-5 mss/year. Query. Length: 1,000-20,000 words. Pays $50-100 subject to funding; pays in copies when funding is limited.

Fiction: Experimental and traditional literary forms. No romance, children's, or inspirational/religious. Buys 10-20 mss/year. Send complete ms. Length: 500-20,000 words. Pays $50-150 subject to funding; sometimes pays in contributor's copies only.

Poetry: Thomas Sexton, poetry editor. Avant-garde, free verse, haiku, and traditional. No light verse. Buys 10-30 poems/year. Submit maximum 10 poems. Length: 2 lines minimum. Pays $10-50 subject to availability funds.

Tips: "All sections are open to freelancers. We rely exclusively on unsolicited manuscripts. *AQR* is a non-profit literary magazine and does not always have funds to pay authors."

AMELIA MAGAZINE, Amelia Press, 329 E St., Bakerfield CA 93304. (805)323-4064. Editor: Frederick A. Raborg Jr. 100% freelance written. Eager to work with new/unpublished writers. "*Amelia* is a quarterly international magazine publishing the finest poetry and fiction available, along with expert criticism and reviews intended for all interested in contemporary literature. *Amelia* also publishes three supplements each year: *Cicada*, which publishes only high quality traditional or experimental haiku and senryu plus fiction, essays and cartoons pertaining to Japan; *SPSM&H*, which publishes the highest quality traditional and experimental sonnets available plus romantic fiction and essays pertaining to the sonnet; and the annual winner of the Charles William Duke long poem contest. Circ. 1,250. Pays on acceptance. Publishes ms an average of 6 months after acceptance. Byline given. Offers 50% kill fee. Buys first North American serial rights. Submit seasonal/holiday material 2 months in advance. Computer printout submissions acceptable; prefers letter-quality to dot-matrix. Reports in 2 months on mss. Sample copy $5.95 (includes postage); writer's guidelines for business size SASE. Sample copy of any supplement $3.50.

Nonfiction: Historical/nostalgic (in the form of belles lettres); humor (in fiction or belles lettres); interview/profile (poets and fiction writers); opinion (on poetry and fiction only); personal experience (as it pertains to poetry or fiction in the form of belles lettres); travel (in the form of belles lettres only); and criticism and book reviews of poetry and small press fiction titles. "Nothing overtly slick in approach. Criticism pieces must have depth; belles lettres must offer important insights into the human scene." Buys 8 mss/year. Send complete ms. Length: 1,000-2,000 words. Pays $25 or by arrangement. "Ordinarily payment for all prose is a flat rate of $25/piece, more for exceptional work." Sometimes pays the expenses of writers on assignment.

Fiction: Adventure; book excerpts (original novel excerpts only); erotica (of a quality seen in Anais Nin or Henry Miller only); ethnic; experimental; fantasy; historical; horror; humorous; mainstream; mystery; novel excerpts; science fiction; suspense; and western. "We would consider slick fiction of the quality seen in *Redbook* and more excellent submissions in the genres—science fiction, wit, Gothic horror, traditional romance, stories with complex *raisons d'être*; avant-garde ought to be truly avant-garde and not merely exercises in vulgarity (read a few old issues of *Evergreen Review* or *Avant-Garde*)." No pornography ("good erotica is not the same thing"). Buys 24-36 mss/year. Send complete ms. Length: 1,000-5,000 words. Pays $35 or by arrangement for exceptional work.

Poetry: Avant-garde, free verse, haiku, light verse and traditional. "No patently religious or stereotypical newspaper poetry." Buys 100-160 poems/year depending on lengths. Prefers submission of at least 3 poems. Length: 3-100 lines. Pays $2-25; additional payment for exceptional work, usually by established professionals. *Cicada* pays $10 each to three "best of issue" poets; *SPSM&H* pays $14 to two "best of issue" sonnets; winner of the long poem contest receives $100 plus copies and publication.

Tips: "*Have something to say* and say it well. If you insist on waving flags or pushing your religion, then do it with subtlety and class. We enjoy a good cry from time to time, too, but sentimentality does not mean we want to see mush. Read our fiction carefully for depth of plot and characterization, then try very hard to improve on it. With the growth of quality in short fiction, we expect to find stories of lasting merit. I also hope to begin seeing more critical essays which, without sacrificing research, demonstrate a more entertaining obliqueness to the style sheets, more 'new journalism' than MLA. In poetry, we also often look for a good 'storyline' so to speak. Above all we want to feel a sense of honesty and value in every piece. As in the first issue of *Amelia*, 'name' writers are used, but newcomers who have done their homework suffer no disadvantage here. So often the problem seems to be that writers feel small press publications allow such a sloughing of responsibility. It is not so."

THE AMERICAN VOICE, Suite 1215, Heyburn Building, Broadway at 4th Ave., Louisville KY 40202. (502)562-0045. Editor: Frederick Smock. Works with small number of new/unpublished writers each year. A quarterly literary magazine "for readers of varying backgrounds and educational levels, though usually college-educated. We aim to be an eclectic reader—to define the American voice by publishing new and established writers from Canada, the U.S., and South America." Circ. 1,500. Pays on publication. Publishes ms an average of 4 months after acceptance. Byline given. Offers 50% kill fee. Buys first North American rights. Photocopied submissions OK. Computer printout submissions acceptable; prefers letter-quality to dot-matrix. Reports in 1 month on queries; 2 months on mss. Sample copy $5.

Nonfiction: Essays, opinion, photo feature and criticism. Buys 15 mss/year. Send complete ms. Length: 10,000 words maximum. Pays $400/essay; $150 to translator. Sometimes pays the expenses of writers on assignment.

Fiction: Buys 30 mss/year. Send complete ms. Pays $400/story; $150 to translator.

Poetry: Avant-garde and free verse. Buys 40 poems/year. Submit maximum 10 poems. Pays $150/poem; $75 to translator.

Tips: "We are looking only for vigorously original fiction, poetry and essays, from new and established writers, and will consider nothing that is in any way sexist, racist or homophobic."

ANTAEUS, The Ecco Press, 26 W. 17th St., New York NY 10011. (212)645-2214. Editor: Daniel Halpern. Managing Editor: Katherine L. Bourne. 100% freelance written. Works with small number of new/unpublished writers each year. "We try to maintain a mix of new and established writers." Semiannual magazine with fiction and poetry. Circ. 5,000. Pays on publication. Publishes ms an average of 1 year after acceptance. Byline given. Buys first North American serial rights. Photocopied submissions OK. Computer printout submissions acceptable; prefers letter-quality to dot-matrix. Reports in 3 weeks on queries; 6 weeks on mss. Sample copy $10; writer's guidelines for SASE.

Nonfiction: General essays and essays for issues devoted to a particular subject.

Fiction: Stories and novel excerpts. Buys 10-15 mss/year. Send complete ms. Length: no minimum or maxi-

mum. Pays $10/printed page.
Poetry: Avant-garde, free verse, light verse and traditional. Buys 30-35 poems/year. Submit maximum 8 poems. Pays $10/printed page.

ANTIOCH REVIEW, Box 148, Yellow Springs OH 45387. Editor: Robert S. Fogarty. 80% freelance written. Quarterly magazine for general, literary and academic audience. Buys all rights. Byline given. Pays on publication. Publishes ms an average of 10 months after acceptance. Computer printout submissions acceptable; prefers letter-quality to dot-matrix. Reports in 6 weeks.
Nonfiction: "Contemporary articles in the humanities and social sciences, politics, economics, literature and all areas of broad intellectual concern. Somewhat scholarly, but never pedantic in style, eschewing all professional jargon. Lively, distinctive prose insisted upon." Length: 2,000-8,000 words. Pays $10/published page.
Fiction: Quality fiction only, distinctive in style with fresh insights into the human condition. No science fiction, fantasy or confessions. Pays $10/published page.
Poetry: Concrete visual imagery. No light or inspirational verse. Contributors should be familiar with the magazine before submitting.

‡ARRIVAL MAGAZINE, A Lively Venture in Politics, Literature and the Arts, Suite 194, 48 Shattuck Square, Berkeley CA 94704. (415)655-0878. Editor: William R. Katovsky. Managing Editor: Emily Zukerberg. 75% freelance written. General interest magazine published quarterly. "A contemporary magazine of American culture. No pretensions, and no axes to grind. Just a sharp new approach to the people, places, events and trends that are making and remaking the American landscape now." Estab. 1987. Circ. 75,000. Pays on publication. Byline given. Buys first North American serial rights or second serial (reprint) rights. Submit seasonal/holiday material 3 months in advance. Simultaneous (if informed), photocopied and previously published submissions OK. Computer printout submissions OK; prefers letter-quality to dot-matrix. Reports in 2 months. Sample copy $2.50; free writer's guidelines.
Nonfiction: Book excerpts, essays, expose, general interest, historical/nostalgic, humor, interview/profile, opinion, personal experience and photo feature. No academic treatises. Buys 30-50 mss/year. Query with published clips or send complete ms. Length: 500-15,000 words. Pays $25-250. Sometimes pays expenses of writers on assignment.
Photos: State availability of photos with submission. Reviews 8x10 prints. Offers $5-75/photo.
Columns/Departments: Book Reviews (literary reviews), 1,200-2,500 words; and Currents (short essays on particular features of American culture), 250-1,500 words. Buys 50-75 mss/year. Query with published clips or send complete ms. Pays $25-250.
Fiction: Confession, ethnic, experimental, historical, humorous, mainstream, novel excerpts. No "pulp, science fiction, romance, adventure or trashy sort of stuff." Buys 10 mss/year. Query with published clips or send complete ms. Length: 2,000-10,000 words. Pays $50-250.
Poetry: Avant-garde, free verse and traditional. Buys 10 poems/year. Submit maximum of 10 poems at one time. Length: 4-100 lines. Pays $25-100.

THE ASYMPTOTICAL WORLD, 341 Lincoln Ave., Box 1372, Williamsport PA 17703. (717)322-7841. Editor: Michael H. Gerardi. 50% freelance written. Works with a small number of new/unpublished writers each year. Annual magazine covering psychodramas, science fiction, fantasy and the experimental. "*The Asymptotical World* is a collection of short tales that attempt to elucidate the moods, sensations and thoughts of a curious world created in the mind of man. The tales touch upon themes of darkness, desolation and death. From each tale, the reader may relive a personal experience or sensation, and he may find relevance or discomfort. The tales were not written to be satanic or sacriligious statements. The stories were penned simply to be dark fantasies which would provide bizarre playgrounds for inquisitive minds." Circ. 1,300. Pays on acceptance. Publishes ms an average of 1 year after acceptance. Byline given. Buys first North American serial rights. Simultaneous queries and photocopied submissions OK. Computer printout submissions acceptable. Reports in 2 months on queries; 4 months on mss. Sample copy $6.95 with 9x12 SAE and 8 first class stamps; writer's guidelines for business size SASE.
Fiction: Experimental, fantasy and psychodrama. Buys 10-15 mss/year. Query with published clips or send complete ms. Length: 1,000-2,500 words. Pays $20-50.
Poetry: Buys 4-6 poems/year. Submit maximum 4 poems. Length: 5-100 lines. Pays $5-50. Would like to see more black and white illustrations.
Tips: "*The Asymptotical World* is definitely unique. It is strongly suggested that a writer review a copy of the magazine to study the format of a psychodrama and the manner in which the plot is left 'open-ended.' The writer will need to study the atmosphere, mood, and plot of published psychodramas before preparing a feature work. The magazine is very young and is willing to explore many fields."

‡BLACK MOUNTAIN REVIEW, Lorien House, Box 1112, Black Mountain NC 28711-1112. (704)669-6211. Editor: David A. Wilson. 80% freelance written. Works with small number of new/unpublished writers each year. A literary, semi-annual magazine of "social, political themes." Estab. 1987. Circ. 300. Pays on publication. Publishes ms an average of 6 months after acceptance. Buys first North American serial rights, first rights and second serial (reprint) rights. Submit seasonal/holiday material 10 months in advance. Photocopied and previously published submissions OK. Computer printout submissions OK. Reports in 1 week on queries; 2 weeks on mss. Sample copy $3.50; writer's guidelines and theme list for business size SASE.

Nonfiction: Essays, well-researched opinion. Special issue features "The Inner Man (#3"), "Mythos" (#4). No diatribes, sex, unresearched opinion. Buys 5 mss/year. Query. Length: 1,000-3,000 words. Pays $2.50/published page.

Photos: State availability of photos with submission. Reviews contact sheets. Offers no additional payment for photos accepted with ms. Identification of subjects required. Buys one-time rights.

Fiction: Experimental, historical, mainstream. Fiction should fit the theme of the issue. No foul language or sex. Buys 2 mss/year. Query. Length 1,000-3,000 words. Pays $2.50/published page.

Poetry: Avant-garde, free verse and traditional. Buys 10 poems/year. Submit maximum 5 poems. Length 4-100 lines. Pays $2.50/published page.

Tips: "Do a well-written, researched piece on a listed theme. It's best to query first so we can work together."

BLACK WARRIOR REVIEW, University of Alabama, Box 2936, University AL 35486. (205)348-4518. Editor: Lynn Domina. Managing Editor: Alan Holmes. 95% freelance written. A semiannual magazine of fiction and poetry. Circ. 1,500. Pays on publication. Publishes ms an average of 6 months after acceptance. Byline given. Buys first rights. Photocopied submissions OK. Computer printout submissions OK; prefers letter-quality to dot-matrix. Reports in 2 weeks on queries; 3 months on mss. Sample copy $3.50; writer's guidelines for #10 SASE.

Nonfiction: Interview/profile and book reviews. Buys 5 mss/year. Query or send complete ms. No limit on length. Payment varies.

Photos: State availability of photos with submission. Offers no additional payment for photos accepted with ms. Identification of subjects required. Buys one-time rights.

Fiction: Ken Walters, fiction editor. Good fiction only. Buys 10 mss/year.

Poetry: Jeff Mock, poetry editor. Good poetry. Submit 4-7 poems. Long poems encouraged. Buys 50 poems/year.

Tips: "Read the *BWR* before submitting."

‡BLOOMSBURY REVIEW, A Book Magazine, Owaissa Communications, Inc. 1028 Bannock, Denver CO 80204. (303)892-0620. Editor: Tom Auer. 75% freelance written. Bimonthly tabloid covering books and book-related matters. "We publish book reviews, interviews with writers and poets, literary essays and original poetry. Our audience consists of educated, literate, *non-specialized* readers." Circ. 10,000. Pays on publication. Publishes ms an average of 4 months after acceptance. Byline given. Buys first rights or one-time rights. Computer printout submissions OK; prefers letter-quality to dot-matrix. Reports in 1 month on queries; 3 months on mss. Sample copy $3.50; writer's guidelines for business size SASE.

Nonfiction: Carol R. Arenberg, articles editor. Essays, interview/profile and book reviews. "Summer issue features reviews, etc. about the American West." No academic or religious articles. Buys 60 mss/year. Query with published clips or send complete ms. Length 500-1,500 words. Pays $10-20. Sometimes pays writers with contributor copies or other premiums "if writer agrees."

Photos: State availability of photos with submissions. Reviews prints. Offers no additional payment for photos accepted with ms. Buys one-time rights.

Columns/Departments: Carol Arenberg, editor. Book reviews and essays. Buys 6 mss/year. Query with published clips or send complete ms. Length: 500-1,500 words. Pays $10-20.

Fiction: John Roberts, fiction editor. Send complete ms. Length: 1,000-3,500 words. Pays $15-25.

Poetry: Ray Gonzalez, poetry editor. Avant-garde, free verse, haiku, light verse and traditional. Buys 20 poems/year. Submit up to 5 poems at one time. Pays $5-10.

Tips: "We appreciate receiving published clips and/or completed manuscripts. Please—no rough drafts. Book reviews should be of new books (within 6 months of publication)."

BOOK FORUM, Hudson River Press, Box 126, Rhinecliff NY 12574. Editor: Marshall Hayes. Editorial Director: Marilyn Wood. 95% freelance written. Works with small number of new/unpublished writers each year. "Serious writers not yet recognized are welcome to query." Quarterly magazine; averages 32 pages (8½x11). Emphasizes contemporary literature, the arts, and foreign affairs for "intellectually sophisticated and knowledgeable professionals: university-level academics, writers, people in government, and the professions." Circ. 5,200. Pays on publication. Publishes ms an average of 6 months after acceptance. Pays 33⅓% kill fee. Byline given. Buys first serial rights. Photocopied submissions OK. No computer printout submissions. Reports in 1 month. Sample copy $3.

Nonfiction: "We seek highly literate essays that would appeal to the same readership as, say, the *London Times Literary Supplement* or *Encounter*. Our readers are interested in professionally written, highly literate and informative essays, profiles and reviews in literature, the arts, behavior, and foreign and public affairs. We cannot use material designed for a mass readership. Think of us as an Eastern establishment, somewhat snobbish literary and public affairs journal and you will have it right." General interest, interview (with select contemporary writers, scientists, educators, artists, film makers), profiles and essays about contemporary innovators. Buys 20-40 unsolicited mss/year. Query. Length: 800-2,000 words. Pays $25-100.

Tips: "To break in, send with the query letter a sample of writing in an area relevant to our interests. If the writer wants to contribute book reviews, send a book review sample, published or not, of the kind of title we are likely to review—literary, social, biographical, art."

THE BOSTON REVIEW, 33 Harrison Ave., Boston MA 02111. (617)350-5353. Editor: Margaret Ann Roth.100% freelance written. Works with a small number of new/unpublished writers each year. Bimonthly magazine of the arts, politics and culture. Circ. 10,000. Pays on acceptance. Publishes an average of 2 months after acceptance. Buys first serial rights. Byline given. Photocopied and simultaneous submissions OK. Computer printout submissions acceptable; prefers letter-quality to dot-matrix. Reports in 2 months. Sample copy $3.

Nonfiction: Critical essays and reviews, natural and social sciences, literature, music, painting, film, photography, dance and theatre. Buys 20 unsolicited mss/year. Length: 1,000-3,000 words. Sometimes pays the expenses of writers on assignment.

Fiction: Length: 2,000-4,000 words. Pays according to length and author, ranging from $50-200.

Poetry: Pays according to length and author.

Tips: "Short (500 words) color pieces are particularly difficult to find, and so we are always on the look-out for them. We look for in-depth knowledge of an area, an original view of the material, and a presentation which makes these accessible to a sophisticated reader who may or may not be informed on that topic. We will be looking for more and better articles which anticipate ideas and trends on the intellectual and cultural frontier."

C.S.P. WORLD NEWS, Editions Stencil, 1307 Bethamy Lane, Gloucester, Ontario K1J 8P3 Canada. Editor-in-Chief: Guy F. Claude Hamel. 100% freelance written. Monthly literary journal emphasizing book reviews. Publishes ms an average of 2 months after acceptance. Buys first serial rights and first North American serial rights. Photocopied submissions OK. Computer printout submissions acceptable; no dot-matrix. SAE, IRCs. Reports in 2 months.

Nonfiction: Sociology and criminology. Buys 12 mss/year. Send complete ms. Length: 2,600 words.

Columns/Departments: Writer's Workshop material. Buys unlimited items/year. Send complete ms. Length: 20-50 words.

Poetry: Publishes avant-garde forms. Submit complete unlimited ms. Length: 6-12 lines.

Fillers: Jokes, gags and anecdotes. Payment negotiated.

Tips: The writer has a better chance of breaking in with short articles and fillers. "We wish to know our writers and give them a chance to know us. A frequent mistake made by writers is their refusal to subscribe—we need their complete support in helping them to publish their work, especially for the first time."

‡CALYX, A Journal of Art & Literature by Women, Calyx, Inc., P.O. Box B, Corvallis OR 97339. (503)753-9384. Editors: Margarita Donnelly et al. Managing Editors: Lisa Domitrovich et al. A literary triannual magazine publishing "Work by women: literature, art, interviews and reviews." Circ. 5,000. Pays on publication. Publishes ms an average of 1 month after acceptance. Byline given. Buys first rights and second serial reprint rights. Photocopied submissions OK. Computer printout submissions OK. Reports in 3 weeks on queries; 1 month on mss. Sample copy for $6.50 plus 75¢ postage; writer's guidelines for business size SASE.

Nonfiction "We are interested in well-crafted writing by women." Essays, interview/profile and book reviews. "We use 10-30 book reviews per issue and 3-6 interviews and essays per year." Send complete ms. Query the editors for book review list. Length for book reviews: 1,000 words; interviews/essays: 3,000 words. Pays in copies or $5/page depending on grant support.

Fiction: Contact: Editorial Board. Serious literary fiction. Buys 10-15 mss/year. Send complete ms. Length: 5,000 words maximum. Pays $5/published page or in copies of journal.

Poetry: Buys 150-250 poems/year. Submit maximum 6 poems. Pays $5/poem or page or in copies of the journal.

Tips: "Send well-crafted writing with SASE and brief biographical statement. Be familiar with our publication."

CANADIAN FICTION MAGAZINE, Box 946, Station F, Toronto, Ontario M4Y 2N9 Canada. Editor: Geoffrey Hancock. Quarterly magazine; 148 pages. Publishes only Canadian fiction, short stories and novel excerpts. Circ. 1,800. Pays on publication. Buys first North American serial rights. Byline given. SASE, IRCs or Canadian stamps. Reports in 6 weeks. Back issue $6 (in Canadian funds); current issue $7.50 (in Canadian funds).

Nonfiction: Interview (must have a definite purpose, both as biography and as a critical tool focusing on problems and techniques) and book reviews (Canadian fiction only). Buys 35 mss/year. Query. Length: 1,000-3,000 words. Pays $10/printed page plus 1-year subscription.

Photos: Purchased on assignment. Send prints. Pays $10 for 5x7 b&w glossy prints; $50 for cover. Model releases required.

Fiction: "No restrictions on subject matter or theme. We are open to experimental and speculative fiction as well as traditional forms. Style, content and form are the author's prerogative. We also publish self-contained sections of novel-in-progress and French-Canadian fiction in translation, as well as an annual special issue on a single author such as Mavis Gallant, Leon Rooke, Robert Harlow or Jane Rule. Please note that *CFM* is an anthology devoted *exclusively* to Canadian fiction. We publish only the works of writers and artists residing in Canada and Canadians living abroad." Pays $10/printed page.
Tips: "Prospective contributors must study several recent issues carefully. *CFM* is a serious professional literary magazine whose contributors include the finest writers in Canada."

‡CANADIAN LITERATURE, University of British Columbia, Vancouver, British Columbia V6T 1W5 Canada. Editor: W.H. New. 70% freelance written. Works with "both new and established writers depending on quality. Quarterly. Circ. 2,000. Not copyrighted. Buys first Canadian rights only. Pays on publication. Publishes ms an average of 2 years after acceptance. Computer printout submissions acceptable; prefers letter-quality to dot-matrix. Query "with a clear description of the project." SAE, IRCs. Sample copy and writer's guidelines for $7.50 (Canadian) and 7x10 SAE with $2.50 Canadian postage.
Nonfiction: Articles of high quality only on Canadian books and writers written in French or English. Articles should be scholarly and readable. Length: 2,000-5,500 words. Pays $5/printed page.

THE CHARITON REVIEW, Northeast Missouri State University, Kirksville MO 63501. (816)785-4499. Editor: Jim Barnes. 100% freelance written. Semiannual (fall and spring) magazine covering contemporary fiction, poetry, translation and book reviews. Circ. 600. Pays on publication. Publishes ms an average of 6 months after acceptance. Byline given. Buys first North American serial rights. Computer printout submissions acceptable; no dot-matrix. Reports in 1 week on queries; 2 weeks on mss. Sample copy for $2 and 7x10 SAE and 63¢ postage.
Nonfiction: Book reviews. Buys 2-5 mss/year. Query or send complete ms. Length: 1,000-5,000. Pays $15.
Fiction: Ethnic, experimental, mainstream, novel excerpts and traditional. "We are not interested in slick material." Buys 6-8 mss/year. Send complete ms. Length: 1,000-6,000 words. Pays $5/page.
Poetry: Avant-garde, free verse and traditional. Buys 50-55 poems/year. Submit maximum 10 poems. Length: open. Pays $5/page.
Tips: "Read *Chariton* and similar magazines. Know the difference between good literature and bad. Know what magazine might be interested in your work. We are not a trendy magazine. We publish only the best. All sections are open to freelancers. Know your market or you are wasting your time—and mine. Do *not* write for guidelines; the only guideline is excellence in all matters."

CONFRONTATION, C.W. Post College of Long Island University, Greenvale NY 11548. (516)299-2391. Editor: Martin Tucker. 90% freelance written. Works with a small number of new/unpublished writers each year. Semiannual magazine; 190 pages. Emphasizes creative writing for a "literate, educated, college-graduate audience." Circ. 2,000. Pays on publication. Pays 50% kill fee. Publishes ms an average of 9 months after acceptance. Byline given. Buys first serial rights. Phone queries, simultaneous and photocopied submissions OK. Query for electronic submissions. Computer printout submissions acceptable; no dot-matrix. Reports in 2 months. Sample copy $2.
Nonfiction: "Articles are, basically, commissioned essays on a specific subject." Memoirs wanted. Buys 6 mss/year. Query. Length: 1,000-3,000 words. Pays $10-100.
Fiction: William Fahey, fiction editor. Experimental, humorous and mainstream. Buys 25-50 mss/year. Submit complete ms. Length: open. Pays $15-100.
Poetry: W. Palmer, poetry editor. Avant-garde, free verse, haiku, light verse and traditional. Buys 60 poems/year. Submit maximum 8 poems. No length requirement. Pays $5-50.
Tips: "We discourage proselytizing literature. We do, however, read all manuscripts. It's rewarding discovering a good manuscript that comes in unsolicited."

THE DENVER QUARTERLY, University of Denver, Denver CO 80208. (303)753-2869. Editor: David Milofsky. 100% freelance written. Works with a small number of new/unpublished writers. Quarterly magazine for generally sophisticated readership. Circ. 1,000. Pays on publication. Publishes ms an average of 6-12 months after acceptance. Buys first North American serial rights. Phone queries OK. Photocopied submissions OK. Computer printout submissions acceptable; no dot-matrix. Reports in 3 months. Sample copy $5.
Nonfiction: "Most reviews are solicited; we do publish a few literary essays in each number." Send complete ms. Pays $5/printed page.
Fiction: Buys 10-15 mss/year. Send complete ms. Pays $5/printed page.
Poetry: Buys 50 poems/year. Send poems. Pays $10/printed page.
Tips: "We decide on the basis of quality only. Prior publication is irrelevant. Promising material, even though rejected, may receive some personal comment from the editor; some material can be revised to meet our standards through such criticism. I receive more good stuff than *DQ* can accept, so there is some subjectivity and a good deal of luck involved in any final acceptance."

DINOSAUR REVIEW,Dinosaur Literary Society, Box 294, Drumheller, Alberta T0l O4O Canada. (403)823-7126. 100% freelance written. Published 2-3 times/year. "A journal of current writing." Circ. 500. Pays on publication. Publishes ms an average of 3 months after acceptance. Byline given. Buys first North American serial rights. Photocopied submissions OK. Computer printout submissions OK; prefers letter-quality to dot-matrix. Reports in 3 weeks on queries; 3 months on mss. Free sample copy and writer's guidelines.
Nonfiction: Book excerpts and essays. No inspirational. Buys 4-6 mss/year. Query. Length: 1,000-4,000 words. Pays $15-100.
Fiction: Aritha Van Herk, fiction editor. Adventure, experimental, humorous, mainstream, novel excerpts and science fiction. Buys 6-8 mss/year. Length: 1,000-5,000 words. Pays $15-125.
Poetry: Mont Reid, poetry editor. Avant-garde, free verse and haiku. No poems about dinosaurs. Buys 50 poems/year. Submit up to 12 poems at one time. Pays $5-75.

ELDRITCH TALES, Magazine in the Weird Tales Tradition, Yith Press, 1051 Wellington Rd., Lawrence KS 66044. (913)843-4341. Editor: Crispin Burnham. 90% freelance written. A quarterly magazine of supernatural horror. Circ. 500. Pays on publication. Byline given. Buys first North American rights. Photocopied and previously published submissions OK. Computer printout submissions acceptable; prefers letter-quality to dot-matrix. Reports in 1 week on queries; 5 months on mss. Sample copy $6; free writer's guidelines.
Nonfiction: Essays and interview/profile. Buys 1-2 mss/year. Send complete ms. Length: 10-500 words. Pays ¼-1¢/word; pays in copies if author prefers.
Photos: State availability of photos with submission.
Columns/Departments: Eldritch Eye (film review columns) and Book Reviews. Buys 1-2 mss/year. Query. Length: 200 words. Pays ¼-1¢/word.
Fiction: Horror, novel excerpts, serialized novels and suspense. No "mad slashers, sword and sorcery, or hard science fiction." Buys 10-12 mss/year. Send complete ms. Length: 50-10,000 words. Pays ¼-1¢/word.
Poetry: Free verse. Buys 5-10 poems/year. Submit maximum 3 poems. Length: 5-20 lines. Pays 10-25¢/line.
Fillers: Facts and newsbreaks. Buys 10/year. Length: 5-25 words. Pays 10-25¢/line.

EPOCH, Cornell University, 251 Goldwin Smith, Ithaca NY 14853. (607)256-3385. Editor: C.S. Giscombe. 50-98% freelance written. Works with a small number of new/unpublished writers each year. Literary magazine of original fiction and poetry published 3 times/year. Circ. 1,000. Pays on publication. Publishes ms 2-12 months after acceptance. Byline given. Buys first North American serial rights. Computer printout submissions OK; prefers letter-quality to dot-matrix. Sample copy $3.50. Send SASE for listing of nearest library carrying *Epoch*.
Fiction: "Potential contributors should *read* a copy or two. There is *no other way* for them to ascertain what we need or like." Buys 15-20 mss/year. Send complete ms. Pays $10/page.
Poetry: "Potential contributors should read magazine to see what type of poetry is used." Buys 20-30 poems/year. Pays $1/line.

EROTIC FICTION QUARTERLY, EFQ Publications, Box 4958, San Francisco CA 94101. Editor: Richard Hiller. 100% freelance written. Small literary magazine for thoughtful people interested in a variety of highly original and creative short fiction with sexual themes. Pays on acceptance. Byline given. Buys all rights. Photocopied submissions OK. Computer printout submissions acceptable; prefers letter-quality to dot-matrix. Writer's guidelines for SASE.
Fiction: Heartful, intelligent erotica, any style. Also, stories—not necessarily erotic—about some aspect of authentic sexual experience. No standard pornography or men's magazine-type stories; no contrived or formula plots or gimmicks; no broad satire or parody; no poetry. Send complete ms. Length: 500-5,000 words, average 1,500 words. Pays $35 minimum.
Tips: "*Erotic Fiction Quarterly* particularly needs graphic erotica. This type of story should be a delight to read (and be neither pretentious nor crude), contain an intense sensuality and an element of natural humor, and be vividly imaginative. It will be a uniquely personal expression. I encourage beginners who have something to say regarding sexual attitudes, emotions, roles, etc. Story ideas should come from real life, not media; characters should be real people. There are essentially no restrictions on content, style, explicitness, etc.; *originality*, *clarity*, and *integrity* are most important."

EVENT, % Douglas College, Box 2503, New Westminster, British Columbia V3L 5B2 Canada. Managing Editor: Vye Flindall. 100% freelance written. Works with a small number of new/unpublished writers each year; eager to work with new/unpublished writers. Triannual magazine (March, July and November) for "those interested in literature and writing." Circ. 1,000. Uses 80-100 mss/year. Small payment and contributor's copy only. Publishes ms an average of 3 months after acceptance. Buys first serial rights. Byline given. Photocopied submissions OK. Computer printout submissions acceptable; prefers letter-quality to dot-matrix. Reports in 4 months. Submit complete ms with IRCs.
Nonfiction: "High quality work." Reviews of Canadian books and essays.
Fiction: Short stories and drama.
Poetry: Submit complete ms. "We are looking for high quality modern poetry."

‡**FACET, A Creative Writing Magazine**, Box 4950, Hualapai AZ 86412. (602)757-7462. Editor: Judith C. Porter. 100% freelance written. Wants to see new work of both new and established writers. A bimonthly literary magazine with work expressing all points of view, except works which feature erotica, slander, horror, pornography, didactic religion or are intended for small children. Estab. 1986. Circ. 500. Pays on publication. Publishes ms an average of 2-4 months after acceptance. Byline given. Copyrighted. Buys one-time rights. Submit seasonal/holiday material 2-4 months in advance. Simultaneous and previously published submissions OK. Computer printout submissions OK; no dot-matrix. Reports in 4-6 weeks on ms. Sample copy $2.25 with 6x9 SAE and 3 first class stamps; writer's guidelines for business size SASE.

Fiction: Adventure, experimental, fantasy, historical, humorous, mainstream, mystery, romance, science fiction, suspense, western, political, philosophical, sports, human dilemma, technology and space. "We prefer strong plots, well-defined characters of any age or socio-economic group. Upbeat endings not a must." No horror stories, erotica, pornography, devotional, didactic religious material, or slanderous pieces mentioning real people. Gay or lesbian theme stories carefully examined. Buys 30 mss/year. Send complete ms and biographical information about your writing career. Length 800-3,500 words. Pays $5-$20.

Poetry: Avant-garde, free verse, haiku, light verse and traditional. No frank erotica, devotional religious, pornographic or horrible themes. Buys 36 poems/year. Submit maximum 10 poems. Length: 1-75 lines. Pays $3-$7.

Tips: "Check your work for plot construction, character presentation, consistency in point of view, and character motivation. Be open to suggested changes in the material if required."

‡**FESSENDEN REVIEW**, The Reginald A. Fessenden Educational Fund, Inc. Box 7272, San Diego CA 92107. (619)488-4991. Editor: Douglas Cruickshank. 20% freelance written. "We read all material submitted by subscribers and contributors to the Fessenden Fund. Ours is a quarterly literate book review magazine which prints some 80-90 book reviews per issue—most with illustrations." Pays on publication. Publishes ms an average of 3-6 months after acceptance. No byline given. Buys one-time rights. Query for electronic submissions. Computer printout submissions OK; no dot-matrix. Reports in 3 months on mss. Sample copy for 9x12 SAE with 9 first-class stamps.

Nonfiction: Reviews. Buys 50 mss/year. Send complete ms. Length: 200-2,000 words. Pays $30/unsolicited article.

Photos: State availability of photos with submission.

Columns/Articles: Brief Reviews (must be in style of H.L. Mencken and his followers: iconoclastic, funny, perceptive, wry, witty), 200-500 words. Buys 25 mss/year. Send complete ms. Length: 200-500 words. Pays $15.

Tips: "We want book reviews by people who (1) know their subject intimately and (2) know our magazine and its iconoclastic style intimately."

FICTION NETWORK MAGAZINE, Fiction Network, Box 5651, San Francisco CA 94101. (415)391-6610. Editor: Jay Schaefer. 100% freelance written. Eager to work with new/unpublished writers. Magazine of short stories. Fiction Network distributes short stories to newspapers, and regional magazines and also publishes *Fiction Network Magazine* (for agents, editors and writers). Circ. 6,000. Pays on publication. Publishes ms an average of 6 months after acceptance. Byline given. Buys first serial rights. "Each story accepted may appear in several newspapers and magazines through our syndicate." Photocopied submissions OK. Computer printout submissions acceptable; prefers letter-quality to dot-matrix. Reports in 3 months. Does not return foreign submissions—notification only with SASE. Sample copy $4 U.S. and Canada; $6.50 elsewhere. Writer's guidelines for business size SASE.

Fiction: All types of stories and subjects are acceptable; novel excerpts will be considered only if they stand alone as stories. Considers unpublished fiction only. No poetry, essays, reviews or interviews. No children's or young adult material. Buys 100 mss/year. Send complete ms. "Do not submit a second manuscript until you receive a response to the first manuscript." Length: 5,000 words maximum (2,000 words preferred). Pays $25 minimum for magazine and 50% of syndicate sales.

Tips: "We will be looking for high-quality, very short fiction in 1988. We offer both known and unknown writers excellent exposure while we open up new markets for stories. Our greatest need is for short-short stories." Contributors include Alice Adams, Max Apple, Ann Beattie, Andre Dubus, Lynne Sharon Schwartz, Marian Thurm, Ken Chowder and Bobbie Ann Mason.

THE FIDDLEHEAD, University of New Brunswick, Old Arts Bldg., Box 4400, Fredericton, New Brunswick E3B 5A3 Canada. (506)454-3591. Editor: Michael Taylor. 90% freelance written. Eager to work with new/unpublished writers. Preference is given to Canadian writers. Quarterly magazine covering poetry, short fiction, drawings and photographs and book reviews. Circ. 1,100. Pays on publication. Publishes ms an average of 6-12 months after acceptance. Not copyrighted. Buys first North American serial rights. Submit seasonal/holiday material 6 months in advance. Simultaneous queries and photocopied submissions (if legible) OK. Computer printout submissions acceptable; no dot-matrix. SAE, IRCs. Reports in 3 weeks on queries; 2 months on mss. Sample copy $4.25, Canada; $4.50, U.S.

Fiction: Kent Thompson, fiction editor. "Stories may be on any subject—acceptance is based on quality alone. Because the journal is heavily subsidized by the Canadian government, strong preference is given to Canadian writers." Buys 20 mss/year. Pays $12/page.

Poetry: Robert Gibbs, poetry editor. "Poetry may be on any subject—acceptance is based on quality alone. Because the journal is heavily subsidized by the Canadian government, strong preference is given to Canadian writers." Buys average of 60 poems/year. Submit maximum 10 poems. Pays $12/page; $100 maximum.

Tips: "Quality alone is the criterion for publication. Return postage (Canadian, or IRCs) should accompany all manuscripts."

‡**THE GAMUT, A Journal of Ideas and Information**, Cleveland State University, RT 1216, Cleveland OH 44115. (216)687-4679. Editor: Louis T. Milic. Managing Editor: Mary Grimm. 50-60% freelance written. Triannual magazine. Circ. 1,000. Pays on publication. Publishes ms an average of 6 months after acceptance. Byline given. Buys one-time rights. Submit seasonal/holiday material 6 months in advance. Simultaneous and photocopied submissions OK. Computer printout submissions acceptable. Reports in 1 month on queries; 3 months on mss. Sample copy $2.50; writer's guidelines for business size SASE.

Nonfiction: Essays, general interest, historic/nostalgic, humor, opinion, personal experience, photo feature and technical.Buys 15-20 mss/year. Query with or without published clips, or send complete ms. Length: 1,000-6,000 words. Pays $25-250. Pays authors associated with the university with contributor copies.

Photos: State availability of photos with submission. Offers no additional payment for photos accepted with ms. Captions, model releases and identification of subjects required. Buys one-time rights.

Columns/Departments: Languages of the World (linguistic). Length: 2,000-4,000. Buys 1-2 mss/year. Query with published clips or send complete ms. Pays $75-125.

Fiction: Ethnic, experimental, historical, humorous, mainstream, novel excerpts and science fiction. No condensed novels or genre fiction. Buys 1-2 mss/year. Send complete ms. Length: 1,000-6,000 words. Pays $25-150.

Poetry: Leonard Trawick, poetry editor. Buys 6-15 poems/year. Submit up to 10 at one time. Pays $25-75.

Tips: "Get a fresh approach to an interesting idea or subject; back it up with solid facts, analysis, and/or research. Make sure you are writing for an educated, but general and not expert reader."

GRAIN, Saskatchewan Writers' Guild, Box 1154, Regina, Saskatchewan S4P 3B4 Canada. (306)522-0811 (daytime). Editor: Brenda Riches. 100% freelance written. Eager to work with new/unpublished writers. A literary quarterly magazine that "seeks to publish the best of traditional and experimental writing and to challenge readers and writers." Circ. 850. Pays on acceptance. Publishes ms an average of 3 months after acceptance. No byline given. Not copyrighted. Buys one-time rights. Photocopied submissions OK. Computer printout submissions acceptable; no dot-matrix. SAE, IRC. Reports in 1 month on queries; 3 months on mss. Sample copy for $4, 8½x11 SAE and $1 postage or IRC.

Nonfiction: Literary essays. Buys up to 4 mss/year. Query. Pays $30-100.

Fiction: Brenda Riches and Bonnie Burnard, fiction editors. "Literary art only. No fiction of a popular nature." Buys 12-15 mss/year. Send complete ms. Length: 300-8,000 words. Pays $30-100.

Poetry: Brenda Riches and Garry Radison, poetry editors. "Only poetry that has substance." Buys 30-60/year. Submit maximum 8 poems. Length: 3-200 lines. Pays $30.

Tips: "Only work of the highest literary quality is accepted. Read several back issues. Get advice from a practicing writer to make sure the work is ready to send. Then send it."

HIBISCUS MAGAZINE, Short Stories, Poetry, Art, Hibiscus Press, Box 22248, Sacramento CA 95822. Editor: Margaret Wensrich. 100% freelance written. Works with a small number of new/unpublished writers each year. Magazine "for people who like to read." Circ. 2,000. Pays on publication. Publishes ms 6-18 months after acceptance. Byline given. Buys first North American serial rights. Photocopied submissions OK. Computer printout submissions OK; no dot-matrix. Reports in 3-4 months on queries. Sample copy $3; writer's guidelines for business size SASE.

Fiction: Adventure, fantasy, humorous, mainstream, mystery, romance, science fiction, slice-of-life vignettes, suspense and western. Buys 9-12 mss/year. Send complete ms. Length: 1,500-3,000 words. Pays $15-25.

Poetry: Joyce Odam, poetry editor. Free verse, haiku, light verse and traditional. No subject or line limit. Buys 20-25 poems/year. Submit maximum 4 poems. Pays $5-25.

Fillers: Short humor. Buys 4-6/year. Length: 25-100 words. Pays $2-5.

Tips: "We receive hundreds of submissions each month. We are slow to read and return manuscripts, but we do serve each writer and poet as fast as we can. We are a limited market. We regret we must return work that ought to be published because we do not have enough space."

THE HUDSON REVIEW, 684 Park Ave., New York NY 10021. Managing Editor: Ronald Koury. Quarterly. Pays on publication. Buys first world serial rights in English. Reports in 6-8 weeks.

Nonfiction: Articles, translations and reviews. Length: 8,000 words maximum.

Fiction: Uses "quality fiction". Length: 10,000 words maximum. Pays 2½¢/word.
Poetry: 50¢/line for poetry.
Tips: Unsolicited mss will be read according to the following schedule: *Nonfiction:* Jan. 1 through March 31, and Oct. 1 through Dec. 31; *Poetry:* April 1 through Sept. 30; *Fiction:* June 1 through Nov. 30.

IMAGE MAGAZINE, A Magazine of the Arts, Cornerstone Press, Box 28048, St. Louis MO 63119. (314)296-9662. Managing Editor: Anthony J. Summers. General Editor: James J. Finnegan. 100% freelance written. "We are backlogged at this time. Send a letter first or query before any work is sent." Triannual literary journal "for the educated, open-minded, thinking person." Circ. 600. Pays on publication. Publishes ms an average of 3-6 months after acceptance. Byline given. Offers negotiable kill fee. Buys one-time rights. Simultaneous queries OK. Computer printout submissions acceptable; prefers letter-quality to dot-matrix. Reports in 9 weeks on queries; 10 weeks on mss. Sample copy $3 and 50¢ postage; free writer's guidelines.
Fiction: Erotica, ethnic, experimental, fantasy, horror, humorous, novel excerpts and science fiction. No "cutesy, self-congratulating material." Buys variable number mss/year. Query or send complete ms. Length: open. Pays $1-100.
Poetry: Avant-garde, free verse, haiku, light verse and traditional. No "overly religious, Elvis poetry, 'the world is neat and happy' type, etc." Submit maximum 10 poems. Length: open. Pays $1-100.
Tips: "We receive very few reviews, interviews, interesting articles on the literary world, as well as plays and experimental material. Try these for a better shot."

‡INDIANA REVIEW, Indiana University, 316 N. Jordan, Bloomington IN 47405. (812)335-3439. Editor: Elizabeth Dodd. 100% freelance written. Magazine published 3 times/year. "We publish fine innovative fiction and poetry. We're interested in energy, originality and careful attention to craft. While we publish many well-known writers, we also publish new and emerging poets and fiction writers." Circ. 700. Pays on acceptance. Byline given. Buys first North American serial rights. Computer printout submissions OK; prefers letter-quality to dot-matrix. Reports in 2 weeks on queries; 2 months on mss. Sample copy $4; free writer's guidelines.
Nonfiction: Essays. No pornographic or strictly academic articles dealing with the traditional canon. Buys 3 mss/year. Query. Length: 5,000 maximum. Pays $25-200.
Fiction: Experimental and mainstream. No pornography. Buys 18 mss/year. Send complete ms. Length: 250-15,000. Pays $25.
Poetry: Avant-garde and free verse. "No pornography and no slavishly traditional poetry." Buys 60 mss/year. Submit up to 8 poems at one time. Length: 5 lines minimum. Pays $5/page.
Tips: "Practice."

THE IOWA REVIEW, 369 EPB, The University of Iowa, Iowa City IA 52242. (319)335-0462. Editor: David Hamilton, with the help of colleagues, graduate assistants, and occasional guest editors. Magazine published 3 times/year. Buys first serial rights. Photocopied submissions OK. Reports in 3 months.
Nonfiction, Fiction and Poetry: "We publish essays, stories and poems and would like for our essays not always to be works of academic criticism." Buys 65-85 unsolicited mss/year. Submit complete ms. Pays $1/line for verse; $10/page for prose.

JAM TO-DAY, 372 Dunstable Rd., Tyngsboro MA 01879. Editors: Judith Stanford and Don Stanford. 90% freelance written. Eager to work with new/unpublished writers. Annual literary magazine featuring high quality poetry, fiction and reviews. Especially interested in unknown or little-known authors. Circ. 300. Pays on publication. Publishes ms an average of 6 months after acceptance. Byline given. Buys first rights and nonexclusive anthology rights. Photocopied submissions OK. Computer printout submissions acceptable; prefers letter-quality to dot-matrix. Reports in 6 weeks. Sample copy $3.50 (includes postage).
Fiction: "We will consider quality fiction of almost any style or genre. However, we prefer not to receive material written to mass-market formulas, or that is highly allegorical, abstruse, or heavily dependent on word play for its effect." Buys 2-4 mss/year. Send complete ms. Length: 1,500-7,500 words. Pays $5/page.
Poetry: Avant-garde, free verse, shaped-concrete, found, haiku and traditional. No light verse. Buys 30-50/year. Submit 5 poems maximum. Length: open. Pays $5/poem; higher payment for poems more than 3 pages in length.

JAPANOPHILE, Box 223, Okemos MI 48864. Editor: Earl Snodgrass. 80% freelance written. Works with a small number of new/unpublished writers each year. Quarterly magazine for literate people who are interested in Japanese culture anywhere in the world. Pays on publication. Publishes ms an average of 5 months after acceptance. Buys first North American serial rights. Previously published submissions OK. Computer printout submissions acceptable; no dot-matrix. Reports in 1 month. Sample copy $3, postpaid; writer's guidelines with SASE.
Nonfiction: "We want material on Japanese culture in *North America or anywhere in the world*, even Japan. We want articles, preferably with pictures, about persons engaged in arts of Japanese origin: a Michigan natu-

ralist who is a haiku poet, a potter who learned raku in Japan, a vivid 'I was there' account of a Go tournament in California. We use some travel articles if exceptionally well-written, but we are *not* a regional magazine about Japan. We are a little magazine, a literary magazine. Our particular slant is a certain kind of culture wherever it is in the world: Canada, the U.S., Europe, Japan. The culture includes flower arranging, haiku, religion, art, photography and fiction. It is important to study the magazine." Buys 8 mss/issue. Query preferred but not required. Length: 1,200 words maximum. Pays $8-15.

Photos: State availability of photos. Pays $10-20 for 8x10 b&w glossy prints.

Fiction: Experimental, mainstream, mystery, adventure, science fiction, humorous, romance and historical. Themes should relate to Japan or Japanese culture. Length: 1,000-10,000 words. Pays $20. Contest each year pays $100 to best short story.

Columns/Departments: Regular columns and features are Tokyo Scene and Profile of Artists. "We also need columns about Japanese culture in other cities." Query. Length: 1,000 words. Pays $20 maximum.

Poetry: Traditional, avant-garde and light verse related to Japanese culture or in a Japanese form such as haiku. Length: 3-50 lines. Pays $1-100.

Fillers: Newsbreaks, puzzles, clippings and short humor of up to 200 words. Pays $1-5.

Tips: "We prefer to see more articles about Japanese culture in the U.S., Canada and Europe." Lack of convincing fact and detail is a frequent mistake.

‡**L'APACHE, An International Journal of Literature & Art**, Kathryn Vilips Studios, Inc., Drawer G, 713 Sietta Vista Drive, Wofford Heights CA 93285. (619)376-3634. Editor: Kathryn Vilips. 50% freelance written. Eager to work with new/unpublished writers. A quarterly literary magazine covering art, literature, history. Estab. 1986. Pays on acceptance. Publishes ms an average of 6 months after acceptance. Byline given. Buys simultaneous rights. Submit seasonal/holiday material 3 months in advance. Photocopied submissions OK. Computer printout submissions OK; prefers letter-quality. Reports in 1 month. Sample copy $5 and 8x10 SAE with 89¢ postage; writer's guidelines for #10 SASE.

Nonfiction: Book excerpts, essays, historical/nostalgic, how-to, interview/profile, new product, photo feature and technical. "We also would like to receive Indian legends and stories of old grandfathers (medicine men), and women in Indian history—early or present history. Absolutely no pornography, science fiction or any story, or poetry written in poor taste." Buys 8-12 mss/year. Send complete ms. "Do not send originals." Length: 3,000 maximum words. Pays $25-50 for unsolicited articles.

Photos: Send photos with submissions. Reviews negatives, 3x5 transparencies and 3x5 prints. Payment negotiable. Captions, model releases, identification of subjects required. Buys one-time and foreign rights.

Columns/Departments: The Write Word (creative writing); The Artist's Voice (substantiated complaints on lost, stolen, damaged art); The Indian Voice (art, poetry, history, Indian causes); and Ars Poetica (poetry for the Indian, not against), all 3,000 maximum words. Buys 8 mss/year. Send complete ms. Pays $25-50.

Fiction: Ethnic, experimental, historical, serialized novels and western. "All manuscripts written in good taste will be considered. A new writer's showcase for unpublished writers only, will be once a year with a $300 first prize and publication. Buys 8 mss/year. Send complete ms. Length: 3,000 maximum words. Pays $25-50.

Poetry: Frank Fitzgerald-Bush, poetry editor. Free verse, haiku and traditional. Buys 20-40 poems/year. Length: 4-20 lines. Pays $5-10.

Fillers: Claudia Craig-Potter, fillers editor. Facts. Buys 4-8/year. Pays $5-10.

Tips: "*L'Apache* cares about the problems of the writer and artist, and is sympathetic to the sensitivity that makes them creative, hence, The Artist's Voice, fighting for artist's rights. As long as an artist or writer is totally honest, with absolutely no exaggeration, the manuscripts will be considered. Professors, archaeologists, anthropologists, historians and teachers have an excellent chance of being published."

‡**LETTERS MAGAZINE**, Maine Writers' Workshop, Box 905, Rd. 1, Stonington ME 04681. (207)367-2484. Editor: Helen Nash. 90% freelance written. A quarterly literary magazine. Circ. 6,500. Pays on acceptance. Publishes ms an average of 1 year after acceptance. No byline given. Buys all rights. Submit seasonal/holiday material 6 months in advance. Simultaneous subissions OK. Reports in 1 month. Sample copy for #10 SAE with 1 first class stamp.

Nonfiction: Essays, general interest, historical/nostalgic, humor and travel. Buys 5 mss/year. Query. Length: 2,000 maximum words. Pays $10-50. Pays expenses of writers on assignment.

Photos: State availability of photos with submission.

Fiction: Historical, humorous, mainstream, novel excerpts and science fiction. Buys 2 mss/year. Query. Length: 2,000-7,000 words. Pay varies.

Poetry: Free verse, light verse and traditional. Buys 10 poems/year. Submit maximum 3 poems. Length: 10-40 lines. Pays $5-50.

Tips: "Write and edit three times before submitting."

‡**LITERARY MAGAZINE REVIEW**, KSU Writers Society, English Dept., Denison Hall, Kansas State University, Manhattan KS 66506. (913)532-6106. Editor: G.W. Clift. 98% freelance written. "Most of our reviewers are recommended to us by third parties." A quarterly literary magazine devoted almost exclusively to

reviews of the current contents of small circulation serials publishing some fiction or poetry. "Most of our reviewers were recommended to us." Circ. 500. Pays on publication. Publishes ms an average of 1 month after acceptance. Byline given. Buys first rights. Photocopied submissions OK. Query for electronic submissions. Computer printout submissions OK; prefers letter-quality. Reports in 2 weeks. Sample copy $3.

Nonfiction: Buys 60 mss/year. Query. Length: 1,500+ words. Pays $20 maximum for assigned articles and two contributor's copies. Sometimes pays expenses of writers on assignment.

Photos: State availability of photos with submission. Identification of subjects required.

Tips: Interested in "omnibus reviews of magazines sharing some quality, editorial philosophy or place of origin."

LITERARY SKETCHES, Box 810571, Dallas TX 75381-0571. (214)243-8776. Editor: Olivia Murray Nichols. 33% freelance written. Works with small number of new/unpublished writers each year and is willing to work with new/unpublished writers. Monthly newsletter for readers with literary interests; all ages. Circ 500. Byline given. Pays on publication. Publishes ms an average of 4-6 months after acceptance. Computer printout submissions acceptable; prefers letter-quality to dot-matrix. Reports in 1 month. Sample copy for business size SAE with 1 first class stamp.

Nonfiction: Interviews of well-known writers and biographical material of more than common knowledge on past writers. Concise, informal style. Centennial pieces relating to a writer's birth, death or famous works. Buys 4-6 mss/year. Submit complete ms. Length: up to 750 words. Pays ½¢/word, plus copies.

Tips: "Articles need not be footnoted, but a list of sources should be submitted with the manuscript. We appreciate fillers of 100 words or less if they concern some little known information on an author or book."

LOS ANGELES TIMES BOOK REVIEW, Times Mirror, Times Mirror Sq., Los Angeles CA 90053. (213)972-7777. Editor: Jack Miles. 70% freelance written. Weekly tabloid reviewing current books. Circ. 1.3 million. Pays on publication. Publishes ms an average of 3 weeks after acceptance. Byline given. Offers variable kill fee. Buys first North American serial rights. Computer printout submissions acceptable; prefers letter-quality to dot-matrix. Accepts no unsolicited book reviews or requests for specific titles to review. "Query with published samples—book reviews or literary features." Buys 500 mss/year. Length: 200-1,500 words. Pays $75-500.

THE MALAHAT REVIEW, The University of Victoria, Box 1700, Victoria, British Columbia V8W 2Y2 Canada. Contact: Editor. 100% freelance written. Eager to work with new/unpublished writers. Magazine published 4 times/year covering poetry, fiction, drama and criticism. Circ. 1,300. Pays on acceptance. Publishes ms up to 1 year after acceptance. Byline given. Offers 100% kill fee. Buys first serial rights. Photocopied submissions OK. Computer printout submissions acceptable; prefers letter-quality to dot-matrix. SASE (Canadian postage or IRC). Reports in 2 weeks on queries; 3 months on mss. Sample copy $6.

Nonfiction: Interview/profile (literary/artistic). Buys 2 mss/year. Send complete ms. Length: 1,000-8,000. Pays $35-175.

Photos: Pays $10-50 for b&w prints. Captions required.

Fiction: Buys 20 mss/year. Send complete ms. Length: no restriction. Pays $35/1,000 words.

Poetry: Avant-garde, free verse and traditional. Buys 100/year. Pays $15/page.

THE MASSACHUSETTS REVIEW, Memorial Hall, University of Massachusetts, Amherst MA 01003. (413)545-2689. Editors: John Hicks and Mary Heath. "As pleased to consider new writers as established ones." Quarterly. Pays on publication. Publishes ms 6-18 months after acceptance. Buys first North American serial rights. Computer printout submissions acceptable; no dot-matrix. Reports in 3 months. Mss will not be returned unless accompanied by SASE. Sample copy for $4 plus 50¢ postage.

Nonfiction: Articles on literary criticism, women, public affairs, art, philosophy, music and dance. Length: 6,500 words average. Pays $50.

Fiction: Short stories or chapters from novels when suitable for independent publication. Length: 15-22 typed pages. Pays $50.

Poetry: 35¢/line or $10 minimum.

Tips: No manuscripts are considered from June to October.

MICHIGAN QUARTERLY REVIEW, 3032 Rackham Bldg., University of Michigan, Ann Arbor MI 48109. Editor: Laurence Goldstein. 75% freelance written. Prefers to work with published/established writers; works with a small number of new/unpublished writers each year. Quarterly. Circ. 2,000. Publishes ms an average of 1 year after acceptance. Pays on publication. Buys first serial rights. Computer printout submissions acceptable; no dot-matrix. Reports in 1 month for mss submitted in September-May; in summer, 2 months. Sample copy $2 with 2 first class stamps.

Nonfiction: "*MQR* is open to general articles directed at an intellectual audience. Essays ought to have a personal voice and engage a significant subject. Scholarship must be present as a foundation, but we are not interested in specialized essays directed only at professionals in the field. We prefer ruminative essays, written in a fresh style and which reach interesting conclusions. We also like memoirs and interviews with significant historical or cultural resonance. " Length: 2,000-5,000 words. Pays $80-150, sometimes more.

Fiction and Poetry: No restrictions on subject matter or language. "We publish about 10 stories a year and are very selective. We like stories which are unusual in tone and structure, and innovative in language." Send complete ms. Pays $8-10/published page.

Tips: "Read the journal and assess the range of contents and the level of writing. We have no guidelines to offer or set expectations; every manuscript is judged on its unique qualities. On essays—query with a very thorough description of the argument and a copy of the first page. Watch for announcements of special issues, which are usually expanded issues and draw upon a lot of freelance writing. Be aware that this is a university quarterly that publishes a limited amount of fiction and poetry; that it is directed at an educated audience, one that has done a great deal of reading in all types of literature."

MID-AMERICAN REVIEW, Dept. of English, Bowling Green State University, Bowling Green OH 43403. (419)372-2725. Editor: Robert Early. 100% freelance written. Eager to work with new/unpublished writers. Semiannual literary magazine of "the highest quality fiction and poetry." Also publishes critical articles and book reviews of contemporary literature. Pays on publication. Publishes ms an average of 3-6 months after acceptance. Byline given. Buys one-time rights. Photocopied submissions OK. Computer printout submissions OK; prefers letter-quality to dot-matrix. Reports in 2 months or less. Sample copy $4.50.

Fiction: Character-oriented, literary. Buys 12 mss/year. Send complete ms; do not query. Pays $5/page up to $75.

Poetry: Strong imagery, strong sense of vision. Buys 60 poems/year. Pays $5/page. Annual prize for best fiction, best poem.

Tips: "Send your best work—submit as you would to any other top-quality literary magazine."

MIDWEST POETRY REVIEW, Box 776, Rock Island IL 61201. Editor: Hugh Ferguson. Managing Editor: Tom Tilford. 100% freelance written. Eager to work with new/unpublished writers. A quarterly magazine of poetry. Pays on acceptance. Publishes ms an average of 3 months after acceptance. Byline given. Buys first North American serial rights. Submit seasonal/holiday material 6 months in advance. Computer printout submissions acceptable; no dot-matrix. Reports in 2 weeks. Sample copy $3; writer's guidelines for business size SASE.

Nonfiction: Poetry reviews and technical (on poetry). Buys 4 mss/year. Query. Length: 800-1,500 words. Pays $10 minimum. Sometimes pays expenses of writers on assignment.

Columns/Departments: Comment (poetry enhancement, improvement) 800-1,500 words. Buys 4 mss/year. Query. Pays $10 minimum.

Poetry: Avant-garde, free verse haiku, light verse, and traditional. No jingles. Buys 400 poems/year. Submit maximum 5 poems; must be subscriber to submit. Pays $5 minimum.

Tips: "We would like authenticated live interviews with known poets."

‡NEW ENGLAND REVIEW/BREAD LOAF QUARTERLY, NER/BLQ, Middlebury College, Middlebury VT 05753. (802)388-3711, Ext 5075. Editors: Sydney Lea and Maura High. Managing Editor: Toni Best. 99% freeelance written. Quarterly magazine covering contemporary literature. "We print a wide range of contemporary poetry, fiction, essays and reviews. Our readers tend to be literary and intellectual, but we're not academic or over-refined or doctrinaire." Circ. 2,500. Pays on publication. Publishes ms an average of 6 months after acceptance. Byline given. Buys first-time rights. Submit seasonal/holiday material 9 months in advance. Photocopied submissions OK. Computer printout submissions OK; prefers letter quality to dot matrix. Reports in 1 weeks on queries; 2 months on ms. Sample copy $4; free writer's guidelines.

Nonfiction: Book excerpts, essays, general interest, humor and personal experience. Buys 10 mss/year. Send complete ms. Length: 500-6,000 words. Pays $10 minimum.

Photos: Send photos with submission. Reviews transparencies and prints. Offers $60 minim per photo. Captions and identification of subjects required. Buys one-time rights.

Fiction: Ethnic, experimental, mainstream, novel excerpts, slice-of-life vignettes. Buys 18 mss/year. Send complete ms. Pays $10 minimum.

Poetry: Avant-garde, free verse and traditional. Buys 50 poems/year. Submit up to 6 at one time. Pays $10 minimum.

Tips: "Read at least one issue to get an idea of our range, standards and style. Don't submit simultaneously to other publications. All sections are open. We look for writing that's intelligent, well informed and well crafted."

the new renaissance, An International Magazine of Ideas and Opinions, Emphasizing Literature and the Arts, 9 Heath Road, Arlington MA 02174. Editor: Louise T. Reynolds. 92% + freelance written. Works with a small number of new/unpublished writers each year. "We are beginning to get backlogged and writers in 1988 might want to query with SASE or IRC, before submitting." International biannual literary magazine covering literature, visual arts, ideas and opinions for a general literate, sophisticated public. Circ.

1,500. Pays after publication. Publishes ms 18-25 months after acceptance. Buys all rights. Photocopied submissions OK. Computer printout submissions acceptable; prefers letter-quality to dot-matrix. Does not read any ms without SASE or IRCs. Answers no queries without SASE, IRCs or stamped postcards. Does not read mss from July 1 through December 31 of any year. Reports in 1 month on queries; 7 months on mss. Sample copy $5.10 for back issues; $5.60 recent issue; $6 current issue (all rates apply to U.S. submission; add 50¢ for foreign requests).

Nonfiction: Interview/profile (literary/performing artists); opinion; and literary/artistic essays. "We prefer expert opinion in a style suitable for a literary magazine (i.e., *not* journalistic). Send complete manuscript or essays. Because we are biannual, we prefer to have writers query us, with outlines, etc., on political/sociological articles and give a sample of their writing." Buys 3-6 mss/year. Query for political/sociological pieces with published clips; SASE and IRC. Length: 11-35 pages. Pays $24-95.

Photos: State availability of photos or send photos with query. Do not send slides; do not send originals without SASE. Pays $5-11 for 5x7 b&w prints. Captions, model releases and identification of subjects required, if applicable. Buys one-time rights.

Fiction: Quality fiction, well-crafted, "serious"; occasionally, experimental or light. No "formula or plotted stories; no pulp or woman's magazine fiction; no academic writing. We are looking for writing with a personal voice and with something to say." Buys 5-12 mss/year. Send complete ms. Length: 2-35 pages. Send only one ms. Pays $20-60.

Poetry: James E. S. Woodbury, poetry editor. No poetry before January 2, 1988. Avant-garde, free verse, light verse, traditional and translations (with originals). No heavily academic poetry; "we publish occasional light verse but do not want to see 'Hallmark Card' writing." Submit maximum 6 average length poems; 2-3 long poems. Reports in 4 months. Buys 20-49 poems/year. Pays $10-30.

Tips: "Know your markets. We still receive manuscripts that, had the writer any understanding of our publication, would have been directed elsewhere. Don't submit to independent small magazines unless you've bought and studied an issue. *tnr* is a unique litmag and should be *carefully* perused. Close reading of one or two issues will reveal that we have a classicist philosophy and want manuscripts that hold up to re-readings. Fiction and poetry are completely open to freelancers. Writers most likely to break in to *tnr* are 'serious' writers, poets, those who feel 'compelled' to write. We don't want to see 'pop' writing, trendy or formula writing. Nor do we want writing where the 'statement' is imposed on the story, or writing where the author shows off his superior knowledge or sensibility. Respect the reader and do not 'explain' the story. If we've rejected your work and our comments make some sense to you, keep on submitting to us. Always send us only your best work. New writers frequently don't know how to structure or organize for greatest impact, or sometimes they attempt ambitious statements that they need more skill or expertise to bring off. Do not submit anything from July 1 through December 31. Submissions during those months will be returned unread. We now are working with a backlog of material."

THE NEW SOUTHERN LITERARY MESSENGER, The Airplane Press, 400 S. Laurel St., Richmond VA 23220. (804)780-1244. Editor: Charles Lohmann. 100% freelance written. Eager to work with new/unpublished writers and works with a small number of new/unpublished writers each year. Quarterly literary tabloid featuring short stories and political satire. Circ. 500. Pays on publication. Publishes ms an average of 6 months after acceptance. Byline given. Buys first serial rights and second (reprint) rights. Queries and previously published submissions OK. Computer printout submissions acceptable; no dot-matrix. Reports in 1 week on queries; 6 weeks on mss. Sample copy for $2 and 6x9 SAE with 3 first class stamps; writer's guidelines for 4x9 SASE.

Fiction: Short prose and humor. Avoid fantasy and science fiction. No formula short stories. Buys 16-20 mss/year. Query. Length: 500-2,500 words. Pays $10 and 6 copies.

Tips: "Inquire first about manuscript needs. Buy a sample copy to see if you like the magazine. If you can't develop a rapport with one edition, try another."

THE NORTH AMERICAN REVIEW, University of Northern Iowa, Cedar Falls IA 50614. (319)273-2681. Editor: Robley Wilson Jr. 50% freelance written. Quarterly. Circ. 4,000. Buys all rights for nonfiction and North American serial rights for fiction and poetry. Pays on acceptance. Publishes ms an average of 1 year after acceptance. Computer printout submissions acceptable; no dot-matrix. Familiarity with magazine helpful. Reports in 10 weeks. Sample copy $2.50.

Nonfiction: No restrictions, but most nonfiction is commissioned by magazine. Query. Rate of payment arranged.

Fiction: No restrictions; highest quality only. Length: open. Pays minimum $10/page. Fiction department closed (no mss read) from April 1 to December 31.

Poetry: Peter Cooley, department editor. No restrictions; highest quality only. Length: open. Pays 50¢/line minimum.

THE OHIO REVIEW, Ellis Hall, Ohio University, Athens OH 45701-2979. (614)593-1900. Editor: Wayne Dodd. 40% freelance written. Published 3 times/year. "A balanced, informed engagement of contemporary

American letters, with special emphasis on poetics." Circ. 2,000. Publishes ms an average of 8 months after acceptance. Rights acquired vary with author and material; usually buys first serial rights or first North American serial rights. Submit complete ms. Unsolicited material will be read only September-May. Computer printout submissions acceptable; prefers letter-quality to dot-matrix. Reports in 10 weeks.

Nonfiction, Fiction and Poetry: Buys essays of general intellectual and special literary appeal. Not interested in narrowly focused scholarly articles. Seeks writing that is marked by clarity, liveliness, and perspective. Interested in the best fiction and poetry. Buys 75 unsolicited mss/year. Pays minimum $5/page, plus copies.

Tips: "Make your query very brief, not gabby—one that describes some publishing history, but no extensive bibliographies. We publish mostly poetry—short fiction, some book reviews. Generally short length material."

THE PARIS REVIEW, 45-39 171st Place, Flushing NY 11358. Submit to 541 E. 72nd St., New York NY 10021. Editor: George A. Plimpton. Quarterly. Buys all rights. Pays on publication. Address submissions to proper department and address. Computer printout submissions acceptable; no dot-matrix.
Fiction: Study publication. No length limit. Pays up to $250. Makes award of $1,000 in annual fiction contest. Awards $1,500 in John Train Humor Prize contest, and $1,000 in Bernard F. Conners, Poetry Prize contest.
Poetry: Jonathan Galassi, poetry editor. Study publication. Pays $35/1-24 lines; $50/25-59 lines; $75/60-99 lines; and $150-175/100 lines and over. Sample copy $6.50.

PARTISAN REVIEW, 141 Bay State Rd., Boston MA 02215. (617)353-4260. Editor: William Phillips. Executive Editor: Edith Kurzweil. 90% freelance written. Works with a small number of new/unpublished writers each year. Quarterly literary journal covering world literature, politics and contemporary culture for an intelligent public with emphasis on the arts and political/social commentary. Circ. 8,200. Pays on publication. Publishes ms an average of 6-12 months after acceptance. Buys first serial rights. Byline given. Photocopied submissions OK. Computer printout submissions acceptable; prefers letter-quality to dot-matrix. Reports in 3-4 months. Sample copy $5 and 75¢ postage; free writer's guidelines.
Nonfiction: Essays; interviews and book reviews. Buys 30-40 mss/year. Send complete ms. Pays $50-250. Sometimes pays expenses of writers on assignment.
Fiction: High quality, serious and contemporary fiction. No science fiction, mystery, confession, romantic or religious material. Buys 8-10 mss/year. Send complete ms. Pays $100-250.
Poetry: Buys 60 poems/year. Submit maximum 6 poems. Pays $50.
Tips: "If, after reading *PR* a writer or poet feels that he or she writes with comparable originality and quality, then of course he or she may well be accepted. Standards of self-watchfulness, originality and hard work apply and reap benefits."

PASSAGES NORTH, William Bonifas Fine Arts Center, Escanaba MI 49829. (906)786-3833. Editor: Elinor Benedict. Managing Editor: Carol R. Hackenbruch. 100% freelance written. Eager to work with new/unpublished writers. A semiannual tabloid of poetry, fiction and graphic arts. Circ. 2,000. Pays on publication. Publishes ms an average of 2-4 months after acceptance. Byline given. Buys first rights. Computer printout submissions acceptable; no dot-matrix. Reports in 1 month on queries; 3 months on manuscripts. Sample copy $1.50; writer's guidelines for business size SASE.
Fiction: "High quality" fiction. Buys 6-8 mss/year. Send complete ms. Length: 4,000 words maximum. Pays 3 copies minimum, $50 maximum.
Poetry: No "greeting card" or sentimental poetry and no song lyrics. Buys 80 poems/year. Submit maximum 4 poems. Length: prefers 40 lines maximum. Pays 3 copies minimum, $15 maximum.
Tips: "We want poems and stories of high quality that make the reader see, imagine and experience."

THE PENNSYLVANIA REVIEW, University of Pittsburgh, English Dept./526 CL, Pittsburgh PA 15260. (412)624-0026. Managing Editor: Kristin Kovacic. 95% freelance written. A semiannual magazine publishing contemporary fiction, poetry and nonfiction. Circ. approximately 1,000. Pays on publication. Publishes ms an average of 6 months after acceptance. Byline given. Photocopied submissions OK. Reports in 10 weeks. Sample copy $5; writer's guidelines for business size SAE.
Nonfiction: Essays, criticism reviews, interviews and book reviews. Buys 5-10 mss/year. Send complete ms. Pays $5/page.
Fiction: Linda Lee Harper, fiction editor. Novel excerpts and drama. "No formula fiction; nothing cute; genre fiction (science fiction, romance, mystery) discouraged." Buys 10-20 mss/year. Send complete ms. Pays $5/page.
Poetry: James Gyure, poetry editor. Free verse and traditional. No light verse. Buys 50-75 poems/year. Submit maximum 6 poems. Length: open. Pays $5/page.

PIG IRON MAGAZINE, Pig Iron Press, Box 237, Youngstown OH 44501. (216)783-1269. Editors-in-Chief: Jim Villani and Rose Sayre. 90% freelance written. Annual magazine emphasizing literature/art for writers, artists and intelligent lay audience interested in popular culture. Circ. 1,500. Buys one-time rights. Pays on publication. Publishes ms an average of 18 months after acceptance. Byline given. Photocopied and previously published submissions OK. Computer printout submissions acceptable. Reports in 4 months. Sample copy $2.50; writer's guidelines with SASE.

Nonfiction: General interest, personal opinion, criticism, new journalism and lifestyle. Buys 3 mss/year. Query. Length: 8,000 words maximum. Pays $2/page minimum.

Photos: Submit photo material with query. Pays $2 minimum for 5x7 or 8x10 b&w glossy prints. Buys one-time rights.

Fiction: Fantasy, avant-garde, experimental, psychological fiction and metafiction and humor. Buys 4-12 mss/issue. Submit complete ms. Length: 8,000 words maximum. Pays $2 minimum.

Poetry: Nate Leslie and Joe Allgren, poetry editors. Avant-garde and free verse. Buys 25-50/issue. Submit in batches of 5 or less. Length: open. Pays $2 minimum.

Tips: "Send one story at a time. Show us your ability to remake the conventions of story telling."

PLOUGHSHARES, Box 529, Dept. M, Cambridge MA 02139. Editor: DeWitt Henry. Eager to work with new/unpublished writers. Quarterly magazine for "readers of serious contemporary literature: students, educators, adult public." Circ. 3,800. Pays on publication. Publishes ms an average of 6 months after acceptance. Rights purchased vary with author and material; usually buys all rights or may buy first North American serial rights. Photocopied submissions OK. Computer printout submissions OK; prefers letter quality to dot-matrix. Reports in 6 months. Sample copy $5; writer's guidelines for SASE.

Nonfiction: Interview and literary essays. Length: 5,000 words maximum. Pays $50. Reviews (assigned). Length: 500 words maximum. Pays $15.

Fiction: Experimental and mainstream. Buys 25-50 unsolicited mss/year. Length: 300-6,000 words. Pays $10-50.

Poetry: Traditional forms, blank verse, free verse and avant-garde. Length: open. Pays $10/poem.

Tips: "Because of our policy of rotating editors, we suggest writers check the current issue for news of upcoming editors and/or themes."

‡PRAIRIE FIRE, A Magazine of Canadian Writing, Manitoba Writers' Guild, Inc., 208-100 Arthur St., Winnipeg, Manitoba R3B 1H3 Canada. (204)943-9066. 90% freelance written. A quarterly literary magazine featuring the contemporary writing of Canada's prairie provinces. Circ. 1,000. Pays on publication. Publishes ms an average of 4 months after acceptance. Offers 25% kill fee. Buys first Canadian rights. Computer printout submissions OK; no dot matrix. Reports in 2 months. Sample copy $5; free writer's guidelines.

Nonfiction: No pornography or evangelical articles. Buys 6 mss/year. Query. Length: 500-5,000 words. Pays $35-200 for assigned articles. Pays $30-150 for unsolicited articles. Sometimes pays the expenses of writers on assignment.

Photos: State availability of photos with submission. Reviews transparencies. Offers $5-25 per photo. Captions and identification of subjects required. Buys one-time rights.

Fiction: Margaret Clarke, fiction editor. Experimental, mainstream and novel excerpts. Buys 10 mss/year. Send complete ms. Length: 500-6,000 words. Pays $30-200.

Poetry: Kristiana Gunnars. Avant-garde, free verse, haiku, light verse and traditional. Buys 40 poems/year. Submit maximum 6 poems. Length: 1-1,000 lines. Pays $10-100.

PRAIRIE SCHOONER, Andrews Hall, University of Nebraska, Lincoln NE 68588. Editor: Hilda Raz. 95% freelance written. Prefers to work with published/established writers, and is eager to work with new/unpublished writers. Quarterly. Pays in copies and annual prizes. Publishes ms an average of 6 months after acceptance. Acquires all rights, but rights will revert to author upon request after publication. Computer printout submissions acceptable; prefers letter-quality to dot-matrix. Reports in 2 months. Sample copy $1; writer's guidelines for business size SASE.

Nonfiction: Uses 1-2 articles/issue. Subjects of literary or general interest. No academic articles. Length: 5,000 words maximum.

Fiction: Uses several stories/issue.

Poetry: Uses 20-30 poems in each issue of the magazine. These may be on any subject, in any style. Occasional long poems are used, but preference is for shorter length. High quality necessary.

Tips: "The mix of established and new writers is part of the *Prairie Schooner* tradition we are eager to maintain."

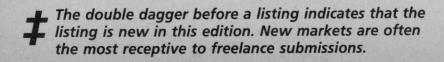

The double dagger before a listing indicates that the listing is new in this edition. New markets are often the most receptive to freelance submissions.

PRISM INTERNATIONAL, Department of Creative Writing, University of British Columbia, Vancouver, British Columbia V6T 1W5 Canada. Editor-in-Chief: Mike Peddie. Managing Editor: Catherine Burke. 100% freelance written. Eager to work with new/unpublished writers. Quarterly magazine emphasizing contemporary literature, including translations. For university and public libraries, and private subscribers. Circ. 1000. Pays on publication. Publishes ms an average of 3 months after acceptance. Buys first North American serial rights. Photocopied submissions OK. Computer printout submissions acceptable; prefers letter-quality to dot-matrix. SAE, IRCs. Reports in 6 weeks. Sample copy $4.
Fiction: Experimental and traditional. Buys 3 mss/issue. Send complete ms. Length: 5,000 words maximum. Pays $25/printed page and 1-year subscription.
Poetry: Avant-garde and traditional. Buys 30 poems/issue. Submit maximum 6 poems. Pays $25/printed page and 1-year subscription.
Drama: One-acts preferred. Pays $25/printed page and 1-year subscription.
Tips: "We are looking for new and exciting fiction. Excellence is still our number one criterion. There will be a special humor theme issue entitled 'Tasteful of Coarse'. Deadline for submissions is Jan. 30, 1988. We will be accepting cartoons for this. As well as poetry and fiction, we are especially open to translations of all kinds, very short fiction pieces and drama which works well on the page."

PULPSMITH magazine, The Smith, 5 Beekman St., New York NY 10038. (212)732-4822. Editor: Harry Smith. Managing Editor: Tom Tolnay. 90% freelance written. A quarterly literary magazine "for a literate audience that seeks entertainment thrills from fiction, essays, articles, poetry of high quality." Circ. 4,000. Pays on acceptance. Byline given. Buys first North American serial rights. Simultaneous and photocopied submissions OK. Computer printout submissions acceptable; prefers letter-quality to dot-matrix. Reports in 1 month on queries; 2 months on mss. Sample copy $3 and 69¢ fourth class postage; writer's guidelines for SASE.
Nonfiction: Essays. Buys 15 mss/year. Query. Length: 5,000 words maximum. Pays $25-100.
Fiction: Nancy Hallinan, fiction editor. Adventure, fantasy, horror, humorous, mainstream, mystery, science fiction, suspense and western. Buys 65 mss/year. Send complete ms. Length: 500-5,000 words. Pays $25-100.
Poetry: Joseph Lazarus, poetry editor. Avant-garde, free verse, haiku and traditional. Buys 100 poems/year. Submit maximum 4 poems. Pays $10-75.

QUARRY, Quarry Press, Box 1061, Kingston, Ontario K7L 4Y5 Canada. (613)376-3584. Editor: Bob Hilderley. 99% freelance written. Eager to work with new/unpublished writers. Quarterly magazine covering poetry, prose, reviews. "We seek high quality new writers who are aware of their genre and who are committed to their art." Circ. 1,000. Pays on publication. Publishes ms an average of 6-8 months after acceptance. Byline given. Buys first North American serial rights. Simultaneous queries and photocopied submissions OK. Computer printout submission acceptable; prefers letter-quality to dot-matrix. Reports in 3 weeks on queries; 3 months on mss. Sample copy $5; writer's guidelines for business size SAE and 65¢ in IRCs.
Nonfiction: Short stories, poetry and book reviews. "We need book reviews of Canadian work. We are not interested in reviews of American or United Kingdom books. No literary criticism." Buys 100 mss/year. Send complete ms. Length: open. Pays $5-$10/page plus 1 year subscription.
Fiction: Any short fiction of high quality. "No nonliterary fiction." Send complete ms. Length: 10-15 pages maximum. Pays $5-10/page.
Poetry: Avant-garde, free verse, haiku, light verse and traditional. "No amateur, derivative poetry." Buys 200 poems/year. Submit maximum 10 poems. Length: open. Pays $5-10/page.
Tips: "Please send IRCs with SAE, not U.S. postage. Try to read a copy of the magazine before submitting. Ask at your library or request a sample copy."

QUEEN'S QUARTERLY, A Canadian Review, Queen's University, Kingston, Ontario K7L 3N6 Canada. (613)547-6968. Editors: Dr. Clive Thomson and Mrs. Marcia Stayer. Quarterly magazine covering a wide variety of subjects, including: science, humanities, arts and letters, politics, and history for the educated reader. 15% freelance written. Circ. 1,900. Pays on publication. Publishes ms an average of 1 year after acceptance. Byline given. Buys first North American serial rights. Photocopied submissions OK. Computer printout submissions acceptable; prefers letter-quality to dot-matrix. Reports in 2 weeks on queries; 3 months on mss. Sample copy $5.00; free writer's guidelines.
Fiction: Fantasy, historical, humorous, mainstream and science fiction. Buys 8-12 mss/year. Send complete ms. Length: 5,000 words maximum. Pays $80-150.
Poetry: Avant-garde, free verse, haiku, light verse and traditional. No "sentimental, religious, or first efforts by unpublished writers". Buys 25/year. Submit maximum six poems. Length: open. Pays $20-35.
Tips: "Poetry and fiction are most open to freelancers. Don't send less than the best. No multiple submissions. No more than 6 poems or one story per submission. We buy just a few freelance submissions."

‡ROOM OF ONE'S OWN, A Feminist Journal of Literature & Criticism, Growing Room Collective, Box 46160, Station G, Vancouver, British Columbia V6R 4G5 Canada. Editors: Gayla Reid, Robin Bellamy, Mary Schendlinger, Eleanor Wachtel, Jeannie Wexler and Jean Wilson. 100% freelance written. Eager to work with new/unpublished writers. Quarterly magazine of original fiction, poetry, literary criticism, and reviews of feminist concern. Circ 1,200. Pays on publication. Publishes ms an average of 3 months after acceptance. By-line given. Buys first serial rights. Photocopied submissions OK. Computer printout submissions acceptable "if readable and not in all caps"; no dot-matrix. Reports in 2 months. Sample copy $2.75.

Nonfiction: Interview/profile (of authors) and literary criticism. Buys 8 mss/year. Send complete ms. Length: 1,500-6,000 words. Pays $50.

Fiction: Quality short stories by women with a feminist outlook. Not interested in fiction written by men. Buys 12 mss/year. Send complete ms. Length: 1,500-6,000 words. Pays $50.

Poetry: Avant-garde, eclectic free verse and haiku. Not interested in poetry from men. Buys 32 poems/year. Submit maximum 10 poems. Length: open. Pays $10-25.

SCRIVENER, Creative Journal, Scrivener, 853 Sherbrooke St. W., Montreal, Quebec H3A 2T6 Canada. (514)398-6588. Editor: Andrew Burgess. 80% freelance written. Works with a small number of new/unpublished writers each year. A semiannual magazine for literary and visual arts. "We publish the best of new material from North American poets, prose writers, graphic artists, photographers and scholars, both established and soon to be established." Circ. 500. Pays on publication. Publishes ms an average of 4 months after acceptance. Byline sometimes given. Not copyrighted. Buys first North American serial rights and simultaneous rights. Simultaneous and photocopied submissions OK. Computer printout submissions acceptable; no dot-matrix. Reports in 2-4 weeks on queries; 4-6 weeks on mss. Sample copy $2.50; writer's guidelines for letter-size SAE with 1 Canadian stamp or IRC.

Nonfiction: Interview/profile, photo feature and scholarly/literary articles on contemporary North American literature. Buys 10-20 mss/year. Send complete ms. Length: 2,000 words maximum. Pays $3-10; pays copies in addition to cash.

Photos: Send photos with submission. Reviews prints. Offers no additional payment for photos accepted with ms. Buys one-time rights.

Columns/Departments: Reviews (scholarly reviews of currently important books, anthologies, etc.), maximum 2,000 words. Buys 5-10 mss/year. Send complete ms. Pays $3-10.

Fiction: Will consider all kinds of fiction, "so long as it is good." Buys 5-10 mss/year. Send complete ms. Length: 4,000 words maximum. Pays $3-10.

Poetry: Tara Spevack, poetry editor. Free verse and traditional. Buys 50 poems/year. Submit maximum 20-25 poems. Maximum length 5 pages. Pays $3-10.

Tips: "Include some biographical data, and some statements about your approach to literature. Be patient with our staff—bitchy letters saying, 'where's my stuff?' will get you nowhere. The areas most open to freelancers are poetry and fiction. *Scrivener* receives a large volume of work, and so is able to pick and choose. We like intensity, craftsmanship and groundedness."

SEWANEE REVIEW, University of the South, Sewanee TN 37375. (615)598-1246. Editor: George Core. "Freelance writing rarely accepted." Works with a small number of new/unpublished writers each year. Quarterly magazine for audience of "variable ages and locations, mostly college-educated and with interest in literature." Circ. 3,400. Pays on publication. Publishes ms an average of 9 months after acceptance. Computer printout submissions acceptable; prefers letter-quality to dot-matrix. Reports in 1 month. Sample copy $4.75, writer's guidelines for business size SASE.

Nonfiction and Fiction: Short fiction (but not drama); essays of critical nature on literary subjects (especially modern British and American literature); and essay-reviews and reviews (books and reviewers selected by the editor). Length: 5,000-7,500 words. Payment varies: averages $12/printed page.

Poetry: Selections of 4 to 6 poems preferred. In general, light verse and translations not acceptable. Maximum payment is 70¢ per line.

THE SHORT STORY REVIEW, (formerly *FM Five*), Box 882108, San Francisco CA 94188. Publisher/Editor: Dwight Gabbard. 80% freelance written. Works with a small number of new/unpublished writers each year; eager to work with new/unpublished writers. Literary tabloid magazine published 4 times/year. "*Short Story Review* offers a forum for issues of concern to short story writers, offering interviews, reviews and essays. *Short Story Review* also publishes short fiction." Circ. 3,000. Publishes ms an average of 5 months after acceptance. Not copyrighted. Acquires first North American serial rights and second serial (reprint) rights. Photocopied and simultaneous submissions OK. Computer printout submissions OK; prefers letter-quality to dot-matrix. Reports in 3 weeks on queries; 3 months on mss. Sample copy $2.50; writer's guidelines for business size SASE.

Nonfiction: Interviews with prominent short story writers and book reviews. Publishes 6-8 mss/year. "We need book reviewers—we review only short story collections and anthologies, so the reviewer should have some background." Query. Length: 2,000-3,000 words. Pays $20/page, $180 maximum.

Fiction: Stephen Woodhams, fiction editor. Literary. No science fiction, fantasy or erotica. Send complete ms. Length: 500-4,000 words. Pays in copies and a one-year subscription.

Tips: "We welcome all kinds of stories as long as they are well-crafted, convincing and, in some way, needing to be told. Though we keep an open mind, we tend to prefer stories with a strong narrative line and focus. We are not much given to stories based on a clever idea, a trick ending, or elaborate plotting if the other elements of short story writing are neglected."

SING HEAVENLY MUSE!, Women's Poetry and Prose, Sing Heavenly Muse! Inc., Box 13299, Minneapolis MN 55414. (612)822-8713. 100% freelance written. Prefers to work with published/established writers; eager to work with new/unpublished writers. A semi-annual journal of women's literature. Circ. 1,500. Pays on publication. Publishes ms an average of 6 months after acceptance. Byline given. Buys first North American serial rights. Photocopied submissions OK. Computer printout submissions acceptable; prefers letter-quality to dot-matrix. Reports in 3 months. Sample copy $3.50; writer's guidelines for #10 SASE.
Fiction: Women's literature, journal pieces, memoir. Buys 15-20 mss/year. Length: 5,000 words maximum. Pays $15-25; contributors receive 2 free copies.
Poetry: Avant-garde, free verse, haiku, light verse and traditional. Accepts 75-100 poems/year. No limit on length. Pays $15-25.
Tips: "To meet our needs, writing must be feminist and women-centered. We read manuscripts generally in April and September. Issues are often related to a specific theme; writer should always query for guidelines and upcoming themes before submitting manuscripts. We occasionally hold contests. Writers should query for contest guidelines."

THE SOUTHERN REVIEW, 43 Allen Hall, Louisiana State University, Baton Rouge LA 70803. (504)388-5108. Editors: James Olney and Fred Hobson. 75% freelance written. Works with a moderate number of new/unpublished writers each year. Quarterly magazine for academic, professional, literary, intellectual audience. Circ. 3,300. Buys first serial rights only. Byline given. Pays on publication. Publishes ms an average of 18 months after acceptance. No queries. Computer printout submissions acceptable; prefers letter-quality to dot-matrix. Reports in 2 to 3 months. Sample copy $5. Writer's guidelines for SASE.
Nonfiction: Essays with careful attention to craftsmanship and technique and to seriousness of subject matter. "Willing to publish experimental writing if it has a valid artistic purpose. Avoid extremism and sensationalism. Essays exhibit thoughtful and sometimes severe awareness of the necessity of literary standards in our time." Emphasis on contemporary literature, especially Southern culture and history. Minimum number of footnotes. Buys 80-100 mss/year. Length: 4,000-10,000 words. Pays $12/page for prose.
Fiction and Poetry: Short stories of lasting literary merit, with emphasis on style and technique. Length: 4,000-8,000 words. Pays $12/page for prose; $20/page for poetry.

SOUTHWEST REVIEW, 6410 Airline Rd., Southern Methodist University, Dallas TX 75275. (214)373-7440. Editor: Willard Spiegelman. 100% freelance written. Works with a small number of new/unpublished writers each year. Quarterly magazine for "adults and college graduates with literary interests and some interest in the Southwest, but subscribers are from all over America and some foreign countries." Circ. 1,400. Pays on publication. Publishes ms an average of 1 year after acceptance. Buys first North American serial rights. Computer printout submissions acceptable; prefers letter-quality to dot-matrix. Byline given. Buys 65 mss/year. Reports immediately or within 3 months. Sample copy $5.
Nonfiction: "Literary essays, social and political problems, history (especially Southwestern), folklore (especially Southwestern), the arts, etc. Articles should be appropriate for literary quarterly; no feature stories. Critical articles should consider writer's whole body of work, not just one book. History should use new primary sources or new perspective, not syntheses of old material." Interviews with writers, historical articles. Query. Length: 3,500-7,000 words.
Fiction: No limitations on subject matter for fiction; high literary quality is only criterion. Prefers stories of experimental and mainstream. Submit complete ms. Length: 1,500-7,000 words. The John H. McGinnis Memorial Award of $1,000 made in alternate years for fiction and nonfiction pieces that appeared in *SWR* during preceding two years.
Poetry: No limitations on subject matter. Not particularly interested in broadly humorous, religious, or sentimental poetry. Free verse, some avant-garde forms; open to all serious forms of poetry. "There are no arbitrary limits on length, but we find shorter poems are easier to fit into our format." The Elizabeth Matchett Stover Memorial Award of $100 made annually for a poem published in *SWR*.
Tips: "The most frequent mistakes we find in work that is submitted for consideration are lack of attention to grammar and syntax and little knowledge of the kind of thing we're looking for. Writers should look at a couple of issues before submitting."

STAR*LINE, Newsletter of the Science Fiction Poetry Association, Science Fiction Poetry Association, Box 1764, Cambridge MA 02238. (617)876-0928. Editor: Elissa Malcohn. 95% freelance written. Eager to work with new/unpublished writers. A bimonthly newsletter covering science fiction, fantasy, horror poetry for association members. Circ. 200. Pays on acceptance. Byline given. Buys one-time rights. Submit seasonal/holiday material 3 months in advance. Photocopied submissions OK. Computer printout submissions acceptable; prefers letter-quality to dot-matrix. Reports in 1 month. Sample copy for $1.50 and 5x7 SAE with 39¢

postage; writer's guidelines for #10 SASE.

Nonfiction: Articles must display familiarity with the genre. How to (write a poem); interview/profile (of science fiction, fantasy and horror poets); opinion (science fiction and poetics); and essays. Buys 4-6 mss/year. Send complete ms. Length: 500-2,000 words. Pays $1-5 plus complimentary copy.

Columns/Department: Reviews (books, chapbooks, magazines, collections of science fiction, fantasy or horror poetry) 50-500 words; and Markets (current markets for science fiction, fantasy or horror poetry) 20-100 words. Buys 40-60 mss/year. Send complete ms. Pays 50¢-$2.

Poetry: Avant-garde, free verse, haiku, light verse and traditional. "Poetry must be related to speculative fiction subjects." Buys 60-80 poems/year. Submit maximum 3 poems. Length: 1-100 lines. Pays $1 for first 10 lines; 5¢/line thereafter plus complimentary copy.

Fillers: Speculative-oriented quotations—prose or poetic. Length: 10-50 words. Pays $1.

STONE COUNTRY, A Magazine of Poetry, Reviews & Graphics, The Nathan Mayhew Seminars of Martha's Vineyard, Box 132, Menemsha MA 02552. (617)693-5832 or (617)645-2829. Editor: Judith Neeld. 98% freelance written. Prefers to work with published/established writers. A semiannual literary magazine. "We look on poetry as disquisition, not exposition. This is not a journal for beginners. Our purpose is to be an outlet for achieving poets whose work deserves serious and growing attention." Circ. 800. Pays on publication. Publishes ms an average of 2-10 months after acceptance. Byline given. Buys one-time rights. Photocopied submissions OK; simultaneous submissions OK if notified. Computer printout submissions acceptable; no dot-matrix. Reports in 1 week on queries 2 months on manuscripts. Sample copy $4; writer's guidelines for SASE.

Nonfiction: Robert Blake Truscott, reviews editor. Judith Neeld, editor (for essays and interview/profiles). Essays (on elements of poetry, currently and historically, only); interview/profile (of current notable poets only); and reviews of poetry books. Buys 2-4 mss/year. Send complete ms. Length: 1,500-2,500 words. Pays $15-25. Poetry contributors receive 1 complimentary copy.

Columns/Departments: Commentary (essays on contemporary poetry and/or poetry from an historical perspective as it relates to contemporary poetry. "Not a column as such, but the section is published in each issue.") Buys 2 mss/year. Send complete ms. Length: 1,500-2,500 words. Pays $15-25.

Poetry: Avant-garde, free verse and traditional. "No light verse or poetry on a soap box." Buys 100-150 poems/year. Submit maximum 5 poems. Length: 5-40 lines. Pays 1 contributor copy.

Tips: "We are most open to poets and their poetry, but welcome reviews and essays of mature quality. Please read a sample copy before submitting."

STORIES, 14 Beacon St., Boston MA 02108. Editor: Amy R. Kaufman. 80% freelance written. Works with a small number of new/unpublished writers each year. Quarterly magazine publishing short fiction. "It is designed to encourage the writing of stories that evoke an emotional response—for which, the editor believes, there is a demand." Circ. 5,000. Pays on publication. Publishes ms an average of 2 months after acceptance. Byline given. Buys first North American serial rights. Photocopied and simultaneous submissions OK (if so marked). Computer printout submissions acceptable; no dot-matrix. Reports in 10 weeks on mss. Sample copy $3 or two for $5 (postpaid); writer's guidelines for business size SASE.

Fiction: Contemporary, ethnic, historical (general), humor/satire, literary, serialized/excerpted novel and translations. "Ordinarily, romance, mystery, fantasy, political pieces and science fiction do not suit our purposes, but we will not exclude any story on the basis of genre; we wish only that the piece be the best of its genre." Buys 30-36 mss/year. Send complete ms. No queries. Length: 750-15,000 words; 4,000-7,000 words average. Pays $150 minimum.

Tips: "We look for characters identifiable not by name, age, profession, or appearance, but by symbolic qualities; timeless themes and styles that are sophisticated but not affected, straightforward but not artless, descriptive but not nearsighted."

‡THE THREEPENNY REVIEW, Box 9131, Berkeley CA 94709. (415)849-4545. Editor: Wendy Lesser. 100% freelance written. Works with small number of new/unpublished writers each year. A quarterly literary tabloid. "We are a general interest, national literary magazine with coverage of politics, the visual arts and the performing arts as well." Circ. 8,000. Pays on acceptance. Publishes ms an average of 9 months after acceptance. Byline given. Buys first North American serial rights. Photocopied submissions OK. Computer printout submissions OK; prefers letter-quality. Reports in 1 month on queries; 2 months on mss. Sample copy $4; writer's guidelines for SASE.

Nonfiction: Essays, expose, historical, interview/profile, personal experience, book, film, theater, dance, music and art reviews. Buys 40 mss/year. Query with or without published clips, or send complete ms. Length: 1,500-4,000 words. Pays $50.

Fiction: No fragmentary, sentimental fiction. Buys 10 mss/year. Send complete ms. Length: 800-4,000 words. Pays $50.

Poetry: Free verse and traditional. No poems "without capital letters or poems without a discernible subject." Buys 30 poems/year. Submit maximum 10 poems. Pays $50.

Tips: Nonfiction (political articles, reviews) is most open to freelancers.

THRESHOLD OF FANTASY, Fandom Unlimited Enterprises, Box 70868, Sunnyvale CA 94086. (415)960-1151. Editor: Randall D. Larson. 95% freelance written. "Semi-backlogged—willing to consider unsolicited submissions from new/unpublished writers but being *very* selective." A magazine published irregularly (1-2 issues/year) covering horror, fantasy, and science fiction in literature and interviews with new and notable writers/artists. Circ. 1,000. Pays 50% on acceptance, 50% on publication. Publishes ms an average of 2 years after acceptance. Byline given. Offers 50% kill fee. Buys first North American serial rights. Photocopied submissions OK. Query for electronic submissions. Computer printout submissions acceptable; prefers letter-quality to dot-matrix. Simultaneous submissions not considered. Submissions without SASE not considered. Reports in 3 weeks on queries; 6 weeks on mss. Sample copy $3.50; writer's guidelines for business size SASE.
Nonfiction: Interview/profile and reviews. Buys 4 mss/year. Query. Length: 1,500-5,000 words for articles; 1,000 words for reviews. Pays $20 for articles; pays in copies for reviews.
Photos: Send photos with submission; required with interview. Offers no additional payment for photos accepted with ms. Identification of subjects required.
Fiction: Fantasy, horror, humorous, mystery and science fiction. "No pastiches of other writers; abstract or 'new wave' writing; stories which *tell* a plot but never *show* the events through effective narrative structure and style; or overly wordy narrations." Buys 30 mss/year. Send complete ms. Length: 500-8,000 words. Pays ¹/₅¢/word.
Tips: Short stories are most open to freelancers.

TRIQUARTERLY, 1735 Benson Ave., Northwestern University, Evanston IL 60201. (312)491-3490. Editor: Reginald Gibbons. 70% freelance written. Eager to work with new/unpublished writers. Published 3 times/year. Publishes fiction, poetry, and essays, as well as artwork. Pays on publication. Publishes ms an average of 1 year after acceptance. Buys first serial rights and nonexclusive reprint rights. Computer printout submissions acceptable; no dot-matrix. Reports in 10 weeks. Study magazine before submitting. Sample copy $4.
Nonfiction: Query before sending essays (no scholarly or critical essays except in special issues).
Fiction and Poetry: No prejudice against style or length of work; only seriousness and excellence are required. Buys 20-50 unsolicited mss/year. Pays $12/page.

UNIVERSITY OF TORONTO QUARTERLY, University of Toronto Press, 63 A St. George Street, Toronto, Ontario M5S 1A6 Canada. Editor-in-Chief: T.H. Adamowski. 66% freelance written. Eager to work with new/unpublished writers. Quarterly magazine emphasizing criticism on literature and the humanities for the university community. Pays on publication. Publishes ms an average of 1 year after acceptance. Acquires all rights. Byline given. Photocopied submissions OK. Computer printout submissions acceptable; prefers letter-quality to dot-matrix. SAE and IRCs. Sample copy $8.95.
Nonfiction: Scholarly articles on the humanities; literary criticism and intellectual discussion. Buys 12 unsolicited mss/year. Pays $50 maximum.

THE UNSPEAKABLE VISIONS OF THE INDIVIDUAL INC., Box 439, California PA 15419. Editors-in-Chief: Arthur Winfield Knight, Kit Knight. 50% freelance written. Annual magazine/book for an adult audience, generally college-educated (or substantial self-education) with an interest in Beat (generation) writing. Circ. 2,000. Payment (if made) on acceptance. Publishes ms an average of 2 months after acceptance. Buys first North American serial rights. Computer printout submissions acceptable; no dot-matrix. Reports in 2 months. Sample copy $3.50.
Nonfiction: Interviews (with Beat writers), personal experience and photo feature. "Know who the Beat writers are—Jack Kerouac, Allen Ginsberg, William S. Burroughs, etc." Uses 20 mss/year. Query or submit complete ms. Length: 300-15,000 words. Pays 2 copies, "sometimes a small cash payment, i.e., $10."
Photos: Used with or without ms or on assignment. Send prints. Pays 2 copies to $10 for 8x10 b&w glossies. Uses 40-50/year. Captions required.
Fiction: Uses 10 mss/year. Submit complete ms. Pays 2 copies to $10.
Poetry: Avant-garde, free verse and traditional. Uses 10 poems/year. Submit maximum 10 poems. Length: 100 lines maximum. Pays 2 copies to $10.

THE VIRGINIA QUARTERLY REVIEW, 1 W. Range, Charlottesville VA 22903. (804)924-3124. Editor: Staige Blackford. 50% freelance written. Quarterly. Pays on publication. Publishes ms an average of 2 years after acceptance. Byline given. Buys first serial rights. Reports in 1 month. Sample copy $5.
Nonfiction: Articles on current problems, economic, historical; and literary essays. Length: 3,000-6,000 words. Pays $10/345-word page.
Fiction: Good short stories, conventional or experimental. Length: 2,000-7,000 words. Pays $10/350-word page. Prizes offered for best short stories and poems published in a calendar year.
Poetry: Generally publishes 15 pages of poetry in each issue. No length or subject restrictions. Pays $1/line.
Tips: Prefers not to see pornography, science fiction or fantasy.

WEBSTER REVIEW, Webster Review, Inc., Webster University, 470 E. Lockwood, Webster Groves MO 63119. (314)432-2657. Editor: Nancy Schapiro. 100% freelance written. A semiannual magazine. *"Webster Review* is an international literary magazine publishing fiction, poetry, essays and translations of writing in those categories. Our subscribers are primarily university and public libraries, and writers and readers of quality fiction and poetry." Circ. 1,000. Pays on publication. Publishes ms an average of 6-8 months after acceptance. Byline given. Buys first North American serial rights. Simultaneous and photocopied submissions OK. Reports in 6 weeks on manuscripts. Sample copy for 9½x6½ SAE with 50¢ postage.
Nonfiction: Essays. Send complete ms.
Fiction: Will consider all types of literature. Buys 6 mss/year. Send complete ms. Pays $25-50, (if funds are available).
Poetry: Pamela White Hadas, poetry editor. Buys 100 poems/year. Pays $10-50 (if funds are available).

‡WEST COAST REVIEW,A Literary Quarterly,West Coast Review Publishing Society, Department of English, Simon Fraser University, Burnaby British Columbia V5A 156 Canada. (604)291-4287. Quarterly magazine covering poetry, fiction, book reviews. "We publish original creative writing regardless of style, subject, etc.; the only criterion is the quality of the writing." Circ. 700. Pays on acceptance. Publishes ms an average of 4 months after acceptance. Byline given. Buys first North American serial rights. Submit seasonal/holiday material 6 months in advance. Photocopied submissions OK. Computer printout submissions OK; prefers letter-quality to dot-matrix. Reports in 2 months. Sample copy $4; writer's guidelines for SAE with 1 Canadian first class stamp or IRC.
Nonfiction: Essays, mainly dealing with literary matters. Buys 15-20 ms/year. Send complete ms. Length: 1,000-5,000 words. Pays $10-15/page for assigned articles; pays $10/page for unsolicited articles.
Photos: State availability of photos with submission. Offers no additional payment for photos accepted with mss. Buys one-time rights.
Fiction: Experimental, mainstream and novel excerpts. Buys 10-12 mss/year. Send complete ms. Length: 2,000-10,000 words. Pays $10-15/page.
Poetry: Avant-garde and traditional. Buys 100-150 poems/year. Submit maximum 10 poems. Length: 4-500 lines. Pays $10-50.

WESTERN HUMANITIES REVIEW, University of Utah, Salt Lake City UT 84112. (801)581-7438. Managing Editor: Scott Cairns. Quarterly magazine for educated readers. Circ. 1,000. Pays on acceptance. Publishes ms an average of 3 months after acceptance. Buys all rights. Phone queries OK. Simultaneous and photocopied submissions OK. Computer printout submissions acceptable; prefers letter-quality to dot-matrix. Reports in 1 month.
Nonfiction: Barry Weller, editor-in-chief. Authoritative, readable articles on literature, art, philosophy, current events, history, religion and anything in the humanities. Interdisciplinary articles encouraged. Departments on film and books. "We commission book reviews." Buys 40 unsolicited mss/year. Pays $50-150.
Fiction: Larry Levis, poetry and fiction editor. Any type or theme. Buys 2 mss/issue. Send complete ms. Pays $25-150.
Poetry: Larry Levis, poetry editor. Avant-garde, free verse and traditional. "We seek freshness and significance. Do not send poetry without having a look at the magazine first." Buys 5-10 poems/issue. Pays $50.
Tips: "The change in editorial staff will probably mean a slight shift in emphasis. We will probably be soliciting more submissions and relying less on uninvited materials. More poetry and scholarly articles (and perhaps less fiction) may be included in the future."

WIDE OPEN MAGAZINE, Wide Open Press, 326 I St., Eureka CA 95501. (707)445-3847. Editor: Clif Simms. 80% freelance written. Eager to work with new/unpublished writers. A quarterly magazine covering solutions to current problems. "Our audience consists of students, teachers, writers, counselors, and other thinking, feeling and doing people. We believe that problems can be solved once narrow, shallow attitudes are dispelled." Circ. 500. Pays on publication. Publishes ms an average of 3 months after acceptance. Byline given. Buys one-time rights; may make work-for-hire assignments. Photocopied and previously published submissions OK. Computer printout submissions acceptable. Reports in 1 month. Sample copy $5; writer's guidelines for #10 SASE.
Nonfiction: Lynn L. Simms, articles editor. Essays; how-to (solve problems); humor; interview/profile (of people who have solved problems); opinion (will consider); and personal experience (of solving problems). "No illogical or unsupported arguments; no arguments from authority, only." Buys up to 8 mss/year. Query or send complete ms. "No clips or biographies." Length: 500-2,500 words. Pays $5-25.
Fiction: Lynn L. Simms, fiction editor. Adventure, experimental, fantasy, historical, humorous, mainstream, mystery, science fiction, suspense and western. "All fiction must have a strong plot and show the characters solving their own problems. No *Deus ex Machina* plots." Buys 4-8 mss/year. Send complete ms. Length: 2,500 words maximum. Pays $5-25.
Poetry: Lynn L. Simms, poetry editor. Avant-garde, free verse, haiku, light verse and traditional. Buys 800 poems/year. Submit maximum 5 poems. Length: 16 lines maximum. No payment.

Tips: "Be logical and find the root causes of problems. Write for a general audience with common sense. And show or tell the process for reaching solutions, too. All areas are open to freelancers."

‡THE YALE REVIEW, 1902A Yale Station, New Haven CT 06520. Editor: Kai T. Erikson. Associate Editor: Penelope Laurans. Managing Editor: Wendy Wipprecht. 20% freelance written. Buys first North American serial rights. Pays on publication. Publishes ms an average of 1 year after acceptance. Computer printout submissions acceptable; no dot-matrix.

Nonfiction and Fiction: Authoritative discussions of politics, literature and the arts. Buys quality fiction. Pays $75-100. Length: 3,000-5,000 words.

YELLOW SILK, Journal of Erotic Arts, verygraphics, Box 6374, Albany CA 94706. (415)841-6500. Editor: Lily Pond. 90% freelance written. Prefers to work with published/established writers; works with a small number of new/unpublished writers each year. A quarterly magazine of erotic literature and visual arts. "Editorial policy: All persuasions; no brutality. Our publication is artistic and literary, not pornographic or pandering. Humans are involved: heads, hearts and bodies—not just bodies alone; and the excellence of art is as important as the erotic content." Circ. 10,000. Pays on publication. Publishes ms an average of 6 months after acceptance. Byline given. Buys all publication rights for one year, at which time they revert to author, reprint and anthology rights for duration of copyright. Photocopied submissions OK. Computer printout submissions acceptable; prefers letter-quality to dot-matrix. Reports in 3 months on manuscripts. Sample copy $4.

Nonfiction: Book excerpts, essays, humor and reviews. "We often have theme issues, but non-regularly and usually not announced in advance." No pornography, romance-novel type writing, sex fantasies. No first-person accounts or blow-by-blow descriptions. No articles. No novels." Buys 5-10 mss/year. Send complete ms. All submissions should be typed, double-spaced, with name, address and phone number on each page; always enclose SASE. No specified length requirements. Pays $10 and 3 contributor copies (plus possible $200 prize.)

Photos: Photos may be submitted independently, not as illustration for submission. Reviews photocopies, contact sheets, transparencies and prints. We can now accept 4-color artwork. Offers varying payment for series of 9-12 used, plus copies. Buys one-time rights and reprint rights.

Columns/Departments: Reviews (book, movie, art, dance, food, anything). "Erotic content and how it's handled is focus of importance. Old or new does not matter. Want to bring readers information of what's out there". Buys 8-10 mss/year. Send complete ms or query. Pays minimum of $10 plus copies.

Fiction: Erotica, including ethnic, experimental, fantasy, humorous, mainstream, novel excerpts and science fiction. "No pornography, romance novel type writing, sex fantasies. No first-person accounts or blow-by-blow descriptions." Buys 12-16 mss/year. Send complete ms. Pays minimum of $10 plus copies and possibility of $200 prize.

Poetry: Avant-garde, free verse, haiku, light verse and traditional. "No greeting-card poetry." Buys 55-80 poems/year. No limit on number of poems submitted, "but don't send book-length manuscripts." Pays minimum of $5 plus copies and possibility of $200 prize.

Tips: "The best way to get into *Yellow Silk* is to be an excellent, well-crafted writer who can approach erotica with freshness and strength of voice, beauty of language, and insight into character. I'll tell you what I'm sick of and have, unfortunately, been seeing more of lately; the products of "How to Write Erotica" classes. This is not brilliant fiction; it is poorly written fantasy and not what I'm looking for. Do not query for submissions or contest. Simply submit work as shown here—there are no further guidelines and you are automatically entered in the contest."

ZYZZYVA, The Last Word: West Coast Writers and Artists, Zyzzyva Inc., Suite 1400, 41 Sutter St., San Francisco CA 94104. (415)387-8389. Editor: Howard Junker. 100% freelance written. Works with a small number of new/unpublished writers each year. Quarterly magazine. "We feature work by West Coast writers only. We are essentially a literary magazine, but of wide-ranging interests and a strong commitment to nonfiction." Circ. 3,000. Pays on acceptance. Publishes ms an average of 3 months after acceptance. Byline given. Buys first North American serial rights and one-time anthology rights. Photocopied submissions OK. Computer printout submissions acceptable; prefers letter-quality to dot-matrix. Reports in 1 week on queries; 2 weeks on mss. Sample copy $8.

Nonfiction: Book excerpts, general interest, historical/nostalgic, humor and personal experience. Buys 15 mss/year. Query. Length: open. Pays $25-100.

Fiction: Ethnic, experimental, humorous, mainstream and mystery. Buys 20 mss/year. Send complete ms. Length: open. Pays $25-100.

Poetry: Buys 20 poems/year. Submit maximum 5 poems. Length: 3-200 lines. Pays $25-50.

❝ The most effective marketing tool for a beginning writer is a well-written query letter. ❞

—*Suzan Ireland Menendez*
Lefthander Magazine

Men's

Men's magazines are becoming more specialized, not general in theme like *Playboy*, and new magazines are showing an increased emphasis on fashion. Magazines that also use material slanted toward men can be found in Business and Finance, Military and Sports sections.

ADAM, Publishers Service, Inc., 8060 Melrose Ave., Los Angeles CA 90046. Monthly for the adult male. General subject: Human sexuality in contemporary society. Circ. 500,000. Buys first North American serial rights. Occasionally overstocked. Pays on publication. Reports in 6 weeks, but occasionally takes longer.
Nonfiction: "On articles, query first. We like hard sex articles, but research must be thorough." Length: 2,500 words. Pays $100-250.
Photos: All submissions must contain model release including parent's signature if under 21; fact sheet giving information about the model, place or activity being photographed, including all information of help in writing a photo story, and SASE. Photo payment varies, depending upon amount of space used by photo set.

CAVALIER, Suite 204, 2355 Salzedo St., Coral Gables FL 33134. (305)443-2370. Editor: Douglas Allen. 80% freelance written. Works with published/established and new/unpublished writers each year. Monthly magazine for "young males, ages 18-29, 80% college graduates, affluent, intelligent, interested in current events, sex, sports, adventure, travel and good fiction." Circ. 250,000. Pays on publication. Publishes ms an average of 3 months after acceptance. Byline given. Buys first serial and second serial (reprint) rights. Buys 44 or more mss/year. See past issues for general approach to take. Submit seasonal material at least 3 months in advance. Computer printout submissions acceptable; prefers letter-quality to dot-matrix. Reports in 3-5 weeks.
Nonfiction: Personal experience, interview, humor, think pieces, exposé and new product. "Be frank—we are open to dealing with controversial issues." No timely material (have 4 months lead time). Prefers 'unusual' subject matter as well as sex-oriented (but serious) articles." Query. Length: 2,800-3,500 words. Pays maximum $500 with photos. Sometimes pays the expenses of writers on assignment.
Photos: Photos purchased with or without captions. No cheesecake.
Fiction: Nye Willden, department editor. Mystery, science fiction, humorous, adventure, and contemporary problems "with at least one explicit sex scene per story." Send complete ms. Length: 2,500-3,500 words. Pays $250 maximum, higher for special.
Tips: "Our greatest interest is in originality—new ideas, new approaches; no tired, overdone stories—both feature and fiction. We do not deal in 'hack' sensationalism but in high quality pieces. Keep in mind the intelligent 18 to 29 year-old male reader. We will be putting more emphasis in articles and fiction on sexual themes. We prefer serious articles. Pornography—fiction can be very imaginative and sensational."

CHIC MAGAZINE, Larry Flynt Publications, Suite 3800, 2029 Century Park E., Los Angeles CA 90067. Executive Editor: Lonn M. Friend. 10% freelance written. Prefers to work with published/established writers. Monthly magazine for men, ages 20-35 years, college-educated and interested in current affairs, entertainment and sports. Circ. 250,000. Pays 1 month after acceptance. Publishes ms an average of 3 months after acceptance. Buys exclusive English and English translation world-wide magazine rights. Pays 20% kill fee. Computer printout submissions acceptable; prefers letter-quality to dot-matrix. Byline given unless writer requests otherwise. Reports in 2 months.
Nonfiction: Sex-related topics of current national interest; interview (personalities in news and entertainment); and celebrity profiles. Buys 12-18 mss/year. Query. Length: 4,500 words. Pays $750. Sometimes pays the expenses of writers on assignment.
Columns/Departments: Sex Life, 2,000 words. Pays $350. Odds and Ends (front of the book shorts; study the publication first) 100-300 words. Pays $50. Third Degree (short Q&As) columns, 1,000 words. Pays $350.
Fiction: "At present we are buying stories with emphasis on erotic themes. These may be adventure, action, mystery, horror or science fiction stories, but the tone and theme must involve sex and eroticism. The erotic nature of the story should not be subordinate to the characterizations and plot; the sex must grow logically from the people and the plot, not be contrived or forced."
Tips: "We do not buy poetry or non-erotic science fiction. Refrain from stories with drug themes, sex with minors, incest and bestiality."

ESQUIRE, 1790 Broadway, New York NY 10019. (212)459-7500. Editor-in-Chief: Lee Eisenberg. 99% freelance written. Monthly. Pays on acceptance. Publishes ms an average of 6 months after acceptance. Usually buys first serial rights. Computer printout submissions acceptable; prefers letter-quality to dot-matrix. Reports in 3 weeks. "We depend chiefly on solicited contributions and material from literary agencies. We are unable to accept responsibility for unsolicited material." Query.

Nonfiction: Articles vary in length, but features usually average 3,000-7,000 words. Articles should be slanted for sophisticated, intelligent readers; however, not highbrow in the restrictive sense. Wide range of subject matter. Rates run roughly between $300 and $3,000, depending on length, quality, etc. Sometimes pays expenses of writers on assignments.

Photos: Temple Smith, photo editor. Payment depends on how photo is used, but rates are roughly $300 for b&w; $500-750 for color. Guarantee on acceptance. Buys first periodical publication rights.

Fiction: L. Rust Hills, fiction editor. "Literary excellence is our only criterion." Length: about 1,000-6,000 words. Payment: $1,500-5,000.

Tips: The writer sometimes has a better chance of breaking in at *Esquire* with short, lesser-paying articles and fillers (rather than with major features) "because we need more short pieces."

FORUM, The International Journal of Human Relations, Penthouse International, 1965 Broadway, New York NY. (212)496-6100. Editor: John Heidery. 100% freelance written. Works with small number of new/unpublished writers each year. A monthly magazine. "*Forum* is the only serious publication in the U.S. to cover human sexuality in all its aspects for the layman—not only the erotic, but the medical, political, legal, etc." Circ. 400,000. Pays on acceptance. Publishes ms an average of 4-6 months after acceptance. Byline given. "Pseudonym mandatory for first-person sex stories." Offers 25% kill fee. Buys all rights. Submit seasonal/holiday material 6 months in advance. Photocopied submissions OK. Query for electronic submissions. Computer printout submissions OK; no dot matrix. Reports in 1 month on queries.

Nonfiction: Book excepts and personal experience "Most of our freelance submissions are true first-person sexual tales." No submissions of a specialized nature, medical, fiction or poetry. Buys 100 mss/year. Query or send complete ms. Length: 2,000-3,000 words. Pays $800-2,500 for assigned articles; pays $800-1,200 for unsolicited articles. Sometimes pays expenses of writers on assignment.

Photos: State availability of photos with submission. Reviews transparencies and 8x11 prints. Offers $40 minimum/photo. Captions, model releases and identification of subjects required.

Tips: "We are interested in true first-person sexual adventures. Pornographic embellishment—that is, mere titillation for the reader—is both discouraged and edited out, though explicit sexual description (there is a difference) is acceptable."

GALLERY MAGAZINE, Montcalm Publishing Corp., 800 2nd Ave., New York NY 10017. (212)986-9600. Editor-in-Chief: Marc Lichter. Managing Editor: Barry Janoff. Design Director: Michael Monte. 30% freelance written. Prefers to work with published/established writers. Monthly magazine "focusing on features of interest to the young American man." Circ. 500,000. Pays 50% on acceptance, 50% on publication. Publishes ms an average of 4 months after acceptance. Byline given. Pays 25% kill fee. Buys first North American serial rights; makes work-for-hire assignments. Submit seasonal/holiday material 6 months in advance. Photocopied submissions OK. Computer printout submissions OK; prefers letter-quality to dot-matrix. Reports in 1 month on queries; 2 months on mss. Sample copy $3.50 plus $1.75 postage and handling. Free writer's guidelines.

Nonfiction: Investigative pieces, general interest, how-to, humor, interview, new products and profile. "We *do not* want to see articles on pornography." Buys 7-9 mss/issue. Query or send complete mss. Length: 1,000-3,000 words. Pays $200-1,500. "Special prices negotiated." Sometimes pays expenses of writers on assignment.

Photos: Send photos with accompanying mss. Pay varies for b&w or color contact sheets and negatives. Buys one-time rights. Captions preferred; model release required.

Fiction: Adventure, erotica, experimental, humorous, mainstream, mystery and suspense. Buys 1 mss/issue. Send complete ms. Length: 500-3,000 words. Pays $250-1,000.

GENT, Suite 204, 2355 Salzedo St., Coral Gables FL 33134. (305)443-2378. Editor: John C. Fox. 75% freelance written. Prefers to work with published/established writers. Monthly magazine for men from every strata of society who enjoy big breasted, full-figured females. Circ. 200,000. Buys first North American serial rights. Byline given. Pays on publication. Publishes ms an average of 2 months after acceptance. Computer printout submissions acceptable; prefers letter-quality to dot-matrix. Reports in 6 weeks. Writer's guidelines for legal size SASE.

Nonfiction: Looking for traditional men's subjects (cars, racing, outdoor adventure, science, gambling, etc.) as well as sex-related topics. Query first. Length: 2,000-3,500 words. Buys 70 mss/year. Pays $100-250.

Photos: B&W photos and color transparencies purchased with mss. Captions (preferred).

Fiction: Erotic. "Stories should contain a huge-breasted female character, as this type of model is *Gent*'s main focus. And this character's endowments should be described in detail in the course of the story." Submit complete ms. No fiction queries. Length: 2,000-4,000 words. Pays $100-200.

Tips: "Our efforts to make *Gent* acceptable to Canadian censors as a conditions for exportation to that country have forced some shifting of editorial focus. Toward this end, we had de-emphasized our editorial coverage of pregnancy, lactation, anal intercourse and all forms of sadism and masochism. Study sample copies of the magazine before trying to write for it. We like custom-tailored stories and articles."

GENTLEMEN'S QUARTERLY, Condé Nast, 350 Madison Ave., New York NY 10017. Editor-in-Chief: Arthur Cooper. Managing Editor: Eliot Kaplan. 60% freelance written. Circ. 607,000. Monthly magazine emphasizing fashion, general interest and service features for men ages 25-45 with a large discretionary income. Pays on acceptance. Byline given. Pays 25% kill fee. Submit seasonal/holiday material 6 months in advance. Computer printout submissions acceptable; prefers letter-quality to dot-matrix. Reports in 1 month.
Nonfiction: Politics, personality profiles, lifestyles, trends, grooming, nutrition, health and fitness, sports, travel, money, investment and business matters. Buys 4-6 mss/issue. Query with published clips. Length: 1,500-4,000 words. Pays $750-3,000.
Columns/Departments: Eliot Kaplan, managing editor. Body & Soul (fitness, nutrition and grooming); Money (investments); Going in Style (travel); Health; Music; Tech (consumer electronics); Dining In (food); Wine & Spirits; Humor; Fiction; Games (sports); Books; The Male Animal (essays by men on life); and All About Adam (nonfiction by women about men). Buys 5-8/issue. Query with published clips or submit complete ms. Length: 1,000-2,500 words. Pays $750-2,000.
Tips: "Major features are usually assigned to well-established, known writers. Pieces are almost always solicited. The best way to break in is through the columns, especially Male Animal, All About Adam, Games, Health or Humor."

‡HIGH SOCIETY, High Society, 801 2nd Ave., New York NY 10017. (212)661-7878. Editor: Louis Montesano. Managing Editor: Ken Kimmel. Articles Editor: Stephen Loshiavo. 80% freelance written. Monthly magazine of erotic adult entertainment. Circ. 300,000. Pays on acceptance. Publishes ms an average of 4 months after acceptance. Byline given. Makes work-for-hire assignments. Submit seasonal/holiday material 6 months in advance. Computer printout submissions acceptable; no dot-matrix. Reports in 2 weeks. Sample copy $3.95; free writer's guidelines.
Nonfiction: Expose (political/entertainment); how-to (sexual, self-help); humor (bawdy); interview/profile (sports, music, politics); opinion (sexual subjects); and personal experience (sexual). Query with published clips. Length: 1,000-1,500 words. Pays $200 minimun: Sometimes pays expenses of writers on assignment.
Photos: State availability of photos or send photo with query. Reviews 1" color transparencies. Model release and identification of subjects required.
Columns/Departments: Silver Spoonfuls: Newsbits, health, reviews. Buys 50 mss/year. Query with published clips. Length: 250-1,000 words. Pays $200-400.
Fiction: Confession (sex oriented), erotica and humorous (sex oriented). Buys 12 mss/year. Query with published clips. Length: 1,000-1,500 words. Pays $150-250.

‡MAGNA, Fashion & Lifestyle Magazine for Big & Tall Men, The Magna Corp., Box 286, Cabin John MD 20818. (301)320-2745. Editor: Jack Shulman. Managing Editor: Marlene Salomon. A quarterly magazine for big and tall men. "We deal with problems particular to large men and to universal interests and problems." Circ. 120,000. Pays on publication. Publishes ms an average of 7 months after acceptance. Byline given. Buys first rights. Submit seasonal/holiday material 9 months in advance. Simultaneous and photocopied submissions OK. Computer printout submissions OK; prefers letter-quality to dot-matrix. Reports in 2 months on queries; 2 weeks on mss. Sample copy $3.50 with $1.35 postage.
Nonfiction: General interest, how-to, humor, interview/profile, personal experience and travel. No fiction or any article that does not treat big or tall men sympathetically. Buys 16 mss/year. Send complete ms. Length: 250-2,500 words. Pays $150-275.
Photos: State availability of photos with submission. Reviews 35mm transparencies. Offers no additional payment for photos accepted with ms. Model releases and identification of subjects required. Buys one-time rights.
Columns/Departments: Gerry Green, column/department editor. Toys for Big Boys (new products of interest), 50-150 words. Buys 24 mss/year. Send complete ms. Length: 50-150 words. Pays $25-100.
Fillers: Facts about big and tall men. Buys 12/year. Length: 75-300 words. Pays $25-60.

‡M/R MAGAZINE, A Magazine About Men, Prometheus Publishing Co., Suite 404, 2600 Dwight Way, Berkeley CA 94704. (415)549-0537. Editor: Sam Julty. 95% freelance written. Prefers to work with published/established writers; works with new/unpublished writers each year. A quarterly magazine with "a focus on men in any aspect of life—work, lifestyle, marriage, fathering, etc.—aimed at men and women readers. *Playboy* is a men's magazine *for* men. *M/r* is a magazine *about* men adapting, reacting or responding to a changing society." Estab. 1986. Circ. 10,000. Pays on acceptance. Publishes ms an average of 3 months after acceptance. Byline given. Buys first or second serial (reprint) rights. Previously published submissions OK. Computer printout submissions OK; prefers letter-quality to dot-matrix. Reports in 2 weeks. Sample copy $1; writer's guidelines for SASE.
Nonfiction: Essays, general interest, humor, interview/profile, opinion and personal experience. "All items

must be *about* men." Special issue on men and war. "We do not want articles on famous men as individuals. We focus on men as a population group and men within subgroups, i.e., black men, Hispanic men, etc." Buys 12 mss/year. Query. Length: 1,200-3,000 words. Pays $100.

Photos: State availability of photos with submission. Reviews 5x7 and 10x12 prints. Offers $3 maximum/photo. Model releases and identification of subjects required. Buys all rights.

Poetry: Avant-garde, free verse, haiku, light verse and traditional. No "poems irrelevant to men's lives, hopes, dreams and regrets." Buys 10 poems/year. Submit maximum 5 poems. Length: 5-25 lines. Pays $10.

Tips: "In any situation, for every social concern, focus on men's views, attitudes and perspectives. What do they think and feel *as men.* Editorial comments and personal perspectives by writers are welcome, but they must be labeled as your analysis. Women writers and women's views on men are especially welcome. Warning: Articulate criticism and commentary is acceptable. Bashing, promotion of sexism, racism and violence is *not* acceptable."

NUGGET, Suite 204, 2355 Salzedo St., Coral Gables FL 33134. (305)443-2378. Editor: John Fox. 75% freelance written. Magazine "primarily devoted to fetishism." Pays on publication. Publishes ms an average of 2 months after acceptance. Byline given. Buys first North American serial rights. Computer printout submissions acceptable; prefers letter-quality to dot-matrix. Reports in 6 weeks.

Nonfiction: Articles on fetishism—every aspect. Buys 20-30 mss/year. Submit complete ms. Length: 2,000-4,000 words. Pays $100-200.

Photos: Erotic pictorials of women and couples—essay types in fetish clothing (leather, rubber underwear, etc.) or women wrestling or boxing other women or men, preferably semi-nude or nude. Captions or short accompanying ms desirable. Reviews color transparencies or b&w photos.

Fiction: Erotic and fetishistic. Should be oriented to *Nugget*'s subject matter. Length: 2,000-4,000 words. Pays $100-200.

Tips: "We require queries on articles only, and the letter should be a brief synopsis of what the article is about. Originality in handling of subject is very helpful. It is almost a necessity for a freelancer to study our magazine first, be knowledgeable about the subject matter we deal with and able to write explicit and erotic fetish material."

‡OPTIONS, The Bi-Monthly, AJA Publishing, Box 470, Pt. Chester NY 10573. (914)939-2111. Editor: Don Stone. Assistant Editor: Diana Sheridan. Mostly freelance written. A bimonthly, sexually explicit magazine for and about bisexuals and homosexuals. "Articles, stories and letters about bisexuality. Positive approach. Safe-sex encounters unless the story clearly pre-dates the AIDS situation." Circ. 100,000. Pays on publication. Publishes ms an average of 4-6 months after acceptance. Byline given. Buys all rights. Submit seasonal/holiday material 6-8 months in advance; buys very little seasonal material. Photocopied submissions OK. Computer printout submissions OK. Reports in 3 weeks. Sample copy $2.95 with 6x9 SAE and 5 first-class stamps. Writers guidelines for SASE.

Nonfiction: Essays (occasional), how-to, humor, interview/profile, opinion and (especially) personal experience. All must be bisexually related. Does not want "anything not bisexually related, anything negative, anything opposed to safe sex, anything dry/boring/ponderous/pedantic, write even serious topics informally if not lightly." Buys 36 mss/year. Send complete ms. Length: 2,000-3,000. Pays $100.

Photos: Reviews transparencies and prints. Pays $10 for b&w photos; $200 for full color. Previously published photos acceptable.

Fiction: "We don't usually get enough true first-person stories and need to buy some from writers. They must be bisexual, usually man/man, hot and believable. They must not read like fiction." Buys 20 ms/year. Send complete ms. Length: 2,000-3,000. Pays $100.

Tips: "We use many more male/male pieces than female/female. Use only 1 serious article per issue. A serious/humorous approach is good here, but only if it's natural to you; don't make an effort for it. We use some serious/hot pieces too."

PLAYBOY, 919 N. Michigan, Chicago IL 60611. 50% freelance written. Prefers to work with published/established writers; works with a small number of new/unpublished writers each year. Monthly. Pays on acceptance. Publishes ms an average of 6 months after acceptance. Offers 20% kill fee. Buys first serial rights and others. Computer printout submissions acceptable; prefers letter-quality to dot-matrix. Reports in 1 month.

Nonfiction: John Rezek, articles editor. "We're looking for timely, topical pieces. Articles should be carefully researched and written with wit and insight. Little true adventure or how-to material. Check magazine for subject matter. Pieces on outstanding contemporary men, sports, politics, sociology, business and finance, music, science and technology, games, all areas of interest to the contemporary urban male." Query. Length: 3,000-5,000 words. Pays $3,000 minimum. *Playboy* interviews run between 10,000 and 15,000 words. After getting an assignment, the freelancer outlines the questions, conducts and edits the interview, and writes the introduction. Pays $4,000 minimum. For interviews contact G. Barry Golson, Executive Editor, 747 3rd Ave., New York NY 10017. Pays expenses of writers on assignment.

Photos: Gary Cole, photography director, suggests that all photographers interested in contributing make a thorough study of the photography currently appearing in the magazine. Generally all photography is done on assignment. While much of this is assigned to *Playboy*'s staff photographers, approximately 50% of the photography is done by freelancers, and *Playboy* is in constant search of creative new talent. Qualified freelancers are encouraged to submit samples of their work and ideas. All assignments made on an all rights basis with payments scaled from $600/color page for miscellaneous features such as fashion, food and drink, etc.; $300/b&w page; $1,000/color page for girl features; cover, $1,500. Playmate photography for entire project: $10,000-13,000. Assignments and submissions handled by senior editor: Jeff Cohen and associate editors: James Larson and Michael Ann Sullivan, Chicago; Marilyn Grabowski and Linda Kenney, Los Angeles. Assignments made on a minimum guarantee basis. Film, processing, and other expenses necessitated by assignment honored.

Fiction: Alice Turner, fiction editor. Both light and serious fiction. "Entertainment pieces are clever, smoothly written stories. Serious fiction must come up to the best contemporary standards in substance, idea and style. Both, however, should be designed to appeal to the educated, well-informed male reader." General types include comedy, mystery, fantasy, horror, science fiction, adventure, social-realism, "problem" and psychological stories. Fiction lengths are 3,000-6,000 words; short-shorts of 1,000 to 1,500 words are used. Pays $2,000; $1,000 short-short. Rates rise for additional acceptances.

Fillers: Party Jokes are always welcome. Pays $50 each. Also interesting items for Playboy After Hours, section (check it carefully before submission). The After Hours front section pays anywhere from $75 for humorous or unusual news items (submissions not returned) to $500 for original reportage. Subject matter should be new trends, fads, personalities and cultural developments. Has regular movie, book and record reviewers. Ideas for Playboy Potpourri pay $75. Query to David Stevens, Chicago. Games, puzzles and travel articles should be addressed to New York office.

SCREW, Box 432, Old Chelsea Station, New York NY 10011. Managing Editor: Manny Neuhaus. 95% freelance written. Eager to work with new/unpublished writers. Weekly tabloid newspaper for a predominantly male, college-educated audience; ages 21 through mid-40s. Circ. 125,000. Pays on publication. Publishes ms an average of 3 months after acceptance. Byline given. Buys all rights. Computer printout submissions acceptable; prefers letter-quality to dot-matrix. Reports in 3 months. Free sample copy and writer's guidelines.

Nonfiction: "Sexually-related news, humor, how-to articles, first-person and true confessions. Frank and explicit treatment of all areas of sex; outrageous and irreverent attitudes combined with hard information, news and consumer reports. Our style is unique. Writers should check several recent issues." Buys 150-200 mss/year. Submit complete ms for first person, true confession. Length: 1,000-3,000 words. Pays $100-200. Will also consider material for Letter From . . . , a consumer-oriented wrap-up of commercial sex scene in cities around the country; and My Scene, a sexual true confession. Length: 1,000-2,500 words. Pays about $40. Sometimes pays the expenses of writers on assignment.

Photos: Reviews b&w glossy prints (8x10 or 11x14) purchased with or without manuscripts or on assignment. Pays $10-50.

Tips: "All mss get careful attention. Those written in *Screw* style on sexual topics have the best chance. I anticipate a need for more aggressive, insightful political humor."

SWANK, GCR Publishing Corp., 888 7th Ave., New York NY 10106. (212)541-7100. Editor: P Katt. 50% freelance written. Eager to work with new/unpublished writers. Monthly magazine on "sex and sensationalism, lurid. High quality adult erotic entertainment." Audience of men ages 18-38, high school and some college education, medium income, skilled blue-collar professionals, union men. Circ. 350,000. Pays on publication. Publishes ms an average of 4 months after acceptance. Byline given; pseudonym, if wanted. Pays 20% kill fee. Buys first North American serial rights. Submit seasonal/holiday material 4 months in advance. Reports in 2 weeks on queries; 1 month on mss. Sample copy $3.50; writer's guidelines for SASE.

Nonfiction: Exposé (researched) and adventure must be accompanied by photographs. "We buy non-sex articles and articles on sex-related topics which don't need to be accompanied by photos." Interested in lifestyle (unusual) pieces. Buys photo pieces on autos. Buys 34 mss/year. Query with or without published clips. Pays $350-500. Sometimes pays the expenses of writers on assignment.

Photos: Bruce Perez, photo editor. State availability of photos. "If you have good photographs of an interesting adventure/lifestyle subject, the writing that accompanies it is bought almost automatically." Model releases required.

Tips: "Don't even bother to send girl photos unless you are a published professional." Looks for "lifestyle and adventure pieces that are accompanied by color 35mm chromes and articles about sex-related topics. We carry one photo/journalism piece about automobiles in issue. "

‡TURN-ON LETTERS, AJA Publishing, Box 470, Port Chester NY 10573. Editor: Julie Silver. Bimonthly magazine covering sex. "Adult material, must be positive, no pain or degradations. No incest, no underage." Circ. 100,000. Pays on publication. Publishes ms. an average of 4-6 months after acceptance. Buys all rights. No byline. No kill fee; "assigned ms are not killed unless they do not fulfill the assignment and/or violate censorship laws." Submit seasonal/holiday material 6 months in advance. Computer printout submissions OK.

Reports in 3 weeks. Sample copy $2.50 with 6x9 SAE and 4 first-class stamps. Writer's guidelines for business size SASE.

Fiction: Sexually explicit material in the format of a letter. Buys 284 "letters"/year. Send complete ms. Length: 500-750 words (2-3 typed pages). Pays $15.

Photos: Reviews transparencies and prints. Buys b&w for $10 and full color for $200. Previously published pictures OK. Buys all rights.

Tips: "When you write, be different, be believable."

‡UNCENSORED LETTERS,Sportomatic Publishers, Box 470, Port Chester NY 10573. Editor: Tammy Simmons. 100% freelance written. Bimonthly magazine covering sex. "Adult material must be positive in approach, no pain or degradation. No incest; no underage." Circ. 100,000. Pays on publication. Publishes ms an average of 4-6 months after acceptance. No byline given. No kill fee; "assigned ms are not killed unless they do not fulfill assignment and/or they violate censorship laws." Buys all rights. Computer printout submissions OK. Reports in 3 weeks. Sample copy $2.95; writer's guidelines for SASE.

Fiction: Sexually explicit material written as true-to-life in the format of a letter. Buys 336 mss/year. Send complete ms. Length: 300-750 (2-3 typed, double-spaced pages). Pays $15.

Photos: Buys b&w's $10 each; full color $200. previously published photos OK. Buys all rights.

Tips: "Read spec sheet, available for SASE. When you write, be different, yet believable."

Military

These publications emphasize military or paramilitary subjects or other aspects of military life. Technical and semitechnical publications for military commanders, personnel and planners, as well as those for military families and civilians interested in Armed Forces activities are listed here.

AMERICAN SURVIVAL GUIDE, McMullen Publishing, Inc., 2145 W. La Palma Ave., Anaheim CA 92801. (714)635-9040. Editor: Jim Benson. 50% freelance written. Monthly magazine covering "self-reliance, defense, meeting day-to-day and possible future threats—survivalism for survivalists." Circ. 89,000. Pays on publication. Publishes ms up to 1 year after acceptance. Byline given. Submit seasonal/holiday material 5 months in advance. Computer printout submissions acceptable; prefers letter-quality to dot-matrix. Sample copy $2.50; writer's guidelines for SASE.

Nonfiction: Expose (political); how-to; interview/profile; personal experience (how I survived); photo feature (equipment and techniques related to survival in all possible situations); emergency medical; health and fitness; communications; transportation; food preservation; water purification; self-defense; terrorism; nuclear dangers; nutrition; tools; shelter; etc. "No general articles about how to survive. We want specifics and single subjects." Buys 60-100 mss/year. Query or send complete ms. Length: 1,500-2,000 words. Pays $140-350. Sometimes pays the expenses of writers on assignment.

Photos: Send photos with ms. "One of the most frequent mistakes made by writers in completing an article assignment for us is sending photo submissions that are inadequate." Captions, model releases and identification of subjects mandatory. Buys all rights.

Tips: "Prepare material of value to individuals who wish to sustain human life no matter what the circumstance. This magazine is a text and reference."

ARMY MAGAZINE, 2425 Wilson Blvd., Arlington VA 22201. (703)841-4300. Editor-in-Chief: L. James Binder. Managing Editor: Mary Blake French. 80% freelance written. Prefers to work with published/established writers; eager to work with new/unpublished writers. Monthly magazine emphasizing military interests. Circ. 171,000. Pays on publication. Publishes ms an average of 6 months after acceptance. Buys all rights. Byline given except for back-up research. Submit seasonal/holiday material 3 months in advance. Photocopied submissions OK. Computer printout submissions acceptable; no dot-matrix. Sample copy and writer's guidelines for 8½x12 SAE with $1 postage.

Nonfiction: Historical (military and original); humor (military feature-length articles and anecdotes); interview; new product; nostalgia; personal experience; photo feature; profile; and technical. No rehashed history. "We would like to see more pieces about interesting military personalities. We especially want material lending itself to heavy, contributor-supplied photographic treatment. The first thing a contributor should recognize is that our readership is very savvy militarily. 'Gee-whiz' personal reminiscences get short shrift, unless they hold their own in a company in which long military service, heroism and unusual experiences are commonplace. At the same time, Army readers like a well-written story with a fresh slant, whether it is about an experience in a foxhole or the fortunes of a corps in battle.'' Buys 12 mss/issue. Submit complete ms. Length: 4,500 words. Pays 12-17¢/word.

Photos: Submit photo material with accompanying ms. Pays $15-50 for 8x10 b&w glossy prints; $35-150 for 8x10 color glossy prints or 2¼x2¼ color transparencies, will also accept 35mm. Captions preferred. Buys all rights.

Columns/Departments: Military news, books, comment (*New Yorker*-type "Talk of the Town" items). Buys 8/issue. Submit complete ms. Length: 1,000 words. Pays $40-150.

ASIA-PACIFIC DEFENSE FORUM, Commander-in-Chief, U.S. Pacific Command, Box 13, Camp H.M. Smith HI 96861. (808)477-5027/6924. Editor-in-Chief: Lt. Col. Paul R. Stankiewicz. Editor: Major Robert Teasdale. 12% (maximum) freelance written. Quarterly magazine for foreign military officers in 51 Asian-Pacific, Indian Ocean and other countries; all services—Army, Navy, Air Force and Marines. Secondary audience—government officials, media and academicians concerned with defense issues. "We seek to keep readers abreast of current status of U.S. forces and of U.S. national security policies, and to enhance international professional dialogue on military subjects.'' Circ. 30,000. Pays on acceptance. Publishes ms an average of 4 months after acceptance. Byline given. Buys simultaneous rights, second serial (reprint) rights or one-time rights. Phone queries OK. Simultaneous, photocopied, and previously published submissions OK. Computer printout submissions OK; prefers letter-quality to dot-matrix. Requires only a self-addressed label. Reports in 3 weeks on queries; 10 weeks on mss. Free sample copy and writer's guidelines (send self-addressed label).

Nonfiction: General interest (strategy and tactics, current type forces and weapons systems, strategic balance and security issues and Asian-Pacific armed forces); historical (occasionally used, if relation to present-day defense issues is clearly apparent); how-to (training, leadership, force employment procedures, organization); interview and personal experience (rarely used, and only in terms of developing professional military skills). "We do not want overly technical weapons/equipment descriptions, overly scholarly articles, controversial policy, and budget matters; nor do we seek discussion of in-house problem areas. We do not deal with military social life, base activities or PR-type personalities/job descriptions.'' Buys 2-4 mss/year. Query or send complete ms. Length: 1,000-3,000 words. Pays $100-300.

Photos: State availability of photos with query or ms. "We provide nearly all photos; however, we will consider good quality photos with manuscripts.'' Reviews 5x7 and 8x10 b&w glossy prints or 35mm color transparencies. Offers no additional payment for photos accompanying mss. Photo credits given. Captions required. Buys one-time rights.

Tips: "The most frequent mistake made by writers is writing in a flashy, Sunday supplement style. Our audience is relatively staid, and fact-oriented articles requiring a newspaper/journalistic approach are used more than a normal magazine style. Develop a 'feel' for our foreign audience orientation. Provide material that is truly audience-oriented and easily illustrated with photos.''

FAMILY MAGAZINE, The Magazine for Military Wives, Box 4993, Walnut Creek CA 94596. (415)284-9093. Editor: Mary Jane Ryan. 100% freelance written. Works with a small number of new/unpublished writers each year. A monthly magazine for military wives who are young, high school educated and move often. Circ. 545,000. Pays on publication. Publishes ms an average of 6-12 months after acceptance. Byline given. Buys first North American serial rights. Submit seasonal/holiday material 6 months in advance. Simultaneous and photocopied submissions OK. Computer printout submissions acceptable; prefers letter-quality to dot-matrix. Reports in 1 month. Sample copy $1.25; writer's guidelines for SASE.

Nonfiction: Humor, personal experience, photo feature and travel, of interest to military wives. No romance, anything to do with getting a man or aging. Buys 30 mss/year. Send complete ms. Length: 2,000 words maximum. Pays $75-200.

Photos: Send photos with submissions. Reviews contact sheets, transparencies and prints. Offers $25-100/photo. Identification of subjects required. Buys one-time rights.

Fiction: Humorous, mainstream and slice-of-life vignettes. No romance or novel excerpts. Buys 5 mss/year. Length: 2,000 words maximum. Pays $75-150.

FOR YOUR EYES ONLY, Military Intelligence Summary, Tiger Publications, Box 8759, Amarillo TX 79114. (806)655-2009. Editor: Stephen V. Cole. 5% freelance written. Eager to work with new/unpublished writers. A biweekly newsletter covering military intelligence (post-1980). Circ. 1,200. Pays on publication. Publishes ms an average of 3 months after acceptance. Byline given. Offers variable kill fee. Buys all rights. Simultaneous queries, and simultaneous, photocopied, and previously published submissions OK. Query for electronic submissions. Computer printout submissions acceptable. Reports in 2 weeks on queries; 1 month on mss. Sample copy $2; writer's guidelines on request with sample copy.

Nonfiction: Exposé, interview/profile, personal experience, technical, how-to, arms sales, tests, current research, wars, battles and military data. "We're looking for technical material presented for nontechnical people. Our emphasis is on how and why things work (and don't work)—not so much what happened as how it happened and what it means." No superficial or humorous material; nothing before 1981. Buys 20 mss/year. Query. Length: 50-1,000 words. Pays 3¢/word.

Photos: State availability of photos or send photos with ms. Pays $5-35 for b&w prints. Captions required. Buys one-time rights or negotiable rights.

Fillers: Newsbreaks. Buys 50-100/year. Length: 30-150 words. Pays $1-5.

Tips: "Read publication and author's guide; be aware of how much we generate internally. Briefings (100-300 words) and Newsnotes (30-150 words) are most open to freelancers."

INFANTRY, Box 2005, Fort Benning GA 31905-0605. (404)545-2350. Editor: Albert N. Garland. 90% freelance written. Eager to work with new/unpublished writers. Bimonthly magazine published primarily for combat arms officers and noncommissioned officers. Circ. 20,000. Not copyrighted. Buys first serial rights. Pays on publication. Payment cannot be made to U.S. government employees. Publishes ms an average of 1 year after acceptance. Computer printout submissions acceptable; prefers letter-quality to dot-matrix. Reports in 1 month. Free sample copy and writer's guidelines.

Nonfiction: Interested in current information on U.S. military organization, weapons, equipment, tactics and techniques; foreign armies and their equipment; lessons learned from combat experience, both past and present; and solutions to problems encountered in the Active Army and the Reserve Components. Departments include Letters, Features and Forum, Training Notes, and Book Reviews. Uses 70 unsolicited mss/year. Recent article example: "The 9mm Story" (January-February 1987). Length of articles: 1,500-3,500 words. Length for Book Reviews: 500-1,000 words. Query with writing sample. Accepts 75 mss/year.

Photos: Used with mss.

Tips: "Start with letters to editor and book reviews to break in."

LIFE IN THE TIMES, Times Journal Co., Springfield VA 22159-0200. (703)750-8672. Editor: Barry Robinson. Managing Editor: Donna Peterson. 30% freelance written. Eager to work with new/unpublished writers. Weekly lifestyle section of Army, Navy and Air Force Times covering current lifestyles and problems of career military families around the world. Circ. 300,000. Pays on acceptance. Publishes ms an average of 2 months after acceptance. Byline given. Offers negotiable kill fee. Buys all rights. Submit seasonal/holiday material 6 months in advance. Query for electronic submissions. Double- or triple-spaced computer printout submissions acceptable; no dot-matrix. Reports in about 2 months. Writer's guidelines for SASE.

Nonfiction: Expose (current military); how-to (military wives); interview/profile (military); opinion (military topic); personal experience (military only); and travel (of military interest). "We accept food articles and short items about unusual things military people and their families are doing." No poetry, cartoons or historical articles. Buys 110 mss/year. Query with published clips. Length: 750-2,000 words. Pays $75-350. Sometimes pays the expenses of writers on assignment.

Photos: State availability of photos or send photos with ms. Reviews 35mm color contact sheets and prints. Captions, model releases, and identification of subjects required. Buys all rights.

Tips: "In your query write a detailed description of story and how it will be told. A tentative lead is nice. Just one good story 'breaks in' a freelancer. Follow the outline you propose in your query letter and humanize articles with quotes and examples."

THE MILITARY ENGINEER, 607 Prince St., Box 21289, Alexandria VA 22320-2289. (703)549-3800. Editor: John J. Kern. 90% freelance written. Prefers to work with published/established writers, but willing to work with new authors. Bimonthly magazine. Circ. 29,000. Pays on publication. Publishes ms an average of 9 months after acceptance. Byline given. Buys all rights. Phone queries OK. Computer printout submissions acceptable. Reports in 1 month. Sample copy and writer's guidelines $4.

Nonfiction: Well-written and illustrated semitechnical articles by experts and practitioners of civil and military engineering, constructors, equipment manufacturers, defense contract suppliers and architect/engineers on these subjects and on subjects of military biography and history. "Subject matter should represent a contribution to the fund of knowledge, concern a new project or method, be on R&D in these fields; investigate planning and management techniques or problems in these fields, or be of militarily strategic nature." Buys 50-70 unsolicited mss/year. Length: 1,000-2,000 words. Query.

Photos: Mss must be accompanied by 6-10 well-captioned photos, maps or illustrations; b&w glossy, generally. Pays approximately $25/page.

MILITARY LIFESTYLE, Downey Communications, Inc., 1732 Wisconsin Ave. NW, Washington DC 20007. Editor: Hope M. Daniels. 80-90% freelance written. Works with equal balance of published and unpublished writers. For military families in the U.S. and overseas. Published 10 times a year. Magazine. Circ. 520,000. Pays on publication. Publishes ms an average of 4-6 months after acceptance. Buys first North American serial rights. Submit seasonal/holiday material at least 6 months in advance. Computer printout submissions acceptable. Reports in approximately 2 months. Sample copy $1.50. Writer's guidelines for SASE.

Nonfiction: "All articles must have special interest for military families. General interest articles are OK if they reflect situations our readers can relate to." Food, humor, profiles, childrearing, health, home decor and travel. "Query letter should name sources, describe focus of article, use a few sample quotes from sources, indicate length, and should describe writer's own qualifications for doing the piece." Length: 800-2,000 words. Pays $200-600/article. Negotiates expenses on a case-by-case basis.

Photos: Purchased with accompanying ms and on assignment. Uses 35mm or larger color transparencies. Captions and model releases are required. Query art director Judi Connelly.

Columns/Departments: It Seems to Me—personal experience pieces by military family members. Also, Your Pet, Your Money and Babystyle. Query. Length: 800-1,200 words. Rates vary.

Fiction: Slice-of-life, family situation, contemporary tableaux. "Military family life or relationship themes only." Buys 6-8 mss/year. Query. Length: 1,500-2,000 words. Pays $200-250.

Tips: "We are a magazine for military families, not just women. Our editorial attempts enthusiastically to reflect that. Our ideal contributor is a military family member who can write. However, I'm always impressed by a writer who has analyzed the market and can suggest some possible new angles for us. Sensitivity to military issues is a must for our contributors, as is the ability to write good personality profiles and/or do thorough research about military family life. We don't purchase household hints, historical articles, WW II-era material or parenting advice that is too personal and limited only to the writer's own experience."

MILITARY LIVING R&R REPORT, Box 2347, Falls Church VA 22042. (703)237-0203. Publisher: Ann Crawford. Bimonthly newsletter for "military consumers worldwide. Please state when sending submission that it is for the *R&R Report Newsletter* so as not to confuse it with our monthly magazine which has different requirements." Pays on publication. Buys first serial rights but will consider other rights. Sample copy $1.

Nonfiction: "We use information on little-known military facilities and privileges, discounts around the world and travel information. Items must be short and concise. Payment is on an honorarium basis, 1-1½¢/word."

MILITARY REVIEW, U.S. Army Command and General Staff College, Fort Leavenworth KS 66027-6910. (913)684-5642. Editor-in-Chief: Col. James A. Rye. Managing Editor: Lt. Col. Thomas Conrad. Associate Editor: Lt. Col. Lynn Havach. 75% freelance written. Eager to work with new/unpublished writers. Monthly journal (printed in three languages; English, Spanish and Brazilian Portuguese), emphasizing the military for military officers, students and scholars. Circ. 27,000. Pays on publication. Publishes ms an average of 8 months after acceptance. Byline given. Buys first serial rights and reserves right to reprint for training purpose. Phone queries and photocopied submissions OK. Query for electronic submission. Computer printout submissions acceptable; prefers letter-quality to dot-matrix. Reports in 1 month. Writer's guidelines for 4x9½ SASE.

Nonfiction: Operational level of war, military history, international affairs, tactics, new military equipment, strategy and book reviews. Prefers not to get poetry or cartoons. Buys 100-120 mss/year. Query. Length: 2,000-3,000 words. Pays $50-200.

Tips: "We need more articles from military personnel experienced in particular specialties. Examples: Tactics from a tactician, military engineering from an engineer, etc. By reading our publication, writers will quickly recognize our magazine as a forum for any topic of general interest to the U.S. Army. They will also discover the style we prefer: concise and direct, in the active voice, with precision and clarity, and moving from the specific to the general."

NATIONAL DEFENSE, American Defense Preparedness Association, Suite 905, 1700 N. Moore St., Arlington VA 22209. (703)522-1820. Editor: Col. D. Ballou. 80% freelance written. Association journal published 10 times annually. "We concentrate on defense technology and focus on defense management executives, engineers and scientists in the defense industry, the Department of Defense, and the military services. Each issue contains departments on small arms, tanks and automotive, space, missiles and aeronautics, sea services, foreign military developments and new developments." Pays on publication. Publishes ms an average of 2 months after acceptance. Byline given. Offers negotiable kill fee. Buys first rights. Submit seasonal/holiday material 3 months in advance. Simultaneous (if advised) and photocopied submissions OK. Computer printout submissions acceptable; prefers letter-quality to dot-matrix. Reports in 2 weeks on queries; 2 months on mss. Free sample copy and writer's guidelines.

Nonfiction: General interest (defense); how-to (defense/management); interview/profile (defense); new product (defense); photo feature (defense); and technical. "Each of our issues focuses on a specific theme for that month. They include: NATO Lifelines, Naval Warfare, Global Warfare, Space and Space Defense, Land Warfare, Air Warfare, and Research and High technology." Buys 50 mss/year. Query. Length: 1,800-2,500 words. Pays $500-1,000. Pays the expenses of writers on assignment.

Photos: State availability of photos with submission. Reviews contact sheets, negatives, 35mm and larger transparencies and 3x5 and larger prints. Offers $50 maximum/photo or by agreement if used. Captions required. Buys one-time rights; if desired, will return photos.

Fillers: Facts and newsbreaks. Length: 50-200 words. Pays $25.

Tips: "Features are most open to freelancers. Study our Theme Calendar."

‡**NATIONAL GUARD**, 1 Massachusetts Ave. NW, Washington DC 20001. (202)789-0031. Editor: Lt. Col. Reid K. Beveridge. 10% freelance written. Monthly magazine for officers of the Army and Air National Guard. Circ. 62,000. Pays on publication. Publishes ms an average of 6 months after acceptance. Rights negotiable. Byline given. Query for electronic submissions. Computer printout submissions acceptable. Query.
Nonfiction: Military policy, strategy, training, equipment, logistics, personnel policies: tactics, combat lessons learned as they pertain to the Army and Air Force (and impact on Army National Guard and Air National Guard). Material must be strictly accurate from a technical standpoint. Does not publish exposes, cartoons or jokes. Buys 10-12 mss/year. Query. Length: 2,000-3,000 words. Payment ($75-500/article) depends on originality, amount of research involved, etc. Sometimes pays expenses of writers on assignment.
Photos: Photography pertinent to subject matter should accompany ms.

NEW BREED, The Magazine for Bold Adventurers, New Breed Publications, Inc., 30 Amarillo Dr., Nanuet NY 10954. (914)623-8426. Editor: Harry Belil. Managing Editor: Richard Schwartzberg. 85% freelance written. Eager to work with new/unpublished writers. Bimonthly magazine covering military adventures, new weapons, survival. For persons interested in "where the action is—hot spots on the globe where the voice of adventure calls." Circ. 60,000. Pays on publication. Publishes ms an average of 6 months after acceptance. Byline given. Buys first serial rights. Photocopied and previously published submissions OK, if so indicated. Computer printout submissions acceptable; prefers letter-quality to dot-matrix. Would rather have typed copy. Reports in 2 weeks on queries; 3 weeks on mss. Sample copy for $3.50, 9x12 SAE, and first class postage; writer's guidelines for SASE.
Nonfiction: "Give us the best possible information on state-of-the-art field weaponry, combat practice and survival techniques for the professional soldier. Material should be slightly right-wing, pro-weapons (including handguns), somewhat hawkish in diplomacy, pro-freedom, pro-constitution, thus, libertarian and capitalist (in the real sense of the term) and consequently anti-totalitarian. Submit mss on all units of the armed forces, as well as soldiers of fortune, police officers and individuals who can be classified as 'New Breed.' " Special annual "combat guns" issue. Buys 80 mss/year. Send complete ms. Length: 3,000-4,000 words. Pays $150-250 for articles with b&w and color photos; pays up to $300 for exceptional stories.
Tips: "The most frequent mistake made by writers in completing an article for us is not studying our publication for format, style and type of material desired. It would help sell the story if some visual material was included."

OFF DUTY, U.S.: Suite C-2, 3303 Harbor Blvd., Costa Mesa CA 92626. Editor: Bruce Thorstad. Europe: Eschersheimer Landstrasse 69, Frankfurt/M, West Germany. Editor: J.C. Couch. Pacific: 14/F Park Commercial Centre, 8 Shelter St., Causeway Bay, Hong Kong. Editor: Jim Shaw. 50% freelance written. Monthly magazine for U.S. military personnel and their families stationed around the world. Most readers ages 18-35. Combined circ. 708,000. Buys first serial rights or second serial (reprint) rights. Pays on acceptance. Publishes ms an average of 6 months after acceptance. Computer printout submissions acceptable. Sample copy and writer's guidelines $1.
Nonfiction: Three editions—American, Pacific and European. "Emphasis is on off-duty travel, leisure, military shopping, wining and dining, sports, hobbies, music, and getting the most out of military life. Overseas editions lean toward foreign travel and living in foreign cultures. In travel articles we like anecdotes, lots of description, color and dialogue. American edition uses more American trends and how-to/service material. Material with special U.S., Pacific or European slant should be sent to appropriate address above; material useful in all editions may be sent to U.S. address and will be forwarded as necessary." Buys 30-50 mss/year for each of three editions. Query. Length: 1,500 words average. Also needs 200-word shorties. Pays 13¢/word for use in one edition; 16¢/word for use in 2 or more. Sometimes pays expenses of writers on assignment.
Photos: Bought with or without accompanying ms. Pays $25 for b&w glossy prints; $50 for color transparencies; $100 for full page color; $200 for covers. "Covers must be vertical format 35mm; larger format transparencies preferred."
Tips: "All material should take into account to some extent our special audience—the U.S. military and their dependents. Our publication is subtitled 'The Military Leisuretime Magazine,' and the stories we like best are about how to get more out of the military experience. That 'more' could range from more fun to more satisfaction to more material benefits. Increasingly, the writer with special knowledge of active-duty military personnel and their families is the writer we need. However, our focus remains on off-duty pursuits and concerns. Query writers very often mistake the basic nature of our magazine. If we do an article on running, we'll get a raft of queries for running articles. That's wrong. We're a general interest magazine; if we've just done running, it's going to be quite a while before we do it again. We've got *dozens* of other subjects to cover."

OVERSEAS!,Military Consumer Today, Inc., Kolpingstr 1, 6906 Leimen, West Germany 06221-25431/32/33. Editorial Director: Charles L. Kaufman. Managing Editor: Greg Ballinger. 95% freelance written. Eager to work with new/unpublished writers; "we don't get enough submissions." Monthly magazine. "*Overseas!* is aimed at the U.S. military in Europe. It is the leading men's lifestyle magazine slanted towards life in Europe, specifically directed to males ages 18-35." Circ. 83,000. Pays on acceptance. Publishes ms an average of 3 months after acceptance. Byline given. Offers kill fee depending on circumstances and writer. Buys one-time rights. Submit seasonal/holiday material at least 4 months in advance. Simultaneous queries, and simultaneous, photocopied, and previously published submissions OK. Computer printout submissions acceptable; prefers letter-quality to dot-matrix. SASE, IRCs. Reports in 2 weeks on queries; 1 month on mss. Sample copy for SAE and 4 IRCs; writer's guidelines for SAE and 1 IRC.

Nonfiction: General interest (lifestyle for men and other topics); how-to (use camera, buy various types of video, audio, photo and computer equipment); humor (no military humor; "we want travel/tourist humor like old *National Lampoon* style. Must be humorous."); interview/profile (music, personality interviews; current music stars for young audience); personal experience (relating to travel in Europe); technical (video, audio, photo, computer; how to purchase and use equipment); travel (European, first person adventure; write toward male audience); men's cooking; and men's fashion/lifestyle. Special issues include Video, Audio, Photo, and Military Shopper's Guide. Needs 250-750 word articles on video, audio, photo and computer products. Published in September every year. No articles that are drug- or sex-related. No cathedrals or museums of Europe stories. Buys 30-50 mss/year "but would buy more if we got better quality and subjects." Query with or without pulished clips or send complete ms. Length: 750-2,000 words. Pays 10¢/word. Usually pays expenses of writers on assignment; negotiable.

Photos: Send photos with accompanying query or ms. Pays $20 minimum, b&w; $35 color transparencies, 35mm or larger. Photos must accompany travel articles—"color slides. Also, we are always looking for photographs of pretty, unposed, dressed, nonfashion, active *women* for our covers." Pays $250 minimum. Identification of subjects required. Buys one-time rights. Buys 12 covers/year.

Columns/Departments: Back Talk—potpourri page of humor, cartoons and other materials relating to life in Europe for Americans. Buys 12-20 mss/year. Query with published clips. Length: 1-150 words. Pays $25-150/piece used. "Would buy more if received more."

Tips: "We would especially like to get submissions on men's cooking—short 25-150 word cooking, food-related tips; needs 4-5 each month. Travel writing humor, men's fashion and articles on video, audio, photo and computer equiptment and use are most open to freelancers. Writing should be lively, interesting, with lots of good information. We anticipate a change in the length of articles. Articles will be shorter with more sidebars, because readers don't have time to read longer articles. *Overseas* magazine is the *Travel and Leisure/GQ/Playboy/Esquire* of this market; any articles that would be suitable for these magazines would probably work in *Overseas!*"

PARAMETERS: JOURNAL OF THE U.S. ARMY WAR COLLEGE, U.S. Army War College, Carlisle Barracks PA 17013. (717)245-4943. Editor: Col. LLoyd J. Matthews, U.S. Army Retired. Quarterly. 100% freelance written. Prefers to work with published/established writers or experts in the field. Readership consists of senior leadership of U.S. defense establishment, both uniformed and civilian, plus members of the media, government, industry and academia interested in national and international security affairs, military strategy, military leadership and management, art and science of warfare, and military history (provided it has contemporary relevance). Most readers possess a graduate degree. Circ. 10,000. Not copyrighted; unless copyrighted by author, articles may be reprinted with appropriate credits. Buys first serial rights. Byline given. Pays on publication. Publishes ms an average of 6 months after acceptance. Computer printout submissions acceptable; no dot-matrix. Reports in 1 month.

Nonfiction: Articles preferred that deal with current security issues, employ critical analysis, and provide solutions or recommendations. Articles on the operational level of war. Liveliness and verve, consistent with scholarly integrity, appreciated. Theses, studies and academic course papers should be adapted to article form prior to submission. Documentation in complete endnotes. Submit complete ms. Length: 4,500 words, preferably less. Pays $150 average (including visuals).

Tips: "Make it short; keep it interesting; get criticism and revise accordingly. Tackle a subject only if your are an authority."

PERIODICAL, Council on America's Military Past, 4970 N. Camino Antonio, Tucson AZ 85718. Editor-in-Chief: Dan L. Thrapp. 90% freelance written. Works with a small number of new/unpublished writers each year. Quarterly magazine emphasizing old and abandoned forts, posts and military installations; military subjects for a professional, knowledgeable readership interested in one-time defense sites or other military installations. Circ. 1,500. Pays on publication. Publishes ms an average of 6 months after acceptance. Buys one-time rights. Simultaneous, photocopied, and previously published (if published a long time ago) submissions OK. Computer printout submissions OK; prefers letter-quality to dot-matrix. Reports in 3 weeks.

Nonfiction: Historical, personal experience, photo feature and technical (relating to posts, their construction/operation and military matters). Buys 4-6 mss/issue. Query or send complete ms. Length: 300-4,000 words. Pays $2/page minimum.

Photos: Purchased with or without ms. Query. Reviews glossy, single-weight 8x10 b&w prints. Offers no additional payment for photos accepted with accompanying ms. Captions required.

‡R&R ENTERTAINMENT DIGEST, R&R Werbe GmbH, 1 Kolpingstrasse, 6906 Leimen, W. Germany 06224-7060. Editor: Marji Hess. 50% freelance written. Monthly entertainment guide for military and government employees and their families stationed in Europe "specializing in travel in Europe, audio/video/photo information, music, and the homemaker scene. Aimed exclusively at military/DoD based in Europe—Germany, Britain and the Mediterranean." Circ. 185,000. Pays on publication. Publishes ms an average of 2-6 months after acceptance. Byline given. "We offer 50% of payment as a kill fee, but this rarely happens—if story can't run in one issue, we try to use it in a future edition." Buys first serial rights for military market in Europe only. "We will reprint stories that have run in stateside publications if applicable to us." Submit seasonal/holiday material 3 months in advance. Computer printout submissions acceptable; prefers letter-quality to dot-matrix. Simultaneous queries, and simultaneous, photocopied, and previously published submissions OK. Reports in 6 weeks. Sample copy and writer's guidelines available for 80¢ in IRCs.

Nonfiction: Humor (limited amount used—dealing with travel experiences in Europe), and travel (always looking for good travel in Europe features). "We buy only articles by writers who have been to or lived in the destination on which they write. Not interested in tourist articles. Our readers live in Europe, average age 26.5, married with 2 children. Over 50% travel by car. August vacation is 1 week or more. Weekend trips are also popular. Should always include restaurant/clubs/hotel recommendations. Looking for bargains." No interviews of singers, historical pieces, album/movie/book reviews, or technical stories. Buys 15 mss/year. Query with published clips or send complete ms. Length: 600-1,000 words. Pays in Deutsche Marks—DM 90 (an estimated $45) /page; full payment for partial page.

Photos: State availablility of photos or send photos with query or mss. Pays DM 80 for 35mm color transparencies. Captions required. "We pay once for use with story but can reuse at no additional cost."

Columns/Departments: Monthly audio, video and photo stories. "We need freelancers with solid background in these areas who can write for general public on a variety of topics." Buys 10 mss/year. Query with published clips or send complete ms. Length: 1,300-1,400 words. Pays DM 90/magazine page.

Fiction: Very little fiction accepted. Query. "It has to be exceptional to be accepted." Length: 600-1,200 words. Pays DM 90/page.

Fillers: Cartoons pertaining to television. Buys 5/year. Pays DM 80/cartoon.

Tips: "Best chance would be a tie-in travel or first-person story with an American holiday: Mother's Day in Paris, Labor Day, Thanksgiving, St. Pat's Day in Europe, etc. Stories must be written with an American military member and family in mind—young married, 2 children with car, 2 weeks annual leave, several 3-day weekends. Sports/adventure travel stories are popular with our readers."

THE RETIRED OFFICER MAGAZINE, 201 N. Washington St., Alexandria VA 22314. (703)549-2311. Editor: Col. Minter L. Wilson, Jr., USA-Ret. 60% freelance written. Prefers to work with published/established writers. Monthly for officers of the 7 uniformed services and their families. Circ. 360,000. Pays on acceptance. Publishes ms an average of 6 months after acceptance. Byline given. Buys all rights or first serial rights. Submit seasonal material (holiday stories with a military theme) at least 6 months in advance. Query for electronic submissions. Reports on material accepted for publication within 2 months. Sample copy and writer's guidelines for 9x12 SAE with $1.07 postage.

Nonfiction: Current military/political affairs, recent military history, humor, hobbies, travel, second-career job opportunities and military family lifestyle. Also, upbeat articles on aging, human interest and features pertinent to a retired military officer's milieu. True military experiences are also useful. "We tend to use articles less technical than a single-service publication. We do not publish poetry or fillers." Buys 48 unsolicited mss/year. Submit complete ms. Length: 750-2,000 words. Pays up to $500 for unsolicited mss.

Photos: Reviews 8x10 b&w photos (normal halftone). Pays $20. Original slides or transparencies must be suitable for color separation. Pays up to $100 for inside color; up to $175 for cover.

Tips: "We're looking for more upbeat articles on Korea and Vietnam."

SOLDIER OF FORTUNE, The Journal of Professional Adventurers, Omega Group, Ltd., Box 693, Boulder CO 80306. (303)449-3750. Editor: Robert K. Brown. 50% freelance written. A monthly magazine covering military, paramilitary, police and combat subjects. "We are an action-oriented magazine; we cover combat hot spots around the world such as Afghanistan, Central America, Angola, etc. We also provide timely features on state-of-the-art weapons and equipment; elite military and police units; and historical military operations. Readership is primarily active-duty military, veterans and law enforcement." Circ. 175,000. Pays on acceptance. Publishes ms an average of 5 months after acceptance. Byline given. Offers 25% kill fee. Buys first North American serial rights. Submit seasonal/holiday material 5 months in advance. Photocopied submissions OK. Computer printout submissions OK; prefers letter-quality. Reports in 3 weeks on queries; 1 month on mss. Sample copy $5; free writer's guidelines.

Nonfiction: Expose; general interest; historical/nostalgic; how-to (on weapons and their skilled use); humor; profile; new product; personal experience; photo feature ("number one on our list"); technical; travel; combat reports; military unit reporters and solid Vietnam history. "No 'How I won the war' pieces; no op-ed pieces *unless* they are fully and factually backgrounded; no knife articles (staff assignments only). *All* submitted articles should have good art; art will sell us on an article. Buys 75 mss/year. Query with or without published clips, or send complete ms. Length: 2,500-5,000 words. Pays $300-1,200 for assigned articles; pays $200-1,000 for unsolicited articles. Sometimes pays the expenses of writers on assgnment.

Photos: Send photos with submission (copies only, no originals). Reviews contact sheets and transparencies. Offers no additional payment for photos accepted with ms. Pays $46 for cover photo. Captions and identification of subjects required. Buys one-time rights.

Columns/Departments: Address to appropriate column editor (i.e., I Was There Editor). Combat weaponcraft (how-to military and police survival skills) and I Was There (first-person accounts of the arcane or unusual based in a combat or law enforcement environment), all 600-800 words. Buys 16 mss/year. Send complete ms. Length: 600-800 words. Combat weaponcraft pays $200; I was There pays $50.

Fillers: Bulletin Board editor. Newsbreaks; military/paramilitary related, "*has* to be documented." Length: 100-250 words. Pays $25.

Tips: "Submit a professionally prepared, complete package. All artwork with cutlines, double-spaced typed manuscript, cover letter including synopsis of article, supporting documentation where applicable, etc. Manuscript must be factual; writers have to do their homework and get all their facts straight. One error means rejection. We will work with authors over the phone or by letter, tell them if their ideas have merit for an acceptable article, and help them fine-tune their work. We actively search for new, old, published or unpublished freelancers from around the world. Good art can sell us an average article. I Was There is a good place for freelancers to start. Vietnam features, if carefully reseached and art heavy, will always get a careful look. Combat reports, again, with good art, are number one in our book and stand the best chance of being accepted. Military unit reports from around the world are well received as are law enforcement articles (units, police in action). If you write for us, be complete and factual; pros read *Soldier of Fortune*, and are *very* quick to let us know if we (and the author) err. If authors hit stumbling blocks in research, call us and perhaps we can help."

‡TUN'S TALES, Geofcom, Ltd., Box 1118, Kulpsville PA 19443. (215)362-8397. Editor: G. Franklin Grimm. 40% freelance written. Eager to work with new/unpublished writers. Bimonthly tabloid for active and reserve Marines. Circ. 112,000. Pays on publication. Publishes ms an average of 2 months after acceptance. Byline given. Buys one-time rights. Submit seasonal/holiday material 2 months in advance. Simultaneous queries, and simultaneous and photocopied submissions OK. Computer printout submissions acceptable; no dot-matrix. Reports in 2 weeks. Sample copy for 8x10 SAE and 8 first class stamps.

Nonfiction: Historical/nostalgic, how-to, humor, interview/profile, personal experience and photo feature, all pertaining to active and reserve Marines. Only articles that deal with the Marine Corps are accepted. Buys 6 mss/year. Send complete ms. Length: 500-3,500 words. Pays $35-150. Sometimes pays the expenses of writers on assignment.

Photos: Send photos with ms. Pays $50-100 for 5x7 b&w prints. Captions, model release, and identification of subjects required. Buys one-time rights.

Tips: "We are open to all articles, both major and fillers that will be of interest to Marines and their spouses."

‡THE VETERAN, Vietnam Veterans of America, Suite 700, 2001 S. Street NW, Washington DC 20009. (202)332-2700. Editor: Mark Perry. Managing Editor: Mokie Pratt Porter. 70% freelance written. A monthly tabloid on the Vietnam war, Viet vets and the Vietnam era. "Writers should be familiar with aspects of America's involvement in Indochina and should be able to write with knowledge on controversies surrounding our involvement there." Estab. 1980. Circ. 33,000. Pays on publication. Publishes ms an average of 1 month after acceptance. Byline given. Offers kill fee of 50% of original fee. Buys first rights. Submit seasonal/holiday material 2 months in advance. Reports in 1 month on queries. Sample copy for 8½x11 SAE with 2 first class stamps.

Nonfiction: Historical and interview/profile. No humor. Buys 24 mss/year. Send complete ms. Length: 1,500-3,000 words. Pays $300-500 for assigned articles; $200-400 for unsolicited articles. Pays expenses of writers on assignment.

Photos: Send photos with submission. Reviews contact sheets. Pays $5-10/photo. Captions required. Buys one-time rights.

Columns/Departments: Update (veterans profiles, interviews, issues), 500-750 words. Buys 12 mss/year. Send complete ms. Pays $100-200.

Tips: "Know our readers, America's Viet vets. I want clean, clear copy, double-spaced."

WORLD WAR II, Empire Press, 105 Loudoun Street SW, Leesburg VA 22075. (703)771-9400. Editor: C. Brian Kelly. 95% freelance written. Prefers to work with published/established writers. A bimonthly magazine covering "military operations in World War II—events, personalities, strategy, national policy, etc." Estab. 1986. Circ. 150,000. Pays on publication. Publishes ms an average of 6-12 months after acceptance. Byline given. Buys first North American serial rights. Submit seasonal/holiday material 6-12 months in advance. Reports in 1 month on queries; 3 months on mss. Sample copy $4; Writer's guidelines for SASE.

Nonfiction: Book excerpts (if in advance of book publication), profile, personal experience, technical, and World War II military history. No fiction. Buys 24 mss/year. Query. Length: 4,000 words. Pays $200. Sometimes pays expenses of writers on assignment.

Photos: State availability of art and photos with submission. (For photos and other art, send photocopies and cite sources. "We'll order.") Offers no additional payment for photos accepted with ms. Captions and identification of subjects required.

Columns/Department: Undercover (espionage, resistance, sabotage, intelligence gathering, behind the lines, etc.); personalities (WW II personalities of interest); and Armaments (weapons, their use and development); all 2,000 words. Book reviews, 300-375 words. Buys 18 mss/year (plus book reviews). Query. Pays $100.

Tips: "List your sources and suggest further readings, in standard format at the end of your piece—as a bibliography for our files in case of factual challenge or dispute. All submissions are on speculation. When the story's right, but the writing isn't, we'll pay a small research fee for use of the information in our own style and language."

Music

Music fans follow the latest music industry news in these publications. Types of music and musicians are the sole focus of some magazines. Publications geared to music industry and professionals can be found in Trade Music section. Additional music and dance markets are included in the Entertainment section.

THE ABSOLUTE SOUND, The Journal of The High End, Box 115, Sea Cliff NY 11579. (516)676-2830. Editor: Harry Pearson, Jr. Managing Editor: Sallie Reynolds. 10% freelance written. Works with a small number of new/unpublished writers each year. Bimonthly magazine covering the music reproduction business, audio equipment and records for "up-scale, high tech men and women between the ages of 20 and 100, serious music lovers." Pays on publication. Byline given. Buys all rights. Query for electronic submissions. Computer printout submissions acceptable; no dot-matrix. Sample copy $7.

Nonfiction: Exposé (of bad commercial audio practices); interview/profile (famous recording engineers, famous conductors); new product (audio); opinion (audio and record reviews); and technical (how to improve your stereo system). Special Recordings Issue. No puff pieces about industry. Query with published clips. Length: 250-5,000 words. Pays $125-1,000. Sometimes pays the expenses of writers on assignment.

Columns/Departments: Audio Musings (satires) and Reports from Overseas (audio fairs, celebrities, record companies). Buys 12 mss/year. Length: 250-750 words. Pays $125-200.

Tips: "Writers should know about audio recordings and the engineering of same—as well as live music. The approach is *literate* witty, investigative—good journalism."

‡BANJO NEWSLETTER,Box 364, Greensboro MD 21639. (301)482-6278. Editor: Hub Nitchie. 10% freelance written. Monthly magazine covering the "instructional and historical treatment of the 5-string banjo. Covers all aspects of the instrument. Tablature is used for musical examples." Circ. 8,000. Pays on publication. Byline given. Buys one-time rights. Query for electronic submissions. Computer printout submissions OK; prefers letter quality. Reports in 1 months on queries. Free sample copy.

Nonfiction: Interviews with 5-string banjo players, banjo builders, shop owners, etc. No humorous fiction from anyone unfamiliar with the popular music field. Buys 6 mss/year. Query. Length: 500-4,000 words. Pays $20-100. Sometimes pays writers with contributor copies or other premiums "if that is what writer wants." Very seldom pays expenses of writers on assignment. "We can arrange for press tickets to musical events."

Photos: State availability of photos with submission. Reviews b&w prints. Offers $10-40/photo. Captions and identification of subjects required whenever possible. Buys one-time rights.

Columns/Departments: Buys 60 mss/year. Query Length: 500-750 words. Payment varies.

Poetry: Poetry Editor: Don Nitchie, General Delivery, West Tisbury, MA 02575. Buys 2 poems/year. Submit maximum 1 poem at one time.

Tips: "The writer should be motivated by being a student of the 5-string banjo or interested in the folk or bluegrass music fields where 5-string banjo is featured. Writers should be able to read and write banjo tablature and know various musicians or others in the field."

BLUEGRASS UNLIMITED, Bluegrass Unlimited, Inc., Box 111, Broad Run VA 22014. (703)361-8992. Editor: Peter V. Kuykendall. 80% freelance written. Prefers to work with published/established writers. Monthly magazine on bluegrass and old-time country music. Circ. 20,000. Pays on publication. Publishes ms an average of 4 months after acceptance. Byline given. Kill fee negotiated. Buys first North American serial rights, one-time rights, all rights, and second serial (reprint) rights. Submit seasonal/holiday material 4 months in advance. Photocopied submissions OK. Computer printout submissions are OK; prefers letter-quality to dot-matrix. Reports in 2 weeks on queries; 2 months on mss. Sample copy and writer's guidelines for 8½x11 or 9x12 SASE.

Nonfiction: General interest, historical/nostalgic, how-to, interview/profile, personal experience, photo feature and travel. No "fan" style articles. Buys 75-80 mss/year. Query with or without published clips. No set word length. Pays 6-8¢/word.

Photos: State availability of photos or send photos with query. Reviews 35mm color transparencies and 3x5, 5x7, and 8x10 b&w and color prints. Pays $25-50 for b&w transparencies; $50-150 for color transparencies; $25-50 for b&w prints; and $50-150 for color prints. Identification of subjects required. Buys one-time rights and all rights.

Fiction: Ethnic and humorous. Buys 3-5 mss/year. Query. No set word length. Pays 6-8¢/word.

Tips: "We would prefer that articles be informational, based on personal experience or an interview with lots of quotes from subject, profile, humor, etc."

CINEMASCORE, The Film Music Journal, Fandom Unlimited Entrps., Box 70868, Sunnyvale CA 94086. (415)960-1151. Editor: Randall D. Larson. 20% freelance written. Works with small number of new/unpublished writers each year. Magazine published twice annually covering music for motion pictures and television, history and criticism. "We are devoted to the review and appreciation of the art and technique of music for motion pictures, emphasizing interviews with industry professionals." Circ. 2,000. Pays 50% on acceptance; 50% on publication. Publishes ms an average of 1 year after acceptance. Byline given. Offers 50% kill fee. Buys first North American serial rights. Photocopied and previously published submissions (rarely) OK. Query for electronic submissions. Computer printout submissions acceptable. Computer printout sumissions OK; prefers letter-quality to dot-matrix. Reports in 3 weeks on queries; 6 weeks on mss. Sample copy $2; writer's guidelines for SAE and 1 first class stamp.

Nonfiction: Interview/profile, technical, critique, musicological analysis and reviews. No general-type reviews. "We want *specific*, in-depth reviews and criticism, and perceptive, though not necessarily technical, analysis." Buys 5-10 mss/year. Query with published clips or send complete ms. Word length open. Pays $15-100 for major research articles; pays in subscriptions for shorter pieces and reviews. Sometimes pays expenses of writers on assignment.

Photos: State availability of photos. Prefers b&w prints. Payment considered part of ms. Identification of subjects required. Buys one-time rights.

Tips: "Have an interest in and knowledge of the use, history, and technique of movie music, and be able to contact industry professionals or insightfully examine their music in an analytical article/profile. Writers should be familiar with the publication before trying to break in. Be willing to buy a copy to ensure writer and publication are compatible."

CREEM, Suite 204, 7715 Sunset Blvd., Los Angeles CA 90046. (213)851-8771. Editors: Bill Holdship and John Kordosh. 80% freelance written. Works with a small number of new/unpublished writers each year. Pays on publication. Publishes ms an average of 2 months after acceptance. Buys all rights. Computer printout submissions acceptable; no dot-matrix. Reports in 6 weeks.

Nonfiction: Short articles, mostly music-oriented. "Feature length stories are mostly staff written, but we're open for newcomers to break in with short pieces. Freelancers are used a lot in the Newbeats section. Please send queries and sample articles to Vicki Arkoff, submissions editor. We bill ourselves as 'America's Only Rock 'n' Roll Magazine'." Query. Pays $50 minimum for reviews, $300 minimum for full-length features. Sometimes pays the expenses of writers on assignment.

Photos: Freelance photos.

Tips: "*Creem* also publishes *Creem Close Up: Metal*, which is directed at readers more interested in heavy metal—it is probably easier for the newcomer to break in to print in that book. You can't study *Creem* too much—our stable of writers have all come from the ranks of our readers. The writer can save his time and ours by studying what we do print and producing similar copy that we can use immediately. Send short stuff—no epics on the first try. We really aren't a good market for the professional writer looking for another outlet—a writer has to be pretty obsessed with music and/or pop culture in order to be published in our magazine. We get people writing in for assignments who obviously have never even read the magazine, and that's totally useless to us."

EAR, Magazine of New Music, New Wilderness Foundation, Inc., Room 208, 325 Spring St., New York NY 10013. (212)807-7944. Publisher/Editor: Carol E. Tuynman. 100% freelance written. Eager to work with new/unpublished writers. A tabloid published 10 times per year for artists interested in the avant-garde. Circ. 20,000. Publishes ms an average of 6 months after acceptance. Byline given. Writer holds rights. Submit seasonal/holiday material 6 months in advance. Query for electronic submission. Computer printout submissions acceptable. Reports in 1 month on queries; 3 months on mss. Sample copy $2.

Nonfiction: Essay; how-to; humor (music related); interview/profile; new product; opinion; personal experience (musicians and composers only); photo feature; and technical. Special issues include Regionalism in New Music, Radio/Audio Art, and Special Edition Instruments. No general opinions or fiction. Buys 5 mss/year. Query. Length: 250-1,000 words. Pays $0-50 for assigned articles; pays $0-25 for unsolicited articles. "Usually we don't pay, or at most, a $25 honorarium is given." All published contributors receive 1 year subscription plus 3 copies of issue they are in.

Photos: Send photos with submission. Reviews 5x7 prints. Offers no additional payment for photos accepted with ms. Captions required. Buys one-time rights.

Columns/Departments: Radio (critical look at radio whether public or commercial, new music U.S. and international), 750 words; Healing Arts (how sound/music and related technologies are interfacing in the healing arts), 750 words; Techno, Video, Info, Citizens of the Cassette Conspiracy, Inside Music. Buys 5 mss/year. Pays $0-100 for radio only.

Fillers: Newsbreaks and short humor. Length: 25-100 words. Pays $0-10.

Tips: "Do not write in *Spin*, or *Rolling Stone* style. Be knowledgable about contemporary music, be a clear writer, don't send poorly edited, messy material. We're not interested in the classical European music tradition."

FRETS MAGAZINE, GPI Publications, 20085 Stevens Creek Blvd., Cupertino CA 95014. (408)446-1105. Editor: Phil Hood. 40% freelance written. Prefers to work with published/established writers. Monthly magazine for amateur and professional acoustic string music enthusiasts; for players, makers, listeners and fans. Country, jazz, classical, blues, pop and bluegrass. For instrumentalists interested in banjo, mandolin, guitar, violin, upright bass, dobro, and others. Circ. open. Pays on acceptance. Publishes ms an average of 6 months after acceptance. Buys first serial rights. Submit seasonal/holiday material 6 months in advance. Computer printout submissions on 8½x11 sheets with legible type acceptable if not a photocopy or multiple submission. "All-caps printout unacceptable." Reports in 6 weeks. Free sample copy and writer's guidelines.

Nonfiction: General interest (artist-oriented); historical (instrument making or manufacture); how-to (instrument craft and repair); interview (with artists or historically important individuals); profile (music performer); and technical (instrument making, acoustics, instrument repair). Prefers not to see humor; poetry; general-interest articles that really belong in a less-specialized publication; articles (about performers) that only touch on biographical or human interest angles, without getting into the 'how-to' nuts and bolts of musicianship. Buys 24 mss/year. Query with published clips or sample lead paragraph. Length: 1,000-2,500 words. Pays $150-350. Experimental (instrument design, acoustics) pays $100-175. Sometimes pays expenses of writers on assignment.

Photos: State availability of photos. Pays $25 minimum for b&w prints (reviews contact sheets); $200 and up for cover shot color transparencies. Captions and credits required. Buys one-time rights.

Columns/Departments: Repair Shop (instrument craft and repair); and *Frets* Visits (on-location visit to manufacturer or major music festival). Buys 10 mss/year. Query. Length: 1,200-1,700 words. Pays $75-175, including photos.

Fillers: Newsbreaks, upcoming events and music-related news.

Tips: "Our focus also includes ancillary areas of string music—such as sound reinforcement for acoustic musicians, using personal computers in booking and management, recording techniques for acoustic music, and so on. We enjoy giving exposure (and encouragement) to talented new writers. We do not like to receive submissions or queries from writers who have only a vague notion of our scope and interest. We do not cover electric guitarists. We want to see more in-depth instructional features and stories on younger artists."

GUITAR PLAYER MAGAZINE, GPI Publications, 20085 Stevens Creek, Cupertino CA 95014. (408)446-1105. Editor: Tom Wheeler. 70% freelance written. Monthly magazine for persons "interested in guitars, guitarists, manufacturers, guitar builders, bass players, equipment, careers, etc." Circ. 180,000. Buys first serial and limited reprint rights. Pays on acceptance. Publishes ms an average of 3 months after acceptance. Byline given. Computer printout submissions acceptable; prefers letter-quality to dot-matrix. Reports in 6 weeks. Free sample copy.

Nonfiction: Publishes "wide variety of articles pertaining to guitars and guitarists: interviews, guitar craftsmen profiles, how-to features—anything amateur and professional guitarists would find fascinating and/or helpful. On interviews with 'name' performers, be as technical as possible regarding strings, guitars, techniques, etc. We're not a pop culture magazine, but a magazine for musicians." Also buys features on such subjects as a guitar museum, role of the guitar in elementary education, personal reminiscences of past greats, technical gadgets and how to work them, analysis of flamenco, etc." Buys 30-40 mss/year. Query. Length: open. Pays $100-300. Sometimes pays expenses of writers on assignment.

Photos: Reviews b&w glossy prints. Pays $50-100. Buys 35mm color transparencies. Pays $250 (for cover only). Buys one time rights.

ILLINOIS ENTERTAINER, Suite 192, 2200 E. Devon, Des Plaines IL 60018. (312)298-9333. Editor: Bill Dalton. 95% freelance written. Prefers to work with published/established writers. Monthly tabloid covering music and entertainment for consumers within 100-mile radius of Chicago interested in music. Circ. 80,000. Pays on publication. Publishes ms an average of 2 months after acceptance. Byline given. Offers 20% kill fee. Buys one-time rights. Submit seasonal/holiday material 2 months in advance. Simultaneous queries OK. Computer printout submissions acceptable "if letters are clear"; no dot-matrix. Reports in 1 month on queries; 2 months on mss. Sample copy $5; style sheet available.

Nonfiction: Interview/profile (of entertainment figures). No Q&A interviews. Buys 75 mss/year. Query with published clips. Length: 500-2,000 words. Pays $15-100. Sometimes pays expenses of writers on assignment.

Photos: State availability of photos. Pays $20 for 5x7 or 8x10 b&w prints; $100 for color cover photo, both on publication only. Captions and identification of subjects required.

Columns/Departments: Software (record reviews stress record over band or genre) and book reviews. Buys 50 mss/year. Query with published clips. Length: 150-250 words. Pays $6-20.

Tips: "Send clips (published or unpublished) with phone number, and be patient. Full staff has seniority, but if you know the ins and outs of the entertainment biz, and can balance that knowledge with a broad sense of humor, then you'll have a chance."

INTERNATIONAL MUSICIAN, American Federation of Musicians, Suite 600, Paramount Building, 1501 Broadway, New York NY 10036. (212)869-1330. Editor: Kelly L. Castleberry II. 10% freelance written. Prefers to work with published/established writers. Monthly for professional musicians. Pays on acceptance. Publishes ms an average of 3 months after acceptance. Byline given. Computer printout submissions OK; no dot-matrix. Reports in 2 months.

Nonfiction: Articles on prominent instrumental musicians (classical, jazz, rock or country). Send complete ms. Length: 1,500-2,000 words.

‡**IT WILL STAND, The Beach Music Magazine**, IWS Communications, Inc., Box 507, Harrisburg NC 28075. (704)455-2014. Editor: Chris Beachley. 30% freelance written. Irregularly published monthly magazine covering beach music (especially soul 1940-present). Circ. 1,700. Pays on acceptance. Publishes ms an average of 3-12 months after acceptance. Byline given. Offers negotiable kill fee. Buys all rights. Submit seasonal/holiday material 2 months in advance. Query for electronic submissions. Computer printout submissions OK; prefers letter-quality to dot-matrix. Sample copy $2.

Nonfiction: Historical/nostalgic, interview/profile, opinion, personal experience and photo feature. Buys 5 mss/year. Query with published clips or send complete ms. Length: open. Pays variable fee. Sometimes pays expenses of writers on assignment.

Photos: State availability of photos. Reviews color and b&w contact sheets and prints.

Tips: "Contact us for direction. We even have artists' phone numbers ready for interviews." Magazine will buy more mss as it becomes a regular monthly publication.

JAM, The Music Magazine, Gwenny Lenny Corporation, Box 110322, Arlington TX 76007. (817)540-2113. Editor: David C. Huff, Jr. Managing Editor: Bev Owens. 25% freelance written. Works with small number of new/unpublished writers each year; eager to work with new/unpublished writers. A monthly music magazine covering national acts in rock, jazz, country and new music. "Write your story so a 12-year-old could understand it, but don't offend the intelligence of a 25-year-old." Circ. 20,000. Pays on acceptance. Publishes ms an average of 2 months after acceptance. Byline given. Buys second serial (reprint) rights or makes work-for-hire assignments. Submit seasonal/holiday material 2 months in advance. Previously published submissions OK. Computer printout submissions acceptable; prefers letter-quality to dot-matrix. Reports in 2 weeks on queries. Sample copy for SAE with 73¢ postage.

Columns/Departments: *Jam* Movie Review (an in-depth look at current releases), and *Jam* Album Review (an in-depth album review of current releases, "intelligently written"). Buys 60 mss/year. Query with published clips. Length: 250-1,500 words. Pays $25.

Tips: "We need in-depth interviews with musicians that you would not find in national publications. Absolutely no *Circus* or *Creem* types of article submissions taken. Well-written, humorous or even funny stories are acceptable. No mindless who, what, where stories. Feature and album reviews are most open to the freelancer. Do not submit material on local music groups or individuals."

‡**KCS, Keyboards, Computers & Software**, KCS, Inc., 299 Main St., Northport NY 11768. (516)754-9311. Editor: Bill Stephen. Managing Editor: Bill Lewis. 65% freelance written. Bimonthly magazine covering computer-generated music and keyboard music. "Our readers are semi-professional/professional musicians with an interest in computer technology and how it applies to music. No general music pieces—everything must have a heavy technical slant." Estab. 1986. Circ. 52,000. Pays on publication. Byline given. Offers 25% kill fee. Buys first North American serial rights. Photocopied submissions OK. Query for electronic submissions. Computer printout submissions OK; prefers letter-quality. Reports in 2 weeks on queries; 3 weeks on mss. Sample copy for 9x10 SAE with $1.41 postage; free writer's guidelines.

Nonfiction: Book excerpts, how-to, interview/profile, new product, opinion and technical. Buys 25 mss/year. Query with published clips. Length: 250-2,500 words. Pays $25-350 for assigned articles. Sometimes pays the expenses of writers on assignment.

Photos: State availability of photos with submission. Reviews 3x5 transparencies and 8x10 prints. Offers $35-250 per photo. Captions and identification of subjects required. Buys one-time rights.

Columns/Departments: Speculations (opinion on music technology evolution), 1,500 words. Buys 4-6 mss/year. Query. Length: 1,200-1,800 words. Pays $120-180.

Tips: "The department most open to freelancers is Running Bytes; it uses short information with a local or national news slant."

KEYBOARD MAGAZINE, GPI Publications, 20085 Stevens Creek Blvd., Cupertino CA 95014. (408)446-1105. Editor: Dominic Milano. 25% freelance written. Prefers to work with published/established writers; works with a small number of new/unpublished writers each year. Monthly magazine for those who play synthesizer, piano, organ, harpsichord, or any other keyboard instrument. All styles of music; all levels of ability. Circ. 70,000. Pays on acceptance. Publishes ms 6 months after acceptance. Byline given. Buys first serial rights and second serial (reprint) rights. Phone queries OK. Electronic submissions OK but "contact our offices for requirements, prefer not to receive unsolicited submissions via modem." Computer printout submissions acceptable; prefers letter-quality to dot-matrix. Reports in 2 weeks. Free sample copy and writer's guidelines.

Nonfiction: "We publish articles on a wide variety of topics pertaining to keyboard players and their instruments. In addition to interviews with keyboard artists in all styles of music, we are interested in historical and analytical pieces, how-to articles dealing either with music or with equipment (including MIDI and computers), profiles on well-known instrument makers and their products. In general, anything that amateur and professional keyboardists would find interesting and/or useful." Buys 20 unsolicited mss/year. Query: letter should mention topic and length of article and describe basic approach. "It's nice (but not necessary) to have a sample first paragraph." Length: approximately 1,000-5,000 words. Pays $150-400. Sometimes pays the expenses of writers on assignment.

Tips: "Query first (just a few ideas at a time, rather than twenty). A musical background helps, and a knowledge of keyboard instruments is valuable."

‡THE MISSISSIPPI RAG, "The Voice of Traditional Jazz and Ragtime," The Mississippi Rag, Inc., 5644 Morgan Ave. S, Minneapolis MN 55419. (612)920-0312. Editor: Leslie Johnson. 70% freelance written. Works with small number of new/unpublished writers each year. A monthly tabloid covering traditional jazz and ragtime. Circ. 2,400. Pays on publication. Publishes ms an average of 4 months after acceptance. Byline given. Buys all rights, "but writer may negotiate if he wishes to use material later." Submit seasonal/holiday material 3 months in advance. Computer printout submissions OK; prefers letter-quality to dot-matrix. Sample copy and writer's guidelines for 9x12 SAE with 56¢ postage.

Nonfiction: Historical/nostalgic, interview/profile, personal experience, photo feature, current jazz news, book reviews and record reviews. Reviews are always assigned. No "long-winded essays on jazz or superficial pieces on local ice-cream social-type Dixieland bands." Buys 24-30 mss/year. Query with or without published clips, or send complete ms. Length: 1,500-4,000 words. Pays 1½¢/word.

Photos: Send photos with submission. Reviews 5x7 or 8x10 prints. Offers $4 minimum per photo. Identification of subjects required. Buys one-time rights.

Columns/Departments: Books and Records reviews. Buys 60 mss/year. Query with or without published clips, or send complete ms. Pays 1½¢/word.

Tips: "Become familiar with the jazz world. The *Rag* is read by musicians, jazz writers, historians, and jazz buffs. We want articles that have depth—solid facts and a good basic grasp of jazz history. Not for the novice jazz writer. Interviews with jazz and ragtime performers are most open to freelancers. It's wise to query first because we have already covered so many performers."

MODERN DRUMMER, 870 Pompton Ave., Cedar Grove NJ 07009. (201)239-4140. Editor-in-Chief: Ronald Spagnardi. Senior Editor: Rick Mattingly. Managing Editor: Rick Van Horn. Monthly for "student, semi-pro and professional drummers at all ages and levels of playing ability, with varied specialized interests within the field." 60% freelance written. Circ. 75,000. Pays on publication. Publishes ms an average of 3 months after acceptance. Buys all rights. Photocopied and previously published submissions OK. Computer printout submissions acceptable; prefers letter-quality to dot-matrix. Reports in 1 month. Sample copy $2.95; free writer's guidelines.

Nonfiction: How-to, informational, interview, new product, personal experience and technical. "All submissions must appeal to the specialized interests of drummers." Buys 20-30 mss/year. Query or submit complete ms. Length: 5,000-8,000 words. Pays $200-500. Pays expenses of writers on assignment.

Photos: Purchased with accompanying ms. Reviews 8x10 b&w prints and color transparencies.

Columns/Departments: Jazz Drummers Workshop, Rock Perspectives, In The Studio, Show Drummers Seminar, Teachers Forum, Drum Soloist, The Jobbing Drummer, Strictly Technique, Book Reviews, and Shop Talk. "Technical knowledge of area required for most columns." Buys 40-50 mss/year. Query or submit complete ms. Length: 500-2,500 words. Pays $25-150.

MODERN PERCUSSIONIST, A Contemporary Magazine for the Serious Drummer/Percussionist, Modern Drummer Publications, Inc., 870 Pompton Ave., Cedar Grove NJ 07009. (201)239-4140. Editor: Rick Mattingly. Managing Editor: Susan Hannum. 50% freelance written. Works with a small number of new/ unpublished writers each year. Quarterly magazine on percussion and percussionists. "Our audience includes percussionists at all levels from student to pro. Writers must have a good general knowledge of the field." Circ. 18,000. Pays on publication. Publishes ms an average of 6 months after acceptance. Byline given. Offers variable kill fee. Buys all rights. Simultaneous queries, and photocopied and previously published submissions OK. Computer printout submissions acceptable; no dot-matrix. Reports in 2 weeks on queries; 1 month on mss. Sample copy $2.25; writer's guidelines for legal size SAE and 1 first class stamp.
Nonfiction: Historical/nostalgic (performers and instruments from the past); how-to (building or repairing percussion instruments); interview/profile (professional players and teachers); new product (new percussion equipment); and technical (percussion techniques). No "fan-magazine" type articles. Buys 20 mss/year. Query with published clips. Length: 4,000-5,000 words. Pays $150-350. Sometimes pays expenses of writers on assignment.
Photos: David Creamer, photo editor. State availability of photos. Reviews b&w contact sheets and 8x10 prints; color transparencies. Pays $10-45 for b&w; $50-100 for color. Captions, model releases, and identification of subjects required.
Columns/Departments: Percussion Today (contemporary and avant-garde); Around The World (instruments and techniques from other countries); and Workshop (care and repair). Buys 12-15 mss/year. Query. Length: 750-1,500 words. Pays $25-100.
Tips: "Feature interviews with prominent performers is the area most open to freelancers."

MUSIC MAGAZINE, Milthril Holdings Inc., 26 Edgewood Cres., Toronto M4W 3A4 Canada. Publisher: W. Michael Fletcher. 90% freelance written. Prefers to work with published/established writers; works with a small number of new/unpublished writers each year. Quarterly magazine emphasizing classical music. Circ. 8,000. Pays on publication. Publishes ms an average of 4 months after acceptance. Byline given. Buys first North American rights, one-time rights, and second serial (reprint) rights. Submit seasonal/holiday material 4 months in advance. Photocopied and previously published submissions (book excerpts) OK. Query for electronic submissions. Computer printout submissions acceptable; prefers letter-quality to dot-matrix. SAE, IRCs (no American stamps). Reports in 2 months. Sample copy and writer's guidelines $2.
Nonfiction: Interview, historical articles, photo feature and profile. "All articles should pertain to classical music and people in that world. We do not want any academic analysis or short pieces of family experiences in classical music." Query with published clips; phone queries OK. Unsolicited articles will not be returned. Length: 1,500-3,500 words. Pays $100-500. Sometimes pays expenses of writers on assignment.
Photos: State availability of photos. Pays $15-25 for 8x10 b&w glossy prints or contact sheets; $100 for color transparencies. No posed promotion photos. "Candid lively material only." Captions required. Buys one-time rights.
Tips: "Send a sample of your writing with suggested subjects. Off-beat subjects are welcome but must be thoroughly interesting to be considered. A famous person or major subject in music are your best bets."

‡MUSICAL AMERICA, (formerly High Fidelity/Musical America), 825 7th Ave., New York NY 10019. Editor: Shirley Fleming. 50% freelance written. Bimonthly. Circ. 20,000. Pays on publication. Publishes ms an average of 3-4 months after acceptance. Buys all rights. Computer printout submissions acceptable; no dot-matrix.
Nonfiction: Articles on music are generally prepared by acknowledged writers and authorities in the field, but uses freelance material. Query with published clips. Length: 1,200 words maximum. Pays $150 minimum.
Photos: New b&w photos of musical personalities, events, etc.

‡ONE SHOT, Attentive Writing for Neglected Rock 'N' Roll, One Shot Enterprises, #3, 3379 Morrison Ave., Cincinnati OH 45220. (513)861-1532. Editor: Steve Rosen. 80% freelance written. Eager to work with new/unpublished writers. *One Shot* is a quarterly magazine dedicated to remembering now-obscure or under-appreciated performers of rock and related musics; especially the one-hit wonders. Uses interviews, essays, poetry and fiction. Estab. 1986. Circ. 115. Pays on publication. Publishes ms an average of 6 months after acceptance. Byline given. Buys one-time, second serial (reprint) or simultaneous rights and makes work-for-hire assignments. Simultaneous, photocopied and previously published submissions OK. Computer printout submissions OK; prefers letter-quality to dot-matrix. Reports in 1 month. Sample copy $2.50; free writer's guidelines.
Nonfiction: Book excerpts, essays, expose, general interest, historical/nostalgic, interview/profile, opinion, personal experience and travel. No religious/inspirational articles. Buys 16 mss/year. Query. Length: 2,500 maximum words. Pays $50 maximum for assigned articles. Pays with copies for nonjournalism work. Sometimes pays expenses of writers on assignment.
Photos: State availability of photos with submission. Reviews contact sheets and 8½x11 prints. Offers no additional payment for photos accepted with ms. Buys one-time rights.
Columns/Departments: Speak, Memory! (personal experiences with now-obscure rock, etc., performers);

and Travel (update on a place which once figured in a rock song, or performer's career, such as "Hitsville USA" studios in Detroit), up to 1,000 words. Buys 10 mss/year. Query with or without published clips or send complete ms. Length: 1,000 maximum words. Pays in "copies, usually."

Fiction: Adventure, condensed novels, confession, erotica, experimental, historical, humorous, mainstream, mystery, novel excerpts and slice-of-life vignettes. No fantasy, sci-fi or religious mss. Buys 4 mss/year. Query with or without published clips or send complete ms. Length: 2,500 maximum words. Pays in "copies, usually."

Poetry: Avant-garde, free verse, haiku, light verse and traditional. Buys 20 poems/year. Pays in "copies usually."

Tips: "*One Shot* needs "Where are They Now" articles on obscure and neglected rock performers who once were popular. Those pieces should include interviews with the performer and others; and provide a sense of "being there". *One Shot* will pay for such stories. Just send me a note explaining your interests, and I'll respond with detailed suggestions. I won't disqualify anyone for not following procedures; I want to encourage a body of work on this topic."

ONLYMUSIC MAGAZINE, 2530 RepublicBank Center, Houston TX 77002. (713)227-0095. Editor: E. Cliff Dittman. 80% freelance written. Prefers to work with published/established writers. A monthly magazine covering progressive music. Circ. 110,000. Pays on publication. Publishes ms an average of 2 months after acceptance. Byline given. Buys all rights. Submit seasonal/holiday material 4 months in advance. Photocopied submissions OK. Query for electronic submissions. Computer printout submissions OK; prefers letter-quality to dot-matrix. Reports in 1 month. Sample copy and writer's guidelines for 10x13 SAE with 5 first class stamps.

Nonfiction: Interview/profile, new product and photo feature. "Nothing political in nature or encouraging drug use glorification." Buys 120 mss/year. Query with resume and published clips. Length: 500-5,000 words. Pays $75-200 for assigned articles; $10-70 for unsolicited articles. May pay writers with concert tickets for concert reviews. Sometimes pays the expenses of writers on assignment.

Photos: Send photos with submission. Reviews 8x10 or 3x5 prints. Offers $10 maximum per photo. Captions, model releases and identification of subjects required. Buys all rights.

Fillers: Facts. Buys 500/year. Length: 10-50 words. Pays $5-20.

Tips: "We cover both Top 40 and underground music."

OPERA CANADA, Suite 433, 366 Adelaide St. E., Toronto, Ontario M5A 3X9 Canada. (416)363-0395. Editor: Ruby Mercer. 80% freelance written. Prefers to work with published/established writers. Quarterly magazine for readers who are interested in serious music; specifically, opera. Circ. 7,000. Pays on publication. Publishes ms an average of 1 year after acceptance. Byline given. Not copyrighted. Buys first serial rights. Photocopied and simultaneous submissions OK. Computer printout submissions acceptable; no dot-matrix. Reports on material accepted for publication within 1 year. Returns rejected material in 1 month. SAE, IRCs. Sample copy $3.50.

Nonfiction: "Because we are Canada's only opera magazine, we like to keep 75% of our content Canadian, i.e., by Canadians or about Canadian personalities and events. We prefer informative and/or humorous articles about any aspect of music theater, with an emphasis on opera. The relationship of the actual subject matter to opera can be direct or indirect. We accept record reviews (*only* operatic recordings); book reviews (books covering any aspect of music theater); and interviews with major operatic personalities. Please, no reviews of performances; we have staff reviewers." Buys 10 mss/year. Query or submit complete ms. Length (for all articles except reviews of books and records): 1,000-3,000 words. Pays $50-200. Length for reviews: 100-500 words. Pays $15.

Photos: Photos with cutlines (i.e. captions) to accompany mss are welcome. No additional payment for photos used with mss. Captions required.

Tips: "We are interested in articles with an emphasis on current or controversial issues in opera."

OVATION, 33 W. 60th St., New York NY 10023. Editor: Frederick Selch. 75% freelance written. Prefers to work with publshed/established writers; works with small number of new/unpublished writers each year. Monthly magazine for classical music listeners covering classical music and the equipment on which to hear it. Average issue includes 4 features plus departments. Pays on publication. Publishes ms an average of 6 months after acceptance. Byline given. Buys all rights. Submit seasonal material 4 months in advance. Computer printout submissions acceptable; no dot-matrix. Reports in 1 month. Sample copy $2.90.

Nonfiction: "We are primarily interested in interviews with and articles about the foremost classical music artists. Historical pieces will also be considered." Buys 5 unsolicited mss/year. Query with published clips. Length: 800-2,500 words. Pays $350-500. Pays expenses of writers on assignment.

Photos: State availability of photos. May offer additional payment for photos accepted with ms. Captions required. Buys one-time rights.

Tips: "Detailed proposals are welcomed with up-to-the-minute facts that make a subject timely and newsworthy. Always include clips. Writers wishing assignments should send resume with clips."

PULSE!, Tower Records, 2500 Del Monte, Building C W., Sacramento CA 95691. (916)321-2450. Editor: Mike Farrace. Contact: Laurie MacIntosh or J.B. Griffith. 80% freelance written. Works with a small number of new/unpublished writers each year. Monthly tabloid covering recorded music. Circ. 150,000. Pays on publication. Publishes ms an average of 2 months after acceptance. Byline given. Buys first serial rights. Simultaneous and photocopied submissions OK. Computer printout submissions acceptable; prefers letter-quality to dot-matrix. Reports in 5 weeks. Free sample copy; writer's guidelines for SAE.
Nonfiction: Feature stories and interview/profile (angled toward artist's taste in music, such as ten favorite albums, first record ever bought, anecdotes about early record buying experiences). Always looking for good hardware reviews, concise news items and commentary about nonpopular musical genres. Buys 200-250 mss/year. Query or send complete ms. Length: 200-2,500 words. Pays $20-500. Sometimes pays expenses of writers on asignment.
Photos: State availability of photos. Color transparencies preferred, but will also review b&w prints. Caption and identification of subjects required. Buys one-time rights.
Fillers: Newsbreaks.
Tips: "Break in with 200 to 500-word news-oriented featurettes on recording artists or on fast breaking, record-related news, personnel changes, unusual match-ups, reissues of great material. Any kind of music. The more obscure genres are the hardest for us to cover, so they stand a good chance of being used. Writers have a better chance writing articles and fillers. Less copy means easier rewrites, and less guilt when we don't like it, thereby making the relationship with the writer easier, more honest and ultimately more productive. We are not only a magazine about records, but one that is owned by a record retailer."

RELIX MAGAZINE, Music for the Mind, Relix Magazine, Inc., Box 94, Brooklyn NY 11229. (212)645-0818. Editor: Toni A. Brown. 60% freelance written. Eager to work with new/unpublished writers. Bimonthly magazine covering rock 'n' roll music and specializing in Grateful Dead, and other San Francisco and 60's related groups for readers ages 15-45. Circ. 20,000. Pays on publication. Publishes ms an average of 6 months after acceptance. Byline given. Buys all rights. Photocopied submissions OK. Computer printout submissions acceptable; prefers letter-quality to dot-matrix. Sample copy $2.50.
Nonfiction: Historical/nostalgic, interview/profile, new product, personal experience, photo feature and technical. Special issues include November photo special. Query with published clips if available or send complete ms. Length open. Pays $1.50/column inch.
Columns/Departments: Query with published clips, if available or send complete ms. Length: open. Pays variable rates.
Fiction: "We are seeking science fiction, rock and roll stories for a potential book." Query with published clips, if available, or send complete ms. Length: open. Pays variable rates.
Tips: "The most rewarding aspects of working with freelance writers are fresh writing and new outlooks."

ROCK & SOUL, Charlton Publications, Suite 808, 441 Lexington Ave., New York NY 10017. (212)370-0986. Editor: Charley Crespo. Managing Editor: Ann Leighton. 80% freelance written. Prefers to work with published/established writers; works with a small number of new/unpublished writers each year; and is eager to work with new/unpublished writers. A monthly magazine covering black music and black entertainment. Circ. 100,000. Pays on publication. Publishes ms an average of 3 months after acceptance. Byline given. 50% kill fee. Buys one-time rights and second serial (reprint) rights. Submit seasonal/holiday material 4 months in advance. Simultaneous, photocopied and previously published submissions OK. Computer printout submissions acceptable; prefers letter-quality to dot-matrix. Reports in 1 month. Free sample copy.
Nonfiction: Book excerpts (music topics), interview/profile (80% of the magazine) and photo feature. No record reviews, articles on unknown recording artists, movie reviews, TV reviews or fiction. Buys 150 mss/year. Query with published clips. Length: 750-2,000 words. Pays $70-225.
Photos: State availability of photos with submission. Reviews transparencies and prints. Offers $30-200 when photos are used. Unused photos are returned. "We do not pay for publicity freebie shots sent by the writer."
Columns/Departments: Newsmakers (stays on a current events topic; not a profile), 750-1,500 words. Buys 25 mss/year. Query with published clips. Pays $70-125.
Tips: "We never use articles that simply flatter a recording artist. Use objectivity when writing about an entertainer. Almost the entire publication is written by freelancers, but most are regular freelancers, contributing every month or almost every month, and many have been with us for years. A writer new to us must submit clips of published work and a strong pitch for a particular idea. We look forward to hearing from writers."

ROLLING STONE, 745 5th Ave., New York NY 10151. Managing Editor: Robert Wallace. 25-50% freelance written. Biweekly tabloid/magazine on contemporary music and lifestyle. "We seldom accept freelance material. All our work is assigned or done by our staff." Byline given. Offers 25% kill fee. Buys first rights only.
Nonfiction: Seeks new general interest topics. Queries must be concise, no longer than 2 pages. Send queries about musicians and music industry to music editor. Writers knowledgable about computers, VCRs, or sound equipment can submit an idea for the technology column that ranges from 50-word picture captions to 750-

word pieces. Does not provide writer's guidelines; recommends reading *Rolling Stone* before submitting query.

THE $ENSIBLE SOUND, 403 Darwin Dr., Snyder NY 14226. Editor/Publisher: John A. Horan. 20% freelance written. Eager to work with new/unpublished writers. Quarterly magazine. "All readers are high fidelity enthusiasts, and many have a high fidelity industry-related job." Circ. 5,900. Pays on acceptance. Publishes ms an average of 3-6 months after acceptance. Byline given. Buys all rights. Simultaneous, photocopied, and previously published submissions OK. Computer printout submissions OK *if triple-spaced*; prefers letter-quality to dot-matrix. Reports in 2 weeks. Sample copy $2.
Nonfiction: Expose; how-to; general interest; humor; historical; interview (people in hi-fi business, manufacturers or retail); new product (all types of new audio equipment); nostalgia (articles and opinion on older equipment); personal experience (with various types of audio equipment); photo feature (on installation, or how-to tips); profile (of hi-fi equipment); and technical (pertaining to audio). "Subjective evaluations of hi-fi equipment make up 70% of our publication. We will accept 10 per issue." Buys 8 mss/year. Submit outline. Pays $25 maximum. Pays expenses of writers on assignment.
Columns/Departments: Bits & Pieces (short items of interest to hi-fi hobbyists); Ramblings (do-it-yourself tips on bettering existing systems); and Record Reviews (of records which would be of interest to audiophiles). Query. Length: 25-400 words. Pays $10/page.

SONG HITS, Charlton Publications, Charlton Bldg., Division St., Derby CT 06418. (203)735-3381. Editor: Mary Jane Canetti. 60% freelance written. Works with a small number of new/unpublished writers each year. A monthly magazine covering recording artists—rock, pop, soul and country. "*Song Hits* readers are between the ages of 10 and 21. Our philosophy in writing is to gear our material toward what is currently popular with our audience." Circ. 175,000. Pays on publication. Publishes ms an average of 3 months after acceptance. Byline given. Offers 25% kill fee. Buys all rights. Simultaneous and photocopied submissions OK. Computer printout submissions acceptable; prefers letter-quality to dot-matrix. Reports in 2 weeks. Free sample copy and writer's guidelines.
Nonfiction: Interview/profile. "We are not interested in articles about pop and rock people that are too adult for our young audience." Buys 60 mss/year. Query with published clips. Length: 1,250-3,000 words. Pays $150. Sometimes pays the expenses of writers on assignment.
Photos: State availability of photos with submission. Reviews contact sheets, 2x2 transparencies and 8x10 prints. Offers $15-30/photo. Identification of subjects required. Buys one-time rights.
Columns/Departments: Concert Review (current reviews of popular touring groups), and Pick of the Litter (album reviews of current and/or up and coming talent; 8-10 per issue). Buys 15 mss/year. Query with published clips. Length: 500-1,000 words. Pays $75.

STEREO REVIEW, CBS Magazines, 1515 Broadway, New York NY 10036. (212)719-6000. Editor-at-large: William Livingstone. Editor-in-Chief: Louise Boundas. Executive Editor: Michael Smolen. 95% freelance written. A monthly magazine. Circ. 550,000. Pays on publication. Publishes ms an average of 5 months after acceptance. Byline given. Buys first North American serial rights, first rights or all rights. Computer printout submissions acceptable; prefers letter-quality to dot-matrix. Sample copy for 9x12 SAE with $1.24 postage.
Nonfiction: Technical and music reviews, and interview/profile. Buys approximately 25 mss/year. Query with published clips. Length: 1,500-3,000 words. Pays $350-750 for assigned articles.
Tips: "Radical change in consumer interest in music reproduction systems (stereo equipment) will impact on the current focus of this magazine."

TRADITION, Prairie Press, 106 Navajo, Council Bluffs IA 51501. (712)366-1136. Editor: Robert Everhart. 20% freelance written. Quarterly magazine emphasizing traditional country music and other aspects of pioneer living. Circ. 2,500. Pays on publication. Not copyrighted. Byline given. Buys one-time rights. Submit seasonal/holiday material 6 months in advance. Simultaneous queries, and simultaneous, photocopied, and previously published submissions OK. Computer printout submissions acceptable. Reports in 1 month. Free sample copy.
Nonfiction: Historical (relating to country music); how-to (play, write, or perform country music); inspirational (on country gospel); interview (with country performers, both traditional and contemporary); nostalgia (pioneer living); personal experience (country music); and travel (in connection with country music contests or festivals). Query. Length: 800-1,200 words. Pays $25-50.
Photos: State availability of photos with query. Payment included in ms price. 5x7 b&w prints. Captions and model releases required. Buys one-time rights.
Poetry: Free verse and traditional. Buys 4 poems/year. Length: 5-20 lines. Submit maximum 2 poems. Pays $2-5.
Fillers: Clippings, jokes and anecdotes. Buys 5/year. Length: 15-50 words. Pays $5-10.
Tips: "Material must be concerned with what we term 'real' country music as opposed to today's 'pop' coun-

try music. Freelancer must be knowledgeable of the subject; many writers don't even know who the father of country music is, let alone write about him."

Mystery

These magazines buy fictional accounts of crime, detective work and mystery. Additional mystery markets can be found in the Literary and "Little" section. Several magazines in the Detective and Crime category also buy mystery fiction. Skim through other sections to identify markets for fiction; many of these will buy mysteries.

ALFRED HITCHCOCK'S MYSTERY MAGAZINE, Davis Publications, Inc., 380 Lexington Ave., New York NY 10017. Editor: Cathleen Jordan. Magazine published 13 times a year emphasizing mystery fiction. Circ. 200,000. Pays on acceptance. Byline given. Buys first serial rights, second serial (reprint) rights and foreign rights. Submit seasonal/holiday material 7 months in advance. Photocopied submissions OK. Reports in 2 months. Writer's guidelines for SASE.
Fiction: Original and well-written mystery and crime fiction. Length: 1,000-14,000 words.

ELLERY QUEEN'S MYSTERY MAGAZINE, Davis Publications, Inc., 380 Lexington Ave., New York NY 10017. Editor: Eleanor Sullivan. 100% freelance written. Magazine published 13 times/year. Circ. 375,000. Pays on acceptance. Publishes ms an average of 6 months after acceptance. Byline given. Buys first serial rights or second serial (reprint) rights. Submit seasonal/holiday material 7 months in advance. Simultaneous, photocopied, and previously published submissions OK. Computer printout submissions acceptable; prefers letter-quality to dot-matrix. Reports in 1 month. Writer's guidelines for SASE.
Fiction: Special consideration will be given to "anything timely and original. We publish every type of mystery: the suspense story, the psychological study, the deductive puzzle—the gamut of crime and detection from the realistic (including stories of police procedure) to the more imaginative (including 'locked rooms' and impossible crimes). We always need detective stories but do not want sex, sadism or sensationalism-for-the-sake-of-sensationalism." No gore or horror; seldom publishes parodies or pastiches. Buys 13 mss/issue. Length: 6,000 words maximum; occasionally higher but not often. Pays 3-8¢/word.
Tips: "We have a department of First Stories to encourage writers whose fiction has never before been in print. We publish an average of 13 first stories a year."

A MATTER OF CRIME, (Formerly *The New Black Mask Quarterly*), Harcourt Brace Jovanovich/Harvest Imprint, 2006 Sumter St., Columbia SC 29201. (803)771-4642. Co-Editors: Matthew J. Bruccoli and Richard Layman. 100% freelance written. A semi-annual "bookazine" publishing spy, mystery and detective fiction. Pays on publication. Publishes ms an average of 4 months after acceptance. Byline given. Buys first serial worldwide rights. Photocopied submissions OK. Computer printout submissions acceptable; prefers letter-quality to dot-matrix. Reports in 3 weeks on queries; 6 weeks on mss.
Fiction: Mystery, spy, detective and suspense and novel excerpts. Buys 25 mss/year. Query with published clips. Length: 2,000-10,000 words. Pays negotiable rates.

Nature, Conservation and Ecology

These publications promote reader awareness of the natural environment, wildlife, nature preserves and ecosystems. They do not publish recreation or travel articles except as they relate to conservation or nature. Other markets for this kind of material can be found in the Regional, Sports, and Travel, Camping and Trailer categories, although the magazines listed there require that nature or conservation articles be slanted to their specialized subject matter and audience. Some juvenile and teen publications also buy nature-related material for young audiences.

AMERICAN FORESTS, American Forestry Association, 1319 18th St. NW, Washington DC 20036. (202)467-5810. Editor: Bill Rooney. 70% freelance written. Bimonthly magazine. "The magazine of trees and forests, published by a citizens' organization for the advancement of intelligent management and use of our forests, soil, water, wildlife, and all other natural resources necessary for an environment of high quality." Circ. 30,000. Pays on acceptance. Publishes ms an average of 8 months after acceptance. Byline given. Buys one-time rights. Phone queries OK but written queries preferred. Submit seasonal/holiday material 5 months in advance. Computer printout submissions acceptable; no dot-matrix. Reports in 2 months. Sample copy $1; writer's guidelines for SASE.
Nonfiction: General interest, historical, how-to, humor and inspirational. All articles should emphasize trees, forests, forestry and related issues. Buys 7-10 mss/issue. Query. Length: 2,000 words. Pays $300-500.
Photos: State availability of photos. Offers no additional payment for photos accompanying ms. Uses 8x10 b&w glossy prints; 35mm or larger color transparencies, originals only. Captions required. Buys one-time rights.
Tips: "Query should have honesty and information on photo support."

‡AMERICAN LAND FORUM, American Land Resource Association, 1319 18th St. N.W., Washington D.C. 20036. (202)331-0637. Editor: Sara Ebenreck. 75% freelance written. Bimonthly magazine covering land-related issues, experiences and achievements. Circ. 4,000. Pays on final acceptance (after any negotiated revisions). Offers variable kill fee. Byline given. Buys first North American serial rights or one-time rights. Submit seasonal/holiday material 6 months in advance. Photocopied and previously published submissions OK. Computer printout submissions OK; prefers letter-quality to dot-matrix. Reports in 1 week on queries; 1 month on mss. Sample copy $5. Writer's guidelines for SASE.
Nonfiction and Fiction: Book excerpts, essays, how-to, humor, interview/profile, personal experience, travel and short fiction. Buys 10 mss/year. Query with published clips or send complete ms. Length: 1,000-3,000. Pays $150-500.
Photos: State availability of photos with submission. Reviews prints. Offers no additional payment for photos accepted with ms. Captions are required. Buys all rights.
Poetry: Poetry Editor: Joe Keser. Land related poetry. Buys 25 poems/year. Submit maximum of 10 poems at one time. Pays $15-75.
Tips: "Incorporate references into the text, rather than footnoting. Good scholarship is essential, but technical terms, notes and approaches are discouraged. Remember that the audience is broad and interdisciplinary."

‡THE AMICUS JOURNAL, Natural Resources Defense Council, 122 E. 42nd St., Rm. 4500, New York NY 10168. (212)949-0049. Editor: Peter Borrelli. 80% freelance written. Quarterly magazine covering national and internatinal environmental policy. "*The Amicus Journal* is intended to provide the general public with a journal of thought and opinion on environmental affairs, particularly those relating to policies of national and international significance." Circ. 65,000. Pays on acceptance. Publishes ms an average of 6 months after acceptance. Byline given. Offers 50% kill fee. Buys first North American serial rights. Submit seasonal/holiday material 6 months in advance. Query for electronic submission. Computer printout submissions OK; prefers letter-quality to dot-matrix. Reports in 6 weeks. Sample copy for 9x12 SAE with $1.07 postage.
Nonfiction: Expose and interview/profile. No articles not concerned with environmental issues of national or international policy significance. Buys 25 mss/year. Query with published clips. Length: 200-1,500 words. Payment negotiable. Sometimes pays expenses of writers on assignment.
Photos: State availability of photos with submssion. Reviews contact sheets, negatives, transparencies and 8x10 prints. Offers negotiable payment for photos. Captions, model releases and identification of subjects required. Buys one-time rights.
Columns/Departments: News and Comment (summary reporting of environmental issues, usually tied to topical items), 200-500 words; Articles (in-depth reporting on issues and personalities), 750-1,500 words; Book Reviews (well-informed essays on books of general interest to environmentalists interested in policy and history), 500-1,000 words. Buys 25 mss/year. Query with published clips. Payment negotiable.
Poetry: Poetry Editor: Brian Swann. Avant-garde and free verse. All poetry should be rooted in nature. Buys 20 poems/year. Pays $25.

Tips: "Except for editorials, all departments are open to freelance writers. Queries should precede manuscripts, and manuscripts should conform to the *Chicago Manual of Style*. Writers are asked to be sensitive to tone. As a policy magazine, we do not publish articles of a personal or satirical nature."

‡APPALACHIAN TRAILWAY NEWS, Appalachian Trail Conference, Box 807, Harpers Ferry WV 25425. (304)535-6331. 50% freelance written. Bimonthly magazine "subject matter must relate to Appalachian Trail." Circ. 21,000. Pays on acceptance. Byline given. Buys first North American serial rights or second serial (reprint) rights. Submit seasonal/holiday material 4 months in advance. Photocopied and previously published submissions OK. Reports in 1 month. Sample copy $2; writer's guidelines for SASE.
Nonfiction: Essays, general interest, historical/nostalgic, how-to, humor, inspirational, interview/profile, personal experience, photo feature, technical and travel. No poetry or religious materials. Buys 15-20 mss/year. Query with or without published clips, or send complete ms. Length: 250-3,000 words. Pays $25-300. Pays expenses of writers on assignment.
Photos: State availability of photos with submission. Reviews contact sheets, negatives and 5x7 prints. Offers $25-100 per photo. Identification of subjects required. Buys one-time rights.
Tips: "Contributors should display an obvious knowledge of or interest in the Appalachian Trail. Those who live in the vicinity of the Trail may opt for an assigned story and should present credentials and subject in which interested to the editor."

THE ATLANTIC SALMON JOURNAL, The Atlantic Salmon Federation, Suite 1030, 1435 St. Alexandre, Montreal, Quebec H3A 2G4 Canada. (514)842-8059. Editor: Joanne Eidinger. 50% freelance written. Works with a small number of new/unpublished writers each year. A quarterly magazine covering conservation efforts for the Atlantic salmon for an "affluent and responsive audience—the dedicated angler and conservationist of the Atlantic salmon." Circ. 20,000. Pays on publication. Publishes ms an average of 3-6 months after acceptance. Byline given. Buys first serial rights to articles and one-time rights to photos. Submit seasonal/holiday material 3 months in advance. Simultaneous queries, and simultaneous and photocopied submissions OK. Electronic submissions OK on Micom floppy disk, but requires hard copy also. Computer printout submissions acceptable; no dot matrix. Reports in 2 months. Sample copy for 9x12 SAE and $1 (Canadian), or SAE with IRC; free writer's guidelines.
Nonfiction: Expose, historical/nostalgic, how-to, humor, interview/profile, new product, opinion, personal experience, photo feature, technical, travel, conservation, cuisine, science and management. "We are seeking articles that are pertinent to the focus and purpose of our magazine, which is to inform and entertain our membership on all aspects of the Atlantic salmon and its environment, preservation and conservation." Buys 15-20 mss/year. Query with published clips and state availability of photos. Length: 1,500-3,000 words. Pays $100-325. Sometimes pays the expenses of writers on assignment.
Photos: State availability of photos with query. Pays $35-50 for 3x5 or 5x7 b&w prints; $35-150 for 2¼x3¼ or 35mm color slides. Captions and identification of subjects required.
Columns/Departments: Adventure Eating (cuisine) and First Person (nonfiction, anecdotal, from first person viewpoint, can be humorous). Buys about 6 mss/year. Length: 1,000-1,500 words. Pays $175.
Fiction: Adventure, fantasy, historical, humorous and mainstream. "We don't want to see anything that does not deal with Atlantic salmon directly or indirectly. Wilderness adventures are acceptable as long as they deal with Atlantic salmon." Buys 3 ms/year. Query with published clips. Length: 3,000 words maximum. Pays $150-325.
Fillers: Clippings, jokes, anecdotes and short humor. Length: 100-300 words average. Does not pay. Cartoons, single or multi-panel, $25-75.
Tips: "We will be buying more consumer oriented articles—travel, equipment. Articles must reflect informed and up-to-date knowledge of Atlantic salmon. Writers need not be authorities, but research must be impeccable. Clear, concise writing is a plus, and submissions must be typed. Anecdote, River Log and photo essays are most open to freelancers. The odds are that a writer without a background in outdoors writing and wildlife reporting will not have the 'informed' angle I'm looking for. Our readership is well-read and critical of simplification and generalization."

BIRD WATCHER'S DIGEST, Pardson Corp., Box 110, Marietta OH 45750. Editor: Mary Beacom Bowers. 60% freelance written. Works with a small number of new/unpublished writers each year. Bimonthly magazine covering natural history—birds and bird watching. "*BWD* is a nontechnical magazine interpreting ornithological material for amateur observers, including the knowledgable birder, the serious novice and the backyard bird watcher; we strive to provide good reading and good ornithology." Circ. 45,000. Pays on publication. Publishes ms an average of 1 year after acceptance. Byline given. Buys one-time rights, first serial rights and second serial (reprint) rights. Submit seasonal/holiday material 6 months in advance. Previously published submissions OK. Computer printout submissions acceptable; no dot-matrix. Reports in 6 weeks. Sample copy $3; writer's guidelines for #10 SASE.
Nonfiction: Book excerpts, how-to (relating to birds, feeding and attracting, etc.), humor, personal experience and travel (limited—we get many). "We are especially interested in fresh, lively accounts of

closely observed bird behavior and displays and of bird watching experiences and expeditions. We often need material on less common species or on unusual or previously unreported behavior of common species." No articles on pet or caged birds; none on raising a baby bird. Buys 75-90 mss/year. Send complete ms. Length: 600-3,500 words. Pays $25-50.

Photos: Send photos with ms. Pays $10 minimum for b&w prints; $25 minimum for color transparencies. Buys one-time rights.

Poetry: Avant-garde, free verse, light verse and traditional. No haiku. Buys 12-18 poems/year. Submit maximum 3 poems. Length 8-20 lines. Pays $10.

Tips: "We are aimed at an audience ranging from the backyard bird watcher to the very knowledgable birder; we include in each issue material that will appeal at various levels. We always strive for a good geographical spread, with material from every section of the country. We leave very technical matters to others, but we want facts and accuracy, depth and quality, directed at the veteran bird watcher and at the enthusiastic novice. We stress the joys and pleasures of bird watching, its environmental contribution, and its value for the individual and society."

FORESTS & PEOPLE, Official Publication of the Louisiana Forestry Association, Louisiana Forestry Association, Drawer 5067, Alexandria LA 71301. (318)443-2558. Editor: John R. Gormley. 50% freelance written. Works with a small number of new/unpublished writers each year. Quarterly magazine covering forests, forest industry, wood-related stories, wildlife for general readers, both in and out of the forest industry. Circ. 8,500, readership 39,000. Pays on acceptance. Publishes ms an average of 6 months after acceptance. Byline given. Not copyrighted. Submit seasonal/holiday material 2 months in advance. Simultaneous queries, and simultaneous, photocopied, and previously published submissions OK. Computer printout submissions OK; no dot-matrix. Reports in 2 weeks on queries; 3 weeks on mss. Sample copy $1.75; free ms guidelines.

Nonfiction: General interest (recreation, wildlife, crafts with wood, festivals); historical/nostalgic (logging towns, historical wooden buildings, forestry legends); interview/profile (of forest industry execs, foresters, loggers, wildlife managers, tree farmers); photo feature (of scenic forest, wetlands, logging operations); and technical (innovative equipment, chemicals, operations, forestland studies, or industry profiles). No research papers. Articles may cover a technical subject but must be understandable to the general public." Buys 12 mss/year. Query with published clips. Length: open. Pays $100.

Photos: State availability of photos. Reviews b&w and color slides. Identification of subjects required.

HIGH COUNTRY NEWS, High Country Foundation, Box 1090, Paonia CO 81428. (303)527-4898. Editor: Betsy Marston. 80% freelance written. Works with a small number of new/unpublished writers each year. Biweekly tabloid covering environment and natural resource issues in the Rocky Mountain states for environmentalists, politicians, companies, college classes, government agencies, etc. Circ. 5,400. Pays on publication. Publishes ms an average of 2 months after acceptance. Byline given. Buys one-time rights. Submit seasonal/holiday material 6 weeks in advance. Computer printout submissions acceptable if "double-spaced (at least) and legible"; prefers letter-quality to dot-matrix. Reports in 1 month. Free sample copy and writer's guidelines.

Nonfiction: Reporting (local issues with regional importance); expose (government, corporate); interview/profile; opinion; personal experience; and centerspread photo feature. Special issues include those on states in the region. Buys 100 mss/year. Query. Length: 3,000 word maximum. Pays 5-10¢/word. Sometimes pays the expenses of writers on assignment.

Photos: Send photos with ms. Reviews b&w contact sheets and prints. Captions and identification of subjects required.

Poetry: Chip Rawlins, poetry editor, Box 51, Boulder WY 82923. Avant-garde, free verse, haiku, light verse and traditional. Pays in contributor copies.

Tips: "We use a lot of freelance material, though very little from outside the Rockies. Start by writing short, 500-word news items of timely, regional interest."

INTERNATIONAL WILDLIFE, National Wildlife Federation, 1412 16th St. NW, Washington DC 20036. Managing Editor: Jonathan Fisher. 85% freelance written. Prefers to work with published/established writers. Bimonthly for persons interested in natural history, outdoor adventure and the environment. Circ. 400,000. Pays on acceptance. Publishes ms an average of 4 months after acceptance. Usually buys all rights to text. "We are now assigning most articles but will consider detailed proposals for quality feature material of interest to a broad audience." Computer printout submissions acceptable; dislikes poor-quality dot-matrix. Reports in 6 weeks.

Nonfiction: Focuses on world wildlife, environmental problems and man's relationship to the natural world as reflected in such issues as population control, pollution, resource utilization, food production, etc. Especially interested in articles on animal behavior and other natural history, first-person experiences by scientists in the field, well-reported coverage of wildlife-status case studies which also raise broader themes about international conservation, and timely issues. Query. Length: 2,000-2,500 words. Also in the market for short, 750-word length "one pagers." Examine past issue for style and subject matter. Pays $750 minimum.

Sometimes pays expenses of writers on assignment.
Photos: Purchases top-quality color photos; prefers packages of related photos and text, but single shots of exceptional interest and sequences also considered. Prefers Kodachrome transparencies. Buys one-time rights.
Tips: "Send us a detailed query that will speak for itself; if we respond favorably, the writer's plugged in."

MICHIGAN NATURAL RESOURCES MAGAZINE, State of Michigan Department of Natural Resources, Box 30034, Lansing MI 48909. (517)373-9267. Editor: N.R. McDowell. Managing Editor: Richard Morscheck. 60% freelance written. Works with a small number of new/unpublished writers each year. Bimonthly magazine covering natural resources in the Great Lakes area. Circ. 125,000. Pays on acceptance. Publishes ms an average of 6 months after acceptance. Byline given. Offers 100% kill fee. Buys first rights. Submit seasonal/holiday material 1 year in advance. Computer printout submissions acceptable; no dot-matrix. Reports in 1 month. Sample copy for $2.50 and 9x12 SAE; writer's guidelines for business size SASE.
Nonfiction: "All material must pertain to this region's natural resources: lakes, rivers, wildlife, flora and special features. No personal experience, domestic animal stories or animal rehabilitation." Buys 24 mss/year. Query with clips of published work. Length: 1,000-4,000 words. Pays $150-400. Sometimes pays the expenses of writers on assignment.
Photos: Gijsbert (Nick) vanFrankenhuyzen, photo editor. "Photos submitted with an article can help sell it, but they must be razor sharp in focus." Send photos with ms. Pays $50-200 for 35mm color transparencies; Kodachrome 64 or 25 preferred. Model releases and identification of subjects required. Buys one-time rights.
Tips: "We hope to exemplify why Michigan's natural resources are valuable to people and vice versa."

NATIONAL PARKS, 1015 31st St., Washington DC 20007. (202)944-8565. Senior Editor: Michele Strutin. 75% freelance written. Prefers to work with published/established writers. Bimonthly magazine for a highly educated audience interested in preservation of National Park System Units, natural areas and protection of wildlife habitat. Circ. 55,000. Pays on acceptance. Publishes ms an average of 6 months after acceptance. Buys first North American serial rights and second serial (reprint) rights. Submit seasonal/holiday material 5 months in advance. Electronic submissions acceptable via IBM XYWrite, but prefers hard copy also. Computer printout submissions acceptable if legible; prefers letter-quality to dot-matrix. Reports in 10 weeks. Sample copy $3; writer's guidelines for SASE.
Nonfiction: Expose (on threats, wildlife problems to national parks); descriptive articles about new or proposed national parks and wilderness parks; brief natural history pieces describing park geology, wildlife, or plants; "adventures" in national parks (crosscountry skiing, bouldering, mountain climbing, kayaking, canoeing, backpacking); and travel tips to national parks. All material must relate to national parks. No poetry or philosophical essays. Buys 6-10 unsolicited mss/year. "We prefer queries rather than unsolicited stories." Length: 1,000-1,500 words. Pays $75-400.
Photos: State availability of photos or send photos with ms. Pays $25-50 for 8x10 b&w glossy prints; $35-100 for color transparencies; offers no additional payment for photos accompanying ms. Captions required. Buys first North American serial rights.

NATIONAL WILDLIFE, National Wildlife Federation, 8925 Leesburg Pike, Vienna VA 22184. (703)790-4510. Editor: John Strohm. Managing Editor: Mark Wexler. 75% freelance written. Works with a small number of new/unpublished writers each year. Bimonthly magazine on wildlife, natural history and environment. "Our purpose is to promote wise use of the nation's natural resources and to conserve and protect wildlife and its habitat. We reach a broad audience that is largely interested in wildlife conservation and nature photography. We avoid too much scientific detail and prefer anecdotal, natural history material." Circ. 850,000. Pays on acceptance. Publishes ms an average of 1 year after acceptance. Offers 25% kill fee. Buys all rights. Submit seasonal/holiday material 8 months in advance. Computer printout submissions acceptable; prefers letter-quality to dot-matrix. Reports in 6 weeks. Sample copy for magazine-size SAE and 4 first class stamps; writer's guidelines for letter size SAE and 1 first class stamp.
Nonfiction: Book excerpts (nature related); general interest (2,500-word features on wildlife, new discoveries, behavior, or the environment); how-to (an outdoor or nature related activity); personal experience (outdoor adventure); photo feature (wildlife); and short 700-word features on an unusual individual or new scientific discovery relating to nature. Buys 50 mss/year. Query with or without published clips. Length: 750-2,500 words. Pays $500-1,750. Sometimes pays expenses of writers on assignment.
Photos: John Nuhn, photo editor. State availability of photos or send photos with query. Reviews 35mm color transparencies. Pays $250-750. Buys one-time rights.
Tips: "Writers can break in with us more readily by proposing subjects (initially) that will take only one or two pages in the magazine (short features)."

‡**NATURAL HISTORY**, Natural History Magazine, 79th and Central Park W., New York NY 10024. Editor: Alan Ternes. Over 75% freelance written. Monthly magazine for well-educated, ecologically aware audience: professional people, scientists and scholars. Circ. 500,000. Pays on publication. Publishes ms an average of 3

months after acceptance. Byline given. Buys first serial rights and becomes agent for second serial (reprint) rights. Submit seasonal material 6 months in advance. Computer printout submissions acceptable. Sample copy $3.

Nonfiction: Uses all types of scientific articles except chemistry and physics—emphasis is on the biological sciences and anthropology. Prefers professional scientists as authors. "We always want to see new research findings in almost all the branches of the natural sciences—anthropology, archeology, zoology and ornithology. We find that it is particularly difficult to get something new in herpetology (amphibians and reptiles) or entomology (insects), and we would like to see material in those fields. We lean heavily toward writers who are scientists. We expect high standards of writing and research. We favor an ecological slant in most of our pieces, but do not generally lobby for causes, environmental or other. The writer should have a deep knowledge of his subject, then submit original ideas either in query or by manuscript. Acceptance is more likely if article is accompanied by high-quality photographs." Buys 60 mss/year. Query or submit complete ms. Length: 2,000-4,000 words. Pays $650-1,000, plus additional payment for photos used.

Photos: Rarely uses 8x10 b&w glossy prints; pays $125/page maximum. Much color is used; pays $300 for inside and up to $500 for cover. Buys one-time rights.

Tips: "Learn about something in depth before you bother writing about it."

OCEANS, Ocean Magazine Associates, Inc., 2001 W. Main St., Stamford CT 06902. Editor: Michael Robbins. 100% freelance written. Prefers to work with published/established writers and works with small number of new/unpublished writers each year. Bimonthly magazine; 72 pages. For people who love the sea. Circ. 50,000. Pays on acceptance. Publishes ms an average of 3 months after acceptance. Byline given. Buys first serial rights; some second serial (reprint) rights. Submit seasonal/holiday material 4 months in advance. Simultaneous and photocopied submissions OK, if identified as such. Query for electronic submissions. Computer printout submissions acceptable if legible. Reports in 2 months. Sample copy $3; writer's guidelines for SASE.

Nonfiction: "We want articles on the worldwide realm of salt water: marine life (biology and ecology), oceanography, maritime history, marine painting and other arts, geography, undersea exploration, voyages, ships, coastal areas including environmental problems, seaports and shipping, islands, aquaculture, peoples of the sea, including anthropological materials. Writing should be direct, factual, very readable; not cute, flippant or tongue-in-cheek. Buys 60 mss/year. Query with SASE. Length: 1,000-6,000 words. Pays $750-1,000. Sometimes pays expenses of writers on assignment.

Tips: "We could use more profiles of important people in the marine world, and more articles of interest to cruise ship passengers."

OCEANUS, The International Magazine of Marine Science and Policy, Woods Hole Oceanographic Institution, Woods Hole MA 02543. (617)548-1400, ext. 2386. Editor: Paul R. Ryan. Assistant Editor: James Hain. 10% freelance written. "*Oceanus* is an international quarterly magazine that monitors significant trends in ocean research, technology and marine policy. Its basic purpose is to encourage wise, environmentally responsible use of the oceans. In addition, two of the magazine's main tasks are to explain the significance of present marine research to readers and to expose them to the substance of vital public policy questions." Circ. 15,000. Pays on publication. Publishes ms an average of 3 months after acceptance. Byline given. Buys all rights. Simultaneous queries OK. Computer printout submissions acceptable; no dot-matrix. Reports in 2 months.

Nonfiction: Interview/profile and technical. *Oceanus* publishes 4 thematic issues/year. Most articles are commissioned. Length: 2,700-3,500 words. Pays $300 minimum. Sometimes pays expenses of writers on assignment.

Photos: State availability of photos. Reviews b&w and color contact sheets and 8x10 prints. Pays variable rates depending on size; $125/full-page b&w print. Captions required. Buys one-time rights.

Tips: The writer has a better chance of breaking in at this publication with short articles and fillers. "Most of our writers are top scientists in their fields."

PACIFIC DISCOVERY, California Academy of Sciences, Golden Gate Park, San Francisco CA 94118. (415)221-5100. Editor: Janet Cox. 100% freelance written. Prefers to work with published/established writers. "A journal of nature and culture around the world read by scientists, naturalists, teachers, students, and others having a keen interest in knowing the natural world more thoroughly." Published quarterly by the California Academy of Sciences. Circ. 25,000. Buys first North American serial rights on articles; one-time rights on photos. Pays on publication. Publishes ms an average of 1 year after acceptance. Query for electronic submissions. Computer printout submissions acceptable; prefers letter-quality to dot-matrix. Usually reports within 3 months.

Nonfiction: "Subjects of articles include behavior and natural history of animals and plants, ecology, evolution, anthropology, geology, paleontology, biogeography, taxonomy, and related topics in the natural sciences. Occasional articles are published on the history of natural science, exploration, astronomy and archaeology. Emphasis is on current research findings. Authors need not be scientists; however, all articles must be based, at least in part, on firsthand fieldwork." Query with 100-word summary of projected article for review before

preparing finished ms. Length: 1,000-3,000 words. Pays 24¢/word.
Photos: Send photos with submission "even if an author judges that his own photos should not be reproduced. Referrals to professional photographers with coverage of the subject will be greatly appreciated." Reviews 35mm, 4x5 or other color transparencies or 8x10 b&w glossy prints. Offers $70-100 and $175 for the cover. Buys one-time rights.

SEA FRONTIERS, 3979 Rickenbacker Causeway, Virginia Key, Miami FL 33149. (305)361-5786. Editor: Gilbert L. Voss. Executive Editor: Jean Bradfisch. 95% freelance written. Works with a small number of new/unpublished writers each year. Bimonthly. "For anyone interested in the sea, its conservation, and the life it contains. Our audience is professional people for the most part; people in executive positions and students." Circ. 30,000. Pays on acceptance. Publishes ms an average of 6-12 months after acceptance. Byline given. Buys first serial rights. Will consider photocopied submissions "if very clear." Computer printout submissions acceptable; no dot-matrix. Reports on submissions in 2 months. Sample copy $3; writer's guidelines for SASE.
Nonfiction: "Articles (with illustrations) covering interesting and little known facts about the sea, marine life, chemistry, geology, physics, fisheries, mining, engineering, navigation, influences on weather and climate, ecology, conservation, explorations, discoveries or advances in our knowledge of the marine sciences, or describing the activities of oceanographic laboratories or expeditions to any part of the world. Emphasis should be on research and discoveries rather than personalities involved." Buys 40-50 mss/year. Query. Length: 500-3,000 words. Pays $50-300.
Photos: Reviews 8x10 b&w glossy prints and 35mm (or larger) color transparencies. Pays $50 for color used on front and $35 for the back cover. Pays $25 for color used on inside covers.
Tips: "Query should include a paragraph or two that tells the subject, the angle or approach to be taken, and the writer's qualifications for covering this subject or the authorities with whom the facts will be checked."

SIERRA, 730 Polk St., San Francisco CA 94109. (415)923-5656. Editor-in-Chief: James Keough. Managing Editor: Jonathan F. King. Associate Editors: Joan Hamilton, Reed McManus, Annie Stine. 80% freelance written. Works with a small number of new/unpublished writers each year. Bimonthly magazine emphasizing conservation and environmental politics for people who are well educated, activist, outdoor-oriented, and politically well informed with a dedication to conservation. Circ. 320,000. Pays on acceptance. Publishes ms an average of 6 months after acceptance. Byline given. Buys first North American serial rights. Photocopied submissions OK. Electronic submissions OK on ASC II files (or XyWrite), but requires hard copy also. Computer printout submissions acceptable; prefers letter-quality to dot-matrix. Reports in 6 weeks. Writer's guidelines for SAE and 3 first class stamps.
Nonfiction: Expose (well-documented on environmental issues of national importance such as energy, wilderness, forests, etc.); general interest (well-researched pieces on areas of particular environmental concern); historical (relevant to environmental concerns); how-to and equipment pieces (on camping, climbing, outdoor photography, etc.); interview (with very prominent figures in the field); photo feature (photo essays on threatened areas); and semi-technical (on energy sources, wildlife management, land use, solid waste management, etc.). No "My trip to . . ." or "why we must save wildlife/nature" articles; no poetry or general superficial essays on environmentalism and local environmental issues. Buys 10-15 mss/issue. Query with published clips. Length: 800-2,500 words. Pays $200-600. Sometimes pays expenses of writers on assignment (up to $50).
Photos: Silvana Nova, art and production manager. State availability of photos. Pays $200 maximum for color or transparencies; $200 for cover photos. Buys one-time rights.
Columns/Departments: Book reviews. Buys 20-25 mss/year. Length: 750-1,000 words. Pays $100; submit queries to Jonathan F. King, managing editor. For Younger Readers, natural history and conservation topics presented for children ages 8 to 13. Pays $200-400; submit queries to Reed McManus, associate editor.
Tips: "Queries should include an outline of how the topic would be covered and a mention of the political appropriateness and timeliness of the article. Familiarity with Sierra Club positions and policies is recommended. Statements of the writer's qualifications should be included. We don't have articles and fillers in our format. Our redesign involves new departments (Afield, and Hot Spots) that use shorter pieces than we've been able to previously use ."

SNOWY EGRET, 205 S. 9th St., Williamsburg KY 40769. (606)549-0850. Editor: Humphrey A. Olsen. 75% freelance written. Works with small number of new/unpublished writers each year; eager to work with new/unpublished writers. Semiannual for "persons of at least high school age interested in literary, artistic, philosophical and historical natural history." Circ. less than 500. Pays on publication. Publishes ms an average of 6 months after acceptance. Byline given. Buys first North American serial rights. Computer printout submissions OK; prefers letter-quality to dot-matrix. Usually reports in 2 months. Sample copy $2; writer's guidelines for SASE.
Nonfiction: Subject matter limited to material related to natural history (preferably living organisms), especially literary, artistic, philosophical and historical aspects. Criticism, book reviews, essays and biographies. No columns. Buys 40-50 mss/year. Pays $2/printed page. Send nonfiction prose mss and books for review to

Humphrey A. Olsen.
Photos: No photos, but drawings acceptable.
Fiction: "We are interested in considering stories or self-contained portions of novels. All fiction must be natural history or man and nature. The scope is broad enough to include such stories as Hemingway's 'Big Two-Hearted River' and Warren's 'Blackberry Winter.' " Length: maximum 10,000 words. Pays $2/printed page. Send mss for consideration and poetry and fiction books for review to Alan Seaburg, poetry and fiction editor, 17 Century St., West Medford MA 02155. "It is preferable to query first."
Poetry: No length limits. Pays $4/printed page, minimum $2.

_____ *Personal Computers*

Personal computer magazines continue to change and evolve. Many add or eliminate computer models that they report on. Many computer magazines have folded. Be sure you see the most recent issue of a magazine before submitting material to it. Business applications for home computers are covered in the Business and Finance section. Magazines on computer games are in the Games and Puzzles category. Publications for data processing personnel are listed in the Trade Information Systems section. Uses of computers in specific professions are covered in the appropriate trade section.

‡**A.N.A.L.O.G. COMPUTING, The Magazine for ATARI Computer Owners**, A.N.A.L.O.G. Magazine Corp., Box 23, Worcester MA 01603. (617)892-9230. Editors: Michael DesChenes and Lee H. Pappas. Managing Editor: Diane L. Gaw. 80% freelance written. Monthly magazine covering the Atari home computer. Pays on publication. Publishes ms an average of 2-6 months after acceptance. Byline given. Buys all rights. Submit seasonal/holiday material 2 months in advance. Photocopied submissions OK. Electronic submissions OK on 300-1200 baud "as long as the disk is prepared with one of the more common Atari word processing programs." Computer printout submissions acceptable; prefers letter-quality to dot-matrix. Reports in 2 weeks. Sample copy $3; writer's guidelines for business size SASE.
Nonfiction: How-to and technical. "We publish beginner's articles, educational programs, utilities, multi-function tutorials, do-it-yourself hardware articles, and games (preferably arcade-style in Basic and/or Assembly language). We also publish reviews of Atari software and hardware." Buys 150 mss/year. Send complete ms. Length: open. Pays $65/typeset magazine page. Sometimes pays expenses of writers on assignment.
Photos: Send photos with ms. Reviews 5x7 b&w prints. Captions required, "clipped to the photo or taped to the back." Buys all rights.
Columns/Departments: Atari software and hardware reviews. Buys 30 mss/year. Send complete ms. Length: open.
Tips: "Almost all submissions are from people who read the magazine regularly and use the Atari home computers. We have published many first-time authors. We have published programs written in BASIC, ASSEMBLY, PILOT, FORTH, LISP, and some information on PASCAL. When submitting any program over 30 lines, authors must send a copy of the program on magnetic media, either cassette or disk. We strive to publish personable, down-to-earth articles as long as the style does not impair the technical aspects of the article. Authors should avoid sterile, lifeless prose. Occasional humor (detailing how the author uses his or her computer or tackles a programming problem) is welcome."

‡**AMIGAWORLD, Exploring the Amiga**, CW/Communications, 80 Elm St., Peterborough NH 03458. (603)924-9471. Editor: Guy Wright. Managing Editor: Shawn Laflamme. 90% freelance written. Eager to work with new/unpublished writers. Bimonthly magazine for users of the Amiga computer from Commodore. "We help people understand the inner workings of the machine so that they can better use and enjoy their computer." Circ. 75,000. Pays on acceptance. Publishes ms an average of 3 months after acceptance. Byline given. Buys all rights. Submit seasonal/holiday material 4 months in advance. Photocopied submissions OK. Query for electronic submissions. Computer printout submissions OK; prefers letter-quality to dot-matrix. Reports in 1 month on queries; 2 months on mss. Writer's guidelines for SASE.
Nonfiction: Bob Ryan, articles editor. General interest, how-to, humor (rarely), personal experience and technical—all related to programming or using Amiga computer. "The magazine features informative, interesting, high quality articles, tutorials, hints and tips, news, and reviews about the Amiga. We don't want to see

any program listings over 20 lines or articles on 'how I got started' or 'why the Amiga computer is so great.' "
Buys 50 mss/year. Query with or without published clips, or send complete ms. Length: 2,000-16,000 words.
Pays $100-1,500 for assigned articles; pays $100-800 for unsolicited articles. Sometimes pays the expenses of
writers on assignment.

Photos: Send photos with submission. Reviews negatives, transparencies and prints. Offers no additional
payment for photos accepted with ms. Captions required. Buys all rights.

Columns/Departments: Linda Barrett, reviews editor. Reviews (hardware and software reviews). "All reviews are assigned by us. Send one page and biography and areas of expertise and we will contact you." Buys
40 mss/year. Length: 500-1,500 words. Pays $50-300.

Tips: "The author should have a good knowledge of the Amiga computer or have access to one. Most of our articles are about the computer itself but we do publish features about famous people using Amigas or unique applications. If you have an idea for an article give us a call first. We are more than happy to discuss on the phone
and even suggest topics. The expected sales of the new Commodore Amiga 500 and Amiga 2000 will mean a
greater swing toward tutorial and beginning computer articles."

ANTIC MAGAZINE, The Atari Resource, Antic Publishing Co., 524 2nd St., San Francisco CA 94107.
(415)957-0886. Editor: Nat Friedland. 25% freelance written. Eager to work with new/unpublished writers.
Monthly magazine for Atari 400/800, 1200XL, 600XL, 800XL, and 1450LXD computer users. Circ.
100,000. Pays on publication. Publishes ms an average of 3 months after acceptance. Byline given. Offers $60
kill fee. Buys all rights. Submit seasonal/holiday material 3 months in advance. Simultaneous queries and photocopied submissions OK. Electronic submissions OK on Atari DOS compatible, but requires hard copy also.
Computer printout submissions acceptable. Reports in 2 weeks on queries; 1 month on mss. Sample copy $3;
free writer's guidelines. Request text files on disks and printout.

Nonfiction: How-to, interview/profile, new product, photo feature and technical. Especially wants article
plus programs—games, utilities, productivity, etc. Special issues include Education (October) and Buyer's
Guide (December). No generalized, nontechnical articles. Buys 250 mss/year. Send complete ms. Length:
500-2,500 words. Pays $50-600. Pays expenses of writers on assignment.

Photos: State availability of photos or send photos with ms. Reviews color transparencies and b&w prints;
b&w should accompany article. Identification of subjects required.

Columns/Departments: Starting Line (beginner's column); Assembly Language (for advanced programmers); Profiles (personalities in the business); and Product Reviews (software/hardware products). Buys 36
mss/year. Send complete ms. Length: 1,500-2,500 words. Pays $120-180.

Tips: "Write for the Product Reviews section. We need 400- to 600-word articles on a new software or hardware product for the Atari 400/800 computers. Give a clear description; personal experience with product;
comparison with other available product; or product survey with charts. The most frequent mistakes made by
writers in completing an article are failure to be clear and specific, and writing overly-long submissions."

A+, THE INDEPENDENT GUIDE TO APPLE COMPUTING, Ziff-Davis, Suite 206, 11 Davis Dr., Belmont
CA 94002. (415)594-2290. Editor-in-Chief: Fred Davis. Managing Editor: Leslie Steere. Senior Editor: Lisa
Raleigh. 95% freelance written. Prefers to work with published/established writers. Monthly magazine covering the Apple Computer product line and related products. "*A+* aims to educate the Apple II, IIe, IIc, and IIGS
owner on professional uses of the various products." Circ. 200,000. Pays 6 weeks after acceptance. Publishes
ms an average of 4 months after acceptance. Byline given. Offers $50-100 kill fee. Buys all rights. Submit sea-
sonal/holiday material 4 months in advance. Query for electronic submission. Computer printout submissions
acceptable.

Nonfiction: How-to, new product and technical. Buys 200 mss/year. Query with published clips. Length:
1,000-2,500 words. Pays negotiable rates. Sometimes pays expenses of writers on assignment.

Tips: "If you know about Apple computers and their uses and have some writing experience, we will consider
you for a freelance assignment."

BYTE MAGAZINE, 70 Main St., Peterborough NH 03458. (603)924-9281. Editor: Philip Lemmons. Monthly
magazine covering personal computers for college-educated, professional users of computers. Circ. 401,500.
Pays on acceptance. Buys all rights. Computer printout submissions acceptable; prefers letter-quality to dot-
matrix. Reports on rejections in 6 weeks; 3 months if accepted. Sample copy $2.95; writer's guidelines for
SASE.

Nonfiction: In-depth discussions of technical topics related to microcomputers or technology that will be
available to micros within 5 years. Buys 160 mss/year. Query. Length: 3,000-5,000 words. Pay is competitive.

Tips: "Many *Byte* authors are regular readers of the magazine, and most readers use a computer either at home
or at work. Back issues of the magazine give prospective authors an idea of the type of article published in *Byte*.
Articles can take one of several forms: tutorial articles on a given subject, how-to articles detailing a specific
implementation of a hardware or software project done on a small computer, survey articles on the future of microcomputers, and sometimes theoretical articles describing work in computer science (if written in an informal, 'friendly' style). You will increase your chances of acceptance if you send a query letter and one to two

outline pages instead of a finished ms."

CLOSING THE GAP, INC., Box 68, Henderson MN 56044. (612)248-3294. Managing Editor: Michael Gergen. 40% freelance written. Eager to work with new/unpublished writers. Bimonthly tabloid covering microcomputers for handicapped readers, special education and rehabilitation professionals. "We focus on currently available products and procedures written for the layperson that incorporate microcomputers to enhance the educational opportunities and quality of life for persons with disabilities." Circ. 10,000. Pays on publication. Publishes ms an average of 2 months after acceptance. Byline given. Buys first serial rights. Simultaneous queries, and simultaneous, photocopied, and previously published submissions OK. Electronic submissions OK via Apple IIe, 64K or Macintosh S12K. Computer printout submissions acceptable (dot-matrix with descenders). Reports in 2 weeks. Free sample copy and writer's guidelines.

Nonfiction: How-to (simple modifications to computers or programs to aid handicapped persons); interview/profile (users or developers of computers to aid handicapped persons); new product (computer products to aid handicapped persons); personal experience (by a handicapped person or on use of microcomputer to aid a handicapped person); articles on current research on projects or microcomputers to aid persons with disabilities; and articles that examine current legislation, social trends and new projects that deal with computer technology for persons with handicaps. No highly technical "computer hobbyist" pieces. Buys 25 mss/year. Query. Length: 500-2,000 words. Pays $25 and up (negotiable). "Many authors' material runs without financial compensation." Sometimes pays expenses of writers on assignment.

Tips: "Knowledge of the subject is vital, but freelancers do not need to be computer geniuses. Clarity is essential; articles must be able to be understood by a layperson. All departments are open to freelancers. We are looking for new ideas. If you saw it in some other computer publication, don't bother submitting. *CTG*'s emphasis is on increasing computer user skills in our area of interest, not developing hobbyist or technical skills. The most frequent mistakes made by writers in completing an article for us is that their submissions are too technical—they associate 'computer'.with hobbyist, often their own perspective—and don't realize our readers are not hobbyists or hackers."

COMMODORE MAGAZINE, Commodore Business Machines, 1200 Wilson Dr., West Chester PA 19380. (215)431-9100. Editor: Carol Minton. 90% freelance written. Monthly magazine for owners of Commodore computers, using them for business, programming, education, communications, art, recreation, etc. Circ. 200,000. Pays on publication. Publishes ms an average of 3 months after acceptance. Byline given. Buys all rights; makes occasional work-for-hire assignments. Submit seasonal/holiday material 5 months in advance. Simultaneous queries and previously published submissions OK. All programs should be submitted on disk with accompanying hardcopy list. Reports in 1 month on queries; 2 months on mss. Free sample copy; writer's guidelines for legal size SASE.

Nonfiction: Book reviews; how-to (write programs, use software); new product (reviews); personal experience; photo feature; and technical. "Write for guidelines." Buys 360 mss/year. Query or send complete ms. Length: 750-2,500 words. Pays $60-100/published page.

Photos: Send photos with ms. Reviews 5x7 b&w and color prints. Captions required. Buys all rights.

Tips: "Write to the editor with several specific ideas. Use Commodore computers. We're open to programming techniques and product reviews."

‡COMPUTER LANGUAGE,Miller Freeman Publications, 500 Howard Street, San Francisco CA 94105. (415)397-1881. Editor: Regina Starr Ridley. Managing Editor: Kathy Kincaide. 100% freelance written. Monthly magazine covering programming languages and software design. Circ. 55,000. Pays on publication. Byline given. Buys all rights. Photocopied submissions OK. Query for electronic submissions. Computer printout submissions OK; prefers letter-quality to dot-matrix. Reports in months. Sample copy $7; free writer's guidelines.

Nonfiction: Interview/profile, new product, technical and product reviews. Buys 150 mss/year. Query. Length: 1,500-4,000. Pays $60-600.

Photos: State availability of photos with submission. Buys one-time rights.

Columns/Departments: Product Wrap-Up (in-depth softwware review); Software Review; Exotic Language (introduction of new computer language); and Computer Visions (interviews with experts in the field). Buys 24 mss/year. Query or send complete ms. Length: 1,500-4,000.

Tips: "Introduce idea for article and/or send manuscripts to editor; propose to become technical reference and/or software reviewer."

COMPUTER SHOPPER, Patch Communications, 5211 S. Washington Ave., Box F, Titusville FL 32780. (305)269-3211. Editor: Stanley Veit. 50% freelance written. Prefers to work with published/established writers; works with a small number of new/unpublished writers each year. A monthly tabloid covering personal computing. "Our readers are experienced computer users. They are interested in using and comparing machines and software, and in saving money." Circ. 283,000. Pays on publication. Publishes ms an average of 2 months after acceptance. Byline given. Offers $25 kill fee. Buys first North American serial rights and 1 reprint right. Submit seasonal/holiday material 4 months in advance. Query for electronic submissions. Computer printout submissions acceptable; prefers letter-quality to dot-matrix. Reports in 1 week on queries; 2 weeks on mss. Sample copy $2.25.

Nonfiction: How-to (computer boards), new product reviews, and technical. "No rank beginner articles." Buys 250 mss/year. Query. Length: 1,500-2,500 words. Pays 6-10¢/word. Sometimes pays expenses of writers on assignment.

Photos: State availability of photos with submission. Reviews b&w prints or line drawings. Offers no additional payment for photos or drawings accepted with ms.

Tips: "We would like to receive spotlights on business and surveys of computer resources and software for particular industries."

COMPUTING NOW!, Canada's Personal Computing Magazine, Moorshead Publications, 1300 Don Mill Rd., Toronto, Ontario, M3B 3M8 Canada. (416)445-5600. Editor: Steve Rimmer. 15-20% freelance written. Eager to work with new/unpublished writers. A monthly magazine covering micro computing, the use of micro computers in small businesses, computer hacking (intermediate to advanced). Circ. 17,000. Pays on publication. Publishes ms an average of 6 months after acceptance. Byline given. Buys first rights. Electronic submissions acceptable; whether hard copy is required depends on the article. Computer printout submissions acceptable; prefers letter-quality to dot-matrix. Free writer's guidelines.

Nonfiction: How-to (on computer hacking); new product (occasional hardware or software review); and technical. No humor, inspirational or general/historical articles. Query. Length: 2,000-3,000 words. Pays 10¢(Canadian)/word. Sometimes pays the expenses of writers on assignment.

Photos: State availability of photos with submission. Reviews prints. Captions, model releases and identification of subjects required.

Tips: "We're getting into electronic (desktop) publishing: page design and layout, graphics integration, scanners and laser printers."

DATA BASED ADVISOR, Featuring Database Management System, Data Based Solutions, Inc., 1975 5th Ave., San Diego CA 92101. (619) 236-1182. David M. Kalman. Technical Editor: David J. Irwin. 80% freelance written. Works with a small number of new/unpublished writers each year. A monthly magazine covering microcomputer software. Circ. 45,000. Pays on publication. Publishes ms an average of 3 months after acceptance. Byline given. Buys all rights. Electronic submissions OK via IBM PC/ and most CP/M formats, but requires hard copy also. Computer printout submissions acceptable. Reports in 6 weeks on queries; 2 months on manuscripts. Free sample copy and writer's guidelines.

Nonfiction: How-to (on optimizing database programs, etc.); new product (reviews); technical (academic discussion of software/database issues); and actual computer programs that can be used by readers. No human interest or corporate submissions. Buys 80 mss/year. Query with published clips. Length: 1,500 words. Pays $350 maximum for assigned articles; pays $150 maximum for unsolicited articles. Pays the expenses of writers on assignment.

Photos: State availability of photos with submission. Offers no additional payment for photos accepted with ms. Captions required. Buys all rights.

Columns/Departments: dBase Program Tips (tutorial or productivity oriented with working programs), 1,500-2,500 words; and Software Reviews (personal experience rather than laboratory testing) 1,500-3,500 words. Buys 25 mss/year. Query with published clips. Pays $150 maximum.

Tips: "Detail your programming experience. We are interested in 'real world' tips based on the experience of database users at all levels."

80 MICRO, 80 Pine St., Peterborough NH 03458. (603)924-9471. Publisher: C.W. Communications/Peterborough. Editor: Eric Maloney. 75% freelance written. Eager to work with new/unpublished writers. Monthly magazine about microcomputing for owners and users of Tandy, TRS DOS and MS DOS microcomputers. Circ. 100,000. Pays on acceptance. Publishes ms an average of 6 months after acceptance. Buys all rights. Written queries preferred. Photocopied submissions OK. Requires hard copy of articles and disk or tape of programs. Computer printout submissions acceptable. Reports in 2 months. Sample copy $4; writer's guidelines for SASE.

Nonfiction: Applications programs for business, education, science, home and hobby; utilities; programming techniques; and tutorials. "We're looking for articles that will help the beginning, intermediate, and advanced Tandy MS DOS user become a better programmer." Buys 5 mss per issue. Query first. Length: 1,000 words average. Pays $75-100/printed page.

Reviews: Writers interested in reviewing current available software are asked to query the review editor, stating areas of interest and equipment owned. Buys 5-8 reviews/issue.

Photos: Offers no additional payment for photos accepted with ms. Buys all rights.

‡THE MACAZINE, The MacIntosh Magazine for the Rest of Us, Hart Graphics, Box 968, 8008 Shaoal Creek Bl., Austin TX 78767. (512)467-4550. Editor: Robert LeVitus. Technical Editor: C.J.

Weigand. 70% freelance written. A monthly magazine for Macintosh computers (Apple) users. Circ. 75,000. Pays on publication. Publishes ms an average of 3 months after acceptance. Byline given. Buys first North American serial rights or second serial (reprint) rights. Simultaneous, photocopied and previously published submissions OK. Query for electronic submissions. Computer printout submissions OK; prefers letter-quality to dot-matrix. Reports in 1 month on queries; 2 months on mss. Sample copy $3.75; writer's guidelines for #10 SASE.

Nonfiction: Book excerpts, essays, how-to, interview/profile, new product, personal experience and technical. Buys 48 mss/year. Query with or without published clips, or send complete ms. Length: 750-4,500 words. Pays 8-10¢/word for assigned articles; pays 5-7¢/word for unsolicited articles.

Photos: State availability of photos with submission. Reviews 4x5 or 8x10 prints. Offers $10-20 per photo. Captions required. Buys one-time rights.

Fillers: Max Vizsla, editor. Facts and mini reviews. Buys 10/year. Length: 50-1,000 words. Pays $50-100.

Tips: "A well-written how-to about something the readers will appreciate knowing always gets my attention. It shows the writer knows our market. Mini Reviews—50-1,000 word reviews—of software or hardware are needed. Must be based on extended usage of the product. Cover both the positive and negative."

‡THE MACINTOSH BUYER'S GUIDE, Redgate Communications Corp., 1660 Beachland Blvd., Vero Beach FL 32963. (305)231-6904. Managing Editor: Jordan Gold. 80% freelance written. Quarterly magazine covering Macintosh software, hardware and peripherals. Circ. 120,000. Pays on acceptance. Publishes ms an average of 1 month after acceptance. Byline given. Buys all rights. Submit seasonal/holiday material 3 months in advance. Query for electronic submissions. Computer printout submissions OK. Reports in 3 weeks on queries. Sample copy $1 with 9x12 SAE.

Nonfiction: General interest, how-to, new product, personal experience and technical. No humor—"we're business related." Buys 35 mss/year. Query with published clips. Length: 600-5,000 words. Pays $100-1,000. Pays expenses of writers on assignment.

Photos: State availability of photos with submission. Reviews transparencies. Offers $25-300 per photo. Buys one-time rights.

Columns/Departments: Quarterly Report (news of interest to the Macintosh computer community) 1500 words; and Reviews (software, hardware and peripherals) 600-800 words. Buys 40 mss/year. Query with published clips. Pays $100-800.

Tips: "Please call the editor or managing editor to ascertain current business topics of interest. By far, most freelancers are users of Macintosh computers." Looking for "feature article writing and new product reviews."

MACWORLD, The Macintosh Magazine, PC World Communications, Inc., Suite 600, 501 Second St., San Francisco CA 94107. (415)546-7822. Editor: Jerry Borrell. 70% freelance written. Works with a small number of new/unpublished writers each year. Monthly magazine covering use of Apple's Macintosh computer. Circ. 175,000. Pays on acceptance. Publishes ms an average of 4 months after acceptance. Byline given. Offers negotiable kill fee. Buys first serial rights. Submit seasonal/holiday material 6 months in advance. Electronic submissions on Macintosh disk with MacWrite or Microsoft Word text files, IBM PC disk with WordStar, Async comm. via modem, but requires hard copy also. Computer printout submissions acceptable. Reports in 2 months. Sample copy $5. Free writer's guidelines.

Nonfiction: How-to, hands-on and practical experiences, interview/profile, new product, opinion, personal experience, photo feature, technical, community and general interest. Buys 120 mss/year. Query with published clips. Length: 500-3,500 words. Pays $50-750. Sometimes pays expenses of writers on assignment.

Photos: State availability of photos or send photos with query. Pays $25-50 for color slides and 5x7 or 8x10 b&w prints. Captions, model releases, and identification of subjects required. Buys one-time rights.

Tips: "We seek clearly written, useful articles. Send in an article proposal first. Short reviews and new items are the best areas to start with. It is important that the writer know the Macintosh and the subject area, e.g., business, graphics, finance."

MICROAGE QUARTERLY, MicroAge Computer Stores, Inc., Box 1920, Tempe AZ 85281. (602)968-3168. Managing Editor: Linnea Maxwell. 65% freelance written. Prefers to work with published/established writers. A quarterly magazine for "new, potential and first-time computer users." Circ. 150,000. Pays on publication. Publishes ms an average of 3 months after acceptance. Byline given. Offers kill fee. Buys first North American serial rights, one-time rights and second serial (reprint) rights. Previously published submissions OK. Query for electronic submissions. Computer printout submissions acceptable. Sample copy and writer's guidelines for 9x12 SAE with $1.07 postage.

Nonfiction: Query with published clips. Length: 800-3,000 words. Pays $200-1,200. Sometimes pays the phone expenses of writers on assignment.

Columns/Departments: Changing Market (changes in uses of business-oriented computer equipment—what affects the market, and how it changes); Changing Technology (changes/improvements in computer technology which affect the business user); and Changing Industry (adaptations in the computer industry); all

1,000-3,000 words. Market Focus (specific "verticals"—construction, accounting, etc.—and how computers are used in these markets), 2,000-2,500 words.

Tips: "We're looking for problem-solving articles on office automation and computer applications oriented toward small and medium size businesses. We're willing to discuss ideas with experienced business or computer-literate writers."

MICROpendium, Covering the TI99/4A and Compatible, Burns-Koloen Communications Inc., Box 1343, Round Rock TX 78664. (512)255-1512. Editor: Laura Burns. 40% freelance written. Eager to work with new/unpublished writers. A monthly tabloid magazine for users of the "orphaned" TI99/4A. "We are interested in helping users get the most out of their home computers." Circ. 6,000. Pays on publication. Publishes ms an average of 2-3 months after acceptance. Byline given. Buys second serial rights. Photocopied and previously published submissions OK. Query for electronic submission. Computer printout submissions acceptable. Reports in 2 weeks on queries; 2 months on manuscripts. Free sample copy and writer's guidelines.

Nonfiction: Book excerpts; how-to (computer applications); interview/profile (of computer "personalities," e.g. a software developer concentrating more on "how-to" than personality); and opinion (product reviews, hardware and software). Interested in reviews of tax software for April issue; query by January. Buys 30-50 mss/year. Query with or without published clips, or send complete ms. "We can do some articles as a series if they are lengthy, yet worthwhile." Pays $10-150, depending on length; may pay with contributor copies or other premiums if writer requests. No pay for product announcements. Sometimes pays the expenses of writers on assignment.

Photos: Send photos with submission. Reviews contact sheets, negatives, transparencies, and prints (b&w preferred). Buys negotiable rights.

Columns/Departments: User Notes (tips and brief routines for the computer) 100 words and up. Buys 35-40 mss/year. Send complete ms. Pays $10.

Tips: "We have more regularly scheduled columnists, which may reduce the amount we accept from others. The area most open to freelancers is product reviews on hardware and software. The writer should be a sophisticated TI99/4A computer user. We are more interested in advising our readers of the availability of good products than in 'panning' poor ones. We are interested in coverage of the Geneva 9640 by Myarc."

‡MORROW OWNER'S REVIEW, The International Magazine for Users of Morrow and Other CP/M Computers, Morrow Owners Review, Box 5487, Berkeley CA 94705. (415)644-2638. Editor: Sypko Andreae. Managing Editor: Serge Timacheff. 85% freelance written. Bimonthly magazine covering personal computing. "We cater to the CP/M and Morrow users. Some general computer articles are published occasionally." Circ. 5,000. Pays on publication. Publishes ms an average of 2-4 months after acceptance. Offers kill fee of ½¢/word. Buys first North American serial rights, first rights or second serial (reprint) rights. Submit seasonal/holiday material 2-3 months in advance. Simultaneous, photocopied and previously published submissions OK. Query for electronic submissions. Computer printout submissions OK; prefers letter-quality to dot-matrix. Reports in 1 month on queries; 4-6 weeks on mss. Sample copy $2 with 8½x11 SAE and 90¢ postage. Free writer's guidelines.

Nonfiction: How-to (programming hardware utilities); humor (limited, in good taste, germaine to the subject); interview/profile (in the CP/M industry); new product (software and hardware); personal experience (software and hardware); and technical (CP/M and Morrow Computers). "An editorial calendar is free upon request. No material in poor taste or non-computer oriented. We publish very few articles relating to DOS-based systems or other non CP/M systems." Buys 50-60 mss/year. Query with or without published clips or send complete ms. Length: 750-2,500 words. Pays 1¢/word. Sometimes pays writers with contributors copies or other premiums "depends upon the situation." Sometimes pays expenses of writers on assignment.

Photos: State availability of photos or send photos with submission. Reviews b&w contact sheets and 3x5 or 5x7 b&w prints. Offers no additional payment for photos accepted with ms (sometimes will pay for film and processing). Captions and identification of subjects required. Buys one-time rights.

Columns/Departments: CP/M Alive! (current status of CP/M); From the Mailbox (various communications about personal computers); Tools for Tyros (a beginner's column about computers); Forever Z (all about the ZCPR3 operating system). Buys 24 mss/year. Query with published clips. Length: 1,000-2,000 words. Pays 1¢/word minimum.

Fillers: Facts and newsbreaks. Buys 10/year. Length: 10-500 words. Pays 1¢/word.

Tips: "We like writers who send us useful, accurate material about CP/M and especally Morrow computers. We welcome queries, and it is easier for writers to ask us about a topic than to spend time with something we won't use. Since the CP/M industry is small, creativity counts. We are more interested in good information than good writing, for the most part. That's why we have editors."

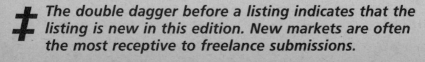

The double dagger before a listing indicates that the listing is new in this edition. New markets are often the most receptive to freelance submissions.

NIBBLE, The Reference for Apple Computing, Micro-SPARC Inc., 52 Domino Dr., Concord MA 01742. (617)371-1660. Editor: David Szetela. Managing Editor: David Krathwohl. 90% freelance written. Eager to work with new/unpublished writers. A monthly magazine for Apple II computer reference. Authors should submit programs that run on Apple computers. Pays on acceptance. Publishes ms an average of 4 months after acceptance. Byline given. Buys all rights. Submit seasonal/holiday material 4 months in advance. Photocopied submissions OK. Query for electronic submissions. Computer printout submissions acceptable. Reports in 1 week on queries; 1 month on manuscripts. Free sample copy and writer's guidelines.
Nonfiction: New product and technical. No product reviews or fiction. Buys 175 mss/year. Query. Length: 500-3,000 words. Pays $50-500. Sometimes pays expenses of writers on assignment.
Photos: State availability of photos with submission. Offers no additional payment for photos accepted with ms. Buys all rights.
Tips: "Authors should submit original Apple programs along with descriptive articles."

PC, The Independent Guide to IBM-Standard Personal Computering, Ziff-Davis Publishing Co., 1 Park Ave., New York NY 10016. (212)503-5255. Editor: Bill Machrone. Executive Editor/Features: Bill Howard. Senior Editor/New Products: Gus Vendetto. 75% freelance written. Prefers to work with published/established writers. Fortnightly magazine for users/owners of IBM Personal Computers and compatible systems. Pays on acceptance. Publishes ms average of 4 months after acceptance. Byline given. Buys all rights. Photocopied submissions OK; electronic copy on floppy disk preferred. Computer printout submissions OK; prefers letter-quality to dot-matrix. Reports in 1 month. Sample copy $5.
Nonfiction: How-to (software and hardware); technical; product evaluations; and programs. Buys 800 mss/year. Query, story proposals should be submitted to the executive editor. Length: 1,000-8,000 words. Sometimes pays expenses of writers on assignment.
Tips: "*PC Magazine* is a computer magazine for business people; however in the coming year we will broaden our coverage of computer products for personal use (i.e. games)."

PCM, The Personal Computing Magazine for Tandy Computer Users, Falsoft, Inc., Falsoft Bldg., 9529 U.S. Highway 42, Box 385, Prospect KY 40059. (502)228-4492. Editor: Lawrence C. Falk. Managing Editor: Kevin Nichols. 75% freelance written. A monthly (brand specific) magazine for owners of the Tandy Model 100, 200 and 600 portable computer and the Tandy 1000, 1200, 2000 and 3000. Circ. 25,000. Pays on publication. Publishes ms an average of 3 months after acceptance. Byline given. Buys full rights, and rights for disk service reprint. Submit seasonal/holiday material 4 months in advance. Photocopied submissions OK. Electronic submissions OK, but requires hard copy also. Computer printout submissions acceptable. Reports in 2 months. Sample copy for SASE; free writer's guidelines.
Nonfiction: Jutta Kapfhammer, submissions editor. How-to. "We prefer articles with programs." No general interest material. Buys 80 mss/year. Send complete ms. "Do not query." Length: 300 words minimum. Pays $40-50/page.
Photos: State availability of photos. Rarely uses photos.
Tips: "At this time we are only interested in submissions for the Tandy MS-DOS and portable computers. Strong preference is given to submissions accompanied by brief program listings. All listings must be submitted on tape or disk as well as in hard copy form."

PERSONAL COMPUTING MAGAZINE, Hayden Publishing Company, Inc., 10 Mulholland Dr., Hasbrouck Heights NJ 07604. (201)393-6187. Editor: Fred Abatemarco. Managing Editor: Peter McKie. 25% freelance written. Monthly magazine on personal computers. "A special-interest magazine that meets the needs of growing users. Editorial content designed to serve business people whose curiosity about the benefits of personal computer use is developing into serious interest and active involvement. Articles and features serve that level of interest without demanding years of experience or advanced knowledge of the technology." Circ. 525,000. Pays on acceptance. Publishes ms an average of 4 months after acceptance. Byline given. Offers 30% kill fee. Buys all rights. Submit seasonal/holiday material 5 months in advance. Simultaneous submissions OK. Computer printout submissions acceptable; prefers letter-quality to dot-matrix. Reports in 2 weeks.
Nonfiction: Peter McKie. Essays, how-to and interview/profile. "We target our articles for managerial-level business executives who use personal computers as a tool in their work. We focus on ways those business people can improve the quality of their work or increase their productivity. In addition, we cover stories on the personal computing industry we deem of merit to readers. No product-based stories, computer neophyte stories or reviews." Query with published clips. Length: 2,500-3,000 words. Pays expenses of writers on assignment.
Fillers: Jack Bell, editor. Any shortcuts readers discover in using applications.
Tips: "Hands-on, applications-oriented features and relevant industry stories are most open to freelancers."

‡**PICO, The Journal of Portable Computing**, Portable Computing International Corp., 7 School St., Box 481, Peterborough NH 03458. (603)924-7859. Editor: Terry Kepner. 80% freelance written. Eager to work with new/unpublished writers. Monthly magazine covering laptop computers, their software and peripherals. Pays on publication. Publishes ms an average of 4 months after acceptance. Byline given. Offers 30% kill fee.

Buys first North American serial rights and the right to use the article again in a yearbook, compendium, or "best of . . ." magazine or book. Submit seasonal/holiday material 6 months in advance. Previously published submissions OK. Query for electronic submissions. Computer printout submissions OK; prefers letter-quality to dot-matrix. Reports in 2 weeks. Sample copy $3.50 with 9x12 SAE and 90¢ postage; writer's guidelines for #10 SASE.

Nonfiction: General interest, humor (April), interview/profile, new product reviews and technical. No articles on how to write programs in BASIC, "my first computer," etc. Buys 120 mss/year. Query with published clips, or send complete ms. Length: 1,000-4,000 words. Pays $80-500 for assigned articles; pays $80-400 for unsolicited articles. Sometimes pays the expenses of writers on assignment.

Photos: Send photos with submission. Especially reviews 8x10 prints; 3x5 prints acceptable. Offers $10-25 per photo. Identification of subjects required. Buys one-time and reprint rights.

Columns/Departments: "Columns are arranged case by case; some are written in-house, some are written by freelance authors." Send complete ms. Length: 700-1,000 words. Pays $80-125.

Fiction: Humorous (April). Buys 2-3 mss/year. Query. Length: 500-1,000 words. Pays $50-100.

Tips: "We want *application* stories: how lap top computers are being integrated into business and society. In general, the easiest way to break in is via a review of some software or hardware. You must write in first person."

PROFILES, The Tutorial Magazine for Microcomputer Users, Kaypro Corporation, 533 Stevens Ave., Solana Beach CA 92075. (619)481-4353. Co-Editors: Diane Ingalls and Terian Tyre. 90% freelance written. "We are trying to build a 'stable' of reliable, competent writers, whether they're 'established' or not." A monthly computer magazine covering MS-DOS & CP/M systems. "Articles must speak to users of micro computers. Interested in how-to articles concerning popular software used on these systems. Technical level of readership ranges from total novice to very advanced." Circ. 100,000. Pays on acceptance. Publishes ms an average of 3-5 months after acceptance. Byline given. Offers 30% kill fee. Buys first world rights. Submit seasonal/holiday material 5 months in advance. Query for information on electronic submissions. Computer printout submissions acceptable. Reports in 1 month. Free sample copy and writer's guidelines.

Nonfiction: How-to (on using specific software/hardware); new product (reviews or evaluations of new hardware or software); and technical (modifications or explanations of specific hardware). No "how I learned to love/hate my computer." Buys 75 mss/year. Query with published clips. Length: 750-3,000 words. Pays $350-500 for assigned articles; pays $350-700 for unsolicited articles. Sometimes pays the expenses of writers on assignment.

Photos: State availability of photos with submission. Reviews negatives. Negotiable payment policy on photos. Model releases and identification of subjects required. Buys one-time rights.

Tips: "We particularly need feature material for beginners and for advanced computer users. Most of the material we now receive is for intermediate/general audiences. Hand-holding instructional material for beginners is appropriate. Advanced users are also seeking how-to material at their level. A lively (but *not* cute) style is welcome, but accuracy, clarity and brevity are more important. No 'think' pieces. We also seek material written by and for those who use computers for business/office applications, as well as programming tutorials with listings (Pascal, assembly language, etc.). Articles should be for both CP/M and MS-DOS users when possible. As Kaypro shifts its focus to MS-DOS computers, we will need more material about that operating environment, but we will continue to support CP/M users. Queries must be complete and specific. Don't make us guess what your article is about."

RAINBOW MAGAZINE, Falsoft, Inc., The Falsoft Bldg., 9529 U.S. Highway 42, Box 385, Prospect KY 40059. (502)228-4492. Editor: Lawrence C. Falk. Managing Editor: James E. Reed. 60% freelance written. Monthly magazine covering the Tandy Color Computer. Circ. 75,000. Pays on publication. Publishes ms an average of 4 months after acceptance. Byline given. Buys full rights and rights for "tape" service reprint. Submit seasonal/holiday material 6 months in advance. Electronic submissions on disk or magnetic tape OK, but requires hard copy also. Computer printout submissions acceptable. Reports in 3 months. Sample copy $3.95; free writer's guidelines.

Nonfiction: Jutta Kapfhammer, submissions editor. Technical (computer programs and articles for Tandy Color Computer. No general "overview" articles. "We want articles *with* programs or tutorials." Buys 300 + mss/year. Send complete ms. Pays $25-50/page.

Fillers: Cartoons (must be Color Computer-related).

SOFT SECTOR, THE PC Compatible Magazine, Falsoft, Inc., The Falsoft Bldg., 9529 U.S. Highway 42, Box 385, Prospect KY 40059. (502)228-4492. Editor: Lawrence C. Falk. Managing Editor: Belinda Kirby. "A monthly bound specific magazine for the Sanyo MS-DOS-based, IBM PC data compatible computer." Pays on publication. Byline given. Buys full rights and rights for disk service reprint. Submit seasonal/holiday material 4 months in advance. Photocopied submissions OK. Electronic submissions OK if ASCII file. Reports in 2 months. Free sample copy; writer's guidelines for SAE.

Nonfiction: Interested only in articles and programs for IBM compatible computers. No general interest or

computer commentary. Buys 120 mss/year. Send complete ms. Length: 200 words minimum. Pays $50 maximum/printed magazine page.
Tips: "Know specific computer or don't submit."

‡ST-LOG, The Magazine for ATARI ST Computer Owners, A.N.A.L.O.G. Magazine Corp., Box 23, Worcester MA 01603. (617)892-9230. Editors: Michael DesChenes and Lee H. Pappas. Managing Editor: Diane L. Gaw. 80% freelance written. Monthly magazine covering the Atari ST home computer. Pays on publication. Publishes ms an average of 2-6 months after acceptance. Byline given. Buys all rights. Submit seasonal/holiday material 2 months in advance. Photocopied submissions OK. Electronic submissions OK on 300-1200 baud "as long as the file is prepared with one of the more common Atari word processing programs." Computer printout submissions acceptable; prefers letter-quality to dot-matrix. Reports in 2 weeks. Sample copy $3; writer's guidelines for business size SASE.
Nonfiction: How-to and technical. "We publish beginner's articles, educational programs, utilities, multi-function tutorials, do-it-yourself hardware articles, and games. We also publish reviews of Atari software and hardware." Buys 150 mss/year. Send complete ms. Length: open. Pays $65/typeset magazine page for regular featues and $120 per page for technical features plus 2¢/byte for source code. Sometimes pays expenses of writers on assignment.
Photos: Send photos with ms. Reviews 5x7 b&w prints. Captions required, "clipped to the photo or taped to the back." Buys all rights.
Columns/Departments: Atari ST software and hardware reviews. Buys 50 mss/year. Send complete ms. Length: open.
Tips: "Almost all submissions are from people who read the magazine regularly and use the Atari ST home computers. We have published many first-time authors. We have published programs written in BASIC, ASSEMBLY, C, PASCAL, and MODULA-2. When submitting any program over 30 lines, authors must send a copy of the program on magnetic media, either cassette or disk. We strive to publish personable, down-to-earth articles as long as the style does not impair the technical aspects of the article. Authors should avoid sterile, lifeless prose. Occasional humor (detailing how the author uses his or her computer or tackles a programming problem) is welcome."

TI PROFESSIONAL COMPUTING, The Magazine for Texas Instruments Computer Users, Publications and Communications, Inc., 12416 Hymeadow Dr., Austin TX 78750. (512)250-9023. Editor: Dean J. Whitehair. Managing Editor: E.M. Kinsfather. 30-40% freelance written. Works with small number of new/unpublished writers each year. A monthly magazine of technical articles relating to Texas Instruments Pro, Business Pro, and 990 series. Circ. 15,000. Pays on publication. Publishes ms an average of 3-4 months after acceptance. Byline given. Buys first North American serial rights and reprints from other PCI magazines. Submit seasonal/holiday material 5 months in advance. Simultaneous submissions and photocopied submissions OK. Query for electronic submissions. Computer printout submissions acceptable; prefers letter-quality to dot-matrix. Free sample copy.
Nonfiction: How-to, interview/profile, new product, opinion and technical. No humor or non-TI-oriented articles. Buys 50 mss/year. Query with or without published clips, or send complete ms. Length 500-4,000 words. Fees negotiable upon assignment, acceptance. Occasionally pays with subscription or other premiums; will negotiate. Sometimes pays the expenses of writers on assignment.
Photos: State availability of photos with submissions. Reviews contact sheets, transparencies, and prints. Offers $10 maximum/photo. Captions, model releases and identification of subjects required. Buys one-time rights.
Tips: "We now accept submissions from Value Added Resellers of TI, and solicit material on all TI computers. We no longer limit coverage to a specific machine—all TI computers are covered."

Photography

Readers of these magazines use their cameras as a hobby and for weekend assignments. Magazines geared to the professional photographer can be found in Photography Trade section.

DARKROOM & CREATIVE CAMERA TECHNIQUES, Preston Publications, Inc., Box 48312, 7800 Merrimac Ave., Niles IL 60648. (312)965-0566. Publisher: Seaton Preston. Editor: David Alan Jay. 75% freelance written. Prefers to work with published/established writers; works with a small number of new/unpublished writers each year and is eager to work with new/unpublished writers. Bimonthly magazine focusing mainly on darkroom techniques, photochemistry, and photographic experimentation and innovation—particularly in the areas of photographic processing, printing and reproduction—plus general user-oriented photography articles aimed at advanced workers and hobbyists. Circ. 45,000. Pays within 1 week of publication. Publishes ms an average of 6 months after acceptance. Byline given. Buys one-time rights. Submit seasonal/holiday material 6 months in advance. Photocopied submissions OK. Query for electronic submissions. Computer printout submissions acceptable (but discouraged). Sample copy $3; writer's guidelines with letter-size SASE.

Nonfiction: General interest articles within above listed topics; how-to, technical product reviews and photo features. Query or send complete ms. Length open, but most features run approximately 2,500 words or 4-5 magazine pages. Pays $100/published page for well-researched technical articles. Sometimes pays expenses of writers on assignment.

Photos: Send photos with ms. Ms payment includes photo payment. Prefers color transparencies and 8x10 b&w prints. Captions, model releases (where appropriate), and identification of subjects required. Buys one-time rights.

Tips: "We would like to receive general photographic articles with a creative or technical bent. Successful writers for our magazine are doing what they write about. They have tried the photo technique and write detailed how-to articles—new twists for use with existing materials, etc."

DARKROOM PHOTOGRAPHY MAGAZINE, Melrose Publishing, #204, 9021 Melrose Ave., Los Angeles CA 90069. (415)989-4360. Editor: Richard Senti. Managing Editor: Ellen Payne. A photography magazine with darkroom emphasis, published 8 times/year for both professional and amateur photographers "interested in what goes on *after* the picture's been taken: processing, printing, manipulating, etc." Circ. 80,000. Pays on publication; pays regular writers on acceptance. Byline given. Buys one-time rights. Photocopied submissions OK. Computer printout submissions acceptable. Reports in 6 weeks. Sample copy and writer's guidelines for SASE.

Nonfiction: Historical/nostalgic (some photo-history pieces); how-to (darkroom equipment build-its); interview/profile (famous photographers); and technical (articles on darkroom techniques, tools, and tricks). No stories on shooting techniques, strobes, lighting, or in-camera image manipulation. Query or send complete ms. Length: varies. Pays $50-500, depending on project.

Photos: State availability or send photos with query or ms. Reviews transparencies and prints. "Supporting photographs are considered part of the manuscript package."

Columns/Departments: Darkroom Basics, Tools & Tricks, Special Effects, Making Money, and Larger Formats. Query or send complete ms. Length: 800-1,200 words. "Published darkroom-related 'tips' receive free one-year subscriptions." Length: 100-150 words.

PETERSEN'S PHOTOGRAPHIC MAGAZINE, Petersen Publishing Co., 8490 Sunset Blvd., Los Angeles CA 90069. (213)854-2200. Publisher: Jackie Augustine. Editor: Bill Hurter. 40% freelance written. Prefers to work with published/established writers; eager to work with new/unpublished writers. Monthly magazine; 100 pages. Emphasizes how-to photography. Circ. 275,000. Pays on publication. Publishes ms an average of 9 months after acceptance. Buys all rights. Submit seasonal/holiday material 5 months in advance. Photocopied submissions OK. Computer printout submissions acceptable. Reports in 2 months. Sample copy $3; free writer's guidelines.

Nonfiction: How-to (equipment reports, darkroom, lighting, special effects, and studio photography). "We don't cover personalities." Buys 12-30 unsolicited mss/year. Send story, photos and captions. Pays $60/printed page.

Photos: With coupon to Photo Contest Editor. Photos purchased with or without accompanying ms. Pays $25-35 for b&w and color photos; offers negotiable rates for covers. Model releases and technical details required.

Tips: "Freelancers should study the easy conversational style of our articles. We are a how-to-do-it magazine which requires clearly detailed text and step-by-step illustration. Write for our free writer's and photographer's guide for details of our requirements."

STRATEGIES, The Self-Promotion Newsletter for Photographers, SG Arts, Inc., Box 838, Montclair NJ 07042. (201)783-5480. Editor: Harold Simon. 10-15% freelance written. Works with a small number of new/unpublished writers each year. Bimonthly newsletter on marketing for fine art photographers. *Strategies* shows fine art photographers how to develop their careers. "We provide first hand information from publishers, photographers, museum curators and gallery directors. Information about every aspect of the fine art photography world—grants, exhibits, portfolios, etc.—is presented." Pays on publication. Publishes ms an average of 2-4 months after acceptance. Byline given. Makes work-for-hire assignments. Simultaneous submissions, photocopied submissions and previously published submissions OK. Electronic submissions OK via Apple Macintosh disks only. Computer printout submissions acceptable. Reports in 1 month. Sample copy $3 with 9x12 SAE and 39¢ postage.

Nonfiction: How-to (about getting exhibits, grants, or being published, putting together portfolios, invitations, or unique promotional experiences); interview/profile; and personal experience. No technical articles about photo equipment, or book/exhibition reviews. Buys 6 mss/year. Query with or without published clips, or send complete ms. Length: 250-1,500 words. Pays $25 plus copies.

WILDLIFE PHOTOGRAPHY, The Wildlife Photography Association, Box 691, Greenville PA 16125. (412)588-3492. Editor: Charles Burchfield, 327 S. Highland St., DuBois PA 15801. (814)371-6818. 90% freelance written. Eager to work with new/unpublished writers. Bimonthly newsletter. "We are dedicated to the pursuit and capture of wildlife on film. Emphasis on how-to and where-to." Circ. 3,000. Pays on acceptance. Publishes ms an average of 6 months after acceptance. Byline given. Buys first rights, one-time rights or second serial (reprint) rights. Submit seasonal/holiday material 4 months in advance. Simultaneous, photocopied and previously published submissions OK. Computer printout submissions acceptable; prefers letter-quality to dot-matrix. Reports in 2 weeks on queries; 6 weeks on mss. Sample copy for $2 and 9x12 SAE; free writer's guidelines.
Nonfiction: Book excerpts; how-to (work with animals to take a good photo); interview/profile (of professionals); new product (of particular interest to wildlife photography); personal experience (with cameras in the field); and travel (where to find superb photo opportunities of plants and animals). No fiction or photography of pets, sports and scenery. Buys 30 mss/year. Query or send complete ms. Length: 200-3,000 words. Pays $10-50.
Photos: Send sharp photos with submission. Reviews contact sheets, negatives, transparencies and 5x7 prints as part of ms package. Photos not accepted separate from ms. Offers no additional payment for photos accepted with ms. Captions and identification of subjects required. Buys one-time rights.
Fillers: Anecdotes and facts. Buys 12/year. Length: 50-200 words. Pays $5-15.
Tips: "Give solid how-to info on how to photograph a specific species of wild animal. Send photos, not only of the subject, but of the photographer and his gear in action. The area of our publication most open to freelancers is feature articles."

____ Politics and World Affairs

These publications cover politics for the reader interested in current events. Other publications that will consider articles about politics and world affairs are listed under Business and Finance, Regional and General Interest. For listings of publications geared toward the professional, see Government and Public Service and International Affairs in the Trade section.

AFRICA REPORT, 833 United Nations Plaza, New York NY 10017. (212)949-5731. Editor: Margaret A. Novicki. 60% freelance written. Prefers to work with published/established writers. A bimonthly magazine for U.S. citizens and residents with a special interest in African affairs for professional, business, academic or personal reasons. Not tourist-related. Circ. 10,500. Pays on publication. Publishes ms an average of 2 months after acceptance. Rights purchased vary with author and material; usually buys all rights, very occasionally first serial rights. Offers negotiable kill fee. Byline given unless otherwise requested. Computer printout submissions OK. Sample copy for $4.50; free writer's guidelines.
Nonfiction: Interested in "African political, economic and cultural affairs, especially in relation to U.S. foreign policy and business objectives. Style should be journalistic but not academic or light. Articles should not be polemical or long on rhetoric but may be committed to a strong viewpoint. I do not want tourism articles." Would like to see in-depth topical analyses of lesser known African countries, based on residence or several months' stay in the country. Buys 15 unsolicited mss/year. Pays $150-250.
Photos: Photos purchased with or without accompanying mss with extra payment. Reviews b&w only. Pays $25. Submit 12x8 "half-plate."
Tips: "Read *Africa Report* and other international journals regularly. Become an expert on an African or Africa-related topic. Make sure your submissions fit the style, length, and level of *Africa Report*."

‡**AMERICAN POLITICS**, The Nation's Magazine of Politics, American Politics, Inc., Suite 802, 810 18th St. N.W., Washington DC 20006. (202)347-1110. Editor: Grant Oliphant. Senior Editor: Jeff Stanton. 80% freelance written. Monthly magazine covering domestic politics, some international. "The magazine accepts articles written from both sides of the political spectrum." Circ. 15,000. Pays on scheduled publication. Publishes ms an average of 2-4 months after acceptance. Byline given. Offers 33% kill fee. Buys first North

American serial rights. Submit seasonal/holiday material 5 months in advance. Query for electronic submissions. Computer printout submissions OK; prefers letter quality to dot matrix. Reports in 2 weeks. Sample copy $2.50 with 8½x11 SAE with 4 first class stamps.
Nonfiction: Essays, expose, historical/nostalgic, humor, interview/profile and opinion. Buys 60 mss/year. Query with published clips. Length: 800-2,500 words. Pays $350-1,000 for assigned articles; pays $300-750 for unsolicited articles. Sometimes pays expenses of writers on assignment.
Photos: State availability of photos with submission.
Tips: "A query that clearly describes a new, punchy angle on a story is the best way to reach us. We want work from people who are interested in politics, appreciate how much of life falls under that description, and want to share their insights with others."

C.L.A.S.S. MAGAZINE, C.L.A.S.S. Promotions, Inc., 27 Union Square West, New York NY 10003. Editor: René John-Sandy. 70% freelance written. Prefers to work with published/established writers; eager to to work with new/unpublished writers. Monthly magazine covering Caribbean/American Third World news and views. Circ. 200,000. Pays on acceptance. Publishes ms an average of 1-2 months after acceptance. Byline given. Buys first rights and second (reprint) rights to material originally published elsewhere. Submit seasonal/holiday material 4 months in advance. Simultaneous queries and previously published submissions OK. Computer printout submissions acceptable; prefers letter-quality to dot-matrix. Reports in 1 month on queries; 6 weeks on mss. Free sample copy and writer's guidelines.
Nonfiction: Features, book excerpts, general interest, historical/nostalgic, inspirational, interview/profile, travel and international news, views and lifestyles in Third World countries. Query or send complete ms. Length: 150-2,500 words. Articles over 700 words must be of international flavor in content. Sometimes pays expenses of writers on assignment.
Poetry: Avant-garde, free verse, haiku, light verse and traditional. Buys 10-20 poems/year. Submit maximum 10 poems. Length: 22-30 lines. Pays $10 minimum.
Tips: "Submit written queries; stick to Afro American/Third World interests and relate to an international audience."

CALIFORNIA JOURNAL, The California Center, 1714 Capitol Ave., Sacramento CA 95814. (916)444-2840. Editor: Richard Zeiger. Managing Editor: A.G. Block. 50% freelance written. Prefers to work with published/established writers. Monthly magazine; 60 pages. Emphasizes analysis of California politics and government. Circ. 20,000. Pays on publication. Publishes ms an average of 2 months after acceptance. Byline given. Buys all rights. Electronic submissions OK via 1200 Baud, IBM PC. Computer printout submissions acceptable; prefers letter-quality to dot-matrix.
Nonfiction: Profiles of state and local government and political analysis. No outright advocacy pieces. Buys 25 unsolicited mss/year. Query. Length: 900-3,000 words. Pays $150-500. Sometimes pays the expenses of writers on assignment.

CRITIQUE: A JOURNAL OF CONSPIRACIES & METAPHYSICS, Box 11368, Santa Rosa CA 95406. (707)525-9401. Editor: Bob Banner. Managing Editor: M. Banovitch. 80% freelance written. Eager to work with new/unpublished writers. Journal published 3 times a year, "that explores conspiracy scenarios, behind-the-scenes news, exposes, and unusual news that frequently create debacles within the ordinary mind set. *Critique* also explores assumptions, beliefs and hypotheses that we use to understand ourselves, our 'world' and the metaphysical crisis of our time." Circ. 5,000. Pays on publication. Publishes ms an average of 2 months after acceptance. Byline given. Submit seasonal material 4 months in advance. Simultaneous queries, and simultaneous, photocopied, and previously published submissions OK. Electronic submissions OK if compatible with Text Files operable in DOS for Apple IIe, but requires hard copy also. Computer printout submissions acceptable. Reports in 4 months. Sample copy $5; free writer's guidelines.
Nonfiction: Book excerpts; book reviews; expose (political, metaphysical, cultural); interview/profile (those in the specified area); and personal experience (as it relates to cultural ideology). Not interested in "anything that gets published in ordinary, established media." Buys 8-25 mss/year. Send complete ms with bio/resume. Length: 200-3,000 words. Pays $30 maximum. "We also publish books. Send us your book proposal."
Tips: "We have published articles, reviews and essays that are difficult to categorize in the simplistic, dualistic Left or Right ideological camps. The material's purpose has been, and will be, to provoke critical thinking; to discriminate between valuable and manipulative information; to incite an awareness of events, trends, phases; and an awareness of our roles and lives within the global psyche that no ordinary consumer of ordinary media could even begin to conceive, let alone use to affect his/her life. Writers have a better chance of breaking in at our publication with short articles and fillers as it gives us the chance to get acquainted, to feel their styles. The most frequent mistakes made by writers in completing an articles are tedious writing and poor organizational structure."

‡**FREEDOM MAGAZINE**, North Star Publishing, Inc., 1301 N. Catalina St., Los Angeles CA 90027. (213)663-2058. Editor: Thomas G. Whittle. Published since 1968 by the Church of Scientology®. 60%

freelance written. Monthly magazine with emphasis on current events and investigative reporting. Circ. 20,000. Pays on acceptance. Publishes ms an average of 3 months after acceptance. Rights purchased vary with author and material. Submit seasonal/holiday material 4 months in advance. Computer printout submissions OK; no dot-matrix. Reports in 1 month.

Nonfiction: Expose and interview/profile. "We welcome articles by government or corporate whistle-blowers. Send documents to fully substantiate the article." Buys at least 40 mss/year. Query with detailed outline, including statement of whether the information has appeared elsewhere. "Enclosing clips of other stories you have published may help your chances of acceptance." Length: 800-5,000 words. Pays $100-350, sometimes more. Sometimes pays the expenses of writers on assignment.

Photos: Send photos with submission. Reviews 35mm color slides, but prefers 2¼ inch transparencies. Reviews 8x10 b&w prints. Offers $10-50 per photo. Captions required. Buys one-time rights.

Columns/Departments: Arts and Entertainment (film and book reviews) 600-1,000 words, pays $75-200; Guest Commentary, 1,000-1,200 words, pays $250.

Fiction: Humor, including political satire. Length: 600-1,200 words. Pays $100-250.

THE FREEMAN, 30 S. Broadway, Irvington-on-Hudson NY 10533. (914)591-7230. Senior Editor: Brian Summers. 75% freelance written. Eager to work with new/unpublished writers. Monthly for "the layman and fairly advanced students of liberty." Buys all rights, including reprint rights. Byline given. Pays on publication. Publishes ms an average of 5 months after acceptance. Computer printout submissions acceptable; prefers letter-quality to dot-maxtrix. Sample copy for 7½x10½ SASE with 4 first class stamps.

Nonfiction: "We want nonfiction clearly analyzing and explaining various aspects of the free market, private enterprise, limited government philosophy, especially as pertains to conditions in the United States. Though a necessary part of the literature of freedom is the exposure of collectivistic cliches and fallacies, our aim is to emphasize and explain the positive case for individual responsibility and choice in a free economy. Especially important, we believe, is the methodology of freedom—self-improvement, offered to others who are interested. We try to avoid name-calling and personality clashes and find satire of little use as an educational device. Ours is a scholarly analysis of the principles underlying a free market economy. No political strategy or tactics." Buys 44 mss/year. Length: 3,500 words maximum. Pays 10¢/word. Sometimes pays expenses of writers on assignment.

Tips: "It's most rewarding to find freelancers with new insights, fresh points of view. Facts, figures, and quotations cited should be fully documented, to their original source, if possible."

GUARDIAN, Independent Radical Newsweekly, Institute for Independent Social Journalism, 33 W. 17th St., New York NY 10011. (212)691-0404. Editor: William A. Ryan. Weekly newspaper covering U.S. and international news and politics for a broad left and progressive audience. Circ. 25,000. Pays on publication. Byline given. Simultaneous queries, and simultaneous and photocopied submissions OK if indicated. Reports in 3 weeks on queries; 1 month on mss. Sample copy for $1, 9x12 SAE and 5 first class stamps; writer's guidelines for business-size SASE.

Nonfiction: Expose (of government, corporations, etc.). "About 90% of our publication is hard news and features on current events." Buys 200 mss/year. Query with published clips. Length: 200-1,800 words. Pays $10-90.

Photos: Anthony Parker, photo editor. State availability of photos. Pays $15 for b&w prints. Captions required.

Columns/Departments: Women, Labor, The Left, and Blacks. Buys 30 mss/year. Query with published clips. Length: 200-700 words. Pays $10-30.

THE INTELLECTUAL ACTIVIST, In Defense of Individual Rights, The Intellectual Activist, Inc., Suite 101, 131 5th Ave., New York NY 10003. (212)982-8357. Editor: Peter Schwartz. 20% freelance written. Works with a small number of new/unpublished writers each year. Bimonthly published newsletter of political and economic analysis. "Our fundamental theme is the defense of individual rights, within the framework of the philosophy of Objectivism. We are especially interested in the exploration of issues in their formative stages, when readers can still influence the outcome by expressing their views in appropriate forums." Pays on publication. Publishes ms an average of 2 months after acceptance. Byline given. Offers 20% kill fee. Buys all rights. Computer printout submissions acceptable; no dot-matrix. Sample copy $2.50. Writer's guidelines for #10 SASE.

Nonfiction: Political/economic analysis. Buys 5 mss/year. Query with or without published clips. Length: 2,000-4,000 words. Pays $250-600. Sometimes pays the expenses of writers on assignment.

Tips: "Read several issues, ask for author's guide, then submit a well-thought-out query. Articles require a firm, pro-individual rights orientation."

THE LIBERTARIAN DIGEST, The Gutenberg Press, 1920 Cedar St., Berkeley CA 94709. (415)548-3776. Editor: Fred Foldvary. 75% freelance written. Eager to work with new/unpublished writers. A bimonthly newsletter which summarizes periodicals of libertarian interest. No original material included. Circ. 200. Pays on acceptance. Publishes ms an average of 2 months after acceptance. Byline given at option of writer. Not copyrighted. Buys all rights. Makes work-for-hire assignments. Simultaneous, photocopied and previously published submissions OK. Electronic submissions OK via 300 Baud, ASCII. Computer printout submissions acceptable "if high quality"; no dot-matrix. Reports in 1 week. Sample copy $2; writer's guidelines and free sample page for SASE.

Nonfiction: Summaries and book reviews. Query. No unsolicited submissions; no original works. Pays 25¢/column inch, no maximum amount. Pays writer with contributor copies or other premiums "if writer desires." Pays expenses of writers on assignment.

Photos: State availability of photos with submissions. Reviews prints. Offers 25¢/column inch. Buys one-time rights.

Fillers: Anecdotes, facts, newsbreaks, and short humor. Variable number of fillers. Pays 25¢/column inch.

Tips: "All copy must be camera-ready. We supply magazines to summarize. Anyone who can submit well-written, camera-ready copy can break in."

‡MOTHER JONES MAGAZINE, The Foundation for National Progress, 1663 Mission St., Second Floor, San Francisco CA 94103. (415)558-8881. Editor: Doug Foster. Managing Editor: Bruce Dancis. 90% freelance written. Monthly magazine of investigative reporting (corporate, governmental). "*Mother Jones* is the largest magazine of political opinion in the United States. Our emphasis is on social change, progressive politics and investigative reporting." Circ. 185,000. Pays on acceptance. Byline given. Offers 25% kill fee. Buys first North American serial rights. Submit seasonal/holiday material 4 months in advance. Computer printout submissions OK; no dot-matrix. Sample copy $3; free writer's guidelines.

Non-fiction: Book excerpts, essays, expose, interview/profile, personal experience and photo feature. Buys 35 mss/year. Query with published clips. Length: 100-7,000 words. Pays $150-2,500. Sometimes pays expenses of writers on assignment.

Photos: State availablility of photos with submission. Reviews contact sheets, negatives, transparencies and prints. Offers $75 minimum/photo. Captions, model releases and identification of subjects required. Buys one-time rights.

Columns/Departments: Global Notebook (international coverage) and The Arts (various topics in popular culture). Buys 25 mss/year. Length: 900-1,500 words. Query with published clips. Pays $450-750.

Fiction: "Please read our magazine to get a feel for our fiction." No western, romance or confession. Buys 3 mss/year. Send complete ms. Length: 1,500-5,000 words. Pays $400-2,000.

Fillers: Frontlines Editor: Bernard Ohanian. Newsbreaks and short humor. Buys 75 mss/year. Length: 100-600 words. Pays $75-200.

Tips: "Frontlines are the best way to break in. Write and ask for Frontlines guideines. Do not telephone."

THE NATION, 72 5th Ave., New York NY 10011. Editor: Victor Navasky. 75% freelance written. Works with a small number of new/unpublished writers each year. Weekly. Buys first serial rights. Query for electronic submission. Computer printout submissions acceptable; prefers letter-quality to dot-matrix.

Nonfiction: "We welcome all articles dealing with the social scene, from a liberal/left perspective." Queries encouraged. Buys 100 mss/year. Length 2,500 words maximum. Modest rates. Sometimes pays expenses of writers on assignment.

Tips: "We are firmly committed to reporting on the issues of labor, national politics, business, consumer affairs, environmental politics, civil liberties and foreign affairs."

‡NATIONAL DEVELOPMENT (DESAROLLO NACIONAL), Intercontinental Publications, Inc., Box 5017, Westport CT 06880. (203)226-7463. Editor-in-Chief: Paul Green. 80% freelance written. Works with a small number of new/unpublished writers each year. Emphasizes Third World infrastructure. For government officials in Third World—technocrats, planners, engineers and ministers. Published 9 times/year; 120 pages. Circ. 60,000. Pays on publication. Publishes ms an average of 6 months after acceptance. Buys all rights. Byline given. Previously published submissions OK. Query for electronic submission. Computer printout submissions acceptable; no dot-matrix. Reports in 1 month. Sample copy and writer's guidelines for 9½x11 SAE with 57¢ postage.

Nonfiction: Technical (construction, government management, planning, power, telecommunications); informational (agriculture, economics, public works, construction management); interview; photo feature; and

ALWAYS submit manuscripts or queries with a self-addressed, stamped envelope (SASE) within your country or International Reply Coupons purchased from the post office for other countries.

technical. Buys 6-10 mss/issue. Query with "inclusion of suggestions for specific article topics; point out your area of expertise." Phone queries OK. Length: 1,800 words. Pays $350.

Photos: B&w and color. Captions required. Query. Total price for ms includes payment for photos.

Columns/Departments: Power technology, telecommunications, computer technology (as applied to infrastructure and development projects), water treatment, financial technology (finances as they might affect Third World governments). Buys 4 mss/issue. Query. Length: 750-1,500 words. Pays $250. Open to suggestions for new columns/departments.

NEWSWEEK, 444 Madison Ave., New York NY 10022. (212)350-4547. My Turn Editor: Phyllis Malamud. Although staff written, accepts unsolicited mss for My Turn, a column of opinion. The 1,000- to 1,100-word essays for the column must be original and contain verifiable facts. Payment is $1,000, on publication, for all rights. Computer printout submissions acceptable; no dot-matrix. Reports in 1 month.

THE PROGRESSIVE, 409 E. Main St., Madison WI 53703. (608)257-4626. Editor: Erwin Knoll. 75% freelance written. Monthly. Pays on publication. Publishes ms an average of 6 weeks after acceptance. Byline given. Buys all rights. Computer printout submissions acceptable "if legible and double-spaced"; prefers letter-quality to dot-matrix. Reports in 2 weeks.

Nonfiction: Primarily interested in articles which interpret, from a progressive point of view, domestic and world affairs. Occasional lighter features. "*The Progressive* is a *political* publication. General-interest material is inappropriate." Query. Length: 3,000 words maximum. Pays $75-250.

Tips: "Display some familiarity with our magazine, its interests and concerns, its format and style. We want query letters that fully describe the proposed article without attempting to sell it—and that give an indication of the writer's competence to deal with the subject."

REASON MAGAZINE, Suite 1062, 2716 Ocean Park Blvd., Santa Monica CA 90405. (213)392-0443. Editor: Mary Zupan. 50% freelance written. Eager to work with new/unpublished writers. A monthly magazine for a readership interested in individual liberty, economic freedom, private enterprise alternatives to government services and individualist cultural and social perspectives. Circ. 32,000. Pays on acceptance. Publishes ms an average of 2 months after acceptance. Rights purchased vary with author and material. Byline given. Offers kill fee by pre-arrangement. Photocopied submissions OK. Computer printout submission OK: double- or triple-spaced mss only. Query for electronic submissions. Reports in 1-2 months. Sample copy for $2 and 9x12 SAE with $1.24 postage.

Nonfiction: "*Reason* deals with social, economic and political issues, supporting both individual liberty and economic freedom. The following kinds of articles are desired: investigative articles exposing government wrongdoing and bungling; investigative articles revealing examples of private (individual, business, or group) ways of meeting needs; individualist analysis of policy issues (e.g., education, victimless crimes, regulation); think pieces exploring implications of individual freedom in economic, political, cultural, and social areas." Query. Buys 50-70 mss/year. Length: 1,000-5,000 words. Sometimes pays expenses of writers on assignment.

‡RIPON FORUM, Ripon Society, 6 Library Ct. SE, Washington DC 20003. (202)546-1292. Editor: William P. McKenzie. 50% freelance written. Eager to work with new/unpublished writers. A bimonthly magazine on progressive Republicanism/GOP politics. Circ. 3,000. Pays on publication. Publishes ms an average of 2-4 months after acceptance. Byline given. Simultaneous and photocopied submissions OK. Computer printout submissions OK. Reports in 1 month on queries; 2 weeks on mss. Free sample copy.

Nonfiction: Essays and opinion. Query with published clips. Length: 800-1,500 words. Pays $80-150. Sometimes pays expenses of writers on assignment.

UTNE READER, The Best of the Alternative Press, LENS Publishing, 2732 W. 43rd St., Minneapolis MN 55410. (612)929-2670. Editors: Helen Cordes, Eric Utne and Jay Walljasper. 5% freelance written; 90% reprints of previously published articles. Works with a small number of new/unpublished writers each year. A bimonthly magazine. "We reprint articles that have already been published, generally in alternative magazines." Circ. 50,000. Pays on publication. Publishes ms an average of 2-6 months after acceptance. Byline given. Buys second serial (reprint) rights. Submit seasonal/holiday material 4 months in advance. Simultaneous, photocopied and previously published submissions OK. Computer printout submissions acceptable; prefers letter-quality to dot-matrix. Reports in 2 months on queries; 3 months on mss. Sample copy $4 with 7x10 SAE and $1.24 postage.

Nonfiction: Book excerpts, essays, humor, interview/profile and opinion. "We don't want to see articles on topics that have been thoroughly hashed through in the mainstream press." Buys 12 mss/year. Send complete ms. Pays $20 minimum; pays premiums rather than a cash payment only if agreed on in advance.

Photos: Send photos with submission. Buys one-time rights.

Tips: "We generally publish only articles that have been published in alternative magazines. Get your article published, and *then* send us a clipping. Be sure to send a copy of the publication in which it appeared."

WASHINGTON MONTHLY, 1711 Connecticut Ave., Washington DC 20009. (202)462-0128. Editor-in-Chief: Charles Peters. 35% freelance written. Works with a small number of new/unpublished writers each year. For "well-educated, well-read people interested in politics, the press and government." Monthly. Circ. 27,000. Rights purchased depend on author and material; buys all rights, first rights, or second serial (reprint) rights. Buys 20-30 mss/year. Pays on publication. Sometimes does special topical issues. Query or submit complete ms. Computer printout submissions acceptable. Tries to report in 2 months. Publishes ms an average of 2-6 weeks after acceptance. Sample copy $3.
Nonfiction: Responsible investigative or evaluative reporting about the U.S. government, business, society, the press and politics. "No editorial comment/essays." Also no poetry, fiction or humor. Length: "average 2,000-6,000 words." Pays 5-10¢/word.
Photos: Buys b&w glossy prints.
Tips: "Best route is to send 1-2 page proposal describing article and angle. The most rewarding aspect of working with freelance writers is getting a solid piece of reporting with fresh ideas that challenge the conventional wisdom."

WORLD POLICY JOURNAL, World Policy Institute, 777 UN Plaza, New York NY 10017. (212)490-0010. Editor: Sherle Schwenninger. 80% freelance written. "We are eager to work with new or unpublished writers as well as more established writers." A quarterly magazine covering international politics, economics and security issues. "We hope to bring a new sense of imagination, principle and proportion, as well as a restored sense of reality and direction to America's discussion of its role in the world." Circ. 10,000. Pays on acceptance. Publishes ms an average of 3 months after acceptance. Byline given. Offers variable kill fee. Buys all rights. Photocopied submissions OK. Computer printout submissions acceptable; prefers letter-quality to dot-matrix. Reports in 2 months. Sample copy for $5.25; free writer's guidelines.
Nonfiction: Articles that "define policies that reflect the shared needs and interests of all nations of the world." Query. Length: 30-40 pages (8,500 words maximum). Pays variable commission rate. Sometimes pays the expenses of writers on assignment.
Tips: "By providing a forum for many younger or previously unheard voices, including those from Europe, Asia, Africa, and Latin America, we hope to replace lingering illusions and fears with new priorities and aspirations. Articles submitted on speculation very rarely suit our particular needs—the writers clearly haven't taken time to study the kind of article we publish."

‡**WORLD'S FAIR**, World's Fair, Inc., Box 339, Corte Madera CA 94925. (415)924-6035. Editor: Alfred Heller. 75% freelance written. Quarterly magazine covering fairs and expositions, (past, present and future). "The people, politics and pageantry of fairs and expositions, in historical perspective; lively, good-humored articles of fact and analysis." Circ. 5,000. Pays on acceptance. Publishes ms an average of 3 months after acceptance. Byline given. Offers 50% kill fee. Buys all rights. Photocopied submissions OK. Computer printout submissions OK; prefers letter-quality to dot-matrix. Reports in 3 weeks. Free writer's guidelines.
Nonfiction: Essays, historical/nostalgic, humor, interview/profile, personal experience and photo feature. Buys 10-12 mss/year. Query with published clips. Length: 750-3,000 words. Pays $50-400. Sometimes pays expenses of writers on assignment.
Photos: State availability of photos or line drawings with submission. Reviews contact sheets and 8x10 b&w prints. Identification of subjects required. Buys one-time rights.
Tips: Looking for "correspondents in cities planning major expositions, in the U.S. and abroad."

Psychology and Self-Improvement

These publications focus on psychological topics, how and why readers can improve their own outlooks, and how to understand people in general. Many General Interest publications also publish articles in these areas.

‡**COA REVIEW, Newsletter for Children of Alcoholics**, Thomas W. Perrin Inc., Box 190, Rutherford NJ 07070. (201)460-7912. Contact: Editor. 50% freelance written. A bimonthly newsletter for children of alco-

holics; also covers co-dependency. "Articles must appeal to both professional therapists and the layperson. They must be well documented and free from jargon." Pays on publication. Byline given. Offers 100% kill fee. Buys first or second serial (reprint) rights. Submit seasonal/holiday material 1 year in advance. Previously published submissions OK. Query for electronic submissions. Computer printout submissions OK. Reports in 3 weeks on queries; 3 months on mss. Sample copy $1; free writer's guidelines.

Nonfiction: Book excerpts, essays, expose, general interest, historical/nostalgic, how-to, humor, interview/ profile, opinion and technical. No poetry, photos or fiction. Buys 6-10 mss/year. Query with or without published clips, or send complete ms. No minimum or maximum length. Pays $25. "Authors receive 6 copies of newsletter in which their work is published."

Tips: "Attitudes of compassion and love toward the alcoholic and the family are essential. Knowledge of the dynamics of self help groups is very important."

‡DAILY DEVELOPMENT, Carlson Learning Network, 12755 State Highway 55, Minneapolis MN 55441. (612)559-2322. Editor: Barbara J. Winter. 80% freelance written. A monthly booklet encouraging personal growth and motivation. "*Daily Development* is a how-to publication focusing on positive thinking, the psychology of winning and self-motivation." Estab. 1986. Pays on publication. Byline given. Buys first and second serial (reprint) rights. Submit seasonal/holiday material 3 months in advance. Simultaneous, photocopied and previously published submissions OK. Reports in 1 month. Free sample copy and writer's guidelines for #10 SAE with 1 first class stamp.

Nonfiction: Essays, how-to, humor, inspirational, interview/profile and personal experience. No "preachy" articles. Buys 250+ mss/year. Send complete ms. Length: 200 words maximum. Pays $35-65.

JOURNAL OF GRAPHOANALYSIS, 111 N. Canal St., Chicago IL 60606. Editor: V. Peter Ferrara. For an audience interested in self-improvement. Monthly. Buys all rights. Pays negotiable kill fee. Byline given. Pays on acceptance. Reports on submissions in 1 month.

Nonfiction: Self-improvement material helpful for ambitious, alert, mature people. Applied psychology and personality studies, techniques of effective living, etc.; all written from intellectual approach by qualified writers in psychology, counseling and teaching, preferably with degrees. Length: 2,000 words. Pays about 5¢/ word.

‡NEW DIMENSIONS, Foundation of Human Understanding, 111 NE Evelyn St., Grants Pass OR 97526. (503)479-0549. 75% freelance written. A monthly magazine for "all ages with a non-denominational, self-help or common-sense perspective on virtually any subject." Circ. 6,500. Pays on publication or acceptance (negotiable). Publishes ms an average of 3 months after acceptance. Byline sometimes given. Buys one-time rights. Submit seasonal/holiday material 2 months in advance. Simultaneous, photocopied and previously published submissions OK. Computer printout submissions OK; prefers letter-quality to dot-matrix. Free sample copy.

Nonfiction: Book excerpts, essays, exposes, general interest, humor, inspirational, interview/profile, opinion, personal experience, photo features and religious. Length: 500 words. Pays $15-50.

Photos: State availability of photos or send photos with submission. Reviews contact sheets, negatives, transparencies (35mm) or prints (8x10). Offers $10-50/photo. Buys one-time rights.

Columns/Departments: Editor: David Kupelian. Point of View (open forum to argue/augment articles in previous issues) 200 words; Forum (open forum on people's opinions on current events/personals) 200 words; Education (insights about learning, alternatives to public schooling) 200-900 words; Science (interesting scientific/nature coincidences) 500+ words; Review (book/movie reviews) 200-400 words; Insights and Outrages (personal stands on various issues) 200-600 words; Political Sense (conservative viewpoints in the political arena) 300-900 words; and Health (reprints usually from other magazines) 300-900 words. Query or send complete ms. No payment.

Fiction: Editor: David Kupelian. Adventure and religious. Query with or without published clips or send complete ms. Length: 500-1,000. Pays $15-50.

Tips: "Areas open to all freelance writers are current event comments, movie reviews, science stories, conservative viewpoints on political subjects, moral value-type articles, and inconoclastic reviews regarding religious subjects—conservative, of course."

NEW FRONTIER, Magazine of Transformation, New Frontier Education Society, 129 N. 13th St., Philadelphia PA 19107. (215)567-1685. Editor: Sw. Virato. 40% freelance written. Prefers to work with published/ established writers; works with a small number of new/unpublished writers each year. Monthly magazine covering the New Age, holistic health and New Age music. "The writer must be consciously aware, holistically oriented, familiar with New Age subjects." Circ. 35,000. Pays on publication. Publishes ms an average of 3 months after acceptance. Byline given. Buys first serial rights, one-time rights and second serial (reprint) rights. Submit seasonal/holiday material 3 months in advance. Simultaneous queries, and simultaneous and photocopied submissions OK. Query for electronic submissions. Computer printout submissions acceptable; prefers letter-quality to dot-matrix. Reports in 3 weeks on queries; 2 months on mss. Sample copy and writer's guidelines for $2 and 10x12 SAE.

Nonfiction: General interest, humor, inspirational, opinion, personal experience, photo feature, parapsychology and self-help material. "Don't send anything aggressive, overtly sexual or negative." Buys 5-10 mss/year. Query with published clips. Length: 750-3,000 words. Pays $35-250. Sometimes pays expenses of writers on assignment.

Photos: Send photos with query. Pays $10-50 for 5x7 b&w prints. Captions, model releases and identification of subjects required.

Tips: "Write a piece to stimulate awareness or expand consciousness. We relish short works that have high impact."

PRACTICAL KNOWLEDGE, 111 N. Canal St., Chicago IL 60606. Editor: Lee Arnold. A monthly self-advancement magazine for active and involved men and women. Buys all rights, "but we are happy to cooperate with our authors." Pays on acceptance. Reports in 2-3 weeks.

Nonfiction and Photos: Uses success stories of famous people, past or present, applied psychology, articles on mental hygiene and personality by qualified writers with proper degrees to make subject matter authoritative. Also human interest stories with an optimistic tone. Length: 5,000 words maximum. Photographs and drawings are used when helpful. Pays 5¢/word minimum; $40 each for illustrations.

PSYCHOLOGY TODAY, American Psychological Association, 1200 17th St. NW, Washington DC 20036. (202)955-7800. Editor: Patrice Horn. Managing Editor: Wray Herbert. 85% freelance written. A monthly magazine covering psychology and the social and behavioral sciences. Circ. 850,000. Pays on acceptance. Publishes ms an average of 5 months after acceptance. Byline given. Offers 20% kill fee. Buys first North American serial rights, one-time rights, second serial (reprint) rights or all rights. Submit seasonal/holiday material 6 months in advance. Photocopied submissions OK. Computer printout submissions acceptable; prefers letter-quality to dot-matrix. Reports in 6 weeks. Sample copy for 8½x11 SAE with 4 first class stamps. Writer's guidelines for letter size SAE with 1 first class stamp.

Nonfiction: Book excerpts, essays, exposé, general interest, interview/profile, opinion, and technical. No inspirational/personal experience. Buys 75 mss/year. Query with published clips. Length: 1,000-3,500 words. Pays $500-2,500. Pays expenses of writers on assignment.

Photos: State availability of photos with submission.

Columns/Departments: Crosstalk (research summaries—contact Richard Camer), and Books (reviews—contact Wray Herbert). Buys 240 mss/year. Query. Length: 300-1,000 words. Pays $150-500. Health/Behavior Dept.: submit query to editor: Joshua Fischman. Length: 1,000-2,000 words. Pays about $750. Work/Business Department: query Elizabeth Stark. Length: 1,000-2,000 words. Pays about $750.

Tips: "Please query first; your chance will be much better."

ROSICRUCIAN DIGEST, Rosicrucian Order, AMORC, Rosicrucian Park, San Jose CA 95191. (408)287-9171, ext. 320. Editor-in-Chief: Robin M. Thompson. 50% freelance written. Works with a small number of new/unpublished writers each year. Bimonthly magazine emphasizing mysticism, science and the arts for "men and women of all ages, seeking answers to life's questions." Circ. 70,000. Pays on acceptance. Publishes ms an average of 5-6 months after acceptance. Buys first serial rights and second serial (reprint) rights. Byline given. Submit seasonal/holiday material 5 months in advance. Photocopied and previously published submissions OK. Computer printout submissions acceptable; no dot-matrix. Reports in 2 months. Free sample copy and writer's guidelines.

Nonfiction: How to deal with life—and all it brings us—in a positive and constructive way. Informational articles—new ideas and developments in science, the arts, philosophy and thought. Historical sketches, biographies, human interest, psychology, philosophical and inspirational articles. No religious, astrological or political material or articles promoting a particular group or system of thought. Buys variable amount of mss each year. Query. Length: 1,000-1,500 words. Pays 6¢/word.

Photos: Purchased with accompanying ms. Send prints. Pays $10/8x10 b&w glossy print.

Fillers: Short inspirational or uplifting (not religious) anecdotes or experiences. Buys 6/year. Query. Length: 25-250 words. Pays 2¢/word.

Tips: "Be specific about what you want to write about—the subject you want to explore—and be willing to work with the editor. Articles should appeal to a worldwide circulation. The most rewarding aspect of working with freelance writers is to see an article 'grow' from the original 'seed' into something that will touch the lives of our readers."

66 *To the maximum extent possible, write only about what interests you, in the way that suits you best; life is too short for allowing much tedium into it.* **99**

—*Poul Anderson, writer*

Regional

Many regional publications rely on staff-written material, but others accept work from freelance writers who live in or know the region. The best regional publication is the one in your hometown, whether it's a city or state magazine or a Sunday magazine in a newspaper. Listed first are general interest magazines slanted toward residents of and visitors to a particular region. Next, regional publications are categorized alphabetically by state, followed by categories for Puerto Rico and Canada. Publications that report on the business climate of a region are grouped in the regional division of the Business and Finance category. Recreation and travel publications specific to a geographical area are listed in the Travel section.

General

INLAND, The Magazine of the Middle West, Inland Steel Co., 18 S. Home Ave., Park Ridge IL 60068. Managing Editor: Sheldon A. Mix. 35-50% freelance written. Prefers to work with published/established writers, and eager to work with new/unpublished writers. Triquarterly magazine; 24 pages. Emphasizes steel products, services and company personnel. Circ. 8,000. Pays on acceptance. "Articles assigned are published within 4 months usually, but pieces in the inventory may remain years without being published." Buys first serial rights and first North American serial rights. "We have always paid the full fee on articles that have been killed." Byline given. Submit seasonal/holiday material at least 1 year in advance. Query for electronic submissions. Computer printout submissions acceptable; prefers letter-quality to dot-matrix. Tries to report in 3 months. Free sample copy.
Nonfiction: Essays, humorous commentaries, profile, historical, think articles, personal opinion and photo essays. "We encourage individuality. At least half of each issue deals with staff-written steel subjects; half with widely ranging nonsteel matter. Articles and essays related somehow to the Midwest (Illinois, Wisconsin, Minnesota, Michigan, Missouri, Iowa, Nebraska, Kansas, North Dakota, South Dakota, Indiana and Ohio) in such subject areas as business, entertainment, history, folklore, sports, humor, current scene generally. But subject is less important than treatment. We like perceptive, thoughtful writing, and fresh ideas and approaches. Please don't send slight, rehashed historical pieces or any articles of purely local interest." Buys 5-10 unsolicited mss/year. Length: 1,200-5,000 words. Payment depends on individual assignment or unsolicited submission (usual range: $300-750). Sometimes pays expenses of writers on assignment.
Photos: Purchased with or without mss. Captions required. "Payment for pictorial essay same as for text feature."
Tips: "We are overstocked with nostalgia and are not looking for folksy treatments of family life and personal experiences. Our publication particularly needs humor that is neither threadbare nor in questionable taste, and shorter pieces (800-1,500 words) in which word-choice and wit are especially important. The most frequent mistake made by writers in completing an article for us is untidiness in the manuscript (inattentiveness to good form, resulting in errors in spelling and facts, and in gaping holes in information). A writer who knows our needs and believes in himself or herself should keep trying." Recently published material: "Canoeing the Crystal," "How Top Executives Use Their Situations to Make Important Decisions" and "Adventures of a Young Balzac."

INTERNATIONAL LIVING, Agora Publishing, 824 E. Baltimore St., Baltimore MD 21202. (301)234-0515. Editor: Bruce Totaro. 60% freelance written. "We prefer established writers and unpublished writers with original, first-hand experience." Monthly newsletter covering international lifestyles, travel, and investment for Americans. Aimed at affluent and not-so-affluent dreamers to whom the romance of living overseas has a strong appeal, especially when it involves money-saving angles. Circ. 65,000. Pays on publication. Publishes ms an average of 6 months after acceptance. Byline given. Buys all rights. Submit seasonal/holiday material 2 months in advance. Electronic submissions acceptable via IBM—Multimate and WordStar. Computer printout submissions acceptable; prefers letter-quality to dot-matrix. Reports in 1 month on queries; 6 weeks on mss. Sample copy $2.50; writer's guidelines for business-size SASE.
Nonfiction: Book excerpts (overseas, travel, retirement investment, save money overseas, invest overseas); historical/nostalgic (travel, lifestyles abroad); how-to (save money, find a job overseas); interview/profile

(famous people and other Americans living abroad); personal experience; travel (unusual, imaginative destinations—give how-to's and costs); and other (humor, cuisine). "We want pithy, fact-packed articles. No vague, long-winded travel articles on well-trodden destinations." Buys 100 mss/year. Query with published clips or send complete ms. Length: 200-1,500 words. Pays $15-200.

Tips: "We are looking for writers who can combine original valuable information with a style that suggests the romance of life abroad. Break in with highly-specific, well-researched material combining subjective impressions of living in a foreign country or city with information on taxes, cost of living, residency requirements, employment and entertainment possibilities. We do heavy rewrites and usually reorganization because of tight space requirements. We are moving toward more how-to and source lists."

MID-ATLANTIC COUNTRY MAGAZINE, A Guide-From the Appalachians to the Atlantic, Country Sun, Inc., Box 246, Alexandria VA 22313. (703)548-6177. Editor: Jim Scott. Managing Editor: Kathy Davis. 90% freelance written. Prefers to work with published/established writers. Monthly magazine of living in the mid-Atlantic region. "Our coverage aims at promoting an appreciation of the region, especially through writing about travel, history, leisure pursuits, outdoor sports, food, nature, the environment, interior decor, gardening, the arts, and people in these states: Virginia, Maryland, Delaware, D.C., West Virginia, North Carolina, Pennsylvania and New Jersey." Circ. 110,000. Pays on publication. Publishes ms an average of 3-6 months after acceptance. Byline given. Buys one-time rights. Submit seasonal/holiday material 6 months in advance. Photocopied submissions OK. Query for electronic submissions. Computer printout submissions (double-spaced) acceptable. Reports in about 2 months. Sample copy for $1 with 9x12 SAE and $1.24 postage; writer's guidelines for business-size SASE.

Nonfiction: Book excerpts (of regional interest); historical (mid-Atlantic history with current news peg); and travel (mid-Atlantic—off the beaten path). "We seek upscale home/decor/garden articles. We are also looking for short articles focusing on regional foods." Buys 120 mss/year. Query with published clips if available. Length: 250-1,500 words. Pays $3.50/column inch minimum; up to $500 for major feature articles. Sometimes pays the expenses of writers on assignment.

Photos: State availability of photos. Pays $35-50 for 35mm color transparencies and 5x7 b&w prints. Captions, model releases and identification of subjects required.

Columns/Departments: People, Places and Pleasures, 250-750 words. Pays $3.50/column inch.

Fiction: Historical, mainstream and novel excerpts of new or about-to-be-published works directly related to region. No nonregional fiction. "We seek top-notch fiction." Query with published clips if available. Length: 1,200-1,500 words. Payment open.

Poetry: "We seldom publish poetry."

Tips: "We are a regional magazine aimed at a mature, active upscale audience who seeks the best in mid-Atlantic living. Articles should reflect the interests of these readers who seek to enrich their lives and experience the good life in the mid-Atlantic. Send us words that sing and articles that capture the romance of the region. Writers should read the magazine before querying."

‡MIDWEST LIVING, A Celebration of the Heartland, Meredith Corp., 1912 Grand Ave., Des Moines IA 50336. (515)284-3006. Editor: Dan Kaercher. Managing Editor: Barbara Humeston. 50% freelance written. Bimonthly regional magazine covering 12 midwest states. Estab. 1986. Circ. 400,000. Pays on acceptance. Publishes ms an average of 2-10 months after acceptance. Byline given. Offers 25% kill fee. Buys first North American serial and all rights. Submit seasonal/holiday material 1 year in advance. Computer printout submissions OK. Reports in 2 months. Free sample copy.

Nonfiction: Essays, general interest, historical/nostalgic, humor, interview/profile, travel, food, crafts, furnishings and gardenings and home decorating. Buys 40 mss/year. Query with published clips. Length: 500-1,800 words. Pays $50-1,600. Pays expenses of writers on assignment.

Photos: State availability of photos with submission. Reviews transparencies. Offers $75-500/photo. Buys one-time rights.

Columns/Departments: Gardening, Viewpoints, Interviews and Humor. Buys 20 mss/year. Query. Length: 750-1,000 words. Pays $350-750.

Poetry: Light verse and traditional (midwestern slant only). Submit maximum 6 poems.

‡NORTHWEST LIVING, Alaska Northwest Publishing, 130 2nd Ave. S., Edmonds WA 98020. (206)774-4111. Editor: Terry W. Sheely. 85% freelance written. A bimonthly magazine publishing information on "people, places of the Northwest from Montana west to Washington, north to Alaska south to Northern Califonria. Country-style information." Circ. 30,000. Pays on acceptance. Publishes ms an average of 1 year after acceptance. Byline given. Buys one-time rights. Submit seasonal/holiday material 6 months in advance. Previously published submissions OK. Computer printout submissions OK; no dot-matrix. Reports in 3 weeks on queries. Writer's guidelines for SASE.

Nonfiction: How-to, interview/profile, photo feature and travel. No poetry or fiction. Buys 120 mss/year. Query. Length: 500-2,000 words. Query for payment rate.

Photos: Send photos with submission. Reviews 35mm transparencies and 5x7 prints. Offers no additional

payment for photos accepted with ms. Buys one-time rights.
Columns/Departments: Query.
Fillers: Facts and short humor. Buys 100/year. Length: 25-300 words. Pays $25 minimum.
Tips: "Query in detail with specific Northwest-oriented material. Include photo support if available. No telephone queries. Allow one-year lead time."

NORTHWEST MAGAZINE, the magazine of *The Oregonian*, 1320 SW Broadway, Portland OR 97201. Editor: Jack Hart. 90% freelance written. Prefers to work with published/established writers. Weekly newspaper Sunday supplement magazine; 24-36 pages. For an upscale, 25-49 year-old audience distributed throughout the Pacific Northwest. Circ. 420,000. Buys first serial rights for Oregon and Washington state. Pays midmonth in the month following acceptance. Publishes ms an average of 4 months after acceptance. Simultaneous submissions considered. Computer printout submissions acceptable; prefers letter-quality to dot-matrix. Electronic submissions OK via modem; call (503)221-8228. Reports in 2 weeks. Free writer's guidelines.
Nonfiction: "Contemporary, regional articles with a strong hook to concerns of the Pacific Northwest. Cover stories usually deal with regional issues and feature 'professional-level' reporting and writing. Personality profiles focus on young, Pacific Northwest movers and shakers. Short humor, personal essays, regional destination travel, entertainment, the arts and lifestyle stories also are appropriate. No history without a contemporary angle, boilerplate features of the type that are mailed out en masse with no specific hook to our local audience, poorly documented and highly opinionated issue stories that lack solid journalistic underpinnings, routine holiday features, or gushy essays that rhapsodize about daisies and rainbows. We expect top-quality writing and thorough, careful reporting. A contemporary writing style that features involving literary techniques like scenic construction stands the best chance." Buys 400 mss/year. Query much preferred, but complete ms considered. All mss on speculation. Length: 800-3,000 words. Pays $75-1,000.
Photos: Photographs should be professional quality Kodachrome slides. Pays $75-150.
Fiction: Address submissions to fiction editor. Short-short stories that reflect the culture and social structure of the Pacific Northwest in a way that relates to contemporary life in the region as well as to the magazine's target audience. New writers welcomed; Northwest writers preferred. Buys 20-24 mss/year. Length: 1,500-2,500 words. Pays $200-225.
Poetry: Paul Pintarich, book review editor. "*Northwest Magazine* seeks poetry with solid imagery, skilled use of language and having appeal to a broad and intelligent audience. We do not accept cutesy rhymes, jingles, doggeral or verse written for a specific season, i.e., Christmas, Valentine's Day, etc. We currently are accepting poems only from poets in the Pacific Northwest region (Oregon, Washington, Idaho, Montana, Northern California, British Columbia and Alaska). Poems from Nevada and Hawaii receive consideration. We are looking for a few fine and distinctive poems each week. Poems on dot-matrix printers accepted if near letter-quality only. No handwritten submissions or threats." Send at least 3 poems for consideration. Length: 23 lines maximum. Pays $10 on acceptance.
Tips: "Pay rates and editing standards are up, and this market will become far more competitive. However, new writers with talent and good basic language skills still are encouraged to try us. Printing quality and flexibility should improve, increasing the magazine's potential for good color photographers and illustrators."

RURALITE, Box 558, Forest Grove OR 97116. (503)357-2105. Editor: Ken Dollinger. 50-70% freelance written. Works with new/unpublished writers each year. Monthly magazine primarily slanted toward small town and rural families, served by consumer-owned electric utilities in Washington, Oregon, Idaho, Nevada, Alaska and northern California. "Ours is an old-fashioned down-home publication, with something for all members of the family." Circ. 223,000. Pays on acceptance. Buys first serial rights and occasionally second serial (reprint) rights. Byline given. Submit seasonal material at least 3 months in advance. Computer printout submissions acceptable; prefers letter-quality to dot-matrix. Sample copy and writer's guidelines for $1.
Nonfiction: Walter J. Wentz, nonfiction editor. Primarily human-interest stories about rural or small-town folk, preferably living in areas (Northwest states and Alaska) served by Rural Electric Cooperatives. Articles emphasize self-reliance, overcoming of obstacles, cooperative effort, hard or interesting work, unusual or interesting avocations, odd or unusual hobbies or histories, public spirit or service and humor. Also considers how-to, advice for rural folk, little-known and interesting Northwest history, people or events. "We are looking specifically for energy (sources, use, conservation) slant and items relating to rural electric cooperatives." No "sentimental nostalgia or subjects outside the Pacific Northwest; nothing racy." Buys 15-20 mss/year. Query. Length: 500-900 words. Pays $30-110, depending upon length, quality, appropriateness and interest, number and quality of photos.
Photos: Reviews b&w negatives with contact sheets. Illustrated stories have better chance for acceptance.
Tips: "Freelance submissions are evaluated and decided upon immediately upon arrival. We need good, solid, well-illustrated 'first-feature' articles to lead off the magazine each month. These receive our best payrate. We are overloaded with second- and third-feature stories already. We will be placing more emphasis on illustrations and layout; good, professional-quality b&w negatives will add to the appeal of any mss. Due to a loss of feature pages, we will be judging freelance submissions much more critically."

‡SOUTHERN MAGAZINE, Arkansas Writers' Project, 200 201 E. Markham 3418, Little Rock AR 72203. (501)375-4114. Editor: Linton Weeks. 95% freelance written. Prefers to work with published/established writers, and works with a small number of new/unpublished writers each year. "This is a magazine for people who live in the South. Each month we probe what it means to be a Southerner today. We examine the culture—high and low—of our region in a critically appreciative way." Estab. 1986. Pays on acceptance. Publishes ms an average of 4-6 months after acceptance. Byline given. Offers 10% kill fee. Buys first North American serial rights. Submit seasonal/holiday material 6 months in advance. Computer printout submissions OK; prefers letter-quality. Reports in 2 months. Sample copy $4; writer's guidelines for business-size SAE.

Nonfiction: Book excerpts, essays, expose, general interest, historical, humor, interview/profile, opinion, photo feature and travel. "No poetry, cartoons, essays on what it feels like to be a Southerner living outside the South, or articles written in dialect." Buys 100-150 mss/year. Query with published clips. Length: 200-4,000 words. Pays $50-2,000. Pays expenses of writers on assignment.

Photos: State availability of photos with submission. Reviews contact sheets. Offers $25-100 per photo. Model release and identification of subjects required. Buys one-time rights.

Columns/Departments: Sense of Place (our keynote column, what it means to be Southern today); Stumping (political story or profile that has resonance beyond county line); Sport (sports in the South); Southern Lit (the world of books in the South; no writer profiles); Bar and Grill (Southern food and drink via essay); Commerce; all 1,200-1,500 words. Buys 72 mss/year. Query with published clips. Pays $400.

Fiction: Southern. No non-Southern fiction. Buys 12 mss/year. Send complete ms. Length: 3,000-5,000 words. Pays $500-1,000.

Tips: "We are looking for stories with an edge, a little topspin, rather than straight-on stories. And, whatever you do, write with compassion. Southern Front, Weekends, South by Design and Southern Lights are most open to freelancers."

YANKEE, Dublin NH 03444. (603)563-8111. Editor-in-Chief: Judson D. Hale. Managing Editor: John Pierce. 50% freelance written. Works with a small number of new/unpublished writers each year. Monthly magazine emphasizing the New England region. Circ. 1,000,000. Pays on acceptance. Publishes ms an average of 10 months after acceptance. Byline given. Buys all rights, first North American serial rights or one-time rights. Submit seasonal/holiday material at least 4 months in advance. Electronic submissions OK via IBM and Xywrite, but requires hard copy also. Computer printout submissions acceptable; no dot-matrix. Reports in 6 weeks. Free sample copy and writer's guidelines.

Nonfiction: Historical (New England history, especially with present-day tie-in); how-to (especially for Forgotten Arts series of New England arts, crafts, etc.); humor; interview (especially with New Englanders who have not received a great deal of coverage); nostalgia (personal reminiscence of New England life); photo feature (prefers color, captions essential); profile; travel (to the Northeast only, with specifics on places, prices, etc.); current issues; antiques; and food. Buys 50 mss/year. Query with brief description of how article will be structured (its focus, etc.); articles must include a New England "hook." Length: 1,500-3,000 words. Pays $150-850. Pays expenses of writers on assignmen.

Photos: Purchased with ms or on assignment; purchased without accompanying ms for This New England feature only; color only. Captions required. Reviews prints or transparencies. Pays $25 minimum for 8x10 b&w glossy prints; $150/page for 2¼x2¼ or 35mm transparencies; 4x5 for cover or centerspread. Total purchase price for ms usually includes payment for photos.

Columns/Departments: Traveler's Journal (with specifics on places, prices, etc.); Antiques to Look For (how to find, prices, other specifics); and At Home in New England (recipes, gardening, crafts). Buys 10-12 mss/year. Query. Length: 1,000-2,500 words. Pays $150-400.

Fiction: Edie Clark, fiction editor. Emphasis is on character development. Buys 12 mss/year. Send complete ms. Length: 2,000-4,000 words. Pays $1,000.

Poetry: Jean Burden, poetry editor. Free verse or traditional. Buys 3-4 poems/issue. Send poems. Length: 32 lines maximum. Pays $50 for all rights, $35 for first magazine rights. Annual poetry contest with awards of $150, $100 and $50 for three best poems during the year.

Alabama

BIRMINGHAM, Birmingham Area Chamber of Commerce, 2027 First Ave. N., Birmingham AL 35203. (205)323-5461. Managing Editor: Ray Martin. 95% freelance written. Prefers to work with published/established writers. A monthly magazine primarily for residents of the Birmingham area, including area Chamber of Commerce members. Circ. 10,000. Pays on publication. Publishes ms an average of 3 months after acceptance. Byline given. Buys first North American serial rights. Submit seasonal/holiday material 4 months in advance. Photocopied submissions OK. Computer printout submissions acceptable; no dot-matrix. Reports in 1 month. Sample copy $2.25 and 9x12 SAE.

Nonfiction: General interest (subject and its relationship to Birmingham, including local individuals who are involved with a particular hobby, business, sport, organization or occupation); historical/nostalgic (focus on the Birmingham of the past, often comparing an area's past history and appearance with its current characteristics); interview/profile (individual's personality in addition to mentioning the person's accomplishments and how the accomplishments were attained; individuals with interesting or unusual occupations are often the subjects of profiles); and personal experience (usually relating the unique experiences of Birmingham residents, often humorous; another type is one which presents the writer's reflections on a specific event or experience). No stories without a direct connection with Birmingham. Buys 144 mss/year. Query with published clips. Length: 4-10 double-spaced typed pages. Pays $50-175. Sometimes pays the expenses of writers on assignment

Tips: "We present Birmingham and its people in an informative, entertaining and positive manner. Rather than reshaping current events and competing with other media on stories having current news value, *Birmingham* prefers to take a deeper look at local individuals who are exceptional in some way. The emphasis of *Birmingham* is always on people rather than things. These people might have an unusual career, hobby or business, but their story always has a tangible connection to our area. *Birmingham* strives for a 50-50 mix of quotes and narrative material. Writers are encouraged to present the atmosphere surrounding their subject as well as descriptions of the individual's physical characteristics."

Alaska

ALASKA, The Magazine of Life on the Last Frontier, Suite 200, 808 E. St., Anchorage AK 99501. (907)272-6070. Editor: Tom Gresham. Managing Editor: Ron Dalby. 60% freelance written. Eager to work with new/unpublished writers. A monthly magazine covering topics "uniquely Alaskan." Circ. 200,000. Pays on acceptance. Publishes ms an average of 6 months after acceptance. Byline given. Buys rights or one-time rights. Submit seasonal/holiday material 1 year in advance. Query for electronic submissions. Computer printout submissions acceptable; prefers letter-quality to dot-matrix. Reports in 2 months on queries; 3 months on manuscripts. Sample copy $3; writer's guidelines for #10 SASE.

Nonfiction: Historical/nostalgic; how-to (on anything Alaskan); humor; interview/profile; personal experience and photo feature. Also travel articles and Alaska destination stories. Does not accept fiction or poetry. Buys 60 mss/year. Query. Length: 100-3,500 words. Pays $100-700. Pays expenses of writers on assignment.

Photos: Send photos with submission. Reviews 35mm transparencies. Captions and identification of subjects required. Offers no additional payment for photos accepted with ms.

NEW ALASKAN, Rt. 1, Box 677, Ketchikan AK 99901. Publisher: R.W. Pickrell. 20% freelance written. Works with a small number of new/unpublished writers each year. Monthly tabloid magazine, 28 pages, for residents of Southeast Alaska. Circ. 5,500. Pays on publication. Publishes ms an average of 6 months after acceptance. Byline given. Rights purchased vary with author and material; buys all rights, first serial rights, one-time rights, simultaneous rights or second serial (reprint) rights. Photocopied submissions OK. Computer printout submissions acceptable. Sample copy $1.50.

Nonfiction: Bob Pickrell, articles editor. Feature material about Southeast Alaska *only*. Emphasis is on full photo or art coverage of subject. Informational, how-to, personal experience, interview/profile, inspirational, humor, historical/nostalgic, personal opinion, travel, successful business operations and new product. Buys 30 mss/year. Submit complete ms. Length: 1,000 words minimum. Pays 2¢/word. Sometimes pays the expenses of writers on assignment.

Photos: B&w photos purchased with or without mss. Minimum size: 5x7. Pays $5 per glossy used; pays $2.50 per negative. Negatives are returned. Captions required.

Fiction: Bob Pickrell, articles editor. Historical fiction related to Southeast Alaska. Length: open. Pays 2¢/word.

WE ALASKANS MAGAZINE, Anchorage Daily News, Box 6616, Anchorage AK 99502. (907)786-4318. Editor: Kathleen McCoy. Managing Editor: Howard C. Weaver. 20-40% freelance written. Prefers to work with published/established writers. Sunday tabloid magazine for daily newspaper. Circ. 60,000. Pays on publication. Publishes ms an average of 30 months after acceptance. Byline given. Buys first North American serial rights. Submit seasonal/holiday material 6 months in advance. Simultaneous queries, and photocopied and previously published submissions OK. Computer printout submissions acceptable. Reports in 2 weeks on queries; 1 month on mss. Sample copy for SAE and 60¢ postage.

Nonfiction: Book excerpts, historical/nostalgic and personal experience. No general interest articles; only material that relates specifically to Alaska. "We prefer warm, human stories." Buys 12 mss/year. Query with published clips. Length: 1,000-2,000 words. Pays $100-300.

Photos: Richard Murphy, photo editor. State availability or send photos with query. Reviews b&w negatives and 35mm color transparencies. Captions, model releases and identification of subjects required. Buys one-time rights.

Tips: "Writers have a better chance of breaking in with articles of approximately 1,000 words. Avoid articles that are too general, clichéd, or don't move the reader."

Arizona

ARIZONA HIGHWAYS, 2039 W. Lewis Ave., Phoenix AZ 85009. (602)258-6641. Editor: Merrill Windsor. 90% freelance written. Prefers to work with published/established writers. State-owned magazine designed to help attract tourists into and through the state. Pays on acceptance. Publishes ms an average of 6 months after acceptance. Computer printout submissions acceptable; no dot-matrix. Sample copy for 98¢ postage; writer's guidelines for SASE.

Nonfiction: Contact managing editor. Subjects include narratives and exposition dealing with contemporary events, popular geography, history, anthropology, nature, special things to see and do, outstanding arts and crafts, travel, etc.; all must be oriented toward Arizona and the Southwest. Buys 6 mss/issue. Buys first serial rights. Query with "a lead paragraph and brief outline of story. We deal with professionals only, so include list of current credits." Length: 1,500-2,000 words. Pays 35-50¢/word. Sometimes pays expenses of writers on assignment.

Photos: "We will use transparencies of 2¼, 4x5 or larger, and 35 mm when it displays exceptional quality or content. We prefer Kodachrome in 35 mm. Each transparency *must* be accompanied by information attached to each photograph: where, when, what. No photography will be reviewed by the editors unless the photographer's name appears on *each* and *every* transparency." Pays $80-350 for "selected" color transparencies. Buys one-time rights.

Tips: "Writing must be of professional quality, warm, sincere, in-depth, well-peopled and accurate. Avoid themes that describe first trips to Arizona, the Grand Canyon, the desert, etc. Emphasis is to be on Arizona adventure and romance and themes that can be photographed. Double check your manuscript for accuracy."

‡ARIZONA LIVING MAGAZINE, AZ Com Publishing, Inc., 5046-C 7th St., Phoenix AZ 85014. (602)264-4295. Editor: Whitney Drake. 70% freelance written. Works with a small number of new/unpublished writers each year. Monthly magazine covering general interest subjects relating to Arizona. "*Arizona Living* magazine is the only statewide general interest magazine in Arizona. Our subscriber base consists of upscale, affluent, on-the-move Arizonans. We don't want to cramp your style, but we demand a solid journalistic approach." Circ. 15,200. Pays on publication. Byline given. Buys first North American serial rights. Submit seasonal/holiday material 4 months in advance. Simultaneous and photocopied submissions OK. Computer printout submissions OK; prefers letter-quality to dot-matrix. Sample copy $1.75 with SAE; writer's guidelines for SASE.

Nonfiction: No "advetorial" submissions. Buys 48 mss/year. Query with published clips or complete ms (preferred). Length: 50-2,500 words. Pays $15-300. Sometimes pays the expenses of writers on assignment.

Photos: State availability of photos or send photos with submission. Reviews contact sheets, negatives, 5x7 transparencies and 5x7 prints. Offers cost of film for photos. Captions, model releases and identification of subjects required.

Fiction: Slice-of-life vignettes (if anything). "We don't generally print fiction."

Fillers: Anecdotes, facts, gags and short humor. Buys 12/year. Length: open. Pays $15-50.

Tips: "Be persistent. Call before you send the manuscript. Call after you've sent it. You can be aggressive without being a pest. Make sure the editor knows your name. Be willing to work for a little less pay on that first job. Remember the editor may be taking a chance on you." Departments most open to freelancers are AZ Best, AZ Flash, Money Talks, Health & Fitness.

‡ARIZONA MONTHLY, Media Horizons, Inc., 3136 N. 3rd Ave., Phoenix AZ 85013. (602)279-7999. Managing Editor: Douglas MacEachern. 80% freelance written. A monthly magazine of general interest features, for the state of Arizona. Estab. 1986. Circ. 30,000. Pays within 45 days of acceptance. Byline given. Offers 25% kill fee. Buys first North American serial rights or all rights. Submit seasonal/holiday material 3 months in advance. Query for electronic submissions. Computer printout submissions OK. Sample copy $2.50; free writer's guidelines.

Nonfiction: Essays, expose, general interest, historical/nostalgic, humor, interview/profile, personal experience and travel. Buys 60 mss/year. Query. Length: 1,500-3,000 words. Pays $500-650. Sometimes pays the expenses of writers on assignment.

Photos: State availability of photos with submission. Reviews contact sheets. Offers negotiable payment for photos. Captions, model releases and identification of subjects required. Buys one-time rights.

Columns/Departments: Arizona at Its Best (items that illustrate the best about Arizonans). Buys 12 mss/year. Query. Length: 750-1,000 words. Pays $50-200.

PHOENIX METRO MAGAZINE, 4707 N. 12th St., Phoenix AZ 85014. (602)248-8900. Editorial Director: Fern Steward Welch. Editor: Robert J. Early. 25% freelance written. Monthly magazine for metropolitan Phoenix and the state of Arizona. "Our publication is edited for residents, visitors and newcomers to the Phoenix area. Of special interest are lifestyle, economy and statewide issue-related stories." Circ. 36,000. Pays on publication. Byline given. Offers 20% kill fee. Buys first rights. Submit special issue material 8 months in advance. Computer printout submissions acceptable; prefers letter-quality to dot-matrix. Reports in 2 weeeks. Sample copy $1.95 with 9x12 SAE and $2.40 postage.
Nonfiction: Expose, general interest, humor, interview/profile, physical sciences and economics. Special issues include Annual Valley Progress Report (August). No pieces without local angle. Buys 100-150 mss/year. Query by phone. Length: 25-10,000 words. Pays $25-1,200 for assigned articles; $25-300 for unsolicited articles. Sometimes pays expenses of writers on assignment.
Photos: State availability of photos with submission. Reviews contact sheets. Offers no additional payment for photos accepted with ms. Offers $25-75/photo. Model releases and identification of subjects required. Buys non-exclusive perpetual rights.
Columns/Departments: Around AZ (anecdotal looks at statewide events, news briefs) and AZ Business (business-related trends, features and personality profiles). Buys 24 mss/year. Query by phone. Length: 400-600 words. Pays $125-600.
Tips: "Telephone the editor with a specific query." Business and health areas are most open to freelancers. "Know subject matter well. Must have multiple sources."

TUCSON LIFESTYLE, Old Pueblo Press, Suite 13, 7000 E. Tangue Verde Rd., Tucson AZ 85715. (602)721-2929. Editor: Sue Giles. 90% freelance written. Prefers to work with published/established writers. A monthly magazine covering city-related events and topics. Circ. 30,000. Pays on acceptance. Publishes ms an average of 6 months after acceptance. Byline given. Buys first rights and second serial (reprint) rights. Submit seasonal/holiday material 1 year in advance. Previously published submissions OK. Computer printout submissions acceptable; prefers letter-quality to dot-matrix. Reports in 6 weeks on queries; 2 months on mss. Sample copy $3; free writer's guidelines.
Nonfiction: Historical/nostalgic, humor, interview/profile, personal experience, travel and local stories. Special Christmas issue (December). "We do not accept *anything* that does not pertain to Tucson or Arizona." Buys 100 mss/year. Query. Length: open. Pays $50-300. Sometimes pays expenses of writers on assignment.
Photos: Reviews contact sheets, 2¼x3¼ transparencies and 5x7 prints. Offers $25-100/photo, Identification of subjects required. Buys one-time rights.
Columns/Departments: HQ Tucson (local business headquartered in Tucson, with national clout); Desert Living (environmental living in Tucson: homes, offices); and Biblioteca (Southwest books and authors). Buys 36 mss/year. Query. Length: open. Pays $100-200.
Tips: Features are most open to freelancers. " 'Style' is not of paramount importance; good, clean copy with interesting leads is a 'musts.' "

Arkansas

ARKANSAS TIMES, Arkansas Writers' Project, Inc., Box 34010, Little Rock AR 72203. (501)375-2985. Editor: Mel White. 25% freelance written. Monthly magazine. "We are an Arkansas magazine. We seek to appreciate, enliven and, where necessary, improve the quality of life in the state." Circ. 30,000. Pays on acceptance. Publishes ms an average of 3 months after acceptance. Byline given. Not copyrighted. Buys first serial rights. Submit seasonal/holiday material 5 months in advance. Simultaneous, photocopied and previously published submissions OK. Computer printout submissions acceptable. Reports in 2 weeks on queries; 1 month on mss. Sample copy $3.25; writer's guidelines for SASE.
Nonfiction: Book excerpts; expose (in investigative reporting vein); general interest; historical/nostalgic; humor; interview/profile; opinion; recreation; and entertainment, all relating to Arkansas. "The Arkansas angle is all-important." Buys 24 mss/year. Query. Length: 250-6,000 words. Pays $100-400. Sometimes pays the expenses of writers on assignment.
Photos: Melissa Thoma, photo editor. State availability of photos. Pays $25-75. Identification of subjects required. Buys one-time rights.
Columns/Departments: Mike Trimble, column editor. I Speak Arkansaw (articles on people, places and things in Arkansas or with special interest to Arkansans). "This is the department that is most open to freelancers." Buys 25 mss/year. Query. Length: 250-1,000 words. Pays $100.
Tips: "The most annoying aspect of freelance submissions is that so many of the writers have obviously never seen our magazine. Only writers who know something about Arkansas should send us mss."

California

BAKERSFIELD LIFESTYLE, 123 Truxtun Ave., Bakersfield CA 93301. (805)325-7124. Editor/Publisher: Steve Walsh. Monthly magazine covering local lifestyles for college educated males and females ages 25-49 in a balanced community of industrial, agricultural and residential areas. Circ. 10,000. Byline and brief bio given. Buys all rights. Simultaneous queries, and simultaneous and photocopied submissions OK. Computer printout submissions acceptable. Reports in 6 months. Sample copy $2.50.
Nonfiction: General interest (topical issues); travel (up to 1,500 words); and articles on former residents who are now successful elsewhere. No investigative reporting, politics or negative editorial. Buys 12-15 mss/year. Length: 2,500 words maximum. Pays $10.
Photos: Send photos with ms. Pays $1/photo used.
Fiction: "Anything in good taste." Buys 20 mss/year. Length: 3,000 words maximum. Pays $10 maximum.

‡THE BERKELEY MONTHLY, Klaber Publishing Co., 1301 59th St., Emeryville CA 94608. (415)658-9811. Editor: Tracy J. Johnston. 90% freelance written. A monthly local, general interest tabloid focusing on good writing and good stories. Circ. 80,000. Pays 15 days after publication. Publishes ms an average of 3 months after acceptance. Byline given. Offers $25 kill fee for features. Buys first North American serial rights. Simultaneous queries, and photocopied and previously published submissions "outside our market" OK. Computer printout submissions OK; prefers letter-quality to dot-matrix. Reports in 1 month on queries; 2 months on mss. Sample copy $2 with 9x12 SAE and 2 first class stamps.
Nonfiction: Book excerpts; expose (local political issues); Berkeley, Oakland); humor; and interview/profile (local personalities). Buys 50 mss/year. Query with published clips. Length: 800-4,000 words. Pays $25-400.

L.A. WEST, (formerly *Previews Magazine*), Santa Monica Bay Printing & Publishing Co., # 245, 919 Santa Monica Blvd., Santa Monica CA 90401. (213)458-3376. Editor: Jan Loomis. 75% freelance written. Works with a small number of new/unpublished writers each year. Monthly magazine of the community of West Los Angeles. "We are a sophisticated magazine with local events and people as our focus, sent free to the entire community." Circ. 45,000. Pays on acceptance. Publishes ms an average of 6-12 months after acceptance. Byline and author bionote given. Buys first North American serial rights and all rights; makes work-for-hire assignments. Submit seasonal/holiday material 6 months in advance. Photocopied submissions OK. Electronic submissions OK on IBM PC/Hayes modem, but requires hard copy also. Computer printout submissions acceptable; prefers letter-quality to dot-matrix. Reports in 1 month on queries. Sample copy and writer's guidelines for 9x12 SAE with $1.24 postage.
Nonfiction: Historical/nostalgic, interview/profile, opinion, lifestyle articles, photo features and travel. No extreme positions, titillation, pornography, etc. Buys 20 mss/year. Query with published clips. Length: 200-1,500 words. Pays $25-500.
Photos: State availability of photos. Reviews color and b&w contact sheets, 4x4 transparencies and 8x10 glossy prints. Pays $35 for b&w; $40 for color.
Tips: "We're looking for well-written articles on subjects that will interest our upscale readers (average income $125,900; average age 39)."

LOS ANGELES READER, 12224 Victory Blvd., North Hollywood CA 91606. (818)763-3555. Features Editor: Anita Newman. Entertainment Editor: Tara Strohmeier. Works with a small number of new/unpublished writers each year. 85% freelance written. Only serious, polished work by experienced writers should be submitted. Weekly tabloid of features and reviews for "affluent young Los Angelenos interested in the arts and popular culture." Circ. 82,000. Pays on publication. Publishes ms an average of 3 months after acceptance. Byline given. Buys one-time rights. Submit seasonal/holiday material 2 months in advance. Simultaneous queries and photocopied submissions OK. Computer printout submissions acceptable; no dot-matrix. Reports in 2 months. Sample copy $1; free writer's guidelines.
Nonfiction: Expose, general interest, journalism, historical/nostalgic, interview/profile, personal experience and photo features—all with strong local slant; moodpieces, possible reprints from other alternative newsweeklies, media analysis—no dull self-analysis. Buys "dozens" of mss/year. Send complete ms. Length: 200-2,000 words. Pays $10-250.
Tips: "Break in with submission for our Cityside page: short news items on Los Angeles happenings/semi-hard news. We are nearly entirely a local publication and want only writing about local themes, topics and people by local writers. Anything exciting."

LOS ANGELES TIMES MAGAZINE, Los Angeles Times, Times Mirror Sq., Los Angeles CA 90053. Editorial Director: Wallace Guenther. Editor: Michael Parrish. 50% freelance written. Weekly magazine of regional general interest. Circ. 1,300,000 + . Payment schedule varies. Publishes ms an average of 2 months after acceptance. Byline given. Buys first North American serial rights. Submit seasonal/holiday material 3 months in advance. Simultaneous queries and submissions OK. Computer printout submissions acceptable; no dot-matrix. Reports in 1 month. Sample copy for 9x12 SAE and 6 first class stamps. Writer's guidelines for SAE and 2 first class stamps.

Nonfiction: General interest, historical/nostalgic, interview/profile, personal experience and photo feature. Must have California tie-in, but no need to be set in California. Query with published clips. "We welcome all queries." Length: 400-1,800 words. Pays $400-2,000. Sometimes pays the expenses of writers on assignment.

Photos: Query first. Reviews color transparencies and b&w prints. Payment varies. Captions, model releases and identification of subjects required. Buys one-time rights.

Tips: "The writer should know the subject well or have researched it adequately. As for style, the best style is when the writer goes to the trouble of employing proper English and self-edits an article prior to submission."

MONTEREY LIFE, The Magazine of California's Spectacular Central Coast, Box 2107, Monterey CA 93942. (408)372-9200. Editor: George Fuller. 70% freelance written. Prefers to work with published/established writers. Monthly magazine covering art, regional affairs, music, sports, environment and lifestyles for "a sophisticated readership in the central California coast area." Circ. 20,000. Pays on publication. Publishes ms an average of 3 months after acceptance. Byline given. Buys first North American serial rights. Submit seasonal/holiday material 4 months in advance. Simultaneous queries, and simultaneous and photocopied submissions OK. Electronic submissions acceptable via Macintosh II, but requires hard copy also. Computer printout submissions acceptable; no dot-matrix. Reports in 3 weeks on queries; 6 weeks on mss. Sample copy for $3.50 and SAE.

Nonfiction: Historical/nostalgic, humor, interview/profile, photo feature and travel. No poetry. "All articles must pertain to issues and lifestyles within the counties of Monterey, Santa Cruz and San Benito except Getaway which covers travel within one day's drive." Buys 75 mss/year. Query with published clips if available. Length: 175-3,000 words. Pays 5-10¢/word. Sometimes pays expenses of writers on assignment.

Photos: State availability of photos. Pays $20-100 for color transparencies; $15-25 for 5x7 and 8x10 b&w prints. Captions, model releases and identification of subjects required. Buys one-time rights.

Columns/Departments: Community Focus. Query with published clips. Length: 250-1,000 words. Pays $25-40.

Tips: "Since we have a core of very capable freelance writers for longer articles, it is easier to break in with short articles and fillers. Ask probing questions."

NORTHCOAST VIEW, Blarney Publishing, Box 1374, Eureka CA 95502. (707)443-4887. Publishers/Editors: Scott K. Ryan and Damon Maguire. 100% freelance written. Works with a small number of new/unpublished writers each year. A monthly magazine covering entertainment, recreation, the arts, consumer news, indepth news, fiction and poetry for Humboldt County audience, mostly 18-50 year olds. Circ. 20,000. Pays on publication. Publishes ms an average of 1-6 months after acceptance. Byline given. Generally buys all rights, but will reassign. Submit seasonal/holiday material 6 months in advance. Simultaneous queries, and simultaneous (so long as not in our area), photocopied, and previously published (so long as rights available) submissions OK. Electronic submissions OK via Compugraphic 7500, 8" disk, hard-sectored. Computer printout submissions acceptable; no dot-matrix. Reports in 6 weeks on queries; 6 months on mss. Sample copy $1; writer's guidelines for SASE.

Nonfiction: Book excerpts (locally written); expose (consumer, government); historical/nostalgic (local); humor; interview/profile (entertainment, recreation, arts or political people planning to visit county); new product (for arts); photo feature (local for art section); and travel (weekend and short retreats accessible from Humboldt County). "Most features need a Humboldt County slant." Special issues include Christmas (December), and St. Patrick's Day (March). Buys 30-40 mss/year. Query with published clips or send complete ms. Length: 1,250-2,500 words. Pays $25-75.

Photos: State availability of photos with query letter or ms and send proof sheet, if available. Pays $5-15 for 5x7 b&w prints; $25-100 for 35mm Ecktachrome slides. Captions, model releases and identification of subjects required. Buys all rights but will reassign.

Columns/Departments: A La Carte (restaurant reviews of county restaurants); Ex Libris (books); Reel Views (film); Vinyl Views (albums); Cornucopia (calendar); Poetry; Rearview (art). Buys 80-100 mss/year. Send complete ms. Length: 500-750 words. Pays $10-25.

Fiction: Adventure, condensed novels, erotica (light), experimental, fantasy, horror, humorous, mystery, novel excerpts (local), science fiction and suspense. "We are open to most ideas and like to publish new writers. Topic and length are all very flexible—quality reading is the only criteria." No cliched, contrived or predictable fiction—"we like a twist to stories." Buys 10-15 mss/year. Send complete ms. Length: 600-4,500 words; "a longer good piece may run 2-3 months consecutively, if it breaks well."

Poetry: Stephen Miller, poetry editor. Avant-garde, free verse, haiku, light verse and traditional. Open to all types. No "sappy, overdone or symbolic poetry." Buys work of 12-20 poets (3-4 poems each)/year. Submit maximum 5 poems. Length: 12-48 lines. Pays $25.

Tips: "Our greatest need always seems to be for reviews—book, album and film. Films need to be fairly current, but remember that some films take a while to get up to Humboldt County. Book and album—we're always looking for somewhat current but lesser known works that are exceptional. The most frequent mistakes made by writers are using too few quotes and too much paraphrasing."

‡ORANGE COAST MAGAZINE, The Magazine of Orange County, O.C.N.L., Inc., 245-D Fischer, Costa Mesa Ca 92626. (714)545-1900. Editor: Janet Eastman. Managing Editor: Palmer Jones. Assignment Editor: John Morell. 95% freelance written. Monthly. "*Orange Coast* is designed to inform and enlighten the educated, upscale residents of affluent Orange Country, California and is highly graphic and well-researched." Circ. 40,000. Pays on acceptance. Publishes ms an average of 5 months after acceptance. Byline given. Buys first serial rights. Submit seasonal/holiday material 6 months in advance. Simultaneous queries, and simultaneous and photocopied submissions OK. Query for electronic submissions. Computer printout submissions acceptable; no dot-matrix. Reports in 2 months. Sample copy $2.50 with 10x12 SAE and $2.25 postage; writer's guidelines for SASE.

Nonfiction: Expose (Orange Country government, refugees, politics, business, crime); general interest (with Orange County focus); historical/nostalgic; guides to activities and services; interview/profile (Orange County prominent citizens); local sports; lifestyle features. and travel. Special issues include Dining (March); Health and Beauty (January); Finance (October); Home and Garden (June); and Holiday (December). Buys 100 mss/year. Query or send complete ms. Length: 1,000-4,000 words. Pays $150 maximum.

Columns/Departments: Local Consumer, Investments, Business, Health, Profiles, Adventure, and Destination. Not open for submission are: Music, Art, Law, Medicine, Film, Restaurant Review ("we have regular reviewers"). Buys 200 mss/year. Query or send complete ms; no phone queries. Length: 1,000-2,000 words. Pays $100 maximum.

Fiction: Buys only under rare circumstances. Send complete ms. Length: 1,000-5,000 words. Must have an Orange County setting. Pays $150 maximum.

Tips: "Most features are assigned to writers we've worked with before. Don't try to sell us 'generic' journalism. *Orange Coast* prefers well-written stories with specific and unusual angles that in some way include Orange County. Be professional and write manuscripts that present you as a stylized, creative writer. A lot of writers miss the Orange County angle. Our writers *must* concentrate on the local angle. We get far too many generalized manuscripts."

‡PALM SPRINGS LIFE, Desert Publications, Inc., 303 N. Indian Ave., Palm Springs CA 92262. (619)325-2333. Editor: Walter H. Bowart. Managing Editor: Becky Kurtz. 50% freelance written. Monthly magazine covering "affluent resort/southern California/Coachella Valley. Printed in full color on the highest quality 70 lb. paper. *Palm Springs Life* is a luxurious magazine aimed at the 'affluence' market. Surveys show that our readership has a median age of 50.1, a median household income of $105,000, a primary home worth $275,150 and a second home worth $190,500." Circ. 75,000. Pays on publication. Publishes ms an average of 3 months after acceptance. Byline given. Buys universal rights. Submit seasonal/holiday material 4 months in advance. Simultaneous, photocopied and previously published submissions OK. Query for electronic submissions. Computer printout submissions OK; prefers letter-quality to dot-matrix. Reports in 2 weeks. Sample copy $5.

Nonfiction: Book excerpts, general interest, historical/nostalgic, humor, interview/profile, new product, photo feature and travel. Special issues include Desert Living Animal/Coachella Valley focus (September); Desert Progress/Luxury Cruises (October); Celebrities/Arts & Culture (November); Holiday Shopping (December). Query with published clips. Length: 700-1,200 words. Pays 15¢/word. Sometimes pays the expenses of writers on assignment.

Photos: Reviews 4x5 and 35mm transparencies. Offers $50-375 (for cover). Captions, model releases and identification of subjects required.

Tips: "*Palm Springs Life* publishes articles about dining, food, wine, beauty, health, sports (especially tennis and golf) and the lifestyle of the powerful, rich and famous. We are always interested in new ways to enjoy wealth, display luxury and consume it. We want to hear what's 'in' and what's 'out,' what's new in Palm Springs and the Coachella Valley, and how to solve problems experienced by our readers."

SACRAMENTO MAGAZINE, Box 2424, Sacramento CA 95811. Editor: Nancy Martin. 60-70% freelance written. Works with a small number of new/unpublished writers each year. Monthly magazine emphasizing a strong local angle on politics, local issues, human interest and consumer items for readers in the middle to high income brackets. Pays on publication. Publishes ms an average of 3 months after acceptance. Rights vary; generally buys first North American serial rights, rarely second serial (reprint) rights. Original mss only (no previously published submissions). Computer printout submissions acceptable; prefers letter-quality to dot-matrix. Reports in 6 weeks. Sample copy $3.50; writer's guidelines for SASE.

Nonfiction: Local issues vital to Sacramento quality of life. Buys 15 unsolicited feature mss/year. Query first; no phone queries. Length: 2,000-3,000 words, depending on author, subject matter and treatment. Sometimes pays expenses of writers on assignment.

Photos: State availability of photos. Payment varies depending on photographer, subject matter and treatment. Captions (including IDs, location and date) required. Buys one-time rights.

Columns/Departments: Media, parenting, first person essays, local travel, gourmet, profile, sports and city arts (850-1,250 words); City Lights (250 words).

SAN DIEGO MAGAZINE, Box 85409, San Diego CA 92138. (619)225-8953. Managing Editor: Winke Self. Editor-in-Chief: Edwin F. Self. 30% freelance written. Prefers to work with published/established writers; works with a small number of new/unpublished writers each year. A monthly magazine emphasizing San Diego; 310 pages. Circ. 60,000. Pays on publication. Publishes ms an average of 3 months after acceptance. Buys all rights, but will negotiate. Byline given. Submit seasonal/holiday material 6 months in advance of issue date. Simultaneous and photocopied submissions OK. Computer printout submissions acceptable; prefers letter-quality to dot-matrix. Reports in 2 months. Sample copy $3.
Nonfiction: Expose (serious, documented); general interest (to San Diego region); historical (San Diego region); interview (with notable San Diegans); nostalgia; photo essays; profile; service guides; and travel. Buys variable number of mss/issue. Prefers query with clips of published work. Send photocopies. Length: 2,000-5,000 words. Pays $600 maximum. Pays the expenses of writers on assignment.
Photos: State availability of photos with query. Fee negotiable. Captions required. Model release required. Buys one-time rights.
Columns/Departments: Topics include Up and Coming (fine and popular arts); Books; Music and Dance; Films; and Urban Eye (San Diego related short items). Length: 500-100 words. Pays $50-75.
Tips: "Write better lead paragraphs; write shorter, with greater clarity; wit and style appreciated; stick to basic magazine journalism principles."

SAN FRANCISCO BAY GUARDIAN, 2700 19th St., San Francisco CA 94110. (415)824-7660. Editor/Publisher: Bruce Brugmann. 60% freelance written. Works with a small number of new/unpublished writers each year. An urban newsweekly specializing in investigative, consumer and lifestyle reporting for a sophisticated, urban audience. Circ. 65,000. Pays 1 month after publication. Publishes ms an average of 2 months after acceptance. Byline given. Buys 200 mss/year. Buys first rights. Photocopied submissions OK; no simultaneous or multiple submissions. Query for electronic submissions. Computer printout submissions acceptable.
Nonfiction: Alan Kay, articles editor. Publishes "incisive local news stories, investigative reports, features, analysis and interpretation, how-to, consumer and entertainment reviews. All stories must have a Bay Area angle." Freelance material should have a "public interest advocacy journalism approach." Sometimes pays the expenses of writers on assignment.
Photos: John Schmitz, photo editor. Purchased with or without mss.
Tips: "Work with our volunteer and intern projects in investigative, political and consumer reporting. We teach the techniques and send interns out to do investigative research. We like to talk to writers in our office before they begin doing a story."

SAN FRANCISCO FOCUS, The City Magazine for the San Francisco Bay Area, 680 8th St., San Francisco CA 94103. (415)553-2800. Editor: Mark K. Powelson. Managing Editor: Judith Kahn. 80% freelance written. Prefers to work with published/established writers. A monthly city/regional magazine. Circ. 200,000. Pays on publication. Publishes ms an average of 2 months after acceptance. Byline given. Offers 33% kill fee. Buys one-time rights. Submit seasonal/holiday material 5 months in advance. Simultaneous queries and previously published submissions OK. Query for electronic submissions. Computer printout submissions acceptable; prefers letter-quality to dot-matrix. Reports in 6 weeks. Sample copy $1.95; free writer's guidelines.
Nonfiction: Expose, humor, interview/profile, the arts, politics, public issues and travel. All stories should relate in some way to the San Francisco Bay Area (travel excepted). Query with published clips or send complete ms. Length: 750-4,000 words. Pays $75-750. Sometimes pays the expenses of writers on assignment.

VALLEY MAGAZINE, World of Communications, Inc., Suite 275, 16800 Devonshire St., Granada Hills CA 91344. (818)368-3353. Editor: Anne Framroze. 90% freelance written. Monthly magazine covering topics and people of interest to the San Fernando Valley. Circ. 40,000. Pays within 2 months of acceptance. Publishes ms an average of 3 months after acceptance. Byline given. Offers 20% kill fee. Buys first North American serial rights. Submit seasonal/holiday material 6 months in advance. Simultaneous, photocopied and previously published submissions OK. Computer printout submissions acceptable; no dot-matrix. Reports in 2 weeks. Free sample copy and writer's guidelines.
Nonfiction: Book excerpts, essays, general interest, how-to, humor, interview/profile, personal experience and travel. "General interest articles range from health to business to personality profiles. There must be a Valley slant. Audience is upscale, mature professionals." Special issues include Health Guide and Local Business. Buys 130 mss/year. Query with published clips. Length: 1,000-3,000 words. Pays $150-500 for assigned articles; pays $100-300 for unsolicited articles. Sometimes pays the expenses of writers on assignment.
Photos: State availability of photos with submission. Reviews transparencies. Captions, model releases and identification of subjects required.
Fiction: Adventure, experimental, historical, humorous, mainstream, mystery, novel excerpts, slice-of-life vignettes, suspense and sociological. Don't submit "badly written personal portraits." Buys variable number of mss/year. Query with published clips. Length: 1,000-2,000 words. Pays $150-300.
Fillers: Anecdotes, facts, gags and short humor. Buys variable number/year. Length: 100-500 words. Pays $50-100.

Tips: "We use published writers only; for beginning writers, send completed manuscript. All articles *must* be tailored for residents of the San Fernando Valley in Los Angeles. Query must be succinct and explain why we would buy the piece and what the specific Valley focus is. We prefer writing that is innovative and possibly experimental in style. Always send clips."

VENTURA COUNTY & COAST REPORTER, The Reporter, VCR Inc., Suite 213, 1583 Spinnaker Dr., Ventura CA 93001. (805)658-2244; (805)656-0707. Editor: Nancy Cloutier. 12% freelance written. Works with a small number of new/unpublished writers each year. Weekly tabloid covering local news. Circ. 35,000. Pays on publication. Publishes ms an average of 2 weeks after acceptance. Byline given. Buys first North American serial rights. Computer printout submissions acceptable; no dot-matrix. Reports in 3 weeks.
Nonfiction: General interest (local slant), humor, interview/profile and travel (local—within 500 miles). Local (Ventura County) slant predominates. Length: 2-5 double-spaced typewritten pages. Pays $10-25.
Photos: State availability of photos with ms. Reviews b&w contact sheet.
Columns/Departments: Boating Experience (Southern California). Send complete ms. Pays $10-25.
Tips: "As long as topics are up-beat with local slant, we'll consider it."

VICTOR VALLEY MAGAZINE, Desert Alive Publishing Company, Box 618, Victorville CA 92392. Editor: Grace Hauser. 90% freelance written. Prefers to work with published/established writers. Bimonthly magazine. Circ. 5,000. Pays within 1 month of publication. Publishes ms an average of 3 months after acceptance. Byline given. Buys first North American serial rights. Submit seasonal/holiday material 3 months in advance. Simultaneous queries, and simultaneous, photocopied, and previously published submissions OK. Computer printout submissions acceptable "if upper and lower case; prefers letter-quality to dot-matrix." Reports in 3 months. Free sample copy; writer's guidelines for 9x12 SAE and 7 first class stamps.
Nonfiction: General interest, historical/nostalgic, how-to, interview/profile, photo feature and local travel. Book reviews, film reviews, controversy and political articles acceptable; also articles on sex and singles. Buys 50 mss/year. Send complete ms. Length: 600-1,000 words. Pays $20-75.
Photos: Send photos with ms. Pays $25-50 for color transparencies; $5-25 for 4x5 b&w prints. Captions, model releases and identification of subjects required. Buys one-time rights.
Columns/Departments: Desert Alive (stories about the animal and plant life in and around the high desert area: what nature enthusiasts can look for, how desert-dwellers can better live with the local wildlife, etc.); History and Lore (stories about the western development of the high desert area); Family Living Today (dealing with family and social relationships, children, self-improvement, popular culture, etc.); and Desert Personalities (interesting locals, not necessarily of prominence).
Tips: "Our readers have expressed a strong interest in local history (Mojave Desert), interesting personalities and living better. Start with wildlife and desert-related activities (rock hounding, prospecting, 4-wheeling, etc.). I'll buy more syndicated material because it's on time, professionally written and costs less."

WEST, 750 Ridder Park Dr., San Jose CA 95190. (408)920-5747. Editor: Jeffrey Klein. For a general audience. 50% freelance written. Prefers to work with published/established writers. Weekly newspaper/magazine, published with the *San Jose Mercury News*. Circ. 300,000. Pays on acceptance. Publishes ms an average of 3 months after acceptance. Byline given. Buys first serial rights, and occasionally second serial (reprint) rights. Submit seasonal material (skiing, wine, outdoor living) 3 months in advance. Will consider photocopied and simultaneous submissions (if the simultaneous submission is out of the area). Computer printout submissions acceptable; prefers letter-quality to dot-matrix. Reports in 1 month. Free sample copy.
Nonfiction: A general newspaper-magazine requiring that most subjects be related to California (especially the Bay Area) and the interests of California. Will consider subjects outside California if subject is of broad or national appeal. Length: 1,000-4,000 words. Query with published clips. Pays $250-600. Sometimes (but infrequently) pays expenses of writers on assignment.
Photos: Carol Doup Maller, photo editor. Payment varies for b&w and color photos purchased with or without mss. Captions required.

WESTWAYS, Automobile Club of Southern California, 3rd Floor, 2890 Terminal Annex, 2601 S. Figueroa St., Los Angeles CA 90007. (213)741-4760. Executive Editor: Mary Ann Fisher. Managing Editor: Bonnie Leslie. 90% freelance written. Prefers to work with published/established writers. Monthly magazine. "*Westways* is a regional publication on travel in the West and world travel. Emphasis is on pleasing and interesting subjects—art, historical and cultural. Our audience is southern California upper-income readers who enjoy leisure and culture." Circ. 475,000. Pays 30 days prior to publication. Publishes ms an average of 6 months after acceptance. Byline given. Offers $75 kill fee. Buys first North American serial rights. Submit seasonal/holiday material 6 months in advance. Photocopied submissions OK. Computer printout submissions acceptable; prefers letter-quality to dot-matrix. Reports in 2 weeks. Sample copy for 9½x12½ SAE and $1; free writer's guidelines.
Nonfiction: General interest, historical, humor, interview/profile, photo feature and travel. "We are always

interested in Christmas/holiday suggestions but need them by May/June prior to season. We do not accept political, controversial or first person articles." Buys 120-130 mss/year. Query with or without published clips or send complete ms. Length: 1,500 words maximum. Pays $150-350. Sometimes pays expenses of writers on assignment.

Photos: Send photos with query or ms. Reviews 35mm color transparencies. Pays $50; $400 for 4-color cover. Captions, model releases, and identification of subjects required. Buys one-time rights.

Columns/Departments: "We have regular monthly columnists for sections/columns except Wit & Wisdom." Buys 24-28 mss/year. Send complete ms. Length: 750-900 words. Pays $100-150.

Connecticut

CONNECTICUT MAGAZINE, Communications International, 789 Reservoir Ave., Bridgeport CT 06606. (203)374-5488. Editor: Sara Cuneo. Managing Editor: Dale Salm. 80% freelance written. Prefers to work with published/established writers. A monthly magazine covering the state of Connecticut. "For an affluent, sophisticated, suburban audience. We want only articles that pertain to living in Connecticut." Circ. 90,000. Pays on publication. Publishes ms an average of 3-4 months after acceptance. Byline given. Offers 20% kill fee. Buys first North American serial rights. Submit seasonal/holiday material 4 months in advance. Photocopied submissions OK. Computer printout submissions acceptable; prefers letter-quality to dot-matrix. Reports in 6 weeks on queries. Writer's guidelines for #10 SASE.

Nonfiction: Book excerpts, expose, general interest, interview/profile and other topics of service to Connecticut readers. No personal essays. Buys 50 mss/year. Query with published clips. Length: 2,500-3,500 words. Pays $500-1,000. Sometimes pays the expenses of writers on assignment.

Photos: State availability of photos with submission. Reviews contact sheets and transparencies. Offers $50 minimum/photo. Model releases and identification of subjects required. Buys one-time rights.

Columns/Departments: Business, Health, Politics, Connecticut Guide, Lively Arts, Gardening, Environment, Education, People, Sports, Law and Courts, Media and From the Past. Buys 50 mss/year. Query with published clips. Length: 1,500-2,500 words. Pays $300-500.

Fillers: Around and About editor—Valerie Schroth, associate editor. Anecdotes and facts. Buys 50/year. Length: 150-400 words. Pays $50 maximum.

Tips: "Make certain that your idea is not something that has been covered to death by the local press and can withstand a time lag of a few months. Freelancers can best break in with Around and About; find a Connecticut story that is offbeat and write it up in a fun, light-hearted, interesting manner. Again, we don't want something that has already gotten a lot of press."

CONNECTICUT TRAVELER, Official Publication of the Connecticut Motor Club/AAA, Connecticut Motor Club/AAA, 2276 Whitney Ave., Hamden CT 06518. (203)281-7505. Editor: Elke Martin. 25% freelance written. Monthly tabloid covering anything of interest to the Connecticut motorist for Connecticut Motor Club members. Circ. 155,000. Pays on publication. Publishes ms an average of 6 months after acceptance. Byline given. Buys first North American serial rights, first serial rights, and second serial (reprint) rights. Submit seasonal/holiday material 4 months in advance. Photocopied and previously published submissions OK. Computer printout submissions acceptable; prefers letter-quality to dot-matrix. Reports in 1 month on queries; 6 weeks on mss. Sample copy for 8½x11 SASE; writer's guidelines for business-size SAE with 39¢ postage.

Nonfiction: How-to (variety, how to make traveling with children fun, etc.); and travel (regional economy or low-budget with specifics, i.e., what accommodations, restaurants, sights, recreation are available). "We are a regional publication and focus on events, traveling and other topics within the New England area. International destination features are written in-house. We do not want to see mechanical or highly complicated automotive how-tos." Buys 20 mss/year. Query. Length: 500-1,500 words. Pays $25-200.

Photos: Send b&w photos with ms. Does not accept color. Buys 8x10 glossies as part of ms package. Captions, model releases and identification of subjects required. Buys one-time rights.

Tips: "If you can get us a story on a travel destination that's unusual and hasn't been beaten to death, and cover the specifics in an interesting and fun-to-read manner, we'll definitely consider the story for publication. We stress a regional slant, suitability (will senior citizens, children, etc., enjoy this trip?), and what makes the particular destination special."

‡**HARTFORD WOMAN, a women's newspaper**,Gamer Publishing, 595 Franklin Ave., Hartford CT 06114. (203)278-3800. Editor: Roberta Burns-Howard. 100% freelance written. Monthly tabloid covering women's issues. "Publication is for and about working women in the Hartford area. Any valid women's issue will be given serious editorial consideration." Circ. 40,000. Pays on publication. Publishes ms an average of 2 months after acceptance. Byline given. Offers $15 kill fee. Not copyrighted. Buys first rights. Submit seasonal/holiday material 3 months in advance. Simultaneous (unless within our geographic area),

photocopied and previously published submissions OK. Reports in 2 weeks on queries; 1 month on mss. Sample copy for 9x12 SASE; postage varies with issue size.

Nonfiction: Expose, general interest (women's), historical/nostalgic, how-to, humor, opinion, jobs and education. All submissions must meet gender and geographic criteria. Special issues include Entrepreneurial (April), Smart Women's Gift Guide (November), Women in Sports (July) and Health (January). Buys 150 mss/year. Query with or without published clips or send complete ms. Length: 500-1,500 words. Pays $25-60. Sometimes pays expenses of writers on assignment.

Photos: Send photos with submission. Offers $7.50-15/photo. Identification of subjects required. Buys one-time rights.

Columns/Departments: Finance (women's financing issues); Autos (women's auto concepts); Careers/Entrepreneurs (experiences, tips and good possibilities); Fashion, and Parenting. Buys 50 mss/year. Query with or without published clips or send complete ms. Length: 800-1,000 words. Pays $35.

Tips: "Telephone the editor. Women writers are given preference over men writers; please don't try the same old angles, we're looking for fresh ideas."

NORTHEAST MAGAZINE, *The Hartford Courant*, 285 Broad St., Hartford CT 06115. (203)241-3700. Editor: Lary Bloom. 50% freelance written. Eager to work with new/unpublished writers. Weekly magazine for a Connecticut audience. Circ. 300,000. Pays on acceptance. Publishes ms an average of 1 month after acceptance. Byline given. Buys one-time rights. Previously published submissions OK. Reports in 3 weeks. Computer printout submissions acceptable; prefers letter-quality to dot-matrix.

Nonfiction: General interest; in-depth investigation of stories behind news; historical/nostalgic; interview/profile (of famous or important people with Connecticut ties); and personal essays (humorous or anecdotal). No poetry. Buys 100-150 mss/year. Length: 750-4,500 words. Pays $200-1,000.

Photos: Most assigned; state availability of photos. "Do not send originals."

Fiction: Well-written, original short stories. Length: 750-4,500 words.

Tips: "Less space available for short fiction means our standards for acceptance will be much higher. We can only print 3-4 short stories a year."

District of Columbia

THE WASHINGTON POST, 1150 15th St. NW, Washington DC 20071. (202)334-6000. Travel Editor: Linda L. Halsey. 60% freelance written. Works with small number of new/unpublished writers each year. Prefers to work with published/established writers. Weekly newspaper travel section (Sunday). Pays on publication. Publishes ms an average of 3 months after acceptance. Byline given. "We are now emphasizing staff-written articles as well as quality writing from other sources. Stories are rarely assigned to freelance writers; all material comes in on speculation; there is no fixed kill fee." Buys first North American serial rights. Query for electronic submissions. Computer printout submissions acceptable if legible; no dot-matrix. Usually reports in 3 weeks.

Nonfiction: Emphasis is on travel writing with a strong sense of place, color, anecdote and history. Query with published clips. Length: 1,500-2,000 words, plus sidebar for practical information.

Photos: State availability of photos with ms.

THE WASHINGTON POST MAGAZINE, *The Washington Post*, 1150 15th St., NW, Washington DC 20071. Managing Editor: Stephen Petranek. 40% freelance written. Prefers to work with published/established writers. Weekly magazine featuring articles of interest to Washington readers. Circ. 1.2 million (Sunday). Average issue includes 4-6 feature articles and 7-10 columns. Pays on acceptance. Publishes ms an average of 2 months after acceptance. Byline given. Buys all rights or first North American serial rights, depending on fee. Submit seasonal material 4 months in advance. Photocopied submissions OK. Computer printout submissions acceptable; no dot-matrix unless near letter-quality. Reports in 6 weeks on queries; 3 weeks on mss. Free sample copy.

Nonfiction: Controversial and consequential articles. Subject areas include children, science, politics, law and crime, media, money, arts, behavior, sports, society, and photo feature. Buys 2 ms/issue. Query with published clips. Length: 1,500-6,500 words. Pays $200-up; competitive with major national magazine rates. Pays expenses of writers on assignment.

Photos: Reviews 4x5 or larger b&w glossy prints and 35 mm or larger color transparencies. Model releases required.

THE WASHINGTONIAN MAGAZINE, 1828 L St. NW, Washington DC 20036. Editor: John A. Limpert. 20% freelance written. Prefers to work with published/established writers who live in the Washington area. For active, affluent and well-educated audience. Monthly magazine; 310 pages. Circ. 144,000. Buys first rights only. Pays on publication. Publishes ms an average of 2 months after acceptance. Simultaneous and photocopied submissions OK. Computer printout submissions acceptable; prefers letter-quality to dot-matrix. Reports in 4-6 weeks.

Close-up

Stephen Petranek
Managing Editor
The Washington Post Magazine

Steve Petranek started his career as a reporter in Rochester, New York, winning the prestigious John Hancock award for finance writing in 1972. In 1977 he moved to Miami, taking on the responsibility for *The Miami Herald*'s *Tropic* magazine. His desire to make that magazine more "controversial and consequential" is evident from the first cover he ran: "a beautiful woman who was deeply suntanned, looking straight up at the bronze globe of the sun. The headline at the bottom of the page was 'Welcome to Skin Cancer Country.' " Petranek came to Washington in 1979 with the same interest in controversy and has worked at *The Washington Post Magazine* ever since.

"I had been looking across the country for a newspaper interested in publishing a magazine that would give *The New York Times* a run for its money," he says. It took longer to achieve this goal than Petranek had hoped, but the new magazine, revamped in 1986, has proven very successful and has increased its staff of writers and editors from 11 to 23.

Petranek, who would rather work directly with writers than through literary agents, says staff members read all of the proposals that come in—although not always all the way through. Very few of the hundreds of proposals and manuscripts he receives each week are well written enough for the magazine, he says. Freelance writers with extraordinary access to a particularly exciting subject have the best chance of being asked to write an article.

Petranek prefers one-paragraph query letters, the equivalent of "a newspaper lead of a magazine article." He looks for proof that a writer is capable of writing the proposed article: either clips from magazines or a list of publications in which the writer's work has appeared. Published stories must be of special interest to Washingtonians, but the writers themselves come from all over the country; the magazine will send "the right writer" wherever the story is.

"We want to touch the emotional values in people rather than the intellectual values," says Petranek about the articles *The Washington Post Magazine* runs. "If we were going to do a story on Lebanon, we would not be likely to send a prototypical magazine writer to Lebanon to soak up the atmosphere. We would probably go to Lebanon and find a family caught in the midst of a city at war with itself, where sons and daughters had ended up on different sides of the battle, and yet the struggle to survive remains." Human values are a constant focus at the magazine—"what motivates people, what makes people do what they do."

A common problem with the articles writers submit is that they are "dramatically underreported." Some writers also have a tendency to "lay their facts out and leave it to the reader to make connections," instead of telling the complete story.

Petranek hopes to see more wit in the magazine in the future, and would also like to find a good columnist on the subject of design. "Writing about the subject of design on a level that raises it above furniture and houses is very difficult to do," he says. The magazine will introduce a column on ethics and ethical situations, in late 1987 or early 1988. Petranek says "the average person makes dozens of ethical decisions every day and never even realizes what's going on."

—Laurie Henry

Nonfiction: *"The Washingtonian* is written for Washingtonians. The subject matter is anything we feel might interest people interested in the mind and manners of the city. The style, as Wolcott Gibbs said, should be the author's—if he is an author, and if he has a style. The only thing we ask is thoughtfulness and that no subject be treated too reverently. Audience is literate. We assume considerable sophistication about the city, and a sense of humor." Buys how-to, personal experience, interview/profile, humor, coverage of successful business operations, think pieces and exposes. Buys 75 mss/year. Length: 1,000-7,000 words; average feature 4,000 words. Pays 30¢/word. Sometimes pays the expenses of writers on assignment. Query or submit complete ms.

Photos: Photos rarely purchased with mss.

Fiction and Poetry: Margaret Cheney, department editor. Must be Washington-oriented. No limitations on length. Pays 20¢/word for fiction. Payment is negotiable for poetry.

Florida

BOCA RATON, J E S Publishing, 114 NE 2nd St., Boca Raton FL 33432. (305)392-3406. Associate Publisher: Tina Loeffler. 20% freelance written. Prefers to work with published/established writers. A bimonthly magazine covering "sophisticated material on Palm Beach County residents." Circ. 13,000. Pays on publication. Byline given. Offers $25 kill fee. Buys first North American serial rights. Submit seasonal/holiday material 6 months in advance. Query for electronic submissions. Computer printout submissions acceptable. Reports in 3 weeks on queries. Sample copy $3.

Nonfiction: Expose, general interest, and interview/profile. No first-person narrative. Buys 50 mss/year. Query with published clips. Length: 1,000-4,000 words. Pays $125-500. Sometimes pays the expenses of writers on assignment.

Photos: State availability of photos with submission. Reviews contact sheets, negatives, transparencies and prints. Captions, model releases and identification of subjects required. Buys one-time rights.

Tips: "Articles should feature Palm Beach County residents. The area of our publication most open to freelancers is features. Be provocative. We use lots of interviews."

CENTRAL FLORIDA MAGAZINE, Central Scene Publications, Inc., 341 N. Maitland Ave., Maitland FL 32751. (305)628-8850. Publisher/Editor: Robert McComas. 5% freelance written. Monthly magazine covering the lifestyles of central Florida. "Our readers are affluent, recreation- and business-oriented residents who enjoy the good life. Content is positive, upbeat." Circ. 25,000. Pays on publication. Publishes ms an average of 3 months after acceptance. Byline given. Offers $25 kill fee. Buys one-time rights; makes work-for-hire assignments. Submit seasonal/holiday material 4 months in advance. Simultaneous queries, and simultaneous, photocopied, and previously published submissions OK. Query for electronic submissions. Computer printout submissions OK; no dot-matrix. Reports in 1 month. Sample copy for $1.50, 9x12 SAE and $1.57 postage; writer's guidelines for business-size SASE.

Nonfiction: General interest (with local slant); historical/nostalgic (local); interview/profile (local); photo feature (local); and travel. Special issues include interior design, boating and shopping (expensive retail). Buys 20-30 mss/year. Query with published clips if available. Length: 750-2,500 words. Pays $35-750. Sometimes pays the expenses of writers on assignment.

Photos: Send photos with query or ms. Pays $25-100 for 35mm color transparencies; $10 for 5x7 and larger b&w prints. Model releases and identification of subjects required. Buys negotiable rights.

Fiction: Humorous and mainstream—"only if it has a local tie-in." Buys 1-2 mss/year. Send complete ms. Length: 1,000-3,500 words. Pays $50-300.

Fillers: Clippings, anecdotes, short humor and newsbreaks—"with a local slant."

Tips: "Focus pieces on the activities of people in central Florida. Query with list of five to ten article ideas."

‡CORAL SPRINGS MONTHLY,Box 8783, Coral Springs FL 33075. (305)344-8090. Editor: Karen King. Managing Editor: Marilyn Tywoniak. Monthly magazine covering people who work and/or live in Coral Springs. "The magazine is distributed to residents and businesses as well as people who plan to move here. 99% positive material." Estab. 1986. Circ. 8,000. Pays on publication. Publishes ms an average of 2-3 months after acceptance. Byline given. Offers $10 kill fee. Buys first rights. Submit seasonal/holiday material 5-6 months in advance. Photocopied submissions OK. Computer printout submissions OK; prefers letter quality to dot matrix. Reports in 1 month. Sample copy $2.50.

Nonfiction: General interest (must interest yuppies or high class), how-to (on home decorating, gardening, fashion and beauty), humor (seasonal), interview/profile (Coral Springs people or celebrities who might frequent here), new products (pertaining to yuppies or high class), technical and travel. "We don't want run-of-the-mill anything. If you can come up with fresh slants or relate something to Coral Springs in any way, we're interested." Buys 60 mss/year. Query with published clips. Length: 500-1,000 words. Pays $25-50. Sometimes pays expenses of writers on assignment.

Photos: State availability of photos with submission. Offer $0-10/photo. Captions, model releases and identification of subjects required. Buys one-time rights.

Columns/Departments: Theatre Insights (area theatre from the inside—not reviews); Business Report (profiles on businesses in the area, or business people); Classic Car (spotlights area classic car owners and their cars); Creative Learning (articles on education—traditional vs experimental); and Cooking (how-to's or profiles on interesting cooks in the area). Buys 34 mss/year. Query with published clips. Length: 500-1,000 words. Pays $25-50.

Filler: Newsbreaks. Buys 12/year. Length: 250-500 words. Pays $10-50.

Tips: "Anything with a fresh angle is welcomed and we'll try to fit it in. Get to know the city and the people here and then query us with your ideas. Cooking, education (creative learning), classic car, personality profile and features are areas most open to freelancers. Keep in mind our family-oriented city and you should be fine. Remember a positive outlook."

FLORIDA GULF COAST LIVING MAGAZINE, Real Estate Magazines, Inc., Suite 109, 1311 N. Westshore Blvd., Tampa FL 33607. Executive Editor: Milana McLead Petty. Magazine published 6 times/year covering real estate and related subjects for "newcomers and local residents looking for new housing in the area we cover." Circ. 420,000 annually. Pays on acceptance. Buys all rights. Submit seasonal/holiday material 3 months in advance. Photocopied submissions OK. Reports in 2 months. Sample copy $2; free writer's guidelines.

Nonfiction: General interest (on housing-related subjects, interior decorating, retirement living, apartment living, moving tips). No personal views. Buys 5-10 mss/year. Query with published clips or send complete ms. Length: 500-1,200 words. Pays $15-125.

Photos: Buys one-time rights or all rights, depending on the subject.

Tips: "Housing features, retirement living, interiors, home marketplace, products and services, and other ideas, are the areas most open to freelancers. Be sure the subject is pertinent to our magazine. Know our magazine's style and write for it."

FLORIDA KEYS MAGAZINE, Crain Communications, Inc., Box 818, 2111 O/S Hwy., Marathon FL 33050. (305)743-3721. Editor: David Ethridge. 90% freelance written. Prefers to work with published/established writers, and works with a small number of new/unpublished writers each year. Monthly general interest magazine covering the Florida Keys for residents and tourists. Circ. 10,000. Pays on publication. Publishes ms an average of 3-4 months after acceptance. Byline given. Buys first serial rights. Submit seasonal/holiday material 3 months in advance. Simultaneous queries and simultaneous and photocopied submissions OK. Computer printout submissions acceptable; prefers letter-quality to dot-matrix. Reports in 1 month. Sample copy $2.

Nonfiction: General interest; historical/nostalgic; how-to (must be Florida Keys related: how to clean a conch; how to catch a lobster); interview/profile; new product; personal experience; photo feature and local travel. Query with published clips. Length: 400-2,000 words. Pays $4/inch. Pays the expenses of writers on assignment.

Photos: State availability of photos. Reviews 35mm transparencies. Pays $5-20 for 5x7 b&w prints; $15-100 for 5x7 color prints. Identification of subjects required.

GULFSHORE LIFE, Gulfshore Publishing Co., Inc., 3620 Tamiami Trail N., Naples FL 33940. (813)262-6425. Managing Editor: Lynn Walker. 25% freelance written. Works with small number of new/unpublished writers. Monthly magazine "for an upper-income audience of varied business and academic backgrounds; actively employed and retired; interested in travel, leisure, business, and sports, as well as local environmental issues." Circ. 18,000. Pays on publication. Publishes ms an average of 6 months after acceptance. Byline given. Buys first serial rights and requests permission for subsequent reprint rights in other publications published by the firm. Submit seasonal material 6 months in advance. Photocopied and simultaneous submissions OK. Computer printout submissions acceptable; no dot-matrix.

Nonfiction: Local personalities, sports, travel, nature, environment, business, boating, fishing and historical pieces. Everything must be localized to the southwest coast of Florida. No political or controversial articles. Query. Length: 1,500-2,500 words. Pays $75-300. Sometimes pays the expenses of writers on assignment.

Tips: "Familiarize yourself with the magazine and the location: Naples, Marco Island, Ft. Myers, Ft. Myers Beach, Sanibel-Captiva, Whiskey Creek, Punta Gorda Isles and Port Charlotte. Submissions accepted at any time."

JACKSONVILLE MAGAZINE, Box 329, Jacksonville FL 32201. (904)353-0300. 75% freelance written. Works with a small number of new/unpublished writers each year. Published 9 times/year. Circ. 15,000. Pays on acceptance. Publishes ms an average of 6 months after acceptance. Buys all rights. Query. Submit seasonal material 3-6 months in advance. Query for electronic submissions. Computer printout submissions acceptable; prefers letter-quality to dot-matrix. Reports in 3 weeks.

Nonfiction: Historical, business and other feature articles mostly pertaining specifically to Jacksonville or Northeast Florida. No fiction or poetry. Buys 30-40 mss/year. Length: usually 1,000-2,000 words. Pays $100-300. Sometimes pays expenses of writers on assignment.

Photos: Reviews b&w glossy prints with good contrast, and color transparencies. Pays $30 minimum for b&w; color terms to be arranged. Sometimes pays the expenses of writers on assignment.
Tips: "Stories with a business/economic and/or northeastern Florida angle are preferred."

JACKSONVILLE TODAY, White Publishing Co., 1032 Hendricks Ave., Box 5610, Jacksonville FL 32207. (904)396-8666. Editor: Carole Caldwell. Managing Editor: Rejeanne Davis Ashley. 90% freelance written. Prefers to work with published/established writers, and works with a small number of new/unpublished writers each year. A monthly city lifestyle magazine "which explores all facets of the North Florida experience—from politics and people to recreation and leisure." Circ. 25,000. Pays on publication. Publishes ms an average of 3 months after acceptance. Byline given. Buys all rights. Submit seasonal/holiday material 3 months in advance. Photocopied submissions OK. Computer printout submissions acceptable; prefers letter-quality to dot-matrix. Reports in 3 weeks on queries; 6 weeks on manuscripts. Sample copy and writer's guidelines for 9x12 SAE and $1.08 postage.
Nonfiction: Exposé, general interest, historical, how-to (general), interview, photo feature and travel. Special issue features golf-oriented material (March material due Jan. 9). No fiction, essays, opinion, religious, non-localized features, humor, or book and film reviews. Buys 60 mss/year. Query with or without published clips, or send complete ms. Length: 600-1,500 words. Pays $150-400. Sometimes pays the expenses of writers on assignment.
Photos: State availability of photos with submission. Reviews contact sheets. Offers $25 minimum per photo. Model releases and identification of subjects required.
Columns/Departments: Living Well (leisure, recreation, home and garden, furnishings, etc.) Ways & Means (personal finance and investment), and Outside (sports and recreation). Buys 72 mss/year. Query with published clips. Length: 800-1,500 words. Pays $150-300.
Tips: "The areas of our publication most open to freelancers are the Escape (travel) and Habitat (leisure, possessions, new trends in consumer purchases) departments. All articles must be localized to the Jacksonville/North Florida area."

MIAMI/SOUTH FLORIDA MAGAZINE, Box 340008, Coral Gables FL 33134. (305)856-5011. Editor: Erica Rauzin. Managing Editor: J.P. Faber. 30-40% freelance written. Works with a small number of new/unpublished writers each year. Monthly magazine for involved, generally well-educated citizens of South Florida. Circ. 36,000 + . Pays on publication. Publishes ms an average of 3 months after acceptance. Rights purchased vary with author and material; usually buys first serial rights. Query for electronic submissions. Computer printout submissions acceptable. Reports in 2-3 months. Sample copy $1.95 and 55¢ postage; writer's guidelines for #10 SASE.
Nonfiction: Investigative pieces on the area; thorough, general features; exciting, in-depth writing. Informational, how-to, interview, profile, local-hook celebrity stories, business stories and repertorial expose. Strong local angle and fresh, opinionated and humorous approach. "No travel stories from freelancers—that's mostly staff generated. We do not like to get freelance manuscripts that are thinly disguised press releases. Writers should read the magazine first—then they'll know what to send and what not to send." Buys about 30 unsolicited mss/year. Query preferred or submit complete ms. Length: 3,000 words maximum (prefers shorter articles). Pays $100-600. Sometimes pays expenses of writers on assignment (with pre-set limit).
Columns/Departments: Humor, business, books, art (all kinds), profiles and home design. Length: 1,500 words maximum. Pays $100-250.
Tips: "We are regional in our outlook, not just Miami, but also Key West, Palm Beach and Ft. Lauderdale. The writer should know, based on an analytical reading, whether his/her work fits our book. We're like most city/regionals: very local, a little brash, a little trendy, and very focused on good writing. We anticipate increased budget consciousness and ever shorter stories. It's time for freelancers and editors to become more businesslike. We welcome your work."

NEW VISTAS, General Development Corp., Corp. Communications Dept., 1111 S. Bayshore Dr., Miami FL 33131. (305)350-1256. Editor: Robert C. Ross. Managing Editor: Otis Wragg. 50% freelance written. Prefers to work with published/established writers. Magazine published 3 times/year on Florida—growth, travel, lifestyle. Reaches residents of General Development's planned communities in Florida (Port Charlotte, Port St. Lucie, Port Malabar, Port LaBelle, Silver Springs Shores, North Port) plus those who own home sites there. Majority of circulation is in Northeast and Midwest U.S. Interested in people, activities, and growth of these communities. Circ. 250,000 + . Pays on publication. Publishes ms an average of 6 months after acceptance. Byline given. Buys first serial rights. Submit seasonal/holiday material 3 months in advance. Computer printout submissions acceptable; prefers letter-quality to dot-matrix. Reports in 2 weeks. Free sample copy.
Nonfiction: General interest, historical/nostalgic, how-to, photo feature, and travel, all Florida-related. Buys 8 mss/year. Query. Length: 500-2,000 words. Pays $100-600. Sometimes pays expenses of writers on assignment.
Photos: State availability of photos or send photos with query. Prefers 35mm color transparencies. Captions required. Buys one-time rights.

Tips: "*New Vista* defines and articulates the dream of living in Florida for a largely out-of-state readership. Stories about Florida living and economics—keyed to General Development's planned communities—are always sought. Familiarity with Florida, and General Development's planned communities is a plus. We usually buy one Florida travel article per issue. Destinations close to General Development communities are best."

SENIOR VOICE NEWSPAPER, Florida's Leading Senior Citizens Newspaper, T.J.L. Publications Inc., Suite 6002, 6541 44th St., Pinellas Park FL 33565. (813)521-4026. Editor: Thomas J. Lubina. Managing Editor: David K. Hollenbeck. 50% freelance written. Prefers to work with published/established writers; works with a small number of new/unpublished writers each year. A monthly newspaper for mature adults fifty years of age and over. Circ. 40,000. Pays on publication. Publishes ms an average of 2 months after acceptance. Byline given. Buys one-time rights. Submit seasonal/holiday material 2 months in advance. Simultaneous and previously published submissions OK. Computer printout submissions acceptable; no dot-matrix. Reports in 1 month. Sample copy $1 with 10x13 SAE and 5 first class stamps.
Nonfiction: Exposé, general interest, historical/nostalgic, how-to, humor, inspirational, interview/profile, opinion, photo feature, travel, health and finance, all slanted to a senior audience. No religious or youth oriented submissions. Buys 40 mss/year. Query or send complete ms. Length: 300-600 words. Pays $15.
Photos: Send photos with submission. Reviews 5x2 prints. Offers $3/photo. Identification of subjects required.
Columns/Departments: Washington Letter (senior citizen legislative interests); Travel (senior slant); V.I.P. Profiles (mature adults). Buys 20 mss/year. Send complete ms. Length: 300-600 words. Pays $15.
Fillers: Anecdotes, facts, political cartoons, gags to be illustrated by cartoonist, and short humor. Buys 10/year. Length: 150-250 words. Pays $15.
Tips: "Travel, political issues, celebrity profiles, and general interest are the areas of our publication most open to freelancers. Keep in mind that *Senior Voice* readers are 50 years of age and older. A working knowledge of issues and problems facing seniors today and a clean precise style will suffice."

SOUTH FLORIDA HOME & GARDEN, Meyer Publications, 75 SW 15 Rd., Miami FL 33129. (305)374-5011. Editor: Erica Rauzin. Managing Editor: Kathryn Howard. 40% freelance written. Works with a small number of new/unpublished writers each year. Monthly magazine of South Florida homes, interior design, architecture, gardening, landscaping, cuisine and home entertainment. "We want beautiful, clever, interesting, practical specific coverage of the subjects listed as they relate to South Florida." Circ. 21,000. Pays 15 days before publication. Publishes ms an average of 5 months after acceptance. Byline given. Offers $25 kill fee by pre-agreement only. Buys first North American serial rights, plus unlimited reuse in our magazine (not resale). Submit seasonal/holiday material 6 months in advance. Electronic submissions OK on Apple IIE or III disk, but requires hard copy also. Computer printout submissions acceptable. Sample copy $2.50; writer's guidelines for #10 SASE.
Nonfiction: General interest (in our subjects); how-to (interior design, cuisine [yes, recipes, but with a South Florida twist] and gardening for southern Florida climate); new product (short); technical (popularized, well-written); and travel (home architecture or garden destinations only). Buys 36 mss/year. Query with or without published clips. Length: 200-1,000 words. Pays $50-300; (rarely more). Pays expenses of writers on assignment by prior agreement only.
Photos: Debra Yates, art director; Virginia Bru, photo editor. State availability of photos or send photos with query. Reviews 35mm, 4x5 or 2" color transparencies or 2" b&w prints. Captions and identification of subjects required. Buys one-time rights plus unlimited editorial re-use of magazine's separations.
Columns/Departments: Homecare—specific home how-to; Garden Care; Ideas; Cuisine; Home Business; Parties; Architecture; and Florida Artists. Buys 36 mss/year. Query with or without published clips. Length: 200-1,000 words. Pays $75-300.
Tips: "We're looking for shorter, more specific stories; more how-to stories; and stronger coverage of antiques, crafts, and other subjects related to design. This is a very specifically focused magazine with an almost parochial local emphasis. The writer must know his/her subject well enough to mesh it with our unique geography, lifestyle and climate. We are increasingly mindful of getting the most for our budget."

SUNSHINE: THE MAGAZINE OF SOUTH FLORIDA, The News & Sun-Sentinel Co., Box 14430, Fort Lauderdale FL 33302. (305)761-4017. Editor: John Parkyn. 50% freelance written. Prefers to work with published/established writers, and works with a small number of new/unpublished writers each year. A general interest Sunday magazine for the *News/Sun-Sentinel's* 750,000 readers in South Florida. Circ. 300,000. Pays within 1 month of acceptance. Publishes ms an average of 2 months after acceptance. Byline given. Offers 25% kill fee. Buys first serial rights or one-time rights in the state of Florida. Submit seasonal/holiday material 2 months in advance. Simultaneous queries, and simultaneous, photocopied, and previously published submissions OK. Computer printout submissions OK; prefers letter-quality to dot-matrix. Reports in 2 weeks on queries; 1 month on mss. Free sample copy and writer's guidelines.
Nonfiction: General interest, how-to, interview/profile and travel. "Articles must be relevant to the interests of adults living in South Florida." Buys about 100 mss/year. Query with published clips. Length: 1,000-3,000

words; preferred length 2,000-3,000 words. Pays 20-25¢/word to $750 maximum (occasionally higher).
Photos: State availability of photos. Pays negotiable rate for 35mm color slides and 8x10 b&w prints. Captions, model releases, and identification of subjects required. Buys one-time rights for the state of Florida.
Tips: "Do not phone—we don't have the staff to handle calls of this type—but do include your phone number on query letter. Keep your writing tight and concise—readers don't have the time to wade through masses of 'pretty' prose. Be as sophisticated and stylish as you can—Sunday magazines have come a long way from the Sunday 'supps' of yesteryear."

TALLAHASSEE MAGAZINE, Marketplace Communications, Inc., Box 12848, Tallahassee FL 32317. (904)385-3310. Editor: William L. Needham. Managing Editor: W.R. Lundquist. 80% freelance written. Prefers to work with published/established writers. Quarterly magazine covering people, events and history in and around Florida's capital city. Circ. 16,000. Pays on publication. Publishes ms an average of 3 months after acceptance. Buys first serial rights. Submit seasonal/holiday material 6 months in advance. Simultaneous queries, and photocopied and previously published submissions OK. Computer printout submissions acceptable; prefers letter-quality to dot-matrix. Reports in 1 month. Sample copy for 9x12 SAE. Query for list of topics.
Nonfiction: General interest (relating to Florida or Southeast); historical/nostalgic (for Tallahassee, North Florida, South Georgia); and interview/profile (related to North Florida, South Georgia). No fiction, poetry or topics unrelated to area. Buys 20 mss/year. Query. Length: 500-1,400 words. Pays 10¢/word.
Photos: State availability of photos with query. Pays $35 minimum for 35mm color transparencies; $20 minimum for b&w prints. Model releases and identification of subjects required. Buys one-time rights.
Tips: "We seek to show positive aspects of life in and around Tallahassee. Know the area. A brief author biographic note should accompany manuscripts."

‡TAMPA BAY, The Suncoast's Magazine, Tampa Bay Publications, 2531 Landmark Dr., Clearwater FL 33519. (813)791-4800. Editor: Gregory L. Snow. Managing Editor: Donald S. Howe. 90% freelance written. Bimonthly magazine. "A lifestyle, 'city' magazine, appealing to upscale, higher income readers. Most editorial needs are local or statewide." Estab. 1986. Circ. 25,000. Pays on publication. Publishes ms an average of 1 month after acceptance. Byline given. Offers 50% kill fee. Buys all rights. Submit seasonal/holiday material 4 months in advance. Simultaneous submissions OK. Query for electronic submissions. Computer printout submissions OK. Reports in 1 month. Sample copy for 9x12 SAE with 11 first class stamps.
Nonfiction: General interest, humor, interview/profile (local), photo feature (local) and travel. Buys 15 mss/year. Query with published clips. Length: 500-3,000 words. Pays $75-300. Sometimes pays the expenses of writers on assignment.
Photos: State availability of photos with submission. Reviews 35mm or 4x5 transparencies and 4x5 prints. Offers no additional payment for photos accepted with ms. Identification of subjects required. Buys one-time rights.
Tips: "Since most of our editorial needs are relatively local (Tampa Bay area), it follows that most of our writers are in the area. For those who are Tampa Bay residents, we are looking for upbeat approaches, fresh ideas, new stories."

‡TROPIC MAGAZINE, Sunday Magazine of the Miami Herald, Knight Ridder, 1 Herald Plaza, Miami FL 33132. (305)376-3432. Editor: Gene Weingarten. 20% freelance written. Works with small number of new/unpublished writers each year. Weekly magazine covering general interest, locally-oriented topics for local readers. Circ. 500,000. Pays on publication. Publishes ms an average of 2 months after acceptance. Byline given. Buys first serial rights. Submit seasonal/holiday material 2 months in advance. Computer printout submission OK; prefers letter-quality to dot matrix. Reports in 6 weeks.
Nonfiction: Tom Shroder, articles editor. General interest; interview/profile (first person); and personal experience. No fiction. Buys 20 mss/year. Query with published clips or send complete ms. Length: 1,500-3,000 words. Pays $200-800/article.
Photos: Philip Brooker, art director. State availability of photos.
Tips: "We would like to receive 500-word essays for the Just A Moment column."

WATERFRONT NEWS, Ziegler Publishing Co., Inc., 1224 S.W. 1st Ave., Ft. Lauderdale FL 33315. (305)524-9450. Editor: John Ziegler. 75% freelance written. Eager to work with new/unpublished writers as well as those who are published and established. A monthly tabloid covering marine and boating topics for the Ft. Lauderdale waterfront community. Circ. 25,000. Pays on publication. Publishes ms an average of 2 months after acceptance. Byline given. Buys first serial rights; second serial (reprint) rights or simultaneous rights. Submit seasonal/holiday material 3 months in advance. Photocopied and previously published submissions OK. Computer printout submissions acceptable; prefers letter-quality to dot-matrix. Reports in 1 month on queries. Sample copy for 9x12 SAE and 73¢ postage; free writer's guidelines.
Nonfiction: Historical/nostalgic (nautical or Southern Florida); new marine products; opinion (on marine topics); technical (on marine topics); and marine travel. Buys 50 mss/year. Query with or without published

clips, or send complete ms. Length: 500-1,500 words. Pays $50-200 for assigned articles; pays $25-200 for unsolicited articles. Sometimes pays the expenses of writers on assignment.

Photos: State availability of photos or send photos with submission. Reviews contact sheets and 3x5 or larger prints. Offers $5/photo. Buys one-time rights.

Columns/Departments: Query with published clips. Length 500-1,500 words. Pays $25-100.

Fiction: Adventure, humorous, and novel excerpts, all with a nautical or South Florida hook. Buys 3 mss/year. Query. Length: 500-1,500 words. Pays $25-200.

Poetry: Avant-garde, free verse, haiku, light verse and traditional. Buys 10 poems/year. Submit maximum 5 poems. Length: 3 lines minimum. Pays $10-200.

Fillers: Anecdotes, facts, nautical one-liners to be illustrated by cartoonist, newsbriefs and short humor. Buys 12/year. Length 100-500 words. Pays $10-200.

Tips: "The writer should be well versed in nautical topics and/or be familiar with the boating scene in Southeastern Florida. If my publication continues to grow as it has, I anticipate buying more and longer articles with more pictures and/or graphics."

Georgia

GEORGIA JOURNAL, Agee Publishers, Inc., Box 526, Athens GA 30603. (404)548-5269. Editor: Jane Agee. 75% freelance written. Works with a small number of new/unpublished writers each year. Quarterly magazine covering the state of Georgia. Circ. 5,000. Pays on acceptance. Publishes ms an average of 3-6 months after acceptance. Byline given. Buys first serial rights. Submit seasonal/holiday material 4-6 months in advance. Photocopied submissions OK. Computer printout submissions acceptable; no dot-matrix. Reports in 1 month. Sample copy $3; writer's guidelines for SASE.

Nonfiction: "We are interested in almost everything going on within the state. Although we specialize in an area, we maintain a general interest format. We do prefer to get pieces that are current that have a human interest slant. We are also very interested in natural science pieces. We do our special focus issues and suggest that writers send for special focus schedule. We are backlogged with historical submissions and prefer not to receive unsolicited historical submissions at this time. We are not interested in sentimental reminiscences, anything risque, specifically political or religious pieces." Buys 30-40 mss/year. Query. Length: 1,200-2,000 words. Pays $25-50. Pays expenses of writers on assignment.

Photos: State availability of photos or send photos with query or ms. Reviews sharp 8x10 b&w glossies. Captions, model releases and identification of subjects required.

Columns/Departments: "We have a short section called Seeing Georgia—a travel column featuring places to go in Georgia."

Fiction: Hugh Agee, fiction editor. "Fiction must be suitable for all ages. Buys 3-4 mss/year. Send complete ms. Length: 1,200-2,000 words. Pays $25.

Poetry: Janice Moore, poetry editor. Free verse, haiku, light verse and traditional. No poetry specifically dealing with another part of the country (out of the South) or anything not suitable for a general audience. "Most of our school-age readers are middle school and older." Uses 20 poems/year. Submit maximum 4 poems. Length: 25 lines. Pays in copies.

Tips: "We are now a quarterly publication, which will limit the number of freelance articles we accept. We have a section of short pieces (3-8 paragraphs) called Under the Chinaberry Tree where we always need good general interest submissions. These pieces are usually on topics not meriting feature article length. See a sample copy for Chinaberry Tree pieces that have been used."

Hawaii

ALOHA, THE MAGAZINE OF HAWAII AND THE PACIFIC, Davick Publishing Co., 828 Fort St. Mall, Honolulu HI 96813. Editor: Cheryl Tsutsumi. 50% freelance written. *Aloha* is a bimonthly regional magazine of international interest. "Most of our readers do not live in Hawaii, although most readers have been to the Islands at least once. Even given this fact, the magazine is directed primarily to residents of Hawaii in the belief that presenting material to an immediate critical audience will result in a true and accurate presentation that can be appreciated by everyone. *Aloha* is not a tourist or travel publication and is not geared to such a readership, although travelers will find it to be of great value." Circ. 80,000. Pays on publication. Publishes ms an average of 8 months after acceptance; unsolicited ms can take a year or more. Byline given. Offers variable kill fee. Buys all rights. Submit seasonal/holiday material 1 year in advance. Photocopied submissions OK. Computer printout submissions acceptable; no dot-matrix. Reports in 2 months. Sample copy $2.95; writer's guidelines for SASE.

Nonfiction: Book excerpts; historical/nostalgic (historical articles must be researched with bibliography); interview/profile; and photo feature. Subjects include the arts, business, people, sports, special places, food, interiors, and history of Hawaii. "We don't want stories of a tourist's experiences in Waikiki or odes to beautiful scenery. We don't want an outsider's impressions of Hawaii, written for outsiders." Buys 24 mss/year. Query with published clips. Length: 1,000-4,000 words. Pays 10¢/word. Sometimes pays expenses of writers on assignment.

Photos: State availability of photos with query. Pays $25 for b&w prints; prefers negatives and contact sheets. Pays $50 for 35mm (minimum size) color transparencies used inside; $150 for color transparencies used as cover art. "*Aloha* features Beautiful Hawaii, a collection of photographs illustrating that theme, in every issue. A second photo essay by a sole photographer on a theme of his/her own choosing is also a regular feature. Queries are essential for the sole photographer essay." Model releases and identification of subjects required. Buys one-time rights.

Fiction: Ethnic and historical. "Fiction depicting a tourist's adventures in Waikiki is not what we're looking for. As a general statement, we welcome material reflecting the true Hawaiian experience." Buys 2 mss/year. Send complete ms. Length: 1,000-2,500 words. Pays 10¢/word.

Poetry: Haiku, light verse and traditional. No seasonal poetry or poetry related to other areas of the world. Buys 6 poems/year. Submit maximum 6 poems. Prefers "shorter poetry." Pays $25.

Tips: "Read *Aloha*. Be meticulous in research and have good illustrative material available, i.e., photos in most cases."

HONOLULU, Honolulu Publishing Co., Ltd., 36 Merchant St., Honolulu HI 96813. (808)524-7400. Editor: Brian Nicol. 20% freelance written. Prefers to work with published/established writers. Monthly magazine covering general interest topics relating to Hawaii. Circ. 35,000. Pays on acceptance. Publishes ms an average of 4 months after acceptance. Byline given. Offers $50 kill fee. Buys first serial rights. Submit seasonal/holiday material 5 months in advance. Simultaneous queries, and simultaneous and photocopied submissions OK. Computer printout submissions acceptable; prefers letter-quality to dot-matrix. Sample copy $2 with 9x11 SAE and $2.30 postage.

Nonfiction: Expose, general interest, historical/nostalgic, and photo feature—all Hawaii-related. "We run regular features on fashion, interior design, travel, etc., plus other timely, provocative articles. No personal experience articles." Buys 10 mss/year. Query with published clips if available. Length: 2,500-5,000 words. Pays $250-400. Sometimes pays expenses of writers on assignment.

Photos: Teresa Black, photo editor. State availability of photos. Pays $15 maximum for b&w contact sheet; $25 maximum for 35mm color transparencies. Captions and identification of subjects required. Buys one-time rights.

Columns/Departments: Calabash (light, "newsy," timely, humorous column on any Hawaii-related subject). Buys 15 mss/year. Query with published clips or send complete ms. Length: 250-1,000 words. Pays $25-35.

RSVP, The Magazine of Good Living, Davick Publications, Suite 640, 828 Fort St. Mall, Honolulu HI 96813. (808)523-9871. Editor: Ceil Sinnex. 30% freelance written. Monthly magazine covering all topics for people who live and desire good life. "*RSVP* is a publication for the upper demographic market of Hawaii. Our readers are affluent, educated, usually professional or entrepreneurial types who have made it big and enjoy the fruits of their labors. Our magazine appeals to society types and aspirants. Articles should be from the perspective of the insider—someone with class and money writing for those with class and money. While the tone is irreverant at times, it is never derogatory of the values of the wealthy." Circ. 8,000. Pays on publication. Publishes ms an average of 10 months after acceptance. Byline given. Offers negotiable kill fee. Buys all rights. Submit seasonal/holiday material 1 year in advance. Photocopied submissions OK. Computer printout submissions acceptable; no dot-matrix. Reports in 2 months.

Nonfiction: General interest, humor, art and collectibles. No articles poking fun at the wealthy or from perspective of the "man in the street." Buys 20 mss/year. Query. Length: 1,000-2,500 words. Pays 10¢/word. Sometimes pays the expenses of writers on assignment.

Photos: State availability of photos with query. Pays $50 for color transparencies. Model releases and identification of subjects required. Buys one-time rights.

Illinois

CHICAGO MAGAZINE, 414 N. Orleans, Chicago IL 60610. Editor: Hillel Levin. Managing Director: Joanne Trestrail. 40% freelance written. Prefers to work with published/established writers; works with a small number of new/unpublished writers each year. Monthly magazine for an audience which is "95% from Chicago area; 90% college-trained; upper income; overriding interests in the arts, dining, good life in the city and suburbs. Most are in 25-50 age bracket, well-read and articulate." Circ. 210,000. Buys first serial rights. Pays on acceptance. Publishes ms an average of 6 months after acceptance. Submit seasonal material 4 months in advance. Computer printout submissions acceptable "if legible." Reports in 2 weeks. Query; indicate "specifics, knowledge of city and market, and demonstrable access to sources." For sample copy, send $3 to Circulation Dept.; writer's guidelines for SASE.

Nonfiction: "On themes relating to the quality of life in Chicago: past, present, and future." Writers should have "a general awareness that the readers will be concerned, influential longtime Chicagoans reading what the writer has to say about their city. We generally publish material too comprehensive for daily newspapers." Personal experience and think pieces, profiles, humor, spot news, historical articles and exposes. Buys about 50 mss/year. Length: 1,000-6,000 words. Pays $100-$2,500. Pays expenses of writers on assignment.

Photos: Reviews b&w glossy prints, 35mm color transparencies or color prints. Usually assigned separately, not acquired from writers.

Tips: "Submit detailed queries, be business-like and avoid cliched ideas."

ILLINOIS MAGAZINE, The Magazine of the Prairie State, Sunshine Park, Box 40, Litchfield IL 62056. (217)324-3425. Editor: Peggy Kuethe. 85% freelance written. Works with a small number of new/unpublished writers each year, and is eager to work with new/unplublished writers. A bimonthly magazine devoted to the heritage of the state. Emphasizes history, current interest, and travel in Illinois for historians, genealogists, students and others who are interested in the state. Circ. 16,000. Pays on publication. Publishes ms an average of 6 months after acceptance. Byline given. Buys first North American serial rigths or one-time rights. Submit seasonal/holiday material 6 months in advance. Photocopied submissions OK. Computer printout submissions acceptable; prefers letter-quality to dot-matrix. Reports in 2 months on queries; 4 months on mss. Sample copy for $1 and 9x12 SAE; writer's guidelines for #10 SASE.

Nonfiction: Essays, general interest, historical/nostalgic, interview/ profile, photo feature and travel. Also, festivals (annual events, county fairs), biography, points of interest, botany, animals, scenic areas that would be of interest to travelers. "We do not want to see family history/family tree/genealogy articles." Buys 75-85 mss/year. Send complete ms. Length: 100-2,000 words. Pays $10-200.

Photos: Send photos with submission. Reviews contact sheets, 35mm or 4x5 transparencies and 3x5, 5x7 and 8x10 prints. Offers $5-50 photo. Captions, model releases, and identification of subjects required. Buys one-time rights.

Fillers: Anecdotes, facts and short humor. Buys 3-5/year. Length: 50-200 words. Pays $10-$25.

Tips: "Be sure to include a phone number where you can be reached during the day. Also, try if at all possible to obtain photographs for the article if it requires them. And don't forget to include sources or references for factual material used in the article."

ILLINOIS TIMES, Downstate Illinois' Weekly Newspaper, Illinois Times, Inc., Box 3524, Springfield IL 62708. (217)753-2226. Editor: Fletcher Farrar Jr. 25% freelance written. Works with a small number of new/unpublished writers each year. Weekly tabloid covering that part of the state outside of Chicago and its suburbs for a discerning, well-educated readership. Circ. 23,000. Pays on publication. Publishes ms an average of 2 months after acceptance. Byline given. Buys first serial rights and second serial (reprint) rights. Submit seasonal/holiday material 1 month in advance. Simultaneous queries, and simultaneous, photocopied, and previously published submissions OK. Computer printout submissions acceptable; prefers letter-quality to dot-matrix. Reports in 3 weeks on queries; 2 months on mss. Sample copy 50¢.

Nonfiction: Book excerpts, expose, general interest, historical, how-to, interview/profile, opinion, personal experience, photo feature, travel ("in our area"), book reviews, politics, environment, energy, etc. "We are not likely to use a story that has no Illinois tie-in." Annual special issues: Lincoln (February); Health & Fitness (March); Gardening (April); Summer (June); Fall Home (September); and Christmas (books). No articles filled with "bureaucratese or generalities; no articles naively glorifying public figures or celebrity stories for celebrity's sake." Buys 50 mss/year. Query or send complete ms. Length: From 1,500 to 2,500 words maximum. Pays 4¢/word; $100 maximum.

Photos: State availability of photos. Pays $15 for 8x10 prints. Identification of subjects required. Buys one-time rights.

Columns/Departments: Guestwork (opinion column, any subject of personal experience with an Illinois angle). Buys 25 mss/year. Send complete ms. Length: 1,500 words maximum. Pays 4¢/word; $60 maximum.

Tips: "The ideal *IT* story is one the reader hates to put down. Good writing, in our view, is not necessarily fancy writing. It is (in the words of a colleague) 'whatever will engage the disinterested reader.' In other words, nothing dull, please. But remember that any subject—even the investment policies of public pension funds—can be made 'engaging.' It's just that some subjects require more work than others. Good illustrations are a plus. As an alternative newspaper we prefer to treat subjects in depth or not at all. Please, no general articles that lack an Illinois angle."

‡INSIDE CHICAGO, Signature Publishing, 2501 W. Peterson Ave., Chicago IL 60659. (312)784-0800. Editor: Deborah Loeser. 90% freelance written. Bimonthly magazine. Estab. 1987. Circ. 50,000. Pays within 30 days of publication. Byline given. Offers 20% kill fee. Buys first rights. Submit seasonal/holiday material 3 months in advance. Query for electronic submissions. Computer printout submissions OK; prefers letter-quality to dot-matrix. Reports in 1 month. Sample copy $2.50; writer's guidelines for SASE.

Nonfiction: Expose, general interest, humor, interview/profile, photo feature, travel, music, art, theatre, design, neighborhood and political. "Do not send anything that does not have a local angle." Buys 60 mss/year. Query with or without published clips, or send complete ms. Length: 1,000-2,500 words. Pays $200 and up. Sometimes pays the expenses of writers on assignment.

Columns/Departments: Snapshots, Music, Art, Performance, Travel, People, Design, Zip Code, Reading and Shopping. Length: approximately 600 words. Pays $100 and up.

Fiction: "We're looking specifically for unpublished short stories by Chicago writers." Send complete ms.

Poetry: "Looking specifically for unpublished work by Chicago poets."

Fillers: Amy Feldman, fillers editor. Needs short pieces for The Front. Buys 30/year. Length: 100-300 words. Pays $25 (no byline).

‡**NEAR WEST GAZETTE**, Near West Gazette Publishing Co., 1335 W. Harrison St., Chicago IL 60607. (312)243-4288. Editor: Mark J. Valentino. Managing Editor: William S. Bike. 50% freelance written. Eager to work with new/unpublished writers. A monthly neighborhood newspaper covering Near West Side of Chicago. News and issues for residents, students and faculty of the neighborhood west of the University of Illinois or Chicago. Circ. 4,500. Pays on publication. Publishes ms an average of 1 month after acceptance. Byline given. Offers 15% kill fee. Not copyrighted. Buys one-time or simultaneous rights. Submit seasonal/holiday material 2 months in advance. Simultaneous, photocopied and previously published submissions OK. Computer printout submissions OK. Reports in 5 weeks. Sample copy for 8½x11 SAE with 3 first class stamps.

Nonfiction: Essays, expose, general interest, historical/nostalgic, humor, inspirational, interview/profile, opinion, personal experience, religious or Near West Side's sports. Publishes a special Christmas issue. Doesn't want to see product promotions. Buys 60 mss/year. Length: 300-1,800 words. Pays $30. Sometimes pays the expenses of writers on assignment.

Photos: Send photos with submission. Reviews 5x7 prints. Offers no additional payment for photos accepted with ms. Identification of subjects required. Buys one-time rights.

Columns/Departments: To Your Health (health/exercise tips), 600 words; Forum (opinion), 750 words; Streets (Near West Side history), 500 words. Buys 12 mss/year. Query. Pays $30.

STYLE, Chicago Tribune, Room 400, 435 N. Michigan Ave., Chicago IL 60011. (312)222-4176. Assistant Features Editor: John Lux. 55% freelance written. Prefers to work with published/established writers. A weekly (Wednesday) lifestyle/fashion tabloid section of the *Chicago Tribune*. Circ. 760,000. Pays on publication. Publishes an average of 1 month after acceptance. Buys first North American serial rights or second serial (reprint) rights. Submit seasonal/holiday material 3 months in advance. Simultaneous, photocopied and previously published submissions OK. Computer printout submissions acceptable. Reports in 3 weeks on mss.

Nonfiction: Essays about some kind of relationship for alternating "He" and "She" column. Buys 50 mss/year. Send complete ms. Length: 800 words. Pays $100.

Photos: Rarely buys photos.

Indiana

INDIANAPOLIS MAGAZINE, 32 E. Washington St., Indianapolis IN 46219. Editor: Nancy Comiskey. Managing Editors: Jane Graham and Brian Smith. 80% freelance written. Prefers to work with published/established writers. A monthly magazine for a "well-educated upscale audience." Circ. 30,000. Pays on publication. Publishes ms an average of 3 months after acceptance. Byline given. Buys all rights. Submit seasonal/holiday material 5 months in advance. Query for electronic submissions. Computer submissions OK; prefers letter-quality to dot-matrix. Reports in 6 weeks on queries. Sample copy $2 with 8½x11 SAE and 39¢ postage; free writer's guidelines.

Nonfiction: Book excerpts, expose, general interest, historical/nostalgic, interview/profile and travel. Buys 85 mss/year. Query with published clips. Length: 500-3,000 words. Pays $40-350 for assigned articles.

Photos: State availability of photos with submission. Offers $30-50 per photo. Model releases and identification of subjects required. Buys one-time rights.

Columns/Departments: General Interest (local slant mandatory), 1,700 words. Pays $125-250.

Tips: "Short 500-word articles are best for new writers. Be professional with the query letter."

INDIANAPOLIS MONTHLY, Mayhill Publications, Suite 225, 8425 Keystone Crossing, Indianapolis IN 46260. (317)259-8222. Editor: Deborah Paul. Associate Editor: Sam Stall. 50% freelance written. Prefers to work with published/established writers. A monthly magazine of "upbeat material reflecting current trends. Heavy on lifestyle, homes and fashion. Material must be regional in appeal." Circ. 45,000. Pays on publication. Publishes ms an average of 2 months after acceptance. Byline given. Offers 50% kill fee. Buys first North American serial rights and makes work-for-hire assignments. Submit seasonal/holiday material 3 months in advance. Computer printout submissions acceptable; prefers letter-quality to dot-matrix. Reports in 1 month. Sample copy $2.04; free writer's guidelines.

Nonfiction: General interest, historical/nostalgic, interview/profile and photo feature. Special issue is the

500 Mile Race issue (May). No poetry, domestic humor or stories without a regional angle. "We prefer stories with a timely or topical angle or 'hook' as opposed to those topics plucked out of thin air." Buys 25 mss/year. Query with published clips, or send complete ms. Length: 200-5,000 words. Pays $35-400. Sometimes pays the expenses of writers on assignment.

Photos: Send photos with submission. Reviews 35mm or 2¼ transparencies. Offers $25 minimum/photo. Identification of subjects required. Buys one-time rights.

Columns/Departments: Business (local made-goods), Sport (heroes, trendy sports), Health (new specialties, technology), and Retrospect (regional history), all 1,000 words. Buys 6-9 mss/year. Query with published clips or send complete mss. Pays $100-300.

Tips: "Monthly departments are open to freelancers. We also run monthly special sections—write for editorial special section lineups."

MICHIANA, Sunday Magazine of *The South Bend Tribune*, Colfax at Lafayette, South Bend IN 46626. (219)233-6161. Editor: Bill Sonneborn. 90% freelance written. Works with a small number of new/unpublished writers each year. Weekly for "average daily newspaper readers; perhaps a little above average since we have more than a dozen colleges and universities in our area." Circ. 125,000. Pays on publication. Publishes ms an average of 3 months after acceptance. Byline given. Buys first North American serial rights or simultaneous rights providing material offered will be used outside of Indiana and Michigan. Will consider photocopied submissions if clearly legible. Computer printout submissions acceptable; prefers letter-quality to dot-matrix. Reports in 3 weeks.

Nonfiction: "Articles of general and unusual interest written in good, clear, simple sentences with logical approach to subject. We use almost no material except that which is oriented to the Midwest, especially Indiana, Michigan, Ohio and Illinois. We avoid all freelance material that supports movements of a political nature. We seldom use first person humor. We use no poetry." Submit complete ms. Buys 100 unsolicited mss/year. Length: 800-3,000 words. Payment is $50-60 minimum, with increases as deemed suitable. Sometimes pays the expenses of writers on assignment.

Photos: "We prefer articles that are accompanied by illustrations, b&w photos or 35mm or larger color transparencies."

RIGHT HERE, The Hometown Magazine, Right Here Publications, Box 1014, Huntington IN 46750. Editor: Emily Jean Carroll. 90% freelance written. Works with a small number of new/unpublished writers each year. Bimonthly magazine of general family interest reaching a northern Indiana audience. Circ. 2,000. Pays 2 weeks after date of issue. Publishes ms an average of 4 months after acceptance. Byline given. Buys first serial rights, one-time rights, simultaneous rights, and second serial (reprint) rights. Submit seasonal/holiday material 5 months in advance. Simultaneous, photocopied, and previously published submissions OK. Computer printout submissions acceptable; prefers letter-quality to dot-matrix. Reports in 2 months on mss. No queries please. Sample copy $1.25; writer's guidelines for SASE.

Nonfiction: General interest, historical/nostalgic, how-to, humor, inspirational, interview/profile, opinion, and travel. "We are looking for short pieces on all aspects of Hoosier living." Profiles, nostalgia, history, recreation, travel, music and various subjects of interest to area readers. Buys 18 mss/year. Send complete ms. Length: 900-2,000 words. Pays $5-30.

Photos: Send photos with ms. Reviews b&w prints. Pays $2-5. Model releases and identification of subjects required. Buys one-time rights.

Columns/Departments: Listen To This (opinion pieces of about 1,000 words); Here and There (travel pieces in or near Indiana); Remember? (nostalgia, up to 2,000 words); Keeping Up (mental, spiritual, self-help, up-lifting, etc., to 2,000 words); and My Space (writers 19 years old and under, to 1,000 words). Buys 30-40 mss/year. Send complete ms. Length: 800-2,000 words. Pays $5-30.

Fiction: Humorous, mainstream, mystery and romance. Needs short stories of about 2,000 words. Buys 6-8 mss/year. Send complete ms. Length: 900-3,000 words. Pays $5-30.

Poetry: Free verse, light verse and traditional. Buys 30-40/year. Submit maximum 6 poems. Length: 4-48 lines. Pays $1-4 for poetry featured separately; pays one copy for poetry used as filler or on poetry page.

Fillers: Anecdotes and short humor. Buys 6-8/year. Length: 300 words maximum. Pays $3 maximum. Pays one copy for material under 300 words.

Tips: "All departments are open. Keep it light—keep it tight. Send short cover letter about yourself."

Iowa

THE IOWAN MAGAZINE, Mid-America Publishing Corp., 214 9th St., Des Moines IA 50309. (515)282-8220. Editor: Charles W. Roberts. 85% freelance written. Quarterly magazine covering history, people, places and points of interest in Iowa. Circ. 24,000. Pays on publication. Publishes ms an average of 1 year after acceptance. Byline given. Buys first serial rights. Submit seasonal/holiday material 5 months in advance. Photocopied and previously published submissions OK. Computer printout submissions acceptable. Reports in 3 months. Sample copy for $3.75, 9x12 SAE and $2 postage; free writer's guidelines.

Nonfiction: General interest, historical (history as in American heritage, not personal reminiscence), interview/profile, and travel. No "articles from nonIowans who come for a visit and wish to give their impression of the state." Buys 32 mss/year. Query with published clips. Length: 750-3,000 words. Pays $75-400. Sometimes pays expenses of writers on assignment.

Photos: Send photos with ms. Pays $20 for b&w; $50 for color transparency. Captions and identification of subjects required.

Tips: "If you are writing about Iowa, write on a specific topic. Don't be *too* general. Write a query letter with maybe two or three ideas."

Kentucky

KENTUCKY HAPPY HUNTING GROUND, Kentucky Dept. of Fish and Wildlife Resources, 1 Game Farm Rd., Frankfort KY 40601. (502)564-4336. Editor: John Wilson. Less than 10% freelance written. Works with a small number of new/unpublished writers each year. A bimonthly state conservation magazine covering hunting, fishing, general outdoor recreation, conservation of wildlife and other natural resources. Circ. 35,000. Pays on publication. Publishes ms an average of 6 months after acceptance. Byline given. Buys one-time rights. Submit seasonal/holiday material 3 months in advance. Previously published submissions OK. Computer printout submissions acceptable. Reports in 3 weeks on queries; 2 months on mss. Free sample copy.

Nonfiction: General interest, historical/nostalgic, how-to, humor, interview/profile, personal experience and photo feature. All articles should deal with some aspect of the natural world, with outdoor recreation or with natural resources conservation or management, and should relate to Kentucky. "No 'Me and Joe' stories (i.e., accounts of specific trips); nothing off-color or otherwise unsuitable for a state publication." Buys 3-6 mss/year. Query or send complete ms. Length: 500-2,000 words. Pays $50-150 (with photos).

Photos: State availability of photos with query; send photos with accompanying ms. Reviews color transparencies (2¼ preferred, 35mm acceptable) and b&w prints (5x7 minimum). No separate payment for photos, but amount paid for article will be determined by number of photos used.

Tips: "We would be much more kindly disposed toward articles accompanied by several good photographs (or other graphic material) than to those without. We will probably be mostly staff-written in 1988 due to budget restraints."

RURAL KENTUCKIAN, Box 32170, Louisville KY 40232. (502)451-2430. Editor: Gary W. Luhr. 75% freelance written. Prefers to work with published/established writers. Monthly feature magazine primarily for Kentucky residents. Circ. 300,000. Pays on acceptance. Publishes ms an average of 8 months after acceptance. Byline given. Not copyrighted. Buys first serial rights for Kentucky. Submit seasonal/holiday material at least 6 months in advance. Will consider photocopied, previously published and simultaneous submissions (if previously published) and/or simultaneous submissions if outside Kentucky. Computer printout submissions acceptable; prefers letter-quality to dot-matrix. Reports in 2 weeks. Free sample copy.

Nonfiction: Prefers Kentucky-related profiles (people, places or events), history, biography, recreation, travel, leisure or lifestyle articles or book excerpts; articles on contemporary subjects of general public interest and general consumer-related features including service pieces. Publishes some humorous and first-person articles of exceptional quality and opinion pieces from qualified authorities. No general nostalgia. Buys 24-36 mss/year. Query or send complete ms. Length: 800-2000 words. Pays $50-$250. Sometimes pays the expenses of writers on assignment.

Photos: State availability of photos. Reviews color slide transparencies and b&w prints. Identification of subjects required. Payment included in payment for ms. Pays extra if photo used on cover.

Tips: "The quality of writing and reporting (factual, objective, thorough) is considered in setting payment price. We prefer well-documented pieces filled with quotes and anecdotes. Avoid boosterism. Writers need not confine themselves to subjects suited only to a rural audience but should avoid subjects of a strictly metropolitian nature. Well-researched, well-written feature articles, particularly on subjects of a serious nature, are given preference over light-weight material. Despite its name, *Rural Kentuckian* is not a farm publication."

Louisiana

NEW ORLEANS MAGAZINE, Box 26815, New Orleans LA 70186. (504)246-2700. Editor: Sherry Spear. 50% freelance written. Monthly magazine; 96 pages. Circ. 37,000. Pays on publication. Buys first-time rights. Byline given. Submit seasonal/holiday material 4 months in advance. Computer printout submissions acceptable; prefers letter-quality to dot-matrix. Reports in 2 months. Publishes ms an average of 4 months after acceptance.

Nonfiction: General interest, interview and profile. Buys 3 mss/issue. Submit complete ms. Length: 1,200-3,000 words. Pays $100-500.

Photos: John Maher, art director. State availability of photos with ms. Captions required. Buys one-time rights. Model releases required.

SUNDAY ADVOCATE MAGAZINE, Box 588, Baton Rouge LA 70821. (504)383-1111, ext. 319. Editor: Larry Catalanello. 5% freelance written. "We are backlogged, but still welcome submissions." Prefers to work with published/established writers; works with a small number of new/unpublished writers each year. Byline given. Pays on publication. Publishes ms an average of 1 month after acceptance. Query for electronic submissions. Computer printout submissions acceptable; prefers letter-quality to dot-matrix.

Nonfiction and Photos: Well-illustrated, short articles; must have local, area or Louisiana angle, in that order of preference. Also interested in travel pieces. Photos purchased with mss. Rates vary. Sometimes pays the expenses of writers on assignment.

Tips: "Styles may vary. Subject matter may vary. Local interest is most important. No more than 4-5 typed, double-spaced pages."

Maine

DOWN EAST MAGAZINE, Camden ME 04843. (207)594-9544. Editor: Davis Thomas. 50% freelance written. Works with a small number of new/unpublished writers each year. Emphasizes Maine people, places, events and heritage. Monthly magazine. Circ. 80,000. Pays on acceptance for text; on publication for photos. Publishes ms an average of 6 months after acceptance. Byline given. Offers 15% kill fee. Buys first North American serial rights. Phone queries OK. Submit seasonal/holiday material 6 months in advance. Computer printout submissions acceptable; prefers letter-quality to dot-matrix. Reports in 1 month. Sample copy $3.50; writer's guidelines with SASE.

Nonfiction: Submit to Manuscript Editor. All material must be directly related to Maine: profiles, biographies, nature, gardening, nautical, travel, recreation, historical, humorous, nostalgic pieces, and photo essays and stories. Buys 40 unsolicited mss/year. Length: 600-2,500 words. Pays up to $400, depending on subject and quality. Sometimes pays the expenses of writers on assignment.

Photos: Purchases on assignment or with accompanying ms. Accepts 35mm color transparencies and 8x10 b&w. Also purchases single b&w and color scenics for calendars. Each photo or transparency must bear photographer's name. Captions and model releases required. Pays page rate of $50.

Columns/Departments: Short Travel (600-1,500 words, tightly written travelogs focusing on small geographic areas of scenic, historical or local interest); I Remember (short personal accounts of some incident in Maine, less than 1,000 words); and It Happened Down East (1-2 paragraphs, humorous Maine anecdotes). Pay depends on subject and quality.

Tips: "We depend on freelance writers for the bulk of our material—mostly on assignment and mostly from those known to us; but unsolicited submissions are valued."

GREATER PORTLAND MAGAZINE, Chamber of Commerce of the Greater Portland Region, 142 Free St., Portland ME 04101. (207)772-2811. Editor: Daniel W. Weeks. 75% freelance written. Works with a small number of new/unpublished writers each year. "We enjoy offering talented and enthusiastic new writers the kind of editorial guidance they need to become professional freelancers." A quarterly magazine covering metropolitan and island lifestyles of Greater Portland. "We cover the arts, night life, islands, people, and progressive business in and around Greater Portland." Circ. 10,000. Pays on acceptance. Publishes ms an average of 2 months after acceptance. Byline given. Buys first serial rights or second serial reprint rights. Submit seasonal/holiday material 6 months in advance. Query for electronic submissions. Computer printout submissions acceptable; prefers letter-quality to dot-matrix. Reports in 1 week on queries; 2 weeks on mss. Free sample copy with $1 postage.

Nonfiction: Articles about people, places, events, institutions and the arts in greater Portland. "*Greater Portland* is largely freelance written. We are looking for well-researched, well-focused essayistic features. First person essays are welcome." Buys 20 mss/year. Query with published clips or send complete ms. Length: 1,500-3,500 words. Pays 10¢/word maximum. Sometimes pays expenses of writers on assignment.

Photos: Buys b&w and color slides with or without ms. Captions required.

Tips: "Send some clips with several story ideas. We're looking for informal, essayistic features structured around a well-defined point or theme. A lively, carefully-crafted presentation is as important as a good subject. We enjoy working closely with talented writers of varying experience to produce a literate (as opposed to slick or newsy) magazine."

‡**LINKING THE DOTS**,Islesboro Publishing, HCR 222, Islesboro ME 04848. (207)734-6745. Publisher/Editor: Agatha Cabaniss. 80% freelance written. Bimonthly magazine on Penobscot Bay islands and

people. Pays on acceptance. Byline given. Buys first rights and second serial (reprint) rights. Computer printout submissions OK. Sample copy $2; writer's guidelines for #10 SASE.

Nonfiction: Articles about contemporary issues on the islands, historical pieces, personality profiles, arts, lifestyles and businesses on the islands. Any story must have a definite Maine island connection. No travel pieces. Query or send complete ms. Pays $20-50.

Photos: State availability of photos with submission.

Tips: "Writers must know the Penobscot Bay Islands. We are not interested in pieces of generic island nature nor do we want 'Vacation on a romantic island. . .' We are interested in development problems, the viability of the islands as year round communities and historical pieces."

MAINE LIFE, 158 Court St., Auburn ME 04210. Publisher: Gary Owen Bowles. Associate Publisher/Editor: Howard L. Kany. 80% freelance written. Bimonthly. For readers of all ages in urban and rural settings. 60% of readers live in Maine; balance are readers in other states who have an interest in Maine. Circ. 30,000. Pays on publication. Publishes ms an average of 3 months after acceptance. Buys first serial rights and second serial (reprint) rights. Submit seasonal/holiday material 6 months in advance. Computer printout submissions acceptable; no dot-matrix. Reports in 3 months. Free sample copy.

Nonfiction: Contemporary Maine issues, Maine travel, home and lifestyles, wildlife and recreation, arts and culture; Maine people, business, and environment. Query. Length: 500-3,000 words. Pays 10¢/word.

Photos: B&w and color slides purchased with or without accompanying ms. Captions required.

Tips: "The writer will notice we accept a variety of styles and also have available short article space under the heading 'Omnibus'. *Maine Life* wants to increase the number of feature articles which deal with contemporary Maine issues. We will consider any speculative submissions—articles and photos."

Maryland

BALTIMORE MAGAZINE, 26 S. Calvert St., Baltimore MD 21202. (301)752-7375. Editor: Stan Heuisler. 40% freelance written. Prefers to work with published/established writers, and works with a small number of new/unpublished writers each year. Monthly magazine; 150 pages. Circ. 56,000. Pays on publication. Publishes ms an average of 3 months after acceptance. Byline given. Buys first serial rights. Submit seasonal/holiday material 3 months in advance. Electronic submission information supplied on request. Computer printout submissions acceptable; prefers letter-quality to dot-matrix. Reports in 6 weeks. Sample copy for 9x12 SAE with $2.84 postage; writer's guidelines for SASE.

Nonfiction: Consumer, profile, lifestyle, issues, narratives and advocacy. Must have local angle. "We do not want to see any soft, nonlocal features." Buys 4 mss/issue. Length: 1,000-5,000 words. Pays $100-700. Sometimes pays expenses of writers on assignment.

Photos: State availability of photos. Reviews color and b&w glossy prints. Captions preferred.

Columns/Departments: Frontlines (local news tips), Tips (local unusual retail opportunities), Class Cars and Tech Talk (high-tech product advice). Query.

CHESAPEAKE BAY MAGAZINE, Suite 200, 1819 Bay Ridge Ave., Annapolis MD 21403. (301)263-2662. Editor: Betty D. Rigoli. 40% freelance written. Works with a small number of new/unpublished writers each year. Monthly magazine; 88 pages. "*Chesapeake Bay Magazine* is a regional publication for those who enjoy reading about the Chesapeake and its tributaries. Our readers are yachtsmen, boating families, fishermen, ecologists—anyone who is part of Chesapeake Bay life." Circ. 30,000. Pays either on acceptance or publication, depending on "type of article, timeliness and need." Publishes ms an average of 14 months after acceptance. Buys first North American serial rights and all rights. Submit seasonal/holiday material 4 months in advance. Simultaneous (if not to magazines with overlapping circulations) and photocopied submissions OK. Computer printout submissions acceptable; no dot-matrix. Reports in 1 month. Sample copy $2; writer's guidelines for SASE.

Nonfiction: "All material must be about the Chesapeake Bay area—land or water." How-to (fishing and sports pertinent to Chesapeake Bay); general interest; humor (welcomed, but don't send any "dumb boater" stories where common safety is ignored); historical; interviews (with interesting people who have contributed in some way to Chesapeake Bay life: authors, historians, sailors, oystermen, etc.); and nostalgia (accurate, informative and well-paced—no maudlin ramblings about "the good old days"); personal experience (drawn from experiences in boating situations, adventures, events in our geographical area); photo feature (with accompanying ms); profile (on natives of Chesapeake Bay); technical (relating to boating, fishing); and Chesapeake Bay folklore. "We do not want material written by those unfamiliar with the Bay area, or general sea stories. No personal opinions on environmental issues or new column (monthly) material and no rehashing of familiar ports-of-call (e.g., Oxford, St. Michaels)." Recent article example: "Getting Away—Norfolk to Duck Point Cove" (Feb. 1987). Buys 25-40 unsolicited mss/year. Query or submit complete ms. Length: 1,000-2,500 words. Pays $75-85. Sometimes pays the expenses of writers on assignment.

Photos: Virginia Leonard, art director. Submit photo material with ms. Reviews 8x10 b&w glossy prints and color transparencies. Pays $100 for 35mm, 2¼x2¼ or 4x5 color transparencies used for cover photos; $15/color photo used inside. Captions and model releases required. Buys one-time rights with reprint permission.

Fiction: "All fiction must deal with the Chesapeake Bay and be written by persons familiar with some facet of bay life." Adventure, fantasy, historical, humorous, mystery and suspense. "No general stories with Chesapeake Bay superimposed in an attempt to make a sale." Buys 3-4 mss/year. Query or submit complete ms. Length: 1,000-2,500 words. Pays $75-90.

Poetry: Attention: Poetry Editor. Free verse and traditional. Must be about Chesapeake Bay. "We want well crafted, serious poetry. Do not send in short, 'inspired' seasick poetry or 'sea-widow' poems." Length: 5-30 lines. Pays $25-35. Poetry used on space available basis only.

Tips: "We are a regional publication entirely about the Chesapeake Bay and its tributaries. Our readers are true 'Bay' lovers, and look for stories written by others who obviously share this love. We are particularly interested in material from the Lower Bay (Virginia) area and the Upper Bay (Maryland/Delaware) area. We are looking for personal experience Chesapeake boating articles/stories."

MARYLAND MAGAZINE, Department of Economic and Community Development, 45 Calvert St., Annapolis MD 21401. (301)269-3507. Publisher: D. Patrick Hornberger. Editor: Bonnie Joe Ayers. 95% freelance written. Prefers to work with published/established writers. Quarterly magazine promoting the state of Maryland. Circ. 45,000. Pays on acceptance. Publishes ms 8-12 months after acceptance. Byline given. Offers 25% kill fee. Buys all rights. Submit seasonal/holiday material 1 year in advance. Photocopied submissions OK. Computer printout submissions acceptable; no dot-matrix. Reports in 2 months. Sample copy $2.25; writer's guidelines for business size SASE.

Nonfiction: General interest, historical/nostalgic, humor, interview/profile, photo feature and travel. Articles on any facet of Maryland life except conservation/ecology. No poetry, fiction or controversial material or any topic *not* dealing with the state of Maryland; no trendy topics, or one that has received much publicity elsewhere. Buys 32 mss/year. Query with published clips or send complete ms. Length: 900-2,200 words. Pays $175-400. Pays expenses of writers on assignment.

Tips: "All sections are open to freelancers. Thoroughly research your topic and give sources (when applicable)."

Massachusetts

BOSTON GLOBE MAGAZINE, *Boston Globe*, Boston MA 02107. Editor-in-Chief: Ms. Ande Zellman. 25% freelance written. Weekly magazine; 64 pages. Circ. 805,099. Pays on publication. Publishes ms an average of 2 months after acceptance. No reprints of any kind. Buys first serial rights. Submit seasonal/holiday material 3 months in advance. Computer printout submissions acceptable; no dot-matrix. SASE must be included with ms or queries for return. Reports in 1 month.

Nonfiction: Expose (variety of issues including political, economic, scientific, medical and the arts); interview (not Q&A); profile; and book excerpts (first serial rights only). No travelogs or personal experience pieces. Buys 65 mss/year. Query. Length: 3,000-5,000 words. Payment negotiable from $750.

Photos: Purchased with accompanying ms or on assignment. Reviews contact sheets. Pays standard rates according to size used. Captions required.

‡**BOSTON MAGAZINE**, 300 Massachusetts Ave., Boston MA 02115. (617)262-9700. Editor: David Rosenbaum. Managing Editor: Betsy Buffington. 30% freelance written. Monthly magazine. "Looks for strong reporting of locally based stories with national interest." Circ. 129,248. Pays on publication. Publishes ms an average of 2 months after acceptance. Byline given. Offers 20% kill fee. Buys first North American serial rights. Submit seasonal/holiday material 3 months in advance. Query for electronic submissions. Reports in 1 month. Sample copy for 9x12 SAE with $2.40 postage.

Nonfiction: General interest, humor, personal experience and photo feature. No fiction or poetry. Buys 75 mss/year. Query with published clips or send complete ms. Length: 1,500-5,000 words. Pays $250-1,500. Sometimes pays the expenses of writers on assignment.

Photos: State availability of photos with submission. Reviews transparencies and prints. Offers no additional payment for photos accepted with ms. Captions, model releases and identification of subjects required. Buys one-time rights.

Columns/Departments: Local Color (odd facts about Boston); Good Spirits (stories about alcohol—wines, beers, drinks, etc.); First Person (experiences of general interest); Sports (Boston short stories). Buys 50 mss/year. Send complete ms. Length: 1,500-2,500 words. Pays $250-500.

Tips: "Query should contain an outline of proposed story structure, including sources and source material. Stories should seek to be controversial. Area most open to freelancers is investigative journalism. Stories concerning newsworthy scandals that are unreported. Look for something everyone believes to be true—then question it."

THE BOSTON PHOENIX, 100 Massachusetts Ave., Boston MA 02115. (617)536-5390. Editor: Richard M. Gaines. 40% freelance written. Weekly alternative newspaper; 140+ pages. For 18-40 age group, educated post-counterculture. Circ. 139,000. Buys first serial rights. Pays on publication. Offers kill fee. Publishes ms an average of 1 month after acceptance. Byline given. Photocopied submissions OK. Computer printout submissions acceptable. Reports in 6 weeks. Sample copy $1.50.

Nonfiction: News (local coverage, national, some international affairs, features, think pieces and profiles); lifestyle (features, service pieces, consumer-oriented tips, medical, food, some humor if topical, etc.); arts (reviews, essays, interviews); and supplements (coverage of special-interest areas, e.g., stereo, skiing, automotive, computers, pro sound, education, home furnishings with local angle). Query section editor. "Liveliness, accuracy, and great literacy are absolutely required." No fiction or poetry. Query letter preferable to ms. Pays 4¢/word and up. Sometimes pays the expenses of writers on assignment.

CAPE COD COMPASS, Quarterdeck Communications, Inc., 935 Main St., Box 375, Chatham MA 02633. (617)945-3542. Editor: Andrew Scherding. Managing Editor: Donald Davidson. 80% freelance written. A semiannual magazine about Cape Cod, Martha's Vineyard and Nantucket (Mass.) region. Circ. 25,000. Pays on acceptance. Publishes ms an average of 6 months after acceptance. Byline given. Offers variable kill fee. Buys first North American serial rights or one-time rights. Photocopied submissions OK. Computer printout submissions acceptable. Reports in 2 weeks on queries; 1 month on mss. Sample copy $4; free writer's guidelines.

Nonfiction: Essays, general interest, historical/nostalgic, interview/profile and photo feature. "Articles must have a theme connected with this region of New England. We rarely publish first-person articles." Buys 30 mss/year. Query with published clips, or send complete ms. Length: 1,500-7,000 words. Pays $300-700 for assigned articles; pays $200-400 for unsolicited articles. Sometimes pays the expenses of writers on assignment.

Photos: Send photos with submission, if any. Reviews transparencies. Offers $60/photo. Model releases and identification of subjects required. Buys one-time rights.

Fiction: Condensed novels, historical, humorous, mainstream, novel excerpts, and slice-of-life vignettes. "No fiction that is not connected with this region." Buys 2 mss/year. Query with published clips or send complete ms. Length: 1,500-3,000 words. Pays $200-400.

Poetry: Buys 4-6 poems/year. Submit maximum 4 poems. Length: open. Pays $35-60.

Tips: "We are quite willing to correspond at length with potential contributors about ideas and potential manuscripts. Telephone calls initiated by the contributor are discouraged. Our magazine is largely nonfiction. We would suggest that the writer become thoroughly knowledgeable about a subject before he or she writes about it with the intention of submitting it to our magazine."

‡CAPE COD LIFE, Including Martha's Vineyard and Nantucket, Cape Cod Life, Inc., Box 222, Osterville MA 02655. (617)428-5706. Editor: Brian F. Shortsleeve. Managing Editor: Joanna M. Phillips. 80% freelance written. Magazine published 6 times/year (weighted toward summer publication), focusing on "area lifestyle, history and culture, people and places, business and industry, and issues and answers." Readers are "year-round and summer residents of Cape Cod as well as non-residents who spend their leisure time on the Cape." Circ. 38,000. Pays within 30 days of publication. Byline given. Offers 20% kill fee. Buys first North American serial rights; makes work-for-hire assignments. Submit seasonal/holiday material 6 months in advance. Simultaneous queries and photocopied submissions OK. Computer printout submissions acceptable; no dot-matrix. Reports in 3 weeks on queries; 1 month on mss. Sample copy $3; writer's guidelines for SASE.

Nonfiction: General interest, historical, gardening, interview/profile, photo feature, travel, marine, nautical, nature, arts and antiques. Buys 20 mss/year. Query with or without published clips. Length: 1,000-4,000 words. Pays $100-400.

Photos: State availability of photos with query. Pays $7.50-20 for photos. Captions and identification of subjects required. Buys first rights with right to reprint.

Columns/Departments: Nature (seasonal articles about nature, flora or fauna native to Cape Cod), 750-800 words. Buys 6 mss/year. Send complete ms. Pays $70-85.

Poetry: Traditional. "We only accept poetry that has a Cape Cod, Martha's Vineyard or Nantucket theme." Buys 12 poems/year. Length: 30 lines maximum. Pays $20.

Tips: "Those freelancers who submit *quality* spec articles generally have a good chance at publication. We do like to see a wide selection of writer's clips before giving assignments. We accept more spec work written about Cape and Islands history than any other area."

LYNN, THE NORTH SHORE MAGAZINE, Hastings Group, 45 Forest Ave., Swampscott MA 01907. (617)592-0160. Editor: Robert Hastings. Associate Editor: Susan Sutherland. 80% freelance written. Prefers to work with published/established writers. A bimonthly magazine covering topics of interest to readers residing on the North shore of Boston. "*Lynn* is a controlled circulation magazine distributed to households with an income over $50,000. All of our articles have a local flavor. We publish articles on money, fashion, sports, medicine, culture, business and humor." Circ. 75,000. Pays on acceptance. Publishes ms an average of 4-6 months after acceptance. Byline given. Buys first rights. Submit seasonal/holiday material 6 months in advance. Photocopied submissions OK. Computer printout submissions acceptable. Reports in 1 month on queries; 3 weeks on mss. Sample copy $2.50; free writer's guidelines.

Nonfiction: Essays, how-to, humor, interview/profile, opinion, personal experience, money, fashion, business, sports, culture and the ocean. Special issues include holidays (December/January) and home guide (April/May). Buys 40 mss/year. Query with published clips. Length: 1,000-2,500 words. Pays $100-400. Pays some expenses of writers on assignment.

Photos: State availability of photos with submission. Reviews contact sheets and negatives. Offers $50-200/photo. Model releases and identification of subjects required. Buys one-time rights.

SUNDAY MORNING magazine, *Worcester Sunday Telegram*, 20 Franklin St., Worcester MA 01613. (617)793-9100. Sunday Morning Editor: Anne Murray. 25-50% freelance written. Eager to work with new/unpublished writers. Sunday supplement serving a broad cross-section of Central Massachusetts residents; 16 pages. Circ. 128,000. Pays on publication. Publishes ms an average of 3 months after acceptance. Buys first North American serial rights. Byline given. Phone queries OK. Submit seasonal/holiday material 2 months in advance. Computer printout submissions OK. Free sample copy.

Nonfiction: Profiles; interviews; beind-the-scenes, informational, first-person, and how-to articles; photo features with a strong New England angle; humor; personal experience (something unusual); and travel with a strong New England angle. Buys 2 mss/issue. Query. Pays $50-100.

Photos: Photos purchased with or without accompanying ms or on assignment. Captions required. Pays $10 for b&w glossy prints, color slides or prints.

Columns/Departments: Open to suggestions for new columns and departments.

Tips: "We place strong emphasis on people stories and on New England."

WHAT'S NEW MAGAZINE, The Good Times Magazine, Multicom 7 Inc., 11 Allen Rd., Boston MA 02135. (617)787-3636. Editor: Bob Leja. 80% freelance written. A monthly magazine covering music, entertainment, sports and lifestyles for the "baby-boom" generation. Circ. 125,000. Pays on publication. Publishes ms an average of 2 months after acceptance. Byline given. Offers 25% kill fee. Buys one-time rights. Submit seasonal/holiday material 4 months in advance. Photocopied submissions OK. Electronic submissions OK; call system operator. Computer printout submissions acceptable; prefers letter-quality to dot-matrix. Reports in 2 months. Sample copy $3 with 9x11 SAE and $1.40 posage.

Nonfiction: Book excerpts, general interest, humor, new product, photo feature and travel. Special issues include motorcycle buyer's guide, consumer elect buyer's guide, and automotive buyer's guide. Buys 120 mss/year. Query with published clips. Length: 150-3,000 words. Pays $25-250 for assigned articles. Sometimes pays the expenses of writers on assignment.

Photos: State availability of photos with submission. Reviews contact sheets. Offers $15 for first photo, $5 for each additional photo published in 1 issue. Captions, model releases and identification of subjects required. Buys one-time rights.

Columns/Departments: Great Escapes (undiscovered or under-explored vacation possibilities); Food Department (new and unusual developments in food and drink); and Fads, Follies and Trends (weird things that everyone is doing—from buying breakdancing accessories to brushing with pump toothpaste). Buys 150 mss/year. Query with published clips. Length: 150-3,000 words. Pays $25-250.

Tips: "*What's New* will remain a unique magazine by continuing to combine informative coverage of established, mainstream artists with reports on the newest bands, movies, fads or trends and by writing about them in the same snappy, witty and irreverent style that has singled it out in the past. The magazine will remain creative enough to find the angle that others fail to see. This calls for some extraordinary talent, and the magazine is fortunate to have such a resource in its national network of freelance writers."

‡WORCESTER MAGAZINE, Box 1000, Worcester MA 01614. (617)799-0511. Editor: Jay Whearley. 10% freelance written. Weekly tabloid, 48 pages emphasizing the central Massachusetts region. Circ. 50,000. Pays on acceptance. Publishes ms an average of 3 weeks after acceptance. Byline given. Buys all rights. Submit seasonal/holiday material 2 months in advance. Simultaneous and photocopied submissions OK. Computer printout submissions acceptable. Reports in 2 weeks. Sample copy $1; free writer's guidelines.

Nonfiction: Expose (area government, corporate); how-to (concerning the area, homes, vacations); interview (local); personal experience; opinion (local); and photo feature. No nonlocal stories. "We leave national and general topics to national and general publications." Buys 30 mss/year. Query with published clips. Length: 1,000-3,500 words. Pays $50-125.

Photos: State availability of photos with query. Pays $25-75 for b&w photos. Captions preferred; model release required. Buys all rights.

Michigan

ANN ARBOR OBSERVER, Ann Arbor Observer Company, 206 S. Main, Ann Arbor MI 48104. Editor: John Hilton. 25% freelance written. Works with a small number of new/unpublished writers each year. Monthly magazine featuring stories about people and events in Ann Arbor. Circ. 48,000. Pays on publication. Publishes ms an average of 2 months after acceptance. Byline given. Buys one-time rights. Query for electronic submissions. Computer printout submissions acceptable. Reports in 3 weeks on queries; 1 month on mss. Sample copy $1.
Nonfiction: Historical/nostalgic, investigative features, profiles and brief vignettes. Must pertain to Ann Arbor. Buys 75 mss/year. Length: 100-7,000 words. Pays up to $1,000/article. Sometimes pays expenses of writers on assignment.
Tips: "If you have an idea for a story, write up a 100-200 word description telling us why the story is interesting. We are most open to intelligent, insightful features of up to 5,000 words about interesting aspects of life in Ann Arbor."

DETROIT MAGAZINE, *The Detroit Free Press*, 321 W. Lafayette Blvd., Detroit MI 48231. (313)222-6446. 20% freelance written. Prefers to work with published/established writers; works with a small number of new/unpublished writers each year. For a general newspaper readership; urban and suburban. Weekly magazine. Circ. 800,000. Pays within 6 weeks of publication. Publishes ms an average of 2-3 months after acceptance. Buys first or second serial rights. Offers kill fee of ⅓ the agreed-upon price. Byline given. Query for electronic submissions. Computer printout submissions acceptable. Reports in 1 month.
Nonfiction: "Seeking quality magazine journalism on subjects of interest to Detroit and Michigan readers: lifestyles and better living, trends, behavior, health and body, business and political intrigue, crime and cops, money, success and failure, sports, fascinating people, arts and entertainment. *Detroit Magazine* is bright and cosmopolitan in tone. Most desired writing style is literate but casual—the kind you'd like to read—and reporting must be unimpeachable." Buys 75-100 mss/year. Query or submit complete ms. "If possible, the letter should be held to one page. It should present topic, organizational technique and writing angle. It should demonstrate writing style and give some indication as to why the story would be of interest to us. It should not, however, be an extended sales pitch." Length: 3,000 words maximum. Pays $125-700. Sometimes pays the expenses of writers on assignment.
Photos: Purchased with or without accompanying ms. Pays $25 for b&w glossy prints or color transparencies used inside; $100 for color used as cover.
Tips: "We will be accepting fewer nostalgia, history and first-person stories than in the past. We are aiming to be more polished, sophisticated and 'slicker' and have recently redesigned our magazine to reflect this. Try to generate fresh ideas, or fresh approaches to older ideas. Always begin with a query letter and not a telephone call. If sending a complete ms, be very brief in your cover letter; we really are not interested in previous publication credits. If the story is good for us, we'll know, and if the most widely published writer sends us something lousy, we aren't going to take it."

DETROIT MONTHLY, Crain Communications, 1400 Woodbridge, Detroit MI 48207. (313)446-0600. Editor: Susan Wyland. 50% freelance written. Monthly magazine. "We are a city magazine for educated, reasonably well-to-do, intellectually curious Detroiters." Circ. 80,000. Pays on acceptance. Byline given. Offers negotiable kill fee. Buys first North American serial rights. Submit seasonal/holiday material 4 months in advance. Query for electronic submissions. Computer printout submissions OK. Reports in 6 weeks.
Nonfiction: Book excerpts, expose and travel. No reminiscenses of childhood. Buys 25 mss/year. Query with published clips. Length: 1,000-5,000 words. Pays $100-1,200. Sometimes pays the expenses of writers on assignment.
Photos: State availability of photos with submission.

GRAND RAPIDS MAGAZINE, Suite 1040, Trust Bldg., 40 Pearl St., NW, Grand Rapids MI 49503. (616)459-4545. Publisher: John H. Zwarensteyn. Editor: Ronald E. Koehler. Managing Editor: Carole Valade Smith. 45% freelance written. Eager to work with new/unpublished writers. Monthly general feature magazine serving western Michigan. Circ. 13,500. Pays on 15th of month of publication. Publishes ms an average of 4 months after acceptance. Buys first serial rights. Phone queries OK. Submit seasonal material 3 months in advance. Photocopied and previously published submissions OK. Electronic submissions OK via IBM 5¼" floppy (MS DOS) or NBI 8" disk (MS DOS), but requires hard copy also. Computer printout submissions acceptable; prefers letter-quality to dot-matrix. Reports in 2 months.
Nonfiction: Western Michigan writers preferred. Western Michigan subjects only: government, labor, education, general interest, historical, interview/profile and nostalgia. Inspirational and personal experience pieces discouraged. No breezy, self-centered "human" pieces or "pieces not only light on style but light on hard information." Humor appreciated but must be specific to region. Buys 5-8 unsolicited mss/year. "If you live here, see the managing editor before you write. If you don't, send a query letter with published clips, or

phone." Length: 500-4,000 words. Pays $25-200. Sometimes pays the expenses of writers on assignment.
Photos: State availability of photos. Pays $15 + /5x7 glossy print and $22 + /35 or 120mm color transparency. Captions and model releases required.
Tips: "Television has forced city/regional magazines to be less provincial and more broad-based in their approach. People's interests seem to be evening out from region to region. The subject matters should remain largely local, but national trends must be recognized in style and content. And we must *entertain* as well as inform."

‡**GREAT LAKES TRAVEL & LIVING**, Great Lakes Publishing Co., 108 West Perry St., Port Clinton OH 43452. (419)734-5774. Editor: David G. Brown. 60-70% freelance written. Works with a small number of new/unpublished writers each year. A monthly magazine covering travel and living in the Great Lakes region—Minnesota, Wisconsin, Illinois, Indiana, Michigan, Ohio and portions of Pennsylvania and New York, as well as southern Ontario. Pays on publication. Publishes ms an average of 5 months after acceptance. Byline given. Offers 50% kill fee. Buys first North American serial rights and one-time rights. Submit seasonal/holiday material 6 months in advance. Photocopied submissions OK. Query for electronic submissions. Computer printout submissions OK. Reports in 3 weeks on queries; 6 weeks on mss. Sample copy for $1 and SAE with $1.24 postage; free writer's guidelines for SAE with 37¢ postage.
Nonfiction: Book excerpts, general interest, historical/nostalgic, interview/profile, photo feature and travel. "Issues are keyed to events during the month of publication." Special Christmas issue (December). No negative expose articles or articles with a negative slant. Buys 100 mss/year. Query. Length: 300-3,500 words. Pays $100-300 for assigned articles; pays $50-300 for unsolicited articles. Sometimes pays the expenses of writers on assignment.
Photos: Send photos with submission. Reviews 2x2 transparencies and 5x7 prints. Offers $50 per photo. Captions, model releases and identification fo subjects required. Buys one-time rights.
Columns/Departments: Joanne Sutton, editor. Calendar (list of events); Events (short stories on specific events occuring during month of publication. Must be events open to the public. Photos desired), 250 words; Food (everything from regional recipes to descriptions of restaurants. "We're always looking for stories about cheese factories, bakeries, wineries, etc. that are open to general public." Photos required), 250-500 words; On The Way ("shorts on places you might stop for an hour or two on the way to a final destination. Small museums, unusual shops, etc. are the typical material for this column, but we would consider stories on little-known scenic lookouts, monuments, etc."), 250-700. Buys 40 mss/year. Query. Pays $50-150.
Fiction: Historical, novel excerpts and slice-of-life vignettes. "We do not want fiction set outside the Great Lakes region. All fiction must pertain to the region and its people." Buys 12 mss/year. Query. Length: 1,000-2,500 words. Pays $100-300.
Fillers: Joanne Sutton, editor. Newsbreaks. Buys 20/year. Length: 50-200 words. Pays $50.
Tips: "Our editorial material is 100% about the Great Lakes region. Beginners should start with shorts on small events, individual destinations, etc. Short features on specific attractions (such as an unusual store, restaurant or person) are always needed and are more likely to be published than long features. We'll work with writers to transform a good idea into a sold story. We need material on Great Lakes regions of western Pennsylvania and upstate New York."

MICHIGAN MAGAZINE, Detroit News, 615 W. Lafayette Blvd., Detroit MI 48231. (313)222-2620. Editor: Cynthia Boal-Janssens. 50% freelance written. Works with a small number of new/unpublished writers each year. Weekly magazine featuring the state of Michigan. "We are a rotogravure magazine published as a Sunday supplement to the *Detroit News*. Our focus continues to be the entire state of Michigan." Circ. 832,000. Pays on publication. Publishes ms an average of 6 months after acceptance. Byline given. Offers 25% kill fee. Buys one-time or second serial (reprint) rights. Submit seasonal/holiday material 5 months in advance. Simultaneous, photocopied and previously published submissions OK. Computer printout submissions OK. Reports in 1 month. Free sample copy and writer's guidelines.
Nonfiction: Essays, expose, general interest, historical/nostalgic, humor, interview/profile and travel (Michigan). No travel out of Michigan. Buys 20 mss/year. Send complete ms. Length: 1,500-3,500 words. Pays $200-650 for assigned articles.
Photos: Send photos with submission. Reviews transparencies and prints. Offers $25-240 per photo. Captions required. Buys one-time rights.
Columns/Departments: Words (columns about language) and Private lives (about person-to-person relationships), all 1,500 words. Buys 6 mss/year. Send complete ms. Length: 1,000-2,000 words. Pays $200-300.
Fiction: Historical, humorous, mystery, science fiction, holiday stories and slice-of-life. Fiction set in Michigan preferred. Buys 12 mss/year. Send complete ms. Length: 1,500-2,500 words. Pays $200-400.

‡**THE MICHIGAN WOMAN**, 20 10 Inc., 31550 Northwestern Highway, Farmington Hills MI 48018. (313)851-5755. Editor: Monica Smiley. 100% freelance written. Bimonthly magazine covering "Michigan women, issues." Circ. 25,000. Pays on publication. Byline given. Free sample copy and writer's guidelines.

Nonfiction: Book excerpts, essays, expose, general interest, historical/nostalgic, how-to, humor, inspirational, interview/profile, new product, opinion, personal experience, photo feature, technical and travel. Query with published clips. Length: 200-3,000 words. Pays 10¢/word. Sometimes pays the expenses of writers on assignment.

Photos: Send photos with submission. Identification of subjects required.

Columns/Departments: Finance, Health, Legal (issues in Michigan affecting women), Cuisine, Book Reviews. Buys 6 mss/year. Query with published clips. Length: 700 words. Pays 10¢/word.

Fiction: Condensed novels, erotica, ethnic, experimental, fantasy, historical, horror, humorous, mainstream, mystery, novel excerpts, religious, romance, science fiction, serialized novels, slice-of-life vignettes, suspense and western. Literary journal published twice/year. Query with published clips. Length: 500-2,000 words. Pays 10¢/word.

Poetry: Pays 10¢/word.

Fillers: Facts and newsbreak. Length: 500-700 words. Pays 10¢/word.

Minnesota

LAKE SUPERIOR MAGAZINE, (formerly Lake Superior Port Cities), Lake Superior Port Cities, Inc., #100, 325 Lake Ave. S., Duluth MN 55802. (218)722-5002. Editor: Paul L. Hayden. 60% freelance written. Works with a small number of new/unpublished writers each year. A bimonthly regional magazine covering contemporary and historical people, places and current events around Lake Superior. Circ. 14,000. Pays on publication. Publishes ms an average of 8 months after acceptance. Byline given. Offers $25 kill fee. Buys first North American serial rights. Submit seasonal/holiday material 8 months in advance. Photocopied submissions OK. Query for electronic submissions. Computer printout submissions acceptable; prefers letter-quality to dot-matrix. Reports in 3 months on manuscripts. Sample copy $3.50 and $1.92 postage; writer's guidelines for SASE.

Nonfiction: Book excerpts, general interest, historical/nostalgic, humor, interview/profile (local), personal experience, photo feature (local), travel (local), regional business. Buys 45 mss/year. Query with published clips. Length 300-5,000 words. Pays $80-300 maximum. Sometimes pays the expenses of writers on assignment.

Photos: State availability of photos with submission. Reviews contact sheets, 2x2 transparencies and 4x5 prints. Offers $15 for b&w and $25 for color transparencies. Captions, model releases, and identification of subjects required.

Columns/Departments: Current events and things to do (for Events Calendar section) short, under 300 words; Shore Lines (letters and short pieces on events and highlights of the Lake Superior Region), up to 150 words; and Book Reviews (Regional targeted or published books), up to 450 words. Direct book reviews to Barbara Landfield, book review editor. Buys 20 mss/year. Query with published clips. Pays $10-35.

Fiction: Ethnic, historical, humorous, mainstream, slice-of-life vignettes and ghost stories. Must be regionally targeted in nature. Buys 5 mss/year. Query with published clips. Length: 300-2,500 words. Pays $1-300.

Tips: "Well-researched queries are attended to. We actively seek queries from writers in Lake Superior communities. Provide enough information on why the subject is important to the region and our readers, or why and how something is unique. We want details. The writer must have a thorough knowledge of the subject and how it relates to our region. We prefer a fresh, unused approach to the subject which provides the reader with an emotional involvement."

MPLS. ST. PAUL MAGAZINE, Suite 1030, 12 S. 6th St., Minneapolis MN 55402. (612)339-7571. Editor: Brian Anderson. Managing Editor: Claude Peck. 90% freelance written. Monthly general interest magazine covering the metropolitan area of Minneapolis/St. Paul and aimed at college-educated professionals who enjoy living in the area and taking advantage of the cultural, entertainment and dining out opportunities. Circ. 50,000. Pays on acceptance. Publishes ms an average of 3 months after acceptance. Byline given. Offers 25% kill fee. Buys first North American serial rights. Submit seasonal/holiday material 5 months in advance. Query for electronic submissions. Computer printout submissions acceptable; prefers letter-quality to dot-matrix. Reports in 1 month. Sample copy $3.50; free writer's guidelines.

Nonfiction: Book excerpts; general interest; historical/nostalgic; interview/profile (local); new product; photo feature (local); and travel (regional). Buys 250 mss/year. Query with published clips. Length: 1,000-4,000 words. Pays $100-800. Sometimes pays expenses of writers on assignment.

Photos: Tara Christopherson, photo editor.

Columns/Departments: Nostalgic—Minnesota historical; Arts—local; Home—interior design, local; Last Page—essay with local relevance. Query with published clips. Length: 750-2,000 words. Pays $100-200.

Tips: People profiles (400 words) and Nostalgia are areas most open to freelancers.

Missouri

KANSAS CITY MAGAZINE, 3401 Main St., Kansas City MO 64111. (816)561-0444. Editor: William R. Wehrman. 80% freelance written. Prefers to work with published/established writers. Monthly; 80-96 pages. Freelance material is considered if it is about Kansas City issues, events or people. Circ. 16,000. Publishes ms an average of 3 months after acceptance. Byline given. Buys all rights. Query for electronic submissions. Computer printout submissions acceptable; prefers letter-quality to dot-matrix. Reports in 1 month. Sample copy for $3 and 9x12 SASE.

Nonfiction: Editorial content is issue- or personality-oriented, arts, investigative reporting, profiles, or lengthy news features with a Kansas City connection. Written queries only; queries and mss should be accompanied by SASE. Longer stories of 2,000-8,000 words pay negotiable depending on story, plus expenses. Sometimes pays expenses of writers on assignment.

Columns/Departments: Short items of 250-350 words considered for City Window column; pays $25. Columns, which include City Windows, dining out, art, theater, sports, music, health and a Postscript essay, are from 1,600-3,000 words and pay $100-200. All material must have a demonstrable connection to Kansas City.

Tips: Freelancers should show some previous reporting or writing experience of a professional nature. "The writer has a better chance of breaking in at our publication with short articles. We like to see their work on easier-to-verify stories, such as City Window, before committing to longer, tougher reporting."

‡ST. LOUIS MAGAZINE, Box 88908, St. Louis MO 63118. (314)231-7200. Editor: Barry Murov. Managing Editor: Steve Friedman. 80% freelance written. A monthly magazine about St. Louisans and St. Louis events. Pays on acceptance. Publishes ms an average of 2 months after acceptance. Byline given. Buys first North American serial rights; makes work-for-hire assignments. Submit seasonal/holiday material 4 months in advance. Computer printout submissions OK; prefers letter-quality. Reports in 2 months on queries; 5 weeks on mss.

Nonfiction: Historical, interview/profile, photo feature and travel. Query with published clips. Length: 250-2,000 words. Pays $25-300. Sometimes pays the expenses of writers on assignment.

Photos: State availability of photos with submission.

Columns/Departments: Travel, Arts, Health For Kids and Family Album. Buys 36 mss/year. Query with published clips. Length: 500-1,250 words. Pays $125 maximum.

Tips: "We are looking for more serious articles this year in addition to service features."

SPRINGFIELD! MAGAZINE, Springfield Communications Inc., Box 4749, Springfield MO 65808. (417)882-4917. Editor: Robert C. Glazier. 85% freelance written. Works with a small number of new/unpublished writers each year; eager to work with new/unpublished writers. Monthly magazine. "This is an extremely local and provincial magazine. No *general* interest articles." Circ. 10,000. Pays on publication. Publishes ms an average of 6 months after acceptance. Byline given. Buys first serial rights. Submit seasonal/holiday material 6-12 months in advance. Simultaneous queries OK. Computer printout submissions acceptable; prefers letter-quality to dot-matrix. Reports in 3 months on queries; 6 months on mss. Sample copy $1.50 and SAE.

Nonfiction: Book excerpts (by Springfield authors only); expose (local topics only); historical/nostalgic (top priority but must be local history); how-to (local interest only); humor (if local angle); interview/profile (needs more on females than on males); personal experience (local angle); photo feature (local photos); and travel (1 page per month). No stock stuff which could appeal to any magazine anywhere. Buys 150+ mss/year. Query with published clips or send complete ms. Length: 500-5,000 words. Pays $25-250. Sometimes pays expenses of writers on assignment.

Photos: State availability of photos or send photos with query or ms. Reviews b&w and color contact sheets; 4x5 color transparencies; and 5x7 b&w prints. Pays $5-35 for b&w; $10-50 for color. Captions, model releases, and identification of subjects required. Buys one-time rights.

Columns/Departments: Buys 250 mss/year. Query or send complete ms. Length varies widely but usually 500-2,500 words. Pays scale.

Tips: "We prefer that a writer read eight or ten copies of our magazine prior to submitting any material for our consideration. The magazine's greatest need is for features which comment on these times in Springfield. We are overstocked with nostalgic pieces right now. We also are much in need of profiles about young women and men of distinction."

Montana

‡MONTANA MAGAZINE, American Geographic Publishing, Box 5630, 3020 Bozeman Ave., Helena MT 59604. (406)443-2842. Managing Editor: Barbara Fifer. Editor: Carolyn Zieg Cunningham. 35% freelance written. Bimonthly magazine; "*Montana Magazine* is a strictly Montana-oriented magazine that features community profiles, personality profiles, contemporary issues, travel pieces." Circ. 85,000. Publishes ms an average of 6-8 months after acceptance. Byline given. Offers $50 kill fee. Buys one-time rights. Submit seasonal material 6 months in advance. Simultaneous submissions OK. Reports in 6 weeks. Sample copy $2.50.

Nonfiction: Essays, general interest, interview/profile, new product, opinion, photo feature and travel. Special features on "summer and winter destination points. Query by January for summer material; July for winter material. No 'me and Joe' hiking and hunting tales; no blood-and-guts hunting stories; no poetry; no fiction; no sentimental essays. Buys 30 mss/year. Query. Length: 300-2,500 words. Pays $75-600 for assigned articles; pays $50-350 for unsolicited articles. Sometimes pays the expenses of writers on assignment.

Photos: Send photos with submission. Reviews contact sheets, 35mm or larger format transparencies; and 5x7 prints. Offers no additional payment for photos accepted with ms. Captions, model releases and identification of subjects required. Buys one-time rights.

Columns/Departments: Over the Weekend (destination points of interest to travelers, family weekends and exploring trips to take), 300 words plus b&w photo; Food and Lodging (great places to eat; interesting hotels, resorts, etc.), 500-700 words plus b&w photo; Made in MT (successful cottage industries), 500-700 words plus b&w photo. Query. Pays $75-125.

Nevada

NEVADA MAGAZINE, Carson City NV 89710. (702)885-5416. Managing Editor: Jim Crandall. 50% freelance written. Works with a small number of new/unpublished writers each year. Bimonthly magazine published by the state of Nevada to promote tourism in the state. Circ. 80,000. Pays on publication. Publishes ms an average of 6 months after acceptance. Byline given. Buys first North American serial rights. Phone queries OK. Submit seasonal/holiday material at least 6 months in advance. Query for electronic submissions. Computer printout submissions acceptable; no dot-matrix. Reports in 2 months. Sample copy $1; free writer's guidelines.

Nonfiction: Nevada topics only. Historical, nostalgia, photo feature, people profile, recreational, travel and think pieces. "We welcome stories and photos on speculation." Buys 40 unsolicited mss/year. Submit complete ms or queries to features editor David Moore. Length: 500-2,000 words. Pays $75-300.

Photos: Send photo material with accompanying ms. Pays $10-50 for 8x10 glossy prints; $15-75 for color transparencies. Name, address and caption should appear on each photo or slide. Buys one-time rights.

Tips: "Keep in mind that the magazine's purpose is to promote tourism in Nevada. Keys to higher payments are quality and editing effort (more than length). Send cover letter, no photocopies. We look for a light, enthusiastic tone of voice without being too cute; articles bolstered by amazing facts and thorough research; and unique angles on Nevada subjects."

THE NEVADAN, *The Las Vegas Review Journal*, Box 70, Las Vegas NV 89101. (702)385-4241. Editor-in-Chief: A.D. Hopkins. 25% freelance written. Works with a small number of new/unpublished writers each year. Weekly tabloid; 16 pages. For Las Vegas and surrounding small town residents of all ages "who take our Sunday paper—affluent, thinking people." Circ. 133,000. Pays on publication. Publishes ms an average of 4 months after acceptance. Byline given. Buys one-time rights and simultaneous rights. Submit seasonal/holiday material 2 months in advance. Photocopied and previously published submissions OK. Computer printout submissions acceptable; prefers letter-quality to dot-matrix. Reports in 3 weeks. Sample copy and writer's guidelines for 9x12 SAE with 3 first class stamps; mention *Writer's Market* in request.

Nonfiction: Historical (more of these than anything else, always linked to Nevada, southern Utah, northern Arizona and Death Valley); personal experience (any with strong pioneer Nevada angle, pioneer can be 1948 in some parts of Nevada). "We also buy contemporary pieces of about 2,400-3,000 words with good photos. An advance query is absolutely essential for these. No articles on history that are based on doubtful sources; no current show business material; and no commercial plugs." Buys 52 mss/year. Query. Phone queries OK. Length: Average 2,500 words (contemporary pieces are longer). Usually pays $100.

Photos: State availability of photos. Pays $15 for 5x7 or 8x10 b&w glossy prints, or 35 or 120mm color transparencies. Captions required. Buys one-time rights on both photos and text.

Tips: "We are shifting emphasis of our main pieces from issues to people. We need strong, several-source pieces about important and interesting people with strong Las Vegas connections—investors, sport figures for example. Offers us in-depth personality pieces about VIPs with Las Vegas angles or articles on little-known interesting incidents in Nevada history and good historic photos. In queries, come to the point. Tell me what sort of photos are available, whether historic or contemporary, black-and-white or color transparency. Be specific in talking about what you want to write."

New Hampshire

‡FOREST NOTES, Society for the Protection of New Hampshire Forests, 54 Portsmouth St., Concord NH 03301. (603)224-9945. Editor: Richard Ober. 25% freelance written. Works with a small number of new/unpublished writers each year. A quarterly non-profit journal covering forestry, conservation, wildlife and protection. "Our readers are concerned with in-depth examinations of natural resource issues in New Hampshire." Circ. 8,000. Pays on acceptance. Publishes ms an average of 3 months after acceptance. Byline given. Buys first or second serial (reprint) rights; makes work-for-hire assignments. Previously published submissions OK. Query for electronic submissions. Computer printout submissions OK; prefers letter-quality to dot-matrix. Reports in 2 weeks on queries; 1 month on mss. Free sample copy.
Nonfiction: Interview/profile (on assignment only); opinion (on the environment); photo feature (black and white photos of New Hampshire) and technical (on forestry). Query. Length: 500-2,000 words. Pays $100-300 or membership in organization. Sometimes pays the expenses of writers on assignment.
Photos: State availability of photos with submission. Reviews 5x7 prints. Offers no additional payment for photos accepted with ms. Captions required. Buys one-time rights.
Columns/Departments: Book review. Buys 1 mss/year. Query. Length: 150-500 words. Pays $25-75.
Tips: "Live in New Hampshire or New England; know your subject."

NEW HAMPSHIRE PROFILES, Goals Communications, Inc., Box 4638, Portsmouth NH 03801. (603)433-1551. Editor: Lynn Harnett. 75% freelance written. Prefers to work with published/established writers; works with small number of new/unpublished writers each year. Monthly magazine; articles concentrate on audience ages 25 and up, consumer-oriented readers who want to know more about the quality of life in New Hampshire. Pays on publication. Publishes ms an average of 6 months after acceptance. Buys first serial rights. Query for electronic submissions. Computer printout submissions acceptable; prefers letter-quality to dot-matrix. Reports in 2 months. Sample copy $2; writer's guidelines for SASE.
Nonfiction: Interview, profile, photo feature and interesting activities for and about the state of New Hampshire and people who live in it. Buys 4-6 mss/issue. Query with published clips or send complete ms. Length varies from 1,000-3,000 words, depending on subject matter. Pays $75-350. Sometimes pays expenses of writers on assignment.
Photos: State availability of photos. Pays $15-25 for 5x7 or 8x10 b&w glossy prints; $25-75 for 2¼x2¼ or 35mm color transparencies used as color photos in magazine.
Tips: "Query before submitting manuscript, and don't send us your only copy of the manuscript—photocopy it. Familiarity with magazine is essential."

‡SEACOAST LIFE, American Marketing Systems, 220 Lafayette Rd., Box 594, North Hampton NH 03862. (603)964-9898. Editor: Lloyd J. Marshall Jr. Managing Editor: Kathy Hargreaves. 85% freelance written. A quarterly magazine covering southern Maine, seacoast New Hampshire and northeast Massachusetts. Circ. 20,000. Pays 30 days after publication. Byline given. Buys first and second rights. Submit seasonal/holiday material 4 months in advance. Simultaneous and photocopied submissions OK. Query for electronic submissions. Computer printout submissions OK; prefers letter-quality. Reports in 2 months. Publishes ms an average of 4 months after acceptance. Sample copy for 9x12 SAE with $1.20 postage; writer's guidelines for #10 SAE with 2 first class stamps.
Nonfiction: Expose, general interest, historical/nostalgic, humor, interview/profile, photo feature. Buys 25 mss/year. Send complete ms. Length: 1,200-4,500 words. Pays $50-1,000. Sometimes pays the expenses of writers on assignment.
Photos: State availability of photos with submission. Reviews contact sheets, transparencies and prints. Offers $25-150 per photo. Captions, model releases and identification of subjects required. Negotiates rights purchased.
Columns/Departments: Food (recipes/seasonal); Health (new developments) and Shopping (new products), all 1,200 words. Busy 150 mss/year. Query. Length: 800-2,000 words. Pays $100-300.
Fiction: Adventure, historical, humorous, mainstream, mystery, romance, slice-of-life vignettes, suspense and other. No erotica. Buys 6 mss/year. Send complete ms. Length: 1,500-4,000 words. Pays $100-350.
Fillers: Phyllis Ring, fillers editor. Anecdotes, facts, gags to be illustrated by cartoonist, newsbreaks and short humor. Buys 100/year. Length: 100-800 words. Pays $100-350.
Tips: "All material must have to do with the seacoast region of New Hampshire or south Maine, or northeast Massachusetts. Areas most open to freelancers are fiction and news stories."

New Jersey

‡ATLANTIC CITY MAGAZINE, 1637 Atlantic Ave., Atlantic City NJ 08401. (609)348-6886. Managing Editor: Ken Weatherford. Editor: Ronnie Polaneczky. 60% freelance written. Works with small number of new/unpublished writers each year. Monthly city magazine covering issues pertinent to the South Jersey area.

Circ. 50,000. Pays on acceptance. Publishes ms an average of 4 months after acceptance. Byline given. Buys one-time rights. Offers variable kill fee. Submit seasonal/holiday material 4 months in advance. Computer printout submissions OK; no dot-matrix. Reports in 1 month. Sample copy $2; free writers guidelines.
Nonfiction: Entertainment, expose, general interest, how-to, interview/profile, photo feature and trends. "No travel pieces or any article without a South Jersey shore area/Atlantic City slant." Query. Length: 100-5,000 words. Pays $50-600 for assigned articles; pays $50-400 for unsolicited articles. Sometimes pays the expenses of writers on assignment.
Photos: State availability of photos. Reviews contact sheets, negatives, 2¼x2¼ transparencies and 8x10 prints. Pay varies. Captions, model releases and identification of subjects required. Buys one-time rights.
Columns/Departments: Art, Business, Entertainment, Environment, Sports and Real Estate. Query with published clips. Length: 500-2,500 words. Pays $150-300.
Tips: "We need more and more stories in 1988 with a strong local angle. Don't approach us with story ideas though, until you have studied two or three issues of the magazine. Try to propose articles that the magazine just can't live without."

‡**NEW JERSEY MONTHLY**, 7 Dumont Place, Morristown NJ 07960. (201)539-8230. Editor: Larry Marscheck. Managing Editor: Patrick Sarver. 85% freelance written. Monthly magazine covering New Jersey. "Almost anything that's New Jersey related." Circ. 105,000. Pays on acceptance. Byline given. Offers 33% kill fee. Buys first rights. Submit seasonal/holiday material 6 months in advance. Query for electronic submissions. Computer printout submissions OK; prefers letter-quality to dot-matrix. Reports in 6 weeks on queries; 2 weeks on mss. Sample copy $2; free writer's guidelines.
Nonfiction: Book excerpts, essays, expose, general interest, historical, humor, interview/profile, opinion, personal experience and travel. Special issue features Health & Fitness/Business Outlook (Jan.); Dining Out and Bridal (Feb.); Real Estate (March); Home & Garden (April); Great Weekends (May); Shore Guide (June); Summer Pleasures (July); Dining Out (Aug.); Financial Strategies (Sept.); Fall Getaways (Oct.); Entertaining (Nov.); Holiday Gala (Dec.). No experience pieces from people who used to live in New Jersey or general pieces that have no New Jersey angle. Buys 180 mss/year. Query with published clips. Length: 2,000-3,000 words. Pays 35¢/word and up. Pays expenses of writers on assignment.
Photos: State availability of photos with submission. Payment negotiated. Identification of subjects required. Buys one-time rights.
Columns/Departments: Business (company profile, trends, individual profiles); Health (trends, how-to, personal experience, service); Politics (perspective pieces from writers working the political beat in Trenton); Home & Garden (homes, gardens, how-tos, trends, profiles, etc.); all 1,500-1,800 words. Buys 60 mss/year. Query with published clips. Length: 1,500-1,800 words. Pays 35¢ and up per word.
Fiction: Adventure, condensed novels, historical, humorous, mystery and novel excerpts. All must relate to New Jersey. Writer must provide condensation, excerpt. Buys 1-5 mss/year. Length: 1,500-3,000 words. Pays 35¢ and up per word.
Fillers: Short humor. Length: 600-1,000 words. Pays 35¢ and up per word.
Tips: "Almost everything here is open to freelancers, since most of the magazine is freelance written. However, to break in, we suggest contributing short items to our front-of-the-book section, "Upfront" (light, off-beat items, trends, people, things; short service items, such as the 10 best NJ-made ice creams; short issue-oriented items; gossip; media notes. We pay 35¢ per published word. This is the only section we pay for on publication."

‡**NEW JERSEY REPORTER, A Journal of Public Issues**, The Center for Analysis of Public Issues (nonprofit), 16 Vandeventer Ave., Princeton NJ 08542. (609)924-9750. Editor: Rick Sinding. 30% freelance written. Prefers to work with published/established writers. Magazine published 10 times/year covering New Jersey politics, public affairs and public issues. "*New Jersey Reporter* is a hard-hitting and highly respected magazine published for people who take an active interest in New Jersey politics and public affairs, and who want to know more about what's going on than what newspapers and television newscasts are able to tell them. We publish a great variety of stories ranging from analysis to exposé." Circ. 3,000. Pays on publication. Publishes ms an average of 2 months after acceptance. Byline given. Buys all rights. Simultaneous queries and submissions, and photocopied and previously published submissions OK. Computer printout submissions acceptable; no dot-matrix. Reports in 1 month. Sample copy $2.50.
Nonfiction: Book excerpts, expose, interview/profile and opinion. "We like articles from specialists (in planning, politics, economics, corruption, etc.), but we reject stories that do not read well because of jargon or too little attention to the actual writing of the piece. Our magazine is interesting as well as informative." Buys 10 mss/year. Query with published clips or send complete ms. Length: 2,000-6,000 words. Pays $100-250. Pays expenses of writers on assignments.
Tips: "Queries should be specific about how the prospective story represents an issue that affects or will affect the people of New Jersey. The writer's resume should be included. Stories—unless they are specifically meant to be opinion—should come to a conclusion but avoid a 'holier than thou' or preachy tone. Allegations should be scrupulously substantiated. Our magazine represents a good opportunity for freelancers to acquire great

clips. Our publication specializes in longer, more detailed, analytical features. The most frequent mistake made by writers in completing an article for us is too much personal opinion versus reasoned advocacy. We are less interested in opinion than in analysis based on sound reasoning and fact. *New Jersey Reporter* is a well-respected publication, and many of our writers go on to nationally respected newspapers and magazines.''

THE SANDPAPER, Newsmagazine of the Jersey Shore, The SandPaper, Inc., 1816 Long Beach Blvd., Surf City NJ 08008. (609)494-2034. Editor: Curt Travers. Managing Editor: Gail Travers. 20% freelance written. Weekly tabloid covering subjects of interest to Jersey shore residents and visitors. *"The Sandpaper* publishes three editions covering many of the Jersey Shore's finest resort communities. Each issue includes a mix of hard news, human interest features, opinion columns and entertainment/calendar listings.'' Circ. 85,000. Pays on publication. Publishes ms an average of 1 month after acceptance. Byline given. Offers 100% kill fee. Buys first rights or all rights. Submit seasonal/holiday material 3 months in advance. Simultaneous, photocopied, and previously published submissions OK. Computer printout submissions acceptable; prefers letter-quality to dot-matrix. Reports in 1 month. Free sample copy.
Nonfiction: Essays, general interest, historical/nostalgic, humor, opinion and environmental submissions relating to the ocean, wetlands and pinelands. Must pertain to New Jersey shore locale. Also, arts and entertainment news and reviews if they have a Jersey shore angle. Buys 25 mss/year. Send complete ms. Length: 200-2,000 words. Pays $15-100. Sometimes pays the expenses of writers on assignment.
Photos: State availability of photos with submission. Offers $6-25/photo. Buys one-time rights or all rights.
Columns/Departments: Speak Easy (opinion and slice-of-life; often humorous); Food for Thought (cooking); and Commentary (forum for social science perspectives); all 500-1,500 words. Buys 50 mss/year. Send complete ms. Pays $15-35.
Fiction: Humorous and slice-of-life vignettes. Buys 25 mss/year. Send complete ms. Length: 500-1,500 words. Pays $15-35.
Tips: "Anything of interest to sun worshippers, beach walkers, nature watchers, water sports lovers is of potential interest to us. The opinion page and columns are most open to freelancers. We are steadily increasing the amount of entertainment-related material in our publication.''

New Mexico

NEW MEXICO MAGAZINE, Joseph Montoya State Bldg., 1100 St. Francis Drive, Santa Fe NM 87503. Editor: Emily Drabanski. Managing Editor: Jon Bowman. 85% freelance written. Monthly magazine; 64-96 pages. Emphasizes New Mexico for a college educated readership, above average income, interested in the Southwest. Circ. 100,000. Pays on acceptance. Publishes ms an average of 6 months after acceptance. Buys first North American serial rights. Submit seasonal/holiday material 8 months in advance. Computer printout submissions acceptable; no dot-matrix. Reports in 8 weeks. Sample copy $1.75; writer's guidelines for SASE.
Nonfiction: New Mexico subjects of interest to travelers. Historical, cultural, humorous, nostalgic and informational articles. "We are looking for more short, light and bright stories for the 'Asi Es Nuevo Mexico' section.'' No columns, cartoons, poetry or non-New Mexico subjects. Buys 5-7 mss/issue. Query with 3 published writing samples. Length: 250-2,000 words. Pays $60-300.
Photos: Purchased with accompanying ms or on assignment. Query or send contact sheet or transparencies. Pays $30-50 for 8x10 b&w glossy prints; $30-75 for 35mm—prefers Kodachrome; (photos in plastic-pocketed viewing sheets). Captions and model releases required. Buys one-time rights.
Tips: "Send a superb short (300 words) manuscript on a little-known event, aspect of history or place to see in New Mexico. Faulty research will immediately ruin a writer's chances for the future. Good style, good grammar. No generalized odes to the state or the Southwest. No sentimentalized, paternalistic views of Indians or Hispanics. No glib, gimmicky 'travel brochure' writing.''

New York

ADIRONDACK LIFE, Route 86, Box 97, Jay NY 12941. Editor: Jeffery G. Kelly. 50% freelance written. Prefers to work with published/established writers; works with a small number of new/unpublished writers each year. Emphasizes the Adirondack region and the North Country of New York State for readers ages 30-60, whose interests include outdoor activities, history, and natural history directly related to the Adirondacks. Bimonthly magazine; 80 pages. Circ. 40,000. Pays on publication. Publishes ms an average of 6 months after acceptance. Buys one-time rights. Byline given. Submit seasonal/holiday material 4 months in advance. Previously published book excerpts OK. Computer printout submissions acceptable; prefers letter-quality to dot-matrix. Reports in 6 weeks. Sample copy $4; free writer's guidelines.
Nonfiction: Outdoor recreation (Adirondack relevance only); natural history, how-to, where-to (should relate to activities and lifestyles of the region); photo feature (all photos must have been taken in the

Adirondacks); profile (Adirondack personality); and historical. "We are seeking articles on flourishing Adirondack businesses, especially small businesses." Buys 24-28 unsolicited mss/year. Query. Length: For features, 3,000 words maximum; for departments, 500-1,000 words. Pays $100-400. Sometimes pays the expenses of writers on assignment.

Photos: Purchased with or without ms or on assignment. All photos must be identified as to subject or locale and must bear photographer's name. Submit color slides or b&w prints. Pays $25 for b&w transparencies; $50 for color transparencies; $300 for cover (color only, vertical in format). Credit line given.

Tips: "We are looking for clear, concise, well-organized manuscripts, written with flair. We are continually trying to upgrade the editorial quality of our publication."

‡**CAPITAL Region Magazine**, Capital District Magazine, Inc., 295 Quail Street, Albany NY 12208. (518)458-2091. Editor: Dardis McNamee. Senior Editor: Peter Golden. 40% freelance written. Prefers to work with published/established writers. A monthly city/regional magazine for New York's capital region. Circ. 35,000. Pays 30 days from acceptance. Publishes ms an average of 3 months after acceptance. Byline given. Offers 25% kill fee. Buys one-time and second serial (reprint) rights. Submit seasonal/holiday material 3 months in advance. Photocopied submissions OK. Electronic submissions OK if IBM compatible in word perfect or ASCII. Computer printout submissions OK; prefers letter-quality to dot-matrix. Reports in 2 months. Sample copy for 8½x11 SAE with $1.20 postage; free writer's guidelines.

Nonfiction: Book excerpts, essays, expose, general interest, historical/nostalgic, humor, interview/profile, arts and culture, photo feature, travel, business and politics. Buys 60 mss/year. Query with published clips (preferred) or send complete ms. Length: 1,500-3,000. Pays $120-400. Fees set at approximately 10¢/word. Pays the expenses of writers on assignment "if agreed upon in advance."

Photos: State availability of photos with submission. Pay $300 plus expenses for covers; $350 plus expenses for features; $500 in usage. Identification of subjects required. Buys one-time rights.

Columns/Departments: Politics, Business, Culture, Food & Wine, Design, Destinations and Media, all 1,000-1,400 words. Buys 30 mss/year. Query with published clips or send complete ms. Length: 1,000-1,4000 words. Pays $120 maximum.

Fiction: "One fiction issue per year, July; short stories, novel excerpts, poetry. Deadline April 15. For writers with a link to the region. Professional quality only; one slot for writers previously unpublished in a general circulation magazine."

Fillers: Vignettes, short essays, newsbreaks and short humor. Buys 30/year. Length: 150-750 words. Pays $25-75.

Tips: "Exclusively local focus, although we welcome pieces seen in larger context. Investigative reporting, profiles, business stories, trend pieces, behind-the-scenes, humor, service features, arts and culture, nitty-gritty. Looking for The Great Read in every story."

CITY LIMITS, News for the Other New York, City Limits Community Information Service, Inc., 40 Prince St., New York NY 10012. (212)925-9820. Editor: Beverly Cheuvront. Managing Editor: Doug Turetsky. 50% freelance written. Works with a small number of new/unpublished writers each year. A monthly magazine covering housing and related urban issues. "We cover news and issues in New York City as they relate to the city's poor, moderate and middle-income residents. We are advocacy journalists with a progressive or 'left' slant." Circ. 5,000. Pays on publication. Publishes ms an average of 1-2 months after acceptance. Byline given. Buys first North American serial rights, one-time rights, or second serial (reprint) rights. Query for electronic submissions. Computer printout submissions acceptable; prefers letter-quality to dot-matrix. Reports in 3 weeks. Sample copy $2.

Nonfiction: Expose, interview/profile, opinion hard news and community profile. "No fluff, no propaganda." Length: 600-2,500 words. Pays $50-150. Sometimes pays expenses of writers on assignment.

Photos: Reviews contact sheets and 5x7 prints. Offers $10-40/photo, cover only. Identification of subjects required. Buys one-time rights.

Columns/Departments: Short Term Notes (brief descriptions of programs, policies, events, etc.), 250-400 words; Book Reviews (housing, urban development, planning, etc.), 250-600 words; Pipeline (covers community organizations, new programs, government policies, etc.), 600-800 words. People (who are active in organizations, community groups, etc.), 600-800 words; and Organize (groups involved in housing, job programs, health care, etc.), 600-800 words. Buys 50-75 mss/year. Query with published clips or send complete ms. Pays $25-35.

Tips: "We are open to a wide range of story ideas that fit our subtitle: 'News for the other New York.' If you don't have particular expertise in housing, urban planning etc., start with a community profile or pertinent book or film review. Short Term Notes is also good for anyone with reporting skills. We're looking for writing that is serious and informed but not academic or heavy handed."

‡**THE GRAPEVINE'S FINGER LAKES MAGAZINE**, Grapevine Press, Inc., 108 S. Albany St., Ithaca NY 14850. (607)272-3470. Editor: Linda McCandless. 95% freelance written. A quarterly magazine covering Finger Lakes Region of New York State. Circ. 20,000. Pays 1 month after publication. Publishes ms an

average of 1 year after acceptance. Byline given. Offers negotiable kill fee. Buys first North American serial rights. Submit seasonal/holiday material 8 months in advance. Simultaneous submissions OK. Computer printout submissions OK; prefers letter-quality. Reports in 1 month on queries; 2 months on mss.

Nonfiction: Expose, general interest, historical/nostalgic, humor, interview/profile and photo feature. Buys 30 mss/year. Query with published clips. Length: 600-2,400 words. Pays $25-100. Pays expenses of writers on assignment.

Columns/Departments: Lake Takes. Query with published clips. Length: 100-300 words. Pays $10-20.

Fiction: Humorous and slice-of-life vignettes. Needs one "Fiend of The Fingerlakes" each quarter; one crime for the past 200 years in Central New York that is reconstructed in colorful detail. Buys 4 mss/year. Query with published clips or send complete ms. Length: 1,200-2,500 words. Pays $30-75.

Poetry: Shawn Mountcastle, poetry editor. Free verse. Buys 4 poems/year. Submit 5 poems maximum. Length: 8-30. Pays $10-25.

HUDSON VALLEY MAGAZINE, Box 425, Woodstock NY 12498. (914)679-5100. Editor: R. B. Dandes. 75% freelance written. Prefers to work with published/established writers; works with small number of new/unpublished writers each year. Monthly. Circ. 26,000. Pays on publication. Publishes ms an average of 6 months after acceptance. Byline given. Buys first North American serial rights, one-time rights, and second serial (reprint) rights. Submit seasonal/holiday material 3 months in advance. Computer printout submissions acceptable; prefers letter-quality to dot-matrix. Reports in 1 month on queries.

Nonfiction: Book excerpts; general interest; historical (Hudson Valley); how-to (home improvement); interview/profile (of area personalities); photo feature. No fiction or personal stories. Length: 1,500-2,000 words. Query. Pays $75-200. Sometimes pays expenses of writers on assignment.

Photos: State availability of photos. Reviews 5x7 b&w prints. Captions required.

Tips: "The writer must live in the region and be familiar with it."

NEW YORK ALIVE, The Magazine of Life and Work in the Empire State, The Business Council of New York State, Inc., 152 Washington Ave., Albany NY 12210. (518)465-7511. Editor: Mary Grates Stoll. 85% freelance written. Works with a small number of new/unpublished writers each year. Bimonthly magazine about New York state—people, places, events, history. "Devoted to promoting the culture, heritage and lifestyle of New York state. Aimed at people who enjoy living and reading about the New York state experience. All stories must be positive in tone and slanted toward promoting the state." Circ. 35,000. Pays within 45 days of acceptance. Publishes ms an average of 8 months after acceptance. Byline given. Offers 25% of agreed-upon purchase price as kill fee. Buys one-time rights. Submit seasonal/holiday material 4 months in advance. Simultaneous queries and previously published submissions OK. Electronic submissions OK via IBM PC Wordstar, but requires hard copy also. Computer printout submissions acceptable. Reports in 3 months on queries; 1 month on mss. Sample copy $2.45; writer's guidelines for legal size SASE.

Nonfiction: Historical/nostalgic, humor, interview/profile, personal experience, photo feature and travel. In all cases subject must be a New York state person, place, event or experience. No stories of general nature (e.g. nationwide trends); political; religious; nonNew York state subjects. Query with published clips. Buys 30-40 mss/year. Length: 1,500-3,000 words. Pays $200-350. Pays expenses of writers on assignment.

Photos: State availability of photos. Reviews b&w contact sheets, 35mm color transparencies, and b&w prints. Pays $15-30 for b&w and $30-250 for color. Model releases and identification of subjects required.

Columns/Departments: Buys 80-100 mss/year. Query with published clips. Length: 500-1,000 words. Pays $50-150.

Tips: "We buy more short articles. The writer should enjoy and feel comfortable with writing straightforward, promotional type of material."

NEW YORK DAILY NEWS, Travel Section, 220 E. 42 St., New York NY 10017. (212)210-1699. Travel Editor: Harry Ryan. 30% freelance written. Prefers to work with published/established writers. Weekly tabloid. Circ. 1.8 million. "We are the largest circulating newspaper travel section in the country and take all types of articles ranging from experiences to service oriented pieces that tell readers how to make a certain trip." Pays on publication. Publishes ms an average of 3 months after acceptance. Byline given. Makes work-for-hire assignments. Submit seasonal/holiday material 4 months in advance. Contact first before submitting electronic submissions; requires hard copy also. Computer printout submissions acceptable "if crisp"; prefers letter-quality to dot-matrix. Reports "as soon as possible." Writer's guidelines for SASE.

Nonfiction: General interest, historical/nostalgic, humor, inspirational, personal experience and travel. "Most of our articles involve practical trips that the average family can afford—even if it's one you can't afford every year. We put heavy emphasis on budget saving tips for all trips. We also run stories now and then for the Armchair Traveler, an exotic and usually expensive trip. We are looking for professional quality work from professional writers who know what they are doing. The pieces have to give information and be entertaining at the same time. No 'How I Spent My Summer Vacation' type articles. No PR hype." Buys 60 mss/year. Query with SASE. Length: 1,500 words maximum. Pays $75-125.

Photos: "Good pictures always help sell good stories." State availability of photos with ms. Reviews contact sheets and negatives. Captions and identification of subjects required. Buys all rights.

Columns/Departments: Short Hops is based on trips to places within a 300 mile radius of New York City. Length: 800-1,000 words. Travel Watch gives practical travel advice.

Tips: "A writer might have some luck gearing a specific destination to a news event or date: In Search of Irish Crafts in March, for example, but do it well in advance."

‡NEW YORK HABITAT, For Co-Op, Condominium and Loft Living, Carol Group Ltd., 928 Broadway, New York NY 10010. (212)505-2030. Editor: Carol Ott. Managing Editor: Tom Soter. 75% freelance written. Publishes 8 issues/year. "*N.Y. Habitat* is a magazine directed to owners, board members, and potential owners of co-ops and condos. All articles should be instructive to these readers, offering them information in an easy-to-read and entertaining manner." Circ. 10,000. Pays on publication. Byline given. Offers 50% kill fee. Buys one-time rights. Submit seasonal/holiday material 6 months in advance. Photocopied submissions OK. Computer printout submissions OK; no dot-matrix. Reports in 2 weeks on queries; 1 month on mss. Sample copy $4; free writer's guidelines.

Nonfiction: How-to (run a co-op); interview/profile (of co-op/condo managers, board members, etc.); personal experience; news stories on trends in co-ops and condos. Special issues include Annual Management Issue (July/August). No articles on lifestyles or apartment furnishings. Buys 30 mss/year. Query with published clips. Length: 2,000-4,500 words. Pays $75-700 for assigned articles; pays $75-500 for unsolicited articles. Pays expenses of writers on assignment.

Photos: State availability of photos with submission. Reviews contact sheets. Offers $50-75 per photo. Captions, model releases and identification of subjects required. Buys one-time rights.

Columns/Departments: Hotline (short, timely news items about co-op and condo living), 500 words; Finances (financial information for buyers and owners), 1000-1,500 words. Westchester Report (news, profiles, management. stories pertaining to Westchester County), 1,000-1,500 words. Buys 15 mss/year. Query with published clips. Pays $75-500.

Tips: "The Hotline section is the most accessible to freelancers. This calls for light (but informative) news and personality pieces pertaining to co-op/condo concerns. If you have ideas for our other columns, however, query, as most of them are completely freelance written."

NEW YORK MAGAZINE, News America Publishing, Inc. 755 2nd Ave., New York 10017. (212)880-0700. Editor: Edward Kosner. Managing Editor: Laurie Jones. 30% freelance written. Weekly magazine emphasizing the New York metropolitan area. Pays on acceptance. Publishes ms an average of 1 month after acceptance. Buys first North American serial rights. Submit seasonal/holiday material 2 months in advance. Photocopied submissions OK. Computer printout submissions acceptable; prefers letter-quality to dot-matrix. Reports in 1 month.

Nonfiction: Expose, general interest, interview, profile, behavior/lifestyle, health/medicine, local politics and entertainment. Query. Pays $850-2,500. Pays expenses of writers on assignment.

Tips: "The writer has a better chance of breaking in with shorter articles. The magazine very rarely assigns a major feature to a new writer."

THE NEW YORK TIMES, 229 W. 43rd St., New York NY 10036. (212)556-1234.

Nonfiction: *The New York Times Magazine* appears in *The New York Times* on Sunday. "Views should be fresh, lively and provocative on national and international news developments, science, education, family life, social trends and problems, arts and entertainment, personalities, sports and the changing American scene. Freelance contributions are invited. Articles must be timely. They must be based on specific news items, forthcoming events or significant anniversaries, or they must reflect trends. Our full-length articles run approximately 4,000 words, and for these we pay from $1,500 to $2,500 on acceptance. Our shorter pieces run from 1,000-2,500 words, and for these we pay from $750 to $1,500 on acceptance." Unsolicited articles and proposals should be addressed to Articles Editor. *Arts and Leisure* section of *The New York Times* appears on Sunday. Wants "to encourage imaginativeness in terms of form and approach—stressing ideas, issues, trends, investigations, symbolic reporting and stories delving deeply into the creative achievements and processes of artists and entertainers—and seeks to break away from old-fashioned gushy, fan magazine stuff." Length: 4,000 words. Pays $100-250, depending on length. *Arts and Leisure* Editor: William H. Honan.

Photos: Send to Photo Editor. Pays $75 minimum for b&w photos.

Tips: "The Op Ed page is always looking for new material and publishes many people who have never been published before. We want material of universal relevance which people can talk about in a personal way. When writing for the Op Ed page, there is no formula, but the writing itself should have some polish. Don't make the mistake of pontificating on the news. We're not looking for more political columnists. Op Ed length runs about 750 words, and pays about $150."

NEW YORK'S NIGHTLIFE AND LONG ISLAND'S NIGHTLIFE, MJC Publications Inc., 1770 Deer Park Ave., Deer Park NY 11729. (516)242-7722. Publisher: Michael Cutino. Managing Editor: Bill Ervolino. 35% freelance written. Eager to work with new/unpublished writers. A monthly entertainment magazine. Circ.

50,000. Pays on publication. Publishes ms an average of 3 months after acceptance. Byline given. Offers $15 kill fee. Buys first North American serial rights and all rights. Submit seasonal/holiday material 10 weeks in advance. Simultaneous queries and photocopied submissions OK. Query for electronic submissions. Computer printout submissions OK; prefers letter-quality to dot-matrix. Reports in 10 weeks. Free sample copy and writer's guidelines.

Nonfiction: General interest, humor, inspirational, interview/profile, new product, photo feature, travel and entertainment. Length: 500-1,500 words. Pays $25-75.

Photos: Send photos with ms. Reviews b&w and color contact sheets. Pays $10 for color transparencies and b&w prints. Captions and model releases required. Buys all rights.

Columns/Departments: Films, Movies, Albums, Sports, Fashion, Entertainment, and Groups. Buys 150 mss/year. Send complete ms. Length: 400-600 words. Pays $25.

Fillers: Clippings, jokes, gags, anecdotes, short humor and newsbreaks. Buys 10/year. Length: 25-100 words. Pays $10.

NEWSDAY, Long Island NY 11747. Viewpoints Editor: Ilene Barth. 75% freelance written. Opinion section of daily newspaper. Byline given. Computer printout submissions acceptable.

Nonfiction: Seeks "opinion on current events, trends, issues—whether national or local government or lifestyle. Must be timely, pertinent, articulate and opinionated. Strong preference for authors within the circulation area. It's best to consult before you start writing." Length: 600-2,000 words. Pays $75-300.

Tips: "The writer has a better chance of breaking in at our publication with short articles since the longer essays are commissioned from experts and well-known writers."

‡OUR TOWN, East Side/West Side Communications Corp., 435 E. 86th St., New York NY 10028. (212)289-8700. Editor: Ed Kayatt. 80% freelance written. Eager to work with new/unpublished writers. Weekly tabloid covering neighborhood news of Manhattan (96th St.-14th St.). Circ. 110,000. Pays on publication. Publishes ms an average of 1 month after acceptance. Byline given. Buys first serial rights. Submit seasonal/holiday material 1 month in advance. Computer printout submission OK; prefer letter-quality to dot-matrix.

Nonfiction: Expose (especially consumer ripoffs); historical/nostalgic (Manhattan, 14th St.-96th St.); interview/profile (of local personalities); photo feature (of local event); and animal rights. "We're looking for local news (Manhattan only, mainly 14th St.-96th St.). We need timely, lively coverage of local issues and events, focusing on people or exposing injustice and good deeds of local residents and business people. (Get *full names, spelled right.*)" Special issues include Education (January, March and August); and Summer Camps (March). Query with published clips. Length: 1,000 words maximum. Pays "70¢/20-pica column-inch as published." Sometimes pays expenses of writers on assignment.

Photos: Pays $2-5 for 8x10 b&w prints. Buys all rights.

Tips: "Come by the office and talk to the editor. (Call first.) Bring samples of writing."

UPSTATE MAGAZINE, *Democrat and Chronicle*, 55 Exchange St., Rochester NY 14614. (716)232-7100. Editor: Peggy Moran. 90-100% freelance written. Works with a small number of new/unpublished writers each year. A Sunday magazine appearing weekly in the *Democrat and Chronicle*. A regional magazine covering topics of local interest written for the most part by area writers. Circ. 260,000. Pays on publication. Publishes ms an average of 4 months after acceptance. Byline given. Buys first North American serial rights and second (reprint) rights to material originally published elsewhere. Submit seasonal/holiday material 3 months in advance. Computer printout submissions acceptable. Computer printout submissions OK; prefers letter-quality to dot-matrix. Reports in 2 month.

Nonfiction: General interest (places and events of local interest); historical/nostalgic; humor; interview/profile (of outstanding people in local area); personal experience; photo feature (with local angle). Buys 100 mss/year. Query. Length: 750-1,500 words; shorter is better. Pays $60-250. Do not send fiction or fillers.

North Carolina

CHARLOTTE MAGAZINE, Box 36639, Charlotte NC 28236. (704)375-8034. Editor: Diane Clemens. 95% freelance written. Eager to work with new/unpublished writers. Monthly magazine emphasizing probing, researched and upbeat articles on local people, places and events. Circ. 20,000. Pays on publication. Publishes ms an average of 3-4 months after acceptance. Buys first serial rights. Query for electronic submissions. Computer printout submissions acceptable; prefers letter-quality to dot-matrix. Reports in 3 weeks. Sample copy $2.50.

Nonfiction: Departments: lifestyles (alternative and typical); business (spotlight successful, interesting businesses and people); town talk (short, local articles of interest); theater, arts, book reviews and sports. No PR promos. "We are seeking articles indicating depth and research in original treatments of subjects. Our eagerness increases with articles that give our well-educated audience significant information through stylish, entertaining prose and uniqueness of perspective. Remember our local/regional emphasis." Query or send complete ms. Length: 1,000-2,000 words. Pays 10¢/word for feature articles.

Photos: State availability of photos. Buys b&w and color prints; pay negotiable. Captions preferred; model release required.

Columns/Departments: "Will consider all types of articles." Buys 6 columns/issue. Query. Length: 1,000-1,500 words. Pays 10¢/word.

SOUTHERN EXPOSURE, Box 531, Durham NC 27702. (919)688-8167. Contact: Editor. Bimonthly magazine, 64-128 pages for Southerners interested in "left-liberal" political perspective and the South; all ages; well-educated. Circ. 7,500. Pays on publication. Buys all rights. Offers kill fee. Byline given. Will consider photocopied and simultaneous submissions. Submit seasonal material 6 months in advance. Reports in 3 months. "Query is appreciated, but not required."

Nonfiction: "Ours is probably the only publication about the South *not* aimed at business or upper-class people; it appeals to all segments of the population. *And*, it is used as a resource—sold as a magazine and then as a book—so it rarely becomes dated." Needs investigative articles about the following subjects as related to the South: politics, energy, institutional power from prisons to universities, women, labor, black people and the economy. Informational interview, profile, historical, think articles, expose, opinion and book reviews. Length: 6,000 words maximum. Pays $50-200. Smaller fee for short items.

Photos: "Very rarely purchase photos, as we have a large number of photographers working for us." 8x10 b&w preferred; no color. Payment negotiable.

THE STATE, *Down Home in North Carolina*, Box 2169, Raleigh NC 27602. Editor: W.B. Wright. 70% freelance written. Publishes material from published and unpublished writers from time to time. Monthly. Buys first serial rights. Pays on acceptance. Deadlines 1 month in advance. Computer printout submissions acceptable; prefers letter-quality to dot-matrix. Sample copy $1.

Nonfiction: General articles about places, people, events, history, nostalgia and general interest in North Carolina. Emphasis on travel in North Carolina, (devotes features regularly to resorts, travel goals, dining and stopping places). Will use humor if related to region. Length: 1,000-1,200 words average. Pays $15-50, including illustrations.

Photos: B&w photos. Pays $3-20, "depending on use."

North Dakota

NORTH DAKOTA REC, North Dakota Association of Rural Electric Cooperatives, Box 727, Mandan ND 58554. (701)663-6501. Managing Editor: Dennis Hill. Monthly magazine. "We cover the rural electric program, primarily funded through the Rural Electrification Administration, and the changes the REA program brought to rural North Dakota. Our focus is on the member/owners of North Dakota's 21 rural electric cooperatives, and we try to report each subject through the eyes of our members." Circ. 75,000. Pays on acceptance. Byline given. Offers one-third of agreed price as kill fee. Buys first North American serial rights. Submit seasonal/holiday material 3-5 months in advance. Simultaneous queries and photocopied submissions OK. Computer printout submissions acceptable; prefers letter-quality to dot-matrix. Reports in 2 weeks on queries; 2 months on mss. Sample copy for 9x12 SAE and $1.39 postage; free writer's guidelines.

Nonfiction: General interest (changes in ND agriculture); historical/nostalgic (on changes REA brought to country); how-to (on efficient use of electricity); and interview/profile (on notable North Dakota rural leaders). No articles that do not show impact/benefit/applicability to rural North Dakotans. Buys 12-15 mss/year. Query. Length: 400-2,000 words. Pays $35-200.

Photos: State availability of photos with query letter or ms. Pays $2.50-5 for b&w contact sheet; $25 maximum for 35mm color transparencies. Captions required. Buys one-time rights.

Fiction: Historical. Buys 2-3 mss/year. Query. Length: 400-1,200 words. Pays $35-150.

Poetry: JoAnn Wimstorfer, family editor. Buys 2-4 poems/year. Submit maximum 8 poems. Pays $5-50.

Tips: "Write about a North Dakotan—one of our members who has done something notable in the ag/energy/rural electric/rural lifestyle areas. Also needs energy efficiency articles on North Dakotans who make wise use of rural electric power."

Ohio

BEACON MAGAZINE, Akron Beacon Journal, 44 E. Exchange St., Akron OH 44328. (216)375-8269. Editor: Ann Sheldon Mezger. 25% freelance written. Eager to work with new/unpublished writers and works with a small number of new/unpublished writers each year. Sunday newspaper magazine of general interest articles with a focus on Northeast Ohio. Circ. 225,000. Pays on publication. Publishes ms an average of 2 months after acceptance. Byline given. Offers 50% kill fee. Buys one-time rights, simultaneous rights, and second serial (reprint) rights. Submit seasonal/holiday material 3 months in advance. Simultaneous queries, and simultaneous and previously published submissions OK. Computer printout submissions acceptable; no dot-matrix. Reports in 1 month. Free sample copy.

Nonfiction: General interest, historical/nostalgic, short humor and interview/profile. Buys 50 mss/year. Query with or without published clips. Include Social Security number with story submission. Length: 500-3,000 words. Pays $75-400. Sometimes pays expenses of writers on assignment.

Photos: State availability of photos. Pays $25-50 for 35mm color transparencies and 8x10 b&w prints. Captions and identification of subjects required. Buys one-time rights.

BEND OF THE RIVER® MAGAZINE, 143 W. Third St., Box 239, Perrysburg OH 43551. (419)874-7534. Publishers: Christine Raizk Alexander and R. Lee Raizk. 90% freelance written. Works with a small number of new/unpublished writers each year, and eager to work with new/unpublished writers. "We buy material that we like whether by an experienced writer or not." Monthly magazine for readers interested in Ohio history, antiques, etc. Circ. 3,000. Pays on publication. Publishes ms an average of 6 months after acceptance. Byline given. Buys one-time rights. Submit seasonal material 2 months in advance; deadline for holiday issue is October 15. Computer printout submissions acceptable; no dot-matrix. Reports in 6 weeks. Sample copy $1.

Nonfiction: "We deal heavily in Ohio history. We are looking for well-researched articles about local history and modern day pioneers doing the unusual. We'd like to see interviews with historical (Ohio) authorities; travel sketches of little-known but interesting places in Ohio; articles about grass roots farmers, famous people from Ohio like Doris Day, Gloria Steinem, etc. and preservation. Our main interest is to give our readers happy thoughts and good reading. We strive for material that says 'yes' to life, past and present." No personal reflection or nostalgia unless you are over 65. Buys 75 unsolicited mss/year. Submit complete ms. Length: 1,500 words. Pays $10-25. Sometimes pays the expenses of writers on assignment.

Photos: Purchases b&w photos with accompanying mss. Pays $1 minimum. Captions required.

Tips: "Any Toledo area, well-researched history will be put on top of the heap. Send us any unusual piece that is either cleverly humorous, divinely inspired or thought provoking. We like articles about historical topics treated in down-to-earth conversational tones. We pay a small amount (however, we're now paying more) but usually use our writers often and through the years. We're loyal."

CINCINNATI MAGAZINE, Suite 300, 35 E. 7th St., Cincinnati OH 45202. (513)421-4300. Editor: Laura Pulfer. Monthly magazine emphasizing Cincinnati living. Circ. 32,000. Pays on acceptance. Byline given. Offers 33% kill fee. Buys all rights. Submit seasonal/holiday material 3 months in advance. Simultaneous, photocopied, and previously published submissions OK. Reports in 5 weeks.

Nonfiction: How-to, informational, interview, photo feature, profile and travel. No humor. Buys 4-5 mss/issue. Query. Length: 2,000-4,000 words. Pays $150-400.

Photos: Thomas Hawley, art director. Photos purchased on assignment only. Model release required.

Columns/Departments: Travel, how-to, sports and consumer tips. Buys 5 mss/issue. Query. Length: 750-1,500 words. Pays $75-150.

Tips: "It helps to mention something you found particularly well done in our magazine. It shows you've done your homework and sets you apart from the person who clearly is not tailoring his idea to our publication. Send article ideas that probe the whys and wherefores of major issues confronting the community, making candid and in-depth appraisals of the problems and honest attempts to seek solutions. Have a clear and well defined subject about the city (the arts, politics, business, sports, government, entertainment); include a rough outline with proposed length; a brief background of writing experience and sample writing if available. We are looking for critical pieces, smoothly written, that ask and answer questions that concern our readers. We do not run features that are 'about' places or businesses simply because they exist. There should be a thesis that guides the writer and the reader. We want balanced articles about the city—the arts, politics, business, etc."

COLUMBUS MONTHLY, 171 E. Livingston Ave., Columbus OH 43215. (614)464-4567. Editorial Director: Lenore E. Brown. 20-40% freelance written. Prefers to work with published/established writers; works with a small number of new/unpublished writers each year. Monthly magazine emphasizing subjects specifically related to Columbus and central Ohio. Pays on publication. Publishes ms an average of 2 months after acceptance. Byline given. Buys all rights. Query for electronic submissions. Computer printout submissions acceptable; prefers letter-quality to dot-matrix. Reports in 1 month. Sample copy $3.20.

Nonfiction: No humor, essays or first person material. "I like query letters which are well-written, indicate the author has some familiarity with *Columbus Monthly*, give me enough detail to make a decision, and include at least a basic biography of the writer." Buys 4-5 unsolicited mss/year. Query. Length: 100-4,500 words. Pays $15-400. Sometimes pays the expenses of writers on assignment.

Photos: State availability of photos. Pay varies for b&w or color prints. Model release required.

Columns/Departments: Art, business, food and drink, movies, politics, sports and theatre. Buys 2-3 columns/issue. Query. Length: 1,000-2,000 words. Pays $100-175.

Tips: "It makes sense to start small—something for our Around Columbus section, perhaps. Stories for that section run between 400-1,000 words."

DAYTON MAGAZINE, Dayton Area Chamber of Commerce, 1980 Kettering Tower, Dayton OH 45423. (513)226-1444. Editor: Linda Lombard. 90% freelance written. Bimonthly magazine covering the Dayton area and its people; "promotes Dayton-area business, people, places and events through informative, timely features and departments." Circ. 10,000. Pays on publication. Publishes ms an average of 2 months after acceptance. Byline given. Buys first serial rights. Submit seasonal/holiday material 4 months in advance. Computer printout submissions acceptable; no dot-matrix. Reports in 2 months. Sample copy for SAE and $1.50 postage.
Nonfiction: General interest, historical/nostalgic, how-to, interview/profile, opinion and photo feature. Must relate to Dayton area. No articles lacking local appeal or slant. Buys approximately 36 mss/year. Query with published clips. Length: 1,400-3,000 words.
Photos: Send photos with ms. Reviews b&w and color contact sheets and color transparencies. Payment "depends on feature." Captions, model releases, and identification of subjects required. Buys one-time rights.
Columns/Departments: Buys 60/year. Query with published clips. Length: 1,000-1,200 words.

‡**THE MAGAZINE**, 4th and Ludlow Sts., Dayton OH 45401. (513)225-2360. Editor: Scott Herron. 30% freelance written. Works with small number of new/unpublished writers each year. Sunday supplement. Circ. 256,000. Byline given. Pays on publication. Publishes ms an average of 3 months after acceptance. Buys first serial rights and second serial (reprint) rights. Query for electronic submissions. Computer printout submissions acceptable. Reports in 2 weeks.
Nonfiction: Magazine focuses on people, places, trends. Few first person articles or essays. Emphasis is on color transparencies supplemented by stories. No travel. Length: open. *"The Daily News* will evaluate articles on their own merits. Average payment per article: $125." Payment varies depending on quality of writing. Sometimes pays expenses of writers on assignment.
Photos: Transparencies and glossy photos. Evaluates photos on their own merit. Payment variable depending on quality.

OHIO MAGAZINE, Ohio Magazine, Inc., Subsidiary of Dispatch Printing Co., 40 S. 3rd St., Columbus OH 43215. Editor-in-Chief: Robert B. Smith. 65% freelance written. Works with a small number of new/unpublished writers each year. Monthly magazine; 96-156 pages. Emphasizes news and feature material of Ohio for an educated, urban and urbane readership. Circ. 103,327. Pays on publication. Publishes ms an average of 5 months after acceptance. Buys all rights, second serial (reprint) rights, one-time rights, first North American serial rights, or first serial rights. Byline given except on short articles appearing in sections. Submit seasonal/holiday material 5 months in advance. Simultaneous, photocopied, and previously published submissions OK. Computer printout submissions acceptable; no dot-matrix. Reports in 2 months. Sample copy $2.50; writer's guidelines for SASE.
Nonfiction: Features: 2,000-8,000 words. Pays $250-700. Cover pieces $600-850; Ohioana and Ohioans (should be offbeat with solid news interest; 50-250 words, pays $15-50); Ohioguide (pieces on upcoming Ohio events, must be offbeat and worth traveling for; 100-300 words, pays $10-15); Diner's Digest ("We are still looking for writers with extensive restaurant reviewing experience to do 5-10 short reviews each month in specific sections of the state on a specific topic. Fee is on a retainer basis and negotiable"); Money (covering business related news items, profiles of prominent people in business community, personal finance—all Ohio angle; 300-1,000 words, pays $50-250); and Living (embodies dining in, home furnishings, gardening and architecture; 300-1,000 words, pays $50-250). Send submissions for features to Robert B. Smith, editor-in-chief, or Ellen Stein Burbach, managing editor; Ohioguide and Diner's Digest to services editor; and Money to Ellen Stein Burbach, managing editor. No political columns or articles of limited geographical interest (must be of interest to all of Ohio). Buys 40 unsolicited mss/year. Sometimes pays expenses of writers on assignment.
Columns/Departments: Ellen Stein Burbach, managing editor. Sports, Last Word, travel, fashion and wine. Open to suggestions for new columns/departments.
Photos: Ellen Stein Burbach, managing editor. Rate negotiable.
Tips: "Freelancers should send a brief prospectus prior to submission of the complete article. All articles should have a definite Ohio application."

‡**PLAIN DEALER MAGAZINE**, Plain Dealer Publishing Co., 1801 Superior Ave., Cleveland OH 44120. (216)344-4546. Editor: Diane Carman. Managing Editor: Norma Conaway. 50% freelance written. A Sunday newspaper magazine covering people and issues relating to Cleveland. Circ. 550,000. Pays on publication. Publishes ms an average of 1 year after acceptance. Byline given. Offers $50 kill fee. Buys first or one-time rights. Submit seasonal/holiday material 3 months in advance. Simultaneous, photocopied and previously published submissions OK. Computer printout submissions OK. Reports in 6 weeks on queries; 3 month on mss. Sample copy 25¢.

Nonfiction: Book excerpts, essays, expose, general interest, historical/nostalgic, humor, interview/profile, personal experience and travel. Buys 20 mss/year. Query with published clips, or send complete ms. Length: 800-5,000 words. Pays $75-750.
Photos: State availability of photos with submission. Buys one-time rights.
Fiction: Adventure, confession, fantasy, humorous, mainstream and slice-of-life vignettes. Buys 5 mss/year. Send complete ms. Length: 1,000-5,000 words. Pays $100-700.

TOLEDO MAGAZINE, The Blade, 541 Superior St., Toledo OH 43660. (419)245-6121. Editor: Sue Stankey. Managing Editor: Edson Whipple. 60% freelance written. Prefers to work with published/established writers and works with a small number of new/unpublished writers each year. Weekly general interest magazine that appears in the Sunday newspaper. Circ. 225,000. Pays on publication. Publishes ms an average of 3 months after acceptance. Byline given. Buys one-time rights. Submit seasonal/holiday material 4-6 months in advance. Simultaneous queries and submissions OK. Computer printout submissions acceptable; no dot-matrix. Reports in 2 weeks on queries; 1 month on mss. Sample copy for 12x9 SAE.
Nonfiction: General interest, historical/nostalgic, humor, interview/profile and personal experience. Buys 100-200 mss/year. Query with or without published clips. Length: 500-6,000 words. Pays $75-500. Sometimes pays expenses of writers on assignment.
Photos: Dave Cron, photo editor. State availability of photos. Reviews b&w and color contact sheets. Payment negotiable. Captions, model release, and identification of subjects required. Buys one-time rights.
Tips: "Submit a well-organized story proposal and include copies of previously published stories."

TRISTATE MAGAZINE, The Cincinnati Enquirer (Gannett), 617 Vine St., Cincinnati OH 45201. (513)369-1938. Editor: Alice Hornbaker. 35-50% freelance written. Eager to work with new/unpublished writers. Sunday newspaper magazine covering a wide range of all local topics. Circ. 750,000. Pays on publication. Publishes ms an average of 4 months after acceptance. Byline given. Buys first serial rights. Submit seasonal/holiday material 6 months in advance. Simultaneous queries, and simultaneous, photocopied, and previously published submissions OK. Query for electronic submissions. Computer printout submissions acceptable; prefers letter-quality to dot-matrix. Reports in 2 weeks on queries. Writer's guidelines for SASE.
Nonfiction: General interest, historical/nostalgic, humor and interview/profile pertaining to the Cincinnati tristate area only. No editorials, how-to, new products, inspirational or technical material. Buys 25-50 mss/year. Query first except for humor and short fiction. Length: 1,000-2,400 words. Pays $100-350.
Fiction: Short-short fiction to 1,000 words, all locally based.
Photos: State availability of photos. Pays $25 per photo. Identification of subjects required. Buys one-time rights.

‡WESTERN RESERVE MAGAZINE, Box 2780, North Canton OH 44720. (216)452-1820. Editor: David Patterson. 60% freelance written. Monthly digest-sized magazine covering local history, house and garden, nature, antiques, historic, preservation. "Articles must be geared to Northeast Ohio and aimed at highly literate, well-educated, well-to-do audience." Circ. 15,000. Pays on publication. Publishes ms an average of 2-6 months after acceptance. Byline given. Buys first or all rights. Submit seasonal/holiday material 4 months in advance. Photocopied submissions OK. Query for electronic submissions. Computer printout submissions OK. Reports in 2 months. Sample copy $2.50 with 6x9 SAE.
Nonfiction: Book excerpts (history); historical/nostalgic; how-to (restoration); interview/profile; photo feature (along with articles); travel (nearby getaways); historic preservations; and house and garden. "No boring first person reminiscenses, far away travel, 'Auntie Mimi's plate collection' articles." Buys 20-30 mss/year. Query with or without published clips, or send complete ms. Length: 1,000-5,000 words. Pays $100 maximum for assigned articles; pays $50 maximum for unsolicited articles.
Photos: Send photos with submission. Reviews 35mm transparencies and 5x7 prints. Offers no additonal payment for photos accepted with ms. Captions, model releases and identification of subjects required. Buys one-time and reprint rights.
Tips: "Know the Northeast Ohio area."

ALWAYS submit manuscripts or queries with a self-addressed, stamped envelope (SASE) within your country or International Reply Coupons purchased from the post office for other countries.

Oklahoma

OKLAHOMA TODAY, Oklahoma Department of Tourism and Recreation, Box 53384, Oklahoma City OK 73152. Editor-in-Chief: Sue Carter. Managing Editor: Susan Tomlinson. 99% freelance written. Works with a small number of new/unpublished writers each year. Bimonthly magazine covering travel and recreation in the state of Oklahoma. "We are interested in showing off the best Oklahoma has to offer; we're pretty serious about our travel slant but will also consider history, nature and personality profiles." Circ. 35,000. Pays on acceptance. Publishes ms an average of 3 months after acceptance. Byline given. Buys first serial rights. Submit seasonal/holiday material 1 year in advance "depending on photographic requirements." Simultaneous queries and photocopied submissions OK. "We don't mind letter-quality computer printout submissions at all, provided they are presented in manuscript format, i.e., double spaced and on 8½x11 sheets, or a size close to that. No scrolls, no dot-matrix." Reports in 2 months. Sample copy $2.50; writer's guidelines with SASE.

Nonfiction: Book excerpts (pre-publication only, on Oklahoma topics); photo feature and travel (in Oklahoma). "We are a specialized market; no first person reminiscences or fashion, memoirs, though just about any topic can be used if given a travel slant." Buys 35-40 mss/year. Query with published clips; no phone queries. Length: 1,000-1,500 words. Pays $150-250.

Photos: High-quality color transparencies, b&w prints. "We are especially interested in developing contacts with photographers who either live in Oklahoma or have shot here. Send samples and price range." Free photo guidelines with SASE. Send photos with ms. Pays $50-100 for b&w and $50-250 for color; reviews 2¼ and 35mm color transparencies. Model releases, identification of subjects, and other information for captions required. Buys one-time rights plus right to use photos for promotional purposes.

Tips: "The best way to become a regular contributor to *Oklahoma Today* is to query us with one or more story ideas, each developed to give us an idea of your proposed slant. We're looking for *lively* writing, writing that doesn't need to be heavily edited and is newspaper style. We have a two-person editorial staff, and freelancers who can write and have done their homework get called again and again. Since we're a magazine interested only in Oklahoma topics, the two big questions are 1)Do I have an Oklahoma query?, and 2) Can I write with authority on that topic?"

Oregon

CASCADES EAST, 716 NE 4th St., Box 5784, Bend OR 97708. (503)382-0127. Editor: Geoff Hill. 100% freelance written. Prefers to work with published/established writers. Quarterly magazine; 64 pages. For "all ages as long as they are interested in outdoor recreation in central Oregon: fishing, hunting, sight-seeing, hiking, bicycling, mountain climbing, backpacking, rockhounding, skiing, snowmobiling, etc." Circ. 8,000 (distributed throughout area resorts and motels and to subscribers). Pays on publication. Publishes ms an average of 6 months after acceptance. Buys all rights. Byline given. Submit seasonal/holiday material 6 months in advance. Computer printout submissions acceptable; no dot-matrix. Reports in 6 weeks. Sample copy $2.

Nonfiction: General interest (first person experiences in outdoor central Oregon—with photos, can be dramatic, humorous or factual); historical (for feature, "Little Known Tales from Oregon History", with b&w photos); and personal experience (needed on outdoor subjects: dramatic, humorous or factual). "No articles that are too general, sight-seeing articles that come from a travel folder, or outdoor articles without the first person approach." Buys 20-30 unsolicited mss/year. Query. Length: 1,000-3,000 words. Pays 3-10¢/word.

Photos: "Old photos will greatly enhance chances of selling a historical feature. First person articles need black and white photos, also." Pays $8-15 for b&w; $15-50 for color transparencies. Captions preferred. Buys one-time rights.

Tips: "Submit stories a year or so in advance of publication. We are seasonal and must plan editorials for summer '89 in the spring of '88, etc., in case seasonal photos are needed."

Pennsylvania

ERIE & CHAUTAUQUA MAGAZINE, Charles H. Strong Bldg., 1250 Tower Ln., Erie PA 16505. (814)452-6070. Editor: K.L. Kalvelage. 100% freelance written. Works with a small number of new/unpublished writers each year. Biannual magazine covering the region of Erie (city), Erie County, Crawford County, Warren County, Pennsylvania and Chautauqua County, New York; for upscale readers with above average education and income. Circ. 30,000. Pays 30 days after publication. Buys all rights. Will reassign rights to author upon written request after publication. Computer printout submissions acceptable; no dot-matrix. Reports in 1 month. Sample copy $2.50; writer's guidelines for SASE.

Nonfiction: Feature articles (usually five per issue) on "key issues affecting our coverage area, lifestyle topics, major projects or events which are of importance to our readership, area history with relevance to life today, preservation and restoration, arts and cultural subjects." Local personality profiles are also needed. Query first. Length: 3,000 words maximum for articles. Pays $35/published page. "All material *must* have relevance to our coverage area." Sometimes pays expenses of writers on assignment.

Photos: Color photos for covers by assignment only to local photographer. Will consider 8x10 b&w glossies with stories. Pays $15 per b&w for all rights 30 days after publication. Model releases and captions required.

Columns/Departments: Business, education, social life, arts and culture and travel (within 100-200 miles of Erie). Will consider new departments on basis of resume showing expertise and two sample columns. Length: 750 words maximum.

Tips: "It's rewarding to see a variety of ideas and styles in freelancers. We enjoy being able to give new writers a start and finding the person with special expertise for a special story. But we regret reviewing inappropriate material and notice a lack of discipline in meeting deadlines and inadequate research—stories without 'meat'."

PENNSYLVANIA, Pennsylvania Magazine Co., Box 576, Camp Hill PA 17011. (717)761-6620. Editor: Albert E. Holliday. Managing Editor: Joan Holliday. 90% freelance written. Bimonthly magazine. Circ. 22,500. Pays on acceptance for assigned articles. Publishes ms an average of 6 months after acceptance. Byline given. Offers 33% kill fee. Buys first North American serial rights. Computer printout submissions acceptable; prefers letter-quality to dot-matrix. Reports in 2 weeks on queries; 3 weeks on mss. Sample copy $2.50; writer's guidelines for #10 SASE.

Nonfiction: General interest, historical/nostalgic, inspirational, personal experience, photo feature, and travel. Nothing on Amish topics, hunting or skiing. Buys 50-75 mss/year. Query. Length: 250-2,500 words. Pays $25-250. Sometimes pays the expenses of writers on assignment.

Photos: Send photocopies of available illustrations with queries. Reviews 35mm and color transparencies and 5x7 b&w prints. Pays $5-50 for b&w; $10-100 for color. Captions and identification of subjects required. Buys one-time rights.

Columns/Departments: Panorama—short items about people, unusual events.

PENNSYLVANIA HERITAGE, Pennsylvania Historical and Museum Commission, Box 1026, Harrisburg PA 17108-1026. (717)787-1396. Editor: Michael J. O'Malley III. 90% freelance written. Prefers to work with published/established writers. Quarterly magazine covering Pennsylvania history and culture. "*Pennsylvania Heritage* introduces readers to Pennsylvania's rich culture and historic legacy, educates and sensitizes them to the value of preserving that heritage and entertains and involves them in such as way as to ensure that Pennsylvania's past has a future. The magazine is intended for intelligent lay readers." Circ. 9,000. Pays on acceptance. Publishes ms an average of 8-12 months after acceptance. Byline given. Buys all rights. Simultaneous queries, and simultaneous and photocopied submissions OK. Computer printout submissions acceptable; prefers letter-quality to dot-matrix. Reports in 3 weeks on queries; 6 weeks on mss. Sample copy for 9x12 SAE and $2.50; free writer's guidelines.

Nonfiction: Art, science, biographies, industry, business, politics, transportation, military, historic preservation, archaeology, photography, etc. No articles which in no way relate to Pennsylvania history or culture. "Our format requires feature-length articles. Manuscripts with illustrations are especially sought for publication." Buys 20-24 mss/year. Query. Length: 2,000-3,500 words. Pays $0-100.

Photos: State availability or send photos with query or ms. Pays $25-100 for color transparencies; $5-10 for b&w photos. Captions and identification of subjects required. Buys one-time rights.

Tips: "We are looking for well-written, interesting material that pertains to any aspect of Pennsylvania history or culture. Potential contributors should realize that, although our articles are popularly styled, they are not light, puffy or breezy; in fact they demand strident documentation and substantiation (sans footnotes). The most frequent mistake made by writers in completing articles for us is making them either too scholarly or too nostalgic. We want material which educates, but also entertains. Authors should make history readable and entertaining."

PHILADELPHIA MAGAZINE, 1500 Walnut St., Philadelphia PA 19102. Editor: Ron Javers. 50% freelance written. Prefers to work with published/established writers; works with a small number of new/unpublished writers each year. Monthly magazine for sophisticated middle- and upper-income people in the Greater Philadelphia/South Jersey area. Circ. 152,272. Pays on acceptance. Publishes ms an average of 2 months after acceptance. Buys first serial rights. Pays 20% kill fee. Byline given. Computer printout submissions acceptable; prefers letter-quality to dot-matrix. Reports in 1 month. Writer's guidelines for SASE.

Nonfiction: Bill Bonelli, articles editor. "Articles should have a strong Philadelphia (city and suburbs) focus but should avoid Philadelphia stereotypes—we've seen them all. Submit lifestyles, city survival, profiles of interesting people, business stories, music, the arts, sports and local politics, stressing the topical or unusual. Intelligent, entertaining essays on subjects of specific local interest. No puff pieces. We offer lots of latitude for style." Buys 50 mss/year. Length: 1,000-7,000 words. Pays $100-1,000. Sometimes pays expenses of writers on assignment.

PITTSBURGH MAGAZINE, Metropolitan Pittsburgh Public Broadcasting, Inc., 4802 5th Ave., Pittsburgh PA 15213. (412)622-1360. Editor-in-Chief: Bruce VanWyngarden. 60% freelance written. Prefers to work with published/established writers; works with a small number of new/unpublished writers each year. "The magazine is purchased on newsstands and by subscription and is given to those who contribute $25 or more a year to public TV in western Pennsylvania." Monthly magazine; 132 pages. Circ. 56,700. Pays on publication. Publishes ms an average of 2 months after acceptance. Buys first North American serial rights and second serial (reprint) rights. Pays kill fee. Byline given. Submit seasonal/holiday material 6 months in advance. Electronic submissions OK via IBM PC. Computer printout submissions acceptable; prefers letter-quality to dot-matrix. Reports in 2 months. Publishes ms an average of 2 months after acceptance. Sample copy $2; free writer's guidelines.
Nonfiction: Expose, lifestyle, sports, informational, service, interview, nostalgia and profile. Query or send complete ms. Length: 2,500 words. Pays $50-500. Query for photos. Model releases required. Sometimes pays the expenses of writers on assignment.
Columns/Departments: Art, books, films, dining, health, sports and theatre. "All must relate to Pittsburgh or western Pennsylvania."

‡**THE PITTSBURGH PRESS SUNDAY MAGAZINE**, The Pittsburgh Press Co., 34 Boulevard of the Allies, Pittsburgh PA 15230. (412)263-1510. Editor: Ed Wintermantel. 10% freelance written. Prefers to work with published/established writers. A weekly general interest newspaper magazine for a general audience. Circ. 625,000. Pays on publication. Publishes ms an average of 2 months after acceptance. Byline given. Not copyrighted. Buys first serial rights in circulation area. Simultaneous queries acceptable. Query for electronic submissions. Computer printout submissions OK. Reports in 1 month. Writer's guidelines for #10 SASE.
Nonfiction: Regional or local interest, humor and interview/profile. No hobbies, how-to or timely events. Buys 40-50 mss/year. Query. "When submitting a manuscript, writer must include his or her social security number. This is a requirement of the Internal Revenue Service since payments for published stories must be reported." Length: 1,000-3,000 words. Pays $100-400.

South Carolina

‡**MYRTLE BEACH MAGAZINE, The Magazine of Grand Strand Lifestyle & Business**, Himmelsbach Communications, Inc., Box 1474, North Myrtle Beach SC 29598. (803)272-8150. Editor: Cynthia L. Clemmer. 60% freelance written. A quarterly covering lifestyles and businesses of Myrtle Beach area (Grand Stand) written "primarily for upper-income Grand Strand residents, including retirees and newcomers, although a number of subscribers are non-residents who have business or property interests or who want in-depth information about the areas." Circ. 15,000. Pays on publication. Publishes ms an average of 3 months after acceptance. Byline given. Buys first serial rights and second serial (reprint) rights, all rights or makes work-for-hire assignments. Submit seasonal/holiday material 6 months in advance. Photocopied and previously published submissions OK. Computer printout submissions OK; prefers letter-quality to dot-matrix. Reports in 1 month on queries; 2 months on mss. Sample copy $2; free writer's guidelines.
Nonfiction: Book excerpts, expose, general interest, historical/nostalgic, how-to (practical ideas for improving local lifestyles), humor, interview/profile (local leaders and personalities), photo feature (local business, sports, arts, entertainment, food, gardening, homes) and travel. "No articles without a local angle or ones geared for tourists rather than residents. Our non-resident readers generally have been visiting here so long and so often that they consider themselves 'second-homers' not tourists." Buys 12-15 mss/year. Query with or without published clips, or send complete ms. Length: 1,500-2,500 words. Pays $75 minimum. Sometimes pays the expenses of writers on assignment.
Photos: State availability of photos with query; send photos with ms. Reviews contact sheets and transparencies. Offers negotiable payment per photo. Captions, model releases and identification of subjects required. Buys one-time rights.
Columns/Departments: Photo Finish (photo story featuring unusual or historic photos), 50-100 words. Buys 20-25 mss/year. Query with published clip or complete ms. Pays $35 minimum.
Poetry: Any kind of poetry if very brief. No poetry without a local angle. Buys 1-2 poems/year. Submit maximum 3 poems. Length: about 30 lines. Pays $5-15.
Tips: "Please don't submit a query/manuscript without first reviewing the magazine itself—then give us a reason for publishing it in *Myrtle Beach Magazine*."

Tennessee

MEMPHIS, MM Corporation, Box 256, Memphis TN 38101. (901)521-9000. Editor: Larry Conley. 60% freelance written. Works with a small number of new/unpublished writers. Circ. 26,500. Pays on publication.

Publishes ms an average of 3 months after acceptance. Byline given. Buys first North American serial rights. Pays $35-100 kill fee. Simultaneous, photocopied, and previously published submissions OK. Computer printout submissions acceptable; prefers letter-quality to dot-matrix. Reports in 6 weeks. Sample copy for 9x12 SAE and $2.50 postage; writer's guidelines for SASE.
Nonfiction: Expose, general interest, historical, how-to, humor, interview and profiles. "Virtually all our material has strong mid-South connections." Buys 25 freelance mss/year. Query or submit complete ms or published clips. Length: 1,500-5,000 words. Pays $100-1,000. Sometimes pays expenses of writers on assignment.
Tips: "The kinds of manuscripts we most need have a sense of story (i.e., plot, suspense, character), an abundance of evocative images to bring that story alive, and a sensitivity to issues at work in Memphis. The most frequent mistakes made by writers in completing an article for us are lack of focus, lack of organization, factual gaps and failure to capture the magazine's style. Tough investigative pieces would be especially welcomed."

MID-SOUTH MAGAZINE, *Commercial Appeal*, Box 334, Memphis TN 38101. (901)529-2794. Editor: Scott Hill. 25% freelance written. Works with small number of new/unpublished writers each year. Sunday newspaper supplement. Circ. 300,000. Pays after publication. Publishes ms an average of 2 months after acceptance. Byline given. Buys one-time rights. Simultaneous queries, and photocopied and previously published submissions (if so indicated) OK. Query for electronic submission. Computer printout submissions acceptable; prefers letter-quality to dot-matrix. Reports in 3 weeks.
Nonfiction: General interest (with regional tie-in). Buys 12 mss/year. Query with published clips. Length: 1,500-2,000 words. Pays $200 maximum.
Photos: State availability of photos. Reviews color transparencies and 5x7 b&w glossy prints. Photos are paid for with payment for ms. Buys one-time rights.

Texas

‡AUSTIN MAGAZINE, American Publishing Corp., Box 4368, Austin TX 78765. (512)339-9955. Managing Editor: Laura Tuma. 60% freelance written. "Hybrid city/business magazine published for Chamber of Commerce. Strong local angle required." Circ. 17,500. Pays on publication. Publishes ms an average of 3 months after acceptance. Byline given. Offers 25% kill fee. Buys first North American serial rights. Submit seasonal/holiday material 6 months in advance. Query for electronic submissions. Computer printout submissions OK. Reports in 1 month. Sample copy $2.25.; free writer's guidelines.
Nonfiction: General interest, interview/profile, photo feature and travel. Buys 40-50 mss/year. Query with published clips. Length: 750-2,500 words. Pays 10¢/word. Sometimes pays the expenses of writers on assignment.
Photos: State availability of photos with submission. Reviews 5x7 prints. Offers $15-50 per photo. Captions, model releases and identification of subjects required. Buys one-time rights.
Tips: "I appreciate clear, well-thought-out queries, with previously published clips to review. Also, since we are strictly a local magazine, some knowledge of Austin is very helpful. Our BusinessLine section uses four to six short (750 words, approximately) articles each month. Articles can be business trips, profiles on successful local business leaders or other related topics."

‡'D' MAGAZINE, Southwest Media Corporation, Suite 1200, 3988 N. Central Expressway, Dallas TX 75204. (214)827-5000. Editor: Ruth Miller Fitzgibbons. 25% freelance written. Monthly magazine. "We are a general interest magazine with emphasis on events occuring in Dallas." Circ. 81,036. Pays on acceptance. Publishes ms an average of 2 months after acceptance. Byline given. Offers 25% kill fee. Buys first North American serial rights. Submit seasonal/holiday material 2 months in advance. Photocopied and previously published submissions OK. Query for electronic submissions. Computer printout submissions OK; prefers letter-quality to dot-matrix. Reports in 1 month. Sample copy $1.95 with SAE and 4 first class stamps; free writer's guidelines.
Nonfiction: Book excerpts, essays, expose, general interest, historical/nostalgic, how-to, humor, interview/profile and travel. Buys 20-30 mss/year. Query with published clips. Length: 1,000-5,000 words. Pays $75-750 for assigned articles; pays $50-500 for unsolicited articles. Pays expenses of writers on assignment.
Photos: State availability of photos with submission. Reviews transparencies and 35mm prints. Offers $50-75 per photo. Captions required. Buys one-time rights.
Columns/Departments: Business; Politics; Travel; and Relationships. Query with published clips or send complete ms. Length: 1,500-2,000 words. Pays $250-350.
Tips: "Tell us something about our city that we have not written about. We realize that is very difficult for someone outside of Dallas to do—that's why 90% of our magazine is written by people who live in the North Texas area."

DALLAS LIFE MAGAZINE, Sunday Magazine of *The Dallas Morning News*, Belo Corporation, Communications Center, Dallas TX 75265. (214)745-8432. Editor: Melissa Houtte. Weekly magazine. "We are a lively, topical, sometimes controversial city magazine devoted to informing, enlightening and entertaining our urban Sunbelt readers with material which is specifically relevant to Dallas lifestyles and interests." Pays on acceptance. Byline given. Buys first North American serial rights or simultaneous rights. Simultaneous queries and submissions OK ("if not competitive in our area"). Computer printout submissions acceptable; prefers letter-quality to dot-matrix. Reports in 1 month on queries; 6 weeks on mss. Sample copy $1.

Nonfiction: General interest; humor (short); interview/profile. "All material must, repeat *must*, have a Dallas metropolitan area frame of reference." Special issues include: Spring and fall home furnishings theme. Buys 15-25 unsolicited mss/year. Query with published clips or send complete ms. Length: 750-3,000 words. Pays $200-650.

Photos: Buys one-time rights.

EL PASO MAGAZINE, El Paso Chamber of Commerce, 10 Civic Center Plaza, El Paso TX 79901. (915)544-7880. Executive Editor: Russell S. Autry. Managing Editor: Brenda Castaneda. 75% freelance written. Prefers to work with published/established writers; works with a small number of new/unpublished writers each year. Monthly magazine that "takes a positive look at El Paso people and businesses. Readers are owners and managers of El Paso businesses." Circ. 5,000. Pays on publication. Publishes ms an average of 2 months after acceptance. Byline given. Buys first North American serial rights. Submit seasonal/holiday material 3 months in advance. Simultaneous queries, and simultaneous and photocopied submissions OK. Computer printout submissions acceptable; prefers letter-quality to dot-matrix. Reports in 2 months. Free sample copy and writer's guidelines.

Nonfiction: General interest, business, historical/nostalgic, interview/profile and photo feature. Buys 75 mss/year. Query with published clips. Length: 1,000-2,500 words. Pays 7¢/word.

Photos: Send photos with ms. Pays $10/photo; $300 for cover photo. Captions, model releases and identification of subjects required. Buys one-time rights.

Tips: "An article for *El Paso Magazine* must talk about an area business and its successes. *El Paso Magazine* will rely more on experienced writers in 1988. Writers must know El Paso."

‡HOUSTON CITY MAGAZINE, Southwest Media Corp., Suite 1450, 1800 W. Loop South, Houston TX 77027. (713)850-7600. Editor: Douglas Milburn. Managing Editor: Joe Phillips. 80% freelance written. Monthly magazine. "We cover the city—the arts, entertainment, business, space, oil, medicine—anything of interest to Houstonians." Circ. 75,000. Pays on publication. Publishes ms an average of 2 months after acceptance. Byline given. Offers 15% kill fee. Buys first North American serial rights. Submit seasonal/holiday material 6 months in advance. Computer printout submissions OK. Reports in 2 weeks on queries; 1 month on mss. Sample copy for 9x12 SAE; writer's guidelines for SASE.

Nonfiction: Essays, expose, general interest, humor, interview/profile, opinion, photo feature and travel. "Everything must have a *strong* Houston hook." Buys 80 mss/year. Query with published clips. Length: 400-3,000 words. Pays $100-1,500 for assigned articles. Sometimes pays the expenses of writers on assignment.

Photos: State availability of photos with submission. Reviews transparencies and prints. Offers $50-300 per photo. Model releases and identification of subjects required. Buys one-time rights.

Columns/Departments: Pat Dougherty, editor. Traffic Rap (interviews while driving in the city), 800 words; City Beats (short newsy takes on the city), 400-600 words; Stepping Out (arts and entertainment shorts), 400-600 words. Buys 96 mss/year. Query with published clips. Pays $100-400.

‡INNER-VIEW, The Newsmagazine of Houston's Innercity, Inner-View Publishing Co., Inc., Box 66156, Houston TX 77266. (713)523-NEWS. Editor: Kit van Cleave. 20% freelance written. Works with small number of new/unpublished writers each year, and is eager to work with new/unpublished writers. Monthly tabloid covering those who live or work inside Loop 610 (half of Houston). "We only print that material which has to do with the lives or careers of those who live and work in our half of Houston. We want to let those writers who may be new in town or are coming here know that we are here and will work with them." Circ. 35,000. Pays on publication. Publishes ms an average of 2 months after acceptance. Byline given. Buys first North American serial rights, first rights or one-time rights. Submit seasonal/holiday material 1 month in advance. Simultaneous and photocopied submissions OK. Computer printout submissions acceptable; no dot-matrix. Reports in 1 month. Sample copy for 8½x11 SAE with $1.20 postage.

Nonfiction: Interview/profile and movie reviews. Plans special holiday issues. Nothing that is "too general to have anything to do with our market; life in New England, for example." Query. Length: 1-2 pages. Pays $20-50.

Photos: State availability of photos with submission. Reviews 8x10 or 5x7 prints. Offers no additional payment for photos accepted with ms. Captions required. Buys one-time rights.

Columns/Departments: Movie Reviews (Innercity, Houston TX; the reviewers must live or work in this area to know what's going on so they can see the film from innercity perspective). Buys 50 mss/year. Query.

Length: 1-2 pages. "We pay tickets or provide press passes."

Tips: "Our publication is part of the new concept of providing a 'small town' community newspaper as part of a major urban area. We are in our eighth year and very successful because we talk about what people in our half of Houston want to know about, and we get advertising from those businesses which are in our market area. Writers should be very familiar with our market area. Our area covers four of the five wealthiest residential areas in Houston, plus all the arts headquarters, plus all the universities in Houston. It's a very upscale area, and 40% of all Houston workers still work in the downtown area, which is the heart of our market area."

SAN ANGELO MAGAZINE, San Angelo Standard Inc., 34 W. Harris, San Angelo TX 76903. (915)653-1221. Editor: Soren W. Nielsen. Executive Editor: Kandis Gatewood. 25% freelance written. Works with a small number of new/unpublished writers each year. Quarterly magazine about San Angelo, Texas and immediate area. "San Angelo magazine is a city magazine, offering a wide variety of features and profiles." Circ. 7,000. Pays on publication. Publishes ms an average of 3-5 months after acceptance. Byline given. Buys first serial rights. Submit seasonal/holiday material 4 months in advance. Query for electronic submissions. Computer printout submissions acceptable; prefers letter-quality to dot-matrix. Reports in 1 month. Sample copy for 9x11 SASE and 4 first class stamps; writer's guidelines for SASE.

Nonfiction: General interest, historical/nostalgic, interview/profile and travel. General interest and historical articles of San Angelo area. No articles not applicable to San Angelo area. Buys 5-6 mss/year. Query with published clips. Pays $25-100. Rarely pays expenses of writers on assignment.

Tips: "Writer should note that first-person articles are not used."

‡SAN ANTONIO MONTHLY, Harte-Hanks Magazines, Inc., Box 17554, San Antonio TX 78217. (512)829-9200. Editor: Jay Rosser. Managing Editor: Christi Phelps. 90% freelance written. A monthly city magazine on lifestyles, issues and politics. "Our readers are basically upper-middle to upper class. They want to take glimpses into the city that don't come packaged in newspapers—issues ranging from politics to home designing, people to travel." Circ. 20,000. Pays on acceptance. Publishes ms an average of 3 months after acceptance. Byline given. Negotiable kill fee. Buys first North American serial rights. Submit seasonal/holiday material 6 months in advance. Simultaneous submissions OK. Computer printout submissions OK; no dot-matrix. Reports in 3 weeks on queries; 6 weeks on mss. Sample copy for 8½x11 SAE with $2.15.

Nonfiction: Expose, interview/profile, photo feature, religious and travel (Texas, Mexico and the Southwest). All submissions must apply to San Antonio or its residents. Buys 20 mss/year. Query. Length: 750-5,000 words. Pays $200-400 for assigned articles; pays $75-400 for unsolicited articles. Sometimes pays the expenses of writers on assignment.

Photos: State availability of photos with submission. Reviews transparencies. Payment negotiable. Captions required. Buys one-time rights.

3RD COAST MAGAZINE, The Magazine of Austin, Third Coast Media Inc., Box 592, Austin TX 78767. (512)472-2016. Editor: David Stansbury. Managing Editor: Kate Berger. 75% freelance written. A monthly magazine covering the city of Austin, Texas. Circ. 20,000. Pays on publication. Publishes ms an average of 3 months after acceptance. Byline given. Offers 25% kill fee. Buys first rights and exclusive periodical resale rights in North America, for a period of one year after publication in *3rd Coast*, the proceeds from any such resale to be divided equally between the author and *3rd Coast*. Submit seasonal/holiday material 6 months in advance. Photocopied submissions OK. Computer printout submissions acceptable; prefers letter-quality to dot-matrix. Sample copy $2; writer's guidelines for SASE.

Nonfiction: Book excerpts, essays, general interest, historical/nostalgic, humor, interview/profile, photo feature and travel. Query with published clips. Length: 500-7,000 words. Pays $100-1,200. Sometimes pays the expenses of writers on assignment.

Photos: Send photos with submissions. Reviews contact sheets and prints. Offers $50-200/photo. Captions, model releases, and identification of subjects required. Buys one-time rights.

Columns/Departments: Craig Hattersley, column/department editor. Art, books, music, performances, profiles, politics, urban affairs, and humor related to Austin, Texas. Buys 30 mss/year. Query with published clips or send complete ms. Length: 800-2,000 words. Pays $150-200.

Vermont

VERMONT LIFE MAGAZINE, 61 Elm St., Montpelier VT 05602. (802)828-3241. Editor-in-Chief: Thomas K. Slayton. 90% freelance written. Prefers to work with published/established writers. Quarterly magazine. Circ. 120,000. Publishes ms an average of 9 months after acceptance. Byline given. Offers kill fee. Buys first serial rights. Submit seasonal/holiday material 1 year in advance. Simultaneous queries, and simultaneous, photocopied, and previously published submissions OK. Computer printout submissions acceptable; prefers letter-quality to dot-matrix. Reports in 1 month. Writer's guidelines on request.

Nonfiction: Wants articles on today's Vermont, those which portray a typical or, if possible, unique aspect of the state or its people. Style should be literate, clear and concise. Subtle humor favored. No Vermont dialect attempts as in "Ayup", outsider's view on visiting Vermont, or "Vermont cliches"—maple syrup, town meetings or stereotyped natives. Buys 60 mss/year. Query by letter essential. Length: 1,500 words average. Pays 20¢/word. Seldom pays expenses of writers on assignment.

Photos: Buys photographs with mss; buys seasonal photographs alone. Prefers b&w contact sheets to look at first on assigned material. Color submissions must be 4x5 or 35mm transparencies. Rates on acceptance: $75 inside, color; $200 for cover. Gives assignments but only with experienced photographers. Query in writing. Captions, model releases, and identification of subjects required. Buys one-time rights, but often negotiates for re-use rights.

Tips: "Writers who read our magazine are given more consideration because they understand that we want Vermontish articles about Vermont. If a writer has a genuine working knowledge of Vermont, his or her work usually shows it. Writers who have only visited the state tend to write in predictable ways on stereotyped subjects."

VERMONT VANGUARD PRESS, Statewide Weekly, Vanguard Publishing, 87 College St., Burlington VT 05401. (802)864-0506. Editor: Joshua Mamis. News Editor: Peter Freyne. Associate Editor: Pamela Polston. 70% freelance written. Works with a small number of new/unpublished writers each year. A weekly alternative newspaper, locally oriented, covering Vermont politics, environment, arts, development, etc. Circ. 20,000. Pays on publication. Publishes ms an average of 1½ months after acceptance. Byline given. Offers 50% kill fee only after written acceptance. Buys first serial rights. Submit seasonal/holiday material 1 month in advance. Simultaneous queries, and simultaneous, photocopied, and previously published submissions OK. Electronic submissions OK via IBM PC or 1200 Baud Modem. Computer printout submissions acceptable; no dot-matrix. Reports in 1 month.

Nonfiction: Expose and humor. Articles should have a Vermont angle. Buys about 12 mss/year. Query with published clips. Length: 500-2,500 words. Pays $20-100. Sometimes pays expenses of writers on assignment.

Photos: Glenn Russell, photo editor. State availability of photos. Pays $10-20 for b&w contact sheets and negatives. Captions, model releases and identification of subjects required. Buys one-time rights.

Tips: "Short news stories are most open to freelancers. Knowledge of Vermont politics is essential."

Virginia

‡NORTHERN VIRGINIAN MAGAZINE, 135 Park St., Box 1177, Vienna VA 22180. (703)938-0666. Editor: Goodie Holden. 80% freelance written. Bimonthly magazine concerning the five counties of northern Virginia. Pays first of month following publication. Publishes ms an average of 3 months after acceptance. Byline given. Buys first serial rights and second serial (reprint) rights. Submit seasonal/holiday material 3 months in advance. Simultaneous queries, and simultaneous, photocopied and previously published submissions OK. Computer printout submissions acceptable. "Send photocopy of manuscript as we can't guarantee its return." Reports in 2 weeks on queries; 1 month on mss. Sample copy $1; free writer's guidelines.

Nonfiction: "Freelance manuscripts welcomed on speculation. We are particularly interested in articles about or related to northern Virginia." Buys 75 mss/year. Query or send complete ms. Length: 2,500 words minimum. Pays 1½¢/word.

Photos: Prefers good, clear b&w glossy photos. Pays $5/photo or photo creditline. Captions, model releases, and identification of subjects required.

Tips: Longer articles preferred, minimum 2,500 words. History articles accepted only if unique.

THE ROANOKER, Leisure Publishing Co., 3424 Brambleton Ave., Box 12567, Roanoke VA 24026. (703)989-6138. Editor: Kurt Rheinheimer. 75% freelance written. Works with a small number of new/unpublished writers each year. Monthly magazine covering people and events of Western Virginia. "*The Roanoker* is a general interest city magazine edited for the people of Roanoke, Virginia, and the surrounding area. Our readers are primarily upper-income, well-educated professionals between the ages of 35 and 60. Coverage ranges from hard news and consumer information to restaurant reviews and local history." Circ. 12,000. Pays on publication. Publishes ms an average of 4 months after acceptance. Byline given. Buys all rights; makes work-for-hire assignments. Submit seasonal/holiday material 4 months in advance. Simultaneous queries OK. Computer printout submissions acceptable. Reports in 2 months. Sample copy for $2 and 9x12 SAE with $1.41 postage.

Nonfiction: Expose; historical/nostalgic; how-to (live better in western Virginia); interview/profile (of well-known area personalities); photo feature; and travel (Virginia and surrounding states). "We are attempting to broaden our base and provide more and more coverage of western Virginia, i.e., that part of the state west of Roanoke. We place special emphasis on consumer-related issues and how-to articles." Periodic special sections on fashion, real estate, media, banking, investing. Buys 100 mss/year. Query with published clips or send complete ms. Length: 3,000 words maximum. Pays $35-200. Sometimes pays expenses of writers on assignment.

Photos: Send photos with ms. Reviews color transparencies. Pays $5-10 for 5x7 or 8x10 b&w prints; $10 maximum for 5x7 or 8x10 color prints. Captions and model releases required. Rights purchased vary.

Tips: "We will look to include more area history pieces in 1988. It helps if freelancer lives in the area. The most frequent mistake made by writers in completing an article for us is not having enough Roanoke area focus: use of area experts, sources, slants, etc."

‡RURAL LIVING, Virginia, Maryland and Delaware Association of Electric Cooperatives, 5061 Chamberlayne Ave., Box 15248, Richmond VA 23227-0648. (804)264-2801. Editor: Richard G. Johnstone, Jr. 35% freelance written. Monthly magazine for members of electric cooperatives. Circ. 225,000. Pays on publication. Publishes ms an average of 3-6 months after acceptance. Byline given. Not copyrighted. Buys one-time rights. Submit seasonal/holiday material 3 months in advance. Simultaneous, photocopied and previously published submissions OK. Computer printout submissions OK; prefers letter-quality to dot-matrix. Reports in 6 weeks. Free sample copy and writer's guidelines.

Nonfiction: General interest, historical/nostalgic, how-to, humor, inspirational, interview/profile, personal experience and travel. Buys 10-15 mss/year. Send complete ms. Length: 500-1,500 words. Pays $100-250 for assigned articles; pays $75-150 for unsolicited articles. Sometimes pays the expenses of writers on assignment.

Photos: State availability of photos with submission. Reviews 4x5 transparencies and 5x7 prints. Offers $50-100 per photo. Buys one-time rights.

Columns/Departments: From the Front Burner (cooking/recipes); Energy Efficiency (helpful ideas and saving energy); Just for Laughs (humor, slice-of-life). Buys 10-12 mss/year. Query or send complete ms. Length: 500-1,000 words. Pays $75-150.

Fiction: Historical, humorous, mainstream, slice-of-life vignettes, cultural on Virginia and Maryland region. Buys 5-7 mss/year. Send complete ms. Length: 500-1,500 words. Pays $75-150.

Tips: "*Rural Living* seeks to provide general articles on the history and culture of the rural areas and small towns in Virginia and Maryland. We also publish articles on crafts (how-to instructions should be incorporated into the article), recipes, lifestyles (rural), etc."

‡VIRGINIA FORESTS MAGAZINE, Virginia Forestry Association, 1205 E. Main St., Richmond VA 23219. (804)644-8462. 75% freelance written. Quarterly magazine covering forestry and conservation. "Our purpose is to get landowners interested in managing their forestland for their own pleasure and profits. We are distributed to our members, the news media, state and federal legislators, all 320 public libraries in Virginia and 900 public and private high schools." Circ. 4,200. "We rarely pay for material." Publishes ms an average of 3 months after acceptance. Byline given. Buys one-time rights. Simultaneous, photocopied and previously published submissions OK. Sample copy for 9x12 SAE with 78¢ postage; sample copy $1.50.

Nonfiction: Historical/nostalgic, how-to (grow timber on a tree farm) and travel (outdoor adventure camping, hiking). Rarely buys mss. Query. Length: 1,000-3,000 words. "We're glad to send 10-20 copies of published work." Sometimes pays the expenses of writers on assignment.

Photos: State availability of photos with submission. Reviews negatives, transparencies and 5x7 and 8x10 prints. Offers no additional payment for photos accepted with ms. Buys one-time rights.

Washington

THE SEATTLE WEEKLY, Sasquatch Publishing, 1931 2nd Ave., Seattle WA 98101. (206)441-5555. Editor: David Brewster. 30% freelance written. Eager to work with new/unpublished writers, especially those in the region. Weekly tabloid covering arts, politics, food, business, sports and books with local and regional emphasis. Circ. 30,000. Pays 3 weeks after publication. Publishes ms an average of 1 month after acceptance. Byline given. Offers variable kill fee. Buys first North American serial rights. Submit seasonal/holiday material 2 months in advance. Simultaneous queries OK. Computer printout submissions acceptable; prefers letter-quality to dot-matrix. Reports in 1 month. Sample copy 75¢; writer's guidelines for #10 SASE.

Nonfiction: Book excerpts; expose; general interest; historical/nostalgic (Northwest); how-to (related to food and health); humor; interview/profile; opinion; travel; and arts-related essays. Buys 25 cover stories/year. Query with resume and published clips. Length: 700-4,000 words. Pays $75-800. Sometimes pays the expenses of writers on assignment.

Fiction: Annual Holiday Short Story Contest. Writers must be residents of the state of Washington. "We prefer that the stories have Northwest locales."

Tips: "The *Weekly* publishes stories on Northwest politics and art, usually written by regional and local writers, for a mostly upscale, urban audience; writing is high quality magazine style. We may decide to publish a new regional magazine, either quarterly or bi-monthly, for a slightly different audience."

WASHINGTON, The Evergreen State Magazine, Evergreen Publishing Co., 901 Lenora, Seattle WA 98121. Editor/Publisher: Kenneth A. Gouldthorpe. Executive Editor: Knute O. Berger. Managing Editor:

David W. Fuller. 70% freelance written. A seven-times-per-year magazine covering all facets of life in Washington for an in-state audience. Circ. 70,000. Pays on acceptance for assigned stories; on publication for "on spec" material. Publishes ms an average of 6 months after acceptance. Byline given. Offers 20% kill fee on accepted stories. Submit seasonal/holiday material 6 months in advance. Electronic submissions OK; call for details. Computer printout submissions acceptable, but leave margins and double-space; prefers letter-quality to dot-matrix. Reports in 1 month on queries; 6 weeks on mss. Sample copy for $2.95; free writer's guidelines.

Nonfiction: Book excerpts (unpublished Washington-related); general interest; historical/nostalgic; humor; interview/profile; personal experience; photo feature; and travel. "Evergreen Publishing Company undertakes book and one-shot publication projects. Washington state ideas encouraged. No political, expose, reviews, or anything not pertaining to Washington or Washingtonians." Query with published clips. Length: features, 1,500-2,500 words; sidebars, 200-600 words. Pays $150-700. Sometimes pays expenses of writers on assignment.

Photos: Carrie Seglin, photo editor. Large format. State availability of photos with query or send photos with query. Pays $50-250 for b&w; $125-325 for 35mm color slides. Captions, model releases, and identification of subjects required. Buys one-time rights.

Columns/Departments: As Others See Us (how Washington is viewed by outsiders); Interiors (homes, architecture, decorating, interiors); State of Mind (thoughts and perspectives on the Evergreen State); Washington Post (our letters column); The Attic (our back page potpourri of pictures, curios etc.); Our Town (where we live, from backwoods to small towns and places you've never seen before); Journeys End (inns, lodges, bed and breakfast hideaways); Players (sports and athletes, games and gamesmen); Statewatch (a round-up from all corners: people, quotes and anecdotes from the lighter side of life); Enterprise (business and commerce); Wildside (wildlife, nature); Open air (outdoors and outdoor activities, from backpacking to picnics, from hang gliding to kite flying); Wordsmith (books, writers and wordsmithing); Repasts (great dining, from grand souffles to small cafes); and Almanac (a compendium of history, weather, wit and wisdom). Buys 75 mss/year. Query with published clips. Length: 600-1,200 words. Pays $150-250.

Fillers: Clippings, jokes, gags, anecdotes, short humor and newsbreaks. Length: 50-250 words. Pays $25-100. Must be Washington related.

Tips: "All areas are open, but the writer has a better chance of breaking in at our publication with short articles and fillers since we buy more departmental material. Our articles emphasize people—sometimes writers get sidetracked. We're also looking for original thinking, not tired approaches."

Wisconsin

FOX RIVER PATRIOT, Weir Publishing, Box 31, Princeton WI 54968. (414)295-6252. Publisher: Barbara J. Weir. 75% freelance written. Eager to work with new/unpublished writers. For country folks of all ages. Monthly tabloid. Circ. 6,000. Pays on publication. Publishes ms an average of 2 months after publication. Buys first North American serial rights and one-time rights. Byline given. Submit seasonal/holiday material 2 months in advance. Simultaneous, photocopied and previously published submissions OK. Computer printout submissions OK; prefers letter-quality to dot-matrix. Reports in 1 month. Sample copy $1.

Nonfiction: Expose, general interest, historical, how-to, humor, interview/profile, nostalgia, personal experience, photo feature, and travel. "In general, we are a country-oriented publication—we stress environment, alternative energy technology, alternative building trends, farming and gardening, etc.—submissions should be in this general area." Buys 4 mss/issue. Send complete ms. Pays $5-25.

Photos: Send photos with ms. Pays $5 for 5x7 b&w prints; $5 for 5x7 color prints. Captions preferred.

Tips: "We are hoping to incorporate a child's learning page. Submissions that are child-oriented will be considered."

MADISON MAGAZINE, Box 1604, Madison WI 53701. Editor: James Selk. 50% freelance written. Prefers to work with published/established writers. Monthly magazine; 100-150 pages. General city magazine aimed at upscale audience. Circ. 24,000. Pays on publication. Publishes ms an average of 2 months after acceptance. Buys all rights. Reports on material accepted for publication 10 days after acceptance. Returns rejected material immediately. Query. Computer printout submissions acceptable; prefers letter-quality to dot-matrix. Sample copy $3.

Nonfiction: General human interest articles with strong local angles. Buys 100 mss/year. Length: 1,000-5,000 words. Pays $25-500. Pays the expenses of writers on assignment.

Photos: Offers no additional payment for b&w photos used with mss. Captions required.

WISCONSIN, *The Milwaukee Journal Magazine*, Box 661, Milwaukee WI 53201. (414)224-2341. Editor: Alan Borsuk. 20% freelance written. Prefers to work with published/established writers. Weekly general interest magazine appealing to readers living in Wisconsin. Circ. 520,000. Pays on publication. Publishes ms an average of 4 months after acceptance. Byline given. Buys first serial rights. Submit seasonal/holiday material 4 months in advance. Simultaneous queries OK. Computer printout submissions acceptable; prefers letter-quality to dot-matrix. Reports in 1 month on queries; 6 months on mss. Sample copy and writer's guidelines for SASE.

Nonfiction: Expose, general interest, humor, interview/profile, opinion, personal experience and photo feature. Special issue planned on fitness. No nostalgic reminiscences. Buys 50 mss/year. Query. Length: 150-2,000 words. Pays $75-500. Sometimes pays expenses of writers on assignment.

Photos: State availability of photos.

Columns/Departments: Opinion, Humor and Essays. Buys 50 mss/year. Query. Length: 150-300 words. Pays $75-150.

Tips: "We are primarily Wisconsin-oriented and are becoming more news-oriented."

WISCONSIN TRAILS, Box 5650, Madison WI 53705. (608)231-2444. Managing Editor: Geri Nixon. 70% freelance written. Prefers to work with published/established writers; works with a small number of new/unpublished writers each year. Bimonthly magazine for readers interested in Wisconsin; its contemporary issues, personalities, recreation, history, natural beauty; and the arts. Circ. 40,000. Buys first serial rights, and one-time rights sometimes. Pays on publication. Submit seasonal material at least 1 year in advance. Publishes ms an average of 6 months after acceptance. Byline given. Photocopied submissions OK. Computer printout submissions acceptable; prefers letter-quality to dot-matrix. Reports in 1 month. Writer's guidelines available.

Nonfiction: "Our articles focus on some aspect of Wisconsin life; an interesting town or event, a person or industry, history or the arts and especially outdoor recreation. We do not use first person essays or biographies about people who were born in Wisconsin but made their fortunes elsewhere. No poetry. No articles that are too local for our regional audience, or articles about obvious places to visit in Wisconsin. We need more articles about the new and little-known." Buys 3 unsolicited mss/year. Query or send outline. Length: 1,000-3,000 words. Pays $100-300 (negotiable), depending on assignment length and quality. Sometimes pays expenses of writers on assignment.

Photos: Purchased with or without mss or on assignment. Prefers 2¼" or larger transparencies, 35mm OK. Color photos usually illustrate an activity, event, region or striking scenery. Prefer photos with people in scenery. B&w photos usually illustrate a given article. Pays $25 each for b&w on publication. Pays $50-75 for inside color; $100-200 for covers. Captions preferred.

Tips: "We're looking for active articles about people, places, events, and outdoor adventures in Wisconsin. We want to publish one in-depth article of state-wide interest or concern per issue, and several short (1,000-word) articles about short trips, recreational opportunities, restaurants, inns, and cultural activities. We will be looking for more articles about out-of-the-way places in Wisconsin that are exceptional in some way."

WOMEN & CO., The Magazine for Women in the La Crosse/Winona Area, MCP Inc., Suite 217, 505 King St., La Crosse WI 54601. (608)782-2130. Editor: Vickie Lojek. 60% freelance written. Works with a samll number of new/unpublished writers each year. A monthly tabloid about working women. "We write for the woman of the '80s who is trying to balance tradition with progress." Circ. 10,500. Pays on publication. Publishes ms an average of 2 months after acceptance. Byline given. Buys first North American serial rights. Submit seasonal/holiday material 3 months in advance. Simultaneous and photocopied submissions OK. Computer printout submissions acceptable; prefers letter-quality to dot-matrix. Reports in 4 weeks. Sample copy for 8x11 SAE.

Nonfiction: General interest, humor, inspirational and personal experience. No Hollywood profiles or international corporate success stories. Buys 36 mss/year. Query. Length: 750-1,500 words. Pays $20-50. Sometimes pays the expenses of writers on assignment.

Photos: Send photos with submission. Reviews contact sheets. Offers $10-30/photo. Model releases required. Buys one-time rights. Sometimes pays the expenses of writers on assignment.

Tips: "To get published in *Women & Co.*, I look for a writer with Midwestern focus. My writers typically live in small cities or towns, have had some writing experience and are pitching a dynamite self-improvement story. Nonfiction articles represent 95% of writing I purchase. Write to me with your story. Why are you interested in archaeology? How did you relate to your midwife? Who do you know who has changed her life? And include past clips."

Puerto Rico

WALKING TOURS OF SAN JUAN, Magazine/Guide, Caribbean World Communications, Inc., First Federal Building, Office 301, Santurce PR 00909. (809)722-1767. Editor: Alfred Dinhofer. Managing Editor: Carmen Merino. 5% freelance written. Prefers to work with published/established writers. Magazine published 2 times/year (January and July). Circ. 22,000. Pays on publication. Publishes ms an average of 3 months after acceptance. Byline given. Buys one-time rights. Computer printout submissions acceptable. Reports in 1 month. Sample copy $3 with 9x12 SAE and $2 postage.

Nonfiction: Historical/nostalgic. "We are seeking historically based articles on San Juan: any aspect of Spanish colonial culture, art, architecture, etc. We must have sources—in fact, we will publish source material at the end of each article for reader reference." Buys 4 mss/year. Query. Length: 2,000-3,000 words. Pays $150. Sometimes pays the expenses of writers on assignment.

Canada

CANADIAN GEOGRAPHIC, 488 Wilbrod St., Ottawa, Ontario K1N 6M8 Canada. Publisher: J. Keith Fraser. Editor: Ross W. Smith. Managing Editor: Ian Darragh. 90% freelance written. Works with a small number of new/unpublished writers each year. Circ. 125,000. Bimonthly magazine. Pays on acceptance. Publishes ms an average of 3 months after acceptance. Buys first Canadian rights; interested only in first time publication. Computer printout submissions acceptable; prefers letter-quality to dot-matrix. Writer's guidelines on request.
Nonfiction: Buys authoritative geographical articles, in the broad geographical sense, written for the average person, not for a scientific audience. Predominantly Canadian subjects by Canadian authors. Buys 30-45 mss/year. Always query first. Length: 1,500-3,000 words. Pays 25¢/word minimum. Usual payment for articles $500-1,500 and up. Higher fees reserved for commissioned articles on which copyright remains with publisher unless otherwise agreed. Sometimes pays the expenses of writers on assignment.
Photos: Reviews 35mm slides, 2¼ transparencies or 8x10 glossies. Pays $60-200 for color photos, depending on published size.

‡**TORONTO LIFE**, 59 Front St. E., Toronto, Ontario M5E 1B3 Canada. (416)364-3333. Editor: Marq de Villiers. 95% freelance written. Prefers to work with published/established writers. Monthly magazine emphasizing local issues and social trends, short humor/satire, and service features for upper income, well educated and, for the most part, young Torontonians. Uses some fiction. Pays on acceptance. Publishes ms an average of 3-4 months after acceptance. Byline given. Buys first North American serial rights. Pays 50% kill fee "for commissioned articles only." Phone queries OK. Reports in 3 weeks. SAE IRCs. Sample copy $2.50.
Nonfiction: Uses most types of articles. Buys 17 mss/issue. Query with published clips. Buys about 40 unsolicited mss/year. Length: 1,000-5,000 words. Pays $800-3,000.
Photos: State availability of photos. Uses good color transparencies and clear, crisp b&w prints. Seldom uses submitted photos. Captions and model release required.
Columns/Departments: "We run about five columns an issue. They are all freelanced, though most are from regular contributors. They are mostly local in concern and cover politics, money, fine art, performing arts, movies and sports." Length: 1,200 words. Pays $400-700.

‡**WESTERN CANADA OUTDOORS**, McIntosh Publishing Company, Ltd., 1132-98th St., Box 430, North Battleford, Saskatchewan S9A 2Y5 Canada. (306)445-4401. Contact: Stanley Nowakowski. 15% freelance written. Bimonthly tabloid covering fish and wildlife. Circ. 42,220. Pays on publication. Publishes ms an average of 2 months after acceptance. Byline given. Buys one-time rights. Submit seasonal/holiday material 1 month in advance. Simultaneous submissions OK. Computer printout submissions OK; prefers letter-quality to dot-matrix. Reports in 3 weeks.
Nonfiction: Expose, general interest, humor, personal experience and photo feature. Buys 4 mss/year. Query with or without published clips, or send complete ms. Length: 200-800 words. Pays $25-50 for assigned articles. Sometimes pays the expenses of writers on assignment.
Photos: State availability of photos with submission. Reviews contact sheets. Offers $10-25 per photo. Captions and identification of subjects required. Buys one-time rights.
Columns/Departments: Buys 18 mss/year. Query. Length: 700-800 words. Pays $25-50.
Fillers: Anecdotes. Buys 6/year.

‡**WESTERN PEOPLE, Supplement to the Western Producer**, Western Producer Publications, Box 2500, Saskatoon, Saskatchewan S7K 2C4 Canada. (306)665-3500. Managing Editor: Mary Gilchrist. Weekly farm newspaper supplement covering rural Western Canada. "Our magazine reflects the life and people of rural Western Canada both in the present and historically." Circ. 135,000. Pays on acceptance. Publishes ms an average of 6 months after acceptance. Byline given. Buys first rights. Submit seasonal/holiday material 3 months in advance. Reports in 2 weeks on queries; 1 month on mss. Sample copy for 9x12 SAE; writer's guidelines for SAE.
Nonfiction: General interest, historical/nostalgic, humor, interview/profile, personal experience and photo feature. Buys 450 mss/year. Send complete ms. Length: 500-2,500 words. Pays $50-250.
Photos: Send photos with submission. Reviews transparencies and prints. Offers $5-25 per photo. Captions and identification of subjects required. Buys one-time rights.
Fiction: Adventure, historical, humorous, mainstream, mystery, novel excerpts, romance, serialized novels, suspense and western stories reflecting life in rural Western Canada. Buys 50 mss/year. Send complete ms.

Length: 1,000-2,000 words. Pays $50-200.

Poetry: Free verse, traditional, haiku and light verse. Buys 75 poems/year. Submit maximum 3 poems. Length: 4-50 lines. Pays $10-35.

Tips: "Western Canada is geographically very large. The approach for writing about an interesting individual is to introduce that person *neighbor-to-neighbor* to our readers."

‡**THE WESTERN PRODUCER**, Western Producer Publications, Box 2500, Saskatoon, Saskatchewan S7K 2C4 Canada. (306)665-3500. Editor: Keith Dryden. Managing Editor: Garry Fairbairn. 30% freelance written. Weekly newspaper covering agriculture and rural life. Publishes "informative material for 135,000 western Canadian farm familes." Pays on acceptance. Byline given. Kill fee varies. Not copyrighted. Buys one-time rights. Submit seasonal/holiday material 2 months in advance. Simultaneous, photocopied and previously published submissions OK. Query for electronic submissions. Computer printout submissions OK; prefers letter-quality to dot-matrix. Reports in 1 week on queries; 3 weeks on mss. Sample copy for 11x14 SAE with IRC; writer's guidelines for 4x9 SAE.

Nonfiction: General interest, historical/nostalgic, how-to (on farm machinery or construction), humor, new product, technical and rural cartoons. Special issue includes Weeds and Chemical issue (March). Nothing "non-Canadian, over 1,500 words." Buys 600 mss/year. Query. Length: 2,000 words. Pays $100-400 for assigned articles; pays $150 maximum for unsolicited articles. Sometimes pays the expenses of writers on assignment.

Photos: Send photos with submission. Reviews contact sheets, negatives, transparencies and prints. Offers $15-50 per photo. Captions required. Buys one-time rights.

Columns/Departments: Mary Gilchrist, editor. Western People (magazine insert focusing on Western Canadian personalities, hobbies, history, fiction), 500-2,000 words. Buys 350 mss/year. Query. Length: 500-2,000 words. Pays $50-500.

Fiction: Ethnic, historical, humorous, slice-of-life vignettes, western and rural settings. No non-western Canadian subjects. Buys 40 mss/year. Query. Length: 500-2,000. Pays $50-500.

Poetry: Free verse, light verse and traditional. Buys 20 poems/year. Length: 10-100 lines. Pays $10-100.

Tips: "Use CP/AP/UPI style and a fresh ribbon." Areas most open to freelancers are "cartoons, on-farm profiles, rural Canadian personalities."

WINDSOR THIS MONTH MAGAZINE, Box 1029, Station A, Windsor, Ontario N9A 6P4 Canada. (519)966-7411. Publisher: J.S. Woloschak. 75% freelance written. "*Windsor This Month* is mailed out in a system of controlled distribution to 24,000 households in the area. The average reader is a university graduate, of middle income, and active in leisure areas." Circ. 24,000. Pays on publication. Buys first North American serial rights. Submit seasonal/holiday material 4 months in advance. "We will accept computer printout submissions or industry compatible magnetic media." SAE, IRCs. Reports in 1 month.

Nonfiction: Windsor-oriented editorial: issues, answers, interviews, lifestyles, profiles, photo essays and opinion. How-to accepted if applicable to readership. Special inserts: design and decor, gourmet and travel featured periodically through the year. Buys 5 mss/issue. Query (phone queries OK). Buys 15 unsolicited mss/year. Length: 500-5,000 words. Pays $64.

Photos: State availability of photos with query. Pays $25. Captions preferred. Buys all rights.

Tips: "If experienced, arm yourself with published work and a list of ten topics that demonstrate knowledge of the Windsor market, and query the editor."

Relationships

These publications focus on lifestyles and relationships of readers. They may offer writers a forum for unconventional views or serve as a voice for particular audiences or causes. These magazines are read, and often written by, single people, gays and lesbians and others interested in alternative outlooks and lifestyles.

ALBUQUERQUE SINGLES SCENE MAGAZINE, 8421-H Osuna NE, Albuquerque NM 87111. (505)299-4401. Editor: Gail Skinner. 90% freelance written. Eager to work with new/unpublished writers. Monthly tabloid covering singles lifestyles. Pays on publication. Publishes ms an average of 6 months after acceptance. Byline given. Buys all rights for one year; first serial rights only under special circumstances. Submit seasonal/

holiday material 3 months in advance. Query for electronic submissions. Computer printout submissions acceptable; prefers letter-quality to dot-matrix. Reports in 3 months. Sample copy $1 with SAE and 4 first class stamps. Free writer's guidelines for SAE and 1 first class stamp.

Nonfiction: General interest; how-to; humor; inspirational; opinion; personal experience; relationships; consumer guide; travel; finance; real estate; parenting; and astrology. All articles must be singles-oriented. No suggestive or pornographic material. Buys 100 mss/year. Send complete ms. "Keep a copy of the manuscript for your file as we do not return them. If you have photo(s) and/or illustration(s) to accompany the article, do not send them with your story unless you do not want them returned." Also publishes some fiction. Length: 800-2,600 words. Pays $36-150. Sometimes pays expenses of writers on assignment.

Photos: State availability of photos with ms. Captions, model releases, and identification of subjects required.

Tips: "We are looking for articles that deal with every aspect of single living—whether on a local or national level. Our readers are of above-average intelligence, income and education. The majority of our articles are chosen from 'relationships' and 'humor' submissions."

ATLANTA SINGLES MAGAZINE & DATEBOOK, Sigma Publications, Inc., Suite 320, 3423 Piedmont Rd. NE., Atlanta GA 30305 and Box 80158, Atlanta GA 30366. (404)239-0642. Editor: Julia Thompson. Associate Editor: Maggie Anthony. 25% freelance written. Works with a small number of new/unpublished writers each year. A monthly magazine for single, widowed or divorced adults, medium to high income level, many business and professionally oriented; single parents, ages 25 to 55. Circ. 15,000. Pays on publication. Publishes ms an average of 6 months after acceptance. Byline given. Buys one-time rights, second serial (reprint) rights and simultaneous rights. Submit seasonal/holiday material 6 months in advance. Simultaneous, photocopied and previously published submissions OK. Computer printout submissions acceptable; prefers letter-quality to dot-matrix. Free sample copy.

Nonfiction: General interest, humor, personal experience, photo feature and travel. No pornography. Buys 12 mss/year. Send complete ms. Length: 600-1,200 words. Pays $100-300 for unsolicited articles; sometimes trades for personal ad.

Photos: Send photos with submission. Cover photos also considered. Reviews prints. Offers no additional payment for photos accepted with ms. Model releases and identification of subjects required. Buys one-time rights.

Columns/Departments: Will consider ideas. Query. Length: 600-800 words. Pays $100-300 per column/department.

Fiction: Confession, fantasy, humorous, mainstream, romance and slice-of-life vignettes. No pornography. Send complete ms. Length: 600-1,200 words. Pays $100-300.

Fillers: Gags to be illustrated by cartoonist and short humor. Length: open. Pays $10-20.

Tips: "We are open to articles on *any* subject that would be of interest to singles, i.e., travel, autos, movies, love stories, fashion, investments, real estate, etc. Although singles are interested in topics like self-awareness, being single again, and dating, they are also interested in many of the same subjects that married people are, such as those listed."

CHANGING MEN, Issues in Gender, Sex and Politics, Feminist Men's Publications, 306 N. Brooks St., Madison WI 53715. Editor: Rick Cote. Managing Editor: Michael Birnbaum. 80% freelance written. Works with a small number of new/unpublished writers each year. A feminist men's journal published two times a year. "We are a forum for anti-sexist men and women to explore issues of masculinity, feminism, sexual orientation, and sex roles." Circ. 4,000. Publishes ms an average of 1 year after acceptance. Byline given. Buys one-time rights. Simultaneous queries, simultaneous, photocopied, and previously published submissions OK. Computer printout submissions acceptable; prefers letter-quality to dot-matrix. Reports in 2 months. Sample copy $4.50; writer's guidelines for business size SAE with 1 first class stamp.

Nonfiction: Book excerpts, humor, interview/profile, opinion, personal experience and photo feature. Plans special issues on male/female intimacy and relationships. Special focus in upcoming issue on male violence. No academic articles or theoretical treatises. Query with published clips. Length: 3,500 words maximum. Pays $25 maximum.

Columns/Departments: Men and War (focus on masculinity and how culture shapes male values), Sports (with a feminist slant), and Book Reviews (focus on sexuality and masculinity). Query with published clips. Length: 500-1,500 words. Pays $15 maximum.

Fiction: Franklin Abbott, fiction editor. Erotica, ethnic, experimental, fantasy, humorous and novel excerpts. Buys 1 ms/year. Query with published clips. Length: 3,500 words maximum. Pays $20 maximum.

Poetry: Free verse, haiku and light verse. Submit maximum 3 poems. Length: 50 lines maximum. No payment for poetry.

Fillers: Clippings, jokes and newsbreaks. Length: 300 words. No payment for fillers.

COLUMBUS SINGLE SCENE, Columbus Single Scene, Inc., Box 30856, Gahanna OH 43230. (614)476-8802. Editor: Jeanne Marlowe. 50% freelance written. A monthly magazine covering information of interest to central Ohio singles of all ages—18 and up—"positive, upbeat approach to single living, but we're neither yuppies nor pollyannas." Circ. 2,000. Pays on acceptance. Publishes ms an average of 1 month after acceptance. Byline given. Offers 40% kill fee. Buys one-time rights, second serial (reprint) rights or simultaneous rights, or makes work-for-hire assignments. Submit seasonal/holiday material 2 months in advance. Simultaneous, photocopied and previously published submissions OK. Computer printout submissions acceptable; prefers letter-quality to dot-matrix. Reports in 2 weeks on queries; 1 month on mss. Sample copy $1.

Nonfiction: Book excerpts; essays; expose; general interest; how-to (related to singles, meeting people, relationships); humor; interview/profile; opinion; personal experience; photofeature; and travel. National Singles Week is 3rd week in September. September issue features singles' achievements and community celebrations. "While we will consider negative personal experiences, the overall attitude toward being single should be positive." Buys 50 mss/year. Query with or without published clips or send complete ms. Length: 500-5,000 words. Pays 10¢/word maximum, $20 maximum/typed page. Sometimes pays in advertising trade. Sometimes pays the expenses of writers on assignment.

Photos: State availability of photos with submission or send photos with submission. Reviews prints (any size). Offers $10 maximum/photo. Model releases and identification of subjects required. Buys one-time rights.

Fiction: Confession, fantasy, humorous, mainstream, mystery, novel excerpts, slice-of-life vignettes. Buys 6 mss/year. Send complete ms. Lenght: 500-5,000 words. Pays 10¢/word maximum; $20 maximum/page.

Poetry: Jennifer Welch, poetry editor. Avant-garde, free verse, haiku, light verse and traditional. Submit maximum 12 poems. Length: 1-50 lines. Pays $5 maximum or advertising trade.

Tips: "We are a low budget, black and white, activities-oriented magazine, best approached as a volunteer. Copy must be concise, well written, and oriented to singles. Writers who prove reliable receive paid assignments. Freelancers' best approach is to answer our reader's most frequent question: 'How and where do you meet potential dates?' "

‡**DRUMMER,**Desmodus, Inc., Box 11314, San Francisco CA 94101. (415)864-3456. Associate Editor: Jim Ed Thompson. 80% freelance written. Gay male leather and related fetish erotica/news. Monthly magazines publishes "erotic aspects of leather and other masculine fetishes for gay men." Circ. 60,000. Pays on publication. Publishes ms an average of 3 months after acceptance. Byline given. Buys first North American serial rights or makes work-for-hire assignments. Submit seasonal/holiday material 6 months in advance. Photocopied and previously published submissions OK. Computer printout submissions OK; prefers letter-quality to dot-matrix. Reports in 1 month on queries; in 2-3 months on mss. Sample copy $5; writer's guidelines for #10 SAE with 1 first class stamp.

Nonfiction: Book excerpts, essays, historical/nostalgic, how-to, humor, interview/profile, new product, opinion, personal experience, photo feature, technical and travel. No feminine slanted pieces. Buys 25 mss/year. Query with or without published clips, or send complete ms. Length: 1,000-15,000 words. Pays $50-200 for assigned articles; $50-100 for unsolicited articles. Sometimes pays writers with contributor copies "if author is willing." Rarely pays expenses of writers on assignment.

Photos: Send photos with submission (photocopies OK). Reviews contact sheets and transparencies. Offers $10-100 per photo. Model releases and identification of subjects required. Buys one-time rights or all rights.

Fiction: Adventure, condensed novels, erotica, ethnic, fantasy, historical, horror, humorous, mystery, novel excerpts, science fiction, slice-of-life vignettes, suspense and western. Must have gay "macho" erotic elements. Buys 60-75 mss/year. Send complete ms. Length: 1,000-20,000 words. Occasionally serializes stories. Pays $100.

Fillers: Anecdotes, facts, gags and newsbreaks. Buys 50/year. Length: 10-100 words. pay $10-50.

Tips: "All they have to do is write—but they must be knowledgeable about some aspect of the scene, While the magazine is aimed at gay men, we welcome contributions from straight men and from straight, bisexual and gay women who understand leather and s/m and kinky erotic fetishes. Fiction is most open to freelancers."

‡**DUNGEON MASTER,**Desmodus Inc., Box 11314, San Francisco CA 94101. (415)864-3456. Editor: Tony DeBlasa. 60% freelance written. Quarterly magazine covering gay male erotic s/m. "Safety is emphasized. This is not a fantasy magazine but is for real how-to articles on equipment, techniques, etc." Circ. 5,000. Most articles are unpaid—except by complimentary subscriptions, ads, etc. Byline given. Buys first North American serial rights, one-time rights, simultaneous rights or makes work-for-hire assignments. Photocopied submissions and previously published submissions OK. Computer printout submissions OK; prefers letter-quality to dot-matrix. Sample copy $4; free writer's guidelines.

Nonfiction: Book excerpts, essays, historical/nostalgic, how-to (mainly), humor, interview/profile, new product, opinion, personal experience, photo feature (may be paid), technical, travel and safety. No fiction or unsafe practices. Buys 40 mss/year. Query with or without published clips, or send complete ms. Length: no limit. Pays $25-200 for assigned articles. Usually pays writers with contributor copies or other premiums rather than a cash payment. Rarely pays expenses of writers on assignment. Send photos with submission. (photocopies OK). Reviews contact sheets and transparencies. Offers $10-100/photo. Model releases and identification of subjects required. Buys one-time rights or all rights.

Fillers: Anecdotes, facts, gags to be illustrated and newbreaks. Busy 10/year. Pays $5-25.

Tips: "Must be knowledgeable in specialized field. While publication is aimed at gay men, submission by straight men and straight and gay women are welcome."

‡**FQ, Foreskin Quarterly**,Desmodus Inc., Box 11314, San Francisco CA 94101. (415)864-3456. Editor: Bud Berkeley. 90% freelance written. Quarterly magazine covering circumcision. "Most writers are anti-circumcision but both sides are solicited and pro—circumcision writers are also invited to submit." Circ. 15,000. Pays on publication. Publishes ms an average of 4-8 months after acceptance. Byline given. Buys first North American serial rights. Photocopied and previously published submissions OK. Computer printout submissions OK; prefers letter-quality to dot-matrix. Reports in 4-6 weekss on queries; 2-4 months on mss. Sample copy $3; writer's guidelines for #10 SAE with 1 first class stamp.

Nonfiction: Book excerpts, essays, expose, historical/nostalgic, how-to, humor, interview/profile, new product, opinion, personal experience, photo feature, technical and travel. Buys 40 mss/year. Query with or without published clips or send complete ms. Length varies. Pays $0-150 for assigned articles; $0-100 for unsolicited material. Pays writers with contributor copies or other premiums "depending on author's willingness."

Photos: Send photos with submission (photocopies OK). Reviews contact sheets and transparencies. Offers $10-100/photo. Model releases and identification of subjects required. Buys one-time rights or all rights.

Fiction: Adventure, confession, erotica, ethnic, fantasy, historical, humorous, religious, science fiction and suspense. Must have foreskin/circumcision slant. Buys 4-8 mss/year. Send complete ms. Length varies. Pays $25-100.

Fillers: Anecdotes, facts, gags to be illustrated. Buys 10-20/year. Pays $10-50.

Tips: "Writers must have genuine interest in subject."

FIRST HAND, Experiences For Loving Men, Firsthand, Ltd., 310 Cedar Lane, Teaneck NJ 07666. (201)836-9177. Editor: Lou Thomas. Publisher: Jackie Lewis. 50% freelance written. Eager to work with new/unpublished writers. Monthly magazine of homosexual erotica. Circ. 70,000. Pays 2 months after acceptance. Publishes ms an average of 8 months after acceptance. Byline given. Buys all rights (exceptions made), and second serial (reprint) rights. Submit seasonal/holiday material 10 months in advance. Photocopied submissions OK. Computer printout submissions acceptable; no dot-matrix. Reports in 2 months. Sample copy $3; writer's guidelines for SASE.

Nonfiction: "We seldom use nonfiction except for our 'Survival Kit' section, but will consider full-length profiles, investigative reports, and so on if they are of information/inspirational interest to gay people. Erotic safe sex stories are acceptable." Length: 3,000 words maximum. Pays $100-150. "We will consider original submissions only." Query.

Columns/Departments: Survival Kit (short nonfiction articles, up to 1,000 words, featuring practical information on safe sex practices, health, travel, books, video, psychology, law, fashion, and other advice/consumer/lifestyle topics of interest to gay or single men). "These should be written in the second or third person." Query. "For this section, we sometimes also buy reprint rights to appropriate articles previously published in local gay newspapers around the country." Pays $35 to $70, depending on length, if original; if reprint, pays half that rate.

Fiction: Erotic fiction up to 5,000 words in length, average 2,000-3,000 words. "We prefer fiction in the first person which is believable—stories based on the writer's actual experience have the best chance. We're not interested in stories which involve underage characters in sexual situations. Other taboos include bestiality, rape—except in prison stories, as rape is an unavoidable reality in prison—and heavy drug use. Writers with questions about what we can and cannot depict should write for our guidelines, which go into this in more detail. We print mostly self-contained stories; we will look at novel excerpts, but only if they stand on their own."

Poetry: Free verse and light verse. Buys 12/year. Submit maximum 5 poems. Length: 10-30 lines. Pays $25.

Tips: "*First Hand* is a very reader-oriented publication for gay men. Half of each issue is comprised by letters from our readers describing their personal experiences, fantasies and feelings. Our readers are from all walks of life, all races and ethnic backgrounds, all classes, all religious and political affiliations, and so on. They are very diverse, and many live in far-flung rural areas or small towns; for some of them, our magazines are the primary source of contact with gay life, in some cases the only support for their gay identity. Our readers are very loyal and save every issue. We return that loyalty by trying to reflect their interests—for instance, by striving to avoid the exclusively big-city bias so common to national gay publications. So bear in mind the diversity of the audience when you write."

GAY CHICAGO MAGAZINE, Ultra Ink, Inc., 1527 N. Wells St., Chicago IL 60606-1305. (312)751-0130. Editor: Dan Di Leo. 50% freelance written. Eager to work with new/unpublished writers. Weekly magazine published for the gay community of metropolitan Chicago. Circ. 19,500. Pays on publication. Publishes ms an average of 2-4 months after acceptance. Byline given. Buys one-time rights. Submit seasonal/holiday material 2 months in advance. Photocopied submissions OK. Computer printout submissions acceptable; prefers letter-

quality to dot-matrix. Reports in 1 month. Sample copy for 6x9 SAE with 56¢ postage.
Nonfiction: General interest and personal experience. "Since our magazine is available in many public places, such as restaurants, clothing stores, record stores, etc., the tone of the articles can be erotic but not X-rated pornographic." Buys 10-12 mss/year. Send complete ms. Length: 1,500 words maximum. Pays $25-50.
Photos: Send photos with ms. Pays $5-15 for 5x7 b&w prints. Captions, model releases, and identification of subjects required.
Columns/Departments: Buys 2-3 mss/year. Send complete ms. Length: 500-1,000 words. Pays $10-40.
Fiction: Erotica, fantasy, historical, humorous, mystery and science fiction. "We seek any type of fiction that would appeal to the gay male or lesbian reader." Buys 2-3 mss/year. Send complete ms. Length: 1,200 words maximum. Pays $10-50.

IN TOUCH FOR MEN, In Touch Publications International, Inc., 7216 Varna, North Hollywood CA 91605. (818)764-2288. Editor-in-Chief: Bob Stanford. 80% freelance written. Works with a small number of new/unpublished writers each year. A monthly magazine covering the gay male lifestyle, gay male humor and erotica. Circ. 70,000. Pays on acceptance. Byline given. Buys one-time rights. Submit seasonal/holiday material 4 months in advance. Simultaneous and photocopied submissions OK. Computer printout submissions acceptable. Reports in 2 weeks on queries; 6 weeks on mss. Sample copy $3.95; free writer's guidelines.
Nonfiction: Buys 36 mss/year. Send complete ms. Length: 1,000-3,500 words. Pays $25-75.
Photos: State availability of photos with submission. Reviews contact sheets, transparencies, and prints. Offers $35/photo. Captions, model releases and identification of subjects required. Buys one-time rights.
Columns/Departments: Touch and Go (brief comments on various items or pictures that have appeared in the media), 50-500 words. Buys 12 mss/year. Send complete ms. Pays $25.
Fiction: Adventure, confession, erotica, historical, horror, humorous, mainstream, mystery, romance, science fiction, slice-of-life vignettes, suspense, and western; all must be gay male erotica. No "heterosexual, heavy stuff." Buys 36 mss/year. Send complete ms. Length: 2,500-3,500 words. Pays $75 maximum.
Fillers: Short humor. Buys 12/year. Length: 1,500-3,500 words. Pays $50-75.
Tips: "Our publication features male nude photos plus three fiction pieces, several articles, cartoons, humorous comments on items from the media, and photo features. We try to present the positive aspects of the gay lifestyle, with an emphasis on humor. Humorous pieces may be erotic in nature. We are open to all submissions that fit our gay male format; the emphasis, however, is on humor and the upbeat. We receive many fiction manuscripts but not nearly enough articles and humor."

‡MACH,Desmodus Inc., Box 11314, San Francisco CA 94101. (415)864-3456. Associate Editor: Jim Ed Thompson. 80% freelance written. Quarterly magazine covering gay male leather erotica. Circ. 10,000. Pays on publication. Byline given. Publishes ms an average of 3-6 months after acceptance. Byline given. Buys first North American serial rights or one-time rights; makes work-for-hire assignments. Submit seasonal/holiday material 6 months in advance. Photocopied submissions and previously published submissions OK. Computer printout submissions OK; prefers letter-quality to dot-matrix. Reports in 3-4 weeks on queries; 1-2 months on mss. Sample copy $6; writer's guidelines for #10 SAE with 2 first class stamps.
Nonfiction: Book excerpts, humor and personal experience. Buys 4-6 mss/year. Query with or without published clips or send complete ms. Length: varies. Pays $50-150 for assigned articles; $100 for unsolicited material. Sometimes pays writers with contributor copies or other premiums rather than a cash payment "if writer/photographer/artist wishes." Rarely pays expenses of writers on assignment.
Photos: Send photos with submission (photocopies OK). Reviews contact sheets and transparencies. Offers $15-100/photo. Model releases and identification of subjects required. Buys one-time rights or all rights.
Fiction: Adventure, confession, erotica, fantasy, historical, horror, humorous, mystery, novel excerpts, science fiction, slice-of-life vignettes, suspense and western. All must involve kinky gay male erotica. No non sexual fiction—note sex per se does not have to occur in the story but it must have an erotic overtone. Buys 25-35 mss/year. Query with published clips or send complete ms. Length: varies. Pays $100.

MANSCAPE 2, First Hand Ltd., Box 1314, Teaneck NJ 07666. (201)836-9177. Editor: Lou Thomas. 75% freelance written. A quarterly magazine focusing on "gay male sexual fetishes, kink and leather sex." Circ. 70,000. Pays two months after acceptance. Publishes ms an average of 9 months after acceptance. Byline given. Buys first North American serial rights or all rights. Submit seasonal/holiday material 9 months in advance. Photocopied submissions OK. "No simultaneous submisions." Computer printout submissions OK; no dot-matrix. Reports in 1 month. Sample copy $4.50; free writer's guidelines.
Nonfiction: Interview/profile and health. "All nonfiction articles must have gay angle." Buys 4 mss/year. Query with or without published clips, or send complete ms. Length: 2,000-3,750. Pays $100-150 for unsolicited articles (no assigned articles).
Fiction: Erotica and novel excerpts. "All fiction must be gay erotica. We don't want to see downbeat attitudes in stories." Buys 30 mss/year. Send complete ms. Length: 2,000-3,750 words. Pays $100-150.
Poetry: Free verse, haiku, light verse, traditional. Must be erotic. Buys 4 poems/year. Submit 5 poems maxi-

mum at one time. Length: 5-20 lines. Pays $25.

Tips: "The fiction section is the best area for freelancers to break in with. Most of the fiction we publish is written in the first person. Stories should be strongly erotic, with at least an edge of kinkiness. And stories should be a celebration of masculinity, of maleness."

METRO SINGLES LIFESTYLES, Metro Publications, Box 28203, Kansas City MO 64118. (816)436-8424. Editor: R.L. Huffstutter. 40% freelance written. Eager to work with new/unpublished writers. A tabloid appearing 9 times/year covering singles lifestyles. Pays on acceptance. Publishes ms an average of 2 months after acceptance. Byline given. Buys one-time rights and second serial (reprint) rights. Submit seasonal/holiday material 3 months in advance. Photocopied submissions OK. Computer printout submissions acceptable; prefers letter-quality to dot-matrix. Reports in 1 month. Sample copy $2 and 9x12 SAE with 90¢ postage.

Nonfiction: Essay, general interest, how-to (on meeting the ideal mate, . . . recovering from divorce, etc.), inspirational, interview/profile, personal experience and photo feature. No sexually-oriented material. Buys 2-6 mss/year. Send complete ms. Length: 700-1,200 words. Pays $100 maximum for assigned articles; pays $20-50 for unsolicited articles. Will pay in copies or other if writer prefers.

Photos: Send photos with submission. Reviews 3x5 prints. Offers no additional payment for photos accepted with ms. Captions, model releases, and identification of subjects required. Buys one-time rights.

Columns/Departments: Movie Reviews, Lifestyles, Singles Events, and Book Reviews (about singles), all 400-1,000 words. Buys 3 mss/year. Send complete ms. Pays $20-50.

Fiction: Confession, humorous, romance and slice-of-life vignettes. No political, religion, ethnic or sexually-oriented material. Buys 6 mss/year. Send complete ms. Length: 700-1,200 words. Pays $20-50.

Poetry: Free verse and light verse. Buys 6 poems/year. Submit maximum 3 poems. Length: 21 lines. Pays $5-10.

Tips: "A freelancer can best approach and break in to our publication with positive articles, photo features about singles and positive fiction about singles. Photos and short bios of singles (blue collar, white collar, and professional) at work needed. Photos and a few lines about singles enjoying recreation (swimming, sports, chess, etc.) always welcome. Color photos, close-up, are suitable."

MOM GUESS WHAT NEWSPAPER, MGW Productions, Inc., Suite 100, 1400 S St., Sacramento CA 95814. (916)441-6397. Editor: Linda Birner. Managing Editor: Judy Powers. 80% freelance written. Works with small number of new/unpublished writers each year. A monthly tabloid covering gay rights and gay lifestyles. Circ. 21,000. Publishes ms an average of 3 months after acceptance. Byline given. Buys all rights. Submit seasonal/holiday material 3 months in advance. Photocopied submissions OK. Computer printout submissions acceptable; no dot-matrix. Reports in 2 months. Sample copy $1; writer's guidelines for 9x12 SAE with 3 first class stamps.

Nonfiction: Interview/profile and photo feature of international, national or local scope. Buys 8 mss/year. Query. Length: 200-1,500 words. Payment depends on article. Pays expenses of writers on special assignment.

Photos: State availability of photos with submission. Reviews 5x7 prints. Offers no additional payment for photos accepted with ms. Captions and identification of subjects required. Buys one-time rights.

Columns/Departments: Restaurants, Political, Health, and Film, Video and Book Reviews. Buys 12 mss/year. Query. Payment depends on article.

R F D, A Country Journal for Gay Men Everywhere, Rt. 1, Box 127-E, Bakersville NC 28705. (704)688-2447. Managing Editor: Ron Lambe. 90% freelance written. Eager to work with new/unpublished writers. Quarterly magazine of rural gay male concerns. "We look for nonsexist, nonexploitation, positive, open-minded explorations of who we are as gay rural men." Circ. 2,000. Pays on publication. Publishes ms an average of 4-6 months after acceptance. Byline given. Not copyrighted. Buys one-time rights. Submit seasonal/holiday material 3 months in advance. Simultaneous queries, and simultaneous, photocopied, and previously published submissions OK. Computer printout submissions acceptable; prefers letter-quality to dot-matrix. Reports in 3 months on queries. Sample copy $4.25 postpaid.

Nonfiction: Richard Chumley, articles editor. Exposé, how-to, humor, inspirational, interview/profile, opinion, personal experience and travel. No common or trendy pieces. Acquires 8-10 mss/year. Send complete ms. Length: 500-5,000 words. Pays in 2 copies of journal.

Photos: Prefers b&w prints, (color of high contrast); of rural, nature, or male themes. Pays in 2 copies of journal. Model releases and identification of subjects required. Buys one-time rights. Pays in 2 copies of journal.

Fiction: Adventure, erotica, fantasy and romance. No sexist or insensitive exploitation. Acquires 8 mss/year. Send complete ms. Length: 1,000-5,000 words. Pays in 2 copies of journal.

Poetry: Franklin Abbott, poetry editor. Advant-garde, free verse, haiku, light verse and traditional. Acquires 40 poems/year. Submit maximum 5 poems. Length: 3-100 lines. Pays in 2 copies of journal.

Tips: "Offer original and thematic work. We prefer simplicity and clarity in style."

SINGLELIFE MAGAZINE, SingleLife Enterprises, Inc., 606 W. Wisconsin Ave., Milwaukee WI 53203. (414)271-9700. Editor: Gail Rose. 30% freelance written. Prefers to work with published/established writers;

works with a small number of new/unpublished writers each year. Bimonthly magazine covering singles life-styles. Circ. 22,000. Pays on publication. Publishes ms an average of 6 months after acceptance. Byline given. Buys one-time rights, second serial (reprint) rights and simultaneous rights. Submit seasonal material 4 months in advance. Simultaneous submissions, photocopies and previously published submissions OK. Query for electronic submissions. Computer printout submissions OK; prefer letter-quality to dot-matrix. Reports in 1-6 weeks. Sample copy and writer's guidelines for $3.50 and 9x11 SAE; writer's guidelines for SAE with 1 first class stamp.

Nonfiction: Leifa Butrick, articles editor. Upbeat and in-depth articles on significant areas of interest to single people such as male/female relationships, travel, health, sports, food, single parenting, humor, finances, places to go and things to do. Prefers third person point of view and ms to query letter. Our readers are between 25 and 50. Length: 1,000-3,000 words. Pays $50-150. Sometimes pays expenses of writers on assignment.

Photos: Send photos with query or ms. Pays $10-100 for b&w contact sheet, 2¼" transparencies and 8x10 prints; pays $20-200 for 2¼" color transparencies and 8x10 prints. Captions, model releases and identification of subjects required.

Fiction and Poetry: Leifa Butrick, editor. Buys 3-4 stories or poems which are well written and cast a new light on what being single means. No simple boy meets girl at the laundromat. Length: not over 2,500 words. Submit any number of poems that pertain to being single. Pays $25-50.

Tips: "The easiest way to get in is to write something light, unusual, but also well-developed."

STALLION MAGAZINE, The Magazine of the Alternate Lifestyle, Charlton Publications, 351 W. 54th St., New York NY 10019. (212)586-4432. Editor: Jerry Douglas. 75% freelance written. Works with a small number of new/unpublished writers each year. Monthly magazine for gay community. Text includes articles and fiction for gay males; pictorially, male nudes. Circ. 80,000. Pays on publication. Publishes ms an average of 4 months after acceptance. Byline given. Buys first North American serial rights. Submit seasonal/holiday material 6 months in advance. Simultaneous queries and simultaneous and photocopied submissions OK; rarely accepts previously published submissions. Computer printout submissions acceptable; no dot-matrix. Reports in 4 months on mss. Free writer's guidelines, but no sample copies.

Nonfiction and Fiction: Book excerpts, exposé, general interest, historical/nostalgic, inspirational, interview/profile, opinion, personal experience and photo feature. "We publish one piece of fiction in each issue, and while we certainly do not avoid erotic content in the stories, the work must have some other quality besides sexual heat. In other words, we are not looking for 'stroke pose' per se. We have accepted a wide range of fiction pieces, the only common denominator being that the work deal with some aspect of the gay experience." Buys 12 fiction/36 nonfiction mss/year. Send complete ms. Length: 2,000-3,000 words. Pays $200.

Tips: "Although the visual content of the magazine is strictly erotic, the textual content is not, and we seek articles and fiction of interest to the gay community, beyond the strictly erotic. We are more interested in articles than fiction."

TORSO, Varsity Communications, 155 Avenue of The Americas, New York NY 10013. (213)850-5400. Editor: Stan Leventhal. 75% freelance written. Works with a small number of new/unpublished writers each year. A monthly magazine for gay men. "Divergent viewpoints are expressed in both feature articles and fiction, which examine values and behavior patterns characteristic of a gay lifestyle. *Torso* has a continuing commitment to well-documented investigative journalism in areas pertaining to the lives and well-being of homosexuals." Circ. 60,000. Pays on publication. Publishes ms an average of 5 months after acceptance. Byline given. Buys first North American serial rights. Submit seasonal/holiday material 3 months in advance. Simultaneous queries, and simultaneous and photocopied submissions OK. Reports in 2 weeks on queries; 1 month on mss. Sample copy $5; writer's guidelines for business size SASE.

Nonfiction: Expose, general interest, humor, interview/profile, opinion, personal experience, photo feature and travel. "*Torso* also regularly reports on cultural and political trends, as well as the arts and entertainment, often profiling the people and personalities who affect them. The tone must be positive regarding the gay experience." Buys 12 mss/year. Query with or without published clips or send complete ms (typewritten and double-spaced). Length: 2,000-4,000 words. Pays $100.

Fiction: Erotica, adventure, fantasy, humorous, novel excerpts and romance. "No long, drawn-out fiction with no form, etc." Buys 35 mss/year. Query with or without published clips or send complete ms. Length: 2,000-4,000 words. Pays $100.

Tips: "Write about what is happening—what you as a gay male (if you are) would care to read."

THE WASHINGTON BLADE, Washington Blade, Inc., 8th Floor, 724 9th St. NW, Washington DC 20001. (202)347-2038. Managing Editor: Lisa M. Keen. 20% freelance written. Works with a small number of new/unpublished writers each year. Weekly news tabloid covering the gay/lesbian community. "Articles (subjects) should be written from or directed to a gay perspective." Circ. 20,000. Pays in 30 days. Publishes ms an average of 1 month after acceptance. Byline given. Offers $15 kill fee. Buys first North American serial rights. Submit seasonal/holiday material 1 month in advance. Photocopied submissions OK. Computer printout submissions acceptable; prefers letter-quality to dot-matrix. Free sample copy and writer's guidelines.

Nonfiction: Exposé (of government, private agency, church, etc., handling of gay-related issues); historical/nostalgic; interview/profile (of gay community/political leaders; persons, gay or nongay, in positions to affect gay issues; outstanding achievers who happen to be gay; those who incorporate the gay lifestyle into their professions); photo feature (on a nationally or internationally historic gay event); and travel (on locales that welcome or cater to the gay traveler). *The Washington Blade* basically covers two areas: news and lifestyle. News coverage of D.C. metropolitan area gay community, local and federal government actions relating to gays, some national news of interest to gays. Section also includes features on current events. Special issues include: Annual gay pride issue (early June), and a monthly style section, "Living". No sexually explicit material. Buys 30 mss/year, average. Query with published clips and resume. Length: 500-1,500 words. Pays 5-10¢/word. Sometimes pays the expenses of writers on assignment.

Photos: "A photo or graphic with feature/lifestyle articles is particularly important. Photos with news stories are appreciated." State availability of photos. Reviews b&w contact sheets and 5x7 glossy prints. Pays $25 minimum. Captions preferred; model releases required. On assignment, photographer paid mutually agreed upon fee, with expenses reimbursed. Publication retains all rights.

Tips: "Send good examples of your writing and know the paper before you submit a manuscript for publication. We get a lot of submissions which are entirely inappropriate." Greatest opportunity for freelancers resides in current events, features, interviews and book reviews.

THE WEEKLY NEWS, The Weekly News Inc., 901 NE 79th St., Miami FL 33138. (305)757-6333. Editor: Joseph McQuay. Managing Editor: Bill Watson. 40% freelance written. Weekly gay tabloid. Circ. 32,000. Pays on publication. Byline given. Buys one-time rights. Submit seasonal/holiday material 2 months in advance. Simultaneous, photocopied and previously published submissions OK. Sample copy for 9½x12½ SAE with $1.50 postage.

Nonfiction: Exposé, humor and interview/profile. Buys 8 mss/year. Send complete ms. Length: 1,000-5,000 words. Pays $25-125. Sometimes pays the expenses of writers on assignment.

Photos: State availability of photos with submission. Reviews 3x5 prints. Offers $5-20/photo. Buys first and future use.

Columns/Departments: Send complete ms. Length: 900 words maximum. Pays $15-30.

Fillers: Anecdotes, gags to be illustrated by cartoonist and short humor. Pays $15-30.

Religious

Religious magazines focus on a variety of subjects, styles and beliefs. Such diversity makes reading each magazine essential for the writer hoping to break in. Educational and inspirational material of interest to church members, workers and leaders within a denomination or religion is needed by the publications in this category. Publications intended to assist professional religious workers in teaching and managing church affairs are classified in Church Administration and Ministry in the Trade section. Religious magazines for children and teenagers can be found in the Juvenile and Teen and Young Adult classifications. Other religious magazines can be found in the Ethnic/Minority section.

AGLOW, Today's Publication for Christian Women, Aglow Publications, Box I, Lynnwood WA 98046-1557. (206)775-7282. Editor: Gwen Weising. 66% freelance written. Works with a small number of new/unpublished writers each year. Bimonthly nondenominational Christian charismatic magazine for women. Pays on acceptance. Publishes ms an average of 1 year after acceptance. Byline given. Buys first North American serial rights, and reprint rights for use in *Aglow* magazine in other countries. Submit seasonal/holiday material 6 months in advance. Simultaneous queries and photocopied submissions acceptable. Computer printout submissions OK; prefers letter-quality to dot-matrix. Reports in 2 months. Writer's guidelines for business size SAE and 1 first class stamp.

Nonfiction: Christian women's spiritual experience articles (first person) and some humor. "Each article should be either a testimony of or teaching about Jesus as Savior, as Baptizer in the Holy Spirit, or as Guide and Strength in everyday circumstances." Queries only. "We would like to see material about 'Women of Vision' who have made and are making an impact on their world for God." Length: 1,000-2,000 words. Pays up to 10¢/word. Sometimes pays expenses of writers on assignment.

‡AMERICA, 106 W. 56th St., New York NY 10019. (212)581-4640. Editor: Rev. George W. Hunt. Published weekly for adult, educated, largely Roman Catholic audience. Pays on acceptance. Byline given. Usually buys all rights. Reports in 2-3 weeks. Free writer's guidelines.
Nonfiction: "We publish a wide variety of material on politics, economics, ecology, and so forth. We are not a parochial publication, but almost all of our pieces make some moral or religious point. We are not interested in purely informational pieces or personal narratives which are self-contained and have no larger moral interest." Articles on literature, current political and social events. Length: 1,500-2,000 words. Pays $50-100.
Poetry: Length: 15-30 lines. Address to Poetry Editor.

THE ANNALS OF SAINT ANNE DE BEAUPRE, Redemptorist Fathers, 9597 St. Anne Blvd., St. Anne De Beaupre, Quebec G0A 3C0 Canada. (418)824-4538. Editor: Bernard Mercier. Managing Editor: Roch Achard. 80% freelance written. Works with a small number of new/unpublished writers each year. "Anyone can submit manuscripts. We judge." Monthly magazine on religion. "Our aim is to promote devotion to St. Anne and Christian family values." Circ. 54,000. Pays on acceptance. Publishes ms an average of 1 year after acceptance. Byline given. Buys first North American serial rights. Submit seasonal/holiday material 2½ months in advance. Simultaneous queries and photocopied submissions OK. Computer printout submissions OK; prefers letter-quality to dot-matrix. Reports in 2 weeks. Free sample copy and writer's guidelines.
Nonfiction: Expose, general interest, inspirational and personal experience. No articles without spiritual thrust. Buys 30 mss/year. Send complete ms. Length: 500-1,200 words. Pays 2-4¢/word.
Fiction: Religious. Buys 15 mss/year. Send complete ms. Length: 500-1,200 words. Pays 3-4¢/word.
Poetry: Traditional. Buys 12/year. Submit maximum 2-3 poems. Length: 12-20 lines. Pays $5-8.
Tips: "Write something educational, inspirational, objective and uplifting. Reporting rather than analysis is simply not remarkable."

THE ASSOCIATE REFORMED PRESBYTERIAN, Associate Reformed Presbyterian General Synod, 1 Cleveland St., Greenville SC 29601. (803)232-8297. Editor: Ben Johnston. 10% freelance written. Works with a small number of new/unpublished writers each year. A Christian publication serving a conservative, evangelical and Reformed denomination, most of whose members are in the Southeast U.S. Circ. 6,300. Pays on acceptance. Publishes ms an average of 3 months after acceptance. Byline given. Not copyrighted. Buys first rights, one-time rights, or second serial (reprint) rights. Submit seasonal/holiday material 4 months in advance. Simultaneous submissions and previously published submissions OK. Computer printout submissions acceptable; prefers letter-quality to dot-matrix. Reports in 1 month. Sample copy $1; writer's guidelines for SASE.
Nonfiction: Book excerpts, essays, inspirational, opinion, personal experience, and religious. Buys 10-15 mss/year. Query. Length: 400-2,000 words. $50 maximum.
Photos: State availability of photos with submission. Reviews 5x7 reprints. Offers $25 maximum per photo. Captions and identification of subjects required. Buys one-time rights. Sometimes pays expenses of writers on assignment.
Fiction: Religious and children's. Buys 5-8 mss/year. Query. Length: 400-1,500 words. Pays $50 maximum. "We expect to resume our contest for writers of children's stories. Contest rules will be available for SASE in January 1988."
Tips: "Feature articles are the area of our publication most open to freelancers. Focus on a contemporary problem and offer Bible-based solutions to it. Provide information that would help a Christian struggling in his daily walk. Writers should understand that we are denominational, conservative, evangelical, Reformed, and Presbyterian. A writer who appreciates these nuances would stand a much better chance of being published here than one who does not."

AXIOS, 800 S. Euclid St., Fullerton CA 92632. (714)526-2131. Editor: David Gorham. 10% freelance written. Eager to work with new/unpublished writers. Monthly journal seeking spiritual articles mostly on Orthodox Christian background, either Russian, Greek, Serbian, Syrian or American. Circ. 6,789. Pays on publication. Publishes ms an average of 6 months after acceptance. Byline given. Offers 50% kill fee. Buys all rights. Submit seasonal/holiday material 4 months in advance. Simultaneous queries, and simultaneous, photocopied, and previously published submissions OK. Query for electronic submissions. Computer printout submissions acceptable; prefers letter-quality to dot-matrix. Reports in 1 month. Sample copy for $2 and 9x12 SAE with $1 postage.
Nonfiction: Book excerpts; expose (of religious figures); general interest; historical/nostalgic; interview/profile; opinion; personal experience; photo feature; and travel (shrines, pilgrimages). Special issues include the persecution of Christians in Iran, Russia, behind Iron Curtain or in Arab lands; Roman Catholic interest in the Orthodox Church. Nothing about the Pope or general "all-is-well-with-Christ" items. Buys 14 mss/year. Send complete ms. Length: 1,000-3,000 words. Pays 4¢/word minimum. Sometimes pays expenses of writers on assignment.
Columns/Departments: Reviews religious books and films. Buys 80 mss/year. Query.
Tips: "We need some hard hitting articles on the 'political' church—the why, how and where of it and why it

lacks the timelessness of the spiritual. Here in *Axios* you can discuss your feelings, your findings, your needs, your growth; give us your outpouring. Don't mistake us for either Protestant or Roman Catholic; we are the voice of Catholics united with the Eastern Orthodox Church, also referred to as the Greek Orthodox Church.''

BAPTIST LEADER, Valley Forge PA 19482-0851. (215)768-2153. Editor: Linda Isham. For pastors, teachers, and leaders in Sunday church schools. 25% freelance written. Works with a small number of new/unpublished writers each year. Monthly; 64 pages. Buys first serial rights. Pays on acceptance. Publishes ms an average of 8 months after acceptance. Deadlines are 8 months prior to date of issue. Computer printout submissions acceptable; prefers letter-quality to dot-matrix. Writer's guidelines for SASE.
Nonfiction: Educational topics. How-to articles for local church school teachers and leaders. Length: 1,500-2,000 words. Pays $25-75.
Tips: "We're planning major changes effective September 1988."

‡BIBLICAL HISTORY, A Chronicle of Faith Through The Ages, Empire Press, 105 Loudoun St., SW, Leesburg VA 22075. (703)771-9400. Executive Editor: C. Brian Kelly. 95% freelance written. Bimonthly magazine covering biblical and religious history. "No devotional material; avoid controversy; popular religious history for largely Christian audience, any denomination." Estab. 1987. Circ. 110,000. Pays on publication. Publishes ms an average of 6-12 months after acceptance. Byline given. Negotiable kill fee. Buys first North American serial rights. Submit seasonal/holiday material 1 year in advance. Photocopied submissions OK. Reports in 1 month on queries; 8-12 weeks on mss. Sample copy $4; writer's guidelines for SAE with 1 first class stamp.
Nonfiction: Historical, religious. Buys 24 mss/year. Query. Length: 4,000 words. Pays $350.
Photos: State availability of art and photos with submission (hardly any photos to be used). Offers no additional payment for photos accepted with ms.
Columns/Departments: Prophets and Believers (biblical figures); His Own Pathway (stories about Jesus Christ); Profiles in Faith (profiles of religious figures in general); Church and the Arts (arts and church relationships). Buys 24 mss/year. Query. Length: 2,000 words. Pays $150.

BIBLICAL ILLUSTRATOR, The Sunday School Board, 127 9th Ave. N., Nashville TN 37234. Editor: Michael J. Mitchell. "Articles are designed to coordinate with other Southern Baptist periodicals. Unsolicited mss are rarely applicable. Inquire first."

CATHOLIC DIGEST, Box 64090, St. Paul MN 55164. Editor: Henry Lexau. Managing Editor: Richard Reece. 50% freelance written. Works with small number of new/unpublished writers each year. Monthly magazine covering the daily living of Roman Catholics for an audience that is 60% female, 40% male; 37% is college educated. Circ. 600,000. Publishes ms an average of 6 months after acceptance. Byline given. Buys first North American serial rights or one-time reprint rights. Submit seasonal material 6 months in advance. Previously published submissions OK, if so indicated. Computer printout submissions acceptable; prefers letter-quality to dot-matrix. Reports in 3 weeks.
Nonfiction: General interest (daily living and family relationships); interview (of outstanding Catholics, celebrities and locals); nostalgia (the good old days of family living); profile; religion; travel (shrines); humor; inspirational (overcoming illness, role model people); and personal experience (adventures and daily living). Buys 25 articles/issue. No queries. Send complete ms. Length: 500-3,000 words, 2,000 average. Pays on acceptance—$200-400 for originals, $100 for reprints.
Columns/Departments: "Check a copy of the magazine in the library for a description of column needs. Payment varies and is made on publication. We buy about 5/issue."
Fillers: Jokes, anecdotes and short humor. Buys 10-15 mss/issue. Length: 10-300 words. Pays $3-50 on publication.

CATHOLIC LIFE, 35750 Moravian Dr., Fraser MI 48026. Editor-in-Chief: Robert C. Bayer. 40% freelance written. Monthly (except July or August) magazine; 32 pages. Emphasizes foreign missionary activities of the Catholic Church in Burma, India, Bangladesh, the Philippines, Hong Kong, Africa, etc., for middle-aged and older audience with either middle incomes or pensions. High school educated (on the average), conservative in both religion and politics. Circ. 18,600. Pays on publication. Publishes ms an average of 3 months after acceptance. Buys all rights. Byline given. Submit seasonal/holiday material 4 months in advance. Simultaneous submissions OK. Computer printout submissions acceptable. Reports in 2 weeks.
Nonfiction: Informational and inspirational foreign missionary activities of the Catholic Church. Buys 20-25 unsolicited mss/year. Query or send complete ms. Length: 1,000-1,500 words. Pays 4¢/word.
Tips: "Query with short, graphic details of what the material will cover or the personality involved in the biographical sketch. Also, we appreciate being advised on the availability of good black-and-white photos to illustrate the material."

CATHOLIC NEAR EAST MAGAZINE, Catholic Near East Welfare Association, 1011 1st Ave., New York NY 10022. (212)826-1480. Editor: Michael Healy. 90% freelance written. Quarterly magazine; 24 pages. For a general audience with interest in the Near East, particularly its religious and cultural aspects. Circ. 130,000. Pays on publication. Publishes ms an average of 4 months after acceptance. Byline given. Buys all rights. Submit seasonal material (Christmas and Easter in different Near Eastern lands or rites) 6 months in advance. Photocopied submissions OK if legible. Computer printout submissions acceptable; no dot-matrix. Reports in 1 month. Sample copy and writer's guidelines for 9½x6½ SASE.

Nonfiction: "Cultural, territorial, devotional material on the Near East, its history, peoples and religions (especially the Eastern Rites of the Catholic Church). Style should be simple, factual, concise. Articles must stem from personal acquaintance with subject matter, or thorough up-to-date research. No preaching or speculations." Length: 1,200-1,800 words. Pays 10¢/word.

Photos: "Photographs to accompany manuscript are always welcome; they should illustrate the people, places, ceremonies, etc. which are described in the article. We prefer color transparencies but occasionally use black and white. Pay varies depending on the quality of the photos."

Tips: "Writers please heed: stick to the people of the Near East, the Balkans through the Middle East to India. Send factual articles; concise, descriptive style preferred, not flowery. Pictures are a big plus; if you have photos to accompany your article, please send them—with captions— at the same time."

CATHOLIC TWIN CIRCLE, Twin Circle Publishing, Suite 900, 6404 Wilshire Blvd., Los Angeles CA 90048. (213)653-2200. Executive Editor: Mary Louise Frawley. 30% freelance written. Prefers to work with published/established writers; works with a small number of new/unpublished writers each year. Weekly tabloid covering Catholic personalities and Catholic interest topics for a mostly Catholic family readership. Circ. 60,000. Pays on publication. Publishes ms an average of 2 months after acceptance. Byline given. Buys all rights. Submit seasonal material 3 months in advance. Photocopied submissions OK. Wants original material. Query for electronic submissions. Computer printout submissions acceptable; prefers letter-quality to dot-matrix. Reports in 2 months on queries; 6 weeks on mss. Writer's guidelines for SASE.

Nonfiction: "We are looking for articles about prominent Catholic personalities in sports, entertainment, politics and business; ethnic stories about Catholics from other countries and topical issues of concern to Catholics. We are interested in writers who are experienced and write on an ongoing basis." Average issue includes 6-7 feature articles. Buys 3-4 mss/issue. Not responsible for unsolicited mss. Length: 250-2,000 words. Pays 10¢/word. Sometimes pays expenses of writers on assignment.

Photos: State availability of photos. Reviews 5x7 or 8x10 b&w glossy prints. Price negotiated. Captions required. Rights vary.

Tips: Writer has a better chance of breaking in with shorter pieces, as "they give a truer example of a writer's style, strengths and weaknesses. Research thoroughly and use quotes from acceptable sources."

‡CHRISTIAN HERALD, 40 Overlook Dr., Chappaqua NY 10514. (914)769-9000. Editor: Dean Merrill. 50% freelance written. A monthly magazine for evangelical Protestants. Circ. 160,000. Pays on acceptance. Byline given. Offers ⅓ kill fee. Buys first North American serial rights or second serial (reprint) rights. Submit seasonal/holiday material 4 months in advance. Reports in 1 month. Sample copy for 9x12 SAE with 2 first class stamps; writer's guidelines for #10 SAE with 1 first class stamp.

Nonfiction: Ruth Chuvala, articles editor. Humor, interview/profile, personal experience and religious. "No articles that tell the reader what to do or how to live." Buys 50 mss/year. Query with published clips, or send complete ms. Length: 100-2,500 words. Pays 10-15¢/word. Sometimes pays the expenses of writers on assignment.

Photos: Send photos with submission. Reviews contact sheets, transparencies and prints. Captions, model releases and identification of subjects required. Buys one-time rights.

Columns/Departments: Kids of the Kingdom (enlightening moments in the course of parenting or teaching children), up to 200 words; The Two of Us (special moments in a Christian marrriage), up to 200 words; One Last Word (personal experiences that pointed out something external), up to 1,000 words. Buys 30 mss/year. Send complete ms. Pays 10-15¢/word.

Tips: "Look around for people who are demonstrating their faith, not just talking about it."

CHRISTIAN HOME & SCHOOL, Christian Schools International, 3350 East Paris Ave. SE, Box 8709, Grand Rapids MI 49508. (616)957-1070. Editor: Gordon L. Bordewyk. Associate Editor: Judy Zylstra. 30% freelance written. Works with a small number of new/unpublished writers each year. Magazine published 8 times/year covering family life and Christian education. "The magazine is designed for parents who support Christian education. We feature material on a wide range of topics of interest to parents." Pays on publication. Publishes ms an average of 4 months after acceptance. Byline given. Buys first North American serial rights. Submit seasonal/holiday material 4 months in advance. Simultaneous queries and photocopied submissions OK. Computer printout submissions acceptable; prefers letter-quality to dot-matrix. Reports in 3 weeks on queries; 1 month on mss. Sample copy for 9x12 SAE and 4 first class stamps.

Nonfiction: Book excerpts, interview/profile, opinion, personal experience, and articles on parenting and school life. "We publish features on issues which affect the home and school and profiles on interesting individuals, providing that the profile appeals to our readers and is not a tribute or eulogy of that person." Buys 40 mss/year. Send complete ms. Length: 500-2,000 words. Pays $25-85. Sometimes pays the expenses of writers on assignment.

Photos: "If you have any black-and-white photos appropriate for your article, send them along."

Tips: "Features are the area most open to freelancers. We are publishing articles that deal with contemporary issues which affect parents; keep that in mind. Use an informal easy-to-read style rather than a philosophical, academic tone. Try to incorporate vivid imagery and concrete, practical examples from real life."

CHRISTIAN SINGLE, Family Ministry Dept., Baptist Sunday School Board, 127 9th Ave. N., Nashville TN 37234. (615)251-2228. Editor: Cliff Allbritton. 50-70% freelance written. Prefers to work with published/established writers; works with a small number of new/unpublished writers each year. Monthly magazine covering items of special interest to Christian single adults. "*Christian Single* is a contemporary Christian magazine that seeks to give substantive information to singles for living the abundant life. It seeks to be constructive and creative in approach." Circ. 105,000. Pays on acceptance "for immediate needs"; on publication "for unsolicited manuscripts." Publishes ms 1-2 years after acceptance. Byline given. Buys all rights; makes work-for-hire assignments. Submit seasonal/holiday material 1 year in advance. Computer printout submissions acceptable; no dot-matrix. Reports in 6 weeks. Sample copy and writer's guidelines for large SASE.

Nonfiction: Humor (good, clean humor that applies to Christian singles); how-to (specific subjects which apply to singles; query needed); inspirational (of the personal experience type); high adventure personal experience (of single adults); photo feature (on outstanding Christian singles; query needed); well researched financial articles targeted to single adults (query needed). No "shallow, uninformative mouthing off. This magazine says something, and people read it cover to cover." Buys 120-150 unsolicited mss/year. Query with published clips. Length: 300-1,200 words. Pays 5¢/word.

Tips: "We look for freshness and creativity, not duplication of what we have already done. Need more upbeat personal experience articles written by Christian *single men*! We are backlogged with submissions by women at this time. We give preference to Christian single adult writers but publish articles by *sensitive* and *informed* married writers also. Remember that you are talking to educated people who attend church."

CHRISTIANITY & CRISIS, 537 W. 121st St., New York NY 10027. (212)662-5907. Editor: Leon Howell. Managing Editor: Gail Hovey. 10% freelance written. Works with a small number of new/unpublished writers each year. Biweekly Protestant journal of opinion. "We are interested in special issues, foreign affairs, liberation theology and other theological developments with social or ethical implications. As an independent religious journal it is part of *C&C*'s function to discuss church policies from a detached and sometimes critical perspective. We carry no 'devotional' material but welcome solid contemplative reflections. Most subscribers are highly educated, well-informed." Circ. 14,000. Pays on publication. Publishes ms an average of 2 months after acceptance. Byline given. Offers variable kill fee. Submit seasonal/holiday material 2 months in advance. Simultaneous queries and photocopied submissions OK. Computer printout submissions acceptable if double-spaced. Reports in 1 month. Sample copy $1.75; free writer's guidelines.

Nonfiction: Buys 150 mss/year. Query with or without published clips. Length: 1,000-4,000 words. Pays 3¢/word. Rarely pays expenses of writers on assignment.

Tips: "We have been publishing more international stories and need to build up reporting on U.S. issues."

CHRISTIANITY TODAY, 465 Gundersen Dr., Carol Stream IL 60188. 80% freelance written. Works with a small number of new/unpublished writers each year. Emphasizes orthodox, evangelical religion. Semimonthly magazine; 55 pages. Circ. 180,000. Publishes ms an average of 6 months after acceptance. Usually buys first serial rights. Submit seasonal/holiday material at least 8 months in advance. Computer printout submissions acceptable; prefers letter-quality to dot-matrix. Reports in 2 months. Sample copy and writer's guidelines for 9x12 SAE and 3 first class stamps.

Nonfiction: Theological, ethical, historical and informational (not merely inspirational). Buys 4 mss/issue. *Query only.* Unsolicited mss not accepted and not returned. Length: 1,000-4,000 words. Pays negotiable rates. Sometimes pays the expenses of writers on assignment.

Columns/Departments: Refiner's Fire (Christian review of the arts). Buys 12 mss/year. Send complete ms. Length: 800-900 words. Pays negotiable rates.

Tips: "We are developing more of our own manuscripts and requiring a much more professional quality of others."

‡CHRISTMAS, The Annual of Literature and Art, Augsburg Publishing, 426 S. 5th St., Box 1209, Minneapolis MN 55440. (612)330-3437. Editor: Leonard Flachman. 100% freelance written. "An annual literary magazine that celebrates Christmas focusing on the effect of the Christmas love of God on the lives of people, and how it colors and shapes traditions and celebrations." Pays on acceptance. Byline given. Buys first rights, one-time rights and all rights; makes work-for-hire assignments. Submit seasonal/holiday material 18 months in advance. Reports in 2 weeks on queries; 3 weeks on mss. Sample copy $6.95.

Nonfiction: Historical/nostalgic (on Christmas customs); inspirational, interview/profile, personal experience and travel. Articles on art and music with Christmas relationships. Buys 6-8 mss/year. Query with published clips, or send complete ms. Length: 2,500-7,500 words. Pays $200-450 for assigned articles; pays $150-300 for unsolicited articles.

Photos: State availability of photos with submission. Reviews transparencies. Offers $15-100 per photo. Captions and identification of subjects required. Buys one-time rights.

Fiction: Karen Walhof, editor. Ethnic, historical and slice-of-life vignettes. "No stories of fictionalized characters at the Bethlehem stable. Fiction should show the effect of God's love on the lives of people." Buys 2 mss/year. Send complete ms. Length: 5,000 words maximum. Pays $150-300.

Poetry: Karen Walhof, editor. Free verse, light verse and traditional. No poetry dealing with Santa Claus. Buys 3 poems/year. Submit maximum 30 poems. Pays $35-40.

CHURCH & STATE, Americans United for Separation of Church and State, 8120 Fenton St., Silver Spring MD 20910. (301)589-3707. Managing Editor: Joseph Conn. 10% freelance written. Prefers to work with published/established writers. Monthly magazine; 24 pages. Emphasizes religious liberty and church/state relations matters. Readership "includes the whole spectrum, but is predominantly Protestant and well-educated." Circ. 50,000. Pays on acceptance. Publishes ms an average of 2 months after acceptance. Buys all rights. Simultaneous, photocopied, and previously published submissions OK. Computer printout submissions OK; prefers letter-quality. Reports in 1 month. Free sample copy and writer's guidelines.

Nonfiction: Expose, general interest, historical and interview. Buys 11 mss/year. Query. Length: 3,000 words maximum. Pays negotiable fee.

Photos: State availability of photos with query. Pays negotiable fee for b&w prints. Captions preferred. Buys one-time rights.

‡THE CHURCH HERALD, 6157 28th St., SE Grand Rapids MI 49506-6999. Editor: Rev. Dr. John Stapert. Managing Editor: Kim Nathan Baker. 20% freelance written. Prefers to work with published/established writers; works with small number of new/unpublished writers each year. Biweekly magazine covering contemporary Christian life. "The *Church Herald* is the denominational publication of the Reformed Church in America, a Protestant denomination in the Presbyterian-Reformed family of churches. We solicit carefully researched and well-written articles on almost any subject, but they all must have a distinctively Christian perspective." Circ. 54,000. Pays on acceptance. Publishes ms an average of 3 months after acceptance. Byline given. Offers 50% kill fee. Buys first rights, one-time rights, second serial (reprint) rights, simultaneous rights and all rights. Submit seasonal/holiday material 3 months in advance. Simultaneous and previously published submissions OK. Query for electronic submission. Computer printout submissions OK; no dot-matrix. Reports in 2 weeks on queries; 4 weeks on mss. Free sample copy and writer's guidelines.

Nonfiction: Essays, general interest, humor, inspirational, personal experience, religious. Buys 30 mss/year. Send complete ms. Length: 400-1,500 words. Pays $45-150 for assigned articles. Pays $45-120 for unsolicited articles. Sometimes pays expenses of writers on assignment.

Photos: State availability of photos with submission. Reviews color transparencies and 8x10 b&w prints. Offers $25-50 per photo. Model releases required. Buys one-time rights.

Fiction: Religious. "We consider good fiction written from a Christian perspective. Avoid pious sentimentality and obvious plots." Buys 15 mss/year. Send complete ms. Length: 400-1,500. Pays $45-120.

Poetry: Free verse and traditional. Buys 20 poems/year. Submit maximum of 10 poems at one time. Length: up to 30 lines. Pays $25-45.

Tips: "Research articles carefully. Superficial articles are immediately recognizable; they cannot be disguised by big words or professional jargon. Writers need not have personally experienced everything they write about, but they must have done careful research. Also, what our readers want are new solutions to recognized problems. If a writer doesn't have any, he or she should try another subject." Sections most open to freelancers are feature articles and poetry.

COLUMBIA, Drawer 1670, New Haven CT 06507. Editor: Elmer Von Feldt. Monthly magazine for Catholic families; caters particularly to members of the Knights of Columbus. Circ. 1,405,411. Pays on acceptance. Buys all rights. Submit seasonal material 6 months in advance. Reports in 1 month. Free sample copy and writer's guidelines.

Nonfiction: Fact articles directed to the Catholic layman and his family dealing with current events, social problems, Catholic apostolic activities, education, ecumenism, rearing a family, literature, science, humor, satire, arts, sports and leisure. Color glossy prints, transparencies or contact prints with negatives are required for illustration. Articles without ample illustrative material are not given consideration. Pays $600 minimum, including photos. Photo stories are also wanted. Buys 30 mss/year. Query or submit complete ms. Length: 2,500-3,500 words. Humor or satire should be directed to current religious, social or cultural conditions. Length: 1,000 words. Pays $200.

Photos: Pays $50 per photo used. Pays 10¢/word.

COMMENTS, From the Friends, Box 840, Stoughton MA 02072. Editor: David A. Reed. 20% freelance written. A quarterly Christian newsletter written especially for "Jehovah's Witnesses, ex-Jehovah's Witnesses and persons concerned about Jehovah's Witnesses, relatives, friends, and neighbors.'' Circ. 2,000. Pays on publication. Publishes ms an average of 3 months after acceptance. Byline sometimes given. Buys second serial (reprint) and simultaneous rights. Submit seasonal/holiday material 4 months in advance. Simultaneous, photocopied and previously published submissions OK. Electronic submissions OK via Macintosh MacWrite. Computer printout submissions acceptable; prefers letter-quality to dot-matrix. Reports in 1 month on mss. Sample copy $1; writer's guidelines for #10 SAE with 2 first class stamps.

Nonfiction: Book excerpts, essays, exposé, how-to (witnessing tips), humor, inspirational, interview/profile, personal experience, religious and book reviews of books on cults only. Special issue topic will be The Next Watchtower President (replacing Fred Franz). ''No general religious material not written specifically for our unique readership.'' Buys 8 mss/year. Send complete ms. Length: 200-1,000 words. Pays $2-20. May pay with contributor copies rather than a cash payment ''when a writer contributes an article as a gift to this ministry.''

Columns/Departments: Witnessing Tips (brief, powerful and effective approaches), 250-300 words; and News Briefs (current events involving Jehovah's Witnesses and ex-Jehovah's Witnesses), 60-240 words. Buys 4 mss/year. Send complete ms. Length: 60-300 words. Pays $2-10.

Fillers: Facts, newsbreaks and quotes. Buys 4/year. Length: 10-50 words. Pays $1-5.

Tips: ''Acquaint us with your background that qualifies you to write in this field. Write well-documented, germane articles in layman's language.''

THE COMPANION OF ST. FRANCIS AND ST. ANTHONY, Conventual Franciscan Friars, Box 535, Postal Station F, Toronto, Ontario M4Y 2L8 Canada. (416)924-6349. Editor-in-Chief: Friar Philip Kelly, OFM Conv. 60% freelance written. Monthly magazine. Emphasizing religious and human values and stressing Franciscan virtues—peace, simplicity, joy. Circ. 10,000. Pays on acceptance. Publishes ms an average of 6 months after acceptance. Buys first North American serial rights. Phone queries OK. Submit seasonal/holiday material 6 months in advance. Computer printout submissions acceptable; prefers letter-quality to dot-matrix. Reports in 3 weeks. Writer's guidelines for SAE, IRCs.

Nonfiction: Historical; how-to (medical and psychological coping); informational; inspirational; interview; nostalgia; profile; and family. No old time religion, antiCatholic or pro-abortion material. No poetry. Buys 6 mss/issue. Send complete ms. Length: 800-1,000 words. Pays 6¢/word, Canadian funds.

Photos: Photos purchased with accompanying ms. Pays $8 for 5x7 (but all sizes accepted) b&w glossy prints. Send prints. Total purchase price for ms includes payment for photos. Captions required.

Fiction: Adventure, humorous, mainstream and religious. Canadian settings preferred. Buys 6 mss/year. Send complete ms. Length: 800-1,000 words. Pays 6¢/word, Canadian funds.

Tips: ''Manuscripts on human interest with photos are given immediate preference. In the year ahead we will be featuring shorter articles, more Canadian and Franciscan themes, and better photos. Use a good typewriter, good grammar and good sense.''

CONFIDENT LIVING, Box 82808, Lincoln NE 68501. (402)474-4567. Editor: Warren Wiersbe. 40% freelance written. Monthly interdenominational magazine for adults from 17 years of age and up. Circ. 125,000. Pays on acceptance. Buys first serial rights or first North American serial rights, or occasionally second serial (reprint) rights. Submit seasonal material at least 1 year in advance. Computer printout submissions acceptable if double spaced; no dot-matrix. Reports in 5 weeks. Sample copy $1.50; writer's guidelines with SASE.

Nonfiction: Managing Editor, Norman A. Olson. Articles which will help the reader learn and apply Christian Biblical principles to his life from the writer's or the subject's own experience. Writers are required ''to affirm agreement with our doctrinal statement. We are especially looking for true, personal experience 'salvation,' church, children's ages 4-10, missions, 'youth' (17 years and over), 'parents', 'how to live the Christian life' articles, reports and interviews regarding major and interesting happenings and people in fundamental, evangelical Christian circles.'' Nothing rambling or sugary sweet, or without Biblical basis. Details or statistics should be authentic and verifiable. Style should be conservative but concise. Prefers that Scripture references be from the *New American Standard Bible* or the *Authorized Version* or the *New Scofield Reference Bible*. Buys approximately 100 mss/year. Length: 1,500 words maximum. Pays 4-10¢/word. ''When you can get us to assign an article to you, we pay nearer the maximum. More manuscripts are now rejected if unaccompanied by photos.'' Sometimes pays expenses of writers on assignment.

Photos: Pays $25 maximum for b&w glossies; $75 maximum for color transparencies. Photos paid on publication.

Tips: ''The basic purpose of the magazine is to explain the Bible and how it is relevant to life because we believe this will accomplish one of two things—to present Christ as Savior to the lost or to promote the spiritual growth of believers, so don't ignore our primary purposes when writing for us. Nonfiction should be Biblical and timely; at the least Biblical in principle. Use illustrations of your own experiences or of someone else's when God solved a problem similar to the reader's. Be so specific that the meanings and significance will be crystal clear to all readers.''

CONSCIENCE, A Newsjournal of Prochoice Catholic Opinion, Catholics for a Free Choice, 2008 17th St. NW, Washington DC 20009. (202)638-1706. Editor: Mary S. Sullivan. 80% freelance written. Eager to work with new/unpublished writers. Bimonthly newsjournal covering reproductive rights, specifically abortion rights. "A feminist, pro-choice perspective is a must, and knowledge of Christianity and specifically Catholicism is helpful." Circ. 10,000. Pays on publication. Publishes ms an average of 4 months after acceptance. Byline given. Buys first North American serial rights; makes work-for-hire assignments. Submit seasonal/holiday material 4 months in advance. Simultaneous queries, and simultaneous, photocopied, and previously published submissions OK. Electronic submissions OK via IBM-XT, Multimate. Computer printout submissions acceptable. Reports in 2 months; free sample copy for #10 SASE with 1 first class stamp; free writer's guidelines for #10 SAE with 1 first class stamp.

Nonfiction: Book excerpts, interview/profile, opinion and personal experience. Especially needs "expose/refutation of antichoice misinformation and specific research into the implications of new reproductive technology and fetal personhood bills/court decisions." Buys 8-12 mss/year. Query with published clips or send complete ms. Length: 1,000-3,500 words. Pays $100-150. "Writers should be aware that we are a nonprofit organization." A substantial number of articles are contributed without payment by writers. Sometimes pays the expenses of writers on assignment.

Photos: State availability of photos with query or ms. Prefers 5x7 b&w prints. Identification of subjects required. Buys all rights.

Columns/Departments: Book reviews. Buys 6-10 mss/year. Send complete ms. Length: 1,000-2,000 words. Pays $50 maximum.

Fillers: Clippings and newsbreaks. Uses 6/year. Length: 25-100 words. No payment.

Tips: "Say something new on the abortion issue. Thoughtful, well-researched and well-argued articles needed. The most frequent mistakes made by writers in completing an article for us are untimeliness and wordiness. When you have shown you can write thoughtfully, we may hire you for other types of articles."

CORNERSTONE, Jesus People USA, 4707 N. Malden, Chicago IL 60640. Editor: Dawn Herrin. 10% freelance written. Works with a small number of new/unpublished writers each year; eager to work with new/unpublished writers. A bimonthly magazine covering contemporary issues in the light of Evangelical Christianity. Circ. 90,000. Pays after publication. Publishes ms an average of 4-6 months after acceptance. Byline given. Buys first serial rights. Submit seasonal/holiday material 6 months in advance. Simultaneous, photocopied and previously published submissions OK. Computer printout submissions acceptable. Reports in 1 month. Sample copy and writer's guidelines for 10x13 SAE with 73¢ postage.

Nonfiction: Essays, personal experience, religious. Buys 3-4 mss/year. Query. Length: 2,700 words maximum. Pays negotiable rate. Sometimes pays the expenses of writers on assignment.

Photos: Send photos with accompanying ms. Reviews 8x10 b&w and color prints and 35mm slides. Identification of subjects required. Buys negotiable rights.

Columns/Departments: Music (interview with artists, mainly rock, focusing on artist's world view and value system as expressed in his/her music); Current Events; Personalities; Film and Book Reviews (focuses on meaning as compared and contrasted to Biblical values). Buys 2-6 mss/year. Query. Length: 100-2,500 words (negotiable). Pays negotiable rate.

Fiction: "Articles may express Christian world view but should not be unrealistic or 'syrupy.' Other than porn, the sky's the limit. We want fiction as creative as the Creator." Buys 1-4 mss/year. Send complete ms. Length: 250-2,500 words (negotiable). Pays negotiable rate.

Poetry: Avant-garde, free verse, haiku, light verse and traditional. No limits *except* for epic poetry ("We've not the room!"). Buys 10-50 poems/year. Submit maximum 10 poems. Payment negotiated.

Fillers: Anecdotes, facts, short humor and newsbreaks. Buys 5-15 year. Length: 20-200 words (negotiable). Payment negotiable.

Tips: "A display of creativity which expresses a biblical world view without cliches or cheap shots at non-Christians is the ideal. We are known as the most avant-garde magazine in the Christian market, yet attempt to express orthodox beliefs in language of the '80s. *Any* writer who does this may well be published by *Cornerstone*. Creative fiction is begging for more Christian participation. We anticipate such contributions gladly. Interviews where well-known personalities respond to the gospel are also strong publication possibilities. Please address all submissions to: Sarah Darden, assistant editor."

THE COVENANT COMPANION, Convenant Press of the Evangelical Covenant Church, 5101 N. Francisco Ave., Chicago IL 60625. (312)784-3000. Editor: James R. Hawkinson. 10-15% freelance written. "As the official monthly organ of The Evangelical Convenant Church, we seek to inform, stimulate, and gather the denomination we serve by putting Convenants in touch with each other and assisting them in interpreting contemporary issues. We also seek to inform them on events in the church. Our background is evangelical and our emphasis is on Christian commitment and life." Circ. 26,500. Publishes ms an average of 2 months after acceptance. Byline given. Buys first or all rights. Submit seasonal/holiday material 4 months in advance. Simultaneous and previously published submissions OK. Query for electronic submissions. Computer printout submissions acceptable; prefers letter-quality. Sample copy $1.50; writer's guidelines for #10 SAE and 1 first class stamp.

Nonfiction: Humor, inspirational and religious. Buys 10-15 mss/year. Send complete ms. Length: 500-2,000 words. Pays $15-50 for assigned articles; pays $15-35 for unsolicited articles.
Photos: Send photos with submissions. Reviews prints. Offers no additonal payment for photos accepted with ms. Identification of subjects required. Buys one-time rights.
Poetry: Traditional. Buys 10-15 poems/year. Submit maximum 10 poems. Pays $10-15.
Tips: "Seasonal articles related to church year and on national holidays are welcome."

DAILY MEDITATION, Box 2710, San Antonio TX 78299. Editor: Ruth S. Paterson. Quarterly. Byline given. Rights purchased vary. Payment on acceptance. Submit seasonal material 6 months in advance. Sample copy 50¢.
Nonfiction: "Inspirational, self-improvement and nonsectarian religious articles, 750-1,600 words, showing the path to greater spiritual growth."
Fillers: Length: 400 words maximum. Pays 1-1½¢/word for prose.
Poetry: Inspirational. Length: 16 lines maximum. Pays 14¢/line.
Tips: "All our material is freelance submission for consideration except our meditations which are staff written. We buy approximately 250 manuscripts a year. We must see finished manuscripts; no queries, please. Checking copy is sent upon publication."

‡DAILY WORD, Unity School of Christianity, Unity Village MO 64065. (816)524-3550. Editor: Colleen Zuck. A monthly magazine of articles, poems, lessons and meditation. Circ. 2.5 million. Pays on acceptance. Publishes ms an average of 6 months after acceptance. Byline given on articles and poetry only. Buys first rights. Submit seasonal/holiday material 8 months in advance. Computer printout submissions OK; prefers letter-quality. Reports in 6 weeks on mss. Free sample copy and writer's guidelines.
Nonfiction: Inspirational and religious. Buys 250 mss/year. Send complete ms. Length: 1,500 words. Pays $20/page.
Poetry: Free verse and traditional. Buys 12-15 poems/year. Pays $1 per line.

DAUGHTERS OF SARAH, 2716 W. Cortland, Chicago IL 60647. (312)252-3344. Editor: Reta Finger. Production Coordinator: Annette Huizenga. 20-30% freelance written. Works with a small number of new/unpublished writers each year. Bimonthly magazine covering Christian feminism. Circ. 5,000. Pays upon acceptance. Publishes ms an average of 9-12 months after acceptance. Byline given. Offers 33-50% kill fee. Buys first serial rights and first North American serial rights. Submit seasonal/holiday material 6 months in advance. Query for electronic submissions. Computer printout submissions acceptable; prefers letter-quality to dot-matrix. Reports in 2 weeks on queries; 2 months on mss. Sample copy $2.50 and 6½x9½ SAE with 3 first class stamps; writer's guidelines for SAE with 1 first class stamp.
Nonfiction: Exegetical-theological articles; book excerpts (book reviews on Christian feminist books); historical (on Christian women); humor (feminist); inspirational (biblical articles about women or feminist issues); personal experience (women's—or men's—experiences from Christian feminist point of view); and issues of social justice relating to women. Special issues include women and the health care system, inclusive language, patriarchy in the Hebrew scriptures, feminist theology, and women and healing. "No general, elementary aspects of Christian feminism; we've gone beyond that. We particularly do not want pieces about women or women's issues that are not written from a feminist and Christian point of view." Buys 10-15 mss/year. Query with or without published clips. Length: 500-2,000 words. (Book reviews on Christian feminist books, 100-500 words). Pays $15-60. Sometimes pays expenses of writers on assignment.
Fiction: Christian feminist. Buys 2-4 mss/year. Query with published clips. Length: 500-2,000 words. Pays $15-60.
Tips: "The writer has a better chance of breaking in at our publication with short articles and fillers. Usually we solicit our feature articles on a particular topic that most freelance writers may not be familiar with. The most frequent mistakes made by writers in completing an article for us are writing too-long articles (we have a small magazine); writing on an unrelated topic; or writing about women but not particularly from a feminist point of view."

‡DECISION, Billy Graham Evangelistic Association, 1300 Harmon Place, Minneapolis MN 55403. (612)338-0500. Editor: Roger C. Palms. Managing Editor: George M. Wilson. 40% freelance written. Works with small number of new/unpublished writers each year. A magazine, published 11 times per year, "to set forth to every reader the Good News of salvation in Jesus Christ with such vividness and clarity that he or she will be drawn to make a commitment to Christ; to encourage, teach and strengthen Christians." Circ. 2 million. Pays on publication. Publishes ms an average of 2 years after acceptance. Byline given. Buys first rights and makes work-for-hire assignments. Include telephone number with submissions. Submit seasonal/holiday material 8 months in advance. Photocopied submissions OK. Computer printout submissions OK; no dot-matrix. Reports in 2 weeks on queries; 2 months on mss. Free sample copy and writer's guidelines.
Nonfiction: How-to, inspirational, personal experience and religious. "No personality-centered articles or articles which are issue oriented or critical of denominations." Buys approximately 100 mss/year. Send com-

plete ms. Length: 100-2,000 words. Pays $10-175. Pays expenses of writers on assignment.
Photos: State availability of photos with submission. Reviews prints. Captions, model releases and identification of subjects required. Buys one-time rights.
Poetry: Free verse and traditional. No long or secular poems. Buys 35 poems/year. Submit maximum 6 poems. Length: 4-20 lines. Pays approximately 30¢ per word.
Fillers: Breck Speers, editor. Anecdotes. Buys 35/year. Length: 100-300 words. Pays $5-25.
Tips: "We are seeking personal conversion testimonies, personal experience articles which show how God intervened in a crisis experience and the way in which Scripture was applied to the experience in helping to solve the problem."

THE DISCIPLE, Box 179, St. Louis MO 63166. Editor: James L. Merrell. 10% freelance written. Monthly published by Christian Board of Publication of the Christian Church (Disciples of Christ). For ministers and church members, both young and older adults. Circ. 58,000. Pays month after publication. Publishes ms an average of 9 months after acceptance. Buys first serial rights. Photocopied and simultaneous submissions OK. Computer printout submissions acceptable; no dot-matrix. Submit seasonal material at least 6 months in advance. Reports in 1 month. Sample copy $1.50; free writer's guidelines for SAE and 1 first class stamp.
Nonfiction: Articles and meditations on religious themes, short pieces, and some humorous. No fiction. Buys 100 unsolicited mss/year. Length: 500-800 words. Pays $10-50.
Photos: Reviews 8x10 b&w glossy prints. Occasional b&w glossy prints, any size, used to illustrate articles. Occasional color. "We are looking for b&w photos of church activities—worship, prayer, dinners, etc." Pays $10-25; $35-100/cover. Pays for photos at end of month after acceptance.
Poetry: Uses 3-5 poems/issue. Traditional forms, blank verse, free verse and light verse. Length: 16 lines maximum. Themes may be seasonal, historical, religious and occasionally humorous. Pays $3-20.
Tips: "We're looking for personality features about lay disciples, churches. Give a good summary of story idea in query. Queries on Christian values in television, radio, film and music desired. We use articles primarily from disciples, ministers and lay persons since our magazine is written to attract the denomination. We are barraged with features that mainly deal with subjects that don't interest our readers; fillers are more general, thus more easily placed. We work with more secular poets than writers and the poets write in religious themes for us."

DISCIPLESHIP JOURNAL, NavPress, a division of The Navigators, Box 6000, Colorado Springs CO 80934. (303)598-1212. Editor: Susan Maycinik. Editorial Director: Don Simpson. 90% freelance written. Works with a small number of new/unpublished writers each year. Bimonthly magazine on Christian discipleship. "The mission of *Discipleship Journal* is to help people examine, understand, and practice the truths of the Bible, so that they may know Jesus Christ, become like Him, and labor for His Kingdom by gathering other men and women into the fellowship of His committed disciples." Circ. 80,000. Pays on acceptance. Publishes ms an average of 4 months after acceptance. Byline given. Buys first North American serial rights and second serial (reprint) rights. Submit seasonal/holiday material 6 months in advance. Simultaneous queries, and simultaneous and previously published submissions OK. Electronic submissions OK via IBM PC-compatible, but requires hard copy also. Computer printout submissions acceptable; prefers letter-quality to dot-matrix. Reports in 4 weeks on queries; 2 months on mss. Sample copy and writer's guidelines for 9x12 SAE and $1.24 postage.
Nonfiction: Book excerpts (rarely); how-to (grow in Christian faith and disciplines; help others grow as Christians; serve people in need; understand and apply the Bible); inspirational; interview/profile (of Christian leaders, focusing on discipleship); personal experience; and interpretation/application of the Bible. No personal testimony; humor; anything not directly related to Christian life and faith; politically partisan articles. Buys 85 mss/year. Query with published clips or send complete ms. Length: 500-3,000 words. Pays 2¢/word reprint; 10-12¢/word first rights. Pays the expenses of writers on assignment.
Tips: "Our articles are meaty, not fluffy. Study writers guidelines and back issues and try to use similar approaches. Don't preach. Polish before submitting. About half of the articles in each issue are related to one theme. Freelancers should write to request theme list. We are looking for more practical articles on ministering to others and more articles dealing with world missions."

ENGAGE/SOCIAL ACTION, 100 Maryland Ave. NE, Washington DC 20002. (202)488-5632. Editor: Lee Ranck. 2% freelance written. Works with a small number of new/unpublished writers each year. Monthly for "United Methodist clergy and lay people interested in in-depth analysis of social issues, with emphasis on the church's role or involvement in these issues." Circ. 4,500. May buy all rights. Pays on publication. Publishes ms an average of 2 months after acceptance. Rights purchased vary with author and material. Photocopied submissions OK, but prefers original. Computer printout submissions acceptable; prefers letter-quality to dot-matrix. Returns rejected material in 4-5 weeks. Reports on material accepted for publication in several weeks. Free sample copy and writer's guidelines.
Nonfiction: "This is the social action publication of the United Methodist Church published by the denomination's General Board of Church and Society. Our publication tries to relate social issues to the church—what the church can do, is doing; why the church should be involved. We only accept articles relating to social is-

sues, e.g., war, draft, peace, race relations, welfare, police/community relations, labor, population problems, drug and alcohol problems." No devotional, 'religious,' superficial material, highly technical articles, personal experiences or poetry. Buys 25-30 mss/year. "Query to show that writer has expertise on a particular social issue, give credentials, and reflect a readable writing style." Query or submit complete ms. Length: 2,000 words maximum. Pays $75-100. Sometimes pays the expenses of writers on assignment.

Tips: "Write on social issues, but not superficially; we're more interested in finding an expert who can write (e.g., on human rights, alcohol problems, peace issues) than a writer who attempts to research a complex issue."

EPIPHANY JOURNAL, Epiphany Press, Box 14727, San Francisco CA 94114. Editor: Philip Tolbert. 10% freelance written. Works with a small number of new/unpublished writers each year. Quarterly magazine covering religious topics for the contemplative Christian. Circ. 3,000. Pays on publication. Publishes ms an average of 6 months after acceptance. Byline given. Buys first serial rights and one-time rights. Submit seasonal/holiday material 6 months in advance. Simultaneous queries, and simultaneous and previously published submissions OK. Computer printout submissions OK; prefers letter-quality to dot-matrix. Reports in 1 month on queries; 2 months on mss. "Sample copy and writer's guidelines available for $5, which will be refunded with payment for your first article." Guidelines only for SAE and 1 first class stamp.

Nonfiction: Essays (applications of traditional patristic spirituality for the practicing Christian in the postmodern world and explorations of the embodiment of traditional Christian culture expressed through literature, craft, art and folklore); interviews with current Christian figures ("Interviews should be topical or issues oriented, not biographical."); and stories from the lives of the Saints and teachers of the Christian tradition. Buys 4-8 mss/year. Query or send complete ms. Length: 2,000-6,000 words. Pays 2¢/word ($100 maximum). Also book excerpts (from forthcoming or recently published spiritual or religious works). No poetry.

Columns/Departments: Book reviews (any current literature of interest to the Christian thinker). Buys 10-15 mss/year. Query or send complete ms. Length: 1,000-2,500 words. Pays 2¢/word ($30 maximum).

Tips: "Get to know our magazine, then send us a query letter or ask for an assignment suggestion. We prefer not to see first person/anecdotal accounts. The writer must have a clear grasp of Christian principles and not merely base their views on sentiment; they must be able to contrast these principles with the modern world view in a way that provides a radical critique of contemporary culture while maintaining a pastoral concern for souls. This perspective must be developed in a writer. The most frequent mistakes made by writers in completing an article for us are unclear thought due to poor grasp of principles, lack of penetration into the subject, lack of relevance to daily spiritual life and contemporary problems, and lack of grounding in the living tradition of orthodox Christianity."

‡EPISCOPAL CHURCH FACTS, From Western New York, Episcopal Diocese of W.N.Y., 1114 Delaware Ave., Buffalo NY 14209. (716)875-8374. Editor: Rev. Donald B. Hill. 35% freelance written. Monthly newspaper covering news and features of interest to Episcopalians. Circ. 11,500. Pays on publication. Publishes an average of 2 months after acceptance. Byline given. Not copyrighted. Buys first rights. Submit seasonal/holiday material 3 months in advance. Simultaneous and photocopied submissions OK. Computer printout submissions OK. Free sample copy.

Nonfiction: General interest, humor, inspirational, and religious. No highly pious generic Christian material. Buys 20 mss/year. Query with or without published clips or send complete ms. Length: 100-3,000 words. Pays $25-50. Sometimes pays expenses of writers on assignment.

Photos: State availability of photos with submission. Reviews 5x7 prints. Offers $10-25 per photo. Captions and identification of subjects required. Buys one-time rights.

Fillers: Anecdotes and short humor. Buys 12/year.

THE EPISCOPALIAN, 1201 Chestnut St., Philadelphia PA 19107. (215)564-2010. Publisher: Richard Crawford. Managing Editor: Judy Mathe Foley. 60% freelance written. Accepts submissions from a small number of new/unpublished writers each year. Monthly tabloid about the Episcopal Church for Episcopalians. Circ. 250,000. Pays on publication. Publishes ms an average of 2 months after acceptance. Byline given. Submit seasonal/holiday material 2 months in advance. Previously published submissions OK. Computer printout submissions acceptable; prefers letter-quality to dot-matrix. Reports in 1 month. Sample copy for 3 first class stamps.

Nonfiction: Inspirational and interview/profile (of Episcopalians participating in church or community activities). "I like action stories about people doing things and solving problems. I like quotes, photos and active voice." No personal experience articles. Buys 24 mss/year. Send complete ms. Length: 1,000-1,500 words. Pays $25-200. Rarely pays expenses of writers on assignment.

Photos: Pays $10 for b&w glossy prints. Identification of subjects required. Buys one-time rights.

Tips: "Stories must have an Episcopal Church connection."

ETERNITY MAGAZINE, The Evangelical Monthly, Evangelical Ministries, Inc., 1716 Spruce St., Philadelphia PA 19103. (215)546-3696. Executive Editor: Donald J. McCrory. Managing Editor: Denise H. Viscuso. A monthly magazine intended "to help readers apply God's Word to all areas of life today." Circ. 40,000. Pays on the 15th of the month previous to issue publication. Byline given. Offers $25-50 kill fee. Buys first North American serial rights. Submit seasonal/holiday material 6 months in advance. Computer printout submissions acceptable; prefers letter-quality to dot-matrix. Reports in 6 weeks. Sample copy $2; writer's guidelines for SAE and 1 first class stamp.

Nonfiction: General interest (the Christian in the culture); how-to (apply Scripture to problems); and interview/profile (well-known evangelicals). No fiction; no short, devotional fillers. Buys 20 mss/year. Query. Length: 500-1,500 words. Pays $35-150.

EVANGEL, Dept. of Christian Education, Free Methodist Headquarters, 901 College Ave., Winona Lake IN 46590. (219)267-7161. Editor: Vera Bethel. 100% freelance written. Weekly magazine; 8 pages. Audience is 65% female, 35% male; married, 25-31 years old, mostly city dwellers, high school graduates, mostly nonprofessional. Circ. 35,000. Pays on publication. Publishes ms an average of 1 year after acceptance. Buys simultaneous rights, second serial (reprint) rights or one-time rights. Submit seasonal/holiday material 3 months in advance. Computer printout submissions acceptable; no dot-matrix. Reports in 4 weeks. Sample copy and writer's guidelines for 6x9 SAE.

Nonfiction: Interview (with ordinary person who is doing something extraordinary in his community, in service to others); profile (of missionary or one from similar service profession who is contributing significantly to society); and personal experience (finding a solution to a problem common to young adults; coping with handicapped child, for instance, or with a neighborhood problem. Story of how God-given strength or insight saved a situation). Buys 100 mss/year. Submit complete ms. Length: 300-1,000 words. Pays $10-25.

Photos: Purchased with accompanying ms. Captions required. Send prints. Pays $5-10 for 8x10 b&w glossy prints; $2 for snapshots.

Fiction: Religious themes dealing with contemporary issues dealt with from a Christian frame of reference. Story must "go somewhere." Buys 50 mss/year. Submit complete ms. Length: 1,200-1,500 words. Pays $35-40.

Poetry: Free verse, haiku, light verse, traditional and religious. Buys 50 poems/year. Submit maximum 6 poems. Length: 4-24 lines. Pays $5.

Tips: "Seasonal material will get a second look (won't be rejected so easily) because we get so little. Write an attention grabbing lead followed by a body of article that says something worthwhile. Relate the lead to some of the universal needs of the reader—promise in that lead to help the reader in some way. Remember that everybody is interested most in himself. Lack of SASE brands author as a nonprofessional; I seldom even bother to read the script. If the writer doesn't want the script back, it probably has no value for me, either."

THE EVANGELICAL BEACON, 1515 E. 66th St., Minneapolis MN 55423. (612)866-3343. Editor: George Keck. 30% freelance written. Works with a small number of new/unpublished writers each year. Denominational magazine of the Evangelical Free Church of America—evangelical Protestant readership; published 17 titles/year (every third Monday, except for a 4 week interval, June-August). Pays on publication. Publishes ms an average of 6 months after acceptance. Rights purchased vary with author and material. Buys first rights or all rights, and some reprints. Computer printout submissions acceptable; prefers letter-quality to dot-matrix. Reports in 8-10 weeks. Sample copy and writer's guidelines for 75¢.

Nonfiction: Articles on the church, Christ-centered human interest and personal testimony articles, well researched on current issues of religious interest. Desires crisp, imaginative, original writing—not sermons on paper. Length: 250-2,000 words. Pays 3¢/word with extra payment on some articles, at discretion of editor.

Photos: Prefers 8x10 b&w photos. Pays $10 minimum.

Fiction: Not much fiction used, but will consider. Length: 100-1,500 words.

Poetry: Very little poetry used. Pays variable rate, $3.50 minimum.

Tips: "Articles need to be helpful to the average Christian—encouraging, challenging, instructive. Also needs material presenting reality of the Christian faith to nonChristians. Some tie-in with the Evangelical Free Church of America is helpful but not required."

EVANGELIZING TODAY'S CHILD, Child Evangelism Fellowship Inc., Warrenton MO 63383. (314)456-4321. Editor: Elsie Lippy. 75% freelance written. Prefers to work with published/established writers. Bimonthly magazine; 72 pages. "Our purpose is to equip Christians to win the world's children to Christ and disciple them. Our readership is Sunday school teachers, Christian education leaders and children's workers in every phase of Christian ministry to children up to 12 years old." Circ. 28,000. Pays within 90 days of acceptance. Publishes ms an average of 6 months after acceptance. Byline given. Offers 30% kill fee if assigned. Buys first serial rights. Submit seasonal/holiday material 6 months in advance. Simultaneous queries and photocopied submissions OK. Computer printout submissions acceptable; no dot-matrix. Reports in 3 weeks on queries; 2 months on mss. Free sample copy; writer's guidelines with SASE.

Nonfiction: Unsolicited articles welcomed from writers with Christian education training or current experience in working with children. Buys 35 mss/year. Query. Length: 1,800-2,000. Pays 6-8¢/word.

Photos: Submissions of photos on speculation accepted. Needs photos of children or related subjects. Pays $20-25 for 8x10 b&w glossy prints; $75-100 for color transparencies.

‡FOCUS ON THE FAMILY, with Dr. James Dobson, Focus on the Family, Inc., 50 E. Foothill Blvd., Arcadia CA 91066. (818)445-1579. Editor: Mike Yorkey. Managing Editor: Mary Alice Parks. 30% freelance written. Works with a small number of new/unpublished writers each year. A monthly non-denominational Christian magazine. Circ. 1,000,000. Pays on publication. Byline given. Offers 33⅓% kill fee. Buys first North American serial rights or second serial (reprint) rights. Submit seasonal/holiday material 5 months in advance. Simultaneous, photocopied and previously published submissions OK. Computer printout submissions OK. Reports in 3 weeks. Sample copy and writer's guidelines for 9x12 SAE with 39¢ postage.
Nonfiction: Book excerpts, how-to (related to family issues), humor, inspirational, personal experience and religious (not overtly). "We are primarily seeking true stories dealing with key family issues and how-to pieces offering sound advice, personal experience, humor and emotion. First person accounts are OK." Buys 12 mss/year. Send complete ms. Length: 500-1,500 words. Pays 5¢/word for reprints; 10¢/word for first submission.
Photos: State availability of photos with submission. Reviews 4x5 transparencies and 8x10 or 4x5 prints. Offers negotiable payment for photos. Model releases required. Buys one-time rights.

FUNDAMENTALIST JOURNAL, Old-Time Gospel Hour, 2220 Langhorne Rd., Lynchburg VA 24514. (804)528-4112. Publisher: Jerry Falwell. Editor: Deborah Wade Huff. 40% freelance written. Works with a small number of new/unpublished writers. A Christian magazine (nonprofit organization) published monthly (July/August combined) covering "matters of interest to all Fundamentalists, providing inspirational articles, features on current issues, human interest stories, profiles, reviews and news reports. Audience is 65% Baptist; 35% other denominations; 30% pastors, 70% other." Circ. 70,000. Pays on publication. Publishes ms an average of 4-12 months after acceptance. Byline given. Offers negotiable kill fee. Buys all rights, first North American serial rights, makes work-for-hire assignments. Submit seasonal/holiday material 6 months in advance. Previously published submissions OK. Computer printout submissions acceptable; prefers letter-quality to dot-matrix. Reports in 3 months. Sample copy for 9x12 SAE with 69¢ postage; writer's guidelines for SAE and 1 first class stamp.
Nonfiction: Earline R. Goodwin, articles editor. Book excerpts; expose (government, communism, education); general interest; historical/nostalgic (regarding the Bible, Christianity, great Christians of old); inspirational, interview/profile; opinion, and personal experience. "Writing must be consistent with Fundamentalist doctrine. We do not want articles that are critical in naming leaders of churches or Christian organizations." Buys 77 mss/year. Query. Length: 500-2,500 words. Pays 10¢/printed word for major articles; 20¢/printed word for shorter articles in special sections. Sometimes pays the expenses of writers on assignment.
Columns/Departments: Length: 300-2,000 words. Pays 10¢/printed word; $10-25 for book reviews.
Tips: "We are looking for more articles to encourage and support the Christian family. We will be asking writers to submit query first. News is usually by assignment; various articles of general interest to Fundamentalist Christian readers, perspective, profiles, missions articles, family living articles and brief articles dealing with pastoring are most open to freelancers."

THE GEM, Churches of God, General Conference, Box 926, Findlay OH 45839. (419)424-1961. Editor: Marilyn Rayle Kern. 98% freelance written. Works with a small number of new/unpublished writers each year. "We are backlogged with submissions but still hope to find new submissions of high quality." Weekly magazine; adult and youth church school take-home paper. "Our readers expect to find true-to-life help for daily living as growing Christians." Circ. 7,500. Pays on publication. Publishes ms an average of 9 months after acceptance. Byline given. Not copyrighted. Buys simultaneous rights, first serial rights or second serial (reprint) rights. Submit seasonal/holiday material 3 months in advance. Simultaneous, photocopied and previously published submissions OK. Query for electronic submission. Computer printout submissions acceptable; prefers letter-quality to dot-matrix. Reports in 6 months. Sample copy and writer's guidelines for 4x9 SAE and 1 first class stamp (unless more than 1 copy).
Nonfiction: General interest, historical/nostalgic, humor, inspirational and personal experience. No preachy, judgmental articles, or use of quotes from other sources. Buys 50 mss/year. Send complete ms. Length: 600-1,600 words. Pays $10-15.
Fiction: Adventure, historical, humorous and religious. No mss which are preachy or inauthentic. Buys 50 mss/year. Send complete ms. Length: 1,000-1,600 words. Pays $10-15.
Fillers: Anecdotes and short humor. Buys 40/year. Length: 100-500 words. Pays $5-7.50.
Tips: "Humor, which does not put down people and leads the reader to understand a valuable lesson, is always in short supply."

GOOD NEWS, The Bimonthly Magazine For United Methodists, Box 150, Wilmore KY 40390. (606)858-4661. Editor: James V. Heidinger II. Executive Editor: James S. Robb. 20% freelance written. Prefers to work with published/established writers; works with a small number of new/unpublished writers each year. Bimonthly magazine for United Methodist lay people and pastors, primarily middle income; conservative and Biblical religious beliefs; broad range of political, social and cultural values. "We are the only evangelical magazine with the purpose of working within the United Methodist Church for Biblical reform and evangelical renewal." Circ. 20,000. Pays on acceptance. Publishes ms an average of 8 months after acceptance. Byline given. Buys first serial rights, simultaneous rights, and second serial (reprint) rights. Submit seasonal/holiday material 6 months in advance. Simultaneous submissions with noncompeting publications OK. Prefers original mss and not photocopies of reprinted material. Computer printout submissions acceptable. Reports in 3 months. Sample copy $2.25; free writer's guidelines.

Nonfiction: Historical (prominent people or churches from the Methodist/Evangelical United Brethren tradition); how-to (build faith, work in local church); humor (good taste); inspirational (related to Christian faith); personal experience (case histories of God at work in individual lives); and any contemporary issues as they relate to the Christian faith and/or the United Methodist Church. No sermons or secular material. Buys 25 mss/year. Must query first with a "brief description of the article, perhaps a skeleton outline. Show some enthusiasm about the article and writing (and research). Tell us something about yourself including whether you or the article has United Methodist tie-in. Send manuscripts % associate editor." Length: 1,500-1,800 words. Pays 5-7¢/word, more on occasion for special assignments. Sometimes pays the expenses of writers on assignment.

Photos: Extra payment for photos with accompanying ms. Uses fine screen b&w prints. Total purchase price for ms includes payment for photos. Payment negotiable. Captions required.

Tips: "Writers must be either United Methodists themselves or intimately familiar with the mindset of our church members. Evangelical slant is a must for all articles, yet we are not fundamentalist or sentimental. We are now moving away from predictable testimony pieces (though there is still room for the fresh testimony which ties in with burning issues, especially when written by Methodists). What we are looking for now are 1,200 word, newspaper style sketches of vibrant, evangelically-oriented United Methodist churches. Photos are a must. We'll hire a pro if we need to. We also need personality profiles of dynamic, unusual United Methodists with accompanying professional quality photo (evidence of vital faith in subject is required)."

‡**GROUP'S JUNIOR HIGH MINISTRY MAGAZINE**, Thom Schultz Publications, Inc., 2890 N. Monroe Ave., Box 481, Loveland CO 80539. (303)669-3836. Editorial Director: Joani Schultz. 90% freelance written (assigned). Magazine published 5 times/year for leaders of junior-high Christian youth groups. "How-to articles for junior high membership building, worship planning, handling specific group problems and improving as a leader; hints for parents of junior highers; special style-formatted junior high group meetings on topics like competition, faith in action, seasonal themes, friendship, dealing with life situations and service projects." Circ. 21,000. Pays on acceptance. Publishes ms an average of 2 months after acceptance. Byline given. Offers $25 kill fee. Buys all rights and makes work-for-hire assignments. Submit seasonal/holiday material 6 months in advance. Query for electronic submission. Computer printout submissions OK; no dot-matrix. Sample copy for 9x12 SAE with $1 postage; writers guidelines for SASE.

Nonfiction: How-to, humor, inspirational/motivational, personal experience, religious/Bible studies, and curriculum. No fiction. Buys 65 assigned mss/year. Query. Length: 500-1,700. Pays $75-100 for assigned articles. Sometimes pays expenses of writers on assignment.

Photos: Send photos with submission. Reviews contact sheets, transparencies and prints. Offers $20-50/b&w photo; $50-150/color photo. Model releases required. Buys one-time rights (occasionally buys additional rights).

Columns/Departments: Parent's Page (brief helps for parents of junior highers; for example, tips on discipline, faith communication, building close family, parent-self understanding, practical help, understanding junior highers and values). Buys 30 mss/year. Send complete ms. Length: 150 words. Pays $25.

Tips: "Writers who are also successful junior high workers or teachers have the best chance of being published in *Jr. High Ministry* simply because they know the kids. We need authors who can give our readers practical tips for ministry with junior highers. We need step-by-step experiential, Bible-oriented, fun meetings for leaders to do with junior high youth groups. The meetings must help the kids apply their Christian faith to life and must follow the standard format in the magazine."

GUIDEPOSTS MAGAZINE, 747 3rd Ave., New York NY 10017. Editor: Van Varner. 30% freelance written. "Works with a small number of new/unpublished writers each year, and reads all unsolicited manuscripts. *Guideposts* is an inspirational monthly magazine for people of all faiths in which men and women from all walks of life tell in first person narrative how they overcame obstacles, rose above failures, handled sorrow, learned to master themselves, and became more effective people through faith in God." Publishes ms an "indefinite" number of months after acceptance. Pays 25% kill fee for assigned articles. Byline given. "Most of our stories are ghosted articles, so the writer would not get a byline unless it was his/her own story." Buys all rights and second serial (reprint) rights. Computer printout submissions acceptable; prefers letter-quality to dot-matrix.

Nonfiction and Fillers: Articles and features should be written in simple, anecdotal style with an emphasis on human interest. Short mss of approximately 250-750 words (pays $25-100) would be considered for such features as Quiet People and general one-page stories. Full-length mss, 750-1,500 words, pays $200-300. All mss should be typed, double-spaced and accompanied by a stamped, self-addressed envelope. Annually awards scholarships to high school juniors and seniors in writing contest. Buys 40-60 unsolicited mss/year. Pays expenses of writers on assignment.

Tips: "Study the magazine before you try to write for it. Each story must make a single spiritual point. The freelancer would have the best chance of breaking in by aiming for a one-page or maybe two-page article. That would be very short, say two and a half pages of typescript, but in a small magazine such things are very welcome. Sensitively written anecdotes are extremely useful. And they are much easier to just sit down and write than to have to go through the process of preparing a query. They should be warm, well-written, intelligent and upbeat. We like personal narratives that are true and have some universal relevance, but the religious element does not have to be driven home with a sledge hammer. A writer succeeds with us if he or she can write a true article in short-story form with scenes, drama, tension and a resolution of the problem presented." Address short items to Rick Hamlin.

HICALL, Gospel Publishing House, 1445 Boonville Ave., Springfield MO 65802. (417)862-2781, ext. 4358. Editor: Rick Knoth. 100% freelance written. Eager to work with new/unpublished writers. Assemblies of God (denominational) weekly magazine of Christian fiction and articles for church-oriented teenagers, 12-17. Circ. 110,000. Pays on acceptance. Publishes ms an average of 6 months after acceptance. Byline given. Buys first North American serial rights, one-time rights, simultaneous rights, and second serial (reprint) rights. Submit seasonal/holiday material 1 year in advance. Simultaneous queries, and simultaneous, photocopied, and previously published submissions OK. Computer printout submissions acceptable; prefers letter-quality to dot-matrix. Reports in 6 weeks. Sample copy for 8x11 SAE and 2 first class stamps; writer's guidelines for SAE.
Nonfiction: Book excerpts; historical; general interest; how-to (deal with various life problems); humor; inspirational; and personal experience. Buys 80-100 mss/year. Send complete ms. Length: 500-2,000 words. Pays 2-3¢/word.
Photos: Photos purchased with or without accompanying ms. Pays $25/8x10 b&w glossy print; $30/35mm.
Fiction: Adventure, humorous, mystery, romance, suspense, western and religious. Buys 80-100 mss/year. Send complete ms. Length: 500-2,000 words. Pays 2-3¢/word.
Poetry: Free verse, light verse and traditional. Buys 30 poems/year. Length: 10-30 lines. Pays 3¢/word; 25¢/line.
Fillers: Clippings, anecdotes, short humor and newsbreaks. Buys 30/year. Pays 2-3¢/word.

‡THE HOME ALTAR, Meditations for Families with Children, The Board of Publication, LCA/Fortress Press, 2900 Queen Lane, Philadelphia PA 19129. (215)848-6800. Editor: M. Elaine Dunham. 100% freelance written. Works with a small number of new/unpublished writers each year. "A quarterly booklet of daily devotions, primarily for Lutheran families. Although the booklet is used by family members of various ages, writing should be geared for an audience of children under 9." Circ. 80,000. Pays on publication. Publishes ms an average of 6 months after acceptance. Byline given. Buys all rights. Computer printout submissions OK "only when printed on manuscript forms supplied." Reports in 1 month on queries. Sample copy for 6x9 SAE with 90¢ postage. Free writer's guidelines.
Nonfiction: Inspirational, personal experience and religious. "No preachy articles." Buys 200 mss/year. Query with published clips. Length: 130-160 words. Pays $7 for assigned articles.
Photos: Send photos with completed assignment. Reviews 5x7 b&w prints. Offers $5 per photo. Model releases required. Buys one-time rights.
Fiction: Religious and slice-of-life vignettes. Buys 165 mss/year. Query with published clips. Length: 130-160 words. Pays $5 per devotion.
Tips: "All writing for this publication is done on assignment. An assignment is given only to a writer who has submitted samples of his or her writing and demonstrated a style suitable for our readership. We're looking for storytellers who can write devotions which closely reflect the central messages of assigned Bible passages. Stories about children, in language accessible to children (9 years old or younger), are preferred. We also look for writers who use inclusive language when writing about human beings or about God."

‡THE JEWISH WEEKLY NEWS, Bennett-Scott Publications Corp., 99 Mill St., Box 1569, Springfield MA 01101. (413)739-4771. 25% freelance written. Eager to work with new/unpublished writers. Jewish news and features, secular and non-secular; World Judaism; arts (New England based). Circ. 2,500. Pays on publication. Publishes ms an average of 2 months after acceptance. Byline given. Not copyrighted. Buys first North American serial rights and second serial (reprint) rights. Submit seasonal/holiday material 2 months in advance. Simultaneous, photocopied and previously published submissions OK. Query for electronic submissions. Computer printout submissions OK. Sample copy for 9x12 SAE with 5 first class stamps.
Nonfiction: Interview/profile, religious and travel. Special issues include Jewish New Year (September); Chanukah (December); Home issues (March); Financial (February). Buys 61 mss/year. Query with published clips. Length: 300-1,000 words. Pays $5.
Photos: Send photos with submission. Reviews 5x7 prints. Offers no additional payment for photos accepted with ms. Identification of subjects required.
Columns/Departments: Jewish Kitchen (Kosher recipes), 300-500 words. Buys 10 mss/year. Query with published clips. Length: 300-5,000 words. Pays 50¢/inch.
Fiction: Sheila Thompson, editor. Slice-of-life vignettes. Buys 5 mss/year. Query with published clips. Length: 750-1,000 words. Pays 50¢/inch.

LIGHT AND LIFE, Free Methodist Church of North America, 901 College Ave., Winona Lake IN 46590. Editor: Bob Haslam. 35% freelance written. Works with a small number of new/unpublished writers each year. Monthly magazine; 36 pages. Emphasizes evangelical Christianity with Wesleyan slant for a cross section of adults. Circ. 43,000. Pays on publication. Publishes ms an average of 6 months after acceptance. Byline given. Prefers first serial rights; sometimes buys second serial (reprint) rights. Submit seasonal/holiday material 6 months in advance. Previously published submissions used occasionally. Computer printout submissions acceptable; no dot-matrix. Reports in 6 weeks. Sample copy $1.50; writer's guidelines for SASE.

Nonfiction: "Each issue includes a mini-theme (two or three articles addressing contemporary topics such as entertainment media, personal relationships, Christians as citizens), so freelancers should request our schedule of mini-theme topics. We also need fresh, upbeat articles showing the average layperson how to be Christ-like at home, work and play." Submit complete ms. Buys 70-80 unsolicited ms/year. Pays 4¢/word. Sometimes pays expenses of writers on assignment.

Photos: Purchased without accompanying ms. Send prints. Pays $5-35 for b&w photos. Offers additional payment for photos accepted with accompanying ms.

LIGUORIAN, Liguori MO 63057. Editor: Rev. Norman Muckerman. 50% freelance written. Prefers to work with published/established writers; works with a small number of new/unpublished writers each year. Monthly. For families with Catholic religious convictions. Circ. 525,000. Pays on acceptance. Publishes ms an average of 3-4 months after acceptance. Byline given "except on short fillers and jokes." Buys all rights but will reassign rights to author *after* publication upon written request. Submit seasonal material 6 months in advance. Query for electronic submissions. Computer printout submissions acceptable; no dot-matrix. Reports in 8 weeks.

Nonfiction: "Pastoral, practical and personal approach to the problems and challenges of people today. No travelogue approach or unresearched ventures into controversial areas. Also, no material found in secular publications—fad subjects that already get enough press, pop psychology, negative or put-down articles." Buys 60 unsolicited mss/year. Length: 400-2,000 words. Pays 7-10¢/word. Sometimes pays expenses of writers on assignment.

Photos: Photographs on assignment only unless submitted with and specific to article.

LIVE, 1445 Boonville Ave., Springfield MO 65802. (417)862-2781. Editor: John T. Maempa. 100% freelance written. Works with a small number of new/unpublished writers each year. Weekly. For adults in Assemblies of God Sunday schools. Circ. 200,000. Pays on acceptance. Publishes ms an average of 1 year after acceptance. Not copyrighted. Submit seasonal material 1 year in advance; do not mention Santa Claus, Halloween or Easter bunnies. Computer printout submissions acceptable; prefers letter-quality to dot-matrix. Reports on material within 3-6 weeks. Free sample copy and writer's guidelines for SASE. Letters without SASE will not be answered.

Nonfiction: Articles with reader appeal emphasizing some phase of Christian living presented in a down-to-earth manner. Biography or missionary material using fiction techniques. Historical, scientific or nature material with spiritual lesson. "Be accurate in detail and factual material. Writing for Christian publications is a ministry. The spiritual emphasis must be an integral part of your material." Prefers not to see material on highly controversial subjects. Buys about 120 mss/year. Length: 1,000-1,600 words. Pays 3¢/word for first serial rights; 2¢/word for second serial (reprint) rights, according to the value of the material and the amount of editorial work necessary. "Please do not send large numbers of articles at one time."

Photos: Color photos or transparencies purchased with mss, or on assignment. Pay open.

Fiction: "Present believable characters working out their problems according to Bible principles; in other words, present Christianity in action without being preachy. We use very few serials, but we will consider three to four-part stories if each part conforms to average word length for short stories. Each part must contain a spiritual emphasis and have enough suspense to carry the reader's interest from one week to the next. Stories should be true to life but not what we would feel is bad to set before the reader as a pattern for living. Stories should not put parents, teachers, ministers or other Christian workers in a bad light. Setting, plot and action should be realistic, with strong motivation. Characterize so that the people will live in your story. Construct your plot carefully so that each incident moves naturally and sensibly toward crisis and conclusion. An element of conflict is necessary in fiction. Short stories should be written from one viewpoint only. We do not accept fiction based on incidents in the Bible." Length: 1,200-1,600 words. Pays 3¢/word for first serial rights; 2¢/word for second serial (reprint) rights. "Please do not send large numbers of articles at one time."

Poetry: Traditional, free and blank verse. Length: 12-20 lines. "Please do not send large numbers of poems at one time." Pays 20¢/line.

Fillers: Brief and purposeful, usually containing an anecdote, and always with a strong evangelical emphasis. Length: 200-600 words.

LIVING WITH TEENAGERS, Baptist Sunday School Board, 127 9th Ave. N, Nashville TN 37234. (615)251-2273. Editor: Jimmy Hester. 50-75% freelance written. Works with a small number of new/unpublished writers each year. Quarterly magazine about teenagers for Baptist parents of teenagers. Circ. 50,000. Pays within 2 months of acceptance. Publishes ms an average of 18 months after acceptance. Buys all rights. Submit seasonal material 1 year in advance. Computer printout submissions OK; prefers letter-quality to dot-matrix. Reports in 2 months. Send 75¢ postage for a sample copy.

Nonfiction: "We are looking for a unique Christian element. We want a genuine insight into the teen/parent relationships." General interest (on communication, emotional problems, growing up, drugs and alcohol, leisure, sex education, spiritual growth, working teens and parents, money, family relationships, and church relationships); inspirational; and personal experience. Buys 60 unsolicited mss/year. Query with clips of previously published work. Length: 600-2,000 words. Pays 5¢/published word.

Fiction: Humorous and religious, but must relate to parent/teen relationship. "No stories from the teen's point of view." Buys 2 mss/issue. Query with clips of previously published work. Length: 600-2,000 words. Pays 5¢/published word.

Poetry: Free verse, light verse, traditional and devotional inspirational; all must relate to parent/teen relationship. Buys 3 mss/issue. Submit 5 poems maximum. Length: 33 characters maximum. Pays $2.10 plus $1.25/line for 1-7 lines; $5.40 plus 75¢/line for 8 lines minimum.

Tips: "A writer can meet our needs if they have something to say to parents of teenagers concerning an issue the parents are confronting with the teenager."

THE LOOKOUT, 8121 Hamilton Ave., Cincinnati OH 45231. (513)931-4050. Editor: Mark A. Taylor. 50-60% freelance written. Eager to work with new/unpublished writers. Weekly for the adult and young adult of Sunday morning Bible school. Pays on acceptance. Publishes ms an average of 4 months after acceptance. Byline given. Buys first serial rights, one-time rights, second serial (reprint) rights, or simultaneous rights. Simultaneous submissions OK. Computer printout submissions acceptable; prefers letter-quality to dot-matrix. Reports in 2 months. Sample copy and writer's guidelines 50¢.

Nonfiction: "Seeks stories about real people or Sunday school classes; items that shed Biblical light on matters of contemporary controversy; and items that motivate, that lead the reader to ask, 'Why shouldn't I try that?' or 'Why couldn't our Sunday school class accomplish this?' Articles should tell how real people are involved for Christ. In choosing topics, *The Lookout* considers timeliness, the church and national calendar, and the ability of the material to fit the above guidelines. Tell us about ideas that are working in your Sunday school and in the lives of its members. Remember to aim at laymen." Submit complete ms. Length: 1,200-1,800 words. Pays 4-6¢/word. We also use inspirational short pieces. "About 600-800 words is a good length for these. Relate an incident that illustrates a point without preaching." Pays 4-5¢/word.

Fiction: "A short story is printed in most issues; it is usually between 1,200-1,800 words long and should be as true to life as possible while remaining inspirational and helpful. Use familiar settings and situations. Most often we use stories with a Christian slant."

Photos: Reviews b&w prints, 4x6 or larger. Pays $5-25. Pays $50-150 for color transparencies for covers and inside use. Needs photos of people, especially adults in a variety of settings.

THE LUTHERAN, 2900 Queen Lane, Philadelphia PA 19129. (215)438-6580. Editor: Edgar R. Trexler. 25% freelance written. Prefers to work with published/established writers. General interest magazine of the Lutheran Church in America published twice monthly, except single issues in July, August and December. Pays on acceptance. Publishes ms an average of 6 months after acceptance. "We need informative, detailed query letters. We also accept manuscripts on speculation only, and we prefer not to encourage an abundance of query letters." Buys one-time rights or first North American serial rights. Electronic submissions OK via IBM PC, but requires hard copy also. Computer printout submissions acceptable; prefers letter-quality to dot-matrix. Free sample copy and writer's guidelines.

Nonfiction: Popularly written material about human concerns with reference to the Christian faith. "We are especially interested in articles in four main fields: Christian ideology; personal religious life, social responsibilities; Church at work; and human interest stories about Lutheran people in whom considerable numbers of other people are likely to be interested. Write primarily to convey information rather than opinions. Every article should be based on a reasonable amount of research or should explore some source of information not readily available. Most readers are grateful for simplicity of style. Sentences should be straightforward with a minimum of dependent clauses and prepositional phrases." Length: 500-2,000 words. Pays $100-300.

Photos: Buys photos submitted with ms. Reviews good 8x10 glossy prints. Pays $15-25. Also color for cover use. Pays up to $300.

Tips: "A great need exists for personal experience writing that is creative, relevant to these times and written for a wide audience."

LUTHERAN FORUM, 308 W. 46th St., New York NY 10036-3894. (212)757-1292. Editor: Glenn C. Stone. 25% freelance written. Works with a small number of new/unpublished writers each year. Quarterly magazine; 40 pages. For church leadership, clerical and lay. Circ. 4,500. Pays on publication. Publishes ms an average of 3 months after acceptance. Byline given. Rights purchased vary with author and material; buys all rights, first North American serial rights, second serial (reprint) rights, and simultaneous rights. Will consider photocopied and simultaneous submissions. Computer printout submissions acceptable; prefers letter-quality to dot-

matrix. Reports in 9 weeks. Sample copy $1.50.
Nonfiction: Articles about important issues and developments in the church's institutional life and in its cultural/social setting. Special interest in articles on the Christian's life in secular vocations. No purely devotional/inspirational material. Buys 8-10 mss/year. Query or submit complete ms. Length: 1,000-3,000 words. Payment varies; $30 minimum. Informational, how-to, interview, profile, think articles and expose. Length: 500-3,000 words. Pays $25-75.
Photos: Purchased with ms and only with captions. Prefers 4x5 prints. Pays $15 minimum.

THE LUTHERAN JOURNAL, 7317 Cahill Rd., Edina MN 55435. Editor: Rev. Armin U. Deye. Quarterly magazine; 32 pages. Family magazine for Lutheran Church members, middle age and older. Circ. 136,000. Pays on publication. Byline given. Will consider photocopied and simultaneous submissions. Reports in 2 months. Free sample copy.
Nonfiction: Inspirational, religious, human interest and historical articles. Interesting or unusual church projects. Informational, how-to, personal experience, interview, humor and think articles. Buys 25-30 mss/year. Submit complete ms. Length: 1,500 words maximum; occasionally 2,000 words. Pays 1-3¢/word.
Photos: B&w and color photos purchased with accompanying ms. Captions required. Payment varies.
Fiction: Mainstream, religious and historical fiction. Must be suitable for church distribution. Length: 2,000 words maximum. Pays 1-1½¢/word.
Poetry: Traditional poetry, blank verse and free verse, related to subject matter.

THE LUTHERAN STANDARD, 426 S. 5th St., Box 1209, Minneapolis MN 55440. (612)330-3300. Acting Editor: Rev. Kenneth Roberts. 30% freelance written. "We look for manuscripts that meet the need of our readers and do not really draw practical distinctions between new and established writers." Published 20 times/year. For families in congregations of the American Lutheran Church. Circ. 540,000. Pays on acceptance. Publishes ms an average of 9 months after acceptance. Byline given. Usually buys one-time rights. Computer printout submissions acceptable; prefers letter-quality to dot-matrix. Reports in 3 weeks. Free sample copy.
Nonfiction: Inspirational articles, especially about members of the American Lutheran Church who are practicing their faith in noteworthy ways, or congregations with unusual programs. Articles "should be written in language clearly understandable to persons with a mid-high school reading ability." Also publishes articles that discuss current social issues and problems (crime, family life, divorce, etc.) in terms of Christian involvement and solutions. No poetry. Buys 30-50 mss/year. Query. Length: limit 1,200 words. Pays 10¢/word. Sometimes pays the expenses of writers on assignment.
Tips: "We are interested in personal experience pieces with a strong first person approach. The manuscript may be on a religious and social issue, but with evident human interest using personal anecdotes and illustrations. How has an individual faced a serious problem and overcome it? How has faith made a difference in a person's life? We prefer letters that clearly describe the proposed project. Excerpts from the project or other samples of the author's work are helpful in determining whether we are interested in dealing with an author. We would appreciate it if more freelance writers seemed to have a sense of who our readers are and an awareness of the kinds of manuscripts we in fact publish. Beginning in 1988, *The Lutheran Standard* will be incorporated into *The Lutheran*, magazine of the New Evangelical Lutheran Church in America, which will have offices in Chicago."

‡**MARIAN HELPERS BULLETIN**, Eden Hill, Stockbridge MA 01263. (413)298-3691. Editor: Rev. Donald J. Van Alstyne, M.I.C. 90% freelance written. Eager to work with new/unpublished writers. Quarterly for average Catholics of varying ages with moderate religious views and general education. Circ. 1,000,000. Pays on acceptance. Publishes ms an average of 5 months after acceptance. Byline given. Submit seasonal material 6 months in advance. Computer printout submissions OK; prefers letter-quality to dot-matrix. Reports in 4-8 weeks. Free sample copy.
Nonfiction: "Subject matter is of general interest on devotional, spiritual, moral and social topics. Use a positive, practical and optimistic approach, without being sophisticated. We would like to see articles on the Blessed Virgin Mary." Buys informational and inspirational articles. Buys 18-24 mss/year. Length: 300-900 words. Pays $40 and up. Sometimes pays expenses of writers on assignment.
Photos: Photos should be sent to complement articles.
Tips: "Human interest stories are very valuable, from which personal reflection is stimulated."

MARRIAGE & FAMILY LIVING, St. Meinrad IN 47577. (812)357-8011. Managing Editor: Kass Dotterweich. 75% freelance written. Monthly magazine. Circ. 40,000. Pays on acceptance. Byline given. Buys first international serial rights, first book reprint option, and control of other reprint rights. Query. Computer printout submissions acceptable; prefers letter-quality to dot-matrix. Reports in 6 weeks. Sample copy $1.
Nonfiction: Articles which affirm marriage and parenting as an awesome vocation created by God; and personal essays relating amusing, heartwarming or insightful incidents which reflect the rich human side of marriage and family life. Length: 1,500-2,000 words maximum. Pays 7¢/word. Pays expenses of writers on assignment.

Photos: Attention, art director. Reviews 8x10 b&w glossy prints and color transparencies or 35mm slides. Pays $150/4-color cover or center spread photo. Uses approximately 6-8 b&w photos and an occasional illustration inside. Pays variable rate on publication. Photos of couples, families and individuals especially desirable. Model releases required.
Poetry: Any style and length. Pays $15 on publication.
Tips: Query with a brief outline of article and opening paragraphs.

MENNONITE BRETHREN HERALD, 3-169 Riverton Ave., Winnipeg, Manitoba R2L 2E5 Canada. Contact: Editor. 25% freelance written. Prefers to work with published/established writers. Family publication "read mainly by people of the Mennonite faith, reaching a wide crosssection of professional and occupational groups, but also including many homemakers. Readership includes people from both urban and rural communities." Biweekly. Circ. 13,500. Pays on publication. Publishes ms an average of 4-6 months after acceptance. Not copyrighted. Byline given. Computer printout submissions OK; no dot-matrix. Sample copy $1. Reports in 3 months. SAE and IRCs.
Nonfiction: Articles with a Christian family orientation; youth directed, Christian faith and life, and current issues. Wants articles critiquing the values of a secular society, attempting to relate Christian living to the practical situations of daily living; showing how people have related their faith to their vocations. Length: 1,500 words. Pays $25-40. Pays the expenses of writers on assignment.
Photos: Photos purchased with mss; pays $5.

THE MESSENGER OF THE SACRED HEART, 661 Greenwood Ave., Toronto, Ontario M4J 4B3 Canada. Editor: Rev. F.J. Power, S.J. For "adult Catholics in Canada and the U.S. who are members of the Apostleship of Prayer." 20% freelance written. Monthly. Circ. 15,000. Buys first rights only. Byline given. Pays on acceptance. Submit seasonal material 3 months in advance. Computer printout submissions acceptable; prefers letter-quality to dot-matrix. Reports in 1 month. SAE and IRCs. Sample copy $1.
Nonfiction: Mary Pujolas, department editor. "Articles on the Apostleship of Prayer and on all aspects of Christian living." Current events and social problems that have a bearing on Catholic life, family life, Catholic relations with nonCatholics, personal problems, the liturgy, prayer and devotion to the Sacred Heart. Material should be written in a popular, nonpious style. "We are not interested in column material." Buys 12 mss/year. Unsolicited manuscripts, unaccompanied by return postage, will not be returned. Length: 1,200-1,500 words. Pays 2¢ word.
Fiction: Mary Pujolas, department editor. Wants fiction which reflects the lives, problems and preoccupations of reading audience. "Short stories that make their point through plot and characters." Length: 1,200-1,500 words. Pays 2¢/word.

THE MIRACULOUS MEDAL, 475 E. Chelten Ave., Philadelphia PA 19144. Editorial Director: Rev. Robert P. Cawley, C.M. 40% freelance written. Quarterly. Pays on acceptance. Publishes ms an average of 2 years after acceptance. Buys first North American serial rights. Buys articles only on special assignment. Computer printout submissions acceptable; no dot-matrix. Free sample copy.
Fiction: Should not be pious or sermon-like. Wants good general fiction—not necessarily religious, but if religion is basic to the story, the writer should be sure of his facts. Only restriction is that subject matter and treatment must not conflict with Catholic teaching and practice. Can use seasonal material; Christmas stories. Length: 2,000 words maximum. Occasionally uses short-shorts from 750-1,250 words. Pays 2¢/word minimum.
Poetry: Maximum of 20 lines, preferably about the Virgin Mary or at least with religious slant. Pays 50¢/line minimum.

MODERN LITURGY, Suite 290, 160 E. Virginia St., San Jose CA 95112. Editor: Kenneth Guentert. 80% freelance written. Magazine; 40-48 pages published 9 times/year for artists, musicians and creative individuals who plan group worship, services; teachers of religion. Circ. 15,000. Buys first serial rights. Pays 3 months after publication. Publishes ms an average of 6 months after acceptance. Byline given. Electronic submissions OK via CPM, but requires hard copy. Computer printout submissions acceptable; prefers letter-quality to dot-matrix. Reports in 6 weeks. Sample copy $4; free writer's guidelines for SAE and 1 first class stamp.
Nonfiction and Fiction: Articles (historical, theological and practical) which address special interest topics in the field of liturgy; example services; and liturgical art forms (music, poetry, stories, dances, dramatizations, etc.). Practical, creative ideas; and art forms for use in worship and/or religious education classrooms. "No material out of our field." Buys 10 mss/year. Query. Length: 750-2,000 words. Pays $5-30.
Tips: "Don't be preachy; use too much jargon; or make articles too long."

‡MOODY MONTHLY, Moody Bible Institute, 820 N. LaSalle Dr., Chicago IL 60610. (312)508-6820. Managing Editor: Mike Umlandt. 20% freelance written. A monthly magazine for evangelical Christianity. "Our readers are conservative, evangelical Christians highly active in their churches and concerned about family living." Circ. 200,000. Pays on acceptance. Publishes ms an average of 6 months after acceptance. Byline given.

Offers $50 kill fee. Buys first North American serial rights. Submit seasonal/holiday material 8 months in advance. Photocopied submissions OK. Query for electronic submissions. Computer printout submissions OK. Reports in 1 month on queries; 2 months on mss. Sample copy for 10x13 SAE; writer's guidelines for business size SAE with 1 first class stamp.

Nonfiction: How-to (on living the Christian life), humor and personal experience. Buys 50 mss/year. Query. Length: 750-2,000 words. Pays 10-15¢/word for assigned articles. Sometimes pays the expenses of writers on assignment.

Photos: State availability of photos with submission. Offers $35-50 per photo. Buys one-time rights.

Columns/Departments: First Person (The only article written for non-Christians; a personal testimony written by the author [we will accept 'as told to's'], the objective is to tell a person's testimony in such a way that the reader will understand the gospel and want to receive Christ as Savior); Parenting (provides practical guidance for parents solidly based on biblical principles); People (write about one aspect of a person's life—employment, family, special interest, school, etc.—showing how he or she lives Christ in that environment and ministers to others; the person's actions must clearly result from personal faith in Christ). Buys 30 mss/year. Query. Length: 750-1,200 words. Pays 10-15¢/word.

NATIONAL CHRISTIAN REPORTER, Box 222198, Dallas TX 75222. (214)630-6495. Editor/General Manager: Spurgeon M. Dunnam III. Managing Editor: John A. Lovelace. 5% freelance written. Prefers to work with published/established writers. Weekly newspaper for an interdenominational national readership. Circ. 25,000. Pays on publication. Publishes ms an average of 1 month after acceptance. Byline given. Not copyrighted. Free sample copy and writer's guidelines.

Nonfiction: "We welcome short features, approximately 500 words. Articles need not be limited to a United Methodist angle but need to have an explicit 'mainstream' Protestant angle. Write about a distinctly Christian response to human need or how a person's faith relates to a given situation. Preferably including evidence of participation in a local Protestant congregation." Send complete ms. Pays 4¢/word. Sometimes pays the expenses of writers on assignment.

Photos: Purchased with accompanying ms. "We encourage the submission of good action photos (5x7 or 8x10 b&w glossy prints) of the persons or situations in the article." Pays $10.

Poetry: "Good poetry welcome on a religious theme; blank verse or rhyme." Length: 4-20 lines. Pays $2.

Tips: "Read our publications before submitting. First person stories seldom fit our needs, but opinion pieces of no more than 500 words will be considered without pay for My Witness and Here I Stand."

‡NEW ENGLAND CHURCH LIFE, Evangelistic Association of New England, Suite 600, 88 Tremont St., Boston MA 02108. (617)523-3579. Editor: Charlene B. Hill. 40% freelance written. Monthly tabloid covering evangelical/charismatic Protestant Christianity. "*New England Church Life* is the community newsmonthly for evangelical and charismatic Christians in six states. Our readers include pastors and lay leaders who network through the resources they find in our pages. Articles demonstrate how believers live out their faith in many situations or help churches and individual Christians in their life and witness." Pays on publication. Publishes ms an average of 3 months after acceptance. Byline given. Offers 50% kill fee. Buys first North American serial rights, second serial (reprint) rights or simultaneous rights. Submits seasonal/holiday material 4 months in advance. Simultaneous and previous published submissions OK. Computer printout submissions OK; prefers letter-quality to dot-matrix. Reports in 6 weeks on queries; 8 weeks on mss. Sample copy $1; writer's guidelines for #10 SAE with 1 first class stamp.

Nonfiction: General interest, how-to, inspirational, interview/profile, and travel. Special issues include Vacations (February); Church Supply and Suppliers (July); and Overseas Missions (November). No articles without regional ties. Where the story is national, local link must be established. No articles on churches, individuals or organizations that lack clear ties to evangelical or charismatic church, group or denomination. Buys 80 mss/year. Query with published clips. Length: 400-1,200 words. Pays $35-50 for assigned articles; $20-40 for unsolicited articles. Sometimes pays expenses of writers on assignment.

Photos: State availability of photos with submission. Reviews contact sheets. Offers $10-35 per photo. Captions and identification of subjects required. Buys one-time rights.

Columns/Departments: Faith on the Job (how a person's Christian lifestyle or commitment was put to the test in the secular workplace, happy ending not required), 350-400 words; Learning in the Church (by and for Christian educators working in the local church, trends, methods, directions for your CE program), 450 words. Buys 70 mss/year. Send complete ms. Pays $5-30.

Fiction: Religious. No preachy, unrealistic stories, full of evangelical/charismatic buzzwords. Buys 4 mss/year. Send complete ms. Length: 800-1,200 words. Pays $25-50.

Tips: "Query with recent clips. Read our publication before contributing. The best way to break in is with a short article (600-800 words) about an effective local church ministry or showing how becoming Christian changed someone's life. Write for all five senses but don't forget facts and figures. Stories that grow out of current news events sell well, too, as long as there's a regional link."

THE NEW ERA, 50 E. North Temple, Salt Lake City UT 84150. (801)531-2951. Managing Editor: Brian K. Kelly. 60% freelance written. "We work with both established writers and newcomers." Monthly magazine; 51 pages. For young people of the Church of Jesus Christ of Latter-day Saints (Mormon); their church leaders and teachers. Circ. 180,000. Pays on acceptance. Publishes ms an average of 1 year after acceptance. Byline given. Buys all rights. Submit seasonal material 1 year in advance. Query for electronic submissions. Computer printout submissions acceptable; prefers letter-quality to dot-matrix. Reports in 1 month. Query preferred. Sample copy 90¢; writer's guidelines for SAE and 1 first class stamp.

Nonfiction: Material that shows how the Church of Jesus Christ of Latter-day Saints is relevant in the lives of young people today. Must capture the excitement of being a young Latter-day Saint. Special interest in the experiences of young Mormons in other countries. No general library research or formula pieces without the *New Era* slant and feel. Uses informational, how-to, personal experience, interview, profile, inspirational, humor, historical, think pieces, travel and spot news. Length: 150-3,000 words. Pays 3-12¢/word. *For Your Information* (news of young Mormons around the world). Pays expenses of writers on assignment.

Photos: Uses b&w photos and color transparencies with mss. Payment depends on use in magazine, but begins at $10.

Fiction: Experimental, adventure, science fiction and humorous. Must relate to young Mormon audience. Pays minimum 3¢/word.

Poetry: Traditional forms, blank verse, free verse, avant-garde forms, light verse and all other forms. Must relate to editorial viewpoint. Pays minimum 25¢/line.

Tips: "The writer must be able to write from a Mormon point of view. We have increased our staff size and anticipate using more staff-produced material. This means freelance quality will have to improve."

NEW WORLD OUTLOOK, Room 1351, 475 Riverside Dr., New York NY 10115. (212)870-3758. Editor: Arthur J. Moore. Executive Editor: George M. Daniels. Associate Editor: Gladys N. Koppole. 70% freelance written. Eager to work with new/unpublished writers. Monthly magazine (combined issues July/August and November/December); 48 pages. For United Methodist lay people; not clergy generally. Circ. 40,000. Pays on publication. Publishes ms an average of 4 months after acceptance. Buys first serial rights. Electronic submissions OK via Wang or IBM PC 5¼ floppy disk, but requires hard copy also. Computer printout submissions acceptable; no dot-matrix. Sample copy for $1 and 9x12 SASE; writer's guidelines for SASE.

Nonfiction: Articles about the involvement of the church around the world, including the U.S. in outreach and social concerns and Christian witness. "Write with good magazine style. Facts and actualities are important. Use quotes. Relate what Christians are doing to meet problems. Use specifics. We have too much on New York and other large urban areas. We need more good journalistic efforts from smaller places in U.S. and articles by freelancers in out-of-the-way places in the U.S. Buys 50-60 mss/year. Query or submit complete ms. Length: 1,000-2,000 words. Usually pays $50-150 but considerably more on occasion. "Writers are encouraged to illustrate their articles photographically if possible." Pays expenses of writers on assignment "if it originates with us or if article is one in which we have a special interest."

Photos: "Generally use b&w but covers (4-color) will be considered. Photos are purchased separately at standard rates."

Tips: "A freelancer should have some understanding of the United Methodist Church, or else know very well a local situation of human need or social problem which the churches and Christians have tried to face. Too much freelance material we get tries to paint with broad strokes about world or national issues. The local story of meaning to people elsewhere is still the best material. Avoid pontificating on the big issues. Write cleanly and interestingly on the 'small' ones. We're interested in major articles and photos (including photo features from freelancers)."

NORTH AMERICAN VOICE OF FATIMA, Fatima Shrine, Youngstown NY 14174. Editor: Rev. Paul M. Keeling, C.R.S.P. 40% freelance written. Works with a small number of new/unpublished writers each year. For Roman Catholic readership. Circ. 3,000. Pays on acceptance. Publishes ms an average of 2 months after acceptance. Not copyrighted. Buys first North American serial rights. Reports in 6 weeks. Computer printout submissions acceptable; no dot-matrix. Free sample copy.

Nonfiction and Fiction: Inspirational, personal experience, historical and think articles. Religious and historical fiction. Length: 700 words. All material must have a religious slant. Pays 2¢/word.

Photos: B&w photos purchased with ms.

OBLATES MAGAZINE, Missionary Association of Mary Immaculate, 15 S. 59th St., Belleville IL 62222. (618)233-2238. Editor of Contributions: Jacqueline Lowery Corn. 30-50% freelance written. Prefers to work with professional writers; but will work with new/unpublished writers. Bimonthly religious magazine for Christian families; audience mainly older adults. Circ. 500,000. Pays on acceptance. Publishes ms an average of 4 months after acceptance. Byline given. Buys first North American serial rights. Submit seasonal/holiday material 6 months in advance. Query for electronic submissions. Computer printout submissions acceptable; no dot-matrix. Reports in 1 month. Sample copy and writer's guidelines for 9x6 or larger SAE with 39¢ postage.

Nonfiction: Inspirational and personal experience with positive spiritual insights. Stories should be inspirational and uplifting. No preachy theological research articles. Avoid current events and controversial topics. Send complete ms. Length: 500 words. Pays $75.

Poetry: Light verse—reverent, well written, perceptive, with traditional rhythym and rhyme. "Emphasis should be on inspiration, insight and relationship with God." Submit maximum 2 poems. Length: 8-16 lines. Pays $25.

Tips: "Our readership is made up mostly of mature Americans who are looking for comfort, encouragement, and a positive sense of applicable Christian direction to their lives. They don't want to spend a lot of time wading through theology laden or personal spiritual journey pieces. Focus on sharing of personal insight to problem (i.e. death or suicide), but must be positive, uplifting, only subtly spiritual."

‡ORT REPORTER, A National Newspaper for the American Jewish Woman, Woman's American ORT, Inc., 315 Park Ave. So., New York NY 10010. (212)505-7700. Editor: Elie Faust-Levy. Associate Editor: Ari Salant. 85% freelance written. Nonprofit journal published by Jewish women's organization. Quarterly tabloid covering "Jewish topics, education, Mideast and women." Circ. 155,000. Payment time varies. Publishes ms. 1-12 months after acceptance. Byline given. Buys first North American serial rights or second serial (reprint) rights. Submit seasonal/holiday material 6 months in advance. Previously published submissions OK. Reports in 2-4 weeks. Free sample copy.

Nonfiction: Book excerpts, essays, general interest, humor, opinion and religious. Plans special issue on Israel's 40th anniversary. No poetry. Buys approximately 40 mss/year. Send complete ms. Length: 500-3000. Pays 8-15¢/word.

Photos: Send photos with submission. Reviews 5x7 prints. Offers $50-85 per photo. Identification of subjects required. Purchases "whatever rights photographer desires."

Columns/Departments: Book Reporter, Film Reporter, Stage Reporter. Buys 4-10 mss/year. Send complete ms. Length: 200-2,000 words. Pays 8-15%/word.

Fiction: Ethnic, novel excerpts, religious. Buys 0-1 ms/year. Send complete ms. Pays 10¢/word.

Tips: "Simply send ms, do not call. First submission must be "on spec". Open Forum (opinion section) is most open to freelancers, although all are open. Looking for well-written essay on relevant topic that makes its point strongly—evokes response from reader."

THE OTHER SIDE, Box 3948, Fredericksburg VA 22402. Editor: Mark Olson. Managing Editor: Kathleen Hayes. Associate Editors: John Linscheid and William O'Brien. 50% freelance written. Prefers to work with published/established writers; works with a small number of new/unpublished writers each year. Magazine published 10 times/year focusing on "peace, justice and economic liberation from a radical Christian perspective." Circ. 15,000. Pays on acceptance. Publishes ms an average of 4 months after acceptance. Byline given. Buys first serial rights. Query for electronic submissions. Computer printout submissions acceptable. Reports in 6 weeks. Sample copy $3; free writer's guidelines.

Nonfiction: Eunice A. Smith, articles editor. Current social, political and economic issues in the U.S. and around the world: personality profiles, interpretative essays, interviews, how-to's, personal experiences and investigative reporting. "Articles must be lively, vivid and down-to-earth, with a radical Christian perspective." Length: 500-6,000 words. Pays $25-300. Sometimes pays expenses of writers on assignment.

Photos: Cathleen Boint, art director. Photos or photo essays illustrating current social, political, or economic reality in the U.S. and Third World. Pays $15-75 for b&w and $50-300 for color.

Fiction: Joseph Comanda, fiction editor. "Short stories, humor and satire conveying insights and situations that will be helpful to Christians with a radical commitment to peace and justice." Length: 300-6,000 words. Pays $25-250.

Poetry: Rod Jellema, poetry editor. "Short, creative poetry that will be thought-provoking and appealing to radical Christians who have a strong commitment to spirituality, peace and justice." Length: 3-50 lines. Pays $15-20.

Tips: "We're looking for tightly written pieces (500-1,000 words) on interesting and unusual Christians (or Christian groups) who are putting their commitment to peace and social justice into action in creative and useful ways. We're also looking for practical, down-to-earth articles (500-6,000 words) for Christian parents who seek to instill in their children their values of personal faith, peace, justice, and a concern for the poor."

OUR FAMILY, Oblate Fathers of St. Mary's Province, Box 249, Battleford, Saskatchewan S0M 0E0 Canada. (306)937-2131, 937-7344. Editor: Nestor Greg Oire. 60% freelance written. Prefers to work with published/established writers; works with a small number of new/unpublished writers each year. Monthly magazine for average family men and women with high school and early college education. Circ. 14,265. Pays on acceptance. Publishes ms an average of 6 months after acceptance. Byline given. Offers 100% kill fee. Generally purchases first North American serial rights; also buys all rights, simultaneous rights, second serial (reprint) rights or one-time rights. Submit seasonal/holiday material 4 months in advance. Simultaneous, photocopied, and previously published submissions OK. Query for electronic submissions. Computer printout submissions acceptable; no dot-matrix. "Writer should inquire with our office before sending letter-quality computer printout or disk submissions." Reports in 1 month. Sample copy $2.50 and SAE, IRC; writer's guidelines for 42¢

(Canadian funds). U.S. postage cannot be used in Canada.

Nonfiction: Humor (related to family life or husband/wife relations); inspirational (anything that depicts people responding to adverse conditions with courage, hope and love); personal experience (with religious dimensions); and photo feature (particularly in search of photo essays on human/religious themes and on persons whose lives are an inspiration to others). Phone queries OK. Buys 72-88 unsolicited mss/year. Pays expenses of writers on assignment.

Photos: Photos purchased with or without accompanying ms. Pays $35 for 5x7 or larger b&w glossy prints and color photos (which are converted into b&w). Offers additional payment for photos accepted with ms (payment for these photos varies according to their quality). Free photo spec sheet with SASE.

Fiction: Humorous and religious. "Anything true to human nature. No romance, he-man adventure material, science fiction, moralizing or sentimentality." Buys 1-2 ms/issue. Send complete ms. Length: 700-3,000 words. Pays 7-10¢/word minimum for original material. Free fiction requirement guide with SASE.

Poetry: Avant-garde, free verse, haiku, light verse and traditional. Buys 4-10 poems/issue. Length: 3-30 lines. Pays 75¢-$1/line.

Fillers: Jokes, gags, anecdotes and short humor. Buys 2-10/issue.

Tips: "Writers should ask themselves whether this is the kind of an article, poem, etc. that a busy housewife would pick up and read when she has a few moments of leisure. We are particularly looking for articles on the spirituality of marriage. We will be concentrating more on recent movements and developments in the church to help make people aware of the new church of which they are a part."

‡**OUR SUNDAY VISITOR MAGAZINE**, Noll Plaza, Huntington IN 46750. (219)356-8400. Editor-in-Chief: Robert Lockwood. 5% freelance written. Works with small number of new/unpublished writers each year. Weekly magazine for general Catholic audience. Circ. 300,000. Pays on acceptance. Publishes ms an average of 2 months after acceptance. Byline given. Submit seasonal material 2 months in advance. Query for electronic submission. Computer printout submissions OK. Reports in 3 weeks. Free sample copy with SASE.

Nonfiction: Uses articles on Catholic-related subjects. Should explain Catholic religious beliefs in articles of human interest; articles applying Catholic principles to current problems, Catholic profiles, etc. Payment varies depending on reputation of author, quality of work, and amount of research required. Buys 25 mss/year. Query. Length: 1,000-1,200 words. Minimum payment for features is $100. Pays expenses of writers on assignment.

Photos: Purchased with mss; with captions only. Reviews b&w glossy prints and color transparencies. Pays minimum of $200/cover photo story; $125/b&w story; $25/color photo; $10/b&w photo.

PARISH FAMILY DIGEST, Our Sunday Visitor, Inc., 200 Noll Plaza, Huntington IN 46750. (219)356-8400. Editor: Louis F. Jacquet. 100% freelance written. Works with small number of new/unpublished writers each year. Bimonthly magazine; 48 pages. "*Parish Family Digest* is geared to the Catholic family and to that family as a unit of the parish." Circ. 150,000. Pays on acceptance. Publishes ms an average of 6 months after acceptance. Byline given. Buys all rights on a work-for-hire basis. Submit seasonal/holiday material 5 months in advance. Photocopied submissions OK; all mss are retyped as edited. Computer printout submissions acceptable; prefers letter-quality to dot-matrix. Reports in 2 weeks on queries; 3 weeks on mss. Sample copy and writer's guidelines for 9½x6½ SAE and 2 first class stamps.

Nonfiction: General interest, historical, inspirational, interview, nostalgia (if related to overall Parish involvement), and profile. No personal essays or preachy first person "thou shalt's or shalt not's." Send complete ms. Buys 72 unsolicited mss/year. Length: 1,000 words maximum. Pays $5-50.

Photos: State availability of photos with ms. Pays $10 for 3x5 b&w prints. Buys one-time rights. Captions preferred; model releases required.

Fillers: Anecdotes and short humor. Buys 6/issue. Length: 100 words maximum.

Tips: "If an article does not deal with some angle of Catholic family life, the writer is wasting time in sending it to us. We rarely use reprints; we prefer fresh material that will hold up over time, not tied to an event in the news. We will be more oriented to families with kids and the problems such families face in the Church and society, in particular, the struggle to raise good Catholic kids in a secular society. Articles on how to overcome these problems will be welcomed."

‡**PARTNERSHIP**, Christianity Today, Inc., 465 Gunderson Dr., Carol Stream IL 60188. (312)260-6200. Editor: Ruth Senter. Managing Editor: Sharon Donohue. 20% freelance written. Bimonthly magazine "that provides thoughtful, provocative and encouraging articles for women who value marriage, ministry and spiritual growth. Has a 50% over-the-shoulder reading by men." Circ. 45,000. Pays on acceptance. Byline given. Buys first serial rights. Submit seasonal/holiday material 7 months in advance. Simultaneous queries and photocopied submissions OK. Reports in 2 weeks on queries; 1 month on mss. Sample copy for 9x12 SAE; free writer's guidelines.

Nonfiction: Personal experience, historical/nostalgic, how-to, humor, inspirational, interview/profile, opinion and photo feature, book reviews. Send queries to managing editor. No unsolicited mss accepted. Pays $15-250.

Photos: State availability of photos with query. Reviews b&w and color transparencies. Identification of subjects required. Buys one-time rights.
Columns/Departments: Buys 30 mss/year. Query. No unsolicited ms.

PENTECOSTAL EVANGEL, The General Council of the Assemblies of God, 1445 Boonville, Springfield MO 65802. (417)862-2781. Editor: Richard G. Champion. 33% freelance written. Works with a small number of new/unpublished writers each year. Weekly magazine; 32 pages. Emphasizes news of the Assemblies of God for members of the Assemblies and other Pentecostal and charismatic Christians. Circ. 288,000. Usually pays on acceptance. Publishes ms an average of 4-6 months after acceptance. Byline given. Buys first serial rights, simultaneous rights, second serial (reprint) rights or one-time rights. Submit seasonal/holiday material 6 months in advance. Simultaneous, photocopied, and previously published submissions OK. Computer printout submissions acceptable; prefers letter-quality to dot-matrix. Reports in 3 months. Free sample copy and writer's guidelines.
Nonfiction: Informational (articles on homelife that convey Christian teachings); inspirational; and personal experience. Buys 5 mss/issue. Send complete ms. Length: 500-2,000 words. Pays 4¢/word maximum. Sometimes pays the expenses of writers on assignment.
Photos: Photos purchased without accompanying ms. Pays $7.50-15 for 8x10 b&w glossy prints; $10-35 for 35mm or larger color transparencies. Total purchase price for ms includes payment for photos.
Poetry: Religious and inspirational. Buys 1 poem/issue. Submit maximum 6 poems. Pays 20-40¢/line.
Tips: "Break in by writing up a personal experience. We publish first person articles concerning spiritual experiences; that is, answers to prayer for help in a particular situation, of unusual conversions or healings through faith in Christ. All articles submitted to us should be related to religious life. We are Protestant, evangelical, Pentecostal, and any doctrines or practices portrayed should be in harmony with the official position of our denomination (Assemblies of God)."

‡THE PENTECOSTAL MESSENGER, Messenger Publishing House, 4901 Pennsylvania, Box 850, Joplin MO 64802. (417)625-7050. Editor: Don Allen. Managing Editor: Peggy Lee Allen. 25% freelance written. Works with small number of new/unpublished writers each year. Monthly (excluding July) magazine covering Pentcostal Christianity. *"The Pentecostal Messenger* is the official organ of the Pentecostal Church of God. Goes to ministers and church members." Circ. 6,500. Pays on publication. Publishes ms an average of 6 months after acceptance. Byline given. Buys second serial (reprint) rights or simultaneous rights. Submit seasonal/holiday material 4 months in advance. Simultaneous, photocopied and previously published submissions OK. Computer printout submissions OK; prefers letter-quality. Reports in 4 weeks on mss. Sample copy for 9x12 SAE and 4 first class stamps; free writer's guidelines.
Nonfiction: Inspirational, personal experience and religious. Special issue includes Sunday School Enlargement (October). Buys 35 mss/year. Send complete ms. Length: 1,800 words. Pays 1½¢/word.
Photos: Send photos with submission. Reviews 2¼x2¼ transparencies and prints. Offers $10-25 per photo. Captions and model releases required. Buys one-time rights.
Tips: "Articles need to be inspirational, informative, written from a positive viewpoint, not extremely controversial."

PLUS, The Magazine of Positive Thinking, Foundation for Christian Living, Box FCL, Route 22, Pawling NY 12564. (914)855-5000. Editor: Eric J. Fellman. 40% freelance written. Prefers to work with published/established writers; works with a small number of new/unpublished writers each year. Magazine published 10 times/year. "Our audience looks for inspiration and practical ways to apply their faith every day." Circ. 900,000. Pays on publication. Publishes ms an average of 5 months after acceptance. Byline given. Buys first North American serial rights, or second serial (reprint) rights. Submit seasonal/holiday material 6 months in advance. Photocopied and previously published submissions OK. Computer printout submissions acceptable; prefers letter-quality to dot-matrix. Reports in 1 month on queries; 6 weeks on mss. Sample copy for SAE with 2 first class stamps; writer's guidelines for SAE with 1 first class stamp.
Nonfiction: Rosemarie Dunn Stokes, articles editor. Book excerpts, inspirational, personal experience and religious. "We look for articles that emphasize a how-to focus—how to take the principles of faith and positive thinking and apply them to daily living. We like well-written, succinct, visual anecdotes in the articles we use. We are not interested in preachy, long-winded articles, nor are we interested in anything resembling a theological treatise. Articles that deal with popular controversial issues are also not our style." Pays "good rates."

PRAIRIE MESSENGER, Catholic Weekly, Benedictine Monks of St. Peter's Abbey, Box 190, Muenster, Saskatchewan S0K 2Y0 Canada. (306)682-5215. Editor: Andrew Britz. Managing Editor: Marian Noll. 10% freelance written. A weekly Catholic journal with strong emphasis on social justice, Third World and ecumenism. Circ. 13,000. Pays on publication. Publishes ms an average of 2-3 months after acceptance. Byline given. Offers 70% kill fee. Not copyrighted. Buys first North American serial rights, first rights, one-time rights, second serial (reprint) rights or simultaneous rights. Submit seasonal/holiday material 3 months in advance. Simultaneous submissions OK. Query for electronic submissions. Computer printout submissions OK;

no dot-matrix. Sample copy for 9x12 SAE with 68¢ Canadian postage; writer's guidelines for 9x12 SAE with 68¢ first class stamps.

Nonfiction: Interview/profile, opinion, and religious. "No articles on abortion or homosexuality." Buys 30 mss/year. Send complete ms. Length: 250-600 words. Pays $40-60. Sometimes pays expenses of writers on assignment.

Photos: Send photos with submission. Review 3x5 prints. Offers $7.50-10/photo. Captions required. Buys all rights.

PRESBYTERIAN RECORD, 50 Wynford Dr., Don Mills, Ontario M3C 1J7 Canada. (416)444-1111. Editor: Rev. James Dickey. 50% freelance written. Eager to work with new/unpublished writers. Monthly magazine for a church-oriented, family audience. Circ. 75,000. Buys 35 mss/year. Pays on publication. Publishes ms an average of 4 months after acceptance. Buys first serial rights, one-time rights, simultaneous rights. Submit seasonal material 3 months in advance. Computer printout submissions acceptable. Reports on ms accepted for publication in 2 months. Returns rejected material in 3 months. SAE and Canadian stamps or IRC. Free sample copy.

Nonfiction: Material on religious themes. Check a copy of the magazine for style. Also, personal experience, interview, and inspirational material. No material solely American in context. Buys 15-20 unsolicited mss/year. Query. Length: 1,000-2,000 words. Pays $45-55 (U.S. funds). Sometimes pays expenses of writers on assignment.

Photos: Pays $15-20 for b&w glossy photos. Uses positive color transparencies for cover. Pays $50. Captions required.

Tips: "There is a trend away from maudlin, first person pieces redolent with tragedy and dripping with simplistic pietistic conclusions."

PRESBYTERIAN SURVEY, Presbyterian Publishing House, Inc., 341 Ponce de Leon Ave. NE, Atlanta GA 30365. (404)873-1549. Editor: Vic Jameson. Managing Editor: Catherine Cottingham. 65% freelance written. Prefers to work with published/established writers; works with a small number of new/unpublished writers each year; willing to work with new/unpublished writers. Denominational magazine published 10 times/year covering religion, denominational activities and public issues for members of the Presbyterian Church (U.S.A.). Pays on acceptance. Publishes ms an average of 9 months after acceptance. Byline given. Offers variable kill fee. Buys first North American serial rights. Submit seasonal/holiday material 8 months in advance. Simultaneous submissions OK. Computer printout submissions acceptable; prefers letter-quality to dot-matrix. Reports in 2 weeks on queries; 1 month on mss. Free sample copy and writer's guidelines.

Nonfiction: Inspirational and Presbyterian programs, issues, people; any subject from a Christian viewpoint. No secular subjects. Buys 50 mss/year. Send complete ms. Length: 800-1,500 words. Pays $50-200. Sometimes pays expenses of writers on assignment.

Photos: Richard Brown, photo editor. State availability of photos. Reviews color transparencies and 8x10 b&w prints. Pays $15-25 for b&w; $25-50 for color. Identification of subjects required. Buys one-time rights.

Columns/Departments: "The only column not by a regular columnist is an op ed page for readers of the magazine (As I See It)." Buys 10 mss/year. Send complete ms. Length: 600-750 words. No payment.

PURPOSE, 616 Walnut Ave., Scottdale PA 15683-1999. (412)887-8500. Editor: James E. Horsch. 95% freelance written. Weekly magazine "for adults, young and old, general audience with interests as varied as there are persons. My particular readership is interested in seeing how Christianity works in tough situations." Circ. 18,800. Pays on acceptance. Publishes ms an average of 8 months after acceptance. Byline given, including city, state/province. Buys one-time rights. Submit seasonal material 6 months in advance. Photocopied and simultaneous submissions OK. Computer printout submissions acceptable if legible; prefers letter-quality to dot-matrix. Submit complete ms. Reports in 6 weeks. Sample copy and writer's guidelines for 6x9 SASE.

Nonfiction: Inspirational articles from a Christian perspective. "I want material that goes to the core of human problems in family, business, politics, religion, sex and any other areas—and shows how the Christian faith resolves them. I want material that's upbeat. *Purpose* is a story paper which conveys truth either through quality fiction or through articles that use the best fiction techniques. Our magazine accents Christian discipleship. Christianity affects all of life, and we expect our material to demonstrate this. I would like to see story-type articles on how individuals, groups and organizations are intelligently and effectively working at some of the great human problems such as overpopulation, hunger, poverty, international understanding, peace, justice, etc., motivated by their faith." Buys 175-200 mss/year. Submit complete ms. Length: 1,100 words maximum. Pays 5¢/word maximum.

Photos: Photos purchased with ms. Pays $5-25 for b&w, depending on quality. Must be sharp enough for reproduction; prefers prints in all cases. Can use color prints. Captions desired.

Fiction: Humorous, religious and historical fiction related to theme of magazine. "Produce the story with specificity so that it appears to take place somewhere and with real people. It should not be moralistic."

Poetry: Traditional poetry, blank verse, free verse and light verse. Length: 12 lines maximum. Pays 50¢-$1/line.

Fillers: Jokes, short humor, and items up to 800 words. Pays 4¢/word maximum.

Tips: "We are looking for articles which show that Christianity is working at issues where people hurt, but stories need to be told and presented professionally. Good photographs help place material with us."

‡QUEEN OF ALL HEARTS,Monfort Missionaries, 26 S. Saxon Ave., Bay Shore NY 11706. (516)665-0726. Managing Editor: Roger Charest, S.M.M. 50% freelance written. Bimonthly magazine covering Marian doctrine and devotion. "Subject: Mary, Mother of Jesus, as seen in the sacred scriptures, tradition, history of the church, the early Christian writers, lives of the saints, poetry, art, music, spiritual writers, apparitions, shrines, ecumenism, etc." Circ. approx 6,000. Pays on acceptance. Publishes ms an average of 6 months after acceptance. Byline given. Not copyrighted. Buys second serial (reprint) rights. Submit seasonal/holiday material 6 months in advance. Reports in 6 weeks. Sample copy $2.

Nonfiction: Essays, inspirational, personal experience and religious. Buys 25 ms/year. Send complete ms. Length: 750-2,500 words. Pays $40-60. Sometimes pays writers in contributor copies or other premiums "by mutual agreement. Poetry paid by contributor copies."

Photos: Send photos with submission. Reviews transparencies and prints. Offers variable payment per photo. Buys one-time rights.

Fiction: Religious. Buys 6 mss/year. Send complete ms. Length: 1500-2500 words. Pays $40-60.

Poetry: Poetry Editor: Joseph Tusiani. Free verse. Buys approx 10 poems/year. Submit 2 poems maximum at one time. Pays in contributor copies.

REVIEW FOR RELIGIOUS, 3601 Lindell Blvd., Room 428, St. Louis MO 63108. (314)535-3048. Editor: Daniel F.X. Meenan, S.J. 100% freelance written. "Each ms is judged on its own merits, without reference to author's publishing history." Bimonthly. For Roman Catholic priests, brothers and sisters. Pays on publication. Publishes ms an average of 9 months after acceptance. Byline given. Buys first North American serial rights and rarely second serial (reprint) rights. Computer printout submissions acceptable; no dot-matrix. Reports in 8 weeks.

Nonfiction: Articles on ascetical, liturgical and canonical matters only; not for general audience. Length: 2,000-8,000 words. Pays $6/page.

Tips: "The writer must know about religious life in the Catholic Church and be familiar with prayer, vows and problems related to them."

ST. ANTHONY MESSENGER, 1615 Republic St., Cincinnati OH 45210. Editor-in-Chief: Norman Perry. 55% freelance written. "Eager to work with new/unpublished writers if their writing is of a professional caliber." Monthly magazine, 59 pages for a national readership of Catholic families, most of which have children in grade school, high school or college. Circ. 420,000. Pays on acceptance. Publishes ms an average of 9 months after acceptance. Byline given. Buys first North American serial rights. Submit seasonal/holiday material 6 months in advance. Electronic submissions OK if compatible with CPT word processor, but requires hard copy also. Computer printout submissions acceptable; no dot-matrix. Free sample copy and writer's guidelines.

Nonfiction: How-to (on psychological and spiritual growth, problems of parenting/better parenting, marriage problems/marriage enrichment); humor; informational; inspirational; interview; personal experience (if pertinent to our purpose); personal opinion (limited use; writer must have special qualifications for topic); and profile. Buys 35-50 mss/year. Length: 1,500-3,500 words. Pays 12¢/word. Sometimes pays the expenses of writers on assignment.

Fiction: Mainstream and religious. Buys 12 mss/year. Submit complete ms. Length: 2,000-3,500 words. Pays 12¢/word.

Tips: "The freelancer should ask why his or her proposed article would be appropriate for us, rather than for *Redbook* or *Saturday Review*. We treat human problems of all kinds, but from a religious perspective. Get authoritative information (not merely library research); we want interviews with experts. Write in popular style. We will be enlarging our type size so word length will be an important consideration."

ST. JOSEPH'S MESSENGER & ADVOCATE OF THE BLIND, Sisters of St. Joseph of Peace, St. Joseph's Home, Box 288, Jersey City NJ 07303. Editor-in-Chief: Sister Ursula Maphet. 30% freelance written. Eager to work with new/unpublished writers. Quarterly magazine; 30 pages. Circ. 35,000. Pays on acceptance. Publishes ms an average of 3 months after acceptance. Buys first serial rights and second serial (reprint) rights, but will reassign rights back to author after publication asking only that credit line be included in next publication. Submit seasonal/holiday material 3 months in advance (no Christmas issue). Computer printout submissions OK; prefers letter-quality to dot-matrix. Simultaneous and previously published submissions OK. Reports in 3 weeks. Free sample copy and writer's guidelines.

Nonfiction: Humor, inspirational, nostalgia, personal opinion and personal experience. Buys 24 mss/year. Submit complete ms. Length: 300-1,500 words. Pays $3-15.

Fiction: Romance, suspense, mainstream and religious. Buys 30 mss/year. Submit complete ms. Length: 600-1,600 words. Pays $6-25.

Poetry: Light verse and traditional. Buys 25 poems/year. Submit maximum 10 poems. Length: 50-300 words. Pays $5-20.

Tips: "It's rewarding to know that someone is waiting to see freelancers' efforts rewarded by 'print'. It's annoying, however, to receive poor copy, shallow material or inane submissions. Human interest fiction, touching on current happenings, is what is most needed."

SCP NEWSLETTER, Spiritual Counterfeits Project, Box 4308, Berkeley CA 94704. (415)540-0300. Editor: Robert J. L. Burrows. 5% freelance written. Prefers to work with published/established writers. "The *SCP Newsletter* is a quarterly newsletter that analyzes new religious movements and spiritual trends from a Christian perspective. Its targeted audience is the educated lay person." Circ. 16,500. Pays on publication. Publishes ms an average of 6 months after acceptance. Byline given. Simultaneous and previously published submissions OK. Computer printout submissions acceptable. Sample copy for 9x13 SAE and $1.58.

Nonfiction: Book excerpts, essays, exposé, historical/nostalgic, inspirational, interview/profile, opinion, personal experience and religious. Buys 10 mss/year. Query with published clips. Length: 2,500-3,500 words. Pays $25-200.

Photos: State availability of photos with submission. Reviews contact sheets and prints. Offers no additional payment for photos accepted with ms. Captions, model releases and identification of subjects required. Buys one-time rights.

Tips: "The area of our publication most open to freelancers is reviews of books relevant to subjects covered by *SCP*. These should be brief and not exceed 3 typewritten, double-spaced pages, 750 words. Send samples of work that are relevant to the *SCP Newsletter*'s area of interest."

SEEK, Standard Publishing, 8121 Hamilton Ave., Cincinnati OH 45231. (513)931-4050, ext. 365. Editor: Eileen H. Wilmoth. 98% freelance written. Prefers to work with published/established writers; works with a small number of new/unpublished writers each year. Sunday school paper; 8 pages. Quarterly, in weekly issues for young and middle-aged adults who attend church and Bible classes. Circ. 45,000. Pays on acceptance. Publishes ms an average of 1 year after acceptance. Byline given. Buys first serial rights and second serial (reprint) rights. Buys 100-150 mss/year. Submit seasonal material 1 year in advance. Computer printout submissions acceptable; prefers letter-quality to dot-matrix. Reports in 10-30 days. Sample copy and writer's guidelines for SASE.

Nonfiction: "We look for articles that are warm, inspirational, devotional, of personal or human interest; that deal with controversial matters, timely issues of religious, ethical or moral nature, or first person testimonies, true-to-life happenings, vignettes, emotional situations or problems; communication problems and examples of answered prayers. Article must deliver its point in a convincing manner but not be patronizing or preachy. They must appeal to either men or women, must be alive, vibrant, sparkling and have a title that demands the article be read. We always need stories of families, marriages, problems on campus and life testimonies." No poetry. Buys 100-150 mss/year. Submit complete ms. Length: 400-1,200 words. Pays 3¢/word.

Photos: B&w photos purchased with or without mss. Pays $20 minimum for good 8x10 glossy prints.

Fiction: Religious fiction and religiously slanted historical and humorous fiction. Length: 400-1,200 words. Pays 3¢/word.

Tips: Submit mss which tell of faith in action or victorious Christian living as central theme. "We select manuscripts as far as one year in advance of publication. Complimentary copies are sent to our published writers immediately following printing."

SHARING THE VICTORY, Fellowship of Christian Athletes, 8701 Leeds Rd., Kansas City MO 64129. (816)921-0909. Editor: Skip Stogsdill. Managing Editor: Randy St. Clair. 20% freelance written. Prefers to work with published/established writers; works with a small number of new/unpublished writers each year. A bimonthly magazine. "We seek to encourage and enable athletes and coaches at all levels to take their faith seriously on and off the 'field.' " Circ. 47,000. Pays on publication. Publishes ms an average of 4 months after acceptance. Byline given. Buys first rights. Submit seasonal/holiday material 4 months in advance. Computer printout submissions acceptable; prefers letter-quality to dot-matrix. Reports in 1 week on queries; 2 weeks on manuscripts. Sample copy $1 with 8½x12 SAE and 3 first class stamps; free writer's guidelines.

Nonfiction: Humor, inspirational, interview/profile, personal experience, and photo feature. No "sappy articles on 'I became a Christian and now I'm a winner.' " Buys 6 mss/year. Query. Length: 500-1,000 words. Pays $50-75 for unsolicited articles.

Photos: State availability of photos with submission. Reviews contact sheets. Pay depends on quality of photo. Model releases required. Buys one-time rights.

Columns/Departments: Sports Conscience (deals with a problem issue in athletics today and some possible solutions or alternatives). Buys 4 mss/year. Query. Length: 700-1,500 words. Pays $50-75.

Poetry: Free verse. Buys 3 poems/year. Pays $30.

Tips: "Profiles and interviews of particular interest to coed athletes, primarily high school and college age. We are redesigning/retooling both our graphics and editorial content to appeal to youth. The area most open to freelancers is profiles on or interviews with well-known athletes or coaches (male, female, minorities or of offbeat sports)."

SIGNS OF THE TIMES, Pacific Press Publishing Association, Box 7000, Boise ID 83707. (208)465-2500. Editor: Kenneth J. Holland. Managing Editor: B. Russell Holt. 40% freelance written. Works with a small number of new/unpublished writers each year. Monthly magazine on religion. "We are a Christian publication encouraging the general public to put into practice the principles of the Bible." Circ. 400,000. Pays on acceptance. Publishes ms an average of 5 months after acceptance. Byline given. Offers $100 kill fee. Buys first North American serial rights and simultaneous rights. Submit seasonal/holiday material 8 months in advance. Simultaneous queries and submissions, and photocopied and previously published submissions OK. Computer printout submissions acceptable; prefers letter-quality to dot-matrix. Reports in 2 weeks on queries; 1 month on mss. Free sample copy and writer's guidelines.

Nonfiction: General interest (home, marriage, health—interpret current events from a Biblical perceptive); how-to (overcome depression, find one's identity, answer loneliness and guilt, face death triumphantly); humor; inspirational (human interest pieces that highlight a Biblical principle); interview/profile; personal experience (overcome problems with God's help); and photo feature. "We want writers with a desire to share the good news of reconciliation with God. Articles should be people-oriented, well-researched and should have a sharp focus and include anecdotes." Buys 150 mss/year. Query with or without published clips, or send complete ms. Length: 500-3,000 words. Pays $100-400. Sometimes pays the expenses of writers on assignment.

Photos: Ed Guthero, photo editor. Send photos with query or ms. Reviews b&w contact sheets; 35mm color transparencies; 5x7 or 8x10 b&w prints. Pays $35-300 for transparencies; $20-50 for prints. Model releases and identification of subjects required (captions helpful). Buys one-time rights.

Tips: "One of the most frequent mistakes made by writers in completing an article assignment for us is trying to cover too much ground. Articles need focus, research, and anecdotes. We don't want essays."

‡SINGLE IMPACT, A Publication Challenging All Singles to Serve Christ, (formerly *Servant*), 7245 College St., Lima NY 14485. (716)582-2790. Editor-in-Chief: Michael P. Cavanaugh. Managing Editor: Susan McCarthy. A quarterly magazine for Christian singles. "We believe in accordance with 1 Corinthians 7:35, that a Christian's singleness is a time to serve God with undistracted devotion. This magazine encourages singles to embrace that vision and launch out into service for God." Circ. 18,000. Pays on publication. Byline given. Not copyrighted. Buys first rights and makes work-for-hire assignments. Submit seasonal/holiday material 6 months in advance. Simultaneous, photocopied and previously published submissions OK. Query for electronic submissions. Computer printout submissions OK. Reports in 2 weeks on queries; 1 month on mss. Free sample copy and writer's guidelines.

Nonfiction: Book excerpt, essays, how-to (on practical Christian teaching, Bibically based); inspirational; interview/profile (of outstanding Christian leaders/singles); personal experience (testimony of how God moved in an area commonly faced by single adults) and religious. No material without Biblical emphasis accepted. Buys 8 mss/year. Query. Length: 250-1,500 words. Pays $12.50-75.

Photos: Send photos with submission. Reviews prints. Pays cost of developing and materials. Identification of subjects required. Buys one-time rights.

Columns/Departments: Single to Single (first person article on how God helped a single person cope—should teach others to do the same). Buys 4 mss/year. Send complete ms. Length: 750-1,500 words. Pays $37-75.

Tips: "Have a potential-oriented attitude toward singleness—and always stress a Christian emphasis. The best section for writers to use to break in to our publication would be our 'Single to Single' column. These are first-person articles about how one single can cope with an issue related to singleness—loneliness, lack of purpose, divorce; can also be written in 'as told to' form."

SISTERS TODAY, The Liturgical Press, St. John's Abbey, Collegeville MN 56321. Editor-in-Chief: Sister Mary Anthony Wagner, O.S.B. Associate Editor: Sister Andre Marthaler, O.S.B. Managing Editor: Sister Dolores Schuh, C.H.M. 80% freelance written. Prefers to work with published/established writers; works with a small number of new/unpublished writers each year. Magazine, published 10 times/year, for religious women of the Roman Catholic Church, primarily. Circ. 9,000. Pays on publication. Publishes ms 1-2 years after acceptance. Byline given. Buys first rights. Submit seasonal/holiday material 4 months in advance. Computer printout submissions acceptable; no dot-matrix. Reports in 3 months. Sample copy $1.50.

Nonfiction: How-to (pray, live in a religious community, exercise faith, hope, charity etc.); informational; and inspirational. Also articles concerning religious renewal, community life, worship, and the role of Sisters in the Church and in the world today. Buys 50-60 unsolicited mss/year. Query. Length: 500-2,500 words. Pays $5/printed page.

Poetry: Free verse, haiku, light verse and traditional. Buys 3 poems/issue. Submit maximum 4 poems. Pays $10.

Tips: "Some of the freelance material evidences the lack of familiarity with *Sisters Today*. We would prefer submitted articles not to exceed eight or nine pages."

SOCIAL JUSTICE REVIEW, 3835 Westminister Place, St. Louis MO 63108. (314)371-1653. Contact: editor. 25% freelance written. Works with a small number of new/unpublished writers each year. Bimonthly.

Publishes ms an average of 3 months after acceptance. Not copyrighted; "however special articles within the magazine may be copyrighted, or an occasional special issue has been copyrighted due to author's request." Buys first serial rights. Computer printout submissions acceptable; prefers letter-quality to dot-matrix.

Nonfiction: Wants scholarly articles on society's economic, religious, social, intellectual and political problems with the aim of bringing Catholic social thinking to bear upon these problems. Query. Length: 2,500-3,500 words. Pays about 2¢/word.

SOLOING, for Christian Singles, Box 15523, West Palm Beach FL 33416. (305)967-7739. Editor: Dennis Lombard. 50-75% freelance written. Eager to work with new/unpublished writers. A monthly tabloid distributed free to singles in churches and the public, geared to all denominations. Circ. 7,000. Pays on publication. Publishes ms an average of 2 months after acceptance. Byline given. Buys first North American serial rights, one-time rights, second serial (reprint) rights, or simultaneous rights, and makes work-for-hire assignments (locally). Submit seasonal/holiday material 2 months in advance. Simultaneous, photocopied, or previously published submissions OK. Computer printout submissions acceptable; prefers letter-quality to dot-matrix. Reports in 1 week. Sample copy $1 with 9x12 SAE; writer's guidelines for #10 SAE with 1 first class stamp.

Nonfiction: Books excerpts and reviews; essays; general interest (Christian subjects); how-to (adjust to singleness); humor; inspirational; interview/profile; opinion; personal experience; photo feature; and religious. "All require inter-denominational, non-doctrinal viewpoint." No critical attitudes. Buys 36 mss/year. Send complete ms. Length: 500-1,500 words. Pays $25-75 for assigned articles; pays $15-35 for unsolicited articles. Sometimes pays expenses of writers on assignment.

Photos: Send photos with submission. Reviews contact sheets and 4x5 b&w glossy prints. Offers $3-5/photo. Captions, model releases, and identification of subjects required. Buys one-time rights.

Fiction: "Have never bought—but will consider" humorous, religious, romance. Must have Christian perspective, but should not be preachy. Send complete ms. Length: 500-1,500 words.

Columns/Departments: Looking for regular singles column—light/humorous. Query with or without published clips, or send complete ms.

Poetry: Light verse and traditional. Buys 15-20 poems/year. Submit maximum 3 poems. Length: 4-60 lines. Pays $5-15. Nothing too abstract or overly sentimental.

Tips: "We will be buying much more as our newspaper expands. We also hope to launch two new papers in 1988. Writer for guidelines. We would like to receive testimonies, how-to for Christian singles, essays, and humor in the single life. New writers are welcome. How-to and personal experience articles are most open to freelancers. Testimonial articles should include an informal b&w photo of subject and subject's signed release. We're looking for the light and inspirational side. Also publish *Good News* and *Neighbor News*. Send for guidelines."

SPIRITUAL LIFE, 2131 Lincoln Rd. NE, Washington DC 20002. (202)832-6622. Co-Editors: Rev. Christopher Latimer, O.C.D. and Rev. Stephen Payne, O.C.D. 80% freelance written. Prefers to work with published/established writers; works with a small number of new/unpublished writers each year. Quarterly. "Largely Catholic, well-educated, serious readers. A few are nonCatholic or nonChristian." Circ. 17,000. Pays on acceptance. Publishes ms an average of 1 year after acceptance. Buys first North American serial rights. "Brief autobiographical information (present occupation, past occupations, books and articles published, etc.) should accompany article." Computer printout submissions OK; prefers letter-quality to dot-matrix. Reports in 2 weeks. Free sample copy and writer's guidelines.

Nonfiction: Serious articles of contemporary spirituality. High quality articles about our encounter with God in the present day world. Language of articles should be college level. Technical terminology, if used, should be clearly explained. Material should be presented in a positive manner. Sentimental articles or those dealing with specific devotional practices not accepted. Buys inspirational and think pieces. No fiction or poetry. Buys 20 mss/year. Length: 3,000-5,000 words. Pays $50 minimum. "Five contributor's copies are sent to author on publication of article." Book reviews should be sent to Rev. Steven Payne, O.C.D.

SPIRITUALITY TODAY, 7200 West Division, River Forest IL 60305. Editor: Rev. Richard Woods, O.P. 25% freelance written. Works with a small number of new/unpublished writers each year. Magazine "for those interested in a more integral and fuller Christian life in the contemporary world." Pays on publication. Publishes ms an average of 14 months after acceptance. Byline given. Buys all rights but reassigned on request without fee. Computer printout submissions acceptable. Sample copy $1; free writer's guidelines.

Nonfiction: Articles that seriously examine important issues concerning the spiritual life, or Christian life, in the context of today's world. Scriptural, biographical, doctrinal, liturgical and ecumenical articles are acceptable. No poetry. Generally Catholic readership, but ecumenically open. Buys 15 unsolicited mss/year. Submit complete ms. Length: 4,000 words. Pays 1¢/word.

Tips: "Examine the journal. It is not a typical devotional or inspirational magazine. Given its characteristics, the style of writing required is deeper and richer than regular freelance writers usually employ."

STANDARD, Nazarene International Headquarters, 6401 The Paseo, Kansas City MO 64131. (816)333-7000, ext. 460. Editor: Sheila Boggess. 95% freelance written. Works with a small number of new/unpublished writers each year. Weekly inspirational "story paper" with Christian leisure reading for adults. Circ. 177,000. Pays on acceptance. Publishes ms an average of 15 months after acceptance. Byline given. Buys one-time rights and second serial (reprint) rights. Submit seasonal/holiday material 9 months in advance. Computer printout submissions acceptable; prefers letter-quality to dot-matrix. Reports in 2 weeks on queries; 6 weeks on mss. Free sample copy; writer's guidelines for SAE with 2 first class stamps.
Nonfiction: How-to (grow spiritually); inspirational; and personal experience (with an emphasis on spiritual growth). Buys 100 mss/year. Send complete ms. Length: 300-1,500 words. Pays 3½¢/word for first rights; 2¢/word for reprint rights.
Photos: Send photos with ms. Pays $15-45 for 8x10 b&w prints. Buys one-time rights.
Fiction: Adventure, religious, romance and suspense—all with a spiritual emphasis. Buys 100 mss/year. Send complete ms. Length: 500-1,500 words. Pays 3½¢/word for first rights; 2¢/word for reprint rights.
Poetry: Free verse, haiku, light verse and traditional. No "lengthy" poetry. Buys 50 poems/year. Submit maximum 5 poems. Length: 50 lines maximum. Pays 25¢/line.
Fillers: Jokes, anecdotes and short humor. Buys 52/year. Length: 300 words maximum. Pays same as nonfiction and fiction.
Tips: "Articles should express Biblical principles without being preachy. Setting, plot and characterization must be realistic. Looking for articles on social issues: How does the church need to respond? How does it? How should Christian parents respond to a homosexual child, or one who becomes pregnant?"

SUNDAY DIGEST, David J. Cook Publishing Co., 850 N. Grove Ave., Elgin IL 60120. Editor: Janette L. Pearson. 75% freelance written. Prefers to work with published/established writers; works with a small number of new/unpublished writers each year. Issued weekly for Christian adults, mainly Protestants. "*Sunday Digest* provides a combination of original articles and reprints, selected to help adult readers better understand the Christian faith, to keep them informed of issues within the Christian community, and to challenge them to a deeper personal commitment to Christ." Pays on acceptance. Publishes ms an average of 9-12 months after acceptance. Buys first serial rights or reprint rights. Computer printout submissions acceptable; no dot-matrix. Reports in 6-8 weeks. Sample copy and writer's guidelines for 6½x9½ SASE (2 first-class stamps.)
Nonfiction: Needs articles applying the Christian faith to personal and social problems, articles of family interest and on church subjects, inspirational self-help, personal experience and anecdotes. Submit complete ms. Length: 500-1,500 words. Pays 10¢/word.
Fiction: Uses true-to-life fiction that is hard-hitting and fast-moving. Christian message should be woven in not tacked on. Pays 10¢/word.
Tips: "It is crucial that the writer is committed to high quality Christian communication. The writer should express an evangelical outlook in a crisp, clear writing style."

SUNDAY SCHOOL COUNSELOR, General Council of the Assemblies of God, 1445 Boonville, Springfield MO 65802. (417)862-2781. Editor: Sylvia Lee. 60% freelance written. Works with small number of new/unpublished writers each year. Monthly magazine on religious education in the local church—the official Sunday school voice of the Assemblies of God channeling programs and help to local, primarily lay, leadership. Circ. 35,000. Pays on acceptance. Publishes ms an average of 9 months after acceptance. Byline given. Offers variable kill fee. Buys first North American serial rights, one-time rights, all rights, simultaneous rights, first serial rights, or second serial (reprint) rights; makes work-for-hire assignments. Submit seasonal/holiday material 7 months in advance. Simultaneous and previously published submissions OK. Computer printout submissions acceptable; prefers letter-quality to dot-matrix. Reports in 2 weeks on queries; 1 month on mss. Sample copy $1; free writer's guidelines.
Nonfiction: How-to, inspirational, interview/profile, personal experience and photo feature. All related to religious education in the local church. Buys 100 mss/year. Send complete ms. Length: 300-1,800 words. Pays $25-90. Sometimes pays expenses of writers on assignment.
Photos: Send photos with ms. Reviews b&w and color prints. Model releases and identification of subjects required. Buys one-time rights.

‡TEACHERS INTERACTION, A Magazine Church School Workers Grow By, Concordia Publishing House, 3558 S. Jefferson, St. Louis MO 63118. Mail submissions to LCMS, 1333 S. Kirkwood Rd., St. Louis MO 63122-7295. Editor: Martha Streufert Jander. 20% freelance written. Quarterly magazine (seven times/year) of practical, inspirational, theological articles for volunteer church school teachers. Material must be true to the doctrines of the Lutheran Church—Missouri Synod. Circ. 17,000. Pays on acceptance. Publishes ms an average of 1 year after acceptance. Byline given. Buys all rights. Submit seasonal/holiday material 7 months in advance. Query for electronic submissions. Computer printout submissions acceptable; prefers letter-quality to dot-matrix. Reports in 1 month on queries; 2 months on mss. Sample copy 90¢; writer's guidelines for 9x12 SAE (with sample copy); for 4½x9½ SAE (without sample copy).
Nonfiction: How-to (practical helps/ideas used successfully in own classroom); inspirational (to the church

school worker—must be in accordance with LCMS doctrine); and personal experience (of a Sunday school classroom nature—growth). No theological articles. Buys 6 mss/year. Send complete ms. Length: 750-1,500 words. Pays $35.

Fillers: Cartoons. Buys 14/year. "*Teachers Interaction* buys short items—activities and ideas planned and used successfully in a church school classroom." Buys 50/year. Length: 200 words maximum. Pays $10.

Tips: "Practical, or 'it happened to me' experiences articles would have the best chance. Also short items— ideas used in classrooms; seasonal and in conjunction with our Sunday school material; New Life in Christ. Our format is changing to include all volunteer church school teachers, not just Sunday school teachers."

THIS PEOPLE MAGAZINE, Reflecting the LDS Lifestyle, This People Publishing, a division of StratAmerica, Suite 500, 5 Triad Center, Salt Lake City UT 84180. (801)575-6900. Editor: Sheri Dew. 75% freelance written. A lifestyle magazine published 8 times annually, geared to members of The Church of Jesus Christ of Latter-day Saints (Mormons). "*This People* is a human interest, consumer publication that profiles the LDS lifestyle and its people. Its tone would be described as upbeat and conservative." Circ. 42,000. Pays on publication. Byline given. Buys first North American serial rights. Submit seasonal/holiday material 6 months in advance. Photocopied submissions OK. Electronic submissions OK. Computer printout submissions acceptable; prefers letter-quality to dot-matrix. Reports in 3 months on queries; 2 months on manuscripts. Sample copy for 9x12 SAE with $1.09 postage; free writer's guidelines.

Nonfiction: Book excerpts, essays, historical/nostalgic, inspirational, interview/profile, personal experience, photo feature and religious. No poetry or travel. Limited fiction. Buys 95 mss/year. Query with published clips. Length: 750-3,500 words. Pays $175-650 for assigned articles; pays $150-300 for unsolicited articles. Sometimes pays the expenses of writers on assignment.

Photos: State availability of photos with submission. Reviews contact sheets, transparencies and prints. Captions and identification of subjects required. Buys all rights.

Fillers: Anecdotes, facts and short humor. Length: 100-350 words. Pays $50-100.

Tips: "Because our magazine is profile-oriented, freelancers will find the most success by becoming familiar with *This People*'s content, then making profile suggestions to the editor. It is imperative that the writer be very familiar with the material *This People* has published in the past."

‡TODAY'S PARISH, Twenty-Third Publications, 185 Willow St., Box 180, Mystic CT 06355. (203)536-2611. Editor: Mary Carol Kendzia. 95% freelance written. A magazine published 7 times/year covering Parish ministry. "Articles must deal with some aspect of parish life." Circ. 16,000. Pays on publication. Publishes ms an average of 6 months after acceptance. Byline given. Buys first rights. Submit seasonal/holiday material 6 months in advance. Photocopied submissions OK. Computer printout submissions OK. Reports in weeks. Free sample copy and writer's guidelines.

Nonfiction: Humor, inspirational, opinion, personal experience and photo feature all related to religion. Buys 45 mss/year. Query with published clips, or send complete ms. Length: 800-1,800 words. Pays $100-150 for assigned articles; pays $60-100 for unsolicited articles. May pay with contributor copies or other premiums at author's request.

Photos: State availability of photos with submission. Reviews contact sheets, negatives, transparencies and prints. Offers no additional payment for photos accepted with ms. Identification of subjects required. Buys one-time rights.

Columns/Departments: Contract author to write 6 columns per year on particular area of interest to our readers. Query. Length: 800-1,200 words. Pays $75-100.

THE UNITED BRETHREN, United Brethren in Christ Church, 302 Lake St., Huntington IN 46750. (219)356-2312. Editor: Steve Dennie. 10% freelance written. A monthly magazine for the United Brethren denomination, having a conservative evangelical slant. Circ. 5,000. Pays on acceptance. Publishes ms an average of 5 months after acceptance. Byline given. Buys one-time rights or second serial (reprint) rights. Submit seasonal/ holiday material 5 months in advance. Photocopied and previously published submissions OK. Computer printout submissions acceptable; prefers letter-quality to dot-matrix. Reports in 8 weeks. Sample copy $2; writer's guidelines for #10 SAE with 1 first class stamp.

Nonfiction: Humor, inspirational, personal experience and religious. Buys 25 mss/year. Send complete ms. Length: 500-2,200 words. Pays $10-45.

Photos: State availability of photos with submissions. Offers $10-15/photo. Identification of subjects required. Buys one-time rights.

Fiction: Humorous and religious. Buys 5 mss/year. Length: 500-2,000 words. Pays $10-45.

Tips: "We like lively, humorous articles which keep the reader interested, yet make a spiritual point. It's helpful if you include a brief note with a few sentences about yourself, especially if it's a first-time submissions. Short articles in the 500-1,200 word range have the best chance. Also, we need well-researched articles on Christian subjects."

UNITED EVANGELICAL ACTION, Box 28, Wheaton IL 60189. (312)665-0500. Editor: Donald R. Brown. Managing Editor: Kevin Piecuch. 50% freelance written. Prefers to work with published/established writers.

Bimonthly magazine; alternating 16-20 pages. Offers "an objective evangelical viewpoint and interpretive analysis of specific issues of consequence and concern to the American Church and updates readers on ways evangelicals are confronting those issues at the grass-roots level." Circ. 10,500. Pays on publication. Publishes ms an average of 2 months after acceptance. Buys first serial rights. Phone queries OK. Query for electronic submission. Computer printout submissions acceptable; prefers letter-quality to dot-matrix. Reports in 1 month. Sample copy and writer's guidelines with SASE.

Nonfiction: Issues and trends in the Church and society that affect the ongoing witness and outreach of evangelical Christians. Content should be well thought through, and should provide practical suggestions for dealing with these issues and trends. Buys 8-10 mss/year. "Always send a query letter before sending an unsolicited manuscript." Length: 900-1,000 words. Pays $50-175. Sometimes pays expenses of writers on assignment.

Tips: Editors would really like to see news (action) items that relate to the National Association of Evangelicals. "We are interested in expanding coverage of NAE activities throughout the country. Send query letter about important topics facing evangelicals or news features about local works by evangelicals. Keep writing terse, to the point, and stress practical over theoretical."

UNITED METHODIST REPORTER, Box 660275, Dallas TX 75266-0275. (214)630-6495. Editor/General Manager: Spurgeon M. Dunnam, III. Managing Editor: John A. Lovelace. Weekly newspaper for a United Methodist national readership. Circ. 475,000. Pays on publication. Byline given. Not copyrighted. Free sample copy and writer's guidelines.

Nonfiction: "We accept occasional short features, approximately 500 words. Articles need not be limited to a United Methodist angle but need to have an explicit Protestant angle, preferably with evidence of participation in a local congregation. Write about a distinctly Christian response to human need or how a person's faith relates to a given situation." Send complete ms. Pays 4¢/word.

Photos: Purchased with accompanying ms. "We encourage the submission of good action photos (5x7 or 8x10 b&w glossy prints) of the persons or situations in the article." Pays $10.

Tips: "Read our publications before submitting. First person stories seldom fit our needs, but opinion pieces of no more than 500 words will be considered without pay for My Witness and Here I Stand."

UNITY MAGAZINE, Unity School of Christianity, Unity Village MO 64065. Editor: Pamela Yearsley. 90% freelance written. A monthly magazine covering metaphysics, spirituality and Christian literature. Circ. 500,000. Pays on acceptance. Publishes ms an average of 7 months after acceptance. Byline given. Buys first North American serial rights. Submit seasonal material 6 months in advance. Photocopied submissions OK. Computer printout submissions acceptable; prefers letter-quality to dot-matrix. Reports in 3 weeks on queries; 2 months on manuscripts. Free sample copy and writer's guidelines.

Nonfiction: Inspirational and metaphysical. Buys 200 mss/year. Submit complete ms. Length: 2,000 maximum words. Pays $10.

Photo: State availability of photos with submission. Reviews 4x5 transparencies. Model releases and identification of subjects required. Buys one-time rights.

Poetry: Any type as long as subject fits the magazine. Buys 120 poems/ year. Submit maximum 10 poems. Length: 30 lines maximum. Pays 50¢/line.

Fillers: Buys 12/year.

THE UPPER ROOM, DAILY DEVOTIONAL GUIDE, The Upper Room, 1908 Grand Ave., Nashville TN 37202. (615)327-2700. World Editor: Janice T. Grana. Managing Editor: Mary Lou Redding. 95% freelance written. Eager to work with new/unpublished writers. Bimonthly magazine "offering a daily inspirational message which includes a Bible reading, text, prayer, 'Thought for the Day,' and suggestion for prayer. Each day's meditation is written by a different person and is usually a personal witness about discovering meaning and power for Christian living through some experience from daily life." Circ. 2,225,000 (U.S.); 385,000 outside U.S. Pays on publication. Publishes ms an average of 1 year after acceptance. Byline given. Buys first North American serial rights and translation rights. Submit seasonal/holiday material 14 months in advance. Computer printout submissions acceptable; prefers letter-quality to dot-matrix. Reports in 6 weeks on mss. Sample copy and writer's guidelines for SAE and 2 first class stamps.

Nonfiction: Inspirational and personal experience. No poetry, lengthy "spiritual journey" stories. Buys 360 unsolicited mss/year. Send complete ms. Length: 250 words maximum. Pays $12.

Tips: "The best way to break into our magazine is to send a well-written manuscript that looks at the Christian faith in a fresh way. Standard stories and sermon illustrations are immediately rejected. We very much want to find new writers and welcome good material. We are particularly interested in meditations based on Old Testament characters and stories. Good repeat meditations can lead to work on longer assignments for our other publications, which pay more. A writer who can deal concretely with everyday situations, relate them to spiritual truths, and write clear, direct prose should be able to write for *The Upper Room*. We want material that provides for more interaction on the part of the reader—meditation suggestions, journaling suggestions, space to reflect and link personal experience with the meditation for the day."

VIRTUE, The Christian Magazine for Women, 548 Sisters Pkwy, Box 850, Sisters OR 97759. (503)549-8261. Editor: Becky Durost Fish. Managing Editor: Ruth Nygren Keller. 75% freelance written. Works with small number of new/unpublished writers each year. A magazine, published 8 times/year, that "encourages women in their development as individuals and provides practical help for them as they minister to their families, churches and communities." Circ. 110,000. Pays on acceptance. Publishes ms an average of 4 months after acceptance. Byline given. Buys first North American serial rights. Submit seasonal/holiday material 9 months in advance. Photocopied submissions OK. Computer printout submissions OK; prefers letter-quality. Reports in 6 weeks on queries; 2 months on mss. Sample copy $3; writer's guidelines for #10 SAE with 1 first class stamp.
Nonfiction: Book excerpts, how-to, humor, inspirational, interview/profile, opinion, personal experience and religious. Buys 70 mss/year. Query. Length: 600-1,800 words. Pays 10¢/word. Sometimes pays the expenses of writers on assignment.
Photos: State availability of photos with submission.
Columns/Departments: In My Opinion (reader editorial); One Woman's Journal (personal experience); Equipped for Ministry (practical how-to for helping others). Buys 25 mss/year. Query. Length: 1,000-1,500. Pays 10¢/word.
Fiction: Fantasy, humorous and religious. Buys 7-10 mss/year. Send complete ms. Length: 1,500-1,800 words. Pays 10¢/word.
Poetry: Free verse, haiku and traditional. Buys 7-10 poems/year. Submit maximum 3 poems. Length: 3-30 lines. Pays $15-50.

VISION LIFESTYLES, A Magazine for Young Adults, (formerly *Aim*), Young Adult Ministries, Box 7259, 1333 Alger SE, Grand Rapids MI 49510. (616)241-5616. Editor: Dale Dielman. 75% freelance written. Prefers to work with published/established writers. A bimonthly magazine that offers articles of general interest to young adults, 18-30 + . Circ. 5,000. Pays on publication. Byline given. Buys one-time or second serial (reprint) rights. Submit seasonal/holiday material 6 months in advance. Photocopied submissions OK. Computer printout submissions acceptable. Reports in 1 month. Sample copy for $1 and SAE with 56¢ postage; writer's guidelines for SASE.
Nonfiction: Human interest articles—with a focus on a person(s) or issue of general interest to young adults. Interview/profile, personal experience, inspirational and humor. Buys 12 mss/year. Query or send complete ms. Length: 700-1,500 words. Pays $40-100 for assigned articles; pays $25-50 for unsolicited articles.
Photos: Offers $25/photo. Model releases and identification of subjects required. Buys one-time rights.
Columns/Departments: Lifestyles (an inspirational/informational column on living a positive Christian life—whether never married, previously married, or a single parent); Budget Briefs (a column addressing financial questions/issues like stock market house buying, retirement, consumer awareness); Work World (a column for the working young adult on issues the young adult faces as a Christian professional); Sports and Leisure (an informational column on leisure-time activities, hobbies); and Creative Christianity (how-to examples of service opportunities for young adults, short-term or long-term, individual or group opportunities). Buys 24 mss/year. Query or send complete ms. Length: 600-700 words. Pays $25-35.
Fiction: Contemporary, slice-of-life vignettes with spiritual/religious slant. Buys 3 mss/year. Query or send complete ms. Length: 700-1,400 words. Pays $25-50.
Poetry: Avant-garde, free verse, haiku, light verse and traditional. Buys 3 poems/year. Submit maximum 3 poems. Pays $15-45.

VISTA, Wesleyan Publishing House, Box 50434, Indianapolis IN 46250-0434. Editor: Patsy Whittenberg. 50% freelance written. Eager to work with new/unpublished writers. Weekly publication of The Wesleyan Church for adults. Circ. 60,000. Pays on acceptance. Publishes ms an average of 10 months after acceptance. Byline given. Not copyrighted. Buys first rights, simultaneous rights, second rights, and reprint rights. Submit seasonal/holiday material 10 months in advance. Computer printout submissions acceptable; prefers letter-quality to dot-matrix. Reports in 1 month.
Nonfiction: Testimonies, how-to's, humor, interviews, opinion pieces from conservative Christian perspective. Length: 500-1,200 words.
Photos: Pays $15-40 for 5x7 or 8x10 b&w glossy print natural looking close-ups of faces in various emotions, groups of people interacting. Various reader age groups should be considered.
Fiction: Believable, quality articles, no Sunday "soaps." Length: 500-1,200 words. Pays 2-4¢/word
Tips: "Short opinion articles (500-700 words) on current religious issues have best chance for publication. Send SASE for current writer's guide. Read it carefully before submitting manuscripts or photos."

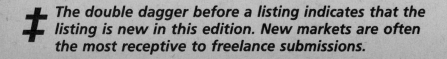

The double dagger before a listing indicates that the listing is new in this edition. New markets are often the most receptive to freelance submissions.

VITAL CHRISTIANITY, Warner Press, Inc., 1200 E. 5th St., Anderson IN 46018. (317)644-7721. Editor-in-Chief: Arlo F. Newell. Managing Editor: Richard L. Willowby. 20-25% freelance written. Prefers to work with published/established writers; works with small number of new/unpublished writers each year. "Always glad to work with talented people—previously published or not." Magazine covering Christian living for people attending local Church of God congregations; published 20 times/year. Circ. 30,000. Pays on acceptance. Byline given. Offers 100% kill fee. Buys one-time rights. Submit seasonal/holiday material 6 months in advance. Query for electronic submissions. Computer printout submissions OK; no dot-matrix. Reports in 6 weeks. Sample copy and writer's guidelines with SASE and $1.
Nonfiction: Humor (with religious point); inspirational (religious—not preachy); interview/profile (of church-related personalities); opinion (religious/theological); and personal experience (related to putting one's faith into practice). Buys 125 mss/year. Query. Length: 1,200 words maximum. Pays $10-100; more for some assigned articles. Sometimes pays the expenses of writers on assignment.
Photos: State availability of photos. Pays $50-300 for 5x7 color transparencies; $20-40 for 8x10 b&w prints. Identification of subjects (when related directly to articles) required. Buys one-time rights. Reserves the right to reprint material it has used for advertising and editorial purposes (pays second rights for editorial re-use).
Tips: "Fillers, personal experience, personality interviews, profiles and good holiday articles are areas of our magazine open to freelancers. All submissions are reviewed. Writers should request our guidelines and list of upcoming topics of interest to determine if they have interest or expertise in writing for us. We will be looking for realistic material to help Christian exercise their political opportunities responsibly."

WAR CRY, The Official Organ of the Salvation Army, 799 Bloomfield Ave., Verona NJ 07044. Editor: Henry Gariepy. 20% freelance written. Prefers to work with published/established writers. Biweekly magazine for "persons with evangelical Christian background; members and friends of the Salvation Army; the 'man in the street.' " Circ. 300,000. Pays on acceptance. Publishes ms an average of 8 months after acceptance. Buys first serial rights and second serial (reprint) rights. Computer printout submissions OK; no dot-matrix. Reports in 2 months. Free sample copy and guidelines.
Nonfiction: Inspirational and informational articles with a strong evangelical Christian slant, but not preachy. In addition to general articles, needs articles slanted toward most of the holidays including Easter, Christmas, Mother's Day, Father's Day, etc. Buys 25 mss/year. Length: approximately 700-1,400 words. Pays 5¢/word.
Photos: Pays $25-35 for b&w glossy prints; $150 for color prints.
Poetry: Religious or nature poems. Length: 8-24 lines. Pays $10-25.

THE WESLEYAN ADVOCATE, The Wesleyan Publishing House, Box 50434, Indianapolis IN 46250-0434. (317)842-0444. Editor: Dr. Wayne E. Caldwell. 10% freelance written. A biweekly magazine by the Wesleyan Church. Circ. 20,000. Pays on publication. Publishes ms an average of 1 year after acceptance. Byline given. Buys first rights or simultaneous rights. Submit seasonal/holiday material 12 months in advance. Simultaneous submissions OK. Query for electronic submissions. Computer printout submission OK; prefers letter-quality to dot-matrix. Reports in 2 weeks. Sample copy for 9x12 SAE with 39¢ postage; writer's guidelines for #10 SAE with 1 first class stamp.
Nonfiction: Humor, inspirational and religious. Buys 5 mss/year. Send complete ms. Length: 250-650 words. Pays $10-40 for assigned articles; $5-25 for unsolicited articles.
Photos: Send photos with submission. Review color transparencies. Buys one-time rights.
Tips: "Write for a guide."

‡WOMAN'S TOUCH, Assemblies of God Women's Ministries Department (GPH), 1445 Boonville, Springfield MO 65802. (417)862-2781. Editor: Sandra Goodwin Clopine. Associate Editor: Nelda E. Ammons. 75-90% freelance written. Eager to work with new/unpublished writers. A bimonthly inspirational magazine for women. "Articles and contents of the magazine should be compatible with Christian teachings as well as human interests. The audience is women, both homemakers and those who are career-oriented." Circ. 21,000. Pays on acceptance. Publishes ms an average of 10-18 months after acceptance. Byline given. Buys one-time rights. Submit seasonal/holiday material 8 months in advance. Photocopied and previously published submissions OK. Computer printout submissions OK; prefers letter-quality to dot-matrix. Reports in 1 week on queries; 1 month on mss. Sample copy and writer's guidelines for SASE.
Nonfiction: General interest, how-to, inspirational, personal experience, religious and travel. Buys 100 mss/year. Send complete ms. Length: 800-1,000 words. Pays $10-35 for unsolicited articles.
Photos: State availability of photos with submission. Reviews negatives, transparencies and 4x6 prints. Offers no additional payment for photos accepted with ms. Identification of subjects required. Buys one-time rights.
Columns/Departments: An Added Touch (special crafts, holiday decorations, family activities); A Personal Touch (articles relating to personal development such as fashion accents, skin care, exercises, etc.). "We've added 'A Lite Touch' for short human interest articles—home and family or career-oriented." Buys 15 mss/year. Query with published clips. Length: 500-1,000 words. Pays $20-35.
Poetry: Free verse, light verse and traditional. Buys 20 poems/year. Submit maximum 6-8 poems. Length: 4-

50 lines. Pays $5-20.

Fillers: Facts. Buys 10/year. Length: 50-200. Pays $5-15.

‡**THE WORD IN SEASON, Daily Devotions**, The Board of Publication, LCA/Fortress Press, 2900 Queen Lane, Philadelphia PA 19129. (215)848-6800. Editor: M. Elaine Dunham. 100% freelance written. Works with a small number of new/unpublished writers each year. A quarterly booklet of daily devotions based on Lutheran lectionary. "Audience is ecumenical, but primarily Lutheran. Inclusive language should be used, whenever referring to human beings or to God. Personal stories or reflections preferred." Circ. 165,000. Pays on acceptance. Publishes ms an average of 6 months after acceptance. Byline given. Buys all rights. Computer printout submissions OK, "only when printed on ms forms supplied." Reports in 1 month on queries. Sample copy for 6x9 SAE with 90¢ postage; free writer's guidelines.

Nonfiction: Humor, inspiration, personal experience and religious. "No preachy tracts and no ideological pronouncements." Buys 20 mss/year. Query with published clips. Length: 120-150 words. Pays $7 for each assigned article.

Tips: "All writing is done on assignment. Review guidelines and sample copies carefully; then submit writing samples. Some prospective writers select a few Bible passages from an old issue and try to create appropriate devotions, which the writers then submit as writing samples. We're looking for sensitive storytellers who can write jargon-free devotions which closely reflect the central message of assigned Bible passages."

Retirement

Retirement magazines have changed to meet the active lifestyles of their readers and dislike the kinds of stereotypes people have of retirement magazines. More people are retiring in their 50s, while others are starting a business or traveling and pursuing hobbies. These publications give readers specialized information on aging, finances and other topics of interest, as well as general articles on travel destinations and recreational activities.

‡**ALBUQUERQUE SENIOR SCENE MAGAZINE**,8421-H Osuna NE, Albuquerque NM 87111. (505)299-4401. Editor: Gail Skinner. 90% freelance written. Eager to work with new/unpublished writers. Quarterly (Spring/Summer/Fall/Winter) 4-color magazine addressing today's modern 50+ adult. Pays on publication. Publishes ms an average of 6 months after acceptance. Byline given. Buys first serial rights, second serial (reprint) rights, or all rights. Submit seasonal/holiday material 6 months in advance. Query for electronic submissions. Computer printout submissions OK; prefers letter-quality to dot-matrix. Reports in 3 months. Sample copy $1 with SAE and 4 first class stamps. Writer's guidelines for SAE and 1 first class stamp.

Nonfiction: General interest, how-to, humor, inspirational, opinion, personal experience, hobbies, health, finance, real estate, travel, retirement, consumer guide, astrology and grandparenting. Buys 50 mss/year. Send complete ms. "Keep a copy of the ms for your file as we do not return them. If you have photo(s) and/or illustration(s) to accompany the article, do not send them with your story unless you do not want them returned." Also publishes some fiction. Length: 600-2,500 words. Pays $35-150. Sometimes pays expenses of writers on assignment.

Photos: State availability of photos with ms. Captions, model releases, identification of subjects required.

Tips: "We are looking for articles that deal with every aspect of life for the active, upbeat, 50+ adult, whether on a local or national level. Our readers are above-average intelligence, income and education."

‡**ELDER STATESMAN**,1201-301 West Pender Street, Vancouver, British Columbia V6E 2V2 Canada. (604)683-1344. Editor: Don McLellan. 50% freelance written. Monthly tabloid. "We cover travel, finance, lifestyles, housing, health, gardening, etc., for 55+ readership. Will accept U.S. writer's submissions if article is applicable to British Columbia seniors." Circ. 40,000+. Pays on publication. Publishes ms an average of 2-3 months after acceptance. Byline given. Offers $25-50 kill fee. Buys first North American serial rights or Western Canadian rights. Submit seasonal/holiday material 3 months in advance. Query for electronic submissions. Computer printout submissions OK; prefers letter-quality to dot-matrix. Reports in 1 month. Free sample copy.

Nonfiction: Book excerpts, expose, general interest, historical/nostalgic, how-to, personal experience and travel. "No rambling so-called 'think pieces', stories that are too long, palm tree/white sand travelogues." Buys 100 mss/year. Query. Length: 300-1,000 words. Pays $100-150. Sometimes pays expenses of writers on assignment.

Photos: Send photos with submission. Offers $10 per photo. Identification of subjects required. Buys all rights.
Fiction: "Annual short story contest in June. Winner gets published plus $200. Amateur, senior writers only."
Tips: Looking for "story on recreational—vehicle travel in U.S., tips for Canadians planning road holiday in U.S., prices, addresses for National listing of Parks for R.V.'s. Must relate to seniors specifically, or at least indirectly; American angle sometimes—but not always—not appropriate."

GOLDEN YEARS MAGAZINE, Golden Years Senior News, Inc., 233 E. New Haven Ave., Melbourne FL 32902-0537. (305)725-4888. Editor: Carol Brenner Hittner. 50% freelance written. Prefers to work with published/established writers. Monthly magazine covering "fantastic Floridians over 50. We serve the needs and interests of Florida's fastest growing generation. Editorial presented in a positive, uplifting, straightforward manner." Circ. 600,000. Pays on publication. Publishes ms an average of 7 months after acceptance. Byline given. Buys first serial rights and first North American serial rights. Submit seasonal/holiday material 1 year in advance. Simultaneous queries, and simultaneous, and photocopied submissions OK. Computer printout submissions acceptable; no dot-matrix. Sample copy $2; writer's guidelines for SAE with 1 first class stamp.
Nonfiction: Profile (Florida senior celebrities), travel, second careers, hobbies, retirement ideas and real estate. Buys 100 mss/year. Query with published clips or send complete ms. Length: 500 words maximum. Pays 70¢/standard one-third-column line.
Photos: "We like to include a lot of photos." Send photos with query or ms. Pays $25 for color transparencies. Captions, model releases, and identification of subjects required. Buys one-time rights. $10 per each b&w photo.
Tips: "We're looking for profiles on Florida people. Our magazine articles are short and special—that's why we are successful."

GRANDPARENTING!, Grandparenting!, 801 Cumberland Hills Dr., Hendersonville TN 37075. (615)822-8586. Editor: Betty Adler. 100% freelance written. Prefers to work with published/established writers. A quarterly tabloid for grandparents covering positive, unique personality of grandparents, and interesting activities. Circ. 5,000. Pays on publication. Publishes ms an average of 3 months after acceptance. Byline given. Submit seasonal/holiday material 3 months in advance. Simultaneous submissions OK. Reports in 6-8 weeks on queries. Sample copy for 9x12 SAE and 50¢ postage and handling.
Nonfiction: Humor, interview/profile, personal experience, and travel for grandparents. No articles about senior citizens, retirees, nursing homes, etc. Query. Length: 500-1,200 words. Pays $50.
Photos: Send photos with submission. Reviews 3x5 prints. Offers no additional payment for photos accepted with ms. Captions and identification of subjects required. Buys all rights.
Columns/Departments: Length: 500 words maximum. Pays $25.
Tips: "Any unsolicited articles, photos or stories will not be returned unless accompanied with a stamped envelope. *Grandparenting!* will not be responsible for unsolicited material."

MATURE LIVING, A Christian Magazine for Senior Adults, Sunday School Board of the Southern Baptist Convention, 127 9th Ave. N., Nashville TN 37209. (615)251-2191. Editor: Jack Gulledge. Assistant Editor: Zada Malugen. 70% freelance written. A monthly leisure reading magazine for senior adults 60 and older. Circ. 330,000. Pays on acceptance. Byline given. Buys all rights and sometimes one-time rights. Submit seasonal/holiday material 18 months in advance. Photocopied submissions OK. Computer printout submissions acceptable; prefers letter-quality to dot-matrix. Reports in 6 weeks. Sample copy for 9x12 SAE with 69¢ postage affixed; writer's guidelines for SAE with 1 first class stamp.
Nonfiction: General interest, historical/nostalgic, how-to, humor, inspirational, interview/profile, personal experience, photo feature and travel. No pornography, profanity, occult; liquor, dancing, drugs, gambling; no book reviews. Buys 100 mss/year. Send complete ms. Length: 1,475 words maximum, prefers 950 words. Pays 5¢/word (accepted).
Photos: State availability of photos with submission. Offers $10-15/photo. Pays on publication. Buys one-time rights.
Fiction: Humorous, mainstream and slice-of-life vignettes. No reference to liquor, dancing, drugs, gambling; no pornography, profanity or occult. Buys 12 mss/year. Send complete ms. Length: 900-1,475 words. Pays 5¢/word.
Poetry: Light verse and traditional. Buys 50 poems/year. Submit maximum 5 poems. Length: open. Pays $5-24.
Fillers: Anecdotes, facts and short humor. Buys 15/year. Length: 50 words maximum. Pays $5.

‡MATURE OUTLOOK, Allstate Enterprises, 3701 W. Lake Ave., Glenview IL 60025. (312)291-4739. Managing Editor: Elizabeth Brewster. 75% freelance written. Works with a small number of new/unpublished writers each year. A bimonthly magazine which focuses on "upbeat travel, health, money and other current subjects geared to the 50+ audience." Circ. 800,000. Pays on acceptance. Publishes ms an average of 6

months after acceptance. Byline given. Offers 10% kill fee. Buys first North American serial rights. Submit seasonal/holiday material 1 year in advance. Computer printout submissions OK; prefers letter-quality to dot-matrix. Reports in 6 weeks. Sample copy for 9x12 SAE with $1 postage and free writer's guidelines.
Nonfiction: Essays, general interest, humor, interview/profile and travel. Query with published clips. Length: 2,000-2,500 words. Pays $1,000 for assigned articles. Pays expenses of writers on assignment.
Photos: State availability of photos with submission. Reviews contact sheets. Buys one-time rights.
Columns/Departments: In Other Words (humorous articles). Query with published clips. Length: 1,000 words maximum. Pays $750 maximum.

MATURE YEARS, 201 8th Ave., S., Nashville TN 37202. Editor: John P. Gilbert. 30% freelance written. Prefers to work with published/established writers; works with a small number of new/unpublished writers each year. Quarterly magazine for retired persons and those facing retirement; persons seeking help on how to handle problems and privileges of retirement. Pays on acceptance. Publishes ms an average of 14 months after acceptance. Rights purchased vary with author and material; usually buys first North American serial rights. Submit seasonal material 14 months in advance. Query for electronic submissions. Computer printout submissions OK. Reports in 6 weeks. Free writer's guidelines.
Nonfiction: "*Mature Years* is different from the secular press in that we like material with a Christian and church orientation. Usually we prefer materials that have a happy, healthy outlook regarding aging. Advocacy (for older adults) articles are at times used; some are freelance submissions. We need articles dealing with many aspects of pre-retirement and retirement living, and short stories and leisure-time hobbies related to specific seasons. Give examples of how older persons, organizations, and institutions are helping others. Writing should be of interest to older adults, with Christian emphasis, though not preachy and moralizing. No poking fun or mushy, sentimental articles. We treat retirement from the religious viewpoint. How-to, humor and travel are also considered." Buys 24 unsolicited mss/year. Submit complete ms. Length: 1,200-1,500 words. Sometimes pays expenses of writers on assignment.
Photos: 8x10 b&w glossy prints, color prints or color transparencies purchased with ms or on assignment.
Fiction: "We buy fiction for adults. Humor is preferred. No children's stories and no stories about depressed situations of older adults." Length: 1,000-1,500 words. Payment varies, usually 4¢/word.
Tips: "We like writing to be meaty, timely, clear and concrete."

MODERN MATURITY, American Association of Retired Persons, 3200 E. Carson, Lakewood CA 90712. Editor-in-Chief: Ian Ledgerwood. 50% freelance written. Prefers to work with published/established writers. Bimonthly magazine for readership of persons 50 years of age and over. Circ. 16 million. Pays on acceptance. Publishes ms an average of 4-6 months after acceptance. Byline given. Buys first North American serial rights. Submit seasonal/holiday material 6 months in advance. Query for electronic submissions. Computer printout submissions acceptable; no dot-matrix. Reports in 6-8 weeks. Free sample copy and writer's guidelines.
Nonfiction: Careers, workplace, practical information in living, investments, financial and legal matters, personal relationships, and consumerism. Query first. Length: up to 2,000 words. Pays up to $3,000. Sometimes pays expenses of writers on assignment.
Photos: Photos purchased with or without accompanying ms. Pays $250 and up for color and $150 and up for b&w.
Fiction: Write for guidelines.
Poetry: All types. Length: 40 lines maximum. Pays $75.
Fillers: Jokes, gags, short anecdotes, puzzles (word search only) and short humor. Pays $50 minimum.
Tips: "The most frequent mistake made by writers in completing an article for us is poor follow-through with basic research. The outline is often more interesting than the finished piece."

NEW ENGLAND SENIOR CITIZEN/SENIOR AMERICAN NEWS, Prime National Publishing Corp., 470 Boston Post Rd., Weston MA 02193. Editor-in-Chief: Eileen F. DeVito. 80% freelance written. For men and women aged 55 and over who are interested in travel, finances, retirement lifestyles, nostalgia, etc. Monthly newspaper; 24-32 pages. Circ. 60,000. Pays on publication. Publishes ms an average of 9 months after acceptance. Buys all rights. Byline given. Submit seasonal/holiday material 3 months in advance. Computer printout submissions acceptable. Reports in 4 months. Sample copy 50¢.
Nonfiction: General interest; how-to (anything dealing with retirement years); inspirational; historical; humor; interview; nostalgia; profile; travel; personal experience; photo features. Buys 10-15 mss/issue. Submit complete ms. Length: 500-1,500 words. Pays $25-50.
Photos: Purchased with ms. Captions required. Pays $5-15/5x7 or 8x10 b&w glossy print. Captions and model releases required.
Tips: "Submit clean, typed, top-quality copy aimed at older tastes, interests, lifestyles and memories."

PRIME TIMES, Grote Deutsch & Co., Suite 120, 2802 International Ln., Madison WI 53704. Managing Editor: Russell H. Grote. Executive Editor: Joan Donovan. 80% freelance written. Prefers to work with published/established writers, but "we will work at times with unpublished writers." Quarterly magazine for people who "are at the height of their careers and planning a dynamic retirement lifestyle, or interested in redefining middle age." The audience is primarily people aged 40-64 who were or are credit union members and want to plan and manage their retirement. Circ. 75,000. Pays on publication. Buys first North American serial rights and second serial (reprint) rights. Publishes ms an average of 6 months after acceptance. Submit seasonal material 6 months in advance. Previously published submissions OK as long as they were not in another national maturity-market magazine. Computer printout submissions acceptable; no dot-matrix. Reports in 2 months. Sample copy only with 9x12 SAE and 5 first class stamps; writer's guidelines for SASE.

Nonfiction: Expose; how-to, new research and updates (related to financial planning methods, consumer activism, preventive health and fitness, travel, and working/dynamic lifestyle after retirement); opinion; profile; travel; popular arts; self-image; personal experience; humor; and photo feature. "No rocking-chair reminiscing." Articles on health and medical issues and research *must* be founded in sound scientific method and must include current, up-to-date data. "Health related articles are an easy sale, but you must do your homework and be able to document your research. Don't waste your time or ours on tired generalizations about how to take care of the human anatomy. If you've heard it before, so have we. We want to know who is doing new research, what the current findings may be, and what scientists on the cutting edge of new research say the future holds, preferably in the next one to five years. Is anyone doing basic research into the physiology of the aging process? If so, who? And what have they found? What triggers the aging process? Why do some people age faster than others? What are the common denominators? Does genetic coding and recombinant DNA research hold the answers to slowing or halting the aging process? Get the picture? Give us the facts, only the facts, and all of the facts. Allow the scientists and our audience to draw their own conclusions." Buys 30-40 mss/year, about half from new talent. Query with published clips. Length: 1,000-3,000 words. Pays $50-1,000. "Be sure to keep a photocopy—just in case gremlins pinch the original." Sometimes pays the expenses of writers on assignment.

Photos: Pays $25-50 for 8x10 glossy high-contrast prints; $25-50 for 35mm color transparency, or according to ASMP guidelines or negotiation; $7.50 for cutline. Will not reproduce color prints. Captions and model releases required. Buys one-time rights. "Do not send irreplaceable *anything*."

Fiction: Length: 1,500-3,500 words. Pays $150-750.

Tips: Query should state qualifications (such as expertise or society memberships). Special issues requiring freelance work include publications on adult friendship; prime-life "passages" (development changes); health and medical research and updates; second careers; money management; continuing education; consequences of the ongoing longevity revolution; and the "creation of new lifestyles for prime-life adults (ages 40-60 primarily) who are well-educated, affluent, and above all, *active*. "Whether urban or rural, male or female, if an attempt at humor, lightness or tongue-in-cheek seems off-target to you, it will to us, too. And we don't gloss over important matters. If you identify a problem, try to identify a solution. Many *Prime Times* readers are not retired but may be interested in planning a dynamic retirement lifestyle; many are well-educated, affluent career professionals or homemakers. About 55% of our readers are women. All are active and redefining the middle years with creative energy and imagination. Age irrelevant writing very desirable. The focus of *Prime Times* in 1988 will be on presenting readers with refreshing and newsworthy material for dynamic middle-agers, people who have a 'forever-forty' mentality."

‡**SENIOR, California Senior Magazine**, Suggs & Lombadi, 3565 S. Higuera St., San Luis Obispo CA 93401. (805)544-8711. Editor: George Brand. Associate Editor: Herb Kamm, A. Brandon. 90% freelance written. Monthly magazine covering senior citizens to inform and entertain the "over-50" audience. Circ. 40,000. Pays on publication. Byline given. Publishes ms an average of 1 month after acceptance. Byline given. Not copyrighted. Buys first rights or second rights. Submit seasonal/holiday material 2 months in advance. Computer printout submissions OK; prefers letter-quality. Reports in 2 weeks. Sample copy for 9x11 SAE and 44¢ postage; free writer's guidelines.

Nonfiction: Historical/nostalgic, humor, inspirational, personal experience and travel. Special issue features War Years (November); Christmas (December); and Travel (April). Buys 30-75 mss/year. Query. Length: 300-900 words. Pays $1.50/inch. Sometimes pays the expenses of writers on assignment.

Photos: Send photos with submission. Reviews 8x10 prints. Offers $10-25 per photo. Captions and identification of subjects required. Buys one-time rights.

Columns/Departments: Finance (investment); Taxes; Auto; Medicare, all 600 words. Length: 300-900 words. Pays $1.50/inch.

Poetry: A. Brandon, editor. Light verse and traditional. Buys 24-30 poems/year. Submit 4-5 poems/year. Pays $1.50/inch.

Fillers: Herb Kamm, editor. Anecdotes and facts. Length: 25-30 words. Pays $1.50/inch.

‡**SENIOR EDITION**, SEI Publishing Corporation, Suite 2240, 1660 Lincoln, Denver CO 80264. (303)837-9100. Editor: Allison St. Claire, 5% freelance written. Monthly tabloid. "Colorado newspaper for seniors(with national distribution) emphasizing legislation, opinion and advice columns, local and national news, features and local calendar aimed at over-55 community." Circ. 12,000. Pays on publication. Publishes ms an average of 1-6 months after acceptance. Byline given. Offer 25-50% kill fee. Buys first North American

serial rights and simultaneous rights. Submit seasonal/holiday material 3 months in advance. Reports in 1-2 weeks on queries; 2-3 weeks on mss. Sample copy $1; writer's guidelines for SASE.

Nonfiction: Historical/nostalgic, humor, inspirational, opinion, personal experience and travel. Does not want "anything aimed at less than age 55-plus market; anything patronizing or condescending to seniors." Buys 6 mss/year. Query with or without published clips, or send complete ms. Length: 50-1,000 words. Pays $5-100 for assigned articles; $5-50 for unsolicited articles. Sometimes pays expenses of writers on assignment.

Photos: Send photos with submission (or photocopies of available pictures). Offers $3-10 per photo. Identification of subjects required. Buys one-time rights.

Columns/Departments: Senior Overlook (opinions of seniors about anything they feel strongly about: finances, grandkids, love, life, social problems, etc. May be editorial, essay, prose or poetry). Buys 12 mss/year. Send complete ms. Length: 50-1,000 words. Pays $10 maximum.

Fillers: Short humor. Buys 4/year. Length: 300 words maximum. Pays $10 maximum.

Tips: Areas most open to freelancers are "Opinion: have a good, reasonable point backed with personal experience and/or researched data. Diatribes, vague or fuzzy logic, or overworked themes not appreciated. Advice: solid information and generic articles accepted. We will not promote any product or business unless it is the only one in existence. Must be applicable to senior lifestyle."

___ Romance and Confession

Listed here are publications that need stories of romance ranging from ethnic and adventure to romantic intrigue and confession. Each magazine has a particular slant; some are written for young adults, others to family-oriented women. Some magazines also are interested in general interest nonfiction on related subjects.

AFFAIRE DE COEUR, Keenan and Rowe Enterprises, 5660 Roosevelt Pl., Fremont CA 94538. (415)656-4804. Editor: Barbara N. Keenan. Editor: Beth Rowe. 56% freelance written. Monthly magazine of book reviews, articles and information on publishing for romance readers and writers. Circ. 18,000. Pays on publication. Publishes ms an average of 6-12 months after acceptance. Byline given. Buys one-time rights. Submit seasonal/holiday material 3 months in advance. Simultaneous, photocopied and previously published submissions OK. Reports in 3-4 months. Sample copy $2; writer's guidelines for #10 SAE and 1 first class stamp.

Nonfiction: Book excerpts, essays, general interest, historical/nostalgic, how-to, interview/profile, personal experience and photo feature. Buys 2 mss/year. Query. Length: 500-2,200 words. Pays $5-15. Sometimes pays writers with contributor copies or other premiums.

Photos: State availability of photos with submission. Review prints. Offers $2/photo. Identification of subjects required. Buys one-time rights.

Columns/Departments: Reviews (book reviews). Query. Length: 125-150 words. Does not pay.

Fiction: Historical, mainstream and romance. Buys 2 mss/year. Query. Length: 1,500-2,200. Pays $15.

Poetry: Light verse. Buys 2 poems/year. Submit 1 poem. Does not pay.

Fillers: Newsbreaks. Buys 2/year. Length: 50-100. Does not pay.

Tips: "Please send clean copy. Do not send material without SASE. Do not expect a return for 2-3 months. Type all information. Send some sample of your work."

‡BLACK CONFESSION, Lexington Library, Inc., 355 Lexington Ave., New York NY 10017. (212)391-1400. Editor: Nathasha Brooks. Associate Editor: Lisa Cochran. See *Jive*.

‡BRONZE THRILLS, Lexington Library, Inc., 355 Lexington Ave., New York NY 10017. (212)391-1400. Editor: Nathasha Brooks. Associate Editor: Lisa Cochran. See *Intimacy/Black Romance*. "Stories can be a bit sexier than in the other magazines."

‡IMTIMACY/BLACK ROMANCE, 355 Lexington Ave., New York NY 10017. (212)391-1400. Editor: Nathasha Brooks. 90% freelance written. Eager to work with new/unpublished writers. A bimonthly magazine covering romance and love. Circ. 100,000. Pays on publication. Publishes ms an average of 3 months after acceptance. Byline given. Buys first and one-time rights. Submit seasonal/holiday material 6 months in advance. Photocopied submissions OK. Computer printout submissions OK. Reports in 2 months on queries; 3

Close-up

Nathasha Brooks
Editor
Black Romance

"I really enjoy the fact that I work with talented beginning writers who have a burning desire to write, lack self-confidence, but are still so determined they won't give up," says Nathasha Brooks of her work as editor of *Jive*, *Black Romance*, *Bronze Thrills*, and *Black Confessions*. "My magazines appeal to women of all ages. Men find our magazines entertaining as well. Our readers are looking for escape. They're looking for glitter, glamour and fantasy."

Although Brooks enjoys working with beginners, she has found some recurring problems in submissions. "Major problems are that the plot isn't thick enough, characters are undefined, the dialogue is flimsy or thin, and there is no conflict or tension. Also, writers are very timid at writing in sex scenes and will often underwrite them. Some white writers seem to have a problem with consistency, making blond-haired, blue-eyed characters live a black existence without bothering to research how black people really live. Struggle, conflict, obstacles, a good sex scene, and romance sprinkled throughout add the most realism to stories. Writers should cover international romance, interracial romance, wealthy characters in love, the 'bitch goddess' who steals someone's man, the woman who keeps her man, and stories about characters who are ultra glamorous and professional. Romance stories seem more real if they are based upon timely events and depict romance as it is now in the '80s. An example is that people in love have sex, they don't just hold hands anymore. The AIDS and crack epidemics have an impact on romance. Not keeping up with the times make for superficial stories.

"Plot development should be in a natural, sequential order. We don't want too many coincidences. If something happens, show us through characterization and dialogue. Stories need a first person point of view. The female lead should be somewhat of a superwoman—glamorous, strong-willed, with a good job. Give quirks to your characters, like rubbing or scratching their heads, smoking, wearing a certain line of clothing or shopping at a certain store. Your characters should be individuals.

"Two of us read stories here during the two weeks between magazines," says Brooks. "We look at them in terms of what the reader would like to see. And it should be so romantic it leaves me in tears. I try to put it on a personal level: Could this happen to me?"

What happens to those stories that do appeal to Brooks? "I'll draw up a synopsis, choose four blurbs for the story and file it under the name of the magazine or category it falls into, such as glamorous or innocent. If we don't let people know their story has been rejected, it's being considered.

"The ideal writer should be able to take criticism and never give up when things aren't going well. He or she should be willing to work with me from the first submission to the tenth rewrite, to actual published piece. They shouldn't be afraid of work, because I usually ask for several rewrites before publication. If they're not serious about their work, this is not the magazine to query."

—*Sheila Freeman*

months on mss. Sample copy for 9x12 SAE with 4-5 first class stamps; free writer's guidelines.

Nonfiction: Historical (Black cultural articles); how-to (relating to romance and love); personal experience (confessions); and feature articles on any aspect of love and romance. "I would not like to see any special features that are overly researched." Buys 100 mss/year. Query with published clips, or send complete ms. Length: 500-1,250 words. Pays $100.

Photos: Send photos with submission. Reviews contact sheets, negatives, transparencies and 8x10 prints. Offers $40 per photo. Model releases required. Buys one-time rights.

Columns/Departments: Beauty (Black skin, hair, foot and hand care); Fashion (any articles about current fashions that our audience may be interested in will be considered). Buys 50 mss/year. Query with published clips or send complete ms. Length: 500-1,250 words. Pays $100.

Fiction: Confession and romance. "I would not like to see anything that stereotypes Black people. Stories which are too sexual in content and lack romance are unacceptable." Buys 300 mss/year. *Bronze Thrills* accepts stories which are a bit sexier than those written for *Jive, Black Confession,* or *Black Romance.* Send complete ms (12-15 typed pages). Pays $75-100.

Poetry: Free verse and haiku. "I do not want cute, rhyming poetry. I prefer free verse." Buys 40 poems/year. Length: 5-25 lines. Pays $10 per poem.

Tips: "This is a great market for beginning, unpublished writers. I am a tough editor because I want quality material and would like to encourage serious writers to submit to us on a regular basis. I discourage sloppiness, carelessness and people who give lip service to wanting to be a writer and not doing the work involved. I would like to emphasize to the writers that writing is not easy, and not to think that they will get a break here. Contemporary issues and timely subjects should be the basis of any stories submitted to us."

‡JIVE, Lexington Library, Inc., 355 Lexington Ave., New York NY 10017. (212)391-1400. Editor: Nathasha Brooks. 90% freelance written. Eager to work with new/unpublished writers. A bimonthly magazine covering romance and love. Circ. 100,000. Pays on publication. Publishes ms an average of 3 months after acceptance. Byline given. Buys first and one-time rights. Submit seasonal/holiday material 6 months in advance. Clear, legible photocopied submissions OK. Computer printout submissions OK; prefers letter-quality to dot-matrix. Reports in 2 months on queries; 3 months on mss. Sample copy for 9x12 SAE with 4 or 5 first class stamps; free writer's guidelines.

Nonfiction: Historical (Black cultural articles); how-to (relating to romance and love); personal experience (confessions); and feature articles on any aspect of love and romance. "I would not like to see any special features that are overly researched." Buys 100 mss/year. Query with published clips, or send complete ms. Length: 500-1,250 words. Pays $100.

Photos: Send photos with submission. Reviews contact sheets, negatives, transparencies and 8x10 prints. Offers $40 per photo. Model releases required. Buys one-time rights.

Columns/Departments: Beauty (Black skin, hair, foot and hand care); Fashion (any articles about current fashions that our audience may be interested in will be considered); how-to special features that deal with romance. Buys 50 mss/year. Query with published clips or send complete ms. Length: 500-1,250 words. Pays $100.

Fiction: Confession and romance. "I would not like to see anything that stereotypes Black people. Stories which are too sexual in content and lack romance are unacceptable. However, all stories must contain one or two sex scenes that are romantic, not lewd." Buys 300 mss/year. Send complete ms (12-15 typed pages). Pays $75-100.

Poetry: Free verse and haiku. "I do not want cute, rhyming poetry. I prefer free verse." Buys 40 poems/year. Length: 5-25 lines. Pays $10 per poem.

Tips: "We reach an audience that is comprised mostly of women who are college students, high school students, housewives, divorcees, and older women. The audience is mainly Black and ethnic. Our slant is Black and should reinforce Black pride. Our philosophy is to show our experiences in as positive a light as possible without addressing any of the common stereotypes that are associated with Black men: lovemaking prowess, penil size, etc. Stereotypes of any kind are totally unacceptable. The fiction section which accepts romance stories and confession stories about love and romance are most open to freelancers. Also, our special features section is very open. We would like to see stories that are set outside the U.S.—perhaps, they should be set in the Caribbean, Europe, Africa, etc. Women should be shown as being professional, assertive, independent, but should still enjoy being romanced and loved by a man. We'd like to see themes that are reflective of things happening around us in the 80's—crack, AIDS, living together, surrogate mothers, etc. The characters should be young, but not the typical 'country bumpkin girl who was turned out by a big city pimp' type story. Cosmopolitan storylines would be great too. Please writers who are not Black, research your story to be sure that it depicts Black people in a positive manner. Do not make Black characters a caricature of a white character. This is totally unacceptable."

MODERN ROMANCES, Macfadden Women's Group, Inc., 215 Lexington Ave., New York NY 10016. Editor: Colleen Brennan. 100% freelance written. Monthly magazine; 80 pages for blue-collar, family-oriented women, ages 18-35 years old. Circ. 200,000. Pays the last week of the month of issue. Buys all

rights. Submit seasonal/holiday material 6 months in advance. Reports in 2 months.
Nonfiction: General interest, baby and child care, how-to (homemaking subjects), humor, inspirational, and personal experience. Submit complete ms. Length: 200-1,500 words. Pay depends on merit. "Confession stories with reader identification and a strong emotional tone. No third person material." Buys 14 mss/issue. Submit complete ms. Length: 1,500-8,500 words. Pays 5¢/word.
Poetry: Light, romantic poetry. Length: 24 lines maximum. Pay depends on merit.

SECRETS, Macfadden Holdings, Inc., 215 Lexington Ave., New York NY 10016. (212)340-7500. Vice President and Editorial Director: Florence J. Moriarty. Editor: Jean Press Silberg. 100% freelance written. Monthly magazine for blue-collar family women, ages 18-35. Pays on publication. Publishes ms an average of 4 months after acceptance. Buys all rights. Submit seasonal material at least 5 months in advance. Reports in 3 months.
Nonfiction and Fiction: Wants true stories of special interest to women: family, marriage and romance themes, "woman-angle articles," or self-help or inspirational fillers. "No pornographic material; no sadistic or abnormal angles. Stories must be written in the first person." Buys 150 mss/year. Submit complete ms. Length: 300-1,000 words for features; 2,500-7,500 words for full-length story. Occasional 10,000-worders. Greatest need: 4,500-6,000 words. Pays 3¢/word for story mss.
Tips: "Know our market. We are keenly aware of all contemporary lifestyles and activities that involve women and family—i.e.; current emphasis on child abuse, or renewed interest in the image of marriage, etc."

TRUE CONFESSIONS, Macfadden Holdings, Inc., 215 Lexington Ave., New York NY 10016. Editor: Helen Vincent. 90% freelance written. Eager to work with new/unpublished writers. For high-school-educated, blue-collar women, teens through maturity. Monthly magazine. Circ. 250,000. Buys all rights. Byline given on some articles. Pays during the last week of month of issue. Publishes ms an average of 6 months after acceptance. Submit seasonal material 6 months in advance. Reports in 4 months. Submit complete ms. Computer printout submissions acceptable; prefers letter-quality to dot-matrix. No simultaneous submissions.
Stories, Articles, and Fillers: Timely, exciting, emotional first-person stories on the problems that face today's young women. The narrators should be sympathetic, and the situations they find themselves in should be intriguing, yet realistic. Every story should have a strong romantic interest and a high moral tone, and every plot should reach an exciting climax. Careful study of a current issue is suggested. Length: 2,000-6,000 words; 5,000 word stories preferred; also book lengths of 8,000-10,000 words. Pays 5¢/word. Also publishes articles and short fillers.

TRUE EXPERIENCE, Macfadden Women's Group, 215 Lexington Ave., New York NY 10016. Editor: Helen Atkocius. Monthly magazine; 80 pages. For young marrieds, blue-collar, high school education. Interests: children, home, arts, crafts, family and self-fulfillment. Circ. 225,000. Pays 30 days after publication. Byline given. Buys all rights. No photocopied or simultaneous submissions. Submit seasonal material 5 months in advance. Reports in 3 months.
Nonfiction: Stories on life situations, e.g., love, divorce, any real-life problems. Romance and confession, first-person narratives with strong identification for readers. Articles on health, self-help or child care. "Remember that we are contemporary. We deal with women's self-awareness and consciousness of their roles in society." Buys 100 mss/year. Submit complete ms. Length: 250-1,500 words for nonfiction; 1,000-7,500 words for personal narrative. Pays 3¢/word.
Poetry: Only traditional forms. Length: 4-20 lines. Payment varies.
Tips: "Study the magazine for style and editorial content."

TRUE LOVE, Macfadden Holdings Inc., 215 Lexington Ave., New York NY 10016. (212)340-7500. Editor: Jean Sharbel. 100% freelance written. Monthly magazine; 80 pages. For young, blue-collar women, teens through mid-30's. Confession stories based on true happenings, with reader identification and a strong emotional tone. No third person material; no simultaneous submissions. Circ. 200,000. Pays the last week of the month of the issue. Byline given. Buys all rights. Submit seasonal material 6 months in advance. Reports in 2 months.
Nonfiction: Confessions, true love stories; problems and solutions; health problems; marital and child-rearing difficulties. Avoid graphic sex. Stories dealing with reality, current problems, everyday events, with emphasis on emotional impact. Buys 14 stories/issue. Submit complete ms. Length: 1,500-8,000 words. Pays 3¢/word. Informational and how-to articles. Length: 250-800 words. Pays 5¢/word minimum.
Poetry: Light romantic poetry. Length: 24 lines maximum. Pay depends on merit.
Tips: "The story must appeal to the average blue-collar woman. It must deal with her problems and interests. Characters—especially the narrator—must be sympathetic."

TRUE ROMANCE, Macfadden Women's Group, 215 Lexington Ave., New York NY 10016. (212)340-7500. Editor: Paula Sciarrino. Monthly magazine. "Our readership ranges from teenagers to senior citizens. The majority are high school educated, married, have young children and also work outside the home. They are concerned with contemporary social issues, yet they are deeply committed to their husbands and children. They have high moral values and place great emphasis on love and romance." Circ. 225,000. Pays 1 month after publication. Buys all rights. Submit seasonal/holiday material at least 5 months in advance. Reports in 3 months.

Nonfiction: How-to and informational. Submit complete ms. Length: 300-1,000 words. Pays 3¢/word, special rates for short features and articles. Confession. "We want *only* true contemporary stories about relationships." Buys 13 stories/issue. Submit complete ms. Length: 2,000-7,500 words. Pays 3¢/word; slightly higher flat rate for short-shorts.

Poetry: Light verse and traditional. Buys 15/year. Length: 4-20 lines. Pays $10 minimum.

Tips: "The freelance writer is needed and welcomed. A timely, well-written story that is told by a sympathetic narrator who sees the central problem through to a satisfying resolution is all that is needed to break into *True Romance*. We are always looking for good love stories."

TRUE STORY, Macfadden Women's Group, 215 Lexington Ave., New York NY 10016. Editor: Susan Weiner. 80% freelance written. For young married, blue-collar women, 20-35; high school education; increasingly broad interests; home-oriented, but looking beyond the home for personal fulfillment. Monthly magazine. Circ. 1,700,000. Buys all rights. Byline given "on articles only." Pays on publication. Submit seasonal material 4 months in advance; make notation on envelope that it is seasonal material. Reports in 4 months.

Nonfiction: Pays a flat rate for columns or departments, as announced in the magazine. Query for fact articles.

Photos: Gus Gazzola, art director. Query about all possible photo submissions.

Fiction: "First-person stories covering all aspects of women's interests: love, marriage, family life, careers, social problems, etc. The best direction a new writer can be given is to carefully study several issues of the magazine; then submit a fresh, exciting, well-written true story. We have no taboos. It's the handling and believability that make the difference between a rejection and an acceptance." Buys about 125 full-length mss/year. Submit only complete mss for stories. Length: 1,500-10,000 words. Pays 5¢/word; $150 minimum.

Rural

Readers may be conservative or liberal, but these publications draw them together with a focus on rural lifestyles. Surprisingly, many readers are from urban centers who dream or plan to build a house or someday move to the country.

COUNTRY JOURNAL, Box 8200, Harrisburg PA 17105. Editor: John Randolph. Managing Editor: David D. Sleeper. 90% freelance written. Works with a small number of new/unpublished writers each year. Monthly magazine featuring country living for people who live in rural areas or who are thinking about moving there. Circ. 320,000. Average issue includes 8-10 feature articles and 10 departments. Pays on acceptance. Publishes ms an average of 1 year after acceptance. Byline given. Buys first North American serial rights. Submit seasonal material 1 year in advance. Photocopied submissions OK. Computer printout submissions acceptable, prefers letter-quality; "dot-matrix submissions are acceptable if double-spaced." Reports in 1 month. Sample copy $2.50; writer's guidelines for SASE.

Nonfiction: Book excerpts; general interest; opinion (essays); profile (people who are outstanding in terms of country living); how-to; issues affecting rural areas; and photo feature. No historical or reminiscence. Query with published clips. Length: 2,000-3,500 words. Sometimes pays the expenses of writers on assignment.

Photos: Lisa Furgatch, photo editor. State availability of photos. Review b&w contact sheets, 5x7 and 8x10 b&w glossy prints and 35mm or larger color transparencies. Captions, model release, and identification of subjects required. Buys one-time rights.

Columns/Departments: Listener (brief articles on country topics, how-to's, current events and updates). Buys 15 mss/year. Query with published clips. Length: 200-400 words. Pays approx. $75.

Poetry: Free verse, light verse and traditional. Buys 1 poem/issue. Pays $2.50/line.

Tips: "Be as specific in your query as possible and explain why you are qualified to write the piece (especially for how-to's and controversial subjects). The writer has a better chance of breaking in at our publication with short articles."

FARM & RANCH LIVING, Reiman Publications, 5400 S. 60th St., Greendale WI 53129. (414)423-0100. Managing Editor: Bob Ottum. 80% freelance written. Eager to work with new/unpublished writers. A bimonthly lifestyle magazine aimed at families engaged full time in farming or ranching. "*F&RL* is *not* a 'how-to' magazine—it deals with people rather than products and profits." Circ. 260,000. Pays on acceptance. Publishes ms an average of 1 year after acceptance. Byline given. Offers 25% kill fee. Buys first serial rights and one-time rights. Submit seasonal/holiday material 6 months in advance. Previously published submissions OK. Computer printout submissions acceptable. Reports in 6 weeks. Sample copy $2; writer's guidelines for business size SAE and 1 first class stamp.

Nonfiction: Interview/profile, photo feature, historical/nostalgic, humor, inspirational and personal experience. No how-to articles or stories about "hobby farmers" (doctors or lawyers with weekend farms), or "hard-times" stories (farmers going broke and selling out). Buys 50 mss/year. Query first with or without published clips; state availability of photos. Length: 1,000-3,000 words. Pays $150-500 for text-and-photos package. Pays expenses of writers on assignment.

Photos: Scenic. Pays $20-40 for b&w photos; $75-200 for 35mm color slides. Buys one-time rights.

Fillers: Clippings, jokes, anecdotes and short humor. Buys 150/year. Length: 50-150 words. Pays $20 minimum.

Tips: "In spite of poor farm economy, most farm families are proud and optimistic, and they especially enjoy stories and features that are upbeat and positive. *F&RL*'s circulation continues to increase, providing an excellent market for freelancers. A freelancer must see *F&RL* to fully appreciate how different it is from other farm publications . . . ordering a sample is strongly advised (not available on newsstands). Query first—we'll give plenty of help and encouragement if story looks promising, and we'll explain why if it doesn't. Photo features (about interesting farm or ranch families); Most Interesting Farmer (or Rancher) I've Ever Met (human interest profile); and Prettiest Place in the Country (tour in text and photos of an attractive farm or ranch) are most open to freelancers. We can make separate arrangements for photography if writer is unable to provide photos."

‡FARM FAMILY AMERICA, The Webb Company, 1999 Shepard Rd., St. Paul MN 55116. (612)690-7200. Editor: George Ashfield. Managing Editor: Rudy Schnasse. 75% freelance written. A quarterly magazine published by American Cyanamid and written to the lifestyle, activities and travel interests of American Farm Families. Estab. 1986. Circ. 295,000. Pays on acceptance. Publishes ms an average of 2 months after acceptance. Byline given. Offers 25% kill fee. Buys first or second serial (reprint) rights. Submit seasonal/holiday material 6 months in advance. Simultaneous and photocopied submissions OK. Query for electronic submissions. Computer printout submissions OK. Reports in 6 weeks. Writer's guidelines for #10 SAE with 1 first class stamp.

Nonfiction: General interest and travel. Buys 24 mss/year. Query with published clips. Length: 1,000-1,800 words. Pays $300-650. Sometimes pays the expenses of writers on assignment.

Photos: State availability of photos with submission. Reviews 35mm transparencies and prints. Offers $160-700 per photo. Model releases and identification of subjects required. Buys one-time rights.

THE MOTHER EARTH NEWS, Box 70, Hendersonville NC 28791. (704)693-0211. Editor: Bruce Woods. 40% freelance written. Bimonthly magazine. Emphasizes "country living and country skills, for both long-time and would-be ruralites." Circ. 700,000. Pays on acceptance. Byline given. Submit seasonal/holiday material 5 months in advance. Computer printout submissions acceptable; prefer letter-quality to dot-matrix. No handwritten mss. Reports within 3 months. Publishes ms an average of 1 year after acceptance. Sample copy $3; writer's guidelines for SASE and 39¢ postage.

Nonfiction: Terry Krautwurst, submissions editor. How-to, home business, alternative energy systems, home building, home retrofit and home maintenance, energy-efficient structures, seasonal cooking, gardening and crafts. Buys 300-350 mss/year. Query or send complete ms. "A short, to-the-point paragraph is often enough. If it's a subject we don't need at all, we can answer immediately. If it tickles our imagination, we'll ask to take a look at the whole piece. No phone queries, please." Length: 300-3,000 words.

Photos: Purchased with accompanying ms. Send prints or transparencies. Uses 8x10 b&w glossies; any size color transparencies. Include type of film, speed and lighting used. Total purchase price for ms includes payment for photos. Captions and credits required.

Columns/Departments: "Contributions to Mother's Down-Home Country Lore and Barters and Bootstraps are paid by subscription."

Fillers: Short how-to's on any subject normally covered by the magazine. Query. Length: 150-300 words. Pays $7.50-25.

Tips: "Probably the best way to break in is to study our magazine, digest our writer's guidelines, and send us a concise article illustrated with color transparencies that we can't resist. When folks query and we give a go-ahead on speculation, we often offer some suggestions. Failure to follow those suggestions can lose the sale for the author. We want articles that tell what real people are doing to take charge of their own lives. Articles should be well-documented and tightly written treatments of topics we haven't already covered. The critical thing is length, and our payment is by space, not word count." No phone queries.

Science

These publications are published for laymen interested in technical and scientific developments and discoveries, applied science and technical or scientific hobbies. Publications of interest to the personal computer owner/user are listed in the Personal Computer section. Journals for scientists, engineers, repairmen, etc., are listed in Trade in various sections.

ALTERNATIVE SOURCES OF ENERGY MAGAZINE, 107 S. Central Ave., Milaca MN 56353. Executive Editor: Donald Marier. 15% freelance written. Monthly magazine emphasizing certain alternative energy sources including windpower, hydropower, photovoltaics, cogeneration, waste-to-energy, district-heating. Audience is predominantly male, age 36, college educated and concerned about energy and environmental limitations. Circ. 23,000. Pays on publication. Publishes ms an average of 4 months after acceptance. Buys first North American serial rights returning full rights after publication. Phone queries OK. Simultaneous, photocopied, and previously published submissions OK, "if specified at time of submission." Computer printout submissions acceptable; prefers letter-quality to dot-matrix. Reports in 6 weeks. Sample copy $4.25.
Nonfiction: "Freelance articles published cover a broad range, but we especially look for pieces which deal with technical innovations in the fields mentioned, company profiles, new approaches to financing renewable energy projects, international news, interviews with innovators in the field, progress reports on unique projects, legislative updates, etc. We insist on full addresses for all companies mentioned (unless irrelevant), solid documentation, and a business style. We also advise tight leads, subheaded body copy and short, relevant conclusions." Length: "Articles accepted are generally between 500 and 2,000 words. We are always interested in short pieces on very specific topics. This would typically be a 500-word piece on a new wind, hydro or pv installation with one quality picture. Unless a SASE is included, your article will not be returned. We strongly urge that you forward a short outline prior to beginning a longer article. We'll let you know our level of interest promptly. Pays 7¢/word and two free author copies. If we like the piece, but feel it must be shortened, payment will be based on the printed version."
Photos: $15 per photo or camera ready graphic and two free author copies.
Tips: "*Alternative Sources of Energy Magazine (ASE)* is 'the magazine of the Independent Power Production industry.' Specifically, we cover those industries involved in the production of electricity from renewable energy, including windpower, hydropower, photovoltaics, biomass and cogeneration projects. Writers have a better chance of breaking in at our publication with short articles and fillers because they're tough to get and assure limited 'fluff.' "

‡BIOLOGY DIGEST,Plexus Publishing Inc., 143 Old Marlton Pike, Medford NJ 08055. (609)654-6500. Editor: Mary S. Hogan. Monthly abstracts journal covering life sciences. Circ. 2,000. Pays "after publication is returned from printer." Byline given. Not copyrighted.
Nonfiction: Thomas H. Hogan, publisher. Essays. "A list of suggested further readings must accompany each article." Buys 9 mss/year. Send complete ms. Length: 18-25 double-spaced ms pages.
Photos: "A minimum of 5 photos and/or finished drawings are required to go along with the feature article. If drawings are used, there should be at least 2 photos. Photos are a must because the feature article is always depicted on the cover of the issue through the use of a photo."
Tips: "Although *Biology Digest* is intended for students at the high school and college levels, the feature articles published are of a serious nature and contain scientifically accurate material—not conjecture or opinion. Articles should be self-contained; i.e. the author should assume no previous knowledge of the subject area, and scientific terms should be defined. However, avoid 'talking down' to the reader—he or she is probably smarter than you think."

‡CQ: THE RADIO AMATEUR'S JOURNAL, 76 N. Broadway, Hicksville NY 11801. (516)681-2922. Editor: Alan Dorhoffer. 50% freelance written. For the amateur radio community. Monthly journal. Circ. 100,000. Pays on publication. Buys first rights. Phone queries OK. Submit seasonal/holiday material 3 months in advance. Computer printout submissions acceptable. Reports in 3 weeks. Publishes ms an average of 1 year after acceptance. Free sample copy.
Nonfiction: "We are interested in articles that address all technical levels of amateur radio. Included would be basic material for newcomers and intermediate and advanced material for oldtimers. Articles may be of a theoretical, practical or anecdotal nature. They can be general interest pieces for all amateurs or they can focus in on specific topics. We would like historical articles, material on new developments, articles on projects you can do in a weekend, and pieces on long-range projects taking a month or so to complete." Length: 6-10 typewritten pages. Pays $35/published page.

‡**THE ELECTRON**, CIE Publishing, 4781 E. 355th St., Willoughby OH 44094. (216)946-9065. Managing Editor: Janice Weaver. 80% freelance written. Prefers to work with published/established writers. Bimonthly tabloid on electronics and high technology. Circ. 50,000. Pays on publication. Publishes ms an average of 2 months after acceptance. Byline given. Buys all rights unless negotiated otherwise. Simultaneous queries, and photocopied and previously published submissions OK. Computer printout submissions acceptable; prefers letter-quality to dot-matrix. Reports in 1 month or earlier.

Nonfiction: How-to, interview/profile, personal experience, photo feature and technical. Query with published clips or send complete ms. Pays $35-1,000. Sometimes pays expenses of writers on assignment.

Photos: State availability of photos. Reviews 8x10 and 5x7 b&w prints. Captions and identification of subjects required.

Tips: "We would like to receive educational electronics/technical articles. They must be written in a manner understandable to the beginning—intermediate electronics student."

ELECTRONICS TODAY, 1300 Don Mills Rd., Don Mills, Toronto, Ontario M3B 3M8 Canada. (416)445-5600. Editor: Bill Markwick. 40-50% freelance written. Eager to work with new/unpublished writers each year. Monthly magazine; 64 pages. Emphasizes audio, science, technology, electronics and personal computing for a wide-ranging readership, both professionals and hobbyists. Circ. 20,000. Pays on publication. Publishes ms an average of 2 months after acceptance. Byline given. Buys all rights. Phone queries OK. Submit seasonal/holiday material 4 months in advance. Photocopied submissions OK. Electronic submissions OK; prefer IBM format disks with ASCII files. Computer printout submissions acceptable. SAE, IRC. Reports in 4 weeks. Free writer's guidelines.

Nonfiction: How-to (technical articles in electronics field); humor (if relevant to electronics); new product (if using new electronic techniques); and technical (on new developments, research, etc.). Buys 10 unsolicited mss/year. Query. Length: 600-3,500 words. Pays $75-100/1,000 words.

Photos: "Ideally we like to publish two photos or diagrams per 1,000 words of copy." State availability of photo material with query. Additional payment for photos accepted with accompanying manuscript. Captions required. Buys all rights.

Tips: "Less computer coverage will result in a shift to general science and hi-tech."

MODERN ELECTRONICS, For electronics and computer enthusiasts, Modern Electronics Publishing, Inc., 76 N. Broadway, Hicksville NY 11801. (516)681-2922. 90% freelance written. Monthly magazine covering consumer electronics, personal computers, electronic circuitry, construction projects, and technology for readers with a technical affinity. Circ. 75,000. Pays on acceptance. Publishes ms an average of 3 months after acceptance. Byline given. Offers 25% kill fee. Buys first North American serial rights. Submit seasonal/holiday material minimum 4 months in advance. Computer printout submissions acceptable; prefers letter-quality to dot-matrix. Reports in 1 week on queries; 3 weeks on mss. Sample copy $2; writer's guidelines for business size SAE and 1 first class stamp.

Nonfiction: General interest (new technology, product buying guides); how-to (construction projects, applications); new product (reviews); opinion (experiences with electronic and computer products); technical (features and tutorials: circuits, applications); includes stereo, video, communications and computer equipment. "Articles must be technically accurate. Writing should be 'loose,' not textbookish." No long computer programs. Buys 75 mss/year. Query. Length: 500-4,000 words. Pays $80-150/published page. Sometimes pays

66 *I prefer one query per letter. The worst ones read 'Are you interested in an article on tomatoes? peppers? cucumbers? How about okra, peas, asparagus?' The only reasonable response to such a letter is 'I'm not interested in anything!'* **99**

—*Pattie Vargas,*
Gurney's Gardening News

expenses of writers on assignment.

Photos: Send photos with query or ms. Reviews color transparencies and 5x7 b&w prints. Captions, model releases, and identification of subjects required. Buys variable rights depending on mss.

Tips: "The writer must have technical or applications acumen and well-researched material. Articles should reflect the latest products and technology. Sharp, interesting photos are helpful, as are rough, clean illustrations for re-drawing. Cover 'hot' subjects (avoid old technology). Areas most open to freelancers include feature articles, technical tutorials, and projects to build. Some writers exhibit problems with longer pieces due to limited technical knowledge and/or poor organization. We can accept more short pieces."

OMNI, 1965 Broadway, New York NY 10023-5965. Editor: Patrice Adcroft. 90% freelance written. Prefers to work with published/established writers; works with a small number of new/unpublished writers each year. Monthly magazine of the future covering science fact, fiction, and fantasy for readers of all ages, backgrounds and interests. Circ. 857,000. Average issue includes 2-3 nonfiction feature articles and 1-2 fiction articles; also numerous columns and 2 pictorials. Pays on acceptance. Publishes ms an average of 5 months after acceptance. Offers 25% kill fee. Buys exclusive worldwide and exclusive first English rights and rights for *Omni* anthologies. Submit seasonal material 4-6 months in advance. Photocopied submissions OK. Computer printout submissions acceptable; prefers letter-quality to dot-matrix. Reports in 6 weeks. Free writer's guidelines with SASE (request fiction or nonfiction).

Nonfiction: "Articles with a futuristic angle, offering readers information on housing, energy, transportation, medicine and communications. People want to know, want to understand what scientists are doing and how scientific research is affecting their lives and their future. *Omni* publishes articles about science in language that people can understand and afford. We seek very knowledgeable science writers who are ready to work with scientists and futurists to produce articles that can inform, interest and entertain our readers with the opportunity to participate in many ground breaking studies." Send query/proposal. Length: 2,500-3,500 words. Pays $1,750-2,000.

Photos: Frank DeVino, graphic director. State availability of photos. Reviews 35mm slides and 4x5 transparencies. Pays the expenses of writers on assignment.

Columns/Departments: Explorations (unusual travel or locations on Earth); Mind (by and about psychiatrists and psychologists); Earth (environment); Space (technology); Arts (theatre, music, film, technology); Interview (of prominent person); Continuum (newsbreaks); Star Tech (new products); Antimatter and UFO Update (unusual newsbreaks, paranormal); Stars (astronomy); First/Last Word (editorial/humor); Artificial Intelligence (computers); The Body (medical). Query with clips of previously published work. Length: 1,500 words maximum. Pays $850; $150 for Continuum and Antimatter items.

Fiction: Contact Ellen Datlow. Fantasy and science fiction. Buys 2 mss/issue. Send complete ms. Length: 10,000 words maximum. Pays $1,250-2,000.

Tips: "To get an idea of the kinds of fiction we publish, check recent back issues of the magazine."

POPULAR MECHANICS, 224 W. 57th St., New York NY 10019. (212)262-4815. Editor: Joe Oldham. Managing Editor: Bill Hartford. 50% freelance written. Monthly magazine; 200 pages. Circ. 1,625,000. Computer printout submissions acceptable; must be letter-quality. Buys all rights. Byline given. Pays "promptly." Publishes ms an average of 6 months after acceptance.

Nonfiction: Principal subjects are cars, woodworking, metalworking, home improvement, home maintenance, new technology, sports, electronics, boats, science, photography, audio and video. Also looking for adventure articles with a technology emphasis. No fiction. Looking for reporting on new and unusual developments. The writer should be specific about what makes it new, different, better, cheaper, etc. Query. Length: 300-2,000 words. Pays $300-1,500.

Photos: Dramatic photos are most important, and they should show people and things in action. Top-notch photos are a must for Home and Shop Section articles. Can also use remodeling of homes, rooms and outdoor structures.

POPULAR SCIENCE, 380 Madison Ave., New York NY 10017. Editor-in-Chief: C.P. Gilmore. 35% freelance written. Prefers to work with published/established writers. Monthly magazine; 150-200 pages. For the well-educated adult, interested in science, technology, new products. Circ. 1,800,000. Pays on acceptance. Publishes ms an average of 4 months after acceptance. Byline given. Buys all rights. Pays negotiable kill fee. Free guidelines for writers. Any electronic submission OK. Computer printout submissions acceptable; prefers letter-quality to dot-matrix. Submit seasonal material 4 months after acceptance. Reports in 3 weeks. Query. Writer's guidelines for SAE and 1 first class postage stamp.

Nonfiction: "*Popular Science* is devoted to exploring (and explaining) to a nontechnical but knowledgable readership the technical world around us. We cover the physical sciences, engineering and technology, and above all, products. We are largely a 'thing'-oriented publication: things that fly or travel down a turnpike, or go on or under the sea, or cut wood, or reproduce music, or build buildings, or make pictures, or mow lawns. We are especially focused on the new, the ingenious and the useful. We are consumer-oriented and are interested in any product that adds to the enjoyment of the home, yard, car, boat, workshop, outdoor recreation. Some of our 'articles' are only a picture and caption long. Some are a page long. Some occupy 4 or more pages. Contributors should be as alert to the possibility of selling us pictures and short features as they are to major articles. Freelancers should study the magazine to see what we want and avoid irrelevant submissions. No biology or life sciences." Buys several hundred mss/year. Pays $200/published page minimum. Uses both color and b&w photos. Pays expenses of writers on assignment.

Tips: "Probably the easiest way to break in here is by covering a news story in science and technology that we haven't heard about yet. We need people to be acting as scouts for us out there and we are willing to give the most leeway on these performances. We are interested in good, sharply focused ideas in all areas we cover. We prefer a vivid, journalistic style of writing, with the writer taking the reader along with him, showing the reader what he saw, through words. Please query first."

RADIO-ELECTRONICS, 500-B Bi-County Blvd., Farmingdale NY 11735. (516)293-3000. Editorial Director: Art Kleiman. For electronics professionals and hobbyists. Monthly magazine, 128 pages. Circ. 242,000. Buys all rights. Byline given. Pays on acceptance. Submit seasonal/holiday material 8 months in advance. Reports in 3 weeks. Send for "Guide to Writing."

Nonfiction: Interesting technical stories on all aspects of electronics, including video, radio, computers, communications, and stereo written from viewpoint of the electronics professional, serious experimenter, or layman with technical interests. Construction (how-to-build-it) articles used heavily. Unique projects bring top dollars. Cost of project limited only by what item will do. Emphasis on "how it works, and why." Much of material illustrated with schematic diagrams and pictures provided by author. Also high interest in how-to articles. Length: 1,000-5,000 words. Pays about $50-500.

Photos: State availability of photos. Offers no additional payment for b&w prints or 35mm color transparencies. Model releases required.

Columns/Departments: Pays $50-200/column.

Fillers: Pays $15-35.

Tips: "The simplest way to come in would be with a short article on some specific construction project. Queries aren't necessary; just send the article, 5 or 6 typewritten pages."

73 FOR RADIO AMATEURS, Peterborough NH 03458. (603)525-4201. Editor/Publisher: Wayne Green. Associate Publisher: Stu Norwood. For amateur radio operators and experimenters. Monthly. Buys all rights. Pays on acceptance. Reports on submissions within a few weeks. Query.

Nonfiction: Articles on anything of interest to radio amateurs, experimenters and computer hobbyists—construction projects. Pays $40-50/page.

Photos: Photos purchased with ms.

Tips: Query letter "should be as specific as possible. Don't hold back details that would help us make a decision. We are not interested in theoretical discussions, but in practical ideas and projects which our readers can use."

SPACE WORLD, 203W, 600 Maryland Ave. SW, Washington DC 20024. (202)484-1111. Editor: Tony Reichhardt. Managing Editor: Helga Onan. 80% freelance written. Prefers to work with published/established writers, but is open to new/unpublished writers. A monthly magazine covering the space program. "We publish non-technical, lively articles about all aspects of international space programs, from shuttle missions to planetary probes to plans for the future." Circ. 20,000. Pays on publication. Publishes ms an average of 3 months after acceptance. Byline given. Buys first North American serial rights. Simultaneous and photocopied submissions OK. Electronic submissions OK via IBM PC computer (Word Perfect Software), Hayes Smartcom 2 Modem, 300 or 1200 baud, but requires hard copy also. Computer printout submissions acceptable; prefers letter-quality. Reports in 2 weeks on queries; 1 month on mss. Sample copy for 9x12 SAE with 2 first class stamps; free writer's guidelines.

Nonfiction: Essays, expose, general interest, historical/nostalgic, how-to, humor, interview/profile, new product, opinion, personal experience, photo feature and technical. No very technical articles. Query with published clips, or send complete ms. Length: 1,000-2,000 words. Pays $150 for features. "Our circulation should go up, due to a new membership recruitment campaign. Pay for articles may rise as well."

Photos: Send photos with submission. Reviews 5x7 prints. Offers no additional payment for photos accepted with ms. Captions required.

Tips: "We're looking for behind-the-scenes, authoritative and accurate articles that aren't overly technical. We cover the whole wide range of space activities—the human side as well as the science. Assume that you are writing for a curious, intelligent lay person."

TECHNOLOGY REVIEW, Alumni Association of the Massachusetts Institute of Technology, Room 10-140, Massachusetts Institute of Technology, Cambridge MA 02139. Editor-in-Chief: John I. Mattill. 20% freelance written. Emphasizes technology and its implications for scientists, engineers, managers and social scientists. Magazine published 8 times/year. Circ. 75,000. Pays on publication. Publishes ms an average of 3-6 months after acceptance. Buys first rights. Phone queries OK. Submit seasonal/holiday material 6 months in advance of issue date. Simultaneous and photocopied submissions OK. Computer printout submissions acceptable. Reports in 6 weeks. Sample copy $2.50.

Nonfiction: General interest, interview, photo feature and technical. Buys 5-10 mss/year. Query. Length: 1,000-6,000 words. Pays $50-750. Sometimes pays the expenses of writers on assignment.

Columns/Departments: Book Reviews; Trend of Affairs; Technology and Economics; and Prospects (guest column). Also special reports on other appropriate subjects. Query. Length: 750-4,000 words. Pays $50-750.

‡**UFO REVIEW**, Global Communications, Box 1994, New York NY 10001. (212)685-4080. Editor: Timothy Beckley. Emphasizes UFOs and space science. 50% freelance written. Published 4 times/year. Tabloid. Circ. 50,000. Pays on publication. Publishes ms an average of 4 months after acceptance. Phone queries OK. Photocopied submissions OK. Reports in 3 weeks. Sample copy $1.25.

Nonfiction: Expose (on government secrecy about UFOs). "We also want articles detailing on-the-spot field investigations of UFO landings, contact with UFOs, and UFO abductions. No lights-in-the-sky stories." Buys 1-2 mss/issue. Query. Length: 1,200-2,000 words. Pays $25-75.

Photos: Send photos with ms. Pays $5-10 for 8x10 b&w prints. Captions required.

Fillers: Clippings. Pays $2-5.

Tips: "Read the tabloid first. We are aimed at UFO fans who have knowledge of the field. Too many submissions are made about old cases everyone knows about. We don't accept rehash. We get a lot of material unrelated to our subject."

Science Fiction, Fantasy and Horror

Additional science fiction, fantasy and horror markets are in the Literary and "Little" section.

AMAZING™ **Stories**, TSR, Inc., Box 110, Lake Geneva WI 53147-0110. Editor: Patrick L. Price. 90% freelance written. Eager to work with a limited number of new/unpublished writers. Bimonthly magazine of science fiction and fantasy short stories. "Audience does not need to be scientifically literate, but the authors must be, where required. *AMAZING* is devoted to the best science fiction and fantasy by new and established writers. There is no formula. We require the writers using scientific concepts be scientifically convincing, and that every story contain believable and interesting characters and some overall point." Circ. 13,000. Pays on acceptance. Publishes ms an average of 18 months after acceptance. Byline given. Buys first North American serial rights; "single, non-exclusive re-use option (with additional pay)." Photocopied submissions OK. Computer printout submissions acceptable; no dot-matrix. Reports in 10 weeks. Sample copy for $2.50; writer's guidelines $2, postpaid.

Nonfiction: Historical (about science fiction history and figures); interview/profile and science articles of interest to science fiction audiences; reviews and essays about major science fiction movies written by big names. No "pop pseudo-science trends: The Unified Field Theory Discovered; How I Spoke to the Flying Saucer People; Interpretations of Past Visits by Sentient Beings, as Read in Glacial Scratches on Granite, etc." Buys 4-8 mss/year. Query with or without published clips. Length: 300-10,000 words. Pays 6¢/word 3,000-6,000 words; 10-12¢/word for 12,000 or more words. Sometimes pays the expenses of writers on assignment.

Fiction: Contemporary and ethnic fantasy; science fiction. "We are looking for hard or speculative science fiction, space fantasy/opera, and fantasy. We don't want horror fiction or fairy tales. No 'true' experiences, media-derived fiction featuring *Star Wars* (etc.) characters, stories based on UFO reports or standard occultism." Buys 50-60 mss/year. Send complete ms. Length: 500-25,000 words. "Anything longer, ask." Pays 8¢/word to 6,000 words; 5¢/word for 12,000 or more words.

Poetry: All types are OK. No prose arranged in columns. Buys 10 poems/year. Submit maximum 3 poems. Length: 30 lines maximum; ideal length, 20 lines or less. Pays $1/line.

Tips: "Short fiction is the best way for freelancers to break in to our publication. We basically want good stories. We look for larger pieces by established writers, because their names help sell our product. Don't try to especially tailor one for our 'slant.' We want original concepts, good writing, and well-developed characters.

Avoid certain obvious clichés: UFO landings in rural areas, video games which become real (or vice-versa), stories based on contemporary newspaper headlines. '*Hard*' science fiction, that is, science fiction which is based on a plausible extrapolation from real science, is increasingly rare and very much in demand. We are moving away from heroic, pseudo-medieval European fantasies, and more toward ethnic (Japanese, Arabian, Central American, etc.) and contemporary fantasies. All sorts of hard, speculative, or militaristic science fiction desired."

ANALOG SCIENCE FICTION/SCIENCE FACT, 380 Lexington Ave., New York NY 10017. Editor: Dr. Stanley Schmidt. 100% freelance written. Eager to work with new/unpublished writers. For general future-minded audience. Monthly. Buys first North American serial rights and nonexclusive foreign serial rights. Pays on acceptance. Publishes ms an average of 6-10 months after acceptance. Byline given. Computer printout submissions (with dark ink) acceptable; prefers letter-quality to dot-matrix. Reports in 1 month. Sample copy $2.50 (no SASE needed); free writer's guidelines for SAE and 1 first class stamp.
Nonfiction: Illustrated technical articles dealing with subjects of not only current but future interest, i.e., with topics at the present frontiers of research whose likely future developments have implications of wide interest. Buys about 12 mss/year. Query. Length: 5,000 words. Pays 6¢/word.
Fiction: "Basically, we publish science fiction stories. That is, stories in which some aspect of future science or technology is so integral to the plot that, if that aspect were removed, the story would collapse. The science can be physical, sociological or psychological. The technology can be anything from electronic engineering to biogenetic engineering. But the stories must be strong and realistic, with believable people doing believable things—no matter how fantastic the background might be." Buys 60-100 unsolicited mss/year. Send complete ms on short fiction; query about serials. Length: 2,000-60,000 words. Pays 5-6¢/word for novelettes and novels; 6-7¢/word for shorts under 7,500 words;$450-550 for intermediate lengths.
Tips: "In query give clear indication of central ideas and themes and general nature of story line—and what is distinctive or unusual about it. We have no hard-and-fast editorial guidelines, because science fiction is such a broad field that I don't want to inhibit a new writer's thinking by imposing 'Thou Shalt Not's.' Besides, a really good story can make an editor swallow his preconceived taboos. I want the best work I can get, regardless of who wrote it—and I need new writers. So I work closely with new writers who show definite promise, but of course it's impossible to do this with *every* new writer. No occult or fantasy."

BEYOND . . ., Science Fiction and Fantasy, Other World Books, Box 1124, Fair Lawn NJ 07410-1124. (201)791-6721. Editor: Shirley Winston. Managing Editor: Roberta Rogow. 80% freelance written. Eager to work with new/unpublished writers. A science fiction and fantasy magazine published 4 times a year. "Our audience is mostly science fiction fans." Circ. 300. Pays on publication. Publishes ms an average of 6-9 months after acceptance. Byline given. Buys first North American serial rights. Submit seasonal/holiday material 6 months in advance. Photocopied submissions OK. Electronic submissions OK via Kaypro II, Wordstar, but requires hard copy also. Computer printout submissions acceptable; prefers letter-quality to dot-matrix. Reports in 3 weeks. Sample copy $4.50; writer's guidelines for SASE.
Nonfiction: Essays and humor. Buys 3 mss/year. Send complete ms. Length: 500-1,500 words. Pays $1.25-3.75 and 1 copy.
Columns/Departments: Reviews (of books and periodicals in science fiction and fantasy area), 500-1,500 words. Buys 3 mss/year. Send complete ms. Length: 500-1,500 words. Pays $1.25-3.75.
Fiction: Fantasy and science fiction only. "We enjoy using stories with a humorous aspect. No horror stories; excessive violence or explicit sex; nothing degrading to women or showing prejudice based on race, religion, or planet of origin. No predictions of universal destruction; we prefer an outlook on the future in which the human race survives and progresses." Buys 20 mss/year. Send complete ms. Length: 500-8,000 words; prefers 4,000-5,000 words. Pays $1.25-20 and 1 copy.
Poetry: Free verse, haiku, light verse and traditional. "Poetry should be comprehensible by an educated reader literate in English, take its subject matter from science fiction or fantasy, need not rhyme but should fall musically on the ear." No poetry unrelated to science fiction or fantasy. Buys 18 poems/year. Submit maximum 3 poems. Length: 4-65 words. Pays 2¢/line and 1 copy.
Tips: Fiction and poetry are most open to freelancers.

FANTASY REVIEW, Owned and operated by Meckler Publishing Corp., 11 Ferry Lane West, Westport CT 06880: Editorial offices at: Florida Atlantic University, 500 NW 20th St., Boca Raton FL 33431. (305)393-3839. Editor: Robert A. Collins. Associate Editor: Catherine Fischer. 50% freelance written. A monthly genre literary magazine about fantasy/horror/science fiction for authors, fans, scholars, editors, publishers, dealers, book store owners and students. Circ. 3,500. Pays on publication. Publishes ms an average of 2 months after acceptance. Byline given. Buys first North American serial rights. Submit seasonal/holiday material 4 months in advance. Simultaneous queries, and simultaneous and photocopied submissions OK. Query for electronic submissions. Computer printout submissions acceptable; prefers letter-quality to dot-matrix. Reports in 3 weeks on queries; 6 weeks on mss. Sample copy $1.25; writer's guidelines for SASE.
Nonfiction: General interest (essays directed to fans); historical/nostalgic (about authors, publishers, artists

in books, films, magazines, art in field); opinion (reviews of books, films, art); photo feature (fantasy and science fiction events); and surveys of foreign fiction, foreign fandom. "We don't want breezy fluff. We need solid research and reasoning, knowledge of field, plus easy style. No 'little green men invade our city' stuff. Writers must know the field." Buys 36 mss/year. Query or send complete ms. Length: 1,000-5,000 words. Pays 2-3¢/word.

Photos: State availability of photos with query letter, send photos with ms. Pays $5-25 for 5x7 or 8x10 b&w prints. Captions, model release, and identification of subjects required. Buys one-time rights.

Poetry: Free verse, haiku, light verse, traditional. "Poems must have a fantasy, horror, or science fiction twist. We don't want conventional topics." Buys 12 poems/year. Submit maximum 5 poems. Length: 3-30 lines. Pays $5-25.

Fillers: Cartoons, jokes, gags, newsbreaks. Fillers must have genre interest. Length: 50-150 words. Pays $5.

Tips: "We especially need good articles (*solid thinking*, entertaining style) on odd or representative authors, trends, topics within the field; also interviews with up-and-coming authors and artists *with* pictures. We are widening our scope to include gaming, films videos and comics. Need thoughtful (or scholarly) essays written in popular style. Good articles on gaming, comics, films now wanted."

HAUNTS, Nightshade Publications, Box 3342, Providence RI 02906. (401)781-9438. Editor: Joseph K. Cherkes. 98% freelance written. Prefers to work with published/established writers; works with small number of new/unpublished writers each year. "We are a literary quarterly geared to those fans of the 'pulp' magazines of the 30's, 40's and 50's, with tales of horror, the supernatural, and the bizzare. We are trying to reach those in the 18-35 age group." Circ. 1,000. Pays on publication. Publishes ms an average of 8 months after acceptance. Byline given. Buys first North American serial rights. Photocopied submissions OK. Computer printout submissions acceptable; prefers letter-quality to dot-matrix. Reports in 3 weeks on queries; 2 months on mss. Sample copy $2.50; free writer's guidelines.

Fiction: Fantasy, horror and suspense. "No fiction involving blow-by-blow dismemberment, explicit sexual scenes, or pure adventure." Buys 36 fiction mss/year. Query. Length: 1,500-10,000 words. Pays $5-33.

Poetry: Free verse, light verse and traditional. Buys 4 poems/year. Submit maximum 3 poems. Offers contributor's copies.

Tips: "Market open from June 1 to December 1 inclusive. How the writer handles revisions often is a key to acceptance."

THE HORROR SHOW, Phantasm Press, 14848 Misty Springs Ln., Oak Run CA 96069-9801. (916)472-3540. Editor: David B. Silva. 95% freelance written. Eager to work with new/unpublished writers. Quarterly horror magazine. Circ. 4,000. Publishes ms an average of 3 months after acceptance. Buys first serial rights. Computer printout submissions OK; prefers letter-quality to dot-matrix. Reports in 3 weeks. Sample copy for $4 and $1 postage; writer's guidelines for SAE and 1 first class stamp.

Columns/Departments: Nightmares (news about the horror field).

Fiction: Contemporary horror. "Articles should *not* splash over into science fiction or fantasy (sword and sorcery). We are specifically looking for material with well-developed characters. Do not over-indulge in sex or violence." Send complete ms. Length: 4,000 words maximum. Pays ½-1½¢/word plus contributor's copy.

Tips: "We enjoy the honor of publishing first stories and new writers, but we always expect a writer's best effort. Read the magazine. Come up with a unique premise, polish every word, then send it our way. A frequent mistake made by writers in completing an article for us is that the article is not directed at the reader. We look for informative articles directly related to the horror genre. In 1988, we will continue to slant each issue toward a specific author or artist in the field of horror."

ISAAC ASIMOV'S SCIENCE FICTION MAGAZINE, Davis Publications, Inc., 380 Lexington Ave., New York NY 10017. (212)557-9100. Editor-in-Chief: Gardner Dozois. 98% freelance written. Works with a small number of new/unpublished writers each year. Emphasizes science fiction. 13 times a year magazine; 192 pages. Circ. 125,000. Pays on acceptance. Buys first North American serial rights, nonexclusive foreign serial rights and occasionally reprint rights. "Clear and dark" photocopied submissions OK but no simultaneous submissions. Legible computer printout submissions acceptable; prefers letter-quality to dot-matrix. Reports in 6 weeks. Writer's guidelines for SASE.

Nonfiction: Science. Query first.

Fiction: Science fiction primarily. Some fantasy and poetry. "It's best to read a great deal of material in the genre to avoid the use of some *very* old ideas." Buys 10 mss/issue. Submit complete ms. Length: 100-20,000 words. Pays 5-8¢/word except for novel serializations at 4¢/word.

Tips: Query letters not wanted, except for nonfiction.

‡**THE NIGHTMARE EXPRESS**,Nocturnal Publications, 262 Sherburne #2, St. Paul MN 55103. (612)290-2068. Editor: Donald L. Miller. 75% freelance written. Bimonthly newsletter covering the markets and interests of horror writers. "*The Nightmare Express* is informing and providing members with a communication link, a way to exchange ideas, information on markets, and informative articles pertaining to the area of horror

Close-up

James Gunn
Author

In fiction writing classes at the University of Kansas, James Gunn tells his students they must learn to think of themselves as professionals. "I'm not doing them any favors if I let them think that editors will look at their stuff and say, 'It's marvelous' . . . when editors will really say, 'It's drivel!' "

An award-winning author of science fiction novels and nonfiction, Gunn also won awards for his work as an editor and as director of public relations for the University of Kansas, a position he held for 12 years before becoming a professor of English. In addition to his insistence on a professional approach, Gunn has a great deal of empathy for aspiring writers. He started writing science fiction in 1948 and was a fulltime freelancer for four years.

Gunn tells his students the only thing they have to sell is themselves. "They have a particular kind of genetic inheritance and a particular set of experiences that nobody else has. If they can manage to put that into good fictional form, it's something nobody else can do."

Gunn believes writers' experiences include more than just what they know. "They can also write about what they imagine, if they imagine it effectively enough. After all, the inside of their heads is unique, too." He encourages students to write about the things that really matter to them and to make those things matter to somebody else.

At the same time, Gunn reminds his students that nobody is really interested in what they write about their souls unless they can express it well. "Any kind of writing that isn't intended to be communication is simply therapeutic. If all you want to do is express your own anger or guilt, you might as well put it in a diary. That's fine for its purpose, but it's not writing. Writing is something that's intended to be read. So you have to express your uniqueness, but express it in a way that moves somebody else."

Gunn doubts that anyone can teach a writer to be more creative. He focuses on teaching his students the skills of criticism and revision. "First, they have to learn what's good and what's bad, particularly in their own writing. Then they have to learn to revise, to go back and rewrite. It's my theory that stories aren't written, they're rewritten."

Occasionally using his own work as an example, Gunn conducts manuscript workshops with his students. "We all start with the understanding that whatever we've written isn't good enough. We don't look for praise or strokes. We ask 'How can I make it better?' "

Gunn has obviously learned the lesson well. He is the author of 80 stories and 18 books, and the editor of six books. He has also written plays, screenplays, radio scripts, articles, verse and criticism.

Gunn summarizes 40 years' worth of insight and experience with characteristic understatement. "Writing is a hard, unrewarding occupation. You can usually make more money and get more satisfaction out of doing other things. But it's not a bad way to spend your spare time," he says with a slow smile, "better than in a saloon or in front of the television."

—*Becky Hall Williams*

fiction." Estab. 1986. Circ. 150. Pays on publication. Publishes ms an average of 4-6 months after acceptance. Byline given. Buys one-time rights and second serial (reprint) rights. Photocopied and previously published submissions OK. Computer printout submissions OK; no dot-matrix Reports in 1 weeks on queries; 2-3 weeks on mss. Sample copy $1.50; writer's guidelines for #10 SASE.

Nonfiction: Essays, general interest, how-to (write, sell, publish horror), interview/profile, opinion. "Plans special fiction issue for summer (each year). Reading for these issues will be between November and June (guidelines will be available). No material that discourages the aspiring author." Buys 10-12 mss/year. Query with or without published clips, or send complete ms. Length: 100-1,500 words. Pays $2-10. Pays for poetry and artwork with contributor copies or other premiums.

Columns/Departments: "Columns are already set, but I am open to new ideas." Buys 2/5 mss/year. Query. Length: 500-1,000 words. Pays $2-10.

Fiction: "The fiction used in *TNE* is accepted from members only." Horror mss and novel excerpts. "No 'cutsey' or fiction that holds back the terror." Buys 10-15 mss/year. Send complete ms. Length: 500-2,000. Pays ¼-½¢/word.

Poetry: Avant-garde, free verse, light verse and traditional. No poetry that doesn't relate to horror. Buys 25-40 poems/year. Submit maximum of 3 poems at one time. Length: 4-25 lines (prefers short poetry). "Payment is in contributor's copies."

Tips: "I am looking for informative articles that the author of horror fiction can touch base with. We also publish an annual special fiction issue. See *TNE* for details."

‡OWLFLIGHT, Science Fiction and Fantasy, Unique Graphics, 1025 55th St., Oakland CA 94608. (415)655-3024. Editor: Millea Kenin. 100% freelance written. Magazine published irregularly. "Science fiction and fantasy—stories, poems, b&w artwork, graphic stories must all be in this genre." Circ. 1500. Pays $10 deposit on acceptance, balance on publication; all on acceptance if $10 or under. Publishes ms an average of 24 month affter acceptance. Byline given. Buys first North American serial rights or second serial (reprint) rights. Simultaneous submisions acceptable if identified; photocopied submissions OK. Previously published submissions OK if over 5 years ago, outside North America and/or outside science fiction/fantasy genre in limited circulation. Computer printout submissions OK; dot-matrix acceptable only if dots are invisible to naked eye. Reports in 1 week on queries; 1-5 weeks on mss. Sample copy $3; free writer's guidelines with sample order. Writer's guidelines for #10 SAE with 2 first class stamps, without sample order.

Nonfiction: Humorous (non-fact articles) and speculative science and other background material for science fiction/fantasy. Buys 1-3 mss/year. Query. Length: 1,000-5,000 words. Pays 1¢/word.

Photos: State availability of photos with submission or send photos with submission. Reviews 4x5 to 8x10 prints. Offers $5-10 per photo. Payment negotiable. Identification of subjects required. Buys one-time rights.

Fiction: Adventure, erotica, experimental, fantasy, horror, humorous, mystery, as long ias it is also fantasy or science fiction. Does not want to see "anything that glorifies war, racism or sexism, or anything that isn't science fiction or fantasy. Buys 12-24 mss/year. Query "only to find out if we're open or overstocked—do not describe story." length: 3,000-10,000 words. Pays 1¢/word. "We also use graphic stories and assigned illustration for fiction; would consider plays."

Poetry: Avant-garde, free verse, haiku, light verse, traditional or any other style or form. Does not want to see "anything that does not have a clear science fiction or fantasy theme." Buys 12-36 poems/year. Submit up to 6 poems at one time. Length: 3-100 lines (8-50 preferred). Pays $1 minimum, 1¢/word.

Tips: "Get our guidelines—they are very detailed. Know proper mss submission formats and procedures. Send us stories and poems that are clearly genre science fiction or fantasy, or that are more experimental than genre science fiction/fantasy—not near-mainstream work with minimal science fiction/fantasy aspects."

PANDORA, Role-Expanding Science Fiction and Fantasy, Empire Books, Box 625, Murray KY 42071. Editors: Jean Lorrah and Lois Wickstrom. 95% freelance written. Works with a small number of new/unpublished writers each year; eager to work with new/unpublished writers. Magazine published 2 times/year covering science fiction and fantasy. Circ. 600. Pays on acceptance. Publishes ms an average of 6-12 months after acceptance. Byline given. Offers $10 kill fee. Buys first North American serial rights and second serial (reprint) rights; one-time rights on some poems. Photocopied submissions OK. Readable computer printout submissions on white 8½x11 paper acceptable. Reports in 6 weeks. Sample copy $3.50; writer's guidelines for SAE with 1 first class stamp.

Columns/Departments: Books Briefly. "We buy 200-word reviews of science fiction and fantasy books that a reader truly loves and feels are being ignored by the regular reviewers. Small press titles as well as major press titles are welcome." Buys 3-4 mss/year. Query or send complete ms. Length: 200-250 words. Pays 1¢/word.

Fiction: Experimental, fantasy, science fiction. "No pun stories. Nothing x-rated. No inaccurate science." Buys 15 mss/year. Send complete ms. Length: 1,000-5,000 words "except for controversial stories which may go to 10,000 words." Pays 1¢/word.

Poetry: Ruth Berman, 5620 Edgewater Blvd., Minneapolis MN 55417. Buys 9 poems/year. Length: open.

Tips: "Send us a complete short story. If we like it, we'll send you a critique with suggestions, if we don't want it just the way it is, but would want it with some more work. You don't have to do exactly what we've suggested, but you should fix weak spots in your story. Inexperienced writers often break in with a book or game review. We use very few articles, basically science articles or articles about writing science fiction. People sometimes submit totally unacceptable things they'd know we'd never touch if they'd been reading the magazine. For example, one writer sent a long gossipy scandal article appropriate to a newsstand scandal sheet, naming names and claiming claims. Definitely not for any magazine of our kind, as he'd have known if he had read previous issues."

SPACE AND TIME, 138 W. 70th St., New York NY 10023. Editor: Gordon Linzner. Biannual magazine covering fantasy fiction, with a broad definition of fantasy that encompasses science fiction, horror, swords and sorcery, etc. Circ. 500. 99% freelance written. Eager to work with new/unpublished writers. Pays on acceptance. Publishes ms an average of 2 years after acceptance. Byline given. Buys first North American serial rights. Photocopied submissions OK. Computer printout submissions acceptable; prefers letter-quality to dot-matrix. Reports in 2 months. Sample copy $4; guidelines for SASE.

Fiction: Fantasy, horror and science fiction. "Submit skillful writing and original ideas. We lean toward strong plot and character. No fiction based on TV shows or movies (*Star Trek*, *Star Wars*, etc.) or popular established literary characters (e.g., Conan) except as satire or other special case. No UFO, gods from space, or material of that ilk, unless you've got a drastically new slant." Buys 24 unsolicited mss/year. Length: 12,000 words maximum. Pays 1/4¢/word plus contributor's copies.

Poetry: Buys 12 poems/year. Submit maximum 5 poems. Length: open. Pays in contributor's copies. "Currently overstocked through 1988 and only interested in narrative poems."

Tips: "All areas are open to freelancers, but we would particularly like to see more hard science fiction, and fantasies set in 'real' historical times. No nonfiction or no fiction that cannot be considered science fiction or fantasy. We particularly enjoy uncovering new talent and offbeat stories for which there are few (if any) markets otherwise; seeing *S&T* authors go on to better paying, wider circulating markets. It seems to us that we're getting an unnaturally high percentage of horror, so our tendency will be to lean toward other science fiction/fantasy genres—and a possible format change may favor shorter works. We regret that we can't publish more material more often. A lot of good, interesting stories have to be passed over, and there are few other markets for genre fiction."

STARLOG MAGAZINE, The Science Fiction Universe, Starlog Group, 8th Floor, 475 Park Ave. South, New York NY 10016. (212)689-2830. Editor: David McDonnell. Managing Editor: Carr D'Angelo. 85% freelance written. Works with a small number of new/unpublished writers each year and is eager to work with new/unpublished writers. Monthly magazine covering "the science fiction-fantasy-adventure genre: its films, TV, books, art and personalities. We explore the fields of science fiction and fantasy with occasional forays into adventure (i.e., the James Bond and Indiana Jones films). We concentrate on the personalities and behind-the-scenes angles of science fiction/fantasy films with comprehensive interviews with actors, directors, screenwriters, producers, special effects technicians and others. Be aware that *sci-fi* is mostly considered a derogatory term by our readers and by us." Pays on publication. Publishes ms an average of 4 months after acceptance. Byline given. All contributors are also credited in masthead. Offers kill fee "only to mss *written* or interviews *done.*" Buys first North American serial rights to material with option to reprint (for an additional fee) certain articles in annual *Best of Starlog*. Buys second serial (reprint) rights to certain other material. Submit seasonal/holiday material 6 months in advance. Simultaneous queries and photocopied submissions OK. Computer printout submissions acceptable; prefers letter-quality to dot-matrix. Reports in 4 weeks on queries; 6 weeks on mss. "We provide an assignment sheet to *all* writers with deadline and other info, thus authorizing a queried piece." Sample copy $3. Writer's guidelines for SASE.

Nonfiction: Interview/profile (actors, directors, screenwriters who have made past or current contributions to science fiction films, and science fiction novelists); photo features; special effects how-tos (on filmmaking only); retrospectives of famous SF films and TV series; occasional pieces on science fiction fandom, conventions, etc. "We also cover animation (especially Disney and WB)." No personal opinion or "my" views of *Star Wars*, *Star Trek* or memories of when the writer first saw some film. *No* first person. "We prefer article format as opposed to question-and-answer interviews." Buys 150 or more mss/year. Query first with published clips. "We prefer queries by mail to phone queries. If we've never talked to you before, avoid making first contact with us by phone." Length: 500-3,000 words. Pays $35 (500-word pieces); $50-225 (1,000-word and up pieces). Avoids articles on horror films/creators—see listing for sister magazine *Fangoria* which covers horror in *Writer's Market* entertainment section.

Photos: State availability of photos. Pays $10-25 for color slide transparencies and 8x10 b&w prints depending on quality. "No separate payment for photos provided by film studios." Captions, model releases, identification of subjects, and credit line on photos required. Photo credit given. Buys all rights.

Columns/Departments: Other Voices (essays by well-known, *published*, science fiction writers on their genre work, the writing life or their opinions, especially needed); Fan Network (articles on science fiction fandom and its aspects—basically staff-written); Booklog (genre book news, mini interviews with authors and book reviews—this material is especially needed); Medialog (news of upcoming science fiction films and TV

projects and mini-interviews with those involved); and Videolog (videocassette and disk releases of genre interest, staff-written). "We also require science fiction news items of note, Comics Scene items (profiles of upcoming genre-oriented comic books/strips), items on fantasy, merchandising items of interest, toys, games and old science fiction film/TV reunion photos/feature material." Buys 24-30 mss/year. Query with published clips. Length: 300-750 words. No kill fee on logs. Payment for department items $35 on publication only.
Fiction: "We do *not* publish any fiction. *Stop* sending it to us."
Tips: "We expect to emphasize literary science fiction much more in 1988 and will need more interviews with writers and coverage of science fiction/fantasy literature. Additionally, we expect to cover science fiction/fantasy TV series, and films of the past in much more detail. A writer can best break in to *Starlog* with short news pieces or by getting an unusual interview that we can't get through normal channels (for example, an interview with Dino De Laurentiis or Stanley Kubrick), or by out—thinking us and coming up with something new on a current film or book before we can think of it. We are always looking for *new* angles on *Star Wars, Star Trek, Doctor Who, Blake's 7* and seek a small number of features investigating aspects (i.e., cast & crew) of series which remain very popular with many readers: *Lost in Space, Space 1999, Battlestar Galactica, The Twilight Zone, The Outer Limits.* Know science fiction media before you try us. Most full-length major assignments go to freelancers with whom we're already dealing. A writer can more easily prove himself with a short item. Discovering new freelancers and helping them to break into print is a special joy. We love it. We're fans of this material—and a prospective writer must be, too—but we were *also* freelancers. And if your love for science fiction shows through, we would love to *help* you break in."

STARWIND, The Starwind Press, Box 98, Ripley OH 45167. (513)392-4549. Editors: David F. Powell and Susannah C. West. 75% freelance written. Eager to work with new/unpublished writers. A quarterly magazine "for the young adult (18-25 or thereabouts) who has an interest in science and technology, and who also enjoys reading well-crafted science fiction and fantasy." Circ. 2,500. Pays on publication. Publishes ms an average of 6-12 months after acceptance. Byline given. Rights vary with author and material; negotiated with author. Usually first serial rights and second serial reprint rights (nonfiction). Photocopied submissions OK. Electronic submissions OK on IBM PC or PC compatible and Apple Macintosh. Computer printout submissions acceptable. Photocopied and dot-matrix submissions OK. "In fact, we encourage disposable submissions; easier for us and easier for the author. Just enclose SASE for our response. We prefer non-simultaneous submissions." Reports in 2-3 months. Sample copy for $3.50 and 9x12 SAE; writer's guidelines for business size SAE and 1 first class stamp.
Nonfiction: How-to (technological interest, e.g., how to build a robot eye, building your own radio receiver, etc.); interview/profile (of leaders in science and technology fields); and technical ("did you know" articles dealing with development of current technology). "No speculative articles, dealing with topics such as the Abominable Snowman, Bermuda Triangle, etc. At present, most nonfiction is staff-written or reprinted from other sources. We hope to use more freelance written work in the future." Query. Length: 1,000-7,000 words. Pays 1-4¢/word.
Photos: Send photos with accompanying query or ms. Reviews b&w contact sheets and prints. Model releases and identification of subjects required. "If photos are available, we prefer to purchase them as part of the written piece." Buys negotiable rights.
Fiction: Fantasy and science fiction. "No stories whose characters were created by others (e.g. *Lovecraft, Star Trek, Star Wars* characters, etc.)." Buys 15-20 mss/year. Send complete ms. Length: 2,000-10,000 words. Pays 1-4¢/word. "We prefer previously unpublished fiction."
Tips: "Our need for nonfiction is greater than for fiction at present. Almost all our fiction and nonfiction is unsolicited. We rarely ask for rewrites, because we've found that rewrites are often disappointing; although the writer may have rewritten it to fix problems, he/she frequently changes parts we liked, too."

THRUST—SCIENCE FICTION AND FANTASY REVIEW, Thrust Publications, 8217 Langport Terrace, Gaithersburg MD 20877. (301)948-2514. Editor: D. Douglas Fratz. 20% freelance written. Prefers to work with published/established writers; works with small number of new/unpublished writers each year. A quarterly literary review magazine covering science fiction and fantasy literature. "*THRUST—Science Fiction and Fantasy Review* is the highly acclaimed, Hugo-Award-nominated magazine about science fiction and fantasy. Since 1973, *THRUST* has been featuring in-depth interviews with science fiction's best known authors and artists, articles and columns by the field's most outspoken writers, and reviews of current science fiction books. *THRUST* has built its reputation on never failing to take a close look at the most sensitive and controversial issues concerning science fiction, and continues to receive the highest praise and most heated comments from professionals and fans in the science fiction field." Circ. 1,800. Pays on publication. Publishes ms an average of 6 months after acceptance. Byline given. Buys first North American serial rights, one-time rights and second serial (reprint) rights. Submit seasonal/holiday material 3-6 months in advance. Simultaneous queries, and simultaneous, photocopied and previously published submissions OK. Electronic submissions OK on IBM compatible-MS-DOS or PC-DOS with WordStar. Computer printout submissions acceptable; prefers letter-quality to dot-matrix. Reports in 2 weeks on queries; 2 months on mss. Sample copy for $2.50; writer's guidelines for SAE and 1 first class stamp.

Nonfiction: Humor, interview/profile, opinion, personal experience and book reviews. Buys 50-100 mss/ year. Query or send complete ms. Length: 200-10,000 words. Pays 1-2¢/word.

Photos: "We publish only photos of writers being interviewed." State availability of photos. Pays $2-15 for smaller than 8x10 b&w prints. Buys one-time rights.

Columns/Departments: Uses science fiction and fantasy book reviews and film reviews. Buys 40-100 mss/ year. Send complete ms. Length: 100-1,000 words. Pays 1¢/word. (Reviews usually paid in subscriptions, not cash.)

Tips: "Reviews are best way to break into *THRUST*. Must be on current science fiction and fantasy books. The most frequent mistake made by writers in completing articles for us is writing to a novice audience; *THRUST*'s readers are science fiction and fantasy experts."

TWILIGHT ZONE, Montcalm Publishing Co., 800 2nd Ave., New York NY 10017. (212)986-9600. Editor-in-chief: Tappan King. Associate Editor: Alan Rodgers. Managing Editor: Peter Emshwiller. 80% freelance written. Bimonthly magazine of fantasy fiction with stories by authors as diverse as Stephen King and Joyce Carol Oates. Circ. 110,000. Pays half on acceptance, half on publication. Publishes ms an average of 9 months after acceptance. Byline given. Buys first North American serial rights, first serial rights and second serial (reprint) rights. Submit seasonal/holiday material 9 months in advance. Simultaneous and photocopied submissions OK. Computer printout submissions acceptable; prefers letter-quality to dot-matrix. Reports in 3-6 months. Sample copy $3.

Fiction: Fantasy, understated horror and some surrealism. No sword and sorcery; hardware-oriented science fiction; vampire, werewolf or deals-with-the-devil stories. Buys 35 mss/year. Send complete ms. Length: 7,500 words maximum. Pays 5-8¢/word; $150 minimum. Sometimes pays expenses of writers on assignment.

‡2 AM MAGAZINE, Box 50444, Chicago IL 60650. (312)652-0013. Editor: Gretta M. Anderson. 100% freelance written. A quarterly magazine of fiction, poetry, articles and art for readers of fantasy, horror and science fiction. Estab. 1986. Circ. 500. Pays on acceptance. Publishes ms an average of 6 months after acceptance. Byline given. Buys first North American serial rights or one-time rights. Submit seasonal/holiday material 9 months in advance. Simultaneous, photocopied and previously published submissions OK. Computer printout submission OK; no dot-matrix. Reports in 1 month on queries; 2-3 months on mss. Sample copy $4.95; writer's guidelines for #10 SAE with 1 first class stamp.

Nonfiction: How-to, interview/profile, opinion. "No essays originally written for high school or college courses." Buys 5 mss/year. Query with or without published clips or send complete ms. Length: 500-2,000 words. Pay ½-1¢/word.

Photos: State availability of photos with submission. Offers no additional payment for photos accepted with ms. Identification of subjects required. Buys one-time rights.

Fiction: Fantasy, horror, mystery, science fiction and suspense. Buys 50 mss/year. Send complete ms. Length: 250-3,000 words. Pays ½-1¢/word.

Poetry: Free verse and traditional. "No haiku/zen or short poems without imagery." Buys 20 poems/year. Submit up to 5 poems at one time. Length: 5-100 lines. Pays $1-5.

Tips: "We are always interested in seeing short fiction under 1,000 words. Short-shorts are incredibly difficult to do well, and when we see a well-written short under 1,000 words we literally leap for joy. We can always find space in an otherwise-filled issue for an excellent story under 1,000 words."

Sports

For the convenience of writers who specialize in one or two areas of sport and outdoor writing, the publications are subcategorized by the sport or subject matter they emphasize. Publications in related categories (for example, Hunting and Fishing; Archery and Bowhunting) often buy similar material. Writers should read through this entire category to become familiar with the subcategories. Publications on horse breeding and hunting dogs are classified in the Animal category, while horse racing is listed here. Publications dealing with automobile or motorcycle racing can be found in the Automotive and Motorcycle category. Markets interested in articles on exercise and fitness are listed in the Health and Fitness section. Outdoor publications that promote the preservation of nature, placing only secondary emphasis on nature as a setting for sport, are in the Nature, Conservation and Ecology category. Regional magazines are frequently interested in sports material with a local angle. Camping publications are classified in the Travel, Camping and Trailer category.

Archery and Bowhunting

‡ARCHERY WORLD, All Season Bowhunter Action, Winter Sports Publishing, Suite 100, 11812 Wayzata Blvd., Minnetonka MN 55343. (612)545-2662. Editor: Rick Sapp. Managing Editor: Tim Dehn. 70% freelance written. A magazine published 8 times/year and written for bowhunting and archery enthusiasts who participate in the sport year-round. Circ. 165,000. Pays on publication. Publishes ms an average of 3 months after acceptance. Byline given. Offers 25% kill fee. Buys first rights. Simultaneous submissions OK. Reports in 2 weeks on queries; 4-6 weeks on mss. Sample copy for 9x12 SAE and 8 first class stamps; writer's guidelines for 9x4 SAE with 1 first class stamp.
Nonfiction: Essays, historical/nostalgic, how-to, humor, interview/profile and personal experience. No product reviews. Buys 50 mss/year. Query or send complete ms. Length: 1,400-3,000 words. Pays $100-250.
Photos: Send photos with submission. Reviews 35mm or 2¼ transparencies and b&w prints. Offers no additional payment for photos accepted with ms. Captions required. Buys one-time rights.
Columns/Departments: Action (hunting tips, hunting experiences: well written, interesting, and supported by at least one clear, well composed photo), 250-500 words. Columns on contract only.
Tips: "Writers should be bowhunters or at least familiar with bowhunting. They should read bowhunting stories published in *Archery World*, *Field & Stream*, *Outdoor Life* and *Sports Afield* to check the quality of writing and the types of subjects that are most used. Articles should come in ready to publish with a minimum of editing, and supported by a variety of good b&w prints and or slides."

BOW AND ARROW HUNTING, Box HH/34249 Camino Capistrano, Capistrano Beach CA 92624. Editorial Director: Roger Combs. 80% freelance written. Eager to work with new/unpublished writers. Bimonthly magazine for bowhunters. Pays on acceptance. Publishes ms an average of 6 months after acceptance. Buys first serial rights. Byline given. Computer printout submissions acceptable; prefers letter-quality to dot-matrix. Reports on submissions in 2 months. Author must have some knowledge of archery terms.
Nonfiction: Articles: bowhunting, techniques used by champs, how to make your own tackle, and off-trail hunting tales. Likes a touch of humor in articles. "No dead animals or 'my first hunt.' " Also uses one technical and how-to article per issue. Submit complete ms. Length: 1,500-2,500 words. Pays $150-300. Sometimes pays the expenses of writers on assignment.
Photos: Purchased as package with ms; 5x7 minimum. Pays $100 for cover chromes, 35mm or larger.
Tips: "Subject matter is more important than style—that's why we have editors and copy pencils. Good b&w photos are of primary importance. Don't submit color prints. We staff-write our shorter pieces."

BOWHUNTER MAGAZINE, 3720 S. Calhoun St., Fort Wayne IN 46807. (219)456-3580. Editor: M. R. James. Executive Editor: Cathy A. Dee. 90% freelance written. Eager to work with new/unpublished writers. Bimonthly magazine; 132 pages. For "readers of all ages, backgrounds and experience who share two common passions—hunting with the bow and arrow and a love of the great outdoors." Circ. 180,000. Buys first publication rights. Pays on acceptance. Publishes ms an average of 6-12 months after acceptance. "We include our Bowhunting Annual as part of the subscription package. This means we have seven issues each year including the Annual (on sale in July) which has been designated a Special Deer Hunting Issue." Submit seasonal material 8 months in advance. Reports in 6 weeks. Query for electronic submissions. Computer printout submissions acceptable; prefers letter-quality to dot-matrix. Sample copy $2; writer's guidelines for SAE with 1 first class stamp.
Nonfiction: "We want articles that inform as well as entertain readers. Writers should anticipate every question a reader may ask and answer questions in the article or accompanying sidebar. Most features deal with big or small game bowhunting (how-to, where-to-go, etc.) The 'Me and Joe' article is still considered here, but we do not cover all aspects of archery—only bowhunting. Unusual experiences are welcome and freshness is demanded, especially when covering common ground. Readers demand accuracy, and writers hoping to sell to us must have a thorough knowledge of bowhunting. No writer should attempt to sell material to us without first studying one or more issues of the magazine. We especially like articles that promote responsible bowhunting and combat anti-hunting attacks. Humor, personal experiences, interviews and personality profiles, nostalgia, personal opinions, and historical articles are good bets. No 'See what animal I bagged—ain't I great' articles." Buys approximately 100 mss/year. Query or submit complete ms. Length: 200-3,500 words. Pays $25-250, sometimes more. Sometimes pays the expenses of writers on assignment.
Photos: Photos purchased with or without accompanying ms. Pays $20-35 for 5x7 or 8x10 b&w prints; $50 minimum for 35mm or 2¼x2¼ color. Captions optional.
Tips: "We are very well stocked with all types of bowhunting articles and so are becoming increasingly selective about what we accept. Keep the reader foremost in mind. Write for him, not yourself. Know the sport

and share your knowledge. Weave helpful information into the storyline (e.g., costs involved, services of guide or outfitter, hunting season dates, equipment preferred and why, tips on items to bring, where to write for information, etc.). We have no set formula per se, but most features are first person narratives and most published material will contain elements mentioned above. We enjoy working with promising newcomers who understand our magazine and our needs. Most writers submit material 'on spec.' We reserve most assignments for staffers. We're upgrading the quality of our photos/illustrations and are editing more tightly. We still encourage submissions from non-professionals, but all should have useful information, hard facts, a slant to the average bowhunter."

Bicycling

BICYCLE GUIDE, Raben Publishing Co., 711 Boylston St., Boston MA 02116. (617)236-1885. Editor: Theodore Costantino. 25% freelance written. "We're equally happy working with established writers and new writers." Magazine published 9 times/year covering "the world of high-performance cycling. We cover racing, touring, and mountain biking from an enthusiast's point of view." Circ. 200,000. Pays on publication. Publishes ms an average of 4 months after acceptance. Byline given. Offers kill fee. Buys first North American serial rights. Submit seasonal/holiday material 6 months in advance. Simultaneous submissions OK. Computer printout submissions acceptable; prefers letter-quality to dot-matrix. Reports in 3 weeks on queries; 1 month on mss. Sample copy for 8½x11 SAE with 2 first class stamps; writer's guidelines for SAE with 1 first class stamp.
Nonfiction: Humor; interview/profile, new product, opinion; photo feature; technical; and travel (short rides in North America only). Buyers' annual published in April. "We need 'how-to-buy' material by preceding November." No entry-level how-to repairs or projects; long overseas tours; puff pieces on sports medicine; or 'my first ride' articles. Buys 18 mss/year. Query. Length: 900-3,500 words. Pays $200-600. Sometimes pays expenses of writers on assignment.
Photos: Send photos with submissions. Reviews transparencies and 5x8 b&w prints. Offers $50-250/photo. Captions, model releases, and identification of subjects required. Buys one-time rights.
Columns/Departments: What's Hot (new product reviews, personalities, events), 100-200 words; En Route (helpful hints for high performance cycling; on-the-road advice) 100 words; and Guest Column (thoughtful essay of interest to our readers) 900-1,200 words. Buys 30 mss/year. Query. Pays $25-450.
Tips: "Freelancers should be cyclists with a thorough knowledge of the sport. Area most open to freelancers are Training Methods (cover specific routines); Rides (75-100-mile loop rides over challenging terrain in continental U.S.); and Technical Pages (covers leading edge, technical innovations, new materials)."

BICYCLE RIDER, TL Enterprises Inc., 29901 Agoura Rd., Agoura CA 91301. (818)991-4980. Editor: Bob Mendel. Managing Editor: Merrill Pierson. 50% freelance written. Published 9 times a year. "A special interest magazine for the enthusiast who enjoys the sport of cycling for recreation, fitness, travel. Emphasis on reader participation rather than competition." Pays on publication. Byline given. Buys first North American serial rights. Submit seasonal/holiday material 5-6 months in advance. Sample copy $2; writer's guidelines for SASE.
Nonfiction: Book excerpts, essays, nostalgic, humor, inspirational, interview/profile, opinion, personal experience, photo feature, technical and travel. Buys 55 mss/year. Query with published clips. Length: 500-3,000 words. Pays $100-400 for assigned articles; pays $75-350 for unsolicited articles.
Photos: Send photos with submission. Reviews color transparencies. Offers no additional payment for photos accepted with ms.
Columns/Departments: How To (technical and technique tips); Maintenance (bicycle repair); For Beginners Only (basic, introductory cycling information). Query with published clips. Length: 500-750 words. Pays $200.

‡BICYCLING, Rodale Press, Inc., 33 E. Minor St., Emmaus PA 18098. Editor and Publisher: James C. McCullagh. 20-25% freelance written. Prefers to work with published/established writers. Publishes 10 issues/year (7 monthly, 3 bimonthly); 104-200 pages. Circ. 252,000. Pays on acceptance or publication. Publishes ms an average of 6 months after acceptance. Byline given. Buys all rights. Submit seasonal/holiday material 5 months in advance. Query for electronic submissions. Computer printout submissions acceptable; prefers letter-quality to dot-matrix. Writer's guidelines for SAE and 1 first class stamp.
Nonfiction: How-to (on all phases of bicycle touring, bike repair, maintenance, commuting, new products, clothing, riding technique, nutrition for cyclists, conditioning). Fitness is more important than ever. Also travel (bicycling must be central here); photo feature (on cycling events of national significance); and technical (component review—query). "We are strictly a bicycling magazine. We seek readable, clear, well-informed pieces. We rarely run articles that are pure humor or inspiration but a little of either might flavor even our most technical pieces. No poetry or fiction." Buys 1-2 unsolicited mss/issue. Send complete ms. Length: 1,500 words average. Pays $25-1,200. Sometimes pays expenses of writers on assignment.

Photos: State availability of photos with query letter or send photo material with ms. Pays $15-50 for b&w prints and $35-250 for color transparencies. Captions preferred; model release required.
Fillers: Anecdotes and news items for Paceline section.
Tips: "We're alway seeking adventurous accounts of bicycle touring."

CYCLING USA, The Official Publication of the U.S. Cycling Federation, 1750 E. Boulder St., Colorado Springs CO 80909. (303)578-4581. Editor: Diane Fritschner. 50% freelance written. Monthly magazine covering reportage and commentary on American bicycle racing, personalities, and sports physiology for USCF licensed cyclists. Circ. 24,000. Pays on publication. Publishes ms an average of 2 months after acceptance. Byline given. Offers 30% kill fee. Buys first serial rights and second serial (reprint) rights. Submit seasonal/holiday material 2 months in advance. Simultaneous queries, and photocopied and previously published submissions OK. Computer printout submissions acceptable; no dot-matrix. Reports in 2 weeks. Sample copy for 10x12 SAE and 60¢ postage.
Nonfiction: How-to (train, prepare for a bike race); interview/profile; opinion; personal experience; photo feature; technical; and race commentary on major cycling events. No comparative product evaluations. Buys 15 mss/year. Query with published clips. Length: 500-2,000 words. Pays 10¢/word.
Photos: State availability of photos. Pays $10-25 for 5x7 b&w prints; $175 for color transparencies used as cover. Captions required. Buys one-time rights.
Columns/Departments: Athlete's Kitchen, Nuts & Bolts, Coaches Column.
Tips: "A background in bicycle racing is important because the sport is somewhat insular, technical and complex. Most major articles are generated inhouse. Race reports are most open to freelancers. Be concise, informative and anecdotal. The most frequent mistake made by writers in completing an article for us is that it is too lengthy; our format is more compatible with shorter (500-800 word) articles than longer features."

VELO-NEWS, A Journal of Bicycle Racing, Box 1257, Brattleboro VT 05301. (802)254-2305. Editor: Geoff Drake. 20% freelance written. Works with a small number of new/unpublished writers each year. Monthly tabloid October-March, biweekly April-September covering bicycle racing. Circ. 14,000. Pays on publication. Publishes ms an average of 1 month after acceptance. Byline given. Buys all rights. Simultaneous queries, and simultaneous, photocopied, and previously published submissions OK. Electronic submissions OK; call first. Computer printout submissions acceptable; prefers letter-quality to dot-matrix. Reports in 2 weeks. Sample copy for 9x12 SAE.
Nonfiction: How-to (on bicycle racing); interview/profile (of people important in bicycle racing); opinion; photo feature; and technical. Buys 50 mss/year. Query. Length: 300-3,000 words. Pays $3/column inch.
Photos: State availability of photos. Pays $15-30 for 8x10 b&w prints. Captions and identification of subjects required. Buys one-time rights.

Boating

BAY & DELTA YACHTSMAN, Recreation Publications, 2019 Clement Ave., Alameda CA 94501. (415)865-7500. Editor: Dave Preston. 45% freelance written. Works with a small number of new/unpublished writers each year. Emphasizes recreational boating for small boat owners and recreational yachtsmen in northern California. Monthly tabloid newspaper; 90-166 pages. Circ. 22,000. Pays on publication. Publishes ms an average of 6 months after acceptance. Byline given. Buys one-time serial rights. Submit seasonal/holiday material 3 months in advance. Photocopied submissions OK. Electronic submissions OK via IBM Wordstar compatible, but requires hard copy also. Computer printout submissions OK. Reports in 1 month. Free writer's guidelines.
Nonfiction: Historical (nautical history of northern California); how-to (modifications, equipment, supplies, rigging, etc., aboard both power and sailboats); humor (no disaster or boating ineptitude pieces); informational (government legislation as it relates to recreational boating); interview; nostalgia; personal experience ("How I learned about boating from this" type of approach); photo feature (to accompany copy); profile; and travel. Buys 5-10 unsolicited mss/issue. Query. Length: 1,200-2,000 words. Pays $1/column inch.
Photos: Photos purchased with accompanying ms. Pays $5 for b&w glossy or matte finish photos. Total purchase price for ms includes payment for photos. Captions required.
Fiction: Adventure (sea stories, cruises, races pertaining to West Coast and points South/Southwest); fantasy; historical; humorous; and mystery. Buys 4 mss/year. Query. Length: 500-1,750 words. Pays $1/column inch.
Tips: "Think of our market area: the waterways of northern California and how, why, when and where the boatman would use those waters. Writers should be able to comprehend the boating and Bay Area references in our magazine. Think about unusual onboard applications of ideas (power and sail), special cruising tips, etc. We're very interested in local boating interviews—both the famous and unknown. Write for a knowledgeable boating public."

BOAT PENNSYLVANIA, Pennsylvania Fish Commission, Box 1673, Harrisburg PA 17105. (717)657-4520. Editor: Art Michaels. 75% freelance written. Quarterly magazine covering motorboating, sailing, canoeing, water skiing, kayaking and rafting in Pennsylvania. Pays 6-8 weeks after acceptance. Publishes ms an average of 8 months after acceptance. Byline given. Buys variable rights. Submit seasonal/holiday material 8 months in advance. Computer printout submissions acceptable; prefers letter-quality to dot-matrix. Reports in 2 weeks on queries; 2 months on manuscript. Writer's guidelines for #10 SAE with 1 first class stamp.

Nonfiction: How-to, photo feature, technical, and historical/nostalgic, all related to water sports in Pennsylvania. No saltwater material. Buys 40+ mss/year. Query. Length: 250-2,000 words. Pays $25-300.

Photos: Send photos with submission. Reviews 35mm and larger color transparencies and 8x10 b&w prints. Captions, model releases, and identification of subjects required. Buys variable rights.

Columns/Departments: Safety (any safety-related subject that directly relates to non-angling boating in Pennsylvania). Buys 8 mss/year. Query. Length: 250-500 words. Pays $25-75.

CANADIAN YACHTING MAGAZINE, Maclean Hunter Bldg., 7th Floor, 777 Bay St., Toronto, Ontario M5W 1A7 Canada. Editor: John Morris. 80% freelance written. Monthly magazine aimed at owners of power and sail pleasure boats, both cruising and racing. Canadian writers usually favored. Circ. 30,000. Pays on acceptance. Publishes ms an average of 6 months after acceptance. Buys first North American serial rights. Previously published submissions OK, but remember "our obligation not to duplicate material published in larger American magazines available in our reader area." Computer printout submissions acceptable.

Nonfiction: "Some of our 'entertainment' coverage of important racing events must be handled by U.S. freelancers. Cruise and humorous stories particularly in powerboats are welcome from anyone." Also uses occasional technical pieces, especially on motor maintenance. No general interest. Buys 20 unsolicited mss/year. Send complete ms. Length: 1,000-2,500 words. Pays $180-500 (Canadian).

Photos: Pays $15-40 for 8x10 b&w prints; $25-200 for 35mm color transparencies.

Tips: "Query should contain writer's experience and reassurance of photo quality (usually sample). In writing for us, stick to the outline, keep it Canadian and keep it relevant to our readers."

CANOE MAGAZINE, Canoe Associates, Box 3146, Kirkland WA 98083. (206)827-6363. Managing Editor: George Thomas. 80-90% freelance written. A bimonthly magazine on canoeing, whitewater kayaking, and kayaking. Circ. 55,000. Pays on publication. Publishes ms an average of 2-3 months after acceptance. Byline given. Offers 25% kill fee (rarely needed). Buys all rights. Submit seasonal/holiday material 4 months in advance. Electronic submissions OK via MS-DOS formatted 5¼" disc or ASCII data file transmitted at 300 or 1,200 Baud, but requires hard copy also. Computer printout submissions acceptable; no dot-matrix. Reports in 1 month. Free sample copy and writer's guidelines.

Nonfiction: Dave Harrison, articles editor. Essays, general interest, historical/nostalgic, how-to, humor, interview/profile, new product, opinion, personal experience, photo feature, technical and travel. Plans a special entry-level guide to canoeing and kayaking. No "trip diaries." Buys 60+ mss/year. Query with or without published clips, or send complete ms. Length: 500-2,500 words. Pays $5/column inch. Pays the expenses of writers on assignment.

Photos: State availability of photos with submission or send photos with submission. Reviews contact sheets, negatives, transparencies and prints. "Some activities we cover are canoeing, kayaking, canoe sailing or poling, canoe fishing, camping, backpacking (when compatible with the main activity,) and occasionally inflatable boats. We are not interested in groups of people in rafts, photos showing disregard for the environment, gasoline-powered, multi-horsepower engines unless appropriate to the discussion, or unskilled persons taking extraordinary risks." Offers $50-150/photo. Model releases and identification of subjects required. Buys one-time rights.

Columns/Departments: Dave Harrison, column/department editor. Competition (racing); Continuum (essay); Counter Currents (environmental); Put-In (short interesting articles)—all 1,500 words. Buys 60 mss/year. Pays $5-5.75/column inch.

Fiction: Uses very little fiction. Buys 5 mss/year.

Fillers: Anecdotes, facts, gags to be illustrated by cartoonist, and newsbreaks. Buys 20/year. Length: 500-1,000 words. Pays $5-5.75/column inch.

Tips: "Start with Put-In articles (short featurettes) of approximately 500 words, book reviews, or short, unique equipment reviews. Or give us the best, most exciting article we've ever seen—with great photos. Short Strokes is also a good entry forum focusing on short trips on good waterways accessible to lots of people. Query for specifics."

CRUISING WORLD, 524 Thames St., Newport RI 02840. (401)847-1588. Editor: George Day. 75% freelance written. Eager to work with new/unpublished writers. For all those who cruise under sail. Monthly magazine; 200 pages. Circ. 125,000. Pays on acceptance. Publishes ms an average of 8 months after acceptance. Rights purchased vary with author and material. Buys first world serial rights. Reports in about 2 months. Electronic submissions OK via IBM-PC, Wordstar, but requires hard copy also. Computer printout submissions acceptable; prefers letter-quality to dot-matrix.

Nonfiction: "We are interested in seeing informative articles on the technical and enjoyable aspects of cruising under sail. Also subjects of general interest to seafarers." Buys 135-140 unsolicited mss/year. Submit complete ms. Length: 500-3,500 words. Pays $50-500. Sometimes pays expenses of writers on assignment.

Photos: 5x7 b&w prints and color transparencies purchased with accompanying ms.

Tips: Interested in "short pieces (500 words) on: marine life; seaports; bird life; specific techniques; news of sailing events. The most frequent mistakes made by writers in completing an article assignment for us are missing our audience; missing our style; missing the point of the whole exercise; typing single-space; supplying unusable photos; writing too much but saying too little."

CURRENTS, Voice of the National Organization for River Sports, 314 N. 20th St., Colorado Springs CO 80904. (303)473-2466. Editor: Eric Leaper. Managing Editor: Mary McCurdy. 25% freelance written. Bimonthly magazine covering river running (kayaking, rafting, river canoeing). Circ. 10,000. Pays on publication. Publishes ms an average of 6 months after acceptance. Byline given. Offers 25% kill fee. Buys first North American serial rights, first rights and one-time rights. Submit seasonal/holiday material 2 months in advance. Simultaneous queries, and simultaneous, photocopied, and previously published submissions OK. Computer printout submissions acceptable; prefers letter-quality to dot-matrix. Reports in 2 weeks on queries; in 1 month on mss. Sample copy for $1 and 9x12 SAE with 73¢ postage; writer's guidelines for #10 SAE and 1 first class stamp.

Nonfiction: How-to (run rivers and fix equipment); in-depth reporting on river conservation and access issues and problems; humor (related to rivers); interview/profile (any interesting river runner); new product; opinion; personal experience; technical; travel (rivers in other countries). "We tell river runners about river conservation, river access, river equipment, how to do it, when, where, etc." No trip accounts without originality; no stories about "my first river trip." Buys 20 mss/year. Query with or without clips of published work. Length: 500-2,500 words. Pays $12-75.

Photos: State availability of photos. Pays $10-35. Reviews b&w or color prints or slides; b&w preferred. Captions and identification of subjects (if racing) required. Buys one-time rights.

Columns/Departments: Book and film reviews (river-related). Buys 5 mss/year. Query with or without clips of published work or send complete ms. Length: 100-500 words. Pays $5-50.

Fiction: Adventure (river). Buys 2 mss/year. Query. Length: 1,000-2,500 words. Pays $25-75.

Fillers: Clippings, jokes, gags, anecdotes, short humor, newsbreaks. Buys 5/year. Length: 25-100 words. Pays $5-10.

Tips: "We need more material on river news—proposed dams, wild and scenic river studies, accidents, etc. If you can provide brief (300-500 words) on these subjects, you will have a good chance of being published. Material must be on whitewater rivers. Go to a famous river and investigate it; find out something we don't know—especially about rivers that are *not* in Colorado or adjacent states—we already know about the ones near us."

LAKELAND BOATING, 1921 St. Johns Ave., Highland Park IL 60035. (312)432-8477. Editor: Brian Callaghan. 70% freelance written. Will work with new/unpublished writers, if they know boating. Prefers to work with published/established writers. Monthly magazine emphasizing pleasure boating in the Great Lakes region—both sail and power, but more emphasis on power. Circ. 46,000. Pays on publication. Publishes ms an average of 6 months after acceptance. Buys first serial rights. Query for electronic submissions. Computer printout submissions acceptable if legible. Reports in 2 months. Sample copy $2 with SAE and 39¢ postage.

Nonfiction: 2 "cruise" stories/issue. May be personal experiences, but reader must get enough details on ports, marinas, dangers, etc. to perform a similar cruise. Include sketches, maps, lists of marinas, access ramps, harbors of refuge. "We need 'people' stories about individuals living a water lifestyle on the Great Lakes or major inland rivers. We also need stories about waterfront developments such as new harbors, condominiums with dockage and tourist-type attractions which can be visited by boat." Query first. Length: 1,500-2,500 words. Fees vary.

Photos: Send photos with ms. Original 35mm or larger transparencies for color stories. Captions required or identification of all pictures, prints or transparencies. "Please stamp every transparency with name and address." Original photo materials are returned.

Tips: "*Lakeland Boating* readers are a mixture of powerboaters and sailers, with the dominate percentage for powerboaters. Writers should keep this in mind when submitting article suggestions and queries. All stories must have a Great Lakes or Midwestern freshwater slant. Cruise stories must give details. We don't want a 'Me 'n Joe' narrative of every breakfast and fuel stop. The waters being cruised and ports being visited are always more important than the people doing the cruising. Much of our editorial material is planned 6 to 12 months in advance. Biggest reason for stories being rejected are failure to meet our regional needs (failure to read our magazine to learn our slant and style), and poor writing. We would rather spend time developing a story right from the beginning than reject an otherwise well-written manuscript."

MOTORBOATING & SAILING, 224 W. 57th St., New York NY 10019. (212)262-8768. Editor: Peter A. Janssen. Monthly magazine covering powerboats and sailboats for people who own their own boats and are active in a yachting lifestyle. Circ. 145,000. Pays on acceptance. Byline given. Buys one-time rights. Reports in 3 months.

Nonfiction: General interest (navigation, adventure, cruising), and how-to (maintenance). Buys 5-6 mss/issue. Average issue includes 8-10 feature articles. Query. Length: 2,000 words.

Photos: Reviews 5x7 b&w glossy prints and 35mm or larger color transparencies. Offers no additional payment for photos accepted with ms. Captions and model releases required.

OFFSHORE, New England's Boating Magazine, Offshore Publications, Inc., 220-9 Reservoir St., Needham MA 02194. (617)449-6204. Editor: Herbert Gliick. 80% freelance written. Eager to work with new/unpublished writers. Monthly magazine (oversize) covering boating and the New England coast for New England boat owners. Circ. 24,000. Pays on acceptance. Publishes ms an average of 2 months after acceptance. Byline given. Offers negotiable kill fee. Buys first North American serial rights. Submit seasonal/holiday material 2 months in advance. Simultaneous queries, and simultaneous, photocopied, and previously published submissions OK. Electronic submissions OK via Kaypro PC disk, ASCI via phone, but requires hard copy also. Computer printout submissions acceptable. Reports in 1 week. Sample copy for 11x14 SAE and 88¢ postage.

Nonfiction: Articles on boats, boating and New England coastal places and people. Coastal history of NJ, NY, CT, RI, MA, NH and ME. Boat-related fiction. Thumbnail and/or outline of topic will elicit immediate response. Buys 125 mss/year. Query with writing sample or send complete ms. Length: 1,000-3,500 words. Pays 6-10¢/word.

Photos: Reviews photocopies of 5x7 b&w prints. Identification of subjects required. Buys one-time rights.

Tips: "Demonstrate familiarity with boats or New England coast and ability to recognize subjects of interest to regional boat owners. Those subjects need not be boats. *Offshore* does not take itself as seriously as most national boating magazines. The most frequent mistake made by writers in completing an article for us is failing to build on a theme (what is the point of the story?)." Also publishes second edition, *Northeast Offshore* serving NY and NJ coast.

PACIFIC YACHTING, Power and Sail in British Columbia, S.I.P. Division, Maclean Hunter, Ltd., 1132 Hamilton St., Vancouver, British Columbia V6B 2S2 Canada. (604)687-1581. Editor: Paul Burkhart. Monthly magazine of yachting and recreational boating. Circ. 20,000. 50-60% freelance written. Pays mostly on publication. Publishes ms an average of 6 months after acceptance. Byline given. Buys first and second serial (reprint) rights and makes work-for-hire assignments. Submit seasonal/holiday material 4 months in advance. Simultaneous queries, and simultaneous, photocopied, and previously published submissions OK. Query for electronic submissions. Computer printout submissions acceptable; prefers letter-quality to dot-matrix. SAE and IRCs. Reports in 2 months on queries; 6 months on mss. Publishes ms an average of 6 months after acceptance. Sample copy $2.

Nonfiction: Book excerpts, how-to, humor, interview/profile, new product, opinion, personal experience, photo feature, technical, travel. "Freelancers can break in with first-person articles about yachting adventures on the west coast of Canada accompanied by good 35mm photos. We're open to 'how-to' pieces by writers with strong technical backgrounds in the marine recreation field." No "poetry, religious, or first sailing experiences." Buys 150 mss/year. Will buy fewer stories in the year ahead. Query. Length: 100-2,000 words. Pays 20¢/word.

Photos: Send photos with ms. Reviews b&w contact sheets, b&w and color negatives, 35mm color transparencies (preferred) and prints. Captions and identification of subjects required. Buys various rights.

Columns/Departments: Scuttlebutt (news and light items, new gear, book reviews) and Boat Care (how-to). Buys 80 mss/year. Send complete ms. Length: 100-400 words. Pays $10-40.

Tips: "In working with freelancers we enjoy discovering fresh new perspectives in our own backyard. We regret, however, their failure to inquire or check out our magazine style."

‡PLEASURE BOATING MAGAZINE, Graphcom Publishing, Inc., 1995 NE 150th St., North Miami FL 33181. (305)945-7403. Publisher: Robert L. Ulrich. 10% freelance written. A monthly magazine covering boating, fishing, diving and sailing. "*Pleasure Boating* is distributed on major airlines and is directed to an audience of boat owners and those interested in sail and powerboating, along the East Coast from New York around the Gulf to Texas." Circ. 20,000. Pays on publication. Byline given. Buys first North American serial rights and all rights. Submit seasonal/holiday material 6 months in advance. Reports in 1 month on queries; 2 months on mss. Sample copy $2 with SAE and $1.58 postage.

Nonfiction: New product and boating experiences. Buys 4 mss/year. Query. Length: 2,500-3,000 words. Pays $250-300 for assigned articles; pays $100-150 for unsolicited articles. Sometimes pays the expenses of writers on assignment.

Photos: State availability of photos with submission. Reviews negatives, transparencies and prints. Offers $25-50 per photo. Captions, model releases and identification of subjects required. Buys all rights.

POWERBOAT MAGAZINE, 15917 Strathern St., Van Nuys CA 91406. Publisher: Bob Nordskog. 60% freelance written. Works with a small number of new/unpublished writers each year. For performance-conscious boating enthusiasts. January, West Coast Runabout Performance Trials; February, East Coast Runabout Performance Trials; March, Offshore Performance Trials; April, Water Ski Issue; May, Awards for Product Excellence; June through November/December, Race reporting and various other features on recreational boating. Circ. 82,000. Pays on publication. Publishes ms an average of 3 months after acceptance. Byline given. Buys all rights or one-time North American serial rights. Reports in 2 weeks. Query for electronic submissions. Computer printout submissions OK; prefers letter-quality to dot-matrix. Free sample copy.

Nonfiction: Uses articles about power boats and water skiing that offer special interest to performance-minded boaters, how-to-do-it pieces with good color slides, developments in boating, profiles on well-known boating and skiing individuals, competition coverage of national and major events. Query required. Length: 1,500-2,000 words. Pays $150-500/article. Sometimes pays the expenses of writers on assignment.

Photos: Photos purchased with mss. Prefers 35mm Kodachrome slides.

Tips: "We are interested in publishing more technical articles, i.e., how to get better performance out of a boat, engine or tow vehicle. When submitting an article, it should be in the area of *high performance* boating only. We *do not* cover sailing, large yachts, fishing boats, etc."

RIVER RUNNER MAGAZINE, Rancher Publications, Box 697, Fallbrook CA 92028. (619)723-8155. Editor: Ken Hulick. 90% freelance written. "Interested in working with new/unpublished writers who understand our needs and who submit material professionally." Seven-time-per-year magazine covering whitewater rafting, canoeing, and kayaking. "Audience is predominately male, college educated, and approximately 20-45 years old. The editorial slant favors whitewater action. Stories reflect the natural beauty and excitement of running rivers." Circ. 20,000. Pays on publication. Publishes ms an average of 4 months after acceptance. Byline given. Buys first North American serial rights. Submit seasonal/holiday material 6 months in advance. Computer printout submissions acceptable; prefers letter-quality to dot-matrix. Reports in 1 month on queries; 2 months on mss. Sample copy $2.50; writer's guidelines for 4x9 SAE and 1 first class stamp.

Nonfiction: Features on running a specific river (or region), with practical information for other paddlers, that convey a sense of place as well as whitewater action. How-to articles on techniques (mostly for immediate-level readers). Equipment overviews of canoes, kayaks, rafts, paddles, clothing and accessories. Occasional features on sea kayaking, competition whitewater racing, historical/personality profile, conservation, and alternative water sports (wave skiing, bathtub racing, etc.). "In 1988 we are going to be focusing a bit more on the whitewater enthusiasts who travel with guides and outfitters." No fiction or poetry. "We focus primarily on the United States, but regularly run features on other North American and international destinations." Buys 40-50 mss/year. Query with or without published clips or send complete ms. Length: 1,500-2,500 words. Pays 5-10¢/word. Sometimes pays the expenses of writers on assignment.

Photos: State availability of photos with query letter or submit with ms. Pays $25-75 for color transparencies; $15-45 for b&w prints. "We need good, sharp photographs that portray the total whitewater experience." Captions required. Buys first North American serial rights.

Columns/Departments: Conservation (focus on nationally relevant threats to rivers); Upfront (short, bright, lively commentary on off-beat aspects of river running; Reviews (cover, relevant books, videos, etc.); Tips (offers technical advice for all paddlers); Guided Whitewater (addresses the needs of guided clients) and Forum (often nonpaid column provided for recognized river spokespersons to voice opinions of interest to the paddling community). Buys 30-40 mss/year. Send complete ms. Length: 500-1,000 words. Pays 5¢/word.

Tips: "Submit fresh, original story ideas with strong supporting photographs. The prime need is for original, well-written river feature stories. Stories should be written for the intermediate-level paddler and display an understanding of our editorial needs."

SAIL, Charlestown Navy Yard, 100 First Ave., Charleston MA 02129-2097. (617)241-9500. Editor: Keith Taylor. 50% freelance written. Works with a small number of new/unpublished writers each year. Monthly magazine for audience that is "strictly sailors, average age 42, above average education." Pays on publication. Publishes ms an average of 6 months after acceptance. Buys first North American serial rights. Submit seasonal or special material at least 3 months in advance. Reports in 8 weeks. Computer printout submissions acceptable; no dot-matrix. Free sample copy.

Nonfiction: Patience Wales, managing editor. Wants "articles on sailing: technical, techniques and feature stories." Interested in how-to, personal experience, profiles, historical and new products. "Generally emphasize the excitement of sail and the human, personal aspect. No logs." Special issues: "Cruising issues, chartering issues, fitting-out issues, special race issues (e.g., America's Cup), boat show issues." Buys 200 mss/year (freelance and commissioned). Length: 1,500-3,000 words. Pays $100-800. Sometimes pays the expenses of writers on assignment.

Photos: Offers additional payment for photos. Uses b&w glossy prints or Kodachrome 64 color transparencies. Pays $600 if photo is used on the cover.

Tips: Request an articles specification sheet.

SAILING MAGAZINE, 125 E. Main St., Port Washington WI 53074. (414)284-3494. Editor and Publisher: William F. Schanen, III. Monthly magazine; 82 pages. For readers ages 25-44, majority professionals. About 75% of them own their own sailboat. Circ. 35,000. Pays on publication. Photocopied and simultaneous submissions OK. Reports in 6 weeks. Free writer's guidelines.
Nonfiction: Micca Leffingwell Hutchins, editor. "Experiences of sailing, whether cruising, racing or learning. We require no special style. We're devoted exclusively to sailing and sailboat enthusiasts, and particularly interested in articles about the trend toward cruising in the sailing world." Informational, personal experience, profile, historical, travel and book reviews. Buys 24 mss/year. Query or submit complete ms. Length: open. Payment negotiable. Must be accompanied by photos.
Photos: B&w and color photos purchased with or without accompanying ms. Captions required. Pays flat fee for article.

SAILING WORLD, North American Publishing Co., 111 East Ave., Norwalk CT 06851. Editor: John Burnham. 40% freelance written. Magazine published 12 times/year; 92 pages. Circ. 53,000. Pays on publication. Publishes ms an average of 4 months after acceptance. Buys first North American serial rights. Byline given. Query for electronic submissions. Computer printout submissions acceptable. Sample copy $1.75.
Nonfiction: How-to for racing and performance-oriented sailors, photo feature, profile, regatta reports, and travel. No travelogs. Buys 5-10 unsolicited mss/year. Query. Length: 750-2,000 words. Pays $50 per column of text.
Tips: "Send query with outline and include your experience. The writer may have a better chance of breaking in at our publication with short articles and fillers such as regatta news reports from his or her own area."

‡SEA, The Magazine of Western Boating, Duncan McIntosh Co., Inc., Box 1337, Newport Beach CA 92664. Editor: Duncan McIntosh Jr. Managing Editor: Cathi Douglas. 70% freelance written. A monthly magazine covering recreational power and sail boating, offshore fishing and recreation, environmental and coastal news of the West Coast. "*Sea* readers are well educated boat owners, knowledgeable about sail and power boating beyond the fundamentals." Circ. 48,000. Pays on publication. Publishes ms an average of 3 months after acceptance. Byline given. Negotiable kill fee. Buys first North American serial rights or second serial (reprint) rights. Submit seasonal/holiday material 6 months in advance. Photocopied and previously published submissions acceptable "occasionally." Query for electronic submissions. Computer printout submissions OK; prefers letter-quality to dot-matrix. Reports in 1 month on queries; 6 weeks on mss. Free sample copy and writer's guidelines.
Nonfiction: General interest (on boating and coastal topics); historical/nostalgic (on maritime lore and port history); how-to (tips on caring for boat, engine, etc.); humor (boating related); interview/profile (of prominent boating personality); opinion (on state of boating/coastal issues); travel (West Coast cruising destination); and racing rules. No extremely technical maintenance articles. Buys 60 mss/year. Query with or without published clips, or send complete ms. Length: 800-3,500 words. Pays $100-450 for assigned articles; pays $75-350 for unsolicited articles. Pays the expenses of writers on assignment.
Photos: Send photos with submission. Reviews contact sheets, transparencies and 5x7 prints. Offers $15-100 maximum per photo. Identification of subjects required. Buys one-time rights.
Columns/Departments: Harbor Hopping(features on West Coast cruising destinations), 1,000-2,500 words; West Coast Focus (West Coast boating news items), 800-1,000 words; Competition—Power, Sail (news items on racing), 800-1,000 words; Nautical Elegance (feature on a well-preserved, renovated antique boat), 800-2,500 words; Interview (feature on a prominent boating personality), 1,500-3,000 words. Buys 80 mss/year. Send complete ms. Pays $75-400.
Fillers: Facts, newsbreaks, short humor. Buys 6-12/year. Length: 250-1,000 words. pays $50-100.
Tips: "First-time contributors should include resume or information about themselves which identifies their knowledge of subject. Features are always welcomed. We will continue running cruising destination pieces, personality profiles and news items, and perhaps will increase coverage of coastal news and ecological/marine and pollution issues. Free deadline schedule available to writers."

SEA KAYAKER, Sea Kayaker, Inc., 1670 Duranleau St., Vancouver, British Columbia V6H 3S4 Canada. (604)263-1471. Editor: John Dowd. Managing Editor: Beatrice Dowd. 50% freelance written. Works with small number of new/unpublished writers each year. A quarterly magazine on the sport of sea kayaking. Circ. 10,000. Pays on publication. Publishes ms. an average of 6 months after acceptance. Byline sometimes given. Offers 20% kill fee. Buys first North American serial rights or second serial (reprint) rights. Submit seasonal/holiday material 6 months in advance. Previously published submissions OK. Computer printout submissions acceptable; prefers letter-quality to dot-matrix. Reports in 2 months. Sample copy $3.45; free writer's guidelines.
Nonfiction: Essays, historical/nostalgic, how-to (on making equipment), humor, inspirational, interview/profile, opinion, personal experience, photo feature, technical and travel. Buys 15 mss/year. Query with or without published clips, or send complete ms. Length: 750-4,000 words. Pays $75-400 for assigned articles; pays $50-200 for unsolicited articles. May negotiate payment with contributor copies or premiums rather than

cash if requested by writer. Sometimes pays the expenses of writers on assignment.

Photos: State availability of photos with submission. Reviews contact sheets. Offers $15-35/photo. Captions, model releases, and identification of subjects required. Buys one-time rights.

Columns/Department: History, Safety, Environment, and Humor. Buys 6 mss/year. Length: 750-4,000 words. Pays $50-400.

Fiction: Adventure, experimental, fantasy, historical, horror, humorous, mainstream, mystery, science fiction, slice-of-life vignettes and suspense. Buys 6 mss/year. Send complete ms. Length: 750-4,000 words. Pays $50-400.

Tips: "We do not accept telephone queries. We consider unsolicited mss that include a SASE, but we give greater priority to brief (several paragraphs) descriptions of proposed articles accompanied by at least two samples—published or unpublished—of your writing. Enclose a statement as to why you're qualified to write the piece and indicate whether photographs or illustrations are available to accompany the piece."

‡SMALL BOAT JOURNAL, S.B. Journal, Inc., Box 1066, Bennington VT 05201. (802)442-3101. Editor: Thomas Baker. Managing Editor: Richard Lebovitz. 95% freelance written. Bimonthly magazine covering recreational boating. "*Small Boat Journal* focuses on the practical and enjoyable aspects of owning and using small boats. *Small Boat Journal* covers all types of watercraft under 30 feet in length—powerboats, sailboats, rowing boats, sea kayaks and canoes. Topics include cruising areas and adventures, boat evaluations, and helpful tips for building, up-grading and maintaining, and safely handling small boats." Circ. 53,000. Pays on acceptance. Publishes ms an average of 6 months after acceptance. Byline given. Offers 50% kill fee. Buys first or second serial (reprint) rights. Submit seasonal/holiday material 4 months in advance. Simultaneous (as long as author agrees to give first rights to *SBJ*) and photocopied submissions OK. Query for electronic submissions. Computer printout submissions OK; prefers letter-quality to dot-matrix. Reports in 1 month on queries; 3 weeks on mss. Sample copy for 8½x11 SAE with 7 first class stamps; writer's guidelines for #10 SAE with 1 first class stamp.

Nonfiction: Book excerpts, essays, historical/nostalgic, how-to (boating, maintenance, restoration and improvements), humor, interview/profile, new product, personal experience, photo feature, technical and travel. Plans special issues on sea kayaking, rowing, electronics, engines, fishing boats and equipment, boatbuilding. Buys 60 mss/year. Query with or without published clips, or send complete ms. Length: 800-4,000 words. Pays $150-600 for assigned articles; pays $75-400 for unsolicited articles. Sometimes pays the expenses of writers on assignment.

Photos: Send photos with submission. Reviews contact sheets, transparencies and prints. Offers $15-200 per photo. Model releases and identification of subjects required. Buys one-time rights.

Columns/Departments: Seamanship (boating safety, piloting and navigation), 1,500 words; Rigs & Rigging (care and improvement of rigging and sails), 1,500 words; Ripples (personal experiences and reflections on boating), 1,000 words; Boatcraft (ideas for improving a boat), 1,500 words; Inside Outboards (care and maintenance of outboard engines), 1,500 words. Buys 40 mss/year. Query with published clips. Length: 900-2,500 words. Pays $50-400.

Fiction: Adventure, humorous and slice-of-life vignettes. Send complete ms. Length: 1,000-2,500 words. Pays $150-400.

Fillers: Anecdotes, facts, gags to be illustrated by cartoonist and short humor. Pays $25-100.

Tips: "Our best stories provide comprehensive, in-depth information about a particular boating subject. *SBJ*'s readers are experienced and sophisticated boating enthusiasts—most own more than one type of boat—and expect well-researched articles with a practical, how-to slant. Excellent photos are a plus, as are stories with engaging tales drawn from the author's experience." Most open to freelances are "topics related to seamanship, engine maintenance and repair, boat handling, boat building, hull maintenance and repair, restoration and historical subjects related to small boats."

SOUNDINGS, The Nation's Boating Newspaper, Pratt St., Essex CT 06426. (203)767-0906. Editorial Director: Christine Born. Eager to work with new/unpublished writers; works with a small number of new/unpublished writers each year. National monthly boating newspaper with nine regional editions. Features "news—hard and soft—for the recreational boating public." Circ. 100,000. Pays after "the 10th of the month of publication." Publishes ms an average of 3 months after acceptance. Byline given. Buys one-time rights. Deadline 5th of month before issue. Simultaneous queries and simultaneous and photocopied submissions OK. Electronic submissions OK via 300 baud. Computer printout submissions acceptable; prefers letter-quality to dot-matrix. Reports in 2 months on queries; 5 weeks on mss. Sample copy for 8½x11 SAE and 7 first class stamps; free writer's guidelines.

Nonfiction: General interest, historical/nostalgic, interview/profile, opinion and photo feature. Race coverage is also used; supply full names, home towns and the full scores for the top 10 winners in each division. No personal experiences. Send complete ms. Length: 250-1,000 words. Pays $10-150. Sometimes pays the expenses of writers on assignment.

Photos: Send photos with ms. Pays $20 minimum for 8x10 b&w prints. Identification of subjects required. Buys one-time rights.

Fillers: Short humor, newsbreaks. Length: 50-100 words. Pays $10-20.

TRAILER BOATS MAGAZINE, Poole Publications, Inc., Box 2307, Gardena CA 90248. (213)323-9040. Editor: Jim Youngs. Managing Editor: Bob Kovacik. 30-40% freelance written. Works with a small number of new/unpublished writers each year. Monthly magazine (November/December issue combined); 100 pages. Emphasizes legally trailerable boats and related activities. Circ. 80,000. Pays on publication. Publishes ms an average of 2 months after acceptance. Byline given. Buys all rights. Submit seasonal/holiday material 3 months in advance. Query for electronic submissions. Computer printout submissions acceptable; prefers letter-quality to dot-matrix. Reports in 1 month. Sample copy $1.25; writer's guidelines for SASE.

Nonfiction: General interest (trailer boating activities); historical (places, events, boats); how-to (repair boats, installation, etc.); humor (almost any boating-related subject); nostalgia (same as historical); personal experience; photo feature; profile; technical; and travel (boating travel on water or highways). No "How I Spent My Summer Vacation" stories, or stories not even remotely connected to trailerable boats and related activities. Buys 18-30 unsolicited mss/year. Query or send complete ms. Length: 500-3,000 words. Pays $50 minimum. Pays expenses of writers on assignment.

Photos: Send photos with ms. Pays $7.50-50 for 5x7 or 8x10 b&w glossy print; $15-100 for 35mm color transparency. Captions required.

Columns/Departments: Boaters Bookshelf (boating book reviews); Over the Transom (funny or strange boating photos); and Patent Pending (an invention with drawings). Buys 2/issue. Query. Length: 100-500 words. Pays 7¢-10¢/word. Mini-Cruise (short enthusiastic approach to a favorite boating spot). Need map and photographs. Length: 500-750 words. Pays $50. Open to suggestions for new columns/departments.

Fiction: Adventure, experimental, historical, humorous and suspense. "We do not use too many fiction stories but we will consider them if they fit the general editorial guidelines." Query or send complete ms. Length: 500-1,500 words. Pays $50 minimum.

Tips: "Query should contain short general outline of the intended material; what kind of photos; how the photos illustrate the piece. Write with authority covering the subject like an expert. Frequent mistakes are not knowing the subject matter or the audience. Use basic information rather than prose, particularly in travel stories. The writer may have a better chance of breaking in at our publication with short articles and fillers if they are typically hard to find articles. We do most major features inhouse."

WATERFRONT MAGAZINE, Southern California's Boating News Magazine, Duncan McIntosh Co. Inc., Suite C-2, 1760 Monrovia Ave., Costa Mesa CA 92627; Box 1579, Newport Beach CA 92663. (714)646-3963. Editor: Duncan McIntosh Jr. Managing Editor: Linda L. Yuskaitis. 60% freelance written. Prefers to work with published/established writers; works with a small number of new/unpublished writers each year. A monthly magazine covering recreational sail and power boating, offshore sportfishing and coastal issues in Southern California. "*Waterfront* readers are well-educated boat owners, and have knowledge of sail and power boating beyond the fundamentals." Circ. 30,000. Pays on publication. Publishes ms an average of 2 months after acceptance. Byline given. Offers negotiable kill fee. Buys first North American serial rights, or second serial (reprint) rights. Submit seasonal/holiday material 4 months in advance. Photocopied submissions OK, but prefers original; previously published submissions OK in some cases. Electronic submissions OK via WordStar word processing format only, but requires hard copy also. Computer printout submissions acceptable; prefers letter-quality to dot-matrix. Reports in 1 month. Free sample copy and writer's guidelines.

Nonfiction: General interest (boating/coastal topics); historical/nostalgic (maritime lore; histories of ports, old ships) how-to (tips on caring for a boat); humor (boating related); interview/profile (of prominent Southern California boating personality); new product (marine-related new products); and opinion (re: state of boating, race rules, coastal issues, etc.). No extremely technical maintenance articles or reviews on the performance of new boats. Buys 75 mss/year. Query with or without published clips, or send complete ms. Length: 250 (news)-2,200 (features). Pays $75-275. Pays some expenses of writers on assignment.

Photos: Send photos with submission. Reviews contact sheets, 2x2 transparencies and 5x7 prints. Offers $20/photo. Identification of subjects required. Buys one-time rights.

Columns/Departments: Channel Islands (coastal news and race results from Santa Barbara/Ventura/Oxnard area); Newport (coastal news and race results from Newport Beach/Oceanside/Dana Pt.); Marina del Rey to Long Beach (coastal news and race results from Marina del Rey/Los Angeles/Long Beach areas); San Diego (coastal news and race results from Oceanside/San Diego/Coronado areas); Fishing (record catches and regulation changes affecting Southern California anglers); Industry (news of promotions and business relocations of marine industry in Southern California); and Waterfront Forum (opinion pieces on issues affecting Southern California boatmen and their environment). Buys 70 mss/year. Send complete ms. All columns 250-750 words, except Waterfront Forum, 500-1,200 words. Pays $2/column inch.

Fillers: Marine facts, cartoons and short humor. Buys 10-20/year. Length: 250-500 words. Pays $25-75.

Tips: "We are most interested in receiving general interest boating articles, i.e. stories that are not limited to just sailboats or just power boats. Articles on how boat owners can enjoy related sports such as snorkeling, diving or beachcombing, for example, also are welcome. We woud like to see stories dealing with all aspects of the Olympic yachting events in Seoul, Korea (sports/personalities/human interest angles), with particular attention paid to Southern California and American sailors. First-time contributors should include resume or some information that identifies their writing qualifications and knowledge about the story subject. All subregional news departments (Channel Islands, Marina del Rey to Long Beach, Newport, San Diego) are very receptive to freelance contributions. Because of news slant here, material must be timely according to our deadlines, which are about six weeks prior to month of issue. Free deadline schedule available to writers."

‡**THE WESTERN BOATMAN**, Poole Publications, Inc., 16427 S. Avalon Blvd., Gardena CA 90248. (213)323-9040. Editor: Ralph Poole. Managing Editor: Elyse Mintey Curwen. 40% freelance written. A bimonthly magazine on pleasure boating. "Informed, authoritative service stories and well-backgrounded travel and how-to pieces are valued; conversational style that shows expert knowledge of the subject is a must." Circ. 30,000. Pays on publication. Publishes ms an average of 4 months after acceptance. Byline given. Buys first North American serial rights and one-time rights. Submit seasonal/holiday material 6 months in advance. Photocopied submissions OK. Computer printout submissions OK; prefers letter-quality. Reports in 6 weeks. Free sample copy and writer's guidelines.
Nonfiction: Historical/nostalgic, how-to, humor, interview/profile, opinion, personal experience, photo feature, technical and travel. "No ship's log (daily entry) style travel stories; limited hard-core sailboat racing." Buys 60-70 mss/year. Query with published clips. Length: 300-1,800 words. Pays $20-250. Sometimes pays the expenses of writers on assignment.
Photos: Send photos with submission. Reviews contact sheets, 2x2 transparencies and 5x7 prints. Offers $7.50-125 per photo. Captions and identification of subjects required. Buys one-time rights.
Columns/Departments: Boating/Travel (unique spots to visit in cruising destinations), 200-250 words; Calendar (all events possible on the water); News Brief (potpourri of happenings in boating), 150-250; Racing Circles (power and sailboat competition news), 200-500 words. Buys 50-60 mss/year. Send complete ms. Pays $150-200.
Tips: "Know the subject matter: boats and boating in the West. This is a special interest magazine for enthusiasts building skills and exploring the territory with their own boats. Query first and send photos with query, if possible—that really helps the editor evaluate the potential of a feature. News items should be written in news style."

WOODENBOAT MAGAZINE, The Magazine for Wooden Boat Owners, Builders, and Designers, WoodenBoat Publications, Inc., Box 78, Brooklin ME 04616. (207)359-4651. Editor: Jon Wilson. Executive Editor: Billy R. Sims. Managing Editor: Jennifer Buckley. Contributing Editor: Peter H. Spectre. 50% freelance written. Works with a small number of new/unpublished writers each year. Bimonthly magazine for wooden boat owners, builders, and designers. "We are devoted exclusively to the design, building, care, preservation, and use of wooden boats, both commercial and pleasure, old and new, sail and power. We work to convey quality, integrity, and involvement in the creation and care of these craft, to entertain, to inform, to inspire, and to provide our varied readers with access to individuals who are deeply experienced in the world of wooden boats." Circ. 110,000. Pays on publication. Publishes ms an average of 6-12 months after acceptance. Byline given. Offers variable kill fee. Buys first North American serial rights. Submit seasonal/holiday material 3 months in advance. Simultaneous queries and submissions (with notification) and photocopied and previously published submissions OK. Query for electronic submissions. Computer printout submissions acceptable. Reports in 3 weeks on queries; 4 weeks on mss. Sample copy $4; writer's guidelines for SASE.
Nonfiction: Technical (repair, restoration, maintenance, use, design and building wooden boats). No poetry, fiction. Buys 100 mss/year. Query with published clips. Length: 1,500-5,000 words. Pays $6/column inch. Sometimes pays expenses of writers on assignment.
Photos: Send photos with query. Negatives must be available. Pays $15-75 for b&w; $25-350 for color. Identification of subjects required. Buys one-time rights.
Columns/Departments: On the Waterfront pays for *information* on wooden boat-related events, projects, boatshop activities, etc. Buys 25/year. "We use the same columnists for each issue." Send complete information. Length: 250-1,000 words. Pays $5-50 for information.
Tips: "We appreciate a detailed, articulate query letter, accompanied by photos, that will give us a clear idea of what the author is proposing. We appreciate samples of previously published work. It is important for a prospective author to become familiar with our magazine first. It is extremely rare for us to make an assignment with a writer with whom we have not worked before. Most work is submitted on speculation. The most common failure is not exploring the subject material in enough depth."

‡**YACHTING**, CBS Magazine Div.; 5 River Rd., Cos Cob CT 06807. (203)629-8300. Editor: Roy Attaway. Editorial Director: John Owens. 30% freelance written. "The magazine is written and edited for experienced, knowledgeable yachtsmen." Circ. 150,000. Pays on acceptance. Byline given. Offers 50% kill fee. Buys first rights. Submit seasonal/holiday material 6 months in advance. Computer printout submissions OK; prefers letter-quality to dot-matrix. Reports in 2 weeks on queries; 1 month on mss.
Nonfiction: Book excerpts, personal experience, photo feature and travel. No cartoons, fiction, poetry. Query with published clips. Length: 250-2,500 words. Pays $250-1,000 for assigned articles. Pays expenses of

writers on assignment.

Photos: Send photos with submission. Reviews 35mm transparencies. Offers no additional payment for photos accepted with ms. Captions, model releases and identification of subjects required.

Columns/Departments: Cruising Yachtsman (stories on cruising; contact Jack Somer, editor); Racing Yachtsman (stories about sail or power racing; contact Guy Gurney). Buys 30 mss/year. Send complete ms. Length: 750 words maximum. Pays $250-500.

Tips: "We require considerable expertise in our writing because our audience is experienced and knowledgeable. Vivid descriptions of quaint anchorages and quainter natives are fine, but our readers want to know how they do it, too."

Bowling

BOWLERS JOURNAL, 101 E. Erie St., Chicago IL 60611. (312)266-7171. Editor-in-Chief: Mort Luby. Managing Editor: Jim Dressel. 30% freelance written. Prefers to work with published/established writers; works with a small number of new/unpublished writers each year. Emphasizes bowling. Monthly magazine; 100 pages. Circ. 22,000. Pays on acceptance. Publishes ms an average of 2 months after acceptance. Buys all rights. Submit seasonal/holiday material 3 months in advance of issue date. Photocopied submissions OK. Computer printout submissions acceptable; prefers letter-quality to dot-matrix. Reports in 6 weeks. Sample copy $2.

Nonfiction: General interest (stories on top pros); historical (stories of old-time bowlers or bowling alleys); interview (top pros, men and women); and profile (top pros). "We publish some controversial matter, seek outspoken personalities. We reject material that is too general; that is, not written for high average bowlers and bowling proprietors who already know basics of playing the game and basics of operating a bowling alley." Buys 15-20 unsolicited mss/year. Query, phone queries OK. Length: 1,200-3,500 words. Pays $75-200.

Photos: State availability of photos with query. Pays $5-15 for 8x10 b&w prints; and $15-25 for 35mm or 2¼x2¼ color transparencies. Buys one-time rights.

‡BOWLING, 5301 S. 76th St., Greendale WI 53129. (414)421-6400, ext. 230. Editor: Dan Matel. 15% freelance written. Official publication of the American Bowling Congress. Monthly. Pays on acceptance. Publishes ms an average of 2 months after acceptance. Byline given. Rights purchased vary with author and material; usually buys all rights. Reports in 1 month. Computer printout submissions acceptable; prefers letter-quality to dot-matrix.

Nonfiction: "This is a specialized field and the average writer attempting the subject of bowling should be well-informed. However, anyone is free to submit material for approval." Wants articles about unusual ABC sanctioned leagues and tournaments, personalities, etc., featuring male bowlers. Nostalgia articles also considered. No first-person articles or material on history of bowling. Length: 500-1,200 words. Pays $25-150 per article. No poems.

Photos: Pays $10-15/photo.

Tips: "Submit feature material on bowlers, generally amateurs competing in local leagues, or special events involving the game of bowling. Should have connection with ABC membership. Queries should be as detailed as possible so that we may get a clear idea of what the proposed story would be all about. It saves us time and the writer time. Samples of previously published material in the bowling or general sports field would help. Once we find a talented writer in a given area, we're likely to go back to him in the future. We're looking for good writers who can handle assignments professionally and promptly." No articles on professionals.

WOMAN BOWLER, 5301 S. 76th St., Greendale WI 53129. (414)421-9000. Editor: Bill Krier. 3% freelance written. Works with a small number of new/unpublished writers each year. Monthly (except for combined July/August) magazine; 64 pages. Circ. 150,000. Emphasizes bowling for women bowlers, ages 18-90. Buys all rights. Pays on acceptance. Publishes ms an average of 3 months after acceptance. Byline given "except on occasion, when freelance article is used as part of a regular magazine department. When this occurs, it is discussed first with the author." Submit seasonal/holiday material 2 months in advance. Photocopied and previously published submissions OK; prefers letter-quality to dot-matrix. Reports in 1 month. Free sample copy and writer's guidelines.

Nonfiction: Interview; profile; and spot news. Buys 25 mss/year. Query. Length: 1,500 words maximum (unless by special assignment). Pays $25-100.

Photos: Purchased with accompanying ms. Query. Pays $25 for b&w glossy prints. Model releases and identification of subjects required.

Gambling

GAMBLING TIMES MAGAZINE, 1018 N. Cole Ave., Hollywood CA 90038. (213)463-4833. Editor: Len Miller. Associate Editor: Adriene Corbin. Monthly magazine; 100 pages. 50% freelance written. Circ. 70,000.

Pays on publication. Buys first North American serial rights. Byline given. Submit seasonal/holiday material 5-6 months in advance of issue date. Computer printout submissions acceptable; prefers letter-quality to dot-matrix. Write for instructions on specific ms preparation for electronic typesetting equipment after query acceptance. Double-space all submissions, maximum 10 pp. Reports in 4-6 weeks. Publishes ms an average of 5 months after acceptance. Free writer's guidelines; mention *Writer's Market* in request.

Nonfiction: How-to (related to gambling systems, betting methods, etc.); humor; photo feature (racetracks, jai alai, casinos); and travel (gambling spas and resort areas). "Also interested in investigative reports focusing on the political, economical and legal issues surrounding gambling in the U.S. and the world and new gambling developments. No cutesy stuff. Keep your style clean, hard-edged and sardonic (if appropriate). Writers may query on any subject which is germane to our format." Buys 100 mss/year; prefers pictures with mss. Query. Pays $50-150.

Fiction: "We only use heavily gambling-related material and prefer fast-paced, humorous stories. Please, no more 'man scores big and dies' stuff." Buys 12 mss/year. Submit complete ms double spaced, maximum 9 pp. Pays $50-100.

Tips: "Know gambling thoroughly. *Pictures with mss will add $50 to the payment.* Action shots—always people shots. Photographs must show something unique to the subject in article. We enjoy the feeling of accomplishment when we've helped an amateur or beginner to make it into print. But we dislike a writer to begin a series of phone inquiries the day after he or she has mailed a submission."

POKER PLAYER, Gambling Times Inc., 1018 N. Cole Ave., Hollywood CA 90038. (213)466-5261. Managing Editor: Gary Thompson. 70% freelance written. Eager to work with new/unpublished writers. Biweekly tabloid covering poker games. (This is the only poker publication in the U.S.) Circ. 27,000. Pays on publication. Publishes ms an average of 1-2 months after acceptance. Byline given. Buys all rights. Query for electronic submissions. Computer printout submissions acceptable; no dot-matrix (except as samples). Reports in 1 month. Sample copy $1; free writer's guidelines.

Nonfiction: Book excerpts; how-to; humor; interview/profile; photo feature; and technical (poker strategy). Also needs articles on tournaments, local club news and regional legislative news. Anecdotes also considered. All articles must be poker related. Query. Length: 150-2,000 words. Pays $50 maximum.

Photos: State availability of photos. Reviews b&w prints.

Tips: "A solid, informative and well-written piece will be accepted regardless of length. Writers tend to think they are writing for a bunch of yahoos. Our readers know poker and want solid information. Vernacular is fine, but it can't be used to hide a lack of substance."

General Interest

CITY SPORTS MAGAZINE, Box 3693, San Francisco CA 94119. Editors: Dan Tobin in northern California; Greg Ptacek in southern California (1120 Princeton Dr., Marina del Rey CA 90291) and Will Balliet in New York (140 West 22nd St., 10th Floor, New York NY 10011). 80% freelance written. Works with a small number of new/unpublished writers each year. Monthly controlled circulation tabloid covering fitness, health and participant sports (such as running, cycling, tennis, skiing, water sports, etc.). Circ. in California 203,000; in NY 100,000. Three editions published monthly—for northern California, southern California and New York. 50% of editorial features run nationally, and 50% run in one of the regional editions. Pays on acceptance for features. Publishes ms an average of 2 months after acceptance. Uses assignment contracts. Pays negotiable kill fee. Buys one-time rights. Simultaneous and previously published submissions OK. Query for electronic submissions. Computer printout submissions OK. Reports in 1 month on queries. Sample copy $3.

Nonfiction: Interview/profile of participant athletes; travel; instructional and service pieces on sports and fitness; health and nutrition articles; humor. "We accept very few first-person sports accounts unless they are very unusual (such as first-time expeditions or sports participation in exotic locale) or humorous." Special issues include: Health Clubs (February); Sports Vacations (April); Running (May); Bicycling and Outdoors (June); Fitness Walking (July); Sports Medicine (October); Downhill Skiing (November); Cross-Country Skiing (December). Buys 70 mss/year. Query with clips of published work. Length: 1,200-2,800 words. Pays $150-350 for regionally run features; $200-700 for national features.

Photos: Pays $40-80 for 35mm color; $200-500 for covers; $20-50 for b&w 8x10 glossy prints. Model releases and identification of subjects required.

Tips: "We are including more articles on general health, fitness, nutrition and travel in addition to our mainstay articles on participant sports."

NEW ENGLAND OUT-OF-DOORS MAGAZINE, (formerly Massachusetts/New Hampshire Out-of-Doors), 510 King St., Box 248, Littleton MA 01460. (617)486-4785. Editor: Bryant "Red" Chaplin. 20% freelance written. A monthly tabloid covering hunting, fishing, camping, shooting: "useful news and information on how to, where to, in New England area, adjoining states and Northeastern Canadian provinces; occasional philosophical pieces." Circ. 21,000. Pays on publication. Publishes on average 3 months after acceptance. Byline given. Buys one-time rights. Submit seasonal/holiday material 3 months in advance. Query for electronic submissions. Computer printout submissions acceptable. Reports in 2 weeks. Sample copy for 9x12 SAE.

Nonfiction: How-to (hunt, fish, camp, shoot, aimed at mature sportsmen who don't need beginner basics); inspirational (*why* we hunt/fish philosophical "mood" pieces); personal experience; and travel (where to). "We do not accept product/service pieces about non-advertisers obviously written to pay off free product or trip writer received." Buys 40-50 mss/year. Length: 800-1,800 words (flexible). Pays $1/typeset column inch.

Photos: Send photos with submissions; 1-5 maximum. Reviews b&w prints only. Offers $10 inside; $25 cover. Captions required. Buys one-time rights.

Tips: "Front-of-book feature articles are most open to freelancers. Context should be set in New England and or must be about New England people, if set elsewhere. Writer should include factual information, costs, how to plan, etc., so the reader can see himself duplicating the trip. Don't expect to write about New England hunting/fishing if you live somewhere else; it won't go. We abhor the writer who thinks he can localize any story by just changing place names. Know your subject first of all—writing is secondary."

OUTDOOR CANADA MAGAZINE, Suite 301, 801 York Mills Rd., Don Mills, Ontario M3B 1X7 Canada. (416)443-8888. Editor-in-Chief: Teddi Brown. 70% freelance written. Works with a small number of new/unpublished writers each year. Emphasizes noncompetitive outdoor recreation in Canada *only*. Magazine published 8 times/year; 72-120 pages. Circ. 141,000. Pays on publication. Publishes ms an average of 6-8 months after acceptance. Buys first rights. Submit seasonal/holiday material 1 year in advance of issue date. Byline given. Originals only. Computer printout submissions acceptable; no dot-matrix. *SASE or IRCs or material not returned.* Reports in 1 month. Mention *Writer's Market* in request for editorial guidelines.

Nonfiction: Adventures, outdoor issues, fishing, exploring, outdoor destinations in Canada, some how-to. Buys 35-40 mss/year, usually with photos. Length: 1,000-2,500 words. Pays $100 and up. Sometimes pays the expenses of writers on assignment.

Photos: Emphasize people in the outdoors. Pays $20-50 for 8x10 b&w glossy prints; $30-150 for 35mm color transparencies; and $300/cover. Captions and model releases required.

News: Short news pieces. Buys 70-80/year. Length: 200-500 words. Pays $6/printed inch.

REFEREE, Referee Enterprises, Inc., Box 161, Franksville WI 53126. (414)632-8855. Editor: Tom Hammill. For well-educated, mostly 26- to 50-year-old male sports officials. 20-25% freelance written. Eager to work with new/unpublished writers; works with a small number of new/unpublished writers each year. Monthly magazine. Circ. 42,000. Pays on acceptance of completed manuscript. Publishes ms an average of 3-6 months after acceptance. Rights purchased varies. Submit seasonal/holiday material 6 months in advance. Photocopied and previously published submissions OK. Computer printout submissions acceptable. Reports in 2 weeks. Free sample copy.

Nonfiction: How-to, informational, humor, interview, profile, personal experience, photo feature and technical. Buys 54 mss/year. Query. Length: 700-3,000 words. Pays 4-10¢/word. "No general sports articles." Recent article example: "Story about a 22-year-old amateur league umpire whose goal was to become a major umpire. He worked for a year in the minor leagues, but was released after the 1983 season. In July 1984 he committed suicide by hanging himself." (May 1986). Sometimes pays the expenses of writers on assignment.

Photos: Purchased with or without accompanying ms or on assignment. Captions preferred. Send contact sheet, prints, negatives or transparencies. Pays $15-25 for each b&w used; $25-40 for each color used; $75-100 for color cover. Sometimes pays the expenses of writers on assignment.

Columns/Departments: Arena (bios); Law (legal aspects); Take Care (fitness, medical). Buys 24 mss/year. Query. Length: 200-800 words. Pays 4¢/word up to $50 maximum for Law and Take Care. Arena pays about $15 each, regardless of length.

Fillers: Jokes, gags, anecdotes, puzzles and referee shorts. Query. Length: 50-200 words. Pays 4¢/word in some cases; others offer only author credit lines.

Tips: "Queries with a specific idea appeal most to readers. Generally, we are looking more for feature writers, as we usually do our own shorter/filler-type material. It is helpful to obtain suitable photos to augment a story. Don't send fluff—we need hard-hitting, incisive material tailored just for our audience. Anything smacking of public relations is a no sale. Don't gloss over the material too lightly or fail to go in-depth looking for a quick sale (taking the avenue of least resistance)."

‡SPORTS HISTORY, Empire Press, 105 Loudon St. SW, Leesburg VA 22075. (203)771-9400. Editor: Mark Farber. 95% freelance written. Bimonthly magazine devoted to "the great athletes and events from our sporting past." Estab. 1987. Circ. 110,000. Pays on publication. Byline given. Offers negotiable kill fee. Buys first North American serial rights. Submit seasonal/holiday material 1 year in advance. Photocopied submissions OK. Reports in 3-4 months. Sample copy $4; writer's guidelines for SAE with 1 first class stamp.

Nonfiction: Historical/nostalgic and personal experience. Buys 24 feature mss/year. Query. Length: 4,000 words. Pays $300. Sometimes pays the expenses of writers on assignment.

Photos: State availability of photos with submission. Offers no additional payment for photos accepted with ms.

Columns/Departments: Personality (profiles); Great Moments (high drama); Stats (faces behind stats). Buys 18 mss/year. Query. Length: 2,000 words. Pays $150.

SPORTSCAN™, Brannigan-Demarco Communications, Inc., 141 5th Ave., New York NY 10010. (212)505-7600. Editor-in-Chief: Kevin McShane. Assistant Editor: Maggie Schwarz. 75% freelance written. A bimonthly magazine covering sports nostalgia and sports training. "*Sportscan* is sponsored by a pharmaceutical company and sent free to doctors and pharmacists." Circ. 75,000. Pays on acceptance. Publishes an average of 4 months after acceptance. Offers 15% kill fee. Buys all rights. Submit seasonal/holiday material 4 months in advance. Photocopied and previously published submissions OK. Computer printout submissions acceptable; prefers letter-quality to dot-matrix. Reports in 2 weeks on queries; 1 month on mss. Free sample copy and writer's guidelines.

Nonfiction: Historical/nostalgic (sports-related); training (especially medical aspects); interview/profile (sports figures, especially nostalgic slant); and analysis of trends in sports. No sports medicine. Buys 40 mss/year. Query with published clips, or send complete ms. Length: 1,000-1,500 words. Pays $500-1,000 for assigned articles; pays $300-1,000 for unsolicited articles.

Photos: State availability of photos with submission. Reviews contact sheets. Offers $50-100/photo. Captions required. Buys one-time rights.

Columns/Departments: Fast Break (sports shorts, trivia, humorous news items, etc.), 200-250 words; Book Scan (book reviews of sports-related topics), 200-250 words; and Where Have You Gone (interviews with sports legends no longer in the public eye), 1,000-1,500 words. Buys 10 mss/year. Query with published clips or send complete ms. Pays $100-500.

Tips: "Send written query outlining the proposed article and any writing sample that might demonstrate the tone or angle. Sports nostalgia features and Fast Break items are most open to freelancers."

SPORTS PARADE, Meridian Publishing Co., Inc., Box 10010, Odgen UT 84409. (801)394-9446. Editor: Robyn Walker. 65% freelance written. Works with a small number of new/unpublished writers each year. A monthly general interest sports magazine distributed by business and professional firms to employees, customers, clients, etc. Readers are predominantly upscale, mainstream, family oriented. Circ. 40,000. Pays on acceptance. Publishes ms an average of 8 months after acceptance. Byline given. Buys first rights, second serial (reprint) rights or nonexclusive reprint rights. Submit seasonal/holiday material 6 months in advance. Simultaneous, photocopied and previously published submissions OK. Computer printout submissions acceptable; prefers letter-quality to dot-matrix. Reports in 6 weeks. Sample copy $1 with 9x12 SAE; writer's guidelines for business size SAE and 1 first class stamp.

Nonfiction: General interest, historical/nostalgic and interview/profile. "General interest articles covering the entire sports spectrum, from the National Football league to horseshoes. Personality profiles on top flight professional and amateur sports figures are used as cover stories. Stories about heroes of the past are also welcome if color photos and/or artwork are available." Buys 20 mss/year. Query. Length: 1,100-1,200 words. Pays 15¢/word.

Photos: Send with query or ms. Pays $35 for color transparencies; $50 for cover. Captions and model releases required.

Tips: "I will be purchasing more articles based on personalities—today's stars as well as yesterday's heroes."

WISCONSIN SILENT SPORTS, Waupaca Publishing Co., Box 152, Waupaca WI 54981. (715)258-7731. Editor: Greg Marr. 75% freelance written. Eager to work with new/unpublished writers. Monthly magazine on running, cycling, cross-country skiing, canoeing, camping, backpacking, hiking. A regional publication aimed at people who run, cycle, cross-country ski, canoe, camp and hike in Wisconsin. Not a "coffee-table" magazine. "Our readers are participants from rank amateur weekend athletes to highly competitive racers." Circ. 10,000. Pays on publication. Publishes ms an average of 2 months after acceptance. Byline given. Offers 20% kill fee. Buys one-time rights. Submit seasonal/holiday material 2 months in advance. Simultaneous queries, and photocopied and previously published submissions OK. Computer printout submissions acceptable; prefers letter-quality to dot-matrix. Reports in 1 month. Sample copy and writer's guidelines for large SAE and 5 first class stamps.

Nonfiction: General interest, how-to, interview/profile, new product, opinion, technical and travel. No first person unless it is of Edward Abbey/Norman Mailer quality. Buys 25 mss/year. Query. Length: 2,500 words maximum. Pays $15-100. Sometimes pays expenses of writers on assignment.

Tips: "Where-to-go, how-to, and personality profiles are areas most open to freelancers. Writers should keep in mind that this is a regional Wisconsin-based publication. We do drift over into border areas occasionally but center on Wisconsin."

WOMEN'S SPORTS AND FITNESS MAGAZINE, Women's Sports Publications, Inc., Suite 400, 501 Second St., San Francisco CA 94107. Editor: Martha Nelson. 80% freelance written. Works with a small number of new/unpublished writers each year. Monthly magazine; 64-100 pages. Emphasizes women's sports, fitness and health. Circ. 300,000. Pays on publication. Publishes ms an average of 3 months after acceptance. Generally buys all rights. Submit seasonal/holiday material 3 months in advance. Computer printout submissions acceptable; no dot-matrix. Reports in 1 month on queries; 6 weeks on mss. Sample copy $2; writer's guidelines for SASE.

Nonfiction: Profile, service piece, interview, how-to, historical, personal experience, personal opinion, travel, new product and reviews. "All articles should pertain to women's sports and fitness or health. All must be of national interest." Buys 5 mss/issue. Length: 2,500-3,000 words. Pays $300-800 for features. Sometimes pays the expenses of writers on assignment.

Photos: State availability of photos. Pays about $25-50 for b&w prints; $100-250 for 35mm color transparencies. Buys one-time rights.

Columns/Departments: Buys 6-8/issue. Query with published clips. Length: 500-1,500 words. Pays $100 minimum.

Fillers: Health and fitness information. Length: 100-250 words.

Tips: "We prefer queries to manuscripts. The best query letters often start with a first paragraph that could be the first paragraph of the article the writer wants to do. Queries should indicate that the writer has done the preliminary research for the article and has an 'angle' or something to give the article personality. Published clips help too. Freelancers can best break into *Women's Sports and Fitness* by submitting short items for the Personal Best and Fast Breaks sections or opinion pieces for End Zone. We are looking for profiles of athletes that demonstrate a real understanding of the athlete; we are looking for items of concern to active women—and we interpret that broadly—from the water she drinks to women to watch or remember, from adventure/travel to event coverage to home exercise equipment."

Golf

GOLF DIGEST, 5520 Park Ave., Trumbull CT 06611. (203)373-7000. Executive Editor: Jerry Tarde. 30% freelance written. Emphasizes golfing. Monthly magazine. Circ. 1.2 million. Pays on acceptance. Publishes ms an average of 6 weeks after acceptance. Buys all rights. Byline given. Submit seasonal/holiday material 4 months in advance. Photocopied submissions OK. Computer printout submissions acceptable; prefers letter-quality to dot-matrix. Reports in 6 weeks.

Nonfiction: How-to, informational, historical, humor, inspirational, interview, nostalgia, opinion, profile, travel, new product, personal experience, photo feature and technical; "all on playing and otherwise enjoying the game of golf." Query. Length: 1,000-2,500 words. Pays $150-1,500 depending on length of edited mss.

Photos: Nick DiDio, art director. Purchased without accompanying ms. Pays $75-150 for 5x7 or 8x10 b&w prints; $100-300/35mm color transparency. Model release required.

Poetry: Lois Hains, assistant editor. Light verse. Buys 1-2/issue. Length: 4-8 lines. Pays $25.

Fillers: Lois Hains, assistant editor. Jokes, gags, anecdotes, and cutlines for cartoons. Buys 1-2/issue. Length: 2-6 lines. Pays $10-25.

GOLF ILLUSTRATED, Family Media, Inc., 3 Park Ave., New York NY 10016. (212)340-9200. Editor: Al Barkow. Managing Editor: David Earl. 60% freelance written. Eager to work with new/unpublished writers. A monthly magazine covering personalities and developments in the sport of golf. Circ. 200,000. Pays on acceptance or publication. Publishes ms an average of 2 months after acceptance. Offers 10% kill fee. Buys all rights. Submit seasonal/holiday material 6 months in advance. Query for electronic submissions. Computer printout submissions acceptable; no dot-matrix. Reports in 3 weeks on queries; 6 weeks on manuscripts.

Nonfiction: Essays, historical/nostalgic, how-to, humor, interview/profile, opinion, personal experience, photo feature, and travel. Buys 70 mss/year. Query with published clips. Length: 750-1,750 words. Pays $500-1,500 for assigned articles; pays $250-1,000 for unsolicited articles. Sometimes pays the expenses of writers on assignment.

Photos: State availability of photos with submission. Reviews contact sheets and transparencies. Offers $50-400/photo. Captions and identification of subjects required. Buys one-time rights.

Columns/Departments: Health and Fitness, Food, and Opinion (all related to golf), approximately 750 words. Query with published clips. Pays $500-1,000.

Fillers: Anecdotes, facts, gags to be illustrated by cartoonist and short humor. Buys 30/year. Length: 100-500 words. Pays $25-300.

Tips: "A freelancer can best break in to our publication by following the personalities—the PGA, LPGA and PGA Senior tour pros and the nature of the game in general."

GOLF MAGAZINE, Times Mirror Magazines, Inc., 380 Madison Ave., New York NY 10017. (212)687-3000. Editor: George Peper. 25% freelance written. Works with a small number of new/unpublished writers each year. Monthly magazine; 150 pages. Golf audience, 95% male, ages 15-80, college-educated, professionals. Circ. 850,000. Pays on acceptance. Publishes an average of 6 months after acceptance. Byline given. Buys all rights. Submit seasonal/holiday material 4 months in advance. Photocopied submissions OK. Dot-matrix submissions acceptable if double-spaced. Reports in 4 weeks. Send mss to specific section editors—feature, instruction, Golf Reports, etc. General mss direct to James A. Frank, Executive Editor. Sample copy $2.

Nonfiction: How-to (improve game, instructional tips); informational (news in golf); humor; profile (people in golf); travel (golf courses, resorts); new product (golf equipment, apparel, teaching aids); and photo feature (great moments in golf—must be special; most photography on assignment only). Buys 4-6 unsolicited mss/year. Query. Length: 1,200-2,500 words. Pays $600-1,000. Sometimes pays expenses of writers on assignment.

Photos: Purchased with accompanying ms or on assignment. Captions required. Query. Pays $50 for 8½x11 glossy prints (with contact sheet and negatives); $75 minimum for 3x5 color prints. Total purchase price for ms includes payment for photos. Captions and model releases required.

Columns/Departments: Golf Reports (interesting golf events, feats, etc.); What's Going On (news of golf tours). Buys 5-10 mss/year. Query. Length: 250 words maximum. Pays $75. Open to suggestions for new columns/departments.

Fiction: Humorous or mystery. Must be golf-related. Buys 1-2 mss/year. Looking to do more in future. Query. Length: 1,200-2,000 words. Pays $500-750.

Tips: "Best chance is to aim for a light piece which is not too long and is focused on a personality. Anything very technical that would require a consummate knowledge of golf, we would rather assign ourselves. But if you are successful with something light and not too long, we might use you for something heavier later. We are looking for detailed knowledge of golf. Shorter items are a good test of knowledge. Probably the best way to break in would be by our Golf Reports section in which we run short items on interesting golf feats, events and so forth. If you send us something like that, about an important event in your area, it is an easy way for us to get acquainted."

GULF COAST GOLFER, Gulf Coast Golfer, Inc., 9182 Old Katy Rd., Houston TX 77055. (713)464-0308. Editor: Bob Gray. 30% freelance written. Prefers to work with published/established writers. Monthly magazine covering results of major area competition, data on upcoming tournaments, reports of new and improved golf courses, and how-to tips for active, competitive golfers in Texas Gulf Coast area. Circ. 33,000. Pays on publication. Publishes ms an average of 1 month after acceptance. Byline given. Buys one-time rights. Submit seasonal/holiday material 3 months in advance. Reports in 3 weeks. Sample copy for 9x12 SAE; free writer's guidelines.

Nonfiction: How-to and personal experience golf articles. No routine coverage. Query first. Length: by arrangement. Pays negotiable rates.

Tips: Especially wants articles on how-to subjects about golf in Gulf Coast area, but only on assignment basis.

NORTH TEXAS GOLFER, GULF COAST GOLFER, Texas, Louisiana Golf Group, Golfer Magazines, Inc., 9182 Old Katy Rd., Houston TX 77055. (713)464-0308. Editor: Bob Gray. 30% freelance written. A monthly tabloid covering golf in Texas and Louisiana. Emphasizes "grass roots coverage of regional golf course activities" and detailed, localized information on tournaments and competition in Texas and Louisiana. Circ. 60,000 (combined). Pays on publication. Byline given. Buys one-time rights. Submit seasonal/holiday material 3 months in advance. Reports in 2 weeks. Free sample copy.

Nonfiction: How-to, humor, interview/profile, personal experience and travel. Nothing outside of Texas or Louisiana. Buys 20 mss/year. Query. Length: 500-1,500 words. Pays $50-250 for assigned articles.

Photos: Send photos with submission. Offers no additional payment for photos accepted with ms. Identification of subjects required.

Tips: "We publish mostly how-to, where-to articles. They're about people and events in Texas and Louisiana. We could use profiles of successful amateur and professional golfers in our two states—but only on a specific assignment basis. Most of the Tour players already have been assigned to the staff or to freelancers. Do *not* approach people, schedule interviews, then tell us about it."

SCORE, Canada's Golf Magazine, Canadian Controlled Media Communications, 287 MacPherson Ave., Toronto, Ontario M4V 1A4 Canada. (416)961-5141. Managing Editor: John Gordon. 90% freelance written. Works with a small number of new/unpublished writers each year. Magazine published 7 times/year covering golf. "*Score* magazine provides seasonal coverage of the Canadian golf scene, professional, amateur, senior and junior golf for men and women golfers in Canada, the U.S. and Europe through profiles, history, travel, editorial comment and instruction." Circ. over 170,000. Pays on publication. Publishes ms an average of 1-3 months after acceptance. Byline given. Offers negotiable kill fee. Buys all rights and second serial (reprint) rights. Submit seasonal/holiday material 8 months in advance. Computer printout submissions acceptable; prefers letter-quality to dot-matrix. SAE with IRCs. Reports within 1 month. Sample copy for $2 (Canadian), 9x12 SAE and IRCs; writer's guidelines for business size SAE and IRC.

Nonfiction: Book excerpts (golf); historical/nostalgic (golf and golf characters); humor (golf); interview/profile (prominent golf professionals); photo feature (golf); and travel (golf destinations only). The yearly April/May issue includes tournament results from Canada, the U.S., Europe, Asia, Australia, etc., history, profile, and regular features. "No personal experience, technical, opinion or general-interest material. Most articles are by assignment only." Buys 25-30 mss/year. Query with published clips or send complete ms. Length: 700-3,500 words. Pays $140-800.

Photos: Send photos with query or ms. Pays $50-100 for 35mm color transparencies (positives) or $30 for 8x10 or 5x7 b&w prints. Captions, model release (if necessary), and identification of subjects required. Buys all rights.

Columns/Departments: Profile (historical or current golf personalities or characters); Great Moments ("Great Moments in Canadian Golf"—description of great single moments, usually game triumphs); New Equipment (Canadian availability only); Travel (golf destinations, including "hard" information such as greens fees, hotel accommodations, etc.); Instruction (by special assignment only; usually from teaching golf professionals); The Mental Game (psychology of the game, by special assignment only); Humor (golf humor); and History (golf equipment collections and collectors, development of the game, legendary figures and events). Buys 17-20 mss/year. Query with published clips or send complete ms. Length: 700-1,700 words. Pays $140-400.

Fiction: Historical (golf only) and humorous (golf only). No science fiction or adventure. Buys 1-3 mss/year. Query with published clips or send complete ms. Length: 700-1,700 words. Pays $140-400.

Fillers: Clippings, jokes, anecdotes, short humor and newsbreaks. Buys 5/year. Length: 50-100 words. Pays $10-25.

Tips: "Only writers with an extensive knowledge of golf and familiarity with the Canadian and/or U.S. golf scene(s) should query or submit in-depth work to *Score*. Golf-oriented humor is the only exception to this rule. Many of our features are written by professional people who play the game for a living or work in the industry. All areas mentioned under Columns/Departments are open to freelancers. Most of our *major* features are done on assignment only. These are given to regular contributors on the basis of past performances and expertise, etc. Writers wishing to break into the magazine best 'prove' their capabilities with shorter work to begin with. On queries and unsolicited material, frequent mistakes made by writers are faulty or poor presentation, showing a lack of definite direction, poor spelling, grammar and sloppy typing. On assignments, providing the writer is willing to listen to what we need and to discipline him/herself to write accurately and tightly, there shouldn't be major problems. Background research is sometimes not as thorough as we would like. *Score* is planning an increased emphasis on Canada and Canadian players."

Guns

AMERICAN HANDGUNNER, Publishers' Development Corp., Suite 200, 591 Camino de la Reina, San Diego CA 92108. (619)297-5352. Editor: Cameron Hopkins. 90% freelance written. Eager to work with new/unpublished writers. A bimonthly magazine covering handguns, handgun sports, and handgun accessories. "Semi-technical publication for handgun enthusiasts of above-average knowledge/understanding of handguns. Writers must have ability to write about technical designs of handguns as well as ability to write intelligently about the legitimate sporting value of handguns." Circ. 180,000. Pays on publication. Publishes ms an average of 5-9 months after acceptance. Byline given. Offers $50 kill fee. Buys first North American serial rights. Submit seasonal/holiday material 7 months in advance. Previously published submissions OK. Computer printout submissions acceptable; prefers letter-quality to dot-matrix. Reports in 1 week. Free sample copy and writer's guidelines.

Nonfiction: How-to, interview/profile, new product, photo feature, technical and "iconoclastic think pieces." Special issue is the *American Handgunner Annual*. No handgun competition coverage. Buys 60-70 mss/year. Query. Length: 500-3,000 words. Pays $175-600 for assigned articles; pays $100-400 for unsolicited articles. Sometimes pays the expenses of writers on assignment.

Photos: Send photos with submission. Reviews contact sheets, 35mm and 4x5 transparencies and 5x7 b&w prints. Offers no additional payment for b&w photos accepted with ms; offers $50-250/color photo. Captions and identification of subjects required. Buys all rights.

Columns/Departments: Combat Shooting (techniques, equipment, accessories for sport of combat shooting—no "blood and guts"), 600-800 words. Buys 40-60 mss/year. Query. Pays $175-200.

Tips: "We are always interested in 'round-up' pieces covering a particular product line or mixed bag of different product lines of the same theme. If vacation/travel takes you to an exotic place, we're interested in, say, 'The Guns of Upper Volta.' We are looking more closely at handgun hunting."

‡**THE AMERICAN SHOTGUNNER**, Box 3351, Reno NV 89505. Publisher: Bob Thruston. Monthly. Circ. 120,000. Pays on publication. Buys all rights. Submit special material (hunting) 4 months in advance. Reports on material accepted for publication in 1 month. Returns rejected material. Free sample copy and writer's guidelines.
Nonfiction: Sue Thruston, managing editor. All aspects of shotgunning—trap and skeet shooting and hunting, reloading, shooting clothing, and shooting equipment. Emphasis is on the how-to and instructional approach. "We give the sportsman actual material that will help him to improve his game, fill his limit, or build that duck blind, etc. Hunting articles are used in all issues, year-round." Buys 20-30 mss/year. Query. Length: open. Pays $75-250.
Photos: Reviews original transparencies. "We also purchase professional cover material." No additional payment for photos used with mss.

FIREPOWER, The Magazine of Exotic Weaponry, Turbo Publishing, Inc., Box 397, Cornville AZ 86325. (602)634-6127. Editor: Everett Moore, Jr. 50% freelance written. A bimonthly magazine. Pays on publication. Byline given. Buys all rights. Previously published submissions usually OK; some exceptions apply. Computer printout submissions acceptable; prefers letter-quality to dot-matrix. Free sample copy and writer's guidelines.
Nonfiction: General interest, historical/nostalgic, how-to, interview/profile, new product, opinion, personal experience and technical. Buys 50 mss/year. Query with published clips. Length: 500-2,000 words. Pays $50-300.
Photos: Send photos with submission. Reviews transparencies and 3x5 and 5x7 prints. Offers no additional payment for photos accepted with ms. Captions, model releases and identification of subjects required.
Columns/Departments: The Firing Line (new products) and Intelligence Briefs (book review). Buys 10-12 mss/year. Query with published clips. Length: 500-800 words. Pays $50-150.

GUN DIGEST, HANDLOADER'S DIGEST, DBI Books, Inc., 4092 Commercial Ave., Northfield IL 60062. (312)441-7010. Editor-in-Chief: Ken Warner. 50% freelance written. Prefers to work with published/established writers and works with a small number of new/unpublished writers each year. Annual journal covering guns and shooting. Pays on acceptance. Publishes ms an average of 20 months after acceptance. Byline given. Buys all rights. Computer printout submissions acceptable if legible; prefers letter-quality to dot-matrix. Reports in 1 month.
Nonfiction: Buys 50 mss/issue. Query. Length: 500-5,000 words. Pays $100-600; includes photos or illustration package from author.
Photos: State availability of photos with query letter. Reviews 8x10 b&w prints. Payment for photos included in payment for ms. Captions required.
Tips: Award of $1,000 to author of best article (juried) in each issue.

GUN WORLD, 34249 Camino Capistrano, Box HH, Capistrano Beach CA 92624. Editorial Director: Jack Lewis. 50% freelance written. For ages that "range from mid-teens to mid-60s; many professional types who are interested in relaxation of hunting and shooting." Monthly. Circ. 136,000. Buys 80-100 unsolicited mss/year. Pays on acceptance. Publishes ms an average of 6 months after acceptance. Buys first rights. Byline given. Submit seasonal material 4 months in advance. Reports in 6 weeks. Computer printout submissions acceptable; prefers letter-quality to dot-matrix. Copy of editorial requirements for SASE.
Nonfiction and Photos: General subject matter consists of "well-rounded articles—not by amateurs—on shooting techniques, with anecdotes; hunting stories with tips and knowledge integrated. No poems or fiction. We like broad humor in our articles, so long as it does not reflect upon firearms safety. Most arms magazines are pretty deadly and we feel shooting can be fun. Too much material aimed at pro-gun people. Most of this is staff-written and most shooters don't have to be told of their rights under the Constitution. We want articles on new developments; off-track inventions, novel military uses of arms; police armament and training techniques; do-it-yourself projects in this field." Buys informational, how-to, personal experience and nostalgia articles. Pays up to $300, sometimes more. Purchases photos with mss and captions required. Wants 5x7 b&w photos. Sometimes pays the expenses of writers on assignment.
Tips: "The most frequent mistake made by writers in completing an article for us is surface writing with no real knowledge of the subject. To break in, offer an anecdote having to do with proposed copy."

SHOTGUN SPORTS, Shotgun Sport, Inc., Box 340, Lake Havasu City AZ 86403. (602)855-0100. Editor: Frank Kodl. Managing Editor: Fredi Kodl. 90% freelance written. Works with a small number of new/unpublished writers each year; eager to work with new/unpublished writers. Monthly magazine covering the sport of shotgunning. Circ. 110,000. Pays on publication. Publishes ms an average of 8 months after acceptance. Byline given. Buys one-time rights. Submit seasonal/holiday material 3 months in advance. Computer printout submissions acceptable; prefers letter-quality to dot-matrix. Reports in 3 months. Free sample copy and writer's guidelines.
Nonfiction: Book excerpts, expose, general interest, historical/nostalgic, how-to, humor, inspirational,

interview/profile, new product, opinion, personal experience, photo feature, technical and travel; "all articles must be related directly to shotgunning to include trap, skeet or hunting, handloading, gun tests and patterning, etc." Buys 50-70 mss/year. Query or send complete mss. Length: open. Pays $50-200.

Photos: State availability of photos or send photos with ms. Reviews 5x7 b&w prints. "Photos included in payment for ms." Captions required.

S.W.A.T.: SPECIAL WEAPONS AND TACTICS, "For the Prepared American", Turbo Publishing, Inc., Box 270, Cornville AZ 86325. (602)634-6127. Editor: Rolland Huff. 50% freelance written. Works with a small number of new/unpublished writers each year. A monthly magazine. Pays on publication. Publishes ms an average of 2-3 months after acceptance. Byline given. Buys all rights. Most previously published sumbissions OK. Computer printout submissions acceptable; prefers letter-quality to dot-matrix. Free sample copy and writer's guidelines.

Nonfiction: General interest, historical/nostalgic, how-to, interview/profile, law enforcement, new product, opinion, personal experience and technical. No fiction. Buys 50 mss/year. Query with published clips. Length: 500-2,000 words. Pays $50-300.

Photos: Send photos with submission. Reviews transparencies and 3x5 and 5x7 prints. Offers no additional payment for photos accepted with ms. Captions, model releases, and identification of subjects required. Buys all rights.

Columns/Departments: FYI (For Your Information—general information), S.W.A.T. Emporium (new products); S.W.A.T. Library (book review). Buys 10-12 mss/year. Query with published clips. Length: 500-800 words. Pays $50-150.

Tips: "The biggest disappointment we often encounter is having to reject good articles because of poor or insufficient photography."

Horse Racing

THE BACKSTRETCH, 19363 James Couzens Hwy., Detroit MI 48235. (313)342-6144. Editor: Ann Moss. Managing Editor: Ruth LeGrove. 40% freelance written. Works with a small number of new/unpublished writers each year. Quarterly magazine; 100 pages. For Thoroughbred horse trainers, owners, breeders, farm managers, track personnel, jockeys, grooms and racing fans who span the age range from very young to very old. Publication of United Thoroughbred Trainers of America, Inc. Circ. 25,000. Publishes ms an average of 3 months after acceptance. Sample copy $2.

Nonfiction: "*Backstretch* contains mostly general information. Articles deal with biographical material on trainers, owners, jockeys, horses and their careers on and off the track, historical track articles, etc. Unless writer's material is related to Thoroughbreds and Thoroughbred racing, it should not be submitted. Articles accepted on speculation basis—payment made after material is used. If not suitable, articles are returned immediately. Articles that do not require printing by a specified date are preferred. There is no special length requirement and amount paid depends on material. It is advisable to include photos, if possible. Articles should be original copies and should state whether presented to any other magazine, or whether previously printed in any other magazine. Submit complete ms. We do not buy crossword puzzles, cartoons, newspaper clippings, fiction or poetry."

THE FLORIDA HORSE, The Florida Horse, Inc., Box 2106, Ocala FL 32678. (904)629-8082. Editor: F.J. Audette. 25% freelance written. Monthly magazine covering the Florida thoroughbred horse industry. "We seek contemporary coverage and feature material on the Florida breeding, racing and sales scene." Circ. 12,000. Pays on publication. Publishes ms an average of 2 months after acceptance. Byline given. Buys first North American serial rights. Computer printout submissions acceptable; prefers letter-quality to dot-matrix. Reports in 2 weeks. Free sample copy.

Nonfiction: Bill Giauque, associate editor. Articles covering horses and people of the Florida thoroughbred industry. Buys 18-24 mss/year. Length: 1,500-3,000 words. Pays $125-200. Sometimes pays expenses of writers on assignment.

Photos: Send photos with ms. Pays $15-25 for sharp, well-composed 8x10 b&w prints. Captions and identification of subjects required. Buys one-time rights.

Columns/Departments: Medically Speaking (veterinarian analysis of equine problems); Legally Speaking (legal analysis of equine legal considerations); and Track Talk (news and features from racetracks—Florida angle only). Buys 24-36 mss/year. Send complete ms. Length: 800-960 words. Pays $35-50.

Tips: "We recommend that writers be at the scene of the action—racetracks, nurseries, provide clean, focused writing from the Florida angle and submit lively, interesting material full of detail and background."

HOOF BEATS, United States Trotting Association, 750 Michigan Ave., Columbus OH 43215. (614)224-2291. Editor: Dean A. Hoffman. 35% freelance written. Works with a small number of new/unpublished writers each year. Monthly magazine covering harness racing for the participants of the sport of harness racing. "We cover all aspects of the sport—racing, breeding, selling, etc." Circ. 26,000. Pays on publication. Publishes ms an average of 3 months after acceptance. Byline given. Buys negotiable rights. Submit seasonal/holiday material 3 months in advance. Computer printout submissions acceptable. Reports in 3 weeks. Free sample copy, postpaid.

Nonfiction: General interest, historical/nostalgic, humor, inspirational, interview/profile, new product, personal experience, photo feature. Buys 15-20 mss/year. Query. Length: open. Pays $100-400. Pays the expenses of writers on assignment "with approval."

Photos: State availability of photos. Pays variable rates for 35mm transparencies and prints. Identification of subjects required. Buys one-time rights.

Fiction: Historical, humorous, interesting fiction with a harness racing theme. Buys 2-3 mss/year. Query. Length: open. Pays $100-400.

HUB RAIL, Hub Rail, Inc., Box 1831, Harrisburg PA 17105. (717)234-5099. Publisher: David M. Dolezal. Editor: Charlotte Maurer, 5 E. Hyde Rd., Yellow Springs OH 45387. (513)767-7184. Eager to work with new/unpublished writers. Bimonthly magazine; 100 pages. Emphasizes harness horse racing or breeding. Circ. 2,500. Pays on publication. Publishes ms an average of 4 months after acceptance. Buys first North American serial rights. Submit seasonal/holiday material 3 months in advance. Photocopied submissions OK. Computer printout submissions acceptable if double-spaced; prefers letter-quality to dot-matrix. Reports in 1 month.

Nonfiction: General interest, historical, humor and nostalgia. Articles must pertain to harness racing. Phone or mail queries to Charlotte Maurer. Length: 1,000-5,000 words. Pays $50-200. Seldom pays expenses of writers on assignment.

Fiction: "We use short stories pertaining to harness racing." Length: 2,500-7,000 words. Pays $50-200.

Tips: "We are specialized and a writer who doesn't understand the harness racing business shows it clearly. Know who our readers are."

SPEEDHORSE MAGAZINE, Speedhorse, Inc., Box 1000, Norman OK 73070. (405)288-2391. Editor: Diane C. Simmons. 20% freelance written. Prefers to work with published/established writers. A monthly journal "devoted to those involved with breeding or racing quarter horses. It is *not* a general circulation horse publication, however available on selected airlines with over 3 million passengers each year." Circ. 9,000. Pays on publication. Publishes ms an average of 4 months after acceptance. Byline given. Offers negotiable kill fee. Buys negotiable rights. Simultaneous queries OK. Computer printout submissions acceptable; prefers letter-quality to dot-matrix. Reports in 1 month. Sample copy $3.

Nonfiction: How-to (directed specifically at racing); interview/profile (of prominent horsemen); and photo feature (of racing). "Our articles address those topics which interest an experienced horseman. Articles dealing with ranch operations, racing bloodlines and race coverage are of special interest." No general interest stories. Special issues include Stallion articles (November, March); Stakes Winner Issue (April); Service Issue, articles on various services offered horsemen, i.e., transportation, trainers, travel, etc. (May); Broodmare Issue (June); Horse sales and auctions (July, August); Racing Wrap-up (September); and Thoroughbred Issue (October). Buys 3 mss/year. Query. Length: 1,000 words minimum. Pays $25-300. Sometimes pays the expenses of writers on assignment.

Photos: Andrew Golden, photo editor. State availability of photos with query or ms. Reviews b&w and color contact sheets. Pays $5-25 for b&w and color. Identification of subjects required. Buys one-time rights.

Columns/Departments: Book Review and Vet Medicine, by assignment only. Buys 1-2 mss/year. Query. Length: 1,000 words. Pays $50-75.

Fiction: Adventure (race related); historical; humorous; and western. "All fiction must appeal to racing industry." Buys 3 mss/year. Query. Length: 1,000 words minimum. Pays $25-200.

Tips: "If the writer has a good working knowledge of the horse industry and access to people involved with the quarter horse racing industry, the writer should call the editor to discuss possible stories. Very few blind articles are accepted. Most stories are assigned with much editorial direction. Most feature stories are assigned to freelance writers who have been regular contributors to *Speedhorse*. They are located in areas of the country with active quarter horse racing. Many are track publicity directors or newspaper sports writers. The most frequent mistake made by writers in completing an article for us is that they do not write for the market. They send general interest articles rather than technical articles."

SPUR, Box 85, Middleburg VA 22117. (703)687-6314. Managing Director: Kerry Phelps. 80% freelance written. Prefers to work with published/established writers; works with a small number of new/unpublished writers each year. Bimonthly magazine covering Thoroughbred horses and the people who are involved in the business and sport of the Thoroughbred industry. Circ. 10,000. Pays on publication. Publishes ms an average of 3 months after acceptance. Byline given. Buys all rights. Computer printout submissions acceptable; prefers letter-quality to dot-matrix. Reports in 1 month on mss and queries. Sample copy $3.50; writer's guidelines for business size SAE and 1 first class stamp.

Nonfiction: Historical/nostalgic, Thoroughbred care, personality profile, farm, special feature, regional, photo essay, steeplechasing and polo. Buys 30 mss/year. Query with clips of published work, "or we will consider complete manuscripts." Length: 300-4,000 words. Payment negotiable. Sometimes pays the expenses of writers on assignment.

Photos: State availability of photos. Reviews color and b&w contact sheets. Captions, model releases and identification of subjects required. Buys all rights "unless otherwise negotiated."

Columns/Departments: Query or send complete ms to Editorial Dept. Length: 100-500 words. Pays $50 and up.

Fillers: Anecdotes, short humor. Length: 50-100 words. Pays $25 and up.

Tips: "Writers must have a knowledge of horses, horse owners, breeding, training, racing, and riding—or the ability to obtain this knowledge from a subject."

Hunting and Fishing

ALABAMA GAME & FISH, Game & Fish Publications, Inc., Box 741, Marietta GA 30061. (404)953-9222. Editor: Rick Lavender. Monthly how-to, where-to, when-to hunting and fishing magazine covering Alabama. Pays 3 months before publication. Byline given. Buys one-time rights. Submit seasonal material 8 months in advance. Simultaneous queries, and simultaneous and photocopied submissions OK. Computer printout submissions acceptable; no dot-matrix. Reports in 2 months. Sample copy for $2.50 and 10x12 SAE; writer's guidelines for SASE.

Nonfiction: How-to (hunting and fishing *only*); humor (on limited basis); interview/profile (of successful hunter/angler); personal experience (hunting or fishing adventure). No hiking, backpacking or camping. No fiction or poems. No "my first deer" articles. Buys 60 mss/year. Query with or without published clips. Length: 2,200-2,500 words. Pays $150.

Photos: State availability of photos. Pays $75 for color leads; $225 for covers; $25 for b&w photos not submitted as part of story package. Captions and identification of subjects required. Buys one-time rights.

Tips: "We have similar requirements for *South Carolina Game & Fish* and *Florida Game & Fish*."

‡AMERICAN HUNTER, Suite 1000, 470 Spring Park Pl., Herndon VA 22070. Editor: Tom Fulgham. 90% freelance written. For hunters who are members of the National Rifle Association. Circ. 1,412,723. Buys first North American serial rights. Byline given. Free sample copy and writer's guidelines. Computer printout submissions acceptable; prefers letter-quality to dot-matrix.

Nonfiction: Factual material on all phases of hunting. Not interested in material on fishing or camping. Prefers queries. Length: 2,000-3,000 words. Pays $250-450.

Photos: No additional payment made for photos used with mss. Pays $25 for b&w photos purchased without accompanying mss. Pays $50-300 for color.

ARKANSAS SPORTSMAN, Game & Fish Publications, Inc., Box 741, Marietta GA 30061. (404)953-9222. Editor: Keith Brooks. 90-95% freelance written. Works with a small number of new/unpublished writers each year. Monthly how-to, where-to and when-to hunting and fishing magazine covering Arkansas. Pays 3 months before publication. Byline given. Buys one-time rights. Submit seasonal material 8 months in advance. Simultaneous queries, and simultaneous and photocopied submissions OK. Computer printout submissions acceptable; prefers letter-quality to dot-matrix. Reports in 2 months. Sample copy for $2.50 and 10x12 SAE; writer's guidelines for SASE.

Nonfiction: How-to (hunting and fishing *only*); humor (on limited basis); interview/profile (of successful hunter/angler); personal experience (hunting or fishing adventure). No hiking, backpacking or camping. No "my first deer" articles. Buys 60 mss/year. Query with or without published clips. Length: 2,200-2,500 words. Pays $150.

Photos: State availability of photos. Pays $75 for full-page, color leads; $225 for covers; $25 for b&w photos not submitted as part of story package. Captions and identification of subjects required. Buys one-time rights.

BADGER SPORTSMAN, Vercauteren Publishing, Inc., 19 E. Main, Chilton WI 53014. (414)849-4651. Editor: Mike Marquardt. Managing Editor: Gary Vercauteren. 80% freelance written. Monthly tabloid covering Wisconsin outdoors. Circ. 26,260. Pays on publication. Publishes ms an average of 1 month after acceptance. Byline given. Buys one-time rights. Submit seasonal/holiday material 2 months in advance. Previously published submissions OK. Computer printout submissions acceptable; prefers letter-quality to dot-matrix. Sample copy for 9x13 SAE with 56¢ postage; free writer's guidelines.

Nonfiction: General interest; how-to (fishing, hunting, etc., in the Midwest outdoors); humor; interview/profile; personal experience; technical. Buys 400-500 mss/year. Query. Length: open. Pays 35¢/column inch ($15-40).

Photos: Send photos with accompanying query or ms. Reviews 3x5 or larger b&w and color prints. Pays by column inch. Identification of subjects required.

Tips: "We publish stories about *Wisconsin* fishing, hunting, camping; outdoor cooking; and general animal stories."

BASSIN', The Official Magazine for the Weekend Angler, National Reporter Publications, Inc. 15115 S. 76th E. Ave., Bixby OK 74008. (918)366-4441. Executive Editor: André Hinds. 90% freelance written. Works with a small number of new/unpublished writers each year; eager to work with new/unpublished writers. Magazine published 8 times/year covering freshwater fishing with emphasis on black bass. Publishes ms an average of 6 months after acceptance. Circ. 250,000. Pays on acceptance. Byline given. Buys first serial rights. Submit seasonal material 6 months in advance. Prefers queries but will examine mss accompanied by SASE. Electronic submissions OK via 300/1200 baud modem (ASCII text) or Macintosh disk. Computer printout submissions acceptable. Reports in 4-6 weeks. Sample copy $2; writer's guidelines available on request.

Nonfiction: How-to and where-to stories on bass fishing. Prefers completed ms. Length: 1,200-2,500 words. Pays $175-300 on acceptance.

Photos: Send photos with ms. Pays $300 for color cover; $75 for color cover inset. Send b&w prints or color transparencies. Buys one-time rights. Photo payment on publication.

Columns/Departments: Send complete ms. Fishing tips, regional lake reports, product reviews. Length: 100-700 words. Pays $30-50 on publication.

Tips: "Reduce the common fishing slang terminology when writing for *Bassin'* (and other outdoor magazines). This slang is usually regional and confuses anglers in other areas of the country. Good strong features will win me over much more quickly than short articles or fillers. We need absolutely no poetry, no women's perspective stories, no oldtimer's perspective stories and no personality pieces. We need stories on fishing tackle and techniques to catch largemouth bass."

BASSMASTER MAGAZINE, B.A.S.S. Publications, Box 17900, Montgomery AL 36141. (205)272-9530. Editor: Dave Precht. 80% freelance written. Prefers to work with published/established writers. Bimonthly magazine (monthly October-May) about largemouth, smallmouth, spotted bass and striped bass for dedicated beginning and advanced bass fishermen. Circ. 400,000. Pays on acceptance. Publication date of ms after acceptance "varies—seasonal material could take years"; average time is 8 months. Byline given. Buys all rights. Submit seasonal material 6 months in advance. Computer printout submissions OK; prefers letter-quality to dot-matrix. Reports in 1 month. Sample copy $2; writer's guidelines for SAE and 1 first class stamp..

Nonfiction: Historical; interview (of knowledgable people in the sport); profile (outstanding fishermen); travel (where to go to fish for bass); how-to (catch bass and enjoy the outdoors); new product (reels, rods and bass boats); and conservation related to bass fishing. "No 'Me and Joe Go Fishing' type articles." Query. Length: 400-2,100 words. Pays $100-300.

Columns/Departments: Short Cast/News & Views (upfront regular feature covering news-related events such as new state bass records, unusual bass fishing happenings, conservation, new products and editorial viewpoints); 250-400 words.

Photos: "We want a mixture of black and white and color photos." Pays $50 minimum for b&w prints. Pays $300-350 for color cover transparencies. Captions required; model releases preferred. Buys all rights.

Fillers: Anecdotes, short humor and newsbreaks. Buys 4-5 mss/issue. Length: 250-500 words. Pays $50-100.

Tips: "Editorial direction continues in the short, more direct how-to article. Compact, easy-to-read information is our objective. Shorter articles with good graphics, such as how-to diagrams, step-by-step instruction, etc., will enhance a writer's articles submitted to *Bassmaster Magazine*. The most frequent mistakes made by writers in completing an article for us are poor grammar, poor writing, poor organization and superficial research."

BC OUTDOORS, SIP Division, Maclean Hunter Ltd., 202-1132 Hamilton St., Vancouver, British Columbia V6B 2S2 Canada. (604)687-1581. Editor: George Will. 80% freelance written. Works with a small number of new/unpublished writers each year. Outdoor recreation magazine published 10 times/year. *BC Outdoors* covers fishing, camping, hunting, and the environment of outdoor recreation. Circ. 40,000. Pays on acceptance. Publishes ms an average of 6 months after acceptance. Byline given. Offers negotiable kill fee. Buys first North American serial rights. Submit seasonal/holiday material 6 months in advance. Query for electronic submissions. Computer printout submissions acceptable; prefers letter-quality to dot-matrix. Reports in 1 month on queries; 2 months on mss. Sample copy and writer's guidelines for 8x10 SAE with $2 postage.

Nonfiction: How-to (new or innovative articles on outdoor subjects); personal experience (outdoor adventure); and outdoor topics specific to British Columbia. "We would like to receive how-to, where-to features dealing with hunting and fishing in British Columbia and the Yukon." Buys 80-90 mss/year. Query. Length: 1,500-2,000 words. Pays $300-450. Sometimes pays the expenses of writers on assignment.

Photos: State availability of photos with query. Pays $10-30 on publication for 5x7 b&w prints; $15-50 for color contact sheets and 35mm transparencies. Captions and identification of subjects required. Buys one-time rights.

Tips: "More emphasis on saltwater angling and less emphasis on self-propelled activity, like hiking and canoeing will affect the types of freelance material we buy in 1988. Subject must be specific to British Columbia. We receive many manuscripts written by people who obviously do not know the magazine or market. The writer has a better chance of breaking in at our publication with short, lesser-paying articles and fillers, because we have a stable of regular writers in constant touch who produce most main features."

‡CALIFORNIA ANGLER, The Journal for Freshwater and Saltwater Anglers in the Golden State, Outdoor Ventures, Ltd., Box 1789, Carlsbad CA 92008. (619)967-1942. Managing Editor: Jim Gilmore/Tom Waters. 80% freelance written. A recreational fishing magazine published 11 times per year with a combined November and December issue. Circ. 16,000. Pays during month prior to publication. Publishes ms an average of 2 months after acceptance. Byline given. Buys first rights, one-time rights, second serial (reprint) rights or makes-for-hire assignments. Submit seasonal/holiday material 3 months in advance. Simultaneous and photocopied submissions OK. Computer printout submissions OK. Reports in 1 month. Sample copy for 9x12 SAE with $1.58 postage. "We believe our magazine is the best and most articulate set of writer's guidelines for our purpose."

Nonfiction: Tom Waters, freshwater pieces editor; Jim Gilmore, saltwater articles editor. How-to, humor, interview/profile, new product, opinion, personal experience ("if a true angler's adventure"), photo feature, technical and travel (where to fish in California). "No 'me and Joe went fishing' articles." Buys 55-65 mss/year. Query with published clips. Length: 1,800-2,500 words. Pays $200-300.

Photos: Send photos with submission. Reviews 1x1⅜ transparencies and 5x7 or 8x10 prints. Offers no additional payment for photos accepted with ms. Captions and identification of subjects required. Buys one-time rights.

Columns/Departments: Fit-to-be-Tied (knots, rigging and fly-tying, photos required); Angler's Adventure (true-life adventures—exceptional angling experiences, photos, illustrations preferred); Clean Wake (California related fisheries management and conservation themes. Send pictures, diagrams, graphics, etc.). Buys 40-60 mss/year. Query with published clips. Length: 800-1,200 words. Pays $100-200.

Tips: "The talented and innovative photographer tends to get our attention quickly. We have several new regular contributors who broke in because they consistently provided imaginative photography—action photos or underwater pictures showing gamefish in their native habitat. Manuscripts, as appropriate, should also be accompanied by where-to maps and how-to illustrations (in rough form, we will produce finished art). Dunc's Barbershop is most open to freelancers because we get so little humor writing that's really good, as well as Fit-To-Be-Tied—knots, rigging or how-to fishing tips presented and illustrated as if it were going to be published in *Popular Mechanics*."

DEER AND DEER HUNTING, The Stump Sitters, Inc., Box 1117, Appleton WI 54912. (414)734-0009. Editors: Al Hofacker and Dr. Rob Wegner. 80% freelance written. Prefers to work with published/established writers. Bimonthly magazine covering deer hunting for individuals who hunt with bow, gun, or camera. Circ. 120,000. Pays on publication. Publishes ms an average of 6 months after acceptance. Byline given. Offers $50 kill fee. Buys first North American serial rights and second serial (reprint) rights. Submit seasonal/holiday material 4 months in advance. Computer printout submissions acceptable; prefers letter-quality to dot-matrix. Reports in 1 week on queries; 2 weeks on mss. Free sample copy and writer's guidelines.

Nonfiction: Historical/nostalgic; how-to (hunting techniques); opinion; personal experience; photo feature; technical. "Our readers desire factual articles of a technical nature that relate deer behavior and habits to hunting methodology. We focus on deer biology, management principles and practices, habitat requirements, natural history of deer, hunting techniques, and hunting ethics." No hunting "Hot Spot" or "local" articles. Buys 40 mss/year. Query with clips of published work. Length: 1,000-4,000 words. Pays $50-400. Sometimes pays the expenses of writers on assignment.

Photos: State availability of photos. Pays $100 for 35mm color transparencies; $350 for front cover; $30 for 8x10 b&w prints. Captions and identification of subjects required. Buys one-time rights.

Columns/Departments: Deer Browse (unusual observations of deer behavior). Buys 20 mss/year.

Length: 200-800 words. Pays $10-50.
Fillers: Clippings, anecdotes, newsbreaks. Buys 20/year. Length: 200-800 words. Pays $10-40.
Tips: "Break in by providing material of a technical nature, backed by scientific research, and written in a style understandable to the average deer hunter. We focus primarily on white-tailed deer."

‡FIELD AND STREAM, 1515 Broadway, New York NY 10036. Editor: Duncan Barnes. 50% freelance written. Eager to work with new/unpublished writers. Monthly. Buys first rights. Byline given. Reports in 2 months. Query. Writer's guidelines for 8x10 SAE with 1 first class stamp.
Nonfiction and Photos: "This is a broad-based service magazine for the hunter and fisherman. Editorial content ranges from very basic how-to stories detailing a useful technique or a device that sportsmen can make to articles of penetrating depth about national hunting, fishing, and related activities. Also humor and person essays, nostalgia, and 'mood pieces' on the hunting or fishing experience." Prefers color photos to b&w. Query first with photos. Length: 1,000-2,000 words. Payment varies depending on the quality of work, importance of the article. Pays $500 and up for features. *Field & Stream* also publishes regional sections with feature articles on hunting and fishing in specific areas of the country. The sections are geographically divided into Northeast, Midwest, Far West, West and South, and appear 12 months a year. Usually buys photos with mss. When purchased separately, pays $450 minimum for color. Buys first rights to photos.
Fillers: Buys "how it's done" fillers of 500-900 words. Must be unusual or helpful subjects. Pays $250 on acceptance.

THE FISHERMAN, LIF Publishing Corp., Bridge St., Sag Harbor NY 11963. (516)725-4200. Editor: Fred Golofaro. Senior Editor: Pete Barrett. 4 regional editions: *Long Island*, *Metropolitan New York*, Fred Golofaro, editor; *New England*, Tim Coleman, editor; *New Jersey*, Ken Freel, editor; and *Delaware-Maryland-Virginia*, Eric Burnley, editor. 75% freelance written. A weekly magazine covering fishing and boating. Combined circ. 82,000. Pays on publication. Byline given. Offers variable kill fee. Buys all rights. Articles may be run in one or more regional editions by choice of the editors. Submit seasonal/holiday material 2 months in advance. Computer printout submissions acceptable; prefers letter-quality to dot-matrix. Reports in 3 weeks. Free sample copy and writer's guidelines.
Nonfiction: Send submission to editor of regional edition. General interest, historical/nostalgic, how-to, interview/profile, personal experience, photo feature, technical and travel. Special issues include Trout Fishing (April), Offshore Fishing (July), Bass Fishing (August), Surf Fishing (September), Tackle (October) and Electronics (November). "No 'me and Joe' tales. We stress how, where, when, why." Buys approx. 400 mss/year, each edition. Length: 1,500-2,400 words. Pays $100-125 for unsolicited feature articles.
Photos: Send photos with submission; also buys single photos for cover use. Offers no additional payment for photos accepted with ms. Identification of subjects required.
Tips: "Freelance feature stories are most open to freelancers."

FISHING WORLD, 51 Atlantic Ave., Floral Park NY 11001. Editor: Keith Gardner. 100% freelance written. Bimonthly. Circ. 335,000. Pays on acceptance. Buys first North American serial rights. Pays on acceptance. Publishes ms an average of 6 months after acceptance. Photocopied submissions OK. Reports in 2 weeks. Free sample copy.
Nonfiction: "Feature articles range from 1,000-2,000 words with the shorter preferred. A good selection of color transparencies should accompany each submission. Subject matter can range from a hot fishing site to tackle and techniques, from tips on taking individual species to a story on one lake or an entire region, either freshwater or salt. However, how-to is definitely preferred over where-to, and a strong biological/scientific slant is best of all. Where-to articles, especially if they describe foreign fishing, should be accompanied by sidebars covering how to make reservations and arrange transportation, how to get there, where to stay. Angling methods should be developed in clear detail, with accurate and useful information about tackle and boats. Depending on article length, suitability of photographs and other factors, payment is up to $300 for feature articles accompanied by suitable photography. Color transparencies selected for cover use pay an additional $300. B&w or unillustrated featurettes are also considered. These can be on anything remotely connected with fishing. Query. Length: 1,000 words. Pays $25-100 depending on length and photos. Detailed queries accompanied by photos are preferred.
Photos: "Cover shots are purchased separately, rather than selected from those accompanying mss. The editor favors drama rather than serenity in selecting cover shots. Underwater horizontal portraits of fish are purchased (one-time rights) for centerfold use at the rate of $300 per transparency."
Tips: Looking for "more saltwater fishing and more West Coast fishing."

FLORIDA SPORTSMAN, Wickstrom Publishers Inc., 5901 S.W. 74 St., Miami FL 33143. (305)661-4222. Editor: Vic Dunaway. Managing Editor: Biff Lampton. 80% freelance written. Eager to work with new/unpublished writers. A monthly magazine covering fishing, boating and related sports— Florida and Caribbean only. Circ. 100,000. Pays on publication. Publishes ms an average of 6 months after acceptance. Byline given. Offers 50% kill fee. Buys first North American serial rights. Submit seasonal/holiday material 6 months in advance. Computer printout submissions acceptable; prefers letter-quality to dot-matrix. Reports in 1 week on queries; 1 month on mss. Free sample copy and writer's guidelines.

Nonfiction: Essays (environment or nature); how-to (fishing, hunting, boating); humor (outdoors angle); personal experience (in fishing, etc.); and technical (boats, tackle, etc., as particularly suitable for Florida specialties). "We use reader service pieces almost entirely—how-to, where-to, etc. One or two environmental pieces per issue as well. Writers *must* be Florida based, or have lengthy experience in Florida outdoors. All articles must have strong Florida emphasis. We do not want to see general how-to-fish-or-boat pieces which might well appear in a national or wide-regional magazine." Buys 120 mss/year. Query with or without published clips, or send complete ms. Length: 1,500-2,500 words. Pays $250-350 for assigned articles; pays $150-300 for unsolicited articles.

Photos: Send photos with submission. Reviews 35mm transparencies and 4x5 and larger prints. Offers no additional payment for photos accepted with ms. Buys one-time rights.

Columns/Departments: Sportsman Scene (news-feature items on outdoors subjects), 100-500 words; Angler's Clinic (short, detailed fishing how-to), 250-750 words; and Sportsman Recipe (recipes for Florida fish and game), 250-1,000 words. Buys 50 mss/year. Send complete ms. Pays $15-100.

Tips: "Feature articles are most open to freelancers; however there is little chance of acceptance unless contributor is an accomplished and avid outdoorsman *and* a competent writer-photographer with considerable experience in Florida."

FLORIDA WILDLIFE, Florida Game & Fresh Water Fish Commission, 620 South Meridian St., Tallahassee FL 32301. (904)488-5563. Editor: John M. Waters, Jr. About 75% freelance written. Bimonthly state magazine covering hunting, fishing and wildlife conservation. "In outdoors sporting articles we seek themes of wholesome recreation. In nature articles we seek accuracy and conservation purpose." Circ. 29,000. Pays on publication. Publishes ms 2 months to 2 years after acceptance. Byline given. Buys first North American serial rights and occasionally second serial (reprint) rights. Submit seasonal/holiday material 6 months in advance. Simultaneous queries, and simultaneous, photocopied, and previously published submissions OK. "Inform us if it is previously published work." Computer printout submissions acceptable if double-spaced. Reports in 6 weeks on queries; variable on mss. Sample copy $1.25; free writer's guidelines.

Nonfiction: General interest (bird watching, hiking, camping, boating); how-to (hunting and fishing); humor (wildlife related; no anthropomorphism); inspirational (conservation oriented); personal experience (wildlife, hunting, fishing, outdoors); photo feature (Florida species: game, nongame, botany); and technical (rarely purchased, but open to experts). "In a nutshell, we buy general interest hunting, fishing and nature stories. No 'me and Joe' stories, stories that humanize animals, or opinionated stories not based on confirmable facts." Buys 50-60 mss/year. Query. Length: 500-2,500 words. Generally pays $50/publisheed page; including use of photos.

Photos: John Roberge, photo editor. State availability of photos with query. Prefers 35mm color slides of hunting, fishing, and natural science series of Florida wildlife species. Pays $10-50 for inside photos; $100 for front cover photos, $50 for back cover. "We like short, specific captions." Buys one-time rights.

Fiction: "We rarely buy fiction, and then only if it is true to life and directly related to good sportsmanship and conservation. No fairy tales, erotica, profanity, or bathroom humor." Buys 2-3 mss/year. Send complete mss and label "fiction." Length: 500-2,500 words. Genrally pays $50/published page.

Tips: "Read and study recent issues for subject matter, style and examples of our viewpoint, philosophy and treatment. The area of hunting is one requiring sensitivity. We look for wholesome recreation, ethics, safety, and good outdoor experience more than bagging the game in our stories. Of special need at this time are well-written hunting and fishing in Florida articles. Unsolicited articles sent to us generally fail to be well writeen, and accurate, and lack reader interest."

FLY FISHERMAN, Historical Times, Inc., 2245 Kohn Rd., Box 8200, Harrisburg PA 17105. (717)657-9555. Editor: John Randolph. Associate Editors: Jack Russell and Philip Hanyok. 85-90% freelance written. Magazine published 6 times/year on fly fishing. Circ. 137,000. Pays on acceptance. Publishes ms an average 10 months after acceptance. Byline given. Buys first North American serial rights and (selectively) all rights. Submit seasonal/holiday material 1 year in advance. Electronic submissions OK on Wang, but requires hard copy also. Computer printout submissions acceptable; prefers letter-quality to dot-matrix. Reports in 3 weeks on queries; 6 weeks on mss. Sample copy for 11x14 SAE and 4 first class stamps. Free writer's guidelines.

Nonfiction: Book excerpts, how-to, humor, interview/profile, technical and essays on fly fishing, fly tying, shorts and fishing technique shorts and features. Where-to. No other types of fishing, including spin or bait. Buys 75 mss/year. Query or send complete ms. Length: 50-3,000 words. Pays $35-500.

Photos: State availability of photos or send photos with query or ms. Reviews b&w contact sheets and 35mm transparencies. Pays $35-100 for contact sheets; $25-200 for transparencies; $400 for cover photos. Captions, model release and identification of subjects required. Buys one-time rights.

Columns/Departments: Fly Fisherman's Bookshelf—500 to 1,000-word book reviews ($75 each); reviews of fly fishing video tapes $75, same length. Buys 8 mss/year. Query. Length: 500-1,000 words. Pays $75.

Fiction: Essays on fly fishing, humorous and serious. No long articles, anything over 3,000 words. Buys 4 mss/year. Query with published clips. Length: 1,200-3,000 words. Pays $125-500.

Fillers: Short humor and newsbreaks. Buys 30/year. Length: 25-1,000 words. Pays $25-250.

Tips: "Our magazine is a tightly focused, technique-intensive special interest magazine. Articles require fly fishing expertise and writing must be tight and in many instances well researched. The novice fly fisher has little hope of a sale with us, although perhaps 30 percent of our features are entry-level or intermediate-level in nature. Fly fishing technique pieces that are broadly focused have great appeal. Both features and departments—short features—have the best chance of purchase. Accompany submissions with excellent color slides (35mm), black and white 8x10 prints or line drawing illustrations."

THE FLYFISHER, 1387 Cambridge, Idaho Falls ID 83401. (208)523-7300. Editor: Dennis G. Bitton. 90% freelance written. Works with a small number of new/unpublished writers each year. "Any good submission gets worked in, and we could use some new writers." Quarterly magazine; 64-72 pages. "*The Flyfisher* is the official publication of The Federation of Fly Fishers, a nonprofit organization of member clubs and individuals in the U.S., Canada, United Kingdom, France, New Zealand, Chile, Argentina, Japan and other nations. It serves an audience of conservation-minded fly fishermen." Circ. 11,000. Pays after publication. Publishes ms an average of 4 months after acceptance. Byline given. Buys first North American serial rights. Submit seasonal/holiday material 60 days in advance. Computer printout submissions acceptable; no dot-matrix. Reports in 2 weeks. Sample copy $3, available from FFF, Box 1088, West Yellowstone MT 59758. Writer's guidelines for SASE; write to 1387 Cambridge, Idaho Falls ID 83401.

Nonfiction: How-to (fly fishing techniques, fly tying, tackle, etc.); general interest (any type including where to go, conservation); historical (places, people, events that have significance to fly fishing); inspirational (looking for articles dealing with Federation clubs on conservation projects); interview (articles of famous fly fishermen, fly tyers, teachers, etc.); nostalgia (articles of reminiscences on flies, fishing personalities, equipment and places); and technical (about techniques of fly fishing in salt and fresh waters). Buys 6-8 mss/issue. Query. Length: 500-2,500 words. Pays $50-200.

Photos: Pays $15-50 for 8x10 b&w glossy prints; $20-80 for 35mm or larger color transparencies for inside use and $100-150 for covers. Captions required. Buys one-time rights. Prefers a selection of transparencies and glossies when illustrating a manuscript, which are purchased as a package.

Fiction: (Must be related to fly fishing). Adventure, conservation, fantasy, historical, humorous, and suspense. Buys 2 mss/issue. Query. Length, 500-2,000 words. Pays $75-200.

Tips: "We make every effort to assist a writer with visuals if the idea is strong enough to develop. We will deal with freelancers breaking into the field. Our only concern is that the material be in keeping with the quality established. We prefer articles submitted by members of FFF, but do not limit our selection of good articles."

GALLANT/CHARGER'S FISHING & BOATING ILLUSTRATED, Gallant/Charger Publications, Inc., Box HH, Capistrano Beach CA 92624. (714)493-2101. Editor: Jack Lewis. Managing Editor: Mark Thiffault. 50% freelance written. A quarterly magazine covering fishing and boating. "*Fishing & Boating Illustrated* is aimed at recreational fishermen and boaters who enjoy both. Geographic coverage is national, with how-to stories on many fish species." Circ. 100,000. Pays on acceptance. Byline given. Buys one-time rights and makes work-for-hire assignments. Need queries by late spring for the coming March edition. Computer printout submissions acceptable. Reports in 1 month. Sample copy $3.

Nonfiction: How-to (catching specific species of fish, maintaining boats) and technical (on boating projects). Buys 20 mss/year. Query. Length: 250-3,000 words. Pays $25-350.

Photos: Send photos with accompanying query or manuscript. Reviews 35mm transparencies and 8x10 prints. Pays $5-10 for prints, $25-100 for transparencies. Captions, model releases and identification of subjects required.

Tips: "We need queries by late spring for editorial planning. If a manufacturer's product tie-in is possible, so state. Photography must be excellent."

‡GAME & FISH MAGAZINE, Game & Fish Publications, Inc., Suite 136, 2121 New Market Pkwy., Marietta GA 30067. (404)953-9222. Editorial Director: David Morris. 90% freelance written. A monthly regional hunting magazine with separate issues for the states of Oklahoma, Louisiana, Missouri, Kentucky, North Carolina, Virginia and West Virginia. (Title example: *Virginia Game & Fish Magazine*). Pays 3 months prior to cover date of issue. Publishes ms an average of 6 months after acceptance.

Byline given. Offers $75 kill fee. Buys first North American serial rights. Submit seasonal/holiday material 8 months in advance. Computer printout submissions OK; no dot-matrix. Reports in 2 months. Sample copy $2; free writer's guidelines.

Nonfiction: Address to editor of particular magazine. Historical/nostalgic, how-to, humor, interview/profile, personal experience, technical, travel (on where to hunt and fish). Buys 3-5 mss/year. Query. Length: 2,200-3,000 words. Pays $150-350.

Photos: State availability of photos with submission. Reviews 35mm transparencies. Offers $25-75 per photo. Buys one-time rights.

Fiction: Humorous fiction related to hunting only. Buys 3-5 mss/year. Send complete ms. Length: 2,200-3,000 words. Pays $150-350.

Tips: "Feature articles are most open to freelancers. Our magazines are very market specific. Be sure submissions are 'on-target.' "

GEORGIA SPORTSMAN, Game & Fish Publications, Box 741, Marietta GA 30061. (404)953-9222. Editor: Rick Lavender. 90-95% freelance written. Works with a number of new/unpublished writers each year. Monthly how-to, where-to, when-to hunting and fishing magazine covering Georgia. Pays 3 months before publication. Byline given. Buys one-time rights. Submit seasonal material 8 months in advance. Simultaneous queries OK; no simultaneous or photocopied submissions. Computer printout submissions acceptable; prefers letter-quality to dot-matrix. Sample copy for $2 and 10x12 SAE; writer's guidelines for SASE.

Nonfiction: Very state-specific approach; how-to (hunting and fishing *only*); humor/nostalgia (on limited basis); interview/profile (of successful hunter/angler); personal experience (hunting or fishing adventure). No hiking, backpacking or camping. No "my first deer" articles. Buys 75-80 mss/year. Query with or without published clips. Length: 2,200-2,500 words. Pays $150.

Photos: State availability of photos. Pays $75 for color leads; $225 for covers; $25 for b&w photos. Captions and identification of subjects required. Buys one-time rights.

GREAT LAKES FISHERMAN, Great Lakes Fisherman Publishing Co., Suite 101, 921 Eastwind Dr., Westerville OH 43081. (614)882-5653. Editor: Ottie M. Snyder, Jr. 95% freelance written. Eager to work with new/unpublished writers. Monthly magazine covering how, when and where to fish in the Great Lakes region. Circ. 50,000. Pays on 15th of month prior to issue date. Publishes ms an average of 8 months after acceptance. Byline given. Offers $40 kill fee. Buys first North American serial rights. Submit seasonal/holiday material 6-8 months in advance. Computer printout submissions acceptable; prefers letter-quality to dot-matrix. Reports in 5 weeks. Free sample copy and writer's guidelines.

Nonfiction: How-to (where to and when to freshwater fish). "No 'me and Joe' or subject matter outside the Great Lakes region." Buys 84 mss/year. Query with clips of published work. "Letters should be tightly written, but descriptive enough to present no surprises when the ms is received. Prefer b&w photos to be used to illustrate ms with query." Length: 1,500-2,500 words. Pays $135-200. Sometimes pays the expenses of writers on assignment.

Photos: Send photos with ms. "Black and white photos are considered part of manuscript package and as such receive no additional payment. We consider b&w photos to be a vital part of a ms package and return more packages because of poor quality photos than any other reason. We look for four types of illustration with each article: scene (a backed off shot of fisherman); result (not the typical meat shot of angler grinning at camera with big stringer but in most cases just a single nice fish with the angler admiring the fish); method (a lure shot or illustration of special rigs mentioned in the text); and action (angler landing a fish, fighting a fish, etc.). Illustrations (line drawings) need not be finished art but should be good enough for our artist to get the idea of what the author is trying to depict." Prefers cover shots to be verticals with fish and fisherman action shots. Pays $150 for 35mm color transparencies. Captions, model releases and identification of subjects required. Buys one-time rights.

Tips: "Our feature articles are 99.9% freelance material. The magazine is circulated in the eight states bordering the Great Lakes, an area where one-third of the nation's licensed anglers reside. All of our feature content is how, when or where, or a combination of all three covering the species common to the region. Fishing is an age-old sport with countless words printed on the subject each year. A fresh new slant that indicates a desire to share with the reader the author's knowledge is a sale. We expect the freelancer to answer any anticipated questions the reader might have (on accommodations, launch sites, equipment needed, etc.) within the ms. We publish an equal mix each month of both warm- and cold-water articles."

GULF COAST FISHERMAN, Harold Wells Gulf Coast Fisherman, Inc., 205 Bowie, Drawer P, Port Lavaca TX 77979. (512)552-8864. Editor: Gary M. Ralston. 95% freelance written. A quarterly magazine covering Gulf Coast saltwater fishing. "All editorial material is designed to expand the knowledge of the Gulf Coast angler and promote saltwater fishing in general. Our audience is composed principally of persons from managerial/professional occupations." Circ 10,000. Pays on publication. Publishes ms an average of 2 months after acceptance. Byline given. Buys first North American serial rights. Submit seasonal/holiday material 2 months in advance. Computer printout submissions acceptable; prefers letter-quality to dot-matrix. Free sample copy and writer's guidelines.

Nonfiction: How-to (any aspect relating to saltwater fishing that provides the reader specifics on use of tackle, boats, finding fish, etc.); interview/profile; new product; personal experience; and technical. Buys 25 mss/year. Query with or without published clips, or send complete ms. Length: 900-1,800 words. Pays $90-150.

Photos: State availability of photos with submission. Offers no additional payment for photos accepted with ms. Captions and identification of subjects required. Buys one-time rights.

Tips: "Features are the area of our publication most open to freelancers. Subject matter should concern some aspect of or be in relation to saltwater fishing in coastal bays or offshore."

THE MAINE SPORTSMAN, Box 365, Augusta ME 04330. Editor: Harry Vanderweide. 100% freelance written. "Eager to work with new/unpublished writers, but because we run over 30 regular columns, it's hard to get into *The Maine Sportsman* as a beginner." Monthly tabloid. Circ. 30,000. Pays "during month of publication." Buys first rights. Publishes ms an average of 3 months after acceptance. Byline given. Computer printout submissions acceptable; prefers letter-quality to dot-matrix. Reports in 2-4 weeks.

Nonfiction: "We publish only articles about Maine hunting and fishing activities. Any well-written, researched, knowledgable article about that subject area is likely to be accepted by us." Expose, how-to, general interest, interview, nostalgia, personal experience, opinion, profile, and technical. Buys 25-40 mss/issue. Submit complete ms. Length: 200-2,000 words. Pays $20-300. Sometimes pays the expenses of writers on assignment.

Photos: "We can have illustrations drawn, but prefer 1-3 b&w photos." Submit photos with accompanying ms. Pays $5-50 for b&w print.

Tips: "It's rewarding finding a writer who has a fresh way of looking at ordinary events. Specific where-to-go about Maine is needed."

MICHIGAN OUT-OF-DOORS, Box 30235, Lansing MI 48909. (517)371-1041. Editor: Kenneth S. Lowe. 50% freelance written. Works with a small number of new/unpublished writers each year. Emphasizes outdoor recreation, especially hunting and fishing, conservation and environmental affairs. Monthly magazine; 116 pages. Circ. 110,000. Pays on acceptance. Publishes ms an average of 6 months after acceptance. Byline given. Buys first North American serial rights. Phone queries OK. Submit seasonal/holiday material 6 months in advance. Computer printout submissions acceptable; prefers letter-quality to dot-matrix. Reports in 1 month. Sample copy $1.50; free writer's guidelines.

Nonfiction: Expose, historical, how-to, informational, interview, nostalgia, personal experience, personal opinion, photo feature and profile. No humor. "Stories *must* have a Michigan slant unless they treat a subject of universal interest to our readers." Buys 8 mss/issue. Send complete ms. Length: 1,000-3,000 words. Pays $75 minimum for feature stories. Pays expenses of writers on assignment.

Photos: Purchased with or without accompanying ms. Pays $15 minimum for any size b&w glossy prints; $60 maximum for color (for cover). Offers no additional payment for photos accepted with accompanying ms. Buys one-time rights. Captions preferred.

Tips: "Top priority is placed on true accounts of personal adventures in the out-of-doors—well-written tales of very unusual incidents encountered while hunting, fishing, camping, hiking, etc. The most rewarding aspect of working with freelancers is realizing we had a part in their development. But it's annoying to respond to queries that never produce a manuscript."

MID WEST OUTDOORS, Mid West Outdoors, Ltd., 111 Shore Drive, Hinsdale (Burr Ridge) IL 60521. (312)887-7722. Editor: Gene Laulunen. Emphasizes fishing, hunting, camping and boating. Monthly tabloid. 100% freelance written. Circ. 57,000. Pays on publication. Buys simultaneous rights. Byline given. Submit seasonal material 2 months in advance. Simultaneous, photocopied and previously published submissions OK. Reports in 3 weeks. Publishes ms an average of 3 months after acceptance. Sample copy $1; free writer's guidelines.

Nonfiction: How-to (fishing, hunting, camping in the Midwest) and where-to-go (fishing, hunting, camping within 500 miles of Chicago). "We do not want to see any articles on 'my first fishing, hunting or camping experiences,' 'Cleaning My Tackle Box,' 'Tackle Tune-up,' or 'Catch and Release.' '' Buys 840 unsolicited mss/year. Send complete ms. Length: 1,000-1,500 words. Pays $15-25.

Photos: Offers no additional payment for photos accompanying ms; uses b&w prints. Buys all rights. Captions required.

Columns/Departments: Fishing, Hunting. Open to suggestions for columns/departments. Send complete ms. Pays $25.

Tips: "Break in with a great unknown fishing hole within 500 miles of Chicago. Where, how, when and why. Know the type of publication you are sending material to."

MINNESOTA SPORTSMAN, Game & Fish Publications, Box 741, Marietta GA 30061. (404)953-9222. Editor: Ken Dunwoody. 85% freelance written. A magazine covering hunting, fishing and outdoors, published 12 times a year. Pays 2½ months prior to publication. Publishes ms an average of 6 months after acceptance. Byline given. Buys first rights. Submit seasonal/holiday material 9 months in advance. Computer printout submissions acceptable. Reports in 1 month on queries; 6 weeks on mss. Sample copy $1.95 with 8½x11 SAE and 95¢ postage; writer's guidelines for SASE.

Nonfiction: Where-to hunting and fishing stories dealing with Minnesota, how-to articles on game and fish species popular in state, information/education articles relating to hunting, fishing and the outdoors, and interview/profile. "The best articles have strong tie-ins with Minnesota." Sidebars often useful. Buys 80 mss/year. Query with published clips. Length: 2,00-2,500 words (feature); 50-1,000 words (shorts). Features pay from $150-250 plus $75 for every color photo used and $25 for every b&w photo. Also buys freelance photos at same rates, plus $250 for cover photos. Pays 5¢/word for short items.

Tips: "Most of our work is done on assignment. We work primarily with in-state writers who can provide detailed, specific information on hunting and fishing in Minnesota. Prospective writers should become familiar with our approach and submit queries at least 9 months prior to season. Quality color slides are a big plus to any ms or query, since topnotch photography is an important part of the magazine. Besides features, we also use short items up to 1,000 words on interesting or unusual topics related to hunting, fishing or conservation in Minnesota."

MISSISSIPPI GAME & FISH, Game & Fish Publications, Box 741, Marietta GA 30061. (404)953-9222. Editor: Rick Lavender. Monthly how-to, where-to, when-to hunting and fishing magazine covering Mississippi. Pays 3 months before publication. Byline given. Buys one-time rights. Submit seasonal material 8 months in advance. Simultaneous queries, and simultaneous and photocopied submissions OK. Reports in 2 months. Sample copy for $2.50 and 10x12 SAE; writer's guidelines for SASE.

Nonfiction: How-to (hunting and fishing *only*); humor (on limited basis); interview/profile (of successful hunter/angler); personal experience (hunting or fishing adventure). No hiking, backpacking, camping. No fiction or poems. No "my first deer" articles. Buys 60 mss/year. Query with or without published clips. Length: 2,200-2,500 words. Pays $150.

Photos: State availability of photos. Pays $75 for color leads; $225 for covers; $25 for b&w photos not submitted as part of story package. Captions and identification of subjects required. Buys one-time rights.

NORTH AMERICAN HUNTER, Official Publication of the North American Hunting Club, North American Hunting Club, Box 35557, Minneapolis MN 55435. (612)941-7654. Editor: Mark La-Barbera. Managing Editor: Bill Miller. 50% freelance written. A bimonthly magazine for members of the North American Hunting Club covering strictly North American hunting. "The purpose of the NAHC is to enhance the hunting skill and enjoyment of its 100,000 members." Circ. 100,000. Pays on acceptance. Publishes ms an average of 6-10 months after acceptance. Byline given. Buys first North American serial rights, first rights, one-time rights, second serial (reprint) rights, or all rights. Submit seasonal/holiday material 1 year in advance. Electronic submissions OK via IBM PC compatible, but requires hard copy also. Computer printout submissions acceptable; prefers letter-quality to dot-matrix. Reports in 3 weeks. Sample copy $3; writer's guidelines for 4x9 SAE with 1 first class stamp.

Nonfiction: Exposé (on hunting issues); how-to (on hunting); humor; interview/profile; new product; opinion; personal experience; photo feature and where-to-hunt. No fiction or "Me and Joe". Buys 18-24 mss/year. Query. Length: 1,000-2,500 words. Pays $200-325 for assigned articles; pays $25-325 for unsolicited articles.

Photos: Send photos with submissions. Reviews transparencies and 5x7 or 8x10 prints. Offers no additional payment for photos accepted with ms. Captions and identification of subjects required. Buys one-time rights.

Tips: "Write stories as if they are from one hunting friend to another."

NORTH AMERICAN WHITETAIL MAGAZINE, Game & Fish Publications, Inc., Suite 136, 2121 Newmarket Pkwy., Marietta GA 30067. (404)953-9222. Editor: David Morris. 90% freelance written.

A hunting magazine published 8 times/year. Circ. 105,000. Pays 3 months prior to cover date of issue. Publishes ms an average of 6 months after acceptance. Byline given. Offers $75 kill fee. Buys first North American serial rights. Submit seasonal/holiday material 8 months in advance. Computer print-out submissions OK; no dot-matrix. Reports in 2 months. Sample copy $2; free writer's guidelines.

Nonfiction: Historical, how-to, humor, interview/profile, personal experience, technical and travel (where to hunt). Buys 3-5 mss/year. Query. Length: 2,200-3,000 words. Pays $150-350.

Photos: State availability of photos with submission. Reviews 35mm transparencies. Offers $25-75 per photo. Buys one-time rights.

Fiction: Humorous fiction related to hunting only. Buys 3-5 mss/year. Send complete ms. Length: 2,200-3,000 words. Pays $150-350.

Tips: "Feature articles are most open to freelancers. Our magazines are very market specific. Be sure submissions are 'on-target'."

OHIO FISHERMAN, Ohio Fisherman Publishing Co., Suite 101, 921 Eastwind Dr., Westerville OH 43081. (614)882-5658. Editor: Ottie M. Snyder, Jr. 95% freelance written. Works with a small number of new/unpublished writers each year. Monthly magazine covering the how, when and where of Ohio fishing. Circ. 45,000. Pays on 15th of month prior to issue date. Publishes ms an average of 4-6 months after acceptance. Byline given. Offers $40 kill fee. Buys first rights. Submit seasonal/holiday material 6-8 months in advance. Computer printout submissions acceptable; prefers letter-quality to dot-matrix. Reports in 5 weeks. Free sample copy and writer's guidelines.

Nonfiction: How-to (also where to and when to fresh water fish). "Our feature articles are 99% freelance material, and all have the same basic theme—sharing fishing knowledge. No 'me and Joe' articles." Buys 84 mss/year. Query with clips of published work. Letters should be "tightly written, but descriptive enough to present no surprises when the ms is received. Prefer b&w photos to be used to illustrate ms with query." Length: 1,500-2,500 words. Pays $135-175. Sometimes pays the expenses of writers on assignment.

Photos: "Need cover photos constantly. Study cover format carefully. 99% of covers purchased are verticals involving fishermen and fish—action preferred." Send photos with query. "We consider b&w photos to be a vital part of a ms package and return more mss because of poor quality photos than any other reason. We look for four types of illustration with each article: scene (a backed off shot of fisherman); result (not the typical meat shot of angler grinning at camera with big stringer, but in most cases just a single nice fish with the angler admiring the fish); method (a lure or illustration of special rigs mentioned in the text); and action (angler landing a fish, fighting a fish, etc.). Illustrations (line drawings) need not be finished art but should be good enough for our artist to get the idea of what the author is trying to depict." Pays $150 for 35mm color transparencies (cover use); buys 8x10 b&w prints as part of ms package—"no additional payments." Captions and identification of subjects required. Buys one-time rights.

Tips: "The specialist and regional markets are here to stay. They both offer the freelancer the opportunity for steady income. Fishing is an age-old sport with countless words printed on the subject each year. A fresh new slant that indicates a desire to share with the reader the author's knowledge is a sale. We expect the freelancer to answer any anticipated questions the reader might have (on accommodations, launch sites, equipment needed, etc.) within the ms. The most frequent mistakes made by writers in completing an article for us are bad photos—sending in color instead of b&w prints to accompany stories; massive re-writing needed; or material is too seasonal and past time for our needs."

ONTARIO OUT OF DOORS, 7th Floor, 777 Bay St., Toronto, Ontario M5W 1A7 Canada. (416)596-5022, Editor-in-Chief: Burton J. Myers. 80% freelance written. "We prefer a blend of both experienced and new writers." Emphasizes hunting, fishing, camping, and conservation. Monthly magazine; 80 pages. Circ. 55,000. Pays on acceptance. Publishes ms an average of 6 months after acceptance. Buys first North American serial rights. Phone queries OK. Computer printout submissions acceptable; no dot-matrix. Submit seasonal/holiday material 5 months in advance of issue date. Reports in 6 weeks. Free sample copy and writer's guidelines; mention *Writer's Market* in request.

Nonfiction: Expose of conservation practices; how-to (improve your fishing and hunting skills); humor; photo feature (on wildlife); travel (where to find good fishing and hunting); and any news on Ontario. "Avoid 'Me and Joe' articles or funny family camping anecdotes." Buys 20-30 unsolicited mss/year. Query. Length: 150-3,500 words. Pays $35-350. Sometimes pays the expenses of writers on assignment.

Photos: Submit photo material with accompanying query. No additional payment for b&w contact sheets and 35mm color transparencies. "Should a photo be used on the cover, an additional payment of $350-500 is made."

Fillers: Outdoor tips. Buys 24 mss/year. Length: 20-50 words. Pays $20.

Tips: "It's rewarding for us to find a freelancer who reads and understands a set of writer's guidelines, but it is annoying when writers fail to submit supporting photography."

OUTDOOR LIFE, Times Mirror Magazines, Inc., 380 Madison Ave., New York NY 10017. (212)687-3000. Editor: Mr. Clare Conley. Executive Editor: Vin T. Sparano. 95% freelance written. A monthly magazine covering hunting and fishing. Circ. 1.5 million. Pays on acceptance. Publishes ms an average of 6-12 months after acceptance. Byline given. Buys first North American serial rights. Submit seasonal/holiday material 6 months in advance. Previously published submissions OK on occasion. Computer printout submissions acceptable; prefers letter-quality to dot-matrix. Reports in 1 month on queries; 2 months on mss. Writer's guidelines for SASE.

Nonfiction: Book excerpts; essays; how-to (must cover hunting, fishing, or related outdoor activities); humor; interview/profile; new product; personal experience; photo feature; technical; and travel. Special issues include Bass and Freshwater Fishing Annual (March), Deer and Big Game Annual (Aug.), and Hunting Guns Annual (Sept.). No articles that are too general in scope—need to write specifically. Buys 400 mss/year. Query or send ms—"either way, photos are *very important*." Length: 800-3,000 words. Pays $350-600 for 1,000-word features and regionals; pays $900-1,200 for 2,000-word or longer national features.

Photos: Send photos with submission. Reviews 35mm transparencies and 8x10 prints. Offers variable payment. Captions and identification of subjects required. Buys one-time rights. "May offer to buy photos after first use if considered good and have potential to be used with other articles in the future (file photos)." Pay for freelance photos is $100 for ¼ page color to $800 for 2-page spread in color; $1,000 for covers.

Columns/Departments: This Happened to Me (true-to-life, personal outdoor adventure, harrowing experience), approximately 300 words. Buys 12 mss/year. Pays $50.

Fillers: Newsbreaks and do-it-yourself for hunters and fishermen. Buys unlimited number/year. Length: 1,000 words maximum. Payment varies.

Tips: "It is best for freelancers to break in by writing features for one of the regional sections—East, Midwest, South, West. These are where-to-go oriented and run from 800-1,500 words. Writers must send one-page query with photos."

PENNSYLVANIA ANGLER, Pennsylvania Fish Commission, Box 1673, Harrisburg PA 17105-1673. (717)657-4518. Editor: Art Michaels. 75% freelance written. Prefers to work with published/established writers. A monthly magazine covering fishing and related conservation topics in Pennsylvania. Circ. 60,000. Pays 2 months after publication. Publishes ms an average of 7-9 months after acceptance. Byline given. Rights purchased vary. Submit seasonal/holiday material 8 months in advance. Computer printout submissions acceptable; prefers letter-quality to dot-matrix. Reports in 3 weeks on queries; 2 months on mss. Sample copy for 9x12 SAE with 4 first class stamps; writer's guidelines for #10 SAE with 1 first class stamp.

Nonfiction: Historical/nostalgic, how-to, where-to and technical. No saltwater or hunting material. Buys 60+ mss/year. Query. Length: 250-2,500 words. Pays $25-300.

Photos: Send photos with submission. Reviews 35mm and larger color transparencies and 8x10 prints. Offers no additional payment for photos accepted with ms. Captions, model releases and identification of subjects required.

Tips: "Our mainstays are how-tos, where-tos, and conservation pieces, but we seek more top-quality fiction, first-person stories, humor, reminiscenses, and historical articles. These pieces must a strong, specific Pennsylvania slant."

PENNSYLVANIA GAME NEWS, Pennsylvania Game Commission, 8000 Derry St., Harrisburg PA 17105-1567. (717)787-3745. Editor: Bob Bell. 60% freelance written. Works with a small number of new/unpublished writers each year. "We have a large inventory; nevertheless, we read everything that comes in." A monthly magazine covering hunting and outdoors in Pennsylvania. Emphasizes sportsmanlike actions of hunters. Circ. 175,000. Pays on acceptance. Publishes ms an average of 8-10 months after acceptance. Byline given. Buys all rights; "we return unused rights after publication." Submit seasonal/holiday material 6 months in advance. Photocopied submissions OK. Computer printout submissions acceptable; prefers letter-quality to dot-matrix. Reports in 3 weeks on queries; 6 weeks on mss. Free sample copy and writer's guidelines.

Nonfiction: General interest and personal hunting experiences. "We consider material on any outdoor subject that can be done in Pennsylvania *except* fishing and boating." Buys 60 mss/year. Query. Length: 2,500 words maximum. Pays $250 maximum.

Photos: Send photos with submission. Offers $5-20/photo. Captions required. Buys all rights.

Fiction: Must deal with hunting or outdoors; no fishing. Buys very few mss/year. Send complete ms.

Tips: "True hunting experiences—'me and Joe' stuff—are best chances for freelancers. Must take place in Pennsylvania."

PETERSEN'S HUNTING, Petersen's Publishing Co., 8490 Sunset Blvd., Los Angeles CA 90069. (213)854-2184. Editor: Craig Boddington. Managing Editor: Jeanne Frissell. 30% freelance written.

Works with a small number of new/unpublished writers each year. A monthly magazine covering sport hunting. "We are a 'how-to' magazine devoted to all facets of sport hunting, with the intent to make our readers more knowledgeable, more successful and safer hunters." Circ. 300,000. Pays on acceptance. Publishes ms an average of 9 months after acceptance. Byline given. Offers $50 kill fee. Buys all rights. Submit seasonal/holiday material 1 year in advance. Computer printout submissions acceptable; prefers letter-quality to dot-matrix. Reports in 2 weeks. Free sample copy and writer's guidelines.

Nonfiction: General interest; historical/nostalgic; how-to (on hunting techniques); humor; and travel. Special issues include Hunting Annual (August) and the Deer Hunting Annual (September). "No 'me and Joe went hunting.' Articles must include how-to and where-to material along with anecdotal material." Buys 30 mss/year. Query. Length: 2,000-3,000 words. Pays $300 minimum.

Photos: Send photos with submission. Reviews 35mm transparencies and 8x10 b&w prints. Offers no additional payment for b&w photos accepted with ms; offers $50-250/color photo. Captions, model releases and identification of subjects required. Buys one-time rights.

POPULAR LURES, National Reporter Publications, Inc., 15115 S. 76 E. Ave., Bixby OK 74008. (918)366-4441. Executive Editor: Andre Hinds. 95% freelance written. Eager to work with new/unpublished writers. Published monthly in one of two formats: magazine (68 pages) 4 issues, February-May; newsletter (12 pages) 8 issues, June-January. Covers freshwater and saltwater fishing, dealing primarily with the proper lures to use. Estab. 1986. Circ. 50,000. Pays on acceptance. Publishes ms an average of 6 months after acceptance. Byline given. Offers 30% kill fee. Not copyrighted. Buys first North American serial rights or second serial (reprint) rights. Submit seasonal/holiday material 6 months in advance. Photocopied and previously published submissions OK. Query for electronic submissions. Computer printout submissions acceptable. Reports in 1 month on mss. Sample copy $2 (cash or check—no SASE); free writer's guidelines.

Nonfiction: Book excerpts; how-to (fishing and tackle techniques); interview/profile; new product; opinion; personal experience; and photo feature. "For magazine format issues, we purchase features of 1,200-3,000 words (pays $175-200). For newsletter format issues, we purchase short how-to articles of 300-1,000 words (pays $10-75)." Buys 45 mss/year. Query with or without published clips, or send complete ms. Pays $200-225 for assigned articles; pays $175-200 for unsolicited articles.

Photos: Send photos with submission. Reviews 35mm transparencies and 5x8 b&w prints. Offers no additional payment for b&w photos accepted with ms. Offers $35-100/color photo. Captions required. Buys one-time rights.

Columns/Departments: How To Make It (step-by-step guide to making lures). Buys 4 mss/year. Length: 1,200-1,800 words. Pays $175-225.

Fillers: Newsbreaks. Buys 100/year. Length: 100-1,000 words. Pays $10-75.

Tips: "We plan to buy more than 100 short articles a year by 1988 (300-1,000 words). Writers should concentrate on how-to and what-to-use, rather than where-to. I need no travel pieces or stories on antique lures or lure collecting. We need good, short how-to articles on fishing with artificial lures to fill eight monthly newsletter issues. Seasonal short articles are also welcome—especially for summer, fall and winter (no ice fishing, though). The writer should have more than just a working knowledge of the subject, he or she must have a fresh, new angle. All areas are open to freelancers. We are particularly looking for beginners and freelance writers who have never written for outdoor magazines before. This, we hope, will give our magazine a fresher look than other outdoor magazines."

SAFARI MAGAZINE, The Journal of Big Game Hunting, Safari Club International, Suite 1680, 5151 E. Broadway, Tucson AZ 85711. (602)747-0260. Editor: William R. Quimby. 90% freelance written. Bimonthly club journal covering international big game hunting and wildlife conservation. Circ. 15,000. Pays on publication. Publishes ms an average of 1 year after acceptance. Byline given. Offers $100 kill fee. Buys all rights. Submit seasonal/holiday material 1 year in advance. Previously published submissions OK under certain circumstances. Computer printout submissions acceptable; prefers letter-quality to dot-matrix. Reports in 2 weeks on queries; 1 month on mss. Sample copy $3.50; writer's guidelines for SAE.

Nonfiction: Doug Fulton; articles editor. Historical/nostalgic (big game hunting); photo feature (wildlife); and technical (firearms, hunting techniques, etc.). Special issues will include hunting and wildlife photos, and stories covering Alaska and Canada. "Contributors should avoid sending simple hunting narratives that do not contain certain new approaches." Buys 36 mss/year. Query or send complete ms. Length: 1,500-2,500 words. Pays $200.

Photos: State availability of photos with query or ms, or send photos with query or ms. Pays $35 for 5x7 or larger b&w prints; $50-150 for 5x9 or larger color prints. Captions, model releases, and identification of subjects required. Buys one-time rights.

Tips: "Study the magazine. Send manuscripts and photo packages with query. Make it appeal to affluent, knowledgable, world-travelled big game hunters. Features on conservation contributions from big game hunters around the world are most open to freelancers. We have enough stories on first-time African safaris, ordinary deer hunts, Alaska dall sheep hunts. We need South American and eastern Canada hunting stories plus stories dealing with hunting and conservation."

SALT WATER SPORTSMAN, 186 Lincoln St., Boston MA 02111. (617)426-4074. Editor-in-Chief: Barry Gibson. Emphasizes saltwater fishing. 85% freelance written. Works with a small number of new/ unpublished writers each year. Monthly magazine; 120 pages. Circ. 150,000. Pays on acceptance. Publishes ms an average of 5 months after acceptance. Byline given. Buys first North American serial rights. Offers 100% kill fee. Submit seasonal material 8 months in advance. Computer printout submissions acceptable; no dot-matrix. Reports in 1 month. Sample copy and writer's guidelines for 8½x11 SAE with $1.41 postage.

Nonfiction: How-to, personal experience, technical and travel (to fishing areas). "Readers want solid how-to, where-to information written in an enjoyable, easy-to-read style. Personal anecdotes help the reader identify with the writer." Prefers new slants and specific information. Query. "It is helpful if the writer states experience in salt water fishing and any previous related articles. We want one, possibly two well-explained ideas per query letter—not merely a listing." Buys 100 unsolicited mss/year. Length: 1,500-2,000 words. Pays $300 and up. Sometimes pays the expenses of writers on assignment.

Photos: Purchased with or without accompanying ms. Captions required. Uses 5x7 or 8x10 b&w prints and color slides. Pays $400 minimum for 35mm, 2¼x2¼ or 8x10 color transparencies for cover. Offers additional payment for photos accepted with accompanying ms.

Columns: Sportsman's Workbench (how to make fishing or fishing-related boating equipment), 100-300 words.

Tips: "There are a lot of knowledgable fishermen/budding writers out there who could be valuable to us with a little coaching. Many don't think they can write a story for us, but they'd be surprised. We work with writers. Shorter articles that get to the point which are accompanied by good, sharp photos are hard for us to turn down. Having to delete unnecessary wordage—conversation, cliches, etc.—that writers feel is mandatory is annoying. Often they don't devote enough attention to specific fishing information."

SOUTHERN OUTDOORS MAGAZINE, B.A.S.S. Publications, Number 1 Bell Rd., Montgomery AL 36141. Editor: Larry Teague. Emphasizes Southern outdoor activities, including hunting, fishing, boating, shooting, camping. 90% freelance written. Prefers to work with published/established writers. Published 9 times/year. Circ. 240,000. Pays on acceptance. Publishes ms an average of 6 months after acceptance. Buys all rights. Computer printout submissions acceptable; no dot-matrix. Reports in 1 month. Sample copy $1.50.

Nonfiction: Articles should be service-oriented, helping the reader excel in outdoor sports. Emphasis is on techniques and trends. Some "where-to" stories purchased on Southern destinations with strong fishing or hunting theme. Buys 120 mss/year. Length: 2,000 words maximum. Pays 15¢/word. Sometimes pays the expenses of writers on assignment.

Photos: Usually purchased with manuscripts. Pays $50-75 for 35mm color transparencies without ms, and $250-400 for covers.

Fillers: Needs short articles (50-500 words) with newsy slant for Southern Shorts. Emphasis on irony and humor. Also needs humorous or thought-provoking pieces (750-1,200 words) for S.O. Essay feature.

Tips: "It's easiest to break in with short features of 500-1,000 words on 'how-to' fishing and hunting topics. We buy very little first person. Query first and send sample of your writing if we haven't done business before. Stories most likely to sell: bass fishing, deer hunting, other freshwater fishing, inshore saltwater fishing, bird and small-game hunting, shooting, camping and boating. The most frequent mistakes made by writers in completing an article for us are first-person usage; clarity of articles; applicability of topic to the South; lack of quotes from qualified sources."

SPORT FISHING, The Magazine of Offshore Fishing, World Publications, Suite H, 809 S. Orlando Ave., Box 2456, Winter Park FL 32790. (305)628-4802. Editor: Pierce Hoover. 60% freelance written. A bimonthly magazine covering offshore fishing for both big game and light-tackle enthusiasts—from the occasional to active fisherman. Readers are sophisticated, well-traveled, with median income of $80,000. Estab. 1986. Circ. 90,000. Pays on acceptance or on publication. Publishes ms an average of 2-6 months after acceptance. Byline given. Offers kill fee. Buys first North American serial rights. Submit seasonal/holiday material 6 months in advance. Computer printout submissions acceptable; prefers letter-quality to dot-matrix. Reports in 1 month. Free sample copy and writer's guidelines.

Nonfiction: Historical/nostalgic; how-to (need to be well-versed on off-shore fishing); humor; interview/profile; new product (area of expertise needed); photo feature; technical; and travel (seasonal, locations, fishing, facilities); and general—worldwide with emphasis on states). Buys 20 mss/year. Query with published clips or query by phone. Length: 400-3,000 words. Pays $200-500 for assigned articles; pays $100-500 for unsolicited articles. Sometimes pays the expenses of writers on assignment.

Photos: State availability of photos with submission, or send photos with submission. Reviews 35mm slides and b&w glossy prints. Offers $35-200/photo. Captions, model releases and identification of subjects required. Buys one-time rights.

Columns/Departments: Rotating Columns; Power Plants and Maintenance, Seamanship, Light Tackle Fishing, Rigging, and Fishing Techniques. Length: 1,000-2,000 words. Pays $150-200.

Fiction: Adventure (as pertains to offshore fishing); and historical. Buys 3 mss/year. Query. Length: 2,000-5,000 words. Pays $200-300.

Fillers: Anecdotes, facts, gags to be illustrated by cartoonist, newsbreaks and short humor. Buys 30/year. Length: 300-900 words. Pays $50-200.

Tips: "We like to work with fishing experts; no writing experience needed. Contributors must be very knowledgeable about boats and offshore fishing."

SPORTING CLASSICS, Indigo Press, Inc., Highway 521 S., Box 1017, Camden SC 29020. (803)425-1003. Executive Editor: Charles A. Wechsler. 50% freelance written. Prefers to work with published/established writers; works with a small number of new/unpublished writers each year. A bimonthly magazine covering hunting and fishing for well-educated and above-average-income sportsmen. Circ. 42,000. Pays within 60 days after publication. Publishes ms an average of 6 months after acceptance. Byline given. Offers $300 kill fee. Buys first North American serial rights. Submit seasonal/holiday material 6 months in advance. Computer printout submissions acceptable; no dot-matrix. Reports in 5 weeks. Free sample copy and writer's guidelines.

Nonfiction: 'Classic" hunting and fishing adventures, historical/nostalgic, humor, personal experience, photo feature, travel. Buys 35 mss/year. Query. Length 2,500-4,500 words. Pays $300-750 for assigned articles; pays $300-500 for unsolicited articles. Sometimes pays expenses of writers on assignment.

Photos: "Excellent photos and/or art essential." Send photos with submissions and state availability of other photos. Reviews 35mm and larger transparencies. Usually offers no additional payment for photos accepted with ms. Captions and model releases required. Buys one-time rights.

Columns/Departments: My View (places, people, events, etc. in the great outdoors). Buys 6 mss/year. Query. Length: 1,000-1,500 words. Pays $300 minimum.

Fillers: Anecdotes, facts, newsbreaks and short humor. Buys 12/year. Length: 25-1,000 words. Pays $50-150.

Tips: "We're always looking for well-written features—about hunting and fishing, exotic or unusual places to hunt and fish; about great sportsmen; conservation issues that affect game species; sporting dogs; wildlife painters, carvers and sculptors; firearms; decoys; knives; and collectible fishing tackle. Material must be fact-laden with unique, high-interest experience and insights."

SPORTS AFIELD, 250 W. 55th St., New York NY 10019. Editor: Tom Paugh. Managing Editor: Fred Kesting. 33% freelance written. Eager to work with new/unpublished writers. For people of all ages whose interests are centered around the out-of-doors (hunting and fishing) and related subjects. Monthly magazine. Circ. 518,010. Buys first North American serial rights for features, and all rights for *SA Almanac*. Pays on acceptance. Publishes ms an average of 6 months after acceptance. Byline given. "Our magazine is seasonal and material submitted should be in accordance. Fishing in spring and summer; hunting in the fall; camping in summer and fall." Submit seasonal material 6 months in advance. Computer printout submissions acceptable; prefers letter-quality to dot-matrix. Reports in 1 month. Query or submit complete ms.

Nonfiction and Photos: "Informative where-to articles and personal experiences with good photos on hunting, fishing, camping, boating and subjects such as conservation and travel related to hunting and fishing. We want first-class writing and reporting." Buys 15-17 unsolicited mss/year. Length: 500-2,500 words. Pays $750 minimum, depending on length and quality. Photos purchased with or without ms. Pays $50 minimum for 8x10 b&w glossy prints. Pays $50 minimum for 35mm or larger transparencies. Sometimes pays the expenses of writers on assignment.

Fiction: Adventure, humor (if related to hunting and fishing).

Fillers: Send to *Almanac* editor. *Almanac* pays $25 and up depending on length, for newsworthy, unusual, how-to and nature items. Payment on publication. Buys all rights.

Tips: "We seldom give assignments to other than staff. Top-quality 35mm slides to illustrate articles a must. Read a recent copy of *Sports Afield* so you know the market you're writing for. Family-oriented features will probably become more important because more and more groups/families are sharing the outdoor experience."

‡**SPORTSMAN MAGAZINE**, Game & Fish Publications, Inc., Suite 136, 2121 Newmarket Parkway, Marietta GA 30067. (404)953-9222. Editor: David Morris. 90% freelance written. A monthly regional hunting magazine with separate issues for the states of Georgia, Texas, Arkansas and Tennessee (title example: *Tennessee Sportsman Magazine*). Pays 3 months before publication. Publishes ms an average of 6 months after ac-

ceptance. Byline given. Offers $75 kill fee. Buys first North American serial rights. Submit seasonal/holiday material 8 months in advance. Computer printout submissions OK; no dot-matrix. Reports in 2 months. Sample copy $2; free writer's guidelines.

Nonfiction: Address to editor of appropriate state magazine. Historical/nostalgic, how-to, humor, interview/profile, personal experience, technical, travel (where to hunt and fish). Buys 3-5 mss/year. Query. Length: 2,200-3,000 words. Pays $150-350.

Photos: State availability of photos with submission. Reviews 35mm transparencies. Offers $25-75/photo. Buys one-time rights.

Fiction: Humorous (fiction related to hunting only). Buys 3-5 mss/year. Send complete ms. Length: 2,200-3,000 words. pays $150-350.

Tips: "Feature articles are most open to freelancers. Our magazines are very market specific. Be sure submissions are 'on target.'"

TEXAS FISHERMAN, 5314 Bingle Rd., Houston TX 77092. Editor/Publisher: Larry Bozka. 80% freelance written. Prefers to work with published/established writers; works with a small number of new/unpublished writers each year. A tabloid published 9 times a year for freshwater and saltwater fishermen in Texas. Circ. 61,152. Rights purchased vary with author and material. Byline given. Usually buys second serial (reprint) rights. Buys 4-6 mss/month. Pays on acceptance. Publishes ms an average of 3 months after acceptance. Electronic submissions OK, but requires hard copy also; contact production manager Tim Stephens at (713)688-8811. Computer printout submissions acceptable; no dot-matrix. Reports in 1 month. Query. Free sample copy and writer's guidelines.

Nonfiction and Photos: General how-to, where-to, features on all phases of fishing in Texas. Strong slant on informative pieces. Strong writing. Good saltwater stories (Texas only). Length: 1,200-1,500 words. Pays $75-250, depending on length and quality of writing and photos. Mss must include 4-7 good action b&w photos or illustrations. Color slides will be considered for cover or inside use.

Tips: "Query should be a short, but complete description of the story that emphasizes a specific angle. When possible, send black and white and/or color photos with queries. Good art will sell us a story that is mediocre, but even a great story can't replace bad photographs, and better than half submit poor quality photos. How-to, location, or personality profile stories are preferred."

THE TRAPPER, Spearman Publishing & Printing, Inc., 213 N. Saunders, Box 550, Sutton NE 68979. (402)773-4343. Editor: Rich Faler, Box 691, Greenville PA 161225. (412)588-3492. 50% freelance written. Eager to work with new/unpublished writers. A monthly tabloid covering trapping, outdoor occupations, fur farming, medicinal roots and herbs, calling predators and fur markets for both novice and pro audience, male and female, all ages. Circ. 51,000. Pays on publication. Publishes ms an average of 10 months after acceptance. Byline given. Buys first North American serial rights, one-time rights, and all rights. Submit seasonal/holiday material at least 4 months in advance. Computer printout submissions acceptable; prefers letter-quality to dot-matrix. Reports in 6 weeks on mss. Sample copy for $2 and 12x15 SAE; writer's guidelines for SAE and 1 first class stamp.

Nonfiction: How-to (trapping, raising fur, etc.); and personal experience (trapping, outdoor-related experiences). "We do not want to see anything that refers to or condones overharvesting, bragging, etc." Buys 120 mss/year. Query. Length: 500-3,000 words. Pays $20-200.

Photos: Send photos with accompanying query or ms. Pays $5-40 for 8x10 b&w and color prints. Captions required. Buys one-time rights and all rights.

Tips: "A good feature with excellent photos is really needed all the time. We stress good outdoor ethics, conservation and public relations. How-to articles are always needed; look for fresh ideas or different slant. The most frequent mistakes made by writers in completing an article for us is that the articles are too thin or basic; the market is missed (audience not targeted). Being a professional writer isn't as important as knowing your subject inside out. We need articles delivering very specific, in-depth information."

TURKEY, 3941 N. Paradise Rd., Flagstaff AZ 86001. (602)774-6913. Editor: Gerry Blair. 60% freelance written. Works with a small number of new/unpublished writers each year. A monthly magazine covering turkey hunting, biology and conservation of the wild turkey, gear for turkey hunters, where to go, etc. for both novice and experienced wild turkey enthusiasts. "We stress wildlife conservation, ethics, and management of the resource." Circ. 30,000. Pays on publication. Publishes ms an average of 1 year after acceptance. Byline given. Computer printout submissions acceptable; prefers letter-quality to dot-matrix.

Nonfiction: Book excerpts (turkey related); how-to (turkey-related); and personal experience (turkey hunting). Buys 75-100 mss/year. "The most frequent mistake made by writers in completing an article for us is inadequate photo support." Query. Length: 500-3,000 words. Pays $20-150.

Photos: Send photos with accompanying query or ms. Pays $5-20 for 8x10 b&w and color prints; $50 for color slides for cover.

Columns/Departments: "Nearly all columns are done inhouse."
Fillers: Clippings and newsbreaks that relate to or could affect turkey hunting or management. Length: 50-200 words. Pays $10-25.
Tips: "How-to articles, using fresh ideas, are most open to freelancers. We also need more short articles on turkey management programs in all states."

TURKEY CALL, Wild Turkey Bldg., Box 530, Edgefield SC 29824. (803)637-3106. Editor: Gene Smith. 50-60% freelance written. Eager to work with new/unpublished writers and photographers. An educational publication for members of the National Wild Turkey Federation. Bimonthly magazine. Circ. 35,000. Buys one-time rights. Byline given. Pays on acceptance. Publishes ms an average of 6 months after acceptance. Reports in 4 weeks. No queries necessary. Submit complete package. Wants original ms only. Computer printout submissions acceptable; prefers letter-quality to dot-matrix. "Double strike dot-matrix OK." Sample copy $2 with 9x12 SAE and $1.45 postage.
Nonfiction and Photos: Feature articles dealing with the hunting and management of the American wild turkey. Must be accurate information and must appeal to national readership of turkey hunters and wildlife management experts. No poetry or first-person accounts of unremarkable hunting trips. May use some fiction that educates or entertains in a special way. Length: 1,500-2,000 words. Pays $25 for items, $50 for short fillers of 400-500 words, $200-300 for illustrated features. "We want quality photos submitted with features." Art illustrations also acceptable. "We are using more and more inside color illustrations." Prefers b&w 8x10 glossies. Color transparencies of any size are acceptable. Wants no typical hunter-holding-dead-turkey photos or setups using mounted birds or domestic turkeys. Photos with how-to stories must make the techniques clear (example: how to make a turkey call; how to sculpt or carve a bird in wood). Pays $10 minimum for one-time rights on b&w photos and simple art illustrations; up to $75 for inside color, reproduced any size. Covers: Most are donated. Any purchased are negotiated.
Tips: The writer "should simply keep in mind that the audience is 'expert' on wild turkey management, hunting, life history and restoration/conservation history. He/she *must know the subject*. We will be buying more third person, more fiction—in an attempt to avoid the 'predictability trap' of a single subject magazine."

VIRGINIA WILDLIFE, Box 11104, Richmond VA 23230. (804)257-1000. Editor: Harry L. Gillam. Send manuscripts to Editor, V. Shepherd. 80% freelance written. Works with a small number of new/unpublished writers each year. For sportsmen and outdoor enthusiasts. Pays on acceptance. Publishes ms an average of 1 year after acceptance. Buys first North American serial rights and reprint rights. Byline given. Computer printout submissions acceptable; prefers letter-quality to dot-matrix. Free sample copy and writer's guidelines for 8½x11 SASE.
Nonfiction: Uses factual outdoor stories, set in Virginia. "Currently need boating subjects. Always need good fishing and hunting stories—not of the 'me and Joe' genre, however. Slant should be to enjoy the outdoors and what you can do to improve it. Material must be applicable to Virginia, sound from a scientific basis, accurate and easily readable. No subjects which are too controversial for a state agency magazine to address; poetry and cartoons; sentimental or humorous pieces (not because they're inherently bad, but because so few writers are good at either); 'how I nursed an abandoned _____ back to health' or stories about wildlife the author has become 'pals' with." Submit photos with ms. Length: prefers approximately 1,500 words. Pays 10¢/word minimum for edited copy.
Photos: Buys photos with mss; "and occasionally buys unaccompanied good photos." Prefers color transparencies, Kodachrome 64. Captions required. Pays $10-25 for color.
Tips: "We give special preference to Virginia writers and those willing to take on special assignments. We are currently receiving too many anecdotes and too few articles with an educational bent—we want instructional, 'how-to' articles on hunting, fishing, boating and outdoor sports, and also want semi-technical articles on wildlife. We are not receiving enough articles with high-quality photographs accompanying them; also, photos are inadequately labeled and protected. Catering to these needs will greatly enhance chances for acceptance of manuscripts. We have more 'backyard bird' articles than we could ever hope to use, and not enough good submissions on boating, trapping or trout fishing. We are cutting back substantially on number of freelance, over-the-transom submissions we purchase, in favor of making assignments to writers with whom we have established relationships and articles written by our own staff. The trend in our magazine is to pay more for fewer, longer, more in-depth, higher-quality stories. As always, a fresh angle sells, especially since we are basically publishing the same topics year after year. We need more ecosystem approach articles which aim to educate the public on the interrelatedness of the environment."

‡**WASHINGTON FISHING HOLES**, 502 E. Fairhaven, Burlington WA 98233. Editor: Brad Stracener. 70% freelance written. Works with small number of new/unpublished writers each year. Magazine published monthly; 80 pages. For Washington anglers from ages 8-80, whether beginner or expert, in-

terested in the where-to and how-to of Washington fishing. Circ. 10,000. Pays on publication. Publishes ms an average of 3-4 months after acceptance. Buys first North American serial rights and second serial (reprint) rights. Submit material 4 months in advance. Computer printout submissions acceptable; no dot-matrix. Reports in 3 weeks. Sample copy and writer's guidelines for 9x12 SAE with 88¢ postage. Query essential.

Nonfiction: How-to (angling only) and informational (how-to). "Articles and illustrations *must* be local, Washington angling or readily available within a short distance for Washington anglers." Buys 120 mss/year. Query. Length: 1,000-1,500 words. Pays approximately $90-120.

Photos: Purchased with accompanying ms at $10 each extra. Buys color and b&w glossy prints or 35mm color transparencies with article. Covers $50. Color transparency, ASA 64 film. Captions and model release required.

WATERFOWLER'S WORLD, Waterfowl Publications, Ltd., Box 38306, Germantown TN 38183. (901)767-7978. Editor: Cindy Dixon. 75% freelance written. Bimonthly magazine covering duck and goose hunting for the serious hunter and experienced waterfowler, with an emphasis on improvement of skills. Circ. 35,000. Pays on publication. Publishes ms an average of 1 year after acceptance. Buys first North American serial rights. Reports in 2 months. Computer printout submissions acceptable; no dot-matrix. Sample copy $2.50; writer's guidelines for $1.

Nonfiction: General interest (where to hunt); how-to written for the serious duck hunter. Query. Length: 1,500 words. Pays $75-200.

Photos: Reviews 8x10 b&w prints and 35mm color transparencies. Pays $50/cover.

Columns/Departments: Fowlweather Gear (outdoor clothes and supplies).

Tips: "The most frequent mistakes made by writers in completing articles for us are not sending SASE for return of manuscript, and not realizing our audience already knows the basics of duck hunting."

WESTERN OUTDOORS, 3197-E Airport Loop, Costa Mesa CA 92626. (714)546-4370. Editor-in-Chief: Burt Twilegar. 75% freelance written. Works with a small number of new/unpublished writers each year. Emphasizes hunting, fishing, camping, boating for 11 Western states only, Baja California, Canada, Hawaii and Alaska. Monthly magazine; 88 pages. Circ. 150,000. Pays on acceptance. Publishes ms an average of 6 months after acceptance. Buys first North American serial rights. Query (in writing). Submit seasonal material 4-6 months in advance. Photocopied submissions OK. Computer printout submissions are acceptable if double-spaced; no dot-matrix. Reports in 4-6 weeks. Sample copy $1.75; writer's guidelines for SASE.

Nonfiction: Where-to (catch more fish, bag more game, improve equipment, etc.); informational; photo feature. "We do not accept fiction, poetry, cartoons." Buys 70 assigned mss/year. Query or send complete ms. Length: 1,000-1,800 words maximum. Pays $300-500.

Photos: Purchased with accompanying ms. Captions required. Uses 8x10 b&w glossy prints; prefers Kodachrome II 35mm slides. Offers no additional payment for photos accepted with accompanying ms. Pays $150-200 for covers.

Tips: "Provide a complete package of photos, map, trip facts and manuscript written according to our news feature format. Stick with where-to type articles. Both b&w and color photo selections make a sale more likely. The most frequent mistake made by writers in completing an article for us is that they don't follow our style. Our guidelines are quite clear."

WESTERN SPORTSMAN, Box 737, Regina, Saskatchewan, S4P 3A8 Canada. (306)352-8384. Editor: Rick Bates. 90% freelance written. For fishermen, hunters, campers and others interested in outdoor recreation. "Note that our coverage area is Alberta and Saskatchewan." Bimonthly magazine; 64-112 pages. Circ. 30,000. Rights purchased vary with author and material. May buy first North American serial rights or second serial (reprint) rights. Byline given. Pays on publication. Publishes ms an average of 2-12 months after acceptance. "We try to include as much information as possible on all subjects in each edition. Therefore, we usually publish fishing articles in our winter issues along with a variety of winter stories. If material is dated, we would like to receive articles 2 months in advance of our publication date." Computer printout submissions OK; no dot-matrix. Reports in 4 weeks. SAE and IRCs. Sample copy $3.50; free writer's guidelines.

Nonfiction: "It is necessary that all articles can identify with our coverage area of Alberta and Saskatchewan. We are interested in mss from writers who have experienced an interesting fishing, hunting, camping or other outdoor experience. We also publish how-to and other informational pieces as long as they can relate to our coverage area. We are more interested in articles which tell about the average guy living on beans, guiding his own boat, stalking his game and generally doing his own thing in our part of Western Canada than a story describing a well-to-do outdoorsman traveling by motorhome, staying at an expensive lodge with guides doing everything for him except catching the fish, or shooting the big game animal. The articles that are submitted to us need to be prepared in a knowledgeable way and include more information than the actual fish catch or animal or bird kill. Discuss the terrain, the people involved on the trip, the water or weather conditions, the costs, the planning that went into the trip, the equipment and other data closely associated with the particular event in a factual manner. We're always looking for new writers." Buys 120 mss/year. Submit complete ms. Length: 1,500-2,000 words. Pays $100-325. Sometimes pays the expenses of writers on assignment.

Photos: Photos purchased with ms with no additional payment. Also purchased without ms. Pays $20-25/5x7 or 8x10 b&w print; $175-250/35mm or larger transparency for front cover.

Martial Arts

AMERICAN KARATE, Condor Books, Inc., 351 W. 54th St., New York NY 10019. (212)586-4432. Editor: Alan Paul. Managing Editor: David Weiss. 80% freelance written. A bimonthly magazine covering martial arts in America and Canada. *"AK* is directed at American and Canadian martial artists and the ways in which they have adapted and changed the oriental fighting arts to better suit our way of life." Estab. 1986. Circ. 100,000. Pays on publication. Byline given. Offers $50-75 kill fee. Buys first North American serial rights. Submit seasonal/holiday material 3 months in advance. Photocopied submissions OK. Computer printout submissions acceptable; prefers letter-quality to dot-matrix. Reports in 2 weeks on queries; 1 month on mss. Sample copy for 9x12 SAE with 5 first class stamps.

Nonfiction: Book excerpts, general interest, historical/nostalgic, how-to, inspirational, interview/profile, new product, personal experience and technical. No articles of an overly general nature on martial arts. Buys 50 mss/year. Query with or without published clips, or send complete ms. Length: 2,000-3,000 words. Pays $100-200. Sometimes pays the expenses of writers on assignment.

Photos: Send photos with submission. Reviews contact sheets, 35mm transparencies and 5x7 or 8x10 prints. Offers no additional payment for b&w photos accepted with ms; offers $35-100/color photo. Captions and identification of subjects required. Buys one-time rights.

Columns/Departments: AK-TV (martial arts videos), 1,500 words; AK Profile (inspirational pieces about martial artists), 1,500 words; State of the Martial Arts (review of martial arts in American states), 2,000-2,500 words; and Fit to Fight (exercise and weight training for martial artists), 1,500-2,000 words. Buys 25 mss/year. Send complete ms. Pays $75-200.

Tips: "Freelancer can break into our publication by concentrating on the *American* approach our magazine has taken. We are not interested in pieces on oriental practitioners or systems. We also are interested in good quality color and b&w photos. Every area is open. We are vey interested in expanding our stable of contributors."

ATA MAGAZINE, Martial Arts and Fitness, ATA Magazine Co., Inc., Box 240835, Memphis TN 38124-0835. (901)761-2821. Editor: Milo Dailey. Managing Editor: Carla Dailey. 30% freelance written. Works with a small number of new/unpublished writers each year. *ATA Magazine* is the official publication of the American Taekwondo Association covering general health and fitness with emphasis on martial arts (Taekwondo), aerobics, and strength training equipment. Circ. 15,000. Pays on publication. Publishes ms an average of 3 months after acceptance. "Most of publication copyrighted." Buys first North American serial rights unless otherwise arranged. Submit seasonal/holiday material at least 6 months in advance. Sometimes accepts previously published submissions. Query for electronic submissions. Computer printout submissions acceptable; dot-matrix submissions OK "if on non-heat-sensitive paper." Reports in 3 weeks. Sample copy $2.25; writer's guidelines for SAE.

Nonfiction: Interview/profile (on persons notable in other fields who train under *ATA* programs). "Special slant is that martial arts are primarily for fitness and personal development. Defense and sports aspects are to reinforce primary aims. Freelancers who are not ATA members should concentrate on non-martial arts aspects of fitness or on ATA martial artists' personalities. *We're not interested in fads, non-ATA martial arts or overt 'sex' orientation.*" Currently articles are staff-written, assigned to ATA experts or ATA member freelancers; would possibly buy 4-6 outside freelance mss. Query. Length: depends on material. Pays $25-150.

Photos: Payment for photos included in payment for ms. Prefers b&w prints of size appropriate to quality reproduction. Model releases and identification of subjects "with enough information for a caption" required.

Fiction: "We would take a look at fiction—but because of the overall magazine subject matter, would be very, very, very leery. It would almost take a writer who is an ATA martial arts member to get the right outlook."

Tips: "We're doing less 'health' material and more material directed to the beginner in martial arts. Recent freelance submissions have included a piece on a deaf Auburn University varsity swimmer who earned an ATA Black Belt and one on an extended family ATA demonstration team. So far *ATA Magazine* has served as a developmental organ for ATA members who are or wish to be writers. We're willing to work with writers on nontechnical coverage of subjects of interest to our readership—which is mostly 'adult' in its approach to martial arts and fitness in general. Most ATA centers have a good story."

Most martial arts and strength-training articles are staff-written or assigned to association experts. This leaves nutrition and special personality pieces most open to freelancers, along possibly with fiction. To get the right slant, proximity to ATA sources (which are currently in about 200 communities coast to coast) is almost mandatory. It seems only freelancers with a current 'ATA connection' can figure the proper slant. A major problem in writing for most magazines today is to have expert knowledge with ability to communicate at the non-expert level. A middle ground is the 'special interest' magazine such as ours which allows presumption of both interest and a basic knowledge of the subject. Still, it's easy to become too technical and forget that emotion retains readers—not just facts. The most blatant mistake is not reading the entry in *Writer's Market*. We do not use karate movie stars or non-ATA martial artists. Other publications answer this interest segment. We're a small staff with a lot of hats to wear. Unsolicited manuscripts may get dumped by default. Handwritten ones certainly are. *If writers actually read all of our listing, it would save all a lot of time*. One well-known martial arts writer queried, determined we're not 'her thing', and we're both happier."

BLACK BELT, Rainbow Publications, Inc., 1813 Victory Place, Burbank CA 91504. (818)843-4444. Executive Editor: Jim Coleman. 80-90% freelance written. Works with a small number of new/unpublished writers each year. Emphasizes martial arts for both practitioner and layman. Monthly magazine; 132 pages. Circ. 110,000. Pays on publication. Publishes ms an average of 3-5 months after acceptance. Buys first North American serial rights, retains right to republish. Submit seasonal/holiday material 6 months in advance. Photocopied submissions OK. Computer printout submissions acceptable; prefers letter-quality to dot-matrix. Reports in 1 month.
Nonfiction: Expose, how-to, informational, interview, new product, personal experience, profile, technical and travel. Also survival-type manuscripts, and how they relate to the martial arts. No biography, material on teachers or on new or Americanized styles. Buys 8-9 mss/issue. Query or send complete ms. Length: 1,200 words minimum. Pays $10-20/page of manuscript.
Photos: Very seldom buys photos without accompanying mss. Captions required. Total purchase price for ms includes payment for photos. Model releases required.
Fiction: Historical and modern day. Buys 2-3 mss/year. Query. Pays $100-175.
Tips: "We also publish an annual yearbook and special issues periodically. The yearbook includes our annual 'Black Belt Hall of Fame' inductees."

‡**THE FIGHTER—INTERNATIONAL**,Professional Martial Arts Association, 1017 Highland Ave., Largo FL 33540. (813)584-0054. Editor: John M. Corcoran. Bimonthly magazine covering martial arts. "We cover the entire spectrum of the industry, but are particularly interested in controversial issues that affect the martial arts masses." Circ. 150,000 (English language). Pays on acceptance. Publishes ms an average of 2-3 months after acceptance. Byline given. Offers $25 kill fee. Buys first rights (worldwide) or second serial (reprint) rights. Simultaneous, photocopied and previously published submissions OK (only if published in mainstream magazines). Computer printout submissions OK; no dot-matrix. Reports in 3 weeks on queries; 2-4 weeks on mss. Sample copy $3.50 with 8½x11 SAE and $1.58 postage; free writer's guidelines.
Nonfiction: Expose, historical/nostalgic, humor, inspirational, interview/profile (on assignment only) and photo feature. No how-to/technical articles. Buys 25-30 mss/year. Query. Length: 1,500 words or what the story requires. Pays $200-400 for assigned articles; $150-200 for unsolicited articles.
Photos: State availability of photos with query. Reviews contact sheets, transparencies (3x5) and prints (8x10). Offers no additional payment for photos accepted with ms. Captions and identification of subjects required. Buys one-time rights.
Tips: "Submit articles ideas of substance and significance. Omit ideas which have been done to death by other martial arts publications. We are the only full-color magazine in the genre; therefore, visual impact can increase chances of acceptance."

FIGHTING WOMAN NEWS, Martial Arts, Self-Defense, Combative Sports Quarterly, Box 1459, Grand Central Station, New York NY 10163. (212)228-0900. Editor: Valerie Eads. 75% freelance written. Prefers to work with published/established writers. Quarterly magazine. "*FWN* combines sweat and philosophy, the deadly reality of street violence and the other worldliness of such eastern disciplines as Zen. Our audience is composed of adult women actually practicing martial arts with an average experience of 4+ years. Since our audience is also 80+% college grads and 40% holders of advanced degrees we are an action magazine with footnotes. Our material is quite different from what is found in newsstand martial arts publications." Circ. 6,734. Pays on publication. "There is a backlog of poetry and fiction—hence a *very* long wait. A solid factual martial arts article would go out 'next issue' with trumpets and pipes." Byline given. Buys one-time rights. Submit seasonal/holiday material 6 months in advance. Simultaneous queries, and simultaneous, photocopied, and previously published submissions OK. "For simultaneous and previously published we *must* be told about it." Query for electronic submissions. Computer printout submissions acceptable; prefers letter-quality to dot-matrix. "If computer printout submissions are unreadable, we throw them out." Reports as soon as possible. Sample copy $3.50; writer's guidelines for business size SAE and 39¢ postage.

Nonfiction: Book excerpts, expose (discrimination against women in martial arts governing bodies); historical/nostalgic; how-to (martial arts, self-defense techniques); humor; inspirational (e.g., self-defense success stories); interview/profile ("we have assignments waiting for writers in this field"); new product; opinion; personal experience; photo feature; technical; travel. "All materials *must* be related to our subject matter. No tabloid sensationalism, no 'sweat is sexy too' items, no fantasy presented as fact, no puff pieces for an instructor or school with a woman champion inhouse." Buys 12 mss/year. Query. Length: 1,000-5,000 words. Pays in copies or $10 maximum. Sometimes pays the expenses of writers on assignment; expenses negotiated in some cases.

Photos: Muskat Buckby, photo editor. State availability of photos with query or ms. Reviews "technically competent" b&w contact sheets and 8x10 b&w prints. "We negotiate photos and articles as a package. Sometimes expenses are negotiated. Captions and identification of subjects required. The need for releases depends on the situation."

Columns/Departments: Notes & News (short items relevant to our subject matter); Letters (substantive comment regarding previous issues); Sports Reports; and Reviews (of relevant materials in any medium). Query or send complete ms. Length: 100-1,000 words. Pays in copies or negotiate payment.

Fiction: Muskat Buckby, fiction editor. Adventure, fantasy, historical and science fiction. "Any fiction must feature a woman skilled in martial arts." Buys 0-1 mss/year. Query. Length: 1,000-5,000 words. "We will consider serializing longer stories." Pays in copies or negotiates payment.

Poetry: Muskat Buckby, poetry editor. "We'll look at all types. Must appeal to an audience of martial artists. Buys 3-4 poems/year. Length: open. Pays in copy or negotiated payment.

Tips: "We still need solid martial arts nonfiction—how-to; what is going on in various organizations, vis-a-vis women; and what is the significance of the rash of discrimination suits (by men) for women who teach self-defense to women, etc. We also need more how-to aimed at beginning or intermediate students, in view of the considerable rise of interest by middle-aged beginners, for instance; what can you expect when you start karate at age 42? The writer may have a better chance of breaking in at our publication with short articles and fillers since it's easier to find a spot for a borderline filler. We are tight on article space."

KARATE/KUNG-FU ILLUSTRATED, Rainbow Publications, Inc., 1813 Victory Place, Burbank CA 91504. (818)843-4444. Publisher: Michael James. 80% freelance written. Eager to work with new/unpublished writers. Emphasizes karate and kung fu from the traditional standpoint and training techniques. Monthly magazine. Circ. 80,000. Pays on publication. Buys all rights. Photocopied submissions OK. Reports in 1-2 weeks. Sample copy for 8½x11 SASE.

Nonfiction: Expose, historical, how-to, informational, interview, new product, opinion, photo feature, technical and travel. Need historical and contemporary Kung Fu pieces, including styles, how-tos, Chinese philosophy. Buys 6 mss/issue. Query or submit complete ms. Pays $100-200.

Photos: Purchased with or without accompanying ms. Submit 5x7 or 8x10 b&w or color transparencies. Total purchase price for ms includes payment for photos.

Fillers: Query.

Tips: "Style must be concise, authoritative and in third person."

OFFICIAL KARATE, 351 W. 54th St., New York NY 10019. Publisher: Al Weiss. Editor: Alan Paul. 80% freelance written. Eager to work with new/unpublished writers. A bimonthly magazine for karatemen or those interested in the martial arts. Circ. 100,000. Pays on publication. Publishes ms an average of 3 months after acceptance. Rights purchased vary with author and material; generally, first publication rights. Pays 50% kill fee. Byline given. Will consider photocopied submissions. Reports in 1 month.

Nonfiction: "Biographical material on leading and upcoming karateka, tournament coverage, controversial subjects on the art ('Does Karate Teach Hate?', 'Should the Government Control Karate?', etc.). We cover the 'little man' in the arts rather than devote all space to established leaders or champions; people and happenings in out-of-the-way areas along with our regular material." Informational, how-to, interview, profile, spot news. Buys 60-70 mss/year. Query or submit complete ms. Length: 1,000-3,000 words. Pays $50-200.

Photos: Reviews b&w contact sheets or prints. Pays $10-15.

Tips: "We need articles on fighting and self-defense techniques; interviews with leading martial artists; exercise/weight training; nutrition; and training pieces for the karate fighter."

Miscellaneous

‡**THE AMATEUR BOXER**, Diversified Periodicals, Box 249, Cobalt CT 06414. (203)342-4730. Editor: Bob Taylor. 50% freelance written. Eager to work with new/unpublished writers. Magazine published 10 times/year for boxers, coaches and officials. Circ. 1,500. Pays on publication. Publishes ms an average of 3 months after acceptance. Byline given. Buys first rights. Submit material 2 months in advance. Simultaneous queries, and simultaneous, photocopied and previously published submissions OK. Computer printout submissions OK. Reports in 2 weeks on queries; 1 month on mss. Sample copy for 9x12 SAE and 56¢ postage.

Nonfiction: Interview/profile (of boxers, coaches, officials); results; tournament coverage; any stories connected with amateur boxing; photo feature; and technical. Buys 35 mss/year. Query. Length: 500-2,500 words. Pays $10-35.

Photos: State availability of photos. Pays $3-15 for b&w prints. Captions and identification of subjects required. Buys one-time rights.

Tips: "We're very receptive to new writers."

BALLS AND STRIKES, Amateur Softball Association, 2801 NE 50th St., Oklahoma City OK 73111. (405)424-5266. Editor: Bill Plummer III. 30% freelance written. Works with a small number of new/unpublished writers each year. "Only national monthly tabloid covering amateur softball." Circ. 270,000. Pays on publication. Publishes ms an average of 2 months after acceptance. Buys first rights. Byline given. Computer printout submissions acceptable; no dot-matrix. Reports in 3 weeks. Free sample copy.

Nonfiction: General interest, historical/nostalgic, interview/profile and technical. Query. Length: 2-3 pages. Pays $50-65.

Tips: "We generally like shorter features because we try to get many different features in each issue. There is a possibility we will be using more freelance material in the future."

FLORIDA RACQUET JOURNAL, Racquetball-Sports, Florida Racquet Journal, Inc., Box 11657, Jacksonville FL 32239. (904)743-0218. Editor: Norm Blum. Managing Editor: Kathy Blum. Monthly tabloid covering racquetball in the Southeast. 50% freelance written. Circ. 20,000. Pays on acceptance. Byline given. Makes work-for-hire assignments and buys second (reprint) rights to material originally published elsewhere. Offers $25 kill fee. Submit seasonal/holiday material 3 months in advance. Simultaneous queries, and simultaneous, photocopied and previously published submissions OK. Computer printout submissions acceptable. Reports in 2 weeks. Sample copy for $1, SAE, and 2 first class stamps.

Nonfiction: Book excerpts (from racquetball books); expose (of racquetball clubs); historical/nostalgic; humor; new product; personal experience. "No how-to or instructional articles." Buys 12-15 mss/year. Query. Length: 400-900 words. Pays $10-40.

Columns/Departments: Horoscope, crossword puzzle, and health items—all for racquetball players. Buys 36 mss/year. Query. Length: 400-800 words. Pays $10-30.

Fiction: Humorous. Buys variable number mss/year. Query. Length: 500-1,500 words. Pays $10-30.

Poetry: Free verse. Buys variable number/year. Length: 30-60 lines. Pays $5-10.

Fillers: Clippings, jokes, gags, anecdotes, short humor, newsbreaks. Length: 30-50 words. Pays $1-5.

Tips: "We don't want your opinion—let the subject tell the story. If we like your first article we'll keep using you."

‡**HOCKEY ILLUSTRATED**, Lexington Library, Inc., 355 Lexington Ave., New York NY 10017. (212)391-1400. Editor: Stephen Ciacciarelli. 90% freelance written. Published 4 times in season. Magazine covering NHL hockey. "Upbeat stories on NHL superstars—aimed at hockey fans, predominantly a younger audience. Pays on acceptance. Publishes ms an average of 1-2 months after acceptance. Byline given. Buys first North American serial rights. Photocopied submissions OK. Computer printout submissions OK; prefers letter-quality to dot-matrix. Reports in 2 weeks. Sample copy $1.95 with 9x12 SASE or 75¢ postage.

Nonfiction: Inspirational and interview/profile. Buys 40-50 mss/year. Query with or without published clips, or send complete ms. Length: 1,500-3,000 words. Pays $75-125 for assigned and unsolicited articles.

Photos: State availability of photos with submission. Reviews transparencies and prints. Offers no additional payment for photos accepted with ms. Identification of subjects required. Buys one-time rights.

INSIDE RUNNING & FITNESS, "The Tabloid Magazine That Runs Texas,", Inside Running, 9514 Bristlebrook Dr., Houston TX 77083. (713)498-3208. Editor: Joanne Schmidt. 50% freelance written. A monthly tabloid covering running and fitness. "Our audience is Texas runners and triathletes who may also be into cross training with biking and swimming." Circ. 10,000. Pays on acceptance. Publishes ms an average of 1-2 months after acceptance. Byline given. Buys first rights, one-time rights, second serial (reprint) rights and all rights. Submit seasonal/holiday material 2 months in advance. Previously published submissions OK; no dot-matrix. Reports in 1 month on queries; 6 weeks on mss. Sample copy $1.50; writer's guidelines for #10 SAE with 1 first class stamp.
Nonfiction: Book excerpts, expose, historical/nostalgic, humor, interview/profile, opinion, photo feature, technical and travel. "We would like to receive controversial and detailed news pieces which cover both sides of an issue, for example, how a race director must deal with city government to put on an event. Problems seen by both sides include cost, traffic congestion, red tape, etc." No personal experience such as "Why I Love to Run," "How I Ran My First Marathon." Buys 18 mss/year. Query with published clips, or send complete ms. Length: 500-2,500 words. Pays $100 maximum for assigned articles; $50 maximum for unsolicited articles. Sometimes pays the expenses of writers on assignments.
Photos: Send photos with submission. Reviews contact sheets and 5x7 prints. Offers $25 maximum/photo. Captions required. Buys one-time rights.
Tips: "General material on running will be replaced in 1988 by specific pieces which cite names, places, costs and references to additional information. Writers should be familiar with the sport and understand race strategies, etc. The basic who, what, where, when and how also applies. The best way to break in to our publication is to submit brief (3 or 4 paragraphs) writeups on road races to be used in the Results section."

INTERNATIONAL OLYMPIC LIFTER, IOL Publications, 3602 Eagle Rock, Box 65855, Los Angeles CA 90065. (213)257-8762. Editor: Bob Hise. Managing Editor: Herb Glossbrenner. 5% freelance written. Quarterly magazine covering the Olympic sport of weightlifting. Circ. 10,000. Pays on publication. Publishes ms an average of 3 months after acceptance. Byline given. Offers $25 kill fee. Buys one-time rights or negotiable rights. Submit seasonal/holiday material 5 months in advance. Photocopied submissions OK; prefers letter-quality to dot-matrix. Reports in 6 weeks. Sample copy $4; writer's guidelines for SAE and 5 first class stamps.
Nonfiction: Training articles, contest reports, diet—all related to Olympic weight lifting. Buys 4 mss/year. Query. Length: 250-2,000 words. Pays $25-100.
Photos: Action (competition and training). State availability of photos. Pays $1-5 for 5x7 b&w prints. Identification of subjects required.
Poetry: Dale Rhoades, poetry editor. Light verse, traditional—related to Olympic lifting. Buys 6-10 poems/year. Submit maximum 3 poems. Length: 12-24 lines. Pays $10-20.
Tips: "First—a writer must be acquainted with Olympic-style weight lifting. Since we are an international publication we do not tolerate ethnic, cultural, religious or political inclusions. With Olympics in Seoul, Korea in 1988, Olympic-slanted articles are good. A new American weightlifting association has been formed. Articles relating to AWA are readily accepted."

NATIONAL RACQUETBALL, Florida Trade Publication, Drawer 6126, Clearwater FL 33518. Publisher: Joe Massarelli. Associate Publisher: Helen Quinn. Editorial Director: Chuck Leve. For racquetball players of all ages. Monthly magazine. 40% freelance written. Eager to work with new/unpublished writers. Circ. 39,000. Pays on publication. Publishes ms an average of 3 months after acceptance. Buys all rights. Byline given. Submit seasonal/holiday material 2-3 months in advance. Computer printout submissions acceptable. Publishes ms an average of 3 months after acceptance; no dot-matrix. Sample copy $2.
Nonfiction: How-to (play better racquetball or train for racquetball); interview (with players or others connected with racquetball business); opinion (usually used in letters but sometimes fullblown opinion features on issues confronting the game); photo feature (on any subject mentioned); profile (short pieces with photos on women or men players interesting in other ways or on older players); health (as it relates to racquetball players—food, rest, eye protection, etc.); and fashion. No material on tournament results. Buys 4 mss/issue. Query with clips of published work. Length: 500-2,500 words. Pays $50/published page. Sometimes pays the expenses of writers on assignment.
Photos: State availability of photos or send photos with ms. Offers no additional payment for photos accompanying ms. Uses b&w prints or color transparencies. Buys one-time rights. Captions and model releases required. Pays $5/b&w photo and $10/color.
Fiction: Adventure, humorous, mystery, romance, science fiction and suspense. "Whatever an inventive mind can do with racquetball." Buys 3 mss/year. Send complete ms. Pays $50/published page.
Tips: "Break in to *National Racquetball* by writing for monthly features—short pieces about racquetball players you know. We need more contributions from all over the country. Our object is national and international coverage of the sport of racquetball."

NEW YORK RUNNING NEWS, New York Road Runners Club, 9 E. 89th St., New York NY 10128. (212)860-2280. Editor: Raleigh Mayer. 75% freelance written. A bimonthly regional sports magazine covering running, racewalking, nutrition and fitness. Material should be of interest to members of the New York Road Runners Club. Circ. 45,000. Pays on publication. Time to publication varies. Byline given. Offers ⅓ kill fee. Buys first North American serial rights. Submit seasonal/holiday material 4 months in advance. Simultaneous submissions and previously published submissions OK. Computer printout submissions acceptable; no dot-matrix. Reports in 1 month. Sample copy for 9x12 SAE with $1.75 postage.

Nonfiction: Running and marathon articles. Special issues include N.Y.C. Marathon (submissions in by August 1). No non-running stories. Buys 25 mss/year. Query. Length: 750-1,750 words. Pays $50-250. Pays documented expenses of writers on assignment.

Photos: Send photos with submission. Reviews 8x10 b&w prints. Offers $35-300/photo. Captions, model releases, and identification of subjects required. Buys one-time rights.

Columns/Departments: Essay (running-related topics). Query. Length: 750 words. Pays $50-125.

Fiction: Running stories. Buys 25 mss/year. Query. Length: 750-1,750 words. Pays $50-150.

Fillers: Anecdotes. Length: 250-500 words. No payment for fillers.

Tips: "Be knowledgeable about the sport of running. Write like a runner."

PRIME TIME SPORTS & FITNESS, GND Prime Time Publishing, Box 6091, Evanston IL 60204. (312)869-6434. Editor: Dennis A. Dorner. Managing Editor: Nicholas J. Schmitz. 80% freelance written. Eager to work with new/unpublished writers. A monthly magazine covering racquet and health club sports and fitness. Circ. 35,000. Pays on publication. Publishes ms an average of 4 months after acceptance. Byline given. Buys all rights; will assign back to author in 85% of cases. Submit seasonal/holiday material 3 months in advance. Photocopied and previously published submissions OK. No simultaneous submissions. Computer printout submissions acceptable; prefers letter-quality to dot-matrix. Reports in 2 weeks. Sample copy for 10x12 SAE and 5 first class stamps; writer's guidelines for business size SAE and 1 first class stamp.

Nonfiction: Book excerpts (fitness and health); expose (in tennis, fitness, racquetball, health clubs, diets); adult (slightly risque and racy fitness); historical/nostalgic (history of exercise and fitness movements); how-to (expert instructional pieces on any area of coverage); humor (large market for funny pieces on health clubs and fitness); inspirational (on how diet and exercise combine to bring you a better body, self); interview/profile; new product; opinion (only from recognized sources who know what they are talking about); personal experience (definitely—humor); photo feature (on related subjects); technical (on exercise and sport); travel (related to fitness, tennis camps, etc.); news reports (on racquetball, handball, tennis, running events). Special issues: Swimsuit and Resort Issue (March); Baseball Preview (April); Summer Fashion (July); Fall Fashion (October); Ski Issue (November); Christmas Gifts and related articles (December). "We love short articles that get to the point. Nationally oriented big events and national championships. No articles on local only tennis and racquetball tournaments without national appeal except when from Chicago/Milwaukee area." Buys 50 mss/year. Length: 2,000 + words maximum. Pays $20-150. Sometimes pays the expenses of writers on assignment.

Photos: Eric Matye, photo editor. Send photos with ms. Pays $5-75 for b&w prints. Captions, model releases and identification of subjects required. Buys all rights, "but returns 75% of photos to submitter."

Columns/Departments: Linda Jefferson, column/department editor. New Products; Fitness Newsletter; Handball Newsletter; Racquetball Newsletter; Tennis Newsletter; News & Capsule Summaries; Fashion Spot (photos of new fitness and bathing suits); related subjects. Buys 100 mss/year. Send complete ms. Length: 50-250 words ("more if author has good handle to cover complete columns"). Pays $5-25.

Fiction: Joy Kiefer, fiction editor. Erotica (if related to fitness club); fantasy (related to subjects); humorous (definite market); religious ("no God-is-my shepherd, but Body-is-God's-temple OK"); romance (related subjects). "No raunchy or talking down exercise stories, upbeat is what we want." Buys 10 mss/year. Send complete ms. Length: 500-2,500 words maximum. Pays $20-150.

Poetry: Free verse, haiku, light verse, traditional on related subjects. Length: up to 150 words. Pays $10-25.

Fillers: Linda Jefferson, fillers editor. Clippings, jokes, gags, anecdotes, short humor, newsbreaks. Buys 400/year. Length: 25-200 words. Pays $5-15.

Tips: "Send us articles dealing with court club sports, exercise and nutrition that exemplify an upbeat 'you can do it' attitude. Pro sports previews 3-4 months ahead of their seasons are also needed. Good short fiction or humorous articles can break in. Expert knowledge of any related subject can bring assignments; any area is open. A humorous/knowledgeable columnist in weight lifting, aerobics, running and nutrition is presently needed. We review the author's work on a nonpartial basis. We consider everything as a potential article, but are turned off by credits, past work and degrees. We have a constant demand for well-written articles on instruction, health and trends in both. Other articles needed are professional sports training techniques, fad diets, tennis and fitness resorts, photo features with aerobic routines. A frequent mistake made by writers is length—articles are too long. When we assign an article, we want it newsy if it's news and opinion if opinion. Too many writers are incapable of this task.''

SIGNPOST MAGAZINE, Suite 518, 305 Fourth Ave., Seattle WA 98101. Publisher: Washington Trails Association. Editor: Ann L. Marshall. 10% freelance written. "We will consider working with both previously published and unpublished freelancers.'' Monthly about hiking, backpacking and similar trail-related activities, mostly from a Pacific Northwest viewpoint. Will consider any rights offered by author. Buys 12 mss/year. Pays on publication. Publishes ms an average of 6 months after acceptance. Free sample copy. Will consider photocopied submissions. Reports in 6 weeks. Query or submit complete ms. Computer printout submissions acceptable; no dot-matrix.
Nonfiction and Photos: "Most material is donated by subscribers or is staff-written. Payment for purchased material is low, but a good way to break in to print and share your outdoor experiences.''
Tips: "We cover only *self-propelled* backcountry sports and won't consider manuscripts about trail bikes, snowmobiles, or power boats. We *are* interested in articles about modified and customized equipment, food and nutrition, and personal experiences in the backcountry (primarily Pacific Northwest, but will consider nation- and world-wide.''

SKYDIVING, Box 1520, Deland FL 32721. (904)736-9779. Editor: Michael Truffer. 25% freelance written. Works with a small number of new/unpublished writers each year. Monthly tabloid featuring skydiving for sport parachutists, worldwide dealers and equipment manufacturers. Circ. 7,600. Average issue includes 3 feature articles and 3 columns of technical information. Pays on publication. Publishes ms an average of 3 months after acceptance. Byline given. Buys one-time rights. Simultaneous, photocopied and previously published submissions OK, if so indicated. Query for electronic submissions. Computer printout submissions acceptable. Reports in 1 month. Sample copy $2; writer's guidelines with 9x12 SAE and 74¢ postage.
Nonfiction: "Send us news and information on equipment, techniques, events and outstanding personalities who skydive. We want articles written by people who have a solid knowledge of parachuting.'' No personal experience or human-interest articles. Query. Length: 500-1,000 words. Pays $25-100. Sometimes pays the expenses of writers on assignment.
Photos: State availability of photos. Reviews 5x7 and larger b&w glossy prints. Offers no additional payment for photos accepted with ms. Captions required.
Fillers: Newsbreaks. Length: 100-200 words. Pays $25 minimum.
Tips: "The most frequent mistake made by writers in completing articles for us is that the writer isn't knowledgable about the sport of parachuting.''

‡VOLLEYBALL MONTHLY, Straight Down, Inc., Box 3137, San Luis Obispo CA 93403. (805)541-2294. Editor: Jon Hastings. 40% freelance written. Monthly magazine covering volleyball. "National publication geared to players, coaches and fans of the sport of volleyball.'' Circ. 31,000. Pays on publication. Publishes ms an average of 2 months after acceptance. Byline given. Buys one-time rights. Submit seasonal/holiday material 3 months in advance. Computer printout submissions OK. Reports in 2 weeks on queries.
Nonfiction: General interest, historical/nostalgic, how-to, humor, inspirational, interview/profile and personal experience. No "USC beat UCLA last week'' articles. Buys 10 mss/year. Send complete ms. Length: 750-3,000 words. Pays $50-250 for assigned articles; pays $50-150 for unsolicited articles. Sometimes pays the expenses of writers on assignment.
Photos: State availability of photos with submission or send photos with submission. Reviews 8x10 prints. Offers $15-75 per photo. Identification of subjects required. Buys one-time rights.
Columns/Departments: Buys 10 mss/year. Send complete ms. Length: 750-2,000 words. Pays $50-150.
Fiction: Buys 2 mss/year. Send complete ms. Pays $50-150.
Fillers: Anecdotes and short humor. Pays $25-50.

‡WRESTLING WORLD, Lexington Library Inc., 355 Lexington Ave., New York NY 10017. (212)391-1400. Editor: Stephen Ciacciarelli. 100% freelance written. Magazine published 8 times/year. "Professional wrestling fans are our audience. We run profiles of top wrestlers and managers and articles on current topics of interest on the mat scene.'' Circ. 100,000. Pays on acceptance. Byline given. Buys first North American serial rights. Photocopied submissions OK. Computer printout submissions OK; prefers letter-quality to dot-matrix. Reports in 2 weeks. Sample copy $3.
Nonfiction: Interview/profile and photo feature. "No general think pieces.'' Buys 100 mss/year. Query with or without published clips or send complete ms. Length: 1,500-2,500 words. Pays $75-125.
Photos: State availability of photos with submision. Reviews 35 mm transparencies and prints. Offers $25-50/photo package. Pays $50-150 for color transparencies. Identification of subjects required. Buys

one-time rights.

Tips: "Anything topical has the best chance of acceptance. Articles on those hard-to-reach wrestlers stand an excellent chance of acceptance."

Skiing and Snow Sports

AMERICAN SKATING WORLD, Independent Publication of the American Ice Skating Community, Business Communications Inc., 2545-47 Brownsville Rd., Pittsburgh PA 15210. (412)885-7600. Editor: Robert A. Mock. Magazine Editor: Doug Graham. 70% freelance written. Eager to work with new/unpublished writers. Monthly tabloid on figure skating. Circ. 15,000. Pays on publication. Publishes ms an average of 2-3 months after acceptance. Byline given. Buys first North American serial rights and occasionally second serial rights. Submit seasonal/holiday material 3 months in advance. Computer printout submissions acceptable; prefers letter-quality to dot-matrix. Reports in 6 weeks. Sample copy and writer's guidelines $2.

Nonfiction: Expose; general interest; historical/nostalgic; how-to (technique in figure skating); humor; inspirational; interview/profile; new product; opinion; personal experience; photo feature; technical and travel. Special issues include recreational (July), classic skaters (August), annual fashion issue (September), adult issue (December). No fiction. AP Style Guidelines are the primary style source. Short, snappy paragraphs desired. Buys 200 mss/year. Send complete ms. "Include phone number; response time longer without it." Length: 600-1,000 words. Pays $25-75.

Photos: Send photos with query or ms. Reviews color transparencies and b&w prints. Pays $5 for b&w; $15 for color. Identification of subjects required. Buys all rights for b&w; one-time rights for color.

Columns/Departments: Buys 60 mss/year. Send complete ms. Length: 500-750 words. Pays $25-50.

Fillers: Clippings and anecdotes. No payment for fillers.

Tips: "The 1988 Olympics will be held in early 1988, and we still need articles related to the current games or past figure skating history." Event coverage is most open to freelancers; confirm with managing editor to ensure event has not been assigned. Questions are welcome, call managing editor 10 a.m. to 5 p.m. EST.

‡**CROSS COUNTRY SKIER**, Rodale Press, Inc., 135 N. 6th St., Emmaus PA 18098. (215)967-5171. Editor: James C. McCullagh. 90% freelance written. A seasonal (October-Spring) magazine on cross-country skiing. Circ. 65,000. Pays on acceptance or publication. Publishes ms an average of 5 months after acceptance. Byline given. Offers 25% kill fee. Buys one-time or all rights. Query for electronic submissions. Computer printout submissions OK; prefers letter-quality. Reports in 2 months. Free sample copy and writer's guidelines.

Nonfiction: Historical/nostalgic, how-to, interview/profile and technical. No product reviews. Buys up to 100 mss/year. Query with published clips. Length: 2,000-4,000 words. Pays $300-600 for assigned features; pays $50-300 for department articles. Pays expenses of writers on assignment.

Photos: Send photos with submission, when possible. Reviews 2x2 transparencies. Offers $35-200 per photo. Captions, model releases and identification of subjects required. Buys one-time or all rights.

Columns/Departments: Kiosk, Ski Prep, Ski School, Health & Fitness, Competition, Vistas, Shortswings, Up Close and Reviews. Buys up to 75 mss/year. Query with published clips. Length: 1,000-2,000. Except Kiosk which is shorter (100-500 words)." Pays $50-250.

Tips: "Know the subject. Be current. Pay attention to the profile of CCS readers in guidelines."

‡**SKATING**, United States Figure Skating Association, 20 First St., Colorado Springs CO 80906. (303)635-5200. Editor: Dale Mitch. Published 10 times a year except August/September. Circ. 31,000. Official Publication of the USFSA. Pays on publication. Publishes ms an average of 3 months after acceptance. Buys all rights. Byline given. Phone queries OK. Reports in 1 month.

Nonfiction: Historical; how-to (photograph skaters, training, exercise); humor; informational; interview; personal opinion; photo feature; historical biographies; profile (background and interests of national-caliber amateur skaters); technical; and competition reports. Buys 4 mss/issue. Query. Length: 500-1,500 words.

Photos: Photos purchased with or without accompanying ms. Pays $15 for 8x10 or 5x7 b&w glossy prints and $35 for color transparencies. Query.

Columns/Departments: European Letter (skating news from Europe); Ice Abroad (competition results and report from outside the U.S.); Book Reviews; People; Club News (what individual clubs are doing); and Music column (what's new and used for music for skating). Buys 4 mss/issue. Query or send complete ms. Length: 100-1,000 words.

Tips: "We want sharp, strong, intelligent writing by persons knowledgeable in the technical and artistic aspects of figure skating with a new slant and outlook on the development of the sport. Special attention leading up to the Olympics and world championships and our focus to include more feature materials than in the past will affect the types of freelance material we buy in 1988. Knowledge and background in technical aspects of figure skating are almost essential to the quality of writing expected. We would also like to receive articles on former national and international competitions; photos from the past national and and international competitions and personalities and humorous features directly related to figure skating. No professional skater material."

SKI MAGAZINE, 380 Madison Ave., New York NY 10017. (212)687-3000. Editor: Dick Needham. Managing Editor: Andrea Rosengarten. 15% freelance written. A monthly magazine on snow skiing. *"Ski* is written and edited for recreational skiers. Its content is intended to help them ski better (technique), buy better (equipment and skiwear), and introduce them to new resort experiences and ski adventures." Circ. 430,000. Pays on acceptance. Publishes ms an average of 3 months after acceptance. Byline given. Offers 15% kill fee. Buys first North American serial rights. Submit seasonal/holiday material 8 months in advance. Photocopied submission OK. Computer printout submissions OK; prefers letter-quality. Reports in 1 week on queries; 2 weeks on ms. Sample copy available on newstands.
Nonfiction: Essays, historical/nostalgic, how-to, humor, interview/profile and personal experience. Buys 5-10 mss/year. Send complete ms. Length: 1,000-3,500 words. Pays $500-1,000 for assigned articles; pays $300-700 for unsolicited articles. Pays the expenses of writer s on assignment.
Photos: Send photos with submission. Offers $75-300/photo. Captions, model releases and identification of subjects required. Buys one-time rights.
Columns/Departments: Ski Life (interesting people, events, oddities with skiing), 150-300 words; Discoveries (neat special products or services available to skiiers that are out of the ordinary), 100-200 words; and Better Way (new ideas invented by writer that make his skiing life easier, more convenient, more enjoyable), 50-150 words. Buys 20 mss/year. Send complete ms. Length: 100-300 words. Pays $50-100.
Fillers: Facts and short humor. Buys 10/year. Length: 60-75 words. Pays $50-75.
Tips: "Writers must have an extensive familiarity with the sport and know what concerns, interests and amuses skiers. Ski Life, Discoveries and Better Way are most open to freelancers."

SKIING, CBS Magazines, 1 Park Ave., New York NY 10016. (212)503-3920. Editor: Bill Grout. 40% freelance written. Works with a small number of new/unpublished writers each year. A magazine published 7 times a year. *"Skiing* is a service magazine for skiing enthusiasts." Circ. 440,000. Pays on publication. Publishes ms an average of 6 months after acceptance. Byline given. Offers ⅓ kill fee. Buys first North American serial rights. Submit seasonal/holiday material 8 months in advance. Computer printout submissions acceptable; prefers letter-quality to dot-matrix. Reports in 6 weeks on queries; 2 months on mss.
Nonfiction: Essays, how-to, humor, interview/profile, personal experience and travel. No fiction, ski equipment evaluations or 'How I Learned to Ski' stories. Buys 35 mss/year. Query with published clips. Length: 500-2,000 words. Pays $50-1,000 for assigned articles; pays $50-750 for unsolicited articles. Pays the expenses of writers on assignment.
Photos: State availability of photos with submission. Reviews contact sheets and negatives. Offers $50-300/photo. Captions, model releases and identification of subjects required. Buys one-time rights.

SNOWMOBILE CANADA, Suite 202, 2077 Dundas St. E., Mississauga, Ontario L4X 1M2 Canada. (416)624-8218. Editor: Reg Fife. Snowmobiling magazine published in September, October and November "to satisfy the needs of Canada's snowmobilers from coast to coast." Circ. 60,000. Pays on publication. Byline given. Buys first rights. Submit seasonal/holiday material "by July for fall publication." Simultaneous queries acceptable. Computer printout submissions acceptable. Reports in 1 month on queries; 2 months on mss. Free sample copy.
Nonfiction: Personal experience (on snowmobiling in Canada); photo feature (nature in winter); technical (new snowmobile developments); travel (snowmobile type). "We look for articles on nature as it relates to snowmobile use; trail systems in Canada; wilderness tips; the racing scene; ice fishing using snowmobiles, maintenance tips and new model designs." Buys 12 mss/year. Query or send complete ms. Length: 800-2,000 words. Pays $75-150.
Photos: Captions required. Buys one-time rights.

‡SNOWMOBILE MAGAZINE, Winter Sports Publishing, Inc., Suite 100, 11812 Wayzata Blvd., Minnetonka MN 55343. (612)545-2662. Editor: Dick Hendricks. Managing Editor: Michael Dapper. 10% freelance written. A seasonal magazine (September, October, November and December) covering recreational snowmobiling. Circ. 500,000. Pays on publication. Byline given. Buys first North American serial rights. Submit seasonal/holiday material 5 months in advance. Computer printout submissions OK. Reports in 1 month. Sample copy $2.50; free writer's guidelines.
Nonfiction: How-to, interview/profile, new product, photo feature and travel. Buys 5-6 mss/year. Query. Length: 300-1,000 words. Pays $150-500. Sometimes pays the expenses of writers on assignment.
Photos: Send photos with submission. Reviews 35mm transparencies and 3x5 prints. Offers no additional payment for photos accepted with ms. Captions and identification of subjects required. Buys one-time rights.
Fillers: Michael Dapper, editor. Gags, newsbreaks, short humor. Buys 6-10/year. Pays $25-75.
Tips: The areas most open to freelancers include "travel and tour stories (with photos) on snowmobiling and snowmobile resorts and event coverage (races, winter festivals, etc.)."

SNOWMOBILE WEST, 520 Park Ave., Box 981, Idaho Falls ID 83402. Editor: Steve Janes. For recreational snowmobile riders and owners of all ages. Magazine; 48 pages. 5% freelance written. Publishes 4 issues each winter. Circ. 200,000. Buys first North American serial rights. Pays kill fee if previously negotiated at time of assignment. Byline given on substantive articles of two pages or more. Buys 5 mss/year. Pays on publication. Publishes ms an average of 3 months after acceptance. Computer printout submissions acceptable. Free sample copy and writer's guidelines. Reports in 2 months. Articles for one season are generally photographed and written the previous season. Query.

Nonfiction and Photos: Articles about snowtrail riding in the Western U.S.; issues affecting snowmobilers; and maps of trail areas with good color photos and b&w. Pays 3¢/word; $5/b&w; $10/color. B&w should be 5x7 or 8x10 glossy print; color should be 35mm transparencies or larger, furnished with mss. With a story of 1,000 words, typically a selection of 5 b&w and 5 color photos should accompany. Longer stories in proportion. Length: 500-2,000 words.

Tips: "It's rewarding finding a freelance writer who understands the nature and personality of our publication. It's annoying when writers say they have the story that we *really need* to use."

Soccer

SOCCER AMERICA, Box 23704, Oakland CA 94623. (415)549-1414. Editor-in-Chief: Lynn Berling-Manuel. 10% freelance written. Works with a small number of new/unpublished writers each year. Weekly tabloid for a wide range of soccer enthusiasts. Circ. 15,000. Pays on publication. Publishes ms an average of 2 months after acceptance. Buys all rights. Byline given. Submit seasonal/holiday material 30 days in advance. Query for electronic submissions. Computer printout submissions OK; prefers letter-quality to dot-matrix. Reports in 2 months. Sample copy and writer's guidelines $1.

Nonfiction: Expose (why a pro franchise isn't working right, etc.); historical; how-to; informational (news features); inspirational; interview; photo feature; profile; and technical. No 'Why I Like Soccer' articles in 1,000 words or less. It's been done. We are very much interested in articles for our 'special issues': fitness, travel, and college selection process. Buys 1-2 mss/issue. Query. Length: 200-1,500 words. Pays 50¢/inch minimum.

Photos: Photos purchased with or without accompanying ms or on assignment. Captions required. Pays $12 for 5x7 or larger b&w glossy prints. Query.

Tips: "Freelancers mean the addition of editorial vitality. New approaches and new minds can make a world of difference. But if they haven't familiarized themselves with the publication . . . total waste of my time and theirs."

Tennis

TENNIS, 5520 Park Ave., Trumbull CT 06611. Publisher: Mark Adorney. Editor: Alexander McNab. 25% freelance written. Works with a small number of new/unpublished writers each year. For persons who play tennis and want to play it better. Monthly magazine. Circ. 500,000. Buys all rights. Byline given. Pays on publication. Publishes ms an average of 6 months after acceptance.

Nonfiction and Photos: Emphasis on instructional and reader service articles, but also seeks lively, well-researched features on personalities and other aspects of the game, as well as humor. Query. Length varies. Pays $200 minimum/article, considerably more for major features. Pays $50-150/8x10 b&w glossies; $75-350/color transparencies.

Tips: "When reading our publication the writer should note the depth of the tennis-expertise in the stories and should note the conversational, informal writing styles that are used."

‡**WORLD TENNIS**, Family Media, 3 Park Ave., New York NY 10016. (212)340-9683. Editor: Neil Amdur. Managing Editor: Steve Flink. Monthly magazine covering tennis and other racket sports. "We are a magazine catering to tennis enthusiasts—both participants and fans—on every level." Circ. 375,000. Pays on acceptance. Byline given. Offers 25% kill fee. Buys all rights. Submit seasonal/holiday material 4 months in advance. Photocopied submissions OK. Query for electronic submissions. Computer printout submissions OK; no dot-matrix. Reports in 2 weeks on queries; 1 month on manuscripts. Sample copy for 8x11 SAE and 5 first class stamps.

Nonfiction: Peter M. Coan, articles editor. Book excerpts (tennis, fitness, nutrition), essays, humor, interview/profile, new product, personal experience, photo feature, travel (tennis resorts). No instruction, poetry or fiction. Buys 30-40 mss/year. Query with published clips. Length: 750-3,000 words. Pays $100 and up. Sometimes pays expenses of writers on assignment.

Photos: State availability of photos with submission. Reviews contact sheets. Payment varies. Requires captions and identification of subjects. Buys one-time rights.

Columns/Departments: Seniority (essays by older players); My Ad (personal opinion on hot topics); About Juniors (short pieces relating to the junior game), all 750-1,000 words. Buys 12-20 mss/year. Query with published clips. Pays $100 and up.

Fillers: Anecdotes, facts, newsbreaks, short humor. Buys 10-15/year. Length: 750-1,000 words. Pays $100 and up.

Tips: "Query before sending manuscripts. Most of our material is commissioned, but we welcome fresh ideas. The Seniority column is most open to freelancers, but About Juniors and My Ad is also open to fresh ideas. Your best bet is to submit a one-page cover letter explaining your articles idea along with a resume and clips. We want to know the credentials of the freelancer as well as the idea submitted."

Water Sports

‡THE DIVER,Diversified Periodicals, Box 249, Cobalt CT 06414. (203)342-4730. Editor: Bob Taylor. 50% freelance written. Magazine published 10 times/year for divers, coaches and officials. Circ. 1,500. Pays on publication. Byline given. Submit material at least 2 months in advance. Simultaneous queries and simultaneous, photocopied and previusly published submissions OK. Reports in 2 weeks on queries; 1 month on mss. Sample copy for 9x12 SAE and 56¢ postage.

Nonfiction: Interview/profile (of divers, coaches, officials); results; tournament coverage; any stories connected with platform and springboard diving; photo features and technical. Buys 35 mss/year. Query. Length: 500-2,500 words. Pays $15-40.

Photos: Pays $5-25 for b&w prints. Captions and identification of subjects required. Buys one-time rights.

Tips: "We're very receptive to new writers."

DIVER, Seagraphic Publications, Ltd., 10991 Shellbridge Way, Richmond, British Columbia V6X 3C6 Canada. (604)273-4333. Publisher: Peter Vassilopoulos. Editor: Neil McDaniel. 75% freelance written. Emphasizes scuba diving, ocean science and technology (commercial and military diving) for a well-educated, outdoor-oriented readership. Published 9 times/year. Magazine; 48-56 pages. Circ. 25,000. Payment "follows publication." Buys first North American serial rights. Byline given. Query (by mail only). Submit seasonal/holiday material 3 months in advance of issue date. Computer printout submissions acceptable; prefers letter-quality to dot-matrix. SAE and IRCs. Reports in 6 weeks. Publishes ms an average of 2 months after acceptance.

Nonfiction: How-to (underwater activities such as photography, etc.); general interest (underwater oriented); humor; historical (shipwrecks, treasure artifacts, archeological); interview (underwater personalities in all spheres—military, sports, scientific or commercial); personal experience (related to diving); photo feature (marine life); technical (related to oceanography, commercial/military diving, etc.); and travel (dive resorts). No subjective product reports. Buys 40 mss/year. Submit complete ms. Length: 800-2,000 words. Pays $2.50/column inch.

Photos: "Features are mostly those describing dive sites, experiences, etc. Photo features are reserved more as specials, while almost all articles must be well illustrated with b&w prints supplemented by color transparencies." Submit photo material with accompanying ms. Pays $7 minimum for 5x7 or 8x10 b&w glossy prints; $15 minimum for 35mm color transparencies. Captions and model releases required. Buys one-time rights.

Columns/Departments: Book reviews. Submit complete ms. Length: 200 words maximum. Pays $2.50/column inch.

Fillers: Anecdotes, newsbreaks and short humor. Buys 8-10/year. Length: 50-150 words. Pays $2.50/column inch.

Tips: "It's rewarding finding a talented writer who can make ordinary topics come alive. But dealing with unsolicited manuscripts that don't even come close to being suitable for *Diver* is the most frustrating aspect of working with freelancers."

SCUBA TIMES, The Active Diver's Magazine, Poseidon Publishing Corp., Box 6268, Pensacola FL 32503. (904)478-5288. Managing Editor: Fred D. Garth. Publisher: M. Wallace Poole. 80% freelance written. Prefers to work with published/established writers. Bimonthly magazine covering scuba diving. "Our reader is the young, reasonably affluent scuba diver looking for a more exciting approach to diving than he could find in the other diving magazines." Circ. 50,000. Pays after publication. Byline given. Buys first world serial rights. Computer printout submissions acceptable. Sample copy $3. Writer's guidelines for business size SAE and 1 first class stamp.

Nonfiction: General interest; how-to; interview/profile ("of 'name' people in the sport, especially if they're currently doing something interesting"); new products (how to more effectively use them); personal experience (good underwater photography pieces); and travel (pertaining to diving). Especially want illustrated articles on avant garde diving and diving travel, such as resorts that offer nude diving, singles only dive clubs, deep diving, new advances in diving technology, etc. No articles without a specific theme. Buys 40 mss/year. Query first with clips of published work. Will not return material unless accompanied with return postage. Length: 1,200-2,000 words. Pay varies with author. Base rate is $75/published page (30 column inches). Sometimes pays the expenses of writers on assignment.

Photos: Blair Director, art director. "Underwater photography must be of the *highest* quality in order to catch our interest. We can't be responsible for unsolicited photo submissions." Pays $25-250 for 35mm color transparencies; reviews 8x10 b&w prints. Captions, model releases, and identification of subjects required. Buys first world rights. Enclose 9x12 SASE and postage if you want material returned.

Tips: "Our current contributors are among the top writers in the diving field. A newcomer must have a style that captures the inherent adventure of scuba diving, leaves the reader satisfied at the end of it, and makes him want to see something else by this same author soon. Writing for diving magazines has become a fairly sophisticated venture. Writers must be able to compete with the best in order to get published. We only use contributors grounded in underwater photojournalism."

SKIN DIVER, Petersen Publishing Co., 8490 Sunset Blvd., Los Angeles CA 90069. (213)854-2960. Executive Editor: Bonnie J. Cardone. Managing Editor: Connie Johnson. 85% freelance written. Eager to work with new/unpublished writers. Monthly magazine on scuba diving. "*Skin Diver* offers broad coverage of all significant aspects of underwater activity in the areas of recreation, ocean exploration, scientific research, commercial diving and technological developments." Circ. 211,794. Pays on publication. Publishes ms an average of 9 months after acceptance. Byline given. Buys one-time rights. Submit seasonal/holiday material 6 months in advance. No simultaneous submissions. Computer printout submissions acceptable. Reports in 3 weeks on queries; 3 months on mss. Sample copy $3; free writer's guidelines.

Nonfiction: How-to (catch game, modify equipment, etc.); interview/profile; personal experience; travel; local diving; adventure and wreck diving. No Caribbean travel; "how I learned to dive." Buys 200 mss/year. Send complete ms. Length: 300-2,000 words; 1,200 preferred. Pays $50/published page.

Photos: Send photos with query or ms. Reviews 35mm transparencies and 8x10 prints. Pays $50/published page. Captions and identification of subjects required. Buys one-time rights.

Fillers: Newsbreaks and cartoons. Length: 300 words. Pays $15 for cartoons; $50/published page.

Tips: "Forget tropical travel articles and write about local diving sites, hobbies, game diving, local and wreck diving."

SURFER, Surfer Publications, 33046 Calle Aviador, San Juan Capistrano CA 92675. (714)496-5922. Editor: Paul Holmes. 20% freelance written. A monthly magazine "aimed at experts and beginners with strong emphasis on action surf photography." Circ. 92,000. Pays on publication. Byline given. Buys all rights. Submit seasonal/holiday material 6 months in advance. Simultaneous and photocopied submissions OK. Electronic submissions OK via WordStar, Microsoft Word (IBM compatible), but requires hard copy also. Computer printout submissions acceptable; prefers letter-quality to dot-matrix. Reports in 1 month on queries; 10 weeks on manuscripts. Sample copy for 8½x11" SAE with $3.50; free writer's guidelines.

Nonfiction: How-to (technique in surfing); humor, inspiratonal, interview/profile, opinion, and personal experience (all surf-related); photo feature (action surf and surf travel); technical (surfboard design); and travel (surf exploration and discovery—photos required). Buys 30-50 mss/year. Query with or without published clips, or send complete ms. Length: 500-2,500 words. Pays 10-15¢/word. Sometimes pays the expenses of writers on assignment.

Photos: Send photos with submission. Reviews 35mm negatives and transparencies. Offers $10-250/photo. Identification of subjects required. Buys one-time and reprint rights.

Columns/Departments: Our Mother Ocean (environmental concerns to surfers), 1,000-1,500 words; Surf Stories (personal experiences of surfing), 1,000-1,500 words; Reviews (surf-related movies, books), 500-1,000 words; and Sections (humorous surf-related items with b&w photos), 100-500 words. Buys 25-50 mss/year. Send complete ms. Pays 10-15¢/word.

Fiction: Surf-related adventure, fantasy, horror, humorous, and science fiction. Buys 10 mss/year. Send complete ms. Length: 750-2,000 words. Pays 10-15¢/word.

Tips: "All sections are open to freelancers but interview/profiles are usually assigned. Stories must be authoritative and oriented to the hard-core surfer."

SURFING MAGAZINE, Western Empire, 2720 Camino Capistrano, San Clemente CA 92672. (714)492-7873. Editor: David Gilovich. 50% freelance written. Works with a small number of new/unpublished writers each year and is eager to work with new/unpublished writers. Monthly magazine covering all aspects of the sport of surfing. "*Surfing Magazine* is a contemporary, beach lifestyle/surfing publication. We reach the entire spectrum of surfing enthusiasts." Circ. 93,000. Pays on publication. Publishes ms an average of 3 months after acceptance. Byline given. Buys all rights. Submit seasonal/holiday material 4 months in advance. Photocopied submissions OK. Query for electronic submissions. Computer printout submissions acceptable; prefers letter-quality to dot-matrix. Reports in 2 weeks. Sample copy and writer's guidelines for SAE.

Nonfiction: Book excerpts (on surfing, beach lifestyle, ocean-related); how-to (surfing-related); interview/profile (of top surfing personality); new product; photo feature (of ocean, beach lifestyle, surfing); travel (to surfing locations only). Buys 50 mss/year. Query with clips of published work or send complete ms. Length: 3,000 words maximum. Pays 10-15¢/word. Sometimes pays the expenses of writers on assignment.

Photos: Larry Moore, photo editor. State availability of photos or send photos with ms. Pays $35-500 for 35mm color transparencies; $20-75 for b&w contact sheets and negatives. Identification of subjects required. Buys one-time rights.

Columns/Departments: Bill Sharp, column/department editor. Currents—mini-features of current topical interest about surfing, beach and ocean environment. This department includes reviews of books, films, etc. Buys 36 mss/year. Query with clips of published work, if available, or send complete ms. Length: 100-500 words. Pays $75-100.

Fiction: Adventure, humorous. No fantasy fiction. Buys 3 mss/year. Send complete ms. Length: 1,000-4,000 words. Pays 10-15¢/word.

Tips: "We will be running 40% more mini-features in our expanded Currents section. This is a good chance for freelance writers to sell pieces of this nature to *Surfing*."

SWIM MAGAZINE, Sports Publications, Inc., Box 45497, Los Angeles CA 90045. (213)674-2120. Editor: Kim A. Hansen. 75% freelance written. Prefers to work with published/selected writers. Bimonthly magazine. "*Swim Magazine* is for adults interested in swimming for fun, fitness and competition. Readers are fitness-oriented adults from varied social and professional backgrounds who share swimming as part of their lifestyle. Readers' ages are evenly distributed from 25 to 90, so articles must appeal to a broad age group." Circ. 8,500. Pays approximately 1 month after publication. Publishes ms an average of 4 months after acceptance. Byline given. Submit seasonal/holiday material 4 months in advance. Simultaneous queries and photocopied submissions OK. Computer printout submissions OK; no dot-matrix. Reports in 1 month on queries; 3 months on mss. Sample copy for $2.50 prepaid and 9x12 SAE with 11 first class stamps. Free writer's guidelines.

Nonfiction: How-to (training plans and techniques); humor (sophisticated adult-oriented humor); interview/profile (people associated with fitness and competitive swimming); new product (articles describing new products for fitness and competitive training); personal experience (related to how swimming has become an integral part of one's lifestyle); travel (articles on vacation spots); diet and health (articles on diet, health and self-help that relate to, or include swimming). "Articles need to be informative as well as interesting. In addition to fitness and health articles, we are interested in exploring fascinating topics dealing with swimming for the adult reader." Buys 30 mss/year. Send complete ms. Length: 1,000-3,500 words. Pays $3/published column inch. "No payment for articles about personal experiences."

Photos: Send photos with ms. Offers no additional payment for photos accepted with ms. Captions, model releases, and identification of subjects required.

Tips: "Our how-to articles and physiology articles best typify *Swim Magazine*'s projected style for fitness and competitive swimmers. *Swim Magazine* will accept medical guideline and diet articles only by M.D.s and Ph.Ds."

UNDERCURRENT, Box 1658, Sausalito CA 94965. Managing Editor: Ben Davison. 20-50% freelance written. Works with a small number of new/unpublished writers each year. Monthly consumer-oriented *scuba diving newsletter*; 12 pages. Circ. 15,000. Pays on publication. Publishes ms an average of 2 months after acceptance. Buys first rights. Pays $50 kill fee. Byline given. Simultaneous (if to other than diving publisher), photocopied and previously published submissions OK. Query for electronic submissions. Computer printout submissions OK. Reports in 4-6 weeks. Free sample copy and writer's guidelines; mention *Writer's Market* in request.

Nonfiction: Equipment evaluation, how-to, general interest, new product, and travel review. Buys 2 mss/issue. Query with brief outline of story idea and credentials. Will commission. Length: 2,000 words maximum. Pays 10¢/word. Sometimes pays the expenses of writers on assignment.

THE WATER SKIER, Box 191, Winter Haven FL 33882. (813)324-4341. Editor: Duke Cullimore. Official publication of the American Water Ski Association. 50% freelance written. Published 7 times/year. Circ. 20,000. Buys North American serial rights only. Byline given. Buys limited amount of freelance material. Query. Pays on acceptance. Publishes ms an average of 3 months after acceptance. Reports on submissions within 10 days. Computer printout submissions acceptable "if double-spaced and standard ms requirements are followed"; prefers letter-quality to dot-matrix.

Nonfiction and Photos: Occasionally buys exceptionally offbeat, unusual text/photo features on the sport of water skiing. Emphasis on technique, methods, etc.

Tips: "Freelance writers should be aware of specializations of subject matter in magazine publishing; need for more expertise in topic; more professional writing ability."

‡WINDRIDER, World Publications, Inc., Suite H, 809 S. Orlando Ave., Winter Park FL 32789. (305)628-4802. Editor: Terry L. Snow. A magazine on windsurfing, published 7 times/year. "WindRider magazine is designed for the beginner to advanced boardsailor. Writers should have a thorough knowledge of the sport." Circ. 50,000. Pays on publication. Byline given. Kill fee varies. Buys first North American serial rights. Submit seasonal/holiday material 3 months in advance. Simultaneous, photocopied and previously published submissions OK. Computer printout submissions OK. Reports in 6 weeks on queries. Sample copy $2.50; free writer's guidelines.
Nonfiction: How-to, humor, new product, photo feature and technical. "We'll consider any piece that (1) relates to windsurfing (2) is thorough and well-written. However, our demand for fiction and poetry is very small." Buys 25 mss/year. Query with or without published clips, or send complete ms. Length: 500-2,000 words. Pays $50-300. Sometimes pays the expenses of writers on assignment.
Photos: State availability of photos with submission. Reviews contact sheets, color transparencies and 3x5 b&w prints. Offers $10-250 per photo. Captions and model releases required. Buys one-time or all rights.
Columns/Departments: Advanced, Intermediate, Beginner and Equipment, 800-1,00 words. Buys 35 mss/year. Send complete ms. Length: 800-1,200 words. Pays $75-100.
Fiction: Slice-of-life vignettes. "We sometimes use fiction in which a boardsailor describes a memorable experience—true or fictional. This is the only fiction we accept." Buys 7 mss/year. Send complete ms. Length: 800-1,200 words. Pays $75-100.
Fillers: Newsbreaks. Length: 200-800 words. Pays $30-100.
Tips: "We rely heavily on freelancers for the bulk of our printed material. Writers must have a thorough knowledge of the sport, be able to write clearly, and be able to work with deadlines."

———— Teen and Young Adult

The publications in this category are for young people ages 13-18. Publications for college students are listed in Career, College and Alumni.

AMERICAN NEWSPAPER CARRIER, American Newspaper Boy Press, Box 15300, Winston-Salem NC 27103. Editor: Marilyn H. Rollins. 50% freelance written. Works with a small number of new/unpublished writers each year. Usually buys all rights but may be released upon request. Pays on acceptance. Publishes ms an average of 3 months after acceptance. Computer printout submissions acceptable. Reports in 30 days.
Fiction: Uses a limited amount of short fiction written for teen-age newspaper carriers, male and female. It is preferable that stories be written around newspaper carrier characters. Humor, mystery and adventure plots are commonly used. No drugs, sex, fantasy, supernatural, crime or controversial themes. Queries not required. Length: 1,200 words. Pays $25.
Tips: "Fillers are staff-written, usually."

BOYS' LIFE, Boy Scouts of America, Magazine Division, 1325 Walnut Hill Lane, Irving TX 75038-3096. (214)580-2352. Editor: William McMorris. 85% freelance written. Monthly magazine covering Boy Scout activities for "ages 8-18—Boy Scouts, Cub Scouts, and others of that age group." Circ. 1.5 million. Pays on acceptance. Publishes ms an average of 6 months after acceptance. Byline given. Computer printout submissions acceptable.
Nonfiction: "Almost all articles are assigned. We prefer queries to a completed, unsolicted ms."
Tips: "The most frequent mistake made by writers is failure to read *Boys' Life*."

BREAD, Nazarene Publishing House, 6401 The Paseo, Kansas City MO 64131. (816)333-7000. Editor: Karen Desollar. 75% freelance written. Works with a small number of new/unpublished writers each year. A monthly magazine for Nazarene teens. Circ. 26,000. Pays on acceptance. Publishes ms an average of 8 months after acceptance. Byline given. Buys one-time rights. Submit seasonal/holiday material 10 months in advance. Simultaneous, photocopied, and previously published submissions OK. Computer printout submissions acceptable; no dot-matrix. Reports in 6 weeks on queries; 2 months on mss. Sample copy and writer's guidelines for 9x12 SAE with 2 first class stamps.

Nonfiction: How-to and personal experience, both involving teens and teen problems and how to deal with them. Buys 70 mss/year. Send complete ms. Length: 1,200-1,500 words. Pays 3-3½¢/word.
Columns/Departments: Pays $10-40.
Fiction: Adventure, humorous and romance, all demonstrating teens living out Christian commitment in real life.
Tips: "In our magazine, we have a 'theme' each month, so it depends on the theme of the particular month that we choose to accept manuscripts."

CAMPUS LIFE MAGAZINE, Christianity Today, Inc., 465 Gundersen Dr., Carol Stream IL 60188. Executive Editor: Scott Bolinder. Senior Editors: Gregg Lewis and Jim Long. Associate Editor: Chris Lutes. Assistant Editor: Diane Eble. 30-40% freelance written. Prefers to work with published/established writers. For a readership of young adults, high school and college age. "Though our readership is largely Christian, *Campus Life* reflects the interests of all young people—music, bicycling, photography, media and sports." Largely staff-written. "*Campus Life* is a Christian magazine that is *not* overtly religious. The indirect style is intended to create a safety zone with our readers and to reflect our philosophy that God is interested in all of life. Therefore, we publish message stories side by side with general interest, humor, etc." Monthly magazine. Circ. 180,000. Pays on acceptance. Publishes ms an average of 3-6 months after acceptance. Buys first serial and one-time rights. Byline given. Submit seasonal/holiday material 6 months in advance. Simultaneous, photocopied and previously published submissions OK. Query for electronic submissions. Computer printout submissions acceptable. Reports in 2 months. Sample copy $2; writer's guidelines for SASE.
Nonfiction: Personal experiences, photo features, unusual sports, humor, short items—how-to, college or career and travel, etc. Query or submit complete manuscript. Length: 500-3,000 words. Pays $100-300. Sometimes pays the expenses of writers on assignment.
Photos: Pays $50 minimum/8x10 b&w glossy print; $90 minimum/color transparency; $250/cover photo. Buys one-time rights.
Fiction: Stories about problems and experiences kids face. Trite, simplistic religious stories are not acceptable.
Tips: "The best ms for a freelancer to try to sell us would be a well-written first-person story (fiction or nonfiction) focusing on a common struggle young people face in any area of life—intellectual, emotional, social, physical or spiritual. Most manuscripts that miss us fail in quality or style. We are always looking for good humor pieces for high school readers. These could be cartoon spreads, or other creative humorous pieces that would make kids laugh."

‡CAREER WORLD, General Learning Corp., 3652 Mandeville Canyon Rd., Los Angeles CA 90049. (213)208-8025. Editor: Bonnie Bekken. Managing Editor: Jill Lewis. 20% freelance written. Monthly magazine for students covering career development and occupational information. "Requires carefully researched occupational information/career development guidelines, written specifically to a high school audience." Circ. 200,000. Pays on publication. Publishes ms an average of 6 months after acceptance. Byline given. Offers 50% kill fee. Buys first North American serial rights or all rights. Submit seasonal/holiday material 6 months in advance. Photocopied submissions OK. Computer printout submissions OK; no dot-matrix. Reports in 6 weeks on queries; 1 month on mss. Sample copy for 9x12 SAE with 3 first class stamps; writer's guidelines for #10 SAE with 1 first class stamp.
Nonfiction: Job information, interview/profile, photo feature and technical. No "personal experience; we require objective reporting of occupations/workers/career development." Query with published clips, or send complete ms. Length: 500-1,500 words. Pays $100-150 for assigned articles; pays $50-100 for unsolicited articles. Sometimes pays the expenses of writers on assignment.
Photos: State availability of photos with submission. Reviews 5x7 prints. Offers $10-15 per photo. Model releases required. Buys one-time rights.
Tips: "Submit a query in which you describe a suggested article, including a tantalizing headline, and methods of research to be used to give the article credibility. Include a recent clip." The area most open to freelancers is "Offbeat Job—unusual occupations in which a specific jobholder or entrepreneur is interviewed; photos must accompany 500-word article. It should be written in a lively, informative manner, with consideration for a high-school-age reader."

CAREERS, The Magazine for Today's Teens, E.M. Guild, Inc., 1001 Avenue of the Americas, New York NY 10018. (212)354-8877. Editor: Roberta Myers. 100% freelance written. Works with a small number of new/unpublished writers each year. A magazine published 3 times a year covering life-coping skills, career choices, and educational opportunities for high school juniors and seniors. "*Careers* is designed to offer a taste of the working world, new career opportunities, and stories covering the best ways to reach those opportunities—through education, etc." Circ. 600,000. Pays 30 days after acceptance. Publishes ms an average of 2-3 months after acceptance. Byline given. Offers 25% kill fee. Buys first North American serial rights. Submit seasonal/holiday material 6 months in advance. Sometimes accepts previously published submissions. Computer printout submissions acceptable; prefers letter-quality to dot-matrix. Reports in 2 months on queries; 3 weeks on

mss. Sample copy $2; writer's guidelines for letter size SAE with 1 first class stamp.
Nonfiction: Book excerpts, how-to, interview/profile, photo feature, travel. No humor manuscripts. Buys 25 mss/year. Query with published clips. Length: 500-1,200 words. Pays $300-800. Sometimes pays the expenses of writers on assignment.
Photos: State availability of photos with submission. Reviews contact sheets and transparencies. Offers $100 minimum/photo. Captions, model releases, and identification of subjects required. Buys one-time rights.
Columns/Departments: Banking On It, Taste Sensations, and Shape Up. Buys 15 mss/year. Length: 500 words. Pays $300-400.

CHRISTIAN ADVENTURER, Messenger Publishing House, Box 850, Joplin MO 64802. (417)624-7050. Editor-in-Chief: Roy M. Chappell, D.D. Managing Editor: Rosmarie Foreman. 75% freelance written. Prefers to work with published/established writers; works with a small number of new/unpublished writers each year. A denominational Sunday School take-home paper for teens, 13-19. Quarterly; 104 pages. Circ. 3,500. Pays quarterly. Publishes ms an average of 1 year after acceptance. Buys simultaneous, second serial (reprint) or one-time rights. Byline given. Submit seasonal/holiday material 1 year in advance. Photocopied and previously published submissions OK. Computer printout submissions OK; prefers letter-quality to dot-matrix. Reports in 6 weeks. Sample copy and writer's guidelines for 50¢ and 8½x11 SAE and 1 first class stamp.
Nonfiction: Historical (related to great events in the history of the church); informational (explaining the meaning of a Bible passage or a Christian concept); inspirational; nostalgia; and personal experience. Send complete ms. Length: 1,500-1,800 words. Pays 1¢/word.
Fiction: Adventure, historical, religious and romance. Length: 1,500-1,800 words. Pays 1¢/word.
Tips: "The most frequent mistake made by writers in completing an article for us is that they forget we are a Christian publication. They also do not follow the guidelines."

CHRISTIAN LIVING FOR SENIOR HIGHS, David C. Cook Publishing Co., 850 N. Grove, Elgin IL 60120. (312)741-2400. Editor: Anne E. Dinnan. 75% freelance written. Prefers to work with published/established writers, and works with a small number of new/unpublished writers each year. Quarterly magazine; 4 pages. "A take-home paper used in senior high Sunday School classes. We encourage Christian teens to write to us." Pays on acceptance. Publishes ms an average of 15 months after acceptance. Buys all rights. Byline given. Query for electronic submissions. Computer printout submissions acceptable; prefers letter-quality to dot-matrix. Reports in 2 months. Sample copy and writer's guidelines for 4x9½ SAE and 1 first class stamp.
Nonfiction: How-to (Sunday School youth projects); historical (with religious base); humor (from Christian perspective); inspirational and personality (nonpreachy); personal teen experience (Christian); poetry written by teens and photo feature (Christian subject). "Nothing not compatible with a Christian lifestyle." Submit complete ms. Length: 900-1,200 words. Pays $100; $40 for short pieces. Sometimes pays expenses of writers on assignment.
Fiction: Adventure (with religious theme); historical (with Christian perspective); humorous; mystery; and religious. Buys 2 mss/issue. Submit complete ms. Length: 900-1,200 words. Pays $100. "No preachy experiences."
Photos: Gail Russell, photo editor. Photos purchased with or without accompanying ms or on assignment. Send contact sheets, prints or transparencies. Pays $25-40 for 8½x11 b&w photos; $50 minimum for color transparencies. "Photo guidelines available."
Tips: "Our demand for manuscripts should increase, but most of these will probably be assigned rather than bought over-the-transom. Our features are always short. A frequent mistake made by writers in completing articles for us is misunderstanding our market. Writing is often not Christian at all, or it's too 'Christian,' i.e. pedantic, condescending and moralistic."

‡CURRENT HEALTH 2, The Continuing Guide to Health Education, General Learning Corp., 3500 Western Ave., Highland Park IL 60035. (312)432-2700. Editor: Laura Ruekberg. Managing Editor: Mary Ellen Sullivan. 90% freelance written. Prefers to work with published/established writers; works with small number of new/unpublished writers each year. A health education magazine published monthly. "Our audience is seventh through twelfth grade health education students. Articles should be written at a ninth grade reading level. The magazine is curriculum supplementary, and should be accurate, timely, accessible, and highly readable." Circ. 200,000. Pays on publication. Publishes ms an average of 5 months after acceptance. Byline given. Offers 50% kill fee. Buys all rights. Sample copy for 8½x11 SAE with 2 first class stamps; writer's guidelines for business size SAE with 1 first class stamp.
Nonfiction: General interest, interview/profile and new product. "No queries or unsolicited articles. All articles are on assignment only; send resume and samples." Buys 100 mss/year. Query with published clips. Length: 900-2,300 words. Pays $100-700 for assigned articles. Sometimes pays the expenses of writers on assignment.
Tips: "We look for writers with a background in the area they are writing about. Drug writers in particular are needed. Articles on disease, fitness and exercise, psychology, safety, sexuality and nutrition are also needed."

EXPLORING MAGAZINE, Boy Scouts of America, 1325 Walnut Hill Ln., Irving TX 75038-3096. (214)580-2365. Executive Editor: Scott Daniels. 85% freelance written. Prefers to work with published/established writers; works with a small number of new/unpublished writers each year. Magazine published 4 times/year—January, March, May, September. Covers the educational teen-age Exploring program of the BSA. Circ. 400,000. Pays on acceptance. Publishes ms an average of 6 months after acceptance. Byline given. Buys one-time and first rights. Submit seasonal/holiday material 6 months in advance. Simultaneous queries OK. Computer printout submissions acceptable; prefers letter-quality to dot-matrix. Reports in 2 weeks. Sample copy for 8½x10 SAE and $1 postage; writer's guidelines for business size SAE and 1 first class stamp. Write for guidelines and "What is Exploring?" fact sheet.

Nonfiction: General interest, how-to (achieve outdoor skills, organize trips, meetings, etc.); interview/profile (of outstanding Explorer); travel (backpacking or canoeing with Explorers). Buys 15-20 mss/year. Query with clips. Length: 800-2,000 words. Pays $300-450. Pays expenses of writers on assignment.

Photos: Gene Daniels, photo editor. State availability of photos with query letter or ms. Reviews b&w contact sheets. Captions required. Buys one-time rights.

Tips: "Contact the local Exploring Director in your area (listed in phone book white pages under Boy Scouts of America). Find out if there are some outstanding post activities going on and then query magazine editor in Irving, Texas. Strive for shorter texts, faster starts and stories that lend themselves to dramatic photographs."

FREEWAY, Box 632, Glen Ellyn IL 60138. Editor: Billie Sue Thompson. For "young Christian adults of high school and college age." 80% freelance written. Works with a small number of new/unpublished writers each year; eager to work with new/unpublished writers. Weekly. Circ. 60,000. Prefers first serial rights but buys some reprints. Purchases 100 mss/year. Byline given. Reports on material accepted for publication in 5-6 weeks. Publishes ms an average of 1 year after acceptance. Returns rejected material in 4-5 weeks. Computer printout submissions acceptable; prefers letter-quality to dot-matrix. Free sample copy and writer's guidelines.

Nonfiction: "*FreeWay*'s greatest need is for personal experience stories showing how God has worked in teens' lives. Stories are best written in first person, 'as told to' author. Incorporate specific details, anecdotes, and dialogue. Show, don't tell, how the subject thought and felt. Weave spiritual conflicts and prayers into entire manuscript; avoid tacked-on sermons and morals. Stories should show how God has helped the person resolve a problem or how God helped save a person from trying circumstances (1,000 words or less). Avoid stories about accident and illness; focus on events and emotions of everyday life. (Examples: How I overcame shyness; confessions of a food addict.) Short-short stories are needed as fillers. We also need self-help or how-to articles with practical Christian advice on daily living, and trend articles addressing secular fads from a Christian perspective. We do not use devotional material, poetry, or fictionalized Bible stories." Pays 4-7¢/word. Sometimes pays the expenses of writers on assignment.

Photos: Whenever possible, provide clear 8x10 or 5x7 b&w photos to accompany mss (or any other available photos). Payment is $5-30.

Fiction: "We use little fiction, unless it is allegory, parables, or humor."

Tips: "Study our 'Tips to Writers' pamphlet and sample copy, then query or send complete ms. In your cover letter, include information about who you are, writing qualifications, and experience working with teens. Include SASE."

GROUP, Thom Schultz Publications, Box 481, Loveland CO 80539. (303)669-3836. Editorial Director: Joani Schultz. 60% freelance written. Prefers to work with published/established writers, and works with a small number of new/unpublished writers each year. For leaders of high-school-age Christian youth groups. Magazine published 8 times/year. Circ. 63,000. Pays on acceptance. Publishes ms an average of 2 months after acceptance. Buys all rights. Byline given. Phone queries OK. Submit seasonal/holiday material 5 months in advance. Special Easter, Thanksgiving and Christmas issues. Computer printout submissions acceptable; prefers letter-quality to dot-matrix. Reports in 1 month. Sample copy for 9x12 SAE and $1 postage; writer's guidelines for SASE.

Nonfiction: How-to (fundraising, membership-building, worship, games, discussions, activities, crowd breakers, simulation games); informational; (drama, worship, youth group projects, service projects); inspirational (ministry encouragement). Buys 7 mss/issue. Query. Length: 500-1,700 words. Pays up to $150. Sometimes pays the expenses of writers on assignment.

Columns/Departments: Try This One (short ideas for games, crowd breakers, discussions, worship, fund raisers, service projects, etc.). Buys 5 mss/issue. Send complete ms. Length: 300 words maximum. Pays $15. News, Trends and Tips (leadership tips). Buys 1 mss/issue. Send complete ms. Length: 500 words maximum. Pays $25.

Tips: "A writer with youth ministry experience and a practical, conversational writing style will be more likely to be published in *Group*."

‡GROUP MEMBERS ONLY, Thom Schultz Publications, Box 481, Loveland CO 80539. Editorial Director: Joani Schultz. 60% freelance written. Prefers to work with published/established writers; works with small number of new/unpublished writers each year. Magazine published 8 times/year. For members of high-school-age Christian youth groups. Circ. 30,000. Pays on acceptance. Publishes ms an average of 2 months after acceptance. Byline given. Buys all rights. Phone queries OK. Submit seasonal/holiday material 5 months in advance. Query for electronic submission requirements. Computer printout submissions acceptable; prefers letter-quality to dot-matrix. Special Easter, Thanksgiving and Christmas issues and college issues. Reports in 1 month. Sample copy and writer's guidelines for 9x12 SAE with $1 postage.

Nonfiction: How-to (improving self-image and relationships, strengthening faith). Buys 2 mss/issue. Query. Length: 500-1,000 words. Pays up to $150. Sometimes pays expenses of writers on assignment.

GUIDE, 55 W. Oak Ridge Dr., Hagerstown MD 21740. Editor: Jeannette Johnson. 90% freelance written. Works with a small number of new/unpublished writers each year. A Seventh-Day Adventist journal for junior youth and early teens. "Its content reflects Seventh-Day Adventist beliefs and standards. Another characteristic which probably distinguishes it from many other magazines is the fact that all its stories are nonfiction." Weekly magazine; 32 pages. Circ. 52,000. Buys first serial rights, simultaneous rights, and second (reprint) rights to material originally published elsewhere. Pays on acceptance. Publishes ms an average of 6-9 months after acceptance. Byline given. Submit seasonal/holiday material 6 months in advance. Query for electronic submissions. Computer printout submissions acceptable; no dot-matrix. Reports in 6 weeks. Sample copy 40¢.

Nonfiction: Wants nonfiction stories of character-building and spiritual value. All stories must be true and include dialogue. Should emphasize the positive aspects of living, obedience to parents, perseverance, kindness, etc. "We use a limited number of stories dealing with problems common to today's Christian youth, such as peer pressure, parents' divorce, chemical dependency, etc. We can always use 'drama in real life' stories that show God's protection and seasonal stories—Christmas, Thanksgiving, special holidays. We do not use stories of hunting, fishing, trapping or spiritualism." Buys about 300 mss/year. Send complete ms (include word count). Length: 1,500-2,000 words. Pays 3-4¢/word. Also buys serialized true stories. Length: 10 chapters.

Tips: "Typical topics we cover in a yearly cycle include choices (music, clothes, friends, diet); friend-making skills; school problems (cheating, peer pressure, new school); death; finding and keeping a job; sibling relationships; divorce; step-families; runaways/throwaways; drugs; communication; and suicide. Write for our story schedule. We often buy short fillers, and an author who does not fully understand our needs is more likely to sell with a short-short. Frequently writers do not understand our unique needs. Our target age is 10-14. Our most successful writers are those who present stories from the viewpoint of a young teen-ager. Stories that sound like an adult's sentiments passing through a young person's lips are *not* what we're looking for. Use believable dialogue."

IN TOUCH, Wesley Press, Box 50434, Indianapolis IN 46250-0434. Editor: James Watkins. 50% freelance written. Eager to work with new/unpublished writers. A weekly Christian teen magazine. Circ. 26,000. Pays on acceptance. Publishes ms an average of 10 months after acceptance. Byline given. Offers 30% kill fee. Not copyrighted. Buys first rights or second serial (reprint) rights. Submit seasonal/holiday material 10 months in advance. Simultaneous, photocopied, and previously published submissions OK. Computer printout submissions acceptable; prefers letter-quality to dot-matrix. Reports in 1 month on manuscripts. Writer's guidelines for business size SAE with 1 first class stamp.

Nonfiction: Book excerpts, essays, how-to, humor, interview/profile, opinion, personal experience, photo feature from Christian perspective. "Our articles are teaching-oriented and contain lots of humor." Also needs true experiences told in fiction style, humorous fiction and allegories. No Sunday "soap." Buys 100 mss/year. Send complete ms. Length: 500-1,000 words. Pays $15-45.

Photos: Send photos with submissions. Reviews contact sheets and 8x10 prints. Pays $15-25/photo. Buys one-time rights.

Tips: "1. Take the editor to lunch. 2. Read writer's guidelines before submitting manuscripts."

KEYNOTER, Key Club International, 3636 Woodview Trace, Indianapolis IN 46268. (317)875-8755, ext. 172. Executive Editor: Jack Brockley. 65% freelance written. Works with a small number of new/unpublished writers each year, and is eager to work with new/unpublished writers willing to adjust their writing styles to *Keynoter*'s needs. A youth magazine published monthly Oct.-May (Dec./Jan. combined issue), distributed to members of Key Club International, a high school service organization for young men and women. Circ. 120,000. Pays on acceptance. Publishes ms an average of 5 months after acceptance. Byline given. Buys first North American serial rights. Submit seasonal/holiday material 7 months in advance. Simultaneous queries and submissions (if advised), photocopied and previously published submissions OK. Computer printout submissions acceptable; prefers letter-quality to dot-matrix. Reports in 1 month. Sample copy for 9x12 SAE and 3 first class stamps; writer's guidelines for 9½x4 SAE and 1 first class stamp.

Nonfiction: Book excerpts (may be included in articles but are not accepted alone); general interest (must be geared for intelligent teen audience); historical/nostalgic (generally not accepted); how-to (if it offers advice on how teens can enhance the quality of lives or communities); humor (accepted very infrequently; if adds to story, OK); interview/profile (rarely purchased, "would have to be on/with an irresistible subject"); new product (only if affects teens); photo feature (if subject is right, might consider); technical (if understandable and interesting to teen audience); travel (sometimes OK, but must apply to club travel schedule); subjects that entertain and inform teens on topics that relate directly to their lives. "We would also like to receive self-help and school-related nonfiction on leadership, community service, and teen issues. Please, no first-person confessions, no articles that are written down to our teen readers." Buys 5-10 mss/year. Query. Length: 1,500-2,500 words. Pays $125-250. Sometimes pays the expenses of writers on assignment.

Photos: State availability of photos. Reviews b&w contact sheets and negatives. Identification of subjects required. Buys one-time rights. Payment for photos included in payment for ms.

Tips: "We want to see articles written with attention to style and detail that will enrich the world of teens. Articles must be thoroughly researched and must draw on interviews with nationally and internationally respected sources. Our readers are 13-15, mature and dedicated to community service. We are very committed to working with good writers, and if we see something we like in a well-written query, we'll try to work it through to publication."

LIGHTED PATHWAY, Church of God, 922 Montgomery Ave., Cleveland TN 37311. (615)476-4512. Editor: Marcus V. Hand. 25% freelance written. A monthly magazine emphasizing Christian living for youth and young marrieds ages 13-25. Circ. 22,000. Pays on acceptance. Publishes ms an average of 3 months after acceptance. Byline given. Buys first North American serial rights and one-time rights. Submit seasonal/holiday material 4 months in advance. Simultaneous queries, and simultaneous, photocopied, and previously published submissions OK. Computer printout submissions acceptable. Reports in 2 weeks on queries; 1 month on mss. Free sample copy and writer's guidelines.

Nonfiction: Inspirational, interview/profile, personal experience, photo feature and travel. "Our primary objective is inspiration, to portray happy, victorious living through faith in God." Buys 40 mss/year. Query or send complete ms. Length: 1,000-2,000 words. Pays 2½-5¢/word.

Photos: State availability of photos or send photos with query or ms. Pays $10-20 for 8x10 b&w prints. Buys one-time rights and all rights.

Fiction: Adventure, historical and religious. No westerns, gothics, mysteries, animal. Buys 24 mss/year. Query or send complete ms. Length: 1,000-2,000 words. Pays 2½-5¢/word.

Tips: "Write to evangelical, conservative audience, about current subjects involving young people today." Fiction and human interest stories are most open to freelancers.

‡THE MAGAZINE FOR CHRISTIAN YOUTH!,The United Methodist Publishing House,201 Eighth Ave. S., Box 801, Nashville TN 37202. (615)749-6463. Editor: Sidney D. Fowler. Monthly magazine. Circ. 50,000. Pays on acceptance. Publishes ms an average of 9 months after acceptance. Byline given. Buys one-time rights. Submit seasonal/holiday material 9 months in advance. Photocopied and previously published submissions OK. Computer printout submissions OK. Writer's guidelines for SASE.

Nonfiction: Book excerpts; general interest; how-to (deal with problems teens have); humor (on issues that touch teens' lives); inspirational; interview/profile (well-known singers, musicians, actors, sports); personal experience; religious and travel (include teen culture of another country). Buys 5-10 mss/year. Send complete ms. Length: 700-2,500 words. Pays $80-110 for assigned articles; 4¢/word for unsolicited articles. Pays expenses of writers on assignment. "Writers should give indication before expenses happen."

Photos: State availability of photos with submission. Reviews transparencies and 8x10 prints. Offers $25-150/photo. Captions and model releases required. Buys one-time rights.

Fiction: Adventure, ethnic, fantasy, historical, humorous, mainstream, mystery, religious, romance, science fiction, suspense and western. No stories where the plot is too trite and predictable—or too preachy. Buys 25 mss/year. Send complete ms. Length: 700-2,000 words. Pays 4¢/word.

Poetry: Free verse, haiku, light verse and traditional. Buys 6-8 poems/year. Submit maximum of 5 poems at one time. Pays $10-100.

Fillers: Gags to be illustrated by cartoonists and short humor. Buys 6-8/year. Length: 10-75 words. Pays $15-80.

Tips: "Stay current with the youth culture so that your writing will reflect an insight into where teenagers are. Be neat, and always proofread and edit your own copy."

‡PIONEER, (formerly *Probe*), Baptist Brotherhood Commission, 1548 Poplar Ave., Memphis TN 38104. (901)272-2461. Editor-in-Chief: Timothy D. Bearden. 5% freelance written. For "boys age 12-14 who are members of a missions organization in Southern Baptist churches." Monthly magazine; 16 pages. Circ. 35,000. Byline given. Pays on acceptance. Publishes ms an average of 6-8 months after acceptance. Buys simultaneous rights. Submit seasonal/holiday material 8 months in advance. Simultaneous submissions OK. Computer printout submissions acceptable; prefers letter-quality to dot-matrix. Reports in 1 month. Sample copy and writer's guidelines for 9x12 SAE with $1.18 postage.

Nonfiction: How-to (crafts, hobbies); informational (youth, religious especially); inspirational (sports/entertainment personalities); photo feature (sports, teen subjects). No "preachy" articles, fiction or excessive dialogue. Submit complete ms. Length: 500-1,500 words. Pays $20-50.

Photos: Purchased with accompanying ms or on assignment. Captions required. Query. Pays $10 for 8x10 b&w glossy prints.

Tips: "The writer has a better chance of breaking in at our publication with short articles and fillers. Most topics are set years in advance. Regulars and fun articles are current. The most frequent mistake made by writers is sending us preachy articles. They don't read the guide carefully. Aim for the mid-teen instead of younger teen."

PURPLE COW Newspaper for Teens, Suite 320, 3423 Piedmont Rd. NE, Atlanta GA 30305. (404)239-0642. Editor: Maggie Anthony. 5% freelance written. Works with a small number of new/unpublished writers each year. A monthly (during school year) tabloid circulated to Atlanta area high schools. Circ. 40,000. Pays on publication. Buys one-time rights. "Manuscripts are accepted on a 'space-available' basis. If space becomes available, we publish the manuscript under consideration 1-12 months after receiving." Byline given. Submit seasonal/holiday material 2 months in advance. Simultaneous queries and photocopied and previously published submissions OK. Computer printout submissions acceptable; prefers letter-quality to dot-matrix. Reports in 1 month. Sample copy for $1 and 9x12 SAE and 2 first class stamps; writer's guidelines for letter size SAE and 1 first class stamp.

Nonfiction: General interest, how-to, humor and anything of interest to teenagers. No opinion or anything which talks down to teens. No fiction. Buys 7-10 mss/year. Send complete ms. Length: 1,000 words maximum. Pays $5-10.

Cartoons and Photos: Must be humorous, teen-related, up-to-date with good illustrations. Buys 10/year. Send photos with ms. Buys one-time rights. Pays $5-10.

Tips: "A freelancer can best break in to our publication with articles which help teens. Examples might be how to secure financial aid for college or how to survive your freshman year of college."

SCHOLASTIC SCOPE, Scholastic Magazines, Inc., 730 Broadway, New York NY 10003. Editor: Fran Claro. 5% freelance written. Works with a small number of new/unpublished writers each year. Weekly. 4-6th grade reading level; 15-18 age level. Circ. 800,000. Publishes ms an average of 8 months after acceptance. Buys all rights. Byline given. Computer printout submissions acceptable; no dot-matrix. Reports in 4-6 weeks. Sample copy for 10x14 SAE with $1.75 postage.

Nonfiction and Photos: Articles with photos about teenagers who have accomplished something against great odds, overcome obstacles, performed heroically, or simply done something out of the ordinary. Prefers articles about people outside New York area. Length: 400-1,200 words. Pays $125 and up.

Fiction and Drama: Problems of contemporary teenagers (drugs, prejudice, runaways, failure in school, family problems, etc.); relationships between people (interracial, adult-teenage, employer-employee, etc.) in family, job, and school situations. Strive for directness, realism, and action, perhaps carried through dialogue rather than exposition. Try for depth of characterization in at least one character. Avoid too many coincidences and random happenings. Although action stories are wanted, it's not a market for crime fiction. Occasionally uses mysteries and science fiction. Length: 400-1,200 words. Uses plays up to 15,000 words. Pays $150 minimum.

SCHOLASTIC UPDATE, Scholastic, Inc., 730 Broadway, New York NY 10003-9538. (212)505-3000. Editor: David Goddy. 50% freelance written. Classroom periodical published 18 times/year (biweekly during the school year). "A public affairs magazine for social studies students in grades 8-12. Each issue covers a specific problem, country, or institution." Circ. 300,000. Pays on publication. Publishes ms an average of 1-3 months after acceptance. Byline given. Offers 50% kill fee. Buys all rights. Submit seasonal/holiday material 4 months in advance. No simultaneous queries, or simultaneous, photocopied or previously published submissions. Computer printout submissions acceptable; prefers letter-quality to dot-matrix. Reports in 2 months. Sample copy $5 and 9x12 SAE.

Nonfiction: Interview/profile. Buys 20 mss/year. Query with clips of published work. Length: 750-1,500 words. Pays $150/printed page. Sometimes pays the expenses of writers on assignment.

SEVENTEEN, 850 3rd Ave., New York NY 10022. Editor-in-Chief: Midge Turk Richardson. Managing Editor: Sarah Crichton. 80% freelance written. Works with a small number of new/unpublished writers each year. Monthly. Circ. 1,700,000. Buys one-time rights for nonfiction and fiction by adult writers; buys full rights for work by teenagers. Pays 25% kill fee. Pays on acceptance. Publishes ms an average of 6 months after acceptance. Byline given. Computer printout submissions acceptable; prefers letter-quality to dot-matrix. Reports in 3 weeks.

Nonfiction: Katherine Russell Rich, articles editor. Articles and features of general interest to young women who are concerned with the development of their own lives and the problems of the world around them; strong emphasis on topicality, and helpfulness. Send brief outline and query, including a typical lead paragraph, summing up basic idea of article. Also like to receive articles and features on speculation. Length: 1,200-2,000 words. Pays $50-150 for articles written by teenagers but more to established adult freelancers. Articles are commissioned after outlines are submitted and approved. Fees for commissioned articles generally range from $650-1,500. Sometimes pays the expenses of writers on assignment.

Photos: Melissa Warner, art director. Photos usually by assignment only.

Fiction: Sara London, fiction editor. Thoughtful, well-written stories on subjects of interest to young women between the ages of 12 and 20. Avoid formula stories—"My sainted Granny," "My crush on Brad," etc.—heavy moralizing, condescension of any sort. Humorous stories and mysteries are welcomed. Best lengths are 1,000-3,000 words. Pays $500-1,000. "Publishes a novelette every June (not to exceed 25 doubled-spaced manuscript pages). Submissions due January 1." Conducts an annual short story contest for teenage writers. Reports in 2 months. "Manuscripts without SASEs will not be returned."

Poetry: Contact teen features editor. By teenagers only. Pays $15. Submissions are nonreturnable unless accompanied by SASE.

Tips: "Writers have to ask themselves whether or not they feel they can find the right tone for a *Seventeen* article—a tone which is empathetic yet never patronizing; lively yet not superficial. Not all writers feel comfortable with, understand or like teenagers. If you don't like them, *Seventeen* is the wrong market for you. The best way for beginning teenage writers to crack the *Seventeen* lineup is for them to contribute suggestions and short pieces to the You Said It! column, a literary format which lends itself to just about every kind of writing: profiles, puzzles, essays, exposes, reportage, and book reviews."

STRAIGHT, Standard Publishing Co., 8121 Hamilton Ave., Cincinnati OH 45231. (513)931-4050. Editor: Dawn B. Korth. 90% freelance written. "Teens, age 13-19, from Christian backgrounds generally receive this publication in their Sunday School classes or through subscriptions." Weekly (published quarterly) magazine; 12 pages. Pays on acceptance. Publishes ms an average of 1 year after acceptance. Buys first rights, second serial (reprint) rights or simultaneous rights. Byline given. Submit seasonal/holiday material 1 year in advance. Reports in 3-6 weeks. Computer printout submissions acceptable. Include Social Security number on ms. Free sample copy; writer's guidelines with SASE.

Nonfiction: Religious-oriented topics, teen interest (school, church, family, dating, sports, part-time jobs), humor, inspirational, personal experience. "We want articles that promote Christian values and ideals." No puzzles. Query or submit complete ms. "We're buying more short pieces these days; 12 pages fill up much too quickly." Length: 800-1,500 words.

Fiction: Adventure, humorous, religious and suspense. "All fiction should have some message for the modern Christian teen." Fiction should deal with all subjects in a forthright manner, without being preachy and without talking down to teens. No tasteless manuscripts that promote anything adverse to the Bible's teachings. Submit complete ms. Length: 1,000-1,500 words. Pays 2-3½¢/word; less for reprints.

Photos: May submit photos with ms. Pays $20-25 for 8x10 b&w glossy prints and $100 for color slides. Model releases should be available. Buys one-time rights.

Tips: "Don't be trite. Use unusual settings or problems. Use a lot of illustrations, a good balance of conversation, narration, and action. Style must be clear, fresh—no sermonettes or sickly-sweet fiction. Take a realistic approach to problems. Be willing to submit to editorial policies on doctrine; knowledge of the *Bible* a must. Also, be aware of teens today, and what they do. Language, clothing, and activities included in mss should be contemporary. We are becoming more and more selective about freelance material and the competition seems to be stiffer all the time."

TEENAGE MAGAZINE, The Magazine for Sophisticated Young Women, Suite 1000, 928 Broadway, New York NY 10010. (212)505-5350. Editor: Jeannie Ralston. Managing Editor: Ellen Lander. 50% freelance written. Works with small number of new/unpublished writers each year. Bimonthly magazine for worldly, college-minded young women. Circ. 200,000. Pays on acceptance. Publishes ms an average of 4 months after acceptance. Byline given. Offers 20% kill fee. Buys first North American serial rights. Submit seasonal/holiday material 6 months in advance. Computer printout submissions acceptable; prefers letter-quality to dot-matrix. Reports in 1 month. Sample copy for $2.50 and 9x12 SAE with 90¢ postage. Writer's guidelines for SAE.

Nonfiction: Contact articles editor. Book excerpts; general interest (to teenagers); how-to (on college, careers, health); humor (shorts); interview/profile (especially of entertainers); opinion (from teenagers only—300 words); and personal experience. Also looking for short articles on teenagers who have made notable accomplishments. No overly general surveys or how-tos. "We need specific information." Buys 25 mss/year. Query with published clips. Length: 300-2,500 words. Pays $50-1,000. Sometimes pays the expenses of writers on assignment.

Columns/Departments: Contact column/department editor. Mind & Body, Careers and College. Buys 6 mss/year. Query with published clips. Length: 800-1,200 words. Pays $100-350.

Fiction: Contact fiction editor. Adventure, humorous, mystery, novel excerpts, suspense, and youth-related issues, plots, and characters. Buys 3 mss/year. Send complete ms. Length: 1,000-2,500 words. Pays $350 maximum.

Tips: Areas most open to freelancers include Minds Over Matters (opinions by teenagers), how-to, health and beauty and entertainer profiles.

TEENS TODAY, Church of the Nazarene, 6401 The Paseo, Kansas City MO 64131. (816)333-7000. Editor: Karen De Sollar. 100% freelance written. Eager to work with new/unpublished writers. For junior and senior high teens, to age 18, attending Church of the Nazarene Sunday School. Weekly magazine; 8 pages. Circ. 70,000. Pays on acceptance. Publishes ms an average of 8 months after acceptance. Byline given. Buys first rights and second rights. Submit seasonal/holiday material 10 months in advance. Simultaneous, photocopied and previously published submissions OK. Computer printout submissions acceptable; no dot-matrix. Reports in 6-8 weeks. Sample copy and writer's guidelines for 9x12 SAE with 2 first class stamps.

Photos: Photos purchased with or without accompanying ms or on assignment. Pays $10-30 for 8x10 b&w glossy prints. Additional payment for photos accepted with accompanying ms. Model releases required.

Fiction: Adventure (if Christian principles are apparent); humorous; religious; and romance (keep it clean). Buys 1 ms/issue. Send complete ms. Length: 1,200-1,500 words. Pays 3½¢/word, first rights; 3¢/word, second rights.

Poetry: "We accept poetry written by teens—no outside poetry accepted." Buys 15 poems/year. Pays 25¢/line.

Tips: "We're looking for quality nonfiction dealing with teen issues: peers, self, parents, vocation, Christian truths related to life, etc."

TIGER BEAT STAR, D.S. Magazines, Inc., 1086 Teaneck Rd., Teaneck NJ 07666. (201)833-1800. Editor: Nancy O'Connell. 25% freelance written. Works with a small number of new/unpublished writers each year. Monthly teenage fan magazine for young adults interested in movie, TV and recording stars. "It differs from other teenage fan magazines in that we feature many soap opera stars as well as the regular teenage TV, movie and music stars." Circ. 400,000. Average issue includes 20 feature interviews, and 2 or 3 gossip columns. "We have to take each article and examine its worth individually—who's popular this month, how it is written, etc. But we prefer shorter articles most of the time." Pays upon publication. Publishes ms an average of 1 month after acceptance. Byline given. Buys all rights. Submit seasonal material 10 weeks in advance. Previously published submissions discouraged. Electronic submissions OK on disk for Victor 9000 system, but requires hard copy also. Computer printout submissions acceptable; no dot-matrix. Reports in 2 weeks.

Nonfiction: Interview (of movie, TV and recording stars). Buys 1-2 mss/issue. Query with clips of previously published work. "Write a good query indicating your contact with the star. Investigative pieces are preferred." Length: 200-400 words. Pays $50-125. Sometimes pays the expenses of writers on assignment.

Photos: State availability of photos. Pays $25 minimum for 5x7 and 8x10 b&w glossy prints. Pays $75 minimum for 35mm and 2¼ color transparencies. Captions and model releases required. Buys all rights.

Tips: "Be aware of our readership (teenage girls, generally ages 9-17); be 'up' on the current TV, movie and music stars; and be aware of our magazine's unique writing style. We are looking for articles that are clearly and intelligently written, factual and fun. Don't talk down to the reader, simply because they are teenaged. We want to give the readers information they can't find elsewhere. Keep in mind that readers are young and try to include subheads and copybreakers."

TQ (TEEN QUEST), (formerly *Young Ambassador*), The Good News Broadcasting Association, Inc., Box 82808, Lincoln NE 68501. (402)474-4567. Editor-in-Chief: Warren Wiersbe. Managing Editor: Nancy Bayne. 50% freelance written. Works with a small number of new/unpublished writers each year. Monthly magazine emphasizing Christian living for Protestant church-oriented teens, ages 12-17. Circ. 80,000. Buys first serial rights or second serial (reprint) rights. Publishes ms an average of 8 months after acceptance. Byline given. Submit seasonal/holiday material 1 year in advance. Previously published submissions OK. Computer printout submissions acceptable; prefers letter-quality to dot-matrix. Reports in 8 weeks. Free sample copy and writer's guidelines.

Nonfiction: Interviews with Christian sports personalities and features on teens making unusual achievements or involved in unique pursuits—spiritual emphasis a must. Buys 1-3 mss/issue. Query or send complete ms. No phone queries. Length: 500-1,800 words. Pays 4-7¢/word for unsolicited mss; 7-10¢ for assigned articles. Sometimes pays expenses of writers on assignment.

Fiction: Needs stories involving problems common to teens (dating, family, alcohol and drugs, peer pressure, school, sex, talking about one's faith to non-believers, standing up for convictions, etc.) in which the resolution (or lack of it) is true to our readers' experiences. "In other words, no happily-ever-after endings, last-page spiritual conversions, or pat answers to complex problems. We are interested in the everyday (though still profound) experiences of teen life. If the story was written just to make a point, or grind the author's favorite axe, we don't want it. Most of our stories feature a protagonist 14-17 years old. The key is the spiritual element—how the protagonist deals with or makes sense of his/her situation in light of Christian spiritual principles and ideals, without being preached to or preaching to another character or to the reader." Buys 30 mss/year. Send complete ms. Length: 800-1,800 words. Pays 4-7¢/word for unsolicited mss; 7-10¢/word for assigned fiction.

Fillers: Short puzzles on Biblical themes. Send complete mss. Pays $3-10.

Tips: "Articles for *TQ* need to be written in an upbeat style attractive to teens. No preaching. Writers must be familiar with the characteristics of today's teenagers in order to write for them."

YOUTH UPDATE, St. Anthony Messenger Press, 1615 Republic St., Cincinnati OH 45210. (513)241-5615. Editor: Carol Ann Morrow. 75% freelance written. Monthly newsletter of faith life for teenagers. Designed to

attract, instruct, guide and challenge Catholics of high school age by applying the Gospel to modern problems/situations. Circ. 60,000. Pays when ready to print. Publishes ms an average of 4 months after acceptance. Byline given. Reports in 8 weeks. Sample copy and writer's guidelines for SAE and 1 first class stamp.
Nonfiction: Inspirational, interview/profile, practical self-help and spiritual. Buys 12 mss/year. Query. Length: 2,300-2,500 words. Pays $300. Sometimes pays expenses of writers on assignment.

___ *Travel, Camping and Trailer*

Travel agencies and tour companies constantly remind consumers of the joys of traveling. But it's usually the travel magazines that tell potential travelers about the negative as well as positive aspects of potential destinations. Publications in this category tell campers and tourists the where-tos and how-tos of travel. Publications that buy how-to camping and travel material with a conservation angle are listed in the Nature, Conservation and Ecology section.

AAA WORLD, Hawaii/Alaska, AAA Hawaii, 730 Ala Moana Blvd., Honolulu HI 96813. (808)528-2600. Editor: Thomas Crosby. 80% freelance written. Prefers to work with published/established writers. Bimonthly magazine of travel, automotive safety and legislative issues. Orientation is toward stories that benefit members in some way. Circ. 20,000. Pays on publication. Publishes ms an average of 6-8 months after acceptance. Byline given. Buys one-time rights. Submit seasonal/holiday material 4 months in advance. Photocopied and previously published submissions OK. Query for electronic submissions. Computer printout submissions acceptable. Reports in 1 week on queries; 3-4 months on mss. Free sample copy.
Nonfiction: How-to (auto maintenance, safety, etc.); and travel (tips, destinations, bargains). Buys 6 mss/year. Send complete ms. Length: 1,500 words. Pays $150 maximum. Sometimes pays the expenses of writers on assignment.
Photos: State availability of photos. Reviews b&w contact sheet. Pays $10-25. Captions required. Buys one-time rights.
Tips: "Find an interesting, human interest story that affects AAA members."

ACCENT, Meridian Publishing Inc., 1720 Washington, Box 10010, Ogden UT 84409. Editor: Robyn C. Walker. (801)394-9446. 60-70% freelance written. Works with a small number of new/unpublished writers each year. A monthly inhouse travel magazine distributed by various companies to employees, customers, stockholders, etc. "Readers are predominantly upscale, mainstream, family oriented." Circ. 110,000. Pays on acceptance. Publishes ms an average of 1 year after acceptance. Byline given. Buys first rights, second serial (reprint) rights and nonexclusive reprint rights. Simultaneous, photocopied and previously published submissions OK. Computer printout submissions are acceptable; dot-matrix submissions are acceptable if readable. Reports in 6 weeks. Sample copy $1 and 9x12 SAE; writer's guidelines for business size SAE and 1 first class stamp.
Nonfiction: "We want upbeat pieces slanted toward the average traveler, but we use some exotic travel. Resorts, cruises, hiking, camping, health retreats, historic sites, sports vacations, national or state forests and parks are all featured. No articles without original color photos, except with travel tips. We also welcome pieces on travel tips and ways to travel." Buys 40 mss/year. Query. Length: 1,200 words. Pays 15¢/word.
Photos: Send photos with ms. Pays $35 for color transparencies; $50 for cover. Captions and model releases required. Buys one-time rights.
Tips: "Write about interesting places. We are inundated with queries for stories on California and the southeastern coast. Super color transparencies are essential. Most rejections are because of poor quality photography or the writer didn't study the market. We are using three times as many domestic pieces as foreign because of our readership."

ADVENTURE MAGAZINE, American Adventure, 12910 Totem Lake Blvd., Kirkland WA 98034. (206)821-7766. Editor: Pam Sather. 35% freelance written. A monthly magazine on camping and RV travel. Circ. 34,000. Pays on publication. Publishes ms an average of 2 months after acceptance. Byline given. Buys first North American serial rights. Submit seasonal/holiday material 3 months in advance. Photocopied submissions and previously published submissions OK. Computer printout submissions OK; no dot-matrix. Reports in 3 months. Sample copy for 9x12 SAE with 3 first class stamps; writer's guidelines for #10 SAE with 1 first class stamp.

Nonfiction: General interest, how-to, humor, personal experience and travel. No opinions, book excerpts or exposes. Query. Length: 1,500-2,500 words. Pays $200-300.

Photos: State availability of photos with submission. Reviews transparencies. Offers no additional payment for photos accepted with ms. Buys one-time rights.

ASU TRAVEL GUIDE, ASU Travel Guide, Inc., 1325 Columbus Ave., San Francisco CA 94133. (415)441-5200. Editor: Brady Ennis. 20% freelance written. Quarterly guidebook covering international travel features and travel discounts for well-traveled airline employees. Circ. 45,000. Payment terms negotiable. Publishes ms an average of 18 months after acceptance. Byline given. Offers kill fee. Buys first North American serial rights, first and second rights to the same material, and second serial (reprint) rights to material originally published elsewhere. Makes work-for-hire assignments. Submit seasonal/holiday material 6 months in advance. Simultaneous queries and simultaneous, photocopied and previously published submissions OK. Computer printout submissions acceptable; prefers letter-quality to dot-matrix. Reports in 1 month. Writer's guidelines for SASE.

Nonfiction: International travel articles "similar to those run in consumer magazines." Not interested in amateur efforts from inexperienced travelers or personal experience articles that don't give useful information to other travelers. Buys 16-20 mss/year. Destination pieces only; no "Tips On Luggage" articles. "We will be accepting fewer manuscripts and relying more on our established group of freelance contributors." Unsolicited ms or queries without SASE will not be acknowledged. No telephone queries. Length: 1,200-1,500 words. Pays $200.

Photos: "Interested in clear, high-contrast photos; we prefer not to receive material without photos." Reviews 5x7 and 8x10 b&w prints. "Payment for photos is included in article price; photos from tourist offices are acceptable."

Tips: "We'll be needing more domestic U.S. destination pieces in 1988 which combine several cities or areas in a logical manner, e.g., Seattle/Vancouver, Savannah/Atlanta. Query with samples of travel writing and a list of places you've recently visited. We appreciate clean and simple style. Keep verbs in the active tense and involve the reader in what you write. Avoid 'cute' writing, excess punctuation (especially dashes and ellipses), coined words and stale cliches. Any article that starts with the name of a country followed by an exclamation point is immediately rejected. The most frequent mistakes made by writers in completing an article for us are: 1) Lazy writing—using words to describe a place that could describe any destination such as 'there is so much to do in (fill in destination) that whole guidebooks have been written about it'; 2) Including fare and tour package information—our readers make arrangements through their own airline."

AWAY, c/o ALA, 888 Worcester St., Wellesley MA 02181. (617)237-5200. Editor: Gerard J. Gagnon. For "members of the ALA Auto & Travel Club, interested in their autos and in travel. Ages range approximately 20-65. They live primarily in New England." Slanted to seasons. 5-10% freelance written. Quarterly. Circ. 162,000. Buys first serial rights. Pays on acceptance. Publishes ms an average of 3 months after acceptance. Submit seasonal material 6 months in advance. Reports "as soon as possible." Although a query is not mandatory, it may be advisable for many articles. Computer printout submissions acceptable; no dot-matrix. Sample copy for 9x12 SAE with 2 first class stamps.

Nonfiction: Articles on "travel, tourist attractions, safety, history, etc., preferably with a New England angle. Also, car care tips and related subjects." Would like a "positive feel to all pieces, but not the chamber of commerce approach." Buys general seasonal travel, specific travel articles, and travel-related articles; outdoor activities, for example, gravestone rubbing; historical articles linked to places to visit; and humor with a point. "Would like to see more nonseasonally oriented material. Most material now submitted seems suitable only for our summer issue. Avoid pieces on hunting and about New England's most publicized attractions, such as Old Sturbridge Village and Mystic Seaport." Length: 800-1,500 words, "preferably 1,000-1,200 words." Pays approximately 10¢/word.

Photos: Photos purchased with mss. Captions required. B&w glossy prints. Pays $5-10/b&w photo, payment on publication based upon which photos are used. Not buying color photos at this time.

Tips: "The most frequent mistakes we find in articles submitted to us are spelling, typographical errors and questionable statements of fact, which require additional research by the editorial staff. We are buying very few articles at this time."

BIKEREPORT, Bikecentennial, Inc., The Bicycle Travel Association, Box 8308, Missoula MT 59807. (406)721-1776. Editor: Daniel D'Ambrosio. 75% freelance written. Works with a small number of new/unpublished writers each year. Bimonthly bicycle touring magazine for Bikecentennial members. Circ. 18,000. Pays on publication. Publishes ms an average of 8 months after acceptance. Byline given. Include short bio with manuscript. Buys first serial rights. Submit seasonal/holiday material 3 months in advance. Simultaneous queries and photocopied submissions OK. Query for electronic submissions. Computer printout submissions acceptable; no dot-matrix. Reports in 2 weeks on queries; 1 month on mss. Sample copy and guidelines for 9x12 SAE with $1 postage.

Nonfiction: Historical/nostalgic (interesting spots along bike trails); how-to (bicycle); humor (touring); inter-

view/profile (bicycle industry people); personal experience ("my favorite tour"); photo feature (bicycle); technical (bicycle); travel ("my favorite tour"). Buys 20-25 mss/year. Query with published clips or send complete ms. Length: 800-2,500 words. Pays 3¢/word. Sometimes pays the expenses of writers on assignment.
Photos: Bicycle, scenery, portraits. State availability of photos. Model releases and identification of subjects required.
Fiction: Adventure, experimental, historical, humorous. Not interested in anything that doesn't involve bicycles. Query with published clips or send complete ms. "I'd like to see more good fiction and essays." Length: 800-2,500 words. Pays 3¢/word.
Tips: "We don't get many good essays. Consider that a hint. But we are still always interested in travelogs."

THE CAMPER TIMES, Royal Productions, Inc., Box 6294, Richmond VA 23230. (804)270-5653. Editor: David A. Posner. 75% freelance written. Prefers to work with published/established writers; works with a small number of new/unpublished writers each year. A bimonthly tabloid. "We supply the camping public with articles and information on outdoor activities related to camping. Our audience is primarily families that own recreational vehicles." Circ. 30,000. Pays on publication. Publishes ms an average of 4-6 months after acceptance. Byline given. Buys one-time rights, second serial (reprint) rights or simultaneous rights. Submit seasonal/holiday material 2 months in advance. Simultaneous, photocopied and previously published submissions OK. Query for electronic submissions. Computer printout submissions acceptable. Reports in 2 months. Sample copy and writer's guidelines for 9x12 SAE with $1.41 postage.
Nonfiction: How-to and travel; information on places to camp and fishing articles. Also "tourist related articles. Places to go, things to see. Does not have to be camping related." Buys 25 mss/year. Query with or without published clips, or send complete ms. Length: 500-2,000 words. Pays $20-65 for unsolicited articles. Sometimes pays the expenses of writers on assignment.
Photos: State availability of photos with submission. Reviews contact sheets and prints. Offers $1-5/photo. Identification of subjects required. Buys one-time rights.
Columns/Departments: RV Doctor (helpful hints on repairing RVs). Buys 12 mss/year. Query. Length: 100-500 words. Pays $20-35.
Fillers: Anecdotes, facts, gags to be illustrated by cartoonist, newsbreaks and short humor. Buys 25/year. Length: 10-500 words. Pays $5-20.
Tips: "Best approach is to call me. All areas of *The Camper Times* are open to freelancers. We will look at all articles and consider for publication."

CAMPERWAYS, 1108 N. Bethlehem Pike, Box 460, Spring House PA 19477. (215)643-2058. Editor-in-Chief: Charles Myers. 75% freelance written. Prefers to work with published/established writers. Emphasis on recreational vehicle camping and travel. Monthly (except Dec. and Jan.) tabloid. Circ. 35,000. Pays on publication. Publishes ms an average of 4-6 months after acceptance. Buys first, simultaneous, second serial (reprint) or regional rights. Byline given. Submit seasonal/holiday material 3-4 months in advance. Simultaneous, photocopied and previously published submissions OK. Computer printout submissions acceptable; prefers letter-quality to dot-matrix. Reports in 1 month. Sample copy for $2 and 9x12 SAE with $2.40 postage; free writer's guidelines.
Nonfiction: Historical (when tied in with camping trip to historical attraction or area); how-to (selection, care, maintenance of RVs, accessories and camping equipment); humor; personal experience; and travel (camping destinations within 200 miles of New York-DC metro corridor). No "material on camping trips to destinations outside stated coverage area." Buys 80-100 unsolicited mss/year. Query. Length: 1,000-2,000 words. Pays $40-85.
Photos: "Good photos greatly increase likelihood of acceptance. Don't send snapshots, Polaroids. We can't use them." Photos purchased with accompanying ms. Captions required. Uses 5x7 or 8x10 b&w glossy prints. Pays $5/photo published.
Columns/Departments: Camp Cookery (ideas for cooking in RV galleys and over campfires—should include recipes). Buys 10 mss/year. Query. Length: 500-1,500 words. Pays $25-75.
Tips: "Articles should focus on single attraction or activity or on closely clustered attractions within reach on the same weekend camping trip rather than on types of attractions or activities in general. We're looking for little-known or offbeat items. Emphasize positive aspects of camping: fun, economy, etc. We want feature items, not shorts and fillers. Acceptance is based on quality of article and appropriateness of subject matter. The most frequent mistakes made by writers in completing an article for us are failure to follow guidelines or failure to write from the camper's perspective."

CAMPING CANADA, CRV Publishing Canada Ltd., Suite 202, 2077 Dundas St. East, Mississauga, Ontario L4X 1M2 Canada. (416)624-8218. Editor: Peter Tasler. 65-80% freelance written. "We have an established group of writers but are always willing to work with newcomers." A magazine published 7 times/year, covering camping and RVing. Circ. 100,000. Pays on publication. Publishes ms an average of 2-3 months after acceptance. Byline given. Buys first rights. Submit seasonal/holiday material 3 months in advance. Computer printout submissions acceptable; no dot-matrix. Reports in 2 months. Free sample copy and writer's guidelines.

Nonfiction: Canadian recreational life, especially as it concerns or interests Canadian RV and camping enthusiasts; historical/nostalgic (sometimes); how-to; new product; personal experience; technical; and travel. Will accept occasional material unrelated to Canada. Buys 35-40 mss/year. Query first. Length: 1,000-2,500 words. Pays $150-300. Sometimes pays the expenses of writers on assignment.
Photos: Will buy occasional photos. Query first. Mss must be accompanied by photos, unless otherwise agreed upon.
Tips: "Deep, accurate, thorough research and colorful detail are required for all features. Travel pieces should include places to camp (contact information, if available). We would like to receive profiles of celebrity RVers, preferably Canadians, but will look at celebrities known in the U.S. and Canada."

CAMPING TODAY, Official Publication of National Campers & Hikers Association, T-A-W Publishing Co., 9425 S. Greenville Road, Greenville MI 48838. (616)754-9179. Editors: David and Martha Higbie. 80% freelance written. Prefers to work with published/established writers. The monthly official membership publication of the NCHA, "the largest nonprofit camping organization in the United States and Canada. Members are heavily oriented toward RV travel, both weekend and extended vacations. A small segment is interested in backpacking. Concentration is on activities of members within chapters, conservation, wildlife, etc." Circ. 30,000. Pays on publication. Publishes ms an average of 6 months after acceptance. Byline given. Buys one-time rights. Submit seasonal/holiday material 3 months in advance. Simultaneous, photocopied, and previously published submissions OK. Computer printout submissions acceptable; prefers letter-quality to dot-matrix. Reports in 1 month. Sample copy and writer's guidelines for SAE.
Nonfiction: Humor (camping or travel related); interview/profile (interesting campers); new product (RVs and related equipment); technical (RVs); and travel (camping, hiking and RV travel). Buys 12-24 mss/year. Send complete ms. Length: 750-1,000 words. Pays $75-100. Sometimes pays the expenses of writers on assignment.
Photos: Send photos with accompanying query or ms. Reviews color transparencies and 5x7 b&w prints. Pays $25 maximum for color transparencies. Color cover every month. Captions required.
Tips: "Freelance material on RV travel, RV technical subjects and items of general camping and hiking interest throughout the United States and Canada will receive special attention."

‡CARIBBEAN TRAVEL AND LIFE, Suite 400, 606 North Washington St., Alexandria VA 22314. (703)683-5496. Editor: Veronica Gould Stoddart. 90% freelance written. Prefers to work with published/established writers. A quarterly magazine covering travel to the Caribbean, Bahamas and Bermuda. Circ. 130,000. Pays on publication. Publishes ms an average of 3 months after acceptance. Byline given. Offers 25% kill fee. Buys first North American serial rights. Submit seasonal/holiday material 6 months in advance. Photocopied submissions OK. Computer printout submissions OK; prefers letter-quality. Reports in 2 months. Sample copy for 9x12 SAE with $1.24 postage; free writer's guidelines.
Nonfiction: General interest, how-to, interview/profile, personal experience and travel. No "guidebook rehashing; superficial destination pieces or critical exposes." Buys 18 mss/year. Query with published clips. Length: 2,000-2,200 words. Pays $550.
Photos: Send photos with submission. Reviews 35mm transparencies. Offers $75-400 per photo. Captions and identification of subjects required. Buys one-time rights.
Columns/Departments: Tradewinds (focus on one particular kind of water sport or sailing/cruising); Island Buys (best shopping for luxury goods, crafts, duty-free); Island Spice (best cuisine and/or restaurant reviews with recipes); Island Business (how-to guide to business/investment opportunities), all 800-1,000 words; Caribbeana (short items on great finds in travel, culture, and special attractions), 500 words. Buys 36 mss/year. Query with published clips or send complete ms. Length: 500-1,250 words. Pays $75-200.
Tips: We are especially looking for stories with a personal touch and lively, entertaining anecdotes, as well as strong insight into people and places being covered. Also prefers stories with focus on people, i.e, colorful personalities, famous people, etc. Writer should demonstrate why he/she is the best person to do that story based on extensive knowledge of the subject, frequent visits to destination, residence in destination, specialty in field."

CHARTERING MAGAZINE, Chartering Inc., 830 Pop Tilton's Place, Jensen Beach FL 33457. (305)334-2003. Editor: Antonia Thomas. 30-50% freelance written. Prefers to work with published/established writers and works with a small number of new/unpublished writers each year. "*Chartering* is a people-oriented travel magazine with a positive approach. Our focus is yacht charter vacations." Circ. 50,000. Pays on publication. Publishes ms an average of 3 months after acceptance. Buys first North American serial rights. Submit seasonal/holiday material at least 5 months in advance. Simultaneous queries and simultaneous and photocopied submissions, and previously published work (on rare occasion) OK. Query for electronic submissions. Computer printout submissions acceptable; prefers letter-quality to dot-matrix. Reports in 2-4 weeks. Writer's guidelines for #SAE and 1 first class stamp.
Nonfiction: General interest (worldwide, charter boat-oriented travel); historical/nostalgic (charter vacation oriented); how-to (bareboating technique); interview/profile (charter brokers, charter skippers, positive); new

product (would have to be a new type of charter); opinion; personal experience (charter boat related, worldwide, positive people-oriented travel); photo feature (charter boat, worldwide, positive, people-oriented travel); technical (bareboat technique; charter boat IRS; charter boat documentation); travel (charter vacation-oriented); and ancillary topics such as fishing, scuba or underwater photography. Special issues will focus on the Caribbean, diving, and sports fishing. Buys 50-85 mss/year. Query with published clips or send complete ms. Length: 600-3,000 words. Pays $50-350. Rarely pays expenses of writers on assignment.

Photos: "We would like to receive quality cover photos reflecting the charter yacht vacation experience, i.e., water, yacht, and people enjoying." State availability of photos or send photos with query or ms. Pays with article for b&w and color negatives, color transparencies (35mm), and b&w and color prints (3x5 or larger), plus buys cover photos. Requires model releases and identification of subjects. Buys one-time rights.

Columns/Departments: Cruising areas, bareboat techniques (all facets), sail training, facilities. Buys 12-20 mss/year. Query with published clips or send complete ms. Length: 500-1,200 words.

Tips: "We will buy fewer, if any, general travel pieces in 1988. We are happy to look at the work of any freelancer who may have something appropriate to offer within our scope—travel with a charter vacation orientation. We prefer submissions accompanied by good, professional quality photography. The best first step is a request for editorial guidelines, accompanied by a typed letter and work sample. *Chartering* will be looking for more articles of 300-600 words."

CHEVRON USA ODYSSEY, Ortho Information Services, Room 3188, 575 Market St., San Francisco CA 94105. (415)894-1952. Editor: Jim Gebbie. 75% freelance written. Prefers to work with published/established writers. A quarterly magazine. "We are a 44-page, four-color magazine published on contract for the Chevron Travel Club." Circ. 460,000. Pays on acceptance. Publishes ms an average of 8 months after acceptance. Byline given. Offers kill fee. Buys first North American serial rights. Submit seasonal/holiday material 1 year in advance. Photocopied submissions OK. Computer printout submissions acceptable; prefers letter-quality to dot-matrix. Reports in 2 months. Free writer's guidelines.

Nonfiction: How-to (on crafts, family activities, hobbies, etc.), travel and recreational activities. No personal accounts of vacation experiences, fiction or poetry. Buys 35 mss/year. Query with published clips. Length: 700-2,000 words. Pays $100-500 for assigned articles; pays $100-400 for articles requested on spec.

Photos: State availability of photos with submissions. Reviews 35mm and larger color transparencies. Offers $50-400/photo. Identification of subjects required. Usually buys one-time rights. "We purchase only top quality original transparencies, mainly from a stable of past contributors. We encourage photographers to submit their stock sheets."

Columns/Departments: Family Activities (crafts and hobbies, unusual forms of recreation); Travel Tips (featurettes on trends such as travel for the disabled or computers for travel); Food (recipes with a theme); Safety and Service (reports of interest to the motoring public); and American (humorous anecdotes on geography, language, history, travel); all 700-800 words. Buys 5 mss/year. Query with published clips. Pays $100-200.

Fillers: Anecdotes and cartoons. Buys 20/year. Length: 200 words maximum; pays $25 maximum. Pays $75 for cartoons.

Tips: "We are a family publication and are looking for travel-oriented stories that the family can take advantage of. We are looking for lively, tightly written articles done by professionals, emphasizing the South, West and Southwest. Our coverage is national in scope, although we occasionally include stories on Canada, Mexico and US overseas territories. Our emphasis is on travel to attractions/destinations and events/activities taking place in America (primarily the Sun Belt)."

‡CHEVY OUTDOORS, A Celebration of American Recreation and Leisure, Ceco Communications, Inc., 30400 Van Dyke, Warren MI 48093. (800)232-6266. Editor: Tom Morrisey. 85% freelance written. Works with a small number of new/unpublished writers each year. A quarterly magazine covering outdoor recreation. Estab. 1986. Circ. 1,000,000. Pays on publication. Publishes ms an average of 6 months after acceptance. Offers 25% kill fee. Byline given. Buys first rights, one-time rights or second serial (reprint) rights. Submit seasonal/holiday material 6 months in advance. Simultaneous and previously published submissions OK. Computer printout submissions OK; no dot-matrix. Reports in 6 weeks. Sample copy for 9x12 SAE with $1.41 postage.

Nonfiction: Book excerpts; historical/nostalgic; how-to (on outdoor topics—camping, fishing, etc.); humor; interview/profile (on outdoors people, such as authorities in their fields); personal experience (must be outdoor or wilderness related); photo feature; technical (new technologies for campers, anglers, hunters, etc.); travel; and stories on new trends in outdoor recreation. "No exposes or negative articles; we like an upbeat, positive approach." Buys 50 mss/year. Query with published clips. Length: 200-3,000 words. Pays $100-750 for assigned articles; pays $100-500 for unsolicited articles. Sometimes pays the expenses of writers on assignment.

Photos: Send photos with submission. Reviews 35mm or larger transparencies. Offers $25-100 per photo. Model releases and identification of subjects required. Buys one-time rights; sometimes all rights.

Columns/Departments: Outdoor Photography (how-tos by established photographers with national reputation in outdoor photography) and Outdoors People (profiles of notable outdoors enthusiasts or exceptional people who do work related to outdoor recreation). Buys 8-12 mss/year. Query with published clips. Length: 800-1,500 words. Pays $400-750.

Fiction: Tall tales for Campfire Classics department. "These can have a humorous, mysterious or even fanta-sy/occult slant. See current issues for examples of what we're using. No material that is unsuitable for a family audience." Buys 4-6 mss/year. Query with published clips or send complete ms. Length: 600-1,200 words. Pays $100-400.

Fillers: Anecdotes, facts and newsbreaks. Buys 25-30/year. Length: 25-200 words.

Tips: "Stories that are dynamic and active, and stories that focus on people will have a better chance of getting in. Focus queries tightly and look beyond the obvious. Use this as a touchstone—Is this a story that I would be compelled to read if I found it on a coffee table or in a waiting room? If the answer is 'yes,' we want to hear from you. Happily enough, our features well is the best freelance target. Travel, personality profiles or activity fea-tures are probably the best ticket in. But the idea has to be fresh and original, and the copy has to sing. New or unpublished writers should write on topics with which they are *very* familiar; expertise can compensate for a lack of experience."

‡CHICAGO TRIBUNE, Travel Section,435 N. Michigan Ave., Chicago IL 60611. (312)222-3999. *Tribune* Editor: James Squires. Executive Travel Editor: Larry Townsend. Managing Editor: Richard Ciccone. Sunday newspaper section. Weekly leisure travel section averaging 24 pages. Aimed at vacation travelers. Circ. 1.2 million. Pays on publication. Publishes ms an average of 1½ months after acceptance. Byline given. Buys one time rights. Submit seasonal/holiday material 2 months in advance. Simultaneous submissions OK. Query for electronic submissions. Computer printout submissions OK; prefers letter-quality to dot-matrix. Reports in 2 weeks. Sample copy for large SAE with $1.25 postage. Writer's guidelines for SASE.

Nonfiction: Essays, general interest, historical/nostalgic, how-to (travel, pack), humor, opinion, personal experience, photo feature and travel. "There will be 16 special issues in the next 18 months." Buys 500+ mss/year. Send complete ms. Length: 500-2,500 words. Pays $100-250.

Photos: State availability of photos with submission. Reviews 35mm transparencies and 8x10 or 5x7 prints. Offers $100-300 for color photos; $25 for b&w photos. Captions required. Buys one-time rights.

Tips: "Be professional. Use a word processor. Make the reader want to go to the area being written about. Our Page 3Reader is a travel essay, hopefully with humor, insight, tear jerking. A great read. Only 1% of mss make it."

COAST MAGAZINE, The Weekly Vacationers Guide, Resort Publications, Ltd., 5000 N. Kings High-way, Box 2448, Myrtle Beach SC 29577. (803)449-5415. Managing Editor: Mona R. Prufer. Published 38 times/year covering tourism. "We reach more than one million readers/tourists. Our slant is vacation articles, beach, North/South Carolina orientation with coastal information." Circ. 29,000. Pays on acceptance. Byline given. Buys one-time rights (regional). Submit seasonal/holiday material at least 2 months in advance. Simul-taneous queries, and simultaneous, photocopied, and previously published submissions OK. Reports in 2 weeks on queries; 1-2 months on mss. Free sample copy and writer's guidelines.

Nonfiction: Historical/nostalgic (low country, South); new product (beach, tourist-related); personal experi-ence (tourist) and articles on music and beach music. Buys 10 mss/year. Send complete ms. Length: 400-1,000 words. Pays $30 minimum.

Photos: Send photos with ms. Pays $25-100 for b&w or 4-color (cover photos) transparencies; $50 minimum for b&w and color prints. Model releases and identification of subjects required. Buys one-time rights (region-al).

Tips: "Freelancer can best break in to our publication by submitting resort-oriented, and Southern historical material."

‡COLORADO OUTDOOR JOURNAL, Continental Divide Publishing Inc., Box 432, Florence CO 81226. (303)275-3166. Editor: Galen L. Geer. Managing Editor: Chas S. Clifton. 60% freelance written. A bimonth-ly family-oriented recreation magazine covering hunting, fishing and camping in Colorado and portions of ad-jacent states. Estab. 1986. Circ. 20,000. Pays on publication. Publishes ms an average of 4 months after ac-ceptance. Byline given. Offers 25% kill fee. Buys first North American serial rights. Submit seasonal/holiday material 6 months in advance. Photocopied submissions OK. Computer printout submissions OK; prefers let-ter-quality. Reports in 1 month on queries; 2 months on mss. Sample copy $2; writer's guidelines for #10 SAE with 1 first class stamp.

Nonfiction: Book excerpts, historical/nostalgic, how-to, humor, new product, opinion, photo feature and travel. Buys 150 mss/year. Query with published clips. Length: 1,200-3,000 words. Pays $150-400. Some-times pays the expenses of writers on assignment.

Photos: Send photos with submission. Reviews 35mm or 2x2 transparencies and 5x7 or 8x10 b&w prints. Of-fers no additional payment for photos accepted with ms. Captions, model releases and identification of subjects required. Buys one-time rights.

Columns/Departments: Issues (topics affecting Colorado's outdoors and recreation), 1,000-1,500 words; and The Last Page (humor, nostalgic, Colorado history), 1,000-1,250 words. Buys 12 mss/year. Query with published clips. Length: 1,000-1,500 words. Pays $75-150.

Fiction: Adventure, historical, humorous and slice-of-life vignettes. Buys 4 mss/year. Send complete ms.

Length: 1,000-3,000 words. Pays $75-400.
Fillers: Facts. Buys 10/year. Length: 50-250 words. Pays $5-25.
Tips: "*Colorado Outdoor Journal* is most in need of feature outdoor articles with b&w photos and/or color slides. Articles should include where-to and how-to information whenever possible, and *must* have a strong Colorado tie-in. Include sources of additional information for the reader whenever practical. *COJ* does not cover downhill skiing, hang gliding, competitive running and bicycling, and other activities of a highly technical or competitive nature."

DISCOVERY, 3701 West Lake Ave., Glenview IL 60025. Editor: Claire McCrea. 75% freelance written. Prefers to work with published/established writers, and works with a small number of new/unpublished writers each year. A quarterly travel magazine for Allstate Motor Club members. Circ. 1,300,000. Buys first North American serial rights. Pays on acceptance. Publishes ms an average of 8 months after acceptance. Computer printout submissions acceptable; no dot-matrix. Submit seasonal queries 8-14 months in advance to allow for photo assignment. Reports in 2-5 weeks. Sample copy for 9x12 SAE and $1 postage; free writer's guidelines.
Nonfiction: "The emphasis is on North America and its people." Emphasizes automotive travel, offering a firsthand look at the people and places, trends and activities that help define the American character. "We're looking for polished magazine articles that are people-oriented and promise insight as well as entertainment—not narratives of peoples' vacations. Destination articles must rely less on the impressions of writers and more on the observations of people who live or work or grew up in the place and have special attachments. We seek ideas for a 'Best of America' department, which is a roundup of particular kinds of places (i.e beaches, national park lodges, space museums) often related to the season." Query. "Submit a thorough proposal suitable for *Discovery*. It must be literate, concise and enthusiastic. Accompany query with relevant published clips and a resume." Buys 12 unsolicited mss/year. Length: 1,500-2,000 words, plus a 500 word sidebar on other things to see and do. Rates vary, depending on assignment and writer's credentials; usual range is $350-850. Sometimes pays the expenses of writers on assignment.
Photography: Color transparencies (35mm or larger). Pays day rate. For existing photos, rates depend on use. Photos should work as story; captions required. Send transparencies by registered mail. Buys one-time rights.
Tips: "No personal narratives, mere destination pieces or subjects that are not particularly visual. We have a strong emphasis on photojournalism and our stories reflect this. The most frequent mistakes made by writers in completing an article for us are: not writing to assignment, which results in a weak focus or central theme and poor organization and a lack of development, which diminishes the substance of the story. Word precision frequently is the difference between a dull and an exciting story. Writers will benefit by studying several issues of the publication before sending queries."

ENDLESS VACATION, Endless Vacation Publications, Inc., Box 80260, Indianapolis IN 46280. (317)871-9500. Editor: Helen A. Wernle. Prefers to work with published/established writers. A bimonthly magazine covering travel destinations, activities and issues that enhance the lives of vacationers. Circ. 550,000. Pays on publication. Publishes ms an average of 3 months after acceptance. Byline given. Buys first worldwide serial rights. Simultaneous and photocopied submissions OK. Query for electronic submissions. Computer printout submissions acceptable; prefers letter-quality to dot-matrix. Reports in 1 month on queries; 3 weeks on manuscripts. Sample copy $1; writer's guidelines for SAE with 1 first class stamp.
Nonfiction: Contact Manuscript Editor. Travel. Buys 24 mss/year (approx). Query with published clips. Length: 1,200-2,000 words. Pays $250-600 for assigned articles; pays $150-600 for unsolicited articles. Sometimes pays the expenses of writers on assignment.
Photos: State availability of photos with submissions. Reviews 4x5 transparencies and 35mm slides. Offers $100-300/photo. Model releases and identification of subjects required. Buys one-time rights.
Columns/Departments: Gourmet on the Go (culinary topics of interest to travelers whether they are dining out or cooking in their condominium kitchens; no reviews of individual restaurants). Buys 4 mss/year. Query with published clips. Length: 800-1,200 words. Pays $100-250. Sometimes pays the expenses of writers on assignment.
Tips: "Articles must be packed with pertinent facts and applicable how-tos. Information—addresses, phone numbers, dates of events, costs—must be current and accurate. We like to see a variety of stylistic approaches, but in all cases the lead must be strong. A writer should realize that we require first-hand knowledge of the subject and plenty of practical information. For further understanding of *Endless Vacations'* direction, the writer should study the magazine and guidelines for writers."

FAMILY MOTOR COACHING, 8291 Clough Pike, Cincinnati OH 45244-2796. (513)474-3622. Editor: Pamela Wisby Kay. Associate Editor: Maura Basile. 75% freelance written. "We prefer that writers be experienced RVers." Emphasizes travel by motorhome, and motorhome mechanics, maintenance and other technical information. Monthly magazine; 240-336 pages. Circ. 50,000. Pays on acceptance. Publishes ms an average of 4 months after acceptance. Buys first-time, 12 months exclusive rights. Byline given. Submit seasonal/holiday material 5 months in advance. Computer printout submissions acceptable; prefers letter-quality to dot-matrix. Reports in 2 months. Sample copy $2; writer's guidelines for SASE.

Nonfiction: Motorhome travel and living on the road; travel (various areas of country accessible by motor coach); how-to (modify motor coach features); bus conversions; and nostalgia. Buys 20 mss/issue. Query. Phone queries discouraged. Length: 1,000-2,000 words. Pays $50-500.

Photos: State availability of photos with query. Offers no additional payment for b&w contact sheets, 35mm or 2¼x2¼ color transparencies. Captions required. B&w glossy photos should accompany nontravel articles. Buys first rights.

Tips: "Keep in mind, stories must have motorhome angle or connection; inclusion of information about FM-CA members enhances any travel article. Stories about an event somewhere should allude to nearby campgrounds, etc. The stories should be written assuming that someone going there would be doing it by motorhome. We need more articles from which to select for publication. We need geographic balance and a blend of travel, technical and incidental stories. No first-person accounts of vacations."

FRANCE TODAY, France Press, Inc., 1051 Divisadero, San Francisco CA 95115. (415)921-5100. Editor: Anne Prah-Perochon. 70% freelance written. Works with a small number of new/unpublished writers each year. A quarterly magazine covering contemporary France: culture, arts, business, travel, food and wine, etc., for a "sophisticated group of well-traveled Americans interested in modern-day France—French thought, culture and lifestyle." Circ. 50,000. Pays on publication. Publishes ms an average of 3 months after acceptance. Byline given. Offers 10% kill fee. Buys first rights and makes work-for-hire assignments. Submit seasonal/holiday material 6 months in advance. Simultaneous, photocopied, and previously published submissions OK. Query for electronic submissions. Computer printout submissions acceptable; prefers letter-quality to dot-matrix. Reports in 1 month on queries. Free writer's guidelines.

Nonfiction: Essays; general interest; historical/nostalgic; how-to (travel with children, start a business in France, become a French citizen); humor; new product; opinion; personal experience; photo feature; and travel. Buys 30 mss/year. Query with or without published clips, or send complete ms. Length: 500-3,000 words. Pays $50-400 for assigned articles; pays $50-300 for unsolicited articles.

Photos: Send photos with submission. Reviews contact sheets, negatives, transparencies and prints. Offers $30-200/photo. Buys one-time rights.

Columns/Departments: Impressions (cross-cultural experience related to France or Franco-American relationships), 1,000-1,500 words. Pays $100-200.

Tips: "Writers should be advised that our readers have traveled many times to France and that we receive many travel articles. Preference is given to articles that combine various aspects of French life—art and society, fashion and business, etc. All areas are open at this time. There are greater opportunities for lifestyle, business, current events and political or socio-political articles."

GREAT EXPEDITIONS, Canada's Adventure and Travel Magazine, Box 46499, Station G, Vancouver, British Columbia V6R 4G7 Canada. Editor: Marilyn Marshall. 90% freelance written. Eager to work with new/unpublished writers. Bimonthly magazine covering adventure and travel "for people who want to discover the world around them (archaeology to climbing volcanoes); basically a how-to *National Geographic*. We focus on travel (not tourism) and adventure. We are much like a society or club—we provide services besides the basic magazine—and encourage articles and information from our readers." Circ. 3,000. Pays on publication. Publishes ms an average of 6 months after acceptance. Byline given. Buys first rights or second (reprint) rights to material originally published elsewhere. Submit seasonal/holiday material 6 months in advance. Simultaneous queries, and simultaneous, photocopied and previously published submissions OK. Computer printout submissions acceptable; no dot-matrix. SASE; IRCs outside of Canada. Reports in 1 month. Sample copy $2; free writer's guidelines.

Nonfiction: Book reviews (travel and adventure); how-to (travel economically, do adventure trips); personal experience (travel or adventure); travel (economy and budget, exotic-*not* touristic). No tourism articles. Buys 30 mss/year. Query or send complete ms. Length: 1,000-3,000 words. Pays $35 maximum.

Photos: "It is important to send photos with the manuscript. Otherwise we are reluctant to accept pieces (how-tos and book reviews excepted)." Pays $10 for any photo used on the cover. "Color reproduced in b&w for magazine." Captions required. Buys one-time rights.

Columns/Departments: Viewpoint—opinion on travel, adventure, outdoor recreation, environment. Photography—for the traveler, adventurer: equipment techniques. Health—for travelers and adventurers: how to keep healthy, be healthy. Money—best buys, best countries to visit. Length: 400-800 words. Pays $25 maximum.

Tips: "Best to send for a copy—we are rather different from most magazines because we are a network of travelers and adventurers and rely on this network for our information. We have a yearly article and photo contest. Prizes are $50 for best article and $25 for best photo."

GUIDE TO THE FLORIDA KEYS, Humm's, Crain Communications Inc., Box 330712, Miami FL 33133. (305)665-2858. Editor: William A. Humm. 80% freelance written. A quarterly travel guide to the Florida Keys. Circ. 50,000. Pays on publication. Byline given. Buys first rights and second serial (reprint) rights. Sub-

mit seasonal/holiday material 6 months in advance. Previously published submissions OK. Computer printout submissions acceptable. Reports in 2 weeks on queries; 3 weeks on manuscripts. Free sample copy.
Nonfiction: General interest, historical/nostalgic, personal experience and travel, all for the Florida Keys area. Buys 30-40 mss/year. Send complete ms. Length: 500-1,500 words. Pays $4.80/column inch. Sometimes pays the expenses of writers on assignment.
Photos: State availability of photos with submission. Reviews negatives, 35mm and 2x2 transparencies, and 5x7 and 8x10 prints. Offers $40-100/photo. Captions and model releases required. Buys one-time rights.
Columns/Departments: Fishing and Diving (primarily about the Florida Keys), 500-1,500 words. Pays $4.80/column inch.

HIDEAWAYS GUIDE, Hideaways International, 15 Goldsmith St., Littleton MA 01460. Editor: Mark T. Hufford. Managing Editor: Betsy Browning. 25% freelance written. Magazine published 2 times/year—January, July. Also publishes 4 quarterly newsletters. Features travel/leisure and real estate information for upscale, affluent, educated, outdoorsy audience. Deals with unique vacation opportunities: vacation home renting, buying, exchanging, yacht/houseboat charters, adventure vacations, country inns and small resorts. Circ. 12,000. Pays on publication. Publishes ms an average of 4 months after acceptance. Byline given. Buys first North American serial rights, one-time rights and second serial (reprint) rights. Submit seasonal/holiday material 6 months in advance. Previously published submissions OK. Query for electronic submissions. Computer printout submissions OK; no dot-matrix. Reports in 1 month on queries; 2 months on mss. Sample copy $10; writer's guidelines for SASE.
Nonfiction: How-to (with focus on personal experience: vacation home renting, exchanging, buying, selling, yacht and house boat chartering); travel (intimate out-of-the-way spots to visit). Articles on "learning" vacations: scuba, sailing, flying, cooking, shooting, golf, tennis, photography, etc. Buys 10 mss/year. Query. Length: 800-1,500 words. Pays $50-100.
Photos: State availability of photos with query letter or ms or send photos with accompanying query or ms. Reviews b&w prints. Pays negotiable fee. Captions and identification of subjects required. Buys one-time rights.
Tips: "The most frequent mistakes made by writers in completing an article for us are that they are too impersonal with no photos and not enough focus or accommodations."

‡HOSTELERS' KNAPSACK, American Youth Hostels, Box 37613, Washington DC 20013-7613. (202)783-6161. Editor: Sally Janecek. 20-50% freelance written. Eager to work with new/unpublished writers. A quarterly travel magazine published by American Youth Hostels, a nonprofit organization. Circ. 100,000. Pays upon availability of funds. Publishes ms an average of 3-4 months after acceptance. Byline given. Buys first or second serial (reprint) rights. Submit seasonal/holiday material 4 months in advance. Simultaneous, photocopied and previously published submissions OK. Computer printout submissions OK; no dot-matrix. Free sample copy and writer's guidelines.
Nonfiction: General interest (hosteling and traveling), personal experience, photo feature and travel. Buys 1-2 mss/year. Query. Length: 800-1,200 words. Pays $25-50 or contributor copies and byline.
Photos: State availability of photos with submission. Reviews transparencies and 5x7 prints. Offers $5 per photo. Captions and identification of subjects required.
Columns/Departments: Houseparent's Corner (profiles of hostel managers; must include b&w photo); Hostel Spotlight (aspect of a hostel that makes it unique or unusual, its architecture, location; must include b&w photo). Buys 0-1 ms/year. Query. Length: 250-400 words. Pays $25.
Tips: "We are looking for material, preferably first-hand hosteling experiences about 'in' places to travel like Australia or New Zealand, as well as the frequently traveled popular places."

‡IN TOUCH, The International Tours Travel Magazine,Go, Inc., 110 Broad St., Boston MA 02110. Editor: Jenny Webster. Managing Editor: Chuck Beckman. 90% freelance written. Bimonthly magazine publishing "enticing articles on U.S. and international travel. Magazine promotes single, couple and family travel to easily bookable destinations." Circ. 400,000. Pays on publication. Byline given. Buys first North American serial rights. Submit seasonal/holiday material 7 months in advance. Computer printout submissions OK; prefers letter-quality to dot-matrix. Reports in 1 month on queries; 6 weeks on mss. Sample copy for $3 with 10x13 SAE and $1.10 postage. Writer's guidelines for #10 SAE with 1 first class stamp.
Nonfiction: How-to, interview/profile, new product, photo feature and travel. Query with published clips. Length: 1,000-1,950 words. Pays $150-600.
Photos: State availability of photos with submission. Payment negotiable. Captions and identification of subjects required. Buys one-time rights.
Columns/Departments: Chuck Beckman, column/department editor. Insider's Touch (short featurettes on relevant, seasonal travel subjects). Buys 6 mss/year. Query. Length: 300-900 words. Pays $50-100.
Tips: "Hit us with a good query that shows your familiarity with a destination and your ability to write an enticing article on it. Don't simply list things to do and see—instead show how a traveler might interact with the area covered. First person writing is OK if not self-serving."

JOURNAL OF CHRISTIAN CAMPING, Christian Camping International, Box 646, Wheaton IL 60189. Editor: Charlyene Wall. 75% freelance written. Prefers to work with published/established writers. Emphasizes the broad scope of organized camping with emphasis on Christian camping. "Leaders of youth camps and adult conferences read our magazine to get practical help in ways to run their camps." Bimonthly magazine; 32-48 pages. Circ. 6,000. Pays on acceptance. Publishes ms an average of 2 months after acceptance. Buys all rights. Offers 25% kill fee. Byline given. Computer printout submissions acceptable; prefers letter-quality to dot-matrix. Reports in 6 weeks. Sample copy $2.50; writer's guidelines for SASE.
Nonfiction: General interest (trends in organized camping in general and Christian camping in particular); how-to (anything involved with organized camping from motivating staff, to programming, to record keeping, to camper follow-up); inspirational (limited use, but might be interested in practical applications of Scriptural principles to everyday situations in camping, no preaching); interview (with movers and shakers in camping and Christian camping in particular; submit a list of basic questions first); and opinion (write a letter to the editor). Buys 30-50 mss/year. Query required. Length: 600-2,500 words. Pays 5¢/word.
Photos: Send photos with ms. Pays $10/5x7 b&w contact sheet or print; price negotiable for 35mm color transparencies. Buys all rights. Captions required.
Tips: "The most frequent mistake made by writers is that they have not read the information in the listing and send articles unrelated to our readers."

MICHIGAN LIVING, AAA Michigan, 17000 Executive Plaza Drive, Dearborn MI 48126. (313)336-1211. Editor: Len Barnes. 50% freelance written. Emphasizes travel and auto use. Monthly magazine; 48 pages. Circ. 950,000. Pays on acceptance. Publishes ms an average of 4 months after acceptance. Buys first North American serial rights. Offers 100% kill fee. Byline given. Submit seasonal/holiday material 3 months in advance. Reports in 4-6 weeks. Free sample copy and writer's guidelines.
Nonfiction: Travel articles on U.S. and Canadian topics, but not on California, Florida or Arizona. Buys 50-60 unsolicited mss/year. Send complete ms. Length: 200-1,000 words. Pays $78-315.
Photos: Photos purchased with accompanying ms. Captions required. Pays $367 for cover photos; $26.25-157.50 for color transparencies; total purchase price for ms includes payment for b&w photos.
Tips: "In addition to descriptions of things to see and do, articles should contain accurate, current information on costs the traveler would encounter on his trip. Items such as lodging, meal and entertainment expenses should be included, not in the form of a balance sheet but as an integral part of the piece. We want the sounds, sights, tastes, smells of a place or experience so one will feel he has been there and knows if he wants to go back."

THE MIDWEST MOTORIST, AAA Auto Club of Missouri, 12901 North Forty Dr., St. Louis MO 63141. (314)851-3315. Editor: Michael J. Right. Managing Editor: Jean Kennedy. 70% freelance written. Bimonthly magazine on travel and auto-related topics. Primarily focuses on travel throughout the world; prefers stories that tell about sights and give solid travel tips. Circ. 351,000. Pays on acceptance. Publishes ms an average of 8 months after acceptance. Byline given. Not copyrighted. Buys one-time rights, simultaneous rights (rarely), and second serial (reprint) rights. Submit seasonal/holiday material 6-8 months in advance. Simultaneous queries, and simultaneous, photocopied and previously published submissions OK. Query for electronic submissions. Computer printout submissions acceptable as long as they are readable and NOT ALL CAPS; no dot-matrix. Reports in 1 month. Sample copy for 9x12 SAE and 4 first class stamps. Free writer's guidelines.
Nonfiction: General interest; historical/nostalgic; how-to; humor (with motoring or travel slant); interview/profile; personal experience; photo feature; technical (auto safety or auto-related); and travel (domestic and international), all travel-related or auto-related. March/April annual European travel issue; September/October annual cruise issue. No religious, philosophical arguments or opinion not supported by facts. Buys 30 mss/year. Query with published clips. Length: 500-2,000 (1,500 preferred) words. Pays $50-200.
Photos: State availability of photos. Prefers color slides and b&w with people, sights, scenery mentioned. Reviews 35mm transparencies and 8x10 prints. Payment included in ms. Captions, model releases and identification of subjects required. Buys one-time rights.
Tips: "Query should be informative and entertaining, written with as much care as the lead of a story. Feature articles on travel destinations and tips are most open to freelancers."

NATIONAL GEOGRAPHIC TRAVELER, National Geographic Society, 17th and M Sts. NW, Washington DC 20036. (202)857-7721. Editor: Joan Tapper. 90% freelance written. A quarterly travel magazine. "*Traveler* highlights mostly U.S. and Canadian subjects, but about 30% of its articles cover other foreign destinations—most often Europe, Mexico, and the Caribbean, occasionally the Pacific." Circ. 775,000. Pays on acceptance. Publishes ms an average of 12-15 months after acceptance. Byline given. Offers 50% kill fee. Computer printout submissions OK; prefers letter-quality to dot-matrix. Reports in 2 months. Sample copy $5.60; writer's guidelines for SASE.
Nonfiction: Travel. Buys 20 mss/year. Query with published clips. Length: 2,000-4,000 words. Pays $1/word. Pays expenses of writers on assignment.
Photos: Reviews transparencies and prints.

‡NATIONAL MOTORIST, Serving the California Motorist and Traveler,National Automobile Club, One Market Plaza, San Francisco CA 94105. (415)777-4000. Editor: Jane M. Offers. 80% freelance written. Bimonthly magazine covering domestic/international travel and automotive news. *"National Motorist* is edited for National Automobile Club members—all in California—and includes stories on travel opportunities in the West and Canada/Mexico/Hawaii and many other international destinations. Also stories on cruise travel and automotive/legislative news." Circ. 180,000. Pays on acceptance. Publishes ms an average of 2-4 months after acceptance. Byline given. Offers 10% kill fee. Buys first rights. Submit seasonal/holiday material 12 months in advance. Computer printout submissions OK; prefers letter-quality. Reports in 1 month. Free sample copy.
Nonfiction: Photo feature, travel and automotive. Annual cruise issue (January-February 1988). No "too-general pieces on national parks and recreation, stories based primarily on East Coast, nostalgic, historical, personal-experience vacations." Buys 18 mss/year. Query with published clips. Length: 750-1,500 words. Pays $150-300 (depends also on accompanying photos).
Photos: State availability of photos with submission. Reviews transparencies. Offers $35-150/photo; cover $400. Model releases and identification of subjects required. Buys one-time rights.
Columns/Departments: Perspective (issues of relevance, opinion on present topic of interest to motoring public, usually is oriented to Californians); One-Tank Trips (short hops within California). Buys 30 mss/year. Query with or without published clips. Length: 750-900 words. Pays $150-200.
Tips: "We are interested in domestic and international travel writers, especially those who are good in the photographic areas and can support submissions with top quality 35 mm or other size transparencies (no color prints accepted). Also consumer-oriented articles about automobiles—both technically and generally oriented—are encouraged, pertaining to today's vehicles, safety, etc. We prefer, also, those travel areas that are retail as in hotels, places to stay and attractions to seek out rather than simply walking in the pretty woods. Bed and breakfasts, Hawaii getaways, resorts, plus short hops are fine."

NEW ENGLAND GETAWAYS, New England Publishing Group, Inc., 21 Pocahontas Dr., Peabody MA 01960. (617)535-4186. Associate Editor: Christine Kole MacLean. 50% freelance written. Works with a small number of new/unpublished writers each year. A monthly magazine covering travel in New England. Circ. 40,000. Pays on publication. Publishes ms an average of 3 months after acceptance. Offers kill fee. Buys all rights or makes work-for-hire assignments. Submit seasonal/holiday material 4 months in advance. Query for electronic submissions. Computer printout submissions acceptable; prefers letter-quality to dot-matrix. Reports in 1 month. Sample copy $3; writer's guidelines for SASE.
Nonfiction: "We are interested in articles that encourage people to see New England, especially those articles that focus on an event that is going on in a town during a specific time period. The writer covers such events, as well as some local points of interest in advance. We then publish the article in the appropriate issue so that readers know the details about the events and sites, and can plan to attend. No nostalgia or general pieces." Query. Length: 1,000-2,000 words. Pays $150-250 for assigned articles. Sometimes pays expenses of writers on assignment.
Photos: State availability of photos with submission. "Writer is expected to furnish photos once article is assigned." Reviews photos and slides. Offers no additional payment for photos accepted with ms. Captions and model releases required. Buys all rights.
Tips: "Be specific about the area or event you wish to cover. All articles must be information-based—readers want to know the times and places of sites and events, how much they cost, what the hours are, and where they can call for more information. Essentially we want specific articles about what to do and where to go in all of New England. Articles should also include information about mid-week and weekend packages offered by local hotels. Seasonal topics, such as New Year's celebrations or foliage, and New England topics, such as factory outlet shopping or antique shopping, are also acceptable. The best way to see what we want is to write for a sample copy."

NEWSDAY, Melville, Long Island NY 11747. (516)454-2980. Travel Editor: Steve Schatt. Assistant Travel Editor: Barbara Shea. 75% freelance written. For general readership of Sunday Travel Section. Newspaper. Weekly. Circ. 680,000. Buys all rights for New York area only. Buys 175 mss/year. Pays on publication. Will consider photocopied submissions. Simultaneous submissions considered if others are being made outside the New York area. Query for electronic submissions. Computer printout submissions acceptable; prefers letter-quality to dot-matrix. Reports in 1 month.
Nonfiction and Photos: Travel articles with strong focus and theme for Sunday Travel Section, but does not accept pieces based on freebies, junkets, discount or subsidies of any sort. Emphasis on accuracy, honesty, service, and quality writing to convey mood and flavor. Destination pieces must involve visit or experience that a typical traveler can duplicate. Skip diaries, "My First Trip Abroad" pieces or laundry lists of activities; downplay first person. Submit complete ms. Length: 600-1,500 words; prefers 800- to 1,000-word pieces. Pays 12-20¢/word. Photos extra. Also, regional "Weekender" pieces of 700-800 words plus service box, but query Barbara Shea first.
Tips: "We look for professional material with a writer's touch, and it makes no difference who produces it. The test is quality, not experience."

NORTHEAST OUTDOORS, Northeast Outdoors, Inc., Box 2180, Waterbury CT 06722. (203)755-0158. Editor: Debora Nealley. 80% freelance written. Works with a small number of new/unpublished writers each year, and is eager to work with new/unpublished writers. A monthly tabloid covering family camping in the Northeastern U.S. Circ. 14,000. Pays on publication. Publishes ms an average of 8 months after acceptance. Byline given. Offers 50% kill fee. Buys first rights, one-time rights, second serial (reprint) rights, simultaneous rights, and regional rights. Submit seasonal/holiday material 5 months in advance. Simultaneous, photocopied and previously published submissions OK. Query for electronic submissions. Computer printout submissions acceptable; no dot-matrix. Reports in 1 month. Sample copy for 9x12 SAE with 6 first class stamps; writer's guidelines for letter size SAE with 1 first class stamp.

Nonfiction: Book excerpts; general interest; historical/nostalgic; how-to (on camping); humor; new product (company and RV releases only); personal experience; photo feature; and travel. "No diaries of trips, dog stories, or anything not camping and RV related." Length: 300-1,500 words. Pays $40-80 for assigned articles; pays $30-75 for unsolicited articles.

Photos: Send photos with submission. Reviews contact sheets and 5x7 prints or larger. Offers $5-10/photo. Captions and identification of subjects required. Buys one-time rights.

Columns/Departments: Mealtime (campground cooking), 300-900 words. Buys 12 mss/year. Query or send complete ms. Length: 750-1,000 words. Pays $30-75.

Fillers: Camping related anecdotes, facts, newsbreaks and short humor. Buys few fillers. Length: 25-200 words. Pays $5-15.

Tips: "We most often need material on campgrounds and attractions in Maine, New Hampshire, Rhode Island and Massachusetts. Go camping and travel in the Northeastern States, especially New England. Have a nice trip, and tell us about it. Travel and camping articles, especially first-person reports on private campgrounds and interviews with owners, are the areas of our publication most open to freelancers."

PACIFIC BOATING ALMANAC, #14, 4051 Glencoe Ave., Marina Del Ray CA 90292. (213)306-2094. Editor: William Berssen. 5% freelance written. Prefers to work with published/established writers. For "Western boat owners." Published in 3 editions to cover the Pacific Coastal area. Circ. 25,000. Buys all rights. Buys 12 mss/year. Pays on publication. Publishes ms an average of 6 months after acceptance. Submit seasonal material 3 to 6 months in advance. Query for electronic submissions. Computer printout submissions OK; prefers letter-quality. Reports in 1 month. Sample copy $11.95.

Nonfiction: "This is a cruising guide, published annually in three editions, covering all of the navigable waters in the Pacific coast. Though we are almost entirely staff-produced, we would be interested in well-written articles on cruising and trailer-boating along the Pacific coast and in the navigable lakes and rivers of the Western states from Baja, California to Alaska inclusive." Query. Pays $50 minimum. Pays expenses of writers on assignment.

Photos: Pays $10/8x10 b&w glossy print.

Tips: "We are also publishers of boating books that fall within the classification of 'where-to' and 'how-to.' Authors are advised not to send manuscript until requested after we've reviewed a two- to four-page outline of the projected books."

‡**SAN FRANCISCO LETTER**, (formerly *Romantic Dining and Travel Letter*), James Dines & Co., Inc., Box 837, Belvedere CA 94920. Editor: James Dines. Monthly newsletter covering food, wine and travel. "In-depth reviews of 'special places' around the world; hotels, restaurants with detailed wine list commentary, with a greater emphasis on the U.S. West Coast. Appeals to a very affluent audience." Pays on publication. Buys all rights. Submit seasonal/holiday material 4 months in advance. Simultaneous queries and simultaneous and photocopied submissions OK. Computer printout submissions acceptable; prefers letter-quality to dot-matrix. Reports in 3 weeks. Sample copy $5; free writer's guidelines.

Nonfiction: Travel and dining (special places only, not tourist traps or student hangouts). No budget tips or human interest articles. Buys 10-20 mss/year. Query with clips. Pays $100-500 ("according to quality, not length.")

Photos: State availability of photos with query letter or ms. Photos with query preferred. Reviews any size b&w or color prints. Pays negotiable fee. Identification of subjects required. Buys one-time rights.

Tips: "We are very specialized; if a writer makes a special 'discovery' of a place—a secluded hideaway, romantic restaurant, or a particularly romantic and elegant hotel—we'll want it. We want our articles to be very detailed and useful in their description. If the quality is there, we will see it." Major travel features are most open to freelancers.

‡**SOUTHERN TRAVEL**, 5520 Park Ave., Box 395, Trumbull CT 06611-0395. (203)373-7000. Publisher: Rebecca McPheters. Editor: Shepherd Campbell. 90% freelance written. Seeks both established and new/unpublished writers. A service magazine that describes the rich variety of travel opportunities that exist in the Southern U.S. and helps readers get the most for their travel dollars. Quarterly magazine. Circ. 180,000. Byline given. Pays on acceptnace. Publishes ms an average of 6 months after acceptance. Buys all rights. Pays on acceptance. Reports in 1 month. Sample copy $2.25; free writer's guidelines.

Nonfiction: Emphasis on big, colorful features about major destinations, sectional roundups, shorter local articles, and practical travel advice. Buys 120 mss/year. Query with published clips. Length varies. Pays $150 minimum for articles, considerably more for major features. Sometimes pays the expenses of writers on assignment.

Photos: State availablility of photos with submission. Pays $50 for 8x10 b&w glossies; $75-200 for color transparencies. Identification of subjects required. Buys one-time rights.

Tips: "Our greatest need is for articles about local attractions or events that may not be worth a special long trip but are fun to see en route to a major destination."

TEXAS HIGHWAYS MAGAZINE, Official Travel Magazine for the State of Texas, State Dept. of Highways and Public Transportation, 11th and Brazos, Austin TX 78701. (512)463-8581. Editor: Franklin T. Lively. Managing Editor: Jack Lowry. 85% freelance written. Prefers to work with published/established writers. A monthly tourist magazine covering travel and history for Texas only. Pays on acceptance. Publishes ms an average of 10 months after acceptance. Byline given. Offers $100 kill fee. Not copyrighted. Buys one-time rights. Submit seasonal/holiday material 1 year in advance. Simultaneous queries and submissions OK. Query for electronic submissions. Computer printout submissions acceptable; no dot-matrix. Reports in 2 weeks on queries; 1 month on mss. Free sample copy and writer's guidelines.

Nonfiction: Historical/nostalgic, photo feature, travel. Must be concerned with travel in Texas. Send material on "what to see, what to do, where to go in *Texas*." Material must be tourist-oriented. "No disaster features." Buys 75 mss/year. Query with published clips. Length: 1,200-1,600 words. Pays $400-700. Sometimes pays expenses of writers on assignment "after we have worked with them awhile."

Photos: Bill Reaves, photo editor. Send photos with query or ms. Pays $80 for less than a page, $160 for a full page, $300 for cover, $200 for back cover. Accepts 4x5, 2¼x2¼, 35mm color transparencies. Captions and identification of subjects required. Buys one-time rights.

Tips: "We are looking for outdoor features this year, such as state parks, lakes, beaches, and dude ranches. We have too many historical homes and buildings stories now."

TOURS & RESORTS, The World-Wide Vacation Magazine, World Publishing Co., 990 Grove St., Evanston IL 60201-4370. (312)491-6440. Editor/Associate Publisher: Bob Meyers. Associate Editor: Ray Gudas. 90% freelance written. A bimonthly magazine covering world-wide vacation travel features. Circ. 250,000. Pays on acceptance. Byline given. Buys first North American serial rights. Submit seasonal/holiday material 6 months in advance. Previously published submissions acceptable, dependent upon publication—local or regional OK. Computer printout submissions acceptable; prefers letter-quality to dot-matrix. Reports in 3 weeks on queries; 6 weeks on mss. Sample copy $2.50 with 9x12 SASE.

Nonfiction: Primarily destination-oriented travel articles, "Anatomy of a Tour" features, and resort/hotel profiles and roundups, but will consider essays, how-to, humor, company profiles, nostalgia, etc.—if travel-related. "It is best to study current contents and query first." Buys 75 mss/year. Average length: 1,500 words. Pays $150-500.

Photos: Top-quality original color slides preferred. Captions required. Buys one-time rights. Prefers photo feature package (ms plus slides), but will purchase slides only to support a work in progress.

Columns/Departments: Travel Views (travel tips; service articles), and World Shopping (shopping guide). Buys 8-12 mss/year. Query or send complete ms. Length: 800-1,500 words. Pays $125-250.

Tips: "Travel features and the Travel Views department are most open to freelancers. Because we are heavily photo-oriented, superb slides are our foremost concern. The most successful approach is to send 2-3 sheets of slides with the query or complete ms. Include a list of other subjects you can provide as a photo feature package."

TRAILS-A-WAY, 9425 S. Greenville Rd., Greenville MI 48838. (616)754-9179. Editor: David Higbie. 25% freelance written. Newspaper published 11 times/year on camping in the Midwest (Michigan, Ohio, Indiana, Illinois and Wisconsin). "Fun and information for campers who own recreational vehicles." Circ. 57,000. Pays on publication. Byline given. Buys first and second rights to the same material, and second (reprint) rights to material originally published elsewhere. Submit seasonal/holiday material 3 months in advance. Simultaneous queries and submissions OK. Computer printout submissions acceptable; no dot-matrix. Reports in 1 month. Sample copy 75¢; writer's guidelines for business size SAE and 2 first class stamps.

Nonfiction: How-to (use, maintain recreational vehicles—5th wheels, travel and camping trailers, pop-up trailers, motorhomes); humor; inspirational; interview/profile; new product (camp products); personal experience; photo feature; technical (on RVs); travel. March/April issue: spring camping; September/October: fall camping. Winter issues feature southern hot spots. "All articles should relate to RV camping in Michigan, Ohio, Indiana, Illinois and Wisconsin—or south in winter. No tenting or backpacking articles." Buys 40-50 mss/year. Send complete ms. Length: 1,000-1,500 words. Pays $60-125.

Photos: Send photos with ms. Pays $5-10 for b&w and color prints. No slides. Captions required. Buys one-time rights.

TRANSITIONS ABROAD, 18 Hulst Rd., Box 344, Amherst MA 01004. (413)256-0373. Editor/Publisher: Prof. Clayton A. Hubbs. 80-90% freelance written. Eager to work with new/unpublished writers. The magazine for low-budget international travel with an educational or work component. Bound magazine. Circ. 13,000. Pays on publication. Buys first rights and second (reprint) rights to material originally published elsewhere. Byline given. Written queries only. Computer printout submissions acceptable; prefers letter-quality to dot-matrix. Reports in 1 month. Samples copy $2.50; writer's guidelines and topics schedule for 9x12 SAE and 4 first class stamps.

Nonfiction: How-to (find courses, inexpensive lodging and travel); interview (information on specific areas and people); personal experience (evaluation of courses, special interest and study tours, economy travel); and travel (what to see and do in specific areas of the world, new learning and travel ideas). Foreign travel only. Few destination ("tourist") pieces. Emphasis on information and on interaction with people in host country. Buys 40 unsolicited mss/issue. Query with credentials. Length: 500-2,000 words. Pays $25-150.

Photos: Send photos with ms. Pays $10-25 for 8x10 b&w glossy prints, higher for covers. No color. Additional payment for photos accompanying ms. Photos increase likelihood of acceptance. Buys one-time rights. Captions required.

Columns/Departments: Study/Travel Program Notes (evaluation of courses or programs); Traveler's Advisory/Resources (new information and ideas for offbeat independent travel); Jobnotes (how to find it and what to expect); and Book Reviews (reviews of single books or groups on one area). Buys 8/issue. Send complete ms. Length: 1,000 words maximum. Pays $20-50.

Fillers: Info Exchange (information, preferably first-hand— having to do with travel, particularly offbeat educational travel and work or study abroad). Buys 10/issue. Length: 1,000 words maximum. Pays $20-50.

Tips: "We like nuts and bolts stuff, practical information, especially on how to work, live and cut costs abroad. Be specific: names, addresses, current costs. We are particularly interested in educational travel and study abroad for adults and senior citizens. More and more readers want information not only on work but retirement possibilities. Writers who learn our needs become regulars quickly."

TRAVEL SMART, Communications House, Inc., Dobbs Ferry NY 10522. (914)693-4208. Editor/Publisher: H.J. Teison. Covers information on "good-value travel." Monthly newsletter. Pays on publication. Buys all rights. Photocopied submissions OK. Computer printout submissions acceptable. Reports in 6 weeks. Sample copy and writer's guidelines for #10 SAE with 27¢ postage.

Nonfiction: "Interested primarily in bargains or little-known deals on transportation, lodging, food, unusual destinations that won't break the bank. No destination stories on major Caribbean islands, London, New York, no travelogs, my vacation, poetry, fillers. No photos or illustrations. Just hard facts. We are not part of 'Rosy fingers of dawn . . .' School. More like letter from knowledgeable friend who has been there." Query first. Length: 100-1,000 words. Pays "up to $150."

Tips: "When you travel, check out small hotels offering good prices, little known restaurants, and send us brief rundown (with prices, phone numbers, addresses). Information must be current. Include your phone number with submission, because we sometimes make immediate assignments."

TRAVEL-HOLIDAY MAGAZINE, Travel Magazine, Inc., 51 Atlantic Ave., Floral Park NY 11001. (516)352-9700. Editor: Scott Shane. 95% freelance written. Prefers to work with published/established writers but works with a small number of new/unpublished writers each year. For the active traveler with time and money to travel several times a year. Monthly magazine; 100 pages. Circ. 816,000. Pays on acceptance. Publishes ms an average of 6 months after acceptance. Buys first North American serial rights. Byline given. Submit seasonal/holiday material 6 months in advance. Query for electronic submissions. Computer printout submissions acceptable if double-spaced; prefers letter-quality to dot-matrix. Reports in 2 months. Sample copy for 9x12 SAE and $1; free writer's guidelines.

Nonfiction: Interested in travel destination articles. Send query letter/outline; clips of previously published work *must* accompany queries. No phone queries. Only the highest quality writing and photography are considered by the staff. "Don't ask if we'd like to see any articles on San Francisco, France or China. Develop a specific story idea and explain why the destination is so special that we should devote space to it. Are there interesting museums, superb restaurants, spectacular vistas, etc.? Tell us how you plan to handle the piece—convey to us the mood of the city, the charm of the area, the uniqueness of the museums, etc. No food and wine, medical, photo tips, poetry or boring travelogs." Buys 100 mss/year. Length: featurettes (800-1,300 words), $250 and up; features (1,600-1,800 words), up to $600; "Here and There" column (575 words), $150. For "Here and There" column use "any upbeat topic that can be covered succinctly (with one piece of b&w art) that's travel related and deserves special recognition. When querying, please send suggested lead and indicate 'Here and There' in the cover letter."

Photos: Send photos with submission. B&w prints $25; color converted to b&w will be paid at $25 rate; color transparencies (35mm and larger) pays $75-400 depending upon use. Pays on publication.

Tips: "Feature stories should be about major destinations: large cities, regions, etc. Featurettes can be about individual attractions, smaller cities, side trips, etc. We welcome sidebar service information. Stimulate reader interest in the subject as a travel destination through lively, entertaining and accurate writing. A good way to break in—if we're not familiar with your writing—is to send us a good idea for a featurette. Convey the mood of a place without being verbose; although we like good anecdotal material, our primary interest is in the destination itself, not the author's adventures. Do not query without having first read several recent issues. We no longer use any broadbased travel pieces. Each article must have a specific angle. We are assigning articles to the best writers we can find and those writers who develop and produce good material and will continue to work with us on a regular basis. We have also become much more service-oriented in our articles. We will be featuring regional editorial, therefore we require additional regional United States featurette length stories."

‡TRAVELING TIMES, INC.,MAI Enterprises Inc., 23929 W. Valencia Blvd., 3rd Floor, Valencia CA 91355. (805)255-0230. Editor-in-Chief: Mirko A. Ilich. 30-50% freelance written. Quarterly tabloid covering leisure travel. "Upscale readers—targeted demographic trip/cruise must be travel agent commissionable and sales oriented." Circ. 1,700,000. Pays 30 days after publication. Byline given. Offers $50 kill fee. Buys first North American serial rights or all rights. Submit seasonal/holiday material 1-2 months in advance. Photocopied submissions OK. Computer printout submissions OK; no dot-matrix. Free writer's guidelines.
Nonfiction: Personal experience, photo feature and travel. No articles that are non-sales-oriented or non-commissionable to the travel agent. Buys 20-30 mss/year. Query with published clips. Length: 450-1,000 words. Pays $125-225 for assigned articles; $50-150 for unsolicited articles. Sometimes pays expenses of writers on assignment.
Photos: Send photos with submission. Reviews prints (5x7 minimum). Offers no additional payment for photos accepted with ms. Captions required. Buys one-time rights.
Columns/Departments: Travelgram, Cruise Bargains and Tour Tips ("destination/service/cruise experience story, sales oriented, quality company featured, travel agent commissionable"). Buys 25-35 mss/year. Query with published clips. Length: 200-300 words. Pays $50-75.

‡TRAVELORE REPORT, Suite #100, 1512 Spruce St., Philadelphia PA 19102. (215)735-3838. Editor: Ted Barkus. For affluent travelers; businessmen, retirees, well-educated readers; interested in specific tips, tours, and bargain opportunities in travel. Monthly newsletter; 8 pages. Buys all rights. Pays on publication. Submit seasonal material 2 months in advance. Computer printout and disk submissions acceptable. Sample copy $2.
Nonfiction: "Brief insights (25-200 words) with facts, prices, names of hotels and restaurants, etc., on off-beat subjects of interest to people going places. What to do, what not to do. Supply information. We will rewrite if acceptable. We're candid—we tell it like it is with no sugar coating. Avoid telling us about places in United States or abroad without specific recommendations (hotel name, costs, rip-offs, why, how long, etc.). No destination pieces which are general with no specific 'story angle' in mind, or generally available through PR departments." Buys 10-20 mss/year. Pays $5-20.

VISTA/USA, Box 161, Convent Station NJ 07961. (201)538-7600. Editor: Kathleen M. Caccavale. Managing Editor: Martha J. Mendez. 90% freelance written. Will consider ms submissions from *unpublished* writers. Quarterly magazine of the Exxon Travel Club. "Our publication uses articles on North American areas without overtly encouraging travel. We strive to help our readers to gain an in-depth understanding of cities, towns and areas as well as other aspects of American culture that affect the character of the nation." Circ. 825,000. Pays on acceptance. Publishes ms an average of 1 year after acceptance. Buys first North American serial rights. Query about seasonal subjects 18 months in advance. Computer printout submissions acceptable; prefers letter-quality to dot-matrix. Reports in 6 weeks. Sample copy for a 9x12 or larger SAE with 5 first-class stamps; free writer's and photographer's guidelines.
Nonfiction: General interest (geographically oriented articles on North America focused on the character of an area; also general articles related to travel and places); humor (related to travel or places); photo features (photo essays on subjects such as autumn, winter, highly photogenic travel subjects; and special interest areas) and some articles dealing with Americana, crafts and collecting. "We buy feature articles on North America, Hawaii, Mexico and the Caribbean that appeal to a national audience." No feature articles that mention driving or follow routes on a map or articles about hotels, restaurants or annual events. Uses 7-15 mss/issue. Query with outline and clips of previously published work. Length: 1,500-2,500 words. Pays $500 minimum for features. Pays the expenses of writers on assignment.
Columns/Departments: "Our new departments need submissions. Minitrips are point to point or loop driving tours of from 50 to 350 miles covering a healthy variety of stops along the way. Close Focus covers new or changing aspects of major attractions, small or limited attractions not appropriate for a feature article (800-1,000 words). American Vignettes covers anything travel related that also reveals a slice of American life, often with a light or humorous touch, such as asking directions from a cranky New Englander, or covering the phenomenon of 'talking license plates.' "
Photos: Dana E. LaGueux, photo researcher. Send photos with ms. Pays $100 minimum for color transparencies. Captions preferred. Buys one-time rights.
Tips: "We are looking for readable pieces with good writing that will interest armchair travelers as much as readers who may want to visit the areas you write about. Articles should have definite themes and should give our readers an insight into the character and flavor of an area or topic. Stories about personal experiences must

impart a sense of drama and excitement or have a strong human-interest angle. Stories about areas should communicate a strong sense of what it feels like to be there. Good use of anecdotes and quotes should be included. Study the articles in the magazine to understand how they are organized, how they present their subjects, the range of writing styles, and the specific types of subjects used. Afterwards, query and enclose samples of your best writing. We continue to seek fillers, department shorts, and inventory articles of a general, nonseasonal nature (1,500 to 1,800 words) at least tangentially related to travel."

WESTERN RV TRAVELER, Recreation Publications, 2019 Clement Ave., Alameda CA 94501. (415)865-7500. Editor: Dave Preston. 85% freelance written. Works with a small number of new/unpublished writers each year. A monthly magazine for Western recreational vehicle owners. Circ. 30,000. Pays on publication. Publishes ms an average of 6 months after acceptance. Byline given. Buys one-time rights. Submit seasonal/holiday material 6 months in advance. Simultaneous, photocopied, and previously published submissions OK. Electronic submissions OK via disks compatible with IBM WordStar, but requires hard copy also. Computer printout submissions acceptable. Reports in several weeks on queries; several months on mss. Free sample copy and writer's guidelines.
Nonfiction: Historical/nostalgic; how-to (fix your RV); new product; personal experience (particularly travel); technical; and travel (destinations for RVs). No non-RV travel articles. Buys 36 mss/year. Query with or without published clips, or send complete ms. Length: 1,000-3,000 words. Pays $1.50/inch.
Photos: Send photos with submissions. Reviews contact sheets, negatives, transparencies and prints. Offers $5 minimum/photo. Identification of subjects required.
Tips: "RV travel/destination stories are most open to freelancers. Include all information of value to RVers, and reasons why they would want to visit the California or western location."

Women's

Today's women's publications are as diverse as a woman's own daily schedule. Magazines that also use material slanted to women's interests can be found in the following categories: Business and Finance; Child Care and Parental Guidance; Hobby and Craft; Home and Garden; Relationships; Religious; Romance and Confession; and Sports.

AMIT, AMIT Women, 817 Broadway, New York NY 10003. (212)477-4720. Editor: Micheline Ratzersdorfer. 10% freelance written. Magazine published 5 times/year "concerned with Jewish and Israeli themes, i.e., Jewish art, Jewish sociology, Jewish communities around the world to an audience with an above average educational level, a commitment to Jewish tradition and Zionism and a concern for the future of the Jewish community the world over." Circ. 50,000. Pays on publication. Publishes ms an average of 3 months after acceptance. Buys all rights. Submit seasonal material 6 months in advance. Computer printout submissions acceptable "as long as it can be read by the human eye and has adequate leading and margins for editing." Prefers letter-quality to dot-matrix. Reports in 1 month. Free sample copy and writer's guidelines.
Nonfiction: General interest; historical; interview (with notable figures in Jewish and Israeli life); nostalgia; travel; and photo feature (particularly Jewish holiday photos). "We do special holiday features for all Jewish holidays." No fiction, no memoirs about "Momma's Chicken Soup" and things of that ilk; no political analyses of the Middle East unless they can stand a six-month delay until publication; no travelogues lauding non-kosher restaurants." Buys 10 unsolicited mss/year. Query. Length: 1,000-2,000 words. Pays $75 maximum.
Photos: State availability of photos. Reviews 5x7 b&w glossy prints. Offers no additional payment for photos accepted with ms. Captions preferred. Buys one-time rights.
Columns/Departments: Public Affairs (1,000-2,000 words); Life in Israel (1,000-2,000 words). Buys 5 mss/year. Query. Length: 1,000-2,000 words. Pays $75 maximum.
Tips: "We are interested in adding to our stable of freelance writers. The best way to break in is to send a detailed query about a subject you would like to handle for the magazine. All queries will be carefully considered and answered. We've been cut from 8 to 5 issues per year for budgetary reasons, so we are buying less material. But we are still reading whatever comes in. How-to articles in our magazine fall in the categories of Jewish-oriented travel and performance of rituals or religious observance. Humorous treatments of coping with life in Israel are also enjoyed by our readers."

BRIDAL GUIDE, "The How-to for I Do", Globe Communications Corp., 441 Lexington Ave., New York NY 10017. (212)949-4040. Editor: Suzanne Kresse. 80% freelance written. Prefers to work with published/established writers; works with a small number of new/unpublished writers each year. A bimonthly magazine covering wedding planning and the first home. *"Bridal Guide* is designed to be used as a wedding planning guide and keepsake for couples soon to be married. Information about modern wedding trends is directed to brides, grooms, and parents." Circ. 300,000. Pays on publication. Publishes ms an average of 2 months after acceptance. Byline given. Offers up to 50% kill fee. Buys first North American serial rights, second serial (reprint) rights and all rights. Submit seasonal/holiday material 6 months in advance. Simultaneous submissions and previously published submissions OK. Query for electronic submissions. Computer printout submissions acceptable; prefers letter-quality to dot-matrix. Reports in 1 month on queries; 2 months on manuscript. Sample copy $2.50.

Nonfiction: How-to, humor, inspirational, interview/profile, personal experience, religious and travel. Buys 132 mss/year. Send complete ms. Length: 1,000-20,000 words. Pays $200-1,000. Sometimes pays the expenses of writers on assignment.

Photos: Send photos with submission. Reviews 2x3 transparencies and prints. Additional payment for photos accepted with ms. Captions, model releases, and identification of subjects required.

Tips: *"Bridal Guide* is now published six times per year. Along with the new bimonthly schedule, our format has increased. You will find sixteen departments and five feature areas in each issue. This means expanded writing opportunities and greater exposure through our national distribution of 300,000 copies. The magazine offers re-marriage features as well as the etiquette of divorce problems in wedding planning. New information on all aspects of the perfect wedding from initial arrangements to the reception festivities is featured in each issue. Special stories include in-depth coverage of fashion, registry, emotions and honeymoons. Planning the first home is highlighted with specific information on major purchases. The areas of our publication most open to freelancers include how-to stories in bridal fashion, ethnic customs, religious ceremonies, remarriage, etiquette, and honeymoons, celebrity weddings, unusual weddings, wedding planning."

BRIDAL TRENDS, (formerly *Bridal Fair*), Meridian Publishing, Inc., Box 10010, Ogden UT 84409. (801)394-9446. Editor: Marjorie H. Rice. 65% freelance written. Monthly magazine with useful articles for today's bride. Circ. 60,000. Pays on acceptance. Publishes ms an average of 10 months after acceptance. Byline given. Buys first rights, second serial (reprint) rights and non-exclusive reprint rights. Simultaneous, photocopied and previously published submissions OK. Reports in 6 weeks. Sample copy for $1 and 9x12 SAE; writer's guidelines for business size SASE. All requests for sample copies and guidelines should be addressed Attn: Editorial Assistant.

Nonfiction: "General interest articles about traditional and modern approaches to weddings. Topics include all aspects of ceremony and reception planning; flowers; invitations; catering; wedding apparel and fashion trends for the bride, groom, and other members of the wedding party, etc. Also featured are honeymoon destinations, how to build a relationship and keep romance alive, and adjusting to married life." Buys approximately 30 mss/year. Query. Length: 1,200 words. Pays 15¢/word for first rights plus non-exclusive reprint rights. Payment for second rights is negotiable.

Photos: State availability of photos with query letter. Color transparencies and 5x7 or 8x10 prints are preferred. Pays $35 for inside photo; pays $50 for cover. Captions, model release, and identification of subjects required.

Tips: "We publish articles that detail each aspect of wedding planning: invitations, choosing your flowers, deciding on the style of your wedding, and choosing a photographer and caterer."

BRIDE'S, Conde Nast Bldg., 350 Madison Ave., New York NY 10017. (212)880-8800. Editor-in-Chief: Barbara D. Tober. 40% freelance written. Eager to work with new/unpublished writers. A bimonthly magazine for the first- or second-time bride, her family and friends, the groom and his family and friends. Circ. 410,000. Pays on acceptance. Publishes ms an average of 2 months after acceptance. Buys all rights. Also buys first and second serial rights for book excerpts on marriage, communication, finances. Offers 20% kill fee, depending on circumstances. Buys 40 unsolicited mss/year. Byline given. Reports in 2 months. Computer printout submissions acceptable; no dot-matrix. Address mss to Features Department. Writer's guidelines for 4x9½ SASE.

Nonfiction: "We want warm, personal articles, optimistic in tone, with help offered in a clear, specific way. All issues should be handled within the context of marriage. How-to features on all aspects of marriage: communications, in-laws, careers, money, sex, housing, housework, family planning, marriage after a baby, religion, interfaith marriage, step-parenting, second marriage, reaffirmation of vows; informational articles on the realities of marriage, the changing roles of men and women, the kind of troubles in engagement that are likely to become big issues in marriage; stories from couples or marriage authorities that illustrate marital problems and solutions to men and women; book excerpts on marriage, communication, finances, sex; and how-to features on wedding planning that offer expert advice. Also success stories of marriages of long duration. We use first-person pieces and articles that are well researched, relying on quotes from authorities in the field, and anecdotes and dialogues from real couples. We publish first-person essays on provocative topics unique to marriage." Query or submit complete ms. Article outline preferred. Length: 1,000-3,000 words. Pays $300-800.

Columns/Departments: The Love column accepts reader love poems, for $25 each. The Something New section accepts reader wedding planning and craft ideas; pays $25.

Tips: "Since marriage rates are up and large, traditional weddings are back in style, and since more women work than ever before, do *not* query us on just living together or becoming a stay-at-home wife after marriage. Send us a query or a well-written article that is both easy to read and offers real help for the bride or groom as she/he adjusts to her/his new role. No first-person narratives on wedding and reception planning, home furnishings, cooking, fashion, beauty, travel. We're interested in unusual ideas, experiences, and lifestyles. No 'I used baby pink rose buds' articles."

CHATELAINE, 777 Bay St., Toronto, Ontario M5W 1A7 Canada. Editor-in-Chief: Mildred Istona. 75% freelance written. Prefers to work with published/established writers. Monthly general-interest magazine for Canadian women, from age 20 and up. "*Chatelaine* is read by one woman in three across Canada, a readership that spans almost every age group but is concentrated among those 25 to 45 including homemakers and working women in all walks of life." Circ. over 1 million. Pays on acceptance. Publishes ms an average of 3 months after acceptance. Byline given. Computer printout submissions OK; prefers letter-quality to dot-matrix. Reports within 2 weeks. All mss must be accompanied by a SASE (IRCs in lieu of stamps if sent from outside Canada). Sample copy $2 and postage; free writer's guidelines.

Nonfiction: Elizabeth Parr, senior editor, articles. Submit a one-page outline/query first. Full-length major pieces run from 1,500 to 3,000 words. Pays minimum $1,200 for acceptable major article. Buys first North American serial rights in English and French (the latter to cover possible use in *Chatelaine*'s sister French-language edition, edited in Montreal for French Canada). "We look for important national Canadian subjects, examining any and all facets of Canadian life, especially as they concern or interest women. For all serious articles, deep, accurate, thorough research and rich detail are required. Writers new to us should query Diane Passa, managing editor, with ideas for upfront columns on nutrition, fitness, relationships, health, and parents and kids." Pays $350 for about 750 words. Prefers queries for nonfiction subjects on initial contact plus a resume and writing samples. Also seeks full-length personal experience stories with deep emotional impact. Pays $750. Pays expenses of writers on assignment.

Tips: Features on beauty, food, fashion and home decorating are supplied by staff writers and editors, and unsolicited material is not considered.

COUNTRY WOMAN, (formerly *Farm Woman*), Reiman Publications, Box 643, Milwaukee WI 53201. (414)423-0100. Editor: Ann Kaiser. Managing Editor: Eleanor Jacobs. 75-85% freelance written. Eager to work with new/unpublished writers. Bimonthly magazine on the interests of country women. "*Country Woman* is for contemporary rural women of all ages and backgrounds and from all over the U.S. and Canada. It includes a sampling of the diversity that makes up rural women's lives—love of home, family, farm, ranch, community, hobbies, enduring values, humor, attaining new skills and appreciating present, past and future all within the content of the lifestyle that surrounds country living." Circ. 330,000. Pays on acceptance. Publishes ms an average of 1 year after acceptance. Byline given. Offers 20% kill fee. Buys first North American serial rights, one-time rights, and second serial (reprint) rights; makes some work-for-hire assignments. Submit seasonal/holiday material 4-5 months in advance. Photocopied and previously published (on occasion) submissions OK. Computer printout submissions acceptable; no dot-matrix. Reports in 1 month on queries; 4-6 weeks on mss. Sample copy for $2.50 and 9x12 SAE; writer's guidelines for SAE and 1 first class stamp.

Nonfiction: General interest, historical/nostalgic, how-to (crafts, community projects, family relations, self-improvement, decorative, antiquing, etc.); humor; inspirational; interview/profile; personal experience; photo feature; and travel, all pertaining to a rural woman's interest. Buys 100+ mss/year. Query, or send complete ms. Length: 1,000 words maximum. Pays $40-300. Pays the expenses of writers on assignment.

Photos: Send photos with query or ms. Reviews 35mm or 2¼ transparencies. Pays $25-100 for b&w; $60-200 for color. Captions, model releases and identification of subjects required. Buys one-time rights.

Columns/Departments: Why Farm Wives Age Fast (humor), I Remember When (nostalgia), Country Decorating, and Shopping Comparison (new product comparisons). Buys 20 mss (maximum)/year. Query or send complete ms. Length: 500-1,000 words. Pays $55-200.

Fiction: Adventure, humorous, mainstream, suspense and western. Buys 5 mss (maximum)/year. Query or send complete ms. Length: 1,000-1,500 words. Pays $75-200.

Poetry: Traditional, avant-garde, free verse, and light verse. Buys 20 poems/year. Submit maximum 6 poems. Length: 5-24 lines. Pays $25-60.

Fillers: Jokes, anecdotes, short humor and consumer news (e.g. safety, tips, etc.). Buys 40/year. Length: 40-250 words. Pays $25-40.

Tips: "We have recently broadened our focus to include 'country' women, not just women on farms and ranches. This allows freelancers a wider scope in material. Write as clearly and with as much zest and enthusiasm as possible. We love good quotes, supporting materials (names, places, etc.) and strong leads and closings. Readers relate strongly to where they live and the lifestyle they've chosen. They want to be informed and entertained, and that's just exactly why they subscribe. Readers are busy—not too busy to read—but when they do sit down, they want good writing, reliable information and something that feels like a reward. How-to, humor, personal experience and nostalgia are areas most open to freelancers. Profiles, to a certain degree, are also open. We are always especially receptive to short items—250 words, 400 words and so on. Be accurate and fresh in approach.''

FAIRFIELD COUNTY WOMAN, NEW HAVEN COUNTY WOMAN, HARTFORD WOMAN, FCW, Inc., Chadwick & Duke, Publishers, 15 Bank St., Stamford CT 06901. (203)323-3105. Editor: Ina B. Chadwick. Regional Editor (New Haven): Tricia Buie, 31 Whitney St., New Haven CT 06501. Regional Editor (Hartford): Roberta Burns-Howard, 595 Franklin Ave., Hartford CT 06114. "Send a query, not an article."

FAMILY CIRCLE GREAT IDEAS, 110 Fifth Ave., New York NY 10011. Managing Editor: Shari E. Hartford. 20-95% freelance written. Published 5 times/year; 128 pages. Circ. 1,000,000. Pays on acceptance. Publishes ms an average of 3 months after acceptance. Buys all rights. Submit Christmas material 5 months in advance. Computer printout submissions acceptable; no dot-matrix. Reports in 2 weeks. Sample copy $2.25. Writer's guidelines upon request with SASE.
Nonfiction: How-to (crafts and food) and new product (for home and family). "Writers have their best chance of breaking in to the *Great Ideas* series with craft ideas. Craft projects are also included in the books not specifically devoted to crafts." Will also review regionally-based features. Article queries should be directed to managing editor; must be accompanied by SASE. Buys 2 mss/issue. Query. Pays $150-350.
Tips: "We do not accept fiction, poetry, or true-life drama."

FAMILY CIRCLE MAGAZINE, 110 Fifth Ave., New York NY 10011. (212)463-1000. Editor-in-Chief and President: Arthur Hettich. 60% freelance written. For women. Published 17 times/year. Usually buys all rights. Offers 25% kill fee. Byline given. Pays on acceptance. "We are a *service* magazine. Query should stress how-to angle; we want articles that will help our readers. We are especially interested in writers who have a solid background in the areas they suggest." Reports in 6-8 weeks.
Nonfiction: Susan Ungaro, articles editor. Women's interest subjects such as family and social relationships, children, physical and mental health, nutrition, self-improvement, travel. Service articles. For travel, interested mainly in local material. "We look for service stories told in terms of people. We want well-researched service journalism on all subjects." Query. Length: 1,000-2,500 words. Pays $250-2,500.
Tips: Query letters should be "concise and to the point. We get some with 10 different suggestions—by the time they're passed on to all possible editors involved, weeks may go by." Also, writers should "keep close tabs on *Family Circle* and other women's magazines to avoid submitting recently run subject matter."

GLAMOUR, Conde Nast, 350 Madison Ave., New York NY 10017. (212)880-8800. Editor-in-Chief: Ruth Whitney. 75% freelance written. Works with a small number of new/unpublished writers each year. For college-educated women, 18-35 years old. Monthly. Circ. 2.3 million; 7 million readers. Pays on acceptance. Offers 20% kill fee. Publishes ms an average of 6-12 months after acceptance. Byline given. Computer printout submissions OK "if the material is easy to read"; prefers letter-quality to dot-matrix. Reports in 5 weeks. Writer's guidelines for SASE.
Nonfiction: Judy Coyne, articles editor. "Editorial approach is 'how-to' with articles that are relevant in the areas of careers, health, psychology, interpersonal relationships, etc. We look for queries that are fresh and include a contemporary, timely angle. Fashion, beauty, decorating, travel, food and entertainment are all staff-written. We use 1,000 word opinion essays for our Viewpoint section. Pays $500. Our His/Hers column features generally stylish essays on relationships or comments on current mores by male and female writers in alternate months. Pays $1,000 for His/Hers mss. Buys first North American serial rights." Buys 10-12 mss/issue. Query "with letter that is detailed, well-focused, well-organized, and documented with surveys, statistics and research, personal essays excepted." Short articles and essays (1,500-2,000 words) pay $1,000 and up; longer mss (2,500-3,000 words) pay $1,500 minimum on acceptance. Sometimes pays the expenses of writers on assignment.
Tips: "We're looking for sharply focused ideas by strong writers and constantly raising our standards. We are interested in getting new writers, and we are approachable, mainly because our range of topics is so broad."

ALWAYS submit manuscripts or queries with a self-addressed, stamped envelope (SASE) within your country or International Reply Coupons purchased from the post office for other countries.

GOOD HOUSEKEEPING, Hearst Corp., 959 8th Ave., New York NY 10019. (212)262-3614. Editor-in-Chief: John Mack Carter. Executive Editor: Mina Mulvey. Managing Editor: Mary Fiore. Prefers to work with published/established writers. Monthly; 250 pages. Circ. 5,000,000. Pays on acceptance. Buys all rights. Pays 25% kill fee. Byline given. Submit seasonal/holiday material 6 months in advance. Computer printout submissions acceptable; no dot-matrix. Reports in 6 weeks. Sample copy $2. Free writer's guidelines with SASE.
Nonfiction: Joan Thursh, articles editor. How-to/informational; investigative stories; inspirational; interview; nostalgia; personal experience; and profile. Buys 4-6 mss/issue. Query. Length: 1,500-2,500 words. Pays $1,500 on acceptance for full articles from new writers. Regional Editor: Shirley Howard. Pays $250-350 for local interest and travel pieces of 2,000 words. Pays the expenses of writers on assignment.
Photos: Herbert Bleiweiss, art director. Photos purchased on assignment mostly. Some short photo features with captions. Pays $100-350 for b&w; $200-400 for color photos. Query. Model releases required.
Columns/Departments: Light Housekeeping & Fillers, edited by Rosemary Leonard. Humorous short-short prose and verse. Jokes, gags, anecdotes. Pays $25-50. The Better Way, edited by Erika Mark. Ideas and in-depth research. Query. Pays $250-500. "Mostly staff written; only outstanding ideas have a chance here."
Fiction: Naome Lewis, fiction editor. Uses romance fiction and condensations of novels that can appear in one issue. Looks for reader identification. "We get 1,500 unsolicited mss/month—includes poetry; a freelancer's odds are overwhelming—but we do look at all submissions." Send complete mss. Length: 1,500 words (short-shorts); novel according to merit of material; average 5,000 words short stories. Pays $1,000 minimum for fiction short-shorts; $1,250 for short stories.
Poetry: Arleen Quarfoot, poetry editor. Light verse and traditional. "Presently overstocked." Poems used as fillers. Pays $5/line for poetry on acceptance.
Tips: "Always send an SASE. We prefer to see a query first. Do not send material on subjects already covered in-house by the Good Housekeeping Institute—these include food, beauty, needlework and crafts."

‡HOMEWORKING MOTHERS, Mothers' Home Business Network, Box 423, East Meadow NY 11554. (516)997-7394. Editor: Georganne Fiumara. 80% freelance written. Eager to work with new/unpublished writers. Quarterly newsletter "written for mothers who have home businesses or would like to. These mothers want to work at home so that they can spend more time with their children." Circ. 10,000. Pays on publication. Publishes ms an average of 3-6 months after acceptance. Byline given. Buys one-time rights. Submit seasonal/holiday material 8 months in advance. Simultaneous, photocopied and previously published submissions OK. Computer printout submissions OK. Reports in 1 month on queries; 6 weeks on mss. Sample copy $2 with #10 SAE and 56¢ postage.
Nonfiction: Book excerpts, essays, how-to, humor, inspirational, personal experience and technical—home business information "all relating to working at home or home-based businesses." Special issues feature excerpts and reviews of books and periodicals about working at home (spring) and tax-related articles (winter). No articles about questionable home business opportunities. Buys 16-20 mss/year. Query with published clips, or send complete ms. Length: 300-1,000 words. Pays 5-10¢/word. Sometimes pays writers with contributor copies or in advertising or promoting a writer's business if applicable. "We would like to receive in-depth descriptions of one home business possibility, i.e., bookkeeping, commercial art, etc.—at least 3,000 words to be published in booklet form. (Pays $150 and buys all rights)."
Columns/Departments: It's My Business (mothers describe their businesses, how they got started, and how they handle work and children at the same time); Advice for Homeworking Mothers (business, marketing and tax basics written by professionals); Considering the Possibilities (ideas and descriptions of legitimate home business opportunities); A Look at a Book (excerpts from books describing some aspect of working at home or popular work-at-home professions); and Time Out for Kids (inspirational material to help mothers cope). Length: Varies, but average is 500 words. Buys 4 mss/year. Send complete ms. Pays 5-10¢/word.
Poetry: Free verse, light verse and traditional. "About being a mother working at home or home business." Submit maximum 5 poems. Pays $10.
Fillers: Facts and newsbreaks "about working at home for 'Take Note' page." Length: 150 words maximum. Pays $10.
Tips: "We prefer that the writer have personal experience with this lifestyle or be an expert in the field when giving general home business information. It's My Business and Time Out for Kids are most open to freelancers. Writers should read *HM* before trying to write for us."

‡THE JOYFUL WOMAN, For and About Bible-believing Women Who Want God's Best, The Joyful Woman Ministries, Inc., Business Office: Box 90028, Chattanooga TN 37412. (615)698-7318. Editor: Elizabeth Handford, 118 Shannon Lake Circle, Greenville SC 29615. 50% freelance written. Works with small number of new/unpublished writers each year. Bimonthly magazine covering the role of women in home and business. "*The Joyful Woman* hopes to encourage, stimulate, teach, and develop the Christian woman to reach the full potential of her womanhood." Circ. 12,000. Pays on publication. Publishes ms an average of 4 months after acceptance. Byline given. Buys first rights. Submit seasonal/holiday material 4 months in advance. Photocopied submissions OK. Computer printout submissions acceptable; prefers letter-quality to dot-matrix. Reports in 3 months. Sample copy for 9x12 SAE with 4 first class stamps; writer's guidelines for #10 with 1 first class stamp.

Nonfiction: Book excerpts, how-to (housekeeping, childrearing, career management, etc.); inspirational; interview/profile (of Christian women); and personal experience. "We publish material on every facet of the human experience, considering not just a woman's spiritual needs, but her emotional, physical, and intellectual needs and her ministry to others." Buys 80-100 mss/year. Send complete ms. Length: 700-2,500 words. Pays about 2¢/word.

Tips: "The philosophy of the woman's liberation movement trends to minimize the unique and important ministries God has in mind for a woman. We believe that being a woman, and a Christian ought to be joyful and fulfilling personally and valuable to God, whatever her situation—career woman, wife, mother, daughter."

LADIES' HOME JOURNAL, Meredith Corporation, 100 Park Ave., New York NY 10017. (212)953-7070. Editor-in-Chief: Myrna Blyth. Executive Editor: Jan Goodwin. 50% freelance written. A monthly magazine focusing on issues of concern to women. "*LHJ* reflects the lives of contemporary mainstream women and provides the information she needs and wants to live in today's world." Circ. 5,000,000. Pays on acceptance. Publishes ms an average of 3 months after acceptance, but varies according to needs. Byline given. Offers 25% kill fee. Rights bought vary with submission. Submit seasonal/holiday material 6 months in advance. Photocopied submissions OK. Computer printout submissions OK; prefers letter-quality to dot-matrix. Reports in 6 weeks. Sample copy $1.50 with SAE and $1.25 postage. Free writer's guidelines.
Nonfiction: Jan Goodwin, executive editor, oversees the entire department, and may be queried directly. In addition, submissions on the following subjects may be directed to the editors listed for each: Psychology and relationships (senior editor Margery Rosen); medical/health (senior editor Beth Weinhouse); investigative reports or exposes (associate editor Diane Salvatore); and celebrities (associate editor Eric Sherman). Any editor may be queried on person ordeal stories, general entertainment, politics, profiles, self-improvement, lifestyles and trends. Travel and career pieces for Prime Showcase may be sent to Connie Leisure. Query with published clips or send complete ms. Length: 2,000-4,500 words. Fees vary; average is between $1,000 and $3,500. Pays expenses of writers on assignment.
Photos: State availability of photos with submission. Offers variable payment for photos accepted with ms. Captions, model releases and identification of subjects required. Rights bought vary with submissions.
Columns/Departments: Query the following editors for column ideas. A Woman Today (Pam Guthrie, associate editor); Money News (Katherine Barrett, contributing editor); Parent News (Mary Mohler, managing editor); and Pet News (Nina Keilin).
Fiction: "We consider any short story or novel that is submitted by an agent or publisher that we feel will work for our audience." Buys 12 mss/year. Length: 4,000 words. Fees vary with submission.

‡LADY'S CIRCLE, Lopez Publications, Inc., 105 East 35th St., New York NY 10016. (212)689-3933. Editor: (Mr.) Adrian B. Lopez. Managing Editor: Mary F. Bemis. 50% freelance written. Bimonthly magazine. "Midwest homemakers. Christian. Middle to low income. A large number of senior citizens read *Lady's Circle*." Circ. 300,000. Pays on publication. Byline given. Submit seasonal/holiday material 6 months in advance. Photocopied and previously published submissions OK. Reports in 2 months on queries; 3 months on mss. Sample copy for 8½x11 SAE with $1.07 postage. Free writer's guidelines.
Nonfiction: Historical/nostalgic, how-to (crafts, cooking, hobbies), humor, inspirational, interview/profile, opinion, personal experience and religious. No travel. Buys 50-75 mss/year. Query. Pays $125 for unsolicited articles. Sometimes pays expenses of writers on assignment.
Photos: State availability of photos with submission. Reviews negatives, transparencies and prints. Offers $10/photo. Model releases and identification of subjects required.
Columns/Departments: Sound Off (pet peeves) 250 words; Readers' Cookbook (readers send in recipes); and Helpful Hints (hints for kitchen, house, etc.) 3-4 lines per hint. Send complete ms. Pays $5-10.
Fiction: Humorous, mainstream, religious, romance, and slice-of-life vignettes. Nothing experimental. No foul language. Buys 3 mss/year. Send complete ms. Pays $125.
Fillers: Contact Adrian B. Lopez. Anecdotes and short humor. Buys 35/year. Length: 100 words. Pays $5-25.
Tips: "Write for guidelines. A good query is always appreciated. Fifty percent of our magazine is open to freelancers."

McCALL'S, 230 Park Ave., New York NY 10169. (212)551-9500. Editor: Elizabeth Sloan. Managing Editor: Lisel Eisenheimer. 90% freelance written. "Study recent issues." Our publication "carefully and conscientiously services the needs of the woman reader—concentrating on matters that directly affect her life and offering information and understanding on subjects of personal importance to her." Monthly. Circ. 5,000,000. Pays on acceptance. Publishes ms an average of 6 months after acceptance. Offers 20% kill fee. Byline given. Buys first or exclusive North American rights. Computer printout submissions acceptable; no dot-matrix. Reports in 2 months. Writer's guidelines for SASE.
Nonfiction: Lisel Eisenheimer, managing editor. No subject of wide public or personal interest is out of bounds for *McCall's* so long as it is appropriately treated. The editors are seeking meaningful stories of personal experience, fresh slants for self-help and relationship pieces, and well-researched articles and narratives dealing with social problems concerning readers. *McCall's* buys 200-300 articles/year, many in the 1,000- to

1,500-word length. Pays variable rates for nonfiction. Helen Del Monte and Andrea Thompson are editors of nonfiction books, from which *McCall's* frequently publishes excerpts. These are on subjects of interest to women: personal narratives, celebrity biographies and autobiographies, etc. Almost all features on food, household equipment and management, fashion, beauty, building and decorating are staff-written. Query. "All manuscripts must be submitted on speculation, and *McCall's* accepts no responsibility for unsolicited manuscripts." Sometimes pays the expenses of writers on assignment.

Columns/Departments: Child Care (edited by Maureen Smith Williams); short items that may be humorous, helpful, inspiring and reassuring. Pays $100 and up. Vital Signs (edited by Denise Webb); short items on health and medical news. Pay varies. VIP-ZIP (edited by Lydia Moss); high-demography regional section. Largely service-oriented, it covers travel, decorating and home entertainment.

Fiction: Helen Del Monte, department editor. Not considering unsolicited fiction. "Again the editors would remind writers of the contemporary woman's taste and intelligence. Most of all, fiction can awaken a reader's sense of identity, deepen her understanding of herself and others, refresh her with a laugh at herself, etc. *McCall's* looks for stories which will have meaning for an adult reader of some literary sensitivity. *No* stories that are grim, depressing, fragmentary or concerned with themes of abnormality or violence. *McCall's* principal interest is in short stories; but fiction of all lengths is considered." Length: about 3,000 words average. Length for short-shorts: about 2,000 words. Payment begins at $1,500; $2,000 for full-length stories.

Poetry: Helen Del Monte, poetry editor. Poets with a "very original way of looking at their subjects" are most likely to get her attention. *McCall's* needs poems on love, the family, relationships with friends and relatives, familiar aspects of domestic and suburban life, Americana, and the seasons. Pays $5/line on acceptance for first North American serial rights. Length: no longer than 30 lines.

Tips: "Except for humor, query first. We are interested in holiday-related pieces and personal narratives. We rarely use essays. We don't encourage an idea unless we think we can use it. Preferred length: 750-2,000 words. Address submissions to Margot Gilman unless otherwise specified."

MADEMOISELLE, 350 Madison Ave., New York NY 10017. Michelle Stacey, executive editor, articles. 95% freelance written. Prefers to work with published/established writers. Columns are written by columnists; "sometimes we give new writers a 'chance' on shorter, less complex assignments." Directed to college-educated, unmarried working women 18-34. Circ. 1,100,000. Reports in 1 month. Buys first North American serial rights. Pays on acceptance; rates vary. Publishes ms an average of 1 year after acceptance. Computer printout submissions are acceptable "but only letter-quality, double-spaced; no dot-matrix."

Nonfiction: Particular concentration on articles of interest to the intelligent young woman, including personal relationships, health, careers, trends, and current social problems. Send health queries to Ellen Welty, health editor. Send entertainment queries to Gini Sikes, entertainment editor. Query with published clips. Length: 1,500-3,000 words.

Art: Kati Korpijaakko, art director. Commissioned work assigned according to needs. Photos of fashion, beauty, travel. Payment ranges from no-charge to an agreed rate of payment per shot, job series or page rate. Buys all rights. Pays on publication for photos.

Fiction: Eileen Schnurr, fiction and books editor. Quality fiction by both established and unknown writers. "We are interested in encouraging and publishing new writers and welcome unsolicited fiction manuscripts. However we are not a market for formula stories, genre fiction, unforgettable character portraits, surprise endings or oblique stream of consciousness sketches. We are looking for well-told stories that speak in fresh and individual voices and help us to understand ourselves and the world we live in. Stories of particular relevance to young women have an especially good chance, but stories need not be by or from the point of view of a woman—we are interested in good fiction on any theme from any point of view." Buys first North American serial rights. Pays $1,500 for short stories (10-25 pages); $1,000 for short shorts (7-10 pages). Allow 3 months for reply. SASE required. In addition to year-round unqualified acceptance of unsolicited fiction manuscripts, *Mademoiselle* conducts a once-a-year fiction contest open to unpublished writers, male and female, 18-30 years old. First prize is $1,000 plus publication in *Mademoiselle*; second prize, $500 with option to publish. Watch magazine for announcement, usually in January or February issues, or send SASE for rules, after Jan 1.

Tips: "We are looking for timely, well-researched manuscripts."

NA'AMAT WOMAN, (formerly *Pioneer Woman*), Magazine of NA'AMAT USA, the Women's Labor Zionist Organization of America, NA'AMAT USA, 200 Madison Ave., New York NY 10016. (212)725-8010. Editor: Judith A. Sokoloff. 80% freelance written. Magazine published 5 times/year covering Jewish themes and issues; Israel; women's issues; Labor Zionism; and occasional pieces dealing with social, political and economic issues. Circ. 30,000. Pays on publication. Byline given. Not copyrighted. Buys first North American serial, one-time and first serial rights; second serial (reprint) rights to book excerpts; and makes work-for-hire assignments. Reports in 1 month on queries, 2 months on mss. Writer's guidelines for SASE.

Nonfiction: Expose; general interest (Jewish); historical/nostalgic; interview/profile; opinion; personal experience; photo feature; travel (Israel); art; and music. "All articles must be of interest to the Jewish community." Buys 35 mss/year. Query with clips of published work or send complete ms. Pays 8¢/word.

Photos: State availability of photos. Pays $10-30 for b&w contact sheet and 4x5 or 5x7 prints. Captions and identification of subjects required. Buys one-time rights.

Columns/Departments: Film and book reviews with Jewish themes. Buys 20-25 mss/year. Query with clips of published work or send complete ms. Pays 8¢/word.

Fiction: Historical/nostalgic, humorous, women-oriented, and novel excerpts. "Good intelligent fiction with Jewish slant. No maudlin nostalgia or trite humor." Buys 3 mss/year. Send complete ms. Length: 1,200-3,000 words. Pays 8¢/word.

NEW WOMAN MAGAZINE, Murdoch Magazines, 215 Lexington Ave., New York NY 10016. (212)685-4790. Editor: Pat Miller. Managing Editor: Karen Walden. 80% freelance written. Prefers to work with published/established writers, and works with a small number of new/unpublished writers each year. A monthly general interest women's magazine for ages 25-35. "We're especially interested in self-help in love and work (career); we also cover food, fashion, beauty, travel, money." Circ. 1.15 million. Pays on acceptance. Publishes ms an average of 6 months after acceptance. Byline given. Offers 20% kill fee. Buys first North American serial rights and second serial (reprint) rights. Submit seasonal/holiday material 8 months in advance. Simultaneous, photocopied and previously published submissions OK. Computer printout submissions acceptable (double space and leave a wide righthand margin); prefers letter-quality to dot-matrix. Reports in 1 month. Writer's guidelines for business size SAE with 1 first class stamp.

Nonfiction: Stephanie von Hirschberg and Donna Jackson, senior editors. Articles or essays on relationships, psychology, personal experience, travel, health, career advice and money. Does one special section on Money, Careers and/or Health every year. No book or movie reviews, advice columns, fashion, food or beauty material. Buys 75-100 mss/year. Query with published clips or send complete ms. Length: 1,000-3,500 words. Pays $500-2,000. Pays the telephone expenses of writers on assignment.

Photos: State availability of photos with submission. Offers no additional payment for photos accepted with ms. Captions, model releases and identification of subjects required. Buys one-time rights.

Fiction: Sarah Medford (book excerpts); Donna Jackson (short stories). No unsolicited ms except through agent. Buys 6-8 mss/year. Length: 2,000-5,000 words.

Poetry: Send to Jean Gibbons. Light verse. Buys 12 poems/year. Length: 4-40 lines. Pays $50-100.

Fillers: Rosemarie Lennon, fillers editor. Facts, newsbreaks and newspaper clips (for Briefing section). Buys 3/year. Length: 200-500 words. Pays $10-200.

Tips: "The best approach for breaking in to our publication is a personal letter, with clippings of published work, telling us what you're interested in, what you really like to write about, and your perceptions of *New Woman*. It counts a lot when a writer loves the magazine, and responds to it on a personal level. Psychology and relationships articles are most open to freelancers. Best tip: *familiarity with the magazine*. We look for originality, solid research, depth, and a friendly, accessible style."

PLAYGIRL, 801 Second Ave., New York NY 10017. (212)986-5100. Editor-in-Chief: Nancie S. Martin. 75% freelance written. Prefers to work with published/established writers. Monthly entertainment magazine for 18-to 34-year-old females. Circ. 850,000. Average issue includes 4 articles and 2 interviews. Pays 1 month after acceptance. Publishes ms an average of 5 months after acceptance. Byline given. Offers 20% kill fee. Buys all rights. Submit seasonal material 4 months in advance. Simultaneous and photocopied submissions OK, if so indicated. Computer printout submissions acceptable; prefers letter-quality to dot-matrix. Reports in 1 month on queries; in 2 months on mss. Sample copy $5. Writer's guidelines for SASE.

Nonfiction: Humor for the modern woman; exposes (related to women's issues); interview (Q&A format with major show business celebrities); articles on sexuality; medical breakthroughs; relationships; coping; and careers; insightful, lively articles on current issues; and investigative pieces particularly geared to *Playgirl*. Buys 6 mss/issue. Query with clips of previously published work. Length: 1,500-2,500 words. Pays $500-1,000. Sometimes pays the expenses of writers on assignment.

Fiction: Mary Ellen Strote, fiction editor. Contemporary romance stories of 2,500 words. Send complete fiction ms. "The important thing to remember is we don't want graphic sex, and no adventure, suspense, science fiction, murder or mystery stories. We want something emotional." Pays $300 and up for fiction.

Tips: "We are not a beginner's nonfiction market. We're looking for major clips and don't really consider non-published writers."

POLITICAL WOMAN, The Non-partisan Journal for the Thinking Woman, United Resource Services, Suite 254, 4521 Campus Dr., Irvine CA 92715. (714)854-3506. Editor: Sally Corngold. Managing Editor: Cynthia K. Horrocks. 95% freelance written. "Prefers to receive well-edited manuscripts from new or established writers. *Political Woman* is a non-partisan quarterly magazine geared to, but not totally about or for, women. The purpose is to publish objective, informative articles of global significance in a sophisticated, readable style." Circ. 2,500. Pays on publication. Publishes ms an average of 2 months after acceptance. Byline given. Offers 50% kill fee. Buys one-time rights. Simultaneous submissions OK. Query for electronic submissions. Computer printout submissions acceptable. Reports within weeks. Sample copy $2; writer's guidelines for #10 SASE.

Nonfiction: Expose, historical/nostalgic, humor, interview/profile, personal experience, photofeature, travel (with political relevance) and political features. "We are interested in topics covered in political platforms of 1988." Buys 30-50 mss/year. Length: 500-3,000 words. Pays $50-1,000. Sometimes pays the expenses of writers on assignment.

Photos: State availability of photos with submission. Reviews 3x5 transparencies. Offers no additional payment for photos accepted with mss. Captions, model releases, and identification of subjects required. Buys one-time rights. Send SASE for annual photo contest information.

Columns/Departments: Julie Forman and Sally Corngold, column/department editors. Facing Off (opposing views on a single topic); Profile (political figures); Election Topics; and Political Issues. Buys 30-50 mss/year. Query. Length: 500-3,000 words. Pays $50-1,000.

Poetry: Joan Jefts, poetry editor. Avant-garde, free verse, haiku, light verse and traditional. Length: 6-24 lines. Pays $10-200. Send SASE for poetry contest information.

Fillers: Gary Brown, fillers editors. Anecdotes, facts, gags to be illustrated by cartoonist, newsbreaks, and short humor. Buys 20/year. Length: 50-500 words. Pays $10-300.

Tips: The area most open to freelancers is "full-length, *well-documented* exposes. These must be footnoted and sources given."

‡**RADIANCE, The Magazine for Large Women**, Box 31703, Oakland CA 94604. (415)482-0680. Editor: Alice Ansfield. 75% freelance written. A quarterly magazine encouraging "self-esteem for large women—the physical, emotional, social, cultural, spiritual aspects." Circ. 12,000. Pays on publication. Publishes ms an average of 3 months after acceptance. Byline given. Offers $15 kill fee. Buys one-time and second serial (reprint) rights. Submit seasonal/holiday material 3 months in advance. Simultaneous, photocopied and previously published submissions OK. Query for electronic submissions. Computer printout submissions OK; no dot-matrix. Reports in 2 weeks. Sample copy $1.50; writer's guidelines for business size SAE with 1 first class stamp.

Nonfiction: Book excerpts (related to large women), essays, expose, general interest, historical/nostalgic, how-to (on health/well-being/growth/awareness/fashion/movement, etc.), humor, inspirational, interview/profile, new product, opinion, personal experience, photo feature and travel. Future issues will focus on children and weight, interviews with large men, fashion update, emerging spirituality, women and the arts, and women in the media. "No diet successes or articles condemning people for being fat." Query with published clips. Length: 700-2,000 words. Pays $35-100. Sometimes pays writers with contributor copies or other premiums—"negotiable with writer and us."

Photos: State availability of photos with submission. Offers $15-50 per photo. Captions and identification of subjects preferred. Buys one-time rights.

Columns/Departments: Up Front and Personal (personal profiles of women in all areas of life); Health and Well-Being (physical/emotional well-being, self care, research); Images (designer interviews, color/style/fashion, features); Inner Journeys (spirituality awareness and growth, methods, interviews); Perspectives (cultural and political aspects of being in a larger body); Heart to Heart (poetry, artwork, inspiring). Buys 32 mss/year. Query with published clips. Length: 800-1,300 words. Pays $35-100.

Fiction: Condensed novels, ethnic, fantasy, historical, humorous, mainstream, novel excerpts, romance, science fiction, serialized novels and slice-of-life vignettes. Buys 15 mss/year. Query with published clips. Length: 800-1,500 words. Pays $35-100.

Poetry: Nothing "too political and jargony." Buys 15 poems/year. Length: 4-45 lines. Pays $20-50.

Fillers: Anecdotes, facts, gags, newsbreaks and short humor. Length: 50-200 words. Pays $10-35.

Tips: "We need talented and sensitive writers in all areas of the country, and now even in Europe and abroad. We want large women to be featured and profiled—we urge writers to look in their local area and begin to give us suggestions for print. We're an open, conscious, light-hearted magazine that's trying to help women live fully now and look at more than their bodies. Departments are most open to freelancers. Especially wanted are profiles of large women in media, arts, science, education, business, home/family, medicine, spirituality, politics."

REDBOOK MAGAZINE, 224 W. 57th St., New York NY 10019. (212)262-8284. Editor-in-Chief: Annette Capone. Managing Editor: Jennifer Johnson. Executive Editor: Judsen Culbreth. 80% freelance written. Monthly magazine; 200 pages. Circ. 4.1 million. Pays on acceptance. Publishes ms an average of 6 months after acceptance. Rights purchased vary with author and material. Computer printout submissions acceptable; prefers letter-quality to dot-matrix. Reports in 2 months. Free writer's guidelines for *Redbook* for SASE.

Nonfiction: Karen Larson, senior editor. Jean Maguire, health editor. "*Redbook* addresses young mothers between the ages of 25 and 44. Most of our readers are married with children under 18; more than half of *Redbook*'s readers work outside the home. The articles in *Redbook* entertain, guide and inspire our readers. A significant percentage of the pieces stress 'how-to,' the ways a woman can solve the problems in her everyday life. Writers are advised to read at least the last *six* issues of the magazine (available in most libraries) to get a better understanding of what we're looking for. We prefer to see queries, rather than complete manuscripts. Please enclose a sample or two of your writing as well as a stamped, self-addressed envelope." Length: articles, 2,500-3,000 words; short articles, 1,000-1,500 words. Also interested in submissions for Young Mother's Story. "We are interested in stories for the Young Mother series offering the dramatic retelling of an experience involving you, your husband or child. Possible topics might include: how you have handled a child's health or school problem, or conflicts within the family. For each 1,500-2,000 words accepted for publication as Young Mother's Story, we pay $750. Mss accompanied by a large, stamped, self-addressed envelope, must be signed, and mailed to: Young Mother's Story, c/o *Redbook Magazine*. Young Mother's reports in 3-4 months." Pays the expenses of writers on assignment.

Fiction: Deborah Purcell, fiction editor. "Out of the 35,000 unsolicited manuscripts that we receive annually, we buy about 50 stories/year. We find many more stories that, for one reason or another, are not suited to our needs but are good enough to warrant our encouraging the author to send others. Sometimes such an author's subsequent submission turns out to be something we can use. *Redbook* looks for stories by and about men and women, realistic stories and fantasies, funny and sad stories, stories of people together and people alone, stories with familiar and exotic settings, love stories and work stories. But there are a few things common to all of them, that make them stand out from the crowd. The high quality of their writing, for one thing. The distinctiveness of their characters and plots; stock characters and sitcom stories are not for us. We look for stories with a definite resolution or emotional resonance. Cool stylistic or intellectual experiments are of greater interest, we feel, to readers of literary magazines than of a magazine like *Redbook* that tries to offer insights into the hows and whys of day-to-day living. And all the stories reflect some aspect of the experience, the interests, or the dreams of *Redbook*'s particular readership." Short-short stories (7-9 pages, 1,400-1,600 words—or less) are always in demand; but short stories of 10-15 pages, (3,000-5,000 words) are also acceptable. Stories 20 pages and over have a "hard fight, given our tight space limits, but we have bought longer stories that we loved. *Redbook* no longer reads unsolicited novels." Manuscripts must be typewritten, double-spaced, and accompanied by SASE the size of the manuscript. Payment begins at $850 for short shorts; $1,000 for short stories.

Tips: "Shorter, front-of-the-book features are usually easier to develop with first-time contributors. It is very difficult to break into the nonfiction section, although we do buy Young Mother's stories, dramatic personal experience pieces (1,500-2,000 words), from previously unpublished writers. The most frequent mistakes made by writers in completing an article for us are 1) Poor organization. A piece that's poorly organized is confusing, repetitive, difficult to read. I advise authors to do full outlines before they start writing so they can more easily spot structure problems and so they have a surer sense of where their piece is headed. 2) Poor or insufficient research. Most *Redbook* articles require solid research and include: full, well-developed anecdotes from real people (not from people who exist only in the writer's imagination); clear, substantial quotes from established experts in a field; and, when available, additional research such as statistics and other information from reputable studies, surveys, etc."

SAVVY, For the Successful Woman, Family Media, 3 Park Ave., New York NY 10016. (212)340-9200. Editor-in-Chief: Annalyn Swan. Managing Editor: Ann Powell. 90% freelance written. A monthly magazine. "*Savvy* articles are written for successful women. We try to use as many women as possible for our sources. The age group of our readers falls primarily between 25 and 45 and we address both their home and office lives." Circ. 400,000. Pays 4-6 weeks after due date. Publishes ms an average of 2-5 months after acceptance. Byline given. Offers 15-20% kill fee. Buys first North American serial rights, and reprint rights. Submit seasonal/holiday material 4 months in advance. Photocopied submissions OK. Computer printout submissions acceptable; prefers letter-quality to dot-matrix. Reports as soon as possible. Free writer's guidelines with SASE.

Nonfiction: Book excerpts, humor, interview/profile, opinion, personal experience and travel. No limit on mss bought/year. Query with published clips. Length: 800-3,000 words ("depends on its position"). Pays $500 minimum. Pays the expenses of writers on assignment.

Columns/Departments: Savvy Money (how to manage, invest and save money), 900-1,000 words; Health (any topics pertaining to health: illnesses, cures, new findings, etc.), 1,000-1,200 words; and Savvy Manager (how to handle career situations, gain ground at work, change jobs, etc.), 900-1,200 words. Query with published clips. Pays $500 minimum.Travel, 1,000-1,200 Words; Dining In/Dining Out, 1,000-1,200 words.

Tips: "The best advice is to read the magazine before querying. We have expanded our Savvy Money and Savvy Manager sections to include several shorter pieces."

SELF, Conde-Nast, 350 Madison Ave., New York NY 10017. (212)880-8834. Editor: Valorie Weaver. Managing Editor: Dianne Partie. 50% freelance written. "We prefer to work with writers—even relatively new ones—with a degree, training or practical experience in specialized areas, psychology to nutrition." Monthly magazine emphasizing self improvement of emotional and physical well-being for women of all ages. Circ. 1,077,090. Average issue includes 12-20 feature articles and 4-6 columns. Pays on acceptance. Publishes ms an average of 6 months after acceptance. Byline given. Offers 20% kill fee. Buys first North American serial rights. Submit seasonal material 4 months in advance. Simultaneous and photocopied submissions OK. Computer printout submissions acceptable; prefers letter-quality to dot-matrix. Reports in 1 month. Writer's guidelines for SASE.

Nonfiction: Well-researched service articles on self improvement, mind, the psychological angle of daily activities, health, careers, nutrition, fitness, medicine, male/female relationships and money. "We try to trans-

Close-up

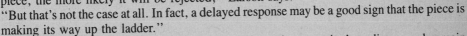

Karen Larson
Senior Editor
Redbook

"Having written freelance articles myself, I am very aware of the writer's need to get some fast feedback," says *Redbook* Senior Editor Karen Astrid Larson. An article or short story sent to the magazine however, may be reviewed by four people before a decision is made. "The writer tends to think that the longer it takes to receive word on a piece, the more likely it will be rejected," Larson says. "But that's not the case at all. In fact, a delayed response may be a good sign that the piece is making its way up the ladder."

As senior editor, Larson says she strives to know the magazine's audience and remain aware of its readers' lifestyles and needs. Freelancers who want to write for *Redbook* will be better prepared if they, too, are familiar with the audience. "Most of our readers are married; most of our readers have children; more than half of our readers work outside the home," Larson says. "They're Baby Boomers in their 20s, 30s, and early 40s whom our advertising department has dubbed the Jugglers because they're juggling home, job and family."

In her position as senior editor, Larson oversees the articles and fiction departments. She began her career at *Ladies' Home Journal* after earning her master's degree in journalism. She was senior editor at *Seventeen* magazine before joining *Redbook* in 1984.

Whether it's *Redbook* or any other magazine, Larson urges writers to be familiar with the publication before sending in a manuscript. "I know writers have heard this again and again, but I will say it still again because it's so important—know the magazine you want to write for. In order for your ideas and manuscripts to have a chance of being accepted, you have to be very familiar with the magazine. You have to have read it—and not just one issue."

In choosing nonfiction articles for *Redbook*, Larson prefers a query with a list of writing credits and "a sample or two of your writing." She says she prefers to have writers include a working title for the article in the query. "The title you come up with needn't be a stellar piece of copywriting, but the better your title, the better you're marketing your idea to the editor," she says. In addition to articles on marriage, sex and health, *Redbook* looks for special reports with a strong human interest angle that can focus on one person's story as a way of shedding light on issues of interest to readers. Parenting is also an important subject but writers should remember that the magazine looks for ideas "that will appeal to parents with older children as well as to parents of babies," Larson says.

In fiction, Larson wants to see the completed story. The magazine is always looking for light, humorous stories and two-part serials "that have strong enough plots to hold a reader's interest from one issue of *Redbook* to the next," Larson says. She prefers to see an outline for serials instead of a completed manuscript.

Larson says she enjoys discovering new writers and "coming up with an exciting idea, working with a good writer who's as excited about the idea as I am, with the result being a great piece published in *Redbook*." Although Larson, like most editors, receives many more articles than she can publish, she urges writers not to become discouraged by rejection. "Sometimes the writers with the most rejection slips end up having the most articles published because they are the ones who didn't give up!"

—Glenda Tennant Neff

late major developments and complex information in these areas into practical, personalized articles." Buys 6-10 mss/issue. Query with clips of previously published work. Length: 1,000-2,500 words. Pays $700-1,800. "We are always looking for any piece that has a psychological or behavioral side. We rely heavily on freelancers who can take an article on contraceptive research, for example, and add a psychological aspect to it. Everything should relate to the whole person." Pays the expenses of writers on assignment "with prior approval."

Photos: Submit to art director. State availability of photos. Reviews 5x7 b&w glossy prints.

Columns/Departments: Self Issues (800-1,200 words on current topics of interest to women such as nutrition and diet scams, finding time for yourself, and personal decision making); Your Health (800-1,200 words on health topics); Your Work (800-1,200 words on career topics); and Your Money (800-1,200 words on finance topics). Buys 4-6 mss/issue. Query. Pays $700-1,200.

Tips: "Original ideas backed up by research, not personal experiences and anecdotes, open our doors. We almost never risk blowing a major piece on an untried-by-us writer, especially since these ideas are usually staff-conceived. It's usually better for everyone to start small, where there's more time and leeway for re-writes. The most frequent mistakes made by writers in completing an article for us are swiss-cheese research (holes all over it which the writer missed and has to go back and fill in) and/or not personalizing the information by applying it to the reader, but instead, just reporting it."

SUNDAY WOMAN PLUS, The King Features Syndicate, 235 E. 45th, New York NY 10017. Editor: Merry Clark. 90% freelance written. Eager to work with new/unpublished writers. A weekly newspaper supplement which runs in more than 80 markets in the U.S. and Canada with circulation of more than 4 million. Publishes ms an average of 2-3 months after acceptance. Buys first rights, and second (reprint) rights to material originally published elsewhere. Computer printout submissions acceptable; no dot-matrix. Sample issue and writer's guidelines for 9x12 SAE with $1 postage.

Nonfiction: Solid, reportorial articles on topics affecting the American family, their lifestyles, relationships, careers, health, money, and business. Also uses celebrity cover stories. No beauty, fashion or pet stories. Length: 1,000-1,200 words. National focus. No poetry, fiction or essays. Pays $50-500 upon acceptance. "We are happy to consider first person stories—reprints only—for Outlook column." Reports in 2 weeks. "Submit previously published pieces for second serial publication by us." Include cover letter with address, phone number, and Social Security number; not responsible for mss submitted without SASE. Manuscripts should be typed and double-spaced. "Query, short and to the point, with clips of published material." No phone calls. Sometimes pays the expenses of writers on assignment.

Tips: "We're looking for offbeat features about people and American life today, and unusual features about people and their accomplishments. We're adding a humor category to the magazine and will be running one piece each week."

‡THE WASHINGTON WOMAN, WW Inc., Suite 1010, 1911 N. Fort Myer Dr., Arlington VA 22209. (703)522-3477. Editor: M.L. Beatty. 90% freelance written. A monthly regional women's magazine. "For the modern woman, on the upward track, dealing with career, family, etc." Circ. 40,000. Pays on publication. Publishes ms an average of 2 months after acceptance. Byline given. Offers 25% kill fee. Buys first rights. Submit seasonal/holiday material 4 months in advance. Photocopied submissions OK. Computer printout submissions OK; prefers letter-quality. Sample copy for 8½x11 with $1.24 postage.

Nonfiction: Book excerpts; essays (women, the human comedy); how-to (on getting ahead); humor (for women); interview/profile (local women—Washington DC and Maryland, and Virginia); health (women's health issues). Special issues include Brides (January); Computers (February); Financial Management (March); Hi-Tech Gadgetry (April); Health Fair (September) and Cars (October). Buys 50 mss/year. Query with published clips. Length: 300-3,000 words. Pays $75-700 for assigned articles; pays $50-350 for unsolicited articles.

Photos: Send photos with submission. Reviews contact sheets. Offers no additional payment for photos accepted with ms. Model releases and identification of subjects required. Buys one-time rights.

Columns/Departments: Speaking Out, A La Carte, Health Watch and Horoscope. Buys 30 mss/year. Send complete ms. Length: 800 words maximum.

WOMAN MAGAZINE, Harris Publishing, 1115 Broadway, New York NY 10010. (212)807-7100. Editor: Sherry Amatenstein. 40% freelance written. Works with a small number of new/unpublished writers each year. Magazine published 9 times/year covering "every aspect of a woman's life. Offers self-help orientation, guidelines on lifestyles, careers, relationships, finances, health, etc." Circ. 500,000. Pays on acceptance. Publishes ms an average of 5 months after acceptance. Byline given. Buys one-time rights. Photocopied and previously published submissions OK. Computer printout submissions acceptable; prefers letter-quality to dot-matrix. Reports in 6 weeks. Sample copy $1.95; writer's guidelines for letter-size SAE and 1 first class stamp.

Nonfiction: Excerpts (most of magazine is book and periodical reprints); how-to; humor; inspirational (how I solved a specific problem); interview/profile (short, 200-1,000 words with successful or gutsy women); round-ups and personal experience (primary freelance need: how a woman took action and helped herself—emotional punch, but not "trapped housewife" material). "The 'woman' reader is evolving into a smarter, cannier woman who wants to reach her full potential." No articles on "10 ways to pep up your marriage"—looking for unique angle. Short medical and legal updates for "Let's Put Our Heads Together" column. Buys 100 mss/year. Query with published clips or send complete ms. Length: 200-1,500 words. Pays $25-125. Sometimes pays the expenses of writers on assignment.

Columns/Departments: Woman in News (200 word pieces on successful women); and Woman Forum (controversial issues regarding women). Query with published clips or send complete ms. Length: 200-1,000 words. Pays $20-200.

Tips: "We're for all women—ones in and out of the home. We don't condescend; neither should you."

WOMAN'S DAY, 1515 Broadway, New York NY 10036. (212)719-6250. Articles Editor: Rebecca Greer. 95% of articles freelance written. 15 issues/year. Circ. over 7,000,000. Buys first and second rights to the same material. Pays negotiable kill fee. Byline given. Pays on acceptance. Computer printout submissions acceptable; no dot-matrix. Reports in 2-4 weeks on queries; longer on mss. Submit detailed queries first to Rebecca Greer.

Nonfiction: Uses articles on all subjects of interest to women—marriage, family life, childrearing, education, homemaking, money management, careers, family health, work and leisure activities. Also interested in fresh, dramatic narratives of women's lives and concerns. "These must be lively and fascinating to read." *Woman's Day* has started a new page called Reflections, a full-page essay running 1,000 words. "We're looking for both tough, strong pieces and softer essays on matters of real concern and relevance to women. We're looking for strong points of view, impassioned opinions, and fresh insights. The topics can be controversial, but they have to be convincing. We look for significant issues—medical ethics and honesty in marriage—rather than the slight and the trivial." Length: 500-3,500 words, depending on material. Payment varies depending on length, type, writer, and whether it's for regional or national use, but rates are high. Sometimes pays the expenses of writers on assignment.

Fiction: Contact Eileen Jordan, department editor. Uses high quality, genuine human interest, romance and humor, in lengths between 1,500 and 3,000 words. Payment varies. "We pay any writer's established rate, however."

Fillers: Neighbors and Tips to Share columns also pay $50/each for brief practical suggestions on homemaking, childrearing and relationships. Address to the editor of the appropriate section.

Tips: "Our primary need is for ideas with broad appeal that can be featured on the cover. We are publishing more articles and devoting more pages to textual material. We're departing from the service format once in a while to print 'some good reads.' We're more interested in investigative journalism than in the past."

THE WOMAN'S NEWSPAPER, New Jersey's largest publication for women, The Woman's Newspaper of Princeton, Inc., Box 1303, Princeton NJ 08542. (609)890-0999. Editor: Arri Parker. 75% freelance written. "We are backlogged but still looking for award-winning stories." Eager to work with new/unpublished writers. Monthly tabloid on anything of interest to women. Circ. 30,000. Pays on publication. Publishes ms an average of 2 months after acceptance. Byline given. Offers $25 kill fee. Buys first rights. Submit seasonal/holiday material 4 months in advance. Simultaneous, photocopied and previously published submissions OK, but not preferred. Query for electronic submissions. Computer printout submissions acceptable. Reports in 2 weeks. Sample copy for $2; writer's guidelines for $1.

Nonfiction: Expose, how-to, interview/profile, and technical. Nothing superficial or incorrect. Buys 180 mss/year. Query by phone. Length: open. Pays $100. Sometimes pays the expenses of writers on assignment.

Photos: State availability of photos. Prefers 5x5 prints. Pays $40. Captions, model releases and identification of subjects required. Buys one-time rights.

Tips: "Our circulation is rapidly extending outside of New Jersey. We are therefore favoring generic topics (not geographically specific) and topics specific to areas outside of New Jersey. We would like to receive more feature stories—people, situations, concepts—from anywhere in the country. No true confessions or fiction."

WOMEN IN BUSINESS, Box 8728, Kansas City MO 64114. (816)361-6621. Editor: Margaret E. Horan. 20% freelance written. Prefers to work with published/established writers, works with small number of new/unpublished writers each year, and is eager to work with new/unpublished writers. Bimonthly magazine for working women in all fields and at all levels; primarily members of the American Business Women's Association; national coverage. Circ. 110,000. Pays on acceptance. Publishes ms an average of 2-12 months after acceptance. Buys all rights. Query for electronic submissions. Sample copy and writer's guidelines for 9x12 SAE with $1 postage.

Nonfiction: General interest, self-improvement, business trends, personal finance, and health and fitness topics. Articles should be slanted toward the average working woman. No articles on women who have made it to the top or "slice of life" opinions/editorials. "We also avoid articles based on first-hand experiences (the 'I' stories)." Query or submit complete ms. Length: 1,000-1,500 words. Pays 15¢/word.

WOMEN'S CIRCLE, 306 E. Parr Rd., Berne IN 46711. Editor: Marjorie Pearl. 100% freelance written. Monthly magazine for women of all ages. Buys all rights. Pays on acceptance. Byline given. Publishes ms an average of 1 year after acceptance. Submit seasonal material 8 months in advance. Reports in 3 months. Sample copy $1. Writer's guidelines for SASE.
Nonfiction: Especially interested in stories about successful, home-based female entrepreneurs with b&w photos or color transparencies. Length: 1,000-2,000 words. Also interesting and unusual money-making ideas. Welcomes good quality crafts and how-to directions in any media - crochet, fabric, etc.

WORKING MOTHER MAGAZINE, McCall's Publishing Co., 230 Park Ave., New York NY 10169. (212)551-9412. Editor: Olivia Buehl. Executive Editor: Mary McLaughlin. 90% freelance written. Prefers to work with published/established writers; works with a small number of new/unpublished writers each year. For women who balance a career with the concerns of parenting. Monthly magazine; 140 pages. Circ. 600,000. Pays on acceptance. Publishes ms an average of 4 months after acceptance. Byline given. Buys all rights. Pays 20% kill fee. Submit seasonal/holiday material 6 months in advance. Computer printout submissions acceptable; no dot-matrix. Reports in 1 month. Sample copy $1.95; writer's guidelines for SASE.
Nonfiction: Service, humor, material pertinent to the working mother's predicament. "Don't just go out and find some mother who holds a job and describe how she runs her home, manages her children and feels fulfilled. Find a working mother whose story is inherently dramatic." Query. Buys 9-10 mss/issue. Length: 750-2,000 words. Pays $300-1,000. "We pay more to people who write for us regularly." Pays the expenses of writers on assignment.
Tips: "The most frequent mistakes made by writers in completing an article for us are not keeping our readers (the working mother) in mind throughout the article; material in the article is not properly organized; and the writing style is stilted or wordy."

WORKING WOMAN, Hal Publications, Inc., 342 Madison Ave., New York NY 10173. (212)309-9800. Executive Editor: Julia Kagan. Editor: Anne Mollegen Smith. 85% freelance written. Works with a small number of new/unpublished writers each year. Monthly magazine for executive, professional and entrepreneurial women. "Readers are ambitious, educated, affluent managers, executives, and business owners. Median age is 34. Material should be sophisticated, witty, not entry-level, and focus on work-related issues." Circ. 770,000. Pays on acceptance. Publishes ms an average of 8 months after acceptance. Byline given. Offers 20% kill fee after attempt at rewrite to make ms acceptable. Buys all rights, first rights for books, and second serial (reprint) rights. Submit seasonal/holiday material 6 months in advance. Computer printout submissions acceptable only if legible; prefers letter-quality to dot-matrix. Sample copy for $2.50 and 8½x12 SAE; writer's guidelines for SAE with 1 first class stamp.
Nonfiction: Julia Kagan, executive editor. Jacqueline Johnson, book excerpts editor. Book excerpts; how-to (management skills, small business); humor; interview/profile (high level executive, political figure or entrepreneur preferred); new product (office products, computer/high tech); opinion (issues of interest to managerial, professional, entrepreneur women); personal experience; technical (in management or small business field); travel (businesswomen's guide); and other (business). No child-related pieces that don't involve work issues; no entry-level topics; no fiction/poetry. Buys roughly 200 mss/year. Query with clips of published work. Length: 250-3,000 words. Pays $50-750. Pays the expenses of writers on assignment.
Photos: State availability of photos with ms.
Columns: Management/Enterprise, Basia Hellwig; Manager's Shoptalk, Walecia Konrad; Lifestyle, Food, Fitness, Freddi Greenberg, Health, Heather Twidale; Business Watch, Michele Morris; Computers, Technology, Roxane Farmanfarmaian. Query with clips of published work. Length: 1,200-1,500 words. Pays $400.
Tips: "Be sure to include clips with queries and to make the queries detailed (including writer's expertise in the area, if any). The writer has a better chance of breaking in at our publication with short articles and fillers as we prefer to start new writers out small unless they're very experienced elsewhere. Columns are more open than features. We do not accept phone submissions."

> 66 *Don't forget a SASE. Lack of a SASE is arrogant or ignorant, or both, because it assumes editors have lots of time to address envelopes; it's also lacking in common courtesy, and no editor wants to work with a writer who exhibits these traits.* 99
>
> —*Richard Busch*
> *editor,* USAir Magazine

Trade, Technical and Professional Journals

Almost every occupation has its own trade journal. Construction workers, doctors, teachers—almost everyone who is employed—can learn about other people with the same jobs and the same problems when they read trade publications.

A trade journal can be the voice of the industry or one of a variety of voices. It usually reports practices that can help or hurt a trade, provides information and job tips that aren't available elsewhere and can even influence the policies of the industry.

Trade journal readers are busy people. They want information conveyed succinctly and specifically about their jobs, and they want to be shown new practices, not just told about them. Because the editors and readers of a trade publication already know about their field, they expect the most accurate and up-to-date information available.

You may be able to write for trade publications if you have training or experience in one or more occupations. Or if you've been writing for consumer magazines, you may have come across an interesting business, an innovative solution to a problem or an employee who can offer special insights on his work. You may be able to write different versions of the same information for both consumer and trade publications.

Boating magazines, for example, are in the Consumer section, while marine navigation journals are listed here. Articles about boats may appear in both categories—but each will have a different audience and a different slant. You'll need to dig deeper for leads into articles for trade journals, but it can be worth the extra effort when you sell two or three articles instead of one.

Like consumer magazines, trade publications are affected by trends and competition. As a result, they are more visually-oriented and dependent on well-written, detailed how-to articles. And, like the occupations they cover, trade magazines are becoming even more specialized.

Although many trade publications are moving in the same direction as consumer magazines, don't expect their editorial requirements and practices to be the same. Sometimes a professional or trade association relies on one person to handle its journal's production plus a variety of other tasks. A few trade journals have large staffs with contributing editors who help evaluate submissions. Some are widely read outside the industry by business reporters who write for the general public. In any case, editors of these journals can't waste time on inappropriate, outdated or inferior submissions.

Trade editors frequently complain about queries that are actually computer-produced form letters. They want queries that show you have studied their magazine. Enclosing your credentials or resume may help you land assignments. The majority of trade editors prefer to assign and discuss an article before it's written. Sometimes the editor will suggest particular questions for the writer to ask.

Don't forget that trade journals within a particular category often compete with one another. You'll want to know which journals are competitors and which ones have cornered the market. An editor won't want a story that his competitor has just published—unless it's a revised version with a fresh slant.

Writing for trade journals can be a good place to start a writing career. Editors like to find reliable freelancers for assignments, and they're often willing to work with writers who know the subject and show promise in communicating it to others.

Advertising, Marketing and PR

Trade journals for advertising executives, copywriters and marketing and public relations professionals are listed in this category. Those whose main interests are the advertising and marketing of specific products, such as home furnishings, are classified under individual product categories. Journals for sales personnel and general merchandisers can be found in the Selling and Merchandising category.

ADVERTISING AGE, 740 N. Rush, Chicago IL 60611. (312)649-5200. Managing Editor: Valorie Mackie. Executive Editor: Robert Goldsborough. Currently staff-produced. Includes weekly sections devoted to one topic (i.e., marketing in southern California, agribusiness/advertising, TV syndication trends). Much of this material is done freelance—on assignment only. Pays kill fee "based on hours spent plus expenses." Byline given "except short articles or contributions to a roundup."

ADVERTISING TECHNIQUES, ADA Publishing Co., 6th Floor, 10 E. 39th St., New York NY 10016. (212)889-6500. Managing Editor: Loren Bliss. 30% freelance written. For advertising executives. Monthly magazine; 50 pages. Circ. 4,500. Pays on acceptance. Not copyrighted. Buys first and second rights to the same material. Reports in 1 month. Publishes ms an average of 2 months after acceptance. Sample copy $1.75.
Nonfiction: Articles on advertising techniques. Buys 10 mss/year. Query. Pays $50-100.

AMERICAN DEMOGRAPHICS, American Demographics, Inc., Box 68, Ithaca NY 14851. (607)273-6343. Editor: Cheryl Russell. Managing Editor: Caroline Arthur. 25% freelance written. Works with a small number of new/unpublished writers each year. For business executives, market researchers, media and communications people, public policymakers. Monthly magazine; 60 pages. Circ. 30,000. Pays on publication. Publishes ms an average of 6 months after acceptance. Buys all rights. Submit seasonal/holiday material 6 months in advance. Query for electronic submissions. Computer printout submissions acceptable; prefers letter-quality to dot-matrix. Reports in 1 month on queries; in 2 months on mss. Include self-addressed stamped postcard for return word that ms arrived safely. Sample copy for $6 and 9x11 SAE with 6 first class stamps.
Nonfiction: General interest (on demographic trends, implications of changing demographics, profile of business using demographic data); and how-to (on the use of demographic techniques, psychographics, understand projections, data, apply demography to business and planning). No anecdotal material or humor. Sometimes pays the expenses of writers on assignment.
Tips: "Writer should have clear understanding of specific population trends and their implications for business and planning. The most important thing a freelancer can do is to read the magazine and be familiar with its style and focus."

ART DIRECTION, Advertising Trade Publications, Inc., 6th Floor, 10 E. 39th St., New York NY 10016. (212)889-6500. Editor: Loren Bliss. 10% freelance written. Prefers to work with published/established writers. Emphasis on advertising design for art directors of ad agencies (corporate, in-plant, editorial, freelance, etc.). Monthly magazine; 100 pages. Circ. 12,000. Pays on publication. Buys one-time rights. Reports in 3 months. Sample copy $3.
Nonfiction: How-to articles on advertising campaigns. Pays $100 minimum.

BARTER COMMUNIQUE, Full Circle Marketing Corp., Box 2527, Sarasota FL 33578. (813)349-3300. Editor-in-Chief: Robert J. Murely. 100% freelance written. Emphasizes bartering for radio and TV station owners, cable TV, newspaper and magazine publishers and select travel and advertising agency presidents. Semiannual tabloid; 48 pages. Circ. 50,000. Pays on publication. Publishes ms an average of 3 months after acceptance. Rights purchased vary with author and material. Phone queries OK. Simultaneous, photocopied and previously published submissions OK. Computer printout submissions acceptable. Reports in 1 month. Free sample copy and writer's guidelines.

Nonfiction: Articles on "barter" (trading products, goods and services, primarily travel and advertising). Length: 1,000 words. "Would like to see travel mss on southeast U.S. and the Bahamas, and unique articles on media of all kinds. Include photos where applicable. No manuscripts on barter for products, goods and services—primarily travel and media—but also excess inventory of business to business." Pays $30-50.
Tips: "Computer installation will improve our ability to communicate."

‡**BPME IMAGE**, Broadcast Promotion and Marketing Executives, Inc., 1528A Granite Hills Dr., El Cajon CA 92019. (619)447-1227. Editor-in-Chief: Robert P. Rimes. Assistant Editor: Bill Strubbe. 80% freelance written. Works with a small number of new/unpublished writers each year. A trade journal for broadcast advertising and promotion executives, published 10 times/year. "*BPME* is a 'how-to' publication that contains editorial material designed to enhance the job performance of broadcast advertising and promotion executives, who constitute the bulk of its readers." Circ. 6,000. Pays on publication. Publishes ms an average of 3 months after acceptance. Byline given. Buys all rights. Submit seasonal/holiday material 3 months in advance. Photocopied submissions OK. Computer printout submissions OK; prefers letter-quality to dot-matrix. Reports in 3 weeks. Sample copy for $7 with 8x10 SAE and $2.35 postage.
Nonfiction: Essays, how-to, humor, interview/profile, personal experience and photo feature. "Each issue has a theme which is available in an editorial listing published in December of each year." Buys 12 mss/year. Query. Length: 800-2,500 words. Pays $300 maximum.
Photos: State availability of photos with submission. Offers $400 maximum per photo. Captions, model releases and identification of subjects required. Buys all rights.
Columns/Departments: Profile (leader in industry); My Turn (opinion). Buys 12 mss/year. Query with published clips. Length: 800-2,500 words. Pays $300 maximum.
Tips: "We would like to receive queries on any subject having to do with broadcast advertising or promotion—stunts, contests, concepts, successful advertising and promotion campaigns, and marketing management tips. Ours is such a specialized audience that it is difficult to break in to print in our publication. A full knowledge of radio and television and/or advertising will help. In short, the more research that goes into the piece, the better. We seem to favor writers who have something to say rather than lightweight puff pieces that are cleverly written. We especially like articles that are based on speeches by well-known persons in radio and TV."

BUSINESS MARKETING, Crain Communications, Inc., 220 E. 42nd St., New York NY 10017. (212)210-0191. Editor: Bob Donath. Monthly magazine covering the advertising, sales and promotion of business and industrial products and services for an audience in marketing/sales middle management and corporate top management. Circ. 50,000. All rights reserved. Send queries first. "Not responsible for unsolicited manuscripts." Sample copy $3.
Nonfiction: Expose (of marketing industry); how-to (advertise, do sales management promotion, do strategy development); interview (of industrial marketing executives); opinion (on industry practices); profile; and technical (advertising/marketing practice). "No self promotion or puff pieces." No material aimed at the general interest reader. Buys 30 mss/year. Query. Length: 1,000-2,000 words.
Photos: State availability of photos. Reviews 8x10 b&w glossy prints and color transparencies. Offers no additional payment for photos accepted with ms. Captions preferred; model release required.
Columns/Departments: Query. Length: 500-1,000 words. "Column ideas should be queried, but generally we have no need for paid freelance columnists."
Fillers: Newsbreaks. Buys 2 mss/issue. Length: 100-500 words.

THE COUNSELOR MAGAZINE, Advertising Specialty Institute, NBS Bldg., 1120 Wheeler Way, Langhorne PA 19047. (215)752-4200. Editor: Catherine A.W. Kuczewski. 25% freelance written. Works with a small number of new/unpublished writers each year. For executives, both distributors and suppliers, in the ad specialty industry. Monthly magazine; 375 pages. Circ. 6,000. Pays on publication. Publishes ms an average of 3 months after acceptance. Buys first rights only. No phone queries. Submit seasonal/holiday material 4 months in advance. Simultaneous, photocopied and previously published submissions OK. Computer printout submissions OK; prefers letter-quality to dot-matrix. Reports in 2-3 months. Sample copy of *Imprint* for 9x12 SAE with 3 first-class stamps.
Nonfiction: Contact managing editor. How-to (promotional case histories); interview (with executives and government figures); profile (of executives); and articles on specific product categories. "Articles almost always have a specialty advertising slant and quotes from specialty advertising practitioners." Buys 30 mss/year. Length: Open. Query with samples. Pays according to assigned length. Sometimes pays the expenses of writers on assignment.
Photos: State availability of photos. B&w photos only. Prefers contact sheet(s) and 5x7 prints. Offers some additional payment for original only photos accepted with ms. Captions and model releases required. Buys one-time rights.
Tips: "If a writer shows promise, we can help him or her modify his style to suit our publication and provide leads. Writers must be willing to adapt or rewrite their material for a specific audience. If an article is suitable

for 5 or 6 other publications, it's probably not suitable for us. The best way to break in is to write for *Imprint*, a quarterly publication we produce for the clients of ad specialty counselors. *Imprint* covers promotional campaigns, safety programs, trade show exhibits, traffic builders and sales incentives—all with a specialty advertising tie-in."

THE FLYING A, Aeroquip Corp., 300 S. East Ave., Jackson MI 49203. (517)787-8121. Editor-in-Chief: Wayne D. Thomas. 10% freelance written. Emphasizes Aeroquip customers and products. Quarterly magazine; 24-32 pages. Circ. 30,000. Pays on acceptance. Buys first or second rights, depending upon circumstances. Simultaneous submissions OK. Reports in 2 months.
Nonfiction: General interest (feature stories with emphasis on free enterprise, business-related or historical articles with broad appeal, human interest.) "An Aeroquip tie-in in a human interest story is helpful." No jokes, no sample copies; no cartoons, no short fillers. Buys 1 mss/issue. Query with biographic sketch and clips. Length: Not to exceed five typewritten pages. Pays $75 minimum.
Photos: Accompanying photos are helpful.
Fillers: Human interest. No personal anecdotes, recipes or how-to articles. "Suggest the writer contact editor by letter with proposed story outline."
Tips: "We publish a marketing-oriented magazine, with a section devoted to employee news. Our products are used in a wide variety of markets, including aerospace, automotive, construction equipment and others. Our primary products are hose lines and fittings for industry."

HIGH-TECH MARKETING, Technical Marketing Corporation, 1460 Post Road East, Westport CT 06880. (203)255-9997. Editor: Candace Port. 75% freelance written. A monthly magazine. "*HTM* is for and about the marketers of high technology." Circ. 20,000. Pays on acceptance. Publishes ms an average of 3 months after acceptance. Byline given. Offers 15% kill fee. Buys first North American serial rights. Submit seasonal/holiday material 4 months in advance. Simultaneous queries and photocopied submissions OK. Electronic submissions OK on IBM PC—Hayes Modem; MCI Mail, but requires hard copy also. Computer printout submissions acceptable; no dot-matrix. Reports in 1 month. Sample copy $3.50; free writer's guidelines.
Nonfiction: Interview/profile (prominent marketers). "We want excellent style—not technical writing. The key word is *marketing—not high tech*." Buys 45 mss/year. Query with published clips. Length: 1,000-3,000 words. Pays $200-700. Sometimes pays the expenses of writers on assignment.
Photos: State availability of photos with submission.
Tips: "We're always looking for personal profiles of high-tech marketers."

HIGH-TECH SELLING, For Electronics, Telecommunications, and Other High-Tech Industries, Bureau of Business Practice/Simon & Schuster, 24 Rope Ferry Rd.,Waterford CT 06385. (800)243-0876. Editor: Michele S. Rubin. Managing Editor: Wayne Muller. 75% freelance written. Prefers to work with published/established writers, but also is eager to work with new/unpublished writers. A monthly training newsletter covering selling. Pays on acceptance. Publishes ms an average of 4 months after acceptance. Byline not given. Buys all rights. Submit seasonal/holiday material 6 months in advance. Photocopied submissions OK. Computer printout submissions acceptable; prefers letter-quality to dot-matrix. Reports in 1 week. Sample copy and writer's guidelines for 4x9½ SAE with 1 first class stamp.
Nonfiction: How-to. Buys 50 mss/year. Query. Length: 1,000-1,500 words. Pays 10-15¢/word. Sometimes pays the expenses of writers on assignment.
Photos: Offers no additional payment for photos accepted with ms.
Tips: "Our entire publication is interview-based."

IMPRINT, The Magazine of Specialty Advertising Ideas, Advertising Specialty Institute, 1120 Wheeler Way, Langhorne PA 19047. (215)752-4200. Editor: Catherine A.W. Kuczewski. 25% freelance written. Works with a small number of new/unpublished writers each year. Quarterly magazine covering specialty advertising. Circ. 60,000+. Pays on publication. Publishes ms an average of 6 months after acceptance. Byline given. Buys one-time rights. Submit seasonal/holiday material 6 months in advance. Simultaneous queries OK. Query for electronic submissions. Computer printout submissions acceptable; prefers letter-quality to dot-matrix. Reports in 3 months. Sample copy for 9x12 SAE with 3 first class stamps.
Nonfiction: How-to (case histories of specialty advertising campaigns); and features (how ad specialties are distributed in promotions). "Emphasize effective use of specialty advertising. Avoid direct-buy situations. Stress the distributor's role in promotions. No generalized pieces on print, broadcast or outdoor advertising." Buys 10-12 mss/year. Query with clips published. Length: varied. Payment based on assigned length. "We pay authorized phone, postage, etc."
Photos: State availability of 5x7 b&w photos. Pays "some extra for *original only* photos." Captions, model release and identification of subjects required.
Tips: "The most frequent mistake writers make is in their misconceptions of what specialty advertising is. Many of them do not understand the medium, or our target audience, which is the end-user and so mistakes

occur. Writers are encouraged to look into the medium before attempting to write any articles. Query with a case history suggestion and writing samples. We can provide additional leads. All articles must be specifically geared to specialty advertising (and sometimes, premium) promotions."

INFORMATION MARKETING, A Direct Marketing Tool for Writers, Publishers, Communicators and Information Marketers, Box 2069, Citrus Heights CA 95611. Editor: Mark Nolan. 25-50% freelance written. Eager to work with new/unpublished writers. A monthly newsletter covering advertising and marketing tips for those who deal "in information of any type." Pays on publication. Publishes ms an average of 3 months after acceptance. Byline given, sometimes depending on length of material. Buys first North American and second serial (reprint) rights. Submit seasonal/holiday material 6 weeks in advance. Simultaneous, photocopied, and previously published submissions OK. Query for electronic submissions. Computer printout submissions acceptable; no dot-matrix. Reports in 3 weeks. Sample copy $1.
Nonfiction: How-to (advertise or market information, press releases, etc); mail order tips, postal tips, directories available, cottage industry success stories, etc., newsletters; and new product (software, word processors). No long dissertations or editorials; only "short, pithy, impact news, tips and sources." Buys 50-100 mss/year (estimated). Recent article: "Bestselling Subject Matter" by Mark Nolan. Send complete ms. Length: 50-150 words. Pays $25-75.
Columns/Departments: New books department: Short reviews on books pertaining to main theme, including those on word processing, advertising techniques, salesmanship, information industry, work-at-home themes, consulting, seminars, etc. Buys 10-25 mss/year. Send complete ms. Length: 50-150 words. Pays $15-25.
Fillers: Clippings and newsbreaks. Buys 10-50/year. Length: 35-75 words. Pays $5.
Tips: "We would love to hear from you if you've studied at least one issue. We need short items most of all. News and tips to help busy nonfiction writers and publishers: how to sell more, save money, choose 'tools', etc. The most frequent mistake made by writers in completing an article for us is too much fine writing. Our subscribers are mostly writers and publishers. They are very busy and want valuable news, tips and sources with a minimum of wasted words. Read some issues to see our style and content."

INSIDE PRINT, Voice of Print Advertising, 6 Riverbend, Box 4949, Stamford CT 06907-0949. (203)358-9900. Editor: Karlene Lukovitz. Managing Editor: Marcia Partch. 30% freelance written. Eager to work with new/unpublished writers. Monthly magazine for advertisers and advertising agencies designed "to examine how they use a wide range of publications, including consumer, business, trade, farm, newspaper, etc." Circ. 32,000. Pays on acceptance. Publishes ms an average of 3 months after acceptance. Buys all rights. Query for electronic submissions. Computer printout submissions acceptable; no dot-matrix. Reports in 2 weeks. Sample copy $4.
Nonfiction: "We are interested in print advertising success stories. We want marketing pieces, case histories, effective use of print advertising and current trends." Buys 4 mss/issue. Query first. Will not respond to handwritten inquiries. Length: 3,000 words maximum. Pays $700 maximum. Pays expenses of writers on assignment.
Tips: "Find an unusual aspect of print advertising."

MORE BUSINESS, 11 Wimbledon Court, Jericho NY 11753. Editor: Trudy Settel. 50% freelance written. "We sell publications material to business for consumer use (incentives, communication, public relations)—look for book ideas and manuscripts." Monthly magazine. Circ. 10,000. Pays on acceptance. Publishes ms an average of 1 month after acceptance. Buys all rights. Computer printout submissions acceptable; no dot-matrix. Reports in 1 month.
Nonfiction: General interest, how-to, vocational techniques, nostalgia, photo feature, profile and travel. Buys 10-20 mss/year. Word length varies with article. Payment negotiable. Query. Pays $4,000-7,000 for book mss.

THE PRESS, The Greater Buffalo Press, Inc., 302 Grote St., Buffalo NY 14207. Managing Editor: Janet Tober. 100% freelance written. Works with a small number of new/unpublished writers each year. Quarterly tabloid for advertising executives at Sunday newspapers, ad agencies, retail chains and cartoonists who create the Sunday funnies. Circ. 4,000. Pays on publication. Publishes ms an average of 6 months after acceptance. Buys all rights. Photocopied submissions and previously published submissions OK. Computer printout submissions acceptable; prefers letter-quality to dot-matrix. Reports in 1 month. Sample copy 50¢; free writer's guidelines.
Nonfiction: Short biographies of people in advertising, retailing, cartooning or unusual occupations. No travel/leisure or personal experience articles. Illustrations or photos must accompany ms. Buys 4-6 mss/issue. Query. Length: 800-1,500 words. Pays $100-125.
Photos: Uses 35mm transparencies or larger (color preferred). Offers no additional payment for photos accepted with ms. Captions optional. Photos are usually returned after publication. "We do not accept photographs or artwork unless they accompany a ms."

SALES & MARKETING MANAGEMENT IN CANADA, Sanford Evans Communications Ltd., Suite 402, 3500 Dufferin St., Downsview, Ontario M3K 1N2 Canada. (416)633-2020. Editor: Ernie Spear. Monthly magazine. Circ. 13,000. Pays on publication. Byline given. Buys first North American serial rights. Simultaneous queries and photocopied submissions OK. Reports in 2 weeks.
Nonfiction: How-to (case histories of successful marketing campaigns). "Canadian articles only." Buys 3 mss/year. Query. Length: 800-1,500 words. Pays $200 maximum.

SIGNCRAFT, The Magazine for the Sign Artist and Commercial Sign Shop, SignCraft Publishing Co., Inc., Box 06031, Fort Myers FL 33906. (813)939-4644. Editor: Tom McIltrot. 30% freelance written. Bimonthly magazine of the sign industry. "Like any trade magazine, we need material of direct benefit to our readers. We can't afford space for material of marginal interest." Circ. 17,500. Pays on publication. Publishes ms an average of 9 months after acceptance. Byline given. Offers negotiable kill fee. Buys first North American serial rights or all rights. Simultaneous queries, and simultaneous, photocopied, and previously published submissions OK. Computer printout submissions acceptable. Reports in 1 month. Free sample copy and writer's guidelines.
Nonfiction: Interviews and profiles. "All articles should be directly related to quality commercial signage. If you are familiar with the sign trade, we'd like to hear from you." Buys 20 mss/year. Query with or without published clips. Length: 500-2,000 words. Pays up to $150.

SIGNS OF THE TIMES, The Industry Journal since 1906, ST Publications, 407 Gilbert Ave., Cincinnati OH 45202. (513)421-2050. Editor: Tod Swormstedt. Managing Editor: Bill Dorsey. 15-30% freelance written. "We are willing to use more freelancers." Magazine published 13 times/year; special buyer's guide between November and December issue. Circ. 18,000. Pays on publication. Publishes ms an average of 3 months after acceptance. Byline given. Buys variable rights. Simultaneous queries, and simultaneous, photocopied and previously published submissions OK. Computer printout submissions acceptable; no dot-matrix. Reports in 1 month. Free sample copy. Writer's guidelines flexible.
Nonfiction: Historical/nostalgic (regarding the sign industry); how-to (carved signs, goldleaf, etc.); interview/profile (usually on assignment but interested to hear proposed topics); photo feature (query first); and technical (sign engineering, etc.). Nothing "nonspecific on signs, an example being a photo essay on 'signs I've seen.' We are a trade journal with specific audience interests." Buys 15-20 mss/year. Query with clips. Pays $150-500. Sometimes pays the expenses of writers on assignment.
Photos: Send photos with ms. "Sign industry-related photos only. We sometimes accept photos with funny twists or misspellings."

TELEMARKETING, The Magazine of Business Telecommunications, Technology Marketing Corporation, 1 Technology Plaza, Norwalk CT 06854. (203)852-6800. Editor: Linda Driscoll. 1% freelance written. Works with a small number of new/unpublished writers each year. A monthly magazine covering telecommunications and marketing via telecommunications. Emphasizes tutorial/how-to information for executives (top management) in or entering the telemarketing field. "Readers have a general understanding of the field and its benefits." Circ. 60,000. Pays on publication. Publishes ms an average of 3 months after acceptance. Byline given. Buys all rights. Query for electronic submissions. Computer printout submissions acceptable; prefers letter-quality to dot-matrix. Reports in 5 weeks. Free sample copy; writer's guidelines for SASE.
Nonfiction: How-to (participate in telecom/telemarketing industry); interview/profile; new product (non-commercial/advertising style); personal experience; and technical. "We need information about current technology in layman's terms/language." No interviews without queries; no broad-based "what is telemarketing" articles. Buys 5-10 mss/year. Query. Length: 500-1,400 words. Pays $15/page-$250 maximum for assigned articles.
Photos: State availability of photos with submission. Reviews contact sheets and negatives. Offers no additional payment for photos accepted with ms. Model releases and identification of subjects required. Buys one-time rights.
Columns/Departments: Telemarketing Q&A (answers to problems faced by telemarketers), 200 words. Also interested in ideas for new columns and departments. Pays $15/page-$250 maximum.
Fillers: Open to queries; request rates.
Tips: "A background in telecommunications and/or telemarketing is desired; general business management helpful. We want very *specific* ideas for articles; i.e. the *area* of telemarketing or telecommunications such as training with audio/visual materials, research of Fortune 50 companies in the field, today's hybrid PBX, etc. Research of the marketplace, i.e.; number of industry participants, future trends, No. 1 companies in the field, is most open to freelancers."

VM & SD (Visual Merchandising and Store Design), ST Publications, 407 Gilbert Ave., Cincinnati OH 45202. Associate Publisher: Pamela Gramke. Editor: Ms. P.K. Anderson. 30% freelance written. Emphasizes store design and merchandise presentation. Monthly magazine; 100-200 pages. Circ. 11,700. Pays on publication. Buys first and second rights to the same material. Simultaneous and previously published submissions OK. Computer printout submissions acceptable. Reports in 1 month. Publishes ms an average of 3 months after acceptance.

Nonfiction: How-to (display); informational (store design, construction, merchandise presentation); interview (display directors and shop owners); profile (new and remodeled stores); new product; photo feature (window display); and technical (store lighting, carpet, wallcoverings, fixtures). No "advertorials" that tout a single company's product or product line. Buys 24 mss year. Query or submit complete ms. Length: 500-3,000 words. Pays $250-400.

Photos: Purchased with accompanying ms or on assignment.

Tips: "Be fashion and design conscious and reflect that in the article. Submit finished manuscripts with photos or slides always. Look for stories on department and specialty store visual merchandisers and store designers (profiles, methods, views on the industry, sales promotions and new store design or remodels). The size of the publication could very well begin to increase in the year ahead. And with a greater page count, we will need to rely on an increasing number of freelancers."

__ *Art, Design and Collectibles*

The businesses of art, art administration, architecture, environmental/package design and antique collectibles are covered in these listings. Art-related topics for the general public are located in the Consumer Art and Contemporary Culture category. Antiques magazines are listed in Consumer Hobby and Craft.

ART BUSINESS NEWS, Myers Publishing Co., 60 Ridgeway Plaza, Stamford CT 06905. (203)356-1745. Editor: Jo Yanow-Schwartz. Managing Editor: Beth Fleckenstein. 25% freelance written. Prefers to work with published/established writers. Monthly tabloid covering news relating to the art and picture framing industry. Circ. 25,000. Pays on publication. Publishes ms an average of 3 months after acceptance. Byline given. Buys all rights. Submit seasonal/holiday material 2 months in advance. Photocopied and simultaneous submissions OK. Computer printout submissions acceptable; prefers letter-quality to dot-matrix. Reports in 2 months.

Nonfiction: General interest; interview/marketing profiles (of dealers, publishers in the art industry); new products; articles focusing on small business people—framers, art gallery management, art trends; and how-to (occasional article on "how-to frame" accepted). Buys 8-20 mss/year. Length: 1,000 words maximum. Query first. Pays $75-250. Sometimes pays the expenses of writers on assignment.

ARTQUEST, International, Box 650W, Livonia NY 14480. Editor: John H. Armstrong. 25% freelance written. Eager to work with new/unpublished writers. A bimonthly newsletter covering freelance commercial art opportunities, ideas for marketing. "*Artquest* is written by freelance artists for freelance artists. Our readers vary in experience from beginners and students to seasoned pros." Circ. 1,000 +. Pays on acceptance. Publishes ms an average of 2 months after acceptance. Byline given. Buys one-time rights. Submit seasonal/holiday material 10 months in advance. Simultaneous and photocopied submissions OK. Computer printout submissions acceptable; no dot-matrix. Reports in 2 weeks on queries; 1 month on mss. Sample copy $5.

Nonfiction: How-to, humor, opinion and personal experience. Especially interested in first-person articles on proven ways (experience) to market freelance art. Special anniversary edition each September; "our largest edition with more articles. We need submission in June to plan space." No unproven suggestions or tips. Buys 6 + mss/year. Query with or without published clips, or send complete ms. Length: 200-400 words. Pays $10-20 for unsolicited articles. Sometimes pays the expenses of writers on assignment.

Photos: State availability of photos with submission. Offers no additional payment for photos accepted with ms.

Columns/Departments: Open Idea File ("How I did it and you can do it also"), 200-400 words, pays $10-20; Book/Product Reviews (content, usability of new items for commercial artists), 100-200 words, pays $10; Art Competitions (entry rules for nationwide commercial art and design contests), 100 words maximum, pays $5 to first contributor. "We need more submissions for Open Idea File. No manuscripts on techniques in art are wanted, instead how you sell what you create." Query or send complete ms; minimum 60 days to entry deadline for contest rules.

Fillers: Anecdotes, facts, newsbreaks. Length: 100 words maximum. Pays $5-10.

Tips: " 'Open Idea File' is most open to freelancers. We need a stimulating article on how freelance artists can make money in their own locale while gaining experience (and a portfolio of published work) to break into the national and international markets."

ARTS MANAGEMENT, 408 W. 57th St., New York NY 10019. (212)245-3850. Editor: A.H. Reiss. For cultural institutions. Published five times/year. 2% freelance written. Circ. 6,000. Pays on publication. Byline given. Buys all rights. Mostly staff-written; uses very little outside material. Computer printout submissions acceptable; no dot-matrix. Query. Reports in "several weeks."
Nonfiction: Short articles, 400-900 words, tightly written, expository, explaining how art administrators solved problems in publicity, fund raising and general administration; actual case histories emphasizing the how-to. Also short articles on the economics and sociology of the arts and important trends in the nonprofit cultural field. Must be fact-filled, well-organized and without rhetoric. Payment is 2-4¢/word. No photographs or pictures.

CALLIGRAPHY IDEA EXCHANGE, Calligraphy Idea Exchange, Inc., Suite 159, 2500 S. McGee, Norman OK 73072-6705. (405)364-8794. Managing Editor: Karyn L. Gilman. 98% freelance written. Eager to work with new/unpublished writers with calligraphic expertise and language skills. A quarterly magazine on calligraphy and related book arts, both historical and contemporary in nature. Circ. 4,000. Pays on publication. Publishes ms an average of 6 months after acceptance. Byline given. Offers 20% kill fee. Buys first rights. Submit seasonal/holiday material 3-4 months in advance. Photocopied submissions OK. Query for electronic submissons. Computer printout submissions acceptable. Sample copy for 9x12 SAE with $1.58 postage; free writer's guidelines.
Nonfiction: Interview/profile, new product, opinion, and technical. Buys 50 mss/year. Query with or without published clips, or send complete ms. Length: 1,000-2,000 words. Pays $50-200 for assigned articles; pays $25-200 for unsolicited articles. Sometimes pays the expenses of writers on assignment.
Photos: State availability of photos with submission. Reviews contact sheets, negatives, transparencies and prints. Pays agreed upon cost. Captions and identification of subjects required. Buys one-time rights.
Columns/Departments: Book Reviews Viewpoint (critical), 500-1,500 words; Ms. (discussion of manuscripts in collections), 1,000-2,000 words; and Profile (contemporary calligraphic figure), 1,000-2,000 words. Query. Pays $50-200.
Tips: "*Calligraphy Idea Exchange*'s primary objective is to encourage the exchange of ideas on calligraphy, its past and present as well as trends for the future. Practical and conceptual treatments are welcomed, as are learning and teaching experiences. Third person is preferred, however first person will be considered if appropriate."

‡THE CRAFTS REPORT, The Newsmonthly of Marketing, Management and Money for Crafts Professionals, The Crafts Report Publishing Co., 3623 Ashworth North, Seattle WA 98103. (206)547-7611. Editor: Michael Scott; Managing Editor: Susan Biskeborn. 50% freelance written. A monthly tabloid covering business subjects for crafts professionals. Circ. 17,000. Pays on publication. Byline given. Offers $50 kill fee. Buys first rights. Photocopied submissions and sometimes previously published submissions OK. Query for electronic submissions. Computer printout submissions OK. Reports in 2 weeks. Sample copy $2.
Nonfiction: Business articles for crafts professionals. No articles on art or crafts techniques. Buys approximately 70 mss/year. Query with published clips. Length: 800-1,200 words. Pays $100-150. Sometimes pays the expenses of writers on assignment.
Photos: State availability of photos with submission or send photos with submission. Reviews 5x7 b&w prints. Identification of subjects required. Buys one-time rights.

‡PAPERCUTTING WORLD, #360, 584 Castro St., San Francisco CA 94114. (415)346-2473. Editor: Joseph W. Bean. 50% freelance written. Eager to work with new/unpublished writers. Quarterly covering cut paper arts and crafts. Estab. 1986. Circ. 1,000. Pays on publication. Publishes ms an average of 3-6 months after acceptance. Byline given. Kill fee negotiable. Buys one-time rights, "except for pieces which, by arrangement with the writer, we might want to reuse. Then we'll pay for *all* rights. Submit seasonal/holiday material 6 months in advance. Simultaneous, photocopied and previously published submissions OK. Computer printout submissions OK; prefers letter-quality. Reports in 3 weeks. Sample copy $5; or free "if writer's letter indicates *any* hope we'll use him or her."
Nonfiction: Book excerpts, historical/nostalgic, how-to, humor, interview/profile, new product, technical and travel; all related to papercutting. "Most of our readers are papercutters or they are collectors or suppliers of materials used by papercutters and collectors." Buys 15-20 mss/year. Query with published clips, or send complete ms. Length: 100-3,000 words. Pays 4-10¢/word. Sometimes pays the expenses of writers on assignment.
Photos: State availability of photos with submission. Reviews contact sheets, negatives and transparencies. Offers variable payment for photos accepted with ms. Captions required. Buys one-time rights.
Fiction: Ethnic, humorous, mainstream, romance, science fiction, slice-of-life vignettes and western, "but

only involving papercutters." Buys 4 mss/year "if I could find them!" Send complete ms. Length: 800-3,000 words. Pays 4-10¢/word.

Poetry: Avant-garde, free verse, haiku, light verse and traditional. "Must be related to paper arts/crafts." Submit maximum 4 poems. Length: open. Pays $5-25.

Fillers: Tricks of the Trade (technical tips); Snippets (anecdotes on papercutting business or traditions). Buys 20 mss/year. Send complete ms. Length: 100-250 words. Pays 4-10¢/word.

Tips: "Except for experts in the field, the best area for a freelance writer would be an assigned feature involving research. Don't try to sell us on a feature about your own work or a friend's, if it isn't already famous, but ask if you want to. Query in great detail."

PROGRESSIVE ARCHITECTURE, 600 Summer St., Box 1361, Stamford CT 06904. Editor: John M. Dixon. 5-10% freelance written. Prefers to work with published/established writers. Monthly. Pays on publication. Publishes ms an average of 4 months after acceptance. Buys all rights for use in architectural press. Query for electronic submissions. Computer printout submissions acceptable.

Nonfiction: "Articles of technical professional interest devoted to architecture, interior design, and urban design and planning and illustrated by photographs and architectural drawings. We also use technical articles which are prepared by technical authorities and would be beyond the scope of the lay writer. Practically all the material is professional, and most of it is prepared by writers in the field who are approached by the magazine for material." Pays $75-300. Sometimes pays the expenses of writers on assignment.

Photos: Buys one-time reproduction rights to b&w and color photos.

Auto and Truck

These journals are geared to automobile, motorcycle and truck dealers; service department personnel; or fleet operators. Publications for highway planners and traffic control experts are listed in the Government and Public Service category.

AMERICAN TRUCKER MAGAZINE, American Trucker Marketing, Box 9159, Brea CA 92622. (714)528-6600. Publisher: David Chinn. Editor: Carl Calvert. 10% freelance written. Eager to work with new/unpublished writers. Monthly magazine for professional truck drivers, owners, management and other trucking personnel. Articles, fillers and other materials should be generally conservative and of particular interest to the readership, of an informative or entertaining nature relating to the trucking industry. Circ. 80,000. Pays on publication. Publishes ms an average of 3 months after acceptance. First-time rights requested. Submit seasonal/holiday material 3 months in advance. Electronic submissions OK via disc, CP/M or MS-DOS. Computer printout submissions acceptable. Reports in 3 weeks. Phone queries OK. Free sample copy and writer's guidelines.

Nonfiction: Realistic articles directed to trucking professionals which promote a positive image of the industry. Photo and features of outstanding rigs, truck maintenance and repair, and business aspects of trucking. 450-2,500 words. Buys 60 articles/year. Pays standard column inch rate. Sometimes pays the expenses of writers on assignment.

Photos: State availability of photos or send captioned photos with ms. Model release required.

Fiction: Realistic, "slice of life" for truckers, adventure and humor. Query. Length: 1,200-2,500 words. Buys 6/year. Pays standard column inch rate.

Tips: Freelance writers offer a balance of writing style throughout the magazine.

AUTO GLASS JOURNAL, Grawin Publications, Inc., Suite 101, 303 Harvard E., Box 12099, Seattle WA 98102-0099. (206)322-5120. Editor: Eric Cosentino. 45% freelance written. Prefers to work with published/established writers. Monthly magazine on auto glass replacement. National publication for the auto glass replacement industry. Includes step-by-step glass replacement procedures for current model cars as well as shop profiles, industry news and trends. Circ. 4,200. Pays on acceptance. Publishes ms an average of 5 months after acceptance. No byline given. Buys all rights. Query for electronic submissions. Computer printout submissions acceptable; prefers letter-quality to dot-matrix. Reports in 2 weeks on queries; 1 week on mss. Sample copy for 6x9 SAE and 56¢ postage. Writer's guidelines for #10 SAE and 1 first class stamp.

Nonfiction: How-to (install all glass in a current model car); and interview/profile. Buys 22-36 mss/year. Query with published clips. Length: 2,000-3,500 words. Pays $75-250, with photos. Sometimes pays the expenses of writers on assignment.

Photos: State availability of photos. Reviews b&w contact sheets and negatives. Payment included with ms. Captions required. Buys all rights.

Tips: "Be willing to visit auto glass replacement shops for installation features."

AUTO LAUNDRY NEWS, Columbia Communications, 370 Lexington Ave., New York NY 10017. (212)532-9290. Publisher/Editor: Ralph Monti. 20% freelance written. Prefers to work with published/established writers, and works with a small number of new/unpublished writers each year. For sophisticated car wash operators. Monthly magazine; 45-100 pages. Circ. 15,000+. Pays on publication. Publishes ms an average of 2 months after acceptance. Buys all rights. Submit seasonal/holiday material 2 months in advance. Query for electronic submissions. Computer printout submissions acceptable; no dot-matrix. Reports in 1 month.

Nonfiction: How-to, historical, humor, informational, new product, nostalgia, personal experience, technical, interviews, photo features and profiles. Buys 15 mss/year. Query. Length: 1,000-2,000 words. Pays $75-175. Sometimes pays the expenses of writers on assignment.

Tips: "The trend toward self-service car washing will affect the types of freelance material we buy in 1988. We would mainly like to receive car wash profiles. Read the magazine; notice its style and come up with something interesting to the industry. Foremost, the writer has to know the industry."

AUTO TRIM NEWS, National Association of Auto Trim Shops (NAATS), 1623 N. Grand Ave., Box 86, Baldwin NY 11510. (516)223-4334. Editor: Nat Danas. Associate Editor: Dani Ben-Ari. 25% freelance written. Monthly magazine for auto trim shops, installation specialists, customizers and restylers, marine and furniture upholsterers as well as manufacturers, wholesalers, jobbers, and distributors serving them. Circ. 8,000. Pays on publication. Byline given. Buys first rights only. Simultaneous and previously published submissions OK. Reports in 1 month. Sample copy $2; free writer's guidelines for SAE and 2 first class stamps.

Nonfiction: How-to, interview/profile, photo feature on customizing, restoration, convertible conversions, and restyling of motor vehicles (cars, vans, trucks, motorcycles, boats and aircraft). Query or send complete ms. Length: 500-1,000 words. Pays $50-200.

Photos: State availability of photos. Pays $5 maximum for b&w print. Reviews b&w contact sheet. Captions and identification of subjects required. Buys one-time rights.

Tips: "No material dealing with engines and engine repairs. We are an aftermarket publication."

AUTOBODY & RECONDITIONED CAR, Key Markets Publishing Co., Box 5867, Rockford IL 61125. Editor: David Mathieu. 50% freelance written. A bimonthly magazine covering autobody repair, reconditioning and refinishing. Audience includes independent body shops; new and used car dealers and fleet operators with body shops; paint, glass and trim shops; and jobbers and manufacturers of automobile straightening equipment and refinishing supplies. Circ. 25,000. Pays on publication. Publishes manuscript an average of 3 months after acceptance. Byline given. Buys first North American serial rights and one-time rights. Submit seasonal/holiday material 3 months in advance. Simultaneous queries, and simultaneous, photocopied, and previously published (if so indicated) submissions OK. Computer printout submissions acceptable; prefers letter-quality to dot-matrix. Reports in 1 month. Sample copy $1. Writer's guidelines for business-size SAE and 1 first class stamp.

Nonfiction: Book excerpts (autobody repair, small business management); how-to (manage an autobody shop, do a specific autobody repair); interview/profile (bodyshop owner); photo feature (step-by-step repair); and technical (equipment, supplies and processes in an autobody shop). Editorial calendar will be provided with writer's guidelines. No personal experience as a customer of an autobody shop, or how *not* to run a shop. Buys 36 mss/year. Query with published clips or send complete ms. Length: 500-2,500 words. Pays $100-200 with photos.

Photos: State availability of photos and send one sample, or send photos with ms. Reviews color negatives and 4x5 transparencies, and 3½x5 b&w and color prints. Payment for photos included in payment for ms. Captions required. Buys one-time rights.

Tips: "Visit 10 autobody shops and ask the owners what they want to read about; find sources, then send in a query; or send in a letter with 10 article topics that you know you can cover and wait for an assignment. Experience in trade publication writing helps. Area most open to freelancers is technical and management how-tos. We want technical, technical, technical articles. Autobody people work with everything from laser beam measuring benches to catalytic thermoreactors. Be willing to learn about such subjects. The most frequent mistakes made by writers are not understanding the audience or the autobody business."

AUTOMOTIVE BOOSTER OF CALIFORNIA, Box 765, LaCanada CA 91011. (213)790-6554. Editor: Don McAnally. 2% freelance written. Prefers to work with published/established writers. For members of Automotive Booster clubs, automotive warehouse distributors, and automotive parts jobbers in California. Monthly. Circ. 3,400. Not copyrighted. Byline given. Pays on publication. Publishes ms an average of 1 month after acceptance. Buys first rights only.

Nonfiction: Will look at short articles and pictures about successes of automotive parts outlets in California.

Also can use personnel assignments for automotive parts people in California. Query first. Pays $1.25/column inch (about 2½¢/word).
Photos: Pays $5 for b&w photos used with mss.

‡**AUTOMOTIVE COOLING JOURNAL, ACJ**, National Automotive Radiator Service Association, 1709 N. Broad St., Box 1307, Lansdale PA 19446. (215)362-5800. Managing Editor: Wayne Juchno. 5% freelance written. Monthly magazine covering automotive heat exchange repair/service. "Service oriented regarding automotive and commercial truck cooling system service." Circ. 7,500. Pays on acceptance. Publishes ms an average of 3 months after acceptance. Byline given. Not copyrighted. Buys one-time rights. Submit seasonal/holiday material 4 months in advance. Photocopied submissions OK. Computer printout submissions OK; prefers letter-quality to dot-matrix. Reports in 3 weeks on queries; 2 weeks on mss. Free sample copy.
Nonfiction: Technical. Special issues include Convention Issue for NARSA (March) and Convention Issue for MACS (January). No soft feature/interviews. Buys 5-10 mss/year. Query with published clips. Payment negotiable. Sometimes pays the expenses of writers on assignment.
Photos: Send photos with submission. Reviews 5x7 prints. Offers no additional payment for photos accepted with ms. Model releases and identification of subjects required. Buys one-time rights.

THE BATTERY MAN, Independent Battery Manufacturers Association, Inc., 100 Larchwood Dr., Largo FL 33540. (813)586-1409. Editor: Celwyn E. Hopkins. 40% freelance written. Emphasizes SLI battery manufacture, applications and new developments. For battery manufacturers and retailers (garage owners, servicemen, fleet owners, etc.). Monthly magazine. Circ. 5,200. Pays on acceptance. Publishes ms an average of 1 year after acceptance. Buys all rights. Byline given. Submit seasonal/holiday material 3 months in advance. Simultaneous, photocopied and previously published submissions OK. Computer printout submissions acceptable; no dot-matrix. Reports in 6 weeks. Sample copy $2.50.
Nonfiction: Technical articles. "Articles about how a company is using batteries as a source of uninterruptable power supply for its computer systems or a hospital using batteries for the same (photos with article are nice) purpose as well as for life support systems, etc." Submit complete ms. Buys 19-24 unsolicited mss/year. Recent article examples: "The Strategic Decision of Leaf vs. Envelope Battery Construction"; "Universal Batteries—Fact or Fad?" and "Acquisitions" (April 1986). Length: 750-1,200 words. Pays 6¢/word.
Tips: "Most writers are not familiar enough with this industry to be able to furnish a feature article. They try to palm off something that they wrote for a hardware store, or a dry cleaner, by calling everything a 'battery store'. We receive a lot of manuscripts on taxes and tax information (such as U.S. income tax). Since this is an international publication, we try to stay away from such subjects, since U.S. tax info is of no use or interest to overseas readers."

‡**BRAKE & FRONT END**, 11 S. Forge St., Akron OH 44304. (216)535-6117. Editor: Jeffrey S. Davis. 5% freelance written. Works with a small number of new/unpublished writers each year. For owners of automotive repair shops engaged in brake, suspension, driveline exhaust and steering repair, including: specialty shops, general repair shops, new car and truck dealers, gas stations, mass merchandisers and tire stores. Monthly magazine; 68 pages. Circ. 28,000. Pays on publication. Publishes ms an average of 3-4 months after acceptance. Byline given. Buys first North American serial rights. Computer printout submissions acceptable; prefers letter-quality to dot-matrix. Reports immediately. Sample copy and editorial schedule $3; guidelines for SASE.
Nonfiction: Specialty shops taking on new ideas using new merchandising techniques; growth of business, volume; reasons for growth and success. Expansions and unusual brake shops. Prefers no product-oriented material. Query. Length: about 800-1,500 words. Pays 7-9¢/word. Sometimes pays expenses of writers on assignment.
Photos: Pays $8.50 for b&w glossy prints purchased with mss.

THE CHEK-CHART SERVICE BULLETIN, Box 6227, San Jose CA 95150. Editor: Mike Calkins. 10% freelance written. Works with a small number of new/unpublished writers each year. Emphasizes trade news and how-to articles on automobile service for professional mechanics. Monthly newsletter; 8 pages. Circ. 20,000. Pays on acceptance. Publishes ms an average of 3 months after acceptance. No byline. Buys all rights. Submit seasonal/holiday material 3-4 months in advance. Query for electronic submissions. Computer printout submissions acceptable. Reports in 2 weeks. Free sample copy and writer's guidelines; mention *Writer's Market* in request.
Nonfiction: "The *Service Bulletin* is a trade newsletter, *not* a consumer magazine. How-to articles and service trade news for professional auto mechanics, also articles on merchandising automobile service. No 'do-it-yourself' articles." Also no material unrelated to car service. Buys 6 unsolicited mss/year. Query with samples. Length: 700-1,100 words. Pays $100-300.
Photos: State availability of photos with query. Offers no additional payment for photos accepted with ms. Uses 8x10 b&w glossy photos. Captions and model release required. Buys all rights.
Tips: "Be willing to work in our style. Ask about subjects we would like to have covered in the future."

COLLISION, Kruza Kaleidoscopix, Inc., Box 389, Franklin MA 02038. Editor: Jay Kruza. For auto dealers, auto body repairmen and managers, and tow truck operators. Magazine published every 5 weeks; 84 pages. Pays on acceptance. Buys all rights. Submit seasonal/holiday material 4 months in advance. Simultaneous, photocopied and previously published submissions OK. Reports in 3 weeks. Sample copy $3; free writer's guidelines and editorial schedule.
Nonfiction: Expose (on government intervention in private enterprise via rule making; also how any business skims the cream of profitable business but fails to satisfy needs of motorist); and how-to (fix a dent, a frame, repair plastics, run your business better). No general business articles such as how to sell more, do better bookkeeping, etc. Query before submitting interview, personal opinion or technical articles. "Journalism of newsworthy material in local areas pertaining to auto body is of interest." Buys 20 or more articles/year. Length: 100-1,500 words. Pays $25-125.
Photos: "Our readers work with their hands and are more likely to be stopped by photo with story." Send photos with ms. Pays $25/first, $7/each additional for 5x7 b&w prints. Captions preferred. Model release required if not news material.
Columns/Departments: Stars and Their Cars, Personalities in Auto Dealerships, Auto Body Repair Shops, Association News and Lifestyle (dealing with general human interest hobbies or pastimes). Almost anything automotive that would attract readership interest. "Photos are very important. Stories that we have purchased are: 'Post office commandeered cars to deliver help during 1906 San Francisco Quake'; 'Bob Salter has rescued 3,000 people with his tow truck'; 'Telnack's design of T-Bird and Sable set new trends in style'; 'Snow increases body shop business for Minnesota shop'; 'Race against the clock with funny wheels on frozen lake.' "

JOBBER TOPICS, 7300 N. Cicero Ave., Lincolnwood IL 60646. (312)588-7300. Articles Editor: Jack Creighton. 10% freelance written. Prefers to work with published/established writers, works with a small number of new/unpublished writers each year, and is eager to work with new/unpublished writers. "A magazine dedicated to helping its readers—auto parts jobbers and warehouse distributors—succeed in their business via better management and merchandising techniques; and a better knowledge of industry trends, sales activities and local or federal legislation that may influence their business activities." Monthly. Pays on acceptance. No byline given. Buys all rights. Computer printout submissions OK; prefers letter-quality to dot-matrix.
Nonfiction: Most editorial material is staff-written. "Articles with unusual or outstanding automotive jobber procedures, with special emphasis on sales, merchandising and machine shop; any phase of automotive parts and equipment sales and distribution. Especially interested in merchandising practices and machine shop operations. Most independent businesses usually have a strong point or two. We like to see a writer zero in on that strong point(s) and submit an outline (or query), advising us of those points and what he intends to include in a feature. We will give him, or her, a prompt reply." Length: 2,500 words maximum. Pay based on quality and timeliness of feature. Pays the expenses of writers on assignment.
Photos: 5x7 b&w glossies or 35mm color transparencies purchased with mss.

MODERN TIRE DEALER, 110 N. Miller Rd., Box 5417, Akron OH 44313. (216)867-4401. Editor: Lloyd Stoyer. 15-20% freelance written. Prefers to work with published/established writers, and works with a small number of new/unpublished writers each year. For independent tire dealers. Monthly tabloid, plus 2 special emphasis issue magazines; 50-page tabloid, 80-page special issues. Published 14 times annually. Buys all rights. Photocopied submissions OK. Computer printout submissions acceptable. Reports in 1 month. Publishes ms an average of 2 months after acceptance. Free writer's guidelines.
Nonfiction: "How independent tire dealers sell tires, accessories and allied services such as brakes, wheel alignment, shocks and mufflers. The emphasis is on merchandising and management. We prefer the writer to zero in on some specific area of interest; avoid shotgun approach." Query. Length: 1,500 words. Pays $300 and up. Sometimes pays the expenses of writers on assignment.
Photos: 8x10, 4x5, 5x7 b&w glossy prints purchased with mss.
Tips: "Changes in the competitive situation among tire manufacturers and/or distributors will affect the types of freelance material we buy in 1988. We want articles for or about tire dealers, not generic articles adapted for our publication."

MOTOR SERVICE, Hunter Publishing Co., 950 Lee, Des Plaines IL 60016. Editor: Jim Holloran. 25% freelance written. Monthly magazine for professional auto mechanics and the owners and service managers of repair shops, garages and fleets. Circ. 131,000. Pays on acceptance. Buys all rights. Pays kill fee. Byline given. Computer printout submissions acceptable. Publishes ms an average of 2 months after acceptance. Free sample copy.
Nonfiction: Technical how-to features in language a mechanic can enjoy and understand; management articles to help shop owners and service managers operate a better business; technical theory pieces on how something works; new technology roundups, etc. No "generic business pieces on management tips, increasing sales, employee motivation or do-it-yourself material, etc." Length: 1,500-2,500 words. Pays $75 for departmental material, $200-$500 for feature articles. Buys 10 mss/year, mostly from regular contributing editors. Query first. "Writers must know our market."

Photos: Photos and/or diagrams must accompany technical articles. Uses 5x7 b&w prints or 35mm transparencies. Offers no additional payment for photos accepted with ms. Captions and model releases required. Also buys color transparencies for cover use. Pays $125-200.
Tips: "We're always looking for new faces but finding someone who is technically knowledgeable in our field who can also write is extremely difficult. Good tech writers are hard to find."

O AND A MARKETING NEWS, Box 765, LaCanada CA 91011. (213)790-6554. Editor: Don McAnally. For "service station dealers, garagemen, TBA (tires, batteries, accessories) people and oil company marketing management." Bimonthly. 5% freelance written. Circ. 9,500. Not copyrighted. Pays on publication. Buys first rights only. Reports in 1 week.
Nonfiction: "Straight news material; management, service and merchandising applications; emphasis on news about or affecting markets and marketers *within the publication's geographic area of the 11 Western states*. No restrictions on style or slant. We could use straight news of our industry from some Western cities, notably Las Vegas, Phoenix, Seattle, and Salt Lake City. Query with a letter that gives a capsule treatment of what the story is about." Buys 25 mss/year. Length: maximum 1,000 words. Pays $1.25/column inch (about 2½¢ a word).
Photos: Photos purchased with or without mss; captions required. No cartoons. Pays $5.

‡REFRIGERATED TRANSPORTER, Tunnell Publications, 1602 Harold St., Houston TX 77006. (713)523-8124. Editor: Gary Macklin. 5% freelance written. Monthly. Not copyrighted. Byline given. Pays on publication. Reports in 1 month. Computer printout submissions acceptable; prefers letter-quality to dot-matrix.
Nonfiction: "Articles on fleet management and maintenance of vehicles, especially the refrigerated van and the refrigerating unit, shop tips, loading or handling systems—especially for frozen or refrigerated cargo, new equipment specifications, conversions of equipment for better handling or more efficient operations. Prefers articles with illustrations obtained from fleets operating refrigerated trucks or trailers." Pays variable rate, approximately $100 per printed page.
Fillers: Buys newspaper clippings. "Do not rewrite."

RENEWS, Kona Communications, Inc., Suite 300, 707 Lake Cook Rd., Deerfield IL 60015. (312)498-3180. Editor: Terry Haller. Managing Editor: Denise L. Rondini. 40% freelance written. Works with a small number of new/unpublished writers each year. Magazine published 12 times/year covering automotive engine/parts rebuilding. Emphasizes technology and management issues affecting automotive rebuilders. Circ. 21,000. Pays on publication. Publishes ms an average of 2 months after acceptance. Byline sometimes given. Buys first rights. Photocopied submissions OK. Computer printout submissions acceptable; prefers letter-quality to dot-matrix. Reports in 1 month.
Nonfiction: Interview/profile, new product, photo feature and technical. "No articles that are too general to be helpful to our readers." Buys 8 mss/year. Query. Length: 1,000-2,500 words. Pays $75-300. Sometimes pays the expenses of writers on assignment.
Photos: Send photos with submission. Reviews contact sheets, transparencies and prints. Offers no additional payment for photos accepted with ms. Captions, model releases and identification of subjects required. Buys one-time rights.
Tips: "A strong automotive technical background or a special expertise in small business management is helpful. Technical and business management sections are most open to freelancers. Most of our writers are thoroughly experienced in the subject they write on. It is difficult for a 'generalist' to write for our audience."

THE SUCCESSFUL DEALER, Kona-Cal, Inc., 707 Lake Cook Rd., Deerfield IL 60015. (312)498-3180. Editor: Terry Haller. Managing Editor: Denise Rondini. 30% freelance written. "We will consider material from both established writers and new ones." Magazine published 6 times/year covering dealership management of medium and heavy duty trucks, construction equipment, forklift trucks, diesel engines and truck trailers. Circ. 19,000. Pays on publication. Byline sometimes given. Buys first serial rights only. Simultaneous queries, and simultaneous and photocopied submissions OK. Computer printout submissions acceptable; prefers letter-quality to dot-matrix. Reports in 2 weeks. Publication date "depends on the article; some are contracted for a specific issue, others on an as need basis."
Nonfiction: How-to (solve problems within the dealership); interview/profile (concentrating on business, not personality); new product (exceptional only); opinion (by readers—those in industry); personal experience (of readers); photo feature (of major events); and technical (vehicle componentry). Special issues include: March-April: American Truck Dealer Convention; September-October: Parts and Service. Query. Length: open. Pays $100-150/page. Sometimes pays the expenses of writers on assignment.
Tips: "Phone first, then follow up with a detailed explanation of the proposed article. Allow two weeks for our response. Articles should be based on real problems/solutions encountered by truck or heavy equipment dealership personnel. We are *not* interested in general management tips."

TOW-AGE, Kruza Kaleidoscopix, Inc., Box 389, Franklin MA 02038. Editor: J. Kruza. For readers who run their own towing service business. 5% freelance written. Prefers to work with published/established writers, and works with a small number of new/unpublished writrs each year. Published every 6 weeks. Circ. 18,000. Buys all rights; usually reassigns rights. Buys about 18 mss/year. Pays on acceptance. Publishes ms an average of 1 month after acceptance. Photocopied and simultaneous submissions OK. Reports in 1-4 weeks. Query for electronic submissions. Computer printout submissions acceptable. Sample copy $3; writer's guidelines for SAE.

Nonfiction: Articles on business, legal and technical information for the towing industry. "Light reading material; short, with punch." Informational, how-to, personal, interview and profile. Query or submit complete ms. Length: 200-800 words. Pays $40-100. Spot news and successful business operations. Length: 100-800 words. Technical articles. Length: 400-1,000 words. Pays expenses of writers on assignment.

Photos: Buys up to 8x10 b&w photos purchased with or without mss, or on assignment. Pays $25 for first photo; $7 for each additional photo in series. Captions required.

Tips: "We would like to receive news items relating to auto body shops and paint wholesalers (with over eight employees) or manufacturers of paints and supplies in the U.S. News items can be developed by knowing where to look. Query with samples of writing, and we may provide leads and assignments to people who can write and use a camera."

TRUCKERS' NEWS, h.e.r. Publications, Ink., 300 N.W. 50th St., Des Moines IA 50333. Owner: Jane Hermann. 10% freelance written. Monthly trucking newspaper for company drivers, owner/operators, owners of large and small trucking firms and persons in allied industries in the Midwest. Circ. 12,500. Pays on publication. Byline given. Not copyrighted. Buys first rights and second (reprint) rights to material originally published elsewhere. Submit seasonal/holiday material 2 months in advance. Simultaneous queries, and simultaneous, photocopied and previously published submissions OK. Computer printout submissions acceptable; no dot-matrix. Reports in 1 month. Publishes ms an average of 2 months after acceptance. Sample copy $1; free writer's guidelines.

Nonfiction: Expose, general interest, historical/nostalgic, how-to, humor, interview/profile, new product, personal experience, photo feature and technical. "Our special May Truckers' Day issue is the largest. Material should be submitted by March 15." Send complete ms. Length: 375-1,250 words. Pays $25-50. Sometimes pays the expenses of writers on assignment.

Photos: Send photos with ms. Pays $10-25 for 5x7 prints. Captions, model release and identification of subjects required.

Tips: "Good, bright features about people in transportation are always welcome, especially when accompanied by a photo."

TRUCKERS/USA, Randall Publishing Co., Box 2029, Tuscaloosa AL 35403. (205)349-2990. Editor: Claude Duncan. 25-50% freelance written. Eager to work with new/unpublished writers. Weekly tabloid for long-haul truck drivers and trucker service industry. "Most of our readers are long-haul truckers. We want stories about these drivers, their trucks, lifestyle and people who serve them, such as truck stops. We want upbeat stories." Circ. 15,000. Pays on acceptance. Publishes ms an average of 1 month after acceptance. Byline given. Offers 100% kill fee. Not copyrighted. Buys first serial rights, one-time rights, second serial (reprint) rights or simultaneous rights. Simultaneous and previously published (updated) submissions OK. Computer printout submissions acceptable; prefers letter-quality to dot-matrix. Reports in 2 weeks. Free sample copy and writer's guidelines.

Nonfiction: General interest (with trucker angle); historical/nostalgic (with trucker angle); humor (with trucker angle); interview/profile (with truckers); personal experience (with truckers); technical (re heavy-duty trucks); and crimes involving long-haul truckers. Buys 100 mss/year. Send complete ms. Length: 250-1,000 words. Pays $10-50. Sometimes pays expenses of writers on assignment.

Photos: Send photos with query or ms. Accepts b&w or color prints; commercially processed accepted if sharp quality. Pays $5. Identification of subjects required.

Tips: "Truckers like to read about other truckers, and people with whom truckers are in frequent contact—truckstop workers, state police, etc. We're looking for localized stories about long-haul truckers. Nothing is too local if it's interesting. We encourage multiple submissions, preferrably with art. Submitting art with copy gives a definite edge. We emphasize subject matter rather than writing style, so any of the articles published can be idea leads to similar stories. We increasingly are running longer articles, which also increases our need for shorter articles to maintain our tabloid newspaper format."

WARD'S AUTO WORLD, 28 W. Adams, Detroit MI 48226. (313)962-4433. Editor-in-Chief: David C. Smith. Editor: James W. Bush. Managing Editor: Burt Stroddard. 10% freelance written. Prefers to work with published/established writers; works with a small number of new/unpublished writers each year. For top and middle management in all phases of auto industry. Also includes heavy-duty vehicle coverage. Monthly magazine; 96 pages. Circ. 85,000. Pays on publication. Pay varies for kill fee. Byline given. Buys all rights. Phone queries OK. Submit seasonal/holiday material 1 month in advance. Electronic submissions OK; phone Mike

Arnolt, managing editor of news operations. Computer printout submissions acceptable; check first before submitting dot-matrix. Reports in 2 weeks. Publishes ms an average of 1 month after acceptance. Free sample copy and writer's guidelines.

Nonfiction: Expose, general interest, international automotive news, historical, humor, interview, new product, photo feature and technical. Few consumer type articles. No "nostalgia or personal history type stories (like 'My Favorite Car')." Buys 4-8 mss/year. Query. Length: 700-5,000 words. Pay $100-600. Sometimes pays the expenses of writers on assignment.

Photos: "We're heavy on graphics." Submit photo material with query. Pay varies for 8x10 b&w prints or color transparencies. Captions required. Buys one-time rights.

Tips: "Don't send poetry, how-to and 'My Favorite Car' stuff. It doesn't stand a chance. This is a business newsmagazine and operates on a news basis just like any other newsmagazine. We like solid, logical, well-written pieces with *all* holes filled."

—————— *Aviation and Space*

In this section are journals for aviation business executives, airport operators and aviation technicians. Publications for professional and private pilots are classified in the Consumer Aviation section.

AG-PILOT INTERNATIONAL MAGAZINE, Bio-Aeronautic Publishers, Inc., Drawer "R", Walla Walla WA 99362. (509)522-4311. Editor: Tom J. Wood. Executive Editor: Rocky Kemp. Emphasizes agricultural aerial application (crop dusting). "This is intended to be a fun-to-read, technical, as well as humorous, and serious publication for the ag pilot and operator. They are our primary target." 20% freelance written. Monthly magazine; 60 pages. Circ. 12,400. Pays on publication. Publishes ms an average of 3 months after acceptance. Buys all rights. Byline given unless writer requests name held. Computer printout submissions acceptable; prefers letter-quality to dot-matrix. Reports in 2 weeks. Sample copy $2.

Nonfiction: Expose (of EPA, OSHA, FAA or any government function concerned with this industry); general interest; historical; interview (of well-known ag/aviation person); nostalgia; personal opinion; new product; personal experience; and photo feature. "If we receive an article, in any area we have solicited, it is quite possible this person could contribute intermittently. The international input is what we desire. Industry-related material is a must. No newspaper clippings." Send complete ms. Length: 800-1,500 words. Pays $25-100. Sometimes pays the expenses of writers on assignment.

Photos: "We would like one color or b&w (5x7 preferred) with the manuscript, if applicable—it will help increase your chance of publication." Four color. Offers no additional payment for photos accepted with ms. Captions preferred, model release required.

Columns/Departments: International (of prime interest, crop dusting-related); Embryo Birdman (should be written, or appear to be written, by a beginner spray pilot); The Chopper Hopper (by anyone in the helicopter industry); Trouble Shooter (ag aircraft maintenance tips); and Catchin' The Corner (written by a person obviously skilled in the crop dusting field of experience or other interest-capturing material related to the industry). Send complete ms. Length: 800-1,500 words. Pays $25-100.

Poetry: Interested in all agri-aviation related poetry. Buys 1/issue. Submit no more than 2 at one time. Maximum length: one 20 inch x 48 picas maximum. Pays $25-50.

Fillers: Short jokes, short humor and industry-related newsbreaks. Length: 10-100 words. Pays $5-20.

Tips: "Writers should be witty and knowledgeable about the crop dusting aviation world. Material *must* be agricultural/aviation-oriented. Crop dusting or nothing!"

AIR LINE PILOT, Magazine of Professional Flight Crews, Air Line Pilots Association, 535 Herndon Parkway, Box 1169, Herndon VA 22069. (703)689-4176. Editor: Esperison Martinez, Jr. 10% freelance written. Prefers to work with published/established writers; works with a small number of new/unpublished writers each year. A monthly magazine for airline pilots covering "aviation industry information—economics, avionics, equipment, systems, safety—that affects a pilot's life in professional sense." Also includes information about management/labor relations trends, contract negotiations, etc. Circ. 42,000. Pays on acceptance. Publishes ms an average of 6 months after acceptance. Offers 35% kill fee. Buys first serial rights and makes work-for-hire assignments. Submit seasonal/holiday material 6 months in advance. Query for electronic submissions. Computer printout submissions acceptable. Reports in 2 months. Sample copy $1; free writer's guidelines.

Nonfiction: Historical/nostalgic, humor, interview/profile, photo feature and technical. "We are backlogged with historical submissions and prefer not to receive unsolicited submissions at this time." Buys 20 mss/year. Query with or without published clips, or send complete ms. Length: 1,000-3,000 words. Pays $100-800 for assigned articles; pays $50-500 for unsolicited articles.

Photos: Send photos with submission. Reviews contact sheets, 35mm transparencies and 8x10 prints. Offers $10-25/photo. Identification of subjects required. Buys one-time rights.

Tips: "For our feature section, we seek aviation industry information that affects the life of a professional airline pilot from a career standpoint. We also seek material that affects his life from a job security and work environment standpoint. Historical material that addresses the heritage of the profession or the advancement of the industry is also sought. Any airline pilot featured in an article must be an Air Line Pilots Association member in good standing."

AIRPORT SERVICES MANAGEMENT, Lakewood Publications, 50 S. 9th St., Minneapolis MN 55402. (612)333-0471. Editor: Gordon Gilbert. 33% freelance written. Emphasizes management of airports, airlines and airport-based businesses. Monthly magazine. Circ. 20,000. Pays on acceptance. Publishes ms an average of 3 months after acceptance. Buys one-time rights, exclusive in our industry. Byline given. Phone queries OK. Submit seasonal/holiday material 3 months in advance. Photocopied submissions OK but must be industry-exclusive. Computer printout submissions acceptable; prefers letter-quality to dot-matrix. Reports in 1 month. Free sample copy and writer's guidelines.

Nonfiction: How-to (manage an airport, aviation service company or airline; work with local governments, etc.); interview (with a successful operator); and technical (how to manage a maintenance shop, snow removal operations, bird control, security operations). "No flying, no airport nostalgia or product puff pieces. We don't want pieces on how one company's product solved everyone's problem (how one airport or aviation business solved its problem with a certain type of product is okay). No descriptions of airport construction projects (down to the square footage in the new restrooms) that don't discuss applications for other airports. Plain 'how-to' story lines, please." Buys 40-50 mss/year, "but at least half are short (250-750 words) items for inclusion in one of our monthly departments." Query. Length: 250-2,500 words. Pays $50 for most department articles, $200-350 for features.

Photos: State availability of photos with query. Payment for photos is included in total purchase price. Uses b&w photos, charts and line drawings.

Tips: "Writing style should be lively, informal and straightforward, but the *subject matter* must be as functional and as down-to-earth as possible. Trade magazines are *business* magazines that must help readers do their jobs better. Frequent mistakes are using industry vendors/suppliers rather than users and industry officials as *sources*, especially in endorsing products or approaches, and directing articles to pilots or aviation consumers rather than to our specialized audience of aviation business managers and airport managers."

JET CARGO NEWS, For Air Shipping Decision-Makers, Box 920952, #398, Houston TX 77292-0952. (713)681-4760. Editor: Rich Hall. 50% freelance written. Works with a small number of new/unpublished writers each year. Designed to serve international industry concerned with moving goods by air. "It brings to shippers and manufacturers spot news of airline and aircraft development, air routes, shipping techniques, innovations and rates." Monthly. Circ. 25,000. Buys all rights. Buys up to 50 mss/year. Pays on publication. Publishes ms an average of 2 months after acceptance. No photocopied or simultaneous submissions. Query for electronic submissions. Computer printout submissions acceptable; prefers letter-quality to dot-matrix. Submit seasonal material 1 month in advance. Reports in 1 month if postage is included. Submit complete ms. Sample copy for 9x12 SAE with 90¢ postage.

Nonfiction: "Direct efforts to the shipper. Tell him about airline service, freight forwarder operations, innovations within the industry, new products, aircraft, packaging, material handling, hazardous materials, computerization of shipping, and pertinent news to the industry. Use a tight magazine style. The writer must know marketing." Buys informational articles, case studies, how-tos, interviews and coverage of successful business operations. Length: 1,500 words maximum. Pays $4/inch. Sometimes pays the expenses of writers on assignment.

Photos: 8x10 b&w glossy prints purchased with and without mss; captions required. Pays $10.

Tips: A frequent mistake is missing target readers and their interests. With short articles and fillers the writer exhibits his/her initiative. "We're moving toward a news orientation in 1988. We hope to generate more case studies of successful shipping solutions and pay a 25 percent premium rate for them. We also hope to see more wrap-ups from a variety of contributors."

————— *Beverages and Bottling*

Manufacturers, distributors and retailers of soft drinks and alcoholic beverages read these publications. Publications for bar and tavern operators and managers of restaurants are classified in the Hotels, Motels, Clubs, Resorts and Restaurants category.

‡BEVERAGE RETAILER WEEKLY, 1661 Rt. 23, Wayne NJ 07470. (201)696-8105. Managing Editor: Jean Marie McKowen. 10% freelance written. Works with a small number of new/unpublished writers each year. Weekly tabloid covering the liquor industry. "We specifically serve retailers, providing news on legal changes, marketing happenings, etc." Circ. 36,000. Pays on publication. Publishes ms an average of 1 month after acceptance. Byline given. Buys one-time rights. Submit seasonal/holiday material 6 weeks in advance. Computer printout submissions acceptable; prefers letter-quality to dot-matrix. Reports in 2 weeks on queries; 1 month on mss. Sample copy and writer's guidelines for 11x17 SAE with 3 first class stamps.
Nonfiction: Expose, historical/nostalgic, how-to, interview/profile, new product, opinion, legislative update, wine, beer, liquor trends, photo feature, technical and travel. Send complete ms. "We would like to receive photos, maps, graphs and charts to accompany the story." Length: 500-2,500 words. Pays $100-200. Sometimes pays the expenses of writers on assignment.
Photos: Contact photo editor. Pays $10-20 for b&w prints. Reviews b&w contact sheets. Identification of subjects required.
Columns/Departments: All About Wine, Marketing Trends, and The Retailers View. Send complete ms. Length: 500-2,500 words. Pays $100-200.
Tips: "Changes in legislative issues affecting the alcoholic beverage industry will affect the type of stories we buy. Call or write, and exhibit satisfactory skills and a knowledge of industry. The more in-depth the article, the more appreciated."

‡MARKET WATCH, Market Intelligence on the Wine, Spirits and Beer Business, M. Shanken Communications, Inc., 400 E. 51st St., New York NY 10022. (212)751-6500. Editor: Marvin R. Shanken. Managing Editor: Michael D. Moaba. 25% freelance written. Monthly magazine covering "wine, spirits and beer marketing, including retailing, wholesaling, latest drinking trends, profiles of successful people in the industry, new product tracking surveys." Pays on publication. Publishes ms an average of 3 months after acceptance. Byline given. Kill fee varies. Buys all rights. Submit seasonal/holiday material 3 months in advance. Photocopied submissions OK. Query for electronic submissions. Computer printout submissions OK. Reports in 1 month. Free sample copy and writer's guidelines.
Nonfiction: Essays, interview/profile and new product. Buys 15 mss/year. Query with published clips. Length: 1,500-2,000 words. Pays $200-500 for assigned articles. Sometimes pays the expenses of writers on assignment.
Photos: State availability of photos with submission. Reviews contact sheets. Identification of subjects required. Buys one-time rights.

MID-CONTINENT BOTTLER, 10741 El Monte, Overland Park KS 66207. (913)341-0020. Publisher: Floyd E. Sageser. 5% freelance written. Prefers to work with published/established writers, and works with a small number of new/unpublished writers each year. For "soft drink bottlers in the 20-state Midwestern area." Bimonthly. Not copyrighted. Pays on acceptance. Publishes ms an average of 2 months after acceptance. Buys first rights only. Reports "immediately." Computer printout submissions acceptable. Sample copy with $1 postage; guidelines with SASE.
Nonfiction: "Items of specific soft drink bottler interest with special emphasis on sales and merchandising techniques. Feature style desired." Buys 2-3 mss/year. Length: 2,000 words. Pays $15-$100. Sometimes pays the expenses of writers on assignment.
Photos: Photos purchased with mss.

SOUTHERN BEVERAGE JOURNAL, Box 561107, Miami FL 33256-1107. (305)233-7230. Senior Editor: Jackie Preston. Managing Editor: Mary McMahon. 5% freelance written. Works with a small number of new/unpublished writers each year, and is eager to work with new/unpublished writers. A monthly magazine for the alcohol beverage industry. Readers are personnel of bars, restaurants, package stores, night clubs, lounges and hotels—owners, managers and salespersons. Circ. 23,000. Pays on publication. Publishes ms an average of 3-4 months after acceptance. Byline given. Buys all rights. Submit seasonal/holiday material 3

months in advance. Computer printout submissions acceptable; no dot matrix. Reports in 1 month.
Nonfiction: Interview/profile and success stories. No canned material. Buys 3 mss/year. Send complete ms. Length: 750-1,250 words. Pays $200 maximum for assigned articles; pays $150 maximum for unsolicited articles. Sometimes pays the expenses of writers on assignment.
Photos: State availability of photos with submission. Reviews 3x5 prints. Offers $10 maximum/photo. Identification of subjects required. Buys all rights.
Tips: "We are interested in legislation having to do with our industry and also views on trends, drinking and different beverages."

TEA & COFFEE TRADE JOURNAL, Lockwood Book Publishing Co., 130 W. 42nd St., New York NY 10036. (212)661-5980. Editor: Jane Phillips McCabe. 50% freelance written. Prefers to work with published/established writers. A monthly magazine covering the international coffee and tea market. "Tea and coffee trends are analyzed; transportation problems, new equipment for plants and packaging are featured." Circ. approximately 10,000. Pays on publication. Publishes ms an average of 2 months after acceptance. Byline given. Makes work-for-hire assignments. Submit seasonal/holiday material 1 month in advance. Simultaneous submissions OK. Computer printout submissions acceptable; no dot-matrix. Free sample copy.
Nonfiction: Exposé, historical/nostalgic, interview/profile, new product, photo feature and technical. Special issue includes the Coffee Market Forecast and Review (January). "No consumer related submissions. I'm only interested in the trade." Buys 60 mss/year. Query. Length: 750-1,500 words. Pays $4.50/published inch.
Photos: State availability of photos with submission. Reviews contact sheets, negatives, transparencies and prints. Pays $4.50/published inch. Captions and identification of subjects required. Buys one-time rights.
Columns/Departments: Office Coffee Service (vending coffee industry/office coffee); Specialties (gourmet trends); and Transportation (shipping lines). Buys 36 mss/year. Query. Pays $4.50/published inch.

‡VINEYARD & WINERY MANAGEMENT, 103 Third St., Box 231, Watkinsglen NY 14891. (607)535-7133. Editor: James McGrath Morris. 80% freelance written. A bimonthly trade journal on winemaking and grape growing. Circ. 3,500. Pays on publication. Byline given. Offers 30% kill fee. Buys first North American serial rights. Submit seasonal/holiday material 4 months in advance. Photocopied submissions OK. Query for electronic submissions. Computer printout submissions OK; prefers letter-quality to dot-matrix. Reports in 3 weeks on queries; 1 month on mss. Free sample copy.
Nonfiction: How-to, interview/profile and technical. Buys 25 mss/year. Query. Length: 300-5,000 words. Pays $20-750 for assigned articles; pays $20-500 for unsolicited articles. Pays expenses of writers on assignment.
Photos: State availability of photos with submission. Reviews contact sheets, negatives and transparencies. Offers no additional payment for photos accepted with ms. Identification of subjects required. Buys one-time rights.

WINES & VINES, 1800 Lincoln Ave., San Rafael CA 94901. Editor: Philip E. Hiaring. 10-20% freelance written. Works with a small number of new/unpublished writers each year. For everyone concerned with the grape and wine industry including winemakers, wine merchants, growers, suppliers, consumers, etc. Monthly magazine. Circ. 5,500. Buy first North American serial rights or simultaneous rights. Pays on acceptance. Publishes ms an average of 3 months after acceptance. Submit special material (water, January; vineyard, February; Man-of-the-Year, March; Brandy, April; export-import, May; enological, June; statistical, July; marketing, September; equipment and supplies, November; champagne, December) 3 months in advance. Computer printout submissions OK; no dot-matrix. Reports in 2 weeks. Sample copy for 10x12 SASE.
Nonfiction: Articles of interest to the trade. "These could be on grape growing in unusual areas; new winemaking techniques; wine marketing, retailing, etc." Interview, historical, spot news, merchandising techniques and technical. No stories with a strong consumer orientation as against trade orientation. Author should know the subject matter, i.e., know proper grape growing/winemaking terminology. Buys 3-4 ms/year. Query. Length: 1,000-2,500 words. Pays 5¢/word. Sometimes pays the expenses of writers on assignment.
Photos: Pays $10 for 4x5 or 8x10 b&w photos purchased with mss. Captions required.
Tips: "Ours is a trade magazine for professionals. Therefore, we do not use 'gee-whiz' wine articles."

——— *Book and Bookstore Trade*

AB BOOKMAN'S WEEKLY, Box AB, Clifton NJ 07015. (201)772-0020. Editor-in-Chief: Jacob L. Chernofsky. Weekly magazine; 160 pages. For professional and specialist booksellers, acquisitions and

academic librarians, book publishers, book collectors, bibliographers, historians, etc. Circ. 8,500. Pays on publication. Byline given. Buys all rights. Phone queries OK. Submit seasonal or holiday material 2-3 months in advance. Simultaneous and photocopied submissions OK. Reports in 1 month. Sample copy $10.
Nonfiction: How-to (for professional booksellers); historical (related to books or book trade or printing or publishing); personal experiences; nostalgia; interviews and profiles. Query. Length: 2,500 words minimum. Pays $60 minimum.
Photos: Photos used with mss.

AMERICAN BOOKSELLER, Booksellers Publishing, Inc., 122 E. 42nd St., New York NY 10168. (212)867-9060. Editor: Ginger Curwen. 10% freelance written. This publication emphasizes the business of retail bookselling and goes to the 6,300 members of the American Booksellers Association and to more than 2,100 other readers nationwide, most of whom are involved in publishing. Monthly magazine; 48 pages. Circ. 8,400. Pays on publication. Publishes ms an average of 4 months after acceptance. Buys first serial rights. Pays 25% kill fee. Byline given. Submit seasonal/holiday material 3 months in advance. Query for electronic submissions. Computer printout submissions acceptable; prefers letter-quality to dot-matrix. Reports in 3 months. Sample copy $3.
Nonfiction: General interest (on bookselling); how-to (run a bookstore, work with publishers); interview (on authors and booksellers); photo feature (on book-related events); bookstore profiles; and solutions to the problems of small businesses. Buys 2 mss/issue. Query with clips of published work and background knowledge of bookselling. Length: 750-2,000 words. Pays $75-300. Sometimes pays the expenses of writers on assignment.
Photos: State availability of photos. Uses b&w 5x7 matte prints and contact sheets. Pays $10-20. Uses 35mm color transparencies. Pays $10-50. Captions and model releases required.
Tips: "While we buy a number of articles for each issue, very few come from freelance writers. Since the focus of the magazine is on the business of bookselling, most of our contributors are booksellers who share their *firsthand* experience with our readers. 85% of these articles are assigned; the rest are unsolicited—but those come mainly from booksellers as well."

THE FEMINIST BOOKSTORE NEWS, Box 882554, San Francisco CA 94188. (415)431-2093. Editor: Carol Seajay. Managing Editor: Christine Chia. 10% freelance written. Works with a small number of new/unpublished writers each year. A bimonthly magazine covering feminist books and the women-in-print industry. "*Feminist Bookstore News* covers 'everything of interest' to the feminist bookstores, publishers and periodicals, books of interest to feminist bookstores, and provides an overview of feminist publishing by mainstream publishers." Circ. 450. Pays on publication. Publishes ms an average of 2 months after acceptance. Byline sometimes given. Buys one-time rights. Simultaneous and photocopied submissions OK. Computer printout submissions acceptable; prefers letter-quality to dot-matrix. Reports in 3 weeks. Sample copy $4.
Nonfiction: Essays, exposé, how-to (run a bookstore); new product; opinion; and personal experience (in feminist book trade only). Special issues include Sidelines issue (May) and University Press issue (fall). No submissions that do not directly apply to the feminist book trade. Query with or without published clips, or send complete ms. Length: 250-2,000 words. Pays $10-25; may pay in copies when appropriate.
Photos: State availability of photos with submission. Model release and identification of subjects required. Buys one-time rights.
Fillers: Anecdotes, facts, newsbreaks and short humor. Length: 100-400 words. Pays $5-15.
Tips: "Have several years experience in the feminist book industry. We publish very little by anyone else."

THE HORN BOOK MAGAZINE, The Horn Book, Inc., 31 St. James Ave., Boston MA 02116. (617)482-5198. Editor: Anita Silvey. 25% freelance written. Prefers to work with published/writers. Bimonthly magazine covering children's literature for librarians, booksellers, professors, and students of children's literature. Circ. 18,000. Pays on publication. Publishes ms an average of 4 months after acceptance. Byline given. Buys one-time rights. Submit seasonal/holiday material 6 months in advance. Simultaneous queries, and simultaneous, photocopied, and previously published submissions OK. Computer printout submissions acceptable; no dot-matrix. Reports in 6 weeks on queries; 2 months on mss. Free sample copy; writer's guidelines for SAE with 1 first class stamp.
Nonfiction: Interview/profile (children's book authors and illustrators). Buys 20 mss/year. Query or send complete ms. Length: 1,000-2,800 words. Pays $25-250.
Tips: "Writers have a better chance of breaking in to our publication with a query letter on a specific article they want to write."

PUBLISHERS WEEKLY, 249 W. 17th St., New York NY 10011. (212)645-0067. Editor-in-Chief: John F. Baker. Weekly. Buys first North American serial rights. Pays on publication. Computer printout submissions acceptable; prefers letter-quality to dot-matrix. Reports "in several weeks."
Nonfiction: "We rarely use unsolicited manuscripts because of our highly specialized audience and their

professional interests, but we can sometimes use news items about publishers, publishing projects, bookstores and other subjects relating to books. We will be paying increasing attention to electronic publishing." No pieces about writers or word processors. Payment negotiable; generally $150/printed page.
Photos: Photos occasionally purchased with and without mss.

WESTERN PUBLISHER, A Trade Journal, WP, Inc., Box 591012, Golden Gate Station, San Francisco CA 94159. (415)661-7964. Publisher: Tony D'Arpino. Editor: Paula von Lowenfeldt. 25% freelance written. Monthly tabloid covering publishing and book industry. Audience includes publishers, booksellers, and librarians in Western United States and Pacific Rim nations. Circ. 10,000. Pays on publication. Publishes ms an average of 1 month after acceptance. Byline given. Kill fee negotiable. Buys one-time rights. Submit seasonal/holiday material 3 months in advance; calendar: 6 months. Simultaneous queries, and simultaneous, photocopied, and previously published submissions OK. Computer printout submissions acceptable; prefers letter-quality to dot-matrix. Reports in 1 week. Sample copy $2.
Nonfiction: Book excerpts (of industry interest), general interest, historical, how-to, interview/profile, new product, opinion, personal experience, photo feature, technical, and short reviews of just published books. No reviews over 500 words. Buys 100 mss/year. Query with or without published clips or send complete ms. Length: open. Pays negotiable rates.
Tips: "The area most open to freelancers is Western Book Round Up (review listings). A freelancer can best break in to our publication with short reviews of forthcoming books, 200-500 words; 250 words, preferred."

____ Brick, Glass and Ceramics

These publications are read by manufacturers, dealers and managers of brick, glass and ceramic retail businesses. Other publications related to glass and ceramics are listed in the Consumer Art and Hobby and Crafts sections.

AMERICAN GLASS REVIEW, Box 2147, Clifton NJ 07015. (201)779-1600. Editor-in-Chief: Donald Doctorow. 10% freelance written. Monthly magazine; 24 pages. Pays on publication. Byline given. Phone queries OK. Buys all rights. Submit seasonal/holiday material 2 months in advance of issue date. Reports in 2-3 weeks. Free sample copy and writer's guidelines; mention *Writer's Market* in request.
Nonfiction: Glass plant and glass manufacturing articles. Buys 3-4 mss/year. Query. Length: 1,500-3,000 words. Pays $40-50.
Photos: State availability of photos with query. No additional payment for b&w contact sheets. Captions preferred. Buys one-time rights.

BRICK AND CLAY RECORD, 6200 S.O.M. Center Rd., Solon OH 44139. (216)349-3060. Editor-in-Chief: Patricia A. Janeway. For "the heavy clay products industry." Monthly. Buys all rights. Pays on publication. Reports in 15 days.
Nonfiction: "News concerning personnel changes within companies; news concerning new plants for manufacture of brick, clay pipe, refractories, drain tile, face brick and abrasives; and news of new products, expansion and new building." Query first. Length: 1,500-2,000 words. Pays minimum $75/published page.
Photos: No additional payment for photos used with mss.
Fillers: "Items should concern only news of brick, clay pipe, refractory or abrasives plant operations and brick distributors. If news of personnel, should be only of top-level personnel. Not interested in items such as patio, motel, or home construction using brick; consumer oriented items; weddings or engagements of clay products people, unless major executives; obituaries, unless of major personnel; or items concerning floor or wall tile (only structural tile); of plastics, metal, concrete, bakelite, or similar products; items concerning people not directly involved in clay plant operation." Pays minimum $6 for "full-length published news item, depending on value of item and editor's discretion. Payment is only for items published in the magazine. No items sent in can be returned."

CERAMIC INDUSTRY, 6200 S.O.M. Center, Solon OH 44139. (216)349-3060. Editor-in-Chief: Patricia A. Janeway. For the ceramic industry; manufacturers of glass, porcelain enamel, whiteware and advanced ceramics (electronic, industrial and high tech). Magazine; 50-60 pages. Monthly. Circ. 7,500. Buys all rights. Byline given. Buys 10-12 mss/year (on assignment only). Pays on publication. Free sample copy on request.

Reports immediately. Query first.

Nonfiction: Semitechnical, informational and how-to material purchased on assignment only. Length: 500-1,500 words. Pays $75/published page.

Photos: No additional payment for photos used with mss. Captions required.

CERAMIC SCOPE, 3632 Ashworth North, Seattle WA 98103. (206)547-7611. Editor: Michael Scott. Managing Editor: Bart Becker. Monthly magazine covering hobby ceramics business. For "ceramic studio owners and teachers operating out of homes as well as storefronts, who have a love for ceramics but meager business education." Also read by distributors, dealers and supervisors of ceramic programs in institutions. Circ. 8,000. Pays on publication. Byline given unless it is a round-up story with any number of sources. Submit seasonal/holiday material 5 months in advance. Computer printout submissions acceptable. Reports in 2 weeks. Sample copy $1.

Nonfiction: "Articles on operating a small business specifically tailored to the ceramic hobby field; photo feature stories with in-depth information about business practices and methods that contribute to successful studio operation."

Photos: State availability of photos or send photos with ms. Pays $5/4x5 or 5x7 glossy b&w print. Captions required.

GLASS DIGEST, 310 Madison Ave., New York NY 10017. (212)682-7681. Editor: Charles B. Cumpston. Monthly. Buys first rights only. Byline given "only industry people—not freelancers." Pays on publication "or before, if ms held too long." Free sample copy on request. Reports "as soon as possible." Enclose SASE for return of submissions.

Nonfiction: "Items about firms in glass distribution, personnel, plants, etc. Stories about outstanding jobs accomplished—volume of flat glass, storefronts, curtainwalls, auto glass, mirrors, windows (metal), glass doors; special uses and values; and who installed it. Stories about successful glass/metal distributors, dealers and glazing contractors—their methods, promotion work done, advertising and results." Length: 1,000-1,500 words. Pays 7¢/word, "usually more. No interest in bottles, glassware, containers, etc., but leaded and stained glass good."

Photos: B&w photos purchased with mss; "8x10 preferred." Pays $7.50, "usually more."

Tips: "Find a typical dealer case history about a firm operating in such a successful way that its methods can be duplicated by readers everywhere."

GLASS MAGAZINE, For the Architectural and Automotive Glass Industries, National Glass Association, Suite 302, 8200 Greensboro Drive, McLean VA 22102. (703)442-4890. Editor: Patricia Mascari. 25% freelance written. Prefers to work with published/established writers; works with a small number of new/unpublished writers each year. A monthly magazine covering the architectural and automotive glass industries for members of the glass and architectural trades. Circ. 13,000. Pays on acceptance. Publishes ms an average of 3-6 months after acceptance. Byline given. Offers varying kill fee. Buys first rights only. Computer printout submissions acceptable; prefers letter-quality to dot-matrix. Reports in 1 month. Sample copy for $4 and 10x13 SAE with $2.40 postage; free writer's guidelines.

Nonfiction: Interview/profile (of various glass businesses; profiles of industry people or glass business owners); and technical (about glazing processes). Buys 20 mss/year. Query with published clips. Length: 1,500 words minimum. Pays $200-600. Sometimes pays the expenses of writers on assignment.

Photos: State availability of photos. Reviews b&w and color contact sheets. Pays $15-30 for b&w; $25-75 for color. Identification of subjects required. Buys one-time rights.

Tips: "We are a growing magazine and do not have a large enough staff to do all the writing that will be required. We need more freelancers."

Building Interiors

MODERN FLOOR COVERINGS, International Thomson Retail Press, 345 Park Ave. S., New York NY 10010. (212)686-7744. Editor: Michael Karol. 15-20% freelance written. Prefers to work with published/established writers. Monthly tabloid featuring profit-making ideas on floor coverings, for the retail community. Circ. 28,000. Pays on acceptance. Publishes ms an average of 3 months after acceptance. Byline given. Buys first rights only. Makes work-for-hire assignments. Electronic submissions OK via IBM PC. Computer printout submissions acceptable; prefers letter-quality submissions to dot-matrix. "Better to write first. Send resume and cover letter explaining your qualifications and business writing experience." Writer's guidelines for SASE.

Nonfiction: Interview and features/profiles. Send complete ms. Length: 1,000-10,000 words. Pays $50-250. Sometimes pays the expenses of writers on assignment.

Tips: "Polished, professional writing is always a plus. Articles on color/design will be more of a focus this year. The most frequent mistake made by writers is that articles are too general to relate to our audience—which is mainly the floor covering retailer/specialty store."

PAINTING AND WALLCOVERING CONTRACTOR, Finan Publishing, Inc., 130 W. Lockwood, St. Louis MO 63119. (314)961-6644. Under license from the Painting and Decorating Contractors of America, 7223 Lee Hwy., Falls Church VA 22046. (703)534-1201. Publisher and Editor: Tom Finan. Executive Editor: Robert D. Richardson. 50% freelance written. Official monthly publication of the PDCA. Circ. 15,000 "with roughly 85% of that number painting contractors/owners." Emphasis on key aspects of the painting and wallcovering contracting business, aiming for complete coverage of tools, techniques, materials, and business management. Freelance by assignment only. Send resume and sample of work. Pays on publication. Publishes ms an average of 1 month after acceptance. Buys first North American serial rights. Electronic submissions OK via 5½in. floppy disks. Computer printout submissions acceptable; prefers letter-quality to dot-matrix.

Nonfiction: How-to, informational, some technical. Buys 20 mss/year. Pays $150-350. Sometimes pays the expenses of writers on assignment.

Photos: Purchased with accompanying ms. Captions required. Pays $15 for professional quality 8x10 glossy b&w prints or color slides. Model release required.

Tips: "We're looking to build long term relations with freelancers around the country. If the writer has no sample clips of the painting/wallcovering contractors, send samples showing familiarity with other aspects of the construction industry. Follow up resume/sample with phone call in 2-3 weeks. The writer sometimes has a better chance of breaking in at our publication with short articles and fillers as we need to be sure the writer understands the market we publish for—sometimes we take a chance on those with inappropriate clips. The most frequent mistake made by writers in completing an article for us is misunderstanding the reader's needs, industry and jargon."

REMODELING, Hanley-Wood, Inc., Suite 475, 655 15th St. NW, Washington DC 20005. (202)737-0717. Editor: Wendy Jordan. 5% freelance written. A monthly magazine covering residential and light commercial remodeling. "We cover the best new ideas in remodeling design, business, construction and products." Circ. 47,000. Pays on publication. Publishes ms an average of 3 months after acceptance. Byline given. Offers 5¢/word kill fee. Buys first North American serial rights. Photocopied submissions OK. Electronic submissions OK, but requires hard copy also. Computer printout submissions acceptable. Reports in 1 month. Free sample copy and writer's guidelines.

Nonfiction: Interview/profile, new product and technical. Buys 6 mss/year. Query with published clips. Length: 250-1,000 words. Pays 20¢/word. Sometimes pays the expenses of writers on assignment.

Photos: State availability of photos with submission. Reviews slides, 4x5 transparencies, and 8x10 prints. Offers $25-100/photo. Captions, model releases, and identification of subjects required. Buys one-time rights.

Tips: "The areas of our publication most open to freelancers are news and new product news."

WALLS & CEILINGS, 14006 Ventura Blvd., Sherman Oaks CA 91423. (213)789-8733. Editor-in-Chief: Lee Rector. Managing Editor: Don Haley. 10% freelance written. Prefers to work with published/established writers, and works with a small number of new/unpublished writers each year. For contractors involved in lathing and plastering, drywall, acoustics, fireproofing, curtain walls, movable partitions together with manufacturers, dealers, and architects. Monthly magazine; 48 pages. Circ. 12,000. Pays on publication. Publishes ms an average of 4-6 months after acceptance. Buys first North American serial rights. Byline given. Phone queries OK. Submit seasonal/holiday material 3 months in advance. Query for electronic submissions. Computer printout submissions OK. Reports in 3 weeks. Sample copy for $5 and 9x12 SASE.

Nonfiction: How-to (drywall and plaster construction and business management); and interview. Buys 12 mss/year. Query. Length: 200-1,000 words. Pays $25-125 maximum. Sometimes pays the expenses of writers on assignment.

Photos: State availability of photos with query. Pays $5 for 8x10 b&w prints. Captions required. Buys one-time rights.

Tips: "We would like to receive wall and ceiling finishing features about unique designs and applications in new buildings (from high-rise to fast food restaurants), fireproofing, and acoustical design with photography (b&w and color)."

Business Management

These publications cover trends, general theory and management practices for business owners and top-level business executives. Publications that use similar material but have a less technical slant are listed in Business and Finance in the Consumer Publications section. Journals dealing with banking, investment and financial management can be found in the Finance category. Journals for middle management, including supervisors and office managers, appear in the Management and Supervision section. Those for industrial plant managers are listed under Industrial Operations and under the sections for specific industries, such as Machinery and Metal. Publications for office supply store operators are included in the Office Environment and Equipment section.

‡**AWARDS SPECIALIST**, DF Publications, 26 Summit St., Box 1230, Brighton MI 48116. (313)227-2614. Editor: James J. Farrell. Managing Editor: Michael J. Davis. 40% freelance written. Prefers to work with published/established writers, and works with a small number of new/unpublished writers each year. A monthly magazine for the recognition industry, especially awards. "_Awards Specialist_ is published for retail business owners and owners involved in the recognition industry. Our aim is to provide solid, down-to-earth information to help them succeed in business, as well as news and ideas about the recognition industry." Pays on acceptance. Publishes ms an average of 4 months after acceptance. Byline sometimes given. Buys all rights or makes work-for-hire assignments. Submit seasonal/holiday material 6 months in advance. Previously published submissions OK "if we are so informed." Query for electronic submissions. Computer printout submissions OK. Reports in 3 weeks. "Sample copy and writer's guidelines sent to those who send us writing samples or query about an article."
Nonfiction: Historical, how-to, interview/profile, new product, photo feature, technical and business and marketing. "Our readers are becoming more involved in the specialty advertising industry. No vague, general articles which could be aimed at any audience. We prefer to receive a query from writers before reviewing a manuscript. Also, a large number of our freelance articles are given to writers on assignment." Buys 20-30 mss/year. Query with clips ("clips do not have to be published, but should give us an indication of writer's ability"). Length: depends on subject matter. Pays $50-225.
Photos: Send photos with submission. Reviews 8x10 prints. Offers no additional payment for photos accepted with ms, "but we take the photos into consideration when deciding rate of compensation for the assignment." Captions, model releases and identification of subjects required. Buys all rights; "semi-exclusive rights may be purchased, for our industry, depending on subject."
Tips: "The best way to work for _Awards Specialist_ is to write to us with information about your background and experience (a resume, if possible), and several samples of your writing. We are most interested in receiving business and marketing articles from freelancers. These would provide solid, down-to-earth information for the smaller business owner. For example, recent articles we have included were on tips for writing good business letters; the proper use of titles for awards; legal and practical considerations of setting up a corporation vs. a sole proprietorship. Articles should be written in clear, plain English with examples and anecdotes to add interest to the subject matter."

COMMON SENSE, Upstart Publishing Company, 50 Mill St., Dover NH 03820. (603)749-5071. Editor: Jean E. Kerr. 25% freelance written. Prefers to work with published/established writers. A monthly newsletter covering small business and personal finance. Pays on acceptance. Publishes ms an average of 2-4 months after acceptance. Byline sometimes given. $20 kill fee. Buys all rights and makes work-for-hire assignments. Simultaneous, photocopied and previously published submissions OK. Computer printout submissions acceptable; prefers letter-quality to dot-matrix. Reports in 1 month. Free sample copy and writer's guidelines.
Nonfiction: How-to, interview/profile and technical. "We are looking for clear, jargon-free information. We often sell our publications in bulk to banks so must avoid subjects and stances that clearly run counter to their interests." No highly technical or pompous language, or politically contentious articles. Buys 15-20 mss/year. Query with published clips. Length: 2,500 words maximum. Pays $250 for assigned articles. "We pay with contributor's copies if there is a significant public relations benefit for the writer."
Columns/Departments: Breakthroughs (technological, medical breakthroughs or innovations, new applications for old materials or products; scientific information of interest to the business communities). Query with published clips. Length: 100-500 words. Pays $10-50.

COMMUNICATION BRIEFINGS, Encoders, Inc., 806 Westminster Blvd., Blackwood NJ 08012. (609)589-3503, 227-7371. Executive Editor: Frank Grazian. 15% freelance written. Prefers to work with published/established writers. A monthly newsletter covering business communication and business management. "Most readers are in middle and upper management. They comprise public relations professionals, editors of company publications, marketing and advertising managers, fund raisers, directors of associations and foundations, school and college administrators, human resources professionals, and other middle managers who want to communicate better on the job." Circ. 25,600. Pays on acceptance. Publishes ms an average of 2-3 months after acceptance. Byline given sometimes on Bonus Items and on other items if idea originates with the writer. Offers 25% kill fee. Buys one-time rights. Submit seasonal/holiday material 2 months in advance. Previously published submissions OK, "but must be rewritten to conform to our style." Computer printout submissions acceptable; prefers letter-quality to dot-matrix. Reports in 1 month. Sample copy and writer's guidelines for #10 SAE and 2 first class stamps.

Nonfiction: "Most articles we buy are of the 'how-to' type. They consist of practical ideas, techniques and advice that readers can use to improve business communication and management. Areas covered: writing, speaking, listening, employee communication, human relations, public relations, interpersonal communication, persuasion, conducting meetings, advertising, marketing, fund raising, telephone techniques, teleconferencing, selling, improving publications, handling conflicts, negotiating, etc. Because half of our subscribers are in the nonprofit sector, articles that appeal to both profit and nonprofit organizations are given top priority." *Short Items*: Articles consisting of one or two brief tips that can stand alone. Length: 40-70 words. *Articles*: A collection of tips or ideas that offer a solution to a communication or management problem or that show a better way to communicate or manage. Examples: "How to produce slogans that work," "The wrong way to criticize employees," "Mistakes to avoid when leading a group discussion," and "5 ways to overcome writer's block." Length: 125-150 words. *Bonus Items:* In-depth pieces that probe one area of communication or management and cover it as thoroughly as possible. Examples: "Producing successful special events," "How to evaluate your newsletter," and "How to write to be understood." Length: 1,300 words. Buys 30-50 mss/year. Pays $15-35 for 40- to 150-word pieces; Bonus Items, $200. Pays the expenses of writers on assignment.

Tips: "Our readers are looking for specific and practical ideas and tips that will help them communicate better both within their organizations and with outside publics. Most ideas are rejected because they are too general or too elementary for our audience. Our style is down-to-earth and terse. We pack a lot of useful information into short articles. Our readers are busy executives and managers who want information dispatched quickly and without embroidery. We omit anecdotes, lengthy quotes and long-winded exposition. The writer has a better chance of breaking in at our publication with short articles and fillers since we buy only six major features (bonus items) a year. We require queries on longer items and bonus items. Writers may submit short tips (40-70 words) without querying. The most frequent mistakes made by writers in completing an article for us are failure to master the style of our publication and to understand our readers' needs."

COMPUTERS IN BANKING, The Computer and Automation Magazine for Bank Management, Dealers Digest Inc., Suite 400, 150 Broadway, New York NY 10038. (212)227-1200. Editor: John Dickinson. Senior Editor: Brian Tracey. Approximately 10-30% freelance written. Prefers to work with published/established writers, and works with a small number of new/unpublished writers each year. A monthly magazine covering bank automation and management. "*Computers in Banking* is for senior bank executives and data processing professionals who make business decisions about computer and automation software and equipment. We cover technology but from an issues and management-oriented perspective." Circ. 42,000. Pays on publication. Publishes ms an average of 2-4 months after acceptance. Byline given for features and some news stories. Offers 25% kill fee. Buys all rights and makes work-for-hire assignments. Photocopied submissions OK. Electronic submissions preferred. Query for electronic submissions. Computer printout submissions acceptable; no dot-matrix. Sample copy for 8½x11 SAE; free writer's guidelines.

Nonfiction: How-to, interview/profile, new product, technical and event coverage. Special issues are staff written. "No one-sided, vendor-oriented pieces. We are a user-oriented magazine." Buys 24-30 mss/year. Query with published clips. Length: 2,500-4,000 words. Pays $200 for news stories, $1,000 for features. Usually pays the expenses of writers on assignment.

Photos: Send photos with submission. Reviews transparencies and any size b&w prints. Offers no additional payment for photos accepted with ms. Identification of subjects required.

Columns/Departments: Case History (one-user, one-vendor, problem/solution), 1,200-2,000 words. Buys 20 mss/year. Query with published clips. Pays $200-400. "We need short news bits for 'upfront' section, which tries to cover installations and product announcements before the official press releases."

Tips: "Writers must have a working knowledge of the computer industry and a good understanding of banking and financial matters. Our standards are very high. Writers should be willing to fill holes, answer specific questions and care about seemingly little details like what a bank paid for a computer system and when it was installed or tested. Publication is national, so focus must be broad. However, we are always looking for regional correspondents. The areas of our publication most open to freelancers are features and short news stories for 'Update' section. There is serious potential for international coverage beginning in 1988."

FARM STORE MERCHANDISING, Miller Publishing, 2501 Wayzata Blvd., Box 67, Minneapolis MN 55440. (612)374-5200. Editor: Margaret Kaeter. Staff Editor: Colleen M. Sauber. 25% freelance written. Eager to work with new/unpublished writers. A monthly magazine for small business owners who sell to farmers. Primary busines lines are bulk and bagged feed, animal health products, grain storage, agricultural chemicals. Pays on publication. Publishes ms an average of 3 months after acceptance. Byline given. Buys first rights or one-time rights. Submit seasonal/holiday material 3 months in advance. Photocopied and previously published submissions OK. Computer printout submissions acceptable; prefers letter-quality to dot-matrix. Reports in 1 month. Free sample copy and writer's guidelines.
Nonfiction: How-to (subjects must be business-oriented, credit, taxes, inventory, hiring, firing, etc.); interview/profile (with successful agribusiness dealers or industry leaders); opinion (on controversial industry issues); personal experiences (good or bad ways to run a business); photo features (people-oriented); and technical (how to maintain sprayers, what's the best fertilizer spreader, etc.). Buys 15 mss/year. Query. Length: 750-2,500 words. Pays $100-300 for assigned articles; pays $25-250 for unsolicited articles. Sometimes pays the expenses of writers on assignment.
Photos: Send photos with submission. Reviews contact sheets. Offers no additional payment for photos accepted with ms. Identification of subjects required. Buys one-time rights.
Columns/Departments: Inside Line (opinion pieces on highly controversial industry issues). Buys 5 mss/year. Query. Length: 1,200-2,000 words. Pays $25-300.
Tips: "The area of our publication most open to freelancers is features on successful farm store dealers. Submit two to three black and white photos. Keep the article under 2,000 words and don't get bogged down in technical details. Tell what sets their business apart and why it works. General business articles also are needed, especially if they have a rural, small-business slant."

‡HISPANIC BUSINESS, Suite 100C, 360 S. Hope Ave., Santa Barbara CA 93105. (805)682-5843. Managing Editor: Forrest Smith. Senior Editor: Steve Beale. Monthly magazine covering Hispanic entrepreneurs, professionals, media, markets. "*Hispanic Business* focuses on topics of interest to Hispanics in the business and professional world, and provides authoritative information on Hispanic markets and the Hispanic business economy." Circ. 110,000. Pays on acceptance. Publishes ms an average of 2 months after acceptance. Byline given. Kill fee "usually ½-⅓ of fee." Buys all rights. Submit seasonal/holiday material 3 months in advance. Photocopied submissions OK. Query for electronic submissions. Computer printout submissions OK; prefers letter-quality to dot-matrix. Reports in 1 month. Sample copy for SASE; free writer's guidelines.
Nonfiction: How-to, interview/profile and travel. "No pure human-interest stories. We are interested in practical articles about business: financing, marketing, management, etc." Buys 10-20 mss/year. Query with published clips. Length: 1,000-6,000 words. Pays $100-600 for assigned articles; pays $100-300 for unsolicited articles. "We prefer to make the assignments. Unsolicited articles have the best shot if short." Pays expenses of writers on assignment.
Photos: State availability of photos with submission. "We usually make our own arrangements for photos. If writer wants to be a photographer, we can negotiate." Reviews contact sheets, transparencies and prints. Offers no additional payment for photos accepted with ms. Identification of subjects required.
Tips: "Writers querying 'out of the cold' should stick to short items with a strong practical 'how-to' flavor (1,000-2,000 words). Feature articles are usually assigned by the editors. We are looking for writers in key cities (L.A., New York, Miami, Chicago, San Antonio, Denver, Houston, Dallas, El Paso, etc.) to whom we can assign major features. We prefer writers who have experience writing about business. We are interested in subjects like how to secure financing, management challenges, marketing, etc. We also do profiles of successful Hispanic-owned businesses. Short features (1,000-2,000 words) are always in demand. As always, they should be practical and oriented toward helping people in the business world."

IN BUSINESS, JG Press, Inc., Box 323, Emmaus PA 18049. (215)967-4135. Editor: Jerome Goldstein. Managing Editor: Ina Pincus. 50% freelance written. Works with a small number of new/unpublished writers each year. Bimonthly magazine covering small businesses, their management and new developments for small business owners or people thinking about starting out. Circ. 60,000. Pays on publication. Publishes ms an average of 4 months after acceptance. Buys first North American serial rights. Submit seasonal material 3 months in advance. Reports in 6 weeks. Sample copy $3; free writer's guidelines.
Nonfiction: Expose (related to small business, trends and economic climate); how-to (advertise, market, handle publicity, finance, take inventory); profile (of an innovative small scale business); and new product (inventions and R&D by small businesses). "Keep how-tos in mind for feature articles; capture the personality of the business owner and the effect of that on the business operations." Buys 5 unsolicited mss/year. Query with clips of published work. Length: 1,000-2,000 words. Pays $75-200. Sometimes pays the expenses of writers on assignment.
Photos: State availability of photos. Pays $25-75. Reviews contact sheets. Captions preferred; model release required.
Tips: "Get a copy of the magazine and read it carefully so you can better understand the editorial focus. Send several specific article ideas on one topic, so we can sharpen the focus. Keep in mind that the reader will be

looking for specifics and transferable information."

MAY TRENDS, George S. May International Company. 111 S. Washington St., Park Ridge IL 60068. (312)825-8806. Editor: John E. McArdle. 20% freelance written. Works with a small number of new/unpublished writers each year. For owners and managers of small and medium-sized businesses, hospitals and nursing homes, trade associations, Better Business Bureaus, educational institutions and newspapers. Magazine published without charge 3 times a year; 28-30 pages. Circulation: 30,000. Buys all rights. Byline given. Buys 10-15 mss/year. Pays on acceptance. Publishes ms an average of 4-6 months after acceptance. Returns rejected material immediately. Query or submit complete ms. Computer printout submissions acceptable; prefers letter-quality to dot-matrix. Reports in 2 weeks. Will send free sample copy to writer on request for SAE with 2 first class stamps.
Nonfiction: "We prefer articles dealing with how to solve problems of specific industries (manufacturers, wholesalers, retailers, service businesses, small hospitals and nursing homes) where contact has been made with key executives whose comments regarding their problems may be quoted. We want problem solving articles, *not* success stories that laud an individual company. We like articles that give the business manager concrete suggestions on how to deal with specific problems—i.e., '5 steps to solve . . .', '6 key questions to ask when . . .', and '4 tell-tale signs indicating . . .'." Focus is on marketing, economic and technological trends that have an impact on medium- and small-sized businesses, not on the "giants"; automobile dealers coping with existing dull markets; and contractors solving cost-inventory problems. Will consider material on successful business operations and merchandising techniques. Length: 2,000-3,000 words. Pays $150-250.
Tips: Query letter should tell "type of business and problems the article will deal with. We specialize in the problems of small (20-500 employees, $500,000-2,500,000 volume) businesses (manufacturing, wholesale, retail and service), plus medium and small health care facilities. We are now including nationally known writers in each issue—writers like the Vice Chairman of the Federal Reserve Bank, the U.S. Secretary of the Treasury; names like George Bush and Malcolm Baldridge; titles like the Chairman of the Joint Committee on Accreditation of Hospitals; and Canadian Minister of Export. This places extra pressure on freelance writers to submit very good articles. Frequent mistakes: 1) Writing for big business, rather than small, 2) using language that is too academic."

‡MEETING NEWS, Facts, News, Ideas For Convention, Meeting and Incentive Planners Everywhere, Gralla Publications, 1515 Broadway, New York NY 10036. (212)869-1300. Editorial Director/Co-Publisher: Peter Shure. Executive Editor: Colleen Davis-Gardephe. A monthly tabloid covering news, facts, ideas and methods in meeting planning; industry developments, legislation, new labor contracts, business practices and costs for meeting planners. Circ. 70,400. Pays on acceptance. Byline given. Buys all rights. Computer printout submissions acceptable; prefers letter-quality to dot-matrix. Reports in 1 month on queries; 2 weeks on mss. Free sample copy.
Nonfiction: Travel; and specifics on how a group improved its meetings or shows, saved money or drew more attendees. "Stress is on business articles—facts and figures." Seven special issues covering specific states as meeting destination—Florida/Colorado/Texas/California/New York and Arizona. No general or philosophical pieces. Buys 25-50 mss/year. Query with published clips. Length: varies. Pays variable rates.
Tips: "Special issues focusing on certain states as meeting sites are most open. Best suggestion—query in writing, with clips, on any area of expertise about these states that would be of interest to people planning meetings there. Example: food/entertainment, specific sports, group activities, etc."

MOBILE MANUFACTURED HOME MERCHANDISER, RLD Group, Inc., Suite 800, 203 N. Wabash, Chicago IL 60601. (312)236-3528. Editor: Jim Mack. Managing Editor: Carrie Allen. 5% freelance written. Prefers to work with published/established writers, and works with a small number of new/unpublished writers each year. A monthly magazine covering the mobile home industry. "Our readers are primarily retailers of mobile/manufactured homes. Our slant is to tell them, through profile stories primarily, how they can do business better and sell more." Circ. approximately 20,000. Pays on publication. Publishes ms an average of 2 months after acceptance. Byline not usually given. Not copyrighted. Buys first North American serial rights and second serial (reprint) rights. Photocopied submissions OK. Computer printout submissions OK. Reports in 2 weeks on queries; 1 month on mss. Sample copy and writer's guidelines for 8x10 SAE with $1.14 postage.
Nonfiction: New product, personal experience, photo feature and technical. No general overview pieces or tax advice. Buys 5-10 mss/year. Query. Length: 1,000-2,000 words. Pays $150-200 for assigned articles; pays $100-200 for unsolicited articles.
Photos: State availability of photos with submission. Reviews contact sheets. Offers no additional payment for photos accepted with ms. Identification of subjects required.
Tips: "Be specific, not general. Focus on a specific area of the business."

NATION'S BUSINESS, Chamber of Commerce of the United States, 1615 H St., NW, Washington DC 20062. (202)463-5650. Editor: Robert Gray. 25% freelance written. Monthly magazine of useful information for business people about managing a business. Audience includes owners and managers of businesses of all sizes, but predominantly smaller to medium-sized businesses. Circ. 850,000. Pays on acceptance. Publishes ms an average of 3 months after acceptance. Byline given. Offers $150 or less kill fee. Buys all rights. Submit seasonal/holiday material 6 months in advance. Simultaneous queries, and simultaneous and photocopied submissions OK, but only for exclusive use upon acceptance. Computer printout submissions acceptable; prefers letter-quality to dot-matrix. Reports in 2 months on queries; 3 months on mss. Sample copy $2.50; free writer's guidelines.

Nonfiction: How-to (run a business); interview/profile (business success stories; entrepreneurs who successfully implement ideas); and business trends stories. Buys 40 mss/year. Query. Length: 650-2,000 words. Pays $175 minimum. Sometimes pays expenses of writers on assignment.

Tips: "Ask for guidelines and read them carefully before making any approach."

‡**NEW MEXICO BUSINESS JOURNAL**, Southwest Publications, Inc., Box 1788, Albuqeurque NM 87120. (505)243-5581. Editor: George Hackler. Managing Editor: Joe Montes. 80% freelance written. A monthly magazine covering the local business community. Circ. 20,000. Pays on acceptance. Publishes ms an average of 3 months after acceptance. Byline given. Buys first rights. Submit seasonal/holiday material 4 months in advance. Simultaneous and photocopied submissions OK. Computer printout submissions OK; prefers letter-quality. Reports in 1 week on queries. Sample copy for 8x11 SAE with 39¢ postage; writer's guidelines for #10 SAE with 1 first class stamp.

Nonfiction: How-to, humor, interview/profile and technical. Buys 100+ mss/year. Query with published clips. Length: 800-2,000 words. Pays $50-1,000 for assigned articles. Sometimes pays the expenses of writers on assignment.

Photos: State availability of photos with submission. Reviews contact sheets, transparencies and prints. Identification of subjects required. Offers $5-25 per photo. Buys one-time rights.

RECORDS MANAGEMENT QUARTERLY, Association of Records Managers and Administrators, Inc., Box 4580, Silver Spring MD 20904. Editor: Ira A. Penn, CRM, CSP. 10% freelance written. Eager to work with new/unpublished writers. Quarterly magazine covering records and information management. Circ. 9,000. Pays on publication. Publishes ms an average of 6 months after acceptance. Byline given. Buys all rights. Photocopied, simultaneous and previously published submissions OK. Computer printout submissions acceptable; prefers letter-quality to dot-matrix. Reports in 1 month on mss. Sample copy $8; free writer's guidelines.

Nonfiction: Professional articles covering theory, case studies, surveys, etc. on any aspect of records and information management. Buys 24-32 mss/year. Send complete ms. Length: 1,500 words minimum. Pays $25-100. Pays a "stipend"; no contract.

Photos: Send photos with ms. Does not pay extra for photos. Prefers b&w prints. Captions required.

Tips: "A writer *must* know our magazine. Most work is written by practitioners in the field. We use very little freelance writing, but we have had some and it's been good. A writer must have detailed knowledge of the subject he/she is writing about. Superficiality is not acceptable."

‡**RISK & BENEFITS MANAGEMENT**, Brentwood Publishing Division of Simon & Schuster, 1640 Fifth St., Box 2178, Santa Monica CA 90401. (213)395-0234. Editor: Kwok-Sze Wong. Managing Editor: Tom Wilhite. 50% freelance written. Prefers to work with published/established writers. Monthly magazine covering risk management and insurance. "We are looking for well-written, pragmatic articles which provide risk managers with new methods and ideas for preventing losses in their organizations." Estab. 1986. Circ. 16,000. Pays on acceptance. Publishes ms an average of 6 months after acceptance. Byline given. Offers $25 kill fee. Buys all rights. Photocopied submissions OK. Computer printout submissions OK; prefers letter-quality to dot-matrix. Reports in 1 month. Sample copy $5.

Nonfiction: No general insurance topics, human interests, profiles (or promotional articles) about insurance companies. Buys 60 mss/year. Query. Length: 500-3,000 words. Pays 10-12¢/word. Sometimes pays the expenses of writers on assignment.

Photos: State availability of photos with submission. Reviews 3x5 prints. Offers no additional payment for photos accepted with ms. Identification of subjects required. Buys all rights.

Columns/Departments: Legislative Watch (update of legislative issues); Legal Perspectives (legal issues in risk management); On Line (computers), all 1,000-1,500 words. Buys 30 mss/year. Query. Length: 1,000-2,000 words. Pays 10-12¢/word.

TOP LINE, An Executive Briefing Service, 13-30 Corporation, 505 Market St., Knoxville TN 37902. (615)521-0600. Associate Editor: Sean Plottner. 60% freelance written. A quarterly magazine covering business management information for owners and CEOs of small and medium-sized firms (under $100 million). Circ. 150,000. Pays on acceptance. Publishes ms an average of 2 months after acceptance. Byline given. Buys first North American serial rights. Computer printout submissions acceptable. Sample copy for 9x12 SAE and 5 first class stamps.

Nonfiction: Topics include human resources, finance and taxes, law and government, marketing strategy, trends, strictly personal. "*Top Line* offers how-to, actionable management information." Buys 8 mss/year. Query with published clips. Length: 4,000 words. Pays $250-1,500.

Tips: "Experience in business writing is a must. Each issue contains one feature article; past topics have included exporting for small companies, planning for profit, new-product development, and doing business with the government."

TRADESHOW AND EXHIBIT MANAGER MAGAZINE, Brentwood Publishing, a Prentice-Hall/Simon & Schuster Co., 1640 5th St., Santa Monica CA 90401. (213)395-0234. Editor: Les Plesko. 75% freelance written. A monthly magazine for the tradeshow industry—for professional exhibit managers, independent show organizers and association tradeshow organizers. Estab. 1986. Circ. 12,000. Pays on acceptance and receipt of phone log and copy of phone bill. Publishes ms an average of 4 months after acceptance. Byline given. Negotiable kill fee. Makes work-for-hire assignments. Computer printout submissions acceptable. Reports in 1 week on queries.

Nonfiction: How-to, interview/profile and new product. No articles written on speculation; accepted articles by assignment only. Buys 50+ mss/year. Query. Length: 1,000 words minimum. Pays $100 minimum for assigned articles or 10-12¢ edited word. Pays the phone expenses of writers on assignment.

Tips: "Business writing experience is helpful; particularly tradeshow experience. We provide story idea, questions, contacts and editorial assistance. Potential freelance writers should write or call—we respond to all legitimate queries. Only Feature section is open to freelancers. Clear, concise business writing is required."

THE TRAVEL BUSINESS MANAGER, Suite 184, 90 West Montgomery Ave., Rockville MD 20850. (301)424-3347. Editor: Eleanor Alexander. 40% freelance written. "Eager to work with new writers who can address our market appropriately." A biweekly newsletter covering operational, strategic, and technical issues relating to retail travel management. Pays on publication. Publishes mss an average of 2 months after acceptance. Byline given. Buys all rights. Computer printout submissions acceptable. Reports in 3 weeks on queries; 6 weeks on mss. Sample copy for SAE with 56¢ postage; writer's guidelines for #SAE with 1 first class stamp.

Nonfiction: Technical and management, with emphasis on the travel industry. No travel—"destination pieces"—of any kind. Buys 30-40 mss/year. Query with published clips. Length: 1,000-1,800 words. Pays $200-500.

Tips: "Know the travel industry well and understand business management. This market includes corporate travel managers, retail travel agents, travel industry suppliers (such as airlines, hotel systems, and car rental vendors), and others with an interest in the travel industry. No material directed toward travelers rather than travel managers. Read the publication first to understand its orientation. Writers may best judge their ability to write for us if they can produce material that addresses its subject authoritatively—with 'The voice of Experience'—rather than on a detached or theoretical level."

Church Administration and Ministry

Publications in this section are written for clergy members, church leaders and teachers. Magazines for lay members and the general public are listed in the Consumer Religious section.

CHRISTIAN EDUCATION TODAY: For teachers, superintendents and other Christian educators, Box 15337, Denver CO 80215. Editor: Edith Quinlan. National Research Editor: Kenneth O. Gangel. 50% freelance written. Works with a small number of new/unpublished writers each year. Quarterly magazine. Pays prior to publication. Publishes ms an average of 6 months after acceptance. Byline given. Buys simultaneous rights with magazines of different circulations. Computer printout submissions acceptable; prefers letter-quality to dot-matrix. Reports in 1 month. Sample copy and writer's guidelines for $1.

Nonfiction: Articles which provide information, instruction and/or inspiration to workers at every level of Christian education. May be slanted to the general area or to specific age-group categories such as preschool, elementary, youth or adult. Simultaneous rights acceptable *only* if offered to magazines which do not have overlapping circulation. Length: 1,000-2,000 words. Payment commensurate with length and value of article to total magazine.

Tips: "Often a submitted short article is followed up with a suggestion or firm assignment for more work from that writer."

CHRISTIAN LEADERSHIP, Board of Christian Education of the Church of God, Box 2458, Anderson IN 46018-2458. (317)642-0257. Acting Editor: Kenneth G. Prunty. 50% freelance written. Works with a small number of new/unpublished writers each year. A monthly magazine (except July and August) covering local Sunday school teachers, church school administrators, youth workers, choir leaders and other local church workers. Circ. 4,000. Pays on publication. Publishes ms an average of 6 months after acceptance. Byline given. Buys first rights and second serial (reprint) rights. Submit seasonal/holiday material 6 months in advance. Simultaneous queries OK. Computer printout submissions acceptable; no dot-matrix. Reports in 4 months. Free sample copy and writer's guidelines.

Nonfiction: General interest, how-to, inspirational, personal experience, guidance for carrying out programs for special days, and continuing ministries. No articles that are not specifically related to local church leadership. Buys 50 mss/year. Send complete ms, brief description of present interest in writing for church leaders, background and experience. Length: 300-1,500 words. Pays 2¢/word ($10 minimum).

Photos: Send photos with ms. Pays $15-25 for 5x7 b&w photos.

Tips: "How-to articles related to Sunday school teaching, program development and personal teacher enrichment or growth, with illustrations of personal experience of the authors, are most open to freelancers."

CHURCH EDUCATOR, Creative Resources for Christian Educators, Educational Ministries, Inc., 2861-C Saturn St., Brea CA 92621. (714)961-0622. Editor: Robert G. Davidson. Managing Editor: Linda S. Davidson. 80% freelance written. Works with a small number of new/unpublished writers each year. A monthly magazine covering religious education. Circ. 5,200. Pays on publication. Publishes manuscript an average of 4 months after acceptance. Byline given. Buys first rights, second serial (reprint) rights, or all rights. "We prefer all rights." Submit seasonal/holiday material 4 months in advance. Simultaneous submissions OK. Computer printout submissions acceptable; prefers letter-quality to dot-matrix. Reports in 3 months. Sample copy for 9x12 SAE and 56¢ postage; free writer's guidelines.

Nonfiction: Book reviews; general interest; how-to (crafts for Church school); inspirational; personal experience; and religious. "Our editorial lines are very middle of the road—mainline Protestant. We are not seeking extreme conservative or liberal theology pieces." No testimonials. Buys 100 mss/year. Send complete ms. Length: 100-2,000 words. Pays 2-4¢/word.

Photos: Send photos with submissions. Reviews 5x7 b&w prints. Offers $5-10/photo. Captions required. Buys one-time rights.

Fiction: Mainstream, religious, and slice-of-life vignettes. Buys 15 mss/year. Send complete ms. Length: 100-2,000 words. Pays 2-4¢/word.

Fillers: Anecdotes and short humor. Buys 15/year. Length: 100-700 words. Pays 2-4¢/word.

Tips: "Send the complete manuscript with a cover letter which gives a concise summary of the manuscript. We are looking for how-to articles related to Christian education. That would include most any program held in a church. Be straightforward and to the point—not flowery and wordy. We're especially interested in youth programs. Give steps needed to carry out the program: preparation, starting the program, continuing the program, conclusion. List several discussion questions for each program."

CHURCH TRAINING, 127 9th Ave. N., Nashville TN 37234. (615)251-2843. Publisher: The Sunday School Board of the Southern Baptist Convention. Editor: Richard B. Sims. 5% freelance written. Works with a small number of new/unpublished writers each year. Monthly. For all workers and leaders in the Church Training program of the Southern Baptist Convention. Circ. 30,000. Pays on acceptance. Publishes ms an average of 18 months after acceptance. Byline given. Buys all rights. Electronic submission OK on ATEX, but requires hard copy also. Computer printout submissions acceptable; no dot-matrix. Reports in 6 weeks. Free sample copy and writer's guidelines.

❝ *The best thing for us is for prospective contributors to follow our guidelines carefully, submit materials that meet those guidelines, and then give us enough time to make a decision.* **❞**

—*Ed Holm*
American History Illustrated

Nonfiction: Articles that pertain to leadership training in the church; success stories that pertain to Church Training; associational articles. Informational, how-to's that pertain to Church Training and personal testimonies. Buys 15 unsolicited mss/year. Query with rough outline. Length: 500-1,500 words. Pays 5¢/word. Sometimes pays the expenses of writers on assignment.
Tips: "Write an article that reflects the writer's experience of personal growth through church training. Keep in mind the target audience: workers and leaders of Church Training organizations in churches of the Southern Baptist Convention. Often subjects and treatment are too general."

CIRCUIT RIDER, A Journal for United Methodist Ministers, United Methodist Publishing House, Box 801, Nashville TN 37202. (615)749-6488. Editor: Keith I. Pohl. Editorial Director: J. Richard Peck. 60% freelance written. Works with a small number of new/unpublished writers each year. A monthly magazine covering professional concerns of clergy. Circ. 48,000. Pays on acceptance. Publishes ms an average of 1 year after acceptance. Byline given. Buys all rights. Submit seasonal/holiday material 6 months in advance. Photocopied submissions OK. Computer printout submissions acceptable; prefers letter-quality to dot-matrix. Reports in 3 weeks.
Nonfiction: How-to (improve pastoral calling, preaching, counseling, administration, etc.). No personal experience articles; no interviews. Buys 50 mss/year. Send complete ms. Length: 600-2,000 words. Pays $30-100. Pays the expenses of writers on assignment.
Photos: State availability of photos. Pays $25-50 for 8x10 b&w prints. Model release required. Buys one-time rights.
Tips: "Know the concerns of a United Methodist pastor. Be specific. Think of how you can help pastors."

THE CLERGY JOURNAL, Church Management, Inc., Box 162527, Austin TX 78716. (512)327-8501. Editor: Manfred Holck, Jr. 20% freelance written. Eager to work with new/unpublished writers. Monthly (except June and December) on religion. Readers are Protestant clergy. Circ. 20,000. Pays on publication. Publishes ms an average of 4 months after acceptance. Byline given. Offers 50% kill fee. Buys all rights. Submit seasonal/holiday material 6 months in advance. Photocopied submissions OK. Computer printout submissions acceptable; prefers letter-quality to dot-matrix. Reports in 2 weeks on queries; 1 month on mss. Sample copy for $2.50 and 9x12 SAE with $3 postage.
Nonfiction: How-to (be a more efficient and effective minister/administrator). No devotional, inspirational or sermons. Buys 20 mss/year. Query. Length: 500-1,500 words. Pays $25-40.

‡LEADERSHIP, A Practical Journal for Church Leaders, Christianity Today, Inc., 465 Gundersen Dr., Carol Stream IL 60188. (312)260-6200. Editor: Terry Muck. Managing Editor: Marshall Shelley. 75% freelance written. Works with a small number of new/unpublished writers each year. A quarterly magazine covering church leadership. Writers must have a "knowledge of and sympathy for the unique expectations placed on pastors and local church leaders. Each article must support points by illustrating from real life experiences in local churches." Circ. 90,000. Pays on acceptance. Publishes ms an average of 6 months after acceptance. Byline given. Buys first North American serial rights. Submit seasonal/holiday material 6 months in advance. Photocopied and previously published submissions OK. Computer printout submissions OK; prefers letter-quality to dot-matrix. Reports in 6 weeks on queries; 2 months on mss. Sample copy $3; free writer's guidelines.
Nonfiction: How-to, humor and personal experience. No "articles from writers who have never read our journal." Buys 50 mss/year. Send complete ms. Length: 100-5,000 words. Pays $30-300. Sometimes pays the expenses of writers on assignment.
Photos: State availability of photos with submission. Offers no additional payment for photos accepted with ms. Identification of subjects required. Buys one-time rights.
Columns/Departments: James D. Berkley, editor. People in Print (book reviews with interview of author), 1,500 words; To Illustrate (short stories or analogies that illustrate a biblical principle), 100 words. Buys 50 mss/year. Send complete ms. Pays $25-100.

MINISTRIES TODAY, Strang Communications Co., 190 N. Westmonte Dr., Altamonte Springs FL 32714. (305)869-5005. Editor: Stephen Strang. Associate Editor: E.S. Caldwell. 20% freelance written. Bimonthly magazine covering Evangelical/Pentecostal/Charismatic ministries. Includes practical articles to help church leaders. Circ. 20,000. Pays on publication. Publishes ms an average of 6 months after acceptance. Byline given. Buys first rights. Photocopied submissions OK. Computer printout submissions acceptable; prefers letter-quality to dot-matrix. Reports in 1 month. Sample copy $3, SAE and 46¢ postage; writer's guidelines for SAE and 22¢ postage.
Nonfiction: How-to (for pastors), and interview/profile. Writers must have personal experience in areas they are writing about. Buys 40 mss/year. Query or send complete ms. Length: 1,700-2,000 words. Pays $50-200. Sometimes pays expenses of writers on assignment.
Photos: Carolyn Kiphuth, photo editor.
Tips: "We need practical, proven ideas with both negative and positive anecdotes. We have a specialized

audience—pastors and leaders of churches. It is unlikely that persons not fully understanding this audience would be able to provide appropriate manuscripts."

PASTORAL LIFE, Society of St. Paul, Route 224, Canfield OH 44406. Editor: Jeffrey Mickler, SSP. 66% freelance written. Works with a small number of new/unpublished writers each year, and is eager to work with new/unpublished writers. Emphasizes priests and those interested in pastoral ministry. Magazine; 64 pages. Monthly. Circ. 6,600. Buys first rights only. Byline given. Pays on publication. Publishes ms an average of 6 months after acceptance. Sample copy to writer on request. Query with a outline before submitting ms. "New contributors are expected to include, in addition, a few lines of personal data that indicate academic and professional background." Computer printout submissions acceptable; no dot-matrix. Reports within 1 month.
Nonfiction: *"Pastoral Life* is a professional review, principally designed to focus attention on current problems, needs, issues and all important activities related to all phases of pastoral work and life." Buys 30 unsolicited mss/year. Length: 2,000-3,400 words. Pays 3¢/word minimum.
Tips: "Projected increase in number of pages will warrant expansion of our material needs."

‡PREACHING, Preaching Resources, Inc., 1529 Cesery Blvd., Jacksonville FL 32211. (904)743-5994. Editor: Dr. Michael Duduit. 75% freelance written. Bimonthly magazine for the preaching ministry. "All articles must deal with preaching. Most articles used offer practical assistance in preparation and delivery of sermons, generally from an evangelical stance." Circ. 5,000. Pays on publication. Publishes ms an average of 1 year after acceptance. Byline given. Buys first rights. Submit seasonal/holiday material 1 year in advance. Photocopied submissions OK. Query for electronic submissions. Computer printout submissions OK. Reports in 6 weeks. Sample copy $2.50; writer's guildeines for SAE with 1 first class stamp.
Nonfiction: How-to (preparation and delivery of sermon; worship leadership) and interview/profile (of significant contemporary preachers). Special issues include Personal Computing in Preaching (September-October); materials/resources to assist in preparation of seasonal preaching (November-December, March-April). Buys 18-24 mss/year. Query. Length: 1,000-2,000 words. Pays $35-50.
Photos: Send photos with submission. Reviews prints. Offers no additional payment for photos accepted with ms. Captions, model releases and identification of subjects required. Buys one-time rights.
Fillers: Buys 6/year. "Buys only completed cartoons." Pays $25.
Tips: "Most desirable are practical, 'how-to' articles on preparation and delivery of sermons."

YOUR CHURCH, The Religious Publishing Co., 198 Allendale Rd., King of Prussia PA 19406. (215)265-9400. Editor: Phyllis Mather Rice. 60% freelance written. Bimonthly magazine for ministers and churches "providing practical, how-to articles on every aspect of administering and leading church congregations." Circ. 186,000. Pays on publication. Publishes ms an average of 1 year after acceptance. Byline given. Offers 50% kill fee. Buys one-time rights. Submit seasonal/holiday material 1 year in advance. Simultaneous queries (if informed) and previously published submissions OK. Computer printout submissions acceptable; no dot-matrix. Reports in 2 months on queries; 3 months on mss. Sample copy $1.50, 9x11 SAE, and 73¢ postage; writer's guidelines for #10 SAE and 22¢ postage.
Nonfiction: How-to (administer and lead church congregations); new product (that churches can use); personal experience (working with congregations); and technical (building churches). No sermons or dissertation-type articles. Buys 60 mss/year. Query or send complete ms. Length: 1,200-3,000 words. Pays $6/typewritten ms page—$100 total maximum.
Tips: "We are interested in topics that would aid our readers. Whether the author is a seasoned or new/unpublished writer is of minor consequence. Freelancers can best break in with articles that have *practical* value to church pastors. We are interested in how-to, readable, interesting copy that flows. We are not interested in dissertation-type articles."

Clothing

KIDS FASHIONS, Larkin-Pluznick-Larkin, 210 Boylston St., Chestnut Hill MA 02167. Editorial offices: Suite 1600, 71 West 35th St., New York NY 10001. (212)594-0880. Editor: Larry Leventhal. 20% freelance written. Works with a small number of new/unpublished writers each year. Magazine covering children's wear industry, with the emphasis on the children's wear retailer. Circ. 18,000. Pays on acceptance. Publishes ms an average of 2 months after acceptance. One byline per writer, per issue. Buys all rights. Submit seasonal/holiday material 9 months in advance. Computer printout submissions acceptable; prefers letter-quality to dot-matrix. Reports in 2 weeks. Free sample copy.

Nonfiction: Merchandising and business how-to; retailer/store profiles and survey articles on merchandising. "Knowledge of retailing and merchandising of apparel helpful, business sense a must." Buys 24-30 mss/year. Query with clips only. Length: 750-2,500 words, or dependent on subject. Pays $150-300.

Photos: State availability of photos. Reviews contacts or prints. Captions and identification of subjects required. Buys one-time rights.

Tips: "We are aiming to be more business oriented—less popcorn and fluff. We like in depth, fully researched articles with lots of attribution. We are not as interested in opinion and razzle-dazzle."

‡T-SHIRT RETAILER AND SCREEN PRINTER, WFC, Inc., 195 Main St., Metuchen NJ 08840. (201)494-2889. Editor: Marsha Parker Cox. Assistant Editor: Deborah Miller. 10% freelance written. A monthly magazine for persons in imprinted garment industry and screen printing. Circ. 25,500. Pays on publication. Publishes ms an average of 3 months after acceptance. Byline given. Buys first North American serial rights. Submit seasonal/holiday material 4 months in advance. Photocopied and previously published submissions OK. Computer printout submissions OK; prefers letter-quality to dot-matrix. Reports in 1 month. Sample copy $7; writer's guidelines for 5x7 SAE with 1 first class stamp.

Nonfiction: How-to, new product, technical and business. Buys 5 mss/year. Query with published clips. Length: 2,000-3,000 words. Pays $100-200 for assigned articles; pays $150 maximum for unsolicited articles.

Photos: Send photos with submission. Reviews contact sheets. Offers no additional payment for photos accepted with ms. Identification of subjects required.

Tips: "We need general business stories: equipment, advertising, store management, etc."

WESTERN & ENGLISH FASHIONS, Bell Publishing, 2403 Champa, Denver CO 80205. (303)296-1600. Editor: Larry Bell. Managing Editor: Lee Darrigrand. 90% freelance written. Prefers to work with published/established writers; works with a small number of new/unpublished writers each year. For "Western and English apparel and equipment retailers, manufacturers and distributors. The magazine features retailing practices such as marketing, merchandising, display techniques, buying and selling to help business grow or improve, etc. Every issue carries feature stories on Western/English/square dance apparel stores throughout the US." Monthly magazine; 50 pages. Circ. 13,000. Pays on publication. Publishes ms an average of 2 months after acceptance. Not copyrighted. Byline given unless extensive rewriting is required. Phone queries OK. Submit seasonal/holiday material 3 months in advance. Simultaneous (to noncompeting publications), photocopied and previously published submissions OK. Computer printout submissions acceptable; no dot-matrix. No fiction or foreign material. Sample copy and writer's guidelines for 9x11½ SAE with $1.50 postage.

Nonfiction: Current trends in fashion of English riding attire, square dance & western; expose (of government as related to industry or people in industry); general interest (pertaining to Western lifestyle); interview (with Western/English store owners); new product (of interest to Western/English clothing retailers—send photo); and photo feature. "We will be doing much more fashion oriented articles and layouts." Buys 20-25/year. Query with outline. Length: 800-3,600 words. Pays $50-150. Sometimes pays the expenses of writers on assignment.

Photos: "We buy photos with manuscripts. Occasionally we purchase photos that illustrate a unique display or store with only a cutline." State availability of photos. Captions required with "names of people or products and locations." Buys one-time rights.

Tips: "We will be highlighting current fashion trends and continuing to feature retail store operations."

⸻ *Coin-Operated Machines*

AMERICAN COIN-OP, 500 N. Dearborn St., Chicago IL 60610. (312)337-7700. Editor: Ben Russell. 30% freelance written. Monthly magazine; 42 pages. For owners of coin-operated laundry and dry cleaning stores. Circ. 18,000. Rights purchased vary with author and material but are exclusive to the field. Pays two weeks prior to publication. Publishes ms an average of 4 months after acceptance. Byline given for frequent contributors. Computer printout submissions acceptable; prefers letter-quality to dot-matrix. Reports as soon as possible; usually in 2 weeks. Free sample copy.

Nonfiction: "We emphasize store operation and use features on industry topics: utility use and conservation, maintenance, store management, customer service and advertising. A case study should emphasize how the store operator accomplished whatever he did—in a way that the reader can apply to his own operation. Manuscript should have a no-nonsense, business-like approach." Uses informational, how-to, interview, profile, think pieces and successful business operations articles. Length: 500-3,000 words. Pays 6¢/word minimum.

Photos: Pays $6 minimum for 8x10 b&w glossy photos purchased with mss. (Contact sheets with negatives preferred.)

Fillers: Newsbreaks and clippings. Length: open. Pays $5 minimum.

Tips: "Query about subjects of current interest. Be observant of coin-operated laundries—how they are designed and equipped, how they serve customers and how (if) they advertise and promote their services. Most general articles are turned down because they are not aimed well enough at audience. Most case histories are turned down because of lack of practical purpose (nothing new or worth reporting). A frequent mistake is failure to follow up on an interesting point made by the interviewee—probably due to lack of knowledge about the industry."

ELECTRONIC SERVICING & TECHNOLOGY, Intertec Publishing Corp., Box 12901, Overland Park KS 66212. (913)888-4664. Editor: Conrad Persson. Managing Editor: Dan Torchia. 90% freelance written. Eager to work with new/unpublished writers. Monthly magazine for professional servicers and electronic enthusiasts who are interested in buying, building, installing and repairing consumer electronic equipment (audio, video, microcomputers, electronic games, etc.) Circ. 60,000. Pays on publication. Publishes ms an average of 6 months after acceptance. Byline given. Buys all rights. Submit seasonal/holiday material 4 months in advance. Simultaneous queries OK. Computer printout submissions acceptable; prefers letter-quality to dot-matrix. Reports in 2 weeks on queries; 1 month on mss. Free sample copy and writer's guidelines.

Nonfiction: How-to (service, build, install and repair home entertainment electronic equipment); personal experience (troubleshooting); and technical (consumer electronic equipment; electronic testing and servicing equipment). "Explain the techniques used carefully so that even hobbyists can understand a how-to article." Buys 36 mss/year. Send complete ms. Length: 1,500 words minimum. Pays $100-200.

Photos: Send photos with ms. Reviews color and b&w transparencies and b&w prints. Captions and identification of subjects required. Buys all rights. Payment included in total ms package.

Columns/Departments: Marge Riggin, column/department editor. Troubleshooting Tips. Buys 12 mss/year. Send complete ms. Length: open. Pays $25.

Tips: "In order to write for *ES&T* it is almost essential that a writer have an electronics background: technician, engineer or serious hobbyist. Our readers want nuts-and-bolts type of information on electronics."

PLAY METER MAGAZINE, Skybird Publishing Co., Inc., Box 24970. New Orleans LA 70184. Publisher: Carol Lally. Editor: Valerie Cognevich. 25% freelance written. "We will work with new writers who are familiar with the amusement industry." Monthly trade magazine, 100 pages, for owners/operators of coin-operated amusement machine companies, e.g., pinball machines, video games, arcade pieces, jukeboxes, etc. Circ. 6,500. Pays on publication. Publishes ms an average of 2 months after acceptance. Byline given. Buys all rights. Submit seasonal/holiday material 2 months in advance. Photocopied and previously published submissions OK. Computer printout submissions acceptable; prefers letter-quality to dot-matrix. Query answered in 2 months. Sample copy $2; free writer's guidelines.

Nonfiction: How-to (get better locations for machines, promote tournaments, evaluate profitability of route, etc.); interview (with industry leaders); new product. "Our readers want to read about how they can make more money from their machines, how they can get better tax breaks, commissions, etc. Also no stories about *playing* pinball or video games. Also, submissions on video-game technology advances; technical pieces on troubleshooting videos, pinballs, and novelty machines (all coin-operated); trade-show coverage (query), submissions on the pay-telephone industry. Our readers don't play the games per se; they buy the machines and make money from them." Buys 48 mss/year. Submit complete ms. Length: 250-3,000 words. Pays $30-215. Sometimes pays expenses of writer's on assignment.

Photos: "The photography should have news value. We don't want 'stand 'em up-shoot 'em down' group shots." Pays $15 minimum for 5x7 or 8x10 b&w prints. Captions preferred. Buys all rights. Art returned on request.

Tips: "We need feature articles more than small news items or featurettes. Query first. We're interested in writers who either have a few years of reporting/feature-writing experience or who know the coin-operated amusement industry well but are relatively inexperienced writers."

VENDING TIMES, 545 8th. Avenue, New York NY 10018. Editor: Arthur E. Yohalem. Monthly. For operators of vending machines. Circ. 14,700. Pays on publication. Buys all rights. "We will discuss in detail the story requirements with the writer."

Nonfiction: Feature articles and news stories about vending operations; practical and important aspects of the business. "We are always willing to pay for good material." Query.

Confectionery and Snack Foods

CANDY INDUSTRY, HBJ Publications, 7500 Old Oak Blvd., Cleveland OH 44130. (216)243-8100. Editor: Pat Magee. 5% freelance written. Monthly. Prefers to work with published/established writers. For confectionery manufacturers. Publishes ms an average of 4 months after acceptance. Buys first serial rights. Computer printout submissions acceptable; prefers letter-quality to dot-matrix. Reports in 1 month.
Nonfiction: "Feature articles of interest to large scale candy manufacturers that deal with activities in the fields of production, packaging (including package design), merchandising; and financial news (sales figures, profits, earnings), advertising campaigns in all media, and promotional methods used to increase the sale or distribution of candy." Length: 1,000-1,250 words. Pays 15¢/word; "special rates on assignments."
Photos: "Good quality glossies with complete and accurate captions, in sizes not smaller than 5x7." Pays $15 b&w; $20 for color.
Fillers: "Short news stories about the trade and anything related to candy and snacks." Pays 5¢/word; $1 for clippings.

PACIFIC BAKERS NEWS, 1809 Sharpe Ave., Walnut Creek CA 94596. (415)932-1256. Publisher: C.W. Soward. 30% freelance written. Eager to work with new/unpublished writers. Monthly business newsletter for commercial bakeries in the western states. Pays on publication. No byline given; uses only one-paragraph news items. Computer printout submissions acceptable.
Nonfiction: Uses bakery business reports and news about bakers. Buys only brief "boiled-down news items about bakers and bakeries operating only in Alaska, Hawaii, Pacific Coast and Rocky Mountain states. We welcome clippings. We need monthly news reports and clippings about the baking industry and the donut business. No pictures, jokes, poetry or cartoons." Length: 10-200 words. Pays 6¢/word for clips and news used.

Construction and Contracting

Builders, architects and contractors learn the latest news of their trade in these publications. Journals targeted for architects are included in the Art, Design and Collectibles section. Those for specialists in the interior aspects of construction are listed under Building Interiors.

AUTOMATION IN HOUSING & MANUFACTURED HOME DEALER, CMN Associates, Inc., Box 120, Carpinteria CA 93013. (805)684-7659. Editor-in-Chief: Don Carlson. 15% freelance written. Monthly magazine; 88 pages. Specializes in management for industrialized (manufactured) housing and volume home builders. Circ. 25,000. Pays on acceptance. Publishes ms an average of 3 months after acceptance. Buys first North American serial rights. Phone queries OK. Computer printout submissions acceptable; no dot-matrix. Reports in 2 weeks. Free sample copy and writer's guidelines.
Nonfiction: Case history articles on successful home building companies which may be 1) production (big volume) home builders; 2) mobile home manufacturers; 3) modular home manufacturers; 4) prefabricated home manufacturers; or 5) house component manufacturers. Also uses interviews, photo features and technical articles. "No architect or plan 'dreams'. Housing projects must be built or under construction." Buys 15 mss/year. Query. Length: 500-1,000 words maximum. Pays $300 minimum.
Photos: Purchased with accompanying ms. Query. No additional payment for 4x5, 5x7 or 8x10 b&w glossies or 35mm or larger color transparencies (35mm preferred). Captions required.
Tips: "Stories often are too long, too loose; we prefer 500 to 750 words. We prefer a phone query on feature articles. If accepted on query, usually article will not be rejected later."

BUILDER/DEALER, (formerly *Log Home and Alternative Housing Builder*, 16 1st Ave., Corry PA 16407-1894. (814)664-8624. Managing Editor: Chuck Mancino. 30% freelance written. Prefers to work with published/established writers but open to new talent. A monthly magazine covering industrialized housing, including log, dome, solar, post and beam, modular, pre cut and panelized homes. Readership consists chiefly of builder/dealers and manufacturers of these homes. Circ. 21,500. Pays on publication. Publishes ms an average of 4 months after acceptance. Byline given. Offers negotiable kill fee. Buys all rights; rights may be re-assigned to author upon request. Submit seasonal/holiday material 5 months in advance. Simultaneous submissions and previously published work OK, "if we're told of the situation." Reports in 1 month on queries. Computer printout submissions acceptable; prefers letter-quality to dot-matrix. Free sample copy and writer's guidelines.

Nonficton: How-to (not how to build—our readers *are* builders; but how to make and increase sales, better market industrialized homes, etc.); new product; technical (new or unique products for industrialized housing); and feature articles. No "puff" pieces or consumer oriented articles. Buys 8-15 ms/year. Query or send complete ms. Length: 1,000-4,000 words. Pays $50-200. Pays expenses of writers on assignment (long distance phone calls).

Photos: Send photos with submission. Reviews 8x10 prints. Captions or other identification of subjects required. Buys all rights; rights may be re-assigned to author upon request.

Columns/Departments: Winner's Circle (interview with a successful builder/dealer); Commercially Speaking (alternative housing in commercial projects); Focus (introducing a manufacturer to the industry); and book reviews. Query or send complete ms. Length: 500-4,000 words (varies according to department). Pays $50-250.

Tips: "A freelancer can best break in to our publication with a good query or article that shows a knowledge of our slant and our readership—'How to increase industrialized housing sales and improve cash flow,' rather than 'How the wife and I built our log home.' We want people knowledgeable in our field, even if they don't have writing experience. Feature articles are most open to freelancers. Come up with detailed pieces on financing, sales, marketing, expanding product lives, etc.—in the log or alternative housing industry. Now and then we'll accept and publish an article over the transom, but more often we assign articles to our freelancers. When we do this we'll provide contacts, suggested slants and interview questions, and other support. If a writer has questions, he/she need only call us."

BUILDER INSIDER, Box 191125, Dallas TX 75219-1125. (214)871-2913. Editor: Mike Anderson. 18% freelance written. Works with a small number of new/unpublished writers each year. Covers the entire north Texas building industry for builders, architects, contractors, remodelers and homeowners. Circ. 8,000. Publishes ms an average of 2 months after acceptance. Photocopied submissions OK. Computer printout submissions OK; prefers letter-quality to dot-matrix. Free sample copy.

Nonfiction: "What is current in the building industry" is the approach. Wants "advertising, business builders, new building products, building projects being developed and helpful building hints localized to the Southwest and particularly to north Texas." Submit complete ms. Length: 100-900 words. Pays $30-50.

CONSTRUCTION SPECIFIER, 601 Madison St., Alexandria VA 22314. (703)684-0200. Editor: Kimberly C. Smith. 50% freelance written. Works with a small number of new/unpublished writers each year. Monthly professional society magazine for architects, engineers, specification writers and project managers. Monthly. Circ. 18,000. Pays on publication. Publishes ms an average of 4 months after acceptance. Deadline: 60 days preceding publication on the 1st of each month. Buys North American serial rights. Computer printout submissions acceptable; prefers letter-quality to dot-matrix. "Call or write first." Model release, author copyright transferral requested. Reports in 3 weeks. Sample copy for 8½x11 SAE $1.50 postage.

Nonfiction: Articles on selection and specification of products, materials, practices and methods used in commercial (nonresidential) construction projects, specifications as related to construction design, plus legal and management subjects. Query. Length: 3,000-5,000 words maximum. Pays 10¢/published word (negotiable), plus art. Pays the expenses of writers on assignment.

Photos: Photos desirable in consideration for publication; line art, sketches, diagrams, charts and graphs also desired. Full color transparencies may be used. 8x10 glossies, 3¼ slides preferred. Payment negotiable.

Tips: "We will get bigger and thus will need good technical articles."

CONTRACTORS MARKET CENTER, Randall Publishing Co., Box 2029, Tuscaloosa AL 35403. (205)349-2990. Editor: Claude Duncan. 25-50% freelance written. Eager to work with new/unpublished writers. Weekly tabloid on heavy-equipment construction industry. "Our readers are contractors including road contractors, and oil and gas industry, who utilize heavy equipment. We write positive, upbeat stories about their work and their personal success. We like personal stories related to large construction projects." Circ. 18,000. Pays on acceptance. Publishes ms an average of 1 month after acceptance. Byline given. Offers 100% kill fee. Not copyrighted. Buys first serial rights, one-time rights, second serial (reprint) rights and simultaneous rights. Submit seasonal/holiday material 1 month in advance. Simultaneous and previously published (updated) submissions OK. Computer printout submissions acceptable; prefers upper and lower case letter-quality to dot-matrix. Reports in 2 weeks. Free sample copy and writer's guidelines.

Nonfiction: General interest (with construction angle); historical/nostalgic (with construction angle); humor (with construction angle); interview/profile (with contractors); personal experience (with construction angle); technical (re: heavy equipment); and business stories related to contractors. Buys 100 mss/year. Send complete ms. Length: 250-1,000 words. Pays $10-50. Sometimes pays the expenses of writers on assignment.

Photos: Send photos with ms. Reviews b&w and color prints; commercially processed OK if sharp. Pays $5. Identification of subjects required.

Tips: "Contractors like to read about other contractors and people with whom they are in frequent contact—suppliers, government regulators, and public works developments. We're primarily looking for people-oriented features. Nothing is too local if it's interesting. Submitting art with copy gives definite edge."

FENCE INDUSTRY/ACCESS CONTROL, (formerly *Fence Industry*), 6255 Barfield Rd., Atlanta GA 30328. (404)256-9800. Editor/Associate Publisher: Bill Coker. 30% freelance written. Prefers to work with published/established writers. Monthly magazine; 54-80 pages. For retailers and installers of fencing and access control equipment. Circ. 16,000. Pays on publication. Publishes ms an average of 2 months after acceptance. Buys all rights. Query for electronic submissions. Computer printout submissions acceptable; no dot-matrix. Reports in 3 months. Free sample copy.

Nonfiction: Case histories, as well as articles on fencing and access control equipment for highways, pools, farms, playgrounds, homes and industries. Surveys and management and sales reports. Interview, profile, historical, successful business operations and articles on merchandising techniques. No how-to articles; "they generally don't apply to installers in our industry." Buys 10-12 unsolicited mss/year. Query. Length: open. Pays 10¢/word.

Photos: Pays $10 for 5x7 b&w photos purchased with mss. Captions required.

Tips: "We will place more focus on access control features in 1988."

FINE HOMEBUILDING, The Taunton Press, Inc., 63 S. Main St., Box 355, Newtown CT 06470. (203)426-8171. Editor: John Lively. Less than 1% freelance written. Bimonthly magazine covering house building, construction, design for builders, architects and serious amateurs. Circ. 210,000. Pays on publication. Publishes ms an average of 6-12 months after acceptance. Byline given. Offers negotiable kill fee. Buys first rights and "use in books to be published." Query for electronic submissions. Computer printout submissions acceptable; prefers letter-quality to dot-matrix. Reports as soon as possible. Sample copy $3.95; free writer's guidelines.

Nonfiction: Technical (unusual techniques in design or construction process). Query. Length: 2,000-3,000 words. Pays $150-900. Pays expenses of writers on assignment.

Columns/Departments: Tools and Materials (products or techniques that are new or unusual); Great Moments in Building History (humorous, embarrassing, or otherwise noteworthy anecdotes); and Reviews (short reviews of books on building or design). Query. Length: 300-1,000 words. Pays $75-150.

‡INLAND ARCHITECT, The Midwestern Magazine for the Building Arts, Inland Architect Press, 10 West Hubbard St., Box 10394, Chicago IL 60610. (312)321-0583. Editor: Cynthia Davidson-Powers. 80% freelance written. Prefers to work with published/established writers. Bimonthly magazine covering architecture and urban planning. "*Inland Architect* is a critical journal covering architecture and design in the midwest for an audience primarily of architects. *Inland* is open to all points of view, providing they are intelligently expressed and of relevance to architecture." Circ. 7,000. Pays on publication. Publishes ms an average of 2 months after acceptance. Byline given. Offers 60% kill fee. Buys first rights. Computer printout submissions OK; no dot-matrix. Reports in 1 month on queries; 2 months on mss. Sample copy $4.

Nonfiction: Book excerpts, essays, historical/nostalgic, interview/profile, criticism and photo feature of architecture. Every summer *Inland* focuses on a midwestern city, its architecture and urban design. Call to find out 1988 city. No new products, "how to run your office," or technical pieces. Buys 40 mss/year. Query with or without published clips, or send complete ms. Length: 750-3,500 words. Pays $100-300 for assigned articles; pays $75-250 for unsolicited articles. Sometimes pays the expenses of writers on assignment.

Photos: Send photos with submission. Reviews 4x5 transparencies and 8x10 prints. Offers no additional payment for photos accepted with ms. Identification of subjects required. Buys one-time rights.

Columns/Departments: Books (reviews of new publications on architecture, design and, occasionally, art), 250-1,000 words. Buys 10 mss/year. Query. Length: 250-1,000 words. Pays $25-100.

Tips: "Propose specific articles, e.g, to cover a lecture, to interview a certain architect. General ideas, such as preservation, are too broad. Articles must be written for an audience primarily consisting of well-educated architects. If an author feels he has a 'hot' timely idea, a phone call is appreciated."

LOUISIANA CONTRACTOR, Rhodes Publishing Co., Inc., 18271 Old Jefferson Hwy., Baton Rouge LA 70817. (504)292-8980. Editor: Joyce Elson. 10% freelance written. Works with Louisiana freelance writers with knowledge of the construction industry. Monthly magazine comprehensive covering heavy commercial, industrial and highway construction in Louisiana, one of the largest construction markets in the U.S. Circ.

6,500. Pays on publication. Publishes ms an average of 2 months after acceptance. Offers negotiable kill fee. Buys all rights. Computer printout submissions OK; prefers letter-quality to dot-matrix. Reports in 2 weeks on queries; 2½ months on mss. Sample copy $1.50.

Nonfiction: "We are particularly interested in writers who can get clearance into a chemical plant or refinery and detail unusual maintenance jobs. Our feature articles are semitechnical to technical, balanced by a lot of name dropping of subcontractors, suppliers and key job personnel. We want quotes, and we never run a story without lots of photos either taken or procured by the writer. Stories on new methods of construction and unusual projects in the state are always wanted. Nothing from anyone unfamiliar with the construction industry in Louisiana." Buys 8-12 mss/year. Query. Length: 1,000-3,500 words. Pays negotiable rate. Sometimes pays the expenses of writers on assignment.

Photos: State availability of photos. Reviews 5x7 or 8x10 b&w glossy prints. Captions and identification of subjects required. "It is absolutely essential that a writer understand construction terms and practices."

MIDWEST CONTRACTOR, Construction Digest, Inc., 3170 Mercier, Box 766, Kansas City MO 64141. (816)931-2080. 5% freelance written. Works with a small number of new/unpublished writers each year. Biweekly magazine covering the public works and engineering construction industries in Iowa, Nebraska, Kansas and western and northeastern Missouri. Circ. 8,426. Pays on publication. Publishes ms an average of 2 months after acceptance. Byline given depending on nature of article. Makes work-for-hire assignments. Query for electronic submissions. Computer printout submissions acceptable; prefers letter-quality to dot-matrix. Reports in 2 weeks. Sample copy for 11x15 SAE with $2 postage.

Nonfiction: How-to, photo feature, technical, "nuts and bolts" construction job-site features. "We seek two- to three-page articles on topics of interest to our readership, including marketing trends, tips, and construction job-site stories. Providing concise, accurate, and original news stories is another freelance opportunity." Buys 4 mss/year. Query with three published clips. Length: 175 typewritten lines, 35 character count, no maximum. Pays $100/published page.

Tips: "We need writers who can write clearly about our specialized trade area. An engineering/construction background is a plus if the person is also an excellent writer. The writer may have a better chance of breaking in at our publication with short articles and fillers because we have very limited space for editorial copy. The most frequent mistake made by writers is that they do not tailor their article to our specific market—the nonresidential construction market in Nebraska, Iowa, Kansas and Missouri. We are not interested in what happens in New York unless it has a specific impact in the Midwest. We will be producing more personality profiles of contractors in 1988."

P.O.B., Point of Beginning, P.O.B. Publishing Co., Box 810, Wayne MI 48184. (313)729-8400. Editor: Edwin W. Miller. 40% freelance written. Prefers to work with published/established writers. Bimonthly magazine featuring articles of a technical, business, professional and general nature for the professionals and technicians of the surveying and mapping community. Circ. 65,500 +. Pays either on acceptance or on publication. Publication date after acceptance "varies with backlog." Byline given "with short biography, if appropriate." Offers 50% kill fee. Buys first serial rights and all rights; makes work-for-hire assignments. Submit seasonal/holiday material 4 months in advance. Simultaneous queries and photocopied submissions OK. Computer printout submissions acceptable (with no right margin justification); no dot-matrix. Reports in 1 month. Sample copy for 9x11 SAE and 8 first class stamps; writer's guidelines for SAE and 1 first class stamp.

Nonfiction: Jeanne M. Helfrick, associate editor. Historical/nostalgic; how-to; business management (particularly for *small* businesses); profiles of firms or individuals; technical discussions; field experiences (of unusual, difficult, and/or special interest projects); and relevant photo features. Buys 24 mss/year. Query with published clips, or send complete ms. Length: 1,000-4,000 words. Pays $150-600. Sometimes pays the expenses of writers on assignment.

Photos: Send captioned photos with ms. Pays $10-50 for color transparencies and prints; $5-25 for 5x7 b&w prints. Model release and identification of subjects required.

Columns/Departments: A Conversation With (interview of people in the field about their professional involvement, point of view); and Picture Profile (profile of people in the field slanted toward their special interest, talent, involvement that is unusual to the profession). Buys 6 mss/year. Query associate editor. Length: 1,000-2,500 words. Payment varies.

REMODELING CONTRACTOR, Maclean Hunter Publishing Co., Suite 500, 300 W. Adams St., Chicago IL 60614. (312)726-2802. Editor: Don Logay. 5% freelance written. A monthly magazine for home-improvement contractors with "business-oriented articles pertaining to remodeling, and emphasis on business ideas for contractor/readers." Circ. 42,000. Pays on publication. Publishes ms an average of 2 months after acceptance. Byline given. Buys first North American serial rights. Submit seasonal/holiday material 3 months in advance. Query for electronic submissions. Computer printout submissions acceptable; no dot-matrix. Reports in 3 weeks on queries. Sample copy for 8½x12 SAE with $1.45 postage. Free writer's guidelines.

Nonfiction: How-to (remodeling project to some degree technical) and photo feature. Buys 6 mss/year. Query with published clips. Length: 750-2,000 words. Pays $75-350 for assigned articles; Pays $200 maximum for unsolicited articles. Sometimes pays the expenses of writers on assignment.

Photos: State availability of photos with submission. Reviews contact sheets, negatives and transparencies. Offers no additional payment for photos accepted with ms. Captions and identification of subjects required.

Tips: "Get copies of the magazine. Study approach, and then call with any suggestion. It is likely that an idea will need to be more tightly focused for a trade magazine's audience." The area most open to freelancers is feature articles.

ROOFER MAGAZINE, D&H Publications, Box 06253, Ft. Myers FL 33906. (813)275-7663. Editor: Shawn Holiday. 10% freelance written. Eager to work with new/unpublished writers, and works with a small number of new/unpublished writers each year. Monthly magazine covering the roofing industry for roofing contractors. Circ. 16,000. Pays on publication. Publishes ms an average of 5 months after acceptance. Byline given. Buys first serial rights and second serial (reprint) rights. Submit seasonal/holiday material 4 months in advance. Computer printout submissions acceptable; no dot-matrix. Reports in 2 weeks on queries; 1 month on mss. Sample copy and writer's guidelines for SAE and 27¢ postage.

Nonfiction: Historical/nostalgic; how-to (solve application problems, overcome trying environmental conditions); interview/profile; and technical. "Write articles directed toward areas of specific interest; don't generalize too much." Buys 7 mss/year. Query. Length: 3,000-7,000 words. Pays $125-250.

Photos: Send photos with accompanying query. Reviews 8x10 b&w prints and standard size transparencies. Identification of subjects required. Buys all rights.

Tips: "We prefer substantial articles (not short articles and fillers). Slant articles toward roofing contractors. Don't embellish too much. Our audience has proven itself to be educated, intelligent and demanding. The submitted freelance article should exemplify those traits. We have little use for generic articles that can appear in any business publication and give little consideration to such material submitted. The tone of articles submitted to us needs to be authoritative but not condescending. Authors of successful freelance articles know the roofing industry."

SHOPPING CENTER WORLD, Communication Channels Inc., 6255 Barfield Rd., Atlanta GA 30328. (404)256-9800. Associate Publisher/Editor: Constance Brittain. 75% freelance written. Prefers to work with published/established writers. A monthly magazine covering the shopping center industry. "Material is written with the shopping center developer and shopping center tenant in mind." Pays on publication. Publishes ms an average of 3 months after acceptance. Byline given. Buys all rights. Submit seasonal/holiday material 3 months in advance. Photocopied submissions OK. Query for electronic submissions. Computer printout submissions acceptable; prefers letter-quality to dot-matrix. Reports in 1 month. Sample copy $4.

Nonfiction: Interview/profile, new product, opinion, photo feature, and technical. Especially interested in renovation case studies on shopping centers. Buys 50 mss/year. Query with or without published clips, or send complete ms. Length: 750-3,000 words. Pays $75-500. Sometimes pays expenses of writers on assignment.

Photos: State availability of photos with submission. Reviews 4x5 transparencies, and 35mm slides. Offers no additional payment for photos accepted with ms. Model releases and identification of subjects required. Buys one-time rights.

Tips: "We are always looking for talented writers to work on assignment. Send resume and published clips. Writers with real estate writing and business backgrounds have a better chance. Product overviews, renovations, and state reviews are all freelance written on an assignment basis."

‡WESTERN ROOFING/INSULATION/SIDING, Dodson Publications, Inc., 27202 Via Burgos, Mission Viejo CA 92691. (714)951-1653. Editor: Marc Dodson. 30% freelance written. Bimonthly magazine. Circ. 12,000. Pays on publication. Publishes ms an average of 2 months after acceptance. Byline given. Buys first rights, one-time rights or simultaneous rights. Submit seasonal/holiday material 4 months in advance. Photocopied submissions OK. Computer printout submissions OK; prefers letter-quality to dot-matrix. Sample copy for $2 or 9x12 SAE with $1.71 postage; writer's guidelines for #10 SASE and one first-class stamp.

Nonfiction: Historical/nostalgic, interview/profile, new product, personal experience and technical articles of interest to "building professionals concerned with the design and specification of roofing, insulation, and siding, and concerned with industry-related news throughout the western United States." Buys 10 mss/year. Send complete ms. Length: 500-2,000 words. Pays $15-150. Sometimes pays with contributor copies depending on quality of article.

Photos: State availability of photos with submission. Reviews contact sheets. Offers no additional payment for photos accepted with ms. Captions and identification of subjects required. Buys one-time rights.

Columns/Departments: Sue Dodson, editor. Industry News (aquisitions, plant openings, legal); People (promotions, new assignments) and Product News (new products/improved products), all 100-300 words. Buys 30 mss/year. Send complete ms. Pays $25 maximum.

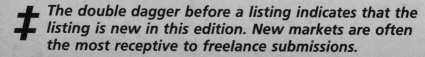

The double dagger before a listing indicates that the listing is new in this edition. New markets are often the most receptive to freelance submissions.

Dental

DENTAL ECONOMICS, Penwell Publishing Co., Box 3408, Tulsa OK 74101. (918)835-3161. Editor: Dick Hale. 50% freelance written. A monthly dental trade journal. "Our readers are actively practicing dentists who look to us for current practice-building, practice-administrative and personal finance assistance." Circ. 103,000. Pays on acceptance. Publishes ms an average of 3-4 months after acceptance. Byline given. Buys first rights. Submit seasonal/holiday material 6 months in advance. Computer printout submissions OK; prefers letter-quality to dot-matrix. Reports in 3 weeks on queries; 1 month on mss. Free sample copy and writer's guidelines.
Nonfiction: General interest, how-to and new product. "No human interest and consumer-related stories." Buys 40 mss/year. Query. Length: 750-3,500 words. Pays $150-500 for assigned articles; pays $75-350 for unsolicited articles. Sometimes pays the expenses of writers on assignment.
Photos: State availability of photos with submission. Reviews contact sheets. Offers no additional payment for photos accepted with ms. Model releases and identification of subjects required. Buys one-time rights.
Columns/Departments: Ron Combs, editor. Tax Q&A (tax tips for dentists), 1,500 words; Capitolgram (late legistlative news—dentistry), 750 words; and Econ Report (national economic outlook), 750 words. Buys 36 mss/year. Pays $50-300.
Tips: "How-to articles on specific subjects such as practice-building, newsletters and collections should be relevant to a busy, solo-practice dentist."

‡DENTIST, Dental Market Network, Stevens Publishing Corp., 225 N. New Rd., Box 7573, Waco TX 76714. (817)776-9000. Editor: Mark S. Hartley. 25% freelance written. Eager to work with new/unpublished writers. A bimonthly trade journal for dentists. Any news or feature story of interest to dentists is considered. Circ. 154,860. Pays 60 days after acceptance. Publishes ms an average of 2 months after acceptance. Byline given. Offers 25% kill fee. Buys first North American serial rights. Submit seasonal/holiday material 1 year in advance. Simultaneous submissions OK. Computer printout submissions OK; prefers letter-quality to dot-matrix. Reports in 1 month on queries; 2 months on mss. Sample copy and writer's guidelines for 12½x15 SASE.
Nonfiction: How-to, humor, interview/profile, new product and technical. Buys 20 mss/year. Query with or without published clips, or send complete ms. Length: 30 inches of copy. Pays $50-200 for assigned articles. Sometimes pays the expenses of writers on assignment
Photos: Send photos with submission. Reviews contact sheets. Offers $10-100 per photo. Captions and identification of subjects required. Buys one-time rights.
Tips: "The emphasis in 1988 will continue to be on obtaining timely, newsworthy editorial pertinent to dentistry."

PROOFS, The Magazine of Dental Sales and Marketing, Box 3408, Tulsa OK 74101. (918)835-3161. Publisher: Joe Bessette. Editor: Mary Elizabeth Good. 10% freelance written. Magazine published 10 times/year; combined issues July/August, November/December. Pays on publication. Byline given. Computer printout submissions acceptable; prefers letter-quality to dot-matrix. Reports in 2 weeks. Free sample copy.
Nonfiction: Uses short articles, chiefly on selling to dentists. Must have understanding of dental trade industry and problems of marketing and selling to dentists and dental laboratories. Query. Pays about $75.
Tips: "The most frequent mistakes made by writers are having a lack of familiarity with industry problems and talking down to our audience."

RDH, The National Magazine for Dental Hygiene Professionals, Stevens Publishing Corp., 225 N. New Rd., Waco TX 76714. (817)776-9000. Editor: Sandra A. Pemberton. 55% freelance written. Eager to work with new/unpublished writers. A monthly magazine covering information relevant to dental hygiene professionals as business-career oriented individuals. "Dental hygienists are highly trained, licensed professionals; most are women. They are concerned with ways to develop rewarding careers, give optimum service to patients and to grow both professionally and personally." Circ. 63,210. Usually pays on publication; sometimes on acceptance. Publishes ms an average of 8 months after acceptance. Byline given. Seldom offers kill fee. Buys first serial rights. Computer printout submissions acceptable; no dot-matrix. Reports in 3 weeks on queries; 2 months on mss. Sample copy for 9x11 SAE; writer's guidelines for SAE with 1 first class stamp.
Nonfiction: Essays, general interest, interview/profile, personal experience, photo feature and technical. "We are interested in any topic that offers broad reader appeal, especially in the area of personal growth (communication, managing time, balancing career and personal life). No undocumented clinical or technical articles; how-it-feels-to-be-a-patient articles; product-oriented articles (unless in generic terms); anything cutesy-unprofessional." Length: 1,500-3,000 words. Pays $100-350 for assigned articles; pays $50-200 for

unsolicited articles. Sometimes pays expenses of writers on assignment.

Photos: Send photos with submission. Reviews 3x5 prints. Model releases required. Buys one-time rights.

Tips: "Freelancers should have a feel for the concerns of today's business-career woman—and address those interests and concerns with practical, meaningful and even motivational messages. We want to see good-quality manuscripts on both personal growth and lifestyle topics. For clinical and/or technical topics, we prefer the writers be members of the dental profession. New approaches to old problems and dilemmas will always get a close look from our editors. *RDH* is also interested in manuscripts for our feature section. Other than clinical information, dental hygienists are interested in all sorts of topics—finances, personal growth, educational opportunities, business management, staff/employer relations, communication and motivation, office rapport and career options. Other than clinical/technical articles, *RDH* maintains an informal tone. Writing style can easily be accommodated to our format."

———— *Drugs, Health Care and Medical Products*

‡NURSING HOMES, And Senior Citizen Care, Centaur & Company, 5 Willowbrook Ct., Potomac MD 20854. (301)983-1152. Editor: William D. Magnes. 60% freelance writen. Bimonthly magazine covering the nursing home industry. "Academic articles (often by RNs and PhDs) and human-interest stories. Most interested in mss on resident/patient care, which can cover a myriad of subjects." Circ. 4,000. Pays on acceptance. Publishes ms an average of 3 months after acceptance. Byline given. Buys all rights. Submit seasonal/holiday material 4 months in advance. Computer printout submissions OK; no dot-matrix. Reports in 2 weeks on queries; 1 month on mss. Sample copy $7.50; free writer's guidelines . "Generally a personal letter."

Nonfiction: Essays, humor, inspirational, new product, opinion and personal experience. No-hyped articles on company or product promotion." Buys 30-40 mss/year. Query with published clips, or send complete ms. Length: 2,500 words maximum. Pays $50-100. Rarely pays the expenses of writers on assignment.

Photos: Send photos with submission. Reviews 3x5 prints. Offers $50 per photo for front cover. Buys all rights.

Columns/Departments: Book Reviews, 250 words. Query with published clips. Pays $30.

Poetry: Light verse and traditional. Buys few poems/year. Pays $25 maximum.

Fillers: Facts, newsbreaks and short humor. Buys few/year.

Tips: "Discuss a problem, how and why it is faced, and the results—but subject must have a thrust about a facility or situation that underscores that is different in some way(s)."

RX HOME CARE, The Journal of Home Health Care and Rehabilitation, Brentwood Publishing, a Simon & Schuster company, 1640 5th St., Santa Monica CA 90401. (213)395-0234. Editor: Les Plesko. 40% freelance written. Monthly magazine covering home health care equipment supply. "The journal addresses the durable medical equipment and health care supply needs of patients being cared for at home. The primary audience is medical supply dealers. The secondary audience is physical therapists, occupational therapists, nurses, physicians, and other medical professionals in the home health care field." Circ. 15,000. Pays on acceptance and receipt of phone log and copy of bill. Publishes ms an average of 6 months after acceptance. Byline given. Buys all rights and makes work-for-hire assignments. Computer printout submissions acceptable. Reports in 1 week. Sample copy by phone request.

Nonfiction: How-to (market durable medical equipment); and technical (on use of non-invasive therapies in the home). "No general articles on health-related topics that are not geared specifically to our readership." Buys 50 mss/year. Query by phone a must. Length: 1,000-2,000 words. Pays 10-12¢/word. Pays expenses of writers on assignment.

Tips: "Writers must conform to our style, which is based on the American Medical Association stylebook. A medical background is not necessary to write for *RX Home Care*, but it is helpful when tackling technical equipment-related topics. All submissions are reviewed by an editorial advisory board of industry professionals."

‡SAFETY COMPLIANCE LETTER, with OSHA Highlights, Bureau of Business Practice, 24 Rope Ferry Rd., Waterford CT 06386. (203)442-4365. Editor: Laurie Beth Roberts. Managing Editor: Wayne Muller. 80% freelance written. Bimonthly newsletter covering occupational safety and health. Publishes interview-based 'how-to' and 'success' stories for personnel in charge of safety and health in manufacturing/industrial environments. Circ. 8,000. Pays on acceptance after editing. Publishes ms an average of 3-6 months after

acceptance. No byline given. Offers 50% kill fee. Buys all rights. Submit seasonal/holiday material 4 months in advance. Reports in 1 week on queries; 1 month on mss. Free sample copy and writer's guidelines.
Nonfiction: How-to (implement an occupational safety/health program) and examples of safety/health programs. No articles that aren't based on an interview. Buys 24 mss/year. Query. Length: 750-1,200 words. Pays 10¢-15¢/word. Sometimes pays the expenses of writers on assignment.

___ *Education and Counseling*

Professional educators, teachers, coaches and counselors—as well as other people involved in training and education—read the journals classified here. Many journals for educators are nonprofit forums for professional advancement; writers contribute articles in return for a byline and contributor's copies. *Writer's Market* includes only education journals that pay for articles. Education-related publications for students are included in the Career, College and Alumni; and Teen and Young Adult sections of Consumer Publications.

‡**ACADEMIC TECHNOLOGY**, Electronic Communications, Inc., Suite 220, 1311 Executive Center Dr., Tallahassee FL 32301. (904)878-4178. Managing Editor: Don Wood. 10% freelance written. Publishes 8 times/school year. "Emphasize trends and innovative computer applications in college and universities." Pays on publication. Publishes ms an average of 3-4 months after acceptance. Byline given. Buys all rights. Submit seasonal/holiday material 6 months in advance. Photocopied and previously published submissions "but say so and where" OK. Computer printout submissions OK; prefers letter-quality to dot-matrix. Reports in 1 month. Sample copy $3.50; free writer's guidelines to serious inquiries.
Nonfiction: Essays, how-to (implement an application, for example), interview/profile (of prominent or expert person in field), opinion (by qualified individual), personal experience (with computers in our field). Buys 8-10 mss/year. Query with or without published clips, or send complete ms. Length: 800-2,100 words. Payment negotiable. Sometimes pays the expenses of writers on assignment.
Photos: Send photos with submission. Reviews transparencies and 5x8 to 8x10 prints. Offers no additional payment for photos accepted with ms. Captions, model releases and identification of subjects required. Buys all rights.
Tips: "Seek out innovative instructional uses of computers among local colleges and universities. Consider all disciplines—English, civics, art, journalism, etc."

THE AMERICAN SCHOOL BOARD JOURNAL, National School Boards Association, 1680 Duke St., Alexandria VA 22314. (703)838-6722. Editor: Gregg Downey. 10% freelance written. "We have no preference for published/unpublished writers; it's the quality of the article and writing that count." Monthly magazine; 52 pages. Emphasizes public school administration and policymaking for elected members of public boards of education throughout U.S. and Canada, and high-level administrators of same. Circ. 42,000. Pays on acceptance. Publishes ms an average of 3 months after acceptance. Buys all rights. Phone queries OK. Photocopied submissions OK. Computer printout submissions acceptable; prefers letter-quality to dot-matrix. Reports in 2 months. Free sample copy and guidelines.
Nonfiction: Publishes how-to articles (solutions to problems of public school operation including political problems). "No material on how public schools are in trouble. We all know that; what we need are *answers*." Buys 20 mss/year. Query. Length: 400-2,000 words. Payment for feature articles varies, "but never less than $100."
Photos: B&w glossies (any size) purchased on assignment. Captions required. Pays $10-50. Model release required.
Tips: "Can you lend a national perspective to a locally observed school program? Do you prefer writing for a general audience or a specific, knowledgeable-on-this-issue audience?"

ARTS & ACTIVITIES, Publishers' Development Corporation, Suite 200, 591 Camino de la Reina, San Diego CA 92108. (619)297-5352. Editor: Dr. Leven C. Leatherbury. Managing Editor: Maryellen Bridge. 95% freelance written. Eager to work with new/unpublished writers. Monthly (except July and August) art education magazine covering art education at levels from preschool through college for educators and therapists engaged in arts and crafts education and training. Circ. 19,466. Pays on publication. Publishes ms an average of 6 months after acceptance. Byline given. Not copyrighted. Buys first serial rights. Submit seasonal/holiday material 4 months in advance. Photocopied submissions OK. Computer printout submissions acceptable; prefers letter-quality to dot-matrix. Reports in 8 weeks. Sample copy for 9x12 envelope and $2 postage; writer's guidelines for business size SAE and 1 first class stamp.

Nonfiction: Historical/nostalgic (arts activities history); how-to (classroom art experiences, artists' techniques); interview/profile (of artists); opinion (on arts activities curriculum, ideas on how to do things better); personal experience ("this ties in with the how-to—we like it to be *personal*, no recipe style"); and articles on exceptional art programs. Buys 50-80 mss/year. Length: 200-2,000 words. Pays $35-150. Sometimes pays the expenses of writers on assignment.

Tips: "Frequently in unsolicited manuscripts writers obviously have not studied the magazine to see what style of articles we publish. The best way to find out if his/her writing style suits our needs is for the author to submit a manuscript on speculation. We are starting to incorporate articles dealing with the performing arts (dance, drama) in addition to our usual editorial focus on visual arts."

CHILDBIRTH EDUCATOR, American Baby, 575 Lexington Ave., New York NY 10022. (212)752-0755. Editor: Marsha Rehns. Managing Editor: Trisha Thompson. 90% freelance written. Works with a small number of new/unpublished writers each year. Quarterly magazine for teachers of prenatal education. "Our audience is teachers of childbirth and baby care classes. Articles should have a firm medical foundation." Circ. 22,000. Pays on acceptance. Publishes ms an average of 6 months after acceptance. Byline given. Offers 25% kill fee. Buys first serial rights for articles and second serial (reprint) rights for book excerpts. Submit seasonal/holiday material 5 months in advance. Computer printout submissions acceptable; no dot-matrix. Reports in 4 months. Free sample copy.

Nonfiction: Book excerpts (obstetrics, child care, teaching, neonatology); how-to (teaching techniques); and technical (obstetrics, child-rearing, neonatology). Buys 24 mss/year. Query with outline, lead and published clips. Length: 1,500-2,500 words. Pays $300-500. Pays expenses of writers on assignment.

Fillers: Newsbreaks. Buys 10/year. Length: 250-750 words. Pays $50-100. No byline.

Tips: "Queries should include a detailed outline, first paragraph, and writer's background. Articles should be serious and directed to an intelligent, specially trained reader. Frequently articles are too superficial in medical terms or lacking practical advice in teaching terms."

CLASSROOM COMPUTER LEARNING, Suite A4, 2169 Francisco Blvd. E., San Rafael CA 94901. Editor: Holly Brady. 50% freelance written. Works with a small number of new/unpublished writers each year. Monthly magazine published during school year emphasizing elementary through high school educational computing topics. Circ. 83,000. Pays on acceptance. Publishes ms an average of 8 months after acceptance. Buys all rights or first serial rights. Submit seasonal/holiday material 6 months in advance. Computer printout submissions acceptable; prefers letter-quality to dot-matrix. Reports in 2 months. Writer's guidelines with SAE and 1 first class stamp; sample copy for SAE and 70¢ postage.

Nonfiction: "We publish manuscripts that describe innovative ways of using computers in the classroom as well as articles that discuss controversial issues in computer education." How-to (specific computer-related activities for children in one of three segments of the school population: Kindergarten-5, 6-9, or 10-12); interviews; and featurettes describing fully developed and tested classroom ideas. Recent article example: "Telecomputing: How to Overcome the Roadblocks" (February 1987). Buys 50 mss/year. Query. Length: 600 words or less for classroom activities; 1,000-1,500 words for classroom activity featurettes; 1,500-2,500 words for major articles. Pays $25 for activities; $100-150 for featurettes; varying rates for longer articles. Educational Software Reviews: Assigned through editorial offices. "If interested, send a letter telling us of your areas of interest and expertise as well as the microcomputer(s) you have available to you." Pays $100 per review. Sometimes pays expenses of writers on assignment.

Photos: State availability of photos with query.

Tips: "The talent that goes in to writing our shorter hands-on pieces is different from that required for features (e.g., interviews, issues pieces, etc.) Write whatever taps your talent best. A frequent mistake is taking too 'novice' or too 'expert' an approach. You need to know our audience well and to understand how much they know about computers. Also, too many manuscripts lack a definite point of view or focus or opinion. We like pieces with clear, strong, well thought out opinions."

COMPUTERS IN EDUCATION, Moorshead Publications, 1300 Don Mills Rd., North York, Toronto, Ontario M3B 3M8 Canada. (416)445-5600. Editor: Roger Allan. 90% freelance written. Eager to work with new/unpublished writers. Magazine published 10 times/year; 48-216 pages. Articles of interest to teachers, computer consultants and administrators working at the kindergarten to 13 level. Circ. 18,000. Pays on publication. Publishes ms an average of 2 months after acceptance. Byline given. Buys first serial rights, first North American serial rights, one time rights, second serial (reprint) rights, and all rights. Phone queries OK. Photocopied submissions OK. Query for electronic submissions. Computer printout submissions acceptable; prefers letter-quality to dot-matrix. Sample copy and writer's guidelines with SASE or IRC.

Nonfiction: Use of computers in education and techniques of teaching using computers; lesson plans, novel applications, anything that is practical for the teacher. Does not want overviews, "Gee Whizzes," and reinventions of the wheel. Length 700-2,000 words. Pays 6-10¢/word. Sometimes pays the expenses of writers on assignment.

Photos: Photos and/or artwork all but mandatory. Pays extra for photos. Captions required.

Tips: "While there will be no change in the editorial mandate (to be practical), there will be more articles on desktop publishing and electronic music in 1988. We would like to receive articles on educational electronic music, educational databases, desktop publishing in the classroom, and on networking. We are looking for practical articles by working teachers. Nothing too general, no overviews, or the same thing that has been said for years."

CURRICULUM REVIEW, Curriculum Advisory Service, 517 S. Jefferson St., Chicago IL 60607. (312)939-3010. Editor-in-Chief: Irene M. Goldman. 80% freelance written. A multidisciplinary magazine for kindergarten-12 principals, department heads, teachers, curriculum planners and superintendents; published 5 times/year. Circ. 10,000. Each issue includes articles in the areas of language arts/reading, mathematics, science, social studies, and the educational uses of computers. A separate feature section varies from issue to issue. Pays on publication. Publishes ms an average of 6 months after acceptance. Byline given. Buys all rights. Photocopies and multiple queries OK, but no multiple submissions. Computer printout submissions acceptable; prefers letter-quality to dot-matrix. Reports in 6 weeks on queries; 4 months on mss.

Nonfiction: Charlotte H. Cox, articles editor. How-to articles should consider primarily an audience of secondary educators and describe successful teaching units or courses with practical applications. Articles of interest to kindergarten-8 educators also welcome. Focus should be on innovative or practical programs, teaching units, new curriculum trends, and controversial or stimulating ideas in education. "While we need articles in all four areas (language arts/reading, math, science, social studies), math and science are especially welcome." Buys 45 mss/year. Length: 1,000-2,000 words. Pays $25-100; sometimes pays in contributor's copies on mutual agreement. Query.

Photos: State availability of photos with query. Prefers 35mm color transparencies or 8x10 b&w or color prints. Model release required. Buys all rights with ms; no additional payment.

Columns/Departments: 600 book reviews/year on an assigned basis with educational vita; textbook, supplements, media, and computer software selection in language arts/reading, mathematics, science and social studies. Emphasizes secondary level. "We are looking for new and lively treatments of educational topics. Description of specific teaching units or courses are welcome if they have broad implications for other schools. Use fresh, descriptive, plain language—no educationalese." Length: 300-600 words.

Tips: "Schedule of featured topics available upon request. The writer has a better chance of breaking in with short articles and fillers since we tend to invite submissions for feature articles to be sure that we have a choice available for feature deadlines."

‡**DANCE EXERCISE TODAY**, International Dance-Exercise Association, 2nd Floor, 2437 Morena Blvd., San Diego CA 92110. (619)275-2450. Editor: Patricia Ryan. Associate Editor: Nancy Lee. 70% freelance written. A trade published nine times/year for the dance-exercise industry. "All articles must be geared to dance-exercise professionals—aerobics instructors and studio owners—covering topics such as aerobics, nutrition, injury prevention, entrepreneurship (in fitness, business), fitness-oriented research and exercise programs." Circ. 12,000. Pays on acceptance. Publishes ms an average of 4 months after acceptance. Byline given. Buys all rights. Simultaneous and photocopied submissions OK. Computer printout submissions OK. Reports in 1 month on queries. Sample copy $4.

Nonfiction: How-to, opinion, personal experience, technical and other. No general information on fitness; our readers are pros who need detailed info. Buys 10 mss/year. Query. Length: 1,000-3,000 words. Pays $100-300.

Photos: State availability of photos with submission. Offers no additional payment for photos with ms. Model releases required. Buys one-time rights.

Columns/Departments: Excercise Technique (detailed, specific info; must be written by expert), 750-1,500 words; Industry News (short reports on research, programs, conferences), 150-300 words; News for Dance-Exercisers (exercise and nutrition info for participants), 750; Book Reviews (exercise, nutrition and busines—reviewer must have expertise), 350 words; Program Spotlight (detailed explanation of specific exercise program), 1,000-1,500 words. Buys 80 mss/year. Query. Length: 150-1,500 words. Pays $15-150.

Tips: Industry News is most open to freelancers. "Writers who have specific knowledge of, or experience working in the fitness industry have an edge. We're looking for short reports on fitness-related conferences and conventions, research, innovative exercise programs, trends, news from countries other than the United States, reports on aerobics competitions and fitness celebrities."

‡**ELECTRONIC EDUCATION**, Electronic Communications, Inc., Suite 220, 1311 Executive Center Dr., Tallahassee FL 32301. (904)878-4178. Editor: Don Wood. Managing Editor: Cindy Whaley. 10-15% freelance written. Magazine published 8 times/school year covering classroom uses of computers in grades K-12. "To help teachers and administrators use computers most effectively for instructional purposes." Circ. 75,000.

Pays on publication. Publishes ms an average of 4 months after acceptance. Byline given. Buys all rights. Submit seasonal/holiday material 6 months in advance. Photocopied and previously published submissions OK "but state so and where." Computer printout submissions OK; prefers letter-quality to dot-matrix. Reports in 1 month. Sample copy $3.50; free writer's guidelines to serious inquiries.

Nonfiction: Essays, how-to (implement an application, for example), interview/profile (of prominent person or expert in field), opinion, personal experience (of application by teacher, for example). Buys 8-10 mss/year. Query with or without published clips, or send complete ms. Length: 800-2,100 words. Payment negotiable; sometimes pays in contributor's copies on mutual agreement. Sometimes pays the expenses of writers on assignment.

Photos: Send photos with submission. Reviews transparencies and 8x10 or 5x8 prints. Offers no additional payment for photos accepted with ms. Captions, model releases and identification of subjects required. Buys all rights.

Tips: "Investigate local schools (k-12) and teachers for innovative instructional uses of computers."

INSTRUCTOR MAGAZINE, 545 5th Ave., New York NY 10017. (212)503-2888. Editor-in-Chief: Leanna Landsmann. 30% freelance written. Eager to work with new/unpublished writers, "especially teachers." Monthly magazine; 180 pages. Emphasizes elementary education. Circ. 255,000. Pays on acceptance. Publishes ms an average of 1 year after acceptance. Buys all rights or first North American serial rights. Submit seasonal/holiday material 6 months in advance. Photocopied submissions OK. Computer printout submissions acceptable; prefers letter-quality to dot-matrix. Reports in 6-8 weeks. Free writer's guidelines; mention *Writer's Market* in request.

Nonfiction: How-to articles on elementary classroom practice—practical suggestions as well as project reports, opinion pieces on professional issues, and current first-person stories by teachers about the teaching experience. Query. Length: 100-2,500 words. Pays $15-100 for short items; $100-350 for articles and features. Send all queries to Jane Schall, associate editor. No poetry.

Tips: "The most frequent mistake writers make is writing to a general audience rather than teachers. We'll be looking for writing that considers the increasing ethnic diversity of classrooms and the greater age-range among elementary teachers."

JOURNAL OF CAREER PLANNING & EMPLOYMENT, College Placement Council, Inc., 62 Highland Ave., Bethlehem PA 18017. (215)868-1421. Managing Editor: Patricia A. Sinnot. 25% freelance written. Published Nov., Jan., March, and May. A magazine for career development professionals who counsel and/or hire prospective college students, graduating students, employees, and job-changers. Circ. 4,000. Pays on acceptance. Publishes ms an average of 4 months after acceptance. Byline given. Buys first rights. Photocopied submissions OK. Computer printout submissions acceptable; no dot-matrix. Reports in 1 month on queries; 2 months on mss. Free writer's guidelines.

Nonfiction: Book excerpts, how-to, humor, interview/profile, opinion, personal experience, photo feature, new techniques/innovative practices and current issues in the field. No articles that speak directly to job candidates. Buys 7-10 mss/year. Query with published clips, or send complete ms. Length: 2,000-4,000 words. Pays $200-400.

Tips: "A freelancer can best break into our publication by sending query with clips of published work, by writing on topics that aim directly at the journal's audience—professionals in the career planning, placement and recruitment field and by using an easy-to-read, narrative style rather than a formal, thesis style. The area of our publication most open to freelancers is nonfiction feature articles only. Make sure that the topic is directly relevant to the career planning and employment field and that the style is crisp and easy to read."

LEARNING 88, 1111 Bethlehem Pike, Springhouse PA 19477. Editor: Maryanne Wagner. 45% freelance written. Published monthly during school year. Emphasizes elementary and junior high school education topics. Circ. 228,000. Pays on acceptance. Buys all rights. Submit seasonal/holiday material 6 months in advance. Photocopied submissions OK. Computer printout submissions acceptable. Reports in 3 months. Sample copy $3; free writer's guidelines.

Nonfiction: "We publish manuscripts that describe innovative, practical teaching strategies or probe controversial and significant issues of interest to kindergarten to 8th grade teachers." How-to (classroom management, specific lessons or units or activities for children—all at the elementary and junior high level, and hints for teaching in all curriculum areas): personal experience (from teachers in elementary and junior high schools); and profile (with teachers who are in unusual or innovative teaching situations). Strong interest in articles that deal with discipline, teaching strategy, motivation and working with parents. Recent article examples: "How to Teach Math Problem Solving Step by Step" (Nov./Dec. 1986) and "A Difficult Student: Marco's Self Image Had Been Battered Too Many Times" (Jan. 1987). Buys 250 mss/year. Query. Length: 1,000-3,500 words. Pays $50-350.

Photos: State availability of photos with query. Model release required. "We are also interested in series of photos that show step-by-step projects or tell a story that will be of interest."

Close-up

Leanna Landsmann
Editor-in-chief, Publisher
Instructor Magazine

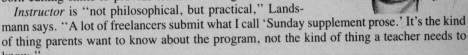

After living with parents who were horticulture writers, Leanna Landsmann says she was convinced that "editing is something you're born with." Later, as a teacher, she discovered that "a good idea will spread quickly." As editor of *Instructor Magazine* for 16 years, she has used those inborn editing skills to provide teachers with good ideas.

Instructor is "not philosophical, but practical," Landsmann says. "A lot of freelancers submit what I call 'Sunday supplement prose.' It's the kind of thing parents want to know about the program, not the kind of thing a teacher needs to know."

Many of *Instructor's* contributors are former teachers or practicing elementary teachers "who write about ideas they've used, or describe a specific motivational technique," Landsmann says. "Non-teachers have few spots because they usually lack knowledge of the subject area. We have a very low percentage of non-teaching articles."

Although the subject matter is specialized, Landsmann says *Instructor* receives about 500-600 unsolicited manuscripts each month, and four people read each manuscript. As editor, Landsmann regularly reviews about 100 manuscripts each month. Her duties are split between editor and publisher roles. About 90% of her editorial time is spent preparing issues. She reserves 10 percent of her time for authors. "We place a big premium on staying in touch with our authors," she says.

Instructor also works to meet special needs of teachers. Four special issues, which Landsmann calls "keepers to use throughout the year," are published each year on topics ranging from educational reform to technology in the classroom. "Hands-On, Minds-On Science: Are you ready to teach it?" was the title of one issue. The issue provided methods for teaching and testing hands-on science lessons, as well as resources for science teachers. The special issue provided what Landsmann calls "a starter kit" for teachers to implement stronger elementary school science programs.

In addition to special issues, *Instructor* now publishes *Early Childhood Teacher*, a seasonal activity guide for teachers of children 3-6 years of age. *Early Childhood Teacher* was started last autumn to meet the needs of preschool and primary teachers who "loved the kindergarten pages in *Instructor* and wanted more."

Landsmann says *Instructor* also deals with trends in education that interest teachers: making research work in the classroom, defining professional status, and determining whether to put an emphasis on factual or thinking skills in the curriculum.

With 950,000 practicing elementary teachers nationwide, writers who "see that something purposeful is going on and believe enough in its success in the classroom" to submit it to *Instructor*, will find, like Landsmann, that good ideas spread quickly.

—Glenda Tennant Neff

MEDIA PROFILES: The Career Development Edition, Olympic Media Information, 550 1st St., Hoboken NJ 07030. (201)963-1600. Editor: Walt Carroll. For colleges, community colleges, libraries, corporate training directors, manpower specialists, education and training services, career development centers, audiovisual specialists and administrators. Serial in magazine format, published every 2 months. Circ. 1,000. Buys all rights. Pays on publication. "Send resume of your experience in human resource development to introduce yourself." Enclose $5 for writer's guidelines and sample issue (refunded with first payment upon publication). Electronic submissions OK if PC DOS. Reports in 2 months.
Nonfiction: "Reviews of instructional films, filmstrips, videotapes, sound/slide programs and the like. We have a highly specialized, rigid format that must be followed without exception. Besides job training areas, we are also interested in the areas of values and personal self-development, upward mobility in the world of work, social change, futuristics, management training, problem solving and adult education. Tell us, above all, about your experience with audiovisuals, and what audiovisual hardware you have access to." Buys 200-240 mss/year. Query. Pays $15/review.
Tips: "Reviewing a film is not the art of sparkling, creative composition. We aim to tell prospective renters or purchasers of off-the-shelf AV programs all they have to know and only what they want to know about a film or tape . . . so they're aware if an entire program may (or may not) be of value to their company. Our purpose is to be accurate, analytical and unbiased. Rather than reviews, we are writing 'profiles'."

MEDIA PROFILES: The Health Sciences Edition, Olympic Media Information, 550 1st St., Hoboken NJ 07030. (201)963-1600. Publisher: Walt Carroll. 100% freelance written. For hospital education departments, nursing schools, schools of allied health, paramedical training units, colleges, community colleges, local health organizations. Serial, in magazine format, published every 2 months. Circ. 1,000 + . Pays on publication. Publishes ms an average of 6 months after acceptance. Buys all rights. Buys 240 mss/year. Electronic submissions OK on PC DOS only. Computer printout submissions acceptable. "Sample copies and writer's guidelines sent on receipt of resume, background, and mention of audiovisual hardware you have access to. Enclose $5 for writer's guidelines and sample issue. (Refunded with first payment upon publication)." Reports in 1 month. Query.
Nonfiction: "Reviews of all kinds of audiovisual media. We are the only review publication devoted exclusively to evaluation of audiovisual aids for hospital and health training. We have a highly specialized, definite format that must be followed in all cases. Samples should be seen by all means. Our writers should first have a background in health sciences; second, have some experience with audiovisuals; and third, follow our format precisely. Writers with advanced degrees and teaching affiliations with colleges and hospital education departments given preference. We are interested in reviews of media materials for nursing education, in-service education, continuing education, personnel training, patient education, patient care and medical problems. We will assign audiovisual aids to qualified writers and send them these to review for us. Unsolicited mss not welcome." Pays $15/review.

MOMENTUM, National Catholic Educational Association, 1077 30th St. NW, Washington DC 20007. Editor: Patricia Feistritzer. 10% freelance written. Quarterly magazine; 56-64 pages. For Catholic administrators and teachers, some parents and students, in all levels of education (preschool, elementary, secondary, higher). Circ. 15,500. Pays on publication. Buys first serial rights. Submit seasonal/holiday material 3 months in advance. Reports in 3 months. Free sample copy.
Nonfiction: Articles concerned with educational philosophy, psychology, methodology, innovative programs, teacher training, research, financial and public relations programs and management systems—all applicable to nonpublic schools. Book reviews on educational/religious topics. Avoid general topics or topics applicable *only* to public education. "We look for a straightforward, journalistic style with emphasis on practical examples, as well as scholarly writing and statistics. All references must be footnoted, fully documented. Emphasis is on professionalism." Buys 28-36 mss/year. Query with outline. Length: 1,500-2,000 words. Pays 2¢/word.
Photos: Pays $7 for b&w glossy photos purchased with mss. Captions required.

NATIONAL BEAUTY SCHOOL JOURNAL, Milady Publishing Corp., 3839 White Plains Rd., Bronx NY 10467. (212)881-3000. Editor: Mary Jane Tenerelli. Associate Editor: Mary Healy. 75% freelance written. Works with a small number of new/unpublished writers each year. A monthly magazine covering cosmetology education. "Articles must address subjects pertinent to cosmetology education (i.e. articles which will assist the instructor in the classroom or the school owner to run his business)." Circ. 6,500 schools. Pays on publication. Publishes ms an average of 2 months after acceptance. Byline given. Buys first rights. Submit seasonal/holiday material 3 months in advance. Simultaneous submissions, photocopied submissions, and previously published submissions OK. Computer printout submissions acceptable; prefers letter-quality to dot-matrix. Free sample copy with writer's guidelines.
Nonfiction: Book excerpts, essays, historical/nostalgic, how-to (on doing a haircut, teaching a technique) humor, inspirational, interview/profile, new product, personal experience, photo feature and technical. No articles geared to the salon owner or operator instead of the cosmetology school instructor or owner. Buys 24

mss/year. Query with or without published clips, or send complete ms. Length: 500-3,000 words. Pays $150 if published.

Photos: Send photos with submissions. Reviews 5x7 b&w prints. Offers no additional payment for photos accepted with ms. Identification of subjects required. Buys first rights.

Columns Departments: Buys 6 mss/year; willing to start new departments. Length: 500-1,000 words. Pays $150.

Fiction: Humorous and slice-of-life vignettes. No fiction relating to anything other than the classroom or the beauty school business. Send complete ms. Length: 500-3,000 words. Pays $150.

Fillers: Facts, gags to be illustrated by cartoonist and newsbreaks. Length: 250-500 words. Pays $150.

Tips: "Talk to school owners and instructors to get a feel for the industry. All areas of our publication are open. Write in clear, simple language."

‡NATIONWIDE CAREERS, The Weekly Guide to Professional Advancement Opportunities, Nationwide Careers, Inc., Box 15727, Little Rock AR 72231-5727. (501)374-4315. Editor: Neva Shelton Bledsoe. 50% freelance written. A weekly specialty tabloid serving the recruitment industry on its regional/national search for mid- and upper-level professionals. Circ. 65,000. Pays on publication. Byline given. Buys first rights. Submit seasonal/holiday material 2 months in advance. Simultaneous, photocopied and previously published submissions OK. Computer printout submissions OK; prefers letter-quality. Reports in 1 month on mss. Free sample copy and writer's guidelines.

Nonfiction: Book excerpts, technical and travel. "Articles must be of interest and/or benefit to the career professional (how to get a job; how to manage effectively on-the-job; related topics such as travel, statistics, etc., with emphasis on leading professionals). Special issues highlight six leading professions—engineering; healthcare; finance/accounting; managerial; data processing/programming; high tech. Also, generic topics concerning the workplace from the executive point of view. No articles unrelated to career growth, advancement, how to prepare resumes, etc." Query and send complete ms "if topics approved." Length: 1,500-3,000 words. Pays $50-250 for assigned articles, or offers ad.

Photos: Uses photos only of subjects featured in profiles; otherwise, photos are not used with articles."

Columns/Departments: Career Doctor (helpful career planning strategies, job search); Climbing the Career Ladder and Another Day at the Office (the politics and expertise of advancement). Buys 50-100 mss/year. Responds to special guidelines. Send complete ms. Length: 400 words. Pays $50-75.

PHI DELTA KAPPAN, Box 789, Bloomington IN 47402-0789. Editor: Robert W. Cole Jr. 2% freelance written. Monthly magazine; 80 pages. For educators—teachers, kindergarten-12 administrators and college professors. All hold BA degrees; one-third hold doctorates. Circ. 150,000. Buys all rights. Pays on publication. Publishes ms an average of 6 months after acceptance. Reports in 2 months. Free sample copy.

Nonfiction: Feature articles on education—emphasizing policy, trends, both sides of issues, controversial developments. Also informational, how-to, personal experience, inspirational, humor, think articles and expose. "Our audience is scholarly but hard-headed." Buys 5 mss/year. Submit complete ms. Length: 500-4,000 words. Pays $250-800. "We pay a fee only occasionally, and then it is usually to an author whom *we* seek out. We do welcome inquiries from freelancers, but it is misleading to suggest that we buy very much from them."

Photos: Pays average photographer's rates for b&w photos purchased with mss, but captions are required. Will purchase photos on assignment. Sizes: 8x10 or 5x7 preferred.

SCHOOL SHOP, Prakken Publications, Inc., Box 8623, Ann Arbor MI 48107. Editor: Alan H. Jones. 100% freelance written. Eager to work with new/unpublished writers. A monthly (except June and July) magazine covering issues, trends and projects of interest to industrial, vocational, technical and technology educators at the secondary and post secondary school levels. Special issue in April deals with varying topics for which mss are solicited. Circ. 45,000. Buys all rights. Pays on publication. Publishes ms an average of 8-12 months after acceptance. Byline given. Prefers authors who have direct connection with the field of industrial and/or technical education. Submit seasonal material 6 months in advance. Simultaneous queries, and simultaneous, photocopied, and previously published submissions OK. Computer printout submissions acceptable; prefers letter-quality to dot-matrix. Reports in 6 weeks. Free sample copy and writer's guidelines.

Nonfiction: Uses articles pertinent to the various teaching areas in industrial education (woodwork, electronics, drafting, machine shop, graphic arts, computer training, etc.). "The outlook should be on innovation in educational programs, processes or projects which directly apply to the industrial/technical education area." Buys general interest, how-to, opinion, personal experience, technical and think pieces, interviews, humor, and coverage of new products. Buys 135 unsolicited mss/year. Length: 200-2,000 words. Pays $25-150.

Photos: Send photos with accompanying query or ms. Reviews b&w and color prints. Payment for photos included in payment for ms.

Columns/Departments: Shop Kinks (brief items which describe short-cuts or special procedures relevant to the industrial arts classroom). Buys 30 mss/year. Send complete ms. Length: 20-100 words. Pays $15 minimum.

Tips: "We are most interested in articles written by industrial, vocational and technical educators about their class projects and their ideas about the field. We need more and more technology-related articles."

SCIENCE PERIODICAL ON RESEARCH AND TECHNOLOGY IN SPORT (formerly *Coaching Review*), Coaching Association of Canada, 333 River Rd., Ottawa, Ontario K1L 8B9 Canada. (613)748-5624. Technical Editor: Terry Shevciw. Technical Editor for other CAC Publications: Steve Newman. Monthly. Circ. 5,000. Buys first North American serial rights "unless copyrighted, CAC reserves the right to grant reprints of material by other sources (e.g. sport organizations, health organizations)." Byline given with biography. Phone queries OK. Query for electronic submissions. Computer printout submissions acceptable; prefers letter-quality to dot-matrix. Sample copy available.
Nonfiction: Geared to medium to elite level coaches. Educational, hands-on, practical topics. Topic areas include testing, psychology, physical training, and sports medicine (diets and nutrition). Material distributed in Canada, US, Europe and Australia. Buys 10-15 unsolicited mss/year. Query with outline. Pays up to $150. Pays some expenses of writers on assignment.
Photos: State availability of photos. Captions required.
Tips: "Well-documented, practical material is desired. Focus on making coaches better coaches by enlightening them."

‡**SIGHTLINES**, Educational Film Library Association, Inc., 45 John St., New York NY 10038. (212)227-5599. Editor: Judith Trojan. 90% freelance written. Prefers to work with published/established writers, "but willing to try new people who have talent and knowledge of the field." Quarterly magazine; 40-48 pages. Journal of the Educational Film Library Association. Emphasizes the nontheatrical film and video world for librarians in university and public libraries, independent filmmakers and video makers, film teachers on the high school and college level, film programmers in community, university and religious organizations and film curators in museums. Circ. 3,000. Pays on publication. Publishes ms an average of 3 months after acceptance. Byline given. Buys first North American serial rights. Phone queries OK. Computer printout submissions acceptable; dot-matrix submissions acceptable "if formatted to our copy paper guidelines." Reports in 2 months. Free sample copy for 9x12 SAE and $1.24 postage.
Nonfiction: Historical (archival work in restoring and programming nontheatrical film and video); how-to (production, distribution, programming); informational (on the production, distribution and programming of nontheatrical films and video); interview (with filmmakers who work in 16mm, video; who make documentary, avant-garde, children's and personal films); new product; and current trends in film, TV or video art. No fanzine material. Buys 15 mss/year. Query with published clips. Length: 1,000-3,500 words. Pays $75-150 per article, "depending on length and if feature article."
Photos: Purchased with accompanying ms. Reviews transparencies and 5x7 or 8x10 (b&w or color) prints. Offers no additional payment for photos accepted with accompanying ms. Captions and model release required. Buys one-time rights.
Columns/Departments: Who's Who in Filmmaking (interview or profile of filmmaker or video artist who works in nontheatrical film and video); Book Reviews (books covering issues related to nontheatrical film/video); Film and Video Reviews; Special Collections (reports on unique media programming and special collections of nontheatrical film and video). Buys 1-2 mss/issue. Query. Pays $100-125. Open to suggestions for new columns or departments. "Other opportunities for freelancers include film/video reviews and media book reviews. Payment for reviews is $10 per review except where multiple titles are covered in one review."
Tips: A frequent mistake made by writers is "not paying attention to the needs of our very special readership."

TEACHER UPDATE, Ideas for Teachers, Teacher Update, Inc., Box 429, Belmont MA 02178. (617)484-7327. Editor: Donna Papalia. 100% freelance written. Eager to work with new/unpublished writers. Monthly (except July and August) newsletter covering early childhood education for preschool teachers. Circ. 10,000. Pays on acceptance. Publishes ms an average of 4 months after acceptance. Byline given. Offers 100% kill fee. Buys all rights. Submit seasonal/holiday material 4 months in advance. Simultaneous queries, and simultaneous, photocopied, and previously published submissions OK. Computer printout submissions acceptable; prefers letter-quality to dot-matrix. Reports in 6 weeks on queries. Sample copy and writer's guidelines for SASE.
Nonfiction: How-to (suggestions for classroom activities). Query. Pays $20/published page.
Columns/Departments: Special Days and Free Materials. Buys 15 mss/year. Query. Pays $20/published page.
Poetry: Children's poems, fingerplays, etc. Buys 6-10/year. Pays $20/published page.
Tips: "Submit original ideas and make sure submissions are in the *Teacher Update* format."

TEACHING/K-8, (formerly Early Years/K-8), The Professional Magazine, Early Years, Inc., 325 Post Rd. W, Box 3330, Westport CT 06880. (203)454-1020. Editor: Allen Raymond. 90% freelance written. "We prefer material from classroom teachers." A monthly magazine covering teaching of kindergarten through eighth grades. Pays on publication. Publishes ms an average of 2-7 months after acceptance. Byline given. Buys all rights. Submit seasonal/holiday material 6 months in advance. Computer printout submissions acceptable; prefers letter-quality to dot-matrix. Reports in 6 weeks on mss. Sample copy $2 with 9x12 SASE; writer's guidelines for #10 SAE with 1 first class stamp.

Nonfiction: Patricia Broderick, articles editor. Classroom curriculum material. Send complete ms. Length: 1,200-1,500 words. Pays $35 maximum.

Photos: Offers no additional payment for photos accepted with ms. Model releases and identification of subjects required.

Columns/Departments: Patricia Broderick, column department editor. Send complete ms. Length: 1,100 word maximum. Pays $25 maximum.

Tips: "Manuscripts should be specifically oriented to a successful teaching strategy, idea, project or program. Broad overviews of programs or general theory manuscripts are not usually the type of material we select for publication. Because of the definitive learning level we cover (pre-school through grade eight) we try to avoid presenting general groups of unstructured ideas. We prefer classroom tested ideas and techniques."

TODAY'S CATHOLIC TEACHER, 26 Reynolds Ave., Ormond Beach FL 32074. (904)672-9974. Editor-in-Chief: Ruth A. Matheny. 40% freelance written. Works with a small number of new/unpublished writers each year. For administrators, teachers and parents concerned with Catholic schools, both parochial and CCD. Circ. 65,000. Pays after publication. Publishes ms an average of 3 months after acceptance. Byline given. Buys all rights. Phone queries OK. Submit seasonal/holiday material 3 months in advance. Sample copy $3; writer's guidelines for SASE; mention *Writer's Market* in request.

Nonfiction: How-to (based on experience, particularly in Catholic situations, philosophy with practical applications); interview (of practicing educators, educational leaders); personal experience (classroom happenings); and profile (of educational leader). Buys 40-50 mss/year. Submit complete ms. Length: 800-2,000 words. Pays $15-75.

Photos: State availability of photos with ms. Offers no additional payment for 8x10 b&w glossy prints. Buys one-time rights. Captions preferred;model release required.

Tips: "We prefer articles based on the author's own expertise, and/or experience, with a minimum of quotations from other sources. We use many one-page features."

Electronics and Communication

These publications are edited for electrical engineers and electrical contractors as well as electronic equipment builders and operators who design and maintain systems connecting and supplying homes, businesses and industries with power. Publications for appliance dealers can be found in the Home Furnishings and Household Goods section.

AV VIDEO, Montage Publishing, Suite 314, 25550 Hawthorne Blvd., Torrance CA 90505. (213)373-9993. Editor: Sam Stalos. Managing Editor: Ed Reid. 25% freelance written. Eager to work with new/unpublished writers. A monthly magazine covering audiovisual and video technology and techniques. "We aim to inform readers who use audiovisuals, video and computer graphics in their professional capacities in business, industry, and government." Circ. 41,500. Pays on acceptance. Publishes ms an average of 6 months after acceptance. Byline given. Offers 50% kill fee. Buys first rights or all rights. Simultaneous and photocopied submissions OK. Query for electronic submissions. Computer printout submissions acceptable; prefers letter-quality to dot-matrix. Reports in 2 months. Free sample copy and writer's guidelines.

Nonfiction: How-to. "In every issue we attempt to publish a wide variety of articles relating to all aspects of audiovisual productions as well as developments in video, interactive video and computer graphics. We welcome all informed, well-written articles pertaining to slides, video, overheads, multi-image, interactive, computer graphics and all attendant applications. No chest thumping. Keep the adjective-to-noun ratio below 50 percent. Nothing related to company profile, personnel or promotions material." Buys 12-20 mss/year. Query with or without published clips, or send complete ms. Pays $200-400 for assigned articles; pays $50-400 for unsolicited articles. Sometimes pays the expenses of writers on assignment.

Photos: Send photos with submission. Reviews negatives, transparencies and prints. Offers no additional payment for photos accepted with ms. Model releases and identification of subjects required. Buys one-time rights.

Tips: "Freelancers should have some direct contact with the industry. Academic research and interview/reportage articles written by professional writers are of less interest to us than pieces written by professionals in our industry who want to share a view, idea or technique with others in the field. The magazine will continue to change with the industry and as the use of computer graphics and video continues to expand, so will our coverage of those fields.''

BROADCAST TECHNOLOGY, Box 420, Bolton, Ontario L0P 1A0 Canada. (416)857-6076. Editor-in-Chief: Doug Loney. 50% freelance written. Monthly (except August, December) magazine; 80 pages. Emphasizes broadcast engineering. Circ. 9,000. Pays on publication. Byline given. Buys all rights. Phone queries OK.
Nonfiction: Technical articles on developments in broadcast engineering, especially pertaining to Canada. Query. Length: 500-1,500 words. Pays $100-300.
Photos: Purchased with accompanying ms. B&w or color. Captions required.
Tips: "Most of our outside writing is by regular contributors, usually employed full-time in broadcast engineering. The specialized nature of our magazine requires a specialized knowledge on the part of a writer, as a rule."

BROADCASTER, 7 Labatt Ave., Toronto, Ontario M5A 3P2 Canada. (416)363-6111. Editor: Daphne Lavers. A monthly trade journal on the broadcasting industry. Pays on publication. Publishes ms an average of 2 months after acceptance. Byline given. Buys all rights. Submit seasonal/holiday material 3 months in advance. Computer printout submissions OK. Free sample copy.
Nonfiction: New product and technical. Query with published clips. Pays $50-400 for assigned articles. Sometimes pays the expenses of writers on assignment.
Photos: Send photos with submission.

CABLE COMMUNICATIONS MAGAZINE, Canada's Authoritative International Cable Television Publication, Ter-Sat Media Publications Ltd., 4 Smetana Dr., Kitchener, Ontario N2B 3B8 Canada. (519)744-4111. Editor: Udo Salewsky. 33% freelance written. Prefers to work with published/established writers. Monthly magazine covering the cable television industry. Circ. 6,300. Pays on acceptance. Publishes ms an average of 2 months after acceptance. Byline given. Buys all rights. Submit seasonal/holiday material 1 month in advance. Photocopied submissions OK. Electronic submissions OK via IBM PC, but requires hard copy also. Computer printout submissions acceptable; no dot-matrix. Reports in 2 weeks on queries; 1 month on mss. Free writer's guidelines; $2 IRCs for sample copy.
Nonfiction: Expose, how-to, interview/profile, opinion, technical articles, and informed views and comments on topical, industry related issues. Also, problem solving-related articles, new marketing and operating efficiency ideas. No fiction. Buys 50 mss/year. Query with published clips or send complete ms. Length: 1,000-4,000 words. Pays $200-800. Pays expenses of writers on assignment.
Columns/Departments: Buys 48 items/year. Query with published clips or send complete ms. Length: 1,000-1,500 words. Pays $200-300.
Tips: "Forward manuscript and personal resume. We don't need freelance writers for short articles and fillers. Break in with articles related to industry issues, events and new developments; analysis of current issues and events. Be able to interpret the meaning of new developments relative to the cable television industry and their potential impact on the industry from a growth opportunity as well as a competitive point of view. Material should be well supported by facts and data. Insufficient research and understanding of underlying issues are frequent mistakes."

CABLE MARKETING, The Marketing/Management Magazine for Cable Television Executives, Jobson Publishing, 352 Park Ave. South, New York NY 10010. (212)685-4848. Editor: Ellis Simon. 10% freelance written. Prefers to work with published/established writers. Monthly magazine for cable industry executives dealing with marketing and management topics, new trends and developments and their impact. Circ. 15,000. Pays on publication. Publishes ms an average of 2 months after acceptance. Byline given. Buys first North American serial rights. Photocopied submissions OK. Computer printout submissions acceptable; prefers letter-quality to dot-matrix. Reports in 1 month. Free sample copy.
Columns/Departments: Cable Tech (technology, engineering and new products); and Cable Scan (news items and marketing featurettes mostly about cable system activities and developments). Buys 20 mss/year. Query with published clips. Length: 200-3,000 words. Pays $50-500. Pays the expenses of writers on assignment.
Tips: "Learn something about the cable TV business before you try to write about it. Have specific story ideas. Have some field of expertise that you can draw upon (e.g., marketing, management or advertising). Short articles and fillers give us a chance to better assess a writer's real abilities without exposing us to undue risk, expense, aggravation, etc. on a feature. Not interested in reviews of programming. Editorial focus is on the *business* of cable television."

CABLE TELEVISION BUSINESS MAGAZINE, Cardiff Publishing Co., #650, 6300 S. Syracuse Way, Englewood CO 80111. (303)220-0600. Editor: Jill Marks. Managing Editor: Chuck Moozakis. 10% freelance written. Prefers writers with telecommunications background. Semimonthly magazine about cable television for CATV system operators and equipment suppliers. Circ. 12,000. Pays on publication. Publishes ms an average of 3 months after acceptance. Byline given. Makes work-for-hire assignments. Phone queries OK. Query for electronic submissions. Computer printout submissions acceptable. Reports in 2 weeks on queries; 1 month on mss. Free sample copy.

Nonfiction: Expose (of industry corruption and government mismanagement); historical (early days of CATV); interview (of important people in the industry); profiles (of people or companies); how-to (manage or engineer cable systems); new product (description and application); and case history. "We use articles on all aspects of cable television from programming through government regulation to technical pieces. We use both color and black and white photos, charts and graphs. A writer should have some knowledge of cable television, then send a letter with a proposed topic." No first person articles. Buys 5 mss/year. Query. Length: 1,800-3,500 words. Pays $100/page of magazine space. Sometimes pays expenses of writers on assignment.

Photos: State availability of photos. Reviews 35mm color transparencies. Pays $50/page of magazine space for contact sheets. Offers no additional payment for photos accepted with ms. Captions required.

Tips: "The most frequent mistake made by writers in completing an article for us is not being specific enough about what the story topic really means to cable management—i.e., dollars and cents, or operational strategy. Freelancers are only used for major features."

‡CINCINNATI BELL MAGAZINE, Cincinnati Bell, Inc., 201 E. Fourth St. 102-520, Cincinnati OH 45201. (513)397-4690. Editor: Mev Soller. 5% freelance written. Magazine covering telecommunications for employees and retirees of Cincinnati Bell Inc., Circ. 7,000. Pays on publication. Publishes ms an average of 3 months after acceptance. Byline given. Not copyrighted. Submit seasonal/holiday material 2 months in advance. Simultaneous, photocopied and previously published submissions OK. Query for electronic submissions. Computer printout submissions OK; prefers letter-quality to dot-matrix. Reports in 2 months on mss. Sample copy for 9x12 SAE with 3 first class stamps.

Nonfiction: Humor, management topics and pop psychology. Buys 12 mss/year. Send complete ms. Length: 2,000-5,000 words. Pays $75-200 for unsolicited articles.

Photos: State availability of photos with submission. Reviews contact sheets. Offers $25-100. Captions, model releases and identification of subjects required. Buys one-time rights.

DVORAK DEVELOPMENTS, Freelance Communications, Box 1895, Upland CA 91785. (818)963-3703. Editor: Randy Cassigham. Managing Editor: Michele Wolf. 20% freelance written. A quarterly newsletter covering business productivity/word processing. "We promote the adoption of the Dvorak keyboard for typewriters and computers. Emphasizes current research studies, case studies, and product overviews (reviews). Readers include individuals, governmental officials, and small and large businesses." Circ. 1,500+. Pays on acceptance. Publishes ms an average of 4 months after acceptance. Byline given. Offers 33% kill fee. Buys first rights; rarely reprint rights. Photocopied submissions OK; previously published materials accepted rarely. Electronic submissions OK via disks in IBM PC format but requires hard copy also. Computer printout submissions acceptable. Reports in 2 weeks. Sample copy and writer's guidelines for SAE with 39¢ postage.

Nonfiction: Interview/profiles (if especially interesting Dvorak user); technical (application notes/case studies); how-to (typically a case study on how a company/agency solved a conversion problem); product overviews (detailed description of a Dvorak-related product/review); book reviews (books which significantly deal with the Dvorak). "We do *not* want to see anything that tries to convince the reader that Dvorak is superior to Qwerty—our readers already believe that. We do not generally care to see stories about an *individual's* experience in changing from Qwerty to Dvorak." Buys 10-15 mss/year. Query, preferably with a recent clip. Length: 200-1,000 words. Pays $25-50. Expenses must be negotiated in advance.

Photos: State availability of photos. Reviews b&w proofs or prints. Offers no additional payment for photos accepted with ms. Captions, model releases, and identification of subjects required. Buys one-time rights.

Tips: "If writers know a lot about the Dvorak, or a specific Dvorak application, they can probably write for us. We desire to get the wider viewpoint a freelancer can provide. Sections most open to freelancers: case studies. There are a lot of Dvorak users out there that we don't know about. We want to hear about them. There will be increased emphasis on companies and governmental agencies that have switched to Dvorak."

‡ELECTRONIC PACKAGING AND PRODUCTION, Cahners Publishing Co., 1350 E. Touhy Ave., Box 5080, Des Plaines IL 60018. (312)635-8800. Editor: Ronald Pound. Managing Editor: Margaret Choudhury. 5% freelance written. Circ. 47,000. Pays on publication. Publishes ms an average of 10 months after acceptance. Byline given. Buys first rights. Computer printout submissions OK; prefers letter-quality. Free sample copy and writer's guidelines.

Nonfiction: Flor Ballate, articles editor. How-to, interview/profile, opinion and technical articles on manufacturing and packaging of electronic components. Buys 2 mss/year. Query. Length: 3,000 words maximum. Pays up to $100/printed page for assigned articles; pays up to $50/printed page for unsolicited articles.

Photos: State availability of photos with submission. Reviews transparencies and prints. Offers no additional payment for photos accepted with ms. Captions, model releases and identification of subjects required. Buys all rights.

Columns/Departments: Susan Crum, editor. News (technical reporting on new products, procedures, company changes, etc.), 15-200 words. Buys 12 mss/year. Query. Pays by contract.

Tips: "Keep informed on the state of the industry—major companies, experts, goals, etc. Talk with the editor about filling in potential editorial calendar voids. Attend exhibitions and conferences in field. The news department is most open to freelancers."

‡**THE INDEPENDENT, Film & Video Monthly**, Foundation for Independent Video & Film, 9th Floor, 625 Broadway, New York NY 10012. (212)473-3400. Editor: Martha Gever. 60% freelance written. Works with a small number of new/unpublished writers each year. Monthly magazine of practical information for producers of independent film and video with focus on low budget, art and documentary work from nonprofit sector. Circ. 5,000. Pays on publication. Publishes ms an average of 4 months after acceptance. Byline given. Buys first serial rights. Submit seasonal/holiday material 4 months in advance. Simultaneous queries OK. Query for electronic submissions. Computer printout submissions acceptable; no dot-matrix. Reports in 1 month. Sample copy for 9x12 SAE and 4 first class stamps.

Nonfiction: Book excerpts ("in our area"); how-to; technical (low tech only); and theoretical/critical articles. No reviews. Buys 60 mss/year. Query with published clips. Length: 1,200-3,500 words. Pays $25-125.

Tips: "Since this is a specialized publication, we prefer to work with writers on short pieces first. A frequent mistake made by writers is unfamiliarity with specific practical and theoretical issues concerning independent film and video."

INFORMATION TODAY, Learned Information Inc., 143 Old Marlton Pike, Medford NJ 08055. (609)654-6266. Publisher: Thomas H. Hogan. Editor: Bev Smith. 30% freelance written. A tabloid for the users and producers of electronic information services, published 11 times per year. Circ. 10,000. Pays on publication. Publishes ms an average of 1 month after acceptance. Byline given. Buys first North American serial rights. Submit seasonal/holiday material 2 months in advance. Computer printout submissions acceptable; prefers letter-quality to dot-matrix. Reports in 2 weeks. Free sample copy and writer's guidelines.

Nonfiction: Book reviews; interview/profile and new product (dealing with information industry); technical (dealing with computerized information services); and articles on library technology, artificial intelligence, database and Videotex services. Buys approximately 25 mss/year. Query with published clips or send complete ms on speculation. Length: 500-1,500 words. Pays $80-200.

Photos: State availability of photos with submission.

Tips: "We look for clearly-written, informative articles dealing with the electronic delivery of information. Writing style should not be jargon-laden or heavily technical."

‡**LIGHTWAVE, The Journal of Fiber Optics**, Howard Rausch Associates, Inc., 235 Bear Hill Rd., Waltham MA 02154. (617)890-2700. Editor: Sharon Scully. Managing Editor: William Ferrall. 15-20% freelance written. Works with a small number of new/unpublished writers each year. A monthly trade journal on fiber optics and its applications for specialists in telecommunications or data communications. Circ. 15,000. Pays on publication. Publishes ms an average of 2 months after acceptance. Byline given. Offers $50 kill fee. Buys all rights. Submit seasonal/holiday material 3 months in advance. Query for electronic submissions. Computer printout submissions OK; prefers letter-quality to dot-matrix. Reports in 2 weeks on queries; 1 week on mss. Sample copy for 14x17 SAE with $1.30 postage; free writer's guidelines.

Nonfiction: Book excerpts, technical book reviews, essays, opinion, photo feature and technical. Buys 2-5 mss/year. Query. Length: 500-2,000 words. Pays $100-2,000 for assigned articles; pays $100-1,000 for unsolicited articles. Sometimes pays the expenses of writers on assignment.

Photos: Send photos with submission. Reviews transparencies and prints. Offers $10-150 per photo. Captions required. Buys all rights.

Tips: "Fiber optics technology will shift in focus from long-distance telephone applications to local and other data markets."

MASS HIGH TECH, Mass Tech Times, Inc., 755 Mt. Auburn St., Watertown MA 02172. (617)924-2422. Editor: Alan R. Earls. Managing Editor: Patrick Porter. 10-20% freelance written. "Interested in queries, samples, proposals especially from writers in the New England region." Bimonthly trade tabloid covering feature news of electronics, computers, biotech, systems analysis, etc., for high-tech professionals in New England; strong regional angle preferred. Circ. 30,000. Pays on publication. Publishes ms an average of 1 month after acceptance. Byline given. Not copyrighted. Buys first North American serial rights. Submit seasonal/holiday material 1 month in advance. Simultaneous queries, and simultaneous, photocopied, and previously published submissions OK "if not in our immediate market." Electronic submissions OK via 300 and/or 1200 baud, Hayes or X modem protocols. Computer printout submissions acceptable; prefers letter-quality to dot-matrix. Reports in 1 month. Sample copy for 9x12 SAE and 5 first class stamps.

Nonfiction: Book excerpts; historical (technology); humor; interview/profile; new product; opinion (qualified scientist); personal experience; and photo feature (needs technical orientation and strong Boston area orientation). Also, Op/Ed pieces of up to 1,200 words relevant to concerns of New England technology firms and employees. "Material should inform without over simplifying. A light, amusing approach is OK." Increasingly oriented toward news and analysis of items impacting market area. Buys 50 mss/year. Send complete ms. Length: 400-1,200 words. Pays $50-250.
Photos: Send photos with ms. Pays $25 for 5x7 b&w prints. Captions and identification of subjects required (if appropriate). Buys one-time rights.
Columns/Departments: Buys 50 mss/year. Query with idea or send one sample ms. Length: 300-900 words. Pays $50 and up.
Fillers: Anecdotes, short humor and newsbreaks. Buys 100 mss/year. Length: 25-100 words. Pays $10 and up.
Tips: "Know the Boston and New England high-tech scene or have knowledgeable contacts. Material should be plausible to trained professionals. Trends in magazine publishing that freelance writers should be aware of include the need for more sophisticated graphics—photos or drawings are often available free from their corporate subjects (in our market)."

MICROWAVES & RF, 10 Mulholland Dr., Hasbrouck Heights NJ 07604. (201)393-6285. Editor: Barry E. Manz. 50% freelance written. Eager to work with new/unpublished writers. Monthly magazine; 200 pages. Emphasizes radio frequency design. "Qualified recipients are those individuals actively engaged in microwave and RF research, design, development, production and application engineering, engineering management, administration or purchasing departments in organizations and facilities where application and use of devices, systems and techniques involve frequencies from HF through visible light." Circ. 60,500. Pays on publication. Publishes ms an average of 6 months after acceptance. Buys all rights. Phone queries OK. Photocopied submissions OK. Query for electronic submissions. Computer printouts acceptable "if legible." Reports in 3 weeks. Free sample copy and writer's guidelines; mention *Writer's Market* in request.
Nonfiction: "We are interested in material on research and development in microwave and RF technology and economic news that affects the industry." How-to (circuit design), new product, opinion, and technical. Buys 100 mss/year. Query. Pays $100.

ON PAGE, The Newsletter Co., Box 439, Sudbury MA 01776. Editor: Stanley J. Kaplan. Managing Editor: Bette Sidlo. 5% freelance written. Eager to work with new/unpublished writers. Monthly newsletter about "the beeper industry (radio pocket paging) for professionals, medical people, sales people, small businessmen, municipal employees and any person whose job takes him/her away from the telephone and who must maintain communications." Circ. 100,000. Pays on acceptance. Publishes ms an average of 4 months after acceptance. Buys all rights. Submit seasonal material 3 months in advance. Phone queries OK. Computer printout submissions acceptable; prefers letter-quality to dot-matrix. Reports in 2 weeks. Free sample copy and writer's guidelines.
Fillers: Clippings, jokes, gags, anecdotes, short humor and newsbreaks. "We are particularly interested in anecdotes for our On Page Forum column in the first person narrative, stories of people and their beeper experiences, and newsbreaks on a variety of communication subjects of interest to people who use beepers. We especially look for seasonal freelance contributions." Buys 5-10 mss/year. Length: 75-150 words. Pays $25-40.
Tips: "Our selection is based more on subject matter and details than on the writer's style. A strong originality is of greatest concern here. Submissions should be geared to beeper users (e.g., subject matter must be related to communications or mobility). No sarcasm or comments insulting those who carry or use a beeper."

‡OUTSIDE PLANT, Box 183, Cary IL 60013. (312)639-2200. Editor: Rick Hoelzer. 10% freelance written. Prefers to work with published/established writers. Trade publication focusing exclusively on the outside plant segment of the telephone industry. Readers are end users and/or specifiers at Bell and Independent operating companies, as well as long distance firms whose chief responsibilities are construction, maintenance, planning and fleet management. Readership also includes telephone contracting firms. Published 8 issues in 1987. Circ. 17,000. Buys first rights. Pays on publication. Publishes ms an average of 3 months after acceptance. Computer printout submissions OK; prefers letter-quality to dot-matrix. Reports in 1 month. Free sample copy and guidelines.
Nonfiction: Must deal specifically with outside plant construction, maintenance, planning and fleet vehicle subjects for the telephone industry. "Case history application articles profiling specific telephone projects are best. Also accepts trend features, tutorials, industry research and seminar presentations. Preferably, features should be by-lined by someone at the telephone company profiled." Pays $35-50/published page, including photographs; pays $35 for cover photos. Sometimes pays the expenses of writers on assignment.
Departments: OSP Tips & Advice (short nuts-and-bolts items on new or unusual work methods); and OSP Tommorrow (significant trends in outside plant), 300-600 word items. Pays $5-50. Other departments include new products, literature, vehicles and fiber optics.
Tips: Submissions should include author bio demonstrating expertise in the subject area."

PRO SOUND NEWS, International News Magazine for the Professional Sound Production Industry, P.S.N. Publications, Inc., 2 Park Ave., New York NY 10016. (212)213-3444. Editor: Randolph P. Savicky. 20% freelance written. Works with a small number of new/unpublished writers each year. Monthly tabloid covering the music recording, sound reinforcement, TV and film sound industry. Circ. 14,500. Pays on publication. Publishes ms an average of 1 month after acceptance. Byline given. Buys first serial rights. Simultaneous queries, and photocopied and previously published submissions OK. Query for electronic submissions. Computer printout submissions acceptable. Reports in 2 weeks.
Nonfiction: Query with published clips. Pays 10¢/word. Sometimes pays the expenses of writers on assignment.

‡RETAILER NEWS, Target Publishing, Suite G, 249 E. Emerson, Orange CA 92665. (714)921-0600. Publisher: Martin Barsky. Managing Editor: Barbara Wexler. 5-10% freelance written. Prefers to work with published/established writers. Monthly tabloid covering consumer electronics and major appliances. For retailers of consumer electronics and major appliances, primarily in the West, but also the rest of the nation." Circ. 22,000. Pays on publication. Publishes ms an average of 2 months after acceptance. Byline given. Buys all rights. Submit seasonal/holiday material 3 months in advance. Simultaneous submissions OK. Computer printout submissions OK; prefers letter-quality. Sample copy for 12x16 SAE with $2.40 postage.
Nonfiction: Interview/profile. Query with published clips. Length: 1,000-2,000 words. Pays $125-175 for assigned articles. Pays expenses of writers on assignment.
Photos: Send photos with submission. Reviews 4x6 prints. Offers no additional payment for photos accepted with ms. Captions and identification of subjects required. Buys all rights.

SATELLITE DIRECT, The Magazine of Direct Broadcast Satellite Communication, (formerly *Satellite Dealer*), CommTek Publishing Co., Box 53, Boise ID 83707. (208)322-2800. Executive Editor: Howard Shippy. 75% freelance written. Monthly magazine covering the satellite television industry. Circ. 19,000. Pays on acceptance. Publishes ms an average of 2 months after acceptance. Byline given. Offers 33% kill fee. Buys first North American serial rights, one-time rights, all rights, first serial rights, and second serial (reprint) rights. Query for electronic submissions. Computer printout submissions acceptable. Reports in 5 weeks on queries. Free sample copy and writer's guidelines.
Nonfiction: Book excerpts (possible from new releases in industry); expose (on government communications policy); how-to (on installation of dishes); humor (if there is an angle); interview/profile (on industry leaders and exceptional dealers); personal experience (from TVRO dealers); photo feature (of unusual dish installations); technical (on radio theory as it pertains to satellite TV); and marketing. Special issues include trade show editions. "We print articles concerning the home satellite television industry. We also touch on SMATV (private cable). Everything we print must in some way be valuable to the satellite television dealer's business. Marketing techniques, installation tips, legal explanations and how-to or technical articles are examples of material we often use. All articles should be analytical in nature. No introductory articles on how great this industry is." Buys at least 120 mss/year. Query with published clips and state availability of photos. Length: 1,200-2,000 words. Pays $200-500. Sometimes pays expenses of writers on assignment.
Photos: State availability of photos with query. Prefers unusual installations, interesting dishes, i.e., landscaped, painted. Reviews contact sheets, and 4x5 and 35mm color transparencies. Pays $10-50 for 8x10 b&w prints; $25-150 for 8x10 color prints. Captions and identification of subjects required. Buys negotiable rights.
Tips: "Well thought out and written queries preferred. Exhibit knowledge of either satellite TV or retail sales and a command of the English language. Quality work gets published, regardless of length (within reason). Not grasping the total picture, usually because of incomplete research, is the most frequent mistake made by writers."

‡TELEVISION BROADCAST, Applying Television Technology, Globecom, Suite 343, 4551 W. 107th St., Overland Park KS 66207. (913)642-6611. Editor: Phil Kurz. Managing Editor: Maureen Waters. 40% freelance written. Monthly magazine covering television stations. "We direct our editorial to TV station general managers, operators, engineers, and news directors. We also serve the production and post-production industry. Our slant is how these people use new technologies for better program quality, greater profit, or better community image." Circ. 25,000. Pays on publication. Publishes ms an average of 3 months after acceptance. Byline given. Offers $100 kill fee. Buys all rights. Submit seasonal/holiday material 4 months in advance. Computer printout submissions OK; no dot-matrix. Reports in 2 weeks on queries; 1 month on mss. Free sample copy and writer's guidelines.
Nonfiction: How-to (on using technology to improve signal quality, profits or community images), interview/profile, personal experience and technical. No articles that appeal mostly to TV viewers. Buys 60 mss/year. Query with published clips. Length: 1,000-2,500 words. Pays $250-500 for assigned articles; pays $100-300 for unsolicited articles. Sometimes pays the expenses of writers on assignment.
Photos: Send photos with submission. Reviews contact sheets. Offers no additional payment for photos accepted with ms. Captions, model releases and identification of subjects required. Buys all rights.
Columns/Departments: Tech Tips (how to solve typical technical problems), News Directions (interviews

with news directors on technology and how it's being used in the news); For GMS Only (interviews with general managers on problems stations face and how they solve these problems), all 500 words. Length: 500-750 words. Pays $75-250.

Fillers: Short humor. Buys 30/year. Length: 25-100 words. Pays $25 maximum.

Tips: "Every city has a leading TV station and a leading television production or post-production company. How do they become leaders, what did they overcome and what do they do to stay a leader? Our general 'how-to' articles department is most open. Query occasionally to stay in tune with what the editor wants, even if it takes a monthly call to figure it out."

VIDEO MANAGER, The Magazine for Decision Makers, Knowledge Industry Publications, Inc., 701 Westchester Ave., White Plains NY 10604. Editor: Fred Schmidt. 85% freelance written. Eager to work with new/unpublished writers. A monthly tabloid covering non-broadcast, private, industrial television. "Our readers are managers of audiovisual, video and communications departments. We stress management, rather than technical and applications stories." Circ. 25,000. Pays on publication. Publishes ms an average of 4 months after acceptance. Byline given. Buys first rights. Computer printout submissions acceptable; prefers letter-quality to dot-matrix. Reports in several weeks on queries. Sample copy available.

Nonfiction: Book excerpts, essays, interview/profile, new product and personal experience. No articles on non-professional activities. Buys 36 mss/year. Query with published clips. Length: 1,500-3,000 words. Pays $50. Sometimes pays the expenses of writers on assignment.

Photos: State availability of photos with submission. Reviews contact sheets, 35mm transparencies and prints. Offers no additional payment for photos accepted with ms. Captions and identification of subjects required.

Columns/Departments: Production Focus (review, how produced, of videotape, non-broadcast, industrial), 1,500 words; Video Manager in Profile (biographic and department information) in detail (standard questionnaire). Buys 70 mss/year. Pays variable rate.

‡VIDEO STORE, The Journal of Video Retailing, HBJ Publications, Suite 250, 1700 E. Dyer Rd., Santa Ana CA 92705. (714)250-8060. Editor: Tom Adams. Managing Editor: Jack Schember. 25% freelance written. Magazine covering video software specialty retailers. "Our readers come to us for: nuts and bolts management articles, financial insight, profiles of other video dealers and trend analysis. Our articles feature retailers telling retailers how to retail from single-store owners to major chain executives." Pays on acceptance. Publishes ms an average of 3 months after acceptance. Byline given. Offers 10-30% kill fee. Buys one-time or all rights; or makes work-for-hire assignments. Query only, no mss. Query for electronic submissions. Computer printout submissions OK; prefers letter-quality to dot-matrix. Reports in 1 month on queries. Sample copy $4 with 9x12 SAE and 11 first class stamps.

Nonfiction: How-to (video retail). No generic retail management articles. Buys 60 mss/year. Query with published clips. Length: 750-2,000 words. Pays $100-750 for assigned articles. Sometimes pays the expenses of writers on assignment.

Photos: State availability of photos with submission. Reviews contact sheets and transparencies. Offers $10 per photo. Identification of subjects required. Buys one-time and all rights.

Columns/Departments: Storefronts (profiles of video retailers), 700-800 words; Spotlight (video retailing in particular cities), 1,200-1,500 words; Marketing Movies (how retailers are marketing particular genre), 1,200-1,500 words; and Celebrity Interviews (interviews with actors, filmmakers whose work is on video), 500-1,000 words. Buys 50 mss/year. Query with published clips. Pays $100-300.

Tips: "Clips *must* show understanding of retail finance and management. Looking for writers to cover local dealers in all markets except New York, Southern California. Don't query with retail stories unless you know your assets from your equity." Looking for "profiles of dealers who are doing well and/or are doing something different. Use numbers."

VIDEO SYSTEMS, Box 12901, Overland Park KS 66212. (913)888-4664. Publisher: Duane Hefner. Editor: Tom Cook. 80% freelance written. Works with a small number of new/unpublished writers each year. Monthly magazine. "International magazine for qualified persons engaged in professional applications of nonbroadcast audio and video who have operating responsibilities and purchasing authority for equipment and software in the video systems field." Circ. 30,000. Pays on acceptance. Publishes ms an average of 2-3 months after acceptance. Buys all rights. Submit seasonal/holiday material 2 months in advance. Photocopied submissions OK. Computer printout submissions OK; prefers letter-quality to dot-matrix. Reports in 2 months. Free sample copy and writer's guidelines.

Nonfiction: General interest (about professional video); how-to (use professional video equipment); historical (on professional video); new product; and technical. No consumer video articles. Buys 2-6 unsolicited mss/year. Submit complete ms. Length: 1,000-3,000 words. Pays $250. Sometimes pays the expenses of writers on assignment.

Photos: State availability of photos with ms. Pay varies for 8x10 b&w glossy prints; $100 maximum for 35mm color transparencies. Model release required.

Tips: "Articles should be written with few or no manufacturers mentioned. Submissions should contain information that will help the reader do his/her job better."

VISUAL COMMUNICATIONS CANADA, (formerly *AV Business Communications*), Maclean Hunter, 5th Floor, 777 Bay St., Toronto, Ontario M5W 1A7 Canada. (416)596-5878. Editor: Cora Golden. 50% freelance written. Prefers to work with writers with a business background. A magazine appearing 10 times a year covering the visual communications industry from an end-user perspective. "Our objective is to provide a non-technical overview of the visual communications industry—news, new products, profiles, etc." The audience is managers of corporate communications in selected Canadian industrial, commercial and financial companies. Circ. 10,322. Pays on acceptance. Publishes ms an average of 2 months after acceptance. Byline given. Offers 50% kill fee. Buys first North American serial rights. Submit seasonal/holiday material 3 months in advance. Simultaneous and photocopied submissions OK. Query for electronic submissions. Computer printout submissions acceptable; prefers letter-quality to dot-matrix. Reports in 1 month on queries; 2 weeks on mss. Sample copy for 9x12 SAE with 2 first class stamps; free writer's guidelines.
Nonfiction: Interview/profile, opinion and technical. All submissions must have a Canadian angle. Buys 50 mss/year. Query with published clips. Length: 1,000-1,500 words. Pays $300-400 for assigned articles. Sometimes pays the expenses of writers on assignment.
Photos: State availability of photos with submission. Reviews contact sheet. Offers $25-150 maximum/photo. Captions, model releases, and identification of subjects required. Buys one-time rights.
Columns/Departments: Newsline (regional, national and international events and trends with a Canadian angle), 600-800 words; and Clips (capsulized information on visual communications programs recently produced. Query. Length: 300-400 words. Pays $25-100.
Tips: "We will be adding more about video and computer graphics in 1988. *Visual Communications Canada* is directed to a business audience. Readers expect information specific to their needs. Our readers have a broad range of skills and knowledge levels. Therefore, submissions must contain sufficient background material for those less familiar with a topic, yet within the interest of more experienced readers. We prefer brief, factual reporting; stories that get right to the point and always answer the question 'What's in it for me?' "

Energy and Utilities

ALTERNATIVE ENERGY RETAILER, Zackin Publications, Inc., Box 2180, Waterbury CT 06722. (203)755-0158. Editor: Ed Easley. 20% freelance written. Prefers to work with published/established writers. Monthly magazine on selling alternative energy products—chiefly solid fuel burning appliances. "We seek detailed how-to tips for retailers to improve business. Most freelance material purchased is about retailers and how they succeed." Circ. 14,000. Pays on publication. Publishes ms an average of 2 months after acceptance. Buys first North American serial rights. Submit seasonal/holiday material 4 months in advance. Computer printout submissions OK; no dot-matrix. Reports in 2 weeks on queries. Sample copy for 8½x11 SAE; writer's guidelines for business size SAE.
Nonfiction: How-to (improve retail profits and business know-how); and interview/profile (of successful retailers in this field). No "general business articles not adapted to this industry." Buys 10-20 mss/year. Query. Length: 1,000 words. Pays $100.
Photos: State availability of photos. Pays $25 maximum for 5x7 b&w prints. Reviews color slide transparencies. Identification of subject required. Buys one-time rights.
Tips: "A freelancer can best break in to our publication with features about readers (retailers). Stick to details about what has made this person a success."

BAROID NEWS BULLETIN, Box 1675, Houston TX 77251. Editor-in-Chief: Virginia Brooks. 50% freelance written. Emphasizes the petroleum industry for a cross-section of ages, education and interests, although most readers are employed by the energy industries. Quarterly magazine; 36 pages. Circ. 20,000. Pays on acceptance. Publishes ms an average of 1 year after acceptance. Buys first North American serial rights. Byline given. Submit seasonal/holiday material 1 year in advance. Computer printout submissions acceptable; prefers letter-quality to dot-matrix. Reports in 2 months. Free sample copy and writer's guidelines.
Nonfiction: General interest and historical. No travel articles or poetry. Buys 12 mss/year. Complete ms preferred. Length: 1,000-3,000 words. Pays 8-10¢/word.
Photos: "Photos may be used in the publication, or as reference for illustration art." Submit b&w prints. No additional payment for photos accepted with ms. Captions preferred. Buys first North American serial rights.
Tips: "We generally publish historical nonfiction written in anecdotal or narrative style. We expect interesting as well as factual articles. Manuscripts accompanied by good quality photos or illustrations stand a much better chance of acceptance. We review on speculation only—no assignments."

ELECTRICAL APPARATUS, The Magazine of the Electrical Aftermarket, Barks Publications, Inc., 400 N. Michigan Ave., Chicago IL 60611-4198. (312)321-9440. Editor: Horace B. Barks. Managing Editor: Kevin N. Jones. Prefers to work with published/established writers. Uses very little freelance material. A monthly magazine for persons working in electrical maintenance, chiefly in industrial plants, who install and service electrical motors, transformers, generators, and related equipment. Circ. 15,000. Pays on publication. Publishes ms an average of 2-3 months after acceptance. Byline given. Buys all rights unless other arrangements made. Electronic submission OK via CP/M disk, or modem. Computer printout submissions acceptable. Reports in 1 week on queries; 1 month on mss. Sample copy $4.

Nonfiction: Elsie Dickson, articles editor. Technical. Buys very few mss/year. Query essential, along with letter outlining credentials. Length: no minimum or maximum. "Some articles lend themselves to serialization, so we set no limit." Pays $250-400/article installment. Pays the expenses of writers on assignment by advance arrangement.

Photos: Send photos with submission. "Photos are important to most articles. We prefer 35mm color slides, but sometimes use color or b&w prints." Offers additional payments, depending on quality and number. Captions and identification of subjects required. Buys one-time rights. "If we reuse photos, we pay residual fee."

Columns/Departments: Address to editor of department. Electrical Manager (items on managing businesses, people), 150-600 words; and Electropix (photo of interest with electrical slant), brief captions. "We are interested in expanding these departments." Pays $25-100.

Tips: "Queries are essential. Technical expertise is absolutely necessary, preferably an E.E. degree, or practical experience. We are also book publishers and some of the material in *EA* is now in book form, bringing the authors royalties."

ELECTRICAL CONTRACTOR, 7315 Wisconsin Ave., Bethesda MD 20814. (301)657-3110. Editor: Larry C. Osius. 10% freelance written. Monthly. For electrical contractors. Circ. 65,000. Publishes ms an average of 3 months after acceptance. Buys first serial rights, second serial (reprint) rights or simultaneous rights. Usually reports in 1 month. Byline given. Free sample copy.

Nonfiction: Installation articles showing informative application of new techniques and products. Slant is product and method contributing to better, faster and more economical construction process. Query. Length: 800-2,500 words. Pays $100/printed page, including photos and illustrative material.

Photos: Photos should be sharp, reproducible glossies, 5x7 and up.

OCEAN INDUSTRY, Gulf Publishing Co., Box 2608, Houston TX 77001. (713)529-4301. Editor: Robert E. Snyder. Associate Editors: Maretta Tubb and Charles McCabe. 5% freelance written. "We prefer to work directly with technical experts, if the freelancer is one; that's OK." "Our readers are generally engineers and company executives in companies with business dealings with off-shore petroleum interests in exploration, drilling and production." Monthly magazine. Circ. 34,000. Pays on publication. Buys all rights. Pays kill fee: "If we assign an article and it is not used, we pay full rate on estimated length." Byline given. Phone queries OK. Photocopied and previously published submissions OK. Computer printout submissions acceptable. Reports in 2 months. Publishes ms an average of 3 months after acceptance. Free sample copy and writer's guidelines.

Nonfiction: Technical and equipment and operations oriented articles relating to hydrocarbon exploration and development, diving and ROVs, electronics, instruments for oil field and offshore applications. No oceanographic, fisheries, aquaculture or mariculture material. Buys 5-10 mss/year. Query. Length: 300-1,500 words. Pays $50-150/published page.

Photos: "Technical concepts are easier to understand when illustrated." State availability of photos with query. No additional payment for 5x7 or 8x10 glossy b&w or color prints. Captions required. Buys all rights.

Tips: "We are going toward more special reports written by experts in their fields. We find nontechnical freelancers do not make good middle men."

PETROLEUM INDEPENDENT, 1101 16th St. NW, Washington DC 20036. (202)857-4775. Editor: Joe W. Taylor. 5% freelance written. Prefers to work with published/established writers. For "college educated men and women involved in high risk petroleum ventures. Our readers drill 90% of all the exploratory oil wells in this country. They pit themselves against the major oil companies, politicians, and a dry hole rate of 9 out of 10 to try to find enough petroleum to offset imports. They are in a highly competitive, extremely expensive business and look to this magazine to help them change the political landscape, read about their friends and the activities of the Independent Petroleum Association of America, and be entertained. Contrary to popular opinion, they are not all Texans. They live in almost every state and are politically motivated. They follow energy legislation closely and involve themselves in lobbying and electoral politics." Bimonthly magazine. Circ. 15,000. Pays on acceptance. Publishes ms an average of 3 months after acceptance. Computer printout submissions acceptable. Buys all rights. Byline given "except if part of a large report compiled in-house." Reports in 2 weeks. Sample copy $2.

Nonfiction: "Articles need not be limited to oil and natural gas—but must tie in nicely." Expose (bureaucratic blunder); informational; historical (energy-related; accurate; with a witty twist); humor (we look for good humor pieces and have found few); and interview (with energy decision makers. Center with questions concerning independent petroleum industry. Send edited transcript plus tape); opinion; profile (of Independent Petroleum Association of America members); and photo feature. Buys 5-10 mss/year. Query with brief outline. Length: 750-3,000 words. Pays $100-500. Longer articles on assignment; pay negotiable. Sometimes pays the expenses of writers on assignment.

Photos: Reviews unusual color transparencies of oil exploration and development. No marketing or refining. Purchased with or without accompanying ms or on assignment. Pay negotiable. Always looking for unusual 4 color material for covers.

Tips: "Call first, then send outline and query. Don't write with a particular slant. Write as if for a mainstream publication."

PIPELINE & UNDERGROUND UTILITIES CONSTRUCTION, Oildom Publishing Co. of Texas, Inc., Box 22267, Houston TX 77027. Editor: Oliver Klinger. Managing Editor: Chris Horner. 5% freelance written. Prefers to work with published/established writers. Monthly magazine covering oil, gas, water, and sewer pipeline construction for contractors and construction workers who build pipelines. Circ. 13,000. No byline given. Not copyrighted. Buys first North American serial rights. Publishes ms an average of 3 months after acceptance. Simultaneous queries and photocopied submissions OK. Computer printout submissions acceptable; prefers letter-quality to dot-matrix. Reports in 2 weeks on queries; 3 weeks on mss. Sample copy for $1 and 9x12 SAE.

Nonfiction: How-to. Query with published clips. Length: 1,500-2,500 words. Pays $100/printed page "unless unusual expenses are incurred in getting the story." Sometimes pays the expenses of writers on assignment.

Photos: Send photos with ms. Reviews 5x7 and 8x10 prints. Captions required. Buys one-time rights.

Tips: "We supply guidelines outlining information we need." The most frequent mistake made by writers in completing articles is unfamiliarity with the field.

PUBLIC POWER, 2301 M St. NW, Washington DC 20037. (202)775-8300. Editor: Vic Reinemer. 20% freelance written. Prefers to work with published/established writers. Bimonthly. Not copyrighted. Pays on publication. Publishes ms an average of 3 months after acceptance. Byline given. Electronic submissions readable on IBM PC OK, but requires hard copy also. Computer printout submissions acceptable. Free sample copy and writer's guidelines.

Nonfiction: Features on municipal and other local publicly-owned electric systems. Payment negotiable. Sometimes pays the telephone expenses of writers on assignment.

Photos: Uses b&w and glossy color prints, and slides.

‡SOONER LPG TIMES, Suite 114-A, 2910 N. Walnut, Oklahoma City OK 73105. (405)525-9386. Editor: John E. Orr. For "dealers and suppliers of LP-gas and their employees." Monthly. Not copyrighted. Pays on publication. Byline given. Reports in 3 weeks.

Nonfiction: "Articles relating to the LP-gas industry, safety, small business practices, and economics; anything of interest to small businessmen." Buys 12 mss/year. Length: 1,000-2,000 words. Pays $10-15.

SUNSHINE SERVICE NEWS, Florida Power & Light Co., Box 29100, Miami FL 33102. (305)552-3887. Editor: L.A. Muniz, Jr. 5% freelance written. Works with a small number of writers each year. Monthly employee newspaper for electrical utility. Circ. 15,000. Pays on publication. Publishes ms an average of 3 months after acceptance. Buys first serial rights. Not copyrighted. Computer printout submissions acceptable. Free sample copy.

Nonfiction: Company news, employee news, general interest, historical, how-to, humor and job safety. Company tie-in preferred. Query. Pays $50-150. Pays expenses of writers on assignment.

_ Engineering and Technology

Engineers and professionals with various specialties read the publications in this section. Publications for electrical and electronics engineers are classified under the Electronics and Communication heading. Magazines for computer professionals are listed in the Information Systems section.

DESIGN GRAPHICS WORLD, Communication Channels, Inc., 6255 Barfield Rd., Atlanta GA 30328. (404)256-9800. Editor: James J. Maivald. 10% freelance written. Works with a small number of new/unpublished writers each year. A monthly magazine covering design graphics in the architecture, engineering and construction community. Circ. 37,000. Pays on publication. Publishes ms an average of 2 months after acceptance. Byline given. 10% kill fee. Buys all rights. Submit seasonal/holiday material 3 months in advance. Computer printout submissions acceptable; no dot-matrix. Reports in 1 month on queries; 2 weeks on mss. Free sample copy and writer's guidelines.
Nonfiction: How-to, interview/profile, new product and technical. "Articles should be knowledgeable, informative and written for professional architects, engineers and designers." No product sales information, brand- or product-specific information features. Buys 8 mss/year. Query with published clips. Length: 500-2,000 words. Pays $50-500 for assigned articles; pays $50-375 for unsolicited articles. Sometimes pays the expenses of writers on assignment.
Photos: Send photos with submission. Reviews 2x2 transparencies and 5x7 prints. Offers no additional payment for photos accepted with ms. Identification of subjects required. Buys all rights.
Tips: "Writers should be capable of dropping consumer-prose writing styles and adopt more technical language and usage."

GRADUATING ENGINEER, McGraw-Hill, 1221 Avenue of the Americas, New York NY 10020. (212)512-4123. Editor: Howard Cohn. Managing Editor: Bill D. Miller. 90% freelance written. Prefers to work with published/established writers. Published September-March "to help graduating engineers make the transition from campus to the working world." Circ. 83,000. Pays on acceptance. Publishes ms an average of 4 months after acceptance. Byline given. Buys first North American serial rights. Reports in 3 weeks. Sample copy for 9x12 SAE and $1 postage.
Nonfiction: General interest (on management, human resources); and career entry and advancement. Special issues include Minority, Women and Computer. Buys 100 mss/year. Query. Length: 2,000-3,000 words. Pays $300-500.
Photos: State availability of photos, illustrations or charts. Reviews 35mm color transparencies, 8x10 b&w glossy prints. Captions and model release required.
Tips: "The editorial 'mix' will generally stay the same, but the individual articles and features will recognize changes and developments in the engineering-employment market."

MACHINE DESIGN, Penton/IPC, 1111 Chester, Cleveland OH 44114. (216)696-7000. Editor: Ronald Khol. Executive Editor: Robert Aronson. 1-2% freelance written. Works with a small number of new/unpublished writers each year. A bimonthly magazine covering technical developments in products or purchases of interest to the engineering community. Circ. 180,000. Pays on publication. Publishes ms an average of 2 months after acceptance. Byline sometimes given. Buys first rights. Computer printout submissions acceptable; prefers letter-quality to dot-matrix. Reports in 1 month. Free sample copy.
Nonfiction: General interest; how-to (on using new equipment or processes); and new product. No non-technical submissions. Buys 10-15 mss/year. Query. Length and payment for articles must be negotiated in advance. Sometimes pays the expenses of writers on assignment.
Photos: State availability of photos with submission. Offers negotiable payment. Captions, model releases, and identification of subjects required.
Columns/Departments: Design International (international news), captions; Backtalk (technical humor) and Personal Computers in Engineering (use of personal computers), both have negotiable word length. Buys 50-200 items/year. Query. Pays $20 minimum.
Tips: "The departments of our publication most open to freelancers are Back Talk, News Trends and Design International. Those without technical experience almost never send in adequate material."

THE MINORITY ENGINEER, An Equal Opportunity Career Publication for Professional and Graduating Minority Engineers, Equal Opportunity Publications, Inc., 44 Broadway, Greenlawn NY 11740. (516)261-8917. Editor: James Schneider. 60% freelance written. Prefers to work with published/established writers. Magazines published 4 times/year (fall, winter, spring, April/May) covering career guidance for minority engineering students and professional minority engineers. Circ. 16,000. Pays on publication. Publishes ms an average of 3-6 months after acceptance. Byline given. Buys first North American serial rights. "Deadline dates: fall, May 1; winter, July 15; spring, October 15; April/May, January 1." Simultaneous, photocopied, and previously published submissions OK. Electronic submissions OK, but requires hard copy also. Computer printout submissions acceptable; no dot-matrix. Sample copy and writer's guidelines for 8x10 SAE with 5 first class stamps.
Nonfiction: Book excerpts; articles (on job search techniques, role models); general interest (on specific minority engineering concerns); how-to (land a job, keep a job, etc.); interview/profile (minority engineer role models); new product (new career opportunities); opinion (problems of ethnic minorities); personal experience (student and career experiences); and technical (on career fields offering opportunities for minority engineers). "We're interested in articles dealing with career guidance and job opportunities for minority engineers." Que-

ry or send complete ms. Length: 1,250-3,000 words. Sometimes pays the expenses of writers on assignment.
Photos: Prefers 35mm color slides but will accept b&w. Captions and identification of subjects required. Buys all rights.
Tips: "Articles should focus on career guidance, role model and industry prospects for minority engineers. Prefer articles related to careers, not politically or socially sensitive."

NSBE JOURNAL, National Society of Black Engineers Official Publication, Journals, Inc., Suite 3, 1240 S. Broad St., New Orleans LA 70125. (504)822-3533. Editor: Bill Bowers. Copy Editor: Sonya Stinson. 50% freelance written. Works with a small number of new/unpublished writers each year. A bimonthly magazine covering engineering, science studies and careers. "The majority of our readers are college students in engineering and other technical fields. Readership also includes professional engineers and academic personnel." Circ. 15,000. Pays on acceptance. Publishes ms an average of 1 month after acceptance. Byline given. Buys all rights. Photocopied and previously published submissions OK. Query for electronic submissions. Computer printout submissions acceptable; no dot-matrix. Reports in 2 weeks. Free sample copy and writer's guidelines.
Nonfiction: Historical/nostalgic, how-to, inspirational, interview/profile, photo feature, technical and travel. No highly technical articles on engineering projects, products, etc. Buys 50 mss/year. Query. Length: 3,500 words maximum. Pays $150. Sometimes pays the expenses of writers on assignment.
Photos: Send photos with submission. Reviews contact sheets. Model releases and identification of subjects required.
Columns/Departments: NSBE Updates (trivia, news on outstanding students and professional engineers, statistical information). Buys 15 mss/year. Query. Length: 150 words maximum. Pays $150.

THE WOMAN ENGINEER, An Equal Opportunity Career Publication for Graduating Women and Experienced Professionals, Equal Opportunity Publications, Inc., 44 Broadway, Greenlawn NY 11740. (516)261-8917. Editor: Anne Kelly. 60% freelance written. Works with a small number of new/unpublished writers each year. Magazine published 4 times/year (fall, winter, spring, April/May) covering career guidance for women engineering students and professional women engineers. Circ. 16,000. Pays on publication. Publishes ms 3-12 months after acceptance. Byline given. Buys first North American rights. Simultaneous queries and submissions OK. Computer printout submissions OK; prefers letter-quality to dot-matrix. Free sample copy and writer's guidelines.
Nonfiction: "Interested in articles dealing with career guidance and job opportunities for women engineers. Looking for manuscripts showing how to land an engineering position and advance professionally. Wants features on job-search techniques, engineering disciplines offering career opportunities to women, problems facing women engineers—and how to cope with such problems, in addition to role-model profiles of successful women engineers." Query. Length: 1,000-2,500 words. Sometimes pays the expenses of writers on assignment.
Photos: Prefers color slides but will accept b&w. Captions, model release and identification of subjects required. Buys all rights.
Tips: "We will be looking for shorter manuscripts (800-1,000 words) on job-search techniques, career opportunities for women engineers, and first-person "Endpage Essay.""

___ *Entertainment and the Arts*

The business of the entertainment/amusement industry in arts, film, dance, theatre, etc. is covered by these publications. Journals that focus on the people and equipment of various music specialites are listed in the Music section, while publications for the general public on these topics can be found in Consumer Entertainment and Music sections.

AMUSEMENT BUSINESS, Billboard Publications, Inc., Box 24970, Nashville TN 37202. (615)748-8120. Managing Editor: Tim O'Brien. 25% freelance written. Works with a small number of new/unpublished writers each year. Weekly tabloid; 32-108 pages. Emphasizes hard news of the amusement, sports business, and mass entertainment industry. Read by top management. Circ. 15,000. Pays on publication. Publishes ms an average of 3 weeks after acceptance. Byline sometimes given; "it depends on the quality of the individual piece." Buys all rights. Submit seasonal/holiday material 3 weeks in advance. Phone queries OK. Computer printout submissions acceptable; no dot-matrix.
Nonfiction: How-to (case history of successful advertising campaigns and promotions); interviews (with

leaders in the areas we cover highlighting appropriate problems and issues of today, i.e. insurance, alcohol control, etc.); new product; and technical (how "new" devices, shows or services work at parks, fairs, auditoriums and conventions). Likes lots of financial support data: grosses, profits, operating budgets and per-cap spending. Also needs in-depth looks at advertising and promotional programs of carnivals, circuses, amusement parks, fairs: how these facilities position themselves against other entertainment opportunities in the area. No personality pieces or interviews with stage stars. Buys 500-1,000 mss/year. Query. Length: 400-700 words. Pays $3/published inch. Sometimes pays the expenses of writers on assignment.
Photos: State availability of photos with query. Pays $3-5 for 8x10 b&w glossy prints. Captions and model release required. Buys all rights.
Columns/Departments: Auditorium Arenas; Fairs, Fun Parks; Food Concessions; Merchandise; Promotion; Shows (carnival and circus); Talent; Tourist Attractions; and Management Changes.
Tips: "Submission must contain the whys and whos, etc. and be strong enough that others in the same field will learn from it and not find it naive. We will be increasing story count while decreasing story length."

BILLBOARD, The International News Weekly of Music and Home Entertainment, 1515 Broadway, New York NY 10036. (212)764-7300. 9107 Wilshire Blvd., Beverly Hills CA 90210. (213)273-7040. Editor-in-Chief: Samuel Holdsworth. Special Issues Editor: Ed Ochs. L.A. Bureau Chief: Sam Sutherland. Albums: Sam Sutherland. (All Los Angeles.) Pro Equipment: Steve Dupler. Deputy Editor: Irv Lichtman. Radio/TV Editor: Kim Freeman. Black Music: Nelson George. Executive/Classical Editor: Is Horowitz. Video Editor: Tony Seideman. Review-Singles/Campus Editor: Nancy Erlich. (All New York.) International Editor: Peter Jones (London). Weekly. Pays on publication. Buys all rights.
Nonfiction: "Correspondents are appointed to send in spot amusement news covering phonograph record programming by broadcasters and record merchandising by retail dealers." Concert reviews, interviews with artists, and stories on video software (both rental and merchandising).

BOXOFFICE MAGAZINE, RLD Publishing Corp., Suite 710, 1800 N. Highland Ave., Hollywood CA 90028. (213)465-1186. Editor: Harley W. Lond. 5% freelance written. Monthly business magazine about the motion picture industry for members of the film industry: theater owners, film producers, directors, financiers and allied industries. Circ. 14,000. Pays on publication. Publishes ms an average of 2-4 months after acceptance. Byline given. Buys one-time rights. Phone queries OK. Submit seasonal material 2 months in advance. Simultaneous, photocopied and previously published submissions OK. Computer printout submissions acceptable. Reports in 2 months. Sample copy for $3 and 8½x11 SAE with 98¢ postage.
Nonfiction: Expose, interview, profile, new product, photo feature and technical. "We are a general news magazine about the motion picture industry and are looking for stories about trends, developments, problems or opportunities facing the industry. Almost any story will be considered, including corporate profiles, but we don't want gossip or celebrity stuff." Query with published clips. Length: 1,500-2,500 words. Pays $75-150.
Photos: State availability of photos. Pays $10 maximum for 8x10 b&w prints. Captions required.
Tips: "Request a sample copy, indicating you read about *Boxoffice* in *Writer's Market*. Write a clear, comprehensive outline of the proposed story and enclose a resume and clip samples. We welcome new writers but don't want to be a classroom. Know how to write."

THE ELECTRIC WEENIE, Box 2715, Quincy MA 02269. (617)749-6900, ext. 248. Editor: Tom Adams. 20% freelance written. Monthly magazine covering "primarily radio, for 'personalities' worldwide (however, mostly English speaking). We mail flyers mainly to radio people, but obviously no one is excepted if he/she wants a monthly supply of first-rate gags, one-liners, zappers, etc." Circ. 1,500. Pays on publication. Publishes ms an average of 6 months after acceptance. No byline given. Buys all rights. Submit seasonal/holiday material 6 months in advance. Computer printout submissions acceptable; prefers letter-quality to dot-matrix. Sample copy $5, business size SAE and 1 first class stamp.
Fillers: Jokes, gags, short humor, one liners, etc. "*Short* is the bottom line." Uses 300/month. Pays $1/gag used.
Tips: "We like to receive in multiples of 100 if possible; not mandatory, just preferred. And a little 'spicy' doesn't hurt."

THE LONE STAR COMEDY MONTHLY, Lone Star Publications of Humor, Suite #103, Box 29000, San Antonio TX 78229. (512)271-2632. Editor: Lauren Barnett. Less than 1% freelance written. Eager to work with new/unpublished writers. Monthly comedy service newsletter for professional humorists—DJs; public speakers, comedians. Includes one-liners and jokes for oral expression. Pays on publication "or before." Publishes ms an average of 4-6 months after acceptance. Byline given if 2 or more jokes are used. Buys all rights, exclusive rights for 6 months from publication date. Submit seasonal/holiday material 1 month in advance. Photocopied submissions OK. Computer printout submissions acceptable; no dot-matrix. Reports in 1 month. Inquire for update on prices of sample copies. Writer's guidelines for business size SAE and 1 first class stamp.

Fillers: Jokes, gags and short humor. Buys 20-60/year. Length: 100 words maximum. "We don't use major features in *The Lone Star Comedy Monthly*." Inquire for update on rates. "Submit several (no more than 20) original gags on one or two subjects only."
Tips: "Writers should inquire for an update on our needs before submitting material."

MIDDLE EASTERN DANCER, Mideastern Connection, Inc., Box 1572, Casselberry FL 32707. (305)788-0301. Editor: Karen Kuzsel. Managing Editor: Tracie Harris. 60% freelance written. Eager to work with new/unpublished writers. A monthly magazine covering Middle Eastern dance and culture (belly dancing). "We provide the most current news and entertainment information available in the world. We focus on the positive, but don't shy away from controversy. All copy and photos must relate to Middle Eastern dance and cultural activities. We do not get into politics." Circ. 2,000. Pays on acceptance. Publishes ms an average of 4 months after acceptance, usually sooner, but it depends on type of article and need for that month. Byline given. Buys first rights, simultaneous rights or second serial (reprint) rights. Submit seasonal/holiday material 3 months in advance. Simultaneous, photocopied and previously published submissions OK, unless printed in another belly dance publication. Computer printout submissions acceptable; prefers letter-quality to dot-matrix. Reports in 2 weeks on queries; 3 weeks on mss. Sample copy for 9x12 SAE with 73¢ postage; writer's guidelines for #10 SAE with 1 first class stamp.
Nonfiction: Essays; general interest; historical/nostalgic; how-to (on costuming, putting on shows, teaching and exercises); humor; inspirational; interview/profile; personal experience; photo features; travel (to the Middle East or related to dancers); and reviews of seminars, movies, clubs, restaurants, and museums. Special issues include costuming (March); and anniversary issue (October). No politics. Buys 60 mss/year. Query. Pays $20 maximum for assigned articles; pays $10 maximum for unsolicited articles. May provide free advertising in trade. Sometimes pays the expenses of writers on assignment.
Photos: Send photos with submission. Offers no additional payment for photos accepted with ms. Identification of subjects required. Buys one-time rights.
Columns/Departments: Critics Corner (reviews of books, videotapes, records, movies, clubs and restaurants, museums and special events); Helpful Hints (tips for finding accessories and making them easier or for less); Putting on the Ritz (describes costume in detail with photo); and Personal Glimpses (autobiographical) and Profiles (biographical—providing insights of benefit to other dancers). Query. Pays $5 maximum.
Fiction: Open to fiction dealing with belly dancers as subject.
Poetry: Avant-garde, free verse, haiku, light verse and traditional. Buys 5 poems/year. Submit maximum 3 poems. Pays $5 maximum.
Tips: "It's easy to break in if you stick to belly dancing related information and expect little or no money (advertising instead). Although we are the second largest in the world in this field, we're still small."

‡OPPORTUNITIES FOR ACTORS & MODELS, "A Guide to Working in Cable TV-Radio-Print Advertising," Copy Group, Suite 315, 1900 N. Vine St., Hollywood CA 90068. Editor: Len Miller. 50% freelance written. Works with a small number of new/unpublished writers each year. A monthly newsletter "serving the interests of those people who are (or would like to be) a part of the cable-TV, radio, and print advertising industries." Circ. 10,000. Pays on acceptance. Publishes ms an average of 3 months after acceptance. Byline given. Buys all rights. Simultaneous queries OK. Computer printout submissions OK; prefers letter-quality to dot-matrix. Reports in 3 weeks. Free sample copy and writer's guidelines.
Nonfiction: How-to, humor, inspirational, interview/profile, local news, personal experience, photo feature and technical (within cable TV). Coverage should include the model scene, little theatre, drama groups, comedy workshops and other related events and places. "Detailed information about your local cable TV station should be an important part of your coverage. Get to know the station and its creative personnel." Buys 120 mss/year. Query. Length: 100-950 words. Pays $50 maximum.
Photos: State availability of photos. Model release and identification of subjects required. Buys one-time or all rights.
Columns/Departments: "We will consider using your material in a column format with your byline." Buys 60 mss/year. Query. Length: 150-450 words. Pays $50 maximum.
Tips: "Good first person experiences, interviews and articles, all related to modeling, acting, little theatre, photography (model shots) and other interesting items" are needed.

PERFORMANCE MAGAZINE, 1020 Currie St., Fort Worth TX 76107. (817)338-9444. Publisher: Don Waitt. 15% freelance written. "We are bringing most of the writing in-house." The international trade weekly for the touring entertainment industry. "*Performance* publishes tour routing information, updated on a weekly basis. These itineraries, along with box office reports, regional news, industry directories, live performance reviews and industry features on the concert industry are of interest to our readers." Weekly magazine; also publishes industry directories once a month. Circ. 20,000. Publishes ms an average of 1 month after acceptance. Buys all rights. Phone queries OK. Submit seasonal/holiday material 2 months in advance. Simultaneous submissions OK. Computer printout submissions acceptable; prefers letter-quality to dot-matrix. Reports in 1 month. Sample copy and writer's guidelines $5.

Nonfiction: "This is a trade publication, dealing basically with the ins and outs of booking live entertainment, doing hard news and spot information on sound, lighting and staging companies, clubs, ticketing, concert venues, promoters, booking agents, personal managers, and college news relevant to the live entertainment industry. We also publish interviews and overviews of touring in the major cities." Interviews, opinion and profile. Needs many short news items, much like a newspaper.

Photos: State availability of photos with ms. B&w photos only. Captions preferred. Buys all rights.

Tips: "You won't make a fortune writing for *Performance*, and you may have to wait awhile for the paycheck; on the other side of the coin, though, there are some benefits to writing for the magazine such as free access to many club shows and area concerts, backstage passes, invites to music related press conferences and parties, and the opportunity to gather information and interviews for possible use in higher-paying consumer publications."

TOURIST ATTRACTIONS & PARKS MAGAZINE, Kane Communications, Inc., Suite 226, 401 N. Broad St., Philadelphia PA 19108. (215)925-9744. Editor: Chuck Tooley. A bimonthly magazine covering mass entertainment and leisure facilities. Emphasizes management articles. Circ. 19,600. Pays on publication. Buys all rights. Computer printout submissions acceptable; prefers letter-quality to dot-matrix. Reports in 3 weeks. Sample copy for 9x12 SAE with $1.50 postage.

Nonfiction: Interview/profile and new product. Buys 10 mss/year. Query. Length: 1,000-2,500 words. Pays $50-250 for assigned articles; sometimes payment arranged individually with publisher. Sometimes pays expenses of writers on assignment.

Photos: State availability of photos with submission. Captions and model releases required.

Tips: "Inquire about covering trade shows for us, such as C.M.A."

‡UPB MAGAZINE, The Voice of the United Polka Boosters, The United Polka Boosters, Box 681, Glastonbury CT 06033. (203)537-1880. Editor: Walter Jedziniak. Managing Editor: Irene Kobelski. 50-60% freelance written. Eager to work with new/unpublished writers. A bimonthly magazine of the Polka Music industry. "Our readers share a common love for polka music and are dedicated to its preservation. They want information-packed pieces to help them understand and perform better in the polka industry." Estab. 1986. Circ. 550. Pays on acceptance. Publishes ms an average of 6 months after acceptance. Byline given. Offers 5% kill fee. Buys first or second serial (reprint) rights. Submit seasonal/holiday material 6 months in advance. Simultaneous, photocopied and previously published submissions OK; prefers letter-quality to dot-matrix. Computer printout submissions OK. Reports in 3 weeks. Sample copy for 9x12 SAE with 4 first class stamps; free writer's guidelines for #10 SAE and 1 first class stamp.

Nonfiction: Historical/nostalgic (polka-related), how-to (have published "How to Make a Polka album," "How to Protect Your Songs," "How to Read Music"), humor (polka-related), interview/profile (polka personalities), opinion (on polka issues), technical and the origins and history of well-known polkas. "No submissions that portray polkas as the dictionary definition "a Bohemian dance in 2/4 time." Articles should be clearly written and easily understandable. Polka music in the U.S.A. is what we want—not old world music." Buys 15 mss/year. Query with or without published clips, or send complete ms. Length: 300-2,000 words. Pays $15-35 for assigned articles; pays $5-30 for unsolicited articles. Sometimes pays the expenses of writers on assignment.

Photos: State availability of photos with submission. Reviews 8x10 or 5x7 prints, b&w only. Offers $1-3 per photo. Model releases and identification of subjects required. Buys one-time rights.

Columns/Departments: Behind the Scenes (in-depth report of 'how' and 'why' a polka-related or music-related process is followed), 1,500 words; Personality Profiles (emphasize the subject's contributions to polka music); 800-2,000 words; Origins of Songs (show dates and facts—pack it with research, tie in a contemporary recording if possible), 300-1,500 words. Buys 16 mss/year. Query or send complete ms. Pays $5-35.

Fillers: Anecdotes, facts, newsbreaks, short humor and puzzles. Buys 30/year. Length: 150-750 words. Pays $2-20 and contributor copy.

Tips: "We'd love to see some round-up pieces—for example, 'What 10 top bandleaders say about—' or 'Polka fans speak out about—'. Know the polka industry! We need info to help our readers survive in the world of performance and business. Articles should be well researched and should reflect the writer's knowledge of the present polka industry. A list of sources should accompany your ms. Our publication serves both industry professionals (musicians, DJs, composers, arrangers and promoters), and polka fans. Articles should be both informative and entertaining. We are very eager to work with freelance writers on a regular basis. We'd like pieces on recording, performing, promoting, composing, dancing—all types of well-written music-oriented pieces."

VANTAGE POINT: ISSUES IN AMERICAN ARTS, American Council for the Arts, 1285 Avenue of the Americas, New York NY 10019. Editor: Bill Keens. 80% freelance written. Published 5 times/year as 16-page editorial supplement in *Horizon Magazine*. Bimonthly magazine. Circ. 3,000. Pays on publication. Publishes ms an average of 1-2 months after acceptance. Byline given. Buys first North American serial rights. No telephone queries. Simultaneous queries and simultaneous and photocopied submissions OK. Computer printout submissions OK; prefer letter-quality to dot-matrix. Reports in 6 weeks. Free sample copy if interested in query or submission—otherwise $2.50, 9x12 SAE and $1 postage.

Nonfiction: Features, profiles, essays and interviews. Buys 12 mss/year. Length: 500-3,000 words. Pays $100-250. Pays expenses of writers on assignment.

Tips: "*Vantage Point* focuses on contemporary issues (social, political, economics and artistic) as they affect the art community on all levels. Readers include high level art executives, trustees, patrons, members of the corporation, foundation and education communities, artists and elected government officials."

Farm

Today's farm publications want more than rewrites of USDA and extension service press releases. Farm magazines reflect this, and the successful freelance farm writer turns his attention to the business end of farming. Do you need to be a farmer to write about the subject? It depends on the topic. For more technical articles, editors feel writers should have a farm background or some technical farm education. But there are writing opportunities for the general freelancer too. The following listings for farm publications are divided into seven categories, each specializing in a different aspect of farm publishing: agricultural equipment; crops and soil management; dairy farming; livestock; management; miscellaneous and regional. Be sure to write for sample copies and writer's guidelines. As more and more farmers experience financial problems, some publications that serve them will struggle for survival too.

Agricultural Equipment

CUSTOM APPLICATOR, Little Publications, Suite 540, 6263 Poplar Ave., Memphis TN 38119. (901)767-4020. Editor: Rob Wiley. 50% freelance written. Works with a small number of new/unpublished writers each year. For "firms that sell and custom apply agricultural fertilizer and chemicals." Circ. 16,100. Pays on publication. Publishes ms an average of 2 months after acceptance. Buys all rights. "Query is best. The editor can help you develop the story line regarding our specific needs." Computer printout submissions acceptable; prefers letter-quality to dot-matrix.

Nonfiction: "We are looking for articles on custom application firms telling others how to better perform jobs of chemical application, develop new customers, handle credit, etc. Lack of a good idea or usable information will bring a rejection." Length: 1,000-1,200 words "with 3 or 4 b&w glossy prints." Pays 20¢/word.

Photos: Accepts b&w glossy prints. "We will look at color slides for possible cover or inside use."

Tips: "We don't get enough shorter articles, so one that is well-written and informative could catch our eyes. Our readers want pragmatic information to help them run a more efficient business; they can't get that through a story filled with generalities."

FARM SUPPLIER, Watt Publishing Co., Sandstone Bldg., Mount Morris IL 61054. (815)734-4171. Editor: Marcella Sadler. Editorial Director: Clayton Gill. 20% freelance written. Prefers writers who have a vast knowledge of agriculture. For retail farm supply dealers and managers over the U.S. Monthly magazine. Circ. 40,000. Pays on acceptance. Publishes ms an average of 2-10 months after acceptance. Byline given. Buys all rights in competitive farm supply fields. Phone queries OK. Submit seasonal material or query 2 months in advance. Computer printout submissions acceptable. Reports in 2 weeks.

Nonfiction: How-to, informational, interview, new product and photo feature. "Articles emphasizing product news and how new product developments have been profitably resold or successfully used. We use material on successful farm, feed and fertilizer dealers." No "general how-to articles that some writers blanket the industry with, inserting a word change here or there to 'customize.'" Buys 10 unsolicited mss/year.

Photos: Purchased with accompanying ms. Submit 5x7 or 8x10 b&w prints; 35mm or larger color transparencies. Total purchase price for a ms includes payment for photos.

Tips: "Because of a constantly changing industry, *FS* attempts to work only two months in advance. Freelancers should slant stories to each season in the farm industry and should provide vertical color photos whenever possible with longer features."

FERTILIZER PROGRESS, The Fertilizer Institute, 1015 18th St. NW, Washington DC 20036. (202)861-4900. Edited and published by TFI Communications. Vice President: Thomas E. Waldinger. Editor: Richard F. Dunn, Jr. Assistant Editor: Becki K. Weiss. 7% freelance written. Eager to work with new/unpublished writers. Bimonthly magazine covering fertilizer, farm chemical and allied industries for business and management, with emphasis on the retail market. Circ. 25,000. Pays on publication. Publishes ms an average of 3 months after acceptance. Byline given. Offers 2½¢/word kill fee for assigned stories. Buys all rights. Submit seasonal/holiday material 2 months in advance. Photocopied submissions OK. Computer printout submissions acceptable; prefers letter-quality to dot-matrix. Reports in 2 weeks on queries; 3 weeks on mss. Free sample copy.
Nonfiction: Articles on sales, services, credit, products, equipment, merchandising, production, regulation, research and environment. Also news about people, companies, trends and developments. No "highly technical or philosophic pieces; we want relevance—something the farm retail dealer can sink his teeth into." No material not related to fertilizer, farm chemical and allied industries, and the retail market. Send complete ms. Length: 400-2,500 words. Pays $35-200. Sometimes pays expenses of writers on assignment.
Photos: Send photos with ms. Pays $5-20 for 5x7 b&w and color prints. Captions and identification of subjects required.
Columns/Departments: Fit to be Tried (ideas that really work); and Worth Repeating (agricultural-related editorial commentary). Send complete ms. Length: 500-750 words. Pays $40-60.
Tips: "Query letter to propose story idea provides best results."

Crops and Soil Management

ONION WORLD, Columbia Publishing, 111C S. 7th Ave., Box 1467, Yakima WA 98907. (509)248-2452. Editor: D. Brent Clement. 90% freelance written. A monthly magazine covering "the world of onion production and marketing" for onion growers and shippers. Circ. 5,500. Pays on publication. Publishes ms an average of 1 month after acceptance. Byline given. Not copyrighted. Buys first North American serial rights. Submit seasonal/holiday material 1 month in advance. Simultaneous submissions OK. Computer printout submisions acceptable; prefers letter-quality to dot-matrix. Reports in several weeks. Sample copy for 8½x11 SAE with 90¢ postage.
Nonfiction: General interest, historical/nostalgic and interview/profile. Buys 60 mss/year. Query. Length: 1,200-1,500 words. Pays $75-100 for assigned articles.
Photos: Send photos with submission. Offers no additional payment for photos accepted with ms unless cover shot. Captions and identification of subjects required. Buys all rights.
Tips: "Writers should be familiar with growing and marketing onions. We use a lot of feature stories on growers, shippers and others in the onion trade—what they are doing, their problems, solutions, marketing plans, etc."

POTATO GROWER OF IDAHO, Harris Publishing, Inc., Box 981, Idaho Falls ID 83402. Editor: Steve Janes. 25% freelance written. Emphasizes material slanted to the potato grower and the business of farming related to this subject—packing, shipping, processing, research, etc. Monthly magazine; 48-96 pages. Circ. 18,000. Pays on publication. Buys first North American serial rights. Byline given. Phone queries OK. Submit seasonal/holiday material 3 months in advance. Simultaneous queries, and photocopied and previously published submissions OK. Computer printout submissions acceptable. Reports in 1 month. Sample copy $1, 8½x11 SAE, and 37¢ postage; writer's guidelines for 5½x7 SAE and 1 first class stamp.
Nonfiction: Expose (facts, not fiction or opinion, pertaining to the subject); how-to (do the job better, cheaper, faster, etc.); informational articles; interviews ("can use one of these a month, but must come from state of Idaho since this is a regional publication; on unique personalities in the potato industry, and telling the nation how Idaho grows potatoes"); all types of new product articles pertaining to the subject; photo features (story can be mostly photos, but must have sufficient cutlines to carry technical information); and technical (all aspects of the industry of growing, storage, processing, packing and research of potatoes in general, but must relate to the Idaho potato industry). Buys 5 mss/year. Query. Length: 1,000-2,000 words. Pays $15-100.
Photos: B&w glossies (any size) purchased with mss or on assignment; use of color limited. Query if photos are not to be accompanied by ms. Pays $5 for 5x7 b&w prints; $10-50 for 35mm color slides. Captions, model release, and identification of subjects required. Buys one-time rights.
Columns/Departments: Buys 2 mss/year. Query. Length: 750-1,000 words. Pays $20-35.
Fillers: Newsbreaks. Buys 5/year. Length: 50-500 words. Pays $5-15.
Tips: "Choose one vital, but small aspect of the industry; research that subject and slant it to fit the readership and/or goals of the magazine. All articles on research must have a valid source for foundation. Material must be general in nature about the subject or specific in nature about Idaho potato growers. Write a query letter, noting what you have in mind for an article; be specific." Articles on advancement in potato-growing methods or technology are most open to freelancers.

SINSEMILLA TIPS, Domestic Marijuana Journal, New Moon Publishing, 217 SW 2nd, Box 2046, Corvallis OR 97339. (503)757-8477. Editor: Thomas Alexander. 50% freelance written. Eager to work with new/unpublished writers. Quarterly magazine tabloid covering the domestic cultivation of marijuana. Circ. 10,000. Pays on publication. Publishes ms an average of 3 months after acceptance. Byline given. "Some writers desire to be anonymous for obvious reasons." Buys first serial rights and second serial (reprint) rights. Submit seasonal/holiday material 2 months in advance. Query for electronic submissions. Computer printout submissions acceptable; no dot-matrix. Reports in 2 months. Sample copy $6.

Nonfiction: Book excerpts and reviews; expose (on political corruption); general interest; how-to; interview/profile; opinion; personal experience; and technical. Send complete ms. Length: 500-2,000 words. Pays 2½¢/word. Sometimes pays the expenses of writers on assignment.

Photos: Send photos with ms. Pays $10-20 for b&w prints. Captions optional; model release required. Buys all rights.

Tips: "Writers have the best chance of publication if article is *specifically* related to the American marijuana industry."

SOYBEAN DIGEST, Box 41309, 777 Craig Rd., St. Louis MO 63141-1309. (314)432-1600. Editor: Gregg Hillyer. 75% freelance written. Works with a small number of new/unpublished writers each year. Emphasizes soybean production and marketing. Published monthly except semi-monthly in February and March, and bimonthly in June/July and August/September. Circ. 200,000. Pays on acceptance. Buys all rights. Byline given. Phone queries OK. Submit seasonal material 2 months in advance. Query for electronic submissions. Computer printout submissions OK; prefers letter-quality to dot-matrix. Reports in 3 weeks. Sample copy $3; mention *Writer's Market* in request.

Nonfiction: How-to (soybean production and marketing); and new product (soybean production and marketing). Buys over 100 mss/year. Query or submit complete ms. Length: 1,000 words. Pays $50-350. Sometimes pays the expenses of writers on assignment.

Photos: State availability of photos with query. Pays $25-100 for 5x7 or 8x10 b&w prints, $50-275 for 35mm color transparencies, and up to $350 for covers. Captions and/or ms required. Buys all rights.

TOBACCO REPORTER, Suite 300, 3000 Highwoods Blvd., Box 95075, Raleigh NC 27625. Editor: Anne Shelton. 5% (by those who *know* the industry) freelance written. International business journal for tobacco processors, exporters, importers, manufacturers and distributors of cigars, cigarettes and other tobacco products. Monthly. Buys all rights. Pays on publication. Computer printout submissions acceptable; no dot-matrix. Publishes ms an average of 2 months after acceptance.

Nonfiction: Uses exclusive original material on request only. Pays 10-15¢/word.

Photos: Pays $25 for photos purchased with mss.

Fillers: Wants clippings on new tobacco product brands, smoking and health, and the following relating to tobacco and tobacco products: job promotions, honors, equipment, etc. Pays $5-10/clipping on use only.

Dairy Farming

BUTTER-FAT, Fraser Valley Milk Producers' Cooperative Association, Box 9100, Vancouver, British Columbia V6B 4G4 Canada. (604)420-6611. Editor: Nancy L. Ryder. Managing Editor: Carol A. Paulson. Eager to work with new/unpublished writers. 50% freelance written. Monthly magazine emphasizing this dairy cooperative's processing and marketing operations for dairy farmers and dairy workers in British Columbia. Circ. 3,500. Pays on acceptance. Publishes ms an average of 4 months after acceptance. Byline given. Buys first rights and first and second rights to the same material. Makes work-for-hire assignments. Phone queries preferred. Submit seasonal material 4 months in advance. Simultaneous, photocopied and previously published submissions OK. Computer printout submissions acceptable. Reports in 1 week on queries; in 1 month on mss. Free sample copy and writer's guidelines.

Nonfiction: Interview (character profile with industry leaders); local nostalgia; opinion (of industry leaders); and profile (of association members and employees).

Photos: Reviews 5x7 b&w negatives and contact sheets and color photos. Offers $10/published photo. Captions required. Buys all rights.

Columns/Departments: "We want articles on the people, products, business of producing, processing and marketing dairy foods in this province." Query first. Buys 3 mss/issue. Length: 500-1,500 words. Pays 7¢/word.

Fillers: Jokes, short humor and quotes. Buys 5 mss/issue. Pays $10.

Tips: "Make an appointment to come by and see us!"

‡DAIRY HERD MANAGEMENT, Miller Publishing Co., Box 67, Minneapolis MN 55440. (612)374-5200. Editor: Sheila Widmer Vikla. Emphasizes dairy farming. Monthly magazine; 60 pages. Circ. 108,000. Pays on acceptance. Buys first North American serial rights. Submit seasonal/holiday material 2 months in advance.

Photocopied and previously published submissions OK. Reports in 6 weeks. Free sample copy and writer's guidelines.
Nonfiction: How-to, informational and technical. Buys 2 mss/year. Query. Length: 1,000-3,000 words. Pays $75-200. "Articles should concentrate on useful management information. Be specific rather than general."

THE DAIRYMAN, Box 819, Corona CA 91718. (714)735-2730. Editor: Dennis Halladay. 10% freelance written. Prefers to work with published/established writers, but also works with a small number of new/unpublished writers each year. Monthly magazine dealing with large herd commercial dairy industry. Circ. 33,000. Pays on acceptance or publication. Publishes ms an average of 2-3 months after acceptance. Byline given. Buys first North American serial rights. Submit seasonal material 3 months in advance. Photocopied submissions OK. Computer printout submissions acceptable. Reports in 2 weeks. Sample copy for 8½x11 SAE with 69¢ postage.
Nonfiction: Humor, interview/profile, new product, opinion, and industry analysis. Special issues: Computer issue (February); herd health issue (August); Feeds and Feeding (May); and Barns and Equipment (November). No religion, nostalgia, politics or 'mom and pop' dairies. Query or send complete ms. Length: 300-5,000 words. Pays $10-200.
Photos: Send photo with query or ms. Reviews b&w contact sheets and 35mm or 2¼x2¼ transparencies. Pays $10-25 for b&w; $25-100 for color. Captions and identification of subjects required. Buys one-time rights.
Columns/Departments: Herd health, taxes and finances, economic outlook for dairying. Buys 25/year. Query or send complete ms. Length: 300-2,000 words. Pays $25-100.
Tips: "Pretend you're an editor for a moment; now would you want to buy a story without any artwork?; neither would I. Writers often don't know modern commercial dairying and they forget they're writing for an audience of *dairymen*. Publications are becoming more and more specialized . . . you've really got to know who you're writing for and why they're different."

Livestock

BEEF, The Webb Co., 1999 Shepard Rd., St. Paul MN 55116. (612)690-7374. Editor-in-Chief: Paul D. Andre. Managing Editor: Joe Roybal. 5% freelance written. Prefers to work with published/established writers. Monthly magazine for readers who have the same basic interest—making a living feeding cattle or running a cow herd. Circ. 125,000. Pays on acceptance. Publishes ms an average of 4 months after acceptance. Buys all rights. Byline given. Phone queries OK. Submit seasonal material 3 months in advance. Computer printout submissions acceptable. Reports in 2 months. Free sample copy and writer's guidelines.
Nonfiction: How-to and informational articles on doing a better job of producing, feeding cattle, market building, managing, and animal health practices. Material must deal with beef cattle only. Buys 8-10 mss/year. Query. Length: 500-2,000 words. Pays $25-300. Sometimes pays the expenses of writers on assignment.
Photos: B&w glossies (8x10) and color transparencies (35mm or 2¼x2¼) purchased with or without mss. Query or send contact sheet, captions and/or transparencies. Pays $10-50 for b&w; $25-100 for color. Model release required.
Tips: "Be completely knowledgeable about cattle feeding and cowherd operations. Know what makes a story. We want specifics, not a general roundup of an operation. Pick one angle and develop it fully. The most frequent mistake is not following instructions on an angle (or angles) to be developed."

‡**THE BRAHMAN JOURNAL**, Sagebrush Publishing Co., Inc., Box 220, Eddy TX 76524. (817)859-5451. Editor: Joe Ed Brockett. 10% freelance written. A monthly magazine covering Brahman cattle. Circ. 6,000. Pays on publication. Publishes ms an average of 2 months after acceptance. Byline given. Not copyrighted. Buys first North American serial rights, one-time rights, second serial (reprint) rights and makes work-for-hire assignments. Submit seasonal/holiday material 3 months in advance. Previously published submissions OK. Computer printout submissions OK; no dot-matrix. Reports in 1 month.
Nonfiction: General interest, historical/nostalgic and interview/profile. Special issues include Herd Bull issue (July) and Texas issue (October). Buys 3-4 mss/year. Query with published clips. Length: 1,200-3,000 words. Pays $100-250 for assigned articles.
Photos: Photos needed for article purchase. Send photos with submission. Reviews 4x5 prints. Offers no additional payment for photos accepted with ms. Captions required. Buys one-time rights.

THE CATTLEMAN MAGAZINE, Texas & Southwestern Cattle Raisers Association, 1301 W. 7th St., Ft. Worth TX 76102. (817)332-7155. Editor: Dale Segraves. Managing Editor: Don C. King. Emphasizes beef cattle production and feeding. "Readership consists of commercial cattlemen, purebred seedstock producers, cattle feeders and horsemen in the Southwest." Monthly magazine; 170 pages. Circ. 19,200. Pays on acceptance. Publishes ms an average of 6 months after acceptance. Byline given. Buys all rights. Computer printout submissions acceptable; prefers letter-quality to dot-matrix. Reports in 3 weeks. Sample copy $2;

writer's guidelines for business size SAE and 1 first class stamp.

Nonfiction: Need informative, entertaining feature articles on specific commercial ranch operations, cattle breeding and feeding, range and pasture management, profit tips, and university research on beef industry. "We feature various beef cattle breeds most months." Will take a few historical western-lore pieces. Must be well-documented. No first person narratives or fiction or articles pertaining to areas outside the Southwest or outside beef cattle ranching. Buys 24 mss/year. Query. Length 1,500-2,000 words. Pays $75-300. Sometimes pays the expenses of writers on assignment.

Photos: Photos purchased with or without accompanying ms. State availability of photos with query or ms. Pays $15-25 for 5x7 b&w glossies; $100 for color transparencies used as cover. Total purchase price for ms includes payment for photos. Captions, model release, and identification of subjects required.

Fillers: Cartoons.

Tips: "Submit an article dealing with ranching in the Southwest. Too many writers submit stories out of our general readership area. Economics may force staff writers to produce more articles, leaving little room for unsolicited articles."

‡GULF COAST CATTLEMAN, Gulf Coast Publishing Corp., 11201 Morning Ct., San Antonio TX 78213. (512)344-8300. Managing Editor: Jimmy Guillot. Monthly magazine covering beef cattle production. "We want articles dealing with specific subjects in beef cattle management or marketing that apply to producers in states from Texas to Florida." Circ. 6,800. Pays on acceptance. Publishes ms an average of 3 months after acceptance. Byline given. Buys first North American serial rights or all rights. Submit seasonal/holiday material 4 months in advance. Computer printout submissions OK; prefers letter-quality to dot-matrix. Reports in 1 month. Sample copy for 9x12 SAE with 8 first class stamps.

Nonfiction: How-to (ways to make beef cattle production easier, more profitable, etc.), technical (new technology as it applies to beef cattle production in our area). No western fiction, humor, light feature material. Buys 12 mss/year. Query with published clips, or send complete ms. Length: 500-2,500 words. Pays $100-250. Sometimes pays the expenses of writers on assignment.

Photos: Send photos with submission. Offers no additional payment for photos accepted with ms. Captions required. Buys one-time rights.

Tips: "Successful contributors to our magazine most often are those who have ranching backgrounds, or at least have a degree in agriculture. Put simply, we need articles that take a fresh approach to an old problem—how to profitably raise beef cattle. Find a beef cattle operation—cow/calf or stocker—in the southern or southeastern U.S. where the operator is doing something new or innovative that would apply to others in the business."

‡HOG FARM MANAGEMENT, Miller Publishing Co., Suite 160, 12400 Whitewater Dr., Box 2400, Minneapolis MN 55343. (612)931-2900. Editor: Kathy Hohmann. 25% freelance written. A monthly trade journal on hog production. "Specialized management-oriented features on hog production: feeding, health, finances." Circ. 75,000. Pays on publication. Publishes ms an average of 2 months after acceptance. Byline given. Offers $25 kill fee. Buys all rights. Submit seasonal/holiday material 3 months in advance. Reports in 2 weeks on queries. Sample copy $1; free writer's guidelines.

Nonfiction: General interest, how-to, interview/profile and new product. No humor or excerpts of any kind. Buys 15-20 mss/year. Query with or without published clips, or send complete ms. Length: 200-1,000 words. Pays $150-350.

Photos: State availability of photos with submission. Reviews contact sheets. Offers $10-40 per photo. Model releases and identification of subjects required. Buys all rights.

LIMOUSIN WORLD, Limousin World, Inc., 6408 S. College Ave., Fort Collins CO 80525. Editor: Wes Ishmael. Managing Editor: Louise Kello. 10% freelance written. "Eager to work with any writers, veteran or new, who can do the job for us." A monthly magazine on the Limousin breed of beef cattle for people who breed and raise them. Circ. 13,000. Pays on acceptance. Publishes ms an average of 2 months after acceptance. Byline given. Buys negotiable rights. Submit seasonal/holiday material 2 months in advance. Simultaneous queries, and photocopied and previously published submissions OK. Computer printout submissions acceptable; prefers letter-quality to dot-matrix. Reports in 2 weeks. Sample copy and writer's guidelines for $2.40.

Nonfiction: How-to (beef herd management equipment); interview/profile (interesting Limousin breeders); new product (limited); and travel (Limousin oriented). "Write interesting, informative, entertaining articles on farm and ranch operations where Limousin breeding has an influence. Management, feeding, breeding, profit producing methods, university research and interesting people are all good topics. Queries should be made on subject for herd features before doing. Short human interest articles on well-known popular personalities who are also breeding Limousin are used." Special issue on Herd Reference. No inflammatory or controversial articles. Query. Length: open. Pays $25-200. Sometimes pays the expenses of writers on assignment.

Photos: Send photos with query or ms. Pays $5-25 for 5x7 and 8x10 b&w prints; $25-100 for 5x7 and 8x10 color prints. Captions and model release required. Buys first-time rights.

Tips: "Our readers are in the cattle breeding and raising business for a living so writing should be directed to an informed, mature audience. What we need are articles geared toward the Limousin breed of cattle specifically."

‡**LLAMAS MAGAZINE, The International Camelid Journal**, Clay Press, Inc., Box 100, Herald CA 95638. (209)748-2620. Editor: Cheryl Dal Porto. A bimonthly magazine covering llamas, alpacas, camels, vicunas and guanacos. Circ. 3,500. Pays on acceptance. Publishes ms an average of 6 months after acceptance. Byline given. Buys first rights, second serial (reprint) rights and makes work-for-hire assignments. Submit seasonal/holiday material 6 months in advance. Simultaneous, photocopied and previously published submissions OK. Computer printout submissions OK. Reports in 2 weeks. Sample copy $4 for SAE with $1 postage; free writer's guidelines.

Nonfiction: How-to (on anything related to raising llamas), humor, interview/profile, opinion, personal experience, photo feature and travel (to countries where there are camelids). "All articles must have a tie in to one of the camelid species." Buys 18 mss/year. Query with published clips. Length: 1,000-5,000 words. Pays $50-250 for assigned articles; pays $50-150 for unsolicited articles. May pay new writers with contributor copies. Sometimes pays the expenses of writers on assignment.

Photos: State availability of photos with submission or send photos with submission. Reviews transparencies and 5x7 prints. Offers $25-100 per photo. Captions, model releases and identification of subjects required. Buys one-time rights.

Fillers: Anecdotes, gags and short humor. Buys 20/year. Length: 100-500 words. Pays $25.

Tips: "Get to know the llama folk in your area and query us with an idea. We are open to any and all ideas involving llamas, alpacas and the rest of the camelids. We are always looking for good photos. You must know about camelids to write for us."

POLLED HEREFORD WORLD, 4700 E. 63rd St., Kansas City MO 64130. (816)333-7731. Editor: Ed Bible. 1% freelance written. For "breeders of Polled Hereford cattle—about 80% registered breeders, 5% commercial cattle breeders; remainder are agribusinessmen in related fields." Monthly. Circ. 11,500. Not copyrighted. Buys "no unsolicited mss at present." Pays on publication. Publishes ms an average of 2 months after acceptance. Photocopied submissions OK. Computer printout submissions acceptable; prefers letter-quality to dot-matrix. Submit seasonal material "as early as possible: 2 months preferred." Reports in 1 month. Query first for reports of events and activities. Query first or submit complete ms for features. Free sample copy. No writer's guidelines.

Nonfiction: "Features on registered or commercial Polled Hereford breeders. Some on related agricultural subjects (pastures, fences, feeds, buildings, etc.). Mostly technical in nature; some human interest. Our readers make their living with cattle, so write for an informed, mature audience." Buys informational articles, how-to's, personal experience articles, interviews, profiles, historical and think pieces, nostalgia, photo features, coverage of successful business operations, articles on merchandising techniques, and technical articles. Length: "varies with subject and content of feature." Pays about 5¢/word ("usually about 50¢/column inch, but can vary with the value of material").

Photos: Purchased with mss, sometimes purchased without mss, or on assignment; captions required. "Only good quality b&w glossies accepted; any size. Good color prints or transparencies." Pays $2 for b&w, $2-25 for color. Pays $25 for color covers.

‡**SHEEP! MAGAZINE**, Rt. 1, Box 78, Helenville WI 53137. (414)674-3029. Editor: Doris Thompson. 50% freelance written. Prefers to work with published/established writers, and works with a small number of new/unpublished writers each year. Monthly magazine. "We're looking for clear, concise, useful information for sheep raisers who have a few sheep to a 1,000 ewe flock." Circ. 8,500. Pays on publication. Byline given. Offers $30 kill fee. Buys all rights. Makes work-for-hire assignments. Submit seasonal/holiday material 3 months in advance. Computer printout submissions acceptable; prefers letter-quality to dot-matrix. Sample copy for 9x12 SAE with postage.

Nonfiction: Book excerpts; information (on personalities and/or political, legal or environmental issues affecting the sheep industry); how-to (on innovative lamb and wool marketing and promotion techniques, efficient record-keeping systems or specific aspects of health and husbandry). "Health and husbandry articles should be written by someone with extensive experience or appropriate credentials (i.e., a veterinarian or animal scientist"); profiles (on experienced sheep producers who detail the economics and management of their operation); features (on small businesses that promote wool products and stories about local and regional sheep producer's groups and their activities); new products (of value to sheep producers; should be written by someone who has used them); and technical (on genetics, health and nutrition). First person narratives. Buys 80 mss/year. Query with published clips or send complete ms. Length: 750-2,500 words. Pays $45-150. Sometimes pays the expenses of writers on assignment.

Photos: "Color—vertical compositions of sheep and/or people—for our cover. Use only b&w inside magazine. B&w, 35mm photos or other visuals improve your chances of a sale." Pays $50 maximum for 35mm color transparencies; $5-30 for 5x7 b&w prints. Identification of subjects required. Buys all rights.

Tips: "Send us your best words and photos!"

SIMMENTAL SHIELD, Box 511, Lindsborg KS 67456. Publisher/Editor: Chester Peterson Jr. 30% freelance written. Eager to work with new/unpublished writers. Readers are breeders of purebred cattle and/or commercial cattlemen. Monthly; 124 pages. Circ. 7,000. Buys all rights. Pays on publication. Publishes ms an average of 3 months after acceptance. Computer printout submissions acceptable. Submit material 4 months in advance. Reports in 1 month. Free sample copy $1.50.

Nonfiction and Fillers: Farmer experience and management articles with emphasis on ideas used and successful management ideas based on cattleman who owns Simmental. Research: new twist to old ideas or application of new techniques to the Simmental or cattle business. Wants articles that detail to reader how to make or save money or pare labor needs. Buys informational, how-to, personal experience, interview, profile, humor and think articles. January is AI issue; July is herd sire issue; December is brood cow issue. Query first or submit complete ms. Rates vary. Sometimes pays the expenses of writers on assignment.

Photos: Photos purchased with accompanying ms with no additional payment. Interest in cover photos; accepts 35mm if sharp, well exposed.

Tips: "Articles must involve Simmental and/or beef breeding cattle. Be conversant with our lingo and community."

Management

ACRES U.S.A., A Voice for Eco-Agriculture, Acres U.S.A., Box 9547, Kansas City MO 64133. (816)737-0064. Editor: Charles Walters, Jr. Monthly tabloid covering biologically sound farming techniques. Circ. 16,000. Pays on acceptance. Byline sometimes given. Buys all rights. Submit seasonal/holiday material 3 months in advance. Computer printout submissions acceptable. Reports in 1 month. Sample copy $2.

Nonfiction: Expose (farm-related); how-to; and case reports on farmers who have adopted eco-agriculture (organic). No philosophy on eco-farming or essays. Buys 80 mss/year. Query with published clips. Length: open. Pays 6¢/word.

Photos: State availability of photos. Reviews b&w photos only. Top quality photos only. Pays $6 for b&w contact sheets, negatives and 7x10 prints.

Tips: "We need on-scene reports of farmers who have adopted eco-farming—good case reports. We must have substance in articles and need details on systems developed. Read a few copies of the magazine to learn the language of the subject."

AGWAY COOPERATOR, Box 4933, Syracuse NY 13221. (315)477-6231. Editor: Jean Willis. 2% freelance written for farmers. Works with a small number of new/unpublished writers each year. Published 9 times/year. Pays on acceptance. Publishes ms an average of 6 months after acceptance. Time between acceptance and publication varies considerably. Usually reports in 1 week. Computer printout submissions acceptable; no dot-matrix.

Nonfiction: Should deal with topics of farm or rural interest in the Northeastern U.S. Length: 1,200 words maximum. Pays $100, usually including photos.

Tips: "We prefer an Agway tie-in, if possible. Fillers don't fit into our format. We do not assign freelance articles."

‡FARM JOURNAL, 230 W. Washington Square, Philadelphia PA 19105. Contact: Editor. "The business magazine of American agriculture" is published 14 times/year with many regional editions. Material bought for one or more editions depending upon where it fits. Buys all rights. Byline given "except when article is too short or too heavily rewritten to justify one." Payment made on acceptance and is the same regardless of editions in which the piece is used.

Nonfiction: Timeliness and seasonableness are very important. Material must be highly practical and should be helpful to as many farmers as possible. Farmers' experiences should apply to one or more of these 8 basic commodities: corn, wheat, milo, soybeans, cotton, dairy, beef and hogs. Technical material must be accurate. No farm nostalgia. Query to describe a new idea that farmers can use. Length: 500-1,500 words. Pays 10-20¢/word published.

Photos: Much in demand either separately or with short how-to material in picture stories and as illustrations for articles. Warm human interest pix for covers—activities on modern farms. For inside use, shots of home-made and handy ideas to get work done easier and faster, farm news photos, and pictures of farm people with interesting sidelines. In b&w, 8x10 glossies are preferred; color submissions should be 2¼x2¼ for the cover, and 35mm for inside use. Pays $50 and up for b&w shot; $75 and up for color.

Tips: "*Farm Journal* now publishes in hundreds of editions reflecting geographic, demographic and economic sectors of the farm market."

‡FARM SHOW MAGAZINE, 20088 Kenwood Trail, Box 1029, Lakeville MN 55044. (612)469-5572. Editor: Mark A. Newhall. 20% freelance written. A bimonthly trade journal covering agriculture. Circ. 150,000. Pays on acceptance. Publishes ms an average of 4 months after acceptance. Byline sometimes given. Buys one-time and second serial (reprint) rights. Previously published submissions OK. Computer printout submissions OK. Reports in 1 week. Free sample copy.

Nonfiction: How-to and new product. No general interest, historic or nostalgic articles. Buys 90 mss/year. Send complete ms. Length: 100-2,000 words. Pays $50-500. Pays expenses of writers on assignment.

Photos: Send photos with submission. Reviews 5x7 prints. Offers no additional payment for photos accepted with ms. Captions required. Buys one-time rights.

Tips: "We're looking for first-of-its-kind, inventions of the nuts and bolts variety for farmers."

THE NATIONAL FUTURE FARMER, Box 15130, Alexandria VA 22309. (703)360-3600. Editor-in-Chief: Wilson W. Carnes. 20% freelance written. Prefers to work with published/established writers, and is eager to work with new/unpublished writers. Bimonthly magazine for members of the Future Farmers of America who are students of vocational agriculture in high school, ranging in age from 14-21 years; major interest in careers in agriculture/agribusiness and other youth interest subjects. Circ. 422,528. Pays on acceptance. Publishes ms an average of 4 months after acceptance. Buys all rights. Byline given. Submit seasonal/holiday material 4 months in advance. Query for electronic submissions. Computer printout submissions acceptable; prefers letter-quality to dot-matrix. Usually reports in 1 month. Sample copy and writer's guidelines for 4x9 SAE with 44¢ postage.

Nonfiction: How-to for youth (outdoor-type such as camping, hunting, fishing); and informational (getting money for college, farming; and other help for youth). Informational, personal experience and interviews are used only if FFA members or former members are involved. "Science-oriented material is being used more extensively as we broaden peoples' understanding of agriculture." Buys 15 unsolicited mss/year. Query or send complete ms. Length: 1,000 words maximum. Pays 4-6¢/word. Sometimes pays the expenses of writers on assignment.

Photos: Purchased with mss (5x7 or 8x10 b&w glossies; 35mm or larger color transparencies). Pays $7.50 for b&w; $30-40 for inside color; $100 for cover.

Tips: "Find an FFA member who has done something truly outstanding that will motivate and inspire others, or provide helpful information for a career in farming, ranching or agribusiness. We are also very interested in stories on the latest trends in agriculture and how those trends may affect our readers. We're accepting manuscripts now that are tighter and more concise. Get straight to the point."

NEW HOLLAND NEWS, Sperry New Holland, Inc., 500 Diller Ave., New Holland PA 17557. Editor: Gary Martin. 50% freelance written. Works with a small number of new/unpublished writers each year. Magazine published 8 times/year on agriculture; designed to entertain and inform farm families. Pays on acceptance. Publishes ms an average of 1 year after acceptance. Byline usually given. Offers negotiable kill fee. Buys first North American serial rights, one-time rights, and second serial (reprint) rights. Submit seasonal/holiday material 6 months in advance. Simultaneous queries and previously published submissions OK. Computer printout submissions acceptable; prefers letter-quality to dot-matrix. Reports in 1 month. Sample copy and writer's guidelines for 4x9½ SAE.

Nonfiction: "We need strong photo support for short articles up to 800 words on farm management, farm human interest and agricultural research." Buys 16-20 mss/year. Query. Length: 800 words. Pays $400-600. Sometimes pays the expenses of writers on assignment.

Photos: Send photos with query when possible. Reviews color transparencies. Pays $25-200. Captions, model release, and identification of subjects required. Buys one-time rights.

Tips: "We thrive on good article ideas from knowlegeable farm writers. The writer must have an emotional understanding of agriculture and the farm family and must demonstrate in the article an understanding of the unique economics that affect farming in North America. We want to know about the exceptional farm managers, those leading the way in use of new technology, new efficiencies—but always with a human touch. Successful writers keep in touch with the editor as they develop the article."

SUCCESSFUL FARMING, 1716 Locust St., Des Moines IA 50336. (515)284-2897. Managing Editor: Loren Kruse. 3% freelance written. Prefers to work with published/established writers. Magazine of farm management published 14 times/year for top farmers. Circ. 605,000. Buys all rights. Pays on acceptance. Publishes ms an average of 2 months after acceptance. Reports in 2 weeks. Computer printout submissions acceptable; no dot-matrix. Sample copy for SAE and 5 first class stamps.

Nonfiction: Semitechnical articles on the aspects of farming with emphasis on how to apply this information to one's own farm. "Most of our material is too limited and unfamiliar for freelance writers, except for the few who specialize in agriculture, have a farm background and a modern agricultural education." Buys 25 unsolicited mss/year. Query with outline. Length: about 1,500 words maximum. Pays $250-600. Sometimes pays the expenses of writers on assignment.

Photos: Jim Galbraith, art director. Prefers 8x10 b&w glossies to contacts; color should be transparencies, not prints. Buys exclusive rights. Assignments are given, and sometimes a guarantee, provided the editors can be sure the photography will be acceptable.

Tips: "We are looking for more farm business stories rather than production stories. A frequent mistake made by writers in completing articles is that the focus of the story is not narrow enough and does not include enough facts, observations, examples, and dollar signs. Short articles and fillers are usually specific and to the point."

Miscellaneous

‡GLEANINGS IN BEE CULTURE, A.I. Root Co., 723 W. Liberty St., Medina OH 44256. (216)725-6677. Editor: Kim Flottum. 20% freelance written. Monthly magazine covering beekeeping. Articles designed to reach beginning and intermediate level beekeepers. Circ. 14,000. Pays on publication. Publishes ms an average of 3 months after acceptance. Byline given. Buys one-time rights. Submit seasonal/holiday material 6 months in advance. Query for electronic submissions. Computer printout submissions OK; prefers letter-quality to dot-matrix. Reports in 2 weeks. Free sample copy; writer's guidelines for SAE with 1 first class stamp.
Nonfiction: How-to (beekeeping), interview/profile and new product. No fiction. Buys 30 mss/year. Send complete ms. Length: 200-3,500 words. Pays $25-100. Pays in contributor copies "upon request/negotiation."
Photos: Send photos with submission. Reviews 5x7 prints. Offers $5-25. Captions required. Buys first rights.
Columns/Departments: Starting right (very basic information for beginners in beekeeping), 1,000 words. Buys 5 mss/year. Query. Length: 500-1,000 words. Pays $25-100.
Tips: "Talk to beekeepers." Subjects most open to freelancers include "environmental issues *directly* affecting bees, beekeeping and/or beekeepers."

THE SUGAR PRODUCER, Harris Publishing, Inc., 520 Park, Box 981, Idaho Falls ID 83402. (208)522-5187. Editor: Steve Janes. 25% freelance written. Bimonthly magazine covering the growing, storage, use and by-products of the sugar beet. Circ. 19,000. Pays on publication. Publishes ms an average of 3 months after acceptance. Buys one-time rights. Byline given. Phone queries OK. Photocopied and previously published submissions OK. Computer printout submissions acceptable. Reports in 1 month. Free sample copy and writer's guidelines.
Nonfiction: "This is a trade magazine, not a farm magazine. It deals with the business of growing sugar beets, and the related industry. All articles must tell the grower how he can do his job better, or at least be of interest to him, such as historical, because he is vitally interested in the process of growing sugar beets, and the industries related to this." Expose (pertaining to the sugar industry or the beet grower); how-to (all aspects of growing, storing and marketing the sugar beet); interview; profile; personal experience; and technical (material source must accompany story—research and data must be from an accepted research institution). Query or send complete ms. Length: 750-2,000 words. Pays 3¢/word.
Photos: Purchased with mss. Pays $5 for any convenient size b&w; $10 for color print or transparency; $25 for color shot used on cover. Captions and model release required.

Regional

AG REVIEW, Farm Resource Center, 16 Grove St., Putnam CT 06260. (203)928-7778. Editor: Lucien Laliberty. Associate Editor: Liz Cabelus. 50% freelance written. Eager to work with new/unpublished writers. A monthly magazine covering Northeast (New England, New York and Pennsylvania) agriculture for dairy, beef, cash and field crop farms: reporting and analyzing trends, research and product developments, and innovative problem-solving. Circ. 6,000. Pays on publication. Publishes ms an average of 2-5 months after acceptance. Byline given. Offers 50% kill fee. Buys one-time rights, second serial (reprint) rights or simultaneous rights. Submit seasonal/holiday material 4 months in advance. Photocopied and previously published submissions OK. Computer printout submissions acceptable. Reports in 1 month on queries; 6 weeks on mss. Sample copy and writer's guidelines for 9x12 SAE with $1.07 postage; free writer's guidelines.
Nonfiction: Essays (current events or agricultural developments or researched techniques); how-to (solving specific farm problems, appropriate to Northeast); and new product (unusual innovations, home adaptations). Writer's guidelines lists theme issues. "No blow-by-blow reports of conferences or meetings; gardening; or description of how some farmer runs his farm if it's ordinary stuff." Buys 10 mss/year. Query with or without published clips, or send complete ms. Length: 500-20,000 words (5,000 words more likely; 20,000 would be printed in parts in several issues). Pays $25-300; sometimes pays in Farm Resource Center data management or marketing services. Sometimes pays the expenses of writers on assignment.
Photos: State availability or send photos with submission. Considers color, vertical-format photos of dairy or Northeast farming for cover. Reviews transparencies or 3x5 minimum prints. Offers $5-10/photo. Captions and identification of subjects required. Buys one-time rights.
Tips: "We are most interested in in-depth features, ranging from 2,000-5,000 words, including photos or other

illustrations, and covering in detail an idea, controversery, technique or trend. We need interviews with successful farmers, profiles of innovative marketers, columns, or specialty crops (berries, bees, maple syrup, Christmas trees, etc.) and feature articles on major events/issues/controversies in the dairy industry."

CALIFORNIA FARMER, The Magazine for Commercial Agriculture, California Farmer Publishing Co., 731 Market St., San Francisco CA 94103. (415)495-3340. Editor: Len Richardson. Managing Editor: Richard Smoley. 70% freelance written. Works with a small number of new/unpublished writers each year. Magazine published semimonthly: once a month in July, August, December covering California agriculture. "We cover all issues of interest to the state's commercial farmers, including production techniques, marketing, politics, and social and economic issues." Circ. 56,000. Pays on acceptance. Publishes ms an average of 1-2 months after acceptance. Byline given. Offers $100 kill fee. Makes work-for-hire assignments. Submit seasonal/holiday material 3 months in advance. Photocopied and previously published submissions OK. Electronic submissions OK, only ASCII text by modem through MCI Mail. Computer printout submissions acceptable, "must be double-spaced"; prefers letter-quality to dot-matrix. Reports in 1 month. Free writer's guidelines.

Nonfiction: How-to (agricultural, livestock); interview/profile; technical (agricultural: weed and pest control; crop and livestock management; cultural and irrigation practices; financial involvement and marketing of farm products.) No "It happened to me"-type stories. Buys 75 mss/year. Query with published clips. Length: 1,000-3,000 words. Pays $100-400 for assigned articles; pays $50-300 for unsolicited artcles. Sometimes pays the expenses of writers on assignment.

Photos: Send photos with submissions. "We expect to emphasize high-quality color photography even more than we do now. We will give strong—preference to well-written, accurate, newsworthy stories that are accompanied by suitable photographs. Reviews 35mm color transparencies and b&w glossy prints (any size). Captions and identification of subjects required.

Tips: "We will give preference to writers with a demonstrated knowledge of California agriculture, but we will consider material from and occasionally give assignments to good writers with an ability to research a story, get the facts right and write in a smooth, easy-to-understand style. We are most interested in stories about technical innovations in farming as they relate to California agriculture. Stories should be clear, concise, and above all, accurate. We especially welcome pictures of California farmers as illustration."

FLORIDA GROWER & RANCHER, F.G.R., Inc., 1331 N. Mills Ave., Orlando FL 32803. (305)894-6522. Editor: Frank Abrahamson. 10% freelance written. A monthly magazine for Florida farmers. Circ. 28,000. Pays on publication. Byline given. Buys one-time rights. Submit seasonal/holiday material 2 months in advance. Query for electronic submissions. Computer printout submissions acceptable; prefers letter-quality to dot-matirx. Reports in 2 weeks on queries; 1 month on mss. Free sample copy and writer's guidelines.

Nonfiction: General interest, historical/nostalgic, how-to, interview/profile, new product, personal experience, photo feature, technical. Articles should coordinate with editorial calendar, determined 1 year in advance. Buys 6 mss/year. Query. Length: 500-1,000 words. Pays 40¢/printed line.

Photos: Send photos with submission. Reviews transparencies and prints. Pays $5/b&w print, $50/color cover. Identification of subjects required. Buys one-time rights.

MAINE ORGANIC FARMER & GARDENER, Maine Organic Farmers & Gardeners Association, Box 2176, Augusta ME 04330. (207)622-3118. Editor: Pam Bell, Box 53, South Hiram ME 04080. 40% freelance written. Prefers to work with published/established writers; works with a small number of new/unpublished writers each year. Bimonthly magazine covering organic farming and gardening for urban and rural farmers and gardeners and nutrition-oriented, environmentally concerned readers. "*MOF&G* promotes and encourages sustainable agriculture and environmentally sound living. Our primary focus is organic sustainable farming, gardening and forestry, but we also deal with local, national and global agriculture, food and environmental issues." Circ. 10,000. Pays on publication. Publishes ms an average of 8 months after acceptance. Byline and bio given. Buys first North American serial rights, one-time rights, first serial rights, or second serial (reprint) rights. Submit seasonal/holiday material 6 months in advance. Simultaneous queries, and simultaneous, photocopied, and previously published submissions OK. Computer printout submissions acceptable. Reports in 2 months. Sample copy $1.50; free writer's guidelines.

Nonfiction: Historical/nostalgic (farming); how-to (farm, garden [organically], forestry, woodlot management and rural skills); interview (farmer, gardener, ag or environmental activist or politician); profile; technical; personal experience (farmer, gardener, environment, food plant, livestock, weed, insect, tree, renewable energy, recycling, nutrition and health, food systems, etc.). Also first person experience, interview, or documented report dealing with environmental problem and/or solution. Buys 30 mss/year. Query with published clips or send complete ms. Length: 1,000-3,000 words. Pays $40-130. Sometimes pays expenses of writers on assignment.

Photos: State availability of photos with query; send photos with ms. Reviews contact sheets and negatives. "We usually work from negatives. Many of our assignment writers send exposed films, and we process and print." Pays $5 for 5x7 b&w prints. Captions, model releases, and identification of subjects required. Buys one-time rights.

Tips: "We are nonprofit organization. Our publication's primary mission is to inform and educate. Our readers want to know how to, but they also want to enjoy the reading and know whom the source/expert/writer is. We don't want impersonal how-to articles that sound like Extension bulletins or textbooks."

‡MISSOURI RURALIST, Harvest Publishing, 2401-A Vandiver, Columbia MO 65202. Editor: Larry Harper. Managing Editor: Joe Link. 20% freelance written. Semimonthly magazine featuring Missouri farming for people who make their living at farming. Pays on acceptance. Publishes ms an average of 6 months after acceptance. Byline given. Buys first North American serial rights and all rights in Missouri. Photocopied submissions OK. Computer printout submissions acceptable; prefers letter-quality to dot-matrix. Reports in 1 month. Sample copy $2.
Nonfiction: "We use articles valuable to the Missouri farmer, discussing Missouri agriculture and people involved in it, including homemakers. Technical articles must be written in an easy-to-read style. The length depends on the topic." No corny cartoons or poems on farmers. Query. Pays $60/published page. Sometimes pays the expenses of writers on assignment.
Photos: State availability of photos. Pays $5-10 for 5x7 b&w glossy prints. Pays $60 maximum for 35mm transparencies for covers. Captions required.
Fillers: Newsbreaks. Length: 100-500 words. Pays $60/printed page.
Tips: "We're mostly staff written. Contributed material must be Missouri farming oriented and writer must know and understand Missouri agriculture. Usually articles we receive are too general."

N.D. REC MAGAZINE, N.D. Association of RECs, Box 727, Mandan ND 58554. (701)663-6501. Managing Editor: Dennis Hill. 10% freelance written. Prefers to work with published/established writers, and works with a small number of new/unpublished writers each year. Monthly magazine covering rural electric program and rural North Dakota lifestyle. "Our magazine goes to the 70,000 North Dakotans who get their electricity from rural electric cooperatives. We cover rural lifestyle, energy conservation, agriculture, farm family news and other features of importance to this predominantly agrarian state. Of course, we represent the views of our statewide association." Circ. 74,000. Pays on publication; "acceptance for assigned features." Publishes ms average of 3 months after acceptance. Byline given. Buys first North American serial rights. Submit seasonal/holiday material 6 months in advance. Simultaneous queries OK. Computer printout submissions acceptable; prefers letter-quality to dot-matrix. Reports in 2 weeks. Sample copy for 9x12 SAE with $1.37 postage.
Nonfiction: Expose (subjects of ND interest dealing with rural electric, agriculture, rural lifestyle); historical/nostalgic (ND events or people only); how-to (save energy, weatherize homes, etc.); interview/profile (on great leaders of the rural electric program, agriculture); and opinion (why family farms should be saved, etc.). No fiction that does not relate to our editorial goals. Buys 10-12 mss/year. Length: open. Pays $35-300. Pays expenses of writers on assignment.
Photos: "We need 5x7 b&w glossy prints for editorial material. Transparencies needed for cover, ag/rural scenes only—ND interest." Pays $25 maximum for 35mm color transparencies; $5 minimum for 5x7 b&w prints. Captions and identification of subjects required. Buys one-time rights.
Columns/Departments: Guest Spot: Guest opinion page, preferably about 700-850 words, about issues dealing with agriculture, rural social issues and the rural electric program. Buys 12 mss/year. Length: 700-1,000 words. Pays $35-75.

NEW ENGLAND FARM BULLETIN, New England Farm & Home Assn., Box 147, Cohasset MA 02025. Editor-in-Chief: V.A. Lipsett. Managing Editor: M.S. Maire. 5% freelance written. Works with a small number of new/unpublished writers each year. A biweekly newsletter covering New England farming. Circ. 11,000. Pays on publication. Publishes ms an average of 2 months after acceptance. Byline given. Buys first North American serial rights. Submit seasonal/holiday material 6 months in advance. Photocopied submissions OK. Computer printout submissions acceptable. Reports in 1 week.
Nonfiction: Essays (farming/agriculture); general interest; historical/nostalgic; how-to; humor; interview/profile (possibly, of New England farm); personal experience; and technical. All articles must be related to New England farming. Buys 6-12 mss/year. Query or send complete ms. Length: 500-1,000 words. Pays 10¢/word.
Tips: "We would probably require the writer to live in New England or to have an unmistakable grasp of what New England is like; must also know farmers." Especially interested in general articles on New England crops/livestocks, specific breeds, crop strains and universal agricultural activity in New England.

‡NEW ENGLAND FARMER, NEF Publishing Co., Box 391, St. Johnsbury VT 05819. (802)748-8908. Editor: Dan Hurley. Managing Editor: Thomas Gilson. 20% freelance written. Monthly tabloid covering New England agriculture for farmers. Circ. 13,052. Pays on publication. Byline given. Buys all rights makes-work-for-hire assignments. Submit seasonal/holiday material 2 months in advance. Computer printout submissions acceptable. Reports in 3 months. Free sample copy.
Nonfiction: How-to, interview/profile, opinion and technical. No romantic views of farming. "We use on-the-farm interviews with good black and white photos that combine technical information with human interest.

No poetics!'' Buys 150 mss/year. Send complete ms. Pays $40-100. Sometimes pays the expenses of writers on assignment.

Photos: Send photos with ms. Payment for photos is included in payment for articles. Reviews b&w contact sheet and 8x10 b&w prints.

Tips: ''Good, accurate stories needing minimal editing, with art, of interest to commercial farmers in New England are welcome. A frequent mistake made by writers is sending us items that do not meet our needs; generally, they'll send stories that don't have a New England focus.''

WYOMING RURAL ELECTRIC NEWS, 340 West B St., Casper WY 82601. (307)234-6152. Editor: Gale Eisenhauer. 10% freelance written. Works with a small number of new/unpublished writers each year; eager to work with new/unpublished writers. For audience of rural people, some farmers and ranchers. Monthly magazine; 20 pages. Circ. 58,500. Not copyrighted. Byline given. Pays on publication. Publishes ms an average of 3 months after acceptance. Buys first serial rights. Will consider photocopied and simultaneous submissions. Submit seasonal material 2 months in advance. Computer printout submissions acceptable; prefers letter-quality to dot-matrix. Reports in 1 month. Free sample copy with SAE and 3 first class stamps.

Nonfiction and Fiction: Wants energy-related material, ''people'' features, historical pieces about Wyoming and the West, and things of interest to Wyoming's rural people. Buys informational, humor, historical, nostalgia and photo mss. Submit complete ms. Buys 12-15 mss/year. Length for nonfiction and fiction: 1,200-1,500 words. Pays $25-50. Buys some experimental, western, humorous and historical fiction. Pays $25-50. Sometimes pays the expenses of writers on assignment.

Photos: Photos purchased with accompanying ms with additional payment, or purchased without ms. Captions required. Pays up to $50 for cover photos. Color only.

Tips: ''Study an issue or two of the magazine to become familiar with our focus and the type of freelance material we're using. Submit entire manuscript. Don't submit a regionally set story from some other part of the country and merely change the place names to Wyoming. Photos and illustrations (if appropriate) are always welcomed.''

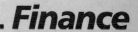

Finance

These magazines deal with banking, investment and financial management. Publications that use similar material but have a less technical slant are listed under the Consumer Business and Finance section.

‡AMERICAN BANKER, 1 State St. Plaza, New York NY 10004. (212)943-0400. Editor: William Zimmerman. Managing Editor: Robert Casey. 30% freelance written. Daily tabloid covering banking and finance for top management of banks, savings banks, savings and loans and other financial service institutions. Circ. 24,000. Pays on publication. Publishes ms an average of 1 month after acceptance. Byline given. Buys all rights. Simultaneous and previously published (depending on where published) submissions OK. Computer printout submissions acceptable; prefers letter-quality to dot-matrix. Reports in 1 month. Feature calendar on request.

Nonfiction: Patricia Stundza, features editor. Book excerpts and technical (relating to banking/finance). No ''nonbanking or nonbusiness-oriented articles—must be specific.'' Query. Length: 1,500-3,000 words. Pays $75-500. Sometimes pays the expenses of writers on assignment.

Photos: State availability of photos. Pays $100 minimum for 8x10 b&w prints. Captions and identification of subjects required. Buys one-time rights.

‡BANK LOAN OFFICERS REPORT, Warren, Gorham & Lamont, 40th Floor, One Penn Plaza, New York NY 10119. (212)971-5000. Editor: Kathy Gevlin. 50% freelance written. A monthly trade newsletter on all aspects of commercial lending. Circ. 2,500. Pays on publication. No byline given. Computer printout submissions OK. Free sample copy.

Nonfiction: How-to (market, analyze, develop, lending products); interview/profile; new product; and technical. Buys 25 mss/year. Query with or without published clips, or send complete ms. Length: 120 lines. Pays $1.20/line. Sometimes pays the expenses of writers on assignment ''when agreed upon in advance.''

‡BANK OPERATIONS REPORT, Warren, Gorham & Lamont, One Penn Plaza, New York NY 10119. (212)971-5000. Managing Editor: Philip Ruppel. 90% freelance written. Prefers to work with published/established writers, and works with a small number of new/unpublished writers each year. A monthly newsletter covering operations and technology in banking and financial services. Circ. 2,000. Pays on publication. Publishes ms an average of 2 months after acceptance. Buys all rights. Computer printout submissions OK; prefers letter-quality to dot-matrix. Free sample copy.
Nonfiction: How-to articles, case histories, practical oriented for bank operations managers" and technical. Buys 60 mss/year. Query with published clips. Length: 500-1,000 words. Pays $1.20/line. Sometimes pays the expenses of writers on assignment.

‡BANK PERSONNEL REPORT, Warren, Gorham & Lamont, One Penn Plaza, New York NY 10119. (212)971-5000. Managing Editor: Philip Ruppel. 90% freelance written. Prefers to work with published/established writers, and works with a small number of new/unpublished writers each year. A monthly newsletter covering personnel and human resources, "specifically as they relate to bankers." Circ. 2,000. Pays on publication. Publishes ms an average of 2 months after acceptance. Buys all rights. Computer printout submissions OK; prefers letter-quality to dot-matrix. Free sample copy.
Nonfiction: Technical. Buys 60 mss/year. Query with published clips. Length: 500-1,000 words. Pays $1.20/line. Sometimes pays the expenses of writers on assignment.

‡BANKING SOFTWARE REVIEW, International Computer Programs, Inc., Suite 200, 9100 Keystone Crossing, Indianapolis IN 46240. (317)844-7461. Editor: Sheila B. Cunningham. Quarterly trade magazine covering the computer software industry as it relates to financial institutions. "Editorial slant includes the selection, implementation and use of software in banks and other financial institutions. The audience comprises data processing and end-user management in medium to large financial institutions." Circ. 15,000. Pays on publication. Publishes ms an average of 2 months after acceptance. Byline sometimes given. Buys first or second serial (reprint) rights. Simultaneous and photocopied submissions OK. Query for electronic submissions. Computer printout submissions OK; prefers letter-quality to dot-matrix. Reports in 2 weeks on queries; 3 weeks on mss.
Nonfiction: How-to (successfully install and use software products), interview/profile, new product and technical. No nonsoftware realted, nonbusiness software or humorous articles. Buys 8-10 mss/year. Query with published clips. Length: 700-2,000 words. Pays $100-350 for assigned articles. Sometimes pays the expenses of writers on assignment. Sometimes pays with contributor copies, "depends on number of copies requested."
Photos: Send photos with submission. Reviews 5x7 prints. Offers no additional payment for photos accepted with ms. Identification of subjects required. Buys all rights.
Columns/Departments: Systems Review (in-depth profile of a specific software product at use in a banking environment; must include comments from a financial institution user (e.g., the benefits of the product, its use within the institution, etc.). Length: 500-700 words. Pays $50-100.

BENEFITS CANADA, Pension Fund Investment and Employee Benefit Management, Maclean Hunter Ltd., 777 Bay St., Toronto, Ontario M5W 1A7 Canada. (416)596-5958. Editor: John Milne. 5% freelance written. Works with a small number of new/unpublished writers each year. Magazine published 10 times/year covering investment management, pension fund administration and employee benefits industry for experts in the field. Circ. 14,000. Pays on acceptance. Publishes ms an average of 2 months after acceptance. Byline given. Buys first North American serial rights. Computer printout submissions acceptable; no dot-matrix. Reports in 2 weeks on queries; 1 month on mss. Free sample copy.
Nonfiction: Interview/profile and opinion (of people in pension fund, investments or employee benefits); and technical (investment or employee benefit administration). Query with published clips or send complete ms. Length: 1,000-2,200 words. Pays $125-300. Sometimes pays the expenses of writers on assignment.

‡CONSUMER LENDING REPORT, Warren Gorham & Lamont, 40th Floor, One Penn Plaza, New York NY 10119. (212)971-5000. Editor: Kathy Gevlin. 50% freelance written. A monthly trade journal covering all aspects of consumer lending. Circ. 3,000. Pays on publication. No byline given. Computer printout submissions OK; prefers letter-quality to dot-matrix. Free sample copy.
Nonfiction: How-to (market, analyze, develop lending products); interview/profile; new product and technical. Buys 25 mss/year. Query with or without published clips, or send complete ms. Length: 120 lines. Pays $1.20/line. Sometimes pays the expenses of writers on assignment "if agreed upon in advance".

EXECUTIVE FINANCIAL WOMAN, Suite 1400, 500 N. Michigan Ave., Chicago IL 60611. (312)661-1700. Editor: Lawrence R. Quinn. 10-30% freelance written. Eager to work with new/unpublished writers. Bimonthly magazine for members of the National Association of Bank Women and paid subscribers covering banking, insurance, financial planning, diversified financials, credit unions, thrifts, investment banking and other industry segments. Circ. 30,000. Publishes ms an average of 2 months after acceptance. Byline given. Buys all rights. Submit seasonal material 3 months in advance. Simultaneous queries and photocopied submissions OK. Computer printout submissions acceptable; no dot-matrix. Reports in approximately 1 month. Sample copy $4.

Nonfiction: "We are looking for articles in the general areas of financial services, career advancement, businesswomen's issues and management. Because the financial services industry is in a state of flux at present, articles on how to adapt to and benefit from this fact, both personally and professionally, are particularly apt." Query with resume and clips of published work. Length: 1,000-4,000 words. Pays variable rates.

Photos: "Photos and other graphic material can make an article more attractive to us." Captions and model release required.

Tips: "We're looking for writers who can write effectively about the people who work in the industry and combine that with hard data on how the industry is changing. We're interested in running more Q&As with top executives in the industry, both men and women."

‡THE FEDERAL CREDIT UNION, National Association of Federal Credit Unions, Suite 700, 111 N. 19th St., Arlington VA 22209. (703)522-4770. Editor: Patrick M. Keefe. 25% freelance written. "Looking for writer with financial, banking or credit union experience, but will work with inexperienced (unpublished) writers based on writing skill." Bimonthly magazine covering credit unions. Circ. 7,000. Pays on publication. Publishes ms an average of 3 months after acceptance. Byline sometimes given. Buys first North American serial rights. Submit seasonal/holiday material 5 months in advance. Simultaneous submissions OK. Query for electronic submissions. Computer printout submissions OK; prefers letter-quality to dot-matrix. Reports in 1 month.

Nonfiction: How-to, interview/profile, new product, legal, technical and credit union operations innovations. Special issues include Technology for financial institutions (summer); Purchasing (winter). Query with published clips. Length: 5,000-20,000 words. Pays $200-1,000 for assigned articles.

Photos: Send photos with submission. Reviews 35mm transparencies and 5x7 prints. Offers no additional payment for photos accepted with ms. Model releases and identification of subjects required. Buys all rights.

Tips: "Provide resume or listing of experience pertinent to subject. We seek tips on better ways for credit unions to operate." Areas most open to freelancers are "technical articles/how-to/reports on credit union operations, innovation."

‡FINANCIAL STRATEGIES, Financial Service Corporation, Suite 1900, 250 Piedmont Ave. NE, Atlanta GA 30365. (404)521-6500. Editor: S. Lee. 10-20% freelance written. Quarterly magazine covering financial planning and investments. "The audience is financial planning and financial services professionals—those who *advise* the consuming public—although there is some pass-along consumer readership." Circ. 53,000. Pays on publication. Publishes ms an average of 2 months after acceptance. Byline given. Offers 30% kill fee. Buys first rights or makes work-for-hire assignments. Submit seasonal/holiday material 4 months in advance. Simultaneous submissions OK, but not preferred. Computer printout submissions OK; prefers letter-quality to dot-matrix. Reports in 3 weeks. Free sample copy and writer's guidelines.

Nonfiction: General interest, how-to, interview/profile, new product and opinion. No "articles that are 'product promotional'—in other words about specific investment products where a company may have hired a freelancer for PR purpose." Buys 6-8 mss/year. Query. Length: 1,000-2,000 words. Pays $500-1,000 for assigned articles; pays $200-600 for unsolicited articles. Sometimes pays the expenses of writers on assignment.

Photos: Send photos with submission. Reviews contact sheets, 2x3 transparencies and 5x7 prints. Offers no additional payment for photos accepted with ms. Identification of subjects required. Buys one-time rights.

Columns/Departments: Look at the Limited (generic article on type(s) of limited partnerships); Economic Forecast (broad or specific economic forecasts as they relate to those in financial services); and The Marketplace (new business/marketing opportunities for financial planners). Buys 2-4 mss/year. Query. Length: 1,000-2,000 words. Pays $500-1,000.

FUTURES MAGAZINE, 219 Parkade, Cedar Falls IA 50613. (319)277-6341. Publisher: Merrill Oster. Editor-in-Chief: Darrell Jobman. 20% freelance written. Monthly magazine; 124-140 pages. For private, individual traders, brokers, exchange members, agribusinessmen, bankers, anyone with an interest in futures or options. Circ. 75,000. Buys all rights. Byline given. Pays on publication. Publishes ms an average of 6 months after acceptance. Photocopied submissions OK. Computer printout submissions acceptable; no dot-matrix. Reports in 1 month. Sample copy for 9x12 SAE with $1.92 postage.

Nonfiction: Articles analyzing specific commodity futures and options trading strategies; fundamental and technical analysis of individual commodities and markets; interviews, book reviews, "success" stories; and news items. Material on new legislation affecting commodities, trading, any new trading strategy ("results must be able to be substantiated"); and personalities. No "homespun" rules for trading and simplistic approaches to the commodities market. Treatment is always in-depth and broad. Informational, how-to, interview, profile, technical. "Articles should be written for a reader who has traded commodities for one year or more; should not talk down or hypothesize. Relatively complex material is acceptable." No get-rich-quick gimmicks, astrology articles or general, broad topics. "Writers must have solid knowledge of the magazine's specific emphasis and be able to communicate well." Buys 30-40 mss/year. Query or submit complete ms. Length: 1,500 words optimum. Pays $50-1,000, depending upon author's research and writing quality. "Rarely" pays the expenses of writers on assignment.

Tips: "Writers must have a solid understanding and appreciation for futures or options trading. We will have more financial and stock index features as well as new options contracts that will require special knowledge and experience. The writer has a better chance of breaking in at our publication with short articles and fillers since they can zero in on a specific idea without having to know the whole broad area we cover. Fluffy leads or trying to describe whole trading world instead of targeting key issues are frequent mistakes made by writers. More articles on trading options and on financial institution's use of futures/options will be published in 1988."

‡THE FUTURES AND OPTIONS TRADER, DeLong—Western Publishing Co., 13618 Scenic Crest Dr., Yucaipa CA 92399. (714)793-5545. Editor: Charles Kreidl. Managing Editor: Jeanne Johnson. 50% freelance written. Monthly newspaper covering futures and options. Publishes "basic descriptions of trading systems or other commodity futures information which would be useful to traders. No hype or sales-related articles." Circ. 3,000. Pays on acceptance. Publishes ms an average of 1 month after acceptance. Not copyrighted. Buys all rights. Simultaneous and photocopied submissions OK. Query for electronic submissions. Computer printout submissions OK; prefers letter-quality to dot-matrix. Sample copy for SAE with 1 first class stamp.

Nonfiction: Technical and general trading-related articles. Buys 35 mss/year. Send complete ms. Length: 250-1,000 words. Pays $10-100 for unsolicited articles.

Columns/Departments: Options Trader; Spread Trader (futures and options spread and arbitrage trading); and Index Trader (stock index trading). Buys 35 mss/year. Send complete ms. Lenght: 250-1,000 words. Pays $10-100.

Tips: "Authors should be active in the markets."

ILLINOIS BANKER, Illinois Bankers Association, Suite 1100, 205 W. Randolph, Chicago IL 60606. (312)984-1500. Director of Communications: Martha Rohlfing. Assistant Publisher: Cindy Altman. Production Assistant: Anetta Gauthier. Marketing Manager: Tiffany Renwick. 20% freelance written. Eager to work with new/unpublished writers. Monthly magazine about banking for top decision makers and executives, bank officers, title and insurance company executives, elected officials and individual subscribers interested in banking products and services. Circ. 3,000. Pays on publication. Publishes ms an average of 4 months after acceptance. Byline given. Buys first serial rights. Phone queries OK. Submit material 6 weeks prior to publication. Simultaneous submissions OK. Computer printout submissions acceptable. Free sample copy, writer's guidelines and editorial calendar.

Nonfiction: Interview (ranking government and banking leaders); personal experience (along the lines of customer relations); and technical (specific areas of banking). "The purpose of the publication is to educate, inform and guide its readers on public policy issues affecting banks, new ideas in management and operations, and banking and business trends in the Midwest. Any clear, fresh approach geared to a specific area of banking, such as agricultural bank management, credit, lending, marketing and trust is what we want." Buys 4-5 unsolicited mss/year. Send complete ms. Length: 825-3,000 words. Pays $50-100.

INDEPENDENT BANKER, Independent Bankers Association of America, Box 267, Sauk Centre MN 56378. (612)352-6546. Editor: Norman Douglas. 15% freelance written. Works with a small number of new/unpublished writers each year. Monthly magazine for the administrators of small, independent banks. Circ. 10,000. Pays on acceptance. Publishes ms an average of 3 months after acceptance. Byline given. Not copyrighted. Buys all rights. Computer printout submissions acceptable; prefers letter-quality to dot-matrix. Reports in 1 week. Sample copy and writer's guidelines for 8½x11 SASE.

Nonfiction: How-to (banking practices and procedures); interview/profile (popular small bankers); technical (bank accounting, automation); and banking trends. "Factual case histories, banker profiles or research pieces of value to bankers in the daily administration of their banks." No material that ridicules banking and finance or puff pieces on products and services. Buys 12 mss/year. Query. Length: 2,000-2,500 words. Pays $300 maximum.

Tips: "In this magazine, the emphasis is on material that will help small banks compete with large banks and large bank holding companies. We look for innovative articles on small bank operations and administration."

OTC REVIEW, OTC Review, Inc., 110 Pennsylvania Ave., Oreland PA 19075. (215)887-9000. Editor: Robert Flaherty. Executive Editor: Michael Woods. 50% freelance written. A monthly magazine covering publicly owned companies whose stocks trade in the over-the-counter market. "We are a financial magazine covering the fastest-growing securities market in the world. We study the management of companies traded over-the-counter and act as critics reviewing their performances. We aspire to be 'The Shareholder's Friend.' " Circ. 27,000. Pays on publication. Publishes ms an average of 2 months after acceptance. Byline given. Buys first rights or reprint rights. Sample copy for 8½x11 SAE with 5 first class stamps.

Nonfiction: New product and technical. Buys 30 mss/year. "We must know the writer first as we are careful about whom we publish. A letter of introduction with resumé and clips is the best way to introduce yourself. Financial writing requires specialized knowledge and a feel for people as well, which can be a tough combination to find." Query with published clips. Length: 300-1,500 words. Pays $150-750 for assigned articles; pays a lot more for investigative stories. Does not want any unsolicited articles. Offers copies or premiums for guest columns by famous money managers who are not writing for cash payments, but to showcase their ideas and approach. Pays expenses of writers on assignment.

Photos: Send photos with submission. Reviews contact sheets, negatives, transparencies and prints. Offers no additional payment for photos accepted with ms. Identification of subjects required.

Columns/Departments: Pays $25-75 for assigned items only.

Tips: "Anyone who enjoys analyzing a business and telling the story of the people who started it, or run it today, is a potential *OTC Review* contributor. But to protect our readers and ourselves, we are careful about who writes for us. Business writing is an exciting area and our stories reflect that. If a writer relies on numbers and percentages to tell his story, rather than the individuals involved, the result will be numbingly dull."

‡SAVINGS INSTITUTIONS, U.S. League of Savings Institutions, 111 E. Wacker Dr., Chicago IL 60601. (312)644-3100. Editor: Mary Nowensnick. 5% freelance written. Prefers to work with published/established writers. A monthly business magazine covering management of savings institutions. Circ. 30,000. Pays on acceptance. Publishes ms an average of 3 months after acceptance. Byline given. Buys negotiable rights. Simultaneous queries and photocopied submissions OK. Query for electronic submissions. Computer printout submissions acceptable; prefers letter-quality to dot-matrix. Reports in 2 months. Free sample copy.

Nonfiction: How-to (manage or improve operations); new products (application stories at savings institutions); and technical (financial management). No opinion or 'puff' pieces. Buys 1-3 mss/year. Query with or without published clips. Length: 3,000-8,000 words. Pays $125/published page. Pays expenses of writers on assignment.

Columns/Departments: Beth Linnen, column/department editor. Operations, Marketing, Personnel, and Secondary Mortgage Market. Buys 10 mss/year. Query with or without published clips. Length: 800-3,000 words. Pays $125/published page.

Tips: "Operations and Marketing departments are most open to freelancers."

Fishing

NATIONAL FISHERMAN, Diversified Communications, 21 Elm St., Camden ME 04843. (207)236-4342. Editor-in-Chief: James W. Fullilove. 25% freelance written. Monthly tabloid; 92 pages. For amateur and professional boat builders, commercial fishermen, armchair sailors, bureaucrats and politicians. Circ. 58,000. Pays in month of acceptance. Publishes ms an average of 2 months after acceptance. Byline given. Buys first serial rights only. Phone or letter queries advised. Photocopied submissions OK if good quality. Computer printout submissions acceptable if double spaced; no dot-matrix. Reports in 1 month. Free sample copy and writer's guidelines; mention *Writer's Market* in request.

Nonfiction: Expose, how-to, general interest, humor, historical, interview, new product, nostalgia, personal experience, opinion, photo feature, profile and technical, but all must be related to commerical fishing in some way. Especially needs articles on commercial fishing techniques (problems, solutions, large catches, busts); gear development; and marine historical and offbeat articles. No articles about sailboat racing, cruising and sportfishing. Buys approximately 35 unsolicited mss/year. Submit query or ms. Length: 100-2,000 words. Sometimes pays the expenses of writers on assignment.

Photos: State availability of photos with ms. "Photos improve chances of being used." Pays $5-15 for 5x7 or 8x10 prints; color cover photo pays $250. Buys one-time rights.

Tips: "We are soliciting historical and human interest articles in addition to business-related articles. The writer may have a better chance of breaking in at our publication with short articles and fillers because our issues are smaller these days, and we can seldom afford to give pages over to lengthy features unless they are exceptionally good. The most frequent mistake made by writers in completing an article for us is failure to provide photos or other relevant illustrations. This is a common occurrence. In some cases, lack of art jeopardizes a story's chance of being published."

PACIFIC FISHING, Special Interest Publications, 1515 NW 51st St., Seattle WA 98107. (206)789-5333. Editor: Ken Talley. 75% freelance written. Eager to work with new/unpublished writers. Monthly business magazine for commercial fishermen and others in the West Coast commercial fishing industry. *Pacific Fishing* views the fisherman as a small businessman and covers all aspects of the industry, including harvesting, processing and marketing. Circ. 10,000. Pays on publication. Publishes ms an average of 2 months after acceptance. Byline given. Offers 10-15% kill fee on assigned articles deemed unsuitable. Buys one-time rights. Queries highly recommended. Computer printout submissions acceptable; prefers letter-quality to dot-matrix. Reports in 1 month. Sample copy and writer's guidelines for SAE and 1 first class stamp.

Nonfiction: Interview/profile and technical (usually with a business hook or slant). "Articles must be concerned specifically with *commercial* fishing. We view fishermen as small businessmen and professionals who are innovative and success-oriented. To appeal to this reader, *Pacific Fishing* offers four basic features: technical, how-to articles that give fisherman hands-on tips that will make their operation more efficient and profitable; practical, well-researched business articles discussing the dollars and cents of fishing, processing and marketing; profiles of a fisherman, processor or company with emphasis on practical business and technical areas; and in-depth analysis of political, social, fisheries management and resource issues that have a direct bearing on West Coast commercial fishermen." Buys 20 mss/year. Query noting whether photos are available, and enclosing samples of previous work. Length: 1,500-3,000 words. Pays 7-10¢/word. Sometimes pays the expenses of writers on assignment.

Photos: "We need good, high-quality photography, especially color, of West Coast commercial fishing. We prefer 35mm color slides. Our rates are $125 for cover; $25-75 for inside color; $15-35 for b&w and $10 for table of contents."

Tips: "Because of the specialized nature of our audience, the editor strongly recommends that freelance writers query the magazine in writing with a proposal. We enjoy finding a writer who understands our editorial needs and satisfies those needs, a writer willing to work with an editor to make the article just right. Most of our shorter items are staff written. Our freelance budget is such that we get the most benefit by using it for feature material. The most frequent mistakes made by writers are not keeping to specified length and failing to do a complete job on statistics that may be a part of the story."

Florists, Nurseries and Landscaping

Readers of these publications are involved in growing, selling or caring for plants, flowers and trees. Magazines geared to consumers interested in gardening are listed in the Consumer Home and Garden section.

‡**FLORAL & NURSERY TIMES**, XXX Publishing Enterprises Ltd., Box 699, Wilmette IL 60091. (312)256-8777. Editor: Barbara Gilbert. 10% freelance written. A bimonthly trade journal covering wholesale and retail horticulture and floriculture. Circ. 15,000. Pays on publication. Byline given. Buys simultaneous rights. Buys seasonal/holiday material 3 months in advance. Simultaneous and photocopied submissions OK. Reports in 2 weeks. Free sample copy.

Nonfiction: General interest and technical. Buys 100 mss/year. Query with or without published clips, or send complete ms. Payment is negotiable.

Photos: State availability of photos with submission. Reviews prints. Offers no additional payment for photos accepted with ms. Captions and identification of subjects required. Buys simultaneous rights.

Columns/Departments: Care & Handling (horticultural products). Query. Payment negotiable.

FLORIST, Florists' Transworld Delivery Association, 29200 Northwestern Hwy., Box 2227, Southfield MI 48037. (313)355-9300. Editor-in-Chief: William P. Golden. Managing Editor: Susan L. Nicholas. 3% freelance written. For retail florists, floriculture growers, wholesalers, researchers and teachers. Monthly magazine; 128 pages. Circ. 25,000. Pays on acceptance. Publishes ms an average of 2 months after acceptance. Buys one-time rights. Pays 10-25% kill fee. Byline given "unless the story needs a substantial rewrite." Phone queries OK. Submit seasonal/holiday material 4 months in advance. Simultaneous, photocopied, and previously published submissions OK. Computer printout submissions acceptable; prefers letter-quality to dot-matrix. Reports in 1 month.

Nonfiction: How-to (more profitably run a retail flower shop, grow and maintain better quality flowers, etc.); general interest (to floriculture and retail floristry); and technical (on flower and plant growing, breeding, etc.). Buys 5 unsolicited mss/year. Query with published clips. Length: 1,200-3,000 words. Pays 20¢/word.

Photos: "We do not like to run stories without photos." State availability of photos with query. Pays $10-25

for 5x7 b&w photos or color transparencies. Buys one-time rights.
Tips: "Send samples of published work with query. Suggest several ideas in query letter."

FLOWER NEWS, 549 W. Randolph St., Chicago IL 60606. (312)236-8648. Editor: Lauren C. Oates. For retail, wholesale florists, floral suppliers, supply jobbers and growers. Weekly newspaper; 32 pages. Circ. 14,500. Pays on acceptance. Byline given. Submit seasonal/holiday material at least 2 months in advance. Photocopied and previously published submissions OK. Reports "immediately."
Nonfiction: How-to (increase business, set up a new shop, etc.; anything floral related without being an individual shop story); informational (general articles of interest to industry); and technical (grower stories related to industry, but not individual grower stories). Submit complete ms. Length: 3-5 typed pages. Pays $10-25.
Photos: "We do not buy individual pictures. They may be enclosed with manuscript at regular manuscript rate (b&w only)."

FLOWERS &, The beautiful magazine about the business of flowers, Suite #260, 12233 W. Olympic Blvd., Los Angeles CA 90064. (213)826-5253. Editor: Marie Moneysmith. Managing Editor: Jane Siblering. 40% freelance written. Prefers to work with published/established writers. A monthly magazine for the retail floristry industry. "We are essentially a small business magazine." Circ. approximately 28,000. Pays on acceptance. Publishes ms an average of 4 months after acceptance. Byline given. Offers 20% kill fee. Buys first North American serial rights and second serial (reprint) rights. Submit seasonal/holiday material 4 months in advance. Simultaneous submissions OK. Query for electronic submissions. Computer printout submissions acceptable; prefers letter-quality to dot-matrix. Reports in 1 month on queries; 3 months on mss. Sample copy for 9½x11 SAE; writer's guidelines for #10 SAE with 1 first class stamp.
Nonfiction: Book excerpts; historical/nostalgic; how-to (improve business, strengthen advertising, put out a newsletter, etc.); interview/profile; new product; and technical. "No articles not geared specifically to the floral industry; no articles about flowers (these are written in-house)." Buys 20 mss/year. Query with published clips. Length: 1,000-3,000 words. Pays $250-500. Sometimes pays the expenses of writers on assignment.
Photos: Reviews contact sheets and 4x5 transparencies. Offers $25-100/photo. Captions, model releases, and identification of subjects required. Buys one-time rights.
Tips: Features are most open to freelancers. Think like a small-businessowner. How can you help them solve day-to-day problems? Come up with good, timely topics, make sure they apply to retail floristry, and write a to-the-point query letter, describing the problem and how you'll approach it in an article."

GARDEN SUPPLY RETAILER, Miller Publishing, Box 2400, Minnetonka MN 55343. (612)931-0211. Editor: Kay Melchisedech Olson. 5% freelance written. Prefers to work with published/established writers but "quality work is more important than experience of the writer." Monthly magazine for lawn and garden retailers. Circ. 40,000 + . Pays on acceptance in most cases. Publishes ms an average of 3-4 months after acceptance. Buys first serial rights, and occasionally second serial (reprint) rights. Previously published submissions "in different fields" OK as long as not in overlapping fields such as hardware, nursery growers, etc. Computer printout submissions acceptable; prefers letter-quality to dot-matrix. Reports in 2 weeks on rejections, acceptance may take longer. Sample copy $2.
Nonfiction: "We aim to provide retailers with management, merchandising, tax planning and computer information. No technical advice on how to care for lawns, plants and lawn mowers. Articles should be of interest to *retailers* of garden supply products. Stories should tell retailers something about the industry that they don't already know; show them how to make more money by better merchandising or management techniques; address a concern or problem directly affecting retailers or the industry." Buys 10-15 mss/year. Send complete ms or rough draft plus clips of previously published work. Length: 800-1,000 words. Pays $150-200.
Photos: Send photos with ms. Reviews color negatives and transparencies, and 5x7 b&w prints. Captions and identification of subjects required.
Tips: "We will not consider manuscripts offered to 'overlapping' publications such as the hardware industry, nursery growers, etc. Query letters outlining an idea should include at least a partial rough draft; lists of titles are uninteresting. We seldom use filler material and would find it a nuisance to deal with freelancers for this. Freelancers submitting articles to our publication will find it increasingly difficult to get acceptance as we will be soliciting stories from industry experts and will not have much budget for general freelance material."

INTERIOR LANDSCAPE INDUSTRY, The Magazine for Designing Minds and Growing Businesses, American Nurseryman Publishing Co., Suite 545, 111 N. Canal St., Chicago IL 60606. (312)782-5505. Editor: Brent C. Marchant. 10% freelance written. Prefers to work with published/established writers. "Willing to work with freelancers as long as they can fulfill the specifics of our requirements." Monthly magazine on business and technical topics for all parties involved in interior plantings, including interior landscapers, growers and allied professionals (landscape architects, architects, and interior designers). "We take a professional approach to the material and encourage our writers to emphasize the professionalism of the industry in their writings." Circ. 10,000. Pays on publication. Publishes ms an average of 5 months after acceptance. Byline given. Buys all rights. Submit material 2 months in advance. Query for electronic submissions. Computer printout submissions acceptable; prefers letter-quality to dot-matrix. Reports in 2 weeks on queries; 1 week on mss. Sample copy for 8½x11 SASE.

Nonfiction: How-to (technical and business topics related to the audience); interview/profile (companies working in the industry); personal experience (preferably from those who work or have worked in the industry); photo feature (related to interior projects or plant producers); and technical. No shallow, consumerish-type features. Buys 30 mss/year. Query with published clips. Length: 3-15 ms pages double spaced. Pays $2/published inch. Sometimes pays expenses of writers on assignment.

Photos: Send photos with query. Reviews b&w contact sheet, negatives, and 5x7 prints; standard size or 4x5 color transparencies. Pays $5-10 for b&w; $15 for color. Identification of subjects required. Buys all rights.

Tips: "Demonstrate knowledge of the field—not just interest in it. Features, especially profiles, are most open to freelancers. We are currently increasing coverage of the design professions, specifically as they relate to interior landscaping."

Government and Public Service

Listed here are journals for people who provide governmental services, either in the employ of local, state or national governments or of franchised utilities. Journals for city managers, politicians, civil servants, firefighters, police officers, public administrators, urban transit managers and utilities managers are also listed in this section. Those for private citizens interested in politics, government and public affairs are classified with the Consumer Politics and World Affairs magazines.

AMERICAN FIRE JOURNAL, The Western Source for the Progressive Fire and Rescue Service, Fire Publications, Inc., Suite 7, 9072 E. Artesia Blvd., Bellflower CA 90706. (213)866-1664. Editor: Carol Carlsen Brooks. 75% freelance written. Works with a small number of new/unpublished writers each year. A monthly magazine covering the fire service. "Our readers are fire service professionals, generally at the management level. We try to pay respect to the long and rich traditions of America's firefighters while advocating that they keep up with the latest technology in the field." Pays on publication. Publishes ms an average of 2-9 months after acceptance. Byline given. Offers 50% kill fee, but rarely makes assignments. Buys first rights. Submit seasonal/holiday material 3 months in advance. Computer printout submissions acceptable; prefers letter-quality to dot-matrix. Reports in 1 month. Sample copy $2; writer's guidelines for SASE.

Nonfiction: How-to (on firefighting techniques); interview/profile (of various fire departments around the country); opinion (guest editorials—non-paid); photo feature (of fire scenes); and technical (on fire science). Buys 84 mss/year. Send complete ms. Length ranges from news shorts to 5-part series. Pays $1.50/published inch. Pays premiums other than cash to fire department members or training officers writing on company time about in-house programs.

Photos: Send photos with submission. Reviews contact sheets, negatives and prints (b&w prints preferred except for cover photos, which are color). Offers $4-30/photo. Captions and identification of subjects required. Buys one-time rights, then photos may be used again from morgue, though photographer may also re-sell.

Columns/Departments: Hot Flashes (news from the fire service), 100-300 words; and Innovations (new ideas in tactics, equipment uses or tricks-of-the-trade), 400-800 words (with photos). Buys 48 mss/year. Send complete ms. Pays $1.50/inch.

Fillers: Anecdotes, facts and cartoons. Buys 12/year. Length: open. Pays $1.50-5/inch.

Tips: "Generally, our contributors are members of or involved with the fire service in some way. Our readers are mostly command-level officers, and they are very knowledgeable about the subject, so writers need to be experts in their fields in order to show them something new. We're always looking for good fireground action photos with accompanying description of the fire dept. tactics used. Non-firefighters may break in with articles on management, health and fitness, stress reduction, finance, etc., if they can be related to firefighters."

CHIEF FIRE EXECUTIVE, The Management Magazine for Fire Service Leaders, Firehouse Communications, 33 Irving Place, New York NY 10003. (212)475-5400. Managing Editor: Alan J. Saly. Associate Editor: John Granito. 25% freelance written. Works with a small number of new/unpublished writers each year. A bimonthly magazine for fire service managers. Pays on publication. Publishes ms an average of 4 months after acceptance. Byline given. Offers negotiable kill fee. Buys first North American serial rights. Photocopied submissions OK. Query for electronic submissions. Computer printout submissions acceptable; prefers letter-quality to dot-matrix. Reports in 1 month. Sample copy $5 with 10x13 SAE and $1.75 postage; writer's guidelines for letter size SAE and 1 first class stamp.
Nonfiction: Book excerpts, expose, how-to, interview/profile and technical. Buys 10 mss/year. Query with published clips. Length: 250-3,000 words. Pays $0-400. May negotiate payment to writers with contributor copies or premiums rather than cash. Sometimes pays the expenses of writers on assignment.
Photos: State availability of photos with submission. Reviews contact sheets, transparencies and prints. Offers no additional payment for photos accepted with ms. Identification of subjects required. Buys one-time rights.
Tips: *Chief Fire Executive* "concentrates on the management concerns of fire service leaders, both emergency and nonemergency, and seeks out unusual, innovative techniques which can serve as an example to others."

‡**CHIEF OF POLICE MAGAZINE**, National Association of Chiefs of Police, 1100 NE 125th St., Miami FL 33161. (305)891-9800. Editor: Gerald S. Arenberg. A bimonthly trade journal for law enforcement commanders (command ranks). Estab. 1986. Circ. 10,000. Pays on acceptance. Publishes ms an average of 4-6 months after acceptance. Byline given. Full payment kill fee offered. Buys first rights. Submit seasonal/holiday material 6 months in advance. Simultaneous, photocopied and previously published submissions OK. Computer printout submissions OK. Reports in 2 weeks. Sample copy $3; writer's guidelines for #10 SAE with 1 first class stamp.
Nonfiction: General interest, historical/nostalgic, how-to, humor, inspirational, interview/profile, new product, personal experience, photo feature, religious and technical. "We want stories about interesting police cases and stories on any law enforcement subject or program that is positive in nature. No expose types. Nothing anti-police." Buys 50 mss/year. Send complete ms. Length: 600-2,000 words. Pays $25-75 for assigned articles; pays $10-50 for unsolicited articles. Sometimes (when pre-requested) pays the expenses of writers on assignment.
Photos: Send photos with submission. Reviews 5x6 prints. Offers $5-75 per photo. Captions required. Buys one-time rights.
Columns/Departments: New Police (police equipment shown and tests), 200-600 words. Buys 6 mss/year. Send complete ms. Pays $5-12.
Fillers: Anecdote and short humor. Buys 100/year. Length: 100-1600 words. Pays $5-15.
Tips: "Writers need only contact law enforcement officers right in their own areas and we would be delighted. We want to recognize good commanding officers from sergeant and above who are involved with the community. Pictures of the subject or the department are essential and can be snapshots."

FIREHOUSE MAGAZINE, Firehouse Communications, Inc., 33 Irving Pl., New York NY 10003. (212)475-5400. Editor: Dennis Smith. Executive Editor: Janet Kimmerly. 85% freelance written. Works with a small number of new/unpublished writers each year. Monthly magazine covering fire service. "*Firehouse* covers major fires nationwide, controversial issues, and trends in the fire service, the latest firefighting equipment and methods of firefighting, historical fires, firefighting history and memorabilia. Fire-related books, firefighters with interesting avocations, fire safety education, hazardous materials incidents and the emergency medical services are also covered." Circ. 115,000. Pays on publication. Publishes ms an average of 2 months after acceptance. Byline given. Buys first North American serial rights. Submit seasonal/holiday material 4 months in advance. Exclusive submissions only. Computer printout submissions acceptable; prefers letter-quality to dot-matrix. Reports ASAP. Sample copy for 8½x11 SAE with 7 first class stamps; free writer's guidelines.
Nonfiction: Book excerpts (of recent books on fire, EMS, and hazardous materials); historical/nostalgic (great fires in history, fire collectibles; the fire service of yesteryear); how-to (fight certain kinds of fires, buy and maintain equipment, run a fire department); interview/profile (of noteworthy fire leader; centers, commissioners); new product (for firefighting, EMS); personal experience (description of dramatic rescue; helping one's own fire department); photo feature (on unusual apparatus, fire collectibles, a spectacular fire); technical (on almost any phase of firefighting; techniques, equipment, training, administration); and trends (controversies in the fire service). No profiles of people or departments that are not unusual or innovative, reports of non-major fires, articles not slanted toward firefighters' interests. Buys 100 mss/year. Query with or without published clips, or send complete ms. Length: 500-3,000 words. Pays $50-400 for assigned articles; pays $50-300 for unsolicited articles. Sometimes pays the expenses of writers on assignment.
Photos: Mike Delia, photo editor. Send photos with query or ms. Pays $15-45 for 8x10 b&w prints; $30-200 for color transparencies and 8x10 color prints. Captions and identification of subjects required. Buys one-time rights.
Columns/Departments: Command Post (for fire service leaders); Training (effective methods); Book Re-

views; Fire Safety (how departments teach fire safety to the public); Communicating (PR, dispatching); Arson (efforts to combat it); Doing Things (profile of a firefighter with an interesting avocation; group projects by firefighters). Buys 50 mss/year. Query or send complete ms. Length: 750-1,000 words. Pays $100-300.
Fillers: Gags to be illustrated by cartoonist, anecdotes, short humor and newsbreaks. Buys 20/year. Length: 50-100 words. Pays $5-15.
Tips: "Read the magazine to get a full understanding of the subject matter, the writing style and the readers before sending a query or manuscript. Send photos with manuscript or indicate sources for photos. Be sure to focus articles on firefighters."

FOUNDATION NEWS, The Magazine of Philanthropy, Council on Foundations, 1828 L St. NW, Washington DC 20036. (202)466-6512. Editor: Arlie Schardt. Managing Editor: Susan Calhoun. 70% freelance written. Prefers to work with published/established writers. Bimonthly magazine covering the world of philanthropy, nonprofit organizations and their relation to current events. Read by staff and executives of foundations, corporations, hospitals, colleges and universities and various nonprofit organizations. Circ. 22,000. Pays on acceptance. Publishes ms an average of 3 months after acceptance. Byline given. Offers negotiable kill fee. Not copyrighted. Buys all rights. Submit seasonal/holiday material 5 months in advance. Simultaneous queries and previously published submissions OK. Computer printout submissions acceptable; prefers letter-quality to dot-matrix. Reports in 6 weeks.
Nonfiction: Book excerpts, expose, general interest, historical/nostalgic, how-to, humor, interview/profile and photo feature. Special issue on the role of religion in American life and how religious giving affects social welfare, culture, health conditions, etc. Buys 25 mss/year. Submit written query; not telephone calls. Length: 500-3,000 words. Pays $200-2,000. Pays expenses of writers on assignment.
Photos: State availability of photos. Pays negotiable rates for b&w contact sheet and prints. Captions and identification of subjects required. Buys one-time rights; "some rare requests for second use."
Columns/Departments: Buys 12 mss/year. Query. Length: 900-1,400 words. Pays $100-750.
Tips: "We have a great interest in working with writers familiar with the nonprofit sector."

‡GRASSROOTS FUNDRAISING JOURNAL, Klein & Honig, Partnership, #206, 517 Union Ave., Knoxville TN 37902. Editors: Kim Klein and Lisa Honig. A bimonthly newsletter covering grassroots fund raising for small social change and social service nonprofit organizations. Circ. 3,000. Pays on publication. Byline given. Buys first serial rights. Submit seasonal/holiday material 2 months in advance. Simultaneous queries, and simultaneous, photocopied, and (occasionally) previously published submissions OK. Reports in 2 weeks on queries; 2 months on mss. Sample copy $3.
Nonfiction: Book excerpts; how-to (all fund raising strategies); and personal experience (doing fund raising). Buys 10 mss/year. Query. Length: 2,000-20,000 words. Pays $35 minimum.

LAW AND ORDER, Hendon Co., 1000 Skokie Blvd., Wilmette IL 60091. (312)256-8555. Editor: Bruce W. Cameron. 90% freelance written. Prefers to work with published/established writers. Monthly magazine covering the administration and operation of law enforcement agencies, directed to police chiefs and supervisors. Circ. 26,000. Pays on publication. Publishes ms an average of 6 months after acceptance. Byline given. Buys first North American serial rights. Submit seasonal/holiday material 3 months in advance. Photocopied submissions OK. No simultaneous queries. Computer printout submissions acceptable; prefers letter-quality to dot-matrix. Reports in 1 month. Sample copy for 9x12 SAE.
Nonfiction: General police interest; how-to (do specific police assignments); new product (how applied in police operation); and technical (specific police operation). Special issues include Buyers Guide (January); Communications (February); Training (March); International (April); Administration (May); Small Departments (June); Police Science (July); Equipment (August); Weapons (September); Mobile Patrol (November); and Working with Youth (December). No articles dealing with courts (legal field) or convicted prisoners. No nostalgic, financial, travel or recreational material. Buys 20-30 mss/year. Length: 2,000-3,000 words. Pays $100-300.
Photos: Send photos with ms. Reviews transparencies and prints. Identification of subjects required. Buys all rights.
Tips: "*L&O* is a respected magazine that provides up-to-date information that chiefs can use. Writers must know their subject as it applies to this field. Case histories are well received. We are upgrading quality for editorial—stories *must* show some understanding of the law enforcement field. A frequent mistake is not getting photographs to accompany article."

MARINE CORPS GAZETTE, Professional Magazine for United States Marines, Marine Corps Association, Box 1775, Quantico VA 22134. (703)640-6161. Editor: Col. John E. Greenwood, USMC (Ret.). Managing Editor: Joseph D. Dodd. Less than 5% freelance written. "Will continue to welcome and respond to queries, but will be selective due to large backlog from Marine authors." Monthly magazine. "*Gazette* serves as a forum in which serving Marine officers exchange ideas and viewpoints on professional military matters." Circ. 33,000. Pays on publication. Publishes ms an average of 6 months after acceptance. Byline given. Buys all rights. Computer printout submissions acceptable. Reports in 3 weeks on queries; 2 months on mss. Sample copy $1; free writer's guidelines.

Nonfiction: Historical/nostalgic (Marine Corps operations only); and technical (Marine Corps related equipment). "The magazine is a professional journal oriented toward hard skills, factual treatment, technical detail—no market for lightweight puff pieces—analysis of doctrine, lessons learned goes well. A very strong Marine Corps background and influence are normally prerequisites for publication." Buys 4-5 mss/year from non-Marine Corps sources. Query or send complete ms. Length: 2,500-5,000 words. Pays $200-400; short features, $50-100.

Photos: "We welcome photos and charts." Payment for illustrative material included in payment forms. "Photos need not be original, nor have been taken by the author, but they must support the article."

Columns/Departments: Book Reviews (of interest and importance to Marines); and Ideas and Issues (an assortment of topical articles, e.g., opinion or argument, ideas of better ways to accomplish tasks, reports on weapons and equipment, strategies and tactics, etc., also short vignettes on history of Corps). Buys 60 book reviews and 120 Ideas and Issues mss/year, most from Marines. Query. Length: 500-1,500 words. Pays $25-50 plus book for 750-word book review; $50-100 for Ideas and Issues.

Tips: "Book reviews or short articles (500-1,500 words) on Marine Corps related hardware or technological development are the best way to break in. Sections/departments most open to freelancers are Book Reviews and Ideas & Issues sections—query first. We are not much of a market for those outside U.S. Marine Corps or who are not closely associated with current Marine activities."

PLANNING, American Planning Association, 1313 E. 60th St., Chicago IL 60637. (312)955-9100. Editor: Sylvia Lewis. 25% freelance written. Emphasizes urban planning for adult, college-educated readers who are regional and urban planners in city, state or federal agencies or in private business or university faculty or students. Monthly. Circ. 25,000. Pays on publication. Publishes ms an average of 3 months after acceptance. Buys all rights or first rights. Byline given. Photocopied and previously published submissions OK. Computer printout submissions acceptable; prefers letter-quality to dot-matrix. Reports in 2 months. Free sample copy and writer's guidelines.

Nonfiction: Expose (on government or business, but on topics related to planning, housing, land use, zoning); general interest (trend stories on cities, land use, government); historical (historic preservation); how-to (successful government or citizen efforts in planning; innovations; concepts that have been applied); and technical (detailed articles on the nitty-gritty of planning, zoning, transportation but no footnotes or mathematical models). Also needs news stories up to 500 words. "It's best to query with a fairly detailed, one-page letter. We'll consider any article that's well written and relevant to our audience. Articles have a better chance if they are timely and related to planning and land use and if they appeal to a national audience. All articles should be written in magazine feature style." Buys 2 features and 1 news story/issue. Length: 500-2,000 words. Pays $50-600. "We pay freelance writers and photographers only, not planners."

Photos: "We prefer that authors supply their own photos, but we sometimes take our own or arrange for them in other ways." State availability of photos. Pays $25 minimum for 8x10 matte or glossy prints and $200 for 4-color cover photos. Captions preferred. Buys one-time rights.

POLICE, Hare Publications, 6200 Yarrow Dr., Carlsbad CA 92008. (619)438-2511. Editor: F. McKeen Thompson. Associate Editor: Alexandra Rockey. 100% freelance written. A monthly magazine covering topics related to law enforcement officials. "Our audience is strictly law enforcement officials, detectives and specialized enforcement divisions." Circ. 40,000. Pays on acceptance. Publishes ms an average of 6 months after acceptance. Buys all rights (returned to author 45 days after publication). Submit theme material 3 months in advance. Simultaneous and photocopied submissions OK. Computer printout submissions acceptable. Reports in 2 months. Sample copy $2; writer's guidelines for business size SAE with 2 first class stamps.

Nonfiction: General interest, expose, humor, inspirational, interview/profile, new product, opinion, personal experience and technical. Buys 60 mss/year. Query or send complete ms. Length: 2,000-4,000 words. Pays $200-450 for assigned articles; $200-250 for unsolicited articles.

Photos: Send photos with submission. Captions required. Buys all rights.

Columns/Departments: The Beat (entertainment section—humor, fiction, first-person drama, professional tips); The Arsenal (weapons and ammunition used in the line of duty); and Officer Survival (theories, skills and techniques used by offices for street survival). Buys 75 mss/year. Query or send complete ms. Length: 1,500-2,500 words. Pays $25-175

Tips: "You are writing for police officers—people who live a dangerous and stressful life. Study the editorial calendar—yours for the asking—and come up with an idea that fits into a specific issue. Present the idea in a query outlining exactly what you intend to cover and why it will fit into that particular month. We are actively seeking talented writers."

POLICE TIMES, American Police Academy, 1100 NE 125th St., North Miami FL 33161. (305)891-1700. Editor: Gerald Arenberg. Managing Editor: Donna Shepherd. 80% freelance written. Eager to work with new/unpublished writers. A monthly tabloid covering "law enforcement (general topics) for men and women engaged in law enforcement and private security, and citizens who are law and order concerned.'' Circ. 55,000. Pays on acceptance. Publishes ms an average of 3-6 months after acceptance. Byline given. Offers 50% kill fee. Buys second serial (reprint) rights. Submit seasonal/holiday material 4 months in advance. Simultaneous, photo-copied and previously published submissions OK. Computer printout submissions acceptable; prefers letter-quality to dot-matrix. Sample copy for 8x11 SAE with 3 first class stamps; writer's guidelines for SAE with 1 first class stamp.

Nonfiction: Book excerpts; essays (on police science); exposé (police corruption); general interest; histori-cal/nostalgic; how-to; humor; interview/profile; new product; personal experience (with police); photo feature; and technical—all police-related. "We produce a special edition on police killed in the line of duty. It is mailed May 15 so copy must arrive six months in advance. Photos required." No anti-police materials. Buys 50 mss/year. Send complete ms. Length: 200-3,000 words. Pays $5-50 for assigned articles; pays $5-25 for unsolicited articles. Sometimes pays the expenses of writers on assignment.

Photos: Send photos with submission. Reviews 5x6 prints. Offers $5-25/photo. Identification of subjects re-quired. Buys all rights.

Columns/Departments: Legal Cases (lawsuits involving police actions); New Products (new items related to police services); and Awards (police heroism acts). Buys variable number of mss/year. Send complete ms. Length: 200-1,000 words. Pays $5-25.

Fillers: Anecdotes, facts, newsbreaks and short humor. Buys 100/year. Length: 50-100 words. Pays $5-10. Fillers are usually humorous stories about police officer and citizen situations. Special stories on police cases, public corruptions, etc. are most open to freelancers.

SUPERINTENDENT'S PROFILE & POCKET EQUIPMENT DIRECTORY, Profile Publications, 220 Central Ave., Box 43, Dunkirk NY 14048. (716)366-4774. Editor: Robert Dyment. 60% freelance written. Prefers to work with published/established writers. Monthly magazine covering "outstanding" town, village, county and city highway superintendents and Department of Public Works directors throughout New York state only. Circ. 2,500. Publishes ms an average of 4 months after acceptance. Pays within 90 days. Byline given for ex-cellent material. Buys first serial rights. Submit seasonal/holiday material 3 months in advance. Simultaneous queries OK. Computer printout submissions acceptable; no dot-matrix. Reports in 2 weeks on queries; 1 month on mss. Sample copy for 9x12 SAE and 4 first class stamps.

Nonfiction: John Powers, articles editor. Interview/profile (of a highway superintendent or DPW director in NY state who has improved department operations through unique methods or equipment); and technical. Spe-cial issues include winter maintenance profiles. No fiction. Buys 20 mss/year. Query. Length: 1,500-2,000 words. Pays $125 for a full-length ms. "Pays more for excellent material. All manuscripts will be edited to fit our format and space limitations." Sometimes pays the expenses of writers on assignment.

Photos: John Powers, photo editor. State availability of photos. Pays $5-10 for b&w contact sheets; reviews 5x7 prints. Captions and identification of subjects required. Buys one-time rights.

Poetry: Buys poetry if it pertains to highway departments. Pays $5-15.

Tips: "We are a widely read and highly respected state-wide magazine, and although we can't pay high rates, we expect quality work. Too many freelance writers are going for the expose rather than the meat and potato type articles that will help readers. We use more major features than fillers. Frequently writers don't read sam-ple copies first. We will be purchasing more material because our page numbers are increasing."

TRANSACTION/SOCIETY, Rutgers University, New Brunswick NJ 08903. (201)932-2280, ext. 83. Editor: Irving Louis Horowitz. 10% freelance written. Prefers to work with published/established writers. For social scientists (policymakers with training in sociology, political issues and economics). Published every 2 months. Circ. 45,000. Buys all rights. Byline given. Pays on publication. Publishes ms an average of 6 months after ac-ceptance. Will consider photocopied submissions. No simultaneous submissions. Electronic submissions OK; "manual provided to authors." Computer printout submissions acceptable; prefers letter-quality to dot-matrix. Reports in 1 month. Query. Free sample copy and writer's guidelines.

Nonfiction: Michele Teitelbaum, articles editor. "Articles of wide interest in areas of specific interest to the social science community. Must have an awareness of problems and issues in education, population and urban-ization that are not widely reported. Articles on overpopulation, terrorism, international organizations. No general think pieces." Payment for articles is made only if done on assignment. *No payment for unsolicited ar-ticles.*

Photos: Joan DuFault, photo editor. Pays $200 for photographic essays done on assignment or accepted for publication.

Tips: "Submit an article on a thoroughly unique subject, written with good literary quality. Present new ideas and research findings in a readable and useful manner. A frequent mistake is writing to satisfy a journal, rather than the intrinsic requirements of the story itself. Avoid posturing and editorializing."

VICTIMOLOGY: An International Journal, 5535 Lee Hwy., Arlington VA 22207. (703)536-1750. Editor-in-Chief: Emilio C. Viano. "We are the only magazine specifically focusing on the victim, on the dynamics of victimization; for social scientists, criminal justice professionals and practitioners, social workers and volunteer and professional groups engaged in prevention of victimization and in offering assistance to victims of rape, spouse abuse, child abuse, incest, abuse of the elderly, natural disasters, etc." Quarterly magazine. Circ. 2,500. Pays on publication. Buys all rights. Byline given. Reports in 2 months. Sample copy $5; free writer's guidelines.

Nonfiction: Expose, historical, how-to, informational, interview, personal experience, profile, research and technical. Buys 10 mss/issue. Query. Length: 500-5,000 words. Pays $50-150.

Photos: Purchased with accompanying ms. Captions required. Send contact sheet. Pays $15-50 for 5x7 or 8x10 b&w glossy prints.

Poetry: Avant-garde, free verse, light verse and traditional. Length: 30 lines maximum. Pays $10-25.

Tips: "Focus on what is being researched and discovered on the victim, the victim/offender relationship, treatment of the offender, the bystander/witness, preventive measures, and what is being done in the areas of service to the victims of rape, spouse abuse, neglect and occupational and environmental hazards and the elderly."

YOUR VIRGINIA STATE TROOPER MAGAZINE, Box 2189, Springfield VA 22152. (703)451-2524. Editor: Kerian Bunch. 90% freelance written. Biannual magazine covering police topics for troopers, police, libraries, legislators and businesses. Circ. 10,000. Pays on acceptance. Publishes ms an average of 3 months after acceptance. Byline given. Buys first North American serial rights and all rights on assignments. Submit seasonal/holiday material 2 months in advance. Simultaneous and photocopied submissions OK. Computer printout submissions acceptable; prefers letter-quality to dot-matrix. Reports in 2 months.

Nonfiction: Book excerpts; expose (consumer or police-related); general interest; nutrition/health; historical/ nostalgic; how-to (energy saving); humor; interview/profile (notable police figures); opinion; personal experience; technical (radar); and other (recreation). Buys 40-45 mss/year. Query with clips or send complete ms. Length: 2,500 words. Pays $250 maximum/article (10¢/word). Sometimes pays expenses of writers on assignment.

Photos: Send photos with ms. Pays $25 maximum/5x7 b&w glossy print. Captions and model release required. Buys one-time rights.

Fiction: Adventure, humorous, mystery, novel excerpts and suspense. Buys 4 mss/year. Send complete ms. Length: 2,500 words minimum. Pays $250 maximum (10¢/word) on acceptance.

Tips: "The writer may have a better chance of breaking in at our publication with short articles and fillers due to space limitations."

THE WASHINGTON TROOPER, Grimm Press and Publishing Co., Inc. Communications Dateline, Box 1523, Longview WA 98632. (206)577-8598. Editor: Ron Collins. Managing Editor: Bruce D. Grimm. Send queries only to editor, *The Washington Trooper*, Box 916, Kelso WA 98626. 10% freelance written. Works with a small number of new/unpublished writers each year. A quarterly law enforcement magazine covering legislation, traffic and highway safety "for members of the Washington State Patrol Troopers Association, state legislators, educators, court officials, and civic minded individuals in the State of Washington." Circ. 3,500. Pays on publication. Publishes ms an average of 3 months after acceptance. Byline given. Buys all rights. Submit seasonal/holiday material 6 months in advance. Simultaneous queries and submissions OK. Computer printout submissions OK; prefers letter-quality to dot-matrix. Reports in 6 weeks on queries; 3 months on mss. Sample copy $3.50; writer's guidelines for #10 SAE and 39¢ postage.

Nonfiction: Marjorie F. Grimm, articles editor. Exposé (on state of Washington government or traffic); interview/profile (Washington state troopers); new products; opinion (on law enforcement or traffic and highway safety); and technical (police equipment). Buys 12-20 mss/year. Query or send complete ms. Length: 500-3,500 words. Pays $5-75.

Photos: State availability of photos with query letter or manuscript. Reviews contact sheets and transparencies. Pays $5-25. Model releases, and identification of subjects required.

Fillers: Short humor and newsbreaks. Buys 15/year. Length: 50-250 words. Pays $5-15.

Tips: "Writers must be familiar with goals and objectives of the Washington State Patrol and with law enforcement in general in the Pacific Northwest. The areas of our publication that are most open to freelancers are feature articles depicting life in the State of Washington familiar to a Washington state trooper."

_ Groceries and Food Products

In this section are journals for grocers, food wholesalers, processors, warehouse owners, caterers, institutional managers and suppliers of grocery store equipment.

‡**AMERICAN AUTOMATIC MERCHANDISER**, HBJ Publications, Cleveland OH 44130. (216)243-8100. Editor: David R. Stone. Managing Editor: Mark L. Dlugoss. 5% freelance written. Prefers to work with published/established writers. A monthly trade journal covering vending machines, contract foodservice and office coffee services. "*AAM*'s readers are owners and managers of these companies; we profile successful companies and report on market trends." Circ. 12,500. Pays on acceptance. Publishes ms an average of 3 months after acceptance. Byline sometimes given. Buys first North American serial rights, all rights or makes work-for-hire assignments. Submit seasonal/holiday material 4 months in advance. Photocopied submissions OK. Computer printout submissions OK; prefers letter-quality. Reports in 1 month. Free sample copy.
Nonfiction: Buys 30 mss/year. Query. Length: 1,000-6,000 words. Pays $150-600. Sometimes pays the expenses of writers on assignment.
Photos: Send photos with submission. Reviews contact sheets, transparencies and prints. Offers $50 maximum per photo. Buys all rights.

CANADIAN GROCER, Maclean-Hunter Ltd., Maclean Hunter Building, 777 Bay St., Toronto, Ontario M5W 1A7 Canada. (416)596-5772. Editor: George H. Condon. 10% freelance written. Prefers to work with published/established writers. Monthly magazine about supermarketing and food retailing for Canadian chain and independent food store managers, owners, buyers, executives, food brokers, food processors and manufacturers. Circ 18,000. Pays on publication. Publishes ms an average of 2 months after acceptance. Byline given. Buys first Canadian rights. Phone queries OK. Submit seasonal material 2 months in advance. Previously published submissions OK. Computer printout submissions acceptable; prefers letter-quality to dot-matrix. Reports in 1 month. Sample copy $4.
Nonfiction: Interview (Canadian trendsetters in marketing, finance or food distribution); technical (store operations, equipment and finance); and news features on supermarkets. "Freelancers should be well versed on the supermarket industry. We don't want unsolicited material. Writers with business and/or finance expertise are preferred. Know the retail food industry and be able to write concisely and accurately on subjects relevant to our readers: food store managers, senior corporate executives, etc. A good example of an article would be 'How a Six Store Chain of Supermarkets Improved Profits 2% and Kept Customers Coming.' " Buys 14 mss/year. Query with clips of previously published work. Pays 21¢/word. Sometimes pays the expenses of writers on assignment.
Photos: State availability of photos. Pays $ 10-25 for 8x10 b&w glossy prints. Captions preferred. Buys one-time rights.
Tips: "Suitable writers will be familiar with sales per square foot, merchandising mixes and direct product profitability."

FANCY FOOD, The Business Magazine for Specialty Foods, Confections & Wine, (formerly *Fancy Food & Candy*), Talcott Publishing, Inc., 1414 Merchandise Mart, Chicago IL 60654. (312)824-7440. Editor: Elizabeth Faulkner. 75% freelance written. Works with a small number of new/unpublished writers each year. A trade magazine covering specialty food and confections. Published 9 times a year. Circ. 24,000. Pays on publication. Publishes an average of 2 months after acceptance. Byline given sometimes. Buys all rights. Submit seasonal/holiday material 2 months in advance. Computer printout submissions acceptable; prefers letter-quality to dot-matrix. Sample copy $4.
Nonfiction: Interview/profile and new product. Buys 50 mss/year. Query with published clips. Length: 1,500-4,000 words. Pays $200-250 for assigned articles. Sometimes pays expenses of writers on assignment.
Photos: Send photos with submission. Reviews transparencies and prints. Offers no additional payment other than for film and development for photos accepted with ms. Captions and identification of subjects required. Buys all rights.
Columns/Departments: Points East & West, Wine & Spirits Review, Coffee, Industry News and Buyer's Mart. Buys 24 mss/year. Query with published clips. Length: 2,000-3,000 words. Pays $100-200.
Tips: "Business reporters with knowlege of food and contacts among gourmet retailers are sought. Multi-source product category overviews are most open to freelancers."

‡**FLORIDA GROCER**, Florida Grocer Publications, Inc., Box 430760, South Miami FL 33143. (305)441-1138. Editor: Dennis Kane. 5% freelance written. "*Florida Grocer* is a 16,000 circulation monthly trade newspaper, serving members of the Florida food industry. Our publication is edited for chain and independent food store owners and operators as well as members of allied industries." Circ. 16,000. Pays on acceptance. Byline given. Buys all rights. Submit seasonal/holiday material 6 months in advance. Sample copy for #10 SAE with $1.50 postage.
Nonfiction: Book excerpts, expose, general interest, humor, features on supermarkets and their owners, new product, new equipment, photo feature and video. Buys variable number of mss/year. Query with or without published clips, or send complete ms. Length: varies. Payment varies. Sometimes pays the expenses of writers on assignment.
Photos: State availability of photos with submission. Terms for payment on photos "included in terms of payment for assignment."

Tips: "We prefer feature articles on new stores (grand openings, etc.), store owners, operators; Florida based food manufacturers, brokers, whole sales, distributors, etc. We also publish a section in Spanish and also welcome the above types of materials in Spanish (Cuban)."

FOOD PEOPLE, Olson Publications, Inc., Box 1208, Woodstock GA 30188. (404)928-8994. Editor: Warren B. Causey. 50% freelance written. Prefers to work with published/established writers, and works with a small number of new/unpublished writers each year. Always willing to consider new writers, but they must have a basic command of their craft. Monthly tabloid covering the retail food industry. Circ. 30,000. Pays on publication. Publishes ms an average 1 month after acceptance. Byline given. Buys all rights. Will reassign subsidiary rights after publication and upon request. Submit seasonal/holiday material 6 weeks in advance. Photocopied submissions OK. Query for electronic submissions. Computer printout submissions acceptable; prefers letter-quality to dot-matrix. Computer-modem submissions encouraged. Reports in 1 month.
Nonfiction: Interview/profile (of major food industry figures); photo feature (of food industry conventions, expos and meetings); and news of store/warehouse openings, ad campaigns, marketing strategies, important new products and services. "We would like to receive feature articles about people and companies that illustrate trends in the food industry. Articles should be informative, tone is upbeat. Do not send recipes or how-to shop articles; we cover food as a *business*." Buys 120-180 mss/year. Query or send complete ms. Length: 200-1,000 words. Pays $2/published inch minimum. Usually pays the expenses of writers on assignment.
Photos: "Photos of people. Photos of displays, or store layouts, etc., that illustrate points made in article are good, too. But stay away from storefront shots." State availability of photos with query or send photos with ms. Pays $10 plus expenses for b&w contact sheets and 5x7 b&w prints; and $30 plus expenses for color transparencies. Captions required. Buys one-time rights.
Columns/Departments: Company News, People, New Products, and Morsels. . . a Smorgasbord of Tidbits in the national stew." Send complete ms. Pays $10.
Tips: "Begin with an area news event—store openings, new promotions. Write that as news, then go further to examine the consequences. We are staffing more conventions, so writers shoud concentrate on features about people, companies, trends, new products, innovations in the food industry in their geographic areas. Talk with decision makers to get 'hows' and 'whys.' Because we are news-oriented, we have short deadlines for a monthly. We look for contributors who work well, quickly and who *always* deliver."

HEALTH FOODS BUSINESS, Howmark Publishing Corp., 567 Morris Ave., Elizabeth NJ 07208. (201)353-7373. Editor: Mary Jane Dittman. Editorial Director: Alan Richman. 40% freelance written. Eager to work with new/unpublished writers if competent and reliable. For owners and managers of health food stores. Monthly magazine; 75-100 pages. Circ. 11,000. Pays on publication. Publishes ms an average of 4 months after acceptance. Byline given "if story quality warrants it." Buys first serial rights and first North American serial rights; "also exclusive rights in our trade field." Phone queries OK. "Query us about a good health food store in your area. We use many store profile stories." Simultaneous and photocopied submissions OK if exclusive to their field. Previously published work OK, but please indicate where and when material appeared previously. Computer printout submissions acceptable if double-spaced and in upper and lower case; no dot-matrix. Reports in 1 month. Sample copy $5; plus $2 for postage and handling.
Nonfiction: Expose (government hassling with health food industry); how-to (unique or successful retail operators); informational (how or why a product works; technical aspects must be clear to laymen); historical (natural food use); interview (must be prominent person in industry or closely related to the health food industry or well-known or prominent person in any arena who has undertaken a natural diet/lifestyle;); and photo feature (any unusual subject related to the retailer's interests). Buys 1-2 mss/issue. Query for interview and photo features. Will consider complete ms in other categories. Length: long enough to tell the whole story without padding. Pays $50 and up for feature stories, $75 and up for store profiles.
Photos: "Most articles must have photos included"; negatives and contact sheet OK. Captions required. No additional payment.
Tips: "A writer may find that submitting a letter with a sample article he/she believes to be closely related to articles read in our publication is the most expedient way to determine the appropriateness of his/her skills and expertise."

HEALTH FOODS RETAILING, Communication Channels, Inc., 6255 Barfield Rd., Atlanta GA 30328. (404)256-9800. Editor: Jerelyn Jordan. 25% freelance written. Works with a small number of new/unpublished writers each year, and is eager to work with new/unpublished writers. A monthly magazine covering the health and natural foods industry primarily for retailers. Circ. 11,017. Pays on publication. Publishes ms an average of 2 months after acceptance. Makes work-for-hire assignments. Submit seasonal/holiday material 6 months in advance. Computer printout submissions acceptable; prefers letter-quality to dot-matrix. Reports in 3 weeks. Free sample copy.
Nonfiction: Interview/profile on retail operations in the health and natural food industry. "We do not use features on manufacturing firms." Buys 15 mss/year. Query with published clips. Length: 500-2,000 words. Pays

$75-250 for assigned articles; pays $50-160 for unsolicited articles. Sometimes pays expenses of writers on assignment.

Photos: State availability of photos with submissions. Reviews contact sheets and 2x2 transparencies. Offers $10-20/photo (interior use, not cover). Model releases and identification of subjects required. Buys one-time rights.

Tips: "An understanding of how to communicate basic retailing concepts is more important than a knowledge of the health and natural foods industry. Strong journalistic talent should be a given. It's better to query first, rather than sending a full manuscript. Our major feature section provides the only area for freelance participation; all else is generated by staff. Contributors should realize that as a business publication, *Health Foods Retailing* is more apt to use articles which support assertions with strong, preferably statistical, analysis. We also require generic articles, not promotional efforts for individual operations."

PRODUCE NEWS, 2185 Lemoine Ave., Fort Lee NJ 07024. Editor: Gordon Hochberg. 10-15% freelance written. Works with a small number of new/unpublished writers each year. For commercial growers and shippers, receivers and distributors of fresh fruits and vegetables, including chain store produce buyers and merchandisers. Weekly. Circ. 9,500. Pays on publication. Publishes ms an average of 1 month after acceptance. Deadline is Tuesday afternoon before Thursday press day. Computer printout submissions acceptable. Free sample copy and writer's guidelines.

Nonfiction: News stories (about the produce industry). Buys profiles, spot news, coverage of successful business operations and articles on merchandising techniques. Query. Pays minimum of $1/column inch for original material. Sometimes pays the expenses of writers on assignment.

Photos: B&w glossies. Pays $8-10 for each one used.

Tips: "Stories should be trade-oriented, not consumer-oriented. As our circulation grows in the next year, we are interested in stories and news articles from all fresh fruit-growing areas of the country."

PROGRESSIVE GROCER, Progressive Grocer Co., 1351 Washington Blvd., Stamford CT 06902. (203)325-3500. Editor: Ed Walzer. Associate Editorial Director: Michael Sansolo. Editorial Director: Larry Schaeffer. 3% freelance written. Monthly magazine covering the retail food industry. "We provide analyses of trends, merchandising ideas and innovations, statistical data, company profiles—all retailer oriented. Audience runs gamut from top executive to department managers." Circ. 87,000. Pays on publication. Publishes ms an average of 3 months after acceptance. Byline given. Buys all rights. Computer printout submissions acceptable; no dot-matrix. Submit seasonal/holiday material 3 months in advance. Simultaneous queries and photocopied submissions OK. Reports in 1 month. Free sample copy.

Nonfiction: General interest, how-to (set up or operate a particular department in supermarket); interview/profile (executive level); and photo feature (interesting store format). No puff pieces or anything in excess of 8 typewritten, double-spaced pages. Buys 3 mss/year. Send complete ms. Length: 500-1,500 words. Pays $200 maximum magazine page. Sometimes pays expenses of writers on assignment.

Photos: State availability of photos with ms. Pays $100 maximum for b&w contact sheets; $300 maximum for color contact sheets. Captions, model release and identification of subjects required.

QUICK FROZEN FOODS INTERNATIONAL, E.W. Williams Publishing Co., 80 8th Ave., New York NY 10011. (212)989-1101. Editor: John M. Saulnier. 20% freelance written. Works with a small number of new/unpublished writers each year. Quarterly magazine covering frozen foods around the world—"every phase of frozen food manufacture, retailing, food service, brokerage, transport, warehousing, merchandising. Especially interested in stories from Europe, Asia and emerging nations." Circ. 13,500. Pays on publication. Publishes ms an average of 3 months after acceptance. Byline given. Offers kill fee; "if satisfactory, we will pay promised amount. If bungled, half." Buys all rights, but will relinquish any rights requested. Submit seasonal/holiday material 6 months in advance. Photocopied submissions OK "if not under submission elsewhere." Computer printout submissions acceptable; prefers letter-quality to dot-matrix. Sample copy $5.

Nonfiction: Book excerpts; general interest; historical/nostalgic; interview/profile; new product (from overseas); personal experience; photo feature; technical; and travel. No articles peripheral to frozen food industry such as taxes, insurance, government regulation, safety, etc. Buys 20-30 mss/year. Query or send complete ms. Length: 500-4,000 words. Pays 5¢/word or by arrangement. "We will reimburse postage on articles ordered from overseas." Sometimes pays the expenses of writers on assignment.

Photos: "We prefer photos with all articles." State availability of photos or send photos with accompanying ms. Pays $7 for 5x7 b&w prints (contact sheet if many shots). Captions and identification of subject required. Buys all rights. Release on request.

Columns/Departments: News or analysis of frozen foods abroad. Buys 20 columns/year. Query. Length: 500-1,500 words. Pays by arrangement.

Fillers: Newsbreaks. Length: 100-500 words. Pays $5-20.

Tips: "We are primarily interested in feature materials, (1,000-3,000 words with pictures). We plan to devote more space to frozen food company developments in Pacific Rim countries. Stories on frozen food merchandising and retailing in foreign supermarket chains in Europe, Japan and Australia/New Zealand are welcome. National frozen food prouduction profiles are also in demand worldwide. A frequent mistake is submitting general interest material instead of specific industry-related stories."

‡**SEAFOOD LEADER**, Waterfront Press Co., 1115 NW 45th St., Seattle WA 98107. (206)789-6506. Editor: Peter Redmayne. Managing Editor: Jody Brannon. 20% freelance written. Works with a small number of new/unpublished writers each year. A trade journal on the seafood business published 5 times/year. Circ. 11,700. Pays on publication. Publishes ms an average of 3 months after acceptance. Byline given. Buys first rights and second serial (reprint) rights. Submit seasonal/holiday material 3 months in advance. Simultaneous, photocopied and previously published submissions OK. Query for electronic submissions. Computer printout submissions OK. Reports in 1 month on queries; 2 months on mss. Sample copy $3 with 8½x11 SAE.
Nonfiction: General seafood interest, marketing/business, historical/nostalgic, interview/profile, opinion and photo feature. Each of *Seafood Leader's* five issues has a slant: international (spring), foodservice (summer), merchandising (autumn), shrimp and aquaculture (winter) and the annual Seafood Buyer's Guide. Still, each issue includes stories outside of the particular focus, particularly shorter features and news items. No recreational fishing; no first person articles. Buys 12-15 mss/year. Query with or without published clips, or send complete ms. Length: 1,500-2,500 words. Pays $200-500. Sometimes pays the expenses of writers on assignment.
Photos: State availability of photos with submission. Reviews contact sheets and transparencies. Offers $20-100 per photo. Buys one-time rights.
Fillers: Newsbreak. Buys 10-15/year. Length: 100-250 words. Pays $50-100.
Tips: "*Seafood Leader* is steadily increasing in size and has a growing need for full-length feature stories and special sections. Articles on innovative, unique and aggressive people or companies involved in seafood are needed. Writing should be colorful, tight and fact-filled, always emphasizing the subject's formula for increased seafood sales. A reader should feel as if he's learned something he might apply to his or her business."

‡**SNACK FOOD**, HBJ Publications, Inc., 131 W. 1st St., Duluth MN 55802. (218)723-9343. Executive Editor: Jerry L. Hess. 15% freelance written. For manufacturers and distributors of snack foods. Monthly magazine; 60 pages. Circ. 10,000. Pays on acceptance. Publishes ms an average of 2 months after acceptance. Buys first serial rights. Occasional byline given. Phone queries OK. Photocopied submissions OK. Computer printout submissions acceptable. Reports in 2 months. Free sample copy and writer's guidelines.
Nonfiction: Informational, interview, new product, nostalgia, photo feature, profile and technical articles. "We use an occasional mini news feature or personality sketch." Length: 300-600 words for mini features; 750-1,200 words for longer features. Pays 12-15¢/word. Sometimes pays the expenses of writers on assignment.
Photos: Purchased with accompanying ms. Captions required. Pays $20 for 5x7 b&w photos. Total purchase price for ms includes payment for photos when used. Buys all rights.
Tips: "Query should contain specific lead and display more than a casual knowledge of our audience. The most frequent mistakes made by writers are not writing to our particular audience, and lack of a grasp of certain technical points on how the industry functions."

‡**THE WISCONSIN GROCER**, Wisconsin Grocers Association, Suite 203, 802 W. Broadway, Madison WI 53713. (608)222-4515. Editor: Russell King. 40% freelance written. Eager to work with new/unpublished writers. Bimonthly magazine covering grocery industry of Wisconsin. Circ. 1,500. Pays on publication. Publishes ms an average of 3 months after acceptance. Byline given. Not copyrighted. Buys first North American serial rights, second serial (reprint) rights or simultaneous rights. Submit seasonal/holiday material 5 months in advance. Simultaneous and previously published submissions OK. Computer printout submissions OK. Reports in 2 weeks on queries; 2 months on mss. Sample copy for 9x12 SAE with 51¢ postage.
Nonfiction: How-to (money management, employee training/relations, store design, promotional ideas); interview/profile (of WGA members and Wisconsin politicians only); opinion; technical (store design or

ALWAYS submit manuscripts or queries with a self-addressed, stamped envelope (SASE) within your country or International Reply Coupons purchased from the post office for other countries.

equipment). No articles about grocers or companies not affiliated with the WGA. Buys 6 mss/year. Query. Length: 500-2,000 words. Pays $15 for unsolicited articles. "Pays in copies if the writer works for a manufacturer or distributor of goods or services relevant to the grocery industry, or if a political viewpoint is expressed.

Photos: Send photos with submission. Reviews 5x7 prints. Offers no additional payment for photos accepted with ms. Identification of subjects required. Buys one-time rights.

Columns/Departments: Security (anti-shoplifting, vendor thefts, employee theft, burglary); Employee Relations (screening, training, management); Customer Relations (better service, corporate-community relations, buying trends); Money Management (DPP programs, bookkeeping, grocery—specific computer applications); Merchandising (promotional or advertising ideas), all 1,000 words. Buys 6 mss/year. Query. Length: 500-1,500 words. Pays $15.

Fillers: Facts and newsbreaks. Buys 6/year. Length: 50-250 words. Pays $5.

Tips: "How-tos are especially strong with our readers. They want to know how to increase sales and cut costs. Cover new management techniques, promotional ideas, customer services and industry trends."

THE WISCONSIN RESTAURATEUR, Wisconsin Restaurant Association, 122 W. Washington, Madison WI 53703. (603)251-3663. Editor: Jan La Rue. 10% freelance written. Eager to work with new/unpublished writers. Emphasizes restaurant industry for restaurateurs, hospitals, institutions, food service students, etc. Monthly magazine (December/January combined). Circ. 3,600. Pays on acceptance. Publishes ms an average of 3 months after acceptance. Buys all rights or one-time rights. Pays 10% kill fee. Byline given. Phone queries OK. Submit seasonal/holiday material 2-3 months in advance. Previously published OK; "indicate where." Computer printout acceptable. Reports in 3 weeks. Sample copy and writer's guidelines with large postpaid envelope.

Nonfiction: Expose, general interest, historical, how-to, humor, inspirational, interview, nostalgia, opinion, profile, travel, new product, personal experience, photo feature and technical articles pertaining to restaurant industry. "Needs more in-depth articles. No features on nonmember restaurants." Buys 1 ms/issue. Query with "copyright clearance information and a note about the writer in general." Length: 700-1,500 words. Pays $10-20.

Photos: Fiction and how-to mss stand a better chance for publication if photos are submitted. State availability of photos. Pays $15 for b&w 8x10 glossy prints. Model release required.

Columns/Departments: Spotlight column provides restaurant member profiles. Buys 6/year. Query. Length: 500-1,500 words. Pays $5-10.

Fiction: Experimental, historical and humorous stories related to food service only. Buys 12 mss/year. Query. Length: 1,000-3,000 words. Pays $10-20.

Poetry: Uses all types of poetry, but must have food service as subject. Buys 6-12/year. Submit maximum 5 poems. Length: 10-50 lines. Pays $5-10.

Fillers: Clippings, jokes, gags, anecdotes, newsbreaks and short humor. No puzzles or games. Buys 12/year. Length: 50-500 words. Pays $$1.50-7.50.

Hardware

Journals for general hardware wholesalers and retailers and retailers of special hardware items are listed in this section. Journals specializing in the retailing of hardware for a certain trade, such as plumbing or automotive supplies, are classified with the other publications for that trade.

CHAIN SAW AGE, 3435 N.E. Broadway, Portland OR 97232. Editor: Ken Morrison. 1% freelance written. "We will consider any submissions that address pertinent subjects and are well-written." For "mostly chain saw dealers (retailers); small businesses—usually family-owned, typical ages, interests and education." Monthly. Circ. 20,000. Pays on acceptance or publication. Publishes ms an average of 4 months after acceptance. Photocopied submissions OK. Computer printout submissions acceptable; no dot-matrix. Free sample copy.

Nonfiction: "Must relate to chain saw use, merchandising, adaptation, repair, maintenance, manufacture or display." Buys informational articles, how-to, personal experience, interview, and profiles, inspirational, personal opinion, photo feature, coverage of successful business operations, and articles on merchandising techniques. Buys very few mss/year. Query first. Length: 500-1,000 words. Pays $20-50 "2½¢/word plus photo fees." Sometimes pays the expenses of writers on assignment.

Photos: Photos purchased with or without mss, or on assignment. For b&w glossies, pay "varies." Captions required.

Tips: Frequently writers have an inadequate understanding of the subject area. "We may be in a position to accept more freelance material on an assignment basis."

‡**HARDWARE AGE**, Chilton Co., Chilton Way, Radnor PA 19089. (215)964-4275. Editor: Terry Gallagher. Managing Editor: Rick Carter. 5% freelance written. Emphasizes retailing, distribution and merchandising of hardware and building materials. Monthly magazine; 180 pages. Circ. 71,000. Buys first North American serial rights. No guarantee of byline. Simultaneous, photocopied and previously published submissions OK, if exclusive in the field. Reports in 1-2 months. Sample copy and writer's guidelines $1; mention *Writer's Market* in request.

Nonfiction: Wendy Ampolsk, managing editor. How-to more profitably run a hardware store or a department within a store. "We particularly want stories on local hardware stores and home improvement centers, with photos. Stories should concentrate on one particular aspect of how the retailer in question has been successful." Also wants technical pieces (will consider stories on retail accounting, inventory management and business management by qualified writers). Buys 5-10 unsolicited mss/year. Submit complete ms. Length: 500-3,000 words. Pays $75-200.

Photos: "We like store features with b&w photos. Usually use b&w for small freelance features." Send photos with ms. Pays $25 for 4x5 glossy b&w prints. Captions preferred. Buys one-time rights.

Columns/Departments: Retailers' Business Tips; Wholesalers' Business Tips; and Moneysaving Tips. Query or submit complete ms. Length: 1,000-1,250 words. Pays $100-150. Open to suggestions for new columns/departments.

HARDWARE MERCHANDISER, The Irving-Cloud Publishing Co., 7300 N. Cicero, Lincolnwood IL 60646. (312)674-7300. Publisher: Howard E. Kittelberger. 5% freelance written. Monthly tabloid covering retailers and wholesalers of hardware and building supply products. Circ. 68,000. Pays on acceptance. Publishes ms an average of 3 months after acceptance. Buys first North American serial rights. Computer printout submissions OK; prefers letter-quality to dot-matrix. Reports in 1 month on queries. Free sample copy.

Nonfiction: Profile (of hardware business). Buys 10 mss/year. Query or send complete ms "on speculation; enough to tell the story." Sometimes pays the expenses of writers on assignment.

Photos: Send photos with ms. Reviews 35mm or larger color transparencies. "Photos are paid for as part of article payment."

Home Furnishings and Household Goods

Readers rely on these publications to learn more about the home furnishings trade. Magazines geared to consumers interested in home furnishings are listed in the Consumer Home and Garden section.

‡**APPLIANCE SERVICE NEWS**, 110 W. Saint Charles Rd., Box 789, Lombard IL 60148. Editor: William Wingstedt. For professional service people whose main interest is repairing major and/or portable household appliances. Their jobs consist of service shop owner, service manager or service technician. Monthly "newspaper style" publication. Circ. 41,000. Buys all rights. Byline given. Pays on publication. Will consider simultaneous submissions. Reports in about 1 month. Sample copy $1.50.

Nonfiction: James Hodl, associate editor. "Our main interest is in technical articles about appliances and their repair. Material should be written in a straightforward, easy-to-understand style. It should be crisp and interesting, with high informational content. Our main interest is in the major and portable appliance repair field. We are not interested in retail sales." Query. Length: open. Pays $200-300/feature.

Photos: Pays $10 for b&w photos used with ms. Captions required.

CHINA GLASS & TABLEWARE, Ebel-Doctorow Publications, Inc., Box 2147, Clifton NJ 07015. (201)779-1600. Editor-in-Chief: Amy Stavis. 60% freelance written. Works with a small number of new/unpublished writers each year. Monthly magazine for buyers, merchandise managers and specialty store owners who deal in tableware, dinnerware, glassware, flatware and other tabletop accessories. Pays on publication. Publishes ms an average of 3-4 months after acceptance. Buys one-time rights. Byline given. Phone queries OK. Submit seasonal/holiday material 3 months in advance. Computer printout submissions acceptable; no dot-matrix. Reports in 3 weeks. Free sample copy and writer's guidelines; mention *Writer's Market* in request.
Nonfiction: General interest (on store successes, reasons for a store's business track record); interview (personalities of store owners; how they cope with industry problems; why they are in tableware); and technical (on the business aspects of retailing china, glassware and flatware). "Bridal registry material always welcomed." No articles on how-to or gift shops. Buys 2-3 mss/issue. Query. Length: 1,500-3,000 words. Pays $40-50/page. Sometimes pays the expenses of writers on assignment.
Photos: State availability of photos with query. No additional payment for b&w contact sheets or color contact sheets. Captions required. Buys first serial rights.
Fillers: Clippings. Buys 2/issue. Pays $3-5.
Tips: "Show imagination in the query; have a good angle on a story that makes it unique from the competition's coverage and requires less work on the editor's part for rewriting a snappy beginning."

ENTREE, Fairchild, 7 E. 12th St., New York NY 10003. (212)741-4009. Editor: Terence Murphy. 30% freelance written. Monthly feature magazine covering "food preparation and presentation products (i.e.: cookware, small electrical appliances, tabletop, etc.) wherever they are sold, including department stores, mass merchants, specialty shops. Also covers gift food products such as specialty coffee." Circ. 15,000. Average issue includes 5-11 features, 3 columns, a calendar, news and 50% advertising. Pays on acceptance. Publishes ms an average of 2½ months after acceptance. Byline given. Kill fee varies. Buys all rights. Phone queries OK. Computer printout submissions acceptable; prefers letter-quality to dot-matrix. Reports in 6 weeks on queries; 1 week on mss. Sample copy $2.
Nonfiction: Corporate profiles (of major retailers and manufacturers); industry news analysis; new product ("hot product categories"); photo feature; and technical (cookware and specialty food in terms retailers can apply to their businesses). No first person, humor, cartoons and unsolicited stories on obscure retailers or general pieces of any kind such as accounting or computer stories. Buys 2-3 mss/issue. Query. Length: 1,500-3,000 words. Pays $250-600. Sometimes pays the expenses of writers on assignment.
Photos: Cindy Sutherland, art director. Always looking for illustrations and photographs.
Tips: "We use two to three freelancers every issue and have established a core of regular writers we rely on. We want writers who can thoroughly analyze a market, whether it be cutlery, drip coffee makers, food processors or cookware and who can do in-depth profiles of major retailers or manufacturers."

FLOORING MAGAZINE, 7500 Old Oak Blvd., Cleveland OH 44130. Editor: Dan Alaimo. 5% freelance written. Prefers to work with published/established writers. Monthly magazine for floor covering retailers, wholesalers, contractors, specifiers and designers. Circ. 22,000. Pays on acceptance. Publishes ms an average of 3 months after acceptance. No byline or credit given. Buys all rights. Computer printout submissions acceptable; prefers letter-quality to dot-matrix. Writer's guidelines for SASE.
Nonfiction: Mostly staff-written. Will not be buying a significant number of manuscripts. However, has frequent need for correspondents skilled in 35mm photography for simple, local assignments. Sometimes pays the expenses of writers on assignment.

GIFTWARE BUSINESS, 1515 Broadway, New York NY 10036. (212)869-1300. Editor: Cheryl Proval. 10% freelance written. Prefers to work with published/established writers. Monthly for "merchants (department store buyers, specialty shop owners) engaged in the resale of giftware, china and glass, and decorative accessories." Monthly. Circ. 37,500. Buys all rights. Byline given "by request only." Pays on publication. Publishes ms an average of 2 months after acceptance. Will consider photocopied submissions. Query for electronic submissions. Computer printout submissions acceptable; prefers letter-quality to dot-matrix.
Nonfiction: "Retail store success stories. Describe a single merchandising gimmick. We are a tabloid format—glossy stock. Descriptions of store interiors are less important than sales performance unless display is outstanding. We're interested in articles on aggressive selling tactics. We cannot use material written for the consumer." Buys coverage of successful business operations and merchandising techniques. Query or submit complete ms. Length: 750 words maximum. Sometimes pays the expenses of writers on assignment.
Photos: Purchased with mss and on assignment; captions required. "Individuals are to be identified." Reviews b&w glossy prints (preferred) and color transparencies.
Tips: "All short items are staff produced. The most frequent mistake made by writers is that they don't know the market. As a trade publication, we require a strong business slant, rather than a consumer angle."

GIFTWARE NEWS, Talcott Corp., 112 Adrossan, Box 5398, Deptford NJ 08096. (609)227-0798. Editor: Anthony DeMasi. 50% freelance written. A monthly magazine covering gifts, collectibles, and tabletops for gift-

ware retailers. Circ. 41,000. Pays on publication. Publishes ms an average of 2 months after acceptance. By-line given. Buys all rights. Submit seasonal/holiday material 4 months in advance. Reports in 2 months on mss. Sample copy $1.50.
Nonfiction: How-to (sell, display) and new product. Buys 50 mss/year. Send complete ms. Length: 1,500-2,500 words. Pays $150-250 for assigned articles; pays $75-100 for unsolicited articles.
Photos: Send photos with submission. Reviews 4x5 transparencies and 5x7 prints. Offers no additional payment for photos accepted with ms. Identification of subjects required.
Columns/Departments: Tabletop, Wedding Market and Display—all for the gift retailer. Buys 36 mss/year. Send complete ms. Length: 1,500-2,500 words. Pays $75-200.

HAPPI, (*Household and Personal Products Industry*), Box 555, 26 Lake St., Ramsey NJ 07446. Editor: Hamilton C. Carson. 5% freelance written. For "manufacturers of soaps, detergents, cosmetics and toiletries, waxes and polishes, insecticides, and aerosols." Circ. 15,000. Not copyrighted. Pays on publication. Publishes ms an average of 2 months after acceptance. Will consider photocopied submissions. Submit seasonal material 2 months in advance. Query. Computer printout submissions acceptable.
Nonfiction: "Technical and semitechnical articles on manufacturing, distribution, marketing, new products, plant stories, etc., of the industries served. Some knowledge of the field is essential in writing for us." Buys informational interview, photo feature, spot news, coverage of successful business operations, new product articles, coverage of merchandising techniques and technical articles. No articles slanted toward consumers. Query with published clips. Buys 3 to 4 mss a year. Length: 500-2,000 words. Pays $10-200. Sometimes pays expenses of writers on assignment.
Photos: 5x7 or 8x10 b&w glossies purchased with mss. Pays $10.
Tips: "The most frequent mistakes made by writers are unfamiliarity with our audience and our industry; slanting articles toward consumers rather than to industry members."

HOME FURNISHINGS, Box 581207, Dallas TX 75258. (214)741-7632. Editor: Tina Berres Filipski. 20% freelance written. "We don't buy much unsolicited material. Hardly ever use a writer I don't know." Quarterly magazine for home furnishings retail dealers, manufacturers, their representatives and others in related fields. Circ. 25,000. Pays on acceptance. Publishes ms an average of 2 months after acceptance. Buys first serial rights. Computer printout submissions acceptable; no dot-matrix.
Nonfiction: Informational articles about retail selling; success and problem solving stories in the home furnishings retail business; economic and legislative-related issues, etc. "No trite, over-used features on trends, lighthearted features and no cartoons." Query. Length: open; appropriate to subject and slant. Photos desirable. Sometimes pays the expenses of writers on assignment.

HOME LIGHTING & ACCESSORIES, Box 2147, Clifton NJ 07015. (201)779-1600. Editor: Peter Wulff. 5% freelance written. Prefers to work with published/established writers. For lighting stores/departments. Monthly magazine. Circ. 7,500. Pays on publication. Publishes ms an average of 4-6 months after acceptance. Buys all rights. Submit seasonal/holiday material 6 months in advance. Computer printout submissions acceptable; no dot-matrix. Free sample copy.
Nonfiction: How-to (run your lighting store/department, including all retail topics); interview (with lighting retailers); personal experience (as a businessperson involved with lighting); profile (of a successful lighting retailer/lamp buyer); and technical (concerning lighting or lighting design). Buys 10 mss/year. Query. Pays $60/published page. Sometimes pays the expenses of writers on assignment.
Photos: State availability of photos with query. Offers no additional payment for 5x7 or 8x10 b&w glossy prints. Pays additional $90 for color transparencies used on cover. Captions required.
Tips: "We don't need fillers—only features."

MART, Business Ideas For Today's Retailers and Distributors, Gordon Publications, Inc., Box 1952, Dover NJ 07801. (201)361-9060. Editor: Bob Ankosko. Associate Editor: Rob Sabin. 30% freelance written. Works with a small number of new/unpublished writers each year. Monthly tabloid on consumer electronics, and major appliances retailing; readership includes retailers, wholesale distributors, and manufacturer district managers and representatives. Circ. 65,000. Pays on acceptance. Publishes ms an average of 1 month after acceptance. Byline given. Offers $50 kill fee. Buys all rights. Submit seasonal/holiday material 2 months in advance. Computer printout submissions acceptable; IBM PC floppy disk preferred. Sample copy $3; free writer's guidelines.
Nonfiction: Industry trends, interview/profile, new product roundups, and retailer how-to (business management, etc). Buys 60 mss/year. Query with published clips. Length: 800-2,000 words. Pays $100-350. Sometimes pays the expenses of writers on assignment.
Tips: "We're looking in the future for more colorful, as opposed to hard news articles (from a style approach). We're looking more for in-depth investigative work on those 'newsy' pieces that we use, i.e., exposes. Writers frequently miss getting facts of particular interest to retailers: store volume, selling area, percentage of sales in major appliances, in consumer electronics, etc. Say something to an electronics/major appliance retailer that will somehow help his business."

‡PROFESSIONAL FURNITURE MERCHANT MAGAZINE, The Business Magazine for Progressive Furniture Retailers, Shore Communications, Inc., Suite 300, South, 180 Allen Rd. NE, Atlanta GA 30328. Editor: J. David Goldman. 35% freelance written. Monthly magazine covering the furniture industry from a retailer's perspective. In-depth features on direction, trends, certain retailers doing outstanding jobs, and analyses of product or service areas in which retailing can improve profits. Circ. 20,000. Pays on publication. Publishes ms an average of 3 months after acceptance. Byline given. Buys first serial rights. Submit seasonal/holiday material 3 months in advance. Computer printout submissions acceptable; prefers letter-quality to dot-matrix. Reports in 6 weeks. Sample copy $3.
Nonfiction: Expose (relating to or affecting furniture industry); how-to (business oriented how to control cash flow, inventory, market research, etc.); interview/profile (furniture retailers); and photo feature (special furniture category). No general articles, fiction or personal experience. Buys 24 mss/year. Send complete ms. Length: 1,000-2,400 words. Pays $150-350. Sometimes pays expenses of writers on assignment.
Photos: State availablity of photos. Pays $5 maximum for 4x5 color transparencies; $5 maximum for 3x5 b&w prints. Captions, model release, and identification of subjects required.
Tips: "Read the magazine. Send manuscript specifically geared to furniture retailers, with art (photos or drawings) specified." Break in with features. "First, visit a furniture store, talk to the owner and discover what he's interested in."

‡RETAILER AND MARKETING NEWS, Box 191105, Dallas TX 75219-1105. (214)871-2930. Editor: Michael J. Anderson. Monthly for retail dealers and wholesalers in appliances, TVs, furniture, consumer electronics, records, air conditioning, housewares, hardware, and all related businesses. Circ. 10,000. Photocopied submissions OK. Free sample copy.
Nonfiction: "How a retail dealer can make more profit" is the approach. Wants "sales promotion ideas, advertising, sales tips, business builders and the like, localized to the Southwest and particularly to north Texas." Submit complete ms. Length: 100-900 words. Pays $30.

‡SEW BUSINESS, 1515 Broadway, New York NY 10036. Editor: Christina Holmes. For retailers of home sewing, quilting and needlework merchandise. "We are the only glossy magazine format in the industry—including home sewing and the *Art Needlework* and *Quilt Quarterly* supplements." Monthly. Circ. 20,000. Not copyrighted. Pays on publication. Publishes ms an average of 3-4 months after acceptance. Computer printout submissions OK; prefers letter-quality to dot-matrix. Reports in 5 weeks on queries; in 6 weeks on ms. Sample copy and writer's guidelines for 8½x11 SAE with $1.20 postage.
Nonfiction: Articles on department store or fabric, needlework, or quilt shop operations, including coverage of art needlework, piece goods, patterns, quilting and sewing notions. Interviews with buyers—retailers on their department or shop. "Stories must be oriented to provide interesting information from a *trade* point of view. Looking for retailers doing something different or offbeat, something that another retailer could put to good use in his own operation. Best to query editor first to find out if a particular article might be of interest to us." Buys 25 unsolicited mss/year. Query. Length: 750-1,500 words. Pays $150 minimum.
Photos: Photos purchased with mss. "Should illustrate important details of the story." Sharp 5x7 b&w glossies. Offers no additional payment for photos accompanying ms.

UNFINISHED FURNITURE MAGAZINE, United States Exposition Corp., 1850 Oak St., Northfield IL 60093. (312)446-8434. Editor: Lynda Utterback. 50% freelance written. Bimonthly magazine for unfinished furniture retailers, distributors and manufacturers throughout the U.S., Canada, England, Australia and Europe. Circ. 10,000. Pays on publication. Publishes ms an average of 2 months after acceptance. Byline given. Buys all rights. Submit seasonal/holiday material 6 months in advance. Simultaneous queries, and simultaneous and photocopied submissions OK. Computer printout submissions acceptable. Reports in 3 weeks on queries; 1 month on mss. Free sample copy and writer's guidelines.
Nonfiction: How-to, interview/profile, new product, personal experience and technical (as these relate to the unfinished furniture industry). Production distribution, marketing, advertising and promotion of unfinished furniture and current happenings in the industry. Buys 10 unsolicited mss/year. Send complete ms. Length: 2,000 words. Pays $50-100.
Photos: Pays $5 for b&w photos.
Tips: "We look for professionals in the field (i.e., accountants to write tax articles) to write articles. A frequent mistake made by writers in completing an article for us is not understanding the audience."

Hospitals, Nursing and Nursing Homes

In this section are journals for nurses, medical and nonmedical nursing home personnel, clinical and hospital staffs and laboratory technicians and managers. Journals publishing technical material on new discoveries in medicine and information for physicians in private practice are listed in the Medical category.

‡**FAMILY THERAPY NEWS**, American Association for Marriage and Family Therapy, 407 1717 K St. NW, Washington DC 20006. (202)429-1825. Editor: William C. Nichols. Managing Editor: Kimberly A. Tilley. 10% freelance written. Newspaper for professional organization covering family therapy, family policy, mental health and behavior sciences. *FT News* is a professional newspaper serving marital and family therapists. Writers should be able to reach both doctoral level and graduate student readers. Circ. 13,000. Pays on acceptance. Publishes ms an average of 3 months after acceptance. Byline given. Buys first North American serial rights. Submit seasonal/holiday material 6 months in advance. Query for electronic submissions. Computer printout submissions OK; prefers letter-quality. Reports in 2 weeks. Free sample copy; writer's guidelines for SAE with 2 first class stamps.
Nonfiction: General interest and opinion. Nothing is not of interet in the field of family therapy, family policy, family research, mental health and behavioral science for professionals. Query with or without published clips, or send complete ms. Length: 300-1,800 words. Pays $25-200.
Photos: State availability of photos with submission. Reviews 8x10 prints. Payment negotiable. Identification of subjects required. Buys one-time rights.
Columns/Departments: Family Therapy Forum (wide variety of topics and slants on family therapy, education, training, practice, service delivery, the therapists, family therapists in various countries, opinion), to 1,800 words; In Focus (interview with outstanding therapists, other leaders), to 1,500 words. Send complete ms. Length: 600-1,800. Pays $25-100.
Fillers: Facts. Length: 100-300 words. Pays $10-25.
Tips: "The annual conference is a major source of good material for writers, such as those of the American Family Therapy Association. Query editor. Also, we are in need of short, well-written features on current developments in the field. Materials could be developed into columns as well for Family Therapy Forum in some instances, but straight news-based features are the best bet."

HOSPITAL GIFT SHOP MANAGEMENT, Creative Age Publications, 7628 Densmore Ave., Van Nuys CA 91406. (818)782-7232. Editor: Barbara Feiner. 25% freelance written. Works with a small number of new/unpublished writers each year. Monthly magazine covering hospital gift shop management. "*HGSM* presents practical and informative articles and features to assist in expanding the hospital gift shop into a comprehensive center generating large profits." Circ. 15,000 + . Pays on acceptance. Publishes ms an average of 4 months after acceptance. Byline given. Buys first North American serial rights. Submit seasonal/holiday material 8 months in advance. Computer printout submissions acceptable; dot-matrix OK "if readable and double-spaced." Reports in 1 month. Sample copy and writer's guidelines for $4 postage.
Nonfiction: How-to, interview/profile, photo feature, and management-themed articles. "No fiction, no poetry, no first-person 'I was shopping in a gift shop' kinds of pieces." Buys 12-25 mss/year. Length: 750-2,500 words. Pays $10-100. Query first.
Photos: State availability of photos with query. "If you are preparing a gift shop profile, think of providing gift shop photos." Reviews 5x7 color or b&w prints; payment depends on photo quality and number used. Captions, model release, and identification of subjects required.
Fillers: Cartoons only. Buys 12/year. Pays $20.
Tips: "A freelancer's best bet is to let us know you're out there. We prefer to work on assignment a lot of the time, and we're very receptive to freelancers—especially those in parts of the country to which we have no access. Call or write; let me know you're available. Visit your nearby hospital gift shop—it's probably larger, more sophisticated than you would imagine. I've noticed that query letters are becoming sloppy and lack direction. I wouldn't mind finding writers who can communicate well, explain story ideas in a one-page letter, spell correctly, and wow me with original ideas. Make your query letter stand out. Convince me that your story is going to be exciting. A boring query usually yields a boring story."

HOSPITAL SUPERVISOR'S BULLETIN, Bureau of Business Practice, 24 Rope Ferry Rd., Waterford CT 06386. Editor: Janice Endresen. 40% freelance written. Works with a small number of new/unpublished writers each year. For non-medical hospital supervisors. Semimonthly newsletter; 8 pages. Circ. 3,300. Pays on acceptance. Publishes ms an average of 5 months after acceptance. Buys all rights. No byline. Submit seasonal/holiday material 6 months in advance. Photocopied submissions OK. Computer printout submissions acceptable; prefers letter-quality to dot-matrix. Reports in 1 month. Sample copy and writer's guidelines for SAE with 2 first class stamps.

Nonfiction: Publishes interviews with non-medical hospital department heads. "You should ask supervisors to pinpoint current problems in supervision, tell how they are trying to solve these problems and what results they're getting—backed up by real examples from daily life." Also publishes interviews on people problems and good methods of management. People problems include the areas of training, planning, evaluating, counseling, discipline, motivation, supervising the undereducated, getting along with the medical staff, dealing with change, layoffs, etc. No material on hospital volunteers. "We prefer six- to eight-page typewritten articles. Articles must be interview-based." Pays 12¢/word after editing.

Tips: "Often stories lack concrete examples explaining general principles. I want to stress that freelancers interview supervisors (not high-level managers, doctors, or administrators) of non-medical departments. Interviews should focus on supervisory skills or techniques that would be applicable in any hospital department. The article should be conversational in tone: not stiff or academic. Use the second person to address the supervisor/reader."

LICENSED PRACTICAL NURSE, Official Publication of the National Federation of LPNs, McClain Publishing Co., 125 Briar Cliff Rd., Durham NC 27707. Editor: John T. Kerr. 40% freelance written. Works with a small number of new/unpublished writers each year. A quarterly magazine on nursing for members of the National Federation of LPN's. Circ. 10,000. Pays on publication. Publishes ms an average of 6 months after acceptance. Byline given. Offers 100% kill fee. Buys first North American serial rights. Submit seasonal/holiday material 6 months in advance. Photocopied submissions OK. Computer printout submissions OK; no dot-matrix. Reports in 1 month. Writer's guidelines for SASE.

Nonfiction: Book excerpts/reviews; historical/nostalgic; how-to (improve basic skills, new methods, etc.); humor; opinion/topics of controversy (such as life support systems, unionization, etc.); personal experience; photo feature; non-technical medical news; nurse/doctor and nurse/patient situations; legal liabilities of nurses; tax update for nurses; nursing ethics; care for the elderly; and continuing education. Special Convention Issue mid-summer each year. No highly technical articles or articles devoted to RN situations that would have no bearing on LPNs. Buys 16 mss/year. Query. Length: 300-1,500 words. Pays $15-125.

Photos: State availability of photos, or send photos with query or ms if available. Reviews b&w and color contact sheets. Pays $10-25 for 5x7 b&w prints; $10-75 for 5x7 color prints and color transparencies. Captions, model release, and identification of subjects required. Buys one-time rights.

Fillers: Clippings, anecdotes, short humor and newsbreaks. Buys 20/year. Length: 50-200 words. Pays $2.50-10.

Tips: "First choice is given to LPN writers, then nurse writers, then all others. Articles are chosen because of their value to LPNs in LPN work situations. Content must be invigorating and readable. Dull, technical material will not be accepted."

MEDICENTER MANAGEMENT, Brentwood Publishing Corp., Box 2178, Santa Monica CA 90406. (213)395-0234. Editor-in-Chief/Publisher: Martin H. Waldman. Editor: Rebecca Morrow. 60% freelance written. Prefers to work with experienced business/medical writers. A monthly magazine covering hospital outpatient and freestanding ambulatory health care centers. Circ. 15,000. Pays on acceptance. Publishes ms an average of 3-4 months after acceptance. Byline given. Makes work-for-hire assignments. Photocopied submissions OK. Query for electronic submissions. Computer printout submissions acceptable; no dot-matrix. Reports in 2 weeks. Sample copy for 8½x11 SAE with 4 first class stamps; writer's guidelines for letter size SAE with 1 first class stamp.

Nonfiction: Feature, how-to articles (associated with the business of running a medicenter), interview/profile, new product and technical. Buys 30 mss/year. Query with published clips. Length: 1,500-3,000 words. Pays 10-12¢/word. Sometimes pays the expenses of writers on assignment. Telephone reimbursement up to $150/article.

Photos: Send photos with submission. Reviews prints. Offers no additional payment for photos accepted with ms. Model releases and identification of subjects required. Buys all rights.

Columns/Departments: Profile (a telephone interview or visit to an ambulatory care center resulting in a feature-type profile of the facility), 2,000-2,500 words. Buys 12 mss/year. Query with published clips. Pays 10-12¢/word.

Tips: "We are looking to build up our national freelancing network. Writers based outside of California are especially desirable. A background in business and/or light medical writing coupled with a willingness to learn about this exciting new field are ideal qualifications. Types of facilities covered include birthing centers, urgent care centers, surgical centers, women's centers, mobile diagnostic and treatment units, imaging units, family practice centers, opthalmology centers, group practices, HMOs and occupational/industrial centers."

_____ *Hotels, Motels, Clubs, Resorts and Restaurants*

These publications offer trade tips to hotel, club and resort, and restaurant managers, owners and operators. Journals for manufacturers and distributors of bar and beverage supplies are listed in the Beverages and Bottling section.

CATERING TODAY, The Professional Guide to Catering Profits, ProTech Publishing and Communications, Inc., Box 222, Santa Claus IN 47579. (812)937-4464. Editor: Mary Jeanne Schumacher. 40% freelance written. Prefers to work with published/established writers. A monthly magazine for the off-premise and on-site catering industry covering food trends, business and management advice and features on successful caterers. Circ. 36,000. Pays on publication. Publishes ms an average of 3 months after acceptance. Byline given. Offers 10-30% kill fee. Buys all rights. Submit seasonal/holiday material 3 months in advance. Simultaneous, photocopied and previously published submissions OK. Computer printout submissions acceptable; prefers letter-quality to dot-matrix. Reports in 2 weeks on queries; 3 weeks on mss. Sample copy and writer's guidelines for 9x12 SAE with $1.07 postage.
Nonfiction: How-to (on ice carving, garnishes, cooking techniques, etc); interview/profile; new product; and photo feature. "Also valuable to caterers are advice and ideas on marketing, advertising, public relations and promotion." No fillers, humor, poetry or fiction. Buys 35-40 mss/year. Query with published clips. Length varies. Pays 8¢/word.
Photos: Send photos with submission. Reviews contact sheets, negatives, 4x5 transparencies, and 5x7 prints. Offers $5-10/photo. Captions required.
Tips: "Write from a viewpoint that a caterer/business person can understand, appreciate and learn from. Submissions should be neat, accurate and not flowery or wordy. Areas of our publication most open to freelancers are food trends and uses, equipment reviews, and feature length profiles of caterers."

FLORIDA HOTEL & MOTEL JOURNAL, The Official Publication of the Florida Hotel & Motel Association, Accommodations, Inc., Box 1529, Tallahassee FL 32302. (904)224-2888. Editor: Mrs. Jayleen Woods. 10% freelance written. Prefers to work with published/established writers. Monthly magazine for managers in the lodging industry (every licensed hotel, motel and resort in Florida). Circ. 6,500. Pays on publication. Publishes ms an average of 2 months after acceptance. Byline given. Offers $50 kill fee. Buys all rights and makes work-for-hire assignments. Submit seasonal/holiday material 3 months in advance. Photocopied submissions OK. Computer printout submissions acceptable; no dot-matrix. Reports in 1 month. Sample copy for 9x12 SAE and 4 first class stamps; writer's guidelines for business size SAE and 1 first class stamp.
Nonfiction: General interest (business, finance, taxes); historical/nostalgic (old Florida hotel reminiscences); how-to (improve management, housekeeping procedures, guest services, security and coping with common hotel problems); humor (hotel-related anecdotes); inspirational (succeeding where others have failed); interview/profile (of unusual hotel personalities); new product (industry-related and non brand preferential); photo feature (queries only); technical (emerging patterns of hotel accounting, telephone systems, etc.); travel (transportation and tourism trends only—no scenics or site visits); and property renovations and maintenance techniques. Buys 10-12 mss/year. Query with clips of published work. Length: 750-2,500 words. Pays $75-250 "depending on type of article and amount of research." Sometimes pays the expenses of writers on assignment.
Photos: Send photos with ms. Pays $25-100 for 4x5 color transparencies; $10-15 for 5x7 b&w prints. Captions, model release and identification of subjects required.
Tips: "We prefer feature stories on properties or personalities holding current membership in the Florida Hotel and Motel Association. Memberships and/or leadership brochures are available (SASE) on request. We're open to articles showing how Mom and Dad management copes with inflation and rising costs of energy systems, repairs, renovations, new guest needs and expectations. The writer may have a better chance of breaking in at our publication with short articles and fillers because the better a writer is at the art of condensation, the better his/her feature articles are likely to be."

FOOD & SERVICE, Texas Restaurant Association, Box 1429, Austin TX 78767. (512)444-6543 (in Texas, 1-800-252-9360). Editor: Bland Crowder. 50% freelance written. Magazine published 11 times/year providing business solutions to Texas restaurant owners and operators. Circ. 5,000. Written queries required. Reports in

1 month. Byline given. Not copyrighted. Buys first and second serial rights to the same material, and second (reprint) rights to material originally published elsewhere. Simultaneous queries, photocopied submissions OK. No previously published submissions. Accepts submissions by modem. Free sample copy and editorial calendar for 9x12 SAE with $1.25 postage. Pays on acceptance; rates vary.

Nonfiction: Features must provide business solutions to problems in the restaurant and food service industries. Topics vary but always have business slant; sometimes particular to Texas. No restaurant critiques, human interest stories, or seasonal copy. Quote experts and other restaurateurs; substantiate with facts and examples. Query. Length: 2,000-2,500 words, features; shorter articles sometimes used; product releases, 300-word maximum. Payment rates vary. Sometimes pays the expenses of writers on assignment.

Photos: State availability of photos, but photos usually assigned.

Columns/Departments: Written in-house only.

HOTEL AND MOTEL MANAGEMENT, Harcourt Brace Jovanovich, Inc., 7500 Old Oak Blvd., Cleveland OH 44130. (216)243-8100. Editor: Michael Deluca. Managing Editor: Robert Nozar. 25% freelance written. Prefers to work with published/established writers. Monthly newsmagazine about hotels, motels and resorts in the continental U.S. and Hawaii for general managers, corporate executives, and department heads (such as director of sales; food and beverage; energy; security; front office; housekeeping, etc.) Circ. 41,000. Pays on acceptance. Publishes ms an average of 2 months after acceptance. Byline given. Buys first North American serial rights. No phone queries. Computer printout submissions acceptable; prefers letter-quality to dot-matrix. Reports in 3 weeks on queries; do not send mss. Free sample copy.

Nonfiction: "A how-to, nuts-and-bolts approach to improving the bottom line through more innovative, efficient management of hotels, motels and resorts in the continental U.S. and Hawaii. Articles consist largely of specific case studies and interviews with authorities on various aspects of the lodging market, including franchising, financing, personnel, security, energy management, package tours, telecommunications, food service operations, architecture and interior design, and technological advances. We use freelance coverage of spot news events (strikes, natural disasters, etc.). Query with published clips. "Write a query letter outlining your idea and be specific." Length: 800-1,000 words. Sometimes pays expenses of writers on assignment.

Photos: State availability of b&w photos. Captions preferred. Buys one-time rights.

Tips: "The writer may have a better chance of breaking in at our publication with short articles and fillers because we are a newsmagazine that covers an industry of people who don't have time to read longer articles. We need 'hands on' articles which explain the topic."

INNKEEPING WORLD, Box 84108, Seattle WA 98124. (206)284-4247. Editor/Publisher: Charles Nolte. 75% freelance written. Eager to work with new/unpublished writers. Emphasizes the hotel industry worldwide. Published 10 times a year; 12 pages. Circ. 2,000. Pays on acceptance. Publishes ms an average of 4 months after acceptance. Buys all rights. No byline. Submit seasonal/holiday material 1 month in advance. Computer printout submissions acceptable; no dot-matrix. Reports in 1 month. Sample copy and writer's guidelines for 9x12 SAE with 56¢ postage.

Nonfiction: Managing—interviews with successful hotel managers of large and/or famous hotels/resorts (600-1,200 words); Marketing—interviews with hotel marketing executives on successful promotions/case histories (length: 300-1,000 words); Sales Promotion—innovative programs for increasing business (100-600 words); Bill of Fare—outstanding hotel restaurants, menus and merchandising concepts (300-1,000 words); and Guest Relations—guest service programs, management philosophies relative to guests (200-800 words). Pays $100 minimum or 15¢/word (whichever is greater) for main topics. Other topics—advertising, creative packages, cutting expenses, frequent guest profile, guest comfort, hospitality, ideas, public relations, reports and trends, special guestrooms, staff relations. Length: 50-500 words. Pays 15¢/word. "If a writer asks a hotel for a complimentary room, the article will not be accepted, nor will *Innkeeping World* accept future articles from the writer."

Tips: "We need more in-depth reporting on successful case histories—results-oriented information."

LODGING HOSPITALITY MAGAZINE, Penton Publishing, 1100 Superior Ave., Cleveland OH 44114. (216)696-7000. Editor: Paul B. Engel. Managing Editor: Robert C. Townsend. 25% freelance written. Prefers to work with published/established writers. A monthly magazine covering the lodging industry. "Our purpose is to inform lodging management of trends and events which will affect their properties and the way they do business. Audience: owners and managers of hotels, motels, resorts." Circ. 44,000. Pays on acceptance. Publishes ms an average of 2 months after acceptance. Byline given. Buys first rights. Submit seasonal/holiday material 2 months in advance. Computer printout submissions OK; no dot-matrix. Reports in 1 month.

Nonfiction: General interest, how-to, interview/profile and travel. Special issues include technology (January); interior design (April); foodservice (May); investments (June); franchising (July); marketing (September); and state of the industry (December). "We do *not* want personal reviews of hotels visited by writer, or travel pieces. All articles are geared to hotel executives to help them in their business." Buys 25 mss/year. Query. Length: 700-2,000 words. Pays $150-600. Sometimes pays the expenses of writers on assignment.

Photos: State availability of photos with submission. Reviews contact sheets and transparencies. Offers no additional payment for photos accepted with ms. Captions and identification of subjects required. Buys one-time rights.

Columns/Departments: Budget Line, Suite Success, Resort Report, Executive on the Spot, Strategies Marketwatch, Report from Washington, Food for Profit, Technology Update—all one-page reports of 700 words. Buys 25 mss/year. Query. Pays $150-250.

‡MARKETING & SALES PROMOTION UPDATE, The Newsletter Group, Inc., 1552 Gilmore St., Box 4044, Mountain View CA 94040. (415)941-7525. Editor: Bill Tillinghast. Associate Editor: Howard Baldwin. A trade newsletter for the lodging industry. "Each four-page issue contains 18 tightly-condensed reports of successful marketing strategies recently undertaken by hotels, motels, resorts or bed-and-breakfast inns. Coverage area is worldwide, though largely U.S. Subscribers are marketing/sales directors, worldwide, though largely U.S. We accept tips from freelancers—no complete mss." Circ. 1,200. Pays on publication. Computer printout submissions OK. Sample copy for #10 SAE with 1 first class stamp.
Nonfiction: Lodging industry sales/marketing. Query. Pays $25 for leads only.
Tips: "We seek tips, leads, suggestions and ideas for 100-150-word articles focusing on an outstanding novel or unusual successful sales/marketing promotion or package offered by a hotel, motel, resort or bed-and-break-fast inn. Writer should furnish lead or tip with query. If lead/tip results in a published article, publication will pay query writer $25 within 30 days. If not used, there is no payment. All published copy is staff written. Manuscripts are not accepted. No exceptions. Written queries only, please."

PIZZA TODAY, The Professional Guide To Pizza Profits,, ProTech Publishing and Communications, Inc., Box 114, Santa Claus IN 47579. (812)937-4464. Editor: Paula Werne. Managing Editor: Danny Bolin. 50% freelance written. Prefers to work with published/established writers. A monthly magazine for the pizza industry, covering trends, features of successful pizza operators, business and management advice, etc. Circ. 36,000. Pays on publication. Publishes ms an average of 2 months after acceptance. Byline given. Offers 10-30% kill fee. Buys all rights and negotiable rights. Submit seasonal/holiday material 3 months in advance. Simultaneous, photocopied and previously published submissions OK. Query for electronic submissions. Computer printout submissons acceptable; prefers letter-quality to dot-matrix. Reports in 2 weeks on queries; 3 weeks on manuscripts. Free sample copy and writer's guidelines for 10x13 SAE with $1.28 postage.
Nonfiction: Interview/profile, new product, entrepreneurial slants, time management, pizza delivery and employee training. No fillers, fiction, humor or poetry. Buys 40-60 mss/year. Query with published clips. Length: 750-2,500 words. Pays 8¢/word. Sometimes pays the expenses of writers on assignment.
Photos: Send photos with submission. Reviews contact sheets, negatives, 4x5 transparencies, color slides and 5x7 prints. Offers $5-10/photo. Captions required.
Tips: "We would like to receive nutritional information for low-cal, low-salt, low-fat, etc. pizza."

RESTAURANT HOSPITALITY, Penton IPC, Penton Plaza, 1111 Chester Ave., Cleveland OH 44114. (216)696-7000. Editor: Stephen Michaelides. 30% freelance written. Prefers to work with published/established writers. Monthly magazine covering the foodservice industry for owners and operators of independent restaurants, hotel foodservices, executives of national and regional restaurant chains and foodservice executives of schools, hospitals, military installations and corporations. Circ. 120,000. Average issue includes 10-12 features. Pays on acceptance. Publishes ms an average of 5 months after acceptance. Byline given. Buys exclusive rights. Computer printout submissions acceptable; prefers letter-quality to dot-matrix. Reports in 1 week. Sample copy for 9x12 SAE and $2.50 postage.
Nonfiction: General interest (articles that advise operators how to run their operations profitably and efficiently); interview (with operators); and profile. Stories on psychology, consumer behavior, managerial problems and solutions, how-to's on buying insurance, investing (our readers have a high degree of disposable income), design elements and computers in foodservice. No restaurant reviews. Buys 30 mss/year. Query with clips of previously published work and a short bio. Length: 500-1,500 words. Pays $100/published page. Pays the expenses of writers on assignment.
Photos: Send color photos with manuscript. Captions required.
Columns/Departments: "We are accepting 100-150 word pieces with photos (slides preferred; will accept b&w) for our Restaurant People department. Should be light, humorous, anecdotal." Byline given. Pays $75.
Tips: "We would like to receive queries for articles on insurance costs (liquor liabilities); new tax reform laws; minimum wage; food trends; shortage of qualified employees; shrinking of labor market; ingredient labelling; neo-Prohibitionism; and nutrition. One hard-hitting, investigative piece on the influence of the 'mob' in food service would be welcome. We're accepting fewer queried stories but assigning more to our regular freelancers. We need new angles on old stories, and we like to see pieces on emerging trends and technologies in the restaurant industry. Our readers don't want to read how to open a restaurant or why John Smith is so successful. We'll be publishing short, snappy profiles—way more than in the past—with fewer major features."

‡**RESTAURANT MANAGEMENT**, HBJ Publications, 7500 Old Oak Blvd., Cleveland OH 44130. (216)243-8100. Editor: Loretta Ivany. Uses freelance written articles "only occasionally." Monthly magazine covering management and marketing of independently owned and operated restaurants. Circ. 102,000. Pays on acceptance. Publishes ms an average of 4 months after acceptance. No byline given. Buys first North American serial rights. Submit seasonal/holiday material 6 months in advance. Photocopied submissions OK. Computer printout submissions acceptable; prefers letter-quality to dot-matrix. Reports in 2 months. Sample copy $3.00.
Nonfiction: How-to (improve management of independent restaurant; marketing techniques, promotions, etc.); and interview/profile (with independent restaurateur; needs a strong angle). "Send us a query on a successful independent restaurateur with an effective marketing program, unusual promotions, interesting design and decor, etc." No restaurant reviews, consumer-oriented material, nonrestaurant-oriented management articles. Buys variable number mss/year. Length: open. Pays variable fee.
Photos: State availability of photos. Captions, model release and identification of subjects required. Buys all rights.

‡**SOUTHWEST HOTEL-MOTEL REVIEW**, Texas Hotel and Motel Association, 8602 Crownhill Blvd., San Antonio TX 78209. (512)828-3566. Editor: Melissa Carroll. Associate Editor: Spencer Derden. "The *Review* is a monthly news and information publication for the Texas hospitality industry. The editorial focus is on newsworthy developments in the industry and on feature-length articles presenting information that will assist management level operators in planning and pursuing their business interests." Circ. 4,000. Pays on publication. Publishes ms an average of 2 months after acceptance. Byline given. Offers 25% kill fee. Not copyrighted. Buys first North American serial rights. Submit seasonal/holiday material 3 months in advance. Query for electronic submissions. Computer printout submissions OK; prefers letter-quality to dot-matrix. Reports in 5 weeks on queries. Free sample copy and writer's guidelines.
Nonfiction: Interview/profile and photo feature. Special issues include Alcohol Awareness issue (February); Hotel Design trends (April); National Tourism month (May). "We cannot use general interest articles. We have a very specific audience." Buys 12 mss/year. Query with published clips. Length: 1,000-2,500 words. Pays $175-325 for assigned articles; newsbriefs at $25/manuscript page. Sometimes pays the expenses of writers on assignment.
Photos: Send photos with submission. Reviews 35mm or 4x5 transparencies and 4x5 prints. Offers $15-275 per photo. Identification of subjects required. Buys one-time rights.
Tips: "We like to think that our magazine helps our readers to stay informed about what is happening in the Texas hospitality industry and to run their business more efficiently. Writers who demonstrate an awareness of our special audience with well-written, fact-filled, and accurate articles get our attention. Most of our articles are assigned. A writer with clips to demonstrate his or her ability at this type of writing will have the best chance to break into our rotation. Good works mean more work. Feature length articles on various aspects of hotel ownership and management are our staple. Approximately every other issue contains a food and beverage related article."

VACATION INDUSTRY REVIEW, Worldex Corp., Box 431920, South Miami FL 33243. (305)667-0202. Managing Editor: George Leposky. 50% freelance written. Prefers to work with published/established writers. A bimonthly magazine covering leisure lodgings (timeshare resorts, RV parks, condo hotels, etc.). Circ. 2,500. Pays on acceptance. Publishes ms an average of 2-4 months after acceptance. Byline given. Buys all rights and makes work-for-hire assignments. Submit seasonal/holiday material 4 months in advance. Photocopied submissions OK. Query for electronic submissions. Computer printout submissions acceptable; prefers letter-quality to dot-matrix. Reports in 1 month. Sample copy $1; writer's guidelines with SASE.
Nonfiction: How-to, interview/profile, new product, opinion, personal experience, technical and travel. No consumer travel or real estate related material. Buys 15 mss/year. Query with published clips. Length: 1,000-2,500 words. Pays $75-175. Pays the expenses of writers on assignment, if previously arranged.
Photos: Send photos with submission. Reviews contact sheets, 35mm transparencies, and 5x7 prints. Offers no additional payment for photos accepted with ms. Captions and identification of subjects required. Buys one-time rights.
Tips: "We want articles about the business aspect of the vacation industry: entrepreneurship, project financing, design and construction, sales and marketing, operations, management—in short, anything that will help our readers plan, build, sell and run a quality vacation property that satisfies the owners/guests while earning a profit for the proprietor. Our destination pieces are trade-oriented, reporting the status of tourism and the development of various kinds of leisure lodging facilities in a city, region or country. You can discuss things to see and do in the context of a resort located near an attraction, but that shouldn't be the main focus or reason for the article."

Industrial Operations

Industrial plant managers, executives, distributors and buyers read these journals. Some industrial management journals are also listed under the names of specific industries, such as Machinery and Metal. Publications for industrial supervisors are listed in Management and Supervision.

APPLIANCE MANUFACTURER, For Managers in Business/Office, Consumer & Commercial Appliances, Corcoran Communications, Inc., 6200 Som Center Rd., C-14, Solon OH 44139. (216)349-3060. Editor: Norman C. Remich, Jr. 5% freelance written. A monthly magazine covering design for manufacturing in high-volume automated manufacturing industries. Circ. 35,000. Pays on publication. Publishes ms an average of 3 months after acceptance. Byline given sometimes. Buys all rights. Simultaneous submissions OK. Computer printout submissions acceptable; prefers letter-quality to dot-matrix. Reports in 3 weeks. Free sample copy.
Nonfiction: How-to; interview/profile (sometimes); new product; and technical. Buys 12 mss/year. Send complete ms. Length: open. Pays $50/published page. Pays expenses of writers on assignment.
Photos: Captions and identification of subjects required.

COMPRESSED AIR, 253 E. Washington Ave., Washington NJ 07882. Editor/Publications Manager: S.M. Parkhill. 75% freelance written. Emphasizes applied technology and industrial management subjects for engineers and managers. Monthly magazine; 48 pages. Circ. 145,000. Buys all rights. Publishes ms an average of 3 months after acceptance. Computer printout submissions acceptable; no dot-matrix. Reports in 6 weeks. Free sample copy, editorial schedule; mention *Writer's Market* in request.
Nonfiction: "Articles must be reviewed by experts in the field." Recent articles: "Return of the Propeller" (May 1987) and "People Problems in Automation" (January 1987). Buys 48 mss/year. Query with published clips. Pays negotiable fee. Sometimes pays expenses of writers on assignment.
Photos: State availability of photos in query. Payment for 8x10 glossy color photos is included in total purchase price. Captions required. Buys all rights.
Tips: "We are presently looking for freelancers with a track record in industrial/technology/management writing. Editorial schedule is developed in the summer before the publication year and relies heavily on article ideas from contributors. Resume and samples help. Writers with access to authorities preferred; and prefer interviews over library research. The magazine's name doesn't reflect its contents. We suggest writers request sample copies."

‡CPI PURCHASING, The Magazine About Buying, Cahners Publishing, 275 Washington St., Newton MA 02158. (617)964-3030. Editor: David Erickson. 10% freelance written. A monthly magazine covering the chemical and process industries. Circ. 30,000. Pays on acceptance. Publishes ms an average of 2 months after acceptance. Byline given. Offers 100% kill fee. Buys all rights. Computer printout submissions OK; prefers letter-quality. Sample copy $7.
Nonfiction: "We assign stories, usually on chemical market developments. Our readers are buyers of chemicals and related process equipment. Freelancers should not submit *anything* on spec." Query. Length: 1,000-3,000 words. Pays $300-1,500 for assigned articles. Pays the expenses of writers on assignment.
Photos: State availability of photos.
Tips: "We prefer writers with some background in chemicals or equipment. Houston/Gulf Coast residents are especially welcome, but, please no PR writers."

‡INDUSTRIAL FABRIC PRODUCTS REVIEW, Industrial Fabrics Assoc., Suite 450, 345 Cedar Bldg., St. Paul MN 55101. (612)222-2508. Editor: Jeff Benson. Director of Publications: Roger Barr. 10% freelance written. Monthly magazine covering industrial textiles for company owners, salespersons and researchers in a variety of industrial textile areas. Circ. 6,000. Pays on publication. Publishes ms an average of 2 months after acceptance. Byline given. Buys all rights. Submit seasonal/holiday material 4 months in advance. Simultaneous queries, and photocopied and previously published submissions OK. Computer printout submissions acceptable; prefers letter-quality to dot-matrix. Reports in 4 weeks. Sample copy free "after query and phone conversation."
Nonfiction: Technical, marketing and other topics related to any aspect of industrial fabric industry from fiber to finished fabric product. Special issues include new products, industrial products and equipment. No historical or apparel oriented articles. Buys 12 mss/year. Query with phone number. Length: 1,200-3,000

words. Pays $75/published page. Sometimes pays the expenses of writers on assignment.

Photos: State availability of photos. Reviews 8x10 b&w glossy and color prints. Pay is negotiable. Model release and identification of subjects required. Buys one-time rights.

Tips: "We have added to our permanent magazine staff which will reduce the amount of money we spend on freelance material. However we are also trying to encourage freelancers to learn our industry and make regular, solicited contributions to the magazine."

INSULATION OUTLOOK, National Insulation Contractors Association, Suite 410, 1025 Vermont NW, Washington DC 20005. (202)783-6278. Editor: Marcia G. Lawson. 50% freelance written. Prefers to work with published/established writers. Monthly magazine about general business, commercial and industrial insulation for the insulation industry in the United States and abroad. Publication is read by engineers, specifiers, owners, contractors and energy managers in the industrial and commercial insulation field. There is also representative distribution to public utilities, and energy-related industries. Pays on publication. Publishes ms an average of 3-4 months after acceptance. Byline given. Buys first rights only. Phone queries OK. Written queries should be short and simple, with samples of writing attached. Submit seasonal material 6 months in advance. Simultaneous, photocopied and previously published submissions OK. Query for electronic submissions. Computer printout submissions acceptable; no dot-matrix. Sample copy $2; free writer's guidelines. "Give us a call. If there seems to be compatibility, we will send a free issue sample so the writer can see directly the type of publication he or she is dealing with."

Nonfiction: Articles on the technical aspects of insulation; case studies. Sometimes pays the expenses of writers on assignment.

Columns/Departments: Query. Pays $50-350.

Tips: "We are looking for articles that are moderately technical in nature."

MANUFACTURING SYSTEMS, The Management Magazine of Integrated Manufacturing, Hitchcock Publishing Co., 25 W 550 Geneva Rd., Wheaton IL 60188. (312)665-1000. Editor:Tom Inglesby. Senior Editors: Mary Emrich and Fred Miller. 10-15% freelance written. "We are backlogged with submissions and are trying to make room for new/unpublished articles with something important to say." A monthly magazine covering computers/information in manufacturing for upper and middle-level management in manufacturing companies. Circ. 131,000. Pays on acceptance. Publishes ms an average of 2 months after acceptance. Byline given. Offers 35% kill fee. Buys all rights. Submit seasonal/holiday material 4 months in advance. Simultaneous and photocopied submissions OK. Query for electronic submissions. Computer printout submissions acceptable; prefers letter-quality to dot-matrix. Reports in 2 weeks. Sample copy for SASE.

Nonfiction: Book excerpts, essays, general interest, interview/profile, new product, opinion, technical, case history—applications of system. "Each issue emphasizes some aspect of manufacturing. Editorial schedule available, usually in September, for next year." Buys 6-8 mss/year. Query with or without published clips, or send complete ms. Length: 500-2,500 words. Pays $150-600 for assigned articles; pays $50/published page for unsolicited articles. Sometimes pays limited, pre-authorized expenses of writers on assignment.

Photos: State availability of photos with submission. Reviews contact sheets, negatives, 2x2 and larger transparencies and 5x7 and larger prints. Offers no additional payment for photos accepted with ms. Captions and identification of subjects required. Buys one-time rights.

Columns/Departments: Forum (VIP-to-VIP, bylined by manufacturing executive), 1,000-1,500 words; and Manufacturing Management (consultant's column, bylined by manufacturing consultant), 500-600 words. Buys 1-2 mss/year. Query. 500-1,000 words. Sometimes pays $100-200. "These are *rarely* paid for but we'd consider ghost written pieces bylined by 'name.' "

Fillers: Barbara Dutton, fillers editor. Anecdotes, facts, gags to be illustrated by cartoonist and newsbreaks. Buys 3-6/year. Length: 25-100 words. Pays $10-50.

Tips: "We are moving more toward personal management issues and away from technical articles—how to manage, not what tools are available. We are interested in direct efforts to apply computers to manufacturing productivity—concepts (just-in-time), zero defects, Japanese management methods, *statistical* quality control or newest whizz-bang hardware/software (artificial intelligence, super computer, robots). Features are the most open area. We will be happy to provide market information and reader profile on request."

OCCUPATIONAL HEALTH & SAFETY MAGAZINE, Stevens Publishing, 225 N. New Road, Box 7573, Waco TX 76714. (817)776-9000. Editor: Carol Mouche. Managing Editor: Elizabeth Juden. 50% freelance written. Works with a small number of new/unpublished writers each year. A monthly magazine covering health and safety in the workplace. Circ. 93,000. Pays on publication. Publishes ms an average of 8 months after acceptance. Byline given. Buys first serial rights and first North American serial rights. Submit seasonal/holiday material 6 months in advance. Simultaneous submissions OK. Query for electronic submissions. Computer printout submissions acceptable; prefers letter-quality to dot-matrix. Reports in 1 month on queries, 2 months on mss. Sample copy with writer's guidelines and editorial calendar for 9½x12 SASE.

Nonfiction: Exposé; how-to (for health/safety professionals); interview/profile. Subjects of interest include product liability; OSHA regulations; interviews with health and safety personnel of interest to general readers; and workplace reproductive hazards. No unsubstantiated material; no advertorials; no first-person articles. Query editors on specific subjects only. Length 1,200-5,000 words. Payment varies. Sometimes pays the expenses of writers on assignment.

Photos: Reviews contact sheets, negatives, 4x5 transparencies and prints—prefer color. Captions, model releases and identification of subjects required.

Tips: "There is an increasing merger between OSHA and EPA regulations regarding employee health and safety that should be reviewed editorially. Writers can judge whether their expertise will suit our needs by noting the technical quality of material in our magazine, reviewing the editorial calendar, and by keeping in mind that we will consider anything occupational health or safety related. Expanding on news events is also a good source of editorial material."

PLANT MANAGEMENT & ENGINEERING, MacLean Hunter Bldg; 777 Bay St., Toronto, Ontario M5W 1A7 Canada. Editor: Ron Richardson. 10% freelance written. Prefers to work with published/established writers. For Canadian plant managers and engineers. Monthly magazine. Circ. 26,000. Pays on acceptance. Publishes ms an average of 2 months after acceptance. Buys first Canadian rights. Computer printout submissions acceptable; prefers letter-quality to dot-matrix. Reports in 3 weeks. Sample copy with SAE only.

Nonfiction: How-to, technical and management technique articles. Must have Canadian slant. No generic articles that appear to be rewritten from textbooks. Buys fewer than 20 unsolicited mss/year. Query. Pays 12¢/word minimum. Sometimes pays the expenses of writers on assignment.

Photos: State availability of photos with query. Pays $25-50 for b&w prints; $50-100 for 2¼x2¼ or 35mm color transparencies. Captions required. Buys one-time rights.

Tips: "Increase emphasis on the use of computers and programmable controls in manufacturing will affect the types of freelance material we buy in 1988. Read the magazine. Know the Canadian readers' special needs. Case histories and interviews only—no theoretical pieces. We will probably be buying even less freelance material because of more staff writers."

PRODUCTION ENGINEERING, 1100 Superior Ave., Cleveland OH 44114. (216)696-7000. Editor: George Weimer. Managing Editor: Tom Hughes. 50% freelance written. Prefers to work with published/established writers. For "men and women in production engineering—the engineers who plan, design and improve manufacturing operations." Monthly magazine; 100 pages. Circ. 95,000. Pays on publication. Publishes ms an average of 6 months after acceptance. Buys exclusive first North American serial rights. Byline given; "if by prior arrangement, an author contributed a segment of a broader article, he might not be bylined." Phone queries OK. Photocopied submissions OK, if exclusive.gineers who plan, design and improve manufacturing operations." Monthly magazine; 100 pages. Circ. 95,000. Pays on publication. Publishes ms an average of 6 months after acceptance. Buys exclusive first North American serial rights. Byline given; "if by prior arrangement, an author contributed a segment of a broader article, he might not be bylined." Phone queries OK. Photocopied submissions OK, if exclusive. Computer printout submissions acceptable; prefers letter-quality to dot-matrix. Reports in 2 weeks. Free sample copy and writer's guidelines.

Nonfiction: How-to (engineering, data for engineers); personal experience (from *very* senior production or manufacturing engineers only); and technical (technical news or how-to). "We're interested in solid, hard hitting technical articles on the gut issues of manufacturing. Case histories, but no-fat treatments of manufacturing concepts, innovative manufacturing methods, and state-of-the-art procedures. Our readers also enjoy articles that detail a variety of practical solutions to some specific, everyday manufacturing headache." Buys 2-3 mss/issue. Query. Length: 800-3,000 words. Pays $100-300.

Tips: "All manuscripts must include photos, graphs or other visual elements necessary to the story."

PURCHASING EXECUTIVE'S BULLETIN, Bureau of Business Practice, 24 Rope Ferry Rd., Waterford CT 06386. (203)442-4365. Editor: Claire Sherman. Managing Editor: Wayne Muller. For purchasing managers and purchasing agents. Semimonthly newsletter; 4 pages. Circ. 5,500. Pays on acceptance. Buys all rights. Submit seasonal/holiday material 3 months in advance. Reports in 2 weeks. Free sample copy and writer's guidelines.

Nonfiction: How-to (better cope with problems confronting purchasing executives); and direct interviews detailing how purchasing has overcome problems and found better ways of handling departments. No derogatory material about a company; no writer's opinions; no training or minority purchasing articles. "We don't want material that's too elementary (things any purchasing executive already knows)." Buys 2-3 mss/issue. Query. Length: 750-1,000 words.

Tips: "Make sure that a release is obtained and attached to a submitted article."

‡QUALITY CONTROL SUPERVISOR'S BULLETIN, National Foremen's Institute, 24 Rope Ferry Rd., Waterford CT 06386. (800)243-0876. Editor: Steven J. Finn. 100% freelance written. Biweekly newsletter for quality control supervisors. Pays on acceptance. No byline given. Buys all rights. Computer printout submissions acceptable. Reports in 2 weeks on queries; 1 month on mss. Free sample copy and writer's guidelines.

Nonfiction: Interview and "articles with a strong how-to slant that make use of direct quotes whenever possible." Buys 70 mss/year. Query. Length: 800-1,100 words. Pays 8-14¢/word.

Tips: "Write for our freelancer guidelines and follow them closely. We're looking for steady freelancers we can work with on a regular basis."

SEMICONDUCTOR INTERNATIONAL, Cahners Publishing Co., 1350 E. Touhy Ave., Box 5080, Des Plaines IL 60018. (312)635-8800. Editor: Donald E. Swanson. 5% freelance written. Monthly magazine covering semiconductor industry processing, assembly and testing technology subjects for semiconductor industry processing engineers and management. "Technology stories that cover all phases of semiconductor product manufacturing and testing are our prime interest." Circ. 36,100. Pays on publication. "News items are paid for upon acceptance." Publishes ms an average of 6 months after acceptance. Byline given. Buys all rights and makes work-for-hire assignments. Computer printout submissions acceptable; no dot-matrix. Reports in 1 month.

Nonfiction: Technical and news pertaining to the semiconductor industry in the U.S. and overseas. No "articles that are commercial in nature or product oriented." Buys 50 mss/year (including feature articles and news). Query with "your interest and capabilities" or send complete ms. Length: 2,500 words maximum.

Photos: State availability of photos or send photos with ms. Reviews 8x10 b&w prints and 35mm color transparencies. Captions and identification of subjects required.

Columns/Departments: "News of the semiconductor industry as it pertains to technology trends is of interest. Of special interest is news of the semiconductor industry in foreign countries such as Japan, England, Germany, France, and the Netherlands." Buys 30-40 mss/year. Query. Length: 200-1,500 words. Pays 20¢/word for accepted, edited copy.

Tips: "The most frequent mistake made by writers in completing an article for us is lack of understanding of the semiconductor fabricating industry."

WASTE AGE, National Solid Wastes Management Association, 1730 Rhode Island Ave. NW, Washington DC 20036. Editor: Joe Salimando. 10% freelance written. A monthly magazine for businessmen and municipal officials who manage organizations which remove and dispose of wastes. Circ. 30,000. Pays on acceptance. Byline sometimes given. Offers 50% kill fee. Buys all rights. Electronic submissions OK via IBM Voluswriter software, but requires hard copy also. Computer printout submissions acceptable; prefers letter-quality to dot-matrix. Reports in 3 weeks on queries.

Nonfiction: Historical/nostalgic, interview/profile, photo feature, technical and case studies. Buys 15 mss/year. Must query. Length: 700-3,000 words. Pays $300 minimum. Sometimes pays the expenses of writers on assignment.

Photos: State availability of photos with submission. Reviews contact sheets. Identification of subjects required. Buys one-time rights.

Columns/Departments: Safety (protecting waste industry workers), and Your Image (promotion ideas—for refuse and hazardous waste). Query. Length: 300-1,000 words. Pays $300-450.

WEIGHING & MEASUREMENT, Key Markets Publishing Co., Box 5867, Rockford IL 61125. (815)399-6970. Editor: David M. Mathieu. For users of industrial scales and meters. Bimonthly magazine; 32 pages. Circ. 15,000. Pays on acceptance. Buys all rights. Pays 20% kill fee. Byline given. Reports in 2 weeks. Free sample copy.

Nonfiction: Interview (with presidents of companies); personal opinion (guest editorials on government involvement in business, etc.); profile (about users of weighing and measurement equipment); and technical. Buys 25 mss/year. Query on technical articles; submit complete ms for general interest material. Length: 750-2,500 words. Pays $45-125.

> **❝ Rather than strive for perfection—which would result in my never letting go of a story—I revise or do additional drafts till I'm satisfied it's at least good enough that I'm willing to sign my name. ❞**
>
> *—Louis Alexander*
> *nonfiction magazine writer*

_____ *Information Systems*

These publications give computer professionals more data about their profession. Consumer publications are listed under Personal Computers.

ABSOLUTE REFERENCE, The Journal For 1-2-3 And Symphony Users, Que Corp., Inc., 7999 Knue Rd., Indianapolis IN 46250. (317)842-7162. Editor-in-Chief: M.E. Green. 100% freelance written. Eager to work with new/unpublished writers. Monthly newsletter covering 1-2-3 and symphony applications, tips, and macros. "Que Corp., is one of the world's leading publishers of microcomputer books. Our audience uses *AR* on the job to solve problems that involve Lotus spreadsheet or integrated software use. These readers work for Fortune 500 companies, as well as small businesses." Circ. 6,900. Payment initiated within 14 days of acceptance. Publishes ms an average of 4 months after acceptance. Byline given. Buys all rights. Submit seasonal/holiday material 2 months in advance. Photocopied submissions OK. Query for electronic submissions. Computer printout submissions acceptable. Reports in 2 weeks on queries; 1 month on mss. Sample copy $6; writer's guidelines for #10 SAE and 1 first class stamp.
Nonfiction: How-to (use 1-2-3 or Symphony). "We like to cover tax planning and tax tips using 1-2-3 or Symphony in the March issue to increase productivity on the job)." No articles on Jazz or other software that is not compatible with the IBM PC. No news. Only 1-2-3 and Symphony application articles. Buys 48 mss/year. Query should detail writer's professional experience as it relates to Lotus products or microcomputers. Length: 1,500-3,000 words. Pays 12¢/word.
Photos: "We use program listings, tables, and PC printer images to illustrate articles. This 'art' is purchased with the article."
Columns/Departments: 1-2-3 Tips: Items on short macros to ease printing, locate files, use pointers, etc.—in short, strings of commands that save the user time and energy while working in a file. Symphony Tips are also needed, covering any streamlined approach to file usage. Macro Of The Month is a department devoted to lengthier, meatier macros covering more involved execution of file commands. Wish List items detail commands and features that readers wish Lotus had supplied in 1-2-3 or Symphony. Product Reviews focus on 1-2-3 or Symphony-related hardware or software. Buys 96 mss/year. Query on reviews; send complete ms if tip, macro, or wish list item. Length: 175-400 words (tips, wish list); 500-800 words for reviews; 700-1,000 words for macros. Pays $25 minimum for tips; 12¢/word for reviews; $50-75 for macros.
Tips: "Know 1-2-3 and/or Symphony inside-out. Test the macros; make sure your submission is complete. Suggest a title; label figures and program listings. Write subheads for text; cutlines for figures and listings. Keep in mind the business user—ranging from neophyte to 'old pro.' We use tip writers again and again and encourage them to graduate to writing articles."

ASHTON-TATE QUARTERLY, Ashton-Tate, 20101 Hamilton Ave., Torrance CA 90502. (213)538-7579. Editor: Patricia Matthews. 80% freelance written. A quarterly company magazine covering all dBASE products, Framework II, and Fred and dBASE programming languages. "The *Ashton-Tate Quarterly* is designed for professional and business users of our software. Our goals are to be an essential business reference for users of Ashton-Tate software by illustrating the benefits of our products in business to increase effectiveness, productivity, and creativity and to provide insights into designing and planning business applications and systems." Circ. 15,000. Pays on acceptance. Publishes ms an average of 3 months after acceptance. Byline given. Buys all rights. Electronic submissions OK via IBM-PC, Word Star preferred—"Call, if other formats are used"—but requires hard copy also. Computer printout submissions acceptable; prefers letter-quality to dot-matrix. Reports in 1 month on queries; 6 weeks on mss. Free writer's guidelines.
Nonfiction: Book excerpts, how-to (use dBASE and Framework in business to increase productivity and effectiveness), technical and case studies of products in use. "No testimonials to Ashton-Tate software." Buys 40 mss/year. Send complete ms. Length: 1,000-3,000 words. Pays 15-20¢/word.
Photos: State availability of photos with submission. Offers no additional payment for photos accepted with ms. Model releases and identification of subjects required.
Columns/Departments: Collector's Corner (macros and other useful tips for using Framework II), 500-1,500 words; and Expert's Corner (business advice on topics of interest to our product users), 1,500-3,000 words. Buys 40 mss/year. Send complete ms. Pays15-20¢/word.
Tips: "We need technical information presented in a way that is accessible and interesting to non-technical computer users. Contact editor with article proposals. Be specific about content and objective of articles."

BUSINESS SOFTWARE, Building Better PC Applications, M&T Publishing, 501 Galveston Dr., Redwood City CA 94063. (415)366-3600. Editor: Jim Fawcette. Managing Editor: Nancy Groth. 50% freelance written. "Will work with new writers if technical expertise is there." Monthly magazine covering the business of computers. "We are not geared toward the prepurchasers—the people thinking about getting computers—or those just getting a start in computers. Ours is a *highly sophisticated* audience comprised of people who have been using computers in their businesses for years, who are at the leading edge of what's happening in the world of business computing and who want the leverage computers provide to them." Circ. 60,000. Pays on acceptance. Publishes ms an average of 2-3 months after acceptance. Byline given. Buys first serial rights plus one reprint right. Simultaneous queries and photocopied submissions OK. Query for electronic submissions. Computer printout submissions acceptable; prefers letter-quality to dot-matrix. Reports in 4 weeks on queries; 8 weeks on mss. Free sample copy and writer's guidelines.
Nonfiction: Book excerpts; how-to (advanced tutorials on practical software use); opinion (reviews); and technical. No humor, game reviews or articles not related to business. "We would like to receive technical esoteric tips and tricks for software applications." Buys 50-75 mss/year. Query with published clips or send complete ms. Length: 750-3,500 words. Pays $75-100/published page. Sometimes pays expenses of writers on assignment.
Photos: Send photo with query or ms. Reviews b&w and color contact sheets; payment included in per-page rate. Captions, model release, and identification of subjects required. Buys one-time rights plus one reprint right.
Tips: "Query first, then call after query answered. Timeliness and technical savvy are a must with us. Feature tutorial section always open to freelancers, but note we are an *advanced* user magazine, not interested in novice, prepurchase, or other introductory material. If articles are technically competent, any length is acceptable to us. Frequent mistakes made by writers are not using enough detailed information about the application being discussed, lack of relevance or inability to relate program to business user and lack of photos, display screen, printouts, reports and sidebars. A recent change in format and editor may result in a few policy changes, but the market the magazine focuses on will remain the same."

COMPAQ MAGAZINE, The Magazine for Compaq Computer Users, 3381 Ocean Dr., Vero Beach FL 32963. (305)231-6904. Editor-in-Chief: Paul Pinella. 70% freelance written. A quarterly magazine covering application stories, software reviews and hardware analyses. "Since our readers are users of Compaq computers, writers should be Compaq users themselves or extremely familiar with these machines." Circ. 100,000+. Pays on publication. Publishes ms an average of 1 month after acceptance. Byline given. Offers 100% kill fee. Buys all rights. Submit seasonal/holiday material 2 months in advance. Query for electronic submissions. Computer printout submissions acceptable. Reports in 3 weeks on queries. Sample copy $1 with 8½x11 SAE and 3 first class stamps.
Nonfiction: Essays, general interest, interview/profile, new product, and software reviews. "Don't send anything without query and conversation with the editor." Buys 15 mss/year. Query. Length: 300-500 words. Pays $200-800. Sometimes pays the expenses of writers on assignment.
Photos: State availability of photos with submission. Reviews any size transparencies and any size color or b&w prints. Offers $5-100/photo. Buys one-time rights.
Columns/Departments: Eye of the Needle (commentary on personal computer industry), 1,000 words; On the Job (short essays of interesting Compaq users), 300 words; and Newswatch (news, important events), 100-300 words. Buys 12 mss/year. Business On-Line (business software questions answered) 900 words. Query. Pays $60-200.
Tips: "Feature articles are most open to freelancers. Be familiar with the Compaq computer, and have an interesting story in mind before contacting the editor."

COMPUTER DEALER, Gordon Publications, Inc., Box 1952, Dover NJ 07801-0952. (201)361-9060. Editor: Tom Farre. 70% freelance written. Eager to work with new/unpublished writers if they know the field. Monthly management and technology magazine for computer resellers, including dealers, VARs, distributors, systems houses, and business equipment dealers. Circ. 45,000. Pays on publication. Publishes ms an average of 3 months after acceptance. Buys all rights. Query for electronic submissions. Computer printout submissions OK; prefers letter-quality to dot-matrix. Reports in 2 months.
Nonfiction: Management and business issues; interviews with top computer industry personnel, and technology explication. "Writers must know microcomputer hardware and software and be familiar with computer reselling—our readers are computer-industry professionals in an extremely competitive field." Buys 3-6 mss/issue. Query with published clips. Length: 1,000-4,000 words. pays 10-20¢/word. Sometimes pays the expenses of writers on assignment.
Photos: B&w photos preferable.
Columns/Departments: Solicited by editor. "If the writer has an idea, query by mail to the editor, with clips."

COMPUTING CANADA, The Newspaper for Information Processing Management, Plesman Publications Ltd., #703, 2 Lansing Sq., Willowdale, Ontario M2J 5A1 Canada. (416)497-9562. Editor: Gordon Campbell. Managing Editor: Martin Slofstra. 10% freelance written. A biweekly tabloid covering data processing/data communications. Circ. 32,000. Pays on publication. Publishes ms an average of 2 months after acceptance. Byline given. Offers $50 kill fee. Buys first North American serial rights. Submit seasonal/holiday material 2 months in advance. Simultaneous and photocopied submissions OK. Electronic submissions OK via modem: text capture or Immedia E-mail diskette; PC or 8-in CP/M or Macintosh or Commodore. Computer printout submissions acceptable; prefers letter-quality to dot-matrix. Reports in 2 weeks on queries; 1 month on mss. Free sample copy and writer's guidelines.
Nonfiction: Opinion, personal experience and technical. Must have relevance to Canadians. Buys 150 mss/year. Query with published clips. Length: 400-1,500 words. Pays $75-350 (Canadian) for assigned articles; pays $50-300 for unsolicited articles; sometimes trades advertising for consultants ("*very* infrequently"). Sometimes pays the expenses of writers on assignment.
Photos: Send photos with submission. Reviews 5x7 prints. Offers $10/photo. Model releases and identification of subjects required. Buys one-time rights.

DATA BASE MONTHLY, For Data General and Compatible Users, Data Base Publications, Suite 385, 8310 Capital of Texas Hwy., Austin TX 78731. (512)343-9066. Editor: Wendell Watson. Managing Editor: S. Elizabeth Brown. 50% freelance written. Works with a small number of new/unpublished writers each year. A monthly magazine covering Data General computer systems. "*Data Base Monthly* is the primary independent source of technical and market-specific information for people who use Data General computer systems or sell to the Data General market." Circ. 25,000. Pays on publication. Publishes ms an average of 3 months after acceptance. Byline given. Buys first North American serial rights and second serial (reprint) rights. Submit seasonal/holiday material 3 months in advance. Query for electronic submissions. Computer printout submissions acceptable; prefers letter-quality to dot-matrix. Reports in 1 month. Free sample copy and writer's guidelines.
Nonfiction: How-to, new product (computer-related), and technical all specific to Data General systems. No articles which cannot be related to Data General. Buys 25 mss/year. Query with published clips. Length: 1,000-3,500 words. Pays $100-500 for assigned articles; pays $0-500 for unsolicited articles. Sometimes pays the expenses of writers on assignment.
Photos: State availability of photos with submission. Reviews contact sheets, transparencies and 5x7 prints. Offers $0-25/photo. Captions, model releases, and identification of subjects required. Buys first serial rights.
Columns/Departments: Technical columns (instructive articles on Data General computer hardware and software, including reviews by users), 1,000-2,500 words. Query with published clips. Pays $0-300.
Tips: "Feature articles are the area of our publication most open to freelancers."

DATAMATION, Cahners Publishing Co., 249 W. 17th St., New York NY 10011. Editor-in-Chief: Tim Mead. 20% freelance written. Works with a small number of new/unpublished writers each year. Twice-monthly magazine for data processing professionals. Circ. 190,000. Pays on publication. Byline given. Offers negotiable kill fee. Buys all rights. Submit seasonal/holiday material 3 months in advance. Photocopied and previously published submissions ("if indicated where") OK. Computer printout submissions acceptable; prefers letter-quality to dot-matrix. Query for electronic submissions; prefers letter-quality to dot-matrix. Reports as soon as possible on queries. Publishes ms an average of 4 months after acceptance. Free sample copy and writer's guidelines. "Request our list of themes for the coming year."
Nonfiction: Covers all aspects of computer industry technical, managerial and sociological concerns, as well as computer industry news analysis. No general articles on computers. Buys 60 mss/year. Query with published clips. Length: 2,000-4,000 words. Pays $300-1,000/article. Pays expenses of writers on assignment.
Photos: Reviews 35mm color transparencies and 8x10 b&w prints. No extra payment for photos—included in payment for manuscript.
Tips: "The most frequent mistake made by writers is failure to read the magazine and figure out what we're about."

HARDCOPY, The Need to Know Magazine for DEC Computers, Seldin Publishing Inc., Suite D, 1061 S. Melrose, Placentia CA 92670. (714)632-6924. Editor: Dan Reese. 25% freelance written. Prefers to work with established technical writers. Monthly magazine covering Digital Equipment Corporation (DEC) and DEC-compatible computer equipment, software and peripherals. Circ. 82,000, U.S. and Europe. Pays 30 days from acceptance. Publishes ms an average of 4 months after acceptance. Byline given. Buys all rights to new material. Occasionally buys second (reprint) rights. Submit seasonal/holiday material 4 months in advance. Query for electronic submissions. All mss must be typed, double-spaced. Reports in 2 weeks on queries; 2 months on mss. Sample copy for 9x12 SAE and $2.30 postage; writer's guidelines for business size SAE and 1 first class stamp.
Nonfiction: How-to (sell product; computer-oriented management and business); interview/profile (DEC or

DEC-compatible manufacturers); and technical (DEC computer-oriented). "We are interested in unique DEC Computer-related experiences or any major road blocks you've overcome such as combining work stations from a variety of vendors on a single LAN or choosing a printer or plotter to do a specific job. We're interested in knowing how you dealt with the problem and the steps you took in finding the right solution." No noncomputer related features or computer-oriented features that do not relate in any way to Digital Equipment Corporation. Buys approximately 36 full-length (feature) mss/year, plus news items, product reviews. Query with published clips. Length: Features, 2,500-3,000 words; news items, 50-150 words; reviews, 800-1,200 words. Pays $50-600. Sometimes pays the expenses of writers on assignment.

Photos: Pays $10-25 for 5x7 b&w prints; $25 for 35mm color transparencies. Identification of subjects required.

Tips: "We need solid technical and how-to features from contributors. Research must be thorough, and the article's main point must relate to DEC. For example, a market trend article should explain how DEC's market will be affected. We suggest you query to receive direction, since our needs are very specific. Frequently writers neglect the technical information and vie for style. We want a fact-filled body. 'Padding' is unacceptable.''

HP DESIGN & MANUFACTURING, Independent Magazine for Hewlett-Packard Technical Computer Users, (formerly *The Chronicle Magazine*), Wilson Publications, Inc., Box 399, Cedar Park TX 78613. (512)250-5518. Editor: Catherine V. Warren. 50% freelance written. Eager to work with new/unpublished writers. A monthly magazine covering Hewlett-Packard technical computers and instruments. "*HP Design & Manufacturing* contains material covering the use of HP technical computers for an engineering audience. This includes HP news, tutorials, reviews and new product announcements. Writers must be technically knowledgeable about their subject." Circ. 30,000. Pays on publication. Publishes ms an average of 2 months after acceptance. Byline given. Offers negotiable percentage of promised payment as kill fee. Buys first North American serial rights. Photocopied submissions OK. Query for electronic submissions. Computer printout submissions acceptable; prefers letter-quality to dot-matrix. Reports in 1 week on queries; 2 weeks on mss. Sample copy for 8½x11 SASE.

Nonfiction: How-to (on hardware and software applications), new product, opinion, and technical. Submissions must be directly related to HP 1000, 9000, series 80 computers and test instruments. Buys 50+ mss/year. Query with or without published clips, or send complete ms. Length: 300-2,000. Pays 10¢/word. Sometimes pays the expenses of writers on assignment.

Photos: State availability of photos with submission. Reviews contact sheets, negatives, transparencies and prints. Captions required.

Tips: "As more freelance writers become adept at covering computers, we will purchase more freelance material. Understand vertical publications in general—in particular how they differ from, say, generic computer publications like *Byte*. Let us know what your expertise is and how it will make you the right person to cover the proposed topic. Write for the engineer. Tell him/her how to get the most out of hardware/software. Let readers know of unusual uses for equipment. Be technical but don't be dry (i.e. don't write in manual style).''

‡IEEE SOFTWARE, IEEE Computer Society, 10662 Los Vagueros Circle, Los Alamitos CA 90720. (714)821-8380. Managing Editor: Angela Burgess. 2% freelance written. Works with a small number of new/unpublished writers each year. A bimonthly magazine on computer software. Circ. 23,500. Pays on publication. Publishes ms an average of 3 months after acceptance. Byline given. Offers 25% kill fee. Buys all rights. Simultaneous and photocopied submissions OK. Query for electronic submissions. Computer printout submissions OK; prefers letter-quality to dot-matrix. Reports in 3 weeks on queries; 5 weeks on mss. Sample copy for 9x12 SAE with 4 first class stamps; writer's guidelines for legal-size SAE with 1 first class stamp.

Nonfiction: Interview/profile and technical. "Our news articles show how the technology is being applied and how it affects people. Examples: costs of new languages, problems in SDI software, copyright law, changes in ways of doing things." Buys 10-12 mss/year. Query with published clips. Length: 300-2,000 words. Pays $100-500 for assigned articles. Sometimes pays the expenses of writers on assignment.

Photos: State availability of photos with submission. Reviews contact sheets. Offers $25-50 per photo. Captions and identification of subjects required. Buys one-time rights.

Tips: "The approach is to pitch an idea. If the idea is good, there's a good chance (budget allowing) a story will follow. Be concise and direct.''

‡INFORM, The Magazine of Information and Image Management, Association for Information and Image Management, 1100 Wayne Ave., Silver Spring MD 20910. (301)587-8202. Editor: Steve Fluty. 30% freelance written. Prefers to work with writers with business/high tech experience. A monthly trade magazine on information system management. "Specifically we feature coverage of office automation, computer systems, electronic imaging and developments in storage and retrieval technology like optical disk, computer-assisted retrieval." Circ. 10,000. Pays on publication. Publishes ms an average of 3 months after acceptance. Byline given. Offers $50 kill fee. Buys first North American serial and second serial (reprint) rights. Submit seasonal/holiday material 2 months in advance. Simultaneous and photocopied submissions OK. Computer printout submissions OK; prefers letter-quality to dot-matrix. Free sample copy and writer's guidelines.

Nonfiction: Interview/profile, new product, photo feature and technical. Buys 4-12 mss/year. Query. Length: 1,500-4,000 words. Pays $200-500 for assigned articles. Sometimes pays the expenses of writers on assignment.

Photos: State availability of photos with submission. Reviews negatives, 4x5 transparencies and prints. Offers no additional payment for photos accepted with ms. Captions and identification of subjects required. Buys all rights.

Columns/Departments: Trends (impact of developments across industry segments); Technology (innovations of specific technology); Management (costs, strategies of managing information), all 500-1,500 words. Query. Length: 500-1,500 words. Pays $250.

Fillers: Facts and newsbreaks. Length: 150-500 words. Pays $50-250.

Tips: "We would encourage freelancers who have access to our editorial calendar to contact us regarding article ideas, inquiries, etc. We also cover numerous trade shows during the year, and the availability of freelancers to cover these events would be valuable to us. Our feature section is the area where the need for quality freelance coverage of our industry is most desirable. The most likely candidate for acceptance is someone who has a proven background in business writing, and/or someone with demonstrated knowledge of high-tech industries as they relate to information management."

‡INFORMATION WEEK, CMP Inc., 600 Community Dr., Manhasset NY 11030. (516)365-4600. Editor: Dennis Eskow. Managing Editor: John McCormick. 20% freelance written. Weekly magazine covering information systems management. "Our readers are busy executives who want excellent information or thoughtful opinion on making computers and associated equipment improve the competiveness of their companies." Circ. 130,000. Pays on publication. Publishes ms an average of 1 month after acceptance. Byline given. Offers 25% kill fee. Buys first North American serial rights and second serial (reprint) rights. Submit seasonal/holiday material 2 months in advance. Previously published submissions rarely OK. Query for electronic submissions. Computer printout submissions OK; prefers letter-quality to dot-matrix. Reports in 2 weeks on queries; 1 week on mss. Sample copy for 8x11 SAE.

Nonfiction: Book excerpts (information management); expose (government computing, big vendors); humor (850 word piece reflecting on our information era and its people); and interview/profile (corporate chief information officers). No software reviews, product reviews, no "gee whiz—computers are wonderful" pieces. Buys 20-30 mss/year. Query with or without published clips. Length: 500-3,500 words. Pays $300-1,500. Pays expenses of writers on assignment.

Photos: Send photos with submission. Reviews negatives and transparencies. Pays negotiable rates. Captions, model releases and identification of subjects required. Buys one-time rights.

Columns/Departments: Final Word (a humorous or controversial, personal opinion page on high level computer-oriented business), 850 words; Chiefs (interview, portrait of chief information officer in Fortune 500 Company), 2,000-3,000 words. Buys 100 mss/year. Query. Length: 800-900 words. Pays $100-1,500.

Tips: "We appreciate a *one paragraph* lead, a headline, a deck and a very brief outline. This evokes the quickest response. Humor is the most difficult thing to create and the one we crave the most. Humor is especially difficult when the subject is management information systems. Good humor is an easy sell with us."

JOURNAL OF INFORMATION SYSTEMS MANAGEMENT, Auerbach Publishers, Inc., 1 Penn Plaza, New York NY 10119. Editor: Peggy Burns. Managing Editor: Kim Horan Kelly. 100% freelance written. Works with a small number of new/unpublished writers each year. A quarterly magazine covering information systems management. "Our journal provides those charged with responsibility for MIS mangement with practical, timely, how-to information addressing problems associated with coordinating line functions, managing technologies, interacting with users, and dealing with corporate management." Circ. 10,000. Pays on acceptance. Publishes ms an average of 6 months after acceptance. Byline given (includes capsule biography). Buys all rights. Simultaneous submissions OK. Computer printout submissions acceptable; prefers letter-quality to dot-matrix. Reports in 2 weeks on queries; 2 months on mss. Free sample copy and writer's guidelines.

Nonfiction: How-to; interview/profile (query); case study (query); and MIS-related issues. Upcoming theme issues include Integration of Emerging Technologies, End-User Computing, Data Security, and Networking. "We do not publish informal or jocular essays, nor do we publish elementary, theoretical, or purely academic material." Buys 20 mss/year. Query or send complete ms. Length: 1,000-6,000 words. Pays $500 maximum.

Columns: Each issue of the journal contains 8-10 of the following columns: Strategic Planning, Managing Micros, Managing End-User Computing, Staff Development, Office Automation, Data Center Operations, Systems Development, Data Communications, MIS Economics, Technology Outlook, Security and Privacy, EDP Auditing, The User Interface, Data Management, In Practice: A Consultant's Viewpoint, Corporate Issues in MIS Management, On MIS: A View from the Top, MIS Industry Trends Analysis, Software Solutions, and Book Review. "We will accept column material with a more informal, opinion-oriented slant than our regular articles." Buys 40 mss/year. Query. Length: 1,000-3,000 words. Pays $100.

Tips: "Writers should keep in mind that our readers possess a high level of sophistication in both technical and management areas. As managers of the MIS function, they have many responsibilities that pit them against myriad problems for which they need direct, practical advice. We welcome knowledgeable writers who can help our readers by telling them something they can use, something they do not already know. We discourage submissions that are too basic in scope or too theoretical to be of practical value to MIS managers in their work environment. All areas are equally open to freelancers. We encourage long-term associations with writers who can produce valuable material for us."

JOURNAL OF SYSTEMS MANAGEMENT, 24587 Bagley Road, Cleveland OH 44138. (216)243-6900. Publisher: James Andrews. 100% freelance written. Prefers to work with published/established writers; works with a small number of new/unpublished writers each year. Monthly. For systems and procedures and management people. Pays on publication. Publishes ms an average of 3 months after acceptance. Byline given. Buys all rights. Computer printout submissions acceptable; prefers letter-quality to dot-matrix. Reports "as soon as possible." Free sample copy.

Nonfiction: Articles on case histories, projects on systems, forms control, administrative practices and computer operations. No computer applications articles, humor or articles promoting a specific product. Query or submit ms in triplicate. Length: 3,000-5,000 words. Pays $25 maximum.

Tips: Frequent mistakes made by writers are choosing the wrong subject and being too specific regarding a product.

MICRO CORNUCOPIA, The Micro Technical Journal, Micro Cornucopia Inc., 155 NW Hawthorne, Bend OR 97701. (503)382-8048. Editor: David J. Thompson. A bimonthly magazine offering in-depth technical coverage of micro computers. Circ. 16,000. Pays on publication. Publishes ms an average of 2 months after acceptance. Byline given. Offers $25 kill fee. Buys first rights. Submit seasonal/holiday material 3 months in advance. Electronic submissions OK via MS-DOS/PC-DOS/CP/M. Computer printout submissions acceptable; prefers letter-quality to dot-matrix. Reports in 1 month on queries; 2 months on mss. Sample copy $3; free writer's guidelines.

Nonfiction: Gary Entsminger, articles editor. How-to (published article examples—How to write a PRO-LOG interpreter, How to build a 68000 computer); new product; personal experience and technical. Buys 60 mss/year. Query with or without published clips, or send complete ms. Length: 2,000-5,000 words. Pays $75 minimum for assigned articles; pays $25 minimum for unsolicited articles. May pay other premiums in addition to fee.

Photos: State availability of photos with submission. Offers no additional payment for photos accepted with ms. Buys one-time rights.

MINI, The Magazine for IBM Systems 34/36/38 Decision Makers, Para Research, Inc., 85 Eastern Ave., Box 61, Gloucester MA 01930. (617)283-3438. Editor: Marlene Comet. 50% freelance written ("would like more.") Works with a small number of new/unpublished writers each year. A quarterly magazine covering IBM Systems 34/36/38 computers. "Our readers are general or financial managers using IBM minicomputers, mostly for accounting purposes. They are not computer professionals." Circ. 34,000. Pays on publication. Publishes ms an average of 4 months after acceptance. Byline given. Offers 10¢/word kill fee. Buys first North American serial rights, first rights, one-time rights, second serial (reprint) rights or simultaneous rights. Simultaneous, photocopied and previously published submissions OK. Computer printout submissions acceptable; no dot-matrix. Reports in 1 week on queries; 2 weeks on mss. Free sample copy.

Nonfiction: Book excerpts, how-to, new product, personal experience and technical. Buys 5-10 mss/year. Query. Length: 2,000-5,000 words. Pays $500-1,500. Sometimes pays the expenses of writers on assignment.

Photos: State availability of photos with submission. Captions, model releases and identification of subjects required. Buys one-time rights.

Tips: "We would like to receive material on micro-to-mini communications."

MINI-MICRO SYSTEMS, Cahners Publishing Co., 275 Washington St., Newton MA 02158. (617)964-3030. Editor-in-Chief: George Kotelly. 25% freelance written. Monthly magazine covering minicomputer and microcomputer industries for manufacturers and users of computers, peripherals and software. Circ. 138,000. Pays on publication. Byline given. Publishes ms an average of 3 months after acceptance. Buys all rights. Simultaneous queries and photocopied submissions OK. Computer printout submissions acceptable; prefers letter-quality to dot-matrix. Reports in 1 month on queries. Free sample copy; writer's guidelines for 4x9 SAE and 1 first class stamp.

Nonfiction: Articles about highly innovative applications of computer hardware and software "firsts". Buys 25-50 mss/year. Query with published clips. Length: 500-2,500 words. Pays $70-100/printed page, including illustrations. Sometimes pays expenses of writers on assignment.

Photos: Send line art, diagrams, photos or color transparencies.

Tips: "The best way to break in is to be affiliated with a manufacturer or user of computers or peripherals."

NEWS/34-38, For Users of IBM Systems 34/36/38, Duke Corporation, Box 3438, Loveland CO 80539. (303)663-4700. Editor: David A. Duke. Managing Editor: David Bernard. 40% freelance written. Eager to work with new/unpublished writers. "We need experienced computer-literate writers." A technically-oriented monthly magazine for data processing users of IBM Systems 34/36/38. Circ. 25,000. Pays on publication. Publishes ms an average of 4 months after acceptance. Byline given. Buys all rights. Simultaneous queries OK. Electronic submissions OK on PC Crosstalk, WordStar and IBM System/36, but requires hard copy also. Computer printout submissions acceptable; prefers letter-quality to dot-matrix. Reports in 1 month. Free sample copy and writer's guidelines.
Nonfiction: How-to (use Systems 34/36/38); interviews (with users); new product (review); opinion; personal experience (as a DP manager); and technical (tips and techniques). No fluff. Buys 50-100 mss/year. Query with or without published clips. Length: 1,000-5,000 words. Pays $100-500. Sometimes pays expenses of writers on assignment.
Photos: State availability of photos. Send photos with query or ms. Pays $5-10 for b&w prints; $5-20 for color transparencies. Captions, model release, and identification of subjects required. Buys all rights.
Columns/Departments: Technical Tips. Buys 12 mss/year. Query. Length: 50-500 words. Pays $10-100.
Fillers: Newsbreaks. Buys 25/year. Length: 50-500 words. Pays $10-100.
Tips: "We are a very targeted magazine going to a technically-oriented audience. Our writers *must* have a working knowledge of the IBM Systems 34/36/38 computers. Tutorial topics, user stories and management topics are most open to freelancers. We are interested in short feature stories as preferred by our readers. Also, all articles must have immediate benefit to our readers (i.e., if a technique is described, the code must be included so readers can implement the procedure immediately)."

OA MAGAZINE, (formerly *Office Management & Automation*), Plesman Publications Ltd., Suite 703, 2 Lansing Sq., Willowdale, Ontario M2J 5A1 Canada. (416)497-9562 or 1-800-387-5012. Editor: Gordon Campbell. Managing Editor: Ian McGugan. 50% freelance written. Works with a small number of new/unpublished writers each year. A monthly tabloid covering business management and computer applications. "Stories about managing technology and people effectively, with a Canadian and end-user focus." Circ. 51,000. Pays 30 days after acceptance. Publishes ms an average of 1 month after acceptance. Byline given. Buys first North American serial rights and other rights. Submit seasonal/holiday material 2 months in advance. Photocopied and previously published submissions sometimes OK. Electronic submissions OK; call for details. Computer printout submissions acceptable; no dot-matrix. Reports in 2 weeks. Sample copy for 9x12 SAE with 4 first class stamps; writer's guidelines for letter size SAE with 1 first class stamp.
Nonfiction: Book excerpts, essays, exposé, general interest, how-to (on business computer applications for business), humor, inspirational, interview/profile, new product, opinion, personal experience, photo feature and technical. "No articles lacking 'hard' facts, 'realistic understanding of business' or articles full of advice, non-attributed quotes, etc." Buys 60 mss/year. Query with published clips, resume, or send complete ms. Length: 1,600-2,500 words. Pays $0-350; up to $1,000 for cover story (with photos). Sometimes pays the expenses of writers on assignment.
Photos: State availability of photos with submission; send photos with submission. Reviews contact sheets, 4x5 transparencies (for covers), and 8x10 prints. Offers $0-500/photo. Captions, model releases, and identification of subjects required. Buys one-time rights and other rights.
Columns/Departments: Compleat Manager (humorous, oratorical, analytical, podium); Quarterly Report (legal, finance/accounting, management consulting); and Micro Manager (end-user computing within corporations). Buys 12 mss/year. Query with or without published clips or send complete ms. Length: 800-1,200 words.
Tips: "Send a resume outlining education and experience, especially business and writing education/experience. We are looking for professional writers interested in realistic, humane stories about people and their changing offices in Canada. Vendor hype or generalities are not wanted."

‡SYSTEMS/3X WORLD, (formerly *Small Systems World*), Hunter Publishing, 950 Lee St., Des Plaines IL 60016. (312)296-0770. Editor: Anne Hedin. 10% freelance written. Works with a small number of new/unpublished writers each year. Monthly magazine covering applications of IBM minicomputers (S/34/36/38/ and IBM PC/AT) in business. Circ. 37,000. Pays on acceptance. Publishes ms an average of 2 months after acceptance. Byline given. Buys all rights. Submit seasonal/holiday material 4 months in advance. Query for electronic submissions. Computer printout submissions acceptable; prefers letter-quality to dot-matrix. Reports in 2 weeks on queries. Sample copy $5.
Nonfiction: How-to (use the computer in business); and technical (organization of a data base or file system). "A writer who submits material to us should be an expert in computer applications. No material on large scale computer equipment." No poetry. Buys 8 mss/year. Query. Length: 3,000-4,000 words. Sometimes pays expenses of writers on assignment.
Tips: "We only buy long features, mostly ones that we commission. Frequent mistakes are not understanding the audience and not having read the magazine (past issues)."

UNIX/WORLD, Multiuser Systems, Tech Valley Publishing, 444 Castro St., Mountain View CA 94041. (415)940-1500. Editor-in-Chief: David L. Flack. 75% freelance written. Prefers to work with established writers or experts in the computer industry. Monthly magazine directed exclusively to the multiuser, multitasking computer industry. Readers are employed in management, engineering, and software development. Circ. 32,000 + . Pays 30 days after publication. Publishes ms an average of 4 months after acceptance. Byline given. Offers kill fee. Buys first North American serial rights and second (reprint) rights. Electronic submissions encouraged if compatible with 300/1200 baud ASCII format, UUCP (UNIX) or via PC/MS DOS format diskettes with ASCII files. Computer printout submissions acceptable; prefers letter-quality to dot-matrix. Reports in 1 month. Sample copy $3. Writer's guidelines sent when article is accepted on spec. Ask for editorial calendar so query can be tailored to the magazine's need; send SASE with 39¢ postage.

Nonfiction: Book excerpts; how-to (technical articles on the Unix system or the C language); new products; technical overviews; and product reviews. Query by phone or with cover letter and published clips. Length: 2,500-3,000 words. Pays $100-1,000. Sometimes pays the expenses of writers on assignment.

Photos: Send photos with queries. Reviews b&w contact sheets. Identification of subjects required. Buys all rights.

Columns/Departments: Publishes 2 guest columns—an alternating column on standards/international issues; and a guest column that exposes a controversal viewpoint. Query by phone. Pays $100 each. Other columns are regular departments written by contributing editors.

Tips: "We are shifting more toward a business and commercial focus and would appreciate knowledge in that area. The best way to get an acceptance on an article is to consult our editorial calendar and tailor a pitch to a particular story."

Insurance

‡BUSINESS INSURANCE, 740 N. Rush Street, Chicago IL 60611. Editor: Kathryn J. McIntyre. 2% freelance written. Prefers to work with experienced financial reporters. For "corporate risk, employee benefit and financial executives, insurance brokers and agents, and insurance company executives interested in commercial insurance, risk and benefit financing, safety, security and employee benefits." Special issues on self insurance, pensions, health and life benefits, brokers, reinsurance and international insurance. Weekly. Circ. 49,000. Buys all rights. Pays negotiable kill fee. Byline given. Buys 50 mss/year. Pays on publication. Publishes ms an average of 1 month after acceptance. Submit seasonal or special material 2 months in advance. Query for electronic submissions. Computer printout submissions OK; prefers letter-quality to dot-matrix. Reports in 2 weeks. Query.

Nonfiction: "We publish material on corporate insurance and employee benefit programs and related subjects. We take everything from the buyer's point of view, rather than that of the insurance company, broker or consultant who is selling something. Items on insurance companies, insurance brokers, property/liability insurance, union contract (benefit) settlements, group life/health/medical plans, of interest—provided the *commercial* insurance or benefits angle is clear. Special emphasis on corporate risk management and employee benefits administration requires that freelancers discuss with us their proposed articles. Length is subject to discussion with contributor." Pays $7/column inch or negotiated fee. Sometimes pays the expenses of writers on assignment.

Tips: "Send a detailed proposal including story angle and description of sources."

COMPASS, Marine Office of America Corporation (MOAC), 180 Maiden Lane, New York NY 10038. (212)440-7720. Editor: Irene E. Lombardo. 75% freelance written. Prefers to work with published/established writers. Semiannual magazine of the Marine Office of America Corporation. Magazine is distributed to persons in marine insurance (agents, brokers, risk managers), employees and the media. Circ. 8,000. Pays half on acceptance, half on publication. Publishes ms an average of 6 months after acceptance. Byline given. Offers $500 kill fee on manuscripts accepted for publication, but subsequently cancelled. Not copyrighted. Buys first North American serial rights. Does not accept previously published work or unsolicited mss. Query first. Simultaneous queries OK. Query for electronic submissions. Computer printout submissions acceptable; no dot-matrix. Reports in 4 weeks on queries. Free sample copy and writer's guidelines.

Nonfiction: General interest, historical/nostalgic and technical. "Historical/nostalgia should relate to ships, trains, airplanes, balloons, bridges, sea and land expeditions, seaports and transportation of all types. General interest includes marine and transportation subjects; fishing industry; and environmental events—improvements relating to inland waterways, space travel and satellites. Articles must have human interest. Technical articles may cover energy exploration and development—offshore oil and gas drilling, developing new sources of electric power and solar energy; usages of coal, water and wind to generate electric power; and special cargo handling such as containerization on land and sea. Articles must not be overly technical and should have reader interest." No book excerpts, first-person, exposes, how-to, humor or opinion. Buys 8 mss/year. Query with published clips. All articles are submitted on speculation. Length: 1,500-2,000 words. Pays $1,000 maximum. Sometimes pays the expenses of writers on assignment.

Photos: Robert A. Cooney, photo editor. (212)838-6200. State availability of photos. Reviews b&w and color transparencies and prints. Captions and identification of subjects required. Buys one-time rights.

Tips: "We want profiles of individuals connected with marine, energy, and transportation fields who are unusual. Send a brief outline of the story idea to editor mentioning also the availability of photographs in b&w and color. All articles must be thoroughly researched and original. Articles should have human interest through the device of interviews. We only publish full-length articles—no fillers."

INSURANCE REVIEW, Insurance Information Institute, 110 William St., New York NY 10038. (212)669-9200. Editor: Colleen Katz. Managing Editor: Joseph Burns. 100% freelance written. A monthly magazine covering property and casualty insurance for agents, brokers, insurers, educators, lawyers, financial analysts and journalists. Circ. 80,000. Pays on acceptance. Publishes ms an average of 2 months after acceptance. Byline given. Offers 25% kill fee. Buys first North American serial rights; rights returned to author 90 days after publication. "We retain right to reprint." Electronic submissions OK via IBM PC Word Perfect, but requires hard copy also. Reports in 1 month. Free sample copy and writer's guidelines.

Nonfiction: How-to (improve agency business), humor, interview/profile, opinion, photo feature, technical, travel and business articles with insurance information. Buys 180 mss/year. Query with published clips. Length: 750-2,500 words. Pays $250-1,000 for assigned articles. Pays expenses of writers on assignment.

Photos: Send photos with submission. Reviews contact sheets and transparencies. Captions, model releases and identification of subjects required.

Columns/Departments: By Line (analysis of one line of business p/c), Analysis (financial aspects of p/c industry), and Discoveries (travel pieces on a city). Query. Length: 750-1,200 words. Pays $200-350.

Fillers: Facts, gags to be illustrated by cartoonist and newsbreaks. Buys 50/year. Length: 75-200 words. Pays $25-100.

Tips: "Become well-versed in issues facing the insurance industry. Find interesting people to write about. Profile successful agents or brokers."

‡INSURANCE SOFTWARE REVIEW, International Computer Programs, Inc., Suite 200, 9100 Keystone Crossing, Indianapolis IN 46240. (317)844-7461. Editor: Sheila B. Cunningham. 50% freelance written. Quarterly magazine covering the computer software industry as it relates to insurance companies and agencies. "Editorial slant includes the selection, implementation and use of software in insurance companies, agencies, and brokerages. Audience comprises data processing and end-user management in medium to large insurance concerns." Circ. 15,000. Pays on publication. Publishes ms an average of 2 months after acceptance. Byline sometimes given. Buys first and second serial (reprint) rights. Simultaneous and photocopied submissions OK. Query for electronic submissions. Computer printout submissions OK; prefers letter-quality to dot-matrix. Reports in 2 weeks on queries; 3 weeks on mss. Free sample copy and writer's guidelines.

Nonfiction: How to (successfully install and use software products), interview/profile, new product and technical. No non-software related, non-business software or humorous articles. Buys 8-10 mss/year. Query with published clips. Length: 1,000-2,000 words. Pays $100-350 for assigned articles. Sometimes pays the expenses of writers on assignment.

Photos: Send photos with submission. Reviews 5x7 prints. Offers no additional payment for photos accepted with ms. Identification of subjects required. Buys all rights.

Columns/Departments: Systems Review (in-depth profile of a specific software product at use in an insurance environment; must include comments from an insurance user [e.g., the benefits of the product, its use within the insurance firm, etc.]). Length: 500-700 words. Pays $50-100.

PROFESSIONAL AGENT MAGAZINE, Professional Insurance Agents, 400 N. Washington St., Alexandria VA 22314. (703)836-9340. Editor: Eric R. Wassyng. 25% freelance written. Prefers to work with published/established writers. Monthly magazine covering insurance/small business for independent insurance agents. Circ. 40,000. Pays on acceptance. Publishes ms an average of 2 months after acceptance. Byline given. Buys exclusive rights in the industry. Query for electronic submissions. Computer printout submissions acceptable; prefers letter-quality to dot-matrix. Reports ASAP. Sample copy for SAE.

Nonfiction: Insurance management for small businesses and self-help. Special issues on life insurance and computer interface. Buys 24 mss/year. Query with published clips or send complete ms. Length: 1,000-3,000 words. Pays $150-500. Sometimes pays the expenses of writers on assignment.

Photos: State availability of photos. Pays $35-200 for 5x7 b&w prints; $50-300 for 35mm color transparencies. Captions, model release, and identification of subjects required. Buys one-time rights.

PULSE, Transamerica Occidental Life Insurance Corp., B9E 1149 S. Broadway, Los Angeles CA 90015. (213)741-7226. Editor: Paul A. Sergios. Managing Editor: Stephanie Burchfield. 20% freelance written. Works with a small number of new/unpublished writers each year. A monthly company magazine covering Transamerica products and developments in life insurance. "*Pulse* contains information for Transamerica's 10,000-member selling force, emphasizing trends in life insurance industry, selling techniques of products, and profiles on top sellers." Circ. 10,000. Pays on acceptance. Publishes ms an average of 1 month after acceptance. Byline given. Offers 25% kill fee. Buys one-time rights. Simultaneous, photocopied, and previously published submissions OK. Query for electronic submissions. Computer printout submissions acceptable; prefers letter-quality to dot-matrix. Reports in 2 weeks on queries; 1 month on mss. Free sample copy and writer's guidelines.

Nonfiction: Interview/profile, new product and sales techniques. Articles must deal directly with sales techniques of Transamerica Life agents. Query with published clips. Length: open. Pays $250-500; sometimes pays in copies to very new writers seeking portfolio material.

Photos: Reviews contact sheets. Offers $25-100. Model releases and identification of subjects required. Buys one-time rights.

Tips: "Keep abreast of current trends in life insurance sales, new product introduction and cross-competitive offerings. A strong marketing orientation and extensive knowledge of today's financial services marketplace is preferred in freelancers. Research the local Transamerica branch in your area and look for newsworthy subject matter. Areas most open to freelancers are profiles of Transamerica's top sellers. Read industry trades and keep track of competitors and selling techniques."

———— International Affairs

These publications cover global relations, international trade, economic analysis and philosophy for business executives and government officials involved in foreign affairs. Consumer publications on related subjects are listed in Politics and World Affairs.

FOREIGN AFFAIRS, 58 E. 68th St., New York NY 10021. (212)734-0400. Editor: William G. Hyland. 100% freelance written. For academics, businessmen (national and international), government, educational and cultural readers especially interested in international affairs of a political nature. Published 5 times/year. Circ. 90,000. Pays on publication. Publishes ms an average of 3 months after acceptance. Buys all rights. Pays kill fee. Byline given. Photocopied submissions OK. Electronic submissions OK via 8" disk: Wang; Modem (300-1200 baud), but requires hard copy also. Computer printout submissions acceptable; prefers letter-quality to dot-matrix. Reports in 6 weeks. Submit complete ms. Sample copy $5 postpaid.

Nonfiction: "Articles dealing with international affairs; political, educational, cultural, economic, scientific, philosophical and social sciences. Develop an original idea in depth, with a strong thesis usually leading to policy recommendations. Serious analyses by qualified authors on subjects with international appeal." Recent article example: "The President's Choice: Star Wars or Arms Control" (Winter 1984/85). Buys 25 unsolicited mss/year. Submit complete ms. Length: 5,000 words. Pays approximately $500.

Tips: "We like the writer to include his/her qualifications for writing on the topic in question (educational, past publications, relevant positions or honors), and a clear summation of the article: the argument (or area examined), and the writer's policy conclusions."

JOURNAL OF DEFENSE & DIPLOMACY, Defense and Diplomacy, Inc., 6819 Elm St., McLean VA 22101. (703)448-1338. Editor: Lois M. Blake. 50% freelance written. Eager to work with new/unpublished writers. "Publication credentials not necessary for consideration." Monthly publication covering international affairs and defense. "The *Journal* is a sophisticated, slick publication that analyzes international affairs for decision-makers—heads of state, key government officials, defense industry executives—who have little time to pore through all the details themselves." Circ. 20,000. Pays on publication. Publishes ms an average of 2 months after acceptance. Byline given. Offers 10% kill fee. Buys first rights and second serial (reprint) rights. Simultaneous queries, and simultaneous, photocopied, and previously published submissions OK. Computer printout submissions acceptable; prefers letter-quality to dot-matrix. Reports in 1 month on queries; 2 months on mss. Sample copy $5 (includes postage); writer's guidelines for business size envelope and 1 first class stamp.

Nonfiction: Book excerpts, general interest (strategy and tactics, diplomacy and defense matters), interview/profile, opinion and photo feature. "Decision-makers are looking for intelligent, straightforward assessments.

We want clear, concise writing on articles with international appeal. While we have accepted articles that deal with U.S. decisions, there is always an international aspect to the subject." No articles that focus solely on the United States. Buys 24 mss/year. Send complete ms. Length: 2,000-4,000 words. Pays $250.

Photos: Reviews color and b&w photos. No additional payment is offered for photos sent with ms.

Columns/Departments: Speaking Out (1,000 to 3,000-word "point of view" piece analyzing any current topic of widespread interest); Materiel (a technical discussion of current and upcoming weapons systems); Books (reviews of books on world politics, history, biography and military matters); interview ("We constantly need interviews with important international figures. We are always looking for the non-U.S. interview."). Buys 12 mss/year. Query with published clips. Length: 1,500-3,000 words. Pays $100-250.

Tips: "We depend on experts in the field for most of the articles that we use. As long as a manuscript demonstrates that the writer knows the subject well, we are willing to consider anyone for publication. The most frequent mistake made by writers in completing an article for us is writing in too technical or too official a style. We want to be very readable. We are looking for writers who are able to digest complex subjects and make them interesting and lively. We need writers who can discuss complicated and technical weapons systems in clear non-technical ways."

Jewelry

AMERICAN JEWELRY MANUFACTURER, 8th Floor, 825 7th Ave., New York NY 10019. (212)245-7555. Editor: Steffan Aletti. 5% freelance written. Works with a small number of new/unpublished writers each year. For jewelry manufacturers, as well as manufacturers of supplies and tools for the jewelry industry; their representatives, wholesalers and agencies. Monthly. Circ. 5,000. Buys all rights (with exceptions). Publishes ms an average of 5 months after acceptance. Byline given. Photocopied submissions OK. Computer printout submissions acceptable; prefers letter-quality to dot-matrix. Submit seasonal/holiday material 3 months in advance. Reports in 1 month. Free sample copy and writer's guidelines.

Nonfiction: "Topical articles on manufacturing; company stories; economics (e.g., rising gold prices). Story must inform or educate the manufacturer. Occasional special issues on timely topics, e.g., gold; occasional issues on specific processes in casting and plating. We reject material that is not specifically pointed at our industry; e.g., articles geared to jewelry retailing or merchandising, not to manufacturers." Informational, how-to, interview, profile, historical, expose, successful business operations, new product, merchandising techniques and technical. "The most frequent mistake made by writers in completing an article for us is unfamiliarity with the magazine—retail or merchandising oriented articles are sent in. Query first; we have accepted some general business articles, but not many." Buys 5-10 unsolicited mss/year. Length: open. Payment "usually around $50/printed page." Sometimes pays the expenses of writers on assignment.

Photos: B&w photos purchased with ms. 5x7 minimum.

Tips: "We plan no changes in focus, but we are sensitive to any trends—precious metal prices or availability, new federal tax or pollution laws—that affect the manufacturer's operations."

CANADIAN JEWELLER, 777 Bay St., Toronto, Ontario M5W 1A7 Canada. Editor: Simon Hally. Monthly magazine for members of the jewelry trade, primarily retailers. Circ. 6,000. Pays on acceptance. Buys first Canadian serial rights.

Nonfiction: Wants "stories on the jewelry industry internationally." Query. Length: 200-2,000 words. Pays $40-500.

Photos: Reviews 5x7 and 8x10 b&w prints and 35mm and 2¼x2¼ color transparencies. "We pay more if usable photos accompany ms. Payment is based on space used in the book including both text and photos."

THE DIAMOND REGISTRY BULLETIN, 30 W. 47th St., New York NY 10036. Editor-in-Chief: Joseph Schlussel. 15% freelance written. Monthly newsletter. Pays on publication. Buys all rights. Submit seasonal/holiday material 1 month in advance. Simultaneous and previously published submissions OK. Computer printout submissions acceptable; prefers letter-quality to dot-matrix. Reports in 3 weeks. Sample copy $5.

Nonfiction: Prevention advice (on crimes against jewelers); how-to (ways to increase sales in diamonds, improve security, etc.); and interview (of interest to diamond dealers or jewelers). Submit complete ms. Length: 50-500 words. Pays $10-150.

Tips: "We seek ideas to increase sales of diamonds."

THE ENGRAVERS JOURNAL, Box 318, 26 Summit St., Brighton MI 48116. (313)229-5725. Co-Publisher and Managing Editor: Michael J. Davis. 15% freelance written. "We are eager to work with published/established writers as well as new/unpublished writers." A bimonthly magazine covering the recognition and identification industry (engraving, marking devices, awards, jewelry, and signage.) "We provide practical information for the education and advancement of our readers, mainly retail business owners." Pays on acceptance. Publishes ms an average of 1 year after acceptance. Byline given "only if writer is recognized authority." Buys all rights (usually). Query with published clips and resume. Photocopied and previously published submissions OK. Query for electronic submissions. Computer printout submissions acceptable; prefers letter-quality to dot-matrix. Reports in 2 weeks. Free writer's guidelines; sample copy to "those who send writing samples with inquiry."

Nonfiction: General interest (industry-related); how-to (small business subjects, increase sales, develop new markets, use new sales techniques, etc.); interview/profile; new product; photo feature (a particularly outstanding signage system); and technical. No general overviews of the industry. Buys 12 mss/year. Query with writing samples "published or not," or "send samples and resume to be considered for assignments on speculation." Length: 1,000-5,000 words. Pays $75-250, depending on writer's skill and expertise in handling subject.

Photos: Send photos with query. Reviews 8x10 prints. Pays variable rate. Captions, model release and identification of subjects required.

Tips: "Articles should always be down to earth, practical and thoroughly cover the subject with authority. We do not want the 'textbook' writing approach, vagueness, or theory—our readers look to us for sound practical information."

‡**FASHION ACCESSORIES**, S.C.M. Publications, Inc., 65 W. Main St., Bergenfield NJ 07621-1696. (201)384-3336. Managing Editor: Samuel Mendelson. Monthly newspaper covering costume or fashion jewelry. "Serves the manufacturers, manufacturers' sales reps., importers and exporters who sell exclusively through the wholesale level in ladies' fashion jewelry, mens' jewelry, gifts and boutiques and related novelties." Circ. 8,000. Pays on acceptance. Byline given. Not copyrighted. Buys first rights. Submit seasonal/holiday material 3 months in advance. Photocopied submissions OK. Computer printout submissions OK; no dot-matrix. Sample copy $2.

Nonfiction: Essays, general interest, historical/nostalgic, how-to, humor, interview/profile, new product and travel. Buys 20 mss/year. Query with published clips. Length: 1,000-2,000 words. Pays $100-300. Sometimes pays the expenses of writers on assignment.

Photos: /Send photos with submission. Reviews 4x5 prints. Offers no additional payment for photos accepted with ms. Identification of subjects required. Buys one-time rights.

Columns/Departments: Fashion Report (interviews and reports of fashion news), 1,000-2,000 words.

Tips: "We are interested in anything that will be of interest to costume jewelry buyers at the wholesale level."

WATCH AND CLOCK REVIEW, 2403 Champa St., Denver CO 80205. (303)296-1600. Managing Editor: Jayne L. Barrick. 20% freelance written. The magazine of watch/clock sales and service. Monthly magazine; 68 pages. Circ. 16,000. Pays on publication. Buys first rights only. Byline given. Submit seasonal/holiday material 3 months in advance. Reports in 3 weeks. Free sample copy.

Nonfiction: Articles on successful watch/clock manufacturers and retailers, merchandising and display, and profiles of industry leaders. Buys 15 mss/year. Query. Length: 1,000-2,000 words. Pays $100-250.

Photos: Submit photo material with accompanying ms. No additional payment for b&w glossy prints. Captions preferred; model release required. Buys first serial rights.

Columns/Departments: Buys 7 mss/issue. Pays $150-200. Open to suggestions for new columns/departments.

Tips: "Brevity is helpful in a query. Find the right subject—an interesting clock shop, a jewelry store with unique watch displays, a street clock of antiquarian interest, etc."

Journalism and Writing

Journalism and writing magazines cover both the business and creative sides of writing. Journalism magazine editors need writers whose experiences will be an inspiration to new writers and can report new trends and writing strategies.

THE AMERICAN SCREENWRITER, Grasshopper Productions, Inc., Box 67, Manchaca TX 78652. (512)282-2749. Editor: Gerald J. LePage. 40% freelance written. Eager to work with new/unpublished writers. A bimonthly newsletter covering scriptwriting for the screen and TV. "We address scriptwriters who ask for help through our script evaluation program. We aim at writers who are struggling to find their place in the market." Pays by arrangement with author. Foreign publication residuals guaranteed. Publishes ms an average of 2 months after acceptance. Byline given. Buys all rights. Submit seasonal/holiday material 2 months in advance. Simultaneous queries OK. Reports in 1 month. Sample copy $3; writer's guidelines for SAE and 1 first class stamp.

Nonfiction: Book excerpts, interview/profile, and personal experience related to scriptwriting. "No sophisticated material that oozes of past films which require reader having seen them." Query with published clips. Length: 300-500 words. Pays 5-10¢/word; interviews pay $50.

Tips: "We welcome journalists with screenwriter interview material. We want 'visual' writing—short, comprehensive articles that bring home a problematical point in less than five minute's reading. Suggest writers study publication."

BOOK DEALERS WORLD, American Bookdealers Exchange, Box 2525, La Mesa CA 92041. (619)462-3297. Editorial Director: Al Galasso. News and Feature Editor: Judy Wiggins. 50% freelance written. Quarterly magazine covering writing, self-publishing and marketing books by mail. Circ. 20,000. Pays on publication. Publishes ms an average of 3 months after acceptance. Byline given. Buys first serial rights and second serial (reprint) rights to material originally published elsewhere. Simultaneous and previously published submissions OK. Computer printout submissions acceptable; no dot-matrix. Reports in 1 month. Sample copy for $1.

Nonfiction: Book excerpts (writing, mail order, direct mail, publishing); how-to (home business by mail, advertising); and interview/profile (of successful self-publishers). Positive articles on self-publishing, new writing angles, marketing, etc. Buys 10 mss/year. Send complete ms. Length: 1,000-1,500 words. Pays $25-50.

Columns/Departments: Print Perspective (about new magazines and newsletters); Small Press Scene (news about small press activities); and Self-Publisher Profile (on successful self-publishers and their marketing strategy). Buys 20 mss/year. Send complete ms. Length: 250-1,000 words. Pays $5-20.

Fillers: Clippings. Fillers concerning writing, publishing or books. Buys 6/year. Length: 100-250 words. Pays $3-10.

Tips: "Query first. Get a sample copy of the magazine."

BOOKS AND RELIGION, Editorial Office, The Divinity School, Duke University, Durham NC 27706. (919)684-3569. Publisher: Dennis Campbell. Editor: Christopher Walters-Bugbee. 75% freelance written. Works with a small number of new/unpublished writers each year. Tabloid published bimonthly except July and August, reviewing religion—ecumenically conceived—and related fields. Circ. 15,000. "We do not pay for reviews. Reviewer keeps book." Publishes ms an average of 2 months after acceptance. Byline given. Submit seasonal/holiday material 3 months in advance. Reports in 1 month. Computer submissions acceptable. Sample copy available from: *Books and Religion*, The Divinity School, Duke University, Durham NC 27706.

Nonfiction: Book reviews. "Submit qualifications for reviewing serious works." Pays the expenses of writers on assignment.

Fiction: Query. "Only religious thematic material, broadly understood and not longer than 2,000 words." Purchases first serial rights and second serial rights for both excerpts.

‡BRILLIANT IDEAS FOR PUBLISHERS, Creative Brilliance Associates, 4709 Sherwood Rd., Box 4237, Madison WI 53711. (608)271-6867. Editor: Naomi K. Shapiro. 3% freelance written. A bimonthly magazine covering the newspaper and shopper industry. "We provide business news and ideas to publishers of the daily, weekly, community, surburban newspaper and shopper publishing industry." Circ. 13,500. Pays on publication. Publishes ms an average of 4 months after acceptance. Byline given. Buys all rights. Photocopied submissions OK. Query for electronic submissions. Computer printout submissions OK; no dot-matrix. Reports in 3 weeks. Sample copy for 9x12 SAE with 56¢ postage.

Nonfiction: General interest, historical/nostalgic, how-to (tips and hints regarding editorial, production, etc.), humor, interview/profile, new product and opinion. Only submit articles related to the newspaper industry, i.e., sales, marketing or management. "The writer has to know and understand the industry." Buys 3 mss/year. Query. Length: 300 words maximum. Pays $10-50 for unsolicited articles. May pay writers with contributor copies or other premiums if writer requests.

Photos: State availability of photos with submission. Offers no additional payment for photos accepted with ms. Captions, model releases and identification of subjects required. Buys all rights.

Columns/Departments: "Any books or brochures related to sales, marketing, management, etc. can be submitted for consideration for our BIFP Press department." Buys 3 mss/year. Query. Length: 200 words maximum. Pays $10-50.

Tips: "We are interested in working with any writer or researcher who has good, solid, documented pieces of interest to this specific industry."

BYLINE, Box 130596, Edmond OK 73013. (405)348-3325. Executive Editor/Publisher: Marcia Preston. Managing Editor: Kathryn Fanning. 80-90% freelance written. Eager to work with new/unpublished writers. Monthly magazine for writers and poets. "We stress encouragement of beginning writers." Publishes ms an average of 6 months after acceptance. Byline given. Buys first North American serial rights. Computer printout submissions OK; prefers letter-quality to dot-matrix. Reports within 1 month. Sample copy $3; writer's guidelines for SASE.

Nonfiction: How-to, humor, inspirational, personal experience, *all* connected with writing and selling. Read magazine for special departments. Buys approximately 72 mss/year. Prefers queries; will read complete mss. Length: 50-2,000 words. Pays $5-100; usual rate for main features is $50, on acceptance.

Fiction: General fiction. Writing or literary slant preferred, but not required. Send complete ms: 1,000-3,000 words. Pays $50 on acceptance.

Poetry: Any style, on a writing theme. Preferred length: 4-36 lines. Pays $3-5 on publication plus free issue.

CALIFORNIA PUBLISHER, Suite 1040, 1127 11th St., Sacramento CA 95814. (916)443-5991. Editor: Wayne Miyao. 5-10% freelance written, but increasing. Monthly tabloid read by publishers, journalism teachers, editors and managers in newspaper publishing in California. Publishes ms an average of 1-2 months after acceptance. Byline given. Buys first and second (reprint) rights. Computer printout submissions acceptable; prefers letter-quality to dot-matrix. Sample copy for 9x12 SAE with 39¢ postage.

Nonfiction: In-depth stories or articles designed to inform and amuse California newspaper publishers. Sample topics include: newsprint shortage, changing role of papers, historical profiles on California journalism greats, success stories, role of minorities in the newspaper field, profiles on California newspapers, and technological advances. No general humorous material. "If it isn't specific to *California* journalism, we don't want it." Query. Length: 2,000 words maximum. Pays $25-30.

Photos: Reviews b&w glossy prints.

Tips: "Go on; query us. Stories used will be read by all the newspaper publishers who count in the state of California. We'd like to showcase first effort, good writing talent."

CANADIAN AUTHOR & BOOKMAN, Canadian Authors Association, Suite 104, 121 Avenue Rd., Toronto, Ontario M5R 2G3 Canada. Contact: Editor. 95% freelance written. Prefers to work with published/established writers. "For writers—all ages, all levels of experience." Quarterly magazine; 32 pages. Circ. 3,000. Pays on publication. Publishes ms an average of 6 months after acceptance. Buys first Canadian rights. Byline given. Written queries only. Computer printout submissions acceptable; prefers letter-quality to dot-matrix. Sample copy $4.50.

Nonfiction: How-to (on writing, selling; the specifics of the different genres—what they are and how to write them); informational (the writing scene—who's who and what's what); interview (on writers, mainly leading ones, but also those with a story that can help others write and sell more often); and opinion. No personal, lightweight writing experiences; no fillers. Query with immediate pinpointing of topic, length (if ms is ready), and writer's background. Length: 800-1,500 words. Pays $25/printed page.

Photos: "We're after an interesting-looking magazine, and graphics are a decided help." State availability of photos with query. Offers $5/photo for b&w photos accepted with ms. Buys one-time rights.

Poetry: High quality. "Major poets publish with us—others need to be as good." Buys 40 poems/year. Pays $10.

Tips: "We dislike material that condescends to its reader and articles that advocate an adversarial approach to writer/editor relationships. We agree that there is a time and place for such an approach, but good sense should prevail. If the writer is writing to a Canadian freelance writer, the work will likely fall within our range of interest."

CANADIAN WRITER'S JOURNAL, Ronald J. Cooke Ltd., 58 Madsen Ave., Beaconsfield, Quebec H9W 4T7 Canada. (514)697-9315. Editor: Ronald S. Cooke. 50% freelance written. Works with a small number of new/unpublished writers each year, and is eager to work with new/unpublished writers. "We will accept well-written articles for and by young or experienced writers." A bimonthly digest-size magazine for writers. Circ. 3,000. Pays on publication. Publishes ms an average of 2-4 months after acceptance. Byline given. Buys one-time rights. "We seldom use anything pertaining to holidays." Computer printout submissions acceptable; no dot-matrix. Reports in 2 weeks on queries; 1 month on mss. Sample copy for $2 and 5x7 SAE with $1 postage (Canadian) or IRC.

Nonfiction: How-to articles for writers. Buys 30-35 mss/year. Query. Length: 500-1,000 words. "Would welcome an article on writing plays."

Tips: "We prefer short, how-to articles; 1,000 words is our limit and we prefer 700 words."

COLLEGE MEDIA REVIEW, Dept. of Journalism, Ball State University, Muncie IN 47306. Contact: Lillian Lodge-Kopenhaver, Dept. of Communication, Florida International University, North Miami FL 33181. 100% freelance written. Eager to work with new/unpublished writers. Quarterly magazine for members of College Media Advisers and staffs, editors and faculty advisers of college publications, journalism professors, and others interested in student communication media. Circ. 1,200. Acquires all rights. No payment. Publishes ms an average of 6 months after acceptance. Photocopied submissions OK. Computer printout submissions acceptable; prefers letter-quality to dot-matrix. Reports in 6 months. Sample copy $2.50; free writer's guidelines.

Nonfiction: Articles by, about and of interest to college publications advisers, staffs and editors. Articles should focus on editing, advising and producing college newspapers, yearbooks and magazines and operating electronic media, including radio, television and cable. "We like to use articles reporting research in publications and journalistic skills and well-thought-out opinion and essays on issues in the student media. Legal research specifically is welcome. Articles should be in a readable style with adequate attribution but without overuse of footnotes." Topical subjects of interest include increasing income, reducing costs, promoting publications, use of new technology, censorship cases at private colleges, tips on purchasing new equipment, how-to articles, and advances in techniques and resources. Book reviews on subjects related to student publications and/or college journalism education are welcomed. Submit them to Richard Wells, North Texas State University, Box 5278, Denton TX 76203-5278. Query or submit complete ms. Submit 2 copies of all mss. Length: 3,000 words maximum.

Photos: B&w glossy photos used with ms. Captions required.

COLUMBIA JOURNALISM REVIEW, 700 Journalism Bldg., Columbia University, New York NY 10027. (212)280-5595. Managing Editor: Gloria Cooper. "We welcome queries concerning media issues and performance. *CJR* also publishes book reviews. We emphasize in-depth reporting, critical analysis and good writing. All queries are read by editors."

CREATIVE YEARS, Coronado Publishers, #24, 5010 N.E. Waldo Rd., Gainesville FL 32609. (904)373-7445. Editor: Eloise Cozens Henderson. Associate Editor: Mary Onkka. 20% freelance written. Bimonthly magazine for new and unpublished writers. Circ. 2,000. Pays on publication. Publishes ms an average of 9 months after acceptance. Acquires one-time rights. Submit seasonal/holiday material 3 months in advance. Simultaneous submissions OK. Reports in 3 weeks on queries; 3 months on mss. Sample copy $2; writer's guidelines for SASE.

Nonfiction: General interest, historical/nostalgic, interview, humor, inspirational, opinion and personal experience. No obscenity, profanity, or liquor/drug related articles. Buys 30 mss/year. Length: 450-500 words. Send complete ms. Pays presently in copies only.

Fiction: Humorous, historical and religious. No obscenity, profanity, liquor/drug related mss. Buys 30 mss/year. Length: 450-500 words. Send complete ms. Pays in copies only.

Poetry: Light verse, traditional. No far out, agnostic, atheist, etc. poetry. Buys 12 poems/year. Pays in copies only.

Tips: "We use mostly material of beginning writers. We especially need Biblical quiz and other puzzle material. We are also seeking short articles about old times in sports (Babe Ruth, Ty Cobb, etc.). We are open for writer's questions and answers. Write to co-publisher Joseph Queiman, Box 1191, Meade MD 28755."

CROSS-CANADA WRITERS' QUARTERLY, The Canadian Literary Writer's Magazine, Cross-Canada Writers, Inc., Box 277, Station F, Toronto, Ontario M4Y 2L7 Canada. (416)690-0917. Editor: Ted Plantos. Associate Editor: Susan Ioannou. 90% freelance written. Prefers to work with published/established writers. A quarterly literary writer's magazine covering Canadian writing within an international context. Circ. 2,500. Pays on publication. Publishes ms an average of 1 year after acceptance. Byline given. Buys first North American serial rights. Submit seasonal/holiday material 6 months in advance. Photocopied submissions OK. Computer printout submissions acceptable; prefers letter-quality to dot-matrix. Reports in 3 weeks on queries; 2 months on mss. Sample copy $3.95, 9x12 SAE, and 85¢ Canadian postage or 2 IRCs.

Nonfiction: Essays, articles on literary aesthetics and interview/profile (established authors, editors, publishers—in-depth with photos). "Articles and interviews must have depth, be thought-provoking and offer insights into the creative and working processes of literature." No how-to's for beginners, or on nonliterary kinds of writing. Buys 4-10 mss/year. Query or send complete ms. "Each case is different. With an interview, a query could save time and work. A straight article we would have to read."

Photos: State availability of accompanying photos with query or send photos with ms, 5x7 b&w prints. Captions, model release, and identification of subjects required. Buys one-time rights.

Fiction: Contact the editor. Mainstream. No slight material—mere anecdotes rather than fully developed stories. Buys 4-8 mss/year. Send complete ms. Length: 1,000-3,000 words. Payment on publication.

Poetry: Poetry Editor. Free verse, haiku and traditional (if well-done). No concrete poetry, "diary excerpts" merely, highly obscure private poems or doggerel. Buys 40-50 poems/year. Submit maximum 10 poems. Length: 100 lines maximum "in exceptional cases." Offers $5/poem as payment.

Tips: "The most frequent mistakes made by writers in completing an article for us are misunderstanding of slant, and missing the opportunity for in-depth analysis. We want greater emphasis in literary essays on the aesthetics of writing."

EDITOR & PUBLISHER, 11 W. 19th St., New York NY 10011. Editor: Robert U. Brown. 10% freelance written. Weekly magazine; 60 pages. For newspaper publishers, editors, executives, employees and others in communications, marketing, advertising, etc. Circ. 29,000. Pays on publication. Publishes ms an average of 2 weeks after acceptance. Buys first serial rights. Computer printout submissions acceptable; prefers letter-quality to dot-matrix. Sample copy $1.
Nonfiction: John P. Consoli, managing editor. Uses newspaper business articles and news items; also newspaper personality features and printing technology. Query.
Fillers: "Amusing typographical errors found in newspapers." Pays $5.

THE EDITORIAL EYE, Focusing on Publications Standards and Practices, Editorial Experts, Inc., Suite 400, 85 S. Bragg St., Alexandria VA 22312. (703)642-3040. Editor: Bruce Boston. Managing Editor: Eleanor Johnson. 5% freelance written. Prefers to work with published/established writers. Monthly professional newsletter on editorial subjects: writing, editing, proofreading, and levels of editing. "Our readers are professional publications people. Use journalistic style." Circ. 2,100. Pays on acceptance. Publishes ms an average of 3 months after acceptance. Byline given. Kill fee determined for each assignment. Buys first North American serial rights. "We retain the right to use articles in our training division and in an anthology of collected articles." Submit seasonal/holiday material 3 months in advance. Computer printout submissions acceptable; prefers letter-quality to dot-matrix. Reports in 1 month. Sample copy for SASE and writer's guidelines for 1 first class stamp.
Nonfiction: Editorial problems, issues, standards, practices, and techniques; publication management; publishing technology; style, grammar and usage. No word games, vocabulary building, language puzzles, or jeremiads on how the English language is going to blazes. Buys 10 mss/year. Query. Length: 300-1,200. Pays $25-100.
Tips: "We seek mostly lead articles written by people in the publications field about the practice of publications work. Our style is journalistic with a light touch (not cute). We are interested in submissions on the craft of editing, levels of edit, editing by computer, publications management, indexing, lexicography, usages, proofreading. Our back issue list provides a good idea of the kinds of articles we run."

EDITORS' FORUM, Editors' Forum Publishing Company, Box 411806, Kansas City MO 64141. (913)236-9235. Editor: Jay H. Lawrence. Managing Editor: William R. Brinton. 50% freelance written. Prefers to work with published/established and works with a small number of new/unpublished writers each year. A monthly newsletter geared toward communicators, particularly those involved in the editing and publication of newsletters and company publications. Circ. 700. Pays on publication. Publishes ms an average of 4 months after acceptance. Byline given. Offers 25% kill fee. Not copyrighted. Buys first North American serial rights, second serial (reprint) rights, and makes work-for-hire assignments. Photocopied submissions OK. Previously published submissions OK depending on content. Computer printout submissions acceptable; no dot-matrix. Reports in 2 weeks on queries. Writer's guidelines for # 10 SAE with 22¢ postage.
Nonfiction: How-to on editing and writing, etc. "With the advent of computer publishing, EF is running a regular high tech column on desk top publishing, software, etc. We can use articles on the latest techniques in computer publishing. Not interested in anything that does not have a direct effect on writing and editing newsletters. This is a how-to newsletter." Buys 22 mss/year. Query. Length: 250-1,000 words. Pays $20/page maximum.
Photos: State availability of photos with submission. Reviews contact sheets. Offers $5/photo. Captions, model releases and identification of subjects required. Buys one-time rights.
Tips: "We are necessarily interested in articles pertaining to the newsletter business. That would include articles involving writing skills, layout and makeup, the use of pictures and other graphics to brighten up our reader's publication, and an occasional article on how to put out a good publication inexpensively."

‡THE FINAL DRAFT, Writer's Refinery, Box 47786, Phoenix AZ 85068-7786. (602)944-5268. Editorial Director: Elizabeth "Libbi" Goodman. Editors: Nolan Anglum and Linda Hilton. A monthly newsletter on writing. "The premise of our publication is to teach and impart useful information to published and aspiring writers. We also provide an opportunity for new writers to get published." Circ. 800 and growing. Pays on publication. Publishes ms an average of 2-6 months after acceptance. Byline given. Buys first North American serial rights, second serial (reprint) rights or makes work-for-hire assignments. Submit seasonal/holiday material 6 months in advance. Photocopied and previously published submissions OK. Computer printout submissions OK; prefers letter-quality to dot-matrix. Reports in 1 month. Sample copy for $1 with #10 SAE and 1 first class stamp; writer's guidelines for #10 SAE with 1 first class stamp.
Nonfiction: Book excerpts, essays, expose, general interest, historical/nostalgic, how-to, humor, motivational, interview/profile (especially with writers of juvenile fiction), new product, opinion, personal experience, technical and travel. "No interviews with people not associated with the craft of writing. No book reviews of fiction. Will accept reviews on books dealing with the craft/writing." Buys 100 mss/year. Send complete ms. Length: 500-3,000 words. Pays $5-20 for unsolicited articles. Pays in contributor's copies if article is of interest "but needs major rewriting author cannot do." Sometimes pays the expenses of writers on assignment.

Fiction: Adventure, experimental, fantasy, historical, horror, humorous, mystery, romance, science fiction, slice-of-life vignettes, suspense and western. "We are open to most fiction that uses writing or writers, as the theme. We do not want to see any fiction not slanted toward writers. Buys 3 mss/year "but looking to buy 12 per year." Send complete ms. Length: 500-1,500 words. Pays $4-15.

Poetry: "Must be of interest to writers. Open to all forms. No religious themes." Buys 20 poems/year. Submit maximum 5 poems. Length: 4-25 lines. Pays $2-5.

Fillers: Anecdotes, facts, gags and short humor. Length: 225-375 words. Pays $2-5.

Tips: "We are anxious to help new writers get started, but that does not mean we accept articles/fiction that are poorly written. Mss should be finely tuned *before* we see them. We are increasing the size of our publication, and are actively looking to purchase a wide variety of articles. The most frequent reason for rejection by our staff is the material submitted is either not suitable for our publication or the writer has not focused the article."

FREELANCE WRITER'S REPORT, Cassell Communications Inc., Box 9844, Fort Lauderdale FL 33310. (305)485-0795. Editor: Dana K. Cassell. 15% freelance written. Prefers to work with published/established writers. Monthly newsletter covering writing and marketing advice for freelance writers. Pays on publication. Publishes ms an average of 6 months after acceptance. Byline given. Buys one-time rights. Submit seasonal/holiday material 2 months in advance. Simultaneous queries, and simultaneous, photocopied, and previously published submissions OK. Computer printout submissions OK; no dot-matrix. Reports in 1 month. Sample copy $2.50.

Nonfiction: Book excerpts (on writing profession); how-to (market, write, research); interview (of writers or editors); new product (only those pertaining to writers); photojournalism; promotion and administration of a writing business. No humor, fiction or poetry. Buys 36 mss/year. Query or send complete ms. Length: 500 words maximum. Also buys longer material (1,500-2,500 words) for Special Reports. Pays 10¢/edited word.

Tips: "Write in terse newsletter style, eliminate flowery adjectives and edit mercilessly. Send something that will help writers increase profits from writing output—must be a proven method."

GOOD NEWS, for Christians In The Media Or For Those Interested In The Media As A Ministry, Crown Creations Associates, Box 11626, St. Paul MN 55111-0626. Editor: Steven Mark Deyo. 50% freelance written. Prefers to work with published/established writers, and works with a small number of new/unpublished writers each year. A quarterly newsletter "addressing Christianity in the news profession, and examining how Christians go about their jobs in journalism. It treats ethics, union dynamics, news issues, constitutional rights, media law and history and profiles Christians who exhibit excellence in their news profession." Circ. 500. Pays on publication. Publishes ms an average of 4 months after acceptance. Byline given. Buys first rights or second serial (reprint) rights. Submit seasonal/holiday material 6 months in advance. Photocopied and previously published submissions OK, originals and clips preferred. Query for electronic submissions. Computer printout submissions acceptable; prefers letter-quality to dot-matrix. Reports in 1 month on queries; 8 weeks on mss. Sample copy for 9½x10 SASE; writer's guidelines for # 10 SASE.

Nonfiction: Essays, exposé, general interest, historical, how-to, humor, inspirational, interview/profile, opinion, personal experience, photo feature, religious and travel. "No articles from folks who aren't journalists or who haven't professionally interviewed/profiled journalist(s). Articles must tie in a living Christian faith." Buys 6-8 mss/year. Query with or without published clips, or send complete ms. Length: 200-800 words. Pays up to 4 copies. Sometimes pays the expenses of writers on assignment.

Photos: Send photos with submission. Reviews contact sheets and 5x7 prints. Offers no additional payment for photos accepted with ms. Buys one-time rights.

Columns/Departments: News File (news rundown of issues/events involving Christianity in journalism), 20-100 words; Bureau Report (Christian-in-Media profile: professionalism on location), 200-800 words; and How Will They Hear . . .? (profile of coverage of Christian news angle missed by secular press), 200-800 words. Buys 6-8 mss/year. Query.

Fillers: Anecdotes, facts and newsbreaks. Acquires 10-20/year. Length: 20-100 words. Pays up to 2 copies.

Tips: "Be as professional as the journalist you profile. Be true to a scriptural Christian faith; use spiritual discernment. Go for issues where the church can have a particular answer the secular press seems to be missing. Be open to seeking out the moral/ethical/religious angle in news events that secular journalists pass by."

JOURNALISM EDUCATOR, School of Journalism, University of North Carolina, Chapel Hill NC 27514. (919)962-4084. Editor: Thomas A. Bowers. 100% freelance written. Quarterly for journalism professors, administrators, and a growing number of professional journalists in the U.S. and Canada. Published by the Association for Education in Journalism and Mass Communication. Founded by the American Society of Journalism School Administrators. Does not pay. Byline given. Publishes ms an average of 10 months after acceptance. Query for electronic submissions. Computer printout submissions acceptable.

Nonfiction: "We do accept some unsolicited manuscripts dealing with our publication's specialized area—problems of administration and teaching in journalism education. Because we receive more articles than we can use from persons working in this field, we do not need to encourage freelance materials, however. A writer, generally, would have to be in journalism/communications teaching or in some media work to have the background to write convincingly about the subjects this publication is interested in. The writer also should become familiar with the content of recent issues of this publication." Nothing not directly connected with journalism education at the four-year college and university level. Length: 2,500 words maximum. No payment.

JOURNALISM QUARTERLY, School of Journalism, Ohio University, Athens OH 45701. (614)594-5013. Editor: Guido H. Stempel III. 100% freelance written. Eager to work with new/unpublished writers. "We have 150-175 writers represented each year." For members of the Association for Education in Journalism and Mass Communication and other academicians and journalists. Quarterly. No payment. Publishes ms an average of 9-12 months after acceptance. Usually acquires all rights. Circ. 4,200. Photocopied submissions OK. Computer printout submissions acceptable; no dot-matrix. Reports in 3 months. Free writer's guidelines.
Nonfiction: Research in mass communication. No essays or opinion pieces. Length: 4,000 words maximum. Submit complete ms in triplicate. No payment.
Tips: "Query letters don't really help either the author or me very much. We can't make commitments on the basis of query letters, and we are not likely to reject or discourage the manuscript either, unless it is clearly outside our scope. Do a good piece of research. Write a clear, well-organized manuscript."

PHILATELIC JOURNALIST, 154 Laguna Court, St. Augustine Shores FL 32086-7031. (904)797-3513. Editor: Gustav Detjen, Jr. 25% freelance written. Bimonthly for "journalists, writers and columnists in the field of stamp collecting. *The Philatelic Journalist* is mainly read by philatelic writers, professionals and amateurs, including all of the members of the Society of Philaticians, an international group of philatelic journalists." Circ. 1,000. Not copyrighted. Pays on publication. Publishes ms an average of 1 month after acceptance. Free sample copy. Submit seasonal material 2 months in advance. Photocopied submissions OK. Computer printout submissions acceptable. Reports in 2 weeks. Query.
Nonfiction: "Articles concerned with the problems of the philatelic journalist, how to publicize and promote stamp collecting, how to improve relations between philatelic writers and publishers and postal administrations. Philatelic journalists, many of them amateurs, are very much interested in receiving greater recognition as journalists, and in gaining greater recognition for the use of philatelic literature by stamp collectors. Any criticism should be coupled with suggestions for improvement." Buys profiles and opinion articles. Length: 250-500 words. Pays $15-30.
Photos: Photos purchased with ms. Captions required.

PUBLISHER'S REPORT, National Association of Independent Publishers, Box 850, Moore Haven FL 33471. (813)946-0283. Editor: Ailsa Dewing. 10% freelance written. Bimonthly newsletter for independent publishers, small press and self-publishers with how-to articles on all aspects of publishing. Circ. 350. Publishes ms an average of 6 months after acceptance. Byline given. Buys one-time rights. Submit seasonal/holiday material 6 months in advance. Computer printout submissions acceptable; prefers letter-quality to dot-matrix. Reports in 3 weeks on queries. Sample copy $2 with SAE and 39¢ postage.
Nonfiction: How-to. Buys 6 mss/year. Send complete ms. Length: 250 words. Payment in contributor copies.

‡PUBLISHING TRADE, Serving Under 100,000 Circulation Publications, Coast Publishing, 1680 SW Bayshore Rd., Port St. Lucie Fl 33452. Editor: Douglas E. Roorback. 50% freelance written. Bimonthly magazine covering magazine publishing. Circulated to approximately 13,000 publishers, editors, ad managers, circulation managers, production managers and art directors of magazines. Circ. 13,000. Publishes ms an average of 2 months after acceptance. Byline given. Buys first North American serial rights. Submit seasonal/holiday material 6 months in advance. Query for electronic submissions. Computer printout submissions OK; prefers letter-quality to dot-matrix. Reports in 2 months on queries. Sample copy and writer's guidelines available for 9x12 SAE with $1.75 postage.
Nonfiction: How-to (write, sell advertising, manage production, manage creative and sales people, etc.); interview/profile (*only* after assignment—must be full of "secrets" of success and how-to detail); personal experiences; new product (no payment); and technical (aspects of magazine publishing). "Features deal with every aspect of publishing, including: creating an effective ad sales team; increasing ad revenue; writing effective direct-mail circulation promotion; improving reproduction quality; planning and implementing ad sales strategies; buying printing; gathering unique information; writing crisp, clear articles with impact; and designing publications with visual impact." No general interest. "Everything must be keyed directly to our typical reader—a 39 year-old publisher/editor producing a trade magazine for 30,000 or more readers." Buys 18-24 mss/year. Query. Length: 900-3,000 words.
Photos: Send photos with ms.
Tips: "Articles must present practical, useful, new information in how-to detail, so readers can do what the articles discuss. Articles that present problems and discuss how they were successfully solved also are welcome. These must carry many specific examples to flesh out general statements. We don't care who you are, just how you write."

‡**RIGHTING WORDS, The Journal of Language and Editing**, Righting Words Corp., Box 6811, F.D.R. Station, New York NY 10150. (718)761-0235. Editor: Jonathan S. Kaufman. 80% freelance written. Eager to work with new/unpublished writers. A bimonthly magazine on language usage, trends and issues. "Our readers include copy editors, book and magazine editors, and journalism and English-teachers—people interested in the changing ways of the langauge and in ways to improve their editing and writing skills." Estab. 1986. Pays on acceptance. Publishes ms an average of 1 month after acceptance. Byline given. Offers $100 kill fee. Buys first North American serial rights. Query for electronic submissions. Computer printout submissions OK; no dot-matrix. Reports in 1 month. Sample copy $4.50 with 9x12 SAE and 3 first class stamps; writer's guidelines for SASE.
Nonfiction: General interest, historical/nostalgic and how-to. Buys 30 mss/year. Send complete ms. Length: 3,000 words. Pays $100 minimum for assigned articles; pays $75 minimum for unsolicited articles.
Tips: "Our contributors have included Rudolf Flesch and Willard Espy, but we welcome freelance submissions on editing and language topics that are well-written, contain hard information of value to editors, and that display wit and style. Yes, the editors read all submissions, and often suggest approaches to writers whose material may be good but whose approach is off. No book reviews, please; other than that, all parts of the magazine are open to freelancers. "

RISING STAR, 47 Byledge Rd., Manchester NH 03104. (603)623-9796. Editor: Scott E. Green. 50% freelance written. A bimonthly newsletter on science fiction and fantasy markets for writers and artists. Circ. 150. Pays on publication. Publishes ms an average of 3 months after acceptance. Byline given. Not copyrighted. Buys first rights. Simultaneous, photocopied and previously published submissions OK. Reports in 2 weeks on queries. Sample copy $1 with #10 SAE with 1 first class stamp; free writer's guidelines.
Nonfiction: Book excerpts, essays, interview/profile and opinion. Buys 8 mss/year. Query. Length: 500-900 words. Pays $3 minimum.

THE ROMANTIST, F. Marion Crawford Memorial Society, Saracinesca House, 3610 Meadowbrook Ave., Nashville TN 37205. (615)292-9695 or 226-1890. Editors: John C. Moran, Don Herron and Steve Eng. 100% freelance written. "Writers' backgrounds not an issue; their grasp of their material, and skill at imparting it, is." Annual magazine emphasizing modern romanticism; especially fantastic literature and art. Circ. 300, controlled. All rights retained but permission always is given an author for reprints. Publishes ms an average of 9 months after acceptance. Byline given. Reports in 1 month. Writer's guidelines with SASE.
Nonfiction: Solid articles or bibliographies on fantasy or horror authors and other romantic authors (or artists or composers). No articles without querying first.
Poetry: Traditional; very little free verse. "We prefer rhymed and metered poems, but no homespun doggerel; prefer the tradition of Swinburne, Poe, Noyes, De la Mare, Millay, Masefield, Clark Ashton Smith; especially weird or fantastic verse." Poetry submissions should be double-spaced. Uses 15 unsolicited poems/year. Closed currently to poetry.

ST. LOUIS JOURNALISM REVIEW, 8380 Olive Blvd., St. Louis MO 63132. (314)991-1699. Editor/Publisher: Charles L. Klotzer. 50% freelance written. Prefers to work with published/established writers. Works with a small number of new/unpublished writers each year; eager to work with new/unpublished writers. Monthly tabloid newspaper critiquing St. Louis media, print, broadcasting, TV and cable primarily by working journalists and others. Also covers issues not covered adequately by dailies. Occasionally buys articles on national media criticism. Circ. 9,000. Buys all rights. Byline given. Computer printout submissions acceptable.
Nonfiction: "We buy material which analyzes, critically, St. Louis metro area media and, less frequently, national media institutions, personalities or trends." No taboos. Payment depends. Sometimes pays the expenses of writers on assignment.

SAN FRANCISCO REVIEW OF BOOKS, Box 33-0090, San Francisco CA 94133. Editor: R.E. Newicki. 60% freelance written. For a college-educated audience interested in books and publishing. Quarterly magazine; 32 pages. Circ. 5,000. Acquires all rights. Byline given. Uses about 180 mss/year. Payment in contributors copies and subscription. Publishes ms an average of 3 months after acceptance. Sample copy $1.50. No photocopied or simultaneous submissions. Reports on material accepted for publication in 4-6 weeks. Query for nonfiction; submit complete ms for book reviews.
Nonfiction: Book reviews and articles about authors, books and their themes. "No glib, slick writing. Primarily serious; humor occasionally acceptable. No restrictions on language provided it is germane to the book or article." Interviews, profiles, historical and think articles. Length: 1,200 words maximum for reviews; 2,000 words maximum for articles.

SCAVENGER'S NEWSLETTER, 519 Ellinwood, Osage City KS 66523. (913)528-3538. Editor: Janet Fox. 25% freelance written. Eager to work with new/unpublished writers. A monthly newsletter covering markets for science fiction/fantasy/horror materials especially with regard to the small press. Circ. 400. Publishes ms an average of 8 months after acceptance. Byline given. Not copyrighted. "Copyright symbol printed with author's name on publication." Buys one-time rights. Submit seasonal/holiday material 2 months in advance. Simultaneous, photocopied and previously published submissions OK. Computer printout submissions acceptable; prefers letter-quality to dot-matrix. Reports in 2 weeks. Sample copy 70¢; writer's guidelines for #10 SASE.

Nonfiction: Essays; general interest; how-to (write, sell, publish sf/fantasy/horror); humor; interview/profile (writers, artists in the field); and opinion. Buys 12-15 mss/year. Send complete ms. Length: 1,000 words maximum. Pays $2.

Poetry: Avant-garde, free verse, haiku and traditional. All related to science fiction/fantasy/horror genres. Buys 24 poems/year. Submit maximum 3 poems. Length: 10 lines maximum. Pays $1.

Tips: "Because this is a small publication, it has occasional overstocks."

SCIENCE FICTION CHRONICLE, Algol Press, Box 4175, New York NY 10163. (718)643-9011. Editor: Andrew Porter. 5% freelance written. Works with a small number of new/unpublished writers each year. Monthly magazine about science fiction and fantasy publishing for readers, editors, writers, et al., who are interested in keeping up with the latest developments and news in science fiction and fantasy. Publication also includes market reports, UK news, letters, reviews, columns. Circ. 4,000. Buys first serial rights. Pays on publication. Publishes ms an average of 2 months after acceptance. Makes work-for-hire assignments. Phone queries OK. Submit seasonal material 4 months in advance. Computer printout submissions acceptable; prefers letter-quality to dot-matrix. Reports in 1 week. Sample copy $2.

Nonfiction: Interviews, new product and photo feature. No articles about UFOs, or "news we reported six months ago." Buys 15 unsolicited mss/year. Send complete ms. Length: 200-2,000 words. Pays 3-5¢/word.

Photos: Send photos with ms. Pays $5-15 for 4x5 and 8x10 b&w prints. Captions preferred. Buys one-time rights.

Tips: "News of publishers, booksellers and software related to is most needed from freelancers."

‡TFR, The Freelancers' Report, Literary Publications Company, Box 93, Poquonock CT 06064. (203)688-5496. Editor: Pat McDonald. 90% freelance written. Monthly magazine covering freelancing illustrators, photographers, writers (all genres). "Our target audience is those who are already working and selling their work or serious beginners, rather than hobbyists, but the latter would enjoy our articles and art." Estab. 1986. Circ. 200. Pays on publication. Publishes ms an average of 2 months after acceptance. Byline given. Buys first North American serial or second serial (reprint) rights. Submit seasonal/holiday material 3 months in advance. Photocopied and previously published submissions OK (please note where, when and current ownership by author). Computer printout submissions OK; prefers letter-quality to dot-matrix. Reports in 6 weeks. Sample copy $2.50; writer's guidelines for SAE with 22¢ postage.

Nonfiction: Book excerpts, essays, expose, general interest, historical/nostalgic, how-to (main focus), humor (instantly accepted if it is good and on theme), inspirational, interview/profile, new product, opinion, photo feature, technical and travel. "Personal experiences just don't fit into this kind of publication. Almost anything else is acceptable." Buys 160 mss/year. Send complete ms. "Photocopies are recommended. We tend to edit directly onto copy whether accepted or not." Length: 1,000 words. Pays $1 (filler); $30 for unsolicited articles. "Contract prior to publication offers the option to receive contributor copies in lieu of payment (any of our four publications)."

Photos: Reviews prints ("any size to 8½x11 if screened and clear better than prints." Pays "maximum per author is $30 total." Buys one-time or reprint rights.

Columns: Writing—any genre (how-to, market searches, humorous, just about any ideas of interest to practicing freelance writer); Photography; Illustration. Buys 36 mss/year. Send complete ms. Length: 1,000 words. Pays $30 maximum.

Fiction: "We are basically a trade magazine. The only fiction we can use is that which features a writer (editor, agent, publisher, etc), photographer, illustrator as the main character." Buys 6 mss/year. Send complete ms. Length: 1,000 words. "More than 1,000 would be accepted but would receive no additional payment at word rate of 3¢/word (1.5¢ reprint)."

Poetry: Poetry Editor: Linda Schlichting. Avant-garde, free verse, haiku, light verse and traditional. Poetry must stay within the theme of the publication. Buys 60 peoms/year. Length 40 lines minimum. Pays $1-10.

Fillers: Anecdotes, facts, gags to be illustrated by cartoonist, newsbreak and short humor. Buys 80/year. Length: 100 words maximum. Pays $1-3.

Tips: "We have a small staff and four monthly publications. We discourage any queries and do not give assignments. We will send your material back, edited as we feel might be helpful, if we reject it. Thus we suggest you *not* send originals. We will notify you by written contract within 60 days (but usually 7-14) if we will use your work. We are a *strongly* themed publication. If you do not keep this in mind, you will be wasting our time and yours. We are new and want to constantly improve our publication. If your work is better than anything we have, you will have the spot."

WAYSTATION, for the SF Writer, % Unique Graphics, 1025 55th St., Oakland CA 94608. (415)655-3024. Editor: Millea Kenin. 99% freelance written. Prefers to work with published/established writers; works with a small number of new/unpublished writers each year. Quarterly magazine covering writing, editing and publishing science fiction and fantasy. "*Waystation*'s aim is to assist, entertain and inform science fiction and fantasy writers." Circ. 1,500. Pays on publication. Publishes ms an average of 6 months after acceptance. Byline given. Buys first English language serial rights, and occasionally second serial (reprint) rights. Simultaneous queries and photocopied submissions OK if simultaneous are so identified. "We are completely receptive to computer printout submissions as long as they are NOT dot-matrix with dots visible to the naked eye. Such printouts will be returned unread." Reports in 1 month or less. Sample copy $2.50, payable to Unique Graphics. Guidelines available for SAE with 39¢ postage.

Nonfiction: Expose (of publishing industry); how-to (on specific writing and marketing techniques and skills for science fiction and fantasy); humor (about the science fiction writer's life; "If you find any, send it to us"); interview/profile (of writers, editors, agents, publishers, filmmakers involved in the SF genre); personal experience ("how I wrote and sold science fiction, fantasy or horror fiction"); and technical (science fact with application to science fiction). "We use articles about writing, editing and publishing *science fiction and fantasy*; our material is written by professional science fiction writers for would-be professional science fiction writers. We are not interested in general articles for the beginning writer, nor articles on coping with failure as a writer. We take a practical nuts-and-bolts approach." Buys 32 mss/year. Query with proposal if you have not previously written for *Waystation*. Length: 1,000-3,500 words. Offers contributor copies as payment and a one-year subscription. Pay negotiable to regular contributors.

Fiction: Crazy Diamonds. "Each issue contains one story which has failed to sell elsewhere and three critiques of the story by professional science fiction writers. We use no other fiction." Buys 4 mss/year. Length: 3,500 words maximum, shorter preferred. Offers contributor copies as payment and subscription.

Poetry: "Short humorous or serious verse about the act of writing science fiction or the science fiction writer's life."

Tips: "If you have not seen a copy of *Waystation* and are not closely involved with the science fiction genre, it is better to query with a proposal rather than submitting an unsolicited article. If you are not a big-name science fiction writer, you must have specific knowledge of interest to writers in this genre or specific *successful*, relevant experiences to share. We're tightening up on relevance; absolutely no general how-to-write stuff will be accepted except if solicited."

WDS FORUM, Writer's Digest School, 1507 Dana Ave., Cincinnati OH 45207. (513)531-2222. Editor: Kirk Polking. 100% freelance written. Quarterly newsletter covering writing techniques and marketing for students of courses in fiction and nonfiction writing offered by Writer's Digest School. Circ. 13,000. Pays on acceptance. Publishes ms an average of 6 months after acceptance. Byline given. Pays 25% kill fee. Buys first serial rights and second serial (reprint) rights. Submit seasonal/holiday material 4 months in advance. Simultaneous, photocopied, and previously published submissions OK. Electronic submissions OK, but requires hard copy also. Computer printout submissions acceptable; no dot-matrix. Reports in 3 weeks. Free sample copy.

Nonfiction: How-to (write or market short stories, articles, novels, poetry, etc.); and interviews (with well-known authors of short stories, novels and books). Buys 12 mss/year. Phone or written query. Length: 500-1,000 words. Pays $10-25.

Photos: Pays $5-10 for 8x10 b&w prints of well-known writers to accompany mss. Captions required. Buys one-time rights.

WEST COAST REVIEW OF BOOKS, Rapport Publishing Co., Inc., 6331 Hollywood Blvd., Hollywood CA 90028. (213)464-2662. Editor: D. David Dreis. Bimonthly magazine for book consumers. "Provocative articles based on specific subject matter, books and author retrospectives." Circ. 80,000. Pays on publication. Byline given. Offers kill fee. Buys one-time rights and second serial (reprint) rights to published author interviews. Sample copy $2.

Nonfiction: General interest, historical/nostalgic, and profile (author retrospectives). "No individual book reviews." Buys 25 mss/year. Query. Length: open.

Tips: "There must be a reason (current interest, news events, etc.) for any article here. Example: 'The Jew-Haters' was about anti-semitism which was written up in six books; all reviewed and analyzed under that umbrella title. Under no circumstances should articles be submitted unless query has been responded to." No phone calls.

THE WRITER, 120 Boylston St., Boston MA 02116. Editor-in-Chief/Publisher: Sylvia K. Burack. 20-25% freelance written. Prefers to work with published/established writers. Monthly. Pays on acceptance. Publishes ms an average of 6-8 months after acceptance. Buys first serial rights. Uses some freelance material. Computer printout submissions acceptable; no dot-matrix. Sample copy $2.50.

Nonfiction: Articles for writers on how to write for publication, and how and where to market manuscripts in various fields. Will consider all submissions promptly. No assignments. Length: approximately 2,000 words.

Tips: "New types of publications and our continually updated market listings in all fields will determine changes of focus and fact."

WRITERS CONNECTION, Suite 180, 1601 Saratoga-Sunnyvale Rd., Cupertino CA 95014. (408)973-0227. Editor: Merra Lester. 60% freelance written. Works with a small number of new/unpublished writers each year. Monthly magazine covering writing and publishing. Circ. 2,500. Pays on publication. Publishes ms an average of 6 months after acceptance for articles, much less for column updates. Byline given. Buys first serial rights or second serial (reprint) rights. Submit seasonal/holiday material 2 months in advance. Simultaneous queries, and simultaneous, photocopied, and previously published submissions OK. Computer printout submissions acceptable; prefers letter-quality to dot-matrix. Prefers telephone queries. Sample copy $2 and writer's guidelines for #10 SASE.

Nonfiction: Book excerpts (on writing/publishing); how-to (write and publish, market writing); interview/ profile (writers and publishers with how-to slant); new product (books, videotapes, etc. on writing and publishing); and travel writing. "All types of writing from technical to romance novels and article writing are treated." Submit material for California writers conferences by January each year. No personal experience or profiles without a strong how-to slant. Buys 36 mss/year. Query, preferably by telephone, between 11 a.m. and noon. Length: 100-2,500 words. Pays $12-80; "pay is in credit for Writers Connection memberships, seminars, subscriptions and advertising only." Sometimes pays the expenses of writers on assignment.

Columns/Departments: Markets/Jobs Update and self-publishing. Buys 24 mss/year. Send complete ms. Length: 100-300 words. Pays $12-25 in subscriptions, ads, or credits on seminars or memberships.

Tips: "We are currently seeking how-to articles that will benefit writers working for business and high-tech companies. The focus for these articles should appeal to the working professional writer. Also find and report on new markets freelancers can break in to, new ways to succeed in the business. We use far more short column items, and we generally have a backlog of features awaiting use."

WRITER'S DIGEST, 1507 Dana Ave., Cincinnati OH 45207. (513)531-2222. Submissions Editor: Bill Strickland. 90% freelance written. Monthly magazine about writing and publishing. "Our readers write fiction, poetry, nonfiction, plays and all kinds of creative writing. They're interested in improving their writing skills, improving their sales ability, and finding new outlets for their talents." Circ. 200,000. Pays on acceptance. Publishes ms an average of 1 year. Buys first North American serial rights for one-time editorial use, microfilm/microfiche use, and magazine promotional use. Pays 20% kill fee. Byline given. Submit seasonal/holiday material 8 months in advance. Previously published and photocopied submissions OK. No unsolicited electronic submissions. "We're able to use electronic submissions only for accepted pieces/and will discuss details if we buy your work. We'll accept computer printout submissions, of course—but they *must* be readable. That's the rule behind any submission to any magazine. We strongly recommend letter-quality. If you don't want your manuscript returned, indicate that on the first page of the manuscript or in a cover letter." Reports in 1 month. Sample copy $2.50; writer's guidelines for SASE.

Nonfiction: "Our mainstay is the how-to article—that is, an article telling how to write and sell more of what you write. For instance, how to write compelling leads and conclusions, how to improve your character descriptions, how to become more efficient and productive. We like plenty of examples, anecdotes and $$$ in our articles—so other writers can actually see what's been done successfully by the author of a particular piece. We like our articles to speak directly to the reader through the use of the first-person voice. Don't submit an article on what five book editors say about writing mysteries. Instead, submit an article on how you cracked the mystery market and how our readers can do the same. But don't limit the article to your experiences; include the opinions of those five editors to give your article increased depth and authority." General interest (about writing); how-to (writing and marketing techniques that work); humor (short pieces); inspirational; interview and profile (query first); new product; and personal experience (marketing and freelancing experiences). "We can always use articles on fiction and nonfiction technique, and solid articles on poetry or scriptwriting are always welcome. No articles titled 'So You Want to Be a Writer,' and no first-person pieces that ramble without giving a lesson or something readers can learn from in the sharing of the story." Buys 90-100 mss/year. Queries are preferred, but complete mss are OK. Length: 500-3,000 words. Pays 10¢/word minimum. Sometimes pays expenses of writers on assignment.

Photos: Used only with interviews and profiles. State availability of photos or send contact sheet with ms. Pays $25 minimum for 5x7 or larger b&w prints. Captions required.

Columns/Departments: Chronicle (first-person narratives about the writing life; length: 1,200-1,500 words; pays 10¢/word); The Writing Life (length: 50-800 words; pays 10¢/word); Tip Sheet (short, unbylined items that offer solutions to writing- and freelance business-related problems that writers commonly face; pays 10¢/word); and My First Sale (an "occasional" department; a first-person account of how a writer broke into print; length: 1,000 words; pays 10¢/word). "For First Sale items, use a narrative, anecdotal style to tell a tale that is both inspirational and instructional. Before you submit a My First Sale item, make certain that your story contains a solid lesson that will benefit other writers." Buys approximately 200 articles/year for Writing Life section, Tip Sheet and shorter pieces. Send complete ms.

Poetry: Light verse about "the writing life"—joys and frustrations of writing. "We are also considering poetry other than short light verse—but related to writing, publishing, other poets and authors, etc." Buys 2/issue. Submit poems in batches of 1-8. Length: 2-20 lines. Pays $10-50/poem.

Fillers: Anecdotes and short humor, primarily for use in The Writing Life column. Uses 2/issue. Length: 50-200 words. Pays 10¢/word.

WRITER'S GAZETTE, (formerly *Short Story Review Club*), Trouvere Company, Rt. 2, Box 290, Eclectic AL 36024. Editor: Brenda Williamson. 95% freelance written. Eager to work with new/unpublished writers. Circ. 1,200. Publishes ms an average of 6 months after acceptance. Byline given. Buys one-time rights. Computer printout submissions acceptable; prefers letter-quality to dot-matrix. Reports in 3 months. Sample copy for $4 and 9x12 SAE with 69¢ postage; writer's guidelines for 25¢ and #10 SAE and 1 first class stamp.

Fiction: Adventure, condensed novels, confession, erotica, ethnic, experimental, fantasy, historical, horror, humorous, mainstream, mystery, novel excerpts, religious, romance, science fiction, serialized novels, suspense and western—any short story. Buys 25 mss/year. Send complete ms.

Tips: "Read guidelines and enjoy what you write. We're open to suggestions; guidelines are to follow, but they're not the law at *WG*. We're open for new imaginative ideas."

WRITER'S INFO, Rhyme Time/Story Time, Box 2377, Coeur d'Alene ID 83814. (208)667-7511. Editor: Linda Hutton. 90% freelance written. Eager to work with new/unpublished writers. Monthly newsletter on writing. "We provide helpful tips and advice to writers, both beginners and old pros." Circ. 200. Pays on acceptance. Publishes ms an average of 6 months after acceptance. Byline given. Buys first North American serial rights and second serial (reprint) rights. Submit seasonal/holiday material 9 months in advance. Simultaneous queries, and simultaneous, photocopied, and previously published submissions OK. Computer printout submissions acceptable; prefers letter-quality to dot-matrix. Reports in 1 month. Sample copy for #10 SAE and 2 first class stamps; writer's guidelines for # 10 SAE and 1 first class stamp.

Nonfiction: How-to, humor and personal experience, all related to writing. No interviews or re-hashes of articles published in other writers magazines. Buys 50-75 mss/year. Send complete ms. Length: 300 words. Pays $1-10.

Poetry: Free verse, light verse and traditional. No avant-garde or shaped poetry. Buys 40-50/year. Submit maximum 6 poems. Length: 4-20 lines. Pays $1-10.

Fillers: Jokes, anecdotes and short humor. Buys 3-4/year. Length: 100 words maximum. Pays $1-10.

Tips: "Tell us a system that worked for you to make a sale or inspired you to write. All departments are open to freelancers."

WRITER'S INSPIRATIONAL MARKETS NEWS, (formerly *The Christian Writer*), Box 5650, Lakeland FL 33807. (813)644-3548. Editor: Thomas A. Noton. Editorial Assistant: Jana Huss. 50% freelance written. Prefers to work with published/established writers. Monthly writing publication aimed at inspirational writers. "We aim to teach the professional approach to writing for the inspirational markets." Circ. 10,000. Publishes ms an average of 4-6 months after acceptance. Acquires first serial rights; no reprints. Submit seasonal/holiday material 4 months in advance. Simultaneous queries and photocopied submissions OK. Computer printout submissions acceptable. Reports in 1 month on queries; 2 months on mss. Sample copy $2.50. Writer's guidelines for #10 SAE with 1 first class stamp.

Nonfiction: How-to (specifics on authoring, selling, related subjects); humor (need more material on how to write humor for the inspirational market); inspirational (limited); interview/profile (top Christian authors); new product (electronic writing); and personal experience (some). "We receive too many 'this is my life as a writer' articles. We want more solid help for overcoming specialized problems in authoring." Buys 36-50 mss/year. Query with writing credits. Length: 800-2,500 words. Fillers are 200-600 words. Pays $10 minimum for fillers to $200 for feature articles. Payment depends on need and content of article. Sometimes pays expenses of writers on assignment.

Tips: "We need articles that deliver solid answers, how-to, and specific help to writers on various levels. We are only interested in professionalism as it applies to the craft of writing. Although we use the Christian influence, we don't accept freelance material that deals with it directly. We want those manuscripts to deal with the craft of writing, its problems and answers. Attention to the style of the regular columnists will give a freelance author a 'feel' for what we like."

WRITER'S JOURNAL, Inkling Publications, Inc., Box 65798, St. Paul MN 55165. (612)221-0326. Editor: Marilyn Bailey. Associate Editor: Betty Ulrich. Managing Editor/Publisher: John Hall. 30% freelance written. Monthly. Circ. 3,000. Pays on publication. Publishes ms an average of 2 months after acceptance. Byline given. Buys first North American serial rights. Submit seasonal/holiday material 4 months in advance. Simultaneous queries OK. Query for electronic submissions. Computer printout submissions acceptable; prefers letter-quality to dot-matrix. Reports in 1 month on queries; 6 weeks on mss. Sample copy $2; writer's guidelines for business size SAE and 1 first class stamp.

Nonfiction: How-to (on the business and approach to writing); motivational; interview/profile; opinion; and personal experience. "*Writer's Journal* publishes articles on style, technique, editing methods, copy writing, research, writing of news releases, writing news stories and features, creative writing, grammar reviews, marketing, the business aspects of writing, copyright law and legal advice for writers/editors, independent book publishing, interview techniques, and more." Also articles on the use of computers by writers and a book review section. Buys 30-40 mss/year. Send complete ms. Length: 500-1,500 words. Pays $15-50.

Poetry: Avant-garde, free verse, haiku, light verse and traditional. "The *Inkling* runs four poetry contests each year—spring and fall: Winner and 2nd place cash prizes and two honorable mentions." Buys 20-30 poems/year. Submit maximum 3 poems. Length: 25 lines maximum. Pays $4-15.

Tips: "Articles must be *well* written and slanted toward the business (or commitment) of writing and/or being a writer. Interviews with established writers should be in-depth, particularly reporting interviewee's philosophy on writing, how (s)he got started, etc. Tape interviews, transcribe, then edit. Monthly 'theme' emphasizes a particular genre or type of writing. Opinion pieces (researched and authoritative) on any of the monthly themes welcomed. (Theme schedule available with guidelines.)"

WRITER'S LIFELINE, Box 1641, Cornwall, Ontario K6H 5V6 Canada. Contact: Editor. 95% freelance written. Eager to work with new/unpublished writers. Bimonthly magazine "aimed at freelance writers of all ages and interests." Buys first serial rights. SAE and IRCs.

Nonfiction: "Articles on all aspects of writing and publishing, also book reviews." Send complete ms. Length: 5,000 words maximum. Payment: 3 free issues in which article appears. Publishes ms an average of 2 months after acceptance.

Fiction: Must be tied in to writing and publishing. Poetry published. Payment: 3 free issues in which story or poem appears.

Tips: "Writer should show evidence of his qualification to write on subject. All articles should be pegged to current concerns of writers: self-publishing, hitting local markets, anecdotes of new writer breaking in, and preparing book reviews are among articles we have published recently."

WRITER'S NEWSLETTER, Writer's Studio, 1530 7th St., Rock Island IL 61201. (309)788-3980. Editor: Betty Mowery. 100% freelance written. Eager to work with new/unpublished writers. A bimonthly newsletter/club publication prepared for the help and exposure of writers. Circ. 350. Byline given. Not copyrighted. Acquires first rights. Publishes ms an average of 2 months after acceptance. Submit seasonal/holiday material 3 months in advance. Simultaneous submissions OK. Computer printout submissions acceptable; prefers letter-quality to dot-matrix. Reports in 1 week. Free sample copy; writer's guidelines for 1 first class stamp.

Nonfiction: Essay, general interest, inspirational, interview/profile, personal experience and anything else pertaining to writing. Buys 12 mss/year. Send complete ms. Length: 500 words maximum. Pays in copies.

Fiction: Adventure, experimental, fantasy, historical, humorous, mainstream, mystery, romance and slice-of-life vignettes. No erotica. Buys 12 mss/year. Send complete ms. Length: 500 words minimum. Pays copies.

Poetry: Avant-garde, free verse, haiku, light verse and traditional. Buys 36 poems/year. Submit maximum 5 poems. Length: 20 lines maximum. Pays in copies.

Fillers: Anecdotes, facts and short humor. Buys 6/year. Length: 250 words maximum. Pays in copies.

WRITER'S YEARBOOK, 1507 Dana Ave., Cincinnati OH 45207. Submissions Editor: Bill Strickland. 90% freelance written. Newsstand annual for freelance writers, journalists and teachers of creative writing. "Please note that the *Yearbook* is currently using a 'best of' format. That is, we are reprinting the best of writing about writing published in the last year: articles, fiction, and book excerpts. The *Yearbook* now uses little original material, so do not submit queries or original manuscripts to the *Yearbook*. We will, however, consider already-published material for possible inclusion." Buys reprint rights. Pays 20% kill fee. Byline given. Pays on acceptance. Publishes ms an average of 6 months after acceptance. High-quality photocopied submissions OK. Computer printout submissions acceptable; prefers letter-quality to dot-matrix. "If you don't want your manuscript returned, indicate that on the first page of the manuscript or in a cover letter."

Nonfiction: "In reprints, we want articles that reflect the current state of writing in America. Trends, inside information and money-saving and money-making ideas for the freelance writer. We try to touch on the various facets of writing in each issue of the *Yearbook*—from fiction to poetry to playwriting, and any other endeavor a writer can pursue. How-to articles—that is, articles that explain in detail how to do something—are very important to us. For example, you could explain how to establish mood in fiction, how to improve interviewing techniques, how to write for and sell to specialty magazines, or how to construct and market a good poem. We are also interested in the writer's spare time—what she/he does to retreat occasionally from the writing wars; where and how to refuel and replenish the writing spirit. 'How Beats the Heart of a Writer' features interest us, if written warmly, in the first person, by a writer who has had considerable success. We also want interviews or profiles of well-known bestselling authors, always with good pictures. Articles on writing techniques that are effective today are always welcome. We provide how-to features and information to help our readers become more skilled at writing and successful at selling their writing." Buys 10-15 mss (reprints only)/year. Length: 750-4,500 words. Pays 2¢1/2¢/word minimum.

Photos: Interviews and profiles must be accompanied by high-quality photos. Reviews b&w photos only, depending on use; pays $20-50/published photo. Captions required.

____ *Laundry and Dry Cleaning*

AMERICAN DRYCLEANER, 500 N. Dearborn St., Chicago IL 60610. (312)337-7700. Editor: Earl V. Fischer. 20% freelance written. "We prefer to work regularly with widely scattered photo-reporters who need little direction, but always open to unsolicited submissions from newcomers." For professional drycleaners. Monthly. Circ. 28,000. Buys first North American serial rights or in some cases industry-exclusive simultaneous rights. Pays on publication. Publishes ms an average of 3 months after acceptance. Will send sample copy to writers with specific queries for 6x9 SAE and 2 first class stamps. Reports "promptly." Computer printout submissions acceptable; prefers letter-quality to dot-matrix.
Nonfiction: Articles on all aspects of running a drycleaning business. "These can be narratives about individual drycleaners and how they are handling, say, advertising, counter service, customer relations, cleaning, spot removal, pressing, inspection, packaging, paperwork, or general business management; interpretive reports about outside developments, such as new fabrics and fashions or government regulations affecting drycleaners; or how-to articles offering practical help to cleaners on any facet of their business. The important thing is that the reader find practical benefit in the article, whichever type submitted." No basic advertising and public relations material. "We have regulars for this who know our industry." Pays a minimum of 6¢/published word. Recent article example: "Updated plant perks along at '65,000 pounds per drum' " (February 1986). Sometimes pays the expenses of writers on assignment.
Photos: Photos purchased with mss; quality 8x10 or 5x7 b&w glossies. Photos should help tell story. Pays $6 minimum.
Tips: "We are happy to receive and frequently publish unsolicited manuscripts. If an advance query is made, it would help to get a theme sentence or brief outline of the proposed article. Also helpful would be a statement of whether (and what sort of) photos or other illustrations are available. Anyone with the type of article that our readers would find helpful can break into the publication. The most frequent mistake made by writers in completing an article for us is writing too superficially on too many aspects of a business. It's better to probe for the really unusual and adaptable practical ideas in practice and find out all about them. Also too many photos are meaningless or their significance is not explained. Find a successful drycleaner—one with unusually satisfied customers, for example, or one that seems to be making a lot of money. Find out what makes that cleaner so successful. Tell us about it in specific, practical terms, so other cleaners will be able to follow suit. Articles should help our readers operate their drycleaning businesses more successfully; the appropriateness and practical value of information given are more important than writing style. We prefer *short* reports about *small* cleaning companies doing *one thing* well enough for others to want to know about it and how they might do the same. Reports can range from less than 250 words up to any length the writer can justify. Our editorial space is steadily increasing; staff help is not. We're glad to use anything suitable for publication (new writers are always welcome). We like to have writer's phone numbers for quick contact."

_____ *Law*

While all of these publications deal with topics of interest to attorneys, each has a particular slant. Be sure that your subject is geared to the specific market—lawyers in a single region, students, paralegals, etc. Publications for law enforcement personnel are listed under Government and Public Service.

ABA JOURNAL, American Bar Association, 750 N. Lake Shore Dr., Chicago IL 60611. (312)988-5000. Editor: Larry Bodine. Articles Editor: Robert Yates. 35% freelance written. Prefers to work with published/established writers. Monthly magazine covering law and laywers. "The content of the *Journal* is designed to appeal to the association's diverse membership with emphasis on the general practitioner." Circ. 350,000. Pays on acceptance. Publishes ms an average of 2 months after acceptance. Byline given. "Editor works with writer until article is in acceptable form." Buys all rights. Submit seasonal/holiday material 3 months in advance. Simultaneous queries, and simultaneous and photocopied submissions OK. Electronic submissions OK via ABA/net (the lawyer's computer network). Computer printout submissions acceptable; no dot-matrix. Contact articles editor about electronic submissions. Reports in 3 weeks. Free sample copy and writer's guidelines.

Nonfiction: Book excerpts; general interest (legal); how-to (law practice techniques); interview/profile (law firms and prominent individuals); and technical (legal trends). "The emphasis of the *Journal* is on the practical problems faced by lawyers in general practice and how those problems can be overcome. Articles should emphasize the practical rather than the theoretical or esoteric. Writers should avoid the style of law reviews, academic journals or legal briefs and should write in an informal, journalistic style. Short quotations from people and specific examples of your point will improve an article." Special issues have featured women and minorities in the legal profession. Buys 30 mss/year. Query with published clips or send complete ms. Length: 1,000-3,000 words. Pays $300-800. Pays expenses of writers on assignment.

Tips: "Write to us with a specific idea in mind and spell out how the subject would be covered. Full length profiles and feature articles are always needed. We look for practical information. Don't send us theory, philosophy or wistful meanderings. Our readers want to know how to win cases and operate their practices more efficiently. We need more writing horsepower on lifestyle, profile and practice pieces for lawyers. If the New York Times or Wall Street Journal would like your style, so will we."

THE ALTMAN & WEIL REPORT TO LEGAL MANAGEMENT, Altman & Weil Publications, Inc., Box 472, Ardmore PA 19003. (215)649-4646. Editor: Robert I. Weil. 15-20% freelance written. Works with a small number of new/unpublished writers each year. Monthly newsletter covering law office purchases (equipment, insurance services, space, etc.). Circ. 2,200. Pays on publication. Publishes ms an average of 3-6 months after acceptance. Byline given. Buys all rights; sometimes second serial (reprint) rights. Photocopied and previously published submissions OK. Query for electronic submissions. Computer printout submissions acceptable; no dot-matrix. Reports in 1 month on queries; 6 weeks on mss. Sample copy for business size SAE and 1 first class stamp.

Nonfiction: How-to (buy, use, repair); interview/profile; and new product. Buys 6 mss/year. Query. Submit a sample of previous writing. Length: 500-2,500 words. Pays $125/published page.

Photos: State availability of photos. Reviews b&w prints; payment is included in payment for ms. Captions and model release required. Buys one-time rights.

BARRISTER, American Bar Association Press, 750 N. Lake Shore Dr., Chicago IL 60611. (312)988-6056. Editor: Anthony Monahan. 75% freelance written. Prefers to work with published/established writers; works with a small number of new/unpublished each year. For young lawyers who are members of the American Bar Association concerned about practice of law, improvement of the profession and service to the public. Quarterly magazine; 64 pages. Circ. 155,000. Pays on acceptance. Publishes ms an average of 3 months after acceptance. Buys all rights, first serial rights, second serial (reprint) rights, or simultaneous rights. Photocopied submissions OK. Query for electronic submissions. Computer printout submissions OK; prefers letter-quality to dot-matrix. Reports in 6 weeks. Sample copy for 9x11 SAE with $1 postage.

Nonfiction: "As a magazine of ideas and opinion, we seek material that will help readers in their interrelated roles of attorney and citizen; major themes in legal and social affairs." Especially needs expository or advocacy articles; position should be defended clearly in good, crisp, journalistic prose. "We would like to see articles on issues such as the feasibility of energy alternatives to nuclear power, roles of women and minorities in law, the power and future of multinational corporations; national issues such as gun control; and aspects of the legal profession such as salary comparisons, use of computers in law practice." No humorous court reporter anecdote material or political opinion articles. Buys 15 unsolicited mss/year. Length: 3,000-4,000 words. Query with a working title and outline of topic. "Be specific." Pays $450-750. Sometimes pays the expenses of writers on assignment.

Photos: Donna Tashjian, photo editor. B&w photos and color transparencies purchased without accompanying ms. Pays $35-150.

Tips: "We urge writers to think ahead about new areas of law and social issues; sexual habits, work habits, corporations, etc. We would like to receive sharply-focused, timely profiles of young lawyers (36 or under) doing important, offbeat, innovative or impactful things."

CALIFORNIA LAWYER, The State Bar of California, 555 Franklin St., San Francisco CA 94102. (415)561-8280. Editor: Ray Reynolds. Managing Editor: Tom Brom. 80% freelance written. Monthly magazine of law-related articles and general interest subjects of appeal to attorneys. Circ. 100,000. Pays on acceptance. Publishes ms an average of 3 months after acceptance. Byline given. Buys all rights. Simultaneous queries, and simultaneous and photocopied submissions OK. Computer printout submissions acceptable; prefers letter-quality to dot-matrix. Reports in 2 weeks on queries; 3 weeks on mss. Sample copy for 8½x11 SAE and $1.50 postage; writer's guidelines for SAE and 1 first class stamp.

Nonfiction: General interest, historical, opinion, technical, and personal effectiveness. "We are interested in concise, well-written and well-researched articles on recent trends in the legal profession, legal aspects of issues of current concern, as well as general interest articles of potential appeal and benefit to the state's lawyers. We would like to see a description or outline of your proposed idea, including a list of possible information sources." Buys 36 mss/year. Query with published clips if available. Length: 2,000-3,000 words (features). Pays $700-900.

Photos: Chris Jensen, production editor. State availability of photos with query letter or manuscript. Reviews prints. Identification of subjects and releases required.
Columns/Departments: Business of Practice; Money; Computing; Writing it Right; Ethics Advisory; and Effectiveness. Buys 100/year. Query with published clips if available. Length: 1,000-1,500 words. Pays $300-400.

COMPUTER USER'S LEGAL REPORTER, Computer Law Group, Inc., 191 Post Rd. W., Westport CT 06880. (203)227-1360. Editor: Charles P. Lickson. 20% freelance written. Prefers to work with published/established writers or "experts" in fields addressed. Newsletter published 9 times per year featuring legal issues and considerations facing users of computer and processed data. "The *Computer User's Legal Reporter* is written by a fully qualified legal and technical staff for essentially nonlawyer readers. It features brief summaries on developments in such vital areas as computer contracts, insurance, warranties, crime, proprietary rights and privacy. Each summary is backed by reliable research and sourcework." Circ. 1,000. Pays on publication. Publishes ms an average of 1 month after acceptance. Offers 50% kill fee. Buys first North American serial rights. Simultaneous queries, and simultaneous, photocopied, and previously published submissions OK. Computer printout submissions acceptable; prefers letter-quality to dot-matrix. Reports in 2 weeks. Sample copy for $10 with #10 SAE and 5 first class stamps.
Nonfiction: Book excerpts; expose; how-to (protect ideas, etc.); humor (computer law . . . according to Murphy); interview/profile (legal or computer personality); and technical. No articles not related to computers or high-tech and society. Buys 15 mss/year. Query with published clips. Length: 250-1,000 words. Pays $50; $150 for scenes.
Columns/Departments: Computer Law . . . according to Murphy (humorous "laws" relating to computers, definitions, etc.). The editor buys all rights to Murphyisms which may be included in his book, *Computer Law . . . According to Murphy*. Buys 10 mss/year. Length: 25-75 words. Pays $10-50.
Tips: "Send materials with a note on your own background and qualifications to write what you submit. We invite intelligently presented and well-argued controversy within our field."

THE LAWYER'S PC, A Newsletter for Lawyers Using Personal Computers, Shepard's/McGraw-Hill, Inc.; editorial office at Box 1108, Lexington SC 29072. (803)359-9941. Editor: Robert P. Wilkins. Managing Editor: Daniel E. Harmon. 70% freelance written. A biweekly newsletter covering computerized law firms. "Our readers are lawyers who want to be told how a particular microcomputer program or type of program is being applied to a legal office task, such as timekeeping, litigation support, etc." Circ. 4,000. Pays end of the month of publication. Publishes ms an average of 1-2 months after acceptance. Byline given. Buys first North American serial rights and the right to reprint. Submit seasonal/holiday material 5 months in advance. Query for electronic submissions. Computer printout submissions acceptable; prefers letter-quality to dot-matrix. Reports in 1 month on queries; 2 months on mss. Sample copy for 9x12 SAE with 56¢ postage.
Nonfiction: How-to (applications articles on law office computerization) and software reviews written by lawyers who have no compromising interests. No general articles on why lawyers need computers or reviews of products written by public relations representatives or vending consultants. Buys 30-35 mss/year. Query. Length: 500-2,500 words. Pays $25-125. Sometimes pays the expenses of writers on assignment.
Tips: "Most of our writers are lawyers. If you're not a lawyer, you need to at least understand why general business software may not work well in a law firm. If you understand lawyers' specific computer problems, write an article describing how to solve one of those problems, and we'd like to see it."

THE LAWYERS WEEKLY, The Newspaper for the Legal Profession in Canada, Butterworth (Canada) Inc., (formerly *Ontario Lawyers Weekly*), Suite 201, 423 Queen St. W., Toronto, Ontario M5V 2A5 Canada. Editor: D. Michael Fitz-James. 20% freelance written. "We will work with any *talented* writer of whatever experience level." Works with a small number of new/unpublished writers each year. A 9-times-per-year tabloid covering law and legal affairs for a "sophisticated up-market readership of lawyers and accountants." Circ. 37,000. Pays on publication. Publishes ms an average of 1 month after acceptance. Byline given. Offers 50% kill fee. Usually buys all rights. Submit seasonal/holiday material 6 weeks in advance. Simultaneous queries and submissions, and photocopied submissions OK. Query for electronic submissions. Computer printout submissions acceptable. Reports in 1 month. Sample copy $1.50 Canadian funds and 8½x11 SAE.
Nonfiction: Book reviews; expose; general interest (law); historical/nostalgic; how-to (professional); humor; interview/profile (lawyers and judges); opinion; technical; news; and case comments. "We try to wrap up the week's legal events and issues in a snappy informal package with lots of visual punch. We especially like news stories with photos or illustrations. We are always interested in feature or newsfeature articles involving current legal issues, but contributors should keep in mind our audience is trained in *English/Canadian Common law*—not U.S. law. That means most U.S. constitutional or criminal law stories will generally not be accepted. Contributors should also keep in mind they're writing for *lawyers* and they don't need to reduce legal stories to simple-minded babble often seen in the daily press." Special Christmas issue. No routine court reporting or fake news stories about commercial products. Buys 200-300 mss/year. Query or send complete ms. Length: 700-1,500 words. Pays $25 minimum, negotiable maximum (have paid up to $250 in the past). Payment in

Canadian dollars. Sometimes pays the expenses of writers on assignment.

Photos: State availability of photos with query letter or ms. Reviews b&w contact sheets, negatives, and 5x7 prints. Identification of subjects required. Buys one-time rights.

Columns/Departments: Buys 90-100 mss/year. Send complete ms. Length: 500-1,000 words. Pays negotiable rate.

Fillers: Clippings, jokes, gags, anecdotes, short humor and newsbreaks. Cartoon ideas will be drawn by our artists. Length: 50-200 words. Pays $10 minimum.

Tips: "Freelancers can best break into our publication by submitting news, features, and accounts of unusual or bizarre legal events. A frequent mistake made by writers is forgetting that our audience is intelligent and learned in law. They don't need the word 'plaintiff' explained to them." No unsolicited mss returned without SASE or IRC to U.S. destinations.

LEGAL ECONOMICS, The Magazine of Law Office Management, A Magazine of the Section of Economics of Law Practice of the American Bar Association, Box 11418, Columbia SC 29211. Managing Editor/Art Director: Delmar L. Roberts. 10% freelance written. For the practicing lawyer. 8 issues/year. Magazine; 80-100 pages. Circ. 28,000. Rights purchased vary with author and material. Usually buys all rights. Byline given. Pays on publication. Publishes ms an average of 8 months after acceptance. Computer printout submissions acceptable. Query. Free writer's guidelines; sample copy $6 (make check payable to American Bar Association). Returns rejected material in 90 days, if requested.

Nonfiction: "We assist the practicing lawyer in operating and managing his or her office by providing relevant articles and departments written in a readable and informative style. Editorial content is intended to aid the lawyer by conveying management methods that will allow him or her to provide legal services to clients in a prompt and efficient manner at reasonable cost. Typical topics of articles include fees and billing; client/lawyer relations; microcomputers and office equipment; mergers; retirement/disability; marketing; compensation of partners and associates; legal data base research; and use of paralegals." No elementary articles on a whole field of technology, such as, "why you need word processing in the law office." Pays $75-300.

Photos: Pays $30-60 for b&w photos purchased with mss; $50-75 for color; $100-125 for cover transparencies.

Tips: "We have a theme for each issue with two to three articles relating to the theme. We publish thematic issues, such as one issue exclusively on computer hardware and another on software."

LOS ANGELES LAWYER, Los Angeles County Bar Association, Box 55020, Los Angeles CA 90055. (213)627-2727, ext. 265. Editor: Susan Pettit. 100% freelance written. Prefers to work with published/established writers. Monthly (except for combined July/August issue) magazine covering legal profession with "journalistic and scholarly articles of interest to the legal profession." Circ. 20,000. Pays on acceptance. Publishes ms an average of 2 months after acceptance. Byline given. Buys first serial rights only. Submit seasonal/holiday material 4 months in advance. Simultaneous queries and photocopied submissions OK. Query for electronic submissions. Computer printout submissions acceptable; prefers letter-quality to dot-matrix. Reports in 1 month on queries; 2 months on mss. Sample copy $1.50; free writer's guidelines.

Nonfiction: How-to (tips for legal practitioners); humor; interview (leading legal figures); opinion (on area of law, lawyer attitudes or group, court decisions, etc.); travel (very occasionally); and consumer-at-law feature articles on topics of interest to lawyers. No first person, nonlegal material. Buys 22 mss/year. Query with published clips. Length: 4,000-4,500 words for feature (cover story); 2,000-2,750 words for consumer article. Pays $500-600 for cover story, $200-225 for consumer article. Sometimes pays the expenses of writers on assignment.

Tips: "Writers should be familiar with the Los Angeles legal community as the magazine has a local focus."

THE NATIONAL LAW JOURNAL, New York Law Publishing Company, 111 8th Ave., New York NY 10011. (212)741-8300. Editor: Timothy Robinson. 15% freelance written. Weekly newspaper for the legal profession. Circ. 50,000. Pays on publication. Publishes ms an average of 2 months after acceptance. Byline given. Offers $75 kill fee. Buys all rights. Simultaneous queries OK. Electronic submissions OK on 300 or 1200 baud. Computer printout submissions acceptable; prefers letter-quality to dot-matrix. Reports in 3 weeks on queries; 5 weeks on mss. Sample copy $2.

Nonfiction: Expose (on subjects of interest to lawyers); and interview/profile (of lawyers or judges of note). "The bulk of our freelance articles are 2,000-2,500 word profiles of prominent lawyers, or trend stories relating to the legal profession. We also buy a steady stream of short, spot-news stories on local court decisions or lawsuits; often, these come from legal affairs writers on local newspapers. No articles without a legal angle." Buys 60 mss/year. Query with published clips or send complete ms. Length: 1,500-3,000 words. Pays $300-500. Sometimes pays the expenses of writers on assignment.

Columns/Departments: "For those who are not covering legal affairs on a regular basis, the best way into *The National Law Journal* is probably through our Exhibit A feature. Every week we print a sort of reporter's notebook on some proceeding currently underway in a courtroom. These stories come from all around the country and range from gory murder trials to a night in small claims court. They usually run about 1,000 words and are stylistically quite flexible. We also use op-ed pieces on subjects of legal interest, many of which come from freelancers. Writers interested in doing an op-ed piece should query first." Pays $150.

THE PARALEGAL, The Publication for the Paralegal Profession, Paralegal Publishing Corp./National Paralegal Association, 10 S. Pine St., Box 629, Doylestown PA 18901. (215)348-5575. Editor: William Cameron. 90% freelance written. Prefers to work with published/established writers; works with a small number of new/unpublished writers each year; eager to work with new/unpublished writers. Bimonthly magazine covering the paralegal profession for practicing paralegals, attorneys, paralegal educators, paralegal associations, law librarians and court personnel. Special and controlled circulation includes law libraries, colleges and schools educating paralegals, law schools, law firms and governmental agencies, etc. Circ. 12,000. Byline given. Buys all rights. Simultaneous queries, and simultaneous, photocopied, and previously published submissions OK. Computer printout submissions acceptable; no dot-matrix. Reports in 2 weeks on queries; 1 month on mss. Writer's guidelines and suggested topic sheet for business-size SAE.
Nonfiction: Book excerpts, expose, general interest, historical/nostalgic, how-to, humor, interview/profile, new product, opinion, personal experience, photo feature, technical and travel. Suggested topics include the paralegal (where do they fit and how do they operate within the law firm in each specialty); the government; the corporation; the trade union; the banking institution; the law library; the legal clinic; the trade or professional association; the educational institution; the court system; the collection agency; the stock brokerage firm; and the insurance company. Articles also wanted on paralegals exploring "Where have they been? Where are they now? Where are they going?" Query or send complete ms. Length: 1,500-3,000 words. Pays variable rates; submissions should state desired fee. Ask amount when submitting ms or other material to be considered. Sometimes pays the expenses of writers on assignment.
Photos: Send photos with query or ms. Captions, model release, and identification of subjects required.
Columns/Departments: Case at Issue (a feature on a current case from a state or federal court which either directly or indirectly affects paralegals and their work with attorneys, the public, private or governmental sector); Humor (cartoons, quips, short humorous stories, anecdotes and one-liners in good taste and germane to the legal profession); and My Position (an actual presentation by a paralegal who wishes to share with others his/her job analysis). Query. Submissions should state desired fee.
Fillers: Clippings, jokes, gags, anecdotes, short humor and newsbreaks.

THE PENNSYLVANIA LAWYER, Pennsylvania Bar Association, 100 South St., Box 186, Harrisburg PA 17108. (717)238-6715. Executive Editor: Francis J. Fanucci. Managing Editor: Donald C. Sarvey. 20% freelance written. Prefers to work with published/established writers. Magazine published 7 times/year as a service to the legal profession. Circ. 27,000. Pays on acceptance. Publishes ms an average of 3-5 months after acceptance. Byline given. Buys negotiable serial rights; generally first rights, occasionally one-time rights or second serial (reprint) rights. Submit seasonal/holiday material 5 months in advance. Simultaneous submissions or queries will be considered, but the practice is not encouraged. If the submission or query is a simultaneous one, it should be so noted. Computer printout submissions acceptable; prefers letter-quality to dot-matrix. Reports in 1 month. Free sample copy.
Nonfiction: General interest, how-to, humor, interview/profile, new product, and personal experience. All features *should* relate in some way to Pennsylvania lawyers or the practice of law in Pennsylvania. Buys 10-12 mss/year. Query. Length: 800-2,000 words. Pays $75-350. Sometimes pays the expenses of writers on assignment.

STUDENT LAWYER, American Bar Association, 750 N. Lake Shore Dr., Chicago IL 60611. (312)988-6048. Editor: Lizanne Poppens. Associate Editor: Sarah Hoban. 95% freelance written. Works with a small number of new/unpublished writers each year. Monthly (September-May) magazine; 48-56 pages. Circ. 40,000. Pays on publication. Buys first serial rights and second serial (reprint) rights. Pays negotiable kill fee. Byline given. Submit seasonal/holiday material 4 months in advance. Photocopied submissions OK. Computer printout submissions acceptable; prefers letter-quality to dot-matrix. Reports in 6 weeks. Publishes ms an average of 3 months after acceptance. Sample copy $2; free writer's guidelines.
Nonfiction: Expose (government, law, education and business); profiles (prominent persons in law-related fields); opinion (on matters of current legal interest); essays (on legal affairs); interviews; and photo features. Recent article examples: "Second-guessing the Jury" and "The Solitary Struggle of Human Rights Lawyers" (April 1987). Buys 5 mss/issue. Query. Length: 3,000-5,000 words. Pays $250-600 for main features. Covers some writer's expenses.
Columns/Departments: Briefly (short stories on unusual and interesting developments in the law); Legal Aids (unusual approaches and programs connected to teaching law students and lawyers); Esq. (brief profiles of people in the law); End Note (very short pieces on a variety of topics; can be humorous, educational, outrageous); Pro Se (opinion slot for authors to wax eloquent on legal issues, civil rights conflicts, the state of the union); and Et Al. (column for short features that fit none of the above categories). Buys 4-8 mss/issue. Length: 250-1,000 words. Pays $75-250.
Fiction: "We buy fiction only when it is very good and deals with issues of law in the contemporary world or

offers insights into the inner workings of lawyers. No mystery or science fiction accepted."

Tips: "*Student Lawyer* actively seeks good new writers. Legal training definitely not essential; writing talent is. The writer should not think we are a law review; we are a feature magazine with the law (in the broadest sense) as the common denominator. Past articles concerned gay rights, prison reform, the media, pornography, capital punishment, and space law. Find issues of national scope and interest to write about; be aware of subjects the magazine—and other media—have already covered and propose something new. Write clearly and well."

VERDICT MAGAZINE, Legal Journal of the Association of Southern California Defense Counsel, American Lifestyle Communications, Inc., 123 Truxtun Ave., Bakersfield CA 93301. (805)325-7124. Editor: Sharon Muir. Managing Editor: Steve Walsh. A quarterly magazine covering defense law (corporate). Circ. 5,000. Pays on publication. Byline given. Buys first North American serial rights. Submit seasonal/holiday material 4 months in advance. Photocopied submissions OK. Computer printout submissions acceptable. Reports in 2 months. Sample copy for $2.50, 9x12 SAE and $2 postage; free writer's guidelines.

Nonfiction: How-to (corporate defense law); interview/profile; personal experience; and technical. Buys 12 mss/year. Send complete ms. Length: 1,500-3,000 words. Pays $20-35.

Photos: Send photos with ms. Pays $5-10 for 3x5 b&w prints. Captions required. Buys all rights.

Columns/Departments: Buys 4 mss/year. Send complete ms. Length: 500-750 words. Pays $15-20.

Fiction: Historical and mystery. Buys 4 mss/year. Send complete ms. Length: 1,500-3,000 words. Pays $20-35.

Leather Goods

‡NSRA NEWS, National Shoe Retailers Association, Suite 400, 9861 Broken Land Pkwy., Columbia MD 21046. (301)381-8282. Editor: Cynthia Emmel. 10% freelance written. Bimonthly newsletter covering footwear/accessory industry. Looks for articles that are "informative, educational, but with wit, interest, and creativity. I hate dry, dusty articles." Circ. 4,000-5,000. Byline sometimes given. Buys one-time rights. Submit seasonal/holiday material 3 months in advance. Photocopied submissions OK. Computer printout submissions OK; no dot-matrix. Reports in 2 weeks.

Nonfiction: How-to, interview/profile, new product and technical. January and July are shoe show issues. Buys 4 mss/year. Length: 450 words. Pays $125 for assigned articles. Pays up to $250 for "full-fledged research—1,000 words on assigned articles.

Photos: State availability of photos with submission. Offers no additional payment for photos accepted with ms. Buys one-time rights.

Columns/Departments: Query. Pays $50-125.

Tips: "We are a trade magazine/newsletter for the footwear industry. Any information pertaining to our market is helpful: ex. advertising/display/how-tos."

SHOE SERVICE, SSIA Service Corp., 112 Calendar Court Mall, La Grange IL 60525. (312)482-8010. Editor: Mitchell Lebovic. 50% freelance written. "We want well-written articles, whether they come from new or established writers." Monthly magazine for business people who own and operate small shoe repair shops. Circ. 17,000. Pays on publication. Publishes ms an average of 3 months after acceptance. Byline given. Buys first serial rights, first North American serial rights, and one-time rights. Submit seasonal/holiday material 3 months in advance. Simultaneous queries, and photocopied and previously published submissions OK. Computer printout submissions acceptable; prefers letter-quality to dot-matrix. Reports in 6 weeks. Sample copy $1.

Nonfiction: How-to (run a profitable shop); interview/profile (of an outstanding or unusual person on shoe repair); and business articles (particularly about small business practices in a service/retail shop). Buys 12-24 mss/year. Query with published clips or send complete ms. Length: 500-2,000 words. Pays 5¢/word.

Photos: "Quality photos will help sell an article." State availability of photos. Pays $10-30 for 8x10 b&w prints. Uses some color photos, but mostly uses b&w glossies. Captions, model release, and identification of subjects required.

Tips: "Visit some shoe repair shops to get an idea of the kind of person who reads *Shoe Service*. Profiles are the easiest to sell to us if you can find a repairer we think is unusual."

Library Science

AMERICAN LIBRARIES, 50 E. Huron St., Chicago IL 60611. (312)944-6780. Editor: Arthur Plotnik. 5-10% freelance written. Works with a small number of new/unpublished writers each year. Magazine published 11 times/year for librarians. "A highly literate audience. They are for the most part practicing professionals with a down-to-earth interest in people and current trends." Circ. 42,500. Buys first North American serial rights. Publishes ms an average of 4 months after acceptance. Pays negotiable kill fee. Byline given. Will consider photocopied submissions if not being considered elsewhere at time of submission. Computer printout submissions acceptable; prefers letter-quality to dot-matrix. Submit seasonal material 6 months in advance. Reports in 10 weeks.

Nonfiction: "Material reflecting the special and current interests of the library profession. Nonlibrarians should browse recent journals in the field, available on request in medium-sized and large libraries everywhere. Topic and/or approach must be fresh, vital, or highly entertaining. Library memoirs and stereotyped stories about old maids, overdue books, fines, etc., are unacceptable. Our first concern is with the American Library Association's activities and how they relate to the 46,000 reader/members. Tough for an outsider to write on this topic, but not to supplement it with short, offbeat or significant library stories and features." No fillers. Recent article example: "The Librarian Behind the Bestseller." profiling the librarian who helped develop *In Search of Excellence* (March 1985). Sometimes pays the expenses of writers on assignment.

Photos: "Will look at all good black and white, well-lit photos of library situations, and at color transparencies and bright prints for inside and cover use." Buys 5-10 mss/year. Pays $25-300 for briefs and articles. Pays $50-150 for photos.

Tips: "You can break in with a sparkling, 300-word report on a true, offbeat library event, use of new technology, or with an exciting color photo and caption. Though stories on public libraries are always of interest, we especially need arresting material on academic and school libraries."

CHURCH MEDIA LIBRARY MAGAZINE,127 9th Ave. N., Nashville TN 37234. (615)251-2752. Editor: Floyd B. Simpson. Quarterly magazine; 50 pages. For adult leaders in church organizations and people interested in library work (especially church library work). Circ. 16,000. Pays on publication. Buys all rights, first serial rights and second serial (reprint) rights. Byline given. Phone queries OK. Submit seasonal/holiday material 14 months in advance. Previously published submissions OK. Reports in 1 month. Free sample copy and writer's guidelines.

Nonfiction: "We are primarily interested in articles that relate to the development of church libraries in providing media and services to support the total program of a church and in meeting individual needs. We publish how-to accounts of services provided, promotional ideas, exciting things that have happened as a result of implementing an idea or service; human interest stories that are library-related; and media education (teaching and learning with a media mix). Articles should be practical for church library staffs and for teachers and other leaders of the church." Buys 10-15 mss/issue. Query. Pays 5¢/word.

EMERGENCY LIBRARIAN, Dyad Services, Box 46258, Stn. G, Vancouver, British Columbia V6R 4G6 Canada. Co-Editors: Carol Ann Haycock and Ken Haycock. Bimonthly magazine. Circ. 5,500. Pays on publication. Photocopied submissions OK. No multiple submissions. SAE and IRCs. Reports in 6 weeks. Free writer's guidelines.

Nonfiction: Emphasis is on improvement of library service for children and young adults in school and public libraries. Also annotated bibliographies. Buys 3 mss/issue. Query. Length: 1,000-3,500 words. Pays $50.

Columns/Departments: Five regular columnists. Also Book Reviews (of professional materials in education, librarianship). Query. Length: 100-300 words. Payment consists of book reviewed.

‡THE LIBRARY IMAGINATION PAPER, Carol Bryan Images, 1000 Byus Dr., Charleston WV 25331. (304)345-2378. 30% freelance written. Quarterly newspaper covering public relations education for librarians, clip art included in each issue. Circ. 3,000. Pays on publication. Publishes ms an average of 6 months after acceptance. Byline given. Buys one-time rights. Submit seasonal/holiday material 3 months in advance. Simultaneous, photocopied and previously published submissions OK. Computer printout submissions OK; prefers letter-quality. Reports in 6 weeks on queries; 3 weeks on mss. Sample copy $4.50; writer's guidelines for SASE.

Nonfiction: How-to (on "all aspects of good library publications—both mental tips and hands-on methods. "We need how-to and tips peices on all aspects of PR, for library subscribers—both school and public libraries. In the past we've featured pieces on taking good photos, promoting an anniversary celebration, working with printers, and producing a slide show." No articles on "what the library means to me." Buys 4-6 mss/year. Query with or without published clips, or send complete ms. Length: 500-2,200 words. Pays $35.

Photos: Send photos with submission. Reviews 5x7 prints. Offers $5 per photo. Captions required. Buys one-time rights.

Tips: "Someone who has worked in the library field and has first hand knowledge of library PR needs, methods and processes will do far better with us. Our readers are people who can not be written down to—but their library training has not always incorporated enough preparation for handling promotion, publicity and the public."

‡LIBRARY JOURNAL, 249 N. 17th St., New York NY 10011. Editor-in-Chief: John N. Berry III. 60% freelance written. Eager to work with new/unpublished writers. For librarians (academic, public, special). 115-page magazine published 20 times/year. Circ. 30,000. Buys all rights. Pays on publication. Publishes ms an average of 12-18 months after acceptance. Computer printout submissions OK; prefers letter-quality to dot-matrix. "Our response time is slow, but improving."

Nonfiction: *"Library Journal* is a professional magazine for librarians. Freelancers are most often rejected because they submit one of the following types of article: 'A wonderful, warm, concerned, loving librarian who started me on the road to good reading and success'; 'How I became rich, famous, and successful by using my public library'; 'Libraries are the most wonderful and important institutions in our society, because they have all of the knowledge of mankind—praise them.' We need material of greater sophistication, dealing with issues related to the transfer of information, access to it, or related phenomena. (Current hot are copyright, censorship, the decline in funding for public institutions, the local politics of libraries, trusteeship, U.S. government information policy, etc.)" Professional articles on criticism, censorship, professional concerns, library activities, historical articles, information technology, automation and management, and spot news. Outlook should be from librarian's point of view. Buys 50-65 unsolicited mss/year. Submit complete ms. Length: 1,500-2,000 words. Pays $50-350. Sometimes pays the expenses of writers on assignment.

Photos: Payment for b&w or color glossy photos purchased without accompanying mss is $30. Must be at least 5x7. Captions required.

Tips: "We're increasingly interested in material on library management, public sector fundraising, and information policy."

SCHOOL LIBRARY JOURNAL, 205 E. 42nd. St., New York NY 10017. Editor: Lillian N. Gerhardt. For librarians in schools and public libraries. Magazine published 10 times/year; 88 pages. Circ. 42,000. Buys all rights. Pays on publication. Reports in 6 months.

Nonfiction: Articles on library services, local censorship problems, and how-to articles on programs that use books, films or microcomputer software. Informational, personal experience, interview, expose, and successful business operations. "Interested in history articles on the establishment/development of children's and young adult services in schools and public libraries." Buys 24 mss/year. Length: 2,500-3,000 words. Pays $100 and up, depending on length.

WILSON LIBRARY BULLETIN, 950 University Ave., Bronx NY 10452. (212)588-8400. Editor: Milo Nelson. 80% freelance written. Monthly (September-June) for professional librarians and those interested in the book and library worlds. Circ. 30,000. Pays on publication. Publishes ms an average of 2 months after acceptance. Buys first North American serial rights. Sample copies may be seen on request in most libraries. "Manuscript must be original copy, double-spaced; additional photocopy or carbon is appreciated." Computer printout submissions acceptable; prefers letter-quality to dot-matrix. Deadlines are a minimum 2 months before publication. Reports in 3 months.

Nonfiction: Uses articles "of interest to librarians throughout the nation and around the world. Style must be lively, readable and sophisticated, with appeal to modern professionals; facts must be thoroughly researched. Subjects range from the political to the comic in the world of media and libraries, with an emphasis on the human as well as the technical aspects of any story. No condescension: no library stereotypes." Buys 30 mss/year. Send complete ms. Length: 2,500-6,000 words. Pays about $100-400, "depending on the substance of article and its importance to readers." Sometimes pays the expenses of writers on assignment.

Tips: "The best way you can break in is with a first-rate black and white photo and caption information on a library, library service, or librarian who departs completely from all stereotypes and the commonplace. Libraries have changed. You'd better first discover what is now commonplace."

ALWAYS submit manuscripts or queries with a self-addressed, stamped envelope (SASE) within your country or International Reply Coupons purchased from the post office for other countries.

Lumber

B.C. LUMBERMAN MAGAZINE, 2000 W. 12th Ave., Vancouver, British Columbia V6J 2G2 Canada. (604)731-1171. Editor: Paul MacDonald. 20% freelance written. Prefers to work with published/established writers. Monthly magazine; 50 pages. For the logging and saw milling industries of western Canada and the Pacific Northwest of the United States. Circ. 8,500. Pays on acceptance. Publishes ms an average of 3 months after acceptance. Buys first Canadian serial rights. Computer printout submissions OK. Reports in 2 weeks.

Nonfiction: How-to (technical articles on any aspect of the forest industry); general interest (anything of interest to persons in forest industries in western Canada or U.S. Pacific Northwest); interview (occasionally related to leading forestry personnel); and technical (forestry). No fiction or history. Query first with published clips. Length: 1,500 words average. Pays 15¢/word (Canadian).

Photos: State availability of photos with query. Pays $5-25 for b&w negatives and $50-80 for 8x10 glossy color prints. Captions required. Buys first Canadian rights.

‡CANADIAN FOREST INDUSTRIES, 1450 Don Mills Rd., Don Mills, Ontario M3B 2X7 Canada. Contact: Editor. 25% freelance written. Monthly magazine for forest companies, loggers, lumber-plywood-board manufacturers. Circ. 15,000. Pays on publication. Publishes ms an average of 6 months after acceptance. Byline given. Buys first North American serial rights. Reports in 1 month. Computer printout submissions acceptable; prefers letter-quality to dot-matrix. SAE and IRCs. Free sample copy.

Nonfiction: Uses "articles concerning industry topics, especially how-to articles that help businessmen in the forest industries. All articles should take the form of detailed reports of new methods, techniques and cost-cutting practices that are being successfully used anywhere in Canada, together with descriptions of new equipment that is improving efficiency and utilization of wood. It is very important that accurate descriptions of machinery (make, model, etc.) always be included and any details of costs, etc., in actual dollars and cents can make the difference between a below-average article and an exceptional one." Query. Length: 1,200-1,500 words. Pays 20¢/word minimum, more with photos. Pays expenses of writers on assignment.

Photos: Buys photos with mss, sometimes with captions only. Should be 8x10, b&w glossies or negatives.

NORTHERN LOGGER AND TIMBER PROCESSOR, Northeastern Loggers' Association, Box 69, Old Forge NY 13420. (315)369-3078. Editor: Eric A. Johnson. 40% freelance written. Monthly magazine of the forest industry in the northern U.S. (Maine to Minnesota and south to Virginia and Missouri). "We are not a purely technical journal, but are more information oriented." Circ. 13,000. Pays on publication. Publishes ms an average of 3 months after acceptance. Byline given. Buys all rights. Submit seasonal/holiday material 3 months in advance. Photocopied and previously published submissions OK. "Any computer printout submission that can be easily read is acceptable." Reports in 2 weeks. Free sample copy.

Nonfiction: Expose, general interest, historical/nostalgic, how-to, interview/profile, new product and opinion. "We only buy feature articles, and those should contain some technical or historical material relating to the forest products industry." Buys 12-15 mss/year. Query. Length: 500-2,500 words. Pays $25-125.

Photos: Send photos with ms. Pays $20-35 for 35mm color transparencies; $5-15 for 5x7 b&w prints. Captions and identification of subjects required.

Tips: "We accept most any subject dealing with this part of the country's forest industry, from historical to logging, firewood, and timber processing."

ROSEBURG WOODSMAN, Roseburg Forest Products Co., % Chevalier Advertising, Suite 101, 4905 SW Griffith Dr., Beaverton OR 97005. Editor: Shirley P. Rogers. 99% (but most rewritten) freelance written. Prefers to work with published/established writers. Monthly magazine for wholesale lumber distributors and other buyers of forest products, such as furniture manufacturers. Emphasis on wood products, especially company products. Publishes a special Christmas issue. Circ. 8,000. Pays on publication. Publishes ms an average of 1 year after acceptance. Buys first serial rights or one-time rights. No byline given. Submit seasonal material 6 months in advance. Computer printout submissions acceptable; prefers letter-quality to dot-matrix. Reports in 1 week. Free sample copy and writer's guidelines.

Nonfiction: Features on the "residential, commercial and industrial applications of wood products, such as lumber, plywood, prefinished wall paneling, and particleboard, particularly Roseburg Lumber Co. products. We are no longer looking for stories on hobbyists or individual craftsmen. No 'clever,' 'wise' or witty contributions unless they tell a fascinating story and are well-illustrated. No fillers, isolated photos or inadequately illustrated articles." Buys 25-30 mss/year. Query or submit complete ms. Length: 250-500 words. Pays $50-$100. Pays expenses of writers on assignment.

Photos: "Photos are essential. Good pictures will sell us on a story." Rarely uses b&w photos or color prints. Prefers color transparencies or 35mm slides. Pays $25-50/color transparency used, more for cover photo.

Photos purchased only with ms.

Tips: "Since everything is rewritten to our style, the writer's style is not vitally important. However, there should be some expertise regarding forest products terms, and an absolute dedication to accuracy. I sometimes hire a freelancer 'on assignment' at a higher rate. Send letter specifying experience, publications, types of stories and geographic area covered."

‡SOUTHERN LUMBERMAN, Greysmith Publishing, Inc., Suite 116, 128 Holiday Ct., Franklin TN 37064. (615)791-1961. Editor: Nanci P. Gregg. 20-30% freelance written. Works with a small number of new/unpublished writers each year. A monthly trade journal for the lumber industry. Circ. 10,000. Pays on publication. Publishes ms an average of 4 months after acceptance. Byline sometimes given. Not copyrighted. Buys all rights. Submit seasonal/holiday material 6 months in advance. Query for electronic submissions. Computer printout submissions OK; prefers letter-quality. Reports in 1 month on queries; 2 months on mss. Sample copy $1 with 9x12 SAE and 4 first class stamps.

Nonfiction: Expose, historical, interview/profile, new product, technical. Buys 20-30 mss/year. Query with or without published clips, or send complete ms. Length: 500-2,000 words. Pays $150-350 for assigned articles; pays $150-250 for unsolicited articles. Sometimes pays the expenses of writers on assignment.

Photos: Send photos with submission. Reviews transparencies and 4x5 prints. Offers $10 per photo. Captions and identification of subjects required.

Tips: "Like most, we appreciate a clearly-worded query listing merits of suggested story—what it will tell our readers they need/want to know. We want quotes, we want opinions to make others discuss the article. Best hint? Find an interesting sawmill operation owner and start asking questions—I bet a story idea develops. We need b&w photos too. Most open is what we call the Sweethart Mill stories. We publish at least one per month, and hope to be printing two or more monthly in the immediate future. Find a sawmill operator and ask questions—what's he doing bigger, better, different. We're interested in new facilities, better marketing, improved production."

TREE TRIMMERS LOG, A Newsletter For Today's Tree Trimmer, Tree Trimmers Log, Box 833, Ojai CA 93023. (805)646-9688. Editor: D. Keith. 10% freelance written. Eager to work with new/unpublished writers. Trade newsletter on tree trimming published 10 times/year. Circ. 400. Pays on acceptance. Publishes ms an average of 2 months after acceptance. Byline given. Offers 25% kill fee. Buys first serial rights. Submit seasonal/holiday material 2 months in advance. Simultaneous queries, and simultaneous, photocopied, and previously published submissions OK. Computer printout submissions acceptable. Reports in 1 month. Free sample copy and writer's guidelines.

Nonfiction: Historical/nostalgic (trees, older trimmer reminiscings); how-to (run small businesses, maintain equipment, be more efficient in work); humor; interview/profile (of a trimmer with a slant: singing trimmer, community concerned trimmer, etc.); new product; personal experience (if you're a working trimmer); photo feature (rescue action); and technical (taking care of equipment, climbing gear). No "cuteness." Buys 12-15 mss/year. Query or send complete ms. Length: 50-800 words. Pays $5-25.

Photos: State availability of photos. Reviews b&w contact sheets and b&w 3½x5 prints. Pays $5 for contact sheets; $5-10 for prints. Identification of subjects required. Buys first serial rights.

Columns/Departments: Chain Saw (or equipment) Corner and First Aid (50-150 words). "We're open to suggestions." Buys 10/year. Query. Length: 150-350 words. Pays $10.

Fillers: Clippings, jokes, anecdotes, short humor, puzzles, newsbreaks and cartoons. Buys 20/year. Pays $5-10.

Tips: "We would like to emphasize more interviews or 'people' stories in 1988. Submit a query for an interview with a tree trimmer, a local college horticulturist (trees), etc. Find someone unique, with a good story to tell, or who can offer tips to his fellow trimmers. Being writers, we work with and encourage writers. Our prices are low now, but we invite writers to grow with us."

——— Machinery and Metal

‡AUTOMATIC MACHINING, 100 Seneca Ave., Rochester NY 14621. (716)338-1522. Editor: Donald E. Wood. For metalworking technical management. Buys all rights. Byline given. Computer printout submissions acceptable.

Nonfiction: "This is not a market for the average freelancer. A personal knowledge of the trade is essential. Articles deal in depth with specific job operations on automatic screw machines, chucking machines, high production metal turning lathes and cold heading machines. Part prints, tooling layouts always required, plus written agreement of source to publish the material. Without personal background in operation of this type of equipment, freelancers are wasting time. No material researched from library sources." Query. Length: no limit. Pays $20/printed page.

Tips: "In the year ahead there will be more emphasis on plant and people news so less space will be available for conventional articles."

CANADIAN MACHINERY & METALWORKING, 777 Bay St., Toronto, Ontario M5W 1A7 Canada. (416)596-5714. Editor: Nick Hancock. 15% freelance written. Monthly. Buys first Canadian rights. Pays on acceptance. Query. Publishes ms an average of 6 weeks after acceptance.

Nonfiction: Technical and semitechnical articles dealing with metalworking operations in Canada and in the U.S., if of particular interest to Canadian readers. Accuracy and service appeal to readers is a must. Pays minimum 25¢/word.

Photos: Purchased with mss and with captions only. Pays $10 minimum for b&w features.

CUTTING TOOL ENGINEERING, 464 Central Ave., Northfield IL 60093. (312)441-7520. Publisher: John William Roberts. Editor: Larry Teeman. 25% freelance written. Prefers to work with published/established writers. For metalworking industry executives and engineers concerned with the metal-cutting/metal and material removal/abrasive machining function in metalworking. Bimonthly. 25% freelance written. Circ. 38,775. Pays on publication. Publishes ms an average of 6 months after acceptance. Byline given. Buys all rights. Electronic submissions OK on IBM PC, but requires hard copy also. Computer printout submissions acceptable; no dot-matrix. Call Larry Teeman before querying or submitting ms. Free sample copy.

Nonfiction: "Intelligently written articles on specific applications of all types of metal cutting tools, mills, drills, reamers, etc. Articles must contain all information related to the operation, such as feeds and speeds, materials machined, etc. Should be tersely written, in-depth treatment. In the Annual Diamond/Superabrasive Directory, published in June, we cover the use of diamond/superabrasive cutting tools and diamond/superabrasive grinding wheels." Length: 1,000-2,500 words. Pays "$35/published page, or about 5¢/published word."

Photos: Purchased with mss. 8x10 color or b&w glossies preferred.

Tips: "The most frequent mistake made by writers in completing an article for us is that they don't know the market."

‡FOUNDRY MANAGEMENT & TECHNOLOGY, Penton Plaza, Cleveland OH 44114. (216)696-7000. Editor: Robert C. Rodgers. 5% freelance written. Monthly. Publishes ms an average of 2 months after acceptance. Byline given. Buys first serial rights only. Computer printout submissions acceptable; no dot-matrix. Reports in 2 weeks.

Nonfiction: Uses articles describing operating practice in foundries written to interest companies producing metal castings. Buys 5-6 unsolicited mss/year. Length: 3,000 words maximum. Pays $50/printed page.

Photos: Uses illustrative photographs with article; uses "a great deal of 4-color photos."

MODERN MACHINE SHOP, 6600 Clough Pike, Cincinnati OH 45244. Editor: Ken Gettelman. 25% freelance written. Monthly. Pays 1 month following acceptance. Publishes ms an average of 6 months after acceptance. Byline given. Electronic submissions OK if IBM compatible, but requires hard copy also. Computer printout submissions acceptable; prefers letter-quality to dot-matrix. Reports in 5 days.

Nonfiction: Uses articles dealing with all phases of metal working manufacturing and machine shop work, with photos. No general articles. "Ours is an industrial publication, and contributing authors should have a working knowledge of the metalworking industry." Buys 10 unsolicited mss/year. Query. Length: 800-3,000 words. Pays current market rate. Sometimes pays the expenses of writers on assignment.

Tips: "The use of articles relating to computers in manufacturing is growing."

> **66** *Writers must have fresh, new angles, must present new trends and new outlooks. It doesn't matter if they've been published before, as long as their writing is skillfully executed.* **99**
>
> **—Peg Angsten**
> **American Fitness Magazine**

—— *Maintenance and Safety*

‡**BUILDING SERVICES CONTRACTOR**, MacNair Publications Inc., 101 W. 31st St., New York NY 10001. (212)279-4455. Editor: Frank C. Falcetta. 0-5% freelance written. Bimonthly magazine covering building services and maintenance. Circ. 8,000. Pays on publication. Publishes ms an average of 2-4 months after acceptance. Byline sometimes given. Buys one-time rights and second serial (reprint) rights. Simultaneous, photocopied and previously published submissions OK "as long as not published in competitive magazine." Computer printout submissions OK; prefers letter-quality to dot-matrix. Reports in 2 weeks. Writer's guidelines for SAE.
Nonfiction: How-to, humor, interview/profile, new product and technical. Buys 1-5 mss/year. Query only. Pays $75 minimum.
Photos: State availability of photos with submission. Reviews contact sheets. Offers no additional payment for photos accepted with ms, but offers higher payment when photos are used." Buys one-time rights.
Tips: "I'd love to do more with freelance, but market and budget make it tough. I do most of it myself."

EQUIPMENT MANAGEMENT, 7300 N. Cicero Ave., Lincolnwood IL 60646. (312)588-7300. Executive Editor: Jim Clemens. 10% freelance written. Prefers to work with published/established writers. "We are interested in material related to the heavy equipment industry." Monthly magazine; 76-110 pages. Circ. 70,000. Pays on publication. Publishes ms an average of 4 months after acceptance. Rights purchased vary with author and material; buys all rights. Computer printout submissions acceptable; no dot-matrix. Reports in 1 month. Free sample copy.
Nonfiction: "Our focus is on the effective management of heavy equipment through proper selection, careful specification, correct application and efficient maintenance. We use job stories, technical articles, safety features, basics and shop notes. No product stories or 'puff' pieces." Buys 12 mss/year. Query with outline. Length: 2,000-5,000 words. Pays $25/printed page minimum, without photos. Sometimes pays the expenses of writers on assignment.
Photos: Uses 35mm and 2¼x2¼ or larger color transparencies with mss. Pays $50/printed page when photos are furnished by author.
Tips: "Know the equipment, how to manage it and how to maintain, service, and repair it."

PEST CONTROL MAGAZINE, 7500 Old Oak Blvd., Cleveland OH 44130. (216)243-8100. Editor: Jerry Mix. For professional pest control operators and sanitation workers. Monthly magazine; 68 pages. Circ. 15,000. Buys all rights. Buys 12+ mss/year. Pays on publication. Submit seasonal material 2 months in advance. Reports in 30 days. Query or submit complete ms.
Nonfiction and Photos: Business tips, unique control situations, personal experience (stories about 1-man operations and their problems) articles. Must have trade or business orientation. No general information type of articles desired. Buys 3 unsolicited mss/year. Length: 4 double-spaced pages. Pays $150 minimum. Regular columns use material oriented to this profession. Length: 8 double-spaced pages. No additional payment for photos used with mss. Pays $50-150 for 8x10 color or transparencies.

SANITARY MAINTENANCE, Trade Press Publishing Co., 2100 W. Florist Ave., Milwaukee WI 53209. (414)228-7701. Managing Editor: Don Mulligan. Associate Editor: Susan M. Netz. 7-8% freelance written. Prefers to work with published/established writers, although all will be considered. A monthly magazine for the sanitary supply industry covering "trends in the sanitary supply industry; offering information concerning the operations of janitor supply distributors and building service contractors; and helping distributors in the development of sales personnel." Circ. 13,756. Pays on publication. Publishes ms an average of 5 months after acceptance. Byline given. Buys first North American serial rights. Photocopied submissions OK. Query for electronic submissions. Computer printout submissions acceptable. Free sample copy and writer's guidelines.
Nonfiction: How-to (improve sales, profitability as it applies to distributors, contractors); and technical. No product application stories. Buys 8-12 mss/year. Query with published clips. Length: 1,500-3,000 words. Pays $75-200.
Photos: State availability of photos with query letter or ms. Reviews 5x7 prints. Payment for photos included in payment for ms. Identification of subjects required.
Tips: Articles on sales and financial information for small businesses are open to freelancers.

SERVICE BUSINESS, Published Quarterly for the Self-Employed Professional Cleaner, Service Business Magazine, Inc., Suite 345, 1916 Pike Place, Seattle WA 98101. (206)622-4241. Publisher: William R. Griffin. Editor: Martha Ireland. Associate Editor: Sandra Tollefson. 80% freelance written. Quarterly magazine covering technical and management information relating to cleaning and self-employment. "We cater to those who are self-employed in any facet of the cleaning and maintenance industry who seek to be top professionals in their field. Our readership is small but select. We seek concise, factual articles, realistic but definitely upbeat." Circ. 5,000 + . Pays 30 days after publication. Publishes ms an average of 3 months after acceptance. Byline given. Buys first serial rights, second serial (reprint) rights, and all rights; makes work-for-hire assignments. Submit seasonal/holiday material 4 months in advance. Simultaneous queries and previously published work (rarely) OK. Computer printout submissions acceptable; prefers letter-quality to dot-matrix. Reports in 3 months. Sample copy $3, 9x7½ SAE and 3 first class stamps; writer's guidelines for business size SAE and 1 first class stamp.

Nonfiction: Expose (safety/health business practices); how-to (on cleaning, maintenance, small business management); humor (clean jokes, cartoons); interview/profile; new product (must be unusual to rate full article—mostly obtained from manufacturers); opinion; personal experience; and technical. Special issues include "What's New?" (Feb. 10). No "wordy articles written off the top of the head, obviously without research, and needing more editing time than was spent on writing." Buys 40 mss/year. Query with or without published clips. Length: 500-3,000 words. Pays $5-80. ("Pay depends on amount of work, research and polishing put into article much more than on length.") Pays expenses of writers on assignment with prior approval only.

Photos: State availability of photos or send photos with ms. Pays $5-25 for "smallish" b&w prints. Captions, model release, and identification of subjects required. Buys one-time rights and reprint rights. "Magazine size is 8½x7—photos need to be proportionate."

Columns/Departments: "Ten regular columnists now sell four columns per year to us. We are interested in adding a Safety & Health column (related to cleaning and maintenance industry). We are also open to other suggestions—send query." Buys 36 columns/year; department information obtained at no cost. Query with or without published clips. Length: 500-1,500 words. Pays $15-85.

Fillers: Jokes, gags, anecdotes, short humor, newsbreaks and cartoons. Buys 40/year. Length: 3-200 words. Pays $1-20.

Tips: "We are constantly seeking quality freelancers from all parts of the country. A freelancer can best break in to our publication with fairly technical articles on how to do specific cleaning/maintenance jobs; interviews with top professionals covering this and how they manage their business; and personal experience. Our readers demand concise, accurate information. Don't ramble. Write only about what you know and/or have researched. Editors don't have time to rewrite your rough draft. Organize and polish before submitting."

Management and Supervision

This category includes trade journals for middle management business and industrial managers, including supervisors and office managers. Journals for business executives and owners are classified under Business Management. Those for industrial plant managers are listed in Industrial Operations.

‡BOARD AND ADMINISTRATOR, CMS, Box 259, Akron IA 51001. (712)568-2418. Editor: John Siefer. 50% freelance written. A monthly newsletter covering nonprofit boards of directors, featuring practical ideas for administrators who work with boards. Circ. 7,000. Pays on acceptance. No byline given. Buys all rights. Query for electronic submissions. Sample copy for #10 SAE with 1 first class stamp.
Nonfiction: General interest, how-to, humor, inspirational and opinion. Buys 120 mss/year. Query with published clips. Length: 500-1,000 words. Pays $75-150.

CONSTRUCTION SUPERVISION & SAFETY LETTER, (CL) Bureau of Business Practice, 24 Rope Ferry Rd., Waterford CT 06386. (203)739-0169. Editor: DeLoris Lidestri. Safety Editor: Winifred Bonney, (203)739-0286. 80% freelance written. "We're willing to work with a few new writers if they're willing to follow guidelines carefully." Semimonthly newsletter; 8 pages. Emphasizes all aspects of construction supervision. Buys all rights. Publishes ms an average of 4 months after acceptance. Phone queries OK. Submit seasonal material at least 4 months in advance. Reports in 6 weeks. Free sample copy and writer's guidelines.
Nonfiction: Publishes solid interviews with construction managers or supervisors on how to improve a single aspect of the supervisor's job. Buys 100 unsolicited mss/year. Length: 360-720 words. Pays 10-15¢/word.

Photos: Purchased with accompanying ms. Pays $10 for head and shoulders photo of person interviewed. Safety interviews do not require photo. Total purchase price for ms includes payment for photo.
Tips: "A writer should call before he or she does anything. We like to spend a few minutes on the phone exchanging information."

EMPLOYEE RELATIONS AND HUMAN RESOURCES BULLETIN, Bureau of Business Practice, 24 Rope Ferry Rd., Waterford CT 06386. Supervisory Editor: Barbara Kelsey. 75% freelance written. Works with a small number of new/unpublished writers each year. For personnel, human resources and employee relations managers on the executive level. Semimonthly newsletter; 8 pages. Circ. 3,000. Pays on acceptance. Publishes ms an average of 3 months after acceptance. Buys all rights. No byline. Phone queries OK. Submit seasonal/holiday material 6 months in advance. Photocopied submissions OK. Computer printout submissions acceptable; prefers letter-quality to dot-matrix. Reports in 1 month. Free sample copy and writer's guidelines.
Nonfiction: Interviews about all types of business and industry such as banks, insurance companies, public utilities, airlines, consulting firms, etc. Interviewee should be a high level company officer—general manager, president, industrial relations manager, etc. Writer must get signed release from person interviewed showing that article has been read and approved by him/her, before submission. Some subjects for interviews might be productivity improvement, communications, compensation, labor relations, safety and health, grievance handling, human relations techniques and problems, etc. No general opinions and/or philosophy of good employee relations or general good motivation/morale material. Buys 3 mss/issue. Query. Length: 700-2,000 words. Pays 10-15¢/word after editing. Sometimes pays the expenses of writers on assignment.

‡THE EXECUTIVE ADMINISTRATOR, CMS, Box 259, Akron IA 51001. (712)568-2418. Editor: John Siefer. 50% freelance written. A monthly newsletter covering the administration of nonprofit organizations featuring "practical management and marketing strategies and interviews with administrators." Circ. 5,000. Pays on acceptance. No byline given. Buys all rights. Query for electronic submissions. Sample copy for #10 SAE with 1 first class stamp.
Nonfiction: How-to, humor, interview/profile and personal experience. Buys 120 mss/year. Query with published clips. Length: 500-1,000 words. Pays $75-150.

HIGH-TECH MANAGER'S BULLETIN, TEM, Bureau of Business Practice, 24 Rope Ferry Rd., Waterford CT 06386. (203)442-4365. Editor: Robert Ellal. 50-75% freelance written. "We work with both new or established writers, and are always looking for fresh talent." Bimonthly newsletter for technical supervisors wishing to improve their managerial skills in high technology fields. Pays on acceptance. Publishes ms on average of 6 weeks after acceptance. No byline given. Buys all rights. Computer printout submissions acceptable; prefers letter-quality to dot-matrix. Reports in 2 weeks on queries, 6 weeks on mss. Free sample copy and writer's guidelines.
Nonfiction: How-to (solve a supervisory problem on the job); and interview (of top-notch supervisors and managers). Sample topics could include: how-to increase productivity, cut costs, achieve better teamwork." No filler or non-interview based copy. Buys 72 mss/year. Query first. "Strongly urge writers to study guidelines and samples." Length: 750-1,000 words. Pays 8-14¢/word.
Tips: "We need interview-based articles that emphasize direct quotes. Each article should include a reference to the interviewee's company (location, size, products, function of the interviewee's department and number of employees under his control). Define a problem and show how the supervisor solved it. Write in a light, conversational style, talking directly to technical supervisors who can benefit from putting the interviewee's tips into practice."

MANAGE, 2210 Arbor Blvd., Dayton OH 45439. (513)294-0421. Editor-in-Chief: Douglas E. Shaw. 60% freelance written. Works with a small number of new/unpublished writers each year. Quarterly magazine; 40 pages. For first-line and middle management and scientific/technical managers. Circ. 75,000. Pays on acceptance. Publishes ms an average of 6 months after acceptance. Buys North American magazine rights with reprint privileges; book rights remain with the author. Computer printout submissions OK; prefers letter-quality to dot-matrix. Reports in 1 month. Free sample copy and writer's guidelines.
Nonfiction: "All material published by *Manage* is in some way management oriented. Most articles concern one or more of the following categories: communications, cost reduction, economics, executive abilities, health and safety, human relations, job status, labor relations, leadership, motivation and productivity and professionalism. Articles should be specific and tell the manager how to apply the information to his job immediately. Be sure to include pertinent examples, and back up statements with facts and, where possible, charts and illustrations. *Manage* does not want essays or academic reports, but interesting, well-written and practical articles for and about management." Buys 6 mss/issue. Phone queries OK. Submit complete ms. Length, 600-2,000 words. Pays 5¢/word.
Tips: "Keep current on management subjects; submit timely work."

‡MANAGEMENT ACCOUNTING, National Association of Accountants, 10 Paragon Dr., Montvale NJ 07645-1760. (201)573-9000. Editor: E.S. Koval. Managing Editor: R.F. Randall. 5% freelance written. A monthly magazine covering corporate and financial accounting. Circ. 85,000. Pays on acceptance. Publishes ms an average of 3 months after acceptance. Byline given. Buys all rights. Query for electronic submissions. Computer printout submissions OK; prefers letter-quality to dot-matrix. Reports in 2 weeks on queries. Sample copy and writer's guidelines for 9x12 SASE.

Nonfiction: How-to (on accomplishing accounting or financing) and interview/profile (of top financial types—controllers, chief financial officers, etc.). "We do not want articles about CPAs, CPA practices or public accounting." Buys 2-3 mss/year. Query. Length: 800-2,500 words. Pays $100 for assigned articles. Sometimes pays the expenses of writers on assignment.

Photos: State availability of photos with submission. Reviews contact sheets. Offers variable payment for photos. Buys one-time rights.

Tips: "We are planning to expand our coverage of corporate accounting/finance field by commissioning a limited number of feature articles. Freelancers must query first and be thoroughly familiar with the business/accounting world."

‡MANAGEMENT REVIEW, American Management Association, 135 West 50th St., New York NY 10020. (212)903-8393. Editor: Anthony Rutligliano. Managing Editor: Rod Willis. Monthly magazine covering all aspects of managing in the workplace—private, public, nonprofit. "We have an audience of well-educated, middle- and high-level executives. They are a sophisticated audience looking for pragmatic, *nontheoretical* information and advice on how to run organizations, manage people and operations, and compete in domestic and global markets. Strong emphasis on case studies." Pays on acceptance. Publishes ms an average of 3-4 months after acceptance. Byline given. Offers 50% kill fee. Buys first North American serial rights, second serial (reprint) rights and all rights. Submit seasonal/holiday material 4 months in advance. Previously published submissions OK. Computer printout submissions OK; no dot-matrix. Reports in 3 weeks. Sample copy $5.

Nonfiction: Book excerpts, essays, general interest (business/trade/economics), how-to (case studies and advice for managers), interview/profile, opinion, personal experience (infrequently), other (management, global business, corporate culture topics). "Write for editorial calendar—monthly themes. No cartoons, academic papers, or short 'humourous' looks at management." Buys 100 mss/year. Query with or without published clips, or send complete ms. Length: 500-3,000 words. Pays $250-1,000 for assigned articles; pays $250-1,000 for unsolicited articles. Pays in contributor's copies "when no pay is requested—happens often." Sometimes pays the expenses of writers on assignment.

Photos: State availability of photos with submission. Reviews 8x10 prints.

Columns/Departments: Management in Practice (case studies of good management—how problems/opportunities were handled); Global Perspective (information/case studies on international business & trade); Perspective (essays on management or business topics-opinion); On-Line (case studies or advice/information on information technology in management); and Decision Makers (profiles of top executives/managers; focus on their management styles). Buys 30-50 mss/year. Query with published clips. Length: 1,000-1,500. Pays $250-750.

Tips: "Don't write down to audience—the average *MR* reader has a graduate degree, and/or years of hands-on business and management experience. Need practical, *detailed* information on 'how-to' manage all kinds of situations, operations, and people. *Don't* rehash others' work—the audience has already read Drucker, Tom Peters, *et. al*. For Decision Makers, Management in Practice, Global Perspective and Perspective columns, we're always looking for good writers. Same goes for features—but always query first. Phone queries okay, but letters preferred."

PERSONNEL ADVISORY BULLETIN, Bureau of Business Practice, 24 Rope Ferry Rd., Waterford CT 06386. (203)442-4365, ext. 355. Editor: Jill Peterson. 75% freelance written. Eager to work with new/unpublished writers. Emphasizes all aspects of personnel practitioners for personnel managers in all types and sizes of companies, both white collar and industrial. Semimonthly newsletter; 8 pages. Pays on acceptance. Publishes ms an average of 4 months after acceptance. Buys all rights. Phone queries OK. Submit seasonal/holiday material 4 months in advance. Computer printout submissions acceptable; prefers letter-quality to dot-matrix. Reports in 2 weeks. Free sample copy and writer's guidelines for 10x13 SAE and 2 first class stamps.

Nonfiction: Interviews with personnel managers or human resource professionals on topics of current interest in the personnel field. No articles on hiring and interviewing, discipline, or absenteeism/tardiness control. Buys 30 mss/year. Query with brief, specific outline. Length: 1,000-1,500 words.

Tips: "We're looking for concrete, practical material on how to solve problems. We're providing information about trends and developments in the field. We don't want filler copy. It's very easy to break in. Just query by phone or letter (preferably phone) and we'll discuss the topic. Send for guidelines first, though, so we can have a coherent conversation."

‡PRODUCTION SUPERVISOR'S BULLETIN, Bureau of Business Practice, 24 Rope Ferry Rd., Waterford CT 06386. (203)442-4365. Editor: Anna Maria Trusky. Managing Editor: Wayne N. Muller. 75% freelance written. Biweekly newsletter. "The audience is primarily first-line production supervisors. Articles are meant to address a common workplace issue faced by such a supervisor, (absenteeism, low productivity, etc) and explain how interviewee dealt with the problem." Estab. 1986. Circ. 2,000 + . Pays on acceptance. Publishes ms an average of 4 months after acceptance. Byline not given. Buys all rights. Computer printout submissions OK; prefers letter-quality to dot-matrix. Reports in 2 weeks on queries; 3 weeks on mss. Free sample copy and writer's guidelines.

Nonfiction: How-to (on managing people, solving workplace problems, improving productivity). No high-level articles aimed at upper management. Buys 60-70 mss/year. Query. Length: 800-1,500 words. Pays 9-15¢/word.

Tips: "Freelancers may call me at (203)442-4365 or (203)739-5200. Or write for further information. Sections of publication most open to freelancers are lead story; inside stories (generally 3 to 4 per issue); and Production Management Clinic (in every other issue). Simply include lots of concrete, how-to steps for dealing effectively with the topic at hand."

PRODUCTIVITY IMPROVEMENT BULLETIN, PIB, Bureau of Business Practice, 24 Rope Ferry Rd., Waterford CT 06386. (203)442-4365. Editor: Shelley Wolf. 75% freelance written. Eager to work with new/unpublished writers. Semimonthly newsletter covering productivity improvement programs and techniques of interest to top and middle management. Pays on acceptance. Publishes ms an average of 4 months after acceptance. No byline given. Buys all rights. Computer printout submissions acceptable; prefers letter-quality to dot-matrix. Reports in 2 weeks on queries; 1 month on mss. Free sample copy and writer's guidelines.

Nonfiction: Interviews with middle managers from business or industry detailing how they solved a particular productivity problem. "Our intent is to offer readers a specific 'success story' that has general applications and to show them how they can put these proven techniques into practice in their own company. That's why stories must combine *case-study information* with *how-to advice*, organized into a series of *steps to follow*." No articles on quality circles or general management theory. Buys 50 mss/year. Query. Length: 1,000-1,300 words. Pays 10-15¢/word "after editing."

Columns/Departments: "Personal Productivity column uses interview-based copy explaining specific measures managers can take to increase their personal effectiveness." Buys 12 mss/year. Query. Length: 800-1,000 words. Pays 10-15¢/word.

Tips: "All articles *must* cover a 'problem/solution/how-to/results' format as described in the writer's guidelines. Be willing to return to source for additional information or to rewrite, if necessary. Topics should be well focused. (Check with us before doing the write-up. We like to talk to freelancers.) Writing should be conversational; use the 'you' approach and speak directly to the readers. Use subheads and questions to guide the reader through your piece. Articles on activities of a specific company are subject to its approval."

SALES MANAGER'S BULLETIN, The Bureau of Business Practice, 24 Rope Ferry Rd., Waterford CT 06386. Editor: Paulette S. Withers. 33% freelance written. Prefers to work with published/established writers. Newsletter published twice a month; 8 pages. For sales managers and salespeople interested in getting into sales management. Pays on acceptance. Publishes ms an average of 3-6 months after acceptance. Written queries only except from regulars. Submit seasonal/holiday material 6 months in advance. Original submissions only. Buys all rights. Computer printout submissions acceptable; prefers letter-quality to dot-matrix. Reports in 2 weeks. Sample copy and writer's guidelines only when accompanied by SAE with 2 first clas stamps.

Nonfiction: How-to (motivate salespeople, cut costs, create territories, etc.); interview (with working sales managers who use innovative techniques); and technical (marketing stories based on interviews with experts). No articles on territory management, saving fuel in the field, or public speaking skills. Break into this publication by reading the guidelines and sample issue. Follow the directions closely and chances for acceptance go up dramatically. One easy way to start is with an interview article ("Here's what sales executives have to say about . . ."). Query is vital to acceptance; "send a simple postcard explaining briefly the subject matter, the interviewees (if any), slant, length, and date of expected completion, accompanied by a SASE." Length: 800-1,500. Pays 10-15¢/word.

Tips: "Freelancers should always request samples and writer's guidelines, accompanied by SASE. Requests without SASE are discarded immediately. Examine the sample, and don't try to improve on our style. Write as we write. Don't 'jump around' from point to point and don't submit articles that are too chatty and with not enough real information. The more time a writer can save the editors, the greater his or her chance of a sale and repeated sales, when queries may not be necessary any longer."

SECURITY MANAGEMENT: PROTECTING PROPERTY, PEOPLE & ASSETS, Bureau of Business Practice, 24 Rope Ferry Rd., Waterford CT 06386. Editor: Alex Vaughn. 75% freelance written. Eager to work with new/unpublished writers. Semimonthly newsletter; 8 pages. Emphasizes security for industry. "All material should be slanted toward security directors, preferably industrial, but some retail and institutional as well." Circ. 3,000. Pays on acceptance. Buys all rights. Phone queries OK. Photocopied submissions OK.

Computer printout submissions acceptable; prefers letter-quality to dot-matrix. Reports in 2 weeks. Free sample copy and writer's guidelines.
Nonfiction: Interview (with security professionals only). "Articles should be tight and specific. They should deal with new security techniques or new twists on old ones." Buys 2-5 mss/issue. Query. Length: 750-1,000 words. Pays 10¢/word.

SUPERVISION, 424 N. 3rd St., Burlington IA 52601. Publisher: Michael S. Darnall. Editorial Supervisor: Doris J. Ruschill. Editor: Barbara Boeding. 95% freelance written. "Not accepting new material until 1988." Prefers to work with published/established writers; works with a small number of new/unpublished writers each year. Monthly magazine; 24 pages. For first-line foremen, supervisors and office managers. Circ. 7,489. Pays on publication. Publishes ms an average of 9-12 months after acceptance. Buys all rights. Computer printout submissions OK; prefers letter-quality to dot-matrix. Reports in 3 weeks. Free sample copy and writer's guidelines; mention *Writer's Market* in request.
Nonfiction: How-to (cope with supervisory problems, discipline, absenteeism, safety, productivity, goal setting, etc.); and personal experience (unusual success story of foreman or supervisor). No sexist material written from only a male viewpoint. Include biography and/or byline with ms submissions. Author photos used. Buys 12 mss/issue. Query. Length: 1,500-1,800 words. Pays 4¢/word.
Tips: "We are particularly interested in writers with first-hand experience—current or former supervisors who are also good writers. Following AP stylebook would be helpful." Uses no advertising.

‡**TRAINING, The Magazine of Human Resources Development**, Lakewood Publications, 50 S. Ninth St., Minneapolis MN 55402. (612)333-0471. Editor: Jack Gordon. Managing Editor: Chris Lee. 10% freelance written. A monthly magazine covering training and employee development in the business world. "Our core readers are managers and professionals who specialize in employee training and development (e.g., corporate training directors, VP-human resource development, etc.). We have a large secondary readership among managers of all sorts who are concerned with improving human performance in their organizations. We take a businesslike approach to training and employee education." Circ. 52,000. Pays on acceptance. Publishes ms an average of 3 months after acceptance. Byline sometimes given. Offers $25 kill fee. Buys first North American serial rights and second serial (reprint) rights. Simultaneous, photocopied and previously published submissions OK. Computer printout submissions acceptable; prefers letter-quality to dot-matrix. Reports in 2 weeks on queries; 6 weeks on mss. Sample copy for 9x11 SAE with 4 first class stamps. Writer's guidelines for letter size SAE with 1 first class stamp.
Nonfiction: Essay; exposé; how-to (on training, management, sales, productivity improvement, etc.); humor; interview/profile; new product; opinion; photo feature; and technical (use of audiovisual aids, computers, etc.). "No puff, no 'testimonials' or disguised ads in any form, no 'gee-whiz' approaches to the subjects." Buys 10-12 mss/year. Query with or without published clips, or send complete ms. Length: 200-3,000 words. Pays $50-500.
Photos: State availability of photos or send with submission. Reviews contact sheets and prints. Offers no additional payment for photos accepted with ms. Identification of subjects required. Buys one-time rights and reprint rights.
Columns/Departments: Training Today (news briefs, how-to tips, reports on pertinant research, trend analysis, etc.), 200-800 words. Buys 6 mss/year. Query or send complete ms. Pays $50-75.
Tips: "We would like to develop a few freelancers to work with on a regular basis. We almost never give firm assignments to unfamiliar writers, so you have to be willing to hit us with one or two on spec to break in. Short pieces for our Training Today section involve least investment on your part, but also are less likely to convince us to assign you a feature. Don't tell us what an important person you are and what a huge favor you're doing us by allowing us to review your article. Let the manuscript do the talking. When studying the magazine, freelancers should look at our staff-written articles for style, approach and tone. Do not concentrate on articles written by people identified as consultants, training directors, etc."

UTILITY SUPERVISION, (US), Bureau of Business Practice, 24 Rope Ferry Rd., Waterford CT 06386. (203)739-0169. Editor: DeLoris Lidestri. 80% freelance written. "We're willing to work with a few new writers if they're willing to follow guidelines carefully." Semimonthly newsletter; 4 pages. Emphasizes all aspects of utility supervision. Pays on acceptance. Publishes ms an average of 4 months after acceptance. Buys all rights. Phone queries OK. Submit seasonal material 4 months in advance. Computer printout submissions OK; no dot-matrix. Reports in 6 weeks. Free sample copy and writer's guidelines.
Nonfiction: Publishes how-to (interview on a single aspect of supervision with utility manager/supervisor concentrating on how reader/supervisor can improve in that area). Buys 100 mss/year. Query. Length: 360-750 words. Pays 10-15¢/word.
Photos: Purchased with accompanying ms. Pays $10 for head and shoulders photo of person interviewed. Total purchase price for ms includes payment for photo.
Tips: "A writer should call before he or she does anything. I like to spend a few minutes on the phone exchanging information."

WAREHOUSING SUPERVISOR'S BULLETIN, WSB, Bureau of Business Practice, 24 Rope Ferry Rd., Waterford CT 06386. (203)442-4365. Editor: Isabel Will Becker. 75-90% freelance written. "We work with a wide variety of writers and are always looking for fresh talent." Biweekly newsletter covering traffic, materials handling and distribution for warehouse supervisors "interested in becoming more effective on the job." Pays on acceptance. Publishes ms an average of 3 months after acceptance. No byline given. Buys all rights. Computer printout submissions acceptable. Reports in 2 weeks on queries; 6 weeks on mss. Free sample copy and writer's guidelines.

Nonfiction: How-to (increase efficiency, control or cut costs, cut absenteeism or tardiness, increase productivity, raise morale); and interview (of warehouse supervisors or managers who have solved problems on the job). No descriptions of company programs, noninterview articles, textbook-like descriptions or union references. Buys 50 mss/year. Query. "A resume and sample of work are helpful." Length: 800-1,200 words. Pays 8-14¢/word. Sometimes pays the expenses of writers on assignment.

Tips: "All articles must be interview-based and emphasize how-to information. They should also include a reference to the interviewee's company (location, size, products, function of the interviewee's department and number of employees under his control). Focus articles on one problem, and get the interviewee to pinpoint the best way to solve it. Write in a light, conversational style, talking directly to warehouse supervisors who can benefit from putting the interviewee's tips into practice."

Marine and Maritime Industries

BOATING INDUSTRY, 850 3rd Ave., New York NY 10022. Editor-in-Chief/Publisher: Charles A. Jones. Editor: Olga Badillo-Sciortino. 15% freelance written. Prefers to work with published/established writers. Monthly for boating retailers and distributors. Circ. 27,200. Pays on publication. Publishes ms an average of 3 months after acceptance. Byline given. Buys all rights. Best practice is to check with editor first on story ideas for go-ahead. Submit seasonal material 4 months in advance. Reports in 2 months.

Nonfiction: Business-oriented pieces about marine management. Interested in good column material, too. Buys 10-15 mss/year. Query. Length: 1,500-4,000 words. No clippings. Pays 9-15¢/word.

Photos: B&w glossy photos purchased with mss; "also some color."

BOATING PRODUCT NEWS, The Product Newspaper for the Marine Industry, Whitney Communications Co., 850 3rd Ave., New York NY 10022. (212)715-2732. Editor: John R. Burger. 20% freelance written. A monthly tabloid covering the "new product and product marketing end of the marine industry for distributors, dealers, manufacturers, marina owners and retailers." Circ. 27,000. Pays on publication. Publishes ms an average of 2 months after acceptance. Byline given. Buys all rights. Simultaneous and previously published submissions OK. Computer printout submissions acceptable; prefers letter-quality to dot-matrix. Reports in several months. Free sample copy and writer's guidelines.

Nonfiction: Interview/profile, new product, photo feature, technical and feature. Buys 40-45 mss/year. Query with published clips. Length: 500 words. Pays $6/printed inch. Sometimes pays the expenses of writers on assignment. State availability of photos with submission.

Photos: Reviews contact sheets and 3x5 prints. Offers $20 minimum/photo. Identification of subjects required. Buys one-time rights.

‡CANADIAN AQUACULTURE, Harrison House Publishers, 4611 William Head Rd., Victoria, British Columbia V8X 3W9 Canada. (604)478-9209. Editor: Peter Chettleburgh. 50% freelance written. Works with a small number of new/unpublished writers each year. A quarterly magazine covering aquaculture in Canada. Circ. 1,500. Pays on publication. Publishes ms an average of 3 months after acceptance. Byline given. Buys first North American serial rights. Submit seasonal/holiday material 5 months in advance. Computer printout submissions OK. Reports in 2 weeks. Free sample copy for 9x12 SAE with 4 first class stamps; free writer's guidelines.

Nonfiction: How-to, interview/profile, new product, opinion and photo feature. Buys 16-20 mss/year. Query. Length: 200-1,500 words. Pays 10-20¢/word for assigned articles; pays 7-15¢/word for unsolicited articles. May pay writers with contributor copies if writer requests. Sometimes pays the expenses of writers on assignment.

Photos: Send photos with submission. Reviews 5x7 prints. Captions required. Buys one-time rights.

‡**THE FISH BOAT**, H.L. Peace Publications, Box 2400, Covington LA 70434. (504)893-2930. Editor: Harry L. Peace. Managing Editor: Roland Sweet. 10% freelance written. Prefers to work with published/established writers. A monthly magazine covering commercial fishing, seafood processing and marketing. Circ. 19,320. Pays on acceptance. Publishes ms an average of 4 months after acceptance. Byline given. Buys one-time rights. Simultaneous, photocopied and previously published submissions OK. Computer printout submissions OK; prefers letter-quality to dot-matrix. Reports in 1 month on queries; 6 weeks on mss. Sample copy $3.
Nonfiction: How-to (on maintaining fishing vessel, engine, hydraulics, other gear); new product (including newly constructed boats and gear innovations); personal experience; technical (related to fishing vessel operation, processing. Special issues include safety and survival (June) and Navigations and Communication (May). Buys 6-10 mss/year. Query. Length: 1,500 words maximum. Pays $150-250 for assigned articles; pays $150-200 for unsolicited articles. Sometimes pays the expenses of writers on assignment.
Photos: Send photos with submission. Reviews contact sheets. Offers no additional payment for photos accepted with ms. Identification of subjects required. Buys one-time rights.
Columns/Departments: "We publish no columns, but are open to appropriate suggestions." Query. Pays $50-100.
Tips: "As U.S. fisheries management changes, we will explore the ways fishermen are adapting to these changes, especially in the areas of boats and gear. The writer must know the commercial fishing field and be familiar with fishing vessels and gear. Spending time with fishermen or reading related trade papers and magazines is helpful. Our freelance needs are geared towards features which, either by regionality or their technical nature, could not have reasonably been prepared in-house. This might include first-person access to a fisheries operation, special understanding of a particular issue of importance to the industry, or a regional slant to an issue or operation worth sharing with a national audience. Whenever possible, we prefer to employ freelancers who can also illustrate their work with suitable photography. Our usual arrangement is to acquire an editorial/photo package."

‡**OCEAN NAVIGATOR, Marine Navigation & Ocean Voyaging**, Navigator Publishing Corp., 18 Danforth St., Portland ME 04101. (207)772-2466. Editor: Greg Walsh. Managing Editor: T.E. Queeney. 50% freelance written. A bimonthly magazine covering marine navigation. Pays on publication. Publishes ms an average of 6 months after acceptance. Byline given. Pays kill fee of a percentage of word count. Buys first North American serial rights. Photocopied submissions. Query for electronic submissions. Computer printout submissions OK; dot-matrix acceptable if double spaced. Reports in 3 weeks on queries; 1 month on mss. Sample copy $3 with SAE and $1.10 postage.
Nonfiction: General interest, how-to (for navigational and voyaging techniques), personal experience (on voyaging stories). Buys 14-16 mss/year. Send complete ms. Length: 800-3,000 words. Pays $450. Sometimes pays the expenses of writers on assignment.
Photos: Send photos with submission. Reviews b&w contact sheets and 5x7 prints. Offers no additional payment for photos accepted with ms. Identification of subjects required. Buys one-time rights.
Tips: "Writing for us requires a certain knowledge of marine topics. Our readers tend to be experienced mariners. They aren't interested in introductory pieces on beginner's topics. Navigation and detailed voyaging stories from which the reader can learn are best. Stories on ocean voyaging are most open to freelancers. Stories should be accounts written by someone who was actually on the voyage. A voyage can be as short as 500 miles or around te world, the main thing is to make the piece interesting and informative."

‡**PROCEEDINGS**, U.S. Naval Institute, Annapolis MD 21402. (301)268-6110. Editor: Fred H. Rainbow. Managing Editor: John G. Miller. 95% freelance written. Eager to work with new/published writers. Monthly magazine covering naval and maritime subjects. Circ. 100,000. Pays on acceptance. Publishes ms an average of 5 months after acceptance. Byline given. Buys all rights. Submit seasonal/holiday material 3 months in advance. Photocopied submissions OK. Computer printout submissions OK; prefers letter-quality. Reports in 2 weeks on queries; 1 month on mss. Free sample copy and writer's guidelines.
Nonfiction: Essays, expose, general interest, historical/nostalgic, how-to (related to sea service professional subjects), humor, interview/profile, new product, opinion, personal experience, photo feature and technical. "*Proceedings* is an unofficial, open forum for the discussion of naval and maritime topics." Special issues include International Navies (March) and Naval Review (May). Buys 250 mss/year. Query or send complete ms. Length: up to 3,500 words. Pays $50-600. Sometimes pays writers with contributor copies or other premiums "if author desires." Sometimes pays the expenses of writers on assignment.
Photos: Send photos with submission. Reviews contact sheets, negatives, transparencies and prints. Offers $10-100 per photo. Buys one-time rights.
Columns/Departments: Book Reviews, Nobody Asked Me About . . ., and Crossword Puzzles (all with naval or maritime slants), all 500-2,000 words. Buys 90 mss/year. Query. Pays $50-200.
Fiction: Adventure, historical and humorous. Buys 4 mss/year. Query. Length: 500-3,000 words. Pays $50-600.
Fillers: Kristine Wilcox, editor. Anecdotes. Buys 50/year. Length: 1,000 words maximum. Pays $25-150.
Tips: "Write about something you know about, either from first-hand experience or based on primary source material. Our letters to the editor column is most open to freelancers."

SEAWAY REVIEW, The International Business Magazine of the Great Lakes/St. Lawrence System, The Seaway Review Bldg., 221 Water St., Boyne City MI 49712. Publisher: Jacques LesStrang. Managing Editor: Michelle Cortright. 10% freelance written. Prefers to work with published/established writers. "For the entire Great Lakes/St. Lawrence region maritime community, executives of companies that ship via the Great Lakes, traffic managers, transportation executives, federal and state government officials and manufacturers of maritime equipment." Quarterly magazine. Circ. 16,000. Pays on publication. Publishes ms an average of 3 months after acceptance. Buys first North American serial rights. Submit seasonal material 2 months in advance. Photocopied submissions OK. Electronic submissions OK via 1200 Baud/MS DOS. Computer printout submissions acceptable. Reports in 3 weeks. Sample copy $5.

Nonfiction: Articles dealing with Great Lakes shipping, shipbuilding, marine technology, economics of eight states in the Seaway region (Michigan, Minnesota, Illinois, Indiana, Ohio, New York, Pennsylvania and Wisconsin), and Canada (Ontario, Quebec), port operation, historical articles dealing with Great Lakes shipping, current events dealing with commercial shipping on lakes, etc. No subjects contrary to our editorial statement. Submit complete ms. Length: 1,000-4,000 words. "Pay varies with value of subject matter and knowledgeability of author, $50-300." Pays expenses of writers on assignment.

Photos: State availability of photos with query. Pays $10-50 for 8x10 glossy b&w prints; $10-100 for 8x10 glossy color prints or transparencies. Captions required. Buys one-time rights. Buys "hundreds" of freelance photos each year for photo file.

Fillers: Clippings and spot news relating to ports and the Great Lakes. Buys 3/issue. Length: 50-500 words. Pays $5-50.

Medical

Through these journals, physicians and mental health professionals learn how other professionals help their patients and manage their medical practices efficiently. Journals for nurses, laboratory technicians and other medical workers are included with the Hospitals, Nursing and Nursing Home journals. Publications for druggists and drug wholesalers and retailers are grouped with the Drugs, Health Care and Medical Products journals. Publications that report on medical trends for the consumer can be found in the Health and Sciences categories.

AMERICAN MEDICAL NEWS, American Medical Association, 535 N. Dearborn St., Chicago IL 60610. (312)645-5000. Editor: Dick Walt. Executive Editor: Barbara Bolsen. 5-10% freelance written. "Prefers writers already interested in the health care field—not clinical medicine." Weekly tabloid providing nonclinical information for physicians—information on socio-economic, political, and other developments in medicine. "*AMN* is a specialized publication circulating to physicians, covering subjects touching upon their profession, practices, and personal lives. This is a well-educated, highly sophisticated audience." Circ. 375,000 physicians. Pays on acceptance. Publishes ms an average of 2 months after acceptance. Byline given. Offers variable kill fee. Buys all rights. Rights sometimes returnable on request after publication. Simultaneous queries OK. Computer printout submissions acceptable. Reports in 1 month. Free sample copy and writer's guidelines.

Nonfiction: Flora Johnson Skelly, assistant executive editor for outside contributions. Interview/profile (occasional); opinion (mainly from physicians); and news and interpretive features. Special issues include "Year in Review" issue published in January. No clinical articles, general-interest articles physicians would see elsewhere, or recycled versions of articles published elsewhere. Buys 200 mss/year. Query. Length: 200-4,000 words. Pays $400-750 for features; $50-100 for opinions and short news items. "We have limited travel budget for freelancers; we pay minimal local expenses."

Tips: "We are trying to create a group of strong feature writers who will be regular contributors."

APA MONITOR, 1200 17th St. NW, Washington DC 20036. (202)955-7690. Editor: Kathleen Fisher. Managing Editor: Laurie Denton. 5% freelance written. Works with a small number of new/unpublished writers each year. Monthly 64-page newspaper for psychologists and other social scientists and professionals interested in behaviorial sciences and mental health area. Circ. 80,000. Pays on acceptance. Publishes ms an average of 3 months after acceptance. Buys first serial rights. Query for electronic submissions. Computer printout submissions acceptable; no dot-matrix. Sample copy $3 and 9x12 SASE.

Nonfiction: News and feature articles about issues facing psychology both as a science and a mental health profession; political, social and economic developments in the behaviorial science area. Interview, profile and occasional historical pieces. No personal views or reminiscences. Buys no mss without query. Length: 300-2,000 words. Pays expenses of writers on assignment.
Tips: "Our writers need to be longtime readers or science writers to strike the paper balance for reaching both the top scientists and practitioners in the country and the beginning graduate student."

‡**APPLIED RADIOLOGY, The Journal of Medical Imaging**, Brentwood Publishing Simon & Schuster, Box 2178, 1640 Fifth St., Santa Monica CA 90406-2178. (213)395-0234. Editor: Betsy Schreiber. 10% freelance written. Monthly magazine covering radiology. "Audience consists of radiologists and radiology technologists. Material is therefore highly technical." Circ. 25,000. Pays on acceptance. Publishes ms an average of 3 months after acceptance. Byline given. Makes work-for-hire assignments. Computer printout submissions OK; prefers letter-quality to dot-matrix. Reports in 2 weeks on queries; 1 month on mss. Writer's guidelines for SAE with 1 first class stamp.
Nonfiction: Interview/profile, new product and technical. No material written for general public. Buys 10 mss/year. Query. Length: 1,500-3,000 words. Pays 15-20¢/word. Sometimes pays the expenses of writers on assignment.
Photos: Send photos with submission. Reviews prints. Offers no additional payment for photos accepted with ms. Identification of subjects required. Buys all rights.
Columns/Departments: Profile (prominent radiologist or technologist), 1,500-2,00 words. Buys 2 mss/year. Query with published clips. Pays 15-20¢/word.
Tips: Subjects most open to freelancers are "topics dealing with management of radiology departments."

‡**CALIFORNIA PHARMACIST**, California Pharmacists Association, Suite 300, 1112 I St., Sacramento CA 95814. (916)444-7811. Managing Editor: Mary Peppers-Johnson. 8% freelance written. Prefers to work with published/established writers. *California Pharmacist*, the official publication of the California Pharmacists Association, is a monthly professional journal for pharmacists. Circ. 7,200. Pays on acceptance. Publishes ms an average of 3 months after acceptance. Byline given. Buys first North American serial rights and first rights. Submit seasonal/holiday material 3 months in advance. Photocopied submissions OK. Computer printout submissions OK; no dot-matrix. Sample copy for 9½x12½ SAE with $1 postage.
Nonfiction: Interview/profile and technical. Annual topics include Home Health Care (February); Poison Prevention (March); Pharmacy Computers (April). Buys 10 mss/year. Query with published clips. Length: 2,250-2,500 words. Pays $150-300 for assigned articles. Sometimes pays the expenses of writers on assignment.
Photos: State availability of photos with submission. Offers $10 maximum per photo. Captions and identification of subjects required. Buys all rights.

‡**CARDIOLOGY MANAGEMENT**, Brentwood Publishing, Box 2178, Santa Monica CA 90406. (213)395-0234. Editor: Rebecca Morrow. Bimonthly magazine covering the business of cardiology. "*Cardiology Management* primarily contains business-oriented articles that focus on the management issues facing cardiology practices, departments and rehab renters. Readership includes cardiologists, cardiology dept. managers, office and center administrators." Estab. 1987. Circ. 14,000. Pays on acceptance. Byline given. Buys all rights. Photocopied submissions OK. Query for electronic submissions. Computer printout submissions OK; no dot-matrix. Reports in 2 months on queries; 4 months on mss. Sample copy for 8½x11 SAE with 4 first class stamps; writer's guidelines for #10 SAE with 1 first class stamp.
Nonfiction: How-to (effectively run and manage a cardiology facility), interview/profile, and new products/technologies. Query with published clips. Length: 1,500-3,000 words. Pays 10¢-12¢/word. Sometimes pays the expenses of writers on assignment.
Photos: Send photos with submission. Reviews prints. Offers no additional payment for photos accepted with ms. Captions and model releases required. Buys all rights.

CARDIOLOGY WORLD NEWS, Medical Publishing Enterprises, Box 1548, Marco Island FL 33937. (813)394-0400. Editor: John H. Lavin. 75% freelance written. Prefers to work with published/established writers. Monthly magazine covering cardiology and the cardiovascular system. "We need short news articles *for doctors* on any aspect of our field—diagnosis, treatment, risk factors, etc." Pays on acceptance. Publishes ms an average of 2 months after acceptance. Byline given "for special reports and feature-length articles." Offers 20% kill fee. Buys first North American serial rights. Photocopied submissions OK. Query for electronic submissions. Computer printout submissions acceptable. Reports in 1 month. Sample copy $1; free writer's guidelines.
Nonfiction: New product and technical (clinical). No fiction, fillers, profiles of doctors or poetry. Query with published clips. Length: 250-1,500 words. Pays $50-300; $50/column for news articles. Pays expenses of writers on assignment.
Photos: State availability of photos with query. Pays $50/published photo. Rough captions, model release,

and identification of subjects required. Buys one-time rights.

Tips: "Submit written news articles of 250-500 words on speculation with basic source material (not interview notes) for fact-checking. We demand clinical or writing expertise for full-length feature. Clinical cardiology conventions/symposia are the best source of news and feature articles."

‡**CINCINNATI MEDICINE**, Academy of Medicine, 320 Broadway, Cincinnati OH 45202. (513)421-7010. Managing Editor: Vicki L. Black. 20% freelance written. Works with a small number of new/unpublished writers each year. Quarterly membership magazine for the Academy of Medicine of Cincinnati. "We cover socioeconomic and political factors that affect the practice of medicine in Cincinnati. For example: How will changes in Medicare policies affect local physicians and what will they mean for the quality of care Cincinnati's elderly patients receive. (Ninety-nine percent of our readers are Cincinnati physicians.)" Circ. 3,000. Pays on acceptance. Publishes ms an average of 3-6 months after acceptance. Byline given. Makes work-for-hire assignments. Simultaneous queries and photocopied submissions OK. Computer printout submissions acceptable; prefers letter-quality to dot-matrix. Reports in 3 weeks on queries; 2 weeks on mss. Sample copy for $2 and 9x12 SAE and 7 first class stamps; writer's guidelines for 4½x9½ SAE with 1 first class stamp.
Nonfiction: Historical/nostalgic (history of, or reminiscences about, medicine in Cincinnati); interview/profile (of nationally known medical figures or medical leaders in Cincinnati); and opinion (opinion pieces on controversial medico-legal and medico-ethical issues). "We do not want: scientific-research articles, stories that are not based on good journalistic skills (no seat-of-the-pants reporting), or why my 'doc' is the greatest guy in the world stories." Buys 8-10 mss/year. Query with published clips or send complete ms. Length: 800-2,500 words. Pays $125-300. Sometimes pays expenses of writers on assignment.
Photos: State availability of photos with query or ms. Captions and identification of subjects required. Buys one-time rights.
Tips: "Send published clips; do some short features that will help you develop some familiarity with our magazine and our audience; and show initiative to tackle the larger stories. First-time writers often don't realize the emphasis we place on solid reporting. We want accurate, well-balanced reporting or analysis. Our job is to *inform* our readers."

DIAGNOSTIC IMAGING, Miller Freeman, 500 Howard St., San Francisco CA 94105. Publisher: Thomas Kemp. Editor: Peter Ogle. 10% freelance written. Monthly news magazine covering radiology, nuclear medicine, magnetic resonance, and ultrasound for physicians in diagnostic imaging professions. Circ. 24,000. Average issue includes 4-5 features. Pays on acceptance. Publishes ms an average of 2-3 months after acceptance. Byline given. Buys all rights. No phone queries. "Written query should be well-written, concise and contain a brief outline of proposed article and a description of the approach or perspective the author is taking." Submit seasonal material 1 month in advance. Simultaneous and photocopied submissions OK. Query for electronic submissions. Computer printout submissions acceptable; no dot-matrix. Reports in 2 weeks. Free sample copy.
Nonfiction: "We are interested in topical news features in the areas of radiology, magnetic resonance imaging, nuclear medicine and ultrasound, especially news of state and federal legislation, new products, insurance, regulations, medical literature, professional meetings and symposia and continuing education." Buys 10-12 mss/year. Query with published clips. Length: 1,000-2,000 words. Pays 22¢/word minimum. Sometimes pays the expenses of writers on assignment.
Photos: Reviews 5x7 b&w glossy prints and 35mm and larger color transparencies. Offers $20 for photos accepted with ms. Captions required. Buys one-time rights.

‡**THE DISPENSING OPTICIAN**, Opticians Association of America, 10341 Democracy Lane, Box 10110, Fairfax VA 22030. (703)691-8355. Editor: James H. McCormick. Managing Editor: Robert E. Rathbone. 75% freelance written. Magazine covering opticianry published 11 times/year. Circ. 10,750. Pays on publication. Publishes ms an average of 2 months after acceptance. Byline given. Usually buys industry rights, including right to reprint. Submit seasonal/holiday material 5 months in advance. Photocopied and previously published submissions (if not printed in optical field) OK. Computer printout submissions OK. Reports in 1 month on queries; 2 months on mss. Free sample copy "if query interests us; otherwise, no."
Nonfiction: How-to (on succeeding in some aspect of dispensing), interview/profile, new product, photo feature and technical (all related to opticianry only) and articles addressed to small business owners in retail field. Buys 10 mss/year. Query "if we know writer's work" or query with published clips "if we don't know writer's work." Length: 500-3,000 words. Pays "up to $250 for assigned articles (and more for photos) for first North American publishing and reprint rights. Pays 6¢/word for optical industry rights to general articles not prepared on assignment. Sometimes pays the expenses of writers on assignment.
Photos: State availability of photos with submission. Reviews contact sheets or 5x7 prints. Buys rights "with author free to sell prints to publications not in optical field."

EMERGENCY, The Journal of Emergency Services, 6200 Yarrow Drive, Carlsbad CA 92009. (619)438-2511. Editor: F. McKeen Thompson. Articles Editor: Laura Gilbert. 100% freelance written. Works with a small number of new/unpublished writers each year. A monthly magazine covering pre-hospital services and emergency care. "Our readership is primarily composed of EMTs, paramedics and ambulance attendants. We prefer a professional, semi-technical approach on pre-hospital subjects." Circ. 35,000. Pays on acceptance. Publishes ms an average of 6 months after acceptance. Byline given. Buys all rights, nonexclusive. Submit seasonal/holiday material 3 months in advance. Photocopied submissions OK. Computer printout submissions acceptable; no dot-matrix. Reports in 1 month on queries, 2 months on mss. Sample copy $5; writer's guidelines for SASE.

Nonfiction: Semi-technical expose, general interest, how-to (on treating pre-hospital emergency patients), interview/profile, new techniques, opinion, personal experience and photo feature. "We do not publish cartoons, color *print* photos, term papers, product promotions disguised as articles or overly-technical manuscripts." Buys 100 mss/year. Query with published clips. Length 1,500-3,000 words. Pays $100-400. Sometimes pays expenses of writers on assignment.

Photos: Send photos with submission. Reviews color transparencies and b&w prints. Offers no additional payment for photos accepted with ms. Offers $5-30/photo without ms. Captions and identification of subjects required.

Columns/Departments: Open Forum (opinion page for EMS professionals), 500 words. Trauma Primer (pre-hospital care topics, treatment of injuries, etc.), 1,000-2,000 words. Buys 40 mss/year. Query first. Length: 500-2,000 words. Pays $0-150.

Fillers: Anecdotes, facts and newsbreaks. Buys 60/year. Length: no more than 500 words. Pays $0-50.

Tips: "Writing style for features and departments should be knowledgeable and lively with a clear theme or story line to maintain reader interest and enhance comprehension. The biggest problem we encounter is dull, lifeless writing with nothing to perk reader interest. Keep in mind we are not a textbook. We appreciate a short, one paragraph biography on the author."

FACETS, American Medical Association Auxiliary, Inc., 535 N. Dearborn St., Chicago IL 60610. (312)645-4470. Editor: Kathleen T. Jordan. Work with both established and new writers; welcome well-written, well-reseached articles from either. For physicians' spouses. 30% freelance written. Magazine published 6 times/year; 32 pages. Circ. 90,000. Pays on acceptance. Publishes ms an average of 6 months after acceptance. Buys first rights. Simultaneous, photocopied and previously published submissions OK. Computer printout submissions acceptable; prefers letter-quality to dot-matrix. Reports in 6 weeks. Free sample copy and writer's guidelines.

Nonfiction: All articles must be related to the experiences of physicians' spouses. Current health issues; financial topics; physicians' family circumstances; business management; volunteer leadership how-to's. Buys 20 mss/year. Query with clear outline of article—what points will be made, what conclusions drawn, what sources will be used. No personal experience or personality stories. Length: 1,000-2,500 words. Pays $300-800. Pays expenses of writers on assignment.

Photos: State availability of photos with query. Uses 8x10 glossy b&w prints and $2^{1}/4x2^{1}/4$ color transparencies.

Tips: Uses "articles only on specified topical matter; with good sources, not hearsay or personal opinion. Since we use only nonfiction and have a limited readership, we must relate factual material."

‡FITNESS MANAGEMENT, The Magazine for Professionals in Adult Physical Fitness, Leisure Publications, Inc., Suite 213, 215 S. Highway 101, Box 1198, Solana Beach CA 92075. (619)481-4155. Editor: Edward H. Pitts. 50% freelance written. Bimonthly magazine covering commercial, corporate and community fitness centers. "Readers are owners, managers, and program directors of physical fitness facilities. *FM* helps them run their enterprises safely, efficiently and profitably. Ethical and professional positions in health, nutrition, sports medicine, management, etc., are consistent with those of established national bodies." Circ. 21,000. Pays on publication. Publishes ms an average of 5 months after acceptance. Byline given. Pays 50% kill fee. Buys all rights. Submit seasonal/holiday material 6 months in advance. Query for electronic submissions. Computer printout submissions OK; prefers letter-quality to dot matrix. Reports in 1 month on queries; 2 months on mss. Writer's guidelines for #10 SAE with 1 first class stamp. Sample copy for $5.

Nonfiction: Book excerpts (prepublication), how-to (manage fitness center and program), new product (no pay), photo feature (facilities-programs), technical and other (news of fitness research and major happenings in fitness industry). No exercise instructions or general ideas without examples of fitness businesses that have used them successfully. Buys 30 mss/year. Query. Length: 750-2,000 words. Pays $60-300 for assigned articles; pays up to $160 for unsolicited articles. Pays expenses of writers on assignment.

Photos: Send photos with submission. Reviews contact sheets, 2x2 and 4x5 transparencies and 5x7 prints. Offers $10 per photo. Captions and model releases required.

Tips: "We seek writers who are expert in a business or science field related to the fitness-service industry or who are experienced in the industry. Be current with the state of the art/science in business and fitness and communicate it in human terms (avoid intimidating academic language; tell the stroy of how this was learned and/or cite examples of quotes of people who have applied the knowledge successfully)."

GERIATRIC CONSULTANT, Medical Publishing Enterprises, Box 1548, Marco Island FL 33937. (813)394-0400. Editor: John H. Lavin. 70% freelance written. Prefers to work with published/established writers. Bimonthly magazine for physicians covering medical care of the elderly. "We're a clinical magazine directed to doctors and physician assistants. All articles must *help* these health professionals to help their elderly patients. We're too tough a market for nonmedical beginners." Circ. 105,000. Pays on acceptance. Publishes ms an average of 3 months after acceptance. Byline given. Offers 20% kill fee. Buys first North American serial rights. Simultaneous queries OK. Query for electronic submissions. Computer printout submissions acceptable. Reports in 1 month. Sample copy for $1; free writer's guidelines.
Nonfiction: How-to (diagnosis and treatment of health problems of the elderly) and technical/clinical. No fiction or articles directed to a lay audience. Buys 20 mss/year. Query. Length: 750-3,000 words. Pays $100-300. Pays expenses of writers on assignment.
Photos: State availability of photos. (Photos are not required.) Model release and identification of subjects required. Buys one-time rights.
Tips: "Many medical meetings are now held in the field of geriatric care. These offer potential sources and subjects for us."

‡GROUP PRACTICE JOURNAL, American Group Practice Association, 1422 Duke St., Alexandria VA 22314. (703)838-0033. Editor: Thomas J. Fiorina. 50% freelance written. A bimonthly trade journal for medical administrators in physician group practices around the country. Editorial content focuses on health care as a business. Circ. 39,000. Pays on acceptance. Publishes ms an average of 2 months after acceptance. Byline given. Offers 25% kill fee. Buys first North American serial rights. Query for electronic submissions. Computer printout submissions OK. Reports in 4 weeks. Free sample copy and writer's guidelines.
Nonfiction: Book excerpts, interview/profile and new product. Buys 30 mss/year. Query. Length: 1,000-3,000 words. Pays $500-1,000. Sometimes pays the expenses of writers on assignment.
Photos: State availability of photos with submission. Reviews contact sheets, 35mm transparencies and 8x10 prints. Offers additional payment for photos accepted with ms. Captions, model releases and identification of subjects required. Buys one-time rights.
Columns/Departments: Book Review (business side of medicine), 750 words. Buys 6 mss/year. Query. Pays $250-500.
Tips: "We will only publish timely articles about competition in health-care field, specifically the group practice market. We need articles about entrepreneurial side of medicine; investing; personality pieces on movers and shakers in business of medicine; computers; and joint ventures. Avoid articles on clinical or diagnostic medicine: new cures for AIDS, physical fitness articles, new surgical procedures, etc."

‡JEMS, Journal of Emergency Medical Services, Suite 100, 215 S. Highway 101, Solana Beach CA 92075. (619)481-1128. Executive Editor: Keith Griffiths. Managing Editor: Rick Minerd. Monthly magazine covering emergency medicine. "*Jems* is circulated to providers and administrators of emergency medical care. We try to cover every facet of EMS." Circ. 33,000. Pays on publication. Publishes ms an average of 4 months after acceptance. Byline sometimes given. Offers 20-40% kill fee. Buys first North American serial rights or second serial (reprint) rights. Submit seasonal/holiday material 6 months in advance. Query for electronic submissions. Computer printout submissions OK; prefers letter-quality. Reports in 1 month on queries; 3 months on mss.
Nonfiction: Book excerpts, how-to (various EMS techniques—immobilization, airways, etc.), new product, opinion, photo feature and technical. Special issues include specialized rescue vehicle articles and winter injuries. No "paramedics were kind to me"—victim oriented, or "A day in the life of . . . articles. Buys 18-20 mss/year. Query with or without published clips, or send complete ms. Length: 1,500-3,000 words. Pays $75. Sometimes pays the expenses of writers on assignment.
Photos: Send photos with submission. Reviews contact sheets, negatives, 35mm transparencies and 5x7 or larger prints. Offers per photo. Buys one-time rights.
Columns/Departments: Inside EMS (news of local or national importance ot EMS); CPR Corner (news of CPR updates or studies). Buys 8-12 mss/year. Send complete ms. Length: 250-1,000 words. Pays 10¢/word.
Tips: "Go on ambulance runs as a 'ride along.' Area of publication most open to freelancers is Inside EMS department. Go beyond a newspaper clipping and find out the importance of the subject to rescue personnel."

THE JOURNAL, Addiction Research Foundation of Ontario, 33 Russell St., Toronto, Ontario M5S 2S1 Canada. (416)595-6053. Editor: Anne MacLennan. 50% freelance written. Prefers to work with published/established writers. Monthly tabloid covering addictions and related fields around the world. "*The Journal* alerts professionals in the addictions and related fields or disciplines to news events, issues, opinions and developments of potential interest and/or significance to them in their work, and provides them an informed context in which to judge developments in their own specialty/geographical areas." Circ. 26,000. Pays on publication. Publishes ms an average of 3 months after acceptance. Byline given. Kill fee negotiable. Not copyrighted. Buys first serial rights and second serial (reprint) rights. Computer printout submissions acceptable. SAE with Canadian postage; IRC. Reports in 2 months on queries; 3 months on mss. Free sample copy and writer's guidelines.

Nonfiction: Only. Query with published clips or send complete ms. Length: 1,000 words maximum. Pays 20¢/word minimum. Sometimes pays the expenses of writers on assignment.
Photos: Terri Etherington, production editor. State availability of photos. Pays $25 and up for 5x7 or 8x10 b&w prints. Captions, model release, and identification of subjects required. Buys one-time rights.
Columns/Departments: Under contract.
Tips: "A freelancer can best break in to our publication with six years reporting experience, preferably with medical/science writing background. We rarely use untried writers."

THE MAYO ALUMNUS, Mayo Clinic, 200 SW 1st St., Rochester MN 55905. (507)284-2511. Editor: Mary Ellen Landwehr. 10% freelance written. "We usually use our own staff for writing, and only occasionally use freelancers." For physicians, scientists and medical educators who trained at the Mayo Clinic. Quarterly magazine; 48 pages. Circ. 12,000. Pays on acceptance. Publishes ms an average of 3 months after acceptance. Buys all rights. Previously published submissions OK. Computer printout submissions acceptable; prefers letter-quality to dot-matrix. Reports in 2 months. Free sample copy; mention *Writer's Market* in request. No writer's guidelines available at this time.
Nonfiction: "We're interested in seeing interviews with members of the Mayo Alumni Association—stories about Mayo-trained doctors/educators/scientists/researchers who are interesting people doing interesting things in medicine, surgery or hobbies of interest, etc." Query with clips of published work. Length: 1,000-3,000 words. Pays 15¢/word, first 1,500 words. Maximum payment is $275. Sometimes pays the expenses of writers on assignment.
Photos: "We need art and must make arrangements if not provided with the story." Pays $50 for each color transparency used. State availability of photos with query. Captions preferred. Buys all rights.
Tips: "I keep a file of freelance writers, and when I need an alumnus covered in a certain area of the country, I contact a freelancer from that area. Those who suit my needs are the writers in the right place at the right time or those who have a story about an interesting alumnus."

MD MAGAZINE, New Horizons for the Physician, MD Publications, 30 E. 60th St., New York NY 10022. (212)355-5432. Editor: A.J. Vogl. Managing Editor: Barbara Guidos. 80% freelance written. Monthly magazine on culture/travel; a general interest magazine for physicians, covering all aspects of human experience. Circ. 140,000. Pays on acceptance. Publishes ms an average of 6 months after acceptance. Byline given. Offers 33⅓% kill fee. Buys first North American serial rights and second serial (reprint) rights. Submit seasonal/holiday material 4 months in advance. Photocopied and previously published submissions OK. Computer printout submissions acceptable; prefers letter-quality to dot-matrix. Reports in 1 month. Sample copy $2; free writer's guidelines.
Nonfiction: Sharon AvRutuick, articles editor. Book excerpts, general interest, historical/nostalgic, interview/profile, photo feature and travel. Buys 100+ mss/year. Query with published clips. Length: 1,000-3,000 words. Pays $350-700. Rarely pays expenses of writers on assignment.
Photos: Doris Brautigan, photo editor. Send photos with ms. Reviews b&w and color transparencies (35mm or larger) and 8x10 prints and b&w contact sheets. Payment varies. Captions and identification of subjects required. Pays $60-175 for b&w photos; $100-225 for color. Buys one-time rights.
Columns/Departments: Buys 50+ mss/year. Query with published clips. Length: 1,000-1,500 words. Pays $300-350.
Tips: "It is fresh ideas and writing that make things and people come alive."

‡THE MEDICAL BUSINESS JOURNAL, Medical Business Publishing Corp., 3461 Rt. 22 E., Somerville NJ 08876. (201)231-9695. Editor: Peter Dorfman. 10% freelance written. "Our authors generally have health care industry credentials." Publishes ms an average of 1-2 months after acceptance. Byline given. Query for electronic submissions. Computer printout submissions OK; prefers letter-quality to dot-matrix.
Nonfiction: Query with published clips, or send complete ms. Length: 1,500 words. Pays for assigned articles. Sometimes pays the expenses of writers on assignment.
Tips: "We would like to receive profiles of health care business segments written for a highly sophisticated audience."

MEDICAL ECONOMICS, Medical Economics Co., Inc., 680 Kinderkamack Rd., Oradell NJ 07649. (201)262-3030. Editor: Don L. Berg. Managing Editor: Richard Service. Less than 5% freelance written. Bi-weekly magazine covering topics of nonclinical interest to office-based private physicians (MDs and DOs only). "We publish practice/management and personal/finance advice for office-based MDs and osteopaths." Circ. 167,000. Pays on acceptance. Publishes ms an average of 3 months after acceptance. Byline given. Offers 25% of full article fee as kill fee. Buys all rights and first serial rights. Computer printout submissions acceptable. Reports in 2 months on queries; 3 weeks on mss. Sample copy for $3 and 9x12 SASE.
Nonfiction: Contact Lilian Fine, chief of Outside Copy Division. How-to (office and personnel management, personal-money management); personal experience (only involving MDs or DOs in private practice); and travel (how-to articles). No clinical articles, hobby articles, personality profiles or office design articles.

Buys 8-10 mss/year. Query with published clips. Length: 1,500-3,000 words. Pays $750-1,800. "The payment level is decided at the time go-ahead is given after query."

Photos: Contact Lilian Fine, chief of Outside Copy Division. State availability of photos. Pays negotiable rates for b&w contact sheets and for 35mm color slides. Model release and identification of subjects required. Buys one-time rights.

Tips: "How-to articles should fully describe techniques, goals, options and caveats—in terms that are clear and *realistic* for the average physician. Use of anecdotal examples to support major points is crucial. Our full-time staff is quite large, and therefore we buy only freelance articles that are not already assigned to staff writers. This puts a premium on unusual and appealing subjects."

‡MEDICAL MEETINGS, The International Guide for Healthcare Meetings Planners, The Laux Co., Inc., 63 Great Rd., Maynard MA 01754. Editor: Betsy Bair Cassidy. 60% freelance written. A bimonthly trade journal covering the medical meetings market. Circ. 13,500. Pays on publication. Publishes ms an average of 2 months after acceptance. Byline given. Offers negotiable kill fee. Makes work-for-hire assignments. Computer printout submissions OK; prefers letter-quality. Reports in 1 month.

Nonfiction: How-to, humor, interview/profile and travel. "Almost all of our articles are assigned according to a specific editorial calendar." Buys 40 mss/year. Query with published clips. Length: 1,000-2,500 words. Pays $150-500 for assigned articles; pays $100-200 for unsolicited articles. Sometimes pays the expenses of writers on assignment.

Photos: State availability of photos with submission. Reviews 5x7 transparencies and 5x7 prints. Captions required. Buys one-time rights.

Tips: "Request our editorial calender and follow up with specific destination or feature articles you would like to write. Knowledge of meetings industry is very helpful."

MEDICAL TIMES, Romaine Pierson Publishers, Inc., 80 Shore Rd., Port Washington NY 11050. (516)883-6350. Editors: A.J. Bollet, M.D., and A.H.Bruckheim, M.D. Executive Editor: Anne Mattarella. 100% freelance written. "Anyone with a good (i.e., applicable) idea and a well-written query letter will be considered for assignment." Monthly magazine covering clinical medical subjects for primary care physicians in private practice. Circ. 120,000. Pays on acceptance. Publishes ms an average of 1 year after acceptance. Byline given. Buys all rights and makes work-for-hire assignments. Submit seasonal/holiday material 6 months in advance. Simultaneous queries OK. Computer printout submissions acceptable; no dot-matrix. Reports in 1 month on queries; 2 months on mss. Sample copy $5; writer's guidelines for business size SASE.

Nonfiction: "We accept only clinical medical and medico-legal material. It is useless to send us any material that is not related directly to medicine. No first person accounts or interviews. We publish articles on the diagnosis and treatment of diseases." Buys 100 mss/year (95% from physicians). Query. Length: 500-2,500 words. Pays $25-300. Sometimes pays the expenses of writers on assignment.

Photos: State availability of photos. Pays variable rates for 2x2 b&w and color transparencies, and 4x5 or 8x10 b&w and color prints. Model release and identification of subjects required.

Fillers: Anecdotes. "Must be true, unpublished and medically oriented." Buys 25/year. Length: 25-200 words.

Tips: "A query letter is a must. 99% of our material is 'invited.' The writer must have a medical or health-related background and be able to write on technical subjects for a sophisticated audience."

MEDICAL WORLD NEWS, HEI Publishing, Suite 112, 7676 Woodway, Houston TX 77063. (713)780-2299. Editor: Annette Oestreicher. Managing Editor: Don Gibbons. 20% freelance written. Works with a small number of new/unpublished writers each year. A biweekly magazine covering the clinical, social, political, and economic aspects of medicine for doctors. Circ. 160,000. Pays on publication. Publishes ms an average of 3 weeks after acceptance. Byline sometimes given. Offers up to 50% kill fee. Buys first U.S. rights, but expects full ownership within the physician market. Computer printout submissions acceptable; prefers letter-quality to dot-matrix. Sample copy and writer's guidelines for 8½x11 SAE.

Nonfiction: "All stories must have at least two sources and news style. No single-source articles. Buys 100 mss/year. Query with published clips. Length: 200-4,000 words. Pays $80-1,800. Sometimes pays the expenses of writers on assignment.

Photos: State availability of photos with submission. Offers $20/photo. Identification of subjects required. Buys one-time rights.

Columns/Department: Query with published clips.

THE NEW PHYSICIAN, 1890 Preston White Dr., Reston VA 22091. Editor: Renie Schapiro. 20% freelance written. Prefers to work with published/established writers. For medical students, interns and residents. Published 9 times/year; 56 pages. Circ. 50,000. Buys first serial rights. Pays on publication. Publishes features an average of 3 months after acceptance; news within 2 months. Will consider simultaneous submissions. Computer printout submissions acceptable; prefers letter-quality to dot-matrix. Reports in 2 months or less. Sample copy for 10x13 SAE with 90¢ minimum postage; writer's guidelines for SASE.

Nonfiction: "Articles on social, political, economic issues in medicine/medical education. Our readers need more than a superficial, simplistic look into issues that affect them. We want skeptical, accurate, professional contributors to do well-researched, comprehensive, incisive reports and offer new perspectives on health care problems." Not interested in material on "my operation," or encounters with physicians, or personal experiences as physician's patient, or highly technical or clinical material. Humorous articles and cartoons for physicians-in-training welcome. Buys about 6 features/year and 5 short news items/year. Query or send complete ms. Length: 500-3,500 words. Pays $75-500 with higher fees for selected investigative pieces. Sometimes pays expenses of writers on assignment.

Tips: "We will be looking in 1988 for a few more practically-oriented articles for physicians-in training—how-tos for young doctors starting out. They must be authoritative, and from objective sources, not a consultant trying to sell his services. We would also like to receive short news items (500-1,000 words) on interesting local events around the country that would be of interest to our national audience. Our magazine demands sophistication on the issues we cover because we are a professional journal for readers with a progressive view on health care issues and a particular interest in improving the health care system. Those freelancers we publish reveal in their queries and ultimately in their manuscripts a willingness and an ability to look deeply into the issues in question and not be satisfied with a cursory review of those issues."

NURSINGLIFE, The magazine for professional growth and fulfillment, Springhouse Corp., 1111 Bethlehem Pike, Springhouse PA 19477. (215)646-8700. Editorial Director: Maryanne Wagner. Managing Editor: Tony DeCrosta. 75% freelance written. Works with a small number of new/unpublished writers each year, and is eager to work with new/unpublished writers. A bimonthly magazine that "addresses all the personal needs of nurses—home, career, psychological, legal, etc." Circ. 200,000. Pays on publication. Publishes ms an average of 6 months after acceptance. Byline given. Offers variable kill fee. Buys all rights and makes work-for-hire assignments. Simultaneous and photocopied submissions OK. Computer printout submissions acceptable. Reports in 6 weeks. Free writer's guidelines.

Nonfiction: Book excerpts (of interest to nurses); how-to (showing nurses how to be better at their jobs); interview/profile; legal; ethical; management; psychology; timely topics; personal experience and technical. "Specific articles cover subjects such as how to avoid legal risks, how to make good ethical decisions, and how to use teamwork for better patient care. We need legal articles—lawyers' advice to help nurses cope with malpractice lawsuits and the legal risks of nursing. 'Difficult Person' articles are first-person narratives by nurses describing the most difficult person they've ever worked with. Practical solutions are important; a good story isn't enough." No fiction, poetry or personal experience articles that simply vent frustration but don't offer advice other nurses can use. Buys 30-40 mss/year. Query with or without published clips, or send complete ms. Length: 750-2,500 words. Pays $50-750. Pays expenses of writers on assignment.

Photos: State availability of photos with submission. Reviews contact sheets and transparencies. Captions, model releases and identification of subjects required. Buys one-time rights.

Tips: "We're moving from a clinical focus to a stict personal one—to help nurses deal with the latest career and family pressures. Call with your idea—we'll give you immediate yes or no. The area of our publication most open to freelancers is Difficult Person feature. We're always looking for nurses who are making a difference and anyone who can help nurses deal with the pressures of balancing their career and family."

NURSINGWORLD JOURNAL, Prime National Publishing Corp., 470 Boston Post Rd., Weston MA 02193. (617) 849-2702. Editor: Ira Alterman. 50% freelance written. A monthly tabloid covering nursing for professional nurses. Circ. 40,000. Pays on publication. Byline given. Buys all rights. Computer printout submissions acceptable; prefers letter-quality to dot-matrix. Reports in 1 month on queries; 2 months on manuscripts. Sample copy $2; free writer's guidelines.

Nonfiction: General interest, historical/nostalgic, how-to and technical. Buys 20-50 mss/year. Send complete ms. Length: 500-2,000 words. Pays $50-100.

Photos: Send photos with submission. Reviews contact sheets and prints. Offers no additional payment for photos accepted with ms. Captions, releases and identification of subjects required.

‡OPTIONS: The Changing World of Medical Practice, Creative Age Publications, 7628 Densmore Ave., Van Nuys CA 91406. (818)782-7328. Managing Editor: Barbara Feiner. Monthly magazine covering the changing world of medicine. "In today's competitive marketplace, physicians are confronted with the challenges of building viable practices. *Options* covers the issues that years of medical school ignore—financial, business, and management themes." Estab. 1986. Circ. 44,000. Pays on acceptance. Byline given. Buys one-time rights. Submit seasonal/holiday material 8 months in advance. Simultaneous submissions OK. Computer printout submissions OK; prefers letter-quality to dot-matrix. Reports in 6 weeks. Sample copy $2.95.

Nonfiction: How-to, opinion and personal experience. Buys 12-36 mss/year. Query with published clips, or send complete ms. Length: 1,000-3,500 words. Pays $50-200.

Photos: State availability of photos with submission. Reviews 2x2 transparencies and 5x7 prints. Offers $25 minimum per photo. Captions, model releases and identification of subjects required. Buys one-time rights.

Columns/Departments: The Bottom Line (financial), 1,250 words. Buys 6-12 mss/year. Query with published clips. Pays $50-100.

Tips: "We're looking for writers who have a familiarity with the medical marketplace."

PERINATAL PRESS, Perinatal Press, Inc., 52nd and F Sts., Sacramento CA 95819. (916)733-1750. Executive Editor: J.M. Schneider, M.D. Managing Editor: K. Mulligan, B.A. A newsletter published 6 times per year for perinatal health care providers. Circ. 5,000. Pays on publication. Publishes ms an average of 8 months after acceptance. Byline given. Buys first North American serial rights. Reports in 3 weeks on queries; 6 weeks on mss. Sample copy $3.

Nonfiction: How-to, humor, opinion, technical and review articles. Buys 4-6 mss/year. Query. Pays $75-150 for assigned articles. May pay with premiums rather than cash for short pieces, such as book reviews.

Photos: State availability of photos with submission. Reviews 3x5 prints. Offers no additional payment for photos accepted with ms. Captions required. Buys one-time rights.

Poetry: "Have never used poetry before but would *consider* for publication. Must be about perinatal health care—for professionals. Would offer $25.

Tips: "Feature articles are most open to freelancers. We have a *professional audience* and need well written articles with nonsexist language, and family-centered care philosophy."

THE PHYSICIAN AND SPORTSMEDICINE, McGraw-Hill, 4530 W. 77th St., Edina MN 55435. (612)835-3222. Features Editor: Cindy Christian Rogers. Managing Editor: Douglas Benson. Executive Editor: Frances Munnings. 30% freelance written. Prefers to work with published/established writers. Monthly magazine covering medical aspects of sports and exercise. "We look in our feature articles for subjects of practical interest to our physician audience." Circ. 130,000. Pays on acceptance. Publishes ms an average of 2 months after acceptance. Byline given. Buys one-time rights. Submit seasonal/holiday material 6 months in advance. Computer printout submissions OK; no dot-matrix. Reports in 1 month. Sample copy for $4; writer's guidelines for #10 SAE and 1 first class stamp.

Nonfiction: Interview (persons active in this field); and technical (new developments in sports medicine). Query. Length: 250-2,500 words. Pays $150-900.

Photos: Marty Duda, photo editor. State availability of photos. Buys one-time rights.

‡PHYSICIAN'S MANAGEMENT, Harcourt Brace Jovanovich Health Care Publications, 7500 Old Oak Blvd., Cleveland OH 44130. (216)243-8100. Editor: Bob Feigenbaum. 25% freelance written. Prefers to work with published/established writers. Monthly magazine emphasizes finances, investments, malpractice, socioeconomic issues, estate and retirement planning, small office administration, practice management, leisure time, computers, travel, automobiles, and taxes for primary care physicians in private practice. Circ. 110,000. Pays on acceptance. Publishes ms an average of 6 months after acceptance. Buys first serial rights only. Submit seasonal or holiday material 5 months in advance. Query for electronic submissions. Computer printout submissions acceptable; prefers letter-quality to dot-matrix. Reports in 1 month. Sample copy $3.50.

Nonfiction: *"Physician's Management* is a practice management/economic publication, not a clinical one." Publishes how-to articles (limited to medical practice management); informational (when relevant to audience); and personal experience articles (if written by a physician). No fiction, clinical material or satire that portrays MD in an unfavorable light; or soap opera, "real-life" articles. Length: 2,000-2,500 words. Buys 10 mss/issue. Query. Pays $125/3-column printed page. Use of charts, tables, graphs, sidebars and photos strongly encouraged. Sometimes pays expenses of writers on assignment.

Tips: "Talk to doctors first about their practices, financial interests, and day-to-day nonclinical problems and then query us. Also, the ability to write a concise, well-structured and well-researched magazine article is essential. Freelancers who think like patients fail with us. Those who can think like MDs are successful. Our magazine is growing significantly. The opportunities for good writers will, therefore, increase greatly."

PODIATRY MANAGEMENT, Box 50, Island Station NY 10044. (212)355-5216. Publisher: Scott C. Borowsky. Editor: Barry Block, D.P.M. Managing Editor: M.J. Goldberg. Business magazine published 8 times/year for practicing podiatrists. "Aims to help the doctor of podiatric medicine to build a bigger, more successful practice, to conserve and invest his money, to keep him posted on the economic, legal and sociological changes that affect him." Circ. 11,000. Pays on publication. Byline given. Buys first North American serial rights and second serial (reprint) rights. Submit seasonal/holiday material 4 months in advance. Simultaneous queries, and simultaneous, photocopied and previously published submissions OK. Reports in 2 weeks. Sample copy $2; free writer's guidelines.

Nonfiction: General interest (taxes, investments, estate planning, recreation, hobbies); how-to (establish and collect fees, practice management, organize office routines, supervise office assistants, handle patient relations); interview/profile; and personal experience. "These subjects are the mainstay of the magazine, but offbeat articles and humor are always welcome." Buys 25 mss/year. Query. Length: 1,000-2,500 words. Pays $150-350.

Photos: State availability of photos. Pays $10 for b&w contact sheet. Buys one-time rights.

‡**PRACTICAL GASTROENTEROLOGY**, Pharmaceutical Communications, Inc., Suite 802, 42-15 Crescent St., Long Island City NY 11101. (718)937-4283. Editor: James Hazlett. Managing Editor: Christine Arax Nemetz. "*Practical Gastroenterology* is a professional clinical journal concerned with the diagnosis, therapy, management of digestive disorders. Edited for the gastroenterologist and internist, each issue consists of articles on topics the practioner encounters in daily practice." Circ. 65,000. Pays on publication. Publishes ms an average of 5 months after acceptance. Byline given. Offers 25% kill fee. Buys all rights. Submit seasonal/holiday material 6 months in advance. Photocopied submissions OK. Reports in 1 week on queries; 2 months on mss. Free sample copy and writer's guidelines.

Nonfiction: How-to, personal experience (clinical) and technical. Buys 2-3 mss/year. Send complete ms. Length: 1,000-2,500 words. Pays $800 maximum for assigned articles. Pays expenses of writers on assignment.

Photos: Send photos with submission. Captions and identification of subjects required. Offers no additional payment for photos accepted with ms. Buys all rights.

Tips: "Call and speak to editor or associate editor, or submit manuscript. Keep the nonspecialist in mind. Focus on information that will be useful and informative and instructive to the primary-care physican. Writing should be practical, pragamatic, chock-full of how-to info."

RESIDENT & STAFF PHYSICIAN, Romaine Pierson Publishers, Inc., 80 Shore Rd., Port Washington NY 11050. (516)883-6350. Editor: Alfred Jay Bollet, M.D. Executive Editor: Anne Mattarella. 5% freelance written. Monthly journal covering clinical medicine and practice management for residents and staff physicians. "*Resident & Staff Physician* goes to hospital-based physicians throughout the country, including practically all residents and the full-time hospital staff responsible for their training." Circ. 100,000. Pays on acceptance. Publishes ms an average of 1 year after acceptance. Byline given. Buys all rights. "However, we may grant permission to reprint if requested by the writer." Submit seasonal/holiday material 1 year in advance. Photocopied submissions OK. Reports in 3 weeks on queries; 4 months on mss. Sample copy for $8; free writer's guidelines.

Nonfiction: Historical/nostalgic (medical); medical humor; medical practice management. No case reports. Buys 2 mss/year. Query. Length: 6-8 typewritten pages. Pays $200-300.

Photos: State availability of photos. "Payment is included in manuscript payment." Captions, model release and identification of subjects required. Buys all rights.

Columns/Departments: Medical Mixups (terms patients mix up, e.g., Cadillacs in the eyes instead of cataracts). Buys 5-10 mss/year. Send complete ms. Length: 50 words. Pays $25 maximum.

Fillers: Jokes, anecdotes, short humor and newsbreaks. Buys 5/year. Length: 25-500 words. Pays $25-$100.

Tips: "A freelancer can best break in to our publication with filler items or humorous anecdotes. Keep the audience in mind. Jokes about high doctor fees are *not* funny to doctors."

‡**RESPONSE! The Magazine of Search, Rescue & Recovery**, Jems Publishing Co., Inc., Suite 100, 215 S. Highway 101, Box 1026, Solana Beach CA 92075. (619)481-1128. Executive Editor: Keith Griffiths. Managing Editor: Dave Beck. 20% freelance written. Bimonthly magazine covering search, rescue and recovery for providers and administrators of emergency care. Circ. 10,000. Pays on publication. Byline given. Offers 20-30% kill fee. Buys first North American serial and one-time rights. Submit seasonal/holiday material 6 months in advance. Query for electronic submissions. Computer printout submissions OK; prefers dot-matrix. Reports in 3 weeks on queries; 3 months on mss. Free sample copy and writer's guidelines.

Nonfiction: Book excerpts, how-to, humor, new product, opinion, photo feature and technical. Special issues include "Winter search and rescue, backcountry vehicles for rescue, tracking, "hasty team" searches, military search and rescue techniques." No "I was saved by a ranger" articles. Buys 6-10 mss/year. Query with or without published clips, or send complete ms. Length: 1,000-3,000 words. Pays 10¢/word. Sometimes pays the expenses of writers on assignment.

Photos: Send photos with submission. Reviews contact sheets, negatives, 2x2 transparencies and 5x7 prints. Offers $10-25 per photo. Buys one-time rights.

Tips: "Read our magazine, spend some time with a search team."

STRATEGIC HEALTH CARE MARKETING, Health Care Communications, 211 Midland Ave., Box 594, Rye NY 10580. (914)967-6741. Editor: Michele von Dambrowski. 20% freelance written. Prefers to work with published/established writers. "Will only work with unpublished writer on a 'stringer' basis initially." A monthly newsletter covering health care services marketing in a wide range of settings including hospitals and medical group practices, home health services and urgent care centers. Emphasizing strategies and techniques employed within the health care field and relevant applications from other service industries. Pays on publication. Publishes ms an average of 2 months after acceptance. Byline sometimes given. Offers 25% kill fee. Buys first North American serial rights. Simultaneous and photocopied submissions OK. Computer printout submissions acceptable; no dot-matrix. Reports in 1 month. Sample copy for 9x12 SAE and 56¢ postage; guidelines sent with sample copy only.

Nonfiction: How-to, interview/profile, new product and technical. Buys 9 mss/year. Query with published clips. Length: 700-2,000 words. Pays $50-250. Sometimes pays the expenses of writers on assignment with prior authorization.

Photos: State availability of photos with submissions. (Photos, unless necessary for subject explanation, are rarely used.) Reviews contact sheets. Offers $10-30/photo. Captions and model releases required. Buys one-time rights.

Fillers: Facts and newsbreaks. Buys 6/year. Length: 50-250 words. Pays $10-50.

Tips: "Writers with prior experience on business beat for newspaper or newsletter will do well. This is not a consumer publication—the writer with knowledge of both health care and marketing will excel. Interviews or profiles are most open to freelancers. Absolutely no unsolicited manuscripts; any received will be returned or discarded unread."

SURGICAL ROUNDS, Romaine Pierson Publishers, Inc., 80 Shore Rd., Port Washington NY 11050. (516)883-6350. Editor: Mark M. Ravitch, M.D. Executive Editor: Roxane Cafferata. Monthly magazine for surgeons and surgical specialists throughout the country, including interns and residents, all surgical faculty in medical schools, plus full-time hospital and private practice surgeons and operating room supervisors. Circ. 70,000. Pays on acceptance. Byline given. Buys all rights. Reports in 1 month. Sample copy $5; free writer's guidelines.

Nonfiction: How-to (practical, everyday clinical applications). "Articles for 'The Surgeon's Laboratory' should demonstrate a particular procedure step-by-step and be amply and clearly illustrated with intraoperative color photographs and anatomical drawings." Buys 80 mss/year. Query with published clips. Length: 1,500-2,000 words. Pays $150-400.

Mining and Minerals

‡COAL AGE, 11 W. 19th St., New York NY 10017. Editor: Joseph F. Wilkinson. For supervisors, engineers and executives in coal mining. Monthly. Circ. 24,000. Pays on publication. Buys all rights. Reports in 3 weeks.

Nonfiction: Uses some technical (operating type) articles; some how-to pieces on equipment maintenance; and management articles. Query. Pays $200/printed page.

GOLD PROSPECTOR, Gold Prospectors Association of America, Box 507, Bonsall CA 92003. (619)728-6620. Editor: Steve Teter. 60% freelance written. Eager to work with new/unpublished writers. Bimonthly magazine covering gold prospecting and mining. "*Gold Prospector* magazine is the official publication of the Gold Prospectors Association of America. The GPAA is an international organization of more than 100,000 members who are interested in recreational prospecting and mining. Our primary audience is people of all ages who like to take their prospecting gear with them on their weekend camping trips, and fishing and hunting trips. Our readers are interested not only in prospecting, but camping, fishing, hunting, skiing, backpacking, etc. And we try to carry stories in each issue pertaining to subjects besides prospecting." Circ. 150,000. Pays on publication. Publishes ms an average of 6 months after acceptance. Byline given. Buys first North American serial rights and second serial (reprint) rights. Submit seasonal/holiday material 6 months in advance. Simultaneous queries and photocopied and previously published submissions OK. Computer printout submission acceptable; no dot-matrix. Reports in 3 weeks. Sample copy for $2 and 9x12 SAE and 5 first class stamps; writer's guidelines for SASE.

Nonfiction: Historical/nostalgic; how-to (prospecting techniques, equipment building, etc.); humor; new product; personal experience; technical; and travel. "One of our publishing beliefs is that our audience would rather experience life than watch it on television—that they would like to take a rough and tumble chance with the sheer adventure of taking gold from the ground or river after it has perhaps lain there for a million years. Even if they don't, they seem to enjoy reading about those who do in the pages of *Gold Prospector* magazine." Buys 75-100 mss/year. Query with or without published clips if available or send complete ms. Length: 1,000-3,000 words. Pays $25-100.

Photos: State availability of photos with query or ms. Pays $2.50-$10 for 3½x5 b&w prints; $5-25 for 3½x5-color prints. Captions, model release, and identification of subjects required. Buys all rights.

Columns/Departments: Precious metals market report, mining news, and dowsing report. Buys 15-25/year. Query with or without published clips if available or send complete ms. Length: 500-1,000 words. Pays $25-100.

Tips: "Articles must deal with gold prospecting as the major topic."

ROCK PRODUCTS, Maclean-Hunter Publishing Corp., 300 W. Adams, Chicago IL 60606. (312)726-2802. Editor: Richard S. Huhta. 1-5% freelance written. Monthly magazine of the nonmetallic mining industry for producers of cement, lime, sand, gravel, crushed stone and lightweight aggregate. Circ. 23,000. Pays on publication. Publishes ms an average of 3-6 months after acceptance. Byline given. Buys first serial rights. Query for electronic submissions. Computer printout submissions OK; prefers letter-quality to dot-matrix. Reports in 2 weeks.

Nonfiction: Technical (maintenance and cement). "All pieces must relate directly to our industry. No general business articles." Buys 5-6 mss/year. Query. Length: 2,000-4,000 words. Pays variable fee. Pays expenses of writers on assignment

Photos: No restrictions. Color transfer a plus. No additional fee for ms accompanied by photos.

Music

THE CHURCH MUSICIAN, 127 9th Ave. N., Nashville TN 37234. (615)251-2961. Editor: William Anderson. 30% freelance written. Works with a small number of new/unpublished writers each year; eager to work with new/unpublished writers. Southern Baptist publication for Southern Baptist church music leaders. Monthly. Circ. 20,000. Buys all rights. Pays on acceptance. Publishes ms an average of 1 year after acceptance. No query required. Reports in 2 months. Free sample copy.

Nonfiction: Leadership and how-to features, success stories and articles on Protestant church music. "We reject material when the subject of an article doesn't meet our needs. And they are often poorly written, or contain too many 'glittering generalities' or lack creativity." Length: maximum 1,300 words. Pays up to 5¢/word.

Photos: Purchased with mss; related to mss content only. "We use only b&w glossy prints."

Fiction: Inspiration, guidance, motivation and morality with Protestant church music slant. Length: to 1,300 words. Pays up to 5¢/word.

Poetry: Church music slant, inspirational. Length: 8-24 lines. Pays $5-15.

Fillers: Short humor. Church music slant. No clippings. Pays $5-15.

Tips: "I'd advise a beginning writer to write about his or her experience with some aspect of church music; the social, musical and spiritual benefits from singing in a choir; a success story about their instrumental group; a testimonial about how they were enlisted in a choir—especially if they were not inclined to be enlisted at first. A writer might speak to hymn singers—what turns them on and what doesn't. Some might include how music has helped them to talk about Jesus as well as sing about Him. We would prefer most of these experiences be related to the church, of course, although we include many articles by freelance writers whose affiliation is other than Baptist. A writer might relate his experience with a choir of blind or deaf members. Some people receive benefits from working with unusual children—retarded, or culturally deprived, emotionally unstable, and so forth."

CLAVIER, A Magazine for Pianists and Organists, The Instrumentalist Co., 200 Northfield Rd., Northfield IL 60093. (312)446-5000. Editor: Barbara Kreader. 95% freelance written. A magazine published 10 times a year covering keyboard teaching and performance. Circ. 22,000. Pays on publication. Publishes ms an average of 1 year after acceptance. Byline given. Buys all rights. Submit seasonal/holiday material 6 months in advance. Computer printout acceptable; prefers letter-quality to dot-matrix. Reports in 1 week on queries; 2 months on manuscripts. Free sample copy and writer's guidelines.

Nonfiction: Essays; historical/nostalgic; how-to (on teaching, keeping a small business running, etc.); humor, interview/profile; personal experience and photo feature. Query with published clips. Length: 1,000-3,000 words. Pays $20-45/printed magazine page.

Photos: Send photos with submission. Reviews contact sheets, negatives, transparencies, and prints. Offers no additional payment for photos accepted with ms; offers $10-20/photo if by major photographers. Captions, model releases and identification of subjects required.

Tips: "Articles should be of interest and direct practical value to our readers, who are studio teachers of piano and organ, church organists, or harpsichordists. Topics may include pedagogy, technique, performance, ensemble playing, and accompanying. Material should be covered clearly and thoroughly but without repetition and unnecessary digressions."

FLUTE TALK, The Instrument Publishing Co., 200 Northfield Rd., Northfield IL 60093. (312)446-5000. Editor: Polly Hansen. 70% freelance written. Prefers to work with published/established writers, and is eager to work with new/unpublished writers. Magazine published 10 times/year covering flute performance. Circ. 12,000. Pays on publication. Publishes ms an average of 6 months after acceptance. Byline given. Buys all rights. Submit seasonal/holiday material 4 months in advance. Computer printout submissions acceptable; no dot-matrix. Reports in several weeks. Sample copy and writer's guidelines for 9½x12 SAE with 90¢ postage.

Nonfiction: How-to (execute certain flute techniques); humor; inspirational; interview/profile; opinion; personal experience; photo feature; and technical (flute repair). "Writing must be educational, but upbeat. A thorough knowledge of flute playing and/or music teaching is necessary." March issue contains listing of flute master classes held in the summer. No unsolicited performance guides or interviews duplicating those already featured. Buys 25 mss/year. Send complete ms. Length: 500-3,000 words. Pays $20-200. Sometimes pays the expenses of writers on assignment.

Photos: Send photos with submission. Reviews contact sheets, 2x2 transparencies and 8x10 prints—for cover only. Identification of subjects required. "For cover photos we pay photographer and buy all rights; for photos within an article, we don't pay and will accept any size."

Columns/Departments: Book Review (review of recently published flute texts), 500-750 words; and Record Reviews (review of recently released flute recordings), 500 words. Buys 6 mss/year. Query with published clips. Length: 250-750 words. Pays $20-45.

Fillers: Anecdotes, facts, gags to be illustrated by cartoonist, newsbreaks and short humor. Buys 20/year. Length: 125-375 words. Pays $15 maximum.

Tips: "We'd like more submissions related to jazz flute: tips for doublers, getting studio work, history of jazz flute, discographies, and tips for improvising, etc. We look for highly informative, knowledgeable, and fun to read articles related to flute performance. It is easy to be published in *Flute Talk* if the article is well-written and applicable. Do *not* send single spaced manuscripts. If a photocopy is sent make sure the copy is dark. Submissions should not be under consideration by another publication. Most open to freelancers are articles related to flute techniques such as breath control, finger technique, tonguing exercises with music included, alternate fingering charts, trill charts, etc. Also book, concert, and record reviews. Because *Flute Talk* is read by both professional flutists and amateurs, we present material for a wide range of ability levels. General interest regardng flute related topics are therefore applicable."

THE INSTRUMENTALIST, Instrumentalist Publishing Company, 200 Northfield Rd., Northfield IL 60093. (312)446-5000. Managing Editor: Elaine Guregian. Approximately 95% freelance written. Works with a small number of new/unpublished writers each year. A monthly magazine covering instrumental music education for school band and orchestra directors, as well as performers and students. Circ. 23,000. Pays on publication. Publishes ms an average of 6-9 months after acceptance. Byline given. Buys all rights. Submit seasonal/holiday material 4 months in advance. Photocopied submissions OK. Computer printout submissions acceptable; prefers letter-quality to dot-matrix. Reports in 2 months. Sample copy $2; free writer's guidelines.

Nonfiction: Book excerpts (rarely); essays (on occasion); general interest (on occasion, music); historical/nostalgic (music); how-to (teach, repair instruments); humor (on occasion); interview/profile (performers, conductors, composers); opinion; personal experience; photo feature; and travel. Buys 35-40 mss/year. Send complete ms. Length: 750-1,750 words. Pays $30-45/published page.

Photos: State availability of photos with submission. Reviews slides and 5x7 prints. Payment varies. Captions and identification of subjects required. Buys variable rights.

Columns/Departments: Challenge (opinions on issues facing music educators), 500-750 words; Personal Perspective (advice and ideas from experienced educators and performers), 500-750 words; Idea Exchange ('how-tos' from educators), 250-500 words; My 2¢ Worth (opinions and humorous viewpoints), 250-500 words. Buys 12-15 mss/year. Send complete ms. Length: 250-500 words. Pays $30-45.

Fillers: Anecdotes and short humor. Buys 12-15/year. Length: 250 words maximum. Pays $25-45.

Tips: "Know the music education field, specifically band and orchestra. Interviews with performers should focus on the person's contribution to education, opinions about it, experience in it, etc. Interviews and features on performers and groups are probably most accessible to non-musicians."

‡INTERNATIONAL BLUEGRASS, International Bluegrass Music Association, 326 St. Elizabeth St., Owensboro KY 42301. (502)684-9025. Editor: Art Menius. 30% freelance written. Bimonthly newsletter covering bluegrass music industry. "We are the business publication for the bluegrass music industry. IBMA believes that our music has growth potential. We are interested in hard news and features concerning how to reach that potential and how to conduct business more effectively." Estab. 1985. Circ. 3,000. Pays on publication. Publishes ms an average of 2 months after acceptance. Byline given. Not copyrighted. Buys one-time rights. Submit seasonal/holiday material 4 months in advance. Simultaneous, photocopied and previously published submissions OK. Query for electronic submissions. Computer printout submissions OK. Reports in 1 month on queries; 6 weeks on mss.

Nonfiction: Book excerpts, essays, how-to (conduct business effectively within bluegrass music), new product and opinion. No interview/profiles of performers (rare exceptions) or fans. Buys 6 mss/year. Query with or without published clips, or send complete ms. Length: 300-1,200 words. Pays $25 maximum for assigned articles. Pays in contributor's copies unless payment in cash agreed at assignment.

Photos: Send photos with submission. Reviews 5x8 prints. Offers no additional payment for photos accepted with ms. Captions and identification fo subjects required. Buys one-time rights.

Columns/Departments: At the Microphone (opinion about the bluegrass music industry). Buys 6 mss/year. Send complete ms. Length: 300-1,200 words. Pays $0-25.

Fillers: Anecdotes, facts, newsbreaks and short humor. Buys 2/year. Length: 60-200 words.

Tips: "The easiest break-in is to submit an article about an organizational member of IBMA—such as a bluegrass association, instrument manufacturer or dealer, or performing venue. We're interested in a slant strongly toward the business end of bluegrass music. At the Microphone is the most open to freelancers. We want considered opinion about the state of the bluegrass industry from people who know either first hand or through close observation/interview."

‡MIX MAGAZINE, The Recording Industry Magazine,Mix Publications, 2608 Ninth St., Berkeley CA 94710. (415)843-7901. Editor: David M. Schwartz. Managing Editor: Blair Jackson. 50% freelance written. A monthly trade journal for audio recording and music technology. Circ. 44,000. Pays on publication. Byline given. 50% kill fee. Buys first North American serial rights. Query for electronic submission. Computer printout submissions OK; prefers letter-quality to dot-matrix. Sample copy for 8½x11 SAE with $1.50 postage; writer's guidelines for #10 SASE.

Nonfiction: How-to and technical. Buys 100 mss/year. Query with or without published clips or send complete ms. Length: 500-3,000 words. Pays $50-500. Sometimes pays writers with contributor copies or other premiums "by negotiation." Sometimes pays expenses of writers on assignment.

Photos: Send photos with submission. Reviews transparencies and prints. Offers no additional payment for photos accepted with ms. Captions and model releases required. Buys one-time rights.

Columns/Departments: Interactivity (optical disc(CD) storage technology), Artist Studios (profile of recording studio owned by major recording artist), and Producer's Desk (profile of popular record producer). Buys 20 mss/year. Query with published clips. Length: 1,000-2,000 words. Pays $100-300.

Tips: "Seek out unique and future thinking topic pieces in music technology. Explore them carefully and thoroughly."

MUSIC & SOUND OUTPUT, The Magazine For Performers and Producers, Testa Communications, Inc., 220 Westbury Ave., Carle Place NY 11514. (516)334-7880. Editor: Robert Seidenberg. 40% freelance written. Works with a small number of new/unpublished writers each year. Monthly magazine of contemporary music and recording. Audience is mostly working musicians. Prefers technical versus sociological slant in coverage of rock, jazz, R&B, country, pop, blues, and ethnic music. Circ. 78,000. Pays on publication. Publishes ms an average of 2-3 months after acceptance. Byline given. Offers 10-20% kill fee. Buys all rights. Photocopied submissions OK. Computer printout submissions acceptable; prefers letter-quality to dot-matrix. Reports in 2 weeks. Sample copy for $2.50.

Nonfiction: Interview/profile (music performers, producers, engineers); technical (recording, and live sound, query first); and reviews of records. No mss written from a fan's point of view, i.e., features on performers without getting an interview. Buys 10-20 mss/year. Query with published clips. Length: 250-3,000 words. Pays $175-500. Sometimes pays expenses of writers on assignment.

Photos: State availability of photos. Prefers exclusive photos. Reviews color transparencies and 8x10 b&w prints. Pays $50-300 for color; $20-200 for b&w. Identification of subjects required. Buys one-time rights.

Columns/Departments: Record reviews (any genre). Buys 10-20 mss/year. Send complete ms. Length: 200-500 words. Pays $40-100.

Tips: "Music-related clips are always impressive. We are seeking writers with experience in the music industry as a performer or with extensive technical background in recording. Areas most open to freelancers include record reviews and short (500-1,000 words), profiles of new bands, established musicians with a new direction, producers, engineers and innovators."

OPERA NEWS, 1865 Broadway, New York NY 10023. Managing Editor: Jane Poole. 75% freelance written. Monthly magazine (May-November); biweekly (December-April). For all people interested in opera; opera singers, opera management people, administrative people in opera, opera publicity people, and artists' agents; people in the trade and interested laymen. Circ. 120,000. Pays on publication. Publishes ms an average of 3 months after acceptance. Buys first serial rights only. Pays negotiable kill fee. Byline given. Computer printout submissions acceptable; prefers letter-quality to dot-matrix. Sample copy $2.50.

Nonfiction: Most articles are commissioned in advance. In summer, uses articles of various interests on opera; in the fall and winter, articles that relate to the weekly broadcasts. Emphasis is on high quality writing and an intellectual interest to the opera-oriented public. Informational, how-to, personal experience, interview, profile, historical, think pieces, personal opinion and opera reviews. Query; no telephone inquiries. Length: 2,500 words maximum. Pays 13¢/word for features; 11¢/word for reviews. Rarely pays the expenses of writers on assignment.

Photos: Pays minimum of $25 for photos purchased on assignment. Captions required.

Office Environment and Equipment

‡AMERICAN OFFICE DEALER,A/S/M Communications, Inc., 49 E. 21st St., 6th Floor, New York NY 10010. (212)529-3344. Editor: Christopher A. Clark. Managing Editor: Ron Gales. 5% freelance written. Trade journal. Monthly magazine covering the office products industry. "For retailers of office supplies, furniture, machines, systems, computers, and peripherals. Heavy emphasis on people, products and industry news." Circ. 28,000. Pays on publication. Publishes ms an average of 1 month after acceptance. Byline given. Offers 25% kill fee. Buys first rights. Photocopied submissions OK. Query for electronic submissions. Computer printout submissions OK; prefers letter-quality to dot-matrix. Reports in 1 week. Free sample copy.
Nonfiction: Interview/profile and new product. "No generic retail 'How to run your business' articles, general business articles on financial management." Buys 10 mss/year. Query with published clips. Length: 500-5,000 words. Pays $50-500. Sometimes pays expenses of writers on assignment.
Photos: Send photos with submission. Reviews contact sheets, negatives, transparencies and prints. Offers no additional payment for photos accepted with ms. (after expenses are paid). Captions required. Buys one-time rights.
Tips: "A background in retail is necessary, as is some understanding of modern office technology. Most of the magazine is staff written, but we take great interest in qualified freelance writers who demonstrate a lively writing style in addition to the aforementioned attributes. Just because it's a trade magazine doesn't mean it has to be boring. Subject most open to freelancers are profiles of office products dealers in U.S."

MODERN OFFICE TECHNOLOGY, Penton Publishing, 1100 Superior Ave., Cleveland OH 44114. (216)696-7000. Editorial Director: John Dykeman. Editor: Lura K. Romei. Production Manager: Vickie Friess. 5-10% freelance written. A monthly magazine covering office automation. "We serve corporate management and corporate personnel, financial management, administrative and operating management, systems and information management, managers and supervisors of support personnel, and purchasing." Circ. 160,000. Pays on publication. Publishes ms an average of 6 months after acceptance. Byline given. Buys first and one-time rights. Photocopied submissions OK. Electronic submissions OK via disk only, Kaypro II, IBM compatible; requires hard copy also. Computer printout submissions acceptable. Reports in 3 weeks. Free sample copy and writer's guidelines.
Nonfiction: New product, opinion and technical. Buys 8 mss/year. Query with or without published clips, or send complete ms. Length: open. Pays $250-500 for assigned articles; pays $250-400 for unsolicited articles. Pays writers with contributor copies or other premiums rather than cash on request. Pays expenses of writers on assignment.
Photos: Send photos with submission. Reviews contact sheets, 4x5 transparencies and prints. Offers no additional payment for photos accepted with ms. Captions and identification of subjects required. Buys one-time rights.
Columns/Departments: Reader's Soapbox (opinions on office-related subjects), 750 words. Buys 3 mss/year. Send complete ms. Pays $75-150.
Tips: "Our readers are always looking for better ways to do the things they have to do daily. Any off-the-beaten-track material has a fairly good chance of being seriously considered. Features, certainly, is our most open area. We're looking for depth, clarity, and applicability to office management."

OFFICE SYSTEMS ERGONOMICS REPORT, The Koffler Group, 3029 Wilshire Blvd., Santa Monica CA 90403. (213)453-1844. Editor: Kathy Potosnak. Managing Editor: Richard Koffler. 5% freelance written. "We will review all submissions." A bimonthly covering computers and human factors: "objective, practical advice on how computers can/should be used by people." Circ. 1,000. Pays on publication. Publishes ms an average of 2 months after acceptance. Byline given. Offers negotiable kill fee. Buys all rights. Simultaneous, photocopied and previously published submissions OK. Query for electronic submissions. Computer printout submissions acceptable. Free sample copy.
Nonfiction: Book excerpts, essays, exposé, general interest, humor, interview/profile, new product, opinion, personal experience and technical. Buys 6-10 mss/year. Query with or without published clips, or send complete ms. Length: open. Pays negotiable rates.
Photos: Send photos with submission. Reviews contact sheets. Offers no additional payment for photos accepted with ms. Captions and model releases required. Buys one-time rights.
Tips: "Writers who can objectively review an issue and related scientific research and then provide practical advice on the topic for managers will suit our needs. Continued emphasis will be placed on usable information with a *firm* basis in research."

Paint

AMERICAN PAINT & COATINGS JOURNAL, American Paint Journal Co., 2911 Washington Ave., St. Louis MO 63103. (314)534-0301. Editor: Chuck Reitter. 10% freelance written. Weekly magazine; 78 pages. For the coatings industry (paint, varnish, lacquer, etc.); manufacturers of coatings, suppliers to coatings industry, educational institutions, salesmen. Circ. 7,300. Publishes ms an average of 3 months after aceptance. Pays on publication. Pays kill fee "depending on the work done." Buys all rights. Phone queries OK. Simultaneous and photocopied submissions OK. Computer printout submissions acceptable. Reports in 3 weeks. Free sample copy and writer's guidelines.
Nonfiction: Informational, historical, interview, new product, technical articles and coatings industry news. Buys 2 mss/issue. Query before sending long articles; submit complete ms for short pieces. Length: 75-1,200 words. Pays $5-100. Sometimes pays expenses of writers on assignment.
Photos: B&w (5x7) glossies purchased with or without mss or on assignment. Query. Pays $3-10.

Paper

BOXBOARD CONTAINERS, Maclean Hunter Publishing Co., 300 W. Adams St., Chicago IL 60606. (312)726-2802. Editor: Charles Huck. Managing Editor: William Turley. A monthly magazine covering box and carton manufacturing for corrugated box, folding carton, setup box manufacturers internationally. Emphasizes technology and management. Circ. 13,000. Pays on publication. Byline given. Buys first North American serial rights. Submit seasonal/holiday material 2 months in advance. Photocopied submissions OK. Electronic submissions OK via XY Write/IBM PC, but requires hard copy also. Computer printout submissions acceptable; no dot-matrix. Reports in 1 month. Free sample copy.
Nonfiction: How-to, interview/profile, new product, opinion, personal experience, photo feature and technical. Buys 10 mss/year. Query. Length: 2,000-6,000 words. Pays $75-350 for assigned articles; pays $50-200 for unsolicited articles. Sometimes pays the expenses of writers on assignment.
Photos: Send photos with submission. Reviews 35mm, 4x5 and 6x6 transparencies and 8x10 prints. Offers no additional payment for photos accepted with ms. Captions, model releases and identification of subjects required. Buys one-time rights.
Tips: Features are most open to freelancers.

PULP & PAPER CANADA, Southam Communications Ltd., Suite 201, 310 Victoria Ave., Montreal, Quebec H3Z 2M9 Canada. (514)487-2302. Editor: Peter N. Williamson. Managing Editor: Graeme Rodden. 5% freelance written. Prefers to work with published/established writers. Monthly magazine. Circ. 8,803. Pays on acceptance. Publishes ms "as soon as possible" after acceptance. Byline given. Offers kill fee according to prior agreement. Buys first North American serial rights. Submit seasonal/holiday material 2 months in advance. Computer printout submissions acceptable; prefers letter-quality to dot-matrix. SAE and IRC. Reports in 2 weeks on queries; 3 weeks on mss. Sample copy $5 (Canada), $7 (other countries); free writer's guidelines.
Nonfiction: How-to (related to processes and procedures in the industry); interview/profile (of Canadian leaders in pulp and paper industry); and technical (relevant to modern pulp and/or paper industry). No fillers, short industry news items, or product news items. Buys 10 mss/year. Query with or without published clips or send complete ms. Articles with photographs (b&w glossy) or other good quality illustrations will get priority review. Length: 1,500-2,000 words (with photos). Pays $150 (Canadian funds)/published page, including photos, graphics, charts, etc. Sometimes pays the expenses of writers on assignment.
Tips: "Any return postage must be in either Canadian stamps or International Reply Coupons only."

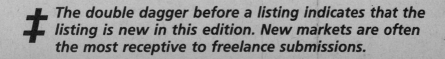

The double dagger before a listing indicates that the listing is new in this edition. New markets are often the most receptive to freelance submissions.

Pets

Listed here are publications for professionals in the pet industry, wholesalers, manufacturers, suppliers, retailers, owners of pet specialty stores, pet groomers, aquarium retailers, distributors and those interested in the fish industry. Publications for pet owners are listed in the Animal section of Consumer Publications.

PET AGE, The Largest Circulation Pet Industry Trade Publication, H.H. Backer Associates, Inc., 207 S. Wabash Ave., Chicago IL 60604. (312)663-4040. Editor: Karen M. Long. 10-20% freelance written. Prefers to work with published/established writers. Monthly magazine about the pet industry for pet retailers and industry. Circ. 17,000. Pays on acceptance. Publishes ms an average of 3 months after acceptance. Byline given. Buys first serial rights, first rights, all rights, or exclusive industry rights. Submit seasonal/holiday material 3-4 months in advance. Query for electronic submissions. Computer printout submissions acceptable; prefers letter-quality to dot-matrix. Reports in 1 month on queries; 2 weeks on mss. Sample copy for $2.50 and 9x12 SASE; free writer's guidelines.
Nonfiction: Book excerpts, profile (of a successful, well-run pet retail operation); how-to; interview; photo feature; and technical—all trade-related. Query first with published clips. Buys 6-12 mss/year. "Query as to the name and location of a pet operation you wish to profile and why it would make a good feature. No general retailing articles or consumer-oriented pet articles." Length: 1,000-3,000 words. Pays $75-200 for assigned articles; $50-150 for unsolicited articles. Sometimes pays the expenses of writers on assignment.
Photos: Reviews 5x7 b&w glossy prints. Captions and identification of subjects required. Offers $5 (negotiable) for photos. Buys one-time rights or all rights.
Tips: "Our readers already know about general animal care and business practices. This is a business publication for busy people, and must be very informative in easy-to-read, as brief as possible style. The type of article we purchase most frequently is the pet shop profile, a story about an interesting/successful pet shop. We need queries on these (we get references on the individual shop from our sources in the industry). We supply typical questions to writers when we answer their queries."

‡PET BUSINESS, 5400 NW 84th Ave., Miami FL 33166. (305)591-1629. Editor: Linda Mills. 10% freelance written. Eager to work with new/unpublished writers. "Our monthly news magazine reaches retailers, distributors and manufacturers of companion animals and pet products. Groomers, veterinarians and serious hobbyists are also represented." Circ. 15,000. Pays on publication. Publishes ms an average of 2 months after acceptance. Byline sometimes given. Not copyrighted. Buys first rights. Submit seasonal/holiday material 2 months in advance. Computer printout submissions OK; no dot-matrix. Sample copy $3. Writer's guidelines for SASE.
Nonfiction: "Articles must be newsworthy and pertain to animals routinely sold in pet stores (dogs, cats, fish, birds, reptiles and small animals). Research, legislative and animal behavior reports are invited. All data must be attributed. No fluff!" Buys 40 mss/year. Send complete ms. "No queries—the news gets old quickly." Length: 50-800 words. Pays $5 per column inch.
Photos: Send photos (slides or prints) with submission. Offers $10-20 per photo. Buys one-time rights.
Tips: "We are open to national and international news written in standard news format. Keep an eye on anti-pet trade forces ('humaniacs' legislators)."

THE PET DEALER, Howmark Publishing Corp., 567 Morris Ave., Elizabeth NJ 07208. (201)353-7373. Editorial Director: Alan Richman. 10% freelance written. Prefers to work with published/established writers; works with a small number of new/unpublished writers each year; and eager to work with new/published writers. "We want writers who are good reporters and clear communicators." Monthly magazine; 80 pages. Emphasizes merchandising, marketing and management for owners and managers of pet specialty stores, departments, and pet groomers and their suppliers. Circ. 11,000. Pays on publication. Publication "may be many months between acceptance of a manuscript and publication." Byline given. Phone queries OK. Submit seasonal/holiday material 3 months in advance. Computer printout submissions acceptable; no dot-matrix. Reports in 1 week. Sample copy and writer's guidelines for 9x12 SAE with 39¢ postage.
Nonfiction: How-to (store operations, administration, merchandising, marketing, management, promotion and purchasing). Consumer pet articles—lost pets, best pets, humane themes—*not* welcome. Emphasis is on *trade* merchandising and marketing of pets and supplies. Buys 8 unsolicited mss/year. Length: 800-1,200 words. Pays $50-100.

Photos: Submit photo material with ms. No additional payment for 5x7 b&w glossy prints. "Six photos with captions required." Buys one-time rights.

Tips: "We're interested in store profiles outside the New York, New Jersey, Connecticut and Pennsylvania metro areas. Photos are of key importance. Articles focus on new techniques in merchandising or promotion. Submit query letter first, with writing background summarized; include samples. We seek one-to-one, interview-type features on retail pet store merchandising. Indicate the availability of the proposed article, your willingness to submit on exclusive or first-in-field basis, and whether you are patient enough to await payment on publication."

PETS/SUPPLIES/MARKETING, Harcourt Brace Jovanovich Publications, 1 E. 1st St., Duluth MN 55802. (218)723-9303. Publisher/Editor: David Kowalski. 10% freelance written. Monthly magazine. For independent pet retailers, chain franchisers, livestock and pet supply wholesalers, and manufacturers of pet products. Circ. 14,200. Pays on publication. Buys first rights only. Phone queries OK. Submit seasonal/holiday material 4 months in advance. Photocopied submissions OK. Computer printout submissions acceptable. Reports in 2 months. Free writer's guidelines. Sample copy $5.

Nonfiction: How-to (merchandise pet products, display, set up window displays, market pet product line); interviews (with pet store retailers); opinion (of pet industry members or problems facing the industry); photo features (of successful pet stores or effective merchandising techniques and in-store displays); profiles (of successful retail outlets engaged in the pet trade); and technical articles (on more effective pet retailing, e.g., building a central filtration unit, constructing custom aquariums or display areas). Business management articles must deal specifically with pet shops and their own unique merchandise and problems. Length: 1,000-2,000 words. Buys 1-2 mss/issue. Query. Pays 10¢/word. Sometimes pays the expenses of writers on assignment.

Photos: Purchased with or without mss or on assignment. "We prefer 5x7 or 8x10 b&w glossies. But we will accept contact sheets and standard print sizes. For color, we prefer 35mm Kodachrome transparencies or 2¼x2¼." Pays $10 for b&w; $25 for color. Captions and model release required.

Columns/Departments: Suggestions for new columns or departments should be addressed to the editor. No clippings, please.

Tips: "We want articles which stress professional retailing, provide insight into successful shops, and generally capture the excitement of an exciting and sometimes controversial industry. All submissions are read. However, an initial query could save time and energy and ensure a publishable article."

Photography Trade

AMERICAN CINEMATOGRAPHER, A.S.C. Holding Corp., Box 2230, Hollywood CA 90078. (213)876-5080. Editor: George Turner. 75% freelance written. Monthly magazine; 112 pages. An international journal of film and video production techniques "addressed to creative, managerial, and technical people in all aspects of production. Its function is to disseminate practical information about the creative use of film and video equipment, and it strives to maintain a balance between technical sophistication and accessibility." Circ. 35,000. Pays on publication. Publishes ms an average of 3 months after acceptance. Buys all rights. Phone queries OK. Simultaneous and photocopied submissions OK. Computer printout submissions acceptable "provided they are adequately spaced."

Nonfiction: Jean Turner, assistant editor. Descriptions of new equipment and techniques or accounts of specific productions involving unique problems or techniques; historical articles detailing the production of a classic film, the work of a pioneer or legendary cinematographer or the development of a significant technique or type of equipment. Also discussions of the aesthetic principles involved in production techniques. Recent article example: "Tales From Silverado," (July, 1985). Length: 1,500 to 5,000 words. Pays according to position and worth. Negotiable. Sometimes pays the expenses of writers on assignment.

Photos: B&w and color purchased with mss. No additional payment.

Tips: "No unsolicited articles. Call first. Doesn't matter whether you are published or new. Queries must describe writer's qualifications and include writing samples."

FUNCTIONAL PHOTOGRAPHY, The Magazine of Visual Documentation and Communication for the Scientific, Technical & Medical Image Maker, PTN Publishing Corp., 210 Crossways Park Dr., Woodbury NY 11797. Senior Editor: David A. Silverman. 70% freelance written. Eager to work with new/unpublished writers. Bimonthly magazine of scientific/medical/technical image producers (doctors, R&D, scientific personnel). Circ. 33,000. Pays on publication. Publishes ms an average of 3-6 months after acceptance. Byline given. Not copyrighted. Computer printout submissions acceptable; prefers letter-quality or double-strike dot-matrix. Reports in 6 weeks. Sample copy $2; writer's guidelines for #10 SAE and 1 first class stamp.

Nonfiction: How-to, photo feature (related to our market), and technical. "Articles must be of instructive value for our particular type of technical reader." Buys 10-20 mss/year. Query with published clips. Pays $150-200.

Photos: Send photos with query. Reviews prints. Captions, model release and identification of subjects required. Buys one-time rights.

‡**THE PHOTO REVIEW**, 301 Hill Ave., Langhorne PA 19047. (215)757-8921. Editor: Stephen Perloff. 50% freelance written. A quarterly magazine on photography with reviews, interviews and articles on art photography. Circ. 750. Pays on publication. Publishes ms an average of 3 months after acceptance. Byline given. Buys one-time rights. Simultaneous, photocopied and previously published submissions OK. Computer printout submissions OK. Reports in 3 weeks on queries; 2 months on mss. Sample copy for 8½x11 SAE with 73¢ postage.

Nonfiction: Essays, historical/nostalgic, interview/profile and opinion. No how-to articles. Buys 10-15 mss/year. Query. Pays $25-200.

Photos: Send photos with submission. Reviews 8x10 prints. Offers no additional payment for photos accepted with ms. Captions and identification of subjects required. Buys one-time rights.

PHOTOFLASH, Models & Photographers Newsletter, Box 7946, Colorado Springs CO 80933. Managing Editor: Ron Marshall. 20% freelance written. Prefers to work with published/established writers; also works with a small number of new/unpublished writers each year. Quarterly newsletter of photographic modeling and glamour photography "for models, photographers, publishers, picture editors, modeling agents, advertising agencies, and others involved in the interrelated fields of modeling and photography." Pays on publication. Publishes ms an average of 3 months after acceptance. Byline given. Buys first North American serial rights and second serial (reprint) rights. Submit seasonal/holiday material 6 months in advance. Simultaneous queries, and simultaneous, photocopied and previously published submissions OK. "If previously published, please tell us when and where." Computer printout submissions acceptable; prefers letter-quality to dot-matrix. Reports in 2 months on queries; 4 months on mss. Sample copy $5.

Nonfiction: Interview/profile (of established and rising professionals in the field, especially models); photo feature; and technical (illustrating/explaining photographic and modeling techniques). Send complete ms. "We prefer photo-illustrated text packages."

Photos: Send photos with ms. "Payment is for the complete photo-text package; it includes a credit line, contributor copies and $15-25 depending on quality, completeness, etc. of the submissions." Reviews 8x10 b&w prints. Captions and model release required.

PHOTO LAB MANAGEMENT, PLM Publishing, Inc., 1312 Lincoln Blvd., Santa Monica CA 90406. (213)451-1344. Editor: Carolyn Ryan. Associate Editor: Arthur Stern. 25% freelance written. Monthly magazine covering process chemistries, process control, process equipment and marketing/administration for photo lab owners, managers and management personnel. Circ. over 16,000. Pays on publication. Publishes ms an average of 4 months after acceptance. Byline and brief bio given. Buys first North American serial rights. Submit seasonal/holiday material 6 months in advance. Query for electronic submissions. Computer printout submissions acceptable. Reports on queries in 6 weeks. Free sample copy and writer's guidelines for business size SAE and 1 first class stamp.

Nonfiction: Personal experience (lab manager); technical; and management or administration. Buys 40-50 mss/year. Query with brief biography. Length: 1,200-1,800 words. Pays $60/published page.

Photos: Reviews 35mm color transparencies and 4-color prints suitable for cover. "We're looking for outstanding cover shots of photofinishing images."

Tips: "Our departments are written in-house and we don't use 'fillers'. Send a query if you have some background in the industry or a willingness to dig out information and research for a top quality article that really speaks to our audience. The most frequent mistakes made by writers in completing an article for us are on the business management side—taking a generic rather than a photo lab approach. Writers must have photofinishing knowledge."

PHOTOLETTER, PhotoSource International, Pine Lake Farm, Osceola WI 54020. (715)248-3800. Editor: Lori Johnson. Managing Editor: H.T. White. 10% freelance written. A monthly newsletter on marketing photographs. "The *Photoletter* pairs photobuyers with photographers' collections." Circ. 780. Pays on acceptance. Publishes ms an average of 6 months after acceptance. Byline given. Buys one-time rights and simultaneous rights. Submit seasonal/holiday material 3 months in advance. Simultaneous, photocopied, and previously published submissions OK. Query for electronic submissions. Computer printout submissions acceptable. Reports in 2 weeks on queries. Sample copy $3; no writer's guidelines.

Nonfiction: Lori Johnson, articles editor. How-to market photos and personal experience in marketing photos. "Our readers expect advice in how-to articles." No submissions that do not deal with selling photos.

Buys 6 mss/year. Query. Length: 300-850 words. Pays $50-100 for unsolicited articles.
Columns/Departments: Jeri Engh, columns department editor. "We would welcome column ideas."
Length: 350 words. Pays $45-75.
Fillers: Facts. Buys 20/year. Length: 30-50 words. Pays $10.
Tips: "Columns are most open to freelancers. Bring an *expertise* on marketing photos or some other aspect of
aid to small business persons."

PHOTOVIDEO, Maclean Hunter, 5th Fl., 777 Bay St. Toronto, Ontario M5W 1A7 Canada. (416)596-5878.
Editor: Don Long. 50-75% freelance written. Prefers to work with published/established writers. A magazine
published 9 times a year for photo and video retailers, and professional photographers. "We seek to provide
information to the trade to help in making better business decisions—news, products, trends, how-to etc."
Circ. 16,500. Pays on acceptance. Publishes ms an average of 2-3 months after acceptance. Byline given.
Offers 50% kill fee. Buys first Canadian serial rights. Submit seasonal/holiday material 3 months in advance.
Simultaneous and photocopied submissions OK. Query for electronic submissions. Computer printout
submissions acceptable; prefers letter-quality to dot-matrix. Reports in 1 month on queries; 2 weeks on
manuscripts. Sample copy for 8½x11 SAE with IRCs.
Nonfiction: Professional how-to, interview/profile, opinion, photo feature (professionally oriented) and
technical. No non-Canadian submissions. Buys 20 mss/year. Query with published clips. Length 200-1,200
words. Pays $100-400 (Canadian) for assigned articles; pays $50-200 (Canadian) for unsolicited articles.
Sometimes pays the expenses of writers on assignment.
Photos: State availability of photos with submission. Reviews contact sheets. Offers $25-150
(Canadian)/photo. Captions, model releases, and identification of subjects required. Buys one-time rights.
Columns/Departments: News and Comment (regional, national and international events), 600-800 words;
and What's Coming Up (Calendar, minimum lead time of 2 months), 100 words. Query. Length: 100-800
words. Pays $25-100 (Canadian).
Tips: "Content is a carefully balanced package for both retailer and professional about photo and video. It
covers such areas as profiles of successful businesses, new technology, professional techniques, marketing and
merchandising ideas, advertising and promotion, business and association news, and economic and market
trends. Our readers have a broad range of skills and knowledge levels. Therefore, submissions must contain
sufficient background material for those less familiar with a topic, yet maintain the interest of more
experienced readers."

PROFESSIONAL PHOTOGRAPHER, The Business Magazine of Professional Photography,
Professional Photographers of America, Inc., 1090 Executive Way, Des Plaines IL 60018. (312)299-8161.
Editor: Alfred DeBat. 80% freelance written. Monthly magazine of professional portrait, wedding,
commercial, corporate and industrial photography. Describes the technical and business sides of professional
photography—successful photo techniques, money-making business tips, legal considerations, selling to new
markets, and descriptions of tough assignments and how completed. Circ. 36,000. Publishes ms an average of
6-9 months after acceptance. Byline given. Buys one-time rights. Submit seasonal/holiday material 6 months
in advance. Simultaneous queries, and photocopied and previously published submissions OK. Computer
printout submissions acceptable; prefers letter-quality to dot-matrix. Reports in 2 months. Sample copy $3.25;
free writer's guidelines.
Nonfiction: How-to. Professional photographic techniques: How I solved this difficult assignment, How I
increased my photo sales, How to buy a studio . . . run a photo business etc. Special issues include February:
Portrait Photography; April: Wedding Photography; May: Commercial Photography; and August: Industrial
Photography. Buys 8-10 ms/issue. Query. Length: 1,000-3,000 words. "We seldom pay, as most writers are
PP of A members and want recognition for their professional skills, publicity, etc."
Photos: State availability of photos. Reviews 35mm color transparencies and 8x10 prints. Captions and
model release required. Buys one-time rights.

THE RANGEFINDER, 1312 Lincoln Blvd., Santa Monica CA 90406. (213)451-8506. Editor: Arthur C.
Stern. Associate Editor: Carolyn Ryan. Monthly magazine; 80 pages. Emphasizes professional photography.
Circ. 55,000. Pays on publication. Publishes ms an average of 3 months after acceptance. Byline given. Buys
first North American serial rights. Phone queries OK. Submit seasonal material 4 months in advance.
Computer printout submissions acceptable; prefers letter-quality to dot-matrix. Reports in 6 weeks. Sample
copy $2.50; writer's guidelines for SASE.
Nonfiction: How-to (solve a photographic problem; such as new techniques in lighting, new poses or
set-ups); profile; and technical. "Articles should contain practical, solid information. Issues should be covered
in depth. Look thoroughly into the topic." No opinion or biographical articles. Buys 5-7 mss/issue. Query with
outline. Length: 800-1,200 words. Pays $60/published page.
Photos: State availability of photos with query. Captions preferred; model release required. Buys one-time
rights.
Tips: "Exhibit knowledge of photography. Introduce yourself with a well-written letter and a great story
idea."

STUDIO PHOTOGRAPHY, PTN Publishing Corp., 210 Crossways Park Dr., Woodbury NY 11797. (516)496-8000. Editor: Jenni Bidner. 85% freelance written. Prefers to work with published/established writers or experienced photographers with writing skills. Monthly magazine. Circ. 65,000. Pays on publication. Publishes ms an average of 6 months after acceptance. Not copyrighted. Buys first serial rights only. Submit seasonal/holiday material 5 months in advance. Computer printout submissions acceptable; prefers letter-quality to dot-matrix. Reports in 6 weeks.
Nonfiction: Interview, personal experience, photo feature, communication-oriented, technical, travel and business-oriented articles. Buys 5-6 mss/issue. Length: 1,000-3,000 words. Pays about $75/page.
Photos: State availability of photos with query. Photos and article in one package.
Tips: "We look for professional quality writing coupled with top-notch photographs. Submit photos with all articles. No original transparencies, only fine quality duplicates. Only people with definite ideas and a sense of who they are need apply for publication. Read the magazine and become familiar with it before submitting work. Write for editorial schedule and writer/photographer's guidelines."

TECHNICAL PHOTOGRAPHY, PTN Publishing Corp., 210 Crossways Park Dr., Woodbury NY 11797. Senior Editor: David A. Silverman. 60% freelance written. Eager to work with new/unpublished writers. Monthly magazine; 64 pages. Publication of the "on-staff (in-house) industrial, military and government still, video and AV professional who must produce (or know where to get) visuals of all kinds." Circ. 60,000. Pays on publication. Publishes ms an average of 3-6 months after acceptance. Buys first North American serial rights. Byline given. Computer printout submissions acceptable; prefers letter-quality or double-strike dot-matrix. Reports in 6 weeks. Sample copy $2; guidelines for #10 envelope and 1 first class stamp.
Nonfiction: How-to; interview; photo feature; profile (detailed stories about in-house operations); and technical. "All manuscripts must relate to industrial, military or government production of visuals." Buys 50 mss/year. Query. Length: "as long as needed to adequately cover the subject matter." Pays $150-200.
Photos: Offers no additional payment for photos purchased with ms. Query. Captions, model release, and subject identification required.

Plumbing, Heating, Air Conditioning and Refrigeration

CONTRACTOR MAGAZINE, 1301 S. Grove Ave., Barrington IL 60010. Executive Editor: Diana Amrein. 15% freelance written. For mechanical contractors and wholesalers. Semimonthly newsmagazine; 50 (11x15) pages. Circ. 46,100. Pays on publication. Publishes ms an average of 3 months after acceptance. Buys first serial rights. Photocopied submissions OK. No simultaneous submissions. Computer printout submissions acceptable. Reports in 1 month. Sample copy $3.
Nonfiction: Articles on materials, use, policies, and business methods of the air conditioning, heating, plumbing, piping, solar, energy management, and contracting industry. Topics covered include news reports, how-to, informational, interview, profile, think articles, expose, spot news, successful business operations, merchandising techniques and labor. Buys 12 mss/year. Query or submit complete ms. Pays $300 maximum. Pays expenses of writers on assignment.
Photos: 5x7 b&w glossies purchased with or without ms. Pays $10. Captions required.
Tips: "We are looking more for news than for features. We're backlogged with features."

DISTRIBUTOR, The Voice of Wholesaling, Technical Reporting Corp., Box 745, Wheeling IL 60090. (312)537-6460. Editorial Director: Steve Read. Managing Editor: James Butschli. 30% freelance written. Prefers to work with published/established writers. Bimonthly magazine on heating, ventilating, air conditioning and refrigeration. Editorial material shows "executive wholesalers how they can run better businesses and cope with personal and business problems." Circ. 10,000. Pays on publication. Publishes ms an average of 1 month after acceptance. Byline sometimes given. Buys one-time rights. Submit seasonal/holiday material 3 months in advance. "We want material exclusive to the field (industry)." Photocopied submissions OK. Query for information on electronic submissions. Computer printout submissions acceptable; prefers letter-quality to dot-matrix. Reports in 1 month. Sample copy $4.

Nonfiction: How-to (run a better business, cope with problems); and interview/profile (the wholesalers). No flippant or general approaches. Buys 6 mss/year. Query with or without published clips or send complete ms. Length: 1,000-2,000 words. Pays $100-200 (10¢ a word). Sometimes pays the expenses of writers on assignment.

Photos: State availability of photos or send photos with query or ms. Pays $5 minimum. Captions and identification of subjects required.

Tips: "Know the industry—come up with a different angle on an industry subject (one we haven't dealt with in a long time). Wholesale ideas and top-quality business management articles are most open to freelancers."

DOMESTIC ENGINEERING MAGAZINE, Construction Industry Press, 385 N. York Rd., Elmhurst IL 60126. Editor: Stephen J. Shafer. Managing Editor: David J. Hanks. 15% freelance written. Prefers to work with published/established writers. Monthly magazine; 100 pages. Emphasizes plumbing, heating, air conditioning and piping for contractors, and for mechanical contractors in these specialties. Gives information on management, marketing and merchandising. Circ. 40,000. Pays on acceptance. Publishes ms an average of 6 months after acceptance. Buys all rights. Simultaneous, photocopied and previously published submissions OK. Computer printout submissions acceptable; prefers letter-quality to dot-matrix. Reports in 1 month. Sample copy $10.

Nonfiction: How-to (some technical in industry areas). Expose, interview, profile, personal experience, photo feature and technical articles are written on assignment only and should be about management, marketing and merchandising for plumbing and mechanical contracting businessmen. Buys 12 mss/year. Query. Pays $25 minimum. Sometimes pays the expenses of writers on assignment.

Photos: State availability of photos. Pays $10 minimum for b&w prints (reviews contact sheets) and color transparencies.

EXPORT, 386 Park Ave. S., New York NY 10016. Editor: R. Weingarten. For importers and distributors in 183 countries who handle hardware, air conditioning and refrigeration equipment and related consumer hardlines. Bimonthly magazine; 60-80 pages in English and Spanish editions. Circ. 38,500. Buys first rights and second (reprint) rights to material originally published elsewhere. Byline given. Buys about 10 mss/year. Pays on acceptance. Publishes ms an average of 5 months after acceptance. Reports in 1 month. Query.

Nonfiction: News stories of products and merchandising of air conditioning and refrigeration equipment, hardware and related consumer hardlines. Informational, how-to, interview, profile and successful business operations. Length: 1,000-3,000 words. Pays $300 maximum.

Tips: "One of the best ways to break in here is with a story originating outside the U.S. or Canada. Our major interest is in new products and new developments—but they must be available and valuable to overseas buyers. We also like company profile stories. Departments and news stories are staff-written."

‡FLORIDA FORUM, FRSA Services Corp., Drawer 4850, Winter Park FL 32793. (305)671-3772. Editor: Gerald Dykhuisen. 10% freelance written. Eager to work with new/unpublished writers. Monthly magazine covering the roofing, sheet metal and air conditioning industries. Circ. 9,800. Pays on publication. Publishes ms an average of 2 months after acceptance. Byline given. Buys one-time rights. Submit seasonal/holiday material 2 months in advance. Simultaneous queries, and simultaneous, photocopied, and previously published submissions OK. Electronic submissions OK on Hewlett Packard 3000 or Apple Macintosh. Computer printout submissions acceptable; prefers letter-quality to dot-matrix. Reports in 2 weeks. Free sample copy and writer's guidelines.

Nonfiction: General interest, historical/nostalgic, humor, interview/profile, new product, opinion, personal experience and technical. Buys 25 mss/year. Send complete ms. Length: open. Pays variable rates.

Photos: Send photos with ms. Pays variable rates for b&w prints.

Columns/Departments: Buys 12/year. Send complete ms. Length: open. Pays variable rates.

HEATING/PIPING/AIR CONDITIONING, 2 Illinois Center, Chicago IL 60601. (312)861-0880. Editor: Robert T. Korte. Monthly. Buys all rights. Pays on publication. Query. Reports in 2 weeks.

Nonfiction: Uses engineering and technical articles covering design, installation, operation, maintenance, etc., of heating, piping and air conditioning systems in industrial plants and large buildings. Length: 3,000-4,000 words maximum. Pays $60/printed page.

Tips: "Query to have facts and an in-depth analysis of unique approaches. Be able to communicate with top level engineers first. Non-engineering trained freelancers really have very little chance of acceptance."

HEATING, PLUMBING, AIR CONDITIONING, 1450 Don Mills Rd., Don Mills, Ontario M3B 2X7 Canada. (416)445-6641. Editor: Ronald H. Shuker. 20% freelance written. Monthly. For mechanical contractors; plumbers; warm air and hydronic heating, refrigeration, ventilation, air conditioning and insulation contractors; wholesalers; architects; consulting and mechanical engineers who are in key management or specifying positions in the plumbing, heating, air conditioning and refrigeration industries in Canada. Circ. 14,500. Pays on publication. Publishes ms an average of 3 months after acceptance. Computer printout submissions acceptable; prefers letter-quality to dot-matrix. Reports in 2 months. For a prompt reply, "enclose a sheet on which is typed a statement either approving or rejecting the suggested article which can either be checked off, or a quick answer written in and signed and returned." Free sample copy.

Nonfiction: News, technical, business management and "how-to" articles that will inform, educate, motivate and help readers to be more efficient and profitable who design, manufacture, install, sell, service, maintain or supply all mechanical components and systems in residential, commercial, institutional and industrial installations across Canada. Length: 1,000-1,500 words. Pays 10-20¢/word. Sometimes pays expenses of writers on assignment.

Photos: Photos purchased with ms. Prefers 4x5 or 5x7 glossies.

Tips: "Topics must relate directly to the day-to-day activities of *HPAC* readers in Canada. Must be detailed, with specific examples, quotes from specific people or authorities—show depth. We specifically want material from other parts of Canada besides southern Ontario. Not really interested in material from U.S. unless specifically related to Canadian readers' concerns. We primarily want articles that show *HPAC* readers how they can increase their sales and business step-by-step based on specific examples of what others have done."

SNIPS MAGAZINE, 407 Mannheim Rd., Bellwood IL 60104. (312)544-3870. Editor: Nick Carter. 2% freelance written. Monthly. For sheet metal, warm air heating, ventilating, air conditioning and roofing contractors. Publishes ms an average of 3 months after acceptance. Buys all rights. "Write for detailed list of requirements before submitting any work."

Nonfiction: Material should deal with information about contractors who do sheet metal, warm air heating, air conditioning, ventilation and roofing work; also about successful advertising campaigns conducted by these contractors and the results. Length: "prefers stories to run less than 1,000 words unless on special assignment." Pays 5¢ each for first 500 words, 2¢ each for additional word.

Photos: Pays $2 each for small snapshot pictures, $4 each for usable 8x10 pictures.

WOOD 'N ENERGY, Energy Publications, Inc., Box 2008, Laconia NH 03247. (603)528-4285. Editor: Jason Perry. 10% freelance written. Works with a small number of new/unpublished writers each year. Monthly magazine covering wood, coal and solar heating (residential). "*Wood 'n Energy* is mailed to retailers, distributors and manufacturers of wood, coal and solar heating equipment in the U.S. and Canada. A majority of our readers are small businessmen who need help in running their businesses and want to learn secrets to prospering in a field that has seen better days when oil embargoes were daily happenings." Circ. 32,000. Pays on publication. Publishes ms an average of 2 months after acceptance. Byline given. Buys one-time rights and all rights. Submit seasonal/holiday material 4 months in advance. Simultaneous queries OK. Electronic submissions OK if compatible with TRS-80, Model III or IV, but requires hard copy also. Computer printout submissions acceptable; prefers letter-quality to dot-matrix. Reports in 2 weeks. Sample copy $2.50.

Nonfiction: Interview/profile (of stove dealers, manufacturers, others); photo feature (of energy stores); and technical (nuts and bolts of stove design and operation). Special issue includes Buyers Guide/Retailers Handbook (annual issue with retail marketing articles), "how to run your business," accounting. "The best times of year for freelancers are in our fall issue (our largest) and also in February and March." No "how wonderful renewable energy is" and experiences with stoves. "This is a *trade* book." Buys 25 mss/year. Query with or without published clips or send complete ms. Pays $25-300. Sometimes pays expenses of writers on assignment.

Photos: State availability of photos or send photos with query or ms. Pays $35 minimum for b&w contact sheets; $125 maximum for color contact sheets. Identification of subjects required. Buys one-time rights.

Columns/Departments: Reports (energy news; potpourri of current incentives, happenings); Regulations (safety and standard news); and Retailers Corner (tips on running a retail shop). "We are also looking for freelancers who could serve in our 'network' around the country. If there's a law passed regulating wood-stove emissions in their town, for example, they could send us a clip and/or rewrite the story. These pay $50 or so, depending on the clip. Contact editor on an individual basis (over the phone is OK) for a green light." Query with or without published clips. Length: 150-500 words. Pays $35-150.

Tips: "Short, hot articles on retailers (500 words and photographs) are desperately needed. We're looking for serious business articles. Freelancers who know the ins and outs of running a business have an excellent shot at being published."

WOODHEAT '88, Energy Publications, Inc., Box 2008, Laconia NH 03247. (603)528-4285. Editor: Jason Perry. 40% freelance written. An annual buyer's guide and sourcebook on wood heat, published in July. Circ. 175,000. Pays on variable schedule. Publishes ms an average of 6 months after acceptance. Byline given. Offers variable kill fee. Buys variable rights. Simultaneous queries and submissions OK. Computer printout submissions acceptable; prefers letter-quality to dot-matrix. Reports in 1 month.

Nonfiction: How-to (installation, etc.); interview/profile (of those in the field, retailers, consumers); new product (new wood energy products); photo feature (of stove installations and/or energy efficient homes); and technical (details on buying and installing). No personal experiences with wood stoves. Buys 5-8 mss/year. Query. Length: 100-2,550 words. Pays $50-500. Pays expenses of writers on assignment.

Photos: State availability of photos with query or ms. Uses all types. Pays $35-250. Captions, model release, and identification of subjects required. Buys variable rights.

Columns/Departments: Reports (potpourri of energy news, wood heat news). Buys 0-10 mss/year. Query. Length: 150-400 words. Pays $35-100.

Tips: "Articles in the magazine must appeal to both current owners and buyers. Personality is a plus in any article; we'd like features on someone who has invented a better burning stove or someone who is handcrafting masonry fireplaces, for example. Article ideas are formulated by mid-January, so query letters should be on hand at that time. Be specific with story ideas. Shorter articles on a wide range of energy issues—in a section called Reports—can be accepted until May. These must be accompanied by a photo. Writing should be spicy, interesting and short. All areas are open to freelancers. We find that freelancers score better with articles with local slants. With 15 million households having wood stoves, there are bound to be many stories to tell."

Printing

GRAPHIC ARTS MONTHLY, Cahners Publishing Co., 875 Third Ave., New York NY 10022. (212)605-9574. Editor: Roger Ynostroza. Managing Editor: Peter Johnston. 15% freelance written. Prefers to work with published/established writers. A monthly magazine covering the printing industry. Circ. 91,000. Pays on publication. Publishes ms an average of 3 months after acceptance. Byline given. Buys all rights. Submit seasonal/holiday material 3 months in advance. Simultaneous queries OK. Computer printout submissions acceptable; prefers letter-quality to dot-matrix. Reports in 1 month. Free sample copy and writer's guidelines for SAE and 2 first class postage stamps.

Nonfiction: New product, photo feature and technical. Buys 15 mss/year. Query. Pays 10¢/word.

Photos: State availability of photos with query or ms. Captions required.

Fillers: Cartoons. Buys 50/year. Pays $15 minimum.

Tips: "The writer may have a better chance of breaking in at our publication with short articles and fillers since a very technical and specialized field means that major features need to be tailored specifically to the audience while shorter pieces can be more general. The most frequent mistakes made by writers in completing an article for us are that topic and writing style are usually much too general to be of direct benefit to our readership. Many freelance writers seem to want to adapt one topic to several different fields and publications. Also, case-study stories are often success-story descriptions that benefit and interest only the subject company, not the bulk of the readership."

HIGH VOLUME PRINTING, Innes Publishing Co., Box 368, Northbrook IL 60062. (312)564-5940. Editor: Dan Witte. 20% freelance written. Eager to work with new/unpublished writers. Bimonthly magazine for book, magazine printers, large commercial printing plants with 20 or more employees. Aimed at telling the reader what he needs to know to print more efficiently and more profitably. Circ. 26,000. Pays on publication. Publishes ms an average of 9 months after acceptance. Byline given. Buys first and second serial rights. Simultaneous queries OK. Query for electronic submissions. Computer printout submissions acceptable. Reports in 2 weeks. Writer's guidelines, sample articles provided.

Nonfiction: How-to (printing production techniques); new product (printing, auxiliary equipment, plant equipment); photo feature (case histories featuring unique equipment); technical (printing product research and development); shipping; and publishing distribution methods. No product puff. Buys 12 mss/year. Query. Length: 700-3,000 words. Pays $50-300. Sometimes pays the expenses of writers on assignment.

Photos: Send photos with ms. Pays $25-100 for 3x5 and larger b&w prints; $25-150 for any size color transparencies and prints. Captions, model release, and identification of subjects required.

Tips: "Feature articles covering actual installations and industry trends are most open to freelancers. Be familiar with the industry, spend time in the field, and attend industry meetings and trade shows where equipment is displayed. We would also like to receive clips and shorts about printing mergers."

IN-PLANT PRINTER AND ELECTRONIC PUBLISHER, (formerly *In-Plant Printer*), Innes Publishing, Box 368, Northbrook IL 60062. (312)564-5940. Editor: Rod Peichowski. 20% freelance written. Works with a small number of new/unpublished writers each year. Bimonthly magazine covering in-house print shops and electronic publishing. Circ. 38,000. Pays on publication. Publishes ms an average of 3 months after acceptance. Byline "usually" given. Buys first and second rights. Submit seasonal/holiday material 4 months in advance. Query for electronic submissions. Computer printout submissions OK; prefers letter-quality to dot-matrix. Reports in 2 weeks. Free sample copy and writer's guidelines.

Nonfiction: Book excerpts, how-to and case history. "More electronic printing articles, we need experts in this area to write technical articles. No nebulous management advice; undetailed stories lacking in concrete information. No human interest material." Buys 18 mss/year. Query or send complete ms. Length: 1,500-3,000 words. Pays $100-250. Pays expenses of writers on assignment.

Photos: Send photos with ms. "No additional payment is made for photos with ms, unless negotiated." Captions required. Buys all rights.

Tips: "We are looking for case studies of in-plants that incorporate electronic publishing."

IN-PLANT REPRODUCTIONS & ELECTRONIC PUBLISHING, North American Publishing Co., 401 N. Broad St., Philadelphia PA 19108. (215)238-5300. Editor: Maria Martino. Associate Editor: Denise Wallace. 40% freelance written. Prefers to work with published/established writers. Works with a small number of new/unpublished writers each year; eager to work with new/unpublished writers. Monthly magazine about in-plant printing management and electronic publishing for printing departments in business, government, education and industry. These graphic arts facilities include art, composition, camera, platemaking, press, and finishing equipment, xerographic and other business communications systems. Circ. 40,000. Pays on publication. Publishes ms an average 6 months after acceptance. Byline given. Buys first North American serial rights or all rights. Phone queries OK. Computer printout submissions acceptable; prefers letter-quality to dot-matrix. Reports in 1 month. Sample copy $5.

Nonfiction: Interview, profile, how-to and technical. Buys 4 mss/issue. Query. Length: 500-2,500 words. Pays $75-200. Sometimes pays the expenses of writers on assignment.

Tips: "We would like to receive articles on how to justify equipment and how to market printing services."

INSTANT AND SMALL COMMERCIAL PRINTER, Innes Publishing, 425 Huehl Rd., Bldg. 11B, Northbrook IL 60062. (312)564-5940. Editor: Daniel Witte. Bimonthly magazine covering the instant/retail and smaller commercial printing industry for owners/operators of print shops. "We are primarily concerned with ways to be successful, ways to make lots of money, new markets and processes, technological innovations. Basically we try to focus on the needs and concerns of the entrepreneurial type." Circ. 24,000. Pays on publication. Byline given. Buys first North American serial rights with option for future use. Submit seasonal/holiday material 6 months in advance. Photocopied and previously published submissions OK. Reports in 2 weeks on queries; 1 month on mss. Sample copy $3; free writer's guidelines.

Nonfiction: Book excerpts (primarily on small business-related or graphic arts-related topics); general interest (anything about marketing, promotion, management); how-to (focus on more efficient ways to do everyday things printers do: and technical, business, financial); interview/profile (case histories of successful printers with angle on unique or special services); personal experience (any small printer who has tried marketing some new or unique service, successful or not); technical (any printing-related topic). Buys 18-25 mss/year. Query with or without published clips or send complete ms. Pays $200 maximum.

Photos: State availability of photos. Pays $50 maximum for b&w contact sheets, slides or 3x5 prints; $100 maximum for color contact sheets, slides or 3x5 prints. Captions, model release and identification of subjects required. Buys all rights.

Columns/Departments: Promotion—about advertising/promotion techniques used by instant printers (with samples), and Computers—information about computers and software for instant printers. Buys 12 mss/year. Query with or without published clips or send complete ms. Length: 1,000 words maximum. Pays $75 maximum.

Fillers: Clippings, anecdotes, newsbreaks, and printing or marketing hints. Pays $10 maximum.

Tips: "I would suggest reading copies of our magazine, as well as related graphic arts magazines, for style."

PLAN AND PRINT, 9931 Franklin Ave., Box 879, Franklin Park IL 60131. (312)671-5356. Editor-in-Chief: Janet A. Thill. 50% freelance written. Prefers to work with published/established writers. Works with a small number of new/unpublished writers each year; eager to work with new/unpublished writers. Monthly magazine for computer-aided design users, commercial reproduction companies, in-plant reproduction, printing, drafting and design departments of business and industry and architects. Circ. 30,000. Pays on publication. Publishes ms an average of 6 months after acceptance. Buys all rights. Byline given. Submit seasonal/holiday material 6 months in advance. Computer printout submissions acceptable; no dot-matrix. Reports in 2 weeks. Free sample copy and writer's guidelines.

Nonfiction: How-to (how certain problems may have been solved; new methods of doing certain kinds of reprographics and/or design/drafting/computer-aided design work); and technical (must relate to industry). "Strong interest in computer-aided design." Buys 60 mss/year. Query with published clips. Length: 250-5,000 words. Pays $75-400. Sometimes pays expenses of writers on assignment.

Photos: State availability of photos with query. Pays $5-10 for 8x10 b&w glossy prints. Captions and model release required. Buys all rights.

Columns/Departments: Open to suggestions for new columns/departments.

Poetry: Light verse related to the industry. Buys 6/year. Length: 4-12 lines. Pays $8 maximum.

‡PRINT & GRAPHICS, Box 25498, Washington DC 20007. (202)337-6815. Editor: Geoff Lindsay. 10% freelance written. Eager to work with new/unpublished writers. Monthly tabloid of the commercial printing industry for owners and executives of graphic arts firms. Circ. 10,000. Pays on publication. Publishes ms an average of 2 months after acceptance. Byline given. Buys one-time rights. Simultaneous queries, and simultaneous, photocopied, and previously published submissions OK. Electronic submissions OK via standard protocols, but requires hard copy also. Computer printout submissions acceptable; prefers letter-quality to dot-matrix. Reports in 1 week. Free sample copy.
Nonfiction: Book excerpts, historical/nostalgic, how-to, interview/profile, new product, opinion, personal experience, photo feature and technical. "All articles should relate to graphic arts management." No opinion pieces. Buys 20 mss/year. Query with published clips. Length: 1,000-2,000 words. Pays $50-150.
Photos: State availability of photos. Pays $20-35 for 5x7 b&w prints. Captions and identification of subjects required.

PRINTING VIEWS, For the Midwest Printer, Midwest Publishing, 8328 N. Lincoln, Skokie IL 60077. (312)539-8540. Editor: Ed Schwenn. 10% freelance written. Prefers to work with published/established writers. Monthly magazine about printing and graphic arts for Midwest commercial printers, typographers, platemakers, engravers and other trade people. Circ. 15,000. Average issue includes 2-3 features. Pays on publication. Publishes ms an average of 2 months after acceptance. Byline given. Buys one-time rights. Phone queries OK. Reports in 2 weeks. Sample copy $1.50.
Nonfiction: Interview (possibly with graphic arts personnel); new product (in graphic arts in a Midwest plant); management/sales success in Midwest printing plant; and technical (printing equipment). Buys 6 feature mss/year. Query with clips of previously published work. "We will entertain query letters; no unsolicited manuscripts." Length: 2-9 typed pages. Pays $200-250 for assigned mss only.
Photos: State availability of photos. Reviews b&w contact sheets. Offers additional payment for photos accepted with ms. Captions preferred. Buys one-time rights.

QUICK PRINTING, The Information Source for Commercial Copyshops and Printshops, Coast Publishing, 3255 South U.S. 1, Ft. Pierce FL 33482. (305)465-9450. Publisher: Robert Schweiger. Editor: Douglas E. Roorbach. 50% freelance written. A monthly magazine covering the quick printing industry. "Our articles tell quick printers how they can be more profitable. We want figures to illustrate points made." Circ. 28,000+. Pays on acceptance. Publishes ms an average of 4 months after acceptance. Byline given. Buys first North American serial rights, all rights. Submit seasonal/holiday material 6 months in advance. Photocopied submissions OK, if identified as such. Rarely uses previously published submissions. Query for electronic submissions. Computer printout submissions acceptable; prefers letter-quality to dot-matrix. Reports in 2 weeks. Sample copy for $3 and 9x12 SAE with $1.75 postage; writer's guidelines for #10 SAE with 1 first class stamp.
Nonfiction: How-to (on marketing products better or accomplishing more with equipment); new product; opinion (on the quick printing industry); personal experience (from which others can learn); technical (on printing). No generic business articles, or articles on larger printing applications. Buys 50 mss/year. Send complete ms. Length: 500-1,500 words. Pays $75.
Photos: State availability of photos with submission. Reviews transparencies and prints. Offers no payment for photos. Captions and identification of subjects required.
Columns/Departments: Viewpoint/Counterpoint (opinion on the industry); QP Profile (shop profiles with a marketing slant); and Management (how to handle employees and/or business strategies), all 500-1,500 words. Buys 10 mss/year. Send complete ms. Pays $75.
Tips: "The use of electronic publishing systems by quick printers is of increasing interest. Show a knowledge of the industry. Try visiting your local quick printer for an afternoon to get to know about us. When your articles make a point, back it up with examples, statistics, and dollar figures. We need good material in all areas, but avoid the shop profile. Technical articles are most needed, but they must be accurate. No puff pieces for a certain industry supplier."

SCREEN PRINTING, 407 Gilbert Ave., Cincinnati OH 45202. (513)421-2050. Editor: Susan Venell. 30% freelance written. Works with a small number of new/unpublished writers each year. Monthly magazine; 150 pages. For the screen printing industry, including screen printers (commercial, industrial and captive shops), suppliers and manufacturers, and ad agencies and allied professions. Circ. 12,000. Pays on publication. Publishes ms an average of 3-4 months after acceptance. Byline given. Buys all rights. Query for electronic submissions. Computer printout submissions acceptable; prefers letter-quality to dot-matrix. Reporting time varies. Free writer's guidelines.
Nonfiction: "Since the screen printing industry covers a broad range of applications and overlaps other fields in the graphic arts, it's necessary that articles be of a significant contribution, preferably to a specific area of screen printing. Subject matter is fairly open, with preference given to articles on administration or technology; trends and developments. We try to give a good sampling of technical business and management articles; articles about unique operations. We also publish special features and issues on important subjects, such as

material shortages, new markets and new technology breakthroughs. While most of our material is nitty-gritty, we appreciate a writer who can take an essentially dull subject and encourage the reader to read on through concise, factual, 'flairful' and creative, expressive writing. Interviews are published after consultation with and guidance from the editor." Interested in stories on unique approaches by some shops. No general, promotional treatment of individual companies. Buys 6-10 unsolicited mss/year. Length: 1,500-3,500 words. Pays minimum of $150 for major features. Sometimes pays the expenses of writers on assignment.

Photos: Cover photos negotiable; b&w or color. Published material becomes the property of the magazine.

Tips: "If the author has a working knowledge of screen printing, assignments are more readily available. General management articles are rarely used."

THE TYPOGRAPHER, Typographers International Association, Suite 101, 2262 Hall Pl. NW, Washington DC 20007. (202)965-3400. Contact: Editor. 10% freelance written. Eager to work with new/unpublished writers. Bimonthly tabloid of the commercial typesetting industry for owners and executives of typesetting firms. Circ. 10,000. Pays on publication. Publishes ms an average of 2 months after acceptance. Byline given. Buys one-time rights. Simultaneous queries, and simultaneous, photocopied, and previously published submissions OK. Query for electronic submissions. Computer printout submissions acceptable; no dot-matrix. Reports in 1 week. Free sample copy.

Nonfiction: Book excerpts, historical/nostalgic, how-to, interview/profile, new product, opinion, personal experience, photo feature and technical. "All articles should relate to typesetting management." No opinion pieces. Buys 20 mss/year. Query with published clips. Length: 1,000-2,000 words. Pays $50-150. Sometimes pays the expenses of writers on assignment.

Photos: State availability of photos. Pays $20-35 for 5x7 b&w prints. Captions and identification of subjects required.

Real Estate

AREA DEVELOPMENT MAGAZINE, 525 Northern Blvd., Great Neck NY 11021. (516)829-8990. Editor-in-Chief: Tom Bergeron. 40% freelance written. Prefers to work with published/established writers. Emphasizes corporate facility planning and site selection for industrial chief executives worldwide. Monthly magazine; 110-190 pages. Circ. 33,000. Pays when edited. Publishes ms an average of 2 months after acceptance. Buys first rights only. Byline given. Photocopied submissions OK. Computer printout submissions acceptable; prefers letter-quality to dot-matrix. Reports in 1-3 weeks. Free sample copy and writer's guidelines.

Nonfiction: How-to (case histories of companies; experiences in site selection and all other aspects of corporate facility planning); historical (if it deals with corporate facility planning); interview (corporate executives and industrial developers); and related areas of site selection and facility planning such as taxes, labor, government, energy, architecture and finance. Buys 8-10 mss/yr. Query. Pays $30-40/ms page; rates for illustrations depend on quality and printed size. Sometimes pays the expenses of writers on assignment.

Photos: State availability of photos with query. Prefer 8x10 or 5x7 b&w glossy prints. Captions preferred.

Tips: "Articles must be accurate, objective (no puffery) and useful to our industrial executive readers. Avoid any discussion of the merits or disadvantages of any particular areas or communities. Writers should realize we serve an intelligent and busy readership—they should avoid 'cute' allegories and get right to the point."

BUSINESS FACILITIES, Business Facilities Publishing Co., 121 Monmouth St., Box 2060, Red Bank NJ 07701. (201)842-7433. Editor: Eric Peterson. Managing Editor: Dora Hatras. 20% freelance written. Prefers to work with published/established writers. A monthly magazine covering economic development and commercial and industrial real estate. "Our audience consists of corporate site selectors and real estate people; our editorial coverage is aimed at providing news and trends on the plant location and corporate expansion field." Circ. 32,000. Pays on publication. Publishes ms an average of 3 months after acceptance. Byline given. Buys all rights. Photocopied and previously published submissions OK. Computer printout submissions acceptable; prefers letter-quality to dot-matrix. Reports in 2 weeks. Free sample copy and writer's guidelines.

Nonfiction: General interest, how-to, interview/profile and personal experience. No news shorts and no clippings; feature material only. Buys 12-15 mss/year. Query. Length: 1,000-3,000 words. Pays $200-1,000 for assigned articles, pays $200-600 for unsolicited articles. Sometimes pays the expenses of writers on assignment.

Photos: State availability of photos with submission. Reviews contact sheets, negatives, transparencies and 8x10 prints. Payment negotiable. Captions and identification of subjects required. Buys one-time rights.

Tips: "First, remember that our reader is a corporate executive responsible for his company's expansion and/or relocation decisions and our writers have to get inside that person's head in order to provide him with something that's helpful in his decision-making process. And second, the biggest turnoff is a telephone query. We're too busy to accept them and must require that all queries be put in writing. Submit major feature articles only; all news departments, fillers, etc., are staff prepared. A writer should be aware that our style is not necessarily dry and business-like. We tend to be more upbeat and a writer should look for that aspect of our approach.''

CD PUBLICATIONS, Community Development Services, Inc., Suite 100, 8555 16th St., Silver Spring MD 20903. (301)588-6380. Managing Editor: Simpson Lawson. Newsletters on urban issues. Pays on publication. Byline not given. Buys one-time rights. Writer's guidelines for #10 SAE with 1 first class stamp.
Nonfiction: Only clips on specified urban issues accepted. Buys 500 clips/year. Query. Pays $3.25/clip used.

FINANCIAL FREEDOM REPORT, 1831 Fort Union Blvd., Salt Lake City UT 84121. (801)943-1280. Chairman of the Board: Mark O. Haroldsen. Managing Editor: Carolyn Tice. 25% freelance written. Eager to work with new/unpublished writers. For "professional and nonprofessional investors, and would-be investors in real estate—real estate brokers, insurance companies, investment planners, truck drivers, housewives, doctors, architects, contractors, etc. The magazine's content is presently expanding to interest and inform the readers about other ways to put their money to work for them." Monthly magazine; 72 pages. Circ. 50,000. Pays on publication. Publishes ms an average of 3 months after acceptance. Buys all rights. Phone queries OK. Simultaneous submissions OK. Query for electronic submissions. Computer printout submissions acceptable; prefers letter-quality to dot-matrix. Reports in 2 weeks. Sample copy $3; free writer's guidelines.
Nonfiction: How-to (find real estate bargains, finance property, use of leverage, managing property, developing market trends, goal setting, motivational); and interviews (success stories of those who have relied on own initiative and determination in real estate market or related fields). Buys 25 unsolicited mss/year. Query with clips of published work or submit complete ms. Length: 1,500-3,000 words. "If the topic warranted a two- or three-parter, we would consider it." Pays 5-10¢/word. Sometimes pays the expenses of writers on assignment.
Photos: Send photos with ms. Uses 8x10 b&w matte prints. Offers no additional payment for photos accepted with ms. Captions required.
Tips: "We would like to find several specialized writers in our field of real estate investments. A writer would need to have had some hands-on experience in the real estate field."

‡JOURNAL OF PROPERTY MANAGEMENT, Institute of Real Estate Management, Suite 600, 430 N. Michigan Ave., Chicago IL 60611. (312)661-1930. 15% freelance written. Bimonthly magazine covering real estate management and development. "The *Journal* has a feature/information slant designed to educate readers in the application of new techniques and to keep them abreast of current industry trends." Circ. 15,000. Pays on acceptance. Publishes ms an average of 3 months after acceptance. Byline sometimes given. Buys all rights. Simultaneous submissions OK. Query for electronic submissions. Computer printout submissions OK; no dot-matrix. Reports in 6 weeks on queries; 3 weeks on mss. Free sample copy and writer's guidelines.
Nonfiction: How-to, interview and technical (building systems/computers. "No non-real estate subjects personality or company, humor." Buys 8-12 mss/year. Query with published clips. Length: 1,500-4,000 words. Pays $100-750 for assigned articles; pays $50-750 for unsolicited articles. Pays in contributor's copies "if so agreed." Sometimes pays the expenses of writers on assignment.
Photos: State availability of photos with submission. Reviews contact sheets. Offers no additonal payment for photos accepted with ms. Model releases and identification of subjects required. Buys one-time rights.
Columns/Departments: Karen McManus, editor. Insurance Insights; Tax Corner; Investment Corner and Legal Corner. Buys 6-8 mss/year. Query. Length: 750-1,500 words. Pays $50-350.

PROFIT, An Investment Opportunity Journal, 13410 East Cypress Forest, Houston TX 77070. (713)890-4329. Facsimile (713)955-2684. Publisher: Wm. Barrie Moore. Editor: Patricia A. Bina. 80% freelance written. Eager to work with new/unpublished writers. A bimonthly tabloid covering industrial, investment and commercial real estate. Circ. 20,000. Pays on publication. Publishes ms an average of 2 months after acceptance. Byline given. Offers 50% kill fee. Buys first North American serial rights, one-time rights, second serial (reprint) rights or simultaneous rights. Submit seasonal/holiday material 2 months in advance. Simultaneous, photocopied and previously published submissions OK. Query for electronic submissions. Computer printout submissions acceptable; prefers letter-quality to dot-matrix. Reports in 2-3 weeks. Sample copy $2 with 9x12 SAE. Writer's guidelines for #10 SASE.
Nonfiction: Book excerpts; essays; historical/nostalgic (real estate); how-to (syndicate investment properties); humor (real estate related); interview/profile (real estate, financial); new product (real estate, financial); personal experience (real estate related); photo feature (development or real estate related) and technical (financial, real estate or computer). Buys 60 mss/year. Send complete ms. Length: 500-3,500 words. Pays $25-300.
Photos: Send photos with submission. Reviews contact sheets and 5x7 or 8x10 prints. Offers $5-25/photo. Captions, model releases and identification of subjects required. Buys one-time rights.

Columns/Departments: Tax Shelters, Estate Building, Tax Havens, Tax-Deferred Exchange, Financing, Syndicating and Developing Desk-Top Publishing Advances. Submissions should be "well-documented and written for the highly sophisticated investor or real estate professional." Buys 100 mss/year. Send complete ms. Length: 600-1,200 words. Pays $30-100.

Fiction: Adventure, experimental, historical, horror, humorous, mainstream, mystery, science fiction, serialized novel and suspense. Stories must be themed around real estate subjects and characters. Buys 10-12 mss/year. Query. Length: 600-3,000 words. Pays $25-250. "Please submit asking price with all articles, etc."

Poetry: Avant-garde, free verse, haiku, light verse and traditional. (All real estate oriented). Buys 20-30 poems/year. Submit maximum 5 poems. Length: 4-80 lines. Pays $5-25.

Fillers: Anecdotes, facts, gags to be illustrated by cartoonist, and short humor. All real estate and/or investment related. Buys 100/year. Length: 10-200 words. Pays $5-25.

Tips: "We are looking for continuing writers and columnists. The writer should offer challenging and creative fresh ideas for real estate professionals and investors. Our readers are highly sophisticated professionals who know the basics. Think of your work as being on the graduate level. Make sure your work is well documented and up-to-date. Each column or article should tackle one topic and guide the reader from starting premise to conclusion. Be positive. Be active. Be aggressive. As a new publication, we are looking for a wide scope of input from a broad national base. Our primary areas cover real estate syndication, developing, tax shelters, financial planning, broker estate building, international real estate, creative finance, investment counseling, new technology for real estate, new investment areas, etc."

‡SKYLINES, News of the Office Building Industry, Building Owners and Managers Association International, 1250 Aye St. NW, Washington DC 20005. (202)289-7000. Editor: Kathryn N. Hamilton. 30% freelance written. Prefers to work with published/established writers. A tabloid for the office building industry focusing on real estate financing, building operation, leasing, and marketing strategies. Circ. 6,100. Pays 30 days after acceptance. Byline not given. Publication not copyrighted. Buys one-time rights. Submit seasonal/holiday material 2 months in advance. Query for electronic submissions. Computer printout submissions OK. Free sample copy.

Nonfiction: Expose, interview/profile, opinion and technical. Plans special issue on financing trends, tenant relations, rehab and remodelling and working with architects. No promotional articles that hype on company or product. Buys 6 mss/year. Query. Length: 500-2,000 words. Pays $1,000 maximum. Sometimes pays the expenses of writers on assignment.

Photos: State availability of photos with submission. Reviews contact sheets. Offers no additional payment for photos accepted with ms. Captions and identification of subjects required. Buys one-time rights.

Tips: "We would like to receive information on exaction fees, the growth of suburban downtowns and energy management."

SOUTHWEST REAL ESTATE NEWS, Communication Channels, Inc., Suite 240, 18601 LBJ Freeway, Mesquite TX 75150. (214)270-6651. Associate Publisher/Editor: Jim Mitchell. Managing Editor: Sheryl Roberts. 40% freelance written. Prefers to work with published/established writers. Monthly tabloid newspaper about commercial and industrial real estate for professional real estate people, including realtors, developers, mortgage bankers, corporate real estate executives, architects, contractors and brokers. Circ. 17,000. Average issue includes 4 columns, 20-50 short news items, 2-5 special articles and 2-10 departments. Pays on publication. Publishes ms an average of 2 months after acceptance. Byline given. Buys all rights. Phone queries OK. Submit seasonal/holiday material 2 months in advance. Photocopied submissions OK. Computer printout submissions acceptable; dot-matrix only if it has ascenders and descenders. Prefers letter-quality. Reports in 4-6 weeks. Sample copy and writer's guidelines for 12x16½ SAE with 50¢ postage.

Nonfiction: "We're interested in hearing from writers in major cities in the states that we cover, which are TX, OK, CO, NM, LA, AZ, AR, NV and CA. We are particularly interested in writers with newspaper experience and real estate background. Assignments are made according to our editorial schedule which we will supply upon request. Most open to freelancers are city reviews. Contact the staff to discuss ideas first. No unsolicited material." Buys 3-5 mss/issue. Query. Pays $100-500.

Columns/Departments: Offices, Shopping Centers, Industrials, Multiplexes, Leases, Sales and Purchases, Mortgage and Financial, Realty Operations, Residentials, and People in the News. No newspaper clippings.

Tips: "We retain resumes from writers for possible future use—particularly in the states we cover. Call us and submit a sample of previous work."

Resources and Waste Reduction

PUMPER PUBLICATIONS, Eastern Pumper, Midwest Pumper and Western Pumper, COLE Inc., Drawer 220, Three Lakes WI 54562. (715)546-3347. Editors: Bob Kendall. 5% freelance written. Eager to work with new/unpublished writers. A monthly tabloid covering the liquid waste hauling industry (portable toilet renters, septic tank pumpers, industrial waste haulers, chemical waste haulers, oil field haulers, and hazardous waste haulers). "Our publication is read by companies that handle liquid waste and manufacturers of equipment." Circ. 15,000. Pays on publication. Publishes ms an average of 1 month after acceptance. Byline given. Offers negotiable kill fee. Buys first serial rights. Submit seasonal/holiday material 3 months in advance. Simultaneous queries, and simultaneous, photocopied, and previously published submissions OK. Computer printout submissions acceptable; no dot-matrix. Reports in 1 month. Free sample copy.
Nonfiction: Expose (government regulations, industry problems, trends, public attitudes, etc.); general interest (state association meetings, conventions, etc.); how-to (related to industry, e.g., how to incorporate septage or municipal waste into farm fields, how to process waste, etc.); humor (related to industry, especially septic tank pumpers or portable toilet renters); interview/profile (including descriptions of business statistics, type of equipment, etc.); new product; personal experience; photo feature; and technical (especially reports on research projects related to disposal). "We are looking for quality articles that will be of interest to our readers; length is not that important. We publish trade journals. We need articles that deal with the trade. Studies on land application of sanitary waste are of great interest." Query or send complete ms. Pays 7½¢/word.
Photos: Send photos with query or ms. Pays $15 for b&w and color prints that are used. "We need good contrast." Captions "suggested" and model release "helpful." Buys one-time rights.
Tips: "We hope to expand the editorial content of our monthly publications. We also have publications for sewer and drainage cleaners with the same format as *The Pumpers*; however, the *Cleaner* has a circulation of 23,000. We are looking for the same type of articles and pay is the same."

RESOURCE RECYCLING, North America's Recycling Journal, Resource Recycling, Inc., Box 10540, Portland OR 97210. (503)227-1319. Editor: Jerry Powell. 25% freelance written. Eager to work with new/unpublished writers. A trade journal published 7 times/year, covering recycling of paper, metals and glass. Circ. 2,500. Pays on publication. Publishes ms an average of 3-9 months after acceptance. Byline given. Buys first rights. Simultaneous, photocopied and previously published submissions OK. Query for electronic submissions. Computer printout submissions OK; prefers letter-quality to dot-matrix. Reports in 1 month on queries. Sample copy and writer's guidelines for SAE with $1.24 postage. "No non-technical or opinion pieces." Buys 15-20 mss/year. Query with published clips. Length: 1,200-1,800 words. Pays $100-150. Pays with contributor copies "if writers are more interested in professional recognition than financial compensation." Sometimes pays the expenses of writers on assignment.
Photos: State availability of photos with submission. Reviews contact sheets, negatives and prints. Offers $5-10. Identification of subjects required. Buys one-time rights.
Tips: "Overviews of one recycling aspect in one state (e.g., oil recycling in Alabama) will receive attention."

Selling and Merchandising

Sales personnel and merchandisers interested in how to sell products successfully consult these journals. Journals in nearly every category of Trade also buy sales-related material if it is slanted to the specialized product or industry with which they deal.

THE AMERICAN SALESMAN, 424 N. 3rd St., Burlington IA 52601. Publisher: Michael S. Darnall. Editorial Supervisor: Doris J. Ruschill. Editor: Barbara Boeding. 95% freelance written. Prefers to work with published/established writers; works with a small number of new/unpublished writers each year. Monthly magazine; 32 pages, (5x7). For distribution through company sales representatives. Circ. 2,233. Pays on publication. Publishes ms an average of 4 months after acceptance. Buys all rights. Computer printout submissions OK; no dot-matrix. Sample copy and writer's guidelines for 5x7 SASE; mention *Writer's Market* in request.

Nonfiction: Sales seminars, customer service and follow-up, closing sales, sales presentations, handling objections, competition, telephone usage and correspondence, managing territory, and new innovative sales concepts. No sexist material, illustration written from only a salesperson's viewpoint. No ms dealing with supervisory problems. Query. Length: 900-1,200 words. Pays 3¢/word. Uses no advertising. Follow AP Stylebook. Include biography and/or byline with ms submissions. Author photos used.

ART MATERIAL TRADE NEWS, The Journal of All Art, Craft, Engineering and Drafting Supplies, Communication Channels Inc., 6255 Barfield Rd., Atlanta GA 30328. (404)256-9800. Editor: Charles Craig. 15% freelance written. Works with a small number of new/unpublished writers each year. Monthly magazine on art materials. "Our editorial thrust is to bring art materials retailers, distributors and manufacturers information they can use in their everyday operations." Circ. 12,000. Pays on publication. Publishes ms an average of 3 months after acceptance. "All assigned manuscripts are published." Buys first serial rights. Submit seasonal/holiday material 3 months in advance. Photocopied submissions OK. Computer printout submissions acceptable; prefers letter-quality to dot-matrix. Reports in 6 weeks. Sample copy for 9x12 SAE and $1 postage; writer's guidelines for 4x9½ SAE and 1 first class stamp.

Nonfiction: How-to (sell, retail/wholesale employee management, advertising programs); interview/profile (within industry); and technical (commercial art drafting/engineering). "We encourage a strong narrative style where possible. We publish an editorial 'theme' calendar at the beginning of each year." Buys 15-30 mss/year. Query with published clips. Length: 1,000-3,000 words (prefers 2,000 words). Pays 10¢/word and expenses with prior approval.

Photos: State availability of photos. Pays $10 maximum for b&w contact sheets. Identification of subjects required.

Columns/Departments: Creative Corner (crafts) and Print & Framing. Buys 12-15 mss/year. Query with published clips. Length: 1,000-2,000 words. Pays $75-200.

Tips: "We are very interested in developing a cadre of writers who know the art materials industry well. We would like to receive articles that show knowledge of the specifics of the art materials industry. We reject many general business articles that are not useful to our readers because they fail to take into account the nature of the industry. A current, solid background in any one of these areas helps—commercial art, retail selling, wholesale selling, business finance, employee management, interviewing or advertising. We frequently need filler items relating to the art industry. We appreciate clean, concise copy. We do dealer profiles throughout U.S. They must be written in good conversational tone with complete, accurate background information."

‡CASUAL LIVING, Columbia Communications, 370 Lexington Ave., New York NY 10164. (212)532-9290. Editor: Ralph Monti. A monthly magazine covering outdoor furniture for outdoor furniture specialists, including retailers, mass merchandiser, and department store buyers. Circ. 11,000. Pays on publication. Buys first North American serial rights. Submit seasonal/holiday material 2 months in advance. Computer printout submissions acceptable. Reports in 1 month. Sample copy and writer's guidelines for 9x12 SAE, and 28¢ postage.

Nonfiction: Interview/profile (case histories of retailers in the industry); new product; opinion; and technical. Buys 12-13 mss/year. Query with or without published clips, then follow up with phone call. Length: 1,000 words average. Pays $200-400.

Photos: State availability of photos with query letter or ms. "Photos are essential with all articles." Reviews b&w contact sheet. Pays $75-100 for b&w prints. Buys all rights.

Tips: "Know the industry, trades and fashions, and what makes a successful retailer."

DEALER COMMUNICATOR, Fichera Publications, 777 S. State Road 7, Margate FL 33068. (305)971-4360. Editor: Dave Kaiser. Publisher: Mike Fichera. 20% freelance written. Works with a small number of new/unpublished writers each year. A monthly magazine covering personnel and news developments for the graphic arts industry. Circ. 10,000. Pays on publication. Publishes ms an average of 1 month after acceptance. Byline given. Not copyrighted. Buys one-time rights. Simultaneous and photocopied submissions OK. Computer printout submissions OK; prefers letter-quality to dot-matrix. Reports in 1 week on queries.

Nonfiction: Interview/profile. Buys a varying number of mss/year. Query with published clips. Length: 500-1,000 words. Pays 3-7¢/word. Pays the expenses of writers on assignment.

Photos: State availability of photos with submissions. Offers $5-10/photo. Captions required.

Fillers: Facts and newsbreaks. Buys a varying number/year. Length: 10-50 words. Pays $1-1.50.

Tips: "We cover a national market. Find out what local printing/graphic arts dealers are doing and what is news in the area."

‡**FOOD & DRUG PACKAGING**, 7500 Old Oak Blvd., Cleveland OH 44140. Editor: Sophia Dilberakis. 20% freelance written. Prefers to work with published/established writers. For packaging decision makers in food, drug, and cosmetic firms. Monthly. Circ. 67,000. Rights purchased vary with author and material. Pays on acceptance. Publishes ms an average of 2-4 months after acceptance. Query for electronic submissions. Computer printout submissions OK; prefers letter-quality to dot-matrix.

Nonfiction and Photos: "Looking for news stories about local and state (not federal) packaging legislation, and its impact on the marketplace. Newspaper style." Query only. Length: 1,000-2,500 words; usually 500-700. Payments vary; usally 5¢/word. Sometimes pays the expenses of writers on assignment.

Photos: Photos purchased with mss. 5x7 glossies preferred. Pays $5.

Tips: "Get details on local packaging legislation's impact on marketplace/sales/consumer/retailer reaction; etc. Keep an eye open to *new* packages. Query when you think you've got one. New packages move into test markets every day, so if you don't see anything new this week, try again next week. Buy it; describe it briefly in a query."

‡**INCENTIVE MARKETING, Incorporating Incentive Travel**, Bill Communications, 633 Third St., New York NY 10017. (212)986-4800. Editor: Bruce Bolger. Managing Editor: Mary A. Riordan. Monthly magazine covering sales promotion and employee motivation. "We serve executives in a wide variety of industries who use premiums and/or incentives as part of their sales and marketing programs." Circ. 41,000. Pays on acceptance. Publishes ms an average of 3 months after acceptance. Byline sometimes given. Buys all rights. Submit seasonal/holiday material 3 months in advance. Query for electronic submissions. Computer printout submissions OK; no dot-matrix. Reports in 1 month on queries; 2 months on mss. Free sample copy.

Nonfiction: General interest (marketing); how-to (types of sales promotion, buying product categories, using destinations), interview/profile (sales promotion executives); and travel (incentive-oriented). Buys up to 60 mss/year. Query with published clips. Length: 500-2,000 words. Pays $100-600 for assigned articles; pays $0-100 for unsolicited articles. Sometimes pays the expenses of writers on assignment.

Photos: Send photos with submission. Reviews contact sheets and transparencies. Offers no additional payment for photos accepted with ms. Identification of subjects required.

Columns/Departments: Measurement Issues (how to measure productivity and performance); Inside Promotions (case studies of trade or consumer promotions). Buys up to 30 mss/year. Query with published clips. Length: 500-800. Pays $75-150.

Tips: "Read the publication; request editorial schedule; read consumer business periodicals; query."

INFO FRANCHISE NEWSLETTER, 9 Duke St., St. Catharines, Ontario L2R 5W1 Canada or 728 Center St., Box 550, Lewiston NY 14092. (716)754-4669. Editor-in-Chief: E.L. Dixon, Jr. Managing Editor: Caroline McCaffery. Monthly newsletter; 8 pages. Circ. 5,000. Pays on publication. Buys all rights. Photocopied submissions OK. Reports in 1 month.

Nonfiction: "We are particularly interested in receiving articles regarding franchise legislation, franchise litigation, franchise success stories, and new franchises. Both American and Canadian items are of interest. We do not want to receive any information which is not fully documented or articles which could have appeared in any newspaper or magazine in North America. An author with a legal background who could comment upon such things as arbitration and franchising or class actions and franchising, would be of great interest to us." Expose, how-to, informational, interview, profile, new product, personal experience and technical. Buys 10-20 mss/year. Length: 25-1,000 words. Pays $10-300.

OPPORTUNITY MAGAZINE, 6 N. Michigan Ave., Chicago IL 60602. Managing Editor: Jack Weissman. 33% freelance written. Eager to work with new/unpublished writers. Monthly magazine "for anyone who is interested in making money, full or spare time, in selling or in an independent business program." Circ. 190,000. Pays on publication. Buys all rights. Byline given. Submit seasonal/holiday material 6 months in advance. Free sample copy and writer's guidelines.

Nonfiction: "We use articles dealing with sales techniques, sales psychology or general self-improvement topics." How-to, inspirational, and interview (with successful salespeople selling products offered by direct selling firms, especially concerning firms which recruit salespeople through *Opportunity Magazine*). Articles on self-improvement should deal with specifics rather than generalities. Would like to have more articles that deal with overcoming fear, building self-confidence, increasing personal effectiveness, and other psychological subjects. Submit complete ms. Buys 35-50 unsolicited mss/year. Length: 250-900 words. Pays $20-35.

Photos: State availability of photos with ms. Offers no additional payment for 8x10 b&w glossy prints. Captions and model release required. Buys all rights.

Tips: "Many articles are too academic for our audience. We look for a free-and-easy style in simple language which is packed with useful information, drama and inspiration. Check the magazine before writing. We can't use general articles. The only articles we buy deal with material that is specifically directed to readers who are opportunity seekers—articles dealing with direct sales programs or successful ventures that others can emulate. Try to relate the article to the actual work in which the reader is engaged. Look for fresh approaches. Too many people write on the same or similar topics."

PROFESSIONAL SELLING, 24 Rope Ferry Rd., Waterford CT 06386. (203)442-4365. Editor: Paulette S. Withers. 33% freelance written. Prefers to work with published/established writers, and works with a small number of new/unpublished writers each year. Bimonthly newsletter for sales professionals covering industrial or wholesale sales. *"Professional Selling* provides field sales personnel with both the basics and current information that can help them better perform the sales function." Pays on acceptance. Publishes ms an average of 4-6 months after acceptance. No byline given. Buys all rights. Submit seasonal/holiday material 4 months in advance. Computer printout submissions acceptable; no dot-matrix. Reports in 2 weeks. Sample copy and writer's guidelines for business size SAE and 2 first class stamps.
Nonfiction: How-to (successful sales techniques); and interview/profile (interview-based articles). "We buy only interview-based material." Buys 12-15 mss/year. No unsolicited manuscripts; written queries only. Length: 800-1,000 words.
Tips: "Only the lead article is open to freelancers. That must be based on an interview with an actual sales professional. Freelancers may occasionally interview sales managers, but the slant must be toward field sales, *not* management."

SELLING DIRECT, Communication Channels, Inc., 6255 Barfield Rd., Atlanta GA 30328. (404)256-9800. Publisher: William Manning. Editor: Robert Rawls. 20% freelance written. For independent businessmen and women who sell door-to-door, store-to-store, office-to-office and by the party plan method as well as through direct mail and telephone solicitation; selling products and services. Monthly magazine; 50-100 pages. Circ. 500,000. Pays on publication. Buys all rights. Byline given. Submit seasonal/holiday material 3 months in advance. Electronic submissions OK if compatible with Decmate or Decmate II. Computer printout submissions acceptable. Reports in 3 months. Publishes ms an average of 1 year after acceptance. Free sample copy and writer's guidelines.
Nonfiction: How-to (sell better; increase profits); historical (related to the history of various kinds of sales pitches, anecdotes, etc.); and inspirational (success stories, "rags to riches" type of stories)—with no additional payment. Buys 30 unsolicited mss/year. Query or submit complete ms. Length: 500-1,500 words. Pays 10¢/word.
Photos: Photos purchased with accompanying ms.
Columns/Departments: Ideas Exchange (generated from our readers). Submit complete ms. Open to suggestions for new columns/departments.
Fillers: Jokes, gags, anecdotes and short humor. Buys 2/issue. Length: 150-500 words. Pays $10 for each published item. Buys 1-2 cartoons/issue. Pays $10 per cartoon.
Tips: No general articles on "How to be a Super Salesperson." Writers should concentrate on one specific aspect of selling and expand on that.

SOUND MANAGEMENT, Radio Advertising Bureau, 304 Park Ave. S., New York NY 10010. (212)254-4800. Editor-in-Chief: Daniel Flamberg. Editor: Andrew Giangola. 15% freelance written. A monthly magazine covering radio sales and marketing. "We write practical business and how-to stories for the owners and managers of radio stations on topics geared toward increasing ad sales and training salespeople." Circ. 10,000. Pays on publication. Publishes ms an average of 4 months after acceptance. Byline given. Buys one-time rights, exclusive rights for the field or makes work-for-hire assignments. Submit seasonal/holiday material 3 months in advance. Previously published submissions OK. Free sample copy and writer's guidelines.
Nonfiction: Essays, how-to, interview/profile and personal experience. No articles on disc jockeys or radio programming. Buys 5-10 mss/year. Query with published clips. Length: 400-750 words. Pays $350-650 for assigned articles; pays $50-150 for unsolicited articles. May pay contributor copies for republished items.
Photos: State availability of photos with submission. Reviews contact sheets, negatives and transparencies. Captions, model releases, and identification of subjects required. Buys one-time rights.
Tips: "Our cover story is most open to freelancers, but proven experience in writing about media advertising and marketing is necessary, with strong interviewing and critical writing skills."

WATERBED MAGAZINE, Bobit Publishing, 2512 Artesia Blvd., Redondo Beach CA 90278. (213)376-8788. Editor: Kathy Drake. 10% freelance written. Prefers to work with published/established writers. A monthly magazine covering waterbeds and accessories for waterbed specialty shop owners, furniture stores, sleep shops and waterbed manufacturers, distributors. Circ. 9,200. Pays on publication. Publishes ms an average of 2 months after acceptance. Byline given. Buys first rights or second serial (reprint) rights. Submit seasonal/holiday material 3 months in advance. Photocopied and previously published submissions OK. Computer printout submissions acceptable; no dot-matrix. Reports in 2 weeks. Free sample copy.
Nonfiction: Book excerpts; essays (health benefits of waterbeds); historical/nostalgic; how-to (business management, display techniques, merchandising tips); humor (if in good taste); interview/profile; new product; personal experience; photo feature; technical; and general features depicting waterbeds in a positive way. "Convention issue published in April or May prior to the Waterbed Manufacturer's Association

Convention is extra large. We need more manuscripts then." No articles depicting waterbeds in a negative manner. "The goal of the waterbed industry and the magazine is to get away from the hippie image associated with waterbeds in the past." Buys 25-30 mss/year. Query with published clips. Length: 1,000-5,000 words. Pays $60-250 for assigned articles; pays $50-200 for unsolicited articles. Sometimes pays the expenses of writers on assignment.

Photos: Send photos with submission. Reviews contact sheets, transparencies and 8x10 prints. Offers $10-25/photo. Captions and identification of subjects required. Buys one-time rights.

Tips: "We need profiles on successful waterbed retailers in all parts of the country. If a large, full-line furniture store in your area also sells waterbeds, we are interested in profiles on those stores and owners as well. We are also always looking for interviews with doctors, chiropractors and other health professionals who recommend waterbeds for their patients. Most of our freelance articles concern business management. We need articles on obtaining credit, display techniques, merchandising, how to be a successful salesperson, attracting new customers, creating effective advertising, how to put together an attractive store window display, hiring employees, etc. Anything that could benefit a salesperson or store owner."

Sport Trade

Retailers and wholesalers of sports equipment and operators of recreation programs read these journals. Magazines about general and specific sports are classified in the Consumer Sports section.

AMERICAN BICYCLIST, Suite 305, 80 8th Ave., New York NY 10011. (212)206-7230. Editor: Konstantin Doren. 40% freelance written. Prefers to work with published/established writers. Monthly magazine for bicycle sales and service shops. Circ. 11,025. Pays on publication. Publishes ms an average of 4 months after acceptance. Only staff-written articles are bylined, except under special circumstances. Buys all rights. Computer printout submissions acceptable; no dot-matrix.

Nonfiction: Typical story describes (very specifically) unique traffic-builder or merchandising ideas used with success by an actual dealer. Articles may also deal exclusively with moped sales and service operation within conventional bicycle shops. Emphasis on showing other dealers how they can follow similar pattern and increase their business. Articles may also be based entirely on repair shop operation, depicting efficient and profitable service systems and methods. Buys 12 mss/year. Query. Length: 1,000-2,800 words. Pays 9¢/word, plus bonus for outstanding manuscript. Pays expenses of writers on assignment.

Photos: Reviews relevant b&w photos illustrating principal points in article purchased with ms; 5x7 minimum. Pays $8/photo. Captions required. Buys all rights.

Tips: "A frequent mistake made by writers is writing as if we are a book read by consumers instead of professionals in the bicycle industry."

AMERICAN FIREARMS INDUSTRY, AFI Communications Group, Inc., 2801 E. Oakland Park Blvd., Ft. Lauderdale FL 33306. 10% freelance written. "Work with writers specifically in the firearms trade." Monthly magazine specializing in the sporting arms trade. Circ. 30,000. Pays on publication. Publishes ms an average of 4 months after acceptance. Buys all rights. Computer printout submissions acceptable. Reports in 2 weeks.

Nonfiction: R.A. Lesmeister, articles editor. Publishes informational, technical and new product articles. No general firearms subjects. Query. Length: 900-1,500 words. Pays $100-150. Sometimes pays the expenses of writers on assignment.

Photos: Reviews 8x10 b&w glossy prints. Manuscript price includes payment for photos.

AMERICAN FITNESS, (formerly *Aerobics & Fitness Journal*), The Official Publication of the Aerobics and Fitness Association of America,Suite 310, 15250 Ventura Blvd. Sherman Oaks CA 91403. (818)905-0040. Editor: Peg Angsten, R.N. Managing Editor: Harlyn Enholm. 80% freelance written. Eager to work with new/unpublished writers. Nine-times-per-year magazine covering exercise and fitness, health and nutrition. "We need timely, in-depth informative articles on health, fitness, aerobic exercise, sports nutrition, sports medicine and physiology." Circ. 20,000. Pays on publication. Publishes ms an average of 6 months after acceptance. Byline given. Buys first North American serial rights, and simultaneous rights (in some cases). Submit seasonal/holiday material 4 months in advance. Simultaneous queries and simultaneous, photocopied, and previously published submissions OK. Query for electronic submissions. Computer printout submissions acceptable; prefers letter-quality to dot-matrix. Reports in 2 weeks. Sample copy for $1 or SAE with 6 first class stamps; writer's guidelines for SAE.

Nonfiction: Book excerpts (fitness book reviews); expose (on nutritional gimmickry); historical/nostalgic (history of various athletic events); humor (personal fitness profiles); inspirational (sports leader's motivational pieces); interview/profile (fitness figures); new product (plus equipment review); opinion (on clubs); personal experience (successful fitness story); photo feature (on exercise, fitness, new sport); and travel (spas that cater to fitness industry). No articles on unsound nutritional practices, popular trends or unsafe exercise gimmicks. Buys 18-25 mss/year. Query. Length: 800-2,500 words. Pays $65-180. Sometimes pays expenses of writers on assignment.

Photos: Sports, action, fitness, aerobic competitions and exercise classes. Pays $30-60 for 8x10 b&w prints; $35 for color transparencies. Captions, model release, and identification of subjects required. Buys one-time rights; other rights purchased depend on use of photo.

Columns/Departments: Fitness Industry News, shorts on health and fitness, and profiles on successful fitness figures. Buys 50 mss/year. Query with published clips or send complete ms. Length: 50-150 words. Pays 1¢/word.

Poetry: Buys 2 poems/year. Submit maximum 1 poem. Length: 20-80 lines. Pays $20.

Fillers: Cartoons, clippings, jokes, short humor and newsbreaks. Buys 12/year. Length: 75-200 words. Pays $20.

Tips: "Cover an athletic event, get a unique angle, provide accurate and interesting findings, and write in a lively, intelligent manner. We are looking for new health and fitness reporters and writers. *A&F* is a good place to get started. I have generally been disappointed with short articles and fillers submissions due to their lack of force. Cover a topic with depth."

AMERICAN HOCKEY MAGAZINE, Amateur Hockey Association of the United States, 2997 Broadmoor Valley Rd., Colorado Springs CO 80906. (303)576-4990. Contact: Publisher. Managing Editor: Mike Schroeder. 80% freelance written. Monthly magazine covering hockey in general (with amateur/youth hockey emphasis) for teams, coaches and referees of the Amateur Hockey Association of the U.S., ice facilities in the U.S. and Canada, buyers, schools, colleges, pro teams, and park and recreation departments. Circ. 35,000. Pays on publication. Publishes ms an average of 1 month after acceptance. Byline given. Buys first serial rights; makes work-for-hire assignments. Phone queries OK. Submit seasonal/holiday material 4 months in advance. Photocopied and previously published submissions OK. Reports in 1 month. Sample copy $2.

Nonfiction: General interest, profile, new product and technical. Query. Length: 500-3,000 words. Pays $50 minimum.

Photos: Reviews 5x7 b&w glossy prints and color slides. Offers no additional payment for photos accepted with ms. Captions preferred. Buys one-time rights.

Columns/Departments: Rebound Shots (editorial); Americans in the Pros (U.S. players in the NHL); College Notes; Rinks and Arenas (arena news); Equipment/Sports Medicine; Referees Crease; Coaches Playbook; For the Record; and Features (miscellaneous). Query.

‡ARCHERY BUSINESS, Wintersports Publishing, Suite 100, 11812 Wayzata Blvd., Minnetonka MN 55343. (612)545-2662. Managing Editor: Tim Dehn. 10% freelance written. Prefers to work with published/established writers. A bimonthly trade journal which covers the business side of the sport of bowhunting/archer, including news of archery manufacturers, distributors, sales reps and dealers. Circ. 15,600. Pays on publication. Publishes ms an average of 4 months after acceptance. Byline given. Offers 50% kill fee. Buys first rights or makes work-for-hire assignments. Computer printout submissions OK; no dot-matrix. Reports in 2 weeks on queries; 3 weeks on mss. Sample copy for 9x12 SAE with 10 first class stamps; writer's guidelines for 4x9 SAE with 1 first class stamp.

Nonfiction: Interview/profile and technical. Buys 5 mss/year. Query. Length: 1,400-3,000 words. Pays $150-250 for assigned articles; pays $100-200 for unsolicited articles. Sometimes pays the expenses of writers on assignment.

Photos: Send photos with submission. Reviews contact sheets and 4x6 prints. Offers no additional payment for photos accepted with ms. Captions required. Buys one-time rights.

Tips: "Writers should be familiar with business and take the time to learn about the sport of bowhunting and archery in its present form before sending a query about a particular manufacturer, distributor, rep or retailer they would like to profile in our magazine."

‡ARMS & OUTDOOR DIGEST, (formerly FFL News), AFI Communications Group Inc., 2801 E. Oakland Park Blvd., Ft. Lauderdale FL 33306. (305)561-3505. Editor: Andrew Molchan. Managing Editor: R.A. Lesmeister. 5% freelance written. Monthly tabloid covering firearms/archery. "Our publication mainly deals with the firearms/archery retailer. We publish industry news and information that affects the industry as well as retail tips, liabilty articles, selling techniques, etc." Circ. 230,000. Pays on publication. Publishes ms an average of 4 months after acceptance. Byline given. Submit seasonal/holiday material 2 months in advance. Simultaneous and photocopied submissions OK. Computer printout submissions OK; prefers letter-quality to dot-matrix. Reports in 1 week on queries; 3 weeks on mss. Sample copy $1.

Nonfiction: Interview/profile, new product, photo feature and technical. Does not want to see "anything dealing with the consumer." Buys 2-5 mss/year. Query. Length: 1,000-2,500 words. Pays $250-300 for assigned articles; pays $150 for unsolicited articles. Sometimes pays the expenses of writers on assignment.

Photos: Send photos with submission. Reviews prints. Offers $10 per photo. Buys all rights.

Fillers: Facts. Buys 1/year. "Most fillers used are statistical charts of varying size."

Tips: Encourages telephone queries. Areas most open to freelancers are "firearms technical areas, interviews with people in the firearms-political field, how-to gunsmithing."

BICYCLE BUSINESS JOURNAL, Box 1570, 1904 Wenneca, Fort Worth TX 76101. Editor: Rix Quinn. Works with a small number of new/unpublished writers each year. 10% freelance written. Monthly. Circ. 10,000. Pays on acceptance. Publishes ms an average of 3 months after acceptance. Buys all rights. Computer printout submissions acceptable.

Nonfiction: Stories about dealers who service what they sell, emphasizing progressive, successful sales ideas in the face of rising costs and increased competition. Length: 3 double-spaced pages maximum. Sometimes pays the expenses of writers on assignment.

Photos: B&w glossy photo a must; vertical photo preferred. Query.

Tips: "We are requesting greater professionalism and more content and research in freelance material."

CORPORATE FITNESS, Brentwood Publishing, (a Simon & Schuster Company), 1640 5th St., Santa Monica CA 90401. (213)395-0234. Publisher: Martin H. Waldman. Editor: Shelly Rondeau. 60% freelance written. Bimonthly magazine on employee fitness. "Our readers are directors of on-site employee fitness and recreation programs." Circ. 12,000. Pays on acceptance. Publishes ms an average of 6 months after acceptance. Byline given. Buys all rights. Submit seasonal/holiday material 6 months in advance. Computer printout submissions acceptable; prefers letter-quality to dot-matrix. Reports in 1 month on queries; 2 months on mss. Free sample copy and writer's guidelines.

Nonfiction: How-to (plan, implement, supervise, and evaluate employee health and wellness programs); interview/profile (of on-site corporate fitness and recreation programs and facilities); technical (regarding sports medicine, exercise, physiology, and lifestyle improvements—stress management, smoking cessation, employee assistance program, etc.); and analysis of studies conducted on the benefits of employee fitness programs. "No general articles on health-related topics that are not geared specifically to our readership." Buys 30 mss/year. Query with published clips. Length: 1,000-2,000 words. Pays $100-240. Pays expenses of writers on assignment.

Columns/Departments: Sports Medicine: Prevention and Treatment of injuries incurred by participants in employee fitness and recreation programs. Writers should have exercise physiology background. Buys 6 mss/year. Query with published clips. Length: 1,500-2,000 words. Pays $150-240.

Tips: "Queries with clips are appreciated. Submissions should conform to American Medical Association style and be written clearly and concisely. A medical or exercise physiology background is not necessary, but is helpful when tackling technical subjects. All submissions are reviewed by an editorial advisory board of industry professionals."

FISHING TACKLE RETAILER, B.A.S.S. Publications, 1 Bell Rd., Montgomery AL 36141. (205)272-9530. Editor: Dave Ellison. 90% freelance written. Prefers to work with published/established writers. Magazine published 10 times/year, "designed to promote the economic health of retail sellers of freshwater and saltwater angling equipment." Circ. 22,000. Byline usually given. Publishes ms an average of 1 year after acceptance. Buys all rights. Submit seasonal/holiday material 6 months in advance. Query for electronic submissions. Computer printout submissions acceptable; prefers letter-quality to dot-matrix. Reports in 6 weeks. Sample copy $2; writer's guidelines for standard size SAE and 1 first class stamp.

Nonfiction: How-to (merchandising and management techniques); technical (how readers can specifically benefit from individual technological advances); and success stories (how certain fishing tackle retailers have successfully overcome business difficulties and their advice to their fellow retailers). Articles must directly relate to the financial interests of the magazine's audience. Buys 100 mss/year. Query with published clips. Length: 50-3,000 words. Pays $10-600. Sometimes pays expenses of writers on assignment.

Photos: State availability of photos. Payment included with ms.

Columns/Departments: Retail Pointers (200-300 words) and Profit Strategy (750-900 words)—how-to tips, should be accompanied by illustration. Buys variable number mss/year.

Tips: "Long stories are usually assigned to writers with whom we have an established relationship. The writer has a better chance of breaking in at our publication with short, lesser-paying articles and fillers."

GOLF COURSE MANAGEMENT, Golf Course Superintendents Association of America, 1617 St. Andrews Dr., Lawrence KS 66046. (913)841-2240. Editor: Clay Loyd. 30% freelance written. Eager to work with new/unpublished writers. Monthly magazine covering golf course and turf management. Circ. 20,000. Byline given. Buys all rights. Submit seasonal/holiday material 6 months in advance. Publishes ms an average of 3 months after acceptance. Simultaneous queries and submissions OK. Computer submissions acceptable; prefers letter-quality to dot-matrix. Reports in 2 weeks on queries; 1 month on mss. Free sample copy and writer's guidelines.

Nonfiction: Book excerpts, historical/nostalgic, interview/profile, personal experience and technical. "All areas that relate to the golf course superintendent—whether features or scholarly pieces related to turf/grass management. We prefer all submissions to be written *simply*." Special issues include January "conference issue"—features on convention cities used each year. Buys 20 mss/year. Query with clips of published work. Length: 1,500-3,000 words. Pays $100-300 or more. Sometimes pays the expenses of writers on assignment.

Photos: Send photos with ms. Pays $50-250 for color, 4x5 transparencies preferred. Captions, model release and identification of subjects required. Buys one-time rights.

Tips: "Call communications department (913)841-2240, offer idea, follow with outline and writing samples. Response from us is immediate."

GOLF SHOP OPERATIONS, 5520 Park Ave., Trumbull CT 06611. (203)373-7232. Editor: Nick Romano. 5% freelance written. Works with a small number of new/unpublished writers each year. Magazine published 8 times/year for golf professionals and shop operators at public and private courses, resorts, driving ranges and golf specialty stores. Circ. 13,200. Pays on publication. Publishes ms an average of 2 months after acceptance. Byline given. Submit seasonal material (for Christmas and other holiday sales, or profiles of successful professionals with how-to angle emphasized) 4 months in advance. Photocopied submissions OK. Computer printout submissions acceptable; prefers letter-quality to dot-matrix. Reports in 1 month. Sample copy free.

Nonfiction: "We emphasize improving the golf retailer's knowledge of his profession. Articles should describe how pros are buying, promoting merchandising and displaying wares in their shops that might be of practical value. Must be aimed only at the retailer." How-to, profile, successful business operation and merchandising techniques. Buys 6-8 mss/year. Phone queries preferred. Pays $175-300. Sometimes pays expenses of writers on assignment.

‡NSGA SPORTS RETAILER, National Sporting Goods Association, Suite 700, 1699 Wall St., Mt. Prospect IL 60056. (312)439-4000. Editor: John S. O'Neill. Managing Editor: Larry Weindruch. 75% freelance written. Works with a small number of new/unpublished writers each year. *NSGA Sports Retailer* serves as a monthly trade journal for presidents, CEOs and owners of more than 18,000 retail sporting goods firms. Circ. 9,500. Pays on publication. Publishes ms an average of 1 month after acceptance. Byline given. Offers 50% kill fee. Buys first and second serial (reprint) rights. Submit seasonal/holiday material 3 months in advance. Photocopied submissions OK. Query for electronic submissions. Computer printout submissions OK; prefers letter-quality. Sample copy for 9x12 SAE with 90¢ postage.

Nonfiction: Essays, interview/profile and photo feature. Special issue includes Co-Op Advertising (Dec.). "No articles written without sporting goods retail businessmen in mind as the audience. In other words, generic articles sent to several industries." Buys 50 mss/year. Query with published clips. Pays $75-500. Sometimes pays the expenses of writers on assignment.

Photos: State availability of photos with submission. Reviews contact sheets, negatives, transparencies and 5x7 prints. Payment negotiable. Buys one-time rights.

Columns/Departments: Personnel Management (to-the-point tips on hiring, motivating, firing, etc.); Tax Advisor (simplified explanation of how tax laws affect retailer); Sales Management (in-depth tips to improve sales force's performance); Retail Management (detailed explanation of merchandising/inventory control); Advertising (case histories of successful ad campaigns/ad critiques); Legal Advisor; Computers; Store Design; Visual Mercandising; all 1,500 words. Buys 40 mss/year. Query. Length: 1,000-1,500 words. Pays $75-250.

‡PGA MAGAZINE, Professional Golfer's Association of America, 100 Avenue of Champions, Palm Beach Gardens FL 33418. (305)626-3600. Editor: William A. Burbaum. 10% freelance written. Monthly magazine about golf for 15,500 club professionals and apprentices nationwide. Circ. 38,000. Average issue includes 6-8 articles and 6 departments. Pays on acceptance. Publishes ms an average of 3 months after acceptance. Byline given. Phone queries OK. Submit seasonal material 3 months in advance. Photocopied and previously published submissions OK. Computer printout submissions OK; prefers letter-quality to dot-matrix. Reports in 3 weeks. Free sample copy.

Nonfiction: Historical (great moments in golf revisited); personality profiles; off-beat (e.g., golf in stamps, unique collections); inspirational (personal success stories); and photo feature (great golf courses). Buys 15 mss/year. Query with outline and published clips. Length: 1,500-3,000 words. Pays $300-500. Sometimes pays the expenses of writers on assignment. "Exhibit knowledge and interest in the professional business and in other needs of today's club professional."

Photos: Pays $25/b&w contact sheets; $75-100/35mm inside color transparencies; $250 for cover photos. Captions and model release required.

POOL & SPA NEWS, Leisure Publications, 3923 W. 6th St., Los Angeles CA 90020. (213)385-3926. Editor-in-Chief: J. Field. 25-40% freelance written. Semimonthly magazine emphasizing news of the swimming pool and spa industry for pool builders, pool retail stores and pool service firms. Circ. 12,000. Pays on publication. Publishes ms an average of 1-2 months after acceptance. Buys all rights. Photocopied submissions OK. Query for electronic submissions. Computer printout submissions acceptable; no dot-matrix. Reports in 2 weeks.

Nonfiction: Interview, new product, profile and technical. Phone queries OK. Length: 500-2,000 words. Pays 10-12¢/word. Pays expenses of writers on assignment.

Photos: Pays $10 per b&w photo used.

SAILBOARD NEWS, The International Trade Journal of Boardsailing, Sports Ink Magazine, Inc., Box 159, Fair Haven VT 05743. (802)265-8153. Editor: Mark Gabriel. 50% freelance written. Works with a small number of new/unpublished writers each year. Monthly boardsailing trade glossy tabloid. Circ. 19,000. Pays 30 days after publication. Publishes ms an average of 2 weeks after acceptance. Byline given. Buys one-time rights. Submit seasonal/holiday material 3 weeks in advance. Simultaneous queries OK. Electronic submissions OK via MacIntosh or Easylink. Computer printout submissions acceptable. Reports in 3 weeks. Free sample copy and writer's guidelines.

Nonfiction: Regional retail reports, book excerpts, expose, general interest, historical/nostalgic, how-to, humor, inspirational, interview/profile, new product, opinion, photo feature, technical, travel. Buys 50 mss/year. Send complete ms. Length: 750 words minimum. Pays $50-200.

Photos: Send photos with ms. Reviews b&w negatives and 8x10 prints. Identification of subjects required.

Columns/Departments: Buys 12 mss/year. Query with published clips or send complete ms.

‡SPORTING GOODS BUSINESS, Gralla Publications, Inc., 1515 Broadway, New York NY 10036. (212)869-1300. Editor: Robert E. Carr. Managing Editor: Mark A. Klionsky. 15% freelance written. Monthly magazine covering sporting goods. "Primary readership is sporting goods retailers, so we look for articles that have some 'threat or benefit' to these readers." Circ. 28,000. Pays on publication. Publishes ms an average of 2 months after acceptance. Byline given. Offers various kill fee. Buys all rights. Submit seasonal/holiday material 4 months in advance. Simultaneous submissions OK. Computer printout submissions OK; prefers letter-quality to dot-matrix. Reports in 2 weeks on queries. Free sample copy.

Nonfiction: Expose, general interest, how-to, interview/profile and new product. Send complete ms. Length: 800-1,200 words. Pays $150-350. Sometimes pays the expenses of writers on assignment.

Photos: State availability of photos with submission. Reviews contact sheets, 4x5 transparencies and 5x7 prints. Offers $10-250 per photo. Buys one-time rights.

Columns/Departments: Management/Finance/Operations. Buys 24 mss/year. Send complete ms. Pays $100-300.

Tips: Sections of publication most open to freelancers are "specialty areas like hunting/fishing."

‡SPORTS MARKETING NEWS, Technical Marketing Corp., 1460 Post Rd., Westport CT 06880. (203)255-9997. Editor: Philip Maher. Managing Editor: Betsy Niesyn. 20% freelance written. A biweekly trade journal on sports marketing. Estab. 1986. Circ. 30,000. Pays on acceptance. Publishes ms an average of 1 month after acceptance. Byline sometimes given. Offers 25% kill fee. Buys first North American serial rights or makes work-for-hire assignments. Query for electronic submissions. Free sample copy and writer's guidelines.

Nonfiction: Buys 50 mss/year. Query with published clips. Length: 500-2,000 words. Pays $50-500. Sometimes pays the expenses of writers on assignment.

Photos: Send photos with submission. Captions, model releases and identification of subjects required. Buys one-time rights.

WOODALL'S CAMPGROUND MANAGEMENT, Woodall Publishing Co., Suite 205, 11 North Skokie Highway, Lake Bluff IL 60044. (312)295-7799. Editor: Mike Byrnes. 66% freelance written. Works with a small number of new/unpublished writers each year. A monthly tabloid covering campground management and operation for managers of private and public campgrounds throughout the U.S. Circ. 16,000. Pays after publication. Publishes ms an average of 4 months after acceptance. Byline given. Buys all rights. Will reassign rights to author upon written request. Submit seasonal/holiday material 4 months in advance. Simultaneous queries OK. Computer printout submissions acceptable; prefers letter-quality to dot-matrix. Reports in 1 month on queries; 2 months on mss. Free sample copy and writer's guidelines.

Nonfiction: How-to, interview/profile and technical. "Our articles tell our readers how to maintain their resources, manage personnel and guests, market, develop new campground areas and activities, and interrelate with the major tourism organizations within their areas. 'Improvement' and 'profit' are the two key words." Buys 48+ mss/year. Query. Length: 500 words minimum. Pays $50-200. Sometimes pays expenses of writers on assignment.

Photos: Send contact sheets and negatives. "We pay for each photo used."

Tips: "Contact us and give us an idea of your ability to travel and your travel range. We sometimes have assignments in certain areas. The best type of story to break in with is a case history type approach about how a campground improved its maintenance, physical plant or profitability."

—— *Stone and Quarry Products*

CONCRETE CONSTRUCTION MAGAZINE, 426 South Westgate, Addison IL 60101. Editorial Director: Ward R. Malisch. Monthly magazine, 80 pages average, for general and concrete contractors, architects, engineers, concrete producers, cement manufacturers, distributors and dealers in construction equipment and testing labs. Circ. 82,000. Pays on acceptance. Bylines used only by prearrangement with author. Buys all rights. Photocopied submissions OK. Reports in 2 months. Free sample copy and writer's guidelines.
Nonfiction: "Our magazine has a major emphasis on cast-in-place and precast concrete. Prestressed concrete is also covered. Our articles deal with tools, techniques and materials that result in better handling, better placing, and ultimately an improved final product. We are particularly firm about not using proprietary names in any of our articles. Manufacturer and product names are never mentioned; only the processes or techniques that might be of help to the concrete contractor, the architect or the engineer dealing with the material. We do use reader response cards to relay reader interest to manufacturers." No job stories or promotional material. Buys 8-10 mss/year. Submit query with topical outline. Pays $200/2-page article. Prefers 1,000-2,000 words with 2-3 illustrations.
Photos: Photos used only as part of complete ms.
Tips: "Condensed, totally factual presentations are preferred."

DIMENSIONAL STONE, Dimensional Stone Institute, Inc., Suite D, 17901 Ventura Blvd., Encino CA 91316. (818)344-4200. Editor: Jerry Fisher. 25% freelance written. A bimonthly magazine covering dimensional stone use for managers of producers, importers, contractors, fabricators and specifiers of dimensional stone. Circ. 14,580. Pays on publication. Publishes ms an average of 2 months after acceptance. Byline given. Buys first rights or second serial (reprint) rights. Photocopied submissions and previously published submissions OK. Computer printout submissions acceptable; prefers letter-quality to dot-matrix. Sample copy available.
Nonfiction: Interview/profile and technical, only on users of dimensional stone. Buys 6-7 mss/year. Send complete ms. Length: 1,000-3,000 words. Pays $100 maximum. Sometimes pays the expenses of writers on assignment.
Photos: Send photos with submission. Reviews any size prints. Offers no additional payment for photos accepted with ms. Identification of subjects required.
Tips: "Articles on outstanding uses of dimensional stone are most open to freelancers."

STONE IN AMERICA, American Monument Association, 6902 N. High St., Worthington OH 43085. (614)885-2713. Managing Editor: Bob Moon. Monthly magazine for the retailers of upright memorials in the U.S. and Canada. Circ. 2,600. Pays on acceptance. Buys interment industry rights. Phone queries preferred. Reports in 1 month. Free sample copy and writer's guidelines.
Nonfiction: How-to (run a monument business); informational (major news within the industry, monuments as an art form); profile (successful retailers); and technical. Buys 30-40 mss/year. Length: 1,500-2,000 words. Query. Pays $100-400.
Photos: Pays $20-50 for 5x7 or 8x10 b&w glossy prints.

‡STONE REVIEW, National Stone Association, 1415 Elliot Place NW, Washington DC 20007. (202)342-1100. Editor: Frank Atlee. Bimonthly magazine covering quarrying and supplying of crushed stone. "Designed to be a communications forum for the stone industry. Publishes information on industry technology, trends, developments and concerns. Audience are quarry operations/management, and manufacturers of equipment, suppliers of services to the industry." Estab. 1985. Circ. 2,100. Pays on publication. Publishes ms an average of 3 months after acceptance. Byline given. Negotiable kill fee. Buys one-time rights. Submit seasonal/holiday material 6 months in advance. Simultaneous, photocopied and previously published submissions OK. Computer printout submissions OK; prefers letter-quality to dot-matrix. Reports in 1 month. Free sample copy.
Nonfiction: Technical. Query with or without published clips, or send complete ms. Length: 1,000-2,500 words. "Note: We have no budget for freelance material, but I'm willing to get monetary payment OK for right material."
Photos: State availability of photos with query, then send photos with submission. Reviews contact sheets, negatives, transparencies and prints. Offers no additional payment for photos accepted with ms. Identification of subjects required. Buys one-time rights.
Tips: "At this point, all features are written by contributors in the industry, but I'd like to open it up. Articles on unique equipment, applications, etc. are good, as are those reporting on trends (e.g., there is a strong push on now for automation of operations)."

_____ *Toy, Novelty and Hobby*

‡**MINIATURES DEALER MAGAZINE**, (formerly *Miniatures and Doll Dealer Magazine*), Boynton & Associates Inc., Clifton House, Clifton VA 22024. (703)830-1000. Editor/Associate Publisher: Geraldine Willems. 50% freelance written. Eager to work with new/unpublished writers. For "retailers in the dollhouse/miniatures trade. Our readers are generally independent, small store owners who don't have time to read anything that does not pertain specifically to their own problems." Monthly magazine; 40 pages. Circ. 2,000. Pays on publication. Publishes ms an average of 3 months after acceptance. Buys all rights. Byline given. Phone queries OK. Submit seasonal/holiday material 4 months in advance. Photocopied, previously published and simultaneous submissions (if submitted to publications in different fields) OK. Computer printout submissions acceptable; prefers letter-quality to dot-matrix. Reports in 3 weeks. Sample copy $1.50; writer's guidelines for SASE.
Nonfiction: How-to (unique articles—e.g., how to finish a dollhouse exterior—are acceptable if they introduce new techniques or ideas; show the retailer how learning this technique will help sell dollhouses); profiles of miniatures shops; and business information pertaining to small store retailers. Buys 2-4 mss/issue. Query or send complete ms. "In query, writer should give clear description of intended article, when he could have it to me plus indication that he has studied the field, and is not making a 'blind' query. Availability of b&w photos should be noted." Pay negotiable.
Photos: "Photos must tie in directly with articles." State availability of photos. Pays $7 for each photo used. Prefers 5x7 b&w glossy prints (reviews contact sheets). Captions and model release preferred.
Tips: "We are interested in articles on full-line miniatures stores. The best way for a freelancer to break in is to study several issues of our magazine, then try to visit a miniatures shop and submit an *M&D Visits . . .* article. This is a regular feature that can be written by a sharp freelancer who takes the time to study and follow the formula this feature uses. Also, basic business articles for retailers—inventory control, how to handle bad checks, etc., that are written with miniatures dealers in mind, are always needed. *M&D* is extremely interested in good business articles."

MODEL RETAILER MAGAZINE, Clifton House, Clifton VA 22024. (703)830-1000. Editor: Geoffrey Wheeler. 30% freelance written. Works with a small number of new/unpublished writers each year. Monthly magazine "for hobby store owners—generally well-established small business persons, fairly well educated, and very busy." Circ. 5,980. Pays on publication. Publishes ms an average of 1-2 months after acceptance. Byline given. Buys one-time rights. Phone queries OK (no collect calls), but prefers written queries. Submit seasonal/holiday material 3 months in advance. Photocopied and previously published submissions OK, but material must not have been previously published in industry magazines. Computer printout submissions acceptable; no dot-matrix. Reports in 3 weeks. Free writer's guidelines and sample copy.
Nonfiction: Retailer profiles; articles on store management, marketing, merchandising, advertising; and photo feature (if photos tie in with marketing techniques or hobby store operation, etc.). No company profiles, 'human interest' stories, self-publicity articles, or reports on trade shows. ("We do those ourselves"). Buys 2-4 mss/issue. Query. Length: 1,200-2,500 words. Pays for complete manuscript package of: main copy, side bars (if needed), working headline, and illustrative material (if needed). Range: $125-350, depending on length and degree of specialization. Sometimes pays the expenses of writers on assignment.
Photos: "Photos that illustrate key points and are of good quality will help the article, particularly if it concerns business operation. Photos are paid for as part of total package."

PLAYTHINGS, Geyer-McAllister, 51 Madison Ave., New York NY 10010. (212)689-4411. Editor: Frank Reysen, Jr. Managing Editor: Barbara McClorey. 20-30% freelance written. A monthly merchandising magazine covering toys and hobbies aimed mainly at mass market toy retailers. Circ. 15,000. Pays on acceptance. Publishes ms an average of 3 months after acceptance. Byline sometimes given. Buys one-time rights. Submit seasonal/holiday material 3 months in advance. Simultaneous and photocopied submissions OK. Reports in 2 weeks. Free sample copy.
Nonfiction: Interview/profile, photo feature and retail profiles of toy and hobby stores and chains. Annual directory, May. Buys 10 mss/year. Query. Length: 900-2,500 words. Pays $100-350. Sometimes pays the expenses of writers on assignment.
Photos: Send photos with submission. Captions and identification of subjects required. Buys one-time rights.
Columns/Departments: Buys 5 mss/year. Query. Pays $50-100.

SOUVENIRS & NOVELTIES MAGAZINE, Kane Communications, Inc., Suite 226, 401 N. Broad St., Philadelphia PA 19108. (215)925-9744. Editor: Chuck Tooley. A magazine published 7 times/year for resort and gift industry. Circ. 20,000. Pays on publication. Byline given. Buys all rights. Computer printout submissions acceptable; prefers letter-quality to dot-matrix. Reports in 3 weeks. Sample copy for 6x9 SAE with $1 postage.

Nonfiction: Interview/profile and new product. Buys 6 mss/year. Query. Length: 700-1,500 words. Pays $25-175 for assigned articles. Sometimes pays the expenses of writers on assignment.

Photos: State availability of photos with submission. Captions, model releases and identification of subjects required.

THE STAMP WHOLESALER, Box 706, Albany OR 97321. Executive Editor: Sherrie Steward. 80% freelance written. Newspaper published 28 times/year; 32 pages. For philatelic businessmen; many are part-time and/or retired from other work. Circ. 6,000. Pays on publication. Byline given. Buys all rights. Computer printout submissions acceptable; prefers letter-quality to dot-matrix. Reports in 10 weeks. Free sample copy.

Nonfiction: How-to information on how to deal more profitably in postage stamps for collections. Emphasis on merchandising techniques and how to make money. Does not want to see any so-called "humor" items from nonprofessionals. Buys 60 ms/year. Submit complete ms. Length: 1,000-1,500 words. Pays $35 and up/article.

Tips: "Send queries on business stories. Send manuscript on stamp dealer stories. We need stories to help dealers make and save money."

Transportation

‡AMERICAN MOVER, American Movers Conference, 2200 Mill Rd., Alexandria VA 22314. (703)838-1938. Editor: Leslie L. Frank. 10% freelance written. Works with a small number of new/unpublished writers each year. A monthly trade journal on the moving and storage industry for moving company executives. Circ. 1,800. Pays on publication. Publishes ms an average of 3 months after acceptance. Byline given. Offers $100 kill fee. Buys first North American serial rights. Submit seasonal/holiday material 3 months in advance. Query for electronic submissions. Computer printout submissions OK; prefers letter-quality to dot-matrix. Reports in 3 weeks on queries. Free sample copy and writer's guidelines.

Nonfiction: How-to, interview/profile, new product, personal experience, photo feature, technical and small business articles. "No fiction or articles geared toward consumers." Buys 6 mss/year. Query with published clips. Length: 1,000-5,000 words. Pays $100-200 for assigned articles. Pays contributor copies at writer's request.

Photos: Send photos with submission. Reviews 5x7 prints. Offers no additional payment for photos accepted with ms. Captions required. Buys one-time rights.

Tips: "We have an editorial calendar available that lists topics we'll be covering. Articles on small business, such as tax tips, insurance, safety, etc., are helpful. Feature articles are most open to freelancers. Articles must slant toward moving company presidents on business-related issues. Timely topics are deregulation, drug testing, computers, insurance, tax reform and marketing."

INBOUND LOGISTICS, Thomas Publishing Co., 1 Penn Plaza, 26th Fl., New York NY 10019. (212)290-7336. Editor: Richard S. Sexton. 50% freelance written. Prefers to work with published/established writers. Bimonthly magazine covering the transportation industry. "*Inbound Logistics* is distributed to people who buy, specify, or recommend inbound freight transportation services and equipment. The editorial matter provides basic explanations of inbound freight transportation, directory listings, how-to technical information, trends and developments affecting inbound freight movements, and expository, case history feature stories." Circ. 45,000. Pays on publication. Publishes ms an average of 3 months after acceptance. Byline given. Buys all rights. Simultaneous queries, and simultaneous and photocopied submission OK. Computer printout submissions acceptable; no dot-matrix. Reports in 2 weeks. Free sample copy and writer's guidelines.

Nonfiction: How-to (basic help for traffic managers) and interview/profile (transportation professionals). Buys 15 mss/year. Query with published clips. Length: 750-1,000 words. Pays $300-1,200. Pays expenses of writers on assignment.

Photos: Paula J. Slomer, photo editor. State availability of photos with query. Pays $100-500 for b&w contact sheets, negatives, transparencies and prints; $250-500 for color contact sheets, negative transparencies and prints. Captions and identification of subjects required.

Columns/Departments: Viewpoint (discusses current opinions on transportation topics). Query with published clips.

Tips: "Have a sound knowledge of the transportation industry; educational how-to articles get our attention."

‡PILOTING CAREERS MAGAZINE, Future Aviation Professionals of America, 4291-J Memorial Dr., Decatur GA 30032. Editor: Carol Vernon. 65-70% freelance written. Prefers to work with published/established writers. "*Piloting Careers* is a monthly magazine which tries to help pilots in their job searches and in reaching their career goals. We tell our members what it's like to work for individual airlines and flight departments, as well as how to get the jobs they seek." Circ. 16,000. Pays on acceptance. Publishes ms an average of 3 months after acceptance. Byline given. Buys all rights and makes work-for-hire assignments. Photocopied and previously published submissions OK. Computer printout submissions OK; prefers letter-quality. Reports in 1 month on queries; 3 months on mss. Sample copy for 9x12 SAE with 95¢ postage; writer's guidelines for 4x9½ SAE and 1 first class stamp.

Nonfiction: How-to and interview/profile. "No historical, personal experience, humor or inspirational pieces. We don't want to hear from pilots writing about their own airlines." Buys 20-24 mss/year. Query with or without published clips, or send complete ms. Length: 1,500 words minimum. Pays 18¢/word. Sometimes pays the expenses of writers on assignment.

Photos: Send photos with submission. Reviews 35mm transparencies and 5x7 and 8x10 prints. Offers no additional payment for photos accepted with ms. Identification of subjects required. . Buys all rights.

Columns/Departments: Low-Time Blues (beginning jobs which help pilots build flight times); Class I Medical (medical issues affecting pilots); Aviation Law (legal issues affecting pilots), all 1,500-2,500 words. Buys 6-12 mss/year. Query. Length: 1,000-2,500 words. Pays $50 maximum.

Tips: "Queries with published clips are appreciated. Writers must know the aviation industry well or specialize in a single aspect of aviation: business, company interview processes, medical certification, aviation law. We look for anything that will help a pilot make a good job decision or prepare for a job with the airlines when it is offered. Full features are the most open. Our lead feature each month, called "Flying For," is about a different airline each issue and is written on assignment only. Writers who prove their knowledge and skill on another feature may later be added to a roster of writers who are assigned "Flying For" articles."

‡TRUCKS MAGAZINE, Dedicated to the People Behind the Wheel, 20 Waterside Plaza, New York NY 10010-2615. (212)532-1392. Editor: John Stevens. Managing Editor: Chris Krieg. 25% freelance written. Magazine covering long haul, heavy-duty trucking. "Trucks magazine is dedicated to the health, safety, image and profitability of long haul, heavy-duty truck drivers and their families." Circ. 50,000. Pays within 30 days of publication. Publishes ms an average of 6-10 months after acceptance. Byline given. Buys first rights. Submit seasonal/holiday material 10 months in advance. Reports in 1 week on queries; sample copy for 8x10 SAE with $1.75 postage.

Nonfiction: Expose, general interest, how-to, inspirational, new product, personal experience and photo feature. Buys 25 mss/year. Send complete ms. Length: 1,500 words maximum. Pays $50/published page.

Photos: Send photos with submission. Reviews transparencies and prints. Offers no additional payment for photos accepted with ms. Captions, model releases and identification of subjects required. Buys one-time rights.

Travel

These publications are designed for travel professionals to learn about trends, tours and types of transportation for their customers. Magazines about vacations and travel for general readers are listed under Travel in the Consumer section.

ABC STAR SERVICE, ABC International, 131 Clarendon St., Boston MA 02116. (617)262-5000. Managing Editor: Kenneth Hale-Wehmann. 100% freelance written. "Eager to work with new/unpublished writers as well as those working from a home base abroad, planning trips that would allow time for hotel reporting, or living in major ports for cruise ships." Worldwide guide to accommodations and cruises founded in 1960 (as *Sloan Travel Reports*) and sold to travel agencies on subscription basis. Pays 15 days prior to publication. Publishes ms an average of 3 months after acceptance. Buys all rights. Query for electronic submissions. Computer printout submissions OK; prefers letter-quality to dot-matrix. Query. Query should include details on

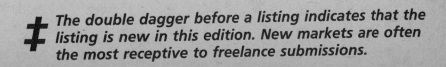

The double dagger before a listing indicates that the listing is new in this edition. New markets are often the most receptive to freelance submissions.

writer's experience in travel and writing, specific forthcoming travel plans, and how much time would be available for hotel or ship inspections. Buys 4,000+ reports/year. Pays $15/report used (higher for ships). "Higher rates of payment and of guaranteed acceptance of set number of reports will be made after correspondent's ability and reliability have been established." Writer's guidelines and list of available assignments for #10 SAE and 1 first class stamp.

Nonfiction: Objective, critical evaluations of hotels and cruise ships suitable for international travelers, based on personal inspections. Freelance correspondents ordinarily are assigned to update an entire state or country. "Assignment involves on-site inspections of all hotels we review; revising and updating published reports; and reviewing new properties. Qualities needed are thoroughness, precision, perservance, and keen judgement. Solid research skills and powers of observation are crucial. Travel and travel writing experience are highly desirable. Reviews should be colorful, clear, and documented with hotel's brochure, tariff sheet, etc. We accept no hotel advertising or payment for listings, so reviews should dispense praise and criticism where deserved."

Tips: "We may require sample hotel or cruise reports on facilities near freelancer's hometown before giving the first assignment. No byline because of sensitive nature of reviews."

‡**AIRFAIR INTERLINE MAGAZINE, The Authority On Interline Travel**, Airline Marketing, Inc., 25 W. 39th St., New York NY 10018. (212)840-6714. Managing Editor: Ratu Kamlani. Bimonthly magazine covering travel information for airline employees; describing travel packages by air, land or ship and including information on hotels and restaurants. Circ. 30,000. Pays on publication. Byline given. Buys first North American serial rights. Submit seasonal/holiday material 2 months in advance. Simultaneous queries, and simultaneous and photocopied submissions OK. Reports in 6 months on queries; 4 months on mss. Free sample copy and writer's guidelines.

Nonfiction: Travel (should concentrate on foreign destinations). Buys 20 mss/year. Query with clips of published work. Length: 2,000 words maximum. Pays $75.

AMERICAS, Organization of American States, Editorial Offices, General Secretariat Bldg., 1889 F. St. NW, Washington DC 20006. Managing Editor: A.R. Williams. 70% freelance written. Official cultural organ of Organization of American States. Audience is persons interested in inter-American topics. Editions published in English and Spanish. Bimonthly. Circ. 75,000. Buys first publication and reprint rights. Byline given. Pays on publication. Publishes ms an average of 6 months after acceptance. Computer printout submissions acceptable; prefers letter-quality to dot-matrix. "They have *got* to be readable." Free sample copy. Queries preferred. Articles received on speculation only. Include cover letter with writer's background. Reports in 3 months. Not necessary to enclose SASE.

Nonfiction: Articles of general New World interest on travel, history, art, literature, theatre, development, archeology, etc. Emphasis on modern, up-to-date Latin America. Taboos are religious and political themes or articles with noninternational slant. "Photos not required, but are a big plus." Buys 36 unsolicited mss/year. Length: 2,500 words maximum. Pays $200 minimum.

Tips: "Send excellent photographs in both color and b&w, address an international readership, not a local or national one. We want something more critically insightful than a Sunday newspaper travel section piece. We read everything that comes in over the transom. We'll publish anything that's good, and we don't much care if the author has been published before or not. In fact, we're getting weary of published authors who don't write very well and whose careers seem to have been propelled along by talented editors providing the authors with marvelous clips."

‡**BUS RIDE**, Friendship Publications, Inc., Box 1472, Spokane WA 99210. (509)328-9181. Editor: William A. Luke. Magazine published 8 times/year covering bus transportation. Circ. 12,500. Byline given. Not copyrighted. Sample copy $3; free writer's guidelines.

Nonfiction: How-to (on bus maintenance, operations, marketing); new product; and technical. Only bus transportation material is acceptable. Query. Length: 500-1,500 words. No payment from publication; "writer may receive payment from company or organization featured."

Photos: State availability of photos. Reviews b&w 8x10 prints. Captions required.

Fillers: Newsbreaks. Length: 50-100 words.

Tips: "A freelancer can contact bus companies, transit authorities, suppliers and products for the bus industry to write articles which would be accepted by our publication."

BUS TOURS MAGAZINE, The Magazine of Bus Tours and Long Distance Charters, National Bus Trader, Inc., 9698 W. Judson Rd., Polo IL 61064. (815)946-2341. Editor: Larry Plachno. Editorial Assistant: Richard Wartenberg. 80% freelance written. Eager to work with new/unpublished writers. Bimonthly magazine for bus companies and tour brokers who design or sell bus tours. Circ. 9,306. Pays as arranged. Publishes ms an average of 6 months after acceptance. Byline given. Not copyrighted. Buys rights as arranged. Submit seasonal/holiday material 9 months in advance. Simultaneous queries OK. Computer printout submissions acceptable; no dot-matrix. Reports in 1 month. Free sample copy and writer's guidelines.

Nonfiction: Historical/nostalgic, how-to, humor, interview/profile, new product, professional, personal experience, and travel; all on bus tours. Buys 10 mss/year. Query. Length: open. Pays negotiable fee. Sometimes pays the expenses of writers on assignment.
Photos: State availability of photos. Reviews 35mm transparencies and 6x9 or 8x10 prints. Caption, model release, and identification of subjects required.
Columns/Departments: Bus Tour Marketing; and Buses and the Law. Buys 15-20 mss/year. Query. Length: 1-1½ pages.
Tips: "Most of our feature articles are written by freelancers under contract from local convention and tourism bureaus. Specifications sent on request. Writers should query local bureaus regarding their interest. Writer need not have extensive background and knowledge of bus tours."

CANADIAN RV DEALER, Suite 202, 2077 Dundas St. E., Mississauga, Ontario L4X 1M2 Canada. (416)624-8218. Editor: Peter Tasler. 20% freelance written. Published 7 times/year "to better the development and growth of Canada's recreational vehicle and camping accessory dealers." Circ. 8,000. Pays on publication. Publishes ms an average of 2 months after acceptance. Byline given. Buys first serial rights. Reports in 2 months. Free sample copy and writer's guidelines.
Nonfiction: All features must pertain to the Canadian RV dealer and marketplace. Will consider occasional U.S. pieces if applicable to Canada or unusual slant. Would also consider dealer-slanted humor. Self-help management-type articles also OK. Query first.

NATIONAL BUS TRADER, The Magazine of Bus Equipment for the United States and Canada, 9698 W. Judson Rd., Polo IL 61064. (815)946-2341. Editor: Larry Plachno. 25% freelance written. Eager to work with new/unpublished writers. Monthly magazine for manufacturers, dealers and owners of buses and motor coaches. Circ. 7,354. Pays on either acceptance or publication. Publishes ms an average of 3 months after acceptance. Byline given. Not copyrighted. Buys rights "as required by writer." Simultaneous queries, and simultaneous, photocopied, and previously published submissions OK. Computer printout submissions acceptable; no dot-matrix. Reports in 1 month. Free sample copy.
Nonfiction: Historical/nostalgic (on old buses); how-to (maintenance repair); new products; photo feature; and technical (aspects of mechanical operation of buses). "We are finding that more and more firms and agencies are hiring freelancers to write articles to our specifications. We are more likely to run them if someone else pays." No material that does *not* pertain to bus tours or bus equipment. Buys 3-5 unsolicited mss/year. Query. Length: varies. Pays variable rate. Sometimes pays the expenses of writers on assignment.
Photos: State availability of photos. Reviews 5x7 or 8x10 prints and 35mm transparencies. Captions, model release, and identification of subjects required.
Columns/Departments: Bus maintenance; Buses and the Law; Regulations; and Bus of the Month. Buys 20-30 mss/year. Query. Length: 1-1½ pages. Pays variable rate.
Tips: "We are a very technical publication. Writers should submit qualifications showing extensive background in bus vehicles. We're very interested in well-researched articles on older bus models and manufacturers, or current converted coaches. We would like to receive history of individual bus models prior to 1953 and history of GMC 'new look' models. Write or phone editors with article concept or outline for comments and approval."

RV BUSINESS, TL Enterprises, Inc., 29901 Agoura Rd., Agoura CA 91301. (818)991-4980. Executive Editor: Katherine Sharma. 60% freelance written. Prefers to work with published/established writers. Semi-monthly magazine covering the recreational vehicle and allied industries for people in the RV industry—dealers, manufacturers, suppliers, campground management, and finance experts. Circ. 25,000. Pays on acceptance. Publishes ms an average of 2 months after acceptance. Byline given. Offers 50% kill fee. Buys first North American serial rights. Submit seasonal/holiday material 6 months in advance. Photocopied submissions OK. Query for electronic submissions. Computer printout submissions acceptable; prefers letter-quality to dot-matrix. Reports in 3 weeks on queries; 6 weeks on mss. Sample copy for 9x12 SAE and 3 first class stamps; writer's guidelines for business size SAE and 1 first class stamp.
Nonfiction: Technical, financial, legal or marketing issues; historical/nostalgic (companies, products or people pertaining to the RV industry itself); how-to (deal with any specific aspect of the RV business); interview/profile (persons or companies involved with the industry—legislative, finance, dealerships, campground management, manufacturing, supplier); new product (no payment for company promo material—Product Spotlight usually requires interview with company spokesperson, first-hand experience with product. Specifics and verification of statistics required—must be factual) opinion (controversy OK); personal experience (must be something of importance to readership—must have a point: it worked for me, it can for you; or this is why it didn't work for me); photo feature (4-color transparencies required with good captions; photo coverage of RV shows, conventions and meetings not appropriate topics for photo feature); and technical (photos required, 4-color preferred). General business articles may be considered. Buys 75 mss/year. Query with published clips. Send complete ms—"but only read on speculation." Length: 1,000-1,500 words. Pays variable rate up to $500. Sometimes pays expenses of writers on assignment.

Photos: State availability of photos with query or send photos with ms. Reviews 35mm transparencies and 8x10 b&w prints. Captions, model release, and identification of subjects required. Buys one-time or all rights; unused photos returned.

Columns/Departments: Guest editorial; News (50-500 words maximum, b&w photos appreciated); and RV People (color photos/4-color transparencies; this section lends itself to fun, upbeat copy). Buys 100-120 mss/year. Query or send complete ms. Pays $10-200 "depending on where used and importance."

Tips: "Query. Phone OK; letter preferable. Send one or several ideas and a few lines letting us know how you plan to treat it/them. We are always looking for good authors knowledgable in the RV industry or related industries. Change of editorial focus requires more articles that are brief, factual, hard hitting, business oriented and in-depth. Will work with promising writers, published or unpublished."

‡**SUCCESSFUL MEETINGS MAGAZINE, The Authority on Meetings and Incentive Travel Management**, Bill Communications, Inc., 633 3rd Ave., New York NY 10017. (212)986-4800. Editor-in-Chief: Mel Hosansky. Executive Editor: Holly Hughes. Monthly magazine on corporate and association meeting planning. Circ. 77,000. Pays on acceptance. Byline given. Offers 100% kill fee. Buys all rights. Submit seasonal/holiday material 3 months in advance. Reports in 2 months. Sample copy $5; free writer's guidelines.

Nonfiction: Book excerpts (about meeting planning); general interest (trends in this industry); how-to (about meeting management); humor (about business travel/meetings); interview/profile (with industry people); technical (audiovisual); and travel (business group travel). No promotional pieces on hotels or other suppliers. Buys 60-70 mss/year. Query with published clips. Length: 150-800 words. Pays $125-500.

Tips: "Experience in meeting planning is useful. Travel writing or business writing (*not* financial) is also useful. We are willing to interview potential freelancers for a regular ongoing relationship. We see too many dry articles by 'experts'—we need writers who can interview experts and fashion their comments into authoritative overview articles." Site reports and feature stories (topics determined in advance—request editorial calendar) are areas most open to freelancers.

‡**TRAVELAGE MIDAMERICA**, Official Airlines Guide, Inc., A Dun & Bradstreet Co., Suite 701, 320 N. Michigan, Chicago IL 60601. (312)346-4952. Editor/Publisher: Martin Deutsch. Managing Editor: Karen Goodwin. 15% freelance written. Weekly magazine "for travel agents in the 13 midAmerica states and in Ontario and Manitoba." Circ. 20,000. Pays on publication. Publishes ms an average of 2 months after acceptance. Buys one-time rights and second serial (reprint) rights. Submit seasonal/holiday material 3 months in advance. Simultaneous, photocopied, and previously published submissions OK. Computer printout submissions acceptable ("but not pleased with"); prefers letter-quality to dot-matrix. Query first. Reports in 1 month. Free sample copy and writer's guidelines.

Nonfiction: "News on destinations, hotels, operators, rates and other developments in the travel business." Also runs human interest features on retail travel agents in the readership area. No stories that don't contain prices; no queries that don't give detailed story lines. No general destination stories, especially ones on "do-it-yourself" travel. Buys 20 mss/year. Query. Length: 400-1,500 words. Pays $1.50/column inch.

Photos: State availability of photos with query. Pays $1.50/column inch for glossy b&w prints.

Tips: "Our major need is for freelance human interest stories with a marketing angle on travel agents in our readership area. Buying freelance destination stories is a much lower priority."

TRAVELAGE WEST, Official Airline Guides, Inc., 100 Grant Ave., San Francisco CA 94108. Executive Editor: Donald C. Langley. 5% freelance written. Prefers to work with published/established writers. Weekly magazine for travel agency sales counselors in the western U.S. and Canada. Circ. 35,000. Pays on publication. Publishes ms an average of 1 month after acceptance. Byline given. Buys all rights. Offers kill fee. Submit seasonal/holiday material 2 months in advance. Query for electronic submissions. Computer printout submissions acceptable; prefers letter-quality to dot-matrix. Reports in 1 month. Free writer's guidelines.

Nonfiction: Travel. "No promotional approach or any hint of do-it-yourself travel. Emphasis is on news, not description. No static descriptions of places, particularly resort hotels." Buys 40 mss/year. Query. Length: 1,000 words maximum. Pays $2/column inch.

Tips: "Query should be a straightforward description of the proposed story, including (1) an indication of the news angle, no matter how tenuous, and (2) a recognition by the author that we run a trade magazine for travel agents, not a consumer book. I am particularly turned off by letters that try to get me all worked up about the 'beauty' or excitement of some place. Authors planning to travel might discuss with us a proposed angle before they go; otherwise their chances of gathering the right information are slim."

Veterinary

‡**ANGUS JOURNAL**,Angus Publications, Inc., 3201 Frederick Blvd., St. Joseph MO 64501. (816)233-0508. Editor: Jim Cotton. 10% freelance written. Monthly (except June/July, which are combined) magazine. "Must be Angus-related or beef cattle with no other breeds mentioned." Circ. 14,000. Pays on acceptance. Byline given. Buys first North American serial rights, second serial(reprint) rights, simultaneous rights and makes work-for-hire assignments. Submit seasonal/holiday material 3 months in advance. Simultaneous submissions, photocopied submissions and previously published submissions OK. Computer printout submissions OK; prefer letter-quality to dot-matrix. Reports in 2 weeks. Samples copy $1.50 wtih 10x13 SAE and 4 first class stamps; writer's guidelines for #10 SASE.

Nonfiction: Historical/nostalgic, how-to, humor, interview/profile and photo feature. Nothing without an angus slant. Buys 1 mss/year. Send complete ms. Length: 1,000-5,000 words. Pays $50-300.

Photos: Send photos with submission. Review contact sheets and transparencies. Offers no additions payment for photos accepted with ms. Identification of subjects required. Buys one-time rights.

Columns/Departments: The Grazier (pasture, fencing, range management). Send complete ms. Length: 500-2,000 words. Pays $25-75.

Fiction: Historical, humorous and western. Must be short, with an angus slant. Send complete ms. Length: 2,000-4,000 words. Pays $100-300.

Poetry: Light verse and traditional. Nothing without an angus, beef cattle, farming or ranching slant. Submit up to 4 poems at one time. Length: 4-20 lines. Pays $10-75.

Fillers: Anecdotes, facts, newbreaks and short humor. Length: 50-200 words. Pays $5-25.

Tips: Areas most open to freelancers are "farm and ranch profiles—breeder interviews."

‡**GROOM & BOARD, For Professional Groomers & Kennel Operators, Incorporating *Groomers Gazette Kennel News*,** H.H. Backer Associates, Inc., Suite 504, 207 S. Wabash Ave., Chicago IL 60604. (312)663-4040. Editor: Karen M. Long. 10-25% freelance written. Works with small number of new/unpublished writers each year. Magazine published 8 times/year covering the grooming and kennel industries. "*Groom & Board* is the only national publication for professional groomers and kennel operators. It covers products, grooming styles, operation of business, animal management." Circ. 14,000. Pays on acceptance. Publishes ms an average of 3 months after acceptance. Byline given. Buys first North American serial or all rights. Submit seasonal/holiday material 4 months in advance. Query for electronic submission. Computer printout submissions OK; prefers letter-quality. Reports in 1 month on queries; 2 weeks on mss. Sample copy for $2.50 and 9x12 SASE; free writer's guidelines.

Nonfiction: Book excerpts, how-to (groom breeds, make money, advertise, promote); interview/profile; opinion; personal business experience; photo feature and technical. No general articles that cover subjects we've covered in depth; animal/pet stories. Buys 4-10 mss/year. Query with published clips. Length: 1,000-3,000 words. Pays $75-200 for assigned articles; pays $50-150 for unsolicited articles. Sometimes pays expenses of writers on assignment.

Photos: Send photos with submission. Reviews contact sheets, transparencies and 5x7 prints. Offers $5 per photo. Captions and identification of subjects required. Buys one-time rights.

Tips: "The type of article we purchase most is the grooming shop/boarding kennel profile, a story about an interesting/successful business. We supply typical questions to writers when we answer their queries."

MODERN VETERINARY PRACTICE, American Veterinary Publications, Inc., 5782 Thornwood Dr., Goleta CA 93117. 5% freelance written. Monthly magazine, 80 pages; for graduate veterinarians. Circ. 22,000. Pays on publication. Publishes ms an average of 3 months after acceptance. Buys all rights. Phone queries OK. Submit seasonal/holiday material 3 months in advance. Computer printout submissions acceptable; prefers letter-quality to dot-matrix. Reports in 1 month. Sample copy $4.25.

Nonfiction: How-to (clinical medicine, new surgical procedures, business management); informational (business management, education, government projects affecting practicing veterinarians, special veterinary projects); interviews (only on subjects of interest to veterinarians; query first); and technical (clinical reports, technical advancements in veterinary medicine and surgery). Buys 12-15 unsolicited mss/year. Submit complete ms, but query first on ideas for pieces other than technical or business articles. Pays $25 for published page.

Photos: B&w glossies (5x7 or larger) and color transparencies (5x7) used with mss. No additional payment.

Tips: "Contact practicing veterinarians or veterinary colleges. Find out what interests the clinician and what new procedures and ideas might be useful in a veterinary practice. Better yet, collaborate with a veterinarian. Most of our authors are veterinarians or those working with veterinarians in a professional capacity. Knowledge of the interests and problems of practicing veterinarians is essential."

VETERINARY COMPUTING, American Veterinary Publications, Inc., Drawer KK, Santa Barbara CA 93102. (800)235-6947 CA, AK or HI (805)963-6561. Editors: Jean Yamamura and Paul Pratt, VMD. 60% freelance written. Prefers to work with writers knowledgable in computers. Monthly magazine department covering computer applications in veterinary medicine and practice management. "Our readers are veterinary practitioners who have computers or are thinking about buying them. They are looking for information on the best and most cost-effective ways to purchase and use computers in their practices." Pays on publication. Publishes ms an average of 4 months after acceptance. Byline given. Buys all rights. Submit seasonal/holiday material 4 months in advance. Simultaneous queries and photocopied submissions OK. Electronic submissions OK if 5¼" single-sided disks with an MS DOS WordStar, or any ASCII file, but requires hard copy also. Computer printout submissions acceptable; prefers letter-quality to dot-matrix. Reports in 3 weeks on queries; 1 month on mss. Sample copy for 9x12 SAE and 3 first class stamps; free writer's guidelines.

Nonfiction: How-to, new product, book and software reviews, and computer-user tips. No profiles or overly philosophical articles. "We want concrete, practical, usable pieces about how practitioners can most effectively use computers in their businesses." Buys 12-24 mss/year. Query or send complete ms (on short articles). Length: 150-2,000 words. Pays $10 (for short tips; $50/first published page, $25 for succeeding full pages for longer articles; printed page equals 3 typed double-spaced pages).

Tips: "Make submissions concise, practical, and usable in plain, nontechnical language. We are especially interested in material on how to use canned software in a veterinary practice. Reviews/articles about canned software and money-saving computer tips are the areas most open to freelancers in our publication. The writer may have a better chance of breaking in short articles and fillers, though length does not matter as much as practicality. The most frequent mistakes made by writers are lack of depth and lack of how-to information (telling what a vet does with the computer without telling how)."

VETERINARY ECONOMICS MAGAZINE, 9073 Lenexa Dr., Lenexa KS 66215. (913)492-4300. Editor: Mike Sollars. 50% freelance written. Prefers to work with published/established writers and works with a small number of new/unpublished writers each year. Monthly magazine for all practicing veterinarians in the U.S. Buys exclusive rights in the field. Pays on publication. Publishes ms an average of 6 months after acceptance. Computer printout submissions acceptable.

Nonfiction: Uses case histories telling about good business practices on the part of veterinarians. Also, articles about financial problems, investments, insurance and similar subjects of particular interest to professionals. "We reject articles with superficial information about a subject instead of carefully researched and specifically directed articles for our field." Pays negotiable rates. Pays expenses of writers on assignment.

VETERINARY PRACTICE MANAGEMENT, Whittle Communications, 505 Market St., Knoxville TN 37902. (615)595-5211. Associate Editor: Rose R. Kennedy. 80% freelance written. Prefers to work with published/established business writers. Semiannual magazine—"a business guide for small animal practitioners." Circ. 33,000. Pays on acceptance. Publishes ms an average of 3-4 months after acceptance. Byline given. Offers kill fee. Buys first serial rights to the same material. Simultaneous queries OK. Query for electronic submissions. Computer printout submissions acceptable; prefers letter-quality to dot-matrix. Writer's guidelines and free sample copy to experienced business writers.

Nonfiction: How-to, and successful business (practice) management techniques supported by veterinary anecdotes and expert advice. No "how to milk more dollars out of your clients" articles. Buys 16 mss/year. Query with published clips; no unsolicited manuscripts. Pays $600-2,0000 (average $1,200). Pays expenses of writers on assignment.

Columns/Departments: Management Briefs, and In the Know. "Most items are written in-house, but we will consider ideas." Query with published clips. Pays up to $400.

> **❝** *A number of our now regularly contributing freelance writers began by submitting a piece that was nearly acceptable—with changes. They proceeded to rework and rewrite their piece as many as ten times to get it right. By sticking with the story, they not only proved their desire to work for us, but learned in the process exactly what we were looking for.* **❞**

> *—Ellen Stein Burbach*
> *managing editor,* **Ohio Magazine**

Scriptwriting

Writing plays for stage or screen has been described as writing with the eye rather than with the pen. As you begin to write scripts, you'll find immediately how different writing fiction and scripts really is. Phrases like "five years earlier," or "meanwhile, back in town," so useful as transitions in prose, cannot be used in plays or screenplays; the changes in time and place must be somehow shown in scenes. And while the audience will be able to take in instantly whatever setting you have chosen, the producers of your play or filmscript must have this information described for them in minute detail.

New writers should read all the scripts they can, and watch and analyze plays, TV programs and movies. If you're writing for the screen or stage, try to write a story that actors will enjoy playing, with a plot touching on subjects likely to be of interest to a large audience. Clarity will be your primary concern when you write business or instructional scripts.

Market research is vital if you hope to have your script produced. A professional attitude, and care in keeping your targeted audience in mind as you write, will increase your chances of success greatly.

Business and Educational Writing

"We're looking for writers with the ability to convert dry information into an interesting conversational style," says the president of one production company, echoing the thoughts of many producers who seek writers for their business and educational scripts. The business subgenre of scriptwriting can be roughly divided into two types: scripts intended to describe a company's product and sell it to consumers, and scripts designed to train or motivate employees of large companies.

Corporations often ask agencies to produce the films they want, and it's unlikely a script you have on hand will meet the exact needs of a particular agency or corporation. The sample screenplay and résumé you send will generally be used to screen *you* and your suitability for future freelance assignments.

Instructors at elementary schools, junior highs and high schools continue to use film strips, movies and overhead transparencies to teach their students. Producers of these materials are often open to queries by freelancers with an interest in writing on specific subjects. "Keep up to date and informed on educational trends," advises one producer, adding, "study the market before starting to work."

Instructional videos on topics like sports, painting and cooking continue to be popular, although the B. Dalton bookstore chain has stopped carrying these videos, cutting an important outlet for these instructional films.

Dependability and a professional attitude are essential, especially if you will be working directly with an agency's clients. As one producer notes, "writers must be highly creative *and* highly disciplined." Equally important is the ability to keep your script produceable within your assigned budget.

Local writers usually have a strong advantage over out-of-town freelancers. A new writer will do best to send résumés or samples to nearby advertising agencies or producers and set up an appointment to talk about possible assignments. Check your phone book for ideas. If you're interested in writing scripts for educational films or film strips, it will be worth your while to watch some produced by the company for which you'd like to work. Check with your local schools or the education department library at a nearby college or university.

The cable TV market continues to grow and new freelancers may have an easier time breaking in now than they would have 10 years ago. A square (□) to the left of a listing denotes firms interested in cable TV scripts.

ADMASTER, INC., 95 Madison Ave., New York NY 10016. (212)679-1134. Director: Charles Corn. Produces sales and training material. Purchases 50-75 scripts/year. Works with 5-10 writers/year. Buys all rights. No previously published material. Reports in 1 month. Free catalog.
Needs: Charts, film loops (16mm), films (35 and 16mm), filmstrips (sound), multimedia kits, overhead transparencies, slides, tapes and cassettes. "We need material for multi-media industrial and financial meetings." Submit synopsis/outline, complete script or résumé. Makes outright purchase of $250-500.
Tips: "We want local writers only."

‡AMERICAN MEDIA INC.,1454 30th St., West Des Moines IA 50265. (515)224-0919. Contact: Art Bauer. Produces material for the business and industry training market (management, motivation, sales). Buys 10+ scripts/year. Buys all rights. Previously produced material OK. Reports in 3 weeks. Catalog for 8½x11 SAE with $1 postage.
Needs: Produces 16mm films and 1-inch videotapes. Submit synopsis/outline or completed script. Payment varies depending on script and quality.
Tips: "Do your homework, don't rush, think a project through. Ask and find out what your client needs, not just what you think. Work long and hard."

‡ARNOLD AND ASSOCIATES PRODUCTIONS, INC., 2159 Powell St., San Francisco CA 94133. (415)989-3490. President: John Arnold. Executive Producers: James W. Morris and Thomas Kennedy. Produces material for the general public (entertainment/motion pictures) and for corporate clients (employees/customers/consumers). Buys 10-15 scripts/year. Works with 3 writers/year. Buys all rights. Previously produced material OK. Reports on mss in 1 month.
Needs: Films (35mm) and videotape. Looking for "upscale image and marketing programs." Dramatic writing for "name narrators and post scored original music; and motion picture. $5-6 million dollar budget. Dramatic or horror." Query with samples or submit completed script. Makes outright purchase of $1,000.
Tips: Looking for "upscale writers that understand corporate image production, and motion picture writer(s) that understands story and dialogue."

A/V CONCEPTS CORP., 30 Montauk Blvd., Oakdale NY 11769. (516)567-7227. Contact: P. Solimene or K. Brennan. Produces material for elementary-high school students, either on grade level or in remedial situations. 100% freelance written. Works with a small number of new/unpublished writers each year. Buys 25 scripts/year from unpublished/unproduced writers. Employs both filmstrip and personal computer media. Computer printout submissions acceptable. Reports on outline in 1 month; on final scripts in 6 weeks. Buys all rights.
Needs: Interested in original educational computer (disk-based) software programs for Apple plus, 48k. Main concentration in language arts, mathematics and reading. "Manuscripts must be written using our lists of vocabulary words and meet our readability formula requirements. Specific guidelines are devised for each level. Length of manuscript and subjects will vary according to grade level for which material is prepared. Basically, we want material that will motivate people to read." Pays $100 and up.
Tips: "Writers must be highly creative and highly disciplined. We are interested in mature content materials."

BARR FILMS, 3490 E. Foothill Blvd., Pasadena CA 91107. (213)793-6153. Vice President, Product Development: George Holland. Produces material for schools, health agencies, libraries, colleges, business and government." Buys 10-20 scripts/year. Buys all rights. Reports in 1 month. Free catalog.
Needs: Films (16mm). Looking for "short, 10-25-minute films on any educational or training subject." Submit synopsis/outline. Makes outright purchase of $1,000-3,000.

SAMUEL R. BLATE ASSOCIATES, 10331 Watkins Mill Dr., Gaithersburg MD 20879-2935. (301)840-2248. President: Samuel R. Blate. Produces audiovisual material for business and nearby Washington, D.C. government. "We work with two to six writers per year—it varies as to business conditions and demand." Buys first rights when possible. Electronic submissions OK via CP/M-80, SSDD, Kaypro II. Computer printout submissions acceptable; prefers letter-quality to dot-matrix. Reports in 1 week on queries; 2 weeks on submissions. **Needs:** Filmstrips (silent and sound), multimedia kits, slides, tapes and cassettes. Especially needs short AV productions produced for specific client needs. Query with samples. Payment "depends on type of contract with principal client." Pays expenses of writers on assignment. **Tips:** "Writers must have a strong track record of technical and aesthetic excellence. Clarity is not next to divinity—it is above it."

‡BNA COMMUNICATIONS, INC., 9439 Key West Ave., Rockville MD 20850. (301)948-0540. Producer/Director: Clifton R. Witt. Produces material primarily for business, industry and government; "client-sponsored films approach specific audiences." 50% freelance written. All scripts produced are unagented submissions. Buys 7-12 scripts, works with 3-4 writers/year. Buys 1 script/year from unpublished/unproduced writer. Buys "usually all rights—but other arrangements have been made." Reports in 1 month. Free catalog. **Needs:** "Our needs are presently under control." Video, films, slide shows and video disks. Query with samples. **Tips:** "We're looking for writers with the ability to grasp the subject and develop a relatively simple treatment, particularly if the client is not motion-savvy. Don't overload with tricks . . . unless the show is about tricks. Most good scripts have some concept of a beginning, middle and end. We are interested in good *dialogue* writers. Currently doing many chemical safety programs (hazardous waste, etc.)"

‡BOSUSTOW VIDEO, 2207 Colby Ave., West Los Angeles CA 90064-1504. (213)478-0821. President: Tee Bosustow. Produces material for corporate, promotional and home-video audiences. Worked with 12 writers last year. Buys all rights "usually." Previously produced material OK. Does not return unsolicited material. "I hire writers for specific projects, never use pre-written material." Reports back "only when job available." **Needs:** Tapes and cassettes. Submit résumé only. Makes outright purchase (average $100/page). **Tips:** Looks for writers with the "ability to convert dry information into interesting conversational style."

CABSCOTT BROADCAST PRODUCTION, INC., 517 7th Ave., Lindenwold NJ 08021. (609)346-3400. Contact: Larry Scott/Anne Foster. Produces industrial and broadcast material. 10% freelance written. Works with a small number of new/unpublished writers each year. Buys 10-12 scripts/year. Buys all rights. No previously produced material. Electronic submissions OK via Apple MacIntosh or Apple III, but requires hard copy also. Computer printout submissions acceptable; prefers letter-quality to dot-matrix. Reports in 1 month. Free catalog. **Needs:** Tapes and cassettes and video. Query with samples. Makes outright purchase. Sometimes pays expenses of writers on assignment.

CATHEDRAL FILMS, INC., Suite I, 5310 Derry, Agoura CA 91301. (818)991-3290. Contact: Scott Miller. Produces material for church and school audiences. Works with variable number of writers/year. Buys all rights and AV rights. Previously produced material OK "except from other AV media." Reports in 1 month on queries; 2 months on mss. Catalog for SAE and 54¢ postage. **Needs:** Various Christian, religious, educational and/or dramatic material. All ages. Produces 16mm films, sound filmstrips and video. Submit synopsis/outline or complete script. Pays variable rates.

‡CHAPPLE FILMS AND VIDEO, Route 198, Chaplin CT 06235. (203)455-9779. President: Wendy Wood. Produces business, educational and general films. Purchases 10 scripts/year. Buys all rights. No previously produced material. Free catalog. **Needs:** "In general, 10-minute scripts on a wide variety of industrial subjects." Produces 16mm films, slides, tapes and cassettes and videotapes. Submit completed script, resume and samples. Makes outright purchase. **Tips:** Looking for "humor and the ability to work fast."

CLEARVUE, INC., 5711 N. Milwaukee Ave., Chicago IL 60646. (312)775-9433. President: W.O. McDermed. Produces material for educational market—grades kindergarten-12. 90% freelance written. Prefers to work with published/established writers; works with a small number of new/unpublished writers each year. Buys 20-50 scripts/year from previously unpublished/unproduced writers. Buys all rights. Previously produced material OK. Electronic submissions OK, but requires hard copy also. Computer printout submissions acceptable; prefers letter-quality to dot-matrix. Reports in 2 weeks on queries; 3 weeks on submissions. Free catalog. **Needs:** Filmstrips (silent), filmstrips (sound), multimedia kits, and slides. "Our filmstrips are 35 to 100 frames—8 to 30 minutes for all curriculum areas." Query. Makes outright purchase, $100-5,000. Sometimes pays the expenses of writers on assignment.

Tips: "Our interests are in filmstrips and video for the elementary and high school markets on all subjects."

‡**COMARK**,1415 Second St., Santa Monica CA 90401. Vice President: Stan Ono. Produces material for corporate/industrial audience. Buys 18 scripts/year. Buys all rights. No previously produced material.

Needs: "Video training, sales/marketing, retail, financial and food services." Produces 16mm films, multimedia kits, slides and video. Submit resume. Makes outright purchase.

COMPASS FILMS, 51 Madison St., Newton NJ 07860. Executive Producer: Robert Whittaker. Produces material for educational, industrial and general adult audiences. Specializes in Marine films, stop motion and special effects with a budget . . . and national and worldwide filming in difficult locations. 60% freelance written. Works with 3 writers/year. Buys 2-4 scripts/year. 80% of scripts are unagented submissions. Buys all rights. Query with samples or submit resume. Computer printout submissions acceptable. Reports in 6 weeks. Buys all rights.

Needs: Scripts for 5- to 30-minute business films, and general documentary and theatrical feature films. "We would like to consider theatrical stories for possible use for feature films. We also would like to review writers to develop existing film treatments and ideas with strong dialogue." Also needs ghost writers, editors and researchers. Produces 16mm and 35mm films and video tape products. Payment negotiable, depending on experience. Pays expenses of writers on assignment.

Tips: Writer/photographers receive higher consideration "because we could also use them as still photographers on location and they could double-up as rewrite men . . . and ladies. Experience in videotape editing supervision an asset. We are producing more high 'fashion-tech' industrial video."

COMPRO PRODUCTIONS, Suite 114, 2080 Peachtree Ind. Court, Atlanta GA 30341. (404)455-1943. Producers: Nels Anderson and Steve Brinson. Audience is general public and specific business audience. Buys 10-25 scripts/year. Buys all rights. No previously produced material. No unsolicited material; submissions will not be returned because "all work is contracted."

Needs: "We solicit writers for corporate films/video in the areas of training, point purchase, sales, how-to, benefit programs, resorts and colleges." Produces 16-35mm films and videotapes. Query with samples. Makes outright purchase or pays cost per minute.

CONDYNE/THE OCEANA GROUP, 75 Main St., Dobbs Ferry NY 10522. (914)693-5944. Vice President: Yvonne Heenan. Produces material for legal market, and business and CPA markets. Works with 10-20 writers/year; buys 20 scripts/year. Buys all rights. No previously produced material. Electronic submissions OK via IBM PC. Dot-matrix submissions acceptable. Reports in 2 weeks on queries; 2 months on submissions. Catalog for 7x10 SAE and 3 first class stamps.

Needs: Tapes and cassettes, and video (VHS). "We are looking for video, ½ hour to one hour length—preview in ½" VHS, practical, how-to for legal market (lawyers in practice, law students)." Query with samples, submit synopsis/outline, resume, or preview tape and synopsis/outline. No phone calls accepted. All submissions must be in writing. Pays royalty or makes outright purchase; $250-500 for audio scripts, depending on qualifications; 10% royalty.

Tips: "We are especially interested in original software programs for lawyers and interactive videodisks (legal how-to) and video."

‡**CONTINENTAL FILM PRODUCTIONS CORPORATION**, Box 5126, 4220 Amnicola Hwy., Chattanooga TN 37406. (615)622-1192. President: James E. Webster. Produces "industrial non theatrical training films." Works with many writers annually. Buys all rights. No previously produced material. Unsolicited submissions not returned. "We don't want them—only assigned requested work." Reports in 1 week. Free catalog.

Needs: "We do need new writers of various types. Please contact us by mail with samples and résumé. Samples will be returned postpaid." Produces 16mm film loops, 8mm and 16mm films, sound filmstrips, multimedia kits, overhead transparencies, slides, tapes and cassettes, teaching machine programs and video. Query with samples and résumé. Outright purchase: $250 minimum; $6,000+ maximum.

Tips: "Send name, samples and résumé." Looks for writers whose work shows " technical understanding, humor, common sense, practicality, simplicity, creativity, etc." Suggests writers "increase use of humor in training films." Also seeking scripts on "human behavior industry" and on "why elementary and high school students should continue their educations."

CORONADO STUDIOS, #150, 4500 Biscayne Blvd., Miami FL 33137. (305)573-7250. President: Fred L. Singer. Produces material for the general public, various specialized audiences. Buys 50 commercials/year; 15 corporate films/year. "We commission custom scripts that have no value to anyone but our clients." Computer printout submissions acceptable. Reports in 2 weeks on queries; 1 month on submissions.

Needs: "We will need an indeterminate number of scripts for commercials and corporate films." Produces 16mm films and videotapes. Query with samples. Pays by outright purchase; "depends on nature of job."

NICHOLAS DANCY PRODUCTIONS, INC., 333 W. 39th St., New York NY 10018. (212)564-9140. President: Nicholas Dancy. Produces media material for corporate communications, the health care field, general audiences, employees, members of professional groups, members of associations and special customer groups. 60% freelance written. Prefers to work with published/established writers. Buys 5-10 scripts/year; works with 5-10 writers/year. None of scripts are unagented submissions. Buys all rights. Reports in 1 month. Electronic submissions OK. Computer printout submissions acceptable; prefers letter-quality to dot-matrix.
Needs: "We use scripts for videotapes or films from 5 minutes to 1 hour for corporate communications, sales, orientation, training, corporate image, medical and documentary." Format: videotape, 16mm films and slide tape. Query with résumé. "No unsolicited material. Our field is too specialized." Pays by outright purchase of $800-5,000. Pays expenses of writers on assignment.
Tips: "Writers should have a knowledge of business and industry and professions, an ability to work with clients and communicators, a fresh narrative style, creative use of dialogue, good skills in accomplishing research, and a professional approach to production. New concept trends are important in business. We're looking for new areas."

DUBOIS/RUDDY, 2145 Crooks, Troy MI 48084. (313)643-0320. Vice President: Chris Ruddy. Produces material for corporations. Works with 20-30 writers/year. Buys all rights. No previously produced material. Query with résumé. No scripts.
Needs: Multi-image and film production. Makes outright purchase; payment negotiable.
Tips: "We will use local writers only. Call and make an appointment."

‡EDUCATIONAL FILMSTRIPS AND VIDEO,1401 19th St., Huntsville TX 77340. (409)295-5767. President: Dr. Kenneth L. Russell. Produces material for junior high, senior high, college and university audiences. Buys "perhaps 20 scripts/year." Buys all rights or pays royalty on gross retail and wholesale. Previously produced material OK. Reports in 1 week on queries; in 1 month on submissions. Free catalog.
Needs: "Filmstrips and video for educational purposes." Produces filmstrips with sound and video. Query. Pays 6% royalty.
Tips: "Photographs on 2x2 slides must have good saturation of color." Looks for writers with the "ability to write and illustrate for educational purposes."

EDUCATIONAL IMAGES LTD., Box 3456, Elmira NY 14905. (607)732-1090. Executive Director: Dr. Charles R. Belinky. Produces material (sound filmstrips, multimedia kits and slide sets) for schools, kindergarten through college and graduate school, public libraries, parks, nature centers, etc. Also produces science-related software material. Buys 50 scripts/year. Buys all AV rights. Computer printout submissions OK. Free catalog.
Needs: Slide sets and filmstrips on science, natural history, anthropology and social studies. "We are looking primarily for complete AV programs; we will consider slide collections to add to our files. This requires high quality, factual text and pictures." Query with a meaningful sample of proposed program. Pays $150 minimum.
Tips: The writer/photographer is given high consideration. "Once we express interest, follow up. Potential contributors lose many sales to us by not following up on initial query. Don't waste our time and yours if you can't deliver."

EDUCATIONAL INSIGHTS,19560 S. Rancho Way, Dominguez Hills CA 90220. (213)637-2131. Director of Development: Dennis J. Graham. Produces material for elementary schools and retail "home-learning" markets. Works with 10 writers/year. Buys all rights. Previously produced material OK. Reports in 2 weeks. Catalog for 9x12 SAE with 27¢ postage.
Needs: Charts, models, multimedia kits, study prints, tapes and cassettes, and teaching machine programs. Query with samples. Pays varied royalties or makes outright purchase.
Tips: "Keep up-to-date information on educational trends in mind. Study the market before starting to work."

EFFECTIVE COMMUNICATION ARTS, INC., 221 W. 57th St., New York NY 10019. (212)333-5656. Vice President: W.J. Comcowich. Produces films, videotapes and interactive videodisks for physicians, nurses and medical personnel. Prefers to work with published/established writers. 80% freelance written. Buys approximately 20 scripts/year. Electronic submissions OK via modem. Computer printout submissions acceptable; prefers letter-quality to dot-matrix. Buys all rights. Reports in 1 month.
Needs: Multimedia kits, 16mm films, television shows/series, videotape presentations and interactive videodisks. Currently interested in about 15 films, videotapes for medical audiences; 6 interactive disks for medical audience, 3 interactive disks for point-of-purchase. Submit complete script and resume. Makes outright purchase or negotiates rights. Pays expenses of writers on assignment.
Tips: "Videotape scripts on technical subjects are becoming increasingly important. Explain what the film accomplishes—how it is better than the typical."

FIRE PREVENTION THROUGH FILMS, INC., Box 11, Newton Highlands MA 02161. (617)965-4444. Manager: Julian Olansky. Produces material for audiences involved with fire prevention and general safety: grades kindergarten through 12; colleges and universities; laboratories; industry and home safety. 50% freelance written. Works with a small number of new/unpublished writers each year. Purchases 1-3 scripts/year. "We work with several local scriptwriters on a yearly basis." Buys all rights. No previously produced material. Computer printout submissions acceptable; prefers letter-quality to dot-matrix. Reports in 3 weeks. Free catalog.
Needs: Films (16mm). "We will need scripts for films dealing with general safety in an office setting (20 minutes). Will consider any script dealing with fire prevention and/or general safety (20-minute film or less)." Query with or without samples. Makes outright purchase.

‡FIRST RING, 15303 Ventura Blvd., #800, Sherman Oaks CA 91403-3155. Assistant Editor: Phil Potters. Estab. 1987. "Audio material only. Humorous telephone answering machine messages. Intended for use by all persons who utilize telephone answering machines." Buys 100 scripts/year. Buys all rights. No previously produced material. Reports in 1 week on queries; 3 months on submissions.
Needs: Write for guidelines. Scripts must not exceed 20 seconds in their finished production; however there is no minimum duration. Produces tapes and cassettes. Query. Outright purchase of $100 upon acceptance.
Tips: Looking for writers with "the ability to write hilarious scripts as set forth in guidelines. All submissions are considered even from writers whose prior work was not accepted. This is a new business and its potential has not yet been tapped."

FLIPTRACK LEARNING SYSTEMS, Division of Mosaic Media, Inc., 999 Main, Glen Ellyn IL 60137. (312)790-1117. Publisher: F. Lee McFadden. Produces training media for microcomputer equipment and business software. Works with a small number of new/unpublished writers each year. 25% freelance written. Buys 3 courses/year; 1-3 from unpublished/unproduced writers. All courses published are unagented submissions. Works with 5-6 writers/year. Buys all rights. Electronic submissions OK via IBM PC, prefers WordStar or Word Perfect; requires hard copy also. Computer printout submissions OK. Reports in 3 weeks. Free product literature.
Needs: Computer courses on disk, video or audio geared to the adult or mature student in a business setting and to the first-time microcomputer user. Produces audio, video, CBT and reference manuals. Query with resumé and samples if available. Pays negotiable royalty; makes some outright purchases. Sometimes pays expenses of writers on assignment.
Tips: "We would like to move from primarily audio-based courseware into audio and computer-based-training. We prefer to work with Chicago-area and midwestern writers."

‡FLORIDA VIDCOM, 3685 N. Federal Highway, Pompano Beach FL 33064. (305)943-5590. President: Joseph M. Carey. Produces material for a corporate audience, and TV commercials for consumers. Buys all rights. Previously produced material OK.
Needs: Slides, tapes and cassette and videotapes. Looking for writers for wide-ranging corporate and individual projects—including sales and marketing pieces and TV commercials.

PAUL FRENCH & PARTNERS, INC., Rt. 5, Gabbettville Rd., LaGrange GA 30240. (404)882-5581. Contact: Gene Byrd. 20% freelance written. Computer printout submissions acceptable. Reports in 2 weeks. Buys all rights.
Needs: Wants to see multi-screen scripts (all employee-attitude related) and/or multi-screen AV sales meeting scripts or résumés. Produces silent and sound filmstrips, videotapes, cassettes and slides. Query or submit resumé. Pays in outright purchase of $500-5,000. Payment is in accordance with Writers Guild standards.

GESSLER PUBLISHING CO., INC., Gessler Educational Software, 900 Broadway, New York NY 10003. (212)673-3113. President: Seth C. Levin. Produces material for students learning ESL and foreign languages. 50% freelance written. Eager to work with new/unpublished writers. Buys about 60-75 scripts/year. 100% of scripts are unagented submissions. Prefers to buy all rights, but will work on royalty basis. Do not send disk submission without documentation. Query for electronic submissions. Computer printout submissions acceptable; prefers letter-quality to dot-matrix. Reports in 3 weeks on queries; 2 months on submissions.
Needs: Video and filmstrips "to create an interest in learning a foreign language and its usefulness in career objectives; also culturally insightful video/filmstrips on French, German, Italian and Spanish speaking countries." Produces sound filmstrips, multimedia kits, overhead transparencies, games, realia, tapes and cassettes, computer software. Also produces scripts for videos. Submit synopsis/outline or software with complete documentation, introduction, objectives. Makes outright purchase and pays royalties.
Tips: "Be organized in your presentation; be creative but keep in mind that your audience is primarily junior/senior high school students. We will be looking for new filmstrips, videotapes, software and videodisks which can be used in foreign language and ESL classes."

‡**BRAD HAGERT**, Box 18642, Irvine CA 92713. (714)261-7266. Produces material for corporate executives. Buys 10 scripts/year. Buys all rights. No previously produced material. Reports in 1 month.
Needs: Films, videotapes, multimedia kits, slides, tapes and cassettes. Query with samples. Makes outright purchase.

HAYES SCHOOL PUBLISHING CO., INC., 321 Pennwood Ave., Wilkinsburg PA 15221. (412)371-2373. 2nd Vice President: Clair N. Hayes, III. Produces material for school teachers, principals, elementary through high school. Also produces charts, workbooks, teacher's handbooks, posters, bulletin board material, educational software and liquid duplicating books (grades kindergarten through 12). 25% freelance written. Prefers to work with published/established writers; works with a small number of new/unpublished writers each year. Buys 5-10 scripts/year from unpublished/unproduced writers. 100% of scripts produced are unagented submissions. Buys all rights. Electronic submissions OK via Apple IIe. Computer printout submissions acceptable; prefers letter-quality to dot-matrix. Catalog for 3 first class stamps.
Needs: Educational material only. Particularly interested in educational material for high school level. Query. Pays $25 minimum.

‡**DENNIS HOMMEL ASSOCIATES, INC.**,3540 Middlefield Road, Menlo Park CA 94025-3025. (415)365-4565. Creative Director/Producer: D. Hommel. Produce material for "employees: employee orientation material, i.e., social security, retirement planning, topics of general appeal to all employees including work habits, safety, etc." Purchases negotiable rights. Previously produced material OK. Reports in 2 weeks.
Needs: Produces slides with audio tape and videotape (7-15 minutes). Submit synopsis/outline or completed script. Payment negotiable.
Tips: "Be concise, do your homework so that content reflects current attitudes. Use plain language, well organized progression of ideas. "

IMPERIAL INTERNATIONAL LEARNING CORP., 329 E. Court St., Kankakee IL 60901. (815)933-7735. Editor: Patsy Gunnels. Material intended for kindergarten through grade 12 audience. 60% freelance written. Prefers to work with published/established writers; works with a small number of new/unpublished writers each year. Buys 2-4 scripts/year from unpublished/unproduced writers. Buys all rights. No previously produced material. Electronic submissions OK via Apple, IBM PC, TRS-80, Commodore 64, with at least 48K. Computer printout submissions acceptable. Reports in 2 weeks on queries; 1 month on submissions. Free catalog.
Needs: "Supplemental learning materials of various lengths in the areas of reading, math, social studies and science with emphasis on using the microcomputer or videotape programs." Produces silent filmstrips, tapes and cassettes, and microcomputer and videotape. Query with samples or submit complete script and resume. Pays negotiable rates.
Tips: "We are interested in software, interactive videodisks, and videotape programs that meet curricular needs in the math, science, language arts, social studies and special education classroom."

INDUSTRIAL MEDIA, INC., 6660 28th St. SE, Grand Rapids MI 49506. (616)949-7770. Contact: Ed Anderson. Produces instructional aids for vocational schools and industrial in-plant training programs. 50% freelance written. Buys 1 script/year from unpublished/unproduced writers. 2 scripts are unagented submissions. Buy all rights "usually, but other arrangements are possible." Computer printout submissions acceptable; prefers letter-quality to dot-matrix. Catalog for 1 first class stamp.
Needs: Slide/cassette and video presentations coordinated with student workbooks and instruction guides for industrial training. "We specialize in materials for training industrial equipment maintenance personnel and apprentices. Topics of particular interest to our customers include: Industrial electricity, electronics, hydraulics, mechanical maintenance, blueprint reading, welding, safety, and management skills for plant supervisors. We will consider any topic with broad application in manufacturing training. We prefer to work with writers who can develop an entire, self-contained package, complete with performance objectives, script, workbooks, instruction guide and testing materials." Pays expenses of writers on assignment.

INSIGHT! INC., 100 E. Ohio St., Chicago IL 60611. (312)467-4350. President: Neal Cochran. Produces material for all audiences, depending on type of client. 90% freelance written. Buys scripts from produced writers only. All scripts produced by contract. Buys over 200 scripts/year from more than 30 writers. Buys all rights. Electronic submissions OK via modem ASCOM CP/M or 5¼" disk Apple II+ or Eagle II. Computer printout submissions acceptable.
Needs: "Our needs depend on contracts awarded to Insight! Films, videotapes, filmstrips and, most important, industrial shows of all types." Produces 16mm films, multimedia and "book" shows. No educational materials. Concentrates entirely on film, video and shows. Query with samples. Pays by outright purchase.

INSTRUCTOR BOOKS, 545 5th Ave., New York NY 10176. Director: Judy Cohn. "U.S. and Canadian school supervisors, principals and teachers purchase items in our line for instructional purposes." 50% freelance written. Buys 6 scripts/year from unpublished/unproduced writers. Most scripts produced are un-agented submissions. Buys all rights. Writer should have "experience in preparing materials for elementary students, including suitable teaching guides to accompany them, and demonstrate knowledge of the appropriate subject areas, or demonstrate ability for accurate and efficient research and documentation." Computer printout submissions acceptable; no dot-matrix. Free catalog.
Needs: Elementary curriculum enrichment—all subject areas. Display material, copy and illustration should match interest and reading skills of children in grades for which material is intended. Production is limited to printed matter: resource handbooks, teaching guides and idea books. Length: 6,000-12,000 words. Query. Standard contract, but fees vary considerably, depending on type of project. Sometimes pays the expenses of writers on assignment.
Tips: "Writers who reflect current educational practices can expect to sell to us."

□ **INTERNATIONAL MEDIA SERVICES INC.**, 718 Sherman Ave., Plainfield NJ 07060. (201)756-4060. President/General Manager: Stuart Allen. Produces varied material depending on assignment or production in house; includes corporate, public relations, sales, radio/TV, CATV, teleconferencing/CCTV, etc. 60-75% freelance written. 90% of scripts produced are unagented submissions. "We normally issue assignments to writers in the freelance market who specialize in appropriate fields of interest." Buys all rights. No previously produced material. Computer printout submissions acceptable. Reporting time varies depending on job requirements and specifications.
Needs: Charts, dioramas, 8/16mm film loops, 16/35mm films, silent and sound filmstrips, kinescopes, multimedia kits, overhead transparencies, phonograph records, slides, tapes and cassettes, television shows/series and videotape presentations. "We routinely hire writers from a freelance resource file." Cable TV needs include educational and entertainment marketplaces. Query with or without samples, or submit synopsis/outline and resume. "All work must be copyrighted and be original unpublished works." Pays in accordance with Writers Guild standards, negotiated contract or flat rate.
Tips: "We are not responsible for unsolicited material and recommend not submitting complete manuscripts for review without prior arrangement."

‡**DAVID J. JACKSON PRODUCTIONS, INC.**, Suite 111, 646 Barrington, Brentwood CA 90049. (213)471-8316. President: David Jackson. Produces interactive video dramas and corporate training films for the commercial market and special markets. Works with 13-14 writers annually. Buys all rights. No previously produced material. Reports in 2 weeks on queries; in 2 weeks on submissions.
Needs: 17-30 minute docudrama programs; 4-10 minute slide programs. Produces multimedia kits, phonograph records, tapes and cassettes. Query with samples or completed scripts. Pays in accordance with Writers Guild standards.
Tips: Looks for "fluid continuity, deep-drawn characterizations in work; for writers who are flexible, easy to work with."

‡**JACOBY/STORM PRODUCTIONS INC.**, 22 Crescent Road, Westport CT 06880. (203)227-2220. Contact: Doris Storm. Produces material for business people, students of all ages, professionals (e.g. medical). Works with 4-6 writers annually. Buys all rights. No previously produced material. Reports in 2 weeks.
Needs: "Short dramatic films on business subjects, educational filmstrips on varied subjects sales and corporate image films." Produces 16mm films, filmstrips (sound), slides, tapes and cassettes, videotapes and videodisks. Query. Makes outright purchase (depends on project).
Tips: "Prefers local people. Looks for experience, creativity, dependability, attention to detail, enthusiasm for project, ability to interface with client. Wants more film/video, fewer filmstrips, more emphasis on creative approaches to material."

□ **PAUL S. KARR PRODUCTIONS**, 2949 W. Indian School Rd., Box 11711, Phoenix AZ 85017. Utah Division: 1024 N. 250 E., Box 1254, Orem UT 84057. (801)226-8209. (602)266-4198. Produces films and videos for industry, business and education. "*Do not submit material unless requested.*" Buys all rights. Works on co-production ventures that have been funded.
Needs: Produces 16mm films and videos. Query. Payment varies.
Tips: "One of the best ways for a writer to become a screenwriter is to come up with a client that requires a film or video. He can take the project to a production company, such as we are, assume the position of an associate producer, work with an experienced professional producer in putting the production into being, and in that way learn about video and filmmaking and chalk up some meaningful credits."

KIMBO EDUCATIONAL-UNITED SOUND ARTS, INC., 10-16 N. 3rd Ave., Box 477, Long Branch NJ 07740. (201)229-4949. Contact: James Kimble or Amy Laufer. Produces materials for the educational market (early childhood, special education, music, physical education, dance, and preschool children 6 months and up). 50% freelance written. Buys approximately 12-15 scripts/year; works with approximately 12-15 writers/year. Buys 5 scripts/year from unpublished/unproduced writers. Most scripts are unagented submissions. Buys all rights or first rights. Previously produced material OK "in some instances." Reports in 1 month. Free catalog.

Needs: "For the next two years we will be concentrating on general early childhood movement oriented products, new albums in the fitness field and more. Each will be an album/cassette with accompanying teacher's manual and, if warranted, manipulatives." Phonograph records and cassettes, "all with accompanying manual or teaching guides." Query with samples and synopsis/outline or completed script. Pays 5-7% royalty on lowest wholesale selling price, and by outright purchase. Both negotiable. Sometimes pays expenses of writers on assignment.

Tips: "We look for creativity first. Having material that is educationally sound is also important. Being organized is certainly helpful. Fitness is growing rapidly in popularity and will always be a necessary thing. Children will always need to be taught the basic fine and gross motor skills. Capturing interest while reaching these goals is the key."

□ **KOCH/MARSCHALL PRODUCTIONS, INC.**, 1718 N. Mohawk St., Chicago IL 60614. (312)664-6482. Executive Producer: Sally E. Marschall. Produces material for general library audience, high school or college, and mass audience. 20% freelance written. "We read more than a hundred scripts a year. We may buy one a year. We work with one writer at a time." Buys all rights. No previously produced material. Reports in 2 months on queries; 3 months on submissions. SASE required.

Needs: Produces 16 and 35mm films. "We are looking for feature film ideas that have comedic potential. These can be historical, comtemporary, musical, theatrical, European, American, romantic, thrilling and/or mysterious." Produces feature-length comedy material for cable TV. "We negotiate payment with each writer."

Tips: "We are looking for original, innovative, nonexploitational, nonderivative screenplays. No first drafts, no student theses. Screenplays must be intelligent, provocative and exciting. Writers must be well-educated, experienced in film writing, and compatible with a team of filmmakers."

BRIEN LEE & COMPANY, 2025 N. Summit Ave., Milwaukee WI 53202. (414)277-7600. President/Creative Director: Brien Lee. Produces custom audiovisual material for business, industry, arts/nonprofit, advertising and public relations agencies, business associations, and special entertainment-oriented projects. Buys 5 scripts/year average. Buys all rights. Computer printout submissions acceptable; disk OK if compatible. Reports in 1 month, sometimes leading to an interview and an assignment.

Needs: "We need people who understand what AV is all about . . . words, pictures, sound. Motivational, informational, clear-cut, straightforward . . . writing that is literate, but never so good it could stand on its own without the pictures or sound. It is usually writing for one narrator, plus additional voices and/or characters. No hype." Produces videotapes, multi-image presentations, and mixed media presentations, slide-sound programs and interactive video. Submit example of scripting ability as well as a résumé.

Recent Productions: *AVL, Milwaukee Journal* and CUNA Mutual.

WILLIAM V. LEVINE ASSOCIATES, INC., 31 E. 28th St., New York NY 10016. (212)683-7177. President: William V. Levine. Presentations for business and industry. 15% freelance written. Prefers to work with established writers. Buys 4 scripts/year. Firm emphasizes "creativity and understanding of the client's goals and objectives." Will interview writers after submission of resume and/or sample AV scripts. Specifically seeks writers with offbeat or humorous flair. Previously produced material OK. Buys all rights. "We prefer New York City area based writers only."

Needs: Business-related scripts *on assignment* for specific clients for use at sales meetings or for desk-top presentations. Also uses theme-setting and inspirational scripts with inherent messages of business interest. Produces 16mm films, multimedia presentations, video, slides and live industrial shows. Query with résumé. Pays $500-2,500.

‡**LORI PRODUCTIONS, INC.**, 3347 Lauren Canyon Blvd., Studio City CA 91604. (213)466-7567. Contact: Jim Wipper. Produces material for industrial clients. 20% freelance written. Buys 5-10 scripts/year. 99% of scripts are unagented submissions. Buys all rights. Computer printout submissions acceptable; prefers letter-quality to dot-matrix. Reports in 3 weeks.

Needs: "We produce industrial films (sales, corporate image, training, safety), which generally run from 30 seconds to 18 minutes in length." Also produces video and cable TV material (varies with customers requirements). Seeks writers with a "clean, concise writing style; a familiarity with film production; and experience with industrial films." Works with Los Angeles area writers *only*. Produces 16mm films, live corporate shows, multi-image presentations, and sales meetings. Query with résumé. Pays by outright purchase of $500-2,000. Sometimes pays expenses of writers on assignment.

‡MANHATTAN VIDEO PRODUCTION INC.,12 W. 27th Street, 11th Floor, New York NY 10001. (212)683-6565. Producer/Partner: George Cauttero. "Videotape material is intended for corporate and commercial clients." Buys approximately 10 scripts/year. Buys all rights. No previously produced material. Reports in 2 weeks.
Needs: Produces tapes and cassettes. Query with samples or send completed ms.
Tips: "Our needs are corporate information pieces, training scripts and corporate image enhancement proposals for videotape programs. We look for originality, clear concepts, knowledge of scriptwriting for videotape and general knowledge of production costs as well as post-production costs in order to conform a script to a specific budget. Corporate television is growing in leaps and bounds, requiring talented writers with a comprehensive knowledge of corporate structures and needs; i.e. training, internal communications."

MARSHFILM ENTERPRISES, INC., Box 8082, Shawnee Mission KS 66208. (816)523-1059. President: Joan K. Marsh. Produces software and filmstrips for elementary and junior/senior high school students. 100% freelance written. Works with a small number of new/unpublished writers each year. Buys 8-16 scripts/year. All scripts produced are unagented submissions. Buys all rights. Computer printout submissions acceptable; prefers letter-quality to dot-matrix.
Needs: 50 frame; 15 minutes/script. Sound filmstrips. Query only. Pays by outright purchase of $250-500/script.

MARYLAND PUBLIC TELEVISION, 11767 Bonita Ave., Owings Mills MD 21117. (301)337-4052. Head Writer: Dick George. Produces material "for general public TV audience. The vast majority of our scripts are staff-written; however, when our staff is too busy to take on a new project, we do occasionally buy freelance material, perhaps 3 times a year." Buys all rights. No previously produced material. Reports in 2 months.
Needs: Films (16mm) and video. "We do documentaries and instructional shows on many different subjects. Right now I need comedy sketches for Crabs, a local satirical comedy show produced and aired live. I'd like more submissions, especially from women and minorities." Send résumé and samples, etc. Makes outright purchase; approximately $100/script minute, with exceptions.
Tips: Send résumé and samples. "I'm *not* looking for program ideas—I'm in occasional need of writers to develop *our* program ideas. For Crabs, send scripts, 3 minutes maximum, produceable live in studio with studio audience."

MEDIA LEARNING SYSTEMS, INC., 120 West Colorado Blvd., Pasadena CA 91105. (818)449-0006. President: Jim Griffith. Produces "custom" material for corporate, industrial, educational, and product promotional audience. 50% freelance written. Buys 12 scripts/year. Buys 1-2 scripts/year from unpublished/unproduced writers. All scripts are unagented submissions. Buys all rights. No previously produced material. Computer printout submissions acceptable. Reports in 1 month.
Needs: Video and video disks. Also produces scripts for video and video disks for kindergarten through grade 12 and college level learning programs. Sometimes pays expenses of writers on assignment.
Tips: "We are seeking generic, curriculum-oriented educational scripts suitable for interactive video disk development."

MERIWETHER PUBLISHING LTD. (Contemporary Drama Service), Box 457, Downers Grove IL 60515. Editor: Arthur Zapel. "We publish how-to materials in book, filmstrip, game and audio cassette formats. We are interested in materials for high school and college level students only. Our contemporary drama division publishes 60-70 plays/year." 95% freelance written. Works with a small number of new/unpublished writers each year; eager to work with new/unpublished writers. Buys 40-60 scripts/year from unpublished/unproduced writers. 95% of scripts are unagented submissions. Computer printout submissions acceptable; no dot-matrix. Reports in 3 weeks on queries; 6 weeks on full-length submissions. Query should include synopsis/outline, résumé of credits, sample of style and SAE. Catalog available for $1 postage. Offers 10% royalty or outright purchase.
Needs: Filmstrips, game and audio cassettes. Christian activity book mss also accepted. We will consider elementary level religious materials and plays. Query. Pays royalty; buys some mss outright. Sometimes pays the expenses of writers on assignment.
Tips: "We publish a wide variety of speech contest materials for high school students. We are publishing more reader's theatre scripts and musicals based on classic literature or popular TV shows, provided the writer includes letter of clearance from the copyright owner."

‡MONAD TRAINER'S AIDE, 163-60 22nd Ave., Whitestone NY 11357. (718)352-3227. CEO: Gene Richman. Produces material for business training market. Buys all rights. Previously produced material OK. Reports in 2 weeks on queries; 6 weeks on submissions. Catalog for SAE and $2 postage.
Needs: Produces 16 mm films and videocassettes. Query or submit synopsis/outline and résumé. Pays by royalty or outright purchase in accordance with Writers Guild standards.
Tips: Writers need "good ability to communicate verbally as well as written." Looks for "short motivational type films applicable to both sexes."

MOTIVATION MEDIA, INC., 1245 Milwaukee Ave., Glenview IL 60025. (312)297-4740. Executive Producer: Frank Stedronsky. Produces customized material for salespeople, customers, corporate/industrial employees and distributors. 90% freelance written. Buys 100 scripts/year from unpublished/unproduced writers. Prefers to work with published/established writers. All scripts produced are unagented submissions. Buys all rights. Computer printout submissions acceptable. Reports in 1 month.
Needs: Material for all audiovisual media—particularly marketing-oriented (sales training, sales promotional, sales motivational) material. Produces sound filmstrips, 16mm films, multimedia sales meeting programs, videotapes, cassettes, and slide sets. Software should be AV-oriented. Query with samples. Pays $150-5,000. Pays the expenses of writers on assignment.

MULTI-MEDIA PRODUCTIONS, INC., Box 5097, Stanford CA 94305. Program Manager: Jim Quinn. Produces audiovisual instructional material for secondary (grades 9-12) schools. 100% freelance written. Prefers to work with published writers, but can work with small number of promising unpublished writers. Buys 20 programs/year; 10-15 from unpublished/unproduced writers. All programs produced are unagented submissions. Buys all rights. Computer printout submissions acceptable; prefers letter-quality to dot-matrix. Reports in 6 weeks. Free catalog.
Needs: Already produced video material suitable for general high school social studies curricula: history, biography, sociology, psychology, student health, anthropology, archeology and economics. "Style should be straightforward, lively, objective and interactive." Approximate specifications (filmstrip): 50 frames, 10-15 minutes/program part; 1- or 2-part programs. Video: 10-40 minutes per program. Writer supplies script, slides for filmstrip, and teacher's manual (per our format). Pays royalties quarterly, starting at 15% of return on each program sold. "Programs with a central academic theme sell best. Program subjects should adhere to secondary curricula and to student-interactive instructional methods." Query with samples.
Recent Production: 8-part video series on adolescent concerns.
Tips: "We are looking for programs that engage the viewer with their controversy, timeliness, and appropriateness to curricula. Sound filmstrips still do best when they challenge the student by presenting conflicting viewpoints or by directly inviting the student to participate in the program. We want to add significantly to our sound filmstrip line and move into distribution of video materials applicable to the educational market. Submit queries and we will offer our suggestions."

BURT MUNK & COMPANY, 666 Dundee Rd., Northbrook IL 60062. (312)564-0855. President: Burton M. Munk. Produces material for industrial, sales training, product information, and education (schools). 100% freelance written. Works with approximately 10 writers/year. All scripts are unagented submissions. "We deal directly with writers but do not receive submissions of scripts." Buys all rights. Electronic submissions OK via Apple II Plus or Apple IIe, 64K, DOS 3.3. Does not return material; "all our work is 'made to order' for specific client needs—we are a custom house."
Needs: Sound filmstrips, slides, tapes and cassettes, 16mm films and videotapes. Also produces scripts for video. Open for software ideas. "We will contact individual writers who seem suitable for our projects." Makes outright purchase. Sometimes pays expenses of writers on assignment.
Tips: "We have published one very successful software program and are open for more. We will accept unsolicited ideas in disk form (Apple II Plus, 64K, DOS 3.3)."

□ **NETWORK COMMUNICATIONS LTD.**, 14524 85th Ave., Edmonton, Alberta T5R 3Z4 Canada. (403)489-1044. President: R. Schwartz. Produces material for advertising, cable TV, government, etc. 50% freelance written. 100% of scripts are unagented submissions. Computer printout submissions acceptable; prefers letter-quality to dot-matrix. Reports in 3 weeks.
Needs: Produces cable programs, industrial films and TV commercials (35mm, 16mm or videotape). Submit résumé and sample concept or script. Pays by hourly rate, percentage of budget depending upon project. Sometimes pays expenses of writers on assignment.

NYSTROM, 3333 N. Elston Ave., Chicago IL 60618. (312)463-1144. Editorial Director: Darrell A. Coppock. Produces material for school audiences (kindergarten through 12th grade). Computer printout and disk submissions OK. Free catalog.
Needs: Educational material on social studies, earth and life sciences, career education, reading, language arts and mathematics. Produces charts, sound filmstrips, models, multimedia kits, overhead transparencies and realia. Required credentials depend on topics and subject matter and approach desired. Query. Pays according to circumstances.

‡**OMNI COMMUNICATIONS**, Suite 207, 101 E. Carmel Dr., Carmel IN 46032. (317)844-6664. Vice President: Dr. Sandra M. Long. Produces commercial, training, educational and documentary material. Buys all rights. No previously produced material. Reports in 2 months.
Needs: "Educational, documentary, commercial, training, motivational." Produces slides, shows and multi-image videotapes. Query. Makes outright purchase.

Tips: "Must have experience as writer and have examples of work. Examples need to include print copy and finished copy of videotape if possible. A résumé with educational background, general work experience and experience as a writer must be included. Especially interested in documentary-style writing. Writers' payment varies, depending on amount of research needed, complexity of project, length of production and other factors."

OUR SUNDAY VISITOR, INC., Religious Education Dept., 200 Noll Plaza, Huntington IN 46750. (219)356-8400. Director of Religious Education: Rev. Vincent Giese. Produces material for students (kindergarten through 12th grade), adult religious education groups and teacher trainees. "We are very concerned that the materials we produce meet the needs of today's church." Free catalog.
Needs: "Proposals for projects should be no more than 2 pages in length, in outline form. Programs should display up-to-date audiovisual techniques and cohesiveness. Broadly speaking, material should deal with religious education, including liturgy and daily Christian living, as well as structured catechesis. It must not conflict with sound Catholic doctrine and should reflect modern trends in education." Produces educational books, charts, sound and filmstrips. "Work-for-hire and royalty arrangements possible."

PHOTO COMMUNICATION SERVICES, INC., 6410 Knapp NE, Ada MI 49301. (616)676-1499. President: Michael Jackson. Produces commercial, industrial, sales, training material etc. 95% freelance written. Buys 25% of scripts from unpublished/unproduced writers. 95% of scripts produced are unagented submissions. Buys all rights and first serial rights. Electronic submissions OK via IBM PC format (disk), 300, 1200 or 2400 Baud Modem, or on the Source, I.D. # BBH782 or MCI Mail I.D. 247-7996 or EasyLink Box No. 62909611. Computer printout submissions acceptable. Reports in 1 month on queries; 2 weeks on scripts. Writer's guidelines for SASE.
Needs: Multimedia kits, slides, tapes and cassettes, and video presentations. Primarily interested in 35mm multimedia, 1-24 projectors and video. Query with samples or submit completed script and résumé. Pays in outright purchase or by agreement.

PIC, 2220 W. Magnolia Blvd., Burbank CA 91506. (818)953-4600. Produces custom scripts for industrial/corporate clientele. Contact: Shelly Schiner. Buys 5 scripts/year. Buys all rights. No previously produced material.
Needs: Films (16mm), slides, multiimage and video. Films are custom-made "per needs of client." Payment is negotiated per project.
Tips: Looking for writers with "experience with scripts, who can represent our company at client meetings."

PREMIER VIDEO FILM & RECORDING CORP., 3033 Locust, St. Louis MO 63103. (314)531-3555. Secretary/Treasurer: Grace Dalzell. Produces material for the corporate community, religious organizations, political arms, and hospital and educational groups. 100% freelance written. Prefers to work with published/established writers. Buys 50-100 scripts/year. All scripts are unagented submissions. Buys all rights; "very occasionally the writer retains rights." Previously produced material OK; "depends upon original purposes and markets." Computer printout submissions acceptable; prefers letter-quality to dot-matrix. Reports "within a month or as soon as possible."
Needs: "Our work is all custom produced with the needs being known only as required." 35mm film loops, super 8mm and 35mm films, silent and sound filmstrips, multimedia kits, overhead transparencies, phonograph records, slides, and tapes and cassettes." Produces TV, training and educational scripts for video. Submit complete script and résumé. Pays in accordance with Writers Guild standards or by outright purchase of $100 or "any appropriate sum." Sometimes pays the expenses of writers on assignment.
Tips: "Always place without fail *occupational pursuit*, name, address and phone number in upper right hand corner of résumé. We're looking for writers with creativity, good background and a presentable image."

□ **PRIMALUX VIDEO**, 30 W. 26th St., New York NY 10010. (212)206-1402. Director: M. Clarke. Produces industrial and training material; promotional pieces. 70% freelance written. Buys 10 scripts/year; works with 2 writers/year. Buys all rights. No previously produced material. Computer printout submissions acceptable.
Needs: Television show/series and videotape presentations. Produces scripts for video and fashion show material for cable TV. Query with samples. Pays royalty or by outright purchase. Pays expenses of writers on assignment.

RHYTHMS PRODUCTIONS, Box 34485, Los Angeles CA 90034. President: Ruth White. Produces children's educational cassette/books. Buys all rights. Previously published material OK "if it is suitable for our market and is not now currently on the market. We also look for tapes that have been produced and are ready for publication." Reports on mss in 3 weeks. Catalog for 8½x11 SAE and 39¢ postage.
Needs: Phonograph records and tapes and cassettes. Looking for children's stories with musical treatments if possible. "Must have educational content or values." Query with samples. Payment is negotiable.

SAXTON COMMUNICATIONS GROUP LTD., 124 E. 40th St., New York NY 10016. (212)867-2210. Produces material for industrial, consumer and sales audiences, AV presentations and meetings. **Needs:** "We work with more than 5 outside writers regularly. We buy copy and scripts for approximately 50 projects a year." Submit résumé.

‡PETER SCHLEGER COMPANY, 135 W. 58th St., New York NY 10019. (212)765-7129. President: Peter R. Schleger. Produces material "primarily for employee populations in corporations and non-profit organizations." Buys all rights, "most work is paid for for a one-time use, and that piece may have no life beyond one project." Previously produced material OK. Reports in 1 month. "Typical programs are customized workshops or specific individual programs from subjects such as listening and presentation skills to medical benefits communication. No program is longer than 10 minutes. If they need to be, they become shorter modules." **Needs:** Produces sound filmstrips, video and printed manuals and leader's guides. Send completed script and résumé. Makes outright purchase; payment "depends on script length." **Tips:** "We are looking to receive and keep on file a résumé and short, completed scripts sample of a program not longer than 10 minutes. The shorter the better to get a sense of writing style and the ability to structure a piece. We would also like to know the fees the writer expects for his/her work. Either per-diem, by project budget or by finished script page. We want communicators with a training background or who have written training programs, modules and the like. We want to know of people who have written print material, as well. We do not want to see scripts that have been written, and are looking for a producer/director. We will look at queries for possible workshops or new approaches for training, but these must be submitted as longshots only; it is not our primary business."

PHOEBE T. SNOW PRODUCTIONS, INC., 240 Madison Ave., New York NY 10016. (212)679-8756. Creative Director: Deborah R. Herr. Produces material for corporate uses, sales force, in-house training, etc. 90% freelance written. Buys 20-40 scripts/year from published/produced writers only. All scripts produced are unagented submissions. Buys all rights. Computer printout submissions acceptable; prefers letter-quality to dot-matrix. Reports in 2 weeks on queries; 1 month on mss. **Needs:** 16mm films, sound filmstrips and slides. Query with samples and resume. Pays by outright purchase. **Tips:** "Have some understanding of AV for corporations. This is not the educational field. We're looking for creative writers who work with speed and can take direction. Be aware of short deadlines and some low budgets."

SPENCER PRODUCTIONS, INC., 234 5th Ave., New York NY 10001. (212)697-5895. General Manager: Bruce Spencer. Produces material for high school students, college students and adults. Occasionally uses freelance writers with considerable talent. **Needs:** 16mm films, prerecorded tapes and cassettes. Satirical material only. Query. Pay is negotiable.

□ E.J. STEWART, INC., 525 Mildred Ave., Primos PA 19018. (215)626-6500. "Our firm is a television production house providing programming for the broadcast, industrial, educational and medical fields. Government work is also handled." 50% freelance written. Buys 50 scripts/year; buys 5% of scripts/year from unpublished/unproduced writers. Buys all rights. Computer printout submissions acceptable. Reports "when needed." **Needs:** "We produce programming for our clients' specific needs. We do not know in advance what our needs will be other than general scripts for commercials and programs depending upon requests that we receive from clients." Cable television material. Videotapes. Submit résumé only. Pays in negotiable outright purchase. Sometimes pays expenses of writers on assignment. **Tips:** "A trend in the audiovisual field freelance writers should be aware of is interactive laser disk programming."

TALCO PRODUCTIONS, 279 E. 44th St., New York NY 10017. (212)697-4015. President: Alan Lawrence. Vice President: Marty Holberton. Produces variety of material for motion picture theatres, TV, radio, business, trade associations, non-profit organizations, etc. Audiences range from young children to senior citizens. 20-40% freelance written. Buys scripts from published/produced writers only. All scripts produced are unagented submissions. Buys all rights. No previously published material. Computer printout submissions acceptable; prefers letter-quality to dot-matrix. Reports in 3 weeks on queries. **Needs:** Films (16-35mm); filmstrips (sound); phonograph records; slides; radio tapes and cassettes; and videotape. "We maintain a file of writers and call on those with experience in the same general category as the project in production. We do not accept unsolicited manuscripts. We prefer to receive a writer's resume listing credits. If his/her background merits, we will be in touch when a project seems right." Makes outright purchase/project and in accordance with Writer's Guild standards (when appropriate). Sometimes pays the expenses of writers on assignment.

TEL-AIR INTERESTS, INC., 1755 N.E. 149th St., Miami FL 33181. (305)944-3268. President: Grant H. Gravitt. Produces material for groups and theatrical and TV audiences. Buys all rights. Submit resume.
Needs: Documentary films on education, travel and sports. Produces films and videotape. Pays by outright purchase.

□ **TELEMATION PRODUCTIONS, INC. AND TELEMATION INTERACTIVE**, 7700 E. Iliff Ave., Denver CO 80231. (303)751-6000. Corporate Sales: Jim Levy. "Telemation is a major video production firm with studios in Denver, Chicago, Phoenix and Seattle. We will forward contacts to the appropriate telemation facility from Denver." Produces material for corporate and industrial video. 90% freelance written. Prefers to work with published/established writers. 100% of scripts produced are unagented submissions. Buys all rights. No previously produced material. Electronic submissions OK via Hayes 1200sm or IBM-XT, IBM-AT, but requires hard copy also. Computer printout submissions acceptable; prefers letter-quality to dot-matrix.
Needs: Videotape; interactive video disk programs for the corporate and industrial market—marketing, sales, training, product rollout, etc. Submit all interactive video programming to Richard Schneider. Produces material—from entertainment to documentary to educational—for cable TV. Query with samples and résumé. "All work is done on assignment. We do not accept unsolicited scripts—assignments only." Makes outright purchase. Pays expenses of writers on assignment.
Tips: "Only writers with solid corporate and industrial video experience should contact us. Also, location near one of Telemation's facilities is important. We have a growing need for scriptwriters in the area of corporate and industrial video or film."

TELETECHNIQUES, INC., 1 W. 19th St., New York NY 10011. (212)206-1475. Contact: Michael Temmer. Works with 3-4 writers/year. Buys all rights. Sometimes accepts previously produced material. Reports in 2 months.
Needs: Material for industrials and TV programs. Produces 35 and 16mm films and videos. Query with samples. Writers are paid in accordance with Writers Guild standards by royalty or outright purchase.
Tips: "Contributors should be flexible and have a knowledge of the video and film media."

‡**TRANSLIGHT MEDIA ASSOCIATES**, 931 W. Liberty, Wheaton IL 60187. (312)690-7780. Producer: John Lorimer. Produces material for business people and religious organizations. Buys 4-8 scripts/year. Buys all rights. No previously produced material. "We like to keep samples as part of file for reference. If writer wants something back they should obtain permission to send it first." Reports as project arises in writer's skill area.
Needs: "We produce primarily slide/tape, multi-image and video programs. Our needs are generally for short (5-10 minute) creative scripts for sales, fund raising, business meeting, or corporate image applications. No commercial or TV shows." Query with samples. Outright purchase $250-3,000.
Tips: "We look for creative concepts, and ability to communicate clearly and concisely. We also look for writers that recognize that often in an audiovisual script the visuals are more important than the words—writers that write a visual concept, not just copy. We prefer to work with local writers (Chicago market). Initial query should include 2 or 3 short scripts or excerpts that show range and style. No phone queries please."

‡**TRANSTAR PRODUCTIONS, INC.**, Suite C, 9520 E. Jewell Ave. Denver CO 80231. (303)695-4207. Producer/Director: Doug Hanes. Produces primarily industrial material. 10% freelance written. Buys 5 scripts/year from unpublished/unproduced writers. 100% of scripts are unagented submissions. Buys 5-6 scripts/year. Buys all rights. No previously produced material. Computer printout submissions acceptable; prefers letter-quality to dot-matrix. Reporting time varies.
Needs: 16mm films, slides, tapes and cassettes, and videotape presentations. Also produces scripts for industrial sales and training. Submit résumé. Pays negotiable rate.

‡**TRI VIDEO TELEPRODUCTION—Lake Tahoe**, Box 8822, Incline Village NV 89450-8822. (702)323-6868. Production Manager: Beth Davidson. Produces material primarily for corporate targets (their sales, marketing and training clients). Works with 3-4 writers each year developing contracted material. Could work with more, and could produce more programs if the right material were available. Buys all rights or negotiable rights. No previously produced material. Does not return material "unless requested from a previous query."
Needs: "Will have a need for writing contract projects; would consider other projects which are either sold to a client and need a producer, or which the writer wishes to sell and have produced. In all cases, corporate sales, marketing and training materials. Perhaps some mass audience (how-to) video programs." Produces videtapes only. Query. Makes outright purchase in accordance with Writers Guild standards; "would consider joint venture."
Tips: "We are strong on production skill; weak on sales, so if your idea needs to be sold to an end user before it is produced, we may not be the right avenue. However give us a try. We might be able to put the right people together." Looks for "creativity, of course, but solid understanding of the buying market. We don't go in for highly symbolic and abstract materials."

TROLL ASSOCIATES, 100 Corporate Dr., Mahwah NJ 07430. (201)529-4000. Contact: M. Schecter. Produces material for elementary and high school students. Buys approximately 200 scripts/year. Buys all rights. Reports in 3 weeks. Free catalog.
Needs: Produces multimedia kits, tapes and cassettes, and (mainly) books. Query or submit outline/synopsis. Pays royalty or by outright purchase.

TUTOR/TAPE, 107 France St., Toms River NJ 08753. President: Richard R. Gallagher. Produces and publishes cassettes, filmstrips, software and visual aids including slides and transparencies for the college market. 50% freelance written. Most scripts produced are unagented submissions. Buys average 5 scripts/year. "We are the largest publisher of prerecorded educational cassettes for the college market. We are capable of handling everything from writer to recording to packaging to marketing in a totally vertically integrated production-marketing publishing organization." Computer printout submissions acceptable. Reports in 1 week.
Needs: 10-25 page scripts for 15-30 minute educational messages on college topics, including business, management, marketing, personnel, advertising, accounting, economics and other related material. We also seek remedial and study skills material useful to college students and suitable for audio presentation. Send brief synopsis or short outline stating credentials, education or experience. Pays 15% royalty or by outright purchase.
Tips: "Writers should submit material relevant to students in college who need assistance in passing difficult courses, or interesting material which supplements college textbooks and enhances class work."

UNIVERSITY OF WISCONSIN STOUT TELEPRODUCTION CENTER, 800 S. Broadway, Menomonie WI 54751. (715)232-2624. Production Manager/TV Coordinator: Tim Fuhrmann. Produces instructional TV programs for primary, secondary, post secondary and specialized audiences. 10% freelance written. Buys scripts from published/produced writers only. All scripts produced are unagented submissions. "We produce ITV programs for national, regional and state distribution to classrooms around the U.S. and Canada." Buys all rights. Computer printout submissions acceptable; prefers letter-quality to dot-matrix.
Needs: "Our clients fund programs in a 'series' format which tend to be 8-12 programs each." Produces only with one-inch broadcast quality. "I need materials from writers who have experience in writing instructional TV. I have an immediate need for writers with secondary teaching experience who can write a secondary level chemical-abuse series. Only the 'pros' need apply. We also have a need for writers in Wisconsin and Minnesota whom we can call on to write one or multi-program/series in instructional television." Query with résumé and samples of TV scripts.
Recent Production: *Story Lords* (2nd grade reading comprehension agency: Wisconsin Educational Communications Board). Sometimes pays the expenses of writers on assignment.
Tips: "Freelance writers should be aware of the hardware advances in broadcast and nonbroadcast. There are new avenues for writers to pursue in adult learning, computer assisted programming and interactive programming."

‡VABS MULTI-IMAGE, 705 Hinman, Evanston IL 60202. (312)328-8697. President: Alan Soell. "We produce material for all levels of corporate, medical, cable, and educational institutions for the purposes of training and development, marketing and meeting presentations. We also are developing programming for the broadcast areas. 75% freelance written. We work with a core of three to five freelance writers from development to final drafts." All scripts published are unagented submissions. Buys all rights. Previously produced material OK. Computer printout submissions acceptable. Reports in 2 weeks on queries.
Needs: Videotape, 16mm films, silent and sound filmstrips, multimedia kits, overhead transparencies, realia, slides, tapes and cassettes, and television shows/series. Currently interested in "sports instructional series that could be produced for the consumer market on tennis, gymnastics, bowling, golf, aerobics, health and fitness, cross-country skiing and cycling. Also home improvement programs for the novice—for around the house—in a series format. These two areas should be 30 minutes and be timeless in approach for long shelf life." Sports audience, age 25-45; home improvement, 25-65. "Cable TV needs include the two groups of programming detailed here. We are also looking for documentary work on current issues, nuclear power, solar power, urban development, senior citizens—but with a new approach." Query or submit synopsis/outline and resume. Pays by contractual agreement.
Tips: "I am looking for innovative approaches to old problems that just don't go away. The approach should be simple and direct so there is immediate audience identification with the presentation. I also like to see a sense of humor used. Trends in the audiovisual field include interactive video with tape and video disk—for training purposes."

□ WREN ASSOCIATES, INC., 5 Independence Way, Princeton NJ 08540. Copy Department Head: Debbie Schnur. Produces material for employees and salespeople, and various sales and corporate presentations for Fortune 500 corporate clients. 20% freelance written. Buys 30-40 scripts/year from previously produced writers only. All scripts produced are unagented submissions. Buys all rights. No previously published material. Electronic submissions OK over CompuServe network, on IBM/Compaq, MS word, and Kaypro II. Computer printout submissions acceptable. Reports in 3 weeks. Catalog for #10 SAE and 1 first class stamp.

Needs: Produces 8mm film loops, 16mm films, sound filmstrips, multimedia kits, slides (multiprojector shows); tapes and cassettes, television shows/series (corporate networks); videotape presentations; interactive video on a project-by-project basis for clients and video scripts for industrial specialists on assignment. Produces scripts for cable TV medical network. "We need freelance writers who can assimilate technical or business-oriented subject matter (e.g., telecommunications services, automotive). They must be able to present this material in a clear, entertaining presentation that *sells* the product." Query with samples. Pays $400-7,000/job. Sometimes pays expenses of writers on assignment.
Tips: "Freelance writers should be aware of interactive video disk, tape trend. It's the coming wave in training and P.O.P. sales."

ZELMAN STUDIOS LTD., 623 Cortelyou Rd., Brooklyn NY 11218. (718)941-5500. General Manager: Jerry Krone. Produces material for business, education and fund-raising audiences. Reports in 1 month. Buys all rights.
Needs: Produces film loops, silent and sound filmstrips, films, videotapes, audiocassettes and slides. Query with samples and résumé. Pays by outright purchase "by agreement, based on talent and turnaround."

ZM SQUARED, Box C-30, Cinnaminson NJ 08077. (609)786-0612. Contact: Pete Zakroff. "We produce AVs for a wide range of clients including education, business, industry and labor organizations." Buys 10 scripts/year; works with 4-5 writers/year. Buys all rights. No previously produced material. Electronic submissions OK via Apple system. Computer printout submissions acceptable. Reports in 2 weeks on queries; 1 month on submissions. Free catalog.
Needs: Silent filmstrips, kinescopes, multimedia kits, overhead transparencies, slides, tapes and cassettes, and videotape presentations. Query with or without samples. Pays 3-10% royalty or by outright purchase $150-750.

Playwriting

Read the following listings carefully and realize that the types of plays theaters produce vary greatly. Theaters in large cities are usually more open to experimental, avant-garde work than theaters in small towns, and many play producers in small towns will be partial to plays set in their own geographic areas. Playwrights may also limit their markets by including language likely to alienate a conservative audience. Most theaters appreciate playwrights who help keep costs down by writing plays that call for small casts and few set changes.

Producers note a common problem among the plays submitted: too many read like TV situation comedies. Many producers share the view of Rick Davis, dramaturge at Center Stage Theatre in Baltimore, who wants "no conventional, highly psychologized renderings of the quotidian problems of uninteresting people." Before sitting down to write, decide first what medium is best suited for the story you want to tell.

Perhaps one of the easier ways to get started selling plays is by writing dramas to be performed by elementary, junior high and high school students in school or church settings. Play publishers (rather than producers), like Lillenas Publishing Co. and Oracle Press, may offer good opportunities to talented new playwrights. Check public libraries for collections of plays meant for these audiences and note that such plays are among the few where large casts (often up to 30) are encouraged.

Payment to playwrights varies greatly. As important as payment are the rights your producer obtains to your script. We've only included opportunities that pay writers for their work here; nonpaying productions, however, can be a good way to get your work before the public. Playwriting conferences often offer opportunities for staged readings and criticism by respected dramaturges and producers.

A useful organization for playwrights, The International Society of Dramatists, publishes *The Dramatist's Bible* and a newsletter, *The Globe* (ISD Fulfillment Center, Box 3470, Fort Pierce FL 22448). *Dramatists Sourcebook* (Theatre Communications Group, 355 Lexington

Ave., New York NY 10017) also lists theaters that consider unsolicited playscripts, play publishers, agents, fellowships, festivals, contests and other playwriting opportunities in film, radio and video. Another useful directory is the Theater Communications Group's *Theatre Directory*, which lists nearly 275 professional nonprofit theaters. The Alliance of Resident Theatres will provide general information to playwrights and consultations for members. The Alliance (Room 315, 325 Spring Street, New York NY 10013) also provides information on its 85 member theaters. Playwrights should also consider joining The Dramatists Guild (234 W. 44th St., New York NY 10036). You need not have sold a script to be a member. Guild members receive the monthly *Dramatists Guild Newsletter* and *The Dramatists Guild Quarterly*; both contain information about marketing plays.

Professional format

Manuscripts you send to publishers or producers should be as readable as possible, separating parenthetical remarks from dialogue in the reader's visual field. Basically you need to center the name of the character who is speaking on the page, separate stage directions from dialogue, and skip three lines or so between speakers. An example of proper manuscript format is available in *Guidelines*, $3 postpaid from Samuel French, Inc., 45 W. 25th Street, New York NY 10010.

‡**ACTORS ALLEY REPERTORY THEATRE**, 4334 Van Nuys Blvd., Sherman Oaks CA 91403. (818)986-7440. Artistic Director: Jordan Charney. Produces 14 plays/year. Equity-waiver theatre. Query with synopsis or submit complete ms. Reports in 6 months.
Needs: No musicals, no young-audience plays.
Tips: "Any full-length play submitted is also considered for our annual playwriting contest. 1st prize $350 and possible production. Actors Alley takes great pride in presenting many world, American and west coast premieres."

ACTORS THEATRE OF LOUISVILLE, 316 West Main St., Louisville KY 40202. (502)584-1265. Producing Director: Jon Jory. Produces/publishes approximately 30 new plays of varying lengths/year. Professional productions are performed for subscription audience from diverse backgrounds. Submit complete ms for one-act plays; agented submissions only for full-length plays. Reports in 6-9 months on submissions. No dot-matrix computer printout submissions. Buys production (in Louisville only) rights. Offers variable royalty.
Needs: "We accept only one-act plays—unsolicited. No children's shows or musicals. We produce both full-lengths and one-acts. National one-act play contest postmark deadline: April 15, 1988."

‡**ACTORS THEATRE OF TULSA, INC.**, Box 2116, Tulsa OK 74101. (918)749-6488. Artistic Director: Clifton R. Justice. Produces 5 plays/year. "Plays will be performed at our home theatre an on tour throught the state of Oklahoma. We are a non-equity, professional theatre company devoted to the production of contemporary theatre and the development of a permanent acting ensemble. Our audience is primarily professional people, with college degrees and a large amount of theatre sophistication." Send query and synopsis or submit complete ms. Reports in 2 months. "Generally we do not retain any rights on the manuscript except for acknowledgment of production if the piece is published." Pays $500-1,000.
Needs: "Productions are usually full-length plays dealing with a wide variety of issues and styles. We have no restrictions concerning language or subject matter. Our current season has ranged from Tina Howe's *The Art of Dining*, to *The Normal Heart*. Theatre facility is a black box and is used most effectively as arena or thrust. Casting always comes from a permanent ensemble that is ususally no larger than 15. We are seeking playwrights who are interested in developing projects with the members of the company. This would involve participating in activities at our home theatre with housing provided. We do not produce any musicals and are not likely to consider historical pieces. The theatre company is extremely limited in ethnic actors although we are not opposed to these pieces—but the playwright should be aware of this fact."
Tips: "We are currently seeking funding to bring a playwright in for a residency. While most writers are being encouraged to develop the commercial aspect of their abilities and playing it safe, we are looking for new perspectives and an individual voice in the theatre. Strength in writing and the ability to work in the theatre as a collabrative art form are essential to our organizaiton. The pieces are judged whether there is any universality as well as unique perspective to what the writer is saying. Additionally, we look to see if the play is theatrical in nature or would be more appropriate for film or television. Does the script go beyond realism and create an event that can only happen in a theatre with live actors and a live audience?"

ALASKA REPERTORY THEATRE, Suite 201, 705 W. 6th Ave., Anchorage AK 99501. (907)276-2327. Artistic Director: Andrew J. Traister. Produces 4-5 plays/year. Professional plays performed for Alaskan audiences. No unsolicited scripts; send synopsis and letter of inquiry *only*. Reports in 5 months. Pays 3% + royalty "depending on work."
Needs: Produces all types of plays.

‡ALLEY THEATRE, 615 Texas Ave., Houston TX 77002. Literary Manager: Robert Strane. A resident professional theatre: large stage seating 798; arena stage seating 296. Unagented submissions accepted. Computer printout submissions acceptable; prefers letter-quality to dot-matrix.
Needs: Plays—one-act and full-length—and musicals (script and cassette); plays for young audiences; adaptations and translations. Makes variable royalty arrangements. Send description/synopsis and letter of inquiry. Reports in 4 months. Produces 10-15 plays/year.
Recent Play Productions: *The Immigrant*, by Mark Harelik
Tips: "Address directly or through parable issues of the present."

‡AMERICAN RENAISSANCE THEATER, 112 Charlton St., New York NY 10014. (212)929-4718. Produces 2-4 plays/year. Off-off Broadway productions in 70-seat theater. Agented submissions only, or membership recommendation. Reports in 6 months. Obtains right of first option to produce; very small percent if other producer picks up option. Makes outright purchase of $100. Does not return unsolicited material.
Needs: American themes and writers.
Tips: "Be original—break new ground."

‡AMERICAN STAGE COMPANY, 211 3rd St. So., St. Petersburg FL 33731. (813)823-1600. Artistic Director: Victoria Holloway. Produces 5 plays/year. Plays performed on "our mainstage, in the park (Shakespeare) or on tour in schools." Submit query and synopsis. Reports in 4 months. Payment varies.
Needs: New American plays for small cast. No musicals.

AMERICAN STAGE FESTIVAL, Box 225, Milford NH 03055. Artistic Director: Larry Carpenter. "The ASF is a central New England professional theatre (professional equity company) with a 3 month summer season (June-August)" for audience of all ages, interests, education and sophistication levels. Query with synopsis. Produces musicals (20%) and nonmusicals (80%). 5 are mainstage and 10 are children's productions; 40% are originals. Royalty option and subsequent amount of gross: optional. Reports in 3 months.
Needs: "The Festival can do comedies, musicals and dramas. However, the most frequent problems are bolder language and action than a general mixed audience will accept. We have a 40-foot proscenium stage with 30-foot wings, but no fly system. Festival plays are chosen to present scale and opportunities for scenic and costume projects far beyond the 'summer theater' type of play." Length: Mainstage: 2-3 acts; children's productions: 50 minutes.
Recent Productions: *Corpse*, by Gerald Mood; *Rhymes with Evil*, by Charles Traeger.
Tips: Writers could improve submissions with "dramatic action, complexity, subplot and a unique statement. Try to get a staged reading of the script before submitting the play to us. Our audiences prefer plays that deal with human problems presented in a conventional manner."

AN CLAIDHEAMH SOLUIS/CELTIC ARTS CENTER, 5651 Hollywood Blvd., Hollywood CA 90028. (213)462-6844. Artistic Director: S. Walsh. Produces 6 plays/year. Equity waiver. Query and synopsis. Reports in 6 weeks. Rights acquired varies. Pays $25-50.
Needs: Scripts of Celtic interest (Scottish, Welsh, Irish, Cornish, Manx, Breton). "This can apply to writer's background or subject matter. We are particularly concerned with works that relate to the survival of cultures and traditions.

‡ANGEL'S TOUCH PRODUCTIONS, 11022 Hesby Street, North Hollywood CA 91601. (818)506-3056. Director of Development: Phil Nemy. Professional Broadway productions for all audiences. Send script and synopsis. Reports in 3-4 months. Rights negotiated between production company and author. Payment negotiated.
Needs: All types, all genres, only full-length plays and screenplays—no one-acts. or pieces involving homosexuality.
Tips: "Keep in mind the costs involved in mounting a Broadway or regional theatre production and try to write accordingly."

ARAN PRESS, 1320 S. 3rd St., Louisville KY 40208. (502)636-0115. Publishes a varying number of professional theatre, community theatre, college and university theatre, dinner theatre and summer stock plays. Query. Reports in 3 weeks. Acquires stage production rights. Pays 10% royalty on book; or 50% of standard royalty (i.e. half of $35 or $50 per performance).
Needs: "Anything the writer deems suitable for one or more of our five targeted markets." No children's plays.

ARENA STAGE, 6th and Maine Ave. SW, Washington DC 20024. (202)554-9066. Artistic Director: Zelda Fichandler. Produces 8-11 plays/year. Works with 1-4 unpublished/unproduced writers annually in "Play Lab," a play development project. Stages professional productions in Washington for intelligent, educated, sophisticated audiences using resident Equity company. Virtually none of the scripts produced are unagented submissions. Works with 2-4 unpublished/unproduced writers annually. Prefers query and synopsis plus the first 10 pages of dialogue, or agented submissions. Reports in 4 months. "We obtain an option to produce for one year or other term; percentage of future earnings." Pays 5% royalty. Computer printout submissions acceptable "as long as they are easily readable; no dot-matrix."

Needs: Produces classical, contemporary European and American plays; new plays, translations and adaptations without restrictions. No sitcoms, blank verse, pseudo-Shakespearean tragedies, movies-of-the-week or soap operas.

Tips: "We can consider large casts, though big plays are expensive and must justify that expense artistically. Be theatrical. Navel-gazing is of little interest. Plays with relevance to the human situation—which cover a multitude of dramatic approaches—are welcome here."

‡ARIZONA THEATRE COMPANY,56 W. Congress, Tucson AZ 85702. (602)884-8210. Director: Gary Gisselman. Produces 7 plays/year. Professional LORT B theatre, performing in Tucson and Phoenix. Send query and synopsis. Reports in 6 months.

Needs: "Full-length plays and musicals. Reasonable technical demands and cast size. All types and topics."

Tips: "Writers should have something to say in an interesting way. No one acts of large cast historical dramas without a purpose or point of view."

THE ARKANSAS ARTS CENTER CHILDREN'S THEATRE, Box 2137, MacArthur Park, Little Rock AR 72203. (501)372-4000. Artistic Director: Bradley Anderson. Produces 5-6 mainstage plays, 3 tours/year. Mainstage season plays performed at The Arkansas Arts Center for Little Rock and surrounding area; tour season by professional actors throughout Arkansas and surrounding states. Mainstage productions perform to family audiences in public performances; weekday performances for local schools in grades K through senior high school. Tour audiences generally the same. Works with 1 unpublished/unproduced writer annually. Submit complete script. Computer printout submissions acceptable; prefers letter-quality to dot-matrix. Reports in several months. Buys negotiable rights. Pays $250-1,500 or negotiable commission.

Needs: Original adaptations of classic and contemporary works. Also original scripts. "This theatre is defined as a children's theatre; this can inspire certain assumptions about the nature of the work. We would be pleased if submissions did not presume to condescend to a particular audience. We are not interested in 'cute' scripts. Submissions should simply strive to be good theatre literature."

Recent Title: *Joan of Arc.*

Tips: "We would welcome scripts open to imaginative production and interpretation. Also, scripts which are mindful that this children's theatre casts adults as adults and children as children. Scripts which are not afraid of contemporary issues are welcome."

ART CRAFT PUBLISHING CO., 232 Dows Bldg., Cedar Rapids IA 52406. (319)364-6311. Publisher: C. McMullen. Publishes plays for the junior and senior high school market. Query with synopsis or send complete ms. Reports in 2 months. Acquires amateur rights only. Makes outright purchase for $100-1,500 or pays royalty.

Needs: One- and three-acts—preferably comedies or mystery comedies. Currently needs plays with a larger number of characters for production within churches and schools. Prefers one-set plays. No "material with the normal 'taboos'—controversial material."

ARTREACH TOURING THEATRE, 3936 Millsbrae Ave., Cincinnati OH 45209. (513)351-9973. Director: Kathryn Schultz Miller. Produces 4 plays/year to be performed in area schools and community organizations. "We are a professional company. Our audience is primarily young people in schools and their families." Submit complete ms. Reports in 6 weeks. Buys exclusive right to produce for 9 months. Pays $4/show (approximately 150 performances).

Needs: Plays for children and adolescents. Serious, intelligent plays about contemporary life or history/legend. "Limited sets and props. Can use scripts with only 2 men and 2 women; 45 minutes long. Should be appropriate for touring." No clichéd approaches, camp or musicals.

Tips: "We look for opportunities to create innovative stage effects using few props, and we like scripts with good acting opportunities."

ASOLO STATE THEATRE, Postal Drawer E, Sarasota FL 33578. (813)355-7115. Artistic Director: John Ulmer. Produces 7 plays/year. 80% freelance written. About 50% of scripts produced are unagented submissions. A LORT theatre with an intimate performing space. "We play to rather traditional middle-class audiences." Works with 2-4 unpublished/unproduced writers annually. "We do not accept unsolicited scripts. Writers must send us a letter and synopsis with self-addressed stamped postcard." Computer printout submissions accepta-

ble; no dot-matrix. Reports in 5 months. Negotiates rights. Negotiates payment.
Needs: Play must be *full length*. "We do not restrict ourselves to any particular genre or style—generally we do a good mix of classical and modern works."
Tips: "We have no special approach—we just want well written plays with clear, dramatic throughlines. Don't worry about trends on the stage. Write honestly and write for the stage, not for a publication."

AT THE FOOT OF THE MOUNTAIN THEATER, 2000 S. 5th St., Minneapolis MN 55454: (612)375-9487. Artistic Director: Phyllis Jane Rose. 25% freelance written. 2-4 scripts are unagented submissions. "Plays will be performed in our 'black box' theatre by a professional acting company. Plays submitted to our *Broadcloth Series* (a sampler of new scripts by women writers) will be given staged readings by our professional ensemble. No unsolicited scripts accepted. Multimedia Crosscultural Alliance of Women is a group of women of color interested in producing work written and performed by people of color." Works with 4-6 unpublished/unproduced writers annually. "Put yourself on our newletter mailing list and watch for when scripts are called for (approx bi-annually)." Submit complete script. Computer printout submissions acceptable; no dot-matrix. Reports in 6 months. Pays $10-30/performance. Submissions returned with SASE.
Needs: All genres: full-length plays, one acts, and musicals by women. Encourages experimental plays. "We are mainly interested in plays by and about women and prefer to produce plays with predominantly female casts. Plays with a feminist approach to the world; plays which work at creating new forms." No sexist or racist plays.
Tips: "The theatre prefers small casts and simple sets."

‡ATLANTA NEW PLAY PROJECT,Box 14252, Atlanta GA 30324. (404)373-8005. Artistic Director: Frank M. Miller. Produces 10 plays/year. "Plays presented as readings in annual, one-week festival, usually second week in June. Target audience is theatre artists and more serious theatre goers." Write for guidelines, which vary with each theatre involved. Reports in 6 months. Obtains rights to 1 or 2 readings. Pays $100-200. "Also we do associate readings with no payment to writers."
Needs: "All types, depending on missions of member theatres. No bad scripts, particularly movie/TV scripts masquerading as stage plays and what I call children's theatre for adults (i.e. plays that preach a moral leson first and tell a story later)."
Tips: "The ANPP is a cooperative venture of 17 local theatre groups, each with its own interests. Writers need to consider more imaginative use of stage, in the vein of Peter Nichols or Arthur Kopit. Get away from one-set drama in which everything is spelled out in dialogue. Learn the value of stage poetry (Williams) and action (Bond)."

‡ATTIC THEATRE, Box 02457, Detroit MI 48202. (313)875-8285. Associate Artistic Director: Ronald Martell. Produces 6 plays/year. Professional resident theatre company. Send query and synopsis or submit through agent. Reports in 3 months. Rights obtained vary. Pay varies widely.
Needs: "Full-length plays and musicals. Prefers 'modern' plays with social and political issues, casts of 4-10 with roles for males and females. We encourage open stage styles rather than typical boxset scripts. We tend to produce works from writers whom we know, whom we have worked with and who know our company's style. We tend to view submissions by writers unknown to us as an introduction only."
Tips: "We engage writers, not product. If we like your work, we may not produce it but may request more material, possibly request a commission."

‡AVILA COLLEGE PERFORMING ARTS DEPT., 11901 Wornall Rd., Kansas City MO 64145. (816)942-8400. Artistic Director: W.J. Louis, PhD. Produces 5 plays/year. Possibility of 1 script produced by unagented submission. Performs collegiate amateur productions (4 main stage, 1 studio productions) for Kansas City audiences. Query with synopsis. Computer printout submissions acceptable; prefers letter-quality to dot-matrix. Reports in 3 months. Buys rights arranged with author. Pays rate arranged with author.
Needs: All genres with wholesome ideas and language—musicals, dramas. Length 1-2 hours. Small casts (2-5 characters), women casts; few props, simple staging. No lewd and crude language and scenes.
Tips: Example of play just done: *Towards The Morning*, by John Fenn. Story: "Mentally confused bag lady and 17-year-old egocentric boy discover they need each other; she regains mental stability; he grows up a bit and becomes more responsible. Trends in the American stage freelance writers should be aware of include (1) point-of-view one step beyond theatre of the absurd—theatre that makes light of self-pity; and (2) need for witty, energetic social satire done without smut in the style of *Kid Purple*, by Don Wollner, The 1984 national competition winner of the Unicorn Theatre, Kansas City, Mo."

RAN AVNI/JEWISH REPERTORY THEATRE, 344 E. 14th St., New York NY 10003. (212)674-7200. Artistic Director: Ran Avni. "We are an Equity non-profit theatre, Mini-contract." Produces 5 plays/year. Query with synopsis. Reports in 1 month. Pays $25-50/performance.
Needs: "Plays in English that relate to the Jewish experience."

BACKSTAGE THEATRE, Box 297, Breckenridge CO 80424. (303)453-0199. Artistic Director: Allyn Mosher. Produces 2-5 plays/year. Plays performed semi-professionally for resort community, tourist market. Submit complete ms. Reports in 3 weeks. Pays $20-40/performance.
Needs: Comedies, mysteries and small cast musicals. Cast should be of fewer than 10, single-level sets.
Tips: "Writers should be aware of theatrical multiple roles in plays like *The Dining Room* and *Greater Tuna*. Avoid sterile TV-like situations."

BAKER'S PLAY PUBLISHING CO., 100 Chauncy St., Boston MA 02111. Editor: John B. Welch. 80% freelance written. Plays performed by amateur groups, high schools, children's theatre, churches and community theatre groups. "We are the largest publisher of chancel drama in the world." 90% of scripts are unagented submissions. Works with 2-3 unpublished/unproduced writers annually. Submit complete script. Submit complete cassette of music or musical submissions. Computer printout submissions acceptable. Publishes 18-25 straight plays and musicals; all originals. Pay varies; outright purchase price to split in production fees. Reports in 4 months.
Needs: "We are finding strong support in our new division—plays for young adults featuring contemporary issue-oriented dramatic pieces for high school production."

MARY BALDWIN COLLEGE THEATRE, Mary Baldwin College, Staunton VA 24401. (703)887-7192. Artistic Director: Dr. Virginia R. Francisco. Produces 5 plays/year. 10% freelance written. 0-1% of scripts are unagented. Works with 0-1 unpublished/unproduced writer annually. An undergraduate women's college theatre with an audience of students, faculty, staff and local community (adult, conservative). Query with synopsis. Electronic submissions OK via IBM-PC DOS Text File, Word Perfect, Word Star, or Multimate File. Computer printout submissions acceptable; prefers letter-quality to dot-matrix. Reports in 3 months. Buys performance rights only. Pays $10-50/performance.
Needs: Full-length and short comedies, tragedies, musical plays, particularly for young women actresses, dealing with women's issues both contemporary and historical. Experimental/studio theatre not suitable for heavy sets. Cast should emphasize women. No heavy sex; minimal explicit language.
Tips: "A perfect play for us has several roles for young women, few male roles, minimal production demands, a concentration on issues relevant to contemporary society, and elegant writing and structure."

‡**BARTER THEATRE**, Box 867, Abingdon VA 24210. (703)628-2281. Artistic Director: Rex Partington. Produces 12 plays/year. "Professional productions. Regional theatre. All types of audiences." Submit complete ms. Reports in 6 months. Pays 5% royalty.
Needs: Produces "contemporary comedies and dramas of relevance, and worthy adaptations of classics." Plays should have casts of 4 to 12, and a single or unit set.
Tips: Looking for "subjects of relevance and significance," with theme of individuals and society coping with universal challenges." No one acts or "lighter than air" scripts.

‡**BEREA COLLEGE THEATRE**, Box 22, Berea KY 40404. (606)986-9341, Ext 6355. Produces 4 full-length and 10 one-act plays/year. "Amateur performances; college audience with community persons in audience also." Send query and synopsis or submit complete ms. Reports in 3 weeks. Obtains negotiable rights. Pays $35-50/performance.
Needs: Medium cast plays (10-20 persons); no musicals.
Tips: "Single-page business letter with synopsis will be good to start with."

BERKELEY JEWISH THEATRE, 1414 Walnut St., Berkeley CA 94709. (415)849-0498. Artistic Director: Barbara Damashek. Produces 4 plays and 6 staged readings/year. Plays performed in an Equity Waiver theatre, 100 seats at Berkeley Jewish Community Center. "Will move end of this year to new 200 seat theatre and cabaret space in redesigned Durkee building in west Berkeley." Submit complete ms. Reports in 1 month. Acquires production rights. Pays $35-50/performance.
Needs: Plays for main stage and cabaret in all genres which embody and express the variety of experience of the American Jewish diaspora.
Tips: "Writers should have a sound general knowledge of American Jewish culture and the problems confronting the largest Jewish community outside of the State of Israel. Avoid the models for plays set by Broadway, Hollywood or television, or risk ruining one's talent and integrity."

BERKSHIRE THEATRE FESTIVAL, INC., E. Main St., Stockbridge MA 01262. Artistic Director: Josephine R. Abady. 25% original scripts. Produces 7-8 plays a year (4 are mainstage and 4 are second spaces). Submissions by agents only.

‡**WALTER L. BORN**, 2 Beaver Place, Aberdeen NJ 07747. (201)566-6985. Produces 4 musicals/year. Produces "only musicals—for non-professional productions in Aberdeen." Submit complete ms. Reports in 1 month. Buys the right to performance on limited basis. Pays $125-150/performance.

Needs: Produces musicals on subject of growing old, problems of living by elderly; people with disabilities. Music can be classical, modern or rock. Maximum length: 2 hours. Cast should be small (6-12); set should be simple "since we cannot fly." Vehicle should be challenging and realistic. "No simplistic mediocrity."
Tips: "We are looking for innovative approaches to musical theatre that do not depend on traditions of any kind."

‡BRISTOL RIVERSIDE THEATRE, Box 1250, Bristol PA 19007. (215)785-6664. Artistic Director: Susan D. Atkinson. Estab. 1986. Produces 5 mainstage, 4 workshops, and 20 readings plus children's theatre/year. "We are a professional regional professional theatre company; we produce new works exclusively in our workshop and reading series. The intention is to develop the works for mainstage productions. Our audience is drawn from Bucks County, Philadelphia, Trenton, Princeton and surrounding New Jersey areas. We also plan a two-show, popular, summer program." Submit complete ms. Reports in 10 months. "Since we are a developmental company and spend a great deal of time on each work selected for reading and/or workshop, we request a percentage of author's revenues for a given period of time and recognition of the theatre and key individuals on subsequent productions, after the reading phase of the development is completed." Offers variable royalty.
Needs: "We produce all genres from dramas, comedies to musicals and operas. We also produce one-acts. We would prefer smaller shows with limited costs, but we have never shied away from larger shows. The quality, not the quantity, is the determining factor in all cases."
Tips: "We are not interested in plays that have as their only goal entertainment. We would hope all works would have this quality, but if there is no other value sought, we would not be interested. We are a company in search of the new mainstream of theatre in America. We aim to entertain, enlighten and elevate our audience. And we are seeking authors who are interested in developing their works, not just presenting them; we view theatre as a process."

BROADWAY PLAY PUBLISHING, INC., 357 W. 20th St., New York NY 10011. (212)627-1055. Publishes 15-20 plays/year. 10% of scripts published are unagented submissions. Works with 5 unpublished/unproduced writers annually. Query with synopsis. Computer printout submissions acceptable. Reports on submitted mss in 3 months. Buys stock, amateur, acting edition publishing rights. Pays 10% on book royalty; 90% stock; 80% amateur.
Needs: New contemporary full-length American plays—use of language. No autobiography, domestic realism, adaptations or translations. No musicals or one-acts.

‡DIANNE BUSCH—THE WESTERN STAGE, 156 Homestead Ave., Salinas CA 93901. Producing Director: Dianne Busch. Produces 12-18 plays (including one acts)/year. "Summer theatre for subscriber audience in Salinas/Monterey/Carmel area. Query with synopsis or submit complete ms (prefer). Reports in 6 weeks. Obtains production rights, sometimes workshop rights. Pays 10% royalty or makes negotiable arrangements with new playwrights, $200 and up.
Needs: Almost anything: one acts, full length—all genres and styles. Would prefer to stay away from complete avant-garde, for audience reasons. Our audiences are not ready for it yet."
Tips: "Our audiences object to plays which are *full* of strong language—I personally don't mind if it is consistent with the theme and characters—but it would be rare for us to produce, for example, a David Mamet play."

CAPITAL REPERTORY COMPANY, Box 399, Albany NY 12201. (518)462-4531. Producing Directors: Peter Clough and Bruce Bouchard. Stages 6 productions/season. 33% freelance written. "We are a professional regional theatre with a subscriber audience (broad mix)." 50% of scripts are unagented submissions. Works with 5-10 unpublished/unproduced writers annually. Submit complete ms. Reports in 3 months. Makes outright purchase. Computer printout submissions acceptable; no dot-matrix. All genres, topics, styles, lengths, etc. are needed.
Tips: Send "bound, typed, clean manuscripts."

CARROLL COLLEGE, Helena MT 59625. (406)442-3450. Director of Theater: Jim Bartruff. Produces 4-6 plays/year. "We produce plays in an educational theatre with amateurs for college and community audiences." Submit query and synopsis or complete ms. Reports in 2 weeks. Pays $10-50/performance.
Needs: American standards, musicals, classics and original scripts. "We are a small group with limited space and production budgets. Gear plays for college students learning the various crafts of the theatre."
Tips: "As a church-related college, we do dismiss certain titles due to language, topic, theme, etc."

CASA MANANA MUSICALS, INC., 3101 W. Lancaster, Box 9054, Fort Worth TX 76107. (817)332-9319. Producer/General Manager: Bud Franks. Assistant Producer: Charles A. Ballinger. "All performances are staged at Casa Manana Theatre and are community funded." Query. Produces 6 summer stock musicals (uses Equity people only), theater-in-the-round. Children's playhouse theatre produces 8 children's shows in the winter season.
Needs: Scripts of all kinds; cassettes acceptable.

THE CAST THEATRE, 804 N. El Centro Ave., Los Angeles CA 90038. (213)462-9872. Producing Artistic Director: Ted Schmitt. Equity Waiver (professional) production either in The CAST Theatre or in The-CAST-at-the-Circle, the two theatres in the complex. The productions are meant for general audience. Submit complete ms. Reports in 4 months. Offers $100-500 advance against royalties.
Needs: "Any style, type or genre of playscript and musical (tape of score must accompany book and lyrics for consideration). ``We look for both comedies and dramas with substance and compelling ideas, that deal with human relationships and with the indomitability of the human spirit. Because of limited staging, we cannot consider elaborate concepts and are inclined to favor limbo or one-unit settings." Maximum cast: 18. No "comedies that smack of TV sit-com situations and writing."

CENTER FOR PUPPETRY ARTS, 1404 Spring St. NW, Atlanta GA 30309. (404)873-3089. Artistic Director: Luis Q. Barroso. Produces 4 plays/year. Professional puppet theatre. Adult audiences. Submit query and synopsis, or submit complete ms. Reports in 6 weeks. Negotiates rights. Pays $15-50/performance.
Needs: Plays that can be produced with puppets or a combination of actors and puppets. Playwright should be "adventurous, willing to deal with the uniqueness of puppetry."
Tips: "Puppetry is becoming an accepted form of theatre, not just for children but also for adults. Writers should acquaint themselves with the different types of puppets (marionette, rod, hand, shadows) and begin to write meaningful scripts for this unique art form."

‡CENTER STAGE, 700 N. Calvert St., Baltimore MD 21202. (301)685-3200. Artistic Director: Stan Wojewodski, Jr. Submit to: Rick Davis, resident dramaturg. Produces 6-9 plays/year. "Professional L.O.R.T 'B' company; audience is both subscription and single-ticket. Wide-ranging audience profile." Query with synopsis or submit through agent. Reports in 6 weeks. Rights negotiated. Payment depending on category of production (e.g., mainstage, playwrights, series, etc.).
Needs: Produces "dramas and comedies, occasional musicals. No restrictions on topics or styles, though experimental work is encouraged. Casts over 30 would give us pause. Be inventive, theatrical, not precious; we like plays with vigorous language and stage image. No conventional, highly psychologized renderings of the quotidian problems of uninteresting people."
Tips: "We are interested in reading adaptations and translations as well as original work."

THE CHANGING SCENE THEATER, 1527½ Champa St., Denver CO 80202. Director: Alfred Brooks. Year-round productions in theatre space. Cast may be made up of both professional and amateur actors. For public audience; age varies, but mostly youthful and interested in taking a chance on new and/or experimental works. No limit to subject matter or story themes. Emphasis is on the innovative. "Also, we require that the playwright be present for at least one performance of his work, if not for the entire rehearsal period. We have a small stage area, but are able to convert to round, semi-round or environmental. Prefer to do plays with limited sets and props." 1-act, 2-act and 3-act. Produces 8-10 nonmusicals a year; all are originals. 90% freelance written. 65% of scripts produced are unagented submissions. Works with 3-4 unpublished/unproduced writers annually. "We do not pay royalties or sign contracts with playwrights. We function on a performance-share basis of payment. Our theatre seats 76; the first 50 seats go to the theatre; the balance is divided among the participants in the production. The performance-share process is based on the entire production run and not determined by individual performances. We do not copyright our plays." Send complete script. Reporting time varies; usually several months.
Recent Title: *Hostages*, by Mary Guzzy.
Tips: "We are experimental: open to young artists who want to test their talents and open to experienced artists who want to test new ideas/explore new techniques. Dare to write 'strange and wonderful' well-thought-out scripts. We want upbeat ones. Consider that we have a small performance area when submitting."

‡DOROTHY CHANSKY, #5R, 107 West 70th St., New York NY 10023. (212)724-2751. Produces 1 play/year. Professional, off-Broadway, Broadway productions. Query with synopsis or send complete ms. Reports in 2 months. Pays royalty.
Needs: Seeks drama, comedies, musicals. "Strictly educational, highly classical work is not useful to me. My bent is serious/commercial."
Tips: "Excellence and the individual voice are what I seek. However, if you send a cover letter with typos, if you misspell my name, if you bury me under stacks of reviews of amateur productions, it will be that much harder to make a good impression with your play. Presentation counts."

CIRCLE IN THE SQUARE THEATRE, 1633 Broadway, New York NY 10019. (212)307-2700. Artistic Director: Theodore Mann. Literary Advisor: Seth Goldman. Produces 3 plays/year. Theatre for subscription audience and New York theatre-going public. Query with 1-page synopsis only. Reports in 3 months. Pays royalty.
Tips: "We produce classics, revivals, full-length new plays and musicals."

CIRCLE REPERTORY CO., 161 Avenue of the Americas, New York NY 10013. (212)691-3210. Associate Artistic Director: Rod Marriott. Produces 5 mainstage plays, 5 Projects in Progress/year. Accepts unsolicited mss for full-length plays only; we no longer produce one-acts.

CIRCUIT PLAYHOUSE/PLAYHOUSE ON THE SQUARE, 51 S. Cooper, Memphis TN 38104. (901)725-0776. Artistic Director: Jackie Nichols. Produces 2 plays/year. 100% freelance written. Professional plays performed for the Memphis/Mid-South area. Member of the Theatre Communications Group. 100% of scripts are unagented submissions. Works with 1 unpublished/unproduced writer annually. A play contest is held each fall. Submit complete ms. Computer printout submissions acceptable. Reports in 3 months. Buys "percentage of royalty rights for 2 years." Pays $500-1,000 in outright purchase.
Needs: All types; limited to single or unit sets. Cast of 20 or fewer.
Tips: "Each play is read by three readers through the extended length of time a script is kept. Preference is given to scripts for the southeastern region of the U.S."

‡CITY THEATRE COMPANY, B39 CL, University of Pittsburgh, Pittsburgh PA 15260. (412)624-1357. Literary Manager: Dennis Kennedy. Produces 4 full productions and readings/year. "We are a small professional theatre, operating under an Equity contact, and committed to twentieth-century American plays. Our seasons are innovative and challenging, both artistically and socially. We perform in a 117-seat thrust stage, playing usually 6 times a week, each production running 5 weeks or more. We have a committed audience following." Query and synopsis or submit through agent. Obtains no rights. Pays 5-6% royalty.
Needs: "No limits on style or subject, but we are most interested in theatrical plays that have something to say about the way we live. No light comedies or TV-issue dramas." Normal cast limit is 8. Plays must be appropriate for small space without flies.
Tips: "American playwrights only. We run a staged reading series of 6 plays a year, choosing work that we wish to consider for full production. Write from need and from commitment."

I.E. CLARK, INC., Saint John's Rd., Box 246, Schulenburg TX 78956. (409)743-3232. Publishes 15 plays/year for educational theatre, children's theatre, religious theatre, regional professional theatre, amateur community theatre. 20% freelance written. 3-4 scripts produced/year are unagented submissions. Works with 2-3 unpublished/unproduced writers annually. Submit complete script. Computer printout submissions acceptable; prefers letter-quality to dot-matrix. Reports in 6 months. Buys all available rights; "we serve as an agency as well as a publisher." Pays standard book and performance royalty, "the amount and percentages dependent upon type and marketability of play."
Needs: "We are interested in plays of all types—short or long. We seldom publish musicals, but audio tapes of music are requested with submissions. We prefer that a play has been produced (directed by someone other than the author); photos and reviews of the production are helpful. No limitations in cast, props, staging, etc.; however, the simpler the staging, the larger the market. Plays with more than one set are difficult to sell. So are plays with only one or two characters. We insist on literary quality. We like plays that give new interpretations and understanding of human nature. Correct spelling, punctuation and grammar (befitting the characters, of course) impress our editors."
Tips: "Entertainment value and a sense of moral responsibility seem to be returning as essential qualities of a good play script. The era of glorifying the negative elements of society seems to be fading rapidly. Literary quality, entertainment value and good craftsmanship rank in that order as the characteristics of a good script in our opinion. 'Literary quality' means that the play must say something; preferably something new and important concerning man's relations with his fellow man; and these 'lessons in living' must be presented in an intelligent, believable and—perhaps—poetic manner."

COACH HOUSE PRESS, INC., Box 458, Morton Grove IL 60053. (312)967-1777. President: David Jewell. Primarily publisher of children's plays. 100% freelance written. Most scripts published are unagented submissions. Works with 3-5 unpublished/unproduced writers annually. Publishes production scripts and trade paperback originals. Averages 3-8 plays/year. Pays 5-15% royalty on book receipts; 50% on performance royalty. Simultaneous and photocopied submissions OK. Electronic submissions OK by special arrangement via ASCII, but requires hard copy also. Computer printout submissions acceptable; prefers letter-quality to dot-matrix. Reports in 3 weeks on queries; 2 months on mss.
Needs: Drama—plays for children's theatre and over-60 adult theatre. Books on theatre production. Publishes for theatre producers and recreation specialists.
Recent Title: *New Plays for Mature Actors* by Bonnie L. Vorenberg.
Tips: "The trend to greater respect for young people is leading toward more intelligent and challenging scripts for children's theatre. A script which has received first-rate production(s) enhances its value to us, because it's more likely the author has tested and strengthened the script with the help of audience response."

‡COMPANY ONE, 94 Allyn St., Hartford CT 06103. (203)278-6347. Artistic Director: Stephen Rust. Produces 10 plays/year. "One-act plays submitted to Company One, if selected, will be performed at the Hartford Arts Center as part of our Lunchtime/Drivetime Theater series. Our audience members are generally downtown employees looking for an entertaining break in their workday. This, however, does not preclude the presentation of thought-provoking material." Submit complete ms. Reports in 6 weeks. Pays 5% royalty, $10-25 per performance.

Needs: "Best suited to the Lunchtime/Drivetime format is the 40 minute, 2 or 3 character, single set, comedy. Although a good play can find its way around limitations, Company One tries to keep its casts small (four or less), its sets and props simple, and special effects to a minimum. Company One now produces 8 one-act plays/year during the Spring and Fall in a month-long festival format. Each play receives about 7 performances. We also now consider full-length original scripts for evening productions."

Tips: "Based on increasing attendance and positive audience response, the one-act play may find a new and growing market beyond the annual festivals. People enjoy Lunchtime Theater, and we need good plays to show them, all the year round. Writers should no longer feel the need to submit only comedies; something more dangerous or sexy may be appropriate in the coming seasons."

‡COMPANY THEATRE, 1768 Dryden Road, Freeville NY 13068. (607)347-4411. Artistic Director: Stuart Scadron-Wattles. Produces 3 plays/year. Semi-professional productions for a general audience. Send query and synopsis. Reports in 3-6 months. Pays $50-100/performance.

Needs: "One-act or full-length; comedy or drama; musical or straight; written from a biblical world view." No cast above 10; prefers unit staging.

Tips: Looks for "non-religious writing from a biblical world view for an audience which loves the theatre. See trends toward shorter scenes. Playwrights should be aware that they are writing for the stage—not television."

CONTEMPORARY DRAMA SERVICE, Meriwether Publishing Ltd., Box 7710, Colorado Springs CO 80933. (303)594-4422. Editor-in-Chief: Arthur Zapel. Publishes 50-60 plays/year. "We publish for the secondary school market and colleges. We also publish for mainline liturgical churches—drama activities for church holidays, youth activities and fundraising entertainments. These may be plays or drama-related books." Query with synopsis or submit complete ms. Reports in 5 weeks. Obtains either amateur or all rights. Pays 10% royalty or outright from $200-750.

Needs: "Most of the plays we publish are 1-acts, 15 to 45 minutes in length. We occasionally publish full-length 3-act plays. We prefer comedies in the longer plays. Musical plays must have name appeal either by prestige author, prestige title adaptation or performance on Broadway or TV. Comedy sketches, monlogues and 2-character plays are welcomed. We prefer simple staging appropriate to high school, college or church performance. We like playwrights who see the world positively and with a sense of humor. Offbeat themes and treatments are accepted if the playwright can sustain a light touch and not take himself (herself) too seriously. In documentary or religious plays we look for good research and authenticity."

CROSSROADS THEATRE COMPANY, 320 Memorial Parkway, New Brunswick NJ 08901. (201)249-5625. Artistic Director: Lee Richardson. Produces 6 plays/year. Regional theatre that stages Equity professional productions. Query with synopsis. Computer printout submissions acceptable. Reports in 6 months. Returns rights to percentage of future productions. Pays royalty.

Needs: "We need plays involving minority experiences by any writer." Black (Afro-American, African, Caribbean) and interracial plays are preferred. Productions should be suited to a 150-seat theatre.

Tips: "We look for well-crafted scripts that deal with minorities in a non-traditional form, providing a new perspective or insight. Cast size and scenic requirements figure prominently in selection process."

‡DAKOTA THEATRE CARAVAN, Box 1014, Spearfish SD 57783. (605)642-8120. Artistic Director: Jeanne-Marie Zeck.Produces 2 plays/year. Professional productions on tour through 8 midwestern states. Query with synopsis. Reports in 6 weeks. Obtains non-exclusive, multi-year rights. Pays $10-100/performance.

Needs: Plays that in some way speak to the human condition, that can be produced in non-traditional performance spaces. Past plays have explored stereotyping, rural vs urban relationships, farm issues, sexual relationships, histories of common people. No more than 7 actors. Sometimes lighting is not required or available on some tours.

‡DALTON LITTLE THEATRE/WORLD CARPETS NEW PLAY PROJECT, Box 841, Dalton GA 30722. (404)226-6618. Coordinator: Bruce Mitchell. Third play produced in August 1987. Amateur productions in summer of each year. Submit complete ms. Reports in 2-3 months. Obtains first performance rights. Pays 100% royalty or outright $400.

Needs: "Any full-length play or musical is accepted." Writers should keep in mind small stage/playing area. No less-than-full-length or previously produced plays.

Tips: Manuscripts accepted Dec. 1 through Jan. 31. Reports on May 1.

DELAWARE THEATRE COMPANY, Box 516, Wilmington DE 19899. (302)594-1104. Artistic Director: Cleveland Morris. Produces 5 plays/year. 10% freelance written. "Plays are performed as part of a five-play subscription season in a 300-seat auditorium. Professional actors, directors and designers are engaged. The

season is intended for a general audience." 10% of scripts are unagented submissions. Works with 1 unpublished/unproduced writer every two years. Query with synopsis. Computer printout submissions acceptable; prefers letter-quality to dot-matrix. Reports in 6 months. Buys variable rights. Pays 5% (variable) royalty.
Needs: "We present comedies, dramas, tragedies and musicals. All works must be full-length and fit in with a season composed of standards and classics. All works have a strong literary element. Plays with a flair for language and a strong involvement with the interests of classical humanism are of greatest interest. Single-set, small-cast works are likeliest for consideration."

DENVER CENTER THEATRE COMPANY, 1050 13th St., Denver CO 80204. (303)893-4200. Artistic Director: Donovan Marley. Produces 12 plays/year. Professional regional repertory (LORT-B) plays performed in the only major regional theatre in the Rocky Mountain West. Also, professional tours possible, both regionally and nationally. Submit complete ms. Computer printout submissions acceptable; no dot-matrix. Reports in 2 months. Negotiates rights. Negotiates royalty.
Needs: "Full-length comedies and dramas. The Denver Center Theatre Company is especially eager to see plays of regional interest. Send SASE for return of ms. We do not accept musicals, children's plays, 1-character plays, translations, adaptations or plays with more than 12 characters."

‡DOBAMA THEATRE, 1846 Coventry Road, Cleveland Heights OH 44118. (216)932-6838. Literary Manager: Jean Cummins. "We maintain our own theatre and our own unpaid non-Equity company. Although not wildly experimental, our company has built a reputation for taking risks with new and unusual works. Our audience is theatrically sophisticated." Submit complete ms. Reports in 3-6 months. "Obtains no rights at present." Pays $35 each performance. Typical run is 9 performances.
Needs: "We produce full-length dramas and comedies and an occasional musical. Most of our plays are intimate, small cast. About once a year we break out with something larger, more theatrical. We are a ¾ arena, 200 seat house; on-screen projections are nearly impossible for us. Also no basement, trap door effects. Our ceilings are pretty low."
Tips: "We are interested in plays with good human values. We look for a chance to help new and emerging playwrights see their vision take shape on stage. We try to comment on every script that we receive."

DORSET THEATRE FESTIVAL, Box 519, Dorset VT 05251. (802)867-2223. Artistic Director: Jill Charles. Produces 6 plays/year. 20% freelance written. A professional (equity) theatre, season June-September or October. Audience is sophisticated, largely tourists and second-home owners from metropolitan New York and Boston areas. Does not accept unsolicited mss or queries; submit via agent only. Computer printout submissions acceptable; prefers letter-quality to dot-matrix. Reports in 4 months. Negotiates rights. Negotiates rate; minimum $250 for 11 performances.
Needs: Full length plays (2 acts); any genre, but should have broad audience appeal; generally realistic, but *not* "kitchen dramas." Will consider musicals; must have accompanying cassette. Cast less than 10; single or unit (flexible) settings preferred. "We produce one new play each season and also have a new play reading series of 5 new scripts. We lean toward *positive* plays, whether comedy or drama. No family melodrama."
Tips: "Best time to have agent submit play is from September to January. (Plays received after March 1 may not be read until fall). Trends on the American stage that freelance writers should be aware of include small casts."

THE DRAMATIC PUBLISHING CO., 311 Washington St., Woodstock IL 60098. (815)338-7170. Publishes about 30 new shows a year. 60% freelance written. 40% of scripts published are unagented submissions. "Current growth market is in plays and musicals for children, plays and small-cast musicals for stock and community theatre." Also has a large market for plays and musicals for schools and other amateur theatre groups. Works with 2-6 unpublished/unproduced writers annually. Reports in 2-6 months. Buys stock and amateur theatrical rights. Pays by usual royalty contract, 10 free scripts and 40% discount on script purchases.
Tips: "Avoid stereotype roles and situations. Submit cassette tapes with musicals whenever possible. Always include SASE if script is to be returned. Only one intermission (if any) in a show running up to two hours."

‡DUBUQUE FINE ARTS PLAYERS, 569 S. Grandview Ave., Dubuque IA 52001. (319)582-5558. Contact: James E. Ryan. Produces 3 one acts, 1 full length, 1 experimental play/year. Amateur productions for a general audience. Submit complete ms. Obtains first production rights. Prizes of $100, $150 and $200.
Needs: "One acts, 3 a year, about 15 to 45 minutes usually. Cast of 5 or 6, single set usually. We have a limited membership, so it is just about 'do-it-yourself' theater."
Tips: "Submissions November 1 to December 31 only. Keep stage directions to a minimum. We get 150-200 submissions/year."

ELDRIDGE PUBLISHING CO., Box 216, Franklin OH 45005. (513)746-6531. Publishes 12-15 plays/year. For elementary, junior high, senior high, church and community audience. Query with synopsis (acceptable) or submit complete ms (preferred). Please send cassette tapes with any operettas. Reports in 2 months. Buys all rights. Pays 35% royalty (3-act royalties approx. $35/$25, 1-act royalty rates usually $10/$10); outright from $100-300 or occasionally offers 10% of copy sale receipts.

Needs: "We are always on the lookout for Xmas plays (religious for our church market or secular for the public school market). Also lighthearted 1-acts and 3-acts. We do like some serious, high caliber plays reflective of today's sophisticated students. Also operettas for jr/sr high school, and more limited, elementary market. We prefer larger casts for our 3-acts and operettas. Staging should be in keeping with school budgets and expertise. We are *not* interested in plays that are highly sexually suggestive or use abusive language."

Tips: "Submissions are welcomed at any time but during our fall season, response will definitely take the 2 months. Authors are paid royalties twice a year. They receive complimentary copies of their published plays, the annual catalog and 50% discount if buying additional copies."

THE EMPTY SPACE, 95 S. Jackson St., Seattle WA 98104. (206)587-3737. Artistic Director: M. Burke Walker. Produces 6 plays/year. 100% freelance written. Professional plays for subscriber base and single ticket Seattle audience. 1 script/year is unagented submission. Works with 5-6 unpublished/unproduced writers annually. Query with synopsis before sending script. Computer printout submissions OK; prefers letter-quality to dot-matrix. Response in 3 months. LOA theatre.

Needs: "Other things besides linear, narrative realism; but we are interested in that as well; no restriction on subject matter. Generally we opt for broader, more farcical comedies and harder-edged, uncompromising dramas. We like to go places we've never been before." No commercial musicals.

EUREKA THEATRE, 2730 16th St., San Francisco CA 94103. (415)558-9811. Artistic Director: Tony Taccone. Produces 6 plays/year. Produces professional plays under Equity small theatre contract for Bay area subscription audience. Accepts agented submissions only. Reports in 6 months. Rights purchased negotiated with agent. Pays 5% minimum royalty.

Needs: Full-length and one-acts—dramas and comedies, some with music—new plays, translations, adaptions, etc. No children's theatre.

Tips: "The Eureka Theatre has a decidedly progressive political bias and is primarily interested in plays that consciously support that concern. We are much more interested in plays which explore social relationships then domestic relationships."

‡FEEDBACK THEATREBOOKS, Box 5187, Bloomington IN 47402-5187. Produces at least 1 play/year. "We do not provide full productions but may offer staged readings by amateur and/or professional performers for a general audience of adults and/or children. Possible subsidy and/or cooperative publishing options to writers." Publishes plays for general readers, libraries, playwrights, literary managers, directors and other theatre artists. Submit complete ms or send work to playwriting contests. Reports in 3-6 months. Usually obtains first publication rights only. Cash award of $200-300.

Needs: "No limitations on length, subject matter or style. If the play is a translation or adaptation of material not in public domain, the author must be able to provide permission in writing from the copyright holder. We are particularly interested in works that can be read with pleasure and staged dramatically. We are open to all kinds of works—as long as the writer is serious and committed."

Tips: "We consider all submissions for possible publication and/or staged readings, but those scripts entered in one of our playwriting competitions stand a better chance. Economy is essential today; only those elements that are necessary to the play should be in the script. By economy, we mean in the number of characters, the technical requirements, and, especially, economy of words. We receive many over-written and self explanatory scripts, wtih too much talked about and too little actually dramatized."

RICHARD FICARELLI, 44 Apollo Lane, Hicksville NY 11801. Produces 1-2 plays/year. Plays are Equity productions performed in NY, Broadway and off-Broadway theatres. Regional possibilities. Submit query and synopsis. Reports in 6 weeks. Acquires DGA (standard) rights. Pays standard royalty.

Needs: Situation comedies *only*. Prefers cast of fewer than 14. No dramas.

THE FIREHOUSE THEATRE, 514 S. 11th St., Omaha NE 68102. (402)346-6009. Artistic Director: Dick Mueller. Produces 7 plays/year. Has produced 4 unagented submissions in 14 years. Computer printout submissions acceptable; prefers letter-quality to dot-matrix.

Needs: "We produce at the Firehouse Dinner Theatre in Omaha. Our interest in new scripts is the hope of finding material that can be proven here at our theatre and then go on from here to find its audience." Submit complete ms. Reporting times vary; depends on work load. Buys negotiable rights. Pays $100/week or negotiable rates.

Tips: "We are a small theatre. Certainly size and cost are a consideration. Quality is also a consideration. We can't use heavy drama in this theatre. We might, however, consider a production if it were a good script and use another theatre."

FLORIDA STUDIO THEATRE, 1241 N. Palm Ave., Sarasota FL 33577. (813)366-9017. Artistic Director: Richard Hopkins. Submit work to Jeff Mousseau, new plays director. Produces 4 established scripts and 3 new plays/year. "*FST* is a professional not-for-profit theatre." Plays are produced in 165-seat theatre for a subscription audience (primarily). *FST* operates under a small professional theatre contract of Actor's Equity. Submit query and synopsis. Reports in 1 month. Pays $200 for workshop production of new script.
Needs: Contemporary plays ("courageous and innovative"). Prefers casts of no more than 8, and single sets.

‡**FMT**, Box 92127, Milwaukee WI 53202. (414)271-8484. Contact: M. Moynihan. Produces 3-5 plays/year. "On tour, sites vary. Summer tour is an outdoor production. Audiences: children and young audiences, family and general adult audiences." Send query and synopsis. Reports in 3-6 months. Obtains first production rights. On scripts commissioned by and developed with the company, FMT shares copyright. Pays $600-2,500 or $10-25/performance.
Needs: Plays for young audiences that can be performed on tour by 2 to 4 performers; work in clown/new vaudeville traditions that can be performed outdoors as part of a traveling revue; satirical musicals that deal with socio/political themes; scripts for short video public service announcements on the subject of peace/violence/conflict resolution (commercials for sanity); scripts that deal with the life and work of Chicago peace activist Joseph Polowsky and other modern or historical peace activists; Christmas holiday family scripts that can tour with 2-4 actors. No racist, sexist, stupid, clichéd work.
Tips: "We more often collaborate with writers than take a play as is. Economy certainly is affecting what gets produced. Strong narratives that are highly theatrical (no literature and not cinema) seem to be needed."

‡**BUD FRANKS, PRODUCER/GENERAL MANAGER**, Box 9054, Fort Worth TX 76107. (817)332-9319. Artistic Director: Bud Franks. Produces 6 plays/summer. Summer stock musicals; professional productions. Query with synopsis.
Needs: Productions for circular stage.

SAMUEL FRENCH, INC., 45 W. 25th St., New York NY 10010. Editor: Lawrence Harbison. 100% freelance written. "We publish about 80-90 new titles a year. We are the world's largest publisher of plays. 10-20% are unagented submissions. In addition to publishing plays, we occasionally act as agents in the placement of plays for professional production—eventually in New York. Pays on royalty basis. Submit complete ms (bound). "Always type your play in the standard, accepted stageplay manuscript format used by all professional playwrights in the U.S. If in doubt, send $3 to the attention of Lawrence Harbison for a copy of 'Guidelines.' We require a minimum of two months to report."
Needs: "We are willing at all times to read the work of freelancers. Our markets prefer simple-to-stage, light, happy romantic comedies or mysteries. If your work does not fall into this category, we would be reading it for consideration for agency representation. No 25-page 'full-length' plays; no children's plays to be performed *by* children; no puppet plays; no adaptations of public domain children's stories; no verse plays; no large-cast historical (costume) plays; no seasonal and/or religious plays; no television, film or radio scripts; no translations of foreign plays."
Recent Title: *I'm Not Rappaport*, by Herb Gardner (Broadway comedy); *The Curate Shakespeare As You Like It*, by Don Nigro; and *Cuba and His Teddy Bear*, by Reinaldo Pavod (Broadway drama).

‡**GASLAMP QUARTER THEATRE**, 547 4th Ave., San Diego CA 92101. (619)232-9608. Artistic Director: Will Simpson. Produces 5 plays/year. "Non-equity professional house producing plays for a local audience and some tourists. Query with synopsis. Pays royalty, "scale depends on author," or $100 and up/week.
Needs: "We have done everything from Shaw to Pinter. We prefer smaller casts, not a too wide range of ages. One or two sets preferred."
Tips: Has been seeing "a little too much introspection on long monologues continually filling us in."

‡**THE WILL GEER THEATRICUM BOTANICUM**, Box 1222, Topanga CA 90290. (213)455-2322. Artistic Director: Ellen Geer. Produces 3 plays/year. Professional summer theater. Query with synopsis. Reports in 6 months. Obtains negotiable rights. Pays royalty.
Needs: Seeks full-length plays appropriate for repertory company in large outdoor arena: musical, political, humanistic. "Not over 10 in cast—we do *not* have a large technical budget."

‡**GEORGE STREET PLAYHOUSE**, 9 Livingston Ave., New Brunswick NJ 08901. (201)846-2895. Artistic Director: Eric Krebs. Produces 8 plays/year. Professional regional theater (LORT D). Submit complete ms or submit through agent. Reports in 3 months. Obtains rights to negotiate with playwright in good faith for regional/off-Broadway rights for 60 days after final performance at Georgia Street Playhouse. Pays royalty or outright from $500.
Needs: "Drama, comedy, lyrical realism and non-realistic; full-length; social relevance. Prefers cast size under 12." No murder mysteries or conventional comedies.
Tips: "We present a series of 12 staged readings each year and two of these plays are chosen for 3-4 week workshop productions."

GEORGETOWN PRODUCTIONS, 7 Park Ave., New York NY 10016. Producers: Gerald Van De Vorst and David Singer. Produces 1-2 plays/year for a general audience. Works with 2-3 unpublished/unproduced writers annually. Dramatist Guild membership required. Submit complete ms only. Standard Dramatists Guild contract.

Needs: Prefers plays with small casts and not demanding more than one set. Interested in new unconventional scripts dealing with contemporary issues, comedies, mysteries, musicals or dramas. No first-drafts; outlines; 1-act plays.

Tips: "The current trend is toward light entertainment, as opposed to meaningful or serious plays."

‡EMMY GIFFORD CHILDREN'S THEATER, 3504 Center St., Omaha NE 68105. (402)345-4849. Artistic Director: James Larson. Poruces 8 plays/year. "Our target audience is children, preshcool—jr. high and their parents." Query with synopsis with SASE or write for guidelines and application. Reports in 9 months. Royalty negotiable and/or $1,000 prize.

Needs: "Plays must be geared to children and parents (PG rating). Titles recognized by the general public have a stronger chance of winning the prize. Cast limit: 25 (8-10 adults). No adult scripts.

Tips: "Unsolicited scripts are not accepted unless they meet Susie Barker playwriting guidelines. Previously produced plays may be accepted only after a letter of inquiry (familiar titles only!!)."

GOLDEN ROD PUPPETS, Box 1464, Weaverville NC 28787. Puppeteer: Hobey Ford. Produces 2 plays/year. Professional productions for tours. Plays are performed solo, using a variety of puppetry techniques, puppeteer in full view. Plays and variety shows are performed at festivals, libraries, elementary schools, theatres, company parties and hotel lobbies for kindergarden through sixth grade, family audiences and adult audiences. Submit query and synopsis or letters of interest for collaboration on special projects. Reports in 1 month. Will pay royalties or upfront user fees: $50-500.

Needs: Narratives introducing action, with optional musical background. Plot unfolds through puppet action. No lengthy dialogues, or limit to a puppet narrator. Also character skits with one character, action and dialogue, comedy. Scenery limited or suggested by music or sound. Characters go into audience and play off environment. "I produce plays, skits and do storytelling, 5 minutes, 10 minutes, 30 minutes and 45 minutes; plays must be simple, written for puppet action, one or two characters at a time. Short animated character storytelling pieces needed. Educational, ecological, historical or cultural themes."

Tips: "Be willing to explore new ways of staging puppetry for a solo puppeteer. Golden Rod Puppets has innovative highly artistic puppets and staging techniques. I see a deterioration of the well-crafted story. I think writers need to remember the importance of good dialogue and action that build the plot. The art of storyteller is essential to my productions. Write what you know and feel most strongly about; then ask yourself very honestly what is essential and interesting for your audience. Puppet theater requires lots of actions, spectacle and fast pace. I rely heavily on musical background. This can be included by writers or I can add it."

‡HEUER PUBLISHING CO., 233 Dows Bldg., Box 248, Cedar Rapids IA 52406. (319)364-6311. Publishes plays for junior and senior high school and church groups. Query with synopsis or submit complete ms. Reports in 2 months. Purchases amateur rights only. Pays royalty or cash.

Needs: "One- and three-act plays suitable for school production. Preferably comedy or mystery comedy. All material should be with the capabilities of high school actors. We prefer material with one set." No "special day material, material with controversial subject matter."

HONOLULU THEATRE FOR YOUTH, Box 3257, Honolulu HI 96801. (808)521-3487. Artistic Director: John Kauffman. Produces 6 plays/year. 50% freelance written. Plays are professional productions in Hawaii, primarily for youth audiences (youth aged 2 to 20). 80% of scripts are unagented submissions. Works with 2 unpublished/unproduced writers annually. Computer printout submissions acceptable; prefers letter-quality to dot-matrix. Reports in 3 months. Buys negotiable rights.

Needs: Contemporary subjects of concern/interest to young people; adaptations of literary classics; fantasy including space, fairy tales, myth and legend. "HTY wants well-written plays, 60-90 minutes in length, that have something worthwhile to say and that will stretch the talents of professional adult actors." Cast not exceeding 8; *no* technical extravaganzas; *no* full-orchestra musicals; simple sets and props, costumes can be elaborate. No plays to be enacted by children or camp versions of popular fairytales. Query with synopsis. Pays $1,000-2,500.

Tips: "Young people are intelligent and perceptive, if anything more so than lots of adults, and if they are to become fans and eventual supporters of good theatre, they must see good theatre while they are young. Trends on the American stage that freelance writers should be aware of include a growing awareness that we are living in a world community. We must learn to share and understand other people and other cultures."

‡HUDSON GUILD THEATRE, 414 West 26th St., New York NY 10001. (212)760-9836. Literary Manager: Steven Ramay. Produces 5 mainstage plays annually, and conducts readings/workshops. "The plays are performed at the Hudson Guild Theatre. Our audiences (largely subscription) are from the greater New York City

area, including parts of New Jersey, Connecticut and all Manhattan boroughs.'' Submit complete ms; prefers synopsis in addition to ms. Reports in 2 months. All rights agreements are worked out individually in production contract negotiations. Pays flat $1,000 fee for mainstage productions.
Needs: ''Our interests are varied and international in scope. Socially and politically aware plays are preferred. We usually limit our casts to no more than 8, although exceptions can be made depending on the project.''
Tips: ''Don't submit your complete works. Submitting one play at a time usually insures a more thoughtful consideration of your material.''

WILLIAM E. HUNT, 801 West End Ave., New York NY 10025. Interested in reading scripts for stock production, off-Broadway and even Broadway production. ''Small cast, youth-oriented, meaningful, technically adventuresome; serious, funny, far-out. Must be about people first, ideas second. No political or social tracts.'' No 1-act, anti-Black, anti-Semitic or anti-Gay plays. ''I do not want 1920, 1930 or 1940 plays disguised as modern by 'modern' language. I do not want plays with 24 characters, plays with 150 costumes, plays about symbols instead of people. I do not want plays which are really movie or television scripts.'' Works with 2-3 unpublished/unproduced writers annually. Pays royalties on production. Off-Broadway, 5%; on Broadway, 5%, 7½% and 10%, based on gross. No royalty paid if play is selected for a showcase production. Reports in ''a few weeks.'' Must have SASE or script will not be returned.
Tips: ''Production costs and weekly running costs in the legitimate theatre are so high today that no play (or it is the very rare play) with more than six characters and more than one set, by a novice playwright, is likely to be produced unless that playwright will either put up or raise the money him or herself for the production.''

HUNTINGTON PLAYHOUSE, 28601 Lake Rd., Bay Village OH 44140. (216)871-8333. Artistic Director: Bud Binns. Produces 7 plays/year. Stages amateur productions at own theatre for an adult community audience. Submit complete ms. Reports in 2 months. Pays $35-40/performance; $75-100/performance on musicals.
Needs: Musicals and straight comedies. No dramas.

‡INNER CITY CULTURAL CENTER,1308 S. New Hampshire Ave., Los Angeles CA 90006. (213)387-1161. Artistic Director: C. Bernard Jackson. Produces 6 plays/year. Professional productions for the general public. Query with synopsis. Reports in 6 months. Obtains subsidiary rights.
Needs: All genres—special interest in plays reflecting experience of people of color (Asians, Blacks, Hispanic and Native American). Normally single set. No previously published plays.
Tips: ''See trends toward smaller cast size, single set, reduced dependency on type casting, touring potential (portability).''

‡INTAR HISPANIC AMERICAN ARTS CENTER,Box 788, New York NY 10108. (212)695-6134. Artistic Director: Max Ferra. Produces 3 plays/year. ''Plays produced in our theater at 420 W. 42nd St., New York NY and developmental work done at INTAR TWO on W. 53rd St.'' Query and synopsis. Reports in 6 weeks. Obtains negotiable rights. Pays outright fee of $1,000-1,500.
Needs: ''We produce plays and musicals by Hispanic-Americans, ususally dealing with themes of import to Hispanic-American community. We also keep up to 13 Hispanic playwrights in residence at our theater labs, paying them a monthly stipend. Our resources are limited, and stage cannot deal with more than 10 actors. Focus is on new work.''
Tips: ''Plays submited to us must be written by Hispanic-Americans.''

INVISIBLE THEATRE, 1400 N. 1st Ave., Tucson AZ 85719. (602)882-9721. Artistic Director: Susan Claassen. Literary Manager: Paul Fisher. Produces 5-7 plays/year. 10% freelance written. Semiprofessional regional theatre for liberal, college-educated audiences. Plays performed in 78-seat non-Equity theatre with small production budget. Works with 1-5 unpublished/unproduced writers annually. Query with synopsis. Computer printout submissions acceptable; prefers letter-quality to dot-matrix. Reports in 6 months. Buys non-professional rights. Pays 10% royalty.
Needs: ''Two act plays, generally contemporary, some historical, comedies, drama, small musicals, wide range of topics. Limited to plays with small casts of 10 or less, strong female roles, simple sets, minimal props.'' No large musicals, complex set designs, casts larger than 15.
Tips: ''Trends in the American stage that will affect the types of scripts we accept include social issues—social conscience—i.e. South Africa, coming to terms with elderly parents, overcoming effects of disease, family relationships, things that the average person can relate to and think about. Challenges we can all relate to, common experiences, because people enjoy people. Our audiences include some older, somewhat conservative, members (although *not* rigid or dogmatic) as well as younger, more liberal groups. We try to have broad appeal—mixing experimental with comedy and drama throughout the year.''

‡IRONBOUND THEATRE INC., 179 Van Buren St., Newark NJ 07105. (201)272-3125. Artistic Director: Steven Gravatt. Produces 3 mainstage and 10 readings/year. ''Original scripts are developed through a process with a staged reading. If selected they are first produced at our theatre playhouse, Newark, NJ, then production travels to New York City." Query with synopsis or submit complete ms. Reports in 4 months. Obtains first production rights. Pays outright purchase of $100 minimum.

Needs: "We produce 'progressive' type plays (not meaning socialist or communist) scripts that risk and induce thought and are entertaining. No imitations."

Tips: "Write from the heart, not the pocketbook."

‡**JEWEL BOX THEATRE**, 3700 North Walker, Oklahoma City OK 73118. (405)521-1786. Artistic Director: Charles Tweed. Produces 6 plays/year. Amateur productions. Intended for 2,500 season subscribers and general public. Submit complete ms. Reports in 3 months. "We would like to have first production rights and 'premiere' the play at Jewel Box Theatre." Pays $500 contest prize.

Needs: "We produce dramas, comedies and musicals. Usually we have two-act plays, but one and three acts are acceptable. Plays usually run two hours. Our theatre is in-the-round, so we adapt plays accordingly. We have not used multi-media projections. We do not use excessive profanity. We will dilute dialogue if necessary."

‡**KAM THEATRE**, 215 North Franklin St., Thunder Bay, Ontario P7C 4J1 Canada. (807)622-5511. Co-Director: Deborah Ratelle. Produces 4 adult, 1 children's play/year. "Professional repertory for Canadian audiences. Interested in plays by Canadian playwrights, with some social relevance." Submit complete ms. Reports in 2 months. Pays 10% royalty of gross, minimum $300.

Needs: "Canadian plays of all genres. Canadian concerns and topics. We have produced a variety of styles from commedia to surrealistic to realistic. Desired length 2 hours; for elementary schools, 45 minutes. We are a small company with limited budgets. Cast size maximum is 6. One to two locations sets or abstract sets, limited props etc."

Tips: Writers should be aware that "the arts are being cut back and asked to compete as a business by governments and other funding bodies. The repercussions will affect not only what we produce but how we choose, and why we exclude."

‡**KUMU KAHUA**, 1770 East-West Rd., Honolulu HI 96822. (808)948-7677. Artistic Director: Dando Kluever. Produces 4 productions, 4 public readings/year. "Plays performed at various theatres for community audiences. Actors are not paid. It's a nonprofit company." Submit complete ms. Royalty is $25 per performance; usually 10 performances of each production.

Needs: "Plays must have some interest for local audiences, preferably by being set in Hawaii or dealing with some aspect of the Hawaiian experience. Prefer small cast, with simple staging demands. We don't like commercial, trivial plays structured and designed for BO success of a Broadway sort. No trivial commercial farces, whodunits, plays like made-for-TV movies or sitcoms."

Tips: "We need some time to evaluate, and may want to hold the script awhile. We're not trendy."

LAMB'S PLAYERS THEATRE, 500 Plaza Blvd., Box 26, National City CA 92050. (619)474-3385. Artistic Director: Robert Smyth. Produces 7 plays/year. 15% freelance written. A professional non-Equity resident company with a year-round production schedule. Audience is varied; high percentage of family and church interest. Works with 1-2 unpublished/unproduced writers annually. Submit synopsis. Computer printout submissions acceptable. Reports in 4 months. Buys first production rights, touring option. Pays $500-5,000.

Needs: "We produce a wide variety of material which, while not necessarily 'religious' in nature often reflects a broad-based Christian perspective." Prefers smaller cast (2-10); adaptable staging (arena stage). "We are not interested in material that is 'preachy,' or material thats intention is to shock or titillate with sex, violence or language."

Tips: "Trends freelance writers should be aware of include productions which offer hope without being clichéd or sentimental; productions needing small cast and imaginative yet inexpensive sets; and an interest in presentational style pieces—acknowledgment and/or interaction with the audience."

LILLENAS PUBLISHING CO., Box 419527, Kansas City MO 64141. (816)931-1900. Editor: Paul M. Miller. "We publish on two levels: (1) Program Builders—seasonal and topical collections of recitations, sketches, dialogues and short plays. (2) Drama Resources. These assume more than one format; (a) Full length scripts, (b) shorter plays and sketches all by one author, (c) Collection of short plays and sketches by various authors. All program and play resources are produced with local church and Christian school in mind. Therefore there are taboos." Queries are encouraged, but synopsis and complete manuscripts are read. Computer printout submissions are acceptable, if highly readable. First rights are purchased for Program Builder manuscripts. For our line of Drama Resources, we purchase all print rights, but this is negotiable.

Needs: 98% of Program Builder materials are freelance written. Manuscripts selected for these publications are outright purchases; verse is 25 cents per line, prose (play scripts) are $5 a double-spaced page. Lillenas Drama Resources is a line of play scripts that are, in the most part, written by professionals with experience in production as well as writing. However, while we do read unsolicited manuscripts, more than half of what we pub-

lish is written by experienced authors whom we have already published. Drama Resources (whether full-length scripts, one-acts, or sketches) are paid on a 10% royalty. There are no advances.
Tips: "All plays need to be presented in standard play script format. We welcome a summary statement of each play. Purpose statements are always desirable. Approximate playing time, cast and prop lists, etc. are important to include. We are interested in fully scripted traditional plays, reader's theatre scripts, choral speaking pieces. Contemporary setting generally have it over biblical settings. Christmas and Easter scripts must have a bit of a twist. Secular approaches to these seasons (Santas, Easter bunnies, and so on, are not considered). We sell our product in 10,000 Christian bookstores. We are probably in the forefront as a publisher of religious drama resources."

‡LONG ISLAND STAGE, Box 190, Hempstead NY 11550. (516)564-4600. Artistic Director: Clinton J. Atkinson. Produces 6 plays/year. Professional productions, September through June, subscription audience. Query and synopsis. Reports in 3 months. Obtains rights of first refusal on subsequent productions, acknowledgment of original production and percentage of royalties for several years. Pays negotiable royalty.
Needs: Realistic, contemporary translations, occasional musicals. "Comedy or serious, no matter." Single set if possible or unit set, small casts—under 10.
Tips: No Broadway-type comedies.

LOS ANGELES THEATRE CENTER, 514 S. Spring St., Los Angeles CA 90013. (213)627-6500. Literary Manager: Mame Hunt. Produces 15-20 plays/year. 90% freelance written. A professional theatre for a multicultural metropolitan audience. 10% of scripts are unagented submissions. Works with 7-10 unproduced writers annually. Query with synopsis plus 10 pages of script. *No unsolicited ms.* Reports in 6 months. Buys first production rights, options to extend and move, subsidiaries. Pays 4-7% royalty. Computer printout submissions acceptable; no dot-matrix.
Needs: Plays with social or political awareness preferred. 10 actors maximum. No "television scripts or movies pretending to be theatre."
Tips: "The most important and exciting new work in the theatre is non-naturalistic. It takes risks with its subject matter and form and, therefore, it is dramatic writing that cannot be easily transferred to another form, i.e., television or film."

‡LOS ANGELES THEATER UNIT, Box 429, Los Angeles CA 90078. Literary Director: Lanny Thomas. Managing Director: Marla Fisher. Produces 2-3 plays/year, 100% freelance written; 50% by unagented writers. "We have an educated, urban audience of mostly professional people and theater professionals. We perform mostly in theatres of 99 seats or less with professional directors and actors who work for free in exchange for the opportunity to do interesting projects in a supportive, non-commercial atmosphere." Submit complete ms. Reports in 2 months. Obtains one-time license to produce for a limited run, with option to extend. Payment varies according to rights obtained, minimum $500.
Needs: "We produce only plays which have never been performed on the West Coast, except in college or workshop productions. We prefer original plays we can 'world premiere.' We generally produce full-length plays, though an outstanding one-act may excite our attention. At the current time our budgets preclude elaborate or expensive sets or changes, unless these problems can be worked out by creative staging."
Tips: "I don't feel writers of any worth write according to trends. I do feel that the theater-going audience of today watches the tube or goes to a movie to be mindlessly entertained or titillated. They attend the theater, the most immediate personal medium, to be disturbed, to be enlightened, to be moved, to be changed. If your play does not achieve this effect, rewrites are in order. Important plays set trends and change society. In order to do this, they must be focused, have a point of view and be true to themselves and their version of reality. Good plays will always find a producer, so keep looking. And remember, if at first you don't succeed, rewrite."

LUNCHBOX THEATRE, Box 9027, Bow Valley Sq., Calgary, Alberta T2P 2W4 Canada. (403)265-4292. Artistic Director: Bartley Bard. Produces 7 plays/year. 12.5% freelance written. Varying number of scripts produced are unagented submissions. Professional company performs at lunchtime for downtown workers, shoppers, school groups—everyone. Submit complete ms. Reports in 6 months. Pays 7% royalties on gross box-office receipts; or pays $25-35/performance. Returns scripts once or twice a year. "In the meantime, we mail out letters."
Needs: One-acts only. "Must be 40-50 minutes in length. Emphasis on fast-paced comedies. Small cast plays given more consideration. Generally, *one* set. No 'dead baby' plays, plays containing overt physical violence, 'prairie dramas' or 'kitchen sink dramas.' We are a lunch-hour theatre: keep it light."

‡MCCARTER THEATRE COMPANY, 91 University Pl., Princeton NJ 08540. (609)683-9100. Artistic Director: Nagle Jackson. Produces 7 plays/year. Professional resident theatre. Submit complete ms. Reports in 2-3 months. Obtains negotiable rights. Payment negotiable:—"professional rates."
Needs: Produces plays that are "large in spirit."
Tips: The writer should "write passionately about the issues which concern her/him and our sophisticated,

aware adult audience." No "pornography, soap opera, conventional documentaries."

MAGIC THEATRE, INC., Bldg. D, Fort Mason, San Francisco CA 94123. (415)441-8001. General Director: John Lion. Administrative Director: Marcia O'Dea. Dramaturg: Martin Esslin. "Oldest experimental theatre in California." For public audience, generally college-educated. General cross-section of the area with an interest in alternative theatre. Plays produced in the off-Broadway manner. Cast is full-Equity. Produces 7 plays/year. 50% of scripts produced are unagented submissions. Works with 4-6 unpublished/unproduced writers annually. Submit complete ms. 1- or 2-act plays considered. "We pay $500 advance against 5% of gross."

MAGNUS THEATRE COMPANY, 137 N. May St., Thunder Bay, Ontario P7C 3N8 Canada. (807)623-5818. Artistic Director: Michael McLaughlin. Produces 6 plays/year. Professional stock theatre produced in 197-seat facility, and performed for a demographically diverse general audience.
Needs: "Fairly general in genres, but with a particular emphasis on new plays, must be full-length. Smaller (i.e. up to seven) casts are viewed favorably; some technical limitations, always, always, budget limitations. No one-act plays or plays with very large casts, multiple settings, plays which are specifically American in theme or content.
Tips: Thunder Bay is very earthy, working city, and we try to reflect that sensibility in our choice of plays. Beyond that, however, Magnus has gained a national reputation for its commitment to the development and production of new plays, including, where possible, workshops. Scripts should be universal (i.e. accessible to Canadian audiences) in theme; should be produceable within realistic budget limitations.

‡MANATEE PLAYERS, INC., 102 Old Main St., Bradenton FL (813)748-0111. Contact: Resident Director. Produces 5 plays in regular season, others as varies. Plays performed at Riverfront Theatre. "Community Theatre audience is retiree/family groups." Query and synopsis. Reports in 3 months or more, Fall submissions suggested. Purchases variable rights. Outright purchase from $100-1,000.
Needs: "Full-length smaller casts and simple sets preferred. Comedy/Drama/Musicals. No material inappropriate for our family/retiree audience."

‡MANHATTAN PUNCH LINE, 3rd Floor, 410 W. 42nd St., New York NY 10036. (212)239-0827. Artistic Director: Steve Kaplan. Produces 6-7 plays/year. Professional off-off Broadway theatre company. Submit complete ms. Reports in 3 months. Pays $325-500.
Needs: "Manhattan Punch Line is devoted to producing comedies of all types. We are a developmental theatre interested in producing serious plays with a comedic point of view."
Tips: "The most important and successful playwrights (Durang, Wasserstein, Innaurato) are all writing comedies. Don't worry about being funny, just try to be honest. Large-cast plays are back in."

MANHATTAN THEATRE CLUB, 453 W. 16th Ave., New York NY 10011. Literary Manager: Tom Szentgyorgyi. Produces 10 plays/year. All freelance written. A very few of scripts produced are unagented submissions. A two-theatre performing arts complex classified as off-Broadway, using professional actors. "We present a wide range of new work, from this country and abroad, to a subscription audience. We want plays about contemporary problems and people. Comedies are welcome. No verse plays or historical dramas or large musicals. Very heavy set shows or multiple detailed sets are out. We prefer shows with casts not more than 15. No skits, but any other length is fine." Computer printout submissions acceptable; no dot-matrix. Query with synopsis. Reports in 6 months. Payment is negotiable.

MERIDIAN GAY THEATRE, Box 294, Village Station, New York NY 10014. Artistic Director: Jerry Campbell. Produces 4-5 mainstage plays and 10-15 staged readings/year. Plays are performed off-off-Broadway to a general audience interested in gay/lesbian themed plays. Submit query and synopsis or complete ms. Obtains New York rights only. pays 6% royalty or $20-25/performance.
Needs: Plays with gay and lesbian major characters or themes of any length or style. "We have a small theatre and budget which makes scripts with small casts and minimal set requirements more likely to be considered."

‡MIAMI BEACH COMMUNITY THEATRE, 2231 Prairie Ave., Miami Beach FL 33139. (305)532-4515. Artistic Director: Jay W. Jensen. Produces 5 plays/year. "Amateur productions performed during the year for the Miami Beach community." Send query and synopsis or submit complete ms. Reports in 3 weeks. Pays $35-75/performance (if published work); does not pay for unpublished plays. "Avoid sex."
Needs: "All types. Interested in Spanish themes—Latin American plots, etc, Interested in new plays dealing with AIDS and short plays dealing wth AIDS that could be used in junior highs and senior highs for motivation—about 30 minutes long."

MIDWEST PLAYLABS, The Playwrights Center, 2301 Franklin Ave. E., Minneapolis MN 55406. (612)332-7481. Executive Director: Joan Patchen. 100% freelance written. "Midwest Playlabs is a 2-week developmental workshop for new plays. The program is held in Minneapolis and is open by script competition to playwrights who have an association with the 13 midwestern states or are a member of the Playwrights' Center. It is an intensive two-week workshop focusing on the development of a script and the playwright. Six plays are given staged readings at the site of the workshop." Works with 60 playwrights annually. In most cases writers should be a member of the Playwrights' Center. Announcements of playwrights by mid-April. Computer printout submissions acceptable; prefers letter-quality to dot-matrix.

Needs: "We are interested in playwrights with talent, ambitions for a professional career in theatre and scripts which could benefit from an intensive developmental process involving professional dramaturgs, directors and actors. A playwright needs to be affiliated with the Midwest (must be documented if they no longer reside in the Midwest) or be a Center member; MPL accepts scripts after first of each year. Full lengths only. No produced materials—"a script which has gone through a similar process which would make our work redundant (O'Neill Conference scripts, for instance)." Submit complete ms. Pays a small stipend; room and travel. Submission deadline March 1, 1988.

Tips: "We do not buy scripts. We are a service organization that provides programs for developmental work on scripts for members."

‡MILWAUKEE REPERTORY THEATER, 929 N. Water St., Milwaukee WI 53202. (414)273-7121. Dramaturg: Tanda Dykes. Produces 12 plays/year. Professional productions for the Milwaukee community. Submit synopsis plus 10 pages. "We are a LORT C theater and do ask a continuing contractual interest in new works we develop, but the participation asked falls within pretty standard LORT practices." Payment negotiable.

Needs: "Classics, new works. We have a resident acting company which limits our ability to present new works that have unusual casting requirements. Our ¾ thrust stage makes multi-media plays difficult."

Tips: "We do 10-12 shows a year." No children's plays, musicals. Looks for "a play with political interest; or with characters based on actual individuals (though obviously this is not always the case)." Notices recent trend toward "starkly realistic drama coming out of the German theatre and reflected in works by Shepard, Norman and Mamet."

NATIONAL ARTS CENTRE-ENGLISH THEATRE CO., Box 1534, Station B, Ottawa, Ontario K1P 5W1 Canada. (613)996-5051. Theatre Producer: Andis Celms. Produces and/or presents 12 plays/year. 0-5% freelance written. Works with 1-2 unpublished/unproduced writers annually. All scripts produced are agented submissions. Professional productions performed in the theatre and studio of the National Arts Centre (also, workshop productions in a rehearsal space). Audience ranges from young/middle-aged professionals (especially civil servants) to students. Computer printout submissions acceptable; prefers letter-quality to dot-matrix.

Tips: "Our 'mainstage' audience likes a solid, well-written play with an intelligible story line and no coarse language. Our 'workshop' audience likes to be challenged, both in language and structure, but not abused. We are interested in the smaller cast, 'human interest' style of theatre and film. For example, last season we produced *Children of a Lesser God*. Our audience likes the combination of having heard of the play and being moved by the emotions."

‡NATIONAL PLAYWRIGHTS SHOWCASE, Mercyhurst College, Erie PA 16546. (814)825-0200. Artistic Director: Paul Iddings. Produces 4 plays/year. "Plays are produced at Mercyhurst College Little Theatre or dinner theater. Full-length plays only. Adult and children's theater." Submit complete ms. Reports "eventually." Playwrights retain rights. Playwright receives travel/accommodations, publicity.

Needs: Full-length dramas, musicals, dinner-theater, children's. No full orchestras. No one-acts or overly explicit plays.

NECESSARY ANGEL THEATRE, #400, 553 Queen St. W., Toronto, Ontario M5V 2B6 Canada (416)365-0533. Artistic Director: Richard Rose. Produces 4 plays/year. Plays are Equity productions in various Toronto theatres and performance spaces for an urban audience between 20-55 years of age. Submit complete ms. Reports in 2 months. Obtains various rights "based on the manuscript (original, translation, adaptation) and the playwright (company member, etc.)." Pays 10% royalty.

Needs: "We are open to new theatrical ideas, environmental pieces, unusual acting styles and large casts. The usual financial constraints exist, but they have never eliminated a work to which we felt a strong commitment." No "vacuous TV-influenced sit-coms and melodramas."

Tips: "Necessary Angel Theatre has a full-time dramaturg, D.D. Kugler. All submissions are considered for a series of one-day readings and/or one-week workshops leading to productions within the company season. Playwrights should be aware of the interdisciplinary approach to performance (music, dance, visual arts, theatre) in which the essence of a piece is revealed in visual and aural images which support the text."

THE NEW CONSERVATORY CHILDREN'S THEATRE COMPANY AND SCHOOL, Zephyr Theater Complex, 25 Van Ness, Lower Level, San Francisco CA 94102. (415)861-4814. Artistic Director: Ed Decker. Produces 4-5 plays/year. "The New Conservatory is a children's theatre school (ages four to nineteen) which operates year-round. Each year we produce several plays, for which the older students (usually eleven and up, but younger depending on the readiness of the child) audition. These are presented to the general public at the Zephyr Theatre Complex San Francisco (50-350 seats). Our audience is approximately age 10 to adult." Send query and synopsis. Reports in 1 month. Pays 5% royalty.

Needs: "We emphasize works in which children play *children*, and prefer relevant and controversial subjects, although we also do musicals. We have a commitment to new plays. Examples of our shows are: Mary Gail's *Nobody Home* (world premiere; about latchkey kids); Brian Kral's *Special Class* (about disabled kids), and *The Inner Circle*, by Patricia Loughrey (commissioned scripts about AIDS prevention for kids). As we are a non-profit group on limited budget, we tend not to have elaborate staging; however, our staff is inventive—includes choreographer and composer. Write innovative theatre that explores topics of concern/interest to young people, that takes risks. We concentrate more on ensemble than individual roles, too. We do *not* want to see fairytales or trite rehashings of things children have seen/heard since the age of two. See theatre as education, rather than 'children are cute'."

Tips: "It is important for young people and their families to explore and confront issues relevant to growing up in the '80s. Theatre is a marvelous teaching tool that can educate while it entertains."

NEW PLAYS INCORPORATED, Box 273, Rowayton CT 06853. (203)866-4520. Publisher: Patricia Whitton. Publishes an average of 4 plays/year. Publishes plays for producers of plays for young audiences and teachers in college courses on child drama. Query with synopsis. Reports in 2 months. Agent for amateur and semi-professional productions, exclusive agency for script sales. Pays 50% royalty on productions; 10% on script sales. Free catalog on request.

Needs: Plays for young audiences with something innovative in form and content. Length: usually 45-90 minutes. "Should be suitable for performance by adults for young audiences." No skits, assembly programs, improvisations or unproduced manuscripts.

NEW PLAYWRIGHTS' THEATRE, 31 Water Street, Ashland OR 97520. (503)482-9236. Artistic Director: Bradford O'Neil. Produces 12 new plays/year. "We facilitate our own black box theatre in Ashland with an in-house acting company of ten non-Equity actors. Guest actors and directors (Equity) are hired with each season. Our audience is both local and out of state." Submit complete ms. Plays 5% royalty.

Needs: Full-length, naturalistic, surrealistic and contemporary. Emphasis is placed on excellent writing (dialogue, structure, and plotting). Single set plays preferred. Will not read plays with casts of more than seven. No children's material or " 'martini' farces—'I'm home, honey, where's my martini?' "

THE NEW PLAYWRIGHTS' THEATRE OF WASHINGTON, 1742 Church St. NW, Washington DC 20036. (202)232-4527. Contact: Literary Manager. Produces 5 musicals and straight plays and 16 readings/year. 100% freelance written. 15% of scripts produced are unagented submissions. "Plays are produced in professional productions in the 125-seat New Playwrights' Theatre in the Dupont Circle area of the city for a subscription audience as well as large single-ticket buying followers. Works with varying number of writers annually; 30% unpublished, 65% unproduced. Will not accept unsolicited mss, only synopsis plus 20 pages of finished script, "typed to form, suitably bound." All musicals must be accompanied by cassette tape recording of songs in proper order. Reports in 2 months on synopsis; 6-8 months on scripts. "Rights purchased and financial arrangements are individually negotiated." SASE, acknowledgement postcard. No rights requested on readings; buys 7% of playwright's future royalties for 7 years, and first production credit requested for plays or musicals offered as full productions. Pays 6% royalty against a $300/week minimum.

Needs: "All styles, traditional to experimental, straight plays to musicals and music-dramas, revues and cabaret shows, and full-lengths only. No verse plays, puppet plays or film scripts. Staging: performance space adaptable.

Tips: "We prefer a strong plot line, be the play realistic, expressionistic or non-realistic, with an emphasis on vital, lively, visceral energy in writing. We look at a wide range of styles from the old-fashioned 'well-made play' to more avant-garde structures. We are a theatre of content with a humanist perspective focusing on the personal and public issues of our time."

NEW TUNERS THEATRE, 1225 W. Belmont Ave., Chicago IL 60657. (312)929-7367. Artistic Director: Byron Schaffer, Jr. Produces 3-4 new musicals/year. 66% freelance written. "Nearly all" scripts produced are unagented submissions. Plays performed in a small off-Loop theatre seating 148 for a general theatre audience, urban/suburban mix. Submit complete ms and cassette tape of the score, if available. Reports in 6 months. Buys exclusive right of production within 80 mile radius. "Submit first, we'll negotiate later." Pays 5-10% of gross. "Authors are given a stipend to cover a residency of at least two weeks." Computer printout submissions acceptable; prefers letter-quality to dot-matrix.

Needs: "We're interested in traditional forms of musical theatre as well as more innovative styles. We have less interest in operetta and operatic works, but we'd look at anything. At this time, we have no interest in non-musical plays unless to consider them for possible adaptation—please send query letter first. We are also seeking comic sketches and songs for a 'New Faces' type revue. Our primary interest is in comedic and up-tempo songs, but we will also consider ballads. Cassette tapes of songs should be sent, if possible. Our production capabilities are limited by the lack of space, but we're very creative and authors should submit anyway. The smaller the cast, the better. We are especially interested in scripts using a younger (35 and under) ensemble of actors. We mostly look for authors who are interested in developing their script through workshops, rehearsals and production. No interest in children's theatre. No casts over 15. No one-man shows."

Tips: "Freelance writers should be aware that musical theatre can be more serious. The work of Sondheim and others who follow demonstrates clearly that musical comedy can be ambitious and can treat mature themes in a relevant way. Probably 90 percent of what we receive would fall into the category of 'fluff.' We have nothing against fluff. We've had some great successes producing it and hope to continue to offer some pastiche and farce to our audience; however, we would like to see the musical theatre articulating something about the world around us, rather than merely diverting an audience's attention from that world."

‡NEW WORLD THEATER, INC., Suite 212, 7600 Red Road, South Miami FL 33143. (305)663-0208. Executive Director: Kenneth A. Cotthoff. Estab. 1986. Produces 7 plays/year. "We are a professional (AEA—LOA) resident theater performing at the Colony Theater in Miami Beach. Our season begins in the Fall with the winners of our annual National New Play Competition which is followed by a season of contemporary off-Broadway format plays. Audience upwardly mobile, average age approximately 40ish." Submit complete ms. "must be typed, bound with address on fly sheet." Reports in 3 months for play competition; 1 month otherwise. "We maintain a six month exclusive limited option on any produced." Pays $1,000 for competition or season.

Needs: Contemporary comedies or dramas. Off-Broadway budgets and sensibilities; also interested in young authors and Florida themes. "Currently limiting to cast of six for competition and season. Prefer one main set and no extraordinary budget-breaking items."

Tips: Prefers contemporary format, standard length, one intermission, intelligent, thought provoking (even if comedy). No high budget, children's plays or musicals (small ones OK). This may change as budget expands.

NEW YORK SHAKESPEARE FESTIVAL/PUBLIC THEATER, 425 Lafayette St., New York NY 10003. (212)598-7100. Producer: Joseph Papp. Plays and Musical Development Director: Gail Merrifield. Interested in plays, musicals, operas, translations, adaptations. No restriction as to style, form, subject matter. Produces 10-15 new works year-round at Public Theater complex housing 5 theaters (100-300 seat capacity): Newman, Anspacher, Shiva, LuEsther Hall, Martinson. Also Delacorte 2100-seat ampitheater, Broadway, Royal Court/London Exchange; film and television. Unsolicited and unagented submissions accepted. Computer printout manuscripts and electronic submissions via VHS or Beta OK with hard copy. Send music cassette with musical work. All scripts: include cast of characters with age and brief description; musical works include vocal ranges. Standard options and production agreements. Reports in 2 months.

‡JACKIE NICHOLS, 51 S. Cooper, Memphis TN 38104. Artistic Director: Jackie Nichols. Produces 16 plays/year. Professional productions. Submit complete ms. Reports in 5 months. Pays $500.

Needs: All types. "Small cast, single or unit set."

Tips: Playwrights from the South will be given preference. South is defined as the following states: Alabama, Florida, Georgia, Kentucky, Louisiana, Mississippi, Missouri, North Carolina, South Carolina, Tennessee, Texas, Virginia and West Virginia. This means we will read all shows and when final decisions are made, every other aspect of the play being equal we will choose a southern author.

‡NINE O'CLOCK PLAYERS, 1367 N. St. Andrews Pl, Los Angeles CA 90028. (213)469-1973. Artistic Director: Marjorie Gaines. Produces 2 plays/year. "Plays produced at Assistance League Playhouse by resident amateur and semi-professional compnay. All plays are musical adaptations of classical children's literature. Plays must be appropriate for children ages 4-12." Query and synopsis. Reports in 1 month. Pays negotiable royalty or per performance.

Needs: "Plays must have at least 15 characters and be 1 hour 15 minutes long. Productions are done on a proscenium stage in classical theater style. All plays must have humor, music, and have good moral values. No audience participation and improvisational plays."

‡THE NORTH CAROLINA BLACK REPERTORY COMPANY, Box 2793, Winston-Salem NC 27012. (919)723-7907. Artistic Director: Larry Leon Hamlin. Produces 4-6 plays/year. Plays produced primarily in North Carolina, New York City, and possible touring throughout the South. Submit complete ms. Reports in 5 months. Obtains negotiable rights. Negotiable payment.

Needs: "Full-length plays and musicals: mostly African-American with special interest in historical or contemporary *statement* genre. A cast of 10 would be a comfortable limit; we discourage multiple sets."

Tips: "The best time to submit manuscript is between September and February."

NORTHLIGHT THEATRE, 2300 Green Bay Rd., Evanston IL 60201. (312)869-7732. Artistic Director: Russell Vandenbroucke. "We are a LORT-D theatre with a subscription audience using professional artistic personnel. Our season runs from September through May. We are committed to developing new plays, translations and adaptations. We produce significant new scripts and second productions from an international repertoire as well as older plays and classics. We are interested in ambitious plays with a broad canvas." Audience is primarily college educated, 35-65 years old, with a broad range of socio-economic backgrounds. Query with synopsis. Computer printout submissions acceptable. Reports in 3 months. Produces 5 mainstage plays a year; 20% are unproduced originals developed inhouse. Rights purchased vary.

Needs: "New works of significant scope; second and third productions. Plays may vary in genre and topic. Full-length and prefer a cast size of 10 or less without doubling. Though accessibility is an issue, we rate substance as a higher concern for our audience. We have a 298-seat house with a small, extended apron proscenium stage allowing for some use of multiple sets but only the suggestion of levels, e.g. a second story home, etc. Our budget and other resources restrict very elaborate staging but we are fortunate to have talented and creative designers. Solely commercial work or dinner theatre material is not appropriate for our audiences. Trends on the American stage that writers should be aware of include adaptations from other literary forms and new translations of foreign work. We emphasize work which speaks to the human condition and is often contemporary."

Recent Title: *West Memphis Mojo* by Martin Jones.

ODYSSEY THEATRE ENSEMBLE, 12111 Ohio Ave., Los Angeles CA 90025. (213)826-1626. Artistic Director: Ron Sossi. Produces 12 plays/year. Plays performed in a 3-theatre facility. "All three theatres are Equity waiver; Odyssey 1 and 2 each have 99 seats, while Odyssey 3 has 72-90 seats. We have a subscription audience of 1,800 who subscribe to a six-play season, and are offered a discount on our remaining non-subscription plays. Remaining seats are sold to the general public." Query with synopsis, cast breakdown and 8-10 pages of sample dialogue to Literary Manager: Jon Lewis. Scripts must be securely bound. Reports in 1 month on queries; 6 months on scripts. Buys negotiable rights. Pays 5-7% royalty or $25-35/performance. "We will *not* return scripts without SASE."

Needs: Full-length plays only with "either an innovative form or extremely provocative subject matter. We desire more theatrical pieces that explore possibilities of the live theatre experience. We are seeking full-length musicals. We are not reading one-act plays or light situation comedies."

‡OFF CENTER THEATER, 436 W. 18th St., New York NY 10011. (212)929-8299. Artistic Director: Tony McGrath. Produces 4 plays/year. Equity showcase productions and non-Equity productions. Submit complete ms. Reports in 3 months. Obtains first professional production righs. Pays 6% of box office receipts, after expenses.

Needs: Issue-oriented comedies.

OLD GLOBE THEATRE, Box 2171, San Diego CA 92112. (619)231-1941. Associate Director: Robert Berlinger. Produces 12 plays/year. "We are a LORT B professional house. Our plays are produced for a single-ticket and subscription audience of 250,000, a large cross section of southern California, including visitors from the LA area." Submit complete ms through agent only. Send one-page letter or synopsis if not represented. Reports in 6 months. Buys negotiable rights. Pays 6-10% royalty.

Needs: "We are looking for contemporary, realistic, theatrical dramas and comedies and request that all submissions be full-length plays at this time." Prefers smaller cast and single sets, and "to have the playwright submit the play he has written rather than to enforce any limitations. No musicals or large cast historical dramas."

Tips: "Get back to theatricality. I am tired of reading screenplays."

O'NEILL THEATER CENTER'S NATIONAL PLAYWRIGHTS CONFERENCE/NEW DRAMA FOR TELEVISION PROJECT, Suite 901, 234 W. 44th St., New York NY 10036. (212)382-2790. Artistic Director: Lloyd Richards. Develops staged readings of 10-12 stage plays, 3-4 teleplays/year for a general audience. "We accept unsolicited mss with no prejudice toward either represented or unrepresented writers. Our theatre is located in Waterford, Connecticut and we operate under an Equity LORT(C) Contract. We have 3 theatres: Barn-250 seats, Amphitheatre-300 seats, Instant Theater-150." Submit complete *bound* ms. Decision by late April. "We have an option on the script from time of acceptance until 60 days *after* the four-week summer conference is completed. After that, all rights revert back to the author." Pays small stipend plus room, board and transportation. Computer printout submissions acceptable. "Interested writers must send us a self-addressed-stamped #10 envelope to request our updated guidelines in September prior to the following summer's conference. We accept script submissions from Sept. 15-Dec. 1 of each year. Conference takes place during four weeks in July each summer."

Needs: "We do staged readings of new American plays. We use modular sets for all plays, minimal lighting, minimal props and no costumes. We do script-in-hand readings with professional actors and directors."

THE OPEN EYE: NEW STAGINGS, (formerly Theatre of the Open Eye), 270 W. 89th St., New York NY 10024. (212)769-4143. Artistic Director: Amie Brockway. Produces 3-4 full-length plays/year plus a series of readings and workshop productions of one-acts. "The Open Eye is a professional, Equity LOA, 105-seat, off-

off Broadway theater. Our audiences include a broad spectrum of ages and backgrounds." Submit complete ms in clean, bound copy with SASE for its return. Reports in 3-6 months. Playwright fee for mainstage: $500.
Needs: New Stagings is particularly interested in one-act and full-length plays that take full advantage of the live performance situation. We tend not to do totally realistic plays. We especially like plays that appeal to young people and adults alike."

ORACLE PRESS, LTD., 5323 Heatherstone Dr., Baton Rouge LA 70820. (504)766-5577. Artistic Director: Cj Stevens. Publishes 10-15 plays/year. 90% freelance written. 90% of scripts produced are unagented submissions. Plays performed by college, high school and other amateur groups. Works with 20-30 unpublished/unproduced writers annually. Query with synopsis. Computer printout submissions acceptable; prefers letter-quality to dot-matrix. Reports in 6 weeks. Copyright in name of playwright; performance rights revert to playwright. Pays 10% royalty.
Needs: "Production must be playable *on stage*. Will not publish gratuitous filth or obscenity."
Tips: "The trend which we find deplorable is that of writing everything for Broadway; hence, small casts, limited sets. College and high school groups frequently desire just the opposite."

‡OREGON SHAKESPEAREAN FESTIVAL ASSOCIATION, Box 158, Ashland OR 97520. (503)482-2111. Artistic Director: Jerry Turner. Produces 10-12 plays/year. "The Angus Bowmer Theater has a thrust stage and seats 600. The Black Swan is an experimental space and seats 150; The Elizabethan Outdoor Theatre seats 1,200 (we do almost exclusively Shakespearean productions there—mid-June through September)." Query and synopsis plus 10 pages of dialogue from unsolicited sources/also resume. Complete scripts from agents only. Reports in 6 months. Negotiates individually for rights with the playwright's agent. "Most plays run within our 10 month season for 6-10 months, so royalties are paid accordingly."
Needs: "A broad range of classic and contemporary scripts. One or two fairly new scripts per season. Also a play readings series which focuses on new work. Plays must fit into our 10 month rotating repertory season. Black Swan shows usually limited to 6 actors." No one-acts or musicals.
Tips: "Send your work through an agent if possible. Send the best examples of your work rather than all of it. Don't become impatient or discouraged if it takes 6 months or more for a response. Don't expect detailed critiques with rejections. As always, I want to see plays with heart and soul, intelligence, humor and wit. I also think theatre is a place for the *word*. So, the word first, then spectacle and high-tech effects."

‡PENNSYLVANIA STAGE COMPANY, 837 Linden St., Allentown PA 18101. (215)437-6110. Artistic Director: Gregory S. Hurst. Produces 7 plays and musicals/year. "We are a LORT C theater and our season runs from October through June. The large majority of our audience comes from the Lehigh Valley. Our audience consists largely of adults. We also offer special student and senior citizen matinees." Query and synopsis; also would like a character breakdown and SASE or card. Reports in 3 months for scripts; 2 weeks for synopsis. Payment negotiable.
Needs: "The PSC produces full-length plays and musicals which are innovative and imaginative and that broaden our understanding of ourselves and society. Looking for wide range of styles and topics." Prefers 12 characters or fewer (will consider up to 18) for musicals; 8 or fewer for plays.
Tips: "Works presented at the Stage Company have a passion for being presented now, should be entertaining and meaningful to our local community, and perpetuate our theatrical and literary heritage. We do not want to limit our options in achieving this artistic mission. No one-acts and material that contains grossly offensive language. We appreciate also receiving a sample of dialogue with the synopsis. We have a staged reading program where a director, actors and the playwright work together during an intensive 3-day rehearsal period. A discussion with the audience follows the staged reading."

PEOPLE'S LIGHT & THEATRE COMPANY, 39 Conestoga Rd., Malvern PA 19355. (215)647-1900. Producing Director: Danny S. Fruchter. Produces 6 full-length plays/year. "LORT D Actors' Equity plays are produced in Malvern 30 miles outside Philadelphia in 350-seat main stage and 150-seat second stage. Our audience is mainly suburban, some from Philadelphia. We do a 6-show subscription season." Query with synopsis and cast list. Computer printout submissions acceptable; prefers letter-quality to dot-matrix. Reports in 10 months. Buys "rights to production in our theatre, sometimes for local touring." Pays 2-5% royalty.
Needs: "We will produce anything that interests us." Prefers single set, maximum cast of 12 (for full length), fewer for one act. No musicals, mysteries, domestic comedies.
Tips: "Writers should be aware of trend away from naturalistic family drama and toward smaller cast size."

ERIC PETERSON, OLDCASTLE THEATRE COMPANY, Box 1555, Bennington VT 05201. (802)447-0564. Artistic Directors: Shelli DuBoff, Richard Howe. Produces 7 plays/year. Plays are performed in a small (104 seat) theatre on a former estate now used by Southern Vermont College, by a professional theatre company (in a season from April through October) for general audiences, including residents of a three-state area and tourists during the vacation season. Submit complete ms. Pays "by negotiation with the playwright. As a not-for-profit theatre company, we do not have large sums available."

Needs: Produces classics, musicals, comedy, drama, most frequently American works. Usual performance time is 2 hours. "With a small stage, we limit to small cast and simple props, though we usually do prefer designed sets and appropriate costumes."

PIER ONE THEATRE, Box 894, Homer AK 99603. (907)235-7333. Artistic Director: Lance Petersen. Produces 5-8 plays/year. "Plays to various audiences for various plays—e.g. children's, senior citizens, adult, family, etc. Plays are produced on Kemai Peninsula." Submit complete ms. Reports in 2 months. Pays $25-125/performance.
Needs: "No restrictions—willing to read *all* genres." No stock reviews, hillbilly or sit-coms.
Tips: "Don't start your play with a telephone conversation. New plays ought to be risky business; they ought to be something the playwright feels is terribly important."

‡PINNWORTH PRODUCTIONS,1545 Amwell Road, Somerset NJ 08873. (201)873-2734. Artistic Director: Lou J. Stalsworth. Produces 2 plays/year. Non-equity performers are used in community theaters booked for independent productions. "Our audiences know theater, but sometimes grow weary of 'tired' restagings offered in community seasons, but are unwilling to drive repeatedly to New York to pay high prices on new works." Submit complete ms. Reports in 2 weeks. Pays $100-250.
Needs: "We look for full-length scripts without any preconceptions. Our budgets are small, so we tend to shy away from large costume shows, though anything is possible. If the author can compromise production values (not standards) all things are posible, though the ever-popular small cast, one-set show is always well received.
Tips: "Too many storytellers think that TV sitcom humor is the same thing as a play written for the stage. It is not. The ability to tell a one-liner or to create a single gag does not make a writer. Compound this with an inability on the part of many writers to use the language—or spell it—(this does not include typing) make play reading a sometimes painful exercise."

PIONEER DRAMA SERVICE, 2171 S. Colorado Blvd., Box 22555, Denver CO 80222. (303)759-4297. Publisher: Shubert Fendrich. 10% freelance written. Plays are performed by high school, junior high and adult groups, colleges, churches and recreation programs for audiences of all ages. "We are one of the largest full-service play publishers in the country in that we handle straight plays, musicals, children's theatre and melodrama." Publishes 10 plays/year; 40% musicals and 60% straight plays. 100% of scripts published are unagented submissions. Query only; no unsolicited manuscripts. Computer printout submissions acceptable; prefers letter-quality to dot-matrix. Buys all rights. Outright purchase only with a few exceptions for major musicals. Reports in 30-60 days.
Needs: "We use the standard 2-act format, 2-act musicals, religious drama, comedies, mysteries, drama, melodrama and plays for children's theater (plays to be done by adult actors for children)." Length: 2-act musicals and 2-act comedies up to 90 minutes; and children's theatre of 1 hour. Prefer many female roles, one simple set. Currently overstocked on one-act plays.
Recent Title: *Luann* by Eleanor and Ray Harder (musical based on the Greg Evans comic strip).
Tips: "Pioneer Drama Service is beginning to recognize developmental drama and contemporary issues in current children's theatre as a worthwhile direction for new plays. We are also exploring the religious theatre market. Plays with a cross-market appeal (i.e., schools, community theatre, semi- and professional theatres), with one set, many female roles, two-act structure are ideal for our needs."

PLAYERS PRESS, INC., Box 1132, Studio City CA 91604. Senior Editor: Robert W. Gordon. "We deal in all areas and handle works for film, television as well as theatre. But all works must be in stage play format for publication." Also produces scripts for video, and material for cable television. 80% freelance written. 10-12 scripts are unagented submissions. Works with 1-10 unpublished/unproduced writers annually. Submit complete ms. "Must have SASE or play will not be returned, and two #10 SASEs for update and correspondence. All submissions must have been produced and should include a flyer and/or program with dates of performance." Reports in 3 months. Buys negotiable rights. "We prefer all area rights." Pays variable royalty "according to area; approximately 10-75% of gross receipts." Also pays in outright purchase of $100-25,000 or $5-5,000/performance.
Needs: "We prefer comedies, musicals and children's theatre, but are open to all genres. We will rework the ms after acceptance. We are interested in the quality, not the format."
Tips: "Send only material requested. Do not telephone."

PLAYS, The Drama Magazine for Young People, 120 Boylston, Boston MA 02116. Editor: Sylvia K. Burack. Publishes approximately 75 1-act plays and dramatic program material each school year to be performed by junior and senior high, middle grades, lower grades. Can use comedies, farces, melodramas, skits, mysteries and dramas, plays for holidays and other special occasions, such as Book Week; adaptations of classic stories and fables; historical plays; plays about black history and heroes; puppet plays; folk and fairy tales; creative dramatics; and plays for conservation, ecology or human rights programs. Mss should follow the general style of *Plays*. Stage directions should not be typed in capital letters or underlined. No incorrect grammar or dialect. Desired lengths for mss are: junior and senior high—20 double-spaced ms pages (25 to 30 minutes playing time). Middle grades—12 to 15 pages (15 to 20 minutes playing time). Lower grades—6 to 10 pages (8 to 15 minutes playing time). Pays "good rates on acceptance." Reports in 2-3 weeks. Sample copy $3; send SASE for manuscript specification sheet. Subscription: $20/year.

PLAYWRIGHTS FUND OF NORTH CAROLINA, INC., Box 646, Greenville NC 27835. (919)758-3628. Artistic Director: Christine Rusch. Send scripts Attn: Literary Director. Produces 10 public workshop productions/year, usually staged readings in non-traditional theatre space for purposes of script development. We do about eight new one-acts each season at the Best Lunch Theatre Ever and Downtown, Downstairs (Sept.-May), with selected work at annual PFNC Southeastern Playwrights' Conference (June). Our audiences are intelligent, sensitive folks who love informal theatre. Each of our plays is followed by a post-performance discussion with the playwright, director, cast and audience. Produces plays by Southeastern writers only. Submit complete ms. "We request program/publishing credit for works we've done." Pays $75, travel and per diem so playwright can attend.
Needs: One-acts written by playwrights residing in the Southeastern U.S. (North Carolina, South Carolina, Virginia, West Virginia, Tennessee, Kentucky, Florida, Georgia, District of Columbia, Maryland); "we look for fresh, vivid language, structured action, manifested values. Most of our productions are staged readings with immediate audience feedback. We are not currently able to accept scripts from outside the Southeastern U.S. region."
Tips: "Our focus is on helping the playwright to develop his/her work to its fullest literary potential. We read and provide written response to everything, so be patient. Plays from NC natives and residents are eligible for annual PFNC Competition for NC playwrights. Deadline for submissions for the regular season by playwrights either from NC or from other states is October 1."

‡PRIMARY STAGES COMPANY, INC., 584 Ninth Ave., New York NY 10036. (212)333-7471. Artistic Director: Casey Childs. Produces 4 plays, 4 workshops, over 100 readings/year. All of the plays are produced professionally off-Broadway at the 45th Street Theatre, 354 West 45th St. Query and synopsis. Reports in 3 months. "If Primary Stages produces the play, we ask for the right to move it for up to six months after the closing performance." Writers paid "same as the actors."
Needs: "We are looking for highly theatrical works that were written exclusively with the stage in mind. We do not want TV scripts or strictly realistic plays."
Tips: No "living room plays, disease-of-the-week plays, back-porch plays, father/son work-it-all-out plays, etc."

‡THE QUARTZ THEATRE, Box 465, Ashland OR 97520. (503)482-8119. Artistic Director: Dr. Robert Spira. Produces 5 plays/year. "Semi-professional mini-theatre. General audience." Send query and synopsis. Reports in 2 weeks. Pays 5% royalty after expenses.
Needs: "Any length, any subject, with or without music. We seek playwrights with a flair for language and theatrical imagination."
Tips: "We look at anything. We do not do second productions unless substantial rewriting is involved. Our theatre is a steppingstone to further production. Our playwrights are usually well-read in comparative religion, philosophy, psychology, and have a comprehensive grasp of human problems. We seek the 'self-indulgent' playwright who pleases him/herself first of all."

RAFT THEATRE, 432 W. 42nd St., New York NY 10036. (212)947-8389. Artistic Director: Martin Zurla. Produces 2-5 plays/year. Plays performed are professional: showcase (AEA), with mini-contract, off-Broadway; intended for general audiences. Submit complete ms. Computer printout submissions OK. Reports in 3 months. Pays on year option and royalty (on individual basis), or makes outright purchase for $500-1,000.
Needs: "We have *no* restrictions on content, theme, style or length. Prefer scripts that have six or *fewer* characters and limited set and scene changes (due to performing space); and scripts that are typed in professional play-script format. No nudity."
Tips: "We are looking for writers that respect their craft and present their work in like manner. We prefer works that set their own trends and not those that follow other trends. We normally look for scripts that deal with human issues and cover a wide scope and audience, and not the so-called commercial property."

‡A RENAISSANCE THEATRE, Box 10088, Pittsburgh PA 15233. (412)441-8900. Artistic Director: David Logan-Morrow. Estab. 1987. Four major productions and staged readings/year. Professional productions for a general audience. Send query and synopsis. Reports in 6-8 weeks. Obtains standard basic agreement with Dramatist's Guild. Pays $300-1,000.
Needs: All types, all genres. We have no specific preference.
Tips: "Looking for good quality writing, audience appeal and originality. We are a theatre organization dedicated solely to producing new works by American playwrights."

SAIDYE BRONFMAN CENTRE, 5170 Cote St. Catherine Rd., Montreal, Quebec H3W 1M7 Canada. (514)739-2301. Director: Harry Gulkin. Coordinator of Performing Arts: Guy Rodgers. Produces 5-7 plays/year. Professional theatre company. Plays performed in 350 seat theatre. Submit complete ms. Reports in 2 months. Rights negotiated. Pays 4-5% royalty ("approximately, depending on the work").
Needs: Canadian plays with Jewish themes or characters. Small cast. "Themes should be current or daily problems, but we are not specific in our requirements, as plays take many forms."
Tips: "Trends seem to be going towards the intimate play, with a theme that affects everyone, especially child-abuse, drug-abuse, medical problems, etc., although there are a number of historical plays that are surfacing showing a deep interest in past history."

‡SEW PRODUCTIONS/LORRAINE HANSBERRY THEATRE, Suite 708, 25 Taylor, San Francisco CA 94102. (415)474-8842. Artistic Director: Stanley E. Williams. Produces 5 full-length productions/year. Submit complete ms. Obtains standard maximum rights. Pays $20-30 per performance. "The theatre is a multi-cultural company devoted primarily to the work of black playwrights, yet which appeal to a broad 'crossover' audience."
Needs: "We produce contemporary plays of original themes pertaining to the black experience. We have produced works by major writers such as Ntozake Shange, Charles Fuller and of course Lorraine Hansberry, and over ⅔ of our productions are World or West Coast premieres. Scripts by new writers are read primarily for our yearly Black Playwrights Workshop, which provides instruction and training from professional playwrights and dramaturgs, as well as two staged readings of the works-in-progress. Our artistic vision centers on the importance of the playwright as the foundation of drama, and part of our mission is to discover and develop young and emerging black and third-world playwrights. Plays can be musicals, dramas, comedies or experimental pieces; we will consider anything that is skillfully written, challenging, perceptive and focuses on the values and aspirations of blacks. Don't be afraid to be controversial. We are looking for plays that will touch as well as challenge the audience, and take them to higher levels of aesthetic satisfaction and enjoyment of the theatrical experience."
Tips: "Keep casts and production requirements to 'manageable' size."

‡THE SHAZZAM PRODUCTION COMPANY, 418 Pier Ave., Santa Monica CA 90405. Artistic Director: Edward Blackoff. Produces 2 plays/year. Equity-waiver productions for adult audience. Query with complete ms and synopsis. Reports in 6 weeks. Obtains negotiable rights. Pays $15-25/performance.
Needs: "Full-length plays dealing with important contemporary social and political human issues. Limit of 2 sets and requiring no more than 12 actors. No musicals or drawing room farces."

RICHMOND SHEPARD THEATRE COMPLEX, 6468 Santa Monica Blvd., Hollywood CA 90038. (213)462-9399. Artistic Director: Richmond Shepard. Produces 4 new plays/year. Has Equity waiver in Hollywood for the general public. "Our shows are reviewed by all the Los Angeles press and have won many awards. Several have been subsequently published and/or optioned for further production." Prefers query and synopsis "but will accept complete ms." Reports in 2 months. Acquires perpetual residual rights for first production. Pays royalty of 6% of gross after initial production has recouped its investment. Must enclose SASE for reply.
Needs: Small casts, few sets preferred. Use *play form* in your writing. No "illiterate soap operas or plays with much exposition. Familiar plays we have produced include *Travesties* by Tom Stoppard; *Cold Storage* by Ron Ribman and *Entertaining Mr. Sloane* by Joe Orton—shows that show a little intellect and wit."

‡FRANK SILVERA WRITERS' WORKSHOP, 317 West 125th St., New York NY 10027. (212)663-8463. Artistic Director: Karen Baxter. Produces up to 4 plays/year. "Plays attended by 90% black audiences." Submit complete ms. Reports in 6 weeks. "All productions originally read here are credited to the Workshop if they are produced outside." Pays royalty.
Needs: "Universal themes, full-length, one-acts."

> 66 *My own approach to rewriting is simple: go over and over and over the work until you are really sick of it, and then go over it again.* 99
>
> —*Stephen Minot*
> *author of the novel* Chill of Dusk
> *and* Crossing, *a collection of short stories*

‡THE SNOWMASS REPERTORY THEATRE, Box 6275, Snowmass Village CO 81615. (303)923-3773. Artistic Director: Michael Yeager. Produces 8 plays/year. "Plays performed at The Snowmass Festival Theatre (253 seats), or The Wheeler Opera House (488 seats). Professional Equity Productions, for both summer and winter visitors and locals." Submit complete ms. Reports anywhere from 6 weeks to 6 months. Obtains rights for first professional production. Pays 6-12% royalty.
Needs: "We produce full-length comedies, dramas and musicals. Prefer casts of 6-12 characters with relatively equal numbers of male and female characters and no limitations on minority casting; single or suggestive settings."

SOHO REPERTORY THEATRE, 80 Varick St., New York NY 10013. (212)925-2588. Co-Artistic Directors: Jerry Engelbach and Marlene Swartz. Produces 4-10 full productions and 8-10 staged readings/year. 25% freelance written. Performances at the Greenwich House Theatre, Greenwich Village. "The audience is well educated, mature and composed of regular theatregoers. Our playwrights have usually been produced, and some published, previously." All scripts are unagented submissions. Works with 5-10 unpublished/unproduced writers annually, including productions and staged readings. Query with description of the play and how it will work as a live theatre piece. "We prefer that queries/descriptions be submitted by a director interested in staging the play, but will accept author queries, too." Computer printout submissions acceptable; prefers letter-quality to dot-matrix. Reports in 90 days. Rights for full-length plays: percentage of author's royalties on future earnings, credit in published script and on future programs; for staged readings: none. Pays $100 and up for limited run performance rights. Pays $500 and up for future right to option.
Needs: "Unusual plays not likely to be seen elsewhere; including rarely produced classics; revivals of superior or modern works; new plays that utilize contemporary theatre techniques; and musicals and mixed media pieces that are noncommercial. Writers should keep in mind that our stage is a thrust, not a proscenium." Desires "full-length works that are physical, three-dimensional and that use heightened language, are witty and sophisticated, and that demonstrate a high quality of dramatic craft. No sitcoms, featherweight pieces for featherbrained audiences, drawing-room plays, pedantic political pieces, works that do not require the audience to think, or pieces more suited to television or the printed page than to the live stage."
Tips: "We go our own way and are not influenced by 'trends,' 'fads' or other commercial, nonartistic considerations. An ideal script for Soho Rep is highly literate, witty, and dramatically sound, and has plenty of scope for imaginative, physically active staging that breaks the fourth wall."

SOUTH COAST REPERTORY, Box 2197, Costa Mesa CA 92628. (714)957-2602. Dramaturg: Jerry Patch. Literary Manager: John Glore. Produces 6 plays/year on mainstage, 5 on second stage. A professional nonprofit theatre; a member of LORT and TCG. "We operate in our own facility which houses a 507-seat mainstage theatre and a 161-seat second stage theatre. We have a combined subscription audience of 24,000." Submit query and synopsis; maunscripts considered if submitted by agent. Reports in 4 months. Acquires negotiable rights. Pays negotiable royalty.
Needs: "We produce mostly full-lengths but will consider one-acts. Our only iron clad restriction is that a play be well written. We prefer plays that address contemporary concerns and are dramaturgically innovative. A play whose cast is larger than fifteen-twenty will need to be extremely compelling and its cast size must be justifiable."
Tips: "We don't look for a writer to write for us—he or she should write for him or herself. We look for honesty and a fresh voice. We're not likely to be interested in writers who are mindful of *any* trends. Originality and craftsmanship are the most important qualities we look for."

SOUTHEASTERN ACADEMY OF THEATRE AND MUSIC INC., DBA ACADEMY THEATRE, Box 77070, Atlanta GA 30359. (404)873-2518. Artistic Director: Frank Wittow. Produces 12-18 plays/year; mainstage subscription series, theatre for youth, first stage new play series, school of performing arts and lab theatre series. Query and/or send synopsis. Reports in 6 months. Buys "usually sole and exclusive right to produce play within a 100-mile radius of the metro Atlanta area for up to 3 years."
Needs: "Full-length, small cast shows which provide interesting challenges for actors. Plays which deal with new approaches to naturalism, transformational plays. One-acts considered for lab theatre (minimal royalty)." Cast: 12 maximum. Minimal or simple sets. "Deal with basic, honest emotions. Delve into social issues in a subtle manner. Provide thought-provoking material which deals with the human condition and allows for greater self-awareness." No frivolous, light comedies.
Tips: "The Academy Theatre is devoted to exploring human behavior, through physical and emotional involvement, for the purpose of greater self-awareness, for the purpose of making people more social, more able to live with each other."

‡SOUTHERN APPALACHIAN REPERTORY THEATRE (SART), Mars Hill College, Box 53, Mars Hill NC 28754. (704)689-1384. Managing Director: James W. Thomas. Produces 5-6 plays/year. "Since 1975 the Southern Appalachian Repertory Theatre has produced 527 performances of 53 plays and played to over 75,000 patrons in the 152-seat Owen Theatre on the Mars Hill College campus. The theatre's goals are quality,

adventurous programming and integrity, both in artistic form and in the treatment of various aspects of human condition. SART is a professional summer theatre company whose audiences range from students to senior citizens." Send query with synopsis. Reports in 2 months. Pays flat fee of $500.
Needs: "Since 1975, one of SART's goals has been to produce at least one original play each summer season. To date, 14 original stories have been produced. Plays by southern Appalachian playwrights or about southern Appalachia are preferred, but by no means exclusively. New scripts, synopses or letters or inquiry welcomed."

‡SPECTRUM THEATRE, 1 East 104th St., New York NY 10029. (212)860-5535. Artistic Director: Benno Haehnel. Produces 4 plays/year. New York City Off-Broadway mini-contract productions. Submit complete ms. Reports in 6 weeks. Obtains future production standard subsidiary rights. Pays 6% royalty.
Needs: Seeks "primarily full-length realistic plays dealing with social and humanistic problems. Prefers casts of 7 or under; no more than two sets. Looks for vivid characterizations and tight structure; key counterpointing of humorous and dramatic elements. Not interested in musicals."

STAGE ONE: The Louisville Children's Theatre, 721 W. Main St., Louisville KY 40202. (502)589-5946. Producing Director: Moses Goldberg. Produces 6-7 plays/year. 20% freelance written. 15-20% of scripts produced are unagented submissions (excluding work of playwright-in-residence). Plays performed by an Equity company for young audiences aged 4-18; usually does different plays for different age groups within that range. Submit complete ms. Computer printout submissions acceptable. Reports in 4 months. Pays negotiable royalty or $25-50/performance.
Needs: "Good plays for young audiences of all types: adventure, fantasy, realism, serious problem plays about growing up or family entertainment." Cast: ideally, 10 or less. "Honest, visual potentiality, worthwhile story and characters are necessary. An awareness of children and their schooling is a plus." No "campy material or anything condescending to children. No musicals unless they are fairly limited in orchestration."

STAGES REPERTORY THEATRE, Suite 101, 3201 Allen Pkwy., Houston TX 77019. (713)527-0240. Artistic Director: Ted Swindley. Produces 12 adult, 5 children's plays/year. Non-profit professional company, operating in two theatres (one arena and one thrust). "We also tour with children's programs in the Houston area. Adult audience is a fairly eclectic urban mix, tending, we hope, towards the adventurous. Our children's shows are for those four to eleven, mostly school groups. All scripts should be accompanied by resume, SASE, and one-page synopsis including casting and technical requirements. No unbound scripts. Reports in 3 months. Rights and payment negotiated."
Needs: Our Mainstage programming tends towards new off-Broadway works, "renovated" classics and towards thought-provoking, issue-oriented theatre. Our children's programming focuses on works that parents will enjoy as much as kids, and we're always looking for children's scripts that lend themselves to the creation of educational materials for distribution to the teachers. Small-scale production requirements preferable.

‡STAGEWRIGHTS, INC., 165 W. 47th St., New York NY 10036. Artistic Director: Richard Holland. Produces 2 plays/year. Professional productions, off and off-off Broadway for all audiences. Query with synopsis. Reports in 3 weeks. "We adhere to the standard Dramatist Guild contracts."
Needs: "All types, one-act and full-length plays. No pornography."

CHARLES STILWILL, Managing Director, Community Playhouse, Box 433, Waterloo IA 50704. (319)235-0367. Plays performed by Waterloo Community Playhouse with a volunteer cast. Produces 11-13 plays (7-8 adult, 4-6 children's); 1-3 musicals and 7-12 nonmusicals/year; 1-4 originals. 17% freelance written. Most scripts produced are unagented submissions. Works with 1-4 unpublished/unproduced writers annually. "We are one of few community theatres with a commitment to new scripts. We do at least one and have done as many as four a year. We are the largest community theatre per capita in the country. We have 4,300 season members." Average attendance at main stage shows is 3,000; at studio shows 1,200. "We try to fit the play to the theatre. We do a wide variety of plays. Looking for good plays with more roles for women than men. Our public isn't going to accept nudity, too much sex, too much strong language. We don't have enough Black actors to do all-Black shows." Theatre has done plays with as few as two characters, and as many as 98. "On the main stage, we usually pay between $300 and $500. In our studio, we usually pay between $50 and $300. We also produce children's theatre. We are looking for good adaptations of name children's shows and very good shows that don't necessarily have a name. We produce children's theatre with both adult and child actors. We also do a small (2-6 actors) cast show that tours the elementary schools in the spring. This does not have to be a name, but it can only be about 35-45 minutes long." Send synopsis or complete script. Computer printout submissions acceptable. "Reports negatively within 1 year, but acceptance takes longer because we try to fit a wanted script into the balanced season."
Recent Titles: *Joe's Friendy*, by Bruce Gadansky (Western U.S. premiere); and *Legacy*, by John Fenn (world premiere in January 1988).

‡KATHRYN TAYLOR, 4350 Transport St. #104, Ventura CA 93003. (805)642-8515. Artistic Director: Kathryn Taylor. Produces 8 plays/year. Plays produced at the Firelite Dinner Theatre, a community theatre. Submit complete ms. Reports in 3 months. Writers receive copy of vieotape and guest tickets (value $100).
Needs: "Light comedy, musicals, some suspense. Two acts preferred, 2 hour best. This is community theatre; our audience is not always the most educated. Approximately 25 in cast. No X-rated or those with multiple 4-letter words (a few OK) or nudity."
Tips: "Dinner theatre does not attract a theatre educated audience. They most prefer light entertainment that does not require much thought. We attempted a full year of previously unpublished works. We had mixed success. It is important that the title be clear. A great deal of time must be spent on explanation. New upbeat comedies did the best; contemporary subject also."

‡TEJAS ART PRESS, 207 Terrell Rd., San Antonio TX 78209. Editor: Robert Willson. Publishes plays relating to the American Indian experience. Submit complete ms. Reports in 2 months. Pays royalty.
Tips: Wants more drama.

‡THEATER ARTISTS OF MARIN, Box 473, San Rafael CA 94915. (415)454-2380. Artistic Director: Charles Brousse. Produces 5-6 plays/year. Professional non-equity productions for a general adult audience. Submit complete ms. Reports in 3 months. Pays outright $250.
Needs: "All types of scripts: comedy, drama, farce. Prefers contemporary setting, with some relevance to current issues in American society." No children's shows, domestic sitcoms, one man shows or commercial thrillers.

THEATER LUDICRUM, INC., Suite 83, 64 Charlesgate E., Boston MA 02215. (617)424-6831. Contact: Director. Produces 2-3 plays/year. Plays are performed in a small, non-Equity theatre in Boston. "Our audience includes minority groups (people of color, gays, women)." Submit complete ms. Reports in 2 weeks. Rights revert to author after production. Pays $15-30/performance.
Needs: "As a small theater with a small budget, we look for scripts with minimal sets, costumes, props and expense in general. We are interested in scripts that emphasize the word and acting."

‡THEATRE CALGARY, 220 9th Ave. SE, Calgary, Alberta T2G 5C4 Canada. (403)294-7440. Artistic Director: Martin Kinch. Produces 6-8 plays/year. Professional productions. Reports in 3 months. Buys production rights usually, "but it can vary with specific contracts." Payments and commissions negotiated under individual contracts.
Needs: "Theatre Calgary is a major Canadian Regional Theatre. Presently there are two series."
Tips: "We welcome the opportunity to peruse new work."

‡THEATRE RAPPORT, 8128 Gould Ave., Hollywood CA 90046. (213)464-2662. Artistic Director: Crane Jackson. Produces 5 plays/year. "Theatre Rapport is an Equity-waiver theatre (50 seats) which produces plays for a contemporary, *aware* audience." Query with synopsis. Obtains amateur/1 time rights. Pays 20% royalty of gross. (Range $200-500). Does not return unsolicited material.
Needs: "We prefer already produced 'new' plays. 1 set (8 people). The subject matter should be unique, yet should relate to current-day problems." No costumes, avant-garde, ego trips for playrights, message plays.
Tips: "Good mysteries are in short supply; intelligent comedies are needed—not silly farces. Real people with characterizations are a must."

THEATRE RHINOCEROS, 2926 16th St., San Francisco CA 94103. (415)552-4100. Artistic Director: Kris Gannon. Produces 6-8 plays/year. Professional productions of plays written by and relevant to gay and lesbian people. Submit complete ms. Reports in 3 months. Acquires production rights—some subsidiary rights for unproduced scripts. Pays $25-35/performance.
Needs: Full-length scripts preferred. "Smaller casts and single sets work best for us."

THEATRE THREE, 2800 Routh, Dallas TX 75201. (214)871-2933. Artistic Director: Norma Young. Produces 7-10 plays/year. 8% freelance written. Plays in an arena house to a general audience using professional actors.
Needs: Full-length plays. "We produce a wide range of genres including musicals. Our house is inappropriate for spectacle-type shows. Multiset and large cast shows can be cost prohibitive. All scripts must be bound with return SASE. Attn: Norma Young. Theatre Three also produces the Playwrights' Project, for the encouragement and development of local and south-southwest regional playwrights only. 6 scripts given "concert readings" and 3 scripts given "staged" readings/year. Submissions must be bound with return SASE. Attn: Sharon Bunn or Jimmy Mullen. All inquiries to the Theatre Three or Playwrights' Project must have SASE. For acknowledgement of script receipt include stamped postcard.

THEATRE VIRGINIA, Boulevard & Grove Ave., Richmond VA 23221. (804)257-0840. Artistic Director: Terry Burgler. Produces 7 plays/year. LORT company. 10-15% freelance written. Submit letter of inquiry, synopsis and generous (15-20 pages) sample; decisions to solicit will be made based on evaluation of these materials. Computer printout submissions acceptable; prefers letter-quality to dot-matrix. Reports on letters and samples in 4-6 weeks; reports on solicited scripts in 2-4 months. Buys negotiable rights, "but usually we share in future earnings from the property, if we produce the premiere." Pays royalty.

Tips: "We look for writing which reflects an appreciation of theatrical values (as opposed to stark realism). We look also for a strong sense of character, both in creation and presentation. And finally, while we prefer theatricality to kitchen-sink realism, we feel strongly that a script must maintain the sense of a story being told."

THEATREWORKS, University of Colorado, Box 7150, Colorado Springs CO 80933. (303)593-3232. Producing Director: Whit Andrews. Produces 4 full-length plays/year and two new one-acts. "New full-length plays produced on an irregular basis. Casts are semi-professional and plays are produced at the university." Submit query and synopsis. One-act plays are accepted as Playwrights' Forum competition entries—submit complete ms. Deadline: December 15; winners announced February 15. Two one-act competition winners receive full production, cash awards and travel allowances. Acquires exclusive regional option for duration of production. Full rights revert to author upon closing. Pays $300-1,200.

Needs: Full lengths and one-acts—no restrictions on subject. "Cast size should not exceed 20; stage area is small with limited wing and fly space. Theatreworks is interested in the exploration of new and inventive theatrical work. Points are scored by imaginative use of visual image. Static verbosity and staid conventionalism not encouraged." No formulaic melodrama or children's plays.

Tips: "Too often, new plays seem far too derivative of television and film writing. We think theatre is a medium which an author must specifically attack. The standard three-act form would appear to be on the way out. Economy, brevity and incisiveness favorably received."

THEATREWORKS/USA, 131 W. 86th St., New York NY 10021. (212)595-7500. Artistic Director: Jay Hamick. Associate Artistic Director: Barbara Pasternack. Produces 3 new plays/season. Produces professional musicals that primarily tour but also play (TYA contract) at an off-Broadway theatre for a young audience. Submit query and synopsis or sample song. Reports in 6 months. Buys all rights. Pays 6% royalty; offers $1,500 advance against future royalties for new, commissioned plays.

Needs: Musicals and plays with music. Historical/biographical themes (ages 9-15), classic literature, fairy tales, and issue-oriented themes suitable for young people ages 9-15. Five person cast, minimal lighting. "We like well-crafted shows with good dramatic structure—a protagonist who wants something specific, an antagonist, a problem to be solved—character development, tension, climax, etc. No Saturday afternoon special-type shows, shows with nothing to say or 'kiddie' theatre shows."

Tips: "Writing for kids is just like writing for adults—only better (clearer, cleaner). Kids will not sit still for unnecessary exposition and overblown prose. Long monologues, soliloquies and 'I Am' songs and ballads should be avoided. Television, movies, video make the world of entertainment highly competitive. Theatre should and must give audiences something they can't get in other mediums. It needs to be real, honest, entertaining and well-crafted—how else can you compete with special effects, stunt men, MTV?"

‡**TRINITY SQUARE ENSEMBLE**, Box 1798, Evanston IL 60204. (312)328-0330. Artistic Director: Karen L. Erickson. Produces 4-6 plays/year. "Professional non-equity company, member of League of Chicago Theatres, ensemble company of artists. We look for scripts adapted from classics suited to our ensemble as well as new works. Writers are encouraged to research our company. We produce new children's pieces—must blend stories with school curriculum." Send query and synopsis. Reports in 4-6 months. Obtains negotiated percentage of rights, usually 10%. "We do not want full ms submissions. If we request, then we'll return."

Needs: Cast: prefer no more than 10. Set: simpler the better.

Tips: "Our ensemble is 70% women/30% men. Keep this in mind as you develop scripts. No male-dominated, fluffy comedies. Get to know us—write for our performers. Looks for strength in female characters."

‡**24th STREET EXPERIMENT**, 411 SW 24th St., San Antonio TX 78285. (512)435-2103. Artistic Director: Richard Slocum. Professional productions. Send query and synopsis and first five pages of ms. Reports in 3 months. Obtains no rights. Pays $15-50/performance.

Needs: Full-length musicals and revue, one-act children's scripts, one-act and full-length contemporary and experimental dramas and comedies. Needs small cast (2-8), prefers unit set or simple staging.

Tips: "We are most interested in psychological dramas with a sense of humor, plays that are experimental in format, content or staging. No large-cast, elaborate sets. A partial list of authors and titles we have already produced includes Joyce Carol Oates, *Medea*, *Little Shop of Horrors*, Beckett, Brecht, Mrozek, Kafka, A. . .*My Name is Alice*, *Agnes of God*, *Jesse and the Bandit Queen*, Strindberg, *Play Strindberg*, Sylvia Plath."

‡**THE VANCOUVER PLAYHOUSE**, 543 West 7th Ave., Vancouver, British Columbia V5Z 1B4 Canada. (604)872-6622. Artistic Director: Walter Learning. Produces 8 plays/year. Professional productions for a general audience. Submit complete ms. Reports in 2 months. Obtains all rights. Pays 4-10% royalties.

VICTORIAN THEATRE, 4201 Hooker, Denver CO 80211. (303)433-5050. Artistic Director: Sterling Jenkins. Produces 5-6 plays/year. Plays are produced at Victorian Theatre, a non-profit, semi-professional organization with a widely varied general audience in Denver. The historic theatre seats 90 people. Agented submissions are preferred; submit query and synopsis, or complete ms. Reports in 4 months. Requires regional exclusivity. Pays $30-40/performance.
Needs: Prefers modern two-act comedies and dramas. No topic restriction. "We have a small, intimate proscenium stage with a trap door, limited wings and no fly space." Prefer simple one-set plays. No large scale musicals or multi-setting, three-act dramas.
Tips: "Because of television, audiences are used to action packed variety in entertainment and have shortening attention spans. Comic relief is an asset in even the most serious drama. Audiences are looking more than ever for escape from stress of life."

‡VIETNAM VETERANS ENSEMBLE THEATRE COMPANY, 314 W. 54th St., New York NY 10019. (212)512-1960. Artistic Director: Thomas A. Bird. Produces 3 plays/year on average. Professional productions, off-off and off Broadway. Submit complete ms. Reports in 2 months. Obtains standard industry rights. Pays advance against percent of box office gross.
Needs: Full-length plays, any style/genre. Looks for "work with a strong center of belief/a moral stance/passion. No melodramas, full-scale 'B'way' musicals; sitcoms masquerading as plays."
Tips: Writers should be aware of "rising costs, lowered standards, lack of moral courage, less risk-taking and shrinking markets in which to fail."

VIRGINIA STAGE COMPANY, Box 3770, Norfolk VA 23514. (804)627-6988. Artistic Director: Charles Towers. Produces 7 plays/year. 20% freelance written. Only agent submitted or professionally recommended scripts are accepted. A professional regional theatre serving the one million people of the Hampton Roads area. Plays are performed in LORT C proscenium mainstage or LORT D flexible second stage. Works with 2 writers annually. Query with synopsis only; "sample scene or dialogue may be included." Negotiates rights and payment.
Needs: "Primarily full-length dramas and comedies which address contemporary issues within a study of broader themes and theatricality. Material must be inherently theatrical in use of language, staging or character. We do not want to see material which offers simplistic solutions to complex concerns, or is more easily suited for television or film."

‡THE VORTEX THEATRE COMPANY, 164 Eleventh Ave., New York NY 10011. Artistic Director: Robert Coles. Off-off-Broadway productions. Submit complete ms. Reports in 6 months. Obtains rights to percentage of author's future income from play; first refusal on rights for Broadway or Off-Broadway production. Pays 5% royalty for Equity contract productions; outright purchase from $10-50 for showcase code productions.
Needs: "Plays of any style and any content will be considered, but we hope for plays that make a serious comment on contemporary life while maintaining entertainment value. We also have a special interest in non-traditional dramatic structure and the opportunity to utilize vivid or unusual scenic design."

‡WALNUT STREET THEATRE, 9th and Walnut Streets, Philadelphia PA 19107. (215)574-3550. Executive Director: Bernard Havard. Produces 5 mainstage and 5 studio plays/year. "Our plays are performed in our own space. WST has 3 theatres—a proscenium (mainstage) audience capacity 1,052; 2 studios audience capacity 79-99. We are a member of the League of Regional Theatres. We have a subscription audience, the fifth largest in the nation." Query with synopsis and 10 pages. Reports in 1 month. Rights negotiated per project. Pays royalty (negotiated per project) or outright purchase.
Needs: "Full-length dramas and comedies, musicals, translations, adaptations and revues. The studio plays must be small cast, simple sets."
Tips: "We will consider anything. Bear in mind on the mainstage we look for plays with mass appeal, Broadway style. The studio spaces are our Off-Broadway. No children's plays. Our mainstage audience goes for work that is entertaining and light. Our studio season is where we look for plays that have bite, are more provocative."

‡WEST COAST ENSEMBLE, Box 38728, Los Angeles CA 90038. (213)871-1052. Artistic Director: Les Hanson. Produces 10 plays/year. Plays will be performed in one of our two theatres in Hollywood in an Equity-waiver situation. Submit complete ms. Reports in 5 months. Obtains the exclusive rights in southern California to present the play for the period specified. All ownership and rights remain with the playwright. Pays $25-45/performance.
Needs: Prefers a cast of 6-12.
Tips: "Submit the manuscript in acceptable dramatic script format."

‡WESTBETH THEATRE CENTER, INC.,151 Bank St., New York NY 10014. (212)691-2272. Artistic Director: Andrew Engelman. Produces 10 readings and 6 productions/year. Professional off-Broadway theatre.

Query and synopsis, submit complete ms or submit through agent. Reports in 2 months. Obtains rights to produce as showcase with option to enter into full option agreement. Writers paid $100 for showcase.
Needs: "Contemporary full-length plays. Production values (i.e. set, costumes, etc.) should be kept to a minimum" No period pieces.

‡WICHITA STATE UNIVERSITY THEATRE, Box 31, Wichita State University, Wichita KS 67208. (316)689-3185. Artistic Director: Richard Welsbacher. Produces 16 plays/year. "College audience." Submit complete ms. Reports in 2 months. Obtains rights to stage one production (4 performances). "Writer's expenses are paid to see final rehearsals and performance."
Needs: For the contest, full-length play of 90 minutes (minimum) or a group of related one-acts.
Tips: "No children's plays. Plays submitted should be original, unpublished and previously unproduced. Authors must be graduate or undergraduate college students." Send SASE for guidelines.

‡THE WO/MAN'S SHOWCASE, INC., 5266 Gate Lake Rd., Fort Lauderdale FL 33319. (305)772-4371. Artistic Director: Ann White. Produces 6 plays/year. "Alternative theatre, professional productions for mature audiences. Plays performed in various settings: libraries, theatres, colleges and universities, hotels and dinner theatres." Conducts annual playwrights' competition and festival. Send mss August through November 15 for productions in Spring. SASE for guidelines. Winning playwright receives $500.

WOMEN'S THEATRE PROJECT, 203 N. Howell, St. Paul MN 55104. (612)647-1953. Artistic Director: Carolyn Levy. Produces 2-3 plays/year. Plays performed in small (140 seat) Black Box theatre. Professional production for general public. Submit complete ms. Reporting time varies. Pays 5-10% royalty or $500-1,000.
Needs: "New plays by women about issues of importance to women, hopefully with good roles for women, although they do *not* need to be plays with all women casts. We are interested in good characters, interesting forms and styles, risk-taking ventures into new ideas and forms."
Tips: "We want to make our audiences think and ask questions. We don't solve problems or prescribe solutions, we raise issues."

WOOLLY MAMMOTH THEATRE COMPANY, Box 32229, Washington DC 20007. (202)393-1224. Artistic Director: Howard Shalwitz. Literary Manager: Neil Steyskal. Produces 5 plays/year. 50% freelance written. Produces professional productions for the general public in Washington, DC. 2-3 scripts/year are unagented submissions. Works with 1-2 unpublished/unproduced writers annually. Query with synopsis. Reports in 2 weeks on synopsis; 6 weeks on scripts; very interesting scripts take much longer. Buys first- and second-class production rights. Pays 5% royalty.
Needs: "We look only for plays that are highly unusual in some way. Apart from an innovative approach, there is no formula. One-acts are not used." Cast limit of 8; no unusually expensive gimmicks.

Screenwriting

The rise of cable TV (HBO, the largest cable company, now has 14 million subscribers) is good news for screenwriters, who now have more potential markets for their work than were available five years ago. Writers interested in screenplays can now consider mini-series as an option as well. Writing two-hour movies produced for video store distribution rather than showings at movie houses is another possibility for screenwriters to consider. Due to the cost, this type of film is easier for new writers to market than films for theater distribution. Hollywood films for theater distribution cost an estimated $10 million to $40 million to produce, while made-for-video films are being produced for $50,000 to $1 million.

Still, scripts for movie or TV producers are one of the most difficult types of work to market. With so much money at stake, producers are hesitant to hire writers without track records. You'll need to be as familiar as possible with what each producer is looking for *before* you query with your ideas. And writers who live outside the Los Angeles area are likely to find sales to major film producers particularly difficult. Finding a good agent can help considerably, especially if you live outside California. See the section on agents for suggestions, and note that we have indicated producers that need cable TV material with the symbol (□).

Screenplay format is complicated; if you're not familiar with it, you'll want to see samples before typing your manuscript. For a working script, you'll need to include directions to the camera operator for every single shot described—about 100 per half hour of film. Ideally, each script describes the size of the shot (medium, close-up, follow shot, etc.); the physical location of the shot (interior—the bedroom, exterior—the swimming pool, etc.); the lighting effects desired; any movement of the camera; the actors in the shot; and any unusual sound effects. This kind of writing can be tedious—but you'll need to learn to do it if you want to be perceived as a professional. Generally the script for a two-hour film or TV program will run from 120 to 150 pages, with plenty of white space on each page for notes by producers and technicians.

You'll notice that some producers here are interested in seeing "treatments" rather than or in addition to full scripts. A treatment, a 5-to 10-page description of scenes that make up the entire script written in the third person and present tense, reads more like a short story than the full script.

Don't assume your script needs to be entirely fiction. Notice how many movies and miniseries are based on real-life events. New novels are frequently optioned by producers, but few of the novels optioned are ever actually made into films. Many of Saul Bellow's novels have been under consideration by producers for years, for example, but none has ever actually been made into a movie. Classics and other works of fiction and nonfiction in the public domain are a source of useful inspiration.

It's a good idea to register your script with the Writers Guild of America (8955 Beverly Blvd., Los Angeles CA 90048 or 555 W. 57th St., New York NY 10019) prior to submitting it. Write to the Writers Guild for more information.

‡ALEXI PRODUCTIONS LTD., Box 8482, Universal City CA 91608. (818)843-3443. Contact: Nikolai Alexandrov. "All of our productions are done in Europe for an international audience. Mostly documentarily oriented, with comedy or drama and little or no violence. Intended first to entertain, and second to educate." Buys 5 scripts/year. To this date, all material has been submitted in London by Europeans. We are just opening up to the idea of using American writers. Buys all rights. No previously produced material. Reports in 4-6 weeks.
Needs: "We do from one-hour to five-hour material. Again, it must be entertaining and educational." Submit synopsis/outline, completed ms and resume.
Tips: "Be honest in evaluating your material's potential." Looks for "originality, humor and the ability to properly research material."

‡BACHNER PRODUCTIONS, INC., 360 First Ave., #5D, New York NY 10010. (212)673-2946. President: Annette Bachner. Produces material for television, home video cassettes, cable TV. Buys 4 scripts/year. Buys all rights. No previously produced material. Does not return unsolicited submissions. "Do not want unsolicited material." Reports on queries in 1 months; on solicited submissions in 2 months.
Needs: 35mm and 16mm films, realia, tapes and cassettes. Natural history subjects only. Query. Pays by outright purchase in accordance with Writers Guild standards.
Tips: Looks for writers with "experience in visual media."

‡□DAVE BELL ASSOCIATES, INC., 3211 Cahuenga Blvd. W., Los Angeles CA 90068. (213)851-7801. Director of Development: Kris Bell. Produces documentaries for HBO and the television networks, movies for television and specials for television. "We don't generally buy scripts; we option several a year (probably somewhere in the neighborhood of 15-20). Then take the scripts to the networks; if they buy, we buy. We also option ideas, proposals and treatments." Buys all rights. Previously published material OK. Does not return unsolicited material. Reports in 2 weeks.
Needs: We need low budget (under $2 million) screenplays for theatrical production and release; scripts or ideas for television movies (this includes true stories) and films (16 and 35mm). Query with samples or submit synopsis/outline, completed scripted and resume. Pays in accordance with Writers Guild standards.
Tips: "Identify whatever original elements your project contains and put them in a letter. If it isn't original, inventive, unique, we won't read any further than page 20. We look for writers who can formulate a complex sentence, know the fundamentals of plotting and executing a story and who can spell and create interesting characters and good dialogue."

□ **Open box preceding a listing indicates a cable TV market.**

‡CALIFORNIA INTERNATIONAL DIVISION OF JOSEPH NICOLETTI PUBLISHING CO., Box 2818, Newport Beach CA 92663. Review Department: Bob Burns. Produces "PG, R and G rated material. No X!" Buys 25-50 scripts/year. Buys negotiable rights. Previously produced material OK. SASE. Reports in 1 month. Catalog for SAE and 10 first class stamps.
Needs: Phonograph records, tapes and cassettes. "Music, thriller, outer-space, family type, 1-2 hrs." Query or send "whatever you feel best shows your work!" Pays in accordance with Writers Guild standards.
Tips: "Send only work *you* believe in!"

‡ANTHONY CARDOZA ENTERPRISES, Box 4163, North Hollywood CA 91607. (818)985-5550. President: Anthony Cardoza. Produces material for "theatre, TV and home." Buys one screenplay/year. Buys all rights. No previously produced material. Reports in 1 month.
Needs: Feature films. Submit completed script. Outright purchase.

◻THE CHAMBA ORGANIZATION, 230 W. 105th St., #2-A, New York NY 10025. President: St. Clair Bourne. Produces material for "the activist-oriented audience; the general audience (PG), and in the educational film market we aim at high school and adult audiences, especially the so-called 'minority' audiences. Assignments are given solely based upon our reaction to submitted material. The material is the credential." 100% freelance written. 100% of scripts produced are unagented submissions. Buys 2-4 scripts/year. Works with 3 unpublished/unproduced writers annually. Computer printout submissions acceptable; prefers letter-quality to dot-matrix.
Needs: "I concentrate primarily on feature film projects and unique feature-length documentary film projects. We prefer ... mission of film treatments first. Then, if the idea interests us, we negotiate the writing of the script." Also needs scripts for music videos and material (film) for cable television. Query with a brief description of plot, thumbnail descriptions of principal characters and any unusual elements. Payment negotiable according to Writers Guild standards.
Tips: Trends in screen include "a critical examination of traditional American values and dissatifaction with 'yuppie ideology.' "

‡THE CHICAGO BOARD OF RABBIS BROADCASTING COMMISSION, 1 South Franklin St., Chicago IL 60606. (312)444-2896. Director of Broadcasting: Mindy Soble. "Television scripts are requested for *The Magic Door*, a children's program produced in conjunction with CBS's WBBM-TV 2 in Chicago." 26 scripts are purchased per television season. Buys all rights. Reports in 1 month. Free writers guidelines.
Needs: *Magic Door*, is a weekly series of 26 shows that contain Jewish content and have universal appeal. The program take place backstage in a theatre where a company of actors brings stories to life for a puppet-child, Mazel. (Mazel is a large hand puppet who is worked by a member of the company, Wendy). The company consists of approximately 15 actors and actresses. Most of the programs utilize 3 or 4 of the above, including Wendy." Submit synopsis/outline, resume or a completed script with the right to reject. Outright purchase of $125.
Tips: "A Judaic background is helpful yet not critical. Writing for children is key. We prefer to use Chicago writers, as script rewrites are paramount."

◻CHRISTIAN BROADCASTING NETWORK, Virginia Beach VA 23463. (804)424-7777. Head Writer, Producers Group: John Faulk. Produces material for a general mass audience as well as Christian audiences. Second largest cable network in the nation. Producer of *700 Club*. "We consider scripts for: women's programs, children's programs, dramas based on Bible characters, holiday shows, etc. Mostly staff-written but will consider freelance treatments." Will works with unpublished/unproduced writers. Previously produced material OK. Computer printout submissions acceptable; prefers letter-quality to dot-matrix. Send to Harry Young, program director, CBN Cable Network. Reports in 2 weeks.
Needs: Secular and Christian. Dramatic, service, educational, children's, feature films, informational shows, film adaptations of books. Query and request release form to submit an idea or script. Buys some ideas outright; flat fee for treatment, outline or script.
Tips: "We're looking for writers with strong television/film background who have screenwriting experience. A basic belief in the *Bible* is necessary."

CINE/DESIGN FILMS, INC., 255 Washington St., Denver CO 80203. (303)777-4222. Producer/Director: Jon Husband. Produces educational material for general, sales-training and theatrical audiences. 75% freelance written. 90% of scripts produced are unagented submissions. "Original solid ideas are encouraged." Computer printout submissions acceptable. Rights purchased vary.
Needs: "Motion picture outlines in the theatrical and documentary areas. We are seeking theatrical scripts in the low-budget area that are possible to produce for under $1,000,000. We seek flexibility and personalities who can work well with our clients." Produces 16mm and 35mm films. Send an 8-10 page outline before submitting ms. Unbound scripts will be returned unread. Pays $100-200/screen minute on 16mm productions. Theatrical scripts negotiable.
Tips: "Understand the marketing needs of film production today."

☐**DA SILVA ASSOCIATES**, 137 E. 38th St., New York NY 10016. Executive Producer: Raul da Silva. 10% freelance written. Produces material for entertainment audiences. Must work with published/established writers. 50% of scripts produced are unagented submissions. Rights purchased vary. "If possible, we share profits with writers, particularly when resale is involved." Computer printout submissions acceptable; prefers letter-quality to dot-matrix.
Needs: "We produce both types of material: on assignment and proprietary." Produces video (entertainment only—drama, comedy, and documentaries) with inspirational and motivational themes only. No "handicapped conquers" plots sought; 35mm films, phonograph records, tapes and cassettes. Also produces material for cable TV (drama/comedy). "Generally we work on assignment only. We have a selection of writers known to us already." Cannot handle unsolicited mail/scripts. Submit resume. Open to credit sheets. Pays in accordance with Writers Guild standards. Pays expenses of writers on assignment.
Tips: "We are planning several series, both drama and documentary."

‡**JOHN DOREMUS, INC./MUSIC IN THE AIR**, Suite 1810, 875 N. Michigan Ave., Chicago IL 60611. (312)664-8944. Director, Global Marketing: Alexis H. Sarkisian. Produces films for an adult/adolescent audience. Buys all rights. No previously produced material. Free catalog.
Needs: Tapes and cassettes. Query.

☐**DSM PRODUCERS**, Suite 1204, 161 W. 54th St., New York NY 10019. (212)245-0006. Produces material for consumer, trade and executive audiences. 96% freelance written. Previously produced material OK. Computer printout submissions acceptable; prefers letter-quality to dot-matrix. Reports in 1 month.
Needs: Phonograph records, tapes and cassettes. Currently interested in commercial material for all segments of the music industry, i.e., record acts; commercials/film/radio-television/industrial/trade. Produces material for cable television. Submit cassette/video or completed script and resume. Pays in royalty or in accordance with Writers Guild standards.

‡**FELINE PRODUCTIONS**, 1125 Veronica Springs Rd., Santa Barbara CA 93105. (805)682-4047. Executive Producer: Deby DeWeese. Produces material for educational institutions, non-profit agencies and home video markets. Number of scripts purchased "varies year to year—rarely more than 10/year." Buys all rights or first rights. Previously produced material OK. Reports in 1 month.
Needs: "Low-budget 30- and 60-minute scripts in dual slide or video format. Fiction or non-fiction. Educational, progressive, radical alternative media scripts encouraged. Particularly interested in feminist slant. Alternative lifestyle topics fine. Prefer single-camera approach. Same approach for radio scripts. Need good 15-30 minute radio sci-fi scripts with more traditional slant." Multimedia kits, slides, tapes and cassettes, videotapes (both ½ inch and ¾ inch). Query.
Tips: "Be real. Be yourself. Write from your heart. Be courageous, adventuresome and willing to take a risk. We hate tech talk."

‡**ROBERT GUENETTE PRODUCTIONS**, 8489 West Third St., Los Angeles CA 90048. (213)658-8450. President: R. Guenette. Vice President: Peter Wood. Produces films for TV and theatrical audiences. Buys 15-20 scripts/year "on the average." Buys all rights. No previously produced material. Reports in 1 week on queries; 1 month on submissions.
Needs: 16mm and 35mm films; tapes and cassettes. Query with samples or submit synopsis/outline and completed ms. Pays in accordance with Writers Guild standards.

‡**HEAPING TEASPOON ANIMATION**, 4002 19th St., San Francisco CA 94114. (415)626-1893. Creative Director: Chuck Eyler. Produces animated material for all ages. Produces 1-2 scripts/year. Rights purchased "depend on material." Previously produced material OK "if not produced in animation and suitable for it." Reports on queries in 2 weeks; on mss in 1 month. Catalog for #10 SAE.
Needs: Films (35mm). Produces "clever 30-second public service announcements, educational film ideas and/or scripts and feature scripts." Query with samples or submit complete script. Payment "depends on situation."
Tips: "Animation has its own world. We prefer to do things that can't be done in live action—those that exploit caricature and exaggeration."

‡**INNERQUEST COMMUNICATIONS**, 6383 Rose Lane, Carpinteria CA 93013. (805)684-9977. Producer: Don L Higley. Estab. 1987. Produces films for "a national television audience of people who are interested in the news of nature and of having a close-to-home wilderness experience of our country's natural resources. Our audience will include those who participate in the field sports and individuals who want to explore and experience the fauna and flora of the great outdoors." Buys all rights. Previously produced material acceptable. Reports in 1 month on queries; in 2 weeks on submissions. Catalog for SASE.
Needs: "We will be producing a weekly hour-long show that will be in two parts. One part will be an 18-minute location segment that will include the adventures of a biologist and a writer exploring the wonders of Moth-

er Nature. The other part will be a 36-minute studio segment in news show setting that will include a potpourri of topical wildlife, conservation, and environmental news and a report on recreational opportunities available to everyone." 16mm films. Query. Outright purchase: $25 minimum, negotiable maximum.

Tips: "Watch the show to see the format that we are producing and submit material that will be suitable for that mode. Since a good part of our show will be news format, the writing should be concise, clear and original. Brevity seems to transmit an idea more powerfully than anything else at a time when the airwaves are jammed with excessive information."

IN-SYNC, 4572 Marston Dr., Encino CA 91316. (818)708-0539. Contact: Jeff Varga. Produces films for youth-oriented audiences. "As a producer of low-budget pictures, we have an extremely competitive market. A writer need only submit intelligent, humorous scripts." Negotiates purchase of rights on an individual basis. No shot-by-shot manuscripts read. Replies only for seriously considered scripts. All need SASE.

Needs: Youth-oriented feature-length screenplays (at least 80 pages). Subject include psychological (not psycho mad slashers) thrillers, action/adventure and science fiction. No pornography. Screenplays must be properly formatted, including a 3-page treatment (double-spaced), and a topic sentence. Produces 35mm films. Submit synopsis/outline and 2 copies of completed script.

Tips: "There are presently films such as *Re-animator*, *The Gods Must Be Crazy*, etc. that can be shot from anywhere from $60,000-$1 million in budget dollars and achieve sometimes 100 times the invested dollar. We need those types of scripts with very minimal amount of locations and not needing a cast of thousands nor $40 million dollar special effects."

‡KOCH MARSCHALL PRODUCTIONS, INC., 1718 N. Mohawk St., Chicago IL 60647. (312)664-6482. Contact: Sally Marschall, Literary Division. Produces material for general film audience. Previously produced plays OK. Reports on queries in 3 months; on mss in 3 weeks.

Needs: Films (35mm). Looking for "film scripts for feature films, 1½-2 hours. Should be either dramatic and/or light comedy. No exploitation or violence." Query with samples or synopsis/outline. Makes outright purchase or pays in accordance with Writers Guild standards. Payment "depends on script."

Tips: "Originality is important. No copy-cat material." Seeks "strong story" with interesting, well developed characters."

□LEE MAGID PRODUCTIONS, Box 532, Malibu CA 90265. (213)858-7282. President: Lee Magid. Produces material for all markets, teenage-adult; commercial—even musicals. 90% freelance written. 70% of scripts produced are unagented submissions. Buys 20 scripts/year; works with 10 writers/year. Works with "many" unpublished/unproduced writers. Buys all rights or will negotiate. No previously produced material. Does not return unsolicited material. Electronic submissions acceptable via VHS video or cassette/audio. Reports in 6 weeks.

Needs: Films, sound filmstrips, phonograph records, television shows/series, videotape presentations. Currently interested in film material, either for video (television) or theatrical. "We deal with cable networks, producers, live-stage productions, etc." Works with musicals for cable TV. Prefers musical forms for video comedy. Submit synopsis/outline and resume. Pays in royalty, in outright purchase, in accordance with Writers Guild standards, or depending on author.

Tips: "We're interested in comedy material. Forget drug-related scripts."

□MEDIACOM DEVELOPMENT CORP., Box 1926, Simi Valley CA 93062. (818)991-5452. Director/Program Development: Felix Girard. 80% freelance written. Buys 10-20 scripts annually from unpublished/unproduced writers. 50% of scripts produced are unagented submissions. Query with samples. Computer printout submissions acceptable. Reports in 1 month. Buys all rights or first rights.

Needs: Produces charts; sound filmstrips; 16mm films; multimedia kits; overhead transparencies; tapes and cassettes; slides and videotape with programmed instructional print materials, broadcast and cable television programs. Publishes software ("programmed instruction training courses"). Negotiates payment depending on project.

Tips: "Send short samples of work. Especially interested in flexibility to meet clients' demands, creativity in treatment of precise subject matter. We are looking for good, fresh projects (both special and series) for cable and pay television markets. A trend in the audiovisual field that freelance writers should be aware of is the move toward more interactive video disk/computer CRT delivery of training materials for corporate markets."

□NICKELODEON MTV NETWORKS, INC., 1775 Broadway, New York NY 10019. (212)713-6409. Director of Creative Planning: Dee LaDuke. Produces material for age-specific audience aged 2-15. Now in 18 million homes. Buys negotiable rights. Reports in 1 month.

Needs: "Full channel children's programming for cable TV. Value-filled, non-violent material desired." Submit resume and programming ideas (2-3 page explanations). Phone first for information and release forms. Pays variable rate. Also utilizes writers with promotional background for short-format, on-air spots for both Nickelodeon and Nick at Nite, our overnight service of "TV for the TV generation." Submit resumes, reels and sample scripts to Betty Cohen, director on-air productions.

◻**PACE FILMS, INC.**, 411 E. 53rd Ave., New York NY 10022. (212)755-5486. President: R. Vanderbes. Produces material for a general theatrical audience. Buys all rights. Reports in 2 months.
Needs: Theatrical motion pictures. Produces 35mm films, cable tapes and cassettes. Query with samples; submit synopsis/outline or completed script. Pays in accordance with Writers Guild standards.

‡**TOM PARKER MOTION PICTURES**, 18653 Ventura Blvd., Tarzana CA 91356. (818)342-9115. President: Tom Parker. Produces material for theatre and home-video audience. Works with 5-10 scripts/year. Buys all rights. No previously produced material. Reports on mss in 3 weeks.
Needs: Films (35mm) and video. "Looking for completed scripts for low budget 'R'-rated theatrical features made for home video and shot in video." Submit synopsis/outline or completed script. Makes outright purchase of $5,000-25,000.
Tips: "Scripts must be comedy or drama. No violence, social commentaries, horror, documentaries. Nothing weird or too far out. Limited dialogue. In the theatrical market, the trend is towards fantasy and escapist films for mass audience." Prefers "R" rated light, sexy comedies and action.

PAULIST PRODUCTIONS, Box 1057, Pacific Palisades CA 90272. (213)454-0688. Contact: Story Department. 100% freelance written. *Family Specials* are geared toward senior high school students. Buys 4-6 half-hour scripts/year. WGA membership required. Computer printout submissions acceptable; no dot-matrix.
Needs: "We are looking for longer form one- to three-hour television specials and theatrical releases on people who have acted boldly on their moral convictions regarding human and/or Christian values." Submit complete script through agent only. "We are not interested in unsolicited manuscripts."
Tips: "Watch our *Family Specials* enough so that you have a strong sense of the sort of material we produce. We look for wit, originality of theme and approach, an unsentimental, yet strong and positive manner of approaching subject matter—intelligent, literate, un-cliché-ridden writing."

‡**SLR PRODUCTIONS**, Box 3266, Los Angeles CA 90078-3266. (213)876-6336. Vice President, Creative Affairs: Roberta Dacks. Produces material for national television-viewing audience. Works with 6 writers/year. Buys all rights. Previously produced material OK. Reports on mss in 3 weeks.
Needs: Films. "We are looking for treatments or screenplays for television movies and motion pictures. Topics range from true stories, dramas, comedies, etc." Submit synopsis/outline, complete script and resume. Pays in accordance with Writers' Guild standards. "For television movies, free options on material until a development deal is procured."

◻**TELEVISION PRODUCTION SERVICES CORP.**, Box 1233, Edison NJ 08818. (201)287-3626. Executive Director/Producer: R.S. Burks. Produces video music materials for major market distributor networks, etc. Buys 50-100 scripts/year. Buys all rights. Computer printout submissions OK; prefers letter-quality to dot-matrix printouts. Reports in 2 weeks.
Needs: "We do video music for record companies, MTV, HBO, etc. We use treatments of story ideas from the groups' management. We also do commercials for over-the-air broadcast and cable." We are now doing internal in-house video for display on disco or internally distributed channels. Submit synopsis/outline or completed script, and resume; include SASE.
Tips: Looks for rewrite flexibility and availability. "We have the capability of transmission electronically over the phone modem to our printer or directly onto disk for storage."

THEME SONG: A Musical and Literary Production House, 396 Watchogue Rd., Staten Island NY 10314. (718)698-4178. Director: Lawrence Nicastro. Produces material for theatre (stage/screen); radio; television (entertainment/educational documentary). Buys 50 scripts/year. Buys first rights. Previously published material OK, if a revision is sought. Reports in 1 month. "I'll answer each query individually. We enjoy newsworthy subjects and investigative/collaborative themes."
Needs: Phonographs records, tapes and cassettes and 3/4" video tape. Query. Pays negotiable royalty.
Tips: "I am interested in political lyrics/songs and in concrete criticism of American life and ways of improving our condition; also international themes or cooperative themes."

‡**BOB THOMAS PRODUCTIONS, INC.**, 60 E. 42nd St., New York NY 10165. President: Robert G. Thomas. 100% freelance written. WGA-East & West membership required.
Needs: Scripts of "mass appeal," acceptable for prime-time television audiences. Submit *only* through registered agents.

‡**VIDEO VACATION GUIDE, INC AND CINEMATRONICS INC.**, 1091 E. Commercial Blvd. (front), Ft. Lauderdale FL 33334. (305)491-8802. President: Jaf Fletcher. Produces "general travel/tourism" material. Buys 30-50 scripts/year. Buys all rights. No previously produced material. Reports in 2 weeks.
Needs: Travel videos on worldwide countries, areas and hotels. Query with samples. Outright purchase of $100-2,000.

With an increase in the number of comedy clubs, more comedians than ever have a chance to perform and most are willing to look at new material. In addition, cartoonists are always ready to approach new magazines with gags slanted to their readers. If you think your sense of humor is something others may want to share, gag writing is a satisfying hobby that can add a few extra dollars to your bank account. Collaboration between gag writers and cartoonists or between comedy writers and comedians isn't unusual. Keep in mind, though, that to comedians and cartoonists, humor is a business. Few writers can live by humor alone.

A professional approach is essential. Sending carbon copies of jokes, handwritten gags or cards bent by repeated submissions will reveal you as an amateur. Type each of your gags or jokes on a separate sheet of paper or on an index card. Submit gags in batches of 10 to 20 and always include a self-addressed, stamped envelope.

Keep careful records of your submissions. Individual cards can easily become separated, so include your name and address on the back of each card. Also include a code number in the upper left corner. A master card in your files should list the text of each joke, its code number, where and when it has been submitted and any response it received. You may also want to keep a file with a submission sheet for each market you've approached. Include the submission date and the code number of each gag sent to that particular market. If you've mailed more than one batch to the same market, keep a separate sheet for each mailing. Number each sheet and write the same number on the back of your return envelope. When your gags are returned, matching the number on the envelope with the number on the submission sheet should make it easier to check your returned material.

Many buyers hold a gag for a year or more while trying to find a market for it. "Be patient. I work from the top markets on down," says one cartoonist. If you're dealing with cartoonists who accept simultaneous submissions, be sure to inform them if a gag they are holding has been sold. If you're dealing with comedians, do not make simultaneous submissions. Wait until you receive a response or your material is returned before sending the gag to another entertainer. Since you may not be sure your material has reached a comedian, you should politely state in your cover letter that if you have not been contacted within four months, you'll assume that the comedian is not buying gags and you will market your material elsewhere.

Before choosing to write for a comedian or a cartoonist, decide which type of presentation is best for your ideas. Know the difference between a gag and a joke: comedians need one-liners and jokes, while cartoonists need material appropriate for visual gags.

If you're interested in writing gags for a cartoonist, your submission does not require an elaborate drawing or even a paragraph to set up the situation. A simple statement like "Woman says to man" usually will be sufficient. Cartoonists like to illustrate without seeing another person's interpretation of the gag. A truly funny line should set an artist's imagination to work without any additional help from the writer.

Captions should be simple and the humor universal. If you study cartoonists' work in books and magazines, you'll find that most cartoonists use timely gags that focus on the audiences' newest crazes. Avoid submitting gags that insult people's religions or nationalities; you're hoping to entertain an audience, not insult them.

Gag writers working with cartoonists are paid after the cartoonist receives a check from the publication. Magazines may pay from $10-300 per cartoon. The writer usually earns 25% commission on the selling price. The commission may go as high as 50% if the cartoonist submits a sketch and sells only the writer's gag line, not the finished cartoon.

Comedians generally buy their material one-liner at a time, although some do buy entire monologues. Payment rates for this type of writing vary greatly. Comedians may pay $10 for a one-liner, but some pay more and others less.

Although comedians are invited to be listed in *Writer's Market*, some decline because they lack the time or staff to handle unsolicited material. Others choose not to be listed because they don't want their audiences to know they don't write all their own material. But don't let the lack of a listing keep you from submitting.

Familiarize yourself with a comedian's style and subject matter and compose several jokes tailored to that performer. Send your material to the comedian in care of the theater, nightclub or TV station where he or she is performing. Remember not to send simultaneous submissions.

There is plenty of coincidental duplication of jokes; don't complicate the problem by sending the same material to different comedians. Some entertainers are hesitant to look at an unfamiliar writer's material, fearing they'll be accused of stealing ideas. If you should hear a joke very similar to one of your own, don't panic. Many jokes and stories are in the public domain and may be used by anyone. Jokes and stories that are truly your own, derived from your own life experiences, may be submitted for copyright protection (see the Appendix).

Cartoonists and comedians are not the only markets humor writers should consider. Read Sol Saks' *The Craft of Comedy Writing* (Writer's Digest Books) for information on humor writing for TV, radio, film and theatre. Many of the listings in *Writer's Market* also will consider humorous material. Some greeting card companies are interested in humorous verse, and many magazines buy short humor, anecdotes and jokes to use as fillers. When it comes to selling, don't limit your sense of humor; there are a lot of markets that could use a good laugh.

‡**BANANA TIME**, Condor Communications, Box 45, Station Z, Toronto, Ontario M5N 2Z3 Canada. Began buying jokes in 1987; buys 300-360 gags/year. Buys 30-40% of gags from freelance writers. Uses gags in magazine distributed to Canadian radio stations. Submit gags on 8½x11 paper; 10 in one batch. Reports in 2 months. Makes outright purchase of $2 (Canadian). Pays upon acceptance.
Needs: "We want zingers about boss, colleagues, wives, kids, girlfriends, etc.; one-liners on any topics suitable for radio; and gags based on current news, trends and fads" No "ethnic, racist or sexist material, 'blue' material, profanity or tasteless jokes based on disasters."
Tips: "As with any writing, know your market. Observe the world around you and lampoon that which you find ridiculous. If you read the paper, watch TV and observe your fellow man, you'll never run out of ideas for jokes. U.S. writers, please send SAE with 1 IRC. U.S. stamps are no good in Canada. A sample issue of *Banana Time* and a set of guidelines are available for $2. Payable to Condor Communications."

EDOUARD BLAIS, 2704 Parkview Blvd., Minneapolis MN 55422. (612)588-5249. Holds 250 gags/year. Works with 10-15 gagwriters/year. Prefers to work with published/established writers. Sells to men's, sports, fitness, health, education, family, outdoor, camping and fishing publications. Recently sold material to *Network*, *Milwaukee Journal*, and *Globe*. Buys 25-50% of the gags received from freelance writers. Submit gags on 3x5 slips; 10-12 in one batch. Reports in 1 week. Sells cartoons for $10-50; pays gagwriters $2-12. Pays 25% commission. Writer's guidelines for SAE and 1 first class stamp.
Needs: Erotic, women's magazines, health, fitness, hobbies, education, family, outdoors, camping, and fishing gags, rural (farm) etc. Looks for sight gags—no captions, or a minimum amount of words. "I accept gags I feel match up well with my style of drawing."
Tips: "I would especially like to receive gags on family—especially young married couples, not necessarily dealing with sex (that's OK, too), but all aspects of young family life. Gag writers should be aware of what's going on in all phases of society, the style of language being used, and new developments (like fast food, microwave, G-spot, etc.). I am relatively new to cartooning (and will complete my sixth year this March)."

Market conditions are constantly changing! If this is 1989 or later, buy the newest edition of Writer's Market *at your favorite bookstore or order directly from* Writer's Digest Books.

DAN BORDERS, 191 Alton Rd., Galloway OH 43119. (614)878-3528. Holds 35 gags/year. Works with 7 gagwriters/year. Sells to computer magazines of all kinds, trade journals, many general interest and electronic gags. Has sold material to *Computer World*, *Info World*, *Dr. Dobb's Journal*, *Radio-Electronics* and *Reader's Digest*. Eager to work with new/unpublished writers. Buys 25% of the gags received from freelance writers. Submit gags on 3x5 cards or slips. Submit 15 gags in one batch. Sells cartoons for $25-50. Pays 25% commission.
Needs: Electronics and computer gags, and environment, family and angel gags. No "girlie gags." Looks for humorists with dry humor.
Tips: "Many computer magazines are buying computer cartoons. Also electronic 'toons' are selling well. I am always ready to see good, well-thought-out ideas."

ASHLEIGH BRILLIANT, 117 W. Valerio St., Santa Barbara CA 93101. Sold about 315 cartoons last year. Self-syndicated and licensed to publications and manufacturers worldwide. Reports in 2 weeks. Pays $25.
Needs: "My work is so different from that of any other cartoonist that it must be carefully studied before any gags are submitted. Any interested writer not completely familiar with my work should first send $2 and SASE for my catalog of 1,000 copyrighted examples. Otherwise, their time and mine will be wasted."

LEONARD BRUCE, AKA "LEO", Leoleen-Durck Creations, Suite 226, Box 2767, Jackson TN 38302. (901)668-1205. Holds 20 gags/month. Works with 4 gagwriters/year. Works with a small number of new/unpublished writers each year; eager to work with new/unpublished writers. Sells to newspapers, charity publications, space publications, science fiction and science fiction movie magazines, comic book publications, and animal care publications. Submit gags on 3x5 cards. Submit 12 gags in one batch. Pays 10% commission. Buys first serial rights. Reports in 2 weeks.
Needs: Looking for gags on science fiction movie themes, comic book hero themes, themes on computers, space travel, UFOs, life on other planets, "aliens" trying to cope with our world. Also a Berry's World theme; one guy in crazy situations. No political, foreign affairs or white collar themes. Will consider gags for cartoon strips: Leotoons (science fiction "alien" themes); Fred (space exploration themes); and It's a Mad World (crazy situations in our insane world). Looks for offbeat gags, weird humor, "taking normal situations and turning them into 'sight gags' or word gags. As an example: Berry's World or Herman gag themes."
Tips: "I look for quality and good typing ability in a gagwriter. Gagwriters should be aware that gags *have* to be very funny or the whole cartoon doesn't work or sell. The gag is the main reason a cartoon sells nowadays. We are a 2 person operation and the gagwriter should have patience in working with me on the artistic and financial part of the business. Also the gag writer should work *with* the artist to help 'sell' his gags also in strip form. I would especially like to receive gags on alien life and science fiction."

DON COLE, 12 Lehigh St., Dover NJ 07801-2510. (201)328-9153. Holds 312 gags/year. Sells to general interest publications; also trade journals. Worked on upcoming Chipmunk movie *The Chipmunks Great Adventure*. Works with 15 gagwriters/year. Buys 5% of the gags received from freelance writers. Submit gags on 3x5 slips; about 12 (or 1 ounce) per batch. Reports in 3 days. Sell cartoons for $10-400; pays gagwriters $2.50-100. Pays 25% commission.
Needs: General; trade journal; comic strip; or single panel gags; "*anything* funny." No off-color gags. Especially wants "topical humor, satire, anything funny, for a general audience or related to a trade."
Tips: "Send *original* work only. No gags from old magazines or cartoon books. Each gag based on its own merit. Realize that a hold is not a sale. Lengthy correspondence and status reports are usually a waste of time and money not budgeted for. I file some gags for later use in making up special batches, drawing the funniest or best slanted gags for a particular market first. After a time, I return gags I no longer want."

THOMAS W. DAVIE, 28815 4th Place S, Federal Way WA 98003. Buys 75 gags/year. Works with 10 gagwriters/year. Has sold to *Medical Economics*, *Sports Afield*, King Features, *Chevron U.S.A.*, *Rotarian*, *Saturday Evening Post*, *Ladies' Home Journal*, *Playgirl* and *Boys' Life*. Buys 30% of the gags received from freelance writers. Gags should be typed on 3x5 slips. Prefers batches of 5-25. Sells cartoons for $10-450. Pays 25% commission. Reports in 1 month. No IRC.
Needs: General gags, medicals, mild girlies, sports (hunting and fishing), business and travel gags. No pornography.
Tips: "I'm often overstocked—please don't flood me with gags."

LEE DeGROOT, Box 115, Ambler PA 19002. Pays 25% on sales.
Needs: Interested in receiving studio greeting card ideas. "I draw up each idea in color before submitting to greeting card publishers, therefore, giving the editors a chance to visualize the idea as it would appear when printed . . . and thus increasing enormously the chances of selling the idea."

‡**STEVE DICKENSON**, 1354 Farmer Road, Conyers GA 30207. "Just initiated buying gags. Work with one syndicate." Recent sales to United Cartoonist Syndicate. Submit gags on 3x5 cards; 12-24 in one batch. Re-

ports in 1 month. Makes outright purchase of $15.

Needs: *"Especially* need material focusing on the pathos of pubescent boys (school, girlfriends, parents, zits, shaving, etc.). Today's teens are sophisticated, like it or not. Keep the humor in the same vein. I am not all opposed to material that is bizarre or a bit off the wall. Just keep it clean and funny. As my client newspaper list increases, so will the fees that I pay."

Tips: "Understatement works well, however, we tend to forget that the art of cartooning entails drawing funny pictures. I love visual humor just as much. Would *love* to see warm and appealing humor regarding senior citizens. Please, no stereotypical 'aches and pains' gags. Keep it in a positive mode, one that best addresses their problems and joys."

NORM DREW, Laurier House, Suite 608-L, 1600 Beach Ave., Vancouver, British Columbia V6G 1Y6 Canada. Sells to general urban magazines and daily and weekly newspapers, trade journals, TV, film, greeting card and novelty companies. Submit 3x5 cards or slips; 12-20 in a batch. Reports in 1 week on submissions. Works with both published and new writers. Pays gagwriters 25%. General gags: 25-40% reprint. Send SAE with IRCs or loose U.S. stamps.

Needs: Subjects include urban lifestyles, consumer, TV viewers, bicycling, photography, home video, media trades—TV, radio, press, entertainment—film, stock market, apartment living, travel, hobbies: model building, model railroads, shortwave radio, collectors: stamps, coins, and flea market hunters, gardening. Young urbans, senior citizens, and contemporary kids views, foibles. No puns, porn, prurience, 'sick' subjects; no religion, racial, or stereotypes. No weak play-on-words or illustrated "jokes". "I look for fresh, original, healthy humor, contemporary urban foibles; subtle, classy observations; accurate inside knowledge of the subject; visual irony, imminent victim gags; good visual situation sense; fresh, zany, slightly irreverent, sassy approach; attuned to current absurdities, timeless universal human frailties. Condense punchline to its punchiest minimal. I may reword/restage gag for stronger visual impact. Gag writer still will get 25%."

‡DUCK & COVER COMEDY GROUP, Box 53236, Philadelphia PA 19105. (215)626-0982. Began buying jokes in 1985; buys 6-8 gags/year. Buys 20% of gags from freelance writers. Recordings sent to client radio stations and distributors of airline in-flight entertainment. Submit gags by scripts or cassette tapes; 1-3 in one batch. Reports in 1 month. Pays $35-50 for each script; negotiable amount for completed tapes. Pays after the piece is produced.

Needs: Short radio scripts—absolutely nothing over 90 seconds, preferably under one minute. Script should stand on its own without a lot of involved production. "No 'wacky' stuff or impersonations. We're looking for thought-provoking socially relevant material. Political and cultural stuff is OK too."

"FRANK", 900 Karlaney Ave., Cayce SC 29033. Holds 200 gags/year. Sells to trade journals and general interest publications. Works with 50 gagwriters/year. Buys 5% of the gags received from freelance writers. Submit on 3x5 slips. Reports in 2 weeks. Sells cartoons for $15-300; pays gagwriters $5-100. Pays 33⅓% commission "upon receipt of my check from the publication." Submit seasonal material 6 months in advance.

Needs: General interest, family, business, medical. No sex. "Let me see really fresh and funny material." Rarely considers word-play or multi-panel cartoons.

Tips: "Know the difference between a gag and a joke. Jokes are for comedians, gags, for cartoonists. I see too many jokes. Also, don't feel pressured to send me a certain number of gags in each batch. And be patient after a ' hold. ' I keep some cartoons circulating for 2 or 3 years."

DAVE GERARD, Box 692, Crawfordsville IN 47933. (317)362-3373. Holds 100 gags/year. Sells 10-20 freelance cartoons per month for magazines and periodicals. Recently sold material to *National Enquirer*, *D.A.C. News*, *Wall Street Journal*, *Good Housekeeping*, *Better Homes & Gardens*, *Medical Economics*, and King Features' *Laff-A-Day*. Receives 500 gags/week and uses approximately 10. Submit gags on 3x5 cards; 10 in one batch. Reports in 2 weeks. Sells cartoons for $50-300. Pays 25% commission.

Needs: General interest and sports, business, family and upbeat gags on pertinent and timely topics, like taxes, inflation, computers, etc. No *"prisoners hanging on wall, kings and queens, talking animals,* or *put-down humor.* I will be frank if material is not what I like. No erotic material."

Tips: "I like good sight gag material and short captions; also no-caption gags. I'm aware that one-liners do sell as cartoons but prefer gags that need a cartoon for full effect."

GLASSMAN, Box 46664, Los Angeles CA 90046. Buys 75 gags/year. Buys 50% of gags from freelance writers. Has performed on talk shows, at nightclubs and at conventions. Will be performing on talk shows, at comedy clubs, and at one night comedy concerts in the next year. Submit gags in one-time form typed on 8½x11 paper. No limit to number submitted on one subject. Reports in 2 weeks. Pays $15 minimum/line. Pays after the gag is performed (in a workshop situation).

Needs: Will specify slant and topic. "I like as many one liners on that specific subject as I can get." Material must be acceptable on network TV.

‡**THE GREAT MIDWESTERN ICE CREAM COMPANY**, Box 1717, Fairfield IA 52556. (515)472-7595. Holds unlimited number of gags/year. Uses in newspaper ads and articles, radio ads and interviews and TV ads and interviews. We are frequently intereviewed by TV, radio and newspapers. Submit gags on 3x5 cards or slips. Reports in 1 week. Makes outright purchase of $25 per joke.
Needs: "Funny and/or clever, highly original quips, jokes, puns, limericks and poems about ice cream in general and great midwestern ice cream in specific. Please don't send the I scream/you scream poem."
Tips: "We love originality."

MEL HELITZER, Scripps Hall of Journalism, Ohio University, Athens OH 45701. (614)594-5608. Buys 100-150/year. Uses gags as a master of ceremonies at banquets. Works with 5-6 gagwriters/year. Eager to work with new/unpublished writers. Buys 1% of the gags received from freelance writers. Submit gags on 3x5 cards; 10 or more in a batch. Reports in 1 week. Pays gagwriters $5-10. Pays on acceptance.
Needs: University-related material from professor's point of view. Subjects include faculty, administration, students, sports and curriculum. Short one-liners or one-paragraph ancedotes. No student drugs, sex or alcohol. "No blue language, but doubles entendres are OK."

CHARLES HENDRICK JR., Old Fort Ave., Kennebunkport ME 04046. (207)967-4412. Buys several gags/year; sold 50-60 cartoons last year. Prefers to work with published/established writers. Sells to newspapers, magazines and local markets. Works with 6 gagwriters/year. Buys 5-10% of the gags received from freelance writers. Submit 8 gags at a time. Sells cartoons for $25-200. Pays 50% of net commission or negotiates commission. Reports in 1 month.
Needs: General family, trade (hotel, motel, general, travel, vacationers), safe travel ideas—any vehicle, and medical. Gags must be clean; no lewd sex. Mild sex OK.

DAVID R. HOWELL, Box 170, Porterville CA 93258. (209)781-5885. Holds 100+ gags/year. Sells to magazines, trade journals, etc. Has sold material to *True Detective*, *TV Guide*, *National Enquirer*, *Woman's World*, King Features, *Cartoons*, etc. Works with 30-40 gagwriters/year. Prefers to work with published/established writers. Buys 5% of gags received from freelance writers. Submit gags on 3x5 cards or slips; 6-12 in one batch. Reports in 1 week. Sells cartoons for $25-300; pays gagwriters $6.25-75. Pays 25% commission.
Needs: Cars, medical, farm, computer, specific topics. "No politics, sex, taboo topics. No old stuff. I need fresh, original approaches."

REAMER KELLER, 4500 S. Ocean Blvd., Palm Beach FL 33480. (305)582-2436.
Needs: Prefers general and visual gags. Pays 25%.

MILO KINN, 1413 SW Cambridge St., Seattle WA 98106. Holds approximately 200 gags/year; sells 100-200 cartoons/year. Has sold to *Medical Economics*, *Machine Design*, *American Machinist*, *Infoworld*, *Review of the News*, *Private Practice* and many farm publications and trade journals, etc. Works with 8-10 writers annually. Buys 25% of the gags received from freelance writers. Sells cartoons for $15-100 "and up, on occasion." Pays 25% commission.
Needs: Medical, machinist, dental, farm, male slant, woman, captionless, adventure and family gags. Sells farm, medical, office, factory, crime and general cartoons.
Tips: "There seem to be fewer markets. Computers seem to be out."

LO LINKERT, 1333 Vivian Pl., Port Coquitlam, British Columbia V3C 2T9 Canada. Works with 20 gagwriters/year. Has sold to most major markets. Prefers batches of 10-15 gags. Sells cartoons for $50-600. Pays 25% commission. Returns rejected material in 1 week. Enclose SAE and 30¢ U.S. postage.
Needs: Clean, general, topical, medical, family, office, outdoors gags; captionless, pro woman sophisticated ideas. "Make sure your stuff is funny. No spreads." Wants "action gags—not two people saying something funny. No puns, dirty sex, drugs, drunks, racial or handicapped. Religion gags must be in good taste."
Tips: "I look for a gagwriter who sends few, but great, gags. I hate to be swamped by one writer who dumps bundles of old gags on me."

ART McCOURT, Box 210346, Dallas TX 75211. (214)339-6865. Began selling cartoons in 1950. Works with 15 gagwriters/year. Sells 700 cartoons/year to general/family, medical, farm and male magazines. Has sold material to *Ford Times*, *Furrow*, *Agway Coop*, *Medical Management*, McNaught Syndicate, *National Enquirer*, *American Legion* and King Features. Prefers to work with published/established writers; works with a small number of new/unpublished writers each year. Buys 50% of the gags received from freelance writers. Submit 15-20 gags at one time on 3x5 cards or slips. Sells cartoons for $10-340. Pays 25% commission. Reports in 2 days.
Needs: Family/general, medical (no gripes about doctors' bills), male, computers, hunting, fishing, and farm gags. "Something unique and up-to-date." No "crowds, ghouls, TV, mothers-in-law, talking animals or desert islands."

Tips: "I look for original, crisp wordage and fresh approach with minimal descriptions. Don't just send a punchline that has no background. Read the newspapers; be topical. Writers shouldn't be impatient; gags can make the rounds for several years."

THERESA McCRACKEN, 910 Constitution NE, Washington DC 20002. (202)547-1373. Holds 100 gags/year. Sells mostly to trade journals, but also to some general interest magazines and newspapers. Recently sold material to *Vegetarian Times*, *Computer Digest*, *American Medical News*, *Legal Times*, *CEO* and the *The Saturday Evening Post*. 10% of cartoons sold uses gagwriters' material. Sells cartoons for $10-100; pays gagwriters $2.50-25. Submit gags on 3x5 cards or slips; 10-20 in one batch. Pays 25% commission.
Needs: "Since I sell mostly to trade journals in one batch, I prefer to receive 10 to 20 gags on one subject at a time. My topic needs change monthly. My favorite cartoons are captionless or ones with very short cut-lines."

REX F. MAY (BALOO), Box 3108, West Lafayette IN 47906. (317)463-3689. Holds 500 gags/year. Works with 15 gagwriters/year. Sells to general interest and some girlie magazines. Has sold material to *Good Housekeeping*, *National Enquirer*, *Hustler*, *Cavalier*, *Woman's World*, *Wall Street Journal*, King Features, *Medical Economics*, *Saturday Evening Post*, *Easyriders*, *Datamation*, *Leadership*, *New Woman*, *Changing Times* and *Christian Science Monitor*. Buys less than 1% of the gags received from freelance writers. Submit gags on 3x5 slips; no more than 100 in a batch. Sells cartoons for $15-300; pays gagwriters $3.75-75. Pays 25% commission. Reports in 2 weeks.
Needs: "I don't need many gags. A top gagwriter myself, I write 15,000 gags a year for many top cartoonists. I still use gags by others if they fit my style. You probably should look my style over before you submit. I don't do much background or use many props. It's a very simple style. What I want is general-to-weird material. I sell weird non-girlie stuff to the girlie magazines, so don't send standard girlies. Simplicity and shortness of caption are the way to go.
Tips: "Cartoonists, be aware that I have plenty of gags on hand. Especially interested in writing for syndicated features, panel or strip. It takes me about three years currently, to try a cartoon from the top to the bottom markets, so be patient."

THOMAS PRISK, Star Rt., Box 52, Michigamme MI 49861. Sells to trade journals, newsletters, magazines, etc. Published in *The Bulletin of The Atomic Scientists*, *Sun*, *Globe*, *National Examiner*, *Byline*, *Medical Economics*, *Creative Computing*. Holds with the *Saturday Evening Post*, *National Enquirer*, *Good Housekeeping*, etc. Submit gags on 3x5 slips, 10 or more to a batch. Pays 25% commission. Reports in 3 weeks. "Foreign writers, use only American postage; I don't have the time or patience for the postal coupons."
Needs: Medical, dental, computer, office, captionless and with short captions. "I would also like to see religious gags with the Christian slant and much more off-beat humor." No porn or racial prejudice slants.
Tips: "Unless gags are legibly handwritten, they should be typed out. The gags I hold are slanted to my style and market needs. Rejected gags are not necessarily considered unsalable. I look for off-beat material that takes an old or popular theme and gives it a special twist. SASE *must* be included in each batch and in *all* inquiries if a response is desired. If requested, a held gag will be returned to the writer, otherwise, I will hold it until sold, or until I reconsider the gag and return it at a later date. Will also create cartoons to illustrate articles. Simply send me a copy of the article prior to publication and I will quickly draw a cartoon to tie-in with its theme. I will do this for a commission of 25%."

‡LARRY ROBERTSON, 7837 SE Harrison, Portland OR 97215. (503)775-5520. Holds approximately 25 gags/year. Sells to trade journals. Recent sales to *Phi Delta Kappan*, *Bureau of Business Practice*, Official Detective Group, and *American Machinist*. Submit gags on 3x5 cards or slips; 10 or more in one batch. Reports in 2 weeks. Pays 25% percentage arrangement.
Needs: "I'm looking for close tight slants for magazines I submit to. The writer should contact me first so I can write in detail what I need instead of just sending me gags he has in stock. I would *not* like to see gags that have been in circulation for a long time. I don't want any erotic or dirty gags."
Tips: "I find too many general gags being sent that will not sell to many trade journals. I would like the writer when first contacting me to describe what publications his gags have been selling to."

DAN ROSANDICH, Pilgrim Route, Box 101A, Houghton MI 49931. (906)482-6234. Holds 250 gags/year. Fulltime magazine cartoonist who will pay 25% of any holds that sell. Has sold and sells to 150 different publications in last 10 years.
Needs: Captionless gags only. "They can be about anything—just try me and we'll take it from there. Please note if you send any ideas which are not captionless, you'll be wasting your time and your postage."

TER SCOTT, Box 305, Lake Nebagamon WI 54849. (715)374-2525. Holds 100-300 gags/year. Works with 15-30 gagwriters/year. Sells to trade journals, newspapers and advertisers. Submit gags on 3x5 slips; 10-25 in one batch. Sells cartoons for $25-100. Pays 25% commission plus occasional bonuses. Reports in 2 weeks.

Needs: "I will look at anything but hardcore, girlies and racial prejudice and prefer general, religious, farm, sales and trade journal material. I provide a list of markets and currently submit cartoons to my regular gagwriters as these accounts become stocked or change often. I always need topical and seasonal material for Classified Comics newspaper strip, sales magazines, and ideas for greeting cards (nothing risque), magazines and trade journals (in subjects such as salesmanship, business) and general family humor, etc."

Tips: "Forget resumes, fancy paper, etc. Humor is what I need. Readable 3x5 cards are fine. Also, I'd like to see a batch on one subject like farming, sales, etc., making sure to pick on the right folks. For instance, a farm magazine shouldn't pick on farmers, they're the heros and the audience. Sales people look at their sales journal and want to see their customers or procedures picked on, not *themselves*. Gags rejected are humor that should be for standup comedians, those submitted on anything other than usual 3x5 cards and those with postage due. Submissions without SASE will not be responded to."

GODDARD SHERMAN, 1214 McRee Dr., Valdosta GA 31602. Holds 200 gags/year. Sells to general, medical and youth publications. Has sold material to *National Enquirer*, *Saturday Evening Post*, *Boys' Life*, *Medical Economics*, *Modern Maturity* and *Woman's World*. Submit gags on 3x5 slips; 15-20 gags in one batch. Reports in 2 weeks. Pays 33⅓% commission.

Needs: Prefers captionless gags, or very short captions; funny action in picture. No overly technical settings. Avoid overworked themes, such as invention of wheel, natives boiling missionaries, desert islands, etc.

JOHN W. SIDE, 335 Wells St., Darlington WI 53530. Interested in "small-town, local happening gags with a general slant." Pays 25% commission. Sample cartoon $1. Returns rejected material "immediately."

STEWART SLOCUM, (signs work Stewart), 18 Garretson Road, White Plains NY 10604. (914)948-6682. Holds about 50 gags/year. Works with 20 gagwriters/year. Sells to general interest, women's and sports publications. Recently sold material to *McCalls*, *Family Circle*, *New Woman*, *Golf Journal*, King Features, *Good Housekeeping* and the *Wall Street Journal*. Sells up to half of the gags held from freelance writers. Submit gags on 3x5 slips; 10-15 in one batch. Sells cartoons for $15-325; pays gagwriters $3.75-81.50. Pays 25% commission. Reports in 2 days.

Needs: General, family, women-in-business, computer and sports gags. The best markets for cartoons/gags in 1988 will be women's magazines and publications that publish general and business humor.

Tips: "I would especially like to receive gags on women in family and business situations, and on golf, baseball, and important holidays."

‡SPANKY, Box 822084, Dallas TX 75382-2084. Began buying jokes in 1984; buys 75-100 gags/year. Buys 15% of gags from freelance writers. Uses gags for comedy clubs and college performances nationwide. Submit gags on 8½x11 paper; no limit to number in one batch. Reports in 1 month. Makes outright purchase of $5-10. Pays upon acceptance.

Needs: "I perform in character, a loveable but very confused, guy (i.e. Jim on 'Taxi'). I use observational humor: a unique view of everyday events." Currently needs material for "Jobs I've been Fired from," "Practical Jokes" and "Questions About Life in America."

Tips: "I demand originality. Don't send anything that even sounds a little familiar to another comic's joke. Although I try to respond in 30 days, I am often on the road and don't get to review the material until weeks after it has been mailed."

SUZANNE STEINIGER, 9373 Whitcomb, Detroit MI 48228. (313)838-5204. Holds 100+ gags/year. Sells to farm magazines, sex-type periodicals, women's and general interest magazines and Charlton Publications. Works with 3-4 gagwriters/year. Prefers to work with published/established writers. Buys 30% of the gags received from freelance writers. Submit gags on 3x5 cards or 3x5 slips. Submit 30 or more gags in one batch. Pays 25% commission. Reports in 1 week.

Needs: "For the present I would like to see gags *National Lampoon* style. I guess you could say general interest, but I'm looking for crazy *new* ideas. I like to see everything except detailed scenes. Writers should simplify their words and scenes. I am working on a cartoon strip. I will not say what the strip is about for fear of someone accidentally getting the same idea. I am looking for a patient writer, someone I can discuss my idea with and someone to *help*. I do like gags that are funny and less detailed. For example, a writer should say 'man to woman in restaurant' instead of 'man in crowded restaurant, waiter looking surprised to the woman next to him.' There should be less confusion. I like quick and simple gags the best. I would especially like to receive greeting card ideas in 1988."

Tips: "Today the gags are funnier visually. The scene should have fewer props. Fewer props made the great comics such as the Marx Brothers very funny and popular, not to mention Peanuts. There should be fewer details and more concentration on the joke, the entire *gag*. I like writers who do a good job of writing and leave the drawing to us (cartoonists). I'm also looking for simple animal gags. Animal gags are my specialty. I'd like them to be slanted for the *New Yorker* and *Saturday Evening Post*. I recently sold to the *Post* and I hope to sell to *The New Yorker*. That's my goal. And another one of my goals is to sell my one panel features to the syndicate of my choice."

‡JOHN STINGER, Box 350, Stewartsville NJ 08886. Interested in general business gags. Would like to see more captionless sight gags. Currently doing a syndicated panel on business. Has sold to major markets. "Index cards are fine, but keep gags short." Pays 25% commission; "more to top writers." Bought about 25 gags last year. Can hold unsold gags for as long as a year.

FRANK TABOR, 2817 NE 292nd Ave., Camas WA 98607. (206)834-3355. Began selling cartoons in 1947. Holds 200 gags/year. Works with 20 gagwriters/year. Sells to trade journals. Recently sold material to *American Medical News*, *American Machinist*, *Management Accounting*, *Computing*, *Chesapeake Bay*, *Tooling & Production*, *True Detective*, *Espionage*, *Medical Tribune*, *Northern Logger*, and *Timber Harvesting*. Works with a small number of new/unpublished writers each year. Buys 5% of the gags received from freelance writers. Submit gags on 3x5 slips; 10-20 in one batch. Sells cartoons for $7.50-150; pays gagwriters $2-25. Pays 25-30% commission. Reports in 2 days.
Needs: Police; detective; fishing; health and fitness; prison situations; salesman; medical (must be funny for the doctor—no gags on big doctor bills); industrial (shop gags OK); machine shop (welding); office and accounting gags. "Cartoon spreads are wide open." No gags on subjects not listed above. "I receive too much material written for the general markets and not nearly enough gags on the subjects I ask for. I look for situations in which the cartoon carries the punch; I don't care for the one-liner or illustrated joke. I need trade gags by writers who know or who will study the trade they're writing about."
Tips: "Not enough writers are trying to write for the trades. They're too easily won over by the big rates at the major markets. I have lots of trades paying $35 to $225, and they're begging for cartoons. I am interested in reviewing ideas on strips and panels for syndication."

ISSAM TEWFIK, #701, 2400 Carling Ave., Ottawa, Ontario K2B 7H2 Canada. (613)828-5239. Holds 300 gags/year. Sells to general interest magazines, trade journals, men's and women's publications and newspapers. Has sold material to *Hospital Supervisor Bulletin* and *Accent on Living*. Works with 20 gagwriters/year. Eager to work with new/unpublished writers. Buys 20% of the gags received from freelance writers. Submit gags on 3x5 slips. Submit 10 or more gags in one batch. Sells cartoons for $25-100; pays gagwriters $3-10. Pays 25% commission. Reports in 1 week.
Needs: General, family, erotic, sports, law, military, insurance, medical, computers, children, detective, cars, old age, management, outdoor, money, trucking, etc. Prefers gags that are slanted towards a specific subject and a magazine. Research the magazine and slant towards its requirements. "I will consider eagerly a well conceived strip or panel with well-defined characters and theme (e.g., family, animal, professional, children and single people)."
Tips: "Identify a need either in a specific magazine or a syndicate and let us work together to produce something marketable. Slanting to the different publications is the key to success."

BOB THAVES, Box 67, Manhattan Beach CA 90266. Pays 25% commission. Returns rejected material in 1-2 weeks. May hold unsold gags indefinitely.
Needs: Gags "dealing with anything except raw sex. Also buys gags for syndicated (daily and Sunday) panel, Frank & Ernest. I prefer offbeat gags for that, although almost any general gag will do."

BARDULF UELAND, Halstad MN 56548. Has sold to over 90 different publications. Works with 12 gagwriters/year. Submit 12-15 gags/batch. Pays 30% commission. Reports in 1-3 days, but holds unsold gags indefinitely unless return is requested.
Needs: General, family, education. No sex.

JOSEPH F. WHITAKER, 2522 Percy Ave., Orlando FL 32818. (305)298-8311. Holds 100 gags/year. Works with 6-7 gagwriters/year. Sells all types of gags. Recently sold material to *Star*, *National Enquirer*, *National Catholic News*, McNaught Syndicate and women's magazines. Prefers to work with published/established writers; works with a small number of new/unpublished writers each year. Buys 60% of the gags received from freelance writers. Submit gags on 3x5 slips; 10-15 in one batch. Sells cartoons for $10-300. Pays 25% commission. Reports in 2 weeks.
Needs: All types of gags. The best markets for cartoons/gags in 1988 will be syndicates, girlie, women, farm, advertising and insurance.
Tips: "I look for captionless gags."

Greeting Card Publishers

There is a great deal of competition in the greeting card market—one publisher estimates his firm receives 200,000 submissions each year and buys only 200. Although the numbers may be discouraging, the alternative card market has experienced a high growth rate in the past few years. And editorial directors at greeting card companies say writers who can deliver the old messages of love, sympathy and congratulations in new ways are still in demand. "We're always looking for a new approach," says Susan Schwartz, editorial director at Carolyn Bean Publishing. "If we like it, we'll try it."

To develop new approaches, greeting card writers should make it a practice to study the market. Industry reports say 80-90% of greeting cards are purchased by women. Cards are most often sent for birthdays and most buyers prefer humorous cards. Companies are reporting an increased use of humor, even in sentiments, and a trend toward more direct statements of sentiments.

In addition to birthdays, card ideas are always needed for life transitions: birth, death, marriage and graduation. The growing alternative card market is also producing cards that deal irreverently with occasions like job promotions, retirements, diets and divorces. Risque, insult and outrageous humor cards are popular. Many card companies also consider ideas for "added dimension" cards with parts ranging from small moving pieces to an electronic piano card with a working keyboard. Another company developed cards in the shape of computer floppy disks.

Contemporary cards also are using more gags and everyday language than rhymes. If you decide to use rhyme, keep your verses short and don't use overworked rhyming words. Reading your verses and puns aloud can help you determine if the rhythms flow smoothly.

If a company that interests you offers guidelines or a market list, send for these before submitting your card ideas. Submission requirements and definitions of the different types of cards may vary slightly from company to company. These guidelines will acquaint you with the company's preferences and requirements. Always include a self-addressed, stamped envelope with your request.

Greeting card companies usually acquire all rights to the verses they buy. A writer may be able to negotiate rights if presenting a complete concept for a promotion series. Such a series incorporates an original character or a special theme in greeting cards and subsidiary product lines. Many companies also require writers to provide a release form, guaranteeing the material submitted is original and has not been sold elsewhere. If a company provides you with a release form, be sure you understand the terms before signing it.

To submit conventional greeting card material, type or neatly print your verses on 4x6 or 3x5 slips of paper or index cards. Don't assume that including your name and address in a cover letter will be sufficient information for your card ideas. The usual submission is 5 to 15 cards, and they can easily become separated from your cover letter. You should type your name and address on the back of each. To avoid sending duplicate submissions to the same publisher, you may want to include an identification code on each card. Establish a master card for each idea and keep track of where and when it was submitted and its purchase or return date. Some writers find it useful to begin their code with a letter signifying the type of card, such as B for birthday. Larry Sandman's *A Guide to Greeting Card Writing* (Writer's Digest Books) suggests following this code with the first letter of each of the first three words of your verse. Keep all the cards you submit to a company in one batch and assign the batch a submission number. Write this number on the back of your return SASE to help you match up your verses if they are returned to you.

To submit humorous or studio card ideas, fold sheets of paper into card dummies about the size and shape of an actual card, or use index cards. Unless your idea relies on a visual gag, or you are artistically inclined, it's best not to sketch in a design for your card. For ideas that use attachments, try to include the item on your dummy. For mechanical card ideas, many of which use pop-ups or sliding parts, you must make a workable mechanical dummy. Although these types of cards are extra work for the writer, most companies pay more for attachment and mechanical card ideas.

Before submitting your card ideas to a company, always consider their latest lines of cards. In addition to the market lists and guidelines many companies offer, study the card racks. Notice the types of cards people buy. You may find clerks in card stores have valuable observations on the types of cards most popular with their customers. If you want to write greeting cards, also think about the type of card and occasion for sending it that would entice you to buy. And most of all, think about the message you would want to receive or give. "Have a specific person or personal experience in mind as you write," counsels Blue Mountain Arts editorial manager Patricia Wayant.

‡ACCORD PUBLICATIONS, 1a Mt. Vernon St., Ridge Field Park NJ 07660. (201)440-3210. 20% freelance written. Buys 60 freelance ideas/samples per year; receives 300 annually. Submit seasonal/holiday material 1½ years in advance. Buys negotiable rights. Pays on publication. Free writer's guidelines/market list. Market list is regularly revised.
Needs: Conventional, humorous and juvenile. Will consider ideas for musical cards, assemble-it-yourself cards or other unusual types of greeting cards. Pays $150/card idea. Pays 5% royalty.
Tips: "Locate an outlet for our cards in your area and study our requirements." We have difficulty finding "cards that are different from the traditional folded-board printed cards. Growth areas are cut-out cards or any cards with an added dimension."

AMBERLEY GREETING CARD CO., 11510 Goldcoast Dr., Cincinnati OH 45249. (513)489-2775. Editor: Ned Stern. 90% freelance written. Bought 250 freelance ideas/samples last year; receives an estimated 25,000 submissions annually. Reports in 1 month. Material copyrighted. Buys all rights. Pays on acceptance. Writer's guidelines for business size SAE and 1 first class stamp. Market list is regularly revised.
Needs: Humorous, informal, sensitive and studio. No seasonal material or poetry. Prefers unrhymed verses/ideas. Humorous cards sell best. Pays $40/card idea.
Tips: "Amberley publishes specialty lines, primarily novelty and humorous studio greeting cards. We accept freelance ideas, including risque and nonrisque. Make it short and to the point. Nontraditional ideas are selling well. Include SASE (with correct postage) for return of rejects."

AMERICAN GREETINGS, 10500 American Rd., Cleveland OH 44144. (216)252-7300. Contact: Director-Creative Recruitment. No unsolicited material. "We like to receive a letter of inquiry describing education or experience, or a resume first. We will then screen those applicants and request samples from those that interest us."

ARGUS COMMUNICATIONS, 1 DLM Park, Allen TX 75002. (214)248-6300. Editor: Mrs. Martee Phillips. 70% freelance written. Buys 200-300 sentiments for line, and 350-400 for test. Bought 200 freelance ideas/samples last year; receives an estimated 20,000 submissions annually. Submit seasonal/holiday material 1 year in advance. Reports in 3-6 weeks. Purchases right for card, poster and postcards. Pays on acceptance. Submission guidelines available for business size SASE.
Needs: Humorous, informal, sensivity, studio, and unique "lifestyle" concepts. No traditional sentiments, rhymed verse or poetry. Prefers humorous sentiments/ideas. Pays $50-110, or may negotiate for a total concept. $25 test fee paid for each sentiment held for testing.
Other Production Lines: Postcards, posters and promotions.
Tips: "Greeting cards are a personalized, 'me-to-you' form of communication that express a wish for the recipient, a greeting, or an expression of endearment. Concentrate on warm humor that supports the relationship. Writers should focus on humorous birthday and friendship material. Target audience is females 18-45."

CAROLYN BEAN PUBLISHING, LTD., 2230 W. Winton Ave., Hayward CA 94545. (415)957-9574. Editorial Director: Susan E. Schwartz. 75% freelance written. Bought 250 freelance ideas/samples last year; receives an estimated 5,000 submissions annually. Submit seasonal/holiday material 18 months in advance. Buys exclusive card rights; negotiates others. Pays on acceptance. Reports in 2 months. Writer's guidelines for SAE and 49¢ postage.
Needs: "Our greatest need is ideas for the cards people send most: birthday and friendship. We are always

looking for a new approach—if we like it, we'll try it. We are not tied down to one look, or tone. Alternative cards should be laugh-out-loud funny—not cute. We also do a complete captioned line of traditional cards for all occasions. Copy for traditional cards should be in rhymed verse that scans easily—it should read as you would say it—don't break a line in a strange place just to make it rhyme." Pays $25 but terms are negotiable.

‡**BLACK & WHITE CARDS**, Box 6250, Grand Central Station, New York NY 10163-6020. Editor: Lawrence Thompson. 25% freelance written. Bought 6 freelance ideas/samples last year; receives 50 annually. Submit seasonal/holiday material 1 year in advance. Reports in 6 weeks. Buys all rights. Pays on publication.
Needs: Announcements, humorous, informal, inspirational, invitations, sensitivity and soft line. Considers ideas for musical cards, assemble-it-yourself cards or other novelty cards. Submit no more than 6 card ideas/batch; prefers composite sheets. Pays 2-5% royalty.
Tips: "Ideal submissions are from a writer/photographer/artist or a team. We presently publish lines ranging from 'fine art' to 'cartoons' marketed individually or in boxed gift sets."

BLUE MOUNTAIN ARTS, INC., Dept. WM, Box 1007, Boulder CO 80306. Contact: Editorial Staff. Buys 50-75 items/year. Reports in 3-5 months. Buys all rights. Pays on publication.
Needs: Inspirational (without being religious); and sensitivity ("primarily need sensitive and sensible writings about love, friendships, families, philosophies, etc.—written with originality and universal appeal"). Pays $150.
Other Product Lines: Calendars, gift books and greeting books. Payment varies.
Tips: "Get a feel for the Blue Mountain Arts line prior to submitting material. Our needs differ from other card publishers; we do not use rhymed verse, preferring instead a more honest person-to-person style. Have a specific person or personal experience in mind as you write. We use unrhymed, sensitive poetry and prose on the deep significance and meaning of life and relationships. A very limited amount of freelance material is selected each year, either for publication on a notecard or in a gift anthology, and the selection prospects are highly competitive. But new material is always welcome and each manuscript is given serious consideration."

BRILLIANT ENTERPRISES, 117 W. Valerio St., Santa Barbara CA 93101. Contact: Editorial Dept. Buys all rights. Submit words and art in black on 5½x3½ horizontal, thin white paper in batches of no more than 15. Reports "usually in 2 weeks." Catalog and sample set for $2.
Needs: Postcards. Messages should be "of a highly original nature, emphasizing subtlety, simplicity, insight, wit, profundity, beauty and felicity of expression. Accompanying art should be in the nature of oblique commentary or decoration rather than direct illustration. Messages should be of universal appeal, capable of being appreciated by all types of people and of being easily translated into other languages. Since our line of cards is highly unconventional, it is essential that freelancers study it before submitting." No "topical references, subjects limited to American culture or puns." Limit of 17 words/card. Pays $40 for "complete ready-to-print word and picture design."

‡**THE CALLIGRAPHY COLLECTION**, 2939 NW 43 Ave., Gainesville FL 32605. (904)378-0748. Editor: Kathy Fisher. Has not used any freelance material in the past. Submit seasonal/holiday material 6 months in advance. Reports in 2 months. Buys all rights. Pays on publication.
Needs: "Ours is a line of framed prints of watercolors with calligraphy." Conventional, humorous, informal, inspirational, sensitivity, soft line and studio. Prefers unrhymed verse, but will consider rhymed. Submit 3 ideas/batch. Pays $50-100/framed print idea.
Other Product Lines: Gift books, greeting books and plaques.
Tips: Sayings for grandfathers are difficult to get. Bestsellers are humorous, sentimental, inspirational and conventional cards—such as wedding announcements, thank you, all occasions, and birthday plaques. "Our audience is women 20 to 50 years of age. Write something they would like to give or receive as a lasting gift."

‡**CARING CARD CO.**, Box 90278, Long Beach CA 90809-0278. Editor: Shirley Hassell. 45% freelance written. Buys 25% freelance ideas/samples per year; receives 65% annually. Reports in 1 month. Buys all rights. Pays on publication. Free writer's guidelines/market list.
Needs: Inspirational, sensitivity and soft line. "Significant loss" cards for people in life/death transitions. Submit 3-6, 6-9, or 9-12 card ideas/batch. Pays $10-25/card idea.
Other Product Lines: Calendars ($25-50); Plaques ($10-30) and Posters (5-25).
Tips: "Writers should be aware of people's inner awareness of who and what they really are. Our cards are for people of all ages in life/death transitions—divorce, terminal illness, aids, etc."

CARLTON CARDS, (formerly Drawing Board Greetings), 8200 Carpenter Freeway, Dallas TX 75247. (214)638-4800. Editor: Jimmie Fitzgerald. 15-20% freelance written. Buys thousands freelance ideas/samples per year. Submit seasonal/holiday material 1 year in advance. Reports in 2 weeks. Buys all rights. Writer's guidelines/market list for SASE.
Needs: Announcements, humorous, inspirational, invitations, juvenile, sensitivity and studio. No porno-

graphic material. Considers ideas for musical cards, assemble-it-yourself cards or novelty cards. Submit 10-20 card ideas/batch. Pays $50-100/card idea.

Other Product Lines: Calendars (500-1,200); postcards ($30-50) and promotions (1,000). 10-20 card ideas each.

Tips: Please send copy on 3x5 cards, with name and address with code number. No more than 10 or 20 per mailing.

‡**COLORTYPE**, 1640 Market St., Corona CA 91720. (714)734-7410. Editor: Mike Gribble. 100% freelance writen. Buys 75 freelance ideas/samples yer year; receives 200 annually. Submit seasonal/holiday material 9 months in advance. Reports in 3 weeks. Buys all rights. Pays on acceptance. Writer's guidelines/market list for 6x9 SASE.

Needs: Humorous, assemble-it-yourself cards or other novelty cards. Prefers to receive 6 "or more" card ideas/batch. Pays $100-150/card idea. Royalty "open for discussion."

Tips: "Prefer humorous. Photos of humorous subjects are difficult to get."

‡**COMSTOCK CARDS**, 1205 Industrial Way, Sparks NV 89431. (702)359-9441. Editor: John Posen. Estab. 1986. "Just starting to purchase freelance material." 25% freelance written. Buys 20 freelance ideas/samples per year; receives 50 annually. Submit seasonal/holiday material 1 year in advance. Reports in 5 weeks. Buys all rights. Pays on acceptance. Free writer's guidelines/market list. Market list issued one time only.

Needs: Humorous, informal, invitations, studio and "puns, put-downs, put ons outrageous humor aimed at a sophisticated, adult female audience. No conventional, soft line or sensitivity hearts and flowers, etc." Prefers to receive 25 cards/batch. Pays $50-75/card idea.

Other Product Lines: Calendars ($300-500) and postcards ($50-75).

Tips: "Always keep holiday occasions in mind and personal me-to-you expressions that relate to today's occurences. Ideas must be simple and concisely delivered. A combination of strong image and strong gag line make a successful greeting card. Consumers relate to themes of work, sex and friendship combined with current social, political and economic issues."

CONTENOVA GIFTS, 1239 Adanac St., Vancouver, British Columbia V6A 2C8 Canada. (604)253-4444. Editor: Jeff Sinclair. 100% freelance written. Bought over 100 freelance ideas/samples last year; receives an estimated 15,000+ submissions annually. Submit ideas on 3x5 cards or small mock-ups in batches of 10-15. Reports same day received. Buys world rights. Pays on acceptance. Current needs list for SAE and IRC.

Needs: Humorous and studio. Both risque and nonrisque. "Short gags with good punch work best." Birthday, belated birthday, get well, anniversary, thank you, congratulations, miss you, new job, etc. Seasonal ideas needed for Christmas by March; Valentine's Day by September. Prefers unrhymed verses/ideas. Risque and birthday cards sell best. Pays $50.

Tips: "Not interested in play-on-words themes. We do not like to follow trends but set them. We're leaning toward more 'cute risque' and no longer using drinking themes. Put together your best ideas and submit them. One great idea sent is much better than 20 poor ideas filling an envelope. We are always searching for new writers who can produce quality work. you need not be previously published. Our audience is 18-65—the full spectrum of studio card readers."

‡**CREATE-A-CRAFT**, Box 330008, Fort Worth TX 76163-0008. (817)292-1855. Editor: Mitchell Lee. 5% freelance written. Buys 2 freelance ideas/samples per year; receives 300 annually. Submit seasonal/holiday material 1 year in advance. Submissions accompanied by SASE not returned—"not enough staff to take time to package up returns." Buys all rights.

Needs: Announcements, conventional, humorous, juvenile and studio. "Payment depends upon the assignment, amount of work involved, and production costs involved in project."

Tips: No unsolicited material. "Send letter of inquiry describing education, experience, or resume with one sample first. We will screen applicants and request samples from those who interest us."

‡**CREATIVE DIRECTIONS, INC.**, 323 S. Franklin Bldg., Ste. W-268, Dept. F, Chicago IL 60606. Editor: Robert Lewis. Estab. 1986. Submit seasonal/holiday material 1 year in advance. Reports back in 6 weeks. Buys exclusive greeting card rights. Pays royalties from purchases.

Needs: Announcements, conventional, humorous, informal, inspirational, invitations, juvenile, sensitivity, soft line and studio. Pays 1% royalty with commission earning opportunities. Other product lines include postcards, calendars and promotions.

Tips: "Length of verse is open. We are not looking for any particular style (conventional, unconventional, rhymed and unrhymed acceptable). We prefer verse that suggests: 'Let us say it for you.' We welcome new writers."

‡**THE CRYSTAL GROUP OF COMPANIES, INC.**, 4375 Brainy Boro Station, Metuchen NJ 08840. (201)654-4400. Submit seasonal/holiday material 6 months in advance. Reports in 3 weeks. Not copyrighted.

Use an up-to-date Market Directory!

Don't let your *Writer's Market* turn old on you.

You may be reluctant to give up this copy of *Writer's Market*. After all, you would never discard on old friend.

But resist the urge to hold onto an old *Writer's Market!* Like your first typewriter or your favorite pair of jeans, the time will come when this copy of *Writer's Market* will have to be replaced.

In fact, if you're still using this *1988 Writer's Market* when the calendar reads 1989, your old friend isn't your best friend anymore. Many of the editors listed here have moved or been promoted. Many of the addresses are now incorrect. Rates of pay have certainly changed, and even the editorial needs are changed from last year.

You can't afford to use an out-of-date book to plan your marketing efforts. But there's an easy way for you to stay current—order the *1989 Writer's Market.* All you have to do is complete the attached post card and return it with your payment or charge card information. Best of all, we'll send you the 1989 edition at the 1988 price—just $21.95. The *1989 Writer's Market* will be published and ready for shipment in September 1988.

Make sure you have the most current marketing information—order the new edition of *Writer's Market* now.

(See other side for more books to help you get published)

These books will also help you get published!

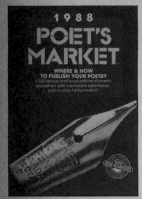

1988 Poet's Market
by Judson Jerome
Writer's Digest magazine poetry columnist Judson Jerome helps you publish your poetry by providing complete contact details for and critiques of each of the 1,700 poetry publishers listed in this annual directory. You'll also find articles on *how* to publish your poetry, interviews with poets and editors, and three indexes to help you find publishers fast.
432 pages/$17.95

1987 Fiction Writer's Market
edited by Laurie Henry
You'll find 1,600 publishing opportunities (including hundreds not found in *Writer's Market*)—from literary/little magazines to commercial periodicals to small presses—to help you sell your short stories and novels, complete with the editors' names/addresses, editorial needs, and special tips. Plus: 23 chapters of fiction writing instruction written by such professionals as Grace Paley and Jay Neugeboren; lists of contests, awards, and agents; and a subject index.
540 pages/$18.95 (1988 edition available March 1988)

Use coupon on other side to order your copies today!

Pays on acceptance. Free writer's guidelines/market list.
Needs: Announcements, conventional, humorous, informal, inspirational, invitations, juvenile, sensitivity, soft line and studio. No risque material. Pays $30-50/card idea.
Other Product Lines: Calendars and gift books.

CURRENT, INC., Box 2559, Colorado Springs CO 80901. (303)594-4100. Editor: Nancy McConnell. 10-15% freelance written. Bought 180 freelance sentiments or manuscripts last year; receives an estimated 300 submissions annually. Submit seasonal/holiday material 18 months in advance. Reports in 6-8 weeks. Buys all rights. Pays on acceptance. "Flat fee only; no royalty." Writer's guidelines for business size SAE and 1 first class stamp.
Needs: All occasion and woman-to-woman cards; short 1-2 line puns for all occasions not too risque; short children's stories, long (6-12 lines) inspirational verse. Pays $15/sentiment; $20-25/verse.
Tips: "Our customer is primarily a married working woman between the ages of 35-44. We pick up trends and create our own. We suggest that writers keep abreast of what's selling at retail. Don't send traditional greeting card verse or off-color humor because we *don't* buy it. Fresh puns for holidays such as Christmas and Easter, are difficult to get. Read our direct mail catalog."

‡EISNER ADVERTISING STUDIO, 2421 Traymore Road, Cleveland OH 44118. Buys 20% freelance written material. Buys 20 freelance/samples per year. Receives 50 submissions/year. Submit seasonal/holiday material 6 months in advance. Buys all rights. Pays on acceptance.
Needs: Informal, inspirational, invitations, sensitivity, soft lines and studio. Prefers unrhymed verse. Submit 8 card ideas/batch. Pays $100-250.
Other Product Lines: Bumper stickers, calendars, gift books, greeting books, plaques, postcards, promotions and puzzles; payment varies. Query.
Tips: Writers should be mindful of the increase of soft line. Humorous and Jewish feminist cards sell best for Eisner Advertising.

FREEDOM GREETING CARD CO., Box 715, Bristol PA 19007. (215)945-3300. Editor: J. Levitt. 90% freelance written. Submit seasonal/holiday material 1 year in advance. Reports in 2 weeks. Pays on acceptance. Free writer's guidelines/market list. Market list available to writer on mailing list basis.
Needs: Announcements, conventional, humorous, inspirational, invitations, juvenile and sensitivity. Payment varies.
Tips: General and friendly cards sell best for Freedom.

‡GRAND SLAM GREETINGS, INC., 35 York St., Brooklyn NY 11201. (718)797-1204. Contact: Editorial Director. Currently we do "captioned" funny tee-shirts. Reports in 2 weeks. Pays on acceptance.
Needs: Humorous ("risque is OK"), soft line and studio. Prefers unrhymed verse. Pays $50/card idea.
Other Product Lines: Tee shirts ($50).

‡HALLMARK CARDS, INC., Box 419580, Kansas City MO 64141-6580. Contact: Carol King. Reports in 2 months. Purchase all social expression rights. Pays on acceptance.
Needs: Humorous and studio cards. No traditional verse.
Tips: "Purchasing humorous card ideas for contemporary and Shoebox lines. Study the lines carefully before submitting. Submissions should be typed on 3x5 cards, or lettered legibly on folded card prototypes. Submit 10-15 ideas with name and address on each. Send SASE."

‡KALAN, INC., 521 Walnut St., Darby PA 19023. (215)586-7122. Editor: D.M. Kingsley. 90% freelance written. Buys 100 freelance ideas/samples per year; receives 500 annually. Submit seasonal/holiday material 8 months in advance. Reports in 1 month. Buys all rights. Pays on acceptance. Writer's guidelines/market list for #10 SAE with 1 first class stamp. Market list regularly revised.
Needs: Humorous, informal and studio. Good humor line needs birthday, friendship, and/or gag type, get well, anniversary, please write, miss you, to keep in touch, relationship, retirement, promotion, new job, and new home or apt. XRATED—an adult x-rated line needs birthday, get well, friendship, anniversary and seasonal—Christmas, Valentine, St. Patrick's Day and Halloween. "Prefers unrhymed verse, but also will use rhymed. Submit 12 card ideas/batch. Pays $15-75/card idea.
Other Product Lines: Bumper stickers, postcards, posters and novelty products/with copy.
Tips: "Humorous every day cards—birthday and friendship—sell best for Kalan. Toned-down risque card ideas with a double-suggestive meaning are hard to get."

MAINE LINE CO., Box 418, Rockport ME 04856. (207)236-8536. Editor: Marjorie MacClennen. 95% freelance written. Buys 200-400 freelance ideas/samples per year. Receives approximately 2,500 submissions/year. Submit photocopies (1 idea per page) or index cards. Please send SASE for return of samples. Reports in 2 months. Submit seasonal/holiday material 1 year in advance. Material copyrighted. Buys greeting card

Close-up

Perri Ardman
Editor-in-Chief
Maine Line Company

"We couldn't find greeting cards that spoke for us," says Perri Ardman when explaining the inception of the company she and partner Joyce Boaz started in 1979. "Since we weren't happy with what we found in the marketplace, we figured others were also ready for something different. Our sense of humor found an audience. We were offbeat and we had very funny captions and sentiments with humorous illustrations."

Although Maine Line developed a reputation for publishing feminist cards, Ardman disagrees with that restrictive reputation. "It doesn't really apply. I don't feel I'm sexist in any way; I'm a humanist. Our cards are written for people who want to have relationships. Our cards poke fun at the differences. I think both men and women have their difficulties. Women may be more in tune, but men can write greeting cards if they are forward thinking and haven't put people into any slot. Although our cards are humorous, they deal with the very real concerns of our audience. That audience is primarily women because women still buy more than 90 percent of all greeting cards. More and more, however, we are producing cards that either men or women can send. Beneath the humor we have very real emotions, attitudes, feelings, and experiences. The humor allows us to stand back and laugh at ourselves and the circumstances of our lives."

Many beginning greeting card writers overlook smaller companies, choosing to submit to the giant firms of the industry. Ardman understands that writers may feel there's more prestige in selling to a large firm, but she knows there are advantages to working with smaller companies. "We have a personal relationship with the writers with whom we work. There's a person for the writer to talk to, to get feedback from, not a large bureaucracy. A small company doesn't have thousands of writers knocking off cards, so we can operate more quickly. We're not working two or three years ahead, so writers see the fruit of their labor sooner. The response is faster, perhaps more considerate."

But don't assume small companies are less selective. "We're hard judges," says Ardman. "If I look at thirty ideas and choose one, that's good. Everything is read by three or four people to start with and then moves on to a dozen or more people. We have meetings to talk about copy. A piece of copy might go through ten edits and be cut on the eleventh. We have to consider what's happening in the market, what we're doing now, what's our backlog, how many illustrations, and how we responded to the idea. The process takes a while.

"Words are really important. Can we rewrite it? Add to it? What can we do? The writer's work is just the beginning. There's a lot of refining. By the time the copy is on a card it's been through a pretty grueling ordeal.

"Think about writing as communication," advises Ardman. "Think about things people want to talk about. Too often, writers look at cards and come up with the same ideas. Don't identify too much with what you're writing; it doesn't say anything about the quality of you as an individual. The writer isn't on the line. It's a piece of copy."

—Sheila Freeman

rights. Pays on acceptance. Writer's guidelines for business size SAE and 3 first class stamps. Market list is regularly revised and issued one time only.

Needs: Humorous, everyday, seasonal, and holiday cards for modern women and men. No juvenile or religious material. Prefers unrhymed verse. Pays $50/card idea.

Other Product Lines: Postcards and notepad ideas.

Tips: "Don't submit traditional-type material. Study our guidelines. We want greeting card copy with particular appeal to contemporary women of all ages, from all walks of life and also unisex copy. Prose is better than verse; humor based on realities of life rather than on word-play most likely to be accepted. Copy that speaks, beneath the humor, a universal truth which people recognize, or copy which articulates attitudes, experiences, and feelings shared by many is most likely to be accepted. Copy that is suggestive, clever and tasteful is OK. Birthday cards and women-to-women friendship cards dealing with women's concerns are always needed. There is a demand for freelance copy from people who have an interesting perspective on modern life, expressed in a unique way, understood by many. Writers need not submit any visuals with copy but may suggest visuals. Lack of drawing ability does not decrease chances of having copy accepted; however, we also seek people who can both write and illustrate. Writers who have a contemporary illustrative style are invited to send samples or tearsheets to illustrate copy they're submitting."

OATMEAL STUDIOS, Box 138W3, Rochester VT 05767. (802)767-3171. Editor: Dawn Abraham. 85% freelance written. Buys 400-500 greeting card lines/year. Pays on acceptance. Reports in 6 weeks. Current market list for self-addressed, business size envelope and 1 first class stamp.

Needs: Birthday, friendship, anniversary, get well cards, etc. Also Christmas, Chanukah, Mother's Day, Father's Day, Easter, Valentine's Day, etc., and humorous invitations, notepad ideas, mug ideas and poster quotes. Humorous material (clever and *very* funny) year-round. "Humor, conversational in tone and format, sells best for us." Prefers unrhymed contemporary humor. Current pay schedule available with guidelines.

Tips: "The greeting card market has become more competitive with a greater need for creative and original ideas. We are looking for writers who can communicate situations, thoughts, and relationships in a funny way and apply them to a birthday, get well, etc., greeting. We don't use studio ideas or word-play (word-picture-play) ideas, and our trend is toward positive humor that relates to life. We suggest that a writer send for our guidelines to get a clear picture of the type of humor we're looking for."

‡PACIFIC PAPER GREETINGS INC., Box 2249, Sidney, British Columbia V8L 3S8 Canada. (604)656-0504. Editor: Louise Rytter. 50% freelance written. Buys 40 freelance ideas/samples per year. Submit seasonal/holiday material 1 year in advance. Reports in 3 weeks. Buys all rights. Pays on acceptance. Writer's guidelines/ market list for SAE with 1 IRC.

Needs: Conventional, inspirational, sensitivity and soft line, romantic. Payment negotiable. No "rude verses; nothing too lengthy and poetic."

RED FARM STUDIO, Box 347, 334 Pleasant St., Pawtucket RI 02862. (401)728-9300. Art Director: Mary M. Hood. Buys 50 ideas/samples per year. Reports in 2 weeks. Buys all rights. Pays on acceptance. Market list for #10 SASE.

Needs: Conventional, inspirational, sensitivity, and soft line cards. "We cannot use risque or insult humor." Submit no more than 10 ideas/samples per batch. Pays $3 per line of copy.

Tips: "Write verses that are direct and honest. Flowery sentiments are not in fashion right now. It is important to show caring and sensitivity, however. Our audience is middle to upper middle class adults of all ages."

REDLETERKARDZ, Box 231015, Pleasant Hill CA 94523. (415)792-1200. Editor: Ed Kennedy. Buys 30-60 freelance sentiments annually. Bought 53 freelance ideas/samples last year; receives an estimated 1,200 submissions annually. Submit seasonal/holiday material 6 months in advance. Reports in 1 month. Pays on acceptance.

Needs: Conventional, humorous, informal, juvenile, sensitivity and soft line. Uses both rhymed and unrhymed verse, but uses more unrhymed. Submit 10-18 card ideas/samples per batch. Pays $50-150.

Tips: "Write 'me to you' messages that are clearly understood and appeal to most people. Material should be creative, original and positive with emotions, feelings or humor."

RENAISSANCE GREETING CARDS, Box 126, Springvale ME 04083. (207)324-4153. Editor: Ronnie Sellers. Purchase minimal freelance submissions. 5% freelance written. Bought 20-50 freelance ideas/samples last year; receives 1,000-1,500 submissions annually. Submit seasonal/holiday material at least 9 months in advance. Reports in 2 months, longer on seasonal submissions. (Ceramic and other gift products, cards, stationery, gift wrap copyrighted). Pays on acceptance or publication, "probably acceptance with writers." Market list for business-size SAE with 1 first class stamp. Market list regularly revised.

Needs: "Most interested in humorous submissions. Always interested in receiving inspirational, but not heavily religious cards." Sensitivity cards are also important. "We publish 'upbeat' positive and sincere greetings that enhance relationships. No off-color material or 'put down' material." Usually pays flat fee of $25-50 (per accepted written submission), more if provided with illustrations or graphics.

Other Product Lines: Calendars, gift books, greeting books, postcards, posters and puzzles. Payment negotiable.

Tips: "Address the specific occasions for which greeting cards are sent (Birthday, Get Well, Friendship, etc.). Be original but be sincere. Be clever but stay upbeat and positive. We are a contemporary card company. Our customers expect written context that is more 'original' than that normally associated with the traditional publishers. Write material that will appeal to younger, 'baby boom' audience. We are interested in expanding our humor lines—no slang or off-color. We prefer occasion-oriented but are open to other ideas."

ROCKSHOTS, INC., 632 Broadway, New York NY 10012. (212)420-1400. Editor: Tolin Greene. "We buy 75 greeting card verse (or gag) lines annually." Submit seasonal/holiday material 1 year in advance. Reports in 1 month. Buys use for greeting cards. Writer's guidelines for SAE and 1 first class stamp.

Needs: Humorous ("should be off-the-wall, as outrageous as possible, preferably for sophisticated buyer"); soft line; combination of sexy and humorous come-on type greeting ("sentimental is not our style"); and insult cards ("looking for cute insults"). No sentimental or conventional material. "Card gag can adopt a sentimental style, then take an ironic twist and end on an off-beat note." Submit no more than 10 card ideas/samples per batch. Pays up to $50. Prefers gag line on 8x11 paper with name, address, and phone and social security numbers in right corner.

Tips: "Think of a concept that would normally be too outrageous to use, give it a cute and clever wording to make it drop-dead funny and you will have commercialized a non-commercial message. It's always good to mix sex and humor. Our emphasis is definitely on the erotic. Hard-core eroticism is difficult for the general public to handle on greeting cards. The trend is toward 'light' sexy humor, even cute sexy humor. 'Cute' has always sold cards, and it's a good word to think of even with the most sophisticated, crazy ideas. 95% of our audience is female. Remember that your gag line will probably be illustrated by a cartoonist, illustrator or photographer. So try to think visually. If no visual is needed, the gag line *can* stand alone, but we generally prefer some visual representation."

ROUSANA CARDS, 28 Sager Place, Hillside NJ 07205. Contact: Editor. Looking for everyday, seasonal, conventional, humor, studio and informal. Short verse and prose. "Professionals only please."

‡THE ROYCE INTERNATIONAL CORP., #106, 6924 Canby Ave., Reseda CA 91335. (818)342-8900. Editor: Barbara Marsh. Submit seasonal/holiday material 4-6 months in advance. Reports in 2 weeks. Purchases all rights. Pays on acceptance.

Needs: Humorous, inspirational, sensitivity and studio. "No material raunchy and in poor taste." Payment varies.

Other Product Lines: Calendars, gift books, postcards, posters, promotions and puzzles. Pay "flexible."

Tips: "We're looking for loveable one-or-two liners relating to art work which is mainly animal related. It can be serious or humorous, sensitive, etc."

‡STRINGS ATTACHED, Box 132, Mill Valley CA 94942-0132. (415)459-5300. Editor: Zai Zatoon. Buys 5% freelance material annually. Bought 50 freelance ideas/samples in the last year. Receives 100 submissions annually. Submit seasonal/holiday material 1 year in advance. Reports in 2 weeks. Buys all rights. Pays on acceptance.

Needs: Novelty cards. Prefers unrhymed verse but wll consider both rhymed and unrhymed. Submit 5-10 card ideas/samples per batch. "Universal humor is difficult to get especially puns for Christmas, Valentine's, Mother's Day, Father's Day and Graduations. No inspirational or religious material." Pays $5-75.

Other Product Lines: Bumper stickers and greeting books.

Tips: "Funny is money and mush sells."

SUNRISE PUBLICATIONS, INC., Box 2699, Bloomington IN 47402. (812)336-9900. Contact: Product Manager. 100% freelance written. Bought 200 freelance ideas/samples last year; receives an estimated 2,000 submissions annually. Reports in 1 month. Acquires greeting card rights only. Pays on acceptance. Free writer's guidelines. Market list is regularly revised.

Needs: Conventional, humorous, informal. No "off-color humor or lengthy poetry." Prefers unrhymed verses/ideas. "We like short one- or two-line captions, sincere or clever. Our customers prefer this to lengthy rhymed verse. Submit ideas for birthday, get well, friendship, wedding, baby congrats, sympathy, thinking of you, anniversary, belated birthday, thank yous, fun and love." Pays $20 per card idea.

Tips: "Think always of the sending situation and both the person buying the card and its intended recipient. Most card purchasers are aged between 18 and 45 years, and are female."

‡TECH STYLES, Box 1877, Winter Haven FL 33880. Editor: Dean Bagley. Estab. 1986. Submit seasonal/holiday material 6 months in advance. Reports in 6 weeks. Buys all rights. Pays on acceptance. Writer's guidelines/market list for #10 SAE with 1 first class stamp.

Needs: Conventional, humorous, informal, invitations, juvenile and studio. Pays 25-150 or royalty to be negotiated.

Tips: "Tech styles has only one focus—computers. The subject matter may vary. Anyone who can combine off-the-wall ideas with computers is desirable. There are two people who buy these cards—computer people who like cartoons and funny phrases about their profession, and non-computer people who know someone who is a computer nerd and would like to buy him/her a funny gift. Am open to all kinds of ideas about computers and humorous slants toward gift products. For example, we have a greeting card that looks exactly like a floppy disk. Would like to see a lot of these ideas combined with the Christmas season, such as the Computerized Twelve Days of Christmas or Santa Claus going computerized. There is a lot to work with if one is creative."

VAGABOND CREATIONS, INC., 2560 Lance Dr., Dayton OH 45409. (513)298-1124. Editor: George F. Stanley, Jr. 30% freelance written. Buys 30-40 ideas annually. Submit seasonal/holiday material 6 months in advance. Reports in 1 week. Buys all rights. Sometimes copyrighted. Pays on acceptance. Writer's guidelines for business size SAE. Market list issued one time only.

Needs: Cute, humorous greeting cards (illustrations and copy) often with animated animals or objects in people-situations with short, subtle tie-in message on inside page only. No poetry. Pays $10-25/card idea.

WARNER PRESS, INC., Box 2499, Anderson IN 46018. (317)644-7721. Product Editor: Cindy M. Grant. 85% freelance written. Buys $3,000-4,000 worth of freelance material/year. Scheduled reading times: everyday verses (March-May); Christmas verses (June-August). Reports in 5 weeks. Prefers to buy all rights. Pays on acceptance. Writer's guidelines for business size SASE. Market list is regularly revised.

Needs: Announcements, conventional, informal, inspirational, juvenile, sensitivity and verses of all types with contemporary Christian message and focus. No off-color humor. "Cards with a definite Christian perspective that is subtly stressed, but not preachy, sell best for us." Uses both rhymed and unrhymed verses/ideas "but we're beginning to move away from 'sing-song' rhyme, toward contemporary prose." Pays $5-40 per card idea.

Other Product Lines: Pays $60-150 for calendars; $30-100 for greeting books; $15-30 for plaques; $5-10 for postcards; $10-50 for posters; $20-50 for short meditations; negotiates payment for coloring books and children's books.

Tips: "Try to avoid use of 'I' or 'we' on card verses. A majority of what we purchase is for box assortments. An estimated 75% of purchases are Christian in focus; 25% good conventional verses. Religious card ideas that are not preachy are difficult to find. The market is moving away from the longer verses in a variety of card types, though there is still a market for good inspirational verses (i.e. like Helen Steiner Rice).Our best sellers are short poems or sensitivity verses that are unique, meaningful and appropriate for many people. We do not purchase verses specifically to one person (such as relative or very close friend) but rather for boxed assortments."

CAROL WILSON FINE ARTS, INC., Box 17394, Portland OR 97217. (503)281-0780. Editor: Gary Spector. 90% freelance written. Buys 100 freelance ideas/samples per year; receives thousands annually. Submit seasonal/holiday material 1 year in advance. Reports in 6 weeks. Buys negotiable rights. Whether payment is made on acceptance or publication varies, with type of agreement. Writer's guidelines/market list for business size SAE and 1 first class stamp.

Needs: Humorous and unrhymed. Pays $40-80/card idea. "Royalties could be considered for a body of work."

Other Product Lines: Postcards.

Tips: "We are looking for laugh-out-loud, unusual and clever ideas for greeting cards. All occasions are needed but most of all birthday cards are needed. It's OK to be outrageous or risque. Cards should be 'personal'— ask yourself—is this a card that someone would buy for a specific person?"

ALWAYS submit manuscripts or queries with a self-addressed, stamped envelope (SASE) within your country or International Reply Coupons purchased from the post office for other countries.

Syndication is one of the most competitive areas a writer can venture into. The biggest evidence of this recently was the response to the *Chicago Sun-Times'* selection of a columnist to replace syndicated columnist Ann Landers. More than 12,000 people applied; two were selected. And yet, each year thousands of editors, staff columnists for newspapers and magazines, established freelancers and beginning writers still hope for the chance.

Rumors of wealth aside, the major advantage of syndication is that a syndicate's marketing efforts can expose a writer's name to millions of readers. The reality is that there are only about 1,700 daily newspapers and a very limited amount of space for syndicated columns. Even those accepted by a syndicate have no guarantee that their exposure will be long-lived. The success of a column depends on the response it draws from readers. If reader interest wanes, the syndicate loses subscribers. And a syndicate will drop a column that fails to make money, even a once-popular column.

Before you approach a syndicate, be ready to prove you can regularly turn out quality material that will appeal to readers. Study the writers currently syndicated, not just in your local daily newspaper, but in papers from other cities as well. Check back issues of newspapers at the library and see how successful columnists keep up with current events and change their approach to reflect social change. Study the structure of the columns; you'll find that syndicated material is short (500-1,000 words), concise and carefully documented. Since syndicates sell primarily to newspapers, terse newspaper style is appropriate even for features.

For your own column, choose a subject that interests you and one you know well. You'll have a better chance at being syndicated if you are an expert in a field that is popular but not overcrowded with writers. Don't make the mistake of imitating a well-known columnist. Newspapers already have an Evans and Novak, a Carl Rowan and a Mike Royko; they don't need any more. It will also be to your advantage to have some experience writing a column for a newspaper. You don't have to be a regular staffer. Columns written free of charge for a local paper will prove that you can produce work on a steady basis. Be sure your tearsheets support your proposal when you send copies to a syndicate. Clips of a local society column won't prove you can write political commentary.

Most syndicate editors prefer a query with about six sample columns and a self-addressed, stamped envelope. If you're dealing with a specialized subject, mention any training or experience that qualifies you to deal with such material. If you have never written a column for a newspaper, be sure to mention any writing experience you do have.

Syndicates handle not only regular columns, but also one-shot features, puzzles, cartoons, fillers and newsbreaks. Some sell only specialized material, such as health, religious or business articles, so be sure your material fits the syndicate you're querying.

Writers are usually paid 40-60% on the syndicate's gross receipts for each column. Syndicates also may offer a salary or pay a flat fee for a one-shot item. In fact, writing freelance one-shots may provide an entry into syndication when a column proposal initially is not accepted. Syndicates usually acquire all rights to accepted material, although a few are now offering writers the option of retaining ownership. If they do acquire all rights, the writer cannot reuse such material without the syndicate's permission.

Some writers choose to self-syndicate, but this option calls for investing time and money in marketing and distributing your work. Payment is usually whatever the newspaper is willing to pay. Small papers pay as little as $5 for a column, while larger dailies may pay up to $15-20. One self-syndicated writer says she and an editor will "generally dicker, and I never know whether I'm making a fair rate or not. Mainly I ask for a flat rate per monthly column—and they offer half what I ask." You may find it necessary to negotiate with some newspapers, offering your material free of charge for a trial period, then agreeing on a fee for later columns if you receive a favorable response.

Self-syndicators also must provide their own copyright protection, as some newspapers are not copyrighted. It's less expensive to copyright columns as a collection, rather than individually. More information on copyright can be found in Rights and the Writer in the Appendix.

For more information on syndicates and syndication markets, consult the *Editor and Publisher Syndicate Directory* (11 W. 19th St., New York NY 10011), the *The Gale Directory of Publications* in the library and *How to Make Money in Newspaper Syndication*, by Susan Lane (Newspaper Syndication Specialists, Suite 326, Box 19654, Irvine CA 92720).

‡**ADVENTURE FEATURE SYNDICATE**, 329 Harvery Dr., Glendale CA 91206. (818)247-1721. Editor: Orpha Harryman Barry. Reports in 1 month. Buys all rights, first North American serial rights and second serial (reprint) rights. Free writer's guidelines.
Needs: Fiction (spies) and fillers (adventure/travel). Submit complete ms.

‡**AMERICA INTERNATIONAL SYNDICATE**, 1324½ North 3rd Street, St. Joseph MO 64501. (816)279-9315. Editor: Gerald Bennett. 100% freelance written by cartoonists on contract. Works with 6 previously unpublished cartoonists/year. "We sell to newspapers, trade magazines, puzzle books and comic books." Reports in 1 month. Buys all rights. Pays 50% of gross on sales. Writer's guidelines for #10 SASE.
Needs: Short fictional stories of "You Are The Detective" type for comic strips, puzzles, crosswords, children games, puzzles, art and stories. Send samples of feature (6-8) with SASE. Pays 50% of gross. Currently syndicates Alfonso by Charles Russo (comic strip).
Tips: "Keep the art simple, and uncluttered as possible; know your subject and strive for humor."

‡**AMERICAN NEWSPAPER SYNDICATE**, 9 Woodrush Dr., Irvine CA 92714. (714)559-8047. Executive Editor: Susan Smith. 50% regular columns by writers under contract; 50% freelance articles and series by writers on a one-time basis. Plan to syndicate up to 7 new U.S. and Canadian columnists this year. Plan to buy 20 one-time articles/series per year. Syndicates to U.S. and Canadian medium-to-large general interest and special interest newspapers. Works with previously unpublished and published writers. Pays 50% of net sales, salary on some contracted columns. Buys first North American serial rights. Computer printout submissions acceptable. Reports in 3 weeks. Writer's guidelines for SASE if material is to be returned.
Needs: "Newspaper columns and one-time articles/series on travel, entertainment, how-to, human interest, business, personal finance, lifestyle, health, legal issues. "Practical, money-saving information on everyday needs such as medicine, insurance, automobiles, education, home decoration and repairs, and travel is always in great demand by newspapers." Columns should be 700 words in length; one-time articles should be 1,500 words.
Tips: "We seek fresh, innovative material that may be overlooked by the other syndicates. Because we know the newspaper syndication market, we feel we can find a place for the previously-unpublished writer if the material is well-executed. Be sure to research your idea thoroughly. Good, solid writing is a must. This is a very tough business to penetrate—but the rewards can be great for those who are successful."

AP NEWSFEATURES, 50 Rockefeller Plaza, New York NY 10020. (212)621-1500. Assistant General Manager: Dan Perkes.
Nonfiction: Buys column ideas "dealing with all areas that can be expanded into book form. Do not buy single features."

ARKIN MAGAZINE SYNDICATE, 761 NE 180th St., North Miami Beach FL 33162. Editor: Joseph Arkin. 20% freelance written by writers on contract; 70% freelance written by writers on a one-time basis. "We regularly purchase articles from several freelancers for syndication in trade and professional magazines." Submit complete ms. Previously published submissions OK, "if all rights haven't been sold." Computer printout submissions acceptable; no dot-matrix. Reports in 3 weeks. Buys all North American magazine and newspaper rights. "SASE required with all submissions."
Needs: Magazine articles (nonfiction, 750-2,200 words, directly relating to business problems common to several (not just one) business firms, in different types of businesses); and photos (purchased with written material). "We are in dire need of the 'how-to' business article." Will not consider article series. Pays 3-10¢/word; $5-10 for photos; "actually, line drawings are preferred instead of photos." Pays on acceptance.
Tips: "Study a representative group of trade magazines to learn style, needs and other facets of the field."

ARTHUR'S INTERNATIONAL, Box 10599, Honolulu HI 96816. (808)955-4969. Editor: Marvin C. Arthur. Syndicates to newspapers and magazines. Computer printout submissions acceptable; prefers letter-quality to dot-matrix. Reports in 1 week. "SASE must be enclosed." Buys all rights.

Needs: Fillers, magazine columns, magazine features, newspaper columns, newspaper features and news items. "We specialize in timely nonfiction and historical stories, and columns, preferably the unusual. We utilize humor. Travel stories utilized in 'World Traveler'." Buys one-shot features and article series. "Since the majority of what we utilize is column or short story length, it is better to submit the article so as to expedite consideration and reply. Do not send any lengthy manuscripts." Pays 50% of net sales, salary on some contracted work and flat rate on commissioned work. Currently syndicates Marv, by Marvin C. Arthur (informative, humorous, commentary); Humoresque, by Don Alexander (humorous); and World Spotlight, by Don Kampel (commentary).
Tips: "We do not use cartoons but we are open for fine illustrators."

THE ARTISTS AND WRITERS SYNDICATE, 1034 National Press Building, Washington DC 20045. (202)882-8882. Vice President: David Steitz. 100% written by writers on contract. Purchases 2 or 3 freelance features annually. Syndicates to newspapers—U.S. and Canada. Computer printout submissions acceptable. Reports in 2 weeks. Writer's guidelines for SASE.
Needs: Newspaper columns (weekly preferred, illustrated). Must be popular subject. "Quality of writing must be first-rate." Query with published clips or photocopies of unpublished work. Pays 50% commission.
Tips: "This is a very difficult field to enter. We suggest trying newspaper syndication only after succeeding (and establishing a good track record) with a newspaper—or two or three newspapers."

BUDDY BASCH FEATURE SYNDICATE, 771 West End Ave., New York NY 10025. (212)666-2300. Editor/Publisher: Buddy Basch. 10% written by writers on contract; 5% freelance written by writers on a one-time basis. Buys 10 features/year; works with 3-4 previously unpublished writers annually. Syndicates to print media: newspapers, magazines, house organs, etc. Computer printout submissions acceptable; no dot-matrix. Reports in 2 weeks or less. Buys first North American serial rights.
Needs: Magazine features, newspaper features, and one-shot ideas that are really different. "Try to make them unusual, unique, real 'stoppers', not the usual stuff." Will consider one-shots and article series on travel, entertainment, human interest—"the latter, a wide umbrella that makes people stop and read the piece. Different, unusual and unique are the key words, not what the *writer* thinks is, but has been done nine million times before." Query. Pays 20-50% commission. Additional payment for photos $10-50. Currently syndicates It Takes a Woman, by Frances Scott (woman's feature), Travel Whirl and Scramble Steps.
Tips: "Never mind what your mother, fiance or friend thinks is good. If it has been done before and is old hat, it has no chance. Do a little research and see if there are a dozen other similar items in the press—and don't just try a very close 'switch' on them. You don't fool anyone with this. There are fewer and fewer newspapers, with more and more people vying for the available space. But there's *always* room for a really good, different feature or story. Trouble is few writers (amateurs especially) know a good piece, I'm sorry to say."

‡**BLACK CONSCIENCE SYNDICATION INC.**,1 Hediger Dr., Wheatley Heights NY 11798. (516)491-7774. Editor: Clyde Davis. Estab. 1987. 65% of material freelance written. Buys 1,000 features annually. Uses material for magazines, newspapers, radio and television. Computer printout submissions OK; no dot-matrix. Reports in 2 weeks. Buys all rights. Free writer's guidelines.
Needs: Magazine columns, magazine features, newspaper columns, newpaper features and news items. Buys single features and aricle series. Query only. Pays 50% commission. Currently syndicates New York Knotes by Niles Davis (entertainment in New York City).
Tips: "The purpose of Black Conscience Syndication Inc., is to provide writers who produce material vital to the well-being of the black community an avenue to have their copy published in black newspapers and trade publications throughout the world. We are interested in all types of material that are informative and enlightening: book reviews, interviews and feature articles."

BUSINESS FEATURES SYNDICATE, Box 9844, Ft. Lauderdale FL 33310. (305)485-0795. Editor: Dana K. Cassell. 100% freelance written. Buys about 100 features/columns a year. Syndicates to trade journal magazines, business newspapers and tabloids. Computer printout submissions acceptable; no dot-matrix. Buys exclusive rights while being circulated. Writer's guidelines for business size SAE and 1 first class stamp. Reports in 1 month.
Needs: Fillers, columns, features and news items. Buys single features and article series on generic business, how-to, marketing, merchandising, security, management and personnel. Length: 250-2,500 words. Query or submit complete ms. Pays 50% commission. Currently syndicates Retail Market Clinic, Security Patrol.
Tips: "We need nonfiction material aimed at the independent retailer or small service business owner. Material must be written for and of value to more than one field, for example: jewelers, drug store owners, and sporting goods dealers. We aim at retail trade journals; our material is more how-to business oriented than that bought by other syndicates."

‡**CARTOON EXPRESS SYNDICATIONS**, 4271 Rockport Bay Way, Oceanside CA 92054-9892. Editor: Bev Seybert. Estab. 1987. Works with 10 artists annually. Syndicates to newspapers, magazines and book publishers. Reports in 1 month. Buys all rights. Free writer's guidelines.
Needs: Magazine features (comic panels covering specific topics: sports, huning, fishing, etc.) and newspa-

per features (comic panels and comic strips in a family entertainment slant). Buys article series. "Cartoon strips/panels should focus around a particular character or characters and should be on a continuous basis. They must be of good taste and may be aimed at certain segments of society." Query with 5-10 samples of unpublished artwork. Pays 50% author percentage. Currently syndicates Major Katastrofee, by J.A. Walley (cartoon strip).

Tips: "The common denominator of the successful features printed today is the cartoonists' ability to consistently, year after year, be able to retain the readers' attention and at the same time to attract new readers to his work. The only prevailing trend that appears to be consistent is that the published work should always keep within well defined lines. It should not be distasteful or offensive in any way."

CONTINUUM BROADCASTING NETWORK/GENERATION NEWS, INC., Suite 46, 345 W. 85th St., New York NY 10024. Submit material to: 3546 84th St., Jackson Heights NY 11372. (212)713-5208 and (212)713-5165. Executive Editor: Donald J. Fass. Associate Editor: Stephen Vaughn. Broadcast Feature Producer: Deanna Baron. 60% freelance written. 45% written by writers on contract; 5% freelance written by writers on a one-time basis. Buys 300 features/interviews/year. Works with 25-30 previously unpublished writers annually. Syndicates to newspapers and radio. Computer printout submissions acceptable; no dot-matrix. Buys all rights. Writer's guidelines for business size SAE and 2 first-class stamps. Reports in 5 weeks.
Needs: Newspaper columns (all kinds of weekly regular features for newspapers); radio broadcast material (90-second and 2½-minute regular daily radio features: lifestyle, comedy, music and interview—scripts as well as taped features); 30-minute and 60-minute specials. One-shot features for radio only-for 30- and 60-minute specials; scripts and completed productions. Query with 1 or 2 clips of published work only and 1 page summary on proposed articles. Demo tape and/or full script for broadcast; not necessary to query on tapes, but return postage must be provided. Pays 25-50% commission or $25-175, depending on length. Offers no additional payment for photos accompanying ms. Currently syndicates The World of Melvin Belli, Getting It Together (weekly youth-oriented music and lifestyle column); Keeping Fit (daily series); Rockweek and Backstage (weekly entertainment series); On Bleecker Street (weekly music/interview series).
Tips: "We seek a unique or contemporary concept with broad appeal that can be sustained indefinitely and for which the writer already has at least some backlog. Unique health, fitness, lifestyle, music, entertainment and trivia material will be emphasized, with a decrease in pop psychology, child psychology, history, seniors and parenting material."

EDITORIAL CONSULTANT SERVICE, Box 524, West Hempstead NY 11552. Editorial Director: Arthur A. Ingoglia. 40% written by writers on contract; 10% freelance written by writers on a one-time basis. "We work with 75 writers in the U.S. and Canada." Previously published writers only. Adds about 3 new columnists/year. Syndicates material to an average of 60 newspapers, magazines, automotive trade and consumer publications, and radio stations with circulation of 50,000-575,000. Computer printout submissions acceptable; letter-quality submissions preferred. Buys all rights. Writer's guidelines for SASE. Reports in 3 weeks.
Needs: Magazine and newspaper columns and features; news items; and radio broadcast material. Prefers carefully documented material with automotive slant. Also considers automotive trade features. Will consider article series. No horoscope, child care, lovelorn or pet care. Query with published clips. Author's percentage varies; usually averages 50%. Additional payment for 8x10 b&w and color photos accepted with ms. Submit 2-3 columns. Currently syndicates Let's Talk About Your Car, by R. Hite.
Tips: "Emphasis is placed on articles and columns with an automotive slant. We prefer consumer-oriented features, i.e., how-to save money on your car, what every woman should know about her car, how to get more miles per gallon, etc."

FICTION NETWORK, Box 5651, San Francisco CA 94101. (415)391-6610. Editor: Jay Schaefer. 100% freelance written by writers on a one-time basis. Syndicates fiction to newspapers and regional magazines. Buys 100 features/year. Works with 25 previously unpublished writers annually. Computer printout submissions acceptable; letter-quality only. Reports in 3 months. Buys first serial rights. Sample catalog of syndicated stories $4; writer's guidelines for SAE with 1 first class stamp.
Needs: All types of fiction (particularly holiday) under 2,000 words. "We specialize in quality literature." Submit complete ms; do not send summaries or ideas. "Send one manuscript at a time; do not send second until you receive a response to the first." Pays 50% commission. Syndicates short fiction only; authors include Alice Adams, Ann Beattie, Max Apple, Andre Dubus, Bobbie Ann Mason, Joyce Carol Oates and others.
Tips: "We seek and encourage previously unpublished authors. Keep stories short, fast-paced and interesting. We need short-short stories under 1,000 words."

‡FOTOPRESS, INDEPENDENT NEWS SERVICE INTERNATIONAL, Box 681, Station A, Downsview, Ontario M3M 3A9 Canada. 50% written by writers on contract; 25% freelance written by writers on a one-time basis. Works with 30% previously unpublished writers. Syndicates to domestic and international magazines, newspapers, radio, TV stations and motion picture industry. Computer printout submissions acceptable; prefers letter-quality. Reports in 6 weeks. Buys variable rights. Writer's guidelines for $3 in IRCs.
Needs: Fillers, magazine columns, magazine features, newspaper columns, newspaper features, news items, radio broadcast material, documentary, travel and art. Buys one-shot and article series for international poli-

tics, scientists, celebrities and religious leaders. Query or submit complete ms. Pays 50-75% author's percentage. Offers $5-150 for accompanying ms.

Tips: "We need all subjects from 500-3,000 words. Photos are purchased with or without features. All writers are regarded respectfully—their success is our success."

‡FREELANCE SYNDICATE, INC., Box 1626, Orem UT 84057. (801)785-1300. Editor: Demas W. Jasper. Estab. 1986. 100% freelance written. Writers, artists and humorists must be members or trial members of FSI. Syndicates to fellow members and printers/publishers. Reports in 10 days. Buys all rights. Writer's guidelines for #10 SAE with 1 first class stamp.

Needs: Fiction, fillers, magazine columns, magazine features, newspaper columns, newspaper features, news items, photos and artwork. Topics include personal finances, political topics, practical how-to's, family and child, AIDS developments, medical insights, first-person stories, and senior citizen topics. Submissions from members only, or with membership application. Query first on membership with SASE. Items must have previously sold with the submitting freelancer retaining reprint-resale rights for assignment to FSI. Value is based on the documented prior-sale value of submitted items and materials. Exchange between members of marketable material is one direct benefit on a straight dollar-value for dollar-value basis. On items syndicated through FSI, FSI retains only the first $5 for its service fee. Membership also provides a directory listing available to printers and publishers as explained in the FSI membership booklet. Query for electronic submissions. Computer printout submissions OK; prefers letter-quality to dot-matrix.

GENERAL NEWS SYNDICATE, 147 W. 42nd St., New York NY 10036. (212)221-0043. 25% written by writers on contract; 12% freelance written by writers on a one-time basis. Works with 12 writers/year; average of 5 previously unpublished writers annually. Syndicates to an average of 12 newspaper and radio outlets averaging 20 million circulation; buys theatre and show business people columns (mostly New York theatre pieces). Computer printout submissions acceptable; prefers letter-quality to dot-matrix. Reports in 3 weeks. Buys one-time rights.

Needs: Entertainment-related material.

GLOBAL PRESS REVIEW, 1307 4th St. NE, Washington DC 20002. (202)543-9428. Editor: Diane Sherwood. Syndicates to domestic and foreign news and features publications, independent journals, specialized newsletters, and electronic and print information services—both domestic and overseas. Send photocopies of ideas or mss which do not need to be returned. Query for electronic submissions. Computer printout submissions acceptable. Reports "as soon as possible."

HARRIS & ASSOCIATES PUBLISHING DIVISION, #34, 5353 La Jolla Blvd., La Jolla CA 92037. (615)488-3851. President: Dick Harris. 20% written by writers on contract; 10% freelance written by writers on a one-time basis. Works with 6 previously unpublished writers annually. Rights purchased vary with author and material. Buys first North American serial rights. Does not purchase many mss per year since material must be in special style. Computer printout submissions OK; no dot-matrix. Pays on acceptance. Reports in less than 1 month.

Nonfiction: Material on driver safety and accident prevention. Not necessary to query. Send sample of representative material. Pays 15¢/word minimum.

Photos: Action, unposed, 8x10 b&w photos are purchased without features or on assignment. Captions are required. Pays $25 minimum/photo.

Humor: Humor for modern women (not women's lib); humor for sports page. "We like to look at anything in our special interest areas. Golf and tennis are our specialties. We'll also look at cartoons in these areas. Will buy or contract for syndication. Everything must be short, terse, with humorous approach."

Tips: "Submit *good* photos or art with text."

HERITAGE FEATURES SYNDICATE, 214 Massachusetts Ave. NE, Washington DC 20002. (202)543-0440. Managing Editor: Andy Seamans. 99% freelance written by writers on contract; 1% freelance written by writers on one-time basis. Buys 3 columns/year. Works with 2-3 previously unpublished writers annually. Syndicates to over 100 newspapers with circulations ranging from 2,000-630,000. Works with previously published writers. Computer printout submissions acceptable; prefers letter-quality to dot-matrix. Buys first North American serial rights. Reports in 3 weeks.

Needs: Newspaper columns (practically all material is done by regular columnists). One-shot features. "We purchase 750-800 word columns on political, economic and related subjects." Query. Pays $50 minimum. Currently syndicates nine columnists, including For the Record by Herb Schmertz; Fed Up, by Don Feder; and The Answer Man, by Andy Seamans.

HISPANIC LINK NEWS SERVICE, 1420 N St. NW, Washington DC 20005. (202)234-0280. Editor/Publisher: Charles A. Ericksen. 50% freelance written by writers on contract; 50% freelance written by writers on a one-time basis. Buys 156 columns and features/year. Works with 50 writers/year; 5 previously unpublished writers. Syndicates to 200 newspapers and magazines with circulations ranging from 5,000 to 300,000. Computer printout submissions acceptable; prefers letter-quality to dot-matrix. Reports in 2 weeks. Buys second serial (reprint) or negotiable rights. Free writer's guidelines.

Needs: Magazine columns, magazine features, newspaper columns, newspaper features. One-shot features and article series. "We prefer 650-700 word op/ed or features geared to a general national audience, but focus on issue or subject of particular interest to Hispanic Americans. Some longer pieces accepted occasionally." Query or submit complete ms. Pays $25-150. Currently syndicates Hispanic Link, by various authors (opinion and/or feature columns).

Tips: "This year we would especially like to get topical material and vignettes relating to Hispanic presence and progress in the United States. Provide insights on Hispanic experience geared to a general audience. Eighty-five to ninety percent of the columns we accept are authored by Hispanics; the Link presents Hispanic viewpoints, and showcases Hispanic writing talent to its 200 subscribing newspapers and magazines. Copy should be submitted in English. We syndicate in English and Spanish."

HOLLYWOOD INSIDE SYNDICATE, Box 49957, Los Angeles CA 90049. (714)678-6237. Editor: John Austin. 10% written by writers on contract; 40% freelance written by writers on a one-time basis. Purchases entertainment-oriented mss for syndication to newspapers in San Francisco, Philadelphia, Detroit, Montreal, London, and Sydney, etc. Works with 2-3 previously unpublished writers annually. Pays on acceptance "but this is also negotiable because of delays in world market acceptance and payment." Previously published submissions OK, if published in the U.S. and Canada only. Computer printout submissions acceptable; prefers letter-quality to dot-matrix. Reports in 6 weeks. Negotiates for first rights or second serial (reprint) rights.

Needs: News items (column items concerning entertainment—motion picture—personalities and jet setters for syndicated column; 750-800 words). Also considers series of 1,500-word articles; "suggest descriptive query first. We are also looking for off-beat travel pieces (with pictures) but not on areas covered extensively in the Sunday supplements. We can always use pieces on 'freighter' travel. Not luxury cruise liners but lower cost cruises. We also syndicate nonfiction book subjects—sex, travel, etc., to overseas markets. No fiction." Query or submit complete ms. Pay negotiable.

Tips: "Study the entertainment pages of Sunday (and daily) newspapers to see the type of specialized material we deal in. Perhaps we are different from other syndicates, but we deal with celebrities. No 'I' journalism such as 'when I spoke to Cloris Leachman.' Many freelancers submit material from the 'dinner theatre' and summer stock circuit of 'gossip type' items from what they have observed about the 'stars' or featured players in these productions—how they act off stage, who they romance, etc. We use this material."

HYDE PARK MEDIA, 7158 Lee St., Chicago IL 60648. (312)967-7666. Editor: Anthony DeBartolo. 50% freelance written by writers on a one-time basis. Syndicates to Chicago area newspapers and magazines. Query for electronic submissions. Computer printout submissions acceptable; prefers letter-quality to dot-matrix. Reports in 2 weeks. Buys first and second serial rights.

Needs: Unusual, off-beat magazine features (1,500-3,000 words) and newspaper features with a local hook (750-1,500 words). Buys single (one-shot) features only. Send complete manuscript and SASE. No phone queries. Pays 50% commission on sale.

Tips: "No more submissions from Indiana housewives wanting to be columnists. We *ain't* Santa Claus."

INTERPRESS OF LONDON AND NEW YORK, 400 Madison Ave., New York NY 10017. (212)832-2839. Editor: Jeffrey Blyth. 50% freelance written by writers on contract; 50% freelance written by writers on a one-time basis. Works with 3-6 previously unpublished writers annually. Buys British and European rights mostly, but can handle world rights. Will consider photocopied submissions. Previously published submissions OK "for overseas." Computer printout submissions acceptable; prefers letter-quality to dot-matrix. Pays on publication, or agreement of sale. Reports immediately or as soon as practicable.

Nonfiction: "Unusual stories and photos for British and European press. Picture stories, for example, on such 'Americana' as a five-year-old evangelist; the 800-pound 'con-man'; the nude-male calendar; tallest girl in the world; interviews with pop celebrities such as Yoko Ono, Michael Jackson, Bill Cosby, Tom Selleck, Cher, Priscilla Presley, Cheryl Tiegs, Eddie Murphy, Liza Minelli, also news of stars on such shows as 'Dynasty'/'Dallas'; cult subjects such as voodoo, college fads, anything amusing or offbeat. Extracts from books such as Earl Wilson's *Show Business Laid Bare*, inside-Hollywood type series ('Secrets of the Stuntmen'). Real life adventure dramas ('Three Months in an Open Boat,' 'The Air Crash Cannibals of the Andes'). No length limits—short or long, but not too long. Query or submit complete ms. Payment varies; depending on whether material is original, or world rights. Pays top rates, up to several thousand dollars, for exclusive material."

Photos: Purchased with or without features. Captions required. Standard size prints. Pay $50 to $100, but no limit on exclusive material.

Tips: "Be alert to the unusual story in your area—the sort that interests the American tabloids (and also the European press)."

KING FEATURES SYNDICATE, INC., 235 E. 45th St., New York NY 10017. (212)682-5600. Contact: Executive Editor. 10% freelance written. Syndicates material to newspapers. Works with 10 previously unpublished writers annually. Submit "brief cover letter with samples of feature proposals." Previously published submissions OK. Computer printout submissions acceptable. Reports in 3 weeks. Buys all rights.

Needs: Newspaper features and columns. No travel, wine or general humor columns; restaurant, theatre or movie reviews; or fad-oriented subjects. Pays "revenue commission percentage" or flat fee. Special single article opportunity is Sunday Woman Plus, a weekly supplement distributed nationally. Buys one-time rights to articles on beauty, health, grooming, fashion, coping, money management for women, career guidance, etc. Query with SASE to Merry Clark, senior editor.

Tips: "Be brief, thoughtful and offer some evidence that the feature proposal is viable. Read newspapers—lots of them in big and small markets—to find out what already is out there. Don't try to buck established columns which newspapers would be reluctant to replace with new and untried material."

LOS ANGELES TIMES SYNDICATE, Times Mirror Square, Los Angeles CA 90053. Vice President/Editor: Don Michel. Special Articles Editor: Dan O'Toole. Syndicates to U.S. and worldwide markets. Usually buys first North American serial rights and world rights, but rights purchased can vary. Submit seasonal material six weeks in advance. Material ranges from 800-2,000 words.

Needs: Reviews continuing columns and comic strips for U.S. and foreign markets. Send columns and comic strips to Don Michel. Also reviews single articles, series, magazine reprints, and book serials. Send these submissions to Dan O'Toole. Send complete mss. Pays 50% commission. Currently syndicates Erma Bombeck, Art Buchwald, Dr. Henry Kissinger, Dr. Jeane Kirkpatrick, William Pfaff, Paul Conrad and Lee Iacocca.

Tips: "We're dealing with fewer undiscovered writers but still do review material."

‡MERCURY SYNDICATIONS, Box 2601, Hutchinson KS 67504-2601. Editor: Gary McMaster. 100% freelance written by writers on contract. Works with 30 writers/year. Syndicates to magazines and newspapers. Computer printout submissions OK; no dot-matrix. Reports in 3 months. Buys first North American serial rights or second serial (reprint) rights.

Needs: Magazine and newspaper columns. Buys article series. Submit complete ms. Pays 70% commission. Currently syndicated The Pen Moves On, by Linda M. McMaster (interview/book preview).

Tips: "Try something new. Don't copy columns already in print and write as if you were talking to the reader. Don't write down to the reader. Well written ideas that are new and different stand a 50/50 chance in our market."

MINORITY FEATURES SYNDICATE, Box 421, Farrell PA 16146. (412)342-5300. Editor: Merry Frable. Reports in 5 weeks. 60% written by freelance writers on contract; 40% freelance written by writers on a one-time basis. Works with 500 previously unpublished writers annually. Buys first North American serial rights. Computer printout submissions acceptable; no dot-matrix. Reports in 5 weeks. Writer's guidelines for 44¢ postage.

Needs: Fillers, magazine features, newspaper features. Also needs comic book writers for Bill Murray Productions. Query with published clips. Pays open commission. Pays $25 minimum for photos. Currently syndicates Sonny Boy, Those Browns and The Candyman, by Bill Murray (newspaper features).

Tips: "We are getting in the comic book market. Writers should write for guidelines."

NATIONAL NEWS BUREAU, 2019 Chancellor St., Philadelphia PA 19103. (215)569-0700. Editor: Harry Jay Katz. "We work with more than 200 writers and buy over 1,000 stories per year." Syndicates to more than 1,000 publications. Reports in 2 weeks. Buys all rights. Writer's guidelines for 9x12 SAE and 54¢ postage.

Needs: Newspaper features; "we do many reviews and celebrity interviews. Only original, assigned material." One-shot features and article series; film reviews, etc. Query with clips. Pays $5-200 flat rate. Offers $5-200 additional payment for photos accompanying ms.

NEW YORK TIMES SYNDICATION SALES CORP., 130 Fifth Ave., New York NY 10111. (212)645-1000. Senior Vice President/Editorial Director: Paula Reichler. 70% written by writers on contract; 30% freelance written by writers on a one-time basis. Syndicates approximately "three books per month plus numerous one-shot articles." Also included in foreign newspapers and magazines. Buys first serial rights, first North American serial rights, one-time rights, second serial (reprint) rights, and all rights. Computer printout submissions acceptable; no dot-matrix.

Needs: Wants magazine and newspaper features; magazine and newspaper columns; and book series. "On syndicated articles, payment to author is 50% of net sales. We only consider articles that have been previously published. Send tearsheets of articles published." Submit approximately 4 samples of articles, 12 samples of columns. Photos are welcome with books and articles.

Tips: "Topics should cover universal markets and either be by a well-known writer or have an off-beat quality. Quizzes are welcomed if well-researched."

‡NEWS AMERICA SYNDICATE, 1703 Kaiser Ave., Irvine CA 92714. (714)250-4000. Editor: Tom Reinken. 25% written by writers on contract; 15% freelance written by writers on a one-time basis. Buys 520 articles annually; works with 500 previously unpublished writers. Syndicates to newspapers and magazines. Computer printout submissions acceptable. Reports in 2 weeks. Buys all rights, first North American serial rights or second serial (reprint) rights. Free writer's guidelines.

Needs: Magazine features, newspaper columns and newspaper features. Buys one-shot features and article series. Submit complete ms. Pays 50% author's percentage. Payment negotiable. Currently syndicates Ann Landers, by Ann Landers (advice column); Inside Report, by Evans/Novak (politics); and Observations, by Pope John Paul II (religion).

Tips: "Look for something no one else is doing, or do something differently. We're one of few syndicates to accept and publish freelance writing on a regular (every week) basis."

NEWS FLASH INTERNATIONAL, INC., 2262 Centre Ave., Bellmore NY 11710. (516)679-9888. Editor: Jackson B. Pokress. 25% written by writers on contract; 25% freelance written by writers on a one-time basis. Supplies material to Observer newspapers and overseas publications. Works with 10-20 previously unpublished writers annually. "Contact editor prior to submission to allow for space if article is newsworthy." Photocopied submissions OK. Computer printout submissions acceptable; no dot-matrix. Pays on publication.

Nonfiction: "We have been supplying a 'ready-for-camera' sports page (tabloid size) complete with column and current sports photos on a weekly basis to many newspapers on Long Island, as well as pictures and written material to publications in England and Canada. Payment for assignments is based on the article. Payments vary from $20 for a feature of 800 words. Our sports stories feature in-depth reporting as well as book reviews on this subject. We are always in the market for good photos, sharp and clear, action photos of boxing, wrestling, football, baseball and hockey. We cover all major league ball parks during the baseball and football seasons. We are accredited to the Mets, Yanks, Jets and Giants. During the winter we cover basketball and hockey and all sports events at the Nassau Coliseum."

Photos: Purchased on assignment; captions required. Uses "good quality 8x10 b&w glossy prints; good choice of angles and lenses." Pays $7.50 minimum for b&w photos.

Tips: "Submit articles which are fresh in their approach on a regular basis with good quality black and white glossy photos if possible; include samples of work. We prefer well-researched, documented stories with quotes where possible."

‡NEWSPAPER ENTERPRISE ASSOCIATION, INC., 200 Park Ave., New York NY 10166. (212)557-5870/(212)692-3700. Editorial Director: David Hendin. Director, International Newspaper Operations: Sidney Goldberg. Executive Editor: D.L. Drake. Director of Comics: Sarah Gillespie. 100% written by writers on contract. "We provide a comprehensive package of features to mostly small- and medium-size newspapers." Computer printout submission acceptable; prefers letter-quality to dot-matrix. Reports in 6 weeks. Buys all rights.

Needs: "Any column we purchase must fill a need in our feature lineup and must have appeal for a wide variety of people in all parts of the country. We are most interested in lively writing. We are also interested in features that are not merely copies of other features already on the market. The writer must know his or her subject. Any writer who has a feature that meets all of those requirements should simply send a few copies of the feature to us, along with his or her plans for the column and some background material on the writer." Current columnists include Bob Walters, Bob Wagman, Chuck Stone, George McGovern, Dr. Peter Gott, Tom Tiede, Ben Wattenberg and William Rusher. Current comics include Alley Oop, Born Loser, Frank & Ernest, Eek and Meek, Kit 'n' Carlyle, Bugs Bunny, Berry's World, Arlo and Janis, Snafu and Captain Easy.

Tips: "We get enormous numbers of proposals for first person columns—slice of life material with lots of anecdotes. While many of these columns are big successes in local newspapers, it's been our experience that they are extremely difficult to sell nationally. Most papers seem to prefer to buy this sort of column from a talented local writer."

‡NUMISMATIC INFORMATION SERVICE, Rossway Rd., Rt. 4, Box 237A, Pleasant Valley NY 12569. Editor: Barbara White. Buys 5 features/year. Query. Computer printout submissions acceptable. Reports in 2 weeks. Buys all rights.

Needs: Newspaper columns (anything related to numismatics and philately, particularly the technical aspects of the avocations); news items (relative to the world of coin and stamp collecting); and fillers (on individual coins or stamps, or the various aspects of the hobbies). No fiction or get rich schemes. Pays $5 for 500-word article; 50¢ additional payment for b&w photos accepted with ms.

‡SINGER COMMUNICATIONS, INC., 3164 Tyler Ave., Anaheim CA 92801. (714)527-5650. Editor: Natalie Carlton. 50% written by writers on contract; 30% freelance written by writers on a one-time basis. Buys 500 features and columns, and 1,000 cartoons/year. Syndicates to magazines, newspapers and book publishers. Computer printout submissions acceptable; prefers letter-quality. Reports in 1 month. Rights negotiable. Writer's guidelines for $1.

Needs: Short stories, crosswords, puzzles, quizzes, interviews, entertainment and psychology features, cartoons, books for serialization and foreign reprints. Buys one-shot features and article series on celebrities. Query with clips of published work or submit complete ms. Pays 50% author's percentage. Currently syndicates Solve a Crime, by B. Gordon (mystery puzzle) and Hollywood Gossip, by N. Carr (entertainment).

Tips: "Good interviews with celebrities, men/women relations, business and real estate features have a good chance with us. Aim at world distribution and therefore have a universal approach."

SYNDICATED WRITERS & ARTISTS INC., 2901 Tacoma Ave., Indianapolis IN 46218. (317)924-4311. Editor: Eunice Trotter. 99% written by writers on contract; 1% freelance written by writers on a one-time basis. Works with 30 writers annually. Syndicates to newspapers. Reports in 6 weeks. Query for electronic submissions. Computer printout submissions acceptable; prefers letter-quality to dot-matrix. Buys all rights. Writer's guidelines for SASE.
Needs: Fillers, newspaper columns, newspaper features and news items. 300 words with minority angle. Query with clips of published work. "Three different samples of your work should be submitted (10 cartoon strips or panels). Submissions should also include brief bio of writer/artists. No material is returned without a SASE. Pays author's percentage of 35-40%. Currently syndicates Into the Groove, by L. Michael Jackson (entertainment); Viewpoint, by Ken Wibecan (editorial); and Political Cartoon, by Dennis Gill (editorial).
Tips: "The kind of writing we seek has a minority angle. Previously, there was no market for material with a minority angle; we believe there now is such a market. More news instead of opinion will be required. Quality requirements."

SYNDICATED WRITERS GROUP, 609 E. Philadelphia Ave., Boyertown PA 19512-2112. Editor: Daniel Grotta. 95% freelance written by writers on contract; 30% written by writers on one-time basis. Works with 1-2 previously unpublished writers/year. "Syndicated Writers Group is somewhat unique in that it is primarily a library of features articles—the editorial equivalent of a stock photo agency. We are not interested in either timely material or columns, since the idea is to have a large file of ready-to-publish 'ever-readies' on almost any subject that we can transmit electronically to client newspapers and magazine on an as-needed basis." Query for electronic submissions. Computer printout submissions preferred from prospective writers. "All those whom we accept as contract writers must eventually be computerized." Writer's guidelines for SASE. "No submissions acknowledged or returned without SASE." Reports in 3 months.
Needs: "We have a need for contract writers with an expertise in certain fields such as technology, medicine, home and garden, autos, pets, lifestyles, computers, consumerism, etc. The best articles are those that can remain fresh for months and, with periodic updating by the author, can continue to sell for years. One-shots OK—but only after a writer has been accepted by SWG as a contract writer. We are looking for established writers who regularly sell their articles to one or two local papers only and wish to reach a wider audience." Absolutely no columns, graphic material or cartoons. Pays 50% commission; 80% when SWG acts as agent for specific assignment; 85% for secondary rights sales, such as books, TV etc. Maintain exclusive rights to individual articles for the length of the contract.
Tips: "Each article must be outstanding—a potential award winner—able to be marketed independently as if the publication never before or again will run anything by the author."

TEENAGE CORNER, INC., 70-540 Gardenia Ct., Rancho Mirage CA 92270. President: David J. Lavin. Buys 122 items/year for use in newspapers. Submit complete ms. Reports in 1 week. Material is not copyrighted.
Needs: 500-word newspaper features. Pays $25.

TRIBUNE MEDIA SERVICES, 64 E Concord St., Orlando FL 32801. (305)422-8181. President: Robert S. Reed. Editor: Michael Argirion. Syndicates to newspapers. Reports in 1 month. Buys all rights, first North American serial rights and second serial (reprint) rights.
Needs: Newspaper columns, comic strips. Query with published clips. Currently syndicates the columns and cartoons of Mike Royko, Bob Greene, Liz Smith, Andy Rooney, Marilyn Beck, Jeff MacNelly and Mike Peters.

UNITED CARTOONIST SYNDICATE, Box 7081, Corpus Christi TX 78415. (512)855-2480. President: Pedro R. Moreno. 10% freelance written by writers on a one-time basis. Works with 12 cartoonists annually. Syndicates to newspapers, newsletters, magazines, books or book publishers, and licensing companies. Reports in 1 week on submissions. Simultaneous submissions OK. Guidelines $5 with copies of artwork or clips of published or unpublished work. Also publishes the newsletter "Cartoonist Market."
Needs: Newspaper features (comic panel and comic strips in a family entertainment slant). Purchases single (one-shot) features and article series. Will consider metaphysical, UFOs, and human and animal interest stories or articles. Query with published clips or 6-12 samples of unpublished artwork (reduced) or articles. Include SASE for their return. Pays author 40%. Additional payment for photos: $10-25. Currently syndicates Brother Simon and Lucus, by Pedro R. Moreno.
Tips: "We do not accept any material that deals with sex, or put down material against anything or anybody. We also sell cartoon books of our syndicated artists at $5 each or request for price list of original comic strips, comic panel or Sunday strip."

‡**UNITED FEATURE SYNDICATE**, 200 Park Ave., New York NY 10166. Editorial Director: David Hendin. Director International Newspaper Operations: Sidney Goldberg. Executive Editor: D.L. Drake. Director of

Comic Art: Sarah Gillespie. 100% freelance written by writers who have signed contract. Supplies features to 1,700 U.S. newspapers, plus Canadian and other international papers. Works with published writers. Query with 4-6 samples and SASE. Computer printout submissions acceptable. Reports in 6 weeks.

Columns, Comic Strips and Puzzles: Current columnists include Jack Anderson, Judith Martin, Donald Lambro, Martin Sloane, June Reinsich. Comic strips include Peanuts, Nancy, Garfield, Drabble, Marmaduke, Rose is Rose and Robotman. Standard syndication contracts are offered for columns and comic strips.

Tips: "We buy the kind of writing similar to major syndicates—varied material, well-known writers. The best way to break in to the syndicate market is for freelancers to latch on with a major newspaper and to develop a following. Also, cultivate new areas and try to anticipate trends."

‡UNITED MEDIA, 200 Park Ave., New York NY 10166. (212)692-3700. Executive Editor: Diana L. Drake. 100% written by writers on contract. Syndicates to newspapers. Computer printout submission acceptable; prefers letter-quality. Reports in 1 month. Writer's guidelines for #10 SAE and 1 first class stamp.

Needs: Newspaper columns and newspaper features. Query with photocopied clips of published work. "Authors under contract have negotiable terms." Currently syndicates Miss Manners, by Judith Martin (etiquette); Dr. Gott, by Peter Gott, M.D. (medical) and Supermarket Shopper, by Martin Sloane (coupon clipping advice).

Tips: "We include tips in our guidelines. We buy very few of the hundreds of submissions we see monthly. We are looking for the different feature as opposed to new slants on established columns."

‡UNIVERSAL PRESS SYNDICATE, 490 Main Street, Kansas City MO 64112. Buys syndication rights. Reports normally in 1 month. Return postage required.

Nonfiction: Looking for features—columns for daily and weekly newspapers. "Any material suitable for syndication in daily newspapers." Currently handling James J. Kilpatrick and others. Payment varies according to contract.

❝ *The first time I receive any material from a writer, I look at the content of the cover letter. If it is written to me about my magazine, my readers, then I am more likely to have an immediate interest in the work. I can only be as interested in them as they are in me!* **❞**

—*Carol Perri*
The California Highway Patrolman

Services and Opportunities

<hr>

Author's Agents

"The best part of agenting is finding new talent," says one agent. Whether you are new in the market or an established freelancer, it's a good idea to become acquainted with the variety of services agents offer, the fees or commissions they charge, and the way they deal with writers and publishers.

In general, agents are a combination of sales representatives and business managers. Agents keep in touch with editors and buyers of subsidiary rights; they know where to sell marketable manuscripts and how to negotiate contracts; they help collect payments from publishers and keep accurate records of earnings.

Of course agents don't decide whether or not a manuscript should be published; that's still a job for editors. Agents can only tell you if they believe your manuscript is ready to be submitted to a publisher.

If you've read the Book Publishers section of *Writer's Market*, you know that the publishing industry has become extremely competitive and cost-conscious. Like any other business, a publishing company that fails to make a profit will not survive. Few publishers can afford to hire a staff of editors or freelance readers to go through hundreds of unsolicited manuscripts; they simply receive too many unpublishable manuscripts for each one that is publishable. For that reason, more and more book publishers will only consider manuscripts submitted through an agent. They rely on agents to do the screening for them.

The greater demand for agented submissions has resulted in an increase in the number of literary agencies. In addition to New York-based agents, many agents settled on the West Coast, primarily to work with film and TV producers. Now more new agencies are opening throughout the U.S., many started by former editors and teachers with an entrepreneurial spirit.

Commissions and fees

Literary agents have always charged a commission on the manuscripts they place with publishers or producers—in much the same way real estate agents charge a commission. The commission, usually 10-20%, is subtracted from the author's advance and royalty payments from the publisher. In other words, the writer doesn't pay the agent a commission until the manuscript has been sold.

Agents rarely charge for general office overhead like the cost of utilities or secretarial services. Instead, they sometimes ask their clients to pay for specific expenses related to selling that writer's manuscript: photocopying, long distance phone calls, messenger service, etc.

Commissions and charges for specific office expenses are regarded as perfectly acceptable in the industry. Additional fees for reading or critiquing manuscripts are becoming more common, although not uniformly accepted. Some agencies charge a reading fee; no comments on improving the manuscript are offered in this case. Other agencies charge a criticism fee in which they often provide several pages of detailed suggestions.

"We regard a reading fee and criticism fee interchangeably since notes from reading are used for the critique," says one agent. Several firms that charge fees regard them as one-time payments; if the writer becomes a client, no more fees will be charged for future manuscripts. Some agencies also reimburse the writer for the original fee when the manuscript is sold.

Understanding fees

Agents' fees continue to be a hotly debated topic. Previous editions of *Writer's Market* sought to protect readers by listing agents who told us they charged only commissions. Since 1987 we have included both commission-only and commission- and fee-charging agents. Why include agents who charge fees? Approximately 80% of all literary agencies now charge some kind of fee. We at *Writer's Market* believe our job is to provide you with the most complete and up-to-date information to allow you to choose an agent. We can't give recommendations or make decisions for you, but we do want to help in your search.

Remember that payment of a reading or criticism fee almost never guarantees that the agency will represent you. Payment of a fee may or may not give you the kind of constructive criticism you need. Read the individual listings carefully. There is no way to generalize about fee-charging agencies.

Likewise, there is no standard when it comes to fees. Some agencies charge criticism fees of $25-75; others charge $200 or more. Reading fees, although less common than criticism fees, are usually less than $50. One fee may apply to a complete manuscript, while another is for an outline and sample chapters. Some agents require fees from unpublished writers only. Sometimes agents refund a fee when the manuscript is sold. A few agents charge a marketing, handling or processing fee to all clients. Several agents offer a consultation service, ranging from $15-200 per hour, to advise writers on book contracts they have received without the help of an agent. If you decide to pay a fee, be sure you know *exactly* what you'll receive in return.

How a literary agent works

Agents do many things to earn their commissions, but it's almost impossible to describe what an "average" agent does. Let's begin by considering what literary agents don't do.

An agent can't sell unsalable work or teach you how to write. An agent won't edit your manuscript; that is an editor's job. An agent can't defend you in a court of law unless he is also an attorney. An agent won't act as your press agent, social secretary or travel agent; you'll have to hire someone else to handle those chores.

As far as what an agent can and will do, each agency is different in the services it offers, the clients if prefers, its contacts in the industry, and the style in which it conducts business. In general, an agent's tasks can be divided into those done before a sale, during a sale and after a sale.

Before the sale, an agent evaluates your manuscript and sometimes make suggestions about revisions. If the agent wants to represent you, you'll usually receive a contract or letter of agreement specifying the agent's commission, fees and the terms of the agreement. When that's signed, the agent begins talking to editors and sending your manuscript out. Your agent can tell you about any marketing problems, give you a list of submissions and even send you copies of rejections if you really want them. The agent repeats this sequence until the manuscript sells, you withdraw it or your agreement expires. Some agents also are involved in book packaging or producing work; this activity is noted in individual listings. See the Book

Producers and Packagers section introduction for more information.

During the sale the agent negotiates with the publisher for you, offering certain rights to the publisher and usually reserving other rights for future sale. The agent examines the contract, negotiates clauses for your benefit and tries to get additional rights, like book jacket approval, for you. Your agent can explain the contract to you and make recommendations, but the final decision is always yours.

After the sale, the agent maintains a separate bank account for you, collects money from the publisher, deducts the appropriate commission and sends you the remainder. The agent examines all royalty statements and requests corrections or an audit when necessary. The agent also checks the publisher's progress on the book and makes sure your copyright has been registered. Sometimes the agent resolves conflicts between a writer and an editor or publisher. If you have retained subsidiary rights to your book, the agent will continue working for additional sales of movie, book club, foreign or video rights, etc. Your agent may even introduce you to an editor who has expressed interest in your future work.

Do you need an agent?

Not everyone needs an agent. Some writers are perfectly capable of handling the placement of their manuscripts and enjoy being involved in all stages of selling, negotiating and checking production of their books. Others have no interest in, or talent for, the business side of writing.

Ask yourself the following questions when evaluating your need for an agent:
- Do you have the skills to handle an agent's usual tasks?
- Can you take care of marketing your book and analyzing your contract?
- Can you afford to pay an agent 10-20% of your royalties?
- Would you like working through a middleman on all aspects of your book's future?
- Will you have more time to write if you have an agent?

No matter how much you want or need an agent, you'll be wasting time and money if your manuscript isn't ready for an agent. Of the manuscripts received by agents, only one in 100 is ready to be submitted to publishers; some agents say one in 1,000 is a better estimate.

Try to be objective about whether or not you have truly polished your manuscript and studied the marketplace for your kind of writing. You should also talk to other writers who have agents and read all you can find about working with an agent. It may sound like a lot of work, but if you want an agent to take you seriously, you'll make every effort to obtain some published credits, enter a literary or journalistic contest, and always correspond in a professional manner.

Making contact

Few agents will look at unsolicited manuscripts. Some will consider queries only if you've been recommended by a client or an editor. But the majority will look at a query and possibly an outline and sample chapters from an unknown writer.

Apparently, many writers make some basic mistakes when approaching agents. "Please, no handwritten or messy typewritten queries," urges one agent. Another says he receives query letters "which do not enclose SASE and are inordinately long, that is they spend most of their length 'describing' their project in jacket blurb terms, and often telling nothing at all of what the book is about." In addition to following the suggestions in each agent's listing, plan your query letter carefully. It should include a brief description of your manuscript, anticipated number of words or pages, whether or not you've been published and your credentials (for nonfiction). "As an agent, I am looking for work I can sell," an agent told us. "The writer should write me a letter that *shows* he can write literate prose, not just *tell* me it's salable."

If the agent asks to see more of your work, consider yourself lucky, but don't assume you now have an agent. Just as you need to find out more about the agent, he has to know more about you and your writing. Don't expect an immediate response to your query or manuscript. On the other hand, if you receive no response or a negative response to your query, don't be discouraged. Continue to contact other agents. It's fine to send simultaneous queries, but never send a manuscript to more than one agent at a time.

Judging an agent

A bad agent can be worse than no agent at all. We've already discussed the expectations agents have for writers. Now it's time for you to decide what your expectations are for an agent. When an agency indicates an interest in representing your work, don't just assume it's the right one for you. If you want to make a knowledgable decision, you'll need more information—and that means asking questions.

While the answers to many of these questions appear in an agency's individual listing, it's a good idea to ask them again. Policies change and reporting time, commission amounts and fees may vary.

● How soon do you report on queries? On manuscripts?
● Do you charge a reading or critiquing fee? If yes, how much? What kind of feedback will I receive? What's the ratio of the agency's income from fees compared to income from marketing books? If the manuscript is accepted, will my fee be returned? Credited against my marketing expenses? Or is it a nonreturnable charge to cover reading/critiquing expenses?
● Do you charge any other fees?
● How many clients do you represent?
● Will you provide me with a list of recent sales, titles published or clients?
● May I contact any of your clients for referrals? [This is the most valuable information you can get, but some agents regard it as a breach of confidentiality.]
● Who will work with me and what kind of feedback can I expect—regular status reports, good news only, copies of informative letters from editors, etc.?
● Who will negotiate my contracts?
● Which subsidiary rights do you market directly? Which are marketed through subagents? Which are handled by the publisher?
● Do you offer any special services—tax/legal consultation, manuscript typing, book promotion or lecture tour coordination, etc.? Which cost extra? Which are covered by commission?
● Do you offer any editorial support? How much?
● Do you offer a written agreement? If yes, how long does it run? What kind of projects are covered? Will (or must) all of my writing be represented? What will your commission be on domestic, foreign and other rights? Which expenses am I responsible for? Are they deducted from earning, billed directly, or paid by initial deposit? How can the agreement be terminated? After it terminates, what happens to work already sold, current submissions, etc.?

If the agency doesn't offer a contract or written agreement of any kind, you should write a letter of your own that summarizes your understanding on all these issues. Ask the agent to return a signed copy to you. A few agents prefer informal verbal agreements. No matter how personal a relationship you have with an agent, it's still a business matter. If the agent refuses to sign a simple letter of understanding, you may want to reconsider your choice of agencies.

Additional resources

The search for an agent can be a frustrating and time-consuming task, especially if you don't know what you're looking for. You can learn more about agents by studying several books on the subject. Check with your library or bookstore for *Literary Agents: How to Get and Work with the Right One for You*, by Michael Larsen (Writer's Digest Books) and *Literary Agents: A Writer's Guide*, by Debby Mayer (Poet's & Writer's, Inc., 201 W. 54th St., New

York NY 10019). *Literary Agents of North America* (Author Aid/Research Associates International, 340 E. 52nd St., New York NY 10022) is a directory of agents indexed by name, geography, subjects and specialities, size and affiliates. The library may also have a copy of *Literary Market Place*, which includes names and addresses of agents.

Remember that agents are not required to have any special training or accreditation. Some are members of a number of professional organizations or writers groups, depending on their special interests. Each of the following three organizations requires its members to subscribe to a code of ethics and standard practices.

• ILAA—Independent Literary Agents Association, Inc., 15th floor, 55 5th Ave., New York NY 10003. Founded in 1977, ILAA is a nationwide association of fulltime literary agents. An informative brochure, list of members and copy of the association's code of ethics is sent on request to writers who enclose #10 SAE with two first class stamps. ILAA does not provide information on specialties of individual members.

• SAR—Society of Author's Representatives, Inc. 39½ Washington Sq. S., New York NY 10012. Founded in 1928, SAR is a voluntary association of New York agents. A brochure and membership list are available for SASE. Members are identified as specializing in literary or dramatic material.

• WGA—Writer's Guild of America. Agents and producers in the TV, radio and motion picture industry can become members or signatories of WGA by signing the guild's basic agreement which outlines minimum standards for treatment of writers. For a list of agents who have signed the WGA agreement, send a money order for $1.30 to one of the WGA offices. If you live east of the Mississippi River, write to WGA East, 555 W. 57th St., New York NY 10019; west of the Mississippi, write WGA West, 8955 Beverly Blvd., Los Angeles CA 90048.

Like *Writer's Market*, these agencies will not make recommendations of agents but provide information to help you in your search.

CAROLE ABEL LITERARY AGENCY, 160 W. 87th St., New York NY 10024. (212)724-1168. President: Carole Abel. Estab. 1978. Member of ILAA. Represents 45 clients. 25% of clients are new/unpublished authors. Prefers to work with published/established writers; works with a small number of new/unpublished authors. Specializes in contemporary women's novels, biographies, thrillers, health, nutrition, medical nonfiction (diet and exercise) and history.
Will Handle: Nonfiction books, novels. Currently handles 50% nonfiction books and 50% novels. Will read—at no charge—unsolicited queries, outlines and mss. Reports in 2 weeks on queries; 6 weeks on mss. "If our agency does not respond within 2 months to your request to become a client, you may submit requests elsewhere."
Terms: Agent receives 15% commission on domestic sales; 15% on dramatic sales; and 20% on foreign sales. Charges for phone, postage, bulk mailing, messenger and photocopying expenses. 100% of income derived from commission on ms sales.
Recent Sales: *Building Dreams*, by Justine Valente (NAL); *St. Anselm's Kidnapping*, by Bill Kennedy (St. Martin's); *First Class*, by Ann Rooth (Berkley).

DOMINICK ABEL LITERARY AGENCY, INC., Suite 12C, 498 West End Ave., New York NY 10024. (212)877-0710. President: Dominick Abel. Estab. 1975. Member of ILAA. Represents 80 clients. 5% of clients are new/unpublished writers. Prefers to work with published/established authors; works with a small number of new/unpublished authors.
Will Handle: Nonfiction books and novels. Currently handles 50% nonfiction books and 50% novels. Will read—at no charge—unsolicited queries and outlines. Reports in 2 weeks on queries. "If our agency does not respond within 2 months to your request to become a client, you may submit requests elsewhere."
Terms: Agent receives 10% commission on domestic sales; 10% on dramatic sales; and 20% on foreign sales. Charges for overseas postage, phone and cable expenses.
Recent Sales: No information given.

EDWARD J. ACTON INC., 928 Broadway, New York NY 10010. (212)675-5400. Contact: Inge Hanson. Estab. 1975. Member of ILAA. Represents 100 clients. Works with a small number of new/unpublished authors. Specializes in politics, celebrities, sports and commercial fiction.

Will Handle: Nonfiction books and novels. Currently handles 5% magazine articles; 40% nonfiction books; 35% novels; 5% movie scripts; 5% TV scripts; 10% video production and software. Will read—at no charge—unsolicited queries and outlines. Reports in 3 weeks on queries.
Terms: Agent receives 15% commission on domestic sales; 15% on dramatic sales; and 19% on foreign sales. Charges for photocopy expenses. 100% of income derived from commission on ms sales.
Recent Sales: *Man of the House*, by Tip O'Neill (Random House); *Ballplayer!*, by Pete Rose (Warner Books); and *The Irish*, by Jason Miller (Simon & Schuster).

LEE ALLAN AGENCY, Box 18617, Milwaukee WI 53218. (414)463-7441. Agent: Lee A. Matthias. Estab. 1983. Member of WGA. Represents 18 clients. 80% of clients are new/unpublished writers. "A writer must have a minimum of one (in our judgment) salable work. Credentials are preferred, but we are open to new writers." Specializes in "screenplays for mass film audience, low to medium budget preferred, but of high quality, not exploitation; and novels of high adventure, genre fiction such as mystery and science fiction—no romance, nonfiction, textbooks, or poetry."
Will Handle: Novels (male adventure, mystery, science fiction, literary) and movie scripts (low to medium budget, mass appeal material). Currently handles 50% novels; 50% movie scripts. Will read—at no charge—unsolicited queries and outlines. Does not read unsolicited mss. Must be queried first. Reports in 2 weeks on queries; 6 weeks on mss. "If our agency does not respond within 1 month to your request to become a client, you may submit requests elsewhere."
Terms: Agent receives 10% commission on domestic sales; 10% on dramatic sales; and 20% on foreign sales. Charges for photocopying, binding.

MARCIA AMSTERDAM AGENCY, Suite 9A, 41 W. 82nd St., New York NY 10024. (212)873-4945. Contact: Marcia Amsterdam. Estab. 1969. Member of WGA. 20% of clients are new/unpublished writers. Eager to work with new/unpublished writers. Specializes in fiction, nonfiction, young adult, TV and movies.
Will Handle: Nonfiction books, novels, juvenile books (young adult), and movie and TV scripts. Will read—at no charge—unsolicited queries, synopsis and outlines. Reports in 2 weeks on queries; 1 month on mss. "If our agency does not respond within 1 month to your request to become a client, you may submit requests elsewhere."
Terms: Agent receives 15% commission on domestic sales; 15% on dramatic sales; and 15% on foreign sales. Charges for telegraph, cable, phone, and legal fees (when client agrees to them). 100% of income is derived from commission on ms sales.
Recent Sales: *Goodbye Forever Tree*, by Rose Blue (NAL); *The Chain Letter*, by Ruby Jean Jensen (Zebra Books); and *Liege-Killer*, by Christopher Hinz (St. Martin's).

‡AUTHOR AID ASSOCIATES, 340 E. 52nd St., New York NY 10022. (212)758-4213; 697-2419. Editorial Director: Arthur Orrmont. Estab. 1967. Represents 150 clients. 10% of clients are new/unpublished writers. Works with a small number of new/unpublished authors.
Will Handle: Magazine fiction, nonfiction books, novels, juvenile books, movie scripts, stage plays, TV scripts and poetry collections. Currently handles 5% magazine fiction; 35% nonfiction books; 38% novels; 5% juvenile books; 5% movie scripts; 2% stage plays; 5% poetry and 5% other. Will read—at no charge—unsolicited queries and outlines. Reports within 1 month on mss.
Terms: Agent receives 10-15% commission on domestic sales; 15% on dramatic sales; and 20% on foreign sales. Charges a reading fee "only to new/unpublished authors. Refundable from commission on sale." 15% of income derived from reading fees. Charges for cable, photocopy and messenger express. Offers a consultation service through which writers not represented can get advice on a contract. 15% of income derived from fees; 85% of income derived from sales of writer's work.
Recent Sales: *Living Your Past Lives*, by Karl Scholotterbeck (Ballantine); *Waylon Jennings*, by R. Serge Denisoff (St. Martin's Press); and *One Day in Dallas, Eyewitness to the Kennedy Assassination*, by Ed Cherryholmes (Texian Press).

AUTHORS MARKETING SERVICES LTD., 217 Degrassi St., Toronto, Ontario M4M 2K8 Canada. (416)463-7200. Vice President: L. Hoffman. Estab. 1978. Represents 22 clients. 60% of clients are new/unpublished writers. Prefers to work with published/established authors; works with a small number of new/unpublished authors. Specializes in contemporary novels, intrigue/adventure, self-help and business.
Will Handle: Nonfiction books and novels. Currently handles 35% nonfiction books; 60% novels; and 5% consultation. Will read—at no charge—unsolicited queries and outlines. Reports in 3 weeks on queries. "If our agency does not respond within 1 month to your request to become a client, you may submit requests elsewhere."
Terms: Agent receives 15% commission on domestic (Canada and US) sales; and 20% on foreign sales. Charges a reading fee; will waive fee if representing the writer. 3% of income derived from reading fees. Sometimes offers a consultation service through which writers not represented can get advice on a contract; charges $35/hour. 5% of income derived from fees; 95% of income derived from commission on ms sales.

Recent Sales: *Voyage to the Whales*, by Dr. Hal Whitehead (Dutton); *Out of the Mouths of Babes*, by Martin Kendrick (Macmillan); *Mind Over Money*, by Dr. Norm Forman (Doubleday).

THE AXELROD AGENCY, INC., 126 5th Ave., New York NY 10011. (212)929-1704. President: Steven Axelrod. Estab. 1983. Represents 45 clients. 15% of our clients are new/unpublished writers. Specializes in hardcover and softcover mainstream and genre fiction, and software.
Will Handle: Nonfiction books, novels and software. Currently handles 45% nonfiction books; 45% novels and 10% software. Will read—at no charge—unsolicited queries, outlines and mss. Reports in 1 week on queries; 5 weeks on mss. "If our agency does not respond within 2 months to your request to become a client, you may submit requests elsewhere."
Terms: Agent receives 10% commission on domestic sales; 10% on dramatic sales; and 20% on foreign sales. Charges for photocopying. 100% of income derived from commission on ms sales.
Recent Sales: *Mayflower Madam*, by Sydney Biddle Barrows, with William Novak (Arbor House); *Nova Calendar (1987)* (Yankee Books); and *The Gamble*, by LaVyrle Spencer (Berkley).

VIRGINIA BARBER LITERARY AGENCY, INC., 353 W. 21st St., New York NY 10011. (212)255-6515. Contact: Virginia Barber or Mary Evans. Estab. 1974. Member of ILAA. Represents 75 clients. "Sometimes we receive such an interesting query letter that we ask to read the manuscript even though the writer lists no publications at all. We have no rigid rules about prior publication. We prefer authors who have tried to publish their work, if only in little magazines or newspapers. No agent could honestly claim to prefer unpublished writers to successfully established ones. If you want to know whether or not we could be enthusiastic about, say a particular novel by an unpublished writer, the answer is emphatically 'yes'." Specializes in general adult fiction and nonfiction. "We represent only a few authors of paperback originals or category novels."
Will Handle: Nonfiction books and novels. "The large majority of our contracts involve adult books, nonfiction and fiction about 50/50." Will read—at no charge—unsolicited queries and outlines. Reports in 2 weeks on queries; 6 weeks on mss. "If our agency does not respond within 2 months to your request to become a client, you may submit requests elsewhere."
Terms: Agent receives 10% commission on domestic sales; 10% on dramatic sales; 20% on foreign sales. 100% of income derived from commission on ms sales.
Recent Sales: "If writers we want to represent request information, we will gladly refer them to various editors we've worked with."

MAXIMILIAN BECKER, 115 E. 82nd St., New York NY 10028. (212)988-3887. President: Maximilian Becker. Estab. 1950. Works with a small number of new/unpublished authors.
Will Handle: Nonfiction books, novels and stage plays. Will read—at no charge—unsolicited queries, outlines and mss, but may charge a criticism fee or service charge for work performed after the initial reading. Reports in 2 weeks on queries; 3 weeks on mss.
Terms: Agent receives 15% commission on domestic sales; and 20% on foreign sales. Charges a criticism fee "if detailed criticism is requested. Writers receive a detailed criticism with suggestions—five to ten pages. No criticism is given if manuscript is hopeless."
Recent Sales: *Goering*, by David Irving (William Morrow); and *Year of the Wild Rose*, by Clara Rising (Villard Books).

‡MEREDITH BERNSTEIN, 33 Riverside Dr., New York NY 10023. (212)799-1007. President: Meredith Bernstein. Estab. 1981. Member of ILAA. Represents about 100 clients. 10% of our clients are new/unpublished writers. Eager to work with new/unpublished writers. Specializes in fiction and nonfiction contemporary novels, mysteries, child care, business and money, romances, sagas, fashion and beauty, humor, visual books and psychology.
Will Handle: Nonfiction books, novels, juvenile books and movie scripts. Currently handles 45% nonfiction books; 45% novels; 5% juvenile books and 5% miscellaneous. Will read unsolicited queries, outlines and mss. Reports in 1 week on queries; 2 weeks on mss. "If our agency does not respond within 1 month to your request to become a client, you may submit requests elsewhere."
Terms: Agent receives 15% commission on domestic sales and 20% on foreign sales. Charges a reading fee. 5% of income derived from reading fees. Charges writers for photocopy expenses. 5% of income derived from fees; 95% of income derived from sales of writer's work.
Recent Sales: *Mating Birds*, by Lewis Nkosi (St. Martin's Press); *Perchance to Dream*, by Maura Seger (Avon); and *The Bloomingdale's Health Style Cookbook* (McGraw-Hill).

THE BLAKE GROUP LITERARY AGENCY, Suite 600, One Turtle Creek Village, Dallas TX 75219. (214)828-2160. Director/Agent: Ms. Lee B. Halff. Estab. 1979. Member of Texas Publishers Association (TPA) and Texas Booksellers Association (TBA). Represents 40 clients. Prefers to work with published/established authors; works with a small number of new/unpublished authors.
Will Handle: Magazine fiction and nonfiction, nonfiction books, novels, textbooks, juvenile books, movie

scripts, radio scripts, stage plays, TV scripts, syndicated material and poetry. Currently handles 13% magazine articles; 30% nonfiction books; 38% novels; 2% textbooks; 7% juvenile books; 2% movie scripts; 2% stage plays; 1% TV scripts; 2% poetry; and 3% science fiction. Will read submissions at no charge, but may charge a criticism fee or service charge for work performed after the initial reading "at author's request." Submit complete ms; no queries please. Reports in 3 months on mss. "If our agency does not respond within 3 months to your request to become a client, you may submit requests elsewhere. Pre-stamped return mailer must accompany submissions; no checks accepted."
Terms: Agent receives 10% commission on domestic sales; 15% on dramatic sales; and 20% on foreign sales. Sometimes offers a consultation service through which writers not represented can get advice on a contract; charges $50/hour. 90% of income derived from commission on ms sales.
Recent Sales: *Strawman*, by Harold Durham (Zebra Books); *Weight Loss To Super Wellness*, by Ted L. Edwards, Jr. M.D. (Human Kinetics); *Do You Have A Secret?*, by Pamela Russell and Beth Stone (Compcare).

THE BOOK PEDDLERS, 18326 Minnetonka Blvd., Deephaven MN 55391. (612)475-3527. Owner/Agent: Vicki Lansky. Estab. 1984. Member of ILAA. Also provides book packaging services. Represents 26 clients. 80% of clients are new/unpublished writers. Prefers to work with published/established writers.
Will Handle: Nonfiction books, novels and syndicated material. Currently handles 80% nonfiction books and 20% novels. Will read—at no charge—unsolicited queries and outlines. Does not read unsolicited mss. Reports in 2 weeks on queries; 3 weeks on mss. "If our agency does not respond within 1 month to your request to become a client, you may submit requests elsewhere."
Terms: Agent receives 15% commission on domestic sales; and 20% on foreign sales. Does not charge reading fee "at this time" (May 1987). Sometimes offers a consultation service through which writers not represented can get advice on a contract; charges $50/hour. 90% of income derived from commission on ms sales.
Recent Sales: *File Don't Pile*, by Pat Dorf (St. Martin's); *Family Bed*, by Tine Thevinin (Avery); and *With Interest*, by Jo Murphy (Dow-Jones/Irwin).

GEORGE BORCHARDT INC., 136 E. 57th St., New York NY 10022. (212)753-5785. President: George Borchardt. Estab. 1967. Member of SAR. Represents 200 clients. 1-2% of our clients are new/unpublished writers. "We do not consider new clients unless highly recommended by someone we trust." Prefers to work with published/established authors; also works with a small number of new/unpublished authors. Specializes in fiction, biography and general nonfiction of unusual interest.
Will Handle: Nonfiction books and novels. Does not read unsolicited mss.
Terms: Agent receives 10% commission on domestic sales; 10% on dramatic sales; and 20% on foreign sales (15% on British). Charges for photocopy expenses. 100% of income derived from commission on ms sales.
Recent Sales: *Memory of an Invisible Man*, by H.F. Saint (Atheneum); *Reagan*, by Edmund Morris (Random House); *The Rabbi of Lud*, by Stanley Elkin (Scribner's).

‡BOSTON LITERARY AGENCY, Suite 404, 333 W. 57th St., New York NY 10019. (212)765-3663. Contact: Justin K. McDonough. Estab 1975. Represents 10 clients. 40% of clients are new/unpublished writers; works with a small number of new/unpublished writers; eager to work with new/unpublished writers.
Will Handle: Nonfiction books, novels, movie and TV scripts. Currently handles 50% novels; 50% nonfiction books. Does not read unsolicited ms. Reports in 2 weeks on queries.
Terms: Agent receives 10% commission on domestic sales; 15% on dramatic sales; and 20% on foreign sales. Charges writers for photocopy and overnight express mail expenses. 100% of income derived from commissions of ms sales.
Recent Sales: *Forensic Fires*, by F. Reid Buckley (Harper and Row); *Paul Manship*, by John Manship (Abbeville Press).

THE BRADLEY-GOLDSTEIN AGENCY, Suite 6E, 7 Lexington Ave., New York NY 10010. (718)672-7924. President: Paul William Bradley. Director: Martha Goldstein. Estab. 1985. Represents 75 clients. 50% of clients have been new/unpublished writers. Will consider taking on a small number of new/unpublished authors. Specializes in "quality" fiction and nonfiction, biographies, politics, science, social science, business, current affairs, and the arts.
Will Handle: Nonfiction books, novels and textbooks. Currently handles 70% nonfiction books; 20% novels; and 10% textbooks. Will read—at no charge—unsolicited query letters and outlines only. "Include SASE." Do not send mss. Reports in 2 months on queries.
Terms: Agent receives 15% commission on domestic sales; and 25% on foreign sales. Charges for postage, photocopying, and telephone expenses. Offers a consultation service through which writers can get advice on a contract; charges $50/hour. 90% of income is derived from commission on ms sales; 10% on consultations.
Recent Sales: *Walt Disney: A Biography*, by Maxine Fisher (Franklin Watts); *Marvel Comics: The Untold Story of the World's Most Successfull Comic Book Empire*, by Ron Whyte (St. Martin's Press); *The Book of Crabs and Lobsters*, by Chris Reaske (Nick Lyons Books).

BRANDT & BRANDT LITERARY AGENTS, INC., 1501 Broadway, New York NY 10036. (212)840-5760. Estab. 1914. Member of SAR. Represents 250 clients. Works with a small number of new/unpublished authors.
Will Handle: Nonfiction books and novels. "We read and answer letters from writers about their work only."
Terms: Agent receives 10% commission on domestic sales; 10% on dramatic sales; and 20% on foreign sales. Charge for photography and phone expenses. 100% of income derived from commission on manuscript sales.
Recent Sales: *The Lebaron Secret*, by Birmingham, (L. Brown); *Move Your Shadow*, by Lelyveld (Times Books); and *Easy In The Islands*, by Shacochis (Crown).

CURTIS BROWN LTD., 10 Astor Pl., New York NY 10003. (212)473-5400. Member of SAR. Prefers to work with published/established authors; works with a small number of new/unpublished authors. Specializes in general fiction and nonfiction.
Will Handle: Nonfiction books, novels and juvenile books. Will read—at no charge—unsolicited queries and outlines accompanied by SASE; does not read unsolicited mss.
Terms: "Will explain to clients when they wish to sign."
Recent Sales: No information given.

‡**NED BROWN INC.**, Box 5020, Beverly Hills CA 90210. (213)276-1131. President: Ned Brown. Estab. 1963. Writer must be previously published or have a recommendation from other client or publisher. Prefers to work with published/established authors.
Will Handle: Magazine fiction, nonfiction books, novels, movie scripts, stage plays and TV scripts. Does not read unsolicited mss.
Terms: Agent receives 10% commission on domestic sales; 15% on dramatic sales; and 20% on foreign sales. Charges writers for "extraordinary expenses."
Recent Sales: No information given.

PEMA BROWNE LTD., 185 E. 85th St., New York NY 10028. (212)369-1925. Treasurer: Perry J. Browne. Estab. 1966. Member of WGA. Represents 25 clients. 25% of clients are new/unpublished writers. "We review only new projects and require that writers have not sent manuscript to publishers or other agents." Eager to work with new/unpublished writers. Specializes in men's adventure, thrillers, mainstream, historical, regencies and contemporary romances; young adult; children's; reference; how-to and other types on nonfiction.
Will Handle: Nonfiction books, novels, juvenile books, movie scripts, TV scripts and syndicated material. Currently handles 25% nonfiction books; 25% novels; 10% juvenile books; 2% movie scripts; 2% TV scripts; 2% syndicated material; and 33% mass-market. Will read—at no charge—unsolicited queries, synopses and mss. Reports in 2 weeks on queries; 1 month on mss. "If our agency does not respond within 2 months to your request to become a client, you may submit requests elsewhere."
Terms: Agent receives 15% commission on domestic sales; 10% on dramatic sales; and 10% on foreign sales. 100% of income derived from commission on ms sales.
Recent Sales: *Encyclopedia of Music*, by Robert Lisauer (Paragon); *Welcome to the Real World*, by Wes Smith and John Sandford (Ballantine); and *Playing Games*, by Barbara Cummings (Silhouette).

SHIRLEY BURKE AGENCY, Suite B-704, 370 E. 76th St., New York NY 10021. (212)861-2309. President: Shirley Burke. Estab. 1948. Represents 15 clients. 15% of our clients are new/unpublished writers. "The most important qualification for writers is talent—not how many books they've sold." Eager to work with new/unpublished writers "if I feel there is real talent there."
Will Handle: Nonfiction books and novels. Currently handles 50% nonfiction books and 50% novels. Will read—at no charge—unsolicited queries and short outlines. Reports in 2 weeks on queries. "Do not send mss. Enclose SASE."
Terms: Agent receives 10% commission on domestic sales; 20% on foreign sales.
Recent Sales: *Mozart* (McGraw-Hill); *Our Father's House* (Putnam); and *Wild Orchids*, (Warner).

‡**JANE BUTLER, ART AND LITERARY AGENT, ASSOCIATE, VIRGINIA KIDD LITERARY AGENTS**,538 E. Harford St., Box 278, Milford PA 18337. (717)296-7266, 491-2045. Associate: Jane Butler. Estab. 1981. "Prefers some published credits, but all queries are welcome; no SASE, no reply." Works with small number of new/upublished writers each year. "The best part of agenting is discovering new talent: writer should be prolific in one of the areas within which I specialize." Specializes in nonfiction (popular natural history, popular soft sciences—anthropology, archaeology; native American and oriental religious history and modern practice; myths and fairy tales; and military history) and fiction (historical, mysteries, science fiction, horror, historical fantasy and fantasy).
Will Handle: Nonfiction books and novels. Currently handles 15% nonfiction books; 80% novels; 5% juvenile books. Will read—at no charge—unsolicited queries, outlines and mss. Reports in 2 weeks on queries; 1 month on mss. "If our agency does not respond within 2 months to your request to become a client, you may submit requests elsewhere."

Terms: Agent receives 10% commission on domestic sales; 15% on dramatic sales; and 20% on foreign sales. 100% of income derived from commission on ms sales.
Recent Sales: *Khamsin*, by Judith Tarr (Bantam Spectra); *Queen of Heaven*, by Alis Rasmussen (Baen Books); and *Wreck Diving Off The New Jersey Coast*, by Gary Gentile (Sea Sports Publications).

CANADIAN SPEAKERS' AND WRITERS' SERVICE LIMITED, 44 Douglas Crescent, Toronto, Ontario M4W 2L7 Canada. (416)921-4443. President: Matie Molinaro. Estab. 1950. Represents 225 clients. 3% of clients are new/unpublished writers. Prefers to work with published/established authors; works with a small number of new/unpublished authors.
Will Handle: Magazine fiction, nonfiction books, novels, juvenile books, movie scripts, radio scripts, stage plays and TV scripts. Currently handles 70% nonfiction books; 5% novels; 5% movie scripts; 10% radio scripts; 5% stage plays; and 5% TV scripts. Does not read unsolicited mss. Reports in 3 weeks on queries; 1 month on mss. "If our agency does not respond within 1 month to your request to become a client, you may submit requests elsewhere."
Terms: Agent receives 15% commission on domestic sales; 15% on dramatic sales; and 20% on foreign sales. Charges a criticism/reading fee: $50, plus $3/one-thousand words. "Each reading/critique is handled by four people and a composite report is sent out to the writer." Offers a consultation service through which writers not represented can get advice on a contract; charges $160/hour. 5% of income derived from fees; 95% of income derived from commission on manuscript sales. Payment of a criticism fee does not ensure that agency will represent a writer.
Recent Sales: *McLuhan Letter*, (Oxford University Press); *Ben Wicks First Treasury*, by Ben Wicks (Methuen Publishers); and *Medical Survival*, by Dr. Gifford Jones (Methuen).

RUTH CANTOR, LITERARY AGENT, Rm. 1133, 156 5th Ave., New York NY 10010. (212)243-3246. Contact: Ruth Cantor. Estab. 1952. Represents 40 clients. Writer must have "a good, sound track record in the publishing field . . . A skimpy one will sometimes get you a reading if I'm convinced that talent might be lurking in the bulrushes." Prefers to work with published/established authors; works with a small number of new/unpublished authors. Specializes in "any good trade book, fiction of quality, good, competent mysteries with new elements, juvenile books above the age of eight, up through young adult."
Will Handle: Nonfiction books, novels and juvenile books. Will read—at no charge—unsolicited queries and outlines. Reports in 1 month on queries; 2 months on mss.
Terms: Agent receives 10% commission on domestic sales; 10% on dramatic sales; and 10% on foreign sales.
Recent Sales: *The Rod of Sybil* (Harcourt); *The Players* (Warner); and *Lady Divine*, by Barbara Sherrod (Warner).

TERRY CHIZ AGENCY, Suite E, 5761 Whitnall Hwy., North Hollywood CA 91601. (818)506-0994. President: Terry Chiz. Vice President: Shan Sia. Estab. 1984. Represents 18 clients. 20% of clients are new/unpublished writers. Prefers to work with published/established authors; works with a small number of new/unpublished authors. Specializes in film and TV.
Will Handle: Novels, movie scripts and TV scripts. No romance or historical. Currently handles 20% novels; 40% movie scripts; and 40% TV scripts. Will read—at no charge—unsolicited queries and outlines. Reports in 2 weeks. "If our agency does not respond within 1 month to your request to become a client, you may submit elsewhere." Will not respond without SASE.
Terms: Agent receives 10% commission.
Recent Sales: "Film deals pending on several properties that are in book and script not for public information."

CONNIE CLAUSEN ASSOCIATES, Suite 16H, 250 E. 87 St., New York NY 10128. (212)427-6135. Contacts: Connie Clausen, Guy Kettelhack. Estab. 1976. Represents approximately 90 clients. 3% of clients are new/unpublished writers. Prefers to work with published/established authors; works with a small number of new/unpublished authors. Considers recommendations from clients and publishers. Specializes in trade nonfiction of all kinds, and some fiction.
Will Handle: Nonfiction books, and novels and juvenile books (sometimes). Handles magazine articles and fiction if client has a book. Currently handles 3% magazine articles; 90% nonfiction books; 5% novels; and 2% juvenile books. Does not read unsolicited mss. Reports in 1 month "when possible (often less)" on queries.
Terms: Agent receives 15% commission on domestic sales; 15% on dramatic sales; and 20% on foreign sales. Charges for photocopying, postage, and messenger expenses.
Recent Sales: *Are You Lonesome Tonight?*, by Lucy DeBarbin and Dary Matera (Villard); *Caught In The Crossfire*, by Jan Goodwin (Dutton); and *Good Girls Don't Eat Dessert*, by Drs. Rosalyn Meadow and Lillie Weiss (Weidenfeld).

HY COHEN LITERARY AGENCY, LTD., Suite 1400, 111 W. 57th St., New York NY 10019. (212)757-5237. President: Hy Cohen. Estab. 1975. Represents 20 clients. 50% of our clients are new/unpublished writers.

Will Handle: Nonfiction books and novels. Currently handles 50% nonfiction books and 50% novels. Will read—at no charge—unsolicited queries, outlines and mss, accompanied by SASE. Reports in 1 week on queries; 1 month on mss. "If our agency does not respond within 1 month to your request to become a client, you may submit requests elsewhere."
Terms: Agent receives 10% commission on domestic sales; 10% on dramatic sales; and 20% on foreign sales. Charges for "unusual" postage and phone expenses. 100% of income derived from commission on ms sales.
Recent Sales: *Let's Go Kill A Neighbor*, by David Goodnough (Walker); *Sidewinder*, by Sharon Zaffirini (Ballantine); and *Wit and Wisdom of Mark Twain*, by Alex Ayers (Harper and Row).

RUTH COHEN, INC., Box 7626, Menlo Park CA 94025. (415)854-2054. President: Ruth Cohen. Estab. 1982. Member of ILAA. Represents 45-60 clients. 30% of clients are new/unpublished writers. Writers must have a book that is well written and preferably have some publishing experience. Prefers to work with published/established authors; eager to work with new/unpublished writers. Specializes in juvenile, young adult nonfiction and genre books.
Will Handle: Nonfiction books for adults, juvenile books (for ages 3-14 and young adult), and genre novels—mystery, Western, contemporary romance, science fiction, fantasy, and historical romance. Currently handles 30% nonfiction books; 30% novels; and 40% juvenile books. Will read—at no charge—unsolicited queries, outlines and partial mss. Reports in 3 weeks on queries; 1 month on mss. "No multiple agency submissions. If our agency does not respond within 3 months to your request to become a client, you may submit requests elsewhere."
Terms: Agent receives 10% commission on domestic sales; 15% on dramatic sales; and 20% on foreign sales. Charges writers for photocopying. 100% of income derived from commission on ms sales.
Recent Sales: *No More Tantrums*, (St. Martin's); *Sundown*, (Walker and Company) and *The Narrow Book*, (Harper and Row).

COLLIER ASSOCIATES, Suite 1003, 875 Avenue of the Americas, New York NY 10001. (212)563-4065. Manager: Oscar Collier. Estab. 1976. Member of SAR and ILAA. Represents 80 clients. Works with a small number of new/unpublished authors. Specializes in fiction trade books (war, crime, and historical novels) and nonfiction trade books on business and finance, biographies, popular psychology, math for general audience, politics, exposes, medicine, nature and outdoors, history, cookbooks by highly qualified experts, and nutrition.
Will Handle: Nonfiction books and novels. Will read—at no charge—unsolicited queries and outlines with SASE. Simultaneous submissions OK. Usually reports in 1 month on queries.
Terms: Agent receives 15% commission on domestic sales; 15% on dramatic sales; and 20% on foreign sales. Charges for books ordered from publishers for rights submissions, Express Mail, and copying expenses.
Recent Sales: *The Search for the Real Nancy Reagan* (Macmillan); *Prairie*, by Anne Lee Waldo (Berkeley Books); *Why the Best Laid Investment Plans Usually Go Wrong*, by Harry Browne (William Morrow and Co., Inc.).

CONNOR LITERARY AGENCY, 640 W. 153rd St., New York NY 10031. (212)491-5233. Owner: Marlene Connor. Estab. 1985. Represents 20 clients. 25% of clients are new/unpublished writers. "I would prefer that my writers have been published at some point (it shows that they have attempted to market themselves). Literary awards are also good." Specializes in commercial fiction leaning toward mysteries, thrillers, romantic suspense, current affairs, and horror. "I am also interested in black and ethnic writers. I am an expert at general nonfiction, how-to, illustrated, and self-help books. I also work with magazine tie-in books, and books that tie-in with an organization or corporation. I work closely with an excellent book producing team for books that are heavily illustrated or have special design needs."
Will Handle: Nonfiction books, novels, illustrated, how-to and self-help. Currently handles 50% nonfiction books and 50% novels. Will read—at no charge—unsolicited queries and outlines. Reports in 2 months on queries. "Material will not be returned without SASE."
Terms: Agent receives 15% commission on domestic sales; and 25% on foreign sales. No criticism fee "unless the author requests a criticism after rejection, then the charge is $50. Because of the volume of submissions I can only answer those I am interested in." Charges for photocopy, postage, telephone and messenger expenses, and special materials for presentation. Sometimes offers a consultation service through which writers can get advice on a contract; charges $75/hour. 2% of income derived from fees; 98% of income derived from commission on ms sales.
Recent Sales: *Simplicity's Simply The Best Sewing Book* (Harper and Row); *Rosalinda*, by Randy Russell (Bantam); and *Street Food*, by Rose Grant (Crossing Press).

‡BEN CONWAY AND ASSOCIATES, Suite 403, 999 N. Doheny Dr., Los Angeles CA 90069. (213)271-8133. President: Ben Conway. Estab. 1968. Represents 75 clients. 7% of clients are new/unpublished writers. Prefers to work with published/established writers; works with small number of new/unpublished writers each year. "Television comedy is our forte, but we also work with a variety of TV and film genres."

Will Handle: Movie and TV scripts. Currently handles 50% movie scripts and 50% TV scripts. Does not read unsolicited manuscripts. Reports in 1 week on queries with enclosed SASE.
Terms: Standard commission 10%. Charges writer for photocopies.
Recent Sales: No information given.

RICHARD CURTIS ASSOCIATES, INC., Suite 1, 164 E. 64th St., New York NY 10021. (212)371-9481. President: Richard Curtis. Associate: Elizabeth Waxse. Estab. 1969. Member of ILAA. Represents 75 clients. 5% of clients are new/unpublished writers. Writer must have some published work and either a finished novel or proposed nonfiction book. Prefers to work with published/established authors; works with a small number of new/unpublished authors. Specializes in commercial fiction of all genres, mainstream fiction and nonfiction.
Will Handle: Nonfiction books, novels, textbooks, juvenile books, and movie scripts. Currently handles 1% magazine articles; 1% magazine fiction; 25% nonfiction books; 65% novels; 5% textbooks; 3% juvenile books. Will read—at no charge—unsolicited queries and outlines. Reports in 2 weeks on queries; 1 month on mss. "If our agency does not respond within 1 month to your request to become a client, you may submit requests elsewhere."
Terms: Agent receives 10% commission on domestic sales; 15% on dramatic sales; and 20% on foreign sales. Charges a reading fee; 1% of income derived from reading fee. Writer receives two to four single-spaced pages of general explanation, line-by-line, and assessment of market and of author's "credentials." Work done by book trade editors. Charges for photocopying, messengers, purchase of books for subsidiary exploitations, cable, air mail and express mail. Offers a consultation service through which writers not represented can get advice on a contract; charges $200/hour. 1% of income derived from fees; 99% of income derived from commission on ms sales.
Recent Sales: *Heiress*, by Janet Dailey (Little, Brown); *Blazewyndham*, by Beatrice Small (NAL); and *Forge of God*, by Greg Bear (TOR).

D.J. ENTERPRISES, 339 S. Franklin St., Allentown PA 18102. (215)437-0723. President: Douglas J. Tomel. Estab. 1980. Member of ILAA. Represents 200 clients. 95% of clients are new/unpublished writers. Writer must send letter of reference before sending ms. Prefers to work with published/established authors. "We handle all material, except gay material."
Will Handle: Magazine articles (true-to-life stories) and movie and TV scripts. Currently handles 5% magazine articles; 90% movie scripts; and 5% TV scripts. Will read—at no charge—unsolicited queries, outlines and mss. Reports in 2 weeks on queries and mss. "If our agency does not respond within 1 month to your request to become a client, you may submit requests elsewhere."
Terms: Agent receives 10% commission on domestic, dramatic, and foreign sales. Charges for postage expenses.
Recent Sales: *Miracle of Melody Malone*, by John Inman; *The Great Sports Caper*, by Doug Tomel.

‡ANITA DIAMANT, THE WRITER'S WORKSHOP, INC., #1508, 310 Madison Ave., New York NY 10017. (212)687-1122. President: Anita Diamant. Estab. 1917. Member of SAR. Represents 100 clients. 30% of clients are new/unpublished writers. Prefers to work with published/established authors; works with a small number of new/unpublished authors. Specializes in general and commercial fiction (hard and soft cover) such as historical romances, general romances, horror and science fiction; and nonfiction such as health, politics and biography.
Will Handle: Magazine articles, nonfiction books and novels. Currently handles 40% nonfiction books; 40% novels; 10% young adult books; and 10% other. Will read—at no charge—unsolicited queries. Reports in 1 month on queries. "If our agency does not respond within 2 months to your request to become a client, you may submit requests elsewhere."
Terms: Agent receives 15% commission for up to $120,000 advance on domestic sales—10% thereafter; 15% on dramatic sales; and 15-20% on foreign sales. Charges for photocopy, messenger, special mailing and telephone expenses. 100% of income derived from sales of writers' work.
Recent Sales: *Dark Angel*, by V.C. Andrews (Poseidon); *New McGarr*, by Bartholemew Gill (Viking/Penguin); and *Reasons of the Heart*, by Henry Giniger (Franklin Watts).

‡SANDRA DIJKSTRA LITERARY AGENCY,Suite 515C, 1237 Camino Del Mar, Del Mar CA 92014. (619)755-3115. Contact: Sandra Dijkstra. Estab. 1981. Member of ILAA. Represents 50 clients. 60% of clients are new/unpublished writers. "We, of course, prefer to take on established authors, but are happy to represent any writer of brilliance or special ability. Most of our sales are nonfiction (self-help, true story, cultural criticism), but we have placed both quality and popular fiction as well."
Will Handle: Nonfiction books (author must have expertise in the field) and novels. Currently handles 75% nonfiction books; 25% novels. Will read—at no charge—unsolicited queries and outlines. Reports in 2-3 weeks on queries. "If our agency does not respond within 6 weeks to your request to become a client, you may submit requests elsewhere."

Terms: Receives 15% commission on domestic sales; 20% on British sales (10% to British agent); and 30% on translation (20% to foreign agent who represents world rights). Charges an evalution and criticism fee. Evaluation fee will be waived if ms is solicited by agency. 10% of income derived from criticism fees; charges $175 for a 300-page ms. Writer receives "a 3-5 page single-spaced critique covering all aspects of a work's literary qualities and marketability." Charges a $150 yearly expense fee to cover phone, postage, photocopy costs incurred in marketing ms.

Recent Sales: *If I'm So Wonderful Why Am I Still Single*, by Susan Page (Viking); *Finally Free: A Woman Doctor's 17-Year Battle with Drug Addiction*, by Martha Morrison, M.D. (Crown); and *The Happy Family*, by Arturo Islas (Morrow).

THE JONATHAN DOLGER AGENCY, Suite 9B, 49 E. 96th St., New York NY 10128. (212)427-1853. President: Jonathan Dolger. Estab. 1980. Represents 70 clients. 25% of clients are new/unpublished writers. Writer must have been previously published if submitting fiction. Prefers to work with published/established authors; works with a small number of new/unpublished writers. Specializes in adult trade fiction and nonfiction, and illustrated books.

Will Handle: Nonfiction books, novels and illustrated books. Will read—at no charge—unsolicited queries and outlines with SASE included.

Terms: Agent receives 10-15% commission on domestic sales; 10% on dramatic sales; and 20-30% on foreign sales. Charges for "standard expenses." Offers a consultation service through which writers not represented can get advice on a contract; charges a negotiable fee. 100% of income derived from commission on ms sales.

Recent Sales: Confidential.

‡DORESE AGENCY LTD., 8A, 41 W. 82nd St., New York NY 10024. (212)580-2855. President: Alyss Dorese. Estab. 1979. Member of WGA. Represents 35 clients. 10% of clients are new/unpublished authors. Writers must have been "published previously, unless recommended by a professional, or else we must be impressed by the material or subject matter." Works with a small number of new/unpublished authors. Specializes in nonfiction, true crime and mass market fiction.

Will Handle: Magazine articles (public affairs); nonfiction books; novels; movie scripts. Currently handles 30% nonfiction books; 20% novels; 60% movie scripts; and 10% TV scripts. Will read—at no charge—unsolicited queries and outlines. Does not read unsolicited mss. Reports in 6 weeks on queries. "If our agency does not respond within 2 months to your request to become a client, you may submit requests elsewhere."

Terms: Agent receives 15% commission on domestic sales; 15% on dramatic sales; and 20% on foreign sales. Charges a reading and criticism fee of $50/250-page ms; $75/350 pages. Fee will be deducted from first monies earned. 10% of incomed derived from reading fees. Charges for legal fees, phone and photocopy expenses. Sometimes offers a consultation service through which writers not represented can get advice on a contract; charges $60/hour. 1% of commission derived from fees; 94% of income derived from sales writer's work; 5% of income derived from criticism services. Payment of a criticism fee does not ensure that agency will represent a writer as the writer's work might not be commercial.

Recent Sales: Confidential.

EDUCATIONAL DESIGN SERVICES, INC., Box 253, Wantagh NY 11793. (718)539-4107/(516)221-0995. Vice President: Edwin Selzer. President: Bertram Linder. Estab. 1979. Represents 18 clients. 90% of clients are new/unpublished writers. Eager to work with new/unpublished writers in the educational field. Specializes in educational materials aimed at the kindergarten through twelfth grade market; primarily textual materials.

Will Handle: Nonfiction books and textbooks. Currently handles 100% textbooks. Reports in 1 month on queries and mss. "If our agency does not respond within 6 weeks to your request to become a client, you may submit requests elsewhere. You must send SASE."

Terms: Agent receives 15% commission on domestic sales; and 25% on foreign sales. Charges for phone, postage and delivery expenses, and retyping "if necessary"; charges $50/hour. 100% of income derived from commission on ms sales.

Recent Sales: *Money* (Schoolhouse Press); *Nueva Historia de Los Estados Unidos* (Minerva Books); and *Comprehensive Social Studies* (Barrons Education Series).

PETER ELEK ASSOCIATES, Box 223, Canal St. Station, New York NY 10013. (212)431-9368. Assistant: Carol Diehl. Estab. 1979. Also provides book packaging services. Represents 15 clients. 15% of our clients are new/unpublished writers. "An applicant must be, or is clearly intending to be self-supporting through their writing." Prefers to work with published/established authors; works with a small number of new/unpublished authors. Specializes in illustrated nonfiction, current affairs, self-help (not pop-psych), contemporary biography/autobiography, food, popular culture (all for adults); and preschool and juvenile illustrated fiction, nonfiction and novelties; and contemporary adventure for adults.

Will Handle: Nonfiction books, novels and juvenile books. No category fiction. Currently handles 60% nonfiction books and 40% juvenile books. Will read—at no charge—unsolicited queries and outlines. Reports in 2 weeks on queries. "If our agency does not respond within 6 weeks to your request to become a client, you may submit requests elsewhere."

Terms: Agent receives 15% commission on domestic sales; 20% on dramatic sales; and 20% on foreign sales. Charges for manuscript retyping, "if required." Sometimes offers a consultation service through which writers not represented can get advice on a contract; charges $75/hour, $125 minimum. 5% of income derived from fees; 33⅓% of income derived from commission on ms sales ("66⅔% derived from sale of finished packaged books"). 100% income derived from sales of writers' work.

Recent Sales: *The Everyday Gourmet*, by Kathleen Perry (Warner); *The Discovery of The Titanic*, by Dr. Robert Ballard (Warner); and *Business Innovators*, by William Davis (AMACOM).

‡THE ERIKSON LITERARY AGENCY,Suite C, 815 De La Vina, Santa Barbara CA 93101. (805)963-8373. Agent: George Erikson. Estab. 1987. Represents 11 clients. 55% of clients are new/unpublished writers. Eager to work with new/unpublished writers.

Will Handle: Nonfiction books, novels and movie scripts. Currently handles 60% nonfiction books; 30% novels and 10% movie scripts. Reports in 1 month on queries; 2 months on mss. "If our agency does not respond within 2 months to your request to becomes a client, you may submit requests elsewhere."

Terms: Receives 15% commission on domestic sales; 15% on dramatic sales and 20% on foreign sales. Charges reading fee of $100 for full ms. Reading fee will be deducted from agency's earned commissions. 10% of income derived from reading fees. Writer receives one page evaluation with marketing advice. Charges for photocopying, mailing and telephone are charged against advances. 90% of income derived from sales of writer's work; 10% of income derived from criticism services.

Recent Sales: "This agency is just starting."

‡FARWESTERN CONSULTANTS, INC., Box 47786, Phoenix AZ 85068-7786. (602)861-3546. President: Elizabeth "Libbi" Goodman. Estab. 1987. Represents 17 clients. 50% of our clients are new/unpublished writers. "We have a strong background in literatures, editing; and cover the NY and regional markets. We devote whatever time is needed to help a writer develop his full potential. We believe a dynamic relationship between author and agent is necessary for success." Eager to work with new/unpublished writers. "We also work with a number of established authors." Specializes in ethnic fiction/nonfiction, all categories of western fiction/nonfiction, regional, women's contemporary fiction and literary novels. Will not handle category romance, juvenile or poetry.

Will Handle: Magazine fiction (literary quarterly); most book-length nonfiction; popular fiction; short story collections and screenplays (must be accompanied by a signed release form and a treatment). Currently handles 5% magazine fiction; 25% nonfiction books; 65% novels; 5% movie scripts and 5% short story collections. Will read—at not charge—unsolicited queries, synopsis and first three chapters when SASE is enclosed. "Will only read complete mss if we have read a partial and request the rest." Reports in 2-3 weeks on queries; 4-6 weeks on partials. "If our agency does not respond within 2 months to your request to become a client, you may submit requests elsewhere.

Terms: Receives 10% commission on domestic sales; 10% on dramatic sales; and 20% on foreign sales. "If a writer is not represented by us and still wants a detailed critique of his ms for rewrite purposes, we will do so as a separate situation. We are not in the critiquing business and do not charge our clients for critiques." Less than 1% of income derived from criticism fees. Critique fee $275 for 300-page, typed double-spaced book ms. A critique would consist of 5-6 pages, single spaced. Ms would be given a line edit as well as an overall evaluation as to plot structure, characterization and writing style. Critiques are done by published novelists who are affiliated with the president of our firm. Charges writers for postage, phone and photocopies. Less than 1% of income is derived from fees charged to writers; 99% of income is derived from commission on manuscript sales.

Recent Sales: "We are a new agency. One screenplay and one novel presently in negotiation."

FLORENCE FEILER LITERARY AGENCY, 1524 Sunset Plaza Dr., Los Angeles CA 90069. (659)652-6920/ 652-0945. Associate: Audrey Rugh. Estab. 1967. Represents 40 clients. No unpublished writers. "Quality is the criterion." Specializes in fiction, nonfiction, essays and screen; very little TV and no short stories.

Will Handle: Textbooks (for special clients), juvenile books, movie scripts. Will read—at no charge— queries and outlines only. Reports in 2 weeks on queries; 10 weeks on mss. "If our agency does not respond within 3 months to your request to become a client, you may submit requests elsewhere."

Terms: Agent receives 10% commission on domestic sales; 10% on dramatic sales; and 20% on foreign sales.

Recent Sales: *Angelic Avengers*, *Out of Africa*, and *Last Magnificent War*.

FRIEDA FISHBEIN LTD., 2556 Hubbard St., Brooklyn NY 11235. (212)247-4398. President: Janice Fishbein. Estab. 1925. Represents 30 clients. 50% of clients are new/unpublished writers. "We agree to represent a writer solely on the basis of a *complete* work." Eager to work with new/unpublished writers. Specializes in historical romance, historical adventure, male adventure, mysteries, thrillers, and family sagas. Books on the environment, nursing and medicine, plays and screenplays.

Will Handle: Nonfiction books, novels, textbooks, juvenile books, movie scripts, stage plays and TV scripts. No poetry or magazine articles. Currently handles 20% nonfiction books; 30% novels; 5% textbooks; 10% juvenile books; 10% movie scripts; 15% stage plays; and 10% TV scripts. Will read—at no charge—unsolicited queries and brief outlines. Reports in 2 weeks on queries; 6 weeks on mss. "If our agency does not respond within 2 months to your request to become a client, you may submit requests elsewhere."

Terms: Agent receives 10% commission on domestic sales; 10% on dramatic sales; and 20% on foreign sales. Charges reading fee; $75/TV script, screenplay or play; $60/50,000 words for manuscripts, $1/each 1,000 additional words. Fee will be waived if representing writer. "Our readers are part-time workers who also serve as editors at magazines and/or publishers. Our reports are always longer for larger manuscripts. The usual reader's report varies between three to five pages, and may or may not include a line-to-line critique, but it always includes an overall evaluation." 20% of income derived from fees; 80% of income derived from commission on ms sales. Payment of a criticism fee does not ensure that agency will represent a writer.

Recent Sales: *The Home Day Care Book*, by Sherry Alexander (Atlantic Monthly Press); *Code of Honor*, by Herbert L. Fisher (Berkley Publishing Co.); and "Double Cross," by Gary Bohlke (play).

‡**FLAMING STAR LITERARY ENTERPRISES**, 320 Riverside Dr., New York NY 10025. (212)222-0083. President: Joseph B. Vallely. Estab. 1985. Represents 30 clients. 50% of clients are new/unpublished writers. Eager to work with new/unpublished writers. Specializes in commercial and literary fiction and nonfiction.

Will Handle: Nonfiction books and novels. Currently handles 50% nonfiction books and 50% novels. Will read submissions at no charge, but may charge a criticism fee or service charge for work performed after the initial reading. Reports in 1 week on queries; 2 weeks on mss. "If our agency does not respond within 1 month to your request to become a client, you may submit requests elsewhere."

Terms: Agent receives 15% commission on domestic sales; 15% on dramatic sales; and 20% on foreign sales. (All rates are for unpublished authors. Commissions are 5% lower for previously published authors.) Charges criticism fee. 10% of income derived from criticism fee. Charges $125 criticism fee for 300-page, typed, double-spaced manuscript. Writer receives line by line and overall evaluation, including marketing advice. Critique is performed by president. Critique runs from 2-6 pages. Charges writers for postage, phone, messenger and photocopies. 10% of income comes from fees charged to writer; 90% comes from commission on ms sales. "I only charge fees when I know I will represent the writer. The fee is deducted from commission if ms is sold."

Recent Sales: Confidential.

ROBERT A. FREEDMAN DRAMATIC AGENCY, INC., (formerly Harold Freedman Brandt & Brandt Dramatic Dept., Inc.), Suite 2310, 1501 Broadway, New York NY 10036. (212)840-5760. President: Robert A. Freedman. Vice President: Selma Luttinger. Member of SAR. Prefers to work with established authors; works with a very small number of new/unpublished authors. Specializes in plays and motion picture and television scripts.

Will Handle: Movie scripts, stage plays and TV scripts. Does not read unsolicited mss. Usually reports in 2 weeks on queries; 6 weeks on mss.

Terms: Agent receives 10% on dramatic sales; "and, as is customary, 20% on amateur rights." Charges for photocopying.

Recent Sales: "We will tell any author directly information on our sales that are relevant to his/her specific script."

SAMUEL FRENCH, INC., 45 W. 25th St., New York NY 10010. (212)206-8990. Editor: Lawrence Harbison. Estab. 1830. Member of SAR. Represents "hundreds" of clients. Prefers to work with published/established authors; works with a small number of new/unpublished authors. Specializes in plays.

Will Handle: Stage plays. Currently handles 100% stage plays. Will read—at no charge—unsolicited queries and mss. Replies "immediately" on queries; decision in 2-8 months regarding publication. "Enclose SASE."

Terms: Agent receives 90% book royalties; 10% professional production royalties; and 20% amateur production royalties.

Recent Sales: No information given.

‡**JAY GARON-BROOKE ASSOCIATES INC.**, 17th Floor, 415 Central Park West, New York NY 10025. (212)866-3654. President: Jay Garon. Established 1952. Member of ILAA and Author's Guild Inc. Represents 100 clients. 15% of clients are new/unpublished writers. Prefers to work with published/established authors; works with small number of new/unpublished authors.

Will Handle: Nonfiction books, novels, juvenile books (young adult), movie scripts and stage plays. Currently handles 25% nonfiction books; 70% novels; 2% juvenile books; 1% movie scripts; 1% stage plays and 1% TV scripts. Does not read unsolicited material. Reports in 1 month. "If our agency does not respont within 3 months to your request to become a client, you may submit requests elsewhere."

Terms: Agent receives 15% commission on domestic sales; 10-15% on dramatic sales; and 30% on foreign sales. Charges criticism fee for unpublished authors; $85 for 300-page, typed, double-spaced manuscript.

Recent Sales: *A Glimpse of Stocking*, by Elizabeth Gage (Simon and Schuster); *Silver Eyed Woman*, by Mary Ann T. Smith (Morrow); and *Candlemas Eve*, by Jeffrey Sackett (Bantam).

MAX GARTENBERG, LITERARY AGENT, 15 W. 44th St., New York NY 10036. (212)860-8451. Contact: Max Gartenberg. Estab. 1954. Represents 30 clients. 10% of clients are new/unpublished writers. "The writer must convince me of his or her professional skills, whether through published or unpublished materials he/she has produced." Prefers to work with published/established authors; works with a small number of new/unpublished authors. Specializes in nonfiction and fiction trade books.
Will Handle: Nonfiction books and novels. Currently handles 75% nonfiction books and 25% novels. Will read—at no charge—unsolicited queries and outlines. Reports in 1 week on queries. "If our agency does not respond within 1 month to your request to become a client, you may submit requests elsewhere. SASE required."
Terms: Agent receives 10% commission on domestic sales; 10% on dramatic sales; and 15% on foreign sales. 100% of income derived from commission on ms sales.
Recent Sales: *The Jungles of New Guinea*, by Edwin P. Hoyt (Presido Press); *Arthritis*, by Dava Sobel and Arthur C. Klein (St. Martin's Press); and *Business to Business Selling*, by Paul J. Kelly (AMACOM).

LUCIANNE S. GOLDBERG LITERARY AGENTS, INC., Suite 6-A, 255 W. 84th St., New York NY 10024. (212)799-1260. Editorial Director: Cyril Hildebrand. Estab. 1974. Represents 65 clients. 10% of clients are new/unpublished writers. "Any author we decide to repesent must have a good idea, a good presentation of that idea and writing skill to compete with the market. Representation depends solely on the execution of the work whether writer is published or unpublished." Specializes in nonfiction works, "but will review a limited number of novels."
Will Handle: Nonfiction books and novels. Currently handles 75% nonfiction books and 25% novels. Will read—at no charge—unsolicited queries and outlines. Reports in 2 weeks on queries; 3 weeks on mss. "If our agency does not respond within 1 month to your request to become a client, you may submit requests elsewhere."
Terms: Agent receives 15% commission on domestic sales; 25% on dramatic sales; and 25% on foreign sales. Charges reading fee on unsolicited mss: $150/full-length ms. Criticism is included in reading. 1% of income derived from reading fees. "Our critiques run three to four pages, single-spaced. They deal with the overall evaluation of the work. Three agents within the organization read and then confer. Marketing advice is included." Payment of fee does not ensure the agency will represent a writer. Charges for phone expenses, cable fees, photocopying and messenger service after the work is sold. 80% of income derived from commission on ms sales.
Recent Sales: *IDOL: The Real Rock Hudson Story*, by Jerry Oppenheimer (Random House); *Sunny: The Life of Martha von Bulow*, by James Southwood (Simon & Schuster); and *One Big Bed*, by John Krich (McGraw-Hill).

GOODMAN ASSOCIATES, LITERARY AGENTS, 500 West End Ave., New York NY 10024. Contact: Arnold or Elise Goodman. Estab. 1976. Member of ILAA. Represents 75 clients. 10% of clients are new/unpublished writers. Specializes in general adult and juvenile trade fiction and nonfiction. No short stories, articles, poetry or computer books.
Will Handle: Will read—at no charge—unsolicited queries and outlines. "Include SASE for response."
Terms: Agent receives 15% commission on domestic sales; 15% on dramatic sales; and 20% on foreign sales. Charges for photocopying, long-distance phone, messenger, telex and book purchases for subsidiary rights submissions.
Recent Sales: No information given.

IRENE GOODMAN LITERARY AGENCY, 521 5th Ave., 17th Floor, New York NY 10017. (212)688-4286. Contact: Irene Goodman, president, Pault Katz, associate, or David Levin, associate. Estab. 1978. Member of ILAA Represeents 132 clients. 20% of clients are new/unpublished writers. Works with a large number of new/unpublished authors. Specializes in women's fiction (mass market, category and historical romance), science fiction, fantasy, popular nonfiction, reference and young adult (romance and series).
Will Handle: Novels and nonfiction books. Currently handles 20% nonfiction books; 80% novels. Will read—at no charge—unsolicited queries and proposals (3 chapters and outline). Reports in 3 weeks. "We prefer a query, brief synopsis and credentials. No reply without SASE. Remember that boring is the first deadly sin. Hook us on the first page and keep us turning those pages."
Terms: Agent receives 15% commission on domestic sales; 15% on dramatic sales; and 20% on foreign sales. Reading fee for complete ms: $65, refundable upon sale of work, includes feedback. 5% of income derived from fees charged to writers; 95% from commission on ms sales.
Recent Sales: *Gentle Vengeance*, by Linda Lael Miller (Pocket); and *Velvet Embrace* (Zebra).

GRAHAM AGENCY, 311 W. 43rd St., New York NY 10036. (212)489-7730. Owner: Earl Graham. Estab. 1971. Member of SAR. Represents 35 clients. 35% of clients are new/unpublished writers. Prefers to work with published/established authors; eager to work with new/unpublished writers. Specializes in full-length stage plays and musicals.

Will Handle: Stage plays and musicals. Currently handles 100% stage plays. Will read—at no charge—unsolicited queries and outlines, and plays and musicals which we agree to consider on the basis of the letters of inquiry. Reports in 1 week on simple queries. Simultaneous submissions OK.
Terms: Agent receives 10% commission on domestic sales; 10% on dramatic sales; and 10% on foreign sales. 100% of income derived from commission on ms sales.
Recent Sales: No information given.

HAROLD R. GREENE, INC., Suite 302, 760 N. La Cienega, Los Angeles CA 90069. (213)855-0824. President: Harold Greene. Estab. 1985. Member of WGA and DGA. Represents 12 clients, primarily screenwriters. Specializes in screenplay writing and novels that are adaptable to films or TV movies.
Will Handle: Novels and movie scripts. Currently handles 5% novels and 95% movie scripts. Does not read unsolicited mss.
Terms: Agent receives 10% commission on domestic sales; 10% on dramatic sales; and 10% on foreign sales.
Recent Sales: *The Long Walk*, by George La Fountaine (Putnam); *Lifter*, by Crawford Kilian (Berkeley); and *Forever And a Day*, by Pamela Wallace (Silhouette).

THOMAS S. HART LITERARY ENTERPRISES, 20 Kenwood St., Boston MA 02124. (617)288-8512. President: Thomas Hart. Estab. 1983. Represents 25 clients. 30% of clients are new/unpublished writers. Prefers to work with published/established authors; works with a small number of new/unpublished authors. Specializes in literary and mainstream fiction, sports, fitness and natural history.
Will Handle: Nonfiction books and novels. Currently handles 5% magazine articles; 35% nonfiction books; and 60% novels. Will read—at no charge—unsolicited queries, outlines and mss. Reports in 3 weeks on queries; 1 month on mss. "If our agency does not respond within 2 months to your request to become a client, you may submit requests elsewhere."
Terms: Agent receives 15% commission on domestic sales; 15% on dramatic sales; and 20% on foreign sales. Doesn't give criticism if project is rejected. Charges for phone and photocopy expenses. Offers a consultation service through which writers not represented can get advice on a contract; charges $150/contract. 100% of income derived from commission on ms sales.
Recent Sales: *Rocket Man*, by Roger Clemens with Pete Gammons (Viking Penguin); *Snap*, by Abby Frucht (Ticknor and Fields); and *Her Own Terms*, by Judith Grussman (Soho Press).

HEACOCK LITERARY AGENCY, INC., Suite 14, 1523 6th St., Santa Monica CA 90401. (213)393-6227. President: Jim Heacock. Vice President: Rosalie Heacock. Estab. 1978. Member of ILAA and the Association of Talent Agents (writers only). Represents 60 clients. 35% of clients are new/unpublished writers. Works with a small number of new/unpublished authors. Specializes in nonfiction on a wide variety of subjects—health, nutrition, diet, exercise, sports, psychology, crafts, women's studies, business expertise, pregnancy and parenting, alternative health concepts, starting a business and celebrity biographies.
Will Handle: Nonfiction books; novels (by authors who have been previously published by major houses); movie scripts (prefer Writer's Guild members); and TV scripts (prefer Writer's Guild members). Currently handles 85% nonfiction books; 5% novels; 5% movie scripts and 5% TV scripts. Will read—at no charge—unsolicited queries and outlines. Reports in 1 month on queries if SASE is included. "If our agency does not respond within 1 month to your request to become a client, you may submit requests elsewhere."
Terms: Agent receives 15% commission on domestic sales; 10% on dramatic sales; 25% on foreign sales (if a foreign agent is used. If we sell direct to a foreign publisher, the commission is 15%). Charges writers for postage, phone and photocopying. Offers a consultation service through which writers not represented can get advice on a contract; charges $125/hour. 2% of income derived from such fees; 98% of income derived from commission on ms sales.
Recent Sales: *Heckedy Peg*, by Don and Audrey Wood (Harcourt Brace Jovanovich); *Successful Sitcom Writing*, by Jurgen Wolff (St. Martin's Press); and *Immune for Life*, by Dr. Arnold Fox and Barry Fox (Medallion Books).

HEINLE + HEINLE ENTERPRISES, INC., 29 Lexington Rd., Concord MA 01742. (617)369-4858. President: Beverly D. Heinle. Estab. 1973. Represents 25 clients. 50% of clients are new/unpublished writers. Prefers previously published writers, but will consider serious new writers. Prefers to work with published/established authors; works with a small number of new/unpublished authors. Specializes in cookbooks. Will read—at no charge—unsolicited queries and outlines. Reports in 2 weeks on queries. "If our agency does not respond within 2 months to your request to become a client, you may submit requests elsewhere."
Terms: Agent receives 10% commission on domestic, dramatic and foreign sales. 100% of income derived from commission on ms sales.
Recent Sales: *The Gourmet Galley*, by Terence Janericco (International Marine); *Cooking by Degrees*, Boston University (Harvard Commons); and *The Chef's Companion*, by Elis Riely (VNR).

HHM LITERARY AGENCY, Box 1153, Rahway NJ 07065. (201)388-8167. Contact: Haes H. Monroe. Estab. 1985. Represents 20 clients. 25% of clients are new/unpublished writers. Prefers to work with published/established authors.
Will Handle: Nonfiction books and novels. Currently handles 25% nonfiction books; 75% novels. Will read—at no charge—unsolicited queries and outlines. Reports in 2 months.
Terms: Agent receives 10% commission on domestic sales; 15% on dramatic sales; and 20% on foreign sales. Charges for phone and photocopying, messenger, cable, "other extraordinary" office expenses. 100% of income derived from commission on ms sales.
Recent Sales: No information given.

FREDERICK HILL ASSOCIATES, 2237 Union St., San Francisco CA 94123. (415)921-2910. Associate: Bonnie Nadell. Estab. 1979. Represents 60 clients. 50% of clients are new/unpublished writers. Specializes in general nonfiction (biography, history, politics, current events, architecture, cooking, the arts, etc.); mainstream fiction and young adult.
Will Handle: Nonfiction books, novels and juvenile books.
Terms: Agent receives 15% commission on domestic sales; 10% on dramatic sales; and 20% on foreign sales. Charges for overseas airmail (books, proofs only), overseas telex, cable, domestic telex. 100% of income derived from commission on ms sales.
Recent Sales: *The Broom of the System*, by David Foster Wallace (Viking); *Eddie Black*, by Walter Shapiro (Arbor House); and *Torch Rat*, by Steve Barr and John Poppy (William Morrow).

ALICE HILTON LITERARY AGENCY, 13131 Welby Way, North Hollywood CA 91606. (818)982-5423/982-2546. Estab. 1986. Member of WGA. Eager to work with new/unpublished writers. Specializes in movie and TV scripts—"any good salable material with quality—although agent's personal taste runs in the genre of 'Cheers,' 'L.A. Law,' 'American Playhouse,' 'Masterpiece Theatre' and Wood Allen vintage humor."
Will Handle: Movie and TV scripts only. Will read—at no charge—unsolicited queries, outlines and manuscripts. Reports in 1 month. "If our agency does not respond within 2 months to your request to become a client, you may submit requests elsewhere."
Terms: Agent receives 10% commission on dramatic sales. Charges for phone, postage and photocpy expenses. 100% of income derived from commission on ms sales. "Send SASE."
Recent Sales: No information given.

HINTZ & FITZGERALD, INC., Suite 211, 207 E. Buffalo St., Milwaukee WI 53202. (414)273-0300. Contact: Sandy Hintz or Colleen Fitzgerald. Estab. 1978. Represents 25 clients. 30% of clients are new/unpublished writers. "Preference is given to writers with some publishing history, e.g., articles in quality publications and books. We also seriously consider anyone (new people) with a good story and writing style." Specializes in most fiction—mysteries, westerns, science fiction, fantasy, how-tos, biographies, general nonfiction, and juvenile fiction and nonfiction. No picture books.
Will Handle: Nonfiction books, novels and juvenile books. Currently handles 25% nonfiction books; 50% novels; 25% juvenile books. Will read—at no charge—unsolicited queries and outlines. Reports in 2 weeks on queries; 1 month on mss.
Terms: Agent receives 10% commission on domestic sales; 15% on foreign sales. Charges for extraordinary postage and phone expenses. ("This is not necessary 95 percent of the time.") Sometimes offers a consultation service through which writers can get advice on a contract. 100% of income derived from commission on ms sales.
Recent Sales: *Highland Laddie Gone*, by Sharyn McCrumb (Avon); *6-Book Space Series*, by Gregory Vogt (Franklin Watts); and *Nathan Phillips Mystery*, by Nick O'Donohue (Paperjacks Press).

JOHN L. HOCHMANN BOOKS, 320 E. 58th St., New York NY 10022. (212)319-0505. President: John L. Hochmann. Estab. 1976. Represents 21 clients. Writer must have demonstrable eminence in field or previous publications for nonfiction, and critically and/or commercially successful books for fiction. Prefers to work with published/established authors; and to "develop new series for established authors of original paperback fiction."
Will Handle: Nonfiction books, novels, and textbooks. Currently handles 60% nonfiction books and 40% novels. Will read—at no charge—unsolicited queries, outlines and solicited mss. Reports in 2 weeks on queries; 1 month on mss.
Terms: Agent receives 15% commission on domestic sales; and additional commission on foreign sales. Sometimes offers a consultation service through which writers not represented can get advice on a contract; "we have sometimes done this without charge, but if the number of inquiries increases, our policy may change." 100% of income derived from commission on ms sales.
Recent Sales: *Trainmaster*, by Noel B. Gerson (Warner); *Clinical Care of the Aged Person*, by David G. Satin, M.D. (Oxford); and *Betty Parsons: A Dealer and Her Artists*, by Lee Hall (Abrams).

‡SCOTT HUDSON TALENT REPRESENTATION, 2B, 215 East 76th St., New York NY 10021. (212)570-9645. President: Scott Hudson. Estab. 1983. Member of WGA. Represents 30 clients. Prefers to work with published/established authors; works with a small number of new/unpublished authors. Specializes in selling for the entertainment field; screenwriters, television writers, playwrights and some book writers.
Will Handle: Movie scripts, stage plays and TV scripts. Currently handles 30% movie scripts; 30% stage plays; and 40% TV scripts. Will read—at no charge—unsolicited queries and outlines with a synopsis and resume. We "only respond if we are interested."
Terms: Agent receives 10% commission on domestic sales; 10% on dramatic sales; and 15% on foreign sales.

INTERNATIONAL LITERATURE AND ARTS AGENCY, 50 E. 10th St., New York NY 10003. (212)475-1999. Director: Bonnie R. Crown. Estab. 1977. Represents 10 clients. 20% of clients are new/unpublished writers. Works with a small number of new/unpublished authors; eager to work with new/unpublished writers in area of specialization, and established translators from Asian languages. Specializes in translations of literary works from Asian languages, arts- and literature-related works, and "American writers who have been influenced by some aspect of an Asian culture, for example, a novel set in Japan, or India, or nonfiction works about Asia. For details of policy, send query with SASE."
Will Handle: Novels, stage plays (related to Asia or Asian American experience), and poetry (translations of Asian classics). Currently handles 50% nonfiction books; 25% novels; and 25% classics from Asian languages. Will read—at no charge—unsolicited queries and brief outlines. Reports in 1 week on queries; 3 weeks on mss. "If our agency does not respond within 2 weeks to your request to become a client, you may submit requests elsewhere. For details of policy, send query with SASE."
Terms: Agent receives 15% commission on domestic sales; and 20% on foreign sales. Sometimes charges a reading fee to new, unpublished writers; waives fee if representing the writer. 2% of income derived from reading fees. "We do not do critiques, as such, but do give the writer a brief evaluation of marketing potential based on my reading. If a reading fee is waived there is a processing fee of $25-45. May charge for phone and photocopy expenses." 2-3% of income derived from fees; 97-98% of income is derived from commission on ms sales.
Recent Sales: *Wings of Stone*, by Linda Ty-Casper (Readers International).

INTERNATIONAL PUBLISHER ASSOCIATES, INC., 746 West Shore, Sparta NJ 07871. (201)729-9321. Executive Vice President: Joe DeRogatis. Estab. 1982. Represents 30 clients. 80% of clients are new/unpublished writers. Eager to work with new/unpublished writers. Specializes in all types of nonfiction.
Will Handle: Nonfiction books and novels. Currently handles 80% nonfiction books and 20% fiction. Will read—at no charge—unsolicited queries and outlines. Reports in 3 weeks on queries. "If our agency does not respond within 1 month to your request to become a client, you may submit requests elsewhere."
Terms: Agent receives 15% commission on domestic sales; and 20% on foreign sales. 100% of income derived from commission on ms sales.
Recent Sales: *Soap Opera Babylon*, by Jason Bonderoff (Putnam); and *Guerilla Tactics for Women Over Forty*, by Anne Cardoza and Mavis Sutton (Mills and Sanderson).

JANUS LITERARY AGENCY, Box 107, Nahant MA 01908. (617)593-0576. Contact: Lenny Cavallaro. Estab. 1980. Represents 5 clients. 20% of clients are new/unpublished writers. "Will gladly consider published and/or unpublished writers." Prefers nonfiction "of popular or controversial slant."
Will Handle: Nonfiction books and novels. Currently handles 80% nonfiction books; and 20% fiction. Will read—at no charge—unsolicited queries and outlines. Must enclose SASE. Reports in 1 week on queries; 2 weeks on mss.
Terms: Agent receives 15% commission on domestic sales; and 15% on foreign sales. Charges reading fee; $50-200, to appraise ms. 22.3% of income derived from reading fees. Reading fee includes critique. "Most critiques run 1-3 typed pages, single spaced. Some very detailed, line-by-line commentary is included. I read everything myself; hold degree in English; was formerly an English teacher; am a published author; was formerly a book critic for *New Haven Register* (newspaper)." Most new clients must pay a reading fee; exceptions are rare. $50-200 is normal fee range. I waive fee for clients whose works I have placed, or if the topic and proposal are absolutely extraordinary. Charges $50-100 handling fee (phone calls, postage, etc.). Sometimes offers a consultation service through which writers not represented can get advice on a contract; charges $25/hour. 31.8% of income derived from fees; 68.2% of income derived from commission on ms sales. Payment of a criticism fee does not ensure that agency will represent writer.
Recent Sales: *Protect Your Children*, by Laura Huchton (Prentice-Hall); and *Ouija: The Most Dangerous Game*, by Stoker Hunt (Harper & Row).

SHARON JARVIS AND CO., INC., 260 Willard Ave., Staten Island NY 10314. (718)273-1066. President: Sharon Jarvis. Estab. 1985 (previously known as Jarvis, Braff Ltd. Established 1979). Member of ILAA. Represents 70 clients. 20% of clients are new/unpublished writers. Prefers to work with published/established authors; works with a small number of new/unpublished authors. Considers types of genre fiction, commercial fiction and nonfiction.

Will Handle: Nonfiction books, novels and juvenile books. Currently handles 20% nonfiction books; 70% novels; and 10% juvenile books. Does not read unsolicited mss. Reports in 1 week on queries. "If our agency does not respond within 1 month to your request to become a client, you may submit requests elsewhere."
Terms: Agent receives 15% commission on domestic sales; extra 10% on dramatic sales; and extra 10% on foreign sales. ("We have sub-agents in ten different foreign markets.") Charges reading fee; $40 per manuscript ("fee goes to outside reader; recommended material then read by agency at no extra charge"). Critique is a one-page analysis "aimed toward agency evaluation of author's talent and marketability." Charges for photocopying. 100% of income derived from commission on ms sales.
Recent Sales: *The Dragon Trilogy* by Melanie Rawn (DAW Books); *The International Encyclopedia of Espionage*, by Michael Kurland (Facts on File); and *Space: The Next 25 Years*, by Thomas R. McDonough (John Wiley and Sons).

‡ASHER D. JASON ENTERPRISES, INC., Suite 3B, 111 Barrow St., New York NY 10014. (212)929-2129. President: Asher D. Jason. Estab. 1983. Represents 25 clients. 15% of clients are new/unpublished writers. "Writers must be either published or have a salable nonfiction idea or an excellent finished fiction ms." Prefers to work with published/established authors; works with a small number of new/unpublished authors. Specializes in fiction, nonfiction, romance, espionage, horror/suspense and mystery.
Will Handle: Nonfiction books and novels. Currently handles 15% magazine articles; 70% nonfiction books; and 15% novels. Will read—at no charge—unsolicited queries and outlines. Reports in 1 week on queries; 3 weeks on mss. "If our agency does not respond within 1 month to your request to become a client, you may submit requests elsewhere."
Terms: Agent receives 15% commission on domestic sales; 15% on dramatic sales; and 20% on foreign sales. Charges for photocopy and foreign postage expenses. 100% of income derived from sales of writers' work.
Recent Sales: *Make Up Book*, by Joey Mills (Villard); *Just Ask*, by Bonnie Hammer and Debbie Cohen (New American Library); and *Taekwondo*, by Werner and Franz Bussen (Simon & Schuster).

JET LITERARY ASSOCIATES, INC., 124 E. 84th St., New York NY 10028. (212)879-2578. President: J. Trupin. Estab. 1976. Represents 85 clients. 5% of clients are new/unpublished writers. Writer must have published articles or books. Prefers to work with published/established authors. Specializes in nonfiction.
Will Handle: Nonfiction books and novels. Currently handles 50% nonfiction books and 50% novels. Does not read unsolicited mss. Reports in 2 weeks on queries; 1 month on mss. "If our agency does not respond within 2 months to your request to become a client, you may submit requests elsewhere."
Terms: Agent receives 15% commission on domestic sales; 15% on dramatic sales; and 25% on foreign sales. Charges for phone and postage expenses. 100% of income derived from commission on ms sales.
Recent Sales: *Imponderables*, by David Feldman (Morrow); *The Good Fat Diet*, (Bantam); and *1913*, by Martin Green (Macmillan).

ALEX KAMAROFF ASSOCIATES, Suite 303 East, 200 Park Ave., Pan Am Bldg., New York NY 10166. (212)557-5557. President: Alex Kamaroff. Associate: Jeremy Shere. Estab. 1985. Member of ILAA. Represents 63 clients. 15% of clients are new/unpublished writers. Specializes in men's adventure, science fiction, mysteries, horror, category and historical romances, contemporary women's fiction.
Will Handle: Novels. Currently handles 5% nonfiction books; 95% novels. Will read—at no charge—unsolicited queries and outlines; no reply without SASE. Reports in 1 week on queries; 3 weeks on mss. Charges $45 reading fee refundable upon sale of ms.
Terms: Agent receives 10% commission on domestic sales; 10% on dramatic sales; and 20% on foreign sales. Charges for phone expenses. Offers a consultation service through which writers can get advice on a contract. 100% of income derived from commission on ms sales.
Recent Sales: *Louis Rukeyser Business Almanac (1988)* (Simon & Schuster); and *The War Virus*, (Pocket's Star Trek Series).

KIDDE, HOYT AND PICARD LITERARY AGENCY, 335 E. 51st St., New York NY 10022. (212)755-9461. Chief Associate: Katharine Kidde. Estab. 1981. Represents 50 clients. "We prefer that a writer be published, with at least a few pieces in magazines, but we will take on a new writer if we feel her or his writing is extraordinary." Works with a small number of new authors. Specializes in mainstream and literary fiction; romantic fiction, some historical, some contemporary; mainstream nonfiction; and "a very little" young adult fiction.
Will Handle: Nonfiction books and "a few" young adult books. Will handle magazine articles and magazine fiction for national magazines, if also handling a book-length ms for the author. Currently handles 1% magazine articles; 2% magazine fiction; 22% nonfiction books; 70% novels; and 5% young adult books. Will read—at no charge—unsolicited queries. Reports in 2 weeks on queries; 1 month on mss. "If our agency does not respond within 6 weeks to your request to become a client, you may submit requests elsewhere."
Terms: Agent receives 15% commission on domestic sales; commission on dramatic sales varies. Sometimes charges for phone, postage and photocopy expenses. 100% of income derived from commission on ms sales.
Recent Sales: *Timeless Towns*, by J.R. Humphreys (St. Martin's); *Beyond Capricorn*, by Frank Sherry (Morrow); and *Twilight Of Innocence*, by Helen Lehr (Sinclair).

‡DANIEL P. KING, LITERARY AGENT, 5125 N. Cumberland Blvd., Whitefish Bay WI 53217. (414)964-2903. President: Daniel P. King. Estab. 1974. Member of Crime Writer's Association. Represents 125 clients. 25% of clients are new/unpublished writers. Eager to work with new/unpublished writers. Specializes in crime and mystery, science fiction, mainstream fiction, short stories, and books in English for foreign sales.
Will Handle: Magazine articles (crime, foreign affairs, economics); magazine fiction (mystery, romance); nonfiction books (crime, politics); novels (mystery, science fiction, romance, mainstream); movie scripts (in cooperation with an agent in California); TV scripts (with California agent); syndicate material (general, politics, economics). Currently handles 5% magazine articles; 10% magazine fiction; 30% nonfiction books; 50% novels; 2% movie scripts; 2% TV scripts; 1% syndicated material. Will read—at no charge—unsolicited queries and outlines. Does not read unsolicited ms. Reports in 1 week. "If our agency does not respond within 1 week to your request to become a client, you may submit requests elsewhere."
Terms: Agent receives 10% commission on domestic sales; 10% on dramatic sales; and 20% on foreign sales. Charges a reading fee "if writer wishes a critique." Charges $35-55 for a 300-page, typed double-spaced book ms. Charges a criticism fee "only if writer wishes a critique of the material and if we think that this will improve the work." Critiques "provide an overall evaluation of the writing skill level, analysis of story line and suggestions for rewriting. The text will be marked throughout with grammatical, spelling, etc., corrections." Charges writers for long distance telephone, telex, and foreign postage. Offers a consultation service through which writers can get advice on a contract. Charges $50/hour. "Less than 1%" of income derived from fees; 99% from commission on ms sales.
Recent Sales: *Sound of Murder*, by John Bonnet (Harper & Row); *Perish the Thought*, by John Bonnet (Hale); *Floodshock*, by Antony Milner (Alan Sutton, Ltd.).

HARVEY KLINGER, INC., 301 W. 53rd St., New York NY 10019. (212)581-7068. President: Harvey Klinger. Estab. 1977. Represents 60 clients. 25% of our clients are new/unpublished writers. "We seek writers demonstrating great talent, fresh writing and a willingness to listen to editorial criticism and learn." Works with a small number of new/unpublished authors. Specializes in mainstream fiction, (not category romance or mysteries, etc.), nonfiction in the medical, social sciences, autobiography and biography areas.
Will Handle: Nonfiction books and novels. Currently handles 60% nonfiction books and 40% novels. Will read—at no charge—unsolicited queries and outlines. Reports in 2 weeks on queries. "If our agency does not respond within 2 months to your request to become a client, you may submit requests elsewhere."
Terms: Agent receives 15% commission on domestic sales; 15% on dramatic sales; and 25% on foreign sales. Charges for photocopy expenses. 100% of income derived from commission on ms sales.
Recent Sales: *Green City In The Sun*, by Barbara Wood (Random); *The Proprietor's Daughter*, by Lewis Orde (Little, Brown); and *How to Make Love All The Time*, by Barbara DeAngelis (Rawson).

PAUL KOHNER, INC., 9169 Sunset Blvd., Los Angeles CA 90069. (213)550-1060. Agent: Gary Salt. Estab. 1939. Represents 100 clients. Writer must have sold material in the market or category in which they are seeking representation. Prefers to work with published/established authors. Specializes in film and TV scripts and related material, and dramatic rights for published or soon-to-be published books—both fiction and nonfiction. No plays, poetry or short stories. "We handle dramatic and performing rights only."
Will Handle: Magazine articles and nonfiction books (if they have film or TV potential); novels (only previously published or with publication deals set); movie scripts; and TV scripts. Currently handles 5% magazine articles; 12½% nonfiction books; 12½% novels; 40% movie scripts; and 30% TV scripts. Will read—at no charge—unsolicited queries only. Reports in 1 week on queries. "If our agency does not respond within 1 month to your request to become a client, you may submit requests elsewhere."
Terms: Agent receives 10% commission on dramatic sales. Charges for photocopy and binding expenses. Sometimes offers a consultation service through which film and TV writers not represented can get advice on a contract; charges varying rate. 100% of income derived from commission on dramatic rights sales.
Recent Sales: *The Flight of The Intruder* (Naval Institute Press); *Men Who Hate Women and The Women Who Love Them*, (Bantam).

BARBARA S. KOUTS, (Affiliated with Philip G. Spitzer Literary Agency), 788 Ninth Ave., New York NY 10019. (212)265-6003. Literary Agent: Barbara S. Kouts. Estab. 1980. Member of ILAA. Represents 50 clients. 75% of clients are new/unpublished writers. Eager to work with new/unpublished writers. Specializes in fiction, nonfiction and children's books.
Will Handle: Nonfiction books, novels and juvenile books. Currently handles 40% nonfiction books; 40% novels; and 20% juvenile books. Will read—at no charge—unsolicited queries and outlines. Reports in 3 weeks on queries; 2 months on mss. "If our agency does not respond within 2 months to your request to become a client, you may submit requests elsewhere."
Terms: Agent receives 10% commission on domestic sales; and 20% on foreign sales. Charges writers for photocopy expenses.
Recent Sales: *The Enchanted Tapestry*, by Robert San Souci (Dial); *Food Festival*, by Alice Geffen and Carole Berglie (Pantheon); *Bed And Breakfast, North America*, by Hal Gieseking (Simon & Schuster).

‡KRATZ AND KOMPANY, 210 Fifth Ave., New York NY 10010. (212)683-9222. Contact: F. Kratz. Established 1982. Member of WGA East. Represents 11 clients. 100% of clients are new/unpublished writers. Eager to work with new/unpublished writers. Specializes in screen plays.
Will Handle: Movie scripts. Currently handles 100% movie scripts. Will read—at no charge—unsolicited queries and outlines. Reports in 2 weeks. "If our agency does not respond within 2 months to your request to become a client, you may submit requests elsewhere."
Terms: Agent receives 10% commission on domestic sales, dramatic sales and foreign sales. Charges a reading fee. 10% of income derived from reading fees. Writer receives "a total breakdown of scripts—chances of sale, demands for re-write, etc." 10% of income derived from fees charged to writer; 90% from commission on ms sales.
Recent Sales: No information given.

‡PETER LAMPACK AGENCY, INC., 2015, 551 Fifth Ave., New York NY 10017. (212)687-9106. President: Peter Lampack. Estab. 1977. Represents 90 clients. 10% of clients are new/unpublished writers. Majority of clients are published/established authors; works with a small number of new/unpublished authors. Specializes in "commercial fiction, particularly contemporary relationships, male-oriented action adventure, mysteries, horror and historical romance; literary fiction; and upscale, serious nonfiction or general interest nonfiction only from a recognized expert in a given field."
Will Handle: Nonfiction books, novels, movie scripts and TV scripts ("but not for espiodic TV series—must lend itself to movie-of-the-week or mini-series format.") Currently handles 15% nonfiction books; 75% novels; 5% movie scripts; 5% TV scripts. Will read—at no charge—unsolicited queries, outlines and mss. Reports in 2 weeks on queries; 6 weeks on mss. "If our agency does not respond within 2 months to your request to become a client, you may submit requests elsewhere."
Terms: Agent receives 15% commission on domestic sales; 15% on dramatic sales; and 20% on foreign sales. Charges for photocopy expenses "although we prefer writers supply copies of their work. Writers are required to supply or bear the cost of copies of books for overseas sales." 100% of income derived from sales of writers' work.
Recent Sales: *First Born*, by Doris Mortman (Bantam Books): *Foe*, by V.M. Coetzee (Viking Press); *Swan Song*, by Robert McCammon (Pocket Books); and *Parallelogram*, by Thomas Caplan (Viking Press).

MICHAEL LARSEN/ELIZABETH POMADA LITERARY AGENTS, 1029 Jones St., San Francisco CA 94109. (415)673-0939. Contact: Mike Larsen or Elizabeth Pomada. Member of ILAA. Represents 150 clients. 50-55% of clients are new/unpublished writers. Eager to work with new/unpublished writers. "We have very catholic tastes and do not specialize. We handle literary, commercial, and genre fiction, and the full range of nonfiction books."
Will Handle: Adult nonfiction books and novels. Currently handles 75% nonfiction books and 25% novels. Will read—at no charge—unsolicited queries, the first 30 pages and synopsis of completed novels, and nonfiction book proposals. Reports in 6 weeks on queries. "Always include SASE. Send SASE for brochure."
Terms: Agent receives 15% commission on domestic sales; 15% on dramatic sales; and 20% on foreign sales. May charge writer for printing, postage for multiple submissions, foreign mail, foreign phone calls, galleys, books, and legal fees. Offers a separate consultation service; charges $100/hour. 100% of income derived from commission on ms sales.
Recent Sales: *Healing With Humor*, by Allen Klein (Tarcher); *Deathspell*, by Katharine Kerr (Doubleday); *The 90-Minute Hour*, by Jan Levinson (Dodd, Mead).

LAW OFFICES OF ROBERT L. FENTON, P.C., Suite 390, 31800 Northwestern Hwy., Farmington Hills MI 48018. (313)855-8780. President: Robert L. Fenton. Estab. 1960. Represents 30 clients. 10% of clients are new/unpublished writers. Prefers to work with published/established authors; works with a small number of new/unpublished writers.
Will Handle: Nonfiction books and novels. Currently handles 50% nonfiction books and 50% novels. Reads solicited queries, outlines and mss for a fee. Reports in 3 weeks on queries. "If our agency does not respond within 2 months to your request to become a client, you may submit requests elsewhere. I package many works into TV movies or feature films. Recently had office at Universal Films (for 3½ years)."
Terms: Agent receives 15% commission on domestic sales and 15% on foreign sales. Charges a reading fee; waives fee if representing writer who has been published twice. 10% of income derived from reading fees. Cri-

ALWAYS submit manuscripts or queries with a self-addressed, stamped envelope (SASE) within your country or International Reply Coupons purchased from the post office for other countries.

tique: oral or written, if written is approximately 2 pages. Charges nominal retainer to unpublished authors. Charges for phone, photocopy and postage expenses. 20% of income derived from fees.
Recent Sales: *Plunderers*, by R. Greenfield and H. Margolis (Simon & Schuster); *Mein Amerika*, by Leo Rutman (Stein and Day); and *Judicial Indiscretion*, by James W. Ellison (St. Martin's).

ELIZABETH LAY, LITERARY AGENT, Box 183, 484 Lake Park Ave., Oakland CA 94610. (415)839-2480. President: Elizabeth Lay. Estab. 1980. Member of ILAA. Represents 20 clients. 30% of clients are new/unpublished writers. Works with a small number of new/unpublished authors. Specializes in fiction (women's mainstream, fantasy, mysteries, historical romances and westerns) and nonfiction (of interest to women, and health and diet).
Will Handle: Nonfiction books and novels. Currently handles 50% nonfiction books and 50% novels. Will read—at no charge—unsolicited queries and outlines. Reports in 2 weeks on queries; 6 weeks on mss. "If our agency does not respond within 2 months to your request to become a client, you may submit requests elsewhere."
Terms: Agent receives 15% commission on domestic sales; 15% on dramatic sales; and 20% on foreign sales. Charges reading fee for first novel mss by unpublished writers. Fees based on length, minimum $50, maximum $200/1,000 pages. Charges writers for postage, overseas telephone and photocopying. 95% of income derived from commission on ms sales.
Recent Sales: *Witch Woman*, by E.E. Allen (Warner Books); *Spit in the Ocean*, by S. Singer (St. Martin's Press); and *Freedom Fire*, by E.E. Allen (Warner Books).

L. HARRY LEE LITERARY AGENCY, Box 203, Rocky Point NY 11778. (516)744-1188. President: L. Harry Lee. Estab. 1979. Member of WGA. Represents 150 clients. 40% of clients are new/unpublished writers. "Mainly interested in screenwriters." Specializes in movies, TV (episodic, movies-of-the-week and sit-coms) and contemporary novels.
Will Handle: Novels, movie scripts, stage plays, and TV scripts (movies, mini-series, MOW's, episodic, and sit-coms). Currently handles 10% novels; 60% movie scripts; 3% stage plays; 27% TV scripts. Will read—at no charge—unsolicited queries and outlines; does not read material submitted without SASE. No dot-matrix. Reports in 2 weeks on queries; 6 weeks on mss.
Terms: Agent receives 15% commission on domestic sales; 15% on dramatic sales; and 20% on foreign sales. Charges a marketing fee; 5% of income derived from marketing fees. Charges for photocopies, line editing, proofing, typing, and postage expenses. Offers a consultation service through which writers not represented can get advice on a contract; charges $75/hour. 5% of income derived from marketing fees; 90% of income derived from commission on ms sales.
Recent Sales: "Snake Check," "Tramp Star," and "War Zone."

THE ADELE LEONE AGENCY, INC., 26 Nantucket Pl., Scarsdale NY 10583. (914)961-2965/3085. Associates: Richard McEnroe and Ralph A. Leone. Estab. 1979. Represents 50 clients. 20% of clients are new/unpublished writers. Prefers to work with published/established authors; works with a number of new/unpublished authors. Specializes in historical, gothic, regency, and contemporary romance; science fiction and fantasy, westerns, horror, war novels, military history, biography and general women's and mainstream fiction, science, physics, health and nutrition, astrology and occult.
Will Handle: Nonfiction books and novels. Currently handles 40% nonfiction books and 60% novels. Will read—at no charge—unsolicited queries and outlines. Reports in 3 months on queries.
Terms: Agent receives 15% commission on domestic sales; 10% on dramatic sales. Charges writer for photocopies, airmail and overnight mail. 100% of income derived from commission on ms sales.
Recent Sales: *Bittersweet Ecstasy*, by Janelle Taylor (Zebra); *The Chaos Theory*, by John Briggs and David Peat (Harper and Row); and *Due East*, by Valerie Sayers (Dolphin/Doubleday).

‡ELLEN LEVINE LITERARY AGENCY, INC., Suite 1205, 432 Park Ave. So., New York NY 10016. (212)889-0620. Contact: Diana Finch. Established 1980. Member of SAR and ILAA. Represents over 100 clients. 10% of clients are new/unpublished writers.
Will Handle: Nonfiction books and novels. Currently handles 40% nonfiction books; 55% novels and 5% juvenile books. Will read—at no charge—unsolicited queries and outlines. Does not read unsolicited manuscripts. Reports in 1 week on queries. "If our agency does not respond within 1 month of receipt of your solicited ms, you may submit requests elsewhere."
Terms: Agent receives 10% commission on domestic sales; 10% on dramatic sales; and 20% on foreign sales. Charges writer for photocopying mss for submissions, overseas calls, cables and postage incurred in representation of foreign rights, cost of books bought to submit for foreign rights and other subsidiary rights. 100% of income derived from commission on ms sales.
Recent Sales: "We do not release this information except by individual request from prospective clients."

WENDY LIPKIND AGENCY, Suite 5K, 225 E. 57th St., New York NY 10022. (212)935-1406. President: Wendy Lipkind. Estab. 1977. Member of ILAA. Represents 50 clients. 20% of clients are new/unpublished writers. Works with a small number of new/unpublished authors. Specializes in nonfiction (social history, adventure, biography, science, sports, history) and fiction ("good story telling. I do not specialize in genre mass-market fiction").
Will Handle: Nonfiction books and novels. Currently handles: 80% nonfiction books and 20% novels. Will read—at no charge—unsolicited queries and outlines. Reports in 2 weeks on queries.
Terms: Agent receives 10% commission on domestic sales; 10-15% on dramatic sales; and 20% on foreign sales. Charges $100 one-time handling fee if sells work. Charges for phone, foreign postage, photocopy, cables and messenger expenses. 100% of income derived from commission on ms sales.
Recent Sales: *The New Crowd* (Simon & Schuster); *Windstar* (Macmillan); and *American Art Deco* (Atlantic Monthly Press).

PETER LIVINGSTON ASSOCIATES, INC., 143 Collier St., Toronto, Ontario M4W 1M2 Canada. (416)928-1010. Associate: David Johnston. Estab. 1982. Member of ILAA. Represents 50 clients. 50% of our clients were new/unpublished writers. Works with a small number of new/unpublished authors. Specializes in hardcover, "front list" fiction—thrillers, mystery, and women's books—and nonfiction by leading authorities or experienced journalists. "In nonfiction, previous magazine publication and/or credentials in the field help. In fiction, short story publications help."
Will Handle: Nonfiction books; novels (hardcover, mainstream); and movie scripts (only if by previously published or produced writers). Currently handles 5% magazine articles; 60% nonfiction books; 25% novels; 5% movie scripts; and 5% TV scripts. Will read—at no charge—unsolicited queries and outlines. Reports in 2 weeks on queries; 5 weeks on mss. "If our agency does not respond within 6 weeks to your request to become a client, you may submit requests elsewhere."
Terms: Agent receives 15% commission on domestic sales; 15% on dramatic sales; and 20% on foreign sales. Charges a reading fee to "unrecommended and previously unpublished authors" of fiction; waives fee if representing writer. 1% of income derived from reading fees. Writer receives "a brief (two to three page) critique of the manuscript for reading fee. Readings are done by inhouse agents and/or professional editors." Charges for photocopy, postage, messenger, telex, and phone expenses.
Recent Sales: *The Christkiller*, by Marcel Montecino (Arbor House); *Savant: Genius Among Us, Genius Within Us*, by Dr. Darold Treffert (Harper & Row); and *The Real Coke: The Real Story*, by T. Oliver (Random House).

DONALD MACCAMPBELL INC., 12 E. 41st St., New York NY 10017. (212)683-5580. Editor: Maureen Moran. Estab. 1940. Represents 50 clients. "The agency does not handle unpublished writers." Specializes in women's book-length fiction in all categories.
Will Handle: Novels. Currently handles 100% novels. Does not read unsolicited mss. Reports in 1 week on queries; 2 weeks on mss. "If our agency does not respond within 1 month to your request to become a client, you may submit requests elsewhere."
Terms: Agent receives 10% commission on domestic sales; and 20% on foreign sales. 100% of income derived from commission on ms sales.
Recent Sales: *Prisoner of Desire*, by Jennifer Blake (Ballantine); *Guadalajara*, by E. Howard Hunt (Stein & Day); and *Sweet Thunder*, by Lynne Scott-Drennan (Doubleday).

‡MARCH TENTH, INC., 4 Myrtle St., Haworth NJ 07641. (201)387-6551. President: Sandra Choron. Estab. 1981. Represents 40 clients. 5% of clients are new/unpublished writers. "Writers must have professional expertise in the field in which they are writing." Prefers to work with published/established writers.
Will Handle: Nonfiction books. Currently handles 100% nonfiction books. Does not read unsolicited mss. Reports in 1 month. "If our agency does not respond within 1 month to your request to become a client, you may submit requests elsewhere."
Terms: Agent receives 15% commission on domestic sales; 20% on dramatic sales; and 20% on foreign sales. Charges writers for postage, photocopy, and overseas phone expenses. Sometimes offers a consultation service through which writer can get advice on a contract; charges $50/hour. 10% of income is derived from fees; 90% of income derived from commission of ms sales.
Recent Sales: *Glory Days*, by Dave Marsh (Pantheon); *American's Favorite Stories by America's Favorite Storytellers*, by Jimmy Neil Smith (Crown); and *How to Marry The Man Of Your Choice*, by Margaret Kent (Warner).

DENISE MARCIL LITERARY AGENCY, INC., 316 W. 82nd St. 5F, New York NY 10024. (212)580-1071. President: Denise Marcil. Estab. 1977. Member of ILAA. Represents 80 clients. Works with a small number of new/unpublished authors. Specializes in "solid, informative nonfiction including such areas as money, business, health, child care, parenting, self-help and how-to's and commercial fiction, especially women's fiction; also mysteries, psychological suspense and horror."

Will Handle: Nonfiction books and novels. Currently handles 40% nonfiction books and 60% novels. Will read—at no charge—unsolicited queries and outlines. Reports in 2 weeks on queries; 3 months on mss. "If our agency does not respond within 4 months to your request to become a client, you may submit requests elsewhere."

Terms: Agent receives 15% commission on domestic sales; 15% on dramatic sales; and 22½% on foreign sales. Charges a reading fee: $30/first 3 chapters and outline. Less than 5% of income derived from reading fees. Charges for disbursements, postage, copying and messenger service. 95% of income derived from commission on ms sales.

Recent Sales: *No More Cravings*, by Dr. Douglas Hunt (Warner); *Let The Buyer Beware*, by Douglas Forde (Viking/Penguin); and *Parent's Guide to Raising Sexually Healthy Children* (Rowson Assoc.).

BETTY MARKS, Suite 9F, 176 E. 77th St., New York NY 10021. (212)535-8388. Contact: Betty Marks. Estab. 1969. Member of ILAA. Represents 35 clients. Prefers to work with published/established authors; works with a small number of new/unpublished authors. Specializes in journalists' nonfiction.

Will Handle: Nonfiction books, cookbooks and novels. Will read—at no charge—unsolicited queries and outlines. Reports in 1 week on queries; 6 weeks on mss. "If our agency does not respond within 6 weeks to your request to become a client, you may submit requests elsewhere."

Terms: Agent receives 15% commission on domestic sales; and 10% on foreign sales (plus 10% to foreign agent). Charges a reading fee for unpublished writers; fee will be waived if representing writer. Charges criticism fee. "Writers receive two page letter covering storyline, plot, characters, dialogue, language, etc." Written by agent. Charges for "extraordinary" postage, phone and messenger expenses. Offers a consultation service through which writers not represented can get advice on a contract; charges $50/hour. 95% of income derived from commission on ms sales. Payment of criticism fee does not ensure that agency will represent a writer.

Recent Sales: *The Death and Life of Dith Pran* (Elizabeth Sifton); *At Any Cost* (Pantheon); *I, Koch* (Dodd Mead); and *High Calcium, Low Calorie Cookbook (Contemporary)*.

CLAUDIA MENZA LITERARY AGENCY, 237 W. 11th St., New York NY 10014. (212)889-6850. President: Claudia Menza. Estab. 1983. Represents 25 clients. 40% of clients are new/unpublished writers. Specializes in unique fiction and nonfiction dealing with serious subjects (i.e. political and medical issues).

Will Handle: Nonfiction books and novels. Currently handles 50% nonfiction books and 50% novels. Will read—at no charge—unsolicited queries and outlines. Does not read unsolicited mss. Reports in 2 weeks on queries; 2 months on mss.

Terms: Agent receives 15% commission on domestic sales; 15% on dramatic sales; and 15% on foreign sales (20% if a foreign agent is also used).

Recent Sales: "Privileged information."

SCOTT MEREDITH, INC., 845 3rd Ave., New York NY 10022. (212)245-5500. Vice President and Editorial Director: Jack Scovil. Estab. 1946. Represents 2,000 clients. 10% of clients are new/unpublished writers. "We'll represent on a straight commission basis writers who've sold one or more recent books to major publishers, or several (three or four) magazine pieces to major magazines, or a screenplay or teleplay to a major producer. We're a very large agency (staff of 51) and handle all types of material except individual cartoons or drawings, though we will handle collections of these as well."

Will Handle: Magazine articles, magazine fiction, nonfiction books, novels, textbooks, juvenile books, movie scripts, radio scripts, stage plays, TV scripts, syndicated material and poetry. Currently handles 5% magazine articles; 5% magazine fiction; 23% nonfiction books; 23% novels; 5% textbooks; 10% juvenile books; 5% movie scripts; 2% radio scripts; 2% stage plays; 5% TV scripts; 5% syndicated material; and 5% poetry. Will read—at no charge—unsolicited queries, outlines, and manuscripts "if from a writer with track record as described previously; charges a fee if no sales." Reports in 2 weeks.

Terms: Agent receives 10% commission on domestic sales; 10% on dramatic sales; and 20% on foreign sales. Charges "a single fee which covers multiple readers, revision assistance or critique as needed. When a script is returned as irreparably unsalable, the accompanying letter of explanation will usually run two single-spaced pages minimum on short stories or articles, or from 4 to 10 single-spaced pages on book-length manuscripts, teleplays, or screenplays. All reports are done by agents on full-time staff. No marketing advice is included, since, if it's salable, we'll market and sell it ourselves." Charges for telex, cables and phone expenses. 10% of income derived from fees; 90% of income derived from commission on mss sales.

Recent Sales: *Tough Guys Don't Dance*, by Norman Mailer (movie rights to Cannon Films); *Nucleus*, by Carl Sagan (Random House); and *Reagan's America*, by Garry Wills (Doubleday).

‡MEWS BOOKS LTD.—Sidney B. Kramer,20 Bluewater Hill, Westport CT 06880. (203)227-1836. Secretary: Fran Pollak. Estab. 1972. Represents 35 clients. Prefers to work with published/established authors; works with small number of new/unpublished authors "producing professional work. No editing services." Specializes in juvenile (pre-school through young adult), cookery, adult nonfiction and fiction, technical and medical.

Will Handle: Nonfiction books, novels, juvenile books, character merchandising and video use of illustrated published books. Currently handles 20% nonfiction; 20% novels; 50% juvenile books and 10% miscellaneous. Will read—at no charge—unsolicited queries and outlines with character description and a few pages of writing sample.

Terms: Agent receives 10% commission on domestic sales for published authors; 15% for unpublished; total 20% on foreign ($500 minimum commission if book is published). Charges writers sales for photocopy and postage expenses and other direct costs. Principle agent is an attorney and former publisher. Offers consultation service through which writers can get advice on a contract or on publishing problems.

THE PETER MILLER AGENCY, INC., Box 764, Midtown Station, New York NY 10018. (212)221-8329. President: Peter Miller. Associate Agent: Mark Connolly. Estab. 1975. Represents 30 clients. 50% of clients are new/unpublished writers. Eager to work with new/unpublished writers, as well as with published/established authors (especially journalists). Specializes in celebrity books (biographies and self-help), true crime accounts, mysteries, mystery thrillers, historical fiction/family sagas, women's fiction, and "fiction with *real* motion picture potential."

Will Handle: Nonfiction books, novels and movie scripts. Currently handles 45% nonfiction books; 35% novels; and 20% movie scripts. Will read—at no charge—unsolicited queries and outlines. Reports in 2 weeks on queries; 1 month on mss.

Terms: Agent receives 15% commission on domestic sales; and 20-25% on foreign sales. Charges a criticism fee for unpublished writers. Fee is refunded if book sells. 5% of income derived from criticism fees. "The agency offers a reading evaluation, usually two to four pages in length, which gives detailed analysis of literary craft, commercial potential and recommendations for improving the work, if necessary." Charges for photocopy expenses. 5% of income derived from fees; 95% of income derived from commission on ms sales.

Recent Sales: *Lullabye and Goodnight*, by Vincent Bugliosi and William Stadiem (NAL); *New Beauty: An Accupressure Facelift*, by Lindsay Wagner and Robert Klein (Prentice Hall Press); and *Accidental Millionaire*, by Lee Butcher (Pargan House Publishers).

MULTIMEDIA PRODUCT DEVELOPMENT, INC., Suite 724, 410 S. Michigan Ave., Chicago IL 60605. (312)922-3063. President: Jane Jordan Browne. Estab. 1971. Member of ILAA. Represents 100 clients. 10% of clients are new/unpublished writers. Works with a small number of new/unpublished authors. "We are generalists, taking on nonfiction and fiction that we believe will be on target for the market."

Will Handle: Nonfiction books ("new idea" books, how-to, science and biography) and novels (mainstream and genre). Currently handles 68% nonfiction books; 30% novels; and 2% juvenile books. Will read—at no charge—unsolicited queries and outlines. Reports in 3 weeks on queries. "We review manuscripts only if we solicit submission and only as 'exclusives.' "

Terms: Agent receives 15% commission on domestic sales; 15% on dramatic sales; and 20% on foreign sales. Charges for photocopying, overseas telegrams and telephone calls, and overseas postage expenses. Sometimes offers a consultation service through which writers not represented can get advice on a contract; charges $100/hour. 100% of income derived from commission on ms sales.

Recent Sales: *The Official Computer Joke Book*, by Larry Wilde and Steve Wozniak (Bantam); *The Echo Vector*, by James Kahn (St. Martin's); and *Gloria And Joe*, by Axel Madsen (Arbor House).

‡JEAN V. NAGGAR LITERARY AGENCY, 336 East 73rd St., New York NY 10021. (212)794-1082. President: Jean Naggar. Estab. 1978. Member of ILAA. Represents 80 clients. "If a writer is submitting a first novel, this must be completed and in final draft form before writing to query the agency." Prefers to work with published/established authors; works with small number of new/unpublished authors. Specializes in mainstream fiction and nonfiction—no category romances, no occult.

Will Handle: Nonfiction books, novels and juvenile books. Handles magazine articles and magazine fiction from authors who also write fiction/nonfiction books. Will read—at no charge—unsolicited queries and outlines. Reports in 2 weeks on queries.

Terms: Agent receives 15% commission on domestic sales; 15% on dramatic sales; 20% on foreign sales. Charges writers for photocopy, long distance telephone, cables and overseas postage expenses.

Recent Sales: *Through A Glass Darkly*, by Karleen Koen (Random House); *China White*, by Tony Kenrick (Little, Brown), and *Harvest of Bittersweet*, by Patricia Leimbach (Harper and Row).

CHARLES NEIGHBORS, INC., Suite 3607A, 7600 Blanco Rd., San Antonio TX 78216. (512)342-5324. Owner: Charles Neighbors. Estab. 1966. Represents 60 clients. 10% of clients are new/unpublished writers. Works with a small number of new/unpublished authors.

Will Handle: Nonfiction books, novels and movie scripts. Currently handles 30% nonfiction books; 60% novels; and 10% movie scripts. Will read—at no charge—unsolicited queries and outlines. Reports in 1 month on queries; 2 months on mss. "If our agency does not respond within 2 months to your request to become a client, you may submit requests elsewhere."

Terms: Agent receives 15% commission on domestic sales; 15% on dramatic sales; and 20% on foreign sales.

Charges for photocopying and foreign postage expenses. 100% of income derived from commission on ms sales.
Recent Sales: *Two Point Conversion*, by Bryce Webster (Amacom); *Hold Back The Dawn*, by Ruth Vaughn (Medallion).

B.K. NELSON LITERARY AGENCY, 10 E. 39th St., New York NY 10016. (212)889-0637. President: Bonita K. Nelson. Estab. 1978. Represents 15 clients. 2% of clients are new/unpublished writers. "A writer has to understand the basics of writing, not just have an idea. We want professionalism. Do the best you can do and we will work with you." Eager to work with new/unpublished writers. Specializes in how-to, computer, business books, historical romances, contemporary romance, software and game show proposals, the college educational market, and motion picture scripts of all kinds.
Will Handle: Nonfiction books, novels, movie scripts, how-to and computer applications. Currently handles 65% nonfiction books; 30% novels; and 5% textbooks. "Will read inquiries and outlines limited to 5 pages and will make a decision at point of inquiry." Does not read unsolicited mss. Reports in 1 week on queries; 2 weeks on mss. "If our agency does not respond within 3 months to your request to become a client, you may submit requests elsewhere."
Terms: Agent receives 15% commission on domestic sales; 15% on dramatic sales; and 10% on foreign sales. Charges a reading fee if the writer "wants a manuscript read, and for us to determine if it is salable." 1% of income derived from reading fees. "If the writer wants a detailed criticism against which to rewrite the book, we will then do it for a fee after having discussed the manuscript with a potential author/client." 1% of income derived from fees; 99% of income derived from commission on ms sales.
Recent Sales: *Marketing to the Fortune 500*, by Jeff Davidson (Dow Jones-Irwin); *Marketer's Direct-Mail Idea Book and Workbook*, by Holtz, Herman; and *The Complete Writer's Reference*, by Holtz (Dow Jones).

‡NEW AGE WORLD SERVICES, 62091 Valley View Circle, Joshua Tree CA 92252. (619)366-2833. Owner: Victoria Vandertuin. Estab. 1957. Member of Academy of Science Fiction, Fantasy and Horror Films. Represents 12 clients. 100% of clients are new/unpublished writers. Eager to work with new/unpublished writers. Specializes in all New Age fields: occult, astrology, metaphysical, yoga, U.F.O., ancient continents, para sciences, mystical, magical, health, beauty, political, and all New Age categories in fiction and nonfiction.
Will Handle: Magazine articles, magazine fiction, nonfiction books, novels and poetry. Currently handles 10% magazine articles; 10% magazine fiction; 40% nonfiction books; 30% novels and 10% poetry. Will read—at no charge— unsolicited queries, outlines and mss; will read submissions at no charge, but may charge a criticism fee or service charge for work performed after the initial reading. Reports in 6 weeks. "If our agency does not respond within 2 month to your request to become a client, you may submit requests elsewhere."
Terms: Receives 15% commission on domestic sales; and 20% on foreign sales. Charges reading fee of $75 for 300-page, typed, double-spaced ms; reading fee waived if representing writer. Charges criticism fee of $85 for 300-page, typed, double-space ms; 10% of income derived from criticism fees. "I personally read all mss for critique or evaluation, they are typed, double-spaced with about four or five or more pages, depending on the ms and the service for the ms the author requests. If requested, marketing advice is included. We charge a representation fee if we represent the author's mss." Charges writer for editorial readings, compiling of query letter and synopsis, printing of same, compiling lists and mailings.
Recent Sales: No information given.

NEW ENGLAND PUBLISHING ASSOCIATES, INC., Box 5, Chester CT 06412. (718)788-6641 or (203)345-4976. President: Elizabeth Frost Knappman. Estab. 1983. Represents 45-50 clients. 25% of clients are new/unpublished writers. Specializes in serious nonfiction.
Will Handle: Nonfiction books. Currently handles 100% nonfiction books. Will read—at no charge—unsolicited queries and outlines. Phone queries are OK. Reports in 1 month on queries. Simultaneous queries OK.
Terms: Agent receives 15% on domestic sales; and 10% on dramatic and foreign sales (plus 10% to co-agent). 100% of income derived from commission on ms sales.
Recent Sales: *Mafia Enforcer*, by Tom Renner and Cecil Kirby (Random House); *Poisoned Blood*, by Philip Ginsburg (Scribner's); and *Bones of Contention*, by Roger Lewin (Simon and Schuster).

THE BETSY NOLAN LITERARY AGENCY, 215 Park Ave. S, New York NY 10003. (212)420-6000. President: Betsy Nolan. Vice President: Michael Powers. Estab. 1980. Represents 26 clients. 50% of clients are new/unpublished writers. Works with a small number of new/unpublished authors.
Will Handle: Nonfiction books and novels. Currently handles 60% nonfiction books and 40% novels. Will read—at no charge—unsolicited queries and outlines. Reports in 2 weeks on queries; 1 month on mss. "If our agency does not respond within 1 month to your request to become a client, you may submit requests elsewhere."
Terms: Agent receives 15% commission on domestic sales; and 20% on foreign sales.
Recent Sales: No information given.

‡THE NORMA-LEWIS AGENCY, 521 Fifth Ave., New York NY 10175. (212)751-4955. Contact: Norma Liebert. Estab. 1980. 50% of clients are new/unpublished writers. Prefers to work with published/established authors; eager to work with new/unpublished writers. Specializes in young adult and children's books.
Will Handle: Novels, textbooks, juvenile books, movie scripts, radio scripts, stage plays and TV scripts. Currently handles 10% nonfiction books; 10% novels; 10% textbooks; 50% juvenile books; 5% movie scripts; 5% radio scripts; 5% stage plays; and 5% TV scripts. Will read—at no charge—unsolicited queries and outlines. Reports in 2 weeks on queries. "If our agency does not respond within 2 weeks to your request to become a client, you may submit requests elsewhere."
Terms: Agent receives 15% commission on domestic sales; 15% on dramatic sales; and 20% on foreign sales. Offers a consultation service through which writers not represented can get advice on a contract. Rate varies. 100% of income derived from commission on ms sales.
Recent Sales: No information given.

‡NUGENT AND ASSOCIATES, INC.,170 Tenth Street, North, Naples FL 33940. (813)262-7562. President: Ray E. Nugent. Estab. 1976. Represents 27 clients. 75% of clients are new/unpublished writers. Eager to work with new/unpublished writers. Specializes in adult fiction and nonfiction—screenplays.
Will Handle: Nonfiction books, novels, movie scripts, stage plays and TV scripts. Currently handles 10% nonfiction books; 70% novels; 5% juvenile books; 5% movie scripts; 3% stage plays; 5% TV scripts; and 2% poetry. Will read—at no charge—unsolicited queries, outlines and mss. Reports in 1 month on queries; 2 months on submissions. "If our agency does not respond within 3 months to your request to become a client, you may submit requests elsewhere."
Terms: Receives 12½% commission on domestic sales; 12½% on dramatic sales and 15% on foreign sales. First book authors are charged $500 to cover ms typing, copies, long distance calls, etc.; balance refundable. Less than 5% of income derived from fees. Charges writers for long distance phone calls, copies, ms typing, any other extraordinary expenses directly associated with the author's specific material. Offers consultation service through which writers can get advice on a contract; charges $60/hour.
Recent Sales:*The Anti-Patriot*, by Gar Mowll, Biblios (England); *Pipes and Strings*, by Bill Ballentine (Richardson and Steerman); and *Disney's World*, by Leonard Mosley (Stein and Day).

FIFI OSCARD ASSOCIATES, 19 W. 44th St., New York NY 10036. (212)764-1100. Contact: Ivy Fischer Stone, Literary Department. Estab. 1956. Member of SAR and WGA. Represents 108 clients. 5% of clients are new/unpublished writers. "Writer must have published articles or books in major markets or have screen credits if movie scripts, etc." Works with a small number of new/unpublished authors. Specializes in literary novels, commercial novels, mysteries and nonfiction, especially celebrity biographies and autobiographies.
Will Handle: Nonfiction books, novels, movie scripts and stage plays. Currently handles 35% nonfiction books; 35% novels; 10% movie scripts; 10% stage plays; and 10% TV scripts. Will read—at no charge—unsolicited queries and outlines. Reports in 1 week on queries if SASE enclosed. "If our agency does not respond within 1 month to your request to become a client, you may submit requests elsewhere."
Terms: Agent receives 15% commission on domestic sales; 10% on dramatic sales; and 20% on foreign sales. Charges for photocopy expenses.
Recent Sales: *Ice Water*, by Hob Broun (Knopf); *Kaffir Boy*, by Mark Mathabane (Macmillan); and *Debbie Reynolds Autobiography* (Morrow).

THE OTTE COMPANY, 9 Goden St., Belmont MA 02178. (617)484-8505. Contact: Jane H. Otte; L. David Otte. Estab. 1973. Represents 25 clients. 33% of clients are new/unpublished writers. Works with a small number of new/unpublished authors. Specializes in quality adult trade books.
Will Handle: Nonfiction books and novels. Currently handles 40% nonfiction books; and 60% novels. Will read—at no charge—unsolicited queries. Reports in 1 week on queries; 1 month on mss. "If our agency does not respond within 1 month to your request to become a client, you may submit requests elsewhere."
Terms: Agent receives 15% commission on domestic sales; 7½% on dramatic sales; and 10% on foreign sales plus 10% to foreign agent. Charges for photocopy, overseas phone and postage expenses. 100% of income derived from commission on ms sales.
Recent Sales: *Jack and Susan in 1933*, by Michael McDowell (Ballantine); *Abbott and Avery*, by Robert Shaw (Viking Penguin); and *Candles Burning*, by Michael McDowell (Berkley).

JOHN K. PAYNE LITERARY AGENCY, INC., Suite 1101, 175 5th Ave., New York NY 10010. (212)475-6447. President: John K. Payne. Estab. 1923 (as Lenniger Literary Agency). Represents 30 clients. 20% of clients are new/unpublished writers. Prefers writers who have one or two books published. Specializes in popular women's fiction, historical romance, biography, sagas.
Will Handle: Nonfiction books, novels, and juvenile books (young adult fiction, nonfiction). Currently publishes 20% nonfiction books and 80% novels. Charges reading fee to unpublished writers; $65 for 60 pages (3 chapters and outline), $25 per ten thousand words thereafter. Charges criticism fee; writer receives 2-3 single-spaced pages for partial scripts, 5 for entire scripts.

Terms: Agent receives 10% commission on domestic sales; 10% on dramatic sales; and 20% on foreign sales. Charges for express mail expenses and photocopies. 5% of income derived from fees charged to writers; 95% of income derived from commission on ms sales.
Recent Sales: *The Will and the Way*, by Rita Clay Estrada (Harlequin); *All the Golden Promises*, by Diana Browning (Fawcett); and *The Man Who Rode Midnight*, by Elmer Kecton (Doubleday).

RAY PEEKNER LITERARY AGENCY INC., 3210 S. 7th St., Milwaukee WI 53215. (414)482-0629. Owner: Ray Puechner and Barbara Berman Peuchner. Estab. 1973. Represents 60 clients. 5% of clients are new/unpublished writers. "New clients are usually referred by an editor or a client already on the list." Prefers to work with published/established authors. Specializes in private-eye novels (hard-boiled), westerns, quality young adult and middle-grades novels. Currently handles 10% nonfiction books; 70% novels; and 20% juvenile books. Does not read unsolicited mss. Reports in 2 weeks on queries.
Terms: Agent receives 10% commission on domestic sales. 100% of income derived from commission on ms sales.
Recent Sales: *Bloody Season*, by Loren D. Estleman (Bantam Books); *Sentries*, by Gary Paulsen (Bradbury Press); and *The Magic Wagon*, by Joe Lausdale (Doubleday).

‡PICKERING ASSOCIATES, INC., (formerly John Pickering Co.), Suite #1500, 225 West 34th St., New York NY 10001. (212)967-5588. President: John Pickering. Vice President: A. Elizabeth Davidson. Estab. 1986. Represents 35 clients. 50% of our clients are new/unpublished writers. "We prefer an author with a successful track record, but the most important criterion is always how well we perceive the author writes: we'll consider any good writer, whether published or not." Specializes in topical nonfiction, contemporary fiction, experimental fiction, historical romances (Regencies), mysteries and thrillers of all sorts.
Will Handle: Nonfiction books (query with proposal and author's backgrond); novels (query with 1-2 sample chapters) and juvenile books. Currently handles 5% magazine articles; 5% magazine fiction; 35% nonfiction books; 42% novels; 1% textbooks; 10% juvenile books; 2% movie scripts. Will read—at no charge—unsolicited queries, outlines and mss. "We report in 1 week on queries; 6 weeks on mss. If our agency does not respond within 2 months to your request to become a client, you may submit requests elsewhere."
Terms: Agent receives 10% commission on domestic sales; and 15-20% on foreign sales. Charges for photocopying, typing, overseas telephone calls. 100% of commission from sales of writers' work.
Recent Sales: *Body and Soul*, by J.P. Smith (Grove Press); *Private Woods*, by Sandra Moore (Harcourt Brace); and *The Other Woman*, by Ellen Lesser (Simon and Schuster).

‡ARTHUR PINE ASSOCIATES, INC., 1780 Broadway, New York NY 10019. (212)265-7330. Contact: Agent. Estab. 1967. Represents 100 clients. 20% of clients are new/unpublished writers. Works with a small number of new/unpublished authors.
Will Handle: Nonfiction books and novels. Currently handles 75% nonfiction books and 25% novels. Does not read unsolicited mss. Reports in 2 weeks on queries.
Terms: Agent receives 15% commission on domestic sales; 15% on dramatic sales; and 15% on foreign sales. Charges a reading fee. .5% of income derived from reading fees. Gives 1-3 pages of criticism. Charges for photocopy expenses. Sometimes offers a consultation service through which writers not represented get advice on a contract; charges $200/hour. .5% of income derived from fees; 99.5% of income derived from sales of writers' work.
Recent Sales: *Please Don't Shoot My Dog*, by Dick Kleiner (William/Morrow/Berkley); *The Survivor of Rape*, by Linda E. Ledray (Holt, Rinehart & Winston); and *The New Thinking Man's Guide to Pro Football*, by Paul Zimmerman (Simon & Schuster).

SIDNEY E. PORCELAIN, Box 1229, Milford PA 18337. (717)296-6420. Manager: Sidney Porcelain. Estab. 1952. Represents 20 clients. 50% of clients are new/unpublished writers. Prefers to work with published/established authors; works with a small number of new/unpublished authors. Specializes in fiction (novels, mysteries, and suspense) and nonfiction (celebrity and exposé).
Will Handle: Magazine articles, magazine fiction, nonfiction books, novels and juvenile books. Currently handles 2% magazine articles; 5% magazine fiction; 5% nonfiction books; 50% novels; 5% juvenile books; 2% movie scripts; 1% TV scripts; and 30% "comments for new writers." Will read—at no charge—unsolicited queries, outlines and mss. Reports in 2 weeks on queries; 3 weeks on mss.
Terms: Agent receives 10% commission on domestic sales; 10% on dramatic sales; and 10% on foreign sales. Sometimes offers a consultation service through which writers not represented can get advice on a contract. 50% of income derived from commission on ms sales.
Recent Sales: No information given.

‡JULIAN PORTMAN AGENCY, Suite 326, 6677 Lincoln Ave., Chicago IL 60645. Branch office: Suite 964, 800 Sunset Blvd., Hollywood CA 90046. (312)676-9815. Senior partner: Julian Portman. Estab. 1969. Represents 35 clients. 25% of our clients are new/unpublished writers. "Our interest is a good writer, storyteller

and plot creator, whether they be a new writer or one who has had a book previously published. Our interest is to find stories that would sell for books and could be turned into potential TV/motion pictures." Works with a small number of new/unpublished authors.
Will Handle: Nonfiction books, novels, movie scripts, TV scripts. Currently handles 30% nonfiction books, 35% novels, 20% movie scripts; 15% TV scripts. Will read—at no charge—unsolicited queries and outlines. Reports in 3 weeks on queries; 7 weeks on mss. "If our agency does not respond within 2 months to your request to become a client, you may submit requests elsewhere."
Terms: Agent receives 15-25% commission on domestic sales; 15% on dramatic sales and 25% on foreign sales. Charges a reading and criticism fee for new writers; reading fee will be waived if represents the writer. 3% of income derived from reading fees. Charges $150-200 for 300-page, typed double-spaced book ms. Writer receives an "overall evaluation of 2-3 pages depending on the quality of the ms. Uses both published authors and journalists on a flat fee arrangement to evaluate mss." Charges a handling fee. 1% of income derived from handling fees. Sometimes offers a consultation service through which writers not represented can get advice on a contract. 15% of income derived from fees. Payment of a criticism fee does not ensure that agency will represent a writer.
Recent Sales: *RKO: The Biggest Little Manor of Them All*, by Betty Lasky (Prentice-Hall); *The Tooth of the Dragon: The Story of General Morris (Two Gun) Cohen*, by Jean Kropfer/Julian Portman (Paperjack).

AARON M. PRIEST LITERARY AGENCY INC., Suite 3902, 122 East 42nd St., New York NY 10168. (212)818-0344. Contact: Aaron Priest, Molly Friedrich.
Will Handle: Fiction and nonfiction books. Currently handles 50% nonfiction and 50% fiction. Will read submissions at no charge. Reports in 1 month on mss. "If our agency does not respond within 1 month to your request to become a client, you may submit requests elsewhere."
Terms: Agency receives 15% commission on domestic sales. Charges for photocopy and foreign postage expenses.
Recent Sales: *Indian Country*, by Philip Caputo; *Joanna's Husband and David's Wife*, by Elizabeth Forsythe Hailey; and *Getting Better All The Time*, by Liz Carpenter.

SUSAN ANN PROTTER LITERARY AGENT, Suite 1408, 110 W. 40th St., New York NY 10018. (212)840-0480. Contact: Susan Protter. Estab. 1971. Member of ILAA. Represents 50 clients. 10% of clients are new/unpublished writers. Writer must have book-length project or manuscript that is ready to be sold. Works with a small number of new/unpublished authors. Specializes in general nonfiction, self-help, psychology, science, health, medicine, novels, science fiction, mysteries and thrillers.
Will Handle: Nonfiction books and novels. Currently handles 5% magazine articles; 60% nonfiction books; 30% novels; and 5% photography books. Will read—at no charge—unsolicited queries and outlines. "Must include SASE." Reports in 2 weeks on queries; 5 weeks on solicited mss. "If our agency does not respond within 2 months to your request to become a client, you may submit requests elsewhere."
Terms: Agent receives 15% commission on domestic sales; 15% on TV, film and dramatic sales; and 25% on foreign sales. Charges for long distance, photocopying, messenger, express mail and airmail expenses. 100% of income derived from commission on ms sales.
Recent Sales: *Fire On The Mountain*, by T. Bisson (Avon); *Mercedes Nights*, by Weaver (St. Martin's); and *Mother: A Collective Portrait*, by Kalergis (Dutton).

HELEN REES LITERARY AGENCY, 308 Commonwealth Ave., Boston MA 02116. (617)262-2401. Contact: Catherine Mahar. Estab. 1982. Member of ILAA. Represents 55 clients. 25% of our clients are new/unpublished writers. Writer must have been published or be an authority on a subject. Prefers to work with published/established authors; works with a small number of new/unpublished authors. Specializes in nonfiction, biographies and business.
Will Handle: Nonfiction books and novels. Currently handles 90% nonfiction books and 10% novels. Will read—at no charge—unsolicited queries and outlines. Reports in 2 weeks on queries; 3 weeks on mss.
Terms: Agent receives 15% commission on domestic sales; and 20% on foreign sales. Occasionally charges a reading fee "for clients who are unpublished and want that service. I don't solicit this." Reading fee will be waived if representing the writer. Charges criticism fee of $250; writer receives criticism of characters, dialogue, plot, style and suggestions for reworking areas of weakness. Sometimes offers a consultation service through which writers not represented can get advice on a contract: no set fee.
Recent Sales: *Price Waterhouse Guide to the New Tax Law* (Bantam); *Senator Barry Goldwater's Autobiography* (Doubleday); and *What Teenagers Want to Know About Sex*, by Boston Children's Hospital (Little, Brown).

RHODES LITERARY AGENCY INC., 140 West End Ave., New York NY 10023. (212)580-1300. President: Joan Lewis. Estab. 1971. Member of ILAA.
Will Handle: Nonfiction books, novels (a limited number), and juvenile books. Will read—at no charge—unsolicited queries and outlines. Include SASE. Reports in 2 weeks on queries.

Terms: Agent receives 10% commission on domestic sales; and 20% on foreign sales.
Recent Sales: No information given.

‡THE RICHLAND AGENCY, Suite 204, 9046 Sunset Blvd., Los Angeles CA 90069. (213)273-9661. Manager: Mark Gray. Estab. 1980. Represents 28 clients. Prefers to work with published/established authors. Specializes in drama and comedy for TV and motion picture.
Will Handle: Novels (in conjunction with screen or teleplay); movie scripts (prefers original material); and TV scripts (in conjunction with original material). Currently handles 20% movie scripts and 80% TV scripts. Does not read unsolicited mss. "If our agency does not respond within 1 month to your request to become a client, you may submit requests elsewhere."
Terms: Agent receives 10% commission on domestic sales; 10% on dramatic sales; and 10% on foreign sales. Charges writers for photocopy expenses. 100% of income derived from fees.
Recent Sales: No information given.

‡MARIE RODELL—FRANCIS COLLIN LITERARY AGENCY, 110 West 40th St., New York NY 10018. (212)840-8664. Contact: Frances Collin. Estab. 1948. Member of SAR. Represents 90 clients. 10% of clients are new/unpublished writers. Prefers to work with published/established authors; works with a small number of new/unpublished authors. Has a "broad general trade list."
Will Handle: Nonfiction books and novels. Currently handles 50% nonfiction books; 40% novels; and 10% juvenile books. Will read—at no charge—unsolicited queries. Reports in 1 week on queries.
Terms: Agent receives 15% commission on domestic sales; 20% on dramatic sales; and 25% on foreign sales. Charges for overseas postage, photocopy and registered mail expenses, and copyright registration fees. 100% of income derived from commission on ms sales.
Recent Sales: Confidential.

ELEANOR ROSZEL ROGERS, LITERARY AGENT, 1487 Generals Hwy., Crownsville MD 21032. (301)987-8166. Agent: Eleanor Rogers. Estab. 1976. Represents 15 clients. "The only qualification a writer must meet is that I like what he sends me—either fiction or nonfiction, for adults or children . . . I have fairly catholic tastes." Eager to work with new/unpublished writers; "I'm interested in seeing what's available, without pre-empting myself, and am interested in working with published *and* nonpublished writers." Specializes in mainstream fiction and nonfiction. "I have no interest whatsoever in 'Harlequin-type' romances, or in science fiction."
Will Handle: Nonfiction books, novels and juvenile books. Currently handles 50% nonfiction books; 49% novels; and 1% juvenile books. Will read—at no charge—unsolicited queries, outlines and mss. Reports in 2 weeks on queries; 3 weeks on mss. "If our agency does not respond within 2 months to your request to become a client, you may submit requests elsewhere. No reply without SASE."
Terms: Agent receives 10% commission on domestic sales and 20% on foreign sales. "I don't offer criticism unless I see weaknesses in a work I hope to represent." Charges for phone, postage, photocopying, and agreed upon travel expenses. 80% of income derived from commission on manuscript sales.
Recent Sales: *Maryland Houses & Gardens*, by Weeks and Foster (Stemmer House); *1941: The Year Our World Began*, by William K. Klingman (Harper and Row); and *Where Time Stands Still*, by Sally Foster (Dodd, Mead).

‡IRENE ROGERS LITERARY REPRESENTATION, Suite #850, 9701 Wilshire Blvd., Beverly Hills CA 90212. (213)837-3511. President: Irene Rogers. Vice President: Paul Pizarro. Estab. 1972. Member of SAR, ILAA and Women in Film. Represents 10 clients. 5% of clients are new/unpublished writers. Prefers to work with published/established authors. Specializes in self-help and contemporary romance novels.
Will Handle: Nonfiction books, novels, movie scripts and TV scripts. Currently handles 45% nonfiction books; 10% novels; 30% movie scripts; and 15% TV scripts. Will read—at no charge—unsolicited queries and outlines. Reports in 3-4 months.
Terms: Receives 10% commission on domestic sales; 5% on dramatic sales; and 5% on foreign sales. 100% of income derived from commission on ms sales.
Recent Sales: Confidential.

STEPHANIE ROGERS AND ASSOCIATES, 3855 Lankershim Blvd.—#218, N. Hollywood CA 91604. (818)509-1010. Owner: Stephanie Rogers. Estab. 1981. Represents 18 clients. 20% of clients are new/unpublished writers. Prefers that the writer has been produced (motion pictures or TV), his/her properties optioned or has references. Prefers to work with published/established authors. Specializes in screenplays—dramas (contemporary), action/adventure, romantic comedies and biographies for motion pictures and TV.
Will Handle: Novels (only wishes to see those that have been published and can translate to screen) and movie and TV scripts (must be professional in presentation and not over 130 pages). Currently handles 10% novels; 50% movie scripts and 40% TV scripts. Does not read unsolicited mss.

Terms: Agent receives 10% commission on domestic sales; 10% on dramatic sales; and 10% on foreign sales. Charges for phone, photocopying and messenger expenses.
Recent Sales: No information given.

‡JANE ROTROSEN AGENCY, 318 East 51st St., New York NY 10022. (212)593-4330. Estab. 1974. Member of ILAA. Represents 100 clients. 90% of clients were new/unpublished writers. Prefers to work with published/established writers; works with small number of new/unpublished writers. Specializes in general trade fiction and nonfiction.
Will Handle: Nonfiction books, novels and juvenile books. Currently handles 30% nonfiction books; 70% novels. Will read—at no charge—unsolicited queries and short outlines. Reports in 2 weeks.
Terms: Receives 15% commission on domestic sales; 15% on dramatic sales; and 20% on foreign sales. Charges writers for photocopies, long-distance/transoceanic telephone, telegraph, telex, messenger service, foreign postage.
Recent Sales "Our client list remains confidential."

JOHN SCHAFFNER ASSOCIATES, INC., Suite 402, 114 E. 28th St., New York NY 10016. (212)689-6888. Contact: Timothy Schaffner or Patrick Delahunt. Estab. 1948. Member of SAR and ILAA. Represents 50-60 clients. 15% of clients are new/unpublished writers. Works with a small number of new/unpublished authors. Specializes in speculative fiction, science fiction, fantasy, celebrity bios, popular self-help, and general nonfiction and fiction.
Will Handle: Nonfiction books and novels. Currently handles 5% magazine fiction; 30% nonfiction books; 60% novels; and 5% juvenile books. Will read—at no charge—unsolicited queries and outlines with SASE or $5 for handling. Reports in 2 weeks on queries; 6 weeks on mss. "If our agency does not respond within 6 weeks to your request to become a client, you may submit requests elsewhere."
Terms: Agent receives 10-15% commission on domestic sales; 15% on dramatic sales; and 20% on foreign sales. Charges writers for "extra services," photocopy expenses, overseas courier, etc. 100% of income derived from commission on ms sales.
Recent Sales: *How to Be Funny*, by Steve Allen (McGraw-Hill); *Menken and Sara: A Life In Letters*, edited by Marion Elizabeth Rodgers (McGraw-Hill); and *A Connoisseur's Guide To Ireland*, by Don Fullington (Henry Holt).

THE SUSAN SCHULMAN LITERARY AGENCY, INC., 454 W. 44th St., New York NY 10036. (212)713-1633/4/5. President: Susan Schulman. Estab. 1978. Member of SAR and ILAA. 10-15% of clients are new/unpublished writers. Prefers to work with published/established authors; works with a small number of new/unpublished authors.
Will Handle: Nonfiction books, novels, movie scripts, treatments for television movies of the week, and dramatic and comedy series. Currently handles 50% nonfiction books; 10% novels; 10% movie scripts; 5% stage plays; and 20% TV scripts. Will read—at no charge—unsolicited queries and outlines. Reports in 2 weeks on queries; 6 weeks on mss. "If our agency does not respond within 1 month to your request to become a client, you may submit request elsewhere."
Terms: Agent receives 15% commission on domestic sales; 10-20% on dramatic sales; and 7½-10% on foreign sales (plus 7½-10% to co-agent). Charges a $50 reading fee if detailed analysis requested; fee will be waived if repesenting the writer. Less than 1% of income derived from reading fees. Charges for foreign mail, special messenger or delivery services, telex and telegrams. Sometimes offers a consultation service through which writers not represented can get advice on a contract; charges $175/hour. Less than 1% of income derived from fees; 99% of income derived from commission on ms sales. Payment of a criticism fee does not ensure that agency will represent writer.
Recent Sales: *Women Who Love Too Much*, by Robin Norwood (Jeremy Tarcher Inc.); *Metamorphosis—Cocoon II*, by David Saperstein (Bantam); and *Drawing From Nature*, (4-part series), by Jim Arnasky to PBS (television); and *21A*, to the Sydney Theatre Festival.

SHORR, STILLE AND ASSOCIATES, Suite 9, 800 S. Robertson Blvd., Los Angeles CA 90035. (213)659-6160. Member of WGA. Writer must have an entertainment industry referral. Works with a small number of new/unpublished authors. Specializes in screenplays, teleplays, high concept action-adventure, romantic comedy.
Will Handle: Movie scripts and TV scripts. Currently handles 50% movie scripts and 50% TV scripts. Will read—at no charge—unsolicited queries. Reports in 1 month on queries; 6 weeks on mss.
Terms: Agent receives 10% commission on domestic sales. Charges for photocopy expenses.
Recent Sales: No information given.

‡SHUMAKER ARTISTS TALENT AGENCY,6533 Hollywood, Hollywood CA 90028. (213)464-0745. Contact: Tim Shumaker. Established 1979. Member of WGA. Represents 40 clients. 30% of clients are new/unpublished writers. "Writer must have proof of reasonable number of sales or must have sufficient training." Prefers to work with published/established authors; works with small number of new/unpublished authors.
Will Handle: Nonfiction books (include author biography with outline, sample chapter, SASE); novels (in-

clude synopsis and outline, SASE); textbooks (include synopsis, table of contents, facts about author); juvenile books (self-help and other); move scripts (include treatment and resume); TV scripts (include treatment and resume); and syndicated material (include complete breakdown in outline form of concept with references). Currently handles 10% novels; 5% textbooks; 5% juvenile books; 25% movie scripts; 5% syndicated material; 35% TV scripts. Does not read unsolicited mss. Reports in 1 months on queries; 2 months on submissions. "If our agency does not respond within 6 months to your request to become a client, you may submit requests elsewhere."

Terms: Receives 10% commission on domestic sales, dramatic sales and foreign sales.

Recent Sales: No information given.

BOBBE SIEGEL, LITERARY AGENCY, 41 W. 83rd St., New York NY 10024. (212)877-4985. Associate: Richard Siegel. Estab. 1975. Represents 60 clients. 40% of clients are new/unpublished writers. "The writer must have a good project, have the credentials to be able to write on the subject and must deliver it in proper fashion. In fiction it all depends on whether I like what I read and if I feel I can sell it." Prefers to work with published/established authors; works with a small number of new/unpublished authors. "Prefer track records, but am eager to work with talent." Specializes in literary fiction, detective and suspense fiction, historicals, how-to, health, woman's subjects, fitness, beauty, feminist sports, biographies and crafts.

Will Handle: Nonfiction books and novels. Currently handles 65% nonfiction books and 35% novels. Does not read unsolicited mss. Reports in 2 weeks on queries; 2 months on mss. "If our agency does not respond within 2 months to your request to become a client, you may submit requests elsewhere."

Terms: Agent receives 15% commission on domestic sales; 10% on dramatic sales; and 10% on foreign sales. If writer wishes critique, will refer to a freelance editor. Charges for photocopying, telephone, overseas mail, express mail expenses. Sometimes offers a consultation service through which writers not represented can get advice on a contract; charges $75/hour. 70% of income derived from commission on ms sales; 30% comes from foreign representation. 100% of income derived from sales of writers' work; "not enough derived from critique to mention as a percentage."

Recent Sales: *The Monkey's Wrench*, by Primo Levi (Summit); *I Never Know What To Say*, by Nina Herrmann Donnelley (Ballantine/Epiphany); and *The Indispensible Writer's Guide*, by Scott Edelstein (Harper and Row).

SINGER COMMUNICATIONS, INC., 3164 Tyler Ave., Anaheim CA 92801. (714)527-5650. Executive Vice President: Natalie Carlton. Estab. 1940. 10% of clients are new/unpublished writers. Prefers to work with published/established authors; works with a small number of new/unpublished authors. Specializes in contemporary romances, nonfiction and biographies.

Will Handle: Magazine articles and syndicated material (submit tearsheets); nonfiction books (query); and romance novels. Currently handles 5% nonfiction books; 20% novels; 75% syndicated material. Will read—at no charge—unsolicited queries and outlines; but may charge a criticism fee or service charge for work performed after the initial reading. Reports in 2 weeks on queries; 6 weeks on mss. "If our agency does not respond within 2 months to your request to become a client, you may submit requests elsewhere."

Terms: Agent receives 15% commission on domestic sales and 20% on foreign sales. Charges a reading fee to unpublished authors which will be credited on sales; .5% of income derived from reading fees. Criticism included in reading fee. "A general overall critique averages three pages. It does not cover spelling or grammar, but the construction of the material. A general marketing critique is also included." Sometimes offers a consultation service through which writers not represented can get advice on a contract. 95% of income derived from sales of writers' work; 5% of income derived from criticism services. "Payment of a criticism fee does not ensure that agency will represent a writer. The author may not be satisfied with our reply, or may need help in making the manuscript marketable."

Recent Sales: "Dozens of magazines, H.H. Allen; Mongadori, Pocketbooks Inc."

EVELYN SINGER LITERARY AGENCY, Box 594, White Plains NY 10602. Agent: Evelyn Singer. Estab. 1951. Represents 75 clients. To be represented, writer must have $20,000 in past sales of freelance works. Prefers to work with published/established authors. Specializes in fiction and nonfiction books, adult and juvenile (picture books only if writer is also the artist).

Will Handle: Nonfiction books (bylined by authority or celebrity); novels (no romances, or pseudo-science, violence or sex); and juvenile books. Currently handles 50% nonfiction books; 25% novels; and 25% juvenile books. Does not read unsolicited mss. "If our agency does not respond within 2 months to your request to become a client, you may submit requests elsewhere."

Terms: Agent receives 15% commission on domestic sales; 20% on dramatic sales; and 20% on foreign sales. Charges for phone and expenses authorized by the author. Sometimes offers a consultation service through which writers not represented can get advice on a contract; charges $100/hour. 100% of income derived from commission on ms sales.

Recent Sales: *Rebuilt Man*, by William Beechcroft (Dodd, Mead); *Snakes*, by Mary Elting (Simon and Schuster); and *How Things Work*, by Mike and Marcia Folsom (Macmillan).

ARE YOU SERIOUS?

About learning to write better? Getting published? Getting paid for what you write?

If you're dedicated to your writing, **Writer's Digest School** can put you on the fast track to writing success.

Study With A Professional

When you enroll in a **Writer's Digest School** course, you get more than writing textbooks and assignments. You get a one-on-one relationship with a professional writer who is currently writing *and selling* the kind of material you're interested in. Your training as a writer is built around this personal guidance from an experienced pro who knows what it takes to succeed in the competitive literary marketplace.

Four Courses Available

Writer's Digest School offers four courses: Writing to Sell Nonfiction (Articles), Writing to Sell Fiction (Short Stories), Elements of Effective Writing, and Advanced Writer's Workshop. Each course is described in more detail on the reverse side.

We've Been Teaching Creative People Since 1920

Writer's Digest School was founded over 60 years ago by the same people who publish **Writer's Digest,** the world's leading magazine for writers, and **Writer's Market,** the indispensable annual reference directory for writers. When you enroll in a **Writer's Digest School** course, you get the quality and expertise that are the hallmarks of the **Writer's Digest** name.

If you're serious about your writing, you owe it to yourself to check out **Writer's Digest School.** Mail the coupon below today for *free* information!

- -

Yes, I'm Serious!

I want to learn to write and sell from the professionals at **Writer's Digest School.** Send me free information about the course I've checked below:

☐ Writing to Sell Nonfiction (Articles)　　　☐ Advanced Writer's Workshop
☐ Writing to Sell Fiction (Short Stories)　　　☐ Elements of Effective Writing

NAME

ADDRESS

CITY　　　　　　　　　　　　　　STATE　　　　　ZIP

Mail this card today! No postage needed

QWM8

Writer's Digest School has been teaching people like you to write for more than 60 years.

Writer's Digest School

1507 Dana Avenue
Cincinnati, Ohio 45207

Four **Writer's Digest School** courses to help you write better and sell more:

- **Writing to Sell Nonfiction.** Master the fundamentals of writing/selling nonfiction articles: finding article ideas, conducting interviews, writing effective query letters and attention-getting leads, targeting your articles to the right publication, and other important elements of a salable article. Course includes writing assignments and one complete article manuscript (and its revision). Your instructor will critique each assignment and help you adapt your article to a particular magazine.

- **Writing to Sell Fiction.** Learn the basics of writing/selling short stories: plotting, characterization, dialogue, theme, conflict, and other elements of a marketable short story. Course includes writing assignments and one complete short story (and its revision). Your instructor will critique each assignment and give you suggestions for selling your story.

- **Advanced Writer's Workshop.** Advanced course open to selected graduates of the Fiction and Nonfiction courses and equally qualified writers. Your professional instructor analyzes and evaluates your four short stories or articles, and gives you specific marketing suggestions. This is an intensive, one-year course for writers serious about publishing their work.

- **Elements of Effective Writing.** Refresher course covers the basics of grammar, punctuation and elements of composition. You review the nine parts of speech and their correct usage, and learn to write clearly and effectively. Course includes 12 lessons with a grammar exercise and editing or writing assignment in each lesson.

Mail this card today for **free** information!

MICHAEL SNELL LITERARY AGENCY, Bridge and Castle Rd., Truro MA 02666. (617)349-3781. President: Michael Snell. Estab. 1980. Represents 100+ clients. 25% of our clients are new/unpublished writers. Eager to work with new unpublished writers. Specializes in business books (from professional/reference to popular trade how-to); college textbooks (in all subjects, but especially business, science and psychology); and how-to and self-help (on all topics, from diet and exercise to sex and personal finance).
Will Handle: Nonfiction books and textbooks. Currently handles 80% nonfiction books; 10% novels; and 10% textbooks. Will read—at no charge—unsolicited queries and outlines. Reports in 3 weeks on queries. "If our agency does not respond within 1 month to your request to become a client, you may submit requests elsewhere: Will not return rejected material unless accompanied by SASE."
Terms: Agent receives 15% commission on domestic sales; 15% on dramatic sales; and 15% on foreign sales. "When a project interests us, we provide a two to three page critique and sample editing, a brochure on *How to Write a Book Proposal*, and a model book proposal at no charge." Charges collaboration, ghostwriting and developmental editing fee "as an increased percentage of manuscript sale—no cash fee." Charges $100/hour. 100% of income derived from commission on sales.
Recent Sales: *Creating Excellence* (New American Library); *Playing Hardball with Soft Skills* (Bantam); and *Hidden Ladders* (Doubleday).

ELYSE SOMMER, INC., 962 Allen Ln., Box E, Woodmere Long Island NY 11598. Also offers book packaging services. Member of ILAA. Represents 20 clients. 20% of clients are new/unpublished writers. Prefers to work with published/established authors; works with a small number of new/unpublished authors.
Will Handle: Nonfiction books. Currently handles 99% nonfiction books. Will read—at no charge—unsolicited queries and outlines. Reports in 2 weeks on queries. "Please include SASE in all correspondence."
Terms: Agent receives 15% commission on domestic sales; 20% on dramatic sales; and 20% on foreign sales.
Recent Sales: *The Crocheter's Quilt Book* (Better Homes and Gardens/Sedgwood Press); and *The Simile Finder*, (Gale Research).

PHILIP G. SPITZER LITERARY AGENCY, 788 9th Ave., New York NY 10019. (212)628-0352. Member of SAR. Represents 50 clients. 10% of clients are new/unpublished writers. Prefers to work with published/established authors; works with a small number of new/unpublished authors. Specializes in general nonfiction (politics, current events, sports, biography) and fiction, including mystery/suspense.
Will Handle: Nonfiction books, novels and movie scripts. Currently handles 45% nonfiction books; 45% novels; and 10% movie scripts. Will read—at no charge—unsolicited queries and outlines. Reports in 2 weeks on queries; 5 weeks on mss. "If our agency does not respond within 1 month to your request to become a client, you may submit requests elsewhere."
Terms: Agent receives 10% commission on domestic sales; 10% on dramatic sales; and 20% on foreign sales. Charges for photocopying expenses. 100% of income derived from commission on ms sales.
Recent Sales: *The Dreams of Ada*, by Robert Mayer (Viking/Penguin); *Neon Rain*, by James Lee Burke (Henry Holt & Co.); and *The Walker Double-Cross*, by Thomas Allen and Norman Polmar (Delacorte).

‡ELLEN LIVELY STEELE AND ASSOCIATES, Drawer 447, Organ NM 88052. (505)382-5449. Contact: Ellen Lively Steele. Estab. 1981. Represents 12 clients. 75% of clients are new/unpublished writers. Accepts writers on referral only. Prefers to work with published/established writers; works with small number of new/unpublished writers. Specializes in occult, science fiction, women's fiction, metaphysical and adventure.
Will Handle: Novels, movie scripts, TV scripts and syndicated material. Currently handles 65% novels; 20% movie scripts; 10% TV scripts; 4% syndicated material; and 1% miscellaneous. Does not read unsolicited material. Reports in 3 weeks on queries. "If our agency does not respond within 2 months to your request to become a client, you may submit requests elsewhere."
Terms: Agent receives 10% commission on domestic sales; 10% on dramatic sales; and 5% on foreign sales. Charges a marketing fee. 10% of income comes from fees charged to writers; 10% of income derived from commission on mss sales.

‡MICHAEL STEINBERG, (formerly Brisk, Rubin and Steinberg Literary Agency), Box 274, Glencoe IL 60022. (312)835-8881. Literary Agent/Attorney: Michael Steinberg. Estab. 1980. Represents 15 clients. 40% of clients are new/unpublished writers. "Not currently accepting new writers except by referral from editors or current authors." Specializes in business and general nonfiction, science fiction and mystery.
Will Handle: Nonfiction books and novels. Currently handles 70% nonfiction books and 30% novels. Does not read unsolicited mss.
Terms: Agent receives 15% commission on domestic sales and 20% on foreign sales. Charges a reading fee when accepting new material; 4% of income derived from reading fees. Charges writers for postage and phone expenses. Offers a consultation service through which writers not represented can get advice on a contract; charges $75/hour, with a minimum of $125. 5% of income derived from fees; 95% of income derived from commission on ms sales.
Recent Sales: *Facts on Futures*, by Jacob Bernstein (Probus Publishing); *Business Without Economists*, by William Hudson (Amacom); and a 3 book mystery series by Dale Gilbert (St. Martin's Press).

‡STEPPING STONE LITERARY AGENCY, 59 West 71st St., New York NY 10023. (212)362-9277. President: Sarah Jane Freymann. Estab. 1974. Member of ILAA. 10% of clients are new/unpublished writers. "The writer has to be good and serious about his/her work. Writers should only send work they are really pleased with. Of course, I prefer published authors—but I am willing to look at unpublished authors' work." Works with a small number of new/unpublished authors. "I do not specialize. But I stress professionalism—I do not want amateurs who write like amateurs."
Will Handle: Nonfiction books and novels. Currently handles 50% nonfiction books and 50% novels. Will read submissions at no charge, but may charge a criticism fee or service charge for work performed after the initial reading. Reports in 2 weeks on queries; 6 weeks on mss. "If our agency does not respond within 6 months to your request to become a client, you may submit requests elsewhere."
Terms: Agent receives 15% commission on domestic sales; 10% on dramatic sales; and 10% on foreign sales. Charges a criticism fee "only if we are asked to critique a work we won't represent." Fee for a 300-page ms $200. Charges for phone, overseas postge and photocopy expenses. Sometimes offers a consultation service through which writers not represented can get advice on contract; less than 10% of income derived from fees. 90-100% of income derived from commission on ms sales.
Recent Sales: No information given.

‡CHARLES M. STERN ASSOCIATES, 319 Coronet, Box 790742, San Antonio TX 78879-0742. (512)349-6141. Owners: Charles M. Stern and Mildred R. Stern. Estab. 1978. 90% of clients are new/unpublished writers. Prefers to work with pubished/established authors; eager to work with new/unpublished writers. Specializes in historical romances, category romances, how-to, mystery and adventure.
Will Handle: Nonfiction books and novels. Currently handles 25% nonfiction books and 75% novels. Does not read unsolicited mss; will handle only a completed mss. Reports in 2 weeks on queries. "If our agency does not respond within 1 month to your request to become a client, you may submit requests elsewhere."
Terms: Agent receives 15% commission on domestic sales; and 20% on foreign sales. Does not charge for photocopy expenses but writer must supply all copies of ms.
Recent Sales: No information given.

GLORIA STERN, Suite 3, 12535 Chandler Blvd., North Hollywood CA 91607. (818)508-6296. Contact: Gloria Stern. Estab. 1984. Represents 18 clients. 65% of clients are new/unpublished writers. Writer must query with project description or be recommended by qualified reader. Prefers to work with published/established authors; works with a number of new/unpublished authors. Specializes in novels and scripts, some theatrical material, dramas or comedy.
Will Handle: Novels, movie scripts and TV scripts (movie of the week). Currently handles 13% novels; 79% movie scripts; and 8% TV scripts. Will read submissions at charge and may charge a criticism fee or service charge for on-going consultation and editing. Reports in 3 weeks on queries; 6 weeks on mss. "If our agency does not respond within 6 weeks to your request to become a client, you may submit requests elsewhere."
Terms: Agent receives 10-15% commission on domestic sales; 10-15% on dramatic sales; and 18% on foreign sales. Occasionally waives fee if representing the writer. Charges criticism fee; $35/hour (may vary). "Initial report averages four or five pages with point by point recommendation. I will work with the writers I represent to point of acceptance." Charges for postage, photocopy, and long distance phone expenses. Percentage of income derived from commission on ms sales varies with sales. Payment of criticism fee usually ensures that agency will represent writer.

GLORIA STERN AGENCY, 1230 Park Ave., New York NY 10128. (212)289-7698. Agent: Gloria Stern. Estab. 1976. Member of ILAA. Represents 30 clients. 2% of our clients are new/unpublished writers. Prefers to work with published/established authors; works with a small number on new/unpublished authors.
Will Handle: Nonfiction books (no how-to; must have expertise on subject); and novels ("serious mainstream", mysteries, accepts very little fiction). Currently handles 90% nonfiction books and 10% novels. Will read—at no charge—unsolicited queries and outlines. Reports in 1 week on queries; 2 months on manuscripts. "If our agency does not respond within 10 weeks to your request to become a client, you may submit request elsewhere."
Terms: Agent receives 15% commission on domestic sales; and 20% on foreign sales. Charges for photocopy exenses. Charges a criticism fee "if the writer makes a request and I think that it could be publishable with help. Criticism include appraisal of style, development of characters and action. Sometimes suggest cutting or building scene. No guarantee that I can represent finished work." Offers a consultation service ("as a courtesy to some authors") through which writers not represented can get advice on a contract; charges $125. .5% of income derived from fee charged to writers; 99.5% of income derived from commission of manuscript sales.
Recent Sales: *How to Learn Math*, by Sheila Tobias (The College Board); *A Taste of Astrology*, by Lucy Ash (Knopf); and *Power Struggle*, by Rudolph and Ridley (Harper & Row).

‡GUNTHER STUHLMANN, AUTHOR'S REPRESENTATIVE, Box 276, Becket MA 01223. (413)623-5170. Associate: Barbara Ward. Estab. 1954. Prefers to work with published/established authors. Specializes in high quality literary material, fiction and nonfiction.

Will Handle: Nonfiction books, novels, young adult, movie and TV rights on established properties (no original screenplays). Will read—at no charge—unsolicited queries and outlines. Reports in 2 weeks on queries. "Include SASE for reply."

Terms: Receives 10% commission on domestic sales; 15% on British sales; 20% on translation.

Recent Sales: *Prisoner's Dilemma*, by Richard Powers (Beech Tree/Morrow); *Henry & June*, by Anais Nin (Harcourt Brace Jovanovich); and *A Literate Passion*, by Henry Miller and Anais Nin (Harcourt Brace Jovanovich).

‡**H.N. SWANSON, INC.**, 8523 Sunset Blvd., Los Angeles CA 90069. (213)652-5385. Contact: Ben Kamsler. Estab. 1934. Represents 125 clients. "We require the writer to be published—such as articles if extensive, novels and/or screenplays." Prefers to work with published/established authors. Specializes in contemporary adventure-thriller fiction.

Will Handle: Novels, movie scripts, stage plays and TV scripts. Currently handles 55% novels; 25% movie scripts; 5% stage plays; and 10% TV scripts. Does not read unsolicited mss. Reports in 6 weeks. "If our agency does not respond within 6 weeks to your request to become a client, you may submit requests elsewhere."

Terms: Agent receives 10% commission on domestic sales; 10% on dramatic sales; and 20% on foreign sales. 75% of income derived from commission on ms sales.

Recent Sales: *Bandits*, by Elmore Leonard (Arbor House); *Fox on the Run*, by Charles Bennett (Warner Books); and *Desperate Justice*, by Richard Speight (Warner Books).

TEAL & WATT, 2036 Vista del Rosa, Fullerton CA 92631. (714)738-8333. Owner: Patricia Teal. Estab. 1978. Member of ILAA and RWA. Represents 40 clients. 20% of clients are new/unpublished writers. "Writer must have honed his skills by virtue of educational background, writing classes, previous publications. Any of these *may* qualify him to submit." Works with a small number of new/unpublished authors. Specializes in category fiction such as mysteries, romances (contemporary and historical), westerns, men's adventure, horror, etc. Also handles nonfiction in all areas, especially self-help and how-to.

Will Handle: Nonfiction books (self-help and how-to) and novels (category only). Currently handles 30% nonfiction books and 70% category novels. Will read—at no charge—unsolicited queries and outlines. No response if not accompanied by SASE. Reports in 3 weeks on queries.

Terms: 15% commission for new, unpublished writers, and 10% for published. Agent receives 10-15% commission on domestic sales; 20% on dramatic sales; and 20% on foreign sales. Charges for phone, postage and photocopy expenses. 5% of total income derived from fees charged to writers; 95% of income derived from commission of mss sales.

Recent Sales: *Murder by Impulse*, by D.R. Meredith (Ballantine); *Sunflower*, by Jill Marie Landis (Berkley); and *Polo, Solo*, by Jerry Kennealy (St. Martin's).

THOMPSON AND CHRIS LITERARY AGENCY, 3926 Sacramento St., San Francisco CA 94118. (415)386-2443. Partner: Teresa Chris. Estab. 1980. Represents 45 clients. 50% of clients are new/unpublished writers. Eager to work with new/unpublished writers. Specializes in "virtually all nonfiction, fiction (mainstream, literary, science fiction, contemporary and historical romance, murder mysteries, etc.), juveniles, picture books, and young adults."

Will Handle: Nonfiction books, novels and juvenile books. Currently handles 60% nonfiction books; 30% novels; 9% juvenile books; and 1% movie scripts. Will read—at no charge—unsolicited queries, outlines and mss. Reports in 1 week on queries; 3 weeks on mss. "If our agency does not respond within 1 month to your request to become a client, you may submit requests elsewhere."

Terms: Agent receives 15% commission on domestic sales; 15-20% on dramatic sales; and 15-20% on foreign sales. Charges writers for phone expenses. 100% of income derived from commission on ms sales.

Recent Sales: *Unquiet Grave*, by Janet Lapierre (St. Martin's); *Collector of Photographs*, by Deborah Valentine (Bantam); and *A Christmas Card for Mr. McFizz*, by Obren Bokich and Dan Lane (Green Tiger).

A TOTAL ACTING EXPERIENCE, Suite 300-C, 6736 Laurel Canyon, North Hollywood CA 91606. (818)765-7244. Agent: Dan A. Bellacicco. Estab. 1984. Member of WGA. Represents 24 clients. 70% of clients are new/unpublished writers. Will accept new and established writers. Specializes in romance, science fiction, mysteries, humor, how-to and self-help books, and audio/visual tapes on all topics.

Will Handle: Nonfiction books, novels, juvenile books, movie scripts, radio scripts, stage plays, TV scripts, syndicated material, lyricists and composers. (No heavy violence, drugs or sex.) Currently handles 2% magazine articles; 2% magazine fiction; 5% nonfiction books; 5% novels; 2% juvenile books; 50% movie scripts; 2% radio scripts; 5% stage plays; 19% TV scripts; and 8% from lyricists/composers. Will read—at no charge— unsolicited queries, outlines and mss. Reports in 2-6 weeks on queries; 3 months on mss. "If our agency does not respond within 3 months to your request to become a client, you may submit requests elsewhere. Your business skills must be sharp: initially do not submit entire work; submit only first 10 pages of your mss; include a one page synopsis of story, resume and letter of introduction with SASE. No exceptions please. No heavy violence, sex or drugs. We seek good people with old fashioned virtues of honesty, sincerity and most of all loyalty—for a long term relationship. We admire strong character development, well written, well motivated, well delineated characters with substance and intelligence. Quality, not quantity. In return you will receive lots of tender loving care. "

Terms: Agent receives 10% commission on domestic sales; 10% on dramatic sales; and 10% on foreign sales. 100% of income derived from commission on ms sales.

Recent Sales: "Confidential."

SUSAN P. URSTADT, INC., Suite 2A, 125 E. 84 St., New York NY 10028. (212)744-6605. President: Susan P. Urstadt. Estab. 1975. Member of ILAA. Represents 35-40 clients. 5% of clients are new/unpublished writers. "Writer must demonstrate writing ability through sample, qualifications through curriculum vitae and reliability through resume or biography." Works with a small number of new/unpublished authors. Looking for writers with a serious long-term commitment to writing. Specializes in literary and commercial fiction, decorative arts and antiques, architecture, sailing, tennis, gardening, cookbooks, biography, performing arts, sports (especially horses), current affairs, lifestyle and current living trends.

Will Handle: Nonfiction books and novels. "We look for serious books of quality with fresh ideas and approaches to current situations and trends." Currently handles 65% nonfiction books; 25% novels; and 10% juvenile books. Will read—at no charge—unsolicited queries, outlines and mss. SASE required. Reports in 1 month on queries; 6 weeks on mss.

Terms: Agent receives 10% commission on domestic sales; 15% on dramatic sales; and 20% on foreign sales. Charges for phone, photocopying, foreign postage and express mail expenses. 100% of income derived from commission on ms sales.

Recent Sales: *Artificial Wilderness*, by Sven Birkerts (Morrow); *The Weekend Refinisher*, by Bruce Johnson (Ballantine); and *Lt. Boruvka Mystery Series*, by Josef Skvorecky (Norton).

‡VICTORIA MANAGEMENT CO., 5C, 222 First Ave., New York NY 10009. (212)529-4750. President: Frank Weimann. Estab. 1985. Represents 2 clients. 100% of clients are new/unpublished writers. "Being a new agency ourselves we will handle unpublished writers. Therefore, we have not set a minimum amount of sales" to be made before we represent a writer. Eager to work with new/unpublished writers. Specializes in films, TV scripts, nonfiction, romance and biography.

Will Handle: Nonfiction books, novels, movie scripts, TV scripts and syndicated material. Currently handles 40% nonfiction books; 10% novels; and 50% movie scripts. Will read—at no charge—unsolicited queries, outlines and mss. Reports in 2 weeks on queries; 1 month on mss. "If our agency does not respond within 6 months to your request to become a client, you may submit requests elsewhere."

Terms: Agent receives 10% commission on domestic sales; 10% on dramatic sales; and 20% on foreign sales. 100% of income derived from commission on ms sales.

CARLSON WADE, Room K-4, 49 Bokee Ct., Brooklyn NY 11223. (718)743-6983. President: Carlson Wade. Estab. 1949. Represents 40 clients. 50% of clients are new/unpublished writers. Eager to work with new/unpublished writers. Will consider all types of fiction and nonfiction.

Will Handle: Magazine articles, magazine fiction, nonfiction books, and novels. Currently handles 10% magazine articles; 10% magazine fiction; 40% nonfiction books; and 40% novels. Will read submissions at no charge, but may charge a criticism fee or service charge for work performed after the initial reading. Reports in 2 weeks. "If our agency does not respond within 1 month to your request to become a client, you may submit requests elsewhere."

Terms: Agent receives 10% commission on domestic sales; 10% on dramatic sales; and 10% on foreign sales. Charges reading fee: $1/1,000 words on short ms; $50/book. 20% of income derived from reading fees. Charges a criticism fee if ms requires extensive work. 10% of income derived from criticism fees. "Short manuscript receives 5 pages of critique, book receives 15 (single space, page by page critique)." 20% of income derived from fees; 80% of income derived from commission on ms sales. Payment of a criticism fee does not ensure that agency will represent a writer. "If a writer revises properly then we take it on. Futher help is available at no cost."

Recent Sales: *Eat Away Illness* (Prentice Hall) and *Nutritional Therapy* (Prentice Hall).

MARY JACK WALD ASSOCIATES, INC., Suite 325, 799 Broadway, New York NY 10003. (212)254-7842. President: Mary Jack Wald. Estab. 1985. Represents 35 authors plus subsidiary rights for publishers. Works with a small number of new/unpublished authors.

Will Handle: Full-length fiction and nonfiction (no computer books); juvenile (authors that are illustrators); movie scripts and TV scripts; magazine articles and short fiction "for authors we represent that have book length mss." Will not read unsolicited mss. Query; submit outline and sample chapters upon request only. Reports in 6 weeks on queries; 10 weeks on mss.

Terms: Agent receives 15% commission on domestic sales; 15% on dramatic sales; and 15% on foreign sales (25-30% if represented by our foreign representative as sub-agent). "If extraordinary expenses are requested (large photocopying expenses, foreign phone calls, long distance trips, etc.) by the author in writing, then bill for same is forwarded to the author. Author must request and agree to these in writing before expenses are incurred." 100% of income derived from commission on ms sales.

Recent Sales: *The Roving Mind*, by Isaac Asimov (The Reader's Digest-excerpt rights); *Pleasant Fieldmouse's Go-To-Bed Tales*, by Jan Wahl (Western Publishing Co., Golden Books); *The Honorable Prison*, by Lyll Becerra de Jenkins (Lodestar Books/E.P. Dutton).

JOHN A. WARE LITERARY AGENCY, 392 Central Park West, New York NY 10025. (212)866-4733. Contact: John Ware. Estab. 1978. Represents 60 clients. 50% of clients are new/unpublished writers. Writers must have appropriate credentials for authorship of proposal (nonfiction) or manuscript (fiction); no publishing track record required. "Open to good writing and interesting ideas, by 'new' or 'old' writers." Specializes in biography; investigative journalism; history; health and psychology (academic credentials required); serious and accessible non-category fiction and mysteries; current issues and affairs; sports; oral history; Americana and folklore.

Will Handle: Nonfiction books and novels. Currently handles 75% nonfiction books; and 25% novels. Will read—at no charge—unsolicited queries and outlines; does not read unsolicited mss. Reports in 2 weeks on queries.

Terms: Agent receives 10% commission on domestic sales; 10% on dramatic sales; and 20% on foreign sales. Charges for messengering, photocopying and extraordinary expenses. 100% of income derived from commission on ms sales.

Recent Sales: *The Doctor's Guide to Instant Stress Relief*, by Drs. Nathan, Staats and Rosch (Putnam); *Fool's Sanctuary*, by Jennifer Johnston (Viking); and *In Concert: Inside the Boston Symphony*, by Carl A. Vigeland (Beech Tree/William Morrow).

‡JAMES WARREN LITERARY AGENCY,13131 Welby Way, North Hollywood CA 91606. (818)982-5423. Agent: James Warren. Editors: James Boston, Audrey Langer, and Bob Carlson. Estab. 1969. Represents 45 clients. 85% of clients are new/unpublished writers. "We are eager to work with select unpublished writers." Specializes in fiction, history, textbooks, professional books, craft books, how-to books, self-improvement books, health books and diet books.

Will Handle: Juvenile books, historical romance novels, movie scripts (especially drama and humor), and TV scripts (drama, humor, documentary). Currently handles 30% nonfiction books; 40% novels; 5% textbooks; 5% juvenile books; 10% movie scripts; and 10% TV scripts. Will read—at no charge—unsolicited queries and outlines. Does not read unsolicited mss. Reports in 1 week on query; 1 month on mss. "If our agency does not respond within 2 month to your request to become a client, you may submit requests elsewhere."

Terms: Receives 15% commission on first domestic sales and 10% on subsequent sales; 20% on foreign sales. Charges reading fee of approximately $2 per thousand words—negotiable according to length of ms; 20% of income derived from reading fees; refunds reading fee if decides to represent writer. "We occasionally encounter a ms that has literary quality but which, in our opinion, does not have commercial punch. In such cases we may decide to submit at the author's expense. Our charge is $15 for an average-sized ms." 20% of total income derived from fees charged to writers; 80% of income derived from commission of ms sales. Payment of fees does not ensure that agency will represent writer.

Recent Sales: *Good Health and Common Sense*, by Dale Alexander (Witkower Press); *Healthy Hair and Common Sense*, by Dale Alexander (Witkower Press); and *A Tax Free America*, by Boris Isaacson (Tomorrow Now Press).

‡RHODA WEYR AGENCY, 216 Vance St., Chapel Hill NC 27514. (919)942-0770. President: Rhoda A. Weyr. Estab. 1983. Member of SAR and ILAA. Prefers to work with published/established authors; works with a small number of new/unpublished authors. Specializes in general nonfiction and fiction of high quality.

Will Handle: Nonfiction books and novels. Will read—at no charge—unsolicited queries, outlines and sample chapters sent with SASE.

Terms: Agent receives 10% commission on domestic sales; 10-15% on dramatic sales; and 20% on foreign sales. 100% of income derived from commission on ms sales.

Recent Sales: Confidential.

WIESER & WIESER, INC., 118 E. 25th St., New York NY 10010. (212)260-0860. President: Olga B. Wieser. Estab. 1976. Represents 60 clients. 10% of clients are new/unpublished writers. Prefers to work with published/established authors; works with a small number of new/unpublished authors. Specializes in literary and mainstream fiction, serious and popular historical fiction, mass market regencies, general nonfiction, business, finance, aviation, sports, photography, Americana, cookbooks, travel books and popular medicine.

Will Handle: Nonfiction books and novels. Currently handles 70% nonfiction books and 30% novels. Will read—at no charge—unsolicited queries and outlines. Reports in 1 week on queries accompanied by SASE.

Terms: Agent receives 15% commission on domestic sales; 15% on dramatic sales; and 20% on foreign sales. Charges for photocopy, cable and overnight postage expenses. Sometimes offers a consultation service

through which writers not represented can get advice on a contract; charges $75/hour. 100% of income derived from commission on ms sales.
Recent Sales: *Hichory Cured*, by Douglas C. Jones (Henry Holt and Co.); *Island of Hope, Island of Tears*, by David M. Brownstone and Irene Frank (Viking/Penguin); and *The Investor's Encyclopedia Tax Reform Edition*, by Chet Currier and The Associated Press (Franklin Watts, Inc.).

‡WINGRA WOODS PRESS/Agenting Division, Suite 3, 33 Witherspoon St., Princeton NJ 08542. (609)683-1218. Agent: Anne Matthews. Estab. 1985. Member of American Booksellers Association and American Book Producers Association. Represents 8 clients. 70% of clients are new/unpublished writers. "Books must be completed, and designed for a distinct market niche." Works with small number of new/unpublished authors. Specializes in cookbooks, travel, children's and how-to books.
Will Handle: Nonfiction books and juvenile books. Currently handles 60% nonfiction books and 40% juvenile books. Will read—at no charge—unsolicited queries, outline and mss. Reports in 3 weeks. "If our agency does not respond within 2 months to your request to become a client, you may submit requests elsewhere."
Terms: Receives 15% commission on domestic sales; 15% on dramatic sales and 15% on foreign sales. Sometimes offers a consultation service through which writers not represented can get advice on a contract; charges $25/hour. 100% of income derived from commission on ms sales.
Recent Sales: *Tapas, Wines and Good Times*, by Don and Marge Foster (Contemporary); and *While I'm Waiting*, by Donna Guthrie (Price-Stern-Sloan).

RUTH WRESCHNER, AUTHOR'S REPRESENTATIVE, 10 W. 74th St., New York NY 10023. (212)877-2605. Agent: Ruth Wreschner. Estab. 1981. Represents 30 clients. 70% of clients are new/unpublished writers. "In fiction, if a client is not published yet, I prefer writers who have written for magazines; in nonfiction, a person well-qualified in his field is acceptable." Prefers to work with published/established authors; works with new/unpublished authors. "I will always pay attention to a writer referred by another client." Specializes in popular medicine, health, how-to books and fiction (no pornography, screenplays or dramatic plays).
Will Handle: Magazine articles (only for commercial magazines); nonfiction books; novels; textbooks; and young adult. Currently handles 5% magazine articles; 80% nonfiction books; 10% novels; 5% textbooks; and 5% juvenile books. Will read—at no charge—unsolicited queries and outlines. Reports in 2 weeks on queries. "Until I am willing to represent a client and he/she has decided to work with me, clients are free to contact other agents; some writers do multiple agent submissions, but they usually state so in their query. Queries must include SASE."
Terms: Agent receives 15% commission on domestic sales; and 20% on foreign sales. Charges for photocopying expenses. "Once a book is placed, I will retain some money from the second advance to cover airmail postage of books, long distance calls, etc. on foreign sales." 100% of income derived from commission on ms sales. "I may consider charging for reviewing contracts in future. In that case I will charge $50/hour plus long distance calls, if any."
Recent Sales: *Life Without Pain* (Addison-Wesley); *The Amino Acid Super Diet* (Putnam's); and *Getting Away With Murder* (New Horizon Press).

ANN WRIGHT REPRESENTATIVES, INC., 136 East 57th St., New York NY 10022. (212)832-0110. Head of Literary Department: Dan Wright. Estab. 1963. Member of WGA. Represents 41 clients. 25% of clients are new/unpublished writers. "Writers must be skilled or have superior material for screenplays, stories or novels that can eventually become motion pictures or television properties." Prefers to work with published/established authors; works with a small number of new/unpublished authors. "Eager to work with any author with material that we can effectively market in the motion picture business worldwide." Specializes in themes that make good motion picture projects.
Will Handle: Novels, movie scripts, stage plays and TV scripts. Currently handles 10% novels; 75% movie scripts; and 15% TV scripts. Will read—at no charge—unsolicited queries and outlines; does not read unsolicited mss. Reports in 2 weeks on queries; 6 weeks on mss. "If our agency does not respond within 2 months to your request to become a client, you may submit requests elsewhere."
Terms: Agent receives 10% commission on domestic sales; 10% on dramatic sales; and 10% on foreign sales. Will critique only works of signed clients. Charges for photocopying expenses. 100% of income derived from commission on ms sales.
Recent Sales: No information given.

WRITERS HOUSE, INC., 21 W. 26 St., New York NY 10010. (212)685-2400. Director of New Clients: Susan Marks. Estab. 1974. Member of ILAA. Represents 140 clients. 5% of clients are new/unpublished writers. Specializes in fiction of all types, adult fiction, juvenile novels, and nonfiction books on business, parenting and popular lifestyles.
Will Handle: Nonfiction books, novels and juvenile books. Currently handles 40% nonfiction books; 30% novels; and 30% juvenile books. Will read—at no charge—unsolicited queries and outlines. Reports in 2 weeks on queries.

Terms: Agent receives 15% commission on sale of adult books, 10% on juvenile and young adult domestic sales; 15% on dramatic sales; and 20% on foreign sales. Charges for overseas postage, Telex, messenger, phone and photocopy expenses. 95% of income derived from commission on ms sales; 5% from scouting for foreign publishers.

Recent Sales: *Lie Down with Lions*, by Ken Follett; *Sweet Valley Summer*, by Francine Pascal; and *The IBM Way*, by F. Buck Rodgers.

‡**WRITER'S CONSULTING GROUP**, Box 492, Burbank CA 91503. (818)841-9294. Director: Robert Barmeier. Estab. 1983. Represents 10 clients. 50% of clients new/unpublished writers. "We prefer to work with established writers unless the author has an unusual true story."

Will Handle: Magazine articles (if written about a true story for which the author has the rights); nonfiction books (celebrity books, true stories, true crime accounts); novels (comedies, sagas, action-adventure only); movie scripts (true stories, comedies, action adventure only. No horror or slasher pictures); and TV scripts (true stories only for movies of the week; no episodic TV). Currently handles 40% nonfiction books; 20% novels; and 40% movie scripts. Will read—at no charge—unsolicited queries, outlines and manuscripts. "They must be accompanied by an SASE or they will be discarded." Reports in 1 month on queries; 3 months on mss. "If our agency does not respond within 1 month to your request to become a client, you may submit requests elsewhere."

Terms: "We will explain our terms to clients when they wish to sign. We receive a 10% commission on domestic sales. We offer ghost writing and other editorial services."

Recent Sales: "We have helped writers sell everything from episodes for children's TV shows (Smurfs) to move-of-the-week options (including the Craig Smith espionage story)."

WRITER'S PRODUCTIONS, Box 630, Westport CT 06881. (203)227-8199. Agent: David L. Meth. Estab. 1981. Eager to work with new/unpublished writers. Specializes in "fiction of literary quality, unique, intriguing nonfiction and photo-essay books. We are especially interested in works of Asian American writers about the Asian American experience, and are specializing in works about the Orient. No historical romances, science fiction, mysteries, westerns, how-to, health works, etc."

Will Handle: Nonfiction books, novels. Currently handles 15% nonfiction books; 85% novels. Will read—at no charge—unsolicited queries, outlines and mss. Reports in 2 weeks on queries; 1 month on mss. "All correspondence must have a SASE for any response, due to the large volume of submissions we receive. No phone calls please."

Terms: Agent receives 15% commission on domestic sales; 20% on dramatic sales; and 20% on foreign sales. 100% of income derived from commission on ms sales.

Recent Sales: No information given.

‡**WRITERS' WORLD FORUM**, Box 20383, Midtown Station, New York NY 10129. (201)664-0263. President: William Parker. Estab. 1985. We represent 8 clients. 75% of clients are new/unpublished writers. "The only qualifications needed for representation are good writing and a well-prepared manuscript. Our advice to writers: Be original. Don't do what everyone else is doing." Eager to work with new/unpublished writers. Specializes in general nonfiction and fiction, "especially literary, ethnic, Third World, women's, etc. We are looking for quality manuscripts on important topics. Always anxious to find new and/or unique voices."

Will Handle: Nonfiction books, novels (no romances) and juvenile books. Currently handles 20% nonfiction books; 70% novels and 10% juvenile books. Will read—at no charge—unsolicited queries and outlines. "Please include SASE." Reports in 2 weeks on queries; 1 month on mss.

Terms: Agent receives 10% commission on domestic sales; 10% on foreign sales.

Recent Sales: No information given.

BARBARA W. YEDLIN, LITERARY AGENT, Pump St., Newcastle ME 04553. (207)563-8335. Agent: Barbara W. Yedlin. Estab. 1981. Represents 8 clients. 100% of clients are new/unpublished writers. "I would like to represent writers with sustained literary talent; they must also display a professional attitude in their dealings with agents and publishers." Works with a small number of new/unpublished authors. Specializes in literary novels and short stories "of high calibre"; juvenile novels (for ages 8-12); mysteries (but no other genre writing); travel; biography and autobiography. No teenage novels or picture books.

Will Handle: Magazine fiction, nonfiction books, novels and juvenile books. No pornography. Currently handles 20% magazine fiction; 10% nonfiction books; 60% novels; and 10% juvenile books. Will read—at no charge—unsolicited queries, outlines and mss. Reports in 2 week on queries; 3 weeks on mss. "If our agency does not respond within 1 month to your request to become a client, you may submit requests elsewhere."

Terms: Agent receives 10% commission on domestic sales. Charges for postal and telephone expenses. 100% of income is derived from commission on ms sales.

Recent Sales: No information given.

SUSAN ZECKENDORF ASSOCIATES, Suite 11B, 171 W. 57th St., New York NY 10019. (212)245-2928. President: Susan Zeckendorf. Estab. 1979. Member of ILAA. Represents 45 clients. 60% of clients are new writers. Specializes in fiction of all kinds—literary, historical, and commercial women's, mainstream thrillers and mysteries, science, music, self-help, and parenting books.
Will Handle: Nonfiction books (by a qualified expert) and novels. Currently handles 40% nonfiction books and 60% novels. Will read—at no charge—unsolicited queries. Reports in 2 weeks on queries; 1 month on mss. "If our agency does not respond within 1 month to your request to become a client, you may submit requests elsewhere."
Terms: Agent receives 15% commission on domestic sales; 15% on dramatic (movie or TV) sales; and 20% on foreign sales. Charges for phone, photocopy and foreign postage expenses. 100% of income derived from commission on ms sales.
Recent Sales: *Scandals*, by Una-Mary Parker (New American Library); *A Long Way to Die*, by James Frey (Bantam); and *Baby Signals*, by Dian Lynch Fraser and Ellen Morris Tiegerman Ph.D. (Walker and Co.).

TOM ZELASKY LITERARY AGENCY, 3138 Parkridge Crescent, Chamblee GA 30341. (404)458-0391. Agent: Tom Zelasky. Estab. 1984. Represents 5 clients. 90% of clients are new/unpublished writers. Prefers to work with published/established authors; works with a small number of new/unpublished authors. Specializes in mainstream fiction or nonfiction, categorical romance, historical romance, historical fiction, westerns, action/detective mysteries, suspense, science fiction.
Will Handle: Nonfiction books, novels, juvenile books, movie scripts, stage plays and TV scripts. Currently handles 20% nonfiction books; 60% novels; and 20% juvenile books. Will read—at no charge—unsolicited queries and outlines. "SASE is compulsory, otherwise, manuscript will be in storage and destroyed after 2 years." Reports in 3 weeks on queries; 3 months on mss. "If our agency does not respond within 3 months to your request to become a client, you should contact me immediately."
Terms: Agent receives 10-15% commission on domestic sales; 10-15% on dramatic sales; and 15-25% on foreign sales. Charges a reading fee; will waive fee if representing the writer. "A critique of one to three pages is mailed to writer when manuscript is rejected. I do my own reading and critique. It is usually a one to three page item, single space, citing craft skills, marketability and overall evaluation." Charges writers for phone calls to writers and publishers and postage. Considering a consultation service to individual writers.
Recent Sales: No information given.

‡**GEORGE ZIEGLER LITERARY AGENCY**, 160 East 97th St., New York NY 10029. (212)348-3637. Proprietor: George Ziegler. Estab. 1977. Represents 20 clients. 50% of clients are new/unpublished writers. Works with small number of new/unpublished writers. Specializes in "nonfiction of strong human interest, or unique consumer books. Genre fiction if it is fresh and original; and mainstream fiction if it is both well written and commercial."
Will Handle: Nonfiction books, novels and stage plays. Currently handles 75% nonfiction books; 24% novels; and 1% stage plays. Will read—at no charge—unsolicited queries and outlines. Reports in 1 week on queries. "If our agency does not respond within 1 month to your request to become a client, you may submit requests elsewhere."
Terms: Receives 15% of commission on domestic sales; and 20% on foreign sales or dramatic sales if a subagent is used.
Recent Sales: *The Dental Consumer*, by Jerry F. Traintor, D.D.S. (Facts on File); *Greifelt Investigation*, by Ken Lawrence (Paperjacks); *Fighting for Tony*, by Mary Callahan, R.N. (Fireside Books).

ALWAYS submit manuscripts or queries with a self-addressed, stamped envelope (SASE) within your country or International Reply Coupons purchased from the post office for other countries.

Contests and Awards

If entering your work in competition sounds appealing, you'll want to explore these listings for contests, grants, fellowships and awards.

Contests enable writers to have their work judged against other writers' work where the same rules apply to everyone. Some competitions focus on a form, like the short story, or a subject, like literacy. In other awards, the theme or approach doesn't matter; the judge's objective is to find the best writing, whether it's an article, play or first-time novel. While editors sometimes judge entries in magazine contests, many contest sponsors hire a panel of professional writers to select winning entries.

Contests offer writers a variety of benefits. Aside from the monetary reward of many writing prizes, there is satisfaction and recognition. Distinction in a playwriting contest may lead to staged readings of a script; a major book award may increase sales of a current novel and interest others in your next book.

Most of the contests listed here are annual competitions. Contests for both published and unpublished work are listed. Some competitions are closed to entries from writers and open only to nominations from the publishing industry. We've included them for their national or literary importance. If you feel your writing meets the requirements of one of these competitions, tell your publisher or editor about the contest.

It's important to follow contest guidelines carefully. Some contests have very detailed instructions and requirements. In contests where writers' names must be concealed in a titled envelope, putting your name on the manuscript will disqualify it from consideration. Another reason for studying contest rules is to find out if you are eligible. Not all contests are for everyone. There are contests specifically for beginning writers and others for professionals, and some contests that allow only students or an organization's members to enter.

Contest rules usually state what is meant by professional or amateur in a particular contest, since there are numerous connotations for these terms. If the rules are not clear, however, send a self-addressed, stamped envelope and a letter asking for clarification. Pose a simple question in the note concerning your eligibility. Don't write or expect to receive a lengthy letter.

Funds for writers are available—the key is knowing where to look. Become familiar with two resources available in most large public libraries: *Annual Register of Grant Support* (National Register Publishing Co., Inc., 3004 Glenview Rd., Wilmette IL 60091) and *Foundation Grants to Individuals* (Foundation Center, 79 5th Ave., New York NY 10003). The *Annual Register* is a guide to grant and fellowship support programs in government, public and private foundations, companies, professional associations, and special interest groups. The detailed subject index will lead you to writing-related programs. The Foundation Center directory lists about 1,000 foundations and application procedures for grants offered to individuals. Included are scholarships, fellowships, residencies, grants to needy writers, and a bibliography of other funding information.

There are opportunities available for writers. Approximately 100 contests have been added to *Writer's Market* listings this year. It's up to you to enter.

The contests are listed by title, address, contact person, type of competition and deadline in 1988. If a contest sounds interesting, send a self-addressed, stamped envelope to the contact person for information, rules and details about prizes. Don't enter any contest without seeking this information.

AAAS PRIZE FOR BEHAVIORAL SCIENCE RESEARCH, American Association for the Advancement of Science, 1333 H. St. NW, Washington DC 20005. Deadline: August 22. Executive Assistant to the Executive Officer: Marge White. Psychology/social sciences/sociology.

HERBERT BAXTER ADAMS PRIZE, Committee Chairman, American Historical Association, 400 A St. SE, Washington DC 20003. European history (first book). Deadline: June 15.

MAUDE ADAMS PLAYWRITING COMPETITION, Stephens College, Columbia MO 65215. (314)876-7193. Artistic Director: Addison Myers. Estab. 1984-85. Full-length plays written by women, dealing with women's issues, with leading roles for women. Deadline: January 15.

JANE ADDAMS PEACE ASSOCIATION CHILDREN'S BOOK AWARD, Jane Addams Peace Association and Women's International League for Peace and Freedom, 5477 Cedonia Ave., Baltimore MD 21206. (301)488-6987. Award Director: Annette Chotin Blank. Previously published book that promotes peace, social justice, and the equality of the sexes and races. Deadline: April 1.

ADRIATIC AWARD, International Society of Dramatists, Box 1310, Miami FL 33153. (305)756-8313. Award Director: A. Delaplaine. Full-length play either unproduced professionally *or* with one professional production (using Equity actors). Deadline: November 1.

‡AIM MAGAZINE SHORT STORY CONTEST, Box 20554, Chicago IL 60619. (312)874-6184. Publisher: Ruth Apilado. Unpublished short stories (4,000 words maximum) "promoting brotherhood among people and cultures." Deadline: Aug. 15.

ALBERTA NEW FICTION COMPETITION, Alberta Culture, Film and Literary Arts, 12th Fl., CN Tower, Edmonton, Alberta T5J 0K5 Canada. (403)427-2554. Open only to Alberta resident authors. Deadline: December 31.

ALBERTA NON-FICTION AWARD, Alberta Culture, Film and Literary Arts, 12 Fl., CN Tower, Edmonton, Alberta T5J 0K5 Canada. (403)427-2554. Nonfiction book by Alberta author published in calendar year. Deadline December 31.

‡AMELIA STUDENT AWARD, *Amelia Magazine*, 329 E St., Bakersfield CA 93304. (805)323-4064. Editor: Frederick A. Raborg, Jr. Previously unpublished poems, essays and short stories by high school students. Deadline: April 15.

AMERICAN ASSOCIATION OF UNIVERSITY WOMEN AWARD, NORTH CAROLINA DIVISION, North Carolina Literary and Historical Association, 109 E. Jones St., Raleigh NC 27611. (919)733-7305. Award Director: Becky Myer. Previously published juvenile literature by a North Carolina author.

THE AMERICAN BOOK AWARDS, Before Columbus Foundation, Suite D, 1446 6th St., Berkeley CA 94710. (415)527-1586. Director: Gundars Strads. Previously published books by contemporary American authors. Deadline: December 31.

‡AMERICAN MINORITY PLAYWRIGHT'S FESTIVAL, The Group Theatre Company, 3940 Brooklyn Ave. NE, Seattle WA 98105. (206)545-4969. Director: Tim Bond. One-act and full-length plays by minority playrights. Honorarium, airfare, housing for 2 playwrights (workshop productions). Deadline: October 15.

‡AMERICAN MUSICAL THEATER FESTIVAL, Box I, Carmel CA 93921. (408)625-9900. Director: Mikel Pippi. Full length musicals with completed scores. Deadline in November.

‡AMERICAN-SCANDINAVIAN FOUNDATION/TRANSLATION PRIZE, American-Scandinavian Foundation, 127 E. 73rd St., New York NY 10021. (212)879-9779. Contact: Publishing Division. Contemporary Scandinavian fiction and poetry translations. Deadline: June 1.

‡AMERICAN SOCIETY OF JOURNALISTS & AUTHORS AWARDS PROGRAM, Room 1907, 1501 Broadway, New York NY 10036. (212)997-0947. Contact: Alexandra S.E. Cantor. Author, article and magazine awards. Deadline: February 1.

AMERICAN SPEECH-LANGUAGE-HEARING ASSOCIATION (ASHA), NATIONAL MEDIA AWARD, 10801 Rockville Pike, Rockville MD 20852. (301)897-5700. Speech-language pathology and audiology (radio, TV, newspaper, magazine). Deadline: June 30.

AMY WRITING AWARDS, The Amy Foundation, Box 16091, Lansing MI 48901. (517)323-3181. President: James Russell. Religious articles previously published in the secular media. Deadline: Jan. 31.

‡ANNUAL INTERNATIONAL NARRATIVE CONTEST, Poets and Patrons, Inc., 839 175th Place, Hammond IN 46324. Director: Dona Lu Goldman. Unpublished poetry. Deadline September 1.

ANNUAL INTERNATIONAL POETRY CONTEST, Poet's Study Club of Terre Haute, Indiana, 826 S. Center, Terre Haute IN 47804. President: Esther Alman. Serious poetry, light verse, and traditional haiku. Deadline: February 1.

ANNUAL INTERNATIONAL SHAKESPEAREAN SONNET CONTEST, Poets Club of Chicago, Agnes Wathall Tatera, 2546 Atlantic St., Franklin Park IL 60131. (312)455-4771. Chairman: Agnes Wathall Tatera. "Classic" Shakespearean sonnet form. Deadline: September 1.

‡ANNUAL JOURNALISM AWARDS COMPETITION, Big Brothers/Big Sisters of America, 230 North 13th St., Philadelphia PA 19107. (215)567-7000. Manager, Public Relations: Colleen Watson. Previously published stories "communicating the difficulties experienced by children from one-parent homes and how such problems are handled." Deadline: April 1.

THE ANNUAL NATIONAL BIBLE WEEK EDITORIAL CONTEST, The Laymen's National Bible Committee Inc., 815 2nd Ave., New York NY 10017. (212)687-0555. Contact: Executive Director. Unpublished editorial (journalism students registered in a college or university only). Deadline: June 3.

ANNUAL NJ POETRY CONTEST, NJIT Alumni Association, NJ Institute of Technology, Newark NJ 07102. (201)596-3441. Contest/Award Director: Dr. Herman A. Estrin. Poetry by elementary, junior high, secondary, and college students who are New Jersey residents.

ANNUAL NORTH AMERICAN ESSAY CONTEST, *The Humanist Magazine*, 7 Harwood Dr., Box 146, Amherst NY 14226. (716)839-5080. Contest/Award Director: Lloyd Morain. Unpublished essay by writers age 29 or younger. Deadline: September 1.

RUBY LLOYD APSEY PLAYWRITING AWARD, University of Alabama, Department of Theater and Dance, University Station, Birmingham AL 35294. (215)934-3236. Contest Director: Dr. Rick J. Plummer. Unpublished full-length plays by new American playwrights. Deadline: January 1.

‡ARTIST'S FELLOWSHIP AWARD, New York Foundation for the Arts, Suite 600, 5 Beekman St., New York NY 10038. (212)233-3900. Contact: Roger Bruce. New York State artists career awards to be used at the artist's discretion to support their work. Deadlines begin in late summer.

THE ARTISTS FELLOWSHIP PROGRAM, The Artists Foundation, Inc., 110 Broad St., Boston MA 02110. (617)482-8100. Award Director: Lucine Ann Folgueras. Fellowships for playwriting, poetry, fiction and nonfiction by Massachusetts residents. Published or unpublished work. Deadlines: October (literary art); March (visual art).

ASSOCIATION FOR EDUCATION IN JOURNALISM AWARDS, Magazine Division, Loyola College, Baltimore MD 21210. Professor of Journalism: Andrew Ciofalo. Awards to enrolled college students for unpublished nonfiction magazine article, research paper on magazine journalism, or magazine design.

‡VINCENT ASTOR MEMORIAL LEADERSHIP ESSAY CONTEST, U.S. Naval Institute, Preble Hall, U.S. Naval Academy, Annapolis MD 21402. (301)268-6110. Award Director: James A. Barber, Jr. Essays on the topic of leadership (junior officers and officer trainees). Deadline: March 1.

‡THE ATHENAEUM OF PHILADELPHIA LITERARY AWARD, The Athenaeum of Philadelphia, 219 S. 6th St., Philadelphia PA 19106. (215)925-2688. Award Director: Nathaniel Burt. Nominated book by a Philadelphia resident. Deadline: December 31.

‡AWARD FOR LITERARY TRANSLATION, American Translators Association, 109 Croton Ave., Ossining NY 10562. (914)941-1500. Contact: Sue Ellen Wright. Previously published book translated from German to English. In even years, Lewis Galentière Prize awarded for translations other than German to English. Deadline: March 15.

BANTA AWARD, Wisconsin Library Association/Banta Foundation of the George Banta Company, Inc., 1922 University Ave., Madison WI 53705. (608)231-1513. Contact: Faith B. Miracle, Administrator, WLA. Book by a Wisconsin author published during the previous year. Deadline: December 31.

GEORGE LOUIS BEER PRIZE, Committee Chairman, American Historical Association, 400 A St. SE, Washington DC 20003. European international history since 1895 (scholarly work). Deadline: June 15.

‡BEST OF BLURBS CONTEST, Writer's Refinery, Box 47786, Phoenix AZ 85068-7786. (602)944-5268. Contest Director: Libbi Goodman. Estab. 1987. "To foster the joy of writing a concise statement of the plot of a novel, write back cover or jacket flap copy for a hypothetical novel." Deadline: September 30. Write "Best of Blurbs/WM" on SASE for rules.

ALBERT J. BEVERIDGE AWARD, Committee Chairman, American Historical Association, 400 A St. SE, Washington DC 20003. American history of U.S., Canada and Latin American (book). Deadline: June 15.

THE BEVERLY HILLS THEATRE GUILD-JULIE HARRIS PLAYWRIGHT AWARD COMPETITION, 2815 N. Beachwood Drive, Los Angeles CA 90068. (213)465-2703. Playwright Award Coordinator: Marcella Meharg. Original full-length plays, unpublished, unproduced, and not currently under option. Deadline: November 1.

BITTERROOT MAGAZINE POETRY CONTEST, Contact: Menke Katz, Editor-in-Chief, *Bitterroot,* Spring Glen NY 12483. Sponsors William Kushner Annual Awards and Heershe Dovid-Badonneh Awards for unpublished poetry. Deadline: December 31.

IRMA SIMONTON BLACK AWARD, Bank Street College of Education, 610 W. 112th St., New York NY 10025. (212)663-7200, ext. 540. Award Director: William H. Hooks. Previously published children's book. Deadline: January 15.

BLACK WARRIOR REVIEW LITERARY AWARDS, *Black Warrior Review*, The University of Alabama, Box 2936, Tuscaloosa AL 35487. (205)348-4518. Contact: Editor. Unpublished poetry and fiction. No deadline.

HOWARD W. BLAKESLEE AWARDS, American Heart Association, 7320 Greenville Ave., Dallas TX 75231. (214)706-1340. Award Director: Howard L. Lewis. Previously published or broadcast reports on cardiovascular diseases. Deadline: Feb. 1.

‡BODY STORY CONTEST, *American Health* Magazine, 80 5th Ave., New York NY 10011. (212)242-2460. Contact: Allegra Holch. 2,000-word fiction or nonfiction story. Deadline: April 1.

BOSTON GLOBE-HORN BOOK AWARDS, Stephanie Loer, Children's Book Editor, *The Boston Globe*, Boston MA 02107. Poetry, nonfiction and illustrated book. Deadline: May 1.

‡BOSTON GLOBE LITERARY PRESS COMPETITION, The Boston Globe, Boston MA 02107. (617)929-2637. Contest Director: Richard Collins. Estab. 1987. Previously published books by small literary presses, submitted by publisher. Deadline: March 30.

BOWLING WRITING COMPETITION, American Bowling Congress, Public Relations, 5301 S. 76th St., Greendale WI 53129. Director: Dave DeLorenzo, Public Relations Manager. Feature, editorial and news. Deadline in December.

‡BRITTINGHAM PRIZE IN POETRY, University of Wisconsin Press, 114 N. Murray, Madison WI 53715. (608)262-4750. Contest Director: Ronald Wallace. Unpublished book-length manuscript of original poetry. Deadline: October 1.

ARLEIGH BURKE ESSAY CONTEST, U.S. Naval Institute, Preble Hall, U.S. Naval Academy, Annapolis MD 21402. (301)268-6110. Award Director: James A. Barber, Jr. Essay that advances professional, literary or scientific knowledge of the naval and maritime services. Deadline: December 1.

‡BUSH ARTIST FELLOWSHIPS, The Bush Foundation, E-900 First Natl. Bank Bldg., St. Paul MN 55101. (612)227-0891. Contact: Sally F. Dixon. Award for Minnesota residents "to buy 6-18 months of time for the applicant to do his/her own work." Deadline: Oct. 31.

‡CALIFORNIA SHORT STORY COMPETITION, Nob Hill Gazette, Pier 5, San Francisco CA 94114. (415)788-3120. Contact: Camille Carew. Previously published or unpublished fiction by California residents. Deadline: Jan. 31.

‡CALIFORNIA WRITERS' CLUB CONFERENCE CONTEST, 2214 Derby St., Berkeley CA 94705. (415)841-1217. Unpublished adult fiction, adult nonfiction, juvenile fiction or nonfiction, poetry and scripts. Deadline: varies in spring.

CANADIAN BOOKSELLERS ASSOCIATION AUTHOR OF THE YEAR AWARD, 49 Laing St., Toronto, Ontario M4L 2N4 Canada. Contact: Board of Directors of the Association. Book by Canadian author.

MELVILLE CANE AWARD, Poetry Society of America, 15 Gramercy Park S., New York NY 10003. (212)254-9268. Contact: Award Director. Published book of poems or prose work on a poet or poetry submitted by the publisher. Deadline: December 31.

‡**CCLM EDITOR'S GRANT AWARDS**, Coordinating Council of Literary Magazines, 666 Broadway, New York NY 10012. (212)614-6551. Contact: Jill Bonart. Awards for editors of noncommercial literary magazines in CCLM. Deadline: Feb. 1.

‡**CCLM SEED GRANTS**, Coordinating Council of Literary Magazines, 666 Broadway, New York NY 10012. (212)614-6551. Contact: Jill Bonart. Literary magazines that have published fewer than 3 issues. Deadline: March 1.

CHILDREN'S SCIENCE BOOK AWARDS, New York Academy of Sciences, 2 E. 63rd St., New York NY 10021. (212)838-0230. Public Relations Director: Ann E. Collins. General or trade science books for children under 17 years. Deadline: November 30.

GERTRUDE B. CLAYTOR MEMORIAL AWARD, Poetry Society of America, 15 Gramercy Park S., New York NY 10003. (212)254-9628. Contact: Award Director. Poem in any form on the American scene or character. Members only. Deadline: December 31.

COLLEGIATE POETRY CONTEST, *The Lyric*, 307 Dunton Dr. SW, Blacksburg VA 24060. Editor: Leslie Mellichamp. Unpublished poems (36 lines or less) by fulltime undergraduates in 4-year U.S. or Canadian colleges. Deadline: June 1.

COMMONWEALTH OF PENNSYLVANIA COUNCIL ON THE ARTS LITERATURE FELLOWSHIPS, 216 Finance Bldg., Harrisburg PA 17120. (717)787-6883. Award Director: Peter Carnahan. Fellowships for Pennsylvania writers of fiction and poetry. Deadline in October.

COMMUNITY CHILDREN'S THEATRE OF KANSAS CITY ANNUAL PLAYWRITING AWARD, 8021 E. 129th Terrace, Grandview MO 64030. (816)761-5775. Award Director: E. Blanche Sellens. Unpublished play for elementary school audiences. Deadline: January 22.

‡**THE BERNARD F. CONNERS PRIZE FOR POETRY**, *The Paris Review*, 541 E. 72nd St., New York NY 10021. Poetry Editor: Editorial Office. Unpublished poetry over 300 lines. Deadline: April 1.

ALBERT B. COREY PRIZE IN CANADIAN-AMERICAN RELATIONS, Office of the Executive Director, American Historical Association, 400 A St. SE, Washington DC 20003. History, Canadian-U.S. relations or history of both countries (book). Deadline: June 15.

‡**COUNCIL FOR WISCONSIN WRITERS, INC. ANNUAL AWARDS COMPETITION**, Box 55322, Madison WI 53705. (414)336-2424. Contact: awards committee. Previously published book-length fiction, short fiction, book-length and short nonfiction, poetry, play, juvenile books, children's picture books and outdoor writing by Wisconsin residents. Deadline: January 15.

‡**CREATIVE ARTISTS GRANT**, Michigan Council for the Arts, 1200 Sixth Ave., Detroit MI 18226. (313)256-3719. Individual Artist Coordinator: Craig Carver. Grants of up to $8,000 for Michigan professional creative writers. Deadline: early April.

‡**CREATIVE ARTS CONTEST**, Women's National Auxiliary Convention, Free Will Baptists, Box 1088, Nashville TN 37202. Contact: Lorene Miley. Unpublished articles, plays, poetry, programs and art from auxiliary members. Deadline: March 1.

CREATIVITY FELLOWSHIP, Northwood Institute Alden B. Dow Creativity Center, Midland MI 48640-2398. (517)832-4478. Award Director: Carol B. Coppage. Ten week summer residency for individuals in any field who wish to pursue a creative idea which has the potential of impact in that field. Deadline: December 31.

GUSTAV DAVIDSON MEMORIAL AWARD, Poetry Society of America, 15 Gramercy Park S., New York NY 10003. (212)254-9628. Contact: Award Director. Sonnet or sequence in traditional forms. Members only. Deadline: December 31.

MARY CAROLYN DAVIES MEMORIAL AWARD, Poetry Society of America, 15 Gramercy Park S., New York NY 10003. (212)254-9628. Contact: Award Director. Unpublished poem suitable for setting to music. Members only. Deadline: December 31.

‡**DEEP SOUTH WRITERS' CONTEST**, Deep South Writer's Conference, Box 44691, University of Southern Louisiana, Lafayette LA 70504. (318)231-6908. Unpublished works of short fiction, nonfiction, novel, poetry, drama and French literature. Deadline: July 15.

‡**DELACORTE PRESS PRIZE FOR AN OUTSTANDING FIRST YOUNG ADULT NOVEL** , Delacorte Press, 245 East 47th St., New York NY 10017. (212)605-3000. Contest Director: Bebe Willoughby. Previously unpublished contemporary young adult fiction. Deadline: December 31. Does not accept unsolicited material.

MARIE-LOUISE D'ESTERNAUX POETRY SCHOLARSHIP CONTEST, The Brooklyn Poetry Circle, 61 Pierrepont St., Brooklyn NY 11201. (718)875-8736. Contest Chairman: Gabrielle Lederer. Poetry by students between 16 and 21 years of age. Deadline: April 15.

ALICE FAY DI CASTAGNOLA AWARD, Poetry Society of America, 15 Gramercy Park S., New York NY 10003. (212)254-9628. Contact: Award Director. Manuscript in progress: poetry, prose on poetry or verse-drama. Members only. Deadline: December 31.

EMILY DICKINSON AWARD, Poetry Society of America, 15 Gramercy Park S., New York NY 10003. (212)254-9628. Contact: Award Director. Poem inspired by Emily Dickinson. Members only. Deadline: December 31.

THE DISCOVERY/NATION 1988, The Poetry Center of the 92nd Street YM-YWHA, 1395 Lexington Ave., New York NY 10128. (212)427-6000, ext. 176 or 208. Poetry (unpublished in book form). Deadline: February 12.

‡**DOG WRITER'S ASSOCIATION OF AMERICA ANNUAL WRITING CONTEST**,c/o H. Sundstrom, President, Box 48, Manassas VA 22110. (703)369-2384. Contest Director: M. Akers-Hanson, Box 301, Kewanee IL 61443. Previously published writing about dogs their rearing, training, care and all aspects of companionship. Deadline varies.

JOHN H. DUNNING PRIZE IN AMERICAN HISTORY, Committee Chairman, American Historical Association, 400 A St. SE, Washington DC 20003. Annual award for U.S. history monograph/book. Deadline: June 15.

‡**EATON LITERARY ASSOCIATES LITERARY AWARDS PROGRAM**, Box 49795, Sarasota FL 33578. (813)355-4561. Editorial Director: Lana Bruce. Previously unpublished short stories and novels. Deadline: March 31 (short story); Aug. 31 (novel).

DAVID JAMES ELLIS MEMORIAL AWARD, Theatre Americana, Box 245, Altadena CA 91001. Contact: Mrs. Leone Jones. Two- or three-act plays, no musicals or children's plays, with a performance time of about 1½-2 hours. Deadline: April 1.

THE RALPH WALDO EMERSON AWARD, Phi Beta Kappa (The United Chapters of Phi Beta Kappa), 1811 Q St. NW, Washington DC 20009. (202)265-3808. Contact: Administrator, Phi Beta Kappa Book Awards. Studies of the intellectual and cultural condition of man, submitted by the publisher. Deadline: May 31.

‡**WILLIAM AND JANICE EPSTEIN AWARD**, National Jewish Book Award—Fiction, Jewish Book Council, 15 E. 26th St., New York NY 10010. (212)532-4949. Director: Paula G. Gottlieb. Novel or collection of short stories of Jewish interest.

JOHN K. FAIRBANK PRIZE IN EAST ASIAN HISTORY, Committee Chairman, American Historical Association, 400 A St. SE, Washington DC 20003. Book on East Asian history. Deadline: June 15.

NORMA FARBER FIRST BOOK AWARD, Poetry Society of America, 15 Gramercy Park S., New York NY 10003. (212)254-9628. Contact: Award Director. Book of original poetry. Publishers only. Deadline: December 31.

FICTION WRITERS CONTEST, Mademoiselle Magazine, 350 Madison Ave., New York NY 10017. Contest Director: Eileen Schnurr. Unpublished short stories by writers aged 18-30. Deadline March 15.

‡**FLORIDA INDIVIDUAL ARTIST FELLOWSHIPS**, Florida Department of State, Bureau of Grants Services, Division of Cultural Affairs, The Capitol, Tallahassee FL 32399-0250. (904)488-3976. Director: Chris Doolin. Fellowship for Florida writers. Deadline: early February.

‡**FOLIO FICTION/POETRY AWARDS**, Folio, Dept. of Literature, American University, Washington DC 20016. (202)885-2971. Fiction and poetry.

CONSUELO FORD AWARD, Poetry Society of America, 15 Gramercy Park S., New York NY 10003. (212)254-9628. Contact: Award Director. Unpublished lyric. Members only. Deadline: Dec. 31.

‡**FOSTER CITY WRITERS CONTEST**, Foster City Committee for the Arts, 650 Shell Blvd., Foster City CA 94404. (415)341-8051. Chairman, Committee for the Arts: Ted Lance. Unpublished fiction, poetry, childrens' stories and humor. Deadline: Aug. 31.

‡**FOURTH ESTATE AWARD**, American Legion National Headquarters, 700 N. Pennsylvania, Indianapolis IN 46204. (317)635-8411. Contact: National Public Relations. Previously published or broadcast piece on an issue of national concern. Deadline: Jan. 31.

‡**THE 49th PARALLEL POETRY CONTEST**, The Signpost Press Inc., 412 N. State St., Bellingham WA 98225. (206)734-9781. Contest Director: Knute Skinner. Unpublished poetry. Deadline: Jan. 1.

GEORGE FREEDLEY MEMORIAL AWARD, Theatre Library Association, 111 Amsterdam Ave., New York NY 10023. (212)870-1670. Award Committee Chair: Martha R. Mahard, Harvard Theatre Collection, Havard College Library, Cambridge MA 02138. Mary Ann Jensen. Published books related to performance in theatre. Deadline: Feb. 26.

DON FREEMAN MEMORIAL GRANT-IN-AID, Society of Children's Book Writers, Box 296 Mar Vista, Los Angeles CA 90066. To enable picture-book artists to further their understanding, training and/or work. Members only. Deadline: Feb. 15.

THE CHRISTIAN GAUSS AWARD, Phi Beta Kappa (The United Chapters of Phi Beta Kappa), 1811 Q St. NW, Washington DC 20009. (202)265-3808. Contact; Administrator, Phi Beta Kappa Book Awards. Works of literary criticism or scholarship submitted by publisher. Deadline: May 31.

‡**GENERAL ELECTRIC FOUNDATION AWARDS FOR YOUNGER WRITERS**, Coordinating Council of Literary Magazines, 666 Broadway, New York NY 10012. (212)614-6551. Contact: Jim Bonart. Previously published poetry, fiction or literary essays in literary magazines. Deadline: April 30.

GOLDEN KITE AWARDS, Society of Children's Book Writers (SCBW), Box 296 Mar Vista Station, Los Angeles CA 90066. (818)347-2849. Coordinator: Sue Alexander. Calendar year published children's fiction, nonfiction and picture illustration books by a SCBW member. Deadline: Dec. 15.

‡**GOODMAN AWARD**, Thorntree Press, 547 Hawthorn Lane, Winnetka IL 60093. (312)446-8099. Contact: John Dickson. Deadline: Feb. 14.

GUIDEPOSTS MAGAZINE YOUTH WRITING CONTEST, Guideposts Associates, Inc., 747 3rd Ave., New York NY 10017. Senior Editor: James McDermott. Memorable true experience of 1,200 words, preferably spiritual in nature. Unpublished first person story by high school juniors or seniors or students in equivalent grades overseas. Deadline: November 28.

‡**VICTORIA CHEN HAIDER MEMORIAL COLLEGE LITERARY MAGAZINE CONTEST**, Coordinating Council of Literary Magazines, 666 Broadway, New York NY 10012. (212)614-6551. Contact: Jill Bonart. College literary magazines that are associate members of CCLM. Deadline: May 30.

NATE HASELTINE MEMORIAL FELLOWSHIPS IN SCIENCE WRITING, Council for the Advancement of Science Writing, Inc., 618 North Elmwood, Oak Park IL 60302. Executive Director: William J. Cromie. Graduate level study in science writing programs.

‡**DRUE HEINZ LITERATURE PRIZE**, University of Pittsburgh Press, 127 N. Bellefield Ave., Pittsburgh PA 15260. (412)624-4110. Collection of short fiction. Award open to writers who have published a book-length collection of fiction or a minimum of three short stories or novellas in commercial magazines or literary journals of national distribution. Deadline: August 31.

ERNEST HEMINGWAY FOUNDATION AWARD, P.E.N. American Center, 568 Broadway, New York NY 10012. First-published novel or short story collection by American author. Deadline: December 31.

CECIL HEMLEY MEMORIAL AWARD, Poetry Society of America, 15 Gramercy Park S., New York NY 10003. (212)254-9628. Contact: Award Director. Unpublished lyric poem on a philosophical theme. Members only. Deadline: December 31.

SIDNEY HILLMAN PRIZE AWARD, Sidney Hillman Foundation, Inc., 15 Union Square, New York NY 10003. (212)242-0700. Executive Director: Joyce D. Miller. Social/economic themes related to ideals of Sidney Hillman (daily or periodical journalism, nonfiction, radio and TV). Deadline: January 15.

‡**HAROLD HIRSCH AWARDS**,United States Ski Writers Association, 514 Franklin St., Denver Co 80218. (303)321-4292. Contest Director: Diane Huntress. Published articles by USSWA members. Deadline: April 25.

‡**HOOVER ANNUAL JOURNALISM AWARDS**, Herbert Hoover Presidential Library Assn., Box 696, West Branch IA 52358. Contact: Tom Walsh. Estab. 1986. Previously published newspaper and magazine journalism that contributes to public awareness and appreciation of the lives of Herbert and Lou Henry Hoover or is based on research at the Herbert Hoover Presidential Library in West Branch, Iowa. Deadline: Jan. 31.

‡**DARRELL BOB HOUSTON PRIZE**,1931 Second Ave., Seattle WA 98101. (206)441-6239. Journalism published within the previous year in Washington State which shows "some soul, some color, some grace, robustness, mirth and generosity," to honor the memory of writer Darrell Bob Houston. Deadline: contact for exact date.

THE ROY W. HOWARD AWARDS,The Scripps Howard Foundation, 1100 Central Trust Tower, Cincinnati OH 45202. (513)977-3036. Public service reporting.

‡**IDAHO WRITER IN RESIDENCE**, Idaho Commission on the Arts, 304 W. State, Boise ID 83720. (208)334-2119. Program Coordinator: Jim Owen. Previously published works by Idaho writers; award offered every two years. Deadline: August 1989.

ILLINOIS STATE UNIVERSITY FINE ARTS PLAYWRITING AWARD, Illinois State University, Theatre Department, Normal IL 61761. (309)438-8783. Director: Dr. John W. Kirk. Previously unproduced full-length plays. No musicals. Deadline: October 15.

INDIVIDUAL ARTIST FELLOWSHIP, Maryland State Arts Council, 15 W. Mulberry St., Baltimore MD 21201. (301)685-6740. Award Director: Oletha De Vane. Grants to Maryland residents for completed works or works in progress. Deadline: mid-January.

‡**MARK H. INGRAHAM PRIZE**,University of Wisconsin Press, 114 N. Murray, Madison WI 53715. (608)262-4750. Contact: Committee of the Press. Unpublished book-length manuscript on the humanities or social sciences. Deadline: September 1.

‡**INKLING FICTION CONTEST**, Inkling Publications, Inc., Box 65798, St. Paul MN 55165. (612)221-0326. Contact: John Hall. Previously unpublished fiction. Deadline: March 15.

‡**INKLING POETRY CONTEST**, Inkling Publications, Inc., Box 65798, St. Paul MN 55165. (612)221-0326. Contact: Esther M. Leiper. Previously unpublished poetry. Deadline: Sept. 15 (fall); April 15 (spring).

INTERNATIONAL IMITATION HEMINGWAY COMPETITION, Harry's Bar & American Grill, 2020 Avenue of the Stars, Los Angeles CA 90067. (213)277-2333. Contest/Award Director: Mark S. Grody, Grody/Tellem Communications, Inc., Suite 840, 11150 W. Olympic Blvd., Los Angeles CA 90064. (213)479-3363. Unpublished one-page parody of Hemingway. Deadline: February 15.

‡**INTERNATIONAL LITERARY CONTEST**,Writer's Refinery, Box 47786, Phoenix AZ 85068-7786. (602)944-5268. Contest Director: Libbi Goodman. Estab. 1986. Unpublished fiction, poetry and essays. Deadline: March 31. Write "International Literary Contest/WM" on SASE for rules.

‡**INTERNATIONAL READING ASSOCIATION CHILDREN'S BOOK AWARD**, International Reading Association, Box 8139, 800 Barksdale Rd., Newark DE 19714-8139. (302)731-1600. Director: IRA Children's Book Award Subcommittee. The *IRA Children's Book Award* will be given for a first or second children's book, either fiction or non fiction, by an author who shows unusual promise in the children's book field. Deadline: Dec 1.

INTERNATIONAL READING ASSOCIATION PRINT MEDIA AWARD, International Reading Association, Box 8139, 800 Barksdale Rd., Newark DE 19714-8139. (302)731-1600. Contact: Patricia Du Bois. Reports by professional journalists from newspapers, magazines and wire services on reading programs. Deadline: Jan. 15.

IOWA ARTS COUNCIL LITERARY AWARDS, Iowa Arts Council, State Capitol Complex, Des Moines IA 50319. (515)281-4451. Director: Iowa Arts Council. Unpublished fiction and poetry by Iowa writers (legal residents). Deadline: July 31.

JOSEPH HENRY JACKSON/JAMES D. PHELAN LITERARY AWARDS, The San Francisco Foundation, 500 Washington St., 8th Floor, San Francisco CA 94111. (415)392-0600. Assistant Coordinator: Adrienne Krug. Jackson: unpublished, work-in-progress fiction (novel or short story), nonfiction, or poetry by author with 3-year consecutive residency in N. California or Nevada prior to submissions. Age 20-35. Phelan: unpublished, work-in-progress fiction, nonfiction, short story, poetry or drama by California-born author. Age 20-35. Deadline: January 15.

JACKSONVILLE UNIVERSITY PLAYWRITING CONTEST, College of Fine Arts, Jacksonville University, Jacksonville FL 32211. (904)744-3950. Director: Davis Sikes. Unproduced one-act and full-length plays. Deadline: January 4.

JAMESTOWN PRIZE, Institute of Early American History and Culture, Box 220, Williamsburg VA 23187. (804)229-5118. Award Director: Philip D. Morgan. Book-length scholarly ms on early American history or culture.

‡THE JAPAN FOUNDATION FELLOWSHIP PROGRAM, Suite 1702, 342 Madison Ave., New York NY 10173. (212)949-6360. Contact: Masayoshi Matsumura. Grants to scholars for research in Japan. Deadline: Nov. 15.

ANSON JONES AWARD, % Texas Medical Association, 1801 N. Lamar Blvd., Austin TX 78701. (512)477-6704. Health (Texas newspaper, magazine—trade, commercial, association, chamber or company, radio and TV). Deadline: January 15.

JUNIOR AND SENIOR AWARDS, International Society of Dramatists, Box 1310, Miami FL 33153. Award Director: A. Delaplaine. Previously unpublished scripts (any media or length) written by high school students (Junior Award) and college students (Senior Awards). Deadline: May 1.

THE JANET HEIDINGER KAFKA PRIZE, English Department/Writers Workshop, 127 Lattimore Hall, University of Rochester, Rochester NY 14627. (716)275-2347. Chairman: Anne Ludlow. Book-length fiction (novel, short story or experimental writing) by U.S. woman citizen submitted by publishers.

‡KANSAS QUARTERLY/KANSAS ARTS COMMISSION AWARDS, SEATON AWARDS, Department of English, Kansas State University, Manhattan KS 66505. (913)532-6716. Editor: Harold Schneider. *KQ/KAC* awards for poetry and fiction published in *KQ*; Seaton awards for Kansas writers whose poetry, fiction and prose appear in *KQ*.

‡ROBERT F. KENNEDY BOOK AWARD, 1031 31st St. NW, Washington DC 20007. (202)333-1880. Executive Director: Caroline Croft. Book which reflects "concern for the poor and the powerless, justice, the conviction that society must assure all young people a fair chance and faith that a free democracy can act to remedy disparities of power and opportunity." Deadline: Jan. 8.

SARAH H. KUSHNER MEMORIAL AWARD, National Jewish Book Award—Scholarship, Jewish Book Council, 15 E. 26th St., New York NY 10010. (212)532-4949. Director: Paula G. Gottlieb. Book which makes an original contribution to Jewish learning.

RUTH LAKE MEMORIAL AWARD, Poetry Society of America, 15 Gramercy Park S., New York NY 10003. (212)254-9628. Contact: Award Director. Unpublished poem of retrospection. Deadline: December 31.

LAMONT POETRY SELECTION, Academy of American Poets, 177 E. 87th St., New York NY 10128. (212)427-5665. Contest/Award Director: Nancy Schoenberger. Second book of unpublished poems by an American citizen, submitted by publisher in manuscript form.

THE HAROLD MORTON LANDON TRANSLATION PRIZE, The Academy of American Poets, 177 E. 87th St., New York NY 10128. (212)427-5665. Award Director: Nancy Schoenberger. Previously published translation of poetry from any language into English by an American translator.

‡LINDEN LANE MAGAZINE ENGLISH-LANGUAGE POETRY CONTEST, Linden Lane Magazine & Press, Inc., Box 2384, Princeton NJ 08543-2384. (609)924-1413. Editor: Belkis Cuza Male. Unpublished Spanish and English poetry, short story and essay prizes. Deadline: May 10.

‡D.H. LAWRENCE FELLOWSHIP, University of New Mexico/English Department, 217 Humanities Bldg., University of New Mexico, Albuquerque NM 87131. (505)277-6347. Contest: Louis Owens. Fellowship for writers of fiction, poetry and/or drama. Deadline: January 31.

‡**STEPHEN LEACOCK MEMORIAL AWARD FOR HUMOUR**, Stephen Leacock Associates, Box 854, Orillia Ontario L3V 6K8 Canada. (705)325-6546. Contest Director: Jean Dickson. Previously published book of humor by a Canadian author. Deadline: Dec. 31.

ELIAS LIEBERMAN STUDENT POETRY AWARD, Poetry Society of America, 15 Gramercy Park S., New York NY 10003. (212)254-9628. Contact: Award Director. Unpublished poem by student (grades 9-12). Deadline: December 31.

‡**LIGHT AND LIFE WRITING CONTEST**,*Light and Life* Magazine, 901 College Ave., Winona Lake IN 46590. (219)267-7656. Editor: Bob Haslam. Unpublished personal experience stories and poetry. Deadline: April 15.

‡**THE RUTH LILLY POETRY PRIZE**, The Modern Poetry Association and The American Council for the Arts, 60 W. Walton St., Chicago IL 60610. (312)413-2210. Contact: Joseph Parisi. Estab. 1986. Annual prize to poet "whose accomplishments in the field of poetry warrant extraordinary recognition." No applicants or nominations are accepted. Deadline: varies.

LINCOLN MEMORIAL ONE-ACT PLAYWRITING CONTEST, International Society of Dramatists, Box 1310, Miami FL 33153. (305)756-8313. Award Director: A. Delaplaine. Unpublished one-act plays, any type, any style. Deadline: January 15.

JOSEPH W. LIPPINCOTT AWARD, Donated by Joseph W. Lippincott, Jr., Administered by American Library Association, 50 E. Huron, Chicago IL 60611. (312)944-6780. For distinguished service to the profession of librarianship (notable published professional writing).

LOCKERT LIBRARY OF POETRY IN TRANSLATION, Princeton University Press, 41 William St., Princeton NJ 08540. (609)452-4900. Poetry Editor: Robert E. Brown. Book-length poetry translation of a single poet. Deadlines: February and August.

‡**LOFT CREATIVE NONFICTION RESIDENCY PROGRAM**.The Loft, 2301 E. Franklin Ave., Minneapolis MN 55406. (612)341-0431. Executive Director: Susan Broadhead. Opportunity to work in month-long seminar with resident writer and cash award to six creative nonfiction writers. "Must live close enough to Minneapolis to participate fully." Deadline: April.

LOFT-MCKNIGHT WRITERS AWARD, The Loft, 2301 E. Franklin Ave., Minneapolis MN 55406. (612)341-0431. Executive Director: Susan Broadhead. Eight awards for Minnesota writers of poetry and creative prose. Deadline: October.

LOFT-MENTOR SERIES, The Loft, 2301 Franklin Ave., Minneapolis MN 55406. (612)341-0431. Executive Director: Susan Broadhead. Opportunity to work with five nationally known writers and cash award available to eight winning poets and fiction writers. "Must live close enough to Minneapolis to participate fully in the series." Deadline: May.

‡**LOUISIANA LITERATURE PRIZE FOR POETRY**, Box 792, Southeastern Louisiana University, Hammond LA 70402. Contest Director: Dr. Tim Gautreaux. Estab. 1987. Unpublished poetry. Deadline: February 15.

‡**MCLEMORE PRIZE**,Mississippi Historical Society. Box 571, Jackson MS 39205. (601)359-1424. Contact: Secretary/Treasurer. Scholarly book on a topic in Mississippi history/biography published in the year of competition. Deadline: Jan. 1.

HOWARD R. MARRARO PRIZE IN ITALIAN HISTORY, Office of the Executive Director, American Historical Association, 400 A St. SE, Washington DC 20003. Work on any epoch of Italian history, Italian cultural history or Italian-American relations. Deadline: June 15.

‡**THE LENORE MARSHALL/NATIONAL PRIZE FOR POETRY**, The New Hope Foundation and *The Nation* Magazine, 72 Fifth Ave., New York NY 10011. (212)242-8400. Administrator: Emily Sack. Book of poems published in the United States during the previous year, and nominated by the publisher. Deadline: June 1.

JOHN MASEFIELD MEMORIAL AWARD, Poetry Society of America, 15 Gramercy Park S., New York NY 10003. (212)254-9628. Contact: Award Director. Unpublished narrative poem in English. No translations. Deadline: December 31.

MASSACHUSETTS ARTISTS FELLOWSHIP, The Artists Foundation, Inc., 110 Broad St., Boston MA 02110. (617)482-8100. Funded by the Massachusetts Council on the Arts and Humanities. Director: Lucine A. Folgueras. Poetry, fiction, nonfiction and playwriting by Massachusetts residents. Oct. 1 (literary art); March 2 (visual art).

THE MAYFLOWER SOCIETY CUP COMPETITION, North Carolina Literary and Historical Association, 109 E. Jones St., Raleigh NC 27611. (919)733-7305. Award Director: Becky Myer. Previously published nonfiction by a North Carolina resident.

LUCILLE MEDWICK MEMORIAL AWARD, Poetry Society of America, 15 Gramercy Park S., New York NY 10003. (212)254-9628. Contact: Award Director. Original poem on a humanitarian theme. Members only. Deadline: December 31.

THE EDWARD J. MEEMAN AWARDS, The Scripps Howard Foundation, 1100 Central Trust Tower, Cincinnati, OH 45202. (513)977-3036. Conservation reporting.

MELCHER BOOK AWARD, Unitarian Universalist Association, 25 Beacon St., Boston MA 02108. Staff Liaison: Rev. Mark W. Harris. Previously published book on religious liberalism. Deadline: December 31.

MENCKEN AWARDS, Free Press Association, Box 15548, Columbus OH 43215. (614)236-1908. FPA Executive Director: Michael Grossberg. Defense of human rights and individual liberties (news story or investigative report, feature story, editorial or op-ed column, editorial cartoon; and book published or broadcast during previous year. Deadline: April 1.

KENNETH W. MILDENBERGER PRIZE, Modern Language Association, 10 Astor Place, New York NY 10003. Contact: Theresa Kirby, Research Programs. Outstanding research publication in the field of teaching foreign languages and literatures. Deadline: May 1.

‡MILL MOUNTAIN THEATRE NEW PLAY COMPETITION, Mill Mountain Theatre, Center in the Square, One Market Sq., Roanoke VA 24011. (703)342-5730. Literary Manager: Jo Weinstein. Previously unpublished plays for up to 10 cast members. Deadline: varies.

‡FELIX MORLEY MEMORIAL PRIZES, Institute for Humane Studies, George Mason University, 4400 University Dr., Fairfax VA 22030. (703)323-1055. Contact: John Blundell. Estab. 1987. Awards for "young writers dedicated to individual liberty." Deadline: June 15.

FRANK LUTHER MOTT-KAPPA TAU ALPHA RESEARCH AWARD IN JOURNALISM, 107 Sondra Ave., Columbia MO 65202. (314)443-3521. Executive Director, Central Office: William H. Taft. Research in journalism (book). Deadline: January 15.

MS PUBLIC EDUCATION AWARDS CONTEST, National Multiple Sclerosis Society, 205 E. 42nd St., New York NY 10017. Contact: Public Affairs Department. Reporting on facts and consequences of multiple sclerosis (newspaper, magazine, radio or TV). Deadline: October 31.

‡NATIONAL JEWISH BOOK AWARD—CHILDREN'S LITERATURE, William (Zev) Frank Memorial Award, Jewish Book Council, 15 E. 26th St., New York NY 10010. (212)532-4949. Director: Paula G. Gottlieb. Children's book on Jewish theme. Deadline: November 25.

‡NATIONAL JEWISH BOOK AWARD—FICTION, William and Janice Epstein Award, 15 E. 26th St., New York NY 10010. (212)532-4949. Director: Paula G. Gottlieb. Jewish fiction (novel or short story collection). Deadline: November 25.

‡NATIONAL JEWISH BOOK AWARD—HOLOCAUST, Leon Jolson Award, Jewish Book Council, 15 E. 26th St., New York NY 10010. (212)532-4949. Contact: Paula G. Gottlieb. Nonfiction book concerning the Holocaust. Deadline: November 25.

‡NATIONAL JEWISH BOOK AWARD—ILLUSTRATED CHILDREN'S BOOK, Marcia and Louis Posner Award, Jewish Book Council, 15 E. 26th St., New York NY 10010. (212)532-4949. Director: Paula G. Gottlieb. Author and illustrator of a children's book on a Jewish theme. Deadline: November 25.

‡NATIONAL JEWISH BOOK AWARD—ISRAEL, Morris J. Kaplun Memorial Award, Jewish Book Council, 15 E. 26th St., New York NY 10010. (212)532-4949. Director: Paula G. Gottlieb. Nonfiction work about the State of Israel. Deadline: November 25.

‡**NATIONAL JEWISH BOOK AWARD—JEWISH HISTORY**, Gerrard and Ella Berman Award, Jewish Book Council, 15 E. 26th St., New York NY 10010. (212)532-4949. Director: Paula G. Gottlieb. Book of Jewish history. Deadline: November 25.

‡**NATIONAL JEWISH BOOK AWARD—JEWISH THOUGHT**, Frank & Ethel S. Cohen Award, Jewish Book Council, 15 E. 26th St., New York NY 10010. (212)532-4949. Director: Paula G. Gottlieb. Book dealing with some aspect of Jewish thought, past or present. Deadline: November 25.

‡**NATIONAL JEWISH BOOK AWARD—SCHOLARSHIP**, Sarah H. Kushner Memorial Award, Jewish Book Council, 15 E. 26th St., New York NY 10010. (212)532-4949. Director: Paula G. Gottlieb. Book which makes an original contribution to Jewish learning.

‡**NATIONAL JEWISH BOOK AWARD—VISUAL ARTS**, Jewish Book Council, 15 E. 26th St., New York NY 10010. (212)532-4949. Director: Paula G. Gottlieb. Book about Jewish art. Deadline: November 25.

NATIONAL ONE-ACT PLAY CONTEST, Actors Theatre of Louisville, 316 W. Main St., Louisville KY 40202. (502)584-1265. Director: Michael Bigelow Dixon. Previously unproduced (professionally) one-act plays. "Entries must *not* have had an Equity or Equity-waiver production." Deadline: April 25.

NATIONAL PLAY AWARD, Box 71011, Los Angeles CA 90071. (213)629-3762. Assistant Literary Manager: David Parrish. Unpublished, nonprofessionally produced plays. Deadline: October 1.

‡**NATIONAL PSYCHOLOGY AWARDS FOR EXCELLENCE IN THE MEDIA**, American Psychological Association/American Psychological Foundation, 1200 17th St. NW, Washington DC 20036. (202)955-7710. Contact: Carolyn Gammon. Newspaper reporting, magazine articles, books/monographs, radio, television/film (news/documentary) and television (entertainment/drama) about psychology. Deadline: April 15.

NATIONAL SOCIETY OF PROFESSIONAL ENGINEERS JOURNALISM AWARDS, 1420 King St., Alexandria VA 22314. (703)684-2852. PR Director: Leslie Collins. Engineering and technology in contemporary life (articles in general interest magazines and newspapers). No deadline.

‡**THE NEBRASKA REVIEW AWARDS IN FICTION AND POETRY**, *The Nebraska Review*, ASH 215, University of Nebraska-Omaha, Omaha NE 68182-0324. (402)554-2771. Contact: Arthur Homer (poetry) and Richard Duggin (fiction). Previously unpublished fiction and a poem or group of poems. Deadline: Nov. 14.

‡**ALLAN NEVINS PRIZE**, Professor Kenneth T. Jackson, Secretary-Treasurer, Society of American Historians, 610 Fayerweather Hall, Columbia University, New York NY 10027. American history (nominated doctoral dissertations on arts, literature, science and American biographies). Deadline: December 31.

‡**NEW LETTERS LITERARY AWARDS**, University of Missouri-Kansas City, Kansas City MO 64110. Unpublished fiction, poetry and essays. Deadline: May 15.

NEW PLAY FESTIVAL, Colony/Studio Theatre, 1944 Riverside Dr., Los Angeles CA 90039. Literary Manager: Todd Nielsen. Unpublished, unproduced play.

‡**NEW PLAYWRIGHTS COMPETITION AND FESTIVAL**, Wo/Man's Showcase, Inc., 5266 Gate Lake Road, Ft. Lauderdale FL 33319. (305)722-4371. Director: Ann White. Unpublished full-length play scripts. Deadline varies.

NEW WRITERS AWARDS, Great Lakes Colleges Association, c/o English Department, Albion College, Albion MI 49224. (517)629-5511. Director: James W. Cook. Published poetry or fiction (first book) submitted by publisher.

NEW YORK STATE HISTORICAL ASSOCIATION MANUSCRIPT AWARD, Box 800, Cooperstown NY 13326. (607)547-2508. Director of Publications: Dr. Wendell Tripp. Unpublished book-length monograph on New York State history. Deadline: February 20.

JOHN NEWBERY MEDAL, Association for Library Service to Children/American Library Association, 50 E. Huron St., Chicago IL 60611. (312)944-6780. Award Director: Susan Roman. Previously published children's literature.

NEWCOMEN AWARDS IN BUSINESS HISTORY, % *Business History Review*, Harvard Business School, Teele 304, Soldiers Field Rd., Boston MA 02163. (617)495-6154. Editor: Richard S. Tedlow. Business history article. Articles must be published in the *Business History Review* to be eligible.

‡**NIMROD, ARTS AND HUMANITIES COUNCIL OF TULSA PRIZES**,2210 South Main, Tulsa OK 74114. (918)584-3333. Director: Francine Ringold. Unpublished fiction (Katherine Anne Porter prize) and poetry (Pablo Neruda Prize). Deadline: April 1.

‡**NISSAN FOCUS AWARDS**, Focus, 5th Floor, 1140 Ave. of the Americas, New York NY 10036. (212)575-0270. Contact: Sam Katz. Screenwriting and 8 other film categories. Deadline: late spring.

NMMA DIRECTORS AWARD, National Marine Manufacturers Association, 353 Lexington Ave., New York NY 10016. (212)684-6622. Boating and allied water sports. Deadline: November 30.

OHIOANA BOOK AWARD, Ohioana Library Association, Room 1105, Ohio Departments Bldg., 65 S. Front St., Columbus OH 43215. (614)466-3831. Award Director: James P. Barry. Books published within the past 12 months by Ohioans or about Ohio and Ohioans.

‡**OKTOBERFEST SHORT FICTION COMPETITION**, Druid Press, 2724 Shades Crest Rd., Birmingham AL 35216. (205)967-6580. Contact: Ann George. Ten previously unpublished short stories. Deadline: Oct. 31.

‡**OMMATION PRESS BOOK CONTEST**, 5548 N. Sawyer, Chicago IL 60625. (312)539-5745. Contact: Effie Mihopoulos. Previously unpublished chapbook manuscripts. Deadline: Dec. 30.

‡**OPR SPRING, SUMMER, FALL AND WINTER COMPETITIONS**, *Odessa Poetry Review*, RR 1, Box 39, Odessa MO 64076. Contact: James Mason Wyzard. Top seven poems received quarterly. Deadline: spring 1988-May 31; summer 1988-Aug. 31; fall 1988-Nov. 30; winter 1988-Feb. 28.

THE C.F. ORVIS WRITING CONTEST, The Orvis Company, Inc., Manchester VT 05254. (802)362-3622. Contest/Award Director: Tom Rosenbauer. Outdoor writing about upland bird hunting and fly fishing (magazine and newspaper). Deadline: February 1.

‡**FRANCIS PARKMAN PRIZE**, Professor Kenneth T. Jackson, Secretary, Society of American Historians, 610 Fayerweather Hall, Columbia University, New York NY 10027. Colonial or national U.S. history (book). Deadline: Jan. 15.

THE ALICIA PATTERSON FOUNDATION FELLOWSHIP PROGRAM FOR JOURNALISTS, The Alicia Patterson Foundation, Suite 320, 655 15th St. NW, Washington DC 20005. (202)639-4203. Contest/Award Director: Helen McMaster Coulson. One-year grants awarded to working journalists with five years of professional experience to pursue independent projects of significant interest.

‡**PEN/JERARD FUND**, PEN American Center, 568 Broadway, New York NY 10012. (212)334-1660. Contact: John Morrone. Estab. 1986. Grant for American woman writer of nonfiction for a booklength work in progress. Deadline: Feb. 15.

PEN MEDAL FOR TRANSLATION, PEN American Center, 568 Broadway, New York NY 10012. (212)334-1660. Translators nominated by the PEN Translation Committee.

PEN/NELSON ALGREN FICTION AWARD, PEN American Center, 568 Broadway, New York NY 10012. (212)334-1660. "For the best uncompleted novel or short story collection by an American writer who needs financial assistance to finish the work." Deadline: Nov. 1.

PEN PUBLISHER CITATION, PEN American Center, 568 Broadway, New York NY 10012. (212)334-1660. "Awarded every two years to a publisher who has throughout his career, given distinctive and continuous service." Nominated by the PEN Executive Board.

PEN/ROGER KLEIN AWARD FOR EDITING, PEN American Center, 568 Broadway, New York NY 10012. (212)334-1660. "Given every two years to an editor of trade books who has an outstanding record of recognizing talents." Nominated by authors, agents, publishers and editors. Deadline: Oct. 1.

PEN TRANSLATION PRIZE, PEN American Center, 568 Broadway, New York NY 10012. Contact: Chairman, Translation Committee. One award to a literary book-length translation into English. (No technical, scientific or reference.) Deadline: Dec. 31.

PEN WRITING AWARDS FOR PRISONERS, PEN American Center, 568 Broadway, New York NY 10012. (212)334-1660. "Awarded to the authors of the best poetry, plays, short fiction and nonfiction received from prison writers in the U.S." Deadline: Sept. 1.

PERKINS PLAYWRITING CONTEST, International Society of Dramatists, Box 1310, Miami FL 33153. (305)756-8313. Award Director: A. Delaplaine. Unproduced full-length plays, any genre, any style. Deadline: Dec. 6.

‡PLAYWRITING FOR CHILDREN AWARD, Community Children's Theatre, 8021 E. 129th Terrace, Grandview MO 64030. (816)761-5775. Unpublished plays for grades 1-6. Deadline: Jan. 22.

‡PLAYWRIGHT'S-IN-RESIDENCE GRANTS, c/o HPRL, INTAR Hispanic-American theater, Box 788, New York NY 10108. (212)695-6134. Residency grant for Hispanic-American playwrights. Deadline: July 30.

‡POETRY ARTS PROJECT CONTEST,Cosponsors: United Resource Services/Political Woman Magazine, Suite 388, 4521 Campus Drive, Irvine CA 92715. Director: Charlene B. Brown. Estab. 1987. Poetry with social commentary by members. Deadline: Nov. 15.

POETRY MAGAZINE POETRY AWARDS, 60 W. Walton St., Chicago IL 60610. (312)413-2210. Contest/Award Director: Joseph Parisi, Editor. All poems published in *POETRY* are automatically considered for prizes. Poems should be submitted to the magazine.

RENATO POGGIOLI TRANSLATION AWARD, PEN American Center, 568 Broadway, New York NY 10012. (212)334-1660. "Given to encourage a beginning and promising translator who is working on a first book length translation from Italian into English." Deadline: Feb. 1.

‡PRESENT TENSE/Joel H. Cavior Literary Awards, Present Tense Magazine, 165 East 56th St., New York NY 10022. Director: Murray Polner. Published fiction, history, religious thought, nonfiction and autobiography with Jewish themes nominated by publisher. Deadline: Nov. 30.

PRINCETON SERIES OF CONTEMPORARY POETS, Princeton University Press, 41 William St., Princeton NJ 08540. (609)452-4900. Poetry Editor: Robert E. Brown. Book-length poetry mss. Deadline: in December.

PRIX ALVINE-BELISLE, ASTED, 7243, rue Saint-Denis, Montreal, Quebec H2R 2E3 Canada. Contact: Jean-Pierre Leduc. French-Canadian literature for children submitted by the publisher.

‡PROMETHEUS AWARDS/HALL OF FAME, Libertarian Futurist Society, 68 Gebhardt Road, Penfield NY 14526. (716)288-6137. Contact: Victoria Varga. Previously published pro-freedom, anti-authoritarian novel of the year. Hall of Fame: one classic libertarian novel at least five years old. Deadline: March 1.

PULITZER PRIZES, Secretary, The Pulitzer Prize Board, 702 Journalism, Columbia University, New York NY 10027. Awards for journalism, letters, drama and music in U.S. newspapers, and in literature, drama and music by Americans. Deadline: February 1 (journalism); March 14 (music and drama) and November 11 (letters).

ERNIE PYLE AWARD, Scripps Howard Foundation, 1100 Central Trust Tower, Cincinnati OH 45202. (513)977-3036. Human-interest reporting.

SIR WALTER RALEIGH AWARD, North Carolina Literary and Historical Association, 109 E. Jones St., Raleigh NC 27611. (919)733-7305. Award Director: Becky Myer. Previously published fiction by a North Carolina writer.

REDBOOK'S SHORT STORY CONTEST, Redbook Magazine, 224 W. 57th St., New York NY 10019. Fiction Editor: Deborah Purcell. Short stories by writers who have not previously published fiction in a major publication. Contest rules appear in the March issue of *Redbook* annually. Deadline: May 31.

‡REUBEN AWARD, National Cartoonists Society, 9 Ebony Ct., Brooklyn NY 11229. (718)743-6510. "Outstanding Cartoonist of the Year" from National Cartoonists Society membership.

RHODE ISLAND STATE COUNCIL ON THE ARTS FELLOWSHIP, 312 Wickenden St., Providence RI 02903. (401)277-3880. Award Director: Edward Holgate. Poetry, fiction or play, must be a resident of Rhode Island. Deadline: March 15.

RHYME TIME CREATIVE WRITING COMPETITION, Rhyme Time/Story Time, Box 2377, Coeur d'Alene ID 83814. (208)667-7511. Award Director: Linda Hutton. Rhymed poetry, fiction and essays. Deadline: first and fifteenth of each month.

‡**THE HAROLD W. RIBALOW PRIZE**,Hadassah Magazine, 50 W. 58th St., New York NY 10019. Executive Editor: Alan M.Tigay. English-language book of fiction on a Jewish Theme. Deadline: March/April.

ROANOKE-CHOWAN AWARD FOR POETRY, North Carolina Literary and Historical Association, 109 E. Jones St., Raleigh NC 27611. (919)733-7305. Award Director: Becky Myer. Previously published poetry by a resident of North Carolina.

FOREST A. ROBERTS PLAYWRITING AWARD, In cooperation with Shiras Institute, Forest A. Roberts Theatre, Northern Michigan University, Marquette MI 49855-5364. (906)227-2553. Award Director: Dr. James A. Panowski. Unpublished, unproduced plays. One-week residency and cash award. Deadline: Nov. 20.

MARY ROBERTS RINEHART FUND, English Department, George Mason University, 4400 University Dr., Fairfax VA 22030. (703)323-2220. Contact: Stephen Goodwin. Grants by nomination to unpublished creative writers for fiction, poetry, drama, biography, autobiography, or history with a strong narrative quality. Grants are given in fiction and poetry in even years, and nonfiction and drama in odd years. Deadline: Nov. 30.

‡**ROLLING STONE COLLEGE JOURNALISM COMPETITION**, Rolling Stone/Smith Corona, Suite 2208, 745 Fifth Ave., New York NY 10151. (212)758-3800. Contact: David M. Rheins. Entertainment reporting, essays and criticism and general reporting among college writers. Deadline: June 1. Must have been published before April 1.

THE CARL SANDBURG LITERARY ARTS AWARDS, The Friends of the Chicago Public Library, 78 E. Washington St., Chicago IL 60602. (312)269-2922. Chicago writers of fiction, nonfiction, poetry, and children's literature.

‡**SCHOLASTIC WRITING AWARDS**, Scholastic Inc., 730 Broadway, New York NY 10003. (212)505-3000. Fiction, nonfiction, poetry and drama (grades 7-12).

THE CHARLES M. SCHULZ AWARD,The Scripps Howard Foundation, Box 5380, Cincinnati OH 45201. (513)977-3035. Cartoonists.

THE SCIENCE AWARD, Phi Beta Kappa (The United Chapters of Phi Beta Kappa), 1811 Q St. NW, Washington DC 20009. (202)265-3808. Contact: Administrator, Phi Beta Kappa Book Awards. Previously published interpretations of the physical or biological sciences or mathematics submitted by the publisher. Deadline: May 31.

‡**SCIENCE IN SOCIETY JOURNALISM AWARDS**, National Association of Science Writers, Box 294, Greenlawn NY 11740. Contact: Diane McGurgan. Newspaper, magazine and broadcast science writing. Deadline: July 1.

‡**SCIENCE-WRITING AWARD IN PHYSICS AND ASTRONOMY**, American Institute of Physics, 335 E. 45th St., New York NY 10017. (212)661-9404. Contact: David Kalson. Previously published articles, booklets or books "that improve public understanding of physics and astronomy." Deadline: Jan. 10.

‡**CHARLES E. SCRIPPS AWARD**,The Scripps Howard Foundation, Box 5380, Cincinnati OH 45201. (513)977-3036. Combatting illiteracy. For newspapers, television and radio stations.

THE EDWARD WILLIS SCRIPPS AWARD, The Scripps Howard Foundation, Box 5380, Cincinnati OH 45201. (513)977-3036. Service to the First Amendment.

‡**THE SENIOR AWARD**, International Society of Dramatists, Box 1310, Miami FL 33153. (305)756-8313. Contact: Andrew Delaplaine. Previously unpublished dramatic writing by college students. Deadline: May 1.

‡*SEVENTEEN MAGAZINE*/Dell Fiction Contest, 850 Third Ave., New York NY 10022. Previously unpublished short stories from writers 13-20 years old. Deadline: Jan. 31.

SFWA NEBULA AWARDS, Science Fiction Writers of America, Inc., Box H, Wharton NJ 07885. Science fiction or fantasy in the categories of novel, novella, novelette and short story recommended by members.

MINA P. SHAUGHNESSY PRIZE, Modern Language Association, 10 Astor Place, New York NY 10003. Contact: Theresa Kirby, Administrative Assistant. Outstanding research publication in the field of teaching English language and literature.

SHELLEY MEMORIAL AWARD, Poetry Society of America, 15 Gramercy Park S., New York NY 10003. (212)254-9628. Contact: Award Director. By nomination only to a living American poet. Deadline: Dec. 31.

‡**SHORT STORY WRITERS COMPETITION**, Hemingway Days Festival, Box 4045, Key West FL 33041. (305)294-4440. Director: Michael Whalton. Unpublished short stories. Deadline: early July. Contact the Hemingway Days Festival for specific date each year.

SIERRA REPERTORY THEATRE, Box 3030, Sonora CA 95370. (209)532-3120. Producer: Dennis C. Jones. Full-length plays. Deadline: May 15.

‡**SILVER GAVEL AWARDS**, American Bar Association, 750 N. Lake Shore Dr., Chicago IL 60611. (312)988-6137. Contact: Marilyn Giblin. Previously published or broadcast works that promote "public understanding of the American system of law and justice." Deadline: Feb. 1.

‡**SIXTH ANNUAL NATIONAL LITERARY CONTEST**, Arizona Authors Association, Box 10492, Phoenix AZ 85064. (602)948-2354. Director: Boye De Mente. Unpublished poetry, short stories and essays. Deadline: July 29.

‡**C.L. SONNICHSEN BOOK AWARD**, Texas Western Press of the University of Texas at El Paso, El Paso TX 79968-0633. (915)747-5688. Press Director: Dale L. Walker. Previously unpublished nonfiction manuscript dealing with the history, literature or cultures of the Southwest. Deadline: April 1.

BRYANT SPANN MEMORIAL PRIZE, History Dept., Indiana State University, Terre Haute IN 47809. Social criticism in the tradition of Eugene V. Debs. Deadline: April 30.

SPUR AWARDS (WESTERN WRITERS OF AMERICA, INC.), WWA, 1753 Victoria, Sheridan WY 82801. (307)672-2079. Director: Barbara Ketcham. Ten categories of western: novel, historical novel, nonfiction book, juvenile nonfiction, juvenile fiction, nonfiction article, fiction short story, best TV script, movie screenplay, cover art. Also, Medicine Pipe Bearer's Award for best first novel. Deadline: Dec. 31.

STANLEY DRAMA AWARD, Wagner College, Staten Island NY 10301. (212)390-3256. Unpublished and nonprofessionally produced full-length plays or related one-acts by American playwrights. Submissions must be accompanied by completed application and written recommendation by theatre professional or drama teacher. Deadline: Aug. 11.

‡**THE AGNES LYNCH STARRETT POETRY PRIZE**, University of Pittsburgh Press, 127 N. Bellefield Ave., Pittsburgh PA 15260. (412)624-4110. First book of poetry for poets who have not had a full-length book published. Deadline. April 30.

THE WALKER STONE AWARDS, The Scripps Howard Foundation, 1100 Central Trust Tower, Cincinnati OH 45202. (513)977-3036. Editorial writing.

‡**SUMMER SOLSTICE THEATRE CONFERENCE CONTEST**, Box 1859, East Hampton NY 11937. (718)237-9303. Director: Zachary Russ. "Summer Solstice presents professional readings of nine new American plays each summer in a unique reading format that is open to the public. Ours is a developmental organization devoted to encouraging and working with new writers and new plays."

MARVIN TAYLOR PLAYWRITING AWARD, Sierra Repertory Theatre, Box 3030, Sonora CA 95370. (209)532-3120. Producing Director: Dennis C. Jones. Full-length plays. Deadline: May 15.

‡**SYDNEY TAYLOR BOOK AWARDS**, Association of Jewish Libraries, Room 1412, 122 East 42nd St., New York NY 10168. (216)991-8847. Director: Merrily F. Hart. Published fiction or nonfiction for children, picture book and body of work. Deadline: approx. Jan. 10.

SYDNEY TAYLOR MANUSCRIPT CONTEST OF AJL, (formerly The Sidney Taylor Children's Book Awards), 15 Goldsmith St., Providence RI 02906. Contact: Lillian Schwartz. Unpublished Jewish book for ages 8-12.

THE TEN BEST "CENSORED" STORIES OF 1987, Project Censored—Sonoma State University, Rohnert Park CA 94928. (707)664-2149. Award Director: Carl Jensen, Ph.D. Current published, nonfiction stories of national social significance that have been overlooked or under-reported by the news media. Deadline: March 1.

THE THEATRE LIBRARY ASSOCIATION AWARD, 111 Amsterdam Ave., New York NY 10023. Awards Committee Chair: Martha R. Mahard, Harvard Theatre Collection, Harvard College Library, Cambridge MA 02138. Book published in the United States in the field of recorded performance, including motion pictures and television. Deadline: Feb. 26.

‡**TOWNGATE THEATRE PLAYWRITING CONTEST**,Oglebay Institute, Wheeling WV 26003. (304)242-4200. Annual award for previously unproduced full-length plays. No musicals. Deadline: Jan. 1.

TOWSON STATE UNIVERSITY PRIZE FOR LITERATURE, College of Liberal Arts, Towson State University, Towson MD 21204. (301)321-2128. Award Director: Dean Annette Chappell. Book or book-length manuscript that has been accepted for publication, written by a Maryland author of no more than 40 years of age. Deadline: May 15.

HARRY S TRUMAN BOOK PRIZE, Harry S Truman Library Institute, Independence MO 64050. Secretary of the Institute: Dr. Benedict K. Zobrist. Previously published book written within a two-year period dealing primarily with the history of the United States between April 12, 1945 and January 20, 1953, or with the public career of Harry S Truman. Deadline: Jan. 20.

‡**UCROSS FOUNDATION RESIDENCY**, Ucross Rt., Box 19, Ucross WY 82835. (307)737-2291. Contact: Heather Burgess. Biannual award for artists' and scholars' resident work program. Deadline: March 1 for August-December program; Oct. 1 for January-May program.

UFO RESEARCH AWARD, Fund for UFO Research, Box 277, Mt. Rainier MD 20712. (301)779-8683. Contact: Executive Committee, Fund for UFO Research. Unscheduled cash awards for published works on UFO phenomena research or public education.

‡**UNDERGRADUATE PAPER COMPETITION IN CRYPTOLOGY**, *Cryptologia*, Rose-Hulman Institute of Technology, Terre Haute IN 47803. Contact: Editor. Unpublished papers on cryptology. Deadline: Jan. 1.

VERBATIM ESSAY COMPETITION , Verbatim, The Language Quarterly, 4 Laurel Heights, Old Lyme CT 06371. (203)434-2104. Award Director: Laurence Urdang. Unpublished articles on topic pertaining to language. Deadline: varies.

‡**VIRGINIA PRIZE FOR LITERATURE**, Virginia Commission for the Arts, 17th Floor, 101 N. 14th St., Richmond VA 23219. (804)225-3132. Contact: Cary Kimble. Unpublished novel, short stories or poetry by Virginia residents. Deadline: Feb. 2 (fiction); April 1 (poetry).

CELIA B. WAGNER AWARD, Poetry Society of America, 15 Gramercy Park St. S., New York NY 10003. (212)254-9628. Contact: Award Director. Unpublished poem. Deadline: Dec. 31.

EDWARD LEWIS WALLANT BOOK AWARD, Mrs. Irving Waltman, 3 Brighton Rd., West Hartford CT 06117. Published fiction with significance for the American Jew (novel or short stories). Deadline: Dec. 31.

‡**WHITING WRITERS' AWARDS**, Mrs. Giles Whiting Foundation, Rm. 3500, 30 Rockefeller Plaza, New York NY 10112. Director: Gerald Freund. Awards for writers nominated by foundation selectors. Direct applications and informal nominations are not accepted by the Foundation.

WICHITA STATE UNIVERSITY PLAYWRITING CONTEST, Wichita State University Theatre, WSU, Box 31, Wichita KS 67208. (316)689-3185. Contest Director: Bela Kiralyfalvi. Two or three short, unpublished, unproduced plays or full-length plays by graduate or undergraduate U.S. college students. Deadline: Feb. 15.

BELL I. WILEY PRIZE, National Historical Society, 2245 Kohn Rd., Box 8200, Harrisburg PA 17105. (717)657-9555, ext. 3301. Civil War and Reconstruction nonfiction (book). Deadline: July 31.

WILLIAM CARLOS WILLIAMS AWARD, Poetry Society of America, 15 Gramercy Park S., New York NY 10003. (212)254-9628. Contact: Award Director. Small press, nonprofit, or university press book of poetry submitted by publisher. Deadline: Dec. 31.

H.W. WILSON LIBRARY PERIODICAL AWARD, donated by H.W. Wilson Company, administered by the American Library Association, 50 E. Huron, Chicago IL 60611. (312)944-6780. Periodical published by a local, state, or regional library, library group, or association in U.S. or Canada.

‡J. J. WINSHIP BOOK AWARD, *The Boston Globe*, 135 Morissey Blvd., Boston MA 02107. (617)929-2649. New England-related book. Deadline: June 30.

WISCONSIN ARTS BOARD FELLOWSHIP PROGRAM, 107 S. Butler St., Madison WI 53703. (608)266-0190. Contact: Grants Coordinator. Literary fellowship in the categories of poetry, drama, fiction and essay/criticism for Wisconsin artists. Deadline: Sept. 12.

WITTER BYNNER FOUNDATION FOR POETRY, INC. GRANTS, Box 2188, Santa Fe NM 87504. (505)988-3251. Award Director: Steven D. Schwartz. Grants for poetry and poetry-related projects. Deadline: Feb. 1.

‡WORD BEAT PRESS FICTION BOOK AWARD, Word Beat Press, Box 22310, Flagstaff AZ 86002. Allen Woodman. Novellas and short story collections. Deadline: March 15.

WORK-IN-PROGRESS GRANT, Society of Children's Book Writers and Judy Blume, Box 296 Mar Vista, Los Angeles CA 90066. Write *SCBW* at preceding address. Two grants-one designated specifically for a contemporary novel for young people—to assist SCBW members in the completion of a specific project.

WORLD HUNGER MEDIA AWARDS, World Hunger Year/Kenny & Marianne Rogers, #1402, 261 W. 35th St., New York NY 10001. (212)226-2714. Director: Bill Ayres. Critical issues of domestic and world hunger (newspaper, periodical, film, TV, radio, photojournalism, book and cartoon, plus special achievement). Deadline: July 31.

WRITERS GUILD OF AMERICA WEST AWARDS, Cheryl Rhoden Public Relations, Writers Guild of America West, 8955 Beverly Blvd., Los Angeles CA 90048. Scripts (screen, TV and radio). Members only. Deadline: September.

‡WRITTEN WORDS COMPETITION/WRITERS-IN-PERFORMANCE INVITATIONAL, Bumbershoot, Seattle's Art Festival, Box 21134, Seattle WA 98111. (206)622-5123. Contact: Louise DiLenge. Published or unpublished poetry or literary short works and published books. Deadline: April 17.

Appendix

The Business of Freelancing

Writing may be your craft, but as a freelancer you'll also have to attend to the business side of writing to be successful. You must, as an independent business person, study the market and be prepared for occasional—or even frequent—disappointment. Freelance writing is a highly competitive profession. Even the most successful writers invest time and money in research, manuscript preparation and marketing with no guarantee their work will sell.

By buying this edition of *Writer's Market*, you have declared that you are serious about the business of freelancing. Management of your writing begins with developing a strategy, gathering ideas, identifying markets and dealing with rejection slips. You'll also need to acquire certain supplies and equipment, and before you put your finished product in the mail, you should know some basic strategies for approaching editors and preparing your queries and manuscripts.

Developing a plan

Some writers decide to write about whatever interests *them* . . . and then look for a publisher. While this is a common approach, it reduces your chances of success. Instead choose a general writing category that interests you. Study the appropriate sections of *Writer's Market*. Pay special attention to the introductions; they describe both general trends and specific details for submissions in each category. Select *several* listings that are good prospects for the writing you want to do. Then follow the suggestions in Approaching Markets later in this Appendix.

Develop *several* ideas. Based on a realistic estimate of getting your work published, make a list of the potential markets for each idea. Make the initial contact with the first market on your list, using its preferred method (query letter, outline/synopsis, manuscript, etc.). As you continue to develop each idea, keep copies of your writing and all correspondence related to it with your list of remaining markets.

If you exhaust your list of possibilities, don't give up. Re-evaluate the idea, revise it or try another angle. If your idea didn't appeal to consumer magazines, it might be right for a trade publication. In freelance writing, your chances of success increase with the number of pieces you send out.

Continue developing ideas and approaching markets. When the first query or manuscript is mailed, begin work on another idea. Identify and rank potential markets for this idea and continue the process, but don't approach a market more than once until you've received a response to your first submission.

Prepare for rejection. When a submission is returned, check the file folder of potential markets for that idea. Cross off the current market and immediately mail an appropriate submission to the next market on your list. Remember, the first editor didn't reject *you*, but simply chose not to buy your product. When you choose not to buy a certain brand of shampoo, you don't intend to personally insult the president of the company that made it. Likewise, a rejection means only that your particular writing did not fit the particular needs of the market at that time. Your job is to find the right publisher for your writing. Submit the work to another market and go back to work on another idea.

Tools of the trade

Like anyone involved in a trade or business, you need certain tools and supplies to produce your product or provide your service. Sharp pencils and yellow pads of paper will get you just so far as a freelance writer. The basic necessities for your writing business, plus some "extras" you may eventually want to have, include:

Typewriters. A well-maintained manual typewriter is adequate for many writers. Those who write fulltime often prefer an electric or electronic typewriter, which usually produce more uniform, clearer characters. Most typewriters are available in either pica or elite type. Pica type has 10 characters to a horizontal inch and elite has 12; both have six single-spaced, or three double-spaced, lines to a vertical inch. The slightly larger pica type is easier to read and many editors prefer it, but they don't object to elite.

Editors dislike, and often refuse to read, manuscripts typed in all caps or in an unusual type styles—such as script, italics or Old English. Reading these manuscripts is hard on the eyes. You should strive for clean, easy-to-read manuscripts and correspondence that reflect pride in your work and consideration for your reader.

Use a good black (never colored) typewriter ribbon and clean the keys frequently. If the enclosures of the letters a, b, d, e, g, etc., become inked in, a cleaning is overdue.

Even the best typists make errors. *Occasional* retyping over erasures is acceptable, but strikeovers give your manuscript a sloppy, careless appearance. Hiding typos with large splotches of correction fluid makes your work look amateurish; use it sparingly. Some writers prefer to use typing correction film for final drafts and correction fluid for rough drafts. Better yet, a self-correcting electric typewriter with a correction tape makes typos nearly invisible. Whatever method you use, it's best to retype a page that has several noticeable corrections. Sloppy typing is taken by many editors as a sign of sloppy work habits—and the likelihood of careless research and writing.

Types of paper. The paper you use must measure 8½x11 inches. That's a standard size and editors are adamant—they don't want unusual colors or sizes. There's a wide range of white 8½x11 papers. The cheaper ones are made from wood pulp. They will suffice, but are not recommended. Editors also discourage the use of erasable bond for manuscripts; typewriter ribbon ink on erasable bond tends to smear when handled. Don't use less than a 16-pound bond paper; 20-pound is preferred. Your best bet is paper with a 25% cotton fiber content. Its texture shows type neatly and it holds up under erasing and corrections.

You don't need fancy letterhead stationery for your correspondence with editors. Plain bond paper is fine; just type your name, address, phone number and the date at the top of the page—centered or in the right-hand corner. If you decide to order letterhead, make it as simple and businesslike as possible. Never use letterhead for typing your manuscript.

Photocopies and carbons. Always make copies of your manuscripts and correspondence before putting them in the mail. Don't learn the hard way—as many writers have—that manuscripts get lost in the mail and publishers sometimes go out of business without returning submissions. While some writers continue to make carbon copies of their correspondence with editors, most depend on photocopy machines for duplicating manuscripts. In general, use carbon copies for your own records; never send a carbon to an editor unless the original correspondence has been lost.

You might want to make several copies of your manuscript while it is still clean and crisp.

Some writers keep their original manuscript as a file copy and submit good quality photocopies. Submitting copies can save you the expense and effort of retyping a manuscript if it becomes lost in the mail. The quality of photocopies varies, so visit print shops in your area until you find one that makes quality photocopies.

If you submit a copy, include a personal note explaining whether or not you are making a simultaneous or multiple submission. Many editors refuse to consider material they think is being submitted simultaneously. See Approaching Markets later in this Appendix.

Some writers include a self-addressed postcard with a photocopied submission; in their cover letter they suggest that if the editor is not interested in the manuscript, it may be tossed out and a reply returned on the postcard. This practice is often recommended for dealing with foreign markets. Submitting disposable photocopies costs the writer some photocopy expense, but saves on large postage bills.

The cost of personal photocopiers is coming down, but they remain much too expensive for most writers. If you need to make a large number of photocopies, you should ask your print shop about quantity discounts. One advantage of a personal computer is that it can quickly print copies of any text you have composed on it.

Computers and accessories. A personal computer can make a writer's work much more efficient. Writing, revising and editing are usually faster and easier on a computer than on a typewriter. Many writers rely on their computers to give them fresh, readable copy as they revise rough drafts into finished manuscripts. When a manuscript is written on a computer, it can come out of the computer in three ways: as hard copy from the computer's printer; stored on a removable electronic disk (often called a "floppy") that can be read by some other computers; or as an electronic transfer over telephone lines using a modem (a device that allows one computer to transmit to another).

● Hard copy—Most editors are receptive to a computer printout submission if it looks like a neatly typed manuscript. Some of the older and less expensive printers produce only a low-quality dot-matrix printout with hard-to-read, poorly shaped letters and numbers. Not many editors are willing to read these manuscripts. New dot-matrix printers can produce letter quality printouts that are almost indistinguishable from a typewritten manuscript. When you submit hard copy to an editor, be sure that you use quality paper. Some computer printers use the standard bond paper you use in a typewriter. Others are equipped with a tractor-feed that pulls continuous form paper with holes along the edges through the machine. If you use continuous form paper, be sure to remove the perforated tabs on each side and separate the pages.

● Disk—You'll find that more publishers are accepting or even requesting electronic submissions on disk. If your disk can be read by the publisher's computer, the publisher won't need to have your manuscript typeset by another person.

● Modem—Some publishers who accept submissions on disk will also accept electronic submissions by modem. This is the fastest method of getting your manuscript to the publisher.

Before sending anything electronically, by either disk or modem, you'll need to query the publisher for details. Your computer and the publisher's must be compatible. When you query about electronic submissions, include the name of your computer, its manufacturer and model; mention the operating system (CPM or MS-DOS) and word processing software you use. Because most editors prefer that you submit hard copy along with any electronic submission, you may wonder why you should even consider using disk or modem. Editors know they can revise manuscripts more quickly on a computer screen as well as save typesetting expenses. Some publishers also pay more for manuscripts submitted on disk or modem.

Assorted supplies. Where will you put all your manuscripts and correspondence? A two- or four-drawer filing cabinet with an ample supply of file folders is the obvious choice—but often too expensive. Many writers make do with manila envelopes and cardboard boxes. The most important thing is to organize and label your correspondence, manuscripts, ideas, submission records, clippings, etc., so you can find them when you need them. See also the sections on Recording Submissions and Bookkeeping in this Appendix.

You will also need stamps and envelopes; see Mailing Submissions and Postage by the Page for the U.S. and Canada. If you decide to invest in a camera to increase your sales of nonfiction manuscripts, you'll find details in the section on Approaching Markets and Mailing Submissions.

Approaching markets

Before submitting a manuscript to a market, be sure you've done the following:
- Familiarize yourself with the publication or other type of market that interests you. Your first sales will probably be to markets you already know through your reading. If you find a listing in *Writer's Market* that seems a likely home for an idea you've been working on, study a sample copy or book catalog to see if your idea fits in with their current topics.
- Always request writer's guidelines, even if you can read a sample copy at the library. Guidelines give a publication's exact requirements for submissions and will help focus your query letter or manuscript. If a publication has undergone editorial changes since this edition of *Writer's Market* went to press, those changes will usually be reflected in its writer's guidelines. The response to your request for guidelines can also tell you if a publication has folded or if it has an unreasonably long response time.
- Check submission requirements. A publication that accepts only queries may not respond at all to a writer who submits a manuscript and cover letter. Don't send an unpublished manuscript to a publication that publishes only reprints. If you're submitting photos, be sure the publication reviews prints or slides, and find out if they require model releases and captions. An editor is impressed when a writer carefully studies a publication before making a submission.
- With submissions or correspondence, enclose a stamped, self-addressed envelope. Editors appreciate the convenience and the savings in postage. Some editorial offices deal with such a large volume of mail that their policies will not allow them to respond to mail that does not include a SASE. If you're submitting to a foreign market, enclose a SAE with IRCs purchased from the post office.

Those are the basics; now you're ready to learn the details of what you should send as you contact an editor.

Query letters. A query letter is a brief, but detailed, letter written to interest an editor in your manuscript. Some beginners are hesitant to query, thinking an editor can more fairly judge an idea by seeing the entire manuscript. Actually most editors of nonfiction prefer to be queried.

Do your best writing when you sit down to compose your query. There is no query formula that will guarantee success, but there are some points to consider before you begin:
- Queries are single-spaced business letters, usually limited to one page. Address the current editor by name, if possible. Do not immediately address an editor by a first name; some editors are offended by unwarranted familiarity. Wait until you receive a response and follow the editor's lead.
- Your major goal is to convince the editor that your idea would be of interest to his readership—and that you are the best writer for the job.
- Be sure you use a strong opening that will pique the editor's interest. Some queries begin with a paragraph that approximates the lead of the intended article.
- Briefly detail the structure of the article. Give some facts and anecdotes, and mention people you intend to interview. Give the editor enough information to make him or her want to know more.
- Mention any special training or experience that qualifies you to write the article.

[date]

Ms. Mary Farrell
Senior Associate Editor
Savvy
3 Park Ave.
New York NY 10016

Dear Ms. Farrell:

   I'd like to propose an executive profile of Frances Grill, owner and founder of Click Model Management, a brash young agency (launched in 1980) which Newsweek magazine credits with having "almost single-handedly changed the face of modeling in this country."

   When other agents were pushing look-alike blondes, Grill créated a quirky, imperfect style emphasizing individuality, with such successes as turning 29-year-old Isabella Rossellini, daughter of Ingrid Bergman, into the record holder for an exclusive modeling contract: $2 million over five years from Lancôme Cosmetics.

   Grill has overcome tremendous odds to succeed. In a poor Sicilian neighborhood in Brooklyn where Grill was raised, her father used to park his children in a local orphanage when times got tight. After spending many years as a photographer's representative, 58-year-old Grill started her agency with a $100,000 investment, undaunted by the market stranglehold of the Big Four agencies—Ford ($30 million a year in billings), Zoli ($25 million), Wilhelmina ($23 million to $28 million), and Elite ($27 million). From $300,000 in billings the first year, Click now bills $8 million a year. Grill is now venturing into film, as well, with a newly created talent agency, Flick.

   I believe this profile would be of great interest to your readers. I'll write it with L. Scott Morgan, who worked with me on a modeling article I just did for Cosmopolitan. My writing credits also include Family Circle, Harper's Magazine, Playgirl, Glamour, Writer's Digest, Publishers Weekly, and 15 other magazines and newspapers. I've also written a book, How to Sell Every Magazine Article You Write (Writer's Digest Books, 1986). I've been a literary agent for the past 12 years, and have taught writing courses at Parson's School of Design.

   I'll look forward to your reaction to this exclusive submision.

                                   Sincerely yours,

                                   Lisa Collier Cool

Magazine query. *This sample query for a magazine article, typed on letterhead stationery, presents information effectively and resulted in an assignment. Reprinted from* How to Write Irresistible Query Letters, *by Lisa Collier Cool (Writer's Digest Books). Copyright ©️ 1987 by Lisa Collier Cool.*

[date]

Ms. Ann Beneduce, Director
Philomel Books
Putnam Publishing Group
200 Madison Ave.
New York NY 10016

Dear Ms. Beneduce:

For seven years the United Nations Conference on the Law of the Sea has been negotiating agreements governing the use of the world's seas and the sharing of their resources. This summer they're meeting again in Geneva on some of the tougher issues.

The Law of the Sea is the subject of a book I'd like to do for young people, and an outline is enclosed.

I have previously published four juveniles with G.P. Putnam in their "Let's Go" series and adult books with Arco (The Private Pilot's Dictionary and Handbook) and Cornerstone Library (How to Make Money in Your Spare Time by Writing). My latest books for Writer's Digest are Law and the Writer (1978) and Jobs for Writers (1980).

The enclosed book idea would seem to have marketing potential not only in schools, but also in tourist attractions such as Planet Ocean in Miami, Sea World in California and other ocean-related locations.

May I have your opinion on this idea at your convenience?

Sincerely,

Kirk Polking

Book query. *This query was accompanied by a three-page outline of the proposed book. The author and book publisher revised the initial proposal and eventually published* Oceans of the World: Our Essential Resource, *addressing the social, political, economic and legal issues in ocean exploration and use. Printed with permission of the author.*

- If you have prior writing experience, you may mention this; if not, there's no need to call attention to the fact. Some editors will also look at clips of your published work. If possible, submit something related to your idea, either in topic or style.
- If photos are available, let the editor know.
- Your closing paragraph may include a direct request to do the article; it may specify the date the manuscript can be completed and an approximate length.
- Don't discuss fees or request advice from the editor.
- Fiction is rarely queried, but if a fiction editor requests a query, briefly describe the main theme and story line, including the conflict and resolution of your story.
- Some writers state politely in their query letter that after a specified date (slightly beyond the listed reporting time), they will assume the editor is not currently interested in their topic and will submit their query elsewhere. For more information about query letters, read *How to Write Irresistible Query Letters*, by Lisa Collier Cool (Writer's Digest Books).

Cover letters. A brief cover letter enclosed with your manuscript is helpful in personalizing a submission. If you have previously queried the editor on the article or book, the note should be a brief reminder: "Here is the piece on the city's missing funds, which we discussed previously. I look forward to hearing from you at your earliest convenience." Don't use the letter to make a sales pitch. Nothing you can say now will make the editor decide in your favor; the manuscript must stand alone.

If you are submitting to a market that considers complete manuscripts, your cover letter should tell the editor something about you—your publishing history, availability to promote the book, and any particular qualifications you have for writing the enclosed manuscript.

If the manuscript you are submitting is a photocopy, indicate whether it is a simultaneous submission. An editor may assume it is, unless you tell him otherwise—and some are offended by writers using this marketing technique. Only send simultaneous submissions to markets that state they will consider such submissions.

Book proposals. Book proposals are some combination of a cover letter, a synopsis, an outline and/or two or three sample chapters. The exact combination of these will depend on the publisher.

Some editors use the terms synopsis and outline interchangeably. If the publisher requests only a synopsis or an outline, not both, be sure you know which format the publisher prefers. Either a synopsis or outline is appropriate for a novel, but you may find an outline is more effective for a nonfiction book.

- A synopsis is a very brief summary of your book. Cover the basic plot or theme of your book and reveal the ending. Make sure your synopsis flows well, is interesting and easy to read.
- An outline covers the highlights of your book chapter-by-chapter. If your outline is for a novel, include all major characters, the main plot, subplots and any pertinent details. An outline may run three to 30 pages, depending upon the complexity and length of your book. Be sure your outline is clearly stated and doesn't become such a tangle of ideas and events that you lose your reader.
- Sample chapters are also requested by many editors. Some editors are interested in the first two or three chapters to see how well you develop your book. Others want a beginning chapter, a chapter from the middle of your book, and the final chapter, so they can see how well you follow through.

Reprints. You can get more mileage—and money—out of your research and writing time by marketing your previously published material for reprint sales. You may use a photocopy of your original manuscript and/or tearsheets from the publication in which it originally appeared. With your reprint submission be sure to inform the editor that you are marketing this article as a reprint, especially if you're sending a photocopy without tearsheets. The editor will need to know when and in what publication it appeared.

If you are marketing for reprint an article that has not yet been published by the original purchaser, inform editors that it may not be used before it has made its initial appearance.

Photographs and slides. The availability of good quality photos can be the deciding factor when an editor is considering a manuscript. Some publications also offer additional pay for photos accepted with a manuscript. When submitting black and white prints, send 8x10 glossies, unless the editor indicates another preference. The universally accepted format for color transparencies is 35mm; few buyers will look at color prints.

On all your photos and slides, you should stamp or print your copyright notice and "Return to:" followed by your name, address and phone number. Rubber stamps are preferred for labeling photos as they are less likely to cause damage; you can order them from many stationery or office supply stores. If using a pen on photos, be careful not to damage them by pressing too hard or allowing ink to bleed through the paper.

● Captions should be typed on a sheet of paper and taped to the bottom of the back of the prints. The caption should fold over the front of the photo so the buyer can fold the paper back for easy reading.

● Submit prints rather than negatives, and consider having duplicates made of your slides. Don't risk having your original negative or slide lost or damaged. Look for a photography lab that can make a high quality copy.

Manuscript mechanics

A unique work may be tossed aside by an editor who refuses to read a handwritten manuscript; and fancy typefaces, coffee stains, or dog-eared pages rarely make a favorable impression. Follow these basic rules of manuscript mechanics and you will present your work in its best form.

Manuscript format. Do not use a cover sheet or title page. Use a binder only if you are submitting a play or a television or movie script. You may use a paper clip to hold pages together, but never use staples.

The upper corners of the first page contain important information about you and your manuscript. This information is always single-spaced. In the upper left corner list your name, address, phone number and Social Security number. In the upper right corner indicate the approximate word count for the manuscript, the rights you are offering for sale and your copyright notice (© 1988 Chris Jones). A handwritten copyright symbol is acceptable. For a book manuscript do not specify the rights you are offering; that will be covered in your contract. Do not number the first page of your manuscript.

Center the title in capital letters one-third of the way down the page. To center, set the tabulator to stop halfway between the right and left edges of the page. Count the letters in the title, including spaces and punctuation, and backspace half that number. Type the title. Set your typewriter to double-space. Type "by" centered one double-space under your title, and type your name or pseudonym centered one double-space beneath that.

After the title and byline, drop down two double-spaces, paragraph indent, and begin the body of your manuscript. Paragraph indentation is five spaces. Margins should be about 1¼ inches on all sides of each full page of typewritten manuscript. You may lightly pencil in a line to remind you when you reach the bottom margin of your page, but be sure to erase it before submitting your manuscript.

On every page after the first, type your last name, a dash and the page number in the upper left corner. The title of your manuscript may, but need not, be typed beneath this. Page number two would read: Jones-2. If you are using a pseudonym, type your real name, followed by your pen name in parentheses, then a dash and the page number: Jones (Smith)-2. Some writers also put the manuscript title on this line. Then drop down two double-spaces and continue typing. Follow this format throughout your manuscript.

If you are submitting novel chapters, leave one-third of the first page of each chapter blank before typing the title. Subsequent pages should include the author's last name, the page number, a shortened form of the book's title, and a chapter number in the upper left margin. Use arabic numerals (1, 2, 3, etc.) for chapter numbers.

When submitting poetry, the poems should be typed single-spaced (double-space between stanzas), one poem per page. For a long poem requiring more than one page, paper clip the pages together.

On the final page of your manuscript, after you've typed your last word and period, skip three double spaces and center the words "The End" or, if it's nonfiction, some writers use the old newspaper telegrapher's symbol —30— which indicates the same thing.

Estimating word count. To estimate word count in manuscripts of up to 25 pages, count the exact number of words on three full pages of your manuscript (not the first or last page). Count abbreviations and short words such as "a" and "by" as one word each. Divide this word count by three and multiply the result by the total number of pages. Round this number to the nearest 100 words. On manuscripts of more than 25 pages, count five pages instead of three and follow the same process, dividing by five.

Mailing submissions

No matter what size manuscript you're mailing, always include sufficient return postage, and a self-addressed envelope large enough to contain your manuscript if it is returned. If you use a postage meter on the SASE instead of stamps, be aware of postal regulations concerning metered postage. If the meter stamp has a date, you must mark the envelope "Postage prepaid by sender" since the SASE may be used to return your manuscript weeks or months later.

A manuscript of fewer than six pages may be folded in thirds and mailed as if it were a letter, using a #10 (business-size) envelope. The enclosed SASE should be a #10 envelope folded in thirds (though these are sometimes torn when a letter opener catches in one of the folds), or a #9 envelope which will slip into the mailing envelope without being folded.

For a manuscript of six or more pages, use 9x12 envelopes for both mailing and return. The return SASE may be folded in half.

A book manuscript should be mailed in a sturdy, well-wrapped box. Your typing paper or envelope box is a suitable mailer. Enclose a self-addressed mailing label and paper clip your return postage stamps to the label.

Always mail photos and slides First Class. The rougher handling received by Fourth Class mail could damage them. If you are concerned about losing prints or slides, send them certified or registered mail. For any photo submission that is mailed separately from a manuscript, enclose a separate self-addressed label, adequate return postage, and an envelope. Never submit photos or slides mounted in glass.

To mail up to 20 prints, use photo mailers that are stamped "Photos—Do Not Bend" and contain two cardboard inserts to sandwich your prints. Or use a 9x12 manila envelope, write "Photos—Do Not Bend" and devise your own cardboard inserts. Some photography supply shops also carry heavy cardboard envelopes that are reusable.

When mailing numerous prints, such as 25 to 50 prints for a photo book, pack them in a sturdy cardboard box. A box for typing paper or photo paper is an adequate mailer. If, after packing both manuscript and photos, there's empty space in the box, slip in enough cardboard inserts to fill the box. Wrap the box securely.

To mail transparencies, first slip them into protective vinyl sleeves, then mail as you would prints. If you're mailing a number of sheets, use a cardboard box as for photos above.

U.S. Postage by the Page

by Carolyn Hardesty

Writers have the satisfaction of "finishing" their work several times. After the relief of completing the first draft, each revision and eventually the final typing give a temporary sensation of being done. But the *finishing* feels most complete when you seal the envelope, write *First Class* on it, and tuck it into the mail slot.

How often is this last stage delayed by a 20-minute wait behind customers who are stamp collectors or who have 10 letters to certify? Writers, who have more ideas than time, don't need that added frustration. Try these suggestions.

For short manuscripts or long queries, use a business-size envelope and up to five pages with a 22¢ stamp. If you are including a business-size SASE (as you should), four pages is the limit. Another option for brief submissions is a 6x9 envelope. With SASE and up to seven sheets, it can be mailed for $.39. (The return envelope will need $.39 also, unless the manuscript is three or fewer pages). Some editors appreciate the ease in handling and reading a manuscript folded once instead of twice.

Another option is Third Class mail, which travels slower but costs less than First Class after the first four ounces.

The chart below can simplify the postal process and save you time. Postage rates are listed by numbers of pages (using 20-lb paper) for First Class packages up to 12 ounces. After the first ounce (22¢), the increments are 17¢. The post office sells a convenient 39¢ stamp and also 17¢ stamps, so a stock of those denominations will allow you to stamp and mail your manuscripts in any dropbox as easily at midnight as noon.

Note: A postal rate increase had been proposed but not implemented when *Writer's Market* went to press. The proposal would raise the price of one First Class stamp from 22¢ to 25¢. Certified and registered mail, along with the cost of insurance, also were slated for increases. Third Class mail would range from 25¢ to $1.50 under the proposal.

First Class Postage Rates

ounces	9x12 envelope, 9x12 SASE number of pages	9x12 SASE (for return trips) number of pages	First Class Postage	Third Class Postage
under 2	. . .	1 to 2	$ .32*	$***
2	1 to 4	3 to 8	.39	.39
3	5 to 10	9 to 12	.56	.56
4	11 to 16	13 to 19	.73	.73
5	17 to 21	20 to 25	.90	.88
6	22 to 27	26 to 30	1.07	.88
7	28 to 32	31 to 35	1.24	.98
8	33 to 38	36 to 41	1.41	.98
9	39 to 44	42 to 46	1.58	1.08
10	45 to 49	47 to 52	1.75	1.08
11	50 to 55	53 to 57	1.92	1.18
12	56 to 61	58 to 63	2.09	1.18

*includes an assessment for over-sized mail that is light in weight

You'll have to go to the post office if your manuscript includes photos and cardboard insert or special cardboard envelope—or if you need any of the following services:

● First Class packages weighing more than 12 ounces are charged according to geographical zones. This is true also for all weights of Fourth Class (or book rate) mail.

● Insurance (for typing and production costs) is 50¢ for $25 liability; $1.10 covers costs to $50; and $1.40 provides insurance to $100.

Carolyn Hardesty, as a freelance writer and graduate student, doesn't have time for post office lines. She is pursuing a Ph.D in American Studies at the University of Iowa and is editor of Iowa Woman.

Canadian Postage by the Page

by Barbara R. Murrin

The following chart is for the convenience of Canadian writers sending domestic mail and American writers sending an SAE with IRCs or Canadian stamps for return of a manuscript from Canadian publishers. For complete postal assistance, use in conjunction with Carolyn Hardesty's U.S. Postage by the Page.

In a #10 (business-size) envelope, you can have up to five pages for $.36 within Canada or $.42 to U.S. If enclosing SASE, four pages is the limit. (If using 9x13 envelopes, send one page less than indicated on chart.)

First Class Postage Rates

Weight up to	9x12 envelope, 9x12 SASE number of pages*	9x12 SASE (for return trips) number of pages	First Class to Canada	U.S.
30 g/1.07 oz.	.....	1 to 3	$ .36	$ .42***
50 g/1.78 oz.	1 to 4	4 to 7	.55	.60
100 g/3.5 oz.	5 to 14	8-18	.73	.91
150 g/5.3 oz.	15 to 25	19-28	.96	1.20
200 g/7.1 oz.	26 to 36	29 to 39	1.20	1.50
250 g/8.9 oz.	37 to 47	40 to 50	1.44	1.80
300 g/10.7 oz.	48 to 57	51 to 61	1.68	2.10
350 g/12.5 oz.	58 to 68	62 to 71	1.93	2.40
400 g/14.2 oz.	69 to 79	72 to 82	2.16	2.70
450 g/16 oz.	80 to 90	83 to 93	2.41	3.00
500 g/17.8 oz.	91 to 101	94 to 104	2.64	3.50
1 kg/2.2 lbs.	102 to 208	105 to 212	**	6.50

			In Canada	Air Parcel to U.S.
1.5 kg	209 to 315	213 to 319	**	$8.00
2.0 kg	316 to 422	320 to 426	**	8.95
2.5 kg	423 to 529	427 to 533	**	9.90

*based on 20 lb. paper and two adhesive labels per envelope

**When mailing parcels 1 kg and over within Canada, rates vary according to destination. Check with post office for each.

***IRCs are work $.42 Canadian postage. Although an IRC is worth $.42 postage in Canada, it will cost you $.80 to buy in the U.S.

Barbara Murrin, *is a business and music teacher and a freelance writer.*

Types of mail service

• First Class is the most expensive way of mailing a manuscript, but many writers prefer it. First Class mail generally receives better handling and is delivered more quickly. Mail sent First Class is forwarded if the addressee has moved, and is returned automatically if it is undeliverable.

• Fourth Class rates are available for packages that weigh 16 ounces or more and are to be delivered within the United States. Pack materials carefully when mailing Fourth Class as they will be handled the same as Parcel Post—roughly. If a letter is enclosed with your Fourth Class package, write "First Class Letter Enclosed" on the package and add adequate First Class postage for your letter. To make sure your package will be returned to you if it is undeliverable, print "Return Postage Guaranteed" under your address.

• Certified Mail must be signed for when it reaches its destination. If requested, a signed receipt is returned to the sender. There is a 75¢ charge for this service, in addition to the required postage.

• Registered Mail is a high security method of mailing. The package is signed in and out of every office it passes through, and a receipt is returned to the sender when the package reaches its destination. This service costs $3.60, in addition to the postage required for the item.

• United Parcel Service may be slightly cheaper than First Class postage if you drop the package off at UPS yourself. UPS cannot legally carry First Class mail, so your cover letter would need to be mailed separately. Check with UPS in your area for current rates. The cost depends on the weight of your package and the distance to its destination.

• Overnight mail services are provided by both the U.S. Postal Service and numerous private firms. These services can be useful if you find yourself in a situation where a manuscript or revisions *must* be at an editor's office. More information on next day service is available from the U.S. Post Office in your area, or check your telephone directory under "Delivery Service."

Other important details

• Money orders should be used if you are ordering sample copies or supplies and do not have checking services available to you. You'll have a receipt and money orders are traceable. Money orders for up to $25 can be purchased from the U.S. Postal Service for 75¢. Banks, savings and loans, and some commercial businesses also carry money orders; their fees vary. *Never* send cash through the mail for sample copies.

• Insurance is available for items handled by the U.S. Postal Service, but is payable only on typing fees or the tangible value of the item in the package—such as typing paper—so your best insurance when mailing manuscripts is to keep a copy of what you send.

• When corresponding with foreign publications and publishers, International Reply Coupons (IRCs) must be used for return postage. Surface rates in foreign countries differ from those in the U.S., and U.S. postage stamps are of no use there. Currently, one IRC costs 80¢ and is sufficient for one ounce traveling at surface rate; two are recommended for air mail return. Many writers dealing with foreign publishers mail photocopies and direct the publisher to dispose of them if they're not appropriate for current editorial needs; when using this method, it's best to also set a deadline for withdrawing your manuscript from consideration.

• International money orders are also available from the post office at a slightly higher fee than those for domestic use.

Recording submissions

An amazing number of writers seem to think once they've mailed a manuscript, the situation is out of their hands. They no longer have control of their work and all they can do is sit and wait. But submitting a manuscript doesn't mean you've lost control of it. Manage your writing business by keeping copies of all manuscripts and correspondence, and by recording the dates of submissions.

One way to keep track of your manuscripts is to use a record of submissions that includes the date sent, title, market, editor and enclosures (such as photos). You should also note the date of the editor's response and—if the manuscript was accepted—the publication date and payment information. You might want to keep a similar record just for queries.

Also remember to keep a separate file for each manuscript or idea along with its list of potential markets. You may want to keep track of expected reporting times on a calendar, too. Then you'll know when a market has been slow to respond.

Bookkeeping

Whether you are profitable in your writing or not, you'll need to keep accurate financial records. Such records are necessary to let you know how you're doing. And, of course, the government is also interested in your financial activities.

If you have another source of income, you should plan to keep separate records for your writing expenses and income. Some writers open separate checking accounts used only for their writing-related expenses.

The best financial records are the ones that get used and usually the simpler the form the more likely it will be used regularly. Get in the habit of recording every transaction related to your writing. You can start at any time; it doesn't need to be on January 1. Because you're likely to have expenses long before you have any income, start keeping your records whenever you make your first purchase related to writing—such as this copy of *Writer's Market*.

A simple bookkeeping system. For most freelance writers, a simple type of "single-entry" bookkeeping is adequate. The heart of the single-entry system is the journal, an accounting book available at any stationery or office supply store. You record in the journal all of the expenses and income of your writing business.

The single-entry journal's form is similar to a standard check register. Instead of withdrawals and deposits, you record expenses and income. You'll need to describe each transaction clearly—including the date; the source of the income (or the vendor of your purchase); a description of what was sold or bought; whether the payment was by cash, check or credit card; and the amount of the transaction.

Your receipt file. Keep all documentation pertaining to your writing expenses or income. This is true whether you have started a bookkeeping journal or not. For every payment you receive, you should have a check stub from the publisher's check, a cover letter stating the amount of payment, or your own bank records of the deposit. For every check you write to pay business expenses, you should have a record in your check register as well as a cancelled check. Keep credit card receipts, too. And for every cash purchase, you should have a receipt from the vendor—especially if the amount is over $25. For small expenses, you can usually keep a list if you don't record them in a journal.

Tax information

Many federal income tax law changes were made last year that affect freelance writers. Income averaging was abolished, home office deductions and estimated tax payment rules changed. In addition, a business had to be profitable two out of five years under the old law to avoid being treated as a hobby. Under the new law, the business has to be profitable three out of five years. While we cannot offer you tax advice or interpretations, we can suggest several sources for the most current information.

● Call your local IRS office. Look in the white pages of the telephone directory under U.S. Government—Internal Revenue Service. Someone will be able to respond to your request for IRS publications and tax forms or other information. Ask about the IRS Tele-tax service, a series of recorded messages you can hear by dialing on a touch-tone phone. If you need answers to complicated questions, ask to speak with a Taxpayer Service Specialist.

● Obtain the basic IRS publications. You can order them by phone or mail from any IRS office; most are available at libraries and some post offices. Start with *Your Federal Income Tax* (Publication 17) and *Tax Guide for Small Business* (Publication 334). These are both comprehensive, detailed guides—you'll need to find the regulations that apply to you and ignore the rest. You may also want to get a copy of *Business Use of Your Home* (Publication 587).

● Consider other information sources. Many public libraries have detailed tax instructions available on tape. Some colleges and universities offer free assistance in preparing tax returns. And if you decide to consult a professional tax preparer, the fee is a deductible business expense on your tax return.

Rights and the writer

We find that writers and editors may define rights in different ways. To eliminate any misinterpretations, read the following definitions of each right—and you'll see the definitions upon which editors updated the *rights* information in their listings.

Every so often, we hear from a writer who is confused because an editor claims to never acquire or buy rights. The truth is, any time an editor buys a story or asks you for permission to publish a story in return for contributor copies, this editor is asking you for *rights* (even when he doesn't use the word rights). Occasionally people start magazines related to their areas of expertise but they don't have extensive knowledge of publishing terms and practices. If you sense that an editor is interested in getting stories but doesn't seem to know what his and the writer's responsibilities are regarding rights, be wary. In such a case, you'll want to explain what rights you're offering (preferably one-time rights only) and that you expect additional payment for subsequent use of your work. Writers may also experience a situation in which they agree to sell first rights, for example, to a magazine but then never receive a check for the manuscript and subsequent inquiries bring no response. In a case like this, we recommend that the writer send a certified letter, return receipt requested, notifying the magazine that the manuscript is being withdrawn from that publication for submission elsewhere. There is no industry standard for how long a writer should wait before using this procedure. The best bet is to check the *Writer's Market* listing for what the magazine lists as its usual reporting time and then, after a reasonable wait beyond that, institute the withdrawal.

Selling rights to your writing. The Copyright Law that went into effect Jan. 1, 1978, said writers were only selling one-time rights to their work unless they—and the publisher—agreed otherwise in writing. In some cases, however, a writer may have little say in the rights sold to an editor. The beginning writer, in fact, can jeopardize a sale by arguing with an editor who is likely to have other writers on call who are eager to please. As long as there are more writers than there are markets, this situation will remain the same.

As a writer acquires skill, reliability, and professionalism on the job, he becomes more valued by editors—and rights become a more important consideration. Though a beginning writer will accept modest payment just to get in print, an experienced writer cannot afford to give away good writing just to see a byline. At this point a writer must become concerned with selling reprints of articles already sold to one market, or using sold articles as chapters in a book on the same topic, or seeking markets for the same material overseas, or offering work to TV or the movies. Such dramatic rights can be meaningful for both fiction and nonfiction writers.

You should strive to keep as many rights to your work as you can from the outset, because before you can resell any piece of writing you must own the rights to negotiate. If you have sold "all rights" to an article, for instance, it can be reprinted without your permission, and without additional payment to you. Many writers will not deal with editors who buy all rights. What an editor buys will determine whether you can resell your own work. Here is a list of the rights most editors and publishers seek. (Book rights will be covered by the contract submitted to the writer by a book publisher. The writer does not indicate any such rights offered on the first page of a book manuscript.)

● First Serial Rights—First serial rights means the writer offers the newspaper or magazine the right to publish the article, story or poem for the first time in any periodical. All other rights to the material belong to the writer. Variations on this right are, for example, first North American serial rights. Some magazines use this purchasing technique to obtain the right to publish first in both the U.S. and Canada since many U.S. magazines are circulated in Canada. If an editor had purchased only first U.S. serial rights, a Canadian magazine could come out with prior or simultaneous publication of the same material. When material is excerpted from a book scheduled to be published and it appears in a magazine or newspaper prior to book publication, this is also called first serial rights.

● First North American Serial Rights—Magazine publishers that distribute in both the United States and Canada frequently buy these first rights covering publication in both countries.

● One-Time Rights—This differs from first serial rights in that the buyer has no guarantee he will be the first to publish the work. One-time rights often apply to photos, but also apply to writing sold to more than one market over a period of time. See also Simultaneous Rights.

● Second Serial (Reprint) Rights—This gives a newspaper or magazine the opportunity to print an article, poem or story after it has already appeared in another newspaper or magazine. The term is also used to refer to the sale of part of a book to a newspaper or magazine after a book has been published, whether or not there has been any first serial publication. Income derived from second serial rights to book material is often shared 50/50 by author and book publisher.

● All Rights—Some magazines buy all rights, either because of the top prices they pay for material, or the fact that they have book publishing interests or foreign magazine connections. A writer who sells an article, story or poem to a magazine under these terms forfeits the right to use his material in its present form elsewhere. If he signs a work-for-hire agreement, he signs away all rights and the copyright to the company making the assignment. If the writer thinks he may want to use his material later (perhaps in book form), he must avoid submitting to such markets or refuse payment and withdraw his material if he discovers it later. Ask the editor whether he is willing to buy only first rights instead of all rights before you agree to an assignment or a sale. Some editors will reassign rights to a writer after a given period, such as one year. It's worth an inquiry in writing.

● Simultaneous Rights—This term covers articles and stories sold to publications (primarily religious magazines) that do not have overlapping circulations. A Catholic publication, for example, might be willing to buy simultaneous rights to a Christmas story they like very much, even though they know a Presbyterian magazine may be publishing the same story in its Christmas issue. Publications that buy simultaneous rights indicate this fact in their listings in *Writer's Market*. Always advise an editor when the material you are sending is a simultaneous submission.

● Foreign Serial Rights—Can you resell a story you have had published in the U.S. or North America to a foreign magazine? If you sold only first U.S. serial rights or first North American rights, yes, you are free to market your story abroad. Of course, you must contact a foreign magazine that buys material that has previously appeared in U.S. or North American periodicals. (See the *International Writers and Artists Yearbook*, distributed by Writer's Digest Books, for foreign markets).

● Syndication Rights—This is a division of serial rights. For example, a book publisher may sell the rights to a newspaper syndicate to print a book in 12 installments in each of 20 U.S. newspapers. If they did this prior to book publication, they would be syndicating first serial rights to the book. If they did this after book publication, they would be syndicating second serial rights to the book. In either case, the syndicate would be taking a commission on the sales it made to newspapers, so the remaining percentage would be split between author and publisher.

● Subsidiary Rights—The rights, other than book publication rights, that should be specified in a book contract. These may include various serial rights, dramatic rights, translation rights, etc. The contract lists what percentage of these sales goes to the author and what percentage to the publisher.

• Dramatic, Television and Motion Picture Rights—This means the writer is selling his material for use on the stage, in television or in the movies. Often a one-year option to buy such rights is offered (generally for 10% of the total price). The interested party then tries to sell the idea to other people—actors, directors, studios or television networks, etc.—who become part of the project, which then becomes a script. Some properties are optioned over and over again, but fail to become dramatic productions. In such cases, the writer can sell his rights again and again—as long as there is interest in the material. Though dramatic, TV and motion picture rights are more important to the fiction writer than to the nonfiction writer, producers today are increasingly interested in nonfiction material; many biographies and articles are being dramatized.

Communicate and clarify. Before submitting material to a market, check its listing in this book to see what rights are purchased. Most editors will discuss rights they wish to purchase before an exchange of money occurs. Some buyers are adamant about what rights they will accept; others will negotiate. In any case, the rights purchased should be stated specifically in writing sometime during the course of the sale, usually in a letter or memo of agreement. If no rights are transferred in writing, and the material is sold for use in a collective work (a work that derives material from a number of contributors), you are authorizing unlimited use of your piece in that work or updates of that work or later collective works in the same series. Thus, you can't collect reprint fees if the rights weren't spelled out in advance, in writing.

Give as much attention to the rights you haven't sold as you do to the rights you have sold. Be aware of the rights you retain, with an eye for additional sales.

Regardless of the rights you sell or don't sell, make sure all parties involved in any sale understand the terms of the sale. Clarify what is being sold *before* any actual sale, and do it in writing. Communication, coupled with these guidelines and some common sense, will preclude misunderstandings with editors over rights.

Keep in mind, too, that if there is a change in editors from the edition of *Writer's Market* you're using, the rights bought may also change.

Copyrighting your writing

The copyright law, effective since Jan. 1, 1978, protects your writing, unequivocally recognizes the creator of the work as its owner, and grants the creator all the rights, benefits and privileges that ownership entails.

In other words, the moment you finish a piece of writing—whether it is a short story, article, novel or poem—the law recognizes that only you can decide how it is to be used.

This law gives writers power in dealing with editors and publishers, but they should understand how to use that power. They should also understand that certain circumstances can complicate and confuse the concept of ownership. Writers must be wary of these circumstances or risk losing ownership of their work. Here are answers to frequently asked questions about copyright law:

To what rights am I entitled under copyright law? The law gives you, as creator of your work, the right to print, reprint and copy the work; to sell or distribute copies of the work; to prepare "derivative works"—dramatizations, translations, musical arrangement, novelizations, etc.; to record the work; and to perform or display literary, dramatic or musical works publicly. These rights give you control over how your work is used, and assure you (in theory) that you receive payment for any use of your work.

If, however, you create the work as a "work-for-hire," you do not own any of these rights. The person or company that commissioned the work-for-hire owns the copyright.

When does copyright law take effect, and how long does it last? A piece of writing is copyrighted the moment it is put to paper and you indicate your authorship with the word Copyright or the ©, the year and your name. Protection lasts for the life of the author plus 50 years, thus allowing your heirs to benefit from your work. For material written by two or more people, protection lasts for the life of the last survivor plus 50 years. The life-plus-50 provision applies if the work was created or registered with the Copyright Office after January 1, 1978, when the updated copyright law took effect. The old law protected works for a 28-year term, and gave the copyright owner the option to renew the copyright for an additional 28 years at the end of that term. Works copyrighted under the old law that are in their second 28-year term automatically receive an additional 19 years of protection (for a total of 75 years). Works in their first term also receive the 19-year extension beyond the 28-year second term, but must still be renewed when the first term ends.

If you create a work anonymously or pseudonymously, protection lasts for 100 years after the work's creation, or 75 years after its publication, whichever is shorter. The life-plus-50 coverage takes effect, however, if you reveal your identity to the Copyright Office any time before the original term of protection runs out.

Works created on a for-hire basis are also protected for 100 years after the work's creation or 75 years after its publication, whichever is shorter. But the copyright is held by the publisher, not the writer.

Must I register my work with the Copyright Office to receive protection? No. Your work is copyrighted whether or not you register it, although registration offers certain advantages. For example, you must register the work before you can bring an infringement suit to court. You can register the work *after* an infringement has taken place, and *then* take the suit to court, but registering after the fact removes certain rights from you. You can sue for actual damages (the income or other benefits lost as a result of the infringement), but you can't sue for statutory damages and you can't recover attorney's fees unless the work has been registered with the Copyright Office *before* the infringement took place. Registering before the infringement also allows you to make a stronger case when bringing the infringement to court.

If you suspect that someone might infringe on your work, register it. If you doubt that an infringement is likely (and infringements are relatively rare), you might save yourself the time and money involved in registering the material.

I have an article that I want to protect fully. How do I register it? Request the proper form from the Copyright Office. Send the completed form, a $10 registration fee, and one copy (if the work is unpublished; two if it's published) of the work to the Register of Copyrights, Library of Congress, Washington, D.C. 20559. You needn't register each work individually. A group of articles can be registered simultaneously (for a single $10 fee) if they meet these requirements: They must be assembled in orderly form (simply placing them in a notebook binder is sufficient); they must bear a single title ("Works by Chris Jones," for example); they must represent the work of one person (or one set of collaborators); and they must be the subject of a single claim to copyright. No limit is placed on the number of works that can be copyrighted in a group.

If my writing is published in a "collective work"—such as a magazine—does the publication handle registration of the work? Only if the publication owns the piece of writing. Although the copyright notice carried by the magazine covers its contents, you must register any writing to which *you* own the rights if you want the additional protection registration provides.

Collective works are publications with a variety of contributors. Magazines, newspapers, encyclopedias, anthologies, etc., are considered collective works. If you sell something to a collective work, state in writing what rights you're selling. If you don't, you are automatically selling the nonexclusive rights to use the writing in the collective work and in any succeeding issues or revisions of it. For example, a magazine that buys your article without specifying in writing the rights purchased can reuse the article in that magazine without paying you. The same is true for other collective works, so always detail in writing what rights you are selling before actually making the sale.

When contributing to a collective work, ask that your copyright notice be placed on or near your published manuscript (if you still own the manuscript's rights). Prominent display of your copyright notice on published work has two advantages: It signals to readers and potential reusers of the piece that it belongs to you, and not to the collective work in which it appears; and it allows you to register all published work bearing such notice with the Copyright Office as a group for a single $10 fee. A published work *not* bearing notice indicating you as copyright owner can't be included in a group registration.

Display of copyright notice is especially important when contributing to an uncopyrighted publication—that is, a publication that doesn't display a copyright symbol and doesn't register with the Copyright Office. You risk losing copyright protection on material that appears in uncopyrighted publication. Also, you have no legal recourse against a person who infringes on something that is published without appropriate copyright notice. That person has been misled by the absence of the copyright notice and can't be held liable for his infringement. Copyright protection remains in force on material published in an uncopyrighted publication without benefit of copyright notice if the notice was left off only a few copies, if you asked in writing that the notice be included and the publisher didn't comply, or if you register the work and make a reasonable attempt to place the notice on any copies that haven't been distributed after the omission was discovered.

Official notice of copyright consists of the symbol ©, the word "Copyright," or the abbreviation "Copr."; the name of the copyright owner or owners; and the year date of first publication (for example, "© 1988 by Chris Jones"). A hand-drawn copyright symbol is acceptable.

Under what circumstances should I place my copyright notice on unpublished works that haven't been registered? Place official copyright notice on the first page of any manuscript. This procedure is not intended to stop a buyer from stealing your material (editorial piracy is very rare, actually), but to demonstrate to the editor that you understand your rights under copyright law, that you own that particular manuscript, and that you want to retain your ownership after the manuscript is published.

How do I transfer copyright? A transfer of copyright, like the sale of any property, is simply an exchange of the property for payment. The law stipulates, however, that the transfer of any exclusive rights (and the copyright is the most exclusive of rights) must be made in writing to be valid. Various types of exclusive rights exist, as outlined above. Usually it is best not to sell your copyright. If you do, you lose control over the use of the manuscript, and forfeit future income from its use.

What is a "work-for-hire assignment"? This is a work that another party commissions you to do. Two types of work-for-hire works exist: Work done as a regular employee of a company, and commissioned work that is specifically called "work-for-hire" in writing at the time of assignment. The phrase "work-for-hire" or something close must be used in the written agreement, though you should watch for similar phrasings. The work-for-hire provision was included in the new copyright law so that no writer could unwittingly sign away his copyright. The phrase "work-for-hire" is a bright red flag warning the writer that the agreement he is about to enter into will result in loss of rights to any material created under the agreement.

Some editors offer work-for-hire agreements when making assignments, and expect writers to sign them routinely. By signing them, you forfeit the potential for additional income from a manuscript through reprint sales, or sale of other rights. Be careful, therefore, in signing away your rights in a "work-for-hire" agreement. Many articles written as works-for-hire or to which all rights have been sold are never resold, but if you retain the copyright, you might try to resell the article—something you couldn't do if you forfeited your rights to the piece.

Can I get my rights back if I sell all rights to a manuscript, or if I sell the copyright itself? Yes. You or certain heirs can terminate the transfer of rights 40 years after creation or 35 years after publication of a work by serving written notice, within specified time limits, to the person to whom you transferred rights. Consult the Copyright Office for the procedural details. This may seem like a long time to wait, but remember that some manuscripts remain popular and earn royalties and other fees for much longer than 35 years.

Must all transfers be in writing? Only work-for-hire agreements and transfers of exclusive rights *must* be in writing. However, getting any agreement in writing before the sale is wise. Beware of other statements about what rights the buyer purchases that may appear on checks, writer's guidelines or magazine mastheads. If the publisher makes such a statement elsewhere, you might insert a phrase like "No statement pertaining to purchase of rights other than the one detailed in this letter—including masthead statements or writer's guidelines—applies to this agreement" into the letter that outlines your rights agreement. Some publishers put their terms in writing on the back of a check that, when endorsed by the writer, becomes in their view a "contract." If the terms on the back of the check do not agree with the rights you are selling, then change the endorsement to match the rights you have sold before signing the check for deposit. Contact the editor to discuss this difference in rights.

Are ideas and titles copyrightable? No. Nor can facts be copyrighted. Only the actual expression of ideas or information can be copyrighted. You can't copyright the idea to do a solar energy story, and you can't copyright lists of materials for building solar energy converters. But you can copyright the article that results from that idea and that information.

Where can I get more information about copyright law? Write the Copyright Office (Library of Congress, Washington, D.C. 20559) for a free Copyright Information Kit. Call (not collect) the Copyright Public Information Office at (202)287-8700 weekdays between 8:30 a.m. and 5 p.m. if you need forms for registration of a claim to copyright. The Copyright Office will answer specific questions but won't provide legal advice. For more information about copyright and other laws, consult the latest edition of *Law and the Writer*, edited by Kirk Polking and Leonard S. Meranus (Writer's Digest Books).

How much should I charge?

Not every writer can experience the joy of winning a Mercedes-Benz in a national advertiser's jingle contest, as one Ohio freelancer did; but there are other income-earning opportunities every writer can tap between acceptances from publishers.

For example, as corporations get "leaner and meaner" under bottom line pressures, more of them are turning to freelancers for their public relations, annual reports, speeches and other writing projects. Freelancers don't get expensive fringe benefits and can be hired on an as-needed basis. Smaller companies, especially many new service firms which can't support an inhouse market research department, are also possible freelance targets.

Are you part ham? Writer Georgelle Hirliman, in an attempt to overcome writer's block on her novel, proposed to the Sante Fe Council for the Arts that she set up her typewriter in a store window so the public could see a writer actually at work. She received a $125 stipend. At the last minute, however, she changed her idea and taped up a pad and pencil to the window inviting audience participation with a writer. They asked questions, she typed out an answer. After the stipend ran out, she took that idea to bookstores in selected cities around the country, taping her questions and answers on bookstore windows. She earned $50 a day, got publicity for the store and increased traffic. Her novel temporarily was put on hold.

What follows is a list of other writing jobs you might want to consider—and rates that have been reported to us by freelancers doing similar work in various parts of the U.S. The rates in your own marketplace may be higher or lower, depending on demand and other local variables. Consider the rates quoted here as guidelines, not fixed fees.

How do you find out what the local going rate is? If possible, contact writers or friends in a related business or agency that employs freelancers to find out what has been paid for certain jobs in the past. Or try to get the prospective client to quote his budget for a specific project before you name your price.

When setting your own fees, keep two factors in mind: (1)how much you think the client is willing or able to pay for the job; and (2)how much you want to earn for your time. For example, if something you write helps a businessman get a $50,000 order or a school board to get a $100,000 grant, that may influence your fees. How much you want to earn for your time should take into consideration not only an hourly rate for the time you spend writing, but also the time involved in travel, meeting with the client, doing research, rewriting and, where necessary, handling details with a printer or producer. One way to figure your hourly rate is to determine what an annual salary might be for a staff person to do the same job you are bidding on, and figure an hourly wage on that. If, for example, you think the buyer would have to pay a staff person $20,000 a year, divide that by 2,000 (approximately 40 hours per week for 50 weeks) and you will arrive at $10 an hour. Then add another 20% to cover the amount of fringe benefits that an employer normally pays in Social Security, unemployment insurance, paid vacations, hospitalization, retirement funds, etc. Then add another dollars-per-hour figure to cover your actual overhead expense for office space, equipment, supplies; plus time spent on professional meetings, readings, and making unsuccessful proposals. (Add up one year's expense and divide by the number of hours per year you work on freelancing. In the beginning you may have to adjust this to avoid pricing yourself out of the market.)

Regardless of the method by which you arrive at your fee for the job, be sure to get a letter of agreement signed by both parties covering the work to be done and the fee to be paid.

You will, of course, from time to time handle certain jobs at less than desirable rates because they are for a cause you believe in, or because the job offers additional experience or exposure to some profitable client for the future. Some clients pay hourly rates; others pay flat fees for the job. Both kinds of rates are listed when the data were available so you have as many pricing options as possible. More details on many of the freelance jobs listed below are contained in *Freelance Jobs for Writers*, edited by Kirk Polking (Writer's Digest Books)— which tells how to get writing jobs, how to handle them most effectively, and how to get a fair price for your work.

Advertising copywriting: Advertising agencies and the advertising departments of large companies need part-time help in rush seasons. Newspapers, radio and TV stations also need copywriters for their small business customers who do not have agencies. Depending on the client and the job, the following rates could apply: $20-75 per hour, $100 and up per day, $200 and up per week, $100-500 as a monthly retainer. Flat-fee-per-ad rates could range from $25-500 depending upon size and kind of client.

Annual reports: A brief report with some economic information and an explanation of figures, $20-35 per hour; a report that must meet Securities and Exchange Commission (SEC) standards and reports that use legal language could bill at $40-65 per hour. Some writers who provide copywriting and editing services charge flat fees ranging from $5,000-10,000.

Anthology editing: Variable advance plus 3-15% of royalties. Flat-fee-per-manuscript rates could range from $500-5,000 or more if it consists of complex, technical material.

Article manuscript critique: 3,000 words, $30.

Arts reviewing: For weekly newspapers, $15-35; for dailies, $45 and up; for Sunday supplements, $100-400; regional arts events summaries for national trade magazines, $35-100.

Associations: Miscellaneous writing projects, small associations, $5-15 per hour; larger groups, up to $60 per hour; or a flat fee per project, such as $250-750 for 10-12 page magazine articles, or $500-1,500 for a 10-page booklet.

Audio cassette scripts: $10-50 per scripted minute, assuming written from existing client materials, with no additional research or meetings; otherwise $75-100 per minute, $750 minimum.

Audiovisuals: For writing; $125-250 per requested scripted minute; includes rough draft, editing conference with client, and final shooting script. For consulting, research, producing, directing, soundtrack oversight, etc., $300-500 per day plus travel and expenses. Writing fee is sometimes 10% of gross production price as billed to client.

Book, as-told-to (ghostwriting): Author gets full advance and 50% of author's royalties; subject gets 50%. Hourly rate for subjects who are self-publishing ($10-35 per hour).

Book, ghostwritten, without as-told-to credit: For clients who are either self-publishing or have no royalty publisher lined up, $5,000 to $30,000 with one-fourth down payment, one-fourth when book half finished, one-fourth at three quarters mark and last fourth of payment when manuscript completed; or chapter by chapter.

Book content editing: $10-50 per hour and up; $600-3,000 per manuscript, based on size and complexity of the project.

Book copyediting: $7.50-20 per hour and up; occasionally $1 per page.

Book indexing: $8-18 per hour; $25 per hour using computer indexing software programs that take fewer hours; $1.50-2 per printed book page; 40-55¢ per line of index; or flat fee.

Book jacket blurb writing: $60-75 for front cover copy plus inside and back cover copy summarizing content and tone of the book.

Book manuscript criticism: $125 for outline and first 20,000 words.

Book manuscript reading, nonspecialized subjects: $20-50 for a half page summary and recommendation. ***Specialized subject:*** $100-350 and up, depending on complexity of project.

Book proofreading: $6.50-20 per hour and up; sometimes 75¢-1 per page.

Book proposal consultation: $25-35 per hour.

Book proposal writing: $300-1,000 or more depending on length and whether client provides full information or writer must do some research.

Book query critique: $50 for letter to publisher and outline.

Book research: $5-20 per hour and up, depending on complexity.

Book reviews: For byline and the book only, on small newspapers; to $25-300 on larger publications.

Book rewriting: $12-30 per hour; sometimes $5 per page. Some writers have combination ghostwriting and rewriting short-term jobs for which the pay could be $350 per day and up. Some participate in royalties on book rewrites.

Brochures: $200-7,500 depending on client (small nonprofit organization to large corporation), length, and complexity of job.

Business booklets, announcement folders: Writing and editing, $25-1,000 depending on size, research, etc.

Business facilities brochure: 12-16 pages, $1,000-4,000.

Business letters: such as those designed to be used as form letters to improve customer relations, $100 per letter for small businesses; $200-500 per form letter for corporations.

Business meeting guide and brochure: 4 pages, $200; 8-12 pages, $400.

Business writing: On the local or national level, this may be advertising copy, collateral materials, speechwriting, films, public relations or other jobs—see individual entries on these subjects for details. General business writing rates could range from $20-50 per hour; $100-200 per day, plus expenses.

Business writing seminars: $10 per person, minimum of 20, for a half-day seminar, plus travel expenses.

Catalogs for business: $25-40 per hour or $60-75 per printed page; more if many tables or charts must be reworked for readability and consistency.

Collateral materials for business: See business booklets, catalogs, etc.

Comedy writing for night club entertainers: Gags only, $2-25 each. Routines, $100-1,000 per minute. Some new comics may try to get a five-minute routine for $150; others will pay $2,500 for a five-minute bit from a top writer.

Commercial reports for businesses, insurance companies, credit agencies: $6-10 per page; $5-20 per report on short reports.

Company newsletters and inhouse publications: Writing and editing 2-4 pages, $200-500; 12-32 pages, $1,000-2,000. Writing, $8-40 per hour; editing, $8-35 per hour.

Church history: $200-1,000 for writing 15 to 50 pages.

College/university history: $35 per hour for research through final ms.

Consultation on communications: $250 per day plus expenses for nonprofit, social service and religious organizations; $400 per day to others.

Consultation on magazine editorial: $1,000-1,500 per day plus expenses.

Consultation to business: On writing, PR, $25-50 per hour.

Consumer complaint letters: $25 each.

Contest judging: Short manuscripts, $5 per entry; with one-page critique, $10-25. Overall contest judging: $100-500.

Copyediting and content editing for other writers: $1 per page. (See also Manuscript consultation and Manuscript criticism.)

Corporate history: $1,000-20,000, depending on length, complexity and client resources.

Corporate profile: Up to 3,000 words, $1,250-2,500.

Dance criticism: $25-400 per article. (See also Arts reviewing.)

Direct-mail catalog copy: $10-50 per page for 3-20 blocks of copy per page of a 24-48 page catalog.

Direct-mail packages: Copywriting direct mail letter, response card, etc., $1,500-5,000 depending on writer's skill, reputation.

Direct response card on a product: $250.

Editing: See book editing, company newsletters, magazines, etc.

Educational consulting and educational grant and proposal writing: $250-750 per day and sometimes up to 5-10% of the total grant funds depending on whether only writing is involved or also research and design of the project itself.

Encyclopedia articles: Entries in some reference books, such as biographical encyclopedias, 500-2,000 words; pay ranges from $60-80 per 1,000 words. Specialists' fees vary.

Executive biography: (based on a resume, but in narrative form): $100.

English teachers—lay reading for: $4-6 per hour.

Family histories: See Histories, family.

Filmstrip script: See Audiovisual.

Financial presentation for a corporation: 20-30 minutes, $1,500-4,500.

Flyers for tourist attractions, small museums, art shows: $25 and up for writing a brief bio, history, etc.

Fund-raising campaign brochure: $5,000 for 20 hours' research and 30 hours to write a major capital campaign brochure, get it approved, lay out and produce with a printer. For a standard fund-raising brochure, many fund-raising executives hire copywriters for $50-75 an hour to do research which takes 10-15 hours and 20-30 hours to write/produce.

Gags: see Comedy writing.

Genealogical research: $5-25 per hour.

Ghostwriting: $15-40 per hour; $5-10 per page, $200 per day plus expenses. Ghostwritten professional and trade journal articles under someone else's byline, $250-3,000. Ghostwritten books: see Book, as-told-to (ghostwriting) and Book, ghostwritten, without as-told-to credit.

Ghostwriting a corporate book: 6 months' work, $13,000-25,000.

Ghostwriting speeches: See Speeches.

Government public information officer: Part-time, with local governments, $10-15 per hour; or a retainer for so many hours per period.

Histories, family: Fees depend on whether the writer need only edit already prepared notes or do extensive research and writing; and the length of the work, $500-15,000.

Histories, local: Centennial history of a local church, $25 per hour for research through final manuscript for printer.

Writer's

DIGEST

THE WORLD'S LEADING MAGAZINE FOR WRITERS

How would you like to get:
- up-to-the-minute reports on new markets for your writing.
- professional advice from editors and writers about what to write and how to write it to maximize your opportunities for getting published.
- in-depth interviews with leading authors who reveal their secrets of success.
- expert opinion about writing and selling fiction, nonfiction, poetry and scripts.
- ...all at a $10.00 discount?

(See other side for details.)

House organ editing: See Company newsletters and Inhouse publications.

Industrial product film: $1,000 for 10-minute script.

Industrial promotions: $15-40 per hour. See also Business writing.

Job application letters: $10-25.

Lectures to local librarians or teachers: $50-100.

Lectures to school classes: $25-75; $150 per day; $250 per day if farther than 100 miles.

Lectures at national conventions by well-known authors: $1,500-20,000 and up, plus expenses; less for panel discussions.

Lectures at regional writers' conferences: $300 and up, plus expenses.

Magazine, city, calendar of events column: $150.

Magazine column: 200 words, $25. Larger circulation publications pay fees related to their regular word rate.

Magazine editing: Religious publications, $200-500 per month.

Magazine stringing: 20¢-1 per word based on circulation. Daily rate: $100-200 plus expenses; weekly rate: $750 plus expenses. Also $7.50-35 per hour plus expenses.

Manuscript consultation: $25-50 per hour.

Manuscript criticism: $20 per 16-line poem; $30 per article or short story of up to 3,000 words; book outlines and sample chapters of up to 20,000 words, $125.

Manuscript typing: 75¢-2.50 per page with one copy; $15 per hour.

Market research survey reports: $10 per report; $15-30 per hour; writing results of studies or reports, $500-1,200 per day.

Medical editing: $15-30 per hour.

Medical proofreading: $10-20 per hour.

Medical writing: $15-80 per hour.

New product release: $300-500 plus expenses.

Newsletters: See Company newsletters and Retail business newsletters.

Newspaper column, local: 80¢ per column inch to $5 for a weekly; $7.50 for dailies of 4,000-6,000 circulation; $10-12.50 for 7,000-10,000 dailies; $15-20 for 11,000-25,000 dailies; and $25 and up for larger dailies.

Newspaper feature: 35¢ to $1.50 per column inch for a weekly.

Newspaper feature writing, part-time: $1,000 a month for an 18-hour week.

Newspaper reviews of art, music, drama: See Arts reviewing.

Newspaper stringing: 50¢-2.50 per column inch up to $7.50 per column inch for some national publications. Also publications like *National Enquirer* pay lead fees up to $250 for tips on page one story ideas.

Newspaper ads for small business: $25 for a small, one-column ad, or $10 per hour and up.

Novel synopsis for film producer: $150 for 5-10 pages typed single-spaced.

Obituary copy: Where local newspapers permit lengthier than normal notices paid for by the funeral home (and charged to the family), $15. Writers are engaged by funeral homes.

Opinion research interviewing: $4-6 per hour or $15-25 per completed interview.

Party toasts, limericks, place card verses: $1.50 per line.

Permission fees to publishers to reprint article or story: $75-500; 10¢-15¢ per word; less for charitable organizations.

Photo brochures: $700-15,000 flat fee for photos and writing.

Poetry criticism: $20 per 16-line poem.

Political writing: See Public relations and Speechwriting.

Press background on a company: $500-1,200 for 4-8 pages.

Press kits: $500-3,000.

Press release: 1-3 pages, $50-200.

Printers' camera-ready typewritten copy: Negotiated with individual printers, but see also Manuscript typing services.

Product literature: Per page, $100-150.

Programmed instruction consultant fees: $300-700 per day; $50 per hour.

Programmed instruction materials for business: $50 per hour for inhouse writing and editing; $500-700 a day plus expenses for outside research and writing. Alternate method: $2,000-5,000 per hour of programmed training provided, depending on technicality of subject.

Public relations for business: $200-500 per day plus expenses.

Public relations for conventions: $500-1,500 flat fee.

Public relations for libraries: Small libraries, $5-10 per hour; larger cities, $35 an hour and up.

Public relations for nonprofit or proprietary organizations: Small towns, $100-500 monthly retainers.

Public relations for politicians: Small town, state campaigns, $10-50 per hour; incumbents, congressional, gubernatorial, and other national campaigns, $25-100 per hour.

Public relations for schools: $10 per hour and up in small districts; larger districts have full-time staff personnel.

Radio advertising copy: Small towns, up to $5 per spot; $20-65 per hour; $100-250 per week for a four- to six-hour day; larger cities, $250-400 per week.

Radio continuity writing: $5 per page to $150 per week, part-time.

Radio documentaries: $200 for 60 minutes, local station.

Radio editorials: $10-30 for 90-second to two-minute spots.

Radio interviews: For National Public Radio, up to 3 minutes, $25; 3-10 minutes, $40-75; 10-60 minutes, $125 to negotiable fees. Small radio stations would pay approximately 50% of the NPR rate; large stations, double the NPR rate.

Readings by poets, fiction writers: $25-600 depending on the author.

Record album cover copy: $100-250 flat fee.

Recruiting brochure: 8-12 pages, $500-1,500.

Research for writers or book publishers: $10-30 an hour and up. Some quote a flat fee of $300-500 for a complete and complicated job.

Restaurant guide features: Short article on restaurant, owner, special attractions, $15; interior, exterior photos, $15.

Résumé writing: $25-150 per résumé.

Retail business newsletters for customers: $175-300 for writing four-page publications. Some writers work with a local printer and handle production details as well, billing the client for the total package. Some writers also do their own photography.

Rewriting: Copy for a local client, $27.50 per hour.

Sales brochure: 12-16 pages, $750-3,000.

Sales letter for business or industry: $150-500 for one or two pages.

Science writing: For newspapers $150-500; magazines $2,000-5,000; encyclopedias $1 per line; textbook editing $40 per hour; professional publications $500-750 for 1,500-3,000 words.

Script synopsis for agent or film producer: $75 for 2-3 typed pages, single-spaced.

Scripts for nontheatrical films for education, business, industry: Prices vary among producers, clients, and sponsors and there is no standardization of rates in the field. Fees include $75-120 per minute for one reel (10 minutes) and corresponding increases with each successive reel; approximately 10% of the production cost of films that cost the producer more than $1,500 per release minute.

Services brochure: 12-18 pages, $1,250-2,000.

Shopping mall promotion: $500 monthly retainer up to 15% of promotion budget for the mall.

Short story manuscript critique: 3,000 words, $30.

Slide film script: See Audiovisuals.

Slide presentation: Including visual formats plus audio, $1,000-1,500 for 10-15 minutes.

Slide/single image photos: $75 flat fee.

Slide/tape script: $75-100 per minute, $750 minimum.

Software manual writing: $15-50 per hour for research and writing.

Special news article: For business submission to trade publication, $250-400/1,000 words.

Special occasion booklet: Family keepsake of a wedding, anniversary, etc., $115 and up.

Speech for government official: $4,000 for 20 minutes plus up to $1,000 travel and miscellaneous expenses.

Speech for owners of a small business: $100 for six minutes.

Speech for owners of larger businesses: $500-3,000 for 10-30 minutes.

Speech for local political candidate: $150-250 for 15 minutes.

Speech for statewide candidate: $500-800.

Speech for national congressional candidate: $1,000 and up.

Syndicated newspaper column, self-promoted: $2-8 each for weeklies; $5-25 per week for dailies, based on circulation.

Teaching adult education course: $10-60 per class hour.

Teaching adult seminar: $350 plus mileage and per diem for a 6- or 7-hour day; plus 40% of the tuition fee beyond the sponsor's breakeven point.

Teaching business writing to company employees: $60 per hour.

Teaching college course or seminar: $15-70 per class hour.

Teaching creative writing in school: $15-60 per hour of instruction, or $1,200 for a 10-session class of 25 students; less in recessionary times.

Teaching elementary and middle school teachers how to teach writing to students: $75-120 for a 1-1½ hour session.

Teaching journalism in high school: Proportionate to salary scale for full-time teacher in the same school district.

Teaching home-bound students: $5 per hour.

Technical typing: $1-4 per double-spaced page.

Technical writing: $35 per ms page or $20-60 per hour, depending on degree of complexity and type of audience.

Trade journal ad copywriting: $250-500.

Trade journal article: For business client, $500-1,500.

Translation, commercial: Final draft in a common European language, 6-20¢/English word.

Translation for government agencies: $27-79 per 1,000 foreign words into English.

Translation, literary: $50-100 per thousand English words.

Translation through translation agencies: Less 33⅓% for agency commission.

TV documentary: 30-minute 5-6 page proposal outline, $250 and up; 15-17 page treatment, $1,000 and up; less in smaller cities.

TV editorials: $35 and up for 1-minute, 45 seconds (250-300 words).

TV information scripts: Short 5-10-minute scripts for local cable TV stations, $10-15/hour.

TV instruction taping: $150 per 30-minute tape; $25 residual each time tape is sold.

TV news film still photo: $3-6 flat fee.

TV news story: $16-25 flat fee.

TV filmed news and features: From $10-20 per clip for 30-second spot; $15-25 for 60-second clip; more for special events.

TV, national and local public stations: $35-100 per minute down to a flat fee of $100-500 for a 30- to 60-minute script.

TV scripts: (Teleplay only), 60 minutes, prime time, Writers Guild rates: $10,584; 30 minutes, $7,846.

Writer-in-schools: Arts council program, $130 per day; $650 per week. Personal charges vary from $25 per day to $100 per hour depending on school's ability to pay.

Writer's workshop: Lecturing and seminar conducting, $50-150 per hour to $500 per day plus expenses; local classes, $50 per student for 10 sessions.

Glossary

Key to symbols and abbreviations follows the **Using Writer's Market** *section at the front of book.*

Advance. A sum of money that a publisher pays a writer prior to the publication of a book. It is usually paid in installments, such as one-half on signing the contract; one-half on delivery of a complete and satisfactory manuscript. The advance is paid against the royalty money that will be earned by the book.

All rights. See "Rights and the Writer" in the Appendix.

Assignment. Editor asks a writer to do a specific article for which he usually names a price for the completed manuscript.

B&W. Abbreviation for black & white photograph.

Bimonthly. Every two months. See also *semimonthly*.

Bionote. A sentence or brief paragraph about the writer at the bottom of the first or last page on which an article or short story appears in a publication. A bionote may also appear on a contributors' page where the editor discusses the writers contributing to that particular edition.

Biweekly. Every two weeks.

Book auction. Selling the rights (i.e. paperback, movie, etc.) of a hardback book to the highest bidder. A publisher or agent may initiate the auction.

Book packager. Draws all the elements of a book together, from the initial concept to writing and marketing strategies, then sells the book package to a book publisher and/or movie producer. Also known as book producer or book developer.

Broadside. An oversized sheet or a one-page poster with illustration and text (poetry, fiction or nonfiction).

Business size envelope. Also known as #10 envelope, it is the standard size used in sending business correspondence.

Caption. Originally a title or headline over a picture but now a description of the subject matter of a photograph, including names of people where appropriate. Also called cutline.

Chapbook. A small booklet, usually paperback, of poetry, ballads or tales.

Clean copy. Free of errors, cross-outs, wrinkles, smudges.

Clippings. News items of possible interest to trade magazine editors.

Clips. Samples, usually from newspapers or magazines, of your *published* work.

Coffee table book. An oversize book, heavily illustrated, that is suitable for display on a coffee table.

Column inch. All the type contained in one inch of a typeset column.

Commissioned work. See *assignment*.

Compatible. The condition which allows one type of computer/word processor to share information or communicate with another type of machine.

Concept. A statement that summarizes a screenplay or teleplay—before the outline or treatment is written.

Contributor's copies. Copies of the issues of a magazine sent to an author in which his/her work appears.

Co-publishing. An arrangement in which author and publisher share publication costs and profits.

Copyediting. Editing a manuscript for grammar, punctuation and printing style, not subject content.

Copyright. A means to protect an author's work. See "Rights and the Writer."

Cover letter. A brief letter, accompanying a complete manuscript, especially useful if responding to an editor's request for a manuscript. A cover letter may also accompany a book proposal. (A cover letter is *not* a query letter; see "Approaching Markets.")

Cutline. See *caption*.

Diorama. An advertising term referring to an elaborate, three-dimensional, miniature display.

Disk. A round, flat magnetic plate on which computer data may be stored.

Docudrama. A fictional film rendition of recent newsmaking events and people.

Dot-matrix. Printed type where individual characters are composed of a matrix or pattern of tiny dots.

El-hi. Elementary to high school.

Epigram. A short, witty, sometimes paradoxical saying.

Erotica. Usually fiction that is sexually-oriented, although it could be art on the same theme.

ESL. Abbreviation for English as a second language.

Fair use. A provision of the copyright law that says short passages from copyrighted material may be used without infringing on the owner's rights.

Feature. An article giving the reader information of human interest rather than news. Also used by magazines to indicate a lead article or distinctive department.

Filler. A short item used by an editor to "fill" out a newspaper column or a page in a magazine. It could be a timeless news item, a joke, an anecdote, some light verse or short humor, a puzzle, etc.

First North American serial rights. See "Rights and the Writer."

Formula story. Familiar theme treated in a predictable plot structure—such as boy meets girl, boy loses girl, boy gets girl.

Genre. Refers either to a general classification of writing, such as the novel or the poem, or to the categories within those classifications, such as the problem novel or the sonnet. Genre fiction describes commercial novels, such as mysteries, romances and science fiction.

Ghostwriter. A writer who puts into literary form an article, speech, story or book based on another person's ideas or knowledge.

Glossy. A black and white photograph with a shiny surface as opposed to one with a non-shiny matte finish.

Gothic novel. One in which the central character is usually a beautiful young girl, the setting is an old mansion or castle; there is a handsome hero and a real menace, either natural or supernatural.

Hard copy. The printed copy of a computer's output.

Hardware. All the mechanically-integrated components of a computer that are not software. Circuit boards, transistors, and the machines that are the actual computer are the hardware.

Honorarium. Token payment—small amount of money, or a byline and copies of a publication.

Illustrations. May be photographs, old engravings, artwork. Usually paid for separately from the manuscript. See also *package sale*.

Interactive fiction. Works of fiction in book or computer software format in which the reader determines the path that the story will take. The reader chooses from several alternatives at the end of a "chapter," and this determines the structure of the story. Interactive fiction features multiple plots and endings.

Invasion of privacy. Writing about persons (even though truthfully) without their consent.

Kill fee. Fee for a complete article that was assigned but which was subsequently cancelled.

Letter-quality submission. Computer printout that looks like a typewritten manuscript.

Libel. A false accusation or any published statement or presentation that tends to expose another to public contempt, ridicule, etc. Defenses are truth; fair comment on the matter of public interest; and privileged communication—such as a report of legal proceedings or a client's communication to his lawyer.

Little magazine. Publications of limited circulation, usually on literary or political subject matter.

LORT. An acronyn for League of Resident Theatres. Letters from A to D follow LORT and designate the size of the theatre.

Mainstream fiction. Fiction that transcends popular novel categories such as mystery, romance or science fiction. Using conventional methods, this kind of fiction tells stories about people and their conflicts with greater depth of characterization, background, etc., than more narrowly focused genre novels.

Mass market. Nonspecialized books of wide appeal directed toward an extremely large audience.

Microcomputer. A small computer system capable of performing various specific tasks with data it receives. Personal computers are microcomputers.

Model release. A paper signed by the subject of a photograph (or his guardian, if a juvenile) giving the photographer permission to use the photograph, editorially or for advertising purposes or for some specific purpose as stated.

Modem. A small electrical box that plugs into the serial card of a computer, used to transmit data from one computer to another, usually via telephone lines.

Monograph. Thoroughly detailed and documented scholarly study concerning a singular subject.

Multiple submissions. Sending the same article, story or poem to several publishers at the same time. Some publishers refuse to consider such submissions. No multiple submission should be made to larger markets unless it is a query on a highly topical article requiring an immediate response and that fact is stated in your letter.

Newsbreak. A newsbreak can be a small newsworthy story added to the front page of a newspaper at press time or a magazine news item of importance to readers.

Novelette. A short novel, or a long short story; 7,000 to 15,000 words approximately. Also known as a novella.

Offprint. Copies of an author's article taken "out of issue" before a magazine is bound and given to the author in lieu of monetary payment. An offprint could then be used by the writer as a published writing sample.

One-time rights. See "Rights and the Writer."

Outline. Of a book is usually a summary of its contents in five to fifteen double-spaced pages; often in the form of chapter headings with a descriptive sentence or two under each one to show the scope of the book. Of a screenplay or teleplay is a scene-by-scene narrative description of the story (10-15 pages for a ½-hour teleplay; 15-25 pages for a 1-hour teleplay; 25-40 pages for a 90-minute teleplay; 40-60 pages for a 2-hour feature film or teleplay).

Over-the-transom. Unsolicited material submitted by a freelance writer.

Package sale. The editor buys manuscript and photos as a "package" and pays for them with one check.

Page rate. Some magazines pay for material at a fixed rate per published page, rather than per word.

Payment on acceptance. The editor sends you a check for your article, story or poem as soon as he reads it and decides to publish it.

Payment on publication. The editor doesn't send you a check for your material until it's published.

Pen name. The use of a name other than your legal name on articles, stories or books where you wish to remain anonymous. Simply notify your post office and bank that you are using the name so that you'll receive mail and/or checks in that name.

Photo feature. Feature in which emphasis is on the photographs rather than accompanying written material.

Photocopied submissions. Submitting *photocopies* of an original manuscript is acceptable to some editors instead of the author sending the original manuscript. Do not assume that an editor who accepts photocopies will also accept multiple or simultaneous submissions.

Plagiarism. Passing off as one's own the expression of ideas and words of another writer.

Public domain. Material which was either never copyrighted or whose copyright term has run out.

Publication not copyrighted. Publication of an author's work in such a publication places it in the public domain, and it cannot subsequently be copyrighted. See "Rights and the Writer."

Query. A letter to an editor aimed to get his interest in an article you want to write.

Rebus. Stories, quips, puzzles, etc., in juvenile magazines that convey words or syllables with pictures, objects or symbols whose names resemble the sounds of the intended words.

Realia. Activities that relate classroom study to real life.

Release. A statement that your idea is original, has never been sold to anyone else, and that you give up all rights to the idea upon payment of the check.

Remainders. Copies of a book that are slow to sell and sometimes purchased from the publisher at a reduced price. Depending on the author's book contract, a reduced royalty or no royalty is paid on remainder books.

Reporting time. The time it takes an editor to report to the author on his query or manuscript.

Reprint rights. See "Rights and the Writer."

Round-up article. Comments from, or interviews with, a number of celebrities or experts on a single theme.

Royalties, standard hardcover book. 10% of the retail price on the first 5,000 copies sold; 12½% on the next 5,000 and 15% thereafter.

Royalties, standard mass paperback book. 4 to 8% of the retail price on the first 150,000 copies sold.

Royalties, trade paperback book. No less than 6% of list price on first 20,000 copies; 7½% thereafter.

Screenplay. Script for a film intended to be shown in theatres.

Second serial rights. See "Rights and the Writer."

Semimonthly. Twice a month.

Semiweekly. Twice a week.

Serial. Published periodically, such as a newspaper or magazine.

Sidebar. A feature presented as a companion to a straight news report (or main magazine article) giving sidelights on human-interest aspects or sometimes elucidating just one aspect of the story.

Simultaneous submissions. See *multiple submissions*.

Slant. The approach or style of a story or article so it will appeal to the readers of a specific magazine. For example, does this magazine always like stories with an upbeat ending?

Slides. Usually called transparencies by editors looking for color photographs.

Slush pile. The stack of unsolicited or misdirected manuscripts received by an editor or book publisher.

Software. Programs and related documentation for use with a particular computer system.

Speculation. The editor agrees to look at the author's manuscript with no assurance that it will be bought.

Style. The way in which something is written—for example, short, punchy sentences or flowing narrative.

Subsidiary rights. All those rights, other than book publishing rights, included in a book contract—such as paperback, book club, movie rights, etc.

Subsidy publisher. A book publisher who charges the author for the cost to typeset and print his book, the jacket, etc., as opposed to a royalty publisher that pays the author.

Syndication rights. See "Rights and the Writer" in the appendix.

Synopsis. A brief summary of a story, novel or play. As part of a book proposal, it is a comprehensive summary condensed in a page or page and a half, single-spaced. See also *outline*.

Tabloids. Newspaper format publication on about half the size of the regular newspaper page, such as the *National Enquirer*.

Tagline. A caption for a photo, or comment added to a filler.

Tearsheet. Page from a magazine or newspaper containing your printed story, article, poem or ad.

Trade. Either a hardcover or paperback book; subject matter frequently concerns a special interest. Books are directed toward the layperson rather than the professional.

Transparencies. Positive color slides; not color prints.

Treatment. Synopsis of a television or film script (40-60 pages for a 2-hour feature film or teleplay).

Unsolicited manuscript. A story, article, poem or book that an editor did not specifically ask to see.

User friendly. Easy to handle and use. Refers to computer hardware designed with the user in mind.

Vanity publisher. See *subsidy publisher*.

Word processor. A computer that produces typewritten copy via automated typing, text-editing, and storage and transmission capabilities.

Work-for-hire. See "Rights and the Writer" in the appendix.

Book Publishers Subject Index

Nonfiction

This index will help you find publishers that consider books on specific subjects—the subjects you choose to write about. Remember that a publisher may be listed here under a general subject category like Art and Architecture, while the company publishes **only** art history or how-to books. Be sure to consult each company's detailed individual listing, its book catalog and several of its books before you send your query or manuscript.

Agriculture/Horticulture. Avi; Delmar; Michigan State University; Stipes; Texas A&M University; University of Nebraska; VGM; Western Producer; Westview.

Americana. Ancestry; Arbor House; Ashley; Atheneum Children's Books; Binford & Mort; John F. Blair; Branden; Brevet; Allen D. Bragdon; Caxton Printers; Cay-Bel; Christopher; Clarion; Arthur H. Clark; Council Oak; Crown; May Davenport; Denlinger's; Devin-Adair; Donning; Down East; Paul S. Eriksson; Faber & Faber; Filter; General Hall; Glenbridge; Golden West; Harcourt Brace Jovanovich; Harper & Row; Harvard Common; Herald Publishing House; Heyday; International Publishers; Interurban Press/Trans Anglo; William Kaufman; Peter Lang; Lexikos; Liberty; McFarland; Madrona; Main Street; Media Productions and Marketing; Meyerbooks; Misty Hill; Monitor; Mosaic; Mott Media; Mustang; New England; Outbooks; Pacific; Paragon; Peter Pauper; Pelican; Pruett; Publishers Associates; Purdue University; Racz; Random House; Renaissance House; Schocken; Second Chance Press; Seven Locks; Shameless Hussy; Shoe String; Shoe Tree; Sierra Club; Silver Burdett; Gibs M. Smith; Stewart, Tabori and Chang; Still Point; Lyle Stuart; Taylor; Ten Speed; Texas Christian University; Transaction; University of Arkansas; University of Illinois; University of Michigan; University of Nebraska; University of Pennsylvania; University Press of Mississippi; University Press of New England; University Press of Virginia; Utah State University; Vestal; Walker; Wallace; Washington State University; Franklin Watts; Westernlore; Winston-Derek; Woodbine; Yankee.

Animals. Alaska Nature; Alpine Productions; Ashley; Canadian Plains Research Center; Carolina Biological Supply; Carolrhoda; Christopher; Coles; Council Oak; Crown; May Davenport; Dembner; Denlinger's; Paul S. Eriksson; Faber & Faber; Facts on File; Fulcrum; Garden Way; Greenhaven; Harper & Row; Homestead; Hounslow; Michael Kesend; Maynard-Thomas; Misty Hill; Mosaic; North Country; Pineapple; Plexus; Raintree; Rocky Top; S.C.E Editions; Charles Scribner's Sons; Shoe Tree; Silver Burdett; Sterling; Tab; Unicorn; Universe; University of Arkansas; Williamson; Willow Creek; Yankee.

Anthropology/Archaelogy. Aristide D. Caratzas; Ohio State University; Rutgers University; Stanford University; University of Alabama; University of Arizona; University of Iowa; University of Nevada; University of Pennsylvania; University of Tennessee; University of Utah; Westernlore; Westview.

Art/Architecture. American Studies; Arbor House; Architectural; Art Direction; Atheneum Children's Books; Atlantic Monthly; Beacon Press; Branden; George Braziller; Cambridge University; Aristide D. Caratzas; Carolrhoda; Chelsea Green; Chelsea House-Edgemont; Christopher; Chronicle; Council Oak; Crown; May Davenport; Davis; Delta; Dodd, Mead;

Douglas & McIntyre; Down East; Dundurn; Paul S. Eriksson; Faber & Faber; Fairleigh Dickinson University; Family Album; Filter; Fitzhenry & Whiteside; Fleet; Forman; Great Ocean; Guernica Editions; Harper & Row; Homestead; Hounslow; Hudson Hills; Intervarsity; William Kaufman; Kent State University; Krantz; Peter Lang; Learning; Loyola University; McFarland; Main Street; Mazda; MIT; William Morrow; Museum of New Mexico; Museum of Northern Arizona; National; National Gallery of Canada; National Textbook; Nimbus; North Light; Noyes Data Corp.; Ohio State University; Pandora; Parnassus Imprints; PBC International; Pennsylvania Historical and Museum Commission; Clarkson N. Potter; Prentice-Hall Canada (trade division); Preservation; Princeton Architectural; Professional; Publishers Associates; Random House; Real Comet; Resource; Rosen; Rutgers University; Abner Schram; Charles Scribner's Sons; Shapolsky; Shoe String; Shoe Tree; Gibbs M. Smith; Sound View; ST; Stewart, Tabori and Chang; Lyle Stuart; Sunstone; Taplinger; Texas Monthly; Twayne; Umi Research; Unicorn; Universe; University of Alberta; University of California; University of Massachusetts; University of Michigan; University of Texas; University Press of America; University Press of New England; Alfred Van Der Marck; Vance; J. Weston Walch; Walker; Wallace; Washington State University; Western Tanager; Whitston; Alan Wofsy; Yee Wen.

Astrology/Psychic. ACS; Llewellyn; Theosophical.

Autobiographies. Adams, Houmes and Ward; Arbor House; Atlantic Monthly; John Daniel; Harcourt Brace Jovanovich; Clarkson N. Potter.

Bibliographies. Borgo; Faber & Faber; Family Album; Floricanto; B. Klein; Oregon State University; Reference Service; Reymont; Scarecrow; University Press of Virginia; Vance; Whitston.

Biography. Adams, Houmes and Ward; Addison-Wesley; Alaska Nature; Alaska Northwest; Alpha; American Atheist; American Studies; Ancestry; Architectural; Ashley; Associated Faculty; Atheneum Children's Books; Atheneum; Atlantic Monthly; Avon; Ballantine/Epiphany; Basil Blackwell; Beaufort; Binford & Mort; John F. Blair; Borgo; Don Bosco; Branden; Cambridge University; Canadian Plains Research Center; Carolrhoda; Carroll & Graf; Catholic University of America; Cay-Bel; CBP; Celestial Arts; Chelsea Green; Chelsea House-Edgemont; China Books and Periodicals; Christopher; Citadel; Clarion; Arthur H. Clark; Contemporary; Council Oak; Credo; Crown; Harry Cuff; John Daniel; Dante University of America; Dillon; Douglas & McIntyre; Down East; Dundurn; Eakin; Enslow; Paul S. Eriksson; Falcon; Family Album; Frederick Fell; Fitzhenry & Whiteside; Fjord; Fleet; Fulcrum; Great Northwest; Great Ocean; Green Hill; Greenhaven; Guernica Editions; Harcourt Brace Jovanovich; Harper & Row; Harvest House; Herald; Here's Life; Hippocrene; Homestead; Houghton Mifflin; Hounslow; Huntington House; Hurtig; ILR; International Publishers; Intervarsity; Kent State University; Michael Kesend; Peter Lang; Lee's Books for Young Readers; Hal Leonard; Liberty; Little, Brown; Loyola University; Madrona; Media Productions and Marketing; Mercer University; Metamorphous; Methuen; Misty Hill; Monitor; William Morrow; Mosaic; Mother Courage; Motorbooks International; Mott Media; Museum of New Mexico; National Press; Naval Institute; New England; New Leaf; New Society; New Victoria; Nimbus; North Country; North Point; Ohio State University; Old Army; Oregon State University; Pacific Press; Pandora; Panjandrum; Paragon; Pelican; Pennsylvania History and Museum Commission; Pineapple; Plexus; Pocket; Poseidon; Clarkson N. Potter; Prairie; Prima; Purdue University; Quill; Racz; Random House; Regnery/Gateway; Renaissance House; Russica; Rutledge Hill; S.C.E. Edition; St. Luke's; St. Martin's; Sandlapper; Santa Barbara; Saybrook; Schirmer; Schocken; Charles Scribner's Sons; Second Chance Press; Seven Locks; Shameless Hussy; Harold Shaw; Shoe String; Silver Burdett; Simon & Schuster; Gibbs M. Smith; Stewart, Tabori and Chang; Still Point; Lyle Stuart; Sherwood Sugden; Sunflower University; Taplinger; Taylor; Texas Monthly; Thunder's Mouth; Times; Transaction; Twayne; Unicorn; Universe; University of Alabama; University of Alberta; University of Arkansas; University of Illinois; University of Massachusetts; University of Nebraska; University of Nevada; University of Pennsylvania; University Press of Mississippi; University Press of New England; Unlimited; Utah State University; Vehicule; Vestal; Walker; Washington State University; Western Producer; Western Tanager; Westernlore; Winston-Derek; Woodbine; Woodsong; Word; Wright; Zebra; Zondervan.

Business/Economics. Adams, Houmes and Ward; Bob Adams; Addison-Wesley; Almar; American Studies; Arbor House; Asher-Gallant; Ashley; Associated Faculty; Atheneum Children's

Books; Avon; Ballinger; Bantam; Basil Blackwell; Beaufort; Benjamin; Betterway; BNA; Brethren; Brevet; Briarcliff; Brick House; Cambridge University; Canadian Plains Research Center; Catholic Health Association; Center for Migration Studies of New York; Chilton; Christopher; Cleaning Consultant Services; Coles; Compact; Consumer Reports; Contemporary; Council Oak; Cynthia; Dartnell; Devin-Adair; Douglas & McIntyre; Enslow; Enterprise; Paul S. Eriksson; ETC; Faber & Faber; Facts on File; Fairleigh Dickinson University; Falcon; Frederick Fell; Fitzhenry & Whiteside; Forman; Fraser Institute; Fulcrum; Gambling Times; General Hall; Glenbridge; Glenmark; Great Ocean; Green Hill; Greenhaven; Gulf; Alexander Hamilton Institute; Harcourt Brace Jovanovich; Harbor House; Harper & Row; Harvard Common; D.C. Heath; Hounslow; Humanics; Industrial; Institute for the Study of Human Issues; Intercultural; International Foundation of Employee Benefit Plans; International Publishers; International Self-Counsel; International Wealth Success; Interurban Press/Trans Anglo; Intervarsity; William Kaufman; Kern International; B. Klein; Knowledge Industry; Robert E. Krieger; Peter Lang; Liberty; Lomond; Longman; McFarland; McGraw-Hill; Mazda; Medical Economics; Melius and Peterson; Menasha Ridge; Metamorphous; Methuen; MGI Management Institute; Michigan State University; MIT; Mosaic; National; National Press; National Publishers of the Black Hills; National Textbook; Oasis; P.A.R; Pacific; Petrocelli; Pilgrim; Pilot; Plenum; Poseidon; Prentice-Hall Canada; Prentice-Hall Canada (secondary school division); Prentice-Hall Canada (trade division); Prentice-Hall, Inc.; Prima; Probus; Professional; Publishers Associates; Purdue University; Racz; Random House; Reference Service; Regnery/Gateway; Reymont; Riverdale; Ross; Rowman & Littlefield; Roxbury; RPM; Rynd; S.C.E. Editions; Saybrook; Schenkman; Self-Counsel; Seven Locks; Shoe String; South End; Sterling; Stipes; Lyle Stuart; Success; Tab; Jeremy P. Tarcher; Teachers College; Ten Speed; Texas A&M University; Texas Monthly; Times; Transaction; Universe; University of Calgary; University of Illinois; University of Michigan; University of Notre Dame; University of Pennsylvania; University of Texas; University Press of America; University Press of Virginia; Wadsworth; J. Weston Walch; Walker; Wallace; Washington State University; Franklin Watts; Western Producer; Westview; John Wiley & Sons; Williamson; Wilshire; Windsor; Wordware; Wright.

Child Guidance/Parenting. Accelerated Development; Bob Adams; Betterway; Delmar; Delta; T.S. Denison; Fortress; Great Ocean; Guidance Centre; Jalmar; John Knox; Learning; Meadowbrook; Octameron; Ohio Psychology; Parenting; Perspectives; Tyndale; Walker; Williamson; Woodbine; Zebra.

Coffee Table Book. Canadian Plains Research Center; Caxton Printers; Chelsea House-Edgemont; China Books and Periodicals; Chronicle; Donning; Dundurn; Faber & Faber; Frederick Fell; Fiddlehead Poetry Books & Goose Lane Editions; Forman; Harbor House; Herald; Homestead; Hounslow; Imagine; Krantz; Hal Leonard; Lexikos; Little, Brown; Llewellyn; Main Street; Multnomah; Museum of Northern Arizona; New York Zoetrope; Nimbus; Pelican; Pennsylvania Historical and Museum Commission; Prima; Princeton Architectural; Racz; Rutledge; Seven Seas; Shapolsky; Stewart; Tabori and Chang; Lyle Stuart; Taylor; Texas Monthly; Unicorn; Alfred Van Der Marck; Vend-O-Books; Willow Creek; Word; Zondervan.

Communications. Steve Davis; Focal; Longman; University of Calgary; Wadsworth.

Community/Public Affairs. Lomond; Pharos.

Computers/Electronics. American Federation of Information Processing; And Books; ARCsoft; Compute!; Computer Science; Dustbooks; Entelek; Gifted Education; Grapevine; H.P.; D.C. Heath; William Kaufman; MGI Management Institute; MIT; National Publishers of the Black Hills; New York Zoetrope; Prentice-Hall; Q.E.D. Information Sciences; Rowman & Littlefield; Sybex; Tab; Teachers College; J. Weston Walch; Wordware.

Consumer Affairs. Almar; Andrews, McMeel & Parker; Benjamin; Brick House; Consumer Reports; Menasha Ridge; National Press.

Cooking/Foods/Nutrition. Alaska Northwest; And Books; Applezaba; Arbor House; Ashley; Atheneum Children's Books; Atheneum; Avi; Ballantine/Epiphany; Bantam; Benjamin; Berkley; Better Homes and Gardens; Betterway; Briarcliff; Allen D. Bragdon; Byls; Cay-Bel; Celestial Arts; Chicago Review; China Books and Periodicals; Christopher; Chronicle; Compact; Consumer Reports; Contemporary; Council Oak; CRCS; Crossing; Crown; John Daniel; Dawn; Donning; Douglas & McIntyre; Down East; Paul S. Eriksson; Evans and Co.; Facts on File; Frederick Fell; Filter; Forman; Garden Way; Glenmark; Golden; Golden West Publishers;

H.P.; Harcourt Brace Jovanovich; Harbor House; Harper & Row; Harvard Common; Hawkes; Herald; Hounslow; Jonathan David; Liberty; Madrona; Marathon International; Mazda; Media Productions; Melius and Peterson; Meyerbooks; Mills & Sanderson; William Morrow; Mosaic; Museum of New Mexico; National; New England; Nimbus; Nitty Gritty Cookbooks; North Point; 101 Productions; Ortho Information Services; Pacific Press; Panjandrum; Parnassus Imprints; Peter Pauper; Peachtree; Pelican; Pennsylvania Historical and Museum Commission; Pineapple; Poseidon; Clarkson N. Potter; Prairie; Prentice-Hall Canada (trade division); Prima; Quill; Random House; Richboro; Rodale; Rutledge; S.C.E. Editions; Sandlapper; Seven Seas; Shapolsky; Shoe Tree; Sterling; Stewart, Tabori and Chang; Still Point; Stoeger; Jeremy P. Tarcher; Taylor; Ten Speed; Texas Monthly; Times; University of North Carolina; Unlimited; Wallace; Western Producer; Williamson; Willow Creek; Wine Appreciation; Woodland; Word; Wright; Yankee.

Counseling/Career Guidance. Pilot; Prakken; Rosen; Teachers College; Ten Speed; VGM.

Crafts. Better Homes and Gardens; Briarcliff; Chilton; Coles; Davis; Doll Reader; Down East; Standard; Sterling; Success; Sunstone; Timber; Troubador; Universe; University of North Carolina; Wallace; Alan Wofsy; Yankee.

Education(al). Accelerated Development; Aztex; Barnes & Noble; Bennett & McKnight; Coles; Communication Skill Builders; T.S. Denison; Dillon; Education Associates; ETC; Fearon; Front Row Experience; Gifted Education; Gryphon House; Guidance Centre; Humanics; Incentive; Interstate Printers & Publishers; Jalmar; Learning; Liberty; Liguori; Longman; Metamorphous; Methuen; Milady; Morehouse-Barlow; New Readers; Octameron; Ohio Psychology; Ohio State University; Oise; Open Court; Oregon State University; P.A.R.; Paulist; Perfection Form; Porter Sargent; Prakken; Regal; Religious Education; Resource; Shining Star; Standard; Stipes; Trillium; University; University Press of America; Wadsworth; J. Weston Walch; Williamson.

Entertainment/Games. Max Hardy-Publisher; Potentials Development for Health & Aging Services; Quill; Scarecrow; Standard; Sterling.

Ethnic. Alpha; Center for Migration Studies of New York; Chelsea House-Edgemont; Ediciones Universal; General Hall; Indiana University; International Publishers; Jonathan David; Kar-Ben Copies; Pelican; Schocken; Thunder's Mouth; Union of American Hebrew Congregations; University of Massachusetts; University of Nebraska; University of Tennessee; University of Texas; University Press of America; University Press of Mississippi.

Fashion/Beauty. Acropolis Books; Facts on File; Fairchild Books & Visuals.

Feminism. Crossing; Firebrand; Press Gang; Shameless Hussy; South End; Spinsters/Aunt Lute.

Film/Cinema/Stage. Borgo; Broadway; Citadel; Coach House; Dembner; Drama; Focal; Imagine; Indiana University; JH; Hal Leonard; McFarland; Main Street; Maynard-Thomas; Meriwether; New York Zoetrope; Pandora; Panjandrum; Players; Rutgers University; Sterling; Taplinger; Theatre Arts; Umi Research; University of Texas.

Gardening. Better Homes and Gardens; Briarcliff; Coles; Garden Way; H.P.; Naturegraph; 101 Productions; Ortho Information Services; Richboro; Symmes; Taylor; Ten Speed; Timber; University of North Carolina; Williamson; Yankee.

Gays/Lesbians. Alyson; Celestial Arts; Crossing; Firebrand; Gay Sunshine; JH; Publishers Associates.

General Nonfiction. American Atheist; American Psychiatric; And Books; Avon Flare; Baen; Holiday; Indiana University; Johnson; Kent State University; Krantz; Lodestar; Lothrop, Lee & Shepard; Media Productions and Marketing; New American Library; Pacific; Pandora; Pocket; Pruett; Renaissance; Ross; St. Martin's; Stein and Day; Thunder's Mouth; University of Wisconsin.

Government/Politics. And Books; Ashley; Atheneum Children's Books; Atheneum; Atlantic Monthly; Basil Blackwell; Beacon Press; BNA; Brook House; Canadian Plains Research Center; Aristide D. Caratzas; Catholic University of America; Center for Migration Studies of New York; Chelsea Green; Chelsea House-Edgemont; Christopher; Council Oak; Crown; Harry Cuff; Delta; Devin-Adair; Douglas & McIntyre; Eakin; Paul S. Eriksson; Fleet; Fraser Institute; Fulcrum; Gambling Times; General Hall; Glenbridge; Great Ocean; Green Hill; Greenhaven; Guernica Editions; Harper & Row; Hounslow; Hurtig; Intercultural; International Publishers; Intervarsity; Krantz; Peter Lang; Life Cycle; Lomond; Madrona; Mazda; Media Productions and Marketing; Michigan State University; Mott Media; National; NC; New Society; Ohio State University; Pacific; Pandora; Pantheon; Paragon; Pennsylvania Historical and Museum Commission; Plenum; Prentice-Hall Canada (trade division); Press Gang; Prima; Publishers Associates; Purdue University; Random House; Real Comet; Regnery/Gateway; Renaissance House; Riverdale; St. Martin's; Saybrook; Schenkman; Second Chance Press; Seven Locks; Shapolsky; Shoe String; South End; Lyle Stuart; Sherwood Sugden; Jeremy P. Tarcher; Taylor; Teachers College; Texas Monthly; Thunder's Mouth; Transaction; Transnational; Universe; University of Alabama; University of Alberta; University of Arkansas; University of Calgary; University of Illinois; University of Massachusetts; University of North Carolina; University of Tennessee; University Press of America; University Press of Mississippi; University Press of New England; University Press of Virginia; Utah State University; Vance; Vehicule; J. Weston Walch; Washington State University; Franklin Watts; Western Producer; Western Tanager; Westview; Word.

Health/Medicine. Acropolis Books; ACS; Addison-Wesley; Almar; American Psychiatric; Arbor House; Ashley; Associated Faculty; Atheneum Children's Books; Augsburg; Avi; Avon; Ballantine/Epiphany; Bantam; Beaufort; Benjamin; Betterway; Bookmakers; Branden; Brethren; Bridge; Brunner/Mazel; Carolina Biological Supply; Catholic Health Association; Celestial Arts; Christopher; Cleaning Consultant Services; Communication Skill Builders; Compact; Consumer Reports; Contemporary; Council Oak; CRCS; Crossing; Crown; Dawn; Delmar; Delta; Dembner; Devin-Adair; Donning; Douglas & McIntyre; Elysium Growth; Enslow; Paul S. Eriksson; Evans and Co.; Faber & Faber; Facts on File; Falcon; Frederick Fell; Fitzhenry & Whiteside; Forman; Glenmark; Great Ocean; Warren H. Green; H.P.; Harper & Row; Hawkes; Health Profession Division; Houghton Mifflin; Hounslow; Humanics; Hunter House; Information Resources; Ishiyaku Euroamerica; William Kaufman; Michael Kesend; Robert E. Krieger; Peter Lang; Life Cycle; Luramedia; Madrona; Meadowbrook; Medical Economics; Merrill; Metamorphous; Meyerbooks; Mills & Sanderson; Mosaic; Mother Courage; National; National Publishers of the Black Hills; Naturegraph; NC; New Harbinger; New Readers; Newcastle; Ohio Psychology; P.P.I.; Pacific Press; Pandora; Panjandrum; Pantheon; Pelican; Perspectives; Prentice-Hall Canada (trade division); Prima; PSG; Publishers Associates; Raintree; Random House; Rodale; Rosen; Rowman & Littlefield; Rynd; S.C.E. Editions; Saybrook; Schocken; Charles Scribner's Sons; Shoe Tree; Sierra Club; Silver Burdett; Speech Bin; Sterling; Stillpoint; Lyle Stuart; Tab; Jeremy P. Tarcher; Teachers College; Theosophical; Times; Transaction; Ultralight; Unicorn; Universe; University of Calgary; University of Pennsylvania; University of Texas; University Press of Virginia; J. Weston Walch; Samuel Weiser; Westview; Williamson; Wilshire; Winston-Derek; Woodbine; Woodland; Word; Wright; Zebra.

History. Academy Chicago; Adams, Hournes and Ward; Addison-Wesley; Alaska Nature; Alaska Northwest; Alpha; American Atheist; American Studies; Ancestry; Appalachian Mountain Club; Arbor House; Architectural; Ashley; Associated Faculty; Atheneum Children's Books; Atheneum; Atlantic Monthly; Aviation; Avon; Aztex; Basil Blackwell; Beacon; Beaufort; Binford & Mort; John F. Blair; Borgo; Boston Mills; Branden; George Braziller; Brethren; Brevet; Cambridge University; Canadian Plains Research Center; Aristide D. Caratzas; Carolrhoda; Catholic University of America; Cay-Bel; Center for Migration Studies of New York; Chatham; Chelsea Green; Chelsea House-Edgemont; Christopher; Citadel; Arthur H. Clark; Copley; Cornell Maritime; Council Oak; Crossway; Crown; Harry Cuff; Dante University of America; Dembner; Devin-Adair; Devonshire; Donning; Douglas & McIntyre; Down East; Dundurn; William B. Eerdmans; Paul S. Eriksson; Faber & Faber; Facts on File; Fairleigh Dickinson University; Falcon; Family Album; Fiddlehead Poetry Books & Goose Lane Editions; Filter; Fitzhenry & Whiteside; Fjord; Fleet; Fulcrum; Glenbridge; Globe Press; Great Ocean; Green Hill; Greenhaven; Guernica Editions; Harcourt Brace Jovanovich; Harper & Row Junior Books; Harper & Row; Hawkes; Heart of the Lakes; D.C. Heath; Herald Publishing House; Heritage; Heyday; Hippocrene; Homestead; Houghton Mifflin; Hounslow; Hunter; Hurtig; Indiana University; Institute for the Study of Human Issues; International Publishing; Interurban Press/Trans Anglo; Johnson; Kaleidoscopix; William Kaufman; Kent State University; Michael Kesend; Robert E. Krieger; Peter Lang; Lee's Books for Young Readers; Lexikos; Liberty; Life Cycle; Little, Brown; Longman; Loyola; McFarland; Madrona; Mazda; Media Productions and Marketing; Mercer University; Methuen; Meyerbooks; Michigan State University; Misty Hill; MIT; Morehouse-Barlow; William Morrow; Mosaic; Motorbooks International; Museum of New Mexico; National; Naturegraph; Naval Institute; NC; New England; New Society; New Victoria; Nimbus; North Point; Northword; Noyes Data; Ohio University; Old Army; Open Court; Oregon State University; Outbooks; Pandora; Pantheon; Paragon; Peachtree; Pelican; Penkevill; Pennsylvania Historical and Museum Commission; Pickwick; Pineapple; Pocket; Poseidon; Prentice-Hall Canada; Preservation; Presidio; Princeton Architectural; Publishers Associates; Purdue University; Quill; Raintree; Random House; Regnery/Gateway; Renaissance; Riverdale; Russica; Rutgers University; S.C.E. Editions; St. Bede's; St. Martin's; Sandlapper; Schenkman; Schocken; Abner Schram; Second Chance Press; Seven Locks; Shameless Hussy; Shapolsky; Harold Shaw; Shoe String; Shoe Tree; Sierra Club; Silver Burdett; Simon & Schuster; Stanford University; Gibbs M.Smith; Still Point; Lyle Stuart; Sherwood Sugden; Sunstone; Taplinger; Teachers College; Ten Speed; Texas A&M University; Texas Western; Three Continents; Timber; Times; Transaction; Twayne; Tyndale; Ultralight; Universe; University of Alabama; University of Alberta; University of Arizona; University of Arkansas; University of Calgary; University of Illinois; University of Iowa; University of Massachusetts; University of Michigan; University of Nebraska; University of Nevada; University of North Carolina; University of Notre Dame; University of Pennsylvania; University of Tennessee; University of Texas; University of Utah; University Press of America; University Press of Mississippi; University Press of New England; University Press of Virginia; Alfred Van Der Marck; Vehicule; Vestal; J. Weston Walch; Walker; Washington State University; Franklin Watts; Western Tanager; Westernlore; Willow Creek; Woodbine; Word; Yankee; Yee Wen; Zebra; Zondervan.

Hobby. Almar; Ancestry; Ashley; Atheneum Children's Books; Bale; Benjamin; Betterway; Allen D. Bragdon; Carstens; Coles; Collector; Council Oak; Crown; Devonshire; Doll Reader; Dundurn; Enslow; Paul S. Eriksson; Faber & Faber; Facts on File; Filter; Glenmark; H.P.; Hawkes; Hounslow; Interurban Press/Trans Anglo; Kalmbach; Michael Kesend; B. Klein; Liberty; Madrona; Main Street; Meadowbrook; Melius and Peterson; Menasha Ridge; Meyerbooks; Mosaic; Mustang; Ortho Information Services; Panjandrum; Racz; Rocky Top; S.C.E. Editions; Charles Scribner's Sons; Shoe Tree; Stackpole; Sterling; Stoeger; Success; Symmes; Tab; Taplinger; Ten Speed; Ultralight; Unlimited; Vestal; Wallace; Western Tanager; Wilderness; Williamson; Wilshire; Woodbine; Woodsong.

House and Home. Better Homes and Gardens; Betterway; Garden Way; Ortho Information Services; Stewart, Tabori and Chang; Williamson.

How-to. AASLH; Abbey; Abbott, Langer & Associates; Acropolis Books; Adams, Houmes and Ward; Addison-Wesley; Alaska Nature; Almar; Alpha; Ancestry; And Books; Andrews, McMeel & Parker; Appalachian Mountain Club; Arbor House; M. Arman; Art Direction; Asher-Gallant; Ashley; Atheneum Children's Books; Avon; Aztex; Ballantine/Epiphany; Bankers; Benjamin; Berkley; Better Homes and Gardens; Betterway; Briarcliff; Brick House; Bridge; Allen D. Bragdon; Byls; CBP; CCC; Chicago Review Press; Chilton; China Books and Periodicals; Chosen; Christian Ed.; Christopher; Cleaning Consultant Services; Compact; Consumer Reports; Contemporary; Cornell Maritime; Council Oak; Craftsman; Credo; Crossing; Dell; Delta; Dembner; Denlinger's; Devin-Adair; Donning; Education Associates; Enslow; Enterprise; Faber & Faber; Falcon; Frederick Fell; Filter; J. Flores; Focal; Forman; Gambling Times; Garden Way; Gay Sunshine; Gifted Education; Glenmark; Grapevine; Great Northwest; Great Ocean; Stephen Green Press/Lewis; Gryphon House; H.P.; Alexander Hamilton Institute; Harper & Row; Harvard Common; Harvest House; Hawkes; Herald; Here's Life; Heyday; Hippocrene; Hounslow; Human Kinetics; Hunter House; Imagine; Intercultural; International Self-Counsel; International Wealth Success; Jonathan David; Kalmbach; William Kaufman; Kern International; Michael Kesend; B. Klein; Krantz; Learning; Leisure Press; Hal Leonard; Liberty; Linch; Little, Brown; Llewellyn; Lone Eagle; Madrona; Main Street; Marathon International; Meadowbrook; Media Productions and Marketing; Melius and Peterson; Menasha Ridge; Meriwether; Metamorphous; MGI Management Institute; Milady; Mills & Sanderson; William Morrow; Mother Courage; Motorbooks International; Mott Media; Mountaineers; Mustang; National Press; New England; Newcastle; Nimbus; North Light; Oasis; OHara; 101 Productions; Ortho Information Services; Pacific Press; Panjandrum; Pantheon; Pelican; Pennsylvania Historical and Museum Commission; Perspectives; Pineapple; Clarkson N. Potter; Prentice-Hall; Prima; Probus; Que; Racz; Rainbow; Resource; Reymont; Richboro; Rocky Top; Rodale; Ross; RPM; S.C.E. Editions; Santa Barbara; Schirmer;

Schocken; Self-Counsel; Seven Seas; Sierra Club; Speech Bin; ST; Standard; Sterling; Stoeger; Stone Wall; Lyle Stuart; Success; Sunstone; Tab; Jeremy P. Tarcher; Ten Speed; Thomas; Travel Keys; Ultralight; Universe; University of Alberta; Unlimited; Vend-O-Books; Vestal; Wallace; Samuel Weiser; Western Marine; Whitaker; Wilderness; John Wiley & Sons; Williamson; Wilshire; Windsor; Wine Appreciation; Woodland; Woodsong; Word; Wright; Writer's Digest; Yankee; Zebra; Zondervan.

Humanities. Duquesne University; Fordham University; Indiana University; McGraw-Hill; Penkevill; Poseidon; Riverdale; Rocky Top; Roxbury; Southern Illinois University; Taplinger; Umi Research; University of Arkansas; University of Calgary; University of Michigan; VGM; Whitston.

Humor. Abbey; American Studies; Andrews, McMeel & Parker; Applezaba; Ashley; Atheneum Children's Books; Ballantine/Epiphany; CBP; CCC; Chicago Review; Citadel; Clarion; Compact; Contemporary; Council Oak; Critic's Choice Paperbacks; Crown; Harry Cuff; John Daniel; Dell; Delta; Donning; Paul S. Eriksson; Faber & Faber; Frederick Fell; Filter; Guernica Editions; H.P.; Hanley & Belfus; Harcourt Brace Jovanovich; Harper & Row; Hounslow; Hurtig; Kaleidoscopix; William Kaufman; Madrona; Main Street; Meadowbrook; Menasha Ridge; Misty Hill; Mosaic; Mustang; New Society; Nimbus; Peter Pauper; Peachtree; Pelican; Pharos; Clarkson N. Potter; Price/Stern/Sloan; Prima; Random House; Real Comet; Russica; Rutledge University; S.C.E. Editions; Sandlapper; Charles Scribner's Sons; Seven Seas; Sterling; Lyle Stuart; Ten Speed; Texas Monthly; Unlimited; Vend-O-Books; Woodbine; Woodsong; Wright; Yankee; Zondervan.

Illustrated Book. Abbey; American Studies; And Books; Appalachian Mountain Club; Atheneum Children's Books; Bear; Betterway; Boston Mills; Branden; Allen D. Bragdon; Canadian Plains Research Center; Carolrhoda; Chelsea House-Edgemont; Christian Ed.; Cleaning Consultant Services; Council Oak; Harry Cuff; Devonshire; Donning; Douglas & McIntyre; Down East; Elysium Growth; Faber & Faber; Falcon; Filter; J. Flores; Great Ocean; Greenhaven; Harcourt Brace Jovanovich; Harbor House; Harvest House; Here's Life; Homestead; Hounslow; Imagine; Michael Kesend; Hal Leonard; Lexikos; Liberty; Meadowbrook; Metamorphous; Methuen; Mosaic; National Press; New England; New Society; Nimbus; Ortho Information Services; Paragon; Parenting; Pelican; Pennsylvania Historical and Museum Commission; Prima; Princeton Architectural; Racz; Random House; Sandlapper; Seven Seas; Speech Bin; Stewart, Tabori and Chang; Lyle Stuart; Texas Monthly; Unicorn; Union of American Hebrew Congregations; Unlimited; Vestal; Williamson; Willow Creek; Woodsong; Wright; Zondervan.

Juvenile. Abbey; Alaska Nature; Atheneum Children's Books; Betterway; Don Bosco; Branden; Byls; Carolrhoda; Chariot; China Books and Periodicals; Christian Ed.; Clarion; Consumer Reports; Crown; Harry Cuff; May Davenport; Dell; Dial Books for Young Readers; Dillon; Dodd, Mead; Douglas & McIntyre; Down East; Dundurn; E.P. Dutton; Eakin; Enslow; Faber & Faber; Farrar, Straus and Giroux; Fleet; C.R. Gibson; Golden; Greenhaven; Harcourt Brace Jovanovich; Harper Junior Books, West Coast; Harvest House; Herald; Homestead; Hounslow; Hunter House; Incentive; Intervarsity; Kaleidoscopix; Kar-Ben Copies; Lee's Books for Young Readers; Margaret K. McElderry; Macmillan; Maynard-Thomas; Mazda; Meadowbrook; Melius and Peterson; Misty Hill; William Morrow; Morrow Junior; Mott Media; National Press; Nimbus; Oddo; P.P.I.; Pacific Press; Panjandrum; Pantheon; Parenting; Pelican; Perspectives; Platt & Munk; Players; Clarkson N. Potter; Prentice-Hall Books for Young Readers; Price/Stern/Sloan; Racz; Raintree; Regnery/Gateway; Review and Herald Publishing; Sandlapper; Shameless Hussy; Harold Shaw; Shoe Tree; Sierra Club; Speech Bin; Standard; Sterling; Success; Troubador; Unicorn; Union of American Hebrew Congregations; Vestal; Walker; Woodsong; Wright; Zondervan.

Labor/Management. Almar; BNA; ILR; MGI Management Institute; Prentice-Hall; RPM; University.

Language and Literature. Beacon Press; George Braziller; Aristide D. Caratzas; Catholic University of America; Coles; Crossing; Dante University of America; Dundurn; Facts on File; Fiddlehead Poetry Books & Goose Lane Editions; Hunter; Indiana University; Longman; Loyola; Merrill; Modern Language Association of America; National Textbook; Oddo; Ohio State University; Ohio University; Oregon State University; Pandora; Paragon; Penkevill; Perfection Form; Clarkson N. Potter; Prentice-Hall Canada; Prentice-Hall/Regents; Rosen; Stanford

University; Texas Christian University; Three Continents; Universe; University of Alabama; University of California; University of Illinois; University of Iowa; University of Nebraska; University of North Carolina; University of Texas; University Press of America; Vehicule; Wadsworth; J. Weston Walch; York.

Law. Anderson; Associated Faculty; Banks-Baldwin Law; Enterprise; Gambling Times; Government Institutes; International Self-Counsel; Linch; Monitor; National Press; Ohio State University; Pantheon; Parker & Son; Rowman & Littlefield; Rutgers University; Rynd; S.C.E. Editions; Transaction; Transnational; University of North Carolina; University of Pennsylvania; University Press of Virginia; Westview.

Literary Criticism. Associated Faculty; Borgo; Dundurn; Fairleigh Dickinson University; Kent State University; Methuen; Mysterious; Purdue University; Rutgers University; Southern Illinois University; Stanford University; Sherwood Sugden; Texas Christian University; Three Continents; Twayne; Umi Research; University of Alabama; University of Arkansas; University of Massachusetts; University of Pennsylvania; University of Tennessee; University Press of Mississippi; York.

Marine Subjects. Cay-Bel; Cornell Maritime; Harbor House; International Marine; Kaleidoscopix; Naval Institute; Oregon State University; PBC International; Seven Seas; Tab.

Military/War. Avon; J. Flores; Old Army; Paladin; Presidio; Shoe String; Stackpole; Sunflower University; Westview.

Money/Finance. Acropolis Books; Allen; Almar; Bale; Ballinger; Bankers; Better Homes and Gardens; Enterprise; Glenmark; International Wealth Success; Kern International; Longman Financial Services.

Music and Dance. American Catholic; And Books; Ashley; Atheneum Children's Books; Beaufort; Branden; Cambridge University; Carolrhoda; Consumer Reports; Contemporary; Council Oak; Crown; Dance Horizons; May Davenport; Delta; Dodd, Mead; Dragon's Teeth; Drama; Paul S. Eriksson; Faber & Faber; Facts on File; Fairleigh Dickinson University; Fjord; Glenbridge; Great Ocean; Guernica Editions; Harper & Row; Indiana University; Robert E. Krieger; Peter Lang; Hal Leonard; McFarland; Mosaic; Museum of New Mexico; National; Ohio State University; Panjandrum; Paragon; Pelican; Pennsylvania Historical and Museum Commission; Prima; Publishers Associates; Quill; Random House; Real Comet; Resource; Rosen; Scarecrow; Schirmer; Shoe String; Shoe Tree; Stipes; Lyle Stuart; Tab; Transaction; Umi Research; Unicorn; Universe; University of Illinois; University of Michigan; University Press of America; University Press of New England; Vestal; Wadsworth; J. Weston Walch; Walker; Samuel Weiser; Writer's Digest.

Nature and Environment. Alaska Nature; And Books; Appalachian Mountain Club; Ashley; Atheneum Children's Books; Bear; Binford & Mort; John F. Blair; Bookmakers Guild; Canadian Plains Research Center; Carolina Biological Supply; Carolrhoda; Chelsea Green; Chronicle; Clarion; Council Oak; Crown; John Daniel; May Davenport; Dawn; Devin-Adair; Devonshire; Down East; Elysium Growth; Paul S. Eriksson; Facts on File; Falcon; Flora and Fauna; Forman; Fulcrum; Golden; Government Institutes; Great Northwest; Stephen Green Press/Lewis; Greenhaven; Harcourt Brace Jovanovich; Harper & Row; Heyday; Homestead; Hounslow; Hurtig; Johnson; Michael Kesend; Lexikos; Melius and Peterson; Meyerbooks; Misty Hill; Mosaic; Museum of New Mexico; Museum of Northern Arizona; New England; Nimbus; North Country; North Point; Northword; Ortho Information Services; Outbooks; Pacific Press; Parnassus Imprints; Pineapple; Platt & Munk; Plexus; Clarkson N. Potter; Raintree; Random House; Review and Herald; Rocky Top; S.C.E. Editions; Charles Scribner's Sons; Seven Locks; Shoe String; Shoe Tree; Sierra Club; Silver Burdett; Stewart, Tabori and Chang; Stone Wall; Stoneydale; Symmes; Jeremy P. Tarcher; Taylor; Ten Speed; Texas A&M University; Texas Monthly; Universe; University of Alberta; University of Arkansas; University of Calgary; University of Nebraska; University Press of New England; Walker; Western Producer; Wilderness; Willow Creek; Woodland; Yankee.

Philosophy. Alba House; Alpha; American Atheist; Appalachian Mountain Club; Aquarian; Ashley; Atheneum Children's Books; Atlantic Monthly; Basil Blackwell; Beacon Press; Berkley; George Braziller; Brethren; Brook House; Canterbury; Catholic University of America; Celestial Arts; Christopher; Council Oak; John Daniel; Donning; Dragon's Teeth; William B. Eerdmans; Elysium Growth; Enslow; Paul S. Eriksson; Facts on File; Fairleigh Dickinson University; Falcon; Frederick Fell; Fulcrum; Garber Communications; Gifted Education;

Glenbridge; Globe; Great Ocean; Greenhaven; Guernica Editions; Harcourt Brace Jovanovich; Harper & Row; Herald; Hounslow; Indiana University; Intercultural; International Publishers; Intervarsity; Robert E. Krieger; Peter Lang; Luramedia; Mercer University; Methuen; Michigan State University; MIT; New Society; North Point; Ohio State University; Ohio University; Open Court; Panjandrum; Paragon; Paulist; Pilgrim; Publishers Associates; Purdue University; Regnery/Gateway; Renaissance; Rocky Top; Rowman & Littlefield; Roxbury; S.C.E. Editions; St. Bede's; Santa Barbara; Saybrook; Schocken; Second Chance Press; Shapolsky; Shoe String; Sierra Club; Simon & Schuster; Stillpoint; Sherwood Sugden; Teachers College; Theosophical; Transaction; University of Alabama; University of Alberta; University of Arizona; University of Calgary; University of Massachusetts; University of Michigan; University of Notre Dame; University of Utah; University Press of America; Valley; Wadsworth; Washington State University; Samuel Weiser; Wingbow; Winston-Derek; Woodsong; Word; Yee Wen; Zondervan.

Photography. Alaska Nature; Appalachian Mountain Club; Atheneum Children's Books; Branden; Chronicle; Contemporary; Council Oak; Crown; Delta; Donning; Elysium Growth; Paul S. Eriksson; Faber & Faber; Fiddlehead Poetry Books & Goose Lane Editions; Filter; Focal; Fulcrum; H.P.; Homestead; Hounslow; Hudson Hills; Krantz; Liberty; Madrona; Motorbooks International; Owl Creek; Pandora; PBC International; Pennsylvania Historical and Museum Commission; Clarkson N. Potter; Raintree; Real Comet; Charles Scribner's Sons; Shapolsky; Sierra Club; Gibbs M. Smith; Sterling; Stewart, Tabori and Chang; Studio; Symmes; Tab; Texas Monthly; Umi Research; Unicorn; University of Michigan; University of Nebraska; University of Texas; Alfred Van Der Marck; Wallace; Western Producer; Writer's Digest; Yankee.

Psychology. Abbey; Accelerated Development; ACS; Addison-Wesley; Affirmation Books; Alba House; American Psychiatric; American Studies; Arbor House; Ashley; Atheneum Children's Books; Atheneum; Augsburg; Avon; Ballantine/Epiphany; Basil Blackwell; Beacon Press; Betterway; Bookmakers Guild; Brethren; Brunner/Mazel; Cambridge University; Celestial Arts; Center for Migration Studies of New York; Christopher; Citadel; Compact; Contemporary; Council Oak; CRCS; Credo; Crown; Dembner; Devonshire; Dimension; Education Associates; William B. Eerdmans; Elysium Growth; Enslow; Paul S. Eriksson; Facts on File; Fairleigh Dickinson University; Falcon; Forman; General Hall; Gifted Education; Glenbridge; Glenmark; Globe; Stephen Greene Press/Lewis; Greenhaven; Guernica Editions; Harcourt Brace Jovanovich; Harper & Row; Hawkes; Hazeldon; Herald; Heroica; Houghton Mifflin; Hounslow; Humanics; Hunter House; Intercultural; International Self-Counsel; Intervarsity; John Knox; Robert E. Krieger; Peter Lang; Learning; Libra; Luramedia; McFarland; Madrona; Metamorphous; Methuen; Mother Courage; National; New Harbinger; New Society; Newcastle; Ohio Psychology; Open Court; Perspectives; Plenum; Poseidon; Prima; Publishers Associates; Quill; Random House; Regnery/Gateway; Riverdale; Rodale; Roxbury; Saybrook; Schenkman; Schocken; Self-Counsel; Shameless Hussy; Harold Shaw; Shoe String; Sigo; Stanford University; Stillpoint; Jeremy P. Tarcher; Theosophical; Transaction; Tyndale; University of Calgary; University of Massachusetts; University of Michigan; University of Nebraska; University Press of America; University Press of New England; J. Weston Walch; Walker; Washington State University; Samuel Weiser; Williamson; Wilshire; Wingbow; Woodsong; Word; Zebra; Zondervan.

Real Estate. Longman Financial Services; Prentice-Hall; Uli.

Recreation. Alaska Nature; And Books; Arbor House; Ashley; Atheneum Children's Books; Beaufort; Chicago Review; Chronicle; Compact; Crown; Down East; Elysium Growth; Enslow; Paul S. Eriksson; Facts on File; Falcon Press Publishing; Frederick Fell; Filter; Fulcrum; Glenmark; Stephen Green Press/Lewis; Guernica Editions; H.P.; Hippocrene; Hounslow; Johnson; Kalmbach; Kern International; Robert E. Krieger; Liberty; Madrona; Meadowbrook; Melius and Peterson; Menasha Ridge; Mountaineers; Mustang; National Press; North Country; Northword; 101 Productions; Outbooks; Pantheon; Peachtree; Pelican; Racz; Riverdale; S.C.E. Editions; Charles Scribner's Sons; Shoe Tree; Sierra Club; Sterling; Stipes; Stoneydale; Jeremy P. Tarcher; Ten Speed; Texas Monthly; University of Michigan; J. Weston Walch; Walker; Wilshire.

Reference. AASLH; Abbott, Langer & Associates; Accelerated Development; Acropolis Books; Bob Adams; Alpha; American Atheist; American Federation of Information Processing; American Psychiatric; American Reference; Ancestry; Appalachian Mountain Club; Architectural; M. Arman; Asher-Gallant; Ashley; Associated Faculty; Avi; Avon; Ballinger; Bankers; Banks-Baldwin Law; Basil Blackwell; Bethany House; Betterway; Binford & Mort; BNA; Bookmakers Guild; Borgo; Branden; Brick House; Broadway; Aristide D. Caratzas; Cay-Bel; Chelsea House-Edgemont; Chicago Review; China Books and Periodicals; Christian Ed.; Christopher; Arthur H. Clark; Coles; Compact; Computer Science; Consumer Reports; Contemporary; Credo; Crown; Harry Cuff; Dante University of America; Steve Davis; Delta; Dharma; Donning; Down East; Drama; Dundurn; William B. Eerdmans; Enslow; Evans and Co.; Facts on File; Fairleigh Dickinson University; Fiddlehead Poetry Books & Goose Lane Editions; Filter; Flora and Fauna; Floricanto; Focal; Genealogical; General Hall; Glenbridge; Government Institutes; Great Ocean; Greenhaven; Guernica Editions; Gulf; Alexander Hamilton Institute; Hanley & Belfus; Harcourt Brace Jovanovich; Harper & Row; Harvard Common; Harvest House; Hazeldon Foundation; Health Profession Division; Herald; Here's Life; Heroica; Heyday; Hippocrene; Homestead; Hounslow; Human Kinetics; Hunter; Hurtig; ILR; Imagine; Industrial; Information Resources; Intercultural; International Foundation of Employee Benefit Plans; International Self-Counsel; Interstate Printers & Publishers; Intervarsity; Ishiyaku Euroamerica; Jonathan David; B. Klein; Krantz; Peter Lang; Learning; Leisure Press; Hal Leonard; Libraries Unlimited; Llewellyn; Lone Eagle; McFarland; McGraw-Hill; Mazda; Meadowbrook; Media Productions and Marketing; Melius and Peterson; Menasha Ridge; Mercer University; Metamorphous; Methuen; Meyerbooks; Michigan State University; Milady; Modern Language Association of America; Monitor; Museum of New Mexico; Museum of Northern Arizona; Mysterious; National; National Press; Thomas Nelson; New York Zoetrope; Octameron; Old Army; Ortho Information Services; Our Sunday Visitor; Pacific; Pandora; Panjandrum; Paragon; Penkevill; Pennsylvania Historical and Museum Commission; Petrocelli; Pharos; Pineapple; Plexus; Pocket; Porter Sargent; Potentials Development for Health & Aging Services; Prentice-Hall; Professional; Prolingua; Que; Racz; Rainbow; Raintree; Reference Service; Rocky Top; Rosen; RPM; Rutledge; Rynd; S.C.E. Editions; St. Martin's; Sandlapper; Schirmer; Schocken; Self-Counsel; Seven Locks; Harold Shaw; Shoe String; Sound View; Speech Bin; ST; Standard; Sterling; Sunflower; Texas Monthly; Thomas; Transaction; Transnational; Ultralight; Universe; University of Alberta; University of Calgary; University of Illinois; University of Michigan; University Press of New England; University Press of Virginia; Unlimited; Vestal; Walker; Wallace; Western Producer; Westview; Whitston; John Wiley & Sons; Windsor; Wingbow; Alan Wofsy; Woodbine; Woodland; Woodsong; Word; Wordware; Writer's Digest; York; Zondervan.

Regional. Alaska Nature; Alaska Northwest; Binford & Mort; John F. Blair; Borealis; Caxton Printers; Chatham; Chicago Review; China Books and Periodicals; Chronicle; Arthur H. Clark; Copley; Cornell Maritime; Harry Cuff; Douglas & McIntyre; Down East; Eakin; William B. Eerdmans; Falcon Press Publishing; Fiddlehead Poetry Books & Goose Lane Editions; Fitzhenry & Whiteside; Golden West Publishers; Green Hill; Guernica Editions; Gulf; Harbor House; Heart of the Lakes; Herald Publishing House; Hurtig; Indiana University; Johnson; Kent State University; Lexikos; Mercer University; Museum of New Mexico; Nimbus; North Country; Ohio University; Oregon State University; Outbooks; Pacific; Parnassus Imprints; Pelican; Pennsylvania Historical and Museum Commission; Pruett; Purdue University; Stoneydale; Sunstone; Syracuse University; Texas A&M University; Texas Monthly; Texas Western; Three Continents; University of Arizona; University of Calgary; University of Nebraska; University of Nevada; University of North Carolina; University of Tennessee; University of Texas; Unviersity of Utah; University Press of Mississippi; Utah State University; Vehicule; Washington State University; Westernlore; Windsor; Yankee.

Religion. Abbey; Abingdon; Accent Books; Affirmation Books; Aglow; Alba House; Alban Institute; Alpha; American Atheist; American Catholic; Aquarian; Ashley; Atheneum Children's Books; Augsburg; Ballantine/Epiphany; Bantam; Basil Blackwell; Beacon Hill Press of Kansas City; Beacon Press; Bear; Bethany House; Binford & Mort; Bookcraft; Don Bosco; Brethren; Bridge; Byls; Aristide D. Caratzas; Catholic Health Association; Catholic University of America; CBP; Chosen; Christian Ed.; Christopher; Compact; Council Oak; Crossway; Dawn; Delta; Devonshire; Dharma; Dimension; William B. Eerdmans; Facts on File; Falcon; Frederick Fell; Fleet; Fortress; Fraser Institute; C.R. Gibson; Glenmark; Great Ocean; Greenhaven; Guernica Editions; Harcourt Brace Jovanovich; Harper & Row; Harvest House; Herald Publishing House; Here's Life; Hounslow; Huntington House; Indiana University; Intervarsity;

John Knox; Robert E. Krieger; Peter Lang; Life Cycle; Liguori; Loyola; McFarland; Mercer University; Meriwether; Methuen; Michigan State University; Misty Hill; Morehouse-Barlow; William Morrow; Mott Media; Multnomah; Thomas Nelson; New Leaf; New Society; Newcastle; Open Court; Orbis; Our Sunday Visitor; Pacific Press; Paragon; Paulist; Peter Pauper; Pelican; Pennsylvania Historical and Museum Commission; Pickwick; Pilgrim; Publishers Associates; Puckerbrush; Purdue University; Random House; Regal; Regnery/Gateway; Religious Education; Resource; Fleming H. Revell; Review and Herald; St. Anthony Messenger; St. Bede's; Santa Barbara; Schocken; Servant; Seven Locks; Shapolsky; Harold Shaw; Shining Star; Shoe String; Silver Burdett; Standard; Sterling; Stillpoint; Sherwood Sugden; Theosophical; Tyndale; Umi Research; Union of American Hebrew Congregations; University of Alabama; University of Calgary; University of North Carolina; University of Notre Dame; University of Tennessee; University Press of America; Alfred Van Der Marck; Wadsworth; Samuel Weiser; Whitaker; Wingbow; Winston-Derek; Word; Yee Wen; Zondervan.

Scholarly. Beacon Press; Birkauser Boston; BNA; Cambridge University; Canadian Plains Research Center; Dante University of America; Duquesne; Fairleigh Dickinson University; Harvard University; ILR; Indiana University; Kent State University; Alfred A. Knopf; Peter Lang; Lomond; McFarland; Mazda; Mercer University; Michigan State University; Mott Media; Nelson-Hall; Ohio State University; Ohio University; Oise; Open Court; Oregon State University; Pacific; Penkevill; Pickwick; Porter Sargent; Purdue University; Religious Education; Rowman & Littlefield; Rutgers University; Schirmer; Southern Illinois; Stanford University; Texas Christian University; Texas Western; Transnational; Twayne; Umi Research; University of Arizona; University of Calgary; University of California; University of Illinois; University of Utah; University of Wisconsin; University Press of America; Washington State University; Westernlore; Whitston; York.

Science/Technology. Addison-Wesley; Almar; American Astronautical Society; Architectural; ARCsoft; Atlantic Monthly; Avi; Ballinger; Bantam; Bear; Birkhauser Boston; Cambridge University; Carolina Biological Supply; Chicago Review; Coles; Computer Science; Crown; Steve Davis; Delta; Dillon; Dodd, Mead; Enslow; Fjord; Flora and Fauna; Grapevine; Warren H. Green; Stephen Greene Press/Lewis; Gulf; Harper & Row Junior Books; Harper & Row; D.C. Heath; Helix; Houghton Mifflin; Industrial; Johnson; William Kaufman; Kent State University; Kern International; John Knox; Krantz; Robert E. Krieger; Little, Brown; McGraw-Hill; Merrill; Metamorphous; Methuen; MIT; Museum of New Mexico; Museum of Northern Arizona; National; Naturegraph; New Readers; Noyes Data; Oddo; Open Court; Oregon State University; Pacific; Plexus; Platt & Munk; Plenum; Prentice-Hall Canada; Prentice-Hall Canada (secondary school division); Quill; Raintree; Regnery/Gateway; Rocky Top; Ross; Rutgers University; St. Martin's; Charles Scribner's Sons; Sierra Club; Simon & Schuster; Stanford University; Stewart, Tabori and Chang; Stipes; Texas Western; Theosophical; Times; Transaction; Twayne; University of Arizona; University of Calgary; University of Michigan; University of Pennsylvania; University of Texas; University Press of New England; Utah State University; VGM; J. Weston Walch; Walker; Westview.

Self-help. AASLH; Abbey; Acropolis Books; ACS; Adams, Houmes and Ward; Affirmation Books; Aglow; Alaska Nature; Allen; American Psychiatric; And Books; Arbor House; Ashley; Atheneum Children's Books; Augsburg; Avon; Ballantine/Epiphany; Benjamin; Betterway; Bookmakers Guild; Bridge; Carolina Biological Supply; CBP; CCC; Celestial Arts; Chicago Review; Chosen; Christopher; Cleaning Consultant Services; Cliffs Notes; Coles; Compact; Consumer Reports; Contemporary; Council Oak; CRCS; Credo; Crown; John Daniel; Dawn; Delta; Dembner; Elysium; Enslow; Enterprise; Paul S. Eriksson; Faber & Faber; Falcon; Frederick Fell; J. Flores; Forman; Fulcrum; Glenmark; Globe; Grapevine; Great Ocean; Stephen Greene Press/Lewis; H.P.; Harcourt Brace Jovanovich; Harper & Row; Harvard Common; Hawkes; Hazeldon Foundation; Herald; Herald Publishing House; Here's Life; Hippocrene; Hounslow; Human Kinetics; Humanics; Hunter House; Huntington House; Intercultural; International Self-Counsel; International Wealth Success; Jonathan David; Kaleidoscopix; Michael Kesend; B. Klein; Krantz; Learning; Liberty; Liguori; Llewellyn; Lone Eagle; Madrona; Main Street; Marathon International; Maynard-Thomas; Media Productions and Marketing; Melius and Peterson; Menasha Ridge; Meriwether; Metamorphous; Methuen; Meyerbooks; Mills & Sanderson; Mother Courage; Mott Media; Multnomah; Mustang; National Press; New Harbinger; New Leaf; New Society; Newcastle; W.W. Norton; Oasis; Ohio

Psychology; Our Sunday Visitor; P.P.I.; Pacific Press; Paladin; Pandora; Parenting; Paulist; Pelican; Perspectives; Poseidon; Clarkson N. Potter; Prentice-Hall; Price/Stern/Sloan; Prima; Racz; Random House; Regal; Rodale; Rutledge; S.C.E. Editions; St. Martin's; Santa Barbara; Self-Counsel; Harold Shaw; Sigo; Spinsters/Aunt Lute; Sterling; Stillpoint; Stoeger; Lyle Stuart; Success; Symmes; Ten Speed; Theosophical; Times; Trillium; Ultralight; Unicorn; University; Unlimited; Walker; Samuel Weiser; Whitaker; John Wiley & Sons; Williamson; Wilshire; Wingbow; Woodbine; Woodsong; Word; Wright.

Social Sciences. Borgo; Cambridge University; Celestial Arts; Chelsea House-Edgemont; Duquesne; McGraw-Hill; Mazda; Merrill; Methuen; National Association of Social Workers; Nelson-Hall; New Readers; Oddo; Ohio University; Oregon State University; Perfection Form; Prentice-Hall Canada; Riverdale; Roxbury; Southern Illinois; Stanford University; Transaction; Universe; University of California; J. Weston Walch; Whitston.

Sociology. Alba House; Alpha; American Psychiatric; Ashley; Associated Faculty; Atheneum Children's Books; Ballantine/Epiphany; Basil Blackwell; Beacon Press; Betterway; Branden; Brethren; Brook House; Canadian Plains Research Center; Canterbury; Center for Migration Studies of New York; Christopher; Compact; Council Oak; Credo; Harry Cuff; Devonshire; William B. Eerdmans; Elysium Growth; Enslow; Paul S. Eriksson; Faber & Faber; Fairleigh Dickinson University; Falcon; Frederick Fell; Fraser Institute; General Hall; Glenbridge; Greenhaven; Harcourt Brace Jovanovich; Harper & Row; Harrow and Heston; Hazeldon Foundation; Herald; Heroica; Humanics; ILR; Institute for the Study of Human Issues; Intercultural; Intervarsity; Robert E. Krieger; Peter Lang; Life Cycle; Lomond; McFarland; Mazda; Media Productions and Marketing; Mercer University; Metamorphous; Mills & Sanderson; Mother Courage; NC; New Society; North Point; Ohio State University; P.P.I.; Pantheon; Penkevill; Perspectives; Pilgrim; Plenum; Poseidon; Publishers Associates; Purdue University; Random House; Real Comet; Regnery/Gateway; Riverdale; Roxbury; Rutgers University; S.C.E. Editions; Santa Barbara; Saybrook; Schenkman; Schocken; Seven Locks; Shameless Hussy; South End; Stanford University; Jeremy P. Tarcher; Teachers College; Thomas; Transaction; Tyndale; University of Alabama; Unviersity of Alberta; University of Arkansas; University of Illinois; University of Massachusetts; University of Michigan; University of Notre Dame; University Press of America; University Press of Mississippi; University Press of New England; Vehicule; J. Weston Walch; Washington State University; Westview; Woodbine; Word; Yee Wen; Zondervan.

Sports. American Studies; Arbor House; Ashley; Atheneum Children's Books; Atheneum; Athletic; Avon; Beaufort; Benjamin; Briarcliff; Coles; Contemporary; Council Oak; Crown; Cynthia; Delta; Dembner; Devin-Adair; Dodd, Mead; Enslow; Paul S. Eriksson; Facts on File; Fleet; Great Northwest; Stephen Greene Press/Lewis; H.P.; Harcourt Brace Jovanovich; Harper & Row Junior Books; Harper & Row; Carl Hungness; Jonathan David; Michael Kesend; Robert E. Krieger; Leisure Press; Liberty; Little, Brown; McFarland; Menasha Ridge; Mosaic; Motorbooks International; Mountaineers; National Press; OHara; Paladin; PBC International; Pennsylvania Historical and Museum Commission; Racz; Random House; S.C.E. Editions; Santa Barbara; Charles Scribner's Sons; Shapolsky; Shoe Tree; Sierra Club; Silver Burdett; Stackpole; Sterling; Stoeger; Stone Wall; Stoneydale; Jeremy P. Tarcher; Taylor; Texas Monthly; Times; University of Illinois; University of Nebraska; J. Weston Walch; Walker; Franklin Watts; Western Marine; Willow Creek; Word; Wright.

Software. Bantam; Career; Dustbooks; Entelek; Kern International; Liberty; Merrill; Michigan State University; National Textbook; Prentice-Hall Canada; Prentice-Hall Canada (secondary school division); Que; Review and Herald; RPM; Schirmer; VGM; J. Weston Walch; Windsor; Wine Appreciation.

Technical. Abbott, Langer & Associates; Almar; Alpha; American Federation of Information Processing; American Psychiatric; ARCsoft; M. Arman; Auto Book; Avi; Aviation; Bankers; Birkhauser Boston; Branden; Brevet; Brick House; Broadway; Canadian Plains Research Center; Aristide D. Caratzas; Carolina Biological Supply; Center for Migration Studies of New York; Chilton; Cleaning Consultant Services; Coles; Computer Science; Consumer Reports; Cornell Maritime; Craftsman; Harry Cuff; Cynthia; Denlinger's; Devonshire; Dustbooks; Enslow; Falcon; Frederick Fell; Flora and Fauna; Focal; Government Institutes; Grapevine; Great Ocean; Gulf; H.P.; Harcourt Brace Jovanovich; Human Kinetics; ILR; Industrial; Information Resources; International Foundation of Employee Benefit Plans; Kern International;

Robert E. Krieger; Learning; Leisure Press; Hal Leonard; Lomond; Lone Eagle; McFarland; Metamorphous; MGI Management Institute; Michigan State University; National; National Publishers of the Black Hills; New York Zoetrope; Noyes Data; Parker & Son; Pennsylvania Historical and Museum Commission; Petrocelli; Prentice-Hall; Probus; Professional; Q.E.D. Information Sciences; Que; Racz; Religious Education; Riverdale; Rocky Top; RPM; Rynd; Schenkman; Seven Seas; Shoe String; ST; Sterling; Stipes; Theatre Arts; Transaction; Uli; Ultralight; Univelt; University of Alberta; University of Calgary; University of Michigan; Unlimited; Vestal; Willow Creek; Windsor; Wordware; Wright.

Textbook. AASLH; Accelerated Development; Alba House; Alpha; American Federation of Information Processing; American Psychiatric; M. Arman; Art Direction; Ashley; Augsburg; Avi; Basil Blackwell; Bennett & McKnight; Birkhauser; Don Bosco; Branden; Brick House; CQ; Canadian Plains Research Center; Aristide D. Caratzas; Career; Center for Migration Studies of New York; Cleaning Consultant Services; Cliffs Notes; Computer Science; Harry Cuff; May Davenport; Delmar; Devonshire; Drama; Education Associates; William B. Eerdmans; ETC; Falcon; Frederick Fell; Fitzhenry & Whiteside; Flora and Fauna; Focal; Fortress; General Hall; Glenbridge; Grapevine; Greenhaven; Guernica Editions; Hanley & Belfus; Max Hardy-Publisher; Harrow and Heston; Health Profession Division; D.C. Heath; Heinle & Heinle; Herald; Heroica; Human Kinetics; Information Resources; Intercultural; International Foundation of Employee Benefit Plans; International Publishers; Interstate Printers & Publishers; Ishiyaku Euroamerica; Jamestown; William Kaufman; Kern International; John Knox; Robert E. Krieger; Peter Lang; Learning; Libraries Unlimited; Llewellyn; Longman; Loyola; McGraw-Hill; Maynard-Thomas; Mazda; Media Productions and Marketing; Mercer University; Meriwether; Metamorphous; Michigan State University; Milady; Mott Media; National; National Publishers of the Black Hills; National Textbook; Nelson-Hall; New York Zoetrope; Ohio Psychology; Oise; P.A.R.; Pacific Press; Paragon; Paulist; Penkevill; Petrocelli; Prentice-Hall Canada; Prentice-Hall Canada (secondary school division); Princeton Architectural; Professional; Prolingua; Pruett; Purdue University; Que; Racz; Prentice-Hall/Regents; Religious Education; Rosen; Roxbury; Rynd; St. Bede's; St. Martin's; Sandlapper; Schenkman; Schirmer; Seven Locks; Shoe String; Speech Bin; ST; Standard; Stanford University; Stipes; Sunflower Unviersity; Thomas; Transaction; Transnational; Trillium; Union of American Hebrew Congregations; University of Alberta; University of Calgary; University of Michigan; University of Notre Dame; University Press of America; Utah State University; VGM; Woodland; Word; Wright; York.

Translation. Alba House; Alyson; M. Arman; Avi; Briarcliff; Chatham; Crossway; Dante University of America; Devin-Adair; Dharma; Dimension; Drama; Enslow; ETC; Fortress; Front Row Experience; Indiana University; Institute for the Study of Human Issues; Peter Lang; Liberty; Open Court; Owl Creek; Pacific; Panjandrum; Paulist; Pickwick; Porter Sargent; Presidio; Resource; Ross; S.C.E. Editions; St. Luke's; Southern Illinois University; Tab; Theosophical; Three Continents; Timber; Transaction; Universe; Unviersity of Massachusetts; University of Nebraska; University of Texas; University of Utah; University of Wisconsin.

Transportation. Golden West; Interurban Press/Trans Anglo.

Travel. Academy Chicago; Alaska Northwest; Almar; American Studies; And Books; Appalachian Mountain Club; Ashley; Atheneum Children's Books; Beaufort; Binford & Mort; Briarcliff; Artistide D. Caratzas; Chelsea Green; Chicago Review; Christopher; Chronicle; Contemporary; Council Oak; John Daniel; Devin-Adair; Dodd, Mead; Donning; Elysium Growth; Paul S. Eriksson; Faber & Faber; Filter; Fodor's Travel; Fulcrum; Glenmark; Harcourt Brace Jovanovich; Harper & Row; Harvard Common; Heyday; Hippocrene; Homestead; Hounslow; Hunter; Intercultural; Interurban Press/Trans Anglo; Johnson; Kaleidoscopix; Michael Kesend; Liberty; Madrona; Marlor; Meadowbrook; Melius and Peterson; Methuen; Mills & Sanderson; Moon; Mosaic; Mustang; National Publishers of the Black Hills; Nimbus; North Point; Octameron; 101 Productions; Outbooks; Passport; Peachtree; Pelican; Pennsylvania Historical and Museum Commission; Pilot; Prentice-Hall Canada (trade division); Prima; Pruett; Riverdale; S.C.E. Editions; Santa Barbara; Shapolsky; Shoe String; Shoe Tree; Sierra Club; Stewart, Tabori and Chang; Ten Speed; Texas Monthly; Travel Keys; University of Michigan; Western Tanager; John Wiley & Sons; Williamson; Wine Appreciation; Yankee.

Women's Issues/Studies. Bantam; Beacon Press; Betterway; Contemporary; Fairleigh Dickinson University; Indiana University; International Publishers; McFarland; New Society; Pandora; Pantheon; Press Gang; Publishers Associates; Rowman & Littlefield; Rutgers University; Saybrook; Scarecrow; Schenkman; Schocken; Spinsters/Aunt Lute; Times; Twayne; Umi Research; University of Massachusetts; University of Tennessee; Westview; Wingbow.

World Affairs. Atlantic Monthly; Ballinger; McFarland.

Young Adult. Philomel; Pineapple; Rosen.

Fiction

This subject index for fiction will help you pinpoint fiction markets without having to scan all the book publishers' listings. As with the nonfiction markets, read the complete individual listings for each publisher for advice on what types of fiction the company buys. For more detailed advice and additional fiction markets that offer a royalty or copies as payment, consult *Fiction Writer's Market* (Writer's Digest Books).

Adventure. Abbey; Alaska Nature; Arbor House; Ashley; Atheneum Children's; Avon; Avon Flare; Baen; Baker Street; Ballantine/Epiphany; Berkley; Branden; Camelot; Canterbury; Carroll & Graf; Chariot; Clarion; Critic's Choice; John Daniel; May Davenport; Dell; Dembner; Dial; Dillon; Donning; Falcon; Fulcrum; Golden Eagle; Harper & Row; Harper & Row Junior; Hounslow; Kaleidoscopix; Kar-Ben Copies; Knights; Lodestar; Misty Hill; Mother Courage; New Victoria; Pandora; Printemps; Quality; Racz; Raintree; Random House; Russica; Charles Scribner's Sons; Second Chance; Shameless Hussy; Sierra Club; Silver Burdett; SOS; Unlimited; Walker; Woodsong Graphics; Wright; Yankee; Zebra.

Confession. Ashley; Falcon; Random House; Second Chance; Shameless Hussy; Wright; Zebra.

Erotica. Devonshire; Falcon; Gay Sunshine; Greenleaf Classics; Hunter House; Knights; New Victoria; Quality; Russica; Thunder's Mouth; Wright; Zebra.

Ethnic. Abbey; Ashley; Atheneum Children's; Avon Flare; Branden; Harry Cuff; John Daniel; May Davenport; Douglas & McIntyre; Ediciones Universal; Faber & Faber; Falcon; Fiction Collective; Fjord; Floricanto; Gay Sunshine; Guernica; Harcourt Brace Jovanovich; Hermes House; Hunter House; Kar-Ben Copies; Knights; Pandora; Press Porcépic; Printemps; Racz; Russica; Second Chance; Shameless Hussy; Shapolsky; Silver Burdett; Still Point; Texas Monthly; Thunder's Mouth; University of Illinois; Winston-Derek; Wright.

Experimental. Applezaba; Atheneum Children's; Avon Flare; Canterbury; John Daniel; Devonshire; Douglas & McIntyre; Faber & Faber; Falcon; Fiction Collective; Fiddlehead; Gay Sunshine; Hermes House; Knights; Panjandrum; Pineapple; Racz; Random House; Second Chance; Shameless Hussy; Thunder's Mouth; University of Illinois; Woodsong Graphics.

Fantasy. Abbey; Ace Science Fiction; Arbor House; Atheneum Children's; Avon; Avon Flare; Baen; Baker Street; Bookmaker's Guild; Camelot; Canterbury; Carroll & Graf; Chariot; Clarion; Crossway; John Daniel; May Davenport; Daw; Del Rey; Dial; Dillon; Donning; Falcon; Harcourt Brace Jovanovich; Harper & Row; Harper & Row Junior; Hunter House; Intervarsity; Iron Crown; Kar-Ben Copies; Knights; Lodestar; Misty Hill; Mother Courage; New Victoria; Printemps; Random House; Sandpiper; Charles Scribner's Sons; Second Chance; Starblaze; Tor; Vend-O-Books; Walker; Woodsong Graphics; Wright.

Feminist. Crossing; Firebrand; Fjord; Hermes House; Mother Courage; New Victoria; Pandora; Press Gang; Shameless Hussy; Spinsters/Aunt Lute.

Gay/Lesbian. Alyson; Ashley; Firebrand; Gay Sunshine; JH Press; Mother Courage; Naiad; New Victoria.

Gothic. Ashley; Atheneum Children's; Avalon; Harlequin; Harper & Row; Knights; Woodsong Graphics; Zebra.

Historical. Abbey; Alaska Nature; Ashley; Atheneum Children's; Avon; Berkley; Branden; Brethren; Carolrhoda; Chariot; Council Oak; Critic's Choice; Harry Cuff; John Daniel; Denlinger's; Devonshire; Dial; Dillon; Eakin; Faber & Faber; Falcon; Fulcrum; Gay Sunshine; Guernica; Harcourt Brace Jovanovich; Harper & Row; Harvest House; Hermes House; Heroica; Houghton Mifflin; Kaleidoscopix; Kar-Ben Copies; Knights; Leisure; Lodestar; Misty Hill; Mother Courage; New England; New Victoria; Pelican; Pineapple; Poseidon; Quality;

Racz; Raintree; Random House; Sandlapper; Charles Scribner's Sons; Second Chance; Shameless Hussy; Sierra Club; Silver Burdett; Still Point; Thunder's Mouth; Tor; Unlimited; Walker; Willow Creek; Woodbine House; Woodsong Graphics; Yankee; Zebra.

Horror. Ashley; Atheneum Children's; Critic's Choice; Dell; Devonshire; Falcon; Leisure; Random House; Russica; Starblaze; Tor; Wright; Yankee; Zebra.

Humor. American Atheist; Andrews, McMeel & Parker; Applezaba; Ashley; Atheneum Children's; Avon Flare; Baker Street; Camelot; Cantebury; Carroll & Graf; Chariot; Clarion; Council Oak; Harry Cuff; John Daniel; Dial; Hounslow; Intervarsity; Kaleidoscopix; Knights; Lodestar; Misty Hill; Mother Courage; New Victoria; North Country; Pandora; Peachtree; Pelican; Prentice-Hall; Printemps; Random House; Russica; Charles Scribner's Sons; Second Chance; Shameless Hussy; Thunder's Mouth; Unlimited; Vend-O-Books; Willow Creek; Woodsong Graphics; Wright; Zebra.

Juvenile. Abingdon; Atheneum Children's; Augsburg; Baker Street; Bantam; Berkley; Bookmaker's Guild; Bradbury; Byls; Carolrhoda; Chariot; Clarion; Crossway; Dawn; Dial; Dillon; Dodd, Mead & Co.; Down East; E.P. Dutton; Eakin; Farras, Straus & Giroux; Floricanto; Golden Books; Harcourt Brace Jovanovich; Harper & Row Junior; Harper & Row Junior West Coast; Kaleidoscopix; Kar-Ben Copies; Lee's Books for Young Readers; Lodestar; Lothrop, Lee & Shepard; Margaret K. McElderry; MacMillan; Melius & Peterson; Misty Hill; Morrow Junior; Oak Tree; Oddo; Pelican; Perspectives; Philomel; Platt & Munk; Press Gang; Press Porcépic; Printemps; Sandlapper; Shoe Tree; Silver Burdett; Speech Bin; Trillium; Unicorn; Western Producer Prairie; Winston-Derek.

Literary. Beaufort; George Braziller; Brook House; Canterbury; Dembner; Douglas & McIntyre; Fiction Collective; Harcourt Brace Jovanovich; Harper & Row; Hermes House; Houghton Mifflin; Michael Kesend; Alfred A. Knopf; Little, Brown & Co.; North Point; Owl Creek; Peachtree; Poseidon; Puckerbrush; Gibbs M. Smith; Texas Western; Thistledown; Thunder's Mouth; University of Arkansas.

Mainstream/Contemporary. Academy Chicago; Applezaba; Ashley; Atheneum Children's; Atlantic Monthly; Avon; Avon Flare; Ballantine/Epiphany; Bantam; Beaufort; Branden; George Braziller; Brook House; Camelot; Carroll & Graf; Chariot; Council Oak; Credo; Critic's Choice; Crossway; Harry Cuff; John Daniel; Delacorte; Delta; Donning; Paul S. Eriksson; Evan & Co.; Faber & Faber; Falcon; Fiddlehead; Fjord; Harper & Row Junior; Hermes House; Heroica; Holiday House; Houghton Mifflin; Hounslow; Intervarsity; Kaleidoscopix; Leisure; Little, Brown & Co.; Lodestar; Methuen; William Morrow; New Readers; W.W. Norton; Ohio State University; Owl Creek; Pandora; Peachtree; Pelican; Perspectives; Pineapple; Poseidon; Clarkson N. Potter; Prentice-Hall; Quality; Racz; Randon House; St. Luke's; St. Martin's; Sandpiper; Saybrook; Charles Scribner's Sons; Second Chance; Sierra Club; Simon & Schuster; Speech Bin; Stein & Day; Still Point; Taplinger; Texas Monthly; University of California; University of Illinois; Franklin Watts; Woodbine House; Woodsong Graphics; Word Beat; Wright; Yankee.

Military/War. Presidio.

Mystery. Abbey; Academy Chicago; Ashley; Atheneum Children's; Avalon; Avon; Avon Flare; Baker Street; Ballantine/Epiphany; Bantam; Beaufort; Camelot; Carroll & Graf; Chariot; Clarion; Cliffhanger; Critic's Choice; John Daniel; Dembner; Dial; Dillon; Dodd, Mead & Co.; Donning; Doubleday; Faber & Faber; Falcon; Fjord; Gay Sunshine; Golden Eagle; Guernica; Harcourt Brace Jovanovich; Harper & Row; Harvest House; Heroica; Knights; Lodestar; Mother Courage; Mysterious; New Victoria; Pantheon; Pocket; Prentice-Hall; Printemps; Racz; Random House; Russica; Charles Scribner's Sons; Second Chance; SOS; Tor; Unlimited; Vend-O-Books; Walker; Franklin Watts; Woodbine House; Woodsong Graphics; Wright; Yankee.

Occult. Berkley; Dell; Methuen; Tor.

Picture Books. Bradbury; Chariot; Dial; Farrar, Straus & Giroux; Golden Books; Green Tiger; Harper & Row Junior; Lothrop, Lee & Shepard; Oak Tree; Philomel; Platt & Munk; Prentice-Hall; Shoe Tree.

Plays. Coach House; Drama Book; Samuel French; JH Press; Meriwether; Players; Printemps.

Poetry. Ahsahta; American Studies; Applezaba; Ashley; Atlantic Monthly; Branden; Chatham; Christopher; Cleveland State; John Daniel; Dragon's Teeth; Ediciones Universal; Fiddlehead; Fjord; International Publishers; Peter Lang; Little, Brown & Co.; William Morrow & Co.;

Ohio State University; Owl Creek; Panjandrum; Paragon House; Press Porcépic; Puckerbrush; Purdue University; Russica; Shameless Hussy; Sparrow; Sunstone; Thistledown; University of Arkansas; University of California; University of Massachusetts; Alfred Van Der Marck; Vehicule; Winston-Derek.

Regional. Alaska Nature; John F. Blair; Borealis; China Books; Harry Cuff; Denlinger's; Faber & Faber; Fjord; Heart of the Lakes; North Country; Peachtree; Pelican; Philomel; Sandlapper; Sunstone; Texas A&M University; Texas Christian University; Texas Monthly; Thistledown; Three Continents; University of Arkansas.

Religious. Abbey; Ashley; Ballantine/Epiphany; Bethany House; Bookcraft; Branden; Brethren; Byls; Chariot; Dawn; Devonshire; Falcon; Harvest House; Herald Press; Intervarsity; Kar-Ben Copies; Meriwether; Resource; Fleming H. Revell; St. Bede's; Shameless Hussy; Shining Star; Standard; Stillpoint; Tyndale House; Winston-Derek; Word Books; Zondervan.

Romances. Alaska Nature; Arbor House; Ashley; Atheneum Children's; Avalon; Avon; Avon Flare; Bantam; Berkley; Branden; Dell; Dial; Dodd, Mead & Co.; Donning; Doubleday; Harlequin; Knights; Leisure; Mother Courage; New Victoria; Pocket; Second Chance at Love; Silhouette; SOS; Walker; Woodsong Graphics; Wright; Zebra.

Science Fiction. Abbey; Ace Science Fiction; Arbor House; Ashley; Atheneum Children's; Avon; Avon Flare; Baen; Berkley; Camelot; Chariot; Contemporary; Critic's Choice; Crossway; Daw; Del Rey; Devonshire; Dillon; Donning; Doubleday; Falcon; Fjord; Gay Sunshine; Harcourt Brace Jovanovich; Harper & Row; Harper & Row Junior; Hermes House; Intervarsity; Iron Crown; Knights; Lodestar; Mother Courage; New Victoria; Pocket; Press Porcépic; Racz; Raintree; Charles Scribner's Sons; Sierra Club; Starblaze; Thunder's Mouth; Vend-O-Books; Walker; Franklin Watts; Woodsong Graphics; Wright.

Short Story Collections. Applezaba; Augsburg; Bookmaker's Guild; Gay Sunshine; Platt & Munk; Press Gang; Still Point; University of Arkansas; Vehicule; Word Beat.

Spiritual. Garber.

Sports. Bantam; Contemporary; Mountaineers; Willow Creek.

Suspense. Alaska Nature; Arbor House; Ashley; Atheneum Children's; Avon; Avon Flare; Ballantine/Epiphany; Beaufort; Berkley; Camelot; Carroll & Graf; Chariot; Clarion; Cliffhanger; Critic's Choice; Dell; Dembner; Dial; Dodd, Mead & Co.; Doubleday; Falcon; Fjord; Golden Eagle; Harcourt Brace Jovanovich; Harper & Row; Knights; Mysterious; Printemps; Racz; Random House; Russica; St. Luke's; Charles Scribner's Sons; Second Chance; SOS; Tor; Vend-O-Books; Walker; Winston-Derek; Woodsong Graphics; Wright; Zebra.

Western. Ashley; Atheneum Children's; Avalon; Avon; Chariot; Critic's Choice; Fulcrum; Green Hill; Harper & Row; Homestead; Knights; Lodestar; New Victoria; Pocket; Quality; Racz; Vend-O-Books; Walker; Woodsong Graphics.

Young Adult. Atheneum Children's; Augsburg; Avon Flare; Bantam; Farrar, Straus & Giroux; Fearon; Harper & Row Junior; Harper & Row Junior West Coast; New Readers; Pelican; Philomel; Prentice-Hall; Printemps; Shoe Tree; Silhouette; Square One; Texas Christian University; Western Producer Prairie.

Index

A

A.N.A.L.O.G. Computing 417
AAA World 616
AAAS Prize for Behavorial Science Research 961
AASLH Press 16
AB Bookman's Weekly 662
ABA Journal 775
Abbey Press 16
Abbott, Langer & Associates 16
ABC Star Service 835
Abel Literary Agency, Carole 924
Abel Literary Agency, Inc., Dominick 924
Abingdon Press 17
Absolute Reference 751
Absolute Sound, The 401
Abyss 286
Academic Technology 685
Academy Chicago 17
Accelerated Development Inc. 17
Accent 616
Accent Books 18
Accent on Living 300
Accord Publications 902
Ace Science Fiction 18
Acres U.S.A. 714
Acropolis Books, Ltd. 18
ACS Publications, Inc. 18
Action 351
Acton Inc., Edward J. 924
Actors Alley Repertory Theatre 857
Actors Theatre of Louisville 857
Actors Theatre of Tulsa, Inc. 857
Adam 388
Adams, Houmes and Ward Book Publishers 18
Adams, Inc., Bob 19
Adams Playwriting Competition, Maude 962
Adams Prize, Herbert Baxter 962
Addams Peace Association Children's Book Award, Jane 962
Addison-Wesley Publishing Co., Inc. 19
Adirondack Life 473
Admaster, Inc. 842
Adriatic Award 962
Advance Publications (see Random House, Inc. 139)
Adventure Feature Syndicate 911

Adventure Magazine 616
Advertising Age 646
Advertising Techniques 646
Aegina Press and University Editions 191
Aero 223
Aerobics & Fitness Journal (see American Fitness 827)
Affaire De Coeur 538
Affirmation Books 19
Africa Report 427
Ag Review 716
Aglow 500
Aglow Publications 19
AG-Pilot International Magazine 659
Agway Cooperator 714
Ahsahta Press 20
AIM (see Vision Lifestyles 532)
AIM Magazine 272
Aim Magazine Short Story Contest 962
AIMplus 300
Air & Space Magazine 224
Air Line Pilot 659
Air Wisconsin 346
Airfair Interline Magazine 836
Airport Services Management 660
Alabama Alumni Magazine 238
Alabama Game & Fish 577
Alaska 439
Alaska Flying Magazine 224
Alaska Nature Press 20
Alaska Northwest Publishing 20
Alaska Quarterly Review 365
Alaska Repertory Theatre 858
Alba House 21
Alban Institute, Inc., The 21
Alberta New Fiction Competition 962
Alberta Non-fiction Award 962
Albuquerque Senior Scene Magazine 534
Albuquerque Singles Scene Magazine 493
Alcalde 239
Alexi Productions Ltd. 888
Alfred Hitchcock's Mystery Magazine 410
Allan Agency, Lee 925
Allen Publishing Co. 21
Alley Theatre 858
Almar Press 21
Aloha, The Magazine of Hawaii and the Pacific 455
Alpha Publishing Company 22

Alpine Publications, Inc. 22
Alternative Energy Retailer 700
Alternative Sources of Energy Magazine 544
Altman & Weil Report to Legal Management, The 776
Alyson Publications, Inc. 22
Amadeus Press (see Timber Press 164)
Amateur Boxer, The 597
Amazing Heroes 253
Amazing Stories 548
Amberley Greeting Card Co. 902
Amelia Magazine 365
Amelia Student Award 962
Amereon Ltd. 191
America 501
America International Syndicate 911
America West Airlines Magazine 347
American Association of University Women Award 962
American Astronautical Society 22
American Atheist 289
American Atheist Press 23
American Automatic Merchandiser 732
American Banker 719
American Bicyclist 827
American Book Awards, The 962
American Book Collector 316
American Bookseller 663
American Brewer 283
American Catholic Press 23
American Cinematographer 811
American Citizen Italian Press, The 273
American Clay Exchange 316
American Coin-Op 676
American Collectors Journal, The 316
American Dane 273
American Demographics 646
American Drycleaner 775
American Farriers Journal 193
American Federation of Information Processing Societies 23
American Film 265
American Fire Journal 726
American Firearms Industry 827
American Fitness 827
American Forests 411

American Glass Review 664
American Greetings 902
American Handgunner 573
American Health Magazine 301
American Heritage 310
American History Illustrated 310
American Hockey Magazine 878
American Hunter 577
American Indian Art Magazine 202
American Jewelry Manufacturer 761
American Karate 594
American Land Forum 411
American Legion Magazine, The 289
American Libraries 781
American Media Inc. 842
American Medical News 794
American Minority Playwright's Festival 962
American Motorcyclist 217
American Mover 834
American Musical Theater Festival 962
American Newspaper Carrier 607
American Newspaper Syndicate 911
American Office Dealer 808
American Paint & Coatings Journal 809
American Politics 427
American Psychiatric Press, Inc., The 23
American References Inc. 24
American Renaissance Theater 858
American Salesman, The 823
American School Board Journal, The 685
American Screenwriter, The 762
American Shotgunner, The 574
American Skating World 601
American Society of Journalists & Authors Award Program 962
American Speech-Language-Hearing Association 962
American Squaredance 265
American Stage Company 858
American Stage Festival 858
American Studies Press, Inc. 24
American Survival Guide 393
American Trucker Magazine 653
American Voice, The 366
American Way 347
American-Scandinavian Foundation/Translation Prize 962
Americas 836
Amicus Journal, The 411
Amigaworld 417
Amit 631
Amsterdam Agency, Marcia 925
Amusement Business 704
Amy Writing Awards 962

An Claidheamh Soluis/Celtic Arts Center 858
Analog Science Fiction/Science Fact 549
Ananda Publications (see Dawn Publications 57)
Ancestry Incorporated 24
Ancestry Newsletter 311
And Books 24
Anderson Publishing Co. 24
Andrews, McMeel & Parker 25
Angel's Touch Productions 858
Angus Journal 839
Animal Kingdom 193
Animals 193
Ann Arbor Observer 466
Annals of Saint Anne De Beaupre, The 501
Annual International Narrative Contest 962
Annual International Poetry Contest 963
Annual International Shakespearean Sonnet Contest 963
Annual Journalism Awards Competition 963
Annual National Bible Week Editorial Contest, The 963
Annual NJ Poetry Contest 963
Annual North American Essay Contest 963
Antaeus 366
Antic Magazine 418
Antioch Review 367
Antiquarian, The 317
Antique Monthly 317
Antique Review 317
Antique Trader Weekly, The 318
Antiques & Auction News 318
AOPA Pilot 224
AP Newsfeatures 911
APA Monitor 794
A+, The Independent Guide to Apple Computing 418
Appalachian Mountain Club 25
Appalachian Trailways News 412
Appaloosa World 194
Applezaba Press 25
Appliance Manufacturer 747
Appliance Service News 737
Applied Radiology 795
Apsey Playwriting Award, Ruby Lloyd 963
Arabian Horse Times 194
Aran Press 858
Ararat 273
Arbor House 25
Archery Business 828
Archery World 556
Architectural Book Publishing Co., Inc. 26
Archon (see The Shoe String Press 151)
ARCsoft Publishers 26
Arctophile, The 318
Area Development Magazine 820

Arena Stage 859
Argus Communications 902
Arizona Highways 440
Arizona Living Magazine 440
Arizona Monthly 440
Arizona Theatre Company 859
Arkansas Arts Center Children's Theatre, The 859
Arkansas Sportsman 577
Arkansas Times 441
Arkin Magazine Syndicate 911
Arman Publishing, Inc., M. 26
Arms & Outdoor Digest 828
Army Magazine 393
Arnold and Associates Productions, Inc. 842
Arrival Magazine 367
Art Business News 651
Art Craft Publishing Co. 859
Art Direction 646
Art Direction Book Company 26
Art Material Trade News 824
Art Times 202
Arthur's International 911
Artilleryman, The 311
Artists and Writers Syndicate, The 912
Artists Fellowship Program, The 963
Artists' Fellowship Award 963
Artist's Magazine, The 202
Artquest 651
Artreach Touring Theatre 859
Arts & Activities 685
Arts Management 652
Artsline 265
Artviews 203
Asher-Gallant Press 26
Ashley Books, Inc. 27
Ashton-Tate Quarterly 751
Asia-Pacific Defense Forum 394
Asolo State Theatre 859
Associate Reformed Presbyterian, The 501
Associated Faculty Press, Inc. 27
Association for Education in Journalism Awards 963
Astor Memorial Leadership Essay Contest, Vincent 963
Astro Signs 214
ASU Travel Guide 617
Asymptotical World, The 367
At the Foot of the Mountain Theater 860
ATA Magazine 594
Athenaeum of Philadelphia Literary Award, The 963
Atheneum Children's Books 28
Atheneum Publishers 28
Athletic Press 28
Atlanta New Play Project 860
Atlanta Singles Magazine & Datebook 494
Atlantic City Magazine 471
Atlantic Monthly Press 28

Atlantic Salmon Journal, The 412
ATO Palm, The 239
Attenzione 273
Attic Theatre 860
ATV Sports Magazine 217
Augsburg Publishing House 29
Austin Homes & Gardens 335
Austin Magazine 485
Author Aid Associates 925
Authors Marketing Services Ltd. 925
Authors' Unlimited 191
Auto Book Press 29
Auto Glass Journal 653
Auto Laundry News 654
Auto Trim News 654
Autobody & Reconditioned Car 654
Automatic Machining 784
Automation in Housing & Manufactured Home Dealer 678
Automotive Booster of California 654
Automotive Cooling Journal 655
AV Business Communications (see Visual Communications Canada 700)
A/V Concepts Corp. 812
AV Video 693
Avalon Books 29
AVI Publishing Co. 29
Aviation Book Co. 29
Aviation/USA 224
Avila College Performing Arts Dept. 860
Avni/Jewish Repertory Theatre, Ran 860
Avon Books 30 (also see Camelot Books 42)
Avon Flare Books 30
Award for Literary Translation 963
Awards Specialist 667
Away 617
Axelrod Agency, Inc., The 926
Axios 501
Aztex Corp. 30

B

B.C. Lumberman Magazine 783
Baby Talk Magazine 247
Bachner Productions, Inc. 888
Backstage Theatre 861
Backstretch, The 575
Backwoodsman Magazine 311
Badger Sportsman 577
Baen Publishing Enterprises 30
Baker Street Productions Ltd. 31
Baker's Play Publishing Co. 861
Bakersfield Lifestyle 442
Baldwin College Theatre, Mary 861
Bale Books 31

Ballantine Books (see Del Rey Books 58)
Ballantine/Epiphany Books 31
Ballinger Publishing Co., 31
Balls and Strikes 597
Baltimore Jewish Times 274
Baltimore Magazine 462
Banana Time 894
Banjo Newsletter 401
Bank Loan Officers Report 719
Bank Note Reporter 319
Bank Operations Report 720
Bank Personnel Report 720
Bankers Publishing Co. 31
Banking Software Review 720
Banks-Baldwin Law Publishing Co. 32
Banta Award 963
Bantam Books, Inc. 32
Baptist Leader 502
Barber Literary Agency, Inc., Virginia 926
Barnes & Noble 32
Baroid News Bulletin 700
Barr Films 842
Barrister 776
Barron's 226
Barter Communique 646
Barter Theatre 861
Basch Feature Syndicate, Buddy 912
Baseball Cards 319
Bassin' 578
Bassmaster Magazine 578
Battery Man, The 655
Bay & Delta Yachtsman 558
BC Business 231
BC Outdoors 578
Beacon Hill Press of Kansas City 32
Beacon Magazine 478
Beacon Press 33
Bean Publishing, Ltd., Carolyn 902
Bear and Co., Inc. 33
Beaufort Books, Publishers 33
Becker, Maximilian 926
Beef 711
Beer Prize, George Louis 963
Bell Associates, Inc., Dave 888
Bend of the River Magazine 479
Benefits Canada 720
Benjamin Company, Inc., The 33
Bennett & McKnight Publishing Co. 34
Berea College Theatre 861
Berkeley Jewish Theatre 861
Berkeley Monthly, The 442
Berkley Publishing Group 34 (also see Ace Science Fiction 18)
Berkshire Theatre Festival, Inc. 861
Berley Publishing Group, The 34
Bernstein, Meredith 926

Best of Blurbs Contest 963
Best of Dell 288
Bestways Magazine 301
Bethany House Publishers 34
Better Business 226
Better Health 301
Better Health & Living 302
Better Homes and Gardens 336
Better Homes and Gardens Books 34
Better Life for You, A 290
Betterway Publications, Inc. 35
Beverage Retailer Weekly 661
Beveridge Award, Albert J. 964
Beverly Hills Theatre Guild-Julie Harris Playwright Award Competition, The 964
Beyond . . . Science Fiction and Fantasy 549
Biblical History 502
Biblical Illustrator 502
Bicycle Business Journal 829
Bicycle Guide 557
Bicycle Rider 557
Bicycling 557
Bikereport 617
Billboard 705
Binford & Mort Publishing 35
Biology Digest 544
Bird Talk 194
Bird Watcher's Digest 412
Birkhäuser Boston 35
Birmingham 438
Bitterroot Magazine Poetry Contest 964
Biworld Publishers, Inc. (see Woodland Books 182)
Black & White Cards 903
Black Award, Irma Simonton 964
Black Belt 595
Black Collegian, The 239
Black Confession 538
Black Conscience Syndication Inc. 912
Black Enterprise Magazine 274
Black Family 275
Black Mountain Review 367
Black Warrior Review 368
Black Warrior Review Literary Awards 964
Blackwell, Inc., Basil 32
Blade Magazine, The 319
Blair, Publisher, John F. 35
Blais, Edouard 894
Blake Group Literary Agency, The 926
Blakeslee Awards, Howard W. 964
Blate Associates, Samuel R. 843
Bloomsbury Review, The 368
Blue & Gray Magazine 312
Blue Mountain Arts, Inc. 903
Bluegrass Unlimited 401
BMX Plus Magazine 217
BNA Books 36

BNA Communications, Inc. 843
B'nai B'rith Jewish Monthly 275
Board and Administrator 787
Boat Pennsylvania 559
Boating Industry 792
Boating Product News 792
Boca Raton 450
Body Press, The (see H.P. Books 80)
Body Story Contest 964
Bon Appetit 283
Book Dealers World 763
Book Forum 368
Book Peddlers, The 927
Bookcraft, Inc. 36
Bookmakers Guild 36
Books and Religion 763
Borchardt Inc., George 927
Borders, Dan 895
Borealis Press, Ltd. 37
Borgo Press, The 37
Born, Walter L. 861
Bosco Publications, Don 37
Boston Business Journal 231
Boston Globe Literary Press Competition 964
Boston Globe Magazine 463
Boston Globe-Horn Book Awards 964
Boston Literary Agency 927
Boston Magazine 463
Boston Mills Press, The 37
Boston Phoenix, The 464
Boston Review, The 369
Bosustow Video 843
Boulder Business Report (see Boulder County Business Report 231)
Boulder County Business Report 231
Bouregy and Co., Inc., Thomas 38
Bow and Arrow Hunting 556
Bowhunter Magazine 556
Bowlers Journal 567
Bowling 567
Bowling Writing Competition 964
Boxboard Containers 809
Boxoffice Magazine 705
Boys' Life 351, 607
BPME Image 647
Bradbury Press 38
Bradley-Goldstein Agency, The 927
Bragdon Publishers, Inc., Allen D. 38
Braham Journal, The 711
Brake & Front End 655
Branden Press, Inc. 38
Brandt & Brandt Dramatic Dept., Inc. Harold Freedman (see Robert A. Freedman Dramatic Agency, Inc. 934)
Brandt & Brandt Literary Agents, Inc. 928

Braziller, Inc., George 38
Bread 607
Brennan Partners, Inc. 290
Brethren Press 39
Brevet Press, Inc. 39
Briarcliff Press Publishers 39
Brick and Clay Record 664
Brick House Publishing Co. 39
Bridal Fair (see Bridal Trends 632)
Bridal Guide 632
Bridal Trends 632
Bride's 632
Bridge Publishing, Inc. 40
Brill Publishing Co., E.J. (see Flora and Fauna Publications 70)
Brilliant, Ashleigh 895
Brilliant Enterprises 903
Brilliant Ideas for Publishers 763
Brisk, Rubin and Steinberg Literary Agency (see Michael Steinberg 953)
Bristol Riverside Theatre 862
Brittingham Prize in Poetry 964
Broadcast Technology 694
Broadcaster 694
Broadman Press 40
Broadway Play Publishing, Inc. 862
Broadway Press 40
Bronfman Centre, Saidye 881
Bronze Thrills 538
Brook House Press 40
Brown Inc., Ned 928
Brown Ltd., Curtis 928
Browne Ltd., Pema 928
Bruce, Leonard 895
Brunner/Mazel, Publishers 41
Brunswick Publishing Company 191
Builder Insider 679
Builder/Dealer 679
Building Services Contractor 786
Burke Agency, Shirley 928
Burke Essay Contest, Arleigh 964
Bus Ride 836
Bus Tours Magazine 836
Busch-The Western Stage, Dianne 862
Bush Artist Fellowships 964
Business Age 226
Business Atlanta 232
Business Facilities 820
Business Features Syndicate 912
Business Insurance 758
Business Marketing 647
Business Month 226
Business Software 752
Business Times, The 232
Business to Business 232
Business Today 257
Business View 233
Business View of SW Florida

(see Business View 233)
Butler, Art and Literary Agent, Jane 928
Butter-Fat 710
Butterworth Publishers (see Focal Press 71)
Byline 764
BYLS Press 41
Byron Preiss Visual Publications, Inc. 187
Byte Magazine 418

C

C&H Publishing Co. (see Cay-Bel Publishing Company 45)
C.L.A.S.S. Magazine 428
C Q Press 41
C.S.P. World News 369
Cable Communications Magazine 694
Cable Marketing 694
Cable Television Business Magazine 695
Cabscott Broadcast Production, Inc. 843
Caddylak Publishing (see Asher-Gallant Press 26)
California Angler 579
California Culinary Academy (see Ortho Information Services 121)
California Farmer 717
California Highway Patrolman 206
California International Division of Joseph Nicoletti Publishing Co. 889
California Journal 428
California Lawyer 776
California Pharmacist 795
California Publisher 764
California Short Story Competition 964
California Traveler (see Western RV Traveler 631)
California Writer's Club Conference Contest 964
Calligraphy Collection, The 903
Calligraphy Idea Exchange 652
Calyx 369
Cambridge University Press 41
Camelot Books 42
Camper Times, The 618
Camperways 618
Camping Canada 618
Camping Today 619
Campion Books (see Loyola University Press 102)
Campus Life Magazine 608
Campus Voice 239
Canadian Aquaculture 792
Canadian Author & Bookman 764
Canadian Booksellers Association Author of the Year

Award 964
Canadian Fiction Magazine 369
Canadian Forest Industries 783
Canadian Geographic 492
Canadian Grocer 732
Canadian Jeweller 761
Canadian Literature 370
Canadian Machinery & Metalworking 785
Canadian Plains Research Center 42
Canadian RV Dealer 837
Canadian Speakers' and Writers' Service Limited 929
Canadian West 312
Canadian Workshop 336
Canadian Writer's Journal 764
Canadian Yachting Magazine 559
Candy Industry 678
Cane Award, Melville 964
Canoe Magazine 559
Canterbury Press 42
Cantor, Literary Agent, Ruth 929
Cape Cod Compass 464
Cape Cod Life 464
Capital 474
Capital Repertory Company 862
Capper's 290
Car and Driver 217
Car Collector/Car Classics 218
Caratzas, Publisher, Aristide D. 43
Cardiology Management 795
Cardiology World News 795
Cardoza Enterprises, Anthony 889
Career Publishing, Inc. 43
Career World 608
Careers 608
Caribbean Travel and Life 619
Caring Card Co. 903
Carlton Cards 903
Carlton Press, Inc. 191
Carnegie-Mellon Magazine 240
Carolina Biological Supply Co. 43
Carolrhoda Books, Inc. 43
Carpenter Publishing House 187
Carroll & Graf Publishers, Inc. 44
Carroll College 862
Carstens Publications, Inc. 44
Cartoon Express Syndications 912
Cartoon World 253
Casa Manana Musicals, Inc. 862
Cascades East 482
Cast Theatre, The 863
Casual Living 824
Cat Fancy 195
Catering Today 743
Cathedral Films, Inc. 843
Catholic Digest 502
Catholic Forester 206

Catholic Health Association, The 44
Catholic Life 502
Catholic Near East Magazine 502
Catholic Twin Circle 503
Catholic University of America Press 44
Cats Magazine 195
Cattleman Magazine, The 711
Cavalier 388
Caxton Printers, Ltd., The 44
Cay-Bel Publishing Company 45
CBIA News 207
CBP Press 45
CCC Publications 45
CCLM Editor's Grant Awards 965
CCLM Seed Grants 965
CD Publications 821
CEDAR Books (see Credo Publishing Corporation 53)
Celestial Arts 45 (also see Ten Speed Press 161)
Center for Migration Studies of New York, Inc. 45
Center for Puppetry Arts 863
Center Stage 863
Central Florida Magazine 450
Ceramic Industry 664
Ceramic Scope 665
Chain Saw Age 736
Chamba Organization, The 889
Changing Men 494
Changing Scene Theater, The 863
Changing Times 257
Chansky, Dorothy 863
Chapple Films and Video 843
Chariot 207
Chariot Books 46
Charlton Review, The 370
Charlotte Magazine 477
Chartering Magazine 619
Chatelaine 633
Chatham Press 46
Chek-Chart Service Bulletin, The 655
Chelsea Green 46
Chelsea House Publishers-Edgemont 46
Chesapeake Bay Magazine 462
Chess Life 287
Chevron USA Odyssey 620
Chevy Outdoors 620
Chic Magazine 388
Chicago Board of Rabbis Broadcasting Commission, The 889
Chicago History 312
Chicago Magazine 456
Chicago Review Press 47
Chicago Tribune 621
Chickadee Magazine 352
Chief Fire Executive 727
Chief of Police Magazine 727
Child 248

Child Life 352
Childbirth Educator 686
Children's Album, The 352
Children's Digest 353
Children's Playmate 353
Children's Science Book Awards 965
Chilton Book Company 47
China Books and Periodicals, Inc. 47
China Glass & Tableware 738
Chiz Agency, Terry 929
Chocolatier 283
Chosen Books Publishing Co., Ltd. 47
Christian Adventurer 609
Christian Broadcasting Network 889
Christian Ed. Publishers 48
Christian Education Today 672
Christian Herald 503
Christian Home & School 503
Christian Leadership 673
Christian Living for Senior Highs 609
Christian Science Monitor, The 291
Christian Single 504
Christian Writer, The (see Writer's Inspirational Market News 773)
Christianity & Crisis 504
Christianity Today 504
Christmas 504
Christopher Publishing House, The 48
Chronicle Books 48
Chronicle Magazine, The (see HP Design & Manufacturing 754)
Chronicle of the Horse, The 195
Church & State 505
Church Educator 673
Church Herald, The 505
Church Media Library Magazine 781
Church Musician, The 805
Church Training 673
Cincinnati Bell Magazine 695
Cincinnati Magazine 479
Cincinnati Medicine 796
Cine/Design Films, Inc. 889
Cinefantastique Magazine 266
Cinemascore 402
Circle in the Square Theatre 863
Circle K Magazine 240
Circle Repertory Co. 864
Circuit Playhouse/Playhouse on the Square 864
Circuit Rider 674
Citadel Press 48
City Limits 474
City Sports Magazine 568
City Theatre Company 864
Civil War Times Illustrated 313
Clarion Books 48
Clark Co., Arthur H. 49

Clark, Inc., I.E. 864
Classroom Computer Learning 686
Clausen Associates, Connie 929
Clavier 805
Claytor Memorial Award, Gertrude B. 965
Cleaning Consultant Services, Inc. 49
Clearvue, Inc. 843
Clergy Journal, The 674
Cleveland State University Poetry Center 49
Cliffhanger Press 49
Cliffs Notes, Inc. 50
Closing the Gap, Inc. 419
Club Costa Magazine 207
Clubhouse 353
COA Review 432
Coach House Press, Inc. 50, 864
Coaching Review (see Science Periodical on Research and Technology 692)
Coal Age 804
Coast Magazine 621
Cobblestone 354
Cohen, Inc., Ruth 930
Cohen Literary Agency, Ltd., Hy 929
Coin Enthusiast's Journal, The 319
Coins 320
Cole, Don 895
Coles Publishing Co., Ltd. 50
Collector Books 50
Collector Editions Quarterly 320
Collectors News & The Antique Reporter 320
College Entertainment Guide 240
College Media Review 764
College Outlook and Career Opportunities 240
College Woman 241
Collegiate Career Woman 241
Collegiate Poetry Contest 965
Collier Associates 930
Collision 656
Colorado Homes & Lifestyles 336
Colorado Outdoor Journal 621
Colortype 904
Columbia 505
Columbia Journalism Review 765
Columbus Monthly 479
Columbus Single Scene 494
Comark 844
Comico, The Comic Company 254
Comments 505
Commodore Magazine 419
Common Ground 214
Common Sense 667
Commonwealth of Pennsylvania Council on the Arts Litera-

ture Fellowships 965
Communication Briefings 668
Communication Skill Builders, Inc. 51
Community Children's Theatre of Kansas City Annual Playwriting Award 965
Compact Books 51
Companion of St. Francis and St. Anthony, The 506
Company One 864
Company Theatre 865
Compaq Magazine 752
Compass 758
Compass Films 844
Compressed Air 747
Compro Productions 844
Compute! Books 51
Computer & Electronics Graduate, The 241
Computer Dealer 752
Computer Gaming World 287
Computer Language 419
Computer Science Press, Inc. 51
Computer Shopper 419
Computer User's Legal Reporter 777
Computers in Banking 668
Computers in Education 686
Computing Canada 753
Computing Now! 420
Comstock Cards 904
Concrete Construction Magazine 832
Condyne/The Oceana/Group 844
Confident Living 506
Confrontation 370
Congress Monthly 275
Connecticut Magazine 447
Connecticut Traveler 447
Conners Prize for Poetry, The Bernard F. 965
Connoisseur, The 291
Connor Literary Agency 930
Conscience 507
Construction Specifier 679
Construction Supervision & Safety Letter 787
Consumer Action News 258
Consumer Lending Report 720
Consumer Reports Books 52
Consumers Digest Magazine 258
Contemporary Books, Inc. 52
Contemporary Drama Service 865
Contenova Gifts 904
Continental Film 844
Continuum Broadcasting Network/Generation News, Inc. 913
Contractor Magazine 814
Contractors Market Center 679
Conway and Associates, Ben 930
Cook Publishing Co., David C. (see Chariot Books 46)

Cook's 284
Copley Books 52
Coral Springs Monthly 450
Corey Prize in Canadian-American Relations, Albert B. 965
Cornell Maritime Press, Inc. 52
Cornerstone 507
Coronado Studies 844
Corporate Fitness 829
Corvette Fever 218
Corvette News 218
Council for Wisconsin Writers, Inc. Annual Awards Competition 965
Council Oak Books 53
Counselor Magazine, The 647
Counted Cross Stitch 334
Country Journal 542
Country Woman 633
Covenant Companion, The 507
CPI Purchasing 747
CQ: The Radio Amateur's Journal 544
Crafts 'N Things 320
Crafts Report, The 652
Craftsman Book Company 53
Crain's Cleveland Business 233
Crain's Detroit Business 234
CRCS Publications 53
Create-A-Craft 904
Creative Artists Grant 965
Creative Arts Contest 965
Creative Directions, Inc. 904
Creative Years 765
Creativity Fellowship 965
Credo Publishing Corporation 53
Creem 402
Cricket 354
Crisis 275
Critic's Choice Paperbacks 53
Critique: A Journal of Conspiracies & Metaphysics 428
Crochet World Omnibook 321
Cross Country Skier 601
Cross-Canada Writers' Quarterly 765
Crossing Press, The 54
Crossroads Theatre Company 865
Crossway Books 54
Crown Publishers, Inc. 54
Cruising World 559
Crystal Group of Companies, Inc., The 904
Cuff Publications Limited, Harry 54
Current Health 1 354
Current Health 2 609
Current, Inc. 905
Currents 560
Curriculum Review 687
Curtis Associates, Inc., Richard 931
Custom Applicator 708
Cutting Tool Engineering 785
Cycle World 219

Cycling USA 558
Cynthia Publishing Company 56

D

D.A.C. News 208
D.J. Enterprises 931
"D" Magazine 485
D&B Reports 227
Da Silva Associates 890
Daily Development 433
Daily Devotional Guide (see
    The Upper Room 531)
Daily Meditation 508
Daily Word 508
Dairy Herd Management 710
Dairyman, The 711
Dakota Theatre Caravan 865
Dallas Life Magazine 486
Dallas Magazine 234
Dallas Observer 266
Dalton Little Theatre/World Car-
    pets New Play Project 865
Dan Sha News 276
Dance Exercise Today 687
Dance Horizons 56
Dance Magazine 266
Dance Teacher Now 266
Dancy Productions, Inc., Nicho-
    las 845
Daniel, Publisher, John 56
Dante University of America
    Press, Inc. 56
Darkroom & Creative Camera
    Techniques 425
Darkroom Photography Maga-
    zine 426
Dartnell Corp. 56
Data Base Monthly 753
Data Based Advisor 420
Datamation 753
Daughters of Sarah 508
Davenport, Publishers, May 57
Davidson Memorial Award,
    Gustav 965
Davie, Thomas W. 895
Davies Memorial Award, Mary
    Carolyn 965
Davis Publications, Inc. 57
Davis Publishing, Steve 57
Daw Books, Inc. 57
Dawn Publications 57
Dayton Magazine 480
Dazzle 302
De Young Press 191
Dealer Communicator 824
Decision 508
Decorative Artist's Workbook
    321
Deep South Writers' Contest
    965
Deer and Deer Hunting 579
DeGroot, Lee 895
Del Ray Books 58
Delacorte Press 58
Delacorte Press Prize for an

Outstanding First Young
    Adult Novel 966
Delaware Theatre Company 865
Dell Crossword Annual 288
Dell Crossword Extravaganza
    288
Dell Crossword Puzzles 288
Dell Crossword Special 288
Dell Crossword Super Special
    288
Dell Crossword Yearbook 288
Dell Crosswords and Variety
    Puzzles 288
Dell Pencil Puzzles & Word
    Games 288
Dell Pencil Puzzles & Word
    Games Yearbook 288
Dell Publishing Co., Inc. 58
Dell Word Search Puzzles 288
Delmar Publishers, Inc. 58
Delta Books 59
Delta Sky 347
Dembner Books 59
Denison & Co., Inc., T.S. 59
Denlinger's Publishers, Ltd. 59
Dental Economics 683
Dentist 683
Denver Center Theatre Compa-
    ny 866
Denver Quarterly, The 370
Design Graphics World 703
D'Esternaux Poetry Scholarship
    Contest, Marie-Louise 966
Detective Cases 260
Detective Dragnet 260
Detective Files 260
Detroit Magazine 466
Detroit Monthly 466
Devin-Adair Publishers, Inc. 60
Devonshire Publishing Co. 60
Di Castagnola, Alice Fay 966
Diagnostic Imaging 796
Dial 267
Dial Books for Young Readers
    60
Dialogue 262
Diamant, Anita 931
Diamond Registry Bulletin, The
    761
Dickenson, Steve 895
Dickinson Award, Emily 966
Dijkstra Literary Agency, San-
    dra 931
Dillon Press, Inc. 60
Dimension Books, Inc. 61
Dimensional Stone 832
Dinosaur Review 371
Dioscorides Press (see Timber
    Press 164)
Disciple, The 509
Discipleship Journal 509
Discoveries 355
Discovery 622
Discovery/Nation, The 966
Dispensing Optician, The 796
Distributor 814
Diver 604

Diver, The 604
Dobama Theatre 866
Dodd, Mead & Co. 61
Dog Fancy 196
Dog Writers' Association of
    America Annual Writing
    Contest 966
Dolger Agency, The Jonathan
    932
Doll Reader 62
Dolls 321
Dolphin Log, The 355
Domestic Engineering Magazine
    815
Donning Company/Publishers,
    Inc, The 62 (also see
    Starblaze 156)
Dorchester Publishing Co., Inc.
    (see Leisure Books 98)
Doremus, Inc./Music In The
    Air, John 890
Dorese Agency Ltd. 932
Dorset Theatre Festival 866
Dossier Quebec (see Vehicule
    Press 174)
Doubleday & Co., Inc. 62
Douglas & McIntyre Publishers
    62
Dow Jones-Irwin 191
Down East Books 62
Down East Magazine 461
Dragon Magazine 287
Dragon's Teeth Press 63
Drama Book Publishers 63
Dramatic Publishing Co., The
    866
Dramatics Magazine 267
Dramatika 267
Drawing Board Greetings (see
    Carlton Cards 903)
Drew, Norm 896
Drummer 495
DSM Producers 890
Dubois/Ruddy 845
Dubuque Fine Arts Players 866
Duck & Cover Comedy Group
    896
Dundurn Press Ltd. 63
Dungeon Master 495
Dunning Prize in American His-
    tory, John H. 966
Dun's Business Month (see
    Business Month 226)
Duquesne University Press 63
Dustbooks 63
Dutton, E.P. 64 (also see Lodes-
    tar Books 101)
Dvorak Developments 695

E

Eagle 254
Eakin Publications, Inc. 64
Ear 402
Early American Life 322
Early Years/K-8 (see Teaching/

K-8 692)
East West 302
Eastern Horse World 196
Eastern Review 348
Eaton Literary Associates Literary Awards Program 966
Echelon 348
Eclipse Comics 254
Economic Facts 258
Edges 322
Ediciones Universal 64
Editor & Publisher 766
Editorial Consultant Service 913
Editorial Eye, The 766
Editors' Forum 766
Education Associates 64
Educational Design Services, Inc. 932
Educational Filmstrips & Video 845
Educational Images Ltd. 845
Educational Insights 845
Educational Methods, Inc. (see Longman Financial Services Publishing 102)
Eedrmans Publishing Co., William B. 65
Effective Communication Arts, Inc. 845
80 Micro 420
El Palacio, The Magazine of the Museum of New Mexico 313
El Paso Magazine 486
Elder Statesman 534
Eldridge Publishing Co. 866
Eldritch Tales 371
Electric Company Magazine, The 355
Electric Weenie, The 705
Electrical Apparatus 701
Electrical Contractor 701
Electron, The 545
Electronic Education 687
Electronic Packaging and Production 695
Electronic Servicing & Technology 677
Electronics Today 545
Elek Associates, Peter 932
Elks Magazine, The 208
Ellery Queen's Mystery Magazine 410
Ellis Memorial Award, David James 966
Elsner Advertising Studio 905
Elysium Growth Press 65
Emergency 797
Emergency Librarian 781
Emerson Award, The Ralph Waldo 966
Emmy Magazine 267
Empire State Books (see Heart of the Lakes Publishing 83)
Employee Relations and Human Resources Bulletin 788
Empty Space, The 867

Endless Vacation 622
Enfantaisie 356
Engage/Social Action 509
Engravers Journal, The 761
Enquirer Magazine, The (see TriState Magazine 481)
Enslow Publishers 65
Entelek 65
Enterprise Publishing Co., Inc. 65
Entree 738
Entrepreneur Magazine 258
Epiphany Journal 510
Episcopal Church Facts 510
Episcopalian, The 510
Epoch 371
Epstein Award, William and Janice 966
Equal Opportunity 242
Equinox: The Magazine of Canadian Discovery 292
Equilibrium 291
Equipment Management 786
Erie & Chautauqua Magazine 482
Erikson Literary Agency, The 933
Eriksson, Publisher, Paul S. 66
Erotic Fiction Quarterly 371
Espionage Magazine 260
Esquire 388
Essence 276
ETC Publications 66
Eternity Magazine 510
Eureka Theatre 867
Evangel 511
Evangelical Beacon, The 511
Evangelizing Today's Child 511
Evans and Co., Inc., M. 66
Evener, The (see Rural Heritage 201)
Event 371
Exceptional Parent, The 248
Executive Administrator,The 788
Executive Female 227
Executive Financial Woman 720
Expecting 248
Exploring Magazine 610
Export 815

F
F Q 496
Faber & Faber, Inc. 66
Faces 356
Facet 372
Facets 797
Fact 227
Facts On File, Inc. 67
Fairbank Prize in East Asian History, John K. 966
Fairchild Books & Visuals 67
Fairfield County Woman 634
Fairleigh Dickinson University Press 67
Falcon Press 67

Falcon Press Publishing Co. 68
Family Album, The 68
Family Circle Great Ideas 634
Family Circle Magazine 634
Family Magazine 394
Family Motor Coaching 622
Family Therapy News 741
Fancy Food 732
F&W Publications (see North Light 118, Writer's Digest Books 184)
Fangoria 268
Fantasy Review 549
Farber First Book Award, Norma 966
Farm & Ranch Living 543
Farm Family America 543
Farm Journal 714
Farm Show Magazine 714
Farm Store Merchandising 669
Farm Supplier 708
Farm Woman (see Country Woman 633)
Farmstead Magazine 336
Farnsworth Publishing (see Longman Financial Services Publishing 102)
Farrar, Straus and Giroux, Inc. 68
Farwestern Consultants, Inc. 933
Fashion Accessories 762
Fast 'n' Fun Crosswords and Variety Puzzles 288
Fate 214
FDA Consumer 258
Fearon Education 68
FEDCO Reporter 208
Federal Credit Union, The 721
Feedback Theatrebooks 867
Feiler Literary Agency, Florence 933
Feline Productions 890
Fell, Publishers, Inc., Frederick 68
Feminist Bookstore News, The 663
Fence Industry (see Fence Industry/Access Control 680)
Fence Industry/Access Control 680
Fertilizer Progress 709
Fessenden Review 372
FFL News (see Arms & Outdoor Digest 828)
Fiberarts 323
Ficarelli, Richard 867
Fiction Collective 69
Fiction Network 913
Fiction Network Magazine 372
Fiction Writers Contest 966
Fiddlehead Poetry Books & Goose Lane Editions 69
Fiddlehead, The 372
Field and Stream 580
Fighter-International, The 595
Fighting Woman News 595

Film Quarterly 268
Filter Press, The 69
Final Draft, The 766
Financial Freedom Report 821
Financial Strategies 721
Fine Homebuilding 680
Finescale Modeler 323
Finnish Connection 246
Fire Prevention Through Films,
    Inc. 846
Firebrand Books 69
Firehouse Magazine 727
Firehouse Theatre, The 867
Firepower 574
First Comics, Inc. 256
First Hand 496
First Ring 846
Fish Boat, The 793
Fishbein Ltd., Frieda 933
Fisherman, The 580
Fishing Tackle Retailer 829
Fishing World 580
Fithian Press (see John Daniel,
    Publisher 56)
Fitness Management 797
Fitzhenry & Whiteside, Ltd. 70
Fjord Press 70
Flaming Star Enterprises 934
Fleet Press Corp. 70
Flight Craft (see Air Wisconsin
    346)
Flight Reports 225
Fliptrack Learning Systems 846
Flooring Magazine 738
Flora and Fauna Publications 70
Floral & Nursery Times 724
Flores Publications, J. 71
Floricanto Press, Inc. 71
Florida Forum 815
Florida Grocer 732
Florida Grower & Rancher 717
Florida Gulf Coast Living Mag-
    azine 451
Florida Horse, The 575
Florida Hotel & Motel Journal
    743
Florida Individual Artist Fellow-
    ships 966
Florida Keys Magazine 451
Florida Leader Magazine 242
Florida Racquet Journal 597
Florida Sportsman 580
Florida Studio Theatre 868
Florida Vidcom 846
Florida Wildlife 581
Florist 724
Flower and Garden Magazine
    337
Flower News 725
Flowers & 725
Flute Talk 805
Fly Fisherman 581
Flyfisher, The 582
Flying A, The 648
FM Five (see The Short Story
    Review 382)
FMT 868

Focal Press 71
Focus on the Family 512
Fodor's Travel Publications, Inc.
    71
Folio Fiction/Poetry Awards 966
Food & Drug Packaging 825
Food & Service 743
Food People 733
For Your Eyes Only 394
Forbes 228
Ford Award, Consuelo 966
Ford Times 292
Fordham University Press 71
Foreign Affairs 760
Forest Notes 471
Forests & People 413
Forman Publishing Inc. 72
Fortress Press 72
49th Parallel Poetry Contest,The
    967
Forum 389
Foster City Writers Contest 967
Fotopress, Independent News
    Service International 913
Foundation News 728
Foundry Management & Tech-
    nology 785
4-H Leader 208
4-Wheel & Off-Road 219
Four Wheeler Magazine 219
Fourth Estate Award 967
Fox River Patriot 490
France Today 623
Frank" 896
Franklin Mint Almanac, The
    323
Franks, Producer, Bud 868
Fraser Institute, The 72
Freedley Memorial Award,
    George 967
Freedman Dramatic Agency,
    Inc., Robert A. 934
Freedom Greeting Card Co. 905
Freedom Magazine 428
Freelance Syndicate, Inc. 914
Freelance Writer's Report 767
Freeman Memorial Grant-in-
    Aid, Don 967
Freeman, The 429
Freeway 610
French & Partners, Inc., Paul
    846
French, Inc., Samuel 72, 868,
    934
Freshwater and Marine Aquari-
    um Magazine 323
Frets Magazine 403
Friday (Of the Jewish Exponent)
    278
Friend, The 356
Friendly Exchange 292
Friends Magazine 220
Front Page Detective 261
Front Row Experience 73
Fulcrum, Inc. 73
Functional Photography 811
Fundamentalist Journal 512

Futures and Options Trader, The
    722
Futures Magazine 721
Futurific Magazine 293

G
Gallant/Charger's Fishing &
    Boating Illustrated 582
Gallery Magazine 389
Gambling Times 73
Gambling Times Magazine 567
Game & Fish Magazine 582
Games 287
Gamut, The 373
Garber Communications, Inc.
    74
Garden Design 337
Garden Magazine 338
Garden Supply Retailer 725
Garden Way Publishing 74
Garon-Brooke Association, Inc.,
    Jay 934
Gartenberg, Literary Agent,
    Max 935
Gaslamp Quarter Theatre 868
Gauss Award, The Christian 967
Gay Chicago Magazine 496
Gay Sunshine Press 74
Geer Theatricum Botanicum,
    The Will 868
Gem, The 512
Genealogical Publishing Co.,
    Inc. 74
General Electric Foundation
    Awards for Younger Writers
    967
General Hall, Inc. 75
General News Syndicate 914
Gent 389
Gentlemen's Quarterly 390
George Street Playhouse 868
Georgetown Productions 869
Georgia Journal 455
Georgia Sportsman 583
Gerard, Dave 896
Geriatric Consultant 798
Gessler Publishing Co., Inc.
    846
Giant Crosswords 288
Gibson Company, The C.R. 75
Gifford Children's Theater, Em-
    my 869
Gifted Children Monthly 248
Gifted Education Press 75
Giftware Business 738
Giftware News 738
Glamour 634
Glass Digest 665
Glass Magazine 665
Glassman 896
Gleanings in Bee Culture 716
Glenbridge Publishing Ltd. 75
Glenmark Publishing 75
Global Press Review 914
Globe 293
Globe Press Books 75

Gold Eagle Books 76
Gold Prospector 804
Goldberg Literary Agents, Inc., Lucianne S. 935
Golden Books 76
Golden Kite Awards 967
Golden Pacific (see Air Wisconsin 346)
Golden Quill Press, The 191
Golden Rod Puppets 869
Golden West Books 76
Golden West Publishers 76
Golden Years Magazine 535
Golf Course Management 829
Golf Digest 571
Golf Illustrated 571
Golf Magazine 572
Golf Shop Operations 830
Good Housekeeping 635
Good News (Kentucky) 512
Good News (Minnesota) 767
Good News Broadcaster (see Confident Living 506)
Good Reading 293
Goodman Associates Literary Agents 935
Goodman Award 967
Goodman Literary Agency, Irene 935
Government Institutes, Inc. 76
Graduating Engineer 703
Graham Agency 935
Grain 373
Grand Rapids Magazine 466
Grand Slam Greetings, Inc. 905
Grandparenting! 535
Grapevine Publications, Inc. 77
Grapevine's Fingerlake Magazine, The 474
Graphic Arts Center Publishing Co. 77
Graphic Arts Monthly 817
Grassroots Fundraising Journal 728
Great American Airways (see Air Wisconsin 346)
Great Expeditions 623
Great Lakes Fisherman 583
Great Lakes Travel & Living 467
Great Midwestern Ice Cream Company, The 897
Great Northwest Publishing and Distributing Company, Inc. 77
Great Ocean Publishers 77
Greater Phoenix Jewish News 278
Greater Portland Magazine 461
Green Hill Publishers, Inc. 77
Green, Inc., Warren H. 78
Green Tiger Press 78
Greene, Inc., Harold R. 936
Greene Press/Lewis Publishing, The Stephen 78
Greenhaven Press, Inc. 78
Greenleaf Classics, Inc. 79

Greyhound Review, The 197
Grit 294
Groom & Board 839
Groundwood Books (see Douglas & McIntyre Publishers 62)
Group 610
Group Members Only 610
Group Practice Journal 798
Group's Junior High Ministry Magazine 513
Growing Parent 249
Grunwald and Radcliff Publishers 187
Gryphon House, Inc. 79
Guardian 429
Guenette Productions, Robert 890
Guernica Editions 79
Guidance Centre 79
Guide 611
Guide to the Florida Keys 623
Guideposts Magazine 513
Guideposts Magazine Youth Writing Contest 967
Guitar Player Magazine 403
Gulf Coast Cattleman 712
Gulf Coast Fisherman 583
Gulf Coast Golfer 572
Gulf Publishing Co. 79
Gulfshore Life 451
Gun Digest 574
Gun World 574
Gurney's Gardening News 338

H

Hadassah Magazine 278
Hagert, Brad 847
Haider Memorial College Literary Magazine Contest, Victoria Chen 967
Hallmark Cards, Inc. 905
Handicap News 263
Handloader's Digest (see Gun Digest 574)
Hands-on Electronics 324
Handwoven 324
Happi 739
Hardcopy 753
Hardware Age 737
Hardware Merchandiser 737
Harper's Magazine 294
Harris & Associate Publishing Division 914
Hart Literary Enterprises, Thomas S. 936
Hartford Woman 447 (also see Fairfield County Woman 634)
Haseltine Memorial Fellowships in Science Writing, Nate 967
Haunts 550
Hayes School Publishing Co., Inc. 847
Heacock Literary Agency, Inc. 936

Headquarters Detective 261
Health Foods Business 733
Health Foods Retailing 733
Healthplex Magazine 303
Heaping Teaspoon Animation 890
Heating, Plumbing, Air Conditioning 815
Heating/Piping/Air Conditioning 815
Heinle + Heinle Enterprises, Inc. 936
Heinz Literature Prize, Drue 967
Helitzer, Mel 897
Helix Press 191
Hemingway Foundation, Ernest 967
Hemley Memorial Award, Cecil 967
Hendrick Jr., Charles 897
Heritage Features Syndicate 914
Heur Publishing Co. 869
HHM Literary Agency 937
Hibiscus Magazine 373
Hicall 514
Hideaways Guide 624
High Adventure 356
High Country News 413
High Fidelity/Musical America (see Musical America 406)
High Society 390
High Times 214
High Volume Printing 817
Highlander, The 279
Highlights for Children 357
High-Tech Manager's Bulletin 788
High-Tech Marketing 648
High-Tech Selling 648
Hill Associates, Frederick 937
Hillman Prize Award, Sidney 967
Hilton Literary Agency, Alice 937
Hintz & Fitzgerald, Inc. 937
Hirsch Awards, Harold 968
HIS Magazine (see U Magazine 247)
Hispanic Business 669
Hispanic Link News Service 914
Hochmann Books, John L. 937
Hockey Illustrated 597
Hog Farm Management 712
Hollywood Inside Syndicate 915
Home Altar, The 514
Home Business News 228
Home Education Magazine 249
Home Furnishings 739
Home Life 249
Home Lighting & Accessories 739
Home Mechanix 324
Homeowner, The 338
Homeworking Mothers 635
Hommel Associates, Inc., Den-

nis 847
Honolulu 456
Honolulu Theatre for Youth 869
Hoof Beats 575
Hoover Annual Journalism
    Awards 968
Horizon Air (see Air Wisconsin
    346)
Horn Book Magazine, The 663
Horoscope Guide 215
Horror Show, The 550
Horse Digest, The 197
Horse Illustrated 197
Horseplay 198
Horses All 198
Horticulture 339
Hospital Gift Shop Management
    741
Hospital Supervisor's Bulletin
    742
Hostelers' Knapsack 624
Hot Bike 220
Hotel and Motel Management
    744
House Beautiful 339
Houston City Magazine 486
Houston Prize, Darrell Bob 968
Howard Awards, The Roy W.
    968
Howell, David R. 897
HP Design & Manufacturing
    754
Hub Rail 576
Hudson Guild Theatre 869
Hudson Review, The 373
Hudson Talent Representation,
    Scott 938
Hudson Valley Magazine 475
Humpty Dumpty's Magazine
    357
Hunt, William E. 870
Huntington Playhouse 870
Hyde Park Media 915

Idaho Writer in Residence 968
Ideals Magazine 294
IEEE Software 754
Illinois Banker 722
Illinois Entertainer 403
Illinois Magazine 457
Illinois State University Fine
    Arts Playwriting Award 968
Illinois Times 457
ILR Press 89
Image Magazine 374
Imagine, Inc. 89
IMC Journal 303
Imperial International Learning
    Corp. 847
Imprint 648
In Business 669
In Touch 611
In Touch for Men 497
IN TOUCH, The International

Tours Travel Magazine 624
Inbound Logistics 834
INC Magazine 228
Incentive Marketing 825
Incentive Publications, Inc. 89
Income Opportunities 259
Independence Press (see Herald
    Publishing House 84)
Independent Banker 722
Independent, The 696
Indiana Business 234
Indiana Review 374
Indiana University Press 89
Indianapolis Magazine 458
Indianapolis Monthly 458
Individual Artist Fellowship 968
Industrial Fabric Products Re-
    view 747
Industrial Media, Inc. 847
Industrial Press Inc. 90
Infantry 395
Info Franchise Newsletter 825
Inform 754
Information Marketing 649
Information Resources Press 90
Information Today 696
Information Week 755
Ingraham Prize, Mark H. 968
Inkling Fiction Contest 968
Inkling Poetry Contest 968
Inland 435
Inland Architect 680
Inner City Cultural Center 870
Inner Light 215
InnerQuest Communications 890
Inner-View 486
Innkeeping World 744
In-Plant Printer (see In-Plant
    Printer and Electronic Pub-
    lisher 817)
In-Plant Printer and Electronic
    Publisher 817
In-Plant Reproductions & Elec-
    tronic Publishing 818
Inside 279
Inside Chicago 457
Inside Detective 261
Inside Print 649
Inside Running & Fitness 598
Insight! Inc. 847
Instant and Small Commercial
    Printer 818
Institute for the Study of Human
    Issues 90
Instructor Books 848
Instructor Magazine 688
Instrumentalist, The 806
Insulation Outlook 748
Insurance Review 759
Insurance Software Review 759
In-Sync 891
INTAR Hispanic-American The-
    ater 870
Intellectual Activist, The 429
Intercultural Press, Inc. 90
Interior Landscape Industry 725
International Advisor, The 228

International Bluegrass 806
International Foundation of Em-
    ployee Benefit Plans 91
International Imitation
    Hemingway Competition
    968
International Literary Contest
    968
International Literature and Arts
    Agency 938
International Living 435
International Marine Publishing
    Co. 91
International Media Services
    Inc. 848
International Musician 404
International Olympic Lifter 598
International Publisher Associ-
    ates, Inc. 938
International Publishers Co.,
    Inc. 91
International Reading Associa-
    tion Children's Book Award
    968
International Reading Associa-
    tion Print Media Award 968
International Self-Counsel Press,
    Ltd. 91
International Wealth Success 92
International Wildlife 413
Interpress of London and New
    York 915
Interstate Printers & Publishers,
    Inc., The 92
Interurban Press/Trans Anglo
    Books 92
Intervarsity Christian Fellowship
    (see Intervarsity Press 92)
Intervarsity Press 92
Intimacy/Black Romance 538
INVESTigate 228
Invisible Theatre 870
Iowa Arts Council Literary
    Awards 968
Iowa Review, The 374
Iowan Magazine, The 459
Iron Crown Enterprises 93
Ironbound Theatre Inc. 870
Isaac Asimov's Science Fiction
    Magazine 550
Ishiyaku Euroamerica, Inc. 93
It Will Stand 404
Italian Times, The 279

J

Jack and Jill 358
Jackson Productions, Inc.,
    David J. 848
Jackson/James D. Phelan Liter-
    ary Awards, Joseph Henry
    969
Jacksonville Magazine 451
Jacksonville Today 452
Jacksonville University Play-
    writing Contest 969

Jacoby/Storm Productions, Inc. 848
Jalmar Press, Inc. 93
Jam 404
Jam To-Day 374
Jamestown Prize 969
Jamestown Publishers, Inc. 94
Janus Literary Agency 938
Japan Foundation Fellowship Program, The 969
Japanophile 374
Jarvis and Co., Inc., Sharon 938
Jason Enterprises, Inc., Asher D. 939
JEMS 798
Jet America (see Air Wisconsin 346)
Jet Cargo News 660
Jet Literary Associates, Inc. 939
Jewel Box Theatre 871
Jewish Monthly, The 280
Jewish News 280
Jewish Weekly News, The 514
JH Press 94
Jive 540
Jobber Topics 656
Johnson Books 94
Jonathan David Publishers 94
Jones Award, Anson 969
Journal of Career Planning & Employment 688
Journal of Christian Camping 625
Journal of Defense & Diplomacy 760
Journal of Graphoanalysis 433
Journal of Information Systems Management 755
Journal of Property Management 821
Journal of Systems Management 756
Journal, The 798
Journalism Educator 767
Journalism Quarterly 768
Joyful Woman, The 635
Juggler's World 325
Junior and Senior Awards 969
Junior Trails 358

K

Kafka Prize, The Janet Heidinger 969
Kalan, Inc. 905
Kaleidoscope 263
Kaleidoscopix Inc., Children's Book Division 94
Kalmbach Publishing co. 95
Kam Theatre 871
Kamaroff Associates, Alex 939
Kansas City Magazine 469
Kansas Quarterly/Kansas Arts Commission Awards, Seaton Awards 969

Karate/Kung-Fu Illustrated 596
Kar-Ben Copies Inc. 95
Karr Productions, Paul S. 848
Kashrus Magazine 284
Kaufman, Inc., William 95
KCS 404
Keller, Reamer 897
Kennedy Book Award, Robert F. 969
Kent State University Press 95
Kentucky Happy Hunting Ground 460
Kern International, Inc. 95
Kesend Publishing, Ltd., Michael 96
Keyboard Magazine 405
Keynoter 611
Kidde, Hoyt and Picard Literary Agency 939
Kids Fashions 675
Kimbo Educational-United Sound Arts, Inc. 848
King Features Syndicate, Inc. 915
King, Literary Agent, David P. 940
Kinn, Milo 897
Kitplanes 225
Kiwanis 209
Klein Publications, B. 96
Klinger, Inc., Harvey 940
Knight-Ridder Press (see H.P. Books 80)
Knights Press 96
Knopf, Inc., Alfred A. 96
Knowledge Industry Publications, Inc. 97
Knox Press, John 97
Koch Marschall Productions, Inc. 849, 891
Kohner, Inc., Paul 940
Korean Culture 280
Kouts, Barbara S. 940
Kratz & Kompany 941
Krieger Publishing Co. Inc., Robert 97
Kumu Kahua 871
Kushner Memorial Award, Sarah H. 969

L

L.A. Parent 250
L.A. West 442
La Crosse CityBusiness 235
Ladies' Home Journal 636
Lady's Circle 636
Lake Memorial Award, Ruth 969
Lake Superior Magazines 468
Lake Superior Port Cities (see Lake Superior Magazine 468)
Lakeland Boating 560
Lamb's Players Theatre 871
Lamont Poetry Selection 969

Lampack Agency, Inc., Peter 941
Landon Translation Prize, The Harold Morton 969
Lang Publishing, Inc., Peter 97
L'Apache 375
Larsen/Elizabeth Pomada Literary Agents, Michael 941
Last Issue 203
Law and Order 728
Law Offices of Robert L. Fenton, P.C. 941
Lawrence Fellowship, D.H. 969
Lawyer's PC, The 777
Lawyers Weekly, The 777
Lay, Literary Agent, Elizabeth 942
Leacock Memorial Award for Humour, Stephen 970
Leadership 674
Learning 88 688
Learning Publications, Inc. 97
Leather Craftsman, The 325
Lector 281
Lee & Company, Brien 849
Lee Literary Agency, L. Harry 942
Lee's Books for Young People 98
Legal Economics 778
Leisure Books 98
Leisure Press 98 (also see Human Kinetics Publishers, Inc. 87)
Leonard Publishing Corp., Hal 98
Leone Agency, Inc., The Adele 942
Let's Live Magazine 303
Letters Magazine 375
Levine Associates, Inc., William V. 849
Levine Literary Agency, Inc., Ellen 942
Lexikos 99
Libertarian Digest, The 429
Liberty Publishing Company, Inc. 99
Libra Publishers, Inc. 99
Libraries Unlimited 99
Library Imagination Paper, The 781
Library Journal 782
Library Professional Publications (see The Shoe String Press 151)
Licensed Practical Nurse 742
Lieberman Student Poetry Award, Elias 970
Life 295
Life Cycle Books 100
Life Enhancement Publications (see Human Kinetics Publishers, Inc. 87)
Life in the Times 395
Light and Life 515
Light and Life Writing

Contest 970
Lighted Pathway 612
Lightwave 696
Liguori Publications 100
Liguorian 515
Lillenas Publishing Co. 871
Lilly Poetry Prize, The Ruth 970
Limousin World 712
Linch Publishing, Inc. 100
Lincoln Memorial One-Act Playwriting Contest 970
Linden Lane Magazine English-Language Poetry Contest 969
Linkert, Lo 897
Linking the DOTS 461
Lion, The 209
Lipkind Agency, Wendy 943
Lippincott Award, Joseph W. 970
Listen Magazine 304
Literary Magazine Review 375
Literary Sketches 376
Little, Brown and Co., Inc. 100
Live 515
Living with Children 250
Living with Preschoolers 250
Living with Teenagers 515
Livingston Associates, Inc., Peter 943
Llamas Magazine 713
Llewellyn Publications 101
Lockert Library of Poetry in Translation 970
Lodestar Books 101
Lodging Hospitality Magazine 744
Loft Creative Nonfiction Residency Program 970
Loft-McKnight Writers Award 970
Loft-Mentor Series 970
Log Home and Alternative Housing Builder (see Builder/Dealer 679)
Log Homes 339
Lomond Publications, Inc. 101
Lone Eagle Publishing Co. 101
Lone Star Comedy Monthly, The 705
Lone Star Horse Report 198
Lone Star Humor 343
Long Island Stage 872
Longman Financial Services Publishing 102
Longman Group, U.S.A. (see Longman Financial Services Publishing 102)
Longman, Inc. 102
Lookout, The 516
Loose Change 325
Loreven Publishing, Inc. (see Critic's Choice Paperbacks 53)
Lori Productions, Inc. 849
Los Angeles Lawyer 778

Los Angeles Reader 442
Los Angeles Theater Unit 872
Los Angeles Theatre Center 872
Los Angeles Times Book Review 376
Los Angeles Times Magazine 442
Los Angeles Times Syndicate 916
Lothrop, Lee & Shepard Books 102
Louisiana Contractor 680
Louisiana Literature Prize for Poetry 970
Loyola University Press 102
Lucas-Evans Books 188
Luna Ventures 188
Lunchbox Theatre 872
LuraMedia 103
Lutheran Forum 516
Lutheran Journal, The 517
Lutheran Standard, The 517
Lutheran, The 516
Lynn, The North Shore Magazine 464

M

MA/AH Publishing (see Sunflower University Press 159)
MACazine, The 420
McCall's 636
MacCampbell Inc., Donald 943
McCarter Theatre Co. 872
McCourt, Art 897
McCracken, Theresa 898
McElderry Books, Margaret K. 103
McFarland & Company, Inc. 103
McGraw-Hill Book Co. 103
Mach 497
Machine Design 703
Macintosh Buyer's Guide, The 421
Maclean's 295
McLemore Prize, Richard A. 970
MacMillan Publishing Company 103
Macworld 421
Mad Magazine 343
Mademoiselle 637
Madison Magazine 490
Madrona Publishers, Inc. 104
Magazine for Christian Youth!, The 612
Magazine, The 480
Magic Theatre, Inc. 873
Magick Theatre 269
Magid Productions, Lee 891
Magna 390
Magnus Theatre Company 873
Main Street Press, The 104
Maine Life 462
Maine Line Co. 905

Maine Organic Farmer & Gardener 717
Maine Sportsman, The 584
Mainstream 264
Malahat Review, The 376
Manage 788
Management Accounting 789
Management Review 789
Manatee Players, Inc. 873
Manhattan Punch Line 873
Manhattan Theatre Club 873
Manhattan Video Production Inc. 850
Manscape 2 497
Manufacturing Systems 748
Manuscripts 325
Marathon International Publishing Company, Inc. 104
March Tenth, Inc. 943
Marcil Literary Agency, Inc., Denise 943
Marian Helpers Bulletin 517
Marine Corps Gazette 728
Market Watch 661
Marketing & Sales Promotion Update 745
Marks, Betty 944
Marlor Press 104
Marraro Prize in Italian History, Howard R. 970
Marriage & Family Living 517
Marshall/National Prize for Poetry, The Lenore 970
Marshfilm Enterprises, Inc. 850
Mart 739
Marvel Comics 256
Maryland Magazine 463
Maryland Public Television 850
Masefield Memorial Award, John 970
Mass High Tech 696
Massachusetts Artists Fellowship 971
Massachusetts Review, The 376
Massachusetts/New Hampshire Out-of-Doors (see New England Out-of-Doors Magazine 568)
Massage Magazine 304
Master Detective 261
Matter of Crime, A 410
Mature Living 535
Mature Outlook 535
Mature Years 536
Maverick Publications 188
May Trends 670
May, Rex F. (Baloo) 898
Mayflower Society Cup Competition, The 971
Maynard-Thomas Publishing, Inc. 104
Mayo Alumnus, The 799
Mazda Publishers 105
MBA 229
md Books (see May Davenport, Publishers 57)
MD Magazine 799

Meadowbrook Press 105
Media History Digest 313
Media Learning Systems, Inc. 850
Media Productions and Marketing, Inc. 105
Media Profiles 690
Mediacom Development Corp. 891
Medical Business Journal, The 799
Medical Economics 799
Medical Economics Books 105
Medical Meetings 800
Medical Times 800
Medical World News 800
Medicenter Management 742
Medwick Memorial Award, Lucille 971
Meeman Awards, The Edward J. 971
Meeting News 670
Melcher Book Award 971
Melius & Peterson Publishing, Inc. 106
Members, Health and Racquet Club Members 304
Memphis 484
Memphis Business Journal 235
Menasha Ridge Press, Inc. 106
Mencken Awards 971
Mennonite Brethren Herald 518
Mennonite Publishing House (see Herald Press 84)
Men's Fitness 304
Menza Literary Agency, Claudia 944
Mercer University Press 106
Mercury Syndications 916
Meredith, Inc., Scott 944
Meridian Gay Theatre 873
Meriwether Publishing Ltd. (Colorado) 106
Meriwether Publishing Ltd. (Illinois) 850
Merrill Publishing Co. 107
Messenger of the Sacred Heart, The 518
Metamorphous Press,Inc. 107
Metapsychology 215
Metheun, Inc 107 (also see Theatre Arts Books 162)
Metro Singles Lifestyles 498
Metropolis 203
Mews Book Ltd. 944
Meyerbooks, Publisher 108
MGI Management Institute, Inc., The 108
Miami Beach Community Theatre 873
Miami/South Florida Magazine 452
Michiana 459
Michigan Living 625
Michigan Magazine 467
Michigan Natural Resources Magazine 414

Michigan Out-of-Doors 584
Michigan Quarterly Review 376
Michigan State University Press 108
Michigan Woman, The 467
Micro Cornucopia 756
Microage Quarterly 421
MICROpendium 422
Microwaves & RF 697
Mid West Outdoors 584
Mid-American Review 377
Mid-Atlantic Country Magazine 436
Mid-Continent Bottler 661
Middle Eastern Dancer 706
Mid-South Magazine 485
Midstate (see Air Wisconsin 346)
Midstream 281
Midway Airlines (see Air Wisconsin 346)
Midway Magazine 348
Midwest Contractor 681
Midwest Living 436
Midwest Motorist, The 625
Midwest Playlabs 873
Midwest Poetry Review 377
Milady Publishing Corporation 108
Mildenberger Prize, Kenneth W. 971
Military Engineer, The 395
Military Images 314
Military Lifestyle 395
Military Living R&R Report 396
Military Review 396
Mill Mountain Theatre New Play Competition 971
Miller Agency, Inc., The Peter 945
Mills & Sanderson, Publishers 108
Milwaukee Journal Magazine, The (see Wisconsin 490)
Milwaukee Repertory Theater 874
Mini 756
Miniature Collector 326
Miniatures & Doll Dealer Magazine (see Miniatures Dealer Magazine 833)
Miniatures Dealer Magazine 833
Mini-Micro Systems 756
Ministries Today 674
Minnesota Sportsman 585
Minority Engineer, The 703
Minority Features Syndicate 916
Miraculous Medal, The 518
Mississippi Game & Fish 585
Mississippi Rag, The 405
Mississippi State University Alumnus 242
Missouri Ruralist 718
Misty Hill Press 109
MIT Press 109
Mix Magazine 807

Mobile Manufactured Home Merchandiser 670
Model Railroader 326
Model Retailer Magazine 833
Modern Drummer 405
Modern Electronics 545
Modern Floor Coverings 665
Modern Language Association of America 109
Modern Liturgy 518
Modern Machine Shop 785
Modern Maturity 536
Modern Office Technology 808
Modern Percussionist 406
Modern Romances 540
Modern Tire Dealer 656
Modern Veterinary Practice 839
Modern Woodmen, The 210
Mom Guess What Newspaper 498
Momentum 690
Monad Trainer's Aide 850
Monitor Book Co., Inc. 109
Mont Chat, Inc. (see Brick House Publishing Co. 39)
Montana Magazine 469
Monterey Life 443
Moody Monthly 518
Moon Publications 191
Moose Magazine 210
More Business 649
Morehouse-Barlow Co., Inc. 110
Morgan Horse, The 198
Morley Memorial Prizes, Felix 971
Morrow and Co., Inc., William 110 (also see Quill 139)
Morrow Junior Books 110
Morrow Owners' Review 422
Mosaic Press Miniature Books 110
Mother Courage Press 110
Mother Earth News, The 543
Mother Jones Magazine 430
Motivation Media, Inc. 851
Motor Service 656
Motorboating and Sailing 560
Motorbooks International Publishers & Wholesalers, Inc. 111
Mott Media, Inc., Publishers 111
Mott Kappa Tau Alpha Research Award in Journalism, Frank Luther 971
Mountain States Collector 326
Mountaineers Books,The 111
Movie Collector's World 269
Movieline Magazine 269
Moving Up 243
Mpls. St. Paul Magazine 468
M/R Magazine 390
MS Public Education Awards Contest 971
Multimedia Product Development, Inc. 945

Multi-Media Productions,Inc. 851
Multnomah Press 111
Munk & Company, Burt 851
Museum of New Mexico Press 112
Museum of Northern Arizona Press 112
Music & Sound Output 807
Music Magazine 406
Musical America 406
Mustang Publishing co. 112
Myrtle Beach Magazine 484
Mysterious Press, The 112

N

N.D. Rec Magazine 718
N.Y. Habitat Magazine 339
Na'Amat Woman 637
Naggar Literary Agency, Jean V. 945
Naiad Press, Inc., The 113
NAL Penguin Inc. (see Dial Books for Young Readers 60)
Nation, The 430
National Arts Centre-English Theatre Co. 874
National Association of Social Workers 113
National Beauty School Journal 690
National Book Company 113
National Bus Trader 837
National Christian Reporter 519
National Defense 396
National Development 430
National Examiner 295
National Fisherman 723
National Forum: The Phi Kappa Phi Journal 243
National Future Farmer, The 715
National Gallery of Canada 113
National Gardening 339
National Geographic Magazine 295
National Geographic Traveler 625
National Geographic World 359
National Guard 397
National Jewish Book Award-Children's Literature 971
National Jewish Book Award-Fiction 971
National Jewish Book Award-Holocaust 971
National Jewish Book Award-Illustrated Children's Book 971
National Jewish Book Award-Israel 971
National Jewish Book Award-Jewish History 972
National Jewish Book Award-Jewish Thought 972
National Jewish Book Award-Scholarship 972

National Jewish Book Award-Visual Arts 972
National Lampoon 345
National Law Journal, The 778
National Literary Guild (see Authors' Unlimited 191)
National Motorist 626
National News Bureau 916
National One-Act Play Contest 972
National Parks 414
National Play Award 972
National Playwrights Showcase 874
National Press, Inc. 114
National Psychology Awards for Excellence in the Media 972
National Publishers of the Black Hills, Inc. 114
National Racquetball 598
National Show Horse 199
National Show Horse News (see National Show Horse 199)
National Society of Professional Engineers Journalism Awards 972
National Textbook Company 114
National Wildlife 414
Nation's Business 670
Nationwide Careers 691
Natural History 414
Naturegraph Publishers, Inc. 114
Naval Institute Press 114
NC Press 115
NCFE Motivator, The 229
Near West Gazette 458
Nebraska Review Awards in Fiction and Poetry, The 972
Necessary Angel Theatre 874
Needlepoint News 326
Neighbors, Inc., Charles 945
Nelson Literary Agency, B.K 946
Nelson Publishers, Thomas 115
Nelson-Hall Publishers 115
Network 251
Network Communications Ltd., 851
Nevada Business Journal 235
Nevada Magazine 470
Nevadan, The 470
Nevins Prize, Allan 972
New Age Journal 296
New Age World Services 946
New Alaskan 439
New American Library 115
New Black Mask Quarterly, The (see A Matter of Crime 410)
New Body 305
New Breed 397
New Business Magazine 235
New Conservatory Children's Theatre Company and School, The 874
New Day (see Greenhaven

Press, Inc. 78)
New Dimensions 433
New England Church Life 519
New England Farm Bulletin 718
New England Farmer 718
New England Getaways 626
New England Out-of-Doors Magazine 568
New England Press, Inc., The 115
New England Publishing Associates, Inc. 946
New England Review/Bread Loaf Quarterly 377
New England Senior Citizen/Senior American News 536
New Era, The 520
New Frontier 433
New Hampshire Alumnus,The 244
New Hampshire Profiles 471
New Harbinger Publications, Inc. 115
New Haven County Woman (see Fairfield County Woman 634)
New Holland News 715
New Jersey Business 236
New Jersey Monthly 472
New Jersey Reporter 472
New Leaf Press, Inc. 116
New Letters Literary Awards 972
New Mexico Business Journal 671
New Mexico Magazine 473
New Orleans Magazine 460
New Physician, The 800
New Play Festival 972
New Plays Incorporated 875
New Playwrights Competition and Festival 972
New Playwrights' Theatre 875
New Playwrights' Theatre of Washington, The 875
New Readers Press 116
new renaissance, the 377
New Society Publishers 116
New Southern Literary Messenger, The 378
New Tuners Theatre 875
New Victoria Publishers 116
New Vistas 452
New Woman Magazine 638
New World Outlook 520
New World Theater, Inc. 876
New Writers Awards 972
New York Alive 475
New York Antique Almanac, The 327
New York Daily News 475
New York Habitat 476
New York Magazine 476
New York Running News 599
New York Shakespeare Festival/Public Theater 876
New York State Historical Asso-

ciation Manuscript Award 972
New York Times, The 476
New York Times Syndication Sales Corp. 916
New York Zoetrope, Inc. 117
New York's Nightlife and Long Island's Nightlife 476
New Yorker, The 296
Newbery Medal, John 972
Newcastle Publishing Co., Inc. 117
Newcomen Awards in Business History 973
News America Syndicate 916
News Flash International, Inc. 917
News/34-38 757
Newsday 477, 626
Newspaper Enterprises Association, Inc. 917
Newsweek 431
Nibble 423
Nichols, Jackie 876
Nickelodeon MTV Networks, Inc. 891
Nightmare Express, The 550
Nightmoves 281
Nimbus Publishing Limited 117
Nimrod, Arts and Humanities Council of Tulsa Prizes 973
Nine O'Clock Players 876
Nissan Discovery 220
Nissan Focus Awards 973
Nitty Gritty Cookbooks 117
NMMA Directors Award 973
Noah's Ark 359
Nolan Literary Agency, The Betsy 946
Norma-Lewis Agency, The 947
North American Hunter 585
North American Review, The 378
North American Voice of Fatima 520
North American Whitetail Magazine 585
North Carolina Black Repertory Company, The 876
North Country Press 118
North Dakota Rec 478
North Light 118
North Point Press 118
North Texas Golfer 572
Northcoast View 443
Northeast Magazine 448
Northeast Outdoors 627
Northern Logger and Timber Processor 783
Northern Virginian Magazine 488
Northlight Theatre 876
Northwest Living 436
Northwest Magazine 437
Northword 118
Norton Co., Inc., W.W. 119
Nostalgiaworld 327

Notre Dame Magazine 244
Now Comics 256
Noyes Data Corp. 119
NSBE Journal 704
NSGA Sports Retailer 830
NSRA News 780
Nugent & Associates, Inc. 947
Nugget 391
Numismatic Information Service 917
Numismatist, The 327
Nursing Homes 684
Nursinglife 801
Nursingworld Journal 801
Nutshell News 328
Nystrom 851

O

O and A Marketing News 657
OA Magazine 757
Oak Tree Publications 119
Oasis Press 119
Oatmeal Studios 907
Oblates Magazine 520
Occupational Health & Safety Magazine 748
Ocean Industry 701
Ocean Navigator 793
Oceans 415
Oceanus 415
Octameron Associates 119
Oddo Publishing, Inc. 119
Odyssey 359
Odyssey Theatre Ensemble 877
Off Center Theatre 877
Off Duty 397
Office Management & Automation (see OA Magazine 757)
Office Systems Ergonomics Report 808
Official Crossword Puzzles 288
Official Crossword Yearbook 288
Official Detective 261
Official Karate 596
Official Pencil Puzzles & Word Games 288
Official Word Search Puzzles 288
Off-Road's Thunder Trucks and Truck Pulls 220
Offshore 561
O'Hara Publications, Inc. 120
Ohio Business 236
Ohio Fisherman 586
Ohio Magazine 480
Ohio Psychology Publishing Co. 120
Ohio Review 378
Ohio State University Press 120
Ohio University Press 120
Ohioana Book Award 973
Oise Press 120
Oklahoma Today 482
Oktoberfest Short Fiction Competition 973

Old Army Press, The 121
Old Bottle Magazine/Popular Archaelogy, The 328
Old Cars Price Guide 328
Old Cars Weekly 328
Old Globe Theatre 877
Old Mill News 314
Old West 314
Ommation Press Book Contest 973
Omni 546
Omni Communications 851
On Page 697
On The Line 360
101 Productions 121
One Shot 406
1,001 Home Ideas 340
O'Neill Theater Center's National Playwright's Conference/New Drama for Television Project 877
Onion World 709
Only Music Magazine 407
Ontario Lawyers Weekly (see The Lawyers Weekly 777)
Ontario Out of Doors 586
Open Court Publishing Co. 121
Open Eye: New Stagings, The 877
Open Wheel Magazine 221
Openers 296
Opera Canada 407
Opera Companion, The 270
Opera News 807
Opportunities for Actors & Models 706
Opportunity Magazine 825
OPR Spring, Summer, Fall and Winter Competitions 973
Optimist Magazine, The 210
Options (California) 801
Options (New York) 391
Oracle Press, Ltd. 878
Orange Coast Magazine 444
Orange County Business Journal 236
Orben's Current Comedy 345
Orbis Books 121
Oregon Business 236
Oregon Shakespearean Festival Associations 878
Oregon State University Press 121
Original Art Report, The 204
Orlando Magazine 237
ORT Reporter 521
Ortho Information Services 121
Orvis Writing Contest, The C.F. 973
Oscard Associates, Fifi 947
Ostomy Quarterly 305
OTC Review 722
Other Side, The 521
Otte Company, The 947
Ottenheimer Publishers, Inc. 188
Our Family 521

Our Little Friend 360
Our Sunday Visitor Magazine 522
Our Sunday Visitor, Inc. 122, 852
Our Town 477
Outbooks Inc. 122
Outdoor Canada Magazine 569
Outdoor Life 587
Outside Plant 697
Ovation 407
Overseas! 397
Owl Creek Press 122
Owl Magazine 360
Owlflight 552

P

P.A.R. Incorporated 122
P.O.B. 681
P.P.I. Publishing 123
P.U.N., The 345
Pace Films, Inc. 892
Pace Magazine 348
Pacific Bakers News 678
Pacific Boating Almanac 627
Pacific Books, Publishers 123
Pacific Coast Journal 199
Pacific Discovery 415
Pacific Fishing 723
Pacific Paper Greetings 907
Pacific Press Publishing Association 123
Pacific Yachting 561
Pagurian Corporation Limited, The 124
Paint Horse Journal 199
Painting and Wallcovering Contractor 666
Paladin Press 124
Palm Springs Life 444
Panache 249
Pandora 552
Pandora Press124
Panjandrum Books 124
Pantheon Books 125
Paperback Press Inc. (see Northword 118)
Papercutting World 652
Parade 296
Paragon House Publishers 125
Paralegal, The 779
Parameters: Journal of the U.S. Army War College 398
Parenting Press, Inc. 125
Paris Review, The 379
Parish Family Digest 522
Parker & Son Publications, Inc. 125
Parker Motion Pictures, Tom 892
Parkman Prize, Francis 973
Parnassus Imprints, Inc. 125
Partisan Review 379
Partnership 522
Passages North 379

Passport Press 126
Pastoral Life 675
Patterson Foundation Fellowship Program for Journalists, The Alicia 973
Paulist Press 126
Paulist Productions 892
Payne Literary Agency, Inc., John K. 947
PBC International, Inc. 126
PC 423
PCM 423
Peachtree Publishers, Ltd. 126
Pediatrics for Parents 251
Peekner Literary Agency, Inc., Ray 948
Pelican Publishing Company 128
Pen Medal for Translation 973
Pen Publisher Citation 973
Pen Translation Prize 973
Pen Writing Awards for Prisoners 974
Pen/Jerard Fund 973
Pen/Nelson Algren Fiction Award 973
Pen/Roger Klein Award for Editing 973
Penkevill Publishing Company, The 128
Pennsylvania 483
Pennsylvania Angler 587
Pennsylvania Game News 587
Pennsylvania Heritage 483
Pennsylvania Historical and Museum Commission 128
Pennsylvania Lawyer, The 779
Pennsylvania Stage Company 878
Pennsylvannia Review, The 379
Pennywhistle Press 361
Pentecostal Evangel 523
Pentecostal Messenger, The 523
People in Action 297
People's Light & Theatre Company 878
Peregrine Smith Books (see Gibbs M. Smith, Inc. 153)
Perfection Form Co., The 129
Performance Magazine 706
Perinatal Press 802
Periodical 398
Perkins Playwriting Contest 974
Persimmon Hill 314
Personal Computing Magazine 423
Personnel Advisory Bulletin 789
Perspective 211
Perspectives Press 129
Pest Control Magazine 786
Pet Age 810
Pet Business 810
Pet Dealer, The 810
Peter Associates, Inc., James 188
Peter Pauper Press, Inc. 126
Petersen's Hunting 587

Peterson, Oldcastle Theatre Company, Eric 878
Peterson's Photographic Magazine 426
Petheric Press (see Nimbus Publishing Limited 117)
Petrocelli Books, Inc. 129
Petroleum Independent 701
Pets/Supplies/Marketing 811
PGA Magazine 830
Pharos Books 129
Phi Delta Kappan 691
Philadelphia Magazine 483
Philatelic Journalist 768
Philomel Books 130
Phoenix Home & Garden 340
Phoenix Metro Magazine 441
Photo Communication Services, Inc. 852
Photo Lab Management 812
Photo Review, The 812
Photoflash 812
Photoletter 812
Photovideo 813
Physician and Sportsmedicine, The 802
Physician's Management 802
PIC 852
Pickering Associates, Inc. 948
Pickering Co., John (see Pickering Associates, Inc. 948)
Pickwick Publications 130
Pico 423
Pier One Theatre 879
Pig Iron Magazine 379
Pilgrim Press, The 130
Pilot Books 130
Piloting Careers Magazine 834
Pine Associates, Inc., Arthur 948
Pineapple Press,Inc. 130
Pinnworth Productions 879
Pioneer 612
Pioneer Drama Service 879
Pioneer Woman (see Na'Amat Woman 637)
Pipe Smoker 329
Pipeline & Underground Utilities Construction 702
Pittsburgh Magazine 484
Pittsburgh Press Sunday Magazine, The 484
Pizza Today 745
Plain Dealer Magazine 480
Plan and Print 818
Planning 729
Plant Management & Engineering 749
Platt & Munk Publishers 131
Play Meter Magazine 677
Playbill 270
Playboy 391
Players Press, Inc. 131, 879
Playgirl 638
Plays 879
Playthings 833
Playwrights Fund of North

Carolina, Inc. 880
Playwright's-In-Residence Grants 974
Playwriting for Children Award 974
Pleasure Boating Magazine 561
Plenum Publishing 131
Plexus Publishing, Inc. 131
Ploughshares 380
Plus 523
Pocket Books 132
Pocket Crossword Puzzles 288
Pockets 361
Podiatry Management 802
Poetry Arts Project 974
Poetry Magazine Poetry Awards 974
Poggioli Translation Award, Renato 974
Poker Chips 288
Poker Player 568
Police 729
Police Bookshelf 190
Police Times 729
Political Woman 638
Polled Hereford World 713
Pool & Spa News 830
Popular Cars 221
Popular Lures 588
Popular Mechanics 546
Popular Science 546
Popular Woodworking 329
Porcelain, Sidney E. 948
Porter Sargent Publishers, Inc. 132
Porter's Personal Finance Magazine, Sylvia 229
Portman Agency, Julian 948
Ports O' Call 211
Poseidon Press 132
Positive Approach, A 264
Postcard Collector 329
Potato Grower of Idaho 709
Potentials Development for Health & Aging Services 132
Potter, Inc., Clarkson N. 132
Power Books (see Fleming H. Revell Co. 141)
Powerboat Magazine 562
Practical Gastroenterology 803
Practical Homeowner 340
Practical Horseman, Performance Horseman 200
Practical Knowledge 434
Prairie Fire 380
Prairie Messenger 523
Prairie Publishing Company, The 133
Prairie Schooner 380
Prakken Publications, Inc. 133
Preaching 675
Premier Video Film & Recording Corp. 852
Prentice-Hall 133
Prentice-Hall Canada, Inc. (College Division) 133

Prentice-Hall Canada, Inc. (Secondary School Division) 133
Prentice-Hall Canada, Inc. (Trade Division) 134
Prentice-Hall, Inc. (Business and Professional Books) 134
Prentice Hall/Regents Publishing Co., Inc 134
Presbyterian Record 524
Presbyterian Survey 524
Present Tense 282
Present Tense/Joel H. Cavior Literary Awards 974
Preservation Press, The 134
Preservation News 314
Presidio Press 134
Press Porcépic 135
Press, The 649
Previews Magazine (see L.A. West 442)
Price/Stern/Sloan Inc., Publishers 135 (see also Troubador Press 165)
Priest Literary Agency, Inc., Aaron M. 949
Prima Publishing and Communications 135
Primalux Video 852
Primary Stages Company, Inc. 880
Primary Treasure (see Our Little Friend 360)
Prime Time Sports & Fitness 599
Prime Times 536
Princeton Alumni Weekly 244
Princeton Architectural Press 135
Princeton Book Company, Publishers (see Dance Horizons 56)
Princeton Parents 245
Princeton Series of Contemporary Poets 974
Print & Graphics 819
Printemps Books, Inc. 136
Printing Views 819
Prisk, Thomas 898
Prism Editions (see Naturegraph Publishers, Inc. 114)
Prism International 381
Private Pilot 225
Prix 974
Pro Sound News 698
Probe (see Pioneer 612)
Probus Publishing Co. 136
Proceedings 793
Produce News 734
Production Engineering 749
Production Supervisor's Bulletin 790
Productivity Improvement Bulletin 790
Professional Agent Magazine 759
Professional Furniture Merchant Magazine 740

Professional Photographer 813
Professional Publications, Inc. 136
Professional Quilter, The 330
Professional Selling 826
Professional Stained Glass 204
Profiles 424
Profit (Florida) 237
Profit (Texas) 821
Progressive Architecture 653
Progressive Grocer 734
Progressive, The 431
Prolingua Associates 136
Prometheus Awards/Hall of Fame 974
Proofs 683
Protter Literary Agent, Susan Ann 949
Pruett Publishing Co. 136
PSA Magazine 349
PSG Publishing Co., Inc. 137
PSI Research (see Oasis Press 119)
Psychic Guide Magazine 216
Psychology Today 434
Public Citizen 259
Public Power 702
Publishers Associates 137
Publisher's Report 768
Publishers Weekly 663
Publishing Trade 768
Puckerbrush Press 137
Pulitzer Prizes 974
Pulp & Paper Canada 809
Pulpsmith Magazine 381
Pulse 760
Pulse! 408
Pumper Publications 823
Purchasing Executive's Bulletin 749
Purdue Alumnus, The 245
Purdue University Press 138
Purple Cow 613
Purpose 524
Purrrr! The Newsletter for Cat Lovers 200
Pyle Award, Ernie 974

Q

Q.E.D. Information Sciences, Inc. 138
Quality Control Supervisor's Bulletin 749
Quality Publications 138
Quarry 381
Quarter Horse Journal, The 200
Quartz Theatre, The 880
Que Corporation 138
Queen of All Hearts 525
Queen's Quarterly 381
Quick Frozen Foods International 734
Quick Printing 819
Quill 139

Quilter's Newsletter Magazine 330
Quiltworld 330
Quinlan Press 190

R

R & E Publishers 191
R F D 498
Racz Publishing Company 139
R-A-D-A-R 361
Radiance 639
Radio-Electronics 547
Raft Theatre 880
Railroad Model Craftsman 330
Rainbow Books 139
Rainbow Magazine 424
Raintree Publishers, Inc. 139
Raleigh Award, Sir Walter 974
Randall Publisher, Peter 191
Random House, Inc. 139 (also see Pantheon Books 125, Time Books 164)
R&R Entertainment Digest 399
R&R Newkirk (see Longman Financial Services Publishing 102)
Rangefinder, The 813
Ranger Rick 361
Rave 270
R/C Modeler Magazine 331
RDH 683
Reader's Digest 297
Readers Review 297
Real Comet Press, The 139
Real Estate Education Co. (see Longman Financial Services Publishing 102)
Reason Magazine 431
Reconstructionist 282
Records Management Quarterly 671
Recreation News 211
Red Farm Studio 907
Redbook Magazine 639
Redbook's Short Story Contest 974
Redleterkardz 907
Rees Literary Agency, Helen 949
Referee 569
Reference Service Press 140
Refrigerated Transporter 657
Regal Books 140
Regardies: The Magazine of Washington Business 237
Regents Publishing Co., Inc. (see Prentice Hall/Regents 134)
Regnery Gateway, Inc. 140
Reipon College Magazine 245
Religious Education Press 140
Relix Magazine 408
Remodeling 666
Remodeling Contractor 681
Renaissance Greeting Cards 907

Renaissance House Publishers 140
Renaissance Theater, A 880
Renegade Press 256
Renews 657
Resident & Staff Physician 803
Resource Publications, Inc. 141
Resource Recycling 823
Response! 803
Restaurant Hospitality 745
Restaurant Management 746
Retailer and Marketing News 740
Retailer News 698
Retired Officer Magazine, The 399
Reuben Award 974
Revell Co., Fleming H. 141 (also see Chosen Books Publishing Co., Ltd. 47)
Review 212
Review and Herald Publishing Association 141
Review for Religious 525
Review Magazine 349
Reymont Associates 141
Rhode Island State Council on the Arts Fellowship 974
Rhodes Literary Agency, Inc. 949
Rhyme Time Creative Writing Competition 975
Rhythms Productions 852
Ribalow Prize, The Harold U. 975
Richboro Press 142
Richland Agency, The 950
Rider 221
Right Here 459
Righting Words 769
Rinehart Fund, Mary Roberts 975
Ripon College Magazine 245
Rising Star 769
Risk & Benefits Management 671
River Runner Magazine 562
Riverdale Company, Inc., Publishers, The 142
Road & Truck 222
Road King Magazine 222
Roanoke-Chowan Award for Poetry 975
Roanoker, The 488
Roberts Playwriting Award, Forest A. 975
Robertson, Larry 898
Rock & Soul 408
Rock Products 805
Rockshots, Inc. 908
Rocky Top Publications 142
Rodale Press 142
Rodell-Francis Collin Literary Agency, Marie 950
Rogers and Associates, Stephanie 950
Rogers Literary Agent, Eleanor

Roszel 950
Rogers Literary Representation, Irene 950
Rolling Stone 408
Rolling Stone College Journalism Competition 975
Romantic Dining & Travel Letter (see San Francisco Letter 627)
Romantist, The 769
Ronin Publishing Inc. 191
Roofer Magazine 682
Room of One's Own 381
Rosandich, Dan 898
Roseburg Woodsman 783
Rosen Publishing Group, The 142
Rosicrucian Digest 434
Ross Books 143
Rotarian, The 212
Rotrosen Agency, Jane 951
Rousana Cards 908
Routledge & Kegan Paul, Inc. (see Methuen, Inc. 107)
Rowman & Littlefield, Publishers 143
Roxbury Publishing Co. 143
Royce International Corp., The 908
RPM Press, Inc. 143
RSVP 456
Rural Heritage 201
Rural Kentuckian 460
Rural Living 489
Ruralite 437
Russica Publishers, Inc. 144
Rutgers University Press 144
Rutledge Hill Press 144
RV Business 837
RX Being Well 306
RX Home Care 684
Rynd Communications 144

S

S.C.E.-Editions L'Etincelle 145
S.W.A.T.: Special Weapons and Tactics 575
Sacramento Magazine 444
Safari Magazine 588
Safety Compliance Letter 684
Sagebrush Journal 331
Sail 562
Sailboard News 831
Sailing Magazine 563
Sailing World 563
St. Anthony Messenger 525
St. Anthony Messenger Press 145
St. Bede's Publications 145
St. Joseph's Messenger & Advocate of the Blind 525
St. Louis Journalism Review 769
St. Louis Magazine 469
St. Luke's Press 145

St. Martin's Press 146
St. Vladimir's Seminary Press 146
Sales & Marketing Management In Canada 650
Sales Manager's Bulletin 790
Salt Water Sportsman 589
Sams and Co., Inc., Howard 191
San Angelo Magazine 487
San Antonio Homes & Gardens 341
San Antonio Monthly 487
San Diego Home/Garden 341
San Diego Magazine 445
San Francisco Bay Guardian 445
San Francisco Focus 445
San Francisco Letter 627
San Francisco Review of Books 769
San Juan Airways (see Air Wisconsin 346)
Sandburg Literary Arts Awards, The Carl 975
Sandlapper Publishing, Inc. 146
Sandpaper, The 473
Sandpiper Press 146
Sanitary Maintenance 786
Santa Barbara Press 147
Satellite Dealer (see Satellite Direct 698)
Satellite Direct 698
Satellite ORBIT 270
Sater's Antiques & Auction News, Joel (see Antiques & Auction News 318)
Saturday Evening Post, The 297
Savings Institutions 723
Savvy 640
Saxton Communications Group Ltd. 853
Saybrook Publishing Co. 147
Scarecrow Press, Inc. 147
Scavenger's Newseltter 769
Scenic Airways (see Air Wisconsin 346)
Schaffner Associates, Inc., John 951
Schenkman Books Inc. 147
Schirmer Books 148
Schleger Company, Peter 853
Schocken Books, Inc. 148
Scholastic Scope 613
Scholastic Update 613
Scholastic Writing Awards 975
School Library Journal 782
School Shop 691
Schram Ltd., Abner 148
Schroeder Publishing Co., Inc. (see Collector Books 50)
Schulman Literary Agency, Inc., The Susan 951
Schulz Award, The Charles M. 975
Science Award, The 975
Science Fiction Chronicle 770

Science in Society Journalism Awards 975
Science Periodical on Research and Technology 692
Science-Writing Award in Physics and Astronomy 975
Score 572
Scorecard 246
Scott Stamp Monthly 331
Scott, Ter 898
Scouting 212
SCP Newsletter 526
Screen Printing 819
Screw 392
Scribner's Sons, Charles 148
Scripps Award, Charles E. 975
Scripps Awards, The Edward Willis 975
Scrivener 332
Scuba Times 604
Sea 563
Sea Frontiers 416
Sea Kayaker 563
Seacoast Life 471
Seafood Leader 735
Seattle Weekly, The 489
Seattle's Child 252
Seaway Review 794
Second Chance at Love 148
Second Chance Press/Permanent Press 149
Secrets 541
Security Management: Protecting Property, People & Assets 790
Seek 526
Select Homes Magazine 341
Selected Reading 298
Self 640
Self-Counsel Press, Inc. 149
Selling Direct 826
Semiconductor International 750
Senior 537
Senior Award, The 975
Senior Edition 537
Senior Voice Newspaper 453
$ensible Sound, The 409
Sertoman, The 213
Servant (see Single Impact 527)
Servant Publications 149
Service Business 786
Seven 298
Seven Locks Press, Inc. 149
Seven Seas Press 149 (also see International Marine Publishing Co. 91)
Seventeen 613
Seventeen Magazine/Dell Fiction Contest 975
73 for Radio Amateurs 547
Sew Business 740
Sew News 331
Sew Productions/Lorraine Hansberry Theatre 881
Sewanee Review 382
SFWA Nebula Awards 975
Shameless Hussy Press 150

Shape 306
Shapolsky Books 150
Sharing the Victory 526
Shaughnessy Prize, Mina P. 976
Shaw Publishers, Harold 150
Shazzam Production Company, The 881
Sheep! Magazine 713
Shelley Memorial Award 976
Shepard Theatre Complex, Richmond 881
Sherman, Goddard 899
Shining Star Publications 151
Shipmate 246
Shoe Service 780
Shoe String Press,The 151
Shoe Tree Press 151
Shopping Center World 682
Shorr, Stille & Associates 951
Short Story Review, The 382
Short Story Review Club (see Writer's Gazette 773)
Short Story Writers Competition 976
Shotgun Sports 574
Shumaker Artists Talent Agency 951
Side, John W. 899
Siegel, Literary Agency, Bobbe 952
Sierra 416
Sierra Club Books 151
Sierra Repertory Theatre 976
Sightlines 692
Signal Editions (see Vehicule Press 174)
Signcraft 650
Signpost Magazine 600
Signs of the Times (Idaho) 527
Signs of the Times (Ohio) 650
Sigo Press 152
Silhouette Books 152 (also see Harlequin Books 87)
Silver Burdett Press 152
Silver Gavel Awards 976
Silvera Writers' Workshop, Frank 881
Simmental Shield 714
Simon & Schuster 152 (also see Poseidon Press 132, Prentice-Hall 133)
Simon & Schuster Supplementary Education Unit (see Silver Burdett Press 152)
Sing Heavenly Muse! 383
Singer Communications, Inc. 917, 952
Singer Literary Agency, Evelyn 952
Single Impact 527
Single Parent, The 252
Singlelife Magazine 498
Sinsemilla Tips 710
Sisters Today 527
Sixth Annual National Literary Contest 976
Skating 601

Ski Magazine 602
Skies America 349
Skiing 602
Skin Diver 605
SKY 349
Skydiving 600
Skylines 822
Slimmer 306
Slocum, Stewart 899
SLR Productions 892
Small Boat Journal 564
Small Systems World (see Systems/3X World 757)
Smith Inc., Gibbs M. 153
Smithsonian Magazine 298
Snack Food 735
Snell Literary Agency, Michael 953
Snips Magazine 816
Snow Productions, Inc., Phoebe T. 853
Snowmass Repertory Theatre, The 882
Snowmobile Canada 602
Snowmobile Magazine 602
Snowmobile West 603
Snowy Egret 416
Soap Opera Digest 271
Soccer America 603
Social Justice Review 527
Soft Sector 424
Soho Repertory Theatre 882
Soldier of Fortune 399
Soloing 528
Sommer, Inc., Elyse 953
Song Hits 409
Sonnichsen Book Award, C.L. 976
Sons of Norway Viking, The 213
Sooner LPG Times 702
SOS Publications 153
Sound Management 826
Sound View Press 153
Soundings 564
South Coast Repertory 882
South End Press 153
South Florida Home & Garden 453
Southeastern Academy of Theatre and Music Inc. 882
Southern Appalachian Repertory Theatre 882
Southern Beverage Journal 661
Southern Exposure 478
Southern Illinois University Press 153
Southern Lumberman 784
Southern Magazine 438
Southern Outdoors Magazine 589
Southern Review, The 383
Southern Travel 627
Southwest Art 204
Southwest Hotel-Motel Review 746
Southwest Real Estate News 822

Southwest Review 383
Southwest Spirit 350
Souvenirs & Novelties Magazine 833
Soybean Digest 710
Space and Time 553
Space World 547
Spanky 899
Spann Memorial Prize, Bryant 976
Sparrow Press 154
Spectrum Theatre 883
Speech Bin, Inc., The 154
Speedhorse Magazine 576
Spencer Productions, Inc. 853
Spin-Off 332
Spinsters/Aunt Lute Books 154
Spire (see Fleming H. Revell Co. 141)
Spiritual Life 528
Spirituality Today 528
Spitzer Literary Agency, Philip G.. 953
Splash 205
Sport Fishing 589
Sporting Classics 590
Sporting Goods Business 831
Sports Afield 590
Sports Collectors Digest 332
Sports Fitness (see Men's Fitness 304)
Sports History 569
Sports Marketing News 831
Sports Parade 570
Sportscan 570
Sportsman Magazine 590
Spring Creek Press (see Johnson Books 94)
Springfield! Magazine 469
Sproutletter, The 341
Spur 576
Spur Awards 976
Square One Publishers 154
ST Publications 155
Stackpole 155
Stage One 883
Stages Repertory Theatre 883
Stagewrights, Inc. 883
Stallion Magazine 499
Stamp Wholesaler, The 834
Standard 529
Standard Publishing 155
Stanford University Press 156
Stanley Drama Award 976
Star, The 299
Starblaze 156
Star*Line 383
Starlog Magazine 553
Starrett Poetry Prize, The Agnes Lynch 976
Startling Detective 262
Starwind 554
State of Art, The 205
State, The 478
Steele & Associates, Ellen Lively 953
Steimatzky Publications of

North America, Inc. (see Shapolsky Books 150)
Stein and Day Publishers 156
Steinberg, Michael 953
Steiniger, Suzanna 899
Stephanus Sons, Publishing, Isidore 190
Stepping Stone Literary Agency 954
Stereo Review 409
Sterling Publishing 156
Stern Agency, Gloria (New York) 954
Stern Associates, Charles M. 964
Stern, Gloria (California) 954
Stewart, Inc., E.J. 853
Stewart, Tabori and Chang 156
Still Point Press 157
Stillpoint Publishing, Inc. 157
Stilwill, Charles 883
Stinger, John 900
Stipes Publishing Co. 157
ST-Log 425
Stock Car Racing Magazine 222
Stoeger Publishing Company 157
Stone Awards, The Walker 976
Stone Country 384
Stone in America 832
Stone Review 832
Stone Wall Press, Inc. §158
Stoneydale Press Publishing Co. 158
Stories 384
Straight 614
Strategic Health Care Marketing 803
Strategies 426
Strings Attached 908
Stuart, Inc., Lyle 158
Student Lawyer 779
Student, The 246
Studio Photography 814
Studio Press 158
Stuhlmann, Author's Representative, Gunther 954
Style 458
Success Publishing 158
Successful Dealer, The 657
Successful Farming 715
Successful Meetings Magazine 838
Sugar Producer, The 716
Sugden & Company, Publishers, Sherwood 159
Summa Publications 191
Summer Solistice Theatre Conference 976
Sunday Advocate Magazine 461
Sunday Digest 529
Sunday Morning magazine 465
Sunday School Counselor 529
Sunday Woman Plus 642
Sunflower University Press 159
Sunrise Publications, Inc. 908
Sunshine Artists USA 332

Sunshine Magazine 299
Sunshine Service News 702
Sunshine: The Magazine of
    South Florida 453
Sunstone Press, The 159
Superintendent's Profile &
    Pocket Equipment Directory
    730
Supervision 791
Surfer 605
Surfing Magazine 605
Surgical Rounds 804
Swallow Press (see Ohio Uni-
    versity Press 120)
Swank 392
Swanson, Inc., H.N. 955
Swim Magazine 606
Sybex, Inc. 159
Symmes Systems 160
Syndicated Writers & Artists
    Inc. 918
Syndicated Writers Group 918
Syracuse University Press 160
Systems/3X World 757

T
T.F.H. Publications, Inc. 190
Tab Books, Inc. 160
Tabor, Frank 900
Talco Productions 853
Tallahassee Magazine 454
Tampa Bay, The Suncoast's
    Magazine 454
Taplinger Publishing Co., Inc.
    160
Tarcher, Inc., Jeremy P. 161
Taylor Book Awards, Sydney
    976
Taylor, Kathryn 884
Taylor Manuscript Contest of
    AJL, Sydney 976
Taylor Playwriting Award, Mar-
    vin 976
Taylor Publishing Company 161
Tea & Coffee Trade Journal 662
Teacher Update 692
Teachers College Press 161
Teachers Interaction 529
Teaching/K-8 692
Teal & Watt 955
Tech Styles 908
Technical Analysis of Stocks
    and Commodities 230
Technical Photography 814
Technology Review 547
Teddy Bear Review 333
Teenage Corner, Inc. 918
Teenage Magazine 614
Teens Today 614
Tejas Art Press 884
Tel-Air Interests, Inc. 854
Telemarketing 650
Telemation Interactive (see Tele-
    mation Productions, Inc.
    854)

Telemation Productions, Inc.
    854
Teletechniques, Inc. 854
Television Broadcast 698
Television Production Services
    Corp. 892
Ten Best "Censored" Stories of
    1987, The 977
Ten Speed Press 161 (also see
    Celestial Arts 45)
Tennis 603
Tensleep Publications (see Me-
    lius & Peterson Publishing,
    Inc. 106)
Tewfik, Issam 900
Texas A&M University Press
    161
Texas Christian University Press
    162
Texas College Student 246
Texas Fisherman 591
Texas Gardener 342
Texas Highways Magazine 628
Texas Monthly Press, Inc. 162
Texas Western Press 162
TFR 770
Thaves, Bob 900
Theater Artists of Marin 884
Theater Ludicrum, Inc. 884
Theatre Arts Books 162
Theatre Calgary 884
Theatre Library Association
    Award, The 977
Theatre of the Open Eye (see
    The Open Eye: New Stag-
    ings 877)
Theatre Rapport 884
Theatre Rhinoceros 884
Theatre Three 884
Theatre Virginia 884
Theatreworks 885
Theatreworks/USA 885
Theme Song 892
Theosophical Publishing House,
    The 163
Third Coast Magazine 487
This People Magazine 530
Thistledown Press 163
Thomas Productions, Inc., Bob
    892
Thomas Publications 163
Thompson and Chris Literary
    Agency 955
Thorndike Press (see North
    Country Press 118)
Three Continents Press 163
3-2-1 Contact 362
3 Wheeling Magazine (see ATV
    Sports Magazine 217)
Threepenny Review, The 384
Threshold of Fantasy 385
Thrust—Science Fiction and
    Fantasy Review 554
Thunder's Mouth Press 164
Ti Professional Computing 425
Tidewater Virginian 237
Tiger Beat Star 615

Timber Press 164
Timeline 315
Times Books 164
Tobacco Reporter 710
Today's Catholic Teacher 693
Today's Parish 530
Toledo Magazine 481
Top Line 671
Tor Books 164
Toronto Life 492
Torso 499
Total Acting Experience, A 955
Total Health 306
Touch 362
Tourist Attractions & Parks
    Magazine 707
Tours & Resorts 628
Tow-Age 658
Towers Club, USA Newsletter
    259
Town and Country 299
Towngate Theatre Playwriting
    Contest 977
Towson State University Prize
    for Literature 977
TQ (TeenQuest) 615
Tradeshow and Exhibit Manager
    Magazine 672
Tradition 409
Trailer Boats Magazine 565
Trails-A-Way 628
Training 791
Transaction Books 164
Transaction/Society 730
Transitions Abroad 629
Translight Media Association
    854
Transnational Publishers, Inc.
    165
Transtar Productions, Inc. 854
Trapper, The 591
Travel & Study Abroad (see
    Transitions Abroad 629)
Travel Business Manager, The
    672
Travel Keys 165
Travel Smart 629
Travel Smart for Business 230
Travel-Holiday Magazine 629
Travelage Midamerica 838
Travelage West 838
Traveling Times, Inc. 630
Travelore Report 630
Tree Trimmers Log 784
Tri Video Teleproduction 854
Tribune Media Services 918
Trifle Magazine 346
Trillium Press 165
Trinity Square Ensemble 885
Triquarterly 385
TriState Magazine 481
Troll Associates 855
Tropic Magazine 454
Tropical Fish Hobbyist 201
Troubador Press 165
Truck Magazine 835
Truckers' News 658

Truckers/USA 658
True Confessions 541
True Detective 262
True Experience 541
True Love 541
True Police Cases 262
True Romance 541
True Story 542
True West 315
Truman Book Prize, Harry S
977
Trumpeter, The 333
T-Shirt Retailer and Screen
Printer 676
Tucson Lifestyle 441
Tun's Tales 400
Turkey 591
Turkey Call 592
Turn-On Letters 392
Turtle Magazine For Preschool
Kids 363
Tutor/Tape 855
TV Guide 271
Twayne Publishers 166
24th Street Experiment 885
Twilight Zone 555
Twins 252
2AM Magazine 555
Tyndale House Publishers, Inc.
166
Typographer, The 820

U

U Magazine 247
Ucross Foundation Residency
977
Ueland, Bardulf 900
UFO Research Award 977
UFO Review 548
Ukrainian Weekly, The 282
ULI-The Urban Land Institute
166
Ultralight Publications, Inc. 166
UMI Research Press 166
Uncensored Letters 393
Undercurrent 606
Undergraduate Paper Competi-
tion in Cryptology 977
Unexplained, The 216
Unfinished Furniture Magazine
740
Unicorn Publishing House, Inc.,
The 167
Union of American Hebrew
Congregations 167
United Brethren, The 530
United Cartoonist Syndicate 918
United Evangelical Action 530
United Feature Syndicate 918
United Media 919
United Methodist Reporter 531
Unity Magazine 531
Univelt, Inc. 167
Universal Press Syndicate 919
Universe Books 167

University Associates, Inc. 168
University Editions (see Aegina
Press 191)
University of Alabama Press
168
University of Alaska Press, 191
University of Alberta Press, The
168
University of Arizona Press 168
University of Arkansas Press,
The 169
University of Calgary Press,
The 169
University of California Press
169
University of Illinois Press 169
University of Iowa Press 170
University of Massachusetts
Press 170
University of Michigan Press
170
University of Nebraska Press
170
University of Nevada Press 171
University of North Carolina
Press, The 171
University of Notre Dame Press
171
University of Pennsylvania Press
171
University of Tennessee Press,
The 171
University of Texas Press 172
University of Toronto Quarterly
385
University of Utah Press 172
University of Wisconsin Press
172
University of Wisconsin Stout
Teleproduction Center 855
University Press of America,
Inc. 172
University Press of Mississippi
172
University Press of New En-
gland 173
University Press of Virginia 173
Unix/World 758
Unlimited Publishing Co. 173
Unspeakable Visions of the In-
dividual, Inc., The 385
UPB Magazine 707
Upper Room, The 531
Upstate Magazine 477
Urstadt, Inc., Susan P 956
USAir Magazine 350
Utah State University Press 173
Utility Supervision 791
Utne Reader 431

V

Vabs Multi-Image 855
Vacation Industry Review 746
Vagabond Creations, Inc. 909
Valley Magazine 445

Valley of the Sun Publishing
Company 174
Van Der Marck Editions, Alfred
174
Vance Bibliographies 174
Vancouver Playhouse, The 885
Vantage Point: Issues in Ameri-
can Arts 707
Vantage Press 191
Vegetarian Journal 307
Vegetarian Times 307
Vehicule Press 174
Velo-News 558
Vending Times 677
Vend-O-Books/Vend-O-Press
175
Venture (Illinois) 363
Venture (New York) 260
Venture County & Coast Re-
porter 446
Verbatim Essay Competition
977
Verdict Magazine 780
Vermont Life Magazine 487
Vermont Vanguard Press 488
Vestal Press, Ltd., The 175
Veteran, The 400
Veterinary Computing 840
Veterinary Economics Magazine
840
Veterinary Practice Management
840
VGM Career Horizons 175
Victimology 730
Victor Valley Magazine 446
Victoria Management Co. 956
Victorian Theatre 886
Video Manager 699
Video Store 699
Video Systems 699
Video Vacation Guide, Inc. and
Cinematronics, Inc. 892
Videomania 271
Vietnam Veterans Ensemble
Theatre Company 886
Vineyard & Winery Manage-
ment 662
Vintage 284
Virginia Camper, The (see The
Camper Times 618)
Virginia Cavalcade 315
Virginia Forests Magazine 489
Virginia Prize for Literature 977
Virginia Quarterly Review, The
385
Virginia Stage Company 886
Virginia Wildlife 592
Virtue 532
Vision Lifestyles 532
Vista (Florida) 282
Vista (Indiana) 532
Vista/USA 630
Visual Communications Canada
700
Vital Christianity 533
VM & SD 650
Volkswagen's World 223

Volleyball Monthly 600
Vortex 257
Vortex Theater Company, The 886

W

Wade, Carlson 956
Wadsworth Publishing Company 175
Wagner Award, Celia B. 977
Walch, Publisher, J. Weston 176
Wald Associates, Inc., Mary Jack 956
Walker and Co. 176
Walking Tours of San Juan 491
Walkways 307
Wallace-Homestead Book Co. 176
Wallant Book Award, Edward Lewis 977
Walls & Ceilings 666
Walnut Street Theatre 886
War Cry 533
Ward's Auto World 658
Ware Literary Agency, John A. 957
Warehousing Supervisor's Bulletin 792
Warner Press, Inc. 909
Warren Literary Agency, James 957
Washington 489
Washington Blade, The 499
Washington Fishing Holes 592
Washington Monthly 432
Washington Post Magazine, The 448
Washington Post, The 448
Washington State University Press 176
Washington Trooper, The 731
Washington Woman, The 642
Washingtonian Magazine, The 448
Waste Age 750
Watch and Clock Review 762
Water Skier, The 606
Waterbed Magazine 826
Waterfowler's World 593
Waterfront Magazine 565
Waterfront News 454
Watts, Inc., Franklin 177
Ways 264
Waystation 771
WDS Forum 771
We Alaskans Magazine 439
Webb Traveler Magazine 299
Webster Review 386
Wee Wisdom 363
Weekly News, The 500
Weighing & Measurement 750
Weight Watchers Magazine 308
Weiser Inc., Samuel 177
Wesleyan Advocate, The 533
West 446

West Air (see Air Wisconsin 346)
West Coast Ensemble 886
West Coast Review 386
West Coast Review of Books 771
Westart 205
Westbeth Theatre Center 886
Western & Eastern Treasures 333
Western & English Fashions 676
Western Boatman, The 566
Western Canada Outdoors 492
Western Horseman, The 201
Western Humanities Review 386
Western Investor 237
Western Marine Enterprises Inc. 177
Western New York Magazine 238
Western Outdoors 593
Western People 492
Western Producer Prairie Books 177
Western Producer, The 493
Western Publisher 664
Western Reserve Magazine 481
Western Roofing/Insulation/Siding 682
Western RV Traveler 631
Western Sportsman 593
Western Tanager Press 178
Westernlore Press 178
Westview Press 178
Westways 446
Weyr Agency, Rhoda 957
What Makes People Successful 300
What's New Magazine 465
Whitaker House 178
Whitaker, Joseph F. 900
Whiting Writers' Awards 977
Whitson Publishing Co., The 178
Whole Life 308
Wholistic Living News 308
Wichita State University Playwriting Contest 977
Wichita State University Theatre 887
Wide Open Magazine 386
Wieser & Wieser, Inc. 957
Wilderness Press 179
Wildlife Photography 427
Wiley & Sons, Inc., John 179
Wiley Prize, Bell I. 977
Williams Award, William Carlos 977
Williamson Publishing Co. 179
Willow Creek Press 179
Wilshire Book Co. 180
Wilson Fine Arts, Inc., Carol 909
Wilson Library Bulletin 782
Wilson Library Periodical Award, H.W. 978
Wimmer Brothers 191

Winch & Associates, B.L. (see Jalmar Press 93)
Wind Rider 607
Windsor Books 180
Windsor Publications 180
Windsor This Month Magazine 493
Wine & Spirits Buying Guide 284
Wine Appreciation Guild Ltd. 180
Wine Spectator, The 285
Wine Tidings 285
Wine World Magazine 285
Wines & Vines 662
Wingbow Press 181
Wingra Woods Press 191
Wingra Woods Press/Agenting Division 958
Wings West (see Air Wisconsin 346)
Winship Book Award, J.J. 978
Winston-Derek Publishers 181
Wisconsin 490
Wisconsin Arts Board Fellowship Program 978
Wisconsin Grocer, The 735
Wisconsin Restaurateur, The 736
Wisconsin Silent Sports 570
Wisconsin Trails 491
Witter Bynner Foundation for Poetry, Inc. Grants 978
Wofsy Fine Arts, Alan 181
Woman Bowler 567
Woman Engineer, The 704
Woman Magazine 642
Woman's Day 643
Woman's Newspaper of Princeton, The (see The Woman's Newspaper 643)
Woman's Newspaper, The 643
Wo/Man's Showcase, Inc., The 887
Woman's Touch 533
Women & Co. 491
Women Artists News 206
Women in Business 643
Women's Circle 644
Women's Circle, Counted Cross Stitch 334
Women's Circle Home Cooking 285
Women's Household Crochet 334
Women's Sports and Fitness Magazine 571
Women's Theatre Project 887
Wonder Time 363
Wood 'N Energy 816
Woodall's Campground Management 831
Woodbine House 182
Woodenboat Magazine 566
Woodheat '88 816
Woodland Books 182
Woodmen of the World Maga-

zine 213
Woodsong Graphics, Inc. 182
Woolly Mammoth Theatre Company 887
Worcester Magazine 465
Word Beat Press 182
Word Beat Press Fiction Book Award 978
Word Books Publisher 183
Word in Season, The 534
Word Beat Press Fiction Book Award 978
Work-in-Progress Grant 978
Workbasket, The 334
Workbench 334
Working Mother Magazine 644
Working Woman 644
Worksteader News, The 230
World Almanac Publications (see Pharos Books 129)
World Coin News 335
World Hunger Media Awards 978
World Market Perspective 231
World Natural History Publications (see Plexus Publishing, Inc. 131)
World Policy Journal 432
World Tennis 603
World War II 400
World's Fair 432
Worldwide Library (see Harlequin Books 81)
WPI Journal 247
Wren Associates, Inc. 855
Wreschner, Author's Representative, Ruth 958
Wrestling World 600
Wright Publishing Company, Inc. 183
Wright Representatives, Inc., Ann 958
Writer, The 771
Writers Connection 772
Writer's Consulting Group 959
Writer's Digest 772
Writer's Digest Books 184
Writer's Gazette 773
Writers Guild of America West Awards 978
Writers House, Inc. 958
Writer's Info 773
Writer's Inspirational Market News 773
Writers' Journal 773
Writer's Lifeline 774
Writer's Newsletter 774
Writer's Productions 959
Writers Publishing Service Co. 191
Writer's Workshop, Inc., The (see Anita Diamant 931)
Writers' World Forum 959
Writer's Yearbook 774
Written Words Competition/ Writers-in-Performance Invitational 978

Wyoming Rural Electric News 719

X-Y-Z

X-It 272
Yachting 566
Yale Review, The 387
Yankee 438
Yankee Books 184
Yankee Homes 342
Yedlin, Literary Agent, Barbara W. 959
Yee Wen Publishing Company 184
Yellow Silk 387
Yesteryear 335
Yoga Journal, The 309
York Press Ltd. 184
Young Ambassador (see TeenQuest 615)
Young American 364
Young Author's Magazine 364
Your Church 675
Your Health 309
Your Health & Fitness 310
Your Home 342
Your Virginia State Trooper Magazine 731
Youth Update 615
Yukon Indian News, The (see Dan Sha News 276)
Zebra Books 184
Zeckendorf Associates, Susan 960
Zelasky Literary Agency, Tom 960
Zelman Studios Ltd. 856
Ziegler Literary Agency, George 960
ZM Squared 856
Zondervan Corp., The 185
ZYZZYVA 387

What Editors Look For

Queries:

1 A fresh, well-focused idea

2. Your point of view on the idea

3. Why you should write on this idea

4. Evidence of research and writing ability

5. How the material might serve their readers and the market

6. Evidence that you've read the company's publications

7. Perfect copy; SASE enclosed.